Official

BASEBALL GUIDE

1987 EDITION

Editor/Baseball Guide
DAVE SLOAN

Associate Editor/Baseball Guide
MIKE NAHRSTEDT

Contributing Editors/Baseball Guide
CRAIG CARTER
BARRY SIEGEL
LARRY WIGGE

President-Chief Executive Officer
RICHARD WATERS

Editor
TOM BARNIDGE

Director of Books and Periodicals
RON SMITH

Published by

1212 North Lindbergh Boulevard
P.O. Box 56 — St. Louis, MO 63166

A Times Mirror Company

IMPORTANT NOTICE

The Official Baseball Guide is protected by copyright. All information, in the form presented here, except playing statistics, was compiled by the publishers and proof is available.

Information from the Official Baseball Guide must not be used elsewhere without special written permission, and then only with full credit to the Official Baseball Guide, published by THE SPORTING NEWS, St. Louis, Missouri.

ISBN 0-89204-237-0 ISSN 0078-3838

TABLE OF CONTENTS

For Index to Contents See Page 523

(Index to Minor League Cities on Page 524)

ON THE COVER: Boston righthander Roger Clemens' fabulous 1986 season included 24 victories, a 2.48 earned-run average, a record 20 strikeouts in one game, the American League's Most Valuable Player and Cy Young awards, the All-Star Game MVP trophy and the Red Sox's first pennant in 11 years.

—Photo by Rich Pilling

Big Individual Performances Highlight Exciting '86 Season

By CLIFFORD KACHLINE

While the rest of the world suffered through several grave tragedies, major league baseball was enjoying a positive and productive 1986 season. Such technological disasters as the crash of the U.S. space shuttle Challenger and the Russian nuclear accident at Chernobyl, combined with the drug-related deaths of two prominent athletes in other sports, left deep scars on the psyches of many persons. As a result, many people looked to America's summer game for relief and received more than they had bargained for.

Not that all was harmony and happiness by any means. Some explosive issues developed between management and the players' union, resulting in what was possibly the most confrontational non-strike year in the game's history. Nevertheless, the 1986 season will be remembered as one of baseball's finest in recent memory.

For the first time since the major leagues went to divisional play in 1969, there were no dramatic, down-to-the-wire races. All four division titles were settled before the season entered its final week. But the absence of exciting chases was offset by impressive individual performances, two spectacular League Championship Series and an equally startling climax to the World Series.

All four divisions crowned new champions. Each of the 1985 winners—the Kansas City Royals, St. Louis Cardinals, Toronto Blue Jays and Los Angeles Dodgers—stumbled and were not factors in their respective races.

After finishing second for two straight seasons, the New York Mets made a shambles of the National League East. Winning 20 of their first 24 games and 44 out of 60, Dave Johnson's crew jumped to a big lead and went on to post the year's best record, 108-54, while finishing a remarkable 21½ games in front of the runnerup Philadelphia Phillies. The Mets clinched on September 17 when Dwight Gooden pitched a six-hit, 4-2 victory over the Chicago Cubs at Shea Stadium.

In the National League West, the surprising San Francisco Giants occupied first place at the All-Star break, one game ahead of Houston. The Astros, however, under the leadership of rookie Manager Hal Lanier, pulled in front on July 21 and

Boston righthander Roger Clemens dominated the 1986 American League season and walked away with both the Most Valuable Player and Cy Young awards.

set the pace the remainder of the way. Mike Scott, Houston's ace, added frosting to the Astros' title cake by throwing a dramatic no-hitter against the Giants on September 25 as Houston clinched the West Division with a 2-0 victory over the Giants at the Astrodome. The Astros finished with a 96-66 record and a 10-game edge over second-place Cincinnati.

The tightest race was the American League West, which still ended with a five-game spread. Like San Francisco, the Texas Rangers surprised everybody by battling the California Angels most of the way. But Gene Mauch's Angels, dubbed "The Last Hurrah Gang" because of their many veterans, began pulling away in late August and clinched with an 8-3 conquest of the Rangers on September 26 at Anaheim Stadium.

Although the Boston Red Sox never fell from the American League East lead after May 15, they were the last division winner to wrap things up. Sparked by hard-throwing righthander Roger Clemens, who won his first 14 decisions, the Red Sox coasted to a seven-game advantage by the All-Star break. But Manager John McNamara watched helplessly as his team played just four games over .500 (39-35) the remainder of the way, finally clinching the division flag on September 28, the next-to-last Sunday of the season, when Dennis (Oil Can) Boyd coasted to a 12-3 victory over Toronto at Fenway Park. The Red Sox's 95-66 regular-season record produced a comfortable 5½-game bulge over the second-place New York Yankees.

Both League Championship Series ranked among the most dramatic post-season clashes ever.

In the American League, California took a 3-1 series lead by registering a stirring 4-3 come-from-behind victory in 11 innings and, one night later, moved within one strike of the first pennant in the Angels' 26-year history. But just as fans and players were ready to pop the champagne corks at Anaheim Stadium, their hopes were dashed. Not only did the Red Sox stage a dramatic, last-ditch rally to win Game 5 in 11 innings, they also won the final two games at Fenway to capture the A.L. pennant. The bitter defeat pushed Mauch's pennantless managing streak to 25 years.

The National League series lasted only six games, but was just as tense and emotional. After Houston's Scott had baffled the Mets twice with his split-fingered fastball to keep the series even at two games apiece, the clubs battled through 12 innings in Game 5 before New York won, 2-1. At the Astrodome the next day, Houston seemed on the verge of knotting the series when Bob Knepper entered the ninth inning with a 3-0 lead. But the Mets staged a stunning rally to tie the score and went on to a dramatic 7-6 victory in 16 innings. Besides earning them the pennant, the uphill triumph helped the Mets avoid a seventh-game showdown against Scott, their nemesis.

The World Series plot was equally improbable. The Red Sox shocked New York rooters and most experts by capturing the first two games at Shea Stadium. The Mets rebounded to win the next pair at Fenway Park before Bruce Hurst, a 1-0 victor in the opener, gave Boston a 3-2 edge with his second victory, 4-2. Like the Angels in the A.L. Championship Series, the Red Sox came within one strike of winning the world championship, only to have their hopes dashed by another dramatic rally. After the Red Sox had forged a 5-3 lead in the 10th inning of Game 6, the Mets staged a shocking comeback that produced a 6-5 victory with the tying and winning runs scoring on a wild pitch and error, respectively. In the decisive seventh game, Hurst, seeking his third victory, blanked the Mets for five innings before running out of gas. The opportunistic New Yorkers jumped on Boston's bullpen and emerged with an 8-5 triumph and the world championship.

As a capper to their memorable season, the Mets received an invitation to visit President Ronald Reagan at the White House. Fourteen of the club's players, along with two coaches and four front-office officials, participated in the November 12 celebration. Fred Wilpon, president of the Mets, headed the delegation, which included catchers Gary Carter, Ed Hearn and John Gibbons, pitchers Dwight Gooden, Bob Ojeda, Rick Aguilera, Roger McDowell, Jesse Orosco, Doug Sisk, Randy Niemann and Rick Anderson, infielders Tim Teufel and Howard Johnson and outfielder Lee Mazzilli.

Despite the lack of close races during the regular season, attendance reached an all-time peak. With all 26 clubs attaining the million mark at the turnstiles for the first time in history, the two leagues drew 47,506,203 fans for the regular season. This surpassed the previous record, set one year earlier, by 681,824. It marked the seventh time in the last 10 seasons that the major leagues had achieved a new attendance high.

The 14 American League teams accounted for 25,172,732 spectators while the

Hard-throwing Mike Scott baffled opposing batters with his split-finger fastball and led Houston to the National League West Division title.

12 National League franchises attracted 22,333,471. Although their attendance was down more than 200,000, the Los Angeles Dodgers topped the 3,000,000 figure for the fifth consecutive year to again lead all clubs. Three teams broke their gate records—the New York Mets, who ranked second behind the Dodgers with 2,767,601; the Kansas City Royals, with 2,320,794, and the Texas Rangers, 1,692,002. Five other clubs exceeded the 2,000,000 level—the Boston Red Sox, California Angels, New York Yankees, Toronto Blue Jays and St. Louis Cardinals.

The continued attendance rise, coupled with the clubs' efforts to put a rein on expenses, notably in the areas of free-agent bidding, roster size and player contracts, brightened the financial outlook of the industry. At the same time, the owners' actions in these and several other matters drew the wrath of the Major League Players Association and led to confrontations that could have a significant impact on the game's future.

Two especially heated issues centered around drug testing and free agency. A program of random drug testing proposed by Commissioner Peter Ueberroth and backed by the clubs was struck down by baseball's impartial arbitrator. Another grievance, charging the clubs with collusion in what the players' union viewed as an attempt to destroy free agency, remained unresolved at year's end. There was strong belief on both sides that the collusion case could be the most important since the 1975 Messersmith-McNally case, which led to free agency.

Ironically, the bitterness between management and the players claimed even the sport's arbitrator as a victim. Thomas Roberts of suburban Los Angeles, who was selected as arbitrator late in 1985, was dismissed in August by the Player Relations Committee, the owners' labor arm, after his drug-testing decision had supported the players. However, a hearing on his ouster subsequently resulted in his reinstatement to complete the hearing on the collusion charge.

The subject of drugs remained a priority concern both inside and outside sports. While the Reagan administration was strengthening efforts to confiscate or destroy sources of cocaine and other mind-altering substances, Commissioner Ueberroth was telling observers that ridding baseball of drugs and getting all clubs on solid financial footing were among his prime objectives.

Although his drug-testing plan was rejected, Ueberroth earned high praise from most quarters for his handling of the players implicated in the 1985 Pittsburgh trial of Curtis Strong, a Philadelphia caterer who was convicted and sentenced to 12 years in federal prison for drug trafficking. That decision was the most difficult of the commissioner's brief tenure atop the baseball world.

Early in the year, Ueberroth conducted separate interviews with the 23 players and one coach who had testified or been implicated in the Pittsburgh trial, or who otherwise were involved with drugs. The only one who declined an invitation to meet Ueberroth was John Milner, a retired outfielder. After lengthy deliberation, Ueberroth announced his verdict on February 28, just as spring training was beginning. In his ruling, he divided the players and their penalties into three groups:

- Group I—Joaquin Andujar, Dale Berra, Enos Cabell, Keith Hernandez, Jeff Leonard, Dave Parker and Lonnie Smith. Each was ordered suspended for one year unless he agreed to (a) donate 10 percent of his 1986 salary to a drug abuse prevention facility or program, (b) participate in a random drug-testing program for the remainder of his career, and (c) perform 100 hours of drug-related community service in each of the next two years. According to the commissioner, the seven were "involved in a prolonged pattern of drug use and . . . in some fashion facilitated the distribution of drugs in baseball."
- Group II—Al Holland, Lee Lacy, Lary Sorensen and Claudell Washington. Each was to be suspended for 60 days without pay unless he agreed to (a) donate five percent of his 1986 salary to a drug abuse prevention facility or program, (b) participate in a random drug-testing program for the remainder of his career, and (c) perform 50 hours of drug-related community service in 1986. Ueberroth charged that the four players "engaged in more limited use of or involvement with drugs."
- Group III—Dusty Baker, Vida Blue, Gary Matthews, Dickie Noles, Tim Raines, Daryl Sconiers, Rod Scurry, Manny Sarmiento, Derrel Thomas and Alan Wiggins. Each was required to agree to participate in a random drug-testing program for the remainder of his career. The commissioner said these were players for whom he found "little or no evidence of drug involvement exists or whose cases have already been handled through other procedures."

Ueberroth also ruled that no major or minor league club could have "any type of relationship" with John Milner until he met with the commissioner and his status was determined. He withheld a ruling on Mike Norris because criminal action was pending in California against the former Oakland pitcher on drug-possession charges. In addition, the commissioner cleared both Bill Madlock and coach Willie Stargell. Berra and Parker had testified at the Pittsburgh trial that Madlock and Stargell gave them amphetamines when they played with the Pirates.

On the basis of their reported 1986 salaries, the penalized players were obligated to donate the following amounts: Group I—Andujar, $115,000; Berra, $51,250; Cabell, $45,000; Hernandez, $135,000; Leonard, $90,000; Parker, $87,500, and Smith, $85,000. Group II—Holland, $20,000; Lacy, $30,000; Sorensen, $10,000, and Washington, $30,000.

While Ueberroth's judgments were stern, observers generally felt they were fair. The penalties were considered harsh enough to leave a lasting impact and establish a precedent, yet they would not affect any team or pennant race by barring a player from playing. The decisions also fit the commissioner's long-standing framework for fighting drugs—prevention rather than punishment—by earmarking the "fines" for drug-prevention programs.

In explaining his ruling, Ueberroth said he rejected outright suspension, with no alternative penalty, for the players in the first two groups because he believed the players could be "a positive force" in combating drugs. "If they put a little of their money and a good portion of their time back into the community where they play ball, it could help others from falling into the same trap," he said.

The reactions of the penalized players ranged from relief to anger. Upon learning of the commissioner's ruling, Hernandez told the media: "Obviously I'm not pleased" and said he would pursue filing a grievance through the Players Association. Hernandez contended that he had been "incorrectly categorized as one who facilitated cocaine use," claiming that while he admitted to using the drug, he never dealt in it or sold it. Several other players at first indicated they, too, might challenge the decision, but all later decided to abide by the ruling and accept the alternate option.

Shortly before the season, Ueberroth sent a five-page letter to all major league players outlining his drug-testing plan. Earlier in the year the Baltimore Orioles had announced development of baseball's first voluntary substance abuse-testing program and said that 26 of the 38 players on their roster had agreed to participate. The other clubs quickly followed the Orioles' lead, including drug-testing clauses in most of the new player contracts.

Ueberroth's drug-testing plan was designed to replace the 18-month-old agreement between the owners and the players' union that management abruptly terminated during the 1985 World Series. It called for each player to submit to urinalysis four times a year for the next two years. Only those players with drug-testing clauses in their contracts, along with those named in the February 28 ruling, would be tested. The letter explained that the tests would check for marijuana, cocaine, morphine and heroin and that the results would be confidential between the doctor and player and would not be accessible to management or the commissioner.

The plan, which was to apply also to umpires and front-office personnel, was to be carried out under the direction of Dr. Anthony F. Daly, who served as Director of Health Services at the 1984 Olympic Games in Los Angeles, and Kim Jasper, a doctor of pharmacology who was Director of Doping Control at the '84 Games. "The program is totally confidential and will have no penalties for those testing positive for the first time," Ueberroth said. "The penalized players, on the other hand, would face immediate suspension if any drug test is positive, if they refuse to submit to a test when asked or if they fail to meet any of the commitments of the penalty."

The commissioner's letter added fuel to the growing dispute between the owners and the athletes. Eugene Orza, associate general counsel of the Players Association, termed the letter "another attempt by the commissioner to deal with the employees directly rather than through the union." Contending drug testing was a matter for collective bargaining, the Players Association filed a grievance against the testing clause as well as a grievance against the commissioner's disciplinary action against the 21 players. In turn, management's Player Relations Committee submitted a grievance of its own against the union's move in challenging Ueberroth's decision.

The two parties' eight-month debate over drug testing was ended, temporarily at least, on July 30 by a ruling handed down by arbitrator Roberts. He declared that in the absence of collective bargaining, the drug-testing clauses in nonguaranteed contracts were in violation of the 1985 Basic Agreement, thus upholding the union's position. A total of 459 players were reported to have a testing clause in their contract. The ruling applied to all except the 44 with guaranteed contracts and to those players disciplined by Ueberroth.

The National Football League had a similar experience three months later when another arbitrator, Richard Kasher, ruled against a mandatory drug-testing program that NFL Commissioner Pete Rozelle had sought to put into effect without union approval.

In the wake of Roberts' verdict, Donald Fehr, executive director of the Players Association, declared the decision "does not change our convictions that a long-term agreement on a joint drug program is in the best interest of everyone in baseball—clubs and players alike. We are persuaded that the Association and the clubs should establish a jointly administered program focusing on education, early diagnosis and treatment by expert medical personnel in confidentiality." Fehr indicated the union would be willing to strike a deal for random testing if it were done through the proper channels.

The first case handled by Roberts early in the year also dealt with a drug-testing clause. Infielder-outfielder Joel Youngblood of the San Francisco Giants, who became a free agent after the 1985 season, reached agreement on a two-year contract with his old club, but the Giants then withdrew the offer when the player declined to sign a drug-testing clause. The matter was submitted for arbitration, and Roberts ruled on March 20 that the Giants could include the clause in Youngblood's contract, as they had done in all new contracts, but added that his decision applied only to Youngblood and "should not be used as a precedent for any other case."

The problem of drugs in sports was magnified by several incidents during the year. The most tragic were the drug-related deaths of Len Bias, a 22-year-old University of Maryland basketball star, on June 19, just two days after he was drafted on the first round by the National Basketball Association champion Boston Celtics, and of Don Rogers, a 23-year-old free safety of the Cleveland Browns National Football League team, on June 27. Another star athlete, Micheal Ray Richardson of the New Jersey Nets, had been permanently banned by the NBA earlier in the year as a three-time drug abuser.

Despite baseball's concerted efforts, it was unable to escape the drug scourge completely. San Diego pitcher LaMarr Hoyt was arrested three times in drug-related episodes. He was first picked up on February 10 by U.S. Customs Service agents at the San Ysidro Port of Entry while returning from Mexico and drew a fine of $620 for having a quantity of marijuana, some Valium tablets and a knife in his possession. Eight days later, the San Diego police stopped him at 12:50 in the morning and found a switchblade and less than an ounce of marijuana in his car.

Hoyt reported to the Padres' spring training camp on February 24, but departed several days later to enter a Minnesota drug and rehabilitation center. His agent said it was an alcohol problem that led the pitcher to enter the treatment facility. Hoyt rejoined the Padres on March 28. At a court appearance four weeks later, he pleaded guilty to a reduced charge in connection with the February 18 arrest and was fined $375 and given three years' probation.

Hoyt's third brush with the law occurred October 28 when he again was arrested by Custom Service agents in San Ysidro. They reported finding plastic bags containing nearly 500 pills concealed under his trousers. In addition, three marijuana cigarettes and approximately two grams of loose marijuana were found in his 1986 Porsche. The car, valued at $33,000, was seized on grounds it was used in the commission of a crime, and Hoyt later was sentenced to 45 days in federal prison. Hoyt's sentence included five years of supervised probation and a $5,025 fine with a stipulation that he would undergo drug testing and alcohol treatment during the probation. The former Cy Young Award winner also faced the possibility of stern discipline from baseball.

Steve Howe, former Los Angeles Dodger and Minnesota Twin southpaw, also experienced pitfalls in his renewed attempt to make a comeback from substance abuse. He and four other players with a prior history of drugs—pitcher Mike Norris, first baseman Daryl Sconiers, third baseman Ken Reitz and infielder-outfielder Derrel Thomas—were signed by the San Jose Bees prior to the start of the California League season. Attitude problems led President-Manager Harry Steve to release Thomas before the season opened, while Norris, who was placed on a two-year drug diversion program on March 27 as a result of a 1985 arrest, was released a few days after the season began before being re-signed by San Jose on June 2. Howe first encountered difficulty when a May 1 drug test given by the commissioner's office proved positive and he was ordered sidelined. When Howe took the mound anyway on May 14, Ueberroth suspended him. Following additional drug rehabilitation therapy, the pitcher was reinstated in late June. Three weeks later, he was suspended again when another test proved positive, even though a second test later the same day showed no trace of drugs.

In an unprecedented move, the Pittsburgh Pirates filed suit against outfielder Dave Parker of the Cincinnati Reds. The suit, filed in Allegheny County Common Pleas Court on April 21, charged that the deterioration of Parker's skills as a baseball player and his failure to stay in good physical condition while under a five-year contract he signed with the Pirates in 1979 were directly related to and caused by his illegal use of cocaine. At the 1985 Pittsburgh drug trial, Parker admitted he began using cocaine in 1976 and was a heavy user until 1982, when he quit because the drug was adversely affecting his performance on the field. Malcolm (Mac) Prine, the Pirates' president, said the club's reason for going to court was to seek to avoid having to pay Parker 20 years of deferred payments totaling $5,312,475. The first installment of $944,445 is due January 10, 1988. Parker's response to the suit was to seek settlement in arbitration rather than court, but U.S. District Judge Glenn Mencer denied the request in August. He held the matter went beyond major league grievance procedures. The suit was not expected to go to trial for two or three years.

Two former players also found themselves in the news because of drug-related incidents. John (Blue Moon) Odom, former Oakland pitcher, was convicted on July 31 of selling $200 worth of cocaine to a co-worker in 1985 and was sentenced to 90 days in jail and five years' probation. Joe Pepitone, former New York Yankees first baseman, was convicted on two misdemeanor counts following a month-long drug trial in Brooklyn. On October 22, Supreme Court Judge Alan Marcus sentenced the 46-year-old Pepitone to a pair of six-month jail terms to be served concurrently.

After more than a decade of watching the Players Association grow into one of the most successful unions in American labor history, there were indications that the owners finally were coming to grips with the situation. Through the free-market system and the fiscal recklessness of management, the union had driven up salaries to what much of the public regarded as obscene levels. But the owners began a concerted effort to slow the rising labor costs in 1985 and '86.

In 1976, the last season before the Messersmith-McNally free-agency ruling became operative, the payrolls of the then-24 clubs amounted to approximately $32 million. They ranged from a low of $876,000 to a high of $1,978,000, and the average salary was approximately $53,500. In 1986, the opening-day payrolls of the 26 teams amounted to almost $284 million, according to figures released by Barry Rona, head of the Player Relations Committee, and the average salary was $431,521, the highest in professional sports.

But, suddenly, the owners refused to bid for free-agent talent, major league rosters were trimmed to 24 players and many clubs set a limit of three years on new contracts. This sudden shift in policy indicated that management had become serious about practicing fiscal prudence. The owners held to the tightened financial practices throughout the year. This was an interesting development because in the past, the owners seldom could agree to act in concert on anything. The media attributed the change to Ueberroth, whose business-wise leadership reportedly convinced the owners of their folly.

As a consequence, players who opted for free agency after the 1985 season failed to reap the financial rewards they expected. In sharp contrast to other years, when such players were in great demand and team-hopping was a regular occurrence, there was no bidding war. Even the top players failed to attract offers from anybody except their old teams. Many clubs, burned by past free-agent mistakes, ascribed the absence of bidding to a shift in strategy—grow your own talent.

Under the Basic Agreement, a team losing a player to free agency can offer to go to salary arbitration with him if the two parties are unable to agree on a new contract. Free agents who reject salary arbitration must re-sign with their old club by midnight January 8 or be ineligible to sign with that team until May 1.

After waiting in vain for offers from other clubs, the three leading free agents—Detroit outfielder Kirk Gibson, California relief pitcher Donnie Moore and Chicago White Sox catcher Carlton Fisk—somewhat reluctantly accepted terms with their old teams shortly before the deadline. Gibson, who reportedly was seeking a five-year, $8 million contract, settled for a three-year, $4 million deal. Moore settled for a three-year, $3 million pact and Fisk signed a two-year, $1.75 million agree-

Detroit outfielder Kirk Gibson reluctantly re-signed with the Tigers after testing the free-agent waters and then suffered an early-season ankle injury that forced him to miss a large chunk of the 1986 season.

ment.

Of the free agents who refused salary arbitration, all but two re-signed with their former team. The exceptions were infielder-outfielder Juan Beniquez, who hooked on with the Baltimore Orioles after California chose not to keep him, and infielder Kurt Bevacqua, who was released by the San Diego Padres.

The absence of bidding prompted Fehr, the player union boss, to file a grievance on February 3 charging that the owners had conspired in their non-pursuit of free agents. He pointed out that the labor agreement prohibits concerted action by either the clubs or players and requested damages and other remedies for any free agent who might have been considered hurt by the alleged collusion.

"It's a troublesome matter and it's pretty apparent to everybody what has been going on," Fehr commented. "If you read the newspapers, you get the impression that somebody's fixed the market."

Fehr expressed hope there would be a decision on the collusion charge "before too much of the season goes by." As it turned out, other grievance proceedings prevented baseball's arbitrator, Roberts, from launching hearings on the free-agent issue until late in June. And then the Player Relations Committee touched off another brouhaha by firing the arbitrator on August 5.

In explaining the surprising move, Rona said he felt it was impossible to continue with Roberts after his "shocking" decision that declared invalid the random drug-testing clauses. "The dismissal of Roberts was based solely on his decision to void drug-testing clauses," Rona added.

The Basic Agreement allows either side to dismiss an arbitrator, something the union had done four times and the PRC once previously. None of the other dismissals, however, occurred in the middle of a hearing, and Fehr promptly filed a grievance against the PRC's action. The problems between the two parties took another odd turn August 21 when the PRC filed unfair labor practices charges against the Players Association because the union had not yet formally signed the new Basic Agreement that was adopted in memorandum form to end the '85 baseball strike.

Richard I. Bloch of Washington, D.C., who was ousted as baseball's impartial arbitrator by the players in 1985, was the choice of both sides to hear the case involving Roberts' dismissal. In his decision announced September 11, Bloch ruled the PRC had acted incorrectly when it fired Roberts in the midst of the proceedings. Roberts subsequently resumed the hearings on the free-agent collusion charge. Meantime, the representatives of the two sides selected George Nicolau of New York City as baseball's new arbitrator on September 8.

In reducing rosters to 24 active players, the clubs claimed the elimination of one player represented a savings of more than $100,000 per team, counting salary, travel expenses, etc. While the Basic Agreement calls for 25-man rosters, it also contains a proviso stating that clubs must have 24 players on the active list at all times. The Players Association contended this provision was meant to be used only on an individual club basis, not on a collective basis, and challenged the move, but the 24-player limit remained in effect from opening day until September 1, when rosters can be expanded to 40.

The hard line mounted by some clubs in seeking to reduce expenses included edicts providing for contracts of no more than one season, elimination of incentives other than possibly the Cy Young or Most Valuable Player awards, no loans, no interest on deferred payments, elimination of non-trade clauses and even the waiving of rights accruing to a player who, during the life of a contract, reaches the 10/5 mark (10 years in the majors, including the last five with the same club).

In midsummer the Kansas City Royals revealed a drastic shift in contract policy. The first indication of a change came when co-Owner Avron Fogelman, who a year earlier had signed George Brett, Willie Wilson and Dan Quisenberry to so-called lifetime contracts that will continue to pay them long after they retire from baseball, conceded that such pacts likely are a thing of the past. "I don't regret doing it, but I don't think of it as being a smart business approach," Fogelman said. "It's just smarter business to pay somebody every year based on what they've accomplished."

The Royals further revised their approach several weeks later when General Manager John Schuerholz announced that Kansas City would offer only one-year contracts in the future. Several other clubs adopted a similar position, especially after the drug-testing clauses were voided.

The owners' attempts to cut back drew support from one unexpected source late in January. Catcher Butch Wynegar, who received a three-year, $2.2 million contract to re-sign as a free agent with the New York Yankees, caused some waves in the players' union when he was quoted as suggesting that baseball salaries were unrealistic and that the clubs' "wild spending" for free agents had to stop for the good of the game. "I agree with the owners," Wynegar said. "The salaries had to stop somewhere. The players are paid too much."

Despite the cost-containment measures, salaries continued to escalate at what management termed "an alarming rate." Information released by the Player Relations Committee pointed out that the opening-day payrolls of $283,941,298 for 658 players, including 34 on the disabled list, represented a 12 percent increase over the previous year's total of $252,720,818. The PRC data also showed the average salary rising from $364,677 a year earlier to $431,521 and disclosed that 15 clubs were spending more than $10 million on player salaries in contrast to 11 teams the year before. The New York Yankees headed the pack with an average salary of $617,000, followed by the Atlanta Braves at $610,116 and the Chicago Cubs at $594,027. The report claimed 55 players were drawing salaries of $1 million or more as compared to 33 the previous season.

Late in the year, USA Today published salary data for all players appearing on a major league roster on August 31. The newspaper said the figures were based on documents filed with the PRC and Players Association plus information obtained from team officials or player agents. It also pointed out that the base salaries shown included deferred payments and prorated signing bonuses. The data revealed a total of 59 players in the million-dollar class for 1986.

Gary Carter of the New York Mets was acknowledged as the highest-paid player at $2,160,714, including $200,000 in incentive bonuses. Mike Schmidt of the Philadelphia Phillies ranked second at $2,136,666, of which $200,000 was a bonus for winning the MVP award. A list of the million-dollar athletes—or the top-salaried player—on each team follows:

American League: Baltimore Orioles—Fred Lynn, $1,190,000; Cal Ripken, $1,150,000; Boston Red Sox—Jim Rice, $1,984,423; Wade Boggs, $1,350,000; Tom Seaver, $1,132,652; Bob Stanley,

$1,060,000; Dwight Evans, $1,017,757; Tony Armas, $1,000,000; California Angels—Doug DeCinces, $1,200,000; Reggie Jackson, $1,102,946; Donnie Moore, $1,000,000; Chicago White Sox—Rich Dotson, $975,000; Cleveland Indians—Andre Thornton, $1,100,000; Detroit Tigers—Kirk Gibson, $1,200,000; Kansas City Royals—George Brett, $1,471,429; Willie Wilson, $1,175,000; Lonnie Smith, $1,000,000; Milwaukee Brewers—Paul Molitor, $1,160,000; Minnesota Twins—Bert Blyleven, $1,450,000; Kent Hrbek, $1,060,000; New York Yankees—Dave Winfield, $1,886,714; Rickey Henderson, $1,570,000; Don Mattingly, $1,375,000; Willie Randolph, $1,060,000; Oakland A's—Joaquin Andujar, $1,233,333; Carney Lansford, $1,200,000; Seattle Mariners—Jim Beattie, $575,000; Texas Rangers—Gary Ward, $865,000; Toronto Blue Jays—Bill Caudill, $1,233,333; Dave Stieb, $1,033,333.

National League: Atlanta Braves—Dale Murphy, $1,825,000; Bob Horner, $1,800,000; Bruce Sutter, $1,729,167; Ken Griffey, $1,050,000; Ted Simmons, $1,000,000; Chicago Cubs—Rick Sutcliffe, $1,530,000; Ron Cey, $1,400,000; Cincinnati Reds—Mario Soto, $1,150,000; John Denny, $1,083,333; Dave Parker, $1,100,000; Pete Rose, $1,000,000; Houston Astros—Nolan Ryan, $1,125,000; Bob Knepper, $1,000,000; Los Angeles Dodgers—Fernando Valenzuela, $1,600,000; Pedro Guerrero, $1,370,000; Jerry Reuss, $1,000,000; Orel Hershiser, $1,000,000; Montreal Expos—Tim Raines, $1,515,000; Andre Dawson, $1,047,000; Jason Thompson (released in July), $1,000,000; New York Mets—Gary Carter, $2,160,714; George Foster (released late in August), $1,800,000; Keith Hernandez, $1,650,000; Dwight Gooden, $1,320,000; Philadelphia Phillies—Mike Schmidt, $2,136,666; Steve Carlton (released in June), $1,000,000; Pittsburgh Pirates—Steve Kemp (released in May), $1,470,000; Tony Pena, $1,225,000; Larry McWilliams, $1,080,000; St. Louis Cardinals—Ozzie Smith, $1,940,000; Jack Clark, $1,300,000; John Tudor, $1,000,000; San Diego Padres—Steve Garvey, $1,250,000; Garry Templeton, $1,103,018; Rich Gossage, $1,046,761; LaMarr Hoyt, $1,000,000; San Francisco Giants—Jeff Leonard, $900,000.

Because of trades and releases, the team payrolls as of August 31 obviously differed from the PRC's opening-day figures. The 1986 total for each club, as well as the average and median salaries, both excluding incentives, were listed by USA Today as follows:

American League

Club	*Players	Total	Average
Baltimore	25	$11,108,300	$444,332
Boston	27	14,702,239	544,527
California	25	11,746,812	469,872
Chicago	30	9,353,040	311,768
Cleveland	29	7,195,000	248,103
Detroit	26	12,254,047	471,309
Kansas City	27	12,706,198	470,599
Milwaukee	24	7,425,475	309,394
Minnesota	25	8,896,000	355,840
New York	27	15,780,880	584,477
Oakland	29	9,318,738	321,335
Seattle	27	4,637,309	171,752
Texas	25	5,768,119	230,724
Toronto	27	11,110,380	411,495
Totals	373	142,002,537	380,703

National League

Club	*Players	Total	Average
Atlanta	26	$15,852,786	$609,722
Chicago	24	13,894,832	578,951
Cincinnati	28	11,171,388	398,978
Houston	24	10,009,576	417,065
Los Angeles	29	14,271,276	492,112
Montreal	31	10,337,464	333,464
New York	25	11,573,714	462,948
Philadelphia	27	9,667,666	358,061
Pittsburgh	26	6,688,000	257,230
St. Louis	27	9,263,902	343,107
San Diego	25	11,609,186	464,367
San Francisco	28	7,594,500	271,232
Totals	320	131,934,290	412,294

*Includes players on disabled list.

The salaries being paid to current performers weren't the only concern of ownership. Financial commitments to players who had been traded or released also weighed heavily on many clubs. A report issued by the Player Relations Committee in June disclosed that major league teams were obligated to pay $56.7 million in long-term contracts to players who no longer were on their rosters. The data indicated there were 117 players being paid from 1983 through 2014 by teams that either swapped or dropped them.

Several months later, USA Today revealed that information it had obtained showed the clubs were shelling out $33,442,500 to 48 players with guaranteed contracts who had been released in the last year alone. The Atlanta Braves, Pittsburgh Pirates, Chicago Cubs and New York Yankees were among those with the heaviest obligations. Shortly before the season opened, the Braves released three pitchers to whom they owed approximately $3.7 million—Len Barker, who was due $2.71 over three years; Rick Camp, who had a $600,000 contract, and Pascual Perez, $350,000. Players cut by the Pirates included outfielder Steve Kemp, whose contract called for $1,470,000 in 1986 and $1,570,000 in '87; infielder Johnny LeMaster, due $400,000 in both 1986 and 1987; outfielders Sixto Lezcano, $500,000, and Lee Mazzilli, $600,000 for both 1986 and 1987, and first baseman

Jason Thompson, who was traded to Montreal just before the season began with the Pirates agreeing to pick up $400,000 of his $1,000,000 contract in both 1986 and '87. The Expos subsequently released Thompson in midseason.

Five players dropped by the Cubs prior to opening day or shortly after the season began had contracts calling for a total of $2 million. They were pitchers Dick Ruthven, whose contract was for $800,000 plus a $250,000 buyout; Warren Brusstar, $475,000, and Matt Keough, $100,000; infielder Richie Hebner, $100,000, and outfielder Gary Woods, $325,000. The New York Yankees still were paying outfielder Omar Moreno, released in August 1985, a salary of $500,000 in 1986 and owed him $600,000 for 1987, while infielder Dale Berra, released in midseason, had a contract calling for $557,500 in 1986, $657,500 in '87 and $757,500 in '88.

Besides eliminating or cutting back on the length of multi-year contracts, management placed incentive and attendance clauses and buyout stipulations under serious review because of costly experiences. When the New York Mets released veteran outfielder George Foster in late August, they not only had to pay the remainder of his $1,800,000 contract, but also were obligated for two buyout provisions of $500,000 each for 1987 and 1988. In the cases of two other veterans, third baseman Ron Cey of the Chicago Cubs and outfielder Reggie Jackson of the California Angels, both profited handsomely from attendance bonuses. Cey collected $400,000 and Jackson earned $127,946 extra based on 1986 turnstile counts. Meanwhile, under terms of the contract that Kent Tekulve brought along from Pittsburgh, the Philadelphia Phillies had to pay the veteran relief specialist $5,000 for each game he pitched beyond 55 appearances in a season—or $90,000 in incentive pay in 1986 above his $800,000 base salary.

While information on player salaries has become readily available in recent years, the fiscal data on club operations continues to be difficult to obtain because most teams are privately held. However, the New York Times secured a financial statement on the New York Mets that was distributed by the investment firm of Dillon, Read & Co. in connection with the August sale of Doubleday & Co., the publishing firm that held majority ownership of the Mets. The figures showed that for the fiscal year ending April 30, 1986, the Mets had a pre-tax profit of $9,564,000. This was after experiencing losses of $2,256,000 and $9,058,000, respectively, for the two preceding years.

At the general managers' annual meeting in November, the executives were presented with a report that pointed out that players generally fall off in performance after signing multi-year deals. The data, which was compiled by the Players Relations Committee, indicated that 51.8 percent of non-pitchers experienced a decrease in performance the first season after getting a multi-year contract while 34.2 percent enjoyed an increase in production and 14 percent did about the same as before. The percentages were 53.8, 37.5 and 8.7, respectively, for the second year and 57.5, 36.3 and 6.3 for the third. During those three seasons, the batting averages of players with multi-year contracts fell from a combined .280 to .261, according to the report.

In the case of pitchers, performances decreased for 37.7 percent the first year while 22.6 percent experienced an increase and 39.6 remained the same. The percentages for the second year were 47.9, 27.1 and 25.0, respectively, and 58.3, 25.0 and 16.7 for the third, the PRC data disclosed.

Salary arbitration also remained a prime concern of management. The large awards by some arbitrators exerted an upward pressure on the overall salary structure, frequently forcing teams to sign players for more than they felt was justified. Eight players who filed for arbitration in January sought salaries of $1 million or more, though five avoided a hearing by reaching agreement on contract terms. Pitcher Orel Hershiser of the Los Angeles Dodgers won his case while Boston teammates Wade Boggs and Rich Gedman lost.

The five who signed prior to the February hearings were Fernando Valenzuela of Los Angeles, who accepted an offer of $5.5 million for three years; John Tudor of St. Louis, who received $3.15 million for three years; Tim Raines of Montreal, $1.5 million for one year; Don Mattingly of the New York Yankees, $1.375 million for one year, and Dwight Gooden of the New York Mets, who at age 21 became baseball's youngest millionaire when he signed for $1.32 million for one year.

Altogether, a record of 159 players filed for salary arbitration, though most agreed to terms before the hearings. Other rich multi-year settlements included: Jody Davis, Chicago Cubs, $2.9 million for three years; Mike Scioscia, Los Angeles, $2.675 million for three years; Mike Scott, Houston, and Glenn Wilson, Philadelphia, both

$2 million for three years, and Jesse Orosco, New York Mets, $1.85 million for two years.

Of the 35 cases that went to arbitration, the players emerged victorious in 15 and the clubs in 20. Although he lost, Boggs set a record for the highest salary ever awarded in baseball arbitration—$1.35 million. The Red Sox third baseman, who a year earlier won a $1 million salary in arbitration, had requested $1.85 million for 1986. The most significant decision in the judgment of some observers involved pitcher Charlie Leibrandt of Kansas City. His was the first of 10 cases involving starting pitchers. When Roberts, one of 12 arbitrators who heard the 35 cases, ruled that Leibrandt should receive his proposed figure of $770,000 and not the $550,000 offered by the Royals, the stage was set for most of the other starters. This included the $925,000 awarded Leibrandt's teammate, Bret Saberhagen, and the $1 million granted to Hershiser.

The 15 players who won their salary arbitration cases, with the club's offer in parentheses, were: Hershiser, $1,000,000 ($600,000); Saberhagen, $925,000 ($625,000); Leibrandt, $770,000 ($500,000); Brett Butler, Cleveland, $850,000 ($600,000); Bryn Smith, Montreal, $700,000 ($500,000); Frank Viola, Minnesota, $674,000 ($525,000); Dave LaPoint, Detroit, $550,000 ($410,000); Ed Lynch, New York Mets, $530,000 ($400,000); Steve Balboni, Kansas City, $525,000 ($350,000); Phil Bradley, Seattle, $475,000 ($375,000); Marty Barrett, Boston, $435,000 ($325,000); Ron Romanick, California, $425,000 ($250,000); Bob Kearney, Seattle, $300,000 ($215,000); Ricky Horton, St. Louis, $275,000 ($215,000); and Dave Van Gorder, Cincinnati, $150,000 ($75,000).

The salaries of the 20 who lost, with the player's rejected figure in parentheses, were: Boggs, $1,350,000 ($1,850,000); Gary Ward, Texas, $865,000 ($930,000); Rich Gedman, Boston, $650,000 ($1,000,000); Julio Franco, Cleveland, $575,000 ($740,000); Gary Gaetti, Minnesota, $515,000 ($675,000); Ron Darling, New York Mets, $440,000 ($615,000); Ron Kittle, Chicago White Sox, $400,000 ($500,000); Mike Moore, Seattle, $400,000 ($530,000); Alvin Davis, Seattle, $400,000 ($550,000); Eddie Milner, Cincinnati, $350,000 ($530,000); Wally Backman, New York Mets, $325,000 ($425,000); Bill Dawley, Houston, $325,000 ($435,000); Greg Brock, Los Angeles, $325,000 ($440,000); Gary Pettis, California, $300,000 ($425,000); Frank DiPino, Houston, $280,000 ($380,000); Kevin McReynolds, San Diego, $275,000 ($450,000); Jeff Dedmon, Atlanta, $200,000 ($270,000); Tim Teufel, New York Mets, $200,000 ($350,000); Tim Laudner, Minnesota, $155,000 ($250,000), and Alan Knicely, Philadelphia, $80,000 ($140,000).

Fortunately for baseball, action on the playing field was good enough to overshadow negative off-field issues.

Roger Clemens provided much of the excitement. Just eight months after undergoing surgery on his pitching shoulder, the 23-year-old Boston Red Sox righthander rocketed his way into the record books when he struck out 20 Seattle batters April 29 in a 3-1 victory at Fenway Park. That sensational performance was merely a portent of things to come. Clemens won 14 of his first 15 starts before Toronto pinned him with his first defeat, a 4-2 decision on July 2. He went on to become the majors leagues' biggest winner with a 24-4 record and also led the American League with a 2.48 earned-run average while striking out 238 batters in 254 innings.

Two ironies marked Clemens' strikeout masterpiece. A fourth-inning error actually worked in Clemens' favor and an old friend was the fireballer's record-tying 19th victim. Don Baylor, subbing at first base, dropped a routine pop foul off Gorman Thomas' bat in the fourth, giving Clemens the unwanted opportunity to come back and fan Thomas. In the ninth inning, Seattle's leadoff batter was Spike Owen. Clemens made his former University of Texas teammate and soon-to-be Red Sox shortstop victim No. 19 and followed by fanning Phil Bradley before Ken Phelps grounded out to end the game.

There were two 1986 no-hitters, both of the unusual variety.

Houston's Mike Scott pitched his masterpiece on September 25, giving an Astrodome crowd of 32,808 more than it had bargained for. The big crowd, anticipating the Astros' West Division title clinching, watched the big righthander strike out 13 batters and permit just three players to reach base in whipping San Francisco, 2-0. It marked the first time in baseball history that a pitcher had thrown a title-clinching no-hitter. Watching from the opposing dugout was Giants Manager Roger Craig, the man who had taught Scott the split-finger fastball, the pitch that turned around his career.

Scott's next start on October 2, his final tuneup prior to the playoffs, also was dramatic. Again pitching against the Giants, but this time in Candlestick Park, Scott

California righthander Don Sutton gets a warm greeting from catcher Bob Boone after recording career victory No. 300 on June 18 against Texas.

pitched perfect baseball through six innings. But in the seventh, his final inning, two doubles produced a San Francisco run. The Astros went on to win in the 10th, 2-1, but Scott wasn't around to improve on his 18-10 record. He finished the regular season with a league-leading 2.22 ERA and struck out 306 batters in 275⅓ innings, thus joining Sandy Koufax, Steve Carlton and J.R. Richard as the only National Leaguers to record 300 strikeouts in a season.

Joe Cowley of the Chicago White Sox threw the other no-hitter, but it wasn't pretty. Cowley's 7-1 victory over the California Angels at Anaheim Stadium September 19 included seven bases on balls. In the sixth inning, Cowley walked the first three Angels and was close to being lifted. But he induced the next batter to pop out and retired Reggie Jackson on a sacrifice fly before recording the third out. Cowley already had entered his name in the record books earlier in the season. On May 28, in his second start after being recalled from Buffalo (American Association), he struck out the first seven Texas batters he faced before Orlando Mercado flied out to snap the streak. Curiously, Cowley fanned only one more batter before being knocked from the mound in the fifth inning of a 6-3 loss.

Cowley's strikeout feat, a modern record for the start of a game, did not stand for long. It was surpassed September 23 by Jim Deshaies, a rookie lefthander with Houston. In a contest at the Astrodome, Deshaies struck out the first eight Los Angeles Dodgers to come to the plate while breezing to a two-hit, 4-0 triumph. A pinch-hitter, rookie Larry See, broke the strikeout string. Deshaies struck out only two more batters the rest of the game.

Don Sutton of the California Angels became the fourth active member of the exclusive 300-victory club. He reached the milestone June 18 by checking Texas on three hits, 5-1, before 37,044 fans at Anaheim Stadium. After the historic victory, the 41-year-old righthander commented: "I've always been an unspectacular grinder, a mechanic," a reference to the fact that he was a 20-game winner only once in his 21 seasons in the majors. Sutton attained another goal September 7 when he made his 700th start, a total topped only by Cy Young with 818. And on closing day, October 5, he boosted his innings pitched over the 5,000 level, making him the 11th pitcher in history to reach that mark. By finishing 15-11 for the season, Sutton boosted his career victory output to 310.

Veteran pitchers Steve Carlton (above) and Tom Seaver donned new uniforms as they approached the conclusion of their spectacular careers.

The other active 300-game winners—Steve Carlton, Tom Seaver and Phil Niekro—all changed clubs during the season. Carlton, in fact, wore the uniforms of three teams. After logging a disappointing 4-8 mark with Philadelphia, he was handed his release on June 24. San Francisco signed him July 4 and, by way of celebration, the 41-year-old lefthander briefly interrupted his long-standing silence by speaking with the media for the first time since 1978. Carlton proceeded to lose three of four decisions with the Giants and was released August 7. Five days later, he joined the Chicago White Sox and went on to record a 4-3 mark, raising his lifetime victory total to 323.

Seaver, also 41, began the season with the White Sox but was traded June 29 to the Boston Red Sox for outfielder Steve Lyons. The swap was made to accommodate Seaver's request to be dealt to a team near his Connecticut home. Several nagging injuries combined to limit him to an overall 7-13 record, giving him 311 career victories.

Niekro, the major leagues' oldest player at 47, went to spring training with the New York Yankees, for whom he had notched win No. 300 on closing day in 1985. But on March 28, 10 days prior to the Yankees' season opener, New York cut him loose while retaining brother Joe. Phil subsequently signed with Cleveland and became the Indians' second-leading winner at 11-11. He finished the season tied with Seaver at 311 victories.

The season also featured a number of noteworthy batting feats.

Bob Horner produced a bright spot in the Atlanta Braves' otherwise dismal season by smashing a record-tying four home runs in a July 6 game against Montreal in Atlanta. The Braves first baseman tagged Expos starter Andy McGaffigan for bases-empty shots in the second and fourth innings and a three-run blast in the fifth. He completed his barrage with a two-out, solo homer off reliever Jeff Reardon in the ninth. Horner became only the 11th player in major league history to hit four homers in a game and the first to do it in a nine-inning contest since Willie Mays in 1961. Even with Horner's prodigious contribution, the Braves lost, 11-8, before a slim Sunday afternoon turnout of 18,153.

At age 40, Reggie Jackson showed that he still possesses some of his old power and flair for the dramatic. On September 18, he blasted three homers, good for seven RBIs, as the Angels routed Kansas City, 18-3, at Anaheim. He drilled a two-run homer off Dennis Leonard in the first inning, delivered a three-run clout against rookie Dave Cone in the fourth and added a two-run drive off Dan Quisenberry in the eighth. Although he batted only .241 for the year, Jackson hit 18 home runs, raising his career total to 548. This enabled him to pass Jimmie Foxx and Mickey Mantle while climbing into sixth place on the all-time home run list.

Wade Boggs overcame adversity to capture his third American League batting championship in four years. The Boston third baseman's misfortunes began June 9 with an unusual accident in his Toronto hotel room. While removing his cowboy boots, he lost his balance, fell and cracked a rib. Eight days later, Boggs' mother was killed in a traffic accident in Tampa, causing him to miss six games. Though the tragedy weighed heavily, Boggs withstood a strong challenge by Yankee slugger Don Mattingly, the A.L.'s 1984 batting leader, to win his second straight crown. An anticipated season-ending, four-game showdown at Fenway Park was voided when a hamstring injury forced Boggs to sit out the series. Mattingly went 8 for 19 as the Yankees swept, but fell five points short of catching Boggs, .357 to .352.

Injury played an even more telling role in the National League batting race. Shortstop Hubie Brooks of Montreal was leading N. L. hitters at .340 when a thumb injury brought his season to an abrupt end August 2, leaving him well short of the 502 official at-bats needed to qualify for a batting title. Teammate Tim Raines, his closest rival at the time, went on to edge Los Angeles second baseman Steve Sax, .334 to .332, for the title.

In addition to Clemens, four other pitchers achieved the 20-victory level. Only one, Detroit's Jack Morris, had done it previously. After a rough start, the Tigers ace came back strong and produced a 21-8 record with a major league-leading six shutouts. Dodgers lefthander Fernando Valenzuela reached the 20-win plateau for the first time on Manager Tommy Lasorda's 59th birthday (September 22) by posting a two-hit, 9-2 decision at Houston. The Dodgers southpaw finished with a 21-11 record. Another lefthanded Mexican, Milwaukee's Ted Higuera, checked in with a 20-11 mark while Mike Krukow of the San Francisco Giants gained victory No. 20 on the final day of the season, beating Los Angeles, 11-2.

Dave Righetti, the New York Yankees' lefthanded relief ace, established a major league record with 46 saves. This broke by one the mark shared by Kansas City's

Boston third baseman Wade Boggs overcame personal problems to win his third American League batting title in the last four seasons.

Quisenberry and former St. Louis ace Bruce Sutter. On the basis of two points for each save and each victory in relief, with one point deducted for every defeat, Righetti's 46 saves and 8-8 record translated into 100 points and earned him the American League's Rolaids Relief Man Award. Don Aase of Baltimore was runnerup with 73 points. In the National League, St. Louis rookie Todd Worrell registered a league-leading 36 saves and a 9-10 record to capture the Relief Man Award with 80 points. Montreal's Reardon finished second with 75.

Toronto outfielder Jesse Barfield was the year's home-run king with 40, while Cleveland outfielder Joe Carter led both leagues with 121 RBIs. Philadelphia third baseman Mike Schmidt paced the National League in home runs (37), RBIs (119) and slugging percentage (.547). Mattingly led all players in slugging (.573), hits (238) and doubles (53). Boggs had the best on-base percentage in the American League (.453), while Raines and New York's Keith Hernandez tied for on-base percentage honors in the N.L. at .413. Vince Coleman of St. Louis and Rickey Henderson of the Yankees repeated as league stolen base champions with 107 and 87, respectively. It marked the seventh consecutive year that Henderson has topped the American League in thefts.

The season was punctuated by some unusual episodes. Stiff disciplinary measures were taken against five players and court actions were brought against several others for off-the-field incidents. The focus of the most celebrated incidents were pitchers Dennis (Oil Can) Boyd of Boston and Rich (Goose) Gossage of San Diego.

Boyd's troubles began in spring training. Severe weight loss (he was down to 138 pounds) and liver trouble that was diagnosed as a non-contagious form of hepatitis sent him to the hospital briefly. Later he was tardy for several workouts and exhibition games, resulting in a fine. Once the season started, however, Boyd settled down. But on July 10 he went into a tirade in the Red Sox clubhouse upon learning he had not been selected for the All-Star Game. After ripping off his uniform and verbally assaulting Manager John McNamara and others, he left Fenway Park before that night's game. When he failed to report the next evening, the Red Sox suspended him and announced he would have to apologize to his teammates before he'd be reinstated. Boyd did apologize on July 13, but the night of the All-Star Game he had a run-in with police near his suburban Chelsea home and was suspended indefinitely by the club. Boyd subsequently entered University of Massachusetts Medical Center in Worcester on July 17 for a week of tests. While he reportedly tested negative for drugs, he was placed on a counseling and support system. The Red Sox finally reinstated Boyd August 1, but his six-week victory drouth didn't end until August 21.

Criticism of Padres Owner Joan Kroc and her son-in-law, team President Ballard Smith, was Gossage's un-doing. The veteran reliever first angered management June 6 by calling Kroc and Smith "gutless, spineless people" and commenting that Smith "doesn't know anything about running a club" after he announced that San Diego players would no longer be allowed to drink beer in the clubhouse. Two months later, after a statement by Smith that the club would not offer multiyear contracts until a form of drug testing was in place, Gossage again popped off publicly in an interview with a New York writer. As a consequence, the Padres announced August 29 that the pitcher was being suspended without pay for the balance of the season. On the basis of his $1.046 million salary, the suspension figured to cost Gossage more than $100,000. His teammates threatened to boycott an August 30 doubleheader at Montreal, but instead drew up a written protest. The Players Association also joined the dispute by filing a grievance contending management did not have the right to suspend a player for speaking his mind. The union urged Gossage to allow the matter to go to arbitration, but on September 18, the eve of the scheduled hearing, the pitcher and the club made peace. In exchange for reinstatement, Gossage agreed to donate $25,000 to a charity—the Ronald McDonald House—and to issue public apologies to Kroc, Smith and the McDonald's fast-food empire, all of which he had slurred.

Outfielder Ken Griffey drew what was believed to be the largest monetary penalty ($10,000) in New York Yankee history when he failed to show up for a June 17 game against Boston. The reason behind the mysterious one-day disappearance reportedly was a personal problem. Griffey, who was back in the lineup the next day, was traded by the Yankees to Atlanta June 30 for outfielder Claudell Washington and shortstop Paul Zuvella.

Dave Kingman, Oakland's designated hitter, was slapped with a $3,500 fine by A's officials after he had a live rat delivered in a box to Susan Fornoff, baseball writer for the Sacramento Bee, in the Kansas City press box on June 23. A note attached to the rat's tail read: "My name is Susan." The incident capped what Fornoff described as a long campaign of harassment waged by Kingman against the female reporter since she started covering the A's a year earlier.

Cincinnati pitcher John Denny also found himself in difficulty after an alleged run-in with a member of the media. Bruce Schoenfeld, a baseball writer for the Cincinnati Post, filed a criminal assault charge May 15 charging that Denny grabbed him around the neck, banged his head against the wall and then threw him to the floor prior to a May 14 game in Philadelphia. Denny, who earlier in the season threw a bat at a dugout TV camera, was placed on rehabilitative probation for six months by the Philadelphia district attorney.

Another celebrated disciplinary case was resolved shortly before the season opened when Ueberroth commuted the suspension of Oakland pitcher Joaquin Andujar. Andujar had drawn a 10-day sentence for bumping umpire Don Denkinger in the seventh game of the 1985 World Series while pitching for St. Louis, but the commissioner, after reviewing the case, reduced the suspension to five days.

Four New York Mets spent the early-morning hours of July 19 in a Houston jail following their arrest for an altercation with off-duty police officers. The four—infielder Tim Teufel and pitchers Ron Darling, Bob Ojeda and Rick Aguilera—were involved in a scuffle outside a popular Houston bar frequented by visiting athletes. Teufel and Darling were charged with aggravated assault and Ojeda and Aguilera with hindering arrest. All four were fined by the Mets, with Teufel and Darling facing possible criminal charges.

Other noteworthy or unusual incidents during the season included:

• President Ronald Reagan helped open the season by delivering the ceremonial first pitch at Baltimore April 7 and watching two innings from the Orioles dugout before heading back to Washington.

• An April 26 game at the Hubert Humphrey Metrodome, home of the Minnesota Twins, was halted briefly in the eighth inning when strong winds tore a hole in the inner roof. As the lights and speakers, suspended from the roof, sagged toward the playing field, players and fans scurried for safety. When all 20 blower fans used to inflate the inner roof were turned on, the roof rose to its accustomed height of about 175 feet above the field and play resumed. But the visiting California Angels further spoiled the night for Minnesota fans by rallying for six ninth-inning runs and a 7-6 victory.

• A skunk that sauntered onto the field delayed a May 3 game at San Diego for seven minutes in the seventh inning. "I saw the crowd standing up and looking past me," first baseman Steve Garvey said. "Then I saw it (the skunk coming toward him) . . . and thought: 'What should I do? I don't want to be sprayed with eau de skunk.' " Groundskeepers quickly, and carefully, escorted the uninvited guest from the field.

• With the Cubs and the parent Chicago Tribune Co. failing in attempts to overturn ordinances banning night baseball at Wrigley Field, National League owners voted unanimously in May to have the Cubs play home games in St. Louis' Busch Stadium if they qualified for the 1986 League Championship Series. Pressure from provisions in baseball's TV contract forced the magnates to act, though the matter became moot when the Cubs failed to challenge for the division title.

• Memorial Day found four N.L. teams enjoying an open date. Just a few years ago, holidays were considered big paydays and regularly featured numerous doubleheaders. However, holidays have become less attractive in recent years, with doubleheaders becoming another casualty of the new economic reality.

• Fog forced termination of a May 27 game in Cleveland with Boston leading, 2-0, and two out in the bottom of the sixth inning. The contest was called after a one-hour, 35-minute wait. "First I couldn't see the scoreboard, and then the center fielder (Tony Armas) disappeared," commented Boston pitcher Mike Brown, who pitched five innings of the abbreviated shutout. "When second base grew dim, I knew we were in trouble."

• Kansas City's gamble in making football star Bo Jackson, the 1985 Heisman Trophy winner as a running back at Auburn, a fourth-round choice in the draft paid off when he signed with the Royals June 20. Jackson, a 23-year-old outfielder, passed up a reported five-year, $5 million-plus contract offer from the National Football League's Tampa Bay Buccaneers in favor of a three-year, $1.066 million package from the Royals. Jackson began his professional baseball career at Memphis (Southern) and was called up to Kansas City in September.

• Marla Collins, a 28-year-old ballgirl at Wrigley Field, was dismissed July 22 when Chicago Cubs officials learned she was featured in an eight-page Playboy magazine spread entitled "Belle of the Ball Club." For the last five years, Collins, attired in shorts and a Cubs shirt, had occupied a seat near the visitors' dugout and kept the umpires supplied with baseballs.

• Catcher Ron Hassey found himself included in a trade for the third time in less than eight months—all involving the same two teams. When the Yankees shipped him to the White Sox with two other players July 30 in what some observers called the Britt Burns payback deal, the New Yorkers received outfielder Ron Kittle, catcher Joel Skinner and infielder Wayne Tolleson. The Yankees originally sent Hassey to the White Sox in a December 1985 trade for Burns, who sat out the entire '86 season because of a chronic right hip problem that was diagnosed as osteoarthritis. Hassey returned to New York in a seven-player February 13 trade that sent pitcher Neil Allen to Chicago.

• The year's most bizarre postponement occurred August 29 in Montreal. Despite perfect weather, that evening's game against San Diego was called off following explosions in the 10-story tower above Olympic Stadium. Welders engaged in construction of the stadium's new retractable roof were working between the eighth and ninth floors when a tank of acetylene gas caught fire that afternoon. Flames spread to other tanks of acetylene and oxygen. Windswept flames and smoke billowed for approximately 90 minutes and some flaming debris fell onto the playing field, leaving burn marks on the artificial turf. Stadium officials claimed the blaze caused no structural damage to the tower and said the retractable roof should be ready for the '87 season.

Nine clubs changed managers during the year, one of them twice.

The San Diego Padres made two managerial changes, the first coming at a hurriedly called early-morning February press conference in San Diego as the team was preparing to begin spring training in Yuma, Ariz. Owner Joan Kroc and Dick Williams both appeared at the media session, which produced an announcement that Williams would not be returning as manager, even though he had one year remaining on a three-year contract. At the same time it was disclosed that Ozzie Virgil, Williams' close friend, had resigned. The next day, the Padres named Steve Boros as their new skipper. He had served the last 15 months as the club's director of minor league instruction.

Earlier in the winter Williams had indicated he was considering quitting when General Manager Jack McKeon dismissed Virgil. In an attempt to smooth over the situation, Mrs. Kroc rehired Virgil, but further evidence of discord surfaced when Williams subsequently dropped coach Harry Dunlop from his staff. Boros' first move on assuming the helm was to rehire Dunlop.

The season was barely a month old when the managerial axe fell again. On May 8, the Seattle Mariners, struggling with a 9-19 record, fired Chuck Cottier. Coach Marty Martinez directed the team that night. The next day it was disclosed that Williams had accepted a three-year contract to become the Mariners' sixth pilot in 10 years. He promptly dropped third base coach Jim Mahoney to make room for Virgil. In taking over the Seattle job, Williams equalled the record held by Jimmie Dykes for most teams managed in this century—six.

Three clubs, including both Chicago teams, dumped their managers in June. Disappointing starts prompted rumors in May that the Cubs' Jim Frey and Tony LaRussa of the White Sox were on thin ice. Frey became the first to go when, with the Cubs at 23-33, he was ousted June 12 along with third base coach Don Zimmer. Another coach, John Vukovich, served as interim pilot that day, and then Gene Michael, who had been third base coach with the Yankees, assumed the reins. Michael doubtless will long remember his June 14 debut: Not only did the Cubs bow to St. Louis, 1-0, to fall into the cellar, but he found himself the victim of an unusual ejection. Prior to the game, umpire Eric Gregg warned both managers about pitchers throwing at batters. When a Scott

Dick Williams took Seattle's managerial reins after leaving San Diego at the beginning of spring training.

Sanderson pitch sent the Cardinals' Terry Pendleton to the dirt, Gregg booted the Cubs pitcher, a move that also meant automatic ejection for the new Cubs manager.

LaRussa fell victim to front-office tinkering. Ken (Hawk) Harrelson, former player and White Sox broadcaster-turned-executive, brought in a high-powered lineup of extra coaches and consultants in the spring, including Willie Horton, Dick Allen, Moe Drabowsky and Don Drysdale. In addition, he ordered the shift of veteran catcher Carlton Fisk to left field. Early in May, amid reports that Harrelson was trying to sign Billy Martin as manager, LaRussa offered his resignation. This was followed May 9 by an unusual press conference in which Harrelson announced that LaRussa would remain and that negotiations with Martin had been called off. That same night Fisk resumed his former catching duties.

However, LaRussa's stay of execution was temporary. On June 20, with the White Sox sporting a 26-38 record, both he and his regular pitching coach, Dave Duncan, were fired. Coach Doug Rader directed the team for two games, and, on June 22, Jim Fregosi moved in as manager. Fregosi, who had been piloting Louisville (American Association), was given a contract through 1988. Like his counterpart with the Cubs, the new White Sox skipper received a surprise in his first day on the job when he discovered his uniform had his name spelled "FERGOSI."

The third manager to walk the plank in June was Jackie Moore of the Oakland A's. He was dismissed June 26 while the club, then 29-44, was visiting Kansas City. Coach Jeff Newman was named interim manager and watched the A's lose eight of 10 games during his tenure. On July 2, 10 days after his ouster in Chicago, LaRussa accepted a three-year contract as Oakland's new manager with the understanding that he'd take over the reins July 7. He brought along Duncan as his pitching coach.

In baseball's most shocking development of the year, Dick Howser was forced to step aside as Kansas City Royals manager July 18 because of a brain tumor. Howser, who led the Royals to the World Series championship the previous fall, had complained for two weeks of a stiff neck and headaches and, according to close associates, was "totally out of it" at the All-Star Game in Houston. When the Royals resumed action at Cleveland July 17 after the All-Star break, the 50-year-old Howser was absent. He entered a hospital that evening for tests that revealed a tumor the size of a golf ball in the left frontal lobe of his brain, an area that controls emotion, personality and speech. Coach Mike Ferraro, who had a malignant tumor removed from a kidney in the spring of 1983 while managing Cleveland, directed the Royals for the remainder of the season.

Howser underwent a three-hour operation in St. Luke's Hospital in Kansas City July 22. Afterward, Dr. Charles Clough, the neurosurgeon who headed the medical team, announced that the tumor was malignant and that it could not be removed completely because Howser's speech could have been affected by probing too deeply into his brain. A series of five weekly radiation treatments was prescribed. On August 12, Howser visited the Royals' clubhouse for the first time since the surgery, and he later watched several games from the stands. After a poor 40-48 showing prior to the All-Star interlude, the Royals played at a 36-38 clip under Ferraro.

To clear the air, General Manager John Schuerholz announced October 9 that the Royals were counting on Howser to return as manager in 1987. At the same time, he announced the release of Ferraro and the signing of Billy Gardner, former Minnesota manager, as the new third base coach. Early in December, after renewed tumor growth was discovered, Howser underwent an innovative three-hour operation in Huntington Memorial Hospital in Pasadena, Calif. The treatment, known as immunotherapy, included the injection of special "killer cells," transformed white blood cells called lymphocytes that attack malignancies.

Four other managers quit or were dismissed in the second half of the season.

The Minnesota Twins became the fifth American League West Division team to change managers when they fired Ray Miller September 12. Under Miller, who took the job in June 1985, the Twins compiled the A.L.'s worst record, 59-80. Coach Tom Kelly was designated to run the team through the end of the season and later was hired for 1987.

After 41 years in baseball, George Bamberger of the Milwaukee Brewers disclosed September 25 that he was retiring. His players gave him a farewell victory that evening as Ted Higuera beat Baltimore, 9-3, to become a 20-game winner. The 61-year-old Bamberger, who had previously retired as Brewers skipper in 1980, was succeeded by coach Tom Trebelhorn. Six days later, the 38-year-old Trebelhorn was officially named Milwaukee's 1987 pilot.

Ironically, he had been slated to pilot the Brewers' Helena (Pioneer) team in '86, but became a Milwaukee coach instead because of a near-tragic episode. At the start of spring training, a natural-gas heater exploded in the Brewers' new facility at Chandler, Ariz., sending a ball of fire roaring through the clubhouse. "It was like somebody dropped a bomb on us," Bamberger recalled. "We're lucky no one was killed." Eight members of the Brewers were injured, with coaches Tony Muser, Herm Starrette and Larry Haney suffering the most serious mishaps. Severe burns idled the trio for weeks and Trebelhorn turned his temporary assignment into a major league managerial opportunity.

Earl Weaver bowed out as Baltimore manager for the second time at the close of the season. He retired in 1982, but was lured back in July 1985 by a $500,000 contract. His latest departure capped one of the worst years in the club's history. After

Former Phillies and Cubs shortstop Larry Bowa guided the Las Vegas Stars to the Pacific Coast League championship and was rewarded with an offer to manage the San Diego Padres.

climbing to within 2½ games of the leading Red Sox on August 5, the Orioles went into a tailspin and wound up in the cellar for the first time in their 33-year history. The 56-year-old Weaver had disclosed privately in mid-August that he intended to quit at season's end, and Owner Edward Bennett Williams confirmed it September 9. The day after the season closed, long-time coach Cal Ripken Sr. was appointed as the new Baltimore manager.

The year's final managerial change, the second made by the San Diego Padres in nine months, occurred October 28. Dismissing Boros, they elevated Larry Bowa to the helm. Early in the year, the 40-year-old Bowa had passed up a lucrative $250,000 contract to serve as utility infielder with the New York Mets in favor of a $28,000 offer to pilot the Padres' Las Vegas farm club. He led that team to the Pacific Coast League championship. After the switch, Boros resumed his previous duties as director of minor league instruction with the Padres.

The leadership role provided by Ueberroth extended into a number of areas beyond those already mentioned. At his urging, the Official Playing Rules Committee voted in March to amend the designated-hitter rule as it applies to the World Series. Instead of employing the DH only in even-numbered years, a practice in effect since 1976, the committee approved the use of the designated hitter each year in the World Series, but only in American League parks.

Seeking to tighten clubhouse security, Ueberroth established new, stricter guidelines prior to the season. The revised regulation limited access to the playing field, clubhouse, etc., to persons officially employed by baseball and the Players Association and to accredited media representatives. Equipment salesmen, vendors and friends, business associates, agents and attorneys of players were banned. "By barring all but essential personnel from the clubhouse and its immediate environs, we will succeed in creating more professional working areas for the players and media and remove distracting elements from the game," Ueberroth said.

Seventy-nine players—the largest number ever—took advantage of the November "window" to file for free agency. The most prominent names on the list were pitcher Jack Morris and catcher Lance Parrish of Detroit, outfielders Tim Raines and Andre Dawson of Montreal and first baseman Bob Horner of Atlanta. Morris removed his name from the list, however, when, after negotiations with four teams, he chose to go to arbitration with the Tigers. The full list of those filing for free agency follows:

American League: Baltimore—Rick Dempsey, Jim Dwyer. Boston—Tony Armas, Rich Gedman, Glenn Hoffman, Joe Sambito, Tom Seaver, Dave Stapleton, Sammy Stewart. California—Bob Boone, Rick Burleson, Doug Corbett, Doug DeCinces, Brian Downing, Terry Forster, Reggie Jackson, Vern Ruhle. Chicago—Steve Carlton. Cleveland—Dickie Noles. Detroit—Larry Herndon, Jack Morris, Lance Parrish. Kansas City—Lynn Jones, Rudy Law, Jamie Quirk, Lonnie Smith. Milwaukee—Rick Cerone, Charlie Moore, Ben Oglivie. Minnesota—Roy Lee Jackson, Frank Pastore. New York—Britt Burns, Mike Fischlin, Ron Guidry, Tommy John, Willie Randolph, Gary Roenicke, Rod Scurry, Claudell Washington. Oakland—Dave Kingman, Lenn Sakata. Seattle—Jim Beattie, Steve Yeager. Texas—Toby Harrah, Darrell Porter, Gary Ward. Toronto—Jim Clancy, Cliff Johnson, Buck Martinez, Ernie Whitt.

National League: Atlanta—Doyle Alexander, Chris Chambliss, Bob Horner, David Palmer, Billy Sample. Chicago—Chris Speier. Cincinnati—Dave Concepcion, John Denny, Joe Price. Houston—Larry Andersen, Alan Ashby, Phil Garner, Dave Lopes. Los Angeles—Enos Cabell. Montreal—Andre Dawson, Wayne Krenchicki, Charlie Lea, Dennis Martinez, Bob Owchinko, Tim Raines. New York—Danny Heep, Ray Knight. Philadelphia—Tom Hume. Pittsburgh—None. St. Louis—Bob Forsch, Clint Hurdle. San Diego—Jerry Royster. San Francisco—Vida Blue, Mike LaCoss, Harry Spilman.

A team of major league all-stars visited Japan for a seven-game series against that country's best players in early November. The U.S. squad, managed by Dave Johnson, won six of the seven contests, many by lopsided scores. The series attracted approximately 239,000 fans, with crowds ranging from 27,000 to 47,000.

Ownership changes on three clubs—the Cleveland Indians, New York Mets and Philadelphia Phillies—were approved at the major leagues' annual meetings in December. Only the Cleveland deal involved a significant switch. The owners of two other teams had formally put their franchises on the block earlier in the year.

The long search for new ownership in Cleveland was climaxed July 2 when two local businessmen, brothers Richard and David Jacobs, signed an agreement to purchase the Indians. The franchise had been for sale since the death three years earlier of F. J. (Steve) O'Neill. The Jacobs brothers' primary business is a real estate development partnership which ranks as one of the largest shopping mall developers in the U.S. The Indians reportedly had an $11.5 million debt as of the fiscal year ending October 15, 1985, and also were committed to between $4 million and $13.5 million in guaranteed deferred salaries through the year 2016.

The Mets' transaction was tied in with the sale of Doubleday & Co., the publishing firm that held 95 percent of the club's stock, to the West German communications firm Bertelsman AG. Nelson Doubleday and Fred Wilpon, board chairman and president, respectively, of the Mets, paid a reported $80.75 million November 14 to acquire full control of the club on a 50-50 basis. Wilpon, who previously owned five percent, and the Doubleday firm shelled out $21.1 million—a record at the time—when they originally bought the franchise in 1980.

Bill Giles, president of the Phillies, and three of his partners purchased the Taft Broadcasting Co.'s 47.3 percent stake of the Philadelphia club late in the year for a reported $24.1 million. Giles, general partner of the group, was joined in the deal by limited partners J.D.B. Associates, Tri-Play Associates and Fitz Eugene Dixon Jr.

The San Diego Padres officially were placed on the block November 20 by Mrs. Kroc. She has headed the club since the 1984 death of her husband, Ray Kroc, founder of the McDonald's fast-food chain who bought the Padres in 1974. San Diego first baseman Steve Garvey disclosed that he was attempting to put together a group to buy the team.

Arrangements for sale of the Texas Rangers were completed early in July, but they fell through when the owners of other American League clubs unanimously rejected the proposed transaction. With his personal fortune tied up in the slumping oil business, Eddie Chiles struck a deal with Edward L. Gaylord, 68-year-old Oklahoma City media magnate. Eighteen months earlier, Gaylord had purchased approximately one-third of Chiles' 90 percent holdings in the Texas club plus five years of TV rights to Ranger games for his Fort Worth-Dallas-based superstation KTVT for a reported $20 million. Under terms of the latest transaction, Gaylord, who owns the Opryland hotel-entertainment complex in Nashville as well as numerous newspapers and radio and television stations, was to acquire the remainder of Chiles' stock and also the lease-purchase agreement on Arlington Stadium and its 140 acres of prime land for an estimated $30 million. In turning down the deal at a September 23-24 meeting in Newport Beach, Calif., American League magnates emphasized that they did not want a superstation owner to gain controlling interest in a team.

After 17 years as president of the National League, Charles (Chub) Feeney retired after the annual meetings in December. He was succeeded by A. Bartlett Giamatti, former president of Yale University. The 48-year-old Giamatti was given a five-year contract following his election at a June 9 meeting of N.L. owners in New York. The 65-year-old Feeney had been associated with the game since starting as an executive with the New York Giants in 1946.

Early in the year, Barry Rona, general counsel to the owners' Player Relations Committee for 10 years, was appointed executive director of that group to succeed Lee MacPhail, who had retired at the end of 1985.

Led by the Chicago White Sox, several clubs experienced major top-level executive changes. Roland Hemond, who was bumped aside as general manager when the White Sox named Harrelson as baseball operations director in October 1985, left the club in May to become assistant on special projects for the commissioner's office. Several weeks later, the White Sox brought in Tom Haller, who had been manager of their Birmingham (Southern) club, to become general manager. However, on September 26, the controversial Harrelson resigned. On October 30, Larry Himes, who had been scouting and player personnel director of the Angels, was appointed vice-president and general manager of the White Sox, succeeding Haller.

Other top-level personnel shifts included: Gene McHale stepped down as president of the New York Yankees in May to establish a sports marketing and consulting firm; John McHale was succeeded as president of the Montreal Expos October 1 by Claude Brochu, but remains as the Expos' chief executive officer through 1987; Woody Woodward was elevated to general manager of the Yankees early in October, replacing Clyde King, who remained as Owner George Steinbrenner's special assistant; Stan Kasten, who headed Ted Turner's Atlanta Hawks basketball team, was named to succeed Turner as president of the Atlanta Braves in November, and the Minnesota Twins hired Ralph Houk November 24 as vice-president for baseball in an advisory capacity and elevated Andy MacPhail to executive vice-president in charge of baseball operations.

New York Yankees first baseman Don Mattingly continued his assault on American League pitchers and finished second in the MVP balloting.

Clemens was the big winner in the post-season honors department. The Boston pitching ace captured both the Most Valuable Player and Cy Young awards in the American League and also was named The Sporting News' Major League Player of the Year. His selection as MVP revived an old debate over whether pitchers should be eligible for that distinction.

With two writers from each city participating, the Most Valuable Player poll of the Baseball Writers' Association found Clemens the top choice on 19 of the 28 American League ballots to pile up 339 points and easily beat Don Mattingly of the Yankees, who was second with 258 points. The National League balloting was a bit closer, but Schmidt of the Phillies, with 15 first-place votes, nosed out Glenn Davis of Houston, 287 points to 231. Results of the MVP voting in both leagues, with each first-place designation worth 14 points, second good for nine, third for eight and on down, follow:

AMERICAN LEAGUE

Player—Club	1	2	3	4	5	6	7	8	9	10	Pts.
Roger Clemens, Bos.	19	5	2	1	—	1	—	—	—	—	339
Don Mattingly, N.Y.	5	14	5	1	1	1	1	—	—	—	258
Jim Rice, Bos.	4	6	11	5	—	1	—	1	—	—	241
George Bell, Tor.	—	2	1	4	6	3	2	2	3	—	125
Jesse Barfield, Tor.	—	—	2	3	3	3	3	5	5	—	107
Kirby Puckett, Minn.	—	—	—	3	7	2	4	3	2	3	105
Wade Boggs, Bos.	—	—	2	2	2	1	7	2	1	4	87
Wally Joyner, Cal.	—	—	1	2	3	4	1	2	1	2	74
Joe Carter, Cle.	—	—	1	2	2	2	—	3	7	5	72
Dave Righetti, N.Y.	—	—	—	1	2	3	4	5	2	2	71
Doug DeCinces, Cal.	—	—	2	3	1	—	1	2	1	1	56
Mike Witt, Cal.	—	—	1	—	—	2	3	—	2	—	34
Don Baylor, Bos.	—	1	—	1	—	1	1	1	1	2	32
Tony Fernandez, Tor.	—	—	—	—	1	2	—	—	—	1	17
Ted Higuera, Mil.	—	—	—	—	—	—	—	1	1	2	7
Gary Gaetti, Minn.	—	—	—	—	—	—	1	—	1	—	6
Pete O'Brien, Tex.	—	—	—	—	—	1	—	—	—	—	5
Scott Fletcher, Tex.	—	—	—	—	—	—	—	1	—	2	5
Marty Barrett, Bos.	—	—	—	—	—	1	—	—	—	—	5
Jose Canseco, Oak.	—	—	—	—	—	—	—	—	—	3	3
Jim Presley, Sea.	—	—	—	—	—	—	—	—	1	—	2
Dick Schofield, Cal.	—	—	—	—	—	—	—	—	—	1	1

NATIONAL LEAGUE

Player—Club	1	2	3	4	5	6	7	8	9	10	Pts.
Mike Schmidt, Phil.	15	5	4	—	—	—	—	—	—	—	287
Glenn Davis, Hous.	6	9	5	3	—	1	—	—	—	—	231
Gary Carter, N.Y.	1	5	7	3	6	1	1	—	—	—	181
Keith Hernandez, N.Y.	2	4	7	2	6	1	1	—	—	—	179
Dave Parker, Cin.	—	—	1	11	6	2	3	—	—	1	144
Tim Raines, Mon.	—	—	—	3	1	6	7	4	—	2	99
Kevin Bass, Hous.	—	—	—	1	4	4	2	4	1	—	73
Von Hayes, Phil.	—	—	—	—	—	2	1	6	4	1	41
Tony Gwynn, S.D.	—	—	—	—	1	—	4	1	3	3	34
Mike Scott, Hous.	—	—	—	1	—	2	2	1	1	3	33
Bill Doran, Hous.	—	1	—	—	—	1	1	3	2	1	32
Eric Davis, Cin.	—	—	—	—	—	2	—	2	—	5	21
Steve Sax, L.A.	—	—	—	—	—	—	1	—	4	1	13
Ray Knight, N.Y.	—	—	—	—	—	—	—	—	4	1	9
Mike Krukow, S.F.	—	—	—	—	—	—	—	2	1	—	8
Todd Worrell, St.L.	—	—	—	—	—	1	—	—	1	—	7
Roger McDowell, N.Y.	—	—	—	—	—	—	—	1	—	2	5
Dave Smith, Hous.	—	—	—	—	—	1	—	—	—	—	5
Fernando Valenzuela, L.A.	—	—	—	—	—	—	—	—	1	2	4
Len Dykstra, N.Y.	—	—	—	—	—	—	1	—	—	—	4
Bob Ojeda, N.Y.	—	—	—	—	—	—	—	—	1	—	2
Dale Murphy, Atl.	—	—	—	—	—	—	—	—	1	—	2
Candy Maldonado, S.F.	—	—	—	—	—	—	—	—	—	2	2

Philadelphia third baseman Mike Schmidt produced big numbers and captured his third National League MVP award.

Clemens was a unanimous choice in the American League's Cy Young balloting, receiving all 28 first-place votes for 140 points. Higuera of Milwaukee finished second with 42. In the National League, Houston's Scott was the top pick of 15 writers and collected 98 points, 10 more than Valenzuela of Los Angeles, who received the nine other first-place votes. A breakdown of the Cy Young poll, with a first-place vote worth five points, second good for three and third for one:

American League

Pitcher—Club	1	2	3	Pts.
Roger Clemens, Boston	28	0	0	140
Ted Higuera, Milwaukee	0	11	9	42
Mike Witt, California	0	9	8	35
Dave Righetti, New York	0	5	5	20
Jack Morris, Detroit	0	3	4	13
Mark Eichhorn, Toronto	0	0	2	2

National League

Pitcher—Club	1	2	3	Pts.
Mike Scott, Houston	15	7	2	98
Fernando Valenzuela, L.A.	9	14	1	88
Mike Krukow, San Fran.	0	2	9	15
Bob Ojeda, New York	0	1	6	9
Ron Darling, New York	0	0	2	2
Rick Rhoden, Pittsburgh	0	0	2	2
Dwight Gooden, New York	0	0	1	1
Sid Fernandez, New York	0	0	1	1

Worrell, St. Louis relief ace, was an easy winner in the BBWAA's National League Rookie of the Year poll, beating out second baseman Robby Thompson of San Francisco. Jose Canseco, Oakland's slugging outfielder, edged first baseman Wally Joyner of California for freshman honors in the American League.

Hal Lanier's impressive leadership prompted BBWAA voters to name the rookie Houston pilot as National League Manager of the Year. Lanier received 19 of 24 first-place votes to handily beat Dave Johnson of the Mets, while John McNamara of Boston, with 13 first-place votes, barely won American League managerial honors over Bobby Valentine of Texas, who was the top pick on 12 ballots.

Besides Clemens, other selections by The Sporting News for honors were: Major League Executive—Frank Cashen of the New York Mets; Major League Manager—Lanier and McNamara (co-winners); Minor League Player—Tim Pyznarski, first baseman with Las Vegas (Pacific Coast); Minor League Manager—Joe Sparks of Indianapolis (American Association); Class AAA Executive—Bob Goughan of Rochester (International); Class AA Executive—Bill Davidson of Midland (Texas), and Class A Executive—Rob Dlugozima of Durham (Carolina). Mattingly and Clemens were designated Player and Pitcher of the Year, respectively, in the American League by The Sporting News, while Schmidt and Scott were selected for similar honors in the National. Worrell and Righetti gained Fireman of the Year designation in their respective leagues, Worrell and Toronto's Mark Eichhorn were picked as Rookie Pitchers of the Year, Canseco and Thompson were TSN's choices as Rookie Players of the Year and John Candelaria of California and Ray Knight of the New York Mets were recognized as the Comeback Players of the Year.

Clemens and Scott earned the new Consort Control Pitcher Awards established by Consort and The Sporting News for starting pitchers.

The annual All-Star Teams chosen by The Sporting News consisted of the following:

American League: 1B—Mattingly, New York; 2B—Tony Bernazard, Cleveland; SS—Tony Fernandez, Toronto; 3B— Boggs, Boston; OF—Jim Rice, Boston; George Bell, Toronto, and Kirby Puckett, Minnesota; C—Rich Gedman, Boston; DH—Don Baylor, Boston; RHP—Clemens, Boston; LHP—Higuera, Milwaukee. National League: 1B—Hernandez, New York; 2B—Sax, Los Angeles; SS—Ozzie Smith, St. Louis; 3B—Schmidt, Philadelphia; OF—Parker, Cincinnati; Raines, Montreal, and Tony Gwynn, San Diego; C—Gary Carter, New York; RHP—Scott, Houston; LHP—Valenzuela, Los Angeles.

The Hillerich & Bradsby Silver Slugger Awards for the best offensive performers at each position, as determined in a poll of managers and coaches conducted by The Sporting News, went to the following: 1B—Mattingly in the American League and Glenn Davis, Houston, in the National League; 2B—Frank White, Kansas City, and Sax, Los Angeles; SS—Cal Ripken, Baltimore, and Brooks, Montreal; 3B—Boggs, Boston, and Schmidt, Philadelphia; OF—Puckett, Minnesota; Bell, Toronto, and Barfield, Toronto, in the American, and Gwynn, San Diego; Raines, Montreal, and Parker, Cincinnati, in the National; C—Lance Parrish, Detroit, and Carter, New York; DH—Baylor, Boston; and P—Rick Rhoden, Pittsburgh.

Winners of the Rawlings Gold Glove Awards for fielding excellence, also selected by the managers and coaches, were: 1B—Mattingly in the American and Hernandez in the National: 2B—White and Ryne Sandberg, Chicago; SS—Fernandez and Smith, St. Louis; 3B—Gary Gaetti, Minnesota, and Schmidt; OF—Gary Pettis, California; Barfield and Puckett in the American and Gwynn, Dale Murphy and Willie McGee, St. Louis, in the National; C—Bob Boone, California, and Jody Davis, Chicago, and P—Ron Guidry, New York and Valenzuela.

NATIONAL LEAGUE

Including

Team Reviews of 1986 Season

Team Day-by-Day Scores

1986 Standings, Home-Away Records

1986 Official N.L. Batting Averages

1986 Official N.L. Fielding Averages

1986 Official N.L. Pitching Averages

1986 Pitching Against Each Club

The addition of lefthander Bob Ojeda to the starting rotation gave the Mets the balance they needed for their 1986 pennant chase.

Dominant Mets Fulfill Dream

By JACK LANG

It was anything a baseball fan could ask for. It was the greatest of seasons, with victories on opening day, closing day and 106 other times in between. For the New York Mets, 1986 was the quintessential season, culminating with eight more victories in the National League Championship Series and the World Series.

At the start of spring training, Manager Davey Johnson had established the goal for his team. "We don't just want to win," he said. "We want to dominate."

When the regular season was over, the Mets had not only dominated, but also overwhelmed the rest of the N.L. East. Their 108 victories were the most for an N.L. team since the Cincinnati Reds won the same number in 1975. Their 21½-game margin over the second-place Philadelphia Phillies was exceeded by only one other team in modern major league history. The 1902 Pittsburgh Pirates finished 27½ games ahead of the Brooklyn Dodgers.

After consecutive second-place finishes under Johnson in his first two years at the helm, the Mets were ready to make a move. Only a couple of holes needed to be filled, and General Manager Frank Cashen supplied the missing parts with two major off-season deals. Without disturbing his major league roster, Cashen obtained pitcher Bob Ojeda from the Boston Red Sox for four minor leaguers and second baseman Tim Teufel from the Minnesota Twins for three minor leaguers.

Ojeda gave the Mets the additional lefthanded starter they needed to face such running teams as St. Louis and Montreal. In Teufel, Johnson had a righthanded hitter to use in his second-base platoon system, which enabled the manager to start Wally Backman exclusively against righthanded pitching.

In spring training, Johnson made two more moves that later benefited the team. The first involved Ray Knight, who was coming off a .218 season in 1985 and was close to being unemployed. Cashen tried to trade the third baseman and then even considered releasing him, but Johnson lobbied for Knight's retention.

Knight responded to his manager's confidence by helping the Mets get off to a fantastic start. Knight hit six home runs in the Mets' first 12 games and batted .306 for the month of April. In May, Knight

Little big men Lenny Dykstra (above) and Wally Backman put zip into the Mets' offense.

SCORES OF NEW YORK METS' 1986 GAMES

APRIL			Winner	Loser
8—At Pitts.	W	4-2	Gooden	Reuschel
11—At Phila.	W	9-7	Ojeda	Gross
12—At Phila.	L	8-9x	Hudson	Niemann
13—At Phila.	L	2-4	Rawley	Aguilera
14—St. Louis	L	2-6§	Perry	Niemann
18—Phila.	W	5-2	Darling	Carlton
19—Phila.	W	3-2	Gooden	Rawley
20—Phila.	W	8-0	Fernandez	Gross
21—Pittsburgh	W	6-5	McDowell	Clements
22—Pittsburgh	W	7-1	Ojeda	Kipper
24—At St. L.	W	5-4*	McDowell	Worrell
25—At St. L.	W	9-0	Gooden	Horton
26—At St. L.	W	4-3	Fernandez	Cox
27—At St. L.	W	5-3	Ojeda	Tudor
29—At Atlanta	W	10-5	Berenyi	McMurtry
30—At Atlanta	W	8-1	Gooden	Johnson

Won 13, Lost 3

MAY			Winner	Loser
1—At Atlanta	L	2-7	Smith	Aguilera
2—At Cinn.	W	8-7	Fernandez	Gullickson
3—At Cinn.	W	4-1	Ojeda	Denny
4—At Cinn.	W	7-2	Darling	Soto
6—Houston	W	4-0	Gooden	Knepper
7—Houston	W	3-2	Fernandez	Ryan
9—Cincinnati	W	2-1	Ojeda	Soto
10—Cincinnati	W	5-1	Darling	Browning
11—Cincinnati	L	2-3	Gullickson	Gooden
12—Atlanta	W	1-0	McDowell	Assenmacher
13—Atlanta	L	3-6	Johnson	Aguilera
14—At Hous.	L	2-6	Knepper	Ojeda
15—At Hous.	W	6-2	Darling	Ryan
16—At L.A.	L	3-4†	Howell	Orosco
17—At L.A.	L	2-6	Niedenfuer	Fernandez
18—At L.A.	W	8-4	Niemann	Reuss
20—At S. Fran.	W	2-1	Ojeda	LaCoss
21—At S. Fran.	W	7-4	Darling	Mason
22—At S. Fran.	L	2-10	Krukow	Gooden
23—At S. Diego	L	4-7	Gossage	Orosco
24—At S. Diego	W	5-4	Berenyi	Thurmond
25—At S. Diego	W	4-2†	Orosco	Lefferts
27—Los Ang.	W	8-1	Darling	Welch
28—Los Ang.	W	4-2	Gooden	Reuss
29—Los Ang.	W	5-2	Fernandez	Valenzuela
30—San Fran.	W	8-7*	Orosco	Davis
31—San Fran.	L	3-7	Garrelts	Ojeda

Won 18, Lost 9

JUNE			Winner	Loser
1—San Fran.	L	3-7	Krukow	Darling
2—San Diego	W	11-2	Gooden	Hoyt
3—San Diego	L	4-5	Hawkins	Fernandez
4—San Diego	W	4-2	McDowell	Walter
5—At Pitts.	W	7-0	Ojeda	Kipper
6—At Pitts.	L	1-7	Rhoden	Darling
6—At Pitts.	W	10-4	McDowell	DeLeon
7—At Pitts.	W	6-4	Gooden	Reuschel
8—At Pitts.	W	4-3	Fernandez	McWilliams
9—Phila.	L	2-3*	Carman	Sisk
10—Phila.	W	8-4†	McDowell	Lerch
11—Phila.	W	5-3	Darling	Carlton
13—Pittsburgh	W	6-5	Orosco	Clements
14—Pittsburgh	W	5-1	Fernandez	Bielecki
15—Pittsburgh	W	4-1	Ojeda	Walk
15—Pittsburgh	W	8-5	Aguilera	Kipper
16—At Mon.	W	4-1*	Sisk	Reardon
17—At Mon.	L	2-4	Hesketh	Berenyi
18—At Mon.	L	4-7	Youmans	Gooden
20—Chicago	W	10-3	Fernandez	Sanderson
21—Chicago	L	6-8	Fontenot	Orosco
22—Chicago	W	4-2	Darling	Sutcliffe
23—Montreal	L	4-5*	Burke	Orosco
24—Montreal	L	2-6	Smith	Berenyi
25—Montreal	W	5-2	Fernandez	McGaffigan
28—At Chicago	W	5-2	McDowell	Fontenot
29—At Chicago	W	7-4	Gooden	Sutcliffe
30—At St. L.	W	7-0	Ojeda	Tudor

Won 19, Lost 9

JULY			Winner	Loser
1—At St. L.	W	2-1	Fernandez	Cox
2—At St. L.	W	4-3	Sisk	Forsch
3—Houston	W	6-5*	Orosco	DiPino
4—Houston	W	2-1	Gooden	Smith
5—Houston	L	1-2	Kerfeld	McDowell
6—Houston	W	5-3	Fernandez	Knudson
7—Cincinnati	L	6-7	Robinson	Niemann
8—Cincinnati	L	4-5*	Franco	McDowell
9—Cincinnati	L	1-11	Browning	Gooden
10—Atlanta	W	5-1	Ojeda	Smith

JULY			Winner	Loser
11—Atlanta	W	11-0	Fernandez	Palmer
12—Atlanta	W	10-1	Aguilera	Mahler
13—Atlanta	W	2-0	Darling	Alexander
17—At Hous.	W	13-2	Ojeda	Ryan
18—At Hous.	L	0-3	Knepper	Darling
19—At Hous.	L	4-5	Smith	McDowell
20—At Hous.	L	8-9y	Knepper	McDowell
21—At Cinn.	W	4-2	Aguilera	Soto
22—At Cinn.	W	6-3x	McDowell	Willis
23—At Cinn.	W	3-2	Darling	Robinson
26—At Atlanta	L	3-4	Assenmacher	McDowell
26—At Atlanta	L	5-8	Acker	Fernandez
27—At Atlanta	W	5-1	Aguilera	Mahler
28—Chicago	W	9-2	Ojeda	Sanderson
29—Chicago	W	3-0	Darling	Trout
29—Chicago	L	1-2	Moyer	Sisk
30—Chicago	L	3-4	Eckersley	Fernandez

Won 16, Lost 11

AUGUST			Winner	Loser
1—Montreal	W	3-1	Gooden	Youmans
2—Montreal	W	4-1	Aguilera	Sebra
3—Montreal	W	4-3*	McDowell	McClure
4—At Chicago	L	2-4	Eckersley	Darling
5—At Chicago	L	5-8	Smith	McDowell
6—At Chicago	W	7-6‡	McDowell	Frazier
6—At Chicago	W	7-6z	Anderson	Trout
7—At Chicago	W	12-3	Aguilera	Sanderson
8—At Mon.	L	3-5	Smith	Ojeda
9—At Mon.	W	10-8	McDowell	Reardon
10—At Mon.	W	7-2	Fernandez	Martinez
11—At Phila.	W	8-4	Gooden	Carman
12—At Phila.	L	1-3	Gross	Aguilera
13—At Phila.	L	4-8	Ruffin	Ojeda
14—St. Louis	W	4-3	McDowell	Worrell
14—St. Louis	L	1-5	Horton	Anderson
15—St. Louis	L	2-4*	Perry	Orosco
16—St. Louis	L	1-3†	Mathews	McDowell
17—St. Louis	L	1-2	Tudor	Aguilera
17—St. Louis	W	9-2	Niemann	Cox
18—At L.A.	W	5-4	Ojeda	Hershiser
19—At L.A.	W	6-4	Darling	Valenzuela
20—At L.A.	W	7-5	Fernandez	Powell
22—At S. Fran.	W	5-3	Gooden	Blue
23—At S. Fran.	W	3-2	Ojeda	Downs
24—At S. Fran.	L	1-10	Krukow	Aguilera
25—At S. Diego	W	5-2	Orosco	Lefferts
26—At S. Diego	W	11-6	Fernandez	Dravecky
27—At S. Diego	W	6-5†	Sisk	Gossage
29—Los Ang.	W	2-1	Ojeda	Honeycutt
30—Los Ang.	W	6-3	Aguilera	Hershiser
31—Los Ang.	L	4-7	Valenzuela	Darling

Won 21, Lost 11

SEPTEMBER			Winner	Loser
1—San Fran.	W	5-2	McDowell	Davis
2—San Fran.	L	3-4	Krukow	Gooden
3—San Fran.	W	4-2	Ojeda	Mulholland
6—San Diego	W	4-3	Orosco	McCullers
7—San Diego	W	7-1	Gooden	LaPoint
7—San Diego	W	6-5	Sisk	Lefferts
8—Montreal	L	1-9	Sebra	Ojeda
9—Montreal	L	7-9	Burke	Orosco
10—Montreal	W	6-1	Darling	Valdez
12—At Phila.	L	3-6	Ruffin	Gooden
13—At Phila.	L	5-6	Schatzeder	McDowell
14—At Phila.	L	0-6	Gross	Fernandez
15—At St. L.	L	0-1§	Worrell	McDowell
16—At St. L.	W	4-2	Aguilera	Conroy
17—Chicago	W	4-2	Gooden	Eckersley
18—Chicago	W	5-0	Anderson	Maddux
19—Phila.	L	3-4	Gross	Fernandez
20—Phila.	W	9-5	Darling	Hume
21—Phila.	L	1-7	Freeman	Mitchell
22—St. Louis	W	5-2	Gooden	Forsch
23—St. Louis	W	9-1	Ojeda	Mathews
24—At Chicago	L	2-8	Hall	Aguilera
25—At Chicago	W	6-5	McDowell	Lynch
26—At Pitts.	W	3-1	Fernandez	Fansler
27—At Pitts.	W	4-2†	Orosco	McWilliams
28—At Pitts.	W	4-1†	Aguilera	Walk
30—At Mon.	L	0-1	Sebra	Darling

Won 16, Lost 11

OCTOBER			Winner	Loser
1—At Mon.	W	6-4*	Orosco	McClure
2—At Mon.	W	8-2	Gooden	Youmans
4—Pittsburgh	W	6-1	Ojeda	Fansler
4—Pittsburgh	W	5-2	Aguilera	Patterson
5—Pittsburgh	W	9-0	Darling	Pena

Won 5, Lost 0

*10 innings. †11 innings. ‡12 innings. §13 innings. x14 innings. y15 innings. zSuspended game, completed August 7.

batted .348. He finished the season with a .298 average and 76 runs batted in and was named the World Series' Most Valuable Player.

It also was in spring training that Johnson was left with no alternative but to open with Lenny Dykstra in center field. Veteran Mookie Wilson was coming off two shoulder operations and then was hit in the eye during a rundown drill and was sidelined for six weeks. Dykstra's response to the full-time job was to hit safely in 12 of his first 15 games, finishing April with a .327 average. He wound up hitting .295 with a team-high 31 stolen bases and played well defensively.

With Knight and Dykstra as the sparks and with Dwight Gooden going 4-0 in April, the Mets were 13-3 at the end of the first month. They were coasting by the end of May, when their 31-12 record put them six games in front, and their lead grew to 13 games by the All-Star break.

Shortly after the intermission, four Mets were involved in a scuffle outside a Houston nightclub. Teufel, Ojeda and pitchers Ron Darling and Rick Aguilera spent the night in jail. Darling and Teufel were later charged with felonious assault against two off-duty police officers working as security guards at the nightclub.

That was not the first time that fisticuffs had put the Mets in the headlines in '86. While they went about the league establishing their superiority, the Mets also irritated opponents with what was perceived by others as arrogance. Shea Stadium fans insisted on curtain calls after every homer, and the Mets responded in theatrical fashion. The high-fives at home plate and the outgoing style of this media-conscious team did nothing to ingratiate the Mets with other N.L. teams, so they were constantly battling the opposition. They were involved in on-field brawls four times in '86.

By the end of July, New York had a 15½-game lead and a new platoon position. A few days earlier, Johnson had announced that Wilson and hard-hitting rookie Kevin Mitchell would platoon in left field. That reduced veteran George Foster to pinch-hitting status. Foster, who batted .227 with only 38 RBIs, was released August 7. Meanwhile, Wilson (.289) and Mitchell (.277) combined for 21 homers and 88 RBIs.

The Mets, who were fortunate to avoid losing any of their regulars for any prolonged period, never lost more than four games in a row. They reached a peak of 22 games over their nearest challenger September 10 and clinched the division title a week later. But still they didn't let up, winning 13 of their last 17 games.

By season's end, it was clear why the Mets ruled the league. Their pitching staff had the league's best earned-run average (3.11) and allowed the fewest homers (103). Offensively, they led the league in several categories, including batting (.263) and runs scored (783), and they were shut out only four times all year.

New York's starting rotation of Gooden, Darling, Ojeda and Sid Fernandez (plus an occasional start by Aguilera) was outstanding. Ojeda led the staff with an 18-5 record and a 2.57 ERA. Gooden was next at 17-6, but that represented a mediocre season for the former Cy Young Award winner. Though his 2.84 ERA and 200 strikeouts would be all-time bests for most pitchers, they were career lows for Gooden.

Darling, a frequent victim of non-support, finished 15-6 with a 2.81 ERA and 184 strikeouts, while Fernandez (16-6, 3.52) tied Gooden by fanning 200 batters. Aguilera did not win a game until June 15 but still went 10-7.

The bullpen was another Met strength. New York's frequent late-inning heroics helped righthander Roger McDowell, who saved a team-high 22 games, win 14 more. Lefthander Jesse Orosco had 21 saves and a 2.33 ERA, while middle reliever Doug Sisk had four victories and a 3.06 ERA.

The offensive backbone of the team was Keith Hernandez, who hit .310, scored 94 runs, knocked in 83 and led the league in walks (94). The Gold Glove first baseman also was a steadying influence on the club.

Catcher Gary Carter batted only .255 but still ranked among the N.L. leaders with 24 homers and 105 RBIs, including a league-high 16 game-winners. Right fielder Darryl Strawberry (.259, 27 homers, 93 RBIs) produced similar numbers.

The Mets' middle infield was effective but not overwhelming. At second base, the fiery Backman hit .320 and scored 67 runs, while Teufel, a defensive liability, batted .247. Shortstop Rafael Santana reduced his errors from 25 in '85 to 16, but his batting average dropped from .257 to .218.

Johnson's frequent use of his backup players kept the team fresh. Among the top players off the bench were outfielder Danny Heep (.282), infielder Howard Johnson (.245) and rookie catcher Ed Hearn (.265).

From a financial standpoint, the Mets were a gold mine. Paid admissions totaled 2,767,601—the largest ever for any New York professional sports team.

Von Hayes played excellent defense at first base and reached the offensive heights that Phillies officials had long predicted.

Slow-Starting Phils Come Alive

By PETER PASCARELLI

Any reasonable hope of challenging for a title disappeared after a 15-24 start left them 12½ games behind the runaway New York Mets. But in the end, the Philadelphia Phillies breathed life into their 1986 season with a strong second half that earned them a solid second-place finish in the National League East.

The Phillies won 27 of 46 games after that slow start to advance from last to third place with a 42-43 record at the All-Star break. They finally moved over .500 July 26 and eventually went 44-32 in the second half to finish with an 86-75 record, 21½ games behind the Mets.

Along the way, the Phils showed a growing team maturity that marked them as future contenders. They had to weather a series of major injuries and personnel moves, including the emotional release of pitcher Steve Carlton and the retirement of outfielders Garry Maddox and Joe Lefebvre. The changes, however, allowed several young Phils to surface as key parts of the club.

"We made some very significant progress as a team this year," Manager John Felske said, "and it is exciting to go into the off-season thinking about how much better this club is and how we are going to keep improving.

"We got great seasons from Mike Schmidt and Von Hayes, which made everybody on the club better. A lot of our young players came into their own. And the way some of our young pitchers performed really became a big part of our season."

No one could have foreseen the upbeat finish to the season during the Phillies' disappointing first several weeks. Their slow on-field start was followed by season-ending injuries to No. 1 catcher Darren Daulton (knee) and pitcher Shane Rawley, who was 11-7 with a 3.54 earned-run average when a shoulder problem forced him to sit.

In addition, rookie righthander Fred Toliver was lost for the season after only five starts. And left fielder Gary Redus, the Phillies' leadoff hitter, missed two months because of elbow surgery.

But these players' absences—most notably those of Rawley and Carlton, who was released after several disappointing starts—led to the discovery of two solid starting pitchers.

One was Don Carman, who had been struggling in the bullpen. The lefthander went 7-3 with a 2.43 ERA as a starter, including the year's epic performance in which he took a perfect game into the ninth inning August 20 in San Francisco before Bob Brenly broke it up with a leadoff double. He finished with a 10-5 record and a 3.22 ERA.

Lefthander Don Carman moved into the Phillies rotation and finished the season with a 10-5 record.

The other was lefthander Bruce Ruffin, who was promoted from Double-A Reading (Eastern) in June. The 22-year-old rookie compiled a 9-4 record and a 2.46 ERA in 21 starts.

"Ruffin and Carman really made a huge difference to our club," Felske said. "They proved to be consistent starters and were very responsible for the way the club turned around."

For a second straight year, righthander Kevin Gross led the Phils in victories, though his 12-12 record and 4.02 ERA fell short of expectations. And the Phils were encouraged by a late-season look at rookie starters Marvin Freeman and Mike Maddux, both of whom had some success.

Meanwhile, the Phils developed one of the league's most potent offenses. The biggest producer was Schmidt, who led the

SCORES OF PHILADELPHIA PHILLIES' 1986 GAMES

APRIL			Winner	Loser
7—At Cinn.	L	4-7	Soto	Carlton
9—At Cinn.	W	5-3‡	Bedrosian	Power
11—New York	L	7-9	Ojeda	Gross
12—New York	W	9-8x	Hudson	Niemann
13—New York	W	4-2	Rawley	Aguilera
14—Pittsburgh	L	1-3†	Guante	Bedrosian
18—At N.Y.	L	2-5	Darling	Carlton
19—At N.Y.	L	2-3	Gooden	Rawley
20—At N.Y.	L	0-8	Fernandez	Gross
22—At Mon.	L	2-8	McGaffigan	Hudson
23—At Mon.	W	5-4	Carlton	Hesketh
24—At Pitts.	W	4-2	Rawley	Rhoden
25—At Pitts.	W	6-3	Gross	Reuschel
26—At Pitts.	W	6-5	Hudson	McWilliams
27—At Pitts.	L	5-13	Bielecki	Carlton
29—Houston	W	12-4	Rawley	Ryan
30—Houston	L	0-1	Scott	Gross

Won 8, Lost 9

MAY			Winner	Loser
2—Atlanta	L	1-7	Palmer	Carlton
3—Atlanta	L	4-10	Mahler	Rawley
4—Atlanta	W	5-1	Gross	Johnson
5—Montreal	L	4-6	Schatzeder	Tekulve
6—Montreal	L	0-8	McGaffigan	Carlton
7—Montreal	L	2-8	Youmans	Rawley
9—At Atlanta	W	7-6	Gross	Johnson
10—At Atlanta	L	1-3	Smith	Hudson
11—At Atlanta	W	2-1	Bedrosian	McMurtry
12—At Hous.	W	5-1	Rawley	Deshaies
13—At Hous.	L	2-3‡	Solano	Rucker
14—Cincinnati	W	8-6	Carman	Franco
15—Cincinnati	L	5-6	Robinson	Bedrosian
16—At S. Fran.	W	3-0	Carlton	Mason
17—At S. Fran.	L	7-12	Krukow	Rawley
18—At S. Fran.	L	1-4	Garrelts	Toliver
20—At S. Diego	L	3-4	Show	Gross
21—At S. Diego	L	2-7	Dravecky	Hudson
22—At S. Diego	L	2-6	Hawkins	Carlton
23—At L.A.	W	8-2	Rawley	Reuss
24—At L.A.	L	0-6	Valenzuela	Toliver
25—At L.A.	L	2-5	Hershiser	Gross
27—San Fran.	W	6-2	Carlton	Robinson
28—San Fran.	W	4-0	Rawley	Garrelts
29—San Fran.	W	5-4	Carman	Minton
30—San Diego	W	2-0	Gross	Show
31—San Diego	W	1-0	Hudson	Dravecky

Won 12, Lost 15

JUNE			Winner	Loser
1—San Diego	W	16-5	Carlton	Hawkins
2—Los Ang.	W	13-2	Rawley	Reuss
3—Los Ang.	L	4-11	Valenzuela	Maddux
4—Los Ang.	W	8-7	Gross	Hershiser
5—At Mon.	W	7-3	Hudson	Tibbs
6—At Mon.	L	9-10†	Burke	Rucker
7—At Mon.	W	3-1	Rawley	McGaffigan
8—At Mon.	L	0-12	Youmans	Maddux
9—At N.Y.	W	3-2†	Carman	Sisk
10—At N.Y.	L	4-8‡	McDowell	Lerch
11—At N.Y.	L	3-5	Darling	Carlton
13—Montreal	W	2-1	Rawley	Burke
14—Montreal	W	7-6	Lerch	Roberge
15—Montreal	L	0-2	McGaffigan	Hudson
16—At Chicago	L	5-7	Moyer	Carlton
17—At Chicago	W	11-8	Tekulve	Fontenot
18—At Chicago	L	4-5†	Smith	Bedrosian
19—St. Louis	W	5-3	Gross	Burris
20—St. Louis	L	2-9	Forsch	Hudson
21—St. Louis	L	6-8	Worrell	Carman
22—St. Louis	L	4-7	Mathews	Maddux
23—Chicago	W	19-1	Rawley	Moyer
24—Chicago	W	7-6†	Bedrosian	Smith
25—Chicago	L	7-10	Hoffman	Hudson
27—At St. L.	W	2-1y	Tekulve	Ownbey
28—At St. L.	W	7-4†	Bedrosian	Perry
29—At St. L.	W	8-7	Bedrosian	Worrell
30—At Pitts.	L	2-3	Walk	Hudson

Won 15, Lost 13

JULY			Winner	Loser
1—At Pitts.	W	5-4§	Hume	McWilliams
2—At Pitts.	L	3-4	Rhoden	Carman
3—Cincinnati	W	7-3	Ruffin	Denny
4—Cincinnati	L	1-4	Browning	Gross
5—Cincinnati	L	2-7	Welsh	Hudson
6—Cincinnati	W	12-5	Hume	Price
7—Atlanta	W	7-3	Rawley	Palmer
8—Atlanta	W	8-2	Ruffin	Mahler
9—Atlanta	L	3-7	Alexander	Gross
10—At Hous.	L	4-11	Knudson	Hudson
11—At Hous.	W	4-1	Carman	Scott
12—At Hous.	L	3-4	Ryan	Rawley
13—At Hous.	W	5-4‡	Bedrosian	Smith
17—At Cinn.	L	6-7‡	Power	Gorman
18—At Cinn.	L	5-6	Browning	Ruffin
19—At Cinn.	L	2-5	Gullickson	Rawley
20—At Cinn.	W	9-3	Hudson	Denny
21—At Atlanta	W	3-1	Tekulve	Dedmon
22—At Atlanta	W	5-4‡	Bedrosian	McMurtry
23—At Atlanta	W	4-2	Ruffin	Alexander
24—Houston	L	3-9	Scott	Rawley
25—Houston	W	4-2	Hudson	Deshaies
26—Houston	W	3-2	Carman	Knudson
27—Houston	L	2-3	Ryan	Gross
28—St. Louis	L	1-3	Cox	Ruffin
29—St. Louis	W	12-7	Hume	Conroy
30—St. Louis	L	3-6	Forsch	Hudson

Won 14, Lost 13

AUGUST			Winner	Loser
1—Chicago	W	4-3‡	Tekulve	DiPino
2—Chicago	W	12-2	Gross	Sanderson
3—Chicago	W	6-2	Bedrosian	DiPino
4—At St. L.	L	2-3	Worrell	Schatzeder
5—At St. L.	L	4-7	Forsch	Maddux
6—At St. L.	L	1-2	Mathews	Carman
7—At St. L.	L	5-6	Tudor	Gross
8—At Chicago	L	1-2	Trout	Ruffin
9—At Chicago	W	4-2	Hudson	Eckersley
10—At Chicago	L	0-4	Lynch	Maddux
11—New York	L	4-8	Gooden	Carman
12—New York	W	3-1	Gross	Aguilera
13—New York	W	8-4	Ruffin	Ojeda
14—Pittsburgh	W	8-7	Tekulve	Jones
15—Pittsburgh	L	5-6	Guante	Schatzeder
15—Pittsburgh	W	3-2	Maddux	Winn
16—Pittsburgh	L	1-6	Rhoden	Gross
16—Pittsburgh	W	6-0	Hume	McWilliams
17—Pittsburgh	W	5-1*	Ruffin	Reuschel
19—At S. Fran.	W	6-5	Tekulve	Garrelts
20—At S. Fran.	W	1-0†	Carman	Krukow
21—At S. Fran.	L	6-7	Davis	Tekulve
22—At S. Diego	W	4-1	Ruffin	Whitson
23—At S. Diego	L	3-4§	McCullers	Tekulve
24—At S. Diego	W	6-5	Tekulve	Gossage
25—At L.A.	L	1-3	Valenzuela	Carman
26—At L.A.	W	6-4	Gross	Vande Berg
27—At L.A.	W	2-1	Ruffin	Welch
29—San Fran.	W	6-4	Maddux	Krukow
30—San Fran.	W	5-3	Carman	LaCoss
31—San Fran.	W	4-3	Tekulve	Blue

Won 19, Lost 12

SEPTEMBER			Winner	Loser
1—San Diego	W	5-4	Tekulve	Lefferts
2—San Diego	L	2-6	LaPoint	Bittiger
3—San Diego	L	5-7	B. Stoddard	Bedrosian
5—Los Ang.	W	4-0	Carman	Hershiser
6—Los Ang.	L	2-3	Valenzuela	Gross
7—Los Ang.	W	2-1	Tekulve	Howell
8—At Chicago	L	4-7	Lynch	Maddux
9—At Chicago	L	6-8†	Smith	Bedrosian
10—At Chicago	L	7-8	Hoffman	Tekulve
12—New York	W	6-3	Ruffin	Gooden
13—New York	W	6-5	Schatzeder	McDowell
14—New York	W	6-0	Gross	Fernandez
15—Pittsburgh	W	5-0	Carman	Rhoden
16—Pittsburgh	W	9-5	Tekulve	Bielecki
17—St. Louis	L	5-8	Forsch	Ruffin
18—St. Louis	W	4-3	Maddux	Mathews
19—At N.Y.	W	4-3	Gross	Fernandez
20—At N.Y.	L	5-9	Darling	Hume
21—At N.Y.	W	7-1	Freeman	Mitchell
22—At Pitts.	W	8-4	Bittiger	Kipper
23—At Pitts.	L	5-6	Jones	Bedrosian
24—At St. L.	L	1-7	Cox	Gross
25—At St. L.	L	4-5	Soff	Schatzeder
26—At Mon.	W	5-0	Freeman	Valdez
27—At Mon.	W	1-0	Carman	Youmans
28—At Mon.	W	5-2	Gross	Martinez
29—Chicago	L	3-8	G. Maddux	M. Maddux
30—Chicago	W	9-2	Ruffin	Hall

Won 16, Lost 12

OCTOBER			Winner	Loser
3—Montreal	L	5-6	McGaffigan	Tekulve
4—Montreal	W	5-4x	Schatzeder	Roberge
5—Montreal	W	2-1†	Schatzeder	Brown

Won 2, Lost 1

*5 innings. †10 innings. ‡11 innings. §12 innings. x14 innings. y17 innings.

Juan Samuel improved his defense at second base and continued to produce big offensive numbers.

league in home runs (37), runs batted in (119) and slugging percentage (.547) while batting .290 and making only six errors at third base all season. Schmidt won his 10th Gold Glove and was named N.L. Most Valuable Player.

Then there was Hayes, who put together a magnificent all-around season. He hit .305 with 19 homers and 98 RBIs, scored 107 runs to tie for the N.L. lead and paced the league with 46 doubles. More remarkable, perhaps, was his solid defensive play at first base, a position at which he had virtually no major league experience entering the season.

Backing up the big two in the lineup was right fielder Glenn Wilson, who was hitting only .181 entering June but bounced back to finish the season with a .271 average, 84 RBIs and a career-high 15 homers. He also led all N.L. outfielders in assists for a second straight year with 20.

Second baseman Juan Samuel became the first N.L. player ever to reach double figures in doubles (36), triples (12), homers (16) and stolen bases (42) in each of his first three seasons. And though defensive problems plagued him, catcher John Russell ended up with 13 homers and 60 RBIs after assuming full-time catching chores in the wake of Daulton's injury.

The Phils' bullpen also developed into a team strength. Steve Bedrosian led the way, establishing a career high and tying the club record with 29 saves in his first season in Philadelphia. The biggest surprise might have been 39-year-old Kent Tekulve, who went 11-5 with a 2.54 ERA in 73 appearances. Tom Hume came back from early-season problems to go 4-1 with four saves.

The one weak link in the starting rotation was righthander Charles Hudson (7-10, 4.94 ERA). Another player who struggled was shortstop Steve Jeltz, who batted .219.

Several part-time players made contributions for the Phils. Jeff Stone (.277), Milt Thompson (.251) and Ron Roenicke (.247, 42 RBIs), all of whom spent time in the minor leagues, filled in capably in the outfield. Infielder Rick Schu batted .274 with eight homers in 208 at-bats.

The Phils' finest hour probably came in mid-September when they hosted the Mets, who arrived needing only one victory to clinch the N.L. East title. But the Phillies delayed New York's celebration with a spine-tingling three-game sweep that helped the Phils become the only N.L. club to beat the Mets more times than they lost to them in 1986.

"Winning the season series from the Mets meant something to us," Felske said. "It showed us and showed them that we can play with them, and it gives us the confidence to believe we are a good team that is only going to get better."

Veteran righthander Bob Forsch won 14 games and provided one of the few bright spots in a dismal Cardinals season.

Cards Fall From Lofty Perch

By RICK HUMMEL

April 24, 1986. It might not rank up there with October 12 (the day the California Angels fell one strike short of winning the American League pennant) or October 25 (the night the Boston Red Sox were one strike shy of a World Series crown) in terms of turning points, but for the St. Louis Cardinals, no day was more significant in their fall from grace in the National League East.

After capturing the N.L. pennant in 1985, the Cardinals resumed their winning ways by getting off to a 7-1 start in 1986. Though they lost their next three games, the Cardinals still were only half a game back when the first-place New York Mets came to Busch Stadium for the start of a four-game series April 24.

St. Louis carried a 4-2 lead into the top of the ninth inning. The Mets had a runner on second with none out, but ace reliever Todd Worrell came on to retire Ray Knight. The Cardinals' second victory over the Mets in as many games appeared to be just moments away.

Howard Johnson had other ideas. The New York shortstop blasted a two-run home run into the right-field seats to tie the score, and the Mets won the game in the 10th inning.

Suddenly, what little momentum that had been created in the young season had been snatched by the Mets, who never let up in their relentless drive to the division title. The Mets swept the next three games from the Cardinals, who then lost five of their next six contests. Thus began a St. Louis tumble into the nether reaches of the N.L. East.

By the All-Star break, St. Louis was in fifth place with a 36-50 record, 24 games behind New York. At that point, the Cardinals' only hope was for a first-division finish, which they attained by going 43-32 in the second half. They wound up third with a 79-82 record.

Actually, that was quite a feat for a team that dropped from first to last in batting in one year. In fact, the Cardinals ranked last in the league in on-base percentage, runs scored, homers and several other offensive categories in '86.

"We had to be a pretty good club to play near .500 as bad as we played," Manager Whitey Herzog said. "I thought we played pretty well with all the injuries we had."

Several pitchers were afflicted. The Cardinals lost righthander Danny Cox for the first 2½ weeks with a broken ankle. Lefthander Rick Horton was on the disabled list for five weeks, lefthander Ken Dayley for nearly three months and righthander Jeff Lahti for virtually the entire season. Lefthander John Tudor missed the last three weeks.

Leg injuries sidelined Gold Glove center fielder Willie McGee, the 1985 N.L. Most Valuable Player, for nearly a month. The biggest injury, however, was that of Jack Clark. The slugging first baseman suffered torn ligaments in his thumb and did not play after June 24.

Clark had only nine homers and 23 runs batted in at the time, but at least he provided some kind of a power threat. When he left the lineup, the Cardinals were left with a bunch of singles hitters—and they weren't even doing that well.

"I honestly thought," Herzog said, "that when Clark got hurt with 94 games to go that we had a chance to lose 100 games. I know what he meant to our attack, and I couldn't see any kind of daylight."

Herzog was most surprised by the Cardinals' season-long batting slump. "It never really did get good," he said.

Several players endured terrible falloffs offensively from the '85 season. McGee went from a league-leading .353 to .256. Left fielder Vince Coleman dropped from .267 to .232. Second baseman Tom Herr fell from .302 and 110 RBIs to .252 and 61 RBIs. Third baseman Terry Pendleton's batting average dropped only one point (to .239), but it was about 40 points below his goal for the season.

The Cardinals' offensive plight was such that Gold Glove shortstop Ozzie Smith, not widely acknowledged as an offensive weapon, led the club in batting at .280.

Right fielder-first baseman Andy Van Slyke batted .270 and was the only player in double figures in homers with 13. The Cardinals never did catch Roger Maris, who set a major league record with 61 homers in 1961. As a team, the Cardinals finished three behind Maris with 58. Two of their everyday players, Smith and Coleman, had no homers. Pendleton hit one and Herr two. That added up to three homers in 2,251 at-bats for that foursome.

Herzog said the biggest disappointment was catcher Mike Heath, who was obtained from Oakland along with pitcher Tim Conroy the previous winter in exchange for 20-game winner Joaquin Andujar. Billed as a tough defensive catcher,

SCORES OF ST. LOUIS CARDINALS' 1986 GAMES

APRIL			Winner	Loser
8—Chicago	W	2-1	Tudor	Sutcliffe
10—Chicago	W	4-2	Ownbey	Eckersley
11—Montreal	W	9-1	Forsch	Hesketh
12—Montreal	W	6-3	Tudor	Youmans
13—Montreal	L	2-3	Smith	Kepshire
14—At N.Y.	W	6-2x	Perry	Niemann
18—At Mon.	W	4-2	Tudor	Hesketh
19—At Mon.	W	9-6y	Conroy	Youmans
20—At Mon.	L	0-2	Tibbs	Horton
22—At Chicago	L	2-3	Baller	Perry
23—At Chicago	L	0-6	Sanderson	Ownbey
24—New York	L	4-5†	McDowell	Worrell
25—New York	L	0-9	Gooden	Horton
26—New York	L	3-4	Fernandez	Cox
27—New York	L	3-5	Ojeda	Tudor
28—At S. Fran.	W	5-4§	Worrell	Davis
29—At S. Fran.	L	0-2	LaCoss	Forsch
30—At S. Diego	L	0-5	Thurmond	Horton

Won 8, Lost 10

MAY			Winner	Loser
1—At S. Diego	L	3-4	Show	Cox
2—At L.A.	L	2-3	Reuss	Tudor
3—At L.A.	L	0-3	Valenzuela	Conroy
4—At L.A.	W	3-1	Forsch	Hershiser
6—San Diego	L	2-3	Walter	Dayley
7—San Diego	W	4-3§	Worrell	Gossage
8—San Diego	W	13-3	Conroy	Dravecky
9—San Fran.	L	1-2†	LaCoss	Worrell
10—San Fran.	W	6-3	Burris	Mason
11—San Fran.	W	4-3	Worrell	Krukow
13—Los Ang.	L	5-6x	Honeycutt	Dayley
14—Los Ang.	L	3-8	Valenzuela	Conroy
16—At Atlanta	L	2-6	Mahler	Forsch
17—At Atlanta	L	0-2	Johnson	Cox
18—At Atlanta	L	2-5	Smith	Tudor
20—Cincinnati	L	3-5	Gullickson	Bargar
21—Cincinnati	W	8-3	Forsch	Denny
22—Cincinnati	L	4-6	Soto	Cox
23—Atlanta	W	3-2	Tudor	Smith
24—Atlanta	W	9-5	Burris	Palmer
25—Atlanta	L	2-6*	Mahler	Conroy
26—Houston	L	1-4	Deshaies	Forsch
27—Houston	L	4-5	Smith	Dayley
28—Houston	L	3-4‡	Kerfeld	Worrell
30—At Cinn.	L	4-6	Price	Burris
31—At Cinn.	W	11-2	Forsch	Browning

Won 9, Lost 17

JUNE			Winner	Loser
1—At Cinn.	W	2-1	Cox	Welsh
2—At Hous.	W	9-2	Tudor	Madden
3—At Hous.	W	3-1	Mathews	Deshaies
4—At Hous.	L	2-4	Scott	Burris
5—Chicago	W	4-3	Forsch	Keough
6—Chicago	L	3-9	Baller	Cox
7—Chicago	W	3-2	Tudor	Sutcliffe
8—Chicago	L	2-14	Trout	Mathews
9—Montreal	L	4-5	Burke	Worrell
10—Montreal	L	2-4	Tibbs	Forsch
11—Montreal	L	3-4†	Reardon	Bargar
13—At Chicago	W	1-0†	Mathews	Sutcliffe
13—At Chicago	L	2-3‡	Smith	Worrell
14—At Chicago	W	1-0	Burris	Sanderson
15—At Chicago	L	3-4‡	Fontenot	Worrell
16—At Pitts.	W	4-2z	Cox	Rhoden
17—At Pitts.	W	7-2	Mathews	Reuschel
18—At Pitts.	L	1-2§	Robinson	Worrell
19—At Phila.	L	3-5	Gross	Burris
20—At Phila.	W	9-2	Forsch	Hudson
21—At Phila.	W	8-6	Worrell	Carman
22—At Phila.	W	7-4	Mathews	Maddux
23—Pittsburgh	W	2-1‡	Worrell	Clements
24—Pittsburgh	W	5-2	Burris	Winn
25—Pittsburgh	W	2-1†	Horton	Clements
27—Phila.	L	1-2y	Tekulve	Ownbey
28—Phila.	L	4-7†	Bedrosian	Perry
29—Phila.	L	7-8	Bedrosian	Worrell
30—New York	L	0-7	Ojeda	Tudor

Won 15, Lost 14

JULY			Winner	Loser
1—New York	L	1-2	Fernandez	Cox
2—New York	L	3-4	Sisk	Forsch
3—At S. Fran.	L	0-1	Krukow	Ownbey
4—At S. Fran.	L	1-6	LaCoss	Burris
5—At S. Fran.	W	7-4†	Worrell	Berenguer
6—At S. Fran.	L	3-8	Garrelts	Cox
7—At L.A.	L	0-1	Pena	Forsch
8—At L.A.	W	1-0	Conroy	Welch
9—At L.A.	L	2-8	Valenzuela	Mathews
10—At S. Diego	L	3-4	Lefferts	Tudor
11—At S. Diego	W	4-2	Cox	Hawkins
12—At S. Diego	W	4-2	Forsch	Whitson
13—At S. Diego	L	6-13	Hoyt	Conroy
17—Los Ang.	W	12-2	Tudor	Hershiser
18—Los Ang.	L	3-4	Valenzuela	Cox
19—Los Ang.	W	2-1	Forsch	Welch
20—Los Ang.	L	2-7	Honeycutt	Conroy
21—San Fran.	W	8-3	Mathews	Carlton
22—San Fran.	W	10-7	Tudor	Blue
23—San Fran.	W	4-3	Cox	LaCoss
25—San Diego	W	3-2	Forsch	Whitson
26—San Diego	W	4-2	Mathews	Hoyt
27—San Diego	W	3-2	Tudor	McCullers
28—At Phila.	W	3-1	Cox	Ruffin
29—At Phila.	L	7-12	Hume	Conroy
30—At Phila.	W	6-3	Forsch	Hudson

Won 14, Lost 12

AUGUST			Winner	Loser
1—At Pitts.	L	0-4	Rhoden	Mathews
2—At Pitts.	W	7-3	Tudor	McWilliams
3—At Pitts.	L	0-3	Reuschel	Cox
4—Phila.	W	3-2	Worrell	Schatzeder
5—Phila.	W	7-4	Forsch	Maddux
6—Phila.	W	2-1	Mathews	Carman
7—Phila.	W	6-5	Tudor	Gross
8—Pittsburgh	W	3-1	Cox	Reuschel
9—Pittsburgh	L	5-8	Walk	Burris
10—Pittsburgh	W	5-4	Forsch	Bielecki
11—At Mon.	W	5-4	Mathews	Youmans
12—At Mon.	L	3-10	Sebra	Tudor
13—At Mon.	W	6-2	Cox	Smith
14—At N.Y.	L	3-4	McDowell	Worrell
14—At N.Y.	W	5-1	Horton	Anderson
15—At N.Y.	W	4-2†	Perry	Orosco
16—At N.Y.	W	3-1‡	Mathews	McDowell
17—At N.Y.	W	2-1	Tudor	Aguilera
17—At N.Y.	L	2-9	Niemann	Cox
19—At Cinn.	L	1-6	Browning	Conroy
20—At Cinn.	L	1-3	Gullickson	Forsch
21—At Cinn.	L	4-9	Welsh	Mathews
22—Houston	W	6-5	Tudor	Ryan
23—Houston	W	7-1	Cox	Scott
24—Houston	L	1-5	Deshaies	Conroy
25—Atlanta	L	2-4	Palmer	Forsch
26—Atlanta	W	7-1	Mathews	Acker
27—Atlanta	W	2-1	Worrell	Mahler
29—Cincinnati	L	0-2	Gullickson	Cox
30—Cincinnati	W	5-2	Conroy	Welsh
31—Cincinnati	W	9-3	Forsch	Browning

Won 19, Lost 12

SEPTEMBER			Winner	Loser
1—At Atlanta	W	5-2	Soff	Acker
2—At Atlanta	L	2-4	Mahler	Tudor
3—At Atlanta	W	5-3	Cox	Smith
5—At Hous.	W	8-5	Soff	Lopez
6—At Hous.	L	6-7	Kerfeld	Worrell
7—At Hous.	L	3-6	Calhoun	Mathews
8—At Pitts.	L	2-3	Patterson	Cox
9—At Pitts.	W	3-1	Horton	Reuschel
10—At Pitts.	W	4-3	Soff	Jones
12—Montreal	L	3-4‡	McGaffigan	Boever
13—Montreal	L	1-5	Martinez	Mathews
14—Montreal	W	10-2	Cox	Sebra
15—New York	W	1-0x	Worrell	McDowell
16—New York	L	2-4	Aguilera	Conroy
17—At Phila.	W	8-5	Forsch	Ruffin
18—At Phila.	L	3-4	Maddux	Mathews
19—At Mon.	L	2-3‡	McClure	Perry
20—At Mon.	W	3-1	Horton	Valdez
21—At Mon.	W	7-2	Conroy	Tibbs
22—At N.Y.	L	2-5	Gooden	Forsch
23—At N.Y.	L	1-9	Ojeda	Mathews
24—Phila.	W	7-1	Cox	Gross
25—Phila.	W	5-4	Soff	Schatzeder
26—Chicago	L	1-4	Sutcliffe	Conroy
27—Chicago	L	3-5†	Lynch	Soff
28—Chicago	W	4-1	Mathews	Trout
30—Pitts.	W	5-3	Cox	Rhoden

Won 14, Lost 13

OCTOBER			Winner	Loser
1—Pittsburgh	L	3-4	McWilliams	Soff
2—Pittsburgh	L	1-5	Kipper	Conroy
4—At Chicago	L	7-8	Lynch	Forsch
5—At Chicago	L	1-8	Hoffman	Cox

Won 0, Lost 4

*5½ innings. †10 innings. ‡11 innings. §12 innings. x13 innings. y17 innings. zSuspended game, completed June 18.

Heath struggled both behind and at the plate. He had just risen above .200 when he was traded to Detroit in August.

"If Heath would have worked out, we might have been better," Herzog said. "We wouldn't have been buried."

Rookie Mike LaValliere was an able replacement for Heath defensively, but his hitting (.234, 30 RBIs) was much like the rest of the club's.

With the exception of infielder Jose Oquendo (.297), the bench provided little help. Utilityman Clint Hurdle (.195) and outfielders Tito Landrum (.210), Curt Ford (.248) and John Morris (.240) struggled.

Ford and Morris, both rookies, contributed to the team's outstanding defense. The Cardinals committed only 123 errors, the N.L. low, and turned 178 double plays (second in the league).

Defense and pitching kept the Cardinals from finishing in the cellar. Though they ranked last in the league in shutouts (four, all combined efforts) and strikeouts, the St. Louis pitching staff compiled a 3.37 earned-run average, No. 4 in the league, and surrendered fewer walks than any other N.L. team.

Righthander Bob Forsch, 36, was the club's top winner at 14-10. He fashioned a 3.25 ERA while pitching 230 innings, the team high.

Tudor, a 21-game winner in '85, was next with a 13-7 record and a 2.92 ERA. Cox, who did not win his first game until June 1, rallied from a 2-7 start to finish 12-13 with a 2.90 ERA and eight complete games.

Conroy, the other half of the Andujar trade, did not live up to expectations. The lefthander went 5-11 with a 5.23 ERA. But another youngster, rookie lefthander Greg Mathews, was 11-8 with a 3.65 ERA after being promoted from Louisville (American Association).

Horton (4-3, 2.24 ERA) and righthander Ray Burris (4-5, 5.60) made spot starts. Burris, who joined the Cardinals in May, was sent to the bullpen before being released in August.

Even without Dayley (five saves) and Lahti for much of the year, the bullpen was strong, mainly because of Worrell. The rookie righthander led the league with 36 saves, won nine games and earned N.L. Fireman of the Year and Rookie of the Year honors. Horton and Pat Perry provided strong middle-inning relief.

The Cardinals' only positive note offensively was that they stole 200 or more bases (262, the league high) for the fifth year in a row. Coleman had a major league-high 107 in 121 attempts, better than his ratio in '85, when he stole 110. But McGee, who had 56 steals in '85, fell to 19.

Overall, the Cardinals offered a pretty sorry defense of their '85 pennant. But as Cox pointed out: "The way we played all year was dismal. Coming in third. . .it could have been a lot worse."

Right fielder Andy Van Slyke improved his average to .270 and led the powerless Cardinals with 13 home runs.

Mitch Webster took over as the Expos center fielder and responded with an impressive .290 batting average.

Injuries Derail Expos Express

By IAN MacDONALD

It's doubtful that the Montreal Expos could have done much to derail the New York Mets' locomotive run to the National League East title in 1986. But they could have made the race interesting if not for an incredible array of critical injuries.

By August 2, Montreal's starting shortstop (cleanup hitter Hubie Brooks) and catcher (Mike Fitzgerald) were through for the year. A month earlier, lefthanded starter Joe Hesketh had thrown his last pitch of the season. By the time the Expos staggered to the finish, righthander Bryn Smith, an 18-game winner the year before, and third baseman Tim Wallach were home with injuries—Smith a damaged elbow that eventually required off-season surgery, Wallach a broken ankle.

And there were other medical maladies. As a result, the Expos finished with a 78-83 record, 29½ games behind the Mets. It was only the club's second losing record since 1978.

The Expos certainly were expecting better results when the season opened.

"We're not on any long-range program here," General Manager Murray Cook said as the team left spring training. "We think we can win it this year."

Manager Buck Rodgers was a little more cautious.

"This could be one of the better pitching staffs in the league ... potentially," he said. "Our strength is going to be our pitching."

With New York running away with the division early, Montreal played like the second-best team in the league for the first three months. Brooks had a fantastic start, challenging the league leaders in average (.333), home runs (14) and runs batted in (54) at the All-Star break. By then, the Expos were 4½ games ahead of the third-place Philadelphia Phillies with a 46-38 record.

"This is about what we expected," Cook said. "If we play to our potential, we're in line for 90 wins."

The Mets were 13 games ahead, though, and realistically, the Expos didn't have much chance of catching up.

"It's going to take a collapse by New York," Rodgers said, "and their pitching staff is too deep for that. We're not in a good position."

Before long, Montreal's position worsened. Hesketh already was gone, having succumbed to shoulder problems after compiling a 6-5 record through early July. Then Brooks, who already was playing in discomfort because of an injured finger on his left hand, was forced to wear a splint on his left thumb shortly after the All-Star break. The shortstop wasn't the same after that. He put up with excruciating pain for several days before going on the disabled list August 2. Brooks was leading the league in hitting (.340) when he was sidelined, but the Expos had long since lost their power threat in the middle of the order.

Young Floyd Youmans survived a shaky start and won 13 games.

The loss of Fitzgerald was almost as devastating. Along with handling the pitchers well and earning the No. 1 catching job, Fitzgerald had raised his average to .282 by the time he suffered a hand injury that placed him on the disabled list the same day as Brooks. Both players underwent surgery.

"The injuries were the last nail in the coffin for any hopes of catching the Mets," Rodgers said at the time. "We've got enough manpower and character on this club to battle for second place, and that's what our new goal is."

The injury-riddled Expos did not reach that goal. A 32-45 second half dropped

SCORES OF MONTREAL EXPOS' 1986 GAMES

APRIL			Winner	Loser
8—At Atlanta	L	0-6	Mahler	Smith
10—At Atlanta	W	6-3	Tibbs	Garber
11—At St. L.	L	1-9	Forsch	Hesketh
12—At St. L.	L	3-6	Tudor	Youmans
13—At St. L.	W	3-2	Smith	Kepshire
15—Chicago	W	4-3†	Reardon	Smith
17—Chicago	L	6-7§	Smith	Reardon
18—St. Louis	L	2-4	Tudor	Hesketh
19—St. Louis	L	6-9y	Conroy	Youmans
20—St. Louis	W	2-0	Tibbs	Horton
22—Phila.	W	8-2	McGaffigan	Hudson
23—Phila.	L	4-5	Carlton	Hesketh
24—At Chicago	L	5-7	Sutcliffe	Smith
25—At Chicago	W	4-2†	Reardon	Keough
26—At Chicago	W	4-2	Burke	Frazier
27—At Chicago	L	10-12	Fontenot	Reardon
29—At Cinn.	W	7-4	Smith	Soto
30—At Cinn.	W	8-0	Tibbs	Browning

Won 9, Lost 9

MAY			Winner	Loser
2—Houston	L	3-6	Knepper	Youmans
3—Houston	W	7-6*	Reardon	DiPino
4—Houston	W	7-6	Reardon	Smith
5—At Phila.	W	6-4	Schatzeder	Tekulve
6—At Phila.	W	8-0	McGaffigan	Carlton
7—At Phila.	W	8-2	Youmans	Rawley
9—Los Ang.	W	8-4	Reardon	Valenzuela
10—Los Ang.	W	3-2†	Schatzeder	Howell
11—Los Ang.	W	4-3	Hesketh	Welch
12—Cincinnati	L	3-4	Power	Roberge
13—Cincinnati	W	4-2	Youmans	Soto
14—Atlanta	W	3-2	B. Smith	Z. Smith
15—Atlanta	L	4-7*	Sutter	Schatzeder
16—At S. Diego	W	3-2	Hesketh	Hawkins
17—At S. Diego	L	3-5	Hoyt	McGaffigan
18—At S. Diego	W	8-3	Youmans	Thurmond
20—At L.A.	L	0-4	Valenzuela	Smith
21—At L.A.	L	1-6	Hershiser	Tibbs
22—At L.A.	W	5-2	Hesketh	Welch
23—At S. Fran.	W	4-3	Youmans	Garrelts
24—At S. Fran.	W	7-4	McGaffigan	Blue
25—At S. Fran.	L	3-11	LaCoss	Smith
26—San Diego	L	6-9	Dravecky	Parrett
27—San Diego	W	5-4	Burke	T. Stoddard
28—San Diego	L	1-10	Hoyt	Youmans
30—At Hous.	W	1-0	Smith	Scott
31—At Hous.	L	3-4	DiPino	Burke

Won 17, Lost 10

JUNE			Winner	Loser
1—At Hous.	L	4-8	Knepper	Hesketh
3—San Fran.	L	6-7	Blue	Youmans
4—San Fran.	L	2-4	Robinson	Reardon
5—Phila.	L	3-7	Hudson	Tibbs
6—Phila.	W	10-9*	Burke	Rucker
7—Phila.	L	1-3	Rawley	McGaffigan
8—Phila.	W	12-0	Youmans	Maddux
9—At St. L.	W	5-4	Burke	Worrell
10—At St. L.	W	4-2	Tibbs	Forsch
11—At St. L.	W	4-3*	Reardon	Bargar
13—At Phila.	L	1-2	Rawley	Burke
14—At Phila.	L	6-7	Lerch	Roberge
15—At Phila.	W	2-0	McGaffigan	Hudson
16—New York	L	1-4*	Sisk	Reardon
17—New York	W	4-2	Hesketh	Berenyi
18—New York	W	7-4	Youmans	Gooden
19—Pittsburgh	L	2-4	Kipper	Smith
20—Pittsburgh	W	7-2	McGaffigan	Walk
21—Pittsburgh	L	1-14	Rhoden	Tibbs
22—Pittsburgh	W	2-1	Hesketh	Reuschel
23—At N.Y.	W	5-4*	Burke	Orosco
24—At N.Y.	W	6-2	Smith	Berenyi
25—At N.Y.	L	2-5	Fernandez	McGaffigan
27—At Pitts.	L	1-7	Rhoden	Tibbs
28—At Pitts.	W	3-2	Hesketh	Reuschel
29—At Pitts.	W	6-4	Youmans	Bielecki
30—At Chicago	W	4-3†	Schatzeder	Smith

Won 15, Lost 12

JULY			Winner	Loser
1—At Chicago	L	0-1z	Gumpert	Schatzeder
2—At Chicago	L	4-5	Smith	McClure
3—At Atlanta	L	1-3	Palmer	Hesketh
4—At Atlanta	W	11-5	Youmans	Mahler
5—At Atlanta	W	12-5	Smith	McMurtry
6—At Atlanta	W	11-8	Burke	Smith
7—Houston	L	1-12	Scott	Martinez
8—Houston	L	1-4	Ryan	Tibbs
9—Houston	W	2-1	Youmans	Knepper
10—Cincinnati	W	8-6	Smith	Welsh
11—Cincinnati	L	2-3	Gullickson	McGaffigan
12—Cincinnati	L	0-2	Denny	Martinez
13—Cincinnati	L	2-10a	Browning	Burke
17—Atlanta	W	4-2	Youmans	Mahler
18—Atlanta	W	5-4	Burke	Dedmon
19—Atlanta	L	2-7	Palmer	Tibbs
21—At Hous.	L	7-8	Kerfeld	Reardon
22—At Hous.	L	0-1*	Smith	Youmans
23—At Hous.	L	3-4†	Lopez	Burke
24—At Cinn.	W	6-5x	Sebra	Willis
25—At Cinn.	L	2-9	Denny	Martinez
26—At Cinn.	L	6-7	Robinson	Sebra
27—At Cinn.	L	7-9	Murphy	Reardon
28—Pittsburgh	L	4-7	Reuschel	Smith
30—Pittsburgh	W	3-2	Tibbs	Winn

Won 9, Lost 16

AUGUST			Winner	Loser
1—At N.Y.	L	1-3	Gooden	Youmans
2—At N.Y.	L	1-4	Aguilera	Sebra
3—At N.Y.	L	3-4*	McDowell	McClure
4—At Pitts.	W	5-4	Tibbs	Jones
5—At Pitts.	W	3-0	Martinez	Bielecki
6—At Pitts.	W	3-2	Youmans	Rhoden
7—At Pitts.	W	5-4	McGaffigan	Robinson
8—New York	W	5-3	Smith	Ojeda
9—New York	L	8-10	McDowell	Reardon
10—New York	L	2-7	Fernandez	Martinez
11—St. Louis	L	4-5	Mathews	Youmans
12—St. Louis	W	10-3	Sebra	Tudor
13—St. Louis	L	2-6	Cox	Smith
14—Chicago	W	5-4*	McGaffigan	Davis
15—Chicago	W	5-2	Martinez	Trout
15—Chicago	W	5-1	Burke	Lynch
16—Chicago	L	0-5	Moyer	Youmans
17—Chicago	L	1-2	Smith	Reardon
19—At S. Diego	L	1-7	Hawkins	Smith
20—At S. Diego	L	2-3	Show	Tibbs
21—At S. Diego	L	0-6	Dravecky	Martinez
22—At L.A.	L	1-2*	Howell	Burke
23—At L.A.	W	7-4	Sebra	Honeycutt
24—At L.A.	L	2-3*	Holton	Burke
25—At S. Fran.	W	6-5	McGaffigan	LaCoss
26—At S. Fran.	L	0-1‡	Garrelts	Roberge
27—At S. Fran.	L	2-3	Downs	McGaffigan
30—San Diego	W	10-1	Smith	Hoyt
30—San Diego	L	4-5	McCullers	McClure
31—San Diego	L	1-4	Wojna	Tibbs

Won 12, Lost 18

SEPTEMBER			Winner	Loser
1—Los Ang.	W	7-6	Reardon	Howell
2—Los Ang.	W	1-0	Youmans	Welch
3—Los Ang.	L	3-5	Honeycutt	Sebra
4—San Fran.	W	4-2	Smith	LaCoss
5—San Fran.	L	4-8	Garrelts	Burke
6—San Fran.	W	3-1	McClure	Williams
7—San Fran.	L	0-1	Krukow	Youmans
8—At N.Y.	W	9-1	Sebra	Ojeda
9—At N.Y.	W	9-7	Burke	Orosco
10—At N.Y.	L	1-6	Darling	Valdez
12—At St. L.	W	4-3†	McGaffigan	Boever
13—At St. L.	W	5-1	Martinez	Mathews
14—At St. L.	L	2-10	Cox	Sebra
15—Chicago	L	3-7	Moyer	Valdez
16—Chicago	W	4-1	Tibbs	Sutcliffe
17—Pittsburgh	W	6-5	St. Claire	Jones
17—Pittsburgh	L	1-4	Kipper	Sebra
18—Pittsburgh	L	1-3	Smiley	Reardon
19—St. Louis	W	3-2†	McClure	Perry
20—St. Louis	L	1-3	Horton	Valdez
21—St. Louis	L	2-7	Conroy	Tibbs
22—At Chicago	W	5-2	Youmans	Eckersley
23—At Chicago	W	10-5	St. Claire	Maddux
24—At Pitts.	L	1-2	Robinson	McClure
25—At Pitts.	W	8-4	Owchinko	Rhoden
26—Phila.	L	0-5	Freeman	Valdez
27—Phila.	L	0-1	Carman	Youmans
28—Phila.	L	2-5	Gross	Martinez
30—New York	W	1-0	Sebra	Darling

Won 15, Lost 14

OCTOBER			Winner	Loser
1—New York	L	4-6*	Orosco	McClure
2—New York	L	2-8	Gooden	Youmans
3—At Phila.	W	6-5	McGaffigan	Tekulve
4—At Phila.	L	4-5x	Schatzeder	Roberge
5—At Phila.	L	1-2*	Schatzeder	Brown

Won 1, Lost 4

*10 innings. †11 innings. ‡12 innings. §13 innings. x14 innings. y17 innings. zSuspended game, completed July 2. aSuspended game, completed July 24.

Jeff Reardon recorded 35 saves but watched his earned-run average rise to 3.94.

them to fourth place in the N.L. East.

Montreal's pitching never lived up to Rodgers' expectations. The staff's 3.78 earned-run average ranked sixth in the league, and the starters managed only 15 complete games. That put a strain on the bullpen, which produced 50 saves (No. 2 in the league) but struggled the last couple of months.

Jeff Reardon finished with 35 saves, only six fewer than his league-leading total in '85, but his ERA was a shaky 3.94. Tim Burke (9-7, 2.93 ERA) was a workhorse again with a team-high 68 appearances, while lefthander Bob McClure, who was purchased from Milwaukee in June, had six saves and a 3.02 ERA. Used both as a starter and a reliever, Andy McGaffigan went 10-5 with a 2.65 ERA.

The best of the starters was righthander Floyd Youmans. The 22-year-old fireballer survived a shaky start to go 13-12 with a 3.53 ERA and 202 strikeouts, making him the first Expo since Steve Rogers in 1977 to fan 200 batters in a season.

Smith was 10-8 when he was sidelined September 9. The other regular starter was righthander Jay Tibbs, who struggled all year, spent some time in the bullpen and finished with a 7-9 record.

Rookie Bob Sebra went 5-5 with a 3.55 ERA after being called up from Indianapolis (American Association) in the second half. Also making several starts was veteran Dennis Martinez (3-6, 4.59), a June acquisition from Baltimore.

Veteran lefthander Dan Schatzeder was dealt to Philadelphia in July after going 3-2 for the Expos. The four-player deal brought Tom Foley to Montreal. With Brooks out, Foley proved himself an asset in the middle of the infield while batting .257 for the Expos.

Foley added a little punch to a generally weak Montreal attack. The Expos tied for fifth in the league with a .254 average but scored only 637 runs (10th in the league).

The major offensive contributors were left fielder Tim Raines and center fielder Mitch Webster. Raines won the N.L. batting crown with a .334 average, scored 91 runs, knocked in 62 and stole 70 bases. His .413 on-base percentage tied for the N.L. high. Webster led the league with 13 triples while hitting .290.

After Raines and Webster, however, there wasn't much to get excited about among the Expos' regulars.

Wallach hit only .233, though he had 18 homers and 71 RBIs. It took a strong finish for right fielder Andre Dawson to rise to .284 with 20 homers and 78 RBIs.

Troubled by his daughter's serious illness, Vance Law had an off year. The second baseman hit a career-low .225. Rookies Al Newman (.200) and Luis Rivera (.205) filled in when necessary at second base and shortstop.

The Expos made a costly mistake at first base early in the season. The plan had been to give rookie Andres Galarraga the job and bring him along slowly, but when the young slugger had trouble with breaking pitches in spring training, the Expos acquired veteran Jason Thompson. As soon as Thompson showed up, Galarraga started to hit. Thompson was released June 30, but the Expos still were responsible for much of the veteran's large salary.

Galarraga was just finding a groove when he suffered the first of two injuries that would disable him for a total of six weeks. The rookie finished with a .271 average and 10 homers.

The Montreal bench was unproductive, as indicated by the club's .188 pinch-hitting average. Utilityman Wally Johnson had the best average (.283) among the club's part-timers, followed by outfielder Jim Wohlford (.266), infielder Wayne Krenchicki (.240) and outfielder Herm Winningham (.216). Dann Bilardello, Fitzgerald's replacement behind the plate, hit only .194.

Montreal's disappointing season was reflected at the gate. The Expos attracted just over 1.1 million fans at home, their lowest attendance in a decade.

Jody Davis gave the Cubs Gold Glove defense behind the plate and tied for the team lead with 21 home runs.

Pitching Problems Doom Cubs

By JOE GODDARD

After a 1985 season in which their entire pitching rotation was felled by injuries, the Chicago Cubs were sure that they would return to the form that brought them a division pennant in 1984.

They didn't. The healthy rotation failed to produce a 10-game winner for the first time this century (excluding the 1981 strike season) as the Cubs finished fifth in the National League East, 37 games out of first place.

With his team out of the running from the first road trip, General Manager Dallas Green fired 1984 N.L. Manager of the Year Jim Frey on June 12. Coach John Vukovich served as interim manager for two games—a June 13 doubleheader split with St. Louis—until New York Yankees coach Gene Michael took over the next day.

At the time Michael became manager, the Cubs had a 24-34 record. Green then questioned Michael's patient methods when the club continued to play at a similar clip (46-56 under Michael) en route to a 70-90 record.

"Offensively, we put up some pretty interesting figures," Green said. "We had three guys with 20 home runs, but it didn't mean a thing for the t-e-a-m. It meant a lot for the 'I.' "

The only impressive part of the pitching staff was big Lee Smith, who became the first N.L. reliever to save 30 games for three straight years. He ranked fourth in the league with 31 saves and tied for the team high in victories with nine, while his 3.09 earned-run average was the Cubs' best.

Eight Cub pitchers threw at least one complete game, but the team total of only 11 was last in the league, as was the staff's 4.49 ERA, the club's worst since 1975.

Rick Sutcliffe, the '84 N.L. Cy Young Award winner, sandwiched eight straight losses around a shoulder ailment to finish with a 5-14 record. Scott Sanderson was the winningest starter with a 9-11 mark, but two came in relief after he had been removed from the rotation late in the season while Michael examined some young pitchers. Workhorse Dennis Eckersley allowed only 1.3 walks per game but paid for his accuracy with a 4.57 ERA as batters waited for their pitches. Lefthander Steve Trout (5-7, 4.75 ERA) was dropped from the rotation in mid-August.

After being obtained from the New York Mets in a June trade, righthander Ed Lynch (7-5, 3.79) performed capably, first as a spot starter and then a reliever. Rookie lefty Jamie Moyer was promoted from the minors the day Michael came aboard and went 7-4 despite a 5.05 ERA.

The middle relievers were ineffective taking leads and ties to Smith. Frank DiPino (2-4) and Ron Davis (0-2) were obtained after the All-Star break from the Houston Astros and the Minnesota Twins, respectively, but neither did better than predecessors George Frazier and Ray Fontenot. Dave Gumpert was 2-0 and inconsistent Guy Hoffman was 6-2, but they were not considered setup men.

On the bright side, the club was pleased with the potential of September call-ups Greg Maddux (2-4) and lefty Drew Hall (1-2).

Though the Cubs made only one more error than St. Louis, the league's top defensive team, they suffered in outfield defense from a lack of speed and skills. That deficiency at least partly accounted for a 28-52 record on the road, where most games were played on artificial turf.

Offensively, the Cubs posted plenty of impressive numbers. They led the league in home runs (155) and ranked third in batting (.256) and fifth in runs (680).

Left fielder Gary Matthews was Chicago's co-leader in homers with 21, but he became a part-time player when Michael decided that his fielding was inadequate. Matthews hit .259 with 46 runs batted in.

Right fielder Keith Moreland led the Cubs with 79 RBIs and 72 runs scored. His RBI total, however, was 27 below his 1985 total and his .271 batting average fell 36 points from the previous year.

Moreland was moved to third base, the weakest spot in the Cubs' lineup, in September to make room for Chico Walker. The 28-year-old Walker tied Bob Dernier's club record for stolen bases in a month with 15 and batted .277 in 101 at-bats.

Dernier, the center fielder, suffered on defense when he tore his rotator cuff while making a catch. He batted just .225.

Ryne Sandberg again played second base impeccably, tying the major league record for his position with only five errors and winning his fourth straight Gold Glove. Although he batted .284 with 14 homers, 76 RBIs and a team-high 34 stolen bases, he had a 3½-month stretch without a game-winning RBI.

SCORES OF CHICAGO CUBS' 1986 GAMES

APRIL			Winner	Loser
8—At St. L.	L	1-2	Tudor	Sutcliffe
10—At St. L.	L	2-4	Ownbey	Eckersley
11—At Pitts.	W	5-4	Trout	McWilliams
12—At Pitts.	L	1-3	Rhoden	Smith
13—At Pitts.	L	0-8	Reuschel	Sutcliffe
15—At Mon.	L	3-4†	Reardon	Smith
17—At Mon.	W	7-6§	Smith	Reardon
18—Pittsburgh	L	0-4	Rhoden	Sutcliffe
19—Pittsburgh	L	8-14	Reuschel	Sanderson
20—Pittsburgh	L	8-10xz	Jones	DiPino
22—St. Louis	W	3-2	Baller	Perry
23—St. Louis	W	6-0	Sanderson	Ownbey
24—Montreal	W	7-5	Sutcliffe	Smith
25—Montreal	L	2-4†	Reardon	Keough
26—Montreal	L	2-4	Burke	Frazier
27—Montreal	W	12-10	Fontenot	Reardon
28—At S. Diego	W	4-3	Keough	Gossage
29—At S. Diego	L	4-5	Lefferts	Fontenot
30—At L.A.	L	0-4	Welch	Eckersley

Won 7, Lost 12

MAY			Winner	Loser
1—At L.A.	L	0-4	Honeycutt	Hoffman
2—At S. Fran.	W	6-5	Keough	Davis
3—At S. Fran.	W	6-5	Frazier	Minton
4—At S. Fran.	L	1-2*	LaCoss	Sutcliffe
4—At S. Fran.	L	1-2	Mason	Frazier
6—Los Ang.	W	7-6	Smith	Niedenfuer
7—Los Ang.	L	4-8	Niedenfuer	Baller
8—Los Ang.	W	6-5	Sanderson	Reuss
9—San Diego	L	2-6	Hawkins	Sutcliffe
10—San Diego	W	6-5	Eckersley	Hoyt
11—San Diego	W	9-5	Trout	Thurmond
13—San Fran.	L	5-6	Minton	Smith
14—San Fran.	L	3-11	LaCoss	Sutcliffe
16—At Hous.	L	6-9	Solano	Baller
17—At Hous.	L	1-5	Scott	Trout
18—At Hous.	W	5-2	Hoffman	Knepper
20—At Atlanta	L	3-8	Palmer	Sanderson
21—At Atlanta	L	8-9§	Dedmon	Frazier
22—At Atlanta	L	0-2	Johnson	Trout
23—Houston	W	4-1	Sutcliffe	Solano
24—Houston	W	4-3	Frazier	Smith
25—Houston	L	1-3†	Kerfeld	Smith
26—Cincinnati	W	9-6	Eckersley	Terry
27—Cincinnati	L	4-5	Browning	Trout
28—Cincinnati	W	5-0	Sutcliffe	Gullickson
30—Atlanta	W	6-1	Sanderson	Mahler
31—Atlanta	L	4-8	Dedmon	Eckersley

Won 12, Lost 15

JUNE			Winner	Loser
1—Atlanta	W	7-3	Hoffman	Smith
2—At Cinn.	W	8-6	Sutcliffe	Gullickson
3—At Cinn.	L	3-5	Power	Baller
4—At Cinn.	L	0-2	Browning	Sanderson
5—At St. L.	L	3-4	Forsch	Keough
6—At St. L.	W	9-3	Baller	Cox
7—At St. L.	L	2-3	Tudor	Sutcliffe
8—At St. L.	W	14-2	Trout	Mathews
9—At Pitts.	L	5-6†	Robinson	Baller
10—At Pitts.	L	4-6	Kipper	Eckersley
11—At Pitts.	L	3-5	Rhoden	Hoffman
13—St. Louis	L	0-1*	Mathews	Sutcliffe
13—St. Louis	W	3-2†	Smith	Worrell
14—St. Louis	L	0-1	Burris	Sanderson
15—St. Louis	W	4-3†	Fontenot	Worrell
16—Phila.	W	7-5	Moyer	Carlton
17—Phila.	L	8-11	Tekulve	Fontenot
18—Phila.	W	5-4*	Smith	Bedrosian
20—At N.Y.	L	3-10	Fernandez	Sanderson
21—At N.Y.	W	8-6	Fontenot	Orosco
22—At N.Y.	L	2-4	Darling	Sutcliffe
23—At Phila.	L	1-19	Rawley	Moyer
24—At Phila.	L	6-7*	Bedrosian	Smith
25—At Phila.	W	10-7	Hoffman	Hudson
28—New York	L	2-5	McDowell	Fontenot
29—New York	L	4-7	Gooden	Sutcliffe
30—Montreal	L	3-4†	Schatzeder	Smith

Won 10, Lost 17

JULY			Winner	Loser
1—Montreal	W	1-0a	Gumpert	Schatzeder
2—Montreal	W	5-4	Smith	McClure
3—At S. Diego	L	1-4	Hoyt	Eckersley
4—At S. Diego	L	1-2	Gossage	Fontenot
5—At S. Diego	W	3-2	Gumpert	Lefferts
6—At S. Diego	L	1-2	Hawkins	Sanderson
8—At S. Fran.	W	4-1	Eckersley	Krukow
9—At S. Fran.	W	4-3*	Smith	Berenguer
10—At L.A.	L	4-11	Hershiser	Moyer
11—At L.A.	W	6-3	Sanderson	Honeycutt
12—At L.A.	W	7-4	Lynch	Niedenfuer
13—At L.A.	L	3-4	Howell	Smith
17—San Fran.	L	4-6	Blue	Lynch
18—San Fran.	W	2-1	Sanderson	LaCoss
19—San Fran.	W	11-6	Hoffman	Krukow
20—San Fran.	L	4-5	Garrelts	Eckersley
21—San Diego	W	6-1	Moyer	Hoyt
22—San Diego	W	6-4	Lynch	McCullers
23—San Diego	L	5-7	Lefferts	Fontenot
25—Los Ang.	W	8-3	Trout	Welch
26—Los Ang.	W	9-4	Eckersley	Honeycutt
27—Los Ang.	L	11-13	Howell	DiPino
28—At N.Y.	L	2-9	Ojeda	Sanderson
29—At N.Y.	L	0-3	Darling	Trout
29—At N.Y.	W	2-1	Moyer	Sisk
30—At N.Y.	W	4-3	Eckersley	Fernandez

Won 15, Lost 11

AUGUST			Winner	Loser
1—At Phila.	L	3-4†	Tekulve	DiPino
2—At Phila.	L	2-12	Gross	Sanderson
3—At Phila.	L	2-6	Bedrosian	DiPino
4—New York	W	4-2	Eckersley	Darling
5—New York	W	8-5	Smith	McDowell
6—New York	L	6-7‡	McDowell	Frazier
6—New York	L	6-7b	Anderson	Trout
7—New York	L	3-12	Aguilera	Sanderson
8—Phila.	W	2-1	Trout	Ruffin
9—Phila.	L	2-4	Hudson	Eckersley
10—Phila.	W	4-0	Lynch	Maddux
11—Pittsburgh	L	7-10	Rhoden	Moyer
12—Pittsburgh	W	3-1	Sanderson	McWilliams
13—Pittsburgh	W	9-8	DiPino	Robinson
14—At Mon.	L	4-5*	McGaffigan	Davis
15—At Mon.	L	2-5	Martinez	Trout
15—At Mon.	L	1-5	Burke	Lynch
16—At Mon.	W	5-0	Moyer	Youmans
17—At Mon.	W	2-1	Smith	Reardon
19—Atlanta	L	2-7	Alexander	Sutcliffe
20—Atlanta	L	3-8	Palmer	Eckersley
21—Atlanta	L	2-5	Acker	Lynch
22—Cincinnati	W	3-2	Moyer	Power
23—Cincinnati	L	3-7	Browning	Sanderson
24—Cincinnati	L	1-7	Gullickson	Davis
25—At Hous.	L	2-3	Kerfeld	Smith
26—At Hous.	W	5-3	Lynch	Darwin
27—At Hous.	L	1-7	Ryan	Moyer
29—At Atlanta	W	7-3	Sanderson	Smith
30—At Atlanta	L	3-4	Alexander	Sutcliffe
31—At Atlanta	L	3-4	Dedmon	Smith

Won 11, Lost 20

SEPTEMBER			Winner	Loser
1—Houston	L	4-6	Darwin	Lynch
2—Houston	L	7-8yc	Darwin	Maddux
3—Houston	L	2-8	Scott	Sanderson
5—At Cinn.	L	2-11	Browning	Sutcliffe
6—At Cinn.	L	1-5	Power	Eckersley
7—At Cinn.	W	11-3	Maddux	Gullickson
8—Phila.	W	7-4	Lynch	Maddux
9—Phila.	W	8-6*	Smith	Bedrosian
10—Phila.	W	8-7	Hoffman	Tekulve
12—At Pitts.	W	9-8*	DiPino	Robinson
13—At Pitts.	L	2-5	Patterson	Maddux
14—At Pitts.	L	2-9	Reuschel	Hall
15—At Mon.	W	7-3	Moyer	Valdez
16—At Mon.	L	1-4	Tibbs	Sutcliffe
17—At N.Y.	L	2-4	Gooden	Eckersley
18—At N.Y.	L	0-5	Anderson	Maddux
19—Pittsburgh	W	8-2	Sanderson	Pena
20—Pittsburgh	W	1-0	Moyer	Rhoden
21—Pittsburgh	W	3-2	Sanderson	Pena
22—Montreal	L	2-5	Youmans	Eckersley
23—Montreal	L	5-10	St. Claire	Maddux
24—New York	W	8-2	Hall	Aguilera
25—New York	L	5-6	McDowell	Lynch
26—At St. L.	W	4-1	Sutcliffe	Conroy
27—At St. L.	W	5-3*	Lynch	Soff
28—At St. L.	L	1-4	Mathews	Trout
29—At Phila.	W	8-3	G. Maddux	M. Maddux
30—At Phila.	L	2-9	Ruffin	Hall

Won 13, Lost 15

OCTOBER			Winner	Loser
4—St. Louis	W	8-7	Lynch	Forsch
5—St. Louis	W	8-1	Hoffman	Cox

Won 2, Lost 0

*10 innings. †11 innings. ‡12 innings. §13 innings. x17 innings. y18 innings. zSuspended game, completed August 11. aSuspended game, completed July 2. bSuspended game, completed August 7. cSuspended game, completed September 3.

Big Lee Smith continued to dominate and became the first National League reliever to record 30 saves in three consecutive seasons.

Gold Glove winner Jody Davis established himself as a premier catcher by nailing 78 baserunners stealing and picking off nine more, but the 24-man roster limitation left him exhausted as the only catcher in the hot months. He drove in 74 runs and tied Matthews with 21 homers.

First baseman Leon Durham hit 20 homers for the fourth time in five years but fell to .262 with only 65 RBIs. Second-year shortstop Shawon Dunston was en route to 80 RBIs when a late-season slump stopped him at 68. Still, he hit 17 homers, the most for a Cub shortstop since Ernie Banks in 1961. Dunston also displayed his strong arm defensively, although his 32 errors showed that he still needs to work out some rough spots.

Age limited Ron Cey's third-base defense, so the 38-year-old veteran shared the position with Manny Trillo and Chris Speier before Moreland moved from right field. Cey finished the season with only 256 at-bats, 13 homers and 36 RBIs, his lowest output as a major leaguer.

The bench was a strong point. Jerry Mumphrey led the team with a .304 average, while Thad Bosley hit over .300 again as a pinch-hitter (.275 overall). Speier and Trillo hit .284 and .296, respectively, in utility infield roles.

But the Cubs still fell far short of their lofty goals, and Green planned an overhaul for 1987.

"I don't want this kind of season to happen again," he said.

Pirates third baseman Jim Morrison surprised everybody with his impressive offensive performance.

Pirates Still Least in East

By CHARLEY FEENEY

Much of the cast was different, but the result was the same for the 1986 Pittsburgh Pirates.

Last place.

The Pirates occupied the cellar in the National League East for the third straight year. Despite many changes, including new ownership, a new general manager, a new field manager and several new faces on the field, the Pirates lost 98 games, six fewer than in 1985 but still the major league high. They finished with a 64-98 record, 44 games out of first place.

Where did the Pirates go wrong?

For starters, they went 1-17 against the division-winning New York Mets. They never got hot, although in April they did win five straight games. They had a pair of six-game losing streaks, and they never won more than 13 games in any month. With a 16-37 mark, the Pirates had the league's worst record in one-run games.

The pitching department was loaded with disappointments. First-year Manager Jim Leyland had counted on pitching to be his new club's strong suit when the season opened, but he quickly found out it was a weak link.

The pitching staff compiled a 3.90 earned-run average, which ranked eighth in the league. The starters turned in only 17 complete games, while the bullpen had 30 saves, the league's second-lowest total.

"We never had depth in pitching throughout the season," first-year General Manager Syd Thrift said.

Rick Rhoden was the club's only effective pitcher. The righthander was a Cy Young Award candidate until he slumped in the last five weeks of the season, losing his last five decisions. He finished with a 15-12 record, a 2.84 ERA, 12 complete games and 253⅔ innings pitched.

The biggest disappointment was Rick Reuschel, the staff ace with 14 victories in '85. The righthander went 9-16 with a 3.96 ERA.

Righthander Bob Walk, who opened the season as a reliever, turned in some creditable performances after joining the rotation but wound up with a 7-8 mark. Walk took the place of lefthander Larry McWilliams, who spent most of the season in the bullpen en route to a 3-11 record. Most of Pittsburgh's other starts came from rookies Mike Bielecki and Bob Kipper, who earned six victories each.

Leyland shuffled his relief pitchers all season but never came up with a solid group. The only bright spot was veteran Don Robinson, who pitched 3⅓ innings before injuring his knee and staying on the disabled list until June 7. Robinson came back to earn a career-high 14 saves in 15 save situations.

Rick Rhoden slumped late in the season, but still finished with a 15-12 record.

"I believe if we had had Robby all season, we would have won 10 more games," Leyland said, "but I hate saying anything like that because it sounds like an excuse."

Some excuse would seem to be in order considering that Leyland's other primary relievers—Cecilio Guante, Jim Winn and Pat Clements—combined for only nine saves and a 3.29 ERA.

Although pitching was the Pirates' main problem, they also had trouble at the plate. Pittsburgh finished with a .250 team batting average, the second-lowest figure in the league, and grounded into more double plays (132) than any other N.L. team.

On the plus side, the Pirates led the

SCORES OF PITTSBURGH PIRATES' 1986 GAMES

APRIL			Winner	Loser
8—New York	L	2-4	Gooden	Reuschel
11—Chicago	L	4-5	Trout	McWilliams
12—Chicago	W	3-1	Rhoden	Smith
13—Chicago	W	8-0	Reuschel	Sutcliffe
14—At Phila.	W	3-1†	Guante	Bedrosian
18—At Chicago	W	4-0	Rhoden	Sutcliffe
19—At Chicago	W	14-8	Reuschel	Sanderson
20—At Chicago	W	10-8xy	Jones	DiPino
21—At N.Y.	L	5-6	McDowell	Clements
22—At N.Y.	L	1-7	Ojeda	Kipper
24—Phila.	L	2-4	Rawley	Rhoden
25—Phila.	L	3-6	Gross	Reuschel
26—Phila.	L	5-6	Hudson	McWilliams
27—Phila.	W	13-5	Bielecki	Carlton
28—At L.A.	L	1-2	Valenzuela	Kipper
29—At L.A.	L	4-5	Hershiser	Patterson
30—At S. Fran.	L	5-6§	Garrelts	Patterson

Won 7, Lost 10

MAY			Winner	Loser
1—At S. Fran.	W	6-2	Walk	Krukow
2—At S. Diego	W	4-0	Bielecki	Dravecky
3—At S. Diego	W	7-6	Guante	Gossage
4—At S. Diego	W	5-2	Winn	Lefferts
6—San Fran.	L	2-7	Krukow	Reuschel
7—San Fran.	L	5-7	Laskey	McWilliams
8—San Fran.	W	8-2	Bielecki	Garrelts
9—Houston	L	2-3	Kerfeld	Winn
10—Houston	L	3-6	Knepper	Rhoden
11—Houston	W	4-3§	DeLeon	Kerfeld
13—San Diego	L	2-4	Show	Bielecki
14—San Diego	L	4-10	Dravecky	Kipper
16—At Cinn.	L	2-7	Denny	Rhoden
17—At Cinn.	W	4-0	Reuschel	Soto
18—At Cinn.	L	3-7	Browning	Bielecki
20—At Hous.	W	4-2	Walk	Ryan
21—At Hous.	W	2-1	Rhoden	Scott
22—At Hous.	L	0-4	Knepper	Reuschel
23—Cincinnati	L	9-12§	Power	DeLeon
24—Cincinnati	L	2-4	Gullickson	Bielecki
25—Cincinnati	L	4-7	Denny	Kipper
26—Atlanta	L	4-9	Assenmacher	Walk
27—Atlanta	L	2-6§	Garber	Walk
28—Atlanta	W	4-3	McWilliams	Palmer
30—Los Ang.	L	4-6‡	Niedenfuer	DeLeon
31—Los Ang.	W	4-0	Kipper	Honeycutt

Won 11, Lost 15

JUNE			Winner	Loser
1—Los Ang.	W	12-3	Rhoden	Welch
2—At Atlanta	W	9-2	Reuschel	Palmer
3—At Atlanta	L	5-8	Mahler	Guante
4—At Atlanta	W	12-3	Bielecki	Johnson
5—New York	L	0-7	Ojeda	Kipper
6—New York	W	7-1	Rhoden	Darling
6—New York	L	4-10	McDowell	DeLeon
7—New York	L	4-6	Gooden	Reuschel
8—New York	L	3-4	Fernandez	McWilliams
9—Chicago	W	6-5‡	Robinson	Baller
10—Chicago	W	6-4	Kipper	Eckersley
11—Chicago	W	5-3	Rhoden	Hoffman
13—At N.Y.	L	5-6	Orosco	Clements
14—At N.Y.	L	1-5	Fernandez	Bielecki
15—At N.Y.	L	1-4	Ojeda	Walk
15—At N.Y.	L	5-8	Aguilera	Kipper
16—St. Louis	L	2-4z	Cox	Rhoden
17—St. Louis	L	2-7	Mathews	Reuschel
18—St. Louis	W	2-1§	Robinson	Worrell
19—At Mon.	W	4-2	Kipper	Smith
20—At Mon.	L	2-7	McGaffigan	Walk
21—At Mon.	W	14-1	Rhoden	Tibbs
22—At Mon.	L	1-2	Hesketh	Reuschel
23—At St. L.	L	1-2‡	Worrell	Clements
24—At St. L.	L	2-5	Burris	Winn
25—At St. L.	L	1-2†	Horton	Clements
27—Montreal	W	7-1	Rhoden	Tibbs
28—Montreal	L	2-3	Hesketh	Reuschel
29—Montreal	L	4-6	Youmans	Bielecki
30—Phila.	W	3-2	Walk	Hudson

Won 12, Lost 18

JULY			Winner	Loser
1—Phila.	L	4-5§	Hume	McWilliams
2—Phila.	W	4-3	Rhoden	Carman
3—At L.A.	L	3-6	Welch	Reuschel
4—At L.A.	W	6-4	Bielecki	Valenzuela
5—At L.A.	W	5-0	Walk	Hershiser
6—At L.A.	L	3-4	Honeycutt	Winn
7—At S. Diego	W	3-1†	Guante	Gossage
8—At S. Diego	L	2-4	Hoyt	Reuschel
9—At S. Diego	W	6-4	Bielecki	McCullers
10—At S. Fran.	L	3-6	Blue	Walk
11—At S. Fran.	W	8-4	Winn	Carlton
12—At S. Fran.	L	1-3	Krukow	Rhoden
13—At S. Fran.	L	4-11	LaCoss	Reuschel
17—San Diego	L	1-2	McCullers	Rhoden
18—San Diego	W	12-7	Reuschel	Hawkins
19—San Diego	W	4-3	Guante	Lefferts
20—San Diego	W	4-2	McWilliams	Dravecky
22—Los Ang.	L	3-4	Powell	Guante
23—Los Ang.	L	5-6	Hershiser	Reuschel
24—Los Ang.	L	2-9	Valenzuela	Walk
25—San Fran.	L	3-7	Mason	Bielecki
26—San Fran.	L	0-9	Carlton	McWilliams
27—San Fran.	W	7-0	Rhoden	Blue
28—At Mon.	W	7-4	Reuschel	Smith
30—At Mon.	L	2-3	Tibbs	Winn

Won 11, Lost 14

AUGUST			Winner	Loser
1—St. Louis	W	4-0	Rhoden	Mathews
2—St. Louis	L	3-7	Tudor	McWilliams
3—St. Louis	W	3-0	Reuschel	Cox
4—Montreal	L	4-5	Tibbs	Jones
5—Montreal	L	0-3	Martinez	Bielecki
6—Montreal	L	2-3	Youmans	Rhoden
7—Montreal	L	4-5	McGaffigan	Robinson
8—At St. L.	L	1-3	Cox	Reuschel
9—At St. L.	W	8-5	Walk	Burris
10—At St. L.	L	4-5	Forsch	Bielecki
11—At Chicago	W	10-7	Rhoden	Moyer
12—At Chicago	L	1-3	Sanderson	McWilliams
13—At Chicago	L	8-9	DiPino	Robinson
14—At Phila.	L	7-8	Tekulve	Jones
15—At Phila.	W	6-5	Guante	Schatzeder
15—At Phila.	L	2-3	Maddux	Winn
16—At Phila.	W	6-1	Rhoden	Gross
16—At Phila.	L	0-6	Hume	McWilliams
17—At Phila.	L	1-5*	Ruffin	Reuschel
18—Houston	L	0-3	Scott	Walk
19—Houston	L	0-1	Deshaies	Bielecki
20—Houston	W	4-1	Rhoden	Knepper
22—Atlanta	W	16-5	Winn	Mahler
23—Atlanta	W	4-3	Reuschel	Smith
24—Atlanta	W	4-3	Walk	Alexander
25—Cincinnati	L	4-5	Robinson	McWilliams
26—Cincinnati	L	4-5	Franco	Krawczyk
27—Cincinnati	L	5-9	Murphy	Robinson
29—At Hous.	L	2-3	Scott	Reuschel
30—At Hous.	W	13-3	Rhoden	Deshaies
31—At Hous.	W	8-2	Walk	Knepper

Won 12, Lost 19

SEPTEMBER			Winner	Loser
1—At Cinn.	L	5-6	Power	Bielecki
2—At Cinn.	L	1-9	Gullickson	Kipper
3—At Cinn.	W	5-3†	Jones	Franco
5—At Atlanta	L	3-4	Assenmacher	Rhoden
6—At Atlanta	L	2-4	Palmer	Fansler
7—At Atlanta	W	3-1	Kipper	Speck
8—St. Louis	W	3-2	Patterson	Cox
9—St. Louis	L	1-3	Horton	Reuschel
10—St. Louis	L	3-4	Soff	Jones
12—Chicago	L	8-9†	DiPino	Robinson
13—Chicago	W	5-2	Patterson	Maddux
14—Chicago	W	9-2	Reuschel	Hall
15—At Phila.	L	0-5	Carman	Rhoden
16—At Phila.	L	5-9	Tekulve	Bielecki
17—At Mon.	L	5-6	St. Claire	Jones
17—At Mon.	W	4-1	Kipper	Sebra
18—At Mon.	W	3-1	Smiley	Reardon
19—At Chicago	L	2-8	Sanderson	Pena
20—At Chicago	L	0-1	Moyer	Rhoden
21—At Chicago	L	2-3	Sanderson	Pena
22—Phila.	L	4-8	Bittiger	Kipper
23—Phila.	W	6-5	Jones	Bedrosian
24—Montreal	W	2-1	Robinson	McClure
25—Montreal	L	4-8	Owchinko	Rhoden
26—New York	L	1-3	Fernandez	Fansler
27—New York	L	2-4‡	Orosco	McWilliams
28—New York	L	1-4‡	Aguilera	Walk
30—At St. L.	L	3-5	Cox	Rhoden

Won 9, Lost 19

OCTOBER			Winner	Loser
1—At St. L.	W	4-3	McWilliams	Soff
2—At St. L.	W	5-1	Kipper	Conroy
4—At N.Y.	L	1-6	Ojeda	Fansler
4—At N.Y.	L	2-5	Aguilera	Patterson
5—At N.Y.	L	0-9	Darling	Pena

Won 2, Lost 3

*5 innings. †10 innings. ‡11 innings. §12 innings. x17 innings. ySuspended game, completed August 11. zSuspended game, completed June 18.

Second baseman Johnny Ray committed only five errors while batting .301 with 78 RBIs.

league with 273 doubles and scored 663 runs, their highest total since 1982.

The Pirates' most productive player was Jim Morrison, who had been considered no more than a journeyman big leaguer. Morrison produced figures second only to Philadelphia's Mike Schmidt among the league's third basemen. Morrison hit .274 with 23 home runs and 88 runs batted in.

The Pirates' leading hitter was Johnny Ray, who batted .301 with 78 RBIs. Ray also tied a major league record for second basemen in 150 or more games by making only five errors all season. At first base, Sid Bream batted .268 with 16 homers, 77 RBIs and a team-high 37 doubles.

Rookie center fielder Barry Bonds was promoted from Hawaii (Pacific Coast) on May 30 and played well enough to be considered a star of the future. Bonds batted only .223 and struck out 102 times in 413 at-bats, but he also hit 16 homers and drove in 48 runs while swinging mostly from the leadoff spot in the order. The son of former major leaguer Bobby Bonds also led all rookies with 36 stolen bases and 65 walks.

Catcher Tony Pena slumped in the first half of the season. A second-half batting surge gave him a .288 average, but his RBI total was 52, including 10 homers. He still displayed one of the game's best throwing arms among catchers.

Leyland got little production out of his shortstops. Sammy Khalifa opened the season as the starter but lost his job to Rafael Belliard, who hit .233. U.L. Washington (.200) was called up from Hawaii when Khalifa was sent down, and all three shortstops combined for only 45 RBIs.

The most frequent custodian of left field was R.J. Reynolds, who hit .269. Leyland had anticipated Mike Brown giving the Pirates batting punch in right field, but Brown (.218) never lived up to expectations and was sent to Hawaii in August.

Joe Orsulak played all three outfield positions and never hurt the team on defense, but his batting average dropped from .300 in '85 to .249.

A pair of rookies performed capably in utility roles. Bobby Bonilla, a July acquisition from the Chicago White Sox, hit .240 while playing all three outfield positions and first and third base. Mike Diaz, who had been a catcher in the Philadelphia and Chicago Cubs organizations, won a job in spring training with his bat. Diaz never started a game behind the plate, instead seeing most of his action in the outfield and at first base. In 209 at-bats, he hit .268 with 12 homers and 36 RBIs.

Diaz and backup catcher Junior Ortiz rate as the Buc bench surprises of '86. Ortiz batted .336 without any power (14 RBIs, no homers in 110 at-bats). Veteran utilityman Bill Almon hit .219.

Leyland did his best to inspire his players during the season. Leyland, who had been third-base coach for the Chicago White Sox for four seasons before he was named manager of the Pirates, lashed out at the players in postgame tirades on a couple of occasions. His first blowup came April 30 after a loss in San Francisco. He kicked food off the table in the clubhouse, screamed at his players and threatened to send some to the minors. The Pirates won their next four games.

Leyland, however, retained the players' respect. When a question arose about whether Leyland would be given a contract for 1987, the players spoke out in defense of their manager. Leyland eventually was asked back for another year.

First baseman Glenn Davis played good defense and gave the Astros a much-needed power boost.

Astros Return to the Fast Lane

By NEIL HOHLFELD

After a five-year slide toward the middle of the pack in the National League, the 1986 Houston Astros went back to the style of play that had served them so well in the late 1970s and early 1980s.

That is, pitching, speed and defense.

Mix in a generous portion of aggressive managing by first-year skipper Hal Lanier and a deft job of acquiring the right blend of young and old players by General Manager Dick Wagner, and the Astros were runaway winners of the N.L. West. They finished with a 96-66 record, 10 games in front of the Cincinnati Reds, and went to the sixth game of the N.L. Championship Series before falling to the New York Mets.

Statistically, Houston's improvement in pitching was most noticeable. The Astros' team earned-run average, a robust 3.66 in '85, when they tied for third place in the division, dropped to 3.15 in '86, second in the league. The Astros led the league with 19 shutouts, 51 saves and 1,160 strikeouts.

A year earlier, the Astros stole just 96 bases. In '86, under Lanier's run-and-gun style of play, they stole 163. Defensively, the Astros' errors dropped from 152 in '85 to 130.

But the numbers only begin to speak of the differences in the two seasons. The driving force behind the switch was N.L. Manager of the Year Lanier, who had served as the top assistant to St. Louis Cardinals Manager Whitey Herzog for five years before replacing Bob Lillis as manager.

From the opening day of spring training, Lanier made it clear that fundamental mistakes—by hitters, fielders and pitchers—would not be tolerated.

"I'm sure they got tired of hearing about it," Lanier said, "but that's the only way I know to play this game. If you continue to make mistakes, you won't be a winning team."

The Astros, who had become a sloppy and slow team, perked to life early in the season. Sparked by five victories from Bob Knepper, eight saves from Dave Smith and .311 hitting from second baseman Bill Doran (a notoriously slow starter), Houston won 15 of its first 21 games and started a run atop the division that lasted nearly all season. A 7-1 record on their first road trip of the year served notice that Lanier's Astros would put up a fight.

Lefthander Bob Knepper won 17 games as part of Houston's top-grade starting rotation.

"I think that proved to the players that they could play with any team in any park," Lanier said. "It built our confidence level to win in April."

Though the Astros played at a .500 clip (13-13) in May, they avoided the long losing streaks that had buried the club in past years. The Astros' longest losing streak of the year was four games.

Another aspect of the Astros' success began to appear in May. Mike Scott, who had never been known as a strikeout pitcher, was starting to fan batters at a head-turning pace.

Helped by the development of a split-finger fastball, Scott finished the season with an 18-10 record and a league-high 306 strikeouts, making him only the fourth N.L. pitcher ever to record more than 300. Scott also led the league with a 2.22 ERA and 275⅓ innings pitched and tied with Knepper for the N.L. lead in shutouts (five). No matter what else happened, the Astros knew they'd have a chance to win whenever Scott, the N.L. Cy Young Award winner, took the mound.

Even though the Astros were 14-15 in June, they led the division at the end of the

SCORES OF HOUSTON ASTROS' 1986 GAMES

APRIL			Winner	Loser
8—San Fran.	L	3-8	Krukow	Ryan
9—San Fran.	L	1-4	Garrelts	Scott
10—San Fran.	W	4-0	Knepper	Blue
11—Atlanta	W	2-1	Kerfeld	Palmer
12—Atlanta	W	4-3	Ryan	Mahler
13—Atlanta	L	7-8	Johnson	Scott
15—At S. Fran.	W	8-3	Knepper	Blue
16—At S. Fran.	W	4-1	Ryan	Mason
18—At Cinn.	W	6-4	Scott	Soto
19—At Cinn.	W	4-3	Knepper	Browning
20—At Cinn.	W	6-4	Madden	Gullickson
21—At Atlanta	L	2-8	Johnson	Ryan
22—At Atlanta	W	3-2	Kerfeld	Ward
23—At Atlanta	W	3-2	Solano	Smith
24—Cincinnati	L	0-3	Soto	Madden
25—Cincinnati	W	3-1	Ryan	Browning
26—Cincinnati	W	1-0	Scott	Gullickson
27—Cincinnati	W	6-0	Knepper	Denny
29—At Phila.	L	4-12	Rawley	Ryan
30—At Phila.	W	1-0	Scott	Gross

Won 14, Lost 6

MAY			Winner	Loser
2—At Mon.	W	6-3	Knepper	Youmans
3—At Mon.	L	6-7*	Reardon	DiPino
4—At Mon.	L	6-7	Reardon	Smith
6—At N.Y.	L	0-4	Gooden	Knepper
7—At N.Y.	L	2-3	Fernandez	Ryan
9—At Pitts.	W	3-2	Kerfeld	Winn
10—At Pitts.	W	6-3	Knepper	Rhoden
11—At Pitts.	L	3-4‡	DeLeon	Kerfeld
12—Phila.	L	1-5	Rawley	Deshaies
13—Phila.	W	3-2†	Solano	Rucker
14—New York	W	6-2	Knepper	Ojeda
15—New York	L	2-6	Darling	Ryan
16—Chicago	W	9-6	Solano	Baller
17—Chicago	W	5-1	Scott	Trout
18—Chicago	L	2-5	Hoffman	Knepper
20—Pittsburgh	L	2-4	Walk	Ryan
21—Pittsburgh	L	1-2	Rhoden	Scott
22—Pittsburgh	W	4-0	Knepper	Reuschel
23—At Chicago	L	1-4	Sutcliffe	Solano
24—At Chicago	L	3-4	Frazier	Smith
25—At Chicago	W	3-1†	Kerfeld	Smith
26—At St. L.	W	4-1	Deshaies	Forsch
27—At St. L.	W	5-4	Smith	Dayley
28—At St. L.	W	4-3†	Kerfeld	Worrell
30—Montreal	L	0-1	Smith	Scott
31—Montreal	W	4-3	DiPino	Burke

Won 13, Lost 13

JUNE			Winner	Loser
1—Montreal	W	8-4	Knepper	Hesketh
2—St. Louis	L	2-9	Tudor	Madden
3—St. Louis	L	1-3	Mathews	Deshaies
4—St. Louis	W	4-2	Scott	Burris
5—At L.A.	L	0-1	Honeycutt	Hernandez
6—At L.A.	L	2-3	Howell	Knepper
7—At L.A.	W	7-5	Lopez	Howell
8—At L.A.	W	3-2	Scott	Valenzuela
9—At S. Diego	W	5-3	Deshaies	Show
10—At S. Diego	W	12-1	Knepper	Dravecky
11—At S. Diego	L	7-11	McCullers	DiPino
12—San Fran.	W	4-1	Hernandez	Krukow
13—San Fran.	L	1-3	Davis	Scott
14—San Fran.	W	7-3	Deshaies	Mulholland
15—San Fran.	L	2-7	Blue	Knepper
17—At Cinn.	L	4-5	Welsh	Hernandez
18—At Cinn.	L	2-3	Robinson	Smith
19—At Cinn.	W	6-2	Deshaies	Soto
20—At S. Fran.	L	1-3	Blue	Knepper
21—At S. Fran.	L	1-2	Garrelts	Knudson
22—At S. Fran.	L	2-4	Krukow	Hernandez
22—At S. Fran.	L	2-3	Berenguer	Smith
23—Cincinnati	W	7-6	Andersen	Power
24—Cincinnati	W	8-4	Ryan	Browning
25—Cincinnati	L	3-4*	Franco	Lopez
27—Los Ang.	W	5-0	Scott	Reuss
28—Los Ang.	W	6-4	Deshaies	Welch
29—Los Ang.	W	2-1	Hernandez	Valenzuela
30—San Diego	L	2-9	Dravecky	Knepper

Won 14, Lost 15

JULY			Winner	Loser
1—San Diego	L	4-7	Show	Knudson
2—San Diego	W	8-1	Scott	Hawkins
3—At N.Y.	L	5-6*	Orosco	DiPino
4—At N.Y.	L	1-2	Gooden	Smith
5—At N.Y.	W	2-1	Kerfeld	McDowell
6—At N.Y.	L	3-5	Fernandez	Knudson
7—At Mon.	W	12-1	Scott	Martinez
8—At Mon.	W	4-1	Ryan	Tibbs
9—At Mon.	L	1-2	Youmans	Knepper
10—Phila.	W	11-4	Knudson	Hudson
11—Phila.	L	1-4	Carman	Scott
12—Phila.	W	4-3	Ryan	Rawley
13—Phila.	L	4-5†	Bedrosian	Smith
17—New York	L	2-13	Ojeda	Ryan
18—New York	W	3-0	Knepper	Darling
19—New York	W	5-4	Smith	McDowell
20—New York	W	9-8§	Knepper	McDowell
21—Montreal	W	8-7	Kerfeld	Reardon
22—Montreal	W	1-0*	Smith	Youmans
23—Montreal	W	4-3†	Lopez	Burke
24—At Phila.	W	9-3	Scott	Rawley
25—At Phila.	L	2-4	Hudson	Deshaies
26—At Phila.	L	2-3	Carman	Knudson
27—At Phila.	W	3-2	Ryan	Gross
28—Atlanta	W	4-2	Knepper	Alexander
29—Atlanta	L	0-1	Palmer	Scott
30—Atlanta	W	4-2	Deshaies	Acker

Won 16, Lost 11

AUGUST			Winner	Loser
1—At S. Diego	W	6-3	Knepper	Hoyt
2—At S. Diego	W	5-4	Scott	Show
3—At S. Diego	L	1-5	Hawkins	Knudson
4—At L.A.	L	3-7	Valenzuela	Kerfeld
5—At L.A.	W	10-2	Lopez	Howell
6—At L.A.	L	4-7	Honeycutt	Keough
8—San Diego	W	5-0	Scott	McCullers
9—San Diego	W	6-2	Deshaies	Hawkins
10—San Diego	L	3-5	Dravecky	Knepper
11—Los Ang.	W	7-6	Smith	Howell
12—Los Ang.	W	3-0	Ryan	Honeycutt
13—Los Ang.	L	3-5	Hershiser	Scott
14—Los Ang.	W	3-2	Andersen	Valenzuela
15—At Atlanta	W	3-0	Knepper	Acker
16—At Atlanta	W	7-4	Keough	Mahler
17—At Atlanta	L	3-4	Speck	Andersen
18—At Pitts.	W	3-0	Scott	Walk
19—At Pitts.	W	1-0	Deshaies	Bielecki
20—At Pitts.	L	1-4	Rhoden	Knepper
22—At St. L.	L	5-6	Tudor	Ryan
23—At St. L.	L	1-7	Cox	Scott
24—At St. L.	W	5-1	Deshaies	Conroy
25—Chicago	W	3-2	Kerfeld	Smith
26—Chicago	L	3-5	Lynch	Darwin
27—Chicago	W	7-1	Ryan	Moyer
29—Pittsburgh	W	3-2	Scott	Reuschel
30—Pittsburgh	L	3-13	Rhoden	Deshaies
31—Pittsburgh	L	2-8	Walk	Knepper

Won 16, Lost 12

SEPTEMBER			Winner	Loser
1—At Chicago	W	6-4	Darwin	Lynch
2—At Chicago	W	8-7xy	Darwin	Maddux
3—At Chicago	W	8-2	Scott	Sanderson
5—St. Louis	L	5-8	Soff	Lopez
6—St. Louis	W	7-6	Kerfeld	Worrell
7—St. Louis	W	6-3	Calhoun	Mathews
8—Cincinnati	W	3-1	Ryan	Welsh
9—Cincinnati	W	9-2	Scott	Browning
10—At L.A.	L	1-5	Hershiser	Deshaies
11—At L.A.	L	6-14	Valenzuela	Knepper
12—At S. Diego	W	5-3	Kerfeld	McCullers
13—At S. Diego	L	3-4	Lefferts	Smith
14—At S. Diego	L	2-3	Lefferts	Scott
16—At Cinn.	W	6-1	Knepper	Gullickson
17—At Cinn.	W	6-1	Darwin	Welsh
18—At Cinn.	W	5-3	Keough	Browning
19—San Diego	W	5-4	Kerfeld	LaPoint
20—San Diego	W	10-6	Scott	Hayward
21—San Diego	L	0-5	Jones	Knepper
22—Los Ang.	L	2-9	Valenzuela	Darwin
23—Los Ang.	W	4-0	Deshaies	Powell
24—San Fran.	W	6-0	Ryan	LaCoss
25—San Fran.	W	2-0	Scott	Berenguer
26—At Atlanta	L	4-5	Alexander	Keough
27—At Atlanta	W	4-0	Darwin	Palmer
28—At Atlanta	W	2-0	Deshaies	Acker
30—At S. Fran.	L	5-6	Davis	Lopez

Won 18, Lost 9

OCTOBER			Winner	Loser
1—At S. Fran.	W	5-0	Darwin	Krukow
2—At S. Fran.	W	2-1*	Keough	Robinson
3—Atlanta	W	6-2	Ryan	Acker
4—Atlanta	W	3-2	Deshaies	Smith
5—Atlanta	W	4-1	Knepper	Mahler

Won 5, Lost 0

*10 innings. †11 innings. ‡12 innings. §15 innings. x18 innings. ySuspended game, completed September 3.

Bill Doran batted .276 and was a model of consistency at second base.

month. Rookie lefthander Jim Deshaies, who finished the season with 12 victories (most among N.L. rookies) and a 3.25 ERA, was 4-1 for the month. Right fielder Kevin Bass, an emerging star, hit .378 with seven home runs in June and finished the year hitting .311 with 20 homers and 79 runs batted in.

Even more so than Bass, first baseman Glenn Davis was showing opponents that the '86 team didn't always have to manufacture runs. Davis, the Astros' first legitimate power hitter in a decade, could win games with one swing, as he did four times with homers in the Astros' final at-bat. His 31 homers was the third-highest total in Astros history, and his 101 RBIs made him the first Astro to reach triple figures since 1976.

In July, the Astros took control of the division. A seven-game winning streak that featured five victories in their final at-bat put the Astros in front for good.

Two veterans, catcher Alan Ashby and left fielder Jose Cruz, provided much of the punch during that hot streak. Ashby, given the No. 1 catching job after the All-Star break, hit .272 in the second half (.257 overall). In that same span, Cruz, who had been slowed by a knee injury early in the year, hit .309 with nine homers and 41 RBIs to finish at .278 with 72 RBIs.

But the most startling comeback of the season belonged to righthander Nolan Ryan. The 39-year-old strikeout king was twice disabled because of a slight tear in the ligament of his right elbow. Before he was sidelined the first time, Ryan was 3-6 with a 5.21 ERA.

Rest, along with Ryan's amazing competitiveness, turned those numbers around. After his first stint on the disabled list, Ryan was 9-2 with a 2.24 ERA and 135 strikeouts in 112⅓ innings.

Knepper turned in his best season since 1978, when he pitched for the San Francisco Giants. The lefthander compiled a 17-12 record, a 3.14 ERA and eight complete games.

Knepper, Scott, Ryan and Deshaies handled the bulk of the starting duties. Lanier used several other pitchers as No. 5 starters, including Danny Darwin, who went 5-2 with a 2.32 ERA after being obtained in an August 15 trade with Milwaukee.

In the bullpen, Smith had a club-record 33 saves, and rookie Charlie Kerfeld, the setup man, won 11 games and saved seven. Veteran Aurelio Lopez was signed as a free agent in June and added seven saves.

One of Houston's most consistent performers was Doran, who played a slick second base, batted .276 and led the club with 92 runs scored and 42 stolen bases. The combination of Phil Garner (.265) and Denny Walling (.312) at third base produced 22 homers and 99 RBIs. At shortstop, Craig Reynolds (.249) and Dickie Thon (.248) combined for 62 RBIs.

Billy Hatcher, one of Wagner's acquisitions, filled the hole in center field and chipped in 38 stolen bases, while backup Davey Lopes stole 25.

A season in which just about everything went right for the Astros was capped with a perfect ending. Scott pitched a no-hitter against San Francisco on September 25 to clinch the division title.

"Somebody pinch me," Lanier said after Scott's no-hitter. "This can't be happening."

It was, of course, because the Astros had reverted to the basic elements of pitching, speed, defense and fundamentals.

"I thought when I took this job last November that this was a good team," Lanier told reporters while celebrating the division championship. "We just needed to play solid baseball, and they did that. They never quit."

Eric Davis survived a slow start and finally emerged as one of the National League's best all-around outfielders.

Early Losses Kill Reds' Hopes

By HAL McCOY

Coming out of spring training, the Cincinnati Reds, a preseason pick to contend for the National League West title, were poised to live up to their press clippings. But a month after the season began, the Reds were on the bottom wondering which way was up.

They eventually did move up in the standings, but by then it was too late. After a 6-19 start put them 10 games out of first place May 10, it took the Reds 3½ months to reach .500 (62-62) in late August. The Reds came on strong to finish second with an 86-76 record, but the division-winning Houston Astros finished 10 games higher—the same deficit the Reds had faced after their terrible start.

"I hope my guys learned a valuable lesson," said Pete Rose, the club's player-manager. "I preached and preached and preached during spring training the importance of a fast start. I thought we were ready. I don't know what happened except that Houston and New York started fast, Cincinnati and Philadelphia started slow. Houston and New York won, Cincinnati and Philadelphia didn't. And that summed it all up for us."

Rose himself began the year on the disabled list with a stomach disorder and contributed little to the team's late-season surge. By midseason Rose was playing sparingly, and by season's end he was not playing at all. Baseball's all-time hits leader finished with only 52 hits in 237 at-bats for a .219 average.

But the Reds regrouped and charged toward the top without Rose in the lineup. They came nearest to first place July 19, when they were four games behind co-leaders Houston and San Francisco despite having a losing record (43-44). The improving Reds still trailed the Astros by eight games but were within reach of the top spot when they went to Houston for a two-game series beginning September 8. They lost both games, though, and when Houston swept a three-game series at Riverfront Stadium a week later, Cincinnati's second-place doom was sealed.

The team that tried to catch Houston in September looked somewhat different from the one that had left spring training with such high hopes.

Veteran shortstop Dave Concepcion was down to third-string status by October. Rookie Barry Larkin was the starter, and

Buddy Bell (above) was impeccable at third base and hit 20 home runs while Dave Parker produced another 100-RBI season.

SCORES OF CINCINNATI REDS' 1986 GAMES

APRIL

			Winner	Loser
7—Phila.	W	7-4	Soto	Carlton
9—Phila.	L	3-5†	Bedrosian	Power
11—At S. Diego	L	3-4†	T. Stoddard	Power
12—At S. Diego	W	3-2	Robinson	T. Stoddard
13—At S. Diego	L	6-7	Gossage	Price
15—At Atlanta	W	5-3	Robinson	Dedmon
16—At Atlanta	W	5-3	Denny	Mahler
18—Houston	L	4-6	Scott	Soto
19—Houston	L	3-4	Knepper	Browning
20—Houston	L	4-6	Madden	Gullickson
23—San Diego	L	4-7	Hawkins	Denny
24—At Hous.	W	3-0	Soto	Madden
25—At Hous.	L	1-3	Ryan	Browning
26—At Hous.	L	0-1	Scott	Gullickson
27—At Hous.	L	0-6	Knepper	Denny
29—Montreal	L	4-7	Smith	Soto
30—Montreal	L	0-8	Tibbs	Browning

Won 5, Lost 12

MAY

			Winner	Loser
2—New York	L	7-8	Fernandez	Gullickson
3—New York	L	1-4	Ojeda	Denny
4—New York	L	2-7	Darling	Soto
5—Atlanta	L	3-4†	Assenmacher	Power
6—Atlanta	W	2-0	Gullickson	Palmer
8—Atlanta	L	5-10	McMurtry	Denny
9—At N.Y.	L	1-2	Ojeda	Soto
10—At N.Y.	L	1-5	Darling	Browning
11—At N.Y.	W	3-2	Gullickson	Gooden
12—At Mon.	W	4-3	Power	Roberge
13—At Mon.	L	2-4	Youmans	Soto
14—At Phila.	L	6-8	Carman	Franco
15—At Phila.	W	6-5	Robinson	Bedrosian
16—Pittsburgh	W	7-2	Denny	Rhoden
17—Pittsburgh	L	0-4	Reuschel	Soto
18—Pittsburgh	W	7-3	Browning	Bielecki
20—At St. L.	W	5-3	Gullickson	Bargar
21—At St. L.	L	3-8	Forsch	Denny
22—At St. L.	W	6-4	Soto	Cox
23—At Pitts.	W	12-9‡	Power	DeLeon
24—At Pitts.	W	4-2	Gullickson	Bielecki
25—At Pitts.	W	7-4	Denny	Kipper
26—At Chicago	L	6-9	Eckersley	Terry
27—At Chicago	W	5-4	Browning	Trout
28—At Chicago	L	0-5	Sutcliffe	Gullickson
30—St. Louis	W	6-4	Price	Burris
31—St. Louis	L	2-11	Forsch	Browning

Won 13, Lost 14

JUNE

			Winner	Loser
1—St. Louis	L	1-2	Cox	Welsh
2—Chicago	L	6-8	Sutcliffe	Gullickson
3—Chicago	W	5-3	Power	Baller
4—Chicago	W	2-0	Browning	Sanderson
6—At S. Fran.	W	5-3	Welsh	Garrelts
7—At S. Fran.	L	2-6	Krukow	Gullickson
8—At S. Fran.	W	7-3	Denny	LaCoss
8—At S. Fran.	L	1-3	Robinson	Power
9—At L.A.	L	5-6	Niedenfuer	Browning
10—At L.A.	L	0-1	Niedenfuer	Franco
11—At L.A.	L	4-5†	Vande Berg	Franco
13—At Atlanta	L	2-3	Mahler	Denny
14—At Atlanta	W	2-1	Robinson	Assenmacher
15—At Atlanta	W	9-7	Browning	Smith
16—At Atlanta	L	3-4*	Garber	Franco
17—Houston	W	5-4	Welsh	Hernandez
18—Houston	W	3-2	Robinson	Smith
19—Houston	L	2-6	Deshaies	Soto
20—Atlanta	W	6-4	Browning	Dedmon
20—Atlanta	W	8-5	Gullickson	Johnson
21—Atlanta	L	6-7	Mahler	Welsh
22—Atlanta	W	5-2	Denny	McMurtry
23—At Hous.	L	6-7	Andersen	Power
24—At Hous.	L	4-8	Ryan	Browning
25—At Hous.	W	4-3*	Franco	Lopez
27—San Fran.	L	6-7‡	Minton	Terry
28—San Fran.	L	1-5	Williams	Denny
29—San Fran.	W	4-3	Robinson	LaCoss
30—Los Ang.	W	6-5†	Willis	Vande Berg

Won 14, Lost 15

JULY

			Winner	Loser
2—Los Ang.	W	4-3*	Franco	Vande Berg
3—At Phila.	L	3-7	Ruffin	Denny
4—At Phila.	W	4-1	Browning	Gross
5—At Phila.	W	7-2	Welsh	Hudson
6—At Phila.	L	5-12	Hume	Price
7—At N.Y.	W	7-6	Robinson	Niemann
8—At N.Y.	W	5-4*	Franco	McDowell
9—At N.Y.	W	11-1	Browning	Gooden
10—At Mon.	L	6-8	Smith	Welsh
11—At Mon.	W	3-2	Gullickson	McGaffigan
12—At Mon.	W	2-0	Denny	Martinez
13—At Mon.	W	10-2y	Browning	Burke
17—Phila.	W	7-6†	Power	Gorman
18—Phila.	W	6-5	Browning	Ruffin
19—Phila.	W	5-2	Gullickson	Rawley
20—Phila.	L	3-9	Hudson	Denny
21—New York	L	2-4	Aguilera	Soto
22—New York	L	3-6x	McDowell	Willis
23—New York	L	2-3	Darling	Robinson
24—Montreal	L	5-6x	Sebra	Willis
25—Montreal	W	9-2	Denny	Martinez
26—Montreal	W	7-6	Robinson	Sebra
27—Montreal	W	9-7	Murphy	Reardon
28—At S. Diego	L	2-5	Hawkins	Browning
29—At S. Diego	L	1-2	Gossage	Robinson
30—At S. Diego	L	3-9	Whitson	Denny

Won 15, Lost 11

AUGUST

			Winner	Loser
1—At L.A.	L	5-9	Honeycutt	Soto
2—At L.A.	L	1-7	Niedenfuer	Robinson
3—At L.A.	L	1-2	Hershiser	Gullickson
4—At S. Fran.	W	2-1	Denny	Mulholland
5—At S. Fran.	W	11-6	Soto	Carlton
6—At S. Fran.	L	1-2x	Robinson	Willis
8—Los Ang.	W	4-0	Gullickson	Hershiser
8—Los Ang.	W	5-1	Welsh	Pena
9—Los Ang.	W	6-2	Denny	Valenzuela
10—Los Ang.	L	0-5	Powell	Soto
11—San Fran.	L	4-13	Davis	Browning
12—San Fran.	L	1-2	Blue	Gullickson
13—San Fran.	W	8-6	Franco	Garrelts
14—San Fran.	W	2-0	Denny	Downs
15—San Diego	W	7-2	Soto	Dravecky
15—San Diego	L	1-7	Show	Browning
16—San Diego	W	4-1	Gullickson	Whitson
17—San Diego	L	5-9	Hoyt	Welsh
18—San Diego	W	6-5	Denny	LaPoint
19—St. Louis	W	6-1	Browning	Conroy
20—St. Louis	W	3-1	Gullickson	Forsch
21—St. Louis	W	9-4	Welsh	Mathews
22—At Chicago	L	2-3	Moyer	Power
23—At Chicago	W	7-3	Browning	Sanderson
24—At Chicago	W	7-1	Gullickson	Davis
25—At Pitts.	W	5-4	Robinson	McWilliams
26—At Pitts.	W	5-4	Franco	Krawczyk
27—At Pitts.	W	9-5	Murphy	Robinson
29—At St. L.	W	2-0	Gullickson	Cox
30—At St. L.	L	2-5	Conroy	Welsh
31—At St. L.	L	3-9	Forsch	Browning

Won 19, Lost 12

SEPTEMBER

			Winner	Loser
1—Pittsburgh	W	6-5	Power	Bielecki
2—Pittsburgh	W	9-1	Gullickson	Kipper
3—Pittsburgh	L	3-5*	Jones	Franco
5—Chicago	W	11-2	Browning	Sutcliffe
6—Chicago	W	5-1	Power	Eckersley
7—Chicago	L	3-11	Maddux	Gullickson
8—At Hous.	L	1-3	Ryan	Welsh
9—At Hous.	L	2-9	Scott	Browning
10—At S. Fran.	W	14-2	Power	Blue
11—At S. Fran.	L	1-2	Downs	Gullickson
12—At L.A.	W	8-3	Welsh	Holton
13—At L.A.	W	3-0	Browning	Welsh
14—At L.A.	W	4-3	Robinson	Niedenfuer
16—Houston	L	1-6	Knepper	Gullickson
17—Houston	L	1-6	Darwin	Welsh
18—Houston	L	3-5	Keough	Browning
19—Los Ang.	L	7-9	Holton	Franco
20—Los Ang.	W	9-5	Murphy	Powell
21—Los Ang.	W	8-4	Terry	Hershiser
22—San Fran.	L	7-10	Williams	Welsh
23—San Fran.	W	6-5	Browning	Davis
24—Atlanta	W	4-1	Power	Mahler
25—Atlanta	W	6-4	Gullickson	Puleo
26—At S. Diego	W	8-6	Murphy	Lefferts
27—At S. Diego	W	7-4†	Franco	McCullers
28—At S. Diego	W	6-3	Power	Vosberg
30—At Atlanta	L	7-8	Mahler	Gullickson

Won 16, Lost 11

OCTOBER

			Winner	Loser
1—At Atlanta	W	6-5	Murphy	Garber
2—At Atlanta	W	6-4§	Murphy	Puleo
3—San Diego	W	6-3	Power	Wojna
4—San Diego	W	10-7	Gullickson	LaPoint
5—San Diego	L	1-2	Hawkins	Welsh

Won 4, Lost 1

*10 innings. †11 innings. ‡12 innings. §13 innings. x14 innings. ySuspended game, completed July 24.

his backup was rookie Kurt Stillwell. The Reds had enough confidence in this duo—particularly Larkin, who hit .283 in 159 at-bats—that they let Concepcion test the free-agent market after the season. Stillwell batted .229 (31 points below Concepcion), but the Reds liked the 21-year-old's potential.

Also by season's end, left field belonged not to Nick Esasky (.230, 12 home runs), but to rookie Kal Daniels, who had been dispatched to Denver (American Association) after the club's 6-19 start. Though he was bitter about the demotion, Daniels returned in late June and finished with a .320 average, six homers and 15 stolen bases in 181 at-bats.

First base was a season-long mess. Rose, Esasky, veteran Tony Perez (.255), Concepcion and rookie Tracy Jones all gave it a try. Jones an outfielder, played only two games at first, but that was long enough to injure his hand while making a tag July 9. The .349 hitter did not swing a bat the rest of the season, even after being reinstated in September.

The starting pitchers were shaky at best, contributing to the league's fourth-worst team earned-run average (3.91). Righthander Bill Gullickson was the top starter with a 15-12 record and a 3.38 ERA. Lefthander Tom Browning, a 20-game winner as a rookie in 1985, languished near .500 all season and finished 14-13 with a 3.81 ERA. Veteran righthander John Denny (11-10) was embroiled in controversy with the media all season and missed the last seven weeks with a mysteriously injured wrist. Lefthander Chris Welsh went 6-9 with a 4.78 ERA and was released after the season.

And there was Mario Soto, once the ace of Cincinnati's staff. The righthander was on the disabled list three times and finally underwent arm surgery, finishing 5-10 with a 4.71 ERA in 19 starts.

The Reds remained close only because their bullpen was outstanding—especially after Ted Power was moved to the starting rotation.

Power, the Reds' stopper in '85 with 27 saves, was abysmal as a reliever through late August, tallying only one save and four victories in 46 appearances. When injuries mounted, Rose started Power out of desperation August 22 in Chicago. The righthander lost, 3-2, but it was his last defeat of the season. In 10 starts, Power went 6-1 with a 2.59 ERA, striking out 52 batters and walking 19.

"Power was our most unpleasant failure and our most pleasant surprise—in one season," General Manager Bill Bergesch said.

Where Power failed, John Franco, Ron Robinson and Rob Murphy succeeded. Franco was 6-6 with 29 saves as the Reds' bullpen finisher, while Robinson, used in both middle and short situations, made 70 appearances and went 10-3 with 14 saves. Murphy, a lefthanded rookie, was called up from Denver after the All-Star break and finished 6-0 with a 0.72 ERA in 34 appearances, mostly as a setup man for Franco.

The Reds could have made an earlier charge for the division title if their bats had not been asleep early in the season. Cincinnati ranked 11th in the league in batting at the All-Star break before finishing tied for fifth with a .254 team average and third with 732 runs.

Dave Parker once again was the club's offensive leader. The 35-year-old right fielder's average dipped to .273, but he hit 31 homers and drove in 116 runs, showing the way for his protege, 24-year-old Eric Davis. After a slow start, Davis emerged as one of the league's best all-around outfielders, hitting .277 with 27 homers, 71 runs batted in, 97 runs scored and 80 stolen bases.

Buddy Bell also started slowly but finished with one of his best seasons (.278, 75 RBIs and a career-high 20 homers). He also was impeccable at third base, making many incredible plays and only 10 errors.

While batting just .259, outfielder Eddie Milner established career highs with 15 homers and 47 RBIs but was riding the bench by October, having lost his job to Davis. Catcher Bo Diaz (.272, 10 homers, 56 RBIs) and second baseman Ron Oester (.258, 44 RBIs) had slightly below-average years.

While the regulars recovered from their sluggish start, the bench remained submerged the entire season. Cincinnati pinch-hitters batted .207 with only one homer—and that was a grand slam by Parker in one of his rare non-starts. Max Venable, one of the league's best pinch-hitters in '85, was 8-for-51 (.157) with no homers and six RBIs in the pinch.

Overall, the Reds looked much better when the season ended than when it began, and youngsters were a major part of that improvement. Five weeks after the season finale, Rose showed his commitment to the club's youth movement by removing himself from the winter roster to make room for a younger player. The Reds could not re-sign him as a player until May 15, 1987.

"I don't know when," Rose said, "but I'll probably play again."

Veteran righthander Mike Krukow provided some much-needed leadership and became the Giants' first 20-game winner since 1973.

Surprising Giants Stand Tall

By NICK PETERS

"Where you are in the standings only counts in October," Houston Manager Hal Lanier said after the Giants swept a June doubleheader from the Astros to take the National League West lead.

Lanier, of course, enjoyed the last laugh when his Astros pulled away in the second half and the Giants finished third, 13 games back. But he was incorrect in assuming that San Francisco's successful first half wasn't significant.

When you lose 100 games in a season, as the Giants did for the first time in franchise history in 1985, any signs of improvement are welcome. Consequently, the club exceeded all expectations in 1986.

The Giants and the 1986 Cleveland Indians became the ninth and 10th major league teams since 1900 to post a winning record following a 100-loss disaster. Credit for that accomplishment belongs to everyone from the front office to the training room, but much of it is attributable to Manager Roger Craig.

When the numerous skeptics doubted it could be done, Craig created a positive club attitude in the spring and brought confidence and direction to a beaten band of players who sorely needed both.

"Before we took the field opening day in Houston, I told the players we had a good chance to win this thing," Craig recalled. "They probably thought I was crazy, but I'm optimistic and I truly believed it.

"The main difference last year was our attitude. The guys never quit. That's why we won so many games in the late innings (26 on their final at-bat) and by coming from behind (40 times). I feel good about a lot of things that happened."

Craig's confidence immediately rubbed off. Despite a lineup that included two rookies and two sophomores in the infield and an unsettled pitching rotation, the Giants posted their first winning April (13-8) since 1973.

Rookie first baseman Will Clark homered off Houston's Nolan Ryan on his first major league at-bat and was off to a quick start. So was left fielder Jeffrey Leonard, who ranked among the leaders in several categories early in the season.

Veteran Mike Krukow, who would become the club's first 20-game winner since Ron Bryant in 1973, demonstrated leadership at the outset. Retread righthander Mike LaCoss, a non-roster pitcher in camp, bolted to a 9-3 getaway.

First baseman Will Clark fought off injury problems and enjoyed an impressive rookie season.

The Giants were the surprise leaders of the N.L. West at the All-Star break for the first time since 1978, and a victory over the Chicago Cubs to start the second half earned a two-game lead over the Astros.

Injuries to Leonard, Clark, third baseman Chris Brown and center fielder Dan Gladden contributed to a second-half slide in which the Giants went 35-39. But that didn't detract from a comeback campaign that gave the club its second-best home attendance in 20 years and a solid founda-

SCORES OF SAN FRANCISCO GIANTS' 1986 GAMES

APRIL			Winner	Loser
8—At Hous.	W	8-3	Krukow	Ryan
9—At Hous.	W	4-1	Garrelts	Scott
10—At Hous.	L	0-4	Knepper	Blue
11—At L.A.	W	9-8‡	Robinson	Niedenfuer
12—At L.A.	W	7-6†	Minton	Powell
13—At L.A.	L	2-3	Hershiser	Garrelts
15—Houston	L	3-8	Knepper	Blue
16—Houston	L	1-4	Ryan	Mason
17—San Diego	W	4-1	Krukow	Hawkins
18—San Diego	W	6-1	Garrelts	Thurmond
19—San Diego	W	6-5	Davis	McCullers
20—San Diego	W	4-0	Blue	Dravecky
21—Los Ang.	W	5-1	Mason	Honeycutt
22—Los Ang.	W	10-3	Krukow	Powell
23—Los Ang.	L	4-6	Valenzuela	Garrelts
25—At S. Diego	L	8-9‡	Lefferts	Minton
26—At S. Diego	W	3-2*	Robinson	Show
27—At S. Diego	L	4-6	Dravecky	Krukow
28—St. Louis	L	4-5‡	Worrell	Davis
29—St. Louis	W	2-0	LaCoss	Forsch
30—Pittsburgh	W	6-5‡	Garrelts	Patterson

Won 13, Lost 8

MAY			Winner	Loser
1—Pittsburgh	L	2-6	Walk	Krukow
2—Chicago	L	5-6	Keough	Davis
3—Chicago	L	5-6	Frazier	Minton
4—Chicago	W	2-1*	LaCoss	Sutcliffe
4—Chicago	W	2-1	Mason	Frazier
6—At Pitts.	W	7-2	Krukow	Reuschel
7—At Pitts.	W	7-5	Laskey	McWilliams
8—At Pitts.	L	2-8	Bielecki	Garrelts
9—At St. L.	W	2-1*	LaCoss	Worrell
10—At St. L.	L	3-6	Burris	Mason
11—At St. L.	L	3-4	Worrell	Krukow
13—At Chicago	W	6-5	Minton	Smith
14—At Chicago	W	11-3	LaCoss	Sutcliffe
16—Phila.	L	0-3	Carlton	Mason
17—Phila.	W	12-7	Krukow	Rawley
18—Phila.	W	4-1	Garrelts	Toliver
20—New York	L	1-2	Ojeda	LaCoss
21—New York	L	4-7	Darling	Mason
22—New York	W	10-2	Krukow	Gooden
23—Montreal	L	3-4	Youmans	Garrelts
24—Montreal	L	4-7	McGaffigan	Blue
25—Montreal	W	11-3	LaCoss	Smith
27—At Phila.	L	2-6	Carlton	Robinson
28—At Phila.	L	0-4	Rawley	Garrelts
29—At Phila.	L	4-5	Carman	Minton
30—At N.Y.	L	7-8*	Orosco	Davis
31—At N.Y.	W	7-3	Garrelts	Ojeda

Won 12, Lost 15

JUNE			Winner	Loser
1—At N.Y.	W	7-3	Krukow	Darling
3—At Mon.	W	7-6	Blue	Youmans
4—At Mon.	W	4-2	Robinson	Reardon
6—Cincinnati	L	3-5	Welsh	Garrelts
7—Cincinnati	W	6-2	Krukow	Gullickson
8—Cincinnati	L	3-7	Denny	LaCoss
8—Cincinnati	W	3-1	Robinson	Power
10—Atlanta	W	3-0	Blue	Smith
11—Atlanta	L	1-2*	Garber	Minton
12—At Hous.	L	1-4	Hernandez	Krukow
13—At Hous.	W	3-1	Davis	Scott
14—At Hous.	L	3-7	Deshaies	Mulholland
15—At Hous.	W	7-2	Blue	Knepper
16—At S. Diego	L	0-4	Hawkins	Laskey
17—At S. Diego	L	5-8	Lefferts	Robinson
18—At S. Diego	W	6-3	LaCoss	Thurmond
19—At S. Diego	L	3-8	Show	Mulholland
20—Houston	W	3-1	Blue	Knepper
21—Houston	W	2-1	Garrelts	Knudson
22—Houston	W	4-2	Krukow	Hernandez
22—Houston	W	3-2	Berenguer	Smith
23—San Diego	W	18-1	LaCoss	Hoyt
24—San Diego	L	0-3	Show	Mulholland
25—San Diego	L	1-3	Dravecky	Blue
27—At Cinn.	W	7-6‡	Minton	Terry
28—At Cinn.	W	5-1	Williams	Denny
29—At Cinn.	L	3-4	Robinson	LaCoss
30—At Atlanta	L	1-5	Mahler	Davis

Won 16, Lost 12

JULY			Winner	Loser
1—At Atlanta	W	9-6*	Robinson	Johnson
2—At Atlanta	L	4-7	Smith	Garrelts
3—St. Louis	W	1-0	Krukow	Ownbey
4—St. Louis	W	6-1	LaCoss	Burris
5—St. Louis	L	4-7*	Worrell	Berenguer
6—St. Louis	W	8-3	Garrelts	Cox
8—Chicago	L	1-4	Eckersley	Krukow
9—Chicago	L	3-4*	Smith	Berenguer
10—Pittsburgh	W	6-3	Blue	Walk
11—Pittsburgh	L	4-8	Winn	Carlton
12—Pittsburgh	W	3-1	Krukow	Rhoden
13—Pittsburgh	W	11-4	LaCoss	Reuschel
17—At Chicago	W	6-4	Blue	Lynch
18—At Chicago	L	1-2	Sanderson	LaCoss
19—At Chicago	L	6-11	Hoffman	Krukow
20—At Chicago	W	5-4	Garrelts	Eckersley
21—At St. L.	L	3-8	Mathews	Carlton
22—At St. L.	L	7-10	Tudor	Blue
23—At St. L.	L	3-4	Cox	LaCoss
25—At Pitts.	W	7-3	Mason	Bielecki
26—At Pitts.	W	9-0	Carlton	McWilliams
27—At Pitts.	L	0-7	Rhoden	Blue
28—At L.A.	L	1-2	Hershiser	LaCoss
29—At L.A.	L	1-2	Valenzuela	Downs
30—At L.A.	L	2-4	Welch	Mulholland
31—Atlanta	W	3-2	Garrelts	Garber

Won 12, Lost 14

AUGUST			Winner	Loser
1—Atlanta	W	3-1	Blue	Mahler
2—Atlanta	W	7-5	Williams	Alexander
3—Atlanta	L	2-4	Palmer	Downs
4—Cincinnati	L	1-2	Denny	Mulholland
5—Cincinnati	L	6-11	Soto	Carlton
6—Cincinnati	W	2-1§	Robinson	Willis
8—At Atlanta	L	6-7	Alexander	LaCoss
9—At Atlanta	W	4-3*	Garrelts	Dedmon
10—At Atlanta	W	4-3	Berenguer	Garber
11—At Cinn.	W	13-4	Davis	Browning
12—At Cinn.	W	2-1	Blue	Gullickson
13—At Cinn.	L	6-8	Franco	Garrelts
14—At Cinn.	L	0-2	Denny	Downs
15—Los Ang.	W	5-1	Krukow	Powell
16—Los Ang.	L	5-6	Welch	LaCoss
17—Los Ang.	L	0-2	Honeycutt	Blue
19—Phila.	L	5-6	Tekulve	Garrelts
20—Phila.	L	0-1*	Carman	Krukow
21—Phila.	W	7-6	Davis	Tekulve
22—New York	L	3-5	Gooden	Blue
23—New York	L	2-3	Ojeda	Downs
24—New York	W	10-1	Krukow	Aguilera
25—Montreal	L	5-6	McGaffigan	LaCoss
26—Montreal	W	1-0‡	Garrelts	Roberge
27—Montreal	W	3-2	Downs	McGaffigan
29—At Phila.	L	4-6	Maddux	Krukow
30—At Phila.	L	3-5	Carman	LaCoss
31—At Phila.	L	3-4	Tekulve	Blue

Won 12, Lost 16

SEPTEMBER			Winner	Loser
1—At N.Y.	L	2-5	McDowell	Davis
2—At N.Y.	W	4-3	Krukow	Gooden
3—At N.Y.	L	2-4	Ojeda	Mulholland
4—At Mon.	L	2-4	Smith	LaCoss
5—At Mon.	W	8-4	Garrelts	Burke
6—At Mon.	L	1-3	McClure	Williams
7—At Mon.	W	1-0	Krukow	Youmans
8—San Diego	W	4-3	Mulholland	Whitson
9—San Diego	W	7-0	LaCoss	Hoyt
10—Cincinnati	L	2-14	Power	Blue
11—Cincinnati	W	2-1	Downs	Gullickson
12—Atlanta	W	11-2	Krukow	Acker
13—Atlanta	L	1-4	Mahler	Mulholland
14—Atlanta	W	7-6	Garrelts	Assenmacher
16—At S. Diego	W	4-1	Krukow	Wojna
17—At S. Diego	L	4-5*	McCullers	Davis
19—At Atlanta	W	4-0	Downs	Mahler
20—At Atlanta	L	1-2	Puleo	LaCoss
21—At Atlanta	W	8-2	Krukow	Alexander
22—At Cinn.	W	10-7	Williams	Welsh
23—At Cinn.	L	5-6	Browning	Davis
24—At Hous.	L	0-6	Ryan	LaCoss
25—At Hous.	L	0-2	Scott	Berenguer
26—Los Ang.	W	3-0	Krukow	Niedenfuer
27—Los Ang.	W	8-3	Blue	Valenzuela
28—Los Ang.	W	6-5x	Minton	Galvez
30—Houston	W	6-5	Davis	Lopez

Won 16, Lost 11

OCTOBER			Winner	Loser
1—Houston	L	0-5	Darwin	Krukow
2—Houston	L	1-2*	Keough	Robinson
3—At L.A.	W	8-2	Downs	Welch
4—At L.A.	L	1-2	Valenzuela	Grant
5—At L.A.	W	11-2	Krukow	Hershiser

Won 2, Lost 3

*10 innings. †11 innings. ‡12 innings. §14 innings. x16 innings.

tion for the future.

Craig somehow managed to field a winner (83-79) despite a relatively punchless lineup down the stretch. He did it with stout pitching. He did it with an exceptional bench featuring the clutch hitting of Candy Maldonado, Harry Spilman and Joel Youngblood. Giants pinch-hitters topped the majors with 10 home runs and 59 runs batted in. He did it with execution, such as 18 successful suicide squeezes and 148 stolen bases, the most by the Giants since 1919. Mainly, he did it with unbridled optimism and enthusiasm, making the players believe in themselves.

The 1986 Giants definitely were overachievers. With two rookies in the lineup, another in the rotation and injuries all around, the club resembled a Triple-A team. Sixty different roster moves had players shuffling back and forth to and from Phoenix (Pacific Coast). Thirteen rookies played for San Francisco in '86, and nine Giants hit their first major league home run.

But it worked. The club developed a spirited attitude in the spring and played with vigor most of the season.

Clark received most of the rookie attention and flashed his potential with a .287 average. But second baseman Robby Thompson was equally impressive, making the jump from Double-A Shreveport, batting .271 and gluing down the infield. Rookie Mike Aldrete batted .250 while platooning in the outfield and at first base.

Brown, who missed the final month with a shoulder problem, finished with a team-high .317 average after taking a .338 mark into his first All-Star Game appearance. Right fielder Chili Davis and Krukow also were All-Stars.

After knocking in 56 runs in 1985, Davis had 55 by the All-Star break. But his statistics dropped appreciably in the second half, no doubt affected by the absence of Leonard, who reluctantly submitted to surgery and missed the final two months.

Leonard was batting over .300 two months into the season and led the league with 11 game-winning runs batted in at the All-Star break. He didn't homer after May 14 because of a wrist injury, yet he didn't leave the lineup for another six weeks.

"Jeff was having an MVP-type season before he got hurt," Craig said. "When he went out of the lineup, it affected our entire offense. I can't say enough about how guys like Jeff, Chili and Robby played hurt."

Maldonado, who had been acquired from the Los Angeles Dodgers for reserve catcher Alex Trevino over the winter, was a pleasant surprise. He established a franchise pinch-hit record with 17 and led the majors with four homers and 20 RBIs as a pinch-hitter.

When Leonard left the lineup, however, it gave Maldonado a chance to play regularly. He finished with a team-leading 18 homers and 85 RBIs in only 405 at-bats.

Catcher Bob Brenly had an off year offensively despite a late rush for 16 homers, but he combined with Krukow and Leonard to provide senior leadership on a club with so many youngsters.

Brenly exemplified the club's comeback spirit with two memorable September performances. On the 14th, he tied a major league record with four errors in one inning while playing third base but came back to belt two homers, including the game-winner in the bottom of the ninth against Atlanta. Two weeks later, his 16th-inning single downed the Dodgers.

Defensively, the club made its fewest errors in a full season (143) since 1967, thanks primarily to the new and efficient double-play combination of Thompson and second-year shortstop Jose Uribe, the least heralded of the regulars.

The Giants' pitchers ranked third in the league with a composite 3.33 earned-run average. Heading the staff was Krukow, who shed his .500-pitcher reputation by going 20-9 with a 3.05 ERA, 10 complete games and 178 strikeouts. He won seven of his last eight decisions, notching No. 20 on the final day.

Whereas Krukow posted his 100th career victory during the season, lefthander Vida Blue (10-10, 3.27 ERA) posted No. 200. The only other double-digit winner among the regular starters was LaCoss, who finished with a 10-13 mark despite his quick start.

Scott Garrelts was in the rotation at the start of the season but returned to the bullpen, finishing with a 3.11 ERA, 13 victories and a team-leading 10 saves.

Roger Mason, who was 3-4 in 11 starts but spent most of the year on the disabled list, and a pair of rookies, Kelly Downs (4-4, 2.75 ERA) and Terry Mulholland (1-7), made occasional starts. Providing bullpen support were Juan Berenguer (2.70 ERA), Mark Davis (2.99), Jeff Robinson (3.36, eight saves) and Greg Minton (five saves).

It was an exciting season for the Giants, the old and new blending into a winning combination against all odds. Suddenly, Candlestick Park wasn't such a big issue because baseball, not bellyaching, dominated the summer scene.

Tony Gwynn was the Padres' top offensive weapon, hitting .329 with a National League-leading 211 hits and 107 runs scored.

Bickering Padres Sink in West

By MARK KREIDLER

The San Diego Padres in 1986 defied Yogi Berra's oft-quoted baseball philosophy. Their season most certainly was over before it was over, and some would say it was over before it started.

After winning the National League pennant in 1984, then tailing off to an 83-79 record and a third-place tie in 1985, the Padres lost all sense of direction. Their 74-88 finish, which put them in fourth place in the N.L. West, was their worst record in a full season since the 1980 team went 73-89 under broadcaster-turned-manager Jerry Coleman.

It was a disaster from the moment in the fall of 1985 that Padres President Ballard Smith and General Manager Jack McKeon decided that Dick Williams' acidic style of managing had run its course in San Diego after four seasons. In time, Williams agreed to a contract buyout, but Owner Joan Kroc pulled the rug from under them—some say she undermined Smith's authority in the process—by negating the deal and claiming Williams would return in 1986.

Williams ultimately resigned on the first day of spring training, and the Padres hurriedly plucked a man out of their minor league system, former Oakland A's skipper Steve Boros, to run the team.

But the Padres did not escape the first week without further turmoil. A few days later, former Cy Young Award winner LaMarr Hoyt entered a rehabilitation center for treatment of alcohol dependency.

Hoyt did not return for a month, and when he did he disputed the notion that he ever was an alcoholic. He also had trouble regaining his pitching form and finished with an 8-11 record and a 5.15 earned-run average.

Hoyt's was the first of a series of pitching maladies to strike down the Padres. At midseason, the team traded away starter Mark Thurmond and reliever Tim Stoddard, both of whom had been ineffective. Thurmond went on to enjoy success in Detroit and Stoddard did well with the New York Yankees. But the pitchers whom the Padres received in return—Dave LaPoint (1-4, 4.26 ERA) and Ed Whitson (1-7, 5.59)—did nothing to reverse the team's slide.

The Padres' top pitchers were righthander Eric Show (9-5, 2.97) and lefthander Dave Dravecky (9-11, 3.07). Both starters, however, went down with season-ending injuries on consecutive days in August. Only one starter, righthander Andy Hawkins (10-8, 4.30), survived the entire year, and the Padres' composite 3.99 ERA ranked 11th in the league. Padre pitchers allowed more home runs (150) and walks (607) than any other N.L. team.

In the meantime, many of the veterans who helped San Diego gain its first-ever N.L. pennant in 1984 began to show their age. Third baseman Graig Nettles, 42, batted only .218, while 37-year-old first baseman Steve Garvey had driven in only 46 runs entering August before finishing with 21 homers and 81 runs batted in. Both had severely limited range on defense.

Catcher Terry Kennedy, admittedly affected by trade talk, drove in only 57 runs, including only 21 after the All-Star break. Shortstop Garry Templeton hovered around .230 for most of the season and finished with a .247 average. Left fielder Carmelo Martinez, who knocked in 66 runs as a rookie in 1984 and 72 in 1985, was benched because of his subpar defensive play and erratic bat. He finished with a .238 average and 25 RBIs.

Veterans Tim Flannery (.280) and Jerry Royster (.257), who were shuttled between second and third base, combined for only 54 RBIs. Rookie Bip Roberts, who had been touted as the answer to San Diego's void at second base and the leadoff spot in the order, contributed only 12 RBIs and 14 stolen bases.

But there were a few bright moments, mostly provided by Gold Glove right fielder Tony Gwynn and center fielder Kevin McReynolds. Gwynn, a model of consistency, batted .329, led the league with 211 hits and tied for the lead with 107 runs scored. He also hit 14 homers, one more than his career total entering the season, and stole 37 bases, a personal best that included a league record-tying five in one game.

McReynolds batted .288 with 26 homers, 96 RBIs and a .504 slugging percentage, by far the best of his three full professional seasons. In the process, McReynolds emerged as the club's top power hitter. Rookie outfielder John Kruk batted .309, outfielder Marvell Wynne hit .264 and righthander Jimmy Jones threw a one-hitter against Houston in his major league debut September 21.

SCORES OF SAN DIEGO PADRES' 1986 GAMES

APRIL

			Winner	Loser
7—At L.A.	L	1-2	Valenzuela	Show
8—At L.A.	W	1-0	Dravecky	Hershiser
9—At L.A.	L	0-1	Welch	Hawkins
10—At L.A.	W	3-2	Thurmond	Honeycutt
11—Cincinnati	W	4-3†	T. Stoddard	Power
12—Cincinnati	L	2-3	Robinson	T. Stoddard
13—Cincinnati	W	7-6	Gossage	Price
14—Los Ang.	W	4-3†	Lefferts	Vande Berg
15—Los Ang.	W	2-1‡	McCullers	Howell
16—Los Ang.	W	2-1	Gossage	Powell
17—At S. Fran.	L	1-4	Krukow	Hawkins
18—At S. Fran.	L	1-6	Garrelts	Thurmond
19—At S. Fran.	L	5-6	Davis	McCullers
20—At S. Fran.	L	0-4	Blue	Dravecky
23—At Cinn.	W	7-4	Hawkins	Denny
25—San Fran.	W	9-8‡	Lefferts	Minton
26—San Fran.	L	2-3*	Robinson	Show
27—San Fran.	W	6-4	Dravecky	Krukow
28—Chicago	L	3-4	Keough	Gossage
29—Chicago	W	5-4	Lefferts	Fontenot
30—St. Louis	W	5-0	Thurmond	Horton

Won 12, Lost 9

MAY

			Winner	Loser
1—St. Louis	W	4-3	Show	Cox
2—Pittsburgh	L	0-4	Bielecki	Dravecky
3—Pittsburgh	L	6-7	Guante	Gossage
4—Pittsburgh	L	2-5	Winn	Lefferts
6—At St. L.	W	3-2	Walter	Dayley
7—At St. L.	L	3-4‡	Worrell	Gossage
8—At St. L.	L	3-13	Conroy	Dravecky
9—At Chicago	W	6-2	Hawkins	Sutcliffe
10—At Chicago	L	5-6	Eckersley	Hoyt
11—At Chicago	L	5-9	Trout	Thurmond
13—At Pitts.	W	4-2	Show	Bielecki
14—At Pitts.	W	10-4	Dravecky	Kipper
16—Montreal	L	2-3	Hesketh	Hawkins
17—Montreal	W	5-3	Hoyt	McGaffigan
18—Montreal	L	3-8	Youmans	Thurmond
20—Phila.	W	4-3	Show	Gross
21—Phila.	W	7-2	Dravecky	Hudson
22—Phila.	W	6-2	Hawkins	Carlton
23—New York	W	7-4	Gossage	Orosco
24—New York	L	4-5	Berenyi	Thurmond
25—New York	L	2-4†	Orosco	Lefferts
26—At Mon.	W	9-6	Dravecky	Parrett
27—At Mon.	L	4-5	Burke	T. Stoddard
28—At Mon.	W	10-1	Hoyt	Youmans
30—At Phila.	L	0-2	Gross	Show
31—At Phila.	L	0-1	Hudson	Dravecky

Won 12, Lost 14

JUNE

			Winner	Loser
1—At Phila.	L	5-16	Carlton	Hawkins
2—At N.Y.	L	2-11	Gooden	Hoyt
3—At N.Y.	W	5-4	Hawkins	Fernandez
4—At N.Y.	L	2-4	McDowell	Walter
5—Atlanta	L	2-4	Smith	Dravecky
6—Atlanta	W	3-2†	Walter	Dedmon
7—Atlanta	L	2-4	Mahler	Hoyt
8—Atlanta	W	4-1	Thurmond	Johnson
9—Houston	L	3-5	Deshaies	Show
10—Houston	L	1-12	Knepper	Dravecky
11—Houston	W	11-7	McCullers	DiPino
13—Los Ang.	L	2-6	Valenzuela	Thurmond
14—Los Ang.	W	12-0	Show	Hershiser
15—Los Ang.	L	0-6	Honeycutt	Dravecky
16—San Fran.	W	4-0	Hawkins	Laskey
17—San Fran.	W	8-5	Lefferts	Robinson
18—San Fran.	L	3-6	LaCoss	Thurmond
19—San Fran.	W	8-3	Show	Mulholland
20—At L.A.	W	5-4	McCullers	Howell
21—At L.A.	W	8-7§	McCullers	Pena
22—At L.A.	W	5-4	Lefferts	Niedenfuer
23—At S. Fran.	L	1-18	LaCoss	Hoyt
24—At S. Fran.	W	3-0	Show	Mulholland
25—At S. Fran.	W	3-1	Dravecky	Blue
27—At Atlanta	L	4-5	Garber	T. Stoddard
28—At Atlanta	L	3-5	Smith	McCullers
29—At Atlanta	L	1-3	Palmer	Thurmond
30—At Hous.	W	9-2	Dravecky	Knepper

Won 14, Lost 14

JULY

			Winner	Loser
1—At Hous.	W	7-4	Show	Knudson
2—At Hous.	L	1-8	Scott	Hawkins
3—Chicago	W	4-1	Hoyt	Eckersley
4—Chicago	W	2-1	Gossage	Fontenot
5—Chicago	L	2-3	Gumpert	Lefferts
6—Chicago	W	2-1	Hawkins	Sanderson
7—Pittsburgh	L	1-3*	Guante	Gossage
8—Pittsburgh	W	4-2	Hoyt	Reuschel
9—Pittsburgh	L	4-6	Bielecki	McCullers
10—St. Louis	W	4-3	Lefferts	Tudor
11—St. Louis	L	2-4	Cox	Hawkins
12—St. Louis	L	2-4	Forsch	Whitson
13—St. Louis	W	13-6	Hoyt	Conroy
17—At Pitts.	W	2-1	McCullers	Rhoden
18—At Pitts.	L	7-12	Reuschel	Hawkins
19—At Pitts.	L	3-4	Guante	Lefferts
20—At Pitts.	L	2-4	McWilliams	Dravecky
21—At Chicago	L	1-6	Moyer	Hoyt
22—At Chicago	L	4-6	Lynch	McCullers
23—At Chicago	W	7-5	Lefferts	Fontenot
25—At St. L.	L	2-3	Forsch	Whitson
26—At St. L.	L	2-4	Mathews	Hoyt
27—At St. L.	L	2-3	Tudor	McCullers
28—Cincinnati	W	5-2	Hawkins	Browning
29—Cincinnati	W	2-1	Gossage	Robinson
30—Cincinnati	W	9-3	Whitson	Denny

Won 12, Lost 14

AUGUST

			Winner	Loser
1—Houston	L	3-6	Knepper	Hoyt
2—Houston	L	4-5	Scott	Show
3—Houston	W	5-1	Hawkins	Knudson
4—Atlanta	L	1-4	Acker	Dravecky
5—Atlanta	L	2-3	Speck	Whitson
6—Atlanta	L	2-4	Assenmacher	Hoyt
8—At Hous.	L	0-5	Scott	McCullers
9—At Hous.	L	2-6	Deshaies	Hawkins
10—At Hous.	W	5-3	Dravecky	Knepper
11—At Atlanta	L	6-11	Mahler	Whitson
12—At Atlanta	W	4-3	Hoyt	Smith
13—At Atlanta	L	7-8	Garber	Gossage
14—At Atlanta	L	3-7	Dedmon	Walter
15—At Cinn.	L	2-7	Soto	Dravecky
15—At Cinn.	W	7-1	Show	Browning
16—At Cinn.	L	1-4	Gullickson	Whitson
17—At Cinn.	W	9-5	Hoyt	Welsh
18—At Cinn.	L	5-6	Denny	LaPoint
19—Montreal	W	7-1	Hawkins	Smith
20—Montreal	W	3-2	Show	Tibbs
21—Montreal	W	6-0	Dravecky	Martinez
22—Phila.	L	1-4	Ruffin	Whitson
23—Phila.	W	4-3‡	McCullers	Tekulve
24—Phila.	L	5-6	Tekulve	Gossage
25—New York	L	2-5	Orosco	Lefferts
26—New York	L	6-11	Fernandez	Dravecky
27—New York	L	5-6†	Sisk	Gossage
30—At Mon.	L	1-10	Smith	Hoyt
30—At Mon.	W	5-4	McCullers	McClure
31—At Mon.	W	4-1	Wojna	Tibbs

Won 11, Lost 19

SEPTEMBER

			Winner	Loser
1—At Phila.	L	4-5	Tekulve	Lefferts
2—At Phila.	W	6-2	LaPoint	Bittiger
3—At Phila.	W	7-5	B. Stoddard	Bedrosian
6—At N.Y.	L	3-4	Orosco	McCullers
7—At N.Y.	L	1-7	Gooden	LaPoint
7—At N.Y.	L	5-6	Sisk	Lefferts
8—At S. Fran.	L	3-4	Mulholland	Whitson
9—At S. Fran.	L	0-7	LaCoss	Hoyt
10—Atlanta	W	9-4	McCullers	Garber
11—Atlanta	W	9-1	Wojna	Palmer
12—Houston	L	3-5	Kerfeld	McCullers
13—Houston	W	4-3	Lefferts	Smith
14—Houston	W	3-2	Lefferts	Scott
16—San Fran.	L	1-4	Krukow	Wojna
17—San Fran.	W	5-4*	McCullers	Davis
19—At Hous.	L	4-5	Kerfeld	LaPoint
20—At Hous.	L	6-10	Scott	Hayward
21—At Hous.	W	5-0	Jones	Knepper
22—At Atlanta	L	8-9	Smith	Hoyt
23—At Atlanta	W	5-2	Booker	Acker
25—At L.A.	L	3-4*	Howell	McCullers
25—At L.A.	W	7-6	McCullers	Howell
26—Cincinnati	L	6-8	Murphy	Lefferts
27—Cincinnati	L	4-7†	Franco	McCullers
28—Cincinnati	L	3-6	Power	Vosberg
29—Los Ang.	L	0-10	Hershiser	Hayward
30—Los Ang.	W	11-8	Hoyt	Howell

Won 11, Lost 16

OCTOBER

			Winner	Loser
1—Los Ang.	W	3-2	Jones	Holton
3—At Cinn.	L	3-6	Power	Wojna
4—At Cinn.	L	7-10	Gullickson	LaPoint
5—At Cinn.	W	2-1	Hawkins	Welsh

Won 2, Lost 2

*10 innings. †11 innings. ‡12 innings. §14 innings.

Kevin McReynolds enjoyed his best offensive season, hitting .288 with 26 home runs and 96 RBIs.

A couple of relievers also enjoyed successful seasons. Lefthander Craig Lefferts led the league with 83 pitching appearances and won nine of 17 decisions while compiling a 3.09 ERA and four saves. Even better was rookie righthander Lance McCullers, who went 10-10 with a 2.78 ERA and five saves.

Otherwise, the news was mostly grim, and the front office commanded the headlines more often than it would have liked. Most prominent was Smith's August 29 suspension of Goose Gossage without pay after the reliever unleashed the second of two verbal tirades against Smith and Kroc, who is Smith's mother-in-law. Gossage was reinstated 20 days later, but he made only two more appearances and, despite leading the team with 21 saves, registered a 4.45 ERA en route to his worst season in years.

Smith also incurred the players' wrath by announcing that the Padres no longer could have beer in their clubhouse after home games, that the club in the future would offer only one-year contracts to players who refused to include a drug-testing clause in their contract, and that the team would not consider signing potential free agent Tim Raines because of the outfielder's former drug problems. Smith later apologized to Raines for that statement, as he did to reporters for calling them "(bleeping) flies" in one angry outburst.

The Padres never won more than four games in a row and sealed their fate by losing 19 of 30 games in August. Boros called it "the most frustrating year I've ever spent in baseball."

Steve Sax made a run at the National League batting title, finishing two points short at .332 with 210 hits and 40 stolen bases.

Dodgers Have Painful Season

By GORDON VERRELL

You knew right off this was no ordinary injury, the one that crippled Pedro Guerrero—and the Los Angeles Dodgers—for all but a month of the 1986 season.

Tending to Guerrero that warm afternoon in Florida as he writhed in pain, holding his left knee, were the team physician, the manager, the club president, the executive vice president, another vice president and half of the team. And when an ambulance took Guerrero away, the Dodgers' hopes went right along with him.

Oh, the Dodgers kept up the brave talk. "Pete's not going to be here, so we can't talk about it; we've just got to go out and play," was the consensus comment. But it was obvious from the start it was going to be a struggle for the Dodgers to repeat as National League West champions.

The first 10 games the Dodgers played were all decided by one run, and they lost seven of them.

"You figure that all those close games we lost, Pete might have made the difference in some of them," right fielder Mike Marshall said.

Guerrero's injury (a ruptured tendon below the knee) was merely the beginning of an agonizing season of injuries. In all, the Dodgers used the disabled list 16 times, a fact that was reflected in the number of lineups—123 in 162 games—Tom Lasorda had to devise during his longest season yet as a manager.

In the spring, Lasorda was rejoicing in his middle lineup of third baseman Bill Madlock, a four-time N.L. batting champion; Guerrero, who had placed third in the N.L. Most Valuable Player voting in 1985, and Marshall, who had slugged 28 homers to go along with Guerrero's 33 the year before. With these three veterans hitting 3-4-5 in the batting order, Lasorda was confident that his team would dominate the division again.

As it developed, there was only one game all season in which all three started and batted 3-4-5.

Guerrero had surgery on his knee April 4, played his first game of the season August 1, later returned to the disabled list and finally hit his first homer September 11, finishing with five. Marshall, who was leading the league in homers near midseason, was ineffective most of the second half because of a nagging back ailment. He wound up with 19 homers and 53 runs batted in. And Madlock, who hit .280 and led the club with only 60 RBIs, appeared on the disabled list twice.

Right fielder Mike Marshall got off to a blazing start but was slowed considerably by a nagging back ailment.

The Dodgers' problems were compounded by a porous bullpen and the major leagues' worst defense (181 errors). It all combined to give Los Angeles its poorest record (73-89) in almost two decades and its lowest finish (fifth) in Lasorda's 18-year managerial career, including the minor leagues.

The Dodgers at least were spared the embarrassment—by half a game—of becoming the first N.L. club to go from first

SCORES OF LOS ANGELES DODGERS' 1986 GAMES

APRIL			Winner	Loser
7—San Diego	W	2-1	Valenzuela	Show
8—San Diego	L	0-1	Dravecky	Hershiser
9—San Diego	W	1-0	Welch	Hawkins
10—San Diego	L	2-3	Thurmond	Honeycutt
11—San Fran.	L	8-9‡	Robinson	Niedenfuer
12—San Fran.	L	6-7†	Minton	Powell
13—San Fran.	W	3-2	Hershiser	Garrelts
14—At S. Diego	L	3-4†	Lefferts	Vande Berg
15—At S. Diego	L	1-2‡	McCullers	Howell
16—At S. Diego	L	1-2	Gossage	Powell
18—At Atlanta	L	3-6	Palmer	Valenzuela
19—At Atlanta	L	0-3	Smith	Hershiser
20—At Atlanta	W	7-3	Welch	Mahler
21—At S. Fran.	L	1-5	Mason	Honeycutt
22—At S. Fran.	L	3-10	Krukow	Powell
23—At S. Fran.	W	6-4	Valenzuela	Garrelts
24—Atlanta	W	6-3	Hershiser	Mahler
25—Atlanta	L	1-4	Johnson	Welch
26—Atlanta	L	4-5*	Sutter	Vande Berg
27—Atlanta	W	7-4	Reuss	Smith
28—Pittsburgh	W	2-1	Valenzuela	Kipper
29—Pittsburgh	W	5-4	Hershiser	Patterson
30—Chicago	W	4-0	Welch	Eckersley

Won 10, Lost 13

MAY			Winner	Loser
1—Chicago	W	4-0	Honeycutt	Hoffman
2—St. Louis	W	3-2	Reuss	Tudor
3—St. Louis	W	3-0	Valenzuela	Conroy
4—St. Louis	L	1-3	Forsch	Hershiser
6—At Chicago	L	6-7	Smith	Niedenfuer
7—At Chicago	W	8-4	Niedenfuer	Baller
8—At Chicago	L	5-6	Sanderson	Reuss
9—At Mon.	L	4-8	Reardon	Valenzuela
10—At Mon.	L	2-3†	Schatzeder	Howell
11—At Mon.	L	3-4	Hesketh	Welch
13—At St. L.	W	6-5§	Honeycutt	Dayley
14—At St. L.	W	8-3	Valenzuela	Conroy
16—New York	W	4-3†	Howell	Orosco
17—New York	W	6-2	Niedenfuer	Fernandez
18—New York	L	4-8	Niemann	Reuss
20—Montreal	W	4-0	Valenzuela	Smith
21—Montreal	W	6-1	Hershiser	Tibbs
22—Montreal	L	2-5	Hesketh	Welch
23—Phila.	L	2-8	Rawley	Reuss
24—Phila.	W	6-0	Valenzuela	Toliver
25—Phila.	W	5-2	Hershiser	Gross
27—At N.Y.	L	1-8	Darling	Welch
28—At N.Y.	L	2-4	Gooden	Reuss
29—At N.Y.	L	2-5	Fernandez	Valenzuela
30—At Pitts.	W	6-4†	Niedenfuer	DeLeon
31—At Pitts.	L	0-4	Kipper	Honeycutt

Won 13, Lost 13

JUNE			Winner	Loser
1—At Pitts.	L	3-12	Rhoden	Welch
2—At Phila.	L	2-13	Rawley	Reuss
3—At Phila.	W	11-4	Valenzuela	Maddux
4—At Phila.	L	7-8	Gross	Hershiser
5—Houston	W	1-0	Honeycutt	Hernandez
6—Houston	W	3-2	Howell	Knepper
7—Houston	L	5-7	Lopez	Howell
8—Houston	L	2-3	Scott	Valenzuela
9—Cincinnati	W	6-5	Niedenfuer	Browning
10—Cincinnati	W	1-0	Niedenfuer	Franco
11—Cincinnati	W	5-4†	Vande Berg	Franco
13—At S. Diego	W	6-2	Valenzuela	Thurmond
14—At S. Diego	L	0-12	Show	Hershiser
15—At S. Diego	W	6-0	Honeycutt	Dravecky
17—At Atlanta	L	3-4*	Assenmacher	Howell
18—At Atlanta	W	5-2	Valenzuela	McMurtry
19—At Atlanta	W	9-4	Hershiser	Smith
20—San Diego	L	4-5	McCullers	Howell
21—San Diego	L	7-8x	McCullers	Pena
22—San Diego	L	4-5	Lefferts	Niedenfuer
23—Atlanta	L	5-6	Dedmon	Howell
24—Atlanta	W	6-2	Hershiser	Palmer
25—Atlanta	L	2-3	Mahler	Honeycutt
27—At Hous.	L	0-5	Scott	Reuss
28—At Hous.	L	4-6	Deshaies	Welch
29—At Hous.	L	1-2	Hernandez	Valenzuela
30—At Cinn.	L	5-6†	Willis	Vande Berg

Won 11, Lost 16

JULY			Winner	Loser
2—At Cinn.	L	3-4*	Franco	Vande Berg
3—Pittsburgh	W	6-3	Welch	Reuschel
4—Pittsburgh	L	4-6	Bielecki	Valenzuela
5—Pittsburgh	L	0-5	Walk	Hershiser
6—Pittsburgh	W	4-3	Honeycutt	Winn
7—St. Louis	W	1-0	Pena	Forsch
8—St. Louis	L	0-1	Conroy	Welch
9—St. Louis	W	8-2	Valenzuela	Mathews
10—Chicago	W	11-4	Hershiser	Moyer
11—Chicago	L	3-6	Sanderson	Honeycutt
12—Chicago	L	4-7	Lynch	Niedenfuer
13—Chicago	W	4-3	Howell	Smith
17—At St. L.	L	2-12	Tudor	Hershiser
18—At St. L.	W	4-3	Valenzuela	Cox
19—At St. L.	L	1-2	Forsch	Welch
20—At St. L.	W	7-2	Honeycutt	Conroy
22—At Pitts.	W	4-3	Powell	Guante
23—At Pitts.	W	6-5	Hershiser	Reuschel
24—At Pitts.	W	9-2	Valenzuela	Walk
25—At Chicago	L	3-8	Trout	Welch
26—At Chicago	L	4-9	Eckersley	Honeycutt
27—At Chicago	W	13-11	Howell	DiPino
28—San Fran.	W	2-1	Hershiser	LaCoss
29—San Fran.	W	2-1	Valenzuela	Downs
30—San Fran.	W	4-2	Welch	Mulholland

Won 15, Lost 10

AUGUST			Winner	Loser
1—Cincinnati	W	9-5	Honeycutt	Soto
2—Cincinnati	W	7-1	Niedenfuer	Robinson
3—Cincinnati	W	2-1	Hershiser	Gullickson
4—Houston	W	7-3	Valenzuela	Kerfeld
5—Houston	L	2-10	Lopez	Howell
6—Houston	W	7-4	Honeycutt	Keough
8—At Cinn.	L	0-4	Gullickson	Hershiser
8—At Cinn.	L	1-5	Welsh	Pena
9—At Cinn.	L	2-6	Denny	Valenzuela
10—At Cinn.	W	5-0	Powell	Soto
11—At Hous.	L	6-7	Smith	Howell
12—At Hous.	L	0-3	Ryan	Honeycutt
13—At Hous.	W	5-3	Hershiser	Scott
14—At Hous.	L	2-3	Andersen	Valenzuela
15—At S. Fran.	L	1-5	Krukow	Powell
16—At S. Fran.	W	6-5	Welch	LaCoss
17—At S. Fran.	W	2-0	Honeycutt	Blue
18—New York	L	4-5	Ojeda	Hershiser
19—New York	L	4-6	Darling	Valenzuela
20—New York	L	5-7	Fernandez	Powell
22—Montreal	W	2-1*	Howell	Burke
23—Montreal	L	4-7	Sebra	Honeycutt
24—Montreal	W	3-2*	Holton	Burke
25—Phila.	W	3-1	Valenzuela	Carman
26—Phila.	L	4-6	Gross	Vande Berg
27—Phila.	L	1-2	Ruffin	Welch
29—At N.Y.	L	1-2	Ojeda	Honeycutt
30—At N.Y.	L	3-6	Aguilera	Hershiser
31—At N.Y.	W	7-4	Valenzuela	Darling

Won 13, Lost 16

SEPTEMBER			Winner	Loser
1—At Mon.	L	6-7	Reardon	Howell
2—At Mon.	L	0-1	Youmans	Welch
3—At Mon.	W	5-3	Honeycutt	Sebra
5—At Phila.	L	0-4	Carman	Hershiser
6—At Phila.	W	3-2	Valenzuela	Gross
7—At Phila.	L	1-2	Tekulve	Howell
8—Atlanta	W	7-0	Welch	Mahler
9—Atlanta	W	9-5	Honeycutt	Smith
10—Houston	W	5-1	Hershiser	Deshaies
11—Houston	W	14-6	Valenzuela	Knepper
12—Cincinnati	L	3-8	Welsh	Holton
13—Cincinnati	L	0-3	Browning	Welch
14—Cincinnati	L	3-4	Robinson	Niedenfuer
16—At Atlanta	L	1-3	Alexander	Hershiser
17—At Atlanta	L	1-4	Dedmon	Valenzuela
18—At Atlanta	L	3-4‡	Assenmacher	Holton
19—At Cinn.	W	9-7	Holton	Franco
20—At Cinn.	L	5-9	Murphy	Powell
21—At Cinn.	L	4-8	Terry	Hershiser
22—At Hous.	W	9-2	Valenzuela	Darwin
23—At Hous.	L	0-4	Deshaies	Powell
25—San Diego	W	4-3*	Howell	McCullers
25—San Diego	L	6-7	McCullers	Howell
26—At S. Fran.	L	0-3	Krukow	Niedenfuer
27—At S. Fran.	L	3-8	Blue	Valenzuela
28—At S. Fran.	L	5-6y	Minton	Galvez
29—At S. Diego	W	10-0	Hershiser	Hayward
30—At S. Diego	L	8-11	Hoyt	Howell

Won 10, Lost 18

OCTOBER			Winner	Loser
1—At S. Diego	L	2-3	Jones	Holton
3—San Fran.	L	2-8	Downs	Welch
4—San Fran.	W	2-1	Valenzuela	Grant
5—San Fran.	L	2-11	Krukow	Hershiser

Won 1, Lost 3

*10 innings. †11 innings. ‡12 innings. §13 innings. x14 innings. y16 innings.

place to last in a single year.

"It was a very tough year," Lasorda said. "We had too many injuries. We just couldn't put enough manpower out there to compete.

"But even though we finished badly, we were in a lot of one-run games (a league-leading 66, of which the Dodgers lost 38), so we weren't getting clobbered a lot. We were in a lot of games . . . games we had the opportunity to win."

But they didn't, either because of an untimely error, or the lack of a timely hit, or because the bullpen went afoul—all three of which hampered the Dodgers throughout the season.

The Dodgers did make one run, winning 13 of 16 games and climbing from last place to third, only 5½ games behind Houston in early August. The Dodgers followed that with four games in Cincinnati, then four in Houston, figuring to keep the ball rolling by winning three of four in both towns.

Instead they lost three of four in both towns and were never heard from again. After climbing over .500 August 4 (53-52) for the first time since they were 2-1, the Dodgers lost 37 of their final 57 games.

On the road, the Dodgers were particularly easy pickings, going 27-54.

Rising above the Dodgers' worst season since 1967 were lefthander Fernando Valenzuela, who won 21 games and his first Gold Glove, and second baseman Steve Sax, who went into the final day of the season still with an eye on the N.L. batting crown.

Sax didn't get it—he finished at .332, just two points behind Montreal's Tim Raines —but he still managed by far his finest season. He stole 40 bases and led the club in virtually every offensive category, including runs scored (91), hits (210), doubles (43) and game-winning RBIs (11).

"It would have meant more if we'd won," Sax said.

Valenzuela said about the same.

"This was my best season, but only because I won 20 games for the first time," he said. "But I didn't pitch any different than last year, when we won."

Valenzuela completed 20 of his 34 starts to lead the league, compiled a 3.14 earned-run average, hurled three shutouts and struck out 242 batters.

"For Fernando to win 21 games on this club is a tremendous accomplishment," Lasorda said.

When Guerrero went down during the Dodgers' final exhibition game in Florida, the immediate beneficiary was Franklin Stubbs, who had been ticketed for another year in Triple A. Stubbs responded well at times—he hit a team-high 23 homers—but other times it was obvious he wasn't quite ready. He also struck out 107 times, tops on the club.

Injuries knocked out the entire infield except for Sax, who missed only five games because of a sore heel. The outfield also was wiped out.

Lasorda used several players to fill the outfield vacancies, including Stubbs, rookie Reggie Williams, whose .277 batting average ranked third on the club, and veterans Ken Landreaux (.261), Len Matuszek (.261) and Bill Russell (.250). Stubbs, Russell and Matuszek also helped out in the infield, where Dave Anderson batted .245 in a utility role.

First baseman Greg Brock hit 16 homers but was limited to 325 at-bats by a knee injury that required arthroscopic surgery. His most frequent replacement was veteran Enos Cabell (.256).

Shortstop Mariano Duncan played in only 109 games because of a fractured ankle and batted just .229 but still led the club with 48 stolen bases. Behind the plate, Mike Scioscia and Alex Trevino combined for a .255 average and 52 RBIs.

All of the injuries and the lack of offensive punch added a heavy burden to the pitching staff, and it showed.

Orel Hershiser, who won 19 games in 1985, came in at 14-14 with a 3.85 ERA, which was almost double his '85 figure (2.03). Bob Welch, whose 3.28 ERA was second to Valenzuela's on the staff, dropped from 14-4 to 7-13 last season, largely because of a lack of support. The Dodgers scored three or fewer runs in 19 of Welch's 33 starts.

Lefthander Rick Honeycutt, who had off-season shoulder surgery, was 11-9 with a 3.32 ERA, but he failed to complete any of his 28 starts.

Jerry Reuss got off slowly, then ran into elbow problems and finished a disappointing 2-6 with a 5.84 ERA. He eventually had arthroscopic surgery. And Alejandro Pena, the league's ERA leader in 1984 before missing virtually all of '85 while recovering from shoulder surgery, posted a 4.89 ERA in 24 appearances.

The bullpen posted a 17-28 record and produced only 25 saves, the second-worst total in the majors. Tom Niedenfuer (11 saves) had a rough start, then ran into some nagging injuries, while Ken Howell (12 saves) slumped after a good start.

Through it all, the fans continued to stream into Dodger Stadium. For the fifth year in a row, the Dodgers surpassed 3 million in attendance.

Center fielder Dale Murphy was not his usual devastating self and the Braves tumbled to the National League West Division basement.

July Swoon Kills Bitter Braves

By GERRY FRALEY

They awoke the morning of the Fourth of July ready to catch San Francisco and take over the lead in the National League West. Three months later, the Atlanta Braves had shown themselves to be pretenders and a team in serious need of introspection.

Just 1½ lengths behind the Giants after games of July 3, the Braves then lost 14 of their next 16 contests to fall to last place, 9½ games back. The Braves never recovered from that swoon, ultimately staggering to a last-place finish with their third straight losing record (72-89).

What happened between the heady first week of July and the bitter end? Have the Braves, after two years of contention earlier in this decade, returned to the famine cycle?

"I still think we have a decent team," General Manager Bobby Cox said. "We're so close right now that it's unbelievable.... This was a year when everybody was just sort of average. I don't know exactly what the reason was.

"I think we were drastically improved, but a lot of clubs in the division improved at the same time. This is going to be a tough year for us. We have to make a lot of decisions."

The Braves did not catch well; they made 141 errors. The Braves did not run well; they finished last in the league with 93 stolen bases in 169 attempts and grounded into 124 double plays. They threw with limited success; their staff was 10th in the league with a 3.97 earned-run average.

Worst of all for the Braves, however, was that they did not hit well. A review of what went wrong for the Atlanta Braves must start with their offense.

In 1986, the myth about the Braves finally died. Contrary to popular wisdom, this is not an intimidating offensive team.

The legend was born in 1973, when the Braves hit 206 home runs and scored 799 runs. A decade later, Atlanta led the league in average (.272) and scoring (746). But over the last three years, only two N.L. teams (Pittsburgh and Montreal) have scored fewer runs than the Braves. In 1986, the Braves finished next to last in scoring (615 runs) and batting (.250).

The production of '83, to which the Braves have pointed as proof that they are a good team, must now be seen as the result of career years that might never be duplicated. Catcher Bruce Benedict hit .298 with 43 runs batted in and made the All-Star team that year. He finished '86 at .225 with 13 RBIs in 160 at-bats. Second baseman Glenn Hubbard batted .263 with 70 RBIs in '83; he batted .230 with 36 RBIs (including only three after August 10) in '86. Shortstop Rafael Ramirez went from .297 and 58 RBIs in '83 to .240 and 33 RBIs.

The career-year theory also must apply to Terry Harper, who went from the left-field starter and 72 RBIs in '85 to 30 RBIs in '86.

"I though we were going to score more runs," said Cox, who had made improving the offense a primary goal in his first year as general manager. "I thought our offense was a little better, but it didn't turn out that way."

Two of Cox's trades helped the offense. One did not.

Cox's first major trade was to acquire catcher Ozzie Virgil from Philadelphia in December 1985. Virgil gave the Braves their best power production from catcher since Earl Williams in 1972, but that is more an indictment of the catchers the Braves have used rather than praise of Virgil's season. He hit .223 with 15 homers and 48 RBIs.

The June 30 acquisition of Ken Griffey from the New York Yankees was more beneficial. Cox gave up right fielder Claudell Washington, who had accumulated only 14 RBIs by that time, and minor league infielder Paul Zuvella to get Griffey, who hit .308 with 12 homers and 32 RBIs as the full-time left fielder.

Cox also helped the Braves by adding Ted Simmons in spring training. Simmons became the spiritual leader of the "Bomb Squad" bench group that became a Braves strength. With Simmons going 11-for-47 with two homers and 18 RBIs as a pinch-hitter, the Braves' bench became a force. Atlanta pinch-hitters batted .277 with seven homers and 53 RBIs. In '85, Atlanta pinch-hitters batted only .209 with four homers and 30 RBIs. Chris Chambliss (20-for-68) was another big contributor off the bench.

Ken Oberkfell reached career highs with five homers and 48 RBIs, but the Braves needed even higher numbers from their third baseman. Rookie shortstop Andres Thomas finished strong to hit .251 in 323 at-bats, but part-time outfielders Billy

SCORES OF ATLANTA BRAVES' 1986 GAMES

APRIL			Winner	Loser
8—Montreal	W	6-0	Mahler	Smith
10—Montreal	L	3-6	Tibbs	Garber
11—At Hous.	L	1-2	Kerfeld	Palmer
12—At Hous.	L	3-4	Ryan	Mahler
13—At Hous.	W	8-7	Johnson	Scott
15—Cincinnati	L	3-5	Robinson	Dedmon
16—Cincinnati	L	3-5	Denny	Mahler
18—Los Ang.	W	6-3	Palmer	Valenzuela
19—Los Ang.	W	3-0	Smith	Hershiser
20—Los Ang.	L	3-7	Welch	Mahler
21—Houston	W	8-2	Johnson	Ryan
22—Houston	L	2-3	Kerfeld	Ward
23—Houston	L	2-3	Solano	Smith
24—At L.A.	L	3-6	Hershiser	Mahler
25—At L.A.	W	4-1	Johnson	Welch
26—At L.A.	W	5-4†	Sutter	Vande Berg
27—At L.A.	L	4-7	Reuss	Smith
29—New York	L	5-10	Berenyi	McMurtry
30—New York	L	1-8	Gooden	Johnson

Won 7, Lost 12

MAY			Winner	Loser
1—New York	W	7-2	Smith	Aguilera
2—At Phila.	W	7-1	Palmer	Carlton
3—At Phila.	W	10-4	Mahler	Rawley
4—At Phila.	L	1-5	Gross	Johnson
5—At Cinn.	W	4-3‡	Assenmacher	Power
6—At Cinn.	L	0-2	Gullickson	Palmer
8—At Cinn.	W	10-5	McMurtry	Denny
9—Phila.	L	6-7	Gross	Johnson
10—Phila.	W	3-1	Smith	Hudson
11—Phila.	L	1-2	Bedrosian	McMurtry
12—At N.Y.	L	0-1	McDowell	Assenmacher
13—At N.Y.	W	6-3	Johnson	Aguilera
14—At Mon.	L	2-3	B. Smith	Z. Smith
15—At Mon.	W	7-4†	Sutter	Schatzeder
16—St. Louis	W	6-2	Mahler	Forsch
17—St. Louis	W	2-0	Johnson	Cox
18—St. Louis	W	5-2	Smith	Tudor
20—Chicago	W	8-3	Palmer	Sanderson
21—Chicago	W	9-8x	Dedmon	Frazier
22—Chicago	W	2-0	Johnson	Trout
23—At St. L.	L	2-3	Tudor	Smith
24—At St. L.	L	5-9	Burris	Palmer
25—At St. L.	W	6-2*	Mahler	Conroy
26—At Pitts.	W	9-4	Assenmacher	Walk
27—At Pitts.	W	6-2§	Garber	Walk
28—At Pitts.	L	3-4	McWilliams	Palmer
30—At Chicago	L	1-6	Sanderson	Mahler
31—At Chicago	W	8-4	Dedmon	Eckersley

Won 18, Lost 10

JUNE			Winner	Loser
1—At Chicago	L	3-7	Hoffman	Smith
2—Pittsburgh	L	2-9	Reuschel	Palmer
3—Pittsburgh	W	8-5	Mahler	Guante
4—Pittsburgh	L	3-12	Bielecki	Johnson
5—At S. Diego	W	4-2	Smith	Dravecky
6—At S. Diego	L	2-3‡	Walter	Dedmon
7—At S. Diego	W	4-2	Mahler	Hoyt
8—At S. Diego	L	1-4	Thurmond	Johnson
10—At S. Fran.	L	0-3	Blue	Smith
11—At S. Fran.	W	2-1†	Garber	Minton
13—Cincinnati	W	3-2	Mahler	Denny
14—Cincinnati	L	1-2	Robinson	Assenmacher
15—Cincinnati	L	7-9	Browning	Smith
16—Cincinnati	W	4-3†	Garber	Franco
17—Los Ang.	W	4-3†	Assenmacher	Howell
18—Los Ang.	L	2-5	Valenzuela	McMurtry
19—Los Ang.	L	4-9	Hershiser	Smith
20—At Cinn.	L	4-6	Browning	Dedmon
20—At Cinn.	L	5-8	Gullickson	Johnson
21—At Cinn.	W	7-6	Mahler	Welsh
22—At Cinn.	L	2-5	Denny	McMurtry
23—At L.A.	W	6-5	Dedmon	Howell
24—At L.A.	L	2-6	Hershiser	Palmer
25—At L.A.	W	3-2	Mahler	Honeycutt
27—San Diego	W	5-4	Garber	T. Stoddard
28—San Diego	W	5-3	Smith	McCullers
29—San Diego	W	3-1	Palmer	Thurmond
30—San Fran.	W	5-1	Mahler	Davis

Won 14, Lost 14

JULY			Winner	Loser
1—San Fran.	L	6-9†	Robinson	Johnson
2—San Fran.	W	7-4	Smith	Garrelts
3—Montreal	W	3-1	Palmer	Hesketh
4—Montreal	L	5-11	Youmans	Mahler
5—Montreal	L	5-12	Smith	McMurtry
6—Montreal	L	8-11	Burke	Smith
7—At Phila.	L	3-7	Rawley	Palmer
8—At Phila.	L	2-8	Ruffin	Mahler
9—At Phila.	W	7-3	Alexander	Gross
10—At N.Y.	L	1-5	Ojeda	Smith
11—At N.Y.	L	0-11	Fernandez	Palmer
12—At N.Y.	L	1-10	Aguilera	Mahler
13—At N.Y.	L	0-2	Darling	Alexander
17—At Mon.	L	2-4	Youmans	Mahler
18—At Mon.	L	4-5	Burke	Dedmon
19—At Mon.	W	7-2	Palmer	Tibbs
21—Phila.	L	1-3	Tekulve	Dedmon
22—Phila.	L	4-5‡	Bedrosian	McMurtry
23—Phila.	L	2-4	Ruffin	Alexander
26—New York	W	4-3	Assenmacher	McDowell
26—New York	W	8-5	Acker	Fernandez
27—New York	L	1-5	Aguilera	Mahler
28—At Hous.	L	2-4	Knepper	Alexander
29—At Hous.	W	1-0	Palmer	Scott
30—At Hous.	L	2-4	Deshaies	Acker
31—At S. Fran.	L	2-3	Garrelts	Garber

Won 7, Lost 19

AUGUST			Winner	Loser
1—At S. Fran.	L	1-3	Blue	Mahler
2—At S. Fran.	L	5-7	Williams	Alexander
3—At S. Fran.	W	4-2	Palmer	Downs
4—At S. Diego	W	4-1	Acker	Dravecky
5—At S. Diego	W	3-2	Speck	Whitson
6—At S. Diego	W	4-2	Assenmacher	Hoyt
8—San Fran.	W	7-6	Alexander	LaCoss
9—San Fran.	L	3-4†	Garrelts	Dedmon
10—San Fran.	L	3-4	Berenguer	Garber
11—San Diego	W	11-6	Mahler	Whitson
12—San Diego	L	3-4	Hoyt	Smith
13—San Diego	W	8-7	Garber	Gossage
14—San Diego	W	7-3	Dedmon	Walter
15—Houston	L	0-3	Knepper	Acker
16—Houston	L	4-7	Keough	Mahler
17—Houston	W	4-3	Speck	Andersen
19—At Chicago	W	7-2	Alexander	Sutcliffe
20—At Chicago	W	8-3	Palmer	Eckersley
21—At Chicago	W	5-2	Acker	Lynch
22—At Pitts.	L	5-16	Winn	Mahler
23—At Pitts.	L	3-4	Reuschel	Smith
24—At Pitts.	L	3-4	Walk	Alexander
25—At St. L.	W	4-2	Palmer	Forsch
26—At St. L.	L	1-7	Mathews	Acker
27—At St. L.	L	1-2	Worrell	Mahler
29—Chicago	L	3-7	Sanderson	Smith
30—Chicago	W	4-3	Alexander	Sutcliffe
31—Chicago	W	4-3	Dedmon	Smith

Won 15, Lost 13

SEPTEMBER			Winner	Loser
1—St. Louis	L	2-5	Soff	Acker
2—St. Louis	W	4-2	Mahler	Tudor
3—St. Louis	L	3-5	Cox	Smith
5—Pittsburgh	W	4-3	Assenmacher	Rhoden
6—Pittsburgh	W	4-2	Palmer	Fansler
7—Pittsburgh	L	1-3	Kipper	Speck
8—At L.A.	L	0-7	Welch	Mahler
9—At L.A.	L	5-9	Honeycutt	Smith
10—At S. Diego	L	4-9	McCullers	Garber
11—At S. Diego	L	1-9	Wojna	Palmer
12—At S. Fran.	L	2-11	Krukow	Acker
13—At S. Fran.	W	4-1	Mahler	Mulholland
14—At S. Fran.	L	6-7	Garrelts	Assenmacher
16—Los Ang.	W	3-1	Alexander	Hershiser
17—Los Ang.	W	4-1	Dedmon	Valenzuela
18—Los Ang.	W	4-3§	Assenmacher	Holton
19—San Fran.	L	0-4	Downs	Mahler
20—San Fran.	W	2-1	Puleo	LaCoss
21—San Fran.	L	2-8	Krukow	Alexander
22—San Diego	W	9-8	Smith	Hoyt
23—San Diego	L	2-5	Booker	Acker
24—At Cinn.	L	1-4	Power	Mahler
25—At Cinn.	L	4-6	Gullickson	Puleo
26—Houston	W	5-4	Alexander	Keough
27—Houston	L	0-4	Darwin	Palmer
28—Houston	L	0-2	Deshaies	Acker
30—Cincinnati	W	8-7	Mahler	Gullickson

Won 11, Lost 16

OCTOBER			Winner	Loser
1—Cincinnati	L	5-6	Murphy	Garber
2—Cincinnati	L	4-6x	Murphy	Puleo
3—At Hous.	L	2-6	Ryan	Acker
4—At Hous.	L	2-3	Deshaies	Smith
5—At Hous.	L	1-4	Knepper	Mahler

Won 0, Lost 5

*5½ innings. †10 innings. ‡11 innings. §12 innings. x13 innings.

Bob Horner produced 27 home runs, far below the 40 Braves officials had envisioned.

Sample and Omar Moreno combined for a .252 average and only 41 RBIs.

The offense needed strong seasons from first baseman Bob Horner and center fielder Dale Murphy. Neither succeeded.

Horner surpassed 500 at-bats for the first time in his career but did not produce the 40-homer, 120-RBI season forecast for him. Horner finished with 27 homers (including four in one July 6 game) and 87 RBIs.

When the Braves faded in July with a 7-19 record, Murphy hit only .220 with two homers and seven RBIs. He surged in the final two months but still had a substandard season (29 homers and 83 RBIs) that gnawed at him.

"I know I had a lot of opportunities to do something," said Murphy, who won his fifth straight Gold Glove. "I wish I could have contributed more. I just never felt comfortable. I felt comfortable for a while, but not for the whole season."

The offensive problems trashed the improvement of a reworked pitching staff. The bullpen lost Bruce Sutter because of a rotator-cuff injury, but Gene Garber filled the void with 24 saves and a 2.54 ERA. Rookie Paul Assenmacher added seven wins and seven saves, while Jeff Dedmon went 6-6 with a 2.98 ERA. The only regular reliever who struggled was Craig McMurtry (1-6, 4.74).

The rotation, boosted by a pair of deals with Toronto, was acceptable. On July 6, Cox sent Joe Johnson, who had gone 6-7 thus far in '86, to the Blue Jays in exchange for Jim Acker. The same day, Cox acquired veteran Doyle Alexander from Toronto in a separate deal. The two righthanders combined for a 9-14 record, but their ERAs (Acker, 3.79; Alexander, 3.84) were bettered by only one member of the rotation. That was righthander David Palmer (3.65), who also set career highs for victories (11), innings (209⅔) and strikeouts (170) and avoided the disabled list for the first time in the '80s.

The rotation lacked a stopper. Righthander Rick Mahler was supposed to take the role, but he led the league in losses (18) and had a 4.88 ERA. Lefthander Zane Smith (8-16) was next to try it, but he was winless in his last 12 starts and dropped out of the rotation.

Though no one was able to stop the Braves' skid, first-year Manager Chuck Tanner was, as always, optimistic about the club.

"We knew it was going to be hard," said Tanner, who had managed last-place clubs in Pittsburgh the previous two years. "Our future will be good. It's going to take a couple of years. I'm not discouraged at all. I'm disappointed, but not discouraged."

National League Averages for 1986

CHAMPIONSHIP WINNERS IN PREVIOUS YEARS

1876—Chicago .788
1877—Boston .646
1878—Boston .683
1879—Providence .705
1880—Chicago .798
1881—Chicago .667
1882—Chicago .655
1883—Boston .643
1884—Providence .750
1885—Chicago .777
1886—Chicago .726
1887—Detroit .637
1888—New York .641
1889—New York .659
1890—Brooklyn .667
1891—Boston .630
1892—Boston .680
1893—Boston .662
1894—Baltimore .695
1895—Baltimore .669
1896—Baltimore .698
1897—Boston .705
1898—Boston .685
1899—Brooklyn .677
1900—Brooklyn .603
1901—Pittsburgh .647
1902—Pittsburgh .741
1903—Pittsburgh .650
1904—New York .693
1905—New York .686
1906—Chicago .763
1907—Chicago .704
1908—Chicago .643
1909—Pittsburgh .724
1910—Chicago .675
1911—New York .647
1912—New York .682
1913—New York .664
1914—Boston .614
1915—Philadelphia .592
1916—Brooklyn .610
1917—New York .636
1918—Chicago .651
1919—Cincinnati .686
1920—Brooklyn .604
1921—New York .614
1922—New York .604
1923—New York .621
1924—New York .608
1925—Pittsburgh .621
1926—St. Louis .578
1927—Pittsburgh .610
1928—St. Louis .617
1929—Chicago .645
1930—St. Louis .597
1931—St. Louis .656
1932—Chicago .584
1933—New York .599
1934—St. Louis .621
1935—Chicago .649
1936—New York .597
1937—New York .625
1938—Chicago .586
1939—Cincinnati .630
1940—Cincinnati .654
1941—Brooklyn .649
1942—St. Louis .688
1943—St. Louis .682
1944—St. Louis .682
1945—Chicago .636
1946—St. Louis* .628
1947—Brooklyn .610
1948—Boston .595
1949—Brooklyn .630
1950—Philadelphia .591
1951—New York† .624
1952—Brooklyn .627
1953—Brooklyn .682
1954—New York .630
1955—Brooklyn .641
1956—Brooklyn .604
1957—Milwaukee .617
1958—Milwaukee .597
1959—Los Angeles‡ .564
1960—Pittsburgh .617
1961—Cincinnati .604
1962—San Francisco§ .624
1963—Los Angeles .611
1964—St. Louis .574
1965—Los Angeles .599
1966—Los Angeles .586
1967—St. Louis .627
1968—St. Louis .599
1969—New York (East) .617
1970—Cincinnati (West) .630
1971—Pittsburgh (East) .599
1972—Cincinnati (West) .617
1973—New York (East) .509
1974—Los Angeles (West) .630
1975—Cincinnati (West) .667
1976—Cincinnati (West) .630
1977—Los Angeles (West) .605
1978—Los Angeles (West) .586
1979—Pittsburgh (East) .605
1980—Philadelphia (East) .562
1981—Los Angeles (West) .573
1982—St. Louis (East) .568
1983—Philadelphia (East) .556
1984—San Diego (West) .568
1985—St. Louis (East) .623

*Defeated Brooklyn, two games to none, in playoff for pennant. †Defeated Brooklyn, two games to one, in playoff for pennant. ‡Defeated Milwaukee, two games to none, in playoff for pennant. §Defeated Los Angeles, two games to one, in playoff for pennant.

STANDING OF CLUBS AT CLOSE OF SEASON

EAST DIVISION

Club	N.Y.	Phil.	St.L.	Mon.	Chi.	Pitt.	Hou.	Cin.	S.F.	S.D.	L.A.	Atl.	W.	L.	Pct.	G.B.
New York	..	8	12	10	12	17	7	8	7	10	9	8	108	54	.667	......
Philadelphia	10	..	6	10	8	11	6	5	9	6	7	8	86	75	.534	21½
St. Louis	6	12	..	9	7	11	5	5	7	7	4	6	79	82	.491	28½
Montreal	8	8	9	..	10	11	4	5	5	4	7	7	78	83	.484	29½
Chicago	6	9	10	8	..	7	4	5	6	6	6	3	70	90	.438	37
Pittsburgh	1	7	7	7	11	..	6	2	4	8	4	7	64	98	.395	44

WEST DIVISION

Club	Hou.	Cin.	S.F.	S.D.	L.A.	Atl.	N.Y.	Phil.	St.L.	Mon.	Chi.	Pitt.	W.	L.	Pct.	G.B.
Houston	..	14	9	10	10	13	5	6	7	8	8	6	96	66	.593	....
Cincinnati	4	..	9	9	10	12	4	7	7	7	7	10	86	76	.531	10
San Francisco	9	9	..	10	10	11	5	3	5	7	6	8	83	79	.512	13
San Diego	8	9	8	..	12	6	2	6	5	8	6	4	74	88	.457	22
Los Angeles	8	8	8	6	..	8	3	5	8	5	6	8	73	89	.451	23
Atlanta	5	6	7	12	10	..	4	4	6	4	9	5	72	89	.447	23½

Championship Series—New York defeated Houston, four games to two.

RECORD AT HOME

EAST DIVISION

Club	N.Y.	Phil.	Chi.	St.L.	Mon.	Pitt.	Hou.	L.A.	S.F.	Cin.	S.D.	Atl.	W.	L.	Pct.
New York	.....	6-3	6-3	4-5	5-4	9-0	5-1	5-1	3-3	2-4	5-1	5-1	55	26	.679
Philadelphia	7-2	.....	6-2	3-6	4-5	6-3	3-3	4-2	6-0	3-3	4-2	3-3	49	31	.613
Chicago	3-6	7-2	.....	6-2	4-5	5-4	2-4	4-2	2-4	3-3	4-2	2-4	42	38	.525
St. Louis	1-8	6-3	5-4	.....	3-6	6-3	2-4	2-4	5-1	3-3	5-1	4-2	42	39	.519
Montreal	4-5	3-6	5-4	3-6	.....	4-5	3-3	5-1	2-4	2-4	2-4	3-2	36	44	.450
Pittsburgh	1-8	4-5	7-2	4-5	2-7	.....	2-4	2-4	2-4	0-6	3-3	4-2	31	50	.383

WEST DIVISION

Club	Hou.	L.A.	S.F.	Cin.	S.D.	Atl.	N.Y.	Phil.	Chi.	St.L.	Mon.	Pitt.	W.	L.	Pct.
Houston	.....	7-2	5-4	7-2	5-4	7-2	4-2	3-3	4-2	3-3	5-1	2-4	52	29	.642
Los Angeles	6-3	.....	5-4	6-3	3-6	5-4	2-4	3-3	4-2	4-2	4-2	4-2	46	35	.568
San Francisco	5-4	6-3	.....	4-5	7-2	6-3	2-4	3-3	2-4	4-2	3-3	4-2	46	35	.568
Cincinnati	2-7	7-2	4-5	.....	5-4	6-3	0-6	4-2	4-2	4-2	3-3	4-2	43	38	.531
San Diego	4-5	6-3	6-3	5-4	.....	4-5	1-5	4-2	4-2	4-2	4-2	1-5	43	38	.531
Atlanta	3-6	6-3	4-5	3-6	7-2	.....	3-3	1-5	5-1	4-2	2-4	3-3	41	40	.506

RECORD ABROAD

EAST DIVISION

Club	N.Y.	Mon.	St.L.	Phil.	Pitt.	Chi.	Hou.	Cin.	S.F.	Atl.	S.D.	L.A.	W.	L.	Pct.
New York	.....	5-4	8-1	2-7	8-1	6-3	2-4	6-0	4-2	3-3	5-1	4-2	53	28	.654
Montreal	4-5	.....	6-3	5-4	7-2	5-4	1-5	3-3	3-3	4-2	2-4	2-4	42	39	.519
St. Louis	5-4	6-3	.....	6-3	5-4	2-6	3-3	2-4	2-4	2-4	2-4	2-4	37	43	.463
Philadelphia	3-6	6-3	3-6	.....	5-4	2-7	3-3	2-4	3-3	5-1	2-4	3-3	37	44	.457
Pittsburgh	0-9	5-4	3-6	3-6	.....	4-5	4-2	2-4	2-4	3-3	5-1	2-4	33	48	.407
Chicago	3-6	4-5	4-5	2-6	2-7	.....	2-4	2-4	4-2	1-5	2-4	2-4	28	52	.350

WEST DIVISION

Club	Hou.	Cin.	S.F.	Atl.	S.D.	L.A.	N.Y.	Mon.	St.L.	Phil.	Pitt.	Chi.	W.	L.	Pct.
Houston	.....	7-2	4-5	6-3	5-4	3-6	1-5	3-3	4-2	3-3	4-2	4-2	44	37	.543
Cincinnati	2-7	.....	5-4	6-3	4-5	3-6	4-2	4-2	3-3	3-3	6-0	3-3	43	38	.531
San Francisco	4-5	5-4	.....	5-4	3-6	4-5	3-3	4-2	1-5	0-6	4-2	4-2	37	44	.457
Atlanta	2-7	3-6	3-6	.....	5-4	4-5	1-5	2-3	2-4	3-3	2-4	4-2	31	49	.388
San Diego	4-5	4-5	2-7	2-7	.....	6-3	1-5	4-2	1-5	2-4	3-3	2-4	31	50	.383
Los Angeles	2-7	2-7	3-6	3-6	3-6	.....	1-5	1-5	4-2	2-4	4-2	2-4	27	54	.333

SHUTOUT GAMES

Club	Hou.	N.Y.	Phil.	Cin.	L.A.	Pitt.	S.F.	Mon.	S.D.	Chi.	Atl.	St.L.	W.	L.	Pct.
Houston	..	1	1	2	3	3	4	1	1	0	3	0	19	6	.760
New York	1	..	1	0	0	2	0	0	0	2	3	2	11	4	.733
Philadelphia	0	1	..	0	1	2	3	2	2	0	0	0	11	7	.611
Cincinnati	1	0	0	..	2	0	1	1	0	1	1	1	8	7	.533
Los Angeles	1	0	1	2	..	0	1	1	3	2	1	2	14	14	.500
Pittsburgh	0	0	0	1	2	..	1	0	1	2	0	2	9	10	.474
San Francisco	0	0	0	0	1	1	..	2	2	0	2	2	10	12	.455
Montreal	1	1	3	1	1	1	0	..	0	0	0	1	9	11	.450
San Diego	1	0	0	0	2	0	2	1	..	0	0	1	7	9	.438
Chicago	0	0	1	1	0	1	0	2	0	..	0	1	6	10	.375
Atlanta	1	0	0	0	1	0	0	1	0	1	..	1	5	10	.333
St. Louis	0	1	0	0	1	0	0	0	0	2	0	..	4	13	.235

OFFICIAL NATIONAL LEAGUE BATTING AVERAGES

Compiled by Elias Sports Bureau

CLUB BATTING

Club	Pct.	G.	AB.	R.	OR.	H.	TB.	2B.	3B.	HR.	RBI.	SH.	SF.	SB.	CS.	LOB.
New York	.263	162	5558	783	578	1462	2229	261	31	148	730	75	53	118	48	1192
San Diego	.261	162	5515	656	723	1442	2139	239	25	136	629	66	35	96	68	1099
Chicago	.256	160	5499	680	781	1409	2186	258	27	155	638	54	51	132	62	1087
Houston	.255	162	5441	654	569	1388	2071	244	32	125	613	53	41	163	75	1113
Montreal	.254	161	5508	637	688	1401	2086	255	50	110	602	53	42	193	95	1137
Cincinnati	.254	162	5536	732	717	1404	2143	237	35	144	670	65	41	177	53	1129
San Fran.	.253	162	5501	698	618	1394	2063	269	29	114	637	101	34	148	93	1132
Philadelphia	.253	161	5483	739	713	1386	2192	266	39	154	696	66	51	153	59	1151
Los Angeles	.251	162	5471	638	679	1373	2023	232	14	130	599	81	39	155	67	1083
Atlanta	.250	161	5384	615	719	1348	2051	241	24	138	575	79	42	93	76	1145
Pittsburgh	.250	162	5456	663	700	1366	2038	273	33	111	618	68	44	152	84	1100
St. Louis	.236	161	5378	601	611	1270	1756	216	48	58	550	108	46	262	78	1129
Totals	.253	969	65730	8096	8096	16643	24977	2991	387	1523	7557	869	519	1842	858	13497

INDIVIDUAL BATTING

(Top Fifteen Qualifiers for Batting Championship—502 or More Plate Appearances)

*Bats lefthanded. †Switch-hitter.

Player and Club	Pct.	G.	AB.	R.	H.	TB.	2B.	3B.	HR.	RBI.	GW.	SH.	SF.	SB.	CS.
Raines, Timothy, Montreal†	.334	151	580	91	194	276	35	10	9	62	8	1	3	70	9
Sax, Stephen, Los Angeles	.332	157	633	91	210	279	43	4	6	56	11	6	3	40	17
Gwynn, Anthony, San Diego*	.329	160	642	107	211	300	33	7	14	59	3	2	2	37	9
Bass, Kevin, Houston†	.311	157	591	83	184	287	33	5	20	79	11	1	4	22	13
Hernandez, Keith, New York*	.310	149	551	94	171	246	34	1	13	83	13	0	3	2	1
Hayes, Von, Philadelphia*	.305	158	610	107	186	293	46	2	19	98	14	1	4	24	12
Ray, Johnny, Pittsburgh†	.301	155	579	67	174	228	33	0	7	78	7	1	7	6	9
Knight, C. Ray, New York	.298	137	486	51	145	206	24	2	11	76	13	3	8	2	1
Webster, Mitchell, Montreal†	.290	151	576	89	167	248	31	13	8	49	8	3	5	36	15
Schmidt, Michael, Philadelphia	.290	160	552	97	160	302	29	1	37	119	13	0	9	1	2
Pena, Antonio, Pittsburgh	.288	144	510	56	147	207	26	2	10	52	8	0	1	9	10
McReynolds, W. Kevin, San Diego	.288	158	560	89	161	282	31	6	26	96	14	5	9	8	6
Dawson, Andre, Montreal	.284	130	496	65	141	237	32	2	20	78	7	1	6	18	12
Sandberg, Ryne, Chicago	.284	154	627	68	178	258	28	5	14	76	5	3	6	34	11
Smith, Osborne, St. Louis†	.280	153	514	67	144	171	19	4	0	54	5	11	3	31	7

DEPARTMENTAL LEADERS: G—Parker, 162; AB—Gwynn, 642; R—Gwynn, Hayes, 107; H—Gwynn, 211; TB—Parker, 304; 2B—Hayes, 46; 3B—Webster, 13; HR—Schmidt, 37; RBI—Schmidt, 119; GW—Carter, Davis (Hou.), 16; SH—Thompson (S.F.), 18; SF—Carter, 15; SB—Coleman, 107; CS—Doran, 19.

(All Players—Listed Alphabetically)

Player and Club	Pct.	G.	AB.	R.	H.	TB.	2B.	3B.	HR.	RBI.	GW.	SH.	SF.	SB.	CS.
Acker, James, Atlanta	.107	21	28	1	3	4	1	0	0	0	0	0	0	0	0
Aguayo, Luis, Philadelphia	.211	62	133	17	28	48	6	1	4	13	0	0	2	1	1
Aguilera, Richard, New York	.157	32	51	4	8	14	0	0	2	6	1	3	0	0	0
Aldrete, Michael, San Francisco*	.250	84	216	27	54	84	18	3	2	25	6	4	1	1	3
Alexander, Doyle, Atlanta	.211	18	38	2	8	9	1	0	0	5	0	6	1	0	0
Almon, William, Pittsburgh	.219	102	196	29	43	75	7	2	7	27	3	1	3	11	4
Amelung, Edward, Los Angeles*	.091	8	11	0	1	1	0	0	0	0	0	0	0	0	0
Andersen, Larry, Phil-Hou	.000	48	6	0	0	0	0	0	0	0	0	1	0	0	0
Anderson, David, Los Angeles	.245	92	216	31	53	65	9	0	1	15	1	2	1	5	1
Anderson, Richard, New York	.091	15	11	1	1	1	0	0	0	0	0	1	0	0	0
Asadoor, Randall, San Diego	.364	15	55	9	20	25	5	0	0	7	0	2	0	1	2
Ashby, Alan, Houston†	.257	120	315	24	81	117	15	0	7	38	6	1	6	1	0
Assenmacher, Paul, Atlanta*	.000	61	6	0	0	0	0	0	0	0	0	0	0	0	0
Backman, Walter, New York†	.320	124	387	67	124	149	18	2	1	27	5	14	3	13	7
Bailey, J. Mark, Houston†	.176	57	153	9	27	44	5	0	4	15	2	0	1	1	1
Baller, Jay, Chicago	.000	36	5	0	0	0	0	0	0	0	0	1	0	0	0
Bargar, Gregory, St. Louis	.000	22	2	0	0	0	0	0	0	0	0	1	0	0	0
Bass, Kevin, Houston†	.311	157	591	83	184	287	33	5	20	79	11	1	4	22	13
Beckwith, T. Joseph, Los Angeles*	.000	15	0	0	0	0	0	0	0	0	0	0	0	0	0
Bedrosian, Stephen, Philadelphia	.200	68	5	0	1	1	0	0	0	0	0	0	0	0	0
Bell, David, Cincinnati	.278	155	568	89	158	253	29	3	20	75	6	3	6	2	8
Belliard, Rafael, Pittsburgh	.233	117	309	33	72	81	5	2	0	31	2	11	1	12	2
Benedict, Bruce, Atlanta	.225	64	160	11	36	48	10	1	0	13	0	4	1	1	0
Berenguer, Juan, San Francisco	.143	46	7	0	1	1	0	0	0	0	0	3	0	0	0
Berenyi, Bruce, New York	.000	14	11	0	0	0	0	0	0	0	0	1	0	0	0
Bielecki, Michael, Pittsburgh	.063	31	48	3	3	3	0	0	0	1	0	4	0	0	0
Bilardello, Dann, Montreal	.194	79	191	12	37	54	5	0	4	17	1	7	0	1	0
Bittiger, Jeffrey, Philadelphia	.333	3	3	1	1	4	0	0	1	1	1	1	0	0	0
Blue, Vida, San Francisco†	.093	28	43	3	4	8	1	0	1	3	0	4	0	0	0
Bochy, Bruce, San Diego	.252	63	127	16	32	65	9	0	8	22	3	1	0	1	0
Bockus, Randy, San Francisco*	.000	6	1	0	0	0	0	0	0	0	0	0	0	0	0
Boever, Joseph, St. Louis	.500	11	2	0	1	1	0	0	0	0	0	0	0	0	0
Bonds, Barry, Pittsburgh*	.223	113	413	72	92	172	26	3	16	48	4	2	2	36	7
Bonilla, Roberto, Pittsburgh†	.240	63	192	28	46	59	6	2	1	17	1	3	0	4	4
Booker, Gregory, San Diego	.000	9	0	0	0	0	0	0	0	0	0	0	0	0	0
Bosley, Thaddis, Chicago*	.275	87	120	15	33	42	4	1	1	9	2	1	0	3	0
Bream, Sidney, Pittsburgh*	.268	154	522	73	140	235	37	5	16	77	9	1	7	13	7
Brenly, Robert, San Francisco	.246	149	472	60	116	190	26	0	16	62	4	5	3	10	6
Brock, Gregory, Los Angeles*	.234	115	325	33	76	137	13	0	16	52	3	1	4	2	5
Brooks, Hubert, Montreal	.340	80	306	50	104	174	18	5	14	58	10	0	5	4	2
Brown, Curtis, Montreal	.000	6	1	0	0	0	0	0	0	0	0	0	0	0	0
Brown, J. Christopher, San Fran	.317	116	416	57	132	175	16	3	7	49	6	0	5	13	9
Brown, Michael C., Pittsburgh	.218	87	243	18	53	72	7	0	4	26	3	0	3	2	3
Browning, Thomas, Cincinnati*	.163	46	86	9	14	14	0	0	0	3	0	7	0	1	0
Bryant, Ralph, Los Angeles*	.253	27	75	15	19	45	4	2	6	13	2	0	1	0	1
Bullock, Eric, Houston*	.048	6	21	0	1	1	0	0	0	1	0	0	0	2	0
Burke, Timothy, Montreal	.000	68	7	0	0	0	0	0	0	1	0	1	0	0	0
Burris, B. Ray, St. Louis	.148	23	27	0	4	7	3	0	0	7	2	0	0	0	0
Butera, Salvatore, Cincinnati	.239	56	113	14	27	41	6	1	2	16	0	2	1	0	0
Cabell, Enos, Los Angeles	.256	107	277	27	71	88	11	0	2	29	2	2	3	10	4
Calhoun, Jeffrey, Houston*	.000	20	0	0	0	0	0	0	0	0	0	0	0	0	0
Candaele, Casey, Montreal†	.231	30	104	9	24	30	4	1	0	6	1	0	1	3	5
Carlton, Steven, Phil-S.F.*	.200	22	45	4	9	13	1	0	1	8	0	1	0	0	0
Carman, Donald, Philadelphia*	.000	50	31	0	0	0	0	0	0	0	0	2	0	0	0
Carter, Gary, New York	.255	132	490	81	125	215	14	2	24	105	16	0	15	1	0
Cedeno, Cesar, Los Angeles	.231	37	78	5	18	22	2	1	0	6	1	2	0	1	1
Cey, Ronald, Chicago	.273	97	256	42	70	130	21	0	13	36	1	1	2	0	0
Chambliss, C. Christopher, Atlanta*	.311	97	122	13	38	52	8	0	2	14	1	0	1	0	2
Childress, Rodney, Philadelphia	.000	2	0	0	0	0	0	0	0	0	0	0	0	0	0
Christmas, Stephen, Chicago*	.111	3	9	0	1	2	1	0	0	2	1	0	0	0	0
Clark, Jack, St. Louis	.237	65	232	34	55	98	12	2	9	23	2	0	1	1	1
Clark, William, San Francisco*	.287	111	408	66	117	181	27	2	11	41	8	9	4	4	7
Clements, Patrick, Pittsburgh	.000	65	6	0	0	0	0	0	0	0	0	0	0	0	0
Coleman, Vincent, St. Louis†	.232	154	600	94	139	168	13	8	0	29	2	3	5	107	14
Concepcion, David, Cincinnati	.260	90	311	42	81	107	13	2	3	30	3	5	4	13	2
Conroy, Timothy, St. Louis*	.138	26	29	2	4	6	2	0	0	6	1	8	0	0	0
Corcoran, Timothy, New York*	.000	6	7	1	0	0	0	0	0	0	0	0	0	0	0
Cox, Danny, St. Louis	.077	32	65	2	5	7	2	0	0	2	2	16	0	0	0
Cruz, Jose, Houston*	.278	141	479	48	133	193	22	4	10	72	12	0	2	3	4
Daniels, Kalvoski, Cincinnati*	.320	74	181	34	58	94	10	4	6	23	3	1	1	15	2
Darling, Ronald, New York	.099	34	81	4	8	10	2	0	0	0	0	10	0	0	0
Darwin, Danny, Houston	.063	12	16	0	1	1	0	0	0	0	0	2	0	0	0
Daulton, Darren, Philadelphia*	.225	49	138	18	31	59	4	0	8	21	2	2	2	2	3
Davis, Charles, San Francisco†	.278	153	526	71	146	219	28	3	13	70	6	2	5	16	13
Davis, Eric, Cincinnati	.277	132	415	97	115	217	15	3	27	71	9	0	3	80	11
Davis, Glenn, Houston	.265	158	574	91	152	283	32	3	31	101	16	0	7	3	1
Davis, Jody, Chicago	.250	148	528	61	132	226	27	2	21	74	5	4	8	0	1
Davis, Mark, San Francisco*	.125	67	8	0	1	2	1	0	0	0	0	0	0	0	0

Player and Club	Pct.	G.	AB.	R.	H.	TB.	2B.	3B.	HR.	RBI.	GW.	SH.	SF.	SB.	CS.
Davis, Ronald, Chicago	.000	17	2	0	0	0	0	0	0	0	0	0	0	0	0
Davis, Trench, Pittsburgh*	.130	15	23	2	3	3	0	0	0	1	0	0	1	0	0
Dawson, Andre, Montreal	.284	130	496	65	141	237	32	2	20	78	7	1	6	18	12
Dayett, Brian, Chicago	.269	24	67	7	18	34	4	0	4	11	3	0	3	0	1
Dayley, Kenneth, St. Louis*	.200	32	5	0	1	1	0	0	0	0	0	0	0	0	0
DeLeon, Jose, Pittsburgh	.000	9	1	0	0	0	0	0	0	0	0	0	0	0	0
Dedmon, Jeffrey, Atlanta*	.125	57	16	2	2	2	0	0	0	1	0	1	0	0	0
Denny, John, Cincinnati	.222	27	54	6	12	12	0	0	0	4	0	5	0	2	3
Dernier, Robert, Chicago	.225	108	324	32	73	101	14	1	4	18	1	5	0	27	2
Deshaies, James, Houston*	.047	26	43	3	2	2	0	0	0	1	0	4	0	0	0
Diaz, Baudilio, Cincinnati	.272	134	474	50	129	180	21	0	10	56	8	2	3	1	1
Diaz, Carlos, Los Angeles	.000	19	1	0	0	0	0	0	0	0	0	0	0	0	0
Diaz, Michael, Pittsburgh	.268	97	209	22	56	101	9	0	12	36	1	0	3	0	1
DiPino, Frank, Hou-Chi*	.167	61	6	0	1	1	0	0	0	0	0	0	0	0	0
Distefano, Benito, Pittsburgh*	.179	31	39	3	7	11	1	0	1	5	0	0	2	0	0
Doran, William, Houston†	.276	145	550	92	152	205	29	3	6	37	5	4	5	42	19
Downs, Kelly, San Francisco	.172	15	29	1	5	5	0	0	0	0	0	0	0	0	1
Dravecky, David, San Diego	.140	35	50	3	7	10	0	0	1	7	0	6	0	1	0
Driessen, Daniel, S.F.-Hou*	.250	32	40	7	10	16	3	0	1	3	0	0	0	0	0
Duncan, Mariano, Los Angeles†	.229	109	407	47	93	124	7	0	8	30	3	5	1	48	13
Dunston, Shawon, Chicago	.250	150	581	66	145	239	37	3	17	68	8	4	2	13	11
Durham, Leon, Chicago*	.262	141	484	66	127	219	18	7	20	65	7	0	5	8	7
Dykstra, Leonard, New York*	.295	147	431	77	127	192	27	7	8	45	7	7	2	31	7
Earley, William, St. Louis	.000	3	0	0	0	0	0	0	0	0	0	0	0	0	0
Eckersley, Dennis, Chicago	.159	33	69	7	11	20	3	0	2	10	2	2	1	0	0
Elster, Kevin, New York	.167	19	30	3	5	6	1	0	0	0	0	0	0	0	0
Esasky, Nicholas, Cincinnati	.230	102	330	35	76	133	17	2	12	41	5	1	4	0	2
Fansler, Stanley, Pittsburgh	.167	5	6	0	1	1	0	0	0	0	0	1	0	0	0
Fernandez, C. Sidney, New York*	.162	32	68	6	11	14	3	0	0	4	2	6	0	1	0
Fimple, John, Los Angeles	.077	13	13	2	1	1	0	0	0	2	0	0	1	0	0
Fitzgerald, Michael, Montreal	.282	73	209	20	59	92	13	1	6	37	6	4	2	3	2
Flannery, Timothy, San Diego*	.280	134	368	48	103	127	11	2	3	28	6	3	2	3	6
Foley, Thomas, Phil-Mtl*	.266	103	263	26	70	94	15	3	1	23	2	2	4	10	3
Fontenot, S. Ray, Chicago*	.167	42	6	1	1	1	0	0	0	0	0	0	0	0	0
Ford, Curtis, St. Louis*	.248	85	214	30	53	78	15	2	2	29	6	1	2	13	5
Forsch, Robert, St. Louis	.171	34	76	7	13	25	4	1	2	12	1	11	1	0	0
Foster, George, New York	.227	72	233	28	53	100	6	1	13	38	5	0	2	1	1
Franco, John, Cincinnati*	.000	74	4	0	0	0	0	0	0	0	0	0	0	0	0
Francona, Terry, Chicago*	.250	86	124	13	31	40	3	0	2	8	3	0	2	0	1
Frazier, George, Chicago	.000	35	4	0	0	0	0	0	0	0	0	0	0	0	0
Freeman, Marvin, Philadelphia	.000	3	6	0	0	0	0	0	0	0	0	1	0	0	0
Funk, Thomas, Houston*	.000	8	1	0	0	0	0	0	0	0	0	0	0	0	0
Gainey, Telmanch, Houston*	.300	26	50	6	15	23	3	1	1	6	1	0	0	3	1
Galarraga, Andres, Montreal	.271	105	321	39	87	130	13	0	10	42	4	1	1	6	5
Galvez, Balvino, Los Angeles	.000	10	2	0	0	0	0	0	0	0	0	0	0	0	0
Garber, H. Eugene, Atlanta	.167	61	6	0	1	1	0	0	0	0	0	1	0	0	0
Garner, Philip, Houston	.265	107	313	43	83	130	14	3	9	41	5	0	3	12	6
Garrelts, Scott, San Francisco	.178	54	45	6	8	12	1	0	1	4	0	7	0	1	0
Garvey, Steven, San Diego	.255	155	557	58	142	227	22	0	21	81	9	0	3	1	2
Gibbons, John, New York	.474	8	19	4	9	16	4	0	1	1	0	0	0	0	0
Gladden, C. Daniel, San Francisco	.276	102	351	55	97	127	16	1	4	29	1	7	0	27	10
Gonzales, Rene, Montreal	.115	11	26	1	3	3	0	0	0	0	0	0	0	0	2
Gonzalez, Jose, Los Angeles	.215	57	93	15	20	33	5	1	2	6	0	2	0	4	3
Gooden, Dwight, New York	.086	33	81	5	7	9	0	1	0	4	0	13	0	0	0
Gorman, Thomas, Philadelphia*	.000	8	1	0	0	0	0	0	0	0	0	0	0	0	0
Gossage, Richard, San Diego	.000	45	7	0	0	0	0	0	0	0	0	0	0	0	0
Gott, James, San Francisco	.000	9	3	0	0	0	0	0	0	0	0	0	0	0	0
Grant, Mark, San Francisco	.000	4	1	0	0	0	0	0	0	0	0	1	0	0	0
Green, Gary, San Diego	.212	13	33	2	7	8	1	0	0	2	0	1	0	0	0
Griffey, G. Kenneth, Atlanta*	.308	80	292	36	90	147	15	3	12	32	2	0	1	12	7
Gross, Gregory, Philadelphia*	.248	87	101	11	25	30	5	0	0	8	0	1	1	1	0
Gross, Kevin, Philadelphia	.188	37	80	6	15	24	4	1	1	5	0	9	0	1	0
Guante, Cecilio, Pittsburgh	.000	52	1	0	0	0	0	0	0	0	0	0	0	0	0
Guerrero, Pedro, Los Angeles	.246	31	61	7	15	33	3	0	5	10	0	0	0	0	0
Gulden, Bradley, San Francisco*	.091	17	22	2	2	2	0	0	0	1	1	0	0	0	0
Gullickson, William, Cincinnati	.076	37	79	3	6	6	0	0	0	2	0	9	0	0	0
Gumpert, David, Chicago	.000	38	5	0	0	0	0	0	0	0	0	0	0	0	0
Gwynn, Anthony, San Diego*	.329	160	642	107	211	300	33	7	14	59	3	2	2	37	9
Hall, Albert, Atlanta†	.240	16	50	6	12	14	2	0	0	1	0	2	0	8	3
Hall, Andrew, Chicago†	.143	5	7	1	1	1	0	0	0	0	0	0	0	0	0
Hamilton, Jeffrey, Los Angeles	.224	71	147	22	33	53	5	0	5	19	3	0	2	0	0
Harper, Terry, Atlanta	.257	106	265	26	68	104	12	0	8	30	6	1	2	3	6
Hatcher, William, Houston	.258	127	419	55	108	149	15	4	6	36	5	6	1	38	14
Hawkins, M. Andrew, San Diego	.149	37	67	2	10	11	1	0	0	2	0	6	0	0	0
Hayes, Von, Philadelphia*	.305	158	610	107	186	293	46	2	19	98	14	1	4	24	12
Hayward, Raymond, San Diego*	.000	4	4	0	0	0	0	0	0	0	0	0	0	0	0
Hearn, Edward, New York	.265	49	136	16	36	53	5	0	4	10	1	2	1	0	1
Heath, Michael, St. Louis	.205	65	190	19	39	61	8	1	4	25	3	1	1	2	3
Heep, Daniel, New York*	.282	86	195	24	55	82	8	2	5	33	2	0	1	1	4
Hensley, Charles, San Francisco*	.000	11	0	0	0	0	0	0	0	0	0	0	0	0	0

Player and Club	Pct.	G.	AB.	R.	H.	TB.	2B.	3B.	HR.	RBI.	GW.	SH.	SF.	SB.	CS.
Hernandez, Keith, New York*	.310	149	551	94	171	246	34	1	13	83	13	0	3	2	1
Hernandez, Manuel, Houston	.000	9	6	0	0	0	0	0	0	1	0	1	0	0	0
Herr, Thomas, St. Louis†	.252	152	559	48	141	185	30	4	2	61	12	6	4	22	8
Hershiser, Orel, Los Angeles	.239	37	71	4	17	20	3	0	0	8	0	10	0	0	1
Hesketh, Joseph, Montreal*	.000	15	23	0	0	0	0	0	0	0	0	3	0	0	0
Hoffman, Guy, Chicago*	.067	33	15	2	1	1	0	0	0	1	0	3	0	0	0
Holton, Brian, Los Angeles	.000	12	5	0	0	0	0	0	0	0	0	0	0	0	0
Honeycutt, Frederick, Los Angeles*	.070	32	43	3	3	4	1	0	0	3	0	6	0	0	0
Horner, J. Robert, Atlanta	.273	141	517	70	141	244	22	0	27	87	11	0	10	1	4
Horton, Ricky, St. Louis*	.056	42	18	0	1	1	0	0	0	0	0	2	0	0	0
Howell, Kenneth, Los Angeles	.000	62	5	0	0	0	0	0	0	0	0	0	0	0	0
Hoyt, D. LaMarr, San Diego	.130	35	46	3	6	7	1	0	0	1	0	3	0	0	0
Hubbard, Glenn, Atlanta	.230	143	408	42	94	124	16	1	4	36	5	6	4	3	2
Hudson, Charles, Philadelphia	.047	36	43	2	2	2	0	0	0	0	0	7	0	0	0
Hume, Thomas, Philadelphia	.000	48	11	0	0	0	0	0	0	0	0	5	0	0	0
Hunt, J. Randall, Montreal	.208	21	48	4	10	16	0	0	2	5	0	0	0	0	0
Hurdle, Clinton, St. Louis*	.195	78	154	18	30	46	5	1	3	15	0	1	2	0	0
Iorg, Dane, San Diego*	.226	90	106	10	24	34	2	1	2	11	1	0	1	0	0
Jackson, Michael, Philadelphia	.000	9	0	0	0	0	0	0	0	0	0	0	0	0	0
James, D. Christopher, Philadelphia	.283	16	46	5	13	19	3	0	1	5	1	1	0	0	0
Jefferson, Stanley, New York†	.208	14	24	6	5	9	1	0	1	3	0	0	0	0	0
Jeltz, L. Steven, Philadelphia†	.219	145	439	44	96	115	11	4	0	36	3	3	2	6	3
Johnson, Howard, New York†	.245	88	220	30	54	98	14	0	10	39	3	1	0	8	1
Johnson, Joseph, Atlanta	.115	17	26	2	3	3	0	0	0	1	0	2	1	0	0
Johnson, Wallace, Montreal†	.283	61	127	13	36	44	3	1	1	10	1	0	0	6	3
Jones, Barry, Pittsburgh	.200	26	5	0	1	1	0	0	0	1	0	1	0	0	0
Jones, Christopher, San Francisco	.000	3	1	0	0	0	0	0	0	0	0	0	0	1	0
Jones, James, San Diego	.167	3	6	1	1	1	0	0	0	0	0	0	0	0	0
Jones, Tracy, Cincinnati	.349	46	86	16	30	39	3	0	2	10	2	0	1	7	1
Kemp, Steven, Pittsburgh*	.188	13	16	1	3	6	0	0	1	1	0	0	0	1	0
Kennedy, Terrence, San Diego*	.264	141	432	46	114	174	22	1	12	57	10	4	1	0	3
Keough, Matthew, Chicago-Hou.	.375	29	16	1	6	7	1	0	0	0	0	0	0	1	0
Kepshire, Kurt, St. Louis*	.000	2	1	0	0	0	0	0	0	0	0	1	0	0	0
Kerfeld, Charles, Houston	.111	61	9	0	1	1	0	0	0	1	0	0	0	0	0
Khalifa, Sam, Pittsburgh	.185	64	151	8	28	34	6	0	0	4	1	3	0	0	2
Kipper, Robert, Pittsburgh	.030	21	33	0	1	1	0	0	0	1	1	3	0	0	0
Knepper, Robert, Houston*	.099	42	91	2	9	13	2	1	0	1	0	4	0	0	0
Knicely, Alan, St. Louis	.195	34	82	8	16	22	3	0	1	6	1	0	1	1	1
Knight, C. Ray, New York	.298	137	486	51	145	206	24	2	11	76	13	3	8	2	1
Knudson, Mark, Houston	.000	9	10	0	0	0	0	0	0	0	0	3	0	0	0
Komminsk, Brad, Atlanta	.400	5	5	1	2	2	0	0	0	1	0	0	0	0	1
Krawczyk, Raymond, Pittsburgh	.000	12	0	0	0	0	0	0	0	0	0	0	0	0	0
Krenchicki, Wayne, Montreal*	.240	101	221	21	53	69	6	2	2	23	1	2	2	2	4
Kruk, John, San Diego*	.309	122	278	33	86	118	16	2	4	38	2	2	2	2	4
Krukow, Michael, San Francisco	.146	35	82	7	12	13	1	0	0	8	1	12	0	1	0
Kutcher, Randy, San Francisco	.237	71	186	28	44	76	9	1	7	16	3	6	0	6	5
LaCoss, Michael, San Francisco	.230	37	61	8	14	22	2	0	2	9	1	5	0	0	0
Laga, Michael, St. Louis*	.217	18	46	7	10	23	4	0	3	8	1	0	0	0	0
Lahti, Jeffrey, St. Louis	.000	4	0	0	0	0	0	0	0	0	0	0	0	0	0
Lake, Steven, Chicago-St. Louis	.294	36	68	8	20	28	2	0	2	14	1	1	0	0	0
Lancellotti, Richard, San Fran.*	.222	15	18	2	4	10	0	0	2	6	0	0	0	0	0
Landreaux, Kenneth, Los Ang.*	.261	103	283	34	74	103	13	2	4	29	4	0	4	10	5
Landrum, T. William, Cincinnati	.000	10	2	0	0	0	0	0	0	0	0	0	0	0	0
Landrum, Terry, St. Louis	.210	96	205	24	43	58	7	1	2	17	4	1	3	3	1
LaPoint, David, San Diego*	.000	24	8	0	0	0	0	0	0	0	0	4	0	0	0
Larkin, Barry, Cincinnati	.283	41	159	27	45	64	4	3	3	19	2	0	1	8	0
Laskey, William, San Francisco	.000	20	1	0	0	0	0	0	0	0	0	0	0	0	0
LaValliere, Michael, St. Louis*	.234	110	303	18	71	94	10	2	3	30	2	10	0	0	1
Law, Vance, Montreal	.225	112	360	37	81	117	17	2	5	44	5	2	2	3	5
Lawless, Thomas, St. Louis	.282	46	39	5	11	12	1	0	0	3	0	2	1	8	1
Leach, Terry, New York	.000	6	0	0	0	0	0	0	0	0	0	0	0	0	0
Lefebvre, Joseph, Philadelphia*	.111	14	18	0	2	2	0	0	0	0	0	0	0	0	0
Lefferts, Craig, San Diego*	.125	84	8	1	1	4	0	0	1	1	1	1	0	0	0
Legg, Gregory, Philadelphia	.450	11	20	2	9	10	1	0	0	1	0	0	0	0	0
Leonard, Jeffrey, San Francisco	.279	89	341	48	95	130	11	3	6	42	11	1	3	16	3
Lerch, Randy, Philadelphia*	.333	4	3	0	1	2	1	0	0	0	0	0	0	0	0
Lindeman, James, St. Louis	.255	19	55	7	14	18	1	0	1	6	0	0	1	1	1
Lopes, David, Chicago-Houston	.275	96	255	49	70	107	10	3	7	35	6	2	2	25	8
Lopez, Aurelio, Houston	.000	45	9	0	0	0	0	0	0	0	0	1	0	0	0
Lynch, Edward, New York-Chicago	.033	24	30	0	1	1	0	0	0	0	0	1	0	0	0
Lyons, Barry, New York	.000	6	9	1	0	0	0	0	0	2	0	0	0	0	0
Madden, Michael, Houston*	.000	13	9	0	0	0	0	0	0	0	0	4	0	0	0
Maddox, Garry, Philadelphia	.429	6	7	1	3	3	0	0	0	1	0	0	0	0	1
Maddux, Gregory, Chicago	.333	6	12	0	4	4	0	0	0	0	0	1	0	0	0
Maddux, Michael, Philadelphia	.045	16	22	0	1	1	0	0	0	1	1	4	0	0	0
Madlock, Bill, Los Angeles	.280	111	379	38	106	153	17	0	10	60	6	1	6	3	3
Magadan, David, New York*	.444	10	18	3	8	8	0	0	0	3	2	0	0	0	0
Mahler, Richard, Atlanta	.193	40	83	8	16	19	3	0	0	7	0	9	0	0	0
Maldonado, Candido, San Fran.	.252	133	405	49	102	193	31	3	18	85	14	0	4	4	4
Manrique, R. Fred, St. Louis	.176	13	17	2	3	6	0	0	1	1	0	0	0	1	0

Player and Club	Pct.	G.	AB.	R.	H.	TB.	2B.	3B.	HR.	RBI.	GW.	SH.	SF.	SB.	CS.
Marshall, Michael A., Los Angeles	.233	103	330	47	77	145	11	0	19	53	9	0	1	4	4
Martin, J. Michael, Chicago*	.077	8	13	1	1	2	1	0	0	0	0	0	0	0	0
Martinez, Carmelo, San Diego	.238	113	244	28	58	95	10	0	9	25	3	1	2	1	1
Martinez, David, Chicago*	.139	53	108	13	15	21	1	1	1	7	0	0	1	4	2
Martinez, J. Dennis, Montreal	.100	19	30	1	3	5	2	0	0	3	0	0	0	0	0
Mason, Roger, San Francisco	.048	11	21	0	1	1	0	0	0	0	0	1	0	0	0
Mathews, Gregory, St. Louis†	.047	23	43	1	2	2	0	0	0	2	0	7	0	0	0
Matthews, Gary, Chicago	.259	123	370	49	96	177	16	1	21	46	4	0	2	3	2
Matuszek, Leonard, Los Angeles*	.261	91	199	26	52	86	7	0	9	28	3	0	1	2	2
Mazzilli, Lee, Pitt.-New York†	.245	100	151	28	37	53	5	1	3	15	0	0	1	4	4
McClure, Robert, Montreal	.250	52	4	0	1	1	0	0	0	0	0	0	0	0	0
McCullers, Lance, San Diego	.091	76	22	4	2	4	2	0	0	3	0	3	0	1	0
McDowell, Roger, New York	.278	75	18	1	5	5	0	0	0	3	0	1	0	0	0
McGaffigan, Andrew, Montreal	.061	50	33	0	2	2	0	0	0	1	0	4	0	0	0
McGee, Willie, St. Louis†	.256	124	497	65	127	184	22	7	7	48	3	0	4	19	16
McMurtry, J. Craig, Atlanta	.125	40	16	3	2	2	0	0	0	0	0	1	0	1	0
McReynolds, W. Kevin, San Diego	.288	158	560	89	161	282	31	6	26	96	14	5	9	8	6
McWilliams, Larry, Pittsburgh*	.138	50	29	2	4	5	1	0	0	0	0	3	0	0	0
Meadows, Michael, Houston*	.333	6	6	1	2	2	0	0	0	0	0	0	0	1	0
Melendez, Francisco, Philadelphia*	.250	9	8	0	2	2	0	0	0	0	0	0	0	0	0
Melvin, Robert, San Francisco	.224	89	268	24	60	93	14	2	5	25	2	3	3	3	2
Milner, Eddie, Cincinnati*	.259	145	424	70	110	189	22	6	15	47	4	1	1	18	11
Minton, Gregory, San Francisco†	.400	48	5	2	2	3	1	0	0	0	0	0	0	0	0
Mitchell, John, New York	.000	4	2	0	0	0	0	0	0	0	0	0	0	0	0
Mitchell, Kevin, New York	.277	108	328	51	91	153	22	2	12	43	7	1	1	3	3
Mizerock, John, Houston*	.185	44	81	9	15	21	1	1	1	6	0	0	1	0	0
Montalvo, Rafael, Houston	.000	1	0	0	0	0	0	0	0	0	0	0	0	0	0
Moore, William, Montreal	.167	6	12	0	2	2	0	0	0	0	0	0	0	0	0
Moreland, B. Keith, Chicago	.271	156	586	72	159	225	30	0	12	79	6	2	11	3	6
Moreno, Omar, Atlanta*	.234	118	359	46	84	126	18	6	4	27	1	6	0	17	16
Morris, John, St. Louis*	.240	39	100	8	24	29	0	1	1	14	3	0	1	6	2
Morrison, James, Pittsburgh	.274	154	537	58	147	259	35	4	23	88	9	0	5	9	8
Motley, Darryl, Atlanta	.200	5	10	1	2	3	1	0	0	0	0	0	0	0	0
Moyer, Jamie, Chicago*	.091	16	22	3	2	2	0	0	0	0	0	4	0	0	0
Mulholland, Terence, San Francisco	.053	15	19	0	1	1	0	0	0	0	0	1	0	0	0
Mumphrey, Jerry, Chicago†	.304	111	309	37	94	124	11	2	5	32	5	1	3	2	3
Murphy, Dale, Atlanta	.265	160	614	89	163	293	29	7	29	83	12	0	1	7	7
Murphy, Robert, Cincinnati*	.000	34	3	0	0	0	0	0	0	0	0	0	0	0	0
Myers, Randall, New York*	.000	10	0	0	0	0	0	0	0	0	0	0	0	0	0
Nettles, Graig, San Diego*	.218	126	354	36	77	134	9	0	16	55	5	0	3	0	1
Newman, Albert, Montreal†	.200	95	185	23	37	43	3	0	1	8	2	4	2	11	11
Niedenfuer, Thomas, Los Angeles	.500	60	4	1	2	2	0	0	0	2	0	1	0	0	0
Niemann, Randy, New York*	.333	31	6	1	2	2	0	0	0	0	0	0	0	0	0
Nieto, Thomas, Montreal	.200	30	65	5	13	21	3	1	1	7	2	0	0	0	1
Oberkfell, Kenneth, Atlanta*	.270	151	503	62	136	181	24	3	5	48	5	4	4	7	4
Oester, Ronald, Cincinnati†	.258	153	523	52	135	186	23	2	8	44	7	7	3	9	2
Ojeda, Robert, New York*	.113	32	71	3	8	8	0	0	0	0	0	8	0	0	0
Olwine, Edward, Atlanta	.333	37	3	0	1	1	0	0	0	0	0	0	0	0	0
O'Neill, Paul, Cincinnati*	.000	3	2	0	0	0	0	0	0	0	0	0	0	0	0
Oquendo, Jose, St. Louis†	.297	76	138	20	41	47	4	1	0	13	2	2	3	2	3
Orosco, Jesse, New York	.000	58	3	1	0	0	0	0	0	1	0	0	1	0	0
Orsulak, Joseph, Pittsburgh*	.249	138	401	60	100	137	19	6	2	19	1	6	1	24	11
Ortiz, Adalberto, Pittsburgh	.336	49	110	11	37	43	6	0	0	14	1	1	2	0	1
Ouellette, Philip, San Francisco†	.174	10	23	1	4	4	0	0	0	0	0	0	0	0	0
Owchinko, Robert, Montreal*	.200	3	5	1	1	1	0	0	0	0	0	0	0	0	0
Ownbey, Richard, St. Louis	.000	17	7	0	0	0	0	0	0	0	0	3	0	0	0
Palmeiro, Rafael, Chicago*	.247	22	73	9	18	31	4	0	3	12	1	0	0	1	1
Palmer, David, Atlanta	.182	35	66	3	12	18	3	0	1	6	1	10	0	0	0
Pankovits, James, Houston	.283	70	113	12	32	43	6	1	1	7	1	0	0	1	1
Parent, Mark, San Diego	.143	8	14	1	2	2	0	0	0	0	0	0	0	0	0
Parker, David, Cincinnati*	.273	162	637	89	174	304	31	3	31	116	12	0	6	1	6
Parrett, Jeffrey, Montreal	.500	12	2	0	1	1	0	0	0	0	0	0	0	0	0
Patterson, Bob, Pittsburgh	.125	11	8	0	1	1	0	0	0	0	0	2	0	0	0
Pena, Adalberto, Houston	.207	15	29	3	6	7	1	0	0	2	0	0	0	1	0
Pena, Alejandro, Los Angeles	.176	24	17	0	3	3	0	0	0	1	0	3	0	0	0
Pena, Antonio, Pittsburgh	.288	144	510	56	147	207	26	2	10	52	8	0	1	9	10
Pena, Hipolito, Pittsburgh*	.000	10	0	0	0	0	0	0	0	0	0	0	0	0	0
Pendleton, Terry, St. Louis*	.239	159	578	56	138	177	26	5	1	59	6	6	7	24	6
Perez, Atanasio, Cincinnati	.255	77	200	14	51	71	12	1	2	29	5	0	3	0	0
Perry, Gerald, Atlanta*	.271	29	70	6	19	27	2	0	2	11	1	1	1	0	1
Perry, W. Patrick, St. Louis*	.000	46	8	0	0	0	0	0	0	0	0	0	0	0	0
Powell, Dennis, Los Angeles*	.214	27	14	1	3	6	3	0	0	0	0	0	0	0	0
Power, Ted, Cincinnati	.125	56	24	3	3	4	1	0	0	1	0	3	0	1	0
Price, Joseph, Cincinnati	.143	25	7	0	1	1	0	0	0	2	0	0	0	0	0
Puhl, Terrance, Houston*	.244	81	172	17	42	61	10	0	3	14	0	4	2	3	2
Puleo, Charles, Atlanta	.333	5	6	0	2	2	0	0	0	3	0	1	0	0	0
Pyznarski, Timothy, San Diego	.238	15	42	3	10	11	1	0	0	0	0	0	0	2	0
Quinones, Luis, San Francisco†	.179	71	106	13	19	26	1	3	0	11	0	4	1	3	1
Raines, Timothy, Montreal†	.334	151	580	91	194	276	35	10	9	62	8	1	3	70	9
Ramirez, Rafael, Atlanta	.240	134	496	57	119	166	21	1	8	33	2	7	3	19	8

Player and Club	Pct.	G.	AB.	R.	H.	TB.	2B.	3B.	HR.	RBI.	GW.	SH.	SF.	SB.	CS.
Rawley, Shane, Philadelphia	.173	23	52	5	9	11	2	0	0	1	0	10	1	0	0
Ray, Johnny, Pittsburgh†	.301	155	579	67	174	228	33	0	7	78	7	1	7	6	9
Ready, Randy, San Diego	.000	1	3	0	0	0	0	0	0	0	0	0	0	0	0
Reardon, Jeffrey, Montreal	.125	62	8	0	1	1	0	0	0	0	0	1	0	0	0
Redus, Gary, Philadelphia	.247	90	340	62	84	147	22	4	11	33	6	1	1	25	7
Renteria, Richard, Pittsburgh	.250	10	12	2	3	4	1	0	0	1	0	0	0	0	0
Reuschel, Ricky, Pittsburgh	.157	43	70	7	11	13	2	0	0	6	0	8	0	0	0
Reuss, Jerry, Los Angeles*	.250	19	20	0	5	6	1	0	0	0	0	0	0	0	0
Reynolds, G. Craig, Houston*	.249	114	313	32	78	109	7	3	6	41	8	1	3	3	1
Reynolds, Robert, Pittsburgh†	.269	118	402	63	108	169	30	2	9	48	4	3	2	16	9
Reynolds, Ronn, Philadelphia	.214	43	126	8	27	40	4	0	3	10	1	0	1	0	0
Rhoden, Richard, Pittsburgh	.278	41	90	9	25	37	9	0	1	10	1	7	1	0	1
Riley, George, Montreal*	.000	10	0	0	0	0	0	0	0	0	0	0	0	0	0
Rivera, Luis, Montreal	.205	55	166	20	34	47	11	1	0	13	2	1	1	1	1
Roberge, Bertrand, Montreal	.000	21	2	0	0	0	0	0	0	0	0	0	0	0	0
Roberts, Leon, San Diego†	.253	101	241	34	61	73	5	2	1	12	0	2	1	14	12
Robinson, Don, Pittsburgh	.667	50	6	1	4	5	1	0	0	1	0	0	0	0	0
Robinson, Jeffrey, San Francisco	.067	65	15	0	1	1	0	0	0	2	0	1	1	0	0
Robinson, Ronald, Cincinnati	.071	70	14	1	1	1	0	0	0	0	0	0	0	0	0
Rodriguez, Ruben, Pittsburgh	.000	2	3	0	0	0	0	0	0	0	0	0	0	0	0
Roenicke, Ronald, Philadelphia†	.247	102	275	42	68	98	13	1	5	42	7	4	3	2	2
Rose, Peter, Cincinnati†	.219	72	237	15	52	64	8	2	0	25	3	0	1	3	0
Rowdon, Wade, Cincinnati	.250	38	80	9	20	27	5	1	0	10	1	1	1	2	0
Royster, Jeron, San Diego	.257	118	257	31	66	93	12	0	5	26	2	6	3	3	5
Rucker, David, Philadelphia*	.000	19	1	0	0	0	0	0	0	0	0	0	0	0	0
Ruffin, Bruce, Philadelphia	.073	21	55	2	4	5	1	0	0	2	0	1	0	0	0
Runge, Paul, Atlanta	.250	7	8	1	2	2	0	0	0	0	0	0	0	0	0
Runnells, Thomas, Cincinnati†	.091	12	11	1	1	2	1	0	0	0	0	0	0	0	0
Russell, John, Philadelphia	.241	93	315	35	76	140	21	2	13	60	5	1	4	0	1
Russell, William, Los Angeles	.250	105	216	21	54	65	11	0	0	18	2	7	2	7	0
Ruthven, Richard, Chicago	.000	6	1	0	0	0	0	0	0	0	0	0	0	0	0
Ryan, L. Nolan, Houston	.102	30	59	1	6	6	0	0	0	5	1	3	0	0	1
St. Claire, Randy, Montreal	.000	11	1	0	0	0	0	0	0	0	0	1	0	0	0
Sample, William, Atlanta	.285	92	200	23	57	86	11	0	6	14	2	2	2	4	2
Samuel, Juan, Philadelphia	.266	145	591	90	157	265	36	12	16	78	11	1	7	42	14
Sandberg, Ryne, Chicago	.284	154	627	68	178	258	28	5	14	76	5	3	6	34	11
Sanderson, Scott, Chicago	.059	38	51	1	3	4	1	0	0	2	1	6	0	0	0
Santana, Rafael, New York	.218	139	394	38	86	100	11	0	1	28	2	1	3	0	0
Santiago, Benito, San Diego	.290	17	62	10	18	29	2	0	3	6	1	0	1	0	1
Sauver, Richard, Pittsburgh*	.333	3	3	0	1	1	0	0	0	0	0	1	0	0	0
Sax, Stephen, Los Angeles	.332	157	633	91	210	279	43	4	6	56	11	6	3	40	17
Schatzeder, Daniel, Mtl.-Phil.*	.385	58	26	5	10	17	2	1	1	2	0	0	0	0	0
Schmidt, Michael, Philadelphia	.290	160	552	97	160	302	29	1	37	119	13	0	9	1	2
Schu, Richard, Philadelphia	.274	92	208	32	57	93	10	1	8	25	1	3	2	2	2
Scioscia, Michael, Los Angeles*	.251	122	374	36	94	129	18	1	5	26	3	6	4	3	3
Scott, Michael, Houston	.126	38	95	7	12	14	2	0	0	3	0	10	0	0	0
Sebra, Robert, Montreal	.207	18	29	2	6	7	1	0	0	0	0	0	0	0	0
See, R. Lawrence, Los Angeles	.250	13	20	1	5	7	2	0	0	2	0	0	0	0	0
Shields, Stephen, Atlanta	.000	6	1	0	0	0	0	0	0	0	0	0	0	0	0
Shipley, Craig, Los Angeles	.111	12	27	3	3	4	1	0	0	4	0	1	0	0	0
Show, Eric, San Diego	.163	24	43	2	7	9	2	0	0	1	0	3	0	0	0
Simmons, Ted, Atlanta†	.252	76	127	14	32	49	5	0	4	25	5	0	4	1	0
Sisk, Douglas, New York	.000	41	4	0	0	0	0	0	0	0	0	0	0	0	0
Smiley, John, Pittsburgh*	.000	12	0	0	0	0	0	0	0	0	0	0	0	0	0
Smith, Bryn, Montreal	.138	30	58	3	8	12	1	0	1	7	0	5	0	0	0
Smith, David, Houston	.000	54	2	0	0	0	0	0	0	0	0	0	0	0	0
Smith, Lee, Chicago	.000	66	5	0	0	0	0	0	0	0	0	0	0	0	0
Smith, Michael, Cincinnati	.000	2	0	0	0	0	0	0	0	0	0	0	0	0	0
Smith, Osborne, St. Louis†	.280	153	514	67	144	171	19	4	0	54	5	11	3	31	7
Smith, Zane, Atlanta*	.085	43	59	2	5	5	0	0	0	3	1	9	0	0	0
Soff, Raymond, St. Louis	.000	30	2	0	0	0	0	0	0	0	0	1	0	0	0
Solano, Julio, Houston	.000	16	6	0	0	0	0	0	0	0	0	1	0	0	0
Soto, Mario, Cincinnati	.111	20	27	2	3	4	1	0	0	1	0	6	0	0	0
Speck, R. Clifford, Atlanta	.000	13	3	0	0	0	0	0	0	0	0	1	0	0	0
Speier, Chris, Chicago	.284	95	155	21	44	70	8	0	6	23	0	4	1	2	2
Spilman, W. Harry, San Francisco*	.287	58	94	12	27	40	7	0	2	22	4	0	0	0	0
Stewart, David, Philadelphia	.000	8	0	0	0	0	0	0	0	0	0	0	0	0	0
Stillwell, Kurt, Cincinnati†	.229	104	279	31	64	72	6	1	0	26	8	4	0	6	2
Stoddard, Robert, San Diego	.000	18	1	0	0	0	0	0	0	0	0	0	0	0	0
Stoddard, Timothy, San Diego	.250	30	4	1	1	4	0	0	1	1	0	0	0	0	0
Stone, Jeffery, Philadelphia*	.277	82	249	32	69	101	6	4	6	19	3	2	0	19	6
Strawberry, Darryl, New York*	.259	136	475	76	123	241	27	5	27	93	15	0	9	28	12
Stubbs, Franklin, Los Angeles*	.226	132	420	55	95	177	11	1	23	58	9	4	2	7	1
Sutcliffe, Richard, Chicago*	.208	29	53	3	11	16	2	0	1	4	0	4	0	0	0
Sutter, H. Bruce, Atlanta	.000	16	1	0	0	0	0	0	0	0	0	0	0	0	0
Tejada, Wilfredo, Montreal	.240	10	25	1	6	7	1	0	0	2	0	0	0	0	0
Tekulve, Kenton, Philadelphia	.000	73	5	1	0	0	0	0	0	0	0	0	0	0	0
Templeton, Garry, San Diego†	.247	147	510	42	126	157	21	2	2	44	4	1	2	10	5
Terry, Scott, Cincinnati	.250	30	4	3	1	1	0	0	0	0	0	1	0	0	0
Teufel, Timothy, New York	.247	93	279	35	69	103	20	1	4	31	3	3	3	1	2

Player and Club	Pct.	G.	AB.	R.	H.	TB.	2B.	3B.	HR.	RBI.	GW.	SH.	SF.	SB.	CS.
Thomas, Andres, Atlanta	.251	102	323	26	81	120	17	2	6	32	3	2	2	4	6
Thompson, Jason, Montreal*	.196	30	51	6	10	14	4	0	0	4	1	0	0	0	1
Thompson, Milton, Philadelphia*	.251	96	299	38	75	102	7	1	6	23	4	4	2	19	4
Thompson, Robert, San Francisco	.271	149	549	73	149	203	27	3	7	47	4	18	1	12	15
Thon, Richard, Houston	.248	106	278	24	69	93	13	1	3	21	3	1	1	6	5
Thurmond, Mark, San Diego*	.250	18	24	0	6	7	1	0	0	6	1	2	0	0	0
Tibbs, Jay, Montreal	.130	36	54	2	7	8	1	0	0	0	0	4	0	0	0
Toliver, Freddie, Philadelphia	.000	5	6	0	0	0	0	0	0	0	0	0	0	1	0
Tomlin, David, Montreal*	.000	7	0	0	0	0	0	0	0	0	0	0	0	0	0
Trevino, Alejandro, Los Angeles	.262	89	202	31	53	78	13	0	4	26	3	2	1	0	0
Trillo, J. Manuel, Chicago	.296	81	152	22	45	58	10	0	1	19	2	2	2	0	2
Trout, Steven, Chicago*	.209	37	43	5	9	10	1	0	0	3	2	4	0	0	0
Tudor, John, St. Louis*	.153	30	72	6	11	12	1	0	0	6	1	13	1	0	0
Uribe, Jose, San Francisco†	.223	157	453	46	101	127	15	1	3	43	2	3	0	22	11
Valdez, Sergio, Montreal	.125	5	8	0	1	1	0	0	0	0	0	0	0	0	0
Valenzuela, Fernando, Los Angeles*	.220	39	109	5	24	28	4	0	0	7	0	6	1	0	0
Vande Berg, Edward, Los Angeles	.000	60	1	0	0	0	0	0	0	0	0	0	0	0	0
Van Gorder, David, Cincinnati	.000	9	10	0	0	0	0	0	0	0	0	0	0	0	0
Van Slyke, Andrew, St. Louis*	.270	137	418	48	113	189	23	7	13	61	9	1	3	21	8
Venable, W. McKinley, Cincinnati*	.211	108	147	17	31	46	7	1	2	15	1	2	2	7	2
Virgil, Osvaldo, Atlanta	.223	114	359	45	80	134	9	0	15	48	6	2	3	1	0
Vosberg, Edward, San Diego*	.000	5	2	0	0	0	0	0	0	0	0	0	0	0	0
Walk, Robert, Pitsburgh	.154	44	39	2	6	9	3	0	0	7	0	1	1	0	2
Walker, Anthony, Houston	.222	84	90	19	20	33	7	0	2	10	1	0	0	11	3
Walker, Cleotha, Chicago†	.277	28	101	21	28	38	3	2	1	7	1	0	1	15	4
Wallach, Timothy, Montreal	.233	134	480	50	112	190	22	1	18	71	9	0	5	8	4
Walling, Dennis, Houston*	.312	130	382	54	119	183	23	1	13	58	10	0	4	1	1
Walter, Gene, San Diego*	.200	57	10	0	2	3	1	0	0	0	0	2	0	0	0
Ward, R. Duane, Atlanta	.000	10	1	0	0	0	0	0	0	0	0	0	0	0	0
Washington, Claudell, Atlanta*	.270	40	137	17	37	63	11	0	5	14	2	1	1	4	7
Washington, U.L., Pittsburgh†	.200	72	135	14	27	35	0	4	0	10	3	4	1	6	0
Wasinger, Mark, San Diego	.000	3	8	0	0	0	0	0	0	1	0	1	0	0	0
Webster, Mitchell, Montreal†	.290	151	576	89	167	248	31	13	8	49	8	3	5	36	15
Welch, Robert, Los Angeles	.105	35	76	2	8	11	0	0	1	4	0	5	0	0	0
Wellman, Brad, San Francisco	.154	12	13	0	2	2	0	0	0	1	0	0	0	0	0
Welsh, Christopher, Cincinnati*	.119	24	42	3	5	10	2	0	1	4	0	4	0	1	0
White, Jerry, St. Louis†	.125	25	24	1	3	6	0	0	1	3	1	1	2	0	0
Whitfield, Terry, Los Angeles*	.071	19	14	0	1	1	0	0	0	0	0	0	0	0	0
Whitson, Eddie, San Diego	.167	17	18	1	3	3	0	0	0	0	0	2	0	0	0
Williams, Frank, San Francisco	.500	36	2	0	1	1	0	0	0	0	0	1	0	0	0
Williams, Reginald, Los Angeles	.277	128	303	35	84	114	14	2	4	32	3	9	1	9	3
Willis, Carl, Cincinnati*	.333	29	3	0	1	1	0	0	0	0	0	1	0	0	0
Wilson, Glenn, Philadelphia	.271	155	584	70	158	241	30	4	15	84	8	0	9	5	1
Wilson, William, New York†	.289	123	381	61	110	164	17	5	9	45	5	0	1	25	7
Wine, Robert, Houston	.250	9	12	2	3	4	1	0	0	0	0	0	0	0	0
Winn, James, Pittsburgh	.063	50	16	1	1	2	1	0	0	0	0	1	0	0	0
Winningham, Herman, Montreal*	.216	90	185	23	40	64	6	3	4	11	2	1	0	12	7
Wohlford, James, Montreal	.266	70	94	10	25	36	4	2	1	11	2	2	1	0	2
Wojna, Edward, San Diego	.143	7	14	1	2	2	0	0	0	0	0	2	0	0	0
Woodard, Michael, San Francisco*	.253	48	79	14	20	27	2	1	1	5	1	1	0	7	2
Worrell, Todd, St. Louis	.143	74	7	0	1	3	0	1	0	0	0	0	0	0	0
Wright, George, Montreal†	.188	56	117	12	22	31	5	2	0	5	0	1	3	1	1
Wynne, Marvell, San Diego*	.264	137	288	34	76	120	19	2	7	37	7	1	3	11	11
Youmans, Floyd, Montreal	.160	33	75	4	12	15	0	0	1	7	0	2	0	0	0
Youngblood, Joel, San Francisco	.255	97	184	20	47	74	12	0	5	28	2	2	3	1	1

AWARDED FIRST BASE ON INTERFERENCE OR OBSTRUCTION: Ray, Pitts. 6 (Diaz, Ashby, Bilardello, Carter, Daulton, Kennedy); Brenly, S.F. 3 (Diaz, Bilardello, Hunt); Benedict, Atl. (Fitzgerald); Clark, St.L. (T. Pena); Hunt, Mtl. (T. Pena); Lawless, St.L. (Diaz); Reynolds, Pitts. (Daulton); Smith, Atl. (Heath); Wilson, N.Y. (Ortiz).

PLAYERS WITH TWO OR MORE CLUBS

(Alphabetically Arranged With Player's First Club on Top)

Player and Club	Pct.	G.	AB.	R.	H.	TB.	2B.	3B.	HR.	RBI.	GW.	SH.	SF.	Tot. BB.	Int. BB.	HP.	SO.	SB.	CS.	GI. DP.
Andersen, Phil.	.000	10	0	0	0	0	0	0	0	0	0	1	0	0	0	0	0	0	0	0
Andersen, Hou.	.000	38	6	0	0	0	0	0	0	0	0	0	0	0	0	0	3	0	0	0
Carlton, Phil.	.206	16	34	3	7	8	1	0	0	5	0	1	0	1	0	0	4	0	0	2
Carlton, S.F.	.182	6	11	1	2	5	0	0	1	3	0	0	0	0	0	0	3	0	0	1
DiPino, Hou.	.200	31	5	0	1	1	0	0	0	0	0	0	0	0	0	0	1	0	0	1
DiPino, Chi.	.000	30	1	0	0	0	0	0	0	0	0	0	0	0	0	0	1	0	0	0
Driessen, S.F.	.188	15	16	2	3	5	2	0	0	0	0	0	0	4	1	0	4	0	0	0
Driessen, Hou.	.292	17	24	5	7	11	1	0	1	3	0	0	0	5	1	0	2	0	0	0
Foley, Phil.	.295	39	61	8	18	22	2	1	0	5	1	0	1	10	1	0	11	2	0	1
Foley, Mtl.	.257	64	202	18	52	72	13	2	1	18	1	2	3	20	5	0	26	8	3	3
Keough, Chi.	.400	19	5	0	2	3	1	0	0	0	0	0	0	0	0	0	2	0	0	0
Keough, Hou.	.364	10	11	1	4	4	0	0	0	0	0	0	0	0	0	0	2	1	0	0

Player and Club	Pct.	G.	AB.	R.	H.	TB.	2B.	3B.	HR.	RBI.	GW.	SH.	SF.	Tot. BB.	Int. BB.	HP.	SO.	SB.	CS.	GI. DP.
Lake, Chi.	.421	10	19	4	8	9	1	0	0	4	1	1	0	1	1	0	2	0	0	1
Lake, St.L.	.245	26	49	4	12	19	1	0	2	10	0	0	0	2	0	0	5	0	0	2
Lopes, Chi.	.299	59	157	38	47	77	8	2	6	22	3	0	1	31	0	2	16	17	6	6
Lopes, Hou.	.235	37	98	11	23	30	2	1	1	13	3	2	1	12	0	0	9	8	2	3
Lynch, N.Y.	.000	1	0	0	0	0	0	0	0	0	0	0	0	0	0	0	0	0	0	0
Lynch, Chi.	.033	23	30	0	1	1	0	0	0	0	0	1	0	2	0	0	17	0	0	0
Mazzilli, Pitt.	.226	61	93	18	21	28	2	1	1	8	0	0	1	26	1	0	25	3	3	2
Mazzilli, N.Y.	.276	39	58	10	16	25	3	0	2	7	0	0	0	12	1	2	11	1	1	1
Schatzeder, Mtl.	.429	33	21	5	9	15	1	1	1	2	0	0	0	5	0	0	8	0	0	0
Schatzeder, Phil.	.200	25	5	0	1	2	1	0	0	0	0	0	0	0	0	0	2	0	0	0

OFFICIAL MISCELLANEOUS NATIONAL LEAGUE

BATTING RECORDS

CLUB MISCELLANEOUS BATTING RECORDS

Club	Slg. Pct.	OB Pct.	Tot. BB.	Int. BB.	HP.	SO.	GIDP.	ShO.
New York	.401	.339	631	68	31	968	122	4
Philadelphia	.400	.327	589	70	40	1154	98	7
Chicago	.398	.318	508	56	15	966	113	10
San Diego	.388	.321	484	74	18	917	130	9
Cincinnati	.387	.325	586	55	18	920	127	7
Atlanta	.381	.319	538	62	24	904	124	10
Houston	.381	.322	536	78	24	916	126	6
Montreal	.379	.322	537	72	33	1016	113	11
San Francisco	.375	.322	536	86	37	1087	83	12
Pittsburgh	.374	.321	569	55	20	929	132	10
Los Angeles	.370	.313	478	58	32	966	109	14
St. Louis	.327	.309	568	69	20	905	83	13
Totals	.380	.322	6560	803	312	11648	1360	113

INDIVIDUAL MISCELLANEOUS BATTING RECORDS

(Top Ten Qualifiers for Slugging Championship)

Player—Club	Slg. Pct.	OB Pct.	Tot. BB.	Int. BB.	HP.	SO.	GI DP.
Schmidt, Phila.	.547	.390	89	25	7	84	8
Strawberry, N.Y.	.507	.358	72	9	6	141	4
McReynolds, S.D.	.504	.358	66	6	1	83	9
Davis, Hou.	.493	.344	64	6	9	72	11
Bass, Hou.	.486	.357	38	11	6	72	15
Morrison, Pitt.	.482	.334	47	5	4	88	6
Hayes, Phila.	.480	.379	74	9	1	77	14
Dawson, Mtl.	.478	.338	37	11	6	79	13
Parker, Cin.	.477	.330	56	16	1	126	18
Murphy, Atl.	.477	.347	75	5	2	141	10

DEPARTMENTAL LEADERS: OB Pct. Raines, .413; TBB—Hernandez, 94; IBB—Schmidt, 25; HP—Wallach, 10; SO—Samuel, 142; GIDP—Carter, T. Pena, Ray, 21.

Player—Club	Slg. Pct.	OB Pct.	Tot. BB.	Int. BB.	HP.	SO.	GI DP.
Acker, Atlanta	.143	.107	0	0	0	21	0
Aguayo, Phil.	.361	.267	8	0	3	26	3
Aguilera, N.Y.	.275	.204	3	0	0	12	0
Aldrete, S.F.	.389	.353	33	4	2	34	3
Alexander, Atl.	.237	.205	0	0	0	8	2
Almon, Pitt.	.383	.319	30	2	0	38	5
Amelung, L.A.	.091	.091	0	0	0	4	1
Andersen, Phil.-Hou.	.000	.000	0	0	0	3	0
Anderson, L.A.	.301	.314	22	1	0	39	11
Anderson, N.Y.	.091	.091	0	0	0	4	0
Asadoor, S.D.	.455	.397	3	1	0	13	0
Ashby, Hou.	.371	.333	39	9	0	56	7
Assenmacher, Atl.	.000	.250	2	0	0	3	0
Backman, N.Y.	.385	.376	36	1	0	32	3
Bailey, Hou.	.288	.302	28	6	0	45	7
Baller, Chi.	.000	.000	0	0	0	1	0
Bargar, St.L.	.000	.000	0	0	0	2	0
Bass, Hou.	.486	.357	38	11	6	72	15
Beckwith, L.A.	.000	.000	0	0	0	0	0
Bedrosian, Phil.	.200	.333	1	0	0	1	0
Bell, Cin.	.445	.362	73	4	5	49	14
Belliard, Pitt.	.262	.298	26	6	3	54	8
Benedict, Atl.	.300	.298	15	1	2	10	9
Berenguer, S.F.	.143	.143	0	0	0	1	0
Berenyi, N.Y.	.000	.000	0	0	0	3	0
Bielecki, Pitt.	.063	.100	2	0	0	26	0
Bilardello, Mtl.	.283	.249	14	3	0	32	5
Bittiger, Phil.	1.333	.333	0	0	0	1	0
Blue, S.F.	.186	.204	6	0	0	20	0
Bochy, S.D.	.512	.326	14	3	0	23	3
Bockus, S.F.	.000	.000	0	0	0	1	0
Boever, St.L.	.500	.500	0	0	0	0	0
Bonds, Pitt.	.416	.330	65	2	2	102	4
Bonilla, Pitt.	.307	.342	29	1	1	39	5
Booker, S.D.	.000	.000	0	0	0	0	0
Bosley, Chi.	.350	.370	18	3	0	24	3
Bream, Pitt.	.450	.341	60	5	1	73	14
Brenly, S.F.	.403	.350	74	10	3	97	4
Brock, L.A.	.422	.309	37	5	0	60	5
Brooks, Mtl.	.569	.388	25	3	2	60	11
Brown, Mtl.	.000	.000	0	0	0	0	0
Brown, S.F.	.421	.376	33	4	9	43	9
Brown, Pitt.	.296	.293	27	3	0	32	9
Browning, Cin.	.163	.172	1	0	0	25	2
Bryant, L.A.	.600	.305	5	0	1	25	1
Bullock, Hou.	.048	.048	0	0	0	3	0
Burke, Mtl.	.000	.125	1	0	0	2	0
Burris, St.L.	.259	.148	0	0	0	9	0
Butera, Cin.	.363	.356	21	3	0	10	5
Cabell, L.A.	.318	.294	14	2	2	26	5
Calhoun, Hou.	.000	.000	0	0	0	0	0
Candaele, Mtl.	.288	.264	5	0	0	15	3
Carlton, Phil.-S.F.	.289	.217	1	0	0	7	3
Carman, Phil.	.000	.000	0	0	0	11	0
Carter, N.Y.	.439	.337	62	9	6	63	21
Cedeno, L.A.	.282	.294	7	0	0	13	0
Cey, Chi.	.508	.384	44	1	3	66	5
Chambliss, Atl.	.426	.384	15	4	0	24	2
Childress, Phil.	.000	.000	0	0	0	0	0
Christmas, Chi.	.222	.111	0	0	0	1	0
Clark, St.L.	.422	.362	45	4	1	61	4
Clark, S.F.	.444	.343	34	10	3	76	3
Clements, Pitt.	.000	.000	0	0	0	3	0
Coleman, St.L.	.280	.301	60	0	2	98	4
Concepcion, Cin.	.344	.314	26	1	0	43	13
Conroy, St.L.	.207	.219	3	0	0	11	0

Player—Club	Slg. Pct.	OB Pct.	Tot. BB.	Int. BB.	HP.	SO.	GI DP.
Corcoran, N.Y.	.000	.222	2	1	0	0	0
Cox, St.L.	.108	.104	2	0	0	32	1
Cruz, Hou.	.403	.351	55	12	0	86	9
Daniels, Cin.	.519	.398	22	1	2	30	4
Darling, N.Y.	.123	.131	3	0	0	29	0
Darwin, Hou.	.063	.063	0	0	0	12	0
Daulton, Phil.	.428	.391	38	3	1	41	1
Davis, S.F.	.416	.375	84	23	1	96	11
Davis, Cin.	.523	.378	68	5	1	100	6
Davis, Hou.	.493	.344	64	6	9	72	11
J. Davis, Chi.	.428	.300	41	4	0	110	14
Davis, S.F.	.250	.125	0	0	0	4	0
R. Davis, Chi.	.000	.000	0	0	0	2	0
Davis, Pitt.	.130	.125	0	0	0	4	1
Dawson, Mtl.	.478	.338	37	11	6	79	13
Dayett, Chi.	.507	.316	6	0	0	10	2
Dayley, St.L.	.200	.333	1	0	0	2	0
DeLeon, Pitt.	.000	.500	0	0	1	1	0
Dedmon, Atl.	.125	.125	0	0	0	7	0
Denny, Cin.	.222	.263	3	0	0	15	1
Dernier, Chi.	.312	.275	2	1	0	41	7
Deshaies, Hou.	.047	.163	6	0	0	31	0
Diaz, Cin.	.380	.327	40	0	0	52	11
Diaz, L.A.	.000	.000	0	0	0	0	0
Diaz, Pitt.	.483	.330	19	0	2	43	5
DiPino, Hou.-Chi.	.167	.167	0	0	0	2	1
Distefano, Pitt.	.282	.190	1	0	0	5	0
Doran, Hou.	.373	.368	81	7	2	57	10
Downs, S.F.	.172	.200	1	0	0	13	0
Dravecky, S.D.	.200	.157	1	0	0	16	1
Driessen, S.F.-Hou.	.400	.388	9	2	0	6	0
Duncan, L.A.	.305	.284	30	1	2	78	6
Dunston, Chi.	.411	.278	21	5	3	114	5
Durham, Chi.	.452	.350	67	16	1	98	6
Dykstra, N.Y.	.445	.377	58	1	0	55	4
Earley, St.L.	.000	.000	0	0	0	0	0
Eckersley, Chi.	.290	.169	1	0	0	34	0
Elster, N.Y.	.200	.242	3	1	0	8	0
Esasky, Cin.	.403	.325	47	0	1	97	8
Fansler, Pitt.	.167	.167	0	0	0	2	0
Fernandez, N.Y.	.206	.197	3	0	0	23	2
Fimple, L.A.	.077	.350	6	1	0	6	0
Fitzgerald, Mtl.	.440	.364	27	6	1	34	4
Flannery, S.D.	.345	.378	54	4	5	61	8
Foley, Phil.-Mtl.	.357	.337	30	6	0	37	4
Fontenot, Chi.	.167	.167	0	0	0	5	0
Ford, St.L.	.364	.318	23	2	0	29	1
Forsch, St.L.	.329	.169	0	0	0	24	1
Foster, N.Y.	.429	.289	21	1	0	53	7
Franco, Cin.	.000	.000	0	0	0	0	0
Francona, Chi.	.323	.286	6	0	1	8	3
Frazier, Chi.	.000	.000	0	0	0	2	0
Freeman, Phil.	.000	.000	0	0	0	3	0
Funk, Hou.	.000	.000	0	0	0	1	0
Gainey, Hou.	.460	.375	6	0	0	19	0
Galarraga, Mtl.	.405	.338	30	5	3	79	8
Galvez, L.A.	.000	.000	0	0	0	1	0
Garber, Atl.	.167	.286	1	0	0	1	0
Garner, Hou.	.415	.329	30	2	1	45	14
Garrelts, S.F.	.267	.196	1	0	0	25	0
Garvey, S.D.	.408	.284	23	5	1	72	18
Gibbons, N.Y.	.842	.545	3	1	0	5	1
Gladden, S.F.	.362	.357	39	3	5	59	5
Gonzales, Mtl.	.115	.179	2	0	0	7	0
Gonzalez, L.A.	.355	.270	7	0	0	29	0
Gooden, N.Y.	.111	.119	2	0	1	16	3
Gorman, Phil.	.000	.000	0	0	0	0	0
Gossage, S.D.	.000	.000	0	0	0	3	1
Gott, S.F.	.000	.250	0	0	1	1	0
Grant, S.F.	.000	.000	0	0	0	1	0
Green, S.D.	.242	.235	1	0	0	11	0
Griffey, Atl.	.503	.351	20	4	0	43	2
G. Gross, Phil.	.297	.379	21	7	1	11	4
K. Gross, Phil.	.300	.198	1	0	0	22	1
Guante, Pitt.	.000	.000	0	0	0	1	0
Guerrero, L.A.	.541	.281	2	0	1	19	1
Gulden, S.F.	.091	.167	2	2	0	5	1
Gullickson, Cin.	.076	.110	3	0	0	15	3
Gumpert, Chi.	.000	.000	0	0	0	4	0
Gwynn, S.D.	.467	.381	52	11	3	35	20
Hall, Atl.	.280	.309	5	0	0	6	0
Hall, Chi.	.143	.250	1	0	0	3	0
Hamilton, L.A.	.361	.232	2	1	0	43	3
Harper, Atl.	.392	.330	29	2	1	39	13
Hatcher, Hou.	.356	.302	22	1	5	52	3
Hawkins, S.D.	.164	.162	1	0	0	23	1
Hayes, Phil.	.480	.379	74	9	1	77	14
Hayward, S.D.	.000	.000	0	0	0	0	1
Hearn, N.Y.	.390	.322	12	0	0	19	4
Heath, St.L.	.321	.293	23	4	1	36	5
Heep, N.Y.	.421	.379	30	5	1	31	3
Hensley, S.F.	.000	.000	0	0	0	0	0
Hernandez, N.Y.	.446	.413	94	9	4	69	14
Hernandez, Hou.	.000	.000	0	0	0	2	0
Herr, St.L.	.331	.342	73	10	5	75	8
Hershiser, L.A.	.282	.250	1	0	0	17	1
Hesketh, Mtl.	.000	.080	2	0	0	18	1
Hoffman, Chi.	.067	.176	2	0	0	4	0
Holton, L.A.	.000	.000	0	0	0	2	0
Honeycutt, L.A.	.093	.216	8	0	0	11	0
Horner, Atl.	.472	.336	52	8	2	72	16
Horton, St.L.	.056	.261	5	0	0	3	0
Howell, L.A.	.000	.000	0	0	0	3	0
Hoyt, S.D.	.152	.149	1	0	0	18	0
Hubbard, Atl.	.304	.340	66	14	4	74	5
Hudson, Phil.	.047	.068	1	0	0	19	0
Hume, Phil.	.000	.000	0	0	0	6	0
Hunt, Mtl.	.333	.283	5	2	0	16	2
Hurdle, St.L.	.299	.311	26	0	1	38	2
Iorg, S.D.	.321	.239	2	0	0	21	2
Jackson, Phil.	.000	.000	0	0	0	0	0
James, Phil.	.413	.298	1	0	0	13	1
Jefferson, N.Y.	.375	.296	2	0	1	8	1
Jeltz, Phil.	.262	.320	65	9	1	97	9
Johnson, N.Y.	.445	.341	31	8	1	64	2
Johnson, Atl.	.115	.143	1	0	0	12	0
Johnson, Mtl.	.346	.321	7	0	0	9	2
Jones, Pitt.	.200	.200	0	0	0	1	0
Jones, S.F.	.000	.000	0	0	0	0	0
Jones, S.D.	.167	.167	0	0	0	4	0
Jones, Cin.	.453	.406	9	1	0	5	2
Kemp, Pitt.	.375	.350	4	0	0	6	1
Kennedy, S.D.	.403	.324	37	7	2	74	10
Keough, Chi.-Hou.	.438	.375	0	0	0	4	0
Kepshire, St.L.	.000	.000	0	0	0	0	0
Kerfeld, Hou.	.111	.200	1	0	0	6	0
Khalifa, Pitt.	.225	.276	19	6	0	28	5
Kipper, Pitt.	.030	.059	1	0	0	11	0
Knepper, Hou.	.143	.099	0	0	0	44	0
Knicely, St.L.	.268	.330	17	0	0	21	1
Knight, N.Y.	.424	.351	40	2	4	63	19
Knudson, Hou.	.000	.091	1	0	0	7	0
Komminsk, Atl.	.400	.400	0	0	0	1	0
Krawczyk, Pitt.	.000	.000	0	0	0	0	0
Krenchicki, Mtl.	.312	.306	22	3	0	32	2
Kruk, S.D.	.424	.403	45	0	0	58	11
Krukow, S.F.	.159	.186	4	0	0	25	1
Kutcher, S.F.	.409	.279	11	0	0	41	3
LaCoss, S.F.	.361	.266	3	0	0	24	0
Laga, St.L.	.500	.308	5	1	1	18	1
Lahti, St.L.	.000	.000	0	0	0	0	0
Lake, Chi.-St.L.	.412	.324	3	1	0	7	3
Lancellotti, S.F.	.556	.222	0	0	0	7	0
Landreaux, L.A.	.364	.313	22	3	1	39	5
Landrum, Cin.	.000	.000	0	0	0	0	0
Landrum, St.L.	.283	.279	20	2	1	41	5
LaPoint, S.D.	.000	.000	0	0	0	1	0
Larkin, Cin.	.403	.320	9	1	0	21	2
Laskey, S.F.	.000	.000	0	0	0	1	0
LaValliere, St.L.	.310	.318	36	5	1	37	7
Law, Mtl.	.325	.298	37	1	1	66	9
Lawless, St.L.	.308	.310	2	0	0	8	0
Leach, N.Y.	.000	.000	0	0	0	0	0
Lefebvre, Phil.	.111	.238	3	0	0	5	3
Lefferts, S.D.	.500	.125	0	0	0	4	0
Legg, Phil.	.500	.450	0	0	0	3	0
Leonard, S.F.	.381	.322	20	1	3	62	4
Lerch, Phil.	.667	.333	0	0	0	1	0

Player—Club	Slg. Pct.	OB Pct.	Tot. BB.	Int. BB.	HP.	SO.	GI DP.
Lindeman, St.L.	.327	.276	2	0	0	10	2
Lopes, Chi.-Hou.	.420	.381	43	0	2	25	9
Lopez, Hou.	.000	.000	0	0	0	6	0
Lynch, N.Y.-Chi.	.033	.094	2	0	0	17	0
Lyons, N.Y.	.000	.100	1	1	0	2	0
Madden, Hou.	.000	.100	1	0	0	8	0
Maddox, Phil.	.429	.556	2	0	0	1	0
Maddux, Chi.	.333	.333	0	0	0	3	0
Maddux, Phil.	.045	.087	1	0	0	7	0
Madlock, L.A.	.404	.336	30	4	5	43	7
Magadan, N.Y.	.444	.524	3	0	0	1	1
Mahler, Atl.	.229	.230	4	0	0	14	2
Maldonado, S.F.	.477	.289	20	4	3	77	12
Manrique, St.L.	.353	.222	1	0	0	1	1
Marshall, L.A.	.439	.298	27	3	4	90	5
Martin, Chi.	.154	.200	2	1	0	4	0
Martinez, S.D.	.389	.333	35	2	1	46	9
Martinez, Chi.	.194	.190	6	0	1	22	1
Martinez, Mtl.	.167	.129	1	0	0	14	0
Mason, S.F.	.048	.048	0	0	0	13	0
Mathews, St.L.	.047	.089	0	0	2	19	1
Matthews, Chi.	.478	.361	60	1	0	59	15
Matuszek, L.A.	.432	.333	21	1	1	47	3
Mazzilli, Pitt.-N.Y.	.351	.401	38	2	2	36	3
McClure, Mtl.	.250	.250	0	0	0	1	0
McCullers, S.D.	.182	.200	3	0	0	11	0
McDowell, N.Y.	.278	.316	1	0	0	4	0
McGaffigan, Mtl.	.061	.088	1	0	0	18	0
McGee, St.L.	.370	.306	37	7	1	82	8
McMurtry, Atl.	.125	.176	1	0	0	9	0
McReynolds, S.D.	.504	.358	66	6	1	83	9
McWilliams, Pitt.	.172	.194	2	0	0	11	0
Meadows, Hou.	.333	.333	0	0	0	0	0
Melendez, Phil.	.250	.250	0	0	0	2	0
Melvin, S.F.	.347	.262	15	1	0	69	7
Milner, Cin.	.446	.317	36	2	0	56	3
Minton, S.F.	.600	.571	2	0	0	3	0
J. Mitchell, N.Y.	.000	.000	0	0	0	1	0
K. Mitchell, N.Y.	.466	.344	33	0	1	61	6
Mizerock, Hou.	.259	.374	24	2	1	16	4
Montalvo, Hou.	.000	.000	0	0	0	0	0
Moore, Mtl.	.167	.167	0	0	0	4	0
Moreland, Chi.	.384	.326	53	10	0	48	15
Moreno, Atl.	.351	.276	21	2	0	77	2
Morris, St.L.	.290	.287	7	2	0	15	2
Morrison, Pitt.	.482	.334	47	5	4	88	6
Motley, Atl.	.300	.273	1	1	0	1	0
Moyer, Chi.	.091	.231	4	0	0	5	1
Mulholland, S.F.	.053	.053	0	0	0	8	0
Mumphrey, Chi.	.401	.355	26	4	0	45	3
Murphy, Atl.	.477	.347	75	5	2	141	10
Murphy, Cin.	.000	.000	0	0	0	1	0
Myers, N.Y.	.000	.000	0	0	0	0	0
Nettles, S.D.	.379	.300	41	8	2	62	6
Newman, Mtl.	.232	.279	21	2	0	20	4
Niedenfuer, L.A.	.500	.500	0	0	0	1	0
Niemann, N.Y.	.333	.429	1	0	0	1	0
Nieto, Mtl.	.323	.278	6	1	1	21	3
Oberkfell, Atl.	.360	.373	83	6	2	40	11
Oester, Cin.	.356	.325	52	16	1	84	18
Ojeda, N.Y.	.113	.125	1	0	0	30	0
Olwine, Atl.	.333	.500	1	0	0	1	0
O'Neill, Cin.	.000	.333	1	0	0	1	0
Oquendo, St.L.	.341	.359	15	4	0	20	3
Orosco, N.Y.	.000	.333	2	0	0	0	0
Orsulak, Pitt.	.342	.299	28	2	1	38	4
Ortiz, Pitt.	.391	.380	9	0	0	13	4
Ouellette, S.F.	.174	.269	3	0	0	3	3
Owchinko, Mtl.	.200	.333	1	0	0	3	0
Ownbey, St.L.	.000	.000	0	0	0	1	0
Palmeiro, Chi.	.425	.295	4	0	1	6	4
Palmer, Atl.	.273	.194	1	0	0	17	1
Pankovits, Hou.	.381	.347	11	1	0	25	4
Parent, S.D.	.143	.200	1	0	0	3	1
Parker, Cin.	.477	.330	56	16	1	126	18
Parrett, Mtl.	.500	.500	0	0	0	1	0
Patterson, Pitt.	.125	.125	0	0	0	6	0
Pena, Hou.	.241	.324	5	2	0	5	3
Pena, L.A.	.176	.176	0	0	0	6	0

Player—Club	Slg. Pct.	OB Pct.	Tot. BB.	Int. BB.	HP.	SO.	GI DP.
A. Pena, Pitt.	.406	356	53	6	1	69	21
H. Pena, Pitt.	.000	.000	0	0	0	0	0
Pendleton, St.L.	.306	.279	34	10	1	59	12
Perez, Cin.	.355	.333	25	2	0	25	6
Perry, Atl.	.386	.342	8	1	0	4	4
Perry, St.L.	.000	.000	0	0	0	4	0
Powell, L.A.	.429	.214	0	0	0	6	0
Power, Cin.	.167	.222	3	0	0	12	0
Price, Cin.	.143	.250	1	0	0	1	0
Puhl, Hou.	.355	.302	15	1	0	24	6
Puleo, Atl.	.333	.333	0	0	0	3	0
Pyznarski, S.D.	.262	.319	4	0	1	11	2
Quinones, S.F.	.245	.207	3	1	1	17	1
Raines, Mtl.	.476	.413	78	9	2	60	6
Ramirez, Atl.	.335	.273	21	1	3	60	16
Rawley, Phil.	.212	.185	1	0	0	18	2
Ray, Pitt.	.394	.363	58	10	3	47	21
Ready, S.D.	.000	.000	0	0	0	1	0
Reardon, Mtl.	.125	.125	0	0	0	6	0
Redus, Phil.	.432	.343	47	4	3	78	2
Renteria, Pitt.	.333	.250	0	0	0	4	0
Reuschel, Pitt.	.186	.192	3	0	0	19	0
Reuss, L.A.	.300	.286	1	0	0	6	0
Reynolds, Hou.	.348	.274	12	5	0	31	8
Reynolds, Pitt.	.420	.335	40	4	1	78	10
Reynolds, Phil.	.317	.242	5	0	0	30	4
Rhoden, Pitt.	.411	.298	3	0	0	13	5
Riley, Mtl.	.000	.000	0	0	0	0	0
Rivera, Mtl.	.283	.285	17	0	2	33	1
Roberge, Mtl.	.000	.000	0	0	0	0	0
Roberts, S.D.	.303	.293	14	1	0	29	2
Robinson, Pitt.	.833	.667	0	0	0	1	0
Robinson, S.F.	.067	.063	0	0	0	7	0
Robinson, Cin.	.071	.071	0	0	0	3	1
Rodriguez, Pitt.	.000	.000	0	0	0	1	0
Roenicke, Phil.	.356	.381	61	4	0	52	4
Rose, Cin.	.270	.316	30	0	4	31	2
Rowdon, Cin.	.338	.330	9	0	1	17	0
Royster, S.D.	.362	.336	32	3	0	45	6
Rucker, Phil.	.000	.000	0	0	0	0	0
Ruffin, Phil.	.091	.073	0	0	0	32	2
Runge, Atl.	.250	.400	2	0	0	4	1
Runnells, Cin.	.182	.091	0	0	0	2	1
Russell, Phil.	.444	.300	25	2	3	103	6
Russell, L.A.	.301	.302	15	2	2	23	6
Ruthven, Chi.	.000	.000	0	0	0	1	0
Ryan, Hou.	.102	.117	1	0	0	22	2
St. Claire, Mtl.	.000	.000	0	0	0	1	0
Sample, Atl.	.430	.338	14	1	3	26	0
Samuel, Phil.	.448	.302	26	3	8	142	8
Sandberg, Chi.	.411	.330	46	6	0	79	11
Sanderson, Chi.	.078	.077	0	0	1	23	0
Santana, N.Y.	.254	.285	36	12	2	43	15
Santiago, S.D.	.468	.308	2	0	0	12	0
Sauver, Pitt.	.333	.333	0	0	0	1	0
Sax, L.A.	.441	.390	59	5	3	58	12
Schatzeder, Mtl-Phi	.654	.484	5	0	0	10	0
Schmidt, Phil.	.547	.390	89	25	7	84	8
Schu, Phil.	.447	.335	18	1	2	44	1
Scioscia, L.A.	.345	.359	62	4	3	23	11
Scott, Hou.	.147	.144	2	0	0	48	0
Sebra, Mtl.	.241	.233	1	0	0	5	1
See, L.A.	.350	.318	2	0	0	7	0
Shields, Atl.	.000	.000	0	0	0	1	0
Shipley, L.A.	.148	.200	2	1	1	5	1
Show, S.D.	.209	.182	1	0	0	14	0
Simmons, Atl.	.386	.313	12	5	1	14	1
Sisk, N.Y.	.000	.000	0	0	0	2	0
Smiley, Pitt.	.000	.000	0	0	0	0	0
Smith, Mtl.	.207	.194	4	0	0	17	0
Smith, Hou.	.000	.000	0	0	0	0	0
Smith, Chi.	.000	.000	0	0	0	5	0
Smith, Cin.	.000	.000	0	0	0	0	0
Smith, St.L.	.333	.376	79	13	2	27	9
Smith, Atl.	.085	.115	2	0	0	19	0
Soff, St.L.	.000	.000	0	0	0	2	0
Solano, Hou.	.000	.000	0	0	0	5	0
Soto, Cin.	.148	.111	0	0	0	6	0
Speck, Atl.	.000	.250	1	0	0	3	0

Player—Club	Slg. Pct.	OB Pct.	Tot. BB.	Int. BB.	HP.	SO.	GI DP.
Speier, Chi.	.452	.349	15	3	1	32	4
Spilman, S.F.	.426	.368	12	3	0	13	0
Stewart, Phil.	.000	.000	0	0	0	0	0
Stillwell, Cin.	.258	.309	30	1	2	47	5
R. Stoddard, S.D.	.000	.000	0	0	0	1	0
T. Stoddard, S.D.	1.000	.250	0	0	0	2	0
Stone, Phil.	.406	.341	20	0	4	52	3
Strawberry, N.Y.	.507	.358	72	9	6	141	4
Stubbs, L.A.	.421	.291	37	11	2	107	9
Sutcliffe, Chi.	.302	.250	2	0	1	13	1
Sutter, Atl.	.000	.000	0	0	0	1	0
Tejada, Mtl.	.280	.296	2	1	0	8	1
Tekulve, Phil.	.000	.167	1	0	0	1	0
Templeton, S.D.	.308	.296	35	21	1	86	12
Terry, Cin.	.250	.400	1	0	0	1	0
Teufel, N.Y.	.369	.324	32	1	1	42	6
Thomas, Atl.	.372	.267	8	2	0	49	14
Thompson, Mtl.	.275	.406	18	2	0	12	0
Thompson, Phil.	.341	.311	26	1	1	62	4
Thompson, S.F.	.370	.328	42	0	5	112	11
Thon, Hou.	.335	.318	29	5	0	49	8
Thurmond, S.D.	.292	.250	0	0	0	3	1
Tibbs, Mtl.	.148	.190	4	0	0	31	0
Toliver, Phil.	.000	.250	1	0	1	1	0
Tomlin, Mtl.	.000	.000	0	0	0	0	0
Trevino, L.A.	.386	.351	27	2	1	35	6
Trillo, Chi.	.382	.359	16	0	0	21	2
Trout, Chi.	.233	.227	1	0	0	15	1
Tudor, St.L.	.167	.162	1	0	0	22	0
Uribe, S.F.	.280	.315	61	19	0	76	2
Valdez, Mtl.	.125	.125	0	0	0	3	0
Valenzuela, L.A.	.257	.218	0	0	0	11	1
Vande Berg, L.A.	.000	.000	0	0	0	1	0
Van Gorder, Cin.	.000	.091	1	0	0	2	1
Van Slyke, St.L.	.452	.343	47	5	1	85	2
Venable, Cin.	.313	.289	17	2	0	24	0
Virgil, Atl.	.373	.343	63	5	4	73	9
Vosberg, S.D.	.000	.000	0	0	0	1	0
Walk, Pitt.	.231	.171	1	0	0	11	0
Walker, Hou.	.367	.307	11	2	0	15	3
Walker, Chi.	.376	.339	10	0	0	20	3
Wallach, Mtl.	.396	.308	44	8	10	72	16
Walling, Hou.	.479	.367	36	5	0	31	8
Walter, S.D.	.300	.273	1	0	0	4	0
Ward, Atl.	.000	.000	0	0	0	0	0
Washington, Atl.	.460	.336	14	0	0	26	4
Washington, Pitt.	.259	.278	15	2	0	27	1
Wasinger, S.D.	.000	.000	0	0	0	2	0
Webster, Mtl.	.431	.355	57	4	4	78	9
Welch, L.A.	.145	.160	4	0	1	23	0
Wellman, S.F.	.154	.214	1	0	0	2	0
Welsh, Cin.	.238	.159	2	0	0	19	0
White, St.L.	.250	.179	2	0	0	3	1
Whitfield, L.A.	.071	.316	5	2	0	2	1
Whitson, S.D.	.167	.167	0	0	0	8	0
Williams, S.F.	.500	.500	0	0	0	1	0
Williams, L.A.	.376	.331	23	9	2	57	8
Willis, Cin.	.333	.333	0	0	0	0	1
Wilson, Phil.	.413	.319	42	1	4	91	15
Wilson, N.Y.	.430	.345	32	5	1	72	5
Wine, Hou.	.333	.308	1	0	0	4	0
Winn, Pitt.	.125	.118	1	0	0	8	1
Winningham, Mtl.	.346	.286	18	3	0	51	4
Wohlford, Mtl.	.383	.327	9	3	0	17	2
Wojna, S.D.	.143	.143	0	0	0	11	1
Woodard, S.F.	.342	.337	10	0	0	9	0
Worrell, St.L.	.429	.143	0	0	0	5	0
Wright, Mtl.	.265	.258	11	0	1	28	3
Wynne, S.D.	.417	.300	15	2	1	45	5
Youmans, Mtl.	.200	.213	5	0	0	29	0
Youngblood, S.F.	.402	.320	18	0	1	34	2

OFFICIAL NATIONAL LEAGUE FIELDING AVERAGES

CLUB FIELDING

Club	Pct.	G.	PO.	A.	E.	TC.	DP.	TP.	PB.
St. Louis	.981	161	4399	1804	123	6326	178	0	9
Chicago	.980	160	4335	1784	124	6243	147	1	17
Montreal	.979	161	4399	1787	133	6319	132	0	21
Houston	.979	162	4369	1565	130	6064	108	0	9
New York	.978	162	4452	1781	138	6371	145	0	8
Atlanta	.978	161	4274	2026	141	6441	181	1	11
Philadelphia	.978	161	4355	1761	137	6253	157	0	23
Cincinnati	.978	162	4404	1809	140	6353	160	0	13
Pittsburgh	.978	162	4352	1918	143	6413	134	0	9
San Diego	.978	162	4330	1629	137	6096	135	0	14
San Francisco	.977	162	4381	1794	143	6318	149	0	12
Los Angeles	.971	162	4363	1801	181	6345	118	0	11
TOTALS	.978	969	52413	21459	1670	75542	1744	2	157

INDIVIDUAL FIELDING

*Throws lefthanded.

FIRST BASEMEN

Leader—Club	Pct.	G.	PO.	A.	E.	DP.
HERNANDEZ, N.Y.*	.996	149	1199	149	5	115

(Listed Alphabetically)

Player—Club	Pct.	G.	PO.	A.	E.	DP.
Aldrete, S.F.*	1.000	37	274	35	0	34
Almon, Pitt.	.923	4	10	2	1	0
Bailey, Hou.	1.000	1	4	0	0	0
Bonilla, Pitt.	.947	4	14	4	1	2
Bream, Pitt.*	.989	153	1320	166	17	107
Brenly, S.F.	.979	19	133	4	3	7
Brock, L.A.	.996	99	726	87	3	46
Cabell, L.A.	.987	61	360	32	5	29
Carter, N.Y.	1.000	9	68	5	0	4
Chambliss, Atl.	.993	20	141	6	1	15
Christmas, Chi.	1.000	1	4	1	0	0
Clark, St.L.	.995	64	623	35	3	66
Clark, S.F.*	.989	102	942	72	11	76
Concepcion, Cin.	1.000	12	45	4	0	6
Corcoran, N.Y.*	1.000	1	8	1	0	1
Davis, Hou.	.992	156	1253	111	11	90
J. Davis, Chi.	.000	1	0	0	0	0
Diaz, Pitt.	.993	20	146	5	1	9
Distefano, Pitt.*	.000	1	0	0	0	0
Driessen, S.F.-Hou.	1.000	16	77	6	0	5
Durham, Chi.*	.995	141	1231	80	7	101
Esasky, Cin.	.991	70	512	30	5	42
Fimple, L.A.	1.000	1	1	0	0	0
Francona, Chi.*	1.000	23	98	7	0	9
Galarraga, Mtl.	.995	102	805	40	4	59
Garvey, S.D.	.994	148	1160	53	7	94
Griffey, Atl.*	1.000	1	0	1	0	0
G. Gross, Phil.*	1.000	5	8	2	0	0

FIRST BASEMAN—Continued

Player—Club	Pct.	G.	PO.	A.	E.	DP.
Guerrero, L.A.	1.000	4	30	0	0	4
Hayes, Phil.	.990	134	1182	96	13	105
Hernandez, N.Y.*	.996	149	1199	149	5	115
Horner, Atl.	.995	139	1378	102	8	138
Hurdle, St.L.	.994	39	301	22	2	31
Iorg, S.D.	1.000	10	39	1	0	3
Johnson, Mtl.	.991	27	204	17	2	15
Jones, Cin.	1.000	2	3	0	0	0
Knicely, St.L.	.995	29	185	16	1	20
Knight, N.Y.	1.000	1	6	0	0	0
Krenchicki, Mtl.	.991	41	305	24	3	22
Kruk, S.D.*	.975	9	37	2	1	3
Laga, St.L.*	1.000	16	109	14	0	9
Lancellotti, S.F.*	1.000	1	2	0	0	0
Law, Mtl.	.990	20	94	9	1	8
Lindeman, St.L.	.992	17	118	10	1	8
Madlock, L.A.	.800	2	7	1	2	1
Magadan, N.Y.	1.000	9	48	5	0	5
Martinez, S.D.	1.000	26	59	9	0	4
Matuszek, L.A.	.977	31	197	20	5	18
Mazzilli, Pitt.-N.Y.	1.000	15	86	2	0	3
Melendez, Phil.*	1.000	2	1	0	0	0
K. Mitchell, N.Y.	.875	2	6	1	1	2
Moore, Mtl.*	1.000	3	22	1	0	1
Moreland, Chi.	1.000	12	92	5	0	10
T. Pena, Pitt.	1.000	4	14	0	0	0
Perez, Cin.	.984	55	398	29	7	46
Perry, Atl.	1.000	1	8	1	0	2
Pyznarski, S.D.	.977	13	118	8	3	11
Reynolds, Hou.	1.000	5	12	1	0	0
Rose, Cin.	.990	61	523	43	6	54
Schmidt, Phil.	.993	35	269	18	2	26
See, L.A.	.979	9	41	6	1	3
Simmons, Atl.	.964	14	124	10	5	13
Spilman, S.F.	.994	19	138	15	1	8
Stubbs, L.A.*	1.000	13	38	4	0	1
Teufel, N.Y.	1.000	3	10	1	0	0
Thompson, Mtl.*	.962	15	121	4	5	7
Trevino, L.A.	1.000	1	0	1	0	0
Trillo, Chi.	1.000	11	80	3	0	7
Van Slyke, St.L.	.996	38	204	23	1	23
Walling, Hou.	1.000	4	30	4	0	2
Youngblood, S.F.	.913	7	18	3	2	3

Triple Plays: Francona, Horner.

FIRST BASEMEN WITH TWO OR MORE CLUBS

Players—Club	Pct.	G.	PO.	A.	E.	DP.
Driessen, S.F.	1.000	4	25	3	0	0
Driessen, Hou.	1.000	12	52	3	0	5
Mazzilli, Pitt.	1.000	7	35	1	0	1
Mazzilli, N.Y.	1.000	8	51	1	0	2

SECOND BASEMEN

Leader—Club	Pct.	G.	PO.	A.	E.	DP.
SANDBERG, Chi.	.994	153	309	492	5	86

(Listed Alphabetically)

Player—Club	Pct.	G.	PO.	A.	E.	DP.
Aguayo, Phil.	.967	31	32	57	3	10
Anderson, L.A.	1.000	5	4	7	0	0
Asadoor, S.D.	1.000	2	1	2	0	0
Backman, N.Y.	.966	113	186	290	17	56
Bell, Cin.	1.000	1	0	1	0	0
Belliard, Pitt.	1.000	23	30	48	0	8
Candaele, Mtl.	.983	24	44	73	2	13
Concepcion, Cin.	.981	10	25	28	1	12
Doran, Hou.	.974	144	262	329	16	62
Fimple, L.A.	.000	1	0	0	0	0
Flannery, S.D.	.993	108	209	246	3	52
Foley, Phil.-Mtl.	.992	26	44	73	1	10
Garner, Hou.	1.000	7	8	11	0	2
Herr, St.L.	.988	152	352	414	9	121
Hubbard, Atl.	.976	142	282	487	19	120
Khalifa, Pitt.	1.000	6	9	5	0	0
Krenchicki, Mtl.	1.000	1	0	1	0	0
Kutcher, S.F.	1.000	3	1	2	0	0
Larkin, Cin.	1.000	3	4	6	0	1
Law, Mtl.	.993	94	170	284	3	50
Lawless, St.L.	1.000	7	4	6	0	0
Legg, Phil.	.941	4	4	12	1	3
Manrique, St.L.	.000	1	0	0	0	0
Morrison, Pitt.	1.000	1	0	1	0	0
Newman, Mtl.	.967	59	76	127	7	25
Oberkfell, Atl.	.977	41	51	77	3	15
Oester, Cin.	.978	151	367	475	19	100
Oquendo, St.L.	.935	21	22	36	4	11
Pankovits, Hou.	.969	26	38	57	3	10
Pena, Hou.	.000	1	0	0	0	0
Quinones, S.F.	1.000	8	8	16	0	2
Ray, Pitt.	.993	151	280	479	5	89
Roberts, S.D.	.971	87	166	172	10	33
Rowdon, Cin.	.929	3	6	7	1	2
Royster, S.D.	.950	21	39	37	4	7
Runge, Atl.	1.000	5	5	12	0	0
Runnells, Cin.	1.000	4	2	5	0	1
Russell, L.A.	.974	8	20	18	1	4
Sample, Atl.	.000	1	0	0	0	0
Samuel, Phil.	.967	143	290	440	25	83
Sandberg, Chi.	.994	153	309	492	5	86
Santana, N.Y.	.000	1	0	0	0	0
Sax, L.A.	.980	154	367	432	16	71
Shipley, L.A.	1.000	1	0	1	0	0
Speier, Chi.	1.000	7	9	18	0	1
Spilman, S.F.	1.000	1	1	1	0	0
Teufel, N.Y.	.971	84	133	173	9	28
Thompson, S.F.	.976	149	255	450	17	97
Trillo, Chi.	.950	6	8	11	1	4
Washington, Pitt.	1.000	3	0	5	0	0
Wasinger, S.D.	1.000	1	1	0	0	0
Wellman, S.F.	.000	1	0	0	0	0
Woodard, S.F.	.986	23	27	42	1	13
Youngblood, S.F.	1.000	4	0	3	0	0

Triple Play: Hubbard.

SECOND BASEMEN WITH TWO OR MORE CLUBS

Player—Club	Pct.	G.	PO.	A.	E.	DP.
Foley, Phil.	1.000	1	0	2	0	1
Foley, Mtl.	.991	25	44	71	1	9

THIRD BASEMEN

Leader—Club	Pct.	G.	PO.	A.	E.	DP.
SCHMIDT, Phil.	.980	124	78	220	6	27

(Listed Alphabetically)

Player—Club	Pct.	G.	PO.	A.	E.	DP.
Aguayo, Phil.	.000	1	0	0	0	0
Almon, Pitt.	.921	28	9	26	3	3
Anderson, L.A.	.976	51	20	63	2	6
Asadoor, S.D.	.889	15	11	29	5	1
Bell, Cin.	.975	151	105	290	10	28
Bonilla, Pitt.	1.000	4	3	9	0	1
Brenly, S.F.	.906	45	37	59	10	9
Brown, S.F.	.933	111	73	177	18	17
Cabell, L.A.	.846	7	6	16	4	2
Candaele, Mtl.	1.000	4	1	1	0	0
Carter, N.Y.	1.000	1	1	3	0	1
Cey, Chi.	.952	77	41	118	8	7
Concepcion, Cin.	1.000	10	9	17	0	3
Diaz, Pitt.	1.000	5	0	1	0	0
Esasky, Cin.	.000	1	0	0	0	0
Flannery, S.D.	.938	23	12	18	2	1
Foley, Phil.-Mtl.	1.000	16	7	23	0	1
Garner, Hou.	.896	84	58	141	23	13
Gonzales, Mtl.	1.000	5	5	8	0	1
Hamilton, L.A.	.968	66	37	85	4	6
Hurdle, St.L.	.909	4	2	8	1	0
Iorg, S.D.	1.000	6	0	1	0	0

THIRD BASEMAN—Continued

Player—Club	Pct.	G.	PO.	A.	E.	DP.
Johnson, N.Y.	.903	45	22	71	10	10
Knight, N.Y.	.948	132	88	204	16	17
Komminsk, Atl.	1.000	2	0	2	0	0
Krenchicki, Mtl.	.947	24	20	34	3	4
Kutcher, S.F.	.000	4	0	0	0	0
Law, Mtl.	1.000	13	9	5	0	1
Lawless, St.L.	.875	12	5	9	2	1
Lindeman, St.L.	.000	1	0	0	0	0
Lopes, Chi.-Hou.	.912	37	21	62	8	4
Madlock, L.A.	.910	101	72	170	24	7
Maldonado, S.F.	1.000	1	0	1	0	0
Manrique, St.L.	1.000	4	1	3	0	0
Martinez, S.D.	.000	1	0	0	0	0
Melvin, S.F.	1.000	1	1	1	0	0
K. Mitchell, N.Y.	.941	7	7	9	1	0
Moreland, Chi.	.917	24	10	34	4	3
Morrison, Pitt.	.946	151	92	257	20	12
Nettles, S.D.	.941	114	83	174	16	14
Oberkfell, Atl.	.976	130	65	258	8	24
Oquendo, St.L.	1.000	1	0	2	0	0
Pena, Hou.	1.000	2	3	2	0	0
Pendleton, St.L.	.962	156	133	371	20	36
Quinones, S.F.	.852	31	5	18	4	2
Ramirez, Atl.	.930	57	18	89	8	6
Ready, S.D.	.667	1	0	2	1	0
Renteria, Pitt.	.600	1	1	2	2	0
Reynolds, Hou.	1.000	4	4	2	0	0
Rowdon, Cin.	.889	7	3	13	2	1
Royster, S.D.	.931	59	25	83	8	9
Runnells, Cin.	1.000	3	2	0	0	0
Russell, L.A.	.000	1	0	0	0	0
Schmidt, Phil.	.980	124	78	220	6	27
Schu, Phil.	.913	58	42	94	13	6
Shipley, L.A.	1.000	1	0	1	0	0
Simmons, Atl.	1.000	9	3	3	0	0
Speier, Chi.	.984	53	21	42	1	3
Spilman, S.F.	.667	5	1	1	1	0
Teufel, N.Y.	.000	1	0	0	0	0
Trillo, Chi.	.949	53	26	49	4	3
Wallach, Mtl.	.958	132	94	270	16	26
Walling, Hou.	.960	102	59	156	9	6
Wasinger, S.D.	.500	3	1	2	3	1
Wellman, S.F.	1.000	1	0	3	0	1
Wohlford, Mtl.	1.000	6	1	5	0	0
Woodard, S.F.	.500	2	0	1	1	0
Youngblood, S.F.	1.000	5	0	1	0	0

THIRD BASEMEN WITH TWO OR MORE CLUBS

Player—Club	Pct.	G.	PO.	A.	E.	DP.
Foley, Phil.	.000	1	0	0	0	0
Foley, Mtl.	1.000	15	7	23	0	1
Lopes, Chi.	.902	32	20	54	8	3
Lopes, Hou.	1.000	5	1	8	0	1

Triple Play: Lopes, Chicago.

SHORTSTOPS

Leader—Club	Pct.	G.	PO.	A.	E.	DP.
SMITH, St.L.	.978	144	229	453	15	96

(Listed Alphabetically)

Player—Club	Pct.	G.	PO.	A.	E.	DP.
Aguayo, Phil.	.967	20	25	33	2	9
Almon, Pitt.	.870	19	8	12	3	1
Anderson, L.A.	.940	34	53	89	9	15
Belliard, Pitt.	.970	96	117	269	12	42
Brooks, Mtl.	.958	80	116	222	15	37
Brown, S.F.	1.000	2	0	4	0	0
Concepcion, Cin.	.965	60	74	174	9	32
Duncan, L.A.	.951	106	172	317	25	46
Dunston, Chi.	.961	149	320	465	32	96
Elster, N.Y.	.962	19	16	35	2	6
Flannery, S.D.	1.000	8	5	11	0	3
Foley, Phil.-Mtl.	.970	53	66	94	5	18
Gonzales, Mtl.	1.000	6	2	11	0	2
Green, S.D.	1.000	13	16	35	0	9
Hamilton, L.A.	1.000	2	3	2	0	0
Jeltz, Phil.	.967	141	229	406	22	81
Johnson, N.Y.	.903	34	28	65	10	14
Khalifa, Pitt.	.961	60	85	163	10	25
Kutcher, S.F.	1.000	13	11	6	0	2
Larkin, Cin.	.976	36	47	119	4	21
Legg, Phil.	1.000	1	0	4	0	0
K. Mitchell, N.Y.	.935	24	31	56	6	7
Morrison, Pitt.	.000	1	0	0	0	0
Newman, Mtl.	.933	22	22	34	4	10
Oquendo, St.L.	.956	29	30	56	4	12
Pena, Hou.	.907	10	17	22	4	2
Quinones, S.F.	.922	33	15	32	4	6
Ramirez, Atl.	.952	86	137	282	21	62
Reynolds, Hou.	.978	98	106	206	7	35
Rivera, Mtl.	.953	55	64	119	9	24
Rowdon, Cin.	.893	6	11	14	3	4
Royster, S.D.	.970	24	19	46	2	7
Russell, L.A.	.962	32	36	64	4	13
Santana, N.Y.	.973	137	203	369	16	68
Shipley, L.A.	.914	10	16	16	3	4
Smith, St.L.	.978	144	229	453	15	96
Speier, Chi.	.975	23	32	46	2	11
Stillwell, Cin.	.951	80	107	205	16	40
Templeton, S.D.	.966	144	207	358	20	60
Thomas, Atl.	.958	97	143	290	19	62
Thompson, S.F.	1.000	1	0	1	0	0
Thon, Hou.	.972	104	142	210	10	39
Uribe, S.F.	.977	156	249	444	16	95
Washington, Pitt.	.947	51	50	92	8	25
Wellman, S.F.	1.000	8	3	7	0	0
Winningham, Mtl.	.000	1	0	0	0	0
Woodard, S.F.	1.000	2	1	0	0	0
Youngblood, S.F.	.857	1	1	5	1	0

SHORTSTOPS WITH TWO OR MORE CLUBS

Player—Club	Pct.	G.	PO.	A.	E.	DP.
Foley, Phil.	.975	24	36	41	2	10
Foley, Mtl.	.965	29	30	53	3	8

OUTFIELDERS

Leader—Club	Pct.	G.	PO.	A.	E.	DP.
McGEE, St.L.	.991	121	325	9	3	0

(Listed Alphabetically)

Player—Club	Pct.	G.	PO.	A.	E.	DP.
Aldrete, S.F.*	.978	31	43	1	1	0
Almon, Pitt.	.983	54	53	5	1	0
Amelung, L.A.*	1.000	4	5	0	0	0
Bass, Hou.	.984	155	303	12	5	4
Bockus, S.F.	.000	1	0	0	0	0
Bonds, Pitt.*	.983	110	280	9	5	2
Bonilla, Pitt.	.974	51	73	3	2	0
Bosley, Chi.*	.969	41	31	0	1	0
Bream, Pitt.*	.000	2	0	0	0	0
Brown, Pitt.	.973	71	107	3	3	2
Bryant, L.A.	.953	26	39	2	2	0
Bullock, Hou.*	.875	6	7	0	1	0
Cabell, L.A.	1.000	16	23	1	0	0
Carter, N.Y.	.833	4	5	0	1	0
Cedeno, L.A.	.944	31	33	1	2	0
Coleman, St.L.	.972	149	300	12	9	2
Cruz, Hou.*	.984	134	237	5	4	1
Daniels, Cin.	.967	47	88	0	3	0
C. Davis, S.F.	.972	148	303	9	9	2
Davis, Cin.	.975	121	274	2	7	0
Davis, Pitt.*	.917	7	10	1	1	0
Dawson, Mtl.	.986	127	200	11	3	2

OUTFIELDERS—Continued

Player—Club	Pct.	G.	PO.	A.	E.	DP.
Dayett, Chi.	1.000	24	31	1	0	0
Dedmon, Atl.	.000	1	0	0	0	0
Dernier, Chi.	.987	105	222	3	3	2
Diaz, Pitt.	.966	38	55	1	2	0
Distefano, Pitt.*	1.000	9	13	0	0	0
Dykstra, N.Y.*	.990	139	283	8	3	2
Esasky, Cin.	1.000	42	73	3	0	2
Ford, St.L.	.975	64	109	7	3	3
Foster, N.Y.	.962	62	96	4	4	1
Francona, Chi.*	1.000	30	25	0	0	0
Gainey, Hou.*	1.000	19	30	0	0	0
Gladden, S.F.	.987	89	226	7	3	2
Gonzalez, L.A.	.924	57	73	0	6	0
Griffey, Atl.*	.986	77	136	1	2	0
G. Gross, Phil.*	1.000	27	32	1	0	0
Guerrero, L.A.	1.000	10	9	1	0	0
Gwynn, S.D.*	.989	160	337	19	4	3
Hall, Atl.	.900	14	26	1	3	0
Harper, Atl.	.970	83	92	5	3	0
Hatcher, Hou.	.983	121	226	7	4	0
Hayes, Phil.	1.000	31	65	4	0	1
Heath, St.L.	1.000	2	1	0	0	0
Heep, N.Y.*	.988	56	83	2	1	1
Hurdle, St.L.	1.000	10	12	0	0	0
Iorg, S.D.	1.000	3	4	0	0	0
James, Phil.	1.000	11	19	0	0	0
Jefferson, N.Y.	1.000	7	13	0	0	0
Johnson, N.Y.	1.000	1	2	0	0	0
Jones, Cin.	1.000	24	43	1	0	0
Kemp, Pitt.*	1.000	4	9	0	0	0
Komminsk, Atl.	1.000	2	1	0	0	0
Krenchicki, Mtl.	.000	1	0	0	0	0
Kruk, S.D.*	.981	74	102	4	2	0
Kutcher, S.F.	.990	51	99	3	1	1
Lancellotti, S.F.*	1.000	1	5	0	0	0
Landreaux, L.A.	.955	85	145	5	7	0
Landrum, St.L.	.993	78	131	6	1	1
Law, Mtl.	.000	1	0	0	0	0
Lawless, St.L.	1.000	1	2	0	0	0
Lefebvre, Phil.	1.000	3	4	0	0	0
Leonard, S.F.	.970	87	158	4	5	1
Lindeman, St.L.	.000	1	0	0	0	0
Lopes, Chi.-Hou.	1.000	41	75	3	0	1
Maddox, Phil.	1.000	3	1	0	0	0
Maldonado, S.F.	.983	101	161	10	3	0
Marshall, L.A.	.963	97	149	8	6	1
Martinez, S.D.	.978	60	83	5	2	0
Martinez, Chi.*	.988	46	77	2	1	1
Matthews, Chi.	.940	105	137	5	9	1
Matuszek, L.A.	1.000	37	38	2	0	0
Mazzilli, Pitt.-N.Y.	1.000	28	42	0	0	0
McDowell, N.Y.	.000	1	0	0	0	0
McGee, St.L.	.991	121	325	9	3	0
McReynolds, S.D.	.977	154	332	9	8	4
Meadows, Hou.*	.000	1	0	0	0	0
Milner, Cin.*	.990	127	292	6	3	0
K. Mitchell, N.Y.	.983	68	114	3	2	1
Moore, Mtl.*	.000	1	0	0	0	0
Moreland, Chi.	.980	121	181	13	4	3
Moreno, Atl.*	.970	97	151	8	5	3
Morris, St.L.*	.986	31	68	0	1	0
Motley, Atl.	1.000	3	5	0	0	0
Mumphrey, Chi.	.982	92	161	3	3	3
Murphy, Atl.	.981	159	303	6	6	1
Oquendo, St.L.	.000	1	0	0	0	0
Orosco, N.Y.*	1.000	1	1	0	0	0
Orsulak, Pitt.*	.981	120	193	11	4	2
Palmeiro, Chi.*	.900	20	34	2	4	1
Pankovits, Hou.	.833	5	4	1	1	0
Parker, Cin.	.970	159	278	9	9	2
Pendleton, St.L.	.000	1	0	0	0	0
Perry, Atl.	.889	21	16	0	2	0
Puhl, Hou.	1.000	47	65	0	0	0
Raines, Mtl.	.979	147	270	13	6	1
Ramirez, Atl.	1.000	3	1	0	0	0
Redus, Phil.	.980	89	185	8	4	2
Reynolds, Hou.	1.000	2	2	0	0	0
Reynolds, Pitt.	.955	112	190	2	9	0
Robinson, S.F.	.000	1	0	0	0	0
Roenicke, Phil.*	.989	83	181	3	2	0
Rowdon, Cin.	1.000	5	2	0	0	0
Royster, S.D.	1.000	7	4	0	0	0
Russell, L.A.	1.000	48	47	2	0	0
Sample, Atl.	.986	56	69	1	1	1
Spilman, S.F.	.000	1	0	0	0	0
Stone, Phil.	.982	58	103	8	2	1
Strawberry, N.Y.*	.975	131	226	10	6	3
Stubbs, L.A.*	.969	124	206	10	7	2
Thompson, Phil.	.991	89	212	1	2	1
Van Slyke, St.L.	.969	110	211	11	7	2
Venable, Cin.	.969	57	63	0	2	0
Walker, Hou.	.986	68	73	0	1	0
Walker, Chi.	.956	26	42	1	2	0
Walling, Hou.	1.000	11	19	1	0	0
Washington, Atl.*	.957	38	44	1	2	0
Webster, Mtl.*	.977	146	325	12	8	3
White, St.L.	1.000	6	5	0	0	0
Whitfield, L.A.	1.000	1	1	0	0	0
Williams, L.A.	.984	124	179	5	3	2
Wilson, Phil.	.989	154	331	20	4	5
Wilson, N.Y.	.979	114	228	7	5	2
Winningham, Mtl.	.980	66	97	2	2	1
Wohlford, Mtl.	1.000	22	21	1	0	0
Worrell, St.L.	.000	2	0	0	0	0
Wright, Mtl.	1.000	32	48	2	0	0
Wynne, S.D.*	.986	125	203	3	3	2
Youngblood, S.F.	1.000	45	49	2	0	1

OUTFIELDERS WITH TWO OR MORE CLUBS

Player—Club	Pct.	G.	PO.	A.	E.	DP.
Lopes, Chi.	1.000	22	31	0	0	0
Lopes, Hou.	1.000	19	44	3	0	1
Mazzilli, Pitt.	1.000	18	26	0	0	0
Mazzilli, N.Y.	1.000	10	16	0	0	0

CATCHERS

Leader—Club	Pct.	G.	PO.	A.	E.	DP.	PB.
BRENLY, S.F.	.995	101	518	55	3	4	10

(Listed Alphabetically)

Player—Club	Pct.	G.	PO.	A.	E.	DP.	PB.
Ashby, Hou.	.985	103	632	43	10	2	7
Bailey, Hou.	.989	53	318	33	4	3	1
Benedict, Atl.	.993	57	252	28	2	1	1
Bilardello, Mtl.	.982	77	391	38	8	3	6
Bochy, S.D.	.991	48	202	22	2	3	2
Brenly, S.F.	.995	101	518	55	3	4	10
Butera, Cin.	.979	53	215	17	5	2	1
Carter, N.Y.	.991	122	869	62	8	13	5
Christmas, Chi.	1.000	1	7	1	0	0	0
Daulton, Phil.	.985	48	244	21	4	6	4
J. Davis, Chi.	.992	145	885	105	8	14	15
Diaz, Cin.	.984	134	732	83	13	10	12
Diaz, Pitt.	1.000	1	1	1	0	0	0
Fimple, L.A.	1.000	7	29	4	0	0	1
Fitzgerald, Mtl.	.993	71	415	35	3	5	3
Gibbons, N.Y.	1.000	8	33	5	0	1	0
Gulden, S.F.	1.000	10	26	1	0	0	0
Hearn, N.Y.	.987	45	223	11	3	1	3
Heath, St.L.	.967	63	259	30	10	4	6
Hunt, Mtl.	.960	21	135	8	6	2	4
Hurdle, St.L.	1.000	5	19	1	0	0	2
Kennedy, S.D.	.990	123	692	70	8	13	9
Knicely, St.L.	1.000	2	2	0	0	0	0
Lake, Chi.-St.L.	.983	36	105	9	2	3	0
LaValliere, St.L.	.988	108	468	47	6	8	1
Lyons, N.Y.	.941	3	16	0	1	0	0
Martin, Chi.	1.000	8	18	5	0	0	1
Melvin, S.F.	.988	84	442	59	6	7	2

CATCHERS—Continued

Leader—Club	Pct.	G.	PO.	A.	E.	DP.	PB.
Mizerock, Hou.	.987	42	221	12	3	0	1
Moreland, Chi.	.984	13	57	6	1	0	1
Nieto, Mtl.	.978	30	123	11	3	1	5
Ortiz, Pitt.	.983	36	165	13	3	2	7
Ouellette, S.F.	1.000	9	42	3	0	0	0
Pankovits, Hou.	.000	1	0	0	0	0	0
Parent, S.D.	.889	3	16	0	2	0	0
T. Pena, Pitt.	.981	139	810	99	18	13	2
Reynolds, Phil.	.991	42	198	16	2	3	2
Rodriguez, Pitt.	1.000	2	6	1	0	0	0
Russell, Phil.	.976	89	498	39	13	10	17
Santiago, S.D.	.946	17	80	7	5	2	3
Scioscia, L.A.	.982	119	756	64	15	4	7
Simmons, Atl.	.978	10	40	5	1	0	2

Player—Club	Pct.	G.	PO.	A.	E.	DP.	PB.
Spilman, S.F.	.000	1	0	0	0	0	0
Tejada, Mtl.	1.000	10	40	8	0	1	3
Trevino, L.A.	.969	63	304	45	11	4	3
Van Gorder, Cin.	1.000	7	20	0	0	0	0
Virgil, Atl.	.984	111	682	93	13	9	8
Wine, Hou.	1.000	8	28	5	0	0	0

CATCHERS WITH TWO OR MORE CLUBS

Player—Club	Pct.	G.	PO.	A.	E.	DP.	PB.
Lake, Chi.	1.000	10	30	3	0	2	0
Lake, St.L.	.976	26	75	6	2	1	0

Triple Play: Virgil.

PITCHERS

Leader—Club	Pct.	G.	PO.	A.	E.	DP.
RHODEN, Pitt.	1.000	34	32	34	0	4

(Listed Alphabetically)

Player—Club	Pct.	G.	PO.	A.	E.	DP.
Acker, Atl.	1.000	21	7	17	0	2
Aguilera, N.Y.	1.000	28	13	26	0	1
Alexander, Atl.	.957	17	8	14	1	2
Andersen, Phil.-Hou.	.913	48	10	11	2	3
Anderson, N.Y.	1.000	15	8	4	0	0
Assenmacher, Atl.*	1.000	61	5	15	0	1
Baller, Chi.	1.000	36	2	4	0	0
Bargar, St.L.	1.000	22	3	7	0	0
Beckwith, L.A.	1.000	15	1	0	0	0
Bedrosian, Phil.	1.000	68	2	10	0	1
Berenguer, S.F.	.900	46	2	7	1	0
Berenyi, N.Y.	1.000	14	3	5	0	0
Bielecki, Pitt.	.971	31	17	16	1	1
Bittiger, Phil.	1.000	3	2	2	0	0
Blue, S.F.*	.931	28	3	24	2	0
Bockus, S.F.	1.000	5	0	4	0	0
Boever, St.L.	1.000	11	1	2	0	0
Booker, S.D.	.667	9	1	1	1	0
Brown, Mtl.	.800	6	1	3	1	0
Browning, Cin.*	.925	39	11	26	3	5
Burke, Mtl.	.963	68	4	22	1	1
Burris, St.L.	1.000	23	4	9	0	1
Butera, Cin.	.000	1	0	0	0	0
Calhoun, Hou.*	1.000	20	2	1	0	0
Carlton, Phil.-S.F.*	1.000	22	3	16	0	1
Carman, Phil.*	1.000	50	4	30	0	2
Childress, Phil.	.000	2	0	0	0	0
Clements, Pitt.*	1.000	65	7	11	0	1
Conroy, St.L.*	.792	25	3	16	5	0
Cox, St.L.	.865	32	22	10	5	0
Darling, N.Y.	.910	34	24	47	7	7
Darwin, Hou.	1.000	12	4	5	0	0
M. Davis, S.F.*	.824	67	3	11	3	1
R. Davis, Chi.	.667	17	1	1	1	0
Dayley, St.L.*	1.000	31	1	7	0	0
DeLeon, Pitt.	.800	9	1	3	1	1
Dedmon, Atl.	.939	57	9	22	2	1
Denny, Cin.	.966	27	16	40	2	2
Deshaies, Hou.*	.917	26	9	13	2	0
Diaz, L.A.*	.875	19	1	6	1	0
DiPino, Hou.-Chi.*	.962	61	8	17	1	1
Downs, S.F.	.950	14	6	13	1	0
Dravecky, S.D.*	.974	26	10	27	1	0
Earley, St.L.*	.000	3	0	0	0	0
Eckersley, Chi.	.936	33	16	28	3	3
Fansler, Pitt.	1.000	5	5	1	0	1
Fernandez, N.Y.*	.955	32	3	18	1	1
Fontenot, Chi.*	.706	42	2	10	5	0
Forsch, St.L.	1.000	33	17	32	0	5
Franco, Cin.*	.875	74	6	22	4	2
Frazier, Chi.	1.000	35	0	2	0	0
Freeman, Phil.	1.000	3	0	1	0	0
Funk, Hou.*	1.000	8	1	1	0	0
Galvez, L.A.	.857	10	3	3	1	1
Garber, Atl.	1.000	61	7	14	0	1
Garrelts, S.F.	.958	53	9	37	2	2

Player—Club	Pct.	G.	PO.	A.	E.	DP.
Gooden, N.Y.	.973	33	36	36	2	5
Gorman, Phil.*	1.000	8	2	2	0	0
Gossage, S.D.	1.000	45	2	5	0	0
Gott, S.F.	1.000	9	0	2	0	0
Grant, S.F.	1.000	4	0	1	0	1
G. Gross, Phil.*	.000	1	0	0	0	0
K. Gross, Phil.	.964	37	25	28	2	2
Guante, Pitt.	.857	52	1	5	1	0
Gullickson, Cin.	.939	37	14	32	3	3
Gumpert, Chi.	1.000	38	3	4	0	0
Hall, Chi.*	1.000	5	0	2	0	0
Hawkins, S.D.	1.000	37	7	28	0	0
Hayward, S.D.*	.500	3	0	1	1	0
Hensley, S.F.*	1.000	11	0	1	0	0
Hernandez, Hou.	1.000	9	1	5	0	0
Hershiser, L.A.	.951	35	22	36	3	6
Hesketh, Mtl.*	.909	15	2	8	1	0
Hoffman, Chi.*	.909	32	1	9	1	0
Holton, L.A.	1.000	12	3	3	0	0
Honeycutt, L.A.*	.978	32	9	35	1	2
Horton, St.L.*	1.000	42	4	24	0	3
Howell, L.A.	.923	62	5	7	1	0
Hoyt, S.D.	.926	35	8	17	2	1
Hudson, Phil.	.970	33	12	20	1	0
Hume, Phil.	.964	48	8	19	1	1
Iorg, S.D.	.000	2	0	0	0	0
Jackson, Phil.	1.000	9	2	0	0	0
Johnson, Atl.	.931	17	5	22	2	1
Jones, Pitt.	.909	26	3	7	1	2
Jones, S.D.	1.000	3	1	2	0	0
Keough, Chi.-Hou.	.900	29	3	6	1	2
Kepshire, St.L.	1.000	2	1	2	0	0
Kerfeld, Hou.	1.000	61	7	9	0	1
Kipper, Pitt.*	.941	20	1	15	1	0
Knepper, Hou.*	.959	40	23	47	3	6
Knudson, Hou.	1.000	9	1	4	0	0
Krawczyk, Pitt.	.667	12	2	0	1	0
Krukow, S.F.	.926	34	17	33	4	1
LaCoss, S.F.	.981	37	19	34	1	2
Lahti, St.L.	.000	4	0	0	0	0
Landrum, Cin.	1.000	10	0	1	0	0
LaPoint, S.D.*	.917	24	3	8	1	1
Laskey, S.F.	.900	20	3	6	1	1
Law, Mtl.	1.000	3	0	1	0	0
Leach, N.Y.	1.000	6	0	2	0	0
Lefferts, S.D.*	1.000	83	3	24	0	3
Lerch, Phil.*	1.000	4	0	1	0	0
Lopez, Hou.	.800	45	2	6	2	0
Lynch, N.Y.-Chi.	1.000	24	7	12	0	2
Madden, Hou.*	1.000	13	1	5	0	0
Maddux, Chi.	.875	6	1	6	1	0
Maddux, Phil.	.882	16	5	10	2	0
Mahler, Atl.	.955	39	23	41	3	2
Martinez, Mtl.	.963	19	3	23	1	0
Mason, S.F.	.909	11	6	4	1	0
Mathews, St.L.*	1.000	23	3	17	0	1
McClure, Mtl.*	.923	52	1	11	1	1
McCullers, S.D.	.917	70	6	16	2	1
McDowell, N.Y.	1.000	75	17	30	0	0
McGaffigan, Mtl.	.821	48	6	17	5	1

PITCHERS—Continued

Player—Club	Pct.	G.	PO.	A.	E.	DP.
McMurtry, Atl.	1.000	37	6	11	0	1
McWilliams, Pitt.*	1.000	49	7	17	0	2
Minton, S.F.	.929	48	7	19	2	1
J. Mitchell, N.Y.	1.000	4	3	1	0	0
Montalvo, Hou.	1.000	1	1	1	0	0
Moyer, Chi.*	1.000	16	2	22	0	0
Mulholland, S.F.*	.769	15	1	9	3	0
Murphy, Cin.*	1.000	34	1	9	0	0
Myers, N.Y.*	1.000	10	0	2	0	0
Niedenfuer, L.A.	.950	60	9	10	1	1
Niemann, N.Y.*	1.000	31	3	9	0	1
Ojeda, N.Y.*	.979	32	9	37	1	3
Olwine, Atl.*	1.000	37	3	5	0	0
Orosco, N.Y.*	1.000	58	4	8	0	0
Owchinko, Mtl.*	1.000	3	0	2	0	0
Ownbey, St.L.	.800	17	4	4	2	0
Palmer, Atl.	1.000	35	18	33	0	3
Parrett, Mtl.	1.000	12	1	2	0	1
Patterson, Pitt.*	1.000	11	1	9	0	1
Pena, L.A.	1.000	24	1	8	0	0
H. Pena, Pitt.*	1.000	10	0	1	0	0
Perry, St.L.*	.955	46	10	11	1	4
Powell, L.A.*	.929	27	7	6	1	1
Power, Cin.	.962	56	7	18	1	1
Price, Cin.*	1.000	25	2	2	0	0
Puleo, Atl.	1.000	5	0	3	0	0
Rawley, Phil.*	.889	23	4	28	4	3
Reardon, Mtl.	1.000	62	8	10	0	1
Reuschel, Pitt.	.971	35	24	44	2	0
Reuss, L.A.*	1.000	19	5	16	0	1
Reynolds, Hou.	.000	1	0	0	0	0
Rhoden, Pitt.	1.000	34	32	34	0	4
Riley, Mtl.*	.000	10	0	0	0	0
Roberge, Mtl.	1.000	21	3	3	0	0
Robinson, Pitt.	1.000	50	6	9	0	0
Robinson, S.F.	.952	64	10	10	1	1
Robinson, Cin.	1.000	70	8	20	0	2
Rucker, Phil.*	1.000	19	1	5	0	1
Ruffin, Phil.*	.966	21	8	20	1	0
Ruthven, Chi.	1.000	6	0	1	0	0
Ryan, Hou.	.931	30	10	17	2	2
St. Claire, Mtl.	1.000	11	1	5	0	0
Sanderson, Chi.	.939	37	11	20	2	0
Sauveur, Pitt.*	1.000	3	1	5	0	1
Schatzeder, Mtl.-Phil.	1.000	55	3	9	0	0
Scott, Hou.	.969	37	24	39	2	2
Sebra, Mtl.	1.000	17	8	8	0	2
Shields, Atl.	1.000	6	1	1	0	0
Show, S.D.	.952	24	6	14	1	1
Sisk, N.Y.	1.000	41	10	6	0	0
Smiley, Pitt.*	1.000	12	1	2	0	0
Smith, Mtl.	.965	30	11	44	2	5
Smith, Hou.	1.000	54	7	6	0	0
Smith, Chi.	1.000	66	1	12	0	2
Smith, Cin.	.000	2	0	0	0	0
Smith, Atl.*	.981	38	7	45	1	4
Soff, St.L.	.929	30	6	7	1	0
Solano, Hou.	.857	16	2	4	1	0
Soto, Cin.	.950	19	3	16	1	0
Speck, Atl.	1.000	13	1	5	0	0
Stewart, Phil.	.000	8	0	0	0	0
B. Stoddard, S.D.	1.000	18	0	3	0	0
T. Stoddard, S.D.	.889	30	1	7	1	1
Sutcliffe, Chi.	.974	28	8	30	1	4
Sutter, Atl.	1.000	16	1	3	0	0
Tekulve, Phil.	.897	73	4	22	3	2
Terry, Cin.	.917	28	2	9	1	2
Thurmond, S.D.*	1.000	17	4	12	0	0
Tibbs, Mtl.	1.000	35	14	24	0	2
Toliver, Phil.	1.000	5	1	4	0	1
Tomlin, Mtl.*	1.000	7	0	4	0	0
Trout, Chi.*	.974	37	7	31	1	3
Tudor, St.L.*	.962	30	10	41	2	4
Valdez, Mtl.	.800	5	3	1	1	1
Valenzuela, L.A.*	.987	34	29	47	1	2
Vande Berg, L.A.*	.913	60	5	16	2	0
Vosberg, S.D.*	.500	5	0	1	1	0
Walk, Pitt.	.942	44	21	28	3	4
Walter, S.D.*	.962	57	8	17	1	1
Ward, Atl.	1.000	10	0	6	0	0
Welch, L.A.	.959	33	21	26	2	2
Welsh, Cin.*	1.000	24	7	23	0	1
Whitson, S.D.	.905	17	6	13	2	1
Williams, S.F.	1.000	36	1	10	0	3
Willis, Cin.	1.000	29	4	10	0	3
Winn, Pitt.	.958	50	8	15	1	1
Wojna, S.D.	.750	7	1	5	2	0
Worrell, St.L.	.867	74	5	8	2	0
Youmans, Mtl.	.900	33	11	16	3	1

PITCHERS WITH TWO OR MORE CLUBS

Player—Club	Pct.	G.	PO.	A.	E.	DP.
Andersen, Phil.	.800	10	2	2	1	1
Andersen, Hou.	.944	38	8	9	1	2
Carlton, Phil.	1.000	16	2	8	0	1
Carlton, S.F.	1.000	6	1	8	0	0
DiPino, Hou.	.929	31	7	6	1	1
DiPino, Chi.	1.000	30	1	11	0	0
Keough, Chi.	.857	19	2	4	1	1
Keough, Hou.	1.000	10	1	2	0	1
Lynch, N.Y.	.000	1	0	0	0	0
Lynch, Chi.	1.000	23	7	12	0	2
Schatzeder, Mtl.	1.000	30	1	6	0	0
Schatzeder, Phil.	1.000	25	2	3	0	0

Triple Play: Lynch, Smith (Atl.).

OFFICIAL NATIONAL LEAGUE PITCHING AVERAGES

CLUB PITCHING

Club	ERA.	G.	CG.	ShO.	Sv.	IP.	H.	BFP.	R.	ER.	HR.	SH.	SF.	HB.	Tot. BB.	Int. BB.	SO.	WP.	Bk.
New York	3.11	162	27	11	46	1484.0	1304	6165	578	513	103	62	43	31	509	29	1083	40	16
Houston	3.15	162	18	19	51	1456.1	1203	6010	569	509	116	82	42	23	523	60	1160	50	11
San Francisco	3.33	162	18	10	35	1460.1	1264	6093	618	541	121	79	44	29	591	78	992	58	15
St. Louis	3.37	161	17	4	46	1466.1	1364	6061	611	549	135	53	54	22	485	73	761	38	13
Los Angeles	3.76	162	35	14	25	1454.1	1428	6199	679	608	115	75	30	26	499	79	1051	51	10
Montreal	3.78	161	15	9	50	1466.1	1350	6208	688	616	119	80	38	33	566	61	1051	49	20
Philadelphia	3.85	161	22	11	39	1451.2	1473	6244	713	621	130	58	47	22	553	71	874	45	17
Pittsburgh	3.90	162	17	9	30	1450.2	1397	6201	700	629	138	66	46	37	570	55	924	59	20
Cincinnati	3.91	162	14	8	45	1468.0	1465	6240	717	638	136	86	60	17	524	81	924	39	5
Atlanta	3.97	161	17	5	39	1424.2	1443	6125	719	629	117	70	34	26	576	63	932	44	11
San Diego	3.99	162	13	7	32	1443.1	1406	6212	723	640	150	82	36	27	607	75	934	38	18
Chicago	4.49	160	11	6	42	1445.0	1546	6248	781	721	143	76	45	19	557	78	962	55	20
Totals	3.72	969	224	113	480	17471.0	16643	74006	8096	7214	1523	869	519	312	6560	803	11648	566	176

NOTE: Total earned runs for eight clubs do not agree with composite total of respective clubs' pitchers due to provisions of Scoring Rule Section 10.18 (i). The following differences are to be noted: Atlanta pitching add to 627 earned runs, Chicago pitchers add to 717, Cincinnati pitchers add to 636; Houston pitchers add to 508; Philadelphia pitchers add to 618; St. Louis pitchers add to 548; San Diego pitchers add to 639; San Francisco pitchers add to 537.

PITCHERS' RECORDS

(Top Fifteen Qualifiers for Earned-Run Leadership—162 or More Innings)

*Throws lefthanded

Pitcher and Club	W.	L.	Pct.	ERA.	G.	GS.	CG.	ShO.	GF.	Sv.	IP.	H.	BFP.	R.	ER.	HR.	SH.	SF.	HB.	Tot. BB.	Int. BB.	SO.	WP.	Bk.
Scott, Michael, Hou.	18	10	.643	2.22	37	37	7	5	0	0	275.1	182	1065	73	68	17	8	6	2	72	6	306	3	0
Ojeda, Robert, N.Y.*	18	5	.783	2.57	32	30	7	2	1	0	217.1	185	871	72	62	15	10	3	2	52	3	148	2	1
Darling, Ronald, N.Y.	15	6	.714	2.81	34	34	4	2	0	0	237.0	203	967	84	74	21	10	6	3	81	2	184	7	3
Rhoden, Richard, Pitt.	15	12	.556	2.84	34	34	12	1	0	0	253.2	211	1015	82	80	17	6	5	2	76	8	159	6	4
Gooden, Dwight, N.Y.	17	6	.739	2.84	33	33	12	2	0	0	250.0	197	1020	92	79	17	10	8	4	80	3	200	4	4
Cox, Danny, St.L.	12	13	.480	2.90	32	32	8	0	0	0	220.0	189	881	85	71	14	8	3	2	60	6	108	3	4
Tudor, John, St.L.*	13	7	.650	2.92	30	30	3	0	0	0	219.0	197	879	81	71	22	9	8	1	53	5	107	2	1
Krukow, Michael, S.F.	20	9	.690	3.05	34	34	10	2	0	0	245.0	204	987	90	83	24	10	5	4	55	4	178	4	0
Garrelts, Scott, S.F.	13	9	.591	3.11	53	18	2	0	27	10	173.2	144	717	65	60	17	10	7	2	74	11	125	9	1
Knepper, Robert, Hou.*	17	12	.586	3.14	40	38	8	5	1	0	258.0	232	1053	100	90	19	22	5	4	62	13	143	5	0
Valenzuela, Fernando, L.A.*	21	11	.656	3.14	34	34	20	3	0	0	269.1	226	1102	104	94	18	15	3	1	85	5	242	13	0
Forsch, Robert, St.L.	14	10	.583	3.25	33	33	3	0	0	0	230.0	211	939	91	83	19	5	9	2	68	11	104	7	0
Welch, Robert, L.A.	7	13	.350	3.28	33	33	7	3	0	0	235.2	227	981	95	86	14	7	8	7	55	6	183	2	1
Honeycutt, Frederick, L.A.*	11	9	.550	3.32	32	28	0	0	2	0	171.0	164	713	71	63	9	6	1	3	45	4	100	4	1
Ryan, L. Nolan, Hou.	12	8	.600	3.34	30	30	1	0	0	0	178.0	119	729	72	66	14	5	4	4	82	5	194	15	0

DEPARTMENTAL LEADERS: W—Valenzuela, 21; L—Mahler, 18; Pct.—Ojeda, .783; G—Lefferts, 83; GS—Browning, Mahler, 39; CG—Valenzuela, 20; ShO—Knepper, Scott, 5; GF—Worrell, 60; Sv.—Worrell, 36; IP—Scott, 275.1; H—Mahler, 283; BFP—Valenzuela, 1,102; R—Mahler, 139; ER—Mahler, 129; HR—K. Gross, 28; SH—Knepper, 22; SF—Gullickson, 13; HB—K. Gross, Reuschel, 8; Tot. BB—Youmans, 118; Int. BB—Worrell, 16; SO—Scott, 306; WP—Ryan, 15; Bk—Deshaies, 7.

(All Pitchers—Listed Alphabetically)

Pitcher and Club	W.	L.	Pct.	ERA.	G.	GS.	CG.	ShO.	GF.	Sv.	IP.	H.	BFP.	R.	ER.	HR.	SH.	SF.	HB.	Tot. BB.	Int. BB.	SO.	WP.	Bk.
Acker, James, Atl.	3	8	.273	3.79	21	14	0	0	3	0	95.0	100	402	47	40	7	6	4	1	26	3	37	2	0
Aguilera, Richard, N.Y.	10	7	.588	3.88	28	20	2	0	2	0	141.2	145	605	70	61	15	6	5	7	36	1	104	5	3
Alexander, Doyle, Atl.	6	6	.500	3.84	17	17	2	0	0	0	117.1	135	496	58	50	9	8	1	0	17	1	74	1	0
Andersen, Larry, Phil.-Hou.	2	1	.667	3.03	48	0	0	0	8	1	77.1	83	323	30	26	2	10	5	1	26	10	42	1	0
Anderson, Richard, N.Y.	2	1	.667	2.72	15	5	0	0	4	1	49.2	45	201	17	15	3	2	4	0	11	3	21	1	1
Assenmacher, Paul, Atl.*	7	3	.700	2.50	61	0	0	0	27	7	68.1	61	287	23	19	5	7	1	0	26	4	56	2	3
Baller, Jay, Chi.	2	4	.333	5.37	36	0	0	0	16	5	53.2	58	248	37	32	7	4	3	2	28	4	42	2	4
Bargar, Gregory, St.L.	0	2	.000	5.60	22	0	0	0	10	0	27.1	36	126	19	7	3	2	2	3	10	1	12	2	0
Beckwith, T. Joseph, L.A.	0	0	.000	6.87	15	0	0	0	4	0	18.1	28	86	16	14	5	0	0	0	6	0	13	0	0
Bedrosian, Stephen, Phil.	8	6	.571	3.39	68	0	0	0	56	29	90.1	79	381	39	34	12	3	3	0	34	10	82	5	2
Berenguer, Juan, S.F.	2	3	.400	2.70	46	4	0	0	17	4	73.1	64	314	23	22	4	2	1	2	44	3	72	4	2
Berenyi, Bruce, N.Y.	2	2	.500	6.35	14	7	0	0	2	0	39.2	47	184	30	28	5	1	3	1	22	0	30	4	0
Bielecki, Michael, Pitt.	6	11	.353	4.66	31	27	0	0	0	0	148.2	149	667	87	77	10	7	6	2	83	3	83	7	5
Bittiger, Jeffrey, Phil.	1	1	.500	5.52	3	3	0	0	0	0	14.2	16	68	10	9	2	1	0	1	7	1	8	2	2
Blue, Vida, S.F.*	10	10	.500	3.27	28	28	0	0	0	0	156.2	137	663	65	57	19	7	6	0	77	3	100	5	1
Bockus, Randy, S.F.	0	0	.000	2.57	5	0	0	0	1	0	7.0	7	36	5	2	1	1	0	0	6	1	4	0	0
Boever, Joseph, St.L.	0	1	.000	1.66	11	0	0	0	4	0	21.2	19	93	5	4	2	0	0	0	11	0	8	1	0
Booker, Gregory, S.D.	1	0	1.000	1.64	9	0	0	0	4	0	11.0	10	47	5	2	0	0	0	0	4	2	7	0	0
Brown, Curtis, Mtl.	0	1	.000	3.00	6	0	0	0	2	0	12.0	15	53	6	4	0	3	1	0	2	2	4	0	0
Browning, Thomas, Cin.*	14	13	.519	3.81	39	39	4	2	0	0	243.1	225	1016	123	103	26	14	12	1	70	6	147	3	0
Burke, Timothy, Mtl.	9	7	.563	2.93	68	2	0	0	25	4	101.1	103	451	37	33	7	6	2	4	46	13	82	4	0
Burris, B. Ray, St.L.	4	5	.444	5.60	23	10	0	0	5	0	82.0	92	361	52	51	13	4	0	4	32	4	34	0	0
Butera, Salvatore, Cin.	0	0	.000	0.00	1	0	0	0	1	0	1.0	0	4	0	0	0	0	0	0	1	0	1	0	0
Calhoun, Jeffrey, Hou.*	1	0	1.000	3.71	20	0	0	0	7	0	26.2	28	119	16	11	3	1	0	0	12	1	14	2	0
Carlton, Steven, Phil.-S.F.*	5	11	.313	5.89	22	22	0	0	0	0	113.0	138	533	90	74	19	6	3	1	61	4	80	5	1
Carman, Donald, Phil.*	10	5	.667	3.22	50	14	2	1	13	1	134.1	113	545	50	48	11	5	3	3	52	11	98	6	2
Childress, Rodney, Phil.	0	0	.000	6.75	2	0	0	0	0	0	2.2	4	12	3	2	0	0	0	0	1	0	1	0	0
Clements, Patrick, Pitt.*	0	4	.000	2.80	65	0	0	0	19	2	61.0	53	256	20	19	1	7	4	2	32	6	31	2	0
Conroy, Timothy, St.L.*	5	11	.313	5.23	25	21	1	0	2	0	115.1	122	513	72	67	15	0	10	3	56	7	79	7	0
Cox, Danny, St.L.	12	13	.480	2.90	32	32	8	0	0	0	220.0	189	881	85	71	14	8	3	2	60	6	108	3	4
Darling, Ronald, N.Y.	15	6	.714	2.81	34	34	4	2	0	0	237.0	203	967	84	74	21	10	6	3	81	2	184	7	3
Darwin, Danny, Hou.	5	2	.714	2.32	12	8	1	0	2	0	54.1	50	222	19	14	3	1	3	0	9	0	40	2	1
Davis, Mark, S.F.*	5	7	.417	2.99	67	2	0	0	20	4	84.1	63	342	33	28	6	5	5	1	34	7	90	3	0
Davis, Ronald, Chi.	0	2	.000	7.65	17	0	0	0	5	0	20.0	31	91	18	17	3	0	1	0	3	0	10	0	1
Dayley, Kenneth, St.L.*	0	3	.000	3.26	31	0	0	0	13	5	38.2	42	170	19	14	1	4	1	1	11	3	33	0	0
DeLeon, Jose, Pitt.	1	3	.250	8.27	9	1	0	0	5	1	16.1	17	83	16	15	2	1	0	1	17	3	11	1	0
Dedmon, Jeffrey, Atl.	6	6	.500	2.98	57	0	0	0	22	3	99.2	90	424	43	33	8	7	2	4	39	5	58	3	2
Denny, John, Cin.	11	10	.524	4.20	27	27	2	1	0	0	171.1	179	731	89	80	15	9	4	4	56	9	115	2	1
Deshaies, James, Hou.*	12	5	.706	3.25	26	26	1	1	0	0	144.0	124	599	58	52	16	4	3	2	59	2	128	0	7
Diaz, Carlos, L.A.*	0	0	.000	4.26	19	0	0	0	9	0	25.1	33	113	14	12	2	1	1	0	7	2	18	2	0
DiPino, Frank, Hou.-Chi.*	3	7	.300	4.37	61	0	0	0	26	3	80.1	74	345	45	39	11	9	3	2	30	6	70	3	0
Downs, Kelly, S.F.	4	4	.500	2.75	14	14	1	0	0	0	88.1	78	372	29	27	5	4	4	3	30	7	64	3	2
Dravecky, David, S.D.*	9	11	.450	3.07	26	26	3	1	0	0	161.1	149	677	68	55	17	12	5	1	54	7	87	0	1
Earley, William, St.L.*	0	0	.000	0.00	3	0	0	0	2	0	3.0	0	11	0	0	0	0	0	0	2	0	2	0	0
Eckersley, Dennis, Chi.	6	11	.353	4.57	33	32	1	0	0	0	201.0	226	862	109	102	21	13	10	3	43	3	137	2	5
Fansler, Stanley, Pitt.	0	3	.000	3.75	5	5	0	0	0	0	24.0	20	99	12	10	2	2	1	0	15	0	13	0	0
Fernandez, C. Sidney, N.Y.*	16	6	.727	3.52	32	31	2	1	1	1	204.1	161	855	82	80	13	9	7	2	91	1	200	6	0
Fontenot, S. Ray, Chi.*	3	5	.375	3.86	42	0	0	0	11	2	56.0	57	241	30	24	5	6	0	0	21	3	24	4	1
Forsch, Robert, St.L.	14	10	.583	3.25	33	33	3	0	0	0	230.0	211	939	91	83	19	5	9	2	68	11	104	7	0
Franco, John, Cin.*	6	6	.500	2.94	74	0	0	0	52	29	101.0	90	429	40	33	7	8	3	2	44	12	84	4	2

Pitcher and Club	W.	L.	Pct.	ERA.	G.	GS.	CG.	ShO.	GF.	Sv.	IP.	H.	BFP.	R.	ER.	HR.	SH.	SF.	HB.	Tot. BB.	Int. BB.	SO.	WP.	Bk.
Frazier, George, Chi.	2	4	.333	5.40	35	0	0	0	12	0	51.2	63	243	36	31	5	2	3	1	34	4	41	3	0
Freeman, Marvin, Phil.	2	0	1.000	2.25	3	3	0	0	0	0	16.0	6	61	4	4	0	0	1	0	10	0	8	1	0
Funk, Thomas, Hou.*	0	0	.000	6.48	8	0	0	0	2	0	8.1	10	41	6	6	1	0	0	0	6	0	2	0	0
Galvez, Balvino, L.A.	0	1	.000	3.92	10	0	0	0	2	0	20.2	19	91	10	9	3	0	0	0	12	2	11	0	2
Garber, H. Eugene, Atl.	5	5	.500	2.54	61	0	0	0	48	24	78.0	76	319	23	22	3	5	1	1	20	7	56	4	0
Garrelts, Scott, S.F.	13	9	.591	3.11	53	18	2	0	27	10	173.2	144	717	65	60	17	10	7	2	74	11	125	9	1
Gooden, Dwight, N.Y.	17	6	.739	2.84	33	33	12	2	0	0	250.0	197	1020	92	79	17	10	8	4	80	3	200	4	4
Gorman, Thomas, Phil.*	0	1	.000	7.71	8	0	0	0	1	0	11.2	21	61	10	10	0	0	1	0	5	1	8	4	0
Gossage, Richard, S.D.	5	7	.417	4.45	45	0	0	0	38	21	64.2	69	281	36	32	8	2	4	2	20	0	63	4	0
Gott, James, S.F.	0	0	.000	7.62	9	2	0	0	3	1	13.0	16	66	12	11	0	1	1	0	13	2	9	1	1
Grant, Mark, S.F.	0	1	.000	3.60	4	1	0	0	3	0	10.0	6	39	4	4	0	0	0	0	5	0	5	0	1
Gross, Gregory, Phil.*	0	0	.000	0.00	1	0	0	0	1	0	0.2	1	4	0	0	0	0	0	0	1	0	2	0	0
Gross, Kevin, Phil.	12	12	.500	4.02	37	36	7	2	0	0	241.2	240	1040	115	108	28	8	5	8	94	2	154	2	1
Guante, Cecilio, Pitt.	5	2	.714	3.35	52	0	0	0	24	4	78.0	65	326	32	29	11	3	2	3	29	3	63	2	1
Gullickson, William, Cin.	15	12	.556	3.38	37	37	6	2	0	0	244.2	245	1014	103	92	24	12	13	2	60	10	121	3	0
Gumpert, David, Chi.	2	0	1.000	4.37	38	0	0	0	12	2	59.2	60	259	32	29	4	4	1	1	28	7	45	3	0
Hall, Andrew, Chi.*	1	2	.333	4.56	5	4	1	0	1	1	23.2	24	101	12	12	3	1	0	0	10	0	21	0	0
Hawkins, M. Andrew, S.D.	10	8	.556	4.30	37	35	3	1	0	0	209.1	218	905	111	100	24	7	6	5	75	7	117	6	2
Hayward, Raymond, S.D.*	0	2	.000	9.00	3	3	0	0	0	0	10.0	16	51	12	10	1	0	0	0	4	0	6	5	1
Hensley, Charles, S.F.*	0	0	.000	2.45	11	0	0	0	2	1	7.1	5	30	2	2	2	0	0	0	2	0	6	0	1
Hernandez, Manuel, Hou.	2	3	.400	3.90	9	4	0	0	1	0	27.2	33	125	15	12	2	4	1	0	12	3	9	1	0
Hershiser, Orel, L.A.	14	14	.500	3.85	35	35	8	1	0	0	231.1	213	988	112	99	13	14	6	5	86	11	153	12	3
Hesketh, Joseph, Mtl.*	6	5	.545	5.01	15	15	0	0	0	0	82.2	92	362	46	46	11	2	2	2	31	4	67	4	3
Hoffman, Guy, Chi.*	6	2	.750	3.86	32	8	1	0	6	0	84.0	92	357	37	36	6	4	3	2	29	7	47	5	1
Holton, Brian, L.A.	2	3	.400	4.44	12	3	0	0	4	0	24.1	28	106	13	12	1	2	1	1	6	2	24	1	0
Honeycutt, Frederick, L.A.*	11	9	.550	3.32	32	28	0	0	2	0	171.0	164	713	71	63	9	6	1	3	45	4	100	4	1
Horton, Ricky, St.L.*	4	3	.571	2.24	42	9	1	0	12	3	100.1	77	387	25	25	7	3	3	1	26	7	49	1	0
Howell, Kenneth, L.A.	6	12	.333	3.87	62	0	0	0	36	12	97.2	86	437	48	42	7	8	3	3	63	9	104	4	0
Hoyt, D. LaMarr, S.D.	8	11	.421	5.15	35	25	1	0	2	0	159.0	170	699	100	91	27	10	3	3	68	8	85	2	2
Hudson, Charles, Phil.	7	10	.412	4.94	33	23	0	0	2	0	144.0	165	638	87	79	20	10	3	0	58	1	82	2	2
Hume, Thomas, Phil.	4	1	.800	2.77	48	1	0	0	9	4	94.1	89	402	37	29	5	5	7	3	34	5	51	6	0
Iorg, Dane, S.D.	0	0	.000	12.00	2	0	0	0	2	0	3.0	5	15	4	4	2	0	0	0	1	0	2	0	0
Jackson, Michael, Phil.	0	0	.000	3.38	9	0	0	0	4	0	13.1	12	54	5	5	2	0	0	2	4	1	3	0	0
Johnson, Joseph, Atl.	6	7	.462	4.97	17	15	2	0	1	0	87.0	101	390	58	48	8	3	1	2	35	4	49	1	1
Jones, Barry, Pitt.	3	4	.429	2.89	26	0	0	0	10	3	37.1	29	159	16	12	3	2	1	0	21	2	29	2	0
Jones, James, S.D.	2	0	1.000	2.50	3	3	1	1	0	0	18.0	10	65	6	5	1	1	0	0	3	0	15	0	0
Keough, Matthew, Chi.-Hou.	5	4	.556	3.94	29	7	0	0	5	0	64.0	58	272	31	28	9	3	1	2	30	4	44	6	2
Kepshire, Kurt, St.L.	0	1	.000	4.50	2	1	0	0	1	0	8.0	8	35	4	4	2	0	0	0	4	0	6	0	1
Kerfeld, Charles, Hou.	11	2	.846	2.59	61	0	0	0	29	7	93.2	71	390	32	27	5	6	7	2	42	3	77	7	2
Kipper, Robert, Pitt.*	6	8	.429	4.03	20	19	0	0	1	0	114.0	123	496	60	51	17	3	3	2	34	3	81	3	3
Knepper, Robert, Hou.*	17	12	.586	3.14	40	38	8	5	1	0	258.0	232	1053	100	90	19	22	5	4	62	13	143	5	0
Knudson, Mark, Hou.	1	5	.167	4.22	9	7	0	0	1	0	42.2	48	191	23	20	5	3	0	1	15	5	20	1	0
Krawczyk, Raymond, Pitt.	0	1	.000	7.30	12	0	0	0	2	0	12.1	17	65	13	10	3	1	1	0	10	0	7	0	0
Krukow, Michael, S.F.	20	9	.690	3.05	34	34	10	2	0	0	245.0	204	987	90	83	24	10	5	4	55	4	178	4	0
LaCoss, Michael, S.F.	10	13	.435	3.57	37	31	4	1	1	0	204.1	179	842	99	81	14	16	3	6	70	8	86	5	5
Lahti, Jeffrey, St.L.	0	0	.000	0.00	4	0	0	0	1	0	2.1	3	10	0	0	0	0	0	0	1	0	3	0	0
Landrum, T. William, Cin.	0	0	.000	6.75	10	0	0	0	4	0	13.1	23	65	11	10	0	1	1	0	4	0	14	0	0
LaPoint, David, S.D.*	1	4	.200	4.26	24	4	0	0	4	0	61.1	67	274	37	29	8	5	1	1	24	4	41	1	4
Laskey, William, S.F.	1	1	.500	4.28	20	0	0	0	7	1	27.1	28	117	14	13	5	1	1	0	13	1	8	0	0

Pitcher and Club	W.	L.	Pct.	ERA.	G.	GS.	CG.	ShO.	GF.	Sv.	IP.	H.	BFP.	R.	ER.	HR.	SH.	SF.	HB.	Tot. BB.	Int. BB.	SO.	WP.	Bk.
Law, Vance, Mtl.	0	0	.000	2.25	3	0	0	0	3	0	4.0	3	16	2	1	0	0	0	0	2	0	0	1	0
Leach, Terry, N.Y.	0	0	.000	2.70	6	0	0	0	1	0	6.2	6	30	3	2	0	0	0	0	3	0	4	0	0
Lefferts, Craig, S.D.*	9	8	.529	3.09	83	0	0	0	36	4	107.2	98	446	41	37	7	9	5	1	44	11	72	1	1
Lerch, Randy, Phil.*	1	1	.500	7.88	4	0	0	0	1	0	8.0	10	42	8	7	0	0	0	0	7	1	5	1	0
Lopez, Aurelio, Hou.	3	3	.500	3.46	45	0	0	0	22	7	78.0	64	321	32	30	6	3	4	0	25	1	44	0	0
Lynch, Edward, N.Y.-Chi.	7	5	.583	3.73	24	13	1	1	3	0	101.1	107	416	48	42	10	5	3	1	23	6	58	0	0
Madden, Michael, Hou.*	1	2	.333	4.08	13	6	0	0	1	0	39.2	47	185	20	18	3	4	1	0	22	3	30	5	0
Maddux, Gregory, Chi.	2	4	.333	5.52	6	5	1	0	1	0	31.0	44	144	20	19	3	1	0	1	11	2	20	2	0
Maddux, Michael, Phil.	3	7	.300	5.42	16	16	0	0	0	0	78.0	88	351	56	47	6	3	3	3	34	4	44	4	2
Mahler, Richard, Atl.	14	18	.438	4.88	39	39	7	1	0	0	237.2	283	1056	139	129	25	10	8	3	95	10	137	5	1
Martinez, J. Dennis, Mtl.	3	6	.333	4.59	19	15	1	1	1	0	98.0	103	416	52	50	11	8	1	3	28	4	63	2	2
Mason, Roger, S.F.	3	4	.429	4.80	11	11	1	0	0	0	60.0	56	262	35	32	5	2	3	3	30	3	43	1	0
Mathews, Gregory, St.L.*	11	8	.579	3.65	23	22	1	0	1	0	145.1	139	591	61	59	15	7	1	2	44	3	67	5	6
McClure, Robert, Mtl.*	2	5	.286	3.02	52	0	0	0	15	6	62.2	53	257	22	21	2	3	2	1	23	2	42	1	1
McCullers, Lance, S.D.	10	10	.500	2.78	70	7	0	0	29	5	136.0	103	550	46	42	12	8	3	4	58	9	92	5	3
McDowell, Roger, N.Y.	14	9	.609	3.02	75	0	0	0	52	22	128.0	107	524	48	43	4	7	3	3	42	5	65	3	3
McGaffigan, Andrew, Mtl.	10	5	.667	2.65	48	14	1	1	8	2	142.2	114	583	49	42	9	10	5	2	55	8	104	5	4
McMurtry, J. Craig, Atl.	1	6	.143	4.74	37	5	0	0	5	0	79.2	82	356	46	42	7	0	2	2	43	5	50	2	0
McWilliams, Larry, Pitt.*	3	11	.214	5.15	49	15	0	0	11	0	122.1	129	545	75	70	16	8	0	7	49	5	80	5	0
Minton, Gregory, S.F.	4	4	.500	3.93	48	0	0	0	28	5	68.2	63	296	35	30	4	7	3	1	34	15	34	3	0
Mitchell, John, N.Y.	0	1	.000	3.60	4	1	0	0	1	0	10.0	10	40	4	4	1	0	0	0	4	0	2	2	0
Montalvo, Rafael, Hou.	0	0	.000	9.00	1	0	0	0	0	0	1.0	1	6	1	1	0	0	0	0	2	0	0	0	0
Moyer, Jamie, Chi.*	7	4	.636	5.05	16	16	1	1	0	0	87.1	107	395	52	49	10	3	3	3	42	1	45	3	3
Mulholland, Terence, S.F.*	1	7	.125	4.94	15	10	0	0	1	0	54.2	51	245	33	30	3	5	1	1	35	2	27	6	0
Murphy, Robert, Cin.*	6	0	1.000	0.72	34	0	0	0	12	1	50.1	26	195	4	4	0	3	3	0	21	2	36	5	0
Myers, Randall, N.Y.*	0	0	.000	4.22	10	0	0	0	5	0	10.2	11	53	5	5	1	0	0	1	9	1	13	0	0
Niedenfuer, Thomas, L.A.	6	6	.500	3.71	60	0	0	0	27	11	80.0	86	345	35	33	11	5	3	1	29	15	55	2	0
Niemann, Randy, N.Y.*	2	3	.400	3.79	31	1	0	0	11	0	35.2	44	158	17	15	2	2	1	0	12	2	18	2	0
Ojeda, Robert, N.Y.*	18	5	.783	2.57	32	30	7	2	1	0	217.1	185	871	72	62	15	10	3	2	52	3	148	2	1
Olwine, Edward, Atl.*	0	0	.000	3.40	37	0	0	0	12	1	47.2	35	189	20	18	5	1	1	1	17	7	37	5	2
Orosco, Jesse, N.Y.*	8	6	.571	2.33	58	0	0	0	40	21	81.0	64	338	23	21	6	2	3	3	35	3	62	2	0
Owchinko, Robert, Mtl.*	1	0	1.000	3.60	3	3	0	0	0	0	15.0	17	62	6	6	1	0	0	0	3	0	6	1	0
Ownbey, Richard, St.L.	1	3	.250	3.80	17	3	0	0	4	0	42.2	47	185	20	18	4	2	2	2	19	0	25	2	0
Palmer, David, Atl.	11	10	.524	3.65	35	35	2	0	0	0	209.2	181	889	98	85	17	4	5	5	102	8	170	9	0
Parrett, Jeffrey, Mtl.	0	1	.000	4.87	12	0	0	0	6	0	20.1	19	91	11	11	3	0	1	0	13	0	21	2	0
Patterson, Bob, Pitt.*	2	3	.400	4.95	11	5	0	0	2	0	36.1	49	159	20	20	0	1	1	0	5	2	20	0	1
Pena, Alejandro, L.A	1	2	.333	4.89	24	10	0	0	6	1	70.0	74	309	40	38	6	3	1	1	30	5	46	1	1
Pena, Hipolito, Pitt.*	0	3	.000	8.64	10	1	0	0	3	1	8.1	7	38	10	8	3	0	0	1	3	1	6	0	0
Perry, W. Patrick, St.L.*	2	3	.400	3.80	46	0	0	0	20	2	68.2	59	288	31	29	5	0	7	0	34	9	29	5	0
Powell, Dennis, L.A.*	2	7	.222	4.27	27	6	0	0	5	0	65.1	65	272	32	31	5	5	2	1	25	7	31	7	2
Power, Ted, Cin.	10	6	.625	3.70	56	10	0	0	30	1	129.0	115	537	59	53	13	9	6	1	52	10	95	5	1
Price, Joseph, Cin.*	1	2	.333	5.40	25	2	0	0	2	0	41.2	49	194	30	25	5	0	5	0	22	2	30	1	0
Puleo, Charles, Atl.	1	2	.333	2.96	5	3	1	0	2	0	24.1	13	97	10	8	4	2	1	1	12	1	18	0	0
Rawley, Shane, Phil.*	11	7	.611	3.54	23	23	7	1	0	0	157.2	166	673	67	62	13	5	2	1	50	4	73	1	1
Reardon, Jeffrey, Mtl.	7	9	.438	3.94	62	0	0	0	48	35	89.0	83	368	42	39	12	9	1	1	26	2	67	0	0
Reuschel, Ricky, Pitt.	9	16	.360	3.96	35	34	4	0	0	0	215.2	232	930	106	95	20	9	10	8	57	2	125	6	1
Reuss, Jerry, L.A.*	2	6	.250	5.84	19	13	0	0	3	1	74.0	96	331	57	48	13	5	0	2	17	4	29	2	0
Reynolds, G. Craig, Hou	0	0	.000	27.00	1	0	0	0	1	0	1.0	3	8	3	3	0	0	0	0	2	0	1	1	0
Rhoden, Richard, Pitt	15	12	.556	2.84	34	34	12	1	0	0	253.2	211	1015	82	80	17	6	5	2	76	8	159	6	4
Riley, George, Mtl*	0	0	.000	4.15	10	0	0	0	4	0	8.2	7	43	4	4	0	0	1	1	8	3	5	0	0

Pitcher and Club	W.	L.	Pct.	ERA.	G.	GS.	CG.	ShO.	GF.	Sv.	IP.	H.	BFP.	R.	ER.	HR.	SH.	SF.	HB.	Tot. BB.	Int. BB.	SO.	WP.	Bk.
Roberge, Bertrand, Mtl	0	4	.000	6.28	21	0	0	0	10	1	28.2	33	128	20	20	2	3	2	1	10	3	20	1	2
Robinson, Don, Pitt	3	4	.429	3.38	50	0	0	0	41	14	69.1	61	295	27	26	5	5	4	2	27	3	53	4	1
Robinson, Jeffrey, S.F.	6	3	.667	3.36	64	1	0	0	22	8	104.1	92	431	46	39	8	1	3	1	32	7	90	11	0
Robinson, Ronald, Cin	10	3	.769	3.24	70	0	0	0	32	14	116.2	110	487	44	42	10	4	3	2	43	8	117	3	0
Rucker, David, Phil*	0	2	.000	5.76	19	0	0	0	5	0	25.0	34	119	19	16	4	2	3	0	14	3	14	2	0
Ruffin, Bruce, Phil*	9	4	.692	2.46	21	21	6	0	0	0	146.1	138	600	53	40	6	2	4	1	44	6	70	0	1
Ruthven, Richard, Chi	0	0	.000	5.06	6	0	0	0	3	0	10.2	12	47	9	6	4	0	0	0	6	0	3	0	0
Ryan, L. Nolan, Hou	12	8	.600	3.34	30	30	1	0	0	0	178.0	119	729	72	66	14	5	4	4	82	5	194	15	0
St. Claire, Randy, Mtl	2	0	1.000	2.37	11	0	0	0	2	1	19.0	13	76	5	5	2	0	0	0	6	1	21	1	0
Sanderson, Scott, Chi	9	11	.450	4.19	37	28	1	1	2	1	169.2	165	697	85	79	21	6	5	2	37	2	124	3	1
Sauver, Richard, Pitt*	0	0	.000	6.00	3	3	0	0	0	0	12.0	17	57	8	8	3	1	0	2	6	0	6	0	2
Schatzeder, Daniel, Mtl-Phil*	6	5	.545	3.26	55	1	0	0	19	2	88.1	81	375	43	32	9	5	3	0	35	9	47	1	0
Scott, Michael, Hou	18	10	.643	2.22	37	37	7	5	0	0	275.1	182	1065	73	68	17	8	6	2	72	6	306	3	0
Sebra, Robert, Mtl	5	5	.500	3.55	17	13	3	1	4	0	91.1	82	377	39	36	9	3	3	3	25	2	66	2	3
Shields, Stephen, Atl	0	0	.000	7.11	6	0	0	0	2	0	12.2	13	55	10	10	4	0	0	0	7	0	6	0	0
Show, Eric, S.D.	9	5	.643	2.97	24	22	2	0	1	0	136.1	109	569	47	45	11	10	1	4	69	4	94	3	2
Sisk, Douglas, N.Y.	4	2	.667	3.06	41	0	0	0	15	1	70.2	77	312	31	24	0	3	0	5	31	5	31	2	1
Smiley, John, Pitt*	1	0	1.000	3.86	12	0	0	0	2	0	11.2	4	42	6	5	2	0	0	0	4	0	9	0	0
Smith, Bryn, Mtl	10	8	.556	3.94	30	30	1	0	0	0	187.1	182	807	101	82	15	10	3	6	63	6	105	4	2
Smith, David, Hou	4	7	.364	2.73	54	0	0	0	51	33	56.0	39	223	17	17	5	4	1	1	22	3	46	2	0
Smith, Lee, Chi	9	9	.500	3.09	66	0	0	0	59	31	90.1	69	372	32	31	7	6	3	0	42	11	93	2	0
Smith, Michael, Cin	0	0	.000	13.50	2	1	0	0	1	0	3.1	7	18	5	5	0	0	0	0	1	0	1	0	0
Smith, Zane, Atl*	8	16	.333	4.05	38	32	3	1	2	1	204.2	209	889	109	92	8	13	6	5	105	6	139	8	0
Soff, Raymond, St.L.	4	2	.667	3.29	30	0	0	0	9	0	38.1	37	162	17	14	4	2	2	0	13	1	22	2	1
Solano, Julio, Hou	3	1	.750	7.59	16	1	0	0	3	0	32.0	39	155	28	27	5	3	1	3	22	2	21	3	1
Soto, Mario, Cin	5	10	.333	4.71	19	19	1	1	0	0	105.0	113	461	61	55	15	6	4	1	46	6	67	3	0
Speck, R. Clifford, Atl	2	1	.667	4.13	13	1	0	0	3	0	28.1	25	123	13	13	2	1	1	1	15	0	21	2	1
Stewart, David, Phil	0	0	.000	6.57	8	0	0	0	2	0	12.1	15	56	9	9	1	0	3	0	4	0	9	1	3
Stoddard, Robert, S.D.	1	0	1.000	2.31	18	0	0	0	5	1	23.1	20	102	7	6	1	1	1	1	11	1	17	2	0
Stoddard, Timothy, S.D.	1	3	.250	3.77	30	0	0	0	9	0	45.1	33	203	20	19	6	4	0	0	34	6	47	2	0
Sutcliffe, Richard, Chi	5	14	.263	4.64	28	27	4	1	0	0	176.2	166	764	92	91	18	6	2	1	96	8	122	13	1
Sutter, H. Bruce, Atl	2	0	1.000	4.34	16	0	0	0	11	3	18.2	17	80	9	9	3	1	0	0	9	2	16	0	0
Tekulve, Kenton, Phil	11	5	.688	2.54	73	0	0	0	34	4	110.0	99	446	35	31	2	4	4	0	25	10	57	3	1
Terry, Scott, Cin	1	2	.333	6.14	28	3	0	0	7	0	55.2	66	258	40	38	8	5	1	0	32	3	32	2	0
Thurmond, Mark, S.D.*	3	7	.300	6.50	17	15	2	1	0	0	70.2	96	328	58	51	7	4	2	0	27	5	32	0	1
Tibbs, Jay, Mtl	7	9	.438	3.97	35	31	3	2	2	0	190.1	181	797	96	84	12	13	4	3	70	3	117	7	2
Toliver, Freddie, Phil	0	2	.000	3.51	5	5	0	0	0	0	25.2	28	112	14	10	0	3	0	0	11	0	20	2	0
Tomlin, David, Mtl*	0	0	.000	5.23	7	0	0	0	6	0	10.1	13	52	8	6	1	2	1	1	7	2	6	1	0
Trout, Steven, Chi*	5	7	.417	4.75	37	25	0	0	3	0	161.0	184	711	88	85	6	9	6	1	78	13	69	6	1
Tudor, John, St.L.*	13	7	.650	2.92	30	30	3	0	0	0	219.0	197	879	81	71	22	9	8	1	53	5	107	2	1
Valdez, Sergio, Mtl	0	4	.000	6.84	5	5	0	0	0	0	25.0	39	120	20	19	2	0	0	1	11	0	20	2	0
Valenzuela, Fernando, L.A.*	21	11	.656	3.14	34	34	20	3	0	0	269.1	226	1102	104	94	18	15	3	1	85	5	242	13	0
Vande Berg, Edward, L.A.*	1	5	.167	3.41	60	0	0	0	29	0	71.1	83	325	32	27	8	4	1	1	33	7	42	1	0
Vosberg, Edward, S.D.*	0	1	.000	6.59	5	3	0	0	0	0	13.2	17	65	11	10	1	0	0	0	9	1	8	0	1
Walk, Robert, Pitt	7	8	.467	3.75	44	15	1	1	7	2	141.2	129	592	66	59	14	6	5	3	64	7	78	12	1
Walter, Gene, S.D.*	2	2	.500	3.86	57	0	0	0	19	1	98.0	89	422	47	42	7	5	3	4	49	7	84	6	0
Ward, R. Duane, Atl	0	1	.000	7.31	10	0	0	0	6	0	16.0	22	73	13	13	2	2	0	0	8	0	8	0	1
Welch, Robert, L.A.	7	13	.350	3.28	33	33	7	3	0	0	235.2	227	981	95	86	14	7	8	7	55	6	183	2	1
Welsh, Christopher, Cin*	6	9	.400	4.78	24	24	1	0	0	0	139.1	163	598	79	74	9	10	4	3	40	4	40	5	0
Whitson, Eddie, S.D.	1	7	.125	5.59	17	12	0	0	0	0	75.2	85	337	48	47	8	2	2	0	37	0	46	1	0

Pitcher and Club	W.	L.	Pct.	ERA.	G.	GS.	CG.	ShO.	GF.	Sv.	IP.	H.	BFP.	R.	ER.	HR.	SH.	SF.	HB.	Tot. BB.	Int. BB.	SO.	WP.	Bk.
Williams, Frank, S.F.	3	1	.750	1.20	36	0	0	0	12	1	52.1	35	194	8	7	0	3	1	4	21	4	33	1	0
Willis, Carl, Cin	1	3	.250	4.47	29	0	0	0	7	0	52.1	54	233	29	26	4	5	1	1	32	9	24	3	1
Winn, James, Pitt	3	5	.375	3.58	50	3	0	0	18	3	88.0	85	377	44	35	9	4	3	2	38	7	70	9	1
Wojna, Edward, S.D.	2	2	.500	3.23	7	7	1	0	0	0	39.0	42	176	19	14	2	2	0	1	16	3	19	0	0
Worrell, Todd, St.L.	9	10	.474	2.08	74	0	0	0	60	36	103.2	86	430	29	24	9	7	6	1	41	16	73	1	0
Youmans, Floyd, Mtl	13	12	.520	3.53	33	32	6	2	1	0	219.0	145	905	93	86	14	6	7	4	118	4	202	10	1

NOTE—Following pitchers combined to pitch shutout games: Atlanta (3)—Johnson and Assenmacher; Johnson and Sutter; Palmer and Garber. Chicago (2)—Moyer, Lynch and Smith; Sanderson, Gumpert and Smith. Cincinnati (2)—Denny and Robinson; Gullickson and Franco. Houston (8)—Ryan and Kerfeld 2; Darwin, Anderson and Kerfeld; Darwin, Lopez, Kerfeld and Smith; Deshaies, Lopez, Kerfeld and Smith; Deshaies and Smith; Ryan and Smith; Scott, DiPino, Kerfeld and Smith. Los Angeles (7)—Honeycutt and Niedenfuer 3; Honeycutt and Howell; Honeycutt, Niedenfuer and Howell; Pena, Diaz, Niedenfuer and Howell; Powell and Howell. Montreal (2)—McGaffigan, McClure and Reardon; Smith and Reardon. New York (4)—Fernandez and McDowell 2; Anderson, J. Mitchell and Myers; Darling and Fernandez. Philadelphia (7)—Carman and Bedrosian 2; Carlton and Tekulve; Carman, Hume and Bedrosian; Freeman and Tekulve; Hudson and Bedrosian; Hume and Tekulve. Pittsburgh (5)—Bielecki, Clements and Winn; Kipper, Walk and Clements; Reuschel, Walk and Winn; Rhoden, Guante, Clements and Winn; Rhoden and Robinson. St. Louis (4)—Burris and Worrell; Conroy and Horton; Mathews and Worrell; Tudor, Horton, Perry and Worrell. San Diego (3)—Dravecky and Walter; Show, Lefferts and Walter; Show, McCullers and Gossage. San Francisco (7)—Blue and Robinson 2; Blue and Garrelts; Carlton, Williams and Berenguer; Downs, M. Davis and Robinson; Krukow and Garrelts; LaCoss and Minton.

PITCHERS WITH TWO OR MORE CLUBS

(Alphabetically Arranged With Pitcher's First Club on Top)

Pitcher and Club	W.	L.	Pct.	ERA.	G.	GS.	CG.	ShO.	GF.	Sv.	IP.	H.	BFP.	R.	ER.	HR.	SH.	SF.	HB.	Tot. BB.	Int. BB.	SO.	WP.	Bk.
Andersen, Phil	0	0	.000	4.26	10	0	0	0	1	0	12.2	19	55	8	6	0	2	1	0	3	0	9	0	0
Andersen, Hou	2	1	.667	2.78	38	0	0	0	7	1	64.2	64	268	22	20	2	8	4	1	23	10	33	1	0
Carlton, Phil	4	8	.333	6.18	16	16	0	0	0	0	83.0	102	393	70	57	15	2	3	0	45	4	62	3	0
Carlton, S.F.	1	3	.250	5.10	6	6	0	0	0	0	30.0	36	140	20	17	4	4	0	1	16	0	18	2	1
DiPino, Hou	1	3	.250	3.57	31	0	0	0	14	3	40.1	27	167	18	16	5	5	1	2	16	1	27	0	0
DiPino, Chi	2	4	.333	5.18	30	0	0	0	12	0	40.0	47	178	27	23	6	4	2	0	14	5	43	3	0
Keough, Chi	2	2	.500	4.97	19	2	0	0	3	0	29.0	36	129	17	16	4	2	0	1	12	2	19	4	2
Keough, Hou	3	2	.600	3.09	10	5	0	0	2	0	35.0	22	143	14	12	5	1	1	1	18	2	25	2	0
Lynch, N.Y.	0	0	.000	0.00	1	0	0	0	0	0	1.2	2	7	0	0	0	0	0	0	0	0	1	0	0
Lynch, Chi	7	5	.583	3.79	23	13	1	1	3	0	99.2	105	409	48	42	10	5	3	1	23	6	57	0	0
Schatzeder, Mtl	3	2	.600	3.20	30	1	0	0	9	1	59.0	53	244	29	21	6	2	2	0	19	2	33	1	0
Schatzeder, Phil	3	3	.500	3.38	25	0	0	0	10	1	29.1	28	131	14	11	3	3	1	0	16	7	14	0	0

1986 N.L. Pitching Against Each Club

ATLANTA—72-89

Pitcher	Chi. W—L	Cin. W—L	Hou. W—L	L.A. W—L	Mtl. W—L	N.Y. W—L	Phil. W—L	Pitt. W—L	St.L. W—L	S.D. W—L	S.F. W—L	Totals W—L
Acker	1—0	0—0	0—4	0—0	0—0	1—0	0—0	0—0	0—2	1—1	0—1	3—8
Alexander	2—0	0—0	1—1	1—0	0—0	0—1	1—1	0—1	0—0	0—0	1—2	6—6
Assenmacher	0—0	1—1	0—0	2—0	0—0	1—1	0—0	2—0	0—0	1—0	0—1	7—3
Dedmon	3—0	0—2	0—0	2—0	0—1	0—0	0—1	0—0	0—0	1—1	0—1	6—6
Garber	0—0	1—1	0—0	0—0	0—1	0—0	0—0	1—0	0—0	2—1	1—2	5—5
Johnson	1—0	0—1	2—0	1—0	0—0	1—1	0—2	0—1	1—0	0—1	0—1	6—7
Mahler	0—1	3—2	0—3	1—3	1—2	0—2	1—1	1—1	3—1	2—0	2—2	14—18
McMurtry	0—0	1—1	0—0	0—1	0—1	0—1	0—2	0—0	0—0	0—0	0—0	1—6
Palmer	2—0	0—1	1—2	1—1	2—0	0—1	1—1	1—2	1—1	1—1	1—0	11—10
Puleo	0—0	0—2	0—0	0—0	0—0	0—0	0—0	0—0	0—0	0—0	1—0	1—2
Smith	0—2	0—1	0—2	1—3	0—2	1—1	1—0	0—1	1—2	3—1	1—1	8—16
Speck	0—0	0—0	1—0	0—0	0—0	0—0	0—0	0—1	0—0	1—0	0—0	2—1
Sutter	0—0	0—0	0—0	1—0	1—0	0—0	0—0	0—0	0—0	0—0	0—0	2—0
Ward	0—0	0—0	0—1	0—0	0—0	0—0	0—0	0—0	0—0	0—0	0—0	0—1
Totals	9—3	6—12	5—13	10—8	4—7	4—8	4—8	5—7	6—6	12—6	7—11	72—89

No Decisions: Olwine, Shields.

CHICAGO—70-90

Pitcher	Atl. W—L	Cin. W—L	Hou. W—L	L.A. W—L	Mtl. W—L	N.Y. W—L	Phil. W—L	Pitt. W—L	St.L. W—L	S.D. W—L	S.F. W—L	Totals W—L
Baller	0—0	0—1	0—1	0—1	0—0	0—0	0—0	0—1	2—0	0—0	0—0	2—4
R. Davis	0—0	0—1	0—0	0—0	0—1	0—0	0—0	0—0	0—0	0—0	0—0	0—2
DiPino	0—0	0—0	0—0	0—1	0—0	0—0	0—2	2—1	0—0	0—0	0—0	2—4
Eckersley	0—2	1—1	0—0	1—1	0—1	2—1	0—1	0—1	0—1	1—1	1—1	6—11
Fontenot	0—0	0—0	0—0	0—0	1—0	1—1	0—1	0—0	1—0	0—3	0—0	3—5
Frazier	0—1	0—0	1—0	0—0	0—1	0—1	0—0	0—0	0—0	0—0	1—1	2—4
Gumpert	0—0	0—0	0—0	0—0	1—0	0—0	0—0	0—0	0—0	1—0	0—0	2—0
Hall	0—0	0—0	0—0	0—0	0—0	1—0	0—1	0—1	0—0	0—0	0—0	1—2
Hoffman	1—0	0—0	1—0	0—1	0—0	0—0	2—0	0—1	1—0	0—0	1—0	6—2
Keough	0—0	0—0	0—0	0—0	0—1	0—0	0—0	0—0	0—1	1—0	1—0	2—2
Lynch	0—1	0—0	1—1	1—0	0—1	0—1	2—0	0—0	2—0	1—0	0—1	7—5
Maddux	0—0	1—0	0—1	0—0	0—1	0—1	1—0	0—1	0—0	0—0	0—0	2—4
Moyer	0—0	1—0	0—1	0—1	2—0	1—0	1—1	1—1	0—0	1—0	0—0	7—4
Sanderson	2—1	0—2	0—1	2—0	0—0	0—3	0—1	3—1	1—1	0—1	1—0	9—11
Smith	0—1	0—0	0—2	1—1	3—2	1—0	2—1	0—1	1—0	0—0	1—1	9—9
Sutcliffe	0—2	2—1	1—0	0—0	1—1	0—2	0—0	0—2	1—3	0—1	0—2	5—14
Trout	0—1	0—1	0—1	1—0	0—1	0—2	1—0	1—0	1—1	1—0	0—0	5—7
Totals	3—9	5—7	4—8	6—6	8—10	6—12	9—8	7—11	10—7	6—6	6—6	70—90

No Decisions: Ruthven.

CINCINNATI—86-76

Pitcher	Atl. W—L	Chi. W—L	Hou. W—L	L.A. W—L	Mtl. W—L	N.Y. W—L	Phil. W—L	Pitt. W—L	St.L. W—L	S.D. W—L	S.F. W—L	Totals W—L
Browning	2—0	4—0	0—5	1—1	1—1	1—1	2—0	1—0	1—2	0—2	1—1	14—13
Denny	2—2	0—0	0—1	1—0	2—0	0—1	0—2	2—0	0—1	1—2	3—1	11—10
Franco	0—1	0—0	1—0	1—3	0—0	1—0	0—1	1—1	0—0	1—0	1—0	6—6
Gullickson	3—1	1—3	0—3	1—1	1—0	1—1	1—0	2—0	3—0	2—0	0—3	15—12
Murphy	2—0	0—0	0—0	1—0	1—0	0—0	0—0	1—0	0—0	1—0	0—0	6—0
Power	1—1	2—1	0—1	0—0	1—0	0—0	1—1	2—0	0—0	2—1	1—1	10—6
Price	0—0	0—0	0—0	0—0	0—0	0—0	0—1	0—0	1—0	0—1	0—0	1—2
Robinson	2—0	0—0	1—0	1—1	1—0	1—1	1—0	1—0	0—0	1—1	1—0	10—3
Soto	0—0	0—0	1—2	0—2	0—2	0—3	1—0	0—1	1—0	1—0	1—0	5—10
Terry	0—0	0—1	0—0	1—0	0—0	0—0	0—0	0—0	0—0	0—0	0—1	1—2
Welsh	0—1	0—0	1—2	2—0	0—1	0—0	1—0	0—0	1—2	0—2	1—1	6—9
Willis	0—0	0—0	0—0	1—0	0—1	0—1	0—0	0—0	0—0	0—0	0—1	1—3
Totals	12—6	7—5	4—14	10—8	7—5	4—8	7—5	10—2	7—5	9—9	9—9	86—76

No Decisions: Butera, Landrum, Smith.

HOUSTON—96-66

Pitcher	Atl. W—L	Chi. W—L	Cin. W—L	L.A. W—L	Mtl. W—L	N.Y. W—L	Phil. W—L	Pitt. W—L	St.L. W—L	S.D. W—L	S.F. W—L	Totals W—L
Andersen	0—1	0—0	1—0	1—0	0—0	0—0	0—0	0—0	0—0	0—0	0—0	2—1
Calhoun	0—0	0—0	0—0	0—0	0—0	0—0	0—0	0—0	1—0	0—0	0—0	1—0
Darwin	1—0	2—1	1—0	0—1	0—0	0—0	0—0	0—0	0—0	0—0	1—0	5—2
Deshaies	3—0	0—0	1—0	2—1	0—0	0—0	0—2	1—1	2—1	2—0	1—0	12—5
DiPino	0—0	0—0	0—0	0—0	1—1	0—1	0—0	0—0	0—0	0—1	0—0	1—3
Hernandez	0—0	0—0	0—1	1—1	0—0	0—0	0—0	0—0	0—0	0—0	1—1	2—3
Keough	1—1	0—0	1—0	0—1	0—0	0—0	0—0	0—0	0—0	0—0	1—0	3—2
Kerfeld	2—0	2—0	0—0	0—1	1—0	1—0	0—0	1—1	2—0	2—0	0—0	11—2
Knepper	3—0	0—1	3—0	0—2	2—1	3—1	0—0	2—2	0—0	2—3	2—2	17—12
Knudson	0—0	0—0	0—0	0—0	0—0	0—1	1—1	0—0	0—0	0—2	0—1	1—5
Lopez	0—0	0—0	0—1	2—0	1—0	0—0	0—0	0—0	0—1	0—0	0—1	3—3

Pitcher	Atl. W—L	Chi. W—L	Cin. W—L	L.A. W—L	Mtl. W—L	N.Y. W—L	Phil. W—L	Pitt. W—L	St.L. W—L	S.D. W—L	S.F. W—L	Totals W—L
Madden	0—0	0—0	1—1	0—0	0—0	0—0	0—0	0—0	0—1	0—0	0—0	1—2
Ryan	2—1	1—0	3—0	1—0	1—0	0—3	2—1	0—1	0—1	0—0	2—1	12—8
Scott	0—2	2—0	3—0	2—1	1—1	0—0	2—1	2—1	1—1	4—1	1—2	18—10
Smith	0—0	0—1	0—1	1—0	1—1	1—1	0—1	0—0	1—0	0—1	0—1	4—7
Solano	1—0	1—1	0—0	0—0	0—0	0—0	1—0	0—0	0—0	0—0	0—0	3—1
Totals	13—5	8—4	14—4	10—8	8—4	5—7	6—6	6—6	7—5	10—8	9—9	96—66

No Decisions: Funk, Montalvo, Reynolds.

LOS ANGELES—73-89

Pitcher	Atl. W—L	Chi. W—L	Cin. W—L	Hou. W—L	Mtl. W—L	N.Y. W—L	Phil. W—L	Pitt. W—L	St.L. W—L	S.D. W—L	S.F. W—L	Totals W—L
Galvez	0—0	0—0	0—0	0—0	0—0	0—0	0—0	0—0	0—0	0—0	0—1	0—1
Hershiser	3—2	1—0	1—2	2—0	1—0	0—2	1—2	2—1	0—2	1—2	2—1	14—14
Holton	0—1	0—0	1—1	0—0	1—0	0—0	0—0	0—0	0—0	0—1	0—0	2—3
Honeycutt	1—1	1—2	1—0	2—1	1—1	0—1	0—0	1—1	2—0	1—1	1—1	11—9
Howell	0—2	2—0	0—0	1—3	1—2	1—0	0—1	0—0	0—0	1—4	0—0	6—12
Niedenfuer	0—0	1—2	3—1	0—0	0—0	1—0	0—0	1—0	0—0	0—1	0—2	6—6
Pena	0—0	0—0	0—1	0—0	0—0	0—0	0—0	0—0	1—0	0—1	0—0	1—2
Powell	0—0	0—0	1—1	0—1	0—0	0—1	0—0	1—0	0—0	0—1	0—3	2—7
Reuss	1—0	0—1	0—0	0—1	0—0	0—2	0—2	0—0	1—0	0—0	0—0	2—6
Valenzuela	1—2	0—0	0—1	3—3	1—1	1—2	4—0	2—1	4—0	2—0	3—1	21—11
Vande Berg	0—1	0—0	1—2	0—0	0—0	0—0	0—1	0—0	0—0	0—1	0—0	1—5
Welch	2—1	1—1	0—1	0—1	0—3	0—1	0—1	1—1	0—2	1—0	2—1	7—13
Totals	8—10	6—6	8—10	8—10	5—7	3—9	5—7	8—4	8—4	6—12	8—10	73—89

No Decisions: Beckwith, Diaz.

MONTREAL—78-83

Pitcher	Atl. W—L	Chi. W—L	Cin. W—L	Hou. W—L	L.A. W—L	N.Y. W—L	Phil. W—L	Pitt. W—L	St.L. W—L	S.D. W—L	S.F. W—L	Totals W—L
Brown	0—0	0—0	0—0	0—0	0—0	0—0	0—1	0—0	0—0	0—0	0—0	0—1
Burke	2—0	2—0	0—1	0—2	0—2	2—0	1—1	0—0	1—0	1—0	0—1	9—7
Hesketh	0—1	0—0	0—0	0—1	2—0	1—0	0—1	2—0	0—2	1—0	0—0	6—5
Martinez	0—0	1—0	0—2	0—1	0—0	0—1	0—1	1—0	1—0	0—1	0—0	3—6
McClure	0—0	0—1	0—0	0—0	0—0	0—2	0—0	0—1	1—0	0—1	1—0	2—5
McGaffigan	0—0	1—0	0—1	0—0	0—0	0—1	4—1	2—0	1—0	0—1	2—1	10—5
Owchinko	0—0	0—0	0—0	0—0	0—0	0—0	0—0	1—0	0—0	0—0	0—0	1—0
Parrett	0—0	0—0	0—0	0—0	0—0	0—0	0—0	0—0	0—0	0—1	0—0	0—1
Reardon	0—0	2—3	0—1	2—1	2—0	0—2	0—0	0—1	1—0	0—0	0—1	7—9
Roberge	0—0	0—0	0—1	0—0	0—0	0—0	0—2	0—0	0—0	0—0	0—1	0—4
St. Claire	0—0	1—0	0—0	0—0	0—0	0—0	0—0	1—0	0—0	0—0	0—0	2—0
Schatzeder	0—1	1—1	0—0	0—0	1—0	0—0	1—0	0—0	0—0	0—0	0—0	3—2
Sebra	0—0	0—0	1—1	0—0	1—1	2—1	0—0	0—1	1—1	0—0	0—0	5—5
Smith	2—1	0—1	2—0	1—0	0—1	2—0	0—0	0—2	1—1	1—1	1—1	10—8
Tibbs	1—1	1—0	1—0	0—1	0—1	0—0	0—1	2—2	2—1	0—2	0—0	7—9
Valdez	0—0	0—1	0—0	0—0	0—0	0—1	0—1	0—0	0—1	0—0	0—0	0—4
Youmans	2—0	1—1	1—0	1—2	1—0	1—2	2—1	2—0	0—3	1—1	1—2	13—12
Totals	7—4	10—8	5—7	4—8	7—5	8—10	8—10	11—7	9—9	4—8	5—7	78—83

No Decisions: Law, Riley, Tomlin.

NEW YORK—108-54

Pitcher	Atl. W—L	Chi. W—L	Cin. W—L	Hou. W—L	L.A. W—L	Mtl. W—L	Phil. W—L	Pitt. W—L	St.L. W—L	S.D. W—L	S.F. W—L	Totals W—L
Aguilera	2—2	1—1	1—0	0—0	1—0	1—0	0—2	3—0	1—1	0—0	0—1	10—7
Anderson	0—0	2—0	0—0	0—0	0—0	0—0	0—0	0—0	0—1	0—0	0—0	2—1
Berenyi	1—0	0—0	0—0	0—0	0—0	0—2	0—0	0—0	0—0	1—0	0—0	2—2
Darling	1—0	2—1	3—0	1—1	2—1	1—1	3—0	1—1	0—0	0—0	1—1	15—6
Fernandez	1—1	1—1	1—0	2—0	2—1	2—0	1—2	3—0	2—0	1—1	0—0	16—6
Gooden	1—0	2—0	0—2	2—0	1—0	2—1	2—1	2—0	2—0	2—0	1—2	17—6
McDowell	1—1	3—1	1—1	0—3	0—0	2—0	1—1	2—0	2—2	1—0	1—0	14—9
J. Mitchell	0—0	0—0	0—0	0—0	0—0	0—0	0—1	0—0	0—0	0—0	0—0	0—1
Niemann	0—0	0—0	0—1	0—0	1—0	0—0	0—1	0—0	1—1	0—0	0—0	2—3
Ojeda	1—0	1—0	2—0	1—1	2—0	0—2	1—1	4—0	3—0	0—0	3—1	18—5
Orosco	0—0	0—1	0—0	1—0	0—1	1—2	0—0	2—0	0—1	3—1	1—0	8—6
Sisk	0—0	0—1	0—0	0—0	0—0	1—0	0—1	0—0	1—0	2—0	0—0	4—2
Totals	8—4	12—6	8—4	7—5	9—3	10—8	8—10	17—1	12—6	10—2	7—5	108—54

No Decisions: Leach, Lynch, Myers.

PHILADELPHIA—86-75

Pitcher	Atl. W—L	Chi. W—L	Cin. W—L	Hou. W—L	L.A. W—L	Mtl. W—L	N.Y. W—L	Pitt. W—L	St.L. W—L	S.D. W—L	S.F. W—L	Totals W—L
Bedrosian	2—0	2—2	1—1	1—0	0—0	0—0	0—0	0—2	2—0	0—1	0—0	8—6
Bittiger	0—0	0—0	0—0	0—0	0—0	0—0	0—0	1—0	0—0	0—1	0—0	1—1
Carlton	0—1	0—1	0—1	0—0	0—0	1—1	0—2	0—1	0—0	1—1	2—0	4—8
Carman	0—0	0—0	1—0	2—0	1—1	1—0	1—1	1—1	0—2	0—0	3—0	10—5
Freeman	0—0	0—0	0—0	0—0	0—0	1—0	1—0	0—0	0—0	0—0	0—0	2—0

Pitcher	Atl. W—L	Chi. W—L	Cin. W—L	Hou. W—L	L.A. W—L	Mtl. W—L	N.Y. W—L	Pitt. W—L	St.L. W—L	S.D. W—L	S.F. W—L	Totals W—L
Gorman	0—0	0—0	0—1	0—0	0—0	0—0	0—0	0—0	0—0	0—0	0—0	0—1
K. Gross	2—1	1—0	0—1	0—2	2—2	1—0	3—2	1—1	1—2	1—1	0—0	12—12
Hudson	0—1	1—1	1—1	1—1	0—0	1—2	1—0	1—1	0—2	1—1	0—0	7—10
Hume	0—0	0—0	1—0	0—0	0—0	0—0	0—1	2—0	1—0	0—0	0—0	4—1
Lerch	0—0	0—0	0—0	0—0	0—0	1—0	0—1	0—0	0—0	0—0	0—0	1—1
Maddux	0—0	0—3	0—0	0—0	0—1	0—1	0—0	1—0	1—2	0—0	1—0	3—7
Rawley	1—1	1—0	0—1	2—2	2—0	2—1	1—1	1—0	0—0	0—0	1—1	11—7
Rucker	0—0	0—0	0—0	0—1	0—0	0—1	0—0	0—0	0—0	0—0	0—0	0—2
Ruffin	2—0	1—1	1—1	0—0	1—0	0—0	2—0	1—0	0—2	1—0	0—0	9—4
Schatzeder	0—0	0—0	0—0	0—0	0—0	2—0	1—0	0—1	0—2	0—0	0—0	3—3
Tekulve	1—0	2—1	0—0	0—0	1—0	0—2	0—0	2—0	1—0	2—1	2—1	11—5
Toliver	0—0	0—0	0—0	0—0	0—1	0—0	0—0	0—0	0—0	0—0	0—1	0—2
Totals	8—4	8—9	5—7	6—6	7—5	10—8	10—8	11—7	6—12	6—6	9—3	86—75

No Decisions: Andersen, Childress, G. Gross, Jackson, Stewart.

PITTSBURGH—64-98

Pitcher	Atl. W—L	Chi. W—L	Cin. W—L	Hou. W—L	L.A. W—L	Mtl. W—L	N.Y. W—L	Phil. W—L	St.L. W—L	S.D. W—L	S.F. W—L	Totals W—L
Bielecki	1—0	0—0	0—3	0—1	1—0	0—2	0—1	1—1	0—1	2—1	1—1	6—11
Clements	0—0	0—0	0—0	0—0	0—0	0—0	0—2	0—0	0—2	0—0	0—0	0—4
DeLeon	0—0	0—0	0—1	1—0	0—1	0—0	0—1	0—0	0—0	0—0	0—0	1—3
Fansler	0—1	0—0	0—0	0—0	0—0	0—0	0—2	0—0	0—0	0—0	0—0	0—3
Guante	0—1	0—0	0—0	0—0	0—1	0—0	0—0	2—0	0—0	3—0	0—0	5—2
Jones	0—0	1—0	1—0	0—0	0—0	0—2	0—0	1—1	0—1	0—0	0—0	3—4
Kipper	1—0	1—0	0—2	0—0	1—1	2—0	0—3	0—1	1—0	0—1	0—0	6—8
Krawczyk	0—0	0—0	0—1	0—0	0—0	0—0	0—0	0—0	0—0	0—0	0—0	0—1
McWilliams	1—0	0—2	0—1	0—0	0—0	0—0	0—2	0—3	1—1	1—0	0—2	3—11
Patterson	0—0	1—0	0—0	0—0	0—1	0—0	0—1	0—0	1—0	0—0	0—1	2—3
H. Pena	0—0	0—2	0—0	0—0	0—0	0—0	0—1	0—0	0—0	0—0	0—0	0—3
Reuschel	2—0	3—0	1—0	0—2	0—2	1—2	0—2	0—2	1—3	1—1	0—2	9—16
Rhoden	0—1	4—1	0—1	3—1	1—0	2—2	1—0	2—2	1—2	0—1	1—1	15—12
Robinson	0—0	1—2	0—1	0—0	0—0	1—1	0—0	0—0	1—0	0—0	0—0	3—4
Smiley	0—0	0—0	0—0	0—0	0—0	1—0	0—0	0—0	0—0	0—0	0—0	1—0
Walk	1—2	0—0	0—0	2—1	1—1	0—1	0—2	1—0	1—0	0—0	1—1	7—8
Winn	1—0	0—0	0—0	0—1	0—1	0—1	0—0	0—1	0—1	1—0	1—0	3—5
Totals	7—5	11—7	2—10	6—6	4—8	7—11	1—17	7—11	7—11	8—4	4—8	64—98

No Decisions: Sauveur.

ST. LOUIS—79-82

Pitcher	Atl. W—L	Chi. W—L	Cin. W—L	Hou. W—L	L.A. W—L	Mtl. W—L	N.Y. W—L	Phil. W—L	Pitt. W—L	S.D. W—L	S.F. W—L	Totals W—L
Bargar	0—0	0—0	0—1	0—0	0—0	0—1	0—0	0—0	0—0	0—0	0—0	0—2
Boever	0—0	0—0	0—0	0—0	0—0	0—1	0—0	0—0	0—0	0—0	0—0	0—1
Burris	1—0	1—0	0—1	0—1	0—0	0—0	0—0	0—1	1—1	0—0	1—1	4—5
Conroy	0—1	0—1	1—1	0—1	1—3	2—0	0—1	0—1	0—1	1—1	0—0	5—11
Cox	1—1	0—2	1—2	1—0	0—1	2—0	0—3	2—0	3—2	1—1	1—1	12—13
Dayley	0—0	0—0	0—0	0—1	0—1	0—0	0—0	0—0	0—0	0—1	0—0	0—3
Forsch	0—2	1—1	3—1	0—1	2—1	1—1	0—2	4—0	1—0	2—0	0—1	14—10
Horton	0—0	0—0	0—0	0—0	0—0	1—1	1—1	0—0	2—0	0—1	0—0	4—3
Kepshire	0—0	0—0	0—0	0—0	0—0	0—1	0—0	0—0	0—0	0—0	0—0	0—1
Mathews	1—0	2—1	0—1	1—1	0—1	1—1	1—1	2—1	1—1	1—0	1—0	11—8
Ownbey	0—0	1—1	0—0	0—0	0—0	0—0	0—0	0—1	0—0	0—0	0—1	1—3
Perry	0—0	0—1	0—0	0—0	0—0	0—1	2—0	0—1	0—0	0—0	0—0	2—3
Soff	1—0	0—1	0—0	1—0	0—0	0—0	0—0	1—0	1—1	0—0	0—0	4—2
Tudor	1—2	2—0	0—0	2—0	1—1	2—1	1—2	1—0	1—0	1—1	1—0	13—7
Worrell	1—0	0—2	0—0	0—2	0—0	0—1	1—2	2—1	1—1	1—0	3—1	9—10
Totals	6—6	7—10	5—7	5—7	4—8	9—9	6—12	12—6	11—7	7—5	7—5	79—82

No Decisions: Earley, Lahti.

SAN DIEGO—74-88

Pitcher	Atl. W—L	Chi. W—L	Cin. W—L	Hou. W—L	L.A. W—L	Mtl. W—L	N.Y. W—L	Phil. W—L	Pitt. W—L	St.L. W—L	S.F. W—L	Totals W—L
Booker	1—0	0—0	0—0	0—0	0—0	0—0	0—0	0—0	0—0	0—0	0—0	1—0
Dravecky	0—2	0—0	0—1	2—1	1—1	2—0	0—1	1—1	1—2	0—1	2—1	9—11
Gossage	0—1	1—1	2—0	0—0	1—0	0—0	1—1	0—1	0—2	0—1	0—0	5—7
Hawkins	0—0	2—0	3—0	1—2	0—1	1—1	1—0	1—1	0—1	0—1	1—1	10—8
Hayward	0—0	0—0	0—0	0—1	0—1	0—0	0—0	0—0	0—0	0—0	0—0	0—2
Hoyt	1—3	1—2	1—0	0—1	1—0	2—1	0—1	0—0	1—0	1—1	0—2	8—11
Jones	0—0	0—0	0—0	1—0	1—0	0—0	0—0	0—0	0—0	0—0	0—0	2—0
LaPoint	0—0	0—0	0—2	0—1	0—0	0—0	0—1	1—0	0—0	0—0	0—0	1—4
Lefferts	0—0	2—1	0—1	2—0	2—0	0—0	0—3	0—1	0—2	1—0	2—0	9—8
McCullers	1—1	0—1	0—1	1—2	4—1	1—0	0—1	1—0	1—1	0—1	1—1	10—10
Show	0—0	0—0	1—0	1—2	1—1	1—0	0—0	1—1	1—0	1—0	2—1	9—5
R. Stoddard	0—0	0—0	0—0	0—0	0—0	0—0	0—0	1—0	0—0	0—0	0—0	1—0
T. Stoddard	0—1	0—0	1—1	0—0	0—0	0—1	0—0	0—0	0—0	0—0	0—0	1—3
Thurmond	1—1	0—1	0—0	0—0	1—1	0—1	0—1	0—0	0—0	1—0	0—2	3—7

Giants righthander Mike Krukow was 4-0 against the New York Mets in 1986, the best record of any pitcher against the league champions last season.

Pitcher	Atl. W—L	Chi. W—L	Cin. W—L	Hou. W—L	L.A. W—L	Mtl. W—L	N.Y. W—L	Phil. W—L	Pitt. W—L	St.L. W—L	S.F. W—L	Totals W—L
Vosberg	0—0	0—0	0—1	0—0	0—0	0—0	0—0	0—0	0—0	0—0	0—0	0—1
Walter	1—1	0—0	0—0	0—0	0—0	0—0	0—1	0—0	0—0	1—0	0—0	2—2
Whitson	0—2	0—0	1—1	0—0	0—0	0—0	0—0	0—1	0—0	0—2	0—1	1—7
Wojna	1—0	0—0	0—1	0—0	0—0	1—0	0—0	0—0	0—0	0—0	0—1	2—2
Totals	6—12	6—6	9—9	8—10	12—6	8—4	2—10	6—6	4—8	5—7	8—10	74—88

No Decisions: Iorg.

SAN FRANCISCO—83-79

Pitcher	Atl. W—L	Chi. W—L	Cin. W—L	Hou. W—L	L.A. W—L	Mtl. W—L	N.Y. W—L	Phil. W—L	Pitt. W—L	St.L. W—L	S.D. W—L	Totals W—L
Berenguer	1—0	0—1	0—0	1—1	0—0	0—0	0—0	0—0	0—0	0—1	0—0	2—3
Blue	2—0	1—0	1—1	2—2	1—1	1—1	0—1	0—1	1—1	0—1	1—1	10—10
Carlton	0—0	0—0	0—1	0—0	0—0	0—0	0—0	0—0	1—1	0—1	0—0	1—3
Davis	0—1	0—1	1—1	2—0	0—0	0—0	0—2	1—0	0—0	0—1	1—1	5—7
Downs	1—1	0—0	1—1	0—0	1—1	1—0	0—1	0—0	0—0	0—0	0—0	4—4
Garrelts	3—1	1—0	0—2	2—0	0—2	2—1	1—0	1—2	1—1	1—0	1—0	13—9
Grant	0—0	0—0	0—0	0—0	0—1	0—0	0—0	0—0	0—0	0—0	0—0	0—1
Krukow	2—0	0—2	1—0	2—2	4—0	1—0	4—0	1—2	2—1	1—1	2—1	20—9
Laskey	0—0	0—0	0—0	0—0	0—0	0—0	0—0	0—0	1—0	0—0	0—1	1—1
LaCoss	0—2	2—1	0—2	0—1	0—2	1—2	0—1	0—1	1—0	3—1	3—0	10—13
Mason	0—0	1—0	0—0	0—1	1—0	0—0	0—1	0—1	1—0	0—1	0—0	3—4
Minton	0—1	1—1	1—0	0—0	2—0	0—0	0—0	0—1	0—0	0—0	0—1	4—4
Mulholland	0—1	0—0	0—1	0—1	0—1	0—0	0—1	0—0	0—0	0—0	1—2	1—7
Robinson	1—0	0—0	2—0	0—1	1—0	1—0	0—0	0—1	0—0	0—0	1—1	6—3
Williams	1—0	0—0	2—0	0—0	0—0	0—1	0—0	0—0	0—0	0—0	0—0	3—1
Totals	11—7	6—6	9—9	9—9	10—8	7—5	5—7	3—9	8—4	5—7	10—8	83—79

No Decisions: Bockus, Gott, Hensley.

AMERICAN LEAGUE

Including

Team Reviews of 1986 Season

Team Day-by-Day Scores

1986 Standings, Home-Away Records

1986 Official A.L. Batting Averages

1986 Official A.L. Fielding Averages

1986 Official A.L. Pitching Averages

1986 Pitching Against Each Club

Boston left fielder Jim Rice managed only 20 home runs, but batted .324 with 200 hits and 110 runs batted in.

Surprising Red Sox Rise in East

By JOE GIULIOTTI

When baseball buffs recall the Boston Red Sox's 1986 season, their first recollection undoubtedly will be of Mookie Wilson's ground ball scooting under Bill Buckner's glove, allowing the winning run to score in Game 6 of the World Series. But such a lasting impression will be unfair to both Buckner and the Red Sox, who had been picked to finish near the bottom of the American League East and yet came within one strike of winning the world championship.

It will be unfair to Buckner, who played heroically on a pair of gimpy ankles. Despite enduring virtually constant pain, the veteran first baseman tallied more at-bats (629) than any of his teammates during the regular season. Buckner also batted .267 with 18 home runs and 102 runs batted in, his second consecutive 100-RBI season.

It also will be unfair to the Red Sox, who effectively dominated baseball's toughest division for most of the season. After moving into sole possession of first place May 15, the Red Sox repulsed challenges from New York, Detroit, Toronto and Baltimore. They survived a 3-10 trip beginning the second half of the season and later all but wrapped up the division title with an 11-game winning streak from August 30 through September 10.

"Every time someone gets close, we turn on the afterburners," second baseman Marty Barrett said in September. "It's like we're sending a message to the league: 'This is our season; don't try and spoil it.' "

Boston finished with a 95-66 record, 5½ games ahead of the New York Yankees, and advanced to the playoffs against California. The Angels won three of the first four games and were one strike away from winning the pennant in Game 5. But center fielder Dave Henderson's dramatic two-out homer in the ninth inning kept the Red Sox alive, and Boston went on to capture its first A.L. flag since 1975 in seven games.

But midnight came for the Cinderella team two weeks later. Boston had the New York Mets on the ropes in Game 6 of the World Series, holding a two-run lead with two out in the bottom of the 10th inning and the bases empty. The next two New York batters singled, but with two strikes on Ray Knight, the Red Sox were one strike away from winning their first world championship since 1918.

Don Baylor hit 31 homers and drove in 94 runs while providing some much-needed leadership in the Red Sox's clubhouse.

Knight also singled, though, to launch a three-run rally that culminated in Wilson's run-scoring grounder between Buckner's legs, tying the Series at three

SCORES OF BOSTON RED SOX' 1986 GAMES

APRIL

			Winner	Loser
7—At Detroit	L	5-6	Morris	Stewart
9—At Detroit	L	5-6†	Hernandez	Stanley
10—At Detroit	W	4-2	Nipper	Petry
11—At Chicago	W	7-2	Clemens	Bannister
12—At Chicago	L	1-3	Seaver	Hurst
13—At Chicago	W	12-2	Lollar	Cowley
14—Kan. City	L	2-8	Leibrandt	Boyd
16—Kan. City	L	0-1	Saberhagen	Nipper
17—Kan. City	W	6-2	Clemens	Gubicza
18—Chicago	W	2-1	Hurst	Seaver
19—Chicago	W	3-2	Boyd	Agosto
20—Chicago	W	6-2	Brown	Bannister
21—Detroit	L	4-5	Terrell	Nipper
22—Detroit	W	6-4	Clemens	Morris
23—Detroit	L	1-3	Tanana	Hurst
25—At Kan. C.	L	0-6	Leibrandt	Boyd
26—At Kan. C.	W	6-1	Nipper	Saberhagen
29—Seattle	W	3-1	Clemens	Moore
30—Seattle	W	9-4	Stewart	Nunez

Won 11, Lost 8

MAY

			Winner	Loser
1—Seattle	W	12-2	Boyd	Swift
2—Oakland	L	1-4	Andujar	Nipper
3—Oakland	W	4-3	Stewart	Codiroli
4—Oakland	W	4-1	Clemens	Langford
5—California	W	3-0	Hurst	Witt
6—California	L	2-6	Forster	Boyd
7—At Seattle	W	11-5	Nipper	Wilcox
8—At Seattle	W	4-2	Brown	Morgan
9—At Oak.	W	9-6†	Stanley	Atherton
10—At Oak.	W	4-2†	Hurst	Ontiveros
11—At Oak.	W	6-5	Boyd	Haas
12—At Calif.	L	1-7	Sutton	Nipper
13—At Calif.	L	4-5	Romanick	Brown
14—At Calif.	W	8-5	Clemens	Bryden
16—Texas	L	1-4	Guzman	Hurst
17—Texas	W	8-2	Boyd	Hough
18—Texas	W	5-4†	Stanley	Harris
19—Minnesota	W	8-7	Sambito	Davis
20—Minnesota	W	17-7	Clemens	Viola
21—Minnesota	W	3-2	Stewart	Portugal
23—At Texas	W	2-1	Boyd	Correa
24—At Texas	L	2-3	Williams	Stanley
25—At Texas	W	7-1	Clemens	Mason
26—At Cleve.	W	5-3	Hurst	Candiotti
27—At Cleve.	W	2-0*	Brown	Heaton
28—At Cleve.	W	13-7	Boyd	Schulze
30—At Minn.	L	5-13	Atherton	Woodward
31—At Minn.	W	7-2	Hurst	Smithson

Won 21, Lost 7

JUNE

			Winner	Loser
1—At Minn.	W	6-3	Clemens	Portugal
2—Cleveland	W	3-1	Boyd	Heaton
3—Cleveland	W	5-1	Brown	Schulze
4—Cleveland	W	6-4	Woodward	Niekro
5—At Milw.	L	5-7	Wegman	Sellers
6—At Milw.	W	3-0	Clemens	Darwin
7—At Milw.	L	0-3	Higuera	Boyd
8—At Milw.	L	3-7	Leary	Brown
9—At Toronto	L	1-5	Stieb	Woodward
10—At Toronto	W	4-3†	Stanley	Eichhorn
11—At Toronto	W	3-2	Clemens	Alexander
13—Milwaukee	W	5-3	Boyd	Higuera
14—Milwaukee	L	0-2	Leary	Brown
15—Milwaukee	L	3-7	Nieves	Sellers
16—At N.Y.	W	10-1	Clemens	Guidry
17—At N.Y.	W	7-6	Stanley	Niekro
18—At N.Y.	W	5-2	Boyd	Shirley
20—Baltimore	L	3-14	Boddicker	Brown
21—Baltimore	W	7-2	Clemens	Dixon
22—Baltimore	L	0-4	Davis	Sellers
23—New York	L	3-11	Fisher	Boyd
24—New York	L	1-8	Rasmussen	Woodward
25—New York	W	5-4	Nipper	Drabek
27—At Balt.	W	5-3	Clemens	Dixon
28—At Balt.	W	7-3	Boyd	Davis
29—At Balt.	W	8-3	Sellers	Boddicker
30— Toronto	W	10-9†	Stanley	Acker

Won 17, Lost 10

JULY

			Winner	Loser
1—Toronto	W	9-7	Seaver	Alexander
2—Toronto	L	2-4	Key	Clemens
3—Toronto	L	5-8	Cerutti	Boyd
4—Seattle	W	6-5	Sellers	Beattie
5—Seattle	L	5-9	Moore	Nipper
6—Seattle	W	7-3	Seaver	Langston
7—Oakland	L	4-6	Stewart	Clemens
8—Oakland	W	8-7	Boyd	Langford
9—Oakland	W	7-6	Sellers	Young
10—California	W	8-7§	Lollar	Cook
11—California	L	0-5	McCaskill	Seaver
12—California	W	3-2	Clemens	Witt
13—California	L	3-12	Candelaria	Sellers
17—At Seattle	L	1-5‡	Ladd	Stanley
18—At Seattle	L	4-10	Moore	Nipper
19—At Seattle	W	9-4	Clemens	Morgan
20—At Seattle	L	5-9	Reed	Sellers
21—At Oak.	L	2-5	Young	Hurst
22—At Oak.	L	2-4	Andujar	Seaver
23—At Oak.	L	2-9	Stewart	Nipper
25—At Calif.	W	8-1	Clemens	Candelaria
26—At Calif.	L	1-4	Witt	Hurst
27—At Calif.	L	0-3	Sutton	Seaver
28—At Chicago	W	3-1	Nipper	Bannister
29—At Chicago	L	1-4	Cowley	Sellers
30—At Chicago	L	2-7	DeLeon	Clemens

Won 10, Lost 16

AUGUST

			Winner	Loser
1—Kan. City	W	5-3	Hurst	Jackson
2—Kan. City	L	2-13	Gubicza	Seaver
3—Kan. City	W	5-3	Nipper	Leibrandt
4—Chicago	L	0-1	DeLeon	Clemens
5—Chicago	L	1-3	Dotson	Boyd
6—Chicago	W	9-0	Hurst	Bannister
8—At Detroit	W	6-1	Seaver	O'Neal
9—At Detroit	W	8-7	Nipper	Tanana
10—At Detroit	W	9-6	Sambito	Campbell
11—At Detroit	L	0-5	Morris	Boyd
12—At Kan. C.	L	1-5	Jackson	Hurst
12—At Kan. C.	L	5-6	Gubicza	Stanley
13—At Kan. C.	W	5-2	Seaver	Leibrandt
14—At Kan. C.	W	11-6	Nipper	Black
15—Detroit	W	8-5	Clemens	Terrell
16—Detroit	L	6-12	Morris	Boyd
17—Detroit	W	7-5	Schiraldi	King
18—At Minn.	W	3-1	Seaver	Viola
19—At Minn.	L	1-5	Portugal	Nipper
20—At Minn.	W	9-1	Clemens	Heaton
21—At Cleve.	W	24-5	Boyd	Swindell
22—At Cleve.	W	6-3	Hurst	Schrom
23—At Cleve.	L	4-5	Camacho	Stanley
24—At Cleve.	L	2-5	Niekro	Nipper
25—At Texas	L	2-4	Mohorcic	Schiraldi
26—At Texas	W	8-1	Boyd	Loynd
27—At Texas	L	1-4	Correa	Hurst
29—Cleveland	L	3-7	Candiotti	Seaver
30—Cleveland	W	7-3	Clemens	Niekro
31—Cleveland	W	4-3	Schiraldi	Wills

Won 17, Lost 13

SEPTEMBER

			Winner	Loser
1—Texas	W	6-4	Hurst	Correa
2—Texas	W	8-6	Stewart	Guzman
3—Texas	W	4-3	Stanley	Mohorcic
5—Minnesota	W	12-2	Clemens	Viola
6—Minnesota	W	3-2	Boyd	Frazier
7—Minnesota	W	9-0	Hurst	Heaton
8—At Balt.	W	9-3‡	Schiraldi	Aase
9—At Balt.	W	7-5	Nipper	Bordi
10—At Balt.	W	9-4	Clemens	Dixon
11—At Balt.	L	6-8	Aase	Crawford
12—At N.Y.	W	7-2	Hurst	Nielsen
13—At N.Y.	L	6-11	Rasmussen	Seaver
14—At N.Y.	L	5-11	Guidry	Nipper
16—Milwaukee	W	2-1	Clemens	Nieves
16—Milwaukee	W	9-3	Schiraldi	Clear
17—Milwaukee	W	4-1	Boyd	Knudson
18—Milwaukee	W	7-1	Hurst	Vuckovich
19—At Toronto	L	4-6	Stieb	Seaver
20—At Toronto	L	2-5	Johnson	Nipper
21—At Toronto	W	3-2	Clemens	Key
23—At Milw.	L	5-8	Leary	Boyd
26—Toronto	L	0-1§	Eichhorn	Schiraldi
27—Toronto	W	2-0	Hurst	Clancy
28—Toronto	W	12-3	Boyd	Ward
29—Baltimore	W	7-5	Nipper	Habyan
30—Baltimore	L	3-6†	Bordi	Stanley

Won 18, Lost 8

OCTOBER

			Winner	Loser
1—Baltimore	W	11-7	Woodward	Arnold
2—New York	L	1-6	Drabek	Hurst
4—New York	L	3-5	Tewksbury	Crawford
4—New York	L	1-3	Rasmussen	Nipper
5—New York	L	0-7	Nielsen	Sellers

Won 1, Lost 4

*6 innings. †10 innings. ‡11 innings. §12 innings.

games apiece. Two nights later, the Mets won Game 7, and New Englanders again were denied a world championship.

But the Red Sox still got farther than anyone had expected, and no one was more responsible for that than Roger Clemens. The A.L. Most Valuable Player and Cy Young Award winner repeatedly put the club back on a winning path, earning 14 victories following a Red Sox defeat.

Clemens, whose 1985 season had ended prematurely when his shoulder required surgery, was brought along slowly in spring training. The righthander proceeded to win his first 14 decisions en route to a 24-4 record, a league-leading 2.48 earned-run average and 238 strikeouts in 254 innings. His 20-strikeout performance April 29 against Seattle established a major league record.

Pitching indeed made the difference for the Red Sox. The Boston staff compiled a 3.93 ERA, the club's best full-season mark since 1978, and walked a league-low 474 batters.

Bruce Hurst may have been the league's best pitcher over the final six weeks. The lefthander won five of his last six decisions to finish 13-8 with a 2.99 ERA, 11 complete games and four shutouts.

The most turbulent member of the rotation was Dennis (Oil Can) Boyd, who was suspended after throwing a tantrum and walking out on the club when he wasn't named to the All-Star team. The righthander also ran into problems with the police and eventually hospitalized himself for testing to clear up whispers of drug involvement. But he bounced back to win a career-high 16 games, going 16-10 with a 3.78 ERA.

Righthander Al Nipper went 10-12 in 26 starts. Boston's most frequent fifth starter was veteran Tom Seaver, who was obtained in a June trade that sent outfielder Steve Lyons to the Chicago White Sox. Seaver, who pitched much better than his 5-7 record indicated, was a big help until a knee injury sidelined him September 19. Rookie Jeff Sellers (3-7) and righthander Mike Brown (4-4 before being sent to Seattle in a multiplayer deal) also were used in the rotation.

A.L. Manager of the Year John McNamara's bullpen was much improved over '85. Bob Stanley (16 saves) and Joe Sambito (12 saves) were McNamara's primary short relievers until Calvin Schiraldi was promoted from Pawtucket (International) after the All-Star break. The 24-year-old righthander became Boston's top stopper while saving nine games, winning four and fashioning a 1.41 ERA.

Long relief was more troublesome for the Red Sox. The top middle reliever was Steve Crawford, who had a 3.92 ERA.

Offensively, Boston had few weak spots. The Red Sox tied for second in the league with a .271 average, led the league with 320 doubles and struck out only 707 times, by far the A.L. low. They were not good baserunners, however, stealing fewer bases (41) than any A.L. team.

Buckner and left fielder Jim Rice were Boston's most consistent clutch hitters. Rice hit only 20 homers—his lowest total ever in a full major league season—but he amassed 200 hits for a .324 average and knocked in 110 runs.

With a .357 average, third baseman Wade Boggs won his third batting title in four years. Boggs also led the league in walks (105) and on-base percentage (.453) and scored a team-high 107 runs.

Marty Barrett was a model of consistency, both at the plate (.286, 60 RBIs and a team-high 15 steals) and at second base (14 errors). Right fielder Dwight Evans smacked 26 homers and drove in 97 runs, while catcher Rich Gedman had 16 homers and 65 RBIs.

Don Baylor, who had been obtained from the Yankees in exchange for Mike Easler before the season, did the job as both a clubhouse leader and the designated hitter. Though he didn't hit for average (.238), Baylor carried the team the first six weeks of the season and wound up with 31 homers and 94 RBIs.

The Red Sox got little production out of their shortstops. Glenn Hoffman was the opening-day starter, but he spent most of the season on the disabled list. Also playing short were rookie Rey Quinones (.237), Ed Romero (.210) and Spike Owen (.183).

Center fielder Tony Armas had his second off year in a row (11 homers, 58 RBIs). When Armas injured his foot in the playoffs, he was replaced by Henderson, who had come to Boston along with Owen in an August trade with Seattle.

Henderson did little to help the Red Sox during the regular season, hitting .196 with only three RBIs in 51 at-bats. But he became an instant hero when he kept the Red Sox alive with his incredible home run in Game 5 of the playoffs.

"When I hit it, I knew it was gone," Henderson said. "I've hit enough homers in my career to know the feeling."

And the feeling that homer created among fans of the Red Sox was one of euphoria, a feeling that persisted even after the Mets ended their dreams of a world championship.

Lefthander Dave Righetti came out of the Yankees bullpen to set a major league record with 46 saves.

Weak Pitching Ruins Yankees

By BILL MADDEN

For all intents and purposes, the New York Yankees' aspirations of joining the New York Mets in a crosstown "Subway Series" were ended March 21. It was on that date in spring training when Yankees Owner George Steinbrenner acknowledged that Britt Burns was suffering from a degenerative hip condition and would miss the entire 1986 season.

So much for the missing cog. The Yankees, who believed after a second-place finish in 1985 that they were one starting pitcher away from winning it all in '86, were thrilled to obtain the lefthander from the Chicago White Sox. The Yankees targeted Burns, an 18-game winner for Chicago in '85, for 18 victories and no less than 200 innings. When Burns went down in spring training, however, the Yankees were back to square one.

Then on March 28, the same day they were trading unhappy designated hitter Don Baylor to the Boston Red Sox for Mike Easler, the Yankees released Phil Niekro, a 16-game winner for New York in each of the previous two years. As it turned out, the Yankees could have used a similar effort from the 47-year-old veteran in '86.

"My starting rotation when spring training opened was supposed to be Ron Guidry, Britt Burns, Joe Niekro, Ed Whitson and Phil Niekro," first-year Manager Lou Piniella said after the season. "How many total wins did we get out of them?"

A whopping 23, four of which were relief wins picked up by Whitson before he finally was traded to the San Diego Padres for middle reliever Tim Stoddard in July.

The only good that came from all this was the emergence of Dennis Rasmussen, who won Burns' spot in the rotation in spring training. The lefthander became the Yankees' ace in '86 with an 18-6 record and a 3.88 earned-run average.

Despite the club's unsettled pitching and the void left by the departure of respected clubhouse leaders Baylor and Niekro, Piniella was able to bring the Yankees out of the starting gate fast. They finished April with a 14-6 mark and on May 25 were 28-15, only half a game behind the American League East-leading Boston Red Sox.

By that time, however, Guidry and Joe Niekro were starting to tumble. After boasting 4-1 and 4-0 records, respectively, on May 10, Guidry and Niekro combined to go 10-21 over the rest of the season.

Mike Pagliarulo carried a big stick and settled into the Yankee third-base job.

The 41-year-old Niekro began to experience shoulder problems and did not pitch after September 6. Guidry, meanwhile,

SCORES OF NEW YORK YANKEES' 1986 GAMES

APRIL			Winner	Loser
8—Kan. City	W	4-2	Guidry	Black
9—Kan. City	L	4-7	Farr	Whitson
10—Kan. City	W	6-5*	Righetti	H'sheimer
11—Milwaukee	W	3-2	Tewksbury	Wegman
12—Milwaukee	W	7-3	Rasmussen	Higuera
13—Milwaukee	W	3-2	Guidry	Cocanower
15—At Cleve.	W	6-2	Niekro	Candiotti
17—At Cleve.	L	4-6	Niekro	Tewksbury
18—At Milw.	L	5-6	Plesac	Fisher
19—At Milw.	L	3-4†	McClure	Scurry
20—At Milw.	W	5-4*	Righetti	Clear
21—At Kan. C.	W	8-4	Whitson	Saberhagen
22—At Kan. C.	W	5-1	Tewksbury	Gubicza
23—At Kan. C.	W	2-1	Rasmussen	Leonard
24—Cleveland	W	2-1	Guidry	Heaton
25—Cleveland	W	10-3	Niekro	Candiotti
26—Cleveland	L	2-3	Schulze	Shirley
27—Cleveland	L	7-9	Bailes	Righetti
29—Minnesota	W	14-11	Whitson	Portugal
30—Minnesota	W	3-2	Niekro	Blyleven

Won 14, Lost 6

MAY			Winner	Loser
1—Minnesota	L	4-7	Agosto	Rasmussen
2—Texas	L	0-7	Correa	Shirley
3—Texas	W	9-4	Tewksbury	Witt
4—Texas	L	3-4	Williams	Guidry
5—At Chicago	W	4-1	Niekro	Dotson
6—At Chicago	W	10-6	Fisher	Dawley
7—At Chicago	W	5-1	John	Bannister
10—At Texas	W	4-3	Guidry	Harris
11—At Texas	L	3-6	Mason	Niekro
11—At Texas	L	1-9	Guzman	Tewksbury
12—At Minn.	W	9-8	Rasmussen	Portugal
13—At Minn.	W	6-4	John	Blyleven
14—Chicago	L	2-3	McKeon	Fisher
15—Chicago	L	1-8	Allen	Guidry
16—Seattle	L	3-7	Langston	Niekro
17—Seattle	W	11-6	Tewksbury	Young
18—Seattle	W	11-3	Rasmussen	Morgan
20—Oakland	L	1-2	Young	Guidry
21—Oakland	W	10-4	Niekro	Plunk
22—Oakland	W	4-3†	Righetti	Howell
23—California	W	10-5	Whitson	Sutton
24—California	W	7-6	Righetti	Moore
25—California	W	8-5	Holland	Corbett
26—California	L	7-8	Witt	Righetti
28—At Seattle	W	6-5	Whitson	Morgan
29—At Seattle	W	2-0	Rasmussen	Wilcox
30—At Oak.	L	3-6	Young	Niekro
31—At Oak.	L	3-4	Ontiveros	Guidry

Won 16, Lost 12

JUNE			Winner	Loser
1—At Oak.	W	7-1	John	Leiper
2—At Calif.	L	7-8	Finley	Righetti
3—At Calif.	L	2-4	Sutton	Rasmussen
4—At Calif.	W	11-0	Niekro	Romanick
6—Baltimore	L	2-5	McGregor	Guidry
7—Baltimore	L	5-7	Boddicker	John
8—Baltimore	L	9-18	Dixon	Whitson
9—At Detroit	W	9-7†	Whitson	Scherrer
10—At Detroit	W	6-3	Niekro	Terrell
11—At Detroit	L	3-9	Tanana	Guidry
12—At Balt.	W	7-5	Fisher	T. Martinez
13—At Balt.	W	3-1	Tewksbury	Davis
14—At Balt.	W	4-2	Rasmussen	McGregor
15—At Balt.	L	3-4	Boddicker	Fisher
16—Boston	L	1-10	Clemens	Guidry
17—Boston	L	6-7	Stanley	Niekro
18—Boston	L	2-5	Boyd	Shirley
19—At Toronto	L	9-10*	Caudill	Righetti
20—At Toronto	W	10-8*	Fisher	Gordon
21—At Toronto	W	4-2*	Righetti	Lamp
22—At Toronto	L	1-15	Key	Niekro
23—At Boston	W	11-3	Fisher	Boyd
24—At Boston	W	8-1	Rasmussen	Woodward
25—At Boston	L	4-5	Nipper	Drabek
27—Toronto	L	7-14	Acker	Fisher
28—Toronto	L	4-7	Key	Niekro
29—Toronto	L	3-6	Cerutti	Fisher
30—Detroit	W	3-2	Rasmussen	Terrell

Won 12, Lost 16

JULY			Winner	Loser
1—Detroit	W	5-4*	Righetti	Hernandez
2—Detroit	L	3-8	LaPoint	Guidry
3—Detroit	W	9-5	Pulido	King
4—At Chicago	L	1-2	Dotson	Tewksbury
5—At Chicago	W	8-0	Rasmussen	Cowley
6—At Chicago	L	2-5	Bannister	Drabek

JULY			Winner	Loser
7—At Texas	W	14-3	Nielsen	Hough
8—At Texas	L	1-6	Mason	Pulido
9—At Texas	W	5-4	Tewksbury	Guzman
10—At Minn.	W	11-1	Rasmussen	Viola
11—At Minn.	W	9-3	Drabek	Heaton
12—At Minn.	W	8-0	Nielsen	Smithson
13—At Minn.	L	0-5	Blyleven	Tewksbury
17—Chicago	W	5-4	Rasmussen	Dotson
18—Chicago	W	8-4	Niekro	Bannister
19—Chicago	L	3-8	Cowley	Nielsen
20—Chicago	L	0-8	Allen	Shirley
21—Texas	W	8-4	Drabek	Witt
22—Texas	W	9-1	Rasmussen	Correa
23—Texas	W	3-2*	Righetti	Hough
25—Minnesota	L	5-9	Heaton	Nielsen
26—Minnesota	L	4-8	Anderson	Drabek
27—Minnesota	W	4-1	Guidry	Blyleven
28—At Milw.	L	4-5	Nieves	Niekro
29—At Milw.	L	4-6	Darwin	Nielsen
30—At Milw.	L	0-5	Higuera	Drabek

Won 14, Lost 12

AUGUST			Winner	Loser
1—At Cleve.	L	3-4	Niekro	Guidry
1—At Cleve.	W	5-3	Fisher	Candiotti
2—At Cleve.	L	5-6*	Noles	Righetti
3—At Cleve.	W	12-8	Scurry	Niekro
4—Milwaukee	L	4-5	Higuera	Drabek
5—Milwaukee	L	1-2*	Plesac	Righetti
6—Milwaukee	W	5-3	Guidry	Nieves
7—Milwaukee	L	2-10	Leary	Niekro
8—Kan. City	W	2-0	John	Leibrandt
9—Kan. City	W	3-2	Fisher	Black
10—Kan. City	L	3-13	Bankhead	Rasmussen
11—Cleveland	W	6-5	Fisher	Wills
12—Cleveland	W	6-4	Stoddard	Yett
13—Cleveland	W	4-0	John	Candiotti
15—At Kan. C.	W	7-4	Drabek	Bankhead
16—At Kan. C.	L	2-4	Jackson	Rasmussen
17—At Kan. C.	L	0-5	Gubicza	Guidry
19—Seattle	L	3-7	Langston	John
20—Seattle	W	5-2	Stoddard	Moore
22—Oakland	W	3-2	Rasmussen	Andujar
23—Oakland	L	1-2	Young	Righetti
24—Oakland	L	4-11	Stewart	Scurry
25—California	L	3-5	Candelaria	Niekro
26—California	L	0-2	Witt	Drabek
28—At Seattle	W	4-2	Rasmussen	Morgan
29—At Seattle	W	13-12	Stoddard	Best
30—At Seattle	L	0-1	Swift	John
30—At Seattle	W	3-0	Niekro	Brown
31—At Seattle	L	2-6	Moore	Drabek

Won 14, Lost 15

SEPTEMBER			Winner	Loser
1—At Oak.	L	8-9	Krueger	Armstrong
2—At Oak.	W	9-8	Fisher	Howell
3—At Oak.	L	3-5	Stewart	Stoddard
5—At Calif.	W	7-4	Drabek	Chadwick
6—At Calif.	L	2-9	Witt	Niekro
7—At Calif.	L	2-7	Sutton	Rasmussen
9—At Toronto	W	3-1	Guidry	Eichhorn
11—At Toronto	W	3-1	Drabek	Key
11—At Toronto	W	7-5	Fisher	Henke
12—Boston	L	2-7	Hurst	Nielsen
13—Boston	W	11-6	Rasmussen	Seaver
14—Boston	W	11-5	Guidry	Nipper
15—Baltimore	W	5-3	Stoddard	Boddicker
16—Baltimore	W	8-1	Drabek	McGregor
17—Baltimore	L	3-8	Bell	Tewksbury
19—At Detroit	L	3-8	Petry	Rasmussen
20—At Detroit	W	5-2	Guidry	Tanana
21—At Detroit	L	1-3	Terrell	Drabek
22—At Balt.	W	4-2	Tewksbury	McGregor
23—At Balt.	W	5-3*	Righetti	Bordi
24—At Balt.	W	4-1	Rasmussen	Flanagan
26—Detroit	L	2-3	Terrell	Guidry
27—Detroit	L	0-1*	Morris	Righetti
28—Detroit	W	10-2	Tewksbury	Kelly
29—Toronto	W	8-1	Rasmussen	Cerutti
30—Toronto	W	5-2	Nielsen	Stieb

Won 16, Lost 10

OCTOBER			Winner	Loser
1—Toronto	L	0-3	Key	Guidry
2—At Boston	W	6-1	Drabek	Hurst
4—At Boston	W	5-3	Tewksbury	Crawford
4—At Boston	W	3-1	Rasmussen	Nipper
5—At Boston	W	7-0	Nielsen	Sellers

Won 4, Lost 1

*10 innings. †11 innings.

missed most of July after being struck on his pitching (left) hand by a line drive and finished the season with his worst record ever (9-12). Though his 3.98 ERA was uncharacteristically high, the Gold Glove winner also was the victim of a lack of support.

By June, however, Piniella could see that pitching wasn't his club's only trouble spot. Two other critical areas, catcher and shortstop, had suddenly become troublesome.

Bobby Meacham, whom Piniella had once predicted "will one day be the shortstop all the others will have to measure up to in this league," collapsed both offensively and defensively and finally was optioned to Columbus (International) in mid-June. Piniella then went through several more shortstops, including Ivan DeJesus, Dale Berra, Mike Fischlin and Paul Zuvella, before finally settling on Wayne Tolleson, who was obtained from the White Sox in a multiplayer trade July 30. Tolleson hit .284 for New York.

At catcher, Butch Wynegar suffered a similar breakdown of skills and eventually was placed on the restricted list after being hospitalized for mental fatigue in early August. Although the Yankees surrendered a solid catcher, Ron Hassey, in the trade for Tolleson, they also got a new catcher, 25-year-old Joel Skinner, in return. Skinner batted .259 in 54 games for the Yankees but was considered more of a long-term prospect than an immediate solution.

Other than Steinbrenner's customary move of firing the pitching coach, which occurred in May when Mark Connor replaced Sammy Ellis, the Yankees did nothing to solve their pitching problems. Forced into a constant patchwork game, Piniella rushed minor leaguers Doug Drabek (7-8) and Scott Nielsen (4-4) into the rotation to replace his injured veterans. And 43-year-old Tommy John made 10 starts. After two months on the disabled list, John finished with a 5-3 record.

Rookie Bob Tewksbury opened the season in the starting rotation but was sent to Columbus in July. The righthander returned in September and finished 9-5 with a 3.31 ERA. Reliever Brian Fisher, who had enjoyed an impressive rookie campaign in '85, went 9-5 with six saves but had a whopping 4.93 ERA.

Despite these problems, the Yankees were only seven games behind the Red Sox at the All-Star break (50-39), and they pulled to within 3½ games August 13. But they won only eight of their next 21 games and slipped to 10½ games back September 7.

At that point, Piniella held a clubhouse meeting and later told reporters: "This club will not quit on me."

The Yankees didn't. They also didn't catch Boston, but they did win 18 of their last 25 games to finish second with a 90-72 mark, 5½ games back.

The Yankees would have finished much lower if not for one of the league's best offenses. They led the league in on-base percentage (.347), tied for second in batting (.271) and ranked third in home runs (188) and fourth in runs scored (797).

Gold Glove first baseman Don Mattingly continued to shine as one of baseball's most outstanding performers. He slugged 31 homers with 113 runs batted in and led the league with 238 hits, 53 doubles and a .573 slugging percentage. He also made a valiant effort to overtake Boston's Wade Boggs, who was sidelined by a hamstring pull, for the A.L. batting title during the Yankees' season-ending, four-game sweep of the Red Sox. He went 8-for-19 but finished with a .352 average, five points behind Boggs.

Right fielder Dave Winfield hit 24 homers and drove in 104 runs to chalk up his fifth straight 100-RBI year. Easler, Baylor's replacement as the DH, was next with 78 RBIs (and a .302 average).

Rickey Henderson again was one of baseball's most versatile performers. The leadoff man stole 87 bases and scored 130 runs, both A.L. highs, and contributed 28 homers and 74 RBIs. The center fielder's batting average dropped 51 points to .263, however, as he became fascinated with the long ball.

Mike Pagliarulo nailed down the third-base job in his second full year in the majors and hit 28 homers with 71 RBIs. Part-time outfielder Dan Pasqua hit 16 homers, and veteran second baseman Willie Randolph hit .276. But Ron Kittle, who was acquired along with Tolleson and Skinner, hit only four homers for the Yankees, while outfielder Claudell Washington, a June acquisition from Atlanta with Zuvella in exchange for veteran Ken Griffey, batted .237.

Perhaps the most extraordinary feat of the year was that of Dave Righetti. Despite the problems with the starting rotation, Righetti was given enough leads to set a major league record with 46 saves.

"It's been a season of a lot of heartbreak," Righetti said after breaking the record shared by Dan Quisenberry and Bruce Sutter, "the biggest being the day the Red Sox clinched the division title. . . . But this has been a great day for me."

Tigers righthander Jack Morris rebounded from a dismal start to record an impressive 21-8 record.

Injuries Quiet Tigers' Roar

By TOM GAGE

Virtually any team that fails to reach its goals can blame injuries to some extent. For the 1986 Detroit Tigers, an elbow, an ankle and a sore back were the major culprits in their second straight third-place finish in the American League East.

Lance Parrish missed the most time. After getting off to an excellent start (22 home runs, 62 runs batted in), the All-Star catcher was sidelined with a chronic back condition and did not play after July 26.

Injuries were old news by then. The season was barely two weeks old when Kirk Gibson went down. The right fielder damaged ligaments in his left ankle April 22 while returning to first base on a pickoff attempt in Boston. He was sidelined until early June.

Dan Petry was the next to go. The righthander underwent arthroscopic surgery to remove bone chips from his elbow June 10. After returning to the starting rotation August 19, Petry won only one more game and finished with a 5-10 record.

"I'm not using injuries as an excuse because other teams have them, too," Manager Sparky Anderson said. "I'm a believer in the theory of 162 games. You are what you are at the end of them. But losing those guys didn't help matters any."

The Tigers never were in serious contention for the division title. They pulled to within 4½ games of the Boston Red Sox on August 7 but got no closer. The Red Sox promptly beat them in five of seven games, and the Tigers were never heard from again. They finished 8½ games back.

But even to climb to within a glimpse of first place after spending much of the first half of the season in last was an accomplishment.

"They never stopped playing hard," Anderson said. "Even when they were 14 down, they played hard. That's all I told them: 'Give it your best and you'll never go home ashamed.' "

The Detroit offense kicked in only sporadically without Gibson, the emotional catalyst of the team, in the lineup. But the Tigers' turnaround could be more directly related to that of Jack Morris. Morris, who gave up four homers in Detroit's season opener—including one to Boston's Dwight Evans on the first pitch of the year—was plagued by severe gopher-ball problems. But the righthander curbed his temper and improved from 7-6 on Independence Day to 21-8 at season's end. In that same span, the Tigers improved from 38-40 to 87-75.

"Through the bad times," Morris said, "I never got down because I relied on experience. I didn't want to sound cocky, but I knew I was too good a pitcher not to turn it around. That's what experience can do for you. I didn't panic; I just waited."

Along the way, Morris compiled a 3.27 earned-run average in 267 innings. He struck out 223 batters and threw 15 complete games and a league-high six shutouts.

Petry's injury forced the Tigers to seek additional pitching help. They found it in rookie Eric King, who was promoted from Nashville (American Association) in May. He quickly worked his way into the starting rotation, where he filled in admirably for Petry, before being returned to the bullpen in September to give Willie Hernandez some late-inning help. The righthander earned the Tigers' season-ending victory in Baltimore to finish 11-4 with a 3.51 ERA.

Anderson started the season with a four-man rotation of Morris, Petry, righthander Walt Terrell (who won 15 games for the second consecutive season) and lefthander Frank Tanana (12-9). The manager called on Dave LaPoint when a fifth starter became necessary in May, but the lefthander was traded to San Diego in July after posting a 5.72 ERA and only three victories in nine decisions. By that time, righthander Randy O'Neal (3-7, 4.33 ERA) already had replaced LaPoint in the rotation.

Mark Thurmond performed well as a middle reliever and spot starter after being obtained in exchange for LaPoint. The lefthander was 4-1 with a 1.92 ERA for Detroit.

Hernandez, the bullpen stopper who had saved 31 games in 1985, saw his save total drop to 24. The former A.L. Most Valuable Player and Cy Young Award winner had a 3.55 ERA, his highest since 1981.

Offensively, the Tigers led the league with 198 homers and ranked third with 798 runs scored. Gibson, despite missing 43 games, sparked the club with his 28 homers, 86 RBIs and 34 stolen bases.

The rest of the outfield, however, made minimal contributions. Pat Sheridan filled in during Gibson's absence and finished with a .237 average. Center fielder

SCORES OF DETROIT TIGERS' 1986 GAMES

APRIL

			Winner	Loser
7—Boston	W	6-5	Morris	Stewart
9—Boston	W	6-5†	Hernandez	Stanley
10—Boston	L	2-4	Nipper	Petry
11—At Cleve.	W	7-2	Terrell	Niekro
12—At Cleve.	L	2-6	Schrom	Morris
13—At Cleve.	L	2-8	Bailes	Tanana
14—At Chicago	W	10-8	Petry	Dotson
16—At Chicago	L	4-10	Bannister	Terrell
17—At Chicago	W	10-6	Morris	Agosto
18—Cleveland	W	6-1	Tanana	Schrom
19—Cleveland	L	6-8	Bailes	Petry
21—At Boston	W	5-4	Terrell	Nipper
22—At Boston	L	4-6	Clemens	Morris
23—At Boston	W	3-1	Tanana	Hurst
25—Chicago	L	7-9	Nelson	O'Neal
26—Chicago	L	4-5‡	James	Campbell
27—Chicago	W	4-1	Morris	Davis
29—Kan. City	W	2-1	Tanana	Leonard
30—Kan. City	L	3-7	Leibrandt	Hernandez

Won 10, Lost 9

MAY

			Winner	Loser
2—Minnesota	L	1-10	Smithson	Morris
3—Minnesota	W	7-4	Terrell	Butcher
4—Minnesota	W	4-1	Tanana	Blyleven
5—At Texas	W	10-3	Petry	Guzman
6—At Texas	L	2-4	Hough	LaPoint
7—At Texas	L	1-2	Henry	Morris
9—At Minn.	L	7-8	Blyleven	O'Neal
10—At Minn.	L	2-12	Viola	Tanana
11—At Minn.	W	4-1	Petry	Smithson
12—At Kan. C.	L	5-6	Jackson	LaPoint
13—At Kan. C.	L	2-4‡	Farr	Hernandez
14—Texas	W	8-2	Terrell	Witt
15—Texas	L	1-8	Mason	Tanana
16—California	L	1-11	Witt	Petry
17—California	W	10-4	LaPoint	Slaton
20—Seattle	W	12-0	Terrell	Moore
21—Seattle	W	6-4	King	Langston
22—Seattle	L	3-5	Young	Petry
23—Oakland	L	1-5	Rijo	LaPoint
24—Oakland	W	4-1	Morris	Codiroli
25—Oakland	W	2-1	Terrell	Young
26—Oakland	W	5-4†	Hernandez	Howell
28—At Calif.	W	4-1	Petry	Slaton
29—At Calif.	W	7-4	LaPoint	Sutton
30—At Seattle	L	7-8§	Huismann	Cary
31—At Seattle	L	4-7	Langston	Terrell

Won 13, Lost 13

JUNE

			Winner	Loser
1—At Seattle	L	1-9	Swift	Tanana
2—At Oak.	L	1-7	Codiroli	Petry
3—At Oak.	L	4-6	Young	LaPoint
4—At Oak.	W	8-5	Morris	Plunk
6—Toronto	L	2-12	Alexander	Terrell
7—Toronto	W	2-1	Tanana	Key
8—Toronto	L	2-4	Eichhorn	O'Neal
9—New York	L	7-9‡	Whitson	Scherrer
10—New York	L	3-6	Niekro	Terrell
11—New York	W	9-3	Tanana	Guidry
12—At Toronto	L	0-9*	Key	LaPoint
13—At Toronto	W	10-4	King	Clancy
14—At Toronto	L	5-6	Henke	Hernandez
15—At Toronto	L	6-9	Lamp	Cary
16—At Balt.	W	5-4	Tanana	Dixon
17—At Balt.	W	6-3	O'Neal	Davis
18—At Balt.	W	6-1	King	McGregor
19—At Balt.	W	7-5	Morris	Aase
20—At Milw.	L	0-1	Leary	Terrell
21—At Milw.	W	4-3	Campbell	Clear
22—At Milw.	L	4-5	Gibson	LaPoint
24—Baltimore	L	1-2†	Aase	Campbell
25—Baltimore	W	11-2	Morris	Boddicker
26—Baltimore	W	8-3	Terrell	Flanagan
27—Milwaukee	W	4-2‡	Hernandez	Plesac
28—Milwaukee	W	8-5	Campbell	Gibson
29—Milwaukee	W	9-5	King	Darwin
29—Milwaukee	L	1-3	Higuera	Morris
30—At N.Y.	L	2-3	Rasmussen	Terrell

Won 14, Lost 15

JULY

			Winner	Loser
1—At N.Y.	L	4-5†	Righetti	Hernandez
2—At N.Y.	W	8-3	LaPoint	Guidry
3—At N.Y.	L	5-9	Pulido	King
4—At Texas	L	1-2	Guzman	Morris
5—At Texas	L	3-9	Correa	Terrell
6—At Texas	W	5-2	Tanana	Witt
7—At Minn.	L	8-10	Smithson	O'Neal
8—At Minn.	W	5-1	King	Blyleven
9—At Minn.	W	7-0	Morris	Anderson
11—At Kan. C.	L	3-4	Farr	Terrell
11—At Kan. C.	W	8-7‡	Hernandez	Gubicza
12—At Kan. C.	L	4-7	Leibrandt	King
13—At Kan. C.	W	5-0	Morris	Bankhead
17—Texas	W	2-1	Terrell	Williams
18—Texas	W	5-0	Morris	Mason
19—Texas	W	5-3§	Hernandez	Harris
20—Texas	W	4-0	King	Guzman
21—Minnesota	L	0-1	Viola	Thurmond
22—Minnesota	W	3-0	Terrell	Blyleven
23—Minnesota	W	12-2	Morris	Anderson
24—Kan. City	L	0-1	Bankhead	O'Neal
25—Kan. City	W	9-2	King	Leonard
26—Kan. City	W	4-3‡	Hernandez	Farr
27—Kan. City	L	4-5	Saberhagen	Hernandez
28—At Cleve.	W	5-1	Morris	Schrom
29—At Cleve.	W	6-3‡	Hernandez	Oelkers
30—At Cleve.	W	11-3	King	Butcher
31—At Cleve.	L	7-8	Bailes	Campbell

Won 17, Lost 11

AUGUST

			Winner	Loser
1—At Chicago	W	5-4	Terrell	Dotson
2—At Chicago	L	3-5	Bannister	Morris
3—At Chicago	L	1-10	Cowley	O'Neal
5—Cleveland	W	6-5	Thurmond	Bailes
5—Cleveland	W	11-9	Tanana	Butcher
7—Cleveland	W	15-1	Morris	Niekro
7—Cleveland	W	6-2	Thurmond	Schrom
8—Boston	L	1-6	Seaver	O'Neal
9—Boston	L	7-8	Nipper	Tanana
10—Boston	L	6-9	Sambito	Campbell
11—Boston	W	5-0	Morris	Boyd
12—Chicago	W	7-3	Thurmond	Carlton
13—Chicago	W	5-2	O'Neal	Cowley
14—Chicago	L	2-8	DeLeon	Tanana
15—At Boston	L	5-8	Clemens	Terrell
16—At Boston	W	12-6	Morris	Boyd
17—At Boston	L	5-7	Schiraldi	King
19—California	L	2-5	McCaskill	Petry
19—California	W	8-3	O'Neal	Ruhle
20—California	W	3-0	Terrell	Candelaria
21—California	L	1-6	Witt	Morris
22—Seattle	W	4-1	King	Morgan
23—Seattle	W	14-0	Tanana	Brown
24—Seattle	L	1-3	Langston	Petry
25—Oakland	L	4-8	Rijo	Terrell
26—Oakland	W	8-7	Thurmond	Von Ohlen
28—At Calif.	L	2-4	Sutton	King
29—At Calif.	L	12-13	Corbett	Hernandez
30—At Calif.	L	4-5	Lucas	Campbell
31—At Calif.	L	3-5	Moore	Terrell

Won 14, Lost 16

SEPTEMBER

			Winner	Loser
1—At Seattle	W	6-5	Morris	Morgan
2—At Seattle	W	7-5	Campbell	Guetterman
3—At Seattle	L	2-3	Trujillo	Kelly
5—At Oak.	W	9-4	Cary	Von Ohlen
6—At Oak.	L	4-5†	Andujar	Campbell
7—At Oak.	L	4-8	Young	Petry
9—Milwaukee	L	1-3	Higuera	Tanana
10—Milwaukee	W	11-7	Terrell	Bosio
11—Milwaukee	W	8-0	Morris	Nieves
12—Baltimore	W	5-3	King	McGregor
13—Baltimore	W	7-2	Hernandez	Flanagan
14—Baltimore	W	7-0	Tanana	Habyan
16—At Toronto	L	4-6	Key	Terrell
17—At Toronto	W	8-6	Morris	Clancy
19—New York	W	8-3	Petry	Rasmussen
20—New York	L	2-5	Guidry	Tanana
21—New York	W	3-1	Terrell	Drabek
22—Toronto	W	2-1	Morris	Clancy
23—Toronto	L	3-6	Eichhorn	Hernandez
24—Toronto	L	2-8	Stieb	Petry
25—Toronto	L	2-4	Johnson	Tanana
26—At N.Y.	W	3-2	Terrell	Guidry
27—At N.Y.	W	1-0†	Morris	Righetti
28—At N.Y.	L	2-10	Tewksbury	Kelly
30—At Milw.	L	0-5	Leary	Petry

Won 14, Lost 11

OCTOBER

			Winner	Loser
1—At Milw.	W	2-1	Tanana	Higuera
2—At Milw.	W	2-1	Morris	Vuckovich
3—At Balt.	W	6-3	Terrell	McGregor
4—At Balt.	W	11-4	Kelly	Bell
5—At Balt.	W	6-3	King	Arnold

Won 5, Lost 0

*7 innings. †10 innings. ‡11 innings. §12 innings.

When Kirk Gibson had to be helped from the field in April with an ankle injury, the Tigers' pennant hopes quickly faded.

Chet Lemon hit .251 with only 53 RBIs, while Dave Collins and Larry Herndon combined for only 64 RBIs.

The Detroit infield, led by shortstop Alan Trammell, was far more productive. Trammell enjoyed his best all-around season, batting .277 with 107 runs and career highs in homers (21) and RBIs (75).

The biggest surprise was Darnell Coles. Acquired in the off-season from Seattle, Coles laid claim to the third-base job and finished with a .273 average, 20 homers and 86 RBIs, tying Gibson for the team high.

First baseman Darrell Evans hit 29 homers and knocked in 85 runs, while second baseman Lou Whitaker had 20 homers and 73 RBIs. With Parrish's 22 homers, the Tigers could boast that their entire infield, plus the catcher, had hit at least 20 homers apiece.

At age 38, designated hitter John Grubb had his best season, hitting .333 with 13 homers and 51 RBIs in just 210 at-bats. Also contributing in part-time roles were infielder Tom Brookens (.270) and catcher Dwight Lowry (.307).

In addition to their potent offensive attack, the Tigers were much improved in the field. After making 143 errors in '85, they committed only 108 miscues, the third-lowest total in the league.

"I'm not ashamed of this team," Trammell said. "To go through what we went through and win as many games as we did was proof that we never gave up. It's good to finish one year looking forward to the next."

Flashy Toronto shortstop Tony Fernandez committed only 13 errors and led the Blue Jays with a .310 average.

Jays Cannot Repeat '85 Magic

By NEIL MacCARL

In climbing from also-ran status to champions of the American League East in 1985, the Toronto Blue Jays relied primarily on their starting pitching. But when they tumbled to fourth place in 1986, pitching proved to be their downfall.

"In some ways, it was a frustrating year," General Manager Pat Gillick said. "We got some overall performance out of areas that we weren't counting on, but we didn't get consistent performances out of some areas that we were counting on."

While first-year Manager Jimy Williams and Gillick had faith in their club's ability to score runs, they were even more sure of their pitching staff, which had paced the league with a 3.29 earned-run average in '85. The central figures in the rotation were righthanders Dave Stieb and Doyle Alexander and lefthander Jimmy Key.

But all three starters fell short of expectations, and the result was a 4.08 staff ERA, No. 7 in the league.

Stieb, the league's ERA champion in 1985, lost his first six decisions and failed to win a game until May 30. But after a brief demotion to the bullpen, he came on to win five of his last seven decisions and finished 7-12 with a 4.74 ERA.

Key got off to a terrible start. He failed to win in his first six games as his ERA rose to 13.27. But he finished the season with a string of 19⅓ scoreless innings to get his ERA down to 3.57. His 14 wins (against 11 losses) tied for the club lead.

Alexander, who had won 17 games in each of the two previous seasons, was 3-1 in April but failed to win a game in May. The club finally satisfied the disgruntled veteran's wish to be traded by sending him to the Atlanta Braves in early July.

Some key relievers also were a disappointment. "We didn't get as much from Bill Caudill and Dennis Lamp as we expected," Gillick said.

Lamp, who had an 11-0 record in long relief in 1985, slipped to 2-6 with a 5.05 ERA. Caudill, who underwent a rigorous off-season weight-reduction program and shed 23 pounds before reporting to spring training, started the season on the disabled list because of a tender shoulder. And for the second year in a row Caudill failed to produce, finishing 2-4 with a 6.19 ERA and two saves.

The Blue Jays were plagued by other injuries as well. Reliever Gary Lavelle and starter Tom Filer, who was 7-0 in nine starts in 1985, both had recurrences of elbow problems in spring training. Surgery sidelined them for the season.

Catcher Buck Martinez made a remarkable recovery from a serious leg fracture in 1985 and won his job back. But he batted only .181 and was released at the end of the season.

Ernie Whitt, who did the bulk of the catching, had a back problem that put him on the disabled list in April, and it took him nearly two months to regain his effectiveness. He finished with a .268 average, 16 home runs and 56 runs batted in.

Veteran Cliff Johnson outhit virtually the entire Toronto designated-hitting squad from 1985, but by mid-July he was having problems with his right hand, causing a second-half slump. Johnson finished with 15 homers and 55 RBIs.

Center fielder Lloyd Moseby hit a career-high 21 homers, knocked in 86 runs and stole a team-high 32 bases, but his average dropped in the second half when he encountered back problems. Second baseman Damaso Garcia (.281) was hampered by tendinitis in his right shoulder.

In addition, the Blue Jays suffered from a lack of production from the infield corners. The third-base platoon of Garth Iorg and Rance Mulliniks knocked in 89 runs but slugged only 14 homers, while first baseman Willie Upshaw contributed only nine homers and 60 RBIs.

But not everything went wrong for Williams, who succeeded Bobby Cox when the latter jumped from the Toronto dugout to the Braves' front office.

Three pitchers who did not figure seriously in Williams' plans at the start of spring training received credit for 30 of Toronto's 86 victories.

Mark Eichhorn, a rookie reliever with an unusual sidearm delivery, was a non-roster player in spring training. The righthander got a chance when Caudill was injured and quickly amazed everybody with his sinker and a baffling changeup.

"I've never seen anybody throw that slow," said veteran Dusty Baker of the Oakland A's.

Eichhorn went 14-6 with 10 saves and 166 strikeouts in 157 innings. His nifty 1.72 ERA was by far the best of any A.L. hurler with more than 60 innings pitched, but he was five innings shy of qualifying for the ERA crown.

Eichhorn often gave righthander Tom

SCORES OF TORONTO BLUE JAYS' 1986 GAMES

APRIL			Winner	Loser
8—At Texas	L	3-6	Guzman	Stieb
9—At Texas	W	3-1	Alexander	Correa
10—At Texas	W	11-10	Henke	Harris
11—At Kan. C.	W	6-2	Clancy	Gubicza
12—At Kan. C.	L	0-1	Leonard	Acker
13—At Kan. C.	L	4-7	Black	Stieb
14—Baltimore	L	1-2	Boddicker	Alexander
17—Baltimore	L	3-5	Flanagan	Key
17—Baltimore	W	7-4	Henke	T. Martinez
18—Kan. City	L	4-6	Leonard	Stieb
19—Kan. City	W	6-5	Alexander	Black
20—Kan. City	L	4-6	Leibrandt	Lamp
21—Texas	W	7-6	Eichhorn	Harris
22—Texas	L	1-10	Witt	Clancy
23—Texas	L	8-9	Williams	Lamp
25—At Balt.	W	2-1†	Eichhorn	Aase
26—At Balt.	L	5-11	Havens	Henke
27—At Balt.	W	8-0	Clancy	Dixon
29—California	L	3-4	Forster	Eichhorn
30—California	W	6-4	Alexander	Moore

Won 9, Lost 11

MAY			Winner	Loser
1—California	L	4-7	Slaton	Key
2—Seattle	L	2-3‡	Ladd	Eichhorn
3—Seattle	L	2-4	Morgan	Acker
4—Seattle	W	3-2	Henke	Moore
5—Oakland	W	10-6	Eichhorn	Krueger
6—Oakland	L	3-17	Haas	Key
7—At Calif.	L	2-6	Sutton	Clancy
8—At Calif.	W	7-6	Eichhorn	Forster
9—At Seattle	L	3-13	Moore	Stieb
10—At Seattle	L	7-8‡	Ladd	Henke
11—At Seattle	W	4-3	Key	Swift
12—At Oak.	W	5-3	Clancy	Andujar
13—At Oak.	L	3-6†	Mooneyham	Lamp
14—At Oak.	L	4-9	Young	Stieb
16—Cleveland	W	7-6	Acker	Candiotti
17—Cleveland	W	11-5	Key	Heaton
18—Cleveland	W	10-2	Clancy	Schulze
19—Cleveland	L	4-6	Niekro	Stieb
20—At Chicago	L	1-2	Davis	Cerutti
21—At Chicago	L	4-5	Nelson	Acker
22—At Chicago	W	5-0	Key	Dotson
23—At Cleve.	L	1-3	Schulze	Clancy
24—At Cleve.	W	9-6	Lamp	Easterly
25—At Cleve.	W	8-1	Cerutti	Schrom
26—At Minn.	L	1-9	Portugal	Alexander
27—At Minn.	L	6-7‡	Pastore	Henke
28—At Minn.	W	14-8	Clancy	Blyleven
30—Chicago	W	6-0	Stieb	Davis
31—Chicago	W	4-3‡	Henke	Nelson

Won 14, Lost 15

JUNE			Winner	Loser
1—Chicago	L	4-6	Dotson	Key
2—Minnesota	W	3-1	Clancy	Blyleven
3—Minnesota	W	6-5	Eichhorn	Atherton
4—Minnesota	L	4-10	Viola	Stieb
6—At Detroit	W	12-2	Alexander	Terrell
7—At Detroit	L	1-2	Tanana	Key
8—At Detroit	W	4-2	Eichhorn	O'Neal
9—Boston	W	5-1	Stieb	Woodward
10—Boston	L	3-4†	Stanley	Eichhorn
11—Boston	L	2-3	Clemens	Alexander
12—Detroit	W	9-0*	Key	LaPoint
13—Detroit	L	4-10	King	Clancy
14—Detroit	W	6-5	Henke	Hernandez
15—Detroit	W	9-6	Lamp	Cary
16—At Milw.	W	9-2	Alexander	Wegman
17—At Milw.	W	2-1§	Henke	Plesac
18—At Milw.	L	1-3	Higuera	Clancy
19—New York	W	10-9†	Caudill	Righetti
20—New York	L	8-10†	Fisher	Gordon
21—New York	L	2-4†	Righetti	Lamp
22—New York	W	15-1	Key	Niekro
23—Milwaukee	L	3-5	Darwin	Stieb
24—Milwaukee	W	8-0	Cerutti	Higuera
25—Milwaukee	W	5-1	Clancy	Leary
27—At N.Y.	W	14-7	Acker	Fisher
28—At N.Y.	W	7-4	Key	Niekro
29—At N.Y.	W	6-3	Cerutti	Fisher
30—At Boston	L	9-10†	Stanley	Acker

Won 17, Lost 11

JULY			Winner	Loser
1—At Boston	L	7-9	Seaver	Alexander
2—At Boston	W	4-2	Key	Clemens
3—At Boston	W	8-5	Cerutti	Boyd
4—California	L	1-9	Sutton	Stieb
5—California	W	7-3	Clancy	Romanick

JULY			Winner	Loser
6—California	L	2-8	McCaskill	Lamp
7—Seattle	W	7-5	Key	Morgan
8—Seattle	L	5-8	Huismann	Cerutti
9—Seattle	W	6-5	Caudill	Moore
10—Oakland	W	8-4	Clancy	Plunk
11—Oakland	W	6-5	Eichhorn	Rijo
12—Oakland	L	3-5	Stewart	Key
13—Oakland	L	5-10	Young	Caudill
17—At Calif.	W	8-5	Key	Sutton
18—At Calif.	W	2-0	Clancy	McCaskill
19—At Calif.	L	3-9	Candelaria	Stieb
20—At Calif.	W	6-3†	Henke	Corbett
21—At Seattle	W	8-3	Cerutti	Huismann
22—At Seattle	L	7-8§	Reed	Caudill
23—At Seattle	W	6-2	Clancy	Moore
25—At Oak.	L	5-6†	Bair	Caudill
26—At Oak.	L	0-2	Plunk	Cerutti
27—At Oak.	L	0-1y	Leiper	Clarke
28—At Kan. C.	W	6-0	Clancy	Leibrandt
29—At Kan. C.	W	5-2	Stieb	Bankhead
30—At Kan. C.	W	7-2	Johnson	Leonard

Won 15, Lost 11

AUGUST			Winner	Loser
1—Baltimore	L	3-7	Dixon	Key
2—Baltimore	L	2-5	McGregor	Clancy
3—Baltimore	W	6-4	Cerutti	Flanagan
4—Baltimore	L	2-12	Boddicker	Johnson
5—Kan. City	L	6-8	Bankhead	Lamp
6—Kan. City	W	8-0	Key	Jackson
7—Kan. City	W	5-4	Eichhorn	Farr
8—At Texas	L	7-9	Harris	Eichhorn
9—At Texas	L	6-7†	Harris	Caudill
10—At Texas	W	8-7†	Eichhorn	Williams
11—At Balt.	L	1-3	Flanagan	Key
12—At Balt.	W	3-0	Clancy	McGregor
13—At Balt.	L	6-7x	Aase	Aquino
15—Texas	W	6-1	Johnson	Correa
16—Texas	W	13-1	Key	Hough
17—Texas	W	8-7‡	Eichhorn	Russell
19—Chicago	W	5-1	Stieb	Cowley
20—Chicago	W	4-1	Johnson	DeLeon
21—Chicago	L	3-4	Schmidt	Key
22—At Minn.	L	3-4	Blyleven	Clancy
23—At Minn.	W	7-4	Cerutti	Smithson
24—At Minn.	W	7-5†	Henke	Atherton
26—At Cleve.	T	6-6	.....	......
27—At Cleve.	W	3-2§	Eichhorn	Oelkers
27—At Cleve.	W	6-3	Cerutti	Wills
28—At Cleve.	W	9-1	Clancy	Schrom
29—Minnesota	W	6-5	Eichhorn	Atherton
30—Minnesota	W	8-1	Johnson	Viola
31—Minnesota	W	7-5	Aquino	Anderson

Won 18, Lost 10, Tied 1

SEPTEMBER			Winner	Loser
1—Cleveland	W	5-4	Henke	Camacho
2—Cleveland	L	5-9	Schrom	Clancy
3—Cleveland	W	3-1	Stieb	Candiotti
5—At Chicago	L	0-5	Dotson	Johnson
6—At Chicago	W	4-0	Key	Bannister
7—At Chicago	L	3-4	Nelson	Clancy
9—New York	L	1-3	Guidry	Eichhorn
11—New York	L	1-3	Drabek	Key
11—New York	L	5-7	Fisher	Henke
12—At Milw.	L	1-4	Johnson	Clancy
13—At Milw.	W	7-1	Johnson	Vuckovich
14—At Milw.	L	0-5	Higuera	Stieb
15—At Milw.	W	5-2	Cerutti	Wegman
16—Detroit	W	6-4	Key	Terrell
17—Detroit	L	6-8	Morris	Clancy
19—Boston	W	6-4	Stieb	Seaver
20—Boston	W	5-2	Johnson	Nipper
21—Boston	L	2-3	Clemens	Key
22—At Detroit	L	1-2	Morris	Clancy
23—At Detroit	W	6-3	Eichhorn	Hernandez
24—At Detroit	W	8-2	Stieb	Petry
25—At Detroit	W	4-2	Johnson	Tanana
26—At Boston	W	1-0§	Eichhorn	Schiraldi
27—At Boston	L	0-2	Hurst	Clancy
28—At Boston	L	3-12	Boyd	Ward
29—At N.Y.	L	1-8	Rasmussen	Cerutti
30—At N.Y.	L	2-5	Nielsen	Stieb

Won 12, Lost 15

OCTOBER			Winner	Loser
1—At N.Y.	W	3-0	Key	Guidry
3—Milwaukee	L	1-4	Wegman	Clancy
5—Milwaukee	L	1-2	Leary	Henke
5—Milwaukee	L	3-4	Nieves	Eichhorn

Won 1, Lost 3

*7 innings. †10 innings. ‡11 innings. §12 innings. x13 innings. y15 innings.

Sidearmer Mark Eichhorn made the most of his opportunity with the Blue Jays, producing a 14-6 record with a sparkling 1.72 earned-run average.

Henke, Toronto's primary closer, a late-inning lead to protect. Henke logged a 9-5 record, a 3.35 ERA and a team-record 27 saves.

"Overall, our bullpen wasn't what we anticipated, although we got excellent performances from Tom Henke and Mark Eichhorn," Gillick said.

Toronto promoted rookie lefthander John Cerutti from Syracuse (International) in mid-May, and he posted a 9-4 record as a starter and middle reliever.

The third surprise contributor to the pitching staff was 24-year-old Joe Johnson, who was obtained from Atlanta in a trade for Jim Acker the same day Alexander was sent to the Braves in a separate deal. Johnson took Alexander's spot in the rotation and posted a 7-2 record.

Toronto's most consistent starter was veteran Jim Clancy, who got off to a 12-5 start. But he lost six starts in September and another in October, primarily due to a lack of support, to finish 14-14.

In addition to these encouraging pitching performances, Williams had to be pleased with his club's hitting and fielding. The Blue Jays exploded for more runs (809) and home runs (181) than they ever had before and also set a club record for fewest errors (100, the A.L. low).

The Toronto attack was led by Gold Glove right fielder Jesse Barfield, who belted a team-record 40 homers, tops in the major leagues, while batting .289. Barfield set team records with 108 RBIs and 107 runs scored and led the league in outfield assists (20) for the second year in a row.

Barfield's .559 slugging percentage was No. 2 in the league, while left fielder George Bell's .532 was fourth. Bell hit .309 with 31 homers, 38 doubles and 101 runs scored, shared the A.L. lead with 15 game-winning RBIs and tied Barfield with 108 RBIs. Bell, Barfield and Moseby together formed one of baseball's best all-around outfields.

One of Toronto's defensive and offensive stalwarts was Gold Glove shortstop Tony Fernandez, who played in every game for the second year in a row. Fernandez lowered his errors from 30 to 13, led the team in batting with a .310 average and became the first Blue Jay to collect more than 200 hits in a season. Williams' move of Fernandez to the leadoff spot in the lineup proved wise.

The most impressive aspect of the Blue Jays' season was their late-season run at the division title. They trailed Boston by 12 games on June 4 but steadily worked their way out of last place. A nine-game winning streak brought them to within 3½ games September 1, and it looked as if the Boston Red Sox could be in trouble. But the Blue Jays lost 18 of their last 30 games to finish fourth with an 86-76 record, 9½ games back.

Indians outfielder Joe Carter developed into one of the top offensive threats in the major leagues while leading the A.L. with 121 RBIs.

Indians on Road to Recovery

By SHELDON OCKER

For the first time in more than two decades, the Cleveland Indians' long-suffering fans can look forward to the coming season with optimism based on the reality of proven performance.

In 1985, the Tribe tied the club record for losses, posting a 60-102 mark and finishing last in the American League East. The 1986 season wasn't supposed to be much better, but the Indians surprised a lot of people by finishing fifth with an 84-78 record. That 24-game turnaround was the best in the team's history.

After a 7-8 start, the Indians won 10 straight games to vault into first place. They then lost nine of their next 10, however, and never returned to the top spot. Nevertheless, the Indians were in third place with a 46-39 record at the All-Star break, and by July 23 they had pulled to within five games of the division-leading Boston Red Sox. The Tribe fell back into the pack during a stretch of 42 games against A.L. East clubs before regaining some ground against the A.L. West in the final 24 games of the year.

Cleveland went 32-46 against East Division clubs but 52-32 against the West, and for the first time since 1959 (excluding the 1981 strike season), the Indians finished fewer than 14 games behind the division/league leader. The Tribe wound up 11½ games behind Boston.

Accompanying the Indians' improvement on the field was a corresponding boost in attendance. The Tribe surpassed 1.4 million, more than double its 1985 total of 655,181 and the most since 1959. Cleveland's attendance increase was the largest in the major leagues.

A strong offensive attack was primarily responsible for Cleveland's improved record. The Indians led the league in several categories, including batting (.284), runs scored (831) and stolen bases (141).

"One thing I don't worry about is offense," Manager Pat Corrales said. "If we can hold a team to four or five runs, we have a chance to win."

The offensive leader of the club was Joe Carter, who paced the league with 121 runs batted in. The outfielder-first baseman also ranked among the leaders with a .302 average, a .514 slugging percentage, 29 home runs, 108 runs, 200 hits, 36 doubles, nine triples and 29 stolen bases. Carter became the first Indian to get 200 hits in a season since Al Rosen in 1953.

Cleveland first baseman Pat Tabler finished fourth in the A.L. batting race with a .326 average.

First baseman Pat Tabler was the league's No. 4 hitter with a .326 average, while shortstop Julio Franco was 10th at .306. Franco added 10 homers and 74 RBIs.

Second baseman Tony Bernazard had his best year ever, batting .301 with 17 homers and 73 RBIs. Third baseman Brook Jacoby (.288, 17 homers, 80 RBIs) completed the Tribe's potent infield.

Cory Snyder, a member of the 1984 U.S. Olympic baseball team, had a tremendous effect on the team after being promoted from Maine (International) on June 12. Used primarily in the outfield, the converted infielder slammed 24 homers and drove in 69 runs while batting .272.

The list of productive hitters was even longer. Center fielder Brett Butler batted .278, stole a team-high 32 bases and hit a league-high 14 triples. Left fielder Mel Hall bounced back from injuries suffered in a May 1985 automobile accident to hit .296 with 18 homers and 77 RBIs. Outfield backup Carmen Castillo batted .278.

A disquieting note was the production of designated hitter Andre Thornton, who endured back and knee problems. Thorn-

SCORES OF CLEVELAND INDIANS' 1986 GAMES

APRIL			Winner	Loser
7—At Balt.	W	6-4	Schrom	Flanagan
9—At Balt.	L	3-4	Aase	Bailes
10—At Balt.	L	1-5	Dixon	Kern
11—Detroit	L	2-7	Terrell	Niekro
12—Detroit	W	6-2	Schrom	Morris
13—Detroit	W	8-2	Bailes	Tanana
15—New York	L	2-6	Niekro	Candiotti
17—New York	W	6-4	Niekro	Tewksbury
18—At Detroit	L	1-6	Tanana	Schrom
19—At Detroit	W	8-6	Bailes	Petry
21—Baltimore	W	7-0	Candiotti	Flanagan
22—Baltimore	L	2-5	Dixon	Niekro
23—Baltimore	W	5-1	Schrom	McGregor
24—At N.Y.	L	1-2	Guidry	Heaton
25—At N.Y.	L	3-10	Niekro	Candiotti
26—At N.Y.	W	3-2	Schulze	Shirley
27—At N.Y.	W	9-7	Bailes	Righetti
29—At Texas	W	6-5	Kern	Harris
30—At Texas	W	6-4	Schulze	Guzman

Won 11, Lost 8

MAY			Winner	Loser
2—At Chicago	W	7-5‡	Camacho	Schmidt
3—At Chicago	W	8-7	Yett	Dawley
4—At Chicago	W	6-4‡	Bailes	James
5—Kan. City	W	5-4‡	Niekro	Quisenberry
6—Kan. City	W	6-1*	Candiotti	Black
7—Kan. City	W	7-1	Heaton	Saberhagen
9—Chicago	L	3-4	Nelson	Bailes
10—Chicago	L	0-4§	Nelson	Bailes
11—Chicago	L	4-5	McKeon	Candiotti
12—Texas	L	2-19	Hough	Heaton
13—Texas	W	3-2‡	Yett	Harris
14—At Kan. C.	L	0-5	Gubicza	Niekro
15—At Kan. C.	L	3-6	Leonard	Bailes
16—At Toronto	L	6-7	Acker	Candiotti
17—At Toronto	L	5-11	Key	Heaton
18—At Toronto	L	2-10	Clancy	Schulze
19—At Toronto	W	6-4	Niekro	Stieb
20—At Milw.	L	9-12	Plesac	Easterly
21—At Milw.	W	4-2	Candiotti	Wegman
22—At Milw.	W	5-4	Heaton	Higuera
23—Toronto	W	3-1	Schulze	Clancy
24—Toronto	L	6-9	Lamp	Easterly
25—Toronto	L	1-8	Cerutti	Schrom
26—Boston	L	3-5	Hurst	Candiotti
27—Boston	L	0-2†	Brown	Heaton
28—Boston	L	7-13	Boyd	Schulze
30—Milwaukee	L	7-11	Nieves	Niekro
31—Milwaukee	W	3-2	Bailes	Plesac

Won 12, Lost 16

JUNE			Winner	Loser
1—Milwaukee	W	9-7	Bailes	McClure
2—At Boston	L	1-3	Boyd	Heaton
3—At Boston	L	1-5	Brown	Schulze
4—At Boston	L	4-6	Woodward	Niekro
6—California	W	3-0	Schrom	McCaskill
7—California	L	2-8	Witt	Candiotti
8—California	W	11-4	Heaton	Slaton
9—Oakland	W	6-5	Bailes	Rijo
10—Oakland	W	8-7	Yett	Rijo
11—Oakland	W	7-4	Schrom	Langford
13—Minnesota	W	11-2	Candiotti	Blyleven
14—Minnesota	L	3-9	Atherton	Heaton
15—Minnesota	L	3-7	Viola	Schulze
17—Seattle	L	2-5	Morgan	Niekro
18—Seattle	W	5-1	Schrom	Beattie
19—Seattle	W	8-1	Candiotti	Moore
20—At Minn.	L	8-9	Viola	Noles
21—At Minn.	W	7-5	Schulze	Portugal
22—At Minn.	W	4-1	Niekro	Smithson
23—At Seattle	W	8-6	Schrom	Beattie
24—At Seattle	L	7-8	Young	Camacho
25—At Seattle	L	1-6	Langston	Butcher
27—At Calif.	W	6-3	Noles	Witt
28—At Calif.	L	3-9	Corbett	Butcher
29—At Calif.	W	6-4	Schrom	Romanick
30—At Oak.	W	8-3	Candiotti	Rijo

Won 15, Lost 11

JULY			Winner	Loser
1—At Oak.	W	9-0	Butcher	Langford
2—At Oak.	W	7-3	Noles	Mooneyham
4—Kan. City	W	10-3	Niekro	Jackson
5—Kan. City	W	10-5	Schrom	Saberhagen
6—Kan. City	W	5-0	Candiotti	Leonard
7—At Chicago	L	3-4	James	Camacho
8—At Chicago	L	2-6	Allen	Oelkers
9—At Chicago	W	6-3	Niekro	Dotson
10—Texas	W	9-6	Schrom	Correa
11—Texas	W	7-2	Candiotti	Witt
12—Texas	L	6-11	Hough	Butcher
13—Texas	L	3-5‡	Williams	Bailes
17—At Kan. C.	L	1-5	Saberhagen	Candiotti
18—At Kan. C.	W	3-2‡	Oelkers	Quisenberry
19—At Kan. C.	W	6-4	Niekro	Bankhead
20—At Kan. C.	L	2-3	Farr	Noles
21—Chicago	W	5-2	Yett	Davis
22—Chicago	W	8-4	Candiotti	Dotson
23—Chicago	W	7-2	Schrom	Bannister
24—At Texas	L	3-7	Loynd	Niekro
25—At Texas	L	5-7	Harris	Bailes
26—At Texas	L	5-8	Witt	Yett
27—At Texas	W	8-3	Candiotti	Correa
28—Detroit	L	1-5	Morris	Schrom
29—Detroit	L	3-6§	Hernandez	Oelkers
30—Detroit	L	3-11	King	Butcher
31—Detroit	W	8-7	Bailes	Campbell

Won 15, Lost 12

AUGUST			Winner	Loser
1—New York	W	4-3	Niekro	Guidry
1—New York	L	3-5	Fisher	Candiotti
2—New York	W	6-5‡	Noles	Righetti
3—New York	L	8-12	Scurry	Niekro
5—At Detroit	L	5-6	Thurmond	Bailes
5—At Detroit	L	9-11	Tanana	Butcher
7—At Detroit	L	1-15	Morris	Niekro
7—At Detroit	L	2-6	Thurmond	Schrom
8—At Balt.	W	3-0	Candiotti	Boddicker
9—At Balt.	W	8-2	Roman	Davis
10—At Balt.	W	6-3	Bailes	Dixon
11—At N.Y.	L	5-6	Fisher	Wills
12—At N.Y.	L	4-6	Stoddard	Yett
13—At N.Y.	L	0-4	John	Candiotti
14—Baltimore	L	2-12	Davis	Roman
15—Baltimore	W	3-2	Wills	Aase
16—Baltimore	W	2-1	Niekro	Flanagan
17—Baltimore	W	11-6	Oelkers	Boddicker
18—Milwaukee	W	10-4	Candiotti	Bosio
19—Milwaukee	L	3-5	Higuera	Roman
20—Milwaukee	L	3-6	Wegman	Bailes
21—Boston	L	5-24	Boyd	Swindell
22—Boston	L	3-6	Hurst	Schrom
23—Boston	W	5-4	Camacho	Stanley
24—Boston	W	5-2	Niekro	Nipper
26—Toronto	T	6-6	....	....
27—Toronto	L	2-3x	Eichhorn	Oelkers
27—Toronto	L	3-6	Cerutti	Wills
28—Toronto	L	1-9	Clancy	Schrom
29—At Boston	W	7-3	Candiotti	Seaver
30—At Boston	L	3-7	Clemens	Niekro
31—At Boston	L	3-4	Schiraldi	Wills

Won 12, Lost 19, Tied 1

SEPTEMBER			Winner	Loser
1—At Toronto	L	4-5	Henke	Camacho
2—At Toronto	W	9-5	Schrom	Clancy
3—At Toronto	L	1-3	Stieb	Candiotti
4—At Milw.	W	15-4	Bailes	Leary
5—At Milw.	W	13-5	Niekro	Wegman
6—At Milw.	W	17-9	Swindell	Nieves
7—At Milw.	L	2-7	Vuckovich	Schrom
9—California	L	1-8	McCaskill	Candiotti
10—California	L	6-7y	Finley	Yett
12—Oakland	W	9-3	Swindell	Krueger
13—Oakland	W	8-6	Oelkers	Mooneyham
14—Oakland	W	5-2	Schrom	Rijo
15—Minnesota	W	4-0	Candiotti	Viola
16—Minnesota	L	3-7	Portugal	Bailes
17—Minnesota	W	5-2	Swindell	Smithson
19—At Oak.	L	1-5	Young	Niekro
20—At Oak.	W	6-5‡	Wills	Howell
21—At Oak.	L	2-4	Andujar	Candiotti
22—At Calif.	L	3-4	Sutton	Bailes
22—At Calif.	W	7-0	Yett	Chadwick
23—At Calif.	W	5-2	Swindell	Witt
25—At Calif.	L	3-6	McCaskill	Wills
26—At Seattle	W	9-7x	Jones	Ladd
27—At Seattle	W	12-4	Schrom	Morgan
28—At Seattle	W	5-4x	Wills	Nunez
29—At Minn.	L	5-6	Blyleven	Swindell
30—At Minn.	L	9-10‡	Portugal	Camacho

Won 15, Lost 12

OCTOBER			Winner	Loser
1—At Minn.	W	12-3	Candiotti	Anderson
3—Seattle	W	6-5	Wills	Trujillo
4—Seattle	W	6-5	Swindell	Langston
5—Seattle	W	4-2	Candiotti	Moore

Won 4, Lost 0

*5 innings. †6 innings. ‡10 innings. §11 innings. x12 innings. y14 innings.

Tom Candiotti brought his knuckleball to Cleveland and led the Indians with a 16-12 record.

ton batted .229 with 17 homers and 66 RBIs and underwent surgery to remove cartilage from his knee after the season.

The only other problem spot was catcher. Though Chris Bando raised his average a whopping 129 points to .268, neither he nor rookie Andy Allanson (.225) offered much run production. They combined for only 55 RBIs.

The Indians' powerful attack was not unexpected. The big surprise was the pitching staff, which had posted a 4.91 earned-run average, worst in the majors, in 1985. A year later, the Indians compiled a 4.58 ERA. Eleven A.L. teams did better, but that slight improvement helped Cleveland achieve a winning record.

"I didn't know (before the season) how the pitchers would be," Corrales said. "But I kept my fingers crossed and some of them worked out a little better than I thought."

A pair of knuckleballers who weren't even on Cleveland's spring training roster were among the club's biggest winners.

Tom Candiotti, who had spent most of the previous seven years struggling in the minors, was given a spring tryout after the Milwaukee Brewers' organization granted him his free agency. He earned a roster spot by showing control of his new knuckleball and proceeded to lead the staff with a 16-12 record. The righthander also compiled a 3.57 ERA, threw three shutouts and led the league with 17 complete games.

Candiotti had an excellent adviser in Phil Niekro, who was signed by the Indians in April after being released by the New York Yankees. The 47-year-old knuckleballer went 11-11 with a 4.32 ERA.

Righthander Ken Schrom, a winter acquisition from Minnesota, rebounded from a 9-12 mark with the Twins in '85 to compile a 14-7 record. The Indians made another trade with Minnesota in June, this time with less favorable results. They swapped Neal Heaton, who had gone 3-6 in 12 starts, for John Butcher, a righthander who went 1-5 with a 6.93 ERA in Cleveland.

Butcher's ineffectiveness and an injury that sidelined Don Schulze (4-4) for several weeks forced Corrales to look at some rookies. Lefthander Scott Bailes was moved from the bullpen and finished 10-10 with seven saves.

On August 21, the Indians received a boost from 21-year-old lefthander Greg Swindell, who three months earlier had been pitching for the University of Texas and then became the Tribe's No. 1 selection in the June draft. Swindell had only three minor league starts, all at Class-A Waterloo (Midwest), when the Indians recalled him. But Indians General Manager Joe Klein and his staff believed he was ready.

"When we drafted Greg, we felt he might help us this year," Klein said.

Swindell didn't disappoint. He posted a 5-2 record and a 4.23 ERA in nine starts.

"He knows more about pitching than anybody on this staff except Phil Niekro," Corrales said after the season.

In the bullpen, Ernie Camacho didn't get much help from his setup men. Of the middle relievers, Bryan Oelkers had the best ERA with a 4.70 mark. Nevertheless, Camacho, whose right elbow was repaired twice by surgeons in 1985, came back to save 20 games.

Surprisingly, Corrales said his club fell short—by one victory, to be exact—of his goal for 1986. The manager had told Klein and a coach during spring training that he wanted the Indians to win 85 games, at which point "they looked at me kind of funny," he recalled.

Eighty-four wins later, Corrales had made them believers.

Lefthander Ted Higuera joined the exclusive 20-victory club while helping the Brewers regain some lost respect.

Young Brewers Are Improving

By **TOM FLAHERTY**

At midseason, the Milwaukee Brewers turned to a page from their past.

Gorman Thomas, the home run-hitting hero who had been traded away in 1983, returned to a hero's welcome after signing as a free agent at the All-Star break.

The storybook return, however, didn't have a happy ending. Thomas batted just .179 with six home runs and 10 runs batted in for the Brewers. He was released after the season.

The signing of Thomas was a rare occasion when the Brewers looked back at the happy days of 1982 and their only American League pennant. For the most part, the Brewers spent 1986 looking ahead.

Thomas saw few familiar faces when he rejoined the Brewers. Only first baseman Cecil Cooper, second baseman Jim Gantner, third baseman Paul Molitor, catcher Charlie Moore, outfielder Ben Oglivie and shortstop-turned-outfielder Robin Yount remained from the 1982 team. Like Thomas, Moore (.260 in '86) and Oglivie (.283) were told at the end of the season that they did not figure in the Brewers' future. Pete Vuckovich, the 1982 A.L. Cy Young Award winner at Milwaukee, received a similar message after going 2-4 in a September stint with the Brewers.

On September 25, with the Brewers' record at 71-81, Manager George Bamberger decided to retire for the third time. Bamberger simply was tired of the strain.

"Managing is a tough job," he said. "There are a lot of good things about it, but it's a tough job. . . . You lose a couple of games, your stomach ties in knots. Why aggravate yourself?"

The young team was turned over to a young manager, 38-year-old Tom Trebelhorn, who had replaced Tony Muser as third-base coach after Muser was injured in a clubhouse explosion during spring training. Trebelhorn originally was named interim manager but then was offered the job for 1987.

Entering the season, the Brewers headed into a youth movement at full throttle. They had a young pitching staff, dubbed "Bambi's Babies," headed by Ted Higuera, a second-year lefthander who became just the third 20-game winner in the team's history. They added three rookie products of their farm system—Billy Jo Robidoux, Glenn Braggs and Dale Sveum—to their lineup, along with 25-year-old outfielder Rob Deer, an off-season acquisition from San Francisco.

The result? The new Brewers finished in the same position (sixth) as the older Brewers of 1985, but much improvement was evident. The Brewers went from 71-90 in '85 to 77-84, 18 games out of first in the A.L. East. Though they never came close to flagging down the Boston Red Sox, the Brewers hovered at or above .500 most of the season. If not for a 5-20 streak in late August and early September, the final record would have been a more accurate assessment of the team's improvement.

Most of the attention was focused on Bambi's Babies, who contributed heavily to the league's fifth-best ERA (4.01). Higuera, the new ace of the staff, claimed a spot among the league's elite with a 20-11 record, a 2.79 ERA, four shutouts, 15 complete games and 207 strikeouts.

The other young pitchers suffered growing pains but enjoyed some success. Juan Nieves, a 21-year-old rookie lefthander who arrived amid much fanfare, got off to a great start, posting a 10-4 record and three shutouts by the end of July. But he then lost eight straight decisions before winning the final game of the season in relief to finish with an 11-12 record and a 4.92 ERA. Righthander Bill Wegman, another rookie, battled the frustrations of 15 no-decisions en route to a 5-12 record and a 5.13 ERA.

The most successful rookie was Dan Plesac. The hard-throwing lefthander teamed with Mark Clear, a veteran righthander obtained from Boston the previous winter, to give the Brewers a strong pair of late-inning stoppers. Plesac had a 10-7 record, a 2.97 ERA and 14 saves, and Clear saved a career-high 16 games while going 5-5 with a 2.20 ERA.

Milwaukee's No. 2 starter was 27-year-old Tim Leary, a former New York Mets prospect who made a fine comeback after arm injuries had threatened a promising career. The righthander won five of his last six decisions to finish 12-12 with a 4.21 ERA. The senior member of the rotation was 30-year-old Danny Darwin (6-8), who was traded to Houston in August.

Offensively, Deer was the Brewers' biggest addition. The powerful right fielder lived up to his reputation of striking out too much by setting a team record with 179, but he also hit 33 homers and knocked in 86 runs.

SCORES OF MILWAUKEE BREWERS' 1986 GAMES

APRIL			Winner	Loser
7—At Chicago	W	5-3	Higuera	Seaver
9—At Chicago	W	4-3	Leary	Dotson
10—At Chicago	W	8-5	Darwin	James
11—At N.Y.	L	2-3	Tewksbury	Wegman
12—At N.Y.	L	3-7	Rasmussen	Higuera
13—At N.Y.	L	2-3	Guidry	Cocanower
14—Texas	L	1-10	Correa	Leary
17—Texas	L	5-7	Harris	Searage
18—New York	W	6-5	Plesac	Fisher
19—New York	W	4-3‡	McClure	Scurry
20—New York	L	4-5†	Righetti	Clear
22—Chicago	L	4-5	Davis	Darwin
23—Chicago	L	1-2	Seaver	Plesac
25—At Texas	W	11-1	Higuera	Guzman
26—At Texas	W	10-2	Leary	Correa
27—At Texas	L	2-6	Witt	Nieves
29—Oakland	W	5-4	McClure	Howell
30—Oakland	W	5-1	Higuera	Rijo

Won 9, Lost 9

MAY			Winner	Loser
1—Oakland	L	2-7	Haas	Leary
2—California	W	5-4	Nieves	Sutton
3—California	W	4-3†	Clear	Moore
4—California	W	5-3	Higuera	McCaskill
5—Seattle	W	3-1	Leary	Langston
6—Seattle	W	10-0	Nieves	Swift
7—At Oak.	L	6-7	Andujar	Wegman
8—At Oak.	L	1-2	Codiroli	Higuera
9—At Calif.	W	16-5	Darwin	McCaskill
10—At Calif.	W	4-2	Nieves	Witt
11—At Calif.	L	1-5	Slaton	Wegman
12—At Seattle	L	0-6	Young	Higuera
13—At Seattle	L	5-8	Morgan	Leary
14—At Seattle	W	9-6	Plesac	Moore
16—Minnesota	W	7-6	Clear	Davis
17—Minnesota	W	4-1*	Higuera	Portugal
18—Minnesota	L	3-5	Blyleven	Leary
20—Cleveland	W	12-9	Plesac	Easterly
21—Cleveland	L	2-4	Candiotti	Wegman
22—Cleveland	L	4-5	Heaton	Higuera
23—At Minn.	L	7-8	Pastore	Plesac
24—At Minn.	W	6-3	Nieves	Viola
25—At Minn.	L	3-4	Smithson	Wegman
26—At Kan. C.	W	4-0	Darwin	Leibrandt
27—At Kan. C.	W	9-1	Higuera	Jackson
28—At Kan. C.	L	3-4	Farr	Clear
30—At Cleve.	W	11-7	Nieves	Niekro
31—At Cleve.	L	2-3	Bailes	Plesac

Won 15, Lost 13

JUNE			Winner	Loser
1—At Cleve.	L	7-9	Bailes	McClure
2—Kan. City	W	7-2	Higuera	Jackson
3—Kan. City	L	1-4	Saberhagen	Leary
4—Kan. City	L	6-8	Leonard	Nieves
5—Boston	W	7-5	Wegman	Sellers
6—Boston	L	0-3	Clemens	Darwin
7—Boston	W	3-0	Higuera	Boyd
8—Boston	W	7-3	Leary	Brown
9—Baltimore	W	3-2	Plesac	Davis
10—Baltimore	W	6-3	Wegman	McGregor
11—Baltimore	L	3-4	Boddicker	Darwin
13—At Boston	L	3-5	Boyd	Higuera
14—At Boston	W	2-0	Leary	Brown
15—At Boston	W	7-3	Nieves	Sellers
16—Toronto	L	2-9	Alexander	Wegman
17—Toronto	L	1-2§	Henke	Plesac
18—Toronto	W	3-1	Higuera	Clancy
20—Detroit	W	1-0	Leary	Terrell
21—Detroit	L	3-4	Campbell	Clear
22—Detroit	W	5-4	Gibson	LaPoint
23—At Toronto	W	5-3	Darwin	Stieb
24—At Toronto	L	0-8	Cerutti	Higuera
25—At Toronto	L	1-5	Clancy	Leary
27—At Detroit	L	2-4‡	Hernandez	Plesac
28—At Detroit	L	5-8	Campbell	Gibson
29—At Detroit	L	5-9	King	Darwin
29—At Detroit	W	3-1	Higuera	Morris
30—At Balt.	L	2-5	McGregor	Leary

Won 13, Lost 15

JULY			Winner	Loser
1—At Balt.	L	3-7	Flanagan	Wegman
2—At Balt.	W	1-0	Nieves	Dixon
4—Oakland	W	5-4	Plesac	Bair
5—Oakland	W	2-1	Darwin	Plunk
6—Oakland	L	3-6	Rijo	Leary
7—California	L	1-3x	Forster	Plesac
8—California	L	3-14	Candelaria	Nieves
9—California	L	1-6	Sutton	Higuera
10—Seattle	L	1-4	Fireovid	Darwin
11—Seattle	L	3-9	Morgan	Leary
12—Seattle	L	9-15	Reed	Wegman
13—Seattle	W	5-0	Nieves	Moore
18—At Oak.	L	1-6	Andujar	Nieves
19—At Oak.	L	2-3	Mooneyham	Clear
20—At Oak.	W	7-2	Higuera	Plunk
20—At Oak.	L	2-4	Rijo	Leary
21—At Calif.	W	5-3	Wegman	Romanick
22—At Calif.	W	6-2	Nieves	Sutton
23—At Calif.	L	2-3†	McCaskill	Darwin
25—At Seattle	W	4-2	Higuera	Morgan
26—At Seattle	L	2-5	Reed	Wegman
27—At Seattle	W	8-1	Leary	Langston
28—New York	W	5-4	Nieves	Niekro
29—New York	W	6-4	Darwin	Nielsen
30—New York	W	5-0	Higuera	Drabek

Won 12, Lost 13

AUGUST			Winner	Loser
1—Texas	L	2-7	Witt	Leary
1—Texas	L	6-8	Correa	Gibson
2—Texas	W	9-8	Plesac	Williams
3—Texas	L	6-7	Russell	Darwin
4—At N.Y.	W	5-4	Higuera	Drabek
5—At N.Y.	W	2-1†	Plesac	Righetti
6—At N.Y.	L	3-5	Guidry	Nieves
7—At N.Y.	W	10-2	Leary	Niekro
8—Chicago	L	6-12	Cowley	Darwin
9—Chicago	W	1-0	Higuera	DeLeon
10—Chicago	W	5-4‡	Clear	Schmidt
11—Chicago	L	1-6	Bannister	Bosio
12—At Texas	W	7-2	Leary	Hough
13—At Texas	L	4-5§	Harris	Johnson
14—At Texas	L	2-8	Loynd	Higuera
15—At Chicago	W	4-3	Plesac	Dawley
16—At Chicago	W	6-5	Johnson	Nelson
17—At Chicago	L	4-7	Carlton	Clutterbuck
18—At Cleve.	L	4-10	Candiotti	Bosio
19—At Cleve.	W	5-3	Higuera	Roman
20—At Cleve.	W	6-3	Wegman	Bailes
22—Kan. City	L	2-4	Jackson	Nieves
23—Kan. City	W	8-4	Plesac	Gubicza
24—Kan. City	W	3-2‡	Clear	Quisenberry
26—Minnesota	W	6-5†	Clear	Atherton
27—Minnesota	L	5-7	Heaton	Nieves
28—Minnesota	L	2-6	Blyleven	Bosio
29—At Kan. C.	W	3-1	Higuera	Leonard
30—At Kan. C.	L	1-10	Gubicza	Birkbeck
31—At Kan. C.	L	1-6	Bankhead	Wegman

Won 15, Lost 15

SEPTEMBER			Winner	Loser
1—At Minn.	L	3-9	Heaton	Nieves
2—At Minn.	L	0-4	Blyleven	Vuckovich
3—At Minn.	L	5-11	Smithson	Higuera
4—Cleveland	L	4-15	Bailes	Leary
5—Cleveland	L	5-13	Niekro	Wegman
6—Cleveland	L	9-17	Swindell	Nieves
7—Cleveland	W	7-2	Vuckovich	Schrom
9—At Detroit	W	3-1	Higuera	Tanana
10—At Detroit	L	7-11	Terrell	Bosio
11—At Detroit	L	0-8	Morris	Nieves
12—Toronto	W	4-1	Johnson	Clancy
13—Toronto	L	1-7	Johnson	Vuckovich
14—Toronto	W	5-0	Higuera	Stieb
15—Toronto	L	2-5	Cerutti	Wegman
16—At Boston	L	1-2	Clemens	Nieves
16—At Boston	L	3-9	Schiraldi	Clear
17—At Boston	L	1-4	Boyd	Knudson
18—At Boston	L	1-7	Hurst	Vuckovich
19—At Balt.	L	1-3	Dixon	Higuera
20—At Balt.	L	3-4	Habyan	Plesac
21—At Balt.	W	5-4‡	Plesac	Havens
23—Boston	W	8-5	Leary	Boyd
25—Baltimore	W	9-3	Higuera	Dixon
26—Baltimore	W	2-0	Vuckovich	Boddicker
27—Baltimore	L	0-7	McGregor	Nieves
28—Baltimore	W	10-2	Birkbeck	Bell
30—Detroit	W	5-0	Leary	Petry

Won 10, Lost 17

OCTOBER			Winner	Loser
1—Detroit	L	1-2	Tanana	Higuera
2—Detroit	L	1-2	Morris	Vuckovich
3—At Toronto	W	4-1	Wegman	Clancy
5—At Toronto	W	2-1	Leary	Henke
5—At Toronto	W	4-3	Nieves	Eichhorn

Won 3, Lost 2

*7 innings. †10 innings. ‡11 innings. §12 innings. x16 innings.

Rob Deer brought power back into vogue in Milwaukee, hitting 33 homers and driving in 86 runs.

Braggs, Robidoux and Sveum had their problems, though.

Braggs, an outfielder who was called up at midseason after tearing up the Pacific Coast League, batted just .237 and drove in only 18 runs. First baseman Robidoux was the team's best clutch hitter for five weeks before he was sidelined with a knee injury. His production started to drop upon his return, and after another several weeks on the disabled list and in the minors, he finished the season at .227 with 21 RBIs. Sveum (.246 in 91 games) had problems defensively, committing 30 errors at three infield positions (26 at third base). And rookie outfielder Mike Felder batted only .239 in 155 at-bats.

Shortstop Ernest Riles, one of the league's top rookies when he batted .286 in '85, saw his average fall to .252. The Brewers also got less than they expected from 27-year-old Bill Schroeder, who was supposed to open the season as the club's starting catcher. Schroeder was on the disabled list at the time, however, and never won his job back. He hit a mere .212 while backing up Moore and Rick Cerone (.259) and filling in at first base.

Most of the familiar faces had familiar problems.

Molitor played in only 105 games because of a hamstring injury and batted .281 with a club-high 20 stolen bases. Yount, who was moved to center field after undergoing his second shoulder operation in two years, led the team with a .312 batting average and 82 runs scored but tallied only 46 RBIs. Cooper, who had elbow surgery before the season, batted just .258. Gantner hit his customary .274, while veteran outfielder Rick Manning knocked in only 27 runs in 205 at-bats.

The result was a weak attack. Milwaukee batted .255, scored 667 runs and hit 127 homers, figures that ranked near the bottom of the league.

The Brewers had more than their share of growing pains in 1986, but their improved record and the emergence of a strong, young pitching staff indicated that the club should blossom in the next couple of years.

Mike Boddicker suffered through an injury-plagued season but still led the Orioles with 14 victories.

Optimistic Orioles Bottom Out

By JIM HENNEMAN

With Manager Earl Weaver back for a full year and Owner Edward Bennett Williams calling his 1986 team the best he'd seen since taking over in 1980, the Baltimore Orioles' season started with high expectations. But Weaver, Williams and countless other shocked observers watched as the team finished last for the first time since the St. Louis Browns moved east.

When it was over, so was Weaver's second reign as skipper. Weaver, who managed the Orioles from 1968-82 and returned to the dugout as a replacement for Joe Altobelli in June 1985, went into a second retirement after finishing below .500 for the first time in an otherwise brilliant major league managerial career. Cal Ripken Sr., who has spent his entire 30-year career with the Orioles' organization, was charged with restoring the club's winning tradition when he was named Weaver's successor the day after the season finale.

The Orioles' troubles started early. Eddie Murray, whose nine previous years had been marked by consistent excellence, was hobbled by an ankle injury when he reported to spring training. The first baseman eventually missed 25 games and had to go on the disabled list for the first time in his career. Murray led the Orioles with a .305 average and 84 runs batted in, but he hit only 17 home runs, his lowest major league total.

As had been the case so often in the past, the Orioles followed Murray's lead.

Newly acquired infielder Jackie Gutierrez spent much of the year on the disabled list and at Rochester (International). He hit .186 in 61 games for Baltimore. Suffering a similar fate was Floyd Rayford, who was expected to start at third base after posting the best year of his career in 1985. But he chipped a bone in his thumb in spring training and never recovered. Rayford batted .176 in 81 games.

Starting pitchers Mike Boddicker, Mike Flanagan and Storm Davis all spent time on the disabled list, where reliever Tippy Martinez was virtually a permanent resident. And center fielder Fred Lynn, who hit .287 with 23 homers, suffered ankle and shoulder injuries that sidelined him for almost a third of the season. Most of Lynn's missed games came during the Orioles' two devastating slumps at midseason and the end of the year.

The Orioles made two strong runs at the American League East champion Boston Red Sox before falling by the wayside. They drew within three games of Boston on June 8, then lost 15 of their next 20 contests. But the Orioles won 13 of their first 19 games after the All-Star break to improve their record to 59-47. That surge left the Orioles 2½ games out of first on August 5, but they lost 42 of their final 56 games and stumbled to last in the division at 73-89, 22½ games back.

Don Aase's 34 saves was one of the few bright spots for the last-place Orioles.

The startling drop was the result of a slump that encompassed every aspect of the team. The Orioles ranked 11th in the league in runs scored (708), 13th in stolen bases (64) and 10th in defense (.978, 135

SCORES OF BALTIMORE ORIOLES' 1986 GAMES

APRIL			Winner	Loser
7—Cleveland	L	4-6	Schrom	Flanagan
9—Cleveland	W	4-3	Aase	Bailes
10—Cleveland	W	5-1	Dixon	Kern
11—At Texas	L	4-5	Wright	Aase
12—At Texas	L	1-2	Harris	Havens
13—At Texas	W	3-2	McGregor	Guzman
14—At Toronto	W	2-1	Boddicker	Alexander
17—At Toronto	W	5-3	Flanagan	Key
17—At Toronto	L	4-7	Henke	T. Martinez
18—Texas	L	3-12	Mason	McGregor
19—Texas	W	10-4	Boddicker	Mahler
20—Texas	W	6-1	Davis	Guzman
21—At Cleve.	L	0-7	Candiotti	Flanagan
22—At Cleve.	W	5-2	Dixon	Niekro
23—At Cleve.	L	1-5	Schrom	McGregor
25—Toronto	L	1-2*	Eichhorn	Aase
26—Toronto	W	11-5	Havens	Henke
27—Toronto	L	0-8	Clancy	Dixon
29—At Chicago	W	8-1	McGregor	Nelson
30—At Chicago	L	6-8	Dotson	Davis

Won 10, Lost 10

MAY			Winner	Loser
2—At Kan. C.	L	0-5	Saberhagen	Flanagan
3—At Kan. C.	W	3-2	Dixon	Gubicza
4—At Kan. C.	L	1-11	Leonard	McGregor
6—At Minn.	W	5-3	Davis	Viola
7—At Minn.	L	2-5	Smithson	Flanagan
9—Kan. City	L	4-7	Black	Dixon
10—Kan. City	W	5-2	Boddicker	Leonard
11—Kan. City	W	4-3	Davis	Leibrandt
12—Chicago	W	4-3	Bordi	James
13—Chicago	W	3-1	Aase	Bannister
14—Minnesota	W	8-3	Dixon	Agosto
15—Minnesota	W	5-3	Boddicker	Viola
16—Oakland	L	4-8	Haas	Davis
17—Oakland	W	8-2	McGregor	Langford
18—Oakland	W	13-4	Bordi	Codiroli
20—California	L	4-6	McCaskill	Boddicker
21—California	W	2-1	Davis	Witt
22—California	W	6-3	McGregor	Slaton
23—At Seattle	W	7-5	Dixon	Morgan
24—At Seattle	W	5-4*	Snell	Huismann
25—At Seattle	W	6-3	Boddicker	Moore
26—At Seattle	L	6-7	Langston	Davis
28—At Oak.	W	9-5	Bordi	Ontiveros
29—At Oak.	W	8-6	Havens	Codiroli
30—At Calif.	W	3-0	Snell	Romanick
31—At Calif.	L	0-2	McCaskill	Davis

Won 18, Lost 8

JUNE			Winner	Loser
1—At Calif.	L	4-7	Witt	McGregor
3—Seattle	W	4-2	Boddicker	Wilcox
4—Seattle	L	1-5	Moore	Dixon
5—Seattle	W	7-1	Davis	Langston
6—At N.Y.	W	5-2	McGregor	Guidry
7—At N.Y.	W	7-5	Boddicker	John
8—At N.Y.	W	18-9	Dixon	Whitson
9—At Milw.	L	2-3	Plesac	Davis
10—At Milw.	L	3-6	Wegman	McGregor
11—At Milw.	W	4-3	Boddicker	Darwin
12—New York	L	5-7	Fisher	T. Martinez
13—New York	L	1-3	Tewksbury	Davis
14—New York	L	2-4	Rasmussen	McGregor
15—New York	W	4-3	Boddicker	Fisher
16—Detroit	L	4-5	Tanana	Dixon
17—Detroit	L	3-6	O'Neal	Davis
18—Detroit	L	1-6	King	McGregor
19—Detroit	L	5-7	Morris	Aase
20—At Boston	W	14-3	Boddicker	Brown
21—At Boston	L	2-7	Clemens	Dixon
22—At Boston	W	4-0	Davis	Sellers
24—At Detroit	W	2-1*	Aase	Campbell
25—At Detroit	L	2-11	Morris	Boddicker
26—At Detroit	L	3-8	Terrell	Flanagan
27—Boston	L	3-5	Clemens	Dixon
28—Boston	L	3-7	Boyd	Davis
29—Boston	L	3-8	Sellers	Boddicker
30—Milwaukee	W	5-2	McGregor	Leary

Won 11, Lost 17

JULY			Winner	Loser
1—Milwaukee	W	7-3	Flanagan	Wegman
2—Milwaukee	L	0-1	Nieves	Dixon
3—At Minn.	L	7-11	Blyleven	Boddicker
4—At Minn.	W	12-7	Havens	Pastore
5—At Minn.	L	6-7	Viola	Flanagan
6—At Minn.	W	1-0	Dixon	Heaton
7—At Kan. C.	W	8-1	Boddicker	Leibrandt
8—At Kan. C.	W	8-4§	Jones	Quisenberry
9—At Kan. C.	L	0-3	Jackson	Bordi
10—At Chicago	W	5-3	Flanagan	Cowley
11—At Chicago	W	4-2	Dixon	Bannister
12—At Chicago	L	3-6	Nelson	Boddicker
13—At Chicago	L	0-7	Allen	McGregor
17—Minnesota	W	6-2	Dixon	Viola
18—Minnesota	L	3-7	Blyleven	McGregor
19—Minnesota	W	1-0	Flanagan	Heaton
20—Minnesota	W	8-3	Boddicker	Smithson
21—Kan. City	L	1-6	Jackson	Dixon
22—Kan. City	W	5-4	Aase	Black
23—Kan. City	L	3-7	Gubicza	McGregor
24—Chicago	W	12-6	Flanagan	Cowley
25—Chicago	W	6-2	Boddicker	Allen
26—Chicago	W	2-1	Bordi	Schmidt
27—Chicago	W	11-3	McGregor	Dotson
28—At Texas	W	4-3	Davis	Hough
29—At Texas	L	5-6‡	Harris	Jones
30—At Texas	L	3-5†	Russell	Snell

Won 16, Lost 11

AUGUST			Winner	Loser
1—At Toronto	W	7-3	Dixon	Key
2—At Toronto	W	5-2	McGregor	Clancy
3—At Toronto	L	4-6	Cerutti	Flanagan
4—At Toronto	W	12-2	Boddicker	Johnson
5—Texas	W	9-2	Davis	Guzman
6—Texas	L	11-13	Williams	Bordi
7—Texas	L	8-9	Russell	Havens
8—Cleveland	L	0-3	Candiotti	Boddicker
9—Cleveland	L	2-8	Roman	Davis
10—Cleveland	L	3-6	Bailes	Dixon
11—Toronto	W	3-1	Flanagan	Key
12—Toronto	L	0-3	Clancy	McGregor
13—Toronto	W	7-6§	Aase	Aquino
14—At Cleve.	W	12-2	Davis	Roman
15—At Cleve.	L	2-3	Wills	Aase
16—At Cleve.	L	1-2	Niekro	Flanagan
17—At Cleve.	L	6-11	Oelkers	Boddicker
19—Oakland	L	1-4	Stewart	Davis
22—California	W	8-7	Bordi	Moore
23—California	W	4-2	Flanagan	Chadwick
24—California	L	3-4	McCaskill	Davis
26—At Seattle	L	2-5	Moore	Dixon
27—At Seattle	L	1-4	Trujillo	Boddicker
28—At Oak.	L	4-5	Leiper	Aase
28—At Oak.	L	7-8	Mooneyham	Aase
29—At Oak.	L	3-4	Plunk	Davis
29—At Oak.	L	0-4	Stewart	Habyan
30—At Oak.	W	5-4	Jones	Rijo
31—At Oak.	L	0-7	Andujar	Boddicker

Won 10, Lost 19

SEPTEMBER			Winner	Loser
1—At Calif.	W	9-3	McGregor	Witt
2—At Calif.	L	1-10	Sutton	Flanagan
3—At Calif.	L	2-5	McCaskill	Jones
5—Seattle	L	2-8	Moore	Dixon
6—Seattle	L	2-6	Morgan	Boddicker
7—Seattle	W	8-0	McGregor	Langston
8—Boston	L	3-9†	Schiraldi	Aase
9—Boston	L	5-7	Nipper	Bordi
10—Boston	L	4-9	Clemens	Dixon
11—Boston	W	8-6	Aase	Crawford
12—At Detroit	L	3-5	King	McGregor
13—At Detroit	L	2-7	Hernandez	Flanagan
14—At Detroit	L	0-7	Tanana	Habyan
15—At N.Y.	L	3-5	Stoddard	Boddicker
16—At N.Y.	L	1-8	Drabek	McGregor
17—At N.Y.	W	8-3	Bell	Tewksbury
19—Milwaukee	W	3-1	Dixon	Higuera
20—Milwaukee	W	4-3	Habyan	Plesac
21—Milwaukee	L	4-5†	Plesac	Havens
22—New York	L	2-4	Tewksbury	McGregor
23—New York	L	3-5*	Righetti	Bordi
24—New York	L	1-4	Rasmussen	Flanagan
25—At Milw.	L	3-9	Higuera	Dixon
26—At Milw.	L	0-2	Vuckovich	Boddicker
27—At Milw.	W	7-0	McGregor	Nieves
28—At Milw.	L	2-10	Birkbeck	Bell
29—At Boston	L	5-7	Nipper	Habyan
30—At Boston	W	6-3*	Bordi	Stanley

Won 8, Lost 20

OCTOBER			Winner	Loser
1—At Boston	L	7-11	Woodward	Arnold
3—Detroit	L	3-6	Terrell	McGregor
4—Detroit	L	4-11	Kelly	Bell
5—Detroit	L	3-6	King	Arnold

Won 0, Lost 4

*10 innings. †11 innings. ‡12 innings. §13 innings.

Larry Sheets made the most of his limited playing time, hitting 18 homers and driving in 60 runs.

errors) and pitching (4.30 earned-run average).

The roster was in a constant state of flux. Weaver utilized 141 different lineups, including nine different leadoff men.

Instead of being a regular, Rayford wound up as one of 10 players who combined to make 40 errors at third base. Rayford was the most frequent starter at third, followed by Tom O'Malley, who batted .254 with 18 RBIs in 181 at-bats.

Six players were used at second base, where Alan Wiggins had been expected to play regularly. Despite stealing 21 bases through late July, Wiggins fell into disfavor with Weaver and was banished to Rochester. Juan Bonilla (.243) and Gutierrez manned second the rest of the way.

Wiggins was joined in Rochester by several others in the disappointing cast, including Mike Young. The outfielder hit 28 homers in '85, but his swing was a mess in '86. Young spent five weeks in Rochester and finished with just nine homers and 42 RBIs.

There were other disappointments. Catcher Rick Dempsey hit .208 with 29 RBIs, while his backup, rookie John Stefero, batted .233. Outfielder John Shelby knocked in 49 runs in 404 at-bats but had a .228 average. Veteran Jim Dwyer tied for the A.L. lead with three pinch-hit homers but batted only .244.

The pitching staff was full of underachievers. With a 3.62 mark, Davis had the best ERA among the starters but finished with a 9-12 record. Flanagan (7-11), Scott McGregor (11-15) and Ken Dixon (11-13) all had losing records and ERAs above 4.20. Boddicker's 4.70 ERA was the worst of the bunch, but the righthander led the staff with a 14-12 record, seven complete games and 175 strikeouts.

With the exception of Don Aase, the bullpen wasn't much better than the starting rotation. Relievers Rich Bordi, Nate Snell, Brad Havens and Odell Jones combined for a 13-10 record, four saves and a 4.23 ERA.

There were few bright spots for the Orioles, but Aase was one of them. The right-handed stopper set a club record with 34 saves, 27 of them by July 28, and earned the save in the American League's All-Star Game triumph as well.

In addition, Cal Ripken had a spectacular year defensively, making only 13 errors and leading the league's shortstops in assists while finishing second in fielding percentage and double plays. Ripken also hit .282 with 25 homers and 81 RBIs.

Designated hitter-outfielder Larry Sheets had 18 homers and 60 RBIs in only 338 at-bats, while right fielder Lee Lacy offered a little better than his normal production (.287, 11 homers, 47 RBIs). Utilityman Juan Beniquez batted .300. And rookie Jim Traber provided a lift when Murray was disabled, hitting 13 homers in 212 at-bats.

But in the final analysis, the Orioles' only significant achievement was drawing the highest attendance ever for a last-place team (1,973,176). That was of little consolation to a club that had grown accustomed to winning.

"We got a lesson in losing, and a lot of these guys couldn't handle it because they weren't used to it," Ripken Sr. said after moving up from third-base coach. "We've had enough lessons in losing."

Young first baseman Wally Joyner came out of nowhere to lead the old Angels to the American League West Division title.

'Old' Angels Enjoy Swan Song

By TOM SINGER

The most frequently made observation about the 1986 California Angels was that they were old, so when the club was on the verge of winning its first American League pennant, those aging veterans were primed for a World Series swan song.

Instead, a dissonant chord was struck, and along came a familiar refrain: Angels blow two-game playoff lead, Gene Mauch goes home empty-handed.

It had happened four years before, although not quite so dramatically. In 1982, with Mauch at the helm, the Angels took a two-games-to-none lead in the best-of-five A.L. Championship Series, then lost the next three games to the Milwaukee Brewers. Mauch, who began his major league managerial career in 1960 but had never won a pennant, took the next two years off from managing.

Mauch returned to the Angel dugout in 1985, and a year later he had his club back in the playoffs, this time against the Boston Red Sox in a seven-game series. The Angels assumed a 3-1 lead in games and carried a 5-2 lead into the ninth inning of Game 5 at Anaheim Stadium. Boston's Don Baylor hit a one-out, two-run home run to make the score 5-4, but with two out, reliever Donnie Moore had two strikes on Dave Henderson. Mauch's elusive pennant was never closer to his grasp.

But Henderson hammered a two-run homer, and the Red Sox went on to win in 11 innings. The next two games were laughers for the Red Sox. Same song, different verse: No flag in Anaheim.

"We worked awful hard for eight months, and we thought we got the job done," said Mauch, who made it an even quarter-century without winning a pennant as a manager. "Then it got away."

And away went a chunk of the club's roster. The last out of the playoffs marked the end of the road for some of the old-timers.

The contracts of 12 Angel veterans ran out in 1986, and club officials indicated that the off-season probably would be a good time to clean house. Like second baseman Bobby Grich, who announced his retirement after the playoffs, some would not return to baseball at all.

"As we were playing the last few innings of that last game, the thought crossed my mind that this would be the last time we'd be together," 36-year-old third baseman Doug DeCinces said.

Center fielder Gary Pettis was superlative on defense and reached base often enough to steal 50 times.

Nevertheless, 1986 was quite a last dance for Grich, DeCinces and the others thrown into limbo: catcher Bob Boone, infielder Rick Burleson, left fielder Brian Downing, right fielder Ruppert Jones, designated hitter Reggie Jackson and

SCORES OF CALIFORNIA ANGELS' 1986 GAMES

APRIL

			Winner	Loser
8—At Seattle	L	4-8*	Ladd	Forsch
9—At Seattle	W	9-5	Slaton	Langston
10—At Seattle	L	2-5	Young	Sutton
11—At Oak.	W	10-3	Romanick	Langford
12—At Oak.	W	9-3	McCaskill	Andujar
13—At Oak.	L	7-11	Codiroli	Witt
14—Seattle	W	7-6	Moore	Ladd
15—Seattle	L	4-9	Young	Sutton
16—Seattle	W	4-0	Romanick	Wilcox
17—Minnesota	L	1-4	Viola	McCaskill
18—Minnesota	W	6-5	Witt	Smithson
19—Minnesota	W	5-4	Slaton	Butcher
20—Minnesota	W	8-5	Forster	Davis
21—Oakland	L	2-6	Andujar	Romanick
22—Oakland	W	5-1	McCaskill	Langford
23—Oakland	W	5-0	Witt	Codiroli
25—At Minn.	L	4-7	Blyleven	Slaton
26—At Minn.	W	7-6	Bryden	Davis
27—At Minn.	W	8-7	Bryden	Smith
29—At Toronto	W	4-3	Forster	Eichhorn
30—At Toronto	L	4-6	Alexander	Moore

Won 13, Lost 8

MAY

			Winner	Loser
1—At Toronto	W	7-4	Slaton	Key
2—At Milw.	L	4-5	Nieves	Sutton
3—At Milw.	L	3-4*	Clear	Moore
4—At Milw.	L	3-5	Higuera	McCaskill
5—At Boston	L	0-3	Hurst	Witt
6—At Boston	W	6-2	Forster	Boyd
7—Toronto	W	6-2	Sutton	Clancy
8—Toronto	L	6-7	Eichhorn	Forster
9—Milwaukee	L	5-16	Darwin	McCaskill
10—Milwaukee	L	2-4	Nieves	Witt
11—Milwaukee	W	5-1	Slaton	Wegman
12—Boston	W	7-1	Sutton	Nipper
13—Boston	W	5-4	Romanick	Brown
14—Boston	L	5-8	Clemens	Bryden
16—At Detroit	W	11-1	Witt	Petry
17—At Detroit	L	4-10	LaPoint	Slaton
20—At Balt.	W	6-4	McCaskill	Boddicker
21—At Balt.	L	1-2	Davis	Witt
22—At Balt.	L	3-6	McGregor	Slaton
23—At N.Y.	L	5-10	Whitson	Sutton
24—At N.Y.	L	6-7	Righetti	Moore
25—At N.Y.	L	5-8	Holland	Corbett
26—At N.Y.	W	8-7	Witt	Righetti
28—Detroit	L	1-4	Petry	Slaton
29—Detroit	L	4-7	LaPoint	Sutton
30—Baltimore	L	0-3	Snell	Romanick
31—Baltimore	W	2-0	McCaskill	Davis

Won 10, Lost 17

JUNE

			Winner	Loser
1—Baltimore	W	7-4	Witt	McGregor
2—New York	W	8-7	Finley	Righetti
3—New York	W	4-2	Sutton	Rasmussen
4—New York	L	0-11	Niekro	Romanick
6—At Cleve.	L	0-3	Schrom	McCaskill
7—At Cleve.	W	8-2	Witt	Candiotti
8—At Cleve.	L	4-11	Heaton	Slaton
9—At Chicago	W	3-0	Sutton	Seaver
10—At Chicago	L	3-7	Allen	Romanick
11—At Chicago	W	12-11	McCaskill	Dotson
12—Kan. City	W	3-2	Witt	Jackson
13—Kan. City	L	2-10	Saberhagen	Slaton
14—Kan. City	W	6-5	Corbett	Black
15—Kan. City	L	5-6	Leibrandt	Romanick
16—Texas	W	2-1	McCaskill	Hough
17—Texas	W	4-0	Witt	Mahler
18—Texas	W	5-1	Sutton	Guzman
20—At Kan. C.	W	6-2	Romanick	Leonard
21—At Kan. C.	W	4-3	McCaskill	Leibrandt
22—At Kan. C.	L	4-7	Bankhead	Witt
23—At Texas	W	6-4	Sutton	Guzman
24—At Texas	W	12-3	Romanick	Correa
25—At Texas	W	7-1	McCaskill	Witt
27—Cleveland	L	3-6	Noles	Witt
28—Cleveland	W	9-3	Corbett	Butcher
29—Cleveland	L	4-6	Schrom	Romanick
30—Chicago	L	3-4	Davis	McCaskill

Won 17, Lost 10

JULY

			Winner	Loser
1—Chicago	L	3-5	Bannister	Cook
2—Chicago	W	4-3	Witt	Allen
4—At Toronto	W	9-1	Sutton	Stieb
5—At Toronto	L	3-7	Clancy	Romanick
6—At Toronto	W	8-2	McCaskill	Lamp
7—At Milw.	W	3-1y	Forster	Plesac
8—At Milw.	W	14-3	Candelaria	Nieves
9—At Milw.	W	6-1	Sutton	Higuera
10—At Boston	L	7-8‡	Lollar	Cook
11—At Boston	W	5-0	McCaskill	Seaver
12—At Boston	L	2-3	Clemens	Witt
13—At Boston	W	12-3	Candelaria	Sellers
17—Toronto	L	5-8	Key	Sutton
18—Toronto	L	0-2	Clancy	McCaskill
19—Toronto	W	9-3	Candelaria	Stieb
20—Toronto	L	3-6*	Henke	Corbett
21—Milwaukee	L	3-5	Wegman	Romanick
22—Milwaukee	L	2-6	Nieves	Sutton
23—Milwaukee	W	3-2*	McCaskill	Darwin
25—Boston	L	1-8	Clemens	Candelaria
26—Boston	W	4-1	Witt	Hurst
27—Boston	W	3-0	Sutton	Seaver
28—At Oak.	W	6-3	McCaskill	Andujar
29—At Oak.	L	2-4	Stewart	Chadwick
30—At Oak.	W	6-2	Candelaria	Leiper
31—At Oak.	W	8-5	Witt	Plunk

Won 15, Lost 11

AUGUST

			Winner	Loser
1—At Seattle	W	3-2	Sutton	Langston
2—At Seattle	L	3-7	Huismann	McCaskill
3—At Seattle	L	3-6	Ladd	Chadwick
4—At Minn.	L	5-6	Pastore	Moore
5—At Minn.	W	13-1	Witt	Anderson
6—At Minn.	L	2-5	Blyleven	Sutton
7—Seattle	W	4-3†	Moore	Ladd
8—Seattle	W	6-4	Ruhle	Swift
9—Seattle	W	5-0	Candelaria	Morgan
10—Seattle	W	4-0	Witt	Langston
11—Minnesota	L	0-2	Blyleven	Sutton
12—Minnesota	W	5-4‡	Lucas	Davis
13—Minnesota	L	2-6	Viola	Ruhle
15—Oakland	W	6-4	Candelaria	Rijo
16—Oakland	W	5-2	Witt	Young
17—Oakland	W	7-3	Sutton	Andujar
19—At Detroit	W	5-2	McCaskill	Petry
19—At Detroit	L	3-8	O'Neal	Ruhle
20—At Detroit	L	0-3	Terrell	Candelaria
21—At Detroit	W	6-1	Witt	Morris
22—At Balt.	L	7-8	Bordi	Moore
23—At Balt.	L	2-4	Flanagan	Chadwick
24—At Balt.	W	4-3	McCaskill	Davis
25—At N.Y.	W	5-3	Candelaria	Niekro
26—At N.Y.	W	2-0	Witt	Drabek
28—Detroit	W	4-2	Sutton	King
29—Detroit	W	13-12	Corbett	Hernandez
30—Detroit	W	5-4	Lucas	Campbell
31—Detroit	W	5-3	Moore	Terrell

Won 19, Lost 10

SEPTEMBER

			Winner	Loser
1—Baltimore	L	3-9	McGregor	Witt
2—Baltimore	W	10-1	Sutton	Flanagan
3—Baltimore	W	5-2	McCaskill	Jones
5—New York	L	4-7	Drabek	Chadwick
6—New York	W	9-2	Witt	Niekro
7—New York	W	7-2	Sutton	Rasmussen
9—At Cleve.	W	8-1	McCaskill	Candiotti
10—At Cleve.	W	7-6§	Finley	Yett
12—At Chicago	L	2-3*	Thigpen	Finley
13—At Chicago	W	3-2x	Lucas	Dawley
14—At Chicago	L	1-3	Cowley	McCaskill
15—At Chicago	W	6-5	Lugo	DeLeon
16—Kan. City	W	6-5	Lucas	Quisenberry
17—Kan. City	W	3-1*	Corbett	Black
18—Kan. City	W	18-3	Witt	Leonard
19—Chicago	L	1-7	Cowley	McCaskill
20—Chicago	W	8-7	Moore	Schmidt
21—Chicago	W	3-0	Candelaria	Dotson
22—Cleveland	W	4-3	Sutton	Bailes
22—Cleveland	L	0-7	Yett	Chadwick
23—Cleveland	L	2-5	Swindell	Witt
25—Cleveland	W	6-3	McCaskill	Wills
26—Texas	W	8-3	Candelaria	Mohorcic
27—Texas	L	0-1	Hough	Sutton
28—Texas	L	3-4	B. Witt	M. Witt
29—At Kan. C.	L	1-2	Gubicza	Lugo
30—At Kan. C.	W	8-4	Finley	Bankhead

Won 17, Lost 10

OCTOBER

			Winner	Loser
1—At Kan. C.	L	0-2	Jackson	Ruhle
2—At Texas	L	9-10	Harris	Lucas
3—At Texas	L	1-6	Witt	McCaskill
4—At Texas	W	2-0	Candelaria	Correa
5—At Texas	L	4-7	Hough	Sutton

Won 1, Lost 4

*10 innings. †11 innings. ‡12 innings. §14 innings. x15 innings. y16 innings.

pitchers Doug Corbett, Don Sutton, Terry Forster, Vern Ruhle and Gary Lucas. The last four had renewable options for 1987, but the club chose to retain only Sutton and Lucas.

The uncertain future bonded the veteran core of a team that showed no outward signs of championship chemistry. This silent commitment took the Angels a long way.

After straddling the .500 level through the season's first two months, the Angels swept by the Texas Rangers into first place in late June, assumed a permanent lead July 7 and led by 10 games when they applied the clincher September 26. They finished with a 92-70 record, five games ahead of Texas.

The Angels didn't play favorites along the way to their third division title in eight years. In season series play, they were bested by only one of 13 teams (Milwaukee), and their sweep of A.L. West clubs included seven straight victories over Texas. They did not lose to the Rangers until after they had clinched the division.

Ironically, the leader of this veteran team was a rookie. First baseman Wally Joyner, whose exploits had given rise to the name Wally World for Anaheim Stadium, had 72 runs batted in by the All-Star break but needed two RBIs in the 162nd game to become the only Angel to reach 100. He also led the club with a .290 average.

But the Angels' domination was a collective effort. Downing (95) and DeCinces (96) closed fast to give the Angels their first trio of 90-RBI men since 1982.

While DeCinces led the club with a modest total of 26 homers, with Joyner (22) and Downing (20) close behind, seven Angels cracked double figures.

Similarly, the pitching staff lacked a 20-game winner, although Mike Witt (18-10), Kirk McCaskill (17-10) and Sutton (15-11) became the first trio of 15-game winners in club history.

Witt was the driving force behind a staff that compiled a 3.84 earned-run average, No. 2 in the league. The righthander ranked among the A.L. leaders with a 2.84 ERA, 14 complete games, three shutouts, 269 innings pitched and 208 strikeouts. McCaskill followed with a 3.36 ERA, 10 complete games and 202 strikeouts, while Sutton had a respectable 3.74 ERA.

The same theme of shared credit also held up in the bullpen, where Moore fell off from 31 saves in 1985 to 21. But with Corbett (10 saves) and Forster (five) making welcome comebacks, Moore's shoulder problems weren't critical.

Comebacks, fadeouts and dramatic improvements were recurring themes.

Burleson conquered a four-year layoff with shoulder injuries to bat .284 as a platooned DH and in his few chances proved that he still was adept on defense. George Hendrick, a .122 hitter the last two months of 1985, batted .272 with 14 homers while sharing right field with Jones (17 homers).

Lefthanders John Candelaria (10-2 with a 2.55 ERA in 16 starts) and Lucas (4-1 with two saves) supplied sparks after missing the first half with injuries.

Jackson, at 40 reduced to handling DH duties against righthanded pitchers, hit 18 homers to raise his career total to 548 but was of little help after the All-Star break (.195). Rob Wilfong, who shared second base with Grich, hit just .219. Righthander Ron Romanick, the club's second-biggest winner over the previous two seasons, struggled to a 5-8 record before being sent to the minors in July.

Gold Glove center fielder Gary Pettis and shortstop Dick Schofield, the vanguards of a youth movement now hitting high gear, became two of the Angels' most consistent clutch performers with 58 and 57 RBIs, respectively. In their 1984 rookie seasons they had combined to drive in 50 runs.

Pettis, who stole 50 bases, and Schofield (23 steals) also anchored the league's second-best defense, which made only 107 errors, a club record.

As befit a club of durable veterans, milestones fell in quick succession.

On May 14, Jackson's 537th homer moved him ahead of Mickey Mantle into sixth place on the all-time list. Within a three-week span in September, Reggie posted both his 2,500th hit and 2,500th strikeout.

On June 18, Sutton became history's 19th 300-game winner with a 5-1 three-hitter against Texas. Sutton went on to reach two other goals, 700 starts and 5,000 innings. On October 2, Boone, who at 38 led all A.L. catchers with 144 games and won his fourth Gold Glove, caught his 1,807th career game to move into second place behind the leader, Al Lopez. Downing ended the season as California's career RBI leader (595).

The Angels' victory total of 92 made the season one of the three best in franchise history, ranking alongside records of 93-69 in 1982 and 90-72 in 1985.

Those were the only other years when the Angels were run solely by Mauch who, faithful to his reputation, remained The Best Manager Who Never Won a Pennant.

Pete Incaviglia had his share of rookie problems, but gave the Rangers 30 home runs and a solid effort.

Youthful Rangers Ride High

By JIM REEVES

Once again, the famous words from "Butch Cassidy and the Sundance Kid" echo through the West.

"Who are those guys, anyway?"

In 1986, "those guys" were the new Texas Rangers.

Greener than a mint julep and as raw as a Montana blizzard, the Rangers pulled off one of the major shocks of the '86 season by finishing second in the American League West with an 87-75 record, matching the second-best performance in club history.

The Houdini-like magic for a team that was expected to finish in a different area code from the rest of the division almost earned Bobby Valentine accolades as A.L. Manager of the Year. He received just one less first-place vote (13-12) than John McNamara, who piloted Boston to the World Series.

No wonder Valentine came so close to scooping up that honor in his first full season as a big-league manager. When the Rangers broke camp in April, the question wasn't how many games they would win, but how many cases of Clearasil clubhouse manager Joe Macko should order.

Young? The team's best pitcher in spring training (Bobby Witt) had never won a professional game. He was one of three rookies to win a spot in the starting rotation.

The Rangers' opening-day cleanup hitter (Pete Incaviglia) was fresh from the Oklahoma State campus. He'd never seen a minor league pitch, much less one in the majors. But he had set a club record with seven spring-training home runs, not to mention another shot that blasted through an outfield fence.

The team's top short reliever from the left side (Mitch Williams) had never pitched above the Double-A level. He had been so wild in spring training a year earlier, the Rangers wouldn't let lefthanders hit against him for fear of someone getting hurt.

But now, as Paul Harvey likes to say, the rest of the story.

After struggling to a 4-9 mark, Witt won his last seven decisions to finish 11-9. He had trouble with his control, walking a club-record 143 batters in 157⅔ innings, but he also fanned 174.

Incaviglia tied Jeff Burroughs' club record for most homers in a season with 30, hit .250 and drove in 88 runs. The right fielder also struck out 185 times to set an A.L. record.

Williams went 8-6 with eight saves and set a major league record for appearances by a rookie pitcher with 80 (the league high).

Those three joined other Ranger heroes to keep the team in either first (46) or second place (112) for 158 of the 181 days in the season. The Rangers held the top spot in the division from May 24 through June 24 and finally settled into second place for good July 7.

In addition, Texas' 51-30 mark matched Boston for the best home record in the league. That, in turn, helped the Rangers draw almost 1.7 million fans to Arlington Stadium, an increase of nearly 600,000 over 1985 and a club record.

"It was a good year, but everyone should be ready to admit that it's just a steppingstone," General Manager Tom Grieve said. "There's a long way to go and a lot to accomplish before we can say we're satisfied. But it's great to see the team come so far and win the imagination of the fans back so quickly."

There were a number of sterling individual performances.

Despite missing a month with a pulled rib muscle, designated hitter Larry Parrish batted .276 with 28 homers and 94 runs batted in. First baseman Pete O'Brien knocked in 90 runs and reached career highs with a .290 average and 23 homers. Flashy rookie outfielder Ruben Sierra, who was called up June 1 from Oklahoma City (American Association), hit .264 with 16 homers and 55 RBIs and showed potential star quality. Outfielder Gary Ward, despite having to cope with misfortune in his family, batted .316. Center fielder Oddibe McDowell hit .266, scored 105 runs, slugged 18 homers and stole 33 bases. Shortstop Scott Fletcher hit .300 and displayed a steady hand on defense. Third baseman Steve Buechele had 18 homers and 54 RBIs in his first full major league season.

At catcher, Don Slaught was off to the finest start of his career when a pitch by Boston's Dennis (Oil Can) Boyd struck him in the face May 17. Slaught returned to the lineup seven weeks later and finished with 13 homers and 46 RBIs.

Orlando Mercado (.235), Geno Petralli (.255) and Darrell Porter (.265, 12 homers) filled in for Slaught behind the plate. Among the other part-time players,

SCORES OF TEXAS RANGERS' 1986 GAMES

APRIL			Winner	Loser
8—Toronto	W	6-3	Guzman	Stieb
9—Toronto	L	1-3	Alexander	Correa
10—Toronto	L	10-11	Henke	Harris
11—Baltimore	W	5-4	Wright	Aase
12—Baltimore	W	2-1	Harris	Havens
13—Baltimore	L	2-3	McGregor	Guzman
14—At Milw.	W	10-1	Correa	Leary
17—At Milw.	W	7-5	Harris	Searage
18—At Balt.	W	12-3	Mason	McGregor
19—At Balt.	L	4-10	Boddicker	Mahler
20—At Balt.	L	1-6	Davis	Guzman
21—At Toronto	L	6-7	Eichhorn	Harris
22—At Toronto	W	10-1	Witt	Clancy
23—At Toronto	W	9-8	Williams	Lamp
25—Milwaukee	L	1-11	Higuera	Guzman
26—Milwaukee	L	2-10	Leary	Correa
27—Milwaukee	W	6-2	Witt	Nieves
29—Cleveland	L	5-6	Kern	Harris
30—Cleveland	L	4-6	Schulze	Guzman

Won 9, Lost 10

MAY			Winner	Loser
2—At N.Y.	W	7-0	Correa	Shirley
3—At N.Y.	L	4-9	Tewksbury	Witt
4—At N.Y.	W	4-3	Williams	Guidry
5—Detroit	L	3-10	Petry	Guzman
6—Detroit	W	4-2	Hough	LaPoint
7—Detroit	W	2-1	Henry	Morris
10—New York	L	3-4	Guidry	Harris
11—New York	W	6-3	Mason	Niekro
11—New York	W	9-1	Guzman	Tewksbury
12—At Cleve.	W	19-2	Hough	Heaton
13—At Cleve.	L	2-3*	Yett	Harris
14—At Detroit	L	2-8	Terrell	Witt
15—At Detroit	W	8-1	Mason	Tanana
16—At Boston	W	4-1	Guzman	Hurst
17—At Boston	L	2-8	Boyd	Hough
18—At Boston	L	4-5*	Stanley	Harris
19—Kan. City	L	4-6	Gubicza	Witt
20—Kan. City	W	4-0	Mason	Leonard
21—Kan. City	W	2-1*	Harris	Farr
22—Kan. City	L	4-5	Jackson	Hough
23—Boston	L	1-2	Boyd	Correa
24—Boston	W	3-2	Williams	Stanley
25—Boston	L	1-7	Clemens	Mason
26—Chicago	W	7-2	Guzman	Schmidt
27—Chicago	W	6-3	Hough	Dotson
28—Chicago	W	6-3	Correa	Cowley
30—At Kan. C.	L	2-12	Leonard	Witt
31—At Kan. C.	L	1-8	Gubicza	Mason

Won 15, Lost 13

JUNE			Winner	Loser
1—At Kan. C.	L	3-5	Leibrandt	Guzman
2—At Chicago	W	1-0	Hough	Cowley
3—At Chicago	W	4-1	Correa	Davis
4—At Chicago	W	5-2	Witt	Seaver
6—Seattle	W	6-5*	Williams	Ladd
7—Seattle	W	7-5	Guzman	Young
7—Seattle	W	3-2	Hough	Guetterman
8—Seattle	W	5-4*	Williams	Best
9—At Minn.	L	2-3*	Atherton	Williams
10—At Minn.	W	14-10	Russell	Davis
11—At Minn.	W	6-2§	Williams	Jackson
13—At Oak.	W	2-1	Guzman	Young
14—At Oak.	L	2-3	Plunk	Correa
15—At Oak.	L	2-9	Codiroli	Witt
16—At Calif.	L	1-2	McCaskill	Hough
17—At Calif.	L	0-4	Witt	Mahler
18—At Calif.	L	1-5	Sutton	Guzman
19—Oakland	W	3-2	Correa	Plunk
20—Oakland	W	10-7	Witt	Codiroli
21—Oakland	W	3-2	Hough	Langford
22—Oakland	W	5-4	Mohorcic	Rijo
23—California	L	4-6	Sutton	Guzman
24—California	L	3-12	Romanick	Correa
25—California	L	1-7	McCaskill	Witt
26—At Seattle	W	10-3	Hough	Guetterman
27—At Seattle	L	5-6	Young	Russell
28—At Seattle	W	5-2	Guzman	Beattie
29—At Seattle	L	3-9	Moore	Correa
30—Minnesota	L	2-5	Viola	Harris

Won 16, Lost 13

JULY			Winner	Loser
1—Minnesota	W	5-0	Hough	Portugal
2—Minnesota	W	10-2	Mason	Smithson
4—Detroit	W	2-1	Guzman	Morris
5—Detroit	W	9-3	Correa	Terrell
6—Detroit	L	2-5	Tanana	Witt
7—New York	L	3-14	Nielsen	Hough
8—New York	W	6-1	Mason	Pulido
9—New York	L	4-5	Tewksbury	Guzman
10—At Cleve.	L	6-9	Schrom	Correa
11—At Cleve.	L	2-7	Candiotti	Witt
12—At Cleve.	W	11-6	Hough	Butcher
13—At Cleve.	W	5-3*	Williams	Bailes
17—At Detroit	L	1-2	Terrell	Williams
18—At Detroit	L	0-5	Morris	Mason
19—At Detroit	L	3-5‡	Hernandez	Harris
20—At Detroit	L	0-4	King	Guzman
21—At N.Y.	L	4-8	Drabek	Witt
22—At N.Y.	L	1-9	Rasmussen	Correa
23—At N.Y.	L	2-3*	Righetti	Hough
24—Cleveland	W	7-3	Loynd	Niekro
25—Cleveland	W	7-5	Harris	Bailes
26—Cleveland	W	8-5	Witt	Yett
27—Cleveland	L	3-8	Candiotti	Correa
28—Baltimore	L	3-4	Davis	Hough
29—Baltimore	W	6-5‡	Harris	Jones
30—Baltimore	W	5-3†	Russell	Snell

Won 12, Lost 14

AUGUST			Winner	Loser
1—At Milw.	W	7-2	Witt	Leary
1—At Milw.	W	8-6	Correa	Gibson
2—At Milw.	L	8-9	Plesac	Williams
3—At Milw.	W	7-6	Russell	Darwin
5—At Balt.	L	2-9	Davis	Guzman
6—At Balt.	W	13-11	Williams	Bordi
7—At Balt.	W	9-8	Russell	Havens
8—Toronto	W	9-7	Harris	Eichhorn
9—Toronto	W	7-6*	Harris	Caudill
10—Toronto	L	7-8*	Eichhorn	Williams
12—Milwaukee	L	2-7	Leary	Hough
13—Milwaukee	W	5-4‡	Harris	Johnson
14—Milwaukee	W	8-2	Loynd	Higuera
15—At Toronto	L	1-6	Johnson	Correa
16—At Toronto	L	1-13	Key	Hough
17—At Toronto	L	7-8†	Eichhorn	Russell
19—At Kan. C.	L	8-9†	Quisenberry	Mohorcic
20—At Kan. C.	W	7-1	Hough	Bankhead
21—At Kan. C.	L	3-4	Leibrandt	Correa
22—Chicago	W	11-3	Russell	Bannister
23—Chicago	W	3-1	Guzman	Carlton
24—Chicago	W	3-2	Hough	Schmidt
25—Boston	W	4-2	Mohorcic	Schiraldi
26—Boston	L	1-8	Boyd	Loynd
27—Boston	W	4-1	Correa	Hurst
28—At Chicago	L	2-6	Carlton	Guzman
29—At Chicago	W	5-2	Hough	Cowley
30—At Chicago	W	6-2	Witt	DeLeon
31—At Chicago	L	1-3	Dotson	Loynd

Won 17, Lost 12

SEPTEMBER			Winner	Loser
1—At Boston	L	4-6	Hurst	Correa
2—At Boston	L	6-8	Stewart	Guzman
3—At Boston	L	3-4	Stanley	Mohorcic
5—Kan. City	W	7-6	Witt	Bankhead
6—Kan. City	W	6-4	Correa	Farr
7—Kan. City	L	2-5	Jackson	Hough
9—Seattle	L	1-3	Nunez	Guzman
10—Seattle	W	3-2*	Harris	Young
11—At Minn.	L	2-6	Viola	Hough
12—At Minn.	L	2-4	Heaton	Correa
13—At Minn.	W	14-1	Mason	Blyleven
14—At Minn.	L	6-7	Frazier	Mohorcic
15—At Oak.	W	6-2	Hough	Stewart
16—At Oak.	W	10-6	Meredith	Von Ohlen
17—At Oak.	W	4-0	Correa	Rodriguez
19—Minnesota	W	4-1	Hough	Blyleven
20—Minnesota	L	2-3	Viola	Williams
21—Minnesota	W	2-1	Witt	Portugal
22—At Seattle	W	2-0	Correa	Langston
23—At Seattle	W	12-6	Hough	Swift
24—At Seattle	L	4-5	Moore	Guzman
26—At Calif.	L	3-8	Candelaria	Mohorcic
27—At Calif.	W	1-0	Hough	Sutton
28—At Calif.	W	4-3	B. Witt	M. Witt
29—Oakland	W	3-0	Correa	Young
30—Oakland	W	9-5	Brown	Rodriguez

Won 15, Lost 11

OCTOBER			Winner	Loser
1—Oakland	L	7-9	Howell	Williams
2—California	W	10-9	Harris	Lucas
3—California	W	6-1	Witt	McCaskill
4—California	L	0-2	Candelaria	Correa
5—California	W	7-4	Hough	Sutton

Won 3, Lost 2

*10 innings. †11 innings. ‡12 innings. §16 innings.

Shortstop Scott Fletcher provided steady defense and surprised everybody by hitting .300.

Tom Paciorek hit .286, Curtis Wilkerson .237 and Toby Harrah .218.

The pitching staff also had its share of heroes. Knuckleballer Charlie Hough missed the first month with a broken finger but won a career-high 17 games while losing 10. Rookie Edwin Correa, who had never pitched above the Double-A level entering the season, won 12 games (the most ever by a Ranger rookie) and had 189 strikeouts. Reliever Greg Harris finished 10-8 with a 2.83 earned-run average and a career-high 20 saves. Dale Mohorcic, a 30-year-old rookie, tallied seven saves and a 2.51 ERA in middle relief.

One youngster who struggled was righthander Jose Guzman, the third rookie member of the starting rotation. Guzman went 9-15 with a 4.54 ERA. Veteran Mike Mason (7-3) had two stints on the disabled list, one of which made possible the quick promotion of rookie Mike Loynd from the minors. Loynd was drafted out of Florida State in June and had only five minor league appearances to his credit when he joined the Rangers. The righthander won his major league debut July 24 but finished 2-2 with a 5.36 ERA.

All told, Texas pitchers struck out more batters (1,059) than any other A.L. team. On the other hand, they also walked the most (736) while compiling a 4.11 ERA.

Still, the Rangers' offense was powerful enough to give their maturing pitchers a chance, and in the end, Texas finished only five games behind California.

"This was a team that did things together," Valentine said. "This was a team by the true definition of the word. It was a team that believed in itself and in each other. It believed in what we were trying to do as a group."

It was definitely a team that didn't know how good it could be after losing 99 games a year earlier.

"If someone had told us in spring training that we might finish a dozen games over .500, we'd have danced in the street," Hough said.

Said Parrish: "We thought we were going in the right direction, and if the kids had struggled and we finished 25 games out, it still would have been the right thing to do. But no one knew how the kids would do."

Obviously, they did just fine.

"We never said we would sacrifice winning for anything," Valentine said. "If I did things early that might have sacrificed a game, it was because I believed it would produce more wins later on. Everything was focused on winning."

And for a change, Texas fans enjoyed a healthy dose of that.

Royals second baseman Frank White was consistent, batting .272 with 22 home runs and 84 runs batted in.

Stunned Royals Lose Crown

By BOB NIGHTENGALE

There was much that was painful for the Kansas City Royals in 1986, but nothing could match the ghastly horror of watching a priest enter their locker room in Baltimore, knowing that their manager needed some divine help.

On July 15, Dick Howser managed the American League to a rare All-Star Game victory. But when the Royals hosted the Cleveland Indians to open the second half of their schedule two nights later, Howser was absent. He spent that evening undergoing tests in a Kansas City hospital.

As the Royals found out the next day, the tests revealed that Howser had a brain tumor about the size of a golf ball. Surgery was scheduled for July 22, by which time the Royals were in Baltimore, awaiting word on their skipper.

The operation lasted three hours. When General Manager John Schuerholz entered the clubhouse before their game with the Orioles, the players could sense that the news would not be good. Schuerholz announced that surgeons had been able to remove only part of Howser's tumor, which was malignant. The manager would have to spend the next several weeks undergoing chemotherapy in an effort to dissolve the tumor.

A priest who served as the Orioles' unofficial chaplain then entered the clubhouse and led the team in a prayer service. The least of the Royals' concerns was the game that night, which they lost, or the ones to follow, many of which they also lost. They were paralyzed by the thought that Howser's All-Star Game triumph might turn out to be the last victory of his managerial career.

"There was a month there when a lot of us wondered if winning a baseball game was all that critical," backup catcher Jamie Quirk said. "It sounds like an excuse, but you're talking about a human being. Losing Dick was an absolute shock.

"The day the priest came in the clubhouse to talk to us, we just kind of looked at each other and said, 'Hey, this is for real.' It was scary. It put some fear in us. You had to wonder if baseball was really that important."

Without Howser, who had led the Royals to their only world championship the year before, the team lacked direction and motivation.

"The steady leadership and synergistic force wasn't there," Schuerholz said. "I don't know if that in itself would have made the difference, but I do believe we would have been more of a factor."

Big first baseman Steve Balboni hit 29 home runs and drove in 88 runs before going to the bench with a back injury.

The Royals hadn't been much of a factor in the A.L. West the first half of the season. Their 40-48 record at the All-Star break left them in fourth place, 8½ games behind the California Angels.

But with Howser's predicament constantly on their minds, the Royals never launched their traditional second-half surge. Never did they make a run for the title, nor even threaten.

SCORES OF KANSAS CITY ROYALS' 1986 GAMES

APRIL

			Winner	Loser
8—At N.Y.	L	2-4	Guidry	Black
9—At N.Y.	W	7-4	Farr	Whitson
10—At N.Y.	L	5-6†	Righetti	H'sheimer
11—Toronto	L	2-6	Clancy	Gubicza
12—Toronto	W	1-0	Leonard	Acker
13—Toronto	W	7-4	Black	Stieb
14—At Boston	W	8-2	Leibrandt	Boyd
16—At Boston	W	1-0	Saberhagen	Nipper
17—At Boston	L	2-6	Clemens	Gubicza
18—At Toronto	W	6-4	Leonard	Stieb
19—At Toronto	L	5-6	Alexander	Black
20—At Toronto	W	6-4	Leibrandt	Lamp
21—New York	L	4-8	Whitson	Saberhagen
22—New York	L	1-5	Tewksbury	Gubicza
23—New York	L	1-2	Rasmussen	Leonard
25—Boston	W	6-0	Leibrandt	Boyd
26—Boston	L	1-6	Nipper	Saberhagen
29—At Detroit	L	1-2	Tanana	Leonard
30—At Detroit	W	7-3	Leibrandt	Hernandez

Won 9, Lost 10

MAY

			Winner	Loser
2—Baltimore	W	5-0	Saberhagen	Flanagan
3—Baltimore	L	2-3	Dixon	Gubicza
4—Baltimore	W	11-1	Leonard	McGregor
5—At Cleve.	L	4-5†	Niekro	Quisenberry
6—At Cleve.	L	1-6*	Candiotti	Black
7—At Cleve.	L	1-7	Heaton	Saberhagen
9—At Balt.	W	7-4	Black	Dixon
10—At Balt.	L	2-5	Boddicker	Leonard
11—At Balt.	L	3-4	Davis	Leibrandt
12—Detroit	W	6-5	Jackson	LaPoint
13—Detroit	W	4-2‡	Farr	Hernandez
14—Cleveland	W	5-0	Gubicza	Niekro
15—Cleveland	W	6-3	Leonard	Bailes
16—At Chicago	L	2-4	Dotson	Leibrandt
17—At Chicago	L	6-7	James	Huismann
18—At Chicago	L	1-5	Bannister	Saberhagen
19—At Texas	W	6-4	Gubicza	Witt
20—At Texas	L	0-4	Mason	Leonard
21—At Texas	L	1-2†	Harris	Farr
22—At Texas	W	5-4	Jackson	Hough
23—Chicago	L	1-4	Cowley	Saberhagen
24—Chicago	W	7-6	Black	James
25—Chicago	W	2-1x	Bankhead	Dawley
26—Milwaukee	L	0-4	Darwin	Leibrandt
27—Milwaukee	L	1-9	Higuera	Jackson
28—Milwaukee	W	4-3	Farr	Clear
30—Texas	W	12-2	Leonard	Witt
31—Texas	W	8-1	Gubicza	Mason

Won 14, Lost 14

JUNE

			Winner	Loser
1—Texas	W	5-3	Leibrandt	Guzman
2—At Milw.	L	2-7	Higuera	Jackson
3—At Milw.	W	4-1	Saberhagen	Leary
4—At Milw.	W	8-6	Leonard	Nieves
5—Minnesota	W	8-2	Bankhead	Smithson
6—Minnesota	W	6-1	Leibrandt	Agosto
7—Minnesota	L	1-4	Blyleven	Jackson
8—Minnesota	L	2-5	Portugal	Saberhagen
9—Seattle	L	3-5	Langston	Leonard
10—Seattle	W	9-5	Farr	Wilcox
11—Seattle	L	2-12	Morgan	Leibrandt
12—At Calif.	L	2-3	Witt	Jackson
13—At Calif.	W	10-2	Saberhagen	Slaton
14—At Calif.	L	5-6	Corbett	Black
15—At Calif.	W	6-5	Leibrandt	Romanick
16—At Oak.	W	3-2‡	Black	Rijo
17—At Oak.	W	2-1	Jackson	Mooneyham
18—At Oak.	L	0-1	Young	Saberhagen
20—California	L	2-6	Romanick	Leonard
21—California	L	3-4	McCaskill	Leibrandt
22—California	W	7-4	Bankhead	Witt
23—Oakland	W	6-3	Jackson	Young
24—Oakland	L	4-8	Plunk	Saberhagen
25—Oakland	W	5-4	Farr	Mooneyham
26—Oakland	W	9-2	Leibrandt	Langford
27—At Minn.	L	4-6	Smithson	Bankhead
28—At Minn.	L	2-7	Blyleven	Jackson
29—At Minn.	L	4-9	Anderson	Saberhagen
30—At Seattle	L	2-3	Langston	Leonard

Won 14, Lost 15

JULY

			Winner	Loser
1—At Seattle	L	5-8	Ladd	Quisenberry
2—At Seattle	L	3-5	Morgan	Bankhead
4—At Cleve.	L	3-10	Niekro	Jackson
5—At Cleve.	L	5-10	Schrom	Saberhagen
6—At Cleve.	L	0-5	Candiotti	Leonard
7—Baltimore	L	1-8	Boddicker	Leibrandt
8—Baltimore	L	4-8§	Jones	Quisenberry
9—Baltimore	W	3-0	Jackson	Bordi
11—Detroit	W	4-3	Farr	Terrell
11—Detroit	L	7-8‡	Hernandez	Gubicza
12—Detroit	W	7-4	Leibrandt	King
13—Detroit	L	0-5	Morris	Bankhead
17—Cleveland	W	5-1	Saberhagen	Candiotti
18—Cleveland	L	2-3†	Oelkers	Quisenberry
19—Cleveland	L	4-6	Niekro	Bankhead
20—Cleveland	W	3-2	Farr	Noles
21—At Balt.	W	6-1	Jackson	Dixon
22—At Balt.	L	4-5	Aase	Black
23—At Balt.	W	7-3	Gubicza	McGregor
24—At Detroit	W	1-0	Bankhead	O'Neal
25—At Detroit	L	2-9	King	Leonard
26—At Detroit	L	3-4‡	Hernandez	Farr
27—At Detroit	W	5-4	Saberhagen	Hernandez
28—Toronto	L	0-6	Clancy	Leibrandt
29—Toronto	L	2-5	Stieb	Bankhead
30—Toronto	L	2-7	Johnson	Leonard

Won 9, Lost 17

AUGUST

			Winner	Loser
1—At Boston	L	3-5	Hurst	Jackson
2—At Boston	W	13-2	Gubicza	Seaver
3—At Boston	L	3-5	Nipper	Leibrandt
5—At Toronto	W	8-6	Bankhead	Lamp
6—At Toronto	L	0-8	Key	Jackson
7—At Toronto	L	4-5	Eichhorn	Farr
8—At N.Y.	L	0-2	John	Leibrandt
9—At N.Y.	L	2-3	Fisher	Black
10—At N.Y.	W	13-3	Bankhead	Rasmussen
12—Boston	W	5-1	Jackson	Hurst
12—Boston	W	6-5	Gubicza	Stanley
13—Boston	L	2-5	Seaver	Leibrandt
14—Boston	L	6-11	Nipper	Black
15—New York	L	4-7	Drabek	Bankhead
16—New York	W	4-2	Jackson	Rasmussen
17—New York	W	5-0	Gubicza	Guidry
19—Texas	W	9-8‡	Quisenberry	Mohorcic
20—Texas	L	1-7	Hough	Bankhead
21—Texas	W	4-3	Leibrandt	Correa
22—At Milw.	W	4-2	Jackson	Nieves
23—At Milw.	L	4-8	Plesac	Gubicza
24—At Milw.	L	2-3‡	Clear	Quisenberry
25—At Chicago	W	2-0	Bankhead	DeLeon
26—At Chicago	W	6-1	Leibrandt	Dotson
27—At Chicago	L	1-3	Bannister	Jackson
29—Milwaukee	L	1-3	Higuera	Leonard
30—Milwaukee	W	10-1	Gubicza	Birkbeck
31—Milwaukee	W	6-1	Bankhead	Wegman

Won 14, Lost 14

SEPTEMBER

			Winner	Loser
1—Chicago	L	0-4	Bannister	Leibrandt
2—Chicago	L	0-3	Carlton	Jackson
3—Chicago	W	2-1†	Black	Nelson
4—Chicago	W	1-0	Farr	Dawley
5—At Texas	L	6-7	Witt	Bankhead
6—At Texas	L	4-6	Correa	Farr
7—At Texas	W	5-2	Jackson	Hough
8—Minnesota	W	5-0	Leonard	Blyleven
9—Minnesota	W	11-3	Gubicza	Smithson
11—Seattle	W	7-6†	Quisenberry	Huismann
12—Seattle	L	2-4†	Langston	Quisenberry
13—Seattle	W	5-4	Leonard	Swift
14—Seattle	W	10-3	Gubicza	Moore
16—At Calif.	L	5-6	Lucas	Quisenberry
17—At Calif.	L	1-3†	Corbett	Black
18—At Calif.	L	3-18	Witt	Leonard
19—At Seattle	L	5-6	Young	Black
20—At Seattle	L	0-3	Trujillo	Saberhagen
21—At Seattle	W	8-1	Leibrandt	Morgan
22—At Minn.	L	1-2	Atherton	Jackson
23—At Minn.	L	2-9	Smithson	Leonard
24—At Minn.	W	2-1	Quisenberry	Blyleven
25—At Minn.	W	8-1	Saberhagen	Viola
27—Oakland	L	3-6	Andujar	Jackson
27—Oakland	L	6-9	Rijo	Black
28—Oakland	W	6-2	Leibrandt	Stewart
29—California	W	2-1	Gubicza	Lugo
30—California	L	4-8	Finley	Bankhead

Won 13, Lost 15

OCTOBER

			Winner	Loser
1—California	W	2-0	Jackson	Ruhle
3—At Oak.	W	8-4	Leibrandt	Andujar
4—At Oak.	W	2-0	Gubicza	Stewart
5—At Oak.	L	0-6	Young	Saberhagen

Won 3, Lost 1

*5 innings. †10 innings. ‡11 innings. §13 innings. x17 innings.

"The bottom just fell out on us," said third baseman George Brett, who struggled along with the rest of the club, hitting only 16 home runs with 73 runs batted in. "It was one of those years when nothing got untracked. Every day when we came to the ball park, we really thought we'd turn this thing around. Every day, we thought we'd start playing like last season. It never happened."

Kansas City went 36-38 under Mike Ferraro, the third-base coach who was named interim manager. By season's end, Royals officials were saying that they expected Howser to return as manager in 1987, and Ferraro was not rehired.

A year after winning the world championship, the Royals were anxious to put the '86 season behind them. It was a year of dubious achievement as well as sadness.

The Royals posted a 76-86 record, their worst mark since 1970, and tied for third place in the American League West, 16 games behind the Angels. It was the first time since 1974 (excluding the 1981 split season) that the Royals had finished lower than second.

Before the All-Star break, the Royals endured an 11-game losing streak, their longest ever. They also suffered their worst loss ever, an 18-3 trouncing by the Angels.

Perhaps nothing better exemplified the Royals' ineptitude in '86 than their individual award winners. Brett was the team batting champion with a .290 average, the lowest by a Royals leader since 1969 (the franchise's first year). And the leading winner on the pitching staff was Charlie Leibrandt, whose 14 victories was the second lowest by a Royals leader since 1972.

Kansas City's pitching staff led the league with a 3.82 earned-run average and 13 shutouts and allowed fewer homers (121) than any other A.L. team. But the individual performances were less impressive. No one took a bigger nose dive than Bret Saberhagen, who battled various injuries while going 7-12 with a 4.15 ERA. The righthander had won the A.L. Cy Young Award with a 20-6 record and a 2.87 ERA in '85.

The Royals' happiest story was Dennis Leonard, who threw a three-hit, 1-0 shutout April 12 in his first major league start after almost three years of inactivity. Despite finishing 8-13 with a 4.44 ERA, the veteran righthander's comeback from four knee operations was remarkable.

Lefthander Danny Jackson (11-12, 3.20 ERA) was perhaps the Royals' finest pitcher, although righthander Mark Gubicza overcame a terrible first half to finish 12-6 with a 3.64 ERA. Rookie Scott Bankhead (8-9, 4.61) made 17 starts.

In the bullpen, Dan Quisenberry, a five-time A.L. Fireman of the Year, saved only 12 games. Bud Black (nine saves) and Steve Farr (eight) frequently got the call in save situations.

With their pitching not quite as sharp, the Royals were unable to get by with a weak offense, as they had in '85. Kansas City's .252 average and 654 runs scored both ranked next to last in the league.

Gold Glove second baseman Frank White was the club's most consistent performer, batting .272 with 22 homers and 84 RBIs. First baseman Steve Balboni led the club with 29 homers and 88 RBIs, but his career was put in jeopardy by a season-ending back injury in September.

Left fielder Lonnie Smith put on a late-season surge to finish with a .287 average and 26 stolen bases. Despite leading the team with 34 steals, center fielder Willie Wilson (.269) struggled through his worst season since his rookie year in 1978.

The Royals got even less production from the rest of the lineup. Catcher Jim Sundberg hit only .212 with 42 RBIs, while Quirk batted .215. Shortstops Argenis Salazar and Buddy Biancalana combined for only 32 RBIs, and designated hitters Hal McRae and Jorge Orta provided 16 homers and 83 RBIs.

Several players were used in right field. Rudy Law (.261) held that spot until a knee injury placed him on the disabled list in July, while Darryl Motley's .203 hitting earned him a trade to Atlanta.

Outfielder Bo Jackson, the 1985 Heisman Trophy winner as a running back at Auburn University, was the most publicized of several promising rookies. After being selected by Kansas City in the fourth round of the June draft, Jackson spurned a multimillion-dollar deal from the Tampa Bay Buccaneers of the National Football League and agreed to terms with the Royals, who recalled him from Memphis (Southern) in September. Though he batted only .207 and struck out 34 times in 82 at-bats, Jackson displayed a strong arm, excellent speed and two mammoth homers.

Infielder Kevin Seitzer (.323) and outfielder Mike Kingery (.258) also showed potential as rookies.

For the most part, though, the Royals had little to be happy about in '86.

"It's been a long season, a frustrating season," Danny Jackson said. "All of our expectations were so high, and nothing was achieved. It'll be one we'll all want to forget."

A's outfielder Jose Canseco finished at the top of an impressive rookie class, hitting 33 home runs and driving in 117 runs.

LaRussa's A's Come to Life

By KIT STIER

When the Athletics who were there look back on the 1986 baseball season, they will remember it for what might have been if....

What if, for example, starters Joaquin Andujar, Moose Haas and Chris Codiroli hadn't missed good portions of the season with injuries? What if bullpen stopper Jay Howell, who saved 29 games in 1985, hadn't been disabled twice? What if the A's hadn't had to use 21 pitchers over the course of the season?

There was a whole stack of ifs awaiting Tony LaRussa when he took over as manager for Jackie Moore in July. It also didn't help that center fielder Dwayne Murphy suffered a back injury in early May. By the time he returned July 5, the outfield was in chaos, Moore had been fired and bullpen coach Jeff Newman was running the club on an interim basis while LaRussa squared away his family and personal belongings.

All the injuries created a situation in which four or five pitchers who hadn't been designated as starters in spring training were in the rotation. Even Howell's best setup man, Steve Ontiveros, who had pitched so brilliantly as a rookie in 1985, fell by the wayside with a sore right arm after collecting his 10th save.

So it was little wonder that the team was in a shambles when LaRussa, who had been fired by the Chicago White Sox in June, finally took the helm July 7, 11 days after Moore had been fired.

LaRussa's first move was to make Dave Stewart, who had been signed by the A's in May, a starter. Stewart, a super prospect first with the Los Angeles Dodgers and then with the Texas Rangers, decided that pitching at home was his cup of tea. The Oakland native won nine of his first 10 decisions before tailing off to 9-5 at season's end.

Stewart started the A's first game under LaRussa. The righthander beat Roger Clemens and the Red Sox at Fenway Park to give the last-place club a 32-52 record. By July 11, the A's had fallen to 24 games under .500 (32-56), five games behind the sixth-place Minnesota Twins in the American League West at the time.

Then, one by one, people started to get healthy, and the A's began to win games for their new boss. Here and there, eyebrows started popping.

Oakland's highly touted left fielder, Jose

Shortstop Alfredo Griffin played excellent defense, batted .285 and stole 33 bases.

Canseco, was named A.L. Rookie of the Year. He hit 33 home runs, drove in 117 runs, stole 15 bases and, like the typical slugger, struck out a lot. He whiffed 175 times, which would have tied an A.L. record had Texas' Pete Incaviglia not established a new mark by striking out 185 times.

Alfredo Griffin left his mark as one of the finest shortstops in the league with a .285 batting average, a career-high 33 steals and spectacular glove work while playing 162 games for the second straight year.

Third baseman Carney Lansford hit .284 with 19 homers and 72 runs batted in, while right fielder Mike Davis slugged 19

SCORES OF OAKLAND ATHLETICS' 1986 GAMES

APRIL

			Winner	Loser
8—Minnesota	L	2-3	Viola	Codiroli
9—Minnesota	L	4-5	Smithson	Howell
10—Minnesota	W	3-0	Haas	Butcher
11—California	L	3-10	Romanick	Langford
12—California	L	3-9	McCaskill	Andujar
13—California	W	11-7	Codiroli	Witt
14—At Minn.	W	7-6	Atherton	Smith
15—At Minn.	W	8-2	Haas	Latham
16—At Minn.	L	5-7*	Davis	Atherton
18—At Seattle	W	4-1	Codiroli	Moore
19—At Seattle	W	7-2	Rijo	Langston
20—At Seattle	W	9-3	Haas	Young
21—At Calif.	W	6-2	Andujar	Romanick
22—At Calif.	L	1-5	McCaskill	Langford
23—At Calif.	L	0-5	Witt	Codiroli
24—Seattle	L	1-3	Langston	Rijo
25—Seattle	W	11-2	Haas	Young
26—Seattle	W	5-3	Andujar	Wilcox
27—Seattle	W	1-0	Langford	Morgan
29—At Milw.	L	4-5	McClure	Howell
30—At Milw.	L	1-5	Higuera	Rijo

Won 11, Lost 10

MAY

			Winner	Loser
1—At Milw.	W	7-2	Haas	Leary
2—At Boston	W	4-1	Andujar	Nipper
3—At Boston	L	3-4	Stewart	Codiroli
4—At Boston	L	1-4	Clemens	Langford
5—At Toronto	L	6-10	Eichhorn	Krueger
6—At Toronto	W	17-3	Haas	Key
7—Milwaukee	W	7-6	Andujar	Wegman
8—Milwaukee	W	2-1	Codiroli	Higuera
9—Boston	L	6-9*	Stanley	Atherton
10—Boston	L	2-4*	Hurst	Ontiveros
11—Boston	L	5-6	Boyd	Haas
12—Toronto	L	3-5	Clancy	Andujar
13—Toronto	W	6-3*	Mooneyham	Lamp
14—Toronto	W	9-4	Young	Stieb
16—At Balt.	W	8-4	Haas	Davis
17—At Balt.	L	2-8	McGregor	Langford
18—At Balt.	L	4-13	Bordi	Codiroli
20—At N.Y.	W	2-1	Young	Guidry
21—At N.Y.	L	4-10	Niekro	Plunk
22—At N.Y.	L	3-4†	Righetti	Howell
23—At Detroit	W	5-1	Rijo	LaPoint
24—At Detroit	L	1-4	Morris	Codiroli
25—At Detroit	L	1-2	Terrell	Young
26—At Detroit	L	4-5*	Hernandez	Howell
28—Baltimore	L	5-9	Bordi	Ontiveros
29—Baltimore	L	6-8	Havens	Codiroli
30—New York	W	6-3	Young	Niekro
31—New York	W	4-3	Ontiveros	Guidry

Won 12, Lost 16

JUNE

			Winner	Loser
1—New York	L	1-7	John	Leiper
2—Detroit	W	7-1	Codiroli	Petry
3—Detroit	W	6-4	Young	LaPoint
4—Detroit	L	5-8	Morris	Plunk
5—At Chicago	L	5-9	Allen	Haas
6—At Chicago	L	4-6	Dotson	Langford
7—At Chicago	L	3-10	Cowley	Codiroli
8—At Chicago	L	5-8	Davis	Young
9—At Cleve.	L	5-6	Bailes	Rijo
10—At Cleve.	L	7-8	Yett	Rijo
11—At Cleve.	L	4-7	Schrom	Langford
13—Texas	L	1-2	Guzman	Young
14—Texas	W	3-2	Plunk	Correa
15—Texas	W	9-2	Codiroli	Witt
16—Kan. City	L	2-3†	Black	Rijo
17—Kan. City	L	1-2	Jackson	Mooneyham
18—Kan. City	W	1-0	Young	Saberhagen
19—At Texas	L	2-3	Correa	Plunk
20—At Texas	L	7-10	Witt	Codiroli
21—At Texas	L	2-3	Hough	Langford
22—At Texas	L	4-5	Mohorcic	Rijo
23—At Kan. C.	L	3-6	Jackson	Young
24—At Kan. C.	W	8-4	Plunk	Saberhagen
25—At Kan. C.	L	4-5	Farr	Mooneyham
26—At Kan. C.	L	2-9	Leibrandt	Langford
27—Chicago	W	8-6	Mooneyham	Nelson
28—Chicago	L	1-4	Dotson	Young
29—Chicago	L	5-6*	James	Bair
30—Cleveland	L	3-8	Candiotti	Rijo

Won 7, Lost 22

JULY

			Winner	Loser
1—Cleveland	L	0-9	Butcher	Langford
2—Cleveland	L	3-7	Noles	Mooneyham
4—At Milw.	L	4-5	Plesac	Bair
5—At Milw.	L	1-2	Darwin	Plunk
6—At Milw.	W	6-3	Rijo	Leary
7—At Boston	W	6-4	Stewart	Clemens
8—At Boston	L	7-8	Boyd	Langford
9—At Boston	L	6-7	Sellers	Young
10—At Toronto	L	4-8	Clancy	Plunk
11—At Toronto	L	5-6	Eichhorn	Rijo
12—At Toronto	W	5-3	Stewart	Key
13—At Toronto	W	10-5	Young	Caudill
18—Milwaukee	W	6-1	Andujar	Nieves
19—Milwaukee	W	3-2	Mooneyham	Clear
20—Milwaukee	L	2-7	Higuera	Plunk
20—Milwaukee	W	4-2	Rijo	Leary
21—Boston	W	5-2	Young	Hurst
22—Boston	W	4-2	Andujar	Seaver
23—Boston	W	9-2	Stewart	Nipper
25—Toronto	W	6-5*	Bair	Caudill
26—Toronto	W	2-0	Plunk	Cerutti
27—Toronto	W	1-0§	Leiper	Clarke
28—California	L	3-6	McCaskill	Andujar
29—California	W	4-2	Stewart	Chadwick
30—California	L	2-6	Candelaria	Leiper
31—California	L	5-8	Witt	Plunk

Won 14, Lost 12

AUGUST

			Winner	Loser
1—At Minn.	L	1-10	Blyleven	Young
2—At Minn.	L	0-8	Smithson	Andujar
3—At Minn.	W	5-4†	Bair	Atherton
4—At Seattle	L	8-9	Best	Mooneyham
5—At Seattle	W	10-4	Young	Beattie
6—At Seattle	W	7-5	Howell	Young
8—Minnesota	W	5-2	Andujar	Smithson
9—Minnesota	L	2-9	Viola	Stewart
10—Minnesota	W	6-2	Young	Heaton
10—Minnesota	W	6-5	Rijo	Atherton
11—Seattle	L	4-6	Ladd	Bair
12—Seattle	W	3-2*	Howell	Ladd
13—Seattle	W	4-1	Stewart	Morgan
15—At Calif.	L	4-6	Candelaria	Rijo
16—At Calif.	L	2-5	Witt	Young
17—At Calif.	L	3-7	Sutton	Andujar
19—At Balt.	W	4-1	Stewart	Davis
22—At N.Y.	L	2-3	Rasmussen	Andujar
23—At N.Y.	W	2-1	Young	Righetti
24—At N.Y.	W	11-4	Stewart	Scurry
25—At Detroit	W	8-4	Rijo	Terrell
26—At Detroit	L	7-8	Thurmond	Von Ohlen
28—Baltimore	W	5-4	Leiper	Aase
28—Baltimore	W	8-7	Mooneyham	Aase
29—Baltimore	W	4-3	Plunk	Davis
29—Baltimore	W	4-0	Stewart	Habyan
30—Baltimore	L	4-5	Jones	Rijo
31—Baltimore	W	7-0	Andujar	Boddicker

Won 17, Lost 11

SEPTEMBER

			Winner	Loser
1—New York	W	9-8	Krueger	Armstrong
2—New York	L	8-9	Fisher	Howell
3—New York	W	5-3	Stewart	Stoddard
5—Detroit	L	4-9	Cary	Von Ohlen
6—Detroit	W	5-4*	Andujar	Campbell
7—Detroit	W	8-4	Young	Petry
9—At Chicago	L	1-4	Cowley	Stewart
10—At Chicago	W	6-2	Rijo	Filson
11—At Chicago	W	2-1	Andujar	Dotson
12—At Cleve.	L	3-9	Swindell	Krueger
13—At Cleve.	L	6-8	Oelkers	Mooneyham
14—At Cleve.	L	2-5	Schrom	Rijo
15—Texas	L	2-6	Hough	Stewart
16—Texas	L	6-10	Meredith	Von Ohlen
17—Texas	L	0-4	Correa	Rodriguez
19—Cleveland	W	5-1	Young	Niekro
20—Cleveland	L	5-6*	Wills	Howell
21—Cleveland	W	4-2	Andujar	Candiotti
22—Chicago	W	5-3	Rijo	Bannister
23—Chicago	W	4-3	Rodriguez	Carlton
24—Chicago	W	4-2	Ontiveros	Cowley
27—At Kan. C.	W	6-3	Andujar	Jackson
27—At Kan. C.	W	9-6	Rijo	Black
28—At Kan. C.	L	2-6	Leibrandt	Stewart
29—At Texas	L	0-3	Correa	Young
30—At Texas	L	5-9	Brown	Rodriguez

Won 13, Lost 13

OCTOBER

			Winner	Loser
1—At Texas	W	9-7	Howell	Williams
3—Kan. City	L	4-8	Leibrandt	Andujar
4—Kan. City	L	0-2	Gubicza	Stewart
5—Kan. City	W	6-0	Young	Saberhagen

Won 2, Lost 2

*10 innings. †11 innings. ‡12 innings. §15 innings.

Injuries slowed Oakland ace Joaquin Andujar early, but he rebounded to record 12 victories.

homers and stole 27 bases. Donnie Hill batted .283 while sharing second base with Tony Phillips, who hit .256.

Designated hitter Dave Kingman crossed the 30-homer mark for the third straight year, hitting 35. His accomplishments were tarnished, however, by a June 23 incident in which he sent a rat to a woman beat writer in the press box at Kansas City. Kingman called it a practical joke, but the A's were not amused. Kingman was fined $3,500 and warned that a second incident would lead to his unconditional release.

Meanwhile, some of the pitching arms began to mend. Andujar recovered from a pulled right hamstring and finished with a 12-7 record and a club-high seven complete games, showing the A's that the two-time 20-game winner with St. Louis was no joke. Howell returned in mid-July and finished with 16 saves.

In addition, lefthander Curt Young turned in his best major league season, going 13-9 with a 3.45 earned-run average. And though Jose Rijo was prone to wildness and finished 9-11 with a 4.65 ERA, the righthander ranked among the league leaders with 176 strikeouts.

But not all was well with the Oakland pitching staff, as the club's 4.31 ERA indicates. Haas, who had gotten off to a quick 7-1 start, added one more loss before a shoulder injury ended his season in July. Codiroli, a 14-game winner in 1985, was 5-8 when elbow problems sidelined him in June. Eric Plunk (4-7, 5.31 ERA), Bill Mooneyham (4-5, 4.52) and Rick Langford (1-10, 7.36) were ineffective.

The A's also had a few weak spots in the lineup. Murphy had career lows with nine homers and 39 RBIs in 329 at-bats. The primary outfield backups, veteran Dusty Baker and rookie Stan Javier, hit .240 and .202, respectively. First baseman Bruce Bochte knocked in only 43 runs. Catchers Mickey Tettleton and Jerry Willard combined for just 61 RBIs.

In the end, however, LaRussa was able to steer the club to a 76-86 record and a third-place tie with Kansas City. The A's went 42-30 after the All-Star break and 45-34 overall under LaRussa. It was clear that the A's had become a better club.

And it wasn't just because some injured players began to regain their health. It was something LaRussa hadn't noticed from across the foul lines when he was managing the White Sox. But he saw it when he joined the A's.

"The basic attitude," LaRussa explained. "There was a real hunger to quit screwing around and start winning games."

Right fielder Harold Baines again led the disappointing White Sox in virtually every offensive category.

Strange White Sox Fall Apart

By DAVE van DYCK

Two words best sum up the 1986 season for the Chicago White Sox: "strange" and "change."

The strangest aspects of the season emanated from the club's front office, while the change was most noticeable on the roster. The result was a season that was "disappointing on and off the field," said Jerry Reinsdorf, the club's co-owner. "A lot of mistakes were made."

On the field, the White Sox struggled to stay out of last place in the American League West. They ultimately finished fifth, 20 games behind the California Angels and only five games ahead of the last-place Seattle Mariners. Their 72-90 record represented a 13-game drop from the year before.

Off the field, the club was engulfed in controversy, much of which involved Ken (Hawk) Harrelson, the former slugger and broadcaster who had stepped into the front office as vice president of baseball operations the previous October. Harrelson quickly began making major changes in the coaching staff and other aspects of the organization.

Manager Tony LaRussa had no choice but to go along with these changes, many of which he didn't like. But on June 20, with the White Sox struggling at 26-38, Harrelson fired LaRussa, the 1983 Manager of the Year. Harrelson, however, admitted botching LaRussa's firing after leaving his status questionable for several weeks.

By the time the season ended, Harrelson himself was gone, having resigned amid the club's internal strife.

But Harrelson certainly left his mark for years to come. When LaRussa brought his Oakland A's to Comiskey Park in September, more than half of the players on the Chicago roster had been added since spring training.

"We're only a couple of hitters away from being a good team," Harrelson said as he departed. "I wouldn't trade pitching staffs with anybody in the league. By 1988, we'll have a club that can compete with anybody."

The pitching statistics certainly gave hope for the future. When Jim Fregosi arrived as the club's new manager June 22, the White Sox had a 4.55 team earned-run average. Fregosi, who had been managing at Louisville (American Association), brought in coach Dick Bosman from Chicago's Triple-A affiliate at Buffalo, and by the end of the season, Chicago had the league's No. 3 ERA (3.93). The White Sox, who were 12 games under .500 when Fregosi took over, went 45-51 under new management.

Jose DeLeon was acquired in a trade with Pittsburgh and showed flashes of brilliance in his late-season stint with the White Sox.

"The pitching was good and the offense was bad," Fregosi said in assessing his team.

The starting pitchers all improved under Fregosi. The club's top winner was righthander Joe Cowley, who went 11-11 with a 3.88 ERA and pitched the season's first no-hitter September 19 against California. Righthander Richard Dotson came off chest and shoulder muscle surgery, and though his final record was 10-17, he pitched more innings (197) than any other member of the staff. Lefthander Floyd Bannister, who had early-season knee surgery, was 10-14 with a 3.54 ERA.

The rotation underwent significant change during the season. Tom Seaver was 2-6 when the unhappy veteran was

SCORES OF CHICAGO WHITE SOX' 1986 GAMES

APRIL			Winner	Loser
7—Milwaukee	L	3-5	Higuera	Seaver
9—Milwaukee	L	3-4	Leary	Dotson
10—Milwaukee	L	5-8	Darwin	James
11—Boston	L	2-7	Clemens	Bannister
12—Boston	W	3-1	Seaver	Hurst
13—Boston	L	2-12	Lollar	Cowley
14—Detroit	L	8-10	Petry	Dotson
16—Detroit	W	10-4	Bannister	Terrell
17—Detroit	L	6-10	Morris	Agosto
18—At Boston	L	1-2	Hurst	Seaver
19—At Boston	L	2-3	Boyd	Agosto
20—At Boston	L	2-6	Brown	Bannister
22—At Milw.	W	5-4	Davis	Darwin
23—At Milw.	W	2-1	Seaver	Plesac
25—At Detroit	W	9-7	Nelson	O'Neal
26—At Detroit	W	5-4†	James	Campbell
27—At Detroit	L	1-4	Morris	Davis
29—Baltimore	L	1-8	McGregor	Nelson
30—Baltimore	W	8-6	Dotson	Davis

Won 7, Lost 12

MAY			Winner	Loser
2—Cleveland	L	5-7*	Camacho	Schmidt
3—Cleveland	L	7-8	Yett	Dawley
4—Cleveland	L	4-6*	Bailes	James
5—New York	L	1-4	Niekro	Dotson
6—New York	L	6-10	Fisher	Dawley
7—New York	L	1-5	John	Bannister
9—At Cleve.	W	4-3	Nelson	Bailes
10—At Cleve.	W	4-0†	Nelson	Bailes
11—At Cleve.	W	5-4	McKeon	Candiotti
12—At Balt.	L	3-4	Bordi	James
13—At Balt.	L	1-3	Aase	Bannister
14—At N.Y.	W	3-2	McKeon	Fisher
15—At N.Y.	W	8-1	Allen	Guidry
16—Kan. City	W	4-2	Dotson	Leibrandt
17—Kan. City	W	7-6	James	Huismann
18—Kan. City	W	5-1	Bannister	Saberhagen
20—Toronto	W	2-1	Davis	Cerutti
21—Toronto	W	5-4	Nelson	Acker
22—Toronto	L	0-5	Key	Dotson
23—At Kan. C.	W	4-1	Cowley	Saberhagen
24—At Kan. C.	L	6-7	Black	James
25—At Kan. C.	L	1-2§	Bankhead	Dawley
26—At Texas	L	2-7	Guzman	Schmidt
27—At Texas	L	3-6	Hough	Dotson
28—At Texas	L	3-6	Correa	Cowley
30—At Toronto	L	0-6	Stieb	Davis
31—At Toronto	L	3-4†	Henke	Nelson

Won 11, Lost 16

JUNE			Winner	Loser
1—At Toronto	W	6-4	Dotson	Key
2—Texas	L	0-1	Hough	Cowley
3—Texas	L	1-4	Correa	Davis
4—Texas	L	2-5	Witt	Seaver
5—Oakland	W	9-5	Allen	Haas
6—Oakland	W	6-4	Dotson	Langford
7—Oakland	W	10-3	Cowley	Codiroli
8—Oakland	W	8-5	Davis	Young
9—California	L	0-3	Sutton	Seaver
10—California	W	7-3	Allen	Romanick
11—California	L	11-12	McCaskill	Dotson
12—At Seattle	W	8-4	Cowley	Guetterman
13—At Seattle	L	10-11	Young	Dawley
14—At Seattle	L	3-7	Langston	Seaver
15—At Seattle	L	5-10	Fireovid	McKeon
17—At Minn.	L	1-4	Smithson	Dotson
18—At Minn.	L	9-10*	Davis	Nelson
19—At Minn.	W	9-8	Bannister	Anderson
20—Seattle	L	3-5	Langston	Seaver
21—Seattle	W	7-6	Allen	Swift
22—Seattle	W	10-4	Dotson	Morgan
23—Minnesota	W	11-2	Cowley	Blyleven
24—Minnesota	L	1-2	Anderson	Davis
25—Minnesota	W	4-3	McKeon	Viola
27—At Oak.	L	6-8	Mooneyham	Nelson
28—At Oak.	W	4-1	Dotson	Young
29—At Oak.	W	6-5*	James	Bair
30—At Calif.	W	4-3	Davis	McCaskill

Won 15, Lost 13

JULY			Winner	Loser
1—At Calif.	W	5-3	Bannister	Cook
2—At Calif.	L	3-4	Witt	Allen
4—New York	W	2-1	Dotson	Tewksbury
5—New York	L	0-8	Rasmussen	Cowley
6—New York	W	5-2	Bannister	Drabek
7—Cleveland	W	4-3	James	Camacho
8—Cleveland	W	6-2	Allen	Oelkers
9—Cleveland	L	3-6	Niekro	Dotson
10—Baltimore	L	3-5	Flanagan	Cowley
11—Baltimore	L	2-4	Dixon	Bannister
12—Baltimore	W	6-3	Nelson	Boddicker
13—Baltimore	W	7-0	Allen	McGregor
17—At N.Y.	L	4-5	Rasmussen	Dotson
18—At N.Y.	L	4-8	Niekro	Bannister
19—At N.Y.	W	8-3	Cowley	Nielsen
20—At N.Y.	W	8-0	Allen	Shirley
21—At Cleve.	L	2-5	Yett	Davis
22—At Cleve.	L	4-8	Candiotti	Dotson
23—At Cleve.	L	2-7	Schrom	Bannister
24—At Balt.	L	6-12	Flanagan	Cowley
25—At Balt.	L	2-6	Boddicker	Allen
26—At Balt.	L	1-2	Bordi	Schmidt
27—At Balt.	L	3-11	McGregor	Dotson
28—Boston	L	1-3	Nipper	Bannister
29—Boston	W	4-1	Cowley	Sellers
30—Boston	W	7-2	DeLeon	Clemens

Won 11, Lost 15

AUGUST			Winner	Loser
1—Detroit	L	4-5	Terrell	Dotson
2—Detroit	W	5-3	Bannister	Morris
3—Detroit	W	10-1	Cowley	O'Neal
4—At Boston	W	1-0	DeLeon	Clemens
5—At Boston	W	3-1	Dotson	Boyd
6—At Boston	L	0-9	Hurst	Bannister
8—At Milw.	W	12-6	Cowley	Darwin
9—At Milw.	L	0-1	Higuera	DeLeon
10—At Milw.	L	4-5†	Clear	Schmidt
11—At Milw.	W	6-1	Bannister	Bosio
12—At Detroit	L	3-7	Thurmond	Carlton
13—At Detroit	L	2-5	O'Neal	Cowley
14—At Detroit	W	8-2	DeLeon	Tanana
15—Milwaukee	L	3-4	Plesac	Dawley
16—Milwaukee	L	5-6	Johnson	Nelson
17—Milwaukee	W	7-4	Carlton	Clutterbuck
19—At Toronto	L	1-5	Stieb	Cowley
20—At Toronto	L	1-4	Johnson	DeLeon
21—At Toronto	W	4-3	Schmidt	Key
22—At Texas	L	3-11	Russell	Bannister
23—At Texas	L	1-3	Guzman	Carlton
24—At Texas	L	2-3	Hough	Schmidt
25—Kan. City	L	0-2	Bankhead	DeLeon
26—Kan. City	L	1-6	Leibrandt	Dotson
27—Kan. City	W	3-1	Bannister	Jackson
28—Texas	W	6-2	Carlton	Guzman
29—Texas	L	2-5	Hough	Cowley
30—Texas	L	2-6	Witt	DeLeon
31—Texas	W	3-1	Dotson	Loynd

Won 12, Lost 17

SEPTEMBER			Winner	Loser
1—At Kan. C.	W	4-0	Bannister	Leibrandt
2—At Kan. C.	W	3-0	Carlton	Jackson
3—At Kan. C.	L	1-2*	Black	Nelson
4—At Kan. C.	L	0-1	Farr	Dawley
5—Toronto	W	5-0	Dotson	Johnson
6—Toronto	L	0-4	Key	Bannister
7—Toronto	W	4-3	Nelson	Clancy
9—Oakland	W	4-1	Cowley	Stewart
10—Oakland	L	2-6	Rijo	Filson
11—Oakland	L	1-2	Andujar	Dotson
12—California	W	3-2*	Thigpen	Finley
13—California	L	2-3‡	Lucas	Dawley
14—California	W	3-1	Cowley	McCaskill
15—California	L	5-6	Lugo	DeLeon
16—At Seattle	L	0-7	Morgan	Dotson
17—At Seattle	W	3-0	Bannister	Langston
18—At Seattle	W	6-4	Carlton	Swift
19—At Calif.	W	7-1	Cowley	McCaskill
20—At Calif.	L	7-8	Moore	Schmidt
21—At Calif.	L	0-3	Candelaria	Dotson
22—At Oak.	L	3-5	Rijo	Bannister
23—At Oak.	L	3-4	Rodriguez	Carlton
24—At Oak.	L	2-4	Ontiveros	Cowley
27—Minnesota	W	5-2	DeLeon	Heaton
27—Minnesota	W	4-3	Schmidt	Portugal
28—Minnesota	L	1-6	Smithson	Bannister
30—Seattle	W	5-4*	Schmidt	Ladd
30—Seattle	W	5-4	Searage	Swift

Won 14, Lost 14

OCTOBER			Winner	Loser
1—Seattle	W	3-1	James	Trujillo
2—At Minn.	W	8-4*	Thigpen	Heaton
3—At Minn.	L	2-9	Smithson	Dotson
4—At Minn.	L	3-7	Blyleven	Bannister
5—At Minn.	L	0-3	Viola	Cowley

Won 2, Lost 3

*10 innings. †11 innings. ‡15 innings. §17 innings.

Shortstop Ozzie Guillen continued to play good defense, but never could find the groove offensively.

traded to Boston in June, but the White Sox signed another veteran, 41-year-old Steve Carlton, who went 4-3 with a 3.69 ERA in Chicago.

A trade with Pittsburgh brought in righthander Jose DeLeon, who showed flashes of greatness while compiling a 4-5 record and a 2.96 ERA. Neil Allen, who had been frustrated in his efforts with the St. Louis Cardinals and the New York Yankees, finally found a home with the White Sox, going 7-2 before injuring his arm. Joel Davis won four of nine decisions in 19 starts.

In the bullpen, stopper Bob James led the club with 14 saves but missed two months with arm troubles. Bobby Thigpen was called up from Birmingham (Southern) for the final two months and went 2-0 with a 1.77 ERA and seven saves. Lefthander Ray Searage came from Milwaukee in July and posted a 0.62 ERA in 29 games. Gene Nelson added six victories and six saves, while Bill Dawley, a Houston castoff who was signed at the beginning of the season, was winless in seven decisions but posted a 3.32 ERA.

White Sox batters, however, provided their pitchers little support. They finished last in the league in batting (.247), on-base percentage (.310), runs (644), home runs (121) and several other categories.

The only bright spot in the lineup was Harold Baines. The right fielder again led the team in virtually every offensive department, including batting (.296), homers (21) and runs batted in (88).

First baseman Greg Walker spent several weeks on the disabled list early in the season and missed the final two months with a broken hand. Despite playing in only 78 games, Walker contributed 13 homers and 51 RBIs. Veteran catcher Carlton Fisk, who started the season in left field and ended up as a part-time designated hitter, was weakened by a summer-long fight against the flu. He finished with a .221 average, 14 homers and 63 RBIs.

Second baseman Julio Cruz (19 RBIs) saw his offensive production continue to fall and was sent home for the last month of the season with toe problems. Shortstop Ozzie Guillen, the A.L. Rookie of the Year in 1985, saw his batting average dip 23 points to .250. The contributions of part-time outfielders Jerry Hairston (26 RBIs), Reid Nichols (18 RBIs), Bobby Bonilla (26 RBIs before being sent to the Pirates in exchange for DeLeon) and Steve Lyons (six RBIs after being obtained in the Seaver trade) were limited.

Outfielder-DH Ron Kittle, the 1983 Rookie of the Year, was sent to the New York Yankees in a multiplayer deal July 30. One of the players the White Sox got in return was sore-kneed catcher Ron Hassey, who spent most of his time as DH. But Hassey proved valuable at the plate, hitting .353 with 20 RBIs in 49 White Sox games.

There were some encouraging signs. Outfielder John Cangelosi stole 50 bases, a record for A.L. rookies. Catcher Ron Karkovice was promoted from Birmingham and showed he was ready defensively to play in the big leagues. Infielder Tim Hulett hit a career-high 17 homers, rookie infielder Russ Morman knocked in 17 runs in 49 games and outfielder Daryl Boston hit .266 with five homers in 56 games.

Despite the disappointing '86 season, club officials were confident that the White Sox would be back in title contention in 1987.

"I don't know why not," Reinsdorf said. "Our division is still not one of powerhouses. And because of our pitching, we don't need to improve our run production too much."

The brightest light in the Twins' dark 1986 season was Kirby Puckett, who emerged as one of the premier players in the game.

Twins Endure Dreary Summer

By PATRICK REUSSE

The 1986 Minnesota Twins hit more home runs than any Twins team in 22 years. Center fielder Kirby Puckett ascended to the level of superstar. Third baseman Gary Gaetti had a spectacular fifth season in Minnesota. Both Puckett and Gaetti won Gold Gloves.

Those were the highlights of an otherwise dreary summer for the Twins, who lost a manager (Ray Miller) and faded to a sixth-place finish in the American League West.

Only two years earlier, the Twins had contended for the division title and looked like the West's team on the rise. What happened?

The Twins finished 21 games out of first place with a 71-91 record. In 26 years of major league baseball in Minnesota, only three Twins teams had lower winning percentages. And never was their pitching worse than it was in 1986.

Numerous statistics indicate that bad pitching was most responsible for the Twins' miserable season. Their 4.77 earned-run average was the highest of any team in the major leagues in '86 as well as the highest of any Twins club ever. They used 18 pitchers during the season and only three—Keith Atherton (3.75), Roy Lee Jackson (3.86) and Neal Heaton (3.98)—finished with ERAs under 4.00 in Minnesota. None of the three opened the season with the Twins.

Minnesota was on a record pace for home runs during much of the season and finished with 196, the second-highest total in the league. But Minnesota pitchers allowed 200 homers, the major league high.

Lefthander Frank Viola issued 37 gopher balls and didn't come close to leading the team. That's because righthander Bert Blyleven established a major league record by giving up 50 homers.

Still, Blyleven and Viola were by far the most productive pitchers on a staff that was in chaos from the opening days of the season. Blyleven finished with a 17-14 record, a 4.01 ERA, 16 complete games, 215 strikeouts and a league-high 271⅔ innings pitched, while Viola went 16-13 with a 4.51 ERA and 191 strikeouts. Righthander Mike Smithson (13-14, 4.77 ERA) was the only other double-digit winner.

The Twins started shuffling pitchers April 15, but Miller, a former Baltimore Orioles pitching coach, never found the right combination. It could have been his downfall.

Miller, who had replaced Billy Gardner as manager in June 1985, was fired 15 months later, on September 12, with the Twins sitting on a 59-80 record. Third-base coach Tom Kelly replaced Miller for the rest of the season.

"I must have been hired to be a god," a bitter Miller said after his dismissal. "Apparently, the organization thought the pitching they had was enough, although it would have taken a guru to make it great."

In '85, Miller had been able to work some magic with Ron Davis, Minnesota's enigmatic reliever. In '86, however, Miller was unable to get a contribution from Davis or anyone else in the bullpen.

The Twins had the fewest saves (24) of any team in the big leagues. Davis earned saves in his first two outings of the season, then went 34 appearances without another save. With his ERA up to 9.08, Davis finally was traded to the Chicago Cubs on August 13 for pitchers George Frazier and Ray Fontenot, neither of whom helped solve the Twins' pitching woes, and a minor league infielder.

The Twins tried to fill the void. Atherton was obtained from Oakland in May and led the staff with just 10 saves. Jackson was promoted from Toledo (International) in May, while Frank Pastore was picked up in April after being released by Cincinnati. They totaled only three saves. Starters Mark Portugal (6-10) and Allan Anderson (3-6) also were used in relief.

Former starter John Butcher had been demoted to relief status long before June 20, when the Twins traded him to Cleveland for Heaton. The newly acquired lefthander made 17 starts and went 4-9.

Minnesota's sorry pitching ruined an excellent offensive effort. The Twins were led at the plate by Puckett, who was voted to the A.L. All-Star team after getting off to a sizzling start that included 11 homers in the first four weeks of the season.

Puckett, who had totaled just four homers in his first two seasons, finished with 31 homers. The stocky outfielder also batted .328 with 223 hits (second in the league to New York's Don Mattingly), 119 runs scored, 96 runs batted in and a team-high 20 stolen bases. Puckett was a solid candidate for A.L. Player of the Year honors until he slowed down near the end of the season as Mattingly was surging.

SCORES OF MINNESOTA TWINS' 1986 GAMES

APRIL			Winner	Loser
8—At Oak.	W	3-2	Viola	Codiroli
9—At Oak.	W	5-4	Smithson	Howell
10—At Oak.	L	0-3	Haas	Butcher
11—Seattle	W	5-1	Blyleven	Wilcox
12—Seattle	L	4-10	Morgan	Viola
13—Seattle	L	2-4	Moore	Smithson
14—Oakland	L	6-7	Atherton	Smith
15—Oakland	L	2-8	Haas	Latham
16—Oakland	W	7-5†	Davis	Atherton
17—At Calif.	W	4-1	Viola	McCaskill
18—At Calif.	L	5-6	Witt	Smithson
19—At Calif.	L	4-5	Slaton	Butcher
20—At Calif.	L	5-8	Forster	Davis
21—At Seattle	W	5-2	Viola	Wilcox
22—At Seattle	W	7-1	Smithson	Morgan
23—At Seattle	L	3-4†	Best	Portugal
25—California	W	7-4	Blyleven	Slaton
26—California	L	6-7	Bryden	Davis
27—California	L	7-8	Bryden	Smith
29—At N.Y.	L	11-14	Whitson	Portugal
30—At N.Y.	L	2-3	Niekro	Blyleven

Won 8, Lost 13

MAY			Winner	Loser
1—At N.Y.	W	7-4	Agosto	Rasmussen
2—At Detroit	W	10-1	Smithson	Morris
3—At Detroit	L	4-7	Terrell	Butcher
4—At Detroit	L	1-4	Tanana	Blyleven
6—Baltimore	L	3-5	Davis	Viola
7—Baltimore	W	5-2	Smithson	Flanagan
9—Detroit	W	8-7	Blyleven	O'Neal
10—Detroit	W	12-2	Viola	Tanana
11—Detroit	L	1-4	Petry	Smithson
12—New York	L	8-9	Rasmussen	Portugal
13—New York	L	4-6	John	Blyleven
14—At Balt.	L	3-8	Dixon	Agosto
15—At Balt.	L	3-5	Boddicker	Viola
16—At Milw.	L	6-7	Clear	Davis
17—At Milw.	L	1-4*	Higuera	Portugal
18—At Milw.	W	5-3	Blyleven	Leary
19—At Boston	L	7-8	Sambito	Davis
20—At Boston	L	7-17	Clemens	Viola
21—At Boston	L	2-3	Stewart	Portugal
23—Milwaukee	W	8-7	Pastore	Plesac
24—Milwaukee	L	3-6	Nieves	Viola
25—Milwaukee	W	4-3	Smithson	Wegman
26—Toronto	W	9-1	Portugal	Alexander
27—Toronto	W	7-6‡	Pastore	Henke
28—Toronto	L	8-14	Clancy	Blyleven
30—Boston	W	13-5	Atherton	Woodward
31—Boston	L	2-7	Hurst	Smithson

Won 11, Lost 16

JUNE			Winner	Loser
1—Boston	L	3-6	Clemens	Portugal
2—At Toronto	L	1-3	Clancy	Blyleven
3—At Toronto	L	5-6	Eichhorn	Atherton
4—At Toronto	W	10-4	Viola	Stieb
5—At Kan. C.	L	2-8	Bankhead	Smithson
6—At Kan. C.	L	1-6	Leibrandt	Agosto
7—At Kan. C.	W	4-1	Blyleven	Jackson
8—At Kan. C.	W	5-2	Portugal	Saberhagen
9—Texas	W	3-2†	Atherton	Williams
10—Texas	L	10-14	Russell	Davis
11—Texas	L	2-6x	Williams	Jackson
13—At Cleve.	L	2-11	Candiotti	Blyleven
14—At Cleve.	W	9-3	Atherton	Heaton
15—At Cleve.	W	7-3	Viola	Schulze
17—Chicago	W	4-1	Smithson	Dotson
18—Chicago	W	10-9†	Davis	Nelson
19—Chicago	L	8-9	Bannister	Anderson
20—Cleveland	W	9-8	Viola	Noles
21—Cleveland	L	5-7	Schulze	Portugal
22—Cleveland	L	1-4	Niekro	Smithson
23—At Chicago	L	2-11	Cowley	Blyleven
24—At Chicago	W	2-1	Anderson	Davis
25—At Chicago	L	3-4	McKeon	Viola
27—Kan. City	W	6-4	Smithson	Bankhead
28—Kan. City	W	7-2	Blyleven	Jackson
29—Kan. City	W	9-4	Anderson	Saberhagen
30—At Texas	W	5-2	Viola	Harris

Won 14, Lost 13

JULY			Winner	Loser
1—At Texas	L	0-5	Hough	Portugal
2—At Texas	L	2-10	Mason	Smithson
3—Baltimore	W	11-7	Blyleven	Boddicker
4—Baltimore	L	7-12	Havens	Pastore
5—Baltimore	W	7-6	Viola	Flanagan
6—Baltimore	L	0-1	Dixon	Heaton
7—Detroit	W	10-8	Smithson	O'Neal

JULY			Winner	Loser
8—Detroit	L	1-5	King	Blyleven
9—Detroit	L	0-7	Morris	Anderson
10—New York	L	1-11	Rasmussen	Viola
11—New York	L	3-9	Drabek	Heaton
12—New York	L	0-8	Nielsen	Smithson
13—New York	W	5-0	Blyleven	Tewksbury
17—At Balt.	L	2-6	Dixon	Viola
18—At Balt.	W	7-3	Blyleven	McGregor
19—At Balt.	L	0-1	Flanagan	Heaton
20—At Balt.	L	3-8	Boddicker	Smithson
21—At Detroit	W	1-0	Viola	Thurmond
22—At Detroit	L	0-3	Terrell	Blyleven
23—At Detroit	L	2-12	Morris	Anderson
25—At N.Y.	W	9-5	Heaton	Nielsen
26—At N.Y.	W	8-4	Anderson	Drabek
27—At N.Y.	L	1-4	Guidry	Blyleven
28—Seattle	W	6-5‡	Atherton	Best
29—Seattle	W	4-2	Viola	Beattie
30—Seattle	L	2-4	Morgan	Heaton

Won 10, Lost 16

AUGUST			Winner	Loser
1—Oakland	W	10-1	Blyleven	Young
2—Oakland	W	8-0	Smithson	Andujar
3—Oakland	L	4-5‡	Bair	Atherton
4—California	W	6-5	Pastore	Moore
5—California	L	1-13	Witt	Anderson
6—California	W	5-2	Blyleven	Sutton
8—At Oak.	L	2-5	Andujar	Smithson
9—At Oak.	W	9-2	Viola	Stewart
10—At Oak.	L	2-6	Young	Heaton
10—At Oak.	L	5-6	Rijo	Atherton
11—At Calif.	W	2-0	Blyleven	Sutton
12—At Calif.	L	4-5§	Lucas	Davis
13—At Calif.	W	6-2	Viola	Ruhle
14—At Seattle	W	14-1	Portugal	Langston
15—At Seattle	L	0-1	Moore	Atherton
16—At Seattle	L	6-7	Ladd	Atherton
17—At Seattle	L	1-11	Morgan	Smithson
18—Boston	L	1-3	Seaver	Viola
19—Boston	W	5-1	Portugal	Nipper
20—Boston	L	1-9	Clemens	Heaton
22—Toronto	W	4-3	Blyleven	Clancy
23—Toronto	L	4-7	Cerutti	Smithson
24—Toronto	L	5-7†	Henke	Atherton
26—At Milw.	L	5-6†	Clear	Atherton
27—At Milw.	W	7-5	Heaton	Nieves
28—At Milw.	W	6-2	Blyleven	Bosio
29—At Toronto	L	5-6	Eichhorn	Atherton
30—At Toronto	L	1-8	Johnson	Viola
31—At Toronto	L	5-7	Aquino	Anderson

Won 12, Lost 17

SEPTEMBER			Winner	Loser
1—Milwaukee	W	9-3	Heaton	Nieves
2—Milwaukee	W	4-0	Blyleven	Vuckovich
3—Milwaukee	W	11-5	Smithson	Higuera
5—At Boston	L	2-12	Clemens	Viola
6—At Boston	L	2-3	Boyd	Frazier
7—At Boston	L	0-9	Hurst	Heaton
8—At Kan. C.	L	0-5	Leonard	Blyleven
9—At Kan. C.	L	3-11	Gubicza	Smithson
11—Texas	W	6-2	Viola	Hough
12—Texas	W	4-2	Heaton	Correa
13—Texas	L	1-14	Mason	Blyleven
14—Texas	W	7-6	Frazier	Mohorcic
15—At Cleve.	L	0-4	Candiotti	Viola
16—At Cleve.	W	7-3	Portugal	Bailes
17—At Cleve.	L	2-5	Swindell	Smithson
19—At Texas	L	1-4	Hough	Blyleven
20—At Texas	W	3-2	Viola	Williams
21—At Texas	L	1-2	Witt	Portugal
22—Kan. City	W	2-1	Atherton	Jackson
23—Kan. City	W	9-2	Smithson	Leonard
24—Kan. City	L	1-2	Quisenberry	Blyleven
25—Kan. City	L	1-8	Saberhagen	Viola
27—At Chicago	L	2-5	DeLeon	Heaton
27—At Chicago	L	3-4	Schmidt	Portugal
28—At Chicago	W	6-1	Smithson	Bannister
29—Cleveland	W	6-5	Blyleven	Swindell
30—Cleveland	W	10-9†	Portugal	Camacho

Won 13, Lost 14

OCTOBER			Winner	Loser
1—Cleveland	L	3-12	Candiotti	Anderson
2—Chicago	L	4-8†	Thigpen	Heaton
3—Chicago	W	9-2	Smithson	Dotson
4—Chicago	W	7-3	Blyleven	Bannister
5—Chicago	W	3-0	Viola	Cowley

Won 3, Lost 2

*7 innings. †10 innings. ‡11 innings. §12 innings. x16 innings.

Bert Blyleven won 17 games for the Twins but surrendered a major league-record 50 home runs in the process.

Gaetti put together his best season ever. The third baseman hit .287 with team-leading totals in homers (34) and RBIs (108). He also finished with a .518 slugging percentage, second on the club to Puckett's .537.

The other big guns in the Minnesota attack were first baseman Kent Hrbek and right fielder Tom Brunansky. Hrbek finished with the lowest average of his five full seasons (.267) but had 91 RBIs and a career-high 29 homers. Brunansky hit .256 with 23 homers and 75 RBIs. In addition, designated hitter Roy Smalley clubbed 20 homers.

A pair of youngsters, rookie second baseman Steve Lombardozzi and shortstop Greg Gagne, manned the middle of the infield for the Twins. Lombardozzi's defense was exceptional, but he tailed off badly at the plate, hitting .227. With a .250 average, 12 homers and 54 RBIs, Gagne had a solid sophomore year.

Lombardozzi's emergence at the end of the '85 season had made possible the off-season trade of incumbent second baseman Tim Teufel. The Twins sent Teufel to the New York Mets, primarily for outfielder Billy Beane. They were counting on Beane, considered one of the hottest prospects in the Mets' rich farm system, to take over the trouble spot in left field. No such luck. Beane spent part of the year at Toledo and batted only .213 in Minnesota.

Randy Bush was used most often in left and batted a career-high .269. Mickey Hatcher also appeared in left as well as other positions and hit .278, although he knocked in only 32 runs.

The Twins even got decent production from their trio of catchers. Mark Salas, Tim Laudner and Jeff Reed combined for 20 homers and 71 RBIs.

But the Twins' cast of sluggers could not compensate for their woeful pitching. The club's disappointing play carried over to the turnstiles, where attendance fell by almost 400,000 to 1.2 million.

Seattle's Jim Presley emerged as one of the top third basemen in the American League, hitting 27 homers and driving in 107 runs.

M's Can't Meet Expectations

By JIM STREET

Expectations were running high when the Seattle Mariners reported to spring training in Arizona. There was a mixture of age and youth that led many to believe that the 10th edition of the Mariners would compile a .500 record at worst, challenge for the American League West title at best.

"We are no longer an expansion team," Mariners Owner George Argyros proclaimed.

Such veterans as designated hitter Gorman Thomas, coming off a 32-home run season, and catcher Steve Yeager, who had been acquired from the Los Angeles Dodgers the previous December, were supposed to provide leadership. Such youngsters as third baseman Jim Presley, second baseman Danny Tartabull and outfielder Phil Bradley would bolster an offense that had set several club hitting records the previous season. Yes, this would be a Mariner team to be reckoned with.

And it was . . . for a week.

Presley, who would become the team's lone All-Star Game representative, hit a game-tying home run in the ninth inning and a game-winning grand slam in the 10th to give Seattle a dramatic 8-4 victory over the California Angels in the season opener. Yeager, who had the task of teaching Seattle's young pitchers to pitch rather than throw, got a big smooch from Morganna, the Kissing Bandit. The Mariners won five of their first eight games, the last victory coming in the wake of an eight-run first inning that featured Tartabull's first major league grand slam. It was his fourth homer in four days, and Thomas already had three homers to his credit. The Mariners' pace certainly set no records, but it was an encouraging start.

The early long-ball success, however, had a negative effect on the team. Batters began swinging from their heels, and the team's slide thus began. Seattle lost 17 of its next 21 games through May 8, and before the last game of that slump, Manager Chuck Cottier and third-base coach Jim Mahoney lost their jobs.

Eleven times in those 21 games, at least nine Mariner batters struck out. Boston's Roger Clemens set a major league record by striking out 20 Seattle batters April 29 in Fenway Park, and by the end of the season, the Mariners had set an A.L. record with 1,148 strikeouts. A nine-game

Danny Tartabull's impressive rookie season included 25 home runs and 96 RBIs.

losing streak to end the season left them in last place with a 67-95 record, 25 games behind California.

The Mariners went 58-75 under Dick Williams, Cottier's replacement. Williams, who had managed Boston, Oakland and San Diego into the World Series, sparked the Mariners to four victories in his first five games and began to make some changes. Harold Reynolds, a slick-fielding second baseman, was promoted from Calgary (Pacific Coast) along with center fielder John Moses. Tartabull was moved to the outfield. Veterans Thomas, Al Cowens and Barry Bonnell were released. Two starters—shortstop Spike Owen and outfielder Dave Henderson, the club's all-time home run leader—were traded to the Boston Red Sox.

In the process, speed became as much of a weapon as the long ball. But without pitching, speed and power aren't enough—and when the Mariners' pitching fell short of expectations, so did the Mariners.

Seattle's staff compiled the league's second-highest earned-run average with a 4.65 mark and tallied only five shutouts, the A.L. low. The biggest disappointment

SCORES OF SEATTLE MARINERS' 1986 GAMES

APRIL			Winner	Loser
8—California	W	8-4*	Ladd	Forsch
9—California	L	5-9	Slaton	Langston
10—California	W	5-2	Young	Sutton
11—At Minn.	L	1-5	Blyleven	Wilcox
12—At Minn.	W	10-4	Morgan	Viola
13—At Minn.	W	4-2	Moore	Smithson
14—At Calif.	L	6-7	Moore	Ladd
15—At Calif.	W	9-4	Young	Sutton
16—At Calif.	L	0-4	Romanick	Wilcox
18—Oakland	L	1-4	Codiroli	Moore
19—Oakland	L	2-7	Rijo	Langston
20—Oakland	L	3-9	Haas	Young
21—Minnesota	L	2-5	Viola	Wilcox
22—Minnesota	L	1-7	Smithson	Morgan
23—Minnesota	W	4-3*	Best	Portugal
24—At Oak.	W	3-1	Langston	Rijo
25—At Oak.	L	2-11	Haas	Young
26—At Oak.	L	3-5	Andujar	Wilcox
27—At Oak.	L	0-1	Langford	Morgan
29—At Boston	L	1-3	Clemens	Moore
30—At Boston	L	4-9	Stewart	Nunez

Won 7, Lost 14

MAY			Winner	Loser
1—At Boston	L	2-12	Boyd	Swift
2—At Toronto	W	3-2†	Ladd	Eichhorn
3—At Toronto	W	4-2	Morgan	Acker
4—At Toronto	L	2-3	Henke	Moore
5—At Milw.	L	1-3	Leary	Langston
6—At Milw.	L	0-10	Nieves	Swift
7—Boston	L	5-11	Nipper	Wilcox
8—Boston	L	2-4	Brown	Morgan
9—Toronto	W	13-3	Moore	Stieb
10—Toronto	W	8-7†	Ladd	Henke
11—Toronto	L	3-4	Key	Swift
12—Milwaukee	W	6-0	Young	Higuera
13—Milwaukee	W	8-5	Morgan	Leary
14—Milwaukee	L	6-9	Plesac	Moore
16—At N.Y.	W	7-3	Langston	Niekro
17—At N.Y.	L	6-11	Tewksbury	Young
18—At N.Y.	L	3-11	Rasmussen	Morgan
20—At Detroit	L	0-12	Terrell	Moore
21—At Detroit	L	4-6	King	Langston
22—At Detroit	W	5-3	Young	Petry
23—Baltimore	L	5-7	Dixon	Morgan
24—Baltimore	L	4-5*	Snell	Huismann
25—Baltimore	L	3-6	Boddicker	Moore
26—Baltimore	W	7-6	Langston	Davis
28—New York	L	5-6	Whitson	Morgan
29—New York	L	0-2	Rasmussen	Wilcox
30—Detroit	W	8-7‡	Huismann	Cary
31—Detroit	W	7-4	Langston	Terrell

Won 11, Lost 17

JUNE			Winner	Loser
1—Detroit	W	9-1	Swift	Tanana
3—At Balt.	L	2-4	Boddicker	Wilcox
4—At Balt.	W	5-1	Moore	Dixon
5—At Balt.	L	1-7	Davis	Langston
6—At Texas	L	5-6*	Williams	Ladd
7—At Texas	L	5-7	Guzman	Young
7—At Texas	L	2-3	Hough	Guetterman
8—At Texas	L	4-5*	Williams	Best
9—At Kan. C.	W	5-3	Langston	Leonard
10—At Kan. C.	L	5-9	Farr	Wilcox
11—At Kan. C.	W	12-2	Morgan	Leibrandt
12—Chicago	L	4-8	Cowley	Guetterman
13—Chicago	W	11-10	Young	Dawley
14—Chicago	W	7-3	Langston	Seaver
15—Chicago	W	10-5	Fireovid	McKeon
17—At Cleve.	W	5-2	Morgan	Niekro
18—At Cleve.	L	1-5	Schrom	Beattie
19—At Cleve.	L	1-8	Candiotti	Moore
20—At Chicago	W	5-3	Langston	Seaver
21—At Chicago	L	6-7	Allen	Swift
22—At Chicago	L	4-10	Dotson	Morgan
23—Cleveland	L	6-8	Schrom	Beattie
24—Cleveland	W	8-7	Young	Camacho
25—Cleveland	W	6-1	Langston	Butcher
26—Texas	L	3-10	Hough	Guetterman
27—Texas	W	6-5	Young	Russell
28—Texas	L	2-5	Guzman	Beattie
29—Texas	W	9-3	Moore	Correa
30—Kan. City	W	3-2	Langston	Leonard

Won 14, Lost 15

JULY			Winner	Loser
1—Kan. City	W	8-5	Ladd	Quisenberry
2—Kan. City	W	5-3	Morgan	Bankhead
4—At Boston	L	5-6	Sellers	Beattie
5—At Boston	W	9-5	Moore	Nipper
6—At Boston	L	3-7	Seaver	Langston
7—At Toronto	L	5-7	Key	Morgan
8—At Toronto	W	8-5	Huismann	Cerutti
9—At Toronto	L	5-6	Caudill	Moore
10—At Milw.	W	4-1	Fireovid	Darwin
11—At Milw.	W	9-3	Morgan	Leary
12—At Milw.	W	15-9	Reed	Wegman
13—At Milw.	L	0-5	Nieves	Moore
17—Boston	W	5-1†	Ladd	Stanley
18—Boston	W	10-4	Moore	Nipper
19—Boston	L	4-9	Clemens	Morgan
20—Boston	W	9-5	Reed	Sellers
21—Toronto	L	3-8	Cerutti	Huismann
22—Toronto	W	8-7‡	Reed	Caudill
23—Toronto	L	2-6	Clancy	Moore
25—Milwaukee	L	2-4	Higuera	Morgan
26—Milwaukee	W	5-2	Reed	Wegman
27—Milwaukee	L	1-8	Leary	Langston
28—At Minn.	L	5-6†	Atherton	Best
29—At Minn.	L	2-4	Viola	Beattie
30—At Minn.	W	4-2	Morgan	Heaton

Won 13, Lost 12

AUGUST			Winner	Loser
1—California	L	2-3	Sutton	Langston
2—California	W	7-3	Huismann	McCaskill
3—California	W	6-3	Ladd	Chadwick
4—Oakland	W	9-8	Best	Mooneyham
5—Oakland	L	4-10	Young	Beattie
6—Oakland	L	5-7	Howell	Young
7—At Calif.	L	3-4†	Moore	Ladd
8—At Calif.	L	4-6	Ruhle	Swift
9—At Calif.	L	0-5	Candelaria	Morgan
10—At Calif.	L	0-4	Witt	Langston
11—At Oak.	W	6-4	Ladd	Bair
12—At Oak.	L	2-3*	Howell	Ladd
13—At Oak.	L	1-4	Stewart	Morgan
14—Minnesota	L	1-14	Portugal	Langston
15—Minnesota	W	1-0	Moore	Atherton
16—Minnesota	W	7-6	Ladd	Atherton
17—Minnesota	W	11-1	Morgan	Smithson
19—At N.Y.	W	7-3	Langston	John
20—At N.Y.	L	2-5	Stoddard	Moore
22—At Detroit	L	1-4	King	Morgan
23—At Detroit	L	0-14	Tanana	Brown
24—At Detroit	W	3-1	Langston	Petry
26—Baltimore	W	5-2	Moore	Dixon
27—Baltimore	W	4-1	Trujillo	Boddicker
28—New York	L	2-4	Rasmussen	Morgan
29—New York	L	12-13	Stoddard	Best
30—New York	W	1-0	Swift	John
30—New York	L	0-3	Niekro	Brown
31—New York	W	6-2	Moore	Drabek

Won 13, Lost 16

SEPTEMBER			Winner	Loser
1—Detroit	L	5-6	Morris	Morgan
2—Detroit	L	5-7	Campbell	Guetterman
3—Detroit	W	3-2	Trujillo	Kelly
5—At Balt.	W	8-2	Moore	Dixon
6—At Balt.	W	6-2	Morgan	Boddicker
7—At Balt.	L	0-8	McGregor	Langston
9—At Texas	W	3-1	Nunez	Guzman
10—At Texas	L	2-3*	Harris	Young
11—At Kan. C.	L	6-7*	Quisenberry	Huismann
12—At Kan. C.	W	4-2*	Langston	Quisenberry
13—At Kan. C.	L	4-5	Leonard	Swift
14—At Kan. C.	L	3-10	Gubicza	Moore
16—Chicago	W	7-0	Morgan	Dotson
17—Chicago	L	0-3	Bannister	Langston
18—Chicago	L	4-6	Carlton	Swift
19—Kan. City	W	6-5	Young	Black
20—Kan. City	W	3-0	Trujillo	Saberhagen
21—Kan. City	L	1-8	Leibrandt	Morgan
22—Texas	L	0-2	Correa	Langston
23—Texas	L	6-12	Hough	Swift
24—Texas	W	5-4	Moore	Guzman
26—Cleveland	L	7-9‡	Jones	Ladd
27—Cleveland	L	4-12	Schrom	Morgan
28—Cleveland	L	4-5‡	Wills	Nunez
30—At Chicago	L	4-5*	Schmidt	Ladd
30—At Chicago	L	4-5	Searage	Swift

Won 9, Lost 17

OCTOBER			Winner	Loser
1—At Chicago	L	1-3	James	Trujillo
3—At Cleve.	L	5-6	Wills	Trujillo
4—At Cleve.	L	5-6	Swindell	Langston
5—At Cleve.	L	2-4	Candiotti	Moore

Won 0, Lost 4

*10 innings. †11 innings. ‡12 innings.

Lefthander Mark Langston struggled to a 12-14 record, but led the A.L. with 245 strikeouts.

was Mike Moore, who dropped from 17-10 in 1985 to 11-13 with a 4.30 ERA. The righthander's first pitch of the season was knocked by California's Bobby Grich into the Kingdome seats. Moore completed 11 games, but he started the season experiencing first-inning woes and then fell into a rut when he had trouble holding late-inning leads.

Seattle's biggest winner was lefthander Mark Langston (12-14, 4.85 ERA). Though those numbers were unimpressive, he seemed to regain the form of his 1984 rookie season, when he led the league in strikeouts. He did so again in '86 with 245.

Righthander Mike Morgan, who came out of spring training as the No. 5 starter, became No. 3 simply by the process of elimination and had a career-high 11 wins—as well as a career-high 17 losses.

The fourth and fifth starting spots were a season-long headache. Lefthander Matt Young, who began the season in the starting rotation, went to the bullpen as the late-inning stopper. Milt Wilcox was 0-8 before being released. Bill Swift was hit hard most of the time and finished 2-9. Jim Beattie was 0-6 after coming back from shoulder problems.

The bullpen, which was hit by injuries to righthanders Edwin Nunez and Karl Best, had periods of excellence, but consistency was a problem. Young finished with a club-leading 13 saves, but none after August 30. Pete Ladd, who was signed to a Triple-A contract before spring training, spent the entire season in Seattle, won eight games and saved six others. Jerry Reed, also picked out of baseball's scrap heap, was 4-0 before suffering a season-ending wrist injury. Mark Huismann went 3-3 with four saves after being obtained in a trade with Kansas City.

The Mariners ranked near the bottom of the league in batting and runs scored, but a few individuals enjoyed successful seasons. Bradley batted .310 after a dreadfully slow start, although his home run production slipped from 26 in '85 to 12 in '86. Presley belted 27 homers with a career-high 107 runs batted in and played well in the field. Tartabull's rookie season resulted in a .270 average, 25 homers and 96 RBIs. First baseman Alvin Davis was slowed by an ankle injury but contributed 18 homers and 72 RBIs while batting .271. Designated hitter-first baseman Ken Phelps hit 24 homers.

The other spots in the lineup were less productive. Yeager batted .208 and caught only 49 games, while Bob Kearney hit .240. A third catcher, Scott Bradley, was acquired from the Chicago White Sox in June and batted .302 for Seattle.

At second base, Reynolds hit .222 but led the club with 30 stolen bases. Center fielder Moses (.256) added 25 steals. Shortstop Rey Quinones, one of the players obtained in the Henderson-Owen deal, batted only .189 in 36 games for Seattle.

The Mariners' season was epitomized by a few key statistics: Their 17-26 record in one-run games was the league's worst. They turned a league-high 191 double plays but also made 156 errors, one shy of the A.L. high. And they had little success on the road. They were 41-41 at home, 26-54 away, and not once did they have a winning road trip.

In short, not much went right for the Mariners in 1986.

"The season was a major disappointment for all of us in the front office, and I would hope the players are also disappointed," General Manager Dick Balderson said. "We had some guys with some respectable statistics, but their individual success is diminished by the fact we didn't function well as a club."

American League Averages for 1986

CHAMPIONSHIP WINNERS IN PREVIOUS YEARS

Year—Club	Pct.
1900—Chicago*	.607
1901—Chicago	.610
1902—Philadelphia	.610
1903—Boston	.659
1904—Boston	.617
1905—Philadelphia	.622
1906—Chicago	.616
1907—Detroit	.613
1908—Detroit	.588
1909—Detroit	.645
1910—Philadelphia	.680
1911—Philadelphia	.669
1912—Boston	.691
1913—Philadelphia	.627
1914—Philadelphia	.651
1915—Boston	.669
1916—Boston	.591
1917—Chicago	.649
1918—Boston	.595
1919—Chicago	.629
1920—Cleveland	.636
1921—New York	.641
1922—New York	.610
1923—New York	.645
1924—Washington	.597
1925—Washington	.636
1926—New York	.591
1927—New York	.714
1928—New York	.656
1929—Philadelphia	.693
1930—Philadelphia	.662
1931—Philadelphia	.704
1932—New York	.695
1933—Washington	.651
1934—Detroit	.656
1935—Detroit	.616
1936—New York	.667
1937—New York	.662
1938—New York	.651
1939—New York	.702
1940—Detroit	.584
1941—New York	.656
1942—New York	.669
1943—New York	.636
1944—St. Louis	.578
1945—Detroit	.575
1946—Boston	.675
1947—New York	.630
1948—Cleveland†	.626
1949—New York	.630
1950—New York	.636
1951—New York	.636
1952—New York	.617
1953—New York	.656
1954—Cleveland	.721
1955—New York	.623
1956—New York	.630
1957—New York	.636
1958—New York	.597
1959—Chicago	.610
1960—New York	.630
1961—New York	.673
1962—New York	.593
1963—New York	.646
1964—New York	.611
1965—Minnesota	.630
1966—Baltimore	.606
1967—Boston	.568
1968—Detroit	.636
1969—Baltimore (East)	.673
1970—Baltimore (East)	.667
1971—Baltimore (East)	.639
1972—Oakland (West)	.600
1973—Oakland (West)	.580
1974—Oakland (West)	.556
1975—Boston (East)	.594
1976—New York (East)	.610
1977—New York (East)	.617
1978—New York (East)	.613
1979—Baltimore (East)	.642
1980—Kansas City (West)	.599
1981—New York (East)	.551
1982—Milwaukee (East)	.586
1983—Baltimore (East)	.605
1984—Detroit (East)	.642
1985—Kansas City (West)	.562

*Not recognized as major league in 1900. †Defeated Boston in one-game playoff for pennant.

STANDING OF CLUBS AT CLOSE OF SEASON

EAST DIVISION

Club	Bos.	N.Y.	Det.	Tor.	Cle.	Mil.	Balt.	Cal.	Tex.	K.C.	Oak.	Chi.	Min.	Sea.	W.	L.	Pct.	G.B.
Boston	..	5	7	7	10	6	9	5	8	6	7	7	10	8	95	66	.590	....
New York	8	..	7	7	8	5	8	5	7	8	5	6	8	8	90	72	.556	5½
Detroit	6	6	..	4	9	8	12	5	7	5	6	6	7	6	87	75	.537	8½
Toronto	6	6	9	..	10	6	5	6	7	7	4	6	8	6	86	76	.531	9½
Cleveland	3	5	4	3	..	8	9	6	6	8	10	7	6	9	84	78	.519	11½
Milwaukee	6	8	5	7	5	..	7	7	4	6	5	7	4	6	77	84	.478	18
Baltimore	4	5	1	8	4	6	..	6	5	6	5	9	8	6	73	89	.451	22½

WEST DIVISION

Club	Cal.	Tex.	K.C.	Oak.	Chi.	Min.	Sea.	Bos.	N.Y.	Det.	Tor.	Cle.	Mil.	Balt.	W.	L.	Pct.	G.B.
California	..	8	8	10	7	7	8	7	7	7	6	6	5	6	92	70	.568	....
Texas	5	..	5	10	11	7	9	4	5	5	5	6	8	7	87	75	.537	5
Kansas City	5	8	..	8	6	6	5	6	4	7	5	4	6	6	76	86	.469	16
Oakland	3	3	5	..	6	7	10	5	7	6	8	2	7	7	76	86	.469	16
Chicago	6	2	7	7	..	6	8	5	6	6	6	5	5	3	72	90	.444	20
Minnesota	6	6	7	6	7	..	6	2	4	5	4	6	8	4	71	91	.438	21
Seattle	5	4	8	3	5	7	..	4	4	6	6	3	6	6	67	95	.414	25

Tie Game—Toronto vs. Cleveland.
Championship Series—Boston defeated California, four games to three.

RECORD AT HOME

EAST DIVISION

Club	Bos.	Det.	Cle.	Tor.	Mil.	N.Y.	Balt.	Tex.	Cal.	Oak.	K.C.	Min.	Chi.	Sea.	W.	L.	Pct.
Boston	.....	3-3	5-1	4-3	5-2	1-6	3-3	5-1	3-3	4-2	3-3	6-0	4-2	5-1	51	30	.630
Detroit	3-4	.....	5-1	2-5	5-2	3-3	5-1	5-1	3-3	4-2	3-3	4-2	3-3	4-2	49	32	.605
Cleveland	2-5	3-4	.....	1-5	3-3	3-3	5-2	3-3	2-3	6-0	6-0	3-3	3-3	5-1	45	35	.563
Toronto	3-3	4-2	5-2	.....	2-4	2-5	2-5	4-2	2-4	3-3	3-3	5-1	4-2	3-3	42	39	.519
Milwaukee	4-1	3-3	2-5	3-4	.....	5-1	5-2	1-5	3-3	4-2	3-3	3-3	2-4	3-3	41	39	.513
New York	2-4	4-3	5-2	2-4	4-3	.....	2-4	4-2	3-3	3-3	4-2	3-3	2-4	3-2	41	39	.513
Baltimore	1-6	0-7	2-4	3-3	4-2	1-6	.....	3-3	4-2	2-2	3-3	5-1	6-0	3-3	37	42	.468

WEST DIVISION

Club	Tex.	Cal.	Oak.	K.C.	Min.	Chi.	Sea.	Bos.	Det.	Cle.	Tor.	Mil.	N.Y.	Balt.	W.	L.	Pct.
Texas	.....	3-4	6-1	4-3	4-2	6-0	5-1	3-3	4-2	3-3	3-3	3-3	3-3	4-2	51	30	.630
California	4-2	.....	5-1	5-2	4-3	3-3	6-1	4-2	4-2	3-4	2-4	2-4	4-2	4-2	50	32	.610
Oakland	2-4	2-5	.....	2-4	4-3	4-2	5-2	3-3	4-2	2-4	5-1	5-1	4-2	5-3	47	36	.566
Kansas City	5-1	3-3	4-3	.....	4-2	4-3	4-3	3-3	4-2	4-2	2-4	3-3	2-4	3-3	45	36	.556
Minnesota	4-3	3-3	3-3	5-2	.....	5-2	3-3	2-4	3-3	3-3	3-3	5-1	1-5	3-3	43	38	.531
Chicago	2-5	3-4	5-2	4-2	4-2	.....	5-1	3-3	3-3	2-4	4-2	1-5	2-4	3-3	41	40	.506
Seattle	3-4	4-2	1-5	5-1	4-3	4-3	.....	3-3	4-2	2-4	3-3	3-3	2-5	3-3	41	41	.500

RECORD ABROAD

EAST DIVISION

Club	N.Y.	Bos.	Tor.	Cle.	Det.	Mil.	Balt.	Cal.	Tex.	Chi.	K.C.	Oak.	Min.	Sea.	W.	L.	Pct.
New York	.....	6-1	5-2	3-3	3-3	1-5	6-1	2-4	3-3	4-2	4-2	2-4	5-1	5-2	49	33	.598
Boston	4-2	.....	3-3	5-2	4-3	1-4	6-1	2-4	3-3	3-3	3-3	3-3	4-2	3-3	44	36	.550
Toronto	4-2	3-4	.....	5-1	5-2	4-3	3-3	4-2	3-3	2-4	4-2	1-5	3-3	3-3	44	37	.543
Cleveland	2-5	1-5	2-5	.....	1-5	5-2	4-2	4-3	3-3	4-2	2-4	4-2	3-3	4-2	39	43	.476
Detroit	3-4	3-3	2-4	4-3	.....	3-3	7-0	2-4	2-4	3-3	2-4	2-4	3-3	2-4	38	43	.469
Milwaukee	3-4	2-5	4-2	3-3	2-5	.....	2-4	4-2	3-3	5-1	3-3	1-5	1-5	3-3	36	45	.444
Baltimore	4-2	3-3	5-2	2-5	1-5	2-5	.....	2-4	2-4	3-3	3-3	3-5	3-3	3-3	36	47	.434

WEST DIVISION

Club	Cal.	Tex.	Chi.	K.C.	Oak.	Min.	Sea.	N.Y.	Bos.	Tor.	Cle.	Det.	Mil.	Balt.	W.	L.	Pct.
California	.....	4-3	4-3	3-3	5-2	3-3	2-4	3-3	3-3	4-2	3-2	3-3	3-3	2-4	42	38	.525
Texas	2-4	.....	5-2	1-5	4-2	3-4	4-3	2-4	1-5	2-4	3-3	1-5	5-1	3-3	36	45	.444
Chicago	3-3	0-6	.....	3-4	2-4	2-5	3-4	4-2	2-4	2-4	3-3	3-3	4-2	0-6	31	50	.383
Kansas City	2-5	3-4	2-4	.....	4-2	2-5	1-5	2-4	3-3	3-3	0-6	3-3	3-3	3-3	31	50	.383
Oakland	1-5	1-6	2-5	3-4	.....	3-3	5-1	3-3	2-4	3-3	0-6	2-4	2-4	2-2	29	50	.367
Minnesota	3-4	2-4	2-4	2-4	3-4	.....	3-4	3-3	0-6	1-5	3-3	2-4	3-3	1-5	28	53	.346
Seattle	1-6	1-5	1-5	3-4	2-5	3-3	.....	2-3	1-5	3-3	1-5	2-4	3-3	3-3	26	54	.325

SHUTOUT GAMES

Club	Det.	Mil.	Tor.	Tex.	Cle.	Oak.	Cal.	K.C.	N.Y.	Chi.	Bos.	Minn.	Balt.	Sea.	W.	L.	Pct.
Detroit	..	1	0	2	0	0	1	1	1	0	1	2	1	2	12	5	.706
Milwaukee	2	..	1	0	0	0	0	1	1	1	2	0	2	2	12	6	.667
Toronto	1	1	..	0	0	0	1	2	1	3	1	0	2	0	12	6	.667
Texas	0	0	0	..	0	2	1	1	1	1	0	1	0	1	8	4	.667
Cleveland	0	0	0	0	..	1	2	1	0	0	0	1	2	0	7	4	.636
Oakland	0	0	2	0	0	..	0	2	0	0	0	1	2	1	8	6	.571
California	0	0	0	2	0	1	..	0	1	2	2	0	1	3	12	10	.545
Kansas City	1	0	1	0	1	1	1	..	1	2	2	1	2	0	13	12	.520
New York	0	0	0	0	1	0	1	1	..	1	1	1	0	2	8	9	.471
Chicago	0	0	1	0	1	0	0	2	1	..	1	0	1	1	8	13	.381
Boston	0	1	1	0	1	0	1	0	0	1	..	1	0	0	6	11	.353
Minnesota	1	1	0	0	0	1	1	0	1	1	0	..	0	0	6	11	.353
Baltimore	0	1	0	0	0	0	1	0	0	0	1	2	..	1	6	13	.316
Seattle	0	1	0	0	0	0	0	1	1	1	0	1	0	..	5	13	.278

OFFICIAL AMERICAN LEAGUE BATTING AVERAGES

Compiled by Sports Information Center

CLUB BATTING

Club	Pct.	G.	AB.	R.	OR.	H.	TB.	2B.	3B.	HR.	RBI.	SH.	SF.	SB.	CS.	LOB.
Cleveland	.284	163	5702	831	841	1620	2451	270	45	157	775	56	49	141	54	1122
New York	.271	162	5570	797	738	1512	2397	275	23	188	745	36	46	139	48	1217
Boston	.271	161	5498	794	696	1488	2282	320	21	144	752	44	52	41	34	1213
Toronto	.269	163	5716	809	733	1540	2438	285	35	181	767	24	49	110	59	1099
Texas	.267	162	5529	771	743	1479	2365	248	43	184	725	31	42	103	85	1038
Detroit	.263	162	5512	798	714	1447	2335	234	30	198	751	52	49	138	58	1164
Minnesota	.261	162	5531	741	839	1446	2369	257	39	196	700	44	38	81	61	1087
Baltimore	.258	162	5524	708	760	1425	2181	223	13	169	669	33	51	64	34	1159
California	.255	162	5433	786	684	1387	2196	236	36	167	743	91	61	109	42	1182
Milwaukee	.255	161	5461	667	734	1393	2105	255	38	127	625	53	53	100	50	1143
Seattle	.253	162	5498	718	835	1392	2191	243	41	158	681	52	29	93	76	1104
Kansas City	.252	162	5561	654	673	1403	2168	264	45	137	618	24	33	97	46	1142
Oakland	.252	162	5435	731	760	1370	2122	213	25	163	683	56	51	139	61	1087
Chicago	.247	162	5406	644	699	1335	1963	197	34	121	605	50	53	115	54	1036
Totals	.262	1134	77376	10449	10449	20237	31563	3520	468	2290	9839	646	656	1470	762	15793

INDIVIDUAL BATTING

(Top Fifteen Qualifiers for Batting Championship—502 or More Plate Appearances)

*Bats lefthanded. †Switch-hitter.

Player and Club	Pct.	G.	AB.	R.	H.	TB.	2B.	3B.	HR.	RBI.	GW.	SH.	SF.	SB.	CS.
Boggs, Wade, Boston*	.357	149	580	107	207	282	47	2	8	71	10	4	4	0	4
Mattingly, Donald, New York*	.352	162	677	117	238	388	53	2	31	113	15	1	10	0	0
Puckett, Kirby, Minnesota	.328	161	680	119	223	365	37	6	31	96	5	2	0	20	12
Tabler, Patrick, Cleveland	.326	130	473	61	154	205	29	2	6	48	8	2	1	3	1
Rice, James, Boston	.324	157	618	98	200	303	39	2	20	110	12	0	9	0	1
Yount, Robin, Milwaukee	.312	140	522	82	163	235	31	7	9	46	8	5	2	14	5
Fernandez, O. Antonio, Toronto†	.310	163	687	91	213	294	33	9	10	65	8	5	4	25	12
Bradley, Philip, Seattle	.310	143	526	88	163	234	27	4	12	50	5	1	2	21	12
Bell, George, Toronto	.309	159	641	101	198	341	38	6	31	108	15	0	6	7	8
Franco, Julio, Cleveland	.306	149	599	80	183	253	30	5	10	74	9	0	5	10	7
Murray, Eddie, Baltimore†	.305	137	495	61	151	229	25	1	17	84	4	0	5	3	0
Easler, Michael, New York*	.302	146	490	64	148	220	26	2	14	78	7	2	5	3	2
Carter, Joseph, Cleveland	.302	162	663	108	200	341	36	9	29	121	11	1	8	29	7
Bernazard, Antonio, Cleveland†	.301	146	562	88	169	256	28	4	17	73	11	7	8	17	8
Fletcher, Scott, Texas	.300	147	530	82	159	212	34	5	3	50	6	10	3	12	11

DEPARTMENTAL LEADERS: G—Fernandez, 163; AB—Fernandez, 687; R—Henderson (N.Y.), 130; H—Mattingly, 238; TB—Mattingly, 388; 2B—Mattingly, 53; 3B—Butler, 14; HR—Barfield, 40; RBI—Carter, 121; GW—Bell, Mattingly, Ripken, 15; SH—Barrett, 18; SF—Joyner, 12; SB—Henderson (N.Y.), 87; CS—Henderson (N.Y.), Moses, 18.

(All Players—Listed Alphabetically)

Player and Club	Pct.	G.	AB.	R.	H.	TB.	2B.	3B.	HR.	RBI.	GW.	SH.	SF.	SB.	CS.
Adduci, James, Milwaukee*	.091	3	11	2	1	2	1	0	0	0	0	1	0	0	0
Allanson, Andrew, Cleveland	.225	101	293	30	66	82	7	3	1	29	1	11	4	10	1
Anderson, Allan, Minnesota*	.000	22	0	0	0	0	0	0	0	0	0	0	0	0	0
Armas, Antonio, Boston	.264	121	425	40	112	174	21	4	11	58	6	0	2	0	3
Baines, Harold, Chicago*	.296	145	570	72	169	265	29	2	21	88	10	0	8	2	1
Baker, Douglas, Detroit†	.125	13	24	1	3	4	1	0	0	0	0	4	0	0	0
Baker, Johnnie, Oakland	.240	83	242	25	58	78	8	0	4	19	1	0	2	0	1
Balboni, Stephen, Kansas City	.229	138	512	54	117	231	25	1	29	88	9	0	6	0	0
Bando, Christopher, Cleveland†	.268	92	254	28	68	83	9	0	2	26	3	10	3	0	1
Barfield, Jesse, Toronto	.289	158	589	107	170	329	35	2	40	108	13	0	5	8	8
Barrett, Martin, Boston	.286	158	625	94	179	238	39	4	4	60	9	18	4	15	7
Bathe, William, Oakland	.184	39	103	9	19	37	3	0	5	11	1	6	0	0	0
Baylor, Donald, Boston	.238	160	585	93	139	257	23	1	31	94	13	0	5	3	5
Beane, William, Minnesota	.213	80	183	20	39	54	6	0	3	15	2	0	0	2	3
Bell, George, Toronto	.309	159	641	101	198	341	38	6	31	108	15	0	6	7	8
Bell, Jay, Cleveland	.357	5	14	3	5	10	2	0	1	4	0	0	0	0	0
Bell, Terence, Kansas City	.000	8	3	0	0	0	0	0	0	0	0	0	0	0	0
Beniquez, Juan, Baltimore	.300	113	343	48	103	136	15	0	6	36	1	2	6	2	3
Bergman, David, Detroit*	.231	65	130	14	30	41	6	1	1	9	3	0	0	0	0
Bernazard, Antonio, Cleveland†	.301	146	562	88	169	256	28	4	17	73	11	7	8	17	8
Berra, Dale, New York	.231	42	108	10	25	38	7	0	2	13	2	2	1	0	0
Biancalana, Roland, Kansas City†	.242	100	190	24	46	64	4	4	2	8	0	4	0	5	1
Bochte, Bruce, Oakland*	.256	125	407	57	104	137	13	1	6	43	5	0	1	3	2
Boggs, Wade, Boston*	.357	149	580	107	207	282	47	2	8	71	10	4	4	0	4
Bonilla, Juan, Baltimore	.243	102	284	33	69	84	10	1	1	18	1	4	0	0	0
Bonilla, Roberto, Chicago†	.269	75	234	27	63	83	10	2	2	26	1	2	1	4	1
Bonnell, R. Barry, Seattle	.196	17	51	4	10	12	2	0	0	4	0	0	1	0	1
Boone, Robert, California	.222	144	442	48	98	135	12	2	7	49	4	12	6	1	0
Boston, Daryl, Chicago*	.266	56	199	29	53	85	11	3	5	22	3	3	1	9	5
Bradley, Philip, Seattle	.310	143	526	88	163	234	27	4	12	50	5	1	2	21	12
Bradley, Scott, Chicago-Seattle*	.300	77	220	20	66	95	8	3	5	28	1	2	2	1	2
Braggs, Glenn, Milwaukee	.237	58	215	19	51	75	8	2	4	18	1	2	3	1	1
Brantley, Michael, Seattle	.196	27	102	12	20	36	3	2	3	7	1	1	0	1	1
Brett, George, Kansas City*	.290	124	441	70	128	212	28	4	16	73	10	0	4	1	2
Brewer, Michael, Kansas City	.167	12	18	0	3	4	1	0	0	0	0	0	0	0	1
Brookens, Thomas, Detroit	.270	98	281	42	76	100	11	2	3	25	1	6	2	11	8
Brower, Robert, Texas	.111	21	9	3	1	2	1	0	0	0	0	0	0	1	2
Browne, Jerome, Texas†	.417	12	24	6	10	12	2	0	0	3	0	0	0	0	2
Brunansky, Thomas, Minnesota	.256	157	593	69	152	251	28	1	23	75	6	1	7	12	4
Buckner, William, Boston*	.267	153	629	73	168	265	39	2	18	102	12	0	8	6	4
Buechele, Steven, Texas	.243	153	461	54	112	189	19	2	18	54	7	9	3	5	8
Burleson, Richard, California	.284	93	271	35	77	106	14	0	5	29	1	6	1	1	3
Bush, R. Randall, Minnesota*	.269	130	357	50	96	150	19	7	7	45	3	1	1	5	3
Butler, Brett, Cleveland*	.278	161	587	92	163	220	17	14	4	51	6	17	5	32	15
Calderon, Ivan, Seattle-Chicago	.250	50	164	16	41	56	7	1	2	15	3	0	0	3	1
Cangelosi, John, Chicago†	.235	137	438	65	103	131	16	3	2	32	3	6	3	50	17
Canseco, Jose, Oakland	.240	157	600	85	144	274	29	1	33	117	14	0	9	15	7
Carter, Joseph, Cleveland	.302	162	663	108	200	341	36	9	29	121	11	1	8	29	7
Castillo, Juan, Milwaukee†	.167	26	54	6	9	11	0	1	0	5	0	2	0	1	1
Castillo, M. Carmelo, Cleveland	.278	85	205	34	57	90	9	0	8	32	1	1	1	2	1
Cerone, Richard, Milwaukee	.259	68	216	22	56	82	14	0	4	18	2	5	5	1	1
Clark, David, Cleveland*	.276	18	58	10	16	26	1	0	3	9	0	2	1	1	0
Cochrane, David, Chicago†	.194	19	62	4	12	17	2	0	1	2	0	1	0	0	0
Coles, Darnell, Detroit	.273	142	521	67	142	236	30	2	20	86	7	7	8	6	2
Collins, David, Detroit†	.270	124	419	44	113	138	18	2	1	27	2	9	2	27	12
Cooper, Cecil, Milwaukee*	.258	134	542	46	140	202	24	1	12	75	6	1	4	1	2
Cotto, Henry, New York	.213	35	80	11	17	23	3	0	1	6	0	0	1	3	0
Cowens, Alfred, Seattle	.183	28	82	5	15	19	4	0	0	6	1	1	1	1	0
Cowley, Joseph, Chicago*	.000	28	0	0	0	0	0	0	0	0	0	0	0	0	0
Craig, Rodney, Chicago†	.200	10	10	3	2	2	0	0	0	0	0	0	0	0	0
Cruz, Julio, Chicago†	.215	81	209	38	45	47	2	0	0	19	2	2	3	7	2
David, Andre, Minnesota*	.200	5	5	0	1	1	0	0	0	0	0	0	0	0	0
Davidson, J. Mark, Minnesota	.118	36	68	5	8	11	3	0	0	2	0	3	0	2	3
Davis, Alvin, Seattle*	.271	135	479	66	130	204	18	1	18	72	8	2	2	0	3
Davis, Michael, Oakland*	.268	142	489	77	131	222	28	3	19	55	5	4	5	27	4
Dawley, William, Chicago	.000	46	2	0	0	0	0	0	0	0	0	0	0	0	0
DeCinces, Douglas, California	.256	140	512	69	131	235	20	3	26	96	13	2	4	2	2
Deer, Robert, Milwaukee	.232	134	466	75	108	230	17	3	33	86	5	2	3	5	2
DeJesus, Ivan, New York	.000	7	4	1	0	0	0	0	0	0	0	0	0	0	0
Dempsey, J. Rikard, Baltimore	.208	122	327	42	68	124	15	1	13	29	5	7	0	1	0
Diaz, Edgar, Milwaukee	.231	5	13	0	3	3	0	0	0	0	0	0	0	0	0
Dodd, Thomas, Baltimore	.231	8	13	1	3	6	0	0	1	2	0	0	0	0	0
Dodson, Patrick, Boston*	.417	9	12	3	5	10	2	0	1	3	0	0	0	0	0
Downing, Brian, California	.267	152	513	90	137	232	27	4	20	95	13	3	8	4	4
Dwyer, James, Baltimore*	.244	94	160	18	39	78	13	1	8	31	3	0	4	0	2

Player and Club	Pct.	G.	AB.	R.	H.	TB.	2B.	3B.	HR.	RBI.	GW.	SH.	SF.	SB.	CS.
Easler, Michael, New York*	.302	146	490	64	148	220	26	2	14	78	7	2	5	3	2
Engle, R. David, Detroit	.256	35	86	6	22	29	7	0	0	4	1	0	0	0	0
Espino, Juan, New York	.162	27	37	1	6	8	2	0	0	5	1	0	1	0	0
Espinoza, Alvaro, Minnesota	.214	37	42	4	9	10	1	0	0	1	0	2	0	0	1
Evans, Darrell, Detroit*	.241	151	507	78	122	224	15	0	29	85	10	0	2	3	2
Evans, Dwight, Boston	.259	152	529	86	137	252	33	2	26	97	8	2	6	3	3
Felder, Michael, Milwaukee†	.239	44	155	24	37	50	2	4	1	13	2	1	5	16	2
Fernandez, C. Antonio, Toronto†	.310	163	687	91	213	294	33	9	10	65	8	5	4	25	12
Fielder, Cecil, Toronto	.157	34	83	7	13	27	2	0	4	13	1	0	0	0	0
Fields, Bruce, Detroit	.279	16	43	4	12	15	1	1	0	6	1	1	2	1	1
Fischlin, Michael, New York	.206	71	102	9	21	23	2	0	0	3	0	5	1	0	1
Fisk, Carlton, Chicago	.221	125	457	42	101	154	11	0	14	63	7	0	6	2	4
Fletcher, Scott, Texas	.300	147	530	82	159	212	34	5	3	50	6	10	3	12	11
Fontenot, S. Ray, Minnesota*	.000	15	1	0	0	0	0	0	0	0	0	0	0	0	0
Foster, George, Chicago	.216	15	51	2	11	18	0	2	1	4	0	0	0	0	0
Franco, Julio, Cleveland	.306	149	599	80	183	253	30	5	10	74	9	0	5	10	7
Gaetti, Gary, Minnesota	.287	157	596	91	171	309	34	1	34	108	12	1	6	14	15
Gagne, Gregory, Minnesota	.250	156	472	63	118	188	22	6	12	54	10	13	3	12	10
Gallego, Michael, Oakland	.270	20	37	2	10	12	2	0	0	4	0	2	0	0	2
Gantner, James, Milwaukee*	.274	139	497	58	136	184	25	1	7	38	4	6	7	13	7
Garcia, Damaso, Toronto	.281	122	424	57	119	159	22	0	6	46	7	2	3	9	6
Gedman, Richard, Boston*	.258	135	462	49	119	196	29	0	16	65	6	1	5	1	0
Gerhart, H. Kenneth, Baltimore	.232	20	69	4	16	21	2	0	1	7	0	0	2	0	1
Gibson, Kirk, Detroit*	.268	119	441	84	118	217	11	2	28	86	12	1	4	34	6
Giles, Brian, Chicago	.273	9	11	0	3	3	0	0	0	1	0	0	0	0	0
Greenwell, Michael, Boston*	.314	31	35	4	11	13	2	0	0	4	0	0	0	0	0
Grich, Robert, California	.268	98	313	42	84	129	18	0	9	30	4	10	1	1	3
Griffey, G. Kenneth, New York*	.303	59	198	33	60	94	7	0	9	26	2	1	4	2	2
Griffin, Alfredo, Oakland†	.285	162	594	74	169	216	23	6	4	51	8	12	6	33	16
Gross, Wayne, Oakland*	.000	3	2	0	0	0	0	0	0	0	0	0	0	0	0
Grubb, John, Detroit*	.333	81	210	32	70	124	13	1	13	51	6	0	3	0	1
Gruber, Kelly, Toronto	.196	87	143	20	28	49	4	1	5	15	0	2	2	2	5
Guillen, Oswaldo, Chicago*	.250	159	547	58	137	170	19	4	2	47	8	12	5	8	4
Gutierrez, Joaquin, Baltimore	.186	61	145	8	27	30	3	0	0	4	0	2	1	3	1
Hairston, Jerry, Chicago†	.271	101	225	32	61	91	15	0	5	26	4	0	1	0	0
Hall, Melvin, Cleveland*	.296	140	442	68	131	218	29	2	18	77	3	0	3	6	2
Harper, Brian, Detroit	.139	19	36	2	5	6	1	0	0	3	0	1	1	0	0
Harrah, Colbert, Texas	.218	95	289	36	63	106	18	2	7	41	0	3	3	2	5
Hassey, Ronald, N. York-Chicago*	.323	113	341	45	110	164	25	1	9	49	4	1	2	1	1
Hatcher, Michael, Minnesota	.278	115	317	40	88	116	13	3	3	32	0	0	4	2	1
Hearron, Jeffrey, Toronto	.217	12	23	2	5	6	1	0	0	4	0	0	0	0	0
Heath, Michael, Detroit	.265	30	98	11	26	41	3	0	4	11	2	0	1	4	1
Henderson, David, Seattle-Boston	.265	139	388	59	103	178	22	4	15	47	4	2	1	2	3
Henderson, Rickey, New York	.263	153	608	130	160	285	31	5	28	74	9	0	2	87	18
Henderson, Stephen, Oakland	.077	11	26	2	2	3	1	0	0	3	0	0	1	0	0
Hendrick, George, California	.272	102	283	45	77	134	13	1	14	47	2	4	3	1	1
Hengel, David, Seattle	.190	21	63	3	12	16	1	0	1	6	1	1	0	0	0
Hernandez, Leonardo, New York	.227	7	22	2	5	10	2	0	1	4	1	0	0	0	0
Herndon, Larry, Detroit	.247	106	283	33	70	109	13	1	8	37	5	0	5	2	1
Hill, Donald, Oakland†	.283	108	339	37	96	128	16	2	4	29	4	4	0	5	2
Hill, Marc, Chicago	.158	22	19	2	3	3	0	0	0	0	0	0	0	0	0
Hoffman, Glenn, Boston	.217	12	23	1	5	7	2	0	0	1	0	0	1	0	0
Householder, Paul, Milwaukee†	.218	26	78	4	17	25	3	1	1	16	0	2	2	1	2
Howell, Jack, California*	.272	63	151	26	41	71	14	2	4	21	3	3	2	2	0
Hrbek, Kent, Minnesota*	.267	149	550	85	147	263	27	1	29	91	11	0	7	2	2
Hudler, Rex, Baltimore	.000	14	1	1	0	0	0	0	0	0	0	0	0	1	0
Hulett, Timothy, Chicago	.231	150	520	53	120	197	16	5	17	44	4	6	4	4	1
Incaviglia, Peter, Texas	.250	153	540	82	135	250	21	2	30	88	11	0	7	3	2
Iorg, Garth, Toronto	.260	137	327	30	85	115	19	1	3	44	2	1	2	3	0
Jackson, Reginald, California*	.241	132	419	65	101	171	12	2	18	58	9	0	3	1	1
Jackson, Vincent, Kansas City	.207	25	82	9	17	27	2	1	2	9	1	0	0	3	1
Jacoby, Brook, Cleveland	.288	158	583	83	168	257	30	4	17	80	9	1	1	2	1
Javier, Stanley, Oakland†	.202	59	114	13	23	31	8	0	0	8	1	0	0	8	0
Johnson, Clifford, Toronto	.250	107	336	48	84	143	12	1	15	55	4	0	2	0	1
Johnson, Rondin, Kansas City†	.258	11	31	1	8	10	0	1	0	2	0	0	0	0	0
Jones, Lynn, Kansas City	.128	67	47	1	6	8	2	0	0	1	0	1	0	0	0
Jones, Richard, Baltimore	.182	16	33	2	6	8	2	0	0	4	0	0	0	0	0
Jones, Robert, Texas*	.095	13	21	1	2	2	0	0	0	3	1	0	0	0	0
Jones, Ross, Seattle	.095	11	21	0	2	2	0	0	0	0	0	0	0	0	1
Jones, Ruppert, California*	.229	126	393	73	90	168	21	3	17	49	3	7	3	10	3
Joyner, Wally, California*	.290	154	593	82	172	271	27	3	22	100	14	10	12	5	2
Karkovice, Ronald, Chicago	.247	37	97	13	24	43	7	0	4	13	1	1	1	1	0
Kearney, Robert, Seattle	.240	81	204	23	49	77	10	0	6	25	2	9	1	0	2
Kiefer, Steven, Milwaukee	.000	2	6	0	0	0	0	0	0	0	0	0	0	0	0
Kingery, Michael, Kansas City*	.258	62	209	25	54	81	8	5	3	14	1	0	2	7	3
Kingman, David, Oakland	.210	144	561	70	118	242	19	0	35	94	10	0	7	3	3
Kittle, Ronald, Chicago-New York	.218	116	376	42	82	158	13	0	21	60	4	0	8	4	1
Kunkel, Jeffrey, Texas	.231	8	13	3	3	6	0	0	1	2	0	0	0	0	0
Lacy, Leondaus, Baltimore	.287	130	491	77	141	192	18	0	11	47	6	4	5	4	6
Laga, Michael, Detroit*	.200	15	45	6	9	19	1	0	3	8	1	0	0	0	0

Player and Club	Pct.	G.	AB.	R.	H.	TB.	2B.	3B.	HR.	RBI.	GW.	SH.	SF.	SB.	CS.
Langford, J. Rick, Oakland	.000	17	0	0	0	0	0	0	0	0	0	0	0	0	0
Lansford, Carney, Oakland	.284	151	591	80	168	249	16	4	19	72	10	1	4	16	7
Laudner, Timothy, Minnesota	.244	76	193	21	47	87	10	0	10	29	5	1	2	1	0
Law, Rudy, Kansas City*	.261	87	307	42	80	119	26	5	1	36	4	2	1	14	6
Leach, Richard, Toronto*	.309	110	246	35	76	107	14	1	5	39	2	0	7	0	0
Lee, Manuel, Toronto†	.205	35	78	8	16	21	0	1	1	7	2	2	1	0	1
Lemon, Chester, Detroit	.251	126	403	45	101	164	21	3	12	53	5	3	4	2	1
Little, R. Bryan, Chi-NY†	.184	34	76	6	14	16	2	0	0	2	0	0	0	0	0
Lollar, W. Timothy, Boston*	1.000	33	1	0	1	1	0	0	0	0	0	0	0	0	0
Lombardi, Phillip, New York	.278	20	36	6	10	19	3	0	2	6	1	0	0	0	0
Lombardozzi, Stephen, Minnesota	.227	156	453	53	103	157	20	5	8	33	1	9	0	3	1
Lowry, Dwight, Detroit*	.307	56	150	21	46	59	4	0	3	18	2	3	0	0	0
Lynn, Fredric, Baltimore*	.287	112	397	67	114	198	13	1	23	67	11	0	4	2	2
Lyons, Stephen, Boston-Chicago*	.227	101	247	30	56	74	9	3	1	20	2	4	4	4	6
Madison, C. Scott, Detroit†	.000	2	7	0	0	0	0	0	0	1	0	0	1	0	0
Manning, Richard, Milwaukee*	.254	89	205	31	52	89	7	3	8	27	2	1	3	5	3
Martinez, John, Toronto	.181	81	160	13	29	43	8	0	2	12	3	4	1	0	0
Mattingly, Donald, New York*	.352	162	677	117	238	388	53	2	31	113	15	1	10	0	0
McDowell, Oddibe, Texas*	.266	154	572	105	152	244	24	7	18	49	5	3	2	33	15
McGriff, Frederick, Toronto*	.200	3	5	1	1	1	0	0	0	0	0	0	0	0	0
McGwire, Mark, Oakland	.189	18	53	10	10	20	1	0	3	9	0	0	0	0	1
McLemore, Mark, California†	.000	5	4	0	0	0	0	0	0	0	0	1	0	0	1
McRae, Harold, Kansas City	.252	112	278	22	70	105	14	0	7	37	6	0	2	0	0
Meacham, Robert, New York†	.224	56	161	19	36	45	7	1	0	10	1	4	0	3	6
Mercado, Orlando, Texas	.235	46	102	7	24	30	1	1	1	7	0	1	2	0	1
Miller, Darrell, California	.228	33	57	6	13	17	2	1	0	4	1	0	1	0	0
Molitor, Paul, Milwaukee	.281	105	437	62	123	186	24	6	9	55	6	2	3	20	5
Moore, Charles, Milwaukee	.260	80	235	24	61	88	12	3	3	39	3	4	3	5	5
Morman, Russell, Chicago	.252	49	159	18	40	57	5	0	4	17	3	1	2	1	0
Moseby, Lloyd, Toronto*	.253	152	589	89	149	246	24	5	21	86	10	2	7	32	11
Moses, John, Seattle†	.256	103	399	56	102	133	16	3	3	34	4	5	4	25	18
Motley, Darryl, Kansas City	.203	72	217	22	44	76	9	1	7	20	2	1	0	0	2
Mulliniks, S. Rance, Toronto*	.259	117	348	50	90	145	22	0	11	45	1	1	2	1	1
Mullins, Francis, Cleveland	.175	28	40	3	7	11	4	0	0	5	0	1	1	0	0
Murphy, Dwayne, Oakland*	.252	98	329	50	83	127	11	3	9	39	6	7	4	3	1
Murray, Eddie, Baltimore†	.305	137	495	61	151	229	25	1	17	84	4	0	5	3	0
Narron, Jerry, California*	.221	57	95	5	21	29	3	1	1	8	0	1	1	0	0
Nelson, Ricky, Seattle*	.167	10	12	2	2	2	0	0	0	1	1	0	0	1	0
Nelson, Robert, Oakland*	.222	5	9	1	2	3	1	0	0	0	0	0	0	0	0
Nichols, Carl, Baltimore	.000	5	5	0	0	0	0	0	0	0	0	0	0	0	0
Nichols, T. Reid, Chicago	.228	74	136	9	31	41	4	0	2	18	5	1	2	5	4
Nixon, Otis, Cleveland†	.263	105	95	33	25	31	4	1	0	8	0	2	0	23	6
Nokes, Matthew, Detroit*	.333	7	24	2	8	12	1	0	1	2	1	0	0	0	0
O'Brien, Peter, Texas*	.290	156	551	86	160	258	23	3	23	90	14	0	3	4	4
Oglivie, Benjamin, Milwaukee*	.283	103	346	31	98	135	20	1	5	53	8	1	7	1	2
O'Malley, Thomas, Baltimore*	.254	56	181	19	46	58	9	0	1	18	1	1	1	0	1
Ontiveros, Steven, Oakland	.000	47	0	0	0	0	0	0	0	0	0	0	0	0	0
Orta, Jorge, Kansas City*	.277	106	336	35	93	138	14	2	9	46	7	0	2	0	3
Owen, Spike, Seattle-Boston†	.231	154	528	67	122	163	24	7	1	45	7	9	3	4	4
Paciorek, Thomas, Texas	.286	88	213	17	61	80	7	0	4	22	1	0	1	1	3
Pagliarulo, Michael, New York*	.238	149	504	71	120	234	24	3	28	71	8	1	2	4	1
Pardo, Alberto, Baltimore†	.137	16	51	3	7	11	1	0	1	3	0	0	0	0	0
Paris, Kelly, Baltimore	.200	5	10	0	2	2	0	0	0	0	0	0	0	0	1
Parrish, Lance, Detroit	.257	91	327	53	84	158	6	1	22	62	8	1	3	0	0
Parrish, Larry, Texas	.276	129	464	67	128	236	22	1	28	94	12	0	6	3	1
Pasqua, Daniel, New York*	.293	102	280	44	82	147	17	0	16	45	7	1	1	2	0
Pecota, William, Kansas City	.207	12	29	3	6	8	2	0	0	2	0	0	1	0	2
Perconte, John, Chicago*	.219	24	73	6	16	17	1	0	0	4	0	1	0	2	0
Peters, Richard, Oakland†	.184	44	38	7	7	8	1	0	0	1	0	0	0	2	2
Petralli, Eugene, Texas†	.255	69	137	17	35	56	9	3	2	18	1	0	0	3	0
Pettis, Gary, California†	.258	154	539	93	139	185	23	4	5	58	6	15	5	50	13
Phelps, Kenneth, Seattle*	.247	125	344	69	85	181	16	4	24	64	6	0	3	2	3
Phillips, K. Anthony, Oakland†	.256	118	441	76	113	152	14	5	5	52	3	9	3	15	10
Pittaro, Christopher, Minnesota†	.095	11	21	0	2	2	0	0	0	0	0	0	0	0	0
Polidor, Gustavo, California	.263	6	19	1	5	6	1	0	0	1	0	0	0	0	0
Porter, Darrell, Texas*	.265	68	155	21	41	83	6	0	12	29	3	0	0	1	1
Presley, James, Seattle	.265	155	616	83	163	285	33	4	27	107	13	3	5	0	4
Pryor, Gregory, Kansas City	.170	63	112	7	19	23	4	0	0	7	0	2	0	1	1
Puckett, Kirby, Minnesota	.328	161	680	119	223	365	37	6	31	96	5	2	0	20	12
Quinones, Rey, Boston-Seattle	.218	98	312	32	68	92	16	1	2	22	1	5	2	4	3
Quirk, James, Kansas City*	.215	80	219	24	47	81	10	0	8	26	3	0	1	0	1
Ramos, Domingo, Seattle	.182	49	99	8	18	20	2	0	0	5	0	2	0	0	1
Randolph, William, New York	.276	141	492	76	136	170	15	2	5	50	9	8	4	15	2
Rayford, Floyd, Baltimore	.176	81	210	15	37	65	4	0	8	19	2	3	0	0	0
Ready, Randy, Milwaukee	.190	23	79	8	15	22	4	0	1	4	1	1	0	2	0
Reed, Jeffrey, Minnesota*	.236	68	165	13	39	53	6	1	2	9	0	3	0	1	0
Reynolds, Harold, Seattle†	.222	126	445	46	99	129	19	4	1	24	2	9	0	30	12
Rice, James, Boston	.324	157	618	98	200	303	39	2	20	110	12	0	9	0	1
Riles, Ernest, Milwaukee*	.252	145	524	69	132	187	24	2	9	47	12	6	3	7	7
Ripken, Calvin, Baltimore	.282	162	627	98	177	289	35	1	25	81	15	0	6	4	2

Player and Club	Pct.	G.	AB.	R.	H.	TB.	2B.	3B.	HR.	RBI.	GW.	SH.	SF.	SB.	CS.
Robidoux, William, Milwaukee*	.227	56	181	15	41	52	8	0	1	21	3	0	1	0	0
Roenicke, Gary, New York	.265	69	136	11	36	50	5	0	3	18	0	0	1	1	1
Rohn, Daniel, Cleveland*	.200	6	10	1	2	2	0	0	0	2	1	0	0	0	0
Romero, Edgardo, Boston	.210	100	233	41	49	66	11	0	2	23	1	7	3	2	0
Romine, Kevin, Boston	.257	35	35	6	9	11	2	0	0	2	0	1	0	2	0
Ryal, Mark, California*	.375	13	32	6	12	18	0	0	2	5	1	0	0	1	0
Sakata, Lenn, Oakland	.353	17	34	4	12	14	2	0	0	5	0	0	1	0	1
Salas, Mark, Minnesota*	.233	91	258	28	60	99	7	4	8	33	2	5	3	3	1
Salazar, Argenis, Kansas City	.245	117	298	24	73	97	20	2	0	24	1	5	1	1	1
Salazar, Luis, Chicago	.143	4	7	1	1	1	0	0	0	0	0	0	0	0	0
Sanchez, Alejandro, Minnesota	.125	8	16	1	2	2	0	0	0	1	0	0	0	0	0
Sax, David, Boston	.455	4	11	1	5	9	1	0	1	1	1	0	0	0	0
Schofield, Richard, California	.249	139	458	67	114	182	17	6	13	57	5	9	9	23	5
Schroeder, A. William, Milwaukee	.212	64	217	32	46	81	14	0	7	19	1	4	1	1	0
Seitzer, Kevin, Kansas City	.323	28	96	16	31	43	4	1	2	11	2	0	0	0	0
Sheets, Larry, Baltimore*	.272	112	338	42	92	165	17	1	18	60	8	1	2	2	0
Shelby, John, Baltimore†	.228	135	404	54	92	147	14	4	11	49	5	2	2	18	6
Shepherd, Ronald, Toronto	.203	65	69	16	14	24	4	0	2	4	0	1	0	0	0
Sheridan, Patrick, Detroit*	.237	98	236	41	56	85	9	1	6	19	1	2	2	9	2
Sierra, Ruben, Texas†	.264	113	382	50	101	182	13	10	16	55	8	1	5	7	8
Skinner, Joel, Chicago-New York	.232	114	315	23	73	99	9	1	5	37	1	2	2	1	4
Slaught, Donald, Texas	.264	95	314	39	83	141	17	1	13	46	4	3	3	3	1
Smalley, Roy, Minnesota†	.246	143	459	59	113	201	20	4	20	57	6	1	2	1	3
Smith, Lonnie, Kansas City	.287	134	508	80	146	209	25	7	8	44	6	2	2	26	9
Snyder, J. Cory, Cleveland	.272	103	416	58	113	208	21	1	24	69	8	1	0	2	3
Spilman, W. Harry, Detroit*	.245	24	49	6	12	23	2	0	3	8	1	1	0	0	0
Stanley, R. Michael, Texas	.333	15	30	4	10	16	3	0	1	1	0	0	0	1	0
Stapleton, David, Boston	.128	39	39	4	5	6	1	0	0	3	0	1	0	0	0
Stefero, John, Baltimore*	.233	52	120	14	28	36	2	0	2	13	0	0	1	0	1
Steinbach, Terry, Oakland	.333	6	15	3	5	11	0	0	2	4	1	0	0	0	0
Stenhouse, Michael, Boston*	.095	21	21	1	2	3	1	0	0	1	1	1	0	0	0
Stieb, David, Toronto	.000	38	0	1	0	0	0	0	0	0	0	0	0	0	0
Sullivan, Marc, Boston	.193	41	119	15	23	30	4	0	1	14	1	3	1	0	0
Sundberg, James, Kansas City	.212	140	429	41	91	138	9	1	12	42	5	2	3	1	1
Sveum, Dale, Milwaukee†	.246	91	317	35	78	116	13	2	7	35	5	5	1	4	3
Tabler, Patrick, Cleveland	.326	130	473	61	154	205	29	2	6	48	8	2	1	3	1
Tartabull, Danilo, Seattle	.270	137	511	76	138	250	25	6	25	96	6	2	3	4	8
Tarver, LaSchelle, Boston*	.120	13	25	3	3	3	0	0	0	1	0	0	0	0	1
Taylor, Dwight, Kansas City*	.000	4	2	1	0	0	0	0	0	0	0	0	0	0	0
Tettleton, Mickey, Oakland†	.204	90	211	26	43	82	9	0	10	35	0	7	4	7	1
Thomas, J. Gorman, Sea.-Milw.	.187	101	315	45	59	117	8	1	16	36	5	3	0	3	4
Thornton, Andre, Cleveland	.229	120	401	49	92	157	14	0	17	66	9	0	8	4	1
Tillman, Kerry, Oakland	.256	22	39	6	10	14	1	0	1	6	1	0	0	2	0
Tolleson, J. Wayne, Chi.-N.Y.†	.265	141	475	61	126	161	16	5	3	43	4	13	4	17	10
Tolman, Timothy, Detroit	.176	16	34	4	6	7	1	0	0	2	0	2	1	1	1
Traber, James, Baltimore*	.255	65	212	28	54	100	7	0	13	44	3	0	5	0	0
Trammell, Alan, Detroit	.277	151	574	107	159	269	33	7	21	75	8	11	4	25	12
Upshaw, Willie, Toronto*	.251	155	573	85	144	211	28	6	9	60	8	4	4	23	5
Valle, David, Seattle	.340	22	53	10	18	36	3	0	5	15	0	0	0	0	0
Walker, Gregory, Chicago*	.277	78	282	37	78	139	10	6	13	51	5	0	3	1	2
Ward, Gary, Texas	.316	105	380	54	120	154	15	2	5	51	5	1	2	12	8
Washington, Claudell, New York*	.237	54	135	19	32	55	5	0	6	16	3	0	0	6	1
Washington, Ronald, Minnesota	.257	48	74	15	19	34	3	0	4	11	0	2	2	1	2
Wegman, William, Milwaukee	.000	37	0	1	0	0	0	0	0	0	0	0	0	0	0
Whitaker, Louis, Detroit*	.269	144	584	95	157	255	26	6	20	73	8	0	4	13	8
White, Devon, California†	.235	29	51	8	12	18	1	1	1	3	0	0	0	6	0
White, Frank, Kansas City	.272	151	566	76	154	263	37	3	22	84	11	2	7	4	4
Whitt, L. Ernest, Toronto*	.268	131	395	48	106	177	19	2	16	56	6	0	3	0	1
Wiggins, Alan, Baltimore†	.251	71	239	30	60	65	3	1	0	11	1	5	4	21	7
Wilfong, Robert, California*	.219	92	288	25	63	89	11	3	3	33	4	8	2	1	4
Wilkerson, Curtis, Texas†	.237	110	236	27	56	72	10	3	0	15	1	0	1	9	7
Willard, Gerald, Oakland*	.267	75	161	17	43	62	7	0	4	26	0	4	4	0	1
Williams, Edward, Cleveland	.143	5	7	2	1	1	0	0	0	1	0	0	0	0	0
Williams, Kenneth, Chicago	.129	15	31	2	4	7	0	0	1	1	0	0	0	1	1
Wilson, Willie, Kansas City†	.269	156	631	77	170	231	20	7	9	44	5	3	1	34	8
Winfield, David, New York	.262	154	565	90	148	261	31	5	24	104	6	2	6	6	5
Woods, Alvis, Minnesota*	.321	23	28	5	9	16	1	0	2	8	1	0	1	0	0
Wright, George, Texas†	.217	49	106	10	23	34	3	1	2	7	1	0	1	3	5
Wright, J. Richard, Texas*	.000	23	0	0	0	0	0	0	0	0	0	0	0	0	0
Wynegar, Harold, New York†	.206	61	194	19	40	67	4	1	7	29	6	0	2	0	0
Yeager, Stephen, Seattle	.208	50	130	10	27	35	2	0	2	12	0	2	1	0	0
Young, Michael, Baltimore†	.252	117	369	43	93	137	15	1	9	42	3	2	3	3	1
Yount, Robin, Milwaukee	.312	140	522	82	163	235	31	7	9	46	8	5	2	14	5
Zuvella, Paul, New York	.083	21	48	2	4	5	1	0	0	2	0	4	0	0	0

AWARDED FIRST BASE ON INTERFERENCE—Allanson, Clev. (Bathe); Beniquez, Balt. (Salas); P. Bradley, Sea. (Salas); Gantner, Mil. (Espino); Jones, Cal. (Hearron); Moore, Mil. (Dempsey); Yeager, Sea. (Salas).

PLAYERS WITH TWO OR MORE CLUBS

(Alphabetically Arranged With Player's First Club on Top)

Player and Club	Pct.	G.	AB.	R.	H.	TB.	2B.	3B.	HR.	RBI.	GW.	SH.	SF.	Tot. BB.	Int. BB.	HP.	SO.	SB.	CS.	GI. DP.
Bradley, Chi.	.286	9	21	3	6	6	0	0	0	0	0	0	0	1	0	2	0	0	2	1
Bradley, Sea.	.302	68	199	17	60	89	8	3	5	28	1	2	2	12	4	2	7	1	0	12
Calderon, Sea.	.237	37	131	13	31	42	5	0	2	13	2	0	0	6	0	1	33	3	1	1
Calderon, Chi.	.303	13	33	3	10	14	2	1	0	2	1	0	0	3	1	0	6	0	0	0
Hassey, N.Y.	.298	64	191	23	57	89	14	0	6	29	2	1	1	24	1	2	16	1	1	8
Hassey, Chi.	.353	49	150	22	53	75	11	1	3	20	2	0	1	22	2	1	11	0	0	7
Henderson, Sea.	.276	103	337	51	93	162	19	4	14	44	4	1	1	37	4	2	95	1	3	5
Henderson, Bos.	.196	36	51	8	10	16	3	0	1	3	0	1	0	2	0	0	15	1	0	1
Kittle, Chi.	.213	86	296	34	63	125	11	0	17	48	3	0	6	28	0	3	87	2	1	10
Kittle, N.Y.	.238	30	80	8	19	33	2	0	4	12	1	0	2	7	1	0	23	2	0	0
Little, Chi.	.171	20	35	3	6	7	1	0	0	2	0	0	0	4	0	0	4	0	0	2
Little, N.Y.	.195	14	41	3	8	9	1	0	0	0	0	0	0	2	0	0	7	0	0	1
Lyons, Bos.	.250	59	124	20	31	45	7	2	1	14	1	1	2	12	2	0	23	2	3	3
Lyons, Chi.	.203	42	123	10	25	29	2	1	0	6	1	3	2	7	0	1	24	2	3	1
Owen, Sea.	.246	112	402	46	99	133	22	6	0	35	5	7	2	34	1	1	42	1	3	11
Owen, Bos.	.183	42	126	21	23	30	2	1	1	10	2	2	1	17	0	1	9	3	1	2
Quinones, Bos.	.237	62	190	26	45	65	12	1	2	15	1	2	1	19	0	3	26	3	2	7
Quinones, Sea.	.189	36	122	6	23	27	4	0	0	7	0	3	1	5	0	0	31	1	1	0
Skinner, Chi.	.201	60	149	17	30	49	5	1	4	20	1	2	1	9	0	1	43	1	0	2
Skinner, N.Y.	.259	54	166	6	43	50	4	0	1	17	0	0	1	7	0	0	40	0	4	4
Thomas, Sea.	.194	57	170	24	33	67	4	0	10	26	3	1	0	27	3	1	55	1	2	2
Thomas, Milw.	.179	44	145	21	26	50	4	1	6	10	2	2	0	31	1	0	50	2	2	3
Tolleson, Chi.	.250	81	260	39	65	87	7	3	3	29	3	9	3	38	0	0	43	13	6	3
Tolleson, N.Y.	.284	60	215	22	61	74	9	2	0	14	1	4	1	14	0	2	33	4	4	3

OFFICIAL MISCELLANEOUS AMERICAN LEAGUE BATTING RECORDS

CLUB MISCELLANEOUS BATTING RECORDS

Club	Slg. Pct.	OB Pct.	Tot. BB.	Int. BB.	HP.	SO.	GIDP.	ShO.
New York	.430	.347	645	52	28	911	142	9
Cleveland	.430	.337	456	26	24	944	129	4
Minnesota	.428	.325	501	33	37	977	123	11
Texas	.428	.331	511	33	35	1088	133	4
Toronto	.427	.329	496	23	33	848	122	6
Detroit	.424	.338	613	35	43	885	99	5
Boston	.415	.346	595	56	66	707	142	11
California	.404	.338	671	45	40	860	134	10
Seattle	.399	.326	572	38	34	1148	125	13
Baltimore	.395	.327	563	26	31	862	159	13
Oakland	.390	.322	553	24	32	983	105	6
Kansas City	.390	.313	474	40	36	919	101	12
Milwaukee	.385	.321	530	26	27	986	122	6
Chicago	.363	.310	487	29	34	940	123	13
Totals	.408	.330	7667	486	500	13058	1759	123

INDIVIDUAL MISCELLANEOUS BATTING RECORDS

(Top Ten Qualifiers for Slugging Championship)

Player—Club	Slg. Pct.	OB Pct.	Tot. BB.	Int. BB.	HP.	SO.	GI DP.
Mattingly, N.Y.	.573	.394	53	11	1	35	17
Barfield, Tor.	.559	.368	69	5	8	146	9
Puckett, Minn.	.537	.366	34	4	7	99	14
Bell, Tor.	.532	.349	41	3	2	62	15
Gaetti, Minn.	.518	.347	52	4	6	108	18
Carter, Clev.	.514	.335	32	3	5	95	8
Parrish, Tex.	.509	.347	52	7	2	114	16
Deer, Milw.	.494	.336	72	3	3	179	4
Gibson, Det.	.492	.371	68	4	7	107	8
Rice, Bos.	.490	.384	62	5	4	78	19
Tartabull, Sea.	.489	.347	61	2	1	157	10
Boggs, Bos.	.486	.453	105	14	0	44	11
Brett, K.C.	.481	.401	80	18	4	45	6
Hrbek, Minn.	.478	.353	71	9	6	81	15
Evans, Bos.	.476	.376	97	4	6	117	11

DEPARTMENTAL LEADERS: OBP—Boggs, .453; Tot. BB—Boggs, 105; Int. BB—Brett, 18; HP—Baylor, 35; SO—Incaviglia, 185; GIDP—Franco, 28.

Player—Club	Slg. Pct.	OB Pct.	Tot. BB.	Int. BB.	HP.	SO.	GI DP.
Adduci, Milw.	.182	.167	1	0	0	2	0
Allanson, Clev.	.280	.260	14	0	1	36	7
Armas, Bos.	.409	.305	24	1	2	77	12
Baines, Chi.	.465	.338	38	9	2	89	14
Baker, Det.	.167	.192	2	0	0	7	0
Baker, Oak.	.322	.314	27	1	0	37	8
Balboni, K.C.	.451	.286	43	2	1	146	8
Bando, Clev.	.327	.325	22	0	1	49	8
Barfield, Tor.	.559	.368	69	5	8	146	9
Barrett, Bos.	.381	.353	65	0	1	31	13
Bathe, Oak.	.359	.208	2	0	1	20	2
Baylor, Bos.	.439	.344	62	8	35	111	12
Beane, Minn.	.295	.258	11	0	0	54	6
Bell, Tor.	.532	.349	41	3	2	62	15
Bell, Clev.	.714	.438	2	0	0	3	0
Bell, K.C.	.000	.400	2	0	0	1	0
Beniquez, Balt.	.397	.372	40	1	3	49	12
Bergman, Det.	.315	.338	21	0	0	16	3
Bernazard, Clev.	.456	.362	53	5	6	77	6

Player—Club	Slg. Pct.	OB Pct.	Tot. BB.	Int. BB.	HP.	SO.	GI DP.
Berra, N.Y.	.352	.294	9	0	1	14	0
Biancalana, K.C.	.337	.298	15	0	0	50	3
Bochte, Oak.	.337	.357	65	3	0	68	9
Boggs, Bos.	.486	.453	105	14	0	44	11
Bonilla, Balt.	.296	.311	25	0	3	21	14
Bonilla, Chi.	.355	.361	33	2	1	49	4
Bonnell, Sea.	.235	.208	1	0	0	13	2
Boone, Cal.	.305	.287	43	1	0	30	15
Boston, Chi.	.427	.335	21	3	0	33	4
P. Bradley, Sea.	.445	.405	77	1	8	134	9
S. Bradley, Chi-Sea.	.432	.347	13	4	4	7	13
Braggs, Milw.	.349	.274	11	0	1	47	6
Brantley, Sea.	.353	.268	10	0	0	21	3
Brett, K.C.	.481	.401	80	18	4	45	6
Brewer, K.C.	.222	.250	2	0	0	6	0
Brookens, Det.	.356	.319	20	0	1	42	4
Brower, Tex.	.222	.111	0	0	0	3	0
Browne, Tex.	.500	.440	1	0	0	4	0
Brunansky, Minn.	.423	.315	53	4	1	98	15
Buckner, Bos.	.421	.311	40	9	4	25	25
Buechele, Tex.	.410	.302	35	1	5	98	10
Burleson, Cal.	.391	.363	33	1	1	32	2
Bush, Minn.	.420	.347	39	2	4	63	7
Butler, Clev.	.375	.356	70	1	4	65	8
Calderon, Sea-Chi	.341	.293	9	1	1	39	1
Cangelosi, Chi.	.299	.349	71	0	7	61	5
Canseco, Oak.	.457	.318	65	1	8	175	12
Carter, Clev.	.514	.335	32	3	5	95	8
Castillo, Milw.	.204	.250	5	0	1	12	2
Castillo, Clev.	.439	.310	9	0	1	48	9
Cerone, Milw.	.380	.304	15	0	1	28	5
Clark, Clev.	.448	.348	7	0	0	11	1
Cochrane, Chi.	.274	.254	5	1	0	22	2
Coles, Det.	.453	.333	45	3	6	84	8
Collins, Det.	.329	.340	44	0	2	49	9
Cooper, Milw.	.373	.310	41	2	1	87	15
Cotto, N.Y.	.288	.229	2	0	0	17	3
Cowens, Sea.	.232	.209	3	0	0	18	3
Craig, Chi.	.200	.333	2	0	0	2	0
Cruz, Chi.	.225	.343	42	0	0	28	4
David, Minn.	.200	.333	0	0	1	2	0
Davidson, Minn.	.162	.189	6	0	0	22	1
Davis, Sea.	.426	.373	76	10	3	68	11
Davis, Oak.	.454	.314	34	2	1	91	7
Dawley, Chi.	.000	.000	0	0	0	0	0
DeCinces, Cal.	.459	.325	52	4	2	74	19
Deer, Milw.	.494	.336	72	3	3	179	4
DeJesus, N.Y.	.000	.200	1	0	0	1	0
Dempsey, Balt.	.379	.309	45	0	3	78	5
Diaz, Milw.	.231	.286	1	0	0	3	0
Dodd, Balt.	.462	.375	2	0	1	2	1
Dodson, Bos.	.833	.533	3	0	0	3	0
Downing, Cal.	.452	.389	90	2	17	84	14
Dwyer, Balt.	.488	.339	23	1	2	31	2
Easler, N.Y.	.449	.362	49	13	0	87	17
Engle, Det.	.337	.312	7	0	0	13	2
Espino, N.Y.	.216	.200	2	0	0	9	0
Espinoza, Minn.	.238	.233	1	0	0	10	0
Evans, Det.	.442	.356	91	5	1	105	6
Evans, Bos.	.476	.376	97	4	6	117	11
Felder, Milw.	.323	.289	13	1	0	16	2
Fernandez, Tor.	.428	.338	27	0	4	52	8
Fielder, Tor.	.325	.222	6	0	1	27	3
Fields, Det.	.349	.283	1	0	0	6	0
Fischlin, N.Y.	.225	.261	8	0	0	29	3
Fisk, Chi.	.337	.263	22	2	6	92	10
Fletcher, Tex.	.400	.360	47	0	4	59	10
Fontenot, Minn.	.000	.000	0	0	0	1	0
Foster, Chi.	.353	.259	3	0	0	8	2
Franco, Clev.	.422	.338	32	1	0	66	28
Gaetti, Minn.	.518	.347	52	4	6	108	18
Gagne, Minn.	.398	.301	30	0	6	108	4
Gallego, Oak.	.324	.289	1	0	0	6	0
Gantner, Milw.	.370	.313	26	2	6	50	13
Garcia, Tor.	.375	.306	13	0	4	32	14
Gedman, Bos.	.424	.315	37	13	4	61	15
Gerhart, Balt.	.304	.267	4	0	0	18	1
Gibson, Det.	.492	.371	68	4	7	107	8
Giles, Chi.	.273	.273	0	0	0	2	1
Greenwell, Bos.	.371	.400	5	0	0	7	1
Grich, Cal.	.412	.354	39	1	3	54	9
Griffey, N.Y.	.475	.349	15	0	1	24	7
Griffin, Oak.	.364	.323	35	6	2	52	5
Gross, Oak.	.000	.333	1	0	0	0	0
Grubb, Det.	.590	.412	28	0	2	28	0
Gruber, Tor.	.343	.220	5	0	0	27	4
Guillen, Chi.	.311	.265	12	1	1	52	14
Gutierrez, Balt.	.207	.207	3	0	1	27	3
Hairston, Chi.	.404	.348	26	3	1	26	9
Hall, Clev.	.493	.346	33	8	2	65	8
Harper, Det.	.167	.200	3	0	0	3	1
Harrah, Tex.	.367	.322	44	0	2	53	7
Hassey, N.Y.-Chi.	.481	.406	46	3	3	27	15
Hatcher, Minn.	.366	.315	19	2	0	26	8
Hearron, Tor.	.261	.308	3	0	0	7	1
Heath, Det.	.418	.291	4	0	0	17	1
Henderson, Sea-Bos	.459	.335	39	4	2	110	6
Henderson, N.Y.	.469	.358	89	2	2	81	12
Henderson, Oak.	.115	.074	0	0	0	5	3
Hendrick, Cal.	.473	.332	26	5	1	41	11
Hengel, Sea.	.254	.215	1	0	1	13	1
Hernandez, N.Y.	.455	.261	1	0	0	8	0
Herndon, Det.	.385	.310	27	2	1	40	3
Hill, Oak.	.378	.329	23	1	0	38	9
Hill, Chi.	.158	.238	1	0	1	3	0
Hoffman, Bos.	.304	.269	2	0	0	3	1
Householder, Milw.	.321	.284	7	0	1	16	1
Howell, Cal.	.470	.349	19	0	0	28	1
Hrbek, Minn.	.478	.353	71	9	6	81	15
Hudler, Balt.	.000	.000	0	0	0	0	0
Hulett, Chi.	.379	.260	21	0	1	91	11
Incaviglia, Tex.	.463	.320	55	2	4	185	9
Iorg, Tor.	.352	.303	20	0	1	47	7
Jackson, Cal.	.408	379	92	11	3	115	14
Jackson, K.C.	.329	.286	7	0	2	34	1
Jacoby, Clev.	.441	.350	56	5	0	137	15
Javier, Oak.	.272	.305	16	0	1	27	2
Johnson, Tor.	.426	.355	52	1	4	57	9
Johnson, K.C.	.323	.258	0	0	0	3	0
Jones, K.C.	.170	.226	6	0	0	5	2
Jones, Balt.	.242	.308	6	0	0	8	0
Jones, Tex.	.095	.174	2	0	0	5	0
Jones, Sea.	.095	.095	0	0	0	4	0
Jones, Cal.	.427	.339	64	5	3	87	8
Joyner, Cal.	.457	.348	57	8	2	58	11
Karkovice, Chi.	.443	.315	9	0	1	37	3
Kearney, Sea.	.377	.281	12	1	0	35	6
Kiefer, Milw.	.000	.000	0	0	0	4	0
Kingery, K.C.	.388	.296	12	2	0	30	4
Kingman, Oak.	.431	.255	33	3	3	126	16
Kittle, Chi.-N.Y.	.420	.284	35	1	3	110	10
Kunkel, Tex.	.462	.231	0	0	0	2	0
Lacy, Balt.	.391	.334	37	2	0	71	12
Laga, Det.	.422	.280	5	1	0	13	0
Lansford, Oak.	.421	.332	39	2	5	51	16
Laudner, Minn.	.451	.333	24	0	3	56	5
Law, K.C.	.388	.327	29	0	2	22	5
Leach, Tor.	.435	.335	13	3	0	24	6
Lee, Tor.	.269	.241	4	0	0	10	5
Lemon, Det.	.407	.326	39	3	8	53	15
Little, Chi.-N.Y.	.211	.244	6	0	0	11	3
Lollar, Bos.	1.000	1.000	0	0	0	0	0
Lombardi, N.Y.	.528	.366	4	0	1	7	2
Lombardozzi, Minn.	.347	.308	52	2	1	76	8
Lowry, Det.	.393	.392	17	0	4	19	4
Lynn, Balt.	.499	371	53	1	2	59	20
Lyons, Bos.-Chi.	.300	.280	19	2	1	47	4
Madison, Det.	.000	.000	0	0	0	3	0
Manning, Milw.	.434	.310	17	2	1	20	5
Martinez, Tor.	.269	.271	20	0	0	25	5
Mattingly, N.Y.	.573	.394	53	11	1	35	17
McDowell, Tex.	.427	.341	65	5	1	112	12
McGriff, Tor.	.200	.200	0	0	0	2	0
McGwire, Oak.	.377	.259	4	0	1	18	0
McLemore, Cal.	.000	.200	1	0	0	2	0
McRae, K.C.	.378	.298	18	4	1	39	9
Meacham, N.Y.	.280	.309	17	0	3	39	6
Mercado, Tex.	.294	.279	6	0	1	13	5

Player—Club	Slg. Pct.	OB Pct.	Tot. BB.	Int. BB.	HP.	SO.	GI DP.
Miller, Cal.	.298	.274	4	0	0	8	3
Molitor, Milw.	.426	.340	40	0	0	81	9
Moore, Milw.	.374	.317	21	1	0	38	6
Morman, Chi.	.358	.324	16	0	2	36	5
Moseby, Tor.	.418	.329	64	3	6	122	7
Moses, Sea.	.333	.311	34	3	0	65	7
Motley, K.C.	.350	.241	11	1	0	31	8
Mulliniks, Tor.	.417	.340	43	1	1	60	12
Mullins, Clev.	.275	.209	2	0	0	11	0
Murphy, Oak.	.386	.364	56	4	4	80	4
Murray, Balt.	.463	.396	78	7	0	49	17
Narron, Cal.	.305	.292	9	0	1	14	5
Nelson, Sea.	.167	.167	0	0	0	4	0
Nelson, Oak.	.333	.300	1	0	0	4	0
Nichols, Balt.	.000	.167	1	1	0	4	0
Nichols, Chi.	.301	.282	11	0	0	23	2
Nixon, Clev.	.326	.352	13	0	0	12	1
Nokes, Det.	.500	.360	1	1	0	1	1
O'Brien, Tex.	.468	.385	87	11	0	66	19
Oglivie, Milw.	.390	.334	30	6	0	33	7
O'Malley, Balt.	.320	.317	17	1	0	21	4
Orta, K.C.	.411	.321	23	3	0	34	9
Owen, Sea.-Bos.	.309	.300	51	1	2	51	13
Paciorek, Tex.	.376	.305	3	0	3	41	5
Pagliarulo, N.Y.	.464	.316	54	10	4	120	10
Pardo, Balt.	.216	.137	0	0	0	14	2
Paris, Balt.	.200	.200	0	0	0	3	1
Parrish, Det.	.483	.340	38	3	5	83	3
Parrish, Tex.	.509	.347	52	7	2	114	16
Pasqua, N.Y.	.525	.399	47	3	3	78	4
Pecota, K.C.	.276	.294	3	0	1	3	1
Perconte, Chi.	.233	.321	11	1	0	10	2
Peters, Oak.	.211	.311	7	1	0	7	2
Petralli, Tex.	.409	.282	5	0	0	14	7
Pettis, Cal.	.343	.339	69	2	0	132	7
Phelps, Sea.	.526	.406	88	6	6	96	4
Phillips, Oak.	.345	.367	76	0	3	82	2
Pittaro, Minn.	.095	.095	0	0	0	8	0
Polidor, Cal.	.316	.300	1	0	0	0	2
Porter, Tex.	.535	.360	22	0	1	51	3
Presley, Sea.	.463	.303	32	3	4	172	18
Pryor, K.C.	.205	.191	3	0	0	14	5
Puckett, Minn.	.537	.366	34	4	7	99	14
Quinones, Bos.-Sea.	.295	.279	24	0	3	57	7
Quirk, K.C.	.370	.273	17	3	1	41	4
Ramos, Sea.	.202	.250	8	0	1	13	7
Randolph, N.Y.	.346	.393	94	0	3	49	11
Rayford, Balt.	.310	.231	15	0	0	50	7
Ready, Milw.	.278	.273	9	0	0	9	3
Reed, Minn.	.321	.308	16	0	1	19	2
Reynolds, Sea.	.290	.275	29	0	3	42	6
Rice, Bos.	.490	.384	62	5	4	78	19
Riles, Milw.	.357	.321	54	0	1	80	14
Ripken, Balt.	.461	.355	70	5	4	60	19
Robidoux, Milw.	.287	.344	33	1	0	36	8
Roenicke, N.Y.	.368	.388	27	0	1	30	1
Rohn, Cleve.	.200	.273	1	0	0	1	0
Romero, Bos.	.283	.270	18	0	2	16	5
Romine, Bos.	.314	.316	3	0	0	9	1
Ryal, Cal.	.563	.412	2	1	0	4	1
Sakata, Oak.	.412	.395	3	0	0	6	1
Salas, Minn.	.384	.282	18	2	1	32	8
Salazar, K.C.	.326	.266	7	0	2	47	3
Salazar, Chi.	.143	.250	1	0	0	3	0
Sanchez, Minn.	.125	.176	1	0	0	8	2
Sax, Bos.	.818	.455	0	0	0	1	0
Schofield, Cal.	.397	.321	48	2	5	55	8
Schroeder, Milw.	.373	.262	9	0	6	59	3
Seitzer, K.C.	.448	.440	19	0	1	14	0
Sheets, Balt.	.488	.317	21	3	2	56	16
Shelby, Balt.	.364	.263	18	0	2	75	3
Shepherd, Tor.	.348	.236	3	0	0	22	1
Sheridan, Det.	.360	.300	21	4	1	57	3
Sierra, Tex.	.476	.302	22	3	1	65	8
Skinner, Chi.-N.Y.	.314	.269	16	0	1	83	6
Slaught, Tex.	.449	.308	16	0	5	59	8
Smalley, Minn.	.438	.342	68	4	0	80	10
Smith, K.C.	.411	.357	46	0	10	78	10
Snyder, Clev.	.500	.299	16	0	0	123	8
Spilman, Det.	.469	.288	3	0	0	8	1
Stanley, Tex.	.533	.394	3	0	0	7	0
Stapleton, Bos.	.154	.171	2	0	0	10	1
Stefero, Balt.	.300	.321	16	0	0	25	1
Steinbach, Oak.	.733	.375	1	0	0	0	0
Stenhouse, Bos.	.143	.424	12	0	0	5	1
Sullivan, Bos.	.252	.260	7	0	4	32	1
Sundberg, K.C.	.322	.303	57	1	0	91	7
Sveum, Milw.	.366	.316	32	0	1	63	7
Tabler, Clev.	.433	.368	29	3	3	75	11
Tartabull, Sea	.489	.347	61	2	1	157	10
Tarver, Bos.	.120	.154	1	0	0	4	0
Taylor, K.C.	.000	.000	0	0	0	0	0
Tettleton, Oak.	.389	.325	39	0	1	51	3
Thomas, Sea.-Milw.	.371	.316	58	4	1	105	5
Thornton, Clev.	.392	.333	65	0	1	67	11
Tillman, Oak.	.359	.310	3	0	0	11	0
Tolleson, Chi.-N.Y.	.339	.338	52	0	2	76	6
Tolman, Det.	.206	.293	6	0	0	4	0
Traber, Balt.	.472	.321	18	2	5	31	6
Trammell, Det.	.469	.347	59	4	5	57	7
Upshaw, Tor.	.368	.341	78	4	2	87	5
Valle, Sea.	.679	.417	7	0	0	7	2
Walker, Chi.	.493	.345	29	4	2	44	4
Ward, Tex.	.405	.372	31	3	4	72	10
Washington, N.Y.	.407	.285	7	0	2	33	3
Washington, Minn.	.459	.278	3	0	0	21	0
Whitaker, Det.	.437	.338	63	5	0	70	20
White, Cal.	.353	.316	6	0	0	8	0
White, K.C.	.465	.322	43	5	2	88	10
Whitt, Tor.	.448	.326	35	3	0	39	11
Wiggins, Balt.	.272	.309	22	0	0	20	0
Wilfong, Cal.	.309	.263	16	2	2	34	4
Wilkerson, Tex.	.305	.273	11	0	1	42	2
Willard, Oak.	.385	.354	22	0	2	28	4
Williams, Clev.	.143	.143	0	0	0	3	0
Williams, Chi.	.226	.182	1	0	1	11	1
Wilson, K.C.	.366	.313	31	1	9	97	6
Winfield, N.Y.	.462	.349	77	9	2	106	20
Woods, Minn.	.571	.375	3	0	0	5	0
G. Wright, Tex.	.321	.250	4	1	1	23	2
Wynegar, N.Y.	.345	.310	30	2	0	21	9
Yeager, Sea.	.269	.273	12	0	0	23	5
Young, Balt.	.371	.342	49	2	3	90	13
Yount, Milw.	.450	.388	62	7	4	73	9
Zuvella, N.Y.	.104	.170	5	0	0	4	1

OFFICIAL AMERICAN LEAGUE DESIGNATED HITTING

CLUB DESIGNATED HITTING

Club	Pct.	AB.	R.	H.	TB.	2B.	3B.	HR.	RBI.	SH.	SF.	BB.	HP.	SO.	SB.	CS.	GI DP.
Baltimore	.298	617	80	184	307	30	3	29	97	1	3	57	2	92	3	1	24
New York	.278	633	78	176	270	30	2	20	97	2	7	64	4	128	7	3	18
Detroit	.275	592	82	163	281	30	2	28	102	4	7	80	0	103	6	7	7
Minnesota	.267	617	84	165	283	27	5	27	78	3	5	71	0	102	1	5	16
Chicago	.266	601	78	160	264	29	3	23	89	0	9	58	5	124	4	6	18
Texas	.263	608	82	160	284	32	1	30	106	0	6	62	2	178	2	4	17
Kansas City	.258	648	64	167	254	35	2	16	84	0	4	44	1	79	1	3	18
Seattle	.254	594	93	151	271	18	6	30	89	2	2	91	4	150	2	7	11
California	.249	602	94	150	249	21	3	24	76	1	5	109	4	142	1	3	15

Club	Pct.	AB.	R.	H.	TB.	2B.	3B.	HR.	RBI.	SH.	SF.	BB.	HP.	SO.	SB.	CS.	GI DP.
Toronto	.242	616	86	149	241	26	3	20	83	0	2	67	5	119	2	4	17
Boston	.240	599	94	144	269	27	1	32	98	0	5	62	34	103	3	5	11
Cleveland	.238	610	81	145	233	22	0	22	93	2	9	81	2	109	5	1	18
Milwaukee	.229	625	64	143	213	24	2	14	73	3	6	66	1	133	4	7	13
Oakland	.221	639	78	141	273	24	0	36	101	0	7	43	3	135	5	4	19
Totals	.256	8601	1138	2198	3692	375	33	351	1266	18	77	955	67	1697	46	60	222

INDIVIDUAL DESIGNATED HITTING

(Listed Alphabetically)

Player and Club	Pct.	G.	AB.	R.	H.	TB.	2B.	3B.	HR.	RBI.	SH.	SF.	BB.	HP.	SO.	SB.	CS.	GI DP.
Armas, Bos.	.000	1	1	0	0	0	0	0	0	0	0	0	0	0	0	0	0	0
Baines, Chi.	.100	3	10	0	1	1	0	0	0	0	0	0	2	0	2	0	0	0
Baker, Oak.	.302	15	53	3	16	21	2	0	1	6	0	0	7	0	6	0	0	2
Baker, Det.	.000	1	1	0	0	0	0	0	0	0	0	0	0	0	0	0	0	0
Baylor, Bos.	.245	143	527	84	129	242	21	1	30	92	0	5	54	34	95	3	5	9
Beane, Minn.	.222	5	9	1	2	2	0	0	0	0	0	0	1	0	1	0	0	1
Bell, Tor.	.289	11	45	8	13	24	6	1	1	6	0	0	4	0	6	0	1	0
Bell, Clev.	.286	2	7	1	2	4	2	0	0	3	0	0	2	0	0	0	0	0
Beniquez, Balt.	.333	16	39	6	13	23	1	0	3	4	0	0	4	0	5	0	0	2
Bergman, Det.	.429	8	7	1	3	3	0	0	0	1	0	0	2	0	0	0	0	0
Berra, N.Y.	.182	4	11	1	2	5	0	0	1	1	0	0	1	1	1	0	0	0
Bochte, Oak.	1.000	1	1	0	1	2	1	0	0	0	0	0	0	0	0	0	0	0
Bonilla, Balt.	.500	2	2	0	1	2	1	0	0	0	0	0	0	0	0	0	0	1
Bonnell, Sea.	.500	2	4	1	2	2	0	0	0	0	0	0	1	0	0	0	1	1
Boston, Chi.	.000	1	0	1	0	0	0	0	0	0	0	0	0	0	0	0	0	0
S. Bradley, Chi-Sea	.280	9	25	2	7	7	0	0	0	0	0	0	1	2	0	0	2	1
Braggs, Milw.	.167	2	6	1	1	1	0	0	0	1	0	0	2	0	1	0	0	0
Brett, K.C.	.222	7	27	4	6	10	1	0	1	6	0	0	2	0	2	0	0	1
Brewer, K.C.	.000	1	0	0	0	0	0	0	0	0	0	0	1	0	0	0	0	0
Brookens, Det.	.324	14	34	7	11	15	2	1	0	2	0	0	4	0	2	1	2	0
Brower, Tex.	.000	1	0	0	0	0	0	0	0	0	0	0	0	0	0	0	0	0
Brunansky, Minn.	.250	2	4	0	1	1	0	0	0	1	0	1	0	0	0	0	0	0
Buckner, Bos.	.200	15	60	8	12	24	6	0	2	6	0	0	5	0	4	0	0	2
Burleson, Cal.	.275	38	131	18	36	49	4	0	3	12	1	0	10	0	18	0	2	0
Bush, Minn.	.267	6	15	3	4	9	2	0	1	3	0	0	3	0	4	0	0	1
Calderon, Chi.	.400	6	20	2	8	12	2	1	0	2	0	0	1	0	5	0	0	0
Cangelosi, Chi.	.000	3	0	0	0	0	0	0	0	0	0	0	0	0	0	1	2	0
Canseco, Oak.	.000	1	3	0	0	0	0	0	0	0	0	0	1	0	1	0	0	0
Castillo, Clev.	.244	35	90	16	22	37	3	0	4	15	0	0	6	0	23	0	0	5
Castillo, Milw.	.000	2	0	2	0	0	0	0	0	0	0	0	0	0	0	0	0	0
Clark, Clev.	.250	7	20	4	5	5	0	0	0	3	2	1	3	0	1	0	0	0
Coles, Det.	.423	7	26	3	11	18	1	0	2	4	0	0	2	0	5	0	1	0
Collins, Det.	.250	24	80	6	20	27	5	1	0	8	2	1	7	0	10	2	1	4
Cooper, Milw.	.254	44	177	18	45	68	6	1	5	28	0	1	15	1	40	1	1	6
Cotto, N.Y.	.000	1	0	0	0	0	0	0	0	0	0	0	0	0	0	0	0	0
Cowens, Sea.	.200	1	5	1	1	1	0	0	0	0	0	0	0	0	2	0	0	0
Cruz, Chi.	.000	3	1	1	0	0	0	0	0	0	0	0	0	0	1	0	0	0
David, Minn.	.500	1	2	0	1	1	0	0	0	0	0	0	0	0	1	0	0	0
Davidson, Minn.	.500	3	4	0	2	4	2	0	0	0	0	0	0	0	1	0	0	0
Davis, Sea.	.294	32	119	14	35	49	2	0	4	14	0	1	9	0	20	0	0	4
DeCinces, Cal.	.250	3	12	2	3	5	2	0	0	0	0	0	0	0	2	0	0	0
Dodd, Balt.	.250	6	12	1	3	6	0	0	1	2	0	0	0	0	2	0	0	1
Downing, Cal.	.243	10	37	6	9	20	3	1	2	5	0	1	6	1	8	0	0	1
Dwyer, Balt.	.343	24	70	13	24	51	7	1	6	19	0	1	12	0	7	0	0	0
Easler, N.Y.	.302	129	450	58	136	199	26	2	11	70	2	5	42	0	81	2	1	16
Engle, Det.	.333	5	12	1	4	6	2	0	0	1	0	0	1	0	2	0	0	1
Evans, Bos.	.333	1	3	1	1	1	0	0	0	0	0	0	1	0	1	0	0	0
Evans, Det.	.234	42	145	21	34	66	5	0	9	24	0	0	25	0	31	1	1	2
Felder, Milw.	.400	1	5	2	2	2	0	0	0	1	0	0	0	0	1	0	0	0
Fielder, Tor.	.161	22	62	5	10	20	1	0	3	8	0	0	5	1	22	0	0	2
Fields, Det.	.000	1	0	1	0	0	0	0	0	0	0	0	0	0	0	0	0	0
Fisk, Chi.	.221	22	86	6	19	30	2	0	3	15	0	2	3	1	26	0	1	2
Fletcher, Tex.	.000	1	0	0	0	0	0	0	0	0	0	0	0	0	0	0	0	0
Foster, Chi.	.111	3	9	0	1	3	0	1	0	1	0	0	0	0	4	0	0	1
Franco, Clev.	.167	3	12	1	2	5	0	0	1	4	0	0	0	0	3	0	0	0
Gantner, Milw.	.000	1	0	1	0	0	0	0	0	0	0	0	0	0	0	0	0	0
Garcia, Tor.	.280	11	25	1	7	7	0	0	0	2	0	0	0	0	6	1	0	1
Gibson, Det.	.067	4	15	4	1	4	0	0	1	1	0	0	4	0	8	1	0	0
Greenwell, Bos.	.400	3	5	1	2	2	0	0	0	0	0	0	1	0	0	0	0	0
Griffey, N.Y.	.000	2	4	1	0	0	0	0	0	0	0	0	1	0	4	0	0	0
Grubb, Det.	.353	52	156	26	55	100	12	0	11	40	0	3	23	0	20	0	1	0
Gruber, Tor.	.000	14	10	3	0	0	0	0	0	0	0	0	1	0	4	0	2	0
Guillen, Chi.	.000	1	0	1	0	0	0	0	0	0	0	0	0	0	0	0	0	0
Gutierrez, Balt.	.000	1	0	0	0	0	0	0	0	0	0	0	0	0	0	0	0	0
Hairston, Chi.	.284	29	102	16	29	49	8	0	4	14	0	0	14	0	11	0	0	3
Hall, Clev.	.182	7	11	0	2	2	0	0	0	0	0	0	0	0	2	0	0	0
Harper, Det.	.222	6	9	1	2	3	1	0	0	2	0	1	0	0	1	0	0	0
Hassey, NY-Chi.	.373	37	126	20	47	67	9	1	3	20	0	1	18	1	8	0	0	5

Player and Club	Pct.	G.	AB.	R.	H.	TB.	2B.	3B.	HR.	RBI.	SH.	SF.	BB.	HP.	SO.	SB.	CS.	GI DP.
Hatcher, Minn.	.316	28	95	17	30	39	4	1	1	11	0	1	6	0	5	0	0	4
Henderson, N.Y.	.111	5	18	4	2	2	0	0	0	0	0	0	4	1	4	3	1	1
Henderson, Oak.	.000	1	0	0	0	0	0	0	0	0	0	0	0	0	0	0	0	0
Henderson, Sea.	.291	22	79	12	23	37	4	2	2	8	1	0	11	0	19	0	1	1
Hendrick, Cal.	.250	4	8	1	2	2	0	0	0	1	0	0	1	0	1	0	0	0
Hengel, Sea.	.147	11	34	1	5	5	0	0	0	2	0	0	1	0	7	0	0	0
Herndon, Det.	.190	18	21	3	4	7	0	0	1	5	0	0	4	0	4	0	0	0
Hill, Oak.	.000	3	6	0	0	0	0	0	0	0	0	0	0	0	0	0	0	0
Householder, Milw.	.231	3	13	0	3	5	2	0	0	4	0	0	0	0	1	0	0	0
Howell, Cal.	.000	2	3	1	0	0	0	0	0	0	0	0	1	0	0	0	0	0
Hrbek, Minn.	.000	1	3	1	0	0	0	0	0	0	0	0	1	0	1	0	0	0
Incaviglia, Tex.	.197	36	132	12	26	44	6	0	4	12	0	0	12	0	54	0	1	2
Jackson, Cal.	.236	121	403	63	95	164	11	2	18	54	0	3	89	3	113	1	1	14
Jackson, K.C.	.250	1	4	0	1	2	1	0	0	0	0	0	0	0	1	0	0	0
Javier, Oak.	.000	2	0	1	0	0	0	0	0	0	0	0	0	0	0	1	0	0
Johnson, Tor.	.248	95	326	48	81	140	12	1	15	51	0	1	49	4	56	0	1	9
Jones, Sea.	.000	1	1	0	0	0	0	0	0	0	0	0	0	0	1	0	0	0
Jones, K.C.	.000	3	3	0	0	0	0	0	0	0	0	0	0	0	0	0	0	0
Kingman, Oak.	.214	140	552	70	118	242	19	0	35	94	0	7	33	3	125	3	3	16
Kittle, Chi-NY	.217	86	299	35	65	128	9	0	18	52	0	8	24	2	86	3	0	7
Kunkel, Tex.	.000	1	1	0	0	0	0	0	0	0	0	0	0	0	0	0	0	0
Lacy, Balt.	.400	3	5	0	2	2	0	0	0	0	0	0	0	0	0	0	0	0
Laga, Det.	.000	2	4	0	0	0	0	0	0	0	0	0	0	0	3	0	0	0
Lansford, Oak.	.333	3	12	1	4	5	1	0	0	1	0	0	0	0	0	0	0	1
Law, K.C.	.286	2	7	1	2	3	1	0	0	1	0	0	1	0	0	0	0	0
Leach, Tor.	.276	42	105	12	29	40	6	1	1	16	0	1	4	0	12	0	0	3
Lynn, Balt.	.000	1	0	1	0	0	0	0	0	0	0	0	1	0	0	0	0	0
Lyons, Chi.	.000	1	0	0	0	0	0	0	0	0	0	0	0	0	0	0	0	0
Madison, Det.	.000	1	4	0	0	0	0	0	0	0	0	0	0	0	1	0	0	0
Manning, Milw.	.000	5	1	1	0	0	0	0	0	0	0	0	0	0	0	0	0	0
Martinez, Tor.	.000	1	1	0	0	0	0	0	0	0	0	0	0	0	0	0	0	0
Mattingly, N.Y.	.250	1	4	1	1	1	0	0	0	0	0	0	0	0	0	0	0	0
McDowell, Tex.	.000	1	4	0	0	0	0	0	0	0	0	0	1	0	1	0	0	1
McGriff, Tor.	.200	2	5	1	1	1	0	0	0	0	0	0	0	0	2	0	0	0
McRae, K.C.	.238	75	244	21	58	89	13	0	6	32	0	2	15	1	37	0	0	7
Miller, Cal.	.667	2	3	1	2	3	1	0	0	0	0	0	1	0	0	0	0	0
Molitor, Milw.	.311	10	45	5	14	21	4	0	1	4	0	0	2	0	7	1	1	0
Moore, Milw.	.250	2	4	0	1	1	0	0	0	2	0	1	0	0	0	0	1	0
Moseby, Tor.	.091	3	11	0	1	1	0	0	0	0	0	0	0	0	4	1	0	0
Moses, Sea.	.364	4	11	3	4	4	0	0	0	0	0	0	0	0	2	0	1	0
Motley, K.C.	.000	2	3	0	0	0	0	0	0	0	0	0	0	0	0	0	0	0
Mulliniks, Tor.	.308	5	13	2	4	4	0	0	0	0	0	0	4	0	0	0	0	1
Mullins, Clev.	.000	1	0	0	0	0	0	0	0	0	0	0	0	0	0	0	0	0
Murphy, Oak.	.000	1	0	0	0	0	0	0	0	0	0	0	0	0	0	0	0	0
Murray, Balt.	.356	16	59	6	21	27	3	0	1	4	0	0	7	0	4	1	0	1
Narron, Cal.	.667	2	3	0	2	2	0	0	0	2	0	1	1	0	0	0	0	0
Nelson, Sea.	.167	4	6	1	1	1	0	0	0	0	0	0	0	0	1	0	0	0
Nelson, Oak.	.200	1	5	1	1	2	1	0	0	0	0	0	0	0	1	0	0	0
Nichols, Chi.	.000	3	0	0	0	0	0	0	0	0	0	0	1	0	0	1	1	0
Nixon, Clev.	.000	5	0	1	0	0	0	0	0	0	0	0	1	0	0	1	0	0
Oglivie, Milw.	.226	42	159	9	36	44	5	0	1	19	0	4	15	0	18	0	2	4
Orta, K.C.	.277	87	318	33	88	130	13	1	9	42	0	2	22	0	33	0	3	9
Paciorek, Tex.	.160	9	25	1	4	4	0	0	0	1	0	0	0	0	11	0	0	0
Pardo, Balt.	.250	1	4	1	1	1	0	0	0	0	0	0	0	0	1	0	0	0
Paris, Balt.	.000	2	1	0	0	0	0	0	0	0	0	0	0	0	0	0	0	1
Parrish, Det.	.300	6	20	2	6	9	0	0	1	3	0	1	1	0	9	0	0	0
Parrish, Tex.	.284	99	359	54	102	188	21	1	21	77	0	6	36	2	89	2	1	11
Pasqua, N.Y.	.333	3	9	1	3	7	1	0	1	2	0	0	1	1	4	0	0	0
Peters, Oak.	.000	4	1	1	0	0	0	0	0	0	0	0	0	0	0	0	0	0
Petralli, Tex.	.000	2	1	0	0	0	0	0	0	0	0	0	0	0	0	1	0	0
Pettis, Cal.	.000	1	0	1	0	0	0	0	0	0	0	0	0	0	0	0	0	0
Phelps, Sea.	.283	52	152	33	43	100	7	4	14	38	0	1	41	2	43	1	1	3
Phillips, Oak.	.250	2	4	1	1	1	0	0	0	0	0	0	1	0	2	0	1	0
Porter, Tex.	.317	19	60	11	19	38	4	0	5	15	0	0	12	0	19	0	1	3
Ramos, Sea.	.000	2	0	2	0	0	0	0	0	0	0	0	0	0	0	0	0	0
Randolph, N.Y.	.000	1	1	0	0	0	0	0	0	1	0	0	0	0	0	0	0	0
Rayford, Balt.	.000	1	1	0	0	0	0	0	0	0	0	0	0	0	0	0	0	0
Ready, Milw.	.000	1	4	0	0	0	0	0	0	0	0	0	0	0	1	0	0	0
Rice, Bos.	.000	1	3	0	0	0	0	0	0	0	0	0	1	0	3	0	0	0
Robidoux, Milw.	.118	10	34	1	4	4	0	0	0	0	0	0	5	0	8	0	0	0
Roenicke, N.Y.	.314	15	35	3	11	18	1	0	2	6	0	0	7	1	9	0	1	0
Ryal, Cal.	.500	2	2	1	1	4	0	0	1	2	0	0	0	0	0	0	0	0
Sakata, Oak.	.000	1	0	0	0	0	0	0	0	0	0	0	0	0	0	0	0	0
Salas, Minn.	.429	8	28	4	12	24	3	0	3	6	0	0	0	0	5	1	0	0
Salazar, Chi.	.200	2	5	1	1	1	0	0	0	0	0	0	1	0	2	0	0	0
Sanchez, Minn.	.182	3	11	1	2	2	0	0	0	1	0	0	1	0	4	0	0	1
Schroeder, Milw.	.297	10	37	6	11	17	3	0	1	4	1	0	1	0	9	0	0	0
Sheets, Balt.	.302	58	205	30	62	105	11	1	10	41	1	0	13	1	32	1	0	11
Shelby, Balt.	.200	2	5	0	1	2	1	0	0	1	0	0	1	0	0	0	0	0

Player and Club	Pct.	G.	AB.	R.	H.	TB.	2B.	3B.	HR.	RBI.	SH.	SF.	BB.	HP.	SO.	SB.	CS.	GI DP.
Shepherd, Tor.	.250	16	12	6	3	4	1	0	0	0	0	0	0	0	6	0	0	1
Sheridan, Det.	.000	5	0	0	0	0	0	0	0	0	0	0	0	0	0	0	0	0
Sierra, Tex.	.143	3	7	0	1	2	1	0	0	0	0	0	0	0	2	0	0	0
Slaught, Tex.	.333	2	9	1	3	3	0	0	0	1	0	0	0	0	1	0	0	0
Smalley, Minn.	.253	114	396	51	100	184	16	4	20	51	1	2	56	0	67	0	3	9
Smith, K.C.	.293	10	41	4	12	20	6	1	0	3	0	0	3	0	6	1	0	1
Snyder, Clev.	.000	1	4	0	0	0	0	0	0	0	0	0	0	0	1	0	0	1
Spilman, Det.	.273	11	33	5	9	19	1	0	3	8	1	0	1	0	6	0	0	0
Stanley, Tex.	.500	3	4	1	2	2	0	0	0	0	0	0	0	0	1	0	0	0
Tabler, Clev.	.333	18	75	10	25	33	5	0	1	8	0	0	4	1	13	0	0	1
Tartabull, Sea.	.250	3	12	1	3	4	1	0	0	1	0	0	1	0	3	0	1	0
Taylor, K.C.	.000	2	1	1	0	0	0	0	0	0	0	0	0	0	0	0	0	0
Thomas, Sea-Mil	.192	88	291	40	56	111	8	1	15	35	3	0	51	1	95	2	4	5
Thornton, Clev.	.223	110	391	48	87	147	12	0	16	60	0	8	65	1	66	4	1	11
Tolleson, Chi.	.000	2	1	1	0	0	0	0	0	0	0	0	0	0	0	1	0	0
Tolman, Det.	.143	9	21	1	3	4	1	0	0	2	1	1	4	0	1	1	1	0
Traber, Balt.	.316	21	76	11	24	42	3	0	5	12	0	1	9	1	10	0	0	2
Trammell, Det.	.000	2	4	0	0	0	0	0	0	1	0	0	2	0	0	0	0	0
Upshaw, Tor.	.000	1	1	0	0	0	0	0	0	0	0	0	0	0	1	0	0	0
Walker, Chi.	.333	1	6	1	2	3	1	0	0	2	0	0	0	0	0	0	0	0
Ward, Tex.	.500	1	6	1	3	3	0	0	0	0	0	0	1	0	0	0	1	0
Washington, Minn.	.229	15	35	4	8	14	0	0	2	2	2	0	2	0	11	0	2	0
Wiggins, Balt.	.000	1	0	0	0	0	0	0	0	0	0	0	0	0	0	0	0	0
Wilkerson, Tex.	.000	2	0	1	0	0	0	0	0	0	0	0	0	0	0	0	0	0
Willard, Oak.	.000	1	2	0	0	0	0	0	0	0	0	0	1	0	0	0	0	0
Williams, Chi.	.000	1	0	0	0	0	0	0	0	0	0	0	0	0	0	0	0	0
Winfield, N.Y.	.111	6	18	0	2	2	0	0	0	0	0	0	1	0	4	0	0	0
Woods, Minn.	.200	7	15	2	3	3	0	0	0	3	0	1	1	0	2	0	0	0
R. Wright, Tex.	.000	1	0	0	0	0	0	0	0	0	0	0	0	0	0	0	0	0
Young, Balt.	.232	38	138	11	32	46	3	1	3	14	0	1	10	0	31	1	1	5
Yount, Milw.	.214	6	14	2	3	6	0	0	1	1	0	0	2	0	4	1	0	0

OFFICIAL AMERICAN LEAGUE FIELDING AVERAGES

CLUB FIELDING

Club	Pct.	G.	PO.	A.	E.	TC.	DP.	TP.	PB.
Toronto	.984	163	4428	1684	100	6212	150	0	9
California	.983	162	4368	1718	107	6193	156	0	12
Detroit	.982	162	4331	1707	108	6146	163	0	12
Chicago	.981	162	4327	1667	117	6111	142	1	14
Minnesota	.980	162	4298	1626	118	6042	168	0	12
Kansas City	.980	162	4322	1757	123	6202	153	0	16
Texas	.980	162	4351	1655	122	6128	160	0	25
New York	.979	162	4330	1672	127	6129	153	0	17
Boston	.979	161	4289	1602	129	6020	146	0	16
Baltimore	.978	162	4310	1651	135	6096	163	0	7
Oakland	.978	162	4299	1597	135	6031	120	0	16
Milwaukee	.976	161	4295	1522	146	5963	146	0	15
Seattle	.975	162	4319	1837	156	6312	191	2	17
Cleveland	.975	163	4343	1703	157	6203	148	0	20
Totals	.979	1134	60610	23398	1780	85788	2159	3	208

INDIVIDUAL FIELDING

FIRST BASEMEN

*Throws lefthanded.

Leader—Club	Pct.	G.	PO.	A.	E.	DP.
MATTINGLY, N.Y.*	.996	160	1377	100	6	132

Player—Club	Pct.	G.	PO.	A.	E.	DP.
Balboni, K.C.	.987	137	1236	98	18	115
Baylor, Bos.	.986	13	65	4	1	7
Beniquez, Balt.	.990	14	96	8	1	14
Bergman, Det.*	.986	41	255	29	4	30
Bochte, Oak.*	.991	115	912	88	9	79
Bonilla, Chi.	.997	30	270	20	1	25
Buckner, Bos.*	.989	138	1067	157	14	104
Carter, Clev.	.993	70	559	47	4	50
Cooper, Milw.*	.988	90	697	61	9	78
Davis, Sea.	.986	101	880	82	14	112
Engle, Det.	1.000	23	173	13	0	20
Evans, Det.	.998	105	808	108	2	85
Grich, Cal.	1.000	11	75	8	0	5
Hairston, Chi.	1.000	19	121	8	0	11
Hatcher, Minn.	.988	22	159	9	2	12
Hrbek, Minn.	.992	147	1218	104	10	137
Joyner, Cal.*	.989	152	1222	139	15	128
Laga, Det.*	1.000	12	98	7	0	10
Lansford, Oak.	.995	60	413	22	2	24
Mattingly, N.Y.*	.996	160	1377	100	6	132
Morman, Chi.	.989	47	342	26	4	31
Murray, Balt.	.989	119	1045	88	13	100
O'Brien, Tex.*	.992	155	1224	115	11	123
Paciorek, Tex.	1.000	23	141	14	0	13
Phelps, Sea.*	.983	55	487	34	9	58
Robidoux, Milw.	.986	43	326	29	5	35
Schroeder, Milw.	1.000	19	117	11	0	10
Seitzer, K.C.	.987	22	210	17	3	17
Stapleton, Bos.	1.000	29	79	7	0	10
Tabler, Clev.	.990	107	846	84	9	87
Traber, Balt.*	.988	29	224	21	3	28
Upshaw, Tor.*	.992	154	1314	131	12	118
Walker, Chi.	.993	77	670	57	5	57

(Fewer Than Ten Games)

Player—Club	Pct.	G.	PO.	A.	E.	DP.
Adduci, Milw.*	1.000	3	25	3	0	1
Baker, Oak.	1.000	3	10	0	0	0
Bonnell, Sea.	.973	8	30	6	1	1

FIRST BASEMAN—Continued

Player—Club	Pct.	G.	PO.	A.	E.	DP.
Bush, Minn.*	1.000	3	15	0	0	2
Deer, Milw.	1.000	4	26	0	0	2
Dodson, Bos.*	1.000	7	25	1	0	6
Dwyer, Balt.*	1.000	1	0	1	0	0
Fielder, Tor.	1.000	7	37	3	0	3
Garcia, Tor.	1.000	1	1	0	0	0
Harper, Det.	1.000	2	7	2	0	2
Hendrick, Cal.	1.000	7	44	3	0	3
Johnson, Tor.	1.000	1	8	1	0	2
Jones, Tex.*	1.000	2	19	1	0	2
Kingman, Oak.	.895	3	17	0	2	2
Leach, Tor.*	.971	7	63	5	2	11
Lowry, Det.*	1.000	1	2	1	0	0
Lyons, Chi.	1.000	1	1	0	0	0
McGriff, Tor.*	1.000	1	3	0	0	0
Moses, Sea.*	.952	7	38	2	2	3
Mullins, Clev.	1.000	1	2	1	0	0
Nelson, Oak.*	.800	2	3	1	1	1
Pasqua, N.Y.*	1.000	5	24	0	0	5
Pryor, K.C.	.000	1	0	0	0	0
Quirk, K.C.	1.000	6	43	6	0	4
Roenicke, N.Y.	1.000	2	6	1	0	0
Ryal, Cal.*	1.000	4	23	2	0	1
Sax, Bos.	1.000	1	4	0	0	0
Sheets, Balt.	.958	4	18	5	1	3
Spilman, Det.	1.000	1	4	0	0	0
Stenhouse, Bos.	1.000	3	18	3	0	3
Thomas, Milw.	.980	6	47	3	1	3
Tolman, Det.	1.000	3	15	0	0	2
Valle, Sea.	.975	4	37	2	1	3
Yount, Milw.	.929	3	13	0	1	1

SECOND BASEMEN

Leader—Club	Pct.	G.	PO.	A.	E.	DP.
LOMBARDOZZI, Minn.	.991	155	289	407	6	102

Player—Club	Pct.	G.	PO.	A.	E.	DP.
Barrett, Bos.	.982	158	303	450	14	104
Bernazard, Clev.	.979	146	351	442	17	95
Biancalana, K.C.	1.000	12	6	13	0	1
Bonilla, Balt.	.981	70	122	140	5	38
Brookens, Det.	.985	31	67	61	2	18
Buechele, Tex.	.992	33	59	66	1	25
Castillo, Milw.	1.000	17	32	32	0	7
Cruz, Chi.	.985	78	132	205	5	45
Espinoza, Minn.	.941	19	12	36	3	7
Fischlin, N.Y.	.970	27	30	34	2	5
Fletcher, Tex.	.975	11	15	24	1	5
Franco, Clev.	.982	13	17	39	1	9
Gallego, Oak.	.986	19	23	50	1	6
Gantner, Milw.	.985	135	304	347	10	87
Garcia, Tor.	.985	106	224	286	8	66
Grich, Cal.	.980	87	127	221	7	49
Gruber, Tor.	.969	14	15	16	1	5
Gutierrez, Balt.	.990	53	93	102	2	29
Harrah, Tex.	.982	93	166	211	7	49
Hill, Oak.	.984	68	92	150	4	27
Hudler, Balt.	.800	13	2	2	1	0
Hulett, Chi.	.987	66	109	187	4	44
Iorg, Tor.	.961	52	61	87	6	10
Johnson, K.C.	1.000	11	14	32	0	5
Jones, Balt.	1.000	11	17	26	0	5
Lee, Tor.	.990	29	32	72	1	10
Little, Chi-N.Y.	.983	26	54	61	2	12
Lombardozzi, Minn.	.991	155	289	407	6	102
Mullins, Clev.	.953	13	14	27	2	4
Perconte, Chi.	.990	24	46	54	1	12
Phillips, Oak.	.976	88	160	290	11	40
Pryor, K.C.	1.000	12	10	20	0	6
Ramos, Sea.	.956	16	19	24	2	6
Randolph, N.Y.	.972	139	313	381	20	94
Reynolds, Sea.	.977	126	278	415	16	111
Sakata, Oak.	.984	16	21	39	1	4
Sveum, Milw.	.981	13	29	23	1	6
Tartabull, Sea.	.947	31	76	101	10	28
Washington, Minn.	.917	16	10	12	2	3
Whitaker, Det.	.984	141	276	421	11	98
White, K.C.	.987	151	316	439	10	91
Wiggins, Balt.	.978	66	121	151	6	40
Wilfong, Cal.	.968	90	135	257	7	48
Wilkerson, Tex.	.968	60	66	114	6	30

Triple Plays—Cruz, Reynolds, Tartabull.

(Fewer Than Ten Games)

Player—Club	Pct.	G.	PO.	A.	E.	DP.
Baker, Det.	1.000	2	4	2	0	0
Bell, Clev.	.778	2	1	6	2	1
Browne, Tex.	.923	8	9	15	2	4
Burleson, Cal.	1.000	6	15	11	0	3
Gaetti, Minn.	.000	1	0	0	0	0
Gagne, Minn.	1.000	4	0	4	0	0
Giles, Chi.	1.000	7	15	11	0	6
Hernandez, N.Y.	1.000	1	1	0	0	0
Jones, Sea.	1.000	3	1	2	0	0
Jones, K.C.	.000	1	0	0	0	0
Lansford, Oak.	1.000	1	0	1	0	0
McLemore, Cal.	1.000	2	3	10	0	1
Moore, Milw.	1.000	1	0	1	0	0
Mulliniks, Tor.	.000	1	0	0	0	0
Nichols, Chi.	1.000	2	0	1	0	0
Peters, Oak.	1.000	1	1	1	0	1
Petralli, Tex.	.000	2	0	0	0	0
Pittaro, Minn.	.969	8	14	17	1	8
Polidor, Cal.	1.000	4	8	8	0	2
Ready, Milw.	.966	7	14	14	1	4
Rohn, Clev.	.900	2	3	6	1	1
Romero, Bos.	1.000	4	0	5	0	1
Salazar, K.C.	1.000	1	0	1	0	0
Stapleton, Bos.	1.000	6	6	7	0	3
Stefero, Balt.	.000	1	0	0	0	0
Tolleson, N.Y.	1.000	3	3	2	0	1

SECOND BASEMAN WITH TWO OR MORE CLUBS

Player—Club	Pct.	G.	PO.	A.	E.	DP.
Little, Chi.	1.000	12	27	21	0	3
Little, N.Y.	.975	14	37	40	2	9

THIRD BASEMEN

Leader—Club	Pct.	G.	PO.	A.	E.	DP.
MULLINIKS, Tor.	.975	110	60	176	6	13

Player—Club	Pct.	G.	PO.	A.	E.	DP.
Beniquez, Balt.	.882	25	13	47	8	1
Berra, N.Y.	.950	18	11	27	2	3
Boggs, Bos.	.953	149	121	267	19	30
Bonilla, Balt.	.918	33	21	35	5	10
Brett, K.C.	.952	115	97	218	16	17
Brookens, Det.	.955	35	26	59	4	4
Buechele, Tex.	.968	137	111	226	11	17
Cochrane, Chi.	.872	18	10	31	6	1
Coles, Det.	.938	133	107	242	23	23
DeCinces, Cal.	.965	132	119	216	12	19
Fletcher, Tex.	1.000	12	5	10	0	2
Gaetti, Minn.	.956	156	118	334	21	36
Gruber, Tor.	.940	42	19	59	5	3
Hill, Oak.	.938	33	12	63	5	4
Howell, Cal.	.977	39	28	56	2	4
Hulett, Chi.	.951	89	70	144	11	10
Iorg, Tor.	.955	90	30	98	6	6
Jacoby, Clev.	.941	158	109	292	25	24
Lansford, Oak.	.982	100	67	147	4	13
McGwire, Oak.	.833	16	10	20	6	1
Molitor, Milw.	.944	91	82	170	15	25
Mulliniks, Tor.	.975	110	60	176	6	13
O'Malley, Balt.	.938	55	37	98	9	8

THIRD BASEMAN—Continued

Player—Club	Pct.	G.	PO.	A.	E.	DP.
Paciorek, Tex.	.927	21	11	27	3	2
Pagliarulo, N.Y.	.953	143	103	283	19	25
Parrish, Tex.	.935	30	23	35	4	2
Pecota, K.C.	.974	12	7	30	1	1
Petralli, Tex.	.846	15	4	7	2	0
Phillips, Oak.	.964	30	20	33	2	3
Presley, Sea.	.965	155	110	308	15	31
Pryor, K.C.	.935	35	15	57	5	8
Quirk, K.C.	.976	24	13	28	1	7
Rayford, Balt.	.912	72	40	115	15	15
Romero, Bos.	.935	18	7	22	2	2
Snyder, Clev.	1.000	11	10	14	0	1
Sveum, Milw.	.865	65	45	122	26	8
Tolleson, Chi-NY	.954	72	42	123	8	11

(Fewer Than Ten Games)

Player—Club	Pct.	G.	PO.	A.	E.	DP.
Bell, Tor.	1.000	2	1	0	0	0
Burleson, Cal.	.857	4	4	2	1	0
Castillo, Milw.	1.000	2	1	0	0	0
Dodd, Balt.	.000	1	0	0	0	0
Evans, Det.	1.000	2	1	1	0	0
Fielder, Tor.	.500	2	0	1	1	0
Gallego, Oak.	1.000	2	0	1	0	0
Gantner, Milw.	1.000	3	5	6	0	0
Grich, Cal.	1.000	2	0	2	0	0
Gross, Oak.	.000	1	0	0	1	0
Gutierrez, Balt.	.818	6	3	6	2	0
Hatcher, Minn.	1.000	3	1	1	0	0
Heath, Det.	.000	1	0	0	1	0
Hernandez, N.Y.	1.000	7	3	10	0	0
Hoffman, Bos.	1.000	1	1	1	0	0
Hudler, Balt.	1.000	1	0	1	0	0
Jones, Balt.	1.000	6	2	12	0	4
Jones, Sea.	1.000	2	3	3	0	1
Lee, Tor.	1.000	2	1	1	0	0
Little, Chi.	1.000	1	1	0	0	0
Lyons, Chi.	1.000	3	1	6	0	0
Madison, Det.	.667	1	1	1	1	1
Mattingly, N.Y.*	.923	3	1	11	1	2
Paris, Balt.	.857	3	0	6	1	1
Polidor, Cal.	1.000	1	1	1	0	0
Ramos, Sea.	.955	8	5	16	1	2
Ready, Milw.	.900	3	2	7	1	0
Roenicke, N.Y.	1.000	3	1	2	0	0
Rohn, Clev.	1.000	2	0	1	0	0
Seitzer, K.C.	1.000	3	0	1	0	0
Sheets, Balt.	1.000	2	2	1	0	0
Smalley, Minn.	1.000	8	3	19	0	1
Spilman, Det.	1.000	2	1	1	0	0
Stanley, Tex.	.857	7	0	6	1	1
Stapleton, Bos.	1.000	2	0	2	0	0
Tartabull, Sea.	1.000	1	0	3	0	0
Washington, Minn.	1.000	3	1	6	0	2
White, K.C.	.000	1	0	0	0	0
Winfield, N.Y.	.000	2	0	0	0	0

Triple Play—Ramos.

THIRD BASEMAN WITH TWO OR MORE CLUBS

Player—Club	Pct.	G.	PO.	A.	E.	DP.
Tolleson, Chi.	.955	65	37	113	7	9
Tolleson, N.Y.	.938	7	5	10	1	2

SHORTSTOPS

Leader—Club	Pct.	G.	PO.	A.	E.	DP.
FERNANDEZ, Tor.	.983	163	294	445	13	103

Player—Club	Pct.	G.	PO.	A.	E.	DP.
Baker, Det.	.970	10	13	19	1	5
Berra, N.Y.	.972	19	29	40	2	8
Biancalana, K.C.	.946	89	102	177	16	40
Brookens, Det.	.974	14	13	24	1	4
Burleson, Cal.	.984	37	43	77	2	12
Espinoza, Minn.	.964	18	11	16	1	4
Fernandez, Tor.	.983	163	294	445	13	103
Fischlin, N.Y.	.955	42	33	73	5	13
Fletcher, Tex.	.973	136	196	354	15	86
Franco, Clev.	.971	134	231	374	18	81
Gagne, Minn.	.959	155	228	377	26	96
Griffin, Oak.	.966	162	282	421	25	85
Guillen, Chi.	.970	157	261	459	22	93
Hoffman, Bos.	.923	11	14	10	2	3
Meacham, N.Y.	.948	56	70	149	12	31
Mullins, Clev.	.926	11	7	18	2	2
Owen, Sea-Bos	.973	154	279	467	21	133
Pryor, K.C.	.941	17	5	11	1	1
Quinones, Bos-Sea	.942	98	143	247	24	54
Ramos, Sea.	.966	21	31	53	3	8
Riles, Milw.	.964	142	212	327	20	76
Ripken, Balt.	.982	162	240	482	13	105
Romero, Bos.	.959	75	102	132	10	29
Salazar, K.C.	.978	115	121	283	9	50
Schofield, Cal.	.972	137	246	389	18	103
Smalley, Minn.	.963	19	11	15	1	4
Snyder, Clev.	.937	34	53	66	8	20
Sveum, Milw.	.945	13	18	34	3	5
Tolleson, Chi-NY	.981	74	100	202	6	38
Trammell, Det.	.969	149	238	445	22	99
Wilkerson, Tex.	.954	56	59	85	7	26
Zuvella, N.Y.	.966	21	30	54	3	12

(Fewer Than Ten Games)

Player—Club	Pct.	G.	PO.	A.	E.	DP.
Brett, K.C.	.000	2	0	0	0	0
Castillo, Milw.	.846	4	8	14	4	3
Cochrane, Chi.	.000	1	0	0	0	0
Coles, Det.	1.000	2	1	0	0	0
DeCinces, Cal.	.000	1	0	0	0	0
DeJesus, N.Y.	.900	7	5	4	1	0
Diaz, Milw.	.875	5	6	8	2	2
Gaetti, Minn.	1.000	2	0	1	0	0
Gallego, Oak.	1.000	1	1	0	0	0
Gantner, Milw.	.000	1	0	0	0	0
Giles, Chi.	.000	1	0	0	0	0
Gruber, Tor.	1.000	5	3	2	0	0
Hill, Oak.	.000	2	0	0	0	0
Iorg, Tor.	1.000	2	1	0	0	0
Jones, Sea.	1.000	4	5	6	0	1
Kiefer, Milw.	1.000	2	7	8	0	2
Kunkel, Tex.	.769	5	4	6	3	0
Lee, Tor.	.857	5	3	3	1	1
Little, Chi.	1.000	7	4	8	0	3
Paciorek, Tex.	1.000	1	0	1	0	0
Pagliarulo, N.Y.	1.000	2	1	0	0	0
Pecota, K.C.	1.000	2	0	1	0	0
Phillips, Oak.	1.000	1	0	3	0	0
Pittaro, Minn.	1.000	4	1	2	0	0
Polidor, Cal.	1.000	1	1	4	0	0
Rohn, Clev.	.800	1	1	3	1	0
Washington, Minn.	1.000	7	1	2	0	1
White, K.C.	1.000	1	1	2	0	1

Triple Play—Ramos.

SHORTSTOPS WITH TWO OR MORE CLUBS

Player—Club	Pct.	G.	PO.	A.	E.	DP.
Owen, Sea.	.972	112	209	372	17	99
Owen, Bos.	.976	42	70	95	4	34
Quinones, Bos.	.940	62	86	150	15	26
Quinones, Sea.	.945	36	57	97	9	28
Tolleson, Chi.	.974	18	13	25	1	3
Tolleson, N.Y.	.981	56	87	177	5	35

OUTFIELDERS

Leader—Club	Pct.	G.	PO.	A.	E.	DP.
YOUNT, Milw.	.997	131	352	9	1	4

Player—Club	Pct.	G.	PO.	A.	E.	DP.
Armas, Bos.	.969	117	247	4	8	0
Baines, Chi.*	.984	141	295	15	5	5
Baker, Oak.	1.000	55	80	4	0	1
Barfield, Tor.	.992	157	368	20	3	8
Beane, Minn.	1.000	67	118	0	0	0
Bell, Tor.	.966	147	269	17	10	1
Beniquez, Balt.	.963	54	102	1	4	0
Bonilla, Chi.	.989	43	91	2	1	1
Boston, Chi.*	.969	53	152	3	5	1
P. Bradley, Sea.	.996	140	250	11	1	0
Braggs, Milw.	.910	56	116	5	12	0
Brantley, Sea.	.983	25	54	3	1	1
Brower, Tex.	1.000	17	9	0	0	0
Brunansky, Minn.	.982	152	315	10	6	1
Bush, Minn.*	.977	102	167	2	4	0
Butler, Clev.*	.993	159	434	9	3	3
Calderon, Sea-Chi	.932	37	64	4	5	1
Cangelosi, Chi.*	.969	129	276	7	9	1
Canseco, Oak.	.958	155	319	4	14	1
Carter, Clev.	.976	104	241	8	6	2
Castillo, Clev.	.939	37	58	4	4	1
Clark, Clev.	1.000	10	26	0	0	0
Collins, Det.*	.995	94	211	2	1	1
Cotto, N.Y.	1.000	29	59	1	0	0
Cowens, Sea.	.971	19	31	2	1	0
Davidson, Minn.	.980	31	48	0	1	0
Davis, Oak.*	.973	139	310	9	9	2
Deer, Milw.	.974	131	286	8	8	1
Downing, Cal.	.989	138	267	5	3	0
Dwyer, Balt.*	1.000	24	33	3	0	1
Easler, N.Y.	.958	11	23	0	1	0
Evans, Bos.	.983	149	280	10	5	3
Felder, Milw.	1.000	42	98	0	0	0
Fields, Det.	.962	14	25	0	1	0
Fisk, Chi.	.947	31	66	5	4	0
Foster, Chi.	1.000	11	19	2	0	0
Gerhart, Balt.	.971	20	34	0	1	0
Gibson, Det.*	.990	114	190	2	2	1
Greenwell, Bos.	1.000	15	18	1	0	1
Griffey, N.Y.*	.971	51	96	5	3	2
Grubb, Det.	1.000	19	26	1	0	0
Hairston, Chi.	1.000	11	11	1	0	0
Hall, Clev.*	.972	126	233	7	7	1
Harper, Det.	.929	11	13	0	1	0
Hatcher, Minn.	.971	46	60	6	2	4
Henderson, N.Y.	.986	146	426	4	6	0
Henderson, Sea-Bos	.980	112	231	11	5	1
Hendrick, Cal.	.968	93	144	6	5	2
Herndon, Det.	.988	83	156	2	2	0
Householder, Milw.	1.000	22	35	1	0	1
Incaviglia, Tex.	.921	114	157	6	14	1
Jackson, K.C.	.886	23	29	2	4	0
Javier, Oak.	1.000	51	118	1	0	1
Jones, Cal.*	.981	121	205	5	4	0
Jones, K.C.	.971	62	34	0	1	0
Kingery, K.C.*	.973	59	102	6	3	2
Kittle, Chi-NY	1.000	21	39	3	0	0
Lacy, Balt.	.992	120	239	8	2	4
Law, K.C.*	.987	77	145	2	2	0
Leach, Tor.*	.978	39	44	0	1	0
Lemon, Det.	.985	124	316	6	5	1
Lynn, Balt.*	.984	107	244	2	4	1
Lyons, Bos-Chi	.978	90	173	5	4	1
Manning, Milw.	.988	83	155	3	2	0
McDowell, Tex.*	.991	148	325	13	3	3
Miller, Cal.	1.000	23	11	0	0	0
Moseby, Tor.	.984	147	371	6	6	1
Moses, Sea.*	.987	93	211	9	3	1
Motley, K.C.	.979	66	92	2	2	1
Murphy, Oak.	.993	97	276	6	2	3
Nichols, Chi.	.989	53	90	3	1	0
Nixon, Clev.	.969	95	90	3	3	0
Oglivie, Milw.*	.991	50	105	4	1	1
Paciorek, Tex.	.967	25	26	3	1	1
Pasqua, N.Y.*	.987	81	148	4	2	1
Peters, Oak.	1.000	27	28	0	0	0
Pettis, Cal.	.985	153	462	9	7	3
Puckett, Minn.	.986	160	429	8	6	3
Ready, Milw.	.950	11	19	0	1	0
Rice, Bos.	.977	156	330	16	8	0
Roenicke, N.Y.	1.000	37	39	3	0	0
Romine, Bos.	1.000	33	45	1	0	1
Sheets, Balt.	.984	32	60	1	1	1
Shelby, Balt.	.978	121	222	5	5	2
Shepherd, Tor.	1.000	32	30	0	0	0
Sheridan, Det.	.977	90	172	1	4	0
Sierra, Tex.	.972	107	200	7	6	1
Smith, K.C.	.965	118	245	5	9	1
Snyder, Clev.	.987	74	150	4	2	1
Tartabull, Sea.	.953	101	157	7	8	0
Tillman, Oak.	.952	17	20	0	1	0
Ward, Tex.	.996	104	237	8	1	3
Washington, N.Y.	.985	39	66	0	1	0
White, Cal.	.961	28	49	0	2	0
Williams, Chi.	1.000	10	18	1	0	1
Wilson, K.C.	.993	155	408	4	3	2
Winfield, N.Y.	.984	145	292	9	5	5
G. Wright, Tex.	.969	42	61	2	2	0
Young, Balt.	.962	69	149	1	6	0
Yount, Milw.	.997	131	352	9	1	4

(Fewer Than Ten Games)

Player—Club	Pct.	G.	PO.	A.	E.	DP.
Baylor, Bos.	1.000	3	6	0	0	0
Bergman, Det.	.000	2	0	0	0	0
Bonnell, Sea.	.941	9	16	0	1	0
Bradley, Chi.	.000	1	0	0	0	0
Brewer, K.C.	1.000	9	9	0	0	0
Brookens, Det.	.000	3	0	0	0	0
Buechele, Tex.	1.000	2	4	0	0	0
Castillo, Milw.	.000	1	0	0	0	0
Coles, Det.	1.000	2	3	0	0	0
Craig, Chi.	.000	2	0	0	0	0
Engle, Det.	1.000	4	1	0	0	0
Fielder, Tor.	.000	1	0	0	0	0
Gaetti, Minn.	1.000	1	2	0	0	0
Gruber, Tor.	.857	9	6	0	1	0
Henderson, Oak.	.800	7	8	0	2	0
Hengel, Sea.	1.000	8	9	1	0	0
Howell, Cal.	1.000	8	10	1	0	1
Jackson, Cal.	.833	4	4	1	1	0
Jones, Tex.	.909	9	10	0	1	0
Lombardi, N.Y.	.867	8	12	1	2	0
Lowry, Det.	1.000	1	2	0	0	0
Molitor, Milw.	1.000	4	4	1	0	0
Moore, Milw.	1.000	4	4	1	0	1
Nelson, Sea.	.667	1	2	0	1	0
Phillips, Oak.	1.000	4	11	0	0	0
Quirk, K.C.	.000	1	0	0	0	0
Romero, Bos.	1.000	1	2	0	0	0
Ryal, Cal.	.900	6	9	0	1	0
Sanchez, Minn.	.000	1	0	0	0	0
Seitzer, K.C.	1.000	5	14	1	0	0
Stanley, Tex.	.000	1	0	0	0	0
Stenhouse, Bos.	1.000	4	5	0	0	0
Tarver, Bos.	1.000	9	16	0	0	0
Taylor, K.C.	.000	1	0	0	0	0
Tolleson, Chi.	1.000	2	2	0	0	0
Tolman, Det.	1.000	4	8	0	0	0
Traber, Balt.	.913	8	19	2	2	0
Williams, Clev.	.000	4	0	0	0	0

Triple Play—Hairston.

OUTFIELDERS WITH TWO OR MORE CLUBS

Player—Club	Pct.	G.	PO.	A.	E.	DP.
Calderon, Sea.	.937	32	55	4	4	1
Calderon, Chi.	.900	5	9	0	1	0
Henderson, Sea.	.979	80	182	9	4	1
Henderson, Bos.	.981	32	49	2	1	0
Kittle, Chi.	1.000	20	37	3	0	0
Kittle, N.Y.	1.000	1	2	0	0	0
Lyons, Bos.	.972	55	100	3	3	1
Lyons, Chi.	.987	35	73	2	1	0

CATCHERS

Leader—Club	Pct.	G.	PO.	A.	E.	DP.	PB.
SUNDBERG, K.C.	.995	134	686	46	4	11	13

Player—Club	Pct.	G.	PO.	A.	E.	DP.	PB.
Allanson, Clev.	.960	99	446	33	20	4	12
Bando, Clev.	.990	86	359	30	4	3	8
Bathe, Oak.	.991	39	211	11	2	1	2
Boone, Cal.	.988	144	812	84	11	16	8
S. Bradley, Sea.	.990	59	281	21	3	5	5
Cerone, Milw.	.991	68	391	44	4	2	7
Dempsey, Balt.	.990	121	659	53	7	9	2
Espino, N.Y.	.987	27	72	6	1	0	2
Fisk, Chi.	.991	71	389	39	4	3	8
Gedman, Bos.	.994	134	866	65	6	10	14
Hassey, NY-Chi	.988	62	318	14	4	4	6
Hearron, Tor.	.980	12	47	3	1	0	1
Heath, Det.	.987	29	145	9	2	1	1
Hill, Chi.	1.000	22	59	7	0	0	0
Karkovice, Chi.	.996	37	227	19	1	4	5
Kearney, Sea.	.989	79	419	46	5	3	4
Laudner, Minn.	.984	68	299	13	5	3	4
Lowry, Det.	.992	55	246	16	2	2	3
Martinez, Tor.	.994	78	289	19	2	6	3
Mercado, Tex.	.996	45	240	25	1	5	6
Miller, Cal.	1.000	10	19	3	0	0	1
Moore, Milw.	.992	72	425	43	4	6	6
Narron, Cal.	.988	51	155	14	2	3	3
Pardo, Balt.	.987	14	70	5	1	1	1
Parrish, Det.	.989	85	483	48	6	5	8
Petralli, Tex.	.988	41	159	7	2	2	2
Porter, Tex.	.994	25	165	9	1	2	3
Quirk, K.C.	.989	41	247	30	3	2	3
Rayford, Balt.	.971	10	32	2	1	0	0
Reed, Minn.	.994	64	332	19	2	5	3
Salas, Minn.	.980	69	358	32	8	5	5
Schroeder, Milw.	.995	35	190	14	1	3	2
Skinner, Chi-NY	.984	114	507	37	9	9	4
Slaught, Tex.	.993	91	533	40	4	1	13
Stefero, Balt.	.984	50	221	20	4	2	3
Sullivan, Bos.	.986	41	203	13	3	1	2
Sundberg, K.C.	.995	134	686	46	4	11	13
Tettleton, Oak.	.984	89	463	32	8	6	11
Valle, Sea.	.982	12	53	1	1	0	1
Whitt, Tor.	.991	129	709	41	7	7	5
Willard, Oak.	.994	71	300	12	2	1	3
Wynegar, N.Y.	.994	57	325	22	2	1	6
Yeager, Sea.	1.000	49	234	22	0	5	7

Triple Plays—Fisk, Kearney.

(Fewer Than Ten Games)

Player—Club	Pct.	G.	PO.	A.	E.	DP.	PB.
Bell, K.C.	1.000	8	7	0	0	0	0
Engle, Det.	1.000	3	11	1	0	0	0
Harper, Det.	1.000	2	5	0	0	0	0
Lombardi, N.Y.	.923	3	10	2	1	0	0
Nichols, Balt.	1.000	5	11	0	0	0	1
Nokes, Det.	1.000	7	43	2	0	2	0
Sax, Bos.	1.000	2	10	1	0	0	0
Sheets, Balt.	.917	6	10	1	1	0	0
Spilman, Det.	1.000	1	2	0	0	0	0
Stanley, Tex.	1.000	4	14	2	0	1	1
Steinbach, Oak.	.962	5	21	4	1	1	0

CATCHERS WITH TWO OR MORE CLUBS

Player—Club	Pct.	G.	PO.	A.	E.	DP.	PB.
Hassey, N.Y.	.985	51	251	9	4	4	6
Hassey, Chi.	1.000	11	67	5	0	0	0
Skinner, Chi.	.988	60	227	15	3	4	1
Skinner, N.Y.	.981	54	280	22	6	5	3

PITCHERS

Leader—Club	Pct.	G.	PO.	A.	E.	DP.
KEY, Tor.*	1.000	36	18	42	0	4

Player—Club	Pct.	G.	PO.	A.	E.	DP.
Aase, Balt.	.944	66	5	12	1	1
Acker, Tor.	1.000	23	9	11	0	2
Agosto, Chi-Minn*	.778	26	3	4	2	0
Alexander, Tor.	.895	17	6	11	2	0
Allen, Chi.	1.000	22	15	10	0	0
Anderson, Minn.*	.947	21	4	14	1	1
Andujar, Oak.	.925	28	16	21	3	4
Arnold, Balt.	1.000	11	4	9	0	0
Atherton, Oak-Minn	.944	60	6	11	1	1
Bailes, Clev.*	.944	62	4	13	1	0
Bair, Oak.	1.000	31	2	7	0	1
Bankhead, K.C.	.958	24	11	12	1	0
Bannister, Chi.*	.962	28	3	22	1	1
Best, Sea.	1.000	26	1	3	0	0
Black, K.C.*	1.000	56	3	21	0	1
Blyleven, Minn.	1.000	36	15	31	0	0
Boddicker, Balt.	.955	33	28	36	3	4
Bordi, Balt.	.957	52	7	15	1	2
Bosio, Milw.	.900	10	4	5	1	1
Boyd, Bos.	.962	30	24	27	2	4
Brown, Bos-Sea	1.000	21	7	12	0	0
Bryden, Cal.	1.000	16	2	4	0	1
Butcher, Minn-Clev	.889	29	9	15	3	2
Camacho, Clev.	.941	51	5	11	1	0
Campbell, Det.	.833	34	6	4	2	1
Candelaria, Cal.*	1.000	16	3	10	0	0
Candiotti, Clev.	.958	36	27	41	3	7
Carlton, Chi.*	1.000	10	1	7	0	1
Cary, Det.*	1.000	22	4	1	0	0
Caudill, Tor.	1.000	40	1	2	0	0
Cerutti, Tor.*	1.000	34	8	21	0	2
Clancy, Tor.	.983	34	34	23	1	2
Clarke, Tor.*	1.000	10	0	3	0	0
Clear, Milw.	.909	59	4	6	1	0
Clemens, Bos.	.923	33	27	21	4	0
Clutterbuck, Milw.	1.000	20	7	5	0	0
Cocanower, Milw.	.857	17	7	11	3	3
Codiroli, Oak.	.848	16	13	15	5	2
Cone, K.C.	1.000	11	4	0	0	0
Corbett, Cal.	1.000	46	8	15	0	3
Correa, Tex.	.947	32	20	34	3	0
Cowley, Chi.	.889	27	16	16	4	0
Crawford, Bos.	.917	40	4	7	1	2
Darwin, Milw.	.903	27	6	22	3	2
Davis, Balt.	.977	25	22	21	1	3
Davis, Chi.	.926	19	7	18	2	1
Davis, Minn.	1.000	36	5	5	0	1
Dawley, Chi.	.941	46	8	8	1	0
DeLeon, Chi.	1.000	13	5	11	0	1
Dixon, Balt.	.943	35	12	21	2	1
Dotson, Chi.	.923	34	13	23	3	0
Drabek, N.Y.	1.000	27	5	13	0	0
Easterly, Clev.*	1.000	13	2	1	0	0
Eichhorn, Tor.	1.000	69	16	21	0	1
Farr, K.C.	1.000	56	8	16	0	1
Finley, Cal.*	1.000	25	8	8	0	1
Fireovid, Sea.	.833	10	3	2	1	0
Fisher, N.Y.	.909	62	3	7	1	1
Flanagan, Balt.*	1.000	29	4	17	0	1
Fontenot, Minn.*	1.000	15	2	3	0	0
Forsch, Cal.	.750	10	0	3	1	1
Forster, Cal.*	1.000	41	2	11	0	2
Frazier, Minn.	1.000	15	3	4	0	0
Gibson, Milw.	1.000	11	4	1	0	0
Gordon, Tor.	.600	14	1	2	2	0
Gubicza, K.C.	1.000	35	17	32	0	3
Guetterman, Sea.*	.895	41	5	12	2	1
Guidry, N.Y.*	.968	30	9	21	1	0
Guzman, Tex.	1.000	29	13	24	0	0
Haas, Oak.	1.000	12	4	8	0	2
Harris, Tex.	.926	73	7	18	2	2
Havens, Balt.*	.944	46	4	13	1	0
Heaton, Clev-Minn*	.974	33	13	24	1	1
Henke, Tor.	1.000	63	2	2	0	1
Henry, Tex.	1.000	19	0	4	0	0
Hernandez, Det.*	1.000	64	6	13	0	0
Higuera, Milw.*	1.000	34	9	26	0	1

PITCHERS—Continued

Player—Club	Pct.	G.	PO.	A.	E.	DP.
Holland, N.Y.*	.500	25	0	2	2	0
Hough, Tex.	.981	33	20	32	1	2
Howell, Oak.	1.000	38	2	6	0	0
Huismann, KC-Sea	.889	46	12	12	3	1
Hurst, Bos.*	.926	25	7	18	2	2
D. Jackson, K.C.*	.946	32	14	21	2	1
Jackson, Minn.	1.000	28	3	6	0	0
James, Chi.	1.000	49	3	6	0	0
John, N.Y.*	.864	13	4	15	3	2
Johnson, Milw.*	.833	19	2	3	1	0
J. Johnson, Tor.	1.000	16	6	7	0	1
Jones, Balt.	1.000	21	2	5	0	0
Jones, Clev.	1.000	11	1	4	0	1
Kern, Clev.	1.000	16	2	6	0	0
Key, Tor.*	1.000	36	18	42	0	4
King, Det.	.971	33	19	15	1	0
Krueger, Oak.*	.909	11	2	8	1	1
Ladd, Sea.	.875	52	2	5	1	0
Lamp, Tor.	.941	40	5	11	1	2
Langford, Oak.	1.000	16	5	1	0	0
Langston, Sea.*	.850	37	7	27	6	3
LaPoint, Det.*	1.000	16	2	8	0	1
Leary, Milw.	.980	33	22	26	1	1
Leibrandt, K.C.*	.983	35	14	43	1	3
Leiper, Oak.*	1.000	33	0	6	0	0
Leonard, K.C.	.909	33	11	29	4	4
Lollar, Bos.*	1.000	32	4	7	0	1
Lucas, Cal.*	1.000	27	6	9	0	0
Mahler, Tex-Tor*	1.000	31	3	9	0	2
T. Martinez, Balt.*	.750	14	0	3	1	0
Mason, Tex.*	1.000	27	9	19	0	1
McCaskill, Cal.	.980	34	24	26	1	0
McClure, Milw.*	1.000	13	1	1	0	0
McGregor, Balt.*	.975	34	12	27	1	2
McKeon, Chi.*	1.000	30	2	2	0	0
Mohorcic, Tex.	1.000	58	5	12	0	3
Mooneyham, Oak.	.917	45	5	17	2	1
Moore, Cal.	.900	49	2	7	1	0
Moore, Sea.	.933	38	23	33	4	1
Morgan, Sea.	.953	37	14	27	2	5
Morris, Det.	.964	35	27	27	2	4
Nelson, Chi.	1.000	54	8	17	0	3
Niekro, N.Y.	.957	25	9	13	1	2
Niekro, Clev.	.911	34	9	32	4	2
Nielsen, N.Y.	1.000	10	0	5	0	2
Nieves, Milw.*	.917	35	4	18	2	2
Nipper, Bos.	.982	26	28	28	1	4
Noles, Clev.	1.000	32	5	8	0	0
Nunez, Sea.	1.000	14	1	1	0	0
Oelkers, Clev.*	1.000	35	5	4	0	0
O'Neal, Det.	.944	37	15	19	2	0
Ontiveros, Oak.	1.000	46	2	10	0	1
Pastore, Minn.	1.000	33	1	5	0	0
Petry, Det.	1.000	20	16	18	0	1
Plesac, Milw.*	1.000	51	1	11	0	0
Plunk, Oak.	.900	26	3	6	1	0
Portugal, Minn.	.950	27	5	14	1	3
Pulido, N.Y.*	1.000	10	1	4	0	1
Quisenberry, K.C.	.966	62	9	19	1	3
Rasmussen, N.Y.*	1.000	31	6	26	0	0
Reed, Sea.	1.000	11	4	3	0	0
Righetti, N.Y.*	1.000	74	1	10	0	2
Rijo, Oak.	.912	39	13	18	3	0
Romanick, Cal.	1.000	18	13	8	0	1
Ruhle, Cal.	.938	16	7	8	1	0
Russell, Tex.	1.000	37	6	17	0	3
Saberhagen, K.C.	.952	30	14	26	2	0
Sambito, Bos.*	1.000	53	1	8	0	1
Scherrer, Det.*	1.000	13	1	3	0	0
Schiraldi, Bos.	1.000	25	2	3	0	0
Schmidt, Chi.	.824	49	7	7	3	0
Schrom, Clev.	.886	34	16	15	4	1
Schulze, Clev.	1.000	19	7	7	0	0
Scurry, N.Y.*	1.000	31	4	5	0	1
Searage, Mil-Chi*	1.000	46	3	8	0	0
Seaver, Chi-Bos.	.943	28	17	16	2	1
Sellers, Bos.	1.000	14	9	9	0	1
Shirley, N.Y.*	.960	39	4	20	1	1
Slaton, Cal-Det	1.000	36	13	18	0	2
Smithson, Minn	.955	34	10	32	2	4
Snell, Balt.	1.000	34	5	14	0	1
Stanley, Bos.	.909	66	6	14	2	0
Stewart, Bos.	1.000	27	6	5	0	0
Stewart, Oak.	.966	29	10	18	1	2
Stieb, Tor.	.980	37	15	33	1	4
Stoddard, N.Y.	.900	24	2	7	1	1
Sutton, Cal.	.941	34	18	14	2	1
Swift, Sea.	.971	29	13	21	1	1
Tanana, Det.*	.957	32	19	26	2	5
Terrell, Det.	1.000	34	30	29	0	6
Tewksbury, N.Y.	.973	23	7	29	1	2
Thigpen, Chi.	1.000	20	2	4	0	1
Thurmond, Det.*	1.000	25	6	3	0	0
Trujillo, Bos-Sea	1.000	14	5	8	0	0
Viola, Minn.*	.906	37	8	21	3	1
Von Ohlen, Oak.*	1.000	24	0	5	0	0
Wegman, Milw.	.975	35	20	19	1	4
Whitson, N.Y.	1.000	14	1	5	0	0
Wilcox, Sea.	1.000	13	4	9	0	1
Williams, Tex.*	.846	80	1	10	2	1
Wills, Clev.	.900	26	3	6	1	0
Witt, Cal.	.984	34	22	39	1	5
Witt, Tex.	.903	31	8	20	3	1
R. Wright, Tex.*	1.000	21	3	7	0	1
Yett, Clev.	1.000	39	2	7	0	0
Young, Oak.*	.911	29	9	32	4	1
Young, Sea.*	.765	65	4	9	4	0

Triple Play—Morgan.

(Fewer Than Ten Games)

Player—Club	Pct.	G.	PO.	A.	E.	DP.
Akerfelds, Oak.	1.000	2	1	1	0	0
Aquino, Tor.	1.000	7	1	1	0	0
Armstrong, N.Y.	.667	7	1	1	1	0
Arnsberg, N.Y.	.000	2	0	0	0	0
Arroyo, Oak.	.000	1	0	0	0	0
Beattie, Sea.	1.000	9	4	6	0	2
Bell, Balt.*	1.000	4	1	0	0	0
Birkbeck, Milw.	1.000	7	1	2	0	0
Birtsas, Oak.*	.000	2	0	0	0	0
Brown, Tex.	1.000	1	0	1	0	0
Burtt, Minn.	.000	3	0	0	0	0
Chadwick, Cal.	1.000	7	3	4	0	0
Clark, Chi.*	1.000	5	2	0	0	0
Cook, Cal.	1.000	5	0	2	0	0
Davis, Tor.*	.000	3	0	0	0	0
Dozier, Oak.	1.000	4	1	0	0	0
Filson, Minn-Chi*	1.000	7	1	0	0	0
Fischer, Cal.	1.000	9	0	2	0	1
Fraser, Cal.	.000	1	0	0	0	0
Gardner, Bos.	.000	1	0	0	0	0
Habyan, Balt.	1.000	6	1	3	0	0
Hargesheimer, K.C.	1.000	5	0	1	0	0
Kelly, Det.	.857	6	2	4	1	0
Kinnunen, Balt.*	1.000	9	1	2	0	0
Knudson, Milw.	1.000	4	3	1	0	0
Latham, Minn.*	.500	7	0	1	1	0
Lazorko, Det.	1.000	3	1	1	0	0
Loynd, Tex.	.909	9	5	5	1	0
Lugo, Cal.	1.000	6	2	2	0	0
D. Martinez, Balt.	1.000	4	1	2	0	0
Meridith, Tex.*	1.000	5	0	2	0	0
Mirabella, Sea.*	1.000	8	0	1	0	0
Montefusco, N.Y.	1.000	4	2	3	0	1
Musselman, Tor.*	1.000	6	1	1	0	0
Pacella, Det.	1.000	5	3	4	0	0
Ritter, Clev.	1.000	5	3	2	0	0
Rodriguez, Oak.	1.000	3	1	4	0	0
Roman, Clev.	.667	6	2	0	1	1
Rozema, Tex.	1.000	6	0	3	0	0
Shields, K.C.	1.000	3	1	1	0	0
Smith, Minn.	1.000	5	0	1	0	0
Swaggerty, Balt.	.000	1	0	0	0	0
Swindell, Clev.*	1.000	9	2	12	0	1
Vuckovich, Milw.	1.000	6	2	7	0	0
Ward, Tor.	1.000	2	1	0	0	0
Woodward, Bos.	1.000	9	5	6	0	0

PITCHERS—Continued

PITCHERS WITH TWO OR MORE CLUBS

Player—Club	Pct.	G.	PO.	A.	E.	DP.
Agosto, Chi	.500	9	1	0	1	0
Agosto, Minn.	.857	17	2	4	1	0
Atherton, Oak.	1.000	13	1	1	0	0
Atherton, Minn.	.938	47	5	10	1	1
Brown, Bos.	1.000	15	7	8	0	0
Brown, Sea.	1.000	6	0	4	0	0
Butcher, Minn.	1.000	16	4	10	0	1
Butcher, Clev.	.769	13	5	5	3	1
Filson, Minn.	.000	4	0	0	0	0
Filson, Chi.	1.000	3	1	0	0	0
Heaton, Clev.	1.000	12	2	11	0	0
Heaton, Minn.	.960	21	11	13	1	1
Huismann, K.C.	.857	10	2	4	1	0
Huismann, Sea.	.900	36	10	8	2	1
Mahler, Tex.	1.000	29	2	8	0	2
Mahler, Tor.	1.000	2	1	1	0	0
Searage, Milw.	1.000	17	2	4	0	0
Searage, Chi.	1.000	29	1	4	0	0
Seaver, Chi.	1.000	12	4	7	0	0
Seaver, Bos.	.917	16	13	9	2	1
Slaton, Cal.	1.000	14	7	12	0	1
Slaton, Det.	1.000	22	6	6	0	1
Trujillo, Bos.	1.000	3	1	3	0	0
Trujillo, Sea.	1.000	11	4	5	0	0

OFFICIAL AMERICAN LEAGUE PITCHING AVERAGES

CLUB PITCHING

Club	ERA.	G.	CG.	ShO.	Sv.	IP.	H.	BFP.	R.	ER.	HR.	SH.	SF.	HB.	Tot. BB.	Int. BB.	SO.	WP.	Bk.
Kansas City	3.82	162	24	13	31	1440.2	1413	6093	673	612	121	51	48	38	479	46	888	43	6
California	3.84	162	29	12	40	1456.0	1356	6066	684	621	153	41	44	27	478	19	955	44	6
Chicago	3.93	162	18	8	38	1442.1	1361	6115	699	630	143	54	43	33	561	28	895	55	3
Boston	3.93	161	36	6	41	1429.2	1469	6102	696	625	167	38	48	26	474	35	1033	55	8
Milwaukee	4.01	161	29	12	32	1431.2	1478	6150	734	638	158	42	49	29	494	22	952	57	9
Detroit	4.02	162	33	12	38	1443.2	1374	6158	714	645	183	47	35	30	571	61	880	50	8
Toronto	4.08	163	16	12	44	1476.0	1467	6264	733	669	164	59	51	45	487	39	1002	38	6
Texas	4.11	162	15	8	41	1450.1	1356	6311	743	662	145	37	42	41	736	37	1059	94	13
New York	4.11	162	13	8	58	1443.1	1461	6173	738	659	175	48	44	24	492	25	878	40	3
Baltimore	4.30	162	17	6	39	1436.2	1451	6164	760	687	177	46	43	21	535	41	954	52	4
Oakland	4.31	162	22	8	37	1433.0	1334	6208	760	686	166	44	55	34	667	35	937	62	19
Cleveland	4.58	163	31	7	34	1447.2	1548	6439	841	736	167	55	60	57	605	34	744	63	13
Seattle	4.65	162	33	5	27	1439.2	1590	6345	835	744	171	41	44	49	585	27	944	46	10
Minnesota	4.77	162	39	6	24	1432.2	1579	6264	839	759	200	43	50	46	503	37	937	58	5
Totals	4.18	1134	355	123	524	20203.1	20237	86852	10449	9373	2290	646	656	500	7667	486	13058	757	113

NOTE—Totals for earned runs for several clubs do not agree with the composite totals for all pitchers of each respective club due to instances in which provisions of Section 10.18 (i) of the Scoring Rules were applied. The following differences are to be noted: Baltimore pitchers add to 688 earned runs, California pitchers add to 622, Chicago pitchers add to 632, Cleveland pitchers add to 744, Milwaukee pitchers add to 642, Minnesota pitchers add to 762, Oakland pitchers add to 687, Seattle pitchers add to 747, Texas pitchers add to 663.

PITCHERS' RECORDS

(Top Fifteen Qualifiers for Earned-Run Leadership—162 or More Innings)

*Throws lefthanded.

Pitcher and Club	W.	L.	Pct.	ERA.	G.	GS.	CG.	ShO.	GF.	Sv.	IP.	H.	BFP.	R.	ER.	HR.	SH.	SF.	HB.	Tot. BB.	Int. BB.	SO.	WP.	Bk.
Clemens, W. Roger, Boston	24	4	.857	2.48	33	33	10	1	0	0	254.0	179	997	77	70	21	4	6	4	67	0	238	11	3
Higuera, Teodoro, Milwaukee*	20	11	.645	2.79	34	34	15	4	0	0	248.1	226	1031	84	77	26	7	11	3	74	5	207	3	0
Witt, Michael, California	18	10	.643	2.84	34	34	14	3	0	0	269.0	218	1071	95	85	22	3	5	3	73	2	208	6	0
Hurst, Bruce, Boston*	13	8	.619	2.99	25	25	11	4	0	0	174.1	169	721	63	58	18	5	3	3	50	2	167	6	0
Jackson, Danny, Kansas City*	11	12	.478	3.20	32	27	4	1	3	1	185.2	177	789	83	66	13	10	4	4	79	1	115	7	0
Morris, John, Detroit	21	8	.724	3.27	35	35	15	6	0	0	267.0	229	1092	105	97	40	7	3	0	82	7	223	12	0
McCaskill, Kirk, California	17	10	.630	3.36	34	33	10	2	1	0	246.1	207	1013	98	92	19	6	5	5	92	1	202	10	2
Young, Curtis, Oakland*	13	9	.591	3.45	29	27	5	2	0	0	198.0	176	826	88	76	19	8	9	7	57	1	116	7	2
Bannister, Floyd, Chicago*	10	14	.417	3.54	28	27	6	1	0	0	165.1	162	688	81	65	17	7	5	2	48	0	92	5	0
Candiotti, Thomas, Cleveland	16	12	.571	3.57	36	34	17	3	1	0	252.1	234	1078	112	100	18	3	9	8	106	0	167	12	4
Key, James, Toronto*	14	11	.560	3.57	36	35	4	2	0	0	232.0	222	959	98	92	24	10	6	3	74	1	141	3	0
Gubicza, Mark, Kansas City	12	6	.667	3.64	35	24	3	2	2	0	180.2	155	765	77	73	8	4	8	5	84	2	118	15	0
Sutton, Donald, California	15	11	.577	3.74	34	34	3	1	0	0	207.0	192	853	93	86	31	3	3	3	49	2	116	4	1
Boyd, Dennis, Boston	16	10	.615	3.78	30	30	10	0	0	0	214.1	222	893	99	90	32	3	6	2	45	1	129	3	0
Hough, Charles, Texas	17	10	.630	3.79	33	33	7	2	0	0	230.1	188	958	115	97	32	9	1	9	89	2	146	16	0

DEPARTMENTAL LEADERS: W—Clemens, 24; L—Dotson, Morgan, 17; Pct.—Clemens, .857; G—Williams (Tex.), 80; GS—Viola, Moore (Sea.), 37; CG—Candiotti, 17; ShO—Morris, 6; GF—Righetti, 68; Sv.—Righetti, 34; IP—Blyleven, 271.2; H—Moore (Sea.), 279; BFP—Moore (Sea.), 1145; R—Langston, 142; ER—Langston, 129; HR—Blyleven, 50; SH—Leibrandt, 14; SF—Schrom, 12; HB—Stieb, 15; Tot. BB—Witt (Tex.), 143; Int. BB—Eichhorn, 14; SO—Langston, 245; WP—Witt (Tex.), 22; Bk.—Plunk, 6.

(All Pitchers—Listed Alphabetically)

Pitcher and Club	W.	L.	Pct.	ERA.	G.	GS.	CG.	ShO.	GF.	Sv.	IP.	H.	BFP.	R.	ER.	HR.	SH.	SF.	HB.	Tot. BB.	Int. BB.	SO.	WP.	Bk.
Aase, Donald, Baltimore	6	7	.462	2.98	66	0	0	0	58	34	81.2	71	837	29	27	6	3	2	0	28	2	67	4	0
Acker, James, Toronto	2	4	.333	4.35	23	5	0	0	6	0	60.0	63	259	34	29	6	6	5	2	22	3	32	3	1
Agosto, Juan, Chi.-Minn.*	1	4	.200	8.64	26	1	0	0	4	1	25.0	49	139	30	24	1	2	0	2	18	0	12	1	0
Akerfelds, Darrell, Oakland	0	0	.000	6.75	2	0	0	0	2	0	5.1	7	26	5	4	2	0	0	0	3	1	5	2	0
Alexander, Doyle, Toronto	5	4	.556	4.46	17	17	3	0	0	0	111.0	120	470	56	55	18	3	3	4	20	1	65	1	0
Allen, Neil, Chicago	7	2	.778	3.82	22	17	2	2	1	0	113.0	101	466	50	48	8	5	7	2	38	1	57	4	0
Anderson, Allan, Minnesota*	3	6	.333	5.55	21	10	1	0	3	0	84.1	106	371	54	52	11	2	3	1	30	3	51	2	2
Andujar, Joaquin, Oakland	12	7	.632	3.82	28	26	7	1	2	1	155.1	139	647	70	66	23	1	4	4	56	1	72	2	4
Aquino, Luis, Toronto	1	1	.500	6.35	7	0	0	0	3	0	11.1	14	50	8	8	2	0	1	0	3	1	5	1	0
Armstrong, Michael, New York	0	1	.000	9.35	7	1	0	0	4	0	8.2	13	42	9	9	4	0	0	0	5	1	8	0	0
Arnold, Tony, Baltimore	0	2	.000	3.55	11	0	0	0	3	0	25.1	25	104	15	10	0	3	0	0	11	3	7	0	0
Arnsberg, Bradley, New York	0	0	.000	3.38	2	1	0	0	1	0	8.0	13	39	3	3	1	0	0	0	1	0	3	0	0
Arroyo, Fernando, Oakland	0	0	.000	......	1	0	0	0	0	0	0.0	0	3	0	0	0	0	0	0	3	0	0	0	0
Atherton, Keith, Oak.-Minn.	6	10	.375	4.08	60	0	0	0	36	10	97.0	100	431	47	44	11	6	6	1	46	4	67	2	0
Bailes, Scott, Cleveland*	10	10	.500	4.95	62	10	0	0	22	7	112.2	123	500	70	62	12	7	4	1	43	5	60	4	2
Bair, C. Douglas, Oakland	2	3	.400	3.00	31	0	0	0	17	4	45.0	37	189	15	15	5	3	3	0	18	0	40	2	0
Bankhead, M. Scott, Kansas City	8	9	.471	4.61	24	17	0	0	2	0	121.0	121	517	66	62	14	5	5	3	37	7	94	1	0
Bannister, Floyd, Chicago*	10	14	.417	3.54	28	27	6	1	0	0	165.1	162	688	81	65	17	7	5	2	48	0	92	5	0
Beattie, James, Seattle	0	6	.000	6.02	9	7	0	0	0	0	40.1	57	188	28	27	7	2	2	3	14	2	24	1	0
Bell, Eric, Baltimore*	1	2	.333	5.01	4	4	0	0	0	0	23.1	23	105	14	13	4	1	1	0	14	0	18	0	0
Best, Karl, Seattle	2	3	.400	4.04	26	0	0	0	15	1	35.2	35	163	19	16	3	2	2	1	21	2	23	2	1
Birkbeck, Michael, Milwaukee	1	1	.500	4.50	7	4	0	0	2	0	22.0	24	97	12	11	0	0	0	0	12	0	13	1	0
Birtsas, Timothy, Oakland*	0	0	.000	22.50	2	0	0	0	2	0	2.0	2	12	5	5	1	1	0	0	4	1	1	0	0
Black, Harry, Kansas City*	5	10	.333	3.20	56	4	0	0	26	9	121.0	100	503	49	43	14	4	4	7	43	5	68	2	2
Blyleven, Rikalbert, Minnesota	17	14	.548	4.01	36	36	16	3	0	0	271.2	262	1126	134	121	50	5	4	10	58	4	215	4	0
Boddicker, Michael, Baltimore	14	12	.538	4.70	33	33	7	0	0	0	218.1	214	934	125	114	30	3	6	11	74	4	175	7	0
Bordi, Richard, Baltimore	6	4	.600	4.46	52	1	0	0	22	3	107.0	105	464	56	53	13	2	3	4	41	5	83	1	0
Bosio, Christopher, Milwaukee	0	4	.000	7.01	10	4	0	0	3	0	34.2	41	154	27	27	9	1	0	0	13	0	29	2	1
Boyd, Dennis, Boston	16	10	.615	3.78	30	30	10	0	0	0	214.1	222	893	99	90	32	3	6	2	45	1	129	3	0
Brown, J. Kevin, Texas	1	0	1.000	3.60	1	1	0	0	0	0	5.0	6	19	2	2	0	0	0	0	0	0	4	0	0
Brown, Michael, Bos.-Sea.	4	6	.400	5.79	21	12	0	0	2	0	73.0	91	334	49	47	14	3	3	1	36	1	41	4	1
Bryden, Thomas, California	2	1	.667	6.55	16	0	0	0	7	0	34.1	38	159	25	25	4	1	4	2	21	0	25	2	0
Burtt, Dennis, Minnesota	0	0	.000	31.50	3	0	0	0	1	0	2.0	7	16	7	7	1	0	0	0	3	1	1	0	0
Butcher, John, Minn.-Clev.	1	8	.111	6.56	29	18	2	1	5	0	120.2	168	554	93	88	17	2	6	4	37	1	45	6	0
Camacho, Ernie, Cleveland	2	4	.333	4.08	51	0	0	0	37	20	57.1	60	267	26	26	1	5	6	2	31	6	36	3	1
Campbell, William, Detroit	3	6	.333	3.88	34	0	0	0	19	3	55.2	46	229	26	24	5	4	3	1	21	5	37	1	0
Candelaria, John, California*	10	2	.833	2.55	16	16	1	1	0	0	91.2	68	365	30	26	4	3	3	3	26	2	81	2	1
Candiotti, Thomas, Cleveland	16	12	.571	3.57	36	34	17	3	1	0	252.1	234	1078	112	100	18	3	9	8	106	0	167	12	4
Carlton, Steven, Chicago*	4	3	.571	3.69	10	10	0	0	0	0	63.1	58	259	30	26	6	2	2	0	25	0	40	2	1
Cary, Charles, Detroit*	1	2	.333	3.41	22	0	0	0	6	0	31.2	33	140	18	12	3	2	2	0	15	4	21	1	1
Caudill, William, Toronto	2	4	.333	6.19	40	0	0	0	20	2	36.1	36	163	25	25	6	2	0	2	17	1	32	0	1
Cerutti, John, Toronto*	9	4	.692	4.15	34	20	2	1	3	1	145.1	150	616	73	67	25	4	5	1	47	2	89	8	0
Chadwick, Ray, California	0	5	.000	7.24	7	7	0	0	0	0	27.1	39	133	26	22	5	1	0	1	15	0	9	1	0
Clancy, James, Toronto	14	14	.500	3.94	34	34	6	3	0	0	219.1	202	913	100	96	24	5	9	4	63	0	126	4	0
Clark, Bryan, Chicago*	0	0	.000	4.50	5	0	0	0	2	0	8.0	8	31	4	4	0	0	0	0	2	0	5	0	0
Clarke, Stanley, Toronto*	0	1	.000	9.24	10	0	0	0	6	0	12.2	18	62	13	13	4	3	1	0	10	1	9	0	2
Clear, Mark, Milwaukee	5	5	.500	2.20	59	0	0	0	52	16	73.2	53	306	23	18	4	1	4	1	36	2	85	8	2
Clemens, W. Roger, Boston	24	4	.857	2.48	33	33	10	1	0	0	254.0	179	997	77	70	21	4	6	4	67	0	238	11	3
Clutterbuck, Bryan, Milwaukee	0	1	.000	4.29	20	0	0	0	7	0	56.2	68	250	32	27	8	1	1	2	16	2	38	2	0

Pitcher and Club	W.	L.	Pct.	ERA.	G.	GS.	CG.	ShO.	GF.	Sv.	IP.	H.	BFP.	R.	ER.	HR.	SH.	SF.	HB.	Tot. BB.	Int. BB.	SO.	WP.	Bk.
Cocanower, James, Milwaukee	0	1	.000	4.43	17	2	0	0	2	0	44.2	40	205	29	22	1	3	1	2	38	0	22	5	0
Codiroli, Christopher, Oakland	5	8	.385	4.03	16	16	1	0	0	0	91.2	91	406	54	41	15	1	1	2	38	2	43	4	0
Cone, David, Kansas City	0	0	.000	5.56	11	0	0	0	5	0	22.2	29	108	14	14	2	0	0	1	13	1	21	3	0
Cook, Michael, California	0	2	.000	9.00	5	1	0	0	1	0	9.0	13	46	12	9	3	0	0	0	7	1	6	0	0
Corbett, Douglas, California	4	2	.667	3.66	46	0	0	0	32	10	78.2	66	312	36	32	11	1	2	1	22	2	36	2	0
Correa, Edwin, Texas	12	14	.462	4.23	32	32	4	2	0	0	202.1	167	886	102	95	15	4	3	3	126	2	189	19	2
Cowley, Joseph, Chicago	11	11	.500	3.88	27	27	4	0	0	0	162.1	133	692	81	70	20	6	4	3	83	1	132	4	0
Crawford, Steven, Boston	0	2	.000	3.92	40	0	0	0	15	4	57.1	69	248	29	25	5	3	2	0	19	7	32	2	0
Darwin, Danny, Milwaukee	6	8	.429	3.52	27	14	5	1	4	0	130.1	120	537	62	51	13	5	6	3	35	1	80	5	0
Davis, George, Baltimore	9	12	.429	3.62	25	25	2	0	0	0	154.0	166	657	70	62	16	3	2	0	49	2	96	5	0
Davis, Joel, Chicago	4	5	.444	4.70	19	19	1	0	0	0	105.1	115	468	64	55	9	3	2	1	51	0	54	4	1
Davis, Ronald, Minnesota	2	6	.250	9.08	36	0	0	0	28	2	38.2	55	198	42	39	7	2	1	4	29	8	30	4	0
Davis, Steven, Toronto*	0	0	.000	17.18	3	0	0	0	0	0	3.2	8	22	7	7	2	0	0	0	5	1	5	1	0
Dawley, William, Chicago	0	7	.000	3.32	46	0	0	0	23	2	97.2	91	405	38	36	10	5	3	1	28	3	66	5	0
DeLeon, Jose, Chicago	4	5	.444	2.96	13	13	1	0	0	0	79.0	49	325	30	26	7	4	1	4	42	0	68	6	0
Dixon, Kenneth, Baltimore	11	13	.458	4.58	35	33	2	0	1	0	202.1	194	874	111	103	33	5	6	1	83	6	170	7	3
Dotson, Richard, Chicago	10	17	.370	5.48	34	34	3	1	0	0	197.0	226	861	125	120	24	4	4	2	69	2	110	10	0
Dozier, Thomas, Oakland	0	0	.000	5.68	4	0	0	0	4	0	6.1	6	30	6	4	1	0	2	0	5	1	4	1	1
Drabek, Douglas, New York	7	8	.467	4.10	27	21	0	0	2	0	131.2	126	561	64	60	13	5	2	3	50	1	76	2	0
Easterly, James, Cleveland*	0	2	.000	7.64	13	0	0	0	4	0	17.2	27	89	16	15	3	1	2	0	12	0	9	2	0
Eichhorn, Mark, Toronto	14	6	.700	1.72	69	0	0	0	38	10	157.0	105	612	32	30	8	9	2	7	45	14	166	2	1
Farr, Steven, Kansas City	8	4	.667	3.13	56	0	0	0	33	8	109.1	90	443	39	38	10	3	2	4	39	8	83	4	1
Filson, W. Peter, Minn.-Chi.*	0	1	.000	6.00	7	1	0	0	4	0	18.0	27	89	13	12	5	0	0	1	7	0	8	1	0
Finley, Charles, California*	3	1	.750	3.30	25	0	0	0	7	0	46.1	40	198	17	17	2	4	0	1	23	1	37	2	0
Fireovid, Stephen, Seattle	2	0	1.000	4.29	10	1	0	0	2	0	21.0	28	89	11	10	1	0	0	1	4	0	10	1	0
Fischer, Todd, California	0	0	.000	4.24	9	0	0	0	5	0	17.0	18	73	8	8	4	1	1	0	8	2	7	0	1
Fisher, Brian, New York	9	5	.643	4.93	62	0	0	0	26	6	96.2	105	424	61	53	14	5	2	1	37	2	67	2	0
Flanagan, Michael, Baltimore*	7	11	.389	4.24	29	28	2	0	0	0	172.0	179	747	95	81	15	10	6	1	66	4	96	8	1
Fontenot, S. Ray, Minnesota*	0	0	.000	9.92	15	0	0	0	7	0	16.1	27	81	19	18	3	0	0	2	4	0	10	2	0
Forsch, Kenneth, California	0	1	.000	9.53	10	0	0	0	4	1	17.0	24	85	21	18	4	1	2	2	10	0	13	0	0
Forster, Terry, California*	4	1	.800	3.51	41	0	0	0	17	5	41.0	47	182	18	16	2	3	1	3	17	1	28	0	0
Fraser, William, California	0	0	.000	8.31	1	1	0	0	0	0	46.1	6	20	4	4	0	1	1	0	1	0	2	0	0
Frazier, George, Minnesota	1	1	.500	4.39	15	0	0	0	10	6	26.2	23	119	13	13	2	1	3	0	16	1	25	1	0
Gardner, Wesley, Boston	0	0	.000	9.00	1	0	0	0	0	0	1.0	1	4	1	1	0	0	1	0	0	0	1	0	0
Gibson, Robert, Milwaukee	1	2	.333	4.73	11	1	0	0	5	0	26.2	23	123	18	14	3	0	1	0	23	1	11	3	0
Gordon, Donald, Toronto	0	1	.000	7.06	14	0	0	0	6	1	21.2	28	102	20	17	1	1	2	1	8	1	13	0	0
Gubicza, Mark, Kansas City	12	6	.667	3.64	35	24	3	2	2	0	180.2	155	765	77	73	8	4	8	5	84	2	118	15	0
Guetterman, A. Lee, Seattle*	0	4	.000	7.34	41	4	1	0	8	0	76.0	108	353	67	62	7	3	5	4	30	3	38	2	0
Guidry, Ronald, New York*	9	12	.429	3.98	30	30	5	0	0	0	192.1	202	809	94	85	28	5	4	1	38	2	140	3	0
Guzman, Jose, Texas	9	15	.375	4.54	29	29	2	0	0	0	172.1	199	757	101	87	23	7	4	6	60	2	87	3	0
Haas, Bryan, Oakland	7	2	.778	2.74	12	12	1	0	0	0	72.1	58	290	23	22	4	2	2	1	19	1	40	0	0
Habyan, John, Baltimore	1	3	.250	4.44	6	5	0	0	1	0	26.1	24	117	17	13	3	2	1	0	18	2	14	1	0
Hargesheimer, Alan, Kansas City	0	1	.000	6.23	5	1	0	0	2	0	13.0	18	61	9	9	1	0	0	1	7	2	4	0	0
Harris, Greg, Texas	10	8	.556	2.83	73	0	0	0	63	20	111.1	103	462	40	35	12	3	6	1	42	6	95	2	1
Havens, Bradley, Baltimore*	3	3	.500	4.56	46	0	0	0	19	1	71.0	64	294	37	36	7	6	1	0	29	1	57	6	0
Heaton, Neal, Clev.-Minn.*	7	15	.318	4.08	33	29	5	0	2	1	198.2	201	850	102	90	26	6	5	2	81	8	90	4	0
Henke, Thomas, Toronto	9	5	.643	3.35	63	0	0	0	51	27	91.1	63	370	39	34	6	2	6	1	32	4	118	3	1
Henry, Dwayne, Texas	1	0	1.000	4.66	19	0	0	0	4	0	19.1	14	93	11	10	1	1	2	1	22	0	17	7	1
Hernandez, Guillermo, Detroit*	8	7	.533	3.55	64	0	0	0	53	24	88.2	87	376	35	35	13	1	3	5	21	1	77	2	1
Higuera, Teodoro, Milwaukee*	20	11	.645	2.79	34	34	15	4	0	0	248.1	226	1031	84	77	26	7	11	3	74	5	207	3	0

Pitcher and Club	W.	L.	Pct.	ERA.	G.	GS.	CG.	ShO.	GF.	Sv.	IP.	H.	BFP.	R.	ER.	HR.	SH.	SF.	HB.	Tot. BB.	Int. BB.	SO.	WP.	Bk.
Holland, Alfred, New York*	1	0	1.000	5.09	25	1	0	0	10	0	40.2	44	177	29	23	5	1	3	0	9	2	37	0	0
Hough, Charles, Texas	17	10	.630	3.79	33	33	7	2	0	0	230.1	188	958	115	97	32	9	1	9	89	2	146	16	0
Howell, Jay, Oakland	3	6	.333	3.38	38	0	0	0	33	16	53.1	53	230	23	20	3	3	1	1	23	4	42	4	0
Huismann, Mark, K.C.-Sea.	3	4	.429	3.79	46	1	0	0	19	5	97.1	98	408	47	41	19	0	3	1	25	0	72	5	0
Hurst, Bruce, Boston*	13	8	.619	2.99	25	25	11	4	0	0	174.1	169	721	63	58	18	5	3	3	50	2	167	6	0
Jackson, Danny, Kansas City*	11	12	.478	3.20	32	27	4	1	3	1	185.2	177	789	83	66	13	10	4	4	79	1	115	7	0
Jackson, Roy Lee, Minnesota	0	1	.000	3.86	28	0	0	0	8	1	58.1	57	249	29	25	7	2	5	3	16	0	32	3	2
James, Robert, Chicago	5	4	.556	5.25	49	0	0	0	40	14	58.1	61	263	36	34	8	4	4	4	23	3	32	5	1
John, Thomas, New York*	5	3	.625	2.93	13	10	1	0	2	0	70.2	73	290	27	23	8	5	3	2	15	1	28	2	0
Johnson, John Henry, Milwaukee*	2	1	.667	2.66	19	0	0	0	5	1	44.0	43	184	15	13	2	3	0	0	10	1	42	5	0
Johnson, Joseph, Toronto	7	2	.778	3.89	16	15	0	0	0	0	88.0	94	368	39	38	3	4	4	3	22	1	39	2	0
Jones, Douglas, Cleveland	1	0	1.000	2.50	11	0	0	0	5	1	18.0	18	79	5	5	0	1	1	1	6	1	12	0	0
Jones, Odell, Baltimore	2	2	.500	3.83	21	0	0	0	12	0	49.1	58	219	22	21	4	2	4	0	23	6	32	2	0
Kelly, Bryan, Detroit	1	2	.333	4.50	6	4	0	0	1	0	20.0	21	88	11	10	4	0	0	0	10	1	18	0	0
Kern, James, Cleveland	1	1	.500	7.90	16	0	0	0	4	0	27.1	34	142	28	24	1	2	0	3	23	0	11	3	0
Key, James, Toronto*	14	11	.560	3.57	36	35	4	2	0	0	232.0	222	959	98	92	24	10	6	3	74	1	141	3	0
King, Eric, Detroit	11	4	.733	3.51	33	16	3	1	9	3	138.1	108	579	54	54	11	6	1	8	63	3	79	4	3
Kinnunen, Michael, Baltimore*	0	0	.000	6.43	9	0	0	0	4	0	7.0	8	31	6	5	1	0	0	0	5	0	1	1	0
Knudson, Mark, Milwaukee	0	1	.000	7.64	4	1	0	0	1	0	17.2	22	82	15	15	7	0	0	0	5	1	9	1	0
Krueger, William, Oakland*	1	2	.333	6.03	11	3	0	0	4	1	34.1	40	149	25	23	4	1	2	0	13	0	10	3	1
Ladd, Peter, Seattle	8	6	.571	3.82	52	0	0	0	33	6	70.2	69	294	33	30	10	0	6	3	18	3	53	2	0
Lamp, Dennis, Toronto	2	6	.250	5.05	40	2	0	0	11	2	73.0	93	329	50	41	5	4	1	0	23	6	30	2	0
Langford, J. Rick, Oakland	1	10	.091	7.36	16	11	0	0	1	0	55.0	69	251	49	45	13	0	2	1	18	0	30	2	0
Langston, Mark, Seattle*	12	14	.462	4.85	37	36	9	0	1	0	239.1	234	1057	142	129	30	5	8	4	123	1	245	10	3
LaPoint, David, Detroit*	3	6	.333	5.72	16	8	0	0	2	0	67.2	85	314	49	43	11	4	1	0	32	3	36	2	1
Latham, William, Minnesota*	0	1	.000	7.31	7	2	0	0	2	0	16.0	24	77	14	13	1	1	2	1	6	0	8	0	0
Lazorko, Jack, Detroit	0	0	.000	4.05	3	0	0	0	2	0	6.2	8	31	3	3	0	0	0	0	4	1	3	0	0
Leary, Timothy, Milwaukee	12	12	.500	4.21	33	30	3	2	2	0	188.1	216	817	97	88	20	4	6	7	53	4	110	7	0
Leibrandt, Charles, Kansas City*	14	11	.560	4.09	35	34	8	1	0	0	231.1	238	975	112	105	18	14	5	4	63	0	108	2	1
Leiper, David, Oakland*	2	2	.500	4.83	33	0	0	0	9	1	31.2	28	136	17	17	3	2	3	2	18	4	15	2	0
Leonard, Dennis, Kansas City	8	13	.381	4.44	33	30	5	2	0	0	192.2	207	821	106	95	22	4	9	4	51	6	114	6	1
Lollar, W. Timothy, Boston*	2	0	1.000	6.91	32	1	0	0	4	0	43.0	51	211	35	33	7	2	4	3	34	3	28	5	1
Loynd, Michael, Texas	2	2	.500	5.36	9	8	0	0	1	1	42.0	49	193	30	25	4	1	2	2	19	1	33	2	0
Lucas, Gary, California*	4	1	.800	3.15	27	0	0	0	11	2	45.2	45	185	19	16	1	0	1	0	6	0	31	5	0
Lugo, Urbano, California	1	1	.500	3.80	6	3	0	0	0	0	21.1	21	86	9	9	4	1	0	0	6	0	9	0	0
Mahler, Michael, Tex-Tor*	0	2	.000	4.08	31	5	0	0	8	3	64.0	72	284	31	29	3	1	4	4	29	2	28	5	0
Martinez, Felix, Baltimore*	0	2	.000	5.63	14	0	0	0	5	1	16.0	18	74	10	10	1	0	1	0	12	1	11	1	0
Martinez, J. Dennis, Baltimore	0	0	.000	6.75	4	0	0	0	1	0	6.2	11	33	5	5	0	0	1	0	2	0	2	1	0
Mason, Michael, Texas*	7	3	.700	4.33	27	22	2	1	2	0	135.0	135	587	71	65	11	3	3	0	56	3	85	5	1
McCaskill, Kirk, California	17	10	.630	3.36	34	33	10	2	1	0	246.1	207	1013	98	92	19	6	5	5	92	1	202	10	2
McClure, Robert, Milwaukee*	2	1	.667	3.86	13	0	0	0	7	0	16.1	18	75	7	7	2	1	1	0	10	1	11	0	0
McGregor, Scott, Baltimore*	11	15	.423	4.52	34	33	4	2	1	0	203.0	216	868	110	102	35	3	6	3	57	0	95	5	0
McKeon, Joel, Chicago*	3	1	.750	2.45	30	0	0	0	5	1	33.0	18	129	10	9	2	1	2	0	17	2	18	0	0
Meridith, Ronald, Texas*	1	0	1.000	3.00	5	0	0	0	0	0	3.0	2	10	1	1	0	1	1	0	1	1	2	0	0
Mirabella, Paul, Seattle*	0	0	.000	8.53	8	0	0	0	2	0	6.1	13	34	7	6	1	0	0	0	3	0	6	1	0
Mohorcic, Dale, Texas	2	4	.333	2.51	58	0	0	0	20	7	79.0	86	325	25	22	5	1	0	1	15	6	29	1	0
Montefusco, John, New York	0	0	.000	2.19	4	0	0	0	1	0	12.1	9	50	3	3	2	0	0	0	5	0	3	0	0
Mooneyham, William, Oakland	4	5	.444	4.52	45	6	0	0	18	2	99.2	103	456	53	50	4	3	2	3	67	4	75	2	0
Moore, Donnie, California	4	5	.444	2.97	49	0	0	0	42	21	72.2	60	295	28	24	10	7	3	0	22	4	53	4	1
Moore, Michael, Seattle	11	13	.458	4.30	38	37	11	1	1	1	266.0	279	1145	141	127	28	10	6	12	94	6	146	4	1

Pitcher and Club	W.	L.	Pct.	ERA.	G.	GS.	CG.	ShO.	GF.	Sv.	IP.	H.	BFP.	R.	ER.	HR.	SH.	SF.	HB.	Tot. BB.	Int. BB.	SO.	WP.	Bk.
Morgan, Michael, Seattle	11	17	.393	4.53	37	33	9	1	2	1	216.1	243	951	122	109	24	7	3	4	86	3	116	8	1
Morris, John, Detroit	21	8	.724	3.27	35	35	15	6	0	0	267.0	229	1092	105	97	40	7	3	0	82	7	223	12	0
Musselman, Jeffrey, Toronto*	0	0	.000	10.13	6	0	0	0	0	0	5.1	8	29	7	6	1	0	0	0	5	1	4	0	0
Nelson, W. Eugene, Chicago	6	6	.500	3.85	54	1	0	0	26	6	114.2	118	488	52	49	7	7	1	3	41	5	70	3	0
Niekro, Joseph, New York	9	10	.474	4.87	25	25	0	0	0	0	125.2	139	571	84	68	15	1	0	1	63	3	59	10	1
Niekro, Philip, Cleveland	11	11	.500	4.32	34	32	5	0	1	0	210.1	241	951	126	101	24	7	2	6	95	1	81	9	2
Nielsen, J. Scott, New York	4	4	.500	4.02	10	9	2	2	1	0	56.0	66	235	29	25	12	0	0	2	12	0	20	0	0
Nieves, Juan, Milwaukee*	11	12	.478	4.92	35	33	4	3	0	0	184.2	224	834	124	101	17	3	5	1	77	0	116	3	1
Nipper, Albert, Boston	10	12	.455	5.38	26	26	3	0	0	0	159.0	186	702	108	95	24	4	5	4	47	2	79	1	1
Noles, Dickie, Cleveland	3	2	.600	5.10	32	0	0	0	9	0	54.2	56	251	33	31	9	3	5	5	30	4	32	1	1
Nunez, Edwin, Seattle	1	2	.333	5.82	14	1	0	0	6	0	21.2	25	93	15	14	5	0	0	0	5	1	17	0	0
Oelkers, Bryan, Cleveland*	3	3	.500	4.70	35	4	0	0	8	1	69.0	70	318	38	36	13	3	2	6	40	2	33	4	0
O'Neal, Randall, Detroit	3	7	.300	4.33	37	11	1	0	9	2	122.2	121	522	69	59	13	3	6	3	44	9	68	8	0
Ontiveros, Steven, Oakland	2	2	.500	4.71	46	0	0	0	27	10	72.2	72	305	40	38	10	1	6	1	25	3	54	4	0
Pacella, John, Detroit	0	0	.000	4.09	5	0	0	0	1	1	11.0	10	51	5	5	0	2	2	0	13	1	5	0	1
Pastore, Frank, Minnesota	3	1	.750	4.01	33	1	0	0	15	2	49.1	54	223	28	22	4	4	4	0	24	6	18	1	0
Petry, Dan, Detroit	5	10	.333	4.66	20	20	2	0	0	0	116.0	122	520	78	60	15	3	3	5	53	3	56	5	0
Plesac, Daniel, Milwaukee*	10	7	.588	2.97	51	0	0	0	33	14	91.0	81	377	34	30	5	6	5	0	29	1	75	4	0
Plunk, Eric, Oakland	4	7	.364	5.31	26	15	0	0	2	0	120.1	91	537	75	71	14	2	3	5	102	2	98	9	6
Portugal, Mark, Minnesota	6	10	.375	4.31	27	15	3	0	7	1	112.2	112	481	56	54	10	5	3	1	50	1	67	5	0
Pulido, Alfonso, New York*	1	1	.500	4.70	10	3	0	0	3	1	30.2	38	135	17	16	8	1	1	0	9	0	13	1	0
Quisenberry, Daniel, Kansas City	3	7	.300	2.77	62	0	0	0	54	12	81.1	92	352	30	25	2	4	5	3	24	12	36	0	0
Rasmussen, Dennis, New York*	18	6	.750	3.88	31	31	3	1	0	0	202.0	160	819	91	87	28	1	5	2	74	0	131	5	0
Reed, Jerry, Seattle	4	0	1.000	3.12	11	4	0	0	4	0	34.2	38	152	13	12	3	0	0	0	13	0	16	1	0
Righetti, David, New York*	8	8	.500	2.45	74	0	0	0	68	46	106.2	88	435	31	29	4	5	4	2	35	7	83	1	0
Rijo, Jose, Oakland	9	11	.450	4.65	39	26	4	0	9	1	193.2	172	856	116	100	24	10	9	4	108	7	176	6	4
Ritter, Reggie, Cleveland	0	0	.000	6.30	5	0	0	0	2	0	10.0	14	48	10	7	1	0	2	1	4	0	6	0	0
Rodriguez, Ricardo, Oakland	1	2	.333	6.61	3	3	0	0	0	0	16.1	17	72	12	12	4	0	0	0	7	0	2	2	1
Roman, Jose, Cleveland	1	2	.333	6.55	6	5	0	0	0	0	22.0	23	105	20	16	3	1	4	1	17	0	9	0	0
Romanick, Ronald, California	5	8	.385	5.50	18	18	1	1	0	0	106.1	124	470	68	65	13	3	5	0	44	0	38	4	0
Rozema, David, Texas	0	0	.000	5.91	6	0	0	0	0	0	10.2	19	52	9	7	1	0	2	0	3	0	3	0	0
Ruhle, Vernon, California	1	3	.250	4.15	16	3	0	0	5	1	47.2	46	197	25	22	5	1	2	1	7	0	23	1	0
Russell, Jeffrey, Texas	5	2	.714	3.40	37	0	0	0	9	2	82.0	74	338	40	31	11	1	2	1	31	2	54	5	0
Saberhagen, Bret, Kansas City	7	12	.368	4.15	30	25	4	2	4	0	156.0	165	652	77	72	15	3	3	2	29	1	112	1	1
Sambito, Joseph, Boston*	2	0	1.000	4.84	53	0	0	0	27	12	44.2	54	200	26	24	4	1	0	2	16	3	30	4	0
Scherrer, William, Detroit*	0	1	.000	7.29	13	0	0	0	8	0	21.0	19	103	19	17	3	2	0	1	22	4	16	1	0
Schiraldi, Calvin, Boston	4	2	.667	1.41	25	0	0	0	21	9	51.0	36	198	8	8	5	2	1	1	15	2	55	1	0
Schmidt, David, Chicago	3	6	.333	3.31	49	1	0	0	21	8	92.1	94	394	37	34	10	3	3	5	27	7	67	5	0
Schrom, Kenneth, Cleveland	14	7	.667	4.54	34	33	3	1	1	0	206.0	217	883	118	104	34	8	12	12	49	3	87	2	1
Schulze, Donald, Cleveland	4	4	.500	5.00	19	13	1	0	1	0	84.2	88	371	48	47	9	0	1	5	34	0	33	6	0
Scurry, Rodney, New York*	1	2	.333	3.66	31	0	0	0	10	2	39.1	38	177	18	16	1	2	0	2	22	1	36	5	0
Searage, Raymond, Milw.-Chi.*	1	1	.500	3.35	46	0	0	0	17	1	51.0	44	220	20	19	7	1	2	1	28	4	36	1	1
Seaver, G. Thomas, Chi.-Bos.	7	13	.350	4.03	28	28	2	0	0	0	176.1	180	759	83	79	17	7	6	7	56	2	103	4	0
Sellers, Jeffrey, Boston	3	7	.300	4.94	14	13	1	0	0	0	82.0	90	366	56	45	13	2	2	3	40	1	51	4	1
Shields, Stephen, Kansas City	0	0	.000	2.08	3	0	0	0	2	0	8.2	3	33	3	2	1	0	2	0	4	1	2	1	0
Shirley, Robert, New York*	0	4	.000	5.04	39	6	0	0	9	3	105.1	108	454	60	59	13	5	8	3	40	1	64	1	0
Slaton, James, Cal-Det.	4	6	.400	5.08	36	12	0	0	13	2	113.1	130	497	70	64	14	1	8	3	40	4	43	2	0
Smith, Leroy, Minnesota	0	2	.000	6.97	5	0	0	0	2	0	10.1	13	50	8	8	1	0	0	1	5	1	8	0	0
Smithson, B. Mike, Minnesota	13	14	.481	4.77	34	33	8	1	1	0	198.0	234	880	123	105	26	5	8	14	57	4	114	15	1
Snell, Nathaniel, Baltimore	2	1	.667	3.86	34	0	0	0	18	0	72.1	69	297	36	31	9	3	3	1	22	4	29	2	0

Pitcher and Club	W.	L.	Pct.	ERA.	G.	GS.	CG.	ShO.	GF.	Sv.	IP.	H.	BFP.	R.	ER.	HR.	SH.	SF.	HB.	Tot. BB.	Int. BB.	SO.	WP.	Bk.
Stanley, Robert, Boston	6	6	.500	4.37	66	1	0	0	50	16	82.1	109	366	48	40	9	2	4	0	22	8	54	1	0
Stewart, David, Oakland	9	5	.643	3.74	29	17	4	1	2	0	149.1	137	644	67	62	15	4	4	3	65	0	102	9	0
Stewart, Samuel, Boston	4	1	.800	4.38	27	0	0	0	5	0	63.2	64	295	33	31	7	1	5	0	48	2	47	5	1
Stieb, David, Toronto	7	12	.368	4.74	37	34	1	1	2	1	205.0	239	919	128	108	29	6	6	15	87	1	127	7	0
Stoddard, Timothy, New York	4	1	.800	3.83	24	0	0	0	6	0	49.1	41	208	23	21	6	6	2	0	23	3	34	3	0
Sutton, Donald, California	15	11	.577	3.74	34	34	3	1	0	0	207.0	192	853	93	86	31	3	3	3	49	2	116	4	1
Swaggerty, William, Baltimore	0	0	.000	18.00	1	0	0	0	0	0	1.0	6	9	2	2	0	0	0	0	1	1	1	1	0
Swift, William, Seattle	2	9	.182	5.46	29	17	1	0	3	0	115.1	148	534	85	70	5	5	3	7	55	2	55	2	1
Swindell, F. Gregory, Cleveland*	5	2	.714	4.23	9	9	1	0	0	0	61.2	57	255	35	29	9	3	1	1	15	0	46	3	2
Tanana, Frank, Detroit*	12	9	.571	4.16	32	31	3	1	1	0	188.1	196	812	95	87	23	8	5	3	65	9	119	7	1
Terrell, C. Walter, Detroit	15	12	.556	4.56	34	33	9	2	1	0	217.1	199	918	116	110	30	2	3	3	98	5	93	5	0
Tewksbury, Robert, New York	9	5	.643	3.31	23	20	2	0	0	0	130.1	144	558	58	48	8	4	7	5	31	0	49	3	2
Thigpen, Robert, Chicago	2	0	1.000	1.77	20	0	0	0	14	7	35.2	26	142	7	7	1	1	1	1	12	0	20	0	0
Thurmond, Mark, Detroit*	4	1	.800	1.92	25	4	0	0	5	3	51.2	44	209	13	11	7	3	1	0	17	2	17	1	0
Trujillo, Michael, Bos-Sea	3	2	.600	3.26	14	4	1	1	5	1	47.0	39	197	17	17	5	3	1	0	21	3	23	1	0
Viola, Frank, Minnesota*	16	13	.552	4.51	37	37	7	1	0	0	245.2	257	1053	136	123	37	4	5	3	83	0	191	12	0
Von Ohlen, David, Oakland*	0	3	.000	3.52	24	0	0	0	3	1	15.1	18	68	7	6	0	1	0	0	7	2	4	1	0
Vuckovich, Peter, Milwaukee	2	4	.333	3.06	6	6	0	0	0	0	32.1	33	139	18	11	3	2	3	2	11	0	12	2	2
Ward, R. Duane, Toronto	0	1	.000	13.50	2	1	0	0	1	0	2.0	3	15	4	3	0	0	0	1	4	0	1	1	0
Wegman, William, Milwaukee	5	12	.294	5.13	35	32	2	0	1	0	198.1	217	836	120	113	32	4	5	7	43	2	82	5	2
Whitson, Eddie, New York	5	2	.714	7.54	14	4	0	0	6	0	37.0	54	189	37	31	5	2	3	0	23	1	27	2	0
Wilcox, Milton, Seattle	0	8	.000	5.50	13	10	0	0	2	0	55.2	74	259	38	34	11	1	3	1	28	1	26	0	1
Williams, Mitchell, Texas*	8	6	.571	3.58	80	0	0	0	38	8	98.0	69	435	39	39	8	1	3	11	79	8	90	5	5
Wills, Frank, Cleveland	4	4	.500	4.91	26	0	0	0	16	4	40.1	43	182	23	22	6	6	2	0	16	4	32	2	0
Witt, Michael, California	18	10	.643	2.84	34	34	14	3	0	0	269.0	218	1071	95	85	22	3	5	3	73	2	208	6	0
Witt, Robert, Texas	11	9	.550	5.48	31	31	0	0	0	0	157.2	130	741	104	96	18	3	9	3	143	2	174	22	3
Woodward, Robert, Boston	2	3	.400	5.30	9	6	0	0	0	0	35.2	46	161	26	21	4	0	2	1	11	0	14	5	1
Wright, J. Richard, Texas*	1	0	1.000	5.03	21	1	0	0	2	0	39.1	44	177	22	22	1	1	0	0	21	0	23	2	0
Yett, Richard, Cleveland	5	3	.625	5.15	39	3	1	1	17	1	78.2	84	350	48	45	10	2	4	1	37	4	50	8	0
Young, Curtis, Oakland*	13	9	.591	3.45	29	27	5	2	0	0	198.0	176	826	88	76	19	8	9	7	57	1	116	7	2
Young, Matthew, Seattle*	8	6	.571	3.82	65	5	1	0	32	13	103.2	108	458	50	44	9	4	3	8	46	2	82	7	1

NOTE—Following pitchers combined to pitch shutout games: Baltimore (4)—Flanagan, Snell, T. Martinez and Aase; Davis and Aase; Dixon and Aase; Flanagan and Aase. Boston (1)—Brown and Crawford. California (4)—Sutton, Lucas and Moore; Witt and Moore; Candelaria and Moore; Candelaria and Ruhle. Chicago (4)—Allen, Nelson and James; DeLeon, James and Schmidt; Carlton and Thigpen; Bannister and Thigpen. Cleveland (1)—Candiotti and Camacho. Detroit (2)—Terrell and Hernandez; Tanana and Campbell. Kansas City (5)—Jackson and Black; Bankhead, Black and Quisenberry; Bankhead and Black; Gubicza and Farr; Gubicza and Black. Milwaukee (2)—Leary and Plesac; Vuckovich, Wegman and Clear. Minnesota (1)—Viola and Atherton. New York (5)—John and Righetti 2; Rasmussen and Righetti; Niekro and Holland; Niekro, Scurry and Righetti. Oakland (4)—Haas and Howell; Langford and Howell; Plunk, Leiper, Stewart and Andujar; Young, Bair, Von Ohlen, Howell and Leiper. Seattle (2)—Wilcox and Young; Swift and Young. Texas (3)—Hough, Williams and Harris; Correa and Williams; Correa and Russell. Toronto (5)—Key and Henke 3; Clancy and Eichhorn; Key, Eichhorn and Henke.

PITCHERS WITH TWO OR MORE CLUBS

(Alphabetically arranged with pitcher's first club on top)

Pitcher and Club	W.	L.	Pct.	ERA.	G.	GS.	CG.	ShO.	GF.	Sv.	IP.	H.	BFP.	R.	ER.	HR.	SH.	SF.	HB.	Tot. BB.	Int. BB.	SO.	WP.	Bk.
Agosto, Chi.	0	2	.000	7.71	9	0	0	0	1	0	4.2	6	24	5	4	0	0	0	0	4	0	3	0	0
Agosto, Minn.	1	2	.333	8.85	17	1	0	0	3	1	20.1	43	115	25	20	1	2	0	2	14	0	9	1	0
Atherton, Oak.	1	2	.333	5.87	13	0	0	0	5	0	15.1	18	75	10	10	2	1	2	0	11	1	8	0	0
Atherton, Minn.	5	8	.385	3.75	47	0	0	0	31	10	81.2	82	356	37	34	9	5	4	1	35	3	59	2	0
Brown, Bos.	4	4	.500	5.34	15	10	0	0	2	0	57.1	72	260	35	34	10	3	3	1	25	1	32	3	0
Brown, Sea.	0	2	.000	7.47	6	2	0	0	0	0	15.2	19	74	14	13	4	0	0	0	11	0	9	1	1
Butcher, Minn.	0	3	.000	6.30	16	10	1	0	1	0	70.0	82	308	50	49	11	1	3	1	24	1	29	4	0
Butcher, Clev.	1	5	.167	6.93	13	8	1	1	4	0	50.2	86	246	43	39	6	1	3	3	13	0	16	2	0
Filson, Minn.	0	0	.000	5.68	4	0	0	0	2	0	6.1	13	35	4	4	1	0	0	1	2	0	4	0	0
Filson, Chi.	0	1	.000	6.17	3	1	0	0	2	0	11.2	14	54	9	8	4	0	0	0	5	0	4	1	0
Heaton, Clev.	3	6	.333	4.24	12	12	2	0	0	0	74.1	73	324	42	35	8	2	0	1	34	4	24	2	0
Heaton, Minn.	4	9	.308	3.98	21	17	3	0	2	1	124.1	128	526	60	55	18	4	5	1	47	4	66	2	0
Huismann, K.C.	0	1	.000	4.15	10	0	0	0	5	1	17.1	18	74	8	8	1	0	1	0	6	0	13	1	0
Huismann, Sea.	3	3	.500	3.71	36	1	0	0	14	4	80.0	80	334	39	33	18	0	2	1	19	0	59	4	0
Mahler, Tex.	0	2	.000	4.14	29	5	0	0	8	3	63.0	71	278	31	29	3	1	4	3	29	2	28	5	0
Mahler, Tor.	0	0	.000	0.00	2	0	0	0	0	0	1.0	1	6	0	0	0	0	0	1	0	0	0	0	0
Searage, Milw.	0	1	.000	6.95	17	0	0	0	8	1	22.0	29	103	17	17	6	1	0	1	9	1	10	1	1
Searage, Chi.	1	0	1.000	0.62	29	0	0	0	9	0	29.0	15	117	3	2	1	0	2	0	19	3	26	0	0
Seaver, Chi.	2	6	.250	4.38	12	12	1	0	0	0	72.0	66	309	37	35	9	2	2	5	27	1	31	1	0
Seaver, Bos.	5	7	.417	3.80	16	16	1	0	0	0	104.1	114	450	46	44	8	5	4	2	29	1	72	3	0
Slaton, Cal.	4	6	.400	5.65	14	12	0	0	1	0	73.1	84	323	52	46	9	1	6	2	29	1	31	1	0
Slaton, Det.	0	0	.000	4.05	22	0	0	0	12	2	40.0	46	174	18	18	5	0	2	1	11	3	12	1	0
Trujillo, Bos.	0	0	.000	9.53	3	0	0	0	1	0	5.2	7	30	6	6	0	1	0	0	6	2	4	1	0
Trujillo, Sea.	3	2	.600	2.40	11	4	1	1	4	1	41.1	32	167	11	11	5	2	1	0	15	1	19	0	0

1986 A.L. Pitching Against Each Club

BALTIMORE—73-89

Pitcher	Bos. W-L	Cal. W-L	Chi. W-L	Clev. W-L	Det. W-L	K.C. W-L	Mil. W-L	Min. W-L	N.Y. W-L	Oak. W-L	Sea. W-L	Tex. W-L	Tor. W-L	Totals W-L
Aase	1-1	0-0	1-0	1-1	1-1	1-0	0-0	0-0	0-0	0-2	0-0	0-1	1-1	6-7
Arnold	0-1	0-0	0-0	0-0	0-1	0-0	0-0	0-0	0-0	0-0	0-0	0-0	0-0	0-2
Bell	0-0	0-0	0-0	0-0	0-1	0-0	0-1	0-0	1-0	0-0	0-0	0-0	0-0	1-2
Boddicker	1-1	0-1	1-1	0-2	0-1	2-0	1-1	2-1	2-1	0-1	2-2	1-0	2-0	14-12
Bordi	1-1	1-0	2-0	0-0	0-0	0-1	0-0	0-0	0-1	2-0	0-0	0-1	0-0	6-4
Davis	1-1	1-2	0-1	1-1	0-1	1-0	0-1	1-0	0-1	0-3	1-1	3-0	0-0	9-12
Dixon	0-3	0-0	1-0	2-1	0-1	1-2	1-2	3-0	1-0	0-0	1-3	0-0	1-1	11-13
Flanagan	0-0	1-1	2-0	0-3	0-2	0-1	1-0	1-2	0-1	0-0	0-0	0-0	2-1	7-11
Habyan	0-1	0-0	0-0	0-0	0-1	0-0	1-0	0-0	0-0	0-1	0-0	0-0	0-0	1-3
Havens	0-0	0-0	0-0	0-0	0-0	0-0	0-1	1-0	0-0	1-0	0-0	0-2	1-0	3-3
Jones	0-0	0-1	0-0	0-0	0-0	1-0	0-0	0-0	0-0	1-0	0-0	0-1	0-0	2-2
T. Martinez	0-0	0-0	0-0	0-0	0-0	0-0	0-0	0-0	0-1	0-0	0-0	0-0	0-1	0-2
McGregor	0-0	2-1	2-1	0-1	0-3	0-2	2-1	0-1	1-3	1-0	1-0	1-1	1-1	11-15
Snell	0-0	1-0	0-0	0-0	0-0	0-0	0-0	0-0	0-0	0-0	1-0	0-1	0-0	2-1
Totals	4-9	6-6	9-3	4-9	1-12	6-6	6-7	8-4	5-8	5-7	6-6	5-7	8-5	73-89

No Decisions—Kinnunen, D. Martinez, Swaggerty.

BOSTON—95-66

Pitcher	Balt. W-L	Cal. W-L	Chi. W-L	Clev. W-L	Det. W-L	K.C. W-L	Mil. W-L	Min. W-L	N.Y. W-L	Oak. W-L	Sea. W-L	Tex. W-L	Tor. W-L	Totals W-L
Boyd	1-0	0-1	1-1	3-0	0-2	0-2	2-2	1-0	1-1	2-0	1-0	3-0	1-1	16-10
Brown	0-1	0-1	1-0	2-0	0-0	0-0	0-2	0-0	0-0	0-0	1-0	0-0	0-0	4-4
Clemens	3-0	3-0	1-2	1-0	2-0	1-0	2-0	4-0	1-0	1-1	2-0	1-0	2-1	24-4
Crawford	0-1	0-0	0-0	0-0	0-0	0-0	0-0	0-0	0-1	0-0	0-0	0-0	0-0	0-2
Hurst	0-0	1-1	2-1	2-0	0-1	1-1	1-0	2-0	1-1	1-1	0-0	1-2	1-0	13-8
Lollar	0-0	1-0	1-0	0-0	0-0	0-0	0-0	0-0	0-0	0-0	0-0	0-0	0-0	2-0
Nipper	2-0	0-1	1-0	0-1	2-1	3-1	0-0	0-1	1-2	0-2	1-2	0-0	0-1	10-12
Sambito	0-0	0-0	0-0	0-0	1-0	0-0	0-0	1-0	0-0	0-0	0-0	0-0	0-0	2-0
Schiraldi	1-0	0-0	0-0	1-0	1-0	0-0	1-0	0-0	0-0	0-0	0-0	0-1	0-1	4-2
Seaver	0-0	0-2	0-0	0-1	1-0	1-1	0-0	1-0	0-1	0-1	1-0	0-0	1-1	5-7
Sellers	1-1	0-1	0-1	0-0	0-0	0-0	0-2	0-0	0-1	1-0	1-1	0-0	0-0	3-7
Stanley	0-1	0-0	0-0	0-1	0-1	0-1	0-0	0-0	1-0	1-0	0-1	2-1	2-0	6-6
Stewart	0-0	0-0	0-0	0-0	0-1	0-0	0-0	1-0	0-0	1-0	1-0	1-0	0-0	4-1
Woodward	1-0	0-0	0-0	1-0	0-0	0-0	0-0	0-1	0-1	0-0	0-0	0-0	0-1	2-3
Totals	9-4	5-7	7-5	10-3	7-6	6-6	6-6	10-2	5-8	7-5	8-4	8-4	7-6	95-66

No Decisions—Gardner.

CALIFORNIA—92-70

Pitcher	Balt. W-L	Bos. W-L	Chi. W-L	Clev. W-L	Det. W-L	K.C. W-L	Mil. W-L	Min. W-L	N.Y. W-L	Oak. W-L	Sea. W-L	Tex. W-L	Tor. W-L	Totals W-L
Bryden	0-0	0-1	0-0	0-0	0-0	0-0	0-0	2-0	0-0	0-0	0-0	0-0	0-0	2-1
Candelaria	0-0	1-1	1-0	0-0	0-1	0-0	1-0	0-0	1-0	2-0	1-0	2-0	1-0	10-2
Chadwick	0-1	0-0	0-0	0-1	0-0	0-0	0-0	0-0	0-1	0-1	0-1	0-0	0-0	0-5
Cook	0-0	0-1	0-1	0-0	0-0	0-0	0-0	0-0	0-0	0-0	0-0	0-0	0-0	0-2
Corbett	0-0	0-0	0-0	1-0	1-0	2-0	0-0	0-0	0-1	0-0	0-0	0-0	0-1	4-2
Finley	0-0	0-0	0-1	1-0	0-0	1-0	0-0	0-0	1-0	0-0	0-0	0-0	0-0	3-1
Forster	0-0	1-0	0-0	0-0	0-0	0-0	1-0	1-0	0-0	0-0	0-0	0-0	1-1	4-1
Forsch	0-0	0-0	0-0	0-0	0-0	0-0	0-0	0-0	0-0	0-0	0-1	0-0	0-0	0-1
Lucas	0-0	0-0	1-0	0-0	1-0	1-0	0-0	1-0	0-0	0-0	0-0	0-1	0-0	4-1
Lugo	0-0	0-0	1-0	0-0	0-0	0-1	0-0	0-0	0-0	0-0	0-0	0-0	0-0	1-1
McCaskill	4-0	1-0	1-3	2-1	1-0	1-0	1-2	0-1	0-0	3-0	0-1	2-1	1-1	17-10
Moore	0-1	0-0	1-0	0-0	1-0	0-0	0-1	0-1	0-1	0-0	2-0	0-0	0-1	4-5
Romanick	0-1	1-0	0-1	0-1	0-0	1-1	0-1	0-0	0-1	1-1	1-0	1-0	0-1	5-8
Ruhle	0-0	0-0	0-0	0-0	0-1	0-1	0-0	0-1	0-0	0-0	1-0	0-0	0-0	1-3
Slaton	0-1	0-0	0-0	0-1	0-2	0-1	1-0	1-1	0-0	0-0	1-0	0-0	1-0	4-6
Sutton	1-0	2-0	1-0	1-0	1-1	0-0	1-2	0-2	2-1	1-0	1-2	2-2	2-1	15-11
Witt	1-2	1-2	1-0	1-2	2-0	2-1	0-1	2-0	3-0	3-1	1-0	1-1	0-0	18-10
Totals	6-6	7-5	7-6	6-6	7-5	8-5	5-7	7-6	7-5	10-3	8-5	8-5	6-6	92-70

No Decisions—Fischer, Fraser.

CHICAGO—72-90

Pitcher	Balt. W-L	Bos. W-L	Cal. W-L	Clev. W-L	Det. W-L	K.C. W-L	Mil. W-L	Min. W-L	N.Y. W-L	Oak. W-L	Sea. W-L	Tex. W-L	Tor. W-L	Totals W-L
Agosto	0-0	0-1	0-0	0-0	0-1	0-0	0-0	0-0	0-0	0-0	0-0	0-0	0-0	0-2
Allen	1-1	0-0	1-1	1-0	0-0	0-0	0-0	0-0	2-0	1-0	1-0	0-0	0-0	7-2
Bannister	0-2	0-4	1-0	0-1	2-0	3-0	1-0	1-2	1-2	0-1	1-0	0-1	0-1	10-14
Carlton	0-0	0-0	0-0	0-0	0-1	1-0	1-0	0-0	0-0	0-1	1-0	1-1	0-0	4-3
Cowley	0-2	1-1	2-0	0-0	1-1	1-0	1-0	1-1	1-1	2-1	1-0	0-3	0-1	11-11
Davis	0-0	0-0	1-0	0-1	0-1	0-0	1-0	0-1	0-0	1-0	0-0	0-1	1-1	4-5
Dawley	0-0	0-0	0-1	0-1	0-0	0-2	0-1	0-0	0-1	0-0	0-1	0-0	0-0	0-7
DeLeon	0-0	2-0	0-1	0-0	1-0	0-1	0-1	1-0	0-0	0-0	0-0	0-1	0-1	4-5
Dotson	1-1	1-0	0-2	0-2	0-2	1-1	0-1	0-2	1-2	2-1	1-1	1-1	2-1	10-17

Pitcher	Balt. W-L	Bos. W-L	Cal. W-L	Clev. W-L	Det. W-L	K.C. W-L	Mil. W-L	Min. W-L	N.Y. W-L	Oak. W-L	Sea. W-L	Tex. W-L	Tor. W-L	Totals W-L
Filson	0-0	0-0	0-0	0-0	0-0	0-0	0-0	0-0	0-0	0-1	0-0	0-0	0-0	0-1
James	0-1	0-0	0-0	1-1	1-0	1-1	0-1	0-0	0-0	1-0	1-0	0-0	0-0	5-4
McKeon	0-0	0-0	0-0	1-0	0-0	0-0	0-0	1-0	1-0	0-0	0-1	0-0	0-0	3-1
Nelson	1-1	0-0	0-0	2-0	1-0	0-1	0-1	0-1	0-0	0-1	0-0	0-0	2-1	6-6
Schmidt	0-1	0-0	0-1	0-1	0-0	0-0	0-1	1-0	0-0	0-0	1-0	0-2	1-0	3-6
Searage	0-0	0-0	0-0	0-0	0-0	0-0	0-0	0-0	0-0	0-0	1-0	0-0	0-0	1-0
Seaver	0-0	1-1	0-1	0-0	0-0	0-0	1-1	0-0	0-0	0-0	0-2	0-1	0-0	2-6
Thigpen	0-0	0-0	1-0	0-0	0-0	0-0	0-0	1-0	0-0	0-0	0-0	0-0	0-0	2-0
Totals	3-9	5-7	6-7	5-7	6-6	7-6	5-7	6-7	6-6	7-6	8-5	2-11	6-6	72-90

No Decisions—Clark.

CLEVELAND—84-78

Pitcher	Balt. W-L	Bos. W-L	Cal. W-L	Chi. W-L	Det. W-L	K.C. W-L	Mil. W-L	Min. W-L	N.Y. W-L	Oak. W-L	Sea. W-L	Tex. W-L	Tor. W-L	Totals W-L
Bailes	1-1	0-0	0-1	1-2	3-1	0-1	3-1	0-1	1-0	1-0	0-0	0-2	0-0	10-10
Butcher	0-0	0-0	0-1	0-0	0-2	0-0	0-0	0-0	0-0	1-0	0-1	0-1	0-0	1-5
Camacho	0-0	1-0	0-0	1-1	0-0	0-0	0-0	0-1	0-0	0-0	0-1	0-0	0-1	2-4
Candiotti	2-0	1-1	0-2	1-1	0-0	2-1	2-0	3-0	0-4	1-1	2-0	2-0	0-2	16-12
Easterly	0-0	0-0	0-0	0-0	0-0	0-0	0-1	0-0	0-0	0-0	0-0	0-0	0-1	0-2
Heaton	0-0	0-2	1-0	0-0	0-0	1-0	1-0	0-1	0-1	0-0	0-0	0-1	0-1	3-6
Jones	0-0	0-0	0-0	0-0	0-0	0-0	0-0	0-0	0-0	0-0	1-0	0-0	0-0	1-0
Kern	0-1	0-0	0-0	0-0	0-0	0-0	0-0	0-0	0-0	0-0	0-0	1-0	0-0	1-1
Niekro	1-1	1-2	0-0	1-0	0-2	3-1	1-1	1-0	2-1	0-1	0-1	0-1	1-0	11-11
Noles	0-0	0-0	1-0	0-0	0-0	0-1	0-0	0-1	1-0	1-0	0-0	0-0	0-0	3-2
Oelkers	1-0	0-0	0-0	0-1	0-1	1-0	0-0	0-0	0-0	1-0	0-0	0-0	0-1	3-3
Roman	1-1	0-0	0-0	0-0	0-0	0-0	0-1	0-0	0-0	0-0	0-0	0-0	0-0	1-2
Schrom	2-0	0-1	2-0	1-0	1-3	1-0	0-1	0-0	0-0	2-0	3-0	1-0	1-2	14-7
Schulze	0-0	0-2	0-0	0-0	0-0	0-0	0-0	1-1	1-0	0-0	0-0	1-0	1-1	4-4
Swindell	0-0	0-1	1-0	0-0	0-0	0-0	1-0	1-1	0-0	1-0	1-0	0-0	0-0	5-2
Wills	1-0	0-1	0-1	0-0	0-0	0-0	0-0	0-0	0-1	1-0	2-0	0-0	0-1	4-4
Yett	0-0	0-0	1-1	2-0	0-0	0-0	0-0	0-0	0-1	1-0	0-0	1-1	0-0	5-3
Totals	9-4	3-10	6-6	7-5	4-9	8-4	8-5	6-6	5-8	10-2	9-3	6-6	3-10	84-78

No Decisions—Ritter.

DETROIT—87-75

Pitcher	Balt. W-L	Bos. W-L	Cal. W-L	Chi. W-L	Clev. W-L	K.C. W-L	Mil. W-L	Min. W-L	N.Y. W-L	Oak. W-L	Sea. W-L	Tex. W-L	Tor. W-L	Totals W-L
Campbell	0-1	0-1	0-1	0-1	0-1	0-0	2-0	0-0	0-0	0-1	1-0	0-0	0-0	3-6
Cary	0-0	0-0	0-0	0-0	0-0	0-0	0-0	0-0	0-0	1-0	0-1	0-0	0-1	1-2
Hernandez	1-0	1-0	0-1	0-0	1-0	2-3	1-0	0-0	0-1	1-0	0-0	1-0	0-2	8-7
Kelly	1-0	0-0	0-0	0-0	0-0	0-0	0-0	0-0	0-1	0-0	0-1	0-0	0-0	1-2
King	3-0	0-1	0-1	0-0	1-0	1-1	1-0	1-0	0-1	0-0	2-0	1-0	1-0	11-4
LaPoint	0-0	0-0	2-0	0-0	0-0	0-1	0-1	0-0	1-0	0-2	0-0	0-1	0-1	3-6
Morris	2-0	3-1	0-1	2-1	2-1	1-0	2-1	2-1	1-0	2-0	1-0	1-2	2-0	21-8
O'Neal	1-0	0-1	1-0	1-2	0-0	0-1	0-0	0-2	0-0	0-0	0-0	0-0	0-1	3-7
Petry	0-0	0-1	1-2	1-0	0-1	0-0	0-1	1-0	1-0	0-2	0-2	1-0	0-1	5-10
Scherrer	0-0	0-0	0-0	0-0	0-0	0-0	0-0	0-0	0-1	0-0	0-0	0-0	0-0	0-1
Tanana	2-0	1-1	0-0	0-1	2-1	1-0	1-1	1-1	1-1	0-0	1-1	1-1	1-1	12-9
Terrell	2-0	1-1	1-1	1-1	1-0	0-1	1-1	2-0	2-2	1-1	1-1	2-1	0-2	15-12
Thurmond	0-0	0-0	0-0	1-0	2-0	0-0	0-0	0-1	0-0	1-0	0-0	0-0	0-0	4-1
Totals	12-1	6-7	5-7	6-6	9-4	5-7	8-5	7-5	6-7	6-6	6-6	7-5	4-9	87-75

No Decisions—Lazorko, Pacella.

KANSAS CITY—76-86

Pitcher	Balt. W-L	Bos. W-L	Cal. W-L	Chi. W-L	Clev. W-L	Det. W-L	Mil. W-L	Min. W-L	N.Y. W-L	Oak. W-L	Sea. W-L	Tex. W-L	Tor. W-L	Totals W-L
Bankhead	0-0	0-0	1-1	2-0	0-1	1-1	1-0	1-1	1-1	0-0	0-1	0-2	1-1	8-9
Black	1-1	0-1	0-2	2-0	0-1	0-0	0-0	0-0	0-2	1-1	0-1	0-0	1-1	5-10
Farr	0-0	0-0	0-0	1-0	1-0	2-1	1-0	0-0	1-0	1-0	1-0	0-2	0-1	8-4
Gubicza	1-1	2-1	1-0	0-0	1-0	0-1	1-1	1-0	1-1	1-0	1-0	2-0	0-1	12-6
H'sheimer	0-0	0-0	0-0	0-0	0-0	0-0	0-0	0-0	0-1	0-0	0-0	0-0	0-0	0-1
Huismann	0-0	0-0	0-0	0-1	0-0	0-0	0-0	0-0	0-0	0-0	0-0	0-0	0-0	0-1
Jackson	2-0	1-1	1-1	0-2	0-1	1-0	1-2	0-3	1-0	2-1	0-0	2-0	0-1	11-12
Leibrandt	0-2	2-2	1-1	1-2	0-0	2-0	0-1	1-0	0-1	3-0	1-1	2-0	1-1	14-11
Leonard	1-1	0-0	0-2	0-0	1-1	0-2	1-1	1-1	0-1	0-0	1-2	1-1	2-1	8-13
Quisenberry	0-1	0-0	0-1	0-0	0-2	0-0	0-1	1-0	0-0	0-0	1-2	1-0	0-0	3-7
Saberhagen	1-0	1-1	1-0	0-2	1-2	1-0	1-0	1-2	0-1	0-3	0-1	0-0	0-0	7-12
Totals	6-6	6-6	5-8	6-7	4-8	7-5	6-6	6-7	4-8	8-5	5-8	8-5	5-7	76-86

No Decisions—Cone, Shields.

MILWAUKEE—77-84

Pitcher	Balt. W-L	Bos. W-L	Cal. W-L	Chi. W-L	Clev. W-L	Det. W-L	K.C. W-L	Min. W-L	N.Y. W-L	Oak. W-L	Sea. W-L	Tex. W-L	Tor. W-L	Totals W-L
Birkbeck	1-0	0-0	0-0	0-0	0-0	0-0	0-1	0-0	0-0	0-0	0-0	0-0	0-0	1-1
Bosio	0-0	0-0	0-0	0-1	0-1	0-1	0-0	0-1	0-0	0-0	0-0	0-0	0-0	0-4

Pitcher	Balt. W-L	Bos. W-L	Cal. W-L	Chi. W-L	Clev. W-L	Det. W-L	K.C. W-L	Min. W-L	N.Y. W-L	Oak. W-L	Sea. W-L	Tex. W-L	Tor. W-L	Totals W-L
Clear	0-0	0-1	1-0	1-0	0-0	0-1	1-1	2-0	0-1	0-1	0-0	0-0	0-0	5-5
Clutterbuck	0-0	0-0	0-0	0-1	0-0	0-0	0-0	0-0	0-0	0-0	0-0	0-0	0-0	0-1
Cocanower	0-0	0-0	0-0	0-0	0-0	0-0	0-0	0-0	0-1	0-0	0-0	0-0	0-0	0-1
Darwin	0-1	0-1	1-1	1-2	0-0	0-1	1-0	0-0	1-0	1-0	0-1	0-1	1-0	6-8
Gibson	0-0	0-0	0-0	0-0	0-0	1-1	0-0	0-0	0-0	0-0	0-0	0-1	0-0	1-2
Higuera	1-1	1-1	1-1	2-0	1-1	2-1	3-0	1-1	2-1	2-1	1-1	1-1	2-1	20-11
Johnson	0-0	0-0	0-0	1-0	0-0	0-0	0-0	0-0	0-0	0-0	0-0	0-1	1-0	2-1
Knudson	0-0	0-1	0-0	0-0	0-0	0-0	0-0	0-0	0-0	0-0	0-0	0-0	0-0	0-1
Leary	0-1	3-0	0-0	1-0	0-1	2-0	0-1	0-1	1-0	0-3	2-2	2-2	1-1	12-12
McClure	0-0	0-0	0-0	0-0	0-1	0-0	0-0	0-0	1-0	1-0	0-0	0-0	0-0	2-1
Nieves	1-1	1-1	3-1	0-0	1-1	0-1	0-2	1-2	1-1	0-1	2-0	0-1	1-0	11-12
Plesac	2-1	0-0	0-1	1-1	1-1	0-1	1-0	0-1	2-0	1-0	1-0	1-0	0-1	10-7
Searage	0-0	0-0	0-0	0-0	0-0	0-0	0-0	0-0	0-0	0-0	0-0	0-1	0-0	0-1
Vuckovich	1-0	0-1	0-0	0-0	1-0	0-1	0-0	0-1	0-0	0-0	0-0	0-0	0-1	2-4
Wegman	1-1	1-0	1-1	0-0	1-2	0-0	0-1	0-1	0-1	0-1	0-2	0-0	1-2	5-12
Totals	7-6	6-6	7-5	7-5	5-8	5-8	6-6	4-8	8-5	5-7	6-6	4-8	7-6	77-84

MINNESOTA—71-91

Pitcher	Balt. W-L	Bos. W-L	Cal. W-L	Chi. W-L	Clev. W-L	Det. W-L	K.C. W-L	Mil. W-L	N.Y. W-L	Oak. W-L	Sea. W-L	Tex. W-L	Tor. W-L	Totals W-L
Agosto	0-1	0-0	0-0	0-0	0-0	0-0	0-1	0-0	1-0	0-0	0-0	0-0	0-0	1-2
Anderson	0-0	0-0	0-1	1-1	0-1	0-2	1-0	0-0	1-0	0-0	0-0	0-0	0-1	3-6
Atherton	0-0	1-0	0-0	0-0	1-0	0-0	1-0	0-1	0-0	0-2	1-2	1-0	0-3	5-8
Blyleven	2-0	0-0	3-0	1-1	1-1	1-3	2-2	3-0	1-3	1-0	1-0	0-2	1-2	17-14
Butcher	0-0	0-0	0-1	0-0	0-0	0-1	0-0	0-0	0-0	0-1	0-0	0-0	0-0	0-3
Davis	0-0	0-1	0-3	1-0	0-0	0-0	0-0	0-1	0-0	1-0	0-0	0-1	0-0	2-6
Frazier	0-0	0-1	0-0	0-0	0-0	0-0	0-0	0-0	0-0	0-0	0-0	1-0	0-0	1-1
Heaton	0-2	0-2	0-0	0-2	0-0	0-0	0-0	2-0	1-1	0-1	0-1	1-0	0-0	4-9
Jackson	0-0	0-0	0-0	0-0	0-0	0-0	0-0	0-0	0-0	0-0	0-0	0-1	0-0	0-1
Latham	0-0	0-0	0-0	0-0	0-0	0-0	0-0	0-0	0-0	0-1	0-0	0-0	0-0	0-1
Pastore	0-1	0-0	1-0	0-0	0-0	0-0	0-0	1-0	0-0	0-0	0-0	0-0	1-0	3-1
Portugal	0-0	1-2	0-0	0-1	2-1	0-0	1-0	0-1	0-2	0-0	1-1	0-2	1-0	6-10
Smith	0-0	0-0	0-1	0-0	0-0	0-0	0-0	0-0	0-0	0-1	0-0	0-0	0-0	0-2
Smithson	1-1	0-1	0-1	3-0	0-2	2-1	2-2	2-0	0-1	2-1	1-2	0-1	0-1	13-14
Viola	1-3	0-3	2-0	1-1	2-1	2-0	0-1	0-1	0-1	2-0	2-1	3-0	1-1	16-13
Totals	4-8	2-10	6-7	7-6	6-6	5-7	7-6	8-4	4-8	6-7	6-7	6-7	4-8	71-91

No Decisions—Burtt, Fontenot.

NEW YORK—90-72

Pitcher	Balt. W-L	Bos. W-L	Cal. W-L	Chi. W-L	Clev. W-L	Det. W-L	K.C. W-L	Mil. W-L	Min. W-L	Oak. W-L	Sea. W-L	Tex. W-L	Tor. W-L	Totals W-L
Armstrong	0-0	0-0	0-0	0-0	0-0	0-0	0-0	0-0	0-0	0-1	0-0	0-0	0-0	0-1
Drabek	1-0	1-1	1-1	0-1	0-0	0-1	1-0	0-2	1-1	0-0	0-1	1-0	1-0	7-8
Fisher	1-1	1-0	0-0	1-1	2-0	0-0	1-0	0-1	0-0	1-0	0-0	0-0	2-2	9-5
Guidry	0-1	1-1	0-0	0-1	1-1	1-3	1-1	2-0	1-0	0-2	0-0	1-1	1-1	9-12
Holland	0-0	0-0	1-0	0-0	0-0	0-0	0-0	0-0	0-0	0-0	0-0	0-0	0-0	1-0
John	0-1	0-0	0-0	1-0	1-0	0-0	1-0	0-0	1-0	1-0	0-2	0-0	0-0	5-3
Niekro	0-0	0-1	1-2	2-0	2-0	1-0	0-0	0-2	1-0	1-1	1-1	0-1	0-2	9-10
Nielsen	0-0	1-1	0-0	0-1	0-0	0-0	0-0	0-1	1-1	0-0	0-0	1-0	1-0	4-4
Pulido	0-0	0-0	0-0	0-0	0-0	1-0	0-0	0-0	0-0	0-0	0-0	0-1	0-0	1-1
Rasmussen	2-0	3-0	0-2	2-0	0-0	1-1	1-2	1-0	2-1	1-0	3-0	1-0	1-0	18-6
Righetti	1-0	0-0	1-2	0-0	0-2	1-1	1-0	1-1	0-0	1-1	0-0	1-0	1-1	8-8
Scurry	0-0	0-0	0-0	0-0	1-0	0-0	0-0	0-1	0-0	0-1	0-0	0-0	0-0	1-2
Shirley	0-0	0-1	0-0	0-1	0-1	0-0	0-0	0-0	0-0	0-0	0-0	0-1	0-0	0-4
Stoddard	1-0	0-0	0-0	0-0	1-0	0-0	0-0	0-0	0-0	0-1	2-0	0-0	0-0	4-1
Tewksbury	2-1	1-0	0-0	0-1	0-1	1-0	1-0	1-0	0-1	0-0	1-0	2-1	0-0	9-5
Whitson	0-1	0-0	1-0	0-0	0-0	1-0	1-1	0-0	1-0	0-0	1-0	0-0	0-0	5-2
Totals	8-5	8-5	5-7	6-6	8-5	7-6	8-4	5-8	8-4	5-7	8-4	7-5	7-6	90-72

No Decisions—Arnsberg, Montefusco.

OAKLAND—76-86

Pitcher	Balt. W-L	Bos. W-L	Cal. W-L	Chi. W-L	Clev. W-L	Det. W-L	K.C. W-L	Mil. W-L	Min. W-L	N.Y. W-L	Sea. W-L	Tex. W-L	Tor. W-L	Totals W-L
Andujar	1-0	2-0	1-3	1-0	1-0	1-0	1-1	2-0	1-1	0-1	1-0	0-0	0-1	12-7
Atherton	0-0	0-1	0-0	0-0	0-0	0-0	0-0	0-0	1-1	0-0	0-0	0-0	0-0	1-2
Bair	0-0	0-0	0-0	0-1	0-0	0-0	0-0	0-1	1-0	0-0	0-1	0-0	1-0	2-3
Codiroli	0-2	0-1	1-1	0-1	0-0	1-1	0-0	1-0	0-1	0-0	1-0	1-1	0-0	5-8
Haas	1-0	0-1	0-0	0-1	0-0	0-0	0-0	1-0	2-0	0-0	2-0	0-0	1-0	7-2
Howell	0-0	0-0	0-0	0-0	0-1	0-1	0-0	0-1	0-1	0-2	2-0	1-0	0-0	3-6
Krueger	0-0	0-0	0-0	0-0	0-1	0-0	0-0	0-0	0-0	1-0	0-0	0-0	0-1	1-2
Langford	0-1	0-2	0-2	0-1	0-2	0-0	0-1	0-0	0-0	0-0	1-0	0-1	0-0	1-10
Leiper	1-0	0-0	0-1	0-0	0-0	0-0	0-0	0-0	0-0	0-1	0-0	0-0	1-0	2-2
Mooneyham	1-0	0-0	0-0	1-0	0-2	0-0	0-2	1-0	0-0	0-0	0-1	0-0	1-0	4-5
Ontiveros	0-1	0-1	0-0	1-0	0-0	0-0	0-0	0-0	0-0	1-0	0-0	0-0	0-0	2-2
Plunk	1-0	0-0	0-1	0-0	0-0	0-1	1-0	0-2	0-0	0-1	0-0	1-1	1-1	4-7
Rijo	0-1	0-0	0-1	2-0	0-4	2-0	1-1	2-1	1-0	0-0	1-1	0-1	0-1	9-11
Rodriguez	0-0	0-0	0-0	1-0	0-0	0-0	0-0	0-0	0-0	0-0	0-0	0-2	0-0	1-2

Pitcher	Balt. W-L	Bos. W-L	Cal. W-L	Chi. W-L	Clev. W-L	Det. W-L	K.C. W-L	Mil. W-L	Min. W-L	N.Y. W-L	Sea. W-L	Tex. W-L	Tor. W-L	Totals W-L
Stewart	2-0	2-0	1-0	0-1	0-0	0-0	0-2	0-0	0-1	2-0	1-0	0-1	1-0	9-5
Von Ohlen	0-0	0-0	0-0	0-0	0-0	0-2	0-0	0-0	0-0	0-0	0-0	0-1	0-0	0-3
Young	0-0	1-1	0-1	0-2	1-0	2-1	2-1	0-0	1-1	3-0	1-0	0-2	2-0	13-9
Totals	7-5	5-7	3-10	6-7	2-10	6-6	5-8	7-5	7-6	7-5	10-3	3-10	8-4	76-86

No Decisions—Akerfelds, Arroyo, Birtsas, Dozier.

SEATTLE—67-95

Pitcher	Balt. W-L	Bos. W-L	Cal. W-L	Chi. W-L	Clev. W-L	Det. W-L	K.C. W-L	Mil. W-L	Min. W-L	N.Y. W-L	Oak. W-L	Tex. W-L	Tor. W-L	Totals W-L
Beattie	0-0	0-1	0-0	0-0	0-2	0-0	0-0	0-0	0-1	0-0	0-1	0-1	0-0	0-6
Best	0-0	0-0	0-0	0-0	0-0	0-0	0-0	0-0	1-1	0-1	1-0	0-1	0-0	2-3
Brown	0-0	0-0	0-0	0-0	0-0	0-1	0-0	0-0	0-0	0-1	0-0	0-0	0-0	0-2
Fireovid	0-0	0-0	0-0	1-0	0-0	0-0	0-0	1-0	0-0	0-0	0-0	0-0	0-0	2-0
Guetterman	0-0	0-0	0-0	0-1	0-0	0-1	0-0	0-0	0-0	0-0	0-0	0-2	0-0	0-4
Huismann	0-1	0-0	1-0	0-0	0-0	1-0	0-1	0-0	0-0	0-0	0-0	0-0	1-1	3-3
Ladd	0-0	1-0	2-2	0-1	0-1	0-0	1-0	0-0	1-0	0-0	1-1	0-1	2-0	8-6
Langston	1-2	0-1	0-3	2-1	1-1	2-1	3-0	0-2	0-1	2-0	1-1	0-1	0-0	12-14
Moore	3-1	2-1	0-0	0-0	0-2	0-1	0-1	0-2	2-0	1-1	0-1	2-0	1-3	11-13
Morgan	1-1	0-2	0-1	1-1	1-1	0-2	2-1	2-1	3-1	0-3	0-2	0-0	1-1	11-17
Nunez	0-0	0-1	0-0	0-0	0-1	0-0	0-0	0-0	0-0	0-0	0-0	1-0	0-0	1-2
Reed	0-0	1-0	0-0	0-0	0-0	0-0	0-0	2-0	0-0	0-0	0-0	0-0	1-0	4-0
Swift	0-0	0-1	0-1	0-3	0-0	1-0	0-1	0-1	0-0	1-0	0-0	0-1	0-1	2-9
Trujillo	1-0	0-0	0-0	0-1	0-1	1-0	1-0	0-0	0-0	0-0	0-0	0-0	0-0	3-2
Wilcox	0-1	0-1	0-1	0-0	0-0	0-0	0-1	0-0	0-2	0-1	0-1	0-0	0-0	0-8
Young	0-0	0-0	2-0	1-0	1-0	1-0	1-0	1-0	0-0	0-1	0-3	1-2	0-0	8-6
Totals	6-6	4-8	5-8	5-8	3-9	6-6	8-5	6-6	7-6	4-8	3-10	4-9	6-6	67-95

No Decisions—Mirabella.

TEXAS—87-75

Pitcher	Balt. W-L	Bos. W-L	Cal. W-L	Chi. W-L	Clev. W-L	Det. W-L	K.C. W-L	Mil. W-L	Min. W-L	N.Y. W-L	Oak. W-L	Sea. W-L	Tor. W-L	Totals W-L
Brown	0-0	0-0	0-0	0-0	0-0	0-0	0-0	0-0	0-0	0-0	1-0	0-0	0-0	1-0
Correa	0-0	1-2	0-2	2-0	0-2	1-0	1-1	2-1	0-1	1-1	3-1	1-1	0-2	12-14
Guzman	0-3	1-1	0-2	2-1	0-1	1-2	0-1	0-1	0-0	1-1	1-0	2-2	1-0	9-15
Harris	2-0	0-1	1-0	0-0	1-2	0-1	1-0	2-0	0-1	0-1	0-0	1-0	2-2	10-8
Henry	0-0	0-0	0-0	0-0	0-0	1-0	0-0	0-0	0-0	0-0	0-0	0-0	0-0	1-0
Hough	0-1	0-1	2-1	4-0	2-0	1-0	1-2	0-1	2-1	0-2	2-0	3-0	0-1	17-10
Loynd	0-0	0-1	0-0	0-1	1-0	0-0	0-0	1-0	0-0	0-0	0-0	0-0	0-0	2-2
Mahler	0-1	0-0	0-1	0-0	0-0	0-0	0-0	0-0	0-0	0-0	0-0	0-0	0-0	0-2
Mason	1-0	0-1	0-0	0-0	0-0	1-1	1-1	0-0	2-0	2-0	0-0	0-0	0-0	7-3
Meridith	0-0	0-0	0-0	0-0	0-0	0-0	0-0	0-0	0-0	0-0	1-0	0-0	0-0	1-0
Mohorcic	0-0	1-1	0-1	0-0	0-0	0-0	0-1	0-0	0-1	0-0	1-0	0-0	0-0	2-4
Russell	2-0	0-0	0-0	1-0	0-0	0-0	0-0	1-0	1-0	0-0	0-0	0-1	0-1	5-2
Williams	1-0	1-0	0-0	0-0	1-0	0-1	0-0	0-1	1-2	1-0	0-1	2-0	1-1	8-6
Witt	0-0	0-0	2-1	2-0	1-1	0-2	1-2	2-0	1-0	0-2	1-1	0-0	1-0	11-9
Wright	1-0	0-0	0-0	0-0	0-0	0-0	0-0	0-0	0-0	0-0	0-0	0-0	0-0	1-0
Totals	7-5	4-8	5-8	11-2	6-6	5-7	5-8	8-4	7-6	5-7	10-3	9-4	5-7	87-75

No Decisions—Rozema.

TORONTO—86-76

Pitcher	Balt. W-L	Bos. W-L	Cal. W-L	Chi. W-L	Clev. W-L	Det. W-L	K.C. W-L	Mil. W-L	Min. W-L	N.Y. W-L	Oak. W-L	Sea. W-L	Tex. W-L	Totals W-L
Acker	0-0	0-1	0-0	0-1	1-0	0-0	0-1	0-0	0-0	1-0	0-0	0-1	0-0	2-4
Alexander	0-1	0-2	1-0	0-0	0-0	1-0	1-0	1-0	0-1	0-0	0-0	0-0	1-0	5-4
Aquino	0-1	0-0	0-0	0-0	0-0	0-0	0-0	0-0	1-0	0-0	0-0	0-0	0-0	1-1
Caudill	0-0	0-0	0-0	0-0	0-0	0-0	0-0	0-0	0-0	1-0	0-2	1-1	0-1	2-4
Cerutti	1-0	1-0	0-0	0-1	2-0	0-0	0-0	2-0	1-0	1-1	0-1	1-1	0-0	9-4
Clancy	2-1	0-1	2-1	0-1	2-2	0-3	2-0	1-3	2-1	0-0	2-0	1-0	0-1	14-14
Clarke	0-0	0-0	0-0	0-0	0-0	0-0	0-0	0-0	0-0	0-0	0-1	0-0	0-0	0-1
Eichhorn	1-0	1-1	1-1	0-0	1-0	2-0	1-0	0-1	2-0	0-1	2-0	0-1	3-1	14-6
Gordon	0-0	0-0	0-0	0-0	0-0	0-0	0-0	0-0	0-0	0-1	0-0	0-0	0-0	0-1
Henke	1-1	0-0	1-0	1-0	1-0	1-0	0-0	1-1	1-1	0-1	0-0	1-1	1-0	9-5
J. Johnson	0-1	1-0	0-0	1-1	0-0	1-0	1-0	1-0	1-0	0-0	0-0	0-0	1-0	7-2
Key	0-3	1-1	1-1	2-2	1-0	2-1	1-0	0-0	0-0	3-1	0-2	2-0	1-0	14-11
Lamp	0-0	0-0	0-1	0-0	1-0	1-0	0-2	0-0	0-0	0-1	0-1	0-0	0-1	2-6
Stieb	0-0	2-0	0-2	2-0	1-1	1-0	1-2	0-2	0-1	0-1	0-1	0-1	0-1	7-12
Ward	0-0	0-1	0-0	0-0	0-0	0-0	0-0	0-0	0-0	0-0	0-0	0-0	0-0	0-1
Totals	5-8	6-7	6-6	6-6	10-3	9-4	7-5	6-7	8-4	6-7	4-8	6-6	7-5	86-76

No Decisions—Davis, Musselman.

1986 CHAMPIONSHIP SERIES

Including

Houston righthander Mike Scott was great, but the New York Mets had too much firepower for the Astros in the N.L. Championship Series.

Mets Outlast Stubborn Astros

By LARRY WIGGE

Mets catcher Gary Carter recalled a meeting of the minds in the 16th inning of Game 6 of the 1986 National League Championship Series. New York was leading Houston, 7-5, with two out, but the Astros had runners on first and third with Glenn Davis at the plate. No one on the Houston roster was more likely to blast a home run and tie the playoffs at three games apiece than the Astros' powerful first baseman.

"Keith Hernandez came to the mound with Jesse Orosco and myself," Carter said. "I could see that Jesse didn't have much left. So Keith said, 'Whatever you do, Gary, don't let Jesse throw Davis a fastball.' "

Hernandez, the Mets' slick-fielding first baseman and team leader, remembered that discussion a little differently.

"I told Kid (Carter), 'If you call for one more fastball, we're going to fight right here, in front of everybody,' " Hernandez recalled. "He said, 'Keith, we're not going to fight.' "

Thus enlightened, Carter called for a breaking ball. The pitch jammed Davis, who had slammed 31 homers and driven in 101 runs in the regular season. The first baseman made contact, though, slapping a single to center that pulled Houston to within one run, 7-6.

Orosco still had to record one more out, and up next was right fielder Kevin Bass, who also feasted on fastballs.

"My adrenaline was flowing," said Bass, who had hit 20 homers with 79 runs batted in that season. "That was a situation I was happy to be in. I felt the pressure was on him (Orosco)."

But Carter never gave Bass the chance to swing at his pitch.

"Jesse reached back for all he had and struck out Kevin Bass using six straight breaking pitches," Carter related in the Mets' victorious locker room in the Houston Astrodome.

While Carter was retelling this story, he had one hand on a bottle of champagne, the other in the vicinity of his back pocket.

"The ball's in there—the last ball from the last strikeout," he said. "And it's not leaving my back pocket. I'm going to have all the guys sign it on the flight home, and I'm never going to let go of it. That had to be the best game that ever lived."

When Orosco struck out Bass to clinch the N.L. pennant for the Mets, the longest game in postseason history was over. And after 16 innings and four hours, 42 minutes, it ended none too soon for the Mets.

"I was afraid he (Davis) was going to hit that pitch and we'd be playing all night," Mets third baseman Ray Knight said. "My legs are still shaking."

Relief also was evident in the Mets' clubhouse. The players knew they would not have to face Astros righthander Mike Scott, who had pitched a five-hit shutout in Game 1 and permitted only one run on three hits in Game 4. Scott, who was named the Most Valuable Player of the playoffs even though the Astros lost, was scheduled to pitch Game 7.

"I feel like I've been pardoned," Mets Manager Davey Johnson said. "We'd have no bullpen left for a seventh game, and I really don't want to see Scott again until next April."

The bullpen was the key advantage for the Mets in the pennant-clinching affair. Starter Bob Ojeda, who yielded the Astros three runs in the first inning on a run-scoring double by third baseman Phil Garner and RBI singles by Davis and left fielder Jose Cruz, departed after five innings. Righthander Rick Aguilera then hurled one-hit, shutout relief from the sixth through the eighth innings, and righthander Roger McDowell permitted just one hit over five innings before Orosco entered the game in the 14th. Aguilera and McDowell, in fact, retired 18 consecutive Houston batters in one stretch.

Astros starter Bob Knepper allowed only two hits and had the Mets shut out until the ninth. But pesky Lenny Dykstra opened that inning with a pinch-hit triple and scored on a single by Mookie Wilson. After Knepper retired Kevin Mitchell on a grounder, Hernandez doubled home another run. It was at that point that Astros Manager Hal Lanier called for relief ace Dave Smith.

"I just kind of fell apart," a forlorn Knepper said. "I should have gone after Dykstra (on a 1-2 count) with a fastball and punched him out right there. But I didn't. I threw a slider and hung it a bit over the plate."

Smith walked Carter and right fielder Darryl Strawberry before Knight hit a fly ball to right field. Hernandez scored after Bass' catch to send the 3-3 game into extra innings.

Smith and righthander Larry Andersen

held the Mets scoreless through the 13th inning. New York then went ahead in the 14th when righthander Aurelio Lopez took the mound for the Astros. A single by Carter, a walk to Strawberry and second baseman Wally Backman's single put New York on top, 4-3. But the Astros came right back to tie the game in their half of the inning when Billy Hatcher belted an Orosco delivery off the screen attached to the left-field foul pole.

Strawberry, who was hitless in four previous at-bats in the game, opened the fateful 16th with a pop-fly double that fell between center fielder Hatcher and second baseman Bill Doran. Hatcher appeared to get a late start on the ball.

"I was playing him to pull," Hatcher said. "When he popped it up, I couldn't get to it."

Knight singled to right to drive in Strawberry and took second on Bass' throw home, then went to third on reliever Jeff Calhoun's wild pitch. After Calhoun walked Backman, both runners advanced on another wild pitch, giving the Mets a 6-4 lead. Dykstra's single provided the Mets with the eventual winning run.

Orosco was to earn his third victory of the playoffs, but not before a scare in the bottom of the 16th.

The threat began when pinch-hitter Davey Lopes drew a one-out walk and went to second on a single by Doran. Hatcher singled to left-center, scoring Lopes. After Denny Walling forced Hatcher at second, Davis pulled the Astros to within one run with his single and set the stage for the Orosco-Bass confrontation and the game-ending strikeout.

"I'm drained, physically and emotionally," Carter said.

The Mets, who set an N.L. Championship Series record by winning with only a .189 batting average, had captured their first pennant since 1973. But most of all, they didn't have to worry about Scott.

Scott was a 14-27 pitcher in all or parts of four seasons with the Mets before being traded to Houston for outfielder Danny Heep in December 1982. After two mediocre seasons with the Astros, Scott learned to throw a split-finger fastball that transformed him into one of the league's best pitchers. The righthander put together back-to-back 18-victory seasons in '85 and '86 to become the Astros' ace.

Not to mention the Mets' tormentor. The N.L. East champs were completely befuddled by Scott's new pitch in the playoff opener, a 1-0 Houston victory.

The only run of the game came when Davis crushed a 1-0 pitch from Dwight

New York's Lenny Dykstra dances around third base after hitting a two-run, ninth-inning home run to beat Houston in Game 3 of the N.L. Championship Series.

Gooden, the previous year's N.L. Cy Young Award winner, over the center-field wall to open the second inning. But Scott made that slim lead stand by allowing only five hits and fanning 14 batters, matching the major league Championship Series record for strikeouts.

The Mets made some noise about Scott scuffing the ball, but they conceded that Scott dominated them. And plate umpire Doug Harvey, when asked by Carter to inspect the ball in the first inning, found no indication of illegal doctoring.

"The umpiring certainly didn't beat us," Johnson said. "Mike Scott beat us. Mike Scott pitched a great ball game. Dwight pitched just a good game."

Pitching continued to dominate the series in Game 2 as Ojeda and Nolan Ryan tossed zeroes through the first three innings. Ryan retired the first 10 batters he faced, including five on strikeouts, but the Mets reached him for two runs in the fourth. Backman and Hernandez singled with one out and Carter drove in the first run of the game with a double. Strawberry followed with a sacrifice fly to give the Mets a 2-0 lead.

The Mets added three more runs and knocked Ryan out of the game in the fifth. With one out, shortstop Rafael Santana singled but was forced at second when Ojeda failed to sacrifice. After Dykstra pulled a long foul ball down the right-field line, Ryan sent the little center fielder a message, whizzing a fastball past Dykstra's head. Dykstra brushed himself off, collected his thoughts and then singled. Backman followed with an RBI single, and Hernandez hit a two-run triple.

Ojeda scattered 10 hits while going the distance in New York's 5-1 triumph. The Astros scored their only run on Garner's run-scoring single in the seventh.

The turning point of the game might have been Ryan's purpose pitch to Dykstra, whose single showed the Mets that they could win a show of strength.

"I think it kind of woke us up," Dykstra said. "I know it woke me up."

Dykstra was a hero again when the teams moved to New York for Game 3. His dramatic two-run homer in the ninth inning lifted the Mets to a 6-5 victory and a 2-1 lead in the series.

The Astros looked like they were off to a cakewalk when they scored two runs in each of the first two innings of Game 3, with Walling and Cruz singling in runs in the first and Doran smashing a two-run homer off righthander Ron Darling in the second. But the Mets, who had been held to four singles in the first five innings by Knepper, rallied for four runs in the sixth to tie the contest.

Mitchell bounced a single over Walling's head at third base and Hernandez followed with a looper to center. Houston shortstop Craig Reynolds committed a costly error when he permitted Carter's grounder to roll under his glove, scoring Mitchell. Strawberry then hit a towering smash over the right-field wall for a three-run homer.

The Astros, however, retaliated in the seventh without getting a hit. Doran walked, ran to third when Knight made a throwing error on Hatcher's bunt and scored on Walling's grounder to second.

After Houston reliever Charlie Kerfeld set the Mets down in order in the eighth, Lanier called on his No. 1 reliever, Smith, to protect the Astros' 5-4 lead.

Leading off, Backman dragged a bunt down the first-base line that was fielded by Davis, but Backman avoided the tag with a sweeping slide. Lanier argued that Backman should be out because he left the basepath to avoid Davis' tag, but umpire Dutch Rennert disagreed and Backman had an infield hit.

With Heep pinch hitting for Santana, the Mets got a break when Houston catcher Alan Ashby had trouble handling one of Smith's deliveries and was charged with a passed ball. Backman advanced to second. After Heep flied out to center, Dykstra swaggered to the plate.

Dykstra fouled the first pitch back. Then he hit the next pitch over the right-field wall and into the Mets' bullpen for a game-winning homer.

Said Johnson: "Lenny does like to swing for the fences. I forgive him today, but he hits too many balls in the air. I keep telling him he could hit .350 if he hit more line drives and ground balls."

Dykstra, who had hit just nine previous big-league homers, danced gleefully around the bases.

"The last time I hit a home run in the bottom of the ninth inning to win a game was in Strat-O-Matic," Dykstra said.

Nevertheless, the impact of Dykstra's unlikely blast will stick forever with Hernandez, who said: "I'll be on my deathbed, dying, delirious, and I'll be yelling, 'Lenny, Lenny.' "

Ashby took the loss hard. He blamed himself for the passed ball in the ninth inning and for calling for Smith's forkball to Dykstra. But he made up for those mistakes in Game 4 by belting a two-run homer that sparked Houston to a 3-1 victory, knotting the series at two games apiece.

It was another exercise in futility for the Mets against Scott, who permitted only three hits and struck out five. Though Scott, returning on three days' rest, was less overpowering than in Game 1, he was no less effective. He did not give up a hit until Knight hit a two-out single in the fifth inning, and New York's only run scored on Heep's sacrifice fly in the eighth.

While Scott was bedeviling New York, Ashby provided more than enough runs in the second. But Ashby needed a break in order to get a chance to hit his two-run homer.

Davis had singled to lead off the second. With two out, Ashby lofted a 3-1 pitch from starter Sid Fernandez toward the seats in shallow left field. Knight had a chance to catch the ball, but Santana called him off at the last second and the ball fell untouched one row into the temporary seats. After fouling off a pitch, Ashby belted Fernandez's next delivery over the left-field fence. The Astros scored their other run in the fifth when shortstop Dickie Thon deposited a Fernandez pitch over the left-field wall.

With the series tied, the Mets once again claimed that Scott scuffed the baseballs. But the fact remained that they couldn't hit the hard-throwing righthander.

"He's been the most dominating pitcher this season," Lanier said. "Over his last six starts, he's been overwhelming."

The weather was overwhelming the next day. Rain forced the postponement of Game 5.

When the rain cleared from the New York area one day later, Lanier switched his scheduled starter from rookie Jim Deshaies to Ryan, baseball's all-time strikeout king. But neither Ryan's two-hit, 12-strikeout performance over nine innings nor Gooden's 10 solid innings was good enough to decide this contest. The game ended in the 12th inning when Carter ended a personal 1-for-21 slump with an RBI single that gave the Mets a 2-1 victory and a 3-2 lead in the series.

The loss might have been a victory for the Astros if not for a miscue by first-base umpire Fred Brocklander. With runners on first and third with one out in the second inning of a scoreless game, Brocklander called Reynolds out at first base to complete a double play. The television replays clearly showed that Reynolds had beaten Santana's relay throw to Hernandez, but Brocklander's call negated a Houston run.

Nonetheless, the Astros jumped on top when Backman took too long to complete a double play with one out in the fifth. Ashby stroked a leadoff double, went to third on a single by Reynolds and scored on a one-out, fielder's-choice grounder to second by Doran. But the Mets tied the game, 1-1, in their half of the fifth on Strawberry's homer, which barely cleared the right-field wall near the foul pole.

Until that hit, Ryan was pitching a perfect game, and the righthander surrendered only one more single and one walk before giving way to Kerfeld in the 10th. Orosco relieved Gooden in the 11th and recorded his second series victory when New York rallied in the bottom of the 12th. With one out, Backman slashed a single off Walling's glove at third and ran to second when Kerfeld's pickoff attempt was wild. Lanier ordered an intentional walk to Hernandez to get to Carter, but the slumping catcher rifled a single up the middle to put the Mets one victory away from the World Series.

GAME OF WEDNESDAY, OCTOBER 8, AT HOUSTON (N)

New York	AB.	R.	H.	RBI.	PO.	A.
Dykstra, cf	3	0	1	0	1	0
Backman, 2b	4	0	0	0	1	1
Hernandez, 1b	4	0	1	0	5	2
Carter, c	4	0	0	0	7	0
Strawberry, rf	4	0	1	0	3	0
Wilson, lf	4	0	0	0	4	0
Knight, 3b	4	0	0	0	1	2
Santana, ss	2	0	1	0	0	2
Mazzilli, ph	1	0	0	0	0	0
Orosco, p	0	0	0	0	0	0
Gooden, p	2	0	0	0	2	0
Heep, ph	1	0	1	0	0	0
Elster, pr-ss	0	0	0	0	0	0
Totals	33	0	5	0	24	7

Houston	AB.	R.	H.	RBI.	PO.	A.
Hatcher, cf	3	0	0	0	1	0
Doran, 2b	4	0	0	0	1	3
Walling, 3b	4	0	0	0	0	1
Davis, 1b	4	1	1	1	6	1
Bass, rf	4	0	2	0	1	0
Cruz, lf	4	0	1	0	2	0
Ashby, c	1	0	1	0	14	0
Reynolds, ss	3	0	2	0	1	0
Thon, ss	0	0	0	0	0	0
Scott, p	3	0	0	0	1	2
Totals	30	1	7	1	27	7

New York	000	000	000—0
Houston	010	000	00x—1

New York	IP.	H.	R.	ER.	BB.	SO.
Gooden (Loser)	7	7	1	1	3	5
Orosco	1	0	0	0	0	1

Houston	IP.	H.	R.	ER.	BB.	SO.
Scott (Winner)	9	5	0	0	1	14

Game-winning RBI—Davis.

Error—Reynolds. Double play—New York 1. Left on bases—New York 7, Houston 8. Two-base hit—Bass. Home run—Davis. Stolen bases—Hatcher, Dykstra, Bass, Strawberry. Umpires—Harvey, Weyer, Pulli, Rennert, West and Brocklander. Time—2:56. Attendance—44,131.

GAME OF THURSDAY, OCTOBER 9, AT HOUSTON (N)

New York	AB.	R.	H.	RBI.	PO.	A.
Dykstra, cf	5	1	2	0	2	0
Backman, 2b	5	2	2	1	5	2
Hernandez, 1b	3	1	2	2	9	0
Carter, c	5	0	1	1	6	0
Strawberry, rf	3	0	0	1	1	0
Wilson, lf	4	0	1	0	1	0
Knight, 3b	3	0	1	0	1	3
Santana, ss	4	0	1	0	1	5
Ojeda, p	4	1	0	0	1	2
Totals	36	5	10	5	27	12

Houston	AB.	R.	H.	RBI.	PO.	A.
Hatcher, cf	5	1	1	0	3	0
Doran, 2b	4	0	1	0	3	2
Garner, 3b	3	0	1	1	1	1
Davis, 1b	4	0	1	0	4	1
Bass, rf	3	0	2	0	1	0
Cruz, lf	4	0	1	0	3	0
Ashby, c	4	0	0	0	9	0
Thon, ss	4	0	2	0	2	2

	AB.	R.	H.	RBI.	PO.	A.
Ryan, p	1	0	0	0	0	1
Pankovits, ph	1	0	0	0	0	0
Andersen, p	0	0	0	0	1	0
Puhl, ph	1	0	1	0	0	0
Lopez, p	0	0	0	0	0	0
Kerfeld, p	0	0	0	0	0	0
Lopes, ph	1	0	0	0	0	0
Totals	35	1	10	1	27	7

New York .... 000 230 000—5
Houston .... 000 000 100—1

New York	IP.	H.	R.	ER.	BB.	SO.
Ojeda (Winner)	9	10	1	1	2	5

Houston	IP.	H.	R.	ER.	BB.	SO.
Ryan (Loser)	5	7	5	5	0	5
Andersen	2	1	0	0	1	2
Lopez	1⅓	2	0	0	2	1
Kerfeld	⅔	0	0	0	0	0

Game-winning RBI—Carter.

Errors—Hatcher, Davis. Double plays—New York 2, Houston 1. Left on bases—New York 8, Houston 9. Two-base hits—Bass, Carter, Dykstra. Three-base hit—Hernandez. Stolen base—Wilson. Sacrifice fly—Strawberry. Umpires—Weyer, Pulli, Rennert, West, Brocklander and Harvey. Time—2:40. Attendance—44,391.

GAME OF SATURDAY, OCTOBER 11, AT NEW YORK

Houston	AB.	R.	H.	RBI.	PO.	A.
Doran, 2b	4	2	2	2	1	1
Hatcher, cf	3	1	2	0	3	0
Walling, 3b	5	1	1	2	0	2
Davis, 1b	3	0	1	0	9	0
Bass, rf	3	0	0	0	4	0
Cruz, lf	3	0	1	1	2	0
Ashby, c	4	0	0	0	4	0
Reynolds, ss	2	1	1	0	2	3
Lopes, ph	1	0	0	0	0	0
Kerfeld, p	0	0	0	0	0	1
Smith, p	0	0	0	0	0	0
Knepper, p	3	0	0	0	0	1
Thon, ss	1	0	0	0	0	0
Totals	32	5	8	5	25	8

New York	AB.	R.	H.	RBI.	PO.	A.
Wilson, cf-lf	4	0	0	0	2	0
Mitchell, lf	4	1	2	0	1	0
Orosco, p	0	0	0	0	0	0
Hernandez, 1b	4	1	2	0	10	2
Carter, c	4	1	0	0	8	1
Strawberry, rf	4	1	2	3	1	0
Knight, 3b	4	0	1	0	0	3
Teufel, 2b	3	0	0	0	2	3
Backman, 2b	1	1	1	0	0	1
Santana, ss	3	0	0	0	2	4
Heep, ph	1	0	0	0	0	0
Darling, p	1	0	0	0	1	2
Mazzilli, ph	1	0	1	0	0	0
Aguilera, p	0	0	0	0	0	0
Dykstra, ph-cf	2	1	1	2	0	0
Totals	36	6	10	5	27	16

Houston .... 220 000 100—5
New York .... 000 004 002—6
One out when winning run scored.

Houston	IP.	H.	R.	ER.	BB.	SO.
Knepper	7	8	4	3	0	3
Kerfeld	1	0	0	0	0	1
Smith (Loser)	⅓	2	2	2	0	0

New York	IP.	H.	R.	ER.	BB.	SO.
Darling	5	6	4	4	2	5
Aguilera	2	1	1	0	2	1
Orosco (Winner)	2	1	0	0	1	2

Game-winning RBI—Dykstra.

Errors—Reynolds, Knight. Double play—New York 1. Left on bases—Houston 7, New York 5. Home runs—Doran, Strawberry, Dykstra. Stolen bases—Hatcher 2, Bass. Sacrifice hit—Hatcher. Hit by pitcher—By Darling (Davis). Wild pitch—Darling. Passed balls—Ashby 2. Umpires—Pulli, Rennert, West, Brocklander, Harvey and Weyer. Time—2:55. Attendance—55,052.

GAME OF SUNDAY, OCTOBER 12, AT NEW YORK (N)

Houston	AB.	R.	H.	RBI.	PO.	A.
Doran, 2b	4	0	0	0	2	3
Hatcher, cf	4	0	0	0	2	0
Garner, 3b	3	0	0	0	0	3
Walling, ph-3b	1	0	1	0	0	0
Davis, 1b	3	1	1	0	14	1
Bass, rf	3	0	0	0	1	0
Cruz, lf	4	0	0	0	1	0
Ashby, c	3	1	1	2	5	0
Thon, ss	3	1	1	1	1	4
Scott, p	3	0	0	0	1	2
Totals	31	3	4	3	27	13

New York	AB.	R.	H.	RBI.	PO.	A.
Dykstra, cf	4	0	1	0	5	0
Backman, 2b	4	0	0	0	2	2
Hernandez, 1b	4	0	0	0	9	0
Carter, c	4	0	0	0	7	0
Strawberry, rf	3	0	0	0	1	0
Wilson, lf	3	1	1	0	2	0
Knight, 3b	3	0	1	0	1	3
Santana, ss	2	0	0	0	0	3
Heep, ph	0	0	0	1	0	0
Sisk, p	0	0	0	0	0	0
Fernandez, p	1	0	0	0	0	0
Mazzilli, ph	1	0	0	0	0	0
McDowell, p	0	0	0	0	0	0
Johnson, ph	1	0	0	0	0	0
Elster, ss	0	0	0	0	0	1
Totals	30	1	3	1	27	9

Houston .... 020 010 000—3
New York .... 000 000 010—1

Houston	IP.	H.	R.	ER.	BB.	SO.
Scott (Winner)	9	3	1	1	0	5

New York	IP.	H.	R.	ER.	BB.	SO.
Fernandez (Loser)	6	3	3	3	1	5
McDowell	2	0	0	0	0	1
Sisk	1	1	0	0	1	0

Game-winning RBI—Ashby.

Error—Scott. Left on bases—Houston 3, New York 3. Two-base hit—Walling. Home runs—Ashby, Thon. Stolen base—Backman. Sacrifice fly—Heep. Umpires—Rennert, West, Brocklander, Harvey, Weyer and Pulli. Time—2:23. Attendance—55,038.

GAME OF TUESDAY, OCTOBER 14, AT NEW YORK

Houston	AB.	R.	H.	RBI.	PO.	A.
Doran, 2b	4	0	1	1	1	2
Hatcher, cf	3	0	1	0	0	0
Walling, 3b	5	0	1	0	1	1
Davis, 1b	5	0	0	0	8	0
Bass, rf	5	0	2	0	6	0
Cruz, lf	5	0	1	0	2	0
Ashby, c	5	1	1	0	15	0
Reynolds, ss	4	0	1	0	1	2
Thon, ph-ss	1	0	0	0	0	0
Ryan, p	3	0	0	0	0	1
Puhl, ph	1	0	1	0	0	0
Kerfeld, p	0	0	0	0	0	0
Totals	41	1	9	1	34	6

New York	AB.	R.	H.	RBI.	PO.	A.
Dykstra, cf	5	0	0	0	1	0
Backman, 2b	5	1	1	0	0	9
Hernandez, 1b	4	0	1	0	14	1
Carter, c	5	0	1	1	6	1
Strawberry, rf	3	1	1	1	2	0
Wilson, lf	4	0	0	0	5	1
Orosco, p	0	0	0	0	0	1
Knight, 3b	4	0	0	0	1	1
Santana, ss	3	0	0	0	6	3
Mazzilli, ph	1	0	0	0	0	0
Elster, ss	0	0	0	0	0	0
Gooden, p	3	0	0	0	1	2
Heep, lf	1	0	0	0	0	0
Totals	38	2	4	2	36	19

Houston .... 000 010 000 000—1
New York..................... 000 010 000 001—2

One out when winning run scored.

Houston	IP.	H.	R.	ER.	BB.	SO.
Ryan	9	2	1	1	1	12
Kerfeld (Loser)	2⅓	2	1	1	1	3

New York	IP.	H.	R.	ER.	BB.	SO.
Gooden	10	9	1	1	2	4
Orosco (Winner)	2	0	0	0	0	2

Game-winning RBI—Carter.

Error—Kerfeld. Double plays—New York 2. Left on bases—Houston 7, New York 4. Two-base hit—Ashby. Home run—Strawberry. Stolen bases—Doran, Puhl. Caught stealing—Bass. Sacrifice hit—Hatcher. Umpires—West, Brocklander, Harvey, Weyer, Pulli and Rennert. Time—3:45. Attendance—54,986.

GAME OF WEDNESDAY, OCTOBER 15, AT HOUSTON

New York	AB.	R.	H.	RBI.	PO.	A.
Wilson, cf-lf	7	1	1	1	2	0
Mitchell, lf	4	0	0	0	2	0
Elster, ss	3	0	0	0	2	2
Hernandez, 1b	7	1	1	1	20	7
Carter, c	5	0	2	0	8	3
Strawberry, rf	5	2	1	0	1	0
Knight, 3b	6	1	1	2	1	7
Teufel, 2b	3	0	1	0	0	5
Backman, ph-2b	2	1	1	1	1	2
Santana, ss	3	0	1	0	4	1
Heep, ph	1	0	0	0	0	0
McDowell, p	1	0	0	0	3	1
Johnson, ph	1	0	0	0	0	0
Orosco, p	0	0	0	0	1	0
Ojeda, p	1	0	0	0	1	2
Mazzilli, ph	1	0	0	0	0	0
Aguilera, p	0	0	0	0	1	1
Dykstra, ph-cf	4	1	2	1	1	0
Totals	54	7	11	6	48	31

Houston	AB.	R.	H.	RBI.	PO.	A.
Doran, 2b	7	1	2	0	1	6
Hatcher, cf	7	2	3	2	2	0
Garner, 3b	3	1	1	1	0	5
Walling, ph-3b	4	0	0	0	2	2
Davis, 1b	7	1	3	2	21	0
Bass, rf	6	0	1	0	3	0
Cruz, lf	6	0	1	1	1	0
Ashby, c	6	0	0	0	12	1
Thon, ss	3	0	0	0	3	3
Reynolds, ph-ss	3	0	0	0	3	3
Knepper, p	2	0	0	0	0	2
Smith, p	0	0	0	0	0	0
Puhl, ph	1	0	0	0	0	0
Andersen, p	0	0	0	0	0	2
Pankovits, ph	1	0	0	0	0	0
Lopez, p	0	0	0	0	0	1
Calhoun, p	0	0	0	0	0	0
Lopes, ph	0	1	0	0	0	0
Totals	56	6	11	6	48	25

N. York..... 000 000 003 000 010 3—7
Houston..... 300 000 000 000 010 2—6

New York	IP.	H.	R.	ER.	BB.	SO.
Ojeda	5	5	3	3	2	1
Aguilera	3	1	0	0	0	1
McDowell	5	1	0	0	0	2
Orosco (Winner)	3	4	3	3	1	5

Houston	IP.	H.	R.	ER.	BB.	SO.
Knepper	8⅓	5	3	3	1	6
Smith	1⅔	0	0	0	3	2
Andersen	3	0	0	0	1	1
Lopez (Loser)	2*	5	3	3	2	2
Calhoun	1	1	1	1	1	0

*Pitched to two batters in sixteenth.

Game-winning RBI—Knight.

Error—Bass. Double plays—Houston 2. Left on bases—New York 9, Houston 5. Two-base hits—Garner, Davis, Hernandez, Strawberry. Three-base hit—Dykstra. Home run—Hatcher. Stolen base—Doran. Caught stealing—Bass 2. Sacrifice hit—Orosco. Sacrifice fly—Knight. Wild pitches—Calhoun 2. Umpires—Brocklander, Harvey, Weyer, Pulli, Rennert and West. Time—4:42. Attendance—45,718.

NEW YORK METS' BATTING AND FIELDING AVERAGES

Player—Position	G.	AB.	R.	H.	TB.	2B.	3B.	HR.	RBI.	B.A.	PO.	A.	E.	F.A.
Dykstra, cf-ph	6	23	3	7	13	1	1	1	3	.304	10	0	0	1.000
Hernandez, 1b	6	26	3	7	10	1	1	0	3	.269	67	12	0	1.000
Mitchell, lf	2	8	1	2	2	0	0	0	0	.250	3	0	0	1.000
Heep, ph-lf	5	4	0	1	1	0	0	0	1	.250	0	0	0	.000
Backman, 2b-ph	6	21	5	5	5	0	0	0	2	.238	9	17	0	1.000
Strawberry, rf	6	22	4	5	12	1	0	2	5	.227	9	0	0	1.000
Mazzilli, ph	5	5	0	1	1	0	0	0	0	.200	0	0	0	.000
Santana, ss	6	17	0	3	3	0	0	0	0	.176	13	18	0	1.000
Knight, 3b	6	24	1	4	4	0	0	0	2	.167	5	19	1	.960
Teufel, 2b	2	6	0	1	1	0	0	0	0	.167	2	8	0	1.000
Carter, c	6	27	1	4	5	1	0	0	2	.148	42	5	0	1.000
Wilson, lf-cf	6	26	2	3	3	0	0	0	1	.115	16	1	0	1.000
Aguilera, p	2	0	0	0	0	0	0	0	0	.000	1	1	0	1.000
Orosco, p	4	0	0	0	0	0	0	0	0	.000	1	1	0	1.000
Sisk, p	1	0	0	0	0	0	0	0	0	.000	0	0	0	.000
Darling, p	1	1	0	0	0	0	0	0	0	.000	1	2	0	1.000
Fernandez, p	1	1	0	0	0	0	0	0	0	.000	0	0	0	.000
McDowell, p	2	1	0	0	0	0	0	0	0	.000	3	1	0	1.000
Johnson, ph	2	2	0	0	0	0	0	0	0	.000	0	0	0	.000
Elster, pr-ss	4	3	0	0	0	0	0	0	0	.000	2	3	0	1.000
Gooden, p	2	5	0	0	0	0	0	0	0	.000	3	2	0	1.000
Ojeda, p	2	5	1	0	0	0	0	0	0	.000	2	4	0	1.000
Totals	6	227	21	43	60	4	2	3	19	.189	189	94	1	.996

HOUSTON ASTROS' BATTING AND FIELDING AVERAGES

Player—Position	G.	AB.	R.	H.	TB.	2B.	3B.	HR.	RBI.	B.A.	PO.	A.	E.	F.A.
Puhl, ph	3	3	0	2	2	0	0	0	0	.667	0	0	0	.000
Reynolds, ss-ph	4	12	1	4	4	0	0	0	0	.333	7	8	2	.882
Bass, rf	6	24	0	7	9	2	0	0	0	.292	16	0	1	.941
Hatcher, cf	6	25	4	7	10	0	0	1	2	.280	11	0	1	.917
Davis, 1b	6	26	3	7	11	1	0	1	3	.269	62	3	1	.985
Thon, ss-ph	6	12	1	3	6	0	0	1	1	.250	6	9	0	1.000
Doran, 2b	6	27	3	6	9	0	0	1	3	.222	9	17	0	1.000
Garner, 3b	3	9	1	2	3	1	0	0	2	.222	1	9	0	1.000
Cruz, lf	6	26	0	5	5	0	0	0	2	.192	11	0	0	1.000
Walling, 3b-ph	5	19	1	3	4	1	0	0	2	.158	3	6	0	1.000
Ashby, c	6	23	2	3	7	1	0	1	2	.130	59	1	0	1.000
Andersen, p	2	0	0	0	0	0	0	0	0	.000	1	2	0	1.000
Calhoun, p	1	0	0	0	0	0	0	0	0	.000	0	0	0	.000
Lopez, p	2	0	0	0	0	0	0	0	0	.000	0	1	0	1.000
Kerfeld, p	3	0	0	0	0	0	0	0	0	.000	0	1	1	.500
Smith, p	2	0	0	0	0	0	0	0	0	.000	0	0	0	.000
Lopes, ph	3	2	1	0	0	0	0	0	0	.000	0	0	0	.000
Pankovits, ph	2	2	0	0	0	0	0	0	0	.000	0	0	0	.000
Ryan, p	2	4	0	0	0	0	0	0	0	.000	0	2	0	1.000
Knepper, p	2	5	0	0	0	0	0	0	0	.000	0	3	0	1.000
Scott, p	2	6	0	0	0	0	0	0	0	.000	2	4	1	.857
Totals	6	225	17	49	70	6	0	5	17	.218	188	66	7	.973

NEW YORK METS' PITCHING RECORDS

Pitcher	G.	GS.	CG.	IP.	H.	R.	ER.	BB.	SO.	HB.	WP.	W.	L.	Pct.	ERA.
McDowell	2	0	0	7	1	0	0	0	3	0	0	0	0	.000	0.00
Aguilera	2	0	0	5	2	1	0	2	2	0	0	0	0	.000	0.00
Sisk	1	0	0	1	1	0	0	1	0	0	0	0	0	.000	0.00
Gooden	2	2	0	17	16	2	2	5	9	0	0	0	1	.000	1.06
Ojeda	2	2	1	14	15	4	4	4	6	0	0	1	0	1.000	2.57
Orosco	4	0	0	8	5	3	3	2	10	0	0	3	0	1.000	3.38
Fernandez	1	1	0	6	3	3	3	1	5	0	0	0	1	.000	4.50
Darling	1	1	0	5	6	4	4	2	5	1	1	0	0	.000	7.20
Totals	6	6	1	63	49	17	16	17	40	1	1	4	2	.667	2.29

No shutouts or saves.

HOUSTON ASTROS' PITCHING RECORDS

Pitcher	G.	GS.	CG.	IP.	H.	R.	ER.	BB.	SO.	HB.	WP.	W.	L.	Pct.	ERA.
Andersen	2	0	0	5	1	0	0	2	3	0	0	0	0	.000	0.00
Scott	2	2	2	18	8	1	1	1	19	0	0	2	0	1.000	0.50
Kerfeld	3	0	0	4	2	1	1	1	4	0	0	0	1	.000	2.25
Knepper	2	2	0	15⅓	13	7	6	1	9	0	0	0	0	.000	3.52
Ryan	2	2	0	14	9	6	6	1	17	0	0	0	1	.000	3.86
Lopez	2	0	0	3⅓	7	3	3	4	3	0	0	0	1	.000	8.10
Smith	2	0	0	2	2	2	2	3	2	0	0	0	1	.000	9.00
Calhoun	1	0	0	1	1	1	1	1	0	0	2	0	0	.000	9.00
Totals	6	6	2	62⅔	43	21	20	14	57	0	2	2	4	.333	2.87

Shutout—Scott. No saves.

COMPOSITE SCORE BY INNINGS

New York	0 0 0	2 4 4	0 1 5	0 0 1	0 1 0	3	—21
Houston	5 5 0	0 2 0	2 0 0	0 0 0	0 1 0	2	—17

Game-winning RBIs—Carter 2, Davis, Dykstra, Ashby, Knight.

Sacrifice hits—Hatcher 2, Orosco.

Sacrifice flies—Strawberry, Heep, Knight.

Stolen bases—Hatcher 3, Bass 2, Doran 2, Dykstra, Strawberry, Wilson, Backman, Puhl.

Caught stealing—Bass 3.

Double plays—Santana, Backman and Hernandez 2; Backman and Hernandez; Thon, Doran and Davis; Knight, Teufel and Hernandez; Backman, Santana and Hernandez; Wilson and Santana; Thon and Davis; Doran, Reynolds and Davis.

Left on bases—New York 7, 8, 5, 3, 4, 9—36; Houston 8, 9, 7, 3, 7, 5—39.

Hit by pitcher—By Darling (Davis).

Passed balls—Ashby 2.

Time of games—First game, 2:56; second game, 2:40; third game, 2:55; fourth game, 2:23; fifth game, 3:45; sixth game, 4:42.

Attendance—First game, 44,131; second game, 44,391; third game, 55,052; fourth game, 55,038; fifth game, 54,986; sixth game, 45,718.

Umpires—Harvey, Weyer, Pulli, Rennert, West and Brocklander.

Official scorers—Red Foley, New York Daily News; John Wilson, Houston Chronicle-retired.

Boston reliever Calvin Schiraldi leaps for joy after recording the final out in the American League Championship Series.

Red Sox Burst Angels' Bubble

By LARRY WIGGE

More than 64,000 people were on their feet, ready to rejoice at a historic moment—the first California Angels pennant in the 26 years of the club's existence and Gene Mauch's first pennant in 25 years of managing.

One more strike. That's all the Angels needed.

The Angels held a three-games-to-one lead over the Boston Red Sox in the 1986 American League Championship Series. Mauch's team also held a 5-4 lead on this October 12 afternoon with one man on base and two out in the top of the ninth inning at Anaheim Stadium.

Angels ace reliever Donnie Moore was pitching to Dave Henderson with a 1-2 count.

Moore's next pitch was low. Ball two. The crowd gasped. The Angels' players, poised on the top step of the dugout and ready to race onto the field, gestured for Moore to get that final out.

Henderson fouled the next pitch to the left of the plate. More suspense. More noise. Then there was another foul ball. Still 2-and-2.

Stepping out of the batter's box, Henderson looked heavenward. The former Seattle Mariners outfielder had been pressed into duty when regular center fielder Tony Armas sprained his ankle earlier in the game. During the regular season with Seattle and Boston, Henderson was a .265 hitter with 15 homers and 47 runs batted in, but only one of those homers and three of those RBIs had come since his August 19 trade to the Red Sox. But this was, without a doubt, the biggest at-bat in the six-year major league career of the Dos Palos, Calif., native.

When Moore sent his third 2-2 delivery to the plate, Henderson took a mighty swing. In a matter of seconds, players were joyously jumping all over the field. But the happy players weren't wearing a halo on their caps.

Henderson had belted a two-run home run into the left-field seats, giving the Red Sox a 6-5 lead. It was poetic justice for Henderson, who had inadvertently knocked Bobby Grich's long drive over the center-field wall to give the Angels a 3-2 lead three innings earlier.

As Henderson did a leaping pirouette before going into his home run trot, you somehow had the feeling this wild and wonderful game was far from over.

Catcher Bob Boone singled off reliever Bob Stanley to start the bottom of the ninth for the Angels. Then pinch-runner Ruppert Jones was sacrificed to second by Gary Pettis. Joe Sambito replaced Stanley on the mound for Boston, but second baseman Rob Wilfong followed with a line single to right, scoring Jones and tying the game. Red Sox Manager John McNamara then called on righthander Steve Crawford, who worked out of a bases-loaded, one-out jam by retiring Doug DeCinces on a fly ball to right field and Grich on a soft liner back to the mound.

Moore was still pitching for California when the game went into the 11th inning. Leading off, designated hitter Don Baylor was hit by a pitch. Dwight Evans followed with a single to center. Rich Gedman, trying to sacrifice, was credited with a bunt single, loading the bases. That's when Henderson stepped up to the plate again.

Once more, Henderson wielded his magic wand, lofting Moore's first pitch into center field for a sacrifice fly. The heavens had frowned on the Angels and smiled on the Red Sox in this 7-6 victory.

"It was like having that guy, Michael Anthony from the 'Millionaire,' come to your door with a check in his hand, only to find out that he had the wrong address," California slugger Reggie Jackson said with a shrug.

"It was like we were on our deathbed and the preacher was reading the last rites," Boston pitcher Roger Clemens said. "Today, the preacher was about halfway through the Lord's Prayer."

By all rights, the Red Sox should have died that day. But they didn't. In fact, they needed no more late-inning heroics in capturing Game 6, 10-4, and Game 7, 8-1, to complete their dramatic comeback.

The Red Sox were a different team after Henderson hit his unforgettable home run. After batting .234 in the first four games of the playoffs, they hit .357 and outscored the Angels, 23-6, from the ninth inning of Game 5 through the last out of the series. The Red Sox had 36 hits and scored 25 runs in those final three games.

This unpredictable series began in Boston's Fenway Park with a dream pitching matchup—Clemens (24-4) for the Red Sox vs. Mike Witt (18-10) for the Angels. Instead of seeing a low-scoring affair, however, the Boston faithful were knocked for a loop when the Angels hammered Cle-

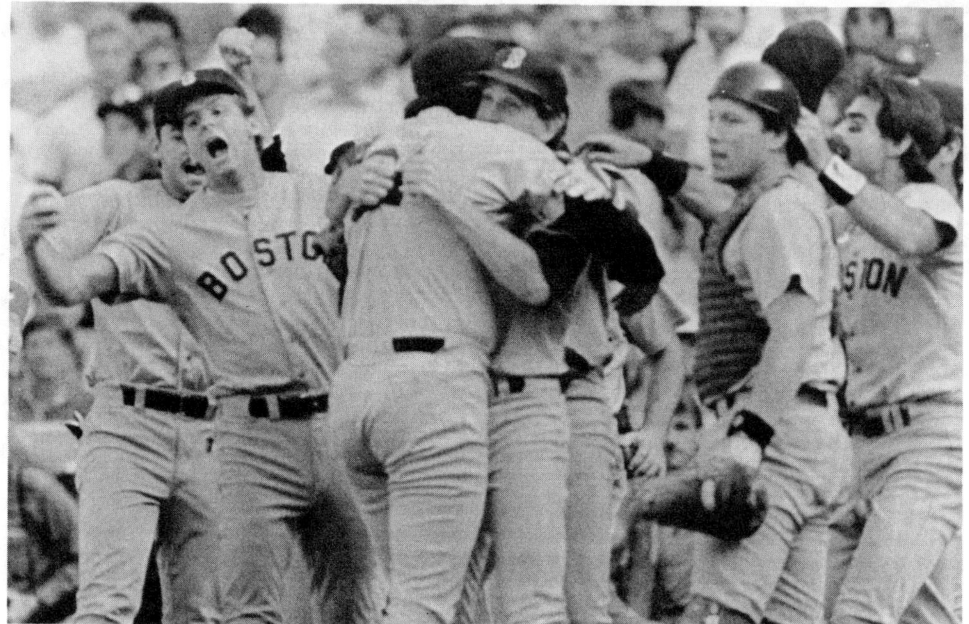

Boston players celebrate after their shocking comeback against California in the crucial fifth game of the A.L. Championship Series.

mens for 10 hits and eight runs in 7⅓ innings. Meanwhile, Witt pitched almost perfect baseball for six innings, retiring 16 batters in succession and not allowing a hit until two were out in the sixth.

Clemens opened the fateful second inning by striking out Wilfong and Dick Schofield. But he followed with a wild streak that included consecutive walks to Boone and Pettis.

Jones, starting in right field against the righthanded Clemens, put the Angels on top when he singled up the middle. Rookie first baseman Wally Joyner made it 2-0 with a double down the left-field line. With a count of 1-and-2 on left fielder Brian Downing, Clemens thought he had escaped further damage when he unleashed a hard slider near the edge of the plate. But umpire Larry Barnett indicated the belt-high pitch was just outside.

"That pitch was too close to take," said Downing, who then singled to left on a 3-2 delivery, scoring two more runs and giving the Angels a four-run cushion.

The Angels added to their lead in the third. Wilfong reached base on Boston shortstop Spike Owen's throwing error and came around on two-out singles by Boone and Pettis, making the score 5-0.

Boston got one run back on second baseman Marty Barrett's run-scoring single in the sixth. But the Angels scored three runs in the eighth on an RBI single by Boone and a two-run single by Downing.

"Even though I don't agree with the call Barnett made on Downing in the second inning, I don't have anyone to blame but myself for walking the eighth and ninth hitters," a dejected Clemens said after the Angels' 8-1 victory. "Walking the eighth and ninth hitters in the lineup will always come back to haunt you."

Meanwhile, Witt went the distance for California, limiting Boston to five hits.

The Red Sox tied the series with a 9-2 triumph in a wacky Game 2.

Third baseman Wade Boggs led off the bottom of the first with a wind-blown triple off the left-field wall and scored on a double by Barrett. The Red Sox made it 2-0 one inning later as Barrett again did the honors with a run-scoring single to left. Barrett's hit followed singles by Gedman, Owen and Boggs, but the nature of two of those hits kept the Red Sox from advancing more than one base at a time. Owen's grounder to short hit a rock and bounced over Schofield's head, while Angels pitcher Kirk McCaskill lost Boggs' chopper in the sun.

The Angels, however, knotted the count at 2-2 on Schofield's RBI single in the fourth and a homer by Joyner in the fifth. Joyner's homer was the first by a rookie in A.L. Championship Series history.

In the Boston half of the fifth, first baseman Bill Buckner hit a one-out single to center. With two out, Baylor walked and Evans followed with a pop fly just behind second base. Second baseman Grich, shortstop Schofield and center fielder Pettis converged on the ball, but it dropped out of Grich's reach when he lost it in the sun. Buckner scored the go-ahead run on Evans' double.

The Angels had a chance to even the count in the sixth when Grich, Schofield and Boone hit consecutive singles. But when Grich rounded third on Boone's hit, third-base coach Moose Stubing failed to indicate whether Grich should hold up or continue home. Grich was caught in a rundown when Boggs cut off left fielder Jim Rice's strong throw home and threw to Owen, who applied the tag.

The Red Sox scored three times in the seventh, thanks largely to fielding errors by Grich, Schofield and third baseman DeCinces. They added three more runs in the eighth on Buckner's sacrifice fly and Rice's two-run homer.

Bruce Hurst scattered 11 hits over nine innings while raising his record to 9-3 at home in '86, an unbelievable mark considering that Fenway Park's left-field wall normally gives lefthanders fits.

For both teams, which combined for five errors plus several other blunders that don't show up in box scores, it was a bizarre afternoon.

"I haven't seen a game like that since I pitched in the Little Leagues," said McCaskill, who was tagged with the loss.

When the scene shifted to Anaheim Stadium for Game 3, righthander Dennis (Oil Can) Boyd was singing much the same tune as Clemens did in Game 1. Boyd held a 1-0 lead going into the bottom of the sixth, but it wasn't the Jacksons or Joyners or Downings who inflicted the damage in California's 5-3 victory.

"The big guys who could hurt me didn't hurt me," Boyd said. "But I let the guys at the bottom of the lineup get me."

After DH Jackson's run-scoring single tied the contest, 1-1, in the sixth, the Angels scored three more runs in the seventh. With two out, Schofield blasted Boyd's first pitch over the fence in left-center field to give California the lead. After Boone singled to right, Pettis smashed a 2-1 delivery from Boyd into the right-field seats for another home run.

Moore replaced winning pitcher John Candelaria on the mound for the Angels in the eighth inning and surrendered two runs, one on a balk and the other on Gedman's run-scoring single. But the Angels increased their lead to 5-3 in their half of the eighth on a sacrifice fly by Jones.

Mauch wasn't in the dugout for any of his team's scoring. He had been ejected in the fourth inning while arguing with umpire Terry Cooney. The arbiter originally called Joyner safe on a play at the plate but later reversed his decision, enraging the California skipper.

"It was the best game I never saw," said Mauch, grinning.

In Game 4, which featured Clemens starting for the first time in his career on three days' rest against veteran Don Sutton, the Angels pulled off a stunning comeback to take a 3-1 lead in the series.

Thanks to Buckner's run-scoring double in the sixth and Barrett's RBI single and some costly California errors in the eighth, Clemens had a 3-0 lead heading into the bottom of the ninth. The righthander was working on a five-hit shutout when DeCinces opened the frame with a towering homer to left-center field. Schofield and Boone then hit consecutive one-out singles to left. With the tying runs on base, McNamara called on his relief ace, rookie Calvin Schiraldi.

Pettis greeted the righthander with a double off the left-field wall that Rice lost in the lights, scoring Schofield and sending Devon White, who was running for Boone, to third. After Jones was walked intentionally to load the bases, Schiraldi fanned Grich for the second out of the inning. Then, when the count reached 1-and-2 on Downing, Schiraldi heaved a pitch that hit Downing in the side, forcing home White with the tying run.

Reserve catcher Jerry Narron opened the Angels' 11th with a single and went to second on a sacrifice by Pettis. Jones again was walked intentionally, bringing Grich to the plate.

Grich, who had committed an error and bobbled another ball in Boston's two-run eighth and was hitless in five at-bats, smacked a fastball from Schiraldi into the left-field corner to score Narron and give the Angels a 4-3 victory.

"I'm just glad Bobby Grich did that because I was getting tired," said righthander Doug Corbett, who earned the victory with 3⅔ innings of shutout relief.

Schiraldi was in tears after the game. He was particularly downcast about hitting Downing with the pitch in the ninth.

"It was the stupidest pitch I ever made in my life," he said. "I screwed up. What else can I say?"

Less than 24 hours later, the Angels were all set to wrap up the series before Henderson pulled off his heroics to rally the Red Sox to a 7-6, 11-inning victory in the pivotal fifth game.

Gedman hit a two-run homer off Witt to put the Red Sox on top in the second inning. But Boone hit a solo homer off Hurst to cut the lead in half in the third. Then, with two out in the sixth, DeCinces doubled and Grich sent a drive to deep center that glanced off Henderson's glove and over the wall, giving the Angels a 3-2 lead.

"I had the ball in the palm of my glove, but then I lost it when my wrist hit the wall," Henderson said. "I should've held it."

The Angels scored two more runs in the seventh, one on an RBI double by Wilfong and another on Downing's sacrifice fly, setting the stage for the dramatic ninth.

Buckner led off that frame with a single. One out later, Baylor hit a two-run homer to cut the California lead to 5-4. Evans popped to DeCinces for the second out, but with Gedman coming up, lefthander Gary Lucas relieved Witt, who had surrendered three hits to the Boston catcher already that afternoon. Lucas hit Gedman with his first pitch.

At that point, Mauch went to his bullpen once again, calling on Moore. The rest is history. Henderson homered and then came back in the 11th with a game-winning sacrifice fly to rescue the Red Sox.

Schiraldi, who saved the victory for reliever Crawford by retiring the Angels in order in the 11th, said: "I really don't know what this does to California, but I know what it does to us. I think the momentum is on our side right now."

Indeed it was.

In Game 6, the Angels jumped on Boyd in the first inning with consecutive run-scoring doubles by Jackson and DeCinces. But the Red Sox, back in the friendly confines of Fenway Park, rallied against McCaskill in their half of the first to tie the game without the benefit of a hit. Boggs and Barrett led off with walks and scored on Boone's passed ball and a run-scoring groundout by Rice.

Boston added five runs on six hits in the third to knock out McCaskill. Barrett doubled home one run and Buckner and Evans contributed RBI singles, while two more runs scored on first baseman Grich's throwing error. The lead swelled to 8-2 in the fifth on an RBI groundout by Henderson, but California tallied on Downing's solo homer in the seventh. The Red Sox then went up, 10-3, in the bottom of the inning on a two-run triple by Owen, whose error accounted for the Angels' fourth and final run in the eighth.

With the momentum clearly on their side and Clemens on the mound for the third time, the Red Sox bombed the Angels, 8-1, in Game 7.

Boston got three unearned runs in the second inning, one scoring on a grounder by Gedman and two more on a single by Boggs. The Red Sox added four more unearned tallies against Candelaria in the fourth. After Pettis muffed a fly ball by Henderson for a three-base error, Owen singled home one run and, later in the inning, Rice clubbed a three-run homer. Right fielder Evans added a solo homer in the seventh.

Meanwhile, Clemens, who was 0-1 in his first two playoff starts, was at his best in limiting the Angels to four singles in seven innings and gaining his first postseason victory. California scored its only run in the eighth, when Clemens allowed a leadoff single to Jones and was relieved by Schiraldi, who gave up DeCinces' run-scoring single. Schiraldi pitched the final two innings, striking out five batters.

The loss was tough for Mauch and the Angels to swallow. Mauch, who managed the Philadelphia Phillies when they blew a big lead down the stretch in 1964, also directed the Angels in 1982, when they went up 2-0 in a best-of-five playoff format only to lose the next three games to the Milwaukee Brewers.

The Angels also had to deal with the loss of Joyner, who was hospitalized with a bacterial infection after Game 3. Joyner hit .455 with one homer and two RBIs in the first three games of the series.

Baylor, who was on the Angel team that lost to the Brewers in '82, said he heard some experts second-guessing Mauch for removing the righthanded Witt in the ninth inning of Game 5.

"The funny thing is we had a similar thing come up in Game 5 in 1982," Baylor said. "I'm not so sure it wasn't on Gene's mind. He had a righthander, Luis Sanchez, pitching in the seventh inning to Cecil Cooper. Everybody thought he should have brought in the lefthander, Andy Hassler. But he didn't, and Cooper got a single to drive in the tying and winning runs.

"This time Mauch brings in the lefthander to get one out. But Lucas has never pitched in a big game for him before. To come in and miss the strike zone by that much is rough. He (Mauch) did the right thing this time, and it backfired."

For the Red Sox, the triumph represented their first trip to the World Series since 1975. One of the players most responsible was Barrett, who batted .367, tied an A.L. playoff record with 11 hits, drove in five runs and was selected the Most Valuable Player of the series.

Another was Henderson, who would have been home watching the playoffs if not for Seattle's decision to trade him, and even so, he might have been in the dugout if not for Armas' injury. And then there was that boost he gave to Grich's homer that almost made him the goat instead of the hero of Game 5.

"I felt bad about it," Henderson admitted. "I was glad to get the chance to make up for not holding onto it."

Did he ever.

GAME OF TUESDAY, OCTOBER 7, AT BOSTON (N)

California	AB.	R.	H.	RBI.	PO.	A.
Jones, rf	4	1	1	1	2	0
Burleson, ph	1	0	0	0	0	0
White, rf	0	0	0	0	2	0
Joyner, 1b	4	1	2	1	8	0
Downing, lf	5	0	2	4	5	0
Jackson, dh	4	0	0	0	0	0
DeCinces, 3b	5	0	1	0	0	4
Wilfong, 2b	5	1	0	0	1	1
Schofield, ss	5	1	1	0	0	1
Boone, c	3	2	2	1	5	0
Pettis, cf	3	2	2	1	4	0
Witt, p	0	0	0	0	0	1
Totals	39	8	11	8	27	7

Boston	AB.	R.	H.	RBI.	PO.	A.
Boggs, 3b	3	0	1	0	2	0
Barrett, 2b	4	0	2	1	0	3
Buckner, 1b	4	0	0	0	9	2
Rice, lf	4	0	0	0	3	0
Baylor, dh	4	0	1	0	0	0
Evans, rf	4	0	0	0	1	0
Gedman, c	3	0	0	0	5	0
Armas, cf	3	0	0	0	4	0
Owen, ss	2	1	1	0	2	4
Clemens, p	0	0	0	0	1	0
Sambito, p	0	0	0	0	0	0
Stanley, p	0	0	0	0	0	0
Totals	31	1	5	1	27	9

California	041 000 030—8
Boston	000 001 000—1

California	IP.	H.	R.	ER.	BB.	SO.
Witt (Winner)	9	5	1	1	2	3

Boston	IP.	H.	R.	ER.	BB.	SO.
Clemens (Loser)	7⅓	10	8	7	3	5
Sambito	⅓	0	0	0	1	0
Stanley	1⅓	1	0	0	0	0

Game-winning RBI—Jones.

Error—Owen. Double play—California 1. Left on bases—California 8, Boston 5. Two-base hits—Joyner 2, Baylor. Stolen base—Schofield. Umpires—Barnett, McCoy, Cooney, Bremigan, Roe and Garcia. Time—2:52. Attendance—32,993.

GAME OF WEDNESDAY, OCTOBER 8, AT BOSTON

California	AB.	R.	H.	RBI.	PO.	A.
Burleson, dh	5	0	1	0	0	0
Joyner, 1b	4	1	2	1	8	1
Downing, lf	4	1	1	0	1	0
DeCinces, 3b	4	0	1	0	1	4
Hendrick, rf	4	0	0	0	1	0
Grich, 2b	4	0	2	0	2	1
Schofield, ss	4	0	2	1	3	3
Boone, c	4	0	1	0	5	1
Pettis, cf	4	0	1	0	2	0
McCaskill, p	0	0	0	0	1	0
Lucas, p	0	0	0	0	0	0
Corbett, p	0	0	0	0	0	0
Totals	37	2	11	2	24	10

Boston	AB.	R.	H.	RBI.	PO.	A.
Boggs, 3b	4	1	2	0	1	4
Barrett, 2b	5	1	3	2	5	1
Buckner, 1b	4	2	1	1	7	1
Stapleton, 1b	0	0	0	0	0	0
Rice, lf	5	2	2	2	0	1
Baylor, dh	2	1	2	0	0	0
Evans, rf	5	0	1	2	4	0
Gedman, c	4	1	1	1	4	0
Armas, cf	4	0	0	0	2	0
Henderson, cf	0	0	0	0	1	0
Owen, ss	3	1	1	0	2	4
Hurst, p	0	0	0	0	1	0
Totals	36	9	13	8	27	11

California	000 110 000—2
Boston	110 010 33x—9

California	IP.	H.	R.	ER.	BB.	SO.
McCaskill (Loser)	7	10	6	3	3	6
Lucas	⅔	1	2	2	1	0
Corbett	⅓	2	1	1	0	0

Boston	IP.	H.	R.	ER.	BB.	SO.
Hurst (Winner)	9	11	2	1	0	4

Game-winning RBI—Evans.

Errors—Owen, Boggs, Grich, DeCinces, Schofield. Double plays—California 1, Boston 1. Left on bases—California 8, Boston 9. Two-base hits—Barrett, Evans. Three-base hit—Boggs. Home runs—Joyner, Rice. Sacrifice hit—Boggs. Sacrifice fly—Buckner. Umpires—McCoy, Cooney, Bremigan, Roe, Garcia and Barnett. Time—2:47. Attendance—32,786.

GAME OF FRIDAY, OCTOBER 10, AT CALIFORNIA (N)

Boston	AB.	R.	H.	RBI.	PO.	A.
Boggs, 3b	4	0	0	0	2	2
Barrett, 2b	5	1	2	0	1	5
Buckner, 1b	5	0	0	0	8	1
Rice, lf	3	2	1	0	3	0
Baylor, dh	3	0	1	0	0	0
Evans, rf	3	0	1	0	0	0
Gedman, c	4	0	3	2	4	1
Armas, cf	4	0	1	0	2	0
Owen, ss	3	0	0	0	3	1
Greenwell, ph	1	0	0	0	0	0
Boyd, p	0	0	0	0	1	2
Sambito, p	0	0	0	0	0	0
Schiraldi, p	0	0	0	0	0	0
Totals	35	3	9	2	24	12

California	AB.	R.	H.	RBI.	PO.	A.
Pettis, cf	3	1	1	2	9	0
Joyner, 1b	3	1	1	0	8	0
Downing, lf	4	0	1	0	3	0
Jackson, dh	3	1	1	1	0	0
DeCinces, 3b	4	0	1	0	0	1
Jones, rf	3	0	0	1	1	0
White, rf	0	0	0	0	0	0
Grich, 2b	4	0	0	0	0	0
Schofield, ss	3	1	2	1	1	1
Boone, c	3	1	1	0	5	1
Candelaria, p	0	0	0	0	0	1
Moore, p	0	0	0	0	0	0
Totals	30	5	8	5	27	4

Boston	010	000	020—3
California	000	001	31x—5

Boston	IP.	H.	R.	ER.	BB.	SO.
Boyd (Loser)	6⅔	8	4	4	2	3
Sambito	⅓	0	0	0	0	0
Schiraldi	1	0	1	0	1	0

California	IP.	H.	R.	ER.	BB.	SO.
Candelaria (Winner)	7	5	1	1	3	5
Moore (Save)	2	4	2	2	1	0

Game-winning RBI—Schofield.

Error—Boggs. Double play—Boston 1. Left on bases—Boston 9, California 5. Two-base hits—Armas, Schofield, Rice. Home runs—Schofield, Pettis. Caught stealing—Pettis. Sacrifice fly—Jones. Balk—Moore. Umpires—Cooney, Bremigan, Roe, Garcia, Barnett, and McCoy. Time—2:48. Attendance—64,206.

GAME OF SATURDAY, OCTOBER 11 AT CALIFORNIA (N)

Boston	AB.	R.	H.	RBI.	PO.	A.
Boggs, 3b	5	0	1	0	1	2
Barrett, 2b	3	1	1	1	1	2
Buckner, 1b	5	0	1	1	10	1
Rice, lf	5	0	0	0	0	0
Baylor, dh	5	0	1	0	0	0
Evans, rf	4	0	0	0	2	0
Gedman, c	5	0	0	0	11	1
Armas, cf	3	1	1	0	2	0
Henderson, cf	1	0	0	0	2	0
Owen, ss	3	1	1	0	2	5
Clemens, p	0	0	0	0	0	1
Schiraldi, p	0	0	0	0	0	0
Totals	39	3	6	2	31	12

California	AB.	R.	H.	RBI.	PO.	A.
Jones, rf	2	0	1	0	2	0
Grich, 2b	6	0	1	1	1	6
Downing, lf	3	0	0	1	1	0
Jackson, dh	5	0	0	0	0	0
DeCinces, 3b	5	1	2	1	2	2
Hendrick, 1b	5	0	0	0	14	2
Schofield, ss	5	1	1	0	3	4
Boone, c	4	0	2	0	4	0
White, pr	0	1	0	0	0	0
Narron, c	1	1	1	0	0	0
Pettis, cf	4	0	3	1	5	0
Sutton, p	0	0	0	0	1	1
Lucas, p	0	0	0	0	0	0
Ruhle, p	0	0	0	0	0	0
Finley, p	0	0	0	0	0	0
Corbett, p	0	0	0	0	0	1
Totals	40	4	11	4	33	16

Boston	000	001	020	00—3
California	000	000	003	01—4

One out when winning run scored.

Boston	IP.	H.	R.	ER.	BB.	SO.
Clemens	8⅓	8	3	3	3	9
Schiraldi (Loser)	2	3	1	1	2	2

California	IP.	H.	R.	ER.	BB.	SO.
Sutton	6⅓	4	1	1	1	2
Lucas	⅓	0	0	0	0	1
Ruhle	⅔	2	2	1	0	0
Finley	0*	0	0	0	0	0
Corbett (Winner)	3⅔	0	0	0	1	1

*Pitched to one batter in eighth.

Game-winning RBI—Grich.

Errors—Owen, Grich, DeCinces. Double play—Boston 1. Left on bases—Boston 7, California 12. Two-base hits—Boggs, Buckner, Baylor, Jones, Pettis. Home run—DeCinces. Caught stealing—Pettis. Sacrifice hits—Barrett, Owen, Pettis. Hit by pitcher—By Schiraldi (Downing). Wild pitch—Ruhle. Passed ball—Boone. Umpires—Bremigan, Roe, Garcia, Barnett, McCoy and Cooney. Time—3:50. Attendance—64,223.

GAME OF SUNDAY, OCTOBER 12, AT CALIFORNIA

Boston	AB.	R.	H.	RBI.	PO.	A.
Boggs, 3b	5	0	1	0	1	2
Barrett, 2b	5	0	0	0	7	4
Buckner, 1b	4	0	1	0	4	0
Stapleton, pr-1b	1	1	1	0	2	1
Rice, lf	5	1	1	0	3	0
Baylor, dh	4	2	1	2	0	0
Evans, rf	5	0	1	0	1	0
Gedman, c	4	2	4	2	8	2
Armas, cf	2	0	0	0	2	0
Henderson, cf	2	1	1	3	3	0
Owen, ss	2	0	0	0	1	0
Greenwell, ph	1	0	1	0	0	0
Romero, pr-ss	2	0	0	0	0	0
Hurst, p	0	0	0	0	0	2
Stanley, p	0	0	0	0	0	1
Sambito, p	0	0	0	0	0	0
Crawford, p	0	0	0	0	1	0
Schiraldi, p	0	0	0	0	0	0
Totals	42	7	12	7	33	12

California	AB.	R.	H.	RBI.	PO.	A.
Burleson, 2b	2	0	0	0	1	3
Wilfong, ph-2b	3	0	2	2	3	3
Schofield, ss	5	0	1	0	3	5
Downing, lf	3	0	0	1	4	0
DeCinces, 3b	5	1	2	0	1	0
Grich, 1b	5	1	1	2	10	2
Jackson, dh	5	0	1	0	0	0
Hendrick, rf	3	0	1	0	1	0
White, pr-rf	2	1	1	0	1	0
Boone, c	3	1	3	1	6	0
Jones, pr	0	1	0	0	0	0
Narron, c	0	0	0	0	0	0
Pettis, cf	3	1	1	0	1	0
Witt, p	0	0	0	0	2	3
Lucas, p	0	0	0	0	0	0
Moore, p	0	0	0	0	0	0
Finley, p	0	0	0	0	0	0
Totals	39	6	13	6	33	16

Boston	020	000	004	01—7
California	001	002	201	00—6

Boston	IP.	H.	R.	ER.	BB.	SO.
Hurst	6	7	3	3	1	4
Stanley	2⅓	4	3	3	2	1
Sambito	0*	1	0	0	0	0
Crawford (Winner)	1⅔	1	0	0	2	1
Schiraldi (Save)	1	0	0	0	0	2

California	IP.	H.	R.	ER.	BB.	SO.
Witt	8⅔	8	4	4	0	5
Lucas	0*	0	1	1	0	0
Moore (Loser)	2	4	2	2	1	0
Finley	⅓	0	0	0	0	0

*Pitched to one batter in ninth.

Game-winning RBI—Henderson.

Double plays—California 2. Left on bases—Boston 6, California 9. Two-base hits—DeCinces 2, Gedman, Wilfong. Home runs—Gedman, Boone, Grich, Baylor, Henderson. Caught stealing—Downing, White. Sacrifice hits—Burleson, Boone, Pettis. Sacrifice flies—Downing, Henderson. Hit by pitcher—By Lucas (Gedman), by Moore (Baylor). Umpires—Roe, Garcia, Barnett, McCoy, Cooney and Bremigan. Time—3:54. Attendance—64,223.

GAME OF TUESDAY, OCTOBER 14, AT BOSTON (N)

California	AB.	R.	H.	RBI.	PO.	A.
Pettis, cf	5	0	1	0	2	0
Jones, rf	4	1	0	0	1	0
Downing, lf	5	1	1	1	1	0
Jackson, dh	5	1	3	1	0	0
DeCinces, 3b	5	0	1	1	1	4
Schofield, ss	4	1	2	0	2	5
Grich, 1b	3	0	1	0	8	0
Wilfong, 2b	4	0	2	0	4	5
Boone, c	3	0	0	0	4	1
Howell, ph	0	0	0	0	0	0
Narron, c	0	0	0	0	1	0
McCaskill, p	0	0	0	0	0	0
Lucas, p	0	0	0	0	0	0
Corbett, p	0	0	0	0	0	0
Finley, p	0	0	0	0	0	0
Totals	38	4	11	3	24	15

Boston	AB.	R.	H.	RBI.	PO.	A.
Boggs, 3b	4	2	1	0	0	1
Barrett, 2b	4	1	3	1	2	1
Buckner, 1b	4	1	2	1	6	0
Stapleton, pr-1b	1	0	1	0	4	0
Rice, lf	5	1	0	1	3	0
Baylor, dh	4	2	1	0	0	0
Evans, rf	4	0	2	1	2	0
Gedman, c	4	1	2	0	5	0
Henderson, cf	3	1	0	1	3	0
Owen, ss	4	1	4	2	1	5
Boyd, p	0	0	0	0	1	0
Stanley, p	0	0	0	0	0	0
Totals	37	10	16	7	27	7

California	2 0 0	0 0 0	1 1 0	— 4
Boston	2 0 5	0 1 0	2 0 x	—10

California	IP.	H.	R.	ER.	BB.	SO.
McCaskill (Loser)	2⅓	6	7	5	2	1
Lucas	1⅓	2	0	0	0	1
Corbett	2⅔	7	3	3	1	1
Finley	1⅔	1	0	0	0	1

Boston	IP.	H.	R.	ER.	BB.	SO.
Boyd (Winner)	7	9	3	3	1	5
Stanley	2	2	1	0	1	0

Game-winning RBI—Barrett.

Errors—Grich, Owen. Double plays—Boston 1, California 3. Left on bases—California 10, Boston 7. Two-base hits—Jackson 2, DeCinces, Barrett. Three-base hit—Owen. Home run—Downing. Hit by pitchers—By Boyd (Grich), by Corbett (Baylor). Passed ball—Boone. Umpires—Garcia, Barnett, McCoy, Cooney, Bremigan and Roe. Time—3:23. Attendance—32,998.

GAME OF WEDNESDAY, OCTOBER 15, AT BOSTON (N)

California	AB.	R.	H.	RBI.	PO.	A.
Jones, rf	4	1	1	0	0	0
Wilfong, 2b	1	0	0	0	0	1
Burleson, 2b	3	0	2	0	2	2
Downing, lf	3	0	1	0	3	0
Jackson, dh	4	0	0	0	0	0
DeCinces, 3b	4	0	1	1	1	3
Schofield, ss	4	0	0	0	1	4
Pettis, cf	4	0	0	0	5	0
Grich, 1b	2	0	0	0	8	0
Howell, ph	1	0	0	0	0	0
Boone, c	2	0	1	0	4	0
Narron, ph	1	0	0	0	0	0
Candelaria, p	0	0	0	0	0	0
Sutton, p	0	0	0	0	0	0
Moore, p	0	0	0	0	0	0
Totals	33	1	6	1	24	10

Boston	AB.	R.	H.	RBI.	PO.	A.
Boggs, 3b	5	0	1	2	0	2
Barrett, 2b	4	0	0	0	3	5
Buckner, 1b	2	0	1	0	5	0
Stapleton, pr-1b	1	1	0	0	6	0
Rice, lf	4	2	1	3	1	0
Baylor, dh	4	1	2	0	0	0
Evans, rf	3	2	1	1	1	0
Gedman, c	4	0	0	1	8	0
Henderson, cf	3	1	0	0	2	0
Owen, ss	4	1	2	1	1	2
Clemens, p	0	0	0	0	0	1
Schiraldi, p	0	0	0	0	0	0
Totals	34	8	8	8	27	10

California	0 0 0	0 0 0	0 1 0	—1
Boston	0 3 0	4 0 0	1 0 x	—8

California	IP.	H.	R.	ER.	BB.	SO.
Candelaria (Loser)	3⅔	6	7	0	3	2
Sutton	3⅓	2	1	1	0	2
Moore	1	0	0	0	0	0

Boston	IP.	H.	R.	ER.	BB.	SO.
Clemens (Winner)	7*	4	1	1	1	3
Schiraldi	2	2	0	0	0	5

*Pitched to one batter in eighth.

Game-winning RBI—Gedman.

Errors—Schofield, Pettis, Owen. Double play—Boston 1. Left on bases—California 8, Boston 5. Two-base hit—Baylor. Home runs—Rice, Evans. Stolen base—Owen. Hit by pitchers—By Clemens (Boone, Grich). Umpires—Barnett, McCoy, Garcia, Bremigan and Roe. Time—2:39. Attendance—33,001.

BOSTON RED SOX'S BATTING AND FIELDING AVERAGES

Player—Position	G.	AB.	R.	H.	TB.	2B.	3B.	HR.	RBI.	B.A.	PO.	A.	E.	F.A.
Stapleton, 1b-pr	4	3	2	2	2	0	0	0	0	.667	12	1	0	1.000
Greenwell, ph	2	2	0	1	1	0	0	0	0	.500	0	0	0	.000
Owen, ss	7	21	5	9	11	0	1	0	3	.429	12	21	5	.868
Barrett, 2b	7	30	4	11	13	2	0	0	5	.367	19	21	0	1.000
Gedman, c	7	28	4	10	14	1	0	1	6	.357	45	4	0	1.000
Baylor, dh	7	26	6	9	15	3	0	1	2	.346	0	0	0	.000
Boggs, 3b	7	30	3	7	10	1	1	0	2	.233	7	13	2	.909
Evans, rf	7	28	2	6	10	1	0	1	4	.214	11	0	0	1.000
Buckner, 1b	7	28	3	6	7	1	0	0	3	.214	49	5	0	1.000
Rice, lf	7	31	8	5	12	1	0	2	6	.161	13	1	0	1.000
Armas, cf	5	16	1	2	3	1	0	0	0	.125	12	0	0	1.000
Henderson, cf	5	9	3	1	4	0	0	1	4	.111	11	0	0	1.000
Schiraldi, p	4	0	0	0	0	0	0	0	0	.000	0	0	0	.000
Clemens, p	3	0	0	0	0	0	0	0	0	.000	1	2	0	1.000
Sambito, p	3	0	0	0	0	0	0	0	0	.000	0	0	0	.000
Stanley, p	3	0	0	0	0	0	0	0	0	.000	0	1	0	1.000
Boyd, p	2	0	0	0	0	0	0	0	0	.000	2	2	0	1.000
Crawford, p	1	0	0	0	0	0	0	0	0	.000	1	0	0	1.000
Hurst, p	2	0	0	0	0	0	0	0	0	.000	1	2	0	1.000
Romero, pr-ss	1	2	0	0	0	0	0	0	0	.000	0	0	0	.000
Totals	7	254	41	69	102	11	2	6	35	.272	196	73	7	.975

CALIFORNIA ANGELS' BATTING AND FIELDING AVERAGES

Player—Position	G.	AB.	R.	H.	TB.	2B.	3B.	HR.	RBI.	B.A.	PO.	A.	E.	F.A.
White, rf-pr	4	2	2	1	1	0	0	0	0	.500	3	0	0	1.000
Narron, c-ph	4	2	1	1	1	0	0	0	0	.500	1	0	0	1.000
Boone, c	7	22	4	10	13	0	0	1	2	.455	33	3	0	1.000
Joyner, 1b	3	11	3	5	10	2	0	1	2	.455	24	1	0	1.000
Pettis, cf	7	26	4	9	13	1	0	1	4	.346	28	0	1	.966
Wilfong, 2b-ph	4	13	1	4	5	1	0	0	2	.308	8	10	0	1.000
Schofield, ss	7	30	4	9	13	1	0	1	2	.300	13	23	2	.947
DeCinces, 3b	7	32	2	9	15	3	0	1	3	.281	6	18	2	.923
Burleson, ph-dh-2b	4	11	0	3	3	0	0	0	0	.273	3	5	0	1.000
Downing, lf	7	27	2	6	9	0	0	1	7	.222	18	0	0	1.000
Grich, 2b-1b	6	24	1	5	8	0	0	1	3	.208	29	9	3	.927
Jackson, dh	6	26	2	5	7	2	0	0	2	.192	0	0	0	.000
Jones, rf-pr	6	17	4	3	4	1	0	0	2	.176	6	0	0	1.000
Hendrick, rf-1b	3	12	0	1	1	0	0	0	0	.083	16	2	0	1.000
Lucas, p	4	0	0	0	0	0	0	0	0	.000	0	0	0	.000
Corbett, p	3	0	0	0	0	0	0	0	0	.000	0	1	0	1.000
Finley, p	3	0	0	0	0	0	0	0	0	.000	0	0	0	.000
Moore, p	3	0	0	0	0	0	0	0	0	.000	0	0	0	.000
Candelaria, p	2	0	0	0	0	0	0	0	0	.000	0	1	0	1.000
McCaskill, p	2	0	0	0	0	0	0	0	0	.000	1	0	0	1.000
Sutton, p	2	0	0	0	0	0	0	0	0	.000	1	1	0	1.000
Witt, p	2	0	0	0	0	0	0	0	0	.000	2	4	0	1.000
Ruhle, p	1	0	0	0	0	0	0	0	0	.000	0	0	0	.000
Howell, ph	2	1	0	0	0	0	0	0	0	.000	0	0	0	.000
Totals	7	256	30	71	103	11	0	7	29	.277	192	78	8	.971

BOSTON RED SOX'S PITCHING RECORDS

Pitcher	G.	GS.	CG.	IP.	H.	R.	ER.	BB.	SO.	HB.	WP.	W.	L.	Pct.	ERA.
Crawford	1	0	0	1⅔	1	0	0	2	1	0	0	1	0	1.000	0.00
Sambito	3	0	0	⅔	1	0	0	1	0	0	0	0	0	.000	0.00
Schiraldi	4	0	0	6	5	2	1	3	9	1	0	0	1	.000	1.50
Hurst	2	2	1	15	18	5	4	1	8	0	0	1	0	1.000	2.40
Clemens	3	3	0	22⅔	22	12	11	7	17	2	0	1	1	.500	4.37
Boyd	2	2	0	13⅔	17	7	7	3	8	1	0	1	1	.500	4.61
Stanley	3	0	0	5⅔	7	4	3	3	1	0	0	0	0	.000	4.76
Totals	7	7	1	65⅓	71	30	26	20	44	4	0	4	3	.571	3.58

No shutouts. Save—Schiraldi.

CALIFORNIA ANGELS' PITCHING RECORDS

Pitcher	G.	GS.	CG.	IP.	H.	R.	ER.	BB.	SO.	HB.	WP.	W.	L.	Pct.	ERA.
Finley	3	0	0	2	1	0	0	0	1	0	0	0	0	.000	0.00
Candelaria	2	2	0	10⅔	11	8	1	6	7	0	0	1	1	.500	0.84
Sutton	2	1	0	9⅔	6	2	2	1	4	0	0	0	0	.000	1.86
Witt	2	2	1	17⅔	13	5	5	2	8	0	0	1	0	1.000	2.55
Corbett	3	0	0	6⅔	9	4	4	2	2	1	0	1	0	1.000	5.40
Moore	3	0	0	5	8	4	4	2	0	1	0	0	1	.000	7.20
McCaskill	2	2	0	9⅓	16	13	8	5	7	0	0	0	2	.000	7.71
Lucas	4	0	0	2⅓	3	3	3	1	2	1	0	0	0	.000	11.57
Ruhle	1	0	0	⅔	2	2	1	0	0	0	1	0	0	.000	13.50
Totals	7	7	1	64	69	41	28	19	31	3	1	3	4	.429	3.94

No shutouts. Save—Moore.

COMPOSITE SCORE BY INNINGS

Boston	3	7	5	4	2	2	6	7	4	0	1—41
California	2	4	2	1	1	3	6	6	4	0	1—30

Game-winning RBIs—Jones, Evans, Schofield, Grich, Henderson, Barrett, Gedman.

Sacrifice hits—Pettis 2, Boggs, Barrett, Owen, Burleson, Boone.

Sacrifice flies—Buckner, Jones, Downing, Henderson.

Stolen bases—Schofield, Owen.

Caught stealing—Pettis 2, Downing, White.

Double plays—DeCinces, Wilfong and Joyner; Joyner, Schofield and McCaskill; Barrett, Owen and Buckner; Boggs, Barrett and Buckner; Owen and Buckner; Barrett and Buckner; Schofield, Wilfong and Grich; DeCinces, Wilfong and Grich 2; Clemens, Barrett and Stapleton.

Left on bases—Boston 5, 9, 9, 7, 6, 7, 5—48; California 8, 8, 5, 12, 9, 10, 8—60.

Hit by pitcher—By Schiraldi (Downing), by Lucas (Gedman), by Moore (Baylor), by Boyd (Grich), by Corbett (Baylor), by Clemens (Boone, Grich).

Passed balls—Boone 2.

Balk—Moore.

Time of games—First game, 2:52; second game, 2:47; third game, 2:48; fourth game, 3:50; fifth game, 3:54; sixth game, 3:23; seventh game, 2:39.

Attendance—First game, 32,993; second game, 32,786; third game, 64,206; fourth game, 64,223; fifth game, 64,223; sixth game, 32,998; seventh game, 33,001.

Umpires—Barnett, McCoy, Cooney, Bremigan, Roe and Garcia.

Official scorers—Ed Munson; Joe Giuliotti, Boston Herald.

1986 WORLD SERIES

Including

Review of 1986 Series

Official Play-by-Play, Each Game

Official Composite Box Score

Relief pitcher Jesse Orosco and catcher Gary Carter celebrate the final out in the Mets' 8-5 victory over Boston in Game 7.

Miraculous Mets Rally To Win

By LARRY WIGGE

After flying to center field for the second out of the 10th inning, New York Mets first baseman Keith Hernandez retired to Manager Dave Johnson's office. It was a nice quiet place to view the Mets' final, World Series-ending out in Game 6 of the 1986 fall classic.

The Boston Red Sox held a 5-3 lead with two out and nobody on base and were ready to break out the champagne.

But, suddenly, fate turned its back on the Red Sox.

Mets catcher Gary Carter started a string of improbable events by lining a single to left. Pinch-hitter Kevin Mitchell singled to center. Ray Knight looped an 0-2 pitch to center, scoring Carter and sending Mitchell to third. With a 2-2 count on Mookie Wilson, Boston reliever Bob Stanley bounced a pitch back to the screen, allowing Mitchell to score and tie the game. As if that wasn't bad enough, Wilson hit a routine bouncer to first baseman Bill Buckner on the next pitch. Buckner let the ball get through his legs and Knight crossed the plate with the winning run.

The unbelievable turn of events shocked millions of baseball fans and even had the Mets wondering about their 1986 comeback magic.

"I went into Davey's office for a beer," Hernandez recalled. "I was very ticked.

"After seeing Gary and Kevin get their hits, I still wasn't sure about our coming back. But, when Ray got the hit to knock in the first run of the inning, I grabbed my hat and glove. I started to go back to the dugout, but then I decided I'd go back to the chair in Davey's room. I figured that chair still had some more hits in it, so I didn't leave."

The unlikely Game 6 rally put the Mets back into a position to win the Series and all but sealed Boston's continued baseball frustration. The Red Sox, who were trying to become the franchise's first team to win a World Series championship since 1918, took a 3-0 lead in Game 7, but then watched helplessly as the Mets fought back for a Series-clinching 8-5 victory. It was the Mets' first World Series title since 1969.

"I don't put stock in history," said Bruce Hurst, Boston's Game 7 starter who was trying to become the first pitcher to win three Series games since Detroit's Mickey Lolich accomplished the feat in 1968. "All that matters is what's in front of us. You can look at this in a lot of ways. We let it slip away or the Mets came and got it."

Whatever the reason, Hurst and other Red Sox faithful couldn't get the 10th inning of Game 6 out of their minds.

"Whoever invented 90 feet between the bases and three outs an inning knew what he was talking about," said Hurst, still shaking his head. "We couldn't get that third out."

The cocky Mets, who were odds-on favorites to win the Series, were stunned when the Red Sox went into Shea Stadium and captured 1-0 and 9-3 Series-opening victories. Their only consolation as they packed their bags and headed to Boston's Fenway Park was that the only team to win a Series after losing the first two games at home was Kansas City, the 1985 champion.

Hurst was the architect of the Game 1 victory, baffling Mets hitters with an assortment of changeups, curves and fastballs, rarely throwing back-to-back pitches the same speed. He had the Mets off-balance and limited them to four hits and no runs over eight innings.

Mets righthander Ron Darling dueled Hurst on even terms through six innings, blanking the Red Sox on three hits. Then came the fateful seventh.

Jim Rice led off with a walk and Darling threw his 10th wild pitch of the season and second of the game. That put Rice on second and, after Dwight Evans grounded out, Rich Gedman hit an innocent-looking grounder toward second baseman Tim Teufel. The ball skipped through Teufel's legs and Rice scored the game's first and only run.

"That run may have been the only run in the game, but that's not what beat us," Darling said in defense of his second baseman. "There hasn't been a team yet that has been shut out and won a game. Hurst's pitching beat us."

Teufel took the brunt of the criticism without making excuses.

"What happened," he said softly, "is every infielder's nightmare. The ball just went through the wickets. No excuses. My job is to field that ball and I didn't field the thing and it cost us the ball game. It's happened to me before, and I have to face it and bounce back. You hate to make an error like that any time, but to make it in the World Series. . . .

"Do I feel terrible? Yes. I missed it and we lost, 1-0. There's not much more you

Jim Rice scores the only run of Game 1 after a seventh-inning error by Mets second baseman Tim Teufel.

can say."

Hurst, who had never batted in the major leagues because of the American League's use of the designated hitter, struck out three times before giving way to pinch-hitter Mike Greenwell in a ninth-inning, bases-loaded situation. Greenwell struck out and reliever Calvin Schiraldi retired the Mets in the bottom of the inning.

"When I came up to the plate the third time, Gary Carter (Mets' catcher) and John Kibler (the home-plate umpire) were laughing," said Hurst. "I told them to stop, that nothing was funny."

Without the benefit of using designated hitter Don Baylor (31 homers, 94 runs batted in during the regular season) in the first two games of the Series, the Red Sox surprised observers in Game 2 by ripping five New York pitchers for 18 hits.

The Bosox jumped on New York starter Dwight Gooden for three runs in the third inning when an error by the usually-reliable Hernandez opened the floodgates. Wade Boggs' double plated one run, while singles by Marty Barrett and Buckner completed the outburst.

After the Mets rallied for two runs in the bottom of the inning, the Red Sox added a run in the fourth on a homer by Dave Henderson and two more in the fifth on a two-run homer by Evans.

Red Sox ace Roger Clemens didn't have his best stuff, either, getting knocked out after surrendering five hits and three runs in 4⅓ innings. Steve Crawford, who had an 0-2 record in 40 games during the regular season but was credited with the victory in Game 5 of the A.L. Championship Series against California, gained credit for this victory with help from Stanley.

There was some criticism when Johnson gave the Mets a day off before Game 3 in Boston. But Johnson gave three reasons for his decision.

"First, we had just gone through an exhausting series with the Astros and we were all drained," he said. "Secondly, I didn't want to have to put my players through the barrage of negative questions they would have been asked about losing the first two games in New York. Nobody needed that. If we hadn't played an exhibition game here (in September), maybe I would have asked them to practice because of the unusual dimensions of this park. But that wasn't the case."

It didn't take long for the refreshed Mets to punch a deep hole in Oil Can Boyd, Boston's Game 3 starter. Lenny Dykstra opened the game by stroking a 1-and-1 pitch into the right-field stands, marking the 14th time in Series history that a game had begun with a home run and the first time since 1978.

Gary Carter hits the first of his two Game 4 home runs in the fourth inning of the Mets' 6-2 victory.

Obviously shaken, Boyd gave up singles to Backman and Hernandez and an RBI double to Carter. With Hernandez on third and Carter on second, Knight hit a squibber down the third-base line. Boggs fielded it and caught Hernandez in a rundown. The Red Sox botched the play, however, allowing both Hernandez and Carter, who was trapped between second and third, to return to their respective bases. Designated hitter Danny Heep followed with a two-run single for a 4-0 Mets lead en route to a 7-1 victory. The Mets' 13-hit explosion was their biggest in postseason play.

"We couldn't afford to go 0-3 in their park. We couldn't afford to get behind early again," said the fiery Dykstra, who went 4 for 5. "We'd been playing catch-up for the entire postseason and we needed to put some pressure on the other people. We had to wake ourselves, shake ourselves. We definitely came out wired."

Meanwhile, Mets starter Bob Ojeda was masterful in his Fenway Park return engagement. He held his old teammates to five hits in seven innings and became the first pitcher in Series history to beat the team he played for the previous season. He also became the first lefthander to beat the Red Sox at Fenway Park in postseason play since Hippo Vaughn did it for the Cubs in 1918.

"Bittersweet victory? No, not at all," said Ojeda, who compiled a 44-39 record in six seasons with the Red Sox. "I'm a New York Met all the way. We went through a lot together. We won 108 (regular-season games) together."

While Ojeda didn't confess to having any special feelings coming back to Boston, Darling, who grew up a Red Sox admirer as a schoolboy at nearby Worchester, Mass., said coming back home was a dream come true.

Darling threw a four-hit shutout at the Red Sox for seven innings in Game 4. He was backed by Carter's two homers and another from Dykstra as the Mets defeated the Red Sox, 6-2, to even the Series at two games apiece. Coupled with his Game

1 performance, Darling's 14 consecutive innings without allowing an earned run were the most in World Series play since Bob Gibson recorded 19 straight shutout innings for the Cardinals in 1967.

"Pitching in your own back yard, where you might never have a chance to pitch again, was fantastic," said an excited Darling. "I've never been so nervous as I was the last two innings watching the game in the locker room.

"Although it's a cliche, it hasn't really sunk in yet. But, by the time I get home, it will be the greatest thing in my career. To have 40 friends from high school here was a great thrill."

The Mets finally got to surprise starter Al Nipper, who hadn't pitched in 18 days, in the fourth inning. Backman singled and went to second on a grounder to short by Hernandez. Carter then launched Nipper's first delivery over the 37-foot wall in left field. Darryl Strawberry doubled and Knight singled him home to complete a three-run inning.

The score was still 3-0 in the seventh when Crawford replaced Nipper. With Wilson at second on a single and a stolen base and two out, Dykstra connected for his second home run in two nights. It was a long drive to right field that deflected over the wall off Evans' glove after he jumped to try to snare the smash.

Carter added to the Mets' lead when he hit his second homer of the night, blasting a Crawford delivery onto the screen above the left-field wall in the eighth.

Boston Manager John McNamara insisted that his strategy of using Nipper, whose 5.38 earned-run average was the highest of any Series starter in 39 years, hadn't backfired. It left him with Hurst, Clemens and Boyd in the next three games pitching on four days rest, while the Mets would have to go with Gooden, Ojeda and Darling on three days.

McNamara was vindicated in Game 5 when Hurst scattered 10 hits in pitching the Red Sox to a 4-2 victory. It marked the first time in the Series that the home team had won.

Until Teufel lofted an eighth-inning home run just inside the right-field foul pole, Hurst had blanked the Mets for 15⅓ innings in two Series games. The Mets scored their only other run in the ninth on Rafael Santana's RBI single.

The Red Sox, meanwhile, nicked Gooden for a run in the second on a triple by Henderson and a sacrifice fly by Spike Owen. They scored again in the third when Buckner reached on an error by Santana, Rice walked and Evans lined a single to right-center.

Gooden was driven from the mound for the second time in the Series when the Red Sox scored two more runs in the fifth. This time, Rice tripled off the right-center field wall and scored on a broken-bat single to right by Baylor. After Evans also singled, Sid Fernandez came in to pitch for the Mets. Rich Gedman struck out, but Henderson smashed a double down the left-field line to score Baylor.

With singles in the fourth and eighth innings, Barrett raised his total to a record 20 hits in 12 postseason games, one more hit than Thurman Munson had for the Yankees in 1976.

The hype for Game 6 centered around the two starting pitchers, Clemens for the Red Sox and Ojeda for the Mets.

"This is not a one-on-one thing," said Ojeda. "I'm not John McEnroe playing Ivan Lendl. If we are going to win this thing, we will win it with a team effort. You have to be realistic. One, two or three guys are not going to decide the game."

The Red Sox touched Ojeda for one run in each of the first two innings, scoring in the first on an infield hit by Boggs and a two-out double by Evans and tallying in the second on singles by Owen, Boggs and Barrett. Meanwhile, Clemens limited the Mets to four hits in his seven innings, two coming in the fifth when the National League champs tied the score with two runs. Knight's RBI single and a double-play grounder by pinch-hitter Heep produced the runs.

The Red Sox took a 3-2 lead in the seventh off reliever Roger McDowell. After Barrett walked and went to second on Buckner's groundout, Rice reached base on a throwing error by Knight. Evans followed with a potential double-play grounder to Backman at second. But, because the Red Sox started Rice on the 3-2 delivery, the throw to second base was too late to retire Rice, Barrett scoring the go-ahead run on the play. Gedman followed with another single, but Rice was thrown out at the plate by Wilson.

Clemens, who had recorded eight strikeouts in seven innings, was forced to leave because of a blister on his pitching hand. It didn't take long for the Mets to strike against reliever Schiraldi.

Lee Mazzilli stroked a pinch single to start the rally. Dykstra then bunted toward the mound and both runners were safe when Schiraldi, a former Mets pitcher, threw low to second. After Backman sacrificed the runners to third and second, Hernandez was walked intentionally. Schiraldi then ran the count to 3-0 on Car-

Series MVP Ray Knight is welcomed home by Howard Johnson as he scores the winning run in the Mets' miraculous 10th-inning rally in Game 6.

ter, who surprisingly took a swing and lined a sacrifice fly to left field, tying the score.

There was enough drama to last a lifetime in the 10th inning. Henderson, whose heroics had given the Red Sox a storybook come-from-behind victory in Game 5 of the A.L. Championship Series, smacked a Rick Aguilera delivery over the left-field wall to give Boston a 4-3 lead. With two out, Boggs lined a double to left-center. Barrett then singled home another run.

Seemingly in the driver's seat, the Red Sox stuck with Schiraldi, who retired the first two batters in the bottom of the 10th, setting up one of the most bizarre turnarounds in World Series history.

Still contemplating his costly error one day later when Game 7 was postponed because of heavy rain, Buckner tried to look for a bright side.

"I never played in the seventh game of a World Series. But I will now," he said. "I hate to say it because I missed a ground ball, but that's the truth. I can't remember the last time I missed a ball like that, but I'll remember that one."

The Red Sox showed no ill effects from the Game 6 disaster when they bolted to a 3-0 lead in the second inning of the Series finale.

Consecutive homers by Evans and Gedman ended Darling's earned-run string at 15. It marked the first time since 1981 that a team had hit back-to-back homers in Series play and only the 10th time in Series history. After Henderson walked and was sacrificed to second, he scored the third run of the inning on a single by Boggs.

Meanwhile, Hurst permitted only one baserunner (a second-inning single by Knight) through five innings. He tired in the sixth, however, and the Mets scored three times to tie the contest.

Mazzilli and Wilson singled to start the rally. After Teufel drew a walk to load the bases, Hernandez lined a single to left-center, scoring Mazzilli and Wilson. The tying run scored when right fielder Evans tried for a diving catch on Carter's blooper, but couldn't control the ball. Pinch-runner Backman scored the run, although Hernandez was forced at second base.

Schiraldi replaced Hurst in the seventh and Knight greeted him by hitting a 2-1 pitch over the left-center field wall to give the Mets a 4-3 lead.

The Mets added two more runs in the seventh. Dykstra got a pinch single, went to second on a wild pitch and scored on a single over the first-base bag by Santana. Walks to Wilson and Backman loaded the bases before Hernandez knocked in his third run of the game with a sacrifice fly.

While the Mets were scoring off Schiraldi and Joe Sambito, Fernandez, who replaced Darling with one on and two out in the fourth, stopped the Red Sox cold. After walking Boggs, Fernandez got Barrett (who had tied Bobby Richardson of the Yankees and Lou Brock of the Cardinals with 13 hits in the Series with a single in the second inning) on a fly ball to right field. The lefthander struck out four of the eight batters he faced in keeping the Red Sox from adding to their early lead.

Though the Red Sox got a two-run double off McDowell in the eighth to cut the lead to 6-5, Orosco came in to shut the door. The Mets got those two runs back in their half of the eighth when Strawberry belted a home run off Nipper and Orosco hit an RBI single through a drawn-in infield expecting a bunt.

"Boston came out here knocking the ball all over the place, but Sid managed to stop it," Wilson said of Fernandez's stellar relief performance.

"No doubt he was the MVP of this game," said Johnson.

The MVP of the Series, however, was Knight, who scored the winning run on Buckner's error in Game 6 and then homered to put the Mets ahead to stay in Game 7.

Game 1

At New York
October 18

Boston (A.L.)	AB.	R.	H.	PO.	A.	E.
Boggs, 3b	4	0	0	1	2	0
Barrett, 2b	4	0	1	2	3	0
Buckner, 1b	4	0	1	4	0	0
Stapleton, 1b	0	0	0	0	1	0
Rice, lf	2	1	1	2	0	0
Evans, rf	3	0	0	2	0	0
Gedman, c	4	0	0	9	0	0
Henderson, cf	4	0	2	5	0	0
Owen, ss	2	0	0	2	0	0
Hurst, p	3	0	0	0	2	0
cGreenwell	1	0	0	0	0	0
Schiraldi, p	0	0	0	0	0	0
Totals	31	1	5	27	8	0

New York (N.L.)	AB.	R.	H.	PO.	A.	E.
Wilson, lf	4	0	1	1	0	0
McDowell, p	0	0	0	0	2	0
Dykstra, cf	3	0	0	4	0	0
Hernandez, 1b	3	0	0	7	0	0
Carter, c	4	0	1	9	0	0
Strawberry, rf	2	0	0	2	0	0
Knight, 3b	3	0	0	1	2	0
Teufel, 2b	3	0	2	0	1	1
aBackman, 2b	1	0	0	0	0	0
Santana, ss	2	0	0	3	2	0
dHeep	1	0	0	0	0	0
Darling, p	2	0	0	0	2	0
bMitchell, lf	1	0	0	0	1	0
Totals	29	0	4	27	10	1

Boston	000	000	100—1
New York	000	000	000—0

Boston	IP.	H.	R.	ER.	BB.	SO.
Hurst (W)	8	4	0	0	4	8
Schiraldi (S)	1	0	0	0	1	1

New York	IP.	H.	R.	ER.	BB.	SO.
Darling (L)	7	3	1	0	3	8
McDowell	2	2	0	0	2	0

Bases on balls—Off Hurst 4 (Dykstra, Hernandez, Strawberry, Knight), off Schiraldi 1 (Strawberry), off Darling 3 (Rice 2, Owen), off McDowell 2 (Evans, Owen).

Strikeouts—By Hurst 8 (Wilson, Dykstra 2, Strawberry 2, Teufel, Darling, Mitchell), by Schiraldi 1 (Heep), by Darling 8 (Boggs, Barrett, Buckner, Gedman, Owen, Hurst 3).

Game-winning RBI—None.

aRan for Teufel in seventh. bCalled out on strikes for Darling in seventh. cFlied out for Hurst in ninth. dStruck out for Santana in ninth. Runs batted in—None. Double plays—Teufel, Santana and Hernandez; Boggs, Barrett and Buckner. Left on bases—Boston 8, New York 8. Stolen bases—Wilson, Strawberry. Sacrifice hit—Santana. Wild pitches—Darling 2. Umpires—Kibler (N.L.) plate, Evans (A.L.) first base, Wendelstedt (N.L.) second base, Brinkman (A.L.) third base, Montague (N.L.) left field, Ford (A.L.) right field. Time—2:59. Attendance—55,076.

FIRST INNING

Boston—Boggs bounced to Knight, who charged the short-hopper and threw to Hernandez at first base for the out. Barrett singled on a grounder that Teufel went far to his left to knock down, but had no play at first. Buckner grounded sharply into a double play, from Teufel to Santana to Hernandez. No runs, one hit, no errors, none left.

New York—Wilson struck out. Dykstra also struck out. Hernandez flied to Henderson. No runs, no hits, no errors, none left.

SECOND INNING

Boston—Rice bounced to Knight. Evans flied deep to Dykstra, one step in front of wall. Gedman popped to Santana. No runs, no hits, no errors, none left.

New York—Carter grounded to Barrett. Strawberry was called out on strikes. Knight walked on four pitches. Teufel lined a single to left, Knight stopping at second. Santana hit a one-hopper back to Hurst, who threw to Buckner for the out. No runs, one hit, no errors, two left.

THIRD INNING

Boston—Henderson flied deep to Dykstra in center. Owen struck out. Hurst, making his first major league appearance at bat, struck out on three pitches. No runs, no hits, no errors, none left.

New York—Darling struck out. Wilson singled sharply up the middle. Wilson stole second. Dykstra walked. Evans made a long run to catch Hernandez' drive deep in the right-field corner, Wilson advancing to third after the catch in foul ground. Carter grounded to Barrett, who threw to Owen at second to force Dykstra. No runs, one hit, no errors, two left.

FOURTH INNING

Boston—Boggs was called out on strikes. Barrett also struck out, giving Darling four consecutive strikeouts. Buckner threw his bat at the ball and looped a single to left. Buckner went to second on a wild pitch. Rice walked on 3-2 pitch. Evans flied to Wilson. No runs, one hit, no errors, two left.

New York—Strawberry walked. Knight popped to Boggs. Teufel struck out, with Strawberry stealing second on the third strike. Henderson made a fine running catch on Santana's sinking liner in short right-center field. No runs, no hits, no errors, one left.

FIFTH INNING

Boston—Gedman struck out. Henderson lined a single to center. Owen flied to Dykstra. Hurst struck out. No runs, one hit, no errors, one left.

New York—Darling lined hard to Henderson in left-center field. Wilson flied to Evans near the right-field line. Dykstra struck out. No runs, no hits, no errors, none left.

SIXTH INNING

Boston—Boggs rapped back to Darling, who threw to Hernandez for the out. Barrett flied to Strawberry. Buckner struck out. No runs, no hits, no errors, none left.

New York—Hernandez walked. Carter broke his bat, grounding a single up the middle, Hernandez stopping at second. Strawberry was called out on strikes. Knight grounded into a double play, Boggs to Barrett to Buckner. No runs, one hit, no errors, one left.

SEVENTH INNING

Boston—Rice walked. With the count 0-2 on Evans, Darling made his second wild pitch of the game, Rice going to second. Evans bounced back to the mound, Darling to Hernandez for the out, Rice holding at second. Gedman jumped on the first pitch and grounded to Teufel, who let the ball go through his legs for an error, Rice scoring and Gedman going to second on Strawberry's throw to the plate. Henderson fouled out to Strawberry in short right field, Gedman holding at second. Owen was walked intentionally. Hurst struck out for the third time. One run, no hits, one error, two left.

New York—Teufel singled to the hole between short and third, Owen fielding the ball but having no play. Backman came in to the game to run for Teufel. Santana sacrificed Backman to second, Hurst fielding the bunt and throwing to Barrett covering first for the out. Mitchell, batting for Darling, was called out on strikes. Boggs made a nice play to his left and threw to Buckner for the out on Wilson's hard smash. No runs, one hit, no errors, one left.

EIGHTH INNING

Boston—Backman stayed in the game and played second, Mitchell remained in the game and played left field and McDowell came in to pitch for the Mets. Boggs lined hard to Santana. Barrett tapped back to the mound, McDowell to Hernandez for the out. Buckner bounced to Santana. No runs, no hits, no errors, none left.

New York—Stapleton came in to play first base for the Red Sox. Dykstra flied to Henderson in right-center. Hernandez flied to Rice. Carter flied to Henderson in left-center. No runs, no hits, no errors, none left.

NINTH INNING

Boston—Rice singled off the glove of McDowell. Evans walked. Rice was forced at third, McDowell to Knight, when Gedman failed to sacrifice. Henderson grounded a single to left, but Evans was out at the plate, Mitchell to Carter, with Gedman advancing to third and Henderson to second on the throw home. Owen was walked intentionally to load the bases. Greenwell batted for Hurst and flied to Dykstra in right-center. No runs, two hits, no errors, three left.

New York—Schiraldi came in to pitch for the Red Sox. Strawberry walked. Strawberry was forced at second, Stapleton to Owen, when Knight failed to sacrifice. Backman flied to Rice near the line in short left field. Heep, batting for Santana, struck out. No runs, no hits, no errors, one left.

Game 2

At New York
October 19

Boston (A.L.)	AB.	R.	H.	PO.	A.	E.
Boggs, 3b	5	1	2	0	4	0
Barrett, 2b	5	0	2	0	1	0
Buckner, 1b	5	0	2	6	1	0
bStapleton, 1b	1	0	0	1	1	0
Rice, lf	6	2	3	2	0	0
Evans, rf	4	2	2	3	0	0
Gedman, c	5	0	1	8	1	0
Henderson, cf	5	2	3	4	0	0
Owen, ss	4	1	3	1	1	0
dRomero, ss	0	0	0	0	0	0
Clemens, p	1	1	0	1	1	0
Crawford, p	1	0	0	0	0	0
aGreenwell	1	0	0	0	0	0
Stanley, p	1	0	0	1	0	0
Totals	44	9	18	27	10	0

New York (N.L.)	AB.	R.	H.	PO.	A.	E.
Dykstra, cf	3	0	1	2	0	0
Backman, 2b	3	1	2	2	4	0
Hernandez, 1b	4	0	1	5	1	1
Carter, c	4	0	1	12	0	0
Strawberry, rf	4	0	0	2	0	0
Heep, lf	2	0	0	1	0	0
Aguilera, p	0	0	0	0	0	0
Orosco, p	0	0	0	0	0	0
cMazzilli	1	0	0	0	0	0
Fernandez, p	0	0	0	0	0	0
Sisk, p	0	0	0	0	0	0
Johnson, 3b	4	0	0	1	0	0
Santana, ss	4	1	2	1	3	0
Gooden, p	2	1	1	0	0	0
Wilson, lf	2	0	0	1	0	0
Totals	33	3	8	27	8	1

Boston	0 0 3	1 2 0	2 0 1	—9
New York	0 0 2	0 1 0	0 0 0	—3

Boston	IP.	H.	R.	ER.	BB.	SO.
Clemens	4⅓	5	3	3	4	3
Crawford (W)	1⅔	1	0	0	0	2
Stanley (S)	3	2	0	0	1	3

New York	IP.	H.	R.	ER.	BB.	SO.
Gooden (L)	5	8	6	5	2	6
Aguilera	1*	5	2	2	1	1
Orosco	2	2	0	0	0	3
Fernandez	⅓	3	1	1	0	1
Sisk	⅔	0	0	0	1	1

*Pitched to five batters in seventh.

Bases on balls—Off Clemens 4 (Backman 2, Hernandez, Heep), off Stanley 1 (Dykstra), off Gooden 2 (Evans, Owen), off Aguilera 1 (Boggs), off Sisk 1 (Barrett).

Strikeouts—By Clemens 3 (Dykstra, Strawberry, Johnson), by Crawford 2 (Strawberry, Wilson), by Stanley 3 (Hernandez, Carter, Santana), by Gooden 6 (Rice, Evans, Gedman 2, Henderson, Owen), by Aguilera 1 (Buckner), by Orosco 3 (Greenwell, Boggs, Gedman), by Fernandez 1 (Stanley), by Sisk 1 (Rice).

Game-winning RBI—Boggs.

aCalled out on strikes for Crawford in seventh. bRan for Buckner in eighth. cFlied out for Orosco in eighth. dRan for Owen in ninth. Runs batted in—Boggs 2, Barrett, Buckner, Evans 2, Henderson 2, Owen, Backman, Hernandez, Carter. Double play—Santana, Backman and Hernandez. Left on bases—Boston 13, New York 9. Two-base hits—Boggs 2. Home runs—Henderson, Evans. Caught stealing—Backman. Sacrifice hits—Dykstra, Clemens. Umpires—Evans (A.L.) plate, Wendelstedt (N.L.) first base, Brinkman (A.L.) second base, Montague (N.L.) third base, Ford (A.L.) left field, Kibler (N.L.) right field. Time—3:36. Attendance—55,063.

FIRST INNING

Boston—Boggs grounded to Backman, who made a nice play to his left and off-balanced throw to first which was dug out by Hernandez for the out. Barrett also bounced to Backman. Buckner lined to Santana. No runs, no hits, no errors, none left.

New York—Dykstra struck out on three pitches. Backman walked. With Hernandez at the plate, Backman was caught stealing, Gedman to Owen. Hernandez then walked. Carter flied to Henderson in left-center field. No runs, no hits, no errors, one left.

SECOND INNING

Boston—Rice struck out. Evans walked. Gedman hit a high bouncer to Backman, who threw to Hernandez for the out, Evans advancing to second on the play. Henderson flied to Dykstra in right-center. No runs, no hits, no errors, one left.

New York—Strawberry struck out. Heep flied to Henderson on the track in dead center field. Johnson struck out. No runs, no hits, no errors, none left.

THIRD INNING

Boston—Owen walked on a 3-2 pitch. Clemens bunted in front of the plate and when Hernandez attempted to get Owen at second, he bounced his throw in front of Santana, both runners were safe and Hernandez was charged with an error. Boggs lined a double down the left-field line, Owen scoring and Clemens stopping at third. Barrett lined a single to right, Clemens scoring and Boggs stopping at third. Buckner grounded a single to right, Boggs scoring and Barrett stopping at second. Rice flied to Strawberry on the track in right field, Barrett going to third after the catch. Evans struck out. Gedman also struck out. Three runs, three hits, one error, two left.

New York—Santana singled off Clemens' glove, beating throw by Owen to first base. Gooden was credited with a single, when he popped his bunt up, but Buckner failed in his attempt to make a diving catch, Santana advancing to second on the play. Dykstra sacrificed Santana to third and Gooden to second, Boggs to Buckner. Backman grounded a single to center, Santana scoring and Gooden stopping at third. Hernandez hit a grounder off Clemens' leg and was thrown out when Boggs fielded the ball and threw to first, Gooden scoring and Backman advancing to second. Boggs made a diving stop of Carter's smash and threw to Buckner at first for the out. Two runs, three hits, no errors, one left.

FOURTH INNING

Boston—Henderson hit a towering home run into the left-center field stands on a 1-0 pitch by Gooden. Owen singled to center. Clemens sacrificed Owen to second, Hernandez to Backman covering first. Boggs hit a grounder to Santana, who threw to Johnson at third to cut down Owen. Barrett singled between Hernandez and the first base bag, Boggs advancing to third. Buckner flied to Heep. One run, three hits, no errors, two left.

New York—Strawberry flied to Evans on the track in right field. Heep walked. Johnson also flied to Evans on the track in deep right. Santana lined a single to center, Heep stopping at second. Buckner made a backhanded stop on Gooden's bouncer over the first base bag and threw to Clemens covering first for the out. No runs, one hit, no errors, two left.

FIFTH INNING

Boston—Rice bounced a single to left. Evans blasted Gooden's first pitch deep into the left-field seats for a home run. Gedman struck out. Henderson also struck out. Gooden then fanned Owen for his third strikeout in succession. Two runs, two hits, no errors, none left.

New York—Evans made a fine running catch on Dykstra's fly ball to right-center field. Backman walked. Hernandez singled off Barrett's glove, Backman advancing to third. Crawford replaced Clemens on the mound for the Red Sox. Carter singled off Owen's glove, Backman scoring and Hernandez stopping at second. Strawberry was called out on strikes. Heep bounced to Barrett. One run, two hits, no errors, two left.

SIXTH INNING

Boston—Aguilera came in to pitch and Wilson went in to play left field for the Mets. Crawford flied to Strawberry in short right field. Boggs walked. With Boggs running, Barrett bounced to Santana, whose off-balanced throw to first retired Barrett. Buckner struck out. No runs, no hits, no errors, one left.

New York—Johnson flied to Rice in short left field. Boggs backhanded Santana's bouncer to third and made a long throw to first for the out. Wilson struck out. No runs, no hits, no errors, none left.

SEVENTH INNING

Boston—Rice grounded a single up the middle. Evans lined a single to center, Rice stopping at second. Gedman looped a single to center to load the bases. Henderson singled to right, scoring Rice with the bases remaining loaded. Owen grounded a single to left, scoring Evans with the bases remaining loaded. Orosco relieved Aguilera for the Mets. Greenwell, batting for Crawford, was called out on strikes. Boggs struck out. Barrett lined to Dykstra in left-center. Two runs, five hits, no errors, three left.

New York—Stanley went to the mound for the Red Sox. Dykstra grounded a single to left. Backman lined a single to left-center, Dykstra stopping at second. Hernandez struck out. Carter also struck out. Strawberry grounded to Owen, who threw to Buckner for the out. No runs, two hits, no errors, two left.

EIGHTH INNING

Boston—Buckner looped a single to right. Stapleton ran for Buckner. Rice singled to left, Stapleton stopping at second. Evans grounded into a double play, Santana to Backman to Hernandez, Stapleton going to third on the play. Gedman was called out on strikes. No runs, two hits, no errors, one left.

New York—Mazzilli batted for Orosco and flied to Henderson. Johnson hit a chopper to Stapleton, who threw to Stanley covering first for the out. Santana struck out. No runs, no hits, no errors, none left.

NINTH INNING

Boston—Fernandez went in to pitch for the Mets. Henderson lined a single to left. Owen grounded a single to center, Henderson stopping at second. Stanley, attempting to sacrifice, bunted foul on the third strike for an out. Boggs lined a double to right-center, Henderson scoring and Owen stopping at third. Romero ran for Owen, when Owen injured his ankle sliding into third. Sisk relieved Fernandez for the Mets. When the count went to 3-0, Sisk intentionally walked Barrett, loading the bases. Stapleton flied to Wilson in short left, runners holding. Rice struck out. One run, three hits, no errors, three left.

New York—Wilson flied to Rice. Dykstra walked on four pitches. Backman grounded to Stapleton, who made the play at first unassisted, Dykstra going to second. Hernandez flied to Henderson, who made the catch on the track in center field. No runs, no hits, no errors, one left.

Game 3

At Boston
October 21

New York (N.L.)	AB.	R.	H.	PO.	A.	E.
Dykstra, cf	5	2	4	0	0	0
Backman, 2b	5	1	1	2	3	0
Hernandez, 1b	4	1	2	11	1	0
Carter, c	5	1	2	7	1	0
Strawberry, rf	4	1	1	2	0	0
Knight, 3b	4	0	1	2	2	0
Heep, dh	3	0	1	0	0	0
aMitchell	0	0	0	0	0	0
bMazzilli	1	0	0	0	0	0
Wilson, lf	4	0	0	1	0	0
Santana, ss	4	1	1	1	5	0
Ojeda, p	0	0	0	0	2	0
McDowell, p	0	0	0	1	1	0
Totals	39	7	13	27	15	0

Boston (A.L.)	AB.	R.	H.	PO.	A.	E.
Boggs, 3b	3	0	1	0	2	0
Barrett, 2b	4	0	2	4	5	0
Buckner, 1b	4	0	0	9	2	0
Rice, lf	3	0	0	1	1	0
Baylor, dh	4	0	1	0	0	0
Evans, rf	4	0	0	2	0	0
Gedman, c	4	0	0	4	1	0
Henderson, cf	2	1	1	4	0	0
Owen, ss	3	0	0	2	3	0
Boyd, p	0	0	0	1	0	0
Sambito, p	0	0	0	0	0	0
Stanley, p	0	0	0	0	1	0
Totals	31	1	5	27	15	0

New York	400	000	210	—7
Boston	001	000	000	—1

New York	IP.	H.	R.	ER.	BB.	SO.
Ojeda (W)	7	5	1	1	3	6
McDowell	2	0	0	0	0	0

Boston	IP.	H.	R.	ER.	BB.	SO.
Boyd (L)	7	9	6	6	1	3
Sambito	0*	2	1	1	0	0
Stanley	2	2	0	0	0	1

*Pitched to two batters in eighth.

Bases on balls—Off Ojeda 3 (Boggs, Rice, Henderson), off Boyd 1 (Hernandez).

Strikeouts—By Ojeda 6 (Buckner, Rice, Evans, Gedman 2, Henderson), by Boyd 3 (Backman, Strawberry, Wilson), by Stanley 1 (Wilson).

Game-winning RBI—Dykstra.

aAnnounced as pinch-hitter for Heep in eighth. bGrounded out for Mitchell in eighth. Runs batted in—Dykstra, Carter 3, Knight, Heep 2, Barrett. Double plays—Backman, Santana, Hernandez; Owen, Barrett and Buckner. Left on bases—New York 6, Boston 6. Two-base hits—Carter, Baylor, Knight. Home run—Dykstra. Wild pitches—

Ojeda, Sambito. Passed ball—Gedman. Umpires—Wendelstedt (N.L.) plate, Brinkman (A.L.) first base, Montague (N.L.) second base, Ford (A.L.) third base, Kibler (N.L.) left field, Evans (A.L.) right field. Time—2:58. Attendance—33,595.

FIRST INNING

New York—Dykstra homered down right-field line on 1-1 pitch from Boyd, giving Mets their first extra-base hit in Series. It was the 14th leadoff home run in Series history. Backman got a broken-bat single to right. Hernandez lined a single to left-center, Backman advancing to third. Carter doubled to the wall in left-center, Backman scoring and Hernandez stopping at third. Strawberry struck out. Knight grounded to Boggs, who threw to Gedman and got Hernandez in a rundown. Gedman chased Hernandez back to third and tossed to Boggs, who then relayed the ball to Owen. However, Hernandez slid into third base safely. Carter, who had advanced to third during the Hernandez rundown, was then chased back to second by Owen. However, when Hernandez faked a dash off third, Owen turned in his direction and Carter reached second base safely, leaving the bases loaded on the fielder's choice. Heep lined a single to center, Hernandez and Carter scoring and Knight stopping at second. Wilson struck out. Santana bounced to Boggs, who threw to Barrett at second to force Heep. Four runs, five hits, no errors, two left.

Boston—Boggs bounced back to the mound, Ojeda to Hernandez for the out. Ojeda made a backhanded stab of Barrett's comebacker and threw to Hernandez for the second out. Buckner flied to Strawberry deep in the right-field corner. No runs, no hits, no errors, none left.

SECOND INNING

New York—Dykstra grounded to Barrett. Backman was called out on strikes. Hernandez hit a chopper to Buckner, who threw to Boyd covering first for the out. No runs, no hits, no errors, none left.

Boston—Rice was called out on strikes. Baylor doubled high off the wall in left field. Evans hit a squibber to Santana, who threw to Hernandez for the out, Baylor holding at second. Gedman was called out on strikes. No runs, one hit, no errors, one left.

THIRD INNING

New York—Carter flied to Henderson in short center. Strawberry flied to Henderson in left-center. Knight popped to Barrett in short right field. No runs, no hits, no errors, none left.

Boston—Henderson lined a single to left. Knight caught Owen's soft check-swing liner. Boggs walked. Barrett grounded a single to right field, Henderson scoring and Boggs stopping at second. Buckner struck out. Santana fielded Rice's shot to short and threw to Backman at second to force Barrett. One run, two hits, no errors, two left.

FOURTH INNING

New York—Heep flied to Henderson. Wilson bounced to Barrett. Santana hit a one-hopper to Boggs, who threw to Buckner for the out. No runs, no hits, no errors, none left.

Boston—Baylor bounced to Santana. Evans hit a chopper in front of the plate and was out Carter to Hernandez. Gedman lined to Wilson, who made a fine running catch. No runs, no hits, no errors, none left.

FIFTH INNING

New York—Dykstra looped a single to left. With Dykstra running on the pitch, Backman hit a high chopper to Buckner, who made the play unassisted at first base. Hernandez flied to Evans just in front of the warning track in right field, Dykstra advancing to third after the catch. Carter popped to Owen in short left field. No runs, one hit, no errors, one left.

Boston—Henderson struck out. Backman made a diving stop of Owen's smash in the hole between first and second and threw to Hernandez for the out. Boggs lined a single to left. Barrett singled sharply up the middle, Boggs stopping at second. Buckner hit a bouncer to Santana, who threw to Backman at second to force Barrett. No runs, two hits, no errors, two left.

SIXTH INNING

New York—Strawberry flied to Henderson in left-center. Knight grounded to Owen, with Buckner making a good pickup of Owen's low throw at first base for the out. Heep flied to Evans in short right field. No runs, no hits, no errors, none left.

Boston—Rice walked. Baylor popped to Knight, who made the catch in front of Santana. Evans struck out. With the count 2-2 on Gedman, Rice went to second on a wild pitch. Gedman was called out on strikes. No runs, no hits, no errors, one left.

SEVENTH INNING

New York—Wilson fouled to Buckner near the stands. Santana singled sharply up the middle. Dykstra looped a single to right, Santana stopping at second. Backman flied to Rice in short left, runners holding. Boyd walked Hernandez on four pitches to load the bases. Carter lined an 0-2 pitch to left for a single, scoring Santana and Dykstra and, when Hernandez stopped at second, Carter was caught between first and second in a rundown and was put out Rice to Gedman to Barrett to Buckner to Owen. Two runs, three hits, no errors, one left.

Boston—Henderson walked. Owen grounded to the hole between first and second, where Backman made a nice play to his left and started a double play, Backman to Santana to Hernandez. Boggs fouled to Carter just behind home plate. No runs, no hits, no errors, none left.

EIGHTH INNING

New York—Sambito replaced Boyd on the mound for the Red Sox. Strawberry lined the first pitch to center for a single. With the count 1-0 to Knight, Sambito uncorked a wild pitch, Strawberry going to second. Gedman was charged with a passed ball on the next pitch, Strawberry advancing to third. Knight hit a smash down the third-base line and into the corner for a double, scoring Strawberry. After Mitchell was announced as a pinch hitter for Heep, Sambito was replaced on the mound by Stanley. Mazzilli, batting for Mitchell, bounced to Barrett, Knight going to third on the play. Wilson struck out. Santana tapped back to the mound, Stanley to Buckner for the out. One run, two hits, no errors, one left.

Boston—McDowell replaced Ojeda on the mound for the Mets. Barrett bounced to Hernandez, who threw to McDowell covering first for the out. McDowell charged over to the first base line to field Buckner's chopper and threw to Hernandez for the out. Rice grounded to Knight. No runs, no hits, no errors, none left.

NINTH INNING

New York—Dykstra grounded the first pitch between short and third, where Owen made a backhanded stop, but had no play at first. Backman bounced to Owen near the second-base bag, with Owen tossing to Barrett to force Dykstra. Hernandez singled past a diving Boggs, Backman stopping at second. Carter grounded into a double play, Owen to Barrett to Buckner. No runs, two hits, no errors, one left.

Boston—Baylor grounded to Knight. Evans flied to Strawberry. Gedman hit a chopper to Backman. No runs, no hits, no errors, none left.

Game 4

At Boston
October 22

New York (N.L.)	AB.	R.	H.	PO.	A.	E.
Dykstra, cf	5	1	1	3	0	0
Backman, 2b	4	1	2	4	1	0
Hernandez, 1b	3	0	0	6	0	0
Carter, c	4	2	3	5	0	0
Strawberry, rf	4	1	2	2	0	0
Knight, 3b	4	0	2	1	0	0
Heep, dh	4	0	0	0	0	0
Wilson, lf	4	1	2	3	1	0
Santana, ss	4	0	0	3	3	0
Darling, p	0	0	0	0	1	0
McDowell, p	0	0	0	0	0	0
Orosco, p	0	0	0	0	0	0
Totals	36	6	12	27	6	0

Boston (A.L.)	AB.	R.	H.	PO.	A.	E.
Boggs, 3b	5	0	0	1	1	0
Barrett, 2b	4	0	2	1	3	0
Buckner, 1b	5	0	0	11	2	0
Rice, lf	4	1	1	2	1	0
Baylor, dh	3	0	0	0	0	0
Evans, rf	3	1	1	3	0	0
Gedman, c	4	0	3	6	1	1
Henderson, cf	3	0	0	1	0	0
Owen, ss	1	0	0	1	3	0
aGreenwell	0	0	0	0	0	0
bRomero, ss	0	0	0	0	0	0
Nipper, p	0	0	0	1	2	0
Crawford, p	0	0	0	0	0	0
Stanley, p	0	0	0	0	1	0
Totals	32	2	7	27	14	1

New York	0 0 0	3 0 0	2 1 0	—6
Boston	0 0 0	0 0 0	0 2 0	—2

New York	IP.	H.	R.	ER.	BB.	SO.
Darling (W)	7	4	0	0	6	4
McDowell	⅔	3	2	2	1	0
Orosco (S)	1⅓	0	0	0	0	1

Boston	IP.	H.	R.	ER.	BB.	SO.
Nipper (L)	6	7	3	3	1	2
Crawford	2	4	3	3	0	2
Stanley	1	1	0	0	0	0

Bases on balls—Off Darling 6 (Barrett, Rice, Baylor, Evans, Owen 2), off McDowell 1 (Greenwell), off Nipper 1 (Hernandez).

Strikeouts—By Darling 4 (Rice, Baylor, Henderson 2), by Orosco 1 (Rice), by Nipper 2 (Carter, Santana), by Crawford 2 (Knight, Santana).

Game-winning RBI—Carter.

aWalked for Owen in eighth. bRan for Greenwell in eighth. Runs batted in—Dykstra 2, Carter 3, Knight, Evans, Henderson. Double plays—Buckner, Owen and Buckner; Rice and Gedman; Gedman and Barrett. Left on bases—New York 4, Boston 11. Two-base hits—Barrett, Gedman, Strawberry, Carter, Rice. Home runs—Carter 2, Dykstra. Stolen bases—Backman, Wilson 2. Caught stealing—Strawberry. Sacrifice fly—Henderson. Umpires—Brinkman (A.L.) plate, Montague (N.L.) first base, Ford (A.L.) second base, Kibler (N.L.) third base, Evans (A.L.) left field, Wendelstedt (N.L.) right field. Time—3:22. Attendance—33,920.

FIRST INNING

New York—Dykstra grounded to Owen, who ranged far to his left to field the smash. Backman bounced to Buckner, who made the play unassisted at first base. Hernandez walked. Carter was called out on strikes. No runs, no hits, no errors, one left.

Boston—Boggs grounded sharply back to the mound, Darling to Hernandez for the out. Barrett lined a double to the wall in left-center. Buckner grounded to Hernandez, who made the play unassisted at first base, Barrett advancing to third. Rice walked. Baylor also walked, loading the bases. Evans bounced to Santana, who threw to Backman at second base to force Baylor. No runs, one hit, no errors, three left.

SECOND INNING

New York—Strawberry bounced to Barrett. Knight grounded a single to left. Heep hit a one-hopper to Buckner who turned it into a double play, Buckner to Owen to Buckner. No runs, one hit, no errors, none left.

Boston—Gedman's smash down the first-base line went into the right-field corner for a double. Henderson struck out. Owen grounded to Backman, who threw to Hernandez for the out, Gedman advancing to third on the play. Boggs flied to Dykstra in right-center. No runs, one hit, no errors, one left.

THIRD INNING

New York—Wilson bounced to Buckner, who threw to Nipper covering first base for the out. Santana tapped back to the mound on a half-swing, Nipper to Buckner for the out. Dykstra bounced to Buckner, who made the play unassisted at first. No runs, no hits, no errors, none left.

Boston—Barrett hit a soft liner to Santana. Buckner fouled to Hernandez. Rice struck out trying to check his swing. No runs, no hits, no errors, none left.

FOURTH INNING

New York—Backman singled up the middle. With Backman running on 1-0 pitch and the Red Sox pitching out, Hernandez threw his bat at the ball and bounced to Owen, who threw to Buckner for the out. Carter drilled a home run into the screen above the left-field wall on a first-pitch delivery from Nipper, Backman scoring ahead of him. Strawberry laced Nipper's next delivery to the left-field wall for a double. Knight lined a 3-2 pitch to center for a single, scoring Strawberry. Heep flied to Evans in short right field. Wilson flied to Henderson in right-center. Three runs, four hits, no errors, one left.

Boston—Baylor struck out. Wilson had trouble with Evans' fly ball, but made the catch in short left field. Gedman popped to Knight on the grass behind third base. No runs, no hits, no errors, none left.

FIFTH INNING

New York—Santana struck out. Nipper made a good play on Dykstra's chopper up the middle and threw to Buckner for the out. Backman grounded a single to left past a diving Boggs. With Hernandez at the plate, Backman stole second. Hernandez bounced to Buckner, who made the play unassisted at first. No runs, one hit, no errors, one left.

Boston—Henderson was called out on strikes. Owen walked, ending Darling's streak of having retired 10 straight batters. Boggs flied to Dykstra one step in front of the wall in left-center field, Owen holding at first. Barrett grounded a single to center, Owen advancing to third. Buckner popped to Backman. No runs, one hit, no errors, two left.

SIXTH INNING

New York—Carter blooped a double down the right-field line. Strawberry flied to Evans against the fence in deep right-center field, Carter advancing to third after the catch. Knight lined a 3-2 pitch to Rice, who made the catch on the run and then threw to Gedman at the plate to tag out Carter attempting to score after the catch for a double play. No runs, one hit, no errors, none left.

Boston—Rice flied to Dykstra in right-center field. Baylor flied to Wilson, who misjudged the ball but recovered to make a one-handed stab one step in front of the wall in the left-field corner. Evans walked on four pitches. Gedman lined a single off the left-field wall on the first pitch from Darling, but was thrown out trying to stretch the hit into a double, Wilson to Backman. No runs, one hit, no errors, one left.

SEVENTH INNING

New York—Crawford replaced Nipper on the mound for the Red Sox. Heep fouled to Boggs in front of the Mets' dugout. Wilson grounded a single up the middle. Santana was called out on strikes. With the count 1-0 on Dykstra, Wilson stole second. Dykstra belted a 1-2 pitch over the right-field fence for a home run, the ball deflecting off Evans' glove and over the wall. Backman bounced to Barrett. Two runs, two hits, no errors, none left.

Boston—Henderson fouled to Wilson, who made the catch deep in the left-field corner. Owen walked. Boggs flied to Strawberry, Owen holding at first. Barrett walked on four pitches. Buckner popped to Santana. No runs, no hits, no errors, two left.

EIGHTH INNING

New York—Hernandez lined to Evans. Carter hit a towering home run over the left-field wall on a 1-2 delivery by Crawford for his second homer of the game. Strawberry grounded a single to right, just out of a diving Barrett's reach. Knight struck out and Strawberry was caught stealing for a double play, Gedman to Barrett. One run, two hits, no errors, none left.

Boston—McDowell replaced Darling on the mound for the Mets. Rice lined a double down the right-field line. Baylor lined to Santana. Evans bounced a single up the middle, scoring Rice. Gedman grounded a single to right on an 0-2 pitch, Evans advancing to third. Henderson hit a sacrifice fly to right, Evans scoring after Strawberry made the catch. Greenwell, batting for Owen, walked on four pitches. Romero went into the game to run for Greenwell. Orosco replaced McDowell on the mound for the Mets. Boggs grounded to Santana, who threw to Backman to force Romero at second. Two runs, three hits, no errors, two left.

NINTH INNING

New York—Romero stayed in the game at shortstop and Stanley replaced Crawford on the mound for the Red Sox. Heep flied to Rice. Wilson grounded a single to center. Wilson stole second on the first pitch to Santana and went on to third when Gedman's throw bounced into center field for an error. Santana bounced back to the mound and Wilson was caught in a rundown between third and home and tagged out, Stanley to Boggs to Gedman, Santana going to second on the play. Dykstra bounced to Barrett. No runs, one hit, one error, one left.

Boston—Barrett grounded to Santana. Buckner hit a shot to Hernandez, who made a backhanded stop and raced to the bag for the unassisted putout. Rice struck out. No runs, no hits, no errors, none left.

Game 5

At Boston
October 23

New York (N.L.)	AB.	R.	H.	PO.	A.	E.
Dykstra, cf	5	0	1	1	0	0
Teufel, 2b	4	1	2	0	2	0
Hernandez, 1b	4	0	1	7	1	0
Carter, c	4	0	0	8	0	0
Strawberry, rf	4	0	1	1	0	0
Knight, 3b	4	0	1	1	0	0
Mitchell, dh	4	0	1	0	0	0
Wilson, lf	4	1	2	4	0	0
Santana, ss	2	0	1	1	1	1
Gooden, p	0	0	0	1	2	0
Fernandez, p	0	0	0	0	0	0
Totals	35	2	10	24	6	1

Boston (A.L.)	AB.	R.	H.	PO.	A.	E.
Boggs, 3b	5	0	2	1	6	0
Barrett, 2b	4	0	2	3	5	0
Buckner, 1b	5	1	1	9	1	0
Stapleton, 1b	0	0	0	2	0	0
Rice, lf	3	1	2	2	0	0
Baylor, dh	3	1	1	0	0	0
Evans, rf	4	0	2	2	0	0
Gedman, c	4	0	0	6	0	0
Henderson, cf	4	1	2	0	0	0
Owen, ss	3	0	0	1	1	0
Hurst, p	0	0	0	1	0	0
Totals	35	4	12	27	13	0

New York	000	000	011—2
Boston	011	020	00x—4

New York	IP.	H.	R.	ER.	BB.	SO.
Gooden (L)	4*	9	4	3	2	3
Fernandez	4	3	0	0	0	5

Boston	IP.	H.	R.	ER.	BB.	SO.
Hurst (W)	9	10	2	2	1	6

*Pitched to three batters in fifth.

Bases on balls—Off Gooden 2 (Barrett, Rice), off Hurst 1 (Santana).

Strikeouts—By Gooden 3 (Baylor, Henderson, Owen), by Fernandez 5 (Rice, Baylor, Gedman 2, Owen), by Hurst 6 (Dykstra 2, Carter, Strawberry, Mitchell, Wilson).

Game-winning RBI—Owen.

Runs batted in—Teufel, Santana, Baylor, Evans, Henderson, Owen. Double play—Boggs, Barrett and Buckner. Left on bases—New York 8, Boston 11. Two-base hits—Teufel, Henderson, Barrett, Wilson. Three-base hits—Henderson, Rice. Home run—Teufel. Sacrifice hit—Santana. Sacrifice fly—Owen. Hit by pitcher—By Gooden (Baylor). Umpires—Montague (N.L.) plate, Ford (A.L.) first base, Kibler (N.L.) second base, Evans (A.L.) third base, Wendelstedt (N.L.) left field, Brinkman (A.L.) right field. Time—3:09. Attendance—34,010.

FIRST INNING

New York—Dykstra grounded to Barrett, who went to his right to field the smash. Teufel doubled up the gap in right-center field. Hernandez bounced to Barrett, who threw to Buckner at first base for the out, Teufel advancing to third on the play. Barrett fielded Carter's slow roller and threw to first for the out. No runs, one hit, no errors, one left.

Boston—Boggs hit a nubber back to the mound, Gooden to Hernandez for the out. Barrett walked. With the count 1-0 to Buckner, Barrett was picked off first base, Gooden to Hernandez. Buckner singled sharply up the middle. Rice was credited with an infield hit when Teufel couldn't come up with his grounder behind second base, Buckner stopping at second. With a 1-2 count, Baylor was hit by a pitch, loading the bases. Evans popped to Wilson in short left. No runs, two hits, no errors, three left.

SECOND INNING

New York—Strawberry hit a chopper to Buckner, who threw to Hurst covering first base for the out. Knight flied to Evans just in front of the track in right. Boggs backhanded Mitchell's grounder near the third-base bag and made a long throw to Buckner for the out. No runs, no hits, no errors, none left.

Boston—Gedman was jammed on a fastball by Hurst and hit a soft popup to Santana. Henderson drilled a 2-2 pitch to the wall in right-center for a triple when Strawberry failed to cut the ball off and Dykstra fell down on the warning track. Owen hit a sacrifice fly to Wilson in left on a 1-1 pitch, scoring Henderson. It was the first time in the Series that the home team had held a lead. Boggs hit a chopper to Hernandez, who threw to Gooden covering first for the out. One run, one hit, no errors, none left.

THIRD INNING

New York—Wilson was called out on strikes. Santana walked. Dykstra blooped a single to center, Santana stopping at second. Teufel flied to Rice near the left-field line, both runners holding. Hernandez also flied to Rice a step in front of the warning track in left. No runs, one hit, no errors, two left.

Boston—Teufel fielded Barrett's bouncer off the mound and threw to Hernandez at first for the out. Santana booted Buckner's grounder to short for an error. Rice walked. Baylor struck out on three pitches. Evans lined a single to center, Buckner scoring ahead of Dykstra's weak throw on a head first slide and Rice stopping at second. Gedman flied to Dykstra. One run, one hit, one error, two left.

FOURTH INNING

New York—Carter was called out on strikes. Strawberry grounded a single to center. Boggs fielded Knight's smash on a short hop and turned it into a double play, Boggs to Barrett to Buckner. No runs, one hit, no errors, none left.

Boston—Henderson struck out. Owen also struck out. Boggs singled up the middle. Barrett also singled up the middle, Boggs advancing to third. Hernandez fielded Buckner's one-hopper and made an unassisted play at first base. No runs, two hits, no errors, two left.

FIFTH INNING

New York—Mitchell blooped a single to right. Wilson grounded a single through the hole between first and second, Mitchell stopping at second. Santana sacrificed Mitchell to third and Wilson to second, Boggs making a barehanded pickup and throwing to Barrett covering first for the out. Dykstra struck out on a high fastball. Teufel bounced to Boggs, who ranged a couple steps to his left to make the play and threw to Buckner for the out. No runs, two hits, no errors, two left.

Boston—Rice hit a 2-2 pitch off the top of the wall in right-center field for a triple. Baylor blooped a single to right, scoring Rice. With Baylor running on a 3-2 delivery, Evans grounded a single to left, Baylor going to third. Fernandez replaced Gooden on the mound for the Mets. Gedman struck out on three pitches. Henderson smashed a double down the left-field line, Baylor scoring and Evans stopping at third. Teufel made a diving stop to his left on Owen's hard shot and threw to Hernandez at first for the out, Evans and Henderson holding their bases on the play. Boggs flied to Wilson. Two runs, four hits, no errors, two left.

SIXTH INNING

New York—Hernandez grounded to Owen, who made a nice play on the one-hop smash and threw to Buckner at first for the out. Boggs went far to his left to field Carter's grounder and threw to Buckner for the out. Strawberry was called out on strikes. No runs, no hits, no errors, none left.

Boston—Barrett popped to Hernandez. Buckner flied to Wilson on the warning track in left-center field. Rice struck out. No runs, no hits, no errors, none left.

SEVENTH INNING

New York—Knight blooped a single to right just in fair territory, Barrett making a quick recovery to hold Knight at first. Mitchell struck out. Wilson flied to Evans in short right field. Santana popped to Barrett in short right field. No runs, one hit, no errors, one left.

Boston—Baylor struck out. Evans bounced to Santana. Gedman struck out on three pitches. No runs, no hits, no errors, none left.

EIGHTH INNING

New York—Dykstra popped to Owen in short left field. Teufel homered into the stands down the right-field line on an 0-2 pitch, the first run off Hurst in 15⅓ innings in the Series. Hernandez looped a single to center. Carter hit a squibber to Barrett, who threw to Buckner at first for the out, Hernandez stopping at second on the play. Strawberry fouled to Boggs. One run, two hits, no errors, one left.

Boston—Henderson flied to Strawberry near the warning track in right. Owen struck out. Boggs was credited with a single when Teufel couldn't come up with his hard smash. Barrett drilled a double off the wall in left-center, Boggs stopping at third. It was Barrett's ninth hit in the Series and his 20th in postseason play, breaking Thurman Munson's record set in 1976. Buckner fouled to Knight. No runs, two hits, no errors, two left.

NINTH INNING

New York—Stapleton went in to play first base for the Red Sox. Knight grounded to Boggs. Mitchell popped to Stapleton. Wilson doubled down the left-field line. Santana singled into the hole between first and second, scoring Wilson. Dykstra struck out on three pitches. One run, two hits, no errors, one left.

Game 6

At New York
October 25

Boston (A.L.)	AB.	R.	H.	PO.	A.	E.
Boggs, 3b	5	2	3	1	0	0
Barrett, 2b	4	1	3	1	4	0
Buckner, 1b	5	0	0	5	0	1
Rice, lf	5	0	0	5	0	0
Evans, rf	4	0	1	1	0	1
Gedman, c	5	0	1	9	0	1
Henderson, cf	5	1	2	5	0	0
Owen, ss	4	1	3	2	2	0
Clemens, p	3	0	0	0	1	0
bGreenwell	1	0	0	0	0	0
Schiraldi, p	1	0	0	0	1	0
Stanley, p	0	0	0	0	0	0
Totals	42	5	13	29	8	3

New York (N.L.)	AB.	R.	H.	PO.	A.	E.
Dykstra, cf	4	0	0	4	0	0
Backman, 2b	4	0	1	0	4	0
Hernandez, 1b	4	0	1	6	1	0
Carter, c	4	1	1	9	0	0
Strawberry, rf	2	1	0	5	0	0
Aguilera, p	0	0	0	0	0	0
eMitchell	1	1	1	0	0	0
Knight, 3b	4	2	2	0	0	1
Wilson, lf	5	0	1	2	1	0
Santana, ss	1	0	0	0	1	0
aHeep	1	0	0	0	0	0
Elster, ss	1	0	0	3	3	1
dJohnson, ss	1	0	0	0	0	0
Ojeda, p	2	0	0	0	0	0
McDowell, p	0	0	0	0	1	0
Orosco, p	0	0	0	0	0	0
cMazzilli, rf	2	1	1	1	0	0
Totals	36	6	8	30	11	2

Boston	110	000	100	2—5
New York	000	020	010	3—6

Two out when winning run scored.

Boston	IP.	H.	R.	ER.	BB.	SO.
Clemens	7	4	2	1	2	8
Schiraldi (L)	2⅔	4	4	3	2	1
Stanley	0*	0	0	0	0	0

New York	IP.	H.	R.	ER.	BB.	SO.
Ojeda	6	8	2	2	2	3
McDowell	1⅔	2	1	0	3	1
Orosco	⅓	0	0	0	0	0
Aguilera (W)	2	3	2	2	0	3

*Pitched to one batter in tenth.

Bases on balls—Off Clemens 2 (Strawberry 2), off Schiraldi 2 (Hernandez, Knight), off Ojeda 2 (Rice, Evans), off McDowell 3 (Barrett 2, Boggs).

Strikeouts—By Clemens 8 (Dykstra 2, Backman, Carter, Knight, Wilson, Santana, Ojeda), by Schiraldi 1 (Johnson), by Ojeda 3 (Rice, Gedman, Clemens), by McDowell 1 (Greenwell), by Aguilera 3 (Rice, Owen, Schiraldi).

Game-winning RBI—None.

aGrounded into double play (with run scoring) for Santana in fifth. bStruck out for Clemens in eighth. cSingled and scored for Orosco in eighth. dStruck out for Elster in ninth. eSingled and scored for Aguilera in tenth. Runs batted in—Barrett 2, Evans 2, Henderson, Carter, Knight 2. Double plays—Barrett, Owen and Buckner; Backman, Elster and Hernandez. Left on bases—Boston 14, New York 8. Two-base hits—Evans, Boggs. Home run—Henderson. Stolen bases—Strawberry 2. Sacrifice hits—Owen, Dykstra, Backman. Sacrifice fly—Carter. Hit by pitcher—By Aguilera (Buckner). Wild pitch—Stanley. Umpires—Ford (A.L.) plate, Kibler (N.L.) first base, Evans (A.L.) second base, Wendelstedt (N.L.) third base, Brinkman (A.L.) left field, Montague (N.L.) right field. Time—4:02. Attendance—55,078.

FIRST INNING

Boston—Boggs singled off Knight's glove, Santana coming up with the deflection but having no play at first base. Barrett lined to Dykstra in right-center field. Buckner flied to Dykstra. Rice walked. Evans lined a 1-1 pitch off the wall in left-center for a double, Boggs scoring and Rice stopping at third. Gedman flied to Strawberry in right-center. One run, two hits, no errors, two left.

New York—Dykstra was called out on strikes. Backman also took a called third strike. Hernandez flied to Henderson in left-center. No runs, no hits, no errors, none left.

SECOND INNING

Boston—Henderson flied to Wilson just in front of the warning track in left field. Owen singled up the middle through the legs of Ojeda. Clemens bunted foul on a third strike. On a 1-1 pitch Owen broke for second and Boggs singled through the vacated spot between first and second, Owen advancing to third on the play. Barrett lined a single to left on a 1-2 pitch, Owen scoring and Boggs stopping at second. Strawberry misjudged Buckner's long fly to right, but recovered to make the catch on the warning track. One run, three hits, no errors, two left.

New York—Carter flied to Henderson. Strawberry walked. Knight struck out swinging, with Strawberry stealing second on the third strike. Wilson was called out on strikes. No runs, no hits, no errors, one left.

THIRD INNING

Boston—Rice was called out on strikes. Evans flied to Strawberry in right-center field. Gedman struck out. No runs, no hits, no errors, none left.

New York—Santana struck out. Ojeda also struck out. Dykstra hit a one-hopper to the left of Owen, who threw to Buckner at first base for the out. No runs, no hits, no errors, none left.

FOURTH INNING

Boston—Henderson flied to Dykstra in short center. Owen singled through the hole between second and third. Clemens, attempting to sacrifice, bunted in the air to Carter in foul territory just to the right of home plate. Boggs hit a high chopper over the mound that Santana fielded and threw to Hernandez at first base for the out. No runs, one hit, no errors, one left.

New York—Backman flied to Rice. Hernandez fouled to Boggs, who reached into the photographer's box to make the catch in foul territory. Carter tapped in front of the plate, Clemens throwing to Buckner at first base for the out. No runs, no hits, no errors, none left.

FIFTH INNING

Boston—Barrett singled past a diving Knight. Buckner flied to Strawberry two steps in front of the fence in right field. Rice flied to Strawberry. Evans walked. Gedman lined to Wilson in short left. No runs, one hit, no errors, two left.

New York—Strawberry walked and then stole second. Knight singled up the middle, Strawberry scoring. Wilson singled through the hole between first and second, Knight going to third when Evans bobbled the ball in right field for an error. Heep, batting for Santana, grounded sharply into a double play, Barrett to Owen to Buckner, Knight scoring on the play. Ojeda grounded to Barrett. Two runs, two hits, one error, none left.

SIXTH INNING

Boston—Elster came in to play at shortstop for the Mets. Henderson grounded to Elster, who made a nice play to his left. Owen was credited with an infield hit when his chopper was fielded by Hernandez, but his off-balanced throw to Ojeda covering first was late and off the mark. Clemens, attempting to sacrifice, bunted in front of the plate and forced Owen at second base, Hernandez to Elster. Boggs bounced to Backman, who threw to Elster at second to force Clemens. No runs, one hit, no errors, one left.

New York—Dykstra was called out on strikes. Owen made a diving stop to his right to field

Backman's smash, but his throw to first was too late for an infield hit. Hernandez lined a single to center and Backman, running with the pitch, continued on to third. Carter was called out on strikes. Strawberry grounded sharply to Barrett, who threw to Owen at second base to force Hernandez. No runs, two hits, no errors, two left.

SEVENTH INNING

Boston—McDowell replaced Ojeda on the mound for the Mets. Barrett walked. With Barrett running on the pitch, Buckner hit a one-hopper to Backman, who threw to Hernandez for the out. Rice hit a chopper to Knight, who threw too high to first for an error, Barrett going to third when the ball went off Hernandez' glove. With Rice running on a 3-2 pitch, Evans grounded to Backman and Rice beat Backman's flip to Elster, who then threw to Hernandez at first to retire Evans, Barrett scoring on the play. Gedman lined a single to left and Rice, trying to score, was thrown out, Wilson to Carter. One run, one hit, one error, one left.

New York—Knight lined to Evans. Wilson bounced to Barrett. Elster flied to Henderson in right-center field. No runs, no hits, no errors, none left.

EIGHTH INNING

Boston—Henderson was credited with a single when his hard smash took a bad hop and went off Elster's shoulder into center field. Owen sacrificed Henderson to second, McDowell to Hernandez. Greenwell, batting for Clemens, struck out on three pitches. After the count reached 2-0, McDowell intentionally walked Boggs. Barrett also walked, loading the bases. Orosco replaced McDowell on the mound for the Mets. Buckner flied to Dykstra on Orosco's first pitch. No runs, one hit, no errors, three left.

New York—Schiraldi came in to pitch for the Red Sox. Mazzilli, batting for Orosco, grounded a single to right. Dykstra sacrificed Mazzilli to second and both runners were safe when Schiraldi bounced his throw to Owen at second in an attempt to force Mazzilli. Backman sacrificed Mazzilli to third and Dykstra to second, Schiraldi to Barrett covering first for the out. Hernandez was walked intentionally, loading the bases. Carter, swinging on a 3-0 pitch, lined hard to Rice in left for a sacrifice fly, Mazzilli scoring after the catch and Dykstra going to third on the throw to the plate. Strawberry flied to Henderson in right-center field. One run, one hit, no errors, two left.

NINTH INNING

Boston—Mazzilli stayed in the game and played right field and Aguilera came in to pitch for the Mets. Rice struck out. Evans was safe at first base when Elster booted his ground ball for an error. Gedman grounded into a double play, Backman to Elster to Hernandez. No runs, no hits, one error, none left.

New York—Knight walked. Wilson bunted in front of the plate and Gedman's throw to second, attempting to force Knight, pulled Owen off the base for an error. Johnson, batting for Elster, was out on strikes when Gedman held his foul tip. Mazzilli chased Rice back to the warning track in left field for his long fly. Dykstra also flied to Rice. No runs, no hits, one error, two left.

TENTH INNING

Boston—Johnson remained in the game and played shortstop for the Mets. Henderson belted an 0-1 pitch into the stands in left field for a home run. Owen struck out. Schiraldi also struck out. Boggs lined a double to the wall in left-center. Barrett grounded a single to center, Boggs scoring and Barrett going to second on Dykstra's throw to the plate. With the count 1-2, Buckner was hit by a pitch. Rice lined to Mazzilli. Two runs, three hits, no errors, two left.

New York—Backman flied to Rice near the left-field line. Hernandez flied to Henderson a step in front of the warning track in center. Carter lined a 2-1 pitch to left for a single. Mitchell, batting for Aguilera, lined an 0-1 pitch to center for a single, Carter stopping at second. Knight looped a single to center on an 0-2 delivery, Carter scoring and Mitchell advancing to third. Stanley replaced Schiraldi on the mound for the Red Sox. Wilson had a 2-2 count on him when Stanley threw a wild pitch, Mitchell scoring and Knight going to second. Wilson grounded a 3-2 delivery over the first-base bag and through Buckner's legs for an error, Knight scoring. Three runs, three hits, one error, none left.

Game 7

At New York
October 27

Boston (A.L.)	AB.	R.	H.	PO.	A.	E.
Boggs, 3b	4	0	1	0	0	0
Barrett, 2b	5	0	1	2	4	0
Buckner, 1b	4	1	2	9	1	0
Rice, lf	4	1	2	2	0	0
Evans, rf	4	1	2	3	1	0
Gedman, c	4	1	1	4	0	0
Henderson, cf	2	1	0	3	0	0
Owen, ss	3	0	0	1	3	0
eBaylor	1	0	0	0	0	0
Nipper, p	0	0	0	0	0	0
Crawford, p	0	0	0	0	0	0
Hurst, p	0	0	0	0	1	0
cArmas	1	0	0	0	0	0
Schiraldi, p	0	0	0	0	0	0
Sambito, p	0	0	0	0	0	0
Stanley, p	0	0	0	0	0	0
Romero, ss	1	0	0	0	1	0
Totals	33	5	9	24	11	0

New York (N.L.)	AB.	R.	H.	PO.	A.	E.
Wilson, cf-lf	3	1	1	3	0	0
Teufel, 2b	2	0	0	3	0	0
bBackman, 2b	1	1	0	1	1	0
Hernandez, 1b	4	0	1	6	0	0
Carter, c	4	0	0	7	0	0
Strawberry, rf	4	1	1	5	0	0
Knight, 3b	4	2	3	0	2	0
Mitchell, lf	2	0	0	0	1	0
dDykstra, cf	2	1	1	0	0	0
Santana, ss	3	1	1	2	2	0
Darling, p	1	0	0	0	1	0
Fernandez, p	0	0	0	0	0	0
aMazzilli	1	1	1	0	0	0
McDowell, p	0	0	0	0	0	0
Orosco, p	1	0	1	0	0	0
Totals	32	8	10	27	7	0

Boston	030	000	020	—5
New York	000	003	32x	—8

Boston	IP.	H.	R.	ER.	BB.	SO.
Hurst	6	4	3	3	1	3
Schiraldi (L)	⅓	3	3	3	0	0
Sambito	⅓	0	0	0	2	0
Stanley	⅓	0	0	0	0	0
Nipper	⅓	3	2	2	1	0
Crawford	⅔	0	0	0	0	0

New York	IP.	H.	R.	ER.	BB.	SO.
Darling	3⅔	6	3	3	1	0
Fernandez	2⅓	0	0	0	1	4
McDowell (W)	1*	3	2	2	0	1
Orosco (S)	2	0	0	0	0	2

*Pitched to three batters in eighth.

Bases on balls—Off Hurst 1 (Teufel), off Sambito 2 (Wilson, Backman), off Nipper 1 (Santana), off Darling 1 (Henderson), off Fernandez 1 (Boggs).

Strikeouts—By Hurst 3 (Teufel, Mitchell, Santana), by Fernandez 4 (Rice, Evans, Gedman, Owen), by McDowell 1 (Armas), by Orosco 2 (Henderson, Barrett).

Game winning RBI—Knight.

aSingled and scored for Fernandez in sixth. bRan for Teufel and scored in sixth. cStruck out for Hurst in seventh. dSingled and scored for Mitchell in seventh. eGrounded out for Owen in eighth. Runs batted in—Boggs, Evans 3, Gedman, Hernandez 3, Carter, Strawberry, Knight, Santana, Orosco. Double plays—None. Left on bases—Boston 6, New York 7. Two-base hit—Evans. Home runs—Evans, Gedman, Knight, Strawberry. Sacrifice hits—Hurst 2, McDowell. Sacrifice fly—Hernandez. Hit by pitcher—By Darling (Henderson), by Crawford (Wilson). Wild pitch—Schiraldi. Umpires—Kibler (N.L.) plate, Evans (A.L.) first base, Wendelstedt (N.L.) second base, Brinkman (A.L.) third base, Montague (N.L.) left field, Ford (A.L.) right field. Time—3:11. Attendance—55,032.

FIRST INNING

Boston—Boggs lined to Santana. Barrett flied to Strawberry in short right field. Buckner grounded a single to right. Rice flied to Strawberry. No runs, one hit, no errors, one left.

New York—Wilson hit a roller to Barrett. Teufel popped to Barrett. Hernandez lined to Henderson. No runs, no hits, no errors, none left.

SECOND INNING

Boston—Evans sent a 3-2 pitch over the wall in left-center field for a homer. Gedman belted a 1-2 delivery over the right-center field wall for a homer, the ball going over the wall off the glove of Strawberry. It was the tenth time in Series history that players hit back-to-back homers. Henderson walked. Owen popped to Santana. Hurst sacrificed Henderson to second, Darling to Teufel covering first on the play. Boggs singled sharply past a diving Santana, Henderson scoring. Barrett got a bunt single down the third-base line. Buckner flied to Wilson in left-center. Three runs, four hits, no errors, two left.

New York—Carter's bunt to the left of the mound was fielded by Hurst, who threw to Buckner at first for the out. Strawberry flied to Rice. Knight lined a single to center. Mitchell's check-swing grounder was fielded by Buckner, who made the play unassisted at first base. No runs, one hit, no errors, one left.

THIRD INNING

Boston—Rice lined a single off the left-field wall, but was thrown out trying to stretch the hit into a double, Mitchell to Teufel. Evans flied to Wilson. Gedman bounced to Hernandez, who made the play unassisted at first. No runs, one hit, no errors, none left.

New York—Santana struck out. Darling chased Evans back to the warning track in right-center field for his long fly. Wilson flied to Evans just in front of the track in right field. No runs, no hits, no errors, none left.

FOURTH INNING

Boston—Henderson was hit by a pitch. Owen lined to Strawberry. Hurst sacrificed Henderson to second, Knight to Teufel covering first on the play. Fernandez replaced Darling on the mound for the Mets. Boggs walked. Barrett flied to Strawberry. No runs, no hits, no errors, two left.

New York—Teufel struck out. Hernandez flied to Evans just short of the warning track in right-center field. Carter hit a roller to Barrett. No runs, no hits, no errors, none left.

FIFTH INNING

Boston—Buckner flied to Strawberry in short right. Rice struck out. Evans also struck out. No runs, no hits, no errors, none left.

New York—Strawberry flied to Henderson on the warning track in right-center. Knight hit a chopper over the mound and was thrown out Owen to Buckner. Mitchell struck out. No runs, no hits, no errors, none left.

SIXTH INNING

Boston—Gedman was called out on strikes. Henderson flied to Wilson in left-center field. Owen was called out on strikes. No runs, no hits, no errors, none left.

New York—Santana hit a chopper over the mound and Owen made a good play to field the ball behind second base and throw to Buckner for the out at first. Mazzilli, batting for Fernandez, grounded a single through the hole between second and third. Wilson lined a single over the head of Boggs, Mazzilli stopping at second. Teufel walked to load the bases. Hernandez lined an 0-1 pitch to left-center for a single, scoring Mazzilli and Wilson and sending Teufel to third. Backman went in to the game to run for Teufel. Carter hit a looper to right field that Evans dived for but could not make the catch, Backman scoring, but Hernandez was forced at second base, Evans to Owen, while Carter was safe at first on the fielder's choice. Strawberry lined to Rice, who made a diving catch. Three runs, three hits, no errors, one left.

SEVENTH INNING

Boston—Backman stayed in the game and played second base and McDowell came in to pitch for the Mets. Armas, batting for Hurst, struck out. Boggs bounced to Knight, with Hernandez making a nice pickup on Knight's low throw to first base. Barrett hit a chopper over the mound to Santana, who threw to Hernandez at first for the out. No runs, no hits, no errors, none left.

New York—Schiraldi came in to pitch for the Red Sox. Knight belted a 2-1 pitch over the wall in left-center field for a home run. Dykstra, batting for Mitchell, grounded a single through the hole between first and second. Dykstra went to second on a wild pitch. Santana grounded a single over the first-base bag on a 2-0 delivery, scoring Dykstra. McDowell sacrificed Santana to second, Buckner to Barrett covering first base on the play. Sambito replaced Schiraldi on the mound for the Red Sox. Wilson was walked intentionally. Backman also walked, loading the bases. Hernandez flied to Henderson in deep left-center field, Santana scoring and Wilson going to third after the catch. Stanley replaced Sambito on the mound for the Red Sox. Carter grounded to Owen, who charged the ball and made an off-balanced throw to Buckner at first for the out. Three runs, three hits, no errors, two left.

EIGHTH INNING

Boston—Dykstra stayed in the game and played center field and Wilson moved from center to left. Buckner looped a single to left. Rice singled past a diving Santana, Buckner stopping at second. Evans lined a double to the wall in right-center field, scoring Buckner and Rice. Orosco replaced McDowell on the mound for the Mets. Gedman lined to Backman. Henderson struck out. Baylor, batting for Owen, bounced to Santana.

Two runs, three hits, no errors, one left.

New York—Romero went in to play shortstop and Nipper replaced Stanley on the mound for the Red Sox. Strawberry blasted a towering home run over the right-center field wall on an 0-2 pitch. Knight also connected on an 0-2 delivery, singling up the middle. Dykstra grounded to Romero, who made the play in front of the second-base bag and threw to Buckner at first for the out. Santana received an intentional walk. After the count reached 1-1, Orosco disdained the bunt and bounced a single up the middle through a drawn-in infield, scoring Knight and sending Santana to third. Crawford replaced Nipper on the mound for the Red Sox. Wilson was hit by a pitch, loading the bases. Backman forced Santana at home plate, Barrett to Gedman. Hernandez grounded to Barrett. Two runs, three hits, no errors, three left.

NINTH INNING

Boston—Romero fouled to Hernandez. Boggs hit a chopper to Backman, who threw to Hernandez at first for the out. Barrett struck out. No runs, no hits, no errors, none left.

NEW YORK METS' BATTING AND FIELDING AVERAGES

Player—Position	G.	AB.	R.	H.	TB.	2B.	3B.	HR.	RBI.	BB.	IBB.	SO.	B.A.	PO.	A.	E.	F.A.
Orosco, p	4	1	0	1	1	0	0	0	1	0	0	0	1.000	0	0	0	.000
Gooden, p	2	2	1	1	1	0	0	0	0	0	0	0	.500	1	2	0	1.000
Teufel, 2b	3	9	1	4	8	1	0	1	1	1	0	2	.444	3	3	1	.857
Mazzilli, ph-rf	4	5	2	2	2	0	0	0	0	0	0	0	.400	1	0	0	1.000
Knight, 3b	6	23	4	9	13	1	0	1	5	2	0	2	.391	5	6	1	.917
Backman, pr-2b	6	18	4	6	6	0	0	0	1	3	0	2	.333	9	13	0	1.000
Dykstra, cf-ph	7	27	4	8	14	0	0	2	3	2	0	7	.296	14	0	0	1.000
Carter, c	7	29	4	8	16	2	0	2	9	0	0	4	.276	57	1	0	1.000
Wilson, lf-cf	7	26	3	7	8	1	0	0	0	1	1	6	.269	15	2	0	1.000
Santana, ss	7	20	3	5	5	0	0	0	2	2	1	5	.250	11	17	1	.966
Mitchell, ph-lf-dh	5	8	1	2	2	0	0	0	0	0	0	3	.250	0	2	0	1.000
Hernandez, 1b	7	26	1	6	6	0	0	0	4	5	1	1	.231	48	4	1	.981
Strawberry, rf	7	24	4	5	9	1	0	1	1	4	0	6	.208	19	0	0	1.000
Heep, ph-lf-dh	5	11	0	1	1	0	0	0	2	1	0	1	.091	1	0	0	1.000
Aguilera, p	2	0	0	0	0	0	0	0	0	0	0	0	.000	0	0	0	.000
Fernandez, p	3	0	0	0	0	0	0	0	0	0	0	0	.000	0	0	0	.000
McDowell, p	5	0	0	0	0	0	0	0	0	0	0	0	.000	1	4	0	1.000
Sisk, p	1	0	0	0	0	0	0	0	0	0	0	0	.000	0	0	0	.000
Elster, ss	1	1	0	0	0	0	0	0	0	0	0	0	.000	3	3	1	.857
Ojeda, p	2	2	0	0	0	0	0	0	0	0	0	1	.000	0	2	0	1.000
Darling, p	3	3	0	0	0	0	0	0	0	0	0	1	.000	0	4	0	1.000
Johnson, 3b-ph-ss	2	5	0	0	0	0	0	0	0	0	0	2	.000	1	0	0	1.000
Totals	7	240	32	65	92	6	0	7	29	21	3	43	.271	189	63	5	.981

Backman—Ran for Teufel in seventh inning of first game; ran and scored for Teufel in sixth inning of seventh game.

Dykstra—Singled for Mitchell in seventh inning of seventh game.

Heep—Struck out for Santana in ninth inning of first game; grounded into double play for Santana in fifth inning of sixth game.

Johnson—Struck out for Elster in ninth inning of sixth game.

Mazzilli—Flied out for Orosco in eighth inning of second game; grounded out for Mitchell in eighth inning of third game; singled for Orosco in eighth inning of sixth game; singled for Fernandez in sixth inning of seventh game.

Mitchell—Struck out for Darling in seventh inning of first game; announced as pinch-hitter for Heep in eighth inning of third game; singled for Aguilera in tenth inning of sixth game.

BOSTON RED SOX' BATTING AND FIELDING AVERAGES

Player—Position	G.	AB.	R.	H.	TB.	2B.	3B.	HR.	RBI.	BB.	IBB.	SO.	B.A.	PO.	A.	E.	F.A.
Barrett, 2b	7	30	1	13	15	2	0	0	4	5	1	2	.433	13	25	0	1.000
Henderson, cf	7	25	6	10	19	1	1	2	5	2	0	6	.400	22	0	0	1.000
Rice, lf	7	27	6	9	12	1	1	0	0	6	0	9	.333	16	2	0	1.000
Evans, rf	7	26	4	8	16	2	0	2	9	4	0	3	.308	16	1	1	.944
Owen, ss	7	20	2	6	6	0	0	0	2	5	2	6	.300	10	13	0	1.000
Boggs, 3b	7	31	3	9	12	3	0	0	3	4	1	2	.290	4	15	0	1.000
Gedman, c	7	30	1	6	10	1	0	1	1	0	0	10	.200	46	3	2	.961
Buckner, 1b	7	32	2	6	6	0	0	0	1	0	0	3	.188	53	7	1	.984
Baylor, dh-ph	4	11	1	2	3	1	0	0	1	1	0	3	.182	0	0	0	.000
Boyd, p	1	0	0	0	0	0	0	0	0	0	0	0	.000	1	0	0	1.000
Nipper, p	2	0	0	0	0	0	0	0	0	0	0	0	.000	1	2	0	1.000
Sambito, p	2	0	0	0	0	0	0	0	0	0	0	0	.000	0	0	0	.000
Armas, ph	1	1	0	0	0	0	0	0	0	0	0	1	.000	0	0	0	.000
Crawford, p	3	1	0	0	0	0	0	0	0	0	0	0	.000	0	0	0	.000
Romero, pr-ss	3	1	0	0	0	0	0	0	0	0	0	0	.000	0	1	0	1.000
Schiraldi, p	3	1	0	0	0	0	0	0	0	0	0	1	.000	0	1	0	1.000
Stanley, p	5	1	0	0	0	0	0	0	0	0	0	1	.000	1	2	0	1.000
Stapleton, 1b-pr	3	1	0	0	0	0	0	0	0	0	0	0	.000	3	2	0	1.000
Greenwell, ph	4	3	0	0	0	0	0	0	0	1	0	2	.000	0	0	0	.000
Hurst, p	3	3	0	0	0	0	0	0	0	0	0	3	.000	1	3	0	1.000
Clemens, p	2	4	1	0	0	0	0	0	0	0	0	1	.000	1	2	0	1.000
Totals	7	248	27	69	99	11	2	5	26	28	4	53	.278	188	79	4	.985

Armas—Struck out for Hurst in seventh inning of seventh game.

Baylor—Grounded out for Owen in eighth inning of seventh game.

Greenwell—Flied out for Hurst in ninth inning of first game; struck out for Crawford in seventh inning of second game; walked for Owen in eighth inning of fourth game; struck out for Clemens in eighth inning of sixth game.

Romero—Ran for Owen in ninth inning of second game; ran for Greenwell in eighth inning of fourth game.

Stapleton—Ran for Buckner in eighth inning of second game.

NEW YORK METS' PITCHING RECORDS

Pitcher	G.	GS.	CG.	IP.	H.	R.	ER.	HR.	BB.	IBB.	SO.	HB.	WP.	W.	L.	Pct.	ERA.
Orosco	4	0	0	5⅔	2	0	0	0	0	0	6	0	0	0	0	.000	0.00
Sisk	1	0	0	⅔	0	0	0	0	1	1	1	0	0	0	0	.000	0.00
Fernandez	3	0	0	6⅔	6	1	1	0	1	0	10	0	0	0	0	.000	1.35
Darling	3	3	0	17⅔	13	4	3	2	10	1	12	1	2	1	1	.500	1.53
Ojeda	2	2	0	13	13	3	3	0	5	0	9	0	1	1	0	1.000	2.08
McDowell	5	0	0	7⅓	10	5	4	0	6	2	2	0	0	1	0	1.000	4.91
Gooden	2	2	0	9	17	10	8	2	4	0	9	1	0	0	2	.000	8.00
Aguilera	2	0	0	3	8	4	4	1	1	0	4	1	0	1	0	1.000	12.00
Totals	7	7	0	63	69	27	23	5	28	4	53	3	3	4	3	.571	3.29

No shutouts. Saves—Orosco 2.

BOSTON RED SOX' PITCHING RECORDS

Pitcher	G.	GS.	CG.	IP.	H.	R.	ER.	HR.	BB.	IBB.	SO.	HB.	WP.	W.	L.	Pct.	ERA.
Stanley	5	0	0	6⅓	5	0	0	0	1	0	4	0	1	0	0	.000	0.00
Hurst	3	3	1	23	18	5	5	1	6	0	17	0	0	2	0	1.000	1.96
Clemens	2	2	0	11⅓	9	5	4	0	6	0	11	0	0	0	0	.000	3.18
Crawford	3	0	0	4⅓	5	3	3	2	0	0	4	1	0	1	0	1.000	6.23
Nipper	2	1	0	6⅓	10	5	5	2	2	1	2	0	0	0	1	.000	7.11
Boyd	1	1	0	7	9	6	6	1	1	0	3	0	0	0	1	.000	7.71
Schiraldi	3	0	0	4	7	7	6	1	3	1	2	0	1	0	2	.000	13.50
Sambito	2	0	0	⅓	2	1	1	0	2	1	0	0	1	0	0	.000	27.00
Totals	7	7	1	62⅔	65	32	30	7	21	3	43	1	3	3	4	.429	4.31

Shutout—Hurst and Schiraldi (combined). Saves—Schiraldi, Stanley.

COMPOSITE SCORE BY INNINGS

New York	4	0	2	3	3	3	7	6	1	3—32
Boston	1	5	5	1	4	0	4	4	1	2—27

Game-winning RBI—Boggs, Dykstra, Carter, Owen, Knight.

Sacrifice hits—Santana 2, Dykstra 2, Hurst 2, Clemens, Owen, Backman, McDowell.

Sacrifice flies—Henderson, Owen, Carter, Hernandez.

Stolen bases—Wilson 3, Strawberry 3, Backman.

Caught stealing—Backman, Strawberry.

Double plays—Teufel, Santana and Hernandez; Boggs, Barrett and Buckner 2; Santana, Backman and Hernandez; Backman, Santana and Hernandez; Owen, Barrett and Buckner; Buckner, Owen and Buckner; Rice and Gedman; Gedman and Barrett; Barrett, Owen and Buckner; Backman, Elster and Hernandez.

Passed ball—Gedman.

Hit by pitcher—By Gooden (Baylor), by Aguilera (Buckner), by Darling (Henderson), by Crawford (Wilson).

Balks—None.

Bases on balls—Off Darling 10 (Owen 3, Rice 3, Barrett, Baylor, Evans, Henderson), off McDowell 6 (Barrett 2, Boggs, Evans, Greenwell, Owen), off Ojeda 5 (Rice 2, Boggs, Evans, Henderson), off Gooden 4 (Barrett, Evans, Owen, Rice), off Aguilera 1 (Boggs), off Fernandez 1 (Boggs), off Sisk 1 (Barrett), off Clemens 6 (Backman 2, Strawberry 2, Heep, Hernandez), off Hurst 6 (Dykstra, Hernandez, Knight, Santana, Strawberry, Teufel), off Schiraldi 3 (Hernandez, Knight, Strawberry), off Nipper 2 (Hernandez, Santana), off Sambito 2 (Backman, Wilson), off Boyd 1 (Hernandez), off Stanley 1 (Dykstra).

Strikeouts—By Darling 12 (Hurst 3, Henderson 2, Barrett, Baylor, Boggs, Buckner, Gedman, Owen, Rice), by Fernandez 10 (Gedman 3, Owen 2, Rice 2, Baylor, Evans, Stanley), by Gooden 9 (Gedman 2, Henderson 2, Owen 2, Baylor, Evans, Rice), by Ojeda 9 (Gedman 3, Rice 2, Buckner, Clemens, Evans, Henderson), by Orosco 6 (Barrett, Boggs, Gedman, Greenwell, Henderson, Rice), by Aguilera 4 (Buckner, Owen, Rice, Schiraldi), by McDowell 2 (Armas, Greenwell), by Sisk 1 (Rice); by Hurst 17 (Dykstra 4, Mitchell 3, Strawberry 3, Teufel 2, Wilson 2, Carter, Darling, Santana), by Clemens 11 (Dykstra 3, Backman, Carter, Johnson, Knight, Ojeda, Santana, Strawberry, Wilson), by Crawford 4 (Knight, Santana, Strawberry, Wilson), by Stanley 4 (Carter, Hernandez, Santana, Wilson), by Boyd 3 (Backman, Strawberry, Wilson), by Nipper 2 (Carter, Santana), by Schiraldi 2 (Heep, Johnson).

Left on bases—New York 50—8, 9, 6, 4, 8, 8, 7; Boston 69—8, 13, 6, 11, 11, 14, 6.

Time of games—First game, 2:59; second game, 3:36; third game, 2:58; fourth game, 3.22; fifth game, 3:09; sixth game, 4:02; seventh game, 3:11.

Attendance—First game, 55,076; second game, 55,063; third game, 33,595; fourth game, 33,920; fifth game, 34,010; sixth game, 55,078; seventh game, 55,032.

Umpires—Kibler (N.L.), Evans (A.L.), Wendelstedt (N.L.), Brinkman (A.L.), Montague (N.L.), Ford (A.L.).

Official scorers—Red Foley, New York Daily News; Dave Nightingale, The Sporting News; Charlie Scoggins, Lowell (Mass.) Sun.

1986 ALL-STAR GAME

Including

Review of 1986 Game

Official Box Score

Official Play-by-Play

Results of Previous Games

Third base coach Mike Ferraro congratulates Frank White after the Kansas City second baseman's seventh-inning homer gave the American League a 3-0 lead.

Clemens Stars in A.L. Victory

By DAVE SLOAN

Thomas Wolfe once said that you can't go home again. But Thomas Wolfe couldn't throw a baseball 95 miles per-hour.

Boston Red Sox righthander Roger Clemens, whose 14-0 start in 1986 was the fourth-best in major-league history, threw three perfect innings and earned Most Valuable Player honors as the American League edged the National League, 3-2, in the 57th All-Star Game July 15 at Houston's Astrodome. Clemens, who was reared in the Houston suburb of Katy and pitched the University of Texas to the College World Series championship in 1983, threw just 25 pitches in his three innings, 21 for strikes, and allowed just two balls to be hit out of the infield en route to receiving credit for the victory.

"It has been like a fantasy camp this season," said Clemens, who entered baseball's All-Star break with a 15-2 record that included a major league-record 20-strikeout performance against Seattle on April 29. "The Red Sox are playing well and I've pitched pretty well this season. Coming home and pitching like this in the All-Star Game with my family here is like a dream come true."

The N.L. squad, which suffered only its second All-Star Game defeat in 15 years, was impressed with the 23-year-old fireballer.

"He throws harder than anyone I've seen in our league," said the New York Mets' Darryl Strawberry, who struck out in his only at-bat against Clemens.

"Some guys throw hard and others throw hard for strikes. Clemens is the latter," said Atlanta's Dale Murphy, who was the only player who came close to getting a hit off the Boston pitcher. Baltimore shortstop Cal Ripken went deep in the hole to throw out Murphy on a close play in the second inning.

Clemens, however, had to share the pitching headlines with Los Angeles Dodgers lefthander Fernando Valenzuela, who tied Hall of Famer Carl Hubbell's 52-year-old All-Star record by striking out five consecutive batters. Valenzuela, who has yet to allow a run in five All-Star appearances, fanned the Yankees' Don Mattingly, Ripken and Toronto's Jesse Barfield in the fourth inning and Detroit's Lou Whitaker and Milwaukee pitcher Ted Higuera in the fifth. Minnesota's Kirby Puckett, who singled off the Mets' Dwight Gooden on the game's first pitch, ended Valenzuela's streak by grounding out to shortstop.

Dodgers pitcher Fernando Valenzuela tied an All-Star Game record with five consecutive strikeouts.

Despite Valenzuela's heroics and a record-tying 12 strikeouts by National League pitchers, this night belonged to Clemens and the American League. For the first time in 24 years, the A.L. was victorious in an N.L. park. It also was the American League's second win in four years and cut the senior circuit's lead in the all-time series to 36-20-1. St. Louis Manager Whitey Herzog was at the helm in both of the N.L.'s latest defeats.

"At least they can't blame me for the '62 defeat," the Cardinals' manager said. "I was playing in the American League that year."

The American League used two home runs by second basemen hitting in the No. 8 spot to post its triumph. Whitaker, the A.L. starter at that position, drilled an 0-2 fastball from Gooden over the right-field wall in the second inning. Dave Winfield of the Yankees had doubled to right before Whitaker delivered his blast.

"That's been a problem all year," said

San Francisco's Chris Brown scores the National League's first run on a passed ball (above) while Detroit's Lou Whitaker crosses the plate after his two-run, second-inning homer.

Gooden, whose record at the All-Star break stood at 10-4 following his phenomenal 1985 record of 24-4."One mistake pitch and I get hurt. I hope I can eliminate that in the second half."

Herzog defended his decision not to walk Whitaker with Clemens coming up next.

"I let my heart manage instead of my brains. But I can't put him (Whitaker) on in an All-Star Game. I know Clemens hasn't been to bat in five years. I said to Tommy (Dodgers Manager Tommy Lasorda) I ought to put him on, but the thing about it is people didn't come to see Clemens hit."

The A.L. increased its advantage to 3-0 in the seventh when Kansas City's Frank White, who replaced Whitaker in the lineup, drilled a solo homer over the left-center field wall off Houston's Mike Scott. Scott, whose 167 strikeouts was tops in the majors at the break, came within one pitch of striking out the side before White's homer.

"The first two pitches he threw me were unhittable," White said. "But with the home crowd cheering him on, I figured he'd be all juiced up and that he wouldn't try to waste a pitch; that he'd try to come back with a third straight fastball—maybe inside, but over the plate. And I knew I was going to take my cut at it; that I wasn't going to cheat myself out of a good swing."

White's pinch-homer was the 14th in All-Star history and the first in six years.

The National League, which didn't have a baserunner until Strawberry's one-out single in the fifth off Higuera, scored its only two runs in the eighth, courtesy of some poor A.L. fielding.

San Francisco's Chris Brown led off the inning with a double against Texas pitcher Charlie Hough. Brown took third base when the next batter, Giants teammate Chili Davis, swung and missed a third strike that got away from Boston catcher Rich Gedman. Gedman recovered the ball, ruled a wild pitch, and threw out Davis at first.

Gedman then had trouble with the third strike to the next batter, Montreal's Hubie Brooks, and was given a passed ball for letting the ball roll away. When Gedman recovered, he threw to Hough, covering home plate, in an unsuccessful attempt to nail Brown crossing the plate. Brooks reached first safely, and subsequently advanced to second on a balk against Hough. The Rangers pitcher then struck out Montreal's Tim Raines for his third strikeout of the inning but only the second out.

The next batter, the Dodgers' Steve Sax, singled to left to score Brooks and cut the A.L. lead to 3-2. American League Manager Dick Howser then lifted Hough in favor of the Yankees' Dave Righetti, who retired pinch-hitter Glenn Davis of the Astros on a pop-up.

The National League threatened in the ninth, putting the tying run on third base and the winning run on first with one out. But Baltimore's Don Aase, whose 22 saves led the majors, snuffed out the rally by getting Brown to bounce into a game-ending double play. White, whose homer proved to be the game-winning run, fielded the ball cleanly, stepped on second and threw to Mattingly at first.

AMERICANS	AB.	R.	H.	RBI.	PO.	A.
Puckett, (Twins) cf......	3	0	1	0	5	0
Henderson, (Yanks) lf.	3	0	0	0	2	0
Moseby, (Blue Jays) lf.	0	0	0	0	0	0
Boggs, (Red Sox) 3b.....	3	0	1	0	0	1
hJacoby, (Indians) 3b..	1	0	0	0	1	1
Parrish, (Tigers) c	3	0	0	0	4	0
iRice (Red Sox)............	1	0	0	0	0	0
Gedman, (Red Sox) c...	0	0	0	0	1	1
Joyner, (Angels) 1b......	1	0	0	0	3	1
bM'ttngly, (Yanks) 1b.	3	0	0	0	7	0
Ripken, (Orioles) ss......	4	0	0	0	0	1
F'rndz, (Blue Jays) ss..	0	0	0	0	0	0
Winfield, (Yanks) rf	1	1	1	0	0	0
cB'rfld, (Blue Jays) rf .	3	0	0	0	2	0
Whitaker, (Tigers) 2b..	2	1	1	2	0	3
fWhite, (Royals) 2b......	2	1	1	1	1	1
Clemens, (Red Sox) p ..	1	0	0	0	1	0
Higuera, (Brewers) p ..	1	0	0	0	0	0
gBaines (White Sox)	1	0	0	0	0	0
Hough, (Rangers) p.....	0	0	0	0	0	0
Righetti, (Yanks) p......	0	0	0	0	0	0
Aase, (Orioles) p	0	0	0	0	0	0
Totals	33	3	5	3	27	9

NATIONALS	AB.	R.	H.	RBI.	PO.	A.
Gwynn, (Padres) lf......	3	0	0	0	1	0
Sax, (Dodgers) 2b.........	1	0	1	1	0	1
Sandberg, (Cubs) 2b	3	0	0	0	0	2
Scott, (Astros) p............	0	0	0	0	0	0
Fernandez, (Mets) p	0	0	0	0	0	0
jG. Davis (Astros)	1	0	0	0	0	0
Krukow, (Giants) p	0	0	0	0	0	1
Hernandez, (Mets) 1b..	4	0	0	0	5	0
Carter, (Mets) c...........	3	0	0	0	9	0
J. Davis, (Cubs) c.........	1	0	1	0	3	0
kPena (Pirates)...........	0	0	0	0	0	0
Strawberry, (Mets) rf .	2	0	1	0	1	0
Parker, (Reds) rf..........	2	0	1	0	0	0
Schmidt, (Phillies) 3b..	1	0	0	0	0	0
Brown, (Giants) 3b	2	1	1	0	1	0
Murphy, (Braves) cf....	2	0	0	0	2	0
C. Davis, (Giants) cf	1	0	0	0	0	0
O. Smith, (Cards) ss.....	1	0	0	0	3	2
dBrooks, (Expos) ss	2	1	0	0	1	0
Gooden, (Mets) p..........	0	0	0	0	0	0
aBass (Astros)...............	1	0	0	0	0	0
V'lnzla, (Dodgers) p.....	0	0	0	0	0	0
eRaines, (Expos) lf	2	0	0	0	1	0
Totals	32	2	5	1	27	6

Americans............................	0 2 0	0 0 0	1 0 0—3
Nationals............................	0 0 0	0 0 0	0 2 0—2

AMERICANS	IP.	H.	R.	ER.	BB.	SO.
Clemens (Red Sox)	3	0	0	0	0	2
Higuera (Brewers).....	3	1	0	0	1	2
Hough (Rangers)	1⅔	2	2	1	0	3
Righetti (Yankees)	⅔	2	0	0	0	0
Aase (Orioles)	⅔	0	0	0	0	0

NATIONALS	IP.	H.	R.	ER.	BB.	SO.
Gooden (Mets)	3	3	2	2	0	2
Valenzuela (Dodgers)	3	1	0	0	0	5
Scott (Astros)	1	1	1	1	0	2
Fernandez (Mets)	1	0	0	0	2	3
Krukow (Giants)	1	0	0	0	0	0

Winning pitcher—Clemens. Losing pitcher—Gooden.

Game-winning RBI—Whitaker.

aGrounded out for Gooden in third. bStruck out for Joyner in fourth. cCalled out on strikes for Winfield in fourth. dGrounded out for O. Smith in fifth. eFlied out for Valenzuela in sixth. fHomered for Whitaker in seventh. gGrounded out for Higuera in seventh. hStruck out for Boggs in eighth. iStruck out for Parrish in eighth. jFouled out for Fernandez in eighth. kRan for J. Davis in ninth. Error—Sandberg. Double play—White and Mattingly. Left on bases—Americans 5, Nationals 4. Two-base hits—Winfield, Brown. Home runs—Whitaker, White. Stolen bases—Puckett, Moseby, Sax. Wild pitch—Hough. Passed ball—Gedman. Balks—Gooden, Hough. Bases on balls—Off Higuera 1 (Schmidt), off Fernandez 2 (Puckett, Moseby). Strikeouts—By Clemens 2 (Sandberg, Strawberry), by Higuera 2 (Gwynn, Sandberg), by Hough 3 (C. Davis, Brooks, Raines), by Gooden 2 (Clemens, Henderson), by Valenzuela 5 (Mattingly, Ripken, Barfield, Whitaker, Higuera), by Scott 2 (Ripken, Barfield), by Fernandez 3 (Jacoby, Rice, Mattingly). Umpires—Froemming (N.L.) plate, Palermo (A.L.) first base, Runge (N.L.) second base, Reed (A.L.) third base, Gregg (N.L.) left field, McClelland (A.L.) right field. Official scorers—Tracy Ringolsby, Dallas Morning News, Ivy McLemore, Houston Post, and Red Foley, New York Daily News.

Players listed on roster but not used: A.L.—Canseco, Hernandez, Murray, Presley, Schrom, Witt; N.L.—Franco, Rawley, Reardon, Rhoden, D. Smith. Time—2:28. Attendance—45,774.

FIRST INNING

Americans—Puckett hit the first pitch of the game up the middle for a single. Henderson also jumped on the first pitch and grounded to Sandberg, who threw to Smith at second to force Puckett. Gooden slipped off the mound while attempting to make a pickoff attempt at first base and was called for a balk, Henderson moving to second on the play. Boggs flied to Gwynn in the left-field corner. Parrish popped to Smith. No runs, one hit, no errors, one left.

Nationals—Gwynn lined to Henderson in left-center field. Sandberg was called out on strikes. Keith Hernandez bounced to Joyner, who threw to Clemens covering first base. No runs, no hits, no errors, none left.

SECOND INNING

Americans—Joyner popped to Smith in short left field. Ripken bounced to Smith. Winfield lined a double off the wall in the right-field corner. Whitaker hit an 0-2 pitch over the right-field fence for a home run to give the A.L. a 2-0 lead. Clemens was called out on strikes. Two runs, two hits, no errors, none left.

Nationals—Carter flied to Puckett. Strawberry struck out. Schmidt also flied to Puckett. No runs, no hits, no errors, none left.

THIRD INNING

Americans—Puckett flied to Strawberry. Henderson struck out. Boggs reached first base safely when Sandberg got a glove on his grounder, but was charged with an error when he couldn't recover in time to make a play at first base. Parrish flied to Murphy. No runs, no hits, one error, one left.

Nationals—Ripken made a backhanded stop of Murphy 's hard grounder in the hole and made the long throw to first for the out. Smith grounded out to Whitaker. Bass, batting for Gooden, grounded to Whitaker. No runs, no hits, no errors, none left.

FOURTH INNING

Americans—Valenzuela came in to pitch for the Nationals. Mattingly, batting for Joyner, struck out. Ripken was called out on strikes. Barfield, batting for Winfield, also was called out on strikes. No runs, no hits, no errors, none left.

Nationals—Mattingly stayed in the game and played first base, Barfield went to right field and Higuera came in to pitch for the Americans. Gwynn was called out on strikes. Sandberg flied to Henderson in short left field. Keith Hernandez flied to Puckett. No runs, no hits, no errors, none left.

FIFTH INNING

Americans—Whitaker was called out on strikes. Higuera also struck out, enabling Valenzuela to tie Carl Hubbell's 1934 All-Star feat of striking out five straight batters. Puckett grounded to Smith. No runs, no hits, no errors, none left.

Nationals—Carter grounded to Boggs. Strawberry lined a single to right for the first N.L. hit. Schmidt walked. Murphy flied to Puckett. Brooks, batting for Smith, grounded to Whitaker. No runs, one hit, no errors, two left.

SIXTH INNING

Americans—Brooks stayed in the game at shortstop, Parker went in to play right field and Brown went in to play third base for the Nationals. Henderson popped to Brooks behind third base. Boggs looped a single to center. Parrish flied to Murphy. Mattingly bounced to Sandberg. No runs, one hit, no errors, one left.

Nationals—Moseby went in to play left field for the Americans. Raines, batting for Valenzuela, flied to Puckett. Gwynn bounced to Mattingly, who made the play unassisted at first base. Sandberg struck out. No runs, no hits, no errors, none left.

SEVENTH INNING

Americans—Raines remained in the game and played left field, Scott went in to pitch, Sax went in to play second base and Chili Davis went in to play center field for the Nationals. Ripken struck out. Barfield also struck out. White, batting for Whitaker, smashed an 0-2 pitch over the left-center field fence for a home run to give the A.L. a 3-0 lead. It was the first All-Star pinch home run since Lee Mazzilli in 1979 and the 14th time the feat had been accomplished. Baines, batting for Higuera, bounced to Sax. One run, one hit, no errors, none left.

Nationals—White stayed in the game at second base and Hough came in to pitch for the Americans. Keith Hernandez flied to Barfield. Carter also flied to Barfield. Parker grounded to Mattingly, who made the play unassisted at first base. No runs, no hits, no errors, none left.

EIGHTH INNING

Americans—Sid Fernandez came in to pitch and Jody Davis went in to catch for the Nationals. Puckett walked. Moseby also walked. Jacoby, batting for Boggs, struck out. Rice batted for Parrish and also struck out, Puckett and Moseby working a successful double steal on the third strike. Mattingly struck out. No runs, no hits, no errors, two left.

Nationals—Jacoby stayed in the game at third base and Gedman went in to catch for the Americans. Brown doubled to the wall in left-center field. Chili Davis struck out on a pitch in the dirt and had to be thrown out at first base, Gedman to Mattingly, with Brown advancing to third on the wild pitch. Brooks also struck out, but was safe at first when the ball got past Gedman for a passed ball; Brown scored on the play, sliding under Hough's tag at the plate. Brooks went to second on a balk by Hough. Raines struck out. Sax lined a single to left-center, scoring Brooks, to cut the A.L. lead to 3-2. Righetti replaced Hough on the mound for the Americans. With Glenn Davis at the plate, batting for Sid Fernandez, Sax stole second base. Davis then fouled to Jacoby. Two runs, two hits, no errors, one left.

NINTH INNING

Americans—Krukow came in to pitch for the Nationals. Ripken bounced back to the mound, Krukow to Keith Hernandez for the out at first base. Barfield popped to Brown. White flied to Raines. No runs, no hits, no errors, none left.

Nationals—Tony Fernandez went in to play shortstop for the Americans. Jacoby had to back up and backhand Hernandez' high chopper and still made a long throw to Mattingly for the out at first base. Jody Davis singled sharply to center. Pena went in to run for Davis. Parker grounded a single to right, Pena advancing to third. Aase replaced Righetti on the mound for the Americans. Brown, trying to check his swing on an outside pitch, bounced into a double play, White to Mattingly. No runs, two hits, no errors, one left.

RESULTS OF PREVIOUS GAMES

1933—At Comiskey Park, Chicago, July 6. Americans 4, Nationals 2. Managers—Connie Mack, John McGraw. Winning pitcher—Lefty Gomez. Losing pitcher—Bill Hallahan. Attendance—47,595.

1934—At Polo Grounds, New York, July 10. Americans 9, Nationals 7. Managers—Joe Cronin, Bill Terry. Winning pitcher—Mel Harder. Losing pitcher—Van Mungo. Attendance—48,363.

1935—At Municipal Stadium, Cleveland, July 8. Americans 4, Nationals 1. Managers—Mickey Cochrane, Frankie Frisch. Winning pitcher—Lefty Gomez. Losing pitcher—Bill Walker. Attendance—69,831.

1936—At Braves Field, Boston, July 7. Nationals 4, Americans 3. Managers—Charlie Grimm, Joe McCarthy. Winning pitcher—Dizzy Dean. Losing pitcher—Lefty Gomez. Attendance—25,556.

1937—At Griffith Stadium, Washington, July 7. Americans 8, Nationals 3. Managers—Joe McCarthy, Bill Terry. Winning pitcher—Lefty Gomez. Losing pitcher—Dizzy Dean. Attendance—31,391.

1938—At Crosley Field, Cincinnati, July 6. Nationals 4, Americans 1. Managers—Bill Terry, Joe McCarthy. Winning pitcher—Johnny Vander Meer. Losing pitcher—Lefty Gomez. Attendance—27,067.

1939—At Yankee Stadium, New York, July 11. Americans 3, Nationals 1. Managers—Joe McCarthy, Gabby Hartnett. Winning pitcher—Tommy Bridges. Losing pitcher—Bill Lee. Attendance—62,892.

1940—At Sportsman's Park, St. Louis, July 9. Nationals 4, Americans 0. Managers—Bill McKechnie, Joe Cronin. Winning pitcher—Paul Derringer. Losing pitcher—Red Ruffing. Attendance—32,373.

1941—At Briggs Stadium, Detroit, July 8. Americans 7, Nationals 5. Managers—Del Baker, Bill McKechnie. Winning pitcher—Ed Smith. Losing pitcher—Claude Passeau. Attendance—54,674.

1942—At Polo Grounds, New York, July 6. Americans 3, Nationals 1. Managers—Joe Cronin, Leo Durocher. Winning pitcher—Spud Chandler. Losing pitcher—Mort Cooper. Attendance—34,178.

1943—At Shibe Park, Philadelphia, July 13 (night). Americans 5, Nationals 3. Managers—Joe McCarthy, Billy Southworth. Winning pitcher—Dutch Leonard. Losing pitcher—Mort Cooper. Attendance—31,938.

1944—At Forbes Field, Pittsburgh, July 11 (night). Nationals 7, Americans 1. Managers—Billy Southworth, Joe McCarthy. Winning pitcher—Ken Raffensberger. Losing pitcher—Tex Hughson. Attendance—29,589.

1945—No game played.

1946—At Fenway Park, Boston, July 9. Americans 12, Nationals 0. Managers—Steve O'Neill, Charlie Grimm. Winning pitcher—Bob Feller. Losing pitcher—Claude Passeau. Attendance—34,906.

1947—At Wrigley Field, Chicago, July 8. Americans 2, Nationals 1. Managers—Joe Cronin, Eddie Dyer. Winning pitcher—Frank Shea. Losing pitcher—Johnny Sain. Attendance—41,123.

1948—At Sportsman's Park, St. Louis, July 13. Americans 5, Nationals 2. Managers—Bucky Harris, Leo Durocher. Winning pitcher—Vic Raschi. Losing pitcher—Johnny Schmitz. Attendance—34,009.

1949—At Ebbets Field, Brooklyn, July 12. Americans 11, Nationals 7. Managers—Lou Boudreau, Billy Southworth. Winning pitcher—Virgil Trucks. Losing pitcher—Don Newcombe. Attendance—32,577.

1950—At Comiskey Park, Chicago, July 11. Nationals 4, Americans 3 (14 innings). Managers—Burt Shotton, Casey Stengel. Winning pitcher—Ewell Blackwell. Losing pitcher—Ted Gray. Attendance—46,127.

1951—At Briggs Stadium, Detroit, July 10. Nationals 8, Americans 3. Managers—Eddie Sawyer, Casey Stengel. Winning pitcher—Sal Maglie. Losing pitcher—Ed Lopat. Attendance—52,075.

1952—At Shibe Park, Philadelphia, July 8. Nationals 3, Americans 2 (five innings—rain). Managers—Leo Durocher, Casey Stengel. Winning pitcher—Bob Rush. Losing pitcher—Bob Lemon. Attendance—32,785.

1953—At Crosley Field, Cincinnati, July 14. Nationals 5, Americans 1. Managers—Chuck Dressen, Casey Stengel. Winning pitcher—Warren Spahn. Losing pitcher—Allie Reynolds. Attendance—30,846.

1954—At Municipal Stadium, Cleveland, July 13. Americans 11, Nationals 9. Managers—Casey Stengel, Walter Alston. Winning pitcher—Dean Stone. Losing pitcher—Gene Conley. Attendance—68,751.

1955—At Milwaukee County Stadium, Milwaukee, July 12. Nationals 6, Americans 5 (12 innings). Managers—Leo Durocher, Al Lopez. Winning pitcher—Gene Conley. Losing pitcher—Frank Sullivan. Attendance—45,643.

1956—At Griffith Stadium, Washington, July 10. Nationals 7, Americans 3. Managers—Walter Alston, Casey Stengel. Winning pitcher—Bob Friend. Losing pitcher—Billy Pierce. Attendance—28,843.

1957—At Busch Stadium, St. Louis, July 9. Americans 6, Nationals 5. Managers—Casey Stengel, Walter Alston. Winning pitcher—Jim Bunning. Losing pitcher—Curt Simmons. Attendance—30,693.

1958—At Memorial Stadium, Baltimore, July 8.

Americans 4, Nationals 3. Managers—Casey Stengel, Fred Haney. Winning pitcher—Early Wynn. Losing pitcher—Bob Friend. Attendance—48,829.

1959 (first game)—At Forbes Field, Pittsburgh, July 7. Nationals 5, Americans 4. Managers—Fred Haney, Casey Stengel. Winning pitcher—Johnny Antonelli. Losing pitcher—Whitey Ford. Attendance—35,277.

1959 (second game)—At Memorial Coliseum, Los Angeles, August 3. Americans 5, Nationals 3. Managers—Casey Stengel, Fred Haney. Winning pitcher—Jerry Walker. Losing pitcher—Don Drysdale. Attendance—55,105.

1960 (first game)—At Municipal Stadium, Kansas City, July 11. Nationals 5, Americans 3. Managers—Walter Alston, Al Lopez. Winning pitcher—Bob Friend. Losing pitcher—Bill Monbouquette. Attendance—30,619.

1960 (second game)—At Yankee Stadium, New York, July 13. Nationals 6, Americans 0. Managers—Walter Alston, Al Lopez. Winning pitcher—Vernon Law. Losing pitcher—Whitey Ford. Attendance—38,362.

1961 (first game)—At Candlestick Park, San Francisco, July 11. Nationals 5, Americans 4 (10 innings). Managers—Danny Murtaugh, Paul Richards. Winning pitcher—Stu Miller. Losing pitcher—Hoyt Wilhelm. Attendance—44,115.

1961 (second game)—At Fenway Park, Boston, July 31. Americans 1, Nationals 1 (nine-inning tie, stopped by rain). Managers—Paul Richards, Danny Murtaugh. Attendance—31,851.

1962 (first game)—At District of Columbia Stadium, Washington, July 10. Nationals 3, Americans 1. Managers—Fred Hutchinson, Ralph Houk. Winning pitcher—Juan Marichal. Losing pitcher—Camilo Pascual. Attendance—45,480.

1962 (second game)—At Wrigley Field, Chicago, July 30. Americans 9, Nationals 4. Managers—Ralph Houk, Fred Hutchinson. Winning pitcher—Ray Herbert. Losing pitcher—Art Mahaffey. Attendance—38,359.

1963—At Municipal Stadium, Cleveland, July 9. Nationals 5, Americans 3. Managers—Alvin Dark, Ralph Houk. Winning pitcher—Larry Jackson. Losing pitcher—Jim Bunning. Attendance—44,160.

1964—At Shea Stadium, New York, July 7. Nationals 7, Americans 4. Managers—Walter Alston, Al Lopez. Winning pitcher—Juan Marichal. Losing pitcher—Dick Radatz. Attendance—50,850.

1965—At Metropolitan Stadium, Bloomington (Minnesota), July 13. Nationals 6, Americans 5. Managers—Gene Mauch, Al Lopez. Winning pitcher—Sandy Koufax. Losing pitcher—Sam McDowell. Attendance—46,706.

1966—At Busch Memorial Stadium, St Louis, July 12. Nationals 2, Americans 1 (10 innings). Managers—Walter Alston, Sam Mele. Winning pitcher—Gaylord Perry. Losing pitcher—Pete Richert. Attendance—49,936.

1967—At Anaheim Stadium, Anaheim (California), July 11. Nationals 2, Americans 1 (15 innings). Managers—Walter Alston, Hank Bauer. Winning pitcher—Don Drysdale. Losing pitcher—Jim Hunter. Attendance—46,309.

1968—At Astrodome, Houston, July 9 (night). Nationals 1, Americans 0. Managers—Red Schoendienst, Dick Williams. Winning pitcher—Don Drysdale. Losing pitcher—Luis Tiant. Attendance—48,321.

1969—At Robert F. Kennedy Memorial Stadium, Washington, July 23. Nationals 9, Americans 3. Managers—Red Schoendienst, Mayo Smith. Winning pitcher—Steve Carlton. Losing pitcher—Mel Stottlemyre. Attendance—45,259.

1970—At Riverfront Stadium, Cincinnati, July 14 (night). Nationals 5, Americans 4 (12 innings). Managers—Gil Hodges, Earl Weaver. Winning pitcher—Claude Osteen. Losing pitcher—Clyde Wright. Attendance—51,838.

1971—At Tiger Stadium, Detroit, July 13 (night). Americans 6, Nationals 4. Managers—Earl Weaver, George (Sparky) Anderson. Winning pitcher—Vida Blue. Losing pitcher—Dock Ellis. Attendance—53,559.

1972—At Atlanta Stadium, Atlanta, July 25 (night). Nationals 4, Americans 3 (10 innings). Managers—Danny Murtaugh, Earl Weaver. Winning pitcher—Tug McGraw. Losing pitcher—Dave McNally. Attendance—53,107.

1973—At Royals Stadium, Kansas City, July 24 (night). Nationals 7, Americans 1. Managers—George (Sparky) Anderson, Dick Williams. Winning pitcher—Rick Wise. Losing pitcher—Bert Blyleven. Attendance—40,849.

1974—At Three Rivers Stadium, Pittsburgh, July 23 (night). Nationals 7, Americans 2. Managers—Yogi Berra, Dick Williams. Winning pitcher—Ken Brett. Losing pitcher—Luis Tiant. Attendance—50,706.

1975—At Milwaukee County Stadium, Milwaukee, July 15 (night). Nationals 6, Americans 3. Managers—Walter Alston, Alvin Dark. Winning pitcher—Jon Matlack. Losing pitcher—Jim Hunter. Attendance—51,480.

1976—At Veterans Stadium, Philadelphia, July 13 (night). Nationals 7, Americans 1. Managers—George (Sparky) Anderson, Darrell Johnson. Winning pitcher—Randy Jones. Losing pitcher—Mark Fidrych. Attendance—63,974.

1977—At Yankee Stadium, New York, July 19 (night). Nationals 7, Americans 5. Managers—Alfred (Billy) Martin, George (Sparky) Anderson. Winning pitcher—Don Sutton. Losing pitcher—Jim Palmer. Attendance—56,683.

1978—At San Diego Stadium, San Diego, July 11 (night). Nationals 7, Americans 3. Managers—Alfred (Billy) Martin, Thomas Lasorda. Winning pitcher—Bruce Sutter. Losing pitcher—Rich Gossage. Attendance—51,549.

1979—At Kingdome, Seattle, July 17. Nationals 7, Americans 6. Managers—Chuck Tanner, Bob Lemon. Winning pitcher—Bruce Sutter. Losing pitcher—Jim Kern. Attendance—58,905.

1980—At Dodger Stadium, Los Angeles, July 8. Nationals 4, Americans 2. Managers—Chuck Tanner, Earl Weaver. Winning pitcher—Jerry Reuss. Losing pitcher—Tommy John. Attendance—56,088.

1981—At Municipal Stadium, Cleveland, August 9 (night). Nationals 5, Americans 4. Managers—Dallas Green, Jim Frey. Winning pitcher—Vida Blue. Losing pitcher—Rollie Fingers. Attendance—72,086.

1982—At Olympic Stadium, Montreal, July 13 (night). Nationals 4, Americans 1. Managers—Thomas Lasorda, Alfred (Billy) Martin. Winning pitcher—Steve Rogers. Losing pitcher—Dennis Eckersley. Attendance—59,057.

1983—At Comiskey Park, Chicago, July 6 (night). Americans 13, Nationals 3. Managers—Harvey Kuenn, Dorrel (Whitey) Herzog. Winning pitcher—Dave Stieb. Losing pitcher—Mario Soto. Attendance—43,801.

1984—At Candlestick Park, San Francisco, July 10 (night). Nationals 3, Americans 1. Managers—Paul Owens, Joseph Altobelli. Winning pitcher—Charlie Lea. Losing pitcher—Dave Stieb. Attendance—57,756.

1985—At Metrodome, Minneapolis, July 16 (night). Nationals 6, Americans 1. Managers—Dick Williams, George (Sparky) Anderson. Winning pitcher—LaMarr Hoyt. Losing pitcher—Jack Morris. Attendance—54,960.

BATTING, PITCHING FEATURES

Including

No-Hit Pitching Performances

Low-Hit Pitching Performances

Top Strikeout Performances

Baseball's Top Firemen

Pitchers Winning 1-0 Games

Multi-Home Run Performances

Batters Hitting Grand Slams

Top One-Game Hitting Performances

Baseball's Top Pinch-Hitters

Top Performances in Debuts

Homers by Parks

Award Winners

Hall of Fame Electees

Hall of Famers List, Years Selected

Major League Draft

Houston manager Hal Lanier douses Mike Scott with champagne after the Astros pitcher's September 25 no-hitter against the Giants clinched the N.L. West title.

Scott, Cowley Pitch No-Hitters

By DAVE SLOAN

Throwing a no-hitter and pitching a division title-clinching victory are dreams that never come true for most major league pitchers. But Houston's Mike Scott accomplished both feats in 1986—in the same game.

Scott, a 31-year-old righthander whose career was on the rocks just two years earlier, pitched a 2-0, no-hit victory over the San Francisco Giants on September 25 as the Astros clinched the National League West title. It marked the first time that a division title or pennant was clinched when a pitcher threw a no-hitter.

"A game like this makes up for every low point in a career," Scott said. "I've never been in the playoffs before and I've never thrown a no-hitter. I'll always cherish this game."

Scott, acquired in a trade with the New York Mets, was just another struggling pitcher in 1984 when he compiled a 5-11 record for the Astros, bringing his major league mark to 29-44. Going nowhere fast, Scott sought help from Roger Craig, who had just resigned as pitching coach of the World Series champion Detroit Tigers.

Craig, known as the master of the split-finger fastball, taught the pitch to Scott prior to the 1985 season. Scott responded by winning 18 games, posting a 3.29 earned-run average and allowing 194 hits in 221⅔ innings. He also struck out 137 batters but gave little indication of what was to follow.

What followed for Scott was a Cy Young Award-winning performance in 1986 and a division title for the Astros, their first since 1980. Scott led the majors with 306 strikeouts, a 2.22 ERA and 275⅓ innings pitched. His no-hit performance was the piece de resistance.

The Giants managed to hit only three of Scott's 102 pitches out of the infield and no great defensive plays were needed to preserve the no-hitter. Scott struck out 13 and allowed only three Giants to reach base safely. His first pitch of the game struck Dan Gladden in the back, Chili Davis walked in the second and Phil Ouellette walked in the eighth. Scott retired Will Clark for the final out, getting the Giants' rookie to tap softly to first baseman Glenn Davis. (Ironically, Clark broke up Scott's bid for a second no-hitter in his next start October 2 with a double leading off the seventh inning.)

"He was throwing the split-finger harder than I've ever seen," said Craig, Scott's former tutor and the Giants' manager. "I've never seen a no-hitter pitched under these circumstances (with a division title on the line). I told one of my coaches in the fourth or fifth inning, 'We're not going to get a hit off him.' "

Scott's gem was the first nine-inning no-hitter in the National League since St. Louis' Bob Forsch no-hit the Montreal Expos on September 26, 1983. It also was the third straight shutout by Astros pitchers, coming one day after Nolan Ryan had pitched 6⅓ innings of hitless ball and struck out 12 Giants in eight innings and two days after Jim Deshaies had set a major league record by striking out the first eight batters in a 4-0 victory over the Los Angeles Dodgers.

Scott's No-Hitter

San Francisco	AB.	R.	H.	RBI.	E.
Gladden, cf	3	0	0	0	0
Thompson, 2b	4	0	0	0	0
Clark, 1b	4	0	0	0	0
Maldonado, lf	3	0	0	0	0
C. Davis, rf	2	0	0	0	0
Brenly, 3b	3	0	0	0	0
Ouellette, c	2	0	0	0	0
Uribe, ss	2	0	0	0	0
Spilman, ph	2	0	0	0	0
Quinones, ss	0	0	0	0	0
Berenguer, p	1	0	0	0	0
Lancellotti, ph	1	0	0	0	0
M. Davis, p	0	0	0	0	0
Aldrete, ph	1	0	0	0	0
Garrelts, p	0	0	0	0	0
Totals	27	0	0	0	0

Houston	AB.	R.	H.	RBI.	E.
Hatcher, cf	4	0	0	0	0
Doran, 2b	4	0	2	0	0
Walling, 3b	4	2	2	1	0
G. Davis, 1b	2	0	1	0	0
Bass, rf	3	0	1	0	0
Cruz, lf	2	0	1	1	0
Ashby, c	4	0	2	0	0
Reynolds, ss	2	0	0	0	0
Thon, ph-ss	2	0	0	0	0
Scott, p	4	0	1	0	0
Totals	31	2	10	2	0

San Francisco	000	000	000—0
Houston	000	010	10x—2

San Francisco	IP.	H.	R.	ER.	BB.	SO.
Berenguer (L. 2-3)	5	8	1	1	4	2
M. Davis	2	2	1	1	1	3
Garrelts	1	0	0	0	0	3

Houston	IP.	H.	R.	ER.	BB.	SO.
SCOTT (W. 18-10)	9	0	0	0	2	13

Game-winning RBI—Walling.

DP—San Francisco 1. LOB—San Francisco 3, Houston 11. HR—Walling. SB—Gladden, Hatcher, C. Davis, Bass. HBP—By Scott (Gladden), by Berenguer (Hatcher). WP—Berenguer, M. Davis. T—2:24. A—32,808.

Cowley's No-Hitter

Chicago	AB.	R.	H.	RBI.	E.
Boston, cf	4	1	2	1	0
Lyons, lf	3	1	1	0	0
Nichols, ph-lf	0	1	0	0	0
Baines, rf	4	0	1	1	0
Hassey, dh	4	1	2	1	0
Morman, 1b	4	0	1	2	0
Guillen, ss	4	0	0	0	0
Hulett, 3b	4	1	1	0	0
Perconte, 2b	4	0	0	0	0
Karkovice, c	3	2	1	1	0
Totals	34	7	9	6	0

California	AB.	R.	H.	RBI.	E.
Pettis, cf	3	0	0	0	0
Joyner, 1b	2	0	0	0	0
Downing, lf	3	0	0	0	0
Jackson, dh	3	0	0	1	0
DeCinces, 3b	4	0	0	0	0
Grich, 2b	3	0	0	0	0
White, rf	3	0	0	0	2
Schofield, ss	2	0	0	0	0
Boone, c	1	1	0	0	1
Totals	24	1	0	1	3

Chicago	000	210	031—7
California	000	001	000—1

Chicago	IP.	H.	R.	ER.	BB.	SO.
COWLEY (W. 11-9)	9	0	1	1	7	8

California	IP.	H.	R.	ER.	BB.	SO.
McCaskill (L. 16-9)	7⅓	6	4	4	1	6
Finley	0*	0	1	1	1	0
Forster	⅔	2	1	0	0	1
Ruhle	1	1	1	1	0	0

Game-winning RBI—Baines.

DP—Chicago 1, California 1. LOB—Chicago 3, California 4. 2B—Boston. HR—Karkovice. SB—Schofield, Hulett. SH—Boston. SF—Jackson. PB—Karkovice. T—2:42. A—28,647.

As Scott enjoyed the flood of superlatives, Chicago White Sox righthander Joe Cowley still was scratching his head over the flood of criticism that was generated by a no-hitter he had thrown six days before.

Cowley, a 28-year-old fireballer acquired by the White Sox in an off-season trade with the Yankees, defeated the California Angels, 7-1, on September 19 in Anaheim. A no-hitter yes, but a masterpiece no. Cowley struck out eight and walked seven. Of the 138 pitches he threw, 69 were strikes and 69 balls. In fact, he was nearly yanked by Manager Jim Fregosi after walking the bases loaded in the sixth inning.

"He was one pitch away from being taken out," said Fregosi, who sent pitching coach Dick Bosman to the mound to visit with his struggling hurler. "When he was 3-1 on Reggie (Jackson), if he'd thrown one more ball he would have come out."

Instead, Cowley coaxed Jackson—who had clubbed three homers in California's 20-hit, 18-3 rout of Kansas City the night before—into hitting a sacrifice fly to deep center field for the second out of the inning. The next batter, Doug DeCinces, popped out.

"I was just glad to be able to finish out the sixth inning," said Cowley, who managed to go the distance for only the sixth time in 70 major league starts.

Cowley's no-hitter was the first in the majors since Mike Witt of the Angels pitched a perfect game against the Texas Rangers on the final day of the 1984 season. And it was the first complete-game no-hitter by a White Sox pitcher in 19 years.

"He got 27 outs, but he wasn't tough to hit at all," said Angels rookie first baseman Wally Joyner, who earlier in the season had foiled no-hit bids by Texas' Charlie Hough (June 16) and Detroit's Walt Terrell (August 20) with ninth-inning hits. "We didn't get a hit; that's all that happened.

"His wildness was what made him so good. He either walked you or you swung at a bad pitch. I'm not even frustrated because it wasn't impressive. I mean, it wasn't."

Many of the 28,647 fans at Anaheim Stadium apparently agreed. After Cowley retired the Angels in order in the eighth inning, about half of those in attendance left the park.

Cowley's early-season pitching performances certainly weren't impressive. He gave up five runs in 2⅓ innings and lost, 12-2, in his Chicago debut April 13 against Boston. Two days later, he was demoted to Chicago's Triple-A club in Buffalo.

Cowley was recalled May 22 and, six days later, set a modern major league record by striking out the first seven batters he faced in a 6-3 loss to Texas. (That record was eclipsed September 23 by Deshaies, a former minor league teammate of Cowley's.)

"I can't believe it happened," said Cowley, whose previous best pitching performance was a three-hitter against Cleveland while pitching for the Yankees in 1984. "It's a great feeling."

The victory improved Cowley's major league record to 33-19 and was his fifth win in five decisions against California.

The closest the Angels came to getting a hit was a line drive to left-center by Jackson in the second inning that was flagged down by Steve Lyons.

For Jackson, the no-hitter was the ninth in which he had played in his 20-year career. But he was not one to find fault with its artistic value.

"It's a no-hitter," he said. "I don't know how strange it was. Give the guy credit."

Angels Play 17 Low-Hit Games

By DAVE SLOAN

When Joe Cowley of the Chicago White Sox left the mound on the night of September 19, he had accomplished something that four other 1986 pitchers could only come close to doing: holding the California Angels hitless. On six occasions opposing pitchers entered the seventh inning against the American League Western Division-champion Angels without having allowed a hit. Only Cowley ended the game that way.

Charlie Hough of the Texas Rangers twice lost no-hit bids against California. On June 16, the veteran knuckleballer was just two outs away from a no-hitter when rookie first baseman Wally Joyner singled to right. Hough lost the no-hitter and the game, 2-1, when Joyner's hit was combined with a three-base error and two passed balls.

On September 27, the Angels' first hit off Hough was Ruppert Jones' seventh-inning single. Hough finished with a two-hitter but won the game this time, 1-0.

Excluding Cowley, Detroit's Walt Terrell came closest to no-hitting the Angels. But Joyner broke that one up, too, tagging Terrell for a two-out double in the ninth inning of an August 20 game at Tiger Stadium.

There were 82 low-hit games (one- and two-hitters) in the major leagues in 1986, but no club participated in more than the Angels. California was involved in 17 of the 41 American League low-hit games, its pitchers throwing eight and its batsmen falling victim nine times— both major-league highs.

In addition to Hough and Terrell, the Yankees' Joe Niekro (June 4) and Kansas City's Danny Jackson (October 1) lost no-hit bids against California. Gary Pettis' double in the eighth inning marred Niekro's attempt and Dick Schofield's ninth-inning single ruined Jackson's.

Kirk McCaskill of the Angels and A.L. Cy Young Award winner Roger Clemens of the Boston Red Sox led the American League with three low-hit pitching performances apiece. McCaskill allowed only a third-inning home run by Steve Buechele in a one-hit, 7-1 victory over Texas on June 25.

McCaskill and Clemens, however, took a back seat to Montreal righthander Floyd Youmans, who pitched five low-hit games. Youmans yielded only a fourth-inning single to Glenn Wilson in a 12-0 win over the Phillies on June 8, a first-inning double to Mike Aldrete in a 1-0 loss to the Giants on September 7 and pitched three two-hitters. Youmans lost two of his low-hit games.

Montreal's Floyd Youmans pitched two one-hitters and three two-hitters to lead the majors in low-hit performances.

Nine times last season, the club pitching the low-hitter lost. Youmans was the only pitcher to lose twice, but on June 16 (against Hough) and October 4 (against Ed Correa), the Angels beat the Rangers with just one and two hits, respectively.

Ironically, on the same day—August 20—that Terrell lost his no-hit bid against California, Philadelphia lefthander Don Carman lost a perfect game against the Giants on Bob Brenly's ninth-inning double. Carman won the game, however, 1-0 on Juan Samuel's 10th-inning homer.

The 1986 season's most unexpected low-hit pitching performance was registered by San Diego righthander Jimmy Jones, who retired 27 of the 28 Houston batters he faced in his September 21 major-league debut at the Astrodome. Ironically, the only hit off Jones was a third-inning triple by Astros pitcher Bob Knepper.

A complete list of one- and two-hit games for the 1986 season follows:

California's Kirk McCaskill tied for the A.L. lead with three low-hit games.

NATIONAL LEAGUE

One-Hit Games

April 30—Thurmond, San Diego vs. St. Louis, 5-0—McGee, single in seventh.

June 4—Browning, Cincinnati vs. Chicago, 2-0—Davis, single in second.

June 8—Youmans, Montreal vs. Philadelphia, 12-0—Wilson, single in fourth.

July 18—Sanderson (seven innings) and Smith (two innings), Chicago vs. San Francisco, 2-1—Leonard, double in fourth.

July 22—Ryan (9⅓ innings) and Smith (⅔ inning), Houston vs. Montreal, 1-0—Fitzgerald, double in fourth.

Aug. 2—Pena (seven innings) and Niedenfuer (two innings), Los Angeles vs. Cincinnati, 7-1—Milner, homer in sixth.

Aug. 16—Hume (six innings) and Tekulve (three innings), Philadelphia vs. Pittsburgh, 6-0—Belliard, single in sixth.

Aug. 20—Carman (nine innings) and Bedrosian (one inning), Philadelphia vs. San Francisco, 1-0—Brenly, double in ninth.

Sept. 7—Youmans (eight innings) and Burke (one inning), Montreal vs. San Francisco, 0-1—Aldrete, double in first.

Sept. 21—Jones, San Diego vs. Houston, 5-0—Knepper, triple in third.

Sept. 26—Freeman (six innings) and Tekulve (three innings), Philadelphia vs. Montreal, 5-0—Raines, single in fourth.

Two-Hit Games

April 8—Sutcliffe (seven innings) and Baller (one inning), Chicago vs. St. Louis, 1-2—Clark, single in fourth; Van Slyke, single in fourth.

April 19—Smith, Atlanta vs. Los Angeles, 3-0—Russell, single in second; Cabell, single in ninth.

April 20—Fernandez (eight innings) and McDowell (one inning), New York vs. Philadelphia, 8-0—Redus, single in first; Schmidt, single in fifth.

May 6—Gooden, New York vs. Houston, 4-0—Davis, single in fifth; Reynolds, single in ninth.

May 20—Valenzuela, Los Angeles vs. Montreal, 4-0—Webster, single in seventh; Wohlford, single in ninth.

May 22—Krukow (eight innings) and Minton (one inning), San Francisco vs. New York, 10-2—Wilson, single in first; Hernandez, homer in first.

May 24—Valenzuela, Los Angeles vs. Philadelphia, 6-0—Hayes, single in first and double in sixth.

May 30—Scott (eight innings) and Kerfeld (one inning), Houston vs. Montreal, 0-1—Fitzgerald, single in second and homer in fifth.

June 4—Berenyi (six innings) and McDowell (three innings), New York vs. San Diego, 4-2—Iorg, single in second; Gwynn, homer in third.

June 5—Honeycutt (eight innings) and Howell (one inning), Los Angeles vs. Houston, 1-0—Bass, single in fifth; Garner, single in eighth.

June 7—Tudor, St. Louis vs. Chicago, 3-2—Sandberg, homer in fourth; Dernier, double in fifth.

June 20—Blue (seven innings) and Berenguer (two innings), San Francisco vs. Houston, 3-1—Cruz, single in second; Bass, homer in seventh.

June 27—Scott, Houston vs. Los Angeles, 5-0—Landreaux, singles in first and fourth.

July 4—Browning (7⅔ innings) and Robinson (1⅓ innings), Cincinnati vs. Philadelphia, 4-1—Hayes, single in seventh; Redus, double in eighth.

July 7—Pena (five innings), Diaz (one inning), Niedenfuer (two innings) and Howell (one inning), Los Angeles vs. St. Louis, 1-0—Van Slyke, single in second; Herr, single in fourth.

July 9—Youmans, Montreal vs. Houston, 2-1—Doran, single in fourth; Meadows, single in eighth.

July 11—Fernandez, New York vs. Atlanta, 11-0—Harper, single in second; Thomas, double in third.

July 12—Denny (six innings) and Robinson (three innings), Cincinnati vs. Montreal, 2-0—Raines, singles in third and ninth.

July 27—Ryan (five innings) and Lopez (four innings), Houston vs. Philadelphia, 3-2—Schmidt, single in first; Wilson, homer in fifth.

Aug. 16—Moyer, Chicago vs. Montreal, 5-0—Wohlford, singles in seventh and ninth.

Aug. 26—Blue (nine innings) and Garrelts (three innings), San Francisco vs. Montreal, 1-0—Dawson, singles in fourth and tenth.

Sept. 2—Youmans, Montreal vs. Los Angeles, 1-0—Scioscia, single in fourth; Sax, single in sixth.

Sept. 6—Fansler (four innings), Smiley (one inning), Walk (one inning), Pena (1⅓ innings) and Robinson (⅔ inning), Pittsburgh vs. Atlanta, 2-4—Hubbard, single in third; Horner, homer in third.

Sept. 7—Krukow, San Francisco vs. Montreal, 1-0—Hunt, single in second; Johnson, single in eighth.

Sept. 22—Gooden, New York vs. St. Louis, 5-2—Smith, single in third; Van Slyke, single in fourth.

Sept. 22—Valenzuela, Los Angeles vs. Houston, 9-2—Lopes, single in first; Garner, triple in seventh.

Sept. 23—Deshaies, Houston vs. Los Angeles, 4-0—Sax, single in fourth; Cabell, single in seventh.

Sept. 24—Ryan (eight innings) and Kerfeld (one inning), Houston vs. San Francisco, 6-0—Aldrete, single in seventh; C. Davis, single in ninth.

Sept. 27—Youmans, Montreal vs. Philadelphia, 0-1—Schmidt, double in fourth; Wilson, single in ninth.

Sept. 30—Sebra, Montreal vs. New York, 1-0—Carter, double in second; Dykstra, single in sixth.

AMERICAN LEAGUE

One-Hit Games

May 22—Key, Toronto vs. Chicago, 5-0—Guillen, single in fifth.

June 4—Niekro (eight innings) and Holland (one inning), New York vs. California, 11-0—Pettis, double in eighth.

June 16—Hough, Texas vs. California, 1-2—Joyner, single in ninth.

June 25—McCaskill, California vs. Texas, 7-1—Buechele, homer in third.

Aug. 20—Terrell, Detroit vs. California, 3-0—Joyner, double in ninth.

Sept. 20—Trujillo, Seattle vs. Kansas City, 3-0—Quirk, single in first.

Oct. 5—Young, Oakland vs. Kansas City, 6-0—Seitzer, single in seventh.

Two-Hit Games

April 16—Romanick, California vs. Seattle, 4-0—Calderon, single in sixth; Thomas, single in ninth.

April 16—Saberhagen, Kansas City vs. Boston, 1-0—Armas, single in second; Baylor, single in fifth.

April 22—McCaskill, California vs. Oakland, 5-1—Griffin, single in third; Tettleton, double in sixth.

April 24—Rijo (8⅓ innings) and Ontiveros (⅔ inning), Oakland vs. Seattle, 1-3—Davis, homer in fourth; Phelps, homer in ninth.

April 27—Langford (seven innings) and Howell (two innings), Oakland vs. Seattle, 1-0—Owen, single in sixth; Calderon, single in ninth.

April 29—Leonard (eight innings), Kansas City vs. Detroit, 1-2—Herndon, single in first; Laga, homer in seventh.

May 23—Schulze, Cleveland vs. Toronto, 3-1—Bell, homer in second; Whitt, single in second.

May 25—Cerutti (eight innings) and Caudill (one inning), Toronto vs. Cleveland, 8-1—Carter, single in first; Tabler, single in second.

May 25—Clemens, Boston vs. Texas, 7-1—McDowell, single in eighth; Porter, homer in ninth.

May 31—McCaskill, California vs. Baltimore, 2-0—Wiggins, single in first; Dwyer, double in ninth.

June 6—Schrom, Cleveland vs. California, 3-0—Pettis, single in first; Howell, single in second.

June 9—Sutton, California vs. Chicago, 3-0—Bonilla, single in fifth; Bradley, single in fifth.

June 22—Niekro, Cleveland vs. Minnesota, 4-1—Puckett, single in first; Hrbek, single in first.

July 5—Clancy (eight innings) and Henke (one inning), Toronto vs. California, 7-3—Burleson, single in fourth; Pettis, single in eighth.

July 18—Morris, Detroit vs. Texas, 5-0—Fletcher, double in first; Slaught, double in second.

July 20—Allen, Chicago vs. New York, 8-0—Winfield, single in fifth; Henderson, double in sixth.

July 25—Clemens, Boston vs. California, 8-1—Jackson, double in fifth; Narron, double in seventh.

July 26—Plunk (six innings), Leiper (⅓ inning), Stewart (1⅓ innings) and Andujar (one inning), Oakland vs. Toronto, 2-0—Moseby, single in third; Leach, double in fourth.

July 29—Cowley (8⅔ innings) and James (⅓ inning), Chicago vs. Boston, 4-1—Rice, singles in second and fourth.

Aug. 1—Blyleven, Minnesota vs. Oakland, 10-1—Bochte, single in fifth; Griffin, homer in eighth.

Aug. 2—Smithson, Minnesota vs. Oakland, 8-0—Murphy, single in seventh; Hill, single in eighth.

Aug. 11—Flanagan (8⅓ innings) and Aase (⅔ inning), Baltimore vs. Toronto, 3-1—Shepherd, double in third; Fernandez, double in ninth.

Aug. 15—Moore, Seattle vs. Minnesota, 1-0—Salas, single in third; Puckett, single in third.

Aug. 16—Witt, California vs. Oakland, 5-2—Murphy, homer in first; Davis, double in eighth.

Aug. 20—Clemens, Boston vs. Minnesota, 9-1—Bush, single in fourth; Gaetti, single in fourth.

Aug. 30—Swift (8⅔ innings) and Young (⅓ inning), Seattle vs. New York, 1-0—Tolleson, single in eighth; Winfield, single in ninth.

Sept. 13—Kelly (6⅓ innings) and Hernandez (2⅔ innings), Detroit vs. Baltimore, 7-2—Young, homer in second and single in seventh.

Sept. 21—Candelaria (seven innings) and Moore (two innings), California vs. Chicago, 3-0—Calderon, single in second; Cochrane, single in eighth.

Sept. 27—McGregor, Baltimore vs. Milwaukee, 7-0—Molitor, single in first; Diaz, single in ninth.

Sept. 27—Hough, Texas vs. California, 1-0—Jones, single in seventh; Narron, single in eighth.

Oct. 1—Jackson, Kansas City vs. California, 2-0—Schofield, single in ninth; DeCinces, single in ninth.

Oct. 4—Correa, Texas vs. California, 0-2—Jones, single in second; Downing, double in second.

Oct. 4—Candelaria (six innings) and Ruhle (three innings), California vs. Texas, 2-0—Mercado, single in third; Incaviglia, single in fourth.

Oct. 5—Viola, Minnesota vs. Chicago, 3-0—Cangelosi, single in fourth; Guillen, single in eighth.

Clemens Tops Strikeout List

By DAVE SLOAN

Boston righthander Roger Clemens was the best pitcher in baseball in 1986. His 24-4 record captured the American League Cy Young Award and led the Red Sox to their first A.L. pennant in 11 years. But Clemens was never better than he was at Fenway Park on April 29, when he retired a record 20 Seattle Mariners on strikes without walking a batter.

Clemens' 20 strikeouts surpassed the nine-inning record of 19 set in modern times by St. Louis Cardinals lefthander Steve Carlton in 1969 and subsequently equaled by Tom Seaver of the New York Mets in 1970 and Nolan Ryan of the California Angels in 1974. Clemens had at least one strikeout in every inning and struck out the side in the first, fourth and fifth frames. Each batter in Seattle's starting lineup fanned at least once, with left fielder Phil Bradley—whose ninth-inning strikeout was Clemens' 20th—whiffing four times.

Clemens' gem was one of 139 10-strikeout performances in the major leagues last season, one of 80 in the American League. Clemens had eight such games overall, tying for the league lead with the Mariners' Mark Langston. The Red Sox, with 14, finished first among A.L. clubs in the 10-K category, while the Mariners and the Detroit Tigers tied for second with 10 each.

The National League West champion Houston Astros led all major league clubs with 18 10-strikeout performances. Mike Scott, whose 306 strikeouts led the majors in 1986, had 11 such games. Ryan, whose shared single-game record was eclipsed by Clemens, had four and rookie Jim Deshaies three.

Ironically, the final 10-strikeout game by each Houston pitcher came on consecutive days late in September as the Astros battled Cincinnati for the division title.

On September 23 against the Los Angeles Dodgers, Deshaies established a modern major league record by fanning the first eight batters of the game. He finished with 10 strikeouts in the Astros' 4-0 victory.

On September 24, Ryan struck out 12 batters in eight innings in a 6-0 triumph over the San Francisco Giants. Ryan, in his 19th complete major league season, extended to 162 his record for most games in a career with 10 or more strikeouts.

Not to be outdone, Scott struck out 13 Giants the next day in a 2-0, no-hit victory that clinched the N.L. West championship for the Astros. It was the first time in major league history that a division title or pennant had been decided with a no-hitter.

Following is a list of all pitchers who achieved at least 10 strikeouts in a game in 1986, with the number of times the feat was accomplished:

AMERICAN LEAGUE: Baltimore (3)—Boddicker 2, Dixon. Boston (14)—Clemens 8, Hurst 5, Boyd. California (6)—McCaskill 4, Candelaria, Witt. Chicago (4)—Dotson 2, Cowley, DeLeon. Cleveland (3)—Candiotti 3. Detroit (10)—Morris 7, Tanana 2, King. Kansas City (2)—Gubicza, Leonard. Milwaukee (5)—Higuera 4, Nieves. Minnesota (7)—Viola 3, Blyleven 2, Heaton, Portugal. New York (1)—Guidry. Oakland (5)—Rijo 4, Plunk. Seattle (10)—Langston 8, Moore 2. Texas (9)—Witt 5, Correa 3, Mason. Toronto (1)—Key.

NATIONAL LEAGUE: Atlanta (2)—Palmer, Smith. Chicago—None. Cincinnati (2)—Denny 2. Houston (18)—Scott 11, Ryan 4, Deshaies 3. Los Angeles (10)—Valenzuela 6, Hershiser 2, Welch 2. Montreal (6)—Youmans 5, Hesketh. New York (11)—Gooden 5, Fernandez 4, Darling, Ojeda. Philadelphia (2)—Carlton, Gross. Pittsburgh (2)—Rhoden 2. St. Louis (1)—Conroy. San Diego (3)—Show 2, Dravecky. San Francisco (2)—Blue, Krukow.

1986 Games With 15 or More Strikeouts

Date	Pitcher—Club—Opp.	Place	IP.	H.	R.	ER.	BB.	SO.	Result
April 29	Clemens, Red Sox vs. Mariners	Boston	9	3	1	1	0	20	W 3-1
April 19	Rijo, A's vs. Mariners	Seattle	8	5	2	2	4	16	W 7-2
June 25	Langston, Mariners vs. Indians	Seattle	9	3	1	0	5	15	W 6-1
Aug. 1	Blyleven, Twins vs. A's	Minnesota	9	2	1	1	1	15	W 10-1
Sept. 27	Youmans, Expos vs. Phillies	Montreal	9	2	1	1	7	15	L 0-1

Righetti, Worrell Top Firemen

By LARRY WIGGE

Dave Righetti didn't agree with New York Yankees' management when he was sent from the starting rotation to the bullpen after he had compiled a 14-8 record in 1983. Now, however, the hard-throwing lefthander realizes it was a good move.

Todd Worrell also was a starting pitcher who was asked to change the course of his career. After the talented righthander confounded the St. Louis Cardinals by not making it to the major leagues after 3½ years in the minors, someone suggested that a move to the bullpen might be in order. The switch finally brought out the talent in Worrell.

Neither started out thinking about the records held by Bruce Sutter, Dan Quisenberry, Goose Gossage, Rollie Fingers and the like, but several of the standards set by those famous relief pitchers were erased by Righetti and Worrell in 1986. In the process, they each earned The Sporting News Fireman of the Year awards, honoring the major leagues top relief pitchers.

Righetti won the American League honor by posting a record 46 saves, one more than the previous major league mark set by Quisenberry in 1983 and equalled by Sutter in '84. Righetti also had eight relief wins for a total of 54 points, far outdistancing Baltimore's Don Aase (34 saves, six wins for 40 points) and Toronto's Tom Henke (27 saves, nine wins for 36 points).

Worrell's National League honor was embellished by the fact that he was a rookie. The 36 saves by Worrell shattered the N.L. rookie mark of 22 by Rawly Eastwick in 1975 and the A.L. record of 23 saves by Doug Corbett in 1980. Worrell also had nine relief wins for a total of 45 points, three better than Montreal's Jeff Reardon (the 1985 Fireman of the Year), who had 35 saves and seven wins. Chicago's Lee Smith was third with 31 saves and nine wins.

Quisenberry, who had won the A.L. Fireman Award five times in the last six seasons, dropped from 45 points in 1985 to 15 (three wins, 12 saves) in 1986.

Righetti became the fourth member of the Yankees to win the Fireman Award since its inception in 1960, following Luis Arroyo (1961), Sparky Lyle (1972) and Gossage (1978). Previous Cardinals winning the award include Lindy McDaniel (1960), Al Hrabosky (1975) and Sutter (1981, '82 and '84).

St. Louis reliever Todd Worrell saved a rookie-record 36 games and captured N.L. Fireman of the Year honors.

Following is a complete list of major league players who recorded saves or relief wins in 1986:

AMERICAN LEAGUE

Pitcher—Club	Saves	Relief Wins	Tot. Pts.
Righetti, New York	46	8	54
Aase, Baltimore	34	6	40
Henke, Toronto	27	9	36
Hernandez, Detroit	24	8	32
Harris, Texas	20	10	30
Moore, California	21	4	25
Eichhorn, Toronto	10	14	24
Plesac, Milwaukee	14	10	24
Camacho, Cleveland	20	2	22
Stanley, Boston	16	6	22
Clear, Milwaukee	16	5	21
Howell, Oakland	16	3	19
James, Chicago	14	5	19
Young, Seattle	13	6	19
Atherton, Oakland-Minnesota	10	6	16
Farr, Kansas City	8	8	16
Williams, Texas	8	8	16
Bailes, Cleveland	7	8	15
Fisher, New York	6	9	15
Quisenberry, Kansas City	12	3	15
Corbett, California	10	4	14
Ladd, Seattle	6	8	14
Sambito, Boston	12	2	14
Black, Kansas City	9	4	13
Schiraldi, Boston	9	4	13
Nelson, Chicago	6	6	12
Ontiveros, Oakland	10	2	12
Schmidt, Chicago	8	3	11
Bordi, Baltimore	3	6	9
Forster, California	5	4	9

Pitcher—Club	Saves	Relief Wins	Tot. Pts.
Mohorcic, Texas	7	2	9
Thigpen, Chicago	7	2	9
Huismann, Seattle	5	3	8
Wills, Cleveland	4	4	8
Frazier, Minnesota	6	1	7
Russell, Texas	2	5	7
Bair, Oakland	4	2	6
Campbell, Detroit	3	3	6
King, Detroit	3	3	6
Lucas, California	2	4	6
Mooneyham, Oakland	2	4	6
Pastore, Minnesota	2	3	5
Thurmond, Detroit	3	2	5
Yett, Cleveland	1	4	5
Caudill, Toronto	2	2	4
Crawford, Boston	4	0	4
Davis, Minnesota	2	2	4
Havens, Baltimore	1	3	4
Lamp, Toronto	2	2	4
McKeon, Chicago	1	3	4
Oelkers, Cleveland	1	3	4
Stewart, Boston	0	4	4
Stoddard, New York	0	4	4
Whitson, New York	0	4	4
Best, Seattle	1	2	3
Cerutti, Toronto	1	2	3
Finley, California	0	3	3
Johnson, Milwaukee	1	2	3
Leiper, Oakland	1	2	3
Mahler, Texas-Toronto	3	0	3
Noles, Cleveland	0	3	3
Portugal, Minnesota	1	2	3
Scurry, New York	2	1	3
Shirley, New York	3	0	3
Slaton, California-Detroit	2	1	3
Acker, Toronto	0	2	2
Agosto, Chicago-Minnesota	1	1	2
Bankhead, Kansas City	0	2	2
Bryden, California	0	2	2
Darwin, Milwaukee	0	2	2
Dawley, Chicago	2	0	2
Fireovid, Seattle	0	2	2
D. Jones, Cleveland	1	1	2
O. Jones, Baltimore	0	2	2
McClure, Milwaukee	0	2	2
Niekro, Cleveland	0	2	2
O'Neal, Detroit	2	0	2
Searage, Milwaukee-Chicago	1	1	2
Snell, Baltimore	0	2	2
Trujillo, Boston-Seattle	1	1	2

One save—Andujar, Oakland; Forsch, California; Gordon, Toronto; Heaton, Cleveland-Minnesota; D. Jackson, Kansas City; R. Jackson, Minnesota; Krueger, Oakland; Loynd, Texas; T. Martinez, Baltimore; Moore, Seattle; Morgan, Seattle; Pacella, Detroit; Pulido, New York; Rijo, Oakland; Ruhle, California; Stieb, Toronto; Von Ohlen, Oakland.

One win—Anderson, Minnesota; Aquino, Toronto; Bannister, Chicago; Cary, Detroit; Gibson, Milwaukee; Gubicza, Kansas City; Henry, Texas; Holland, New York; Kern, Cleveland; Lollar, Boston; Meridith, Texas; Nieves, Milwaukee; Reed, Seattle; Saberhagen, Kansas City; Schulze, Cleveland; Woodward, Boston; R. Wright, Texas; Young, Oakland.

NATIONAL LEAGUE

Pitcher—Club	Saves	Relief Wins	Tot. Pts.
Worrell, St. Louis	36	9	45
Reardon, Montreal	35	7	42
Smith, Chicago	31	9	40
Bedrosian, Philadelphia	29	8	37
Smith, Houston	33	4	37
McDowell, New York	22	14	36
Franco, Cincinnati	29	6	35
Garber, Atlanta	24	5	29
Orosco, New York	21	8	29
Gossage, San Diego	21	5	26
Robinson, Cincinnati	14	10	24
Garrelts, San Francisco	10	8	18
Howell, Los Angeles	12	6	18
Kerfeld, Houston	7	11	18
Niedenfuer, Los Angeles	11	6	17
Robinson, Pittsburgh	14	3	17
Tekulve, Philadelphia	4	11	15
Assenmacher, Atlanta	7	7	14
McCullers, San Diego	5	9	14
Robinson, San Francisco	8	6	14
Lefferts, San Diego	4	9	13
Burke, Montreal	4	8	12
Lopez, Houston	7	3	10
M. Davis, San Francisco	4	5	9
Dedmon, Atlanta	3	6	9
Guante, Pittsburgh	4	5	9
Minton, San Francisco	5	4	9
McClure, Montreal	6	2	8
Schatzeder, Montreal-Philadelphia	2	6	8
Baller, Chicago	5	2	7
Hume, Philadelphia	4	3	7
McGaffigan, Montreal	2	5	7
Murphy, Cincinnati	1	6	7
Berenguer, San Francisco	4	2	6
DiPino, Houston-Chicago	3	3	6
Jones, Pittsburgh	3	3	6
Winn, Pittsburgh	3	3	6
Dayley, St. Louis	5	0	5
Fontenot, Chicago	2	3	5
Sisk, New York	1	4	5
Sutter, Atlanta	3	2	5
Carman, Philadelphia	1	3	4
Gumpert, Chicago	2	2	4
Hoffman, Chicago	0	4	4
Horton, St. Louis	3	1	4
Perry, St. Louis	2	2	4
Power, Cincinnati	0	4	4
Soff, St. Louis	0	4	4
Walk, Pittsburgh	2	2	4
Williams, San Francisco	1	3	4
Andersen, Philadelphia-Houston	1	2	3
Keough, Chicago-Houston	0	3	3
Lynch, New York-Chicago	0	3	3
St. Claire, Montreal	1	2	3
Sanderson, Chicago	1	2	3
Solano, Houston	0	3	3
Walter, San Diego	1	2	3
Clements, Pittsburgh	2	0	2
DeLeon, Pittsburgh	1	1	2
Frazier, Chicago	0	2	2
Holton, Los Angeles	0	2	2
Laskey, San Francisco	1	1	2
McWilliams, Pittsburgh	0	2	2
Smith, Atlanta	1	1	2
B. Stoddard, San Diego	1	1	2

One save—Anderson, New York; Fernandez, New York; Gott, San Francisco; Hall, Chicago; Hensley, San Francisco; Olwine, Atlanta; A. Pena, Los Angeles; H. Pena, Pittsburgh; Reuss, Los Angeles; Roberge, Montreal.

One win—Aguilera, New York; Berenyi, New York; Booker, San Diego; Calhoun, Houston; Conroy, St. Louis; Darwin, Houston; Hawkins, San Diego; Hernandez, Houston; Honeycutt, Los Angeles; Hoyt, San Diego; Hudson, Philadelphia; Knepper, Houston; Lerch, Philadelphia; Madden, Houston; McMurtry, Atlanta; Niemann, New York; Ojeda, New York; Patterson, Pittsburgh; Powell, Los Angeles; Price, Cincinnati; Sebra, Montreal; Smiley, Pittsburgh; Speck, Atlanta; T. Stoddard, San Diego; Terry, Cincinnati; Trout, Chicago; Vande Berg, Los Angeles; Willis, Cincinnati.

Expos Play in Eight 1-0 Games

By DAVE SLOAN

When Kansas City's Dennis Leonard took the mound at Royals Stadium on April 12 against the Toronto Blue Jays, it marked his first major league starting assignment since May 28, 1983.

That was the day the Royals righthander suffered a torn tendon below his left kneecap while delivering a pitch to Baltimore's Cal Ripken. It took 1,048 days, four operations and countless hours of therapy before Leonard was able to pitch again.

But the three-time 20-game winner didn't waste any time in his post-rehabilitation debut showing the baseball world that he was back. He was, in a word, spectacular. Leonard allowed just three hits and retired 20 batters in succession after an infield single by Lloyd Moseby in the third inning. The Royals won, 1-0, after pushing across an eighth-inning run against Toronto starter Jim Acker.

Leonard's triumph was one of 46 1-0 games played in 1986. Twenty-six of those games were played in the National League and all major league teams except Cleveland were involved in at least one. The Montreal Expos played in eight 1-0 games and lost five, both figures tops in the majors.

Home runs accounted for the game's only run 19 times, with three of those homers coming in extra innings.

On July 22 at Houston, the Astros' Glenn Davis blasted a 10th-inning homer off Expos righthander Floyd Youmans to give reliever Dave Smith the victory. On August 20 at San Francisco, Juan Samuel of the Phillies tagged the Giants' Mike Krukow for a 10th-inning homer to make a winner of Don Carman, who had lost a bid for a perfect game in the ninth inning. On September 26 at Boston, Toronto's Jesse Barfield belted a homer off Calvin Schiraldi in the 12th to give Mark Eichhorn a win in relief.

Of the eight extra-inning 1-0 games, the longest took 15 innings. On July 27 at Oakland, Alfredo Griffin of the A's walked with two out and the bases loaded against Toronto reliever Stan Clarke.

Carman, Krukow, Houston's Mike Scott and Texas' Charlie Hough led the majors with two 1-0 victories apiece. Scott and Minnesota's Neal Heaton lost two 1-0 games, but the leader in losses was Youmans, who allowed just six hits in his three 1-0 defeats.

The Los Angeles Dodgers played in consecutive 1-0 games twice last season. On April 8-9, the Dodgers split a pair against the San Diego Padres. They split another pair against St. Louis on July 7-8.

The complete list of 1-0 games, including the winning and losing pitchers and the inning in which the run was scored, follows:

AMERICAN LEAGUE (20)

Date	Winner	Loser	Inning
APRIL—			
12	Leonard, K.C.	*Acker, Tor.	8
16	Saberhagen, K.C.	Nipper, Bos.	2
27	*Langford, Oak.	Morgan, Sea.	2
JUNE—			
2	*Hough, Tex.	Cowley, Chi.	1
18	Young, Oak.	Saberhagen, K.C.	2
20	Leary, Mil.	Terrell, Det.	4
JULY—			
2	Nieves, Mil.	Dixon, Bal.	4
6	*Dixon, Bal.	Heaton, Minn.	5
19	*Flanagan, Bal.	Heaton, Minn.	2
21	*Viola, Minn.	*Thurmond, Det.	6
24	*Bankhead, K.C.	*O'Neal, Det.	8
27	*Leiper, Oak.	*Clarke, Tor.	15
AUGUST—			
4	*DeLeon, Chi.	Clemens, Bos.	8
9	Higuera, Mil.	*DeLeon, Chi.	3
15	Moore, Sea.	*Atherton, Minn.	9
30	*Swift, Sea.	John, N.Y.	8
SEPTEMBER—			
4	*Farr, K.C.	*Dawley, Chi.	8
26	*Eichhorn, Tor.	*Schiraldi, Bos.	12
27	Hough, Tex.	*Sutton, Cal.	4
27	Morris, Det.	*Righetti, N.Y.	10

NATIONAL LEAGUE (26)

Date	Winner	Loser	Inning
APRIL—			
8	Dravecky, S.D.	Hershiser, L.A.	3
9	Welch, L.A.	*Hawkins, S.D.	4
26	Scott, Hou.	Gullickson, Cin.	9
30	*Scott, Hou.	*Gross, Phil.	4
MAY—			
12	*McDowell, N.Y.	*Assenmacher, Atl.	9
30	*Smith, Mon.	*Scott, Hou.	5
31	*Hudson, Phil.	*Dravecky, S.D.	7
JUNE—			
5	*Honeycutt, L.A.	*Hernandez, Hou.	6
10	*Niedenfuer, L.A.	*Franco, Cin.	9
13	*Mathews, St. L.	Sutcliffe, Chi.	10
14	*Burris, St. L.	*Sanderson, Chi.	2
JULY—			
1	*Gumpert, Chi.	*Schatzeder, Mon.	8
3	Krukow, S.F.	*Ownbey, St. L.	6
7	*Pena, L.A.	*Forsch, St. L.	1
8	*Conroy, St. L.	*Welch, L.A.	7
22	*Smith, Hou.	Youmans, Mon.	10
29	*Palmer, Atl.	*Scott, Hou.	7
AUGUST—			
19	*Deshaies, Hou.	*Bielecki, Pitt.	2
20	*Carman, Phil.	Krukow, S.F.	10
26	*Garrelts, S.F.	*Roberge, Mon.	12
SEPTEMBER—			
2	Youmans, Mon.	Welch, L.A.	9
7	Krukow, S.F.	*Youmans, Mon.	1
15	*Worrell, St.L.	*McDowell, N.Y.	13
20	*Moyer, Chi.	Rhoden, Pitt.	6
27	*Carman, Phil.	Youmans, Mon.	4
30	Sebra, Mon.	*Darling, N.Y.	1

*Did not pitch complete game.

Horner Joins Four-Homer Club

By DAVE SLOAN

When Bob Horner of the Atlanta Braves belted four home runs in a game against Montreal on July 6, he became only the 11th player in major league history to accomplish the feat.

Not since Mike Schmidt of the Philadelphia Phillies hit four in a 10-inning game against the Chicago Cubs on April 17, 1976, had a player hit four homers in a single game. And it was the first time in 25 years that four homers had been hit in a nine-inning game.

Unfortunately for Horner, the Braves lost the game, 11-8, as the Expos scored three runs in the fourth inning and six in the fifth. It marked the first time in this century and only the second time in history that the club of the four-homer hitter lost the game. Ed Delahanty's Philadelphia Phillies lost his four-homer game on July 13, 1896.

Horner belted solo homers in the second and fourth innings and a three-run blast in the fifth, all off Expos starter Andy McGaffigan. The Braves' first baseman closed his big day with a two-out solo shot in the ninth off Jeff Reardon. Horner finished with six runs batted in.

"I had a good week today," Horner said afterward.

Ironically, of the eight games in 1986 in which one player hit three or more homers, that player's club lost four times.

On June 12, the Baltimore Orioles' Juan Beniquez—who had hit just one homer all season coming into the game—blasted three solo shots in consecutive at-bats in a 7-5 loss to the New York Yankees. The Braves' Ken Griffey, who had been obtained from the Yankees just three weeks before, hit three homers in a 5-4 loss to the Phillies on July 22, just 16 days after Horner's four-homer feat. On September 1, the Seattle Mariners' Jim Presley clubbed three homers in a 6-5 loss to Detroit.

Including the eight four- and three-homer games, there were 209 multi-homer performances in the big leagues last season, with every club having at least one. American League batters accounted for a whopping 137 such performances, 30 more than in 1985. The Detroit Tigers, whose 198 homers led the majors last season, led all clubs with 18 multi-homer games, one more than the Minnesota Twins.

Kirk Gibson of the Tigers, Gary Gaetti of the Twins and Toronto's Jesse Barfield tied for individual honors with five multi-homer games each. Gibson blasted two homers in the Tigers' 6-5, opening-day victory over Boston on April 7 for the season's first multi-homer game.

Fourteen times in 1986, two players had multi-homer performances in the same game. It happened 13 times in the American League, with three of Barfield's five multi-homer performances being matched in the same game by another player.

On May 6 at Toronto, Barfield and Oakland's Dave Kingman hit two homers apiece in the A's 17-3 victory. On July 3 at Boston, Barfield and teammate Rance Mulliniks each hit two homers in the Blue Jays' 8-5 triumph over the Red Sox. On July 21 at Seattle, Barfield and George Bell of the Blue Jays hit two homers each in an 8-3 victory over the Mariners.

Following is a list of players who had multi-homer games in '86 and the number of times they did it:

AMERICAN LEAGUE: Baltimore (10)—Murray 2, Shelby 2, Beniquez, Dempsey, Lacy, Lynn, Sheets, Traber. Boston (6)—Buckner 2, Evans 2, Armas, Baylor. California (11)—Jackson 3, DeCinces 2, Downing 2, Joyner 2, Howell, Jones. Chicago (7)—Kittle 4, Baines, Hulett, Walker. Cleveland (12)—Carter 3, Snyder 3, Bernazard 2, Hall 2, Jacoby, Thornton. Detroit (18)—Gibson 5, Parrish 4, Evans 3, Whitaker 2, Coles, Grubb, Lemon, Trammell. Kansas City (7)—Brett 2, Balboni, Motley, Orta, Sundberg, White. Milwaukee (7)—Deer 3, Braggs, Cooper, Molitor, Oglivie. Minnesota (17)—Gaetti 5, Brunansky 3, Smalley 3, Gagne 2, Hrbek 2, Puckett, Salas. New York (7)—Mattingly 2, Pagliarulo 2, Henderson, Pasqua, Winfield. Oakland (10)—Davis 3, Kingman 3, Lansford 2, Bathe, Canseco. Seattle (7)—Presley 2, Davis, Henderson, Kearney, Phelps, Tartabull. Texas (8)—Incaviglia 2, Parrish 2, McDowell, O'Brien, Porter, Sierra. Toronto (10)—Barfield 5, Bell 2, Moseby 2, Mulliniks.

NATIONAL LEAGUE: Atlanta (7)—Murphy 3, Horner 2, Griffey, Thomas. Chicago (8)—Davis 2, Matthews 2, Cey, Moreland, Sandberg, Speier. Cincinnati (9)—Davis 3, Bell, Concepcion, Daniels, Milner, Oester, Parker. Houston (6)—Davis 2, Walling 2, Cruz, Garner. Los Angeles (8)—Marshall 3, Brock 2, Stubbs 2, Matuszek. Montreal (3)—Wallach 2,

Bob Horner is welcomed back to the Braves' dugout after hitting the first of his four home runs in a July 6 game against Montreal.

Dawson. New York (9)—Carter 3, Foster 2, Strawberry 2, Johnson, Knight. Philadelphia (8)—Schmidt 3, Redus 2, Hayes, Samuel, Schu. Pittsburgh (2)—Diaz, Morrison. St. Louis (1)—McGee. San Diego (6)—McReynolds 2, Nettles 2, Gwynn, Wynne. San Francisco (5)—Maldonado 2, Brenly, Clark, Davis.

A recap of the four- and three-homer games:

Date	Player—Club—Opp.	Place	AB.	R.	H.	2B.	3B.	HR.	RBI.	Result
July 6	Horner, Braves vs. Expos	H	5	4	4	0	0	4	6	L 8-11
June 8	Lacy, Orioles vs. Yankees	A	6	4	4	0	0	3	6	W 18-9
June 12	Beniquez, Orioles vs. Yankees	H	5	3	3	0	0	3	3	L 5-7
July 22	Griffey, Braves vs. Phillies	H	5	3	3	0	0	3	3	L 4-5
Aug. 29	Carter, Indians vs. Red Sox	A	5	3	5	0	0	3	4	W 7-3
Sept. 1	Presley, Mariners vs. Tigers	H	4	3	3	0	0	3	4	L 5-6
Sept. 10	Davis, Reds vs. Giants	A	5	5	4	0	0	3	4	W 14-2
Sept. 18	Jackson, Angels vs. Royals	H	4	4	3	0	0	3	7	W 18-3

Schofield Slams Tigers Twice

By DAVE SLOAN

When the California Angels entered the bottom of the ninth inning of a game against Detroit on August 29, they had little reason for optimism. The Tigers led, 12-5, and were simply putting the wraps on an easy victory.

Dick Schofield opened the ninth with a single off Tigers pitcher Randy O'Neal. Rick Burleson flied out, but Wally Joyner walked and Brian Downing singled to load the bases.

A two-run double by Jack Howell chased O'Neal and the Tigers brought ace reliever Willie Hernandez into the game. George Hendrick and Bobby Grich greeted Hernandez with run-scoring singles, cutting the Tigers' advantage to 12-9.

Hernandez retired Gary Pettis on a force play for the second out, but walked Ruppert Jones on a 3-2 pitch to load the bases again. He got two quick strikes on the next batter, Schofield, before the Angels shortstop—who had hit just 15 major league home runs prior to 1986—blasted the next pitch over the wall for a game-winning grand slam.

There were 82 grand slams hit in the major leagues last season—50 in the American League—but none were as dramatic as Schofield's blast off Hernandez. Ironically, it was Schofield's second slam of the '86 season and second against the Tigers, both coming at Anaheim Stadium.

Schofield was one of 11 major leaguers (nine in the A.L.) to hit two grand slams in 1986.

Seattle's Jim Presley added a little spice to his two grand slams. Both came in extra innings and produced Mariner victories in the Kingdome. He was the only A.L. player last season to hit an extra-inning slam.

On April 8, Presley became the eighth player in American League history to hit a grand slam on opening day when his 10th-inning homer off California's Ken Forsch gave the Mariners an 8-4 triumph. On July 17, Presley tagged Boston's Bob Stanley for a grand slam in the 11th inning, producing a 5-1 Seattle victory.

Eddie Murray's two grand slams—on April 19 and May 18—gave the Baltimore first baseman 14 slams in his major league career. Oakland's Dave Kingman, however, retained the career lead among active players with his 16th off Detroit's Dave LaPoint on June 3.

Seven of the 82 slams last season were hit by pinch-hitters. Tim Teufel's 11th-inning blast off Philadelphia's Tom Hume on June 10 propelled the Mets to an 8-4 victory. Craig Reynolds' sixth-inning slam off Rick Mahler on April 12 accounted for all the Astros' runs in a 4-3 win over Atlanta.

All major league clubs except Milwaukee hit at least one grand slam, with the Orioles, Red Sox and Angels tying for team honors with seven each. It marked the fifth straight season in which Baltimore either led or tied for the major league lead in that category.

Except for the Mets and Astros, all clubs yielded at least one slam. No pitcher gave up more than two, but Oakland's Eric Plunk was hit for two slams faster than any other hurler.

On July 31 against California, Brian Downing blasted a third-inning slam off Plunk to give the Angels a 4-2 lead. The following inning, Bob Boone tagged Plunk for another slam to put California ahead, 8-2, en route to an 8-5 victory. It was the 35th time in major league history that one club had hit two slams in the same game.

Larry Sheets and Jim Dwyer of the Orioles topped that feat on August 6 by hitting grand slams in the fourth inning of a game against Texas. Baltimore scored nine runs in the inning but lost the game, 13-11. Toby Harrah hit a second-inning grand slam for the Rangers.

One of the more dramatic grand slams was hit at St. Louis on June 29. With the Cardinals leading Philadelphia, 7-4, and two out and two men on in the ninth inning, the Phillies Greg Gross hit a harmless grounder to short. Slick-fielding Ozzie Smith fielded the ball cleanly but his throw to first pulled Alan Knicely off the bag. Gross was safe, the bases were loaded and the next batter, Juan Samuel, drilled St. Louis reliever Todd Worrell's next pitch over the left-field fence for a game-winning homer.

The complete list of grand slams, with the inning in which each was hit in parentheses, follows:

AMERICAN LEAGUE (50)

APRIL—

8 —Presley, Seattle vs. Forsch, California (10)
11 —Downing, California vs. Birtsas, Oakland (9)
15 —Tartabull, Seattle vs. Sutton, California (1)
17 —Baylor, Boston vs. Farr, Kansas City (8)
19 —Murray, Baltimore vs. Rozema, Texas (5)

MAY—

3 —Evans, Detroit vs. Butcher, Minnesota (4)
8 —Joyner, California vs. Acker, Toronto (3)
9 —Spilman, Detroit vs. Blyleven, Minnesota (3)
9 —Davis, Seattle vs. Gordon, Toronto (7)

Philadelphia's Juan Samuel (center) hit one of the more dramatic grand slams of 1986, a ninth-inning game-winning blow against reliever Todd Worrell and the St. Louis Cardinals.

11 —Dempsey, Baltimore vs. Leibrandt, Kansas City (5)
15 —White, Kansas City vs. Yett, Cleveland (8)
17 —Winfield, New York vs. Young, Seattle (2)
18 —Murray, Baltimore vs. Rijo, Oakland (7)
22 —Whitt, Toronto vs. Dotson, Chicago (4)
23 —Lynn, Baltimore vs. Young, Seattle (8)
25 —Boggs, Boston vs. Mason, Texas (2)
29 —Schofield, California vs. LaPoint, Detroit (7)
31 —Coles, Detroit vs. Langston, Seattle (8)

JUNE—
3 —Kingman, Oakland vs. LaPoint, Detroit (1)
20 —Bell, Toronto vs. Righetti, New York (9)
20 —Carter, Cleveland vs. Viola, Minnesota (6)
23 —Walker, Chicago vs. Blyleven, Minnesota (2)

JULY—
2 —Thornton, Cleveland vs. Mooneyham, Oakland (1)
5 —Gaetti, Minnesota vs. Flanagan, Baltimore (1)
8 —Hendrick, California vs. Nieves, Milwaukee (5)
11 —*Sundberg, Kansas City vs. Tanana, Detroit (3)
17 —Presley, Seattle vs. Stanley, Boston (11)
23 —Grubb, Detroit vs. Pastore, Minnesota (6)
25 —Gedman, Boston vs. Ruhle, California (5)
27 —Traber, Baltimore vs. Dawley, Chicago (4)
31 —Downing, California vs. Plunk, Oakland (3)
31 —Boone, California vs. Plunk, Oakland (4)

AUGUST—
1 —*Incaviglia, Texas vs. Gibson, Milwaukee (1)
6 —Harrah, Texas vs. Dixon, Baltimore (2)
6 —Sheets, Baltimore vs. Witt, Texas (4)
6 —Dwyer, Baltimore vs. Russell, Texas (4)
10 —Motley, Kansas City vs. Rasmussen, New York (4)
10 —Evans, Detroit vs. Lollar, Boston (7)
10 —Gedman, Boston vs. Hernandez, Detroit (8)
11 —Tartabull, Seattle vs. Bair, Oakland (7)
16 —Herndon, Detroit vs. Sambito, Boston (8)
21 —Armas, Boston vs. Roman, Cleveland (6)
29 —Schofield, California vs. Hernandez, Detroit (9)
31 —Moseby, Toronto vs. Portugal, Minnesota (3)

SEPTEMBER—
4 —Carter, Cleveland vs. Johnson, Milwaukee (4)
5 —Rice, Boston vs. Viola, Minnesota (3)
5 —Porter, Texas vs. Cone, Kansas City (5)
7 —Rice, Boston vs. Heaton, Minnesota (3)
28 —Incaviglia, Texas vs. Witt, California (7)

OCTOBER—
3 —Lombardozzi, Minnesota vs. Dotson, Chicago (4)

NATIONAL LEAGUE (32)

APRIL—
12 —Reynolds, Houston vs. Mahler, Atlanta (6)
19 —Reynolds, Pittsburgh vs. Sanderson, Chicago (4)
23 —Parker, Cincinnati vs. Hawkins, San Diego (3)
27 —Davis, Chicago vs. McGaffigan, Montreal (4)

MAY—
4 —Puhl, Houston vs. Smith, Montreal (3)
7 —Sax, Los Angeles vs. Baller, Chicago (7)
18 —Brooks, Montreal vs. Thurmond, San Diego (1)
27 —Foster, New York vs. Niedenfuer, Los Angeles (6)
27 —Harper, Atlanta vs. Walk, Pittsburgh (12)

JUNE—
1 —Morrison, Pittsburgh vs. Niedenfuer, L.A. (5)
3 —Simmons, Atlanta vs. Guante, Pittsburgh (6)
8 —Raines, Montreal vs. Rucker, Philadelphia (8)
10 —Teufel, New York vs. Hume, Philadelphia (11)
14 —Garner, Houston vs. Robinson, San Francisco (7)
29 —Samuel, Philadelphia vs. Worrell, St. Louis (9)

JULY—
7 —Bass, Houston vs. Schatzeder, Montreal (9)
11 —Carter, New York vs. Palmer, Atlanta (2)
24 —Parker, Cincinnati vs. McClure, Montreal (8)
29 —Hayes, Philadelphia vs. Burris, St. Louis (4)

AUGUST—
1 —Brock, Los Angeles vs. Soto, Cincinnati (1)
2 —Cabell, Los Angeles vs. Franco, Cincinnati (8)
5 —Hatcher, Houston vs. Powell, Los Angeles (9)
10 —Forsch, St. Louis vs. Bielecki, Pittsburgh (5)
13 —Maldonado, San Francisco vs. Welsh, Cinn. (3)
14 —Griffey, Atlanta vs. Lefferts, San Diego (8)
27 —Davis, Cincinnati vs. Robinson, Pittsburgh (9)

SEPTEMBER—
6 —Horner, Atlanta vs. Fansler, Pittsburgh (3)
12 —Thompson, San Francisco vs. Acker, Atlanta (4)
22 —Gladden, San Francisco vs. Terry, Cincinnati (6)

OCTOBER—
4 —McReynolds, San Diego vs. Gullickson, Cinn. (3)
5 —Strawberry, New York vs. Krawczyk, Pitts. (5)
5 —Maldonado, San Francisco vs. Hershiser, L.A. (7)

*Second game of doubleheader.

Joe Carter Tops Five-Hit List

By DAVE SLOAN

Pitching well may be the key to winning baseball, but a little robust hitting also can produce positive results.

Such was the case with the 29 five-hit performances produced by major leaguers during the 1986 season. The team with the five-hit player won 24 of those games (82.8 percent). Ironically, three of the five losses occurred in the season's first three five-hit games—by Shawon Dunston and Davey Lopes of the Chicago Cubs on April 19 and 20 against Pittsburgh, and by Minnesota's Billy Beane against the New York Yankees on April 29.

Another came on August 11 when Cincinnati Player-Manager Pete Rose, baseball's all-time hits leader, stroked four singles and a double in a 13-4 loss to San Francisco. The five-hit performance was the 10th of Rose's 24-year major league career, a National League record.

Cleveland's Joe Carter led the majors with three five-hit games. On June 10, Carter cracked three singles and two doubles in an 8-7 win over Oakland; on August 29, he hit three homers and two singles in a 7-3 triumph over Boston, and on September 6, Carter lashed two homers, two doubles and a single in a 17-9 victory over Milwaukee.

The only other player with more than one five-hit performance was Boston's Wade Boggs, who did it twice against the Minnesota Twins in late May. On May 20 at Fenway Park, Boggs' four singles and double paced the Red Sox to a 17-7 victory. On May 31 at the Metrodome, Boggs again had four singles and a double in a 7-2 win over the Twins.

Boggs, whose .357 average led the major leagues, also led in multi-hit (four or more) performances with eight. Minnesota's Kirby Puckett followed with seven while the Indians' Carter had six. San Diego's Tony Gwynn paced the N.L. with five multi-hit games.

Overall, there were 279 multi-hit games last season, three fewer than in '85. American League batters accounted for 157 of the total, six more than the previous year. The Indians and Twins tied for team honors with 18 multi-hit games; the Red Sox and Royals had 17 each. The Atlanta Braves (with 15) led the senior circuit.

Bob Horner of the Braves hit four homers in five at-bats on July 6 against Montreal to become only the 11th player in big-league history to perform the feat.

Boston third baseman Wade Boggs led the major leagues in 1986 with eight multi-hit (four or more) games.

On two occasions, doubles accounted for all of a player's hits in a four-hit game, tying another major league record. On June 27, Toronto's Damaso Garcia hit four doubles in a 14-7 triumph over the Yankees. Rafael Ramirez's four doubles helped Atlanta to a 9-8, 13-inning win over the Cubs on May 21. In the same game, teammate Ken Oberkfell singled five times in seven at-bats. The Braves third baseman was one of only three players who failed to drive in a run in a five-hit game last year.

Tony Phillips of the A's (in an 8-4 win over Baltimore on May 16) and Puckett of the Twins (in a 10-1 triumph over Oakland on August 1) were the only players to hit for the cycle (single, double, triple, homer).

Twenty-four players compiled hitting

streaks of 15 or more games. The Dodgers' Steve Sax produced the season's longest streak, a 25-game string from September 1-27. Yankee slugger Don Mattingly's 24-game streak from August 30 to September 26 was the longest in the A.L.

Besides Sax and Mattingly, the following players compiled hitting streaks of 15 or more games in 1986: 21 games—Carter, Indians; 20 games—Kevin Bass, Astros; Boggs, Red Sox; Eddie Milner, Reds; 19 games—Phil Bradley, Mariners; Scott Fletcher, Rangers; 18 games—Garcia, Blue Jays; 17 games—Bill Buckner, Red Sox; Eric Davis, Reds; Tim Raines, Expos; Cal Ripken, Orioles; Cory Snyder, Indians; 16 games—Buddy Bell, Reds; Mike Marshall, Dodgers; Tony Pena, Pirates; Puckett, Twins; Lou Whitaker, Tigers; 15 games—George Bell, Blue Jays; Gwynn, Padres; Billy Hatcher, Astros; Lee Lacy, Orioles; Willie Randolph, Yankees.

The complete list of players with four or more hits in one game follows:

AMERICAN LEAGUE: Baltimore (7) —Lacy 2, Bonilla, Lynn, Murray, Ripken, Traber. Boston (17)—Boggs 8, Armas 2, Buckner 2, Rice 2, Barrett, Gedman, Owen. California (5)—Burleson, Downing, Hendrick, Pettis, Schofield. Chicago (9)—Baines 4, Calderon, Cangelosi, Guillen, Hulett, Walker. Cleveland (18)—Carter 6, Franco 3, Hall 2, Thornton 2, Allanson, Castillo, Jacoby, Snyder, Tabler. Detroit (9)—Gibson 3, Coles 2, Trammell 2, Evans, Parrish. Kansas City (17)—Wilson 4, Smith 3, Brett 2, Kingery 2, White 2, Balboni, Jackson, Orta, Sundberg. Milwaukee (8)—Yount 3, Molitor 2, Cooper, Riles, Sveum. Minnesota (18)—Puckett 7, Gaetti 4, Hatcher 2, Hrbek 2, Beane, Brunansky, Washington. New York (11) —Mattingly 4, Tolleson 2, Griffey, Hassey, Pagliarulo, Roenicke, Wynegar. Oakland (9)—Phillips 3, Griffin 2, Lansford 2, Canseco, Davis. Seattle (11)—Tartabull 3, Davis 2, Owen 2, Phelps 2, Presley, Reynolds. Texas (12)—Fletcher 3, Paciorek 2, Browne, Harrah, O'Brien, Parrish, Sierra, Ward, Wright. Toronto (6)—Fernandez 2, Garcia 2, Bell, Moseby.

NATIONAL LEAGUE: Atlanta (15)—Horner 3, Oberkfell 3, Harper 2, Murphy 2, Moreno, Ramirez, Simmons, Thomas, Washington. Chicago (8)—Dunston 2, J. Davis, Lopes, Moreland, Mumphrey, Trillo, Walker. Cincinnati (9)—Concepcion, Davis, Diaz, Jones, Larkin, Oester, Parker, Rose, Rowdon. Houston (9)—Walling 3, Hatcher 2, Bass, Cruz, Garner, Pankovits. Los Angeles (6)—Landreaux 2, Sax 2, Brock, Scioscia. Montreal (7)—Webster 2, Brooks, Galarraga, Raines, Wallach, Winningham. New York (13)—Dykstra 4, Backman 2, Knight 2, Strawberry 2, Gibbons, Teufel, Wilson. Philadelphia (11)—Samuel 4, Schu 2, Hayes, Redus, Roenicke, Schmidt, Wilson. Pittsburgh (14)—Morrison 4, Bream 3, Orsulak 2, Almon, Bonds, Ortiz, Pena, Ray. St. Louis (9)—Herr 3, McGee 2, Pendleton 2, Smith, Van Slyke. San Diego (13)—Gwynn 5, Kruk 2, McReynolds 2, Asadoor, Flannery, Kennedy, Roberts. San Francisco (8)—Thompson 3, C. Davis 2, Brown, Clark, LaCoss.

The records of all players with five hits in a game follow:

Date	Player—Club—Opp.	Place	AB.	R.	H.	2B.	3B.	HR.	RBI.	Result
April 19	Dunston, Cubs vs. Pirates	H	5	2	5	1	0	1	2	L 8-14
April 20	Lopes, Cubs vs. Pirates (17 innings)	H	5	2	5	1	1	0	3	L 8-10
April 29	Beane, Twins vs. Yankees	A	5	2	5	0	0	1	4	L 11-14
April 30	Strawberry, Mets vs. Braves	A	5	2	5	1	0	1	3	W 8-1
May 12	Paciorek, Rangers vs. Indians	A	6	2	5	0	0	0	2	W 19-2
May 16	Phillips, A's vs. Orioles	A	5	2	5	1	1	1	4	W 8-4
May 20	Boggs, Red Sox vs. Twins	H	6	3	5	1	0	0	3	W 17-7
May 21	Oberkfell, Braves vs. Cubs (13 innings)	H	7	1	5	0	0	0	0	W 9-8
May 23	Wilson, Mets vs. Padres	A	5	1	5	1	1	0	2	L 4-7
May 31	Boggs, Red Sox vs. Twins	A	5	2	5	1	0	0	1	W 7-2
June 7	Hrbek, Twins vs. Royals	A	5	2	5	1	0	1	2	W 4-1
June 10	Carter, Indians vs. A's	H	5	1	5	2	0	0	4	W 8-7
June 10	Brett, Royals vs. Mariners	H	5	3	5	1	0	0	1	W 9-5
June 17	Davis, Mariners vs. Indians	A	5	2	5	1	0	0	0	W 5-2
June 23	Herr, Cardinals vs. Pirates (11 innings)	H	5	0	5	1	0	0	2	W 2-1
July 6	Webster, Expos vs. Braves	A	6	2	5	1	0	1	3	W 11-8
July 9	Franco, Indians vs. White Sox	A	5	2	5	0	0	0	0	W 6-3
July 9	Rowdon, Reds vs. Mets	A	5	2	5	1	0	0	3	W 11-1
July 24	Bass, Astros vs. Phillies	A	5	2	5	0	0	0	2	W 9-3
Aug. 6	Harrah, Rangers vs. Orioles	A	5	3	5	1	0	1	4	W 13-11
Aug. 11	Rose, Reds vs. Giants	H	5	0	5	1	0	0	3	L 4-13
Aug. 13	Moreno, Braves vs. Padres	H	5	2	5	1	0	1	2	W 8-7
Aug. 21	Buckner, Red Sox vs. Indians	A	6	2	5	0	0	0	3	W 24-5
Aug. 22	Bream, Pirates vs. Braves	H	5	4	5	0	0	1	5	W 16-5
Aug. 29	Carter, Indians vs. Red Sox	A	5	3	5	0	0	3	4	W 7-3
Sept. 6	Carter, Indians vs. Brewers	A	6	5	5	2	0	2	4	W 17-9
Sept. 18	Baines, White Sox vs. Mariners	A	5	1	5	1	0	0	3	W 6-4
Sept. 21	Thompson, Giants vs. Braves	A	5	0	5	0	0	0	1	W 8-2
Oct. 2	Fletcher, Rangers vs. Angels	H	6	2	5	1	0	0	2	W 10-9

Maldonado Led in Pinch-Hitting

By DAVE SLOAN

When Candy Maldonado of the San Francisco Giants strolled to the plate in the ninth inning of a May 13 game at Chicago's Wrigley Field, the Giants trailed, 5-4, after a five-run Cubs rally in the eighth inning. Chicago's ace reliever, Lee Smith, was on the mound, one out away from securing the save.

But Maldonado, pinch-hitting for pitcher Greg Minton, would have none of it. On a 1-0 count, he drilled a Smith slider over the left-field wall with a man aboard, giving the Giants a 6-5 victory. It was Maldonado's fifth homer of the year—matching his totals of each of the past two seasons—and his third as a pinch-hitter. He did it again July 1 in a 9-6 triumph over the Atlanta Braves, connecting for a game-tying, ninth-inning homer off Joe Johnson.

Maldonado's four homers and 20 runs batted in as a pinch-hitter were tops in the majors in 1986. The former Los Angeles Dodgers farmhand hit 18 homers in his first season with San Francisco, seven more than he accumulated in parts of five seasons with the Dodgers.

While Maldonado was baseball's most productive pinch-hitter last season, other players also produced in the clutch. Ron Hassey, who split his season between the Yankees and White Sox, compiled a .556 average with 10 hits in 18 at-bats. Larry Herndon of the Tigers and Jim Dwyer of the Orioles each hit three homers, driving in 12 and 11 runs, respectively, in pinch-hitting roles.

Luis Aguayo of the Phillies paced the National League with a .500 average (7 of 14) while Atlanta's Chris Chambliss led all players with 20 pinch-hits. Hal McRae of the Royals led the A.L. with 15 hits.

Following is a list of all pinch-hitters with at least 10 at-bats in 1986:

AMERICAN LEAGUE PINCH-HITTING
(Compiled by Sports Information Center)

Club Pinch-Hitting

Club	AB.	H.	HR.	RBI.	Pct.
Oakland	86	26	3	14	.302
New York	160	46	7	37	.288
Toronto	155	43	4	32	.277
Boston	50	13	3	12	.260
Kansas City	150	39	2	18	.260
California	125	32	4	22	.256
Baltimore	170	43	5	34	.253
Minnesota	195	49	4	31	.251
Detroit	146	35	6	32	.240
Cleveland	88	21	2	20	.239
Texas	113	26	4	14	.230
Chicago	126	27	2	21	.214
Seattle	94	18	4	19	.191
Milwaukee	31	4	0	4	.129
Totals	1689	422	50	310	.250

Individual Pinch-Hitting
(10 or More At-Bats)

Player-Club	AB.	H.	HR.	RBI.	Pct.
Hassey, N.Y.-Chi.	18	10	1	6	.556
Woods, Minn.	16	8	2	7	.500
Beniquez, Balt.	19	9	0	6	.474
Bush, Minn.	30	13	2	7	.433
C. Johnson, Tor.	12	5	1	6	.417
Thornton, Clev.	12	5	1	6	.417
Nichols, Chi.	16	6	0	4	.375
Grich, Cal.	14	5	1	5	.357
Iorg, Tor.	28	10	1	9	.357
Motley, K.C.	12	4	0	1	.333
Roenicke, N.Y.	18	6	1	5	.333
Leach, Tor.	31	10	1	9	.323
McRae, K.C.	47	15	1	6	.319
Pasqua, N.Y.	22	7	1	9	.318
Hall, Clev.	19	6	1	6	.316
Shelby, Balt.	19	6	1	3	.316
Hairston, Chi.	46	14	0	6	.304
Spilman, Det.	10	3	0	0	.300
S. Bradley, Chi-Sea	17	5	1	7	.294
Griffey, N.Y.	14	4	2	5	.286
Jackson, Cal.	14	4	0	2	.286
Orta, K.C.	21	6	0	4	.286
Paciorek, Tex.	18	5	0	1	.278
Porter, Tex.	18	5	1	3	.278
Smalley, Minn.	18	5	0	5	.278
Burleson, Cal.	11	3	0	2	.273
Hendrick, Cal.	11	3	0	3	.273
Lacy, Balt.	11	3	0	1	.273
Whitt, Tor.	11	3	0	2	.273
Hill, Oak.	15	4	0	0	.267
Grubb, Det.	19	5	1	7	.263
Howell, Cal.	16	4	0	1	.250
Jones, Cal.	12	3	2	4	.250
Young, Balt.	12	3	0	3	.250
Martinez, Tor.	17	4	1	2	.235
Herndon, Det.	26	6	3	12	.231
Bergman, Det.	22	5	0	2	.227
Washington, N.Y.	22	5	1	2	.227
Dwyer, Balt.	42	9	3	11	.214
Easler, N.Y.	19	4	0	2	.211
Baker, Oak.	15	3	0	0	.200
Quirk, K.C.	20	4	0	2	.200
Salas, Minn.	25	5	0	0	.200
Washington, Minn.	10	2	0	1	.200
Phelps, Sea.	16	3	2	5	.188
Narron, Cal.	11	2	0	1	.182
Petralli, Tex.	22	4	1	3	.182
Greenwell, Bos.	12	2	0	1	.167
Kittle, Chi.-N.Y.	12	2	0	2	.167
Hatcher, Minn.	38	6	0	6	.158
Bando, Clev.	13	2	0	0	.154
Sheets, Balt.	13	2	0	0	.154
Castillo, Clev.	21	3	0	3	.143
Laudner, Minn.	15	2	0	0	.133
Mulliniks, Tor.	16	2	0	0	.125
Beane, Minn.	11	1	0	0	.091
Collins, Det.	11	1	0	0	.091
G. Thomas, Se-Mil	12	0	0	0	.000

Candy Maldonado (above) and Ron Hassey were two of baseball's best pinch-hitters last season.

NATIONAL LEAGUE PINCH-HITTING

(Compiled by Elias Sports Bureau)

Club Pinch-Hitting

Club	AB.	H.	HR.	RBI.	Pct.
Houston	239	67	7	39	.280
Atlanta	260	72	7	53	.277
Philadelphia	224	60	6	32	.268
San Francisco	274	73	10	59	.266
Chicago	216	54	3	27	.250
San Diego	296	74	8	52	.250
New York	193	41	2	24	.212
Cincinnati	208	43	1	27	.207
St. Louis	196	38	3	26	.194
Pittsburgh	283	54	3	28	.191
Montreal	240	45	2	27	.188
Los Angeles	299	55	5	31	.184
Totals	2928	676	57	425	.231

Individual Pinch-Hitting

(10 or more At-Bats)

Player-Club	AB.	H.	HR.	RBI.	Pct.
Aguayo, Philadelphia	14	7	1	2	.500
Daniels, Cincinnati	23	11	0	4	.478
Kennedy, San Diego	23	11	1	7	.478
Maldonado, S.F.	40	17	4	20	.425
Schatzeder, Mon-Phil.	12	5	0	0	.417
Speier, Chicago	17	7	0	2	.412
Reynolds, Houston	22	9	1	7	.409
Spilman, S.F.	32	13	0	9	.406
Walling, Houston	31	12	1	6	.387
Bochy, San Diego	20	7	2	6	.350
Wilson, New York	20	7	0	3	.350
Mumphrey, Chicago	29	10	1	8	.345
Backman, New York	15	5	0	0	.333
Diaz, Pittsburgh	33	11	1	10	.333
Stone, Philadelphia	21	7	1	3	.333
Russell, L.A.	31	10	0	3	.323
Bosley, Chicago	51	16	1	6	.314
Lancellotti, S.F.	13	4	2	6	.308
Heep, New York	30	9	0	8	.300
Stillwell, Cincinnati	20	6	0	2	.300
Johnson, Montreal	37	11	1	5	.297
Chambliss, Atlanta	68	20	1	9	.294
Pankovits, Houston	38	11	1	2	.289
Dykstra, New York	14	4	0	0	.286
Puhl, Houston	28	8	0	3	.286
Moreno, Atlanta	25	7	1	4	.280
Youngblood, S.F.	58	16	1	10	.276
Hurdle, St. Louis	22	6	1	7	.273
Morris, St. Louis	11	3	0	0	.273
Ortiz, Pittsburgh	11	3	0	1	.273
Perry, Atlanta	11	3	0	2	.273
Sample, Atlanta	33	9	1	3	.273
Nettles, San Diego	19	5	1	5	.263
Aldrete, S.F.	16	4	0	3	.250
Driessen, S.F.-Hou	12	3	1	1	.250
G. Gross, Phil.	52	13	0	6	.250
Kruk, San Diego	32	8	0	3	.250
Royster, San Diego	32	8	0	5	.250
Thon, Houston	20	5	1	4	.250
Wynne, San Diego	12	3	1	5	.250
Schu, Philadelphia	29	7	2	4	.241
Foley, Phil.-Mon.	21	5	0	1	.238
Simmons, Atlanta	47	11	2	18	.234
Cedeno, L.A.	13	3	0	5	.231
Cey, Chicago	13	3	1	3	.231
Perez, Cincinnati	22	5	0	6	.227
Krenchicki, Mon.	31	7	1	5	.226
Trevino, L.A.	31	7	0	5	.226
Martinez, San Diego	36	8	2	6	.222
Oquendo, St. Louis	27	6	0	2	.222
Trillo, Chicago	14	3	0	1	.214
Lopes, Chi.-Hou	19	4	0	6	.211
Brown, Pittsburgh	20	4	0	0	.200
Ford, St. Louis	25	5	0	7	.200
Milner, Cincinnati	15	3	0	0	.200
Van Slyke, St.L.	10	2	0	0	.200
Wohlford, Montreal	41	8	0	7	.195
Landreaux, L.A.	31	6	1	3	.194
Francona, Chicago	42	8	0	0	.190
Roenicke, Phil.	21	4	0	6	.190
Woodard, S.F.	21	4	0	2	.190
Flannery, San Diego	16	3	0	3	.188
Garner, Houston	16	3	1	5	.188
Harper, Atlanta	32	6	1	3	.188
Teufel, New York	16	3	2	7	.188
Iorg, San Diego	70	13	1	7	.186
Bonilla, Pitt.	11	2	1	3	.182
Garvey, San Diego	11	2	0	0	.182
Orsulak, Pitt.	22	4	0	0	.182
Reynolds, Pitt.	11	2	0	0	.182
Almon, Pittsburgh	28	5	0	2	.179
Landrum, St. Louis	28	5	0	3	.179
Guerrero, L.A.	17	3	1	5	.176
Brock, L.A.	23	4	0	0	.174
Washington, Pitt.	29	5	0	1	.172
Jones, Cincinnati	12	2	0	3	.167
Lawless, St. Louis	12	2	0	1	.167
Matuszek, L.A.	25	4	1	5	.160
Venable, Cincinnati	51	8	0	6	.157
Ashby, Houston	20	3	0	1	.150
Distefano, Pitt.	20	3	1	5	.150
Mitchell, New York	20	3	0	2	.150
Mazzilli, Pitt.-N.Y.	54	8	0	4	.148
Newman, Montreal	14	2	0	0	.143
Rowdon, Cincinnati	15	2	0	0	.133
Winningham, Mon.	23	3	0	1	.130
Cabell, L.A.	34	4	0	1	.118
Johnson, New York	17	2	0	0	.118
White, St. Louis	19	2	1	1	.105
Scioscia, L.A.	10	1	0	0	.100
Thompson, Phil.	10	1	0	0	.100
Williams, L.A.	11	1	0	0	.091
Thompson, Mon.	12	1	0	1	.083
Whitfield, L.A.	12	1	0	0	.083
Kutcher, S.F.	13	1	0	0	.077
Wright, Montreal	26	1	0	1	.038
Matthews, Chicago	16	0	0	0	.000
Stubbs, L.A.	12	0	0	0	.000

PINCH-HOMERS FOR 1986

AMERICAN LEAGUE: Baltimore (5)—Dwyer 3, Lynn, Shelby. Boston (3)—Dodson, Gedman, Lyons. California (4)—Jones 2, Grich, Ryal. Chicago (2)—Fisk, Walker. Cleveland (2)—Hall, Thornton. Detroit (6)—Herndon 3, Evans 2, Grubb. Kansas City (2)—McRae, Sundberg. Milwaukee (0)—None. Minnesota (4)—Bush 2, Woods 2. New York (7)—Griffey 2, Hassey, Lombardi, Pasqua, Roenicke, Washington. Oakland (3)—Davis, McGwire, Steinbach. Seattle (4)—Phelps 2, S. Bradley, Valle. Texas (4)—Buechele, McDowell, Petralli, Porter. Toronto (4)—Iorg, C. Johnson, Leach, Martinez.

NATIONAL LEAGUE: Atlanta (7)—Simmons 2, Chambliss, Harper, Moreno, Murphy, Sample. Chicago (3)—Bosley, Cey, Mumphrey. Cincinnati (1)—Parker. Houston (7)—Driessen, Gainey, Garner, Pankovits, Reynolds, Thon, Walling. Los Angeles (5)—Bryant 2, Guerrero, Landreaux, Matuszek. Montreal (2)—Johnson, Krenchicki. New York (2)—Teufel 2. Philadelphia (6)—Schu 2, Aguayo, Reynolds, Samuel, Stone. Pittsburgh (3)—Bonilla, Diaz, Distefano. St. Louis (3)—Hurdle, Manrique, White. San Diego (8)—Bochy 2, Martinez 2, Iorg, Kennedy, Nettles, Wynne. San Francisco (10)—Maldonado 4, Lancellotti 2, Clark, C. Davis, Leonard, Youngblood.

Three Hit Homers in Debuts

By DAVE SLOAN

Of the 164 players who made their major league debuts in 1986, nobody received more publicity or stirred as much interest as Kansas City outfielder Vincent Edward (Bo) Jackson.

Jackson, who won the 1985 Heisman Trophy as a 6-foot-1, 220-pound running back at Auburn University, spurned the National Football League's Tampa Bay Buccaneers to pursue his first athletic love—baseball. Though the Bucs dangled a multi-million dollar contract before his eyes, Jackson chose to sign a baseball contract with the Royals, who took a chance and selected him on the fourth round of the June free-agent draft.

"We didn't draft Bo Jackson to attract attention," said Kansas City General Manager John Schuerholz. "We think he has the potential to be an outstanding baseball player."

After hitting .277 in 53 games with the Royals' Double-A club at Memphis (Southern), Jackson was called up to Kansas City when rosters were expanded September 1. The following day, he made his major league debut in Royals Stadium against the Chicago White Sox, beating out an infield grounder for a single in his first at-bat. Jackson, who hit a 425-foot shot just foul prior to his single off Chicago lefty Steve Carlton, finished with one hit in three at-bats and played flawlessly in right field.

Jackson's debut might have grabbed more headlines, but Russ Morman's August 3 debut with the White Sox earned the 24-year-old a spot in the record books.

In a 10-1 victory over Detroit, Morman homered and singled in a six-run fourth inning off Tiger pitchers Randy O'Neal and Jim Slaton. Morman's two hits tied Billy Martin's major league record for most hits in one inning of a major league debut (Martin set the mark on April 18, 1950, with the Yankees). Morman finished the day with three hits in four at-bats and two runs batted in.

Eighty-five debuts were made in the American League and 79 in the National. Pitchers accounted for 76 and non-pitchers 88. Outfielder Pete Incaviglia's April 8 debut with the Texas Rangers was the former Oklahoma State University star's first professional game.

Three players homered in their first at-bats. On opening day (April 8), Giants first baseman Will Clark homered off Houston's Nolan Ryan in San Francisco's 8-3 win at the Astrodome. On September 12 at Cleveland, Oakland catcher Terry Steinbach hit a first-at-bat homer off Indians starter Greg Swindell in a 9-3 Cleveland victory. On September 29 at the Metrodome, Indians second baseman Jay Bell homered off Twins starter Bert Blyleven in a 6-5 Minnesota victory.

Besides being the Indians' pitcher of record when Steinbach and Bell hit their debut homers, Swindell's own major league debut on August 21 was forgettable.

Swindell, a collegiate standout at the University of Texas and the second player selected overall in the June free-agent draft, lasted just 3⅔ innings in a 24-5 loss to eventual American League champion Boston. He yielded six runs (four earned), six hits and three walks, balked once and failed to strike out a batter. Swindell rebounded, however, to finish the season with a 5-2 record.

The pitcher with the best debut was San Diego's Jimmy Jones, who yielded only one hit in a 5-0 victory over Houston on September 21, four days before the Astros clinched the N.L. West Division title on Mike Scott's no-hitter. The only hit off the 22-year-old righthander was a third-inning triple by Astros pitcher Bob Knepper. Jones struck out five and didn't walk a batter.

On two occasions in 1986, two pitchers made their major league debut for the same club on the same day.

On April 12 at Houston, Atlanta's Paul Assenmacher and Duane Ward pitched in relief of Rick Mahler in a 4-3 loss to the Astros. On May 29 at California, Chuck Finley and Todd Fischer of the Angels relieved Don Sutton in a 7-4 loss to Detroit.

A pair of brothers also made their pitching debuts. On June 3 at Philadelphia, Phillies righthander Mike Maddux lasted just 1⅓ innings in dropping an 11-4 decision to the Dodgers. Exactly three months later, on September 3, Greg Maddux of the Cubs yielded a homer to Houston's Billy Hatcher in the 18th inning and was tagged with an 8-7 loss in the season's longest game.

Greg Maddux, at age 20, was one of a major league-record 53 players used in the game and the youngest player to make his big-league debut in 1986.

An alphabetical list of the players who made their debuts in '86 follows:

Bo Jackson spurned professional football and made a well-publicized major league debut in Kansas City.

Player	Pos.	Club	Date and Place of Birth	Debut
Akerfelds, Darrel Wayne	P	Oakland	6-12-62—Denver, Colo.	8- 1
Aldrete, Michael Peter	1B	San Francisco	1-29-61—Carmel, Calif.	5-28
Allanson, Andrew Neal	C	Cleveland	12-22-61—Richmond, Va.	4- 7
Anderson, Allan Lee	P	Minnesota	1- 7-64—Lancaster, O.	6-11
Anderson, Richard Arlen	P	New York N.L.	11-29-56—Everett, Wash.	6- 9

Player	Pos.	Club	Date and Place of Birth	Debut
Aquino, Luis Antonio	P	Toronto	5-19-65—Rio Piedras, P.R.	8- 8
Arnold, Tony Dale	P	Baltimore	5- 3-59—El Paso, Tex.	8- 9
Arnsberg, Bradley James	P	New York A.L.	8-20-63—Seattle, Wash.	9- 6
Asadoor, Randall Carl	3B	San Diego	10-20-62—Fresno, Calif.	9-14
Assenmacher, Paul Andre	P	Atlanta	12-10-60—Detroit, Mich.	4-12
Bailes, Scott Alan	P	Cleveland	12-18-61—Chillicothe, O.	4- 9
Bankhead, Michael Scott	P	Kansas City	7-31-63—Raleigh, N.C.	5-25
Bathe, William David	C	Oakland	10-14-60—Downey, Calif.	4-12
Bell, Jay Stuart	2B	Cleveland	12-11-65—Elgin AFB, Fla.	9-29
Bell, Terence William	C	Kansas City	10-27-62—Dayton, O.	9- 3
Birkbeck, Michael Lawrence	P	Milwaukee	3-10-61—Orrville, O.	8-17
Bittiger, Jeffrey Scott	P	Philadelphia	4-13-62—Jersey City, N.J.	9- 2
Bockus, Randy Walter	P	San Francisco	10- 5-60—Canton, O.	9-10
Bonds, Barry Lamar	OF	Pittsburgh	7-24-64—Riverside, Calif.	5-30
Bonilla, Roberto M.A.	PH	Chicago A.L.	2-23-63—New York, N.Y.	4- 9
Bosio, Christopher Louis	P	Milwaukee	4- 3-63—Rancho Cordova, Calif.	8- 3
Braggs, Glenn Erick	OF	Milwaukee	10-17-62—San Bernardino, Calif.	7-18
Brantley, Michael Charles	OF	Seattle	6-17-61—Catskill, N.Y.	8- 9
Brewer, Michael Quinn	OF	Kansas City	10-24-59—Shreveport, La.	6-11
Brower, Robert Richard	PR	Texas	1-10-60—Queens, N.Y.	9- 3
Brown, James Kevin	P	Texas	3-14-65—McIntyre, Ga.	9-30
Browne, Jerome Austin	2B	Texas	2-13-66—St. Croix, Virgin Is.	9- 6
Bryden, Thomas Ray	P	California	1-17-59—Moses Lake, Wash.	4-10
Candaele, Casey Todd	PH	Montreal	1-12-61—Lompoc, Calif.	6- 5
Castillo, Juan	2B	Milwaukee	1-25-62—S.P. de Macoris, D.R.	4-12
Chadwick, Ray Charles	P	California	11-17-62—Durham, N.C.	7-29
Clark, David Earl	OF	Cleveland	9- 3-62—Tupelo, Miss.	9- 3
Clark, William Nuschler	1B	San Francisco	3-17-64—New Orleans, La.	4- 8
Clutterbuck, Bryan Richard	P	Milwaukee	12-17-59—Detroit, Mich.	7-18
Cochrane, David Carter	3B	Chicago A.L.	1-31-63—Riverside, Calif.	9- 2
Cone, David Brian	P	Kansas City	1- 2-63—Kansas City, Mo.	6- 8
Cook, Michael Horace	P	California	8-14-63—Charleston, S.C.	7- 1
Daniels, Kalvoski	PH	Cincinnati	8-20-63—Vienna, Ga.	4- 9
Davidson, John Mark	OF	Minnesota	2-15-61—Knoxville, Tenn.	6-20
Diaz, Edgar Serrano	SS	Milwaukee	2- 8-64—Santurce, P.R.	9-16
Dodd, Thomas Marion	PH	Baltimore	8-15-58—Portland, Ore.	7-25
Dodson, Patrick Neal	1B	Boston	10-11-59—Santa Monica, Calif.	9- 5
Downs, Kelly Robert	P	San Francisco	10-25-60—Ogden, Utah	7-29
Dozier, Thomas Dean	P	Oakland	9- 5-61—Richmond, Calif.	5-17
Drabek, Douglas Dean	P	New York A.L.	7-25-62—Victoria, Tex.	5-30
Earley, William Albert	P	St. Louis	1-30-56—Cincinnati, O.	9-22
Elster, Kevin Daniel	SS	New York N.L.	8- 3-64—San Pedro, Calif.	9- 2
Fansler, Stanley Robert	P	Pittsburgh	2-12-65—Elkins, W. Va.	9- 6
Fields, Bruce Alan	OF	Detroit	10- 6-60—Cleveland, O.	9- 3
Finley, Charles Edward	P	California	11-26-62—Monroe, La.	5-29
Fischer, Todd Richard	P	California	9-15-60—Columbus, O.	5-29
Fraser, William Patrick	P	California	5-26-64—Newburgh, N.Y.	9-10
Freeman, Marvin	P	Philadelphia	4-10-63—Chicago, Ill.	9-16
Funk, Thomas James	P	Houston	3-13-62—Gladstone, Mo.	7-24
Galvez, Balvino	P	Los Angeles	3-31-64—S.P. de Macoris, D.R.	5- 7
Gerhart, Harold Kenneth	OF	Baltimore	5-19-61—Charleston, S.C.	9-14
Gordon, Donald Thomas	P	Toronto	10-10-59—New York, N.Y.	4-10
Green, Gary Allan	SS	San Diego	1-14-62—Pittsburg, Calif.	9-14
Hall, Andrew Clark	P	Chicago N.L.	3-27-63—Louisville, Ky.	9-14
Hamilton, Jeffrey Robert	3B	Los Angeles	3-19-64—Flint, Mich.	6-28
Hayward, Raymond Alton	P	San Diego	4-27-61—Enid, Okla.	9-20
Hearn, Edward John	C	New York N.L.	8-23-60—Stuart, Fla.	5-17
Hengel, David Lee	DH	Seattle	12-18-61—Oakland, Calif.	9- 3
Hensley, Charles Floyd	P	San Francisco	3-11-59—Tulare, Calif.	5-10
Hernandez, Manuel Antonio	P	Houston	5- 7-61—La Romana, D.R.	6- 5
Incaviglia, Peter Joseph	OF	Texas	4- 2-64—Pebble Beach, Calif.	4- 8
Jackson, Michael Ray	P	Philadelphia	12-22-64—Houston, Tex.	8-11
Jackson, Vincent Edward	OF	Kansas City	11-30-62—Bessemer, Ala.	9- 2
James, Donald Christopher	OF	Philadelphia	10- 4-62—Rusk, Tex.	4-23
Jefferson, Stanley	OF	New York N.L.	12- 4-62—New York, N.Y.	9- 7
Johnson, Rondin Allen	2B	Kansas City	12-16-58—Bremerton, Wash.	9- 3
Jones, Barry Louis	P	Pittsburgh	2-15-63—Centerville, Ind.	7-18
Jones, James Condia	P	San Diego	4-20-64—Dallas, Tex.	9-21
Jones, Richard Miron	2B	Baltimore	6- 4-59—Tupelo, Miss.	9- 3
Jones, Tracy Donald	OF	Cincinnati	3-31-61—Inglewood, Calif.	4- 7
Joyner, Wallace Keith	1B	California	6-16-62—Atlanta, Ga.	4- 8
Karkovice, Ronald Joseph	C	Chicago A.L.	8- 8-63—Union, N.J.	8-17
Kelly, Bryan Keith	P	Detroit	2-24-59—Silver Spring, Md.	9- 2
King, Eric Steven	P	Detroit	4-10-64—Oxnard, Calif.	5-15
Kingery, Michael Scott	OF	Kansas City	3-29-61—St. James, Minn.	7- 7
Kruk, John Martin	PH	San Diego	2- 9-61—Charleston, W. Va.	4- 9
Kutcher, Randy Scott	OF	San Francisco	4-20-60—Anchorage, Alas.	6-19
Landrum, Thomas William	P	Cincinnati	8-17-57—Columbia, S.C.	8-31
Larkin, Barry Louis	PH	Cincinnati	4-28-64—Cincinnati, O.	8-13

Player	Pos.	Club	Date and Place of Birth	Debut
Legg, Gregory Lynn	2B	Philadelphia	4-21-60—San Jose, Calif.	4-18
Lindeman, James William	1B	St. Louis	1-10-62—Evanston, Ill.	9- 3
Lombardi, Phillip Arden	C	New York A.L.	2-20-63—Granada Hills, Calif.	4-26
Loynd, Michael Wallace	P	Texas	3-26-64—St. Louis, Mo.	7-24
Lyons, Barry Stephen	C	New York N.L.	6- 3-60—Biloxi, Miss.	4-19
Maddux, Gregory Alan	P	Chicago N.L.	4-14-66—San Angelo, Tex.	9- 3
Maddux, Michael Ausley	P	Philadelphia	8-27-61—Dayton, O.	6- 3
Magadan, David Joseph	PH	New York N.L.	9-30-62—Tampa, Fla.	9- 7
Martin, Joseph Michael	C	Chicago N.L.	12- 3-58—Portland, Ore.	8-15
Martinez, David	OF	Chicago N.L.	9-26-64—Manhattan, N.Y.	6-15
Mathews, Gregory Inman	P	St. Louis	5-17-63—Harbor City, Calif.	6- 3
McGriff, Frederick Stanley	1B	Toronto	10-31-63—Tampa, Fla.	5-17
McGwire, Mark David	3B	Oakland	10- 1-63—Claremont, Calif.	8-22
McKeon, Joel Jacob	P	Chicago A.L.	2-25-63—Covington, Ky.	5- 6
McLemore, Mark Tremell	PR	California	10- 4-64—San Diego, Calif.	9-13
Meadows, Michael Ray	PH	Houston	4-29-61—Onslow County, N.C.	7- 3
Mitchell, John Kyle	P	New York N.L.	8-11-65—Dickson, Tenn.	9- 8
Mohorcic, Dale Robert	P	Texas	1-25-56—Cleveland, O.	5-31
Montalvo, Rafael Edgardo	P	Houston	3-31-64—Santurce, P.R.	4-13
Mooneyham, William Craig	P	Oakland	8-16-60—Livermore, Calif.	4-19
Moore, William Ross	PH	Montreal	10- 6-60—Los Angeles, Calif.	7-19
Morman, Russell Lee	1B	Chicago A.L.	4-28-62—Independence, Mo.	8- 3
Morris, John Daniel	OF	St. Louis	2-23-61—Freeport, N.Y.	8- 5
Moyer, Jamie	P	Chicago N.L.	11-18-62—Sellersville, Pa.	6-16
Mulholland, Terence John	P	San Francisco	3- 9-63—Uniontown, Pa.	6- 8
Musselman, Jeffrey Joseph	P	Toronto	6-21-63—Doylestown, Pa.	9- 2
Nelson, Robert Augustus	PH	Oakland	5-17-64—Pasadena, Calif.	9- 9
Nichols, Carl Edward	C	Baltimore	10-14-62—Los Angeles, Calif.	9-14
Nielsen, Jeffrey Scott	P	New York A.L.	12-18-58—Salt Lake City, Utah	7- 7
Nieves, Juan Manuel	P	Milwaukee	1- 5-65—Santurce, P.R.	4-10
Olwine, Edward R.	P	Atlanta	5-28-58—Greenville, O.	6- 2
Ouellette, Philip Roland	C	San Francisco	11-10-61—Salem, Ore.	9-10
Palmeiro, Rafael Corrales	OF	Chicago N.L.	9-24-64—Havana, Cuba	9- 8
Parent, Mark Alan	PH	San Diego	9-16-61—Ashland, Ore.	9-20
Parrett, Jeffrey Dale	P	Montreal	8-26-61—Indianapolis, Ind.	4-11
Pecota, William Joseph	3B	Kansas City	2-16-60—Redwood City, Calif.	9-19
Pena, Hipolito	P	Pittsburgh	1-30-64—Cotui, D.R.	9- 1
Plesac, Daniel Thomas	P	Milwaukee	2- 4-62—Gary, Ind.	4-11
Plunk, Eric Vaughn	P	Oakland	9- 3-63—Wilmington, Calif.	5-12
Pyznarski, Timothy Matthew	1B	San Diego	2- 4-60—Chicago, Ill.	9-14
Quinones, Rey Francisco	SS	Boston	11-11-63—Rio Piedras, P.R.	5-17
Renteria, Richard Avina	PH	Pittsburgh	12-25-61—Harbor City, Calif.	9-14
Ritter, Reggie Blake	P	Cleveland	1-23-60—Malvern, Ark.	5-17
Rivera, Luis Antonio	SS	Montreal	1- 3-64—Cidra, P.R.	8- 3
Roberts, Leon Joseph	2B	San Diego	10-27-63—Berkeley, Calif.	4- 7
Rodriguez, Ricardo	P	Oakland	9-21-60—Oakland, Calif.	9-17
Rodriguez, Ruben Dario	C	Pittsburgh	8- 4-64—Cabrera, D.R.	9-15
Ruffin, Bruce Wayne	P	Philadelphia	10- 4-63—Lubbock, Tex.	6-28
Santiago, Benito	C	San Diego	9- 3-65—Ponce, P.R.	9-14
Sauveur, Richard Daniel	P	Pittsburgh	11-23-63—Arlington, Va.	7- 1
See, Ralph Lawrence	PH	Los Angeles	6-20-60—Norwalk, Calif.	9- 3
Seitzer, Kevin Lee	OF-3B	Kansas City	3-26-62—Springfield, Ill.	9- 3
Shipley, Craig Barry	SS	Los Angeles	1- 7-63—Parramatta, Australia	6-22
Sierra, Ruben Angel	OF	Texas	10- 6-65—Rio Piedras, P.R.	6- 1
Smiley, John Patrick	P	Pittsburgh	3-17-65—Phoenixville, Pa.	9- 1
Snyder, James Cory	OF	Cleveland	11-11-62—Canyon Country, Calif.	6-13
Soff, Raymond John	P	St. Louis	10-31-58—Adrian, Mich.	7-17
Speck, Robert Clifford	P	Atlanta	8- 8-56—Portland, Ore.	7-30
Stanley, Robert Michael	C	Texas	5-25-63—Fort Lauderdale, Fla.	6-24
Steinbach, Terry Lee	C	Oakland	3- 2-62—New Ulm, Minn.	9-12
Stillwell, Kurt Andrew	SS	Cincinnati	6- 4-65—Glendale, Calif.	4-13
Sveum, Dale Curtis	3B	Milwaukee	11-23-63—Richmond, Calif.	5-12
Swindell, Forest Gregory	P	Cleveland	1- 2-65—Austin, Tex.	8-21
Tarver, LaSchelle	OF	Boston	1-30-59—Modesto, Calif.	7-12
Taylor, Dwight Bernard	PR-DH	Kansas City	3-24-60—Los Angeles, Calif.	4-14
Tejeda, Wilfredo Aristades	C	Montreal	11-12-62—Santo Domingo, D.R.	9- 9
Terry, Scott Ray	P	Cincinnati	11-11-59—Hobbs, N.M.	4- 9
Tewksbury, Robert Alan	P	New York A.L.	11-30-60—Concord, N.H.	4-11
Thigpen, Robert Thomas	P	Chicago A.L.	7-17-63—Tallahassee, Fla.	8- 6
Thompson, Robert Randall	2B	San Francisco	5-10-62—West Palm Beach, Fla.	4- 8
Valdez, Sergio Sanchez	P	Montreal	9- 7-64—Elias Pina, D.R.	9-10
Vosberg, Edward John	P	San Diego	9-28-61—Tucson, Ariz.	9-17
Walker, Anthony Bruce	OF	Houston	7- 1-60—San Diego, Calif.	4-12
Ward, Roy Duane	P	Atlanta	5-28-64—Parkview, N.M.	4-12
Wasinger, Mark Thomas	3B	San Diego	8- 4-61—Monterey, Calif.	5-27
Williams, Edward Laquan	OF	Cleveland	11- 1-64—Shreveport, La.	4-18
Williams, Kenneth Royal	OF	Chicago A.L.	4- 6-64—Berkeley, Calif.	9- 2
Williams, Mitchell Steven	P	Texas	11-17-64—Santa Ana, Calif.	4-11
Wine, Robert Paul	C	Houston	7-13-62—Norristown, Pa.	9- 2
Witt, Robert Andrew	P	Texas	5-11-64—Canton, Mass.	4-10

Homers by Parks for 1986

National League

	At Atl.	At Chi.	At Cin.	At Hou.	At L.A.	At Mont.	At N.Y.	At Phil.	At Pitt.	At St.L.	At S.D.	At S.F.	Totals 1986	Totals 1985
Atlanta	77	7	13	5	5	3	1	2	6	3	7	9	138	126
Chicago	7	89	4	6	4	7	8	4	6	9	6	5	155	150
Cincinnati	9	1	86	3	4	2	4	6	8	4	11	6	144	114
Houston	5	5	12	49	8	6	3	3	8	3	13	10	125	121
Los Angeles	8	8	6	5	57	3	5	6	8	7	9	8	130	129
Montreal	7	11	8	4	2	42	5	8	5	6	7	5	110	118
New York	9	11	5	7	5	6	77	6	7	9	4	2	148	134
Philadelphia	4	8	4	4	5	6	5	86	12	10	3	7	154	141
Pittsburgh	5	12	3	4	3	7	4	4	49	7	7	6	111	80
St. Louis	1	3	3	5	0	5	3	5	4	27	1	1	58	87
San Diego	6	5	6	7	4	8	6	4	6	2	80	2	136	109
San Francisco	10	8	9	6	6	3	3	1	5	3	10	50	114	115
1986 Totals	148	168	159	105	103	98	124	135	124	90	158	111	1523	....
1985 Totals	145	202	114	94	101	90	116	129	92	75	141	125	....	1424

AT ATLANTA (148): Atlanta (77)—Horner 20, Murphy 17, Griffey 9, Virgil 6, Hubbard 4, Harper 3, Moreno 3, Simmons 3, Washington 3, Chambliss 2, Oberkfell 2, Perry 2, Ramirez, Sample, Thomas. **Chicago (7)**—Dunston 2, J. Davis, Dernier, Durham, Matthews, Moreland. **Cincinnati (9)**—Parker 3, Concepcion 2, Bell, Butera, Daniels, Davis. **Houston (5)**—Ashby, Bass, Davis, Mizerock, Walling. **Los Angeles (8)**—Marshall 3, Stubbs 2, Brock, Scioscia, Trevino. **Montreal (7)**—Wallach 2, Dawson, Galarraga, Newman, Smith, Webster. **New York (9)**—Strawberry 3, Carter 2, Hernandez, Johnson, K. Mitchell, Wilson. **Philadelphia (4)**—Hayes 2, Samuel, Schu. **Pittsburgh (5)**—Morrison 2, Bonds, Diaz, Reynolds. **St. Louis (1)**—Van Slyke. **San Diego (6)**—Gwynn, Kruk, McReynolds, Nettles, Royster, Wynne. **San Francisco (10)**—Maldonado 2, Thompson 2, Aldrete, Brenly, Clark, C. Davis, Lancellotti, Youngblood.

AT CHICAGO (168): Atlanta (7)—Horner 2, Murphy 2, Ramirez, Sample, Virgil. **Chicago (89)**—J. Davis 14, Durham 13, Matthews 11, Dunston 10, Moreland 8, Sandberg 8, Cey 4, Lopes 4, Mumphrey 4, Dayett 3, Dernier 2, Eckersley 2, Speier 2, Martinez, Palmeiro, Sutcliffe, Trillo. **Cincinnati (1)**—Parker. **Houston (5)**—Cruz, Davis, Hatcher, Thon, Walling. **Los Angeles (8)**—Brock 2, Sax 2, Duncan, Hamilton, Matuszek, Welch. **Montreal (11)**—Brooks 3, Dawson 2, Bilardello, Fitzgerald, Hunt, Law, Raines, Wallach. **New York (11)**—Carter 3, Hernandez 2, Foster, Heep, Johnson, K. Mitchell, Strawberry, Wilson. **Philadelphia (8)**—Schmidt 3, Aguayo, Hayes, Russell, Stone, Thompson. **Pittsburgh (12)**—Bonds 2, Bream 2, Morrison 2, Almon, Bonilla, Diaz, Kemp, Orsulak, Reynolds. **St. Louis (3)**—Herr, Laga, Van Slyke. **San Diego (5)**—Flannery, Kennedy, Kruk, McReynolds, Nettles. **San Francisco (8)**—Blue, Brenly, C. Davis, Gladden, Kutcher, Leonard, Maldonado, Spilman.

AT CINCINNATI (159): Atlanta (13)—Horner 3, Murphy 3, Thomas 2, Virgil 2, Harper, Oberkfell, Sample. **Chicago (4)**—Dunston, Durham, Sandberg, Walker. **Cincinnati (86)**—Parker 18, Bell 14, Davis 13, Esasky 9, Diaz 8, Milner 8, Oester 6, Daniels 3, Larkin 3, Perez 2, Jones, Venable. **Houston (12)**—Garner 3, Ashby 2, Cruz 2, Davis 2, Bass, Hatcher, Walling. **Los Angeles (6)**—Brock 3, Anderson, Madlock, Sax. **Montreal (8)**—Wallach 4, Brooks, Dawson, Fitzgerald, Raines. **New York (5)**—Strawberry 2, Hernandez, Johnson, K. Mitchell. **Philadelphia (4)**—Schmidt 3, Russell. **Pittsburgh (3)**—Morrison 2, Distefano. **St. Louis (3)**—Van Slyke 2, Heath. **San Diego (6)**—Garvey, Gwynn, Kruk, McReynolds, Roberts, Royster. **San Francisco (9)**—Maldonado 3, Brenly 2, Gladden, LaCoss, Lancellotti, Melvin.

AT HOUSTON (105): Atlanta (5)—Griffey, Horner, Murphy, Ramirez, Sample. **Chicago (6)**—J. Davis 2, Cey, Francona, Moreland, Speier. **Cincinnati (3)**—Davis 2, Esasky. **Houston (49)**—Davis 17, Bass 5, Cruz 5, Walling 5, Reynolds 4, Doran 3, Garner 2, Hatcher 2, Walker 2, Ashby, Bailey, Driessen, Puhl. **Los Angeles (5)**—Madlock 2, Bryant, Guerrero, Stubbs. **Montreal (4)**—Dawson 2, Fitzgerald, Raines. **New York (7)**—Carter 2, Dykstra, Heep, Hernandez, K. Mitchell, Strawberry. **Philadelphia (4)**—Schmidt 2, Hayes, Wilson. **Pittsburgh (4)**—Bonds, Bream, Brown, Diaz. **St. Louis (5)**—Clark, Lake, Lindeman, Manrique, Van Slyke. **San Diego (7)**—McReynolds 3, Garvey, Gwynn, Santiago, Templeton. **San Francisco (6)**—C. Davis 2, Brenly, Brown, Clark, Leonard.

AT LOS ANGELES (103): Atlanta (5)—Moreno, Murphy, Ramirez, Sample, Washington. **Chicago (4)**—Matthews 3, Durham. **Cincinnati (4)**—Davis, Diaz, Milner, Parker. **Houston (8)**—Davis 2, Hatcher 2, Walling 2, Bass, Gainey. **Los Angeles (57)**—Marshall 13, Stubbs 12, Matuszek 7, Brock 5, Madlock 4, Cabell 2, Duncan 2, Hamilton 2, Scioscia 2, Trevino 2, Bryant, Gonzalez, Guerrero, Landreaux, Sax, Williams. **Montreal (2)**—Wallach, Wohlford. **New York (5)**—Foster 2, Hernandez, K. Mitchell, Strawberry. **Philadelphia (5)**—Russell 2, Daulton, Schmidt, Wilson. **Pittsburgh (3)**—Bonds, Diaz, Reynolds. **St. Louis**—None. **San Diego (4)**—Flannery, Kennedy, Martinez, McReynolds. **San Francisco (6)**—Leonard 2, Maldonado 2, Melvin, Youngblood.

AT MONTREAL (98): Atlanta (3)—Thomas 2, Oberkfell. **Chicago (7)**—Bosley, Cey, J. Davis, Dunston, Durham, Francona, Sandberg. **Cincinnati (2)**—Davis, Milner. **Houston (6)**—Davis 3, Bass, Puhl, Walling. **Los Angeles (3)**—Bryant 2, Brock. **Montreal (42)**—Dawson 11, Wallach 6, Galarraga 4, Raines 4, Brooks 3, Law 3, Webster 2, Bilardello, Fitzgerald, Foley, Johnson, Krenchicki, Nieto, Schatzeder, Winningham, Youmans. **New York (6)**—Strawberry 3, Carter 2, Wilson. **Philadelphia (6)**—Daulton 2, Wilson 2, Samuel, Schmidt. **Pittsburgh (7)**—Bream 2, Almon, Bonds, Diaz, Morrison, T. Pena. **St. Louis (5)**—Clark, Ford, Heath, Lavalliere, Van Slyke. **San Diego (8)**—Garvey 3, McReynolds 2, Kennedy, Nettles, Royster. **San Francisco (3)**—C. Davis, Garrelts, Maldonado.

AT NEW YORK (124): Atlanta (1)—Washington. **Chicago (8)**—Cey 2, Sandberg 2, Lopes, Matthews, Moreland, Palmeiro. **Cincinnati (4)**—Bell, Butera, Milner, Parker. **Houston (3)**—Garner 2, Bass. **Los Angeles (5)**—Duncan, Landreaux, Marshall, Sax, Williams. **Montreal (5)**—Bilardello, Dawson, Fitzgerald, Galarraga, Webster. **New York (77)**—Carter 13, Strawberry 11, Foster 9, Knight 7,

Hernandez 6, Johnson 5, Dykstra 4, Hearn 4, K. Mitchell 4, Wilson 4, Heep 3, Teufel 2, Aguilera, Backman, Gibbons, Jefferson, Mazzilli. **Philadelphia (5)**—Hayes 2, Redus, Schmidt, Thompson. **Pittsburgh (4)**—Bream, Brown, Morrison, Ray. **St. Louis (3)**—Lake, Pendleton, Van Slyke. **San Diego (6)**—Garvey 2, Gwynn, Iorg, Martinez, McReynolds. **San Francisco (3)**—Brenly, C. Davis, Thompson.

AT PHILADELPHIA (135): Atlanta (2)—Harper 2. **Chicago (4)**—J. Davis 2, Dunston, Matthews. **Cincinnati (6)**—Davis 2, Esasky, Milner, Oester, Welsh. **Houston (3)**—Ashby, Davis, Reynolds. **Los Angeles (6)**—Brock 3, Stubbs 2, Duncan. **Montreal (8)**—Winningham 2, Bilardello, Brooks, Dawson, Law, Raines, Webster. **New York (6)**—Dykstra 2, Knight 2, Carter, Mazzilli. **Philadelphia (86)**—Schmidt 20, Hayes 11, Samuel 10, Redus 8, Russell 8, Wilson 7, Daulton 4, Roenicke 4, Stone 4, Thompson 4, Aguayo 3, K. Gross, Reynolds, Schu. **Pittsburgh (4)**—Bonds, Bream, T. Pena, Ray. **St. Louis (5)**—Clark, Ford, Knicely, Laga, Lavalliere. **San Diego (4)**—McReynolds 2, Kennedy, Martinez. **San Francisco (1)**—Brown.

AT PITTSBURGH (124): Atlanta (6)—Harper 2, Virgil 2, Murphy, Thomas. **Chicago (6)**—Cey 2, Durham 2, Dunston, Lopes. **Cincinnati (8)**—Davis 4, Parker 3, Bell. **Houston (8)**—Bailey 2, Bass 2, Davis 2, Cruz, Thon. **Los Angeles (8)**—Stubbs 3, Brock, Hamilton, Landreaux, Madlock, Williams. **Montreal (5)**—Brooks, Dawson, Galarraga, Hunt, Wallach. **New York (7)**—Strawberry 2, Aguilera, Foster, Johnson, K. Mitchell, Wilson. **Philadelphia (12)**—Schmidt 4, Schu 3, Wilson 2, Bittiger, James, Russell. **Pittsburgh (49)**—Morrison 11, Bonds 9, Diaz 6, Reynolds 6, Bream 5, T. Pena 5, Almon 4, Ray 2, Brown. **St. Louis (4)**—Clark 2, Hurdle 2. **San Diego (6)**—Garvey 2, Bochy, Gwynn, Iorg, Wynne. **San Francisco (5)**—Brown, Clark, Maldonado, Uribe, Youngblood.

AT ST. LOUIS (90): Atlanta (3)—Griffey, Ramirez, Sample. **Chicago (9)**—Matthews 2, Speier 2, Dayett, Durham, Moreland, Palmeiro, Sandberg. **Cincinnati (4)**—Bell, Daniels, Jones, Parker. **Houston (3)**—Bailey, Bass, Walling. **Los Angeles (7)**—Stubbs 2, Duncan, Marshall, Matuszek, Sax, Williams. **Montreal (6)**—Galarraga 2, Webster 2, Wallach, Winningham. **New York (9)**—Knight 2, K. Mitchell 2, Dykstra, Johnson, Strawberry, Teufel, Wilson. **Philadelphia (10)**—Redus 2, Reynolds 2, Schu 2, Hayes, Roenicke, Samuel, Wilson. **Pittsburgh (7)**—Bream 2, Ray 2, Morrison, T. Pena, Rhoden. **St. Louis (27)**—McGee 7, Van Slyke 6, Clark 4, Forsch 2, Landrum 2, Heath, Herr, Laga, Lavalliere, Morris, White. **San Diego (2)**—Garvey, Gwynn. **San Francisco (3)**—Brenly, Carlton, Youngblood.

AT SAN DIEGO (158): Atlanta (7)—Murphy 3, Virgil 2, Oberkfell, Ramirez. **Chicago (6)**—Matthews 2, Cey, J. Davis, Dernier, Speier. **Cincinnati (11)**—Milner 2, Parker 2, Bell, Concepcion, Daniels, Diaz, Esasky, Oester, Venable. **Houston (13)**—Bass 4, Doran 2, Ashby, Cruz, Davis, Lopes, Reynolds, Thon, Walling. **Los Angeles (9)**—Duncan 2, Bryant, Gonzalez, Guerrero, Hamilton, Madlock, Scioscia, Stubbs. **Montreal (7)**—Brooks 3, Fitzgerald, Krenchicki, Raines, Webster. **New York (4)**—Carter, Santana, Strawberry, Teufel. **Philadelphia (3)**—Samuel 2, Schmidt. **Pittsburgh (7)**—Morrison 2, Almon, Bream, Orsulak, T. Pena, Ray. **St. Louis (1)**—Hurdle. **San Diego (80)**—McReynolds 14, Nettles 13, Garvey 11, Gwynn 8, Kennedy 7, Bochy 6, Martinez 6, Wynne 5, Royster 2, Santiago 2, Dravecky, Flannery, Kruk, Lefferts, T. Stoddard, Templeton. **San Francisco (10)**—Maldonado 2, Brenly, Brown, Clark, Gladden, Kutcher, Melvin, Uribe, Youngblood.

AT SAN FRANCISCO (111): Atlanta (9)—Ramirez 2, Virgil 2, Griffey, Horner, Murphy, Palmer, Simmons. **Chicago (5)**—Cey 2, Dunston, Mumphrey, Sandberg. **Cincinnati (6)**—Davis 3, Bell, Milner, Parker. **Houston (10)**—Bass 3, Garner 2, Ashby, Davis, Doran, Pankovits, Puhl. **Los Angeles (8)**—Guerrero 2, Bryant, Landreaux, Madlock, Marshall, Scioscia, Trevino. **Montreal (5)**—Brooks 2, Wallach 2, Galarraga. **New York (2)**—Hernandez, Strawberry. **Philadelphia (7)**—Daulton, Hayes, Samuel, Schmidt, Schu, Stone, Wilson. **Pittsburgh (6)**—Bream, Brown, Diaz, Mazzilli, Morrison, T. Pena. **St. Louis (1)**—Heath. **San Diego (2)**—Bochy, Kennedy. **San Francisco (50)**—Brenly 8, Clark 7, C. Davis 7, Maldonado 6, Kutcher 5, Thompson 4, Brown 3, Leonard 2, Melvin 2, Aldrete, Gladden, LaCoss, Spilman, Uribe, Woodard.

American League

	At Balt.	At Bos.	At Cal.	At Chi.	At Clev.	At Det.	At K.C.	At Mil.	At Min.	At N.Y.	At Oak.	At Sea.	At Tex.	At Tor.	Totals 1986	Totals 1985
Baltimore	91	2	6	6	5	1	4	5	9	10	10	6	4	10	169	214
Boston	15	55	5	5	9	12	4	3	6	10	4	4	5	7	144	162
California	2	5	88	3	5	8	3	7	12	4	10	10	5	5	167	153
Chicago	5	4	5	51	2	11	2	9	8	8	3	6	2	5	121	146
Cleveland	4	8	9	2	80	4	4	11	7	5	7	7	3	6	157	116
Detroit	13	8	10	5	7	96	5	2	11	7	12	11	4	7	198	202
Kansas City	11	7	10	5	5	4	60	6	4	7	2	5	7	4	137	154
Milwaukee	4	4	4	5	7	5	2	63	10	7	5	3	5	3	127	101
Minnesota	10	6	8	6	8	5	4	5	116	12	1	6	2	7	196	141
New York	10	6	7	10	5	11	2	3	11	93	6	12	4	8	188	176
Oakland	1	9	8	4	8	4	3	6	5	7	75	10	9	14	163	155
Seattle	6	7	4	2	6	4	3	4	4	4	8	97	6	3	158	171
Texas	8	10	3	7	4	5	3	13	14	4	8	8	87	10	184	129
Toronto	9	9	5	3	9	9	7	5	6	11	5	11	5	87	181	158
1986 Totals	189	140	172	114	160	179	106	142	223	189	156	196	148	176	2290	....
1985 Totals	190	135	168	157	128	201	110	136	154	159	137	172	178	153	....	2178

AT BALTIMORE (189): Baltimore (91)—Lynn 13, Ripken 10, Sheets 10, Murray 9, Traber 9, Dempsey 7, Dwyer 5, Lacy 5, Rayford 5, Shelby 5, Young 5, Beniquez 4, Stefaro 2, Gerhart, O'Malley. **Boston (15)**—Evans 4, Buckner 3, Armas 2, Gedman 2, Rice 2, Baylor, Henderson. **California (2)**—Boone, Downing. **Chicago (5)**—Baines, Cangelosi, Hulett, Tolleson, Walker. **Cleveland (4)**—Butler, Carter, Franco, Snyder. **Detroit (13)**—Gibson 4, Herndon 2, Whitaker 2, Brookens, Coles, Heath, Nokes, Trammell. **Kansas City (11)**—Balboni 3, Brett 2, Motley 2, McRae, Sundberg, White, Wilson. **Milwaukee (4)**—Cooper 2, Riles, Schroeder. **Minnesota (10)**—Puckett 4, Smalley 3, Gaetti 2, Hrbek. **New York (10)**—Henderson 2, Winfield 2, Easler, Griffey, Lombardi, Mattingly, Pasqua, Randolph. **Oakland (1)**—Phillips. **Seattle (6)**—Phelps 2, P. Bradley, Davis, Moses, Presley. **Texas (8)**—Buechele 2, O'Brien 2, Harrah, Incaviglia, Porter, Ward. **Toronto (9)**—Barfield 3, Johnson 2, Bell, Fielder, Mulliniks, Upshaw.

AT BOSTON (140): Baltimore (2)—Dempsey, Ripken. **Boston (55)**—Rice 10, Baylor 9, Buckner 8, Evans 8, Armas 5, Barrett 4, Boggs 3, Gedman 2, Quinones 2, Romero 2, Lyons, Sullivan. **California (5)**—Jackson 2, Downing, Pettis, Schofield. **Chicago (4)**—Baines 2, Fisk, Kittle. **Cleveland (8)**—Carter 3, Castillo, Franco, Hall, Snyder, Thornton. **Detroit (8)**—Evans 3, Coles 2, Herndon, Laga, Lemon. **Kansas City (7)**—Balboni 5, McRae, Sundberg. **Milwaukee (4)**—Molitor, Oglivie, Schroeder, Yount. **Minnesota (6)**—Gaetti 2, Hrbek 2, Brunansky, Gagne. **New York (6)**—Mattingly 2, Cotto, Hassey, Pagliarulo, Randolph. **Oakland (9)**—Kingman 4, Canseco 3, Bochte, Griffin. **Seattle (7)**—Presley 2, Tartabull 2, Phelps, G. Thomas, Yeager. **Texas (10)**—Parrish 3, Buechele 2, Incaviglia 2, McDowell 2, Porter. **Toronto (9)**—Barfield 3, Bell 2, Moseby 2, Mulliniks 2.

AT CALIFORNIA (172): Baltimore (6)—Shelby 3, Lynn, Murray, Young. **Boston (5)**—Gedman 3, Boggs, Evans. **California (88)**—DeCinces 14, Downing 13, Jackson 11, Joyner 11, Jones 10, Hendrick 8, Schofield 7, Grich 5, Wilfong 3, Burleson 2, Boone, Howell, Pettis, Ryal. **Chicago (5)**—Hulett 2, Baines, Karkovice, Walker. **Cleveland (9)**—Snyder 3, Hall 2, Carter, Clark, Jacoby, Thornton. **Detroit (10)**—Evans 3, Trammell 2, Coles, Grubb, Lemon, Parrish, Whitaker. **Kansas City (10)**—Balboni 3, Biancalana 2, Smith 2, Jackson, McRae, White. **Milwaukee (4)**—Cooper 2, Deer, Gantner. **Minnesota (8)**—Puckett 3, Hrbek 2, Brunansky, Gaetti, Salas. **New York (7)**—Easler 2, Pagliarulo 2, Winfield 2, Griffey. **Oakland (8)**—Canseco 2, Murphy 2, Davis, Hill, Lansford, Tettleton. **Seattle (4)**—Tartabull 2, Calderon, Henderson. **Texas (3)**—Incaviglia 2, Parrish. **Toronto (5)**—Bell 3, Moseby, Mulliniks.

AT CHICAGO (114): Baltimore (6)—Ripken 2, Dempsey, Murray, Pardo, Rayford. **Boston (5)**—Baylor 3, Evans, Rice. **California (3)**—DeCinces, Downing, Jones. **Chicago (51)**—Baines 8, Hulett 7, Walker 6, Fisk 5, Kittle 5, Hairston 3, Hassey 3, Bonilla 2, Nichols 2, Boston, Cangelosi, Cochrane, Foster, Guillen, Karkovice, Morman, Skinner, Tolleson, Williams. **Cleveland (2)**—Hall, Jacoby. **Detroit (5)**—Evans, Gibson, Parrish, Spilman, Whitaker. **Kansas City (5)**—Brett 2, Balboni, White, Wilson. **Milwaukee (5)**—Deer 3, Riles 2. **Minnesota (6)**—Gaetti 2, Beane, Bush, Hatcher, Puckett. **New York (10)**—Pagliarulo 3, Henderson 2, Hassey, Pasqua, Washington, Winfield, Wynegar. **Oakland (4)**—Canseco, Davis, Hill, McGwire. **Seattle (2)**—P. Bradley, Presley. **Texas (7)**—Sierra 2, Harrah, Incaviglia, McDowell, O'Brien, Porter. **Toronto (3)**—Bell, Johnson, Whitt.

AT CLEVELAND (160): Baltimore (5)—Sheets 2, Murray, Ripken, Traber. **Boston (9)**—Armas 3, Baylor 3, Boggs, Buckner, Owen. **California (5)**—DeCinces 2, Jones, Joyner, Schofield. **Chicago (2)**—Hulett, Kittle. **Cleveland (80)**—Carter 14, Snyder 12, Thornton 12, Jacoby 10, Bernazard 9, Hall 8, Tabler 5, Castillo 4, Franco 4, Bando, Clark. **Detroit (7)**—Trammell 3, Gibson 2, Grubb, Lowry. **Kansas City (5)**—Orta 2, Balboni, Sundberg, White. **Milwaukee (7)**—Molitor 3, Deer, Manning, Riles, Sveum. **Minnesota (8)**—Brunansky 2, Gaetti 2, Beane, Gagne, Hrbek, Smalley. **New York (5)**—Pagliarulo 2, Easler, Henderson, Mattingly. **Oakland (8)**—Canseco 2, Kingman 2, Davis, Griffin, Lansford, Steinbach. **Seattle (6)**—P. Bradley, Hengel, Kearney, Presley, G. Thomas, Valle. **Texas (4)**—Fletcher, Parrish, Petralli, Sierra. **Toronto (9)**—Bell 2, Whitt 2, Fernandez, Garcia, Iorg, Mulliniks, Shepherd.

AT DETROIT (179): Baltimore (1)—Young. **Boston (12)**—Baylor 3, Gedman 3, Boggs 2, Evans 2, Rice 2. **California (8)**—Boone 2, Joyner 2, DeCinces, Howell, Pettis, Schofield. **Chicago (11)**—Baines 4, Kittle 3, Hulett 2, Boston, Hairston. **Cleveland (4)**—Bernazard, Castillo, Franco, Snyder. **Detroit (96)**—Evans 15, Gibson 15, Coles 12, Grubb 8, Parrish 8, Trammell 8, Whitaker 8, Lemon 7, Herndon 4, Heath 3, Sheridan 3, Brookens 2, Laga 2, Lowry. **Kansas City (4)**—Smith 2, Brett, Quirk. **Milwaukee (5)**—Deer 2, Cerone, Moore, Sveum. **Minnesota (5)**—Gaetti 2, Puckett 2, Lombardozzi. **New York (11)**—Mattingly 4, Easler, Griffey, Hassey, Henderson, Kittle, Pasqua, Winfield. **Oakland (4)**—Kingman, Lansford, McGwire, Tettleton. **Seattle (4)**—S. Bradley, Davis, Presley, G. Thomas. **Texas (5)**—Slaught 2, Incaviglia, O'Brien, Parrish. **Toronto (9)**—Barfield 4, Fernandez 2, Fielder, Garcia, Whitt.

AT KANSAS CITY (106): Baltimore (4)—Dwyer, Lynn, Rayford, Ripken. **Boston (4)**—Armas, Buckner, Evans, Gedman. **California (3)**—Jones, Narron, Ryal. **Chicago (2)**—Fisk, Morman. **Cleveland (4)**—Bernazard, Butler, Carter, Thornton. **Detroit (5)**—Collins, Gibson, Grubb, Trammell, Whitaker. **Kansas City (60)**—White 12, Balboni 10, Brett 8, Orta 5, Quirk 5, Sundberg 5, Wilson 5, Motley 3, Smith 2, Jackson, Kingery, Law, McRae, Seitzer. **Milwaukee (2)**—Deer 2. **Minnesota (4)**—Hrbek 2, Brunansky, Gaetti. **New York (2)**—Skinner, Winfield. **Oakland (3)**—Lansford 2, Kingman. **Seattle (3)**—Henderson, Kearney, Phelps. **Texas (3)**—Harrah, Parrish, Sierra. **Toronto (7)**—Bell 2, Barfield, Fernandez, Garcia, Moseby, Whitt.

AT MILWAUKEE (142): Baltimore (5)—Murray 2, Dempsey, Rayford, Young. **Boston (3)**—Baylor, Evans, Gedman. **California (7)**—Joyner 3, Hendrick 2, Burleson, Grich. **Chicago (9)**—Baines 2, Fisk 2, Hulett 2, Boston, Hairston, Morman. **Cleveland (11)**—Carter 3, Jacoby 3, Snyder 3, Bernazard, Franco. **Detroit (2)**—Bergman, Trammell. **Kansas City (6)**—Balboni 3, McRae 2, Kingery. **Milwaukee (63)**—Deer 19, Cooper 6, Molitor 5, Gantner 4, Manning 4, Sveum 4, Yount 4, Cerone 3, Braggs 2, Moore 2, Oglivie 2, Riles 2, Schroeder 2, Thomas 2, Felder, Householder. **Minnesota (5)**—Gaetti 2, Hrbek, Salas, Smalley. **New York (3)**—Griffey, Henderson, Winfield. **Oakland (6)**—Baker 3, Canseco 2, Murphy. **Seattle (4)**—P. Bradley, Henderson, Tartabull, G. Thomas. **Texas (13)**—Buechele 3, O'Brien 3, McDowell 2, Harrah, Incaviglia, Parrish, Porter, Slaught. **Toronto (5)**—Upshaw 2, Bell, Fernandez, Whitt.

AT MINNESOTA (223): Baltimore (9)—Lynn 4, Ripken 2, Bonilla, Lacy, Murray. **Boston (6)**—Baylor 2, Evans 2, Gedman, Rice. **California (12)**—DeCinces 2, Jackson 2, Jones 2, Joyner 2, Boone, Burleson, Hendrick, Schofield. **Chicago (8)**—Kittle 3, Boston 2, Fisk 2, Karkovice. **Cleveland (7)**—Carter 3, Bando, Bell, Butler, Hall. **Detroit (11)**—Parrish 4, Whitaker 2, Coles, Evans, Gibson, Sheridan, Spilman. **Kansas City (4)**—Smith, Sundberg, White, Wilson. **Milwaukee (10)**—Deer 3, Oglivie 2, Gantner, Riles, Schroeder, Thomas, Yount. **Minnesota (116)**—Hrbek 18, Gaetti 16, Brunansky 15, Puckett 14, Gagne 10, Laudner 9, Smalley 9, Bush 6, Lombardozzi 6, Salas 5, Washington 4, Woods 2, Hatcher, Reed. **New York (11)**—Henderson 2, Pagliarulo 2, Pasqua 2, Wynegar 2, Easler, Mattingly, Winfield. **Oakland (5)**—Bochte, Canseco, Griffin, Hill, Kingman. **Seattle (4)**—Tartabull 2, Phelps, G. Thomas. **Texas (14)**—Incaviglia 2, O'Brien 2, Porter 2, Sierra 2, Slaught 2, Buechele, McDowell, Paciorek, Stanley. **Toronto (6)**—Barfield 2, Moseby 2, Bell, Leach.

AT NEW YORK (189): Baltimore (10)—Lacy 3, Sheets 2, Shelby 2, Dempsey, Lynn, Ripken. **Boston (10)**—Buckner 4, Evans 2, Rice 2, Baylor, Dodson. **California (4)**—DeCinces 2, Hendrick, Joyner. **Chicago (8)**—Kittle 2, Skinner 2, Walker 2, Baines, Hulett. **Cleveland (5)**—Bernazard, Butler, Carter, Franco, Jacoby. **Detroit (7)**—Evans 3, Grubb, Lemon, Trammell, Whitaker. **Kansas City (7)**—Brett 2, Sundberg 2, Balboni, McRae, Motley. **Milwaukee (7)**—Manning 2, Yount 2, Cooper, Gantner, Thomas.

Minnesota (12)—Gaetti 3, Puckett 3, Hrbek 2, Beane, Hatcher, Laudner, Lombardozzi. **New York (93)**—Mattingly 17, Pagliarulo 14, Henderson 13, Winfield 12, Pasqua 9, Easler 6, Griffey 5, Washington 4, Roenicke 3, Wynegar 3, Berra 2, Hassey 2, Randolph 2, Kittle. **Oakland (7)**—Lansford 3, Canseco 2, Bathe, Tettleton. **Seattle (4)**—Tartabull 2, P. Bradley, Presley. **Texas (4)**—Slaught 2, Buechele, Paciorek. **Toronto (11)**—Barfield 4, Moseby 2, Whitt 2, Fernandez, Iorg, Upshaw.

AT OAKLAND (156): Baltimore (10)—Sheets 3, Ripken 2, Dwyer, Lacy, Murray, Traber, Young. **Boston (4)**—Baylor 2, Evans, Gedman. **California (10)**—Boone 2, Downing 2, Jackson 2, DeCinces, Grich, Pettis, Schofield. **Chicago (3)**—Fisk, Karkovice, Kittle. **Cleveland (7)**—Bernazard 2, Hall 2, Jacoby, Snyder, Thornton. **Detroit (12)**—Gibson 3, Parrish 3, Lemon 2, Coles, Evans, Trammell, Whitaker. **Kansas City (2)**—Quirk, White. **Milwaukee (5)**—Riles 2, Ready, Sveum, Thomas. **Minnesota (1)**—Smalley. **New York (6)**—Winfield 3, Hernandez, Lombardi, Pagliarulo. **Oakland (75)**—Kingman 15, Canseco 14, Davis 11, Lansford 10, Murphy 5, Bathe 4, Tettleton 4, Bochte 3, Phillips 3, Willard 2, Baker, Griffin, McGwire, Tillman. **Seattle (8)**—Davis 2, Phelps 2, Tartabull 2, P. Bradley, Brantley. **Texas (8)**—Parrish 3, Incaviglia 2, McDowell, O'Brien, Paciorek. **Toronto (5)**—Barfield, Johnson, Moseby, Mulliniks, Whitt.

AT SEATTLE (196): Baltimore (6)—Dempsey 2, Lynn 2, Ripken 2. **Boston (4)**—Baylor, Buckner, Evans, Rice. **California (10)**—Downing 2, Hendrick 2, DeCinces, Grich, Jackson, Jones, Joyner, Schofield. **Chicago (6)**—Baines, Fisk, Guillen, Kittle, Morman, Walker. **Cleveland (7)**—Bernazard 2, Allanson, Castillo, Clark, Hall, Snyder. **Detroit (11)**—Trammell 3, Coles 2, Whitaker 2, Evans, Grubb, Sheridan, Spilman. **Kansas City (5)**—Kingery, Orta, Seitzer, Sundberg, Wilson. **Milwaukee (3)**—Schroeder 2, Deer. **Minnesota (6)**—Puckett 3, Smalley 2, Salas. **New York (12)**—Henderson 4, Mattingly 4, Pasqua 2, Easler, Pagliarulo. **Oakland (10)**—Kingman 6, Canseco, Hill, Murphy, Tettleton. **Seattle (97)**—Presley 16, Phelps 15, Davis 14, Tartabull 13, Henderson 10, P. Bradley 5, G. Thomas 5, S. Bradley 4, Kearney 4, Valle 4, Brantley 2, Moses 2, Calderon, Reynolds, Yeager. **Texas (8)**—Buechele 2, Sierra 2, McDowell, O'Brien, Paciorek, Parrish. **Toronto (11)**—Barfield 5, Bell 2, Fielder, Martinez, Moseby, Upshaw.

AT TEXAS (148): Baltimore (4)—Beniquez 2, Lacy, Ripken. **Boston (5)**—Baylor 3, Boggs, Evans. **California (5)**—DeCinces 2, Jones, Pettis, White. **Chicago (2)**—Hulett, Walker. **Cleveland (3)**—Carter, Hall, Tabler. **Detroit (4)**—Parrish 3, Lowry. **Kansas City (7)**—White 3, Balboni, Orta, Quirk, Smith. **Milwaukee (5)**—Braggs 2, Deer, Robidoux, Thomas. **Minnesota (2)**—Brunansky, Smalley. **New York (4)**—Easler, Mattingly, Pagliarulo, Washington. **Oakland (9)**—Canseco 2, Kingman 2, Bochte, Davis, Steinbach, Tettleton, Willard. **Seattle (6)**—Presley 4, Henderson, Phelps. **Texas (87)**—Incaviglia 17, Parrish 14, O'Brien 11, McDowell 8, Sierra 8, Buechele 6, Porter 6, Slaught 5, Harrah 3, Ward 3, Fletcher 2, Kunkel, Mercado, Petralli, G. Wright. **Toronto (5)**—Barfield, Bell, Fielder, Gruber, Upshaw.

AT TORONTO (176): Baltimore (10)—Ripken 2, Traber 2, Dodd, Dwyer, Lynn, Murray, Sheets, Shelby. **Boston (7)**—Baylor 2, Gedman 2, Evans, Rice, Sax. **California (5)**—Howell 2, Burleson, Grich, Joyner. **Chicago (5)**—Baines, Fisk, Skinner, Tolleson, Walker. **Cleveland (6)**—Carter, Castillo, Franco, Hall, Snyder, Thornton. **Detroit (7)**—Parrish 2, Evans, Gibson, Herndon, Sheridan, Whitaker. **Kansas City (4)**—Balboni, Brett, Motley, White. **Milwaukee (3)**—Cooper, Manning, Yount. **Minnesota (7)**—Brunansky 2, Smalley 2, Gaetti, Puckett, Reed. **New York (8)**—Henderson 2, Kittle 2, Hassey, Pagliarulo, Randolph, Wynegar. **Oakland (14)**—Davis 4, Canseco 3, Kingman 3, Lansford, Phillips, Tettleton, Willard. **Seattle (3)**—P. Bradley, Phelps, Tartabull. **Texas (10)**—McDowell 2, Parrish 2, Buechele, Incaviglia, O'Brien, Slaught, Ward, G. Wright. **Toronto (87)**—Barfield 16, Bell 15, Johnson 11, Moseby 11, Whitt 7, Mulliniks 5, Fernandez 4, Gruber 4, Leach 4, Garcia 3, Upshaw 3, Iorg, Lee, Martinez, Shepherd.

THE SPORTING NEWS AWARDS

THE SPORTING NEWS MVP AWARDS

	AMERICAN LEAGUE		NATIONAL LEAGUE	
Year	Player Club	Points	Player Club	Points
1929	Al Simmons, Philadelphia, of	40	No selection	
1930	Joseph Cronin, Washington, ss	52	William Terry, New York, 1b	47
1931	H. Louis Gehrig, New York, 1b	40	Charles Klein, Philadelphia, of	40
1932	James Foxx, Philadelphia, 1b	46	Charles Klein, Philadelphia, of	46
1933	James Foxx, Philadelphia, 1b	49	Carl Hubbell, New York, p	64
1934	H. Louis Gehrig, New York, 1b	51	Jerome Dean, St. Louis, p	57
1935	Henry Greenberg, Detroit, 1b	64	J. Floyd Vaughan, Pittsburgh, ss	42
1936	H. Louis Gehrig, New York, 1b	55	Carl Hubbell, New York, p	61
1937	Charles Gehringer, Detroit, 2b	78	Joseph Medwick, St. Louis, of	70
1938	James Foxx, Boston, 1b	304	Ernest Lombardi, Cincinnati, c	229
1939	Joseph DiMaggio, New York, of	280	William Walters, Cincinnati, p	303
1940	Henry Greenberg, Detroit, of	292	Frank McCormick, Cincinnati, 1b	274
1941	Joseph DiMaggio, New York, of	291	Adolph Camilli, Brooklyn, 1b	300
1942	Joseph Gordon, New York, 2b	270	Morton Cooper, St. Louis, p	263
1943	Spurgeon Chandler, New York, p	246	Stanley Musial, St. Louis, of	267
1944	Robert Doerr, Boston, 2b		Martin Marion, St. Louis, ss	
1945	Edward J. Mayo, Detroit, 2b		Thomas Holmes, Boston, of	

THE SPORTING NEWS PLAYER, PITCHER OF YEAR

AMERICAN LEAGUE

1948—Louis Boudreau, Cleveland, ss
Robert Lemon, Cleveland, p
1949—Theodore Williams, Boston, of
Ellis Kinder, Boston, p
1950—Philip Rizzuto, New York, ss
Robert Lemon, Cleveland, p
1951—Ferris Fain, Philadelphia, 1b
Robert Feller, Cleveland, p
1952—Luscious Easter, Cleveland, 1b
Robert Shantz, Philadelphia, p
1953—Albert Rosen, Cleveland, 3b
Erv (Bob) Porterfield, Washington, p
1954—Roberto Avila, Cleveland, 2b
Robert Lemon, Cleveland, p
1955—Albert Kaline, Detroit, of
Edward Ford, New York, p
1956—Mickey Mantle, New York, of
W. William Pierce, Chicago, p
1957—Theodore Williams, Boston, of
W. William Pierce, Chicago, p
1958—Jack Jensen, Boston, of
Robert Turley, New York, p
1959—J. Nelson Fox, Chicago, 2b
Early Wynn, Chicago, p
1960—Roger Maris, New York, of
Charles Estrada, Baltimore, p
1961—Roger Maris, New York, of
Edward Ford, New York, p
1962—Mickey Mantle, New York, of
Richard Donovan, Cleveland, p
1963—Albert Kaline, Detroit, of
Edward Ford, New York, p
1964—Brooks Robinson, Baltimore, 3b
Dean Chance, Los Angeles, p
1965—Pedro (Tony) Oliva, Minnesota, of
James Grant, Minnesota, p
1966—Frank Robinson, Baltimore, of
James Kaat, Minnesota, p
1967—Carl Yastrzemski, Boston, of
Jim Lonborg, Boston, p
1968—Ken Harrelson, Boston, of
Denny McLain, Detroit, p
1969—Harmon Killebrew, Minnesota, 1b-3b
Denny McLain, Detroit, p
1970—Harmon Killebrew, Minnesota, 3b
Sam McDowell, Cleveland, p
1971—Pedro (Tony) Oliva, Minnesota, of
Vida Blue, Oakland, p
1972—Richie Allen, Chicago, 1b
Wilbur Wood, Chicago, p
1973—Reggie Jackson, Oakland, of
Jim Palmer, Baltimore, p

NATIONAL LEAGUE

1948—Stanley Musial, St. Louis, of-1b
John Sain, Boston, p
1949—Enos Slaughter, St. Louis, of
Howard Pollet, St. Louis, p
1950—Ralph Kiner, Pittsburgh, of
C. James Konstanty, Philadelphia, p
1951—Stanley Musial, St. Louis, of
Elwin Roe, Brooklyn, p
1952—Henry Sauer, Chicago, of
Robin Roberts, Philadelphia, p
1953—Roy Campanella, Brooklyn, c
Warren Spahn, Milwaukee, p
1954—Willie Mays, New York, of
John Antonelli, New York, p
1955—Edwin Snider, Brooklyn, of
Robin Roberts, Philadelphia, p
1956—Henry Aaron, Milwaukee, of
Donald Newcombe, Brooklyn, p
1957—Stanley Musial, St. Louis, 1b
Warren Spahn, Milwaukee, p
1958—Ernest Banks, Chicago, ss
Warren Spahn, Milwaukee, p
1959—Ernest Banks, Chicago, ss
Samuel Jones, San Francisco, p
1960—Richard Groat, Pittsburgh, ss
Vernon Law, Pittsburgh, p
1961—Frank Robinson, Cincinnati, of
Warren Spahn, Milwaukee, p
1962—Maurice Wills, Los Angeles, ss
Donald Drysdale, Los Angeles, p
1963—Henry Aaron, Milwaukee, of
Sanford Koufax, Los Angeles, p
1964—Kenton Boyer, St. Louis, 3b
Sanford Koufax, Los Angeles, p
1965—Willie Mays, San Francisco, of
Sanford Koufax, Los Angeles, p
1966—Roberto Clemente, Pittsburgh, of
Sanford Koufax, Los Angeles, p
1967—Orlando Cepeda, St. Louis, 1b
Mike McCormick, San Francisco, p
1968—Pete Rose, Cincinnati, of
Bob Gibson, St. Louis, p
1969—Willie McCovey, San Francisco, 1b
Tom Seaver, New York, p
1970—Johnny Bench, Cincinnati, c
Bob Gibson, St. Louis, p
1971—Joe Torre, St. Louis, 3b
Ferguson Jenkins, Chicago, p
1972—Billy Williams, Chicago, of
Steve Carlton, Philadelphia, p
1973—Bobby Bonds, San Francisco, of
Ron Bryant, San Francisco, p

PLAYER, PITCHER OF YEAR—Continued

AMERICAN LEAGUE

1974—Jeff Burroughs, Texas, of
Jim Hunter, Oakland, p
1975—Fred Lynn, Boston, of
Jim Palmer, Baltimore, p
1976—Thurman Munson, New York, c
Jim Palmer, Baltimore, p
1977—Rod Carew, Minnesota, 1b
Nolan Ryan, California, p
1978—Jim Rice, Boston, of
Ron Guidry, New York, p
1979—Don Baylor, California, of
Mike Flanagan, Baltimore, p
1980—George Brett, Kansas City, 3b
Steve Stone, Baltimore, p
1981—Tony Armas, Oakland, of
Jack Morris, Detroit, p
1982—Robin Yount, Milwaukee, ss
Dave Stieb, Toronto, p
1983—Cal Ripken, Baltimore, ss
LaMarr Hoyt, Chicago, p
1984—Don Mattingly, New York, 1b
Willie Hernandez, Detroit, p
1985—Don Mattingly, New York, 1b
Bret Saberhagen, Kansas City, p
1986—Don Mattingly, New York, 1b
Roger Clemens, Boston, p

NATIONAL LEAGUE

1974—Lou Brock, St. Louis, of
Mike Marshall, Los Angeles, p
1975—Joe Morgan, Cincinnati, 2b
Tom Seaver, New York, p
1976—George Foster, Cincinnati, of
Randy Jones, San Diego, p
1977—George Foster, Cincinnati, of
Steve Carlton, Philadelphia, p
1978—Dave Parker, Pittsburgh, of
Vida Blue, San Francisco, p
1979—Keith Hernandez, St. Louis, 1b
Joe Niekro, Houston, p
1980—Mike Schmidt, Philadelphia, 3b
Steve Carlton, Philadelphia, p
1981—Andre Dawson, Montreal, of
Fernando Valenzuela, Los Angeles, p
1982—Dale Murphy, Atlanta, of
Steve Carlton, Philadelphia, p
1983—Dale Murphy, Atlanta, of
John Denny, Philadelphia, p
1984—Ryne Sandberg, Chicago, 2b
Rick Sutcliffe, Chicago, p
1985—Willie McGee, St. Louis, of
Dwight Gooden, New York, p
1986—Mike Schmidt, Philadelphia, 3b
Mike Scott, Houston, p

FIREMAN (Relief Pitcher) OF THE YEAR

Year	Player, Club	Player, Club
1960	Mike Fornieles, Boston	Lindy McDaniel, St. Louis
1961	Luis Arroyo, New York	Stu Miller, San Francisco
1962	Dick Radatz, Boston	Roy Face, Pittsburgh
1963	Stu Miller, Baltimore	Lindy McDaniel, Chicago
1964	Dick Radatz, Boston	Al McBean, Pittsburgh
1965	Eddie Fisher, Chicago	Ted Abernathy, Chicago
1966	Jack Aker, Kansas City	Phil Regan, Los Angeles
1967	Minnie Rojas, California	Ted Abernathy, Cincinnati
1968	Wilbur Wood, Chicago	Phil Regan, L.A.-Chicago
1969	Ron Perranoski, Minnesota	Wayne Granger, Cincinnati
1970	Ron Perranoski, Minnesota	Wayne Granger, Cincinnati
1971	Ken Sanders, Milwaukee	Dave Giusti, Pittsburgh
1972	Sparky Lyle, New York	Clay Carroll, Cincinnati
1973	John Hiller, Detroit	Mike Marshall, Montreal
1974	Terry Forster, Chicago	Mike Marshall, Los Angeles
1975	Rich Gossage, Chicago	Al Hrabosky, St. Louis
1976	Bill Campbell, Minnesota	Rawly Eastwick, Cincinnati
1977	Bill Campbell, Boston	Rollie Fingers, San Diego
1978	Rich Gossage, New York	Rollie Fingers, San Diego
1979	Mike Marshall, Minnesota Jim Kern, Texas	Bruce Sutter, Chicago
1980	Dan Quisenberry, Kansas City	Rollie Fingers, San Diego Tom Hume, Cincinnati
1981	Rollie Fingers, Milwaukee	Bruce Sutter, St. Louis
1982	Dan Quisenberry, Kansas City	Bruce Sutter, St. Louis
1983	Dan Quisenberry, Kansas City	Al Holland, Philadelphia Lee Smith, Chicago
1984	Dan Quisenberry, Kansas City	Bruce Sutter, St. Louis
1985	Dan Quisenberry, Kansas City	Jeff Reardon, Montreal
1986	Dave Righetti, New York	Todd Worrell, St. Louis

THE SPORTING NEWS ROOKIE AWARDS

1946—Combined selection—Delmer Ennis, Philadelphia, N. L., of
1947—Combined selection—Jack Robinson, Brooklyn, 1b
1948—Combined selection—Richie Ashburn, Philadelphia, N. L., of

Year	AMERICAN LEAGUE Player, Club	NATIONAL LEAGUE Player, Club
1949	Roy Sievers, St. Louis, of	Donald Newcombe, Brooklyn, p
1950	Combined selection—Edward Ford, New York, A. L., p	
1951	Orestes Minoso, Chicago, of	Willie Mays, New York, of
1952	Clinton Courtney, St. Louis, c	Joseph Black, Brooklyn, p
1953	Harvey Kuenn, Detroit, ss	James Gilliam, Brooklyn, 2b
1954	Robert Grim, New York, p	Wallace Moon, St. Louis, of
1955	Herbert Score, Cleveland, p	William Virdon, St. Louis, of

THE SPORTING NEWS ROOKIE AWARDS—Continued

Year	AMERICAN LEAGUE	NATIONAL LEAGUE
1956	Luis Aparicio, Chicago, ss	Frank Robinson, Cincinnati, of
1957	Anthony Kubek, New York, inf-of	Edward Bouchee, Philadelphia, 1b
	(No pitcher named)	Jack Sanford, Philadelphia, p
1958	Albert Pearson, Washington, of	Orlando Cepeda, San Francisco, 1b
	Ryne Duren, New York, p	Carlton Willey, Milwaukee, p
1959	W. Robert Allison, Washington, of	Willie McCovey, San Francisco, 1b
1960	Ronald Hansen, Baltimore, ss	Frank Howard, Los Angeles, of
1961	Richard Howser, Kansas City, ss	Billy Williams, Chicago, of
	Donald Schwall, Boston, p	Kenneth Hunt, Cincinnati, p
1962	Thomas Tresh, New York, of-ss	Kenneth Hubbs, Chicago, 2b
1963	Peter Ward, Chicago, 3b	Peter Rose, Cincinnati, 2b
	Gary Peters, Chicago, p	Raymond Culp, Philadelphia, p
1964	Pedro (Tony) Oliva, Minnesota, of	Richard Allen, Philadelphia, 3b
	Wallace Bunker, Baltimore, p	William McCool, Cincinnati, p
1965	Curtis Blefary, Baltimore, of	Joseph Morgan, Houston, 2b
	Marcelino Lopez, California, p	Frank Linzy, San Francisco, p
1966	Tommie Agee, Chicago, of	Tommy Helms, Cincinnati, 3b
	James Nash, Kansas City, p	Donald Sutton, Los Angeles, p
1967	Rod Carew, Minnesota, 2b	Lee May, Cincinnati, 1b
	Tom Phoebus, Baltimore, p	Dick Hughes, St. Louis, p
1968	Del Unser, Washington, of	Johnny Bench, Cincinnati, c
	Stan Bahnsen, New York, p	Jerry Koosman, New York, p
1969	Carlos May, Chicago, of	Coco Laboy, Montreal, 3b
	Mike Nagy, Boston, p	Tom Griffin, Houston, p
1970	Roy Foster, Cleveland, of	Bernie Carbo, Cincinnati, of
	Bert Blyleven, Minnesota, p	Carl Morton, Montreal, p
1971	Chris Chambliss, Cleveland, 1b	Earl Williams, Atlanta, c
	Bill Parsons, Milwaukee, p	Reggie Cleveland, St. Louis, p
1972	Carlton Fisk, Boston, c	Dave Rader, San Francisco, c
	Dick Tidrow, Cleveland, p	Jon Matlack, New York, p
1973	Al Bumbry, Baltimore, of	Gary Matthews, San Francisco, of
	Steve Busby, Kansas City, p	Steve Rogers, Montreal, p
1974	Mike Hargrove, Texas, 1b	Greg Gross, Houston, of
	Frank Tanana, California, p	John D'Acquisto, San Francisco, p
1975	Fred Lynn, Boston, of	Gary Carter, Montreal, of-c
	Dennis Eckersley, Cleveland, p	John Montefusco, San Francisco, p
1976	Butch Wynegar, Minnesota, c	Larry Herndon, San Francisco, of
	Mark Fidrych, Detroit, p	Butch Metzger, San Diego, p
1977	Mitchell Page, Oakland, of	Andre Dawson, Montreal, of
	Dave Rozema, Detroit, p	Bob Owchinko, San Diego, p
1978	Paul Molitor, Milwaukee, 2b	Bob Horner, Atlanta, 3b
	Rich Gale, Kansas City, p	Don Robinson, Pittsburgh, p
1979	Pat Putnam, Texas, 1b	Jeff Leonard, Houston, of
	Mark Clear, California, p	Rick Sutcliffe, Los Angeles, p
1980	Joe Charboneau, Cleveland, of	Lonnie Smith, Philadelphia, of
	Britt Burns, Chicago, p	Bill Gullickson, Montreal, p
1981	Rich Gedman, Boston, c	Tim Raines, Montreal, of
	Dave Righetti, New York, p	Fernando Valenzuela, Los Angeles, p
1982	Cal Ripken, Baltimore, ss-3b	Johnny Ray, Pittsburgh, 2b
	Ed Vande Berg, Seattle, p	Steve Bedrosian, Atlanta, p
1983	Ron Kittle, Chicago, of	Darryl Strawberry, New York, of
	Mike Boddicker, Baltimore, p	Craig McMurtry, Atlanta, p
1984	Alvin Davis, Seattle, 1b	Juan Samuel, Philadelphia, 2b
	Mark Langston, Seattle, p	Dwight Gooden, New York, p
1985	Ozzie Guillen, Chicago, ss	Vince Coleman, St. Louis, of
	Teddy Higuera, Milwaukee, p	Tom Browning, Cincinnati, p
1986	Jose Canseco, Oakland, of	Robby Thompson, San Francisco, 2b
	Mark Eichhorn, Toronto, p	Todd Worrell, St. Louis, p

MAJOR LEAGUE EXECUTIVE

Year	Executive	Club
1936	Branch Rickey	St. Louis NL
1937	Edward Barrow	New York AL
1938	Warren Giles	Cincinnati NL
1939	Larry MacPhail	Brooklyn NL
1940	W. O. Briggs, Sr.	Detroit AL
1941	Edward Barrow	New York AL
1942	Branch Rickey	St. Louis NL
1943	Clark Griffith	Washington AL
1944	Wm. O. DeWitt	St. Louis AL
1945	Philip K. Wrigley	Chicago NL
1946	Thomas A. Yawkey	Boston AL
1947	Branch Rickey	Brooklyn NL
1948	Bill Veeck	Cleveland AL
1949	Robt. Carpenter	Phila'phia NL
1950	George Weiss	New York AL
1951	George Weiss	New York AL
1952	George Weiss	New York AL
1953	Louis Perini	Milwaukee NL
1954	Horace Stoneham	N. York NL
1955	Walter O'Malley	Brooklyn NL
1956	Gabe Paul	Cincinnati NL
1957	Frank Lane	St. Louis NL
1958	Joe L. Brown	Pittsburgh NL
1959	E. J. (Buzzie) Bavasi	L.A. NL
1960	George Weiss	New York AL
1961	Dan Topping	New York AL
1962	Fred Haney	Los Angeles AL
1963	Vaughan (Bing) Devine	St.L.NL
1964	Vaughan (Bing) Devine	St.L.NL
1965	Calvin Griffith	Minnesota AL

MAJOR LEAGUE EXECUTIVE—Continued

Year Executive Club
1966—Lee MacPhail, Commissioner's Office
1967—Dick O'Connell, Boston AL
1968—James Campbell, Detroit AL
1969—John Murphy, New York NL
1970—Harry Dalton, Baltimore AL
1971—Cedric Tallis, Kansas City AL
1972—Roland Hemond, Chicago AL
1973—Bob Howsam, Cincinnati NL
1974—Gabe Paul, New York AL
1975—Dick O'Connell, Boston AL

Year Executive Club
1976—Joe Burke, Kansas City AL
1977—Bill Veeck, Chicago AL
1978—Spec Richardson, San Fran. NL
1979—Hank Peters, Baltimore AL
1980—Tal Smith, Houston NL
1981—John McHale, Montreal NL
1982—Harry Dalton, Milwaukee AL
1983—Hank Peters, Baltimore AL
1984—Dallas Green, Chicago NL
1985—John Schuerholz, Kansas City AL
1986—Frank Cashen, New York NL

MAJOR LEAGUE MANAGER

Year Manager Club
1936—Joe McCarthy, New York AL
1937—Bill McKechnie, Boston NL
1938—Joe McCarthy, New York AL
1939—Leo Durocher, Brooklyn NL
1940—Bill McKechnie, Cincinnati NL
1941—Billy Southworth, St. Louis NL
1942—Billy Southworth, St. Louis NL
1943—Joe McCarthy, New York AL
1944—Luke Sewell, St. Louis AL
1945—Ossie Bluege, Washington AL
1946—Eddie Dyer, St. Louis NL
1947—Bucky Harris, New York AL
1948—Bill Meyer, Pittsburgh NL
1949—Casey Stengel, New York AL
1950—Red Rolfe, Detroit AL
1951—Leo Durocher, New York NL
1952—Eddie Stanky, St. Louis NL
1953—Casey Stengel, New York AL
1954—Leo Durocher, New York NL
1955—Walter Alston, Brooklyn NL
1956—Birdie Tebbetts, Cincinnati NL
1957—Fred Hutchinson, St. Louis NL
1958—Casey Stengel, New York AL
1959—Walter Alston, Los Angeles NL
1960—Danny Murtaugh, Pitts. NL
1961—Ralph Houk, New York AL

Year Manager Club
1962—Bill Rigney, Los Angeles AL
1963—Walter Alston, Los Angeles NL
1964—Johnny Keane, St. Louis NL
1965—Sam Mele, Minnesota AL
1966—Hank Bauer, Baltimore AL
1967—Dick Williams, Boston AL
1968—Mayo Smith, Detroit AL
1969—Gil Hodges, New York NL
1970—Danny Murtaugh, Pittsb'gh NL
1971—Charlie Fox, San Francisco NL
1972—Chuck Tanner, Chicago AL
1973—Gene Mauch, Montreal NL
1974—Bill Virdon, New York AL
1975—Darrell Johnson, Boston AL
1976—Danny Ozark, Philadelphia NL
1977—Earl Weaver, Baltimore AL
1978—George Bamberger, Milw'kee AL
1979—Earl Weaver, Baltimore AL
1980—Bill Virdon, Houston NL
1981—Billy Martin, Oakland AL
1982—Whitey Herzog, St. Louis NL
1983—Tony LaRussa, Chicago AL
1984—Jim Frey, Chicago NL
1985—Bobby Cox, Toronto AL
1986—John McNamara, Boston AL
Hal Lanier, Houston NL

MAJOR LEAGUE PLAYER

Year Player Club
1936—Carl Hubbell, New York NL
1937—Johnny Allen, Cleveland AL
1938—Johnny Vander Meer, Cinn. NL
1939—Joe DiMaggio, New York AL
1940—Bob Feller, Cleveland AL
1941—Ted Williams, Boston AL
1942—Ted Williams, Boston AL
1943—Spud Chandler, New York AL
1944—Marty Marion, St. Louis NL
1945—Hal Newhouser, Detroit AL
1946—Stan Musial, St. Louis NL
1947—Ted Williams, Boston AL
1948—Lou Boudreau, Cleveland AL
1949—Ted Williams, Boston AL
1950—Phil Rizzuto, New York AL
1951—Stan Musial, St. Louis NL
1952—Robin Roberts, Philadelphia NL
1953—Al Rosen, Cleveland AL
1954—Willie Mays, New York NL
1955—Duke Snider, Brooklyn NL
1956—Mickey Mantle, New York AL
1957—Ted Williams, Boston AL
1958—Bob Turley, New York AL
1959—Early Wynn, Chicago AL
1960—Bill Mazeroski, Pittsburgh NL
1961—Roger Maris, New York AL

Year Player Club
1962—Maury Wills, Los Angeles NL
Don Drysdale, Los Angeles NL
1963—Sandy Koufax, Los Angeles NL
1964—Ken Boyer, St. Louis NL
1965—Sandy Koufax, Los Angeles NL
1966—Frank Robinson, Baltimore AL
1967—Carl Yastrzemski, Boston AL
1968—Denny McLain, Detroit AL
1969—Willie McCovey, San Fran. NL
1970—Johnny Bench, Cin. NL
1971—Joe Torre, St. Louis NL
1972—Billy Williams, Chicago NL
1973—Reggie Jackson, Oakland AL
1974—Lou Brock, St. Louis NL
1975—Joe Morgan, Cincinnati NL
1976—Joe Morgan, Cincinnati NL
1977—Rod Carew, Minnesota AL
1978—Ron Guidry, New York AL
1979—Willie Stargell, Pittsburgh NL
1980—George Brett, Kansas City AL
1981—Fernando Valenzuela, Los Angeles NL
1982—Robin Yount, Milwaukee AL
1983—Cal Ripken, Baltimore AL
1984—Ryne Sandberg, Chicago NL
1985—Don Mattingly, New York AL
1986—Roger Clemens, Boston AL

MINOR LEAGUE EXECUTIVE (HIGHER CLASSIFICATIONS)

(Restricted to Class AAA Starting in 1963)

Year Executive Club
1936—Earl Mann, Atlanta, Southern
1937—Robt. LaMotte, Savannah, Sally

Year Executive Club
1938—Louis McKenna, St. Paul, A.A.
1939—Bruce Dudley, Louisville, A.A.

MINOR LEAGUE EXECUTIVE (HIGHER CLASSIFICATIONS)—Continued

Year Manager Club
1940—Roy Hamey, Kansas City, A.A.
1941—Emil Sick, Seattle, PCL
1942—Bill Veeck, Milwaukee, A.A.
1943—Clar. Rowland, Los Angeles, PCL
1944—William Mulligan, Seattle, PCL
1945—Bruce Dudley, Louisville, A.A.
1946—Earl Mann, Atlanta, Southern
1947—Wm. Purnhage, Waterloo, I.I.I.
1948—Ed. Glennon, Bir'ham, Southern
1949—Ted Sullivan, Indianapolis, A.A.
1950—Cl. (Brick) Laws, Oakland, PCL
1951—Robert Howsam, Denver, West.
1952—Jack Cooke, Toronto, Int.
1953—Richard Burnett, Dallas, Texas
1954—Edward Stumpf, Indpls., A.A.
1955—Dewey Soriano, Seattle, PCL
1956—Robert Howsam, Denver, A.A.
1957—John Stiglmeier, Buffalo, Int.
1958—Ed. Glennon, Bir'ham, Southern
1959—Ed. Leishman, Salt Lake, PCL
1960—Ray Winder, Little Rock, Sou.
1961—Elten Schiller, Omaha, A.A.
1962—Geo. Sisler, Jr., Rochester, Int.
1963—Lewis Matlin, Hawaii, PCL

Year Manager Club
1964—Ed. Leishman, San Diego, PCL
1965—Harold Cooper, Columbus, Int.
1966—John Quinn, Jr., Hawaii, PCL
1967—Hillman Lyons, Richmond, Int.
1968—Gabe Paul, Jr., Tulsa, PCL
1969—Bill Gardner, Louisville, Int.
1970—Dick King, Wichita, A.A.
1971—Carl Steinfeldt, Jr., Roch'ter, Int.
1972—Don Labbruzzo, Evansville, A.A.
1973—Merle Miller, Tucson, PCL
1974—John Carbray, Sacramento, PCL
1975—Stan Naccarato, Tacoma, PCL
1976—Art Teece, Salt Lake City, PCL
1977—George Sisler, Jr., Col'bus, Int.
1978—Willie Sanchez, Albu'que, PCL
1979—George Sisler, Jr., Col'bus, Int.
1980—Jim Burris, Denver, A.A.
1981—Pat McKernan, Albuquerque, PCL
1982—A. Ray Smith, Louisville, A.A.
1983—A. Ray Smith, Louisville, A.A.
1984—Mike Tamburro, Pawtucket, Int.
1985—Patty Cox Hampton, Okla City, A.A.
1986—Bob Goughan, Rochester, Int.

MINOR LEAGUE EXECUTIVE (LOWER CLASSIFICATIONS)

(Separate Awards for Class AA and Class A Started in 1963)

Year Executive Club
1950—H. Cooper, Hutch'son, West. A.
1951—O. W. (Bill) Hayes, T'ple, B.S.
1952—Hillman Lyons, Danville, MOV
1953—Carl Roth, Peoria, III
1954—James Meaghan, Cedar R., III
1955—John Petrakis, Dubuque, MOV
1956—Marvin Milkes, Fresno, Calif.
1957—Richard Wagner, L'coln, West.
1958—Gerald Waring, Macon, Sally
1959—Clay Dennis, Des Moines, III
1960—Hubert Kittle, Yakima, Northw.
1961—David Steele, Fresno, California
1962—John Quinn, Jr., S. Jose, Calif.
1963—Hugh Finnerty, Tulsa, Texas
Ben Jewell, M. Valley, Pioneer
1964—Glynn West, Birmingham, Sou.
Jas. Bayens, Rock Hill, W. Car.
1965—Dick Butler, Dallas-Ft.W., Tex.
Ken. Blackman, Quad C., Midw.
1966—Tom Fleming, Evansville, South.
Cappy Harada, Lodi, California
1967—Robt. Quinn, Reading, East.
Pat Williams, Spar'burg, W. C.
1968—Phil Howser, Charlotte, South.
Merle Miller, Burlington, Midw.
1969—Charlie Blaney, Albuq., Texas
Bill Gorman, Visalia, Calif.
1970—Carl Sawatski, Arkansas, Texas
Bob Williams, Bakersfield, Calif.
1971—Miles Wolff, Savannah, Dixie A.
Ed Holtz, Appleton, Midwest

Year Executive Club
1972—John Begzos, S. Antonio, Texas
Bob Piccinini, Modesto, Calif.
1973—Dick Kravitz, Jacksonville, Sou.
Fritz Colschen, Clinton, Midw.
1974—Jim Paul, El Paso, Texas
Bing Russell, Portland, N'west
1975—Jim Paul, El Paso, Texas
Cordy Jensen, Eugene, N'west
1976—Woodrow Reid, Chat'ooga, Sou.
Don Buchheister, Ced. Rap., Mid.
1977—Jim Paul, El Paso, Texas
Harry Pells, Quad Cities, Midw.
1978—Larry Schmittou, Nashville, Sou.
Dave Hersh, Appleton, Midwest
1979—Bill Rigney Jr., Midland, Tex.
Tom Romenesko, G'sboro, W.C.
1980—Frances Crockett, C'lotte, Sou.
Tom Romenesko, G'sboro, W.C.
1981—Allie Prescott, Memphis, Southern
Dan Overstreet, Hagerstown, Caro.
1982—Art Clarkson, Birmingham, Sou.
Bob Carruesco, Stockton, Calif.
1983—Edward Kenney, New Britain, East.
Terry Reynolds, Vero Beach, Fla. St.
1984—Bruce Baldwin, Greenville, Sou.
Dave Tarrolly, Beloit, Midwest
1985—Ben Bernard, Albany-Colonie, Eastern
Pete Vonachen, Peoria, Midwest
1986—Bill Davidson, Midland, Texas
Rob Dlugozima, Durham, Carolina

MINOR LEAGUE MANAGER

Year Manager Club
1936—Al Sothoron, Milwaukee, A.A.
1937—Jake Flowers, Salis'y, East. Sh.
1938—Paul Richards, Atlanta, South.
1939—Bill Meyer, Kansas City, A.A.
1940—Larry Gilbert, Nashville, South.
1941—Burt Shotton, Columbus, A.A.
1942—Eddie Dyer, Columbus, A.A.
1943—Nick Cullop, Columbus, A.A.
1944—Al Thomas, Baltimore, Int.
1945—Lefty O'Doul, San Fran., PCL
1946—Clay Hopper, Montreal, Int.
1947—Nick Cullop, Milwaukee, A.A.
1948—Casey Stengel, Oakland, PCL

Year Manager Club
1949—Fred Haney, Hollywood, PCL
1950—Rollie Hemsley, Columbus, A.A.
1951—Charlie Grimm, Milw., A.A.
1952—Luke Appling, Memphis, South.
1953—Bobby Bragan, Hollywood, PCL
1954—Kerby Farrell, Indpls., A.A.
1955—Bill Rigney, Minneapolis, A.A.
1956—Kerby Farrell, Indpls., A.A.
1957—Ben Geraghty, Wichita, A.A.
1958—Cal Ermer, Birmingham, South.
1959—Pete Reiser, Victoria, Texas
1960—Mel McGaha, Toronto, Int.
1961—Kerby Farrell, Buffalo, Int.

MINOR LEAGUE MANAGER—Continued

Year Manager Club
1962—Ben Geraghty, Jackson'le, Int.
1963—Rollie Hemsley, Indpls., Int.
1964—Harry Walker, Jacks'vle., Int.
1965—Grady Hatton, Okla. City, PCL
1966—Bob Lemon, Seattle, PCL
1967—Bob Skinner, San Diego, PCL
1968—Jack Tighe, Toledo, Int.
1969—Clyde McCullough, Tide., Int.
1970—Tom Lasorda, Spokane, PCL
1971—Del Rice, Salt Lake City, PCL
1972—Hank Bauer, Tidewater, Int.
1973—Joe Morgan, Charleston, Int.
1974—Joe Altobelli, Rochester, Int.

Year Manager Club
1975—Joe Frazier, Tidewater, Int.
1976—Vern Rapp, Denver, A.A.
1977—Tommy Thompson, Arkan., Tex.
1978—Les Moss, Evansville, A.A.
1979—Vern Benson, Syracuse, Int.
1980—Hal Lanier, Springfield, A.A.
1981—Del Crandall, Albuquerque, PCL
1982—George Scherger, Indianapolis, A.A.
1983—Bill Dancy, Reading, East.
1984—Bob Rodgers, Indianapolis, A.A.
1985—Jim Fregosi, Louisville, A.A.
1986—Joe Sparks, Indianapolis, A.A.

MINOR LEAGUE PLAYER

Year Player Club
1936—Jn. Vander Meer, Durham, Pied.
1937—Charlie Keller, Newark, Int.
1938—Fred Hutchinson, Seattle, PCL
1939—Lou Novikoff, Tulsa-Los A'les.
1940—Phil Rizzuto, Kansas City, A.A.
1941—John Lindell, Newark, Int.
1942—Dick Barrett, Seattle, PCL
1943—Chet Covington, Scranton, East.
1944—Rip Collins, Albany, Eastern
1945—Gil Coan, Chattanooga, South.
1946—Sibby Sisti, Indianapolis, A.A.
1947—Hank Sauer, Syracuse, Int.
1948—Gene Woodling, S. F., PCL
1949—Orie Arntzen, Albany, Eastern
1950—Frank Saucier, San Ant'o, Tex.
1951—Gene Conley, Hartford, Eastern
1952—Bill Skowron, Kans. City, A.A.
1953—Gene Conley, Toledo, A.A.
1954—Herb Score, Indianapolis, A.A.
1955—John Murff, Dallas, Texas
1956—Steve Bilko, Los Angeles, PCL
1957—Norm Siebern, Denver, A.A.
1958—Jim O'Toole, Nashville, South.
1959—Frank Howard, Victoria-Spok.
1960—Willie Davis, Spokane, PCL
1961—Howie Koplitz, Bir'ham, South.

Year Player Club
1962—Bob Bailey, Columbus, Int.
1963—Don Buford, Indianapolis, Int.
1964—Mel Stottlemyre, Richm'd., Int.
1965—Joe Foy, Toronto, International
1966—Mike Epstein, Rochester, Int.
1967—Johnny Bench, Buffalo, Int.
1968—Merv Rettenmund, Roch'ter, Int.
1969—Danny Walton, Okla. City, A.A.
1970—Don Baylor, Rochester, Int.
1971—Bobby Grich, Rochester, Int.
1972—Tom Paciorek, Albuq'que, PCL
1973—Steve Ontiveros, Phoenix, PCL
1974—Jim Rice, Pawtucket, Int.
1975—Hector Cruz, Tulsa, A.A.
1976—Pat Putnam, Asheville, W. Car.
1977—Ken Landreaux, S.L.C., PCL-El Paso, Tex.
1978—Champ Summers, Indi'polis, A.A.
1979—Mark Bomback, Vancouver, PCL
1980—Tim Raines, Denver, A.A.
1981—Mike Marshall, Albuquerque, PCL
1982—Ron Kittle, Edmonton, PCL
1983—Kevin McReynolds, Las Vegas, PCL
1984—Alan Knicely, Wichita, A.A.
1985—Jose Canseco, Hunt., Sou.-Tac., PCL
1986—Tim Pyznarski, Las Vegas, PCL

Major League All-Star Teams

1925

Bottomley, St. Louis NL 1B
Hornsby, St. Louis NL 2B
Wright, Pittsburgh NL .... SS
Traynor, Pittsburgh NL 3B
Cuyler, Pittsburgh NL .... OF
Carey, Pittsburgh NL .... OF
Goslin, Washington AL .... OF
Cochrane, Philadelphia AL C
Johnson, Washington AL .... P
Rommel, Philadelphia AL .... P
Vance, Brooklyn NL .... P

1926

G. Burns, Cleve. AL
Hornsby, St. Louis NL
J. Sewell, Cleve. AL
Traynor, Pittsburgh NL
Goslin, Wash'ton AL
Mostil, Chicago AL
Ruth, New York AL
O'Farrell, St. Louis NL
Pennock, N. Y. AL
Uhle, Cleveland AL
Alexander, St. L. NL

1927

1B—Gehrig, N. Y. AL
2B—Hornsby, N. Y. NL
SS—Jackson, N. Y. NL
3B—Traynor, Pitts. NL
OF—Ruth, New York AL
OF—Simmons, Phila. AL
OF—P. Waner, Pitts. NL
C—Hartnett, Chicago NL
P—Root, Chicago NL
P—Lyons, Chicago AL

1928

Gehrig, New York AL 1B
Hornsby, Boston NL 2B
Jackson, New York NL .... SS
Lindstrom, N. Y. NL 3B
Ruth, New York AL .... OF
Manush, St. Louis AL .... OF
P. Waner, Pittsburgh NL .... OF
Cochrane, Philadelphia AL C
Grove, Philadelphia AL .... P
Hoyt, New York AL .... P

1929

Foxx, Phila'phia AL
Hornsby, Chicago NL
Jackson, N. Y. NL
Traynor, Pittsb'gh NL
Simmons, Phila. AL
L. Wilson, Chi. NL
Ruth, New York AL
Cochrane, Phila. AL
Grove, Phila'phia AL
Grimes, Pittsburgh NL

1930

1B—Terry, New York NL
2B—Frisch, St. Louis NL
SS—Cronin, Wash'ton AL
3B—Lindstrom, N. Y. NL
OF—Simmons, Phila. AL
OF—L. Wilson, Chi. NL
OF—Ruth, New York AL
C—Cochrane, Phila AL
P—Grove, Phila'phia AL
P—W. Ferrell, Cleve. AL

1931

Gehrig, New York AL ... 1B
Frisch, St. Louis NL ... 2B
Cronin, Washington AL ... SS
Traynor, Pittsburgh NL ... 3B
Simmons, Philadelphia AL ... OF
Averill, Cleveland AL ... OF
Ruth, New York AL ... OF
Cochrane, Philadelphia AL ... C
Grove, Philadelphia AL ... P
Earnshaw, Philadelphia AL ... P

1932

Foxx, Phila'phia AL
Lazzeri, N. Y. AL
Cronin, Wash'ton AL
Traynor, Pittsb'gh NL
O'Doul, Brooklyn NL
Averill, Cleveland AL
Klein, Philadelphia NL
Dickey, New York AL
Grove, Phila'phia AL
Warneke, Chicago NL

1933

1B—Foxx, Phila'phia AL
2B—Gehringer, Det. AL
SS—Cronin, Wash'ton AL
3B—Traynor, Pitts. NL
OF—Simmons, Chi. AL
OF—Berger, Boston NL
OF—Klein, Phila'phia NL
C—Dickey, N. Y. AL
P—Crowder, Wash. AL
P—Hubbell, N. Y. NL

1934

Gehrig, New York AL ... 1B
Gehringer, Detroit AL ... 2B
Cronin, Washington AL ... SS
Higgins, Philadelphia AL ... 3B
Simmons, Chicago AL ... OF
Averill, Cleveland AL ... OF
Ott, New York NL ... OF
Cochrane, Detroit AL ... C
Gomez, New York AL ... P
Rowe, Detroit AL ... P
J. Dean, St. Louis NL ... P

1935

Greenberg, Det. AL
Gehringer, Det. AL
Vaughan, Pitts. NL
J. Martin, St. L. NL
Medwick, St. L. NL
Cramer, Phila. AL
Ott, New York NL
Cochrane, Detroit AL
Hubbell, N. Y. NL
J. Dean, St. Louis NL

1936

1B—Gehrig, New York AL
2B—Gehringer, Det. AL
SS—Appling, Chicago AL
3B—Higgins, Phila. AL
OF—Medwick, St. L. NL
OF—Averill, Cleve. AL
OF—Ott, New York NL
C—Dickey, N. Y. AL
P—Hubbell, N. Y. NL
P—J. Dean, St. Louis NL

1937

Gehrig, New York AL ... 1B
Gehringer, Detroit AL ... 2B
Bartell, New York NL ... SS
Rolfe, New York AL ... 3B
Medwick, St. Louis NL ... OF
J. DiMaggio, New York AL ... OF
P. Waner, Pittsburgh NL ... OF
Hartnett, Chicago NL ... C
Hubbell, New York NL ... P
Ruffing, New York AL ... P

1938

Foxx, Boston AL
Gehringer, Detroit AL
Cronin, Boston AL
Rolfe, New York AL
Medwick, St. Louis NL
J. DiMaggio, N. Y. AL
Ott, New York NL
Dickey, New York AL
Ruffing, New York AL
Gomez, New York AL
Vander Meer, Cin. NL

1939

1B—Foxx, Boston AL
2B—Gordon, N. Y. AL
SS—Cronin, Boston AL
3B—Rolfe, New York AL
OF—Medwick, St. L. NL
OF—J. DiMaggio, N. Y. AL
OF—Williams, Boston AL
C—Dickey, N. Y. AL
P—Ruffing, N. Y. AL
P—Feller, Cleveland AL
P—Walters, Cin. NL

1940

F. McCormick, Cin. NL ... 1B
Gordon, New York AL ... 2B
Appling, Chicago AL ... SS
Hack, Chicago NL ... 3B
Greenberg, Detroit AL ... OF
J. DiMaggio, New York AL ... OF
Williams, Boston AL ... OF
Danning, New York NL ... C
Feller, Cleveland AL ... P
Walters, Cincinnati NL ... P
Derringer, Cincinnati NL ... P

1941

Camilli, Brooklyn NL
Gordon, N. Y. AL
Travis, Wash'ton, AL
Hack, Chicago NL
Williams, Boston AL
J. DiMaggio, N. Y. AL
Reiser, Brooklyn NL
Dickey, New York AL
Feller, Cleveland AL
Wyatt, Brooklyn NL
Lee, Chicago NL

1942

1B—Mize, New York NL
2B—Gordon, N. Y. AL
SS—Pesky, Boston AL
3B—Hack, Chicago NL
OF—Williams, Boston AL
OF—J. DiMaggio, N. Y. AL
OF—Slaughter, St. L. NL
C—Owen, Brooklyn NL
P—M. Cooper, St. L. NL
P—Bonham, N. Y. AL
P—Hughson, Boston AL

1943

York, Detroit AL ... 1B
Herman, Brooklyn NL ... 2B
Appling, Chicago AL ... SS
Johnson, New York AL ... 3B
Wakefield, Detroit AL ... OF
Musial, St. Louis NL ... OF
Nicholson, Chicago NL ... OF
W. Cooper, St. Louis NL ... C
Chandler, New York AL ... P
M. Cooper, St. Louis NL ... P
Sewell, Pittsburgh NL ... P

1944

Sanders, St. Louis NL
Doerr, Boston AL
Marion, St. Louis NL
Elliott, Pittsburgh NL
Musial, St. Louis NL
Wakefield, Detroit AL
F. Walker, Brkn, NL
W. Cooper, St. L. NL
Newhouser, Det. AL
M. Cooper, St. L. NL
Trout, Detroit AL

1945

1B—Cavarretta, Chi. NL
2B—Stirnweiss, N. Y. AL
SS—Marion, St. Louis NL
3B—Kurowski, St. L. NL
OF—Holmes, Boston NL
OF—Pafko, Chicago NL
OF—Rosen, Brooklyn NL
C—Richards, Detroit AL
P—Newhouser, Det. AL
P—Ferriss, Boston AL
P—Borowy, Chicago NL

1946

Musial, St. Louis NL ... 1B
Doerr, Boston AL ... 2B
Pesky, Boston AL ... SS
Kell, Detroit AL ... 3B
Williams, Boston AL ... OF
D. DiMaggio, Boston AL ... OF
Slaughter, St. Louis NL ... OF
Robinson, New York AL ... C
Newhouser, Detroit AL ... P
Feller, Cleveland AL ... P
Ferriss, Boston AL ... P

1947

Mize, New York NL
Gordon, Cleveland AL
Boudreau, Cleve. AL
Kell, Detroit AL
Williams, Boston AL
J. DiMaggio, N. Y. AL
Kiner, Pittsburgh NL
W. Cooper, N. Y. NL
Blackwell, Cin. NL
Feller, Cleveland AL
Branca, Brooklyn NL

1948

1B—Mize, New York NL
2B—Gordon, Cleve. AL
SS—Boudreau, Cleve. AL
3B—Elliott, Boston NL
OF—Williams, Boston AL
OF—J. DiMaggio, N. Y. AL
OF—Musial, St. Louis NL
C—Tebbetts, Boston AL
P—Sain, Boston NL
P—Lemon, Cleveland AL
P—Brecheen, St. L. NL

1949

Henrich, New York AL 1B
Robinson, Brooklyn NL 2B
Rizzuto, New York AL............ SS
Kell, Detroit AL 3B
Williams, Boston AL .... OF
Musial, St. Louis NL................ OF
Kiner, Pittsburgh NL................ OF
Campanella, Brooklyn NL....... C
Parnell, Boston AL .... P
Kinder, Boston AL .... P
Page, New York AL .... P

1950

Dropo, Boston AL
Robinson, Brkn. NL
Rizzuto, New York AL
Kell, Detroit AL
Musial, St. Louis NL
Kiner, Pittsburgh NL
Doby, Cleveland AL
Berra, New York AL
Raschi, New York AL
Lemon, Cleveland AL
Konstanty, Phila. NL

1951

1B—Fain, Phila. AL
2B—Robinson, Brkn. NL
SS—Rizzuto, N. Y. AL
3B—Kell, Detroit AL
OF—Musial, St. Louis NL
OF—Williams, Boston AL
OF—Kiner, Pittsburgh NL
C—Campanella, Brkn. NL
P—Maglie, N. Y. NL
P—Roe, Brooklyn NL
P—Reynolds, N. Y. AL

1952

Fain, Philadelphia AL 1B
Robinson, Brooklyn NL 2B
Rizzuto, New York AL............. SS
Kell, Boston AL 3B
Musial, St. Louis NL................ OF
Sauer, Chicago NL................... OF
Mantle, New York AL .... OF
Berra, New York AL................ C
Roberts, Philadelphia NL .... P
Shantz, Philadelphia AL.......... P
Reynolds, New York AL.......... P

1953

Vernon, Wash'ton AL
Schoendienst, St. L. NL
Reese, Brooklyn NL
Rosen, Cleveland AL
Musial, St. Louis NL
Snider, Brooklyn NL
Furillo, Brooklyn NL
Campanella, Brkn. NL
Roberts, Phila'phia NL
Spahn, Milwaukee NL
Porterfield, Wash. AL

1954

1B—Kluszewski, Cin. NL
2B—Avila, Cleveland AL
SS—Dark, New York NL
3B—Rosen, Cleveland AL
OF—Mays, New York NL
OF—Musial, St. Louis NL
OF—Snider, Brooklyn NL
C—Berra, New York AL
P—Lemon, Cleveland AL
P—Antonelli, N. Y. NL
P—Roberts, Phila. NL

1955

Kluszewski, Cincinnati NL...... 1B
Fox, Chicago AL...................... 2B
Banks, Chicago NL.................. SS
Mathews, Milwaukee NL......... 3B
Snider, Brooklyn NL .... OF
Williams, Boston AL .... OF
Kaline, Detroit AL................... OF
Campanella, Brooklyn NL....... C
Roberts, Philadelphia NL .... P
Newcombe, Brooklyn NL........ P
Ford, New York AL .... P

1956

Kluszewski, Cin. NL
Fox, Chicago AL
Kuenn, Detroit AL
Boyer, St. Louis NL
Mantle, New York AL
Aaron, Milwaukee NL
Williams, Boston AL
Berra, New York AL
Newcombe, Brkn. NL
Ford, New York AL
Pierce, Chicago AL

1957

1B—Musial, St. Louis NL
2B—Scho'st, N.Y.-Mil. NL
SS—McDougald, N. Y. AL
3B—Mathews, Milw. NL
OF—Mantle, N. Y. AL
OF—Williams, Boston AL
OF—Mays, New York NL
C—Berra, New York AL
P—Spahn, Milw. NL
P—Pierce, Chicago NL
P—Bunning, Detroit AL

1958

Musial, St. Louis NL................ 1B
Fox, Chicago AL...................... 2B
Banks, Chicago NL.................. SS
Thomas, Pittsburgh NL 3B
Williams, Boston AL .... OF
Mays, San Francisco NL......... OF
Aaron, Milwaukee NL .... OF
Crandall, Milwaukee NL C
Turley, New York AL .... P
Spahn, Milwaukee NL .... P
Friend, Pittsburgh NL............. P

1959

Cepeda, San Fran. NL
Fox, Chicago AL
Banks, Chicago NL
Mathews, Milw. NL
Minoso, Cleveland AL
Mays, San Fran. NL
Aaron, Milwaukee NL
Lollar, Chicago AL
Wynn, Chicago AL
S. Jones, S. Fran. NL
Antonelli, S. Fran. NL

1960

1B—Skowron, N. Y. AL
2B—Mazeroski, Pitts. NL
SS—Banks, Chicago NL
3B—Mathews, Milw. NL
OF—Minoso, Chicago AL
OF—Mays, San Fran. NL
OF—Maris, New York AL
C—Crandall, Milw. NL
P—Law, Pittsburgh NL
P—Spahn, Milw. NL
P—Broglio, St. Louis NL

1961—National

1B—Orlando Cepeda, S.F.
2B—Frank Bolling, Milw.
SS—Maury Wills, L.A.
3B—Ken Boyer, St. Louis
OF—Willie Mays, S.F.
OF—Frank Robinson, Cin.
OF—Roberto Clemente, Pitts.
C—Smoky Burgess, Pitts.
P—Joey Jay, Cincinnati
P—Warren Spahn, Milw.

1961—American

1B—Norm Cash, Detroit
2B—Bobby Richardson, N.Y.
SS—Tony Kubek, N.Y.
3B—Brooks Robinson, Balt.
OF—Mickey Mantle, N.Y.
OF—Roger Maris, N.Y.
OF—Rocky Colavito, Detroit
C—Elston Howard, N.Y.
P—Whitey Ford, N.Y.
P—Frank Lary, Detroit

1962—National

1B—Orlando Cepeda, S.F.
2B—Bill Mazeroski, Pitts.
SS—Maury Wills, L.A.
3B—Ken Boyer, St. Louis
OF—Tommy Davis, L.A.
OF—Willie Mays, S.F.
OF—Frank Robinson, Cin.
C—Del Crandall, Milw.
P—Don Drysdale, L.A.
P—Bob Purkey, Cin.

1962—American

1B—Norm Siebern, K.C.
2B—Bobby Richardson, N.Y.
SS—Tom Tresh, N.Y.
3B—Brooks Robinson, Balt.
OF—Leon Wagner, L.A.
OF—Mickey Mantle, N.Y.
OF—Al Kaline, Detroit
C—Earl Battey, Minnesota
P—Ralph Terry, N.Y.
P—Dick Donovan, Cleve.

1963—National

1B—Bill White, St. Louis
2B—Jim Gilliam, L.A.
SS—Dick Groat, St. Louis
3B—Ken Boyer, St. Louis
OF—Tommy Davis, L.A.
OF—Willie Mays, S.F.
OF—Hank Aaron, Milw.
C—John Edwards, Cin.
P—Sandy Koufax, L.A.
P—Juan Marichal, S.F.

1963—American

1B—Joe Pepitone, N.Y.
2B—Bobby Richardson, N.Y.
SS—Luis Aparicio, Balt.
3B—Frank Malzone, Boston
OF—Carl Yastrzemski, Boston
OF—Albie Pearson, L.A.
OF—Al Kaline, Detroit
C—Elston Howard, N.Y.
P—Whitey Ford, N.Y.
P—Gary Peters, Chicago

1964—American
1B—Dick Stuart, Boston
2B—Bobby Richardson, N.Y.
SS—Jim Fregosi, L.A.
3B—Brooks Robinson, Balt.
OF—Harmon Killebrew, Minn.
OF—Mickey Mantle, N.Y.
OF—Tony Oliva, Minn.
C—Elston Howard, N.Y.
P—Dean Chance, L.A.
P—Gary Peters, Chicago

1964—National
1B—Bill White, St. Louis
2B—Ron Hunt, New York
SS—Dick Groat, St. Louis
3B—Ken Boyer, St. Louis
OF—Billy Williams, Chicago
OF—Willie Mays, San Fran.
OF—Roberto Clemente, Pitts.
C—Joe Torre, Milwaukee
P—Sandy Koufax, L.A.
P—Jim Bunning, Phila.

1965—American
1B—Fred Whitfield, Cleveland
2B—Bobby Richardson, N.Y.
SS—Zoilo Versalles, Minnesota
3B—Brooks Robinson, Balt.
OF—Carl Yastrzemski, Boston
OF—Jimmie Hall, Minnesota
OF—Tony Oliva, Minnesota
C—Earl Battey, Minnesota
P—Jim Grant, Minnesota
P—Mel Stottlemyre, N.Y.

1965—National
1B—Willie McCovey, S.F.
2B—Pete Rose, Cincinnati
SS—Maury Wills, Los Angeles
3B—Deron Johnson, Cincinnati
OF—Willie Stargell, Pitts.
OF—Willie Mays, San Fran.
OF—Hank Aaron, Milwaukee
C—Joe Torre, Milwaukee
P—Sandy Koufax, L.A.
P—Juan Marichal, S.F.

1966—American
1B—Boog Powell, Baltimore
2B—Bobby Richardson, N.Y.
SS—Luis Aparicio, Baltimore
3B—Brooks Robinson, Balt.
OF—Frank Robinson, Balt.
OF—Al Kaline, Detroit
OF—Tony Oliva, Minnesota
C—Paul Casanova, Wash.
P—Jim Kaat, Minnesota
P—Earl Wilson, Detroit

1966—National
1B—Felipe Alou, Atlanta
2B—Pete Rose, Cincinnati
SS—Gene Alley, Pittsburgh
3B—Ron Santo, Chicago
OF—Willie Stargell, Pittsburgh
OF—Willie Mays, San Fran.
OF—Roberto Clemente, Pitts.
C—Joe Torre, Atlanta
P—Sandy Koufax, L.A.
P—Juan Marichal, S.F.

1967—American
1B—Harmon Killebrew, Minn.
2B—Rod Carew, Minnesota
SS—Jim Fregosi, California
3B—Brooks Robinson, Balt.
OF—Carl Yastrzemski, Boston
OF—Al Kaline, Detroit
OF—Frank Robinson, Balt.
C—Bill Freehan, Detroit
P—Jim Lonborg, Boston
P—Earl Wilson, Detroit

1967—National
1B—Orlando Cepeda, St. Louis
2B—Bill Mazeroski, Pittsburgh
SS—Gene Alley, Pittsburgh
3B—Ron Santo, Chicago
OF—Hank Aaron, Atlanta
OF—Jim Wynn, Houston
OF—Roberto Clemente, Pitts.
C—Tim McCarver, St. Louis
P—Mike McCormick, S.F.
P—Ferguson Jenkins, Chi.

1968—American
1B—Boog Powell, Baltimore
2B—Rod Carew, Minnesota
SS—Luis Aparicio, Chicago
3B—Brooks Robinson, Balt.
OF—Ken Harrelson, Boston
OF—Willie Horton, Detroit
OF—Frank Howard, Wash.
C—Bill Freehan, Detroit
P—Dave McNally, Balt.
P—Denny McLain, Detroit

1968—National
1B—Willie McCovey, S.F.
2B—Tommy Helms, Cincinnati
SS—Don Kessinger, Chicago
3B—Ron Santo, Chicago
OF—Billy Williams, Chicago
OF—Curt Flood, St. Louis
OF—Pete Rose, Cincinnati
C—Johnny Bench, Cincinnati
P—Bob Gibson, St. Louis
P—Juan Marichal, S.F.

1969—American
1B—Boog Powell, Baltimore
2B—Rod Carew, Minnesota
SS—Rico Petrocelli, Boston
3B—Harmon Killebrew, Minn.
OF—Frank Howard, Wash.
OF—Paul Blair, Baltimore
OF—Reggie Jackson, Oak.
C—Bill Freehan, Detroit
RHP—Denny McLain, Detroit
LHP—Mike Cuellar, Baltimore

1969—National
1B—Willie McCovey, S.F.
2B—Glenn Beckert, Chicago
SS—Don Kessinger, Chicago
3B—Ron Santo, Chicago
OF—Cleon Jones, New York
OF—Matty Alou, Pittsburgh
OF—Hank Aaron, Atlanta
C—Johnny Bench, Cincinnati
RHP—Tom Seaver, New York
LHP—Steve Carlton, St. Louis

1970—American
1B—Boog Powell, Baltimore
2B—Dave Johnson, Baltimore
SS—Luis Aparicio, Chicago
3B—Harmon Killebrew, Minn.
OF—Frank Howard, Wash.
OF—Reggie Smith, Boston
OF—Tony Oliva, Minnesota
C—Ray Fosse, Cleveland
RHP—Jim Perry, Minnesota
LHP—Sam McDowell, Cleve.

1970—National
1B—Willie McCovey, S.F.
2B—Glenn Beckert, Chicago
SS—Don Kessinger, Chicago
3B—Tony Perez, Cincinnati
OF—Billy Williams, Chicago
OF—Bobby Tolan, Cincinnati
OF—Hank Aaron, Atlanta
C—Johnny Bench, Cincinnati
RHP—Bob Gibson, St. Louis
LHP—Jim Merritt, Cincinnati

1971—American
1B—Norm Cash, Detroit
2B—Cookie Rojas, K.C.
SS—Leo Cardenas, Minnesota
3B—Brooks Robinson, Balt.
OF—Merv Rettenmund, Balt.
OF—Bobby Murcer, N.Y.
OF—Tony Oliva, Minnesota
C—Bill Freehan, Detroit
RHP—Jim Palmer, Baltimore
LHP—Vida Blue, Oakland

1971—National
1B—Lee May, Cincinnati
2B—Glenn Beckett, Chicago
SS—Bud Harrelson, New York
3B—Joe Torre, St. Louis
OF—Willie Stargell, Pittsburgh
OF—Willie Davis, Los Angeles
OF—Hank Aaron, Atlanta
C—Manny Sanguillen, Pitts.
RHP—Ferguson Jenkins, Chi.
LHP—Steve Carlton, St. Louis

1972—American
1B—Dick Allen, Chicago
2B—Rod Carew, Minnesota
SS—Luis Aparicio, Boston
3B—Brooks Robinson, Balt.
OF—Joe Rudi, Oakland
OF—Bobby Murcer, N.Y.
OF—Richie Scheinblum, K.C.
C—Carlton Fisk, Boston
RHP—Gaylord Perry, Cleveland
LHP—Wilbur Wood, Chicago

1972—National
1B—Willie Stargell, Pittsburgh
2B—Joe Morgan, Cincinnati
SS—Chris Speier, San Fran.
3B—Ron Santo, Chicago
OF—Billy Williams, Chicago
OF—Cesar Cedeno, Houston
OF—Roberto Clemente, Pitts.
C—Johnny Bench, Cincinnati
RHP—Ferguson Jenkins, Chi.
LHP—Steve Carlton, Phila.

1973—American

1B—John Mayberry, K.C.
2B—Rod Carew, Minnesota
SS—Bert Campaneris, Oak.
3B—Sal Bando, Oakland
OF—Reggie Jackson, Oak.
OF—Amos Otis, Kansas City
OF—Bobby Murcer, N.Y.
C—Thurman Munson, N.Y.
RHP—Jim Palmer, Baltimore
LHP—Ken Holtzman, Oakland

1973—National

1B—Tony Perez, Cincinnati
2B—Dave Johnson, Atlanta
SS—Bill Russell, Los Angeles
3B—Darrell Evans, Atlanta
OF—Bobby Bonds, San Fran.
OF—Cesar Cedeno, Houston
OF—Pete Rose, Cincinnati
C—Johnny Bench, Cincinnati
RHP—Tom Seaver, New York
LHP—Ron Bryant, San Fran.

1974—American

1B—Dick Allen, Chicago
2B—Rod Carew, Minnesota
SS—Bert Campaneris, Oak.
3B—Sal Bando, Oakland
OF—Joe Rudi, Oakland
OF—Paul Blair, Baltimore
OF—Jeff Burroughs, Texas
C—Thurman Munson, N.Y.
DH—Tommy Davis, Baltimore
RHP—Jim Hunter, Oakland
LHP—Mike Cuellar, Baltimore

1974—National

1B—Steve Garvey, Los Angeles
2B—Joe Morgan, Cincinnati
SS—Dave Concepcion, Cin.
3B—Mike Schmidt, Phila.
OF—Lou Brock, St. Louis
OF—Jim Wynn, Los Angeles
OF—Richie Zisk, Pittsburgh
C—Johnny Bench, Cincinnati
RHP—Andy Messersmith, L.A.
LHP—Don Gullett, Cincinnati

1975—American

1B—John Mayberry, K.C.
2B—Rod Carew, Minnesota
SS—Toby Harrah, Texas
3B—Graig Nettles, New York
OF—Jim Rice, Boston
OF—Fred Lynn, Boston
OF—Reggie Jackson, Oakland
C—Thurman Munson, N.Y.
DH—Willie Horton, Detroit
RHP—Jim Palmer, Baltimore
LHP—Jim Kaat, Chicago

1975—National

1B—Steve Garvey, Los Ang.
2B—Joe Morgan, Cincinnati
SS—Larry Bowa, Philadelphia
3B—Bill Madlock, Chicago
OF—Greg Luzinski, Phila.
OF—Al Oliver, Pittsburgh
OF—Dave Parker, Pittsburgh
C—Johnny Bench, Cincinnati
RHP—Tom Seaver, New York
LHP—Randy Jones, San Diego

1976—American

1B—Chris Chambliss, N.Y.
2B—Bobby Grich, Baltimore
3B—George Brett, K.C.
SS—Mark Belanger, Balt.
OF—Joe Rudi, Oakland
OF—Mickey Rivers, N.Y.
OF—Reggie Jackson, Balt.
C—Thurman Munson, N.Y.
DH—Hal McRae, Kansas City
RHP—Jim Palmer, Baltimore
LHP—Frank Tanana, Calif.

1976—National

1B—Willie Montanez, S.F.-Atl.
2B—Joe Morgan, Cincinnati
3B—Mike Schmidt, Phila.
SS—Dave Concepcion, Cin.
OF—George Foster, Cincinnati
OF—Cesar Cedeno, Houston
OF—Ken Griffey, Cincinnati
C—Bob Boone, Philadelphia
RHP—Don Sutton, Los Angeles
LHP—Randy Jones, San Diego

1977—American

1B—Rod Carew, Minn.
2B—Willie Randolph, N.Y.
3B—Graig Nettles, N.Y.
SS—Rick Burleson, Boston
OF—Jim Rice, Boston
OF—Larry Hisle, Minn.
OF—Bobby Bonds, Calif.
C—Carlton Fisk, Boston
DH—Hal McRae, K.C.
RHP—Nolan Ryan, Calif.
LHP—Frank Tanana, Calif.

1977—National

1B—Steve Garvey, L.A.
2B—Joe Morgan, Cincinnati
3B—Mike Schmidt, Phila.
SS—Garry Templeton, St. L.
OF—George Foster, Cin.
OF—Dave Parker, Pitts.
OF—Greg Luzinski, Phila.
C—Ted Simmons, St. Louis
RHP—Rick Reuschel, Chicago
LHP—Steve Carlton, Phila.

1978—American

1B—Rod Carew, Minnesota
2B—Frank White, K.C.
3B—Graig Nettles, N.Y.
SS—Robin Yount, Milw.
OF—Jim Rice, Boston
OF—Larry Hisle, Milw.
OF—Fred Lynn, Boston
C—Jim Sundberg, Texas
DH—Rusty Staub, Detroit
RHP—Jim Palmer, Balt.
LHP—Ron Guidry, N.Y.

1978—National

1B—Steve Garvey, L.A.
2B—Dave Lopes, Los Angeles
3B—Pete Rose, Cincinnati
SS—Larry Bowa, Phila.
OF—George Foster, Cin.
OF—Dave Parker, Pitts.
OF—Jack Clark, San Fran.
C—Ted Simmons, St. Louis
RHP—Gaylord Perry, S.D.
LHP—Vida Blue, San Fran.

1979—American

1B—Cecil Cooper, Milw.
2B—Bobby Grich, Calif.
3B—George Brett, K.C.
SS—Roy Smalley, Minn.
OF—Jim Rice, Boston
OF—Fred Lynn, Boston
OF—Ken Singleton, Balt.
C—Darrell Porter, K.C.
DH—Don Baylor, Calif.
RHP—Jim Kern, Texas
LHP—Mike Flanagan, Balt.

1979—National

1B—Keith Hernandez, St. L.
2B—Dave Lopes, Los Angeles
3B—Mike Schmidt, Phila.
SS—Garry Templeton, St. L.
OF—Dave Kingman, Chicago
OF—Omar Moreno, Pittsburgh
OF—Dave Winfield, San Diego
C—Ted Simmons, St. Louis
RHP—Joe Niekro, Houston
LHP—Steve Carlton, Phila.

1980—American

1B—Cecil Cooper, Milw.
2B—Willie Randolph, N.Y.
3B—George Brett, K.C.
SS—Robin Yount, Milw.
OF—Ben Oglivie, Milw.
OF—Al Bumbry, Baltimore
OF—Reggie Jackson, N.Y.
DH—Reggie Jackson, N.Y.
C—Rick Cerone, N.Y.
RHP—Steve Stone, Balt.
LHP—Tommy John, N.Y.

1980—National

1B—Keith Hernandez, St. L.
2B—Manny Trillo, Phila.
3B—Mike Schmidt, Phila.
SS—Garry Templeton, St. L.
OF—Dusty Baker, L.A.
OF—Cesar Cedeno, Houston
OF—George Hendrick, St. L.
C—Gary Carter, Montreal
RHP—Jim Bibby, Pittsburgh
LHP—Steve Carlton, Phila.

1981—American

1B—Cecil Cooper, Milw.
2B—Bobby Grich, Calif.
3B—Buddy Bell, Texas
SS—Rick Burleson, Calif.
OF—Rickey Henderson, Oak.
OF—Dwayne Murphy, Oak.
OF—Tony Armas, Oak.
C—Jim Sundberg, Texas
DH—Richie Zisk, Seattle
RHP—Jack Morris, Detroit
LHP—Ron Guidry, N.Y.

1981—National

1B—Pete Rose, Phila.
2B—Manny Trillo, Phila.
3B—Mike Schmidt, Phila.
SS—Dave Concepcion, Cin.
OF—George Foster, Cin.
OF—Andre Dawson, Mon.
OF—Pedro Guerrero, L.A.
C—Gary Carter, Montreal
RHP—Tom Seaver, Cincinnati
LHP—Fernando Valenzuela, L.A.

1982—American
1B—Cecil Cooper, Milw.
2B—Damaso Garcia, Tor.
3B—Doug DeCinces, Calif.
SS—Robin Yount, Milw.
OF—Dave Winfield, N.Y.
OF—Gorman Thomas, Milw.
OF—Dwight Evans, Boston
C—Lance Parrish, Detroit
DH—Hal McRae, K.C.
RHP—Dave Stieb, Toronto
LHP—Geoff Zahn, Calif.

1982—National
1B—Al Oliver, Montreal
2B—Manny Trillo, Phila.
3B—Mike Schmidt, Phila.
SS—Ozzie Smith, St. Louis
OF—Lonnie Smith, St. Louis
OF—Dale Murphy, Atlanta
OF—Pedro Guerrero, L.A.
C—Gary Carter, Montreal
RHP—Steve Rogers, Montreal
LHP—Steve Carlton, Phila.

1983—American
1B—Eddie Murray, Balt.
2B—Lou Whitaker, Detroit
3B—Wade Boggs, Boston
SS—Cal Ripken, Balt.
OF—Jim Rice, Boston
OF—Dave Winfield, N.Y.
OF—Lloyd Moseby, Toronto
C—Carlton Fisk, Chicago
DH—Greg Luzinski, Chicago
RHP—LaMarr Hoyt, Chicago
LHP—Ron Guidry, New York

1983—National
1B—George Hendrick, St. L.
2B—Glenn Hubbard, Atlanta
3B—Mike Schmidt, Phila.
SS—Dickie Thon, Houston
OF—Dale Murphy, Atlanta
OF—Andre Dawson, Montreal
OF—Tim Raines, Montreal
C—Tony Pena, Pittsburgh
RHP—John Denny, Phila.
LHP—Larry McWilliams, Pitts.

1984—American
1B—Don Mattingly, N.Y.
2B—Lou Whitaker, Detroit
3B—Buddy Bell, Texas
SS—Cal Ripken, Baltimore
OF—Tony Armas, Boston
OF—Dwight Evans, Boston
OF—Dave Winfield, N.Y.
C—Lance Parrish, Detroit
DH—Dave Kingman, Oak.
RHP—Mike Boddicker, Balt.
LHP—Willie Hernandez, Det.

1984—National
1B—Keith Hernandez, N.Y.
2B—Ryne Sandberg, Chicago
3B—Mike Schmidt, Phila.
SS—Ozzie Smith, St. Louis
OF—Dale Murphy, Atlanta
OF—Jose Cruz, Houston
OF—Tony Gwynn, S.D.
C—Gary Carter, Montreal
RHP—Rick Sutcliffe, Chicago
LHP—Mark Thurmond, S.D.

1985—American
1B—Don Mattingly, N.Y.
2B—Damaso Garcia, Tor.
3B—Wade Boggs, Boston
SS—Cal Ripken, Balt.
OF—Rickey Henderson, N.Y.
OF—Harold Baines, Chicago
OF—Phil Bradley, Seattle
C—Carlton Fisk, Chicago
DH—Don Baylor, New York
RHP—Bret Saberhagen, K.C.
LHP—Ron Guidry, New York

1985—National
1B—Keith Hernandez, N.Y.
2B—Tom Herr, St. Louis
3B—Tim Wallach, Mon.
SS—Ozzie Smith, St. L.
OF—Dave Parker, Cin.
OF—Willie McGee, St. L.
OF—Dale Murphy, Atlanta
C—Gary Carter, N.Y.
RHP—Dwight Gooden, N.Y.
LHP—John Tudor, St. Louis

1986—American
1B—Don Mattingly, N.Y.
2B—Tony Bernazard, Cleve.
3B—Wade Boggs, Boston
SS—Tony Fernandez, Tor.
OF—Jim Rice, Boston
OF—George Bell, Toronto
OF—Kirby Puckett, Minn.
C—Rich Gedman, Boston
DH—Don Baylor, Boston
RHP—Roger Clemens, Boston
LHP—Teddy Higuera, Milw.

1986—National
1B—Keith Hernandez, N.Y.
2B—Steve Sax, L.A.
3B—Mike Schmidt, Phila.
SS—Ozzie Smith, St. Louis
OF—Tim Raines, Montreal
OF—Tony Gwynn, San Diego
OF—Dave Parker, Cincinnati
C—Gary Carter, New York
RHP—Mike Scott, Houston
LHP—Fernando Valenzuela, L.A.

Gold Glove Fielding Teams

1957 Majors
P—Shantz, N.Y. AL
C—Lollar, Chicago AL
1B—Hodges, Brooklyn
2B—Fox, Chicago AL
3B—Malzone, Boston
SS—McMillan, Cin.
OF—Minoso, Chicago AL
OF—Mays, N.Y. NL
OF—Kaline, Detroit

1958 American
P—Shantz, New York
C—Lollar, Chicago
1B—Power, Cleveland
2B—Bolling, Detroit
3B—Malzone, Boston
SS—Aparicio, Chicago
OF—Siebern, New York
OF—Piersall, Boston
OF—Kaline, Detroit

1958 National
P—Haddix, Cincinnati
C—Crandall, Milwaukee
1B—Hodges, Los Angeles
2B—Mazeroski, Pitt.
3B—Boyer, St. Louis
SS—McMillan, Cin.
OF—Robinson, Cin.
OF—Mays, San Fran.
OF—Aaron, Milwaukee

1959 American
P—Shantz, New York
C—Lollar, Chicago
1B—Power, Cleveland
2B—Fox, Chicago
3B—Malzone, Boston
SS—Aparicio, Chicago
OF—Minoso, Cleveland
OF—Kaline, Detroit
OF—Jensen, Boston

1959 National
P—Haddix, Pittsburgh
C—Crandall, Milwaukee
1B—Hodges, Los Angeles
2B—Neal, Los Angeles
3B—Boyer, St. Louis
SS—McMillan, Cincinnati
OF—Brandt, San Fran.
OF—Mays, San Francisco
OF—Aaron, Milwaukee

1960 American
P—Shantz, New York
C—Battey, Washington
1B—Power, Cleveland
2B—Fox, Chicago
3B—Robinson, Baltimore
SS—Aparicio, Chicago
OF—Minoso, Chicago
OF—Landis, Chicago
OF—Maris, New York

1960 National
P—Haddix, Pittsburgh
C—Crandall, Milwaukee
1B—White, St. Louis
2B—Mazeroski, Pittsburgh
3B—Boyer, St. Louis
SS—Banks, Chicago
OF—Moon, Los Angeles
OF—Mays, San Francisco
OF—Aaron, Milwaukee

1961 American
P—Lary, Detroit
C—Battey, Chicago
1B—Power, Cleveland
2B—Richardson, N.Y.
3B—Robinson, Baltimore
SS—Aparicio, Chicago
OF—Kaline, Detroit
OF—Piersall, Cleveland
OF—Landis, Chicago

1961 National
P—Shantz, Pittsburgh
C—Roseboro, Los Angeles
1B—White, St. Louis
2B—Mazeroski, Pittsburgh
3B—Boyer, St. Louis
SS—Wills, Los Angeles
OF—Mays, San Francisco
OF—Clemente, Pittsburgh
OF—Pinson, Cincinnati

1962 American
P—Kaat, Minnesota
C—Battey, Minnesota
1B—Power, Minnesota
2B—Richardson, N.Y.
3B—Robinson, Baltimore
SS—Aparicio, Chicago
OF—Landis, Chicago
OF—Mantle, New York
OF—Kaline, Detroit

1962 National
P—Shantz, St. Louis
C—Crandall, Milwaukee
1B—White, St. Louis
2B—Hubbs, Chicago
3B—Davenport, S.F.
SS—Wills, Los Angeles
OF—Mays, San Francisco
OF—Clemente, Pittsburgh
OF—Virdon, Pittsburgh

1963 American
P—Kaat, Minnesota
C—Howard, New York
1B—Power, Minnesota
2B—Richardson, N.Y.
3B—Robinson, Baltimore
SS—Versalles, Minnesota
OF—Kaline, Detroit
OF—Yastrzemski, Boston
OF—Landis, Chicago

1963 National
P—Shantz, St. Louis
C—Edwards, Cincinnati
1B—White, St. Louis
2B—Mazeroski, Pittsburgh
3B—Boyer, St. Louis
SS—Wine, Philadelphia
OF—Mays, San Francisco
OF—Clemente, Pittsburgh
OF—Flood, St. Louis

1964 American
P—Kaat, Minnesota
C—Howard, New York
1B—Power, Los Angeles
2B—Richardson, N.Y.
3B—Robinson, Baltimore
SS—Aparicio, Baltimore
OF—Kaline, Detroit
OF—Landis, Chicago
OF—Davalillo, Cleveland

1964 National
P—Shantz, Philadelphia
C—Edwards, Cincinnati
1B—White, St. Louis
2B—Mazeroski, Pittsburgh
3B—Santo, Chicago
SS—Amaro, Philadelphia
OF—Mays, San Francisco
OF—Clemente, Pittsburgh
OF—Flood, St. Louis

1965 American
P—Kaat, Minnesota
C—Freehan, Detroit
1B—Pepitone, New York
2B—Richardson, N.Y.
3B—Robinson, Baltimore
SS—Versalles, Minnesota
OF—Kaline, Detroit
OF—Tresh, New York
OF—Yastrzemski, Boston

1965 National
P—Gibson, St. Louis
C—Torre, Atlanta
1B—White, St. Louis
2B—Mazeroski, Pittsburgh
3B—Santo, Chicago
SS—Cardenas, Cincinnati
OF—Mays, San Francisco
OF—Clemente, Pittsburgh
OF—Flood, St. Louis

1966 American
P—Kaat, Minnesota
C—Freehan, Detroit
1B—Pepitone, New York
2B—Knoop, California
3B—B. Robinson, Balt.
SS—Aparicio, Baltimore
OF—Kaline, Detroit
OF—Agee, Chicago
OF—Oliva, Minnesota

1966 National
P—Gibson, St. Louis
C—Roseboro, Los Angeles
1B—White, Philadelphia
2B—Mazeroski, Pittsburgh
3B—Santo, Chicago
SS—Alley, Pittsburgh
OF—Mays, San Francisco
OF—Flood, St. Louis
OF—Clemente, Pittsburgh

1967 American
P—Kaat, Minnesota
C—Freehan, Detroit
1B—Scott, Boston
2B—Knoop, California
3B—B. Robinson, Balt.
SS—Fregosi, California
OF—Yastrzemski, Boston
OF—Blair, Baltimore
OF—Kaline, Detroit

1967 National
P—Gibson, St. Louis
C—Hundley, Chicago
1B—Parker, Los Angeles
2B—Mazeroski, Pittsburgh
3B—Santo, Chicago
SS—Alley, Pittsburgh
OF—Clemente, Pittsburgh
OF—Flood, St. Louis
OF—Mays, San Francisco

1968 American
P—Kaat, Minnesota
C—Freehan, Detroit
1B—Scott, Boston
2B—Knoop, California
3B—B. Robinson, Balt.
SS—Aparicio, Chicago
OF—Stanley, Detroit
OF—Yastrzemski, Boston
OF—Smith, Boston

1968 National
P—Gibson, St. Louis
C—Bench, Cincinnati
1B—Parker, Los Angeles
2B—Beckert, Chicago
3B—Santo, Chicago
SS—Maxvill, St. Louis
OF—Mays, San Francisco
OF—Clemente, Pittsburgh
OF—Flood, St. Louis

1969 American
P—Kaat, Minnesota
C—Freehan, Detroit
1B—Pepitone, New York
2B—Johnson, Baltimore
3B—B. Robinson, Balt.
SS—Belanger, Baltimore
OF—Blair, Baltimore
OF—Stanley, Detroit
OF—Yastrzemski, Boston

1969 National
P—Gibson, St. Louis
C—Bench, Cincinnati
1B—Parker, Los Angeles
2B—Millan, Atlanta
3B—Boyer, Atlanta
SS—Kessinger, Chicago
OF—Clemente, Pittsburgh
OF—Flood, St. Louis
OF—Rose, Cincinnati

1970 American
P—Kaat, Minnesota
C—Fosse, Cleveland
1B—Spencer, California
2B—Johnson, Baltimore
3B—B. Robinson, Balt.
SS—Aparicio, Chicago
OF—Stanley, Detroit
OF—Blair, Baltimore
OF—Berry, Chicago

1970 National
P—Gibson, St. Louis
C—Bench, Cincinnati
1B—Parker, Los Angeles
2B—Helms, Cincinnati
3B—Rader, Houston
SS—Kessinger, Chicago
OF—Clemente, Pittsburgh
OF—Agee, New York
OF—Rose, Cincinnati

1971 American
P—Kaat, Minnesota
C—Fosse, Cleveland
1B—Scott, Boston
2B—Johnson, Baltimore
3B—B. Robinson, Balt.
SS—Belanger, Baltimore
OF—Blair, Baltimore
OF—Otis, Kansas City
OF—Yastrzemski, Boston

1971 National
P—Gibson, St. Louis
C—Bench, Cincinnati
1B—Parker, Los Angeles
2B—Helms, Cincinnati
3B—Rader, Houston
SS—Harrelson, New York
OF—Clemente, Pittsburgh
OF—Bonds, San Francisco
OF—Davis, Los Angeles

1972 American
P—Kaat, Minnesota
C—Fisk, Boston
1B—Scott, Milwaukee
2B—Griffin, Boston
3B—Robinson, Baltimore
SS—Brinkman, Detroit
OF—Blair, Baltimore
OF—Murcer, New York
OF—Berry, California

1972 National
P—Gibson, St. Louis
C—Bench, Cincinnati
1B—Parker, Los Angeles
2B—Millan, Atlanta
3B—Rader, Houston
SS—Bowa, Philadelphia
OF—Clemente, Pittsburgh
OF—Cedeno, Houston
OF—Davis, Los Angeles

1973 American
P—Kaat, Chicago
C—Munson, New York
1B—Scott, Milwaukee
2B—Grich, Baltimore
3B—Robinson, Baltimore
SS—Belanger, Baltimore
OF—Blair, Baltimore
OF—Otis, Kansas City
OF—Stanley, Detroit

1973 National
P—Gibson, St. Louis
C—Bench, Cincinnati
1B—Jorgensen, Montreal
2B—Morgan, Cincinnati
3B—Rader, Houston
SS—Metzger, Houston
OF—Bonds, San Francisco
OF—Cedeno, Houston
OF—Davis, Los Angeles

1974 American
P—Kaat, Chicago
C—Munson, New York
1B—Scott, Milwaukee
2B—Grich, Baltimore
3B—Robinson, Baltimore
SS—Belanger, Baltimore
OF—Blair, Baltimore
OF—Otis, Kansas City
OF—Rudi, Oakland

1974 National
P—Messersmith, L.A.
C—Bench, Cincinnati
1B—Garvey, Los Angeles
2B—Morgan, Cincinnati
3B—Rader, Houston
SS—Concepcion, Cincinnati
OF—Cedeno, Houston
OF—Geronimo, Cincinnati
OF—Bonds, San Francisco

1975 American
P—Kaat, Chicago
C—Munson, New York
1B—Scott, Milwaukee
2B—Grich, Baltimore
3B—Robinson, Baltimore
SS—Belanger, Baltimore
OF—Blair, Baltimore
OF—Rudi, Oakland
OF—Lynn, Boston

1975 National
P—Messersmith, L.A.
C—Bench, Cincinnati
1B—Garvey, Los Angeles
2B—Morgan, Cincinnati
3B—Reitz, St. Louis
SS—Concepcion, Cincinnati
OF—Cedeno, Houston
OF—Geronimo, Cincinnati
OF—Maddox, Philadelphia

1976 American
P—Palmer, Baltimore
C—Sundberg, Texas
1B—Scott, Milwaukee
2B—Grich, Baltimore
3B—Rodriguez, Detroit
SS—Belanger, Baltimore
OF—Rudi, Oakland
OF—Evans, Boston
OF—Manning, Cleveland

1976 National
P—Kaat, Philadelphia
C—Bench, Cincinnati
1B—Garvey, Los Angeles
2B—Morgan, Cincinnati
3B—Schmidt, Philadelphia
SS—Concepcion, Cincinnati
OF—Cedeno, Houston
OF—Geronimo, Cincinnati
OF—Maddox, Philadelphia

1977 American
P—Palmer, Baltimore
C—Sundberg, Texas
1B—Spencer, Chicago
2B—White, Kansas City
3B—Nettles, New York
SS—Belanger, Baltimore
OF—Beniquez, Texas
OF—Yastrzemski, Boston
OF—Cowens, Kansas City

1977 National
P—Kaat, Philadelphia
C—Bench, Cincinnati
1B—Garvey, Los Angeles
2B—Morgan, Cincinnati
3B—Schmidt, Philadelphia
SS—Concepcion, Cincinnati
OF—Geronimo, Cincinnati
OF—Maddox, Philadelphia
OF—Parker, Pittsburgh

1978 American
P—Palmer, Baltimore
C—Sundberg, Texas
1B—Chambliss, New York
2B—White, Kansas City
3B—Nettles, New York
SS—Belanger, Baltimore
OF—Lynn, Boston
OF—Evans, Boston
OF—Miller, California

1978 National
P—Niekro, Atlanta
C—Boone, Philadelphia
1B—Hernandez, St. Louis
2B—Lopes, Los Angeles
3B—Schmidt, Philadelphia
SS—Bowa, Philadelphia
OF—Maddox, Philadelphia
OF—Parker, Pittsburgh
OF—Valentine, Montreal

1979 American
P—Palmer, Baltimore
C—Sundberg, Texas
1B—Cooper, Milwaukee
2B—White, Kansas City
3B—Bell, Texas
SS—Burleson, Boston
OF—Evans, Boston
OF—Lezcano, Milwaukee
OF—Lynn, Boston

1979 National
P—Niekro, Atlanta
C—Boone, Philadelphia
1B—Hernandez, St. Louis
2B—Trillo, Philadelphia
3B—Schmidt, Philadelphia
SS—Concepcion, Cincinnati
OF—Maddox, Philadelphia
OF—Parker, Pittsburgh
OF—Winfield, San Diego

1980 American
P—Norris, Oakland
C—Sundberg, Texas
1B—Cooper, Milwaukee
2B—White, Kansas City
3B—Bell, Texas
SS—Trammell, Detroit
OF—Lynn, Boston
OF—Murphy, Oakland
OF—Wilson, Kansas City

1980 National
P—Niekro, Atlanta
C—Carter, Montreal
1B—Hernandez, St. Louis
2B—Flynn, New York
3B—Schmidt, Philadelphia
SS—Smith, San Diego
OF—Dawson, Montreal
OF—Maddox, Philadelphia
OF—Winfield, San Diego

1981 American
P—Norris, Oakland
C—Sundberg, Texas
1B—Squires, Chicago
2B—White, Kansas City
3B—Bell, Texas
SS—Trammell, Detroit
OF—Murphy, Oakland
OF—Evans, Boston
OF—Henderson, Oakland

1981 National
P—Carlton, Philadelphia
C—Carter, Montreal
1B—Hernandez, St. Louis
2B—Trillo, Philadelphia
3B—Schmidt, Philadelphia
SS—Smith, San Diego
OF—Dawson, Montreal
OF—Maddox, Philadelphia
OF—Baker, Los Angeles

1982 American
P—Guidry, New York
C—Boone, California
1B—Murray, Baltimore
2B—White, Kansas City
3B—Bell, Texas
SS—Yount, Milwaukee
OF—Evans, Boston
OF—Winfield, New York
OF—Murphy, Oakland

1982 National
P—Niekro, Atlanta
C—Carter, Montreal
1B—Hernandez, St. Louis
2B—Trillo, Philadelphia
3B—Schmidt, Philadelphia
SS—O. Smith, St. Louis
OF—Dawson, Montreal
OF—Murphy, Atlanta
OF—Maddox, Philadelphia

1983 American
P—Guidry, New York
C—Parrish, Detroit
1B—Murray, Baltimore
2B—Whitaker, Detroit
3B—Bell, Texas
SS—Trammell, Detroit
OF—Evans, Boston
OF—Winfield, New York
OF—Murphy, Oakland

1983 National
P—Niekro, Atlanta
C—Pena, Pittsburgh
1B—Hernandez, St.L.-N.Y.
2B—Sandberg, Chicago
3B—Schmidt, Philadelphia
SS—O. Smith, St. Louis
OF—Dawson, Montreal
OF—Murphy, Atlanta
OF—McGee, St. Louis

1984 American
P—Guidry, New York
C—Parrish, Detroit
1B—Murray, Baltimore
2B—Whitaker, Detroit
3B—Bell, Texas
SS—Trammell, Detroit
OF—Evans, Boston
OF—Winfield, New York
OF—Murphy, Oakland

1984 National
P—Andujar, St. Louis
C—Pena, Pittsburgh
1B—Hernandez, New York
2B—Sandberg, Chicago
3B—Schmidt, Philadelphia
SS—O. Smith, St. Louis
OF—Murphy, Atlanta
OF—Dernier, Chicago
OF—Dawson, Montreal

1985 American
P—Guidry, New York
C—Parrish, Detroit
1B—Mattingly, New York
2B—Whitaker, Detroit
3B—Brett, Kansas City
SS—Griffin, Oakland
OF—Pettis, California
OF—Winfield, New York
OF—Evans, Boston (tie)
—Murphy, Oakland (tie)

1985 National
P—Reuschel, Pittsburgh
C—Pena, Pittsburgh
1B—Hernandez, New York
2B—Sandberg, Chicago
3B—Wallach, Montreal
SS—O. Smith, St. Louis
OF—McGee, St. Louis
OF—Murphy, Atlanta
OF—Dawson, Montreal

1986 American
P—Guidry, New York
C—Boone, California
1B—Mattingly, New York
2B—White, Kansas City
3B—Gaetti, Minnesota
SS—Fernandez, Toronto
OF—Pettis, California
OF—Barfield, Toronto
OF—Puckett, Minnesota

1986 National
P—Valenzuela, Los Angeles
C—Davis, Chicago
1B—Hernandez, New York
2B—Sandberg, Chicago
3B—Schmidt, Philadelphia
SS—Smith, St. Louis
OF—Gwynn, San Diego
OF—Murphy, Atlanta
OF—McGee, St. Louis

Silver Slugger Teams

1980 American
1B—Cecil Cooper, Milw.
2B—Willie Randolph, N.Y.
3B—George Brett, K.C.
SS—Robin Yount, Milw.
OF—Ben Oglivie, Milw.
OF—Al Oliver, Texas
OF—Willie Wilson, K.C.
C—Lance Parrish, Detroit
DH—Reggie Jackson, N.Y.

1980 National
1B—Keith Hernandez, St.L.
2B—Manny Trillo, Phila.
3B—Mike Schmidt, Phila.
SS—Garry Templeton, St.L.
OF—Dusty Baker, Los Angeles
OF—Andre Dawson, Montreal
OF—George Hendrick, St.L.
C—Ted Simmons, St. Louis
P—Bob Forsch, St. Louis

1981 American
1B—Cecil Cooper, Milw.
2B—Bobby Grich, Calif.
3B—Carney Lansford, Bos.
SS—Rick Burleson, Calif.
OF—Rickey Henderson, Oak.
OF—Dwight Evans, Boston
OF—Dave Winfield, N.Y.
C—Carlton Fisk, Chicago
DH—Al Oliver, Texas

1981 National
1B—Pete Rose, Philadelphia
2B—Manny Trillo, Phila.
3B—Mike Schmidt, Phila.
SS—Dave Concepcion, Cin.
OF—Andre Dawson, Montreal
OF—George Foster, Cincinnati
OF—Dusty Baker, Los Angeles
C—Gary Carter, Montreal
P—Fernando Valenzuela, L.A.

1982 American
1B—Cecil Cooper, Milw.
2B—Damaso Garcia, Tor.
3B—Doug DeCinces, Calif.
SS—Robin Yount, Milw.
OF—Dave Winfield, N.Y.
OF—Willie Wilson, K.C.
OF—Reggie Jackson, Calif.
C—Lance Parrish, Detroit
DH—Hal McRae, K.C.

1982 National
1B—Al Oliver, Montreal
2B—Joe Morgan, S.F.
3B—Mike Schmidt, Phila.
SS—Dave Concepcion, Cin.
OF—Dale Murphy, Atlanta
OF—Pedro Guerrero, L.A.
OF—Leon Durham, Chicago
C—Gary Carter, Montreal
P—Don Robinson, Pittsburgh

1983 American

1B—Eddie Murray, Balt.
2B—Lou Whitaker, Detroit
3B—Wade Boggs, Boston
SS—Cal Ripken, Baltimore
OF—Jim Rice, Boston
OF—Dave Winfield, N.Y.
OF—Lloyd Moseby, Toronto
C—Lance Parrish, Detroit
DH—Don Baylor, New York

1983 National

1B—George Hendrick, St.L.
2B—Johnny Ray, Pittsburgh
3B—Mike Schmidt, Phila.
SS—Dickie Thon, Houston
OF—Andre Dawson, Montreal
OF—Dale Murphy, Atlanta
OF—Jose Cruz, Houston
C—Terry Kennedy, San Diego
P—Fernando Valenzuela, L.A.

1984 American

1B—Eddie Murray, Balt.
2B—Lou Whitaker, Detroit
3B—Buddy Bell, Texas
SS—Cal Ripken, Baltimore
OF—Tony Armas, Boston
OF—Jim Rice, Boston
OF—Dave Winfield, N.Y.
C—Lance Parrish, Detroit
DH—Andre Thornton, Cleve.

1984 National

1B—Keith Hernandez, N.Y.
2B—Ryne Sandberg, Chicago
3B—Mike Schmidt, Phila.
SS—Garry Templeton, S.D.
OF—Dale Murphy, Atlanta
OF—Jose Cruz, Houston
OF—Tony Gwynn, San Diego
C—Gary Carter, Montreal
P—Rick Rhoden, Pittsburgh

1985 American

1B—Don Mattingly, N.Y.
2B—Lou Whitaker, Detroit
3B—George Brett, K.C.
SS—Cal Ripken, Baltimore
OF—Rickey Henderson, N.Y.
OF—Dave Winfield, N.Y.
OF—George Bell, Toronto
C—Carlton Fisk, Chicago
DH—Don Baylor, New York

1985 National

1B—Jack Clark, St. Louis
2B—Ryne Sandberg, Chi.
3B—Tim Wallach, Montreal
SS—Hubie Brooks, Montreal
OF—Willie McGee, St. Louis
OF—Dale Murphy, Atlanta
OF—Dave Parker, Cincinnati
C—Gary Carter, New York
P—Rick Rhoden, Pittsburgh

1986 American

1B—Don Mattingly, N.Y.
2B—Frank White, K.C.
3B—Wade Boggs, Boston
SS—Cal Ripken, Baltimore
OF—George Bell, Toronto
OF—Kirby Puckett, Minn.
OF—Jesse Barfield, Toronto
C—Lance Parrish, Detroit
DH—Don Baylor, Boston

1986 National

1B—Glenn Davis, Houston
2B—Steve Sax, L.A.
3B—Mike Schmidt, Phila.
SS—Hubie Brooks, Montreal
OF—Tony Gwynn, San Diego
OF—Tim Raines, Montreal
OF—Dave Parker, Cincinnati
C—Gary Carter, New York
P—Rick Rhoden, Pittsburgh

Baseball Writers' Association Awards

Most Valuable Player Citations

CHALMERS AWARD

Year	AMERICAN LEAGUE Player, Club	Points	NATIONAL LEAGUE Player, Club	Points
1911	Tyrus Cobb, Detroit, of	64	Frank Schulte, Chicago, of	29
1912	Tristram Speaker, Boston, of	59	Lawrence Doyle, New York, 2b	48
1913	Walter Johnson, Washington, p	54	Jacob Daubert, Brooklyn, 1b	50
1914	Edward Collins, Philadelphia, 2b	63	John Evers, Boston, 2b	50

LEAGUE AWARDS

Year	AMERICAN LEAGUE Player, Club	Points	NATIONAL LEAGUE Player, Club	Points
1922	George Sisler, St. Louis, 1b	59	No selection	
1923	George Ruth, New York, of	64	No selection	
1924	Walter Johnson, Washington, p	55	Arthur Vance, Brooklyn, p	74
1925	Roger Peckinpaugh, Washington, ss	45	Rogers Hornsby, St. Louis, 2b	73
1926	George Burns, Cleveland, 1b	63	Robert O'Farrell, St. Louis, c	79
1927	H. Louis Gehrig, New York, 1b	56	Paul Waner, Pittsburgh, of	72
1928	Gordon Cochrane, Philadelphia, c	53	James Bottomley, St. Louis, 1b	76
1929	No selection		Rogers Hornsby, Chicago, 2b	60

BASEBALL WRITERS' ASSOCIATION MVP AWARDS

Year	AMERICAN LEAGUE Player, Club	Points	NATIONAL LEAGUE Player, Club	Points
1931	Robert Grove, Philadelphia, p	78	Frank Frisch, St. Louis, 2b	65
1932	James Foxx, Philadelphia, 1b	75	Charles Klein, Philadelphia, of	78
1933	James Foxx, Philadelphia, 1b	74	Carl Hubbell, New York, p	77
1934	Gordon Cochrane, Detroit, c	67	Jerome Dean, St. Louis, p	78
1935	Henry Greenberg, Detroit, 1b	*80	Charles Hartnett, Chicago, c	75
1936	H. Louis Gehrig, New York, 1b	73	Carl Hubbell, New York, p	60
1937	Charles Gehringer, Detroit, 2b	78	Joseph Medwick, St. Louis, of	70
1938	James Foxx, Boston, 1b	305	Ernest Lombardi, Cincinnati, c	229
1939	Joseph DiMaggio, New York, of	280	William Walters, Cincinnati, p	303
1940	Henry Greenberg, Detroit, of	292	Frank McCormick, Cincinnati, 1b	274
1941	Joseph DiMaggio, New York, of	291	Adolph Camilli, Brooklyn, 1b	300
1942	Joseph Gordon, New York, 2b	270	Morton Cooper, St. Louis, p	263
1943	Spurgeon Chandler, New York, p	246	Stanley Musial, St. Louis, of	267
1944	Harold Newhouser, Detroit, p	236	Martin Marion, St. Louis, ss	190
1945	Harold Newhouser, Detroit, p	236	Philip Cavarretta, Chicago, 1b	279
1946	Theodore Williams, Boston, of	224	Stanley Musial, St. Louis, 1b	319
1947	Joseph DiMaggio, New York, of	202	Robert Elliott, Boston, 3b	205
1948	Louis Boudreau, Cleveland, ss	324	Stanley Musial, St. Louis, of	303
1949	Theodore Williams, Boston, of	272	Jack Robinson, Brooklyn, 2b	264
1950	Philip Rizzuto, New York, ss	284	C. James Konstanty, Philadelphia, p	286
1951	Lawrence Berra, New York, c	184	Roy Campanella, Brooklyn, c	243
1952	Robert Shantz, Philadelphia, p	280	Henry Sauer, Chicago, of	226
1953	Albert Rosen, Cleveland, 3b	*336	Roy Campanella, Brooklyn, c	297
1954	Lawrence Berra, New York, c	230	Willie Mays, New York, of	283
1955	Lawrence Berra, New York, c	218	Roy Campanella, Brooklyn, c	226
1956	Mickey Mantle, New York, of	*336	Donald Newcombe, Brooklyn, p	223
1957	Mickey Mantle, New York, of	233	Henry Aaron, Milwaukee, of	239
1958	Jack Jensen, Boston, of	233	Ernest Banks, Chicago, ss	283
1959	J. Nelson Fox, Chicago, 2b	295	Ernest Banks, Chicago, ss	232½
1960	Roger Maris, New York, of	225	Richard Groat, Pittsburgh, ss	276
1961	Roger Maris, New York, of	202	Frank Robinson, Cincinnati, of	219
1962	Mickey Mantle, New York, of	234	Maurice Wills, Los Angeles, ss	209
1963	Elston Howard, New York, c	248	Sanford Koufax, Los Angeles, p	237
1964	Brooks Robinson, Baltimore, 3b	269	Kenton Boyer, St. Louis, 3b	243
1965	Zoilo Versalles, Minnesota, ss	275	Willie Mays, San Francisco, of	224
1966	Frank Robinson, Baltimore, of	*280	Roberto Clemente, Pittsburgh, of	218
1967	Carl Yastrzemski, Boston, of	275	Orlando Cepeda, St. Louis, 1b	*280
1968	Dennis McLain, Detroit, p	*280	Robert Gibson, St. Louis, p	242
1969	Harmon Killebrew, Minnesota, 1-3b	294	Willie McCovey, San Francisco, 1b	265
1970	John (Boog) Powell, Baltimore, 1b	234	Johnny Bench, Cincinnati, c	326
1971	Vida Blue, Oakland, p	268	Joseph Torre, St. Louis, 3b	318
1972	Richie Allen, Chicago, 1b	321	Johnny Bench, Cincinnati, c	263
1973	Reggie Jackson, Oakland, of	*336	Pete Rose, Cincinnati, of	274
1974	Jeff Burroughs, Texas, of	248	Steve Garvey, Los Angeles, 1b	270
1975	Fred Lynn, Boston, of	326	Joe Morgan, Cincinnati, 2b	321½
1976	Thurman Munson, New York, c	304	Joe Morgan, Cincinnati, 2b	311
1977	Rod Carew, Minnesota, 1b	273	George Foster, Cincinnati, of	291
1978	Jim Rice, Boston, of	352	Dave Parker, Pittsburgh, of	320
1979	Don Baylor, California, of	347	Willie Stargell, Pittsburgh, 1b	216
			Keith Hernandez, St. Louis, 1b	216

BASEBALL WRITERS' ASSOCIATION MVP AWARDS—Cont.

Year	AMERICAN LEAGUE Player, Club	Points	NATIONAL LEAGUE Player, Club	Points
1980	George Brett, Kansas City, 3b	335	Mike Schmidt, Philadelphia, 3b	*336
1981	Rollie Fingers, Milwaukee, p	319	Mike Schmidt, Philadelphia, 3b	321
1982	Robin Yount, Milwaukee, ss	385	Dale Murphy, Atlanta, of	283
1983	Cal Ripken, Baltimore, ss	322	Dale Murphy, Atlanta, of	318
1984	Willie Hernandez, Detroit, p	306	Ryne Sandberg, Chicago, 2b	326
1985	Don Mattingly, New York, 1b	367	Willie McGee, St. Louis, of	280
1986	Roger Clemens, Boston, p	339	Mike Schmidt, Philadelphia, 3b	287

*Unanimous selection.

BASEBALL WRITERS' ASSOCIATION ROOKIE AWARDS

1947—Combined selection—Jack Robinson, Brooklyn, 1b.
1948—Combined selection—Alvin Dark, Boston, N. L., ss.

Year	AMERICAN LEAGUE Player, Club	Votes	NATIONAL LEAGUE Player, Club	Votes
1949	Roy Sievers, St. Louis, of	10	Donald Newcombe, Brooklyn, p	21
1950	Walter Dropo, Boston, 1b	15	Samuel Jethroe, Boston, of	11
1951	Gilbert McDougald, New York, 3b	13	Willie Mays, New York, of	18
1952	Harry Byrd, Philadelphia, p	9	Joseph Black, Brooklyn, p	19
1953	Harvey Kuenn, Detroit, ss	23	James Gilliam, Brooklyn, 2b	11
1954	Robert Grim, New York, p	15	Wallace Moon, St. Louis, of	17
1955	Herbert Score, Cleveland, p	18	William Virdon, St. Louis, of	15
1956	Luis Aparicio, Chicago, ss	22	Frank Robinson, Cincinnati, of	*24
1957	Anthony Kubek, New York, inf-of	23	John Sanford, Philadelphia, p	16
1958	Albert Pearson, Washington, of	14	Orlando Cepeda, San Francisco, 1b	*†21
1959	W. Robert Allison, Washington, of	18	Willie McCovey, San Francisco, 1b	*24
1960	Ronald Hansen, Baltimore, ss	22	Frank Howard, Los Angeles, of	12
1961	Donald Schwall, Boston, p	7	Billy Williams, Chicago, of	10
1962	Thomas Tresh, New York, of-ss	13	Kenneth Hubbs, Chicago, 2b	19
1963	Gary Peters, Chicago, p	10	Peter Rose, Cincinnati, 2b	17
1964	Pedro (Tony) Oliva, Minnesota, of	19	Richard Allen, Philadelphia, 3b	18
1965	Curtis Blefary, Baltimore, of	12	James Lefebvre, Los Angeles, 2b	13
1966	Tommie Agee, Chicago, of	16	Tommy Helms, Cincinnati, 3b	12
1967	Rod Carew, Minnesota, 2b	19	Tom Seaver, New York, p	11
1968	Stan Bahnsen, New York, p	17	Johnny Bench, Cincinnati, c	10½
1969	Lou Piniella, Kansas City, of	9	Ted Sizemore, Los Angeles, 2b	14
1970	Thurman Munson, New York, c	23	Carl Morton, Montreal, p	11
1971	Chris Chambliss, Cleveland, 1b	11	Earl Williams, Atlanta, c	18
1972	Carlton Fisk, Boston, c	*24	Jon Matlack, New York, p	19
1973	Al Bumbry, Baltimore, of	13½	Gary Matthews, San Francisco, of	11
1974	Mike Hargrove, Texas, 1b	16½	Bake McBride, St. Louis, of	16
1975	Fred Lynn, Boston, of	23	John Montefusco, San Francisco, p	12
1976	Mark Fidrych, Detroit, p	22	Butch Metzger, San Diego, p	11
			Pat Zachry, Cincinnati, p	11
1977	Eddie Murray, Baltimore, dh-1b	12½	Andre Dawson, Montreal, of	10
1978	Lou Whitaker, Detroit, 2b	21	Bob Horner, Atlanta, 3b	12½
1979	John Castino, Minnesota, 3b	7	Rick Sutcliffe, Los Angeles, p	20
	Alfredo Griffin, Toronto, ss	7		
1980	Joe Charboneau, Cleveland, of	103	Steve Howe, Los Angeles, p	80
1981	Dave Righetti, New York, p	127	Fernando Valenzuela, Los Angeles, p	107
1982	Cal Ripken, Baltimore, ss-3b	132	Steve Sax, Los Angeles, 2b	63
1983	Ron Kittle, Chicago, of	104	Darryl Strawberry, New York, of	109
1984	Alvin Davis, Seattle, 1b	134	Dwight Gooden, New York, p	118
1985	Ozzie Guillen, Chicago, ss	101	Vince Coleman, St. Louis, of	*120
1986	Jose Canseco, Oakland, of	110	Todd Worrell, St. Louis, p	118

*Unanimous selection. †Three writers did not vote.

Steve Carlton won four Cy Young Awards as a member of the Philadelphia Phillies before the club released him last June 24.

CY YOUNG MEMORIAL AWARD

Year	Pitcher	Club	Votes
1956—	Donald Newcombe, Brooklyn		10
1957—	Warren Spahn, Milwaukee		15
1958—	Robert Turley, New York, A.L.		5
1959—	Early Wynn, Chicago, A.L.		13
1960—	Vernon Law, Pittsburgh		8
1961—	Edward Ford, New York, A.L.		9
1962—	Don Drysdale, Los Angeles, N.L.		14
1963—	Sanford Koufax, Los Angeles, N.L.		*20
1964—	Dean Chance, Los Angeles, A.L.		17
1965—	Sanford Koufax, Los Angeles, N.L.		*20
1966—	Sanford Koufax, Los Angeles, N.L.		*20
1967—	A. L.—Jim Lonborg, Boston		18
	N. L.—M. McCormick, San Francisco		18
1968—	A. L.—Dennis McLain, Detroit		*20
	N. L.—Bob Gibson, St. Louis		*20
1969—	A. L.—Dennis McLain, Detroit		10
	Mike Cuellar, Baltimore		10
	N. L.—Tom Seaver, New York		23
1970—	A. L.—Jim Perry, Minnesota		†55
	N. L.—Bob Gibson, St. Louis		†118
1971—	A. L.—Vida Blue, Oakland		†98
	N. L.—Fergy Jenkins, Chicago		†97
1972—	A. L.—Gaylord Perry, Cleveland		†64
	N. L.—Steve Carlton, Philadelphia		*†120
1973—	A. L.—Jim Palmer, Baltimore		†88
	N. L.—Tom Seaver, New York		†71
1974—	A. L.—Jim Hunter, Oakland		†90
	N. L.—Mike Marshall, Los Angeles		†96
1975—	A. L.—Jim Palmer, Baltimore		†98
	N. L.—Tom Seaver, New York		†98
1976—	A. L.—Jim Palmer, Baltimore		†108
	N. L.—Randy Jones, San Diego		†96
1977—	A. L.—Sparky Lyle, New York		†56½
	N. L.—Steve Carlton, Philadelphia		*†104
1978—	A. L.—Ron Guidry, New York		*†140
	N. L.—Gaylord Perry, San Diego		‡116
1979—	A. L.—Mike Flanagan, Baltimore		†136
	N. L.—Bruce Sutter, Chicago		†72
1980—	A. L.—Steve Stone, Baltimore		100
	N. L.—Steve Carlton, Philadelphia		118
1981—	A. L.—Rollie Fingers, Milwaukee		126
	N. L.—Fernando Valenzuela, Los Ang.		70
1982—	A. L.—Pete Vuckovich, Milwaukee		87
	N. L.—Steve Carlton, Philadelphia		112
1983—	A. L.—LaMarr Hoyt, Chicago		116
	N. L.—John Denny, Philadelphia		103
1984—	A. L.—Willie Hernandez, Detroit		88
	N. L.—Rick Sutcliffe, Chicago		*120
1985—	A. L.—Bret Saberhagen, Kansas City		127
	N. L.—Dwight Gooden, New York		*120
1986—	A. L.—Roger Clemens, Boston		*140
	N. L.—Mike Scott, Houston		98

*Unanimous selection. †Point system used.

Williams, Hunter Voted into Hall

By LARRY WIGGE

Billy Williams, accustomed to being in the lineup every day, had to wait six years in the on-deck circle to gain election to baseball's Hall of Fame. However, the former Chicago Cub great said the wait was worthwhile when he got the word that he and former star righthander Jim (Catfish) Hunter had gained enshrinement at Cooperstown.

"Being elected to the Hall of Fame is like an Oscar for an actor or actress, a Pulitzer for a writer and a Nobel Prize for a scientist," he said. "I don't know whether to laugh or cry right now."

Williams, on the ballot for the sixth time after missing by just four votes in 1986, was named on 354 of 413 ballots for 85.7 percent, well above the required 75 percent for induction. Hunter got 315 votes, five over the minimum, in his third try for election.

Jim Bunning was next on the list with 289 votes, 21 short of election, followed by Orlando Cepeda with 179, Roger Maris 166 and Tony Oliva 160.

Williams, a sweet-swinging lefthanded hitter from Whistler, Ala., had a career average of .290 with 426 homers, 1,476 runs batted in and 2,711 hits in an 18-year career. He spent his first 16 seasons as an outfielder for the Cubs (1959-74) and played his last two seasons with the Oakland A's. He held the National League record for most consecutive games played (1,117) before it was surpassed by Steve Garvey (1,207) in 1983.

Though he never played in a World Series, Williams gained plenty of recognition. He was voted the National League's Rookie of the Year in 1961, when he batted .278 with 25 homers and 86 RBIs. In 1972, he was named Major League Player of the Year by The Sporting News when he led the league in hitting with a .333 average and had 37 homers and 122 RBIs.

Hunter, often recognized as one of the better pressure pitchers in the game, was on World Series winners with Oakland in 1972, '73 and '74, going 21-7, 21-5 and 25-12 in those years. He also contributed to World Series titles with the New York Yankees in 1977 and '78. His 15-year major league record was 224-166 with a 3.26 earned-run average.

Hunter, who never pitched in the minors before joining the Kansas City A's in 1965, pitched a perfect game against Minnesota in 1968, becoming the first pitcher in the

Billy Williams (above) and Jim (Catfish) Hunter are baseball's latest Hall of Fame inductees.

A.L. to toss a perfect game since Charlie Robertson accomplished the feat with the Chicago White Sox in 1922. He won more than 20 games in five consecutive years from 1971-75 and in 1974, his final year with the A's, he won 25 games and was named the American League's Cy Young Award winner.

Hunter, who had signed a two-year contract worth $100,000 a year with the A's prior to the '74 season, became the first of the modern, high-priced free agents on December 16, 1974, when an arbitration panel ruled the A's had purged his contract. Fifteen days later, Hunter accepted a five-year, $2.892 million contract from the Yankees after negotiating with 22 clubs.

Born in Hertford, N.C., Hunter got the nickname "Catfish" from A's Owner Charles O. Finley shortly after he signed with the club. However, his love for hunting and fishing caused an anxious moment when he was 17 years old. While out on a hunt with his brother, Pete, Pete's shotgun accidentally discharged. A bullet blasted through Catfish's right shoe, causing him to lose his small toe while the bones on several other toes were broken. Though he never had much feeling in his toes throughout his career and 15 pellets remained lodged in them, Hunter's control on the mound was exemplary. He walked only 954 batters in 3,449 major league innings.

The complete 1987 Hall of Fame voting totals follow: Williams, 354; Hunter, 315; Bunning, 289; Cepeda, 179; Maris, 166; Oliva, 160; Harvey Kuenn, 144; Bill Mazeroski, 124; Maury Wills, 113; Ken Boyer, 96; Lew Burdette, 96; Mickey Lolich, 84; Minnie Minoso, 82; Elroy Face, 78; Ron Santo, 78; Richie Allen, 55; Curt Flood, 50; Vada Pinson, 48; Joe Torre, 47; Elston Howard, 44; Don Larsen, 30; Thurman Munson, 28; Wilbur Wood, 26; Bobby Bonds, 24; Mike Marshall, 6; Sal Bando, 3. Failing to receive votes were Jerry Grote and Steve Stone.

Following is a complete list of those enshrined in the Hall of Fame prior to 1984 with the vote by which each enrollee was elected:

1936—Tyrus Cobb (222), John (Honus) Wagner (215), George (Babe) Ruth (215), Christy Mathewson (205), Walter Johnson (189), named by Baseball Writers' Association of America. Total ballots cast, 226.

1937—Napoleon Lajoie (168), Tristram Speaker (165), Denton (Cy) Young (153), named by the BBWAA. Total ballots cast, 201. George Wright, Morgan G. Bulkeley, Byron Bancroft Johnson, John J. McGraw, Cornelius McGillicuddy (Connie Mack), named by Centennial Commission.

1938—Grover C. Alexander (212), named by BBWAA. Total ballots, 262. Henry Chadwick, Alexander J. Cartwright, named by Centennial Commission.

1939—George Sisler (235), Edward Collins (213), William Keeler (207), Louis Gehrig, named by BBWAA (Gehrig by special election after retirement from game was announced). Total ballots cast, 274. Albert G. Spalding, Adrian C. Anson, Charles A. Comiskey, William (Buck) Ewing, Charles Radbourn, William A. (Candy) Cummings, named by committee of old-time players and writers.

1942—Rogers Hornsby (182), named by BBWAA. Total ballots cast, 233.

1944—Judge Kenesaw M. Landis, named by committee on old-timers.

1945—Hugh Duffy, Jimmy Collins, Hugh Jennings, Ed Delahanty, Fred Clarke, Mike Kelly, Wilbert Robinson, Jim O'Rourke, Dennis (Dan) Brouthers and Roger Bresnahan, named by committee on old-timers.

1946—Jesse Burkett, Frank Chance, Jack Chesbro, Johnny Evers, Clark Griffith, Tom McCarthy, Joe McGinnity, Eddie Plank, Joe Tinker, Rube Waddell and Ed Walsh, named by committee on old-timers.

1947—Carl Hubbell (140), Frank Frisch (136), Gordon (Mickey) Cochrane (128) and Robert (Lefty) Grove (123), named by BBWAA. Total ballots, 161.

1948—Herbert J. Pennock (94) and Harold (Pie) Traynor (93), named by BBWAA. Total ballots cast, 121.

1949—Charles Gehringer (159), named by BBWAA in runoff election. Total ballots cast, 187. Charles (Kid) Nichols and Mordecai (Three-Finger) Brown, named by committee on old timers.

1951—Mel Ott (197) and Jimmie Foxx (179), named by BBWAA. Total ballots cast, 226.

1952—Harry Heilmann (203) and Paul Waner (195), named by BBWAA. Total ballots cast, 234.

1953—Jerome (Dizzy) Dean (209) and Al Simmons (199), named by BBWAA. Total ballots cast, 264. Charles Albert (Chief) Bender, Roderick (Bobby) Wallace, William Klem, Tom Connolly, Edward G. Barrow and William Henry (Harry) Wright, named by the new Committee on Veterans.

1954—Walter (Rabbit) Maranville (209), William Dickey (202) and William Terry (195), named by BBWAA. Total ballots cast, 252.

1955—Joe DiMaggio (223), Ted Lyons (217), Arthur (Dazzy) Vance (205) and Charles (Gabby) Hartnett (195), named by BBWAA. Total ballots cast, 251. J. Franklin (Home Run) Baker and Ray

Schalk, named by Committee on Veterans.

1956—Hank Greenberg (164) and Joe Cronin (152), named by BBWAA. Total ballots cast, 193.

1957—Joseph V. McCarthy and Sam Crawford, named by Committee on Veterans.

1959—Zachariah (Zack) Wheat, named by Committee on Veterans.

1961—Max Carey and William Hamilton, named by Committee on Veterans.

1962—Bob Feller (150) and Jackie Robinson (124), named by BBWAA. Total ballots cast, 160. Bill McKechnie and Edd Roush, named by Committee on Veterans.

1963—Eppa Rixey, Edgar (Sam) Rice, Elmer Flick and John Clarkson, named by Committee on Veterans.

1964—Luke Appling (189), named by BBWAA in runoff election. Total ballots cast, 225. Urban (Red) Faber, Burleigh Grimes, Tim Keefe, Heinie Manush, Miller Huggins and John Montgomery Ward, named by Committee on Veterans.

1965—James (Pud) Galvin, named by Committee on Veterans.

1966—Ted Williams (282), named by BBWAA. Total ballots cast, 302. Casey Stengel, named by Committee on Veterans.

1967—Charles (Red) Ruffing (266), named by BBWAA in runoff election. Total ballots cast, 306. Branch Rickey and Lloyd Waner, named by Committee on Veterans.

1968—Joseph (Ducky) Medwick (240), named by BBWAA. Total ballots cast, 283. Leon (Goose) Goslin and Hazen (Kiki) Cuyler, named by Committee on Veterans.

1969—Stan (The Man) Musial (317) and Roy Campanella (270), named by BBWAA. Total ballots cast, 340. Stan Coveleski and Waite Hoyt, named by Committee on Veterans.

1970—Lou Boudreau (232), named by BBWAA. Total ballots cast, 300. Earle Combs, Jesse Haines and Ford Frick, named by Committee on Veterans.

1971—Chick Hafey, Rube Marquard, Joe Kelley, Dave Bancroft, Harry Hooper, Jake Beckley and George Weiss, named by Committee on Veterans. Satchel Paige, named by Special Committee on Negro Leagues.

1972—Sandy Koufax (344), Yogi Berra (339) and Early Wynn (301), named by BBWAA. Total ballots cast, 396. Lefty Gomez, Will Harridge and Ross Youngs, named by Committee on Veterans. Josh Gibson and Walter (Buck) Leonard, named by Special Committee on Negro Leagues.

1973—Warren Spahn (316), named by BBWAA. Total ballots cast, 380. Roberto Clemente (393), in special election by BBWAA in which 424 ballots were cast. Billy Evans, George Kelly and Mickey Welch, named by Committee on Veterans. Monte Irvin, named by Special Committee on Negro Leagues.

1974—Mickey Mantle (322) and Whitey Ford (284), named by BBWAA. Total ballots cast, 365. Jim Bottomley, Sam Thompson and Jocko Conlan, named by Committee on Veterans. James (Cool Papa) Bell, named by Special Committee on Negro Leagues.

1975—Ralph Kiner (273), named by BBWAA. Total ballots cast, 362. Earl Averill, Bucky Harris and Billy Herman, named by Committee on Veterans. William (Judy) Johnson, named by Special Committee on Negro Leagues.

1976—Robin Roberts (337) and Bob Lemon (305), named by BBWAA. Total ballots cast, 388. Roger Connor, Cal Hubbard and Fred Lindstrom, named by Committee on Veterans. Oscar Charleston, named by Special Committee on Negro Leagues.

1977—Ernie Banks (321), named by BBWAA. Total ballots cast, 383. Joe Sewell, Al Lopez and Amos Rusie, named by Committee on Veterans. Martin Dihigo and John Henry Lloyd, named by Special Committee on Negro Leagues.

1978—Eddie Mathews (301), named by BBWAA. Total ballots cast, 379. Larry MacPhail and Addie Joss, named by Committee on Veterans.

1979—Willie Mays (409), named by BBWAA. Total ballots cast, 432. Hack Wilson and Warren Giles, named by Committee on Veterans.

1980—Al Kaline (340) and Duke Snider (333), named by BBWAA. Total ballots cast, 385. Chuck Klein and Tom Yawkey, named by Committee on Veterans.

1981—Bob Gibson (337), named by BBWAA. Total ballots cast, 401. Johnny Mize and Rube Foster, named by Committee on Veterans.

1982—Henry Aaron (406) and Frank Robinson (370), named by BBWAA. Total ballots cast, 415. Albert B. (Happy) Chandler and Travis Jackson, named by Committee on Veterans.

1983—Brooks Robinson (344) and Juan Marichal (313), named by BBWAA. Total ballots cast, 374. George Kell and Walter Alston, named by Committee on Veterans.

1984—Luis Aparicio (341), Harmon Killebrew (335) and Don Drysdale (316), named by BBWAA. Total ballots cast, 403. Rick Ferrell and Pee Wee Reese, named by Committee on Veterans.

1985—Hoyt Wilhelm (331) and Lou Brock (315), named by BBWAA. Total ballots cast, 395. Enos Slaughter and Joseph (Arky) Vaughn, named by Committee on Veterans.

1986—Willie McCovey (346), named by BBWAA. Total ballots cast, 425. Bobby Doerr and Ernie Lombardi, named by Committee on Veterans.

Pitching Help Sought In Draft

By DAVE SLOAN

Pitchers were at a premium December 8 when baseball executives, meeting in Hollywood, Fla., looked for bargains in the annual major league draft.

Eight of the 10 players selected were pitchers, including lefthander Tony Ferreira, taken first overall by the Seattle Mariners, and righthander Bob Gibson, drafted second by the Chicago White Sox.

Ferreira, a 24-year-old former Kansas City farmhand, was acquired by the Mets prior to the '86 season in exchange for shortstop Argenis Salazar. He spent the entire 1986 season with the Mets' Triple-A affiliate at Tidewater (International), compiling a 7-5 record and 3.69 earned-run average in 112⅓ innings.

Gibson, a 29-year-old veteran with a Hall of Fame name, has labored the past eight years in the Brewers' organization. His 1986 season was split between Milwaukee and Vancouver (Pacific Coast), the Brewers' Triple-A affiliate before an off-season switch to Denver. Gibson went 10-4 in 16 games at Vancouver before finishing the season with a 1-2 mark at Milwaukee, dropping his overall major league record to 12-18.

The first non-pitcher selected was outfielder Bob Simonson, drafted third by the Montreal Expos off the Brewers' Denver club. Simonson spent the '86 season at Beloit (Midwest), hitting .278 with 27 homers and 95 RBIs in 133 games.

Each player selected in the draft costs $50,000, and if that player fails to make the season-opening roster, he must be returned to his old club for half the draft price.

The Mariners were the only club to make two selections, with eight other teams drafting one player each. The Brewers, Toronto Blue Jays and Pittsburgh Pirates were the only clubs to lose two players apiece.

Draft choices in order of selection:

Mariners—Pitcher Tony Ferreira from Tidewater (International) of the Mets' organization.

White Sox—Pitcher Bob Gibson from Denver (Pacific Coast) of the Brewers' organization.

Expos—Outfielder Bob Simonson from Denver (Pacific Coast) of the Brewers' organization.

A's—Pitcher Cliff Young from Syracuse (International) of the Blue Jays' organization.

Blue Jays—Pitcher Jose Nunez from Omaha (American Association) of the Royals' organization.

Rangers—Outfielder Cecil Espy from Vancouver (Pacific Coast) of the Pirates' organization.

Astros—Pitcher Jeff Edwards from Albuquerque (Pacific Coast) of the Dodgers' organization.

Mets—Pitcher Charlie Corbell from Phoenix (Pacific Coast) of the Giants' organization.

Mariners—Pitcher Stan Clarke from Syracuse (International) of the Blue Jays' organization.

Brewers—Pitcher Vicente Palacios from Vancouver (Pacific Coast) of the Pirates' organization.

Major League Attendance for 1986

NATIONAL LEAGUE

	Home	Road
Atlanta	1,387,181	1,837,380
Chicago	1,859,102	1,879,706
Cincinnati	1,692,432	1,849,888
Houston	1,734,276	1,816,220
Los Angeles	3,023,208	2,074,970
Montreal	1,128,981	1,926,119
New York	2,767,601	2,176,615
Philadelphia	1,933,335	1,721,147
Pittsburgh	1,000,917	1,651,057
St. Louis	2,471,974	1,695,738
San Diego	1,805,716	1,779,829
San Francisco	1,528,748	1,924,802
Total	22,333,471	22,333,471

AMERICAN LEAGUE

	Home	Road
Baltimore	1,973,176	1,737,994
Boston	2,147,641	2,266,765
California	2,655,872	1,685,439
Chicago	1,424,313	1,852,893
Cleveland	1,471,805	1,727,486
Detroit	1,899,437	1,821,142
Kansas City	2,320,794	1,909,566
Milwaukee	1,265,041	1,707,552
Minnesota	1,255,453	1,707,440
New York	2,268,030	2,196,697
Oakland	1,314,646	1,614,837
Seattle	1,029,045	1,558,546
Texas	1,692,002	1,670,132
Toronto	2,455,477	1,716,243
Total	25,172,732	25,172,732

MAJOR LEAGUE TRANSACTIONS

NECROLOGY

Gorman Dealt Sox Into Series

By DAVE SLOAN

The Boston Red Sox narrowly missed winning the 1986 World Series when they were unable to hold a two-run lead with two outs in the 10th inning of Game 6, eventually falling to the New York Mets in seven games.

Even though they lost, the 1986 season was quite an accomplishment for the Red Sox, who had finished 18½ games behind Toronto in the American League East Division in 1985. They came as close as they did in 1986 because of four key trades made by General Manager Lou Gorman.

On March 28, Gorman dealt designated hitter Mike Easler, who had hit 43 home runs and driven in 165 runs in his two seasons in Boston, to the New York Yankees for designated hitter Don Baylor, who had averaged 24 homers and 88 runs batted in in his three years in New York. Gorman gave up 17 months in age but gained a much-needed clubhouse leader. The 37-year-old Baylor hit 31 homers, drove in 94 runs and kept the Red Sox in contention through the first six weeks of the season.

Baylor followed up his big regular season by batting .346 in Boston's seven-game triumph over California in the American League Championship Series.

Gorman's second acquisition came midway through the season, on June 29, when he picked up righthanded pitcher Tom Seaver in a deal with the Chicago White Sox. Seaver, a 306-game winner in 19-plus major league campaigns, provided veteran leadership on an otherwise youthful Red Sox staff. Seaver won five games for Boston, primarily as a fifth starter, before a knee injury on September 19 sidelined him for the rest of the year. Seaver's absence was keenly felt in postseason play, when Red Sox Manager John McNamara was forced to rely on just three proven starters.

Gorman's third deal of the year brought veteran outfielder Dave Henderson and shortstop Spike Owen to Boston from Seattle August 19 for four players.

Although Henderson hit just .196 in 51 regular-season at-bats, his dramatic, two-out homer in the ninth inning of Game 5 of the Championship Series kept the Red Sox, down three games to one to the California Angels, alive. In the 11th inning of the same game, Henderson hit a bases-loaded sacrifice fly to drive home the winning run in Boston's 7-6 victory.

Ironically, a deal between the Red Sox and Mets prior to the '86 season played a big part in both clubs' success.

On November 13, 1985, Gorman traded four pitchers—Bob Ojeda, Tom McCarthy, John Mitchell and Chris Bayer—to the Mets for pitchers Calvin Schiraldi and Wes Gardner and outfielders John Christensen and LaSchelle Tarver. Ojeda, who had never won more than 12 games in any of his six years with the Red Sox, led all Mets starting pitchers with 18 regular-season wins and two postseason triumphs —including a 7-1 victory over his former teammates in Game 3 of the World Series. Schiraldi, who started the season with the Red Sox's Triple-A Pawtucket (International) affiliate, won four games, posted nine saves and compiled a 1.41 earned-run average in 25 appearances for Boston after his July 19 recall. Prior to his poor Series performance—including losses in Games 6 and 7—Schiraldi had given the Sox their only reliable bullpen stopper.

A number of prominent players were released during the '86 season and, in some cases, were signed by other clubs.

On June 24, the Philadelphia Phillies let go of veteran lefthander Steve Carlton, a four-time Cy Young Award recipient and winner of 318 major league games. Carlton, at age 41, had just four wins in 16 starts and had yielded 102 hits and 57 earned runs in 83 innings before his release.

On July 4, the San Francisco Giants, leaders of the N.L. West, signed Carlton, releasing him one month later after just one win in six starts. Less than a week later, the Chicago White Sox signed Carlton for the remainder of the season. Carlton went 4-3 with a 3.69 ERA in the only 10 American League appearances of his 22-year big-league career.

Another release that garnered more than a few headlines came on August 7, when the Mets dumped veteran outfielder George Foster. A star of Cincinnati's Big Red Machine championship teams of the mid-'70s, Foster was a major disappointment in 4½ seasons in New York after signing a five-year, $10 million contract in 1982. Foster, who had hit just .227 with 13 homers and 38 RBIs prior to his release, didn't help his cause by alleging that Mets management was racist in making player moves.

Foster was signed by the White Sox one week later and hit .216 in 51 at-bats. Like Carlton, the late-season stint with the Sox

The acquisition of designated hitter Don Baylor was a big part of Boston's American League championship last season.

was the only A.L. experience of Foster's 18-year pro career.

The Atlanta Braves, who finished last in the N.L. West despite having baseball's best-paid club ($657,657 per player) in 1986, began the season by releasing pitchers Len Barker, Pascual Perez, Rick Camp and Terry Forster on April 1. The April Fools Day Massacre cost the Braves $3.6 million in contracts, $2.85 million alone for Barker, who had been acquired from Cleveland for Brook Jacoby and Brett Butler in 1983.

A number of former stars received unconditional releases from their teams after the season ended. Among those were Los Angeles shortstop Bill Russell, the last remaining Dodger from the club's long-running infield of Steve Garvey, Davey Lopes, Russell and Ron Cey of the 1970s, and San Diego third baseman Graig Nettles, a three-year member of the Padres whose greatest seasons were with the Yankees' championship clubs of the late

'70s.

Four off-season deals made late in the year stand out as perhaps the most important:

• The Pirates finally traded veteran pitcher Rick Rhoden, who had been on Pittsburgh's trading block for years. Rhoden was traded to the Yankees on November 26 along with Cecilio Guante and Pat Clements for Doug Drabek, Brian Fisher and Logan Easley. All six players are pitchers, but Rhoden—who figures to do well with a good offensive team behind him—was the key player involved.

• The Dodgers made two deals December 10, trading pitcher Dennis Powell to Seattle for pitcher Matt Young and dealing first baseman Greg Brock to Milwaukee for pitchers Tim Leary and Tim Crews. The Dodgers need pitching and Brock was never able to escape Steve Garvey's shadow in Los Angeles.

• The Royals believe they found the slugging outfielder they need when they acquired 24-year-old Danny Tartabull from Seattle December 10. To get Tartabull, who hit 25 homers and drove in 96 runs for the Mariners last season, the Royals gave up pitchers Scott Bankhead and Steve Shields and outfielder Mike Kingery.

• The world-champion Mets, baseball's dominant team in 1986, figures to be even stronger in '87 after pulling off the biggest trade at the Hollywood, Fla., winter meetings. On December 11, the Mets traded five of their best young prospects—infielder-outfielder Kevin Mitchell, outfielders Stanley Jefferson and Shawn Abner and pitchers Kevin Armstrong and Kevin Brown—to the Padres for slugging outfielder Kevin McReynolds, pitcher Gene Walter and a minor leaguer. The Mets traded the future for the present, believing McReynolds, who hit 26 homers with 96 RBIs last season, is just what they need to retain their status as baseball's best club.

Following is a list of all player transactions for the 1986 calendar year:

January 7—Astros re-signed shortstop Dickie Thon, a free agent.

January 7—Twins traded pitchers Ken Schrom and Bryan Oelkers to Indians for pitchers Roy Smith and Ramon Romero.

January 8—Indians re-signed pitcher Jamie Easterly and second baseman Tony Bernazard, both free agents.

January 8—Yankees re-signed pitchers Phil Niekro and Joe Niekro and catcher Butch Wynegar, all free agents.

January 8—Tigers re-signed outfielder Kirk Gibson and third baseman Tom Brookens, both free agents.

January 8—Angels re-signed pitcher Donnie Moore, a free agent.

January 8—White Sox re-signed catcher Carlton Fisk, a free agent.

January 13—Cardinals signed infielder Vic Rodriguez, a free agent.

January 15—Cubs signed catcher Steve Christmas, a free agent.

January 15—Orioles signed infielder Juan Bonilla, a free agent, and assigned him to Rochester.

January 16—Rangers signed pitcher Mickey Mahler, a free agent.

January 16—Tigers released catcher-infielder Marty Castillo.

January 16—Twins traded second baseman Tim Teufel and outfielder Pat Crosby to Mets for outfielder Billy Beane and pitchers Bill Latham and Joe Klink; Mets assigned Crosby to Little Falls and Twins assigned Klink to Orlando.

January 16—Mets traded catcher Ronn Reynolds and pitcher Jeff Bittiger to Phillies for pitcher Rodger Cole and first baseman Ronnie Gideon; Phillies assigned Reynolds and Bittiger to Portland and Mets assigned Cole to Tidewater and Gideon to Lynchburg.

January 16—Reds signed pitcher Derek Botelho, a free agent, and assigned him to Denver.

January 16—Twins traded catcher Dave Engle to Tigers for infielder Chris Pittaro and outfielder Alex Sanchez.

January 17—Rangers re-signed outfielder Duane Walker, a free agent.

January 17—Cubs re-signed first baseman Richie Hebner, a free agent.

January 18—Mariners signed pitchers Pete Ladd and Steve Fireovid and infielders Lorenzo Gray and Jerry Dybzinski, all free agents, and all assigned to Calgary.

January 20—A's re-signed designated hitter Dave Kingman, a free agent.

January 20—Reds re-signed first baseman Tony Perez, a free agent.

January 21—Angels signed outfielder Mark Ryal, a free agent.

January 22—Expos re-signed infielder Wally Johnson, a free agent.

January 23—Orioles released outfielder Dan Ford.

January 23—Indians purchased infielder Fran Mullins from Giants.

January 26—Cubs re-signed pitcher Lary Sorensen, a free agent.

January 27—Giants' Phoenix affiliate signed pitcher Jon Perlman, a free agent.

January 28—Orioles signed first baseman-outfielder Juan Beniquez, a free agent formerly with the Angels.

January 28—Rangers signed catcher Darrell Porter, a free agent formerly with the Cardinals.

January 28—Padres signed first baseman-outfielder Dane Iorg, a free agent formerly with the Royals.

January 29—A's Tacoma affiliate signed pitcher Bob Stoddard, a free agent.

January 31—Tigers signed pitcher Bill Campbell, a free agent formerly with the Cardinals.

January 31—Red Sox' Pawtucket affiliate signed pitcher Joe Sambito, a free agent.

February 1—Cubs signed pitcher Matt Keough, a free agent formerly with the Cardinals.

February 1—A's Tacoma affiliate signed infielder Lenn Sakata, a free agent formerly with the Orioles.

February 3—Giants re-signed outfielder Randy Kutcher and signed pitchers Rick Waits and Mike LaCoss and outfielder Chris Jones, all free agents, and assigned them to Phoenix.

February 4—Expos signed shortstop Ivan DeJesus, a free agent formerly with the Cardinals, and assigned him to Indianapolis.

February 5—Mariners' Calgary affiliate signed pitcher Milt Wilcox, a free agent.

February 5—Orioles re-signed outfielder Jim Dwyer, a free agent.

February 6—Yankees signed pitcher Al Holland, a free agent formerly with the Angels, and assigned him to Columbus.

February 7—Mets released infielder Ross Jones.

February 7—Mariners re-signed outfielder Al Cowens, a free agent.

February 8—Indians' Maine affiliate signed pitcher Dickie Noles, a free agent.

February 10—Tigers' Nashville affiliate signed outfielder Tim Tolman, a free agent.

February 10—Cardinals purchased pitcher Greg Bargar from Expos' Indianapolis affiliate and assigned him to Louisville.

February 10—Indians released catcher Butch Benton.

February 13—Pirates' Hawaii affiliate signed pitcher Ed Farmer, a free agent.

February 13—White Sox traded catchers Ron Hassey and Chris Alvarez, pitcher Eric Schmidt and outfielder Matt Winters to Yankees for pitcher Neil Allen, catcher Scott Bradley, outfielder Glen Braxton and cash.

February 13—Braves signed pitcher David Palmer, a free agent.

February 14—Expos re-signed pitcher Bert Roberge, a free agent, and assigned him to Indianapolis.

February 14—Expos sold pitcher Luis Sanchez to Yomiuri Giants of Japanese Baseball.

February 18—Tigers' Nashville affiliate signed first baseman Harry Spilman, a free agent formerly with the Astros.

February 18—Mariners' Chattanooga affiliate signed infielder Ross Jones, a free agent.

February 20—Orioles signed pitcher Luis DeLeon, a free agent, and assigned him to Rochester.

February 25—Indians' Maine affiliate signed pitcher Jim Kern, a free agent.

February 27—Expos purchased catcher Randy Hunt from Cardinals.

March 4—Mets signed first baseman-outfielder Tim Corcoran, a free agent, and assigned him to Tidewater.

March 5—Brewers traded catcher Ted Simmons to Braves for catcher Rick Cerone, pitcher David Clay and shortstop Flavio Alfaro.

March 14—Blue Jays' Syracuse affiliate signed outfielder-first baseman Cesar Cedeno, a free agent formerly with the Cardinals.

March 17—Phillies released catcher-first baseman Alan Knicely.

March 17—Yankees re-signed pitcher John Montefusco, a free agent.

March 18—Angels re-signed pitcher Ken Forsch, a free agent.

March 18—Tigers released infielder Doug Flynn.

March 19—Red Sox released infielder Ed Jurak.

March 20—Giants re-signed outfielder Joel Youngblood, a free agent.

March 20—Mariners released pitcher Frank Wills and catcher Donnie Scott.

March 21—A's released infielder Barbaro Garbey.

March 21—Cardinals' Louisville affiliate signed catcher-first baseman Alan Knicely, a free agent.

March 21—Angels released pitcher Frank LaCorte.

March 23—Padres released pitcher Roy Lee Jackson.

March 23—Twins signed pitcher Roy Lee Jackson, a free agent, and assigned him to Toledo.

March 24—Giants released infielder Dave Owen.

March 25—Padres released shortstop Mario Ramirez.

March 25—Mariners released outfielder Al Chambers.

March 26—Cubs released pitcher Lary Sorensen.

March 26—Expos released pitcher Jack O'Connor.

March 27—Rangers released pitcher Burt Hooton and outfielder Duane Walker.

March 27—Rangers signed infielder Dave Owen, a free agent, and assigned him to Oklahoma City.

March 27—Indians signed pitcher Frank Wills, a free agent, and assigned him to Maine.

March 28—Indians released pitchers Jeff Barkley and Dave Von Ohlen.

March 28—Indians released pitcher Ron Musselman.

March 28—Royals released outfielders Pat Sheridan and Mike Jones and pitcher Joe Beckwith.

March 28—Yankees released pitcher Phil Niekro.

March 28—Red Sox traded designated hitter Mike Easler to Yankees for designated hitter Don Baylor.

March 30—Brewers traded pitcher Moose Haas to A's for infielder Steve Kiefer, pitchers Mike Fulmer and Pete Kendrick and catcher Charlie O'Brien; Brewers assigned O'Brien to Vancouver.

March 31—Blue Jays' Syracuse affiliate signed pitcher Ron Musselman, a free agent.

March 31—Cardinals traded catcher Tom Nieto to Expos for infielder Fred Manrique.

March 31—Cubs released outfielder Gary Woods and pitcher Reggie Patterson.

March 31—Reds traded infielder Wayne Krenchicki to Expos for pitcher Norm Charlton and a player to be named; Reds acquired second baseman Tim Barker on April 2.

March 31—Mariners released infielder Jerry Dybzinski.

April 1—Braves signed outfielder Omar Moreno, a free agent, and assigned him to Richmond.

April 1—Mariners released second baseman Jack Perconte.

April 1—Cardinals released outfielder Brian Harper.

April 1—Braves released pitchers Pascual Perez, Len Barker, Rick Camp and Terry Forster.

April 1—Cubs released first baseman Richie Hebner.

April 1—Indians released catcher Jerry Willard and pitcher Jerry Reed.

April 1—Astros released pitcher Bill Dawley.

April 1—Expos released outfielder Terry Francona, pitcher John Stuper and catcher Ned Yost.

April 1—Brewers released outfielder David Green and pitcher Ray Burris.

April 1—Royals traded pitcher Tony Ferreira to Mets for shortstop Argenis Salazar; Mets assigned Ferreira to Tidewater.

April 1—Mets released pitcher Tom Gorman.

April 1—Royals released shortstop Onix Concepcion.

April 1—White Sox released outfielder Rudy Law.

April 1—Giants released outfielder Ron Roenicke.

April 2—Braves traded pitcher Mike Santiago to Mets for pitcher Ed Olwine; Mets assigned Santiago to Jackson and Braves assigned Olwine to Richmond.

April 2—Dodgers released infielder Bob Bailor and pitcher Bobby Castillo.

April 3—Blue Jays released outfielder-first baseman Cesar Cedeno.

April 3—Royals reclaimed pitcher Jose DeJesus from Blue Jays, who had selected him from Omaha in the 1985 major league draft; Royals assigned DeJesus to Omaha.

April 3—Pirates traded outfielder Marvell Wynne to Padres for pitcher Bob Patterson.

April 3—Orioles released infielder Wayne Gross.

April 3—Astros' Tucson affiliate signed outfielder Duane Walker, a free agent.

April 3—Miami (Independent) signed pitcher Dave Von Ohlen, a free agent.

April 3—Indians signed pitcher Phil Niekro, a free agent.

April 4—Pirates released outfielder Sixto Lezcano and shortstop Johnnie LeMaster.

April 4—Pirates traded first baseman Jason Thompson to Expos for two players to be named; Pirates acquired outfielder Ben Abner and infielder Ronnie Giddens on April 7. Pirates assigned both to Macon.

April 4—Yankees released pitcher Al Holland.

April 4—Reds released pitcher Frank Pastore.

April 4—Reds signed pitcher Chris Welsh, a free agent, and assigned him to Denver.

April 4—A's signed catcher Jerry Willard, a free agent, and assigned him to Tacoma.

April 4—Royals signed outfielder Rudy Law, a free agent.

April 6—Reds reclaimed pitcher Carl Willis from Angels, who had selected him from Denver in the 1985 major league draft; Reds assigned Willis to Denver.

April 7—Cubs released pitcher Warren Brusstar.

April 7—A's signed outfielder Ron Roenicke, a free agent, and assigned him to Tacoma.

April 7—Expos released first baseman-outfielder Scot Thompson.

April 10—Dodgers signed outfielder-first baseman Cesar Cedeno, a free agent.

April 10—Yankees' Columbus affiliate re-signed pitcher Al Holland, a free agent.

April 11—Mariners' Calgary affiliate signed pitcher Jerry Reed, a free agent.

April 11—Cardinals' Louisville affiliate signed pitcher Ray Burris, a free agent.

April 11—San Jose (Independent) signed pitcher Fernando Arroyo, a free agent.

April 15—White Sox signed pitcher Bill Dawley, a free agent.

April 16—Angels signed pitcher Terry Forster, a free agent.

April 18—A's traded pitcher Bob Stoddard and outfielder Kevin Russ to Padres for outfielder Kerry Tillman; A's assigned Tillman to Tacoma and Padres assigned Stoddard to Las Vegas and Russ to Charleston.

April 19—Phillies signed pitcher Tom Gorman, a free agent, and assigned him to Portland.

April 24—Pirates signed infielder U.L. Washington, a free agent formerly with the Expos, and assigned him to Hawaii.

April 25—Tigers signed outfielders Brian Harper and Pat Sheridan, both free agents.

April 28—Twins signed pitcher Frank Pastore, a free agent.

April 29—Tigers released outfielder Nelson Simmons.

April 30—Twins purchased pitcher Juan Agosto from White Sox in exchange for loaning pitcher Pete Filson to White Sox' Buffalo affiliate; Filson was returned to Twins and traded to White Sox for pitcher Kurt Walker, September 3. Twins assigned Walker to Orlando.

May 1—Giants released first baseman Dan Driessen.

May 1—Yankees' Columbus affiliate signed shortstop Ivan DeJesus, a free agent.

May 2—Cubs signed first baseman-outfielder Terry Francona, a free agent, and assigned him to Iowa.

May 2—Yankees signed pitcher Tommy John, a free agent formerly with the A's.

May 4—Orioles' Rochester affiliate signed outfielder Nelson Simmons, a free agent.

May 5—Phillies' Portland affiliate signed pitcher Lary Sorensen, a free agent.

May 5—San Jose (Independent) released pitcher Fernando Arroyo.

May 6—Cubs released pitcher Dick Ruthven.

May 6—Rangers released pitcher Dave Rozema.

May 7—Phillies placed outfielder Garry Maddox on voluntarily retired list.

May 7—White Sox signed infielder Jack Perconte, a free agent, and assigned him to Buffalo.

May 8—Pirates released outfielder Steve Kemp.

May 9—Phillies released pitcher Dave Stewart.

May 9—Phillies purchased outfielder Ron Roenicke from A's Tacoma affiliate.

May 12—A's Tacoma affiliate signed third baseman Wayne Gross, a free agent.

May 13—Phillies released pitcher Larry Andersen.

May 16—Astros signed pitcher Larry Andersen, a free agent.

May 19—A's signed pitcher Doug Bair, a free agent, and assigned him to Tacoma.

May 20—A's traded pitcher Keith Atherton to Twins for a player to be named and cash; A's Tacoma affiliate acquired pitcher Eric Broersma on May 23.

May 20—White Sox' Buffalo affiliate signed pitcher Dave Rozema, a free agent.

May 21—Royals traded pitcher Mark Huismann to Mariners for catcher Terry Bell; Royals assigned Bell to Memphis.

May 23—A's Tacoma affiliate signed pitcher Dave Stewart, a free agent.

May 24—San Jose (Independent) signed pitcher Vern Ruhle, a free agent.

May 24—Dodgers released outfielder Terry Whitfield.

May 25—Angels released pitcher Ken Forsch.

May 27—Phillies placed outfielder Joe Lefebvre on voluntarily retired list.

May 27—White Sox released catcher Marc Hill.

May 29—A's released outfielder Steve Henderson.

May 29—A's Modesto affiliate signed pitcher Fernando Arroyo, a free agent.

June 1—A's Tacoma affiliate purchased pitcher Dave Von Ohlen from Miami (Independent).

June 2—Astros signed first baseman Dan Driessen, a free agent, and assigned him to Tucson.

June 3—Astros signed pitcher Aurelio Lopez, a free agent formerly with the Tigers.

June 5—Dodgers released outfielder-first baseman Cesar Cedeno.

June 5—San Jose (Independent) released pitcher Vern Ruhle.

June 5—Angels' Edmonton affiliate signed pitcher Vern Ruhle, a free agent.

June 8—Expos purchased pitcher Bob McClure from Brewers.

June 9—Mets released first baseman-outfielder Tim Corcoran.

June 12—Tigers released infielder Harry Spilman.

June 12—Cardinals released outfielder Jerry White.

June 12—Brewers traded infielder Randy Ready to Padres for a player to be named; Brewers acquired infielder Tim Pyznarski on October 29. Brewers assigned Pyznarski to Denver.

June 12—Mariners released outfielder Al Cowens.

June 13—A's signed pitcher Bobby Castillo, a free agent, and assigned him to Tacoma.

June 13—Giants signed infielder Harry Spilman, a free agent.

June 14—Cubs released pitcher Matt Keough.

June 14—Mariners released pitcher Milt Wilcox.

June 16—Orioles traded pitcher Dennis Martinez to Expos for a player to be named; Orioles acquired infielder Rene Gonzales on December 16.

June 17—Indians released pitcher Jim Kern.

June 18—Rangers traded outfielder George Wright to Expos for a player to be named or cash.

June 20—Indians traded pitcher Neal Heaton to Twins for pitcher John Butcher.

June 20—White Sox signed outfielder Steve Henderson, a free agent, and assigned him to Buffalo.

June 23—Padres' Las Vegas affiliate signed outfielder Steve Kemp, a free agent.

June 24—Yankees released shortstop Ivan DeJesus.

June 24—Phillies released pitcher Steve Carlton.

June 25—Mariners released outfielder-designated hitter Gorman Thomas.

June 26—Phillies released pitcher Randy Lerch.

June 26—White Sox traded catcher Scott Bradley to Mariners for a player to be named; White Sox acquired outfielder Ivan Calderon on July 1. White Sox assigned Calderon to Buffalo.

June 29—White Sox traded pitcher Tom Seaver to Red Sox for outfielder Steve Lyons.

June 30—Astros' Tucson affiliate signed pitcher Matt Keough, a free agent.

June 30—Yankees traded outfielder Ken Griffey to Braves for outfielder Claudell Washington and shortstop Paul Zuvella.

June 30—Expos released first baseman Jason Thompson.

June 30—Mets traded pitcher Ed Lynch to Cubs for pitcher Dave Lenderman and catcher David Liddell; Mets assigned Lenderman to Jackson and Liddell to Columbia.

June 30—Angels released pitcher Jim Slaton.

July 2—Yankees purchased infielder Bryan Little from White Sox and assigned him to Columbus.

July 4—Giants signed pitcher Steve Carlton, a free agent.

July 6—Blue Jays traded pitcher Doyle Alexander to Braves for pitcher Duane Ward; Blue Jays assigned Ward to Syracuse.

July 6—Blue Jays traded pitcher Jim Acker to Braves for pitcher Joe Johnson.

July 9—Padres traded pitcher Mark Thurmond to Tigers for pitcher Dave LaPoint.

July 9—Padres traded pitcher Tim Stoddard to Yankees for pitcher Ed Whitson.

July 12—San Jose (Independent) signed outfielder Terry Whitfield, a free agent.

July 12—Mariners' Calgary affiliate signed pitcher Ken Forsch, a free agent.

July 14—Tigers signed pitcher Jim Slaton, a free agent.

July 15—Cubs released catcher Steve Lake.

July 16—Reds' Vermont affiliate signed shortstop Ivan DeJesus, a free agent.

July 16—Brewers signed outfielder-designated hitter Gorman Thomas, a free agent.

July 18—A's released pitcher Rick Langford.

July 19—Cardinals' Louisville affiliate signed outfielder-first baseman Cesar Cedeno, a free agent.

July 21—Mariners released outfielder Barry Bonnell.

July 21—Astros traded pitcher Frank DiPino to Cubs for outfielder Davey Lopes.

July 21—San Jose (Independent) signed outfielder Jerry White, a free agent.

July 23—White Sox traded pitcher Al Jones and outfielder Tom Hartley to Brewers for pitcher Ray Searage.

July 23—Pirates traded pitcher Jose DeLeon to White Sox for outfielder Bobby Bonilla; White Sox assigned DeLeon to Buffalo.

July 23—Pirates released outfielder Lee Mazzilli.

July 24—Cubs traded pitcher Steve Engel to Astros, completing deal in which Astros traded outfielder Jerry Mumphrey to Cubs for outfielder Billy Hatcher and a player to be named, December 16, 1985. Astros assigned Engel to Tucson.

July 24—Expos traded pitcher Dan Schatzeder and infielder Skeeter Barnes to Phillies for infielder Tom Foley and pitcher Lary Sorensen; Phillies assigned Barnes to Portland and Expos assigned Sorensen to Indianapolis.

July 24—Cardinals' Louisville affiliate signed catcher Steve Lake, a free agent.

July 26—Cubs traded pitcher Ron Meridith to Rangers for pitcher Bryan Dial and a player to be named; Cubs acquired pitcher Rick Surhoff on July 28. Cubs assigned Surhoff to Iowa.

July 27—Yankees released infielder Dale Berra.

July 27—A's released outfielder Ricky Peters.

July 28—Reds' Vermont affiliate released

shortstop Ivan DeJesus.

July 30—White Sox traded outfielder-designated hitter Ron Kittle, infielder Wayne Tolleson and catcher Joel Skinner to Yankees for catcher Ron Hassey, shortstop Carlos Martinez and a player to be named; White Sox organization acquired catcher Bill Lindsey on December 24.

July 31—Dodgers purchased pitcher Joe Beckwith from Blue Jays' Syracuse affiliate.

August 1—Brewers re-signed pitcher Pete Vuckovich, a free agent, and assigned him to Vancouver.

August 1—Astros released outfielder Duane Walker.

August 3—Mets signed outfielder Lee Mazzilli, a free agent, and assigned him to Tidewater.

August 3—Cardinals' Louisville affiliate signed outfielder Duane Walker, a free agent.

August 4—Astros signed infielder Dale Berra, a free agent, and assigned him to Tucson.

August 7—Giants released pitcher Steve Carlton.

August 7—Mets released outfielder George Foster.

August 8—Yankees released pitcher Al Holland.

August 10—Cardinals traded catcher Mike Heath to Tigers for pitcher Ken Hill and a player to be named; Cardinals acquired first baseman Mike Laga on September 2. Cardinals assigned Hill to Arkansas.

August 10—Tigers released catcher Dave Engle.

August 12—White Sox signed pitcher Steve Carlton, a free agent.

August 13—Twins traded pitchers Ron Davis and Dewayne Coleman to Cubs for pitchers George Frazier and Ray Fontenot and shortstop Julius McDougal; Cubs assigned Coleman to Winston-Salem and Twins assigned McDougal to Orlando.

August 15—Brewers traded pitcher Danny Darwin to Astros for pitcher Don August and a player to be named; Brewers acquired pitcher Mark Knudson on August 21. Brewers assigned Knudson to Vancouver.

August 15—White Sox signed outfielder George Foster, a free agent.

August 19—Mariners traded infielder Spike Owen and outfielder Dave Henderson to Red Sox for infielder Rey Quinones, a player to be named and cash; as part of deal, Mariners claimed pitchers Mike Brown and Mike Trujillo on waivers from Red Sox, August 22, and acquired outfielder John Christensen on September 25.

August 27—Cardinals released pitcher Ray Burris.

September 1—Blue Jays purchased pitcher Mickey Mahler from Rangers' Oklahoma City affiliate.

September 7—White Sox released outfielder George Foster.

September 23—Royals traded outfielder Darryl Motley to Braves for pitcher Steve Shields.

September 30—Brewers released pitcher Chuck Porter.

October 2—White Sox re-signed catcher Marc Hill, a free agent.

October 2—Royals claimed outfielder Jim Eisenreich on waivers.

October 7—Expos released pitcher Bert Roberge.

October 8—White Sox released catcher Marc Hill.

October 8—Blue Jays released pitcher Mickey Mahler.

October 9—Padres released outfielder Dane Iorg.

October 13—Braves released outfielder Omar Moreno and pitcher Mike Payne.

October 15—Yankees released outfielder Leo Hernandez and second baseman Bryan Little.

October 15—Tigers released pitchers Bill Campbell and Jim Slaton.

October 16—Brewers released designated hitter Gorman Thomas.

October 16—Tigers released outfielder Dave Collins.

October 16—Giants released catcher Brad Gulden and pitcher Chuck Hensley.

October 20—Dodgers released pitcher Carlos Diaz.

October 20—Blue Jays released pitcher Dennis Lamp.

October 21—Brewers released pitcher Pete Vuckovich.

October 21—Expos released pitcher Dave Tomlin.

October 24—Astros released first baseman Dan Driessen, pitcher Matt Keough and catcher John Mizerock.

October 29—Indians released outfielder Jim Weaver.

October 30—Padres traded catcher Terry Kennedy and pitcher Mark Williamson to Orioles for pitcher Storm Davis.

October 31—Cardinals released first baseman Alan Knicely.

November 1—Expos released outfielder Jim Wohlford.

November 1—Padres released pitcher Bob Stoddard.

November 3—Dodgers released pitcher Joe Beckwith and infielder Enos Cabell.

November 7—Pirates released infielder U. L. Washington.

November 7—Indians released infielder Fran Mullins.

November 10—Giants released pitcher Bill Laskey, outfielder Rick Lancellotti and infielder Luis Quinones.

November 11—Reds released first baseman Pete Rose as a player, pitcher Chris Welsh and catcher Dave Van Gorder.

November 12—Mets traded shortstop Ron Gardenhire to Twins for a player to be named; Twins assigned Gardenhire to Portland.

November 12—Orioles released infielder Juan Bonilla.

November 12—Pirates released pitcher Ray Krawczyk.

November 12—Dodgers released shortstop Bill Russell.

November 12—Phillies released pitcher Dave Rucker.

November 13—Expos signed outfielder Dave Collins, a free agent.

November 15—Royals signed pitchers Bill Swaggerty, Jerry Don Gleaton and Craig Pippin, first baseman Joe DeSa, and catcher Jamie Nelson, all free agents and all assigned to Memphis.

November 16—Phillies traded pitcher Rocky Childress to Astros for a player to be named.

November 17—Braves signed catcher Al Pardo, pitcher Chuck Hensley and outfielder Trench Davis, all free agents, and all assigned to Richmond.

November 20—Orioles re-signed outfielder Jim Dwyer, a free agent.

November 26—Pirates traded pitchers Rick Rhoden, Cecilio Guante and Pat Clements to Yankees for pitchers Doug Drabek, Brian Fisher and Logan Easley.

December 1—Reds traded pitcher Mike (Mississippi) Smith to Expos for a player to be named; Reds organization acquired pitcher Bill Cutshall on December 9.

December 3—Rangers signed infielder Tom O'Malley, catcher Alan Knicely and pitcher Dave Rucker, all free agents, and all assigned to Oklahoma City.

December 5—Red Sox re-signed pitcher Joe Sambito, a free agent.

December 5—Rangers re-signed catcher Darrell Porter, a free agent.

December 5—Reds re-signed shortstop Dave Concepcion, a free agent.

December 5—Pirates traded second baseman Rich Renteria to Mariners for a player to be named; Pirates acquired pitcher Bob Siegel on December 10.

December 6—Yankees re-signed pitcher Rod Scurry, a free agent.

December 7—Yankees re-signed outfielder Claudell Washington, a free agent.

December 8—Orioles traded catcher John Stefero to Expos for a player to be named; Orioles acquired infielder Rene Gonzales on December 16.

December 8—Tigers re-signed outfielder Larry Herndon, a free agent.

December 8—Royals re-signed outfielder Rudy Law and catcher Jamie Quirk, both free agents.

December 8—A's released third baseman Wayne Gross.

December 8—Phillies released pitcher Jeff Bittiger.

December 9—Expos signed pitcher Mike Madden and catcher John Mizerock, both free agents, and assigned them to Indianapolis.

December 9—Giants re-signed pitcher Mike LaCoss and infielder Harry Spilman, both free agents.

December 10—Dodgers traded pitcher Dennis Powell and infielder Mike Watters to Mariners for pitcher Matt Young.

December 10—Giants signed infielder Chris Speier, a free agent formerly with the Cubs.

December 10—Dodgers traded first baseman Greg Brock to Brewers for pitchers Tim Leary and Tim Crews.

December 10—Mariners traded outfielder Danny Tartabull and pitcher Rick Luecken to Royals for pitchers Scott Bankhead and Steve Shields and outfielder Mike Kingery.

December 11—Yankees traded outfielder Mike Easler and infielder Tom Barrett to Phillies for pitcher Charles Hudson and pitcher Jeff Knox.

December 11—A's traded infielder Donnie Hill to White Sox for pitcher Gene Nelson and a player to be named; A's acquired pitcher Bruce Tanner on December 18 and assigned him to Tacoma.

December 11—Mets traded outfielders Shawn Abner and Stanley Jefferson, third baseman Kevin Mitchell and pitchers Kevin Armstrong and Kevin Brown to Padres for outfielder Kevin McReynolds, pitcher Gene Walter and infielder Adam Ging.

December 15—Astros re-signed infielder-outfielder Davey Lopes, a free agent.

December 16—Rangers released pitcher Ricky Wright.

December 16—Yankees signed infielder Lenn Sakata, a free agent formerly with the A's.

December 17—Orioles traded outfielder Juan Beniquez to Royals for shortstop Joe Jarrell and pitcher Jimmy Daniels; Orioles assigned Jarrell and Daniels to Rochester.

December 17—Mets traded catcher Doug Gwosdz to Mariners for outfielder Ricky Nelson; Mets assigned Nelson to Tidewater and Mariners assigned Gwosdz to Calgary.

December 17—Dodgers released pitcher Ed Vande Berg and catcher Jack Fimple.

December 17—Cardinals released pitcher Ken Dayley.

December 18—Royals released outfielder Mike Brewer.

December 18—Padres released third baseman Graig Nettles and pitcher Dave LaPoint.

December 19—Orioles released pitcher Nate Snell.

December 19—Angels released second baseman Bobby Grich and outfielder Rufino Linares.

December 19—Yankees traded catcher Butch Wynegar to Angels for pitcher Ron Romanick and a player to be named; Yankees assigned Romanick to Columbus.

December 19—Mariners released pitcher Roy Thomas.

December 19—Astros re-signed pitcher Larry Andersen and catcher Alan Ashby, both free agents.

December 19—Cardinals re-signed pitcher Bob Forsch, a free agent.

December 19—Tigers re-signed pitcher Jack Morris, a free agent.

December 19—Braves re-signed pitcher David Palmer, a free agent.

December 19—Twins released pitchers Juan Agosto, Ray Fontenot and Roy Smith.

December 19—Expos released pitcher Bryn Smith, catcher Dann Bilardello and outfielder George Wright.

December 19—Giants released pitchers Juan Berenguer, Atlee Hammaker and Jim Gott.

December 20—Red Sox' Pawtucket affiliate re-signed infielder Glenn Hoffman, a free agent.

December 20—White Sox released pitcher Dave Schmidt and infielders Jack Perconte and Luis Salazar.

December 22—Cardinals traded infielder Fred Manrique to White Sox for pitcher Bill Dawley.

December 22—Pirates released pitcher Lee Tunnell.

December 22—A's signed pitcher Carlos Diaz, a free agent.

December 22—Yankees released pitchers Mike Armstrong and Bob Shirley.

December 22—Royals released pitchers Al Hargesheimer and Dennis Leonard, first baseman Steve Balboni and outfielder Jorge Orta.

December 23—Indians released pitcher John Butcher.

December 23—Brewers released pitcher Jaime Cocanower.

December 23—Mariners signed infielder Dave Stapleton, a free agent formerly with the Red Sox.

December 24—A's signed outfielder Reggie Jackson, a free agent formerly with the Angels.

December 24—Yankees signed outfielder Gary Ward, a free agent formerly with the Rangers.

December 26—Phillies re-signed pitcher Tom Hume, a free agent.

Veeck's Death Saddens Baseball

By RON SMITH

Bill Veeck, the maverick, promotions-minded owner who once sent a midget to the plate in a major league game, and Hall of Famers Hank Greenberg, Ted Lyons and Red Ruffing were the most notable baseball personalities who died in 1986.

The energetic Veeck regarded baseball as entertainment and worked himself into a position to put his outlandish theories into practice, much to the delight of fans and the chagrin of his more serious-minded fellow owners.

Following in the footsteps of his father, Bill Sr., who was president of the Chicago Cubs, Veeck worked his way up in the Cubs organization from stockboy to club treasurer before striking out on his own in the early 1940s, joining with long-time buddy Charley Grimm to buy the down-and-out Milwaukee Brewers, a minor league club languishing at the bottom of the American Association standings.

Veeck quickly showed a promotional genius that soon would become the trademark of his colorful career.

Using a gimmick called "Veeck's Verities," a series of giveaways ranging from a 200-pound block of ice to live lobsters, Veeck began putting people in the Milwaukee park and the Brewers responded by playing winning baseball, capturing Association pennants the last three years that Veeck and Grimm operated the club. That association ended after the 1945 season when Veeck, who had returned on crutches six weeks earlier from World War II duty in the South Pacific after his lower right leg had been crushed by a piece of artillery, sold his controlling interest in the club.

The leg eventually had to be amputated, but that didn't stop Veeck from pursuing his dream—a major league franchise. He found that franchise in Cleveland, where the woebegone Indians had been put on the block. Veeck headed a syndicate that purchased the team, raising most of the $2.2 million through an innovative stock debenture deal. And with Veeck pulling the strings, Cleveland's attendance doubled the first season and the Indians began their climb up the American League standings.

The Indians won the A.L. pennant in 1948 in a one-game playoff against the Boston Red Sox and then defeated the Boston Braves in the World Series. But Veeck's biggest claim to fame in Cleveland was the 1947 signing of infielder Larry Doby, breaking the American League color barrier.

Veeck sold the Indians in 1949 and then took on the St. Louis Browns two years later. The Browns were floundering at the bottom of the A.L. standings and fighting a losing battle in St. Louis against the more popular Cardinals. Veeck used every trick and promotional gimmick he could conceive to turn that around, but never quite succeeded. His most outlandish gimmick occurred in 1951 when he hired midget Eddie Gaedel to pop out of a birthday cake between games of a doubleheader against Detroit and then shocked the baseball world by sending Gaedel, dressed in a Browns uniform bearing the number ⅛ on its back, to the plate as a pinch-hitter in the first inning of the nightcap.

After much discussion, Gaedel was allowed to bat and walked on four pitches. A.L. President Will Harridge banned Gaedel from baseball the next day, but Veeck was laughing all the way to the bank.

He wasn't laughing, however, in 1952 when he tried to move the Browns to Baltimore and was given permission—provided he sell out first. He did and remained in self-imposed banishment until 1958 when he joined with Hank Greenberg to buy the Chicago White Sox. In 1959, Veeck's first season of ownership, his innovative exploding scoreboard was introduced to baseball and the White Sox captured the A.L. pennant.

Veeck was forced into retirement again in 1961 because of his health but emerged again in 1975 to head a group that saved the financially struggling White Sox. Unable to compete in the free-agent market, however, Veeck sold the team in 1980 to a group headed by Jerry Reinsdorf and Eddie Einhorn, the current owners.

He remained in retirement until he died January 2 of cardiac arrest in a Chicago hospital. The 71-year-old Veeck had been admitted three days earlier, suffering from respiratory problems. He had undergone surgery in 1984 for the removal of a tumor in one lung.

The 6-foot-3½, 215-pound Greenberg was the son of Romanian Jewish immigrants who became one of the most feared power hitters in baseball history. After honing his early skills on the playgrounds of New York City, the 19-year-old youngster signed with the Detroit Tigers in 1930

Bill Veeck (center) had reason to celebrate in 1948 after his Indians, led by player-Manager Lou Boudreau (right), had dispatched the Boston Braves in the World Series.

and reached the major leagues three years later as a 22-year-old rookie first baseman. He didn't disappoint.

Sometimes awkward around the first-base bag, Greenberg more than made up for any fielding deficiencies with his lively bat. In 117 games in his rookie season he batted .301 with 12 home runs and 87 runs batted in. He was just warming up.

Greenberg followed that up in 1934 by leading the American League with 63 doubles while his RBI total swelled to 139. The Tigers, under Manager Mickey Cochrane, captured the A.L. pennant before losing to the St. Louis Cardinals in the World Series.

The Tigers repeated as A.L. champions in 1935 and Greenberg won the first of his two MVP awards. He batted .328 and led the league with 36 home runs and 170 RBIs but broke his wrist in the second game of the World Series against the Chicago Cubs and was not a factor in the Tigers' six-game victory.

Greenberg got off to a blazing start in the first 12 games of the 1936 season but broke the same wrist in a first-base collision and was forced to sit out the remainder of the campaign. He rebounded in 1937 with a 183-RBI season (one short of the A.L. record) and blasted a league-leading 58 home runs in 1938. He captured his second MVP in 1940 with a 41-homer, 150-RBI campaign in which he batted .340.

Greenberg's career was put on hold when he enlisted in the Army Air Corps and went on to earn four battle stars during World War II. He returned to baseball with a vengence midway through the 1945 season and capped his storybook comeback in the final game of the season by hitting a pennant-clinching grand slam against the St. Louis Browns. He went on to hit .304 with two homers and seven RBIs in the Tigers' seven-game World Series conquest of the Cubs.

Greenberg's average dipped to .277 in 1946, but he still hit 44 homers and drove in 127 runs. He was shocked to learn during the off-season that he had been waived out of the A.L. and sold to the Pittsburgh Pirates.

After holding out for weeks, Greenberg finally relented and signed the first

Hall of Famer Hank Greenberg delighted Detroit Tigers fans with his raw power and consistency.

$100,000 contract in baseball history. The Pirates installed a temporary fence in front of the left-field wall at Forbes Field to create the famous Greenberg Gardens, but the big slugger managed only 25 homers and 74 RBIs in his final campaign.

Greenberg remained in baseball through 1963 in front-office jobs with the Cleveland Indians and Chicago White Sox, working in both cities under Veeck.

His career .313 batting average, 331 home runs, four home-run championships and two MVPs were more than enough to persuade Hall of Fame voters to honor Greenberg in 1956. The 75-year-old former slugger died of cancer September 4 in his Beverly Hills, Calif., home.

Lyons was a workhorse righthander who compiled a 260-230 career record in 21 seasons with the Chicago White Sox. The record is deceiving because Lyons worked for a White Sox team that finished in the first division only five times during his career.

Lyons joined the White Sox off the Baylor University campus in 1923 and won his last game in 1946. He was a 20-game winner three times, pitched a no-hitter in 1926 and in 1942, at age 41, started and finished 20 games, posting a 14-6 record and A.L.-leading 2.10 earned-run average. He left his mark as a hitter, too, tying a major league mark by doubling twice in the same inning of a July 28, 1935 game.

Lyons' best seasons were 1930, when he recorded a 22-15 record for the seventh-place Sox (62-92) and 1927, when he shared the A.L. lead with 22 victories while pitching for a fifth-place team. One of his more amazing performances occurred in 1929 when he battled George Uhle for 21 innings in a marathon eventually won by the Detroit Tigers, 6-5.

A sore arm limited Lyons to four victories in 1931 and forced him to turn to the knuckleball, which he used effectively throughout the remainder of his career. After spending three seasons in the South Pacific during World War II, Lyons returned to baseball in 1946 and took over in May for Jimmy Dykes as White Sox manager. When the Sox skidded to a 51-101 mark in 1948, Lyons was replaced.

He served as Tigers pitching coach from 1949 to '53 and was pitching coach for the Dodgers in 1954, Walter Alston's first year as manager in Brooklyn. He completed his baseball career as a White Sox scout in 1966.

The 85-year-old Lyons, who was elected to the Hall of Fame in 1955, died July 25 in a nursing home in Sulphur, La., after a six-month battle with cancer.

Nobody could have predicted the direction of Ruffing's career when the righthander was acquired by the New York Yankees on May 6, 1930. Between 1924 and 1930, Ruffing had compiled a not-too-spectacular 39-96 record for the Boston Red Sox, twice leading the American League in losses. But to say that the change of scenery proved beneficial is something of an understatement.

Ruffing combined with Lefty Gomez to give the Yankees an almost unbeatable 1-2 punch in the 1930s. He put together four straight 20-victory seasons (1936-39), coinciding with four straight World Series championships for the Yankees.

His 273-225 career record was remarkable considering his early lack of success and he punctuated that with a 7-2 mark in World Series competition.

Also amazing was the fact that Ruffing pitched for 22 seasons without four toes on his left foot, the result of a mining accident when he was a teen-ager. He said the pain from the injury never left him.

Ruffing would have been a 25-year man if not for 2½ years of Army service in World War II. He came out of the Army and rejoined the Yankees midway through the 1945 season at age 40 and proceeded to compile a 7-3 record and 2.90 ERA. He jumped off to a 5-1 record the next spring but suffered a broken ankle and was released. He caught on with the White Sox in 1947, but appeared in only nine games before suffering a knee injury that ended his career.

Ruffing maintained his connections with baseball long after his retirement. He scouted for the White Sox in 1948, managed in the minors for two summers and served as a superscout for the Indians from 1951 to mid-1959. He was one of the New York Mets' early scouts and the club's first pitching coach in 1962.

In 1967, after several near-misses, he was elected to the Hall of Fame in his last year of eligibility. In September 1973, Ruffing suffered a stroke that left him confined to a wheelchair. But his mind remained clear and he was a familiar figure at a number of Hall of Fame induction ceremonies in Cooperstown, N.Y.

Ruffing, also regarded as one of the best hitting pitchers ever to play the game (he hit 36 career home runs), died of heart failure February 17 in the emergency room of Hillcrest Hospital in Cleveland at age 80.

Among the other baseball personalities who died in 1986 were Paul Richards, the innovative manager and general manager who is considered the architect of the Baltimore Orioles' success during the 1960s; Norm Cash, the 1961 A.L. batting champion and long-time slugging first baseman for the Detroit Tigers; Vince DiMaggio, the oldest of the three baseball-playing DiMaggio brothers; Mike Garcia, a two-time 20-game winner and a member of Cleveland's exceptional pitching staffs in the 1950s; Pat Seerey, a former Chicago White Sox player who is one of 11 major leaguers to hit four home runs in one game; Joe Oeschger, the former Boston Braves righthander who dueled Brooklyn's Leon Cadore for 26 innings and a 1-1 tie in a 1920 Boston marathon; Roberto Maduro, the principal figure in the development of professional baseball in Cuba; Milt Richman, an award-winning baseball writer for United Press International; and Si Burick, the only sportswriter in a city without a major league team ever to be elected to the writers' wing of the Baseball Hall of Fame.

Red Ruffing (above) combined with Lefty Gomez during the 1930s to give the Yankees an almost unbeatable 1-2 pitching punch.

An alphabetical list of baseball deaths in 1986 follows:

Harold W. Arlin, 90, the announcer for the first major league baseball and college football games broadcast on commercial radio, at Mansfield, O., on March 15; worked at KDKA, the Pittsburgh Westinghouse Company's experimental station, as a time study foreman and engineer before his pioneer play-by-play performance in calling the Pittsburgh-Philadelphia National League game on August 21, 1921; described the Pittsburgh-West Virginia college football game at a KDKA microphone three months later at Pittsburgh's Forbes Field and followed that up by calling a Pittsburgh-Nebraska football game later that fall; was concerned with other broadcast areas in addition to sports and introduced such voices as Will Rogers, Lillian Gish, Lloyd George, William Jennings Bryan and Herbert Hoover to radio audiences through interviews; left KDKA after five years to pursue other interests; was recognized by the London Times as "the best known American voice in Europe."

John M. Boozer, 47, a righthanded relief pitcher with a 14-16 major league record in seven seasons with the Philadelphia Phillies in the 1960s, of Hodgkin's disease at Lexington, S.C., on January 27; signed by the Phillies in 1958, the sometimes-wild 6-foot-3 fireballer made the major league roster in 1962 but was relegated to bullpen duty; spent the next seven seasons shuffling up and down between the major and minor leagues, but still managed to appear in 171 big-league contests with a career 4.09 earned-run average; was outrighted to the minors in 1970 and never pitched in the majors again.

Dick Bray, 83, a former play-by-play announcer for the Cincinnati Reds and college football and basketball official, at Cincinnati; teamed with Red Barber and Waite Hoyt in the Reds' radio broadcast booth from 1937 to 1943 and then hosted a popular fan-in-the-stands show on radio until 1954; officiated for 12 years prior to his broadcast career, mostly in the Big Ten Conference.

Richard (Hobe) Brummette, 89, who managed Elizabethton (Tenn.) to five consecutive Appalachian League pennants in the late 1930s and early '40s after a long minor league playing career, at Knoxville on December 8; was a second baseman-outfielder with a good-hit, no-field reputation; led the Piedmont League with a .397 average in 1928 and batted .377 in 1937 as a player-manager for Elizabethton; won another Appalachian League pennant as manager of Kingsport in 1945.

William E. (Bill) Bryson, 70, a baseball writer for the Des Moines Register and Tribune for more than 40 years and a former correspondent for The Sporting News, at Des Moines on January 31; joined the sports department of the Des Moines papers in 1937 and wrote about a variety of sports until his retirement in 1978; covered minor league teams stationed in Des Moines and followed the major league scene closely, attending 32 consecutive World Series as a writer and columnist beginning in 1942; co-authored a baseball dictionary and contributed a chapter on baseball slang to H.L. Mencken's book, "The American Language, Supplement II."

Simon (Si) Burick, 77, the only sportswriter in a city with no major league team ever to be elected to the writers' wing of the Baseball Hall of Fame, at Dayton, O., on December 10; the son of an emigrant Russian cantor, Burick began his newspaper career in the sports department of the Dayton Daily News and went on to serve that publication for almost 58 years while earning a reputation that spread well beyond the Dayton area; became sports editor at age 19 and began writing a daily column in 1928; covered the Cincinnati Reds when they played at Redlands Field, Crosley Field and Riverfront Stadium, rarely missing an opening game; covered five Summer Olympics and wrote about hockey, boxing, auto racing, basketball and football as well as his first love, baseball; was widely known for his wit and conversational manner and was prized as an after-dinner speaker in the latter stages of his career; passed up numerous lucrative offers from major newspapers to remain loyal to his native Dayton; was active in numerous local civic causes and hosted a 15-minute sports program on radio station WHIO in Dayton for 26 years; authored three books, two of them autobiographies of baseball managers Sparky Anderson and Walter Alston; was inducted into the Hall of Fame as a recipient of the J.G. Taylor Spink Award in 1983; was still writing an occasional column for the Daily News at the time of his death.

Joseph F. Burns, 85, a catcher who appeared in eight games for the 1924 Chicago White Sox, at Trenton, N.J., on January 7; managed just two hits in 19 at-bats during his eight-game stay in Chicago and then played another 10 years in the minors before retiring.

John P. Carmichael, 83, a nationally syndicated sports columnist for the Chicago Daily News whose work earned him a spot in baseball's Hall of Fame, at Chicago on June 6; began his journalism career as a police reporter for the Milwaukee Journal and as a reporter and drama critic for the Milwaukee Leader before taking a job on the Chicago Herald and Examiner sports desk in 1927; moved to the Daily News in 1932 and began writing his column, "The Barber Shop," two years later; became Daily News sports editor in 1943 and held that position for 29 years; his nationally acclaimed column ran until 1972 and helped earn him induction into the writers' wing in the library of the baseball Hall of Fame in 1975 as the J.G. Taylor Spink Award winner; a popular after-dinner speaker in Chicago after retirement, Carmichael was among the first inductees into the Chicago Press Club Journalism Hall of Fame in 1980.

Harry P. Creighton, 75, an announcer who worked alongside Jack Brickhouse, Vince Lloyd and Jack Rosenberg in early telecasts of Chicago Cubs games over WGN-TV, at Chicago on November 25; was a familiar face on the screen during Cubs' telecasts in the 1950s, doing beer commercials and relieving Brickhouse as play-by-play commentator; broadcast radio sports before the 1950s and left the television booth in 1956 to operate a beer distributorship on Chicago's South Side.

Norman Dalton (Norm) Cash, 51, a former first baseman for the Detroit Tigers and the 1961 American League batting champion, in a drowning accident on Lake Michigan on October 12; was drafted by the Chicago Bears of the National Football League after graduation from Sul Ross State College in Alpine, Tex., but opted for baseball in 1955 and signed a contract with the Chicago White Sox; appeared with the White Sox at the end of the 1958 season and played 58 games in '59, when he pinch-hit four times for Chicago in the World Series; was traded to Cleveland in 1959 and then was dealt to Detroit one week into the 1960 season; enjoyed a fabulous 1961 season, hitting 41 home runs, driving in 132 runs and batting a league-leading .361, but never batted .300 or drove in 100 runs again; finished his major league career with a .271 average, 377 home runs and 1,103 RBIs; twice led A.L. first basemen in fielding percentage and set a Tigers record with a .997 mark in 1964; hit .385 in the Tigers' 1968 World Series victory over the St. Louis Cardinals, tying a

Series record by delivering two hits in one inning; the free-spirited Cash, who suffered a stroke a few years after his 1974 retirement, was named to The Sporting News' A.L. All-Star teams in 1961 and 1971 and was picked as TSN's Comeback Player of the Year in 1965 and '71.

John P. (Jocko) Collins, 80, a long-time major league baseball scout and former supervisor of officials of the National Basketball Association, at Philadelphia on March 2; worked as a collegiate and professional basketball and football official before joining the NBA for seven years; began scouting for the 76ers and Phillies and remained with the Phils from 1940 to 1966; later scouted for Houston, San Francisco, Baltimore, the New York Yankees and Milwaukee until his retirement in 1981.

John W. (Johnny) Cooney, 85, a versatile performer who spent 20 years in the major leagues as a pitcher, outfielder and first baseman for the Boston Braves, Brooklyn Dodgers and New York Yankees from 1921 to 1944, at Sarasota, Fla., on July 8; born in Providence, R.I., the lefthanded thrower and righthanded batter made his debut with the Braves and compiled a 34-44 record in nine seasons before bone chips in his elbow forced him to make a successful transition to the outfield; was traded to the Dodgers in 1935 after a four-year stint in the minors and impressed Manager Casey Stengel with his outstanding play in center field; was one of five players traded to St. Louis after the 1937 season for shortstop Leo Durocher, but was released and returned to Boston, where he played the outfield and first base for the Braves through the 1942 season; after his retirement in 1944 with a career .286 average in 1,172 games, Cooney coached for the Braves from 1946-55 and then served as pitching coach for the Chicago White Sox from 1957 until his retirement in 1965; was the son of Chicago Cubs shortstop Jimmy Cooney (1890-92) and the brother of Jimmy E. Cooney, a major league infielder with six clubs from 1917-28.

Joe DeSa, 27, a first baseman who spent most of his 10 professional seasons in the minor leagues, in a head-on automobile crash in Puerto Rico on December 20; was returning to San Juan following a Puerto Rican winter league game at Ponce when the accident occurred on an expressway at 4 a.m.; was drafted by the St. Louis Cardinals in 1977 and reached the majors with the Cardinals in 1980, batting .273 in seven games; after three more minor-league seasons, he was signed by the Chicago White Sox as a free agent and played in 28 games with the Sox in 1985, batting .182; was signed on November 8 by the Kansas City Royals and was scheduled to report to their 1987 spring training camp as a non-roster player.

George Diehl, 68, a righthander who appeared in two games with no decisions for the Boston Braves in 1942 and '43, of a heart attack at Kingsport, Tenn., on August 24; spent the remainder of a long playing career in the minors with stops at Hartford, Evansville, Indianapolis, Louisville, Atlanta and New Orleans.

Vincent P. (Vince) DiMaggio, 74, the eldest of the three DiMaggio brothers who spent his major league career playing the outfield for various National League teams while his more famous brothers were performing in the American League, at North Hollywood, Calif., on October 3; spent five years in the Pacific Coast League before breaking in with the Boston Braves in 1937, a year after younger brother Joe had become the regular center fielder for the New York Yankees; played two seasons with Boston before moving to Cincinnati and then joining the Pittsburgh Pirates in 1940, the same year that brother Dominic began playing with the Boston Red Sox; enjoyed his most productive season (21 homers and 100 runs batted in) with the Pirates in 1941, the same season that brother Joe compiled his record 56-game hitting streak, drove in 125 runs and captured A.L. Most Valuable Player honors; the free-swinging righthander, who led the N.L. in strikeouts six times and set a record by whiffing 134 times with Boston in 1938, finished his career in 1946 and 1947 with the Philadelphia Phillies and New York Giants; returned to the PCL in 1947 and spent a couple of seasons with Oakland; finished his baseball career in 1951 when he managed a team in the California League.

Taylor Lee Douthit, 85, one of the last two surviving members of the 1926 St. Louis Cardinals, the first Cardinals team to win a World Series, at Freemont, Calif., on May 30; nicknamed "The Ballhawk" because of his defensive abilities in the outfield, Douthit signed with the Cardinals after his graduation from the University of California and reached the major leagues in 1923; played center field for Cardinal pennant-winners in 1926, '28 and '30 before spending his last three major league seasons with the Cincinnati Reds and Chicago Cubs; compiled a career .291 batting average in 1,074 games and enjoyed seasons of .308 (1926), .336 (1929) and .303 (1930); his brother Bob also was a former professional baseball player; the only player from the 1926 Cardinals still alive is catcher Bob O'Farrell.

Jimmy Esposito, 69, a groundskeeper at Yankee Stadium since 1960, at New York on October 7.

Edward L. (Itzy) Feinberg, 68, a retired Philadelphia-area bar and restaurant owner who appeared in 16 games for the Phillies in 1938 and '39, at Hollywood, Fla., on April 20; after being used sparingly as a utilityman by the Phillies, Feinberg was sold to Washington after the 1939 season; refused to report to the Senators, claiming he could make more money playing semipro ball near his home; batted only 38 times in the major leagues, compiling a .184 average.

Paul R. Florence, 86, who spent 60 years in professional baseball as a player, executive and scout, at Gainesville, Fla., on May 28; the Georgetown University graduate spent 16 years as a player, but only appeared in 46 games in the major leagues, all in 1926 with the New York Giants; became president and general manager of the Cincinnati Reds' Durham, N.C., farm team in 1937 and was moved to Birmingham three years later in the same capacity; became a scout for the Reds before moving into Cincinnati's front office as an assistant to General Manager Gabe Paul, where he remained until 1961; scouted for the Houston Astros from 1961-76 and continued as a consultant after his retirement.

Edward Miguel (Mike) Garcia, 62, a member of Cleveland's outstanding pitching staffs during the 1950s and a two-time 20-game winner, at Fairview Park, O., on January 13; nicknamed the "Big Bear" because of his burly stature, the hard-throwing righthander of Mexican-Indian descent signed with the Indians in 1942 and, after three years of Army service during World War II, won 22 games for Cleveland's Bakersfield club in 1946; reached the major leagues to stay in 1949 and posted a 14-5 record as a rookie; dropped to 11-11 in 1950 when he was distracted by personal problems, but won 20 games in 1951 and 22 in '52; finished 19-8 in 1954 with an American League-leading 2.64 earned-run average, helping the Indians to 111 wins and the A.L. pennant; was knocked out in his only World Series appearance as the Giants swept the Indians; pitched in a rotation with future Hall of Famers Early Wynn, Bob Lemon and Bob Feller in the early 1950s; pitched effectively until 1958 when a back injury forced the Indians to put him on waivers; was re-signed by Cleveland in 1959 and compiled a 3-6 record; finished his career with the Chicago White Sox and Washington, failing to record another victory; compiled a 142-97 career record with a 3.27 ERA and 1,117 strikeouts in 2,175 innings; threw 27 shutouts and twice led the A.L. in that category.

George E. (Eddie) Gilliland, 86, who played a major role in the formation of the Florida State League and served as its first president in 1936, at Deland, Fla., on January 23; enjoyed a long baseball career at both the major and minor league levels; was vice-president for player development with the St. Louis Browns (1932-42), president-general manager of the Toledo Mud Hens (1942-46) and general manager of Miami's Florida State League team in the late 1940s; designed and supervised the construction of the baseball stadium in Miami; served as field representative for the National Association of Professional Baseball Leagues from 1959 until his retirement in 1965.

Arthur J. (Artie) Gore, 78, a former National League umpire whose unexpected dismissal after the 1956 season helped lay the groundwork for the establishment of a major league umpires' union, at Wolfeboro, N.H., on September 29; played shortstop in the Boston Red Sox chain briefly in the late 1920s and early '30s before turning to umpiring; started in the Canadian-American League in 1937 and made stops in the Eastern League and International League before reaching the major leagues in 1947; worked 10 years in the N.L., including two World Series and two All-Star Games, before being dismissed unexpectedly in 1956, a month after his 49th birthday, to make room for younger umpires and because he "didn't fit the pattern"; campaigned in the press for the next several years for what he called the umpires' bill of rights, bringing to light many of the problems that later were corrected through union efforts; worked as a Massachusetts deputy sheriff after dismissal.

Tom Gorman, 67, a National League umpire for 26 years, of a heart attack at Closter, N.J., on August 12; a 6-foot-3 lefthander, Gorman pitched in the New York Giants' organization from 1937-41, appearing in four major league games in 1939; returned home after serving in the Army from 1941-45 and became an umpire in the New England League; was promoted to the International League in 1949 and was called up to the National League before the 1952 season; worked five World Series, two N.L. Championship Series and four All-Star Games before retiring after the 1976 season.

Henry E. Grampp, 82, a righthanded relief pitcher who compiled an 0-1 record in four appearances with the Chicago Cubs in 1927 and 1929, at New York on March 24; valued as a batting practice pitcher by the Cubs because of his ability to imitate the motions and styles of other pitchers and because he could pitch with either arm; pitched in the minors for Reading, Buffalo and Springfield, Mass., and was an East Coast scout for the Cubs from 1946-61.

George A. Grant, 83, a righthander plagued by arm problems during his career with the St. Louis Browns, Cleveland Indians and Pittsburgh Pirates, at Montgomery, Ala., on March 25; played at Auburn University before being signed by the Browns in 1923; developed a sore arm and struggled to a seven-season 15-20 record that covered 113 appearances and 346 innings; umpired in the Southern and Southeastern leagues before retiring from baseball.

Henry Benjamin (Hank) Greenberg, 75, the son of Romanian Jewish immigrants who captured two American League Most Valuable Player awards en route to the Hall of Fame, of cancer at Beverly Hills, Calif., on September 4; the 6-foot-3, 215-pounder was signed off the New York City playgrounds in 1930 by the Detroit Tigers and reached the major leagues in 1933; helped the Tigers win a pennant in 1934, leading the A.L. with 63 doubles and driving in 139 runs; captured the first of his MVP awards in 1935 by batting .328 and leading the league with 36 homers and 170 RBIs as the Tigers won another pennant and followed that up with a World Series win over the Cubs; broke his wrist in the Series and, after getting off to a blazing start in 1936, broke the same wrist and had to miss the rest of the season; hit 40 homers, scored 137 runs and drove in 183—the second highest total in A.L. history, in 1937 and followed that up with a 58-homer, .683 slugging percentage 1938 season; captured his second MVP in 1940 after making the defensive switch from first base to the outfield and hitting .340 with 41 homers and 150 RBIs; career was interrupted for 4½ seasons when he served in the Army Air Corps during World War II, earning four battle stars; returned to the Tigers midway through the 1945 season and led them to another pennant by hitting .311 and driving in 60 runs, capping his comeback with a pennant-winning grand slam home run on the final day of the season; enjoyed a 44-homer, 127-RBI season in 1946 but was unexpectedly sold to the Pittsburgh Pirates during the off-season; bitter, he refused to report and finally was lured into action by a $100,000 contract; drove in 74 runs in 125 games for the last-place Pirates and retired to take a front-office position with the Cleveland Indians; later served as farm director and general manager of the Indians and vice-president of the Chicago White Sox; compiled a career average of .313 with 331 home runs and 1,276 RBIs in 1,394 games; his career .605 slugging percentage ranks fifth on the all-time list; won four home run titles, leading the A.L. in RBIs four times and doubles twice; batted .318 in 23 World Series games with a .624 slugging percentage, seventh highest in Series history; was elected to the baseball Hall of Fame in 1956.

Tom Greenwade, 81, a longtime baseball scout who signed Mickey Mantle to his first New York Yankees contract, at Ashboro, Mo., on August 10; pitched in the minor leagues from 1922-35 before beginning his scouting career with the St. Louis Browns in 1936; was lured to the Brooklyn organization in 1941 and played a role in convincing Branch Rickey to sign black stars Jackie Robinson and Roy Campanella; moved to the Yankees organization in 1945 and signed such future standouts as Bill Virdon, Elston Howard, Jerry Lumpe and Bobby Murcer; worked for the Yankees until his retirement in 1985.

Daniel (Bud) Hafey, 73, an outfielder who played briefly with the Chicago White Sox, Pittsburgh Pirates, Cincinnati Reds and Philadelphia Phillies between 1935 and 1939, at Sierra City, Calif., on July 27; batted .213 in 123 games over three major league seasons; was the nephew of Hall of Fame outfielder Chick Hafey.

Loy V. Hanning, 68, a righthanded pitcher who appeared in 15 games for the St. Louis Browns in 1939 and 1942, at St. Clair, Mo., on June 24; compiled a 1-2 record in 15 appearances, all but one of which was in relief.

Luther Harvel, 80, an outfielder who played 40 games with the 1928 Cleveland Indians, at Kansas City on April 10; batted .221 in his short stint with Cleveland; later managed three minor league teams and scouted from 1964-74 for Philadelphia, Kansas City, Oakland, Cleveland and Los Angeles.

Minor W. (Mickey) Heath, 82, a standout first baseman for the old Hollywood Stars of the Pacific Coast League in the late 1920s who was dogged by health problems and never got a chance to play regularly in the major leagues, at Dallas on July 30; led the Stars to a pennant in 1929 and was named the PCL's Most Valuable Player; enjoyed another big season in 1930 and was sold to the Cincinnati Reds; began the 1931 season as the Reds' starting first baseman but suffered a broken arm in his sixth game and, while recovering, came down with rheumatic fever; was badly burned during the off-season when his home caught on fire and was prohibited from taking advantage of his next shot with the Reds in 1933 when the rheumatic fever returned; played several more years in the minor leagues before becoming manager of the American Association's Milwaukee Brewers in 1940; became vice-president in charge of player personnel for the Brewers and later broadcasted their games until 1951.

Salvador Jose (Chico) Hernandez, 69, a catcher-infielder who appeared in 90 games for the Chicago Cubs during the 1942 and '43 seasons, at his native Havana, Cuba, on January 3; broke into professional baseball as a third baseman and was converted to catcher in 1938; joined the Cubs late in 1941, but did not appear in a game; caught 84 games over the next two seasons and batted .250; returned to Havana in 1944 to play and manage in the Cuban League.

William T. (Wild Bill) Higdon, 61, an outfielder who played in 11 games with the 1949 Chicago White Sox, at Montgomery, Ala., on August 30; signed with the Philadelphia Phillies in 1946 and was acquired by the White Sox in the minor league draft after the 1948 season; batted .304 in 1949 and spent the ends of the 1950, '51 and '52 seasons with the White Sox without appearing in a game; retired from baseball in 1953.

Daniel T. Holden, 60, an infielder, outfielder and pitcher who spent 17 seasons in the minor leagues, at Eugene, Ore., on May 14; spent most of his career in the Dodgers' and Braves' farm systems.

Brooks R. Holder, 71, who spent most of his 16-year professional career in the Pacific Coast League, at Pinole, Calif., on June 7; played for the San Francisco Seals, Hollywood Stars, Oakland Oaks and Portland Beavers between 1936 and 1951, compiling a .295 batting average in 2,404 games; never made it to the major leagues.

Roy (Hardrock) Johnson, 90, who pitched briefly with the 1918 Philadelphia Athletics and spent most of the remainder of a long career as a coach and scout for the Chicago Cubs, at Scottsdale, Ariz., on January 10; compiled a 1-5 record in 1918 and then drifted back to the minor leagues, where he picked up his nickname in 1929 while managing and pitching for a team in Arizona; joined the Cubs as a coach in 1935 and managed the team for one game in 1944 on an interim basis; later scouted for the Cubs in the Southwest and California.

Richard J. (Dick) Kokos, 58, an outfielder who appeared in 475 games in five years with the St. Louis Browns and Baltimore Orioles between 1948 and 1954, at Chicago on April 9; compiled a .263 career average and hit 59 major league home runs; hit 23 of those homers and drove in 77 runs for the Browns in 1949, his best big-league season.

William Lorenz Kopf, 95, a 10-year major league infielder who appeared in all eight games of the 1919 World Series for Cincinnati against the Chicago White Sox in the year of the Black Sox scandal, at Cincinnati on October 15; compiled a .249 career average in 850 big-league games and was Cincinnati's regular shortstop from 1917-1920, with the exclusion of 1918, when he quit baseball to work for a tire and rubber company; began his professional career in 1910 under the name King Brady while continuing to participate in collegiate sports at Fordham College under his real name; played for the Cleveland Indians in 1913 using the name Fred Brady and then spent two seasons with the Philadelphia Athletics; joined the Redlegs in 1916 and remained in Cincinnati until he was traded to the Boston Braves in 1922; spent two seasons in Boston, retired again in 1924 and then returned for one more season in the American Association; batted .222 with two RBIs in the 1919 Series, which resulted in eight Chicago players being banned from baseball for participating in a game-fixing scandal.

Walter O. (Walt) Lanfranconi, 69, a right-handed pitcher who compiled a 4-5 record with the 1941 Chicago Cubs and 1947 Boston Braves, at Barre, Vt., on August 18; dogged by injuries throughout his career, Lanfranconi broke into baseball in 1937 and joined the Cubs in 1941, losing his only decision; spent three years in the Army after a season at Milwaukee of the American Association and returned to Milwaukee in 1946; spent the entire 1947 season with the Braves, compiling a 4-4 record and 2.95 earned-run average.

Jack Layton, 60, the former stadium announcer for the Kansas City Athletics and Royals, at Kansas City on July 26; served as announcer for the A's from 1963 through 1967, after which the team was moved to Oakland; worked 16 years for the Royals, a 1969 expansion team, before retiring in 1986.

Harry (Peanuts) Lowrey, 67, who played 13 seasons with four National League teams between 1942 and '55 before spending 18 seasons as a major league coach, of heart failure at Los Angeles on July 2; primarily an outfielder, though he played every position but pitcher, catcher and first base; compiled a .273 career average with the Chicago Cubs (1942-49), Cincinnati Reds (1949-50), St. Louis Cardinals (1951-54) and Philadelphia Phillies (1955); best season was 1951 when he hit .303 with the Cardinals; batted .310 in his only World Series appearance with the Cubs in 1945; batted .481 as a pinch-hitter in 1952 and collected 22 pinch-hits the following season, setting a St. Louis club record; also set a major league record with seven consecutive pinch-hits, a mark later broken by Dave Philley and Rusty Staub; managed in the minors at New Orleans, Austin and Idaho Falls after his retirement as a player in 1955; coached third base for the Phillies from 1960-66 and followed that with coaching stints for the San Francisco Giants (1967-68), the Montreal Expos (1969), the Cubs (1970-71), the California Angels (1972) and the Cubs again from 1977-81.

Hugh Luby, 72, associated with professional baseball for 45 years as a player, minor league manager, general manager and league president, at Eugene, Ore., on May 11; played 24 seasons in the minor leagues and appeared in a record 866 consecutive Pacific Coast League games with the Oakland Oaks between April 1, 1939, and September 12, 1943; his streak was broken when he was drafted by the New York Giants and spent the 1944 season in New York as a utility infielder, appearing in 111 games and batting .254; only other major league experience came in 1936, when he spent the final nine games of the season playing second base for the Philadelphia Athletics; first managing opportunity came in 1949 for New Orleans in the Pittsburgh chain; served as player-manager through the 1950 season, batting .290 for the Southern Association club; served as player-manager-general manager for Salem of the Western International League from 1951-55, batting .357 in 1954 at age 41; managed from 1957-59 for Eugene of the Northwest League before becoming the team's general manager; after a two-year absence from baseball, Luby returned to Eugene in 1965 as manager-general manager and became president of the Northwest League in 1966; helped lure a Triple-A team to Eugene in 1969 and served as president and general manager of the Phillies' farm team for the first three years of its five-year existence; again served as a manager-general manager in 1974 when Eugene returned to the Northwest League.

Charles Fred (Red) Lucas, 84, a righthanded pitcher who compiled a 157-135 major league record with four teams between 1923 and 1938, at Inglewood, Tenn., on July 9; enjoyed his best seasons with Cincinnati, winning 18 games in 1927 and 19 in 1929 for weak Redlegs teams; led the National League in complete games (28) in 1929 and pitched a modern major league-record 250⅓ consecutive innings without being relieved from August 13, 1931, to July 15, 1932; also a premier pinch-hitter, the lefthander collected 114 career pinch-hits, a major league record until Smoky Burgess broke the mark during the 1960s; his pinch-hit total still ranks fifth on the all-time list; also played for the New York Giants (1923), Boston Braves (1924) and Pittsburgh Pirates (1934-38); finished his major league career with a .281 career average and 3.72 earned-run average; returned to the minors in 1939 as a manager, coach and pinch-hitter until 1949; batted .423 in 1945 as a player-coach for Nashville.

Roy Luebbe, 84, a well-traveled minor league catcher in the 1920s who played in eight games for the New York Yankees in 1925, at Omaha, Neb., on August 21; made more than a dozen stops along the minor league trail and went hitless in 15 at-bats in his only major league stint.

Theodore Amar (Ted) Lyons, 85, a Hall of Fame pitcher who won 260 games for the Chicago White Sox over 21 years, at Sulphur, La., on July 25; came off the Baylor University campus to join the White Sox in 1923 and then spent his entire playing career with the Chicago team before becoming its manager in 1946; compiled a 260-230 record for weak White Sox teams in a career that included three 20-win seasons, a no-hitter and an earned-run average title (2.10) when he compiled a 14-6 record at age 41; was 22-15 in 1930 when the Sox finished in seventh place with a 62-92 record and shared the A.L. lead with 22 victories in 1927 while pitching for a fifth-place team; was limited to four victories in 1931 by a sore arm but developed a knuckleball and went on to win 130 more games over the next 12 seasons; after spending three years in the South Pacific during World War II, Lyons returned to baseball in 1946 and became manager of the White Sox; was replaced after the 1948 season and later coached for the Detroit Tigers and Brooklyn Dodgers; tied a major league record by doubling twice in the same inning in a 1935 game; posted a career 3.67 ERA and pitched 4,161 innings in 594 games; elected to baseball's Hall of Fame in 1955.

Clarence Maddern, 65, an outfielder who appeared in 104 games with the Chicago Cubs and Cleveland Indians from 1946-51, at Tucson, Ariz., in July; the righthanded hitter spent three seasons in the minors and three years in military service during World War II, where he earned three battle stars as an infantryman and participated in the Battle of the Bulge, before joining the Cubs near the end of the 1946 season; returned to Chicago for the 1948 and 1949 seasons and ended his major league career with an 11-game stint in Cleveland in 1951; compiled a .248 career average.

Roberto (Bobby) Maduro, 70, the principal figure in the development of professional baseball in Cuba, at Miami; was the son of a wealthy Havana sugar cane plantation owner who used his resources and influence to establish a system of youth baseball leagues while supplying most of the equipment, money and grounds for playing fields; built Cuba's only first-class baseball facility and in 1946 became owner and operator of a Triple-A club, the Havana Sugar Kings of the International League; his dream of attracting a major league expansion franchise to Havana was burst when Fidel Castro rose to power and effectively put an end to organized baseball on the island; when the new regime took over the family holdings, Maduro managed to escape with his family to the U.S. where he lived 25 years in exile; relocated his Havana club in Jersey City with the help of close friends Gabe Paul Sr. and Walter O'Malley, but couldn't draw the fans so the team was moved to Jacksonville; sold the club in 1963 and went to work for the Commissioner's office as coordinator of Inter-American baseball; left that position in 1981 to establish the short-lived Inter-American League, which operated for only one year with teams in Latin America and Miami; worked in recent years with exiled Cuban players in Miami and remained a member of the Cuban baseball hall of fame committee.

Harl Warren Maggert, 72, an outfielder-third baseman who played in 66 games for the 1938 Boston Braves, at Citrus Heights, Calif., on July 10; compiled a .281 average with three home runs and 19 RBIs in his one-season major league career; was the son of Harl Vess Maggert, who played 75 major league games with the 1907 Pittsburgh Pirates and 1912 Philadelphia A's.

Oland Alexander (Dixie) McArthur, 94, a righthander who pitched in one major league game for the Pittsburgh Pirates in 1914, at Columbus, Miss., on May 31; pitched only one inning in his brief appearance without allowing a run or getting a decision.

William G. (Bill) McCahan, 65, a righthander who pitched a no-hitter and compiled a 16-14 record for the Philadelphia Phillies from 1946-49, at Fort Worth, Tex.; was discovered by legendary A's Manager Connie Mack, who payed his way through Duke University; was in the Army Air Corps from 1943-45 and joined the A's upon his release from active duty; threw his no-hitter against the Washington Senators on September 3, 1947, technically his rookie season, and missed a perfect game only because of a teammate's error; was 10-5 in 1947 but suffered arm problems because of an off-season job lifting heavy oil barrels; played his last major league season in 1949 and then managed a Brooklyn Dodgers' farm club at Pueblo for one season.

Gordon McLendon, an innovative radio personality who pioneered the process of re-creating baseball and football games for broadcast off of wire service ticker tape reports and then put together a network of more than 450 stations to carry those games in the 1950s, of throat cancer at Lewisville, Tex., on September 14; after attending Yale and spending time in the South Pacific during World War II, McLendon was given a downtrodden Texas radio station as a gift from his father; reversed the station's fortunes through the re-creation of sporting events, beginning with the broadcast of the Detroit Lions-Chicago Cardinals football game in 1947; began re-creating major league baseball games in Dallas in 1948 from the accounts teletyped to him from New York; began slowly adding stations and built his Liberty Broadcasting System; handled the re-creation broadcasts himself, adding sound effects, and branched into other areas, such as interviews, music shows and soap opera whodunits; with the advent of television, McLendon began to sell off his network stations in the early 1960s, finally getting rid of the final one in the late 1970s.

Ernie Mehl, 85, a former sports editor of the

Kansas City Star and the man largely responsible for the advent of major league baseball in Kansas City in 1955 and its return in 1969 after a one-year absence, at Sun City, Ariz., on November 11; served as sports editor from 1950 to 1965 and waged a continuing editorial campaign for a major league team in Kansas City; was instrumental in influencing a group led by Arnold Johnson to buy the Philadelphia A's from Connie Mack and move the club to Kansas City; when Johnson died of a stroke in 1960 and the team was put up for sale, Mehl was a member of a group that was outbid by Charles O. Finley; used his influence to persuade the American League to award an expansion franchise to Kansas City in 1969 after Finley had moved the A's to Oakland.

Cliff Melton, 74, a lanky lefthander who in 1937 became the first rookie in baseball history to win 20 games, at Baltimore on July 28; the 6-foot-5, 200-pounder joined the New York Giants in 1937 and helped them win the National League pennant with a 20-9 record and 2.61 earned-run average before losing twice in the World Series to the New York Yankees; pitched seven more years for the Giants but never won more than 14 games in another season; finished his career with an 86-80 record and 3.42 ERA; was born in Black Mountain, N.C., and was nicknamed "Mountain Music" because of his penchant for guitar picking; also dubbed "Rabbit Ears" and "Mickey Mouse" by opponents because of his floppy ears and had to deal with an unusual amount of taunting; made his final appearances in baseball with the San Francisco Seals of the Pacific Coast League in 1946 and '47.

John Wayne Middleton, 86, a lefthanded pitcher in the Cleveland Indians' organization between 1922 and 1925, at Amarillo, Tex., on November 3; pitched briefly for Des Moines and Coffeyville and was batting practice pitcher for Cleveland's 1920 world champions.

David B. Morey, 96, a two-time Walter Camp All-America as a halfback at Dartmouth College who pitched in two major league games with no decisions for the Philadelphia Athletics in 1913, at Oak Bluffs, Mass.; after leaving baseball, spent the next 40 years coaching football, baseball, hockey and lacrosse at several Eastern colleges; received the National Football Foundation's Distinguished American Award in 1981.

Emmett Jerome (Heinie) Mueller, 74, a switch-hitting infielder-outfielder who compiled a .253 career average in 441 major league games with the 1938-41 Philadelphia Phillies, at Orlando, Fla., on October 3; his best season was 1939 when he hit .279 with nine home runs and 43 RBIs.

Joe Mulligan, 72, who won the first game he started in the major leagues but never had another decision in 14 appearances with the 1934 Boston Red Sox, of cancer at Boston on June 5; was signed off the Holy Cross campus, where he was a three-sport star and a baseball All-America; after leaving the Red Sox, he pitched in the minors at Toronto, Syracuse and Oakland.

Joe Oeschger, 95, who pitched all 26 innings for the Boston Braves against Brooklyn on May 1, 1920, in the longest game in major league history, at Santa Rosa, Calif., on July 28; remembered primarily for his 1920 marathon battle with Brooklyn pitcher Leon Cadore, who also pitched all 26 innings in the 1-1 tie game; allowed nine hits in the game and set a major league record by pitching 21 consecutive scoreless innings in one game; pitched a three-hitter and won, 1-0, when the game was made up later in the 1920 season; earned a degree in civil engineering and starred in three sports for St. Mary's College before signing with the Phillies in 1914 for a then-high bonus of $5,000; went on to play for four National League teams in a 12-year career that resulted in an 83-116 record and 3.81 earned-run average; fashioned a 20-14 mark for Boston in 1921, his best major league season; roomed in 1919 with the legendary Jim Thorpe, a Braves teammate; taught physical education and hygiene for 27 years at a junior high school in San Francisco after his baseball retirement.

Frank J. (Blackie) O'Rourke, 94, who spent three-quarters of a century as a player, minor league manager and major league scout, at Union, N.J., on May 14; played in 14 major league seasons with six different clubs between 1912 and 1931; compiled a .254 average in 1,131 games while playing second base, shortstop, third base, outfield and first base for the Boston Braves, Brooklyn Dodgers, Washington Senators, Boston Red Sox, Detroit Tigers and St. Louis Browns; later managed and coached in the minors at Milwaukee, Montreal and Charlotte; became a full-time scout for the Cincinnati Reds in 1941 and joined the Yankees 11 years later, staying with New York until 1983.

Milton E. Price, 83, a Texas League official for 28 years, at Dallas on October 20; became secretary and vice-president of the Texas League in 1931 when his employer at a Texas oil-drilling firm was named the league president; also served as president of the West Texas-New Mexico League in the late 1930s; became a member of the Texas baseball hall of fame in 1979.

Grover S. Resinger, 70, whose baseball career spanned 45 years as a minor league player, coach and manager and major league coach and scout, at St. Louis on January 11; was a third baseman who spent 15 years in the minor leagues without getting a shot at a big-league job; spent 10 years out of baseball before becoming a manager and coach in the St. Louis Cardinals' farm system; became a coach for the Atlanta Braves in 1966 and later coached for the Chicago White Sox, Detroit Tigers and California Angels; later served as a minor league instructor for the Oakland A's and a scout for the New York Yankees.

Robert T. (Bob) Rice, 86, who spent almost half of his 49-year career in Organized Baseball as the traveling secretary of the Pittsburgh Pirates, at Elizabethtown, Pa., on February 20; began his baseball association as an infielder in the St. Louis Cardinals' organization in 1920 and reached the major leagues with the Philadelphia Phillies in 1926, hitting .148 in 19 games; served as a minor league manager from 1929-38 before becoming business manager for a minor league team; became director of the Pirates' farm system in 1941 and was named traveling secretary in 1947, holding that position until his retirement after the 1969 season.

Paul Richards, 77, a highly regarded innovator who loved to face challenges in his role as a major league manager and general manager in the 1950s and '60s, at Waxahachie, Tex., on May 4; compiled a .227 career average in 523 major league games as a shortstop and catcher for the Brooklyn Dodgers (1932), New York Giants (1933-35), Philadelphia Athletics (1935-36) and Detroit Tigers (1943-46); had served as a minor league manager with the old Atlanta Crackers from 1936-42 and then piloted at Buffalo and Seattle after the war; became the manager of the Chicago White Sox in 1951 and enjoyed four straight winning seasons before becoming manager-general manager of the Baltimore Orioles after the 1954 season; took a weak Orioles team (57-97 in 1955) and laid some solid groundwork for what soon became a top American League challenger; moved on to Houston and became general manager of the expansion Colt 45s; helped that club reach respectability before moving to

Atlanta in 1966 as vice-president of baseball operations for the Braves, newly arrived from Milwaukee; had philosophical differences with Braves' ownership and was fired after the 1972 season; returned to baseball in 1976 at age 67 as manager of the Chicago White Sox; retired after that season with a career managerial record of 923-901; later served as a scout and special consultant for the Texas Rangers; was credited while in Baltimore with getting Oriole catchers to use the oversize mitt when knuckleballer Hoyt Wilhelm was pitching, an idea that still is in use today.

Milton (Milt) Richman, 64, who turned a childhood love of baseball into a lifetime of award-winning sports reporting, editing and commentary for United Press and, later, United Press International, of a heart attack at New York on June 9; was a native of the Bronx who could not make it as a baseball player and turned to sports reporting as an alternative, hiring on with United Press in New York after his release from the Army in 1944; gravitated to the sports department and was named UPI's sports columnist in 1964; became the wire service's sports editor in 1972 and was named a senior editor in 1985; continued to write his popular "Today's Sports Parade" column, distributed to UPI's subscribers four times per week, right up until his death in his Manhattan apartment; was known for his honesty, integrity and complimentary style, which earned him the respect of the sports community and resulted in a number of "scoops"; was also known for his powers of retention and ability to recall word-for-word statements without use of notebooks or tape recorders; his first love was baseball, but he was a familiar face at all major sporting events and received many honors during his career with UPI; was inducted into the writers' wing of the baseball Hall of Fame in 1981 as the winner of the J.G. Taylor Spink Award; brother of Arthur Richman, a former sportswriter and currently a front-office official of the New York Mets.

Oscar Roettger, 86, a former pitcher, outfielder and first baseman who was better known later as a tailor of major league uniforms in his capacity as manager of Rawlings Sporting Goods' professional division, of a heart attack at St. Louis on July 4; spent almost two decades in the minor leagues, beginning in the early 1920s, and was on the New York Yankees' roster in 1923 and '24, earning no decisions in six relief appearance with two at-bats; received a full World Series share when the Yankees won their first World Series title in '23, though he did not appear in the postseason classic; was up briefly with the Brooklyn Dodgers as an outfielder in 1927 and with the Philadelphia Athletics as a first baseman early in the 1932 season; compiled a .212 average in 37 at-bats; was a player-manager for Montreal of the International League in 1933 and ended his baseball career as a manager at Birmingham of the Southern Association in 1941; went to work for Rawlings prior to World War II and remained on the job in a limited capacity until his death.

Charles (Red) Ruffing, 80, a baseball Hall of Famer who won 20 games four straight seasons with championship New York Yankees teams in his 22-year career, at Cleveland on February 17; lost four toes in a mining accident as a teen-ager but still pitched well enough in the minor leagues at Danville to attract the attention of the Boston Red Sox, who bought his contract in 1923; pitched five full seasons in Boston, compiling a not-too-impressive 39-96 record and twice led the American League in losses; was traded to the Yankees in 1930 and proceeded to become one of baseball's top pitchers; the righthander combined with Lefty Gomez to give the Yankees an almost unbeatable combination in the 1930s; compiled 20-victory seasons from 1936-39, coinciding with four straight World Series championships for the Yankees; his 273-225 career record (231-124 with the Yankees), 3.80 earned-run average and 7-2 World Series mark were remarkable considering his early lack of success and physical handicap; spent 22 years in the major leagues, even though his career was interrupted for 2½ years by World War II; rejoined the Yankees in 1945 at age 40 and compiled a 7-3 record and 2.90 ERA; jumped off to a 5-1 mark in 1946 before suffering a broken ankle and getting his release from the Yankees; caught on with the Chicago White Sox but appeared in only nine games before suffering a knee injury and calling it a career; was regarded as one of the best hitting pitchers ever to play the game, compiling a .269 career average with 36 home runs and 273 runs batted in; later scouted for the White Sox, managed in the minors, scouted for the Indians and New York Mets and served as the Mets' first pitching coach in 1962; was elected to the baseball Hall of Fame in 1967.

Sidney Salomon Jr., 76, a life insurance magnate and politician who was best known for his sports connections in St. Louis with the baseball Cardinals and Browns and hockey Blues, of a heart attack at Rockledge, Fla., on May 24; was serving as assistant to Postmaster General Robert Hannegan after World War II when Hannegan purchased the Cardinals and made Salomon a vice-president of the club; sold his interest in the Cardinals when Hannegan died in 1947 and bought into the Browns, serving as executive vice-president under Bill Veeck; owned Sportsman's Park in St. Louis, which he sold to August A. Busch Jr. when Anheuser Busch bought the Cardinals in 1953; later bought the Syracuse minor league team, which he moved to Miami as a member of the International League; bought the Blues as a National Hockey League expansion franchise in 1965 and sold the team to the Ralston Purina Co. in 1977.

Leonard W. (Len) Schulte, 69, an infielder who played in 124 games for the St. Louis Browns between 1944 and 1946, at Orlando, Fla., on May 6; batted .247 in 119 games for the Browns in 1945 while serving as a utility infielder; was the younger brother of Herman (Ham) Schulte, an infielder with the Philadelphia Phillies in 1940; managed for several years in the minors after his retirement.

Carl Webb Schultz, 88, a righthanded pitcher who made one major league appearance with the Chicago White Sox in 1924, on July 26; pitched only one inning in his brief curtain call, allowing one run with no decision.

Ed (Packy) Schwartz, 80, a trainer for hockey, football and baseball teams in Chicago before and after World War II, at Thiensville, Wis.; was a trainer for the Chicago Black Hawks, Chicago Cardinals and Chicago White Sox for most of his career, though his last baseball association was with the Philadelphia A's in 1953.

James P. (Pat) Seerey, 63, a righthanded-hitting outfielder with the Cleveland Indians and Chicago White Sox in the 1940s who was one of 11 major league players to hit four home runs in a single game, at Jennings, Mo., on April 28; enjoyed his four-homer game against the Philadelphia Athletics on July 18, 1948, connecting in the fourth, fifth, sixth and 11th innings to help the White Sox to a 12-11 victory at Philadelphia's Shibe Park; managed only a .224 batting average in all or parts of seven major league seasons; led American League batters in strikeouts four times; produced the best at-bat/home run ratio in the A.L. in 1946 for Cleveland when he hit 26 homers in 404 official plate appearances.

Charles J. Sheerin, 75, a utility infielder for the 1936 Philadelphia Phillies and a member of the Fordham University hall of fame, at Long Island, N.Y., on September 27; was signed out of Fordham by the Brooklyn Dodgers, but went to the Phillies in a minor league trade; batted .264 in his 39 major league games.

Donald Silverman, 62, vice-president of the Iowa Cubs and the American Association, at Des Moines on November 23; had acted as general manager of the Cubs for the 1985 and '86 seasons.

Eddie (Buddy) Solomon, 34, a righthanded pitcher who compiled a 36-42 record for six major league clubs between 1973 and 1982, in an automobile accident at Macon, Ga., on January 12; signed with the Los Angeles Dodgers in 1969 and reached the major leagues with short stints in 1973 and '74, getting no decisions; was traded to Chicago and appeared in six games with the Cubs without a decision in '75; went on to pitch for the St. Louis Cardinals (1976), Atlanta Braves (1977-79), Pittsburgh Pirates (1980-82) and Chicago White Sox (1982), compiling a 36-42 career record in 191 games; returned to the minors for one season after his 1982 release before retiring to sell automobiles.

Joe Sparma, 44, a righthander who compiled a 52-56 major league record and pitched the game that clinched the 1968 American League pennant for the Detroit Tigers, at Columbus, O., on May 14; was the starting quarterback at Ohio State University in 1961 and '62 before leaving the team over differences with Coach Woody Hayes and signing a bonus contract with the Tigers; joined the major league team after one season in the minors and enjoyed spotty success over the next six seasons; finished 13-8 in 1965 but enjoyed his best season in 1967, finishing 16-9 with a 3.76 earned-run average; had a run-in in '68 with Manager Mayo Smith and was relegated to the bullpen, but filled in for ailing starter Earl Wilson to pitch the pennant clincher; remained in Smith's doghouse, however, and did not pitch in the World Series against St. Louis; was traded to Montreal after the 1969 season and spent most of 1970 in the minors, compiling an 0-4 mark in his nine games with the Expos; was released and made an unsuccessful comeback attempt with the Tigers.

Max Surkont, 64, a burly righthander who once held the major league record for consecutive strikeouts in a game, at Largo, Fla., on October 8; spent 11 seasons in the minors and three more years in military service before getting his first major league chance in 1949 with the Chicago White Sox; went on to compile a 61-76 record over nine seasons with the Sox, Boston Braves (1950-52), Milwaukee (1953), Pittsburgh (1954-56), St. Louis Cardinals (1956) and New York Giants (1956-57); struck out eight consecutive Cincinnati batters—the last one after a 35-minute rain delay— while pitching for Milwaukee in 1953, establishing a major league record that since has been broken; returned to the minors after his final season in New York and played for Phoenix, Seattle and Buffalo before becoming a Bisons coach in 1963, his final year in baseball.

George (Good Kid) Susce Sr., 77, a catcher who played in 146 major league games over eight seasons before spending nearly 30 years as a big-league coach, at Sarasota, Fla., on February 25; was up and down with the Philadelphia Phillies, Detroit Tigers, Pittsburgh Pirates, St. Louis Browns and Cleveland Indians between 1929 and 1944, compiling a .228 career batting average; signed with Cleveland as a player-coach in 1941 and served the Indians four years as batting practice pitcher, bullpen coach and physical fitness specialist; went on to coach for the Boston Red Sox, Kansas City A's and Milwaukee Braves before beginning a long association with the Washington Senators, who later became the Texas Rangers.

Roy T. (Dixie) Upright, 60, a successful minor-league first baseman-outfielder who had eight at-bats as a pinch-hitter for the 1953 St. Louis Browns, at Kannapolis, N.C., on November 20; earned a good-hit, no-field reputation in his 12 years in the minor leagues; batted over .300 six times and enjoyed three 100-RBI seasons; managed two hits in his brief major league stay, one of them a home run.

Russell (Sheriff) Van Atta, 80, a lefthanded pitcher with the New York Yankees and St. Louis Browns from 1933-39, at Andover, N.J., on October 10; compiled a 33-41 record in his seven-year career with a 5.60 ERA; broke into the major leagues with the Yankees in 1933 and recorded a 12-4 mark; cut his pitching hand during the next off-season and was nothing more than a journeyman pitcher the rest of the way.

William L. (Bill) Veeck, 71, an energetic, flamboyant promotions-minded owner of three major league baseball teams, at Chicago on January 2; was best known for his maverick promotions that included such stunts as signing a midget to a contract and sending him up to bat in a major league game, letting the fans in attendance manage the team for one game, burying a pennant and saluting an average, everyday fan with a night in his honor; began his baseball career as a stockboy-vendor-groundcrew member in the late 1920s for the Chicago Cubs, the team for which his father, Bill Sr., was president; left Kenyon College in Ohio to work full time in the Cubs ticket office after his father's death in 1933 and worked his way up to club treasurer by the early 1940s; struck out on his own shortly thereafter and bought the Milwaukee Braves, a nearly bankrupt team in the American Association; using a series of giveaways ranging from a 200-pound block of ice to live lobsters, Veeck began putting people into the Milwaukee park and the team responded by winning three pennants; spent World War II in the South Pacific where an artillery piece crushed his lower right leg, eventually resulting in amputation; continued his energetic ways, however, and sold his controlling interest in the Brewers after the 1945 season; headed a syndicate that purchased the Cleveland Indians through a radical stock debenture deal and became the youngest owner in major league history; a World Series title in 1948 and the signing of Larry Doby, the American League's first black player, were his biggest accomplishments in Cleveland; sold the Indians for a tidy profit in 1949 and bought the struggling St. Louis Browns two years later; ran promotions for every home game but attendance remained down and the Browns continued to lose; pulled off his biggest promotion between games of a 1951 doubleheader against the Detroit Tigers when midget Eddie Gaedel popped out of a cake and then proceeded to bat in the nightcap, much to the chagrin of unamused officials throughout the baseball establishment who already viewed the maverick owner with contempt; team continued to lose money and Veeck finally won approval to move it to Baltimore—if he sold out first; stayed out of baseball until 1958, when he and Hank Greenberg combined to buy the Chicago White Sox; Sox won the A.L. pennant in 1959 and Veeck continued his radical ways; introduced the exploding scoreboard in 1959; forced to sell by ill health, Veeck returned to baseball one more time, heading up a group that saved the financially ailing White Sox in 1975 and prevented the team's move to Seattle; couldn't compete with the free-agent market and was forced to sell in 1980; suffered constantly throughout his career because of his bad leg and had to undergo several operations to shorten the stump; died from cardiac arrest in a Chicago hospital.

Sammy Vick, 91, a New York Yankees outfielder who in 1920 lost his job to a converted pitcher named Babe Ruth, at Batesville, Miss., on August 17; hit .322 at Memphis before joining the Yankees in 1917 and appeared in only two games the next season because of military duty in World War I; became a regular in 1919, appearing in 106 games and hitting .248; when the Yanks acquired Ruth from the Boston Red Sox in 1920, Vick was limited to 51 games; pinch hit for Ruth, who had suffered a minor arm injury, that season and tripled with the bases loaded; was traded to the Red Sox in 1921 and, after refusing at first to report, appeared in only 41 games; a knee injury forced him out of the major leagues and he eventually ended his career in 1930 in the minor leagues.

William K. (Bill) Walters, 60, president of the Midwest League for the last 13 years and a member of the National Association of Professional Baseball Leagues executive committee, at Burlington, Ia., on February 10; never played professional baseball but became interested in team front-office operations and joined the board of directors of the Midwest League's Burlington team in the 1960s; served as general manager of the Burlington operation for two years and as club president for six; became president of the eight-member Midwest League in 1974 and helped it expand to 12 teams with two more scheduled to be added in 1987; received the Warren Giles Award as the top administrator in the minor leagues in 1985; was scheduled to become chairman of the National Association's executive committee, the governing body of minor league baseball, in 1987.

John R. (Jack) Warner, 82, a third baseman and shortstop with the Detroit Tigers, Brooklyn Dodgers and Philadelphia Phillies between 1925 and '33 who spent more than 60 years in baseball as a player, coach, scout and minor league manager, at Mount Vernon, Ill., on March 13; compiled a career .250 average in 478 games; won a $25 bet from Ty Cobb in 1926 by beating the future Hall of Famer in a footrace; played seven more seasons in the minors after his final major league season with the Phillies and managed two different minor league teams during World War II; coached for the Chicago Cubs' Los Angeles farm team for 12 years after which he scouted for the Dodgers, New York Yankees and Montreal Expos.

James L. (Skeeter) Webb, 78, a smooth-fielding utility infielder who played 12 major league seasons with five different teams, at Meridian, Miss., on July 8; managed only a .219 career average but made up for hitting deficiencies with his glove; appeared in one game for the 1932 St. Louis Cardinals and then spent the next five seasons in the minors before being signed by the Cleveland Indians in 1938; went on to play for the Chicago White Sox, Detroit Tigers and Philadelphia A's before ending his career in 1948; started all seven games of the 1945 World Series for the Tigers, batting .185; coached and managed in the minors from 1950-52 and later did some scouting work.

Edwin Lee (Ed) Wells, 85, a lefthanded pitcher who was believed to be the last man alive to have been a teammate of both Ty Cobb and Babe Ruth, at Birmingham, Ala., on May 1; compiled a 68-69 major league record between 1923 and 1934 while pitching for the Detroit Tigers, New York Yankees and St. Louis Browns; his best season was with the Yankees in 1930, when he recorded a 12-3 record despite a 5.20 earned-run average; collected a World Series check in New York after the 1932 season, though he did not pitch in the postseason classic; pitched for the Browns in 1933 and '34, returned to the minors in '35 and pitched until the middle of the 1937 season before calling it quits.

Joyner C. (Jo Jo) White, 77, who spent 42 years in Organized Baseball as a major league player, coach and scout and as a minor league manager and general manager, at Tacoma, Wash., on October 8; broke into baseball in 1928 and joined the Detroit Tigers near the end of the 1931 season; a leadoff batter with good speed, White enjoyed his best major league season in 1934 when he batted .313 and scored 97 runs for the American League-champion Tigers; spent seven years in Detroit and his final two with the Philadelphia A's and Cincinnati Reds, compiling a .256 career average; played in two World Series with the Tigers (1934 and '35), batting .190; tore up the Pacific Coast League at age 36 while playing for Sacramento in 1945, posting league-leading figures with a .355 average, 162 runs scored, 244 hits and 313 total bases; served as Seattle (PCL) player-manager from 1947-49; also managed five other minor league teams and served as general manager at Sacramento in 1950; scouted for the Cleveland Indians from 1953-58 and then coached for Cleveland, the Kansas City A's, the Milwaukee Braves, the Atlanta Braves and the expansion Kansas City Royals; spent one more season as a minor league manager and scouted for Kansas City for a year before retiring from baseball; was the father of Mike White, who played parts of three seasons (1963-65) with the Houston Astros and later managed in the minors.

James Alger Wilson, 64, a righthanded pitcher who compiled an 86-89 record in the 1940s and '50s with six different major league teams, at Newport Beach, Calif., on September 2; began his 12-year career with the Boston Red Sox and later pitched for the St. Louis Browns, Philadelphia A's, the Boston-Milwaukee Braves, Baltimore Orioles and Chicago White Sox; his best season was 1957 for the White Sox when he compiled a 15-8 record with a 3.48 ERA and 12 complete games.

Jesse (T-Bone) Winters, 92, a righthanded relief pitcher who compiled a 13-24 record over five seasons with the New York Giants and Philadelphia Phillies after World War I, at Abilene, Tex., on June 5; was 1-2 with the Giants from 1919-20 and 12-22 with Philadelphia from 1921-23; compiled a 5.05 earned-run average in 110 appearances, 79 of which were in relief; was mayor of Abilene in the 1950s.

John B. Wyrostek, 67, a two-time National League All-Star outfielder who spent all or parts of 11 seasons with three clubs between 1942 and 1954, at St. Louis on December 12; was signed out of high school by the St. Louis Cardinals in 1937 and went on to play with the Pittsburgh Pirates, Philadelphia Phillies and Cincinnati Reds in a major league career that covered 1,221 games; best season was 1951 when he hit .311 with 61 RBIs for the Reds; finished with a career average of .271.

Eddie Yuhas, 61, a righthander who compiled a 12-2 record as a rookie reliever for the St. Louis Cardinals in 1952 before he developed a mysterious arm ailment and never won another game, at Winston-Salem, N.C., on July 6; joined the Cardinals as a 28-year-old rookie in '52 and combined with veteran Al Brazle to form the most effective bullpen combination in the National League; the pair combined to appear in 100 of the team's 154 games and produced a 24-7 record; Yuhas fashioned a 2.72 earned-run average; arm and shoulder troubles surfaced during spring training in 1953 and doctors diagnosed the problem as tendinitis; appeared in two 1953 games before being placed on the disabled list and retiring after the season.

LEAGUE AND CLUB INFORMATION

Including

Major League Directory

American League Directory

American League Team Directories

National League Directory

National League Team Directories

Major League Players Association Directory

Minor League Presidents

Major League Farm Systems

Directory of Organized Baseball

MAJOR LEAGUES

COMMISSIONER—Peter V. Ueberroth
SECRETARY-TREASURER & GENERAL COUNSEL—Edwin M. Durso
DEPUTY COMMISSIONER & SPECIAL PROJECTS—Alexander H. Hadden
HEADQUARTERS—350 Park Avenue
New York, N. Y. 10022
Telephone—371-7800 (area code 212)
Teletype—910-380-9482

EXECUTIVE COUNCIL—Peter V. Ueberroth, Commissioner; Robert W. Brown, President of American League; A. Bartlett Giamatti, President of National League; Peter Bavasi, Roy Eisenhardt, Peter Hardy and Jerry Reinsdorf, representatives of American League, and Charles Bronfman, Nelson Doubleday, Bill Giles and John McMullen, representatives of National League.

ADMINISTRATOR—William A. Murray
EXECUTIVE VICE-PRESIDENT OF BROADCASTING—Bryan L. Burns
NEWS DEPARTMENT—Richard Levin
DIRECTOR OF SECURITY—Kevin Hallinan
CONTROLLER—Donald C. Marr, Jr.
ASSISTANTS TO ADMINISTRATIVE OFFICER—
George E. Pfister, Miguel A. Rodriguez
(Winter League Baseball Coordinators)
ASSISTANT COUNSEL—Thomas Ostertag
DIRECTOR OF BROADCAST ADMINISTRATION—David Alworth
MANAGER OF BROADCAST OPERATIONS—Leslie Lawrence
PERSONNEL ADMINISTRATION MANAGER—Barbara Ernst
OFFICE MANAGER—Mary Ann Burns
BOOKKEEPER—Rita Datz

NATIONAL ASSOCIATION REPRESENTATIVES—John H. Johnson, President of the National Association, and members of National Association Executive Committee.

NATIONAL ASSOCIATION OF PROFESSIONAL BASEBALL LEAGUES

PRESIDENT-TREASURER—John H. Johnson
ADMINISTRATOR—Sal Artiaga
VICE-PRESIDENT—John H. Moss
LEGAL COUNSEL—Charles J. Crist, Jr.
DIRECTOR OF PROMOTIONS—Bob Sparks
HEADQUARTERS—201 Bayshore Dr. S.E., P. O. Box A
St. Petersburg, Fla. 33731
Telephone—822-6937 (area code 813)
Teletype—810-863-0361

EXECUTIVE COMMITTEE—John H. Moss, Chairman, President of the South Atlantic League; Harold Cooper, President of the International League; and Charles Eshbach, President of the Eastern League.

American League

Organized 1900

ROBERT W. BROWN, M.D.
President

JOHN E. FETZER, GENE AUTRY, CALVIN R. GRIFFITH
Vice-Presidents

ROBERT O. FISHEL
Executive Vice President

MARTIN J. SPRINGSTEAD
Chief Supervisor of Umpires

RICHARD BUTLER
Special Assistant

PHYLLIS MERHIGE
Director of Public Relations

TIM McCLEARY
Manager, Waivers & Player Records

TESS BASTA, CAROLYN COEN
Administrators

Headquarters—350 Park Avenue, New York, N. Y. 10022

Telephone—371-7600 (area code 212)

ASSISTANT SUPERVISORS OF UMPIRES—Henry Soar, Larry Napp, Jerry Neudecker.

UMPIRES—Lawrence Barnett, Nicholas Bremigan, Joseph Brinkman, Alan Clark, Drew Coble, Terrance Cooney, Derryl Cousins, Donald Denkinger, James Evans, Dale Ford, Richard Garcia, Ted Hendry, John Hirschbeck, Mark Johnson, Kenneth Kaiser, Greg Kosc, Tim McClelland, Larry McCoy, James McKean, Durwood Merrill, Dan Morrison, Stephen Palermo, David Phillips, Rick Reed, Michael Reilly, John (Rocky) Roe, Dale Scott, John Shulock, Tim Tschida, Vic Voltaggio, Tim Welke, Larry Young.

OFFICIAL STATISTICIANS—Sports Information Center, 1776 Heritage Drive, No. Quincy, Mass. 02171. Telephone—(617) 328-4674.

BALTIMORE ORIOLES

Chairman of the Board and President—Edward Bennett Williams

Executive Vice-President, General Manager—Henry J. Peters
Vice-President, Secretary, General Counsel—Lawrence Lucchino
Vice-President, Stadium Operations—Jack Dunn, III
Vice-President, Finance—Joseph P. Hamper, Jr.
Treasurer—Robert J. Flanagan
Club Counsel—Lon Babby
Directors—Edward Bennett Williams, Joseph P. DiMaggio, Jack Dunn, III, Jay Emmett, Robert J. Flanagan, Gerald T. Gabrys, Charles H. Hoffberger, Jerold C. Hoffberger, Zanvyl Krieger, Lawrence Lucchino, Henry J. Peters, Peter P. Weidenbruch, Jr.
Vice-President of Business Affairs—Robert R. Aylward
Special Asst. & Executive Vice-President—Doug Melvin
Director of Public Relations—Robert W. Brown
Executive Director, Minor Leagues and Scouting—Thomas A. Giordano
Traveling Secretary—Philip E. Itzoe
Executive Director of Sales and Tickets—Louis I. Michaelson
Director of Corporate Marketing—Martin Conway
Promotions Manager—Jeff Urban
Community Relations Manager—Julia A. Wagner
Ticket Office Manager—Roy Sommerhof
Director, Scouting—Fred B. Uhlman
Administrator, Business Affairs, Minor Leagues & Scouting—John J. McCall
Admin. Asst., Minor Leagues & Scouting—Daniel J. O'Dowd
Assistant Public Relations Director—Richard L. Vaughn
Assistant Ticket Manager—Joseph B. Codd
Director of Broadcast Relations—Kenneth E. Nigro
Director of Computer Services—James L. Kline
Manager—Cal Ripken, Sr.
Club Physicians—Drs. Sheldon Goldgeir and Charles Silverstein
Executive Offices—Memorial Stadium, Baltimore, Md. 21218
Telephone—243-9800 (area code 301)

SCOUTS—(Major League)—Jim Russo, John Stokoe, Bill Werle. (Regular)—Lefty Bagg, Jack Baker, Carlos Bernhart, Joe Bowman, Art Brophy, Ray Crone, Ed Crosby, Joe DeLucca, Jim Gilbert, Jesus Halabi, Len Johnston, Bill Lawlor, George Lauzerique, Mike Ledna, Minnie Mendoza, Bill Miller, Carl Moesche, Lamar North, Jim Pamlanye, Jack Sanford, Fay Thompson, Jerry Zimmerman.

PARK LOCATION—Memorial Stadium, 33rd Street, Ellerslie Avenue, 36th Street and Ednor Road.

Seating capacity—54,002.

FIELD DIMENSIONS—Home plate to left field at foul line, 309 feet; to center field, 405 feet; to right field at foul line, 309 feet.

BOSTON RED SOX

President—Jean R. Yawkey

Chief Executive Officer/Chief Operating Officer—Haywood C. Sullivan
General Partner—Edward G. LeRoux, Jr.
Vice-President, General Manager—James (Lou) Gorman
Chief Financial Officer/Treasurer—Robert C. Furbush
V. P., Player Development Director—Edward F. Kenney
Minor League Administrative Assistant—Edward Kenney, Jr.
Scouting Director—Edward M. Kasko
Public Relations and Publicity Director—Richard L. Bresciani
Traveling Secretary—John J. Rogers
Broadcasting Director—James P. Healey
Executive Assistant—Joseph F. McDermott
Marketing Director—Lawrence C. Cancro
Controller—John J. Reilly
Ticket Director—Arthur J. Moscato
Assistant Publicity Director—Josh S. Spofford
Publicity Assistant—James A. Samia
Asst. to Marketing Director—Thomas L. Queenan, Jr.
Group Sales—Michael L. Silva
Superintendent, Grounds & Maintenance—Joseph Mooney
Manager—John F. McNamara
Club Physician—Dr. Arthur M. Pappas
Executive Offices—4 Yawkey Way, Boston, Mass. 02215
Telephone—267-9440 (area code 617)

SCOUTS—Rafael Batista, Milton Bolling, Ray Boone, Wayne Britton, George Digby, Howard (Danny) Doyle, Bill Enos, Larry Flynn, Charles Koney, Jack Lee, Wilfrid (Lefty) Lefebvre, Don Lenhardt, Howard McCullough, Felix Maldonado, Frank Malzone, Sam Mele, Willie Paffen, Peter Randall, Philip Rossi, Edward Scott, Matt Sczesny, Joe Stephenson, Larry Thomas, Charlie Wagner.

PARK LOCATION—Fenway Park, Yawkey Way, Lansdowne Street and Ipswich Street.

Seating capacity—33,569.

FIELD DIMENSIONS—Home plate to left field at foul line, 315 feet; to center field, 420 feet; to right field at foul line, 302 feet; average right-field distance, 382 feet.

CALIFORNIA ANGELS

President and Chairman of the Board—Gene Autry

Sr. Vice-President and General Manager—Mike Port
Vice-President—Jackie Autry
Vice-President/Secretary-Treasurer—Michael Schreter
Sr. Vice-President, Marketing—John Hays
Sr. Vice-President, Finance and Administration—James Wilson
Vice-President, Public Relations—Tom Seeberg
Assistant to General Manager—Preston Gomez
Director Publicity—Tim Mead
Director Publications—John Sevano
Controller—Jim Kaczmarek
Director Scouting & Player Development—Bob Fontaine
Director Minor League Operations—Bill Bavasi
Adm. Asst., Player Personnel & Development—Frank Marcos
Director Ticket Department—Carl Gordon
Asst. Ticket Manager—Gen Linhoff
Manager, Data Operations—Bob Terzes
Manager, Data Processing—Ron Moore
Director Group Sales & Promotions—Lynn Kirchmann Biggs
Asst. Dir., Group Sales & Promotions—Bob Wagner
Assistant Director Marketing—Jean (Corky) Lippert
Traveling Secretary—Frank Sims
Manager Stadium Operations—Kevin Uhlich
Medical Director—Dr. Robert Kerlan
General Medicine—Dr. Jules Rasinski
Orthopedist—Dr. Lewis Yocum
Trainers—Rick Smith, Ned Bergert
Physical Therapist—Roger Williams
Manager—Gene Mauch
Executive Offices—Anaheim Stadium, 2000 State College Blvd., Anaheim, Calif. 92806
Telephone—937-6700 (area code 714) or 625-1123 (area code 213)

SCOUTS—Edmundo Borrome, George Bradley, Joe Carpenter, Pompeyo Davalillo, Cliff Ditto, Preston Douglas, Jesse Flores, Jimmy Fox, Bob Gardner, Al Geddes, Steve Gruwell, Bruce Hines, Rick Ingalls, Nick Kamzic, Kevin Malone, Jon Neiderer, Eusebio Perez, Vic Power, Phil Rizzo, Paul Robinson, Cooke Rojas, Rich Schlenker, Mark Wiedemaier.

PARK LOCATION—Anaheim Stadium, 2000 State College Blvd.

Seating capacity—64,573.

FIELD DIMENSIONS—Home plate to left field at foul line, 333 feet; to center field, 404 feet; to right field at foul line, 333 feet.

CHICAGO WHITE SOX

Chairman, Board of Directors—Jerry M. Reinsdorf

President—Eddie M. Einhorn
Executive Vice-President—Howard C. Pizer
Vice-President/General Manager—Larry Himes
Vice-President, Baseball Administration—Jack Gould
Vice-President, Marketing—Michael D. McClure
Vice-President/Finance—Timothy L. Buzard
Assistant Vice-President, Marketing—Stephen M. Schanwald
Director of Scouting & Player Development—Al Goldis
Director of Public Relations—Paul H. Jensen
Sales Manager—Millie Johnson
Asst. to the V.P., Marketing/Sales and Promotions—Jeff Overton
Director of Broadcast Sales—Edwin M. Doody
Controller—Terry Savarise
Director of Purchasing—Don Esposito
Traveling Secretary—Glen Rosenbaum
Ticket Manager—Robert K. Devoy
Coordinator of Promotions and Special Events—Christine Makowski
Assistant Director of Scouting & Player Development—Steve Noworyta
Minor League Administrator—Mitch Lukevics
Player Personnel Administrator—Daniel Evans
Administrative Assistant/Baseball Operations—Jeff Chaney
Accounting Manager—Sandra Grobarcik
Assistant Director of Public Relations—Tim Clodjeaux
Broadcast Coordinator—Laura Jane Hyde
Administrative Assistant/Sales & Promotions—Jeff Cieply
Director of ChiSox Fan Club—Karen McDevitt
Sales Representatives—John McCartney, Paul Reis, Chuck Johnsen, John Furrer, Doak Ewing
General Counsel—Allan B. Muchin
Trainer—Herman Schneider
Director of Physical Fitness—Al Vermeil
Team Physicians—Drs. James B. Boscardin, Hugo Cuadros, David Orth
Manager—Jim Fregosi
Equipment/Club House Mgr., White Sox—Willie Thompson
Director of Park Operations—David M. Schaffer
Groundskeepers—Gene and Roger Bossard
Organist—Nancy Faust
Executive Offices—Comiskey Park, 324 W. 35th Street, Chicago, Ill. 60616
Telephone—924-1000 (area code 312)

SCOUTS—(Advance)—Ellis Clary, Bart Johnson. (Supervisors)—Danny Monzon, Duane Shaffer, Lou Snipp. (Full-time scouts)—Juan Ramon Bernhardt, Mark Bernstein, Tom Caldano, Alex Cosmidis, Rod Fridley, Leo Labossiere, Larry Maxie, Larry Monroe, Gary Pellant, Ed Pebley, Mark Snipp, Ken Stauffer, Ron Vaughn, Walt Widmayer. (Part-time scouts)—Alvin Dark, Ed Ford, Eric Gluck, Mike Harris, Edward Ben Hays, Joe Ingalls, Dario Lodigiani, Jose Ortega, Cucho Rodriguez, Craig Wallenbrock.

PARK LOCATION—Comiskey Park, Dan Ryan at 35th Street, Chicago, Ill. 60616.

Seating capacity—44,087.

FIELD DIMENSIONS—Home plate to left field at foul line, 347 feet; to center field, 409 feet; to right field at foul line, 347 feet.

CLEVELAND INDIANS

Board of Directors—Richard E. Jacobs, Chairman; David H. Jacobs, Vice-Chairman; Martin J. Cleary, Gary L. Bryenton

Chairman of the Board and Chief Executive Officer—Richard E. Jacobs
Vice-Chairman of the Board—David H. Jacobs
Senior V.P., Baseball Administration & Player Relations—Dan O'Brien
Vice-President, Administration—Terry Barthelmas
Vice-President, Baseball Operations—Joe Klein
Vice-President, Finance—Gregg Olson
Vice-President—Martin J. Cleary
Director, Publication/Advertising Sales—Valerie Arcuri
Director, Ticket Services—Joan Eppich
Director, Sales/Promotions—Jeff Gregor
Director, Operations—Carl Hoerig
Director, Public Relations—Rick Minch
Director, Player Development & Scouting—Jeff Scott
Director, Team Travel—Mike Seghi
Director, Ticket Sales—Gary Sherwood
Administrator, Player Personnel—Phil Thomas
Controller—Barb Cully
Manager, Indians Gift Shop—Kevin Lynch
Manager, Box Office—Connie Minadeo
Manager, Promotions/Publications—Jon Starrett
Manager, Stadium Operations—Dan Zerbey
Account Executives, Ticket Sales—Tim Needles, Tony Seghy
Speakers Bureau—Bob Feller
Coordinator, Season/Group Sales—Lori Krzeminski
Coordinator, Community Relations—Norm LaFlamme
Coordinator, Computer Ticketing/Data Processing—Candy Ward
Assistant to Director, Public Relations—Susie Gharrity
Manager—Pat Corrales
Indians Equipment & Clubhouse Manager—Cy Buynak
Visiting Clubhouse Manager—Bill Sheridan
Medical Director—William T. Wilder, M.D.
Orthopedic Specialist—John Bergfeld, M.D.
Head Trainer—Jim Warfield
Assistant Trainer—Paul Spicuzza
Team Physicians—Drs. Tom Anderson, James R. Conforto, Godofredo Domingo, Mark Frankel, K.V. Gopal, Peter Greenwalt, Gus A. Kious
Executive Offices—Cleveland Stadium, Cleveland, Ohio 44114
Telephone—861-1200 (area code 216)

SCOUTS—Hector Acevedo, Rick Adair, Eddie Bane, Tom Chandler, Tom Couston, Connie Dettling, Red Gaskill, Orlando Gomez, Luis Issac, Dave Koblentz, Joe Lewis, Bobby Malkmus, Bill Meyer, Jim Miller, Dave Roberts, Woody Smith, Dale Sutherland, Gary Sutherland, Birdie Tebbetts.

PARK LOCATION—Cleveland Stadium, Boudreau Blvd.

Seating capacity—74,208.

FIELD DIMENSIONS—Home plate to left field at foul line, 320 feet; to center field, 400 feet; to right field at foul line, 320 feet.

DETROIT TIGERS

Board of Directors
John E. Fetzer, Thomas S. Monaghan, James A. Campbell

Chairman of the Board—John E. Fetzer
Vice-Chairman and Owner—Thomas S. Monaghan
President & Chief Executive Officer—James A. Campbell
Vice-President & General Manager—William R. Lajoie
Vice-President, Operations—William E. Haase
V.P., Player Procurement & Development—Joseph A. McDonald
V.P., Secretary/Treasurer—Alexander C. Callam
Director of Press & Public Relations—Dan Ewald
Director of Radio & TV—Neal Fenkell
Director of Stadium Operations—Ralph E. Snyder
Director of Ticket Sales—William H. Willis
Administrator of Player Development—Dave Miller
Executive Secretary/Baseball—Alice Sloane
Executive Secretary/Operations—Hazel McLane
Data Processing Manager—Mary Lamphier
Traveling Secretary—Bill Brown
Executive Consultant—Rick Ferrell
Special Assignment Scouts—Walter A. Evers, Jerry Walker
Scouting Coordinator—Bill Schudlich
Eastern Scouting Supervisor—Jax Robertson
Western Scouting Supervisor—Dick Wiencek
Assistant Director of Public Relations—Bob Miller
Director of Marketing—Lew Matlin
Assistant Director of Public Relations/Community Relations—Vince Desmond
Group Sales Coordinator—Irwin Cohen
Assistant Director of Stadium Operations/Grounds Maintenance—Frank Feneck
Assistant Director of Stadium Operations/Grounds Maintenance—Ed Goward
Manager—Sparky Anderson
Club Physician—Clarence S. Livingood M.D.
Orthopedic Consultant—David Collon M.D.
Executive Offices—Tiger Stadium, Detroit, Mich. 48216
Telephone—962-4000 (area code 313)

SCOUTS—Mateo Alou, Rick Arnold, Ray Bellino, Jim Bierman, Wayne Blackburn, Charlie Gault, Joe Lewis, Kenneth Madeja, Rick Magnante, Orlando Pena, Ramon Pena, Dee Phillips, Mike Wallace, Richard Wilson, Marti Wolever.

PARK LOCATION—Tiger Stadium, Michigan Avenue, Cochrane Avenue, Kaline Drive and Trumbull Avenue.

Seating capacity—52,806.

FIELD DIMENSIONS—Home plate to left field at foul line, 340 feet; to center field, 440 feet; to right field at foul line, 325 feet.

KANSAS CITY ROYALS

Board of Directors
Joe Burke, William Deramus, III, Avron Fogelman, Charles Hughes,
Ewing Kauffman, Mrs. Ewing Kauffman, Earl Smith

Chairman of the Board (co-owner)—Ewing Kauffman
Vice Chairman of the Board (co-owner)—Avron Fogelman
President—Joe Burke
Executive Vice-President and General Manager—John Schuerholz
Executive Vice-President, Administration—Spencer (Herk) Robinson
Vice-President, Controller—Dale Rohr
Vice-President and Legal Counsel—Phil Koury
Vice-President, Public Relations—Dean Vogelaar
Director of Marketing and Broadcasting—Dennis Cryder
Traveling Secretary—Will Rudd
Assistant Director of Public Relations—Jeff Coy
Director of Scouting—Art Stewart
Director of Player Development—John Boles
Adm. Asst., Scouting & Player Development—Bob Hegman
Assistant to General Manager—Dean Taylor
Assistant Director of Marketing—Kevin Gray
Director of Ticket Operations—Stacy Sherrow
Director of Season Ticket Sales—Joe Grigoli
Director of Group Sales/Lancer Coordinator—Chris Muehlbach
Director of Event Personnel—Jay Hinrichs
Stadium Engineer—Duane Robinson
Stadium Maintenance Coordinator—Dave Owen
Data Processing Manager—Loretta Kratzberg
Accountants—Tom Pfannenstiel, Ken Willeke
Exec. Secretary/Baseball—Peggy Mathews
Manager—Dick Howser
Equipment Manager—Al Zych
Groundskeeper—George Toma
Team Physician—Dr. Paul Meyer
Trainers—Mickey Cobb, Paul McGannon
Organist—Rick Janssen
Executive Offices—Royals Stadium, Harry S Truman Sports Complex
Mailing Address—P. O. Box 419969, Kansas City, Mo. 64141
Telephone—921-2200 (area code 816)

SCOUTS—Carl Blando, Al Diez, Tom Ferrick, Rosey Gilhousen, Ken Gonzales, Guy Hansen, Ron Hopkins, Gary Johnson, Al Kubski, Tony Levato, Chuck McMichael, Jim Moran, Brian Murphy, George Noga, Herb Raybourn, Jerry Stephens, Roy Tanner.

PARK LOCATION—Royals Stadium, Harry S Truman Sports Complex.

Seating capacity—40,625.

FIELD DIMENSIONS—Home plate to left field at foul line, 330 feet; to center field, 410 feet; to right field at foul line, 330 feet.

MILWAUKEE BREWERS

President, Chief Executive Officer—Allan H. (Bud) Selig

Executive Vice-President, General Manager—Harry Dalton
Vice-President, Marketing—Richard Hackett
Vice-President, Broadcast Operations—William Haig
Vice-President, Finance—Richard Hoffmann
Vice-President, Stadium Operations—Gabe Paul, Jr.
Assistant General Manager—Walter Shannon
Special Assistants to the General Manager—Dee Fondy, Sal Bando
Traveling Secretary—Jimmy Bank
Farm Director—Bruce Manno
Scouting Coordinator—Dan Duquette
Special Assignments—Ray Poitevint
Coordinator of Player Development—Bob Humphreys
Director of Publicity—Tom Skibosh
Assistant Director of Stadium Operations and Advertising—Jack Hutchinson
Director of Community Relations—John Counsell
Director of Publications and Assistant Director of Publicity—Mario Ziino
Ticket Sales Director—Tim Trovato
Ticket Office Manager—John Barnes
Director of Ticket Office Computer Operations—Alice Boettcher
Manager—Tom Trebelhorn
Club Physician—Dr. Paul Jacobs
Trainers—John Adam, Freddie Frederico
Superintendent of Grounds and Maintenance—Harry Gill
Assistant Groundskeeper—Gary Vandenberg
Equipment Manager—Tony Migliaccio
P.A. Announcer—Bob Betts
Executive Offices—Milwaukee Brewers Baseball Club
Milwaukee County Stadium, Milwaukee, Wis. 53214
Telephone—933-4114 (area code 414)

SCOUTS—Supervisors: Julio Blanco-Herrera, Ken Bracey, Felix Delgado, Roland LeBlanc, Walter Youse. Regulars: Fred Beene, Tom Bourque, Nelson Burbrink, Ken Califano, Bill Castro, Lou Cohenour, Warren Dewey, Dick Foster, Jim Gabella, Dave Garcia, Gene Kerns, Phil Long, Steve McAllister, Cal McLish, Ed Mathes, Johnny Neun, Frank Pena, Frank Piet, Reuben Rodriguez, Art Schuerman, Lee Sigman, Earl Silverthorn, Harry Smith, Mike Stafford, John Stearns, Sam Suplizio, Tommy Thompson, Paul Tretiak, Edward Whitsett, Mike Woten.

PARK LOCATION—Milwaukee County Stadium, S. 46th St. off Bluemound Rd.

Seating capacity—53,192.

FIELD DIMENSIONS—Home plate to left field at foul line, 315 feet; to center field, 402 feet; to right field at foul line, 315 feet.

MINNESOTA TWINS

Owner—Carl R. Pohlad

President—Jerry Bell
Chairman of Executive Committee—Howard Fox
Consultant—Calvin R. Griffith
Directors—Donald E. Benson, Paul R. Christen, James O. Pohlad, Robert E. Woolley
Exec. Vice-President, Baseball Operations—Andy MacPhail
Vice-President, Baseball—Ralph Houk
Vice-President, Finance—Jim McHenry
Vice-President, Operations—Dave Moore
Director of Major League Personnel—Bob Gebhard
Director of Minor Leagues—Jim Rantz
Director of Scouting—Terry Ryan
Director of Media Relations—Tom Mee
Traveling Secretary—Laurel Prieb
Manager—Tom Kelly
Club Physicians—Dr. Leonard J. Michienzi, Dr. Harvey O'Phelan
Executive Offices—Hubert H. Humphrey Metrodome, 501 Chicago Ave. South,
Minneapolis, Minn. 55415
Telephone—375-1366 (area code 612)

SCOUTS—Floyd Baker, Vern Borning, Enrique Brito, Ellsworth Brown, Edward Dunn, Dan Durst, Marty Esposito, Jesse Flores, Jr., Jesse Flores, Sr., Angelo Giuliani, Lee Irwin, Hank Izquierdo, Bill Lohr, Bobby Morgan, Spencer (Red) Robbins, Cobby Saatzer, Johnny Sierra, Dennis Sommers, Herb Stein, Fred Waters.

PARK LOCATION—Hubert H. Humphrey Metrodome, 501 Chicago Ave. South.

Seating capacity—55,244.

FIELD DIMENSIONS—Home plate to left field at foul line, 343 feet; to center field, 408 feet; to right field at foul line, 327 feet.

NEW YORK YANKEES

Principal Owner—George M. Steinbrenner

Partners—Harold M. Bowman, Daniel M. Crown, James S. Crown, Lester Crown, Michael Friedman, Marvin Goldklang, Barry Halper, Harvey Leighton, Daniel McCarthy, Harry Nederlander, James Nederlander, Robert Nederlander, William Rose Sr., Edward Rosenthal, Jack Satter, Joan Z. Steinbrenner, Charlotte Witkind, Richard Witkind

Administrative Vice President and Treasurer—M. David Weidler
Vice-President, General Counsel—William F. Dowling
Vice-President, Stadium Operations—Patrick Kelly
Vice-President, Public Relations—Richard Kraft
Vice-President, Publications—David S. Szen
Vice President—Ed Weaver
Special Advisor to Ownership—Clyde King
Vice President and General Manager—Woody Woodward
Vice-President, Baseball Administration—Bob Quinn
Director of Player Development—Bobby Hofman
Director of Scouting—Brian Sabean
Executive Director of Ticket Operations—Frank Swaine
Ticket Director—Mike Rendine
Traveling Secretary—Bill Kane
Director of Group & Season Sales—Debbie Tymon
Assistant Player Development Director—Pete Jameson
Assistant Scouting Director—Roy Krasik
Director of Media Relations—Harvey Greene
Assistant Media Relations Director—Lou D'Ermilio
Executive Marketing Advisor—John C. Fugazy
Director of Customer Services—Joel S. White
Director of Scoreboard Operations—Betsy Leesman
Speakers Bureau—Bob Pelegrino
Editor/Yankees Magazine—Tom Bannon
Sales Manager—Robert Zeig
Director of Accounting—Warren Atkinson
Video Coordination Director—Mike Barnett
Computer Statistics Director—Kevin Elfering
Spring Training Coordinator—Marsh Samuel
Director, Alumni Association—Jim Ogle
Team Physician—Dr. John J. Bonamo
Manager—Lou Piniella
Stadium Superintendent—Tom Colluzzi
Public Address Announcer—Bob Sheppard
Organist—Eddie Layton
Executive Offices—Yankee Stadium, Bronx, N.Y. 10451
Telephone—293-4300 (area code 212)

SCOUTS—Luis Arroyo, Mark Batchko, Hank Bauer, Hop Cassady, Al Cuccinello, Joe DiCarlo, Bill Emslie, Fred Ferreira, Orrin Freeman, Jack Gillis, Dick Groch, Jim Gruzdis, Bob Hartsfield, Bob Lemon, Don Lindeberg, Bill Livesey, Eddie Lopat, Jim Naples, Sr., Ramon Naranjo, Greg Orr, Meade Palmer, Roberto Rivera, Joe Robison, Lou Saban, Stan Saleski, Rudy Santin, Charlie Silvera, Jeff Taylor, Dick Tidrow, Paul Turco, Frank Verdi, Mickey Vernon, Jeff Zimmerman.

PARK LOCATION—Yankee Stadium, E. 161st St. and River Ave., Bronx, N.Y. 10451.

Seating capacity—57,545.

FIELD DIMENSIONS—Home plate to left field at foul line, 312 feet; to center field, 410 feet; to right field at foul line, 310 feet.

OAKLAND A's

President—Roy Eisenhardt

Executive Vice-President—Walter J. Haas
Vice-President, Baseball Operations—Sandy Alderson
Vice-President, Business Operations—Andy Dolich
Vice-President, Finance—Kathleen McCracken
Director of Scouting—Dick Bogard
Special Asst. to V.P., Baseball Operations—Ron Schueler
Director of Player Development—Karl Kuehl
Director of Baseball Administration—Walt Jocketty
Assistant to the President, Baseball Matters—Bill Rigney
Director of Latin American Scouting—Juan Marichal
Director of Team Travel—Mickey Morabito
Director of Broadcasting—David Rubinstein
Director of Public Relations—Jay Alves
Director of Ticket Operations—Raymond B. Krise Jr.
Director of Stadium Operations—Jorge Costa
Director of Publications—Art Worthington
Director of Community Affairs—Dave Perron
Director of Ticket Sales—Steve Page
Director of Advertising Sales—Tom Cordova
Director of Season Sales—Doris Messina
Director of Group Sales—Bettina Flores
Assistant Director of Public Relations—Kathy Jacobson
Business Oper. Coord/Dir. of Promotions—Sharon Kelly
Executive Assistant—Sharon Jones
Manager—Tony LaRussa
Team Physician—Dr. Allan Pont
Team Orthopedist—Dr. Rick Bost
Trainers—Barry Weinberg, Larry Davis
Equipment Manager—Frank Ciensczyk
Visiting Clubhouse Manager—Steve Vucinich
Executive Offices—Oakland-Alameda County Coliseum, Oakland, Calif. 94621
Telephone—638-4900 (area code 415)

SCOUTS—Mark Conkin, Larry Corrigan, Bruce Cudmore, Grady Fuson, Bill Gayton, Marty Miller, Mel Nelson, Camilo Pascual, John Ricciardi, Mike Sgobba, Mike Squires.

PARK LOCATION—Oakland-Alameda County Coliseum, Nimitz Freeway and Hegenberger Road.

Seating capacity—50,219.

FIELD DIMENSIONS—Home plate to left field at foul line, 330 feet; to center field, 397 feet; to right field at foul line, 330 feet.

SEATTLE MARINERS

Chairman of the Board & Chief Executive Officer—George L. Argyros

President & Chief Operating Officer—Charles G. Armstrong
Vice President, Baseball Operations—Dick Balderson
Vice President, Finance & Administration—Brian Beggs
Vice President, Sales and Marketing—Bill Knudsen
Director of Marketing & Broadcasting—Randy Adamack
Director of Player Development—Bill Haywood
Director of Community & Public Relations—Bob Porter
Director of Scouting—Roger Jongewaard
Director of Promotional Sales—Larry Sindall
Director of Ticket Services—Doug Hopkins
Director of Team Travel—Lee Pelekoudas
Director of Stadium Operations—Jeff Klein
Asst. to V.P., Baseball Operations & Special Assignments—Bob Harrison
Assistant Director of Public Relations—Craig Detwiler
Assistant Director of Marketing—Ross Skinner
Assistant Director of Community Relations—Randy Stearnes
Assistant Director of Ticket Services—John Ross Karnoski
Accounting Assistant—Shirley Shreve
Controller—Denise Podosek
Manager—Dick Williams
Trainer—Rick Griffin
Home Clubhouse & Equipment Manager—Henry Genzale
Club Physicians—Dr. Larry Pedegana, Dr. Mitchel Storey
Club Dentist—Dr. Richard Leshgold
Head Groundskeeper—Wilbur Loo
P.A. Announcers—Gary Spinnell, Bill Rice
Executive Offices—P.O. Box 4100
411 First Ave. S., Suite 480, Seattle, Washington 98104
Telephone—628-3555 (area code 206)

SCOUTS—Bill Barkley, Roy Clark, Bill Griffin, Dave Kariff, Joe Henderson, Ken Houp, Bill Kearns, Benny Looper, Jeff Malinoff, Jerry Merik, Tom Mooney, Joe Nigro, Francis Onetta, Whitey Piurek, Cananea Reyes, Mike Roberts, Rick Sweet, Bill Tracy, Rip Tutor, Steve Vrablik, Luke Wrenn.

PARK LOCATION—The Kingdome, 201 South King Street, Seattle, Washington.

Seating capacity—59,438.

FIELD DIMENSIONS—Home plate to left field at foul line, 316 feet; to center field, 410 feet; to right field at foul line, 316 feet.

TEXAS RANGERS

Board of Directors—Eddie Chiles, Edward L. Gaylord, Fran Chiles, Michael H. Stone, Glenn Stinchcomb

Chairman of the Board, Chief Executive Officer—Eddie Chiles
President, Chief Operating Officer—Michael H. Stone
Vice President, General Manager—Thomas A. Grieve
Vice President, Finance and Secretary-Treasurer—Charles F. Wangner
General Counsel—John B. McAdams
Financial Consultant—Weldon Asten
Assistant G.M., Player Personnel and Scouting—Sandy Johnson
Assistant General Manager—Wayne Krivsky
Director, Player Development—Marty Scott
Director, Media Relations—John Blake
Director, Public Relations and Speakers Bureau—Bobby Bragan
Director, Sales, Broadcasting and Producer, Diamond Vision—Chuck Morgan
Director, Promotions and Director, Diamond Vision—Dave Fendrick
Director, Ticket Sales and Management—Mary Ann Bosher
Stadium Manager—Mat Stolley
Traveling Secretary—Dan Schimek
Controller—John McMichael
General Manager, Charlotte County Operations—Jay Miller
Assistant Director, Media Relations—Jim Small
Assistant Director, Ticket Sales & Management—John Schriever
Medical Director—Dr. Mike Mycoskie
Manager—Bobby Valentine
Field Superintendent—Jim Anglea
Assistant Field Superintendent—Brad Richards
Spring Training Director—John Welaj
Home Clubhouse and Equipment Manager—Joe Macko
Visiting Clubhouse Manager—Mike Wallace
Executive Offices—1250 Copeland Road, 11th Floor, Arlington, Tex. 76011
Arlington Stadium—1500 Copeland Road, Arlington, Tex. 76010
Mailing Address—P.O. Box 1111, Arlington, Tex. 76010
Telephone—273-5222 (area code 817)

SCOUTS—Joe Branzell, Jose Casino, Paddy Cottrell, Amado Dinzey, Bill Earnhart, Doug Gassaway, Mark Giegler, Tim Hallgren, Andy Hancock, Jack Hays, Dean Jongewaard, Bryan Lambe, John Metro, Omar Minaya, Omer Monoz, Triny Rivera, Luis Rosa, Eddie Santiago, Bill Schmidt, Rick Schroeder, Mike Snyder, Danilo Troncoso, John Young.

PARK LOCATION—Arlington Stadium, 1500 Copeland Road, Arlington, Tex.

Seating capacity—43,508.

FIELD DIMENSIONS—Home plate to left field at foul line, 330 feet; to center field, 400 feet; to right field at foul line, 330 feet.

TORONTO BLUE JAYS

Vice-Chairman, Chief Executive Officer—N. E. Hardy

Board of Directors—John Craig Eaton, W. Ferguson, L. G. Greenwood, N. E. Hardy, R. Howard Webster, P. N. T. Widdrington
Chairman of the Board—R. Howard Webster
Executive Vice-President, Business—Paul Beeston
Executive Vice-President, Baseball—Pat Gillick
Vice-Presidents, Baseball—Bobby Mattick, Al LaMacchia
Vice-President, Finance & Administration—Bob Nicholson
Director, Public Relations—Howard Starkman
Director, Operations—Ken Erskine
Director, Ticket Operations—George Holm
Director of Marketing—Paul Markle
Controller—Phil Martin
Director, Florida Operations—Ken Carson
Director, Group Sales—Maureen Haffey
Director, Canadian Scouting—Bob Prentice
Manager, Promotions & Community Events—John Brioux
Coordinator & Administrator, Promotions—Colleen Burns
Assistant Director, Public Relations—Gary Oswald
Administrator, Player Personnel—Gord Ash
Assistant Director of Operations—Len Frejlich
Assistant Director, Ticket Operations—Randy Low
Assistant Controller—Sue Sostarich
Director, Security—Fred Wootton
Administrative Aides, Baseball—Susan Allen, Janet Donaldson, Ellen Harrigan
Equipment Manager—Jeff Ross
Coordinator, Promotions & Group Services—Mark Edwards
Supervisor, Grounds—Brad Bujold
Manager—Jimy Williams
Team Physician—Dr. Ron Taylor
Executive Offices—Exhibition Stadium, Exhibition Place, Toronto, Ontario
Mailing Address—Box 7777, Adelaide St. P. O., Toronto, Ont. M5C 2K7
Telephone—595-0077 (area code 416)

SCOUTS—David Blume, Christopher Bourjos, Ellis Dungan, Robert Engle (Eastern Regional Scouting Director), Joe Ford, Epy Guerrero (Coordinator, Latin American Scouting), Tom Hinkle, Jim Hughes, Moose Johnson (Special Assignment), Gordon Lakey (Special Assignment), Duane Larson, Mike McAlphin, Ben McLure, Steve Minor, Wayne Morgan (Western Regional Scouting Director), Paul Ricciarini, Don Welke, Tim Wilken, Dave Yoakum.

PARK LOCATION—Exhibition Stadium on the grounds of Exhibition Place. Entrances to Exhibition Place via Lakeshore Boulevard, Queen Elizabeth Way Highway and Dufferin and Bathurst Streets.

Seating capacity—43,737.

FIELD DIMENSIONS—Home plate to left field at foul line, 330 feet; to center field, 400 feet; to right field at foul line, 330 feet.

National League

Organized 1876

A. BARTLETT GIAMATTI
President and Treasurer

PHYLLIS B. COLLINS
Vice-President & Secretary

KATY FEENEY
Director of Media & Public Affairs

MARY LOU RISLEY
Executive Secretary & Office Manager

CATHY DAVIS
Administrative Assistant

NANCY CROFTS
Manager of Player Records

Headquarters—350 Park Avenue, New York, N. Y. 10022

Telephone—371-7300 (area code 212)

UMPIRES—Greg Bonin, Fred Brocklander, Gerald Crawford, Robert Davidson, Gerry Davis, Dana DeMuth, Robert Engel, Bruce Froemming, Eric Gregg, Tom Hallion, H. Douglas Harvey, John Kibler, Randall Marsh, John McSherry, Edward Montague, David Pallone, Frank Pulli, James Quick, Lawrence (Dutch) Rennert, Steve Rippley, Paul Runge, Richard Stello, Terry Tata, Harry Wendelstedt, Joseph West, Lee Weyer, Charles Williams, William Williams.

OFFICIAL STATISTICIANS—Elias Sports Bureau, Inc., 500 5th Ave., Suite 2114, New York, N. Y. 10036. Telephone (212) 869-1530.

ATLANTA BRAVES

Chairman of the Board—William C. Bartholomay

President—Stan Kasten
Executive Vice-President—Allison Thornwell, Jr.
General Manager—Robert J. Cox
Assistant General Manager—John W. Mullen
Vice-President and Business Manager—Charles S. Sanders
Vice-President, Player Development—Henry L. Aaron
Assistant Vice-President, Scouting—Paul L. Snyder, Jr.
Assistant Scouting Director—Rod Gilbreath
Director of Broadcasting/Marketing—Wayne Long
Ticket Distribution Manager—Ed Newman
Director of Public Relations—Bob DiBiasio
Director of Promotions—Miles McRea
Assistant Public Relations Director—Jim Schultz
Director of Stadium Operations and Security—Ken Little
Director of Matrix Operations—Bob Larson
Assistant Controller—Martin Mathews
Traveling Secretary and Equipment Manager—Bill Acree
Director of Ticket Sales—Andre DeLorenzo
Manager—Chuck Tanner
Club Physician—Dr. David T. Watson
Executive Offices—P.O. Box 4064, Atlanta, Ga. 30302
Telephone—522-7630 (area code 404)

SCOUTS—Mike Arbuckle, Sam Berry, Cloyd Boyer, Forrest (Smoky) Burgess, Jim Busby, Stu Cann, Joe Caputo, Harold Cronin, Tony DeMacio, Dutch Dorman, Lou Fitzgerald, Pedro Gonzalez, Larry Grefer, John Groth, John Hageman, Gene Hassell, Herb Hippauf, Ray Holton, Jim Johnson, Burney R. (Dickey) Martin, Bob Mavis, Red Murff, Umberto Oropeza, Ernie Pedersen, Rance Pless, Jorge Posada, Harry Postove, Jose Salado, Bill Serena, Fred Shaffer, Charles Smith, Tony Stiel, Bob Turzilli, Bob Wadsworth, Wesley Westrum, William R. Wight, Don Williams, Bobby Wine, H.F. (Red) Wooten.

PARK LOCATION—Atlanta-Fulton County Stadium, on Capitol Avenue at the junction of Interstate Highways 20, 75 and 85.

Seating capacity—51,970.

FIELD DIMENSIONS—Home plate to left field at foul line, 330 feet; to center field, 402 feet; to right field at foul line, 330 feet.

CHICAGO CUBS

Board of Directors—Thomas G. Ayers, Stanton R. Cook, Dallas Green, John W. Madigan, Andrew J. McKenna
President and General Manager—Dallas Green
Executive Vice-President, Business Operations—Don Grenesko
Vice-President of Minor Leagues and Scouting—Gordon Goldsberry
Vice-President of Finance—Mark McGuire
Vice-President—E.R. Saltwell
Assistant General Manager—John Cox
Special Player Consultant—Charlie Fox
Special Player Consultant—Hugh Alexander
Controller—Keith Bode
General Counsel—Geoff Anderson
Secretary—Stan Gradowski
Director of Broadcasting and Merchandising—Jeff Odenwald
Director of Marketing—John McDonough
Director of Media Relations—Ned Colletti
Director of Minor League Operations—Bill Harford
Director of Player Development—Pete MacKanin
Director of Publications—Bob Ibach
Director of Scouting—Scott Reid
Director of Stadium Operations—Tom Cooper
Director of Ticket Sales—Frank Maloney
Director of Ticket Services—Lamar Vernon
Traveling Secretary—Peter Durso
Manager of Accounting Systems and Taxes—Joe Kirchen
Manager of Financial Accounting—Tom Luptowski
Assistant Director of Marketing and Publications—Bill Galante
Assistant Director of Media Relations—Sharon Pannozzo
Assistant Director of Promotions and Community Services—Connie Kowal
Assistant Director of Scouting—Scott Nelson
Assistant Director of Stadium Operations/Event Personnel—Paul Rathje
Assistant Director of Stadium Operations/Facilities—Lubie Veal
Assistant Director of Ticket Services—Larry Regan
Assistant Director of Ticket Services—Frank Baltrusaitis
Team Photographer—Steve Green
Team Physician—Jacob Suker, M.D.
Trainer—John Fierro
Equipment Manager—Yosh Kawano
Manager—Gene Michael
Executive Offices—Wrigley Field, 1060 West Addison Street, Chicago, Ill. 60613
Telephone—281-5050 (area code 312)

SCOUTS—Francisco Acevedo, Billy Blitzer, Bill Capps, Billy Champion, Tom Davis, Ed DiRamio, Nino Espinosa, Bobby Gardner, John Gracio, Gene Handley, John Hennessy, Ron Hollingsworth, John (Spider) Jorgensen, Doug Lauman, John (Buck) O'Neil, Luis Peraza, Andy Pienovi, Joaquin Velilla, H.D. (Rube) Wilson, Earl Winn, Harold Younghans.

PARK LOCATION—Wrigley Field, Addison Street, N. Clark Street, Waveland Avenue and Sheffield Avenue.

Seating capacity—38,040.

FIELD DIMENSIONS—Home plate to left field at foul line, 355 feet; to center field, 400 feet; to right field at foul line, 353 feet.

CINCINNATI REDS

General Partner—Marge Schott

President and Chief Executive Officer—Marge Schott
Executive Vice-President & General Manager—Bill Bergesch
Vice-President/Business & Marketing—Don Breen
Vice-President, Player Personnel—Sheldon Bender
Vice-President, Publicity—Jim Ferguson
Director, Scouting—Larry Doughty
Controller—Chris Krabbe
Director, Stadium Operations—Tim O'Connell
Director, Promotions—Cal Levy
Director, Ticket Department—Bill Stewart
Director, Season Tickets—Pat McCaffrey
Director, Group Sales—Tony Harris
Director of Speakers Bureau—Gordy Coleman
Traveling Secretary—Brad Del Barba
Advance Scout—Jim Stewart
Assistant, Player Development and Scouting—Brian Granger
Assistant Publicity Director—Jon Braude
Assistant Ticket Director—John O'Brien
Chief Administrative Assistant—Joyce Pfarr
Manager—Pete Rose
Executive Offices—100 Riverfront Stadium, Cincinnati, O. 45202
Telephone—421-4510 (area code 513)

SCOUTS—Larry Barton, Jr., Gene Bennett, Cameron Bonifay, Dave Calaway, Bill Clark, Martin Daily, Roger Ferguson, Edwin Howsam, Chuck LaMar, Jeff McKay, Sam Mejias, Don Mitchell, Julian Mock, Chet Montgomery, Ed Roebuck, Tom Severtson, Neil Summers, Robert Szymkowski, Mickey White, George Zuraw.

PARK LOCATION—Riverfront Stadium, downtown Cincinnati, bounded by Pete Rose Way to the Ohio River and from Walnut Street to Broadway.

Seating capacity—52,392.

FIELD DIMENSIONS—Home plate to left field at foul line, 330 feet; to center field, 404 feet; to right field at foul line, 330 feet.

HOUSTON ASTROS

Board of Directors—Dr. John J. McMullen, Chairman. Owners—Dr. John J. McMullen, Mrs. R.E. (Bob) Smith, Mrs. Thomas E. (Mimi) Dompier, James A. Elkins, Jr., Alfred C. Glassell, Jr., Bob Marco, Don Sanders, Jack T. Trotter, H.L. Brown and Jacqueline, Peter, Catherine and John, Jr. McMullen.

President and General Manager—Dick Wagner
Vice-President, Baseball Operations—Fred Stanley
Assistant General Manager—William J. Wood
Director of Minor League Operations—Fred Nelson
Director of Scouting—Dan O'Brien, Jr.
Director of Public Relations—Rob Matwick
Traveling Secretary—Barry Waters
Director of Marketing—Ted Haracz
Director of Broadcasting—Art Elliott
Director of Promotions—Karen Williams
Special Assistant to the President—Donald Davidson
Assistant Director of Public Relations—Chuck Pool
Assistant to the Dirs., Minor Leagues/Scouting—Lew Temple
Scoreboard Operations—Paul Darst
Broadcast and Promotions Sales—Hugh Pickett, Art Bradshaw
Ticket Manager—Charles Wall
Manager, Group & Season Ticket Sales—Veronica Stalica
Administrative Asst., Major League Operations—Chris Rice
Secretary, Public Relations—Cinda Donovan
Club Physician—Dr. William Bryan
Public Address Announcer—J. Fred Duckett
Manager—Hal Lanier
Executive Offices—The Astrodome, P.O. Box 288
Houston, Tex. 77001
Telephone—799-9500 (area code 713)
HOUSTON SPORTS ASSOCIATION, INC.
President and Chief Operating Officer—Robert G. Harter
Executive Vice-President—Neal Gunn
Executive Vice-President, Astrodome-Astrohall Stadium Corporation—Jimmie Fore
Vice-President, Operations—W. Gary Keller
Vice-President, Public Affairs—Jim Weidler
Treasurer—Gary Brooks
General Counsel—Frank Rynd
Controller—Adam C. Richards

SCOUTS—Clary Anderson, Stan Benjamin, Jack Bloomfield, Joe Campise, Gerry Craft, Walter Cress, Clark Crist, C.V. Davis, Shug DeFord, Doug Deutsch, Jim Fleming, Ben Galante, Carl Greene, Bill Hallauer, Red Hayworth, Dan Hutson, David Lakey, Julio Linares, Walter Matthews, Hal Newhouser, Tony Pacheco, Joe Pittman, Pico Prado, Ross Sapp, Lynwood Stallings, Reggie Waller, Paul Weaver, Tom Wheeler.

PARK LOCATION—The Astrodome, Kirby and Interstate Loop 610

Seating capacity—45,000.

FIELD DIMENSIONS—Home plate to left field at foul line, 330 feet; to center field, 400 feet; to right field at foul line, 330 feet.

LOS ANGELES DODGERS

Board of Directors—Peter O'Malley, President; Harry M. Bardt;
Roland Seidler, Jr., Vice-President and Treasurer;
Mrs. Roland (Terry) Seidler, Secretary

President—Peter O'Malley
Executive Vice-President—Fred Claire
Vice-President, Player Personnel—Al Campanis
Vice-President, Minor League Operations—William P. Schweppe
Vice-President, Marketing—Merritt Willey
Controller and Assistant Treasurer—Ken Hasemann
Assistant Secretary & General Counsel—Santiago Fernandez
Director, Dodgertown—Charles Blaney
Director, Financial Projects—Bob Graziano
Director, Stadium Operations—Bob Smith
Director, Ticket Department—Walter Nash
Director, Stadium Club and Transportation—Bob Schenz
Director, Dodger Network—David Van de Walker
Director, Scouting—Ben Wade
Director, Publicity—Steve Brener
Director, Publications—Toby Zwikel
Director, Community Relations—Don Newcombe
Community Relations—Roy Campanella, Lou Johnson
Director, Ticket Marketing and Promotions—Barry Stockhamer
Director, Community Services and Special Events—Bill Shumard
Assistant to the President—Ike Ikuhara
Traveling Secretary—Billy DeLury
Auditor—Michael Strange
Manager—Tom Lasorda
Club Physicians—Dr. Frank Jobe, Dr. Michael F. Mellman
Executive Offices—Dodger Stadium, 1000 Elysian Park Avenue,
Los Angeles, Calif. 90012
Telephone—224-1500 (area code 213)

SCOUTS—Eleodoro Arias, Rafael Avila, Boyd Bartley, Bob Bishop, Gib Bodet, Flores Bolivar, Mike Brito, Bob Darwin, Mel Didier, Paul Duval, Eddie Fajardo, Jim Garland, Rafael Gonzalez, Dick Hanlon, Dennis Haren, Gail Henley, Goldie Holt, Victor Horacio, Elvio Jimenez, Tony John, Tim Johnson, Hank Jones, John Keenan, Ron King, Don LeJohn, Steve Lembo, Ed Liberatore, Carl Loewenstine, Don McMahon, Dale McReynolds, Bob Miske, Tommy Mixon, Luis Montalvo, Regie Otero, Pablo Peguero, Bill Pleis, Glen Van Proyen, Phil Regan, Jose Santiago, Jerry Stephenson, Dick Teed, Corito Varona, Miguel Villaran, Guy Wellman.

PARK LOCATION—Dodger Stadium, 1000 Elysian Park Avenue.

Seating capacity—56,000.

FIELD DIMENSIONS—Home plate to left field at foul line, 330 feet; to center field, 395 feet; to right field at foul line, 330 feet.

MONTREAL EXPOS

Board of Directors—Charles R. Bronfman, Lorne C. Webster, John J. McHale, Hugh Hallward, Sen. E. Leo Kolber, Arnold Ludwick

Honorary Directors—Louis R. Desmarais, Sydney Maislin

Chairman of the Board—Charles R. Bronfman
Deputy Chairman and Chief Executive Officer—John J. McHale
President & Chief Operating Officer—Claude R. Brochu
Honorary Treasurer—Arnold Ludwick
Vice-President and General Manager—Murray Cook
Vice-President, Baseball Administration—Bill Stoneman
Group Vice-President—Pierre Gauvreau
Vice-President, Business Operations—Gerry Trudeau
Director of Minor League Clubs—David Dombrowski
Director of Scouting—Gary Hughes
Director, Team Travel—Dan Lunetta
Controller—Raymond St. Pierre
Assistant Director, Scouting—Frank Wren
Executive Asst., Minor Leagues—Marilyn Elzer
Publicists—Monique Giroux, Richard Griffin
Coordinator, Spring Training—Kevin McHale
Manager—Buck Rodgers
Club Physician—Dr. Robert Brodrick
Club Orthopedist—Dr. Larry Coughlin
Mailing Address—P. O. Box 500, Station M, Montreal, Quebec, Canada H1V 3P2
Telephone—253-3434 (area code 514)

SCOUTS—Jesus Alou, Kelvin Bowles, Lloyd Christopher, Ed Creech, Pat Daugherty, Richard DeHart, Manny Estrada, Joseph Frisina, Eddie Haas, Whitey Lockman, Eddie Lyons, Bill MacKenzie, Jethro McIntyre, Roy McMillan, Bob Oldis, Earl Rapp, Mark Servais, Greg Zunino.

PARK LOCATION—Olympic Stadium, 4545 Pierre de Coubertin, Montreal, Quebec, Canada H1V 3N7.

Seating capacity—59,123.

FIELD DIMENSIONS—Home plate to left field at foul line, 325 feet; to center field, 404 feet; to right field at foul line, 325 feet.

NEW YORK METS

Chairman of the Board—Nelson Doubleday

Directors—Nelson Doubleday, Fred Wilpon, J. Frank Cashen, Saul Katz, Marvin Tepper
Special Consultant to the Board of Directors—Richard Cummins
President & Chief Executive Officer—Fred Wilpon
Exec. Vice-President, G.M. & Chief Operating Officer—J. Frank Cashen
Vice-President, Operations—Bob Mandt
Vice-President, Baseball Administration—Alan E. Harazin
Vice-President, Baseball Operations—Joseph McIlvaine
Vice-President, Treasurer—Harold W. O'Shaughnessy
Director of Public Relations—Jay Horwitz
Director of Broadcasting—Mike Ryan
Executive Asst. to General Manager—Jean Coen
Special Asst. to the G.M. & Team Travel Director—Arthur Richman
Director of Marketing—Drew Sheinman
Ticket Manager—Bill Ianniciello
Controller—William Grundel
Director of Minor League Operations—Stephen Schryver
Director of Scouting—Roland Johnson
Stadium Manager—John McCarthy
Director of Amateur Baseball Relations—Tommy Holmes
Manager—Dave Johnson
Club Physician—Dr. James C. Parkes II
Team Trainer—Steve Garland
Executive Offices—William A. Shea Stadium, Roosevelt Avenue and 126th Street, Flushing, N.Y. 11368
Telephone—507-6387 (area code 718)

SCOUTS—Phil Favia, Carmen Fusco, Dick Gernert, Rob Guzik, Marty Harvat, Buddy Kerr, Joe Mason, Bob Minor, Harry Minor, Julian Morgan, Roy Partee, Carlos Pascual, Junior Roman, Marv Scott, Eddy Toledo, Terry Tripp, Bob Wellman, Jim Woodward, Len Zanke, Jack Zduriencik.

PARK LOCATION—William A. Shea Stadium, Roosevelt Avenue and 126th Street, Flushing, N. Y. 11368.

Seating capacity—55,300.

FIELD DIMENSIONS—Home plate to left field at foul line, 338 feet; to center field, 410 feet; to right field at foul line, 338 feet.

PHILADELPHIA PHILLIES

President—Bill Giles

Partners—John Drew Betz Associates, Tri-Play Associates,
Fitz Eugene Dixon Jr., Mrs. Rochelle Levy
Assistant to President—Paul Owens
Executive Vice-President—David Montgomery
Vice-President, Finance—Jerry Clothier
Vice-President, Baseball Administration—Tony Siegle
Vice-President, Public Relations—Larry Shenk
Secretary and Counsel—William Y. Webb
Financial Consultant—Robert D. Hedberg
Vice-President, Player Development and Scouting—Jim Baumer
Director of Planning, Development & Super Boxes—Tom Hudson
Director of Promotions—Frank Sullivan
Traveling Secretary—Eddie Ferenz
Director of Sales and Ticket Operations—Richard Deats
Director of Scouting—Jack Pastore
Director of Community Relations—Chris Wheeler
Director of Marketing—Dennis Lehman
Director of Stadium Operations—Mike DiMuzio
Director of Operations—Pat Cassidy
Director of Management Information—Jeff Eisenberg
Controller—Mike Kent
Director of Publicity—Vince Nauss
Director of Group Sales—Bettyanne Joyce
Director of Season Ticket Sales—Dennis Mannion
Assistant Director of Promotions—Chris Legault
Assistant Director of Marketing—Jo-Anne Levy
Executive Secretary—Nancy Connor
Executive Secretary to Minor Leagues—Bill Gargano
Club Physician—Dr. Phillip Marone
Club Trainer—Jeff Cooper
Strength and Flexibility Instructor—Gus Hoefling
Manager—John Felske
Executive Offices—Philadelphia Veterans Stadium
Mailing Address—P.O. Box 7575, Philadelphia, Pa. 19101
Telephone—463-6000 (area code 215)

SCOUTS—(Special assignment)—Paul Owens and Ray Shore. (Regular)—Bill Adair, Oliver Bidwell, Edward Bockman, Wilfredo Calvino, Carlos Cervo, George Farson, Tom Ferguson, Bill Harper, Jerry Jordan, Jerry Lafferty, Dick Lawlor, Anthony Lucadello, Fred Mazuca, Jose Perez, Bob Poole, Bob Reasonover, Larry Reasonover, Joe Reilly, Jay Robertson, Tony Roig, Rudy Terrasas, Randy Waddill, Don Williams.

PARK LOCATION—Philadelphia Veterans Stadium, Broad Street and Pattison Avenue.

Seating capacity—64,538.

FIELD DIMENSIONS—Home plate to left field at foul line, 330 feet; to center field, 408 feet; to right field at foul line, 330 feet.

PITTSBURGH PIRATES

President & Chief Executive Officer—Malcolm Prine

Senior V.P. & G.M./Baseball Operations—Syd Thrift
Senior Vice-President, Business Development—Bernard J. Mullin
Vice-President, Stadium Operations and Administration—Richard L. Andersen
Vice-President, Finance—Ken Curcio
Vice-President, Marketing—Steve Greenberg
Vice-President, Ticket Operations—Norman DeLuca
Vice-President—Harvey Walker
Secretary & General Counsel—Carl F. Barger
Director of Media Relations—Greg Johnson
Asst. Dir. of Media Relations/Publications Dir.—Jim Lachimia
Asst. Director of Public Relations—Sally O'Leary
Director of Scouting—Elmer Gray
Director of Minor League Clubs—Branch B. Rickey
Asst. Dir. of Minor Leagues & Scouting—James G. Bowden IV
Traveling Secretary—Charles Muse
Radio and TV Coordinator—Greg Brown
Community Relations Director—Patty Paytas
Manager—Jim Leyland
Club Physician—Dr. Joseph Coroso
Team Orthopedist—Dr. Jack Failla
Team Trainer—Kent Biggerstaff
Equipment Manager—John Hallahan
Executive Offices—Three Rivers Stadium, 600 Stadium Circle, Pittsburgh, Pa. 15212
Telephone—323-5000 (area code 412)

SCOUTS—(Scouting Supervisors)—Gene Baker, Jack Bowen, Bart Braun, Joe L. Brown, Bill Bryk, Joe Consoli, Pablo Cruz, Larry D'Amato, Angel Figueroa, Frank Franchi, Jerry Gardner, Pete Gebrian, Fred Goodman, Howie Haak, Terry Logan, Bob Rossi, Lenny Yochim, Bob Zuk. (Associate Scouts)—George Detore, Jose Luna, Boyd Odom, Steve Oleschuk, Bob Whalen.

PARK LOCATION—Three Rivers Stadium, 600 Stadium Circle.

Seating capacity—58,437.

FIELD DIMENSIONS—Home plate to left field at foul line, 335 feet; to center field, 400 feet; to right field at foul line, 335 feet.

ST. LOUIS CARDINALS

Chairman of the Board, President and Chief Executive Officer—
August A. Busch, Jr.

Executive Vice-President, Chief Operating Officer—Fred L. Kuhlmann
Vice-Presidents—August A. Busch, III, Margaret S. Busch
Senior Vice-President—Stan Musial
Director of Business Administration—Mark Gorris
Controller—John McMinn
Board of Directors—Adolphus A. Busch, IV, August A. Busch, Jr.,
August A. Busch, III, Margaret S. Busch, Frederic E. Giersch, Jr., Louis B. Hager,
John Hayward, Ben Kerner, Fred L. Kuhlmann, Stanley F. Musial,
W.R. Persons, Walter C. Reisinger, Louis B. Susman, John Valentine
General Manager—Dal Maxvill
Manager—Whitey Herzog
Assistant to General Manager—Jim Toomey
Administrative Assistant to G.M.—Judy Lovelace
Director of Marketing—Marty Hendin
Administrative Asst. to Director of Marketing—Nancy McElroy
Director of Player Development—Lee Thomas
Director of Scouting—Fred McAlister
Director of Minor League Operations—Paul Fauks
Director of Public Relations—Kip Ingle
Assistant Director of Public Relations—To Be Announced
Director of Promotions—Dan Farrell
Director of Community Relations & Group Sales—Joe Cunningham
Director of Season Ticket Sales—Sue Ann McClaren
Manager of Group Sales—Bridget Wynn
Director of Tickets and Stadium Operations—Mike Bertani
Assistant Director of Tickets—Josephine Arnold
Traveling Secretary—C.J. Cherre
Club Physician—Dr. Stan London
Secretary and Treasurer—John L. Hayward
Assistant Secretary—Richard Schwartz
Executive Offices—Busch Stadium, 250 Stadium Plaza,
St. Louis, Mo. 63102
Telephone—421-3060 (area code 314)

SCOUTS—(Chief Scout)—Mo Mozzali. (Supervisors)—Jim Belz, Vern Benson, Steve Flores, Jim Johnston, Hank Kelly, Marty Keough, Marty Maier, Tom McCormack, Mike Roberts, Hal Smith, Charles (Tam) Thompson, Rube Walker (special assignment). (Part-time)—Jorge Aranzamendi, James Brown, Roberto Diaz, Cecil Espy, Manuel Guerra, Ray King, Juan Melo, Virgil Melvin, Ramon Ortiz, Bob Parks, Joe Popek, Kenneth Thomas.

PARK LOCATION—Busch Stadium, Broadway, Walnut Street, Stadium Plaza and Spruce Street.

Seating capacity—53,138.

FIELD DIMENSIONS—Home plate to left field at foul line, 330 feet; to center field, 414 feet; to right field at foul line, 330 feet.

SAN DIEGO PADRES

Board of Directors—Joan Kroc, Ballard F. Smith, Jr., Anthony J. Zulfer, Jr.

President and Treasurer—Ballard F. Smith, Jr.
Exec. Vice-President, Chief Operating Officer—Dick Freeman
Senior Vice-President, Business Operations—Elten F. Schiller
Vice-President, Baseball Operations—Jack McKeon
Administrative Assistant—Rhoda Polley
Accounting Dept. Supervisor—Bob Wells
Major League Scout, Special Assignments—Dick Hager
Director, Minor Leagues and Scouting—Tom Romenesko
Director of Media Relations—Bill Beck
Assistant Director of Media Relations—Mike Swanson
Administrative Assistant—Mil Chipp
Administrative Assistant—Be Barnes
Director of Broadcasting—Jim Winters
Director of Group Sales—Tom Mulcahy
Director of Marketing—Andy Strasberg
Director of Ticket Sales—Dave Gilmore
Traveling Secretary—John Mattei
Manager—Larry Bowa
Club Physician—Scripps Clinic
Executive Offices—P. O. Box 2000, San Diego, Calif. 92120
Telephone—283-7294 (area code 619)

SCOUTS—Santos Alomar, Dave Bartosch, Billy Castell, Ray Coley, Jose Cora, Manny Crespo, David Freeland, Denny Galehouse, Jose Garcia, Jose Gonzales, Donald Hennelly, Ken Hennelly, Pete Jones, Harvey Koepf, John Kosciak, Don LaBossiere, Joe Lutz, Jim Marshall, Abe Martinez, Bill McKeon, Cotton Nix, Tom Roberts, Ernie Sierra, Brad Sloan, Ed Stevens, Vince Valecce, Bob Warner, Henry Weaver, Hank Zacharias.

PARK LOCATION—San Diego Jack Murphy Stadium, 9949 Friars Road.

Seating capacity—58,402.

FIELD DIMENSIONS—Home plate to left field at foul line, 330 feet; to center field, 405 feet; to right field at foul line, 330 feet.

SAN FRANCISCO GIANTS

Chairman—Robert A. Lurie

President & General Manager—Al Rosen
Executive Vice-President, Administration—Corey Busch
Vice-President, Baseball Operations—Bob Kennedy
Vice-President, Business Operations—Pat Gallagher
Assistant General Manager—Ralph Nelson Jr.
Director of Player Personnel and Scouting—Bob Fontaine
Director of Minor League Operations—Carlos Alfonso
Assistant Director of Minor Leagues/Scouting—Dave Nahabedian
Director of Travel—Dirk Smith
Special Assistants to the President and G.M.—Willie Mays, Willie McCovey
Administrative Assistant—Florence Myers
Director of Public Relations—Duffy Jennings
Director of Marketing—Mario Alioto
Director of Sales—Bob Gaillard
Director of Stadium Operations—Don Foreman
Director of Graphics and Photography—Dennis Desprois
Ticket Manager—Arthur Schulze
Accounting Manager—Jeannie Adamo
Promotions Manager—Carlos Deza
Community Services Manager—Dave Craig
Retail Sales Manager—Dave Alioto
Group Sales Manager—Pennie Lundberg
Assistant Director of Public Relations—David Aust
Assistant Director of Stadium Operations—Gene Telucci
Assistant to the Executive Vice-President—Michael Shapiro, Esq.
Community Representative—Mike Sadek
Speakers Bureau—Joe Orengo
Director of Operations, GiantsVision—Karen Sisco
Director of Affiliate Relations, GiantsVision—Bob Hartzell
Manager—Roger Craig
Executive Offices—Candlestick Park, San Francisco, Calif. 94124
Telephone—468-3700 (area code 415)

SCOUTS—Harry Craft, Nino Escalera, Jim Fairey, Jack French, George M. Genovese, Milt Graff, Grady Hatton, Carl Hubbell, Herman Hannah, Al Heist, Richard Klaus, Andy Korenek, Jim Lyke, Alan Marr, T. McCarthy, D. McMillan, Frank Ontiveros, Jack Paepke, Bill Parese, Ken (Squeaky) Parker, Andy Rodriguez, Hank Sauer, John Shafer, George Silvey, George Sobek, Marvin Stendel, Bill Teed, Gene Thompson, Mike Toomey, Jack Uhey, John Van Ornum, Joe Winstead, Tom Zimmer.

PARK LOCATION—Candlestick Point, Bayshore Freeway.

Seating capacity—58,000.

FIELD DIMENSIONS—Home plate to left field at foul line, 335 feet; to center field, 400 feet; to right field at foul line, 330 feet.

The Sporting News No. 1 MEN of 1986

ROGER CLEMENS
• BOSTON RED SOX •
MAJOR LEAGUE
PLAYER OF THE YEAR

FRANK CASHEN
• NEW YORK METS •
MAJOR LEAGUE EXECUTIVE

HAL LANIER
• HOUSTON ASTROS •
CO-MAJOR LEAGUE
MANAGER

JOHN McNAMARA
• BOSTON RED SOX •
CO-MAJOR LEAGUE
MANAGER

TIM PYZNARSKI
• LAS VEGAS •
MINOR LEAGUE PLAYER

JOE SPARKS
• INDIANAPOLIS •
MINOR LEAGUE MANAGER

BOB GOUGHAN
• ROCHESTER •
MINOR LEAGUE EXECUTIVE
IN CLASS AAA

BILL DAVIDSON
• MIDLAND •
MINOR LEAGUE EXECUTIVE
IN CLASS AA

ROB DLUGOZIMA
• DURHAM •
MINOR LEAGUE EXECUTIVE
IN CLASS A

Major League Players Association

805 Third Avenue
New York, N.Y. 10022
Telephone—(212) 826-0808

Executive Director & General Counsel—Donald Fehr
Special Assistant—Mark Belanger
Associate General Counsel—Eugene Orza
Assistant General Counsel—Lauren Rich
Counsel—Arthur Schack
Legal Assistant—Laura Sigal
Staff—Bonnie White, Tracy Freireich and Virginia Carballo

EXECUTIVE BOARD

Don Baylor—American League Representative
Brett Butler—Alternate American League Representative
Bob Horner—National League Representative
Vance Law—Alternate National League Representative
Orel Hershiser—Pension Committee
Jimmy Key—Pension Committee Alternate
Rick Honeycutt—Pension Committee
Rick Horton—Pension Committee Alternate
Plus all remaining player representatives

NATIONAL LEAGUE PLAYER REPRESENTATIVES

Bob Horner—Atlanta Braves
Scott Sanderson—Chicago Cubs
Ron Robinson—Cincinnati Reds
Bob Knepper—Houston Astros
Dave Anderson—Los Angeles Dodgers
Jim Wohlford—Montreal Expos
Keith Hernandez—New York Mets
Shane Rawley—Philadelphia Phillies
Jim Morrison—Pittsburgh Pirates
Danny Cox—St. Louis Cardinals
Dave Dravecky—San Diego Padres
Jim Gott—San Francisco Giants

AMERICAN LEAGUE PLAYER REPRESENTATIVES

Scott McGregor—Baltimore Orioles
Rich Gedman—Boston Red Sox
Mike Witt—California Angels
Rich Dotson—Chicago White Sox
Joe Carter—Cleveland Indians
Frank Tanana—Detroit Tigers
Danny Jackson—Kansas City Royals
Paul Molitor—Milwaukee Brewers
Bert Blyleven—Minnesota Twins
Dave Winfield—New York Yankees
Chris Codiroli—Oakland A's
Jim Beattie—Seattle Mariners
Geno Petralli—Texas Rangers
Willie Upshaw—Toronto Blue Jays

Minor League Presidents for '87

CLASS AAA

American Association—Joe Ryan, P.O. Box 382, Wichita, Kan. 67201

International League—Harold Cooper, P.O. Box 608, Grove City, Ohio 43123

Mexican League—Pedro Treto Cisneros, Angel Pola No. 16 Col. Periodista C.P. 11220, Mexico, D.F.

Pacific Coast League—Bill Cutler, 2101 E. Broadway Rd., Tempe, Ariz. 85282

CLASS AA

Eastern League—Charles Eshbach, P.O. Box 716, Plainville, Conn. 06062

Southern League—Jimmy Bragan, 235 Main St., Suite 103, Trussville, Ala. 35173

Texas League—Carl Sawatski, 10201 W. Markham St., Little Rock, Ark. 72205

CLASS A

California League—Joe Gagliardi, P.O. Box 26400, San Jose, Calif. 95159

Carolina League—John Hopkins, 4241 United Street, Greensboro, N.C. 27407

Florida State League—George MacDonald, Jr., P.O. Box 414, Lakeland, Fla. 33802

Midwest League—George Spelius, P.O. Box 936, Beloit, Wis. 53511

New York-Pennsylvania League—Leo A. Pinckney, 168 E. Genesee St., Auburn, N.Y. 13021

Northwest League—Jack Cain, P.O. Box 30025, Portland, Ore. 97230

South Atlantic League—John H. Moss, P.O. Box 49, Kings Mountain, N.C. 28086

ROOKIE CLASSIFICATION

Appalachian League—Bill Halstead, 157 Carson Lane, Bristol, Va. 24201

Gulf Coast League—Thomas J. Saffell, 11 Sunset Drive, Suite 501, Sarasota, Fla. 33577

Pioneer League—Ralph C. Nelles, P.O. Box 1144, Billings, Mont. 59103

Major League Farm Systems for '87

AMERICAN LEAGUE

BALTIMORE (5): AAA—Rochester. AA—Charlotte. A—Hagerstown, Newark. Rookie—Bluefield.

BOSTON (5): AAA—Pawtucket. AA—New Britain, Conn. A—Elmira, Greensboro, Winter Haven.

CALIFORNIA (5): AAA—Edmonton. AA—Midland. A—Quad Cities, Palm Springs, Salem, Ore.

CHICAGO (5): AAA—Hawaii. AA—Birmingham. A—Daytona Beach, Peninsula. Rookie—Sarasota.

CLEVELAND (5): AAA—Buffalo. AA—Waterbury. A—Kinston, Waterloo. Rookie—Burlington, N.C.

DETROIT (5): AAA—Toledo. AA—Glens Falls. A—Lakeland, Fayetteville. Rookie—Bristol, Va.

KANSAS CITY (6): AAA—Omaha. AA—Memphis. A—Appleton, Eugene, Fort Myers. Rookie—Sarasota.

MILWAUKEE (5): AAA—Denver. AA—El Paso. A—Beloit, Stockton. Rookie—Helena.

MINNESOTA (5): AAA—Portland. AA—Orlando. A—Kenosha, Visalia. Rookie—Elizabethton.

NEW YORK (6): AAA—Columbus, O. AA—Albany-Colonie, N.Y. A—Fort Lauderdale, Oneonta, Prince William. Rookie—Sarasota.

OAKLAND (5): AAA—Tacoma. AA—Huntsville. A—Medford, Modesto, Madison.

SEATTLE (5): AAA—Calgary. AA—Chattanooga. A—Wausau, Salinas, Bellingham.

TEXAS (5): AAA—Oklahoma City. AA—Tulsa. A—Port Charlotte, Gastonia. Rookie—Sarasota.

TORONTO (6): AAA—Syracuse. AA—Knoxville. A—Myrtle Beach, Dunedin, St. Catharines, Ont. Rookie—Medicine Hat.

NATIONAL LEAGUE

ATLANTA (7): AAA—Richmond. AA—Greenville. A—Sumter, Durham. Rookie—Bradenton, Idaho Falls, Pulaski.

CHICAGO (6): AAA—Iowa. AA—Pittsfield. A—Geneva, Peoria, Winston-Salem. Rookie—Wytheville.

CINCINNATI (6): AAA—Nashville. AA—Vermont. A—Cedar Rapids, Tampa. Rookie—Billings, Sarasota.

HOUSTON (6): AAA—Tucson. AA—Columbus, Ga. A—Asheville, Auburn, Osceola, Fla. Rookie—Sarasota.

LOS ANGELES (6): AAA—Albuquerque. AA—San Antonio. A—Bakersfield, Vero Beach. Rookie—Great Falls, Sarasota.

MONTREAL (6): AAA—Indianapolis. AA—Jacksonville. A—Jamestown, West Palm Beach, Burlington, Ia. Rookie—Bradenton.

NEW YORK (6): AAA—Tidewater. AA—Jackson. A—Columbia, S.C., Little Falls, Lynchburg. Rookie—Kingsport.

PHILADELPHIA (5): AAA—Williamsport. AA—Reading. A—Clearwater, Spartanburg, Utica.

PITTSBURGH (6): AAA—Vancouver. AA—Harrisburg. A—Salem, Va., Macon, Watertown. Rookie—Bradenton.

ST. LOUIS (7): AAA—Louisville. AA—Arkansas. A—Erie, St. Petersburg, Savannah, Springfield. Rookie—Johnson City.

SAN DIEGO (5): AAA—Las Vegas. AA—Wichita. A—Charleston, S.C., Reno, Spokane.

SAN FRANCISCO (6): AAA—Phoenix. AA—Shreveport. A—Clinton, Fresno, Everett. Rookie—Pocatello.

OFFICIAL MINOR LEAGUE AVERAGES

Including

Official Averages of All Class AAA, Class AA, Class A and Rookie Leagues

National Association President John Johnson.

American Association

CLASS AAA

Leading Batter
BRUCE FIELDS
Nashville

League President
JOE RYAN

Leading Pitcher
PETE FILSON
Buffalo

CHAMPIONSHIP WINNERS IN PREVIOUS YEARS

Year	Club	Pct.
1902	Indianapolis	.683
1903	St. Paul	.657
1904	St. Paul	.646
1905	Columbus	.658
1906	Columbus	.615
1907	Columbus	.584
1908	Indianapolis	.601
1909	Louisville	.554
1910	Minneapolis	.637
1911	Minneapolis	.600
1912	Minneapolis	.636
1913	Milwaukee	.599
1914	Milwaukee	.590
1915	Minneapolis	.597
1916	Louisville	.605
1917	Indianapolis	.588
1918	Kansas City	.589
1919	St. Paul	.610
1920	St. Paul	.701
1921	Louisville	.583
1922	St. Paul	.641
1923	Kansas City	.675
1924	St. Paul	.578
1925	Louisville	.635
1926	Louisville	.629
1927	Toledo	.601
1928	Indianapolis	.593
1929	Kansas City	.665
1930	Louisville	.608
1931	St. Paul	.623
1932	Minneapolis	.595
1933	Columbus*	.604
	Minneapolis	.562
1934	Minneapolis	.570
	Columbus*	.556
1935	Minneapolis	.591
1936	Milwaukee†	.584
1937	Columbus†	.584
1938	St. Paul	.596
	Kansas City (2nd)‡	.556
1939	Kansas City	.695
	Louisville (4th)‡	.490
1940	Kansas City	.625
	Louisville (4th)‡	.500
1941	Columbus†	.621
1942	Kansas City	.549
	Columbus (3rd)‡	.532
1943	Milwaukee	.596
	Columbus (3rd)‡	.532
1944	Milwaukee	.667
	Louisville (3rd)‡	.574
1945	Milwaukee	.604
	Louisville (3rd)‡	.545
1946	Louisville†	601
1947	Kansas City	.608
	Milwaukee (3rd)‡	.513
1948	Indianapolis	.649
	St. Paul (3rd)‡	.558
1949	St. Paul	.608
	Indianapolis (2nd)‡	.604
1950	Minneapolis	.584
	Columbus (3rd)‡	.549
1951	Milwaukee†	.623
1952	Milwaukee	.656
	Kansas City (2nd)‡	.578
1953	Toledo	.584
	Kansas City (2nd)‡	.571
1954	Indianapolis	.625
	Louisville (2nd)‡	.556
1955	Minneapolis†	.597
1956	Indianapolis†	.597
1957	Wichita	.604
	Denver (2nd)‡	.584
1958	Charleston	.589
	Minneapolis (3rd)‡	.536
1959	Louisville§	.599
	Omaha§	.516
	Minneapolis (2nd)‡	.586
1960	Denver	.571
	Louisville (2nd)‡	.556
1961	Indianapolis	.573
	Louisville (2nd)‡	.533
1962	Indianapolis	.605
	Louisville (4th)‡	.486
1963-1968	Did not operate.	
1969	Omaha	.607
1970	Omaha*	.529
	Denver	.504
1971	Indianapolis	.604
	Denver*	.521
1972	Wichita	.621
	Evansville*	.593
1973	Iowa	.610
	Tulsa*	.504
1974	Indianapolis	.578
	Tulsa*	.567
1975	Evansville*	.566
	Denver	.596
1976	Denver*	.632
	Omaha	.574
1977	Omaha	.563
	Denver*	.522
1978	Indianapolis	.578
	Omaha*	.489
1979	Evansville*	.574
	Oklahoma City	.533
1980	Denver	.676
	Springfield*	.551
1981	Omaha	.581
	Denver*	.559
1982	Indianapolis*	.551
	Omaha	.518
1983	Louisville	.578
	Denver‡	.545
1984	Denver	.513
	Louisville‡	.510
1985	Oklahoma City	.556
	Louisville*	.521

*Won playoff (East vs. West). †Won championship and four-team playoff. ‡Won four-team playoff. §Respective Eastern and Western division winners.

STANDING OF CLUBS AT CLOSE OF SEASON, SEPTEMBER 1

EASTERN DIVISION

Club	W.	L.	T.	Pct.	G.B.
Indianapolis (Expos)	80	62	1	.563	....
Buffalo (White Sox)	71	71	0	.500	9
Nashville (Tigers)	68	74	1	.479	12
Louisville (Cardinals)	64	78	0	.451	16

WESTERN DIVISION

Club	W.	L.	T.	Pct.	G.B.
Denver (Reds)	76	66	0	.535	....
Iowa (Cubs)	74	68	0	.521	2
Omaha (Royals)	72	70	0	.507	4
Oklahoma City (Rangers)	63	79	0	.444	13

COMPOSITE STANDING OF CLUBS AT CLOSE OF SEASON, SEPTEMBER 1

Club	Ind.	Den.	Iowa	Oma	Buf	Nash	Lou	O.C.	W.	L.	T.	Pct.	G.B.
Indianapolis (Expos)	....	6	10	8	15	14	17	10	80	62	1	.563	....
Denver (Reds)	10	....	14	16	6	7	8	15	76	66	0	.535	4
Iowa (Cubs)	6	12	....	14	10	9	8	15	74	68	0	.521	6
Omaha (Royals)	8	10	12	....	9	6	12	15	72	70	0	.507	8
Buffalo (White Sox)	11	10	6	7	....	14	12	11	71	71	0	.500	9
Nashville (Tigers)	12	9	7	10	12	....	11	7	68	74	1	.479	12
Louisville (Cardinals)	9	8	8	4	14	15	....	6	64	78	0	.451	16
Oklahoma City (Rangers)	6	11	11	11	5	9	10	....	63	79	0	.444	17

Iowa club represented Des Moines, Ia.

Major league affiliations in parentheses.

Playoffs—Indianapolis defeated Denver, four games to three, to win league championship.

Regular-Season Attendance—Buffalo, 425,113; Denver, 301,787; Indianapolis, 220,285; Iowa, 257,986; Louisville, 660,200; Nashville, 364,614; Oklahoma City, 282,752; Omaha, 255,290. Total—2,768,027. Playoffs—43,912.

Managers—Buffalo, Jim Marshall; Denver, Jack Lind; Indianapolis, Joe Sparks; Iowa, Larry Cox; Louisville, Jim Fregosi (thru June 21), Dyer Miller (interim manager June 22-25), Dave Bialas (June 27 thru end of season); Nashville, Leon Roberts; Oklahoma City, Dave Oliver; Omaha, John Boles (thru June 25), Frank Funk (from June 27 thru end of season).

All-Star Team—1B—Joe DeSa, Buffalo; 2B—Casey Candaele, Indianapolis; 3B—German Rivera, Nashville; SS—Barry Larkin, Denver; OF—Bruce Fields, Nashville; Kevin Seitzer, Omaha; Bob Brower, Oklahoma City; Daryl Boston, Buffalo; Chico Walker, Iowa; DH—Lloyd McClendon, Denver; C—Terry McGriff, Denver; Mike Stanley, Oklahoma City; RHP—Al Hargesheimer, Omaha; LHP—Pete Filson, Buffalo; Most Valuable Player—Barry Larkin, Denver; Rookie of the Year—Barry Larkin, Denver; Manager of the Year—Joe Sparks, Indianapolis.

(Compiled by Howe News Bureau, Boston, Mass.)

CLUB BATTING

Club	Pct.	G.	AB.	R.	OR.	H.	TB.	2B.	3B.	HR.	RBI.	GW.	SH.	SF.	HP.	BB.	Int. BB.	SO.	SB.	CS.	LOB.
Denver	.278	142	4659	694	648	1294	1994	254	52	114	636	67	37	46	28	497	29	615	94	35	1018
Oklahoma City	.275	142	4793	725	784	1320	1914	218	47	94	656	58	46	44	42	584	25	800	176	60	1094
Nashville	.274	143	4635	654	682	1271	1836	236	37	85	600	63	34	54	28	505	26	653	163	85	970
Omaha	.270	142	4563	579	580	1234	1691	183	62	50	520	58	47	44	32	460	42	659	192	77	1006
Indianapolis	.269	143	4787	705	672	1290	1939	240	44	107	652	72	53	42	35	543	32	729	168	68	1036
Buffalo	.266	142	4584	660	645	1218	1868	207	28	129	601	60	45	42	52	567	30	741	119	61	1037
Louisville	.262	142	4572	644	634	1199	1767	218	40	90	588	57	26	41	32	479	25	724	137	64	915
Iowa	.259	142	4584	645	661	1187	1865	244	43	116	588	69	33	50	17	570	34	781	205	83	988

INDIVIDUAL BATTING

(Leading Qualifiers for Batting Championship—383 or More Plate Appearances)

*Bats lefthanded. †Switch-hitter.

Player and Club	Pct.	G.	AB.	R.	H.	TB.	2B.	3B.	HR.	RBI.	GW.	SH.	SF.	HP.	BB.	Int. BB.	SO.	SB.	CS.
Fields, Bruce, Nashville*	.368	116	383	57	141	185	31	5	1	53	5	2	4	1	44	3	51	22	7
Hammond, Steven, Iowa*	.330	120	430	62	142	214	45	0	9	73	6	1	10	1	42	3	46	3	4
Larkin, Barry, Denver	.329	103	413	67	136	217	31	10	10	51	4	4	7	2	31	1	43	19	6
Seitzer, Kevin, Omaha	.319	129	432	86	138	219	20	11	13	74	9	1	9	9	89	4	57	20	13
Boston, Daryl, Buffalo*	.303	96	360	57	109	146	16	3	5	41	6	5	3	1	42	4	45	38	10
Schulz, Jeffrey, Omaha*	.303	123	400	40	121	154	19	4	2	61	8	2	8	2	37	9	51	0	2
Candaele, Casey, Indianapolis†	.302	119	480	77	145	195	32	6	2	42	3	11	2	1	46	6	29	16	10
Rivera, German, Nashville	.298	140	506	86	151	227	30	2	14	84	11	0	8	4	48	1	80	13	5
Walker, Cleotha, Iowa†	.298	138	530	97	158	258	30	11	16	65	11	1	6	0	62	2	68	67	22
Tolman, Timothy, Nashville	.298	139	484	68	144	208	23	4	11	71	9	0	8	4	67	2	61	11	4
McGriff, Terence, Denver	.291	108	340	54	99	150	22	1	9	54	9	2	6	2	41	4	71	0	0
Dunbar, Thomas, Oklahoma City*	.290	135	490	77	142	206	20	7	10	91	9	3	8	1	85	7	72	21	5
Parsons, Casey, Louisville*	.289	123	394	61	114	186	22	4	14	60	5	1	7	4	51	8	60	4	2
Johnson, Rondin, Omaha†	.289	127	484	57	140	186	15	14	1	60	5	8	2	1	25	4	52	13	7
Williams, Dallas, Indianapolis*	.289	124	429	66	124	184	20	5	10	64	10	5	2	1	42	5	39	16	8

Departmental Leaders: G—Brower, G. Rivera, 140; AB—Brower, 550; R—Brower, 130; H—Brower, C. Walker, 158; TB—C. Walker, 258; 2B—Hammond, 45; 3B-R. Johnson, 14; HR—McClendon, 24; RBI—Lindeman, 96; GWRBI—Dayett, G. Rivera, C. Walker, 11; SH—Candaele, 11; SF—Dayett, 11; HP—Maler, W. Moore, Seitzer, 9; BB—Brower, 94; IBB—Schulz, 9; SO—Hicks, 130; SB—D. Taylor, C. Walker, 67; CS—C. Walker, 22.

(All Players—Listed Alphabetically)

Player and Club	Pct.	G.	AB.	R.	H.	TB.	2B.	3B.	HR.	RBI.	GW.	SH.	SF.	HP.	BB.	Int. BB.	SO.	SB.	CS.
Abrego, Johnny, Iowa	.500	6	4	1	2	3	1	0	0	2	0	0	0	0	0	0	1	0	0
Ayer, Jonathan, Louisville	.259	84	255	36	66	98	10	2	6	35	5	0	1	2	29	0	36	1	1
Baker, Derrell, Indianapolis	.284	96	268	32	76	98	11	1	3	47	8	1	4	3	38	0	26	11	2
Baker, Douglas, Nashville†	.274	112	369	46	101	133	14	6	2	40	7	8	4	2	32	0	62	14	8
Baller, Jay, Iowa	.000	27	1	0	0	0	0	0	0	0	0	1	0	0	0	0	1	0	0
Barker, Leonard, Indianapolis	.000	13	2	1	0	0	0	0	0	0	0	0	0	0	0	0	1	0	0
Barnes, William, Indianapolis	.267	85	300	40	80	123	18	5	5	40	2	4	3	5	26	2	28	16	10
Barrett, Timothy, Indianapolis*	.000	21	2	0	0	0	0	0	0	0	0	0	0	0	0	0	0	0	0
Bathe, Robert, Iowa	.224	73	161	23	36	71	6	1	9	25	1	1	2	1	31	1	36	0	3
Bernstine, Nehames, Iowa†	.239	85	255	34	61	74	1	3	2	20	2	2	1	2	18	0	44	18	7
Bilardello, Dann, Indianapolis	.600	2	5	1	3	5	0	1	0	0	0	0	0	0	0	0	2	0	0
Bockhorn, Glen, Buffalo	.229	78	205	33	47	73	5	0	7	26	2	2	1	3	36	0	40	4	1
Boever, Daniel, Denver	.192	11	26	2	5	6	1	0	0	2	0	0	0	0	0	0	4	0	0
Booker, Roderick, Louisville*	.280	78	289	51	81	105	11	5	1	30	1	2	1	0	32	1	27	18	6
Boston, Daryl, Buffalo*	.303	96	360	57	109	146	16	3	5	41	6	5	3	1	42	4	45	38	10
Botelho, Derek, Denver	.071	23	14	2	1	1	0	0	0	1	0	4	0	0	1	0	2	0	0
Bradley, Scott, Buffalo*	.333	33	126	14	42	66	3	3	5	20	1	0	2	0	6	0	6	2	0

Player and Club	Pct.	G.	AB.	R.	H.	TB.	2B.	3B.	HR.	RBI.	GW.	SH.	SF.	HP.	BB.	Int. BB.	SO.	SB.	CS.
Braun, Stephen, Louisville*	.273	50	143	18	39	59	8	0	4	26	1	0	2	1	41	5	23	0	0
Brewer, Michael, Omaha	.254	108	389	47	99	163	20	4	12	57	7	0	1	4	37	3	86	30	8
Brooks, Fred, Iowa	.185	97	260	28	48	77	11	0	6	20	2	2	2	0	40	2	45	7	3
Brower, Robert, Oklahoma City	.287	140	550	130	158	236	25	7	13	72	8	4	3	1	94	2	105	53	14
Brown, Curtis, Indianapolis	.333	48	3	1	1	1	0	0	0	0	0	1	0	0	0	0	1	0	0
Brown, Darrell, Oklahoma City†	.296	15	54	7	16	18	2	0	0	3	0	1	0	0	3	1	5	2	1
Brumley, Michael, Iowa†	.225	139	458	74	103	164	21	5	10	44	4	5	4	0	63	3	102	35	14
Buchanan, Robert, Denver*	.250	36	4	0	1	1	0	0	0	0	0	0	0	0	0	0	0	0	0
Calderon, Ivan, Buffalo	.219	27	105	11	23	47	9	0	5	22	3	0	2	2	9	2	28	0	0
Candaele, Casey, Indianapolis†	.302	119	480	77	145	195	32	6	2	42	3	11	2	1	46	6	29	16	10
Capra, Nick, 36 Buf-72 OkC	.259	108	406	68	105	148	18	2	7	31	4	8	4	2	66	1	49	32	15
Cedeno, Cesar, Louisville	.169	20	65	5	11	17	3	0	1	4	0	0	0	0	3	0	12	0	2
Chavez, Pedro, Nashville	.258	122	414	55	107	139	20	3	2	43	2	8	5	2	36	0	42	24	16
Christmas, Stephen, Iowa*	.300	62	180	22	54	77	11	0	4	25	2	1	1	0	19	2	19	1	2
Citari, Joseph, Omaha	.230	117	382	48	88	126	13	2	7	38	4	1	4	2	39	2	79	3	5
Clark, Bryan, Buffalo*	.000	37	2	1	0	0	0	0	0	0	0	0	0	0	0	0	2	0	0
Cochrane, David, Buffalo†	.226	38	124	15	28	53	7	0	6	16	1	2	2	0	11	1	45	0	1
Colbert, Richard, Louisville	.220	46	123	10	27	37	5	1	1	13	3	2	0	1	11	0	32	1	1
Cole, Alexander, Louisville*	.250	63	200	25	50	63	2	4	1	16	4	0	1	1	17	0	30	24	13
Cole, Rodger, Indianapolis	.214	30	14	5	3	3	0	0	0	3	0	2	0	0	1	0	3	0	0
Concepcion, Onix, Omaha	.284	57	183	14	52	62	6	2	0	20	3	2	1	0	15	1	17	4	2
Corey, Mark, Indianapolis	.071	7	14	0	1	2	1	0	0	1	0	0	0	0	1	0	2	0	0
Cornell, Jeffery, Iowa*	.000	46	4	0	0	0	0	0	0	0	0	0	0	0	1	0	3	0	0
Craig, Rodney, Buffalo†	.271	112	402	79	109	186	28	8	11	60	4	6	4	6	56	4	61	29	13
Cusack, David, Nashville	.186	22	59	9	11	18	1	0	2	8	0	0	1	0	9	0	18	1	0
Cutshall, William, Indianapolis*	.400	11	5	0	2	2	0	0	0	0	0	1	0	0	0	0	1	0	0
Daniels, Kalvoski, Denver*	.371	42	132	33	49	89	12	2	8	32	1	0	1	2	34	3	20	12	2
Davidson, Jackie, Iowa†	.143	15	7	1	1	1	0	0	0	0	0	1	0	0	1	0	2	0	0
Davis, Joel, Buffalo*	.000	7	1	0	0	0	0	0	0	0	0	0	0	0	0	0	0	0	0
Dayett, Brian, Iowa	.281	121	409	69	115	213	29	6	19	87	11	0	11	4	66	4	66	0	2
DeSa, Joseph, Buffalo*	.284	130	450	65	128	206	21	3	17	83	4	1	6	8	61	2	45	0	2
Dunbar, Thomas, Oklahoma City*	.290	135	490	77	142	206	20	7	10	91	9	3	8	1	85	7	72	21	5
Earl, Scott, Nashville	.239	128	406	65	97	141	14	3	8	41	3	5	3	3	52	5	51	30	12
Engel, Steven, Iowa	.000	33	4	1	0	0	0	0	0	0	0	1	0	0	1	0	1	0	0
Engle, David, Nashville	.167	8	24	5	4	10	0	0	2	7	0	0	0	1	6	0	4	1	1
Fields, Bruce, Nashville*	.368	116	383	57	141	185	31	5	1	53	5	2	4	1	44	3	51	22	7
Fitzgerald, Michael, Indianapolis	.344	10	32	4	11	14	3	0	0	4	0	0	0	0	5	0	1	0	0
Foley, Marvis, Buffalo*	.325	50	123	22	40	71	7	0	8	24	0	2	2	2	22	1	15	0	0
Fontenot, Ray, Iowa*	.000	2	3	0	0	0	0	0	0	0	0	0	0	0	0	0	2	0	0
Ford, Curtis, Louisville*	.295	53	200	47	59	84	9	2	4	31	5	0	3	0	28	0	16	24	7
Francona, Terry, Iowa*	.250	17	60	7	15	22	3	2	0	8	0	0	0	0	4	2	5	1	0
Garcia, Leonard, Denver*	.278	139	528	81	147	203	32	6	4	57	4	1	3	2	41	2	36	34	6
Giles, Brian, Buffalo	.286	30	98	10	28	44	5	1	3	9	1	2	0	2	10	0	15	4	0
Gonzales, Rene, Indianapolis	.273	116	395	57	108	135	14	2	3	43	5	7	4	2	41	0	47	8	6
Gonzalez, Orlando, Denver	.267	115	345	35	92	121	8	0	7	51	7	3	5	0	25	1	31	1	5
Grubb, John, Nashville*	.179	8	28	4	5	9	1	0	1	3	0	0	0	0	6	0	10	1	1
Hammond, Steven, Iowa*	.330	120	430	62	142	214	45	0	9	73	6	1	10	1	42	3	46	3	4
Hansen, Roger, Omaha	.253	73	194	24	49	66	5	0	4	13	2	1	1	0	19	0	29	0	0
Hardy, John, Buffalo	.000	26	6	1	0	0	0	0	0	0	0	1	0	0	0	0	2	0	0
Harper, Brian, Nashville	.262	95	317	41	83	129	11	1	11	45	5	1	5	2	26	1	27	3	8
Hayes, William, Omaha	.239	90	247	23	59	76	11	0	2	18	0	1	2	1	27	2	54	1	1
Hegman, Robert, Omaha	.234	34	47	6	11	13	2	0	0	3	2	0	0	0	1	0	4	1	0
Henderson, Stephen, Buffalo	.288	72	240	37	69	94	8	1	5	39	6	2	3	2	37	2	47	1	1
Henika, Ronald, Denver*	.320	51	147	20	47	64	8	3	1	11	1	0	0	3	7	1	13	0	0
Hicks, Joseph, Iowa	.223	115	359	48	80	156	18	2	18	60	8	0	2	2	55	6	130	1	5
Hill, Orsino, Denver*	.282	120	354	56	100	172	25	7	11	41	0	1	0	3	64	7	78	2	1
Hinshaw, George, Denver	.254	58	185	29	47	78	6	2	7	29	6	1	0	3	17	0	24	2	1
Hobbs, Rodney, Nashville	.256	116	312	50	80	116	15	3	5	33	3	3	4	1	29	0	56	20	12
Hocutt, Michael, Indianapolis*	.256	127	410	65	105	186	21	3	18	63	6	1	5	1	72	6	113	10	4
Hoffman, Guy, Iowa*	.125	9	8	0	1	1	0	0	0	0	0	2	0	0	0	0	2	0	0
Hunt, Randy, Indianapolis	.248	68	206	34	51	76	9	2	4	30	2	7	1	0	22	2	41	3	0
Johnson, Rondin, Omaha†	.289	127	484	57	140	186	15	14	1	60	5	8	2	1	25	4	52	13	7
Johnson, Wallace, Indianapolis†	.258	61	225	27	58	81	15	4	0	26	3	4	1	0	22	3	16	7	1
Jones, Robert, Oklahoma City*	.252	90	318	31	80	116	16	1	6	50	5	0	6	1	46	6	60	0	2
Kemp, Hubert, Denver*	.200	29	15	0	3	3	0	0	0	0	0	1	0	0	0	0	4	0	0
Kingery, Michael, Omaha*	.332	79	298	47	99	138	14	8	3	47	4	1	4	2	39	8	30	22	7
Knicely, Alan, Louisville	.283	67	233	36	66	101	8	0	9	52	8	0	5	1	41	3	39	0	2
Knox, Michael, Denver	.231	27	13	1	3	4	1	0	0	0	0	4	0	0	1	0	3	0	0
Konderla, Michael, Denver	.000	41	4	0	0	0	0	0	0	0	0	0	0	0	0	0	1	0	0
Krauss, Timothy, Buffalo*	.282	114	426	63	120	183	20	2	13	50	6	5	1	4	47	0	60	6	5
Kunkel, Jeffrey, Oklahoma City	.244	111	409	50	100	157	16	4	11	51	5	6	4	5	18	0	101	10	6
Laga, Michael, Nashville*	.220	12	41	4	9	18	3	0	2	7	1	0	0	0	4	1	7	0	0
Lake, Steven, 49 Iowa-49 Lou	.245	33	98	5	24	30	6	0	0	13	0	1	0	2	2	0	20	0	0
Landrum, William, Denver	.000	24	1	0	0	0	0	0	0	0	0	1	0	0	0	0	0	0	0
Lansford, Joseph, Buffalo	.220	48	109	17	24	44	5	0	5	13	2	0	0	0	22	0	36	2	1
Larkin, Barry, Denver	.329	103	413	67	136	217	31	10	10	51	4	4	7	2	31	1	43	19	6
Layton, Thomas, Iowa*	.000	11	1	0	0	0	0	0	0	0	0	0	0	0	0	0	0	0	0
Lee, Terry, Denver	.240	34	104	10	25	35	2	1	2	10	3	0	2	0	4	0	24	0	1
LeMaster, Johnnie, Indianapolis	.333	7	12	1	4	4	0	0	0	0	0	0	0	0	1	0	2	0	0
Lindeman, James, Louisville	.251	139	509	82	128	236	38	5	20	96	7	0	4	4	39	2	97	9	6
Little, Bryan, Buffalo†	.284	30	109	20	31	43	3	0	3	17	3	1	2	2	12	0	12	2	3
Loggins, Michael, Omaha†	.727	6	11	2	8	13	2	0	1	5	0	0	1	0	3	0	1	1	1
Lombarski, Thomas, Iowa*	.309	96	269	46	83	131	19	1	9	45	7	1	2	1	45	3	24	15	6
Long, William, Buffalo	.333	23	6	1	2	2	0	0	0	0	0	0	0	0	0	0	2	0	0
Lowry, Dwight, Nashville*	.246	18	57	5	14	18	1	0	1	6	0	1	1	0	5	0	14	1	2
Lozado, William, Oklahoma City	.205	43	127	16	26	35	4	1	1	11	2	4	1	1	20	0	25	1	2
Lyons, Stephen, Buffalo*	.297	20	74	18	22	38	5	1	3	8	2	1	0	1	16	1	14	5	1
Lyons, William, Louisville	.250	74	216	32	54	84	10	1	6	32	2	3	2	3	36	1	47	18	2
Maddux, Gregory, Iowa	.200	19	15	3	3	6	0	0	1	1	0	0	0	0	0	0	4	0	0
Madison, Scott, Nashville†	.257	106	354	52	91	144	15	4	10	41	7	2	4	2	51	5	49	3	2
Maler, James, Oklahoma City	.261	96	337	45	88	131	15	2	8	49	4	2	3	9	15	0	31	0	0
Manrique, Fred, Louisville	.285	133	520	79	148	206	19	6	9	51	2	5	2	3	24	4	85	15	6

Player and Club	Pct.	G.	AB.	R.	H.	TB.	2B.	3B.	HR.	RBI.	GW.	SH.	SF.	HP.	BB.	Int. BB.	SO.	SB.	CS.
Manuel, Jerry, Indianapolis	.390	22	41	4	16	21	2	0	1	9	3	0	0	0	2	0	5	0	0
Martinez, Carlos, Buffalo	.296	17	54	6	16	23	1	0	2	6	1	0	2	2	2	0	12	0	0
Martinez, David, Iowa*	.289	83	318	52	92	128	11	5	5	32	6	4	3	1	36	1	34	42	5
McClendon, Lloyd, Denver	.259	132	433	75	112	216	30	1	24	88	9	0	4	2	70	1	75	2	4
McGriff, Terence, Denver	.291	108	340	54	99	150	22	1	9	54	9	2	6	2	41	4	71	0	0
Mercado, Orlando, Oklahoma City	.273	48	172	20	47	69	11	1	3	25	1	0	1	0	26	1	21	0	1
Meridith, Ronald, 26 Iowa-9 OkC*	.000	35	6	0	0	0	0	0	0	0	0	2	0	0	0	0	1	0	0
Miley, David, Denver*	.239	17	46	3	11	16	0	1	1	9	1	0	1	0	4	1	6	0	0
Miller, Michael, Omaha	.212	18	52	3	11	14	3	0	0	3	0	1	2	0	7	0	9	0	0
Mills, Bradley, Iowa*	.302	18	53	6	16	22	6	0	0	7	1	0	0	0	10	1	4	0	0
Montgomery, Jeff, Denver	.167	30	12	2	2	4	0	1	0	1	0	1	0	0	2	0	1	0	0
Moore, William, Indianapolis	.256	122	407	70	104	196	23	0	23	82	9	0	5	9	80	3	93	0	3
Morman, Russell, Buffalo	.266	106	365	52	97	157	17	2	13	57	7	0	3	5	54	4	58	3	1
Moronko, Jeffrey, Oklahoma City	.280	120	428	60	120	175	20	7	7	44	1	4	4	7	42	1	70	23	6
Morris, John, Louisville*	.235	60	213	30	50	80	13	7	1	24	3	0	3	7	23	0	33	11	3
Mota, Jose, Oklahoma City†	.278	71	255	38	71	82	9	1	0	20	4	5	0	3	24	1	43	7	5
Motley, Darryl, Omaha	.234	23	77	10	18	24	4	1	0	8	1	0	1	0	9	0	11	1	1
Moyer, Jamie, Iowa*	.000	6	4	0	0	0	0	0	0	0	0	0	0	0	0	0	3	0	0
Murphy, Robert, Denver*	1.000	27	1	0	1	1	0	0	0	0	0	0	0	0	0	0	0	0	0
Nieto, Thomas, Indianapolis	.299	53	167	21	50	75	16	0	3	19	1	3	1	1	24	3	45	0	0
Noce, Paul, Iowa	.200	7	5	1	1	4	0	0	1	1	0	0	0	0	1	0	2	0	0
Nokes, Matthew, Nashville*	.285	125	428	55	122	185	25	4	10	71	3	0	3	5	30	6	41	2	0
Nyman, Christopher, 18 Buf-53 Nash	.210	71	200	20	42	64	14	1	2	15	4	1	2	2	24	2	44	4	1
O'Neill, Paul, Denver*	.254	55	193	20	49	77	9	2	5	27	5	0	2	2	9	3	28	1	1
Oliver, Scott, Iowa	.000	33	2	0	0	0	0	0	0	0	0	0	0	0	0	0	2	0	0
Owchinko, Robert, Indianapolis*	.000	28	10	1	0	0	0	0	0	0	0	1	0	0	0	0	3	0	0
Owen, Dave, Oklahoma City†	.250	64	188	33	47	69	8	4	2	22	3	1	4	4	43	0	36	9	3
Pacella, John, Nashville	.000	43	1	0	0	0	0	0	0	0	0	0	0	0	0	0	1	0	0
Pacillo, Patrick, Denver	.111	25	18	1	2	2	0	0	0	2	0	3	0	0	1	0	8	0	0
Pagnozzi, Thomas, Louisville	.292	30	106	12	31	38	4	0	1	18	2	0	0	1	6	0	21	0	0
Parmenter, Gary, Iowa	.333	6	3	0	1	1	0	0	0	1	0	0	0	0	0	0	0	0	0
Parrett, Jeffrey, Indianapolis	.000	25	1	0	0	0	0	0	0	0	0	0	0	0	0	0	1	0	0
Parsons, Casey, Louisville*	.289	123	394	61	114	186	22	4	14	60	5	1	7	4	51	8	60	4	2
Pecota, William, Omaha	.264	139	474	48	125	167	26	2	4	54	4	7	3	8	37	3	45	21	8
Perconte, John, Buffalo*	.264	67	231	32	61	74	11	1	0	15	2	5	1	0	31	0	21	9	6
Pettini, Joseph, Louisville	.225	85	236	28	53	79	17	0	3	20	2	2	3	2	26	0	32	4	4
Pevey, Marty, Louisville*	.162	12	37	6	6	9	3	0	0	0	0	0	0	0	4	0	4	0	1
Pino, Rolando, Buffalo	.000	4	8	1	0	0	0	0	0	0	0	1	0	1	1	0	4	0	0
Potestio, Douglas, Iowa	.091	35	11	2	1	1	0	0	0	2	0	1	0	1	0	0	4	0	0
Pryce, Kenneth, Iowa	.000	31	4	0	0	0	0	0	0	0	0	0	0	0	0	0	1	0	0
Pujols, Luis, Oklahoma City	.229	51	192	16	44	67	7	2	4	26	1	0	1	1	9	2	25	0	1
Ramos, Roberto, Iowa	.244	101	303	27	74	97	12	1	3	23	3	0	0	0	45	2	44	7	4
Rivera, German, Nashville	.298	140	506	86	151	227	30	2	14	84	11	0	8	4	48	1	80	13	5
Rivera, Luis Antonio, Indianapolis	.246	108	407	60	100	148	17	5	7	43	5	1	6	4	29	0	68	18	8
Roadcap, Steve, Iowa†	.178	34	73	7	13	18	5	0	0	6	0	1	0	0	14	0	19	0	0
Roberge, Bertrand, Indianapolis	.000	22	1	0	0	0	0	0	0	0	0	0	0	0	0	0	1	0	0
Rodriguez, Victor, Louisville	.272	56	191	13	52	64	9	0	1	18	2	1	0	0	10	0	22	0	1
Rollin, Rondal, Buffalo	.318	8	22	3	7	8	1	0	0	2	0	0	0	0	0	0	6	0	0
Romano, Thomas, Indianapolis	.265	136	480	69	127	194	25	3	12	63	6	0	4	2	47	1	66	35	13
Roof, Eugene, Nashville†	.277	59	141	18	39	49	8	1	0	12	3	3	0	0	19	1	19	6	2
Rowdon, Wade, Denver	.333	55	180	36	60	104	12	4	8	37	6	1	2	0	20	0	16	5	1
Runnells, Thomas, Denver†	.228	95	298	34	68	97	12	4	3	28	1	5	1	0	25	1	27	1	3
Sabo, Christopher, Denver	.273	129	432	83	118	178	26	2	10	60	8	3	6	3	48	2	53	9	2
Santovenia, Nelson, Indianapolis	.211	18	57	6	12	16	1	0	1	2	1	1	0	0	5	0	13	0	0
Schulz, Jeffrey, Omaha*	.303	123	400	40	121	154	19	4	2	61	8	2	8	2	37	9	51	0	2
Scranton, James, Omaha†	.224	112	299	33	67	77	3	2	1	13	1	10	0	2	10	2	48	6	3
Sebra, Robert, Indianapolis	.125	20	8	0	1	1	0	0	0	0	0	1	0	0	1	0	2	0	0
Seitzer, Kevin, Omaha	.319	129	432	86	138	219	20	11	13	74	9	1	9	9	89	4	57	20	13
Sheridan, Patrick, Nashville*	.286	9	35	4	10	15	2	0	1	5	0	0	0	0	5	0	7	2	0
Shines, Raymond, Indianapolis†	.264	38	125	17	33	53	2	0	6	23	5	0	1	4	14	1	13	1	1
Sierra, Ruben, Oklahoma City†	.296	46	189	31	56	98	11	2	9	41	5	1	4	0	15	3	27	8	2
Simmons, Nelson, Nashville†	.200	14	45	5	9	11	2	0	0	4	2	0	0	0	11	0	12	0	0
Sinatro, Matthew, Buffalo	.250	11	32	4	8	11	3	0	0	3	0	1	0	0	1	0	6	0	0
Slaught, Donald, Oklahoma City	.333	3	12	2	4	5	1	0	0	1	0	0	0	0	0	0	3	0	0
Smith, Michael, 30 Den-10 Ind	.200	40	5	1	1	2	1	0	0	1	0	0	0	0	0	0	2	0	0
Snider, Van, Omaha*	.308	4	13	5	4	8	2	1	0	3	1	0	0	0	2	0	3	0	0
Sorensen, Lary, Indianapolis	.000	9	2	0	0	0	0	0	0	0	0	0	0	0	0	0	1	0	0
Springer, Gary, Nashville*	.234	35	94	8	22	29	7	0	0	13	0	0	2	0	12	0	15	5	4
St. Claire, Randy, Indianapolis	.000	57	2	0	0	0	0	0	0	0	0	0	0	0	0	0	1	0	0
Stanley, Michael, Oklahoma City	.366	56	202	37	74	108	13	3	5	49	4	1	1	1	44	0	42	1	1
Stephans, Russell, Omaha	.202	35	84	4	17	20	3	0	0	9	0	1	2	0	9	2	13	0	0
Stephens, Carl Ray, Louisville	.194	12	31	2	6	10	1	0	1	2	1	0	1	1	1	0	13	0	0
Stillwell, Kurt, Denver†	.233	10	30	2	7	7	0	0	0	2	0	0	0	0	2	0	4	2	0
Stoll, Richard, Indianapolis	.214	26	14	1	3	4	1	0	0	2	0	0	1	0	0	0	7	0	0
Stryffeler, Daniel, Louisville*	.263	57	156	25	41	51	4	0	2	14	0	3	2	0	22	1	24	5	4
Surhoff, Richard, 38 OkC-15 Iowa	.000	53	1	0	0	0	0	0	0	0	0	0	0	0	0	0	1	0	0
Tabor, Gregory, Oklahoma City	.284	104	401	50	114	145	19	0	4	51	1	7	2	4	27	0	59	14	4
Tanner, Edwin, Louisville†	.268	43	157	17	42	49	5	1	0	10	2	2	2	1	9	0	8	1	1
Taylor, Dwight, Omaha*	.259	114	428	75	111	145	12	11	0	23	5	11	3	1	47	1	58	67	19
Thompson, Tommy, Buffalo*	.263	108	342	40	90	134	18	1	8	46	4	5	5	3	33	4	43	1	3
Thurman, Gary, Omaha	.500	3	2	1	1	1	0	0	0	0	0	0	0	0	2	0	0	2	0
Tolman, Timothy, Nashville	.298	139	484	68	144	208	23	4	11	71	9	0	8	4	67	2	61	11	4
Tomlin, David, Indianapolis*	.000	39	7	0	0	0	0	0	0	0	0	0	0	0	0	0	4	0	0
Treadway, Jeffrey, Denver*	.328	72	204	20	67	95	11	4	3	23	0	1	2	1	19	2	12	3	1
Valdez, Julio, Iowa†	.237	100	325	29	77	112	11	6	4	39	5	5	6	2	15	2	48	7	6
Van Blaricom, Mark, Omaha	.333	5	3	2	1	1	0	0	0	0	0	0	0	0	1	0	1	0	0
Van Gorder, David, Denver	.228	66	180	26	41	52	6	1	1	19	1	0	4	3	31	0	28	1	1
Velarde, Randy, Buffalo	.200	9	20	2	4	5	1	0	0	2	0	0	0	1	2	0	4	1	0
Walker, Cleotha, Iowa†	.298	138	530	97	158	258	30	11	16	65	11	1	6	0	62	2	68	67	22
Walker, Duane, Louisville*	.271	32	107	18	29	49	7	2	3	12	2	1	0	0	13	0	24	2	2
Wallace, Timothy, Louisville	.225	44	142	9	32	46	8	0	2	13	0	4	2	0	11	0	32	0	0
Welsh, Christopher, Denver*	.250	10	4	0	1	1	0	0	0	1	1	1	0	0	0	0	1	0	0
Werner, Donald, Oklahoma City	.285	66	186	28	53	82	5	3	6	28	1	1	0	2	27	1	39	1	1

Player and Club	Pct.	G.	AB.	R.	H.	TB.	2B.	3B.	HR.	RBI.	GW.	SH.	SF.	HP.	BB.	Int. BB.	SO.	SB.	CS.
Wilkerson, Martin, Omaha*	.234	32	64	4	15	18	3	0	0	11	2	0	0	0	5	1	11	0	0
Williams, Dallas, Indianapolis*	.289	124	429	66	124	184	20	5	10	64	10	5	2	1	42	5	39	16	8
Williams, Kenneth, Buffalo	.212	50	189	21	40	60	4	2	4	15	2	1	0	5	6	0	53	5	4
Willis, Carl, Denver*	.000	20	1	0	0	0	0	0	0	0	0	0	0	0	0	0	1	0	0
Winningham, Herman, Indianapolis*	.269	51	201	35	54	85	5	7	4	24	3	1	1	0	14	0	47	23	2
Winters, Matthew, Buffalo*	.088	14	34	4	3	6	0	0	1	3	0	0	1	0	9	1	8	0	0
Wright, George, Indianapolis†	.327	14	52	9	17	35	3	0	5	21	0	1	1	2	10	0	6	4	0
Yastrzemski, Michael, Buffalo†	.385	7	26	4	10	14	1	0	1	1	0	0	0	0	1	0	4	0	0
Yobs, David, Buffalo*	.220	35	109	10	24	35	5	0	2	12	1	0	0	1	9	2	16	1	0
Zwolensky, Mitchell, Iowa	.000	29	9	2	0	0	0	0	0	0	0	0	0	0	1	0	4	1	0

The following pitchers, listed alphabetically by club, with games in parentheses, had no plate appearances, primarily through use of designated hitters:

BUFFALO—Brizzolara, Anthony (28); Burroughs, Darren (7); Cowley, Joseph (6); Filson, Peter (36); Gleaton, Jerry Don (46); Hall, Gardner (12); Jones, Alfornia (27); McCatty, Steven (8); McKeon, Joel (5); Rozema, David (13); Tanner, Bruce (23); Wehrmeister, David (32).

DENVER—Dibble, Robert (5); Jefferson, James (2); Reynolds, Timothy (1); Scott, Timothy (13); Terry, Scott (12).

INDIANAPOLIS—Chiffer, Floyd (5); Dopson, John (4); Graybill, David (4); Groves, Larry (7); Price, Kevin (2); Riley, George (5); Silva, Mark (3).

IOWA—Bell, Gregory (13); Gumpert, David (28).

LOUISVILLE—Bargar, Gregory (25); Boever, Joseph (52); Buonantony, Richard (23); Burris, Ray (4); Cherry, Paul (11); Citarella, Ralph (18); Conroy, Timothy (2); Dunn, Gregory (10); Dunne, Michael (28); Earley, William (52); Kepshire, Kurt (13); Lerch, Randy (8); Magrane, Joseph (15); Martin, John (3); Martinez, Alfredo (10); Mathews, Gregory (7); Ownbey, Richard (10); Perry, Patrick (5); Rajsich, David (25); Shade, Michael (5); Soff, Raymond (21); Young, Scott (5).

NASHVILLE—Breining, Fred (11); Cary, Charles (22); Conner, Jeffrey (31); Denman, Brian (31); Fallon, Robert (5); Gibson, Paul (30); Heinkel, Donald (9); Henneman, Michael (31); Kelly, Bryan (21); King, Eric (6); Lazorko, Jack (29); O'Neal, Randall (4); Robinson, Jeffrey (25); Scherrer, William (31).

OKLAHOMA CITY—Anderson, Scott (48); Barkley, Jeffrey (18); Brennan, Thomas (21); Clark, Robert (28); Cook, Glen (28); Geisel, David (18); Henry, Dwayne (28); Hough, Charles (1); Mahler, Michael (6); Mason, Michael (1); Mohorcic, Dale (16); Moore, Robert (15); Parrott, Michael (7); Russell, Jeffrey (11); Shimp, Tommy (25); Surhoff, Richard (38); Taylor, William (16); Welchel, Donald (25); Williams, Matthew (11); Wright, Richard (8).

OMAHA—Bankhead, Scott (7); Cato, Keefe (21); Cone, David (39); Davis, John (2); Gordon, Thomas (1); Griffin, Michael (28); Hargesheimer, Alan (23); Martin, Renie (21); Mullen, Thomas (27); Rajsich, David (12); Reyes, Jose (18); Sanchez, Israel (1); Schuler, David (32); Shaw, Theodore (21); Strode, Lester (28); Tabor, Scott (19); Warren, Michael (7).

GRAND SLAM HOME RUNS—Craig, Dayett, Dunbar, Parsons, 2 each; Calderon, Christmas, DeSa, Hammond, Hayes, Hocutt, R. Jones, Lindeman, Little, Maler, D. Martinez, McClendon, W. Moore, Romano, Schulz, G. Wright, 1 each.

AWARDED FIRST BASE ON CATCHER'S INTERFERENCE—De. Baker 2 (Colbert, Thompson); Hocutt 2 (Stanley, Thompson); Moronko 2 (Hammond, Harper), Pecota 2 (McGriff, Werner); Scranton 2 (McGriff, Mercado); Do. Baker (Sinatro); R. Jones (Madison); Kingery (McGriff); Sabo (Werner).

CLUB FIELDING

Club	Pct.	G.	PO.	A.	E.	DP.	PB.
Omaha	.979	142	3567	1317	103	111	8
Denver	.974	142	3569	1577	135	157	16
Iowa	.974	142	3627	1545	139	118	10
Louisville	.971	142	3567	1544	152	147	24
Buffalo	.970	142	3590	1466	154	138	16
Oklahoma City	.970	142	3662	1453	158	138	11
Nashville	.970	143	3643	1543	163	133	18
Indianapolis	.969	143	3751	1553	172	148	20

Triple Play—Nashville.

INDIVIDUAL FIELDING

*Throws lefthanded.

FIRST BASEMEN

Player and Club	Pct.	G.	PO.	A.	E.	DP.
Ayer, Louisville	.944	2	14	3	1	2
Barnes, Indianapolis	1.000	1	4	1	0	1
Bathe, Iowa	.938	2	12	3	1	0
Bockhorn, Buffalo	1.000	4	16	0	0	2
Christmas, Iowa	.986	28	197	9	3	20
Citari, Omaha	.9968	115	878	83	3	73
Corey, Indianapolis	1.000	2	2	0	0	0
Cusack, Nashville	1.000	17	132	13	0	14
DESA, Buffalo*	.9971	114	971	62	3	96
Earl, Nashville	1.000	1	1	0	0	0
Foley, Buffalo	1.000	3	22	0	0	1
Francona, Iowa*	.986	9	70	2	1	4
Hammond, Iowa	.989	12	79	8	1	5
Hansen, Omaha	1.000	2	11	0	0	3
Harper, Nashville	.986	15	66	7	1	6
Henika, Denver	.989	43	346	20	4	43
Hicks, Iowa	.990	100	802	48	9	62
Hocutt, Indianapolis	.982	109	899	77	18	95
Johnson, Indianapolis	.990	20	175	14	2	15
Jones, Oklahoma City*	.991	24	207	16	2	25
Knicely, Louisville	.985	67	539	64	9	63
Laga, Nashville*	.984	12	109	16	2	10
Lansford, Buffalo	.988	23	152	13	2	10
Lee, Denver	.996	33	240	25	1	20
Lindeman, Louisville	.992	74	666	47	6	67
Lombarski, Iowa	1.000	16	105	16	0	7
Lowry, Nashville	1.000	1	4	1	0	0
Lozado, Oklahoma City	.958	6	41	5	2	2
Lyons, Buffalo	1.000	1	8	0	0	0
Madison, Nashville	.987	38	286	20	4	29
Maler, Oklahoma City	.994	96	807	67	5	76
McClendon, Denver	.987	72	621	40	9	67
Miley, Denver	.983	7	57	2	1	7
Moore, Indianapolis	.988	15	76	5	1	11
Nokes, Nashville	.974	25	169	21	5	20
Nyman, 10 Buf-36 Nashville	.991	46	323	23	3	24
Owen, Oklahoma City	1.000	2	20	1	0	0
Rivera, Nashville	.917	2	10	1	1	2
Roof, Nashville	.941	2	16	0	1	0
Rowdon, Denver	.947	2	16	2	1	1
Scherrer, Nashville*	1.000	1	1	0	0	0
Seitzer, Omaha	.995	27	186	16	1	18
Shines, Indianapolis	1.000	9	91	9	0	8
Stanley, Oklahoma City	.975	14	103	13	3	7
Thompson, Buffalo	1.000	3	6	1	0	1
Tolman, Nashville	.995	24	182	17	1	19
VanGorder, Denver	1.000	1	1	0	0	0
Werner, Oklahoma City	.968	8	54	6	2	11
Wilkerson, Omaha	.984	8	60	3	1	4

Triple Play—Madison.

SECOND BASEMEN

Player and Club	Pct.	G.	PO.	A.	E.	DP.
Bockhorn, Buffalo	1.000	14	26	23	0	7
Booker, Louisville	.972	52	104	137	7	29
Brooks, Iowa	.977	93	177	207	9	44
Candaele, Indianapolis	.980	101	219	318	11	68
Capra, Buffalo	.975	17	30	48	2	10
Chavez, Nashville	.964	49	98	117	8	26
Concepcion, Omaha	.857	2	3	3	1	0
Earl, Nashville	.974	98	190	260	12	64
Gonzales, Indianapolis	.964	40	86	99	7	29
Gonzalez, Denver	.978	28	54	79	3	19
Hardy, Buffalo	1.000	1	0	1	0	0
Hegman, Omaha	.966	11	9	19	1	4
JOHNSON, Omaha	.9845	125	239	333	9	57
Krauss, Buffalo	.955	42	81	109	9	29
Larkin, Denver	.923	2	4	8	1	1
LeMaster, Indianapolis	.889	4	4	12	2	1

SECOND BASEMEN—Continued

Player and Club	Pct.	G.	PO.	A.	E.	DP.
Little, Buffalo	1.000	10	25	20	0	5
Lozado, Oklahoma City	1.000	10	21	38	0	8
Lyons, Louisville	.960	12	31	17	2	7
Manrique, Louisville	.987	12	31	46	1	9
Manuel, Indianapolis	1.000	4	4	2	0	1
Miller, Omaha	.971	8	17	16	1	2
Mota, Oklahoma City	.959	67	129	201	14	40
Noce, Iowa	1.000	2	3	2	0	0
Owen, Oklahoma City	.985	14	28	38	1	9
Perconte, Buffalo	.983	58	114	180	5	31
Pettini, Louisville	.9837	73	155	208	6	68

Player and Club	Pct.	G.	PO.	A.	E.	DP.
Pino, Buffalo	1.000	2	2	3	0	2
Rodriguez, Louisville	1.000	2	1	2	0	1
Runnells, Denver	.985	81	148	240	6	61
Springer, Nashville	1.000	8	8	9	0	1
Tabor, Oklahoma City	.965	54	118	133	9	37
Thompson, Buffalo	.927	12	19	19	3	5
Treadway, Denver	.974	45	71	150	6	34
Valdez, Iowa	.961	64	125	146	11	27
VanBlaricom, Omaha	1.000	2	1	1	0	0
Walker, Iowa	.956	8	21	22	2	7
Wilkerson, Omaha	1.000	4	2	2	0	1

Triple Play—Earl.

THIRD BASEMEN

Player and Club	Pct.	G.	PO.	A.	E.	DP.
Baker, Indianapolis	.946	23	28	42	4	3
Barnes, Indianapolis	.923	73	69	134	17	16
Bathe, Iowa	.855	39	8	45	9	0
Bockhorn, Buffalo	.900	5	2	7	1	0
Booker, Louisville	1.000	1	0	1	0	0
Chavez, Nashville	.972	27	14	56	2	5
Christmas, Iowa	1.000	2	2	5	0	2
Cochrane, Buffalo	.951	33	24	54	4	4
Earl, Nashville	.667	1	1	1	1	1
Gonzales, Indianapolis	.967	42	37	81	4	7
Gonzalez, Denver	.923	15	10	14	2	3
Hammond, Iowa	.962	37	25	76	4	10
Hegman, Omaha	1.000	4	0	3	0	0
Hinshaw, Denver	1.000	1	0	1	0	0
Hocutt, Indianapolis	1.000	1	0	1	0	0
Krauss, Buffalo	.667	1	0	2	1	1
Lansford, Buffalo	.500	1	1	1	2	0
Lindeman, Louisville	.881	39	34	62	13	8
Lombarski, Iowa	.934	52	44	97	10	11
Lozado, Oklahoma City	.912	22	10	42	5	3
S. Lyons, Buffalo	.913	9	6	15	2	2
W. Lyons, Louisville	.957	46	37	75	5	3
Madison, Nashville	.988	29	25	60	1	6

Player and Club	Pct.	G.	PO.	A.	E.	DP.
Manuel, Indianapolis	.857	4	1	5	1	2
Martinez, Buffalo	1.000	1	1	1	0	1
McClendon, Denver	1.000	1	0	1	0	0
Mills, Iowa	.964	16	11	42	2	3
Morman, Buffalo	.920	92	64	199	23	23
Moronko, Oklahoma City	.931	101	113	185	22	19
Owen, Oklahoma City	.625	4	1	4	3	0
Pecota, Omaha	.967	130	109	217	11	15
Rivera, Nashville	.909	97	80	170	25	12
Rodriguez, Louisville	.859	30	18	43	10	6
Roof, Nashville	1.000	1	0	1	0	0
Rowdon, Denver	.917	23	17	38	5	6
Runnells, Denver	1.000	1	0	1	0	0
SABO, Denver	.969	117	83	202	9	14
Seitzer, Omaha	.906	16	8	21	3	1
Shines, Indianapolis	.769	11	2	8	3	0
Springer, Nashville	.714	4	2	3	2	0
Stanley, Oklahoma City	.930	15	5	35	3	5
Tabor, Oklahoma City	.800	4	2	6	2	1
Tanner, Louisville	.966	40	24	88	4	7
Treadway, Denver	1.000	3	4	3	0	0
Valdez, Iowa	.971	38	18	50	2	5
Yastrzemski, Buffalo	1.000	3	1	1	0	0

Triple Play—Rivera.

SHORTSTOPS

Player and Club	Pct.	G.	PO.	A.	E.	DP.
BAKER, Nashville	.971	111	208	291	15	61
Booker, Louisville	.974	24	47	67	3	17
Brumley, Iowa	.966	139	177	400	20	55
Chavez, Nashville	.939	36	64	104	11	21
Cochrane, Buffalo	1.000	1	1	4	0	0
Concepcion, Omaha	.961	43	51	95	6	19
Earl, Nashville	1.000	2	1	1	0	0
Giles, Buffalo	.947	30	44	82	7	16
Gonzales, Indianapolis	.944	41	85	117	12	31
Gonzalez, Denver	.957	41	54	124	8	30
Hegman, Omaha	.941	14	7	9	1	2
Krauss, Buffalo	.956	70	105	175	13	36
Kunkel, Oklahoma City	.955	101	135	272	19	60
Larkin, Denver	.963	91	168	279	17	65
LeMaster, Indianapolis	1.000	2	3	2	0	2
Little, Buffalo	.951	18	22	56	4	16
Lazado, Oklahoma City	.957	4	9	13	1	3

Player and Club	Pct.	G.	PO.	A.	E.	DP.
Lyons, Buffalo	.955	8	16	26	2	4
Manrique, Louisville	.957	122	177	375	25	86
Martinez, Buffalo	.894	12	23	19	5	3
Moronko, Olahoma City	.969	6	12	19	1	3
Owen, Oklahoma City	.952	37	43	76	6	17
Pecota, Omaha	1.000	13	15	21	0	4
Pettini, Louisville	1.000	3	3	2	0	0
Pino, Buffalo	.750	2	2	4	2	0
Rivera, Indianapolis	.955	107	178	330	24	75
Rowdon, Denver	.857	4	4	8	2	2
Runnells, Denver	.875	7	7	7	2	2
Scranton, Omaha	.939	101	145	222	24	46
Springer, Nashville	.909	5	3	7	1	1
Stillwell, Denver	.875	9	14	21	5	6
Valdez, Iowa	.978	13	20	24	1	5
VanBlaricom, Omaha	1.000	1	1	1	0	1
Velarde, Buffalo	.925	9	9	28	3	3

OUTFIELDERS

Player and Club	Pct.	G.	PO.	A.	E.	DP.
Ayer, Louisville	.976	50	80	1	2	0
Baker, Indianapolis	.972	52	68	1	2	0
Barnes, Indianapolis	.960	13	22	2	1	1
Bernstine, Iowa	.978	75	130	2	3	2
Bockhorn, Buffalo	.943	49	80	3	5	0
Boever, Denver	.938	11	15	0	1	0
Boston, Buffalo*	.977	93	210	1	5	1
Bradley, Buffalo	1.000	4	9	0	0	0
Brewer, Omaha	.980	96	240	6	5	1
Brower, Oklahoma City	.979	140	366	8	8	1
Brown, Oklahoma City	.944	12	32	2	2	0
Calderon, Buffalo	.861	22	30	1	5	0
Candaele, Indianapolis	.917	17	21	1	2	0
Capra, 16 Buf-71 OkC	.981	87	201	10	4	2
Cedeno, Louisville	1.000	5	10	0	0	0
Cole, Louisville*	.940	62	135	6	9	2
Corey, Indianapolis	1.000	2	3	0	0	0
Craig, Buffalo	.973	112	208	6	6	0
Daniels, Denver	.965	41	78	4	3	0
Dayett, Iowa	.981	104	193	10	4	3
DeSa, Buffalo*	1.000	9	6	3	0	1
Dunbar, Oklahoma City*	.975	127	260	9	7	3
Earl, Nashville	1.000	17	25	1	0	0
Engle, Nashville	1.000	6	10	1	0	0
Fields, Nashville	.979	99	177	10	4	3
Foley, Buffalo	1.000	3	4	0	0	0
Ford, Louisville	.992	53	120	2	1	1

Player and Club	Pct.	G.	PO.	A.	E.	DP.
Francona, Iowa*	1.000	8	12	1	0	1
Garcia, Denver*	.982	137	317	10	6	3
Gonzalez, Denver	.971	25	32	1	1	0
Grubb, Nashville	.900	4	7	2	1	1
Hammond, Iowa	.982	56	100	9	2	2
Hardy, Buffalo	1.000	2	1	0	0	0
Harper, Nashville	.976	25	38	2	1	1
Hayes, Omaha	1.000	3	5	0	0	0
Henderson, Buffalo	.968	34	60	1	2	1
Hill, Denver	.955	115	180	13	9	1
Hinshaw, Denver	1.000	54	82	4	0	1
Hobbs, Nashville	.972	113	232	9	7	5
Johnson, Indianapolis	.929	8	13	0	1	0
Jones, Oklahoma City*	1.000	6	15	0	0	0
Kingery, Omaha*	.995	79	171	10	1	4
Lindeman, Louisville	1.000	13	18	1	0	0
Loggins, Omaha*	1.000	4	6	0	0	0
S. Lyons, Buffalo	1.000	3	6	0	0	0
W. Lyons, Louisville	1.000	10	17	1	0	1
Madison, Nashville	1.000	16	21	0	0	0
Martinez, Iowa*	.991	82	214	7	2	2
McClendon, Denver	.970	19	29	3	1	0
Miller, Omaha	1.000	1	0	1	0	0
Moore, Indianapolis	.972	105	161	11	5	3
Morman, Buffalo	.962	14	23	2	1	0
Moronko, Oklahoma City	1.000	12	27	0	0	0
Morris, Louisville*	.986	58	132	6	2	3

OUTFIELDERS—Continued

Player and Club	Pct.	G.	PO.	A.	E.	DP.
Motley, Omaha	.917	5	11	0	1	0
Nokes, Nashville	1.000	7	6	0	0	0
Nyman, Nashville	1.000	8	6	0	0	0
O'Neill, Denver*	.963	54	98	7	4	1
Owen, Oklahoma City	1.000	1	8	0	0	0
Parsons, Louisville	.979	114	175	11	4	1
Pecota, Omaha	1.000	4	1	0	0	0
Rivera, Nashville	.927	31	46	5	4	0
Rollin, Buffalo	.909	6	10	0	1	0
Romano, Indianapolis	.968	133	298	8	10	1
Roof, Nashville	1.000	27	35	0	0	0
Rowdon, Denver	.864	16	19	0	3	0
Runnells, Denver	.667	4	4	0	2	0
Schulz, Omaha	.961	66	119	5	5	0
Seitzer, Omaha	.967	66	144	2	5	1
Sheridan, Nashville	1.000	9	16	0	0	0
Sierra, Oklahoma City	.983	46	114	4	2	2
Simmons, Nashville	1.000	13	25	3	0	1
Snider, Omaha	1.000	4	7	0	0	0
Springer, Nashville	1.000	5	7	3	0	1
Stryffeler, Louisville	.988	49	83	2	1	0
Tabor, Oklahoma City	1.000	15	27	2	0	0
Tanner, Louisville	1.000	5	4	2	0	0
TAYLOR, Omaha*	.986	114	339	6	5	1
Thompson, Buffalo	1.000	5	8	0	0	0
Thurman, Omaha	1.000	1	2	0	0	0
Tolman, Nashville	.975	111	189	6	5	1
Valdez, Iowa	1.000	3	4	0	0	0
C. Walker, Iowa	.979	124	265	16	6	2
D. Walker, Louisville*	.969	32	60	2	2	1
Wallace, Louisville	1.000	3	5	0	0	0
D. Williams, Indianapolis*	.968	87	141	9	5	4
K. Williams, Buffalo	.991	50	100	8	1	4
Winningham, Indianapolis	.991	49	106	3	1	1
Winters, Buffalo	1.000	13	23	1	0	1
Wright, Indianapolis	.970	14	30	2	1	0
Yastrzemski, Buffalo	1.000	4	5	0	0	0
Yobs, Buffalo*	.842	10	16	0	3	0

CATCHERS

Player and Club	Pct.	G.	PO.	A.	E.	DP.	PB.
Bilardello, Indianapolis	1.000	2	6	0	0	0	0
Bradley, Buffalo	1.000	26	156	9	0	0	5
Christmas, Iowa	1.000	5	34	6	0	1	0
Colbert, Louisville	.980	46	218	33	5	1	6
Engle, Nashville	1.000	1	7	1	0	0	1
Fitzgerald, Indianapolis	.984	10	58	5	1	1	3
Foley, Buffalo	.989	35	159	20	2	7	1
Hammond, Iowa	.900	15	42	3	5	0	2
Hansen, Omaha	.982	60	246	23	5	2	4
Harper, Nashville	.961	55	273	46	13	2	7
HAYES, Omaha	.988	84	374	30	5	2	4
Hunt, Indianapolis	.979	67	375	42	9	2	9
Lake, 17 Iowa-15 Louisville	.988	32	140	21	2	0	2
Lowry, Nashville	.989	17	87	5	1	0	2
Madison, Nashville	.956	20	93	15	5	3	4
McClendon, Denver	.875	2	6	1	1	0	1
McGriff, Denver	.977	91	411	59	11	8	10
Mercado, Oklahoma City	.970	42	234	29	8	4	2
Miley, Denver	.968	6	29	1	1	0	0
Nieto, Indianapolis	.973	52	295	25	9	2	5
Nokes, Nashville	.965	63	327	29	13	4	4
Pagnozzi, Louisville	.984	28	160	19	3	3	6
Pevey, Louisville	.972	12	69	1	2	0	3
Pujols, Oklahoma City	.992	45	204	32	2	6	3
Ramos, Iowa	.976	95	440	50	12	6	6
Roadcap, Iowa	.981	32	137	17	3	4	2
Roof, Nashville	1.000	1	1	0	0	0	0
Santovenia, Indianapolis	.989	18	80	14	1	2	2
Shines, Indianapolis	1.000	6	30	4	0	1	1
Sinatro, Buffalo	.944	11	60	7	4	2	1
Slaught, Oklahoma City	1.000	2	6	1	0	0	0
Stanley, Oklahoma City	.972	18	98	7	3	2	3
Stephans, Omaha	.982	14	48	6	1	0	0
Stephens, Louisville	.978	12	38	6	1	0	2
Thompson, Buffalo	.982	87	427	51	9	4	9
VanGorder, Denver	1.000	55	268	29	0	3	5
Wallace, Louisville	.975	39	219	19	6	3	5
Werner, Oklahoma City	.960	41	177	17	8	2	3
Wilkerson, Omaha	.968	8	30	0	1	0	0

PITCHERS

Player and Club	Pct.	G.	PO.	A.	E.	DP.
Abrego, Iowa	1.000	6	1	7	0	0
Anderson, Oklahoma City	.941	48	7	9	1	0
Baller, Iowa	1.000	27	3	5	0	0
Bankhead, Omaha	1.000	7	2	10	0	0
Bargar, Louisville	.955	25	4	17	1	3
Barker, Indianapolis	1.000	13	1	5	0	1
Barkley, Oklahoma City	1.000	18	2	0	0	0
Barrett, Indianapolis	.900	21	2	7	1	1
Bell, Iowa*	1.000	13	0	3	0	0
Boever, Louisville	.923	52	4	8	1	1
Botelho, Denver	.931	23	10	17	2	1
Breining, Nashville	1.000	11	1	5	0	0
Brennan, Oklahoma City	1.000	21	6	11	0	3
Brizzolara, Buffalo	.955	28	7	14	1	2
Brown, Indianapolis	.960	48	3	21	1	1
Buchanan, Denver*	1.000	36	4	10	0	1
Buonantony, Louisville	.955	23	7	14	1	1
Burris, Louisville	.875	4	1	6	1	0
Burroughs, Buffalo*	.800	7	1	3	1	1
Cary, Nashville*	1.000	22	2	4	0	0
Cato, Omaha	1.000	21	7	14	0	0
Cherry, Louisville*	1.000	11	2	6	0	0
Citarella, Louisville	.769	18	7	3	3	0
B. Clark, Buffalo*	.917	34	6	27	3	2
R. Clark, Oklahoma City*	.957	28	6	16	1	2
Cole, Indianapolis	.872	25	14	20	5	0
Cone, Omaha	1.000	39	3	2	0	0
Conner, Nashville*	.938	31	11	34	3	3
Cook, Oklahoma City	1.000	28	4	23	0	3
Cornell, Iowa	.706	46	3	9	5	1
Cowley, Buffalo	.909	6	4	6	1	1
Cutshall, Indianapolis	1.000	11	6	5	0	0
Davidson, Iowa	.950	15	9	10	1	1
Joe. Davis, Buffalo	1.000	6	3	3	0	0
Denman, Nashville	.978	31	13	32	1	7
Dibble, Denver	.500	5	0	1	1	0
Dopson, Indianapolis	1.000	4	2	0	0	0
Dunn, Louisville	1.000	10	1	1	0	0
Dunne, Louisville	.981	28	17	35	1	2
Earley, Louisville*	.938	52	6	9	1	0
Engel, Iowa*	1.000	33	3	12	0	1
Fallon, Nashville*	1.000	5	1	4	0	0
Filson, Buffalo*	1.000	36	5	16	0	1
Fontenot, Iowa*	1.000	2	0	1	0	0
Geisel, Oklahoma City	1.000	18	5	7	0	0
Gibson, Nashville*	1.000	30	3	10	0	1
Gleaton, Buffalo*	.926	46	2	23	2	0
Graybill, Indianapolis	1.000	3	1	4	0	1
Griffin, Omaha	1.000	28	10	12	0	1
Groves, Indianapolis	1.000	7	0	2	0	0
Gumpert, Iowa	1.000	28	5	12	0	0
Hall, Buffalo*	.857	12	5	7	2	0
Hardy, Buffalo	.900	21	5	4	1	0
Hargesheimer, Omaha	.976	23	12	28	1	3
Heinkel, Nashville	.955	9	7	14	1	1
Henneman, Nashville	.889	31	3	13	2	0
Henry, Oklahoma City	1.000	28	1	6	0	0
Hoffman, Iowa*	1.000	9	2	7	0	0
Jefferson, Denver	.500	2	1	0	1	0
Jones, Buffalo	1.000	27	6	5	0	1
Kelly, Nashville	.944	21	12	22	2	3
Kemp, Denver	.967	29	12	17	1	1
Kepshire, Louisville	.947	13	8	10	1	0
King, Nashville	.900	6	3	6	1	0
Knox, Denver	.974	27	13	25	1	2
Konderla, Denver	1.000	41	1	7	0	0
Landrum, Denver	1.000	24	0	7	0	1
Layton, Iowa	1.000	11	0	1	0	0
Lazorko, Nashville	.973	29	15	21	1	3
Lerch, Louisville*	1.000	8	0	4	0	0
Long, Buffalo	.941	22	10	22	2	0
Lozado, Oklahoma City	1.000	1	1	0	0	0
MADDUX, Iowa	1.000	18	11	37	0	1
Magrane, Louisville*	.895	15	6	28	4	1
Mahler, Oklahoma City*	1.000	6	3	2	0	0
J. Martin, Louisville	1.000	3	1	0	0	0
R. Martin, Omaha	1.000	21	3	8	0	2
Martinez, Louisville	.800	10	1	3	1	0
Mathews, Louisville*	.833	7	1	9	2	1
McCatty, Buffalo	1.000	8	1	8	0	2
McKeon, Buffalo*	.500	5	0	1	1	0
Meridith, 25 Iowa-9 OkC*	.960	34	3	21	1	1
Mohorcic, Oklahoma City	.933	16	6	8	1	1
Montgomery, Denver	1.000	30	13	15	0	2
Moore, Oklahoma City	1.000	15	2	3	0	0
Moyer, Iowa*	1.000	6	4	6	0	0
Mullen, Omaha	.955	27	9	12	1	1
Murphy, Denver*	1.000	27	2	11	0	2
O'Neal, Nashville	.889	4	2	6	1	1
Oliver, Iowa	.818	33	4	5	2	0
Owchinko, Indianapolis*	.909	28	8	12	2	1
Ownbey, Louisville	.938	10	6	9	1	1

PITCHERS—Continued

Player and Club	Pct.	G.	PO.	A.	E.	DP.
Pacella, Nashville	1.000	43	4	7	0	1
Pacillo, Denver	.955	25	13	29	2	2
Parmenter, Iowa	1.000	5	1	5	0	0
Parrett, Indianapolis	.875	25	3	4	1	0
Parrott, Oklahoma City	.857	7	2	4	1	0
Perry, Louisville*	.800	5	2	2	1	0
Potestio, Iowa	.925	27	11	26	3	2
Pryce, Iowa	.875	31	4	10	2	2
Rajsich, 25 Lou-12 Omaha*	.850	37	5	12	3	1
Reyes, Omaha	.846	17	3	8	2	0
Riley, Indianapolis*	1.000	5	0	2	0	0
Roberge, Indianapolis	1.000	22	3	5	0	0
Robinson, Nashville	1.000	25	19	24	0	1
Roof, Nashville	1.000	5	0	1	0	0
Rozema, Buffalo	1.000	13	3	9	0	0
Russell, Oklahoma City	.913	11	9	12	2	1
Sanchez, Omaha*	1.000	1	1	0	0	0
Scherrer, Nashville*	.917	31	3	8	1	1
Schuler, Omaha*	1.000	32	2	7	0	2
Scott, Denver	1.000	13	1	2	0	0
Sebra, Indianapolis	.933	20	11	17	2	2
Shade, Louisville	1.000	5	1	1	0	0
Shaw, Omaha	.964	21	15	12	1	1
Shimp, Oklahoma City	.938	25	5	10	1	1
Smith, 30 Den-10 Ind	.944	40	5	12	1	0
Soff, Louisville	.950	21	4	15	1	2
Sorensen, Indianapolis	.867	9	4	9	2	0
St. Claire, Indianapolis	.935	57	7	22	2	1
Stoll, Indianapolis	.933	26	10	18	2	1
Strode, Omaha*	1.000	28	7	22	0	1
Surhoff, 38 OkC-15 Iowa	.909	53	3	17	2	4
Tabor, Omaha	1.000	19	3	12	0	2
Tanner, Buffalo	.955	23	7	35	2	1
Taylor, Oklahoma City	.941	16	10	6	1	0
Terry, Denver	.889	10	2	6	1	2
Tomlin, Indianapolis*	1.000	39	3	13	0	1
Warren, Omaha	.941	7	4	12	1	0
Wehrmeister, Buffalo	.944	32	6	11	1	1
Welchel, Oklahoma City	.880	25	8	14	3	2
Welsh, Denver*	1.000	10	5	12	0	0
M. Williams, Oklahoma City	.944	11	3	14	1	0
Willis, Denver	1.000	20	3	12	0	1
Wright, Oklahoma City*	1.000	8	1	4	0	0
Young, Louisville	1.000	5	1	2	0	1
Zwolensky, Iowa	.976	26	14	26	1	0

The following players do not have any recorded accepted chances at the positions indicated; therefore, are not listed in the fielding averages for those particular positions: Bockhorn, c; Chiffer, p; Cochrane, of; Conroy, p; Joh. Davis, p; Earl, p; Foley, 2b; Gordon, p; Hough, p; Hunt, of; Little, 3b; Mason, p; Mills, 2b; Perconte, ss; Price, p; Reynolds, p; Roof, 2b, ss; Scranton, p; Silva, p; Springer, p; Wilkerson, 3b, ss; D. Williams, p; Winningham, 3b.

CLUB PITCHING

Club	ERA.	G.	CG.	ShO.	Sv.	IP.	H.	R.	ER.	HR.	HB.	BB.	Int. BB.	SO.	WP.	Bk.
Omaha	3.91	142	38	12	25	1189.0	1135	580	517	101	25	489	26	647	46	16
Indianapolis	4.07	143	10	6	38	1250.1	1235	672	566	109	24	571	33	794	53	21
Denver	4.12	142	22	8	35	1189.2	1246	648	545	77	20	520	18	681	59	20
Buffalo	4.14	142	34	9	20	1196.2	1235	645	551	125	38	460	36	763	67	12
Louisville	4.16	142	23	9	30	1189.0	1194	634	550	72	41	552	31	713	66	28
Nashville	4.25	143	25	7	27	1214.1	1293	682	574	106	49	573	50	755	75	10
Iowa	4.38	142	15	10	38	1209.0	1268	661	588	75	48	537	41	685	76	24
Oklahoma City	5.17	142	10	4	30	1220.2	1407	784	701	120	21	503	8	664	63	19

PITCHERS' RECORDS

(Leading Qualifiers for Earned-Run Average Leadership — 114 or More Innings)

*Throws lefthanded.

Pitcher—Club	W.	L.	Pct.	ERA.	G.	GS.	CG.	GF.	ShO.	Sv.	IP.	H.	R.	ER.	HR.	HB.	BB.	Int. BB.	SO.	WP.
Filson, Buffalo*	14	3	.824	2.27	36	12	4	22	1	6	139.0	116	46	35	12	5	32	4	81	2
Maddux, Iowa	10	1	.909	3.02	18	18	5	0	2	0	128.1	127	49	43	3	12	30	3	65	4
Lazorko, Nashville	8	6	.571	3.20	29	18	7	8	2	1	154.2	146	63	55	12	7	72	7	119	3
B. Clark, Buffalo*	7	6	.538	3.25	34	13	6	14	2	3	122.0	124	54	44	10	2	54	3	85	9
Cole, Indianapolis	12	4	.750	3.29	25	25	2	0	0	0	158.2	145	74	58	8	2	64	1	75	2
Hargesheimer, Omaha	13	6	.684	3.29	23	22	8	0	1	0	150.1	131	63	55	7	3	59	0	71	0
Sebra, Indianapolis	9	2	.818	3.43	20	20	2	0	0	0	126.0	108	59	48	11	2	70	3	91	5
Botelho, Denver	11	7	.611	3.67	23	23	3	0	1	0	147.0	131	70	60	11	4	59	0	91	3
Long, Buffalo	9	9	.500	3.88	22	22	5	0	0	0	146.0	159	73	63	15	1	44	2	86	4
Welchel, Oklahoma City	12	9	.571	3.99	25	25	1	0	0	0	160.0	159	80	71	5	2	74	1	95	9
Knox, Denver	9	12	.429	4.02	27	27	4	0	2	0	170.0	197	91	76	4	2	38	1	50	5

Departmental Leaders: G—St. Claire, 57; W—Filson, 14; L—Dunne, Knox, 12; Pct.—Maddux, .909; GS—Dunne, Griffin, Kemp, 28; CG—Hargesheimer, Magrane, 8; GF—Earley, 42; ShO—Several pitchers with 2; Sv.—Pacella, 17; IP—Dunne, 185.2; H—Denman, 207; R—Denman, 108; ER—Dunne, 94; HR—Strode, 19; HB—Maddux, 12; BB—Strode, 88; IBB—Conner, 11; SO—Lazorko, 119; WP—Meridith, 13.

(All Pitchers—Listed Alphabetically)

Pitcher—Club	W.	L.	Pct.	ERA.	G.	GS.	CG.	GF.	ShO.	Sv.	IP.	H.	R.	ER.	HR.	HB.	BB.	Int. BB.	SO.	WP.
Abrego, Iowa	3	2	.600	5.90	6	6	1	0	0	0	29.0	32	19	19	3	3	18	1	13	4
Anderson, Oklahoma City	5	7	.417	2.96	48	0	0	39	0	15	82.0	82	36	27	6	1	28	3	51	1
Baller, Iowa	3	7	.300	4.40	27	5	1	20	1	9	59.1	63	32	29	1	6	32	6	51	2
Bankhead, Omaha	2	2	.500	1.49	7	7	2	0	0	0	48.1	31	11	8	2	0	14	1	34	1
Bargar, Louisville	3	4	.429	3.56	25	5	0	9	0	2	68.1	56	31	27	3	3	35	2	65	4
Barker, Indianapolis	3	2	.600	3.32	13	10	1	2	0	0	57.0	53	29	21	4	0	31	0	39	4
Barkley, Oklahoma City	2	1	.667	8.90	18	1	0	3	0	1	30.1	46	36	30	6	1	28	0	18	6
Barrett, Indianapolis	0	1	.000	4.00	21	2	0	12	0	4	45.0	40	22	20	5	0	22	0	25	3
Bell, Iowa*	0	0	.000	4.60	13	0	0	1	0	0	15.2	14	8	8	1	1	12	0	22	1
Boever, Louisville	4	5	.444	2.25	51	0	0	26	0	5	88.0	71	25	22	1	2	48	6	75	10
Botelho, Denver	11	7	.611	3.67	23	23	3	0	1	0	147.0	131	70	60	11	4	59	0	91	3
Breining, Nashville	2	3	.400	6.18	11	7	0	2	0	0	39.1	43	31	27	5	0	21	3	24	3
Brennan, Oklahoma City	3	3	.500	5.43	21	7	0	3	0	0	64.2	85	42	39	9	1	15	0	24	2
Brizzolara, Buffalo	6	6	.500	5.40	28	17	5	5	2	0	116.2	131	79	70	14	4	54	1	70	11
Brown, Indianapolis	11	3	.786	3.21	48	2	0	26	0	9	95.1	101	37	34	5	1	22	6	51	1
Buchanan, Denver*	3	7	.300	5.38	36	6	1	12	0	3	77.0	95	53	46	7	0	37	1	29	4
Buonantony, Louisville	7	6	.538	5.58	23	16	2	2	0	0	108.0	106	74	67	9	7	53	2	81	6
Burris, Louisville	1	1	.500	2.41	4	4	0	0	0	0	18.2	18	5	5	1	0	2	0	9	0
Burroughs, Buffalo*	1	3	.250	7.03	7	6	0	0	0	0	24.1	34	23	19	1	2	15	1	13	3
Cary, Nashville*	1	4	.200	5.47	22	0	0	13	0	0	26.1	29	21	16	3	0	15	2	19	2
Cato, Omaha	6	7	.462	4.78	21	16	6	4	1	0	116.2	128	68	62	12	2	24	2	51	1
Cherry, Louisville*	2	4	.333	5.47	11	6	0	1	0	1	51.0	67	35	31	0	0	22	1	22	1
Chiffer, Indianapolis	0	2	.000	15.00	5	0	0	1	0	0	9.0	14	17	15	3	0	8	1	6	0
Citarella, Louisville	3	4	.429	4.87	18	12	0	3	0	0	68.1	79	42	37	2	3	37	1	31	0
B. Clark, Buffalo*	7	6	.538	3.25	34	13	6	14	2	3	122.0	124	54	44	10	2	54	3	85	9
R. Clark, Oklahoma City*	5	7	.417	5.54	28	13	1	5	0	2	113.2	140	76	70	16	1	25	1	47	4

Pitcher—Club	W.	L.	Pct.	ERA.	G.	GS.	CG.	GF.	ShO.	Sv.	IP.	H.	R.	ER.	HR.	HB.	BB.	Int. BB.	SO.	WP.
Cole, Indianapolis	12	4	.750	3.29	25	25	2	0	0	0	158.2	145	74	58	8	2	64	1	75	2
Cone, Omaha	8	4	.667	2.79	39	2	2	33	0	14	71.0	60	23	22	3	3	25	4	63	6
Conner, Nashville*	3	10	.231	5.09	31	15	4	6	0	1	123.2	148	78	70	12	6	57	11	48	11
Conroy, Louisville*	1	0	1.000	2.25	2	2	0	0	0	0	8.0	6	2	2	0	0	6	0	6	0
Cook, Oklahoma City	8	9	.471	6.04	28	23	4	4	1	0	135.2	187	102	91	15	1	47	1	61	6
Cornell, Iowa	4	7	.364	5.69	46	7	0	23	0	7	93.1	110	70	59	9	2	47	6	63	7
Cowley, Buffalo	1	3	.250	3.96	6	5	2	1	0	0	36.1	34	18	16	2	0	26	1	30	8
Cutshall, Indianapolis	5	2	.714	5.60	11	11	0	0	0	0	53.0	50	36	33	6	1	41	0	37	4
Davidson, Iowa	4	5	.444	4.87	15	15	2	0	0	0	92.1	117	58	50	9	3	32	2	48	7
Joe. Davis, Buffalo	1	4	.200	4.58	6	6	1	0	0	0	39.1	41	24	20	5	1	11	1	30	3
Joh. Davis, Omaha	0	0	.000	4.50	2	0	0	2	0	1	2.0	2	1	1	0	1	1	0	1	0
Denman, Nashville	10	10	.500	4.80	31	23	2	4	0	1	163.0	207	108	87	15	8	66	2	62	8
Dibble, Denver	1	0	1.000	5.40	5	0	0	3	0	0	6.2	9	4	4	0	0	2	0	3	0
Dopson, Indianapolis	0	3	.000	4.50	4	4	0	0	0	0	16.0	18	12	8	0	0	11	0	6	2
Dunn, Louisville	0	0	.000	3.27	10	0	0	5	0	2	11.0	8	4	4	1	0	15	0	12	3
Dunne, Louisville	9	12	.429	4.56	28	28	7	0	1	0	185.2	182	102	94	11	5	82	7	94	11
Earl, Nashville	0	0	.000	36.00	1	0	0	1	0	0	1.0	3	4	4	2	0	2	0	0	0
Earley, Louisville*	4	6	.400	3.20	52	0	0	42	0	15	70.1	60	29	25	4	3	32	3	43	4
Engel, Iowa*	6	6	.500	5.94	33	6	1	14	0	2	63.2	68	49	42	4	1	47	5	49	9
Fallon, Nashville*	1	4	.200	5.84	5	5	0	0	0	0	24.2	36	18	16	2	2	17	0	15	1
Filson, Buffalo*	14	3	.824	2.27	36	12	4	22	1	6	139.0	116	46	35	12	5	32	4	81	2
Fontenot, Iowa*	1	0	1.000	1.80	2	2	0	0	0	0	15.0	10	3	3	1	0	8	0	9	0
Geisel, Oklahoma City	1	5	.167	6.34	18	6	0	6	0	2	55.1	76	42	39	10	0	18	0	31	3
Gibson, Nashville*	5	6	.455	3.97	30	14	2	9	0	2	113.1	121	58	50	12	2	40	5	91	8
Gleaton, Buffalo*	4	3	.571	3.22	46	3	1	24	0	7	78.1	79	34	28	5	1	35	4	77	0
Gordon, Omaha	0	0	.000	47.25	1	0	0	0	0	0	1.1	6	7	7	0	0	2	0	3	0
Graybill, Indianapolis	1	0	1.000	5.79	3	3	0	0	0	0	14.0	17	9	9	2	0	5	0	7	0
Griffin, Omaha	8	11	.421	4.08	28	28	6	0	0	0	183.0	186	90	83	17	4	56	2	105	6
Groves, Indianapolis	0	1	.000	5.84	7	0	0	2	0	0	12.1	18	8	8	1	0	8	1	6	0
Gumpert, Iowa	2	1	.667	2.23	28	0	0	24	0	14	44.1	36	13	11	2	2	7	1	33	1
Hall, Buffalo*	4	5	.444	6.06	12	12	2	0	1	0	71.1	84	52	48	13	2	27	0	37	4
Hardy, Buffalo	2	2	.500	5.73	21	0	0	10	0	0	22.0	26	17	14	4	2	20	2	17	1
Hargesheimer, Omaha	13	6	.684	3.29	23	22	8	0	1	0	150.1	131	63	55	7	3	59	0	71	0
Heinkel, Nashville	5	2	.714	2.73	9	8	3	0	0	0	59.1	48	18	18	4	5	14	2	32	1
Henneman, Nashville	2	5	.286	2.95	31	0	0	18	0	1	58.0	57	27	19	5	4	23	1	39	5
Henry, Oklahoma City	2	1	.667	5.89	28	1	0	16	0	3	44.1	51	30	29	3	0	27	0	41	7
Hoffman, Iowa*	4	0	1.000	2.12	9	9	1	0	1	0	59.1	50	14	14	2	1	20	1	48	1
Hough, Oklahoma City	0	1	.000	9.00	1	1	0	0	0	0	5.0	7	5	5	1	0	1	0	3	0
Jefferson, Denver	0	0	.000	3.00	2	0	0	1	0	0	3.0	1	2	1	0	0	4	0	3	0
Jones, Buffalo	2	4	.333	4.56	27	0	0	13	0	4	47.1	52	27	24	6	1	25	3	31	4
Kelly, Nashville	5	5	.500	4.62	21	18	2	1	0	0	101.1	106	72	52	6	9	77	4	74	12
Kemp, Denver	10	7	.588	4.11	29	28	5	0	1	0	171.0	180	89	78	16	2	80	4	106	7
Kepshire, Louisville	1	9	.100	6.48	13	13	2	0	0	0	66.2	82	57	48	7	2	35	1	46	3
King, Nashville	3	2	.600	3.52	6	6	1	0	0	0	38.1	29	16	15	1	1	16	2	38	2
Knox, Denver	9	12	.429	4.02	27	27	4	0	2	0	170.0	197	91	76	4	2	38	1	50	5
Konderla, Denver	6	2	.750	4.67	41	0	0	20	0	2	61.2	74	37	32	6	2	40	3	43	8
Landrum, Denver	1	3	.250	3.47	24	2	0	19	0	8	36.1	36	20	14	1	0	25	2	36	3
Layton, Iowa	1	1	.500	5.48	11	0	0	2	0	0	21.1	25	16	13	0	1	17	0	9	2
Lazorko, Nashville	8	6	.571	3.20	29	18	7	8	2	1	154.2	146	63	55	12	7	72	7	119	3
Lerch, Louisville*	4	2	.667	3.89	8	8	0	0	0	0	41.2	48	21	18	2	0	24	0	15	6
Long, Buffalo	9	9	.500	3.88	22	22	5	0	0	0	146.0	159	73	63	15	1	44	2	86	4
Lozado, Oklahoma City	0	0	.000	0.00	1	0	0	1	0	0	1.2	0	0	0	0	0	0	0	2	0
Maddux, Iowa	10	1	.909	3.02	18	18	5	0	2	0	128.1	127	49	43	3	12	30	3	65	4
Magrane, Louisville*	9	6	.600	2.06	15	15	8	0	2	0	113.1	93	34	26	4	5	33	1	72	7
Mahler, Oklahoma City*	1	4	.200	4.79	6	6	2	0	1	0	35.2	38	20	19	5	0	17	0	20	1
J. Martin, Louisville	2	1	.667	4.26	3	3	0	0	0	0	19.0	23	9	9	1	0	5	0	7	0
R. Martin, Omaha	0	4	.000	5.71	21	0	0	9	0	1	41.0	45	26	26	6	3	35	1	28	4
Martinez, Louisville	0	5	.000	7.02	10	7	0	1	0	0	33.1	40	29	26	5	1	25	0	18	2
Mason, Oklahoma City*	0	1	.000	3.00	1	1	0	0	0	0	3.0	2	5	1	0	0	3	0	1	0
Mathews, Louisville*	3	3	.500	2.58	7	7	2	0	2	0	45.1	44	19	13	2	0	14	0	20	0
McCatty, Buffalo	0	3	.000	9.64	8	3	1	3	0	0	23.1	29	26	25	0	1	18	1	8	2
McKeon, Buffalo*	1	0	1.000	0.00	5	0	0	3	0	0	8.1	1	4	0	0	0	6	2	8	0
Meridith, 25 Iowa-9 OkC*	7	7	.500	4.42	34	17	0	10	0	3	118.0	125	63	58	6	0	52	1	60	13
Mohorcic, Oklahoma City	4	4	.500	2.39	16	0	0	13	0	3	37.2	34	16	10	2	2	11	1	24	1
Montgomery, Denver	11	7	.611	4.39	30	22	2	4	1	0	151.2	162	88	74	13	3	57	0	78	11
Moore, Oklahoma City	0	2	.000	5.82	15	2	0	1	0	0	34.0	40	23	22	7	2	7	0	26	2
Moyer, Iowa*	3	2	.600	2.55	6	6	2	0	0	0	42.1	25	14	12	2	0	11	0	25	0
Mullen, Omaha	7	7	.500	3.49	27	13	4	7	2	1	113.1	112	50	44	10	2	34	5	41	0
Murphy, Denver*	3	4	.429	1.90	27	0	0	16	0	7	42.2	33	12	9	0	0	24	1	36	0
O'Neal, Nashville	1	2	.333	4.76	4	4	1	0	0	0	28.1	28	16	15	4	0	9	1	15	1
Oliver, Iowa	2	3	.400	5.01	33	1	0	16	0	1	59.1	73	42	33	3	1	31	5	36	5
Owchinko, Indianapolis*	11	7	.611	4.18	28	24	1	2	1	0	150.2	156	89	70	18	1	59	2	104	6
Ownbey, Louisville	3	3	.500	4.42	10	10	2	0	0	0	59.0	59	31	29	11	3	25	1	27	0
Pacella, Nashville	7	6	.538	2.90	43	0	0	33	0	17	68.1	63	28	22	3	2	39	2	55	7
Pacillo, Denver	11	6	.647	4.32	25	25	4	0	2	0	148.0	135	81	71	9	2	85	0	111	6
Parmenter, Iowa	0	4	.000	7.48	5	5	0	0	0	0	27.2	36	23	23	1	0	15	1	20	1
Parrett, Indianapolis	2	5	.286	4.96	25	8	0	7	0	2	69.0	54	44	38	6	0	35	2	76	7
Parrott, Oklahoma City	0	3	.000	13.50	7	1	0	2	0	1	9.1	20	17	14	0	1	5	0	4	1
Perry, Louisville*	1	0	1.000	3.27	5	0	0	3	0	1	11.0	8	6	4	0	0	6	1	7	4
Potestio, Iowa	12	9	.571	4.09	27	24	2	0	1	0	160.2	189	85	73	14	3	61	4	64	8
Price, Indianapolis	1	0	1.000	9.00	2	0	0	0	0	0	5.0	9	6	5	1	0	1	0	1	0
Pryce, Iowa	3	8	.273	4.71	31	8	0	4	0	0	78.1	68	41	41	3	5	50	2	34	10
Rajsich, 25 Lou-12 Omaha*	7	3	.700	4.71	37	4	1	16	0	1	80.1	95	54	42	11	5	33	3	38	7
Reyes, Omaha	1	0	1.000	6.06	17	0	0	6	0	0	35.2	50	26	24	3	1	17	0	21	4
Reynolds, Denver	0	0	.000	0.00	1	0	0	1	0	0	1.0	0	0	0	0	0	0	0	1	0
Riley, Indianapolis*	0	2	.000	6.00	5	1	0	0	0	0	9.0	13	6	6	0	1	6	1	4	0
Roberge, Indianapolis	3	0	1.000	2.49	22	0	0	13	0	4	43.1	47	12	12	5	3	17	3	32	5
Robinson, Nashville	10	7	.588	4.38	25	24	3	0	0	0	150.0	162	85	73	12	2	72	6	72	9
Roof, Nashville	0	0	.000	1.69	5	0	0	4	0	0	5.1	4	1	1	1	0	4	0	3	0
Rozema, Buffalo	4	4	.500	3.95	13	11	1	1	0	0	68.1	72	32	30	6	2	5	0	39	0
Russell, Oklahoma City	4	1	.800	3.95	11	11	1	0	0	0	70.2	63	32	31	5	2	38	0	34	1
Sanchez, Omaha*	0	1	.000	9.00	1	1	0	0	0	0	3.0	4	3	3	2	0	2	0	2	0
Scherrer, Nashville*	5	2	.714	5.06	31	1	0	18	0	4	58.2	60	36	33	7	1	28	2	49	2

Pitcher—Club	W.	L.	Pct.	ERA.	G.	GS.	CG.	GF.	ShO.	Sv.	IP.	H.	R.	ER.	HR.	HB.	BB.	Int. BB.	SO.	WP.
Schuler, Omaha*	3	5	.375	3.49	32	0	0	22	0	7	38.2	35	17	15	4	1	12	5	23	0
Scott, Denver	0	2	.000	3.42	13	0	0	6	0	3	23.2	23	10	9	2	0	11	2	20	2
Scranton, Omaha	0	0	.000	0.00	2	0	0	2	0	0	1.1	2	0	0	0	0	1	0	1	0
Sebra, Indianapolis	9	2	.818	3.43	20	20	2	0	0	0	126.0	108	59	48	11	2	70	3	91	5
Shade, Louisville	1	0	1.000	10.24	5	0	0	3	0	0	9.2	14	11	11	1	1	14	1	4	1
Shaw, Omaha	5	9	.357	3.84	21	16	2	2	0	0	98.1	82	51	42	7	1	70	2	62	5
Shimp, Oklahoma City	2	3	.400	5.77	25	6	0	10	0	0	53.0	66	40	34	6	2	24	0	14	7
Silva, Indianapolis	0	0	.000	24.00	3	0	0	1	0	0	3.0	4	8	8	1	0	8	0	1	1
Smith, 30 Den-10 Ind	6	3	.667	5.40	40	5	0	20	0	2	76.2	95	54	46	2	3	44	3	50	6
Soff, Louisville	3	2	.600	1.69	21	0	0	14	0	3	42.2	34	13	8	0	0	15	2	31	1
Sorensen, Indianapolis	2	3	.400	3.16	9	9	3	0	1	0	57.0	51	25	20	6	1	17	1	20	0
Springer, Nashville	0	0	.000	27.00	1	0	0	1	0	0	0.2	3	2	2	0	0	1	0	0	0
St. Claire, Indianapolis	5	7	.417	3.99	57	0	0	35	0	15	99.1	105	49	44	10	6	29	4	72	4
Stoll, Indianapolis	5	11	.313	5.08	26	19	1	3	0	0	118.2	134	80	67	14	4	52	2	47	2
Strode, Omaha*	9	11	.450	4.14	28	27	5	0	2	0	169.2	154	87	78	19	3	88	0	73	9
Surhoff, 38 OkC-15 Iowa	7	8	.467	5.46	53	1	0	35	0	5	85.2	92	57	52	8	2	37	3	42	3
Tabor, Omaha	1	0	1.000	3.31	19	0	0	11	0	1	32.2	34	15	12	1	0	12	2	19	3
Tanner, Buffalo	8	10	.444	4.16	23	23	6	0	1	0	158.0	165	83	73	18	8	53	2	81	12
Taylor, Oklahoma City	5	5	.500	4.60	16	16	1	0	0	0	101.2	94	56	52	7	1	57	0	68	4
Terry, Denver	1	2	.333	2.33	10	1	0	4	0	2	19.1	22	13	5	0	0	8	0	13	2
Tomlin, Indianapolis*	7	5	.583	2.72	38	0	0	23	0	4	72.2	56	24	22	2	0	38	4	70	5
Warren, Omaha	5	1	.833	3.19	7	7	2	0	1	0	48.0	32	19	17	2	0	20	1	31	3
Wehrmeister, Buffalo	7	6	.538	3.94	32	9	0	12	0	0	96.0	88	53	42	14	6	35	9	70	4
Welchel, Oklahoma City	12	9	.571	3.99	25	25	1	0	0	0	160.0	159	80	71	5	2	74	1	95	9
Welsh, Denver*	5	2	.714	4.02	10	7	3	1	0	0	53.2	58	26	24	4	3	14	1	18	2
D. Williams, Indianapolis*	0	1	.000	4.50	4	0	0	3	0	0	4.0	8	2	2	0	0	3	1	1	0
M. Williams, Oklahoma City	1	4	.200	5.70	11	11	0	0	0	0	60.0	78	41	38	7	1	23	0	36	3
Willis, Denver	1	3	.250	4.68	20	1	0	16	0	8	32.2	29	22	17	3	1	16	1	16	2
Wright, Oklahoma City*	1	1	.500	6.92	8	5	0	2	0	0	26.0	28	22	20	3	2	16	0	18	0
Young, Louisville	0	4	.000	7.40	5	5	0	0	0	0	24.1	42	24	20	2	2	8	0	8	0
Zwolensky, Iowa	9	5	.643	5.13	26	18	0	5	0	0	112.1	119	68	64	10	6	49	1	40	3

BALKS—Dunne, 9; Cole, 7; Taylor, 6; Maddux, Stoll, 5 each; Cowley, Magrane, Mathews, Pacella, Parmenter, 4 each; Abrego, Bankhead, Cutshall, R. Martin, Montgomery, Oliver, Robinson, Sebra, Strode, Tanner, Zwolensky, 3 each; Baller, Botelho, Buonantony, Citarella, Cook, Hargesheimer, Kemp, Konderla, Mohorcic, Pacillo, Shimp, Soff, Welsh, 2 each; Bell, Boever, Brennan, Buchanan, Cato, Cherry, Chiffer, B. Clark, R. Clark, Cone, Denman, Dibble, Dopson, Dunn, Filson, Geisel, Gumpert, Hardy, Henneman, Henry, Jones, Kelly, Knox, Landrum, Lerch, Meridith, Murphy, Potestio, Reyes, Russell, Smith, St. Claire, Tabor, Warren, Wehrmeister, Welchel, Willis, Wright, Young, 1 each.

COMBINATION SHUTOUTS—Clark-Wehrmeister, Burroughs-Jones, Buffalo; Botelho-Murphy, Denver; Cole-St. Claire, Sebra-Barrett, Owchinko-Brown, Cole-Parrett, Indianapolis; Meridith-Zwolensky, Abrego-Engel, Moyer-Gumpert, Meridith-Cornell-Engel-Baller, Hoffman-Bell-Surhoff, Iowa; Burris-Dunn-Rajsich, Cherry-Earley, Conroy-Citarella, Lerch-Boever, Louisville; King-Scherrer, Denman-Scherrer, Denman-Henneman, Gibson-Kelly-Cary, Scherrer-Roof-Denman, Nashville; Cook-Parrott, Williams-Surhoff, Oklahoma City; Strode-Cone 2, Hargesheimer-Martin, Shaw-Schuler, Griffin-Cone, Omaha.

NO-HIT GAMES—None.

International League

CLASS AAA

Leading Batter
ANDRE DAVID
Toledo

League President
HAROLD COOPER

Leading Pitcher
DOUG JONES
Maine

CHAMPIONSHIP WINNERS IN PREVIOUS YEARS

Year—Club	Pct.
1884—Trenton	.520
1885—Syracuse	.584
1886—Utica	.646
1887—Toronto	.644
1888—Syracuse	.723
1889—Detroit	.649
1890—Detroit	.617
1891—Buffalo (reg. season)	.727
Buffalo (supplem'l)	.680
1892—Providence	.615
Binghamton*	.667
1893—Erie	.606
1894—Providence	.696
1895—Springfield	.687
1896—Providence	.602
1897—Syracuse	.632
1898—Montreal	.586
1899—Rochester	.624
1900—Providence	.616
1901—Rochester	.642
1902—Toronto	.669
1903—Jersey City	.642
1904—Buffalo	.657
1905—Providence	.638
1906—Buffalo	.607
1907—Toronto	.619
1908—Baltimore	.593
1909—Rochester	.596
1910—Rochester	.601
1911—Rochester	.645
1912—Toronto	.595
1913—Newark	.625
1914—Providence	.617
1915—Buffalo	.632
1916—Buffalo	.586
1917—Toronto	.604
1918—Toronto	.693
1919—Baltimore	.671
1920—Baltimore	.719
1921—Baltimore	.717
1922—Baltimore	.689
1923—Baltimore	.677
1924—Baltimore	.709
1925—Baltimore	.633
1926—Toronto	.657
1927—Buffalo	.667
1928—Rochester	.549
1929—Rochester	.613
1930—Rochester	.629
1931—Rochester	.601
1932—Newark	.649
1933—Newark	.622
Buffalo (4th)†	.494
1934—Newark	.608
Toronto (3rd)†	.559
1935—Montreal	.597
Syracuse (2nd)†	.565
1936—Buffalo‡	.610
1937—Newark‡	.717
1938—Newark‡	.684
1939—Jersey City	.582
Rochester (2nd)†	.556
1940—Rochester	.611
Newark (2nd)†	.594
1941—Newark	.649
Montreal (2nd)†	.584
1942—Newark	.601
Syracuse (3rd)†	.513
1943—Toronto	.625
Syracuse (3rd)†	.536
1944—Baltimore‡	.553
1945—Montreal	.621
Newark (2nd)†	.582
1946—Montreal‡	.649
1947—Jersey City	.610
Syracuse (3rd)†	.575
1948—Montreal‡	.614
1949—Buffalo	.584
Montreal (3rd)†	.545
1950—Rochester	.609
Baltimore (3rd)†	.556
1951—Montreal‡	.617
1952—Montreal	.629
Rochester (3rd)†	.619
1953—Rochester	.630
Montreal (2nd)†	.586
1954—Toronto	.630
Syracuse (4th)§	.510
1955—Montreal	.617
Rochester (4th)†	.497
1956—Toronto	.566
Rochester (2nd)†	.553
1957—Toronto	.575
Buffalo (2nd)†	.571
1958—Montreal‡	.588
1959—Buffalo	.582
Havana (3rd)†	.523
1960—Toronto‡	.649
1961—Columbus	.597
Buffalo (3rd)†	.559
1962—Jacksonville	.610
Atlanta (3rd)†	.539
1963—Syracuse x	.533
Indianapolis‡	.562
1964—Jacksonville	.589
Rochester (4th)†	.532
1965—Columbus	.582
Toronto (3rd)†	.556
1966—Rochester	.565
Toronto (2nd-tied)†	.558
1967—Richmond	.574
Toledo (3rd)†	.525
1968—Toledo	.565
Jacksonville (4th)†	.514
1969—Tidewater	.563
Syracuse (3rd)†	.536
1970—Syracuse‡	.600
1971—Rochester‡	.614
1972—Louisville	.563
Tidewater (3rd)†	.545
1973—Charleston	.586
Pawtucket y†	.534
1974—Memphis	.613
Rochester x‡	.611
1975—Tidewater‡	.610
1976—Rochester	.638
Syracuse (2nd)†	.590
1977—Pawtucket	.571
Charleston (2nd)‡	.557
1978—Charleston	.607
Richmond (4th)†	.511
1979—Columbus‡	.612
1980—Columbus‡	.593
1981—Columbus‡	.633
1982—Tidewater (3rd)†	.540
Rochester	.514
1983—Richmond	.576
Tidewater†	.511
1984—Maine	.566
Pawtucket†	.536
1985—Tidewater†	.540
Columbus	.540

*Won split-season playoff. †Won four-team playoff. ‡Won championship and four-team playoff. §Defeated Havana in game to decide fourth place, then won four-team playoff. xLeague was divided into Northern, Southern divisions. yLeague divided into American, National divisions. (NOTE—Known as Eastern League in 1884, New York State League in 1885, International League in 1886-87, International Association in 1888, International League in 1889-90, Eastern Association in 1891, and Eastern League from 1892 until 1912.)

STANDING OF CLUBS AT CLOSE OF SEASON, SEPTEMBER 1

Club	Rich.	Roch.	Paw.	Tide.	Syr.	Tol.	Col.	Me.	W.	L.	T.	Pct.	G.B.
Richmond (Braves)	....	14	9	7	14	11	9	16	80	60	0	.571	....
Rochester (Orioles)	6	....	10	12	11	13	12	11	75	63	0	.543	4
Pawtucket (Red Sox)	11	9	....	12	9	9	13	11	74	65	0	.532	5½
Tidewater (Mets)	13	8	8	....	7	16	9	13	74	66	0	.529	6
Syracuse (Blue Jays)	6	9	11	13	....	10	10	13	72	67	0	.518	7½
Toledo (Twins)	9	7	11	4	9	....	14	8	62	77	0	.446	17½
Columbus (Yankees)	11	7	7	11	10	6	....	10	62	77	0	.446	17½
Maine (Indians)	4	9	9	7	7	12	10	....	58	82	0	.414	22

Maine club represented Old Orchard Beach, Me.

Tidewater club represented Norfolk and Portsmouth, Va.

Major league affiliations in parentheses.

Playoffs—Richmond defeated Tidewater, three games to none; Rochester defeated Pawtucket, three games to one; Richmond defeated Rochester, three games to two, to win Governor's Cup.

Regular-Season Attendance—Columbus, 548,417; Maine, 105,578; Pawtucket, 186,517; Richmond, 381,364; Rochester, 308,807; Syracuse, 187,758; Tidewater, 171,589; Toledo, 145,909. Total—2,035,759. Playoffs, 43,912.

Managers—Columbus, Barry Foote; Maine, Jim Napier; Pawtucket, Ed Nottle; Richmond, Roy Majtyka; Rochester, John Hart; Syracuse, Doug Ault; Tidewater, Sam Perlozzo; Toledo, Charlie Manuel.

All-Star Team—1B—Pat Dodson, Pawtucket; 2B—Mike Sharperson, Syracuse; 3B—Dave Magadan, Tidewater; SS—Paul Zuvella, Richmond-Columbus; OF—Mike Greenwell, Pawtucket; Gerald Perry, Richmond; LaSchelle Tarver, Pawtucket; C—Pat Dempsey, Toledo; DH—Pete Dalena, Columbus; Starting Pitcher—John Mitchell, Tidewater; Relief Pitcher—Randy Myers, Tidewater; Rookie of the Year—Orestes Destrade, Columbus; Most Valuable Player—Pat Dodson, Pawtucket; Most Valuable Pitcher—John Mitchell, Tidewater; Manager of the Year—John Hart, Rochester.

(Compiled by Howe News Bureau, Boston, Mass.)

CLUB BATTING

Club	Pct.	G.	AB.	R.	OR.	H.	TB.	2B.	3B.	HR.	RBI.	GW.	SH.	SF.	HP.	BB.	Int. BB.	SO.	SB.	CS.	LOB.
Tidewater	.273	140	4667	594	564	1275	1724	210	37	55	541	66	51	43	15	480	32	715	105	34	1041
Pawtucket	.272	139	4515	633	598	1229	1805	210	21	108	592	69	52	36	32	500	20	657	124	59	995
Syracuse	.270	139	4619	623	574	1247	1849	211	38	105	572	69	31	38	33	481	24	774	80	69	968
Toledo	.263	139	4609	561	638	1213	1762	194	14	109	520	58	31	36	27	401	26	661	72	42	948
Rochester	.261	138	4514	619	575	1176	1843	218	31	129	568	69	27	47	22	500	31	710	91	47	976
Richmond	.260	140	4463	648	581	1159	1705	216	30	90	590	77	46	45	27	603	28	716	195	67	992
Maine	.257	140	4486	539	592	1153	1747	217	19	113	505	53	51	42	18	479	23	722	99	72	946
Columbus	.254	139	4564	566	661	1161	1731	208	52	86	509	57	41	33	28	430	19	692	88	59	935

INDIVIDUAL BATTING

(Leading Qualifiers for Batting Championship—378 or More Plate Appearances)

*Bats lefthanded. †Switch-hitter.

Player and Club	Pct.	G.	AB.	R.	H.	TB.	2B.	3B.	HR.	RBI.	GW.	SH.	SF.	HP.	BB.	Int. BB.	SO.	SB.	CS.
David, Andre, Toledo*	.328	111	348	55	114	164	18	1	10	44	5	0	3	3	53	8	19	0	0
Perry, Gerald, Richmond*	.326	107	384	69	125	195	30	5	10	75	17	0	3	4	58	8	41	22	11
Tarver, LaSchelle, Pawtucket*	.320	97	375	68	120	149	19	2	2	26	4	7	2	3	42	1	51	31	11
Magadan, David, Tidewater*	.311	133	473	68	147	195	33	6	1	64	10	2	9	3	84	5	45	2	2
Zuvella, Paul, Columbus	.302	89	334	56	101	122	13	1	2	31	3	6	1	1	41	0	19	11	2
Dempsey, Patrick, Toledo	.300	107	363	47	109	166	21	0	12	46	5	1	1	1	14	2	40	0	3
Pedrique, Alfredo, Tidewater	.293	112	379	49	111	128	13	2	0	41	7	9	8	2	28	1	31	7	0
Gallagher, David, Maine	.292	132	497	59	145	202	23	5	8	44	5	12	2	1	41	1	41	19	12
Jefferson, Stanley, Tidewater†	.290	95	369	60	107	140	19	4	2	37	3	2	1	2	41	4	65	25	7
Sharperson, Michael, Syracuse	.289	133	519	86	150	198	18	9	4	45	6	4	1	7	69	1	67	17	13
Carreon, Mark, Tidewater	.289	115	426	62	123	180	23	2	10	64	8	1	2	3	50	5	42	12	4

Departmental Leaders: G—Runge, 138; AB—Hernandez, 522; R—Sharperson, 86; H—Sharperson, 150; TB—Gerhart, 232; 2B—Hernandez, 35; 3B—Sharperson, 9; HR—Gerhart, 28; RBI—Dodson, 102; GWRBI—Perry, 17; SH—Gallagher, 12; SF—Mata, 10; HP—D. Williams, 9; BB—Runge, 92; IBB—David, McGriff, Perry, 8; SO—Komminsk, 124; SB—Hall, 72; CS—Hall, 16.

(All Players—Listed Alphabetically)

Player and Club	Pct.	G.	AB.	R.	H.	TB.	2B.	3B.	HR.	RBI.	GW.	SH.	SF.	HP.	BB.	Int. BB.	SO.	SB.	CS.
Aikens, Willie, Tidewater*	.133	4	15	2	2	2	0	0	0	0	0	0	0	0	2	0	3	0	0
Allen, Roderick, Maine	.266	73	252	33	67	106	7	1	10	52	10	1	4	1	31	0	46	4	4
Anderson, Richard, Tidewater	.000	22	2	0	0	0	0	0	0	0	0	1	0	0	0	0	0	0	0
Armstrong, Michael, Columbus	.500	31	2	0	1	3	0	1	0	0	0	0	0	0	0	0	1	0	0
Arnsberg, Bradley, Columbus	.000	29	1	0	0	0	0	0	0	0	0	0	0	0	0	0	1	0	0
Barrett, Thomas, Columbus†	.333	2	9	0	3	3	0	0	0	1	0	0	0	0	0	0	3	0	0
Beane, William, Toledo	.294	32	126	17	37	57	5	0	5	17	3	0	0	2	4	2	16	7	0
Beauchamp, Kash, Syracuse	.263	55	198	23	52	86	11	1	7	21	2	1	0	1	13	0	44	6	4
Benzinger, Todd, Pawtucket†	.252	90	314	41	79	129	13	2	11	32	4	1	3	1	23	2	76	7	5
Berenyi, Bruce, Tidewater	.000	10	2	0	0	0	0	0	0	0	0	1	0	0	0	0	2	0	0
Blocker, Terry, Tidewater*	.288	117	434	53	125	175	13	5	9	47	4	4	2	0	30	4	69	21	6
Brunenkant, Barry, Maine	.262	18	42	1	11	15	1	0	1	5	1	2	0	0	5	0	4	0	0
Buckley, Kevin, Maine	.234	109	342	34	80	147	23	1	14	51	2	1	4	0	43	4	84	1	0
Cannizzaro, Chris, Pawtucket†	.268	118	407	65	109	138	19	2	2	36	4	8	2	2	76	2	41	8	4
Carmichael, Alan, Tidewater	.375	3	8	1	3	3	0	0	0	1	1	1	1	0	1	0	2	0	0
Carreon, Mark, Tidewater	.289	115	426	62	123	180	23	2	10	64	8	1	2	3	50	5	42	12	4
Castillo, Martin, Toledo	.251	124	423	48	106	156	26	0	8	45	9	2	3	3	32	1	67	1	2
Castro, Jose, Syracuse	.288	122	413	52	119	180	19	3	12	54	6	5	5	1	45	3	34	0	8
Cecchetti, George, Maine*	.197	71	152	10	30	42	3	0	3	9	0	3	0	1	20	1	36	1	1
Chiffer, Floyd, Richmond	.000	37	2	0	0	0	0	0	0	0	0	0	0	0	0	0	0	0	0
Christensen, John, Pawtucket	.234	62	175	27	41	56	0	0	5	22	4	2	2	4	33	2	38	5	4
Clark, David, Maine*	.279	106	355	56	99	177	17	2	19	58	4	2	2	3	52	5	70	6	5
Clary, Martin, Richmond	.143	24	7	0	1	1	0	0	0	0	0	2	0	0	0	0	2	0	0
Colbert, Richard, Toledo	.286	3	7	0	2	2	0	0	0	1	0	0	0	0	0	0	4	1	0
Corcoran, Timothy, Tidewater*	.260	86	273	21	71	88	10	2	1	24	2	3	1	1	22	3	24	2	1
Cotto, Henry, Columbus	.248	97	359	45	89	139	17	6	7	48	4	1	1	4	19	1	53	16	6
Curry, Stephen, Richmond	.091	4	11	2	1	1	0	0	0	0	0	0	0	0	0	0	2	0	0
Dalena, Peter, Columbus*	.260	123	435	54	113	184	27	4	12	72	10	1	7	2	44	3	48	4	1
David, Andre, Toledo*	.328	111	348	55	114	164	18	1	10	44	5	0	3	3	53	8	19	0	0
Davidson, Mark, Toledo	.248	108	383	55	95	143	16	1	10	38	5	1	4	4	37	0	91	4	6

Player and Club	Pct.	G.	AB.	R.	H.	TB.	2B.	3B.	HR.	RBI.	GW.	SH.	SF.	HP.	BB.	Int. BB.	SO.	SB.	CS.
Davis, Michael, Tidewater	.230	74	217	17	50	68	10	1	2	20	2	1	2	0	14	0	24	0	0
DeFrancesco, Anthony, Pawtucket	.159	20	44	6	7	10	3	0	0	4	1	2	0	0	5	0	9	0	0
DeJesus, Ivan, Columbus	.262	25	84	10	22	27	3	1	0	15	2	2	3	0	10	0	10	4	3
Dempsey, Patrick, Toledo	.300	107	363	47	109	166	21	0	12	46	5	1	1	1	14	2	40	0	3
Destrade, Orestes, Columbus†	.276	98	359	59	99	185	21	4	19	56	4	0	3	0	40	5	88	1	4
Diaz, Jose, Syrcause	.000	12	9	1	0	0	0	0	0	0	0	0	0	0	1	0	2	0	1
Dodd, Thomas, Rochester	.163	17	49	7	8	17	1	1	2	6	0	1	0	1	9	0	10	0	0
Dodson, Patrick, Pawtucket*	.269	120	416	60	112	218	23	1	27	102	12	2	4	2	59	3	93	4	3
Dugas, Shanie, Maine*	.262	69	195	25	51	84	9	0	8	32	0	0	2	1	19	1	38	3	0
Edens, Thomas, Tidewater	.500	11	2	1	1	1	0	0	0	0	0	1	0	0	1	0	0	0	0
Eichelberger, Juan, Richmond	.000	32	2	0	0	0	0	0	0	0	0	0	0	0	0	0	2	0	0
Escobar, Jose, Syracuse	.245	62	143	12	35	46	5	0	2	14	2	5	0	1	4	0	14	2	1
Espino, Juan, Columbus	.302	53	179	21	54	76	5	1	5	21	3	2	0	4	14	1	17	1	3
Espinoza, Alvaro, Toledo	.281	73	253	18	71	87	8	1	2	27	2	7	1	0	6	1	30	1	1
Estes, Frank, Richmond*	.255	103	302	37	77	103	12	4	2	35	4	1	5	1	43	5	22	2	9
Evans, Barry, Maine	1.000	1	1	0	1	1	0	0	0	0	0	0	0	0	0	0	0	0	0
Falcone, David, Rochester*	.333	4	15	4	5	9	1	0	1	4	0	0	0	0	3	0	4	0	0
Ferreira, Anthony, Tidewater*	.200	24	5	1	1	2	1	0	0	1	0	1	0	0	3	0	1	0	0
Fielder, Cecil, Syracuse	.280	88	325	47	91	164	13	3	18	68	15	0	3	3	32	3	91	0	0
Frobel, Douglas, Tidewater*	.249	109	354	49	88	147	18	4	11	53	4	1	3	1	28	5	107	6	1
Funderburk, Mark, Toledo	.168	47	149	14	25	40	3	0	4	15	1	0	2	1	14	1	32	0	1
Gallagher, David, Maine	.292	132	497	59	145	202	23	5	8	44	5	12	2	1	41	1	41	19	12
Gardenhire, Ronald, Tidewater	.276	96	323	41	89	119	10	4	4	33	4	5	1	0	44	1	48	11	5
Geren, Robert, Columbus	.254	68	205	24	52	94	15	3	7	25	4	1	0	2	21	0	60	1	2
Gerhart, Kenneth, Rochester	.274	124	453	73	124	232	18	3	28	72	7	0	2	3	39	2	105	8	9
Gibbons, John, Tidewater	.246	96	317	42	78	103	16	0	3	27	3	4	2	1	41	2	69	0	0
Glavine, Thomas, Richmond*	.000	7	1	0	0	0	0	0	0	0	0	0	0	0	0	0	0	0	0
Glynn, Edward, Tidewater	.000	45	2	0	0	0	0	0	0	0	0	0	0	0	0	0	2	0	0
Graham, Lee, Richmond*	.223	40	121	15	27	36	4	1	1	14	0	2	0	1	10	0	15	4	1
Green, Otis, Syracuse*	.281	122	480	66	135	190	24	8	5	53	6	3	5	6	32	0	62	12	10
Greenwell, Michael, Pawtucket*	.300	89	320	62	96	173	21	1	18	59	8	0	7	2	43	4	20	6	2
Gulliver, Glenn, Rochester*	.118	11	17	4	2	6	1	0	1	1	0	0	0	0	7	1	0	0	0
Gutierrez, Joaquin, Rochester	.303	54	198	29	60	74	7	2	1	22	2	2	0	1	20	0	19	5	0
Gwosdz, Douglas, Tidewater	.063	5	16	0	1	1	0	0	0	1	0	1	1	0	0	0	4	0	0
Hall, Albert, Richmond†	.270	125	441	73	119	152	18	3	3	41	6	5	3	4	70	6	48	72	16
Hart, Michael, Rochester*	.256	123	438	63	112	180	25	2	13	50	5	2	4	2	74	4	57	8	4
Hawkins, Johnny, Columbus	.000	4	10	1	0	0	0	0	0	0	0	0	0	0	2	0	2	0	0
Hearn, Edward, Tidewater	.265	22	83	7	22	29	4	0	1	12	1	0	2	0	10	0	13	0	0
Hearron, Jeffrey, Syracuse	.247	92	320	31	79	121	19	1	7	36	2	1	3	3	25	2	56	0	1
Heath, Kelly, Richmond	.267	102	300	46	80	134	17	2	11	47	3	2	4	2	50	0	51	9	3
Hernandez, Leonardo, Columbus	.272	136	522	62	142	212	35	1	11	64	4	1	1	0	16	1	50	5	5
Hinshaw, George, Maine	.316	39	117	18	37	55	10	1	2	9	3	2	2	0	11	0	20	5	0
Holman, Dale, 37 Syr-12 Rich*	.279	49	147	18	41	56	9	0	2	21	1	1	1	1	10	0	15	0	0
Holmes, Stanley, Toledo	.239	24	71	12	17	31	2	0	4	14	1	0	1	0	7	0	8	1	0
Horn, Samuel, Pawtucket*	.195	20	77	8	15	26	2	0	3	14	3	0	0	0	5	1	23	0	1
Howe, Gregory, Toledo	.333	22	81	16	27	45	6	0	4	7	2	3	0	0	12	0	21	5	5
Hudler, Rex, Rochester	.260	77	219	29	57	81	12	3	2	13	3	3	0	0	16	1	32	12	4
Hughes, Keith, Columbus*	.125	2	8	0	1	1	0	0	0	0	0	0	0	0	0	0	2	0	0
Infante, Alexis, Syracuse	.275	57	193	27	53	63	6	2	0	15	1	3	0	1	15	1	20	6	2
Ingle, Randy, Richmond	.318	8	22	1	7	10	1	1	0	1	0	0	0	0	1	0	5	0	0
Jefferson, Stanley, Tidewater†	.290	95	369	60	107	140	19	4	2	37	3	2	1	2	41	4	65	25	7
Johnston, Christopher, Syracuse	.285	117	414	58	118	208	33	3	17	68	6	0	6	3	48	1	105	1	2
Jones, Michael, Richmond*	.000	25	2	0	0	0	0	0	0	0	0	0	0	0	0	0	2	0	0
Jones, Ricky, Rochester	.251	123	443	49	111	169	25	3	9	56	13	1	7	4	15	0	54	1	2
Komminsk, Brad, Richmond	.234	133	465	67	109	178	22	4	13	65	8	1	5	2	69	1	124	29	3
Lane, Eric, Maine	.000	3	3	1	0	0	0	0	0	0	0	0	0	0	0	0	2	0	0
Leach, Terry, Tidewater	.000	34	1	1	0	0	0	0	0	0	0	0	0	0	1	0	0	0	0
Lee, Manuel, Syracuse†	.246	76	236	34	58	69	6	1	1	19	3	3	0	0	21	0	39	7	9
Little, Bryan, Columbus†	.267	50	176	16	47	58	8	0	1	17	3	9	2	0	17	1	8	3	4
Lomastro, Gerardo, Toledo	.178	46	118	9	21	34	4	0	3	12	0	0	1	0	9	0	22	0	0
Lombardi, Phillip, Columbus	.292	75	277	43	81	125	12	4	8	28	4	2	1	3	32	1	40	5	5
Lyden, Mitchell, Columbus	.000	2	7	0	0	0	0	0	0	0	0	0	0	0	1	0	1	0	0
Lyons, Barry, Tidewater	.295	61	234	28	69	97	16	0	4	46	10	2	7	1	18	2	32	0	0
Magadan, David, Tidewater*	.311	133	473	68	147	195	33	6	1	64	10	2	9	3	84	5	45	2	2
Marte, Alexis, Toledo*	.202	36	94	13	19	22	0	0	1	3	0	1	0	1	11	0	15	11	6
Mata, Victor, Columbus	.275	105	375	37	103	138	19	5	2	41	7	4	10	1	18	1	66	5	6
Mazzilli, Lee, Tidewater†	.300	6	20	3	6	10	1	0	1	1	0	0	0	0	3	0	2	2	0
McCarthy, Thomas, Tidewater	.000	22	3	0	0	0	0	0	0	0	0	1	0	0	1	0	2	0	0
McGriff, Frederick, Syracuse*	.259	133	468	69	121	209	23	4	19	74	12	0	8	4	83	8	119	0	3
McNealy, Derwin, Columbus*	.269	119	428	58	115	138	10	5	1	29	3	6	2	1	49	0	48	24	13
McPhail, Marlin, Tidewater	.250	42	104	16	26	36	2	1	2	8	1	0	0	0	8	0	17	2	1
Meacham, Robert, Columbus†	.140	46	150	14	21	31	0	5	0	11	1	4	1	3	16	0	30	2	2
Mesh, Michael, Pawtucket	.256	93	270	36	69	90	9	3	2	25	4	6	1	2	28	0	37	16	6
Miller-Jones, Gary, Pawtucket†	.227	108	343	45	78	111	12	3	5	41	2	4	3	0	23	5	43	8	1
Milligan, Randy, Tidewater	.083	21	60	3	5	5	0	0	0	3	0	0	0	0	9	0	15	0	0
Mitchell, John, Tidewater	.167	27	6	1	1	1	0	0	0	0	0	2	0	0	0	0	4	0	0
Mitchell, Robert, Syracuse*	.276	93	228	43	63	92	12	1	5	25	2	2	2	0	48	3	29	6	5
Morhardt, Gregory, Toledo*	.253	88	293	32	74	100	14	0	4	27	2	2	3	3	14	1	25	0	0
Mullins, Francis, Maine	.271	30	107	9	29	42	8	1	1	8	0	1	1	1	14	1	15	0	5
Niemann, Randy, Tidewater	.500	7	4	1	2	2	0	0	0	0	0	0	0	0	1	0	1	0	0
Noboa, Milciades, Maine	.286	108	399	44	114	149	21	1	4	32	3	8	3	2	15	0	33	10	14
O'Malley, Thomas, Rochester*	.307	59	212	36	65	102	10	0	9	30	1	0	4	0	41	3	24	0	1
Olson, Gregory, Tidewater	.327	19	55	11	18	19	1	0	0	7	0	1	1	0	5	0	7	1	0
Owen, Lawrence, Richmond	.196	98	265	32	52	74	13	0	3	21	5	6	0	0	44	2	49	3	2
Pardo, Alberto, Rochester†	.213	76	253	34	54	92	12	1	8	34	5	0	2	0	31	1	57	0	0
Paris, Kelly, Rochester	.249	87	309	43	77	130	16	2	11	48	6	2	5	1	22	2	35	9	8
Pasqua, Daniel, Columbus*	.291	32	110	25	32	59	3	3	6	20	2	0	0	0	32	0	29	1	1
Pastornicky, Clifford, Maine	.220	34	91	14	20	35	6	0	3	14	2	2	1	0	5	0	10	0	0
Pedrique, Alfredo, Tidewater	.293	112	379	49	111	128	13	2	0	41	7	9	8	2	28	1	31	7	0
Perry, Gerald, Richmond*	.326	107	384	69	125	195	30	5	10	75	17	0	3	4	58	8	41	22	11
Pittaro, Christopher, Toledo†	.256	107	418	50	107	151	14	3	8	37	6	3	3	3	42	3	55	10	8
Poole, Mark, Syracuse	.000	2	3	0	0	0	0	0	0	0	0	0	0	0	1	0	0	0	0
Puleo, Charles, Richmond	.000	27	5	0	0	0	0	0	0	0	0	0	0	0	0	0	1	0	0

Player and Club	Pct.	G.	AB.	R.	H.	TB.	2B.	3B.	HR.	RBI.	GW.	SH.	SF.	HP.	BB.	Int. BB.	SO.	SB.	CS.
Quinones, Rey, Pawtucket	.264	24	87	12	23	37	2	0	4	18	3	2	0	1	8	0	12	2	0
Rabb, John, Richmond	.266	123	414	73	110	198	19	6	19	78	8	0	6	2	57	5	101	9	5
Ralston, Robert, Toledo	.240	73	204	18	49	54	5	0	0	14	0	4	1	1	9	0	20	6	1
Ramirez, Mario, Toledo	.219	16	32	3	7	7	0	0	0	4	0	0	0	0	3	0	4	0	0
Rayford, Floyd, Rochester	.285	38	137	17	39	62	11	0	4	17	3	0	0	1	18	0	23	1	0
Reddish, Michael, Rochester	.295	58	149	24	44	65	9	0	4	18	0	1	1	3	28	1	36	4	2
Reed, Jeffrey, Toledo*	.310	25	71	10	22	36	5	3	1	14	0	3	1	0	17	0	9	0	0
Reed, Jody, Pawtucket	.282	69	227	27	64	78	11	0	1	30	3	7	4	1	31	0	18	8	2
Robertson, Andre, 38 Col-52 Rich	.187	90	262	25	49	66	6	1	3	15	0	7	0	3	21	1	43	3	2
Rohn, Daniel, Maine*	.217	82	276	38	60	74	14	0	0	12	2	6	2	0	48	0	31	9	6
Romine, Kevin, Pawtucket	.292	71	257	30	75	101	8	3	4	32	2	1	3	1	15	0	30	11	4
Runge, Paul, Richmond	.275	138	458	76	126	173	27	1	6	59	9	9	8	3	92	0	57	16	6
Sanchez, Alejandro, Toledo	.272	99	349	47	95	146	19	1	10	47	6	2	4	2	19	2	68	17	4
Sax, David, Pawtucket	.289	99	322	31	93	141	19	1	9	49	5	4	2	0	43	0	49	0	2
Scott, Donald, Rochester†	.272	59	173	17	47	59	7	1	1	16	2	2	2	1	16	2	18	1	1
Scott, Richard, Columbus	.270	58	159	20	43	65	12	2	2	16	1	0	0	2	15	0	35	6	3
Sharperson, Michael, Syracuse	.289	133	519	86	150	198	18	9	4	45	6	4	1	7	69	1	67	17	13
Sheaffer, Danny, Pawtucket	.340	79	265	34	90	114	16	1	2	30	2	3	1	1	10	0	24	9	6
Shepherd, Ronald, Syracuse	.211	34	128	14	27	40	4	0	3	17	0	0	1	0	11	1	24	3	4
Shields, Stephen, Richmond	.000	21	14	0	0	0	0	0	0	0	0	0	0	0	0	0	5	0	0
Simmons, Nelson, Rochester†	.273	89	304	33	83	130	13	5	8	37	7	5	5	0	27	2	53	4	1
Sinatro, Matthew, Richmond	.197	28	66	8	13	21	2	0	2	7	2	2	1	0	5	0	12	0	2
Sisk, Douglas, Tidewater	.000	9	1	0	0	0	0	0	0	0	0	0	0	0	0	0	0	0	0
Smajstrla, Craig, Maine†	.292	90	319	42	93	108	9	3	0	20	3	2	1	1	32	0	29	13	8
Smith, Kenneth, Rochester*	.154	40	91	16	14	28	3	1	3	6	2	2	0	0	17	0	19	4	1
Smith, Keith, Columbus†	.163	18	49	5	8	11	1	1	0	0	0	1	0	0	3	0	9	0	0
Snyder, Cory, Maine	.302	49	192	25	58	104	19	0	9	32	3	1	3	1	17	1	39	2	3
Soper, Michael, Columbus	.196	55	179	11	35	42	3	2	0	12	3	4	0	3	7	0	13	3	1
Sorce, Samuel, Toledo	.000	3	10	0	0	0	0	0	0	0	0	0	0	0	0	0	1	0	0
Sosa, Miguel, Columbus	.154	4	13	3	2	2	0	0	0	0	0	0	0	1	0	0	3	0	0
Speck, Clifford, Richmond	.000	24	4	0	0	0	0	0	0	0	0	0	0	0	0	0	2	0	0
Springer, Steven, Tidewater	.273	117	440	52	120	163	19	6	4	46	5	5	0	1	30	0	74	10	5
Stefero, John, Rochester*	.258	25	62	8	16	23	1	0	2	7	0	0	0	0	13	2	20	0	1
Stegman, David, Columbus	.176	67	187	22	33	54	8	2	3	15	1	1	1	0	42	3	40	1	0
Stenhouse, David, Syracuse	.284	68	197	13	56	67	8	0	1	18	2	2	0	0	11	0	22	0	1
Stenhouse, Michael, Pawtucket*	.259	49	166	28	43	71	9	2	5	23	5	0	1	2	35	0	23	3	2
Strucher, Mark, Richmond	.252	78	206	24	52	83	16	0	5	32	2	1	4	1	16	0	35	3	0
Tabler, Patrick, Maine	.250	3	12	5	3	4	1	0	0	1	0	0	1	0	2	0	1	0	0
Tarver, LaSchelle, Pawtucket*	.320	97	375	68	120	149	19	2	2	26	4	7	2	3	42	1	51	31	11
Thornton, Louis, Syracuse*	.260	64	231	34	60	74	4	2	2	28	3	1	3	2	14	1	33	20	5
Tiburcio, Fredrick, Richmond*	.267	84	247	33	66	87	8	2	3	25	4	1	1	2	15	0	39	16	5
Tingley, Ronald, 9 Rich-49 Maine	.201	58	174	13	35	48	2	1	3	13	1	3	1	0	12	0	36	2	0
Torve, Kelvin, Rochester*	.242	109	356	39	86	116	16	1	4	41	9	0	4	0	37	0	43	5	2
Traber, James, Rochester*	.279	87	323	46	90	149	19	2	12	55	0	0	7	3	21	6	38	11	4
Treadway, Andre, Richmond	.000	15	1	0	0	0	0	0	0	0	0	2	0	0	0	0	1	0	0
Tremblay, Gary, Pawtucket	.200	29	80	10	16	27	2	0	3	8	1	0	0	1	4	0	29	0	0
Tumpane, Robert, Richmond*	.256	81	242	27	62	97	11	0	8	48	6	0	4	3	29	1	44	0	0
Ullger, Scott, Toledo	.262	121	413	50	108	167	10	2	15	57	5	0	4	2	51	0	63	0	0
Vaughn, DeWayne, Tidewater	.000	25	6	0	0	0	0	0	0	0	0	0	0	0	1	0	3	0	0
Washington, Randy, Maine	.211	104	285	37	60	97	13	0	8	29	0	4	3	2	48	2	55	1	2
Washington, Ronald, Toledo	.268	49	198	22	53	70	6	1	3	19	1	2	2	0	12	2	32	8	5
Weaver, James, Maine*	.239	100	293	42	70	118	11	2	11	28	3	0	2	1	41	5	61	21	10
Wiggins, Alan, Rochester†	.205	17	44	2	9	11	2	0	0	3	0	1	1	0	1	0	3	3	1
Wilborn, Thaddeus, Rochester†	.289	52	152	28	44	62	7	4	1	10	0	4	1	1	18	2	30	9	5
Williams, Dana, Pawtucket	.268	101	370	43	99	136	22	0	5	41	2	3	1	9	17	0	41	6	6
Williams, Jeffrey, Rochester*	.100	17	20	4	2	2	0	0	0	1	1	1	0	0	5	1	5	0	0
Wilson, James, Maine	.232	116	405	33	94	143	20	1	9	57	11	2	8	3	23	2	80	3	2
Wilson, William, Tidewater†	.258	9	31	4	8	9	1	0	0	4	1	0	0	0	3	0	7	4	2
Winters, Matthew, Columbus*	.291	33	86	14	25	33	3	1	1	9	1	0	1	0	12	1	11	1	0
Woods, Alvis, Toledo*	.268	72	205	24	55	84	12	1	5	32	5	0	2	1	35	3	19	0	0
Wyatt, David, Tidewater	.500	23	2	0	1	1	0	0	0	1	0	2	0	0	1	0	0	0	0
Yost, Edgar, Richmond	.294	8	17	0	5	5	0	0	0	0	0	0	0	0	0	0	4	0	0
Young, Michael, Rochester†	.278	32	97	14	27	44	2	0	5	21	3	0	2	1	22	1	25	6	1
Ziem, Stephen, Richmond	.286	15	7	0	2	2	0	0	0	0	0	0	0	0	0	0	3	0	0
Zuvella, Paul, 66 Rich-23 Col	.302	89	334	56	101	122	13	1	2	31	3	6	1	1	41	0	19	11	2

The following pitchers, listed alphabetically by club, with games in parentheses, had no plate appearances, primarily through use of designated hitters:

COLUMBUS—Augustine, Gerald (34); Bradley, Bert (17); Byron, Timothy (16); Bystrom, Martin (13); Christiansen, Clay (7); Drabek, Douglas (8); Faulk, Kelly (21); Fisher, Brian (6); Frey, Steven (11); Fulton, William (12); Graham, Randle (44); Holland, Alfred (11); Nielsen, Scott (19); Patterson, Scott (38); Pries, Jeffrey (8); Pulido, Alfonso (23); Rijo, Jesus (3); Schmidt, Eric (5); Silva, Mark (5); Tewksbury, Robert (2); Tirado, Aristarco (8).

MAINE—Creel, Keith (27); Hagen, Kevin (28); Jones, Douglas (43); Murphy, Michael (7); Noles, Dickie (3); Oelkers, Bryan (9); Pippin, Craig (45); Ritter, Reggie (29); Roberts, Scott (35); Roman, Jose (16); Rowe, Thomas (33); Schulze, Donald (3); Waddell, Thomas (3); Wardle, Curtis (35); Wills, Frank (22); Yett, Richard (1).

PAWTUCKET—Bolton, Thomas (29); Brown, Michael (7); Crawford, Steven (5); Dalton, Michael (37); Davis, Charles (6); Ellsworth, Steven (15); Johnson, Mitchell (18); Leister, John (23); Mecerod, George (32); Rochford, Michael (28); Schiraldi, Calvin (31); Sellers, Jeffrey (15); Trujillo, Michael (42); Woodward, Robert (18).

RICHMOND—Alvarez, Evelio (5); Beard, David (45); Gnacinski, Paul (3); Hodge, Eddie (16); Long, Robert (10); Olwine, Edward (20); Ward, Duane (6).

ROCHESTER—Arnold, Tony (38); Augustine, Gerald (5); Ballard, Jeffrey (2); Bell, Eric (11); DeLeon, Luis (49); Fowlkes, Alan (2); Habyan, John (26); Huffman, Phillip (24); Jones, Odell (17); Kinnunen, Michael (47); Kucharski, Joseph (3); Martinez, Dennis (4); Martinez, Felix (3); Rasmussen, Eric (31); Skinner, Michael (26); Snell, Nathaniel (16); Stranski, Scott (3); Swaggerty, William (26); Wilson, Roger (6).

SYRACUSE—Alba, Gibson (28); Aquino, Luis (43); Beckwith, Joseph (23); Carlucci, Richard (37); Cerutti, John (7); Clarke, Stanley (31); Cooper, Donald (32); Davis, Steven (23); Gilliam, Keith (33); Gordon, Donald (25); Howard, Dennis (2); Hudson, Anthony (28); Leal, Luis (34); McLaughlin, Colin (6); Musselman, Ronald (33); Peraza, Oswald (2); Ward, Duane (14); Wells, David (3).

TIDEWATER—Burns, Thomas (54); Fultz, William (7); Lynch, Edward (4); Myers, Randall (45).

TOLEDO—Agosto, Juan (21); Anderson, Allan (11); Broersma, Eric (10); Brown, Mark (3); Burtt, Dennis (24); Christiansen, Clay (11); Clay, Danny (31); Eufemia, Frank (43); Heimueller, Gorman (32); Hodge, Eddie (5); Latham, William (21); Leggatt, Richard (33); Mitchell, Charles (41); Portugal, Mark (6); Romero, Ramon (5); Smith, Leroy (9); Straker, Lester (20).

GRAND SLAM HOME RUNS—Dodson, Ullger, Young, 2 each; Blocker, Christensen, Clark, Dalena, David, Dugas, Gallagher, Gardenhire, Horn, Lyons, Magadan, Noboa, Perry, Rabb, Sax, Sheaffer, Strucher, 1 each.

AWARDED FIRST BASE ON CATCHER'S INTERFERENCE—Frobel 3 (Owen 2, Espino); Dalena 2 (Buckley, Owen); Paris 2 (Buckley, Gibbons); Edens (Owen); Infante (Buckley); Pedrique (Buckley); Runge (Gibbons); Sosa (Buckley).

CLUB FIELDING

Club	Pct.	G.	PO.	A.	E.	DP.	PB.
Rochester	.976	138	3545	1490	125	162	7
Maine	.975	140	3549	1439	126	140	16
Syracuse	.975	139	3624	1524	134	125	17
Richmond	.974	140	3559	1381	130	125	12
Pawtucket	.973	139	3512	1402	135	128	18
Tidewater	.973	140	3633	1643	146	162	8
Toledo	.972	139	3585	1517	149	155	14
Columbus	.967	139	3584	1455	173	143	15

INDIVIDUAL FIELDING

*Throws lefthanded.

FIRST BASEMEN

Player and Club	Pct.	G.	PO.	A.	E.	DP.
Aikens, Tidewater	1.000	3	24	3	0	4
Benzinger, Pawtucket	1.000	3	21	0	0	3
Buckley, Maine	1.000	8	51	1	0	2
Castillo, Toledo	1.000	3	13	2	0	1
Cecchetti, Maine*	.994	67	448	34	3	38
Corcoran, Tidewater*	.998	59	495	32	1	60
Curry, Richmond	1.000	1	7	0	0	0
Delena, Columbus	.996	59	496	37	2	50
David, Toledo*	1.000	1	2	0	0	0
Davis, Tidewater	.988	30	228	16	3	26
Destrade, Columbus	.986	79	697	63	11	77
Dodson, Pawtucket*	.987	120	983	77	14	100
Estes, Richmond*	.989	29	168	6	2	21
Falcone, Rochester	.957	3	21	1	1	4
Fielder, Syracuse	1.000	7	59	3	0	3
Funderburk, Toledo	.960	3	24	0	1	1
Geren, Columbus	.963	3	23	3	1	3
Hearn, Tidewater	.993	14	137	10	1	14
Holmes, Toledo	.800	1	7	1	2	1
Horn, Pawtucket*	1.000	6	61	4	0	5
Johnston, Syracuse	.900	1	8	1	1	0
Jones, Rochester	1.000	1	4	1	0	1
Lyons, Tidewater	.985	35	314	15	5	25
Magadan, Tidewater	1.000	1	5	1	0	0
Mazzilli, Tidewater	1.000	3	25	0	0	2
McGRIFF, Syracuse*	.992	131	1219	85	10	108
McPhail, Tidewater	1.000	1	2	0	0	1
Milligan, Tidewater	.985	7	60	4	1	6
Morhardt, Toledo*	.990	83	725	50	8	71
Pedrique, Tidewater	1.000	5	42	1	0	7
Perry, Richmond	.990	42	270	21	3	28
Reddish, Rochester	1.000	13	81	3	0	6
Sax, Pawtucket	1.000	8	57	3	0	5
Stenhouse, Pawtucket	.984	7	61	1	1	7
Strucher, Richmond	.993	21	129	18	1	8
Torve, Rochester	.992	71	555	51	5	75
Traber, Rochester*	.997	65	557	54	2	65
Tumpane, Richmond*	.995	75	565	44	3	49
Ullger, Toledo	.994	61	455	38	3	67
Weaver, Maine*	1.000	1	12	1	0	0
Wilson, Maine	.990	89	723	71	8	92

SECOND BASEMEN

Player and Club	Pct.	G.	PO.	A.	E.	DP.
Barrett, Columbus	1.000	1	3	2	0	0
Cannizzaro, Pawtucket	.978	49	85	140	5	23
Curry, Richmond	.889	2	3	5	1	1
DeJesus, Columbus	1.000	3	5	13	0	3
Diaz, Syracuse	1.000	3	2	1	0	0
Dugas, Maine	1.000	9	7	18	0	2
Escobar, Syracuse	.909	7	3	7	1	1
Espinoza, Toledo	1.000	3	11	7	0	2
Gardenhire, Tidewater	.959	45	91	141	10	39
Gulliver, Rochester	.968	9	12	18	1	2
Heath, Richmond	1.000	5	8	9	0	1
Hudler, Rochester	.964	61	125	171	11	48
Jones, Rochester	.971	75	148	223	11	63
Lee, Syracuse	.980	17	45	52	2	16
Little, Columbus	.986	45	86	121	3	30
McPhail, Tidewater	1.000	2	3	3	0	1
Meacham, Columbus	.956	17	37	50	4	16
MILLER-JONES, Pawtucket	.9839	97	166	263	7	65
Noboa, Maine	.966	62	111	169	10	38
O'Malley, Rochester	1.000	1	1	1	0	0
Paris, Rochester	1.000	1	1	2	0	0
Pedrique, Tidewater	1.000	2	6	10	0	1
Pittaro, Toledo	.994	33	69	106	1	30
Ralston, Toledo	.959	60	135	169	13	44
Ramirez, Toledo	.974	14	15	23	1	2
Robertson, Columbus	.959	31	46	93	6	20
Rohn, Maine	.500	1	0	1	1	0
Runge, Richmond	.9834	135	269	383	11	85
Scott, Columbus	.931	33	63	85	11	20
Sharperson, Syracuse	.974	122	249	348	16	63
Smajstrla, Maine	.976	76	134	226	9	47
Smith, Columbus	.978	10	19	26	1	8
Sosa, Columbus	1.000	3	4	10	0	3
Springer, Tidewater	.963	99	222	317	21	86
Ullger, Toledo	.981	24	42	60	2	10
Washington, Toledo	.976	25	58	66	3	19
Wiggins, Rochester	.974	9	18	20	1	6
Wilborn, Rochester	1.000	1	1	4	0	0
Zuvella, Columbus	1.000	1	2	7	0	3

THIRD BASEMEN

Player and Club	Pct.	G.	PO.	A.	E.	DP.
Barrett, Columbus	1.000	1	0	3	0	1
Brunenkant, Maine	1.000	2	0	6	0	1
Cannizzaro, Pawtucket	.852	32	21	54	13	7
Castillo, Toledo	.912	83	57	151	20	21
Castro, Syracuse	.928	119	74	222	23	24
Diaz, Syracuse	1.000	4	0	1	0	0
Dugas, Maine	.957	30	24	66	4	5
Escobar, Syracuse	.951	23	7	32	2	1
Greenwell, Pawtucket	.826	8	5	14	4	2
Heath, Richmond	.905	30	22	54	8	5
Hernandez, Columbus	.931	134	102	265	27	25
Hinshaw, Maine	.000	1	0	0	1	0
Holman, Syracuse	1.000	2	1	2	0	0
Holmes, Toledo	.818	6	2	7	2	0
Hudler, Rochester	.826	9	5	14	4	2
Ingle, Richmond	.900	3	3	6	1	0
Komminsk, Richmond	.911	113	90	198	28	19
MAGADAN, Tidewater	.934	130	73	283	25	31
McPhail, Tidewater	.867	6	4	9	2	0
Mesh, Pawtucket	.943	52	38	78	7	10
Noboa, Maine	.941	19	9	23	2	4
O'Malley, Rochester	.951	57	45	110	8	11
Paris, Rochester	.927	50	32	95	10	14
Pastornicky, Maine	.905	33	28	39	7	6
Pedrique, Tidewater	.909	4	2	8	1	1
Pittaro, Toledo	1.000	12	9	18	0	2
Ralston, Toledo	1.000	8	3	8	0	0
Rayford, Rochester	.972	28	20	50	2	4
Rohn, Maine	1.000	5	7	5	0	0
Sax, Pawtucket	.902	67	43	95	15	8
D. Scott, Rochester	1.000	1	1	0	0	0
R. Scott, Columbus	1.000	7	3	7	0	0
Sharperson, Syracuse	.949	12	8	28	2	2
Smajstrla, Maine	.867	9	11	15	4	3
Smith, Columbus	1.000	4	0	1	0	0
Snyder, Maine	.943	49	46	86	8	10
Springer, Tidewater	1.000	5	3	13	0	0
Stegman, Columbus	1.000	2	1	3	0	0
Ullger, Toledo	.961	25	19	54	3	8
Washington, Toledo	.918	23	18	38	5	6

SHORTSTOPS

Player and Club	Pct.	G.	PO.	A.	E.	DP.
Cannizzaro, Pawtucket	.955	24	30	34	3	13
Davis, Tidewater	1.000	1	0	2	0	0
DeJesus, Columbus	.938	19	31	59	6	8
Diaz, Syracuse	1.000	2	0	1	0	0
Dugas, Maine	.957	14	16	29	2	10
Escobar, Syracuse	.972	28	46	92	4	12
Espinoza, Toledo	.967	70	159	198	12	58
Gardenhire, Tidewater	.960	45	70	147	9	27
Gutierrez, Rochester	.948	54	93	146	13	39
Heath, Richmond	.949	27	37	56	5	13
Hudler, Rochester	1.000	1	2	6	0	2
Infante, Syracuse	.946	57	73	172	14	29
Ingle, Richmond	.938	6	5	10	1	1
Jones, Rochester	.942	52	73	140	13	35
Lee, Syracuse	.944	58	87	185	16	34
Little, Columbus	.909	3	4	6	1	2
Meacham, Columbus	.941	27	44	83	8	18
Mesh, Pawtucket	.922	32	58	72	11	18
Mullins, Maine	.972	30	37	100	4	17
Noboa, Maine	.990	28	40	60	1	17
Paris, Rochester	.965	37	59	107	6	34
PEDRIQUE, Tidewater	.962	101	139	321	18	74
Pittaro, Toledo	.962	66	98	202	12	37
Quinones, Pawtucket	.962	24	35	67	4	18
Ralston, Toledo	1.000	4	6	15	0	3
Reed, Pawtucket	.966	69	115	222	12	40
Robertson, 7 Col-51 Rich	.956	59	82	134	10	30
Rohn, Maine	.959	75	119	208	14	47
Runge, Richmond	.762	4	6	10	5	1
Scott, Columbus	.929	9	10	29	3	9
Smajstrla, Maine	.889	1	3	5	1	1
Smith, Columbus	.824	5	7	7	3	0
Snyder, Maine	1.000	1	0	1	0	0
Soper, Columbus	.959	55	101	157	11	42
Springer, Tidewater	.917	1	3	8	1	1
Washington, Toledo	.917	2	3	8	1	2
Zuvella, 66 Rich-20 Col	.974	86	147	224	10	51

OUTFIELDERS

Player and Club	Pct.	G.	PO.	A.	E.	DP.
Allen, Maine	1.000	40	64	2	0	1
Beane, Toledo	.944	26	68	0	4	0
Beauchamp, Syracuse	.970	55	126	3	4	3
Benzinger, Pawtucket	.986	66	135	4	2	0
Blocker, Tidewater*	.974	115	249	11	7	2
Buckley, Maine	1.000	4	3	1	0	0
Cannizzaro, Pawtucket	1.000	1	2	0	0	0
Carreon, Tidewater*	.971	112	192	6	6	2
Castillo, Toledo	.951	22	38	1	2	0
Castro, Syracuse	1.000	8	10	1	0	0
Christensen, Pawtucket	1.000	48	83	2	0	0
Clark, Maine	.963	84	150	4	6	2
Corcoran, Tidewater*	1.000	13	20	2	0	1
Cotto, Columbus	.965	96	215	5	8	3
David, Toledo*	.981	81	150	9	3	2
Davidson, Toledo	.974	107	290	8	8	1
Davis, Tidewater	.979	32	45	1	1	0
Dodd, Rochester	1.000	5	8	0	0	0
Estes, Richmond*	1.000	51	88	1	0	0
Fielder, Syracuse	.984	38	58	2	1	0
Frobel, Tidewater	.942	43	61	4	4	0
Funderburk, Toledo	1.000	12	18	1	0	1
GALLAGHER, Maine	.997	129	341	14	1	0
Gerhart, Rochester	.970	119	216	11	7	2
Graham, Richmond*	.978	38	83	4	2	0
Green, Syracuse*	.968	119	226	13	8	3
Greenwell, Pawtucket	.970	63	125	6	4	0
Hall, Richmond	.975	120	264	8	7	0
Hart, Rochester*	.986	122	283	6	4	1
Heath, Richmond	.966	41	81	5	3	3
Hinshaw, Maine	.976	20	38	3	1	2
Holman, 33 Syr-10 Rich	.983	43	54	3	1	0
Holmes, Toledo	1.000	2	4	0	0	0
Howe, Toledo	.983	22	58	1	1	1
Hudler, Rochester	1.000	4	3	0	0	0
Hughes, Columbus*	.857	2	6	0	1	0
Jefferson, Tidewater	.991	93	219	5	2	0
Johnston, Syracuse	.957	28	43	1	2	0
Komminsk, Richmond	.951	24	37	2	2	1
LoMastro, Toledo	.947	33	50	4	3	0
Lombardi, Columbus	.967	29	58	0	2	2
Marte, Toledo*	.966	31	55	1	2	1
Mata, Columbus	.931	103	195	6	15	0
Mazzilli, Tidewater	1.000	2	3	1	0	0
McNealy, Columbus*	.976	116	358	4	9	1
McPhail, Tidewater	1.000	19	29	1	0	0
Mesh, Pawtucket	.971	13	30	4	1	0
Mitchell, Syracuse*	1.000	87	173	3	0	1
Morhardt, Toledo*	.889	4	8	0	1	0
Pasqua, Columbus*	.954	32	62	0	3	0
Perry, Richmond	.970	73	124	4	4	2
Rabb, Richmond	.989	42	85	3	1	0
Reddish, Rochester	1.000	5	12	0	0	0
Romine, Pawtucket	.988	64	162	2	2	2
Sanchez, Toledo	.949	95	176	9	10	3
Scott, Columbus	1.000	3	5	0	0	0
Shepherd, Syracuse	.976	34	80	3	2	1
Simmons, Rochester	.986	88	134	8	2	1
Springer, Tidewater	.875	3	7	0	1	0
Stegman, Columbus	.955	26	40	2	2	2
Stenhouse, Pawtucket	1.000	2	1	0	0	0
Tarver, Pawtucket*	.972	81	205	6	6	2
Thornton, Syracuse	.967	61	114	5	4	0
Tiburcio, Richmond*	.973	69	141	4	4	0
Traber, Rochester*	.974	21	35	2	1	0
Tumpane, Richmond*	1.000	1	1	0	0	0
Ullger, Toledo	1.000	16	20	0	0	0
Washington, Maine	.976	95	158	5	4	0
Weaver, Maine*	.967	68	143	5	5	2
Wilborn, Rochester	.948	32	52	3	3	0
D. Williams, Pawtucket	.995	92	183	6	1	2
J. Williams, Rochester*	1.000	12	9	0	0	0
Wilson, Tidewater	1.000	8	19	1	0	0
Winters, Columbus	1.000	27	56	2	0	0
Young, Rochester	.968	27	58	3	2	1

CATCHERS

Player and Club	Pct.	G.	PO.	A.	E.	DP.	PB.
Brunenkant, Maine	1.000	13	54	2	0	0	0
Buckley, Maine	.976	88	433	45	12	5	12
Carmichael, Tidewater	1.000	3	13	3	0	0	0
Castillo, Toledo	.990	20	91	10	1	0	2
Colbert, Toledo	1.000	3	13	1	0	0	0
DeFrancesco, Pawtucket	.977	19	81	5	2	0	2
Dempsey, Toledo	.980	99	432	52	10	5	7
Espino, Columbus	.980	53	227	16	5	1	5
Geren, Columbus	.986	58	247	33	4	2	7
GIBBONS, Tidewater	.993	92	483	51	4	6	5
Gwosdz, Tidewater	.969	5	29	2	1	0	1
Hawkins, Columbus	1.000	4	11	0	0	0	0
Hearn, Tidewater	1.000	6	33	5	0	1	0
Hearron, Syracuse	.984	90	502	53	9	7	10
Lane, Maine	1.000	2	6	0	0	0	1
Lombardi, Columbus	.973	33	164	16	5	2	3
Lyden, Columbus	1.000	1	1	0	0	0	0
Lyons, Tidewater	.992	23	109	10	1	3	1
Olson, Tidewater	.975	18	104	13	3	1	1
Owen, Richmond	.978	97	511	69	13	11	5
Pardo, Rochester	.991	62	321	27	3	4	3
Poole, Syracuse	.857	2	6	0	1	0	0
Rayford, Rochester	.978	7	40	4	1	0	1
Reed, Toledo	.985	25	108	22	2	4	5
Sax, Pawtucket	.985	33	125	7	2	0	4
Scott, Rochester	.991	57	305	22	3	5	2
Sheaffer, Pawtucket	.988	78	380	39	5	6	4
Sinatro, Richmond	.986	24	124	18	2	2	0
Sorce, Toledo	1.000	3	6	1	0	0	0
Stefero, Rochester	1.000	24	117	13	0	0	1
Stenhouse, Syracuse	.988	62	283	36	4	2	7
Strucher, Richmond	.984	28	110	13	2	2	7
Tingley, 9 Rich-48 Maine	.981	57	280	23	6	5	3
Tremblay, Pawtucket	.975	29	146	7	4	2	8
Yost, Richmond	1.000	7	26	2	0	0	0

PITCHERS

Player and Club	Pct.	G.	PO.	A.	E.	DP.
Agosto, Toledo*	1.000	21	1	9	0	0
Alba, Syracuse*	1.000	28	0	5	0	0
Alvarez, Richmond	1.000	5	1	2	0	1
A. Anderson, Toledo*	.889	11	1	7	1	2
R. Anderson, Tidewater	1.000	22	2	20	0	1
Aquino, Syracuse	1.000	43	2	4	0	0
Armstrong, Columbus	1.000	31	7	8	0	0
Arnold, Rochester	.955	38	5	16	1	2
Arnsberg, Columbus	.940	28	21	26	3	3
Augustine, 5 Roch-34 Col*	1.000	39	3	8	0	0
Ballard, Rochester*	1.000	2	0	1	0	0
Beard, Richmond	1.000	45	4	7	0	1
Beckwith, Syracuse	.964	23	7	20	1	2
Bell, Rochester*	1.000	11	2	12	0	1
Berenyi, Tidewater	.667	10	3	3	3	0
Bolton, Pawtucket*	.973	29	6	30	1	2
Bradley, Columbus	1.000	17	2	4	0	0
Broersma, Toledo	1.000	10	3	2	0	1
Mi. Brown, Pawtucket	.909	7	2	8	1	1
Burns, Tidewater	.818	54	1	8	2	1
Burtt, Toledo	.921	24	5	30	3	3
Byron, Columbus	.933	16	6	8	1	4
Bystrom, Columbus	.909	13	6	4	1	2
Carlucci, Syracuse	1.000	37	5	8	0	0
Cerutti, Syracuse*	.889	7	3	5	1	0
Chiffer, Richmond	1.000	37	3	10	0	1
Christiansen, 7 Col-11 Tol	.917	18	5	6	1	1
Clarke, Syracuse*	.952	31	6	14	1	1
Clary, Richmond	1.000	24	17	13	0	0
Clay, Toledo	1.000	29	13	15	0	2
Cooper, Syracuse	1.000	32	4	7	0	0
Crawford, Pawtucket	1.000	5	1	0	0	0
Creel, Maine	.955	27	13	29	2	4
Dalena, Columbus	1.000	1	0	1	0	0
Dalton, Pawtucket*	.947	37	5	13	1	0
C. Davis, Pawtucket	1.000	6	4	2	0	0
S. Davis, Syracuse*	1.000	23	3	7	0	0
DeLeon, Rochester	1.000	49	3	18	0	1
Drabek, Columbus	1.000	8	4	6	0	1
Edens, Tidewater	1.000	11	4	6	0	1
Eichelberger, Richmond	1.000	32	5	4	0	0
Ellsworth, Pawtucket	1.000	15	3	15	0	0
Eufemia, Toledo	1.000	43	6	8	0	0
Faulk, Columbus	.870	21	7	13	3	1
Ferreira, Tidewater*	.923	24	2	22	2	2
Fisher, Columbus	1.000	6	0	1	0	1
Frey, Columbus*	1.000	11	0	4	0	1
Fulton, Columbus	.810	12	5	12	4	1
Fultz, Tidewater	1.000	7	1	1	0	0
Gilliam, Syracuse*	1.000	33	2	9	0	1
Glavine, Richmond*	1.000	7	2	4	0	0
Glynn, Tidewater*	.909	45	1	9	1	1
Gnacinski, Richmond	1.000	3	0	1	0	1
GORDON, Syracuse	1.000	25	12	20	0	2
Graham, Columbus	1.000	44	11	12	0	0
Habyan, Rochester	.967	26	12	17	1	1
Hagen, Maine	.964	27	14	39	2	6
Heimueller, Toledo*	1.000	32	2	23	0	2
Hodge, 5 Tol-16 Rich*	1.000	21	0	4	0	1
Holland, Columbus*	1.000	11	0	4	0	0
Howard, Syracuse	1.000	2	0	2	0	0
Hudson, Syracuse	1.000	28	7	14	0	3
Huffman, Rochester	1.000	24	10	11	0	3
Johnson, Pawtucket	.895	18	10	7	2	0
D. Jones, Maine	.970	43	14	18	1	3
M. Jones, Richmond*	.926	25	5	20	2	1
O. Jones, Rochester	1.000	17	6	6	0	0
Kinnunen, Rochester*	.864	47	7	12	3	0
Kucharski, Rochester	1.000	3	2	1	0	0
Latham, Toledo*	.970	21	9	23	1	0
Leach, Tidewater	.882	34	6	9	2	1
Leal, Syracuse	.850	34	4	13	3	2
Leggatt, Toledo	1.000	33	3	6	0	1
Leister, Pawtucket	1.000	23	10	15	0	2
Long, Richmond	1.000	10	1	3	0	0
Lynch, Tidewater	1.000	4	2	2	0	0
D. Martinez, Rochester	.714	4	2	3	2	0
F. Martinez, Rochester*	1.000	3	1	2	0	0
McCarthy, Tidewater	.964	22	13	14	1	3
McLaughlin, Syracuse	1.000	6	1	0	0	0
Mecerod, Pawtucket	.962	32	11	14	1	1
C. Mitchell, Toledo	1.000	41	9	15	0	2
J. Mitchell, Tidewater	.932	27	13	28	3	2
Murphy, Maine	1.000	7	3	6	0	0
Musselman, Syracuse	.974	33	5	32	1	3
Myers, Tidewater*	1.000	45	3	8	0	0
Nielsen, Columbus	.941	19	10	22	2	3
Niemann, Tidewater*	1.000	7	2	13	0	0
Noles, Maine	1.000	3	1	1	0	0
Oelkers, Maine*	1.000	9	0	7	0	0
Olwine, Richmond*	1.000	20	2	4	0	0
Patterson, Columbus	1.000	38	5	4	0	1
Pippin, Maine	1.000	45	7	9	0	1
Portugal, Toledo	.833	6	4	6	2	0
Pries, Columbus	1.000	8	4	3	0	0
Puleo, Richmond	.964	27	13	14	1	2
Pulido, Columbus*	.967	23	6	23	1	0
Rasmussen, Rochester	.947	31	8	10	1	0
Rios, Columbus	.500	3	0	1	1	0
Ritter, Maine	1.000	29	12	11	0	2
Roberts, Maine	.875	35	2	5	1	0
Rochford, Pawtucket*	1.000	28	5	23	0	0
Roman, Maine	.750	16	5	10	5	1
Romero, Toledo*	.333	5	0	1	2	0
ROWE, Maine	1.000	29	12	20	0	3
Schiraldi, Pawtucket	1.000	31	4	2	0	0
Schmidt, Columbus	1.000	5	2	0	0	0
Schulze, Maine	1.000	3	0	1	0	0
Sellers, Pawtucket	.941	15	5	27	2	2
Shields, Richmond	.963	21	11	15	1	1
Silva, Columbus	1.000	5	1	2	0	0
Sisk, Tidewater	1.000	9	2	4	0	1
Skinner, Rochester	1.000	26	16	15	0	1
Smith, Toledo	.917	9	4	7	1	0
Snell, Rochester	.909	16	5	5	1	1
Speck, Richmond	1.000	24	6	16	0	0
Straker, Toledo	.923	18	6	18	2	0
Swaggerty, Rochester	.982	26	16	38	1	4
Tewksbury, Columbus	1.000	2	1	4	0	1
Tirado, Columbus	.667	8	2	0	1	1
Treadway, Richmond	1.000	15	3	2	0	2
Trujillo, Pawtucket	.955	42	3	18	1	3
Vaughn, Tidewater	.926	25	9	16	2	1
Waddell, Maine	1.000	3	0	2	0	0
Ward, 6 Rich-14 Syr	.960	20	13	11	1	1
Wardle, Maine*	.955	35	8	13	1	1
Wells, Syracuse*	1.000	3	1	1	0	0
Wills, Maine	1.000	22	2	2	0	0
Wilson, Rochester*	.909	6	3	7	1	0
Woodward, Pawtucket	.957	18	6	16	1	1
Wyatt, Tidewater*	.929	23	6	20	2	1
Yett, Maine	1.000	1	0	1	0	0
Ziem, Richmond	1.000	15	3	16	0	0

The following players do not have any recorded accepted chances at the positions indicated; therefore, are not listed in the fielding averages for those particular positions: Ma. Brown, p; Buckley, p; Byron, of; Cecchetti, of; Dalena, c; M. Davis, 3b, p; Estes, p; Evans, 2b; Fowlkes, p; Gulliver, 3b; Hagen, of; Komminsk, 1b; McGriff, of; Miller-Jones, p; Peraza, p; Rohn, of; Sheaffer, of; Sinatro, 3b; Smajstrla, of; D. Stenhouse, 1b; Stranski, p; Strucher, 2b, 3b, of.

CLUB PITCHING

Club	ERA.	G.	CG.	ShO.	Sv.	IP.	H.	R.	ER.	HR.	HB.	BB.	Int. BB.	SO.	WP.	Bk.
Tidewater	3.60	140	15	10	39	1211.0	1183	564	484	97	27	474	22	737	37	8
Richmond	3.73	140	37	11	25	1186.1	1129	581	492	83	26	573	20	785	73	5
Syracuse	3.75	139	13	10	38	1208.0	1151	574	503	103	27	478	15	761	50	14
Maine	3.84	140	18	7	27	1183.0	1230	592	505	99	25	428	27	705	73	5
Rochester	3.94	138	28	6	39	1181.2	1197	575	517	103	24	467	37	730	54	5
Pawtucket	4.06	139	26	10	32	1170.2	1189	598	528	109	19	480	35	692	32	10
Columbus	4.19	139	12	6	33	1194.2	1253	661	556	111	32	474	23	621	38	14
Toledo	4.26	139	25	8	25	1195.0	1281	638	566	90	22	500	24	616	61	7

PITCHERS' RECORDS

(Leading Qualifiers for Earned-Run Average Leadership—112 or More Innings)

*Throws lefthanded.

Pitcher—Club	W.	L.	Pct.	ERA.	G.	GS.	CG.	GF.	ShO.	Sv.	IP.	H.	R.	ER.	HR.	HB.	BB.	Int. BB.	SO.	WP.
D. Jones, Maine	5	6	.455	2.09	43	3	0	21	0	9	116.1	105	35	27	6	0	27	5	98	4
Shields, Richmond	9	8	.529	2.59	21	20	6	1	0	0	149.1	133	55	43	5	2	55	2	124	9

Pitcher—Club	W.	L.	Pct.	ERA.	G.	GS.	CG.	GF.	ShO.	Sv.	IP.	H.	R.	ER.	HR.	HB.	BB.	Int. BB.	SO.	WP.
Speck, Richmond	8	5	.615	2.77	24	13	6	5	2	1	120.1	98	43	37	5	2	51	1	102	8
Musselman, Syracuse	9	7	.563	3.03	33	20	1	2	0	1	145.2	125	60	49	5	5	55	2	90	7
Woodward, Pawtucket	9	6	.600	3.17	18	18	8	0	4	0	127.2	114	55	45	11	2	42	1	73	3
Hagen, Maine	8	11	.421	3.28	27	23	4	0	2	0	164.2	181	75	60	7	8	55	2	62	12
J. Mitchell, Tidewater	12	9	.571	3.39	27	27	5	0	2	0	172.1	162	78	65	10	6	59	2	83	7
Nielsen, Columbus	11	7	.611	3.47	19	19	4	0	0	0	116.2	123	52	45	13	4	38	0	44	2
Puleo, Richmond	14	7	.667	3.49	27	27	9	0	3	0	170.0	166	80	66	13	6	76	0	124	12
Rochford, Pawtucket*	11	10	.524	3.53	28	25	3	0	1	0	170.2	178	76	67	20	1	50	2	70	6

Departmental Leaders: G—Burns, 54; W—Puleo, 14; L—Arnsberg, Creel, 12; Pct.—Bell, O. Jones, Ritter, .700; GS—Arnsberg, 28; CG—Puleo, Swaggerty, 9; GF—Trujillo, 36; ShO—Woodward, 4; Sv.—DeLeon, 13; IP—Arnsberg, 177.1; H—Swaggerty, 204; R—Arnsberg, 106; ER—Arnsberg, Clay, Swaggerty, 83; HR—Skinner, 23; HB—Hagen, 8; BB—Clay, 93; IBB—Six pitchers with six; SO—Puleo, Shields, 124; WP—Pippin, 19.

(All Pitchers—Listed Alphabetically)

Pitcher—Club	W.	L.	Pct.	ERA.	G.	GS.	CG.	GF.	ShO.	Sv.	IP.	H.	R.	ER.	HR.	HB.	BB.	Int. BB.	SO.	WP.
Agosto, Toledo*	4	3	.571	2.31	21	0	0	18	0	6	35.0	33	11	9	0	1	14	0	29	4
Alba, Syracuse*	2	1	.667	4.62	28	0	0	15	0	2	37.0	36	21	19	5	1	28	0	27	1
Alvarez, Richmond	0	0	.000	2.89	5	0	0	0	0	0	9.1	9	5	3	0	1	4	0	6	1
A. Anderson, Toledo*	2	5	.286	4.57	11	11	2	0	0	0	67.0	78	39	34	3	0	31	2	37	3
R. Anderson, Tidewater	7	2	.778	2.68	22	8	1	5	1	0	84.0	76	26	25	8	0	16	0	56	1
Aquino, Syracuse	3	7	.300	2.88	43	6	0	27	0	10	84.1	70	30	27	7	1	34	2	60	5
Armstrong, Columbus	6	9	.400	4.08	31	14	0	12	0	4	106.0	103	54	48	8	1	53	2	103	2
Arnold, Rochester	4	3	.571	1.95	38	1	0	21	0	8	87.2	92	25	19	3	2	14	4	49	2
Arnsberg, Columbus	8	12	.400	4.21	28	28	6	0	2	0	177.1	168	106	83	15	1	53	1	96	4
Augustine, 5 Roch-34 Col*	3	6	.333	4.14	39	2	0	18	0	6	63.0	63	32	29	5	0	24	2	35	0
Ballard, Rochester*	0	2	.000	7.11	2	2	0	0	0	0	6.1	11	6	5	1	1	3	0	7	0
Beard, Richmond	6	6	.500	3.92	45	0	0	20	0	6	64.1	65	40	28	3	1	29	3	62	2
Beckwith, Syracuse	9	6	.600	3.88	23	23	1	0	1	0	125.1	123	59	54	8	0	46	0	97	3
Bell, Rochester*	7	3	.700	3.05	11	11	4	0	0	0	76.2	68	26	26	3	0	35	1	59	7
Berenyi, Tidewater	2	6	.250	6.61	10	9	1	1	0	0	47.0	55	46	36	8	0	27	0	48	3
Bolton, Pawtucket*	3	4	.429	2.72	29	7	1	11	0	2	86.0	80	30	26	6	0	25	2	58	1
Bradley, Columbus	1	1	.500	6.30	17	2	0	7	0	0	30.0	38	21	21	4	0	6	1	5	2
Broersma, Toledo	1	2	.333	3.13	10	0	0	6	0	0	23.0	17	9	8	3	1	9	1	12	0
Ma. Brown, Toledo	0	1	.000	9.00	3	2	0	0	0	0	11.0	16	12	11	3	0	7	0	8	1
Mi. Brown, Pawtucket	1	4	.200	4.68	7	7	1	0	0	0	42.1	51	27	22	4	0	16	0	27	0
Buckley, Maine	0	0	.000	2.25	3	0	0	2	0	0	4.0	5	1	1	0	0	0	0	1	0
Burns, Tidewater	3	4	.429	2.80	54	0	0	35	0	11	74.0	62	28	23	3	3	40	6	39	1
Burtt, Toledo	9	10	.474	4.62	24	19	5	1	2	0	134.1	151	78	69	4	1	52	0	46	7
Byron, Columbus	1	2	.333	3.86	16	7	0	6	0	1	56.0	67	27	24	6	0	22	1	30	4
Bystrom, Columbus	4	1	.800	3.42	13	9	0	3	0	1	55.1	63	24	21	6	3	20	1	28	1
Carlucci, Syracuse	5	3	.625	2.05	37	0	0	17	0	8	61.1	37	19	14	2	2	23	0	45	6
Cerutti, Syracuse*	1	3	.250	4.12	7	7	2	0	1	0	43.2	44	27	20	5	0	16	0	22	1
Chiffer, Richmond	4	1	.800	2.29	37	0	0	23	0	5	74.2	67	22	19	2	0	24	3	51	1
Christiansen, 7 Col-11 Tol	5	4	.556	5.24	18	7	1	6	0	0	77.1	88	49	45	6	1	29	1	42	3
Clarke, Syracuse*	8	9	.471	3.89	31	18	2	9	1	4	138.2	138	68	60	14	5	57	2	64	6
Clary, Richmond	7	6	.538	4.35	24	22	3	1	1	0	132.1	118	72	64	12	1	82	1	56	9
Clay, Toledo	8	11	.421	4.93	29	25	3	1	1	0	151.2	147	92	83	15	3	93	0	105	8
Cooper, Syracuse	5	5	.500	3.80	32	6	0	14	0	4	68.2	64	30	29	11	0	28	1	42	4
Crawford, Pawtucket	1	1	.500	6.00	5	0	0	4	0	2	6.0	10	4	4	1	0	1	0	2	0
Creel, Maine	6	12	.333	3.92	27	27	6	0	1	0	172.0	181	97	75	19	6	49	3	85	2
Dalena, Columbus	0	0	.000	0.00	1	0	0	1	0	0	2.0	0	0	0	0	0	2	0	2	0
Dalton, Pawtucket*	6	2	.750	5.02	37	6	0	22	0	1	71.2	84	43	40	4	4	34	3	49	7
C. Davis, Pawtucket	2	3	.400	7.33	6	6	0	0	0	0	27.0	33	29	22	7	2	25	2	12	0
M. Davis, Tidewater	0	0	.000	18.00	1	0	0	1	0	0	1.0	4	5	2	2	0	1	0	0	0
S. Davis, Syracuse*	5	7	.417	5.59	23	19	1	1	0	0	104.2	104	67	65	15	2	57	0	80	5
DeLeon, Rochester	4	8	.333	3.48	49	0	0	34	0	13	75.0	68	31	29	5	3	32	6	53	2
Drabek, Columbus	1	4	.200	7.29	8	8	0	0	0	0	42.0	50	36	34	9	0	25	0	23	0
Edens, Tidewater	5	3	.625	4.55	11	11	2	0	1	0	61.1	71	33	31	5	1	28	1	31	4
Eichelberger, Richmond	7	4	.636	4.09	32	0	0	22	0	6	44.0	40	22	20	3	0	25	4	44	8
Ellsworth, Pawtucket	6	2	.750	3.36	15	13	2	1	0	0	83.0	82	33	31	9	0	19	2	43	3
Estes, Richmond*	0	0	.000	27.00	1	0	0	1	0	0	1.0	1	3	3	0	0	5	0	0	0
Eufemia, Toledo	3	7	.300	4.32	43	3	0	27	0	10	91.2	104	51	44	8	2	35	6	44	3
Faulk, Columbus	8	4	.667	4.38	21	14	0	1	0	1	96.2	94	58	47	6	7	56	3	41	7
Ferreira, Tidewater*	7	5	.583	3.69	24	17	0	2	0	0	112.1	123	59	46	6	0	40	1	65	2
Fisher, Columbus	0	0	.000	4.15	6	0	0	5	0	2	8.2	8	4	4	0	0	3	0	4	1
Fowlkes, Rochester	0	1	.000	15.00	2	0	0	1	0	0	3.0	3	5	5	1	1	2	0	3	1
Frey, Columbus*	0	2	.000	8.05	11	0	0	2	0	0	19.0	29	17	17	3	0	10	1	11	0
Fulton, Columbus	4	6	.400	3.84	12	12	2	0	0	0	75.0	89	42	32	7	1	25	2	36	2
Fultz, Tidewater	1	1	.500	4.82	7	0	0	2	0	0	18.2	26	10	10	2	0	5	0	14	0
Gilliam, Syracuse*	6	2	.750	2.96	33	0	0	15	0	6	48.2	44	18	16	3	1	24	3	17	1
Glavine, Richmond*	1	5	.167	5.63	7	7	1	0	1	0	40.0	40	29	25	4	2	27	0	12	3
Glynn, Tidewater*	3	4	.429	2.56	45	0	0	18	0	3	63.1	33	22	18	11	0	34	5	63	3
Gnacinski, Richmond	0	0	.000	4.63	3	0	0	0	0	0	11.2	14	7	6	3	0	11	0	8	0
Gordon, Syracuse	8	5	.615	2.89	25	13	2	6	1	2	109.0	105	42	35	3	7	21	1	62	2
Graham, Columbus	4	1	.800	2.64	44	1	0	28	0	3	81.2	75	34	24	8	1	19	3	35	2
Habyan, Rochester	12	7	.632	4.29	26	25	5	0	1	0	157.1	168	82	75	13	1	69	2	93	10
Hagen, Maine	8	11	.421	3.28	27	23	4	0	2	0	164.2	181	75	60	7	8	55	2	62	12
Heimueller, Toledo*	3	8	.273	6.15	32	11	0	12	0	3	79.0	105	61	54	6	3	36	5	39	2
Hodge, 5 Tol-16 Rich*	3	5	.375	7.71	21	3	0	9	0	2	39.2	58	41	34	4	2	14	4	16	2
Holland, Columbus*	1	1	.500	1.45	11	0	0	10	0	6	18.2	15	5	3	1	0	7	0	13	0
Howard, Syracuse	0	0	.000	5.40	2	0	0	0	0	0	3.1	4	3	2	0	0	4	1	3	1
Hudson, Syracuse	2	3	.400	4.70	28	4	1	12	0	0	61.1	62	39	32	9	0	18	2	38	1
Huffman, Rochester	10	9	.526	5.11	24	23	1	0	0	0	130.1	139	78	74	12	5	56	4	84	8
Johnson, Pawtucket	4	5	.444	5.21	18	10	2	1	0	0	84.2	101	53	49	10	1	28	2	36	1
D. Jones, Maine	5	6	.455	2.09	43	3	0	21	0	9	116.1	105	35	27	6	0	27	5	98	4
M. Jones, Richmond*	7	6	.538	4.99	25	21	6	3	0	0	119.0	127	76	66	13	2	66	0	66	5
O. Jones, Rochester	7	3	.700	3.66	17	11	4	1	1	0	83.2	73	38	34	7	1	42	2	69	2
Kinnunen, Rochester*	1	3	.250	2.35	47	1	0	24	0	10	53.2	41	18	14	0	1	29	4	43	5
Kucharski, Rochester	0	2	.000	21.13	3	2	0	1	0	0	7.2	16	18	18	3	0	7	0	3	2
Latham, Toledo*	6	5	.545	3.57	21	21	5	0	3	0	133.2	155	64	53	8	1	43	2	48	3
Leach, Tidewater	4	4	.500	2.49	34	4	1	15	0	7	79.2	69	30	22	8	2	21	1	55	1

Pitcher—Club	W.	L.	Pct.	ERA.	G.	GS.	CG.	GF.	ShO.	Sv.	IP.	H.	R.	ER.	HR.	HB.	BB.	Int. BB.	SO.	WP.
Leal, Syracuse	3	4	.429	4.14	34	9	0	3	0	0	76.0	87	40	35	7	1	32	1	47	3
Leggatt, Toledo	1	4	.200	3.69	33	3	0	10	0	1	107.1	109	46	44	12	2	34	0	58	6
Leister, Pawtucket	8	7	.533	4.08	23	22	4	0	2	0	134.2	125	68	61	11	3	81	3	78	2
Long, Richmond	0	0	.000	5.21	10	0	0	3	0	1	19.0	13	11	11	2	1	16	1	12	0
Lynch, Tidewater	1	0	1.000	5.00	4	4	0	0	0	0	18.0	22	10	10	1	2	5	0	7	0
D. Martinez, Rochester	2	1	.667	6.05	4	4	0	0	0	0	19.1	18	14	13	5	0	9	0	14	0
F. Martinez, Rochester*	0	1	.000	6.00	3	2	0	0	0	0	6.0	7	4	4	0	0	3	0	4	1
McCarthy, Tidewater	3	2	.600	4.04	22	8	1	4	0	3	84.2	89	43	38	7	1	37	1	30	3
McLaughlin, Syracuse	0	0	.000	0.79	6	0	0	4	0	1	11.1	8	1	1	0	0	1	0	13	0
Mecerod, Pawtucket	4	5	.444	7.04	32	10	2	11	0	3	101.0	127	82	79	14	2	53	5	64	4
Miller-Jones, Pawtucket	0	0	.000	0.00	1	0	0	1	0	0	1.1	1	0	0	0	0	0	0	2	0
C. Mitchell, Toledo	6	6	.500	3.78	41	0	0	33	0	5	64.1	70	32	27	3	5	25	6	27	10
J. Mitchell, Tidewater	12	9	.571	3.39	27	27	5	0	2	0	172.1	162	78	65	10	6	59	2	83	7
Murphy, Maine	1	2	.333	3.82	7	5	0	1	0	0	37.2	36	22	16	2	0	19	0	15	2
Musselman, Syracuse	9	7	.563	3.03	33	20	1	2	0	1	145.2	125	60	49	5	5	55	2	90	7
Myers, Tidewater*	6	7	.462	2.35	45	0	0	35	0	12	65.0	44	19	17	2	2	44	3	79	2
Nielsen, Columbus	11	7	.611	3.47	19	19	4	0	0	0	116.2	123	52	45	13	4	38	0	44	2
Niemann, Tidewater*	3	1	.750	3.23	7	7	1	0	1	0	39.0	38	14	14	5	3	18	0	18	1
Noles, Maine	0	1	.000	4.50	3	3	0	0	0	0	10.0	11	6	5	1	0	4	0	4	0
Oelkers, Maine*	4	4	.500	2.42	9	9	2	0	1	0	52.0	49	18	14	3	0	17	0	28	3
Olwine, Richmond*	2	0	1.000	0.73	20	0	0	14	0	4	24.2	18	2	2	1	1	9	0	15	1
Patterson, Columbus	3	5	.375	5.13	38	0	0	22	0	6	54.1	69	37	31	4	7	26	2	26	5
Peraza, Syracuse	0	0	.000	11.57	2	0	0	0	0	0	2.1	3	3	3	0	0	4	0	2	0
Pippin, Maine	3	8	.273	4.95	45	3	0	30	0	3	87.1	88	54	48	8	1	41	6	66	19
Portugal, Toledo	5	1	.833	2.60	6	6	3	0	1	0	45.0	34	15	13	2	2	23	0	30	1
Pries, Columbus	1	3	.250	8.28	8	7	0	1	0	0	25.0	33	27	23	5	2	19	0	13	1
Puleo, Richmond	14	7	.667	3.49	27	27	9	0	3	0	170.0	166	80	66	13	6	76	0	124	12
Pulido, Columbus*	5	8	.385	2.92	23	10	0	5	0	3	95.2	93	41	31	6	2	25	1	28	1
Rasmussen, Rochester	4	3	.571	1.98	31	5	2	11	1	4	91.0	74	24	20	7	3	25	4	77	2
Rios, Columbus	0	1	.000	7.90	3	2	0	0	0	0	13.2	18	14	12	3	2	8	0	11	0
Ritter, Maine	7	3	.700	4.98	29	14	2	13	0	1	97.2	118	60	54	9	0	37	0	57	5
Roberts, Maine	4	7	.364	4.25	35	3	0	24	0	7	65.2	63	38	31	9	0	20	4	48	1
Rochford, Pawtucket*	11	10	.524	3.53	28	25	3	0	1	0	170.2	178	76	67	20	1	50	2	70	6
Roman, Maine	4	5	.444	4.23	16	16	1	0	0	0	95.2	95	50	45	10	2	52	0	76	5
Romero, Toledo*	0	1	.000	11.45	5	1	0	2	0	0	11.0	23	14	14	3	0	11	0	6	1
Rowe, Maine	5	9	.357	4.11	29	12	2	8	0	1	111.2	117	52	51	11	3	31	3	60	11
Schiraldi, Pawtucket	4	3	.571	2.86	31	0	0	26	0	12	44.0	32	19	14	2	0	20	4	59	0
Schmidt, Columbus	0	2	.000	9.58	5	1	0	1	0	0	10.1	15	12	11	1	0	8	1	5	0
Schulze, Maine	0	1	.000	6.30	3	3	0	0	0	0	10.0	12	7	7	1	0	4	0	7	0
Sellers, Pawtucket	7	4	.636	3.74	15	15	3	0	1	0	106.0	95	50	44	5	4	59	3	74	3
Shields, Richmond	9	8	.529	2.59	21	20	6	1	0	0	149.1	133	55	43	5	2	55	2	124	9
Silva, Columbus	0	1	.000	7.11	5	1	0	1	0	0	12.2	11	10	10	2	0	15	1	6	2
Sisk, Tidewater	2	3	.400	4.20	9	4	0	3	0	2	30.0	34	16	14	2	1	9	0	19	2
Skinner, Rochester	10	8	.556	4.18	26	26	3	0	1	0	161.1	166	87	75	23	4	58	1	96	0
Smith, Toledo	2	1	.667	1.51	9	9	1	0	0	0	53.2	42	12	9	4	0	16	0	39	4
Snell, Rochester	2	2	.500	4.44	16	0	0	11	0	4	24.1	25	13	12	3	0	12	4	9	0
Speck, Richmond	8	5	.615	2.77	24	13	6	5	2	1	120.1	98	43	37	5	2	51	1	102	8
Straker, Toledo	6	7	.462	3.44	18	18	5	0	0	0	107.1	102	46	41	10	0	44	2	50	5
Stranski, Rochester	0	0	.000	0.00	3	0	0	1	0	0	2.0	1	0	0	0	0	2	0	3	0
Swaggerty, Rochester	12	7	.632	4.25	26	25	9	0	0	0	175.2	204	92	83	15	2	52	2	56	9
Tewksbury, Columbus	1	0	1.000	2.70	2	2	0	0	0	0	10.0	6	3	3	0	0	2	0	4	0
Tirado, Columbus	0	0	.000	2.25	8	0	0	2	0	0	16.0	17	5	4	0	1	6	0	13	2
Treadway, Richmond	4	3	.571	5.53	15	9	0	2	0	0	53.2	64	36	33	2	1	25	0	28	6
Trujillo, Pawtucket	8	9	.471	2.66	42	0	0	36	0	12	84.2	76	29	25	5	0	27	6	45	2
Vaughn, Tidewater	6	8	.429	3.82	25	19	0	3	0	1	125.0	128	56	53	12	2	41	0	58	4
Waddell, Maine	0	0	.000	6.75	3	2	0	0	0	0	8.0	12	6	6	0	0	3	0	4	1
Ward, 6 Rich-14 Syr	7	5	.583	3.98	20	20	3	0	0	0	117.2	125	56	52	9	3	52	0	67	4
Wardle, Maine*	7	10	.412	4.14	34	15	1	6	0	0	113.0	113	58	52	8	4	57	3	71	7
Wells, Syracuse*	0	1	.000	9.82	3	0	0	1	0	0	3.2	6	4	4	0	0	1	0	2	0
Wills, Maine	4	3	.571	2.87	22	1	0	17	0	6	31.1	37	10	10	4	1	10	1	21	1
Wilson, Rochester*	0	0	.000	2.45	6	0	0	4	0	0	14.2	12	7	4	0	0	14	3	7	3
Woodward, Pawtucket	9	6	.600	3.17	18	18	8	0	4	0	127.2	114	55	45	11	2	42	1	73	3
Wyatt, Tidewater*	9	7	.563	4.04	23	22	3	1	0	0	133.2	147	69	60	5	4	49	2	72	3
Yett, Maine	0	0	.000	4.50	1	1	0	0	0	0	6.0	7	3	3	1	0	2	0	2	0
Ziem, Richmond	8	5	.615	3.08	15	15	6	0	1	0	96.1	88	38	33	12	3	34	1	48	6

BALKS—Arnsberg, 5; Clary, Faulk, 4 each; Alba, Cerutti, Clarke, Clay, S. Davis, Ferreira, Gordon, Heimueller, Niemann, Rochford, Wyatt, 2 each; A. Anderson, Arnold, Beckwith, Bolton, Cooper, C. Davis, Eufemia, Habyan, Hagen, Huffman, Johnson, Leach, Leister, J. Mitchell, Musselman, Nielsen, Patterson, Pippin, Pries, Ritter, Roman, Rowe, Schiraldi, Schmidt, Sellers, Skinner, Straker, Tewksbury, Trujillo, Ward, Wilson, Woodward, Ziem, 1 each.

COMBINATION SHUTOUTS—Arnsberg-Armstrong, Arnsberg-Frey-Graham-Patterson, Bystrom-Pulido, Bystrom-Graham, Columbus; Roberts-Jones-Wills, Wardle-Ritter, Rowe-Ritter, Maine; Dalton-Bolton-Schiraldi, Bolton-Schiraldi, Pawtucket; Clary-Beard, Shields-Olwine-Beard, Puleo-Chiffer-Beard, Richmond; Huffman-Snell, Bell-Arnold, Rochester; Clarke-Aquino, Davis-Carlucci-Leal-Alba-Gordon, Leal-Hudson-Gilliam, Beckwith-Hudson-Aquino, Aquino-Leal-Gilliam, Cooper-McLaughlin, Syracuse; Vaughn-Myers 2, Mitchell-Leach-Myers, Anderson-Myers, Leach-Wyatt, Tidewater; R. Smith-Clay-Agosto, Toledo.

NO-HIT GAME—Cooper-McLaughlin, Syracuse, defeated Richmond, 4-0 (second game), August 16.

Mexican League

CLASS AAA

CHAMPIONSHIP WINNERS IN PREVIOUS YEARS

Year	Club	Pct.
1955	Mexico City Tigers*	.539
1956	Mexico City Reds	.692
1957	Yucatan	.567
	Mex. C. Reds (2nd)†	.550
1958	Nuevo Laredo	.625
1959	Poza Rica	.575
	Mex. C. Reds (3rd)†	.507
1960	Mexico City Tigers	.538
1961	Veracruz	.575
1962	Monterrey	.592
1963	Puebla	.606
1964	Mexico City Reds	.586
1965	Mexico City Tigers	.590
1966	Mexico City Tigers‡	.614
	Mexico City Reds	.571
1967	Jalisco	.607
1968	Mexico City Reds	.586
1969	Reynosa	.591
1970	Aguila§	.580
	Mexico City Reds	.607
1971	Jalisco§	.558
	Saltillo	.593
1972	Saltillo	.636
	Cordoba§	.541
1973	Saltillo	.656
	Mexico City Reds x	.590
1974	Jalisco	.627
	Mexico City Reds x	.551
1975	Tampico x	.541
	Cordoba	.649
1976	Mexico City Reds x	.543
	Union Laguna	.547
1977	Mexico City Reds	.623
	Nuevo Laredo x	.507
1978	Aguascalientes x	.589
	Union Laguna	.523
1979	Saltillo	.704
	Puebla x	.628
1980	No champion y	
1981	Mexico City Reds	.615
	Reynosa	.492
1982	Ciudad Juarez x	.570
	Mexico City Tigers	.508
1983	Campeche z	.614
	Ciudad Juarez	.535
1984	Yucatan z	.560
	Ciudad Juarez	.509
1985	Mexico City Reds z	.606
	Nuevo Laredo	.5275

*Defeated Nuevo Laredo, two games to none, in playoff for pennant. †Won four-team playoff. ‡Won split-season playoff. §League divided into Northern, Southern divisions; won two-team playoff. xLeague divided into Northern, Southern zones; sub-divided into Eastern, Western divisions, won eight-team playoff. yA players strike on July 1 forced the cancellation of the regular season and playoff schedule. zLeague divided into Northern, Southern zones; four clubs from each zone qualified for postseason play. Won final series for league championship.

STANDING OF CLUBS AT CLOSE OF SEASON

NORTHERN ZONE

Club	Mva	Mon	Ags	N.L.	S.L.	U.L.	Leo	Sal	Pue	M.T.	Cam	M.R.	Yuc	Cor	Tab	Ver	W.	L.	T.	Pct.	G.B.
Monclova	....	7	5	7	8	9	12	8	2	2	1	2	4	4	2	3	76	51	1	.598	....
Monterrey	7	....	7	7	8	8	9	7	0	3	3	2	3	1	3	4	72	56	2	.558	4½
Aguascalientes	6	7	....	6	6	7	13	10	3	1	0	2	3	1	1	4	70	56	3	.556	5½
Nuevo Laredo	7	8	8	....	5	8	6	9	2	0	3	1	3	2	2	3	67	57	2	.540	7½
San Luis	6	6	7	9	....	6	8	10	1	2	0	2	2	3	2	2	66	63	2	.512	11
Union Laguna	7	6	7	3	7	....	8	8	1	1	1	3	2	2	2	2	60	65	1	.480	15
Leon	1	5	3	8	6	4	....	8	1	2	0	3	2	2	3	3	51	75	2	.405	24½
Saltillo	6	7	4	4	6	5	6	....	0	1	1	0	3	2	4	3	52	78	0	.400	25½

SOUTHERN ZONE

Club	Mva	Mon	Ags	N.L.	S.L.	U.L.	Leo	Sal	Pue	M.T.	Cam	M.R.	Yuc	Cor	Tab	Ver	W.	L.	T.	Pct.	G.B.
Puebla	2	2	1	2	3	3	3	4	....	8	9	9	9	10	10	13	88	41	1	.682	....
Mexico City Tigers	2	1	2	3	2	3	2	3	6	....	7	10	7	9	9	9	75	48	3	.610	10
Campeche	3	1	3	1	4	3	2	3	5	7	....	5	8	6	7	12	70	57	2	.551	17
Mexico City Reds	1	2	2	2	2	1	1	4	5	6	9	....	8	7	8	10	68	60	1	.531	19½
Yucatan	0	1	1	1	2	2	2	1	5	6	8	5	....	9	8	10	61	68	1	.473	27
Cordoba	0	3	3	2	1	2	1	2	6	4	7	6	5	....	6	11	59	69	1	.461	28½
Tabasco	2	1	3	2	1	2	1	0	3	3	6	6	5	8	....	9	52	74	1	.413	34½
Veracruz	1	0	0	0	2	2	1	1	1	2	2	4	4	3	7	....	30	98	1	.234	57½

Playoffs—Monterrey defeated Monclova, four games to two, in Northern Zone finals. Puebla defeated Mexico City Tigers, four games to one, in Southern Zone finals. Puebla defeated Monterrey, four games to one, in final series to capture league championship.

Managers—Aguascalientes, Roberto Castellon; Campeche, Francisco Estrada; Cordoba, Victor Ramirez, Manuel Castillo; Leon, Jack Pierce, Miguel Gaspar, Alberto Joachin; Mexico City Reds, Benjamin Reyes Chavez; Mexico City Tigers, Roberto Mendez Navarro; Monclova, Alfredo Rios; Monterrey, Vinicio Garcia, Miguel Sotelo; Nuevo Laredo, Jorge Calvo, Jose Guerrero; Puebla, Rodolfo Sandoval; Saltillo, Juan Navarette, Javier Espinosa, Victor Fabela; San Luis, Gregorio Luque Flores; Tabasco, Eduardo Gavilan, Domingo Cruz; Union Laguna, Ramon Conde, Gerardo Gutierrez; Veracruz, Francisco Rodriquez, A. Ortiz, Ramon Arano, Jesus Paredes; Yucatan, Carlos Paz.

(Compiled by Ana Luisa Perea Talarico, League Statistician, Mexico, D.F.)

CLUB BATTING

Club	Pct.	G.	AB.	R.	OR.	H.	TB.	2B.	3B.	HR.	RBI.	GW.	SH.	SF.	HP.	BB.	Int. BB.	SO.	SB.	CS.	LOB.
Puebla	.347	130	4511	959	684	1564	2394	256	35	168	907	81	54	50	29	530	37	510	130	65	998
Aguascalientes	.325	129	4358	824	816	1415	2078	235	34	120	756	59	40	54	42	470	49	461	76	65	905
Monclova	.314	128	4299	894	760	1350	2251	230	31	203	810	65	36	43	40	617	40	722	56	47	959
Yucatan	.313	130	4237	691	714	1322	1936	196	23	124	630	52	43	35	39	410	32	574	88	50	899
Leon	.312	128	4295	729	913	1342	1952	228	17	116	652	45	54	29	33	493	42	519	58	59	948
San Luis	.312	131	4422	879	779	1381	2118	255	28	142	800	50	64	46	34	602	54	721	58	54	990
Mexico City Reds	.307	129	4254	796	706	1304	2040	203	31	157	730	58	26	45	26	483	27	516	47	42	856
Mexico City Tigers	.305	126	4161	780	638	1270	1908	212	36	118	701	69	50	35	29	528	38	600	71	68	910
Union Laguna	.304	126	4218	688	738	1282	1840	193	34	99	618	50	63	29	33	380	52	613	120	67	873
Monterrey	.303	131	4399	772	626	1331	2008	210	40	129	689	59	37	47	39	566	41	657	131	68	1002
Campeche	.297	129	4239	632	602	1259	1757	188	26	86	555	63	38	31	29	392	28	501	81	32	913
Cordoba	.295	129	4143	590	605	1221	1637	152	18	76	544	52	48	32	40	411	22	472	79	54	908
Nuevo Laredo	.294	126	4121	680	626	1212	1925	195	31	152	619	57	34	37	32	462	31	577	89	55	881
Tabasco	.293	127	4173	578	720	1221	1691	191	30	73	518	42	43	39	28	369	24	542	86	45	885
Saltillo	.292	130	4282	693	883	1252	1873	174	27	131	651	47	48	28	36	480	34	584	89	82	878
Veracruz	.245	129	3926	393	768	962	1290	129	14	57	357	26	48	15	27	314	11	637	65	45	742

INDIVIDUAL BATTING

(Leading Qualifiers for Batting Championship—356 or More Plate Appearances)

*Bats lefthanded. †Switch-hitter.

Player and Club	Pct.	G.	AB.	R.	H.	TB.	2B.	3B.	HR.	RBI.	GW.	SH.	SF.	HP.	BB.	Int. BB.	SO.	SB.	CS.
Aikens, Willie Mays, Puebla*	.454	129	445	134	202	384	38	3	46	154	6	0	6	4	117	13	68	0	2
Castaneda, Nicolas, San Luis*	.412	121	396	141	163	358	36	0	53	147	15	0	4	3	128	30	60	3	2
Gray, Gary, Aguascalientes	.406	125	451	120	183	337	31	3	39	123	9	0	6	5	75	19	40	12	5
Sanchez, Orlando, Puebla*	.402	114	425	103	171	285	38	2	24	113	9	1	5	1	44	6	32	1	3
Bronson, Eddie, Union Laguna	.394	113	432	94	170	265	27	4	20	85	7	1	2	5	36	9	45	11	5
Bryant, Derek, Monterrey	.385	128	478	91	184	288	25	5	23	100	6	0	9	1	76	12	50	12	9
Pierce, Jack, Leon*	.381	128	475	111	181	372	27	1	54	148	11	0	2	4	70	14	83	3	3
McDonald, Anthony, Aguascalientes	.380	130	489	94	186	326	31	3	11	101	8	4	7	2	42	2	39	13	12
Collins, James, 91 Leon-35 S Luis*	.367	126	474	102	174	252	41	8	7	73	5	3	3	1	71	7	59	7	10
Bundy, Lorenzo, Mexico City Reds*	.364	128	442	126	161	320	31	4	40	134	11	0	9	6	91	9	36	7	2

Departmental Leaders: G—Carter, Navarrete, 130; AB—Carter, 529; R—N. Castaneda, 141; H—Aikens, 202; TB—Aikens, 384; 2B—Collins, 41; 3B—Ri. Herrera, 13; HR—Pierce, 54; RBI—Aikens, 154; GWRBI—N. Castaneda, Stockstill, Je. Gonzalez, 15; SH—Carter, Briones, 16; SF—Aguilar, 11; HP—An. Lopez, 16; BB—A. Greene, 152; IBB—N. Castaneda, 30; SO—L. Cruz, 95; SB—Carter, 95; CS—Carter, 28.

(All Players—Listed Alphabetically)

Player and Club	Pct.	G.	AB.	R.	H.	TB.	2B.	3B.	HR.	RBI.	GW.	SH.	SF.	HP.	BB.	Int. BB.	SO.	SB.	CS.
Acosta, Martin, Campeche	.222	9	9	0	2	2	0	0	0	1	0	0	0	0	0	0	1	0	0
Adams, Calvin, 27 Veracruz-44 Tab.	.323	71	248	39	80	98	9	0	3	32	7	3	4	2	32	2	22	14	6
Aguilar, Anrique, Aguascalientes	.327	125	504	106	165	258	26	2	21	106	12	4	11	10	28	0	33	3	3
Aguilera, Antonio, Yucatan	.270	78	152	29	41	52	1	2	2	17	2	3	1	2	24	1	44	4	1
Aikens, Willie Mays, Puebla*	.454	129	445	134	202	384	38	3	46	154	6	0	6	4	117	13	68	0	2
Aispuro, Juan, Yucatan	.000	2	4	1	0	0	0	0	0	0	0	0	0	0	1	0	2	1	0
Allen, Broderick, Nuevo Laredo	.292	20	72	10	21	31	4	0	2	10	1	0	1	2	6	0	14	3	1
Almodobar, Ricardo, MC Tigers	.254	80	193	31	49	59	8	1	0	13	0	8	0	2	18	0	41	2	7
Alonso, Hermilo, Puebla	.308	72	185	27	57	71	8	3	0	23	2	3	3	1	6	0	12	0	2
Alvarado, Natanael, Veracruz	.194	22	62	3	12	16	1	0	1	5	1	1	0	0	6	0	8	0	1
Alvarez, Jose Luis, San Luis	.224	59	116	14	26	29	3	0	0	10	1	5	0	3	9	0	15	1	0
Alvarez, Juan Carlos, San Luis	.271	96	277	43	75	96	15	0	2	38	2	4	1	1	33	2	67	2	2
Amador, Jose Luis, Cordoba	.103	17	29	1	3	3	0	0	0	5	0	0	1	1	1	0	6	0	0
Andrade, Reynaldo, Monterrey*	.298	124	426	96	127	183	25	5	7	54	6	5	4	6	83	3	69	5	8
Antunez, Martin, Monterrey*	.000	1	3	1	0	0	0	0	0	0	0	0	0	0	1	0	0	0	0
Arce, Javier, Leon	.297	115	357	38	106	148	19	1	7	54	2	3	5	6	33	1	44	4	4
Arzate, Martin, Aguascalientes	.267	110	296	45	79	94	11	2	0	37	3	7	2	2	30	1	28	4	6
Avila, Ruben, Union Laguna	.289	101	322	33	93	133	9	2	9	57	4	1	7	5	28	4	76	0	2
Ayala, Javier, Leon	.233	68	172	26	40	61	10	1	3	22	4	7	1	2	14	0	32	1	2
Baca, Manuel, Nuevo Laredo	.288	108	330	48	95	160	20	3	13	47	2	0	1	1	22	0	49	0	2
Bajeca, Eleazar, Veracruz	.167	40	108	5	18	19	1	0	0	5	0	3	0	0	3	0	20	1	3
Barandica, Alberto, Union Laguna	.255	71	161	27	41	49	4	2	0	12	0	3	0	0	7	0	22	4	3
Barragan, Gerardo, MC Reds*	.167	24	66	6	11	13	2	0	0	2	1	1	1	0	4	1	14	0	1
Barrera, Jesus Antonio, N Laredo	.192	23	73	5	14	16	2	0	0	8	1	0	1	2	7	0	11	0	2
Barrera, Nelson, MC Reds	.350	129	486	102	170	318	27	5	37	125	8	2	10	2	36	2	66	8	4
Bazan, Pedro, Yucatan*	.319	124	379	57	121	183	21	4	11	58	4	2	4	10	50	5	29	4	2
Bellazetin, Jose Juan, MC Tigers*	.342	114	427	110	146	218	29	8	9	59	6	4	4	2	98	9	41	7	9
Benitez, Julio Cesar, Union Laguna	.230	74	196	17	45	60	5	2	2	22	1	1	0	0	20	1	24	0	0
Bobadilla, Manuel, Monclova	.334	114	287	56	96	129	14	2	5	46	2	3	4	2	52	4	26	3	1
Bocardo, M., 3 MCR-21 SLP-21 Cor	.361	45	108	18	39	60	6	3	3	20	0	1	1	0	9	0	18	3	2
Briones, Antonio, Union Laguna	.294	113	384	81	113	131	12	3	0	25	0	16	1	2	60	0	34	43	20
Bronson, Eddie, Union Laguna	.394	113	432	94	170	265	27	4	20	85	7	1	2	5	36	9	45	11	5
Bruno, Joseph 5 MR-12 Agu-30 Ags.	.324	47	176	43	57	72	8	2	1	22	0	1	1	0	25	2	22	3	5
Bryant, Derek, Monterrey	.385	128	478	91	184	288	25	5	23	100	6	0	9	1	76	12	50	12	9
Buenrostro, Jose Luis, Yucatan	.000	4	6	1	0	0	0	0	0	0	0	0	0	0	0	0	2	0	0
Bundy, Lorenzo, MC Reds*	.364	128	442	126	161	320	31	4	40	134	11	0	9	6	91	9	36	7	2
Burke, Norberto, 24 Pue-92 Agu	.242	116	363	36	88	121	18	0	5	35	4	6	6	3	52	0	59	2	4
Cabrales, Sergio, Campeche	.222	18	36	3	8	11	3	0	0	1	0	0	0	0	3	0	9	0	0
Cabrera, Jorge, Monclova	.299	76	211	42	63	87	12	0	4	20	2	2	1	2	27	0	28	2	7
Calderon, Francisco, Campeche	.200	11	5	1	1	1	0	0	0	2	0	0	1	0	2	0	0	0	0
Chavez, Jose Angel, Veracruz	.254	53	189	18	48	59	11	0	0	7	0	3	0	0	15	0	29	5	6
Chavez, Jose Santos, MC Reds*	.279	84	233	46	65	118	11	3	12	38	2	1	3	4	45	6	48	2	2
Chavez, Juan de Dios, Veracruz	.225	49	151	11	34	43	3	0	2	7	0	3	0	0	7	1	26	0	0
Chavez, Ricardo, Campeche	.237	96	349	44	92	104	6	0	2	28	1	8	0	1	23	1	41	4	0
Camacho, Adulfo, MC Tigers	.319	113	379	75	121	156	24	4	1	44	3	6	3	4	55	3	48	13	7
Camarena, Asuncion, Union Laguna	.177	6	17	0	3	3	0	0	0	2	0	0	0	0	0	0	2	0	0
Campos, Rosendo, Tabasco	.251	74	215	43	54	81	12	3	3	17	0	2	1	3	20	1	37	8	4
Canady, Chuckie, MC Reds	.223	34	121	16	27	43	4	0	4	17	1	1	1	1	15	0	21	0	0
Canedo, Donald, Monclova*	.306	114	333	77	102	153	24	0	9	42	4	4	3	0	79	4	42	7	11
Cano, Guadalupe, Aguascalientes	.299	38	117	12	35	50	7	1	2	21	1	0	5	2	13	0	25	2	2
Cano, Javier, Saltillo	.287	110	370	64	106	126	6	4	2	31	0	4	0	0	62	2	46	25	16
Carrillo, Matias, MC Tigers*	.324	60	216	39	70	120	15	5	11	64	5	2	1	0	24	0	47	8	1
Carter, Donald, Puebla*	.355	130	529	122	188	215	16	4	1	53	2	16	1	2	66	3	59	95	28
Castaneda, Antonio, San Luis	.225	77	147	28	33	46	10	0	1	12	1	2	4	3	16	0	34	2	0
Castaneda, Nicolas, San Luis*	.412	121	396	141	163	358	36	0	53	147	15	0	4	3	128	30	60	3	2
Castelan, Miguel Angel, Puebla*	.324	108	376	61	122	173	21	3	8	81	6	4	5	0	28	4	54	10	10
Castillo, Esteban, Cordoba	.348	129	489	79	170	256	29	0	19	111	9	3	9	4	42	8	26	5	4
Castillo, Roberto, Monterrey	.000	2	0	1	0	0	0	0	0	0	0	1	0	0	0	0	0	0	0
Castro, Antonio, MC Tigers*	.281	102	342	67	96	152	20	3	10	55	8	3	4	0	35	3	42	6	3
Castro, Jose Antonio, Tabasco	.400	3	10	3	4	5	1	0	0	1	0	0	0	0	0	0	3	1	0
Cazarin, Manuel, Cordoba	.318	84	258	40	82	115	15	0	6	43	5	3	1	3	9	1	32	6	2
Clayton, Leonardo, 84 Sal-42 SLP†	.275	126	404	71	111	187	19	6	15	82	5	4	7	1	80	8	70	13	15
Clements, West, Union Laguna	.211	23	71	8	15	24	3	0	2	9	0	0	0	0	11	1	22	0	1
Cole, Michael, Cordoba*	.372	45	156	40	58	73	5	5	0	17	0	0	1	3	37	1	20	25	8
Collins, James, 91 Leon-35 S Luis*	.367	126	474	102	174	252	41	8	7	73	5	3	3	1	71	7	59	7	10
Cosey, Donald Ray, Campeche	.334	124	485	77	162	265	25	6	22	91	11	0	5	2	32	8	53	4	1
Cotes, E., 53 Cor-26 Agu-31 MCR*	.313	110	412	76	129	215	23	0	21	76	4	1	2	1	44	3	53	8	7
Covarrubias, Hector, Puebla	.000	2	1	1	0	0	0	0	0	0	0	0	0	0	1	0	1	0	0
Cruz, Fernando, Puebla	.259	67	139	12	36	41	2	0	2	16	4	0	1	1	8	0	19	0	2
Cruz, Javier 25 MCT-49 San Luis	.246	74	175	28	43	61	5	5	1	19	3	7	1	0	22	1	27	4	5
Cruz, Luis Alfonso, San Luis	.323	118	452	87	146	255	29	1	26	113	6	7	5	7	29	5	95	5	4
Darkis, Willie, Saltillo*	.306	52	196	35	60	135	8	2	21	69	1	0	0	0	13	0	49	1	3
Daut, Manuel, 65 Vera-12 Mon	.216	77	218	25	47	69	6	2	4	23	1	5	0	3	18	0	57	5	1

Player and Club	Pct.	G.	AB.	R.	H.	TB.	2B.	3B.	HR.	RBI.	GW.	SH.	SF.	HP.	BB.	Int. BB.	SO.	SB.	CS.
DeFreites, Arturo, Yucatan	.321	117	442	84	142	248	24	2	26	96	9	0	1	2	32	4	67	3	5
Delgado, Tomas, Yucatan	.300	96	307	46	92	136	17	3	7	46	3	5	3	2	24	1	57	7	6
De Los Santos, Carlos E., Cordoba	.232	113	345	40	80	86	4	1	0	23	5	13	1	7	25	0	24	2	4
Diaz, Albino, Leon	.296	87	280	49	83	119	12	0	8	56	6	5	1	1	42	3	36	4	5
Diaz, Gustavo, Tabasco	.267	7	15	1	4	4	0	0	0	0	0	0	0	0	0	0	1	0	0
Diaz, Jesus, Leon	.214	8	14	1	3	3	0	0	0	0	0	0	0	0	3	1	1	0	0
Diaz, Luis Fernando, Nuevo Laredo	.307	92	241	40	74	106	16	2	4	26	4	2	0	4	22	4	39	1	3
Dimas, Rodolfo, San Luis	.000	1	1	0	0	0	0	0	0	0	0	0	0	0	0	0	0	0	0
Dominguez, David, San Luis	.342	34	111	17	38	57	7	0	4	24	2	3	4	0	15	0	17	1	0
Duran, Oscar, 39 Lar-13 Cor-25 Tab	.251	77	247	36	62	117	10	0	15	46	3	0	1	1	36	3	44	0	3
Duran, Oscar Omar, 43 MCR-1 Cor	.252	44	127	17	32	43	3	4	0	14	1	0	1	1	12	0	29	2	3
Elizondo, Fernando, Saltillo	.306	117	457	69	140	193	32	0	7	45	3	7	4	2	37	1	43	1	4
Escalante, Isidro, Aguascalientes	.320	13	25	5	8	9	1	0	0	4	0	1	0	0	2	0	3	0	0
Estrada, Francisco, Campeche	.304	88	286	30	87	112	14	1	3	32	5	1	1	3	28	2	15	7	3
Estrada, Hector, Puebla	.000	4	2	0	0	0	0	0	0	0	0	0	0	0	0	0	0	0	0
Evans, J., 31 Mon-43 Agu 10 Cor*	.280	84	271	52	76	136	18	0	14	63	5	0	4	6	68	5	34	0	1
Fabela, Lorenzo, Veracruz	.197	47	137	4	27	31	1	0	1	10	1	0	1	2	6	0	28	3	1
Felix, Rodrigo, Campeche	.000	11	3	3	0	0	0	0	0	0	0	0	0	0	0	0	1	0	0
Fernandez, Daniel, Mexico City Reds*	.240	62	204	38	49	66	12	1	1	12	1	4	0	1	49	0	26	7	4
Fierro, Armando, Monterrey	.500	3	2	1	1	1	0	0	0	1	0	0	0	0	0	0	0	0	0
Figueroa, Leobardo, 29 Yuc-7 Cor	.247	36	93	11	23	27	2	1	0	10	1	1	0	4	19	0	11	2	2
Figueroa, Miguel, Veracruz	.200	5	10	1	2	3	1	0	0	0	0	0	0	0	0	0	4	0	0
Ford, Ken, Mexico City Reds	.320	7	25	7	8	15	1	0	2	4	2	0	0	0	3	0	1	1	0
Gage, Ralph, 25 Sal-10 Ags*	.224	35	116	16	26	37	5	0	2	14	1	0	0	0	29	3	17	0	2
Garbey, Barbaro, Nuevo Laredo	.288	22	66	3	19	22	1	1	0	5	1	0	2	1	11	1	8	1	1
Garcia, Jesus, Monclova	.281	33	32	12	9	17	1	2	1	8	0	1	1	0	4	0	10	0	1
Garcia, Jose Luis, San Luis	.311	69	177	41	55	81	10	2	4	29	2	4	0	2	27	0	36	3	4
Garcia, Martin, Monterrey	.232	56	99	15	23	28	5	0	0	9	0	0	2	3	8	0	15	2	2
Garibay, Guy, Nuevo Laredo	.274	36	113	18	31	53	5	1	5	22	3	0	0	0	4	0	19	0	1
Garza, Adolfo, Monclova*	.312	123	442	74	138	251	26	0	29	92	9	0	4	5	40	1	84	3	3
Garza, Gerardo, Nuevo Laredo	.225	33	49	9	11	13	0	1	0	6	0	1	1	0	6	0	13	0	1
Garzon, Felix, Cordoba	.297	126	408	49	121	144	14	0	3	56	6	1	4	5	60	2	59	1	1
Gastelum, Carlos, Mexico City Reds	.222	15	27	2	6	6	0	0	0	0	0	0	0	0	2	0	2	0	1
Gomez, Alejandro, Tabasco	.306	117	389	48	119	151	17	3	3	39	6	4	2	1	14	0	24	19	5
Gomez, Graciano, Leon	.294	116	428	54	126	176	20	3	8	49	5	5	3	9	19	0	28	3	4
Gonzalez, Juan, Saltillo	.250	12	16	3	4	6	0	1	0	1	0	0	0	0	0	0	3	0	0
Gonzalez, Jesus, Puebla	.316	127	519	106	164	236	19	4	15	93	15	5	3	5	55	2	29	3	1
Gonzalez, Mario Angel, Monclova	.212	20	33	1	7	8	1	0	0	3	0	0	0	0	2	0	12	0	0
Gonzalez, Noe, Monterrey	.296	99	324	50	96	151	18	2	11	44	6	3	1	0	46	4	66	3	2
Gray, Gary, Aguascalientes	.406	125	451	120	183	337	31	3	39	123	9	0	6	5	75	19	40	12	5
Greene, Altar, Monclova*	.336	124	393	127	132	269	14	3	39	122	10	0	4	3	152	12	69	8	0
Greene, David, Monterrey*	.391	48	151	41	59	105	11	1	11	38	5	0	1	2	45	6	25	2	0
Guerrero, Francisco, Union Laguna	.274	115	354	54	97	132	20	3	3	35	3	8	2	4	50	0	78	23	14
Guerrero, Leobardo, Aguascalientes	.291	85	330	51	96	122	23	0	1	23	2	0	1	2	41	1	26	5	4
Gutierrez, Jose Luis, Yucatan	.231	9	13	2	3	5	2	0	0	0	0	0	0	1	2	0	7	0	0
Guzman, Andres, Tabasco	.283	99	350	41	99	153	20	2	10	52	2	1	4	2	21	1	47	2	1
Guzman, Marco Antonio, Campeche	.316	128	450	65	142	204	24	1	12	82	8	0	6	4	66	6	47	2	4
Heras, Roberto, Monterrey	.293	97	335	43	98	154	18	1	12	72	5	1	3	3	10	2	55	1	3
Hernandez, Javier, Leon	.310	65	129	14	40	43	3	0	0	16	1	0	2	0	15	1	20	1	2
Hernandez, Jorge Luis, Puebla	.301	63	186	33	56	78	14	1	2	21	1	1	5	9	10	0	27	2	0
Hernandez, Ju., 47 Ca-26 Ve-16 Co	.252	89	302	38	76	107	12	2	5	28	3	4	0	1	37	0	59	9	9
Hernandez, Miguel, Cordoba	.307	119	394	54	121	138	12	1	1	35	4	9	3	3	43	0	54	8	8
Hernandez, Rodolfo, Yucatan	.356	99	323	59	115	189	16	2	18	71	7	4	4	5	48	0	45	1	0
Herrera, Calixto, Veracruz	.196	101	260	16	51	64	8	1	1	15	0	2	0	2	3	0	85	3	1
Herrera, Rene, Cordoba	.285	77	284	50	81	86	2	0	1	26	2	6	3	1	34	0	36	20	4
Herrera, Ricardo, Monterrey*	.331	125	489	109	162	223	20	13	5	33	6	4	2	3	73	1	50	48	20
Herring, Paul, 91 SLP-35 Leon	.323	126	471	90	152	246	28	6	18	103	4	4	8	2	51	7	41	4	8
Huerta, Luis Enrique, Nuevo Laredo	.000	1	1	0	0	0	0	0	0	0	0	0	0	0	0	0	1	0	0
Isales, Orlando, Tabasco	.200	17	55	4	11	19	5	0	1	2	0	0	0	0	5	0	12	1	0
Jacobsen, Kenneth, Yucatan	.125	4	16	0	2	2	0	0	0	0	0	0	0	0	0	0	0	0	0
Jimenez, Eduardo, Leon	.260	16	50	10	13	20	4	0	1	9	0	1	1	1	9	0	9	1	0
Jimenez, Leopoldo, Campeche	.275	57	131	19	36	55	11	1	2	17	3	2	0	0	23	0	19	1	0
Jones, Kenneth, Nuevo Laredo	.229	23	96	11	22	28	1	1	1	4	0	0	0	0	4	0	12	2	3
Lara, Hugo, Veracruz	.500	2	8	0	4	6	2	0	0	1	0	0	0	0	0	0	4	0	0
Lavagnino, Jose Ernesto, San Luis	.200	6	10	0	2	3	1	0	0	1	0	0	0	0	2	0	3	0	0
Lela, Guadalupe, Monclova*	.280	109	304	64	85	139	12	3	12	41	1	3	1	2	44	7	62	10	5
Limon, Salvador, Tabasco	.233	60	176	18	41	54	6	2	1	11	0	3	0	0	5	0	28	0	0
Lizarraga, Alejandro, Union Laguna	.321	124	489	66	157	223	28	1	12	82	11	12	3	1	21	3	36	2	2
Lizarraga, Raul, Leon	.222	9	9	2	2	3	1	0	0	0	0	1	0	0	4	0	1	0	0
Lopez, Alfonso, Mexico City Tigers	.347	104	357	48	124	155	15	2	4	54	8	6	2	1	21	2	16	2	7
Lopez, Antonio, Saltillo	.354	130	497	107	176	304	18	4	34	131	14	0	5	16	35	8	40	7	5
Lopez, Fernando, Saltillo	.211	43	57	7	12	14	2	0	0	3	0	1	0	0	9	0	11	0	0
Lopez, Jaime, Union Laguna*	.298	75	235	27	70	99	12	1	5	36	3	3	5	0	21	14	13	0	0
Lora, Luis, Yucatan*	.333	121	454	76	151	197	23	1	7	61	5	3	5	1	41	4	34	30	10
Luna, Jose Luis, Saltillo	.259	102	301	25	78	102	12	0	4	34	2	6	2	3	22	1	26	0	1
Machiria, Pablo, Mexico City Tigers	.303	102	294	61	89	151	14	3	14	61	6	3	4	5	25	4	55	2	3
Madero, Carlos, Yucatan	.118	13	17	0	2	2	0	0	0	2	0	0	0	0	2	0	4	0	0
Marquez, Francisco, Leon	.279	84	262	25	73	98	14	1	3	39	1	0	2	2	19	1	46	0	2
Martinez, Francisco, 44 Cor-45 Agu	.276	89	286	22	79	95	10	0	2	23	0	6	2	3	14	0	37	2	4
Martinez, Oscar, Saltillo	.212	44	118	10	25	33	2	0	2	19	1	1	2	4	13	0	14	0	2
Martinez, Raul, Monterrey	.278	97	345	44	96	148	14	1	12	59	4	5	3	3	32	1	64	0	4
Mayer, Danny, Mexico City Reds*	.344	41	154	28	53	75	5	1	5	27	2	0	1	1	20	3	12	0	0
Maza, Celerino, 5 Lag-84 SLP	.269	89	294	45	79	89	10	0	0	29	1	1	1	3	38	2	50	2	6
McDonald, Anthony, Aguascalientes	.380	129	489	94	186	256	31	3	11	101	8	4	7	2	42	2	39	13	12
Mendoza, Luis Alonso, Aguascalientes	.320	84	269	39	86	110	15	0	3	35	0	4	1	2	34	0	32	2	2
Mendoza, P., 21 Pu-21 Ve-75 Cam	.288	117	382	67	110	165	20	4	9	49	5	3	1	0	48	0	51	11	6
Meza, Leonel, 24 Agu-59 Mon	.241	83	216	33	52	73	5	2	4	19	3	4	1	0	20	0	30	2	1
Miller, Eddie, Monterrey*	.335	100	364	74	122	199	20	3	17	73	4	3	3	13	45	4	55	44	13
Miller, Lemmie, Saltillo	.336	88	333	66	112	156	16	5	6	41	3	2	3	2	40	2	56	16	9
Monroy, Victor Hugo, Monclova	.320	101	331	50	106	161	23	1	10	64	4	4	7	5	13	0	33	3	6
Mora, Andres, Nuevo Laredo	.355	122	420	86	149	274	20	3	33	117	14	1	7	1	66	11	42	2	6
Morales, Isidro, Mexico City Reds	.000	1	0	1	0	0	0	0	0	0	0	0	0	0	0	0	0	0	0
Morales, Manuel, Mexico City Tigers	.268	95	321	44	86	95	5	2	0	35	1	9	0	0	33	3	25	7	6

Player and Club	Pct.	G.	AB.	R.	H.	TB.	2B.	3B.	HR.	RBI.	GW.	SH.	SF.	HP.	BB.	Int. BB.	SO.	SB.	CS.
Morfin, Jorge, 41 MCR-15 Cor	.278	56	115	23	32	35	1	1	0	10	0	2	2	0	14	0	11	1	4
Moya, Ramon, Tabasco	.000	1	0	1	0	0	0	0	0	0	0	0	0	0	0	0	0	0	0
Navarrete, Juan, Saltillo*	.337	130	517	92	174	218	29	3	3	52	5	9	0	2	44	8	19	19	15
Navarro, Jose Angel, Saltillo	.333	8	6	0	2	2	0	0	0	1	0	0	0	0	0	0	1	0	0
Navarro, Ruben, 11 Mon-83 Agu	.265	94	302	35	80	113	6	3	7	29	1	1	1	2	24	1	59	5	0
Nunez, Arturo, Veracruz	.148	13	27	3	4	6	0	1	0	2	0	0	0	0	3	0	12	0	0
Olivares, Oswaldo, Campeche*	.333	129	502	92	167	211	27	4	3	40	2	10	1	5	59	6	31	27	6
Ontiveros, Juan, San Luis	.000	2	0	1	0	0	0	0	0	0	0	0	0	0	0	0	0	0	0
Ortiz, Alejandro, Nuevo Laredo	.293	123	420	94	123	249	19	1	35	101	7	2	7	10	75	2	78	7	2
Ortiz, Alfredo, 2 Agu-11 Yuc	.143	13	28	2	4	4	0	0	0	4	0	1	1	0	6	1	5	0	0
Ortiz, Jose Manuel, Monclova	.091	13	11	2	1	1	0	0	0	1	0	1	0	0	1	0	5	0	0
Pacho, Juan Jose, Yucatan	.325	130	526	78	171	210	28	1	3	54	2	13	1	2	32	0	36	21	14
Palacios, Vicente, Veracruz	.167	5	6	1	1	1	0	0	0	0	0	0	0	0	0	0	2	0	0
Paredes, Jesus, Veracruz	.211	23	76	7	16	19	3	0	0	2	1	0	0	1	6	0	12	3	3
Payton, Eric, Union Laguna*	.335	121	462	105	155	259	18	1	28	97	10	6	4	6	46	9	77	19	5
Peralta, Amado, Mexico City Tigers*	.279	94	247	52	69	110	13	2	8	46	7	2	0	2	51	4	58	3	6
Perez, Jose Luis, Aguascalientes*	.312	118	372	80	116	193	25	2	16	75	6	4	4	1	72	15	49	8	9
Perez, Julian, San Luis	.359	59	220	47	79	114	11	0	8	45	3	0	1	2	37	0	26	7	4
Perkins, Broderick, 76 MCR-11 Cor*	.330	87	309	70	102	183	17	2	20	63	5	0	0	2	30	4	45	3	1
Perkins, Harold, Nuevo Laredo*	.341	119	464	106	158	229	32	6	9	59	3	5	2	6	64	3	67	55	16
Pierce, Jack, Leon*	.381	128	475	111	181	372	27	1	54	148	11	0	2	4	70	14	83	3	3
Placencia, Juan, San Luis*	.235	10	17	2	4	5	1	0	0	1	0	1	0	0	1	0	2	0	0
Ponce, Hector, Puebla	.296	97	169	40	50	68	9	0	3	29	5	3	1	0	27	0	23	9	6
Puente, Hugo, Yucatan	.259	23	54	4	14	16	2	0	0	7	1	0	0	0	6	0	12	0	1
Puente, Juan, Aguascalientes	.232	42	56	10	13	17	2	1	0	4	0	0	2	1	5	0	6	3	1
Quintero, Guadalupe, MC Reds	.275	67	189	19	52	72	6	1	4	26	0	0	2	2	12	1	22	0	2
Quintero, Victor, 24 Agu-98 Pue	.341	122	449	65	153	196	26	4	3	70	4	11	2	0	27	0	27	2	3
Quiroz, Jose Julian, Union Laguna*	.308	120	435	70	134	191	27	6	6	67	6	3	3	4	27	8	62	4	9
Ramirez, Enrique, Nuevo Laredo	.273	95	264	31	72	94	14	1	2	23	3	7	2	1	14	0	43	2	2
Ramirez, Manuel, Tabasco	.319	120	432	61	138	179	23	3	4	57	5	5	7	6	35	3	28	6	3
Raygoza, Martin, Campeche	.000	1	0	1	0	0	0	0	0	0	0	0	0	0	0	0	0	0	0
Rendon, Jose, Saltillo	.304	79	263	42	80	136	14	0	14	65	5	1	3	0	49	4	59	2	6
Reyes, Enrique, Nuevo Laredo	.234	93	303	28	71	95	6	0	6	27	3	6	2	2	27	0	30	1	3
Reyes, Gerado, San Luis	.354	75	277	59	98	126	23	1	1	34	3	5	2	2	28	0	17	16	6
Reyes, Gustavo, Monterrey	.400	6	5	0	2	2	0	0	0	1	0	0	0	0	0	0	0	0	0
Reyes, Juan, 39 Agu-60 Yuc	.366	99	333	57	122	192	22	0	16	54	3	2	2	0	30	10	61	1	1
Rios, Carlos, 41 Agu-56 Cam	.270	97	344	44	93	114	18	0	1	29	5	6	0	2	7	1	33	5	0
Rivera, Angel, Tabasco	.253	46	95	12	24	39	6	0	3	14	0	1	1	2	15	2	28	0	0
Rivera, Carlos, Campeche	.242	118	413	49	100	152	11	4	11	50	4	4	3	3	25	3	66	12	4
Rivera, Eduardo, 7 Sal-38 Leon	.230	45	126	13	29	39	7	0	1	12	1	3	1	2	12	2	13	0	0
Rivera, Eleazar, Monterrey	.000	8	8	0	0	0	0	0	0	0	0	0	0	0	0	0	2	0	0
Rivera, Jesus, Monterrey	.314	33	118	21	37	68	4	0	9	30	2	0	2	1	17	3	23	1	1
Rivero, Gener, Leon	.284	122	402	65	114	122	8	0	0	29	2	8	1	0	52	0	12	9	5
Robles, Eduardo, Nuevo Laredo	.200	4	5	1	1	1	0	0	0	0	0	0	0	0	1	0	0	0	0
Robles, Humberto, 18 Mon-14 Pue	.206	32	63	14	13	16	3	0	0	6	0	0	2	0	17	1	19	0	0
Robles, Ruben, Aguascalientes	.182	6	22	6	4	5	1	0	0	1	0	0	0	2	3	0	4	0	1
Robles, Sergio, Mexico City Reds	.285	74	239	18	68	74	6	0	0	33	6	3	1	3	7	0	37	1	1
Rodriguez, Genaro, Monterrey	.280	109	379	64	106	160	17	2	11	64	4	6	5	0	27	2	40	7	3
Rodriguez, Guillermo, Puebla	.326	128	494	95	161	297	28	3	34	121	11	4	7	2	30	8	75	1	2
Rodriguez, Jaime, Tabasco	.272	86	283	29	77	101	7	1	5	40	4	2	5	2	11	0	23	6	4
Rodriguez, Juan Francisco, Leon	.332	127	485	98	161	189	24	2	0	34	4	14	3	2	62	1	19	16	14
Rodriguez, Pilar, Cordoba	.333	1	3	0	1	1	0	0	0	0	0	0	0	0	0	0	1	0	0
Rodriguez, Rodolfo, Cordoba*	.231	23	78	6	18	23	2	0	1	10	1	2	1	0	8	0	7	0	1
Rojas, Homar, Mexico City Tigers	.319	114	420	76	134	237	30	2	23	89	10	1	9	1	29	0	52	4	4
Romero, Marco Antonio, Puebla	.217	23	23	3	5	5	0	0	0	4	0	0	0	0	3	0	4	0	0
Rosado, Luis, Veracruz	.319	22	72	3	23	24	1	0	0	8	0	2	0	0	3	0	3	0	2
Rosario, Alfonso, Monclova*	.344	125	508	121	175	296	25	12	24	110	7	2	6	15	44	5	72	4	4
Rosas, Clemente, Aguascalientes	.325	29	80	11	26	41	6	0	3	22	1	3	2	0	3	0	19	0	0
Roys, Luis, 49 Cor-45 Ags*	.278	94	352	55	98	175	9	1	22	73	5	2	3	3	24	7	39	3	5
Rubio, Mauricio, Saltillo	.217	101	180	27	39	47	2	3	0	12	1	4	0	0	24	0	36	2	2
Ruiz, Demetrio, Tabasco	.298	110	393	49	117	135	10	4	0	28	2	6	1	0	34	1	26	10	6
Ruiz, Porfirio, Veracruz	.209	84	235	17	49	59	6	2	0	16	3	3	2	2	17	0	19	4	2
Saenz, Ricardo, Saltillo	.186	41	140	15	26	31	5	0	0	11	0	1	1	0	8	0	17	0	3
Saiz, Herminio, Union Laguna	.298	119	440	71	131	170	20	5	3	51	6	9	1	5	34	0	63	12	4
Salava, Randy, Mexico City Tigers*	.357	113	384	82	137	217	18	4	18	89	5	1	4	7	80	10	70	9	9
Salinas, Luis, Tabasco*	.273	45	150	21	41	68	7	1	6	31	2	0	2	1	16	1	46	0	1
Samaniego, Manuel, Campeche	.284	96	334	52	95	127	14	3	4	51	7	2	5	2	22	1	49	5	1
Sanchez, Andres, 4 Agu-27 MCR	.238	31	63	4	15	18	3	0	0	5	1	0	0	0	7	0	15	1	0
Sanchez, Armando, MC Reds*	.322	119	447	97	144	194	21	7	5	60	4	3	6	2	61	2	17	8	4
Sanchez, Carlos, Saltillo	.000	1	1	0	0	0	0	0	0	0	0	0	0	0	0	0	0	0	0
Sanchez, Gerardo, Nuevo Laredo	.293	125	522	88	153	211	28	9	4	44	3	7	2	0	31	0	43	12	6
Sanchez, Gustavo, Leon	.270	32	37	5	10	11	1	0	0	2	0	1	0	0	2	0	6	0	1
Sanchez, Hector, Monclova	.266	44	94	17	25	31	4	1	0	14	1	5	0	1	10	0	24	1	2
Sanchez, Orlando, Puebla*	.402	114	425	103	171	285	38	2	24	113	9	1	5	1	44	6	32	1	3
Santana, Blas, Yucatan	.279	127	523	76	146	196	19	2	9	54	7	4	3	2	20	0	56	5	6
Sarabia, Antonio, 1 MVA-97 Tab	.311	98	328	50	102	134	15	4	3	43	6	2	2	2	36	3	65	3	6
Sarmiento, Manuel, Cordoba	.250	1	4	0	1	1	0	0	0	0	0	0	0	0	0	0	0	0	0
Scott, Rodney, Tabasco	.276	54	210	38	58	81	11	0	4	26	1	3	2	1	36	1	27	16	5
Serna, Joel, Monclova	.295	120	420	78	124	193	17	2	16	61	6	3	4	3	59	3	71	3	3
Serratos, Miguel, Campeche	.281	119	449	59	126	170	14	0	10	62	10	5	5	7	12	1	63	2	2
Smith, Robert, 56 Agu-60 Cam*	.331	116	408	77	135	190	15	5	10	61	6	1	5	0	59	2	53	15	12
Sommers, Jesus, Leon	.356	116	450	100	160	248	30	2	18	86	4	2	3	1	53	6	50	7	4
Sosa, Arturo, San Luis	.192	56	151	19	29	41	5	2	1	15	0	4	0	1	23	2	41	0	2
Soto, Carlos, Nuevo Laredo	.336	103	342	56	115	219	15	1	29	78	9	0	7	1	59	9	46	1	1
Soto, Gregorio, 32 Cor-40 Veracruz	.252	72	218	21	55	70	9	3	0	21	3	5	2	3	15	0	32	1	3
Stockstill, David, Puebla*	.358	117	430	121	154	281	27	5	30	103	15	3	5	2	78	2	47	2	1
Suarez, Miguel, Veracruz*	.237	89	274	25	65	71	3	0	1	14	0	4	1	2	17	2	32	1	2
Sutton, Leonardo, Leon	.260	17	50	9	13	20	4	0	1	7	0	1	0	0	4	0	16	2	0
Tapia, Noe, Tabasco	.221	84	213	24	47	81	10	0	8	27	0	3	2	1	19	0	31	3	2
Thomas, Darell, Tabasco	.466	24	73	18	34	56	8	1	4	14	1	1	1	0	19	0	7	2	2
Tirado, Francisco, Mexico City Tigers	.000	2	0	0	0	0	0	0	0	0	0	0	0	0	0	0	0	0	0
Tirado, Victor, Yucatan	.167	27	36	3	6	9	1	1	0	1	0	0	0	0	2	0	10	0	0
Torres, Eduardo, Saltillo	.282	108	337	59	95	174	10	0	23	56	4	4	3	6	44	2	73	4	5

Player and Club	Pct.	G.	AB.	R.	H.	TB.	2B.	3B.	HR.	RBI.	GW.	SH.	SF.	HP.	BB.	Int. BB.	SO.	SB.	CS.
Torres, Efrain, Nuevo Laredo	.276	22	29	3	8	8	0	0	0	1	0	1	0	0	4	0	4	0	1
Torres, Nemesio, Tabasco	.305	98	341	46	104	140	15	6	3	39	2	8	4	3	12	1	31	2	2
Torres, Rafael, Aguascalientes	.317	75	224	39	71	93	9	5	1	35	1	1	3	0	33	2	34	3	4
Torres, Raymundo, Yucatan	.325	126	412	88	134	252	19	3	31	92	7	2	7	9	65	4	74	6	2
Ulin, Sergio Trinidad, Nuevo Laredo	.247	65	170	23	42	48	4	1	0	13	2	2	2	0	24	0	31	2	2
Uribe, Fernando, Puebla	.278	32	54	10	15	19	2	1	0	6	0	0	1	1	2	0	12	0	0
Uzcanga, Ali, Mexico City Reds	.278	127	454	74	126	159	17	2	4	57	3	7	5	1	38	0	43	3	4
Valdez, Baltazar, Monclova	.338	117	405	73	137	263	22	1	34	120	12	2	3	1	32	1	90	3	0
Valdez, Luis Alberto, Monterrey	.248	104	318	32	79	93	7	2	1	34	2	4	7	2	28	0	46	2	3
Valencia, Carlos, Aguascalientes	.307	125	518	97	159	222	23	11	6	66	5	5	4	8	36	1	62	13	5
Valenzuela, Horacio, MC Tigers*	.309	99	291	52	90	149	10	2	15	55	5	1	0	3	25	0	42	4	3
Valenzuela, Leonardo, Monclova*	.309	124	469	99	145	248	35	4	20	66	7	5	5	0	54	3	86	7	4
Valenzuela, Ricardo, MC Tigers	.186	77	188	25	35	55	8	0	4	22	3	2	3	2	25	3	44	1	0
Valladolid, Jesus, Cordoba	.294	9	17	4	5	5	0	0	0	1	0	0	0	0	1	0	2	0	0
Valle, Guadalupe, San Luis	.322	121	457	87	147	187	21	2	5	82	2	7	6	4	69	1	86	2	2
Valverde, Raul, Saltillo	.154	15	13	3	2	2	0	0	0	0	0	0	0	0	2	0	0	0	0
Vargas, Antonio, 12 MCT-72 Lag	.257	84	241	34	62	109	9	4	10	43	3	0	2	1	20	3	65	3	2
Vargas, Ignacio, Yucatan	.000	3	6	0	0	0	0	0	0	0	0	0	0	0	0	0	3	0	0
Vargas, Leonel, Mexico City Reds	.333	119	454	78	151	235	28	1	18	83	9	1	2	2	29	1	61	2	6
Vargas, Trinidad, Yucatan	.203	47	74	8	15	19	1	0	1	5	0	1	0	0	2	0	24	0	0
Vattimon, Jose C., 3 MCT-15 Cor	.277	18	47	4	13	13	0	0	0	4	1	1	0	0	4	2	2	0	0
Vega, Ramon, Aguascalientes	.304	85	299	45	91	125	16	3	4	42	6	5	2	2	19	2	30	3	4
Velazquez, Guillermo, Monterrey	.267	62	146	19	39	60	8	2	3	21	4	1	0	0	8	0	24	1	0
Vergara, Salvador, 13 Cor-38 Agu	.235	51	119	11	28	33	3	1	0	9	2	2	1	0	16	0	20	1	2
Vidana, Alejandro, Tabasco	.000	2	3	0	0	0	0	0	0	0	0	0	0	0	0	0	0	0	0
Villa, Victor, Puebla	.588	48	17	12	10	12	0	1	0	5	0	1	1	0	3	0	0	3	0
Villaescusa, Fernando, Yucatan*	.351	59	191	30	67	79	10	1	0	15	1	3	3	1	18	3	15	4	2
Villagomez, David, Cordoba	.308	119	435	60	134	202	25	2	13	73	11	1	5	4	35	3	48	1	1
Villalobos, Enrique, 38 Leon-45 Sal	.258	83	217	21	56	93	10	0	9	40	4	4	2	2	13	3	57	0	1
Villegas, David, Yucatan	.250	5	8	0	2	2	0	0	0	3	0	0	0	0	2	0	1	0	0
Villela, Carlos, San Luis	.300	128	510	96	153	218	26	6	9	55	3	10	5	1	45	0	67	5	6
Vizcarra, Roberto, Leon	.074	28	27	2	2	3	1	0	0	0	0	0	0	0	2	0	6	0	0
Vizcarra, Sergio, San Luis	.250	10	8	5	2	5	0	0	1	2	0	1	0	0	1	0	0	0	0
Whittemore, Reggie, Tabasco*	.330	61	221	34	73	106	9	0	8	40	4	0	0	3	39	7	52	0	0
Wong, Julian, Aguascalientes	.000	1	0	0	0	0	0	0	0	0	0	0	0	0	0	0	0	0	0
Yucupicio, J. Javier, Veracruz	.000	3	5	0	0	0	0	0	0	0	0	0	0	0	0	0	4	0	0
Zambrano, Rosario, Cordoba*	.276	105	301	48	83	122	6	3	9	29	2	2	1	3	29	1	28	3	4
Zepeda, Alejandro, Mexico City Reds.	.000	3	2	0	0	0	0	0	0	0	0	0	0	0	0	0	0	0	0
Zuniga, Armando, Mexico City Tigers	.250	15	36	5	9	11	2	0	0	5	0	0	0	0	1	0	5	1	2
Zuniga, Rafael, Monterrey	.278	28	72	7	20	27	4	0	1	13	1	1	0	1	10	1	13	1	0

The following pitchers, listed alphabetically by club, with games in parentheses, had no plate appearances, primarily through use of designated hitters:

AGUASCALIENTES—Alapizco, Molecio (10); Delgadillo, Gustavo (31); Grajales, Francisco (1); Granillo, Carlos (38); Lopez, Hector (37); MacKenzie, Doug (10); Matus, Nelson (10); Montano, Francisco (18); Munoz, Miguel (31); Rodriguez, Mario Alberto (28); Rojo, Gonzalo (32); Villanueva, Luis (31); Villegas, Mike (38).

CAMPECHE—Barraza, Ernesto (7); Baruch, Matias (8); Berenguer, Francisco (1); Divison, Julio Cesar (45); Dominguez, Herminio (26); Duran, Jesus (2); Flores, Jose Alberto (25); Gaxiola, Fernando (5); Hernandez, Angel (28); Ochoa, Domingo (1); Rodriguez, Ramon (12); Romo, Ruben (5); Sandate, Ricardo (31); Valdez, Humberto (11); Valdez, Rodolfo (29); Williams, Albert (2).

CORDOBA—Aponte, Luis (5); Colorado, Salvador (23); Felix, Antonio (6); Feola, Larry (11); Gaxiola, Fernando (6); Guzman, Gelacio (21); Harper, DeVallon (6); Inzunza, Sergio (17); Leal, Bernabe (28); Luna, Jose Manuel (22); Menendez, Rolando (10); Morales, Isidro (3); Romo, Vicente (10); Sanchez, Leo (1); Serafin, Hector (26); Silva, Eduardo (42); Torres, Martin (28); Vazquez, Marco A. (6); Veliz, Francisco (2).

LEON—Armenta, Martin (7); Calderon, Jose (12); Castro, Eduardo (8); Diaz, Anibal (5); Duarte, Florentino (14); Elvira, Narciso (31); Enriquez, Martin (29); Felix, Antonio (17); Lunar, Luis (18); Menendez, Rolando (26); Meza, Rigoberto (8); Miranda, Francisco (18); Moncada, Mario (2); Morales, Isidro (10); Moreno, Abel (5); Osuna, Roberto (39); Peralta, Alvaro (4); Perez, Leonardo (20); Ramirez, Alfonso (6); Rios, Hector (18); Sanchez, Pablo (9); Taylor, Johnny (9); Valenzuela, Guillermo (28).

MEXICO CITY REDS—Armenta, Martin (1); Barojas, Salome (28); Duarte, Florentino (3); Franco, Francisco (23); Leon, Maximino (21); Lomeli, Jorge Elias (42); Mendez, Luis Fernando (25); Osuna, Ricardo (2); Pulido, Antonio (41); Rios, Hector (14); Solis, Miguel (10); Solis, Ricardo (34); Tejeda, Gregorio (33); Villarreal, Ricardo (9); Villela, Martin (3); Zamudio, Aurelio (10).

MEXICO CITY TIGERS—Alvarado, Jose (12); Alvarez, Refugio (5); Buitimea, Martin (4); Contreras, Roberto (3); Cruz, Jesus (27); Greer, Mike (2); Ibarra, Carlos (29); Jaime Granillo, Ismael (2); Moreno, Angel (25); Renteria, Hilario (4); Retes, Lorenzo (35); Rios, Jesus (28); Rivas, Martin (49); Sarmiento, Walfredo (16); Urrea, John (6); Valdez, Armando (28); Valencia, Miguel Angel (7); Villegas, Ramon (24).

MONCLOVA—Cano, Ezequiel (28); Garcia, Jose Luis (27); Garcia, Rogelio (41); Garza, Adrian (17); Guzman, Ramon (44); Heredia, Ubaldo (24); Keine, Marty (22); Ledon, Juan Carlos (5); Mundo, Jesus (27); Pruneda, Armando (21); Ruiz, Pablo (25); Salas, Ernesto (5); Vazquez, Florentino (25); Velazquez, Luis Alfonso (21).

MONTERREY—Angulo, Pedro (1); Bass, Barry (25); Castro, Rodrigo (2); Cordova, Ernesto (9); Esquer, Mercedes (26); Garza, Adrian (9); Gutierrez, Porfirio (25); Guzman, Gelacio (1); Ledon, Juan Carlos (8); Murillo, Felipe (12); Rice, Woosley (6); Sanchez, Pablo (13); Sanchez, Policarpo (4); Serafin, Hector (15); Serna, Ramon (21); Telechea, Gonzalo (2); Urrea, Leonel (11); Veliz, Francisco (24).

NUEVO LAREDO—Carranza, Javier (37); Castillo, Luis Trinidad (15); Evans, Gary (9); Fuson, F. Robin (22); Hann, Dewayne (7); Kibbe, Jay (7); Martinez, Jose Antonio (13); Mattson, Curt A. (7); Moreno, Jesus (26); Navarro, Adolfo (30); Ochoa, Porfirio (50); Patterson, Reginald (16); Tinoco, Ruben (2); Vaqueiro, Danny (12); Vizcarra, Faustino (22).

PUEBLA—Antunez, Martin (9); Camarena, Martin (34); Castaneda, Aurelio (9); Jimenez, German (24); Jimenez, Isaac (19); Ontiveros, Juan (2); Orozco, Jaime (24); Orozco, Octavio (23); Perez, Cipriano (28); Quijano, Enrique (24); Rincon, Juan (13); Sanchez, Pablo (6); Soto, Alvaro (44); Villarreal, Ricardo (3).

SALTILLO—Alvarez, Martin (31); Beltran, Eleazar (8); Cartagena, Ruben (31); Castaneda, Mario A. (6); Duarte, Florentino (7); Franco, David (24); Franco, Francisco (8); Garcia, Rafael (28); Garces, Robinson (23); Garibaldi, Ramon (6); Inzunza, Sergio (4); Jaime Granillo, Ismael (33); Padilla, Raymundo (38); Pollorena, Oscar (41); Robles, Arturo (5); Rodriguez, Eulogio (31); Rojo, Gustavo (4); Sanchez, Felipe (7); Solis, Miguel (20); Valenzuela, Adan (10); Valenzuela, Jairo (25).

SAN LUIS—Beltran, Eleazar (18); Chavez, Guadalupe (40); Casas, Arturo (15); Contreras, Roberto (15); Cota, Francisco (1); Diaz, Octavio (6); Espinosa, Javier (3); Guzman, Benjamin (3); Herman, Dave (43); Kibbe, Jay (14); Lizarraga, Hugo (3); Marquez, Isidro (25); Purata, Julio (26); Romero, Emigdio (30); Ruiz, Francisco (12); Valdez, Efrain (26).

TABASCO—Aguilar, Miguel (24); Castillejos, Jose Marcos (33); Feola, Larry (13); Garcia, Jorge Luis (28); Gonzalez, Fernando (9); Matus, Nelson (16); Menendez, Willie (17); Rivas, Lorenzo (1); Rojo, Gonzalo (20); Salas, Ernesto (18); Senteney, Steve (15); Soto, Fernando (11); White, Larry (5); Zamberino, Jesus (3).

UNION LAGUNA—Acosta, Cecilio (26); Alvarado, Jose (14); Buces, Leonardo (4); Castaneda, Maximiliano (5); Castillo, Humberto (1); Contreras, Roberto (9); Diaz, Octavio (5); Gaynor, Richie (10); Low, Gabriel (24); Lunar, Luis (8); Palafox, Juan Manuel (23); Rios, Sergio (10); Rivera, Juan Carlos (10); Romo, Manuel (29); Saldana, Egardo (24); Sombra, Francisco (24); Sosa, Carlos (21); Vargas, Miguel Angel (51); Vazquez, Marco A. (2).

VERACRUZ—Arano, Ramon (17); Baruch, Matias (18); Burke, Norberto (1); Castaneda, Aurelio (6); Duarte, Florentino (4); Felix, Antonio (11); Gaxiola, Fernando (6); Guzman, Jose Roberto (9); Luna, Jose Manuel (10); Lunar, Luis (13); Manzanillo, Ravelo (5); Mariscal, Tomas (2); Morales, Isidro (1); Moreno, Abel (14); Ochoa, Domingo (12); Ochoa, Julio (2); Ontiveros, Francisco (5); Ramirez, Roberto (13); Rincon, Juan (8); Rondon, Gilberto (2); Soto, Jose Luis (10); Toledo, Jose Manuel (2); Valdez, Humberto (9); Vazquez, Marco A. (5); Zamudio, Aurelio (30).

YUCATAN—Angulo, Kenneth (22); Belman, Andres (26); Brito, Oscar (6); Cordova, Ernesto (10); Diaz, Cesar (25); Diaz, Octavio (2); Escarrega, Ernesto (10); Montano, Nicolas (30); Pacheco, Alejandro (1); Palacios, Raul (11); Romo, Vicente (1); Ruiz, Cecilio (34); Sauceda, Ramiro (4); Urrea, Leonel (24); Uribe, Juan Carlos (21); Velazquez, Ildefonso (28).

GRAND SLAM HOME RUNS—B. Valdez, 6; L.A. Cruz, Gu. Rodriguez, 3 each; Bobadilla, N. Castaneda, An. Lopez, McDonald, Jo.L. Perez, Rojas, Ray. Torres, Villalobos, 2 each; Aikens, Avila, Bryant, Bundy, G. Cano, Evans, Garibay, A. Garza, Je. Gonzalez, D. Greene, Heras, Machiria, R. Martinez, Meza, Mora, Peralta, Pierce, Rosario, Roys, Uzcanga, L. Valenzuela, Vega, Velazquez, Whittemore, 1 each.

AWARDED FIRST BASE ON CATCHER'S INTERFERENCE—Ar. Sanchez 2 (A. Guzman, Vega); Herring (L. Mendoza); Mora (Vega); Ju. Perez (Villalobos).

CLUB FIELDING

Club	Pct.	G.	PO.	A.	E.	DP.	PB.
Cordoba	.978	129	3173	1325	103	128	9
Mexico City Tigers	.975	126	3170	1287	112	106	8
Mexico City Reds	.975	129	3182	1512	119	158	10
Yucatan	.975	130	3191	1417	117	122	7
Nuevo Laredo	.974	126	3146	1393	121	114	14
Leon	.973	128	3191	1404	129	142	13
Union Laguna	.971	126	3172	1421	136	135	17
Campeche	.971	129	3219	1375	137	110	10
Puebla	.971	130	3266	1486	142	116	22
San Luis	.970	131	3278	1637	150	158	27
Tabasco	.970	127	3132	1349	137	96	15
Monterrey	.970	131	3327	1457	149	125	42
Saltillo	.969	130	3268	1441	150	140	18
Aguascalientes	.969	129	3253	1413	150	96	16
Veracruz	.967	129	3110	1397	156	121	20
Monclova	.966	128	3204	1412	161	145	29

Triple Plays—Campeche, Leon, Saltillo, Yucatan.

INDIVIDUAL FIELDING

*Throws lefthanded.

FIRST BASEMEN

Player and Club	Pct.	G.	PO.	A.	E.	DP.
Whittemore, Tabasco*	1.000	51	405	30	0	31
J. Cruz, San Luis	1.000	30	244	11	0	27
H. Puente, Yucatan	1.000	16	92	6	0	11
Sommers, Leon	.998	51	400	23	1	39
R. Hernandez, Yucatan	.997	38	300	12	1	25
Mora, Nuevo Laredo	.994	116	992	67	6	91
Garzon, Cordoba	.994	125	1165	58	7	110
Cosey, Campeche*	.994	20	157	10	1	8
Bundy, Mexico City Reds*	.994	114	1084	70	7	128
Lora, Yucatan*	.994	58	452	22	3	45
J. Lopez, Union Laguna*	.993	16	145	6	1	21
G. Soto, Veracruz	.992	11	121	5	1	10
Sosa, San Luis	.992	48	351	18	3	45
B. Perkins, 13 MC Reds 1-Cor*	.991	14	106	10	1	22
Salinas, Tabasco*	.991	43	407	25	4	29
M.A. Guzman, Campeche	.991	79	696	55	7	75
A. Garza, Monclova*	.991	16	99	6	1	9
B. Valdez, Monclova	.990	12	93	10	1	13
Clayton 56 Saltillo-42 San Luis	.990	98	894	72	10	86
C. Rivera, Campeche	.990	36	272	16	3	25
Velazquez, Monterrey	.989	52	353	11	4	38
Pierce, Leon	.989	78	672	49	8	91
Gu. Rodriguez, Puebla	.989	127	1178	72	14	100
L.A. Cruz, San Luis	.989	21	169	9	2	22
An. Lopez, Saltillo	.988	77	698	31	9	73
Evans, Veracruz*	.988	38	232	8	3	22
A. Greene, Monclova*	.987	90	672	34	9	89
L.F. Diaz, Nuevo Laredo	.987	10	71	4	1	6
F. Martinez, Veracruz	.987	11	69	6	1	6
R. Valenzuela, MC Tigers	.987	11	72	2	1	10
H. Valenzuela, MC Tigers	.986	45	340	24	5	30
Tapia, Tabasco	.986	10	67	5	1	6
J. Reyes, 37 Vera-26 Yuc*	.986	63	544	31	8	61
Heras, Monterrey	.986	35	267	8	4	24
Al. Lopez, Mexico City Tigers	.985	84	629	40	10	48
Cabrera, Monclova	.983	42	291	7	5	26
Gray, Aguascalientes	.981	103	905	45	18	71
Quiroz, Union Laguna*	.981	108	905	58	19	89
Ge. Rodriguez, Monterrey	.980	72	601	33	13	54
McDonald, Aguascalientes	.978	15	125	8	3	11
A. Rivera, Tabasco	.978	28	162	15	4	15
O. Duran, 3 Lar-3 Cor-6 Tab	.973	12	103	6	3	9
P. Ruiz, Veracruz	.971	30	189	11	6	12
J.L. Perez, Aguascalientes*	.969	13	88	6	3	8

(Fewer Than Ten Games)

Player and Club	Pct.	G.	PO.	A.	E.	DP.
Payton, Union Laguna	1.000	5	50	0	0	5
Fabela, Veracruz	1.000	7	47	0	0	5
Rosado, Veracruz	1.000	5	36	4	0	5
O. Sanchez, Puebla	1.000	4	27	1	0	3
Lavagnino, San Luis	1.000	4	25	2	0	3
C. Soto, Nuevo Laredo	1.000	3	25	1	0	3
Jacobsen, Yucatan	1.000	3	25	1	0	2
Lara, Veracruz	1.000	2	20	1	0	5
Daut, Veracruz	1.000	3	20	0	0	0
Villagomez, Cordoba	1.000	5	18	0	0	1
Alf. Ortiz, Yucatan*	1.000	2	18	0	0	4
Valle, San Luis	1.000	2	17	1	0	0
Saiz, Union Laguna	1.000	3	17	0	0	2
Peralta, Mexico City Tigers	1.000	3	16	1	0	0
Rios, Campeche	1.000	3	17	0	0	0
C. Herrera, Veracruz	1.000	2	16	0	0	2
Avila, Union Laguna	1.000	3	14	1	0	2
Mayer, Mexico City Reds*	1.000	2	12	3	0	3
Benitez, Union Laguna	1.000	2	14	0	0	2
Ja. Hernandez, Leon	1.000	5	12	0	0	1
Amador, Cordoba	1.000	3	10	1	0	1
H. Robles, Puebla	1.000	3	11	0	0	2
Rendon, Saltillo	1.000	2	9	0	0	0
Ju. Alvarez, San Luis	1.000	1	9	0	0	1
O. Martinez, Saltillo	1.000	3	8	0	0	3
Rojas, Mexico City Tigers	1.000	3	6	0	0	2
J.M. Ortiz, Monclova	1.000	2	4	1	0	0
G. Soto, Cordoba	1.000	1	4	0	0	0
Nunez, Veracruz	1.000	1	4	0	0	0
F. Cruz, Puebla	1.000	2	4	0	0	1
L.A. Mendoza, Aguascalientes	1.000	1	2	0	0	0
Villalobos, Leon	1.000	1	1	1	0	0
Rosas, Aguascalientes	1.000	1	2	0	0	1
A. Vargas, Union Laguna	1.000	1	2	0	0	0
Luna, Saltillo	1.000	1	1	0	0	0
Palacios, Veracruz	1.000	1	1	0	0	0
Burke, Veracruz	.977	4	38	4	1	5
Clements, Union Laguna	.974	4	36	1	1	8
Placencia, San Luis	.964	5	25	2	1	2
Vergara, Veracruz	.959	7	47	0	2	3
DeFreites, Yucatan	.949	4	34	3	2	5

Triple Plays—Clayton, Alf. Ortiz, Pierce, C. Rivera.

SECOND BASEMAN

Player and Club	Pct.	G.	PO.	A.	E.	DP.
Barandica, Union Laguna	1.000	29	43	79	0	18
J.A. Barrera, Nuevo Laredo	1.000	11	37	35	0	6
J.F. Rodriguez, Leon	.988	127	376	396	9	107
Villaescusa, Yucatan	.988	52	108	139	3	28
Campos, Tabasco	.988	53	109	136	3	21
Ju. Hernandez, Cordoba	.987	16	37	37	1	10
Je. Gonzalez, Puebla	.984	126	285	375	11	77
Re. Herrera, Cordoba	.981	57	130	177	6	41
Raf. Torres, Aguascalientes	.980	54	135	165	6	33
An. Sanchez, Mexico City Reds	.980	13	20	30	1	7
M. Garcia, Monterrey	.980	25	41	57	2	14
Ar. Sanchez, Mexico City Reds	.980	117	281	393	14	106
L.A. Valdez, Monterrey	.980	104	202	324	11	70
Serna, Monclova	.979	117	300	363	14	91
R. Hernandez, Yucatan	.978	62	131	137	6	37
F. Martinez, 41 Cor-21 Vera	.978	62	152	156	7	45

SECOND BASEMEN—Continued

Player and Club	Pct.	G.	PO.	A.	E.	DP.
Ju. Chavez, Veracruz	.975	45	103	134	6	44
Ge. Sanchez, Nuevo Laredo	.975	112	272	315	15	69
R. Chavez, Campeche	.974	95	224	306	14	65
Navarrete, Saltillo	.973	130	279	370	18	103
Villela, San Luis	.973	129	372	486	24	116
Briones, Union Laguna	.972	108	215	279	14	62
Camacho, Mexico City Tigers	.971	105	237	304	16	67
Bajeca, Veracruz	.969	28	63	63	4	17
Vattimon, 2 MC Tig-14 Cor	.967	16	29	30	2	6
Almodobar, Mexico City Tigers	.965	25	49	62	4	13
R. Zuniga, Monterrey	.964	25	46	62	4	12
L. Guerrero, Aguascalientes	.963	79	184	209	15	38
Scott, Tabasco	.963	44	121	141	10	31
T. Vargas, Yucatan	.963	31	47	56	4	13
Rios, 39 Vera-35 Cam	.957	74	145	214	16	43
N. Torres, Tabasco	.929	33	70	75	11	16
Alonso, Puebla	.895	10	8	9	2	2

(Fewer Than Ten Games)

Player and Club	Pct.	G.	PO.	A.	E.	DP.
Bobadilla, Monclova	1.000	8	17	22	0	5
A. Castaneda, San Luis	1.000	7	14	19	0	5
Barragan, Mexico City Reds	1.000	3	7	11	0	2
Valladolid, Cordoba	1.000	5	4	10	0	1
Aispuro, Yucatan	1.000	2	5	5	0	0
J.A. Chavez, Veracruz	1.000	1	5	3	0	2
Burke, Veracruz	1.000	1	2	3	0	1
DeFreites, Yucatan	1.000	2	1	3	0	0
V. Quintero, Veracruz	1.000	1	3	1	0	0
Calderon, Campeche	1.000	4	1	2	0	0
Je. Garcia, Monclova	1.000	1	2	0	0	0
R. Lizarraga, Leon	1.000	1	0	2	0	0
Uribe, Puebla	1.000	1	0	1	0	0
Rubio, Saltillo	1.000	1	1	0	0	0
E. Ramirez, Nuevo Laredo	.976	9	19	21	1	4
Fabela, Veracruz	.971	8	18	16	1	4
E. Castillo, Cordoba	.938	3	8	7	1	0
Cabrera, Monclova	.938	5	9	6	1	3
Gu. Sanchez, Leon	.923	8	7	5	1	2
J.L. Hernandez, Puebla	917	7	13	20	3	3
A. Zuniga, Mexico City Tigers	.917	9	16	6	2	4
J.M. Ortiz, Monclova	.909	4	6	4	1	2
Pacho, Yucatan	.857	3	3	3	1	2
J. Cano, Saltillo	.857	1	2	4	1	0
J.A. Castro, Tabasco	.800	2	1	3	1	0
C. Rivera, Campeche	.800	1	2	2	1	0
Escalante, Aguascalientes	.667	3	2	2	2	1

Triple Plays—R. Chavez, J.F. Rodriguez, T. Vargas.

THIRD BASEMEN

Player and Club	Pct.	G.	PO.	A.	E.	DP.
Limon, Tabasco	.985	50	50	82	2	8
Santana, Yucatan	.981	126	120	300	8	20
V. Quintero, 5 Agu-46 Pue	.978	51	41	90	3	2
Saiz, Union Laguna	.971	118	110	258	11	19
E. Castillo, Cordoba	.968	126	101	266	12	25
N. Torres, Tabasco	.960	63	61	130	8	11
Ale. Ortiz, Nuevo Laredo	.955	120	100	199	14	25
Ju. Perez, San Luis	.952	59	41	139	9	12
Rios, 7 Veracruz-6 Campeche	.952	13	11	9	1	0
Rendon, Saltillo	.951	13	12	27	2	9
N. Barrera, Mexico City Reds	.950	128	129	272	21	26
Peralta, Mexico City Tigers	.950	82	66	105	9	11
Aguilar, Aguascalientes	.946	125	95	255	22	19
Alonso, Puebla	.945	66	48	108	9	16
Rubio, Saltillo	.944	84	50	102	9	10
A. Castaneda, San Luis	.943	40	26	74	6	13
Meza, 21 Veracruz-58 Mon	.941	79	41	133	11	18
R. Valenzuela, MC Tigers	.939	64	46	78	8	6
Bobadilla, Monclova	.939	80	26	81	7	7
Burke, 24 Puebla-85 Veracruz	.937	109	76	219	20	28
Barandica, Union Laguna	.929	12	6	20	2	1
Romero, Puebla	.929	18	5	8	1	1
Saenz, Saltillo	.925	56	21	90	9	6
Serratos, Campeche	.925	40	29	57	7	6
Sommers, Leon	.922	21	13	34	4	4
N. Gonzalez, Monterrey	.921	96	78	179	22	17
B. Valdez, Monclova	.918	100	68	144	19	14
L.A. Cruz, San Luis	.918	32	24	65	8	9
M. Ramirez, Tabasco	.917	19	18	37	5	2
Fabela, Veracruz	.913	11	6	15	2	1
C. Rivera, Campeche	.913	85	47	162	20	17
Je. Garcia, Monclova	.905	17	10	9	2	2
Arce, Leon	.896	111	87	180	31	26
O. Martinez, Saltillo	.885	32	28	49	10	5
Maza, San Luis	.848	19	13	26	7	3

(Fewer Than Ten Games)

Player and Club	Pct.	G.	PO.	A.	E.	DP.
R. Hernandez, Yucatan	1.000	3	3	8	0	1
Sarabia, Tabasco	1.000	4	4	7	0	0
Camacho, Mexico City Tigers	1.000	7	2	8	0	1
Ju. Gonzalez, Saltillo	1.000	6	1	8	0	2
G. Soto, Veracruz	1.000	2	2	5	0	0
Cazarin, Cordoba	1.000	3	1	6	0	0
Uribe, Puebla	1.000	4	1	5	0	0
Valle, San Luis	1.000	1	1	4	0	0
H. Robles, Puebla	1.000	1	1	3	0	0
DeFreites, Yucatan	1.000	1	3	1	0	0
Gu. Sanchez, Leon	1.000	2	1	2	0	0
Je. Gonzalez, Puebla	1.000	1	2	1	0	0
Campos, Tabasco	1.000	3	2	1	0	0
R. Lizarraga, Leon	1.000	3	0	2	0	0
Zepeda, Mexico City Reds	1.000	1	1	1	0	0
T. Vargas, Yucatan	1.000	1	1	1	0	1
L. Guerrero, Aguascalientes	1.000	1	1	1	0	0
Villaescusa, Yucatan	1.000	1	0	1	0	0
Valladolid, Cordoba	1.000	2	1	0	0	0
Alvarado, Veracruz	1.000	1	0	1	0	0
Clements, Union Laguna	1.000	2	1	0	0	0
Ulin, Nuevo Laredo	.958	9	8	15	1	2
Bajeca, Veracruz	.944	7	6	11	1	2
J.A. Barrera, Nuevo Laredo	.933	6	13	15	2	6
A. Vargas, Union Laguna	.933	8	4	10	1	0
R. Vizcarra, Leon	.875	3	5	2	1	1
McDonald, Aguascalientes	.800	3	1	3	1	1
Stockstill, Puebla	.714	6	3	2	2	0
An. Sanchez, Veracruz	.500	1	0	1	1	0
Darkis, Saltillo	.429	4	2	1	4	0

Triple Plays—Rendon, Santana, Serratos.

SHORTSTOPS

Player and Club	Pct.	G.	PO.	A.	E.	DP.
Re. Herrera, Cordoba	.990	22	34	63	1	15
RIVERO, Leon	.985	122	190	383	9	82
Elizondo, Saltillo	.983	117	242	390	11	87
Limon, Tabasco	.974	11	13	25	1	1
M. Garcia, Monclova	.973	18	20	52	2	7
G. Cano, Aguascalientes	.972	38	63	113	5	16
Cabrales, Campeche	.969	16	21	42	2	6
Rios, 8 Veracruz-4 Campeche	.968	12	21	40	2	5
Rubio, Saltillo	.967	13	22	36	2	9
Campos, Tabasco	.966	11	11	17	1	1
M. Morales, Mexico City Tigers	.965	95	142	273	15	53
Trinidad, Ulin, Nuevo Laredo	.964	55	71	146	8	29
V. Quintero, 18 Agu-72 Pue	.963	90	106	236	13	45
De Los Santos, Cordoba	.963	111	192	327	20	73
Pacho, Yucatan	.963	130	239	407	25	83
Mendoza, 21 P-21 Agu-74 Cam	.962	116	170	315	19	66
Uzcanga, Mexico City Reds	.961	126	225	399	25	115
Uribe, Puebla	.958	23	22	46	3	6
F. Guerrero, Union Laguna	.956	113	239	398	29	83
A. Gomez, Tabasco	.954	117	167	347	25	58
E. Ramirez, Nuevo Laredo	.952	82	113	247	18	37
J.L. Hernandez, Puebla	.952	53	80	180	13	29
Canedo, Monclova	.950	110	165	313	25	75
McDonald, Aguascalientes	.947	94	179	317	28	55
J.A. Chavez, Veracruz	.946	50	89	140	13	22
Valle, San Luis	.946	120	216	413	36	91
Barandica, Union Laguna	.944	19	33	52	5	15
Ri. Herrera, Monterrey	.940	124	212	368	37	85
Bobadilla, Monclova	.938	47	63	119	12	23
Almodobar, Mexico City Tigers	.933	40	57	110	12	22
Gu. Sanchez, Leon	.926	13	10	15	2	5
Ju. Hernandez, 41 Cam-26 Agu	.925	67	100	209	25	46
R. Vizcarra, Leon	.806	14	12	13	6	2

(Fewer Than Ten Games)

Player and Club	Pct.	G.	PO.	A.	E.	DP.
Escalante, Aguascalientes	1.000	6	7	12	0	1
Camacho, Mexico City Tigers	1.000	7	9	6	0	1
Ju. Gonzalez, Saltillo	1.000	4	9	4	0	0
Saiz, Union Laguna	1.000	5	3	8	0	1
Ju. Chavez, Veracruz	1.000	1	4	2	0	1
Maza, San Luis	1.000	2	2	2	0	0
Je. Garcia, Monclova	1.000	1	1	3	0	1
Gu. Reyes, Monterrey	1.000	3	1	2	0	1
Tapia, Tabasco	1.000	1	2	1	0	0
An. Sanchez, Mexico City Reds	.967	5	11	18	1	3
T. Vargas, Yucatan	.950	8	6	13	1	3
S. Vizcarra, San Luis	.889	4	1	7	1	1
R. Valenzuela, MC Tigers	.875	3	3	4	1	1
A. Castaneda, San Luis	.867	7	10	16	4	3
Fabela, Veracruz	.850	8	12	22	6	4
J.A. Barrera, Nuevo Laredo	.806	5	11	14	6	1

Triple Plays—Ju. Hernandez, Rivero.

OUTFIELDERS

Player and Club	Pct.	G.	PO.	A.	E.	DP.
Whittemore, Tabasco	1.000	16	24	0	0	0
Ge. Sanchez, Nuevo Laredo	1.000	14	20	2	0	0
R. Rodriguez, Cordoba*	1.000	13	21	0	0	0
F. Lopez, Saltillo	1.000	31	19	1	0	1
M.A. Gonzalez, Monclova	1.000	10	15	1	0	0
Quiroz, Union Laguna*	1.000	13	14	0	0	0
H. Robles, Puebla	1.000	10	8	2	0	0
Ef. Torres, Nuevo Laredo	1.000	18	9	0	0	0
A. Castro, Mexico City Tigers*	.994	82	151	11	1	3
Carrillo, Mexico City Tigers*	.992	55	123	6	1	0
J.S. Chavez, Mexico City Reds*	.992	72	114	13	1	4
Machiria, Mexico City Tigers	.992	74	120	3	1	0
Bruno, 6 MCR-12 Agu-28 Ags*	.992	46	115	5	1	0
Bellazetin, Mexico City Tigers*	.991	79	99	7	1	1
Cole, Cordoba	.991	45	104	2	1	0
Arzate, Aguascalientes	.990	104	191	15	2	2
L. Valenzuela, Monclova*	.988	124	246	11	3	0
E. Miller, Monterrey*	.988	89	165	4	2	1
Cosey, Campeche	.987	107	219	9	3	2
Duran, 41 MCR-1 Cordoba	.986	42	69	3	1	0
Darell, Tabasco	.986	22	70	0	1	0
Carter, Puebla*	.986	130	249	28	4	2
Suarez, Veracruz*	.985	45	60	4	1	2
Bryant, Monterrey	.983	119	171	6	3	2
Collins, 91 Leon-33 San Luis*	.982	124	204	11	4	4
Maza, San Luis	.980	58	96	4	2	0
Canady, Mexico City Reds	.980	32	46	3	1	0
Ge. Rodriguez, Monterrey	.980	33	45	4	1	1
Leal, Monclova*	.979	107	183	8	4	1
L.A. Cruz, San Luis	.979	72	131	10	3	3
Garibay, Nuevo Laredo	.978	32	42	3	1	1
Smith, 54 Agu-59 Cam*	.976	113	240	1	6	0
G. Gomez, Leon	.976	107	183	17	5	3
A. Lizarraga, Union Laguna	.975	118	149	7	4	0
Salava, Mexico City Tigers*	.974	110	218	10	6	0
D. Ruiz, Tabasco	.974	74	142	8	4	2
Jones, Nuevo Laredo	.974	23	36	1	1	0
A. Greene, Monclova*	.973	57	68	4	2	2
Andrade, Monterrey*	.972	99	170	6	5	2
Morfin, 36 MCR-12 Cordoba	.972	48	64	5	2	0
Bronson, Union Laguna	.970	95	185	12	6	1
DeFreites, Yucatan	.970	99	183	12	6	0
Adams, 26 Veracruz-43 Tab	.969	69	155	3	5	1
H. Perkins, Nuevo Laredo	.968	119	255	19	9	2
Villagomez, Cordoba	.968	74	115	5	4	2
E. Jimenez, Leon	.968	15	28	2	1	0
Fabela, Veracruz	.968	10	27	3	1	0
Ed. Torres, Saltillo	.967	96	228	10	8	1
Ge. Reyes, San Luis	.967	67	108	9	4	2
Cazarin, Cordoba	.967	47	55	3	2	0
Serratos, Campeche	.966	67	108	5	4	1
Ray. Torres, Yucatan	.966	118	244	9	9	1
Payton, Union Laguna	.965	119	263	16	10	2
R. Navarro, 8 Mon-77 Agu	.965	85	140	11	6	1
Herring, 89 San Luis-36 Leon	.965	125	237	13	9	6
Rendon, Saltillo	.964	48	79	2	3	0
Ja. Hernandez, Leon	.964	16	26	1	1	1
A. Diaz, Leon	.964	72	101	5	4	0
L.F. Diaz, Nuevo Laredo	.963	55	73	5	3	1
Ja. Rodriguez, Tabasco	.963	76	152	3	6	1
Baca, Nuevo Laredo	.962	104	171	7	7	0
Fernandez, Mexico City Reds*	.962	58	121	4	5	2
J.L. Garcia, San Luis	.962	57	68	7	3	2
Garbey, Nuevo Laredo	.960	19	22	2	1	1
Ponce, Puebla	.959	87	85	9	4	0
Olivares, Campeche*	.958	125	213	16	10	4
Valencia, Aguascalientes*	.958	126	218	11	10	3
Darkis, Saltillo	.957	22	43	2	2	0
Castelan, Puebla*	.957	109	212	11	10	2
Lora, Yucatan*	.957	73	129	4	6	1
J.L. Perez, Aguascalientes*	.957	92	126	6	6	0
Vergara 10 Cor-39 Veracruz	.957	49	83	5	4	1
G. Soto, 39 Cor-28 Veracruz	.955	67	102	4	5	0
Alvarado, Veracruz	.955	17	20	1	1	1
Dominguez, San Luis	.954	33	59	3	3	2
D. Greene, Monterrey*	.954	36	60	2	3	1
Sarabia, 1 Monclova-89 Tab	.952	90	154	6	8	1
Allen, Nuevo Laredo	.952	19	20	0	1	0
H. Robles, Monterrey	.952	15	20	0	1	0
Gage, 19 Saltillo-2 Ags	.950	21	35	3	2	1
Zambrano, Cordoba*	.950	95	144	7	8	1
Cotes, 19 Cor-37 Agu-27 MCR	.950	83	146	5	8	3
L. Vargas, Mexico City Reds	.948	108	187	14	11	0
J. Cano, Saltillo	.946	104	108	15	7	5
Ayala, Leon	.944	53	67	1	4	0
J. Puente, Aguascalientes	.944	24	47	4	3	1
L. Jimenez, Campeche	.944	17	17	0	1	0
Rosario, Monclova*	.944	125	189	14	12	3
Aguilera, Yucatan	.939	69	118	6	8	2
Delgado, Yucatan	.935	48	83	4	6	0
Barragan, Mexico City Reds	.935	20	27	2	2	1
Stockstill, Puebla	.935	117	178	15	8	2
Roys, 49 Cordoba-45 Ags*	.935	94	195	6	14	1
M.A. Guzman, Campeche	.933	14	22	6	2	2
C. Herrera, Veracruz	.931	89	139	10	11	1
O. Duran, 6 Lar-10 Cor-14 Tab	.930	30	39	1	3	0
Isales, Tabasco	.930	15	39	1	3	0
L. Miller, Saltillo	.926	75	119	7	10	4
Tapia, Tabasco	.917	63	73	4	7	1
Sutton, Leon	.917	16	22	0	2	0
L. Figueroa, 14 Yuc-7 Cor	.914	21	31	1	3	0
J. Rivera, Monterrey	.909	12	20	0	2	0
Clayton, Saltillo	.905	30	37	1	4	0
Scott, Tabasco	.900	10	15	3	2	1
A. Vargas, 1 MCT-38 Lar	.898	39	53	0	6	0
J. Cruz, 7 MCT-14 SLP	.889	21	16	0	2	0

(Fewer Than Ten Games)

Player and Club	Pct.	G.	PO.	A.	E.	DP.
R. Robles, Aguascalientes	1.000	6	17	0	0	0
Almodobar, Mexico City Tigers	1.000	8	11	0	0	0
Ju. Hernandez, Campeche	1.000	7	8	2	0	0
B. Perkins, Mexico City Reds	1.000	7	9	0	0	0
L. Guerrero, Aguascalientes	1.000	2	8	0	0	0
Gutierrez, Yucatan	1.000	8	7	0	0	0
Camarena, Union Laguna	1.000	4	6	0	0	0
Sosa, San Luis	1.000	5	5	0	0	0
M. Figueroa, Veracruz	1.000	3	5	0	0	0
Clements, Union Laguna	1.000	5	4	0	0	0
Aikens, Puebla*	1.000	1	4	0	0	0
An. Sanchez, Mexico City Reds	1.000	3	4	0	0	0
Valverde, Saltillo	1.000	7	4	0	0	0
Burke, Veracruz	1.000	1	2	1	0	0
N. Castaneda, San Luis*	1.000	1	3	0	0	0
Palacios, Veracruz	1.000	2	2	0	0	0
Acosta, Campeche	1.000	2	1	0	0	0
Felix, Campeche	1.000	1	1	0	0	0
Covarrubias, Puebla	1.000	2	1	0	0	0
Ford, Mexico City Reds	.889	7	7	1	1	0
Bajeca, Veracruz	.867	8	12	1	2	1
Buenrostro, Yucatan	.667	3	2	0	1	0
I. Vargas, Yucatan	.667	2	0	2	1	0
Gu. Rodriguez, Puebla	.500	1	1	0	1	0

CATCHERS

Player and Club	Pct.	G.	PO.	A.	E.	DP.	PB.
Gastelum, Mexico City Reds	1.000	15	41	4	0	0	1
L.A. Mendoza, Ags	.995	35	171	21	1	0	5
D. Ruiz, Tabasco	.993	30	112	25	1	1	3
Ed. Rivera, 8 Sal-37 Leon	.993	45	239	28	2	6	6
C. Soto, Nuevo Laredo	.991	21	103	11	1	1	1
Ju. C. Alvarez, San Luis	.991	96	379	60	4	7	12
E. Reyes, Nuevo Laredo	.991	93	489	48	5	15	9
R. Martinez, Monterrey	.989	93	536	79	7	6	30
H. Sanchez, Monclova	.988	40	147	11	2	2	7
Heras, Monterrey	.984	46	230	21	4	4	10
Rojas, Mexico City Tigers	.984	109	603	68	11	5	8
Avila, Union Laguna	.984	80	368	58	7	11	8
M.A. Guzman, Campeche	.984	34	163	19	3	2	2
Vega, Aguascalientes	.983	79	357	55	7	5	8

CATCHERS—Continued

Player and Club	Pct.	G.	PO.	A.	E.	DP.	PB.
M. Hernandez, Cordoba	.983	116	490	37	9	4	7
Rosas, Aguascalientes	.983	21	108	9	2	0	3
Jo. L. Alvarez, San Luis	.982	59	197	27	4	5	11
Samaniego, Campeche	.981	33	147	12	3	2	3
Al. Lopez, Mexico City Tigers	.981	26	96	10	2	2	0
F. Estrada, Campeche	.981	72	386	33	8	9	5
Luna, Saltillo	.981	94	397	71	9	7	8
A. Guzman, Tabasco	.980	93	434	59	10	5	12
G. Quintero, Mexico City Reds	.980	59	220	25	5	2	5
S. Robles, Mexico City Reds	.980	76	301	41	7	2	3
Villalobos, 31 Leon-37 Sal	.980	68	284	52	7	9	9
Bazan, Yucatan	.979	123	517	83	13	6	8
P. Ruiz, Veracruz	.979	42	168	16	4	1	3
Marquez, Leon	.977	78	322	60	9	5	3
V. Tirado, Yucatan	.976	20	37	3	1	0	1
Rosado, Veracruz	.975	15	75	3	2	1	2
Benitez, Union Laguna	.974	49	199	24	6	0	4
Monroy, Monclova	.970	97	437	43	15	5	22
O. Sanchez, Puebla	.969	103	487	36	17	3	18
An. Lopez, Saltillo	.968	11	28	2	1	1	5
Madero, Yucatan	.963	10	19	7	1	0	0
Daut, 53 Veracruz-12 Mon	.968	65	280	54	11	3	12
G. Garza, Nuevo Laredo	.959	19	66	5	3	1	2
F. Cruz, Puebla	.957	34	150	26	8	2	3
Villa, Puebla	.950	14	17	2	1	0	1
Bocardo, 1 MR-20 SL-12 Co	.941	33	100	12	7	1	9
A. Vargas, Union Laguna	.941	14	43	5	3	0	5

(Fewer Than Ten Games)

Player and Club	Pct.	G.	PO.	A.	E.	DP.	PB.
Nunez, Veracruz	1.000	8	40	4	0	0	2
Amador, Cordoba	1.000	8	25	2	0	0	0
M. Ramirez, Tabasco	1.000	4	19	4	0	0	0
Ale. Ortiz, Nuevo Laredo	1.000	4	13	5	0	0	1
C. Herrera, Veracruz	1.000	7	13	2	0	0	1
J.A. Chavez, Veracruz	1.000	4	11	1	0	0	0
El. Rivera, Monterrey	1.000	5	9	2	0	0	2
Clements, Union Laguna	1.000	1	9	0	0	0	0
Sarabia, Tabasco	1.000	3	6	2	0	0	0
J.A. Navarro, Saltillo	1.000	9	6	1	0	1	0
Cazarin, Cordoba	1.000	5	6	0	0	0	0
J. Diaz, Leon	1.000	2	3	0	0	0	0
E. Robles, Nuevo Laredo	1.000	3	1	0	0	0	1
N. Barrera, Mexico City Reds	.909	2	9	1	1	0	0

Triple Play—Villalobos.

PITCHERS

Player and Club	Pct.	G.	PO.	A.	E.	DP.
Colorado, Cordoba	1.000	23	4	41	0	0
R. Solis, Mexico City Reds*	1.000	34	7	32	0	1
G. Jimenez, Puebla*	1.000	24	6	33	0	4
Raygoza, Campeche	1.000	30	8	29	0	2
An. Moreno, MC Tigers*	1.000	25	8	28	0	2
I. Velazquez, Yucatan	1.000	28	10	25	0	3
Silva, Cordoba	1.000	42	8	23	0	0
Ibarra, Mexico City Tigers	1.000	29	8	23	0	1
J. Orozco, Puebla	1.000	24	4	26	0	1
Purata, San Luis*	1.000	24	55	25	0	4
Elvira, Leon*	1.000	31	6	23	0	1
Carranza, Nuevo Laredo*	1.000	37	4	24	0	1
Leon, Mexico City Reds	1.000	21	5	22	0	1
Vargas, Union Laguna	1.000	51	7	19	0	1
Delgadillo, Aguascalientes	1.000	31	5	21	0	0
Luna, 10 Veracruz-22 Cordoba	1.000	32	7	19	0	3
Dimas, San Luis	1.000	30	3	22	0	2
Sombra, Union Laguna	1.000	24	2	23	0	3
M. Rivas, Mexico City Tigers	1.000	49	8	14	0	2
Herman, San Luis	1.000	43	7	15	0	1
Yucupicio, Veracruz	1.000	38	3	19	0	1
Alvarado, 12 MCT-14 Lag	1.000	26	7	15	0	1
F. Montano, Aguascalientes	1.000	18	2	19	0	2
Salas, 18 Tabasco-15 Monclova	1.000	23	8	12	0	0
Torres, Cordoba	1.000	28	4	14	0	0
Castillejos, Tabasco	1.000	33	2	15	0	1
R. Castillo, Monterrey	1.000	33	5	12	0	0
F. Franco, 23 MCR-8 Sal	1.000	31	3	14	0	0
Baruch, 8 Cam-18 Agu	1.000	26	3	14	0	0
Gaxiola, 6 Cor-6 Agu-5 Cam	1.000	17	5	12	0	2
L.T. Castillo, Nuevo Laredo*	1.000	15	9	8	0	1
Retes, Mexico City Tigers*	1.000	35	5	10	0	0
Quijano, Puebla	1.000	24	2	12	0	1
Saldana, Union Laguna	1.000	24	5	9	0	0
W. Sarmiento, MC Tigers	1.000	16	6	8	0	1
J.L. Soto, Veracruz	1.000	10	3	11	0	1
R. Guzman, Monclova	1.000	44	7	6	0	0
Belman, Yucatan	1.000	26	5	8	0	1
C. Diaz, Yucatan	1.000	25	1	12	0	2
Marquez, San Luis	1.000	25	3	9	0	1
Escarrega, Yucatan	1.000	10	3	9	0	1
L. Urrea, 11 Mon-24 Yuc	1.000	35	4	7	0	0
Hernandez, Campeche	1.000	28	5	6	0	0
M.A. Rodriguez, Aguascalientes	1.000	28	1	10	0	1
Pollorena, Saltillo	1.000	41	1	9	0	1
Low, Union Laguna	1.000	24	5	5	0	3
Keine, Monclova	1.000	22	4	6	0	0
Ortiz, 2 Veracruz-8 Yucatan*	1.000	10	2	8	0	0
Vidana, Tabasco	1.000	29	2	7	0	0
Morales, 14 MR-1 V-3 Co-10 L	1.000	28	4	5	0	0
Padilla, Saltillo	1.000	38	2	6	0	0
Camarena, Puebla	1.000	34	1	7	0	2
Inzunza, 17 Cordoba-4 Saltillo*	1.000	21	1	7	0	0
Arano, Veracruz	1.000	17	3	5	0	0
R. Ramirez, Veracruz	1.000	13	2	6	0	0
A. Castaneda, 6 Agu-9 Pue	1.000	15	0	8	0	1
Vazquez, 6 Cor-5 Agu-2 Lag	1.000	13	1	7	0	0
Villarreal, 3 Pue-9 MCR*	1.000	12	3	5	0	0
M. Alvarez, Saltillo	1.000	31	1	6	0	1
Sosa, Union Laguna	1.000	21	1	6	0	0
Miranda, Leon	1.000	18	3	3	0	0
Casas, San Luis	1.000	15	2	4	0	0
Calderon, Leon	1.000	12	1	5	0	1
Garza, 9 Mon-17 Monclova	1.000	26	0	5	0	0
H. Valdez, 11 Cam-9 Agu	1.000	20	1	4	0	0
Ab. Moreno, 5 Leon-14 Agu	1.000	19	1	4	0	0
Senteney, Tabasco	1.000	15	2	3	0	1
R. Palacios, Yucatan	1.000	11	0	5	0	0
F. Soto, Tabasco	1.000	11	0	4	0	0
Lopez, Aguascalientes	1.000	37	0	3	0	0
Martinez, Nuevo Laredo	1.000	13	0	3	0	0
Murillo, Monterrey	1.000	12	0	3	0	0
R. Rodriguez, Campeche	1.000	12	0	3	0	0
F. Ruiz, San Luis	1.000	12	0	3	0	0
Vaqueiro, Nuevo Laredo	1.000	12	0	2	0	0
Alapizco, Aguascalientes	1.000	10	2	0	0	0
G. Guzman, 1 Mon-20 Cor	1.000	21	0	1	0	0
D. Ochoa, 12 Agu-1 Cam	1.000	13	0	1	0	0
Ledon, 5 Monclova-8 Monterrey	1.000	13	1	0	0	0
D. Villegas, Yucatan	1.000	11	0	1	0	0
P. Rodriguez, Cordoba	1.000	11	0	1	0	0
S. Rios, Union Laguna	1.000	10	0	1	0	0
Matus, 10 Ags-16 Tab	.979	26	13	34	1	0
Bass, Monterrey	.976	25	5	35	1	2
C. Ruiz, Yucatan*	.973	34	5	31	1	1
G. Valenzuela, Leon	.972	28	11	24	1	3
P. Ochoa, Nuevo Laredo	.972	50	4	31	1	0
M. Villegas, Aguascalientes	.971	38	7	27	1	0
Zamudio, 30 Agu-10 MCR	.970	40	4	28	1	2
E. Valdez, San Luis	.969	26	8	23	1	1
Fuson, Nuevo Laredo	.962	22	13	37	2	3
Rincon, 8 Veracruz-13 Puebla	.962	21	7	18	1	0
Mundo, Monclova	.960	27	14	34	2	5
C. Perez, Puebla*	.960	28	4	20	1	1
J. Rios, Mexico City Tigers	.958	28	4	19	1	2
Go. Rojo, 20 Tab-32 Ags	.957	52	5	17	1	3
Heredia, Monclova	.955	24	5	37	2	4
O. Orozco, Puebla	.955	23	5	16	1	0
Mendez, Mexico City Reds	.955	25	7	14	1	0
Ro. Garcia, Monclova	.955	41	2	19	1	2
Ra. Garcia, Saltillo	.952	28	19	21	2	2
Navarro, Nuevo Laredo	.952	30	2	18	1	2
Lomeli, Mexico City Reds	.952	42	5	15	1	2
L. Perez, Leon	.950	20	7	12	1	1
Uribe, Yucatan	.950	21	5	14	1	1
A. Soto, Puebla	.950	44	4	15	1	0
Sandate, Campeche*	.947	31	6	30	2	1
P. Ruiz, Monclova*	.947	25	6	30	2	4
Aguilar, Tabasco	.947	24	4	14	1	1
Divison, Campeche	.947	45	7	11	1	1
Ro. Osuna, Leon	.947	39	7	11	1	2
Munoz, Aguascalientes	.947	31	6	12	1	1
MacKenzie, Aguascalientes	.947	10	3	15	1	0
R. Valdez, Campeche	.944	29	14	37	3	1
J. Valenzuela, Saltillo	.944	25	4	13	1	3
Duarte, 14 Le-4 Ve-3 MR-7 Sa	.943	28	9	24	2	2
Gutierrez, Monterrey	.941	25	4	12	1	1
A. Valdez, Mexico City Tigers	.941	28	4	12	1	0
Dominguez, Campeche*	.939	26	6	25	2	2
Contreras, 15 SL-3 MT-9 UL	.938	27	3	12	1	2
J. Ontiveros, 2 Pue-26 SLP	.938	28	3	12	1	0
Serafin, 26 Cor-15 Mon	.938	41	5	10	1	0
Acosta, Union Laguna	.938	26	4	11	1	0
Granillo, Aguascalientes*	.938	38	3	12	1	1
Chavez, San Luis	.935	40	7	22	2	0
K. Angulo, Yucatan	.933	22	6	22	2	2

PITCHERS—Continued

Player and Club	Pct.	G.	PO.	A.	E.	DP.
V. Palacios, Veracruz	.933	23	4	24	2	0
V. Romo, 10 Cor-1 Yuc	.933	11	3	11	1	0
Leal, Cordoba	.933	28	3	11	1	1
D. Franco, Saltillo	.933	24	3	11	1	2
Barojas, Mexico City Reds	.932	28	13	55	5	4
Serna, Monterrey	.929	21	7	19	2	1
Moya, Tabasco	.929	27	6	20	2	1
N. Montano, Yucatan	.929	30	2	11	1	1
Palafox, Union Laguna	.929	23	3	10	1	0
Antunez, 9 Pue-24 Mon*	.923	33	2	10	1	0
M. Sarmiento, Cordoba	.923	11	2	10	1	0
Villanueva, Aguascalientes*	.923	31	3	9	1	0
Beltran, 18 San Luis-8 Saltillo	.919	26	5	29	3	1
R. Menendez, 26 Leon-10 Cor	.917	36	8	14	2	2
Jaime Granillo, 2 MT-33 Mon	.917	35	3	8	1	0
Veliz, 2 Cordoba-24 Monterrey	.917	26	0	11	1	0
Esquer, Monterrey*	.914	26	6	26	3	0
J. Moreno, Nuevo Laredo	.906	26	10	38	5	0
I. Jimenez, Puebla*	.903	19	1	27	3	4
Sanchez, 13 Mon-6 Pu-9 Le*	.900	28	2	7	1	2
Kibbe, 7 Lar-14 SLP	.897	21	13	22	4	2
Flores, Campeche	.895	25	1	16	2	0
M. Solis, 20 Sal-10 MCR	.889	30	10	30	5	3
F. Vazquez, Monclova	.889	25	4	20	3	5
H. Rios, 18 Leon-14 MCR	.889	32	5	19	3	1
Huerta, Nuevo Laredo	.889	21	8	8	2	2
Felix, 11 Agu-6 Cor-17 Leon	.889	34	2	6	1	0
R. Villegas, Mexico City Tigers	.889	24	4	4	1	0
Je. Cruz, Mexico City Tigers*	.889	27	0	8	1	0
Garces, Saltillo	.889	23	3	5	1	0
Enriquez, Leon	.880	29	8	14	3	2
Tejeda, Mexico City Reds	.875	33	2	12	2	0
Figueroa, Veracruz	.875	26	0	7	1	0
Cartagena, Saltillo	.875	31	0	7	1	0
Lunar, 13 Agu-18 Leon-8 Lag	.872	39	6	35	6	2
Feola, 13 Tabasco-11 Cordoba	.872	24	7	27	5	2
Patterson, Nuevo Laredo	.870	16	6	14	3	2
Jor. L. Garcia, Tabasco	.865	28	10	22	5	3
Cano, Monclova	.857	28	3	9	2	0
Vizcarra, Nuevo Laredo	.857	22	1	5	1	0
Pulido, Mexico City Reds	.846	41	2	9	2	0
W. Menendez, Tabasco	.833	17	0	10	2	0
Jos. L. Garcia, Monclova*	.833	27	1	4	1	2
Gaynor, Union Laguna	.824	10	2	12	3	1
Pruneda, Monclova	.813	21	0	13	3	0
Romero, 22 Lag-8 SLP	.800	30	1	7	2	0
O. Diaz, 5 Lag-6 SLP-2 Yuc	.800	13	2	2	1	0
Rivera, Union Laguna	.800	10	1	3	1	0
M. Romo, Union Laguna	.778	29	1	6	2	0
E. Rodriguez, Saltillo	.769	31	4	6	3	1
L.A. Velazquez, Monclova	.727	21	4	12	6	1
A. Valenzuela, Saltillo*	.667	10	0	4	2	1
Cordova, 10 Yuc-10 Mon	.667	20	0	2	1	1

(Fewer Than Ten Games)

Player and Club	Pct.	G.	PO.	A.	E.	DP.
F. Ontiveros, Veracruz	1.000	5	0	7	0	0
Evans, Nuevo Laredo	1.000	9	1	5	0	0
Renteria, Mexico City Tigers	1.000	4	2	3	0	0
J. Urrea, Mexico City Tigers	1.000	6	3	2	0	0
Rice, Monterrey	1.000	6	1	3	0	0
Manzanillo, Veracruz	1.000	5	1	3	0	0
Mattson, Nuevo Laredo	1.000	7	1	2	0	0
Hann, Nuevo Laredo	1.000	7	2	1	0	0
Armenta, 1 MC Reds-7 Leon	1.000	8	1	1	0	0
Harper, Cordoba	1.000	6	0	2	0	0
Buitimea, Mexico City Tigers	1.000	4	0	2	0	0
Rondon, Veracruz	1.000	2	0	2	0	0
R. Castro, Monterrey	1.000	2	0	2	0	0
Taylor, Leon	1.000	9	0	1	0	0
M.A. Castaneda, Saltillo	1.000	6	0	1	0	0
Garibaldi, Saltillo	1.000	6	0	1	0	0
A. Ramirez, Leon	1.000	6	0	1	0	0
R. Romo, Campeche	1.000	5	1	0	0	0
Aponte, Cordoba	1.000	5	1	0	0	0
Gu. Rojo, Saltillo	1.000	4	0	1	0	1
J. Ochoa, Veracruz	1.000	2	0	1	0	0
L. Sanchez, Cordoba	1.000	1	1	0	0	0
Valencia, Mexico City Tigers	.857	7	0	6	1	1
Brito, Yucatan	.800	6	0	4	1	0
R. Alvarez, Mexico City Tigers	.667	5	0	2	1	0
Gonzalez, Tabasco	.667	9	0	2	1	0
Meza, Leon	.667	8	1	1	1	0
Barraza, Campeche	.500	7	0	1	1	0
A. Diaz, Leon	.000	5	0	0	1	0

CLUB PITCHING

Club	ERA.	G.	CG.	ShO.	Sv.	IP.	H.	R.	ER.	HR.	HB.	BB.	Int. BB.	SO.	WP.	Bk.
Monterrey	4.25	131	30	8	15	1109.0	1193	626	524	69	37	447	35	724	62	2
Campeche	4.51	129	47	9	20	1073.0	1215	602	538	103	21	379	22	623	44	3
Nuevo Laredo	4.68	126	44	7	14	1048.2	1193	626	545	110	20	471	36	628	45	6
Cordoba	4.70	129	44	9	13	1057.2	1169	605	552	111	25	399	28	516	50	0
Mexico City Tigers	4.87	126	30	4	33	1056.2	1240	638	572	109	30	400	36	634	42	1
Puebla	5.03	130	48	5	19	1088.2	1366	684	608	101	34	415	37	574	62	4
Mexico City Reds	5.37	129	35	7	21	1060.2	1282	706	633	108	34	457	18	515	64	0
Tabasco	5.43	127	32	5	17	1044.0	1259	720	630	123	31	444	21	531	46	4
Yucatan	5.43	130	45	8	7	1063.2	1316	714	642	132	44	469	17	510	57	1
Monclova	5.46	128	39	8	14	1068.0	1276	760	648	131	30	524	55	576	61	5
Union Laguna	5.46	126	18	2	17	1057.1	1312	738	642	131	45	544	39	508	52	3
San Luis	5.61	131	26	3	9	1092.2	1321	779	681	138	29	535	41	610	56	1
Veracruz	5.74	129	30	6	8	1036.2	1296	768	661	109	41	513	34	537	79	1
Aguascalientes	5.85	129	24	4	27	1084.1	1422	816	705	168	36	363	24	567	38	3
Saltillo	6.60	130	26	2	18	1089.1	1410	883	799	184	44	546	39	569	48	1
Leon	6.79	128	16	1	16	1063.2	1418	913	802	124	35	601	80	584	61	2

PITCHERS' RECORDS

(Leading Qualifiers for Earned-Run Average Leadership—106 or More Innings)

*Throws lefthanded.

Pitcher—Club	W.	L.	Pct.	ERA.	G.	GS.	CG.	GF.	ShO.	Sv.	IP.	H.	R.	ER.	HR.	HB.	BB.	Int. BB.	SO.	WP.
Bass, Monterrey	14	4	.778	2.03	25	24	10	1	3	1	181.1	146	59	41	9	7	53	3	87	5
Fuson, Nuevo Laredo	15	4	.789	2.61	22	20	14	2	3	1	162.0	148	56	47	7	1	45	4	114	4
Colorado, Cordoba	12	7	.632	3.16	23	23	16	0	3	0	170.2	177	67	60	13	1	26	3	96	0
G. Jimenez, Pueblo*	17	6	.739	3.37	24	24	14	0	3	0	170.2	183	76	64	9	5	37	2	115	9
Dominguez, Campeche*	15	9	.625	3.39	26	24	10	2	1	0	175.1	167	73	66	11	3	44	1	124	5
R. Valdez, Campeche	17	7	.708	3.44	29	29	12	0	3	0	204.0	207	90	78	14	1	76	3	131	7
Sandate, Campeche*	13	13	.500	3.47	31	26	14	5	4	3	197.0	212	86	76	12	1	48	1	107	5
F. Montano, Aguascalientes	12	3	.800	3.57	18	17	3	1	1	0	111.0	134	64	44	9	4	30	2	47	5
K. Angulo, Yucatan	14	6	.700	3.61	22	21	15	1	4	0	167.0	154	72	67	12	4	74	0	145	15
Serna, Monterrey	12	8	.600	3.88	21	21	8	0	0	0	148.1	161	76	64	8	4	40	2	94	4

Departmental Leaders: G—Go. Rojo, 52; W—G. Jimenez, C. Ruiz, R. Valdez, 17; L—Jor. L. Garcia, V. Palacios, I. Velazquez, 14; Pct.—O. Orozco, .867; GS—R. Solis, R. Valdez, 29; CG—Colorado, 16; GF—Go. Rojo, 52; ShO—K. Angulo, Esquer, Sandate, 4; Sv.—M. Rivas, 23; IP—R. Valdez, 204; H—M. Solis, 261; R—M. Solis, 143; ER—M. Solis, 131; HR—Ra. Garcia, 30; HB—M. Solis, 12; BB—Barojas, 99; IBB—Ro. Osuna, 14; SO—Ra. Garcia, 155; WP—K. Angulo, Felix, Lunar, An. Moreno, 15.

(All Pitchers—Listed Alphabetically)

Pitcher—Club	W.	L.	Pct.	ERA.	G.	GS.	CG.	GF.	ShO.	Sv.	IP.	H.	R.	ER.	HR.	HB.	BB.	Int. BB.	SO.	WP.
Acosta, Union Laguna	11	11	.500	4.78	26	26	4	0	0	0	143.0	191	85	76	13	8	50	0	59	2
Aguilar, Tabasco*	5	8	.385	6.70	24	14	2	10	1	0	98.0	133	81	73	8	5	62	1	44	1
Aguilera, Yucatan	0	0	.000	5.25	3	0	0	3	0	0	12.0	11	7	7	2	0	6	0	2	1
Alapizco, Aguascalientes	0	1	.000	21.11	10	1	0	9	0	0	18.1	52	44	43	8	2	7	0	8	3
Alvarado, 12 MCT-14-Lag	11	8	.579	4.43	26	22	2	4	0	0	126.0	157	82	62	7	5	72	3	66	12
M. Alvarez, Saltillo	1	1	.500	5.29	31	1	0	30	0	1	34.0	37	22	20	3	0	39	1	35	9
R. Alvarez, MC Tigers	0	0	.000	6.97	5	0	0	5	0	0	10.1	12	8	8	2	1	7	0	5	0
Andrade, Monterrey*	0	0	.000	9.00	1	0	0	1	0	0	2.0	1	2	2	0	0	4	0	1	0
K. Angulo, Yucatan	14	6	.700	3.61	22	21	15	1	4	0	167.0	154	72	67	12	4	74	0	145	15
P. Angulo, Monterrey	0	0	.000	45.00	1	0	0	1	0	0	1.0	4	5	5	0	0	2	0	0	0
Antunez, 9 Pueblo-24 Mon*	6	7	.462	5.08	33	16	0	17	0	0	117.0	153	82	66	6	0	49	5	85	9
Aponte, Cordoba	1	1	.500	2.86	5	0	0	5	0	1	7.1	10	6	3	2	1	3	0	5	1
Arano, Veracruz	5	8	.385	4.97	17	13	2	4	2	2	67.0	87	39	37	6	1	14	2	22	3
Armenta, 1 MCR-7 Leon	1	0	1.000	9.00	8	0	0	8	0	0	18.0	31	20	18	5	1	12	1	7	1
Arzate, Aguascalientes	0	0	.000	27.00	1	0	0	1	0	0	1.0	3	3	3	1	0	1	0	2	0
Baca, Nuevo Laredo	0	0	.000	0.00	1	0	0	1	0	0	1.0	0	0	0	0	0	1	0	1	0
Barojas, Mexico City Reds	11	9	.550	4.86	28	28	10	0	1	0	181.2	205	113	98	18	6	99	0	88	8
Barraza, Campeche	0	0	.000	7.36	7	0	0	7	0	0	14.2	19	17	12	0	0	10	0	7	4
Baruch, 8 Cam-18 Veracruz	4	7	.364	7.75	26	9	1	17	0	1	76.2	117	73	66	14	0	28	2	33	6
Bass, Monterrey	14	4	.778	2.03	25	24	10	1	3	1	181.1	146	59	41	9	7	53	3	87	5
Belman, Yucatan	3	4	.429	5.64	26	9	0	17	0	0	89.1	121	60	56	17	3	38	1	24	1
Beltran, 18 San Luis-8 Saltillo	12	12	.500	5.28	26	26	6	0	0	0	163.2	196	105	96	21	6	62	6	78	2
Berenguer, Campeche	0	1	.000	15.43	1	1	0	0	0	0	2.1	5	4	4	0	0	4	0	0	0
Brito, Yucatan	0	2	.000	10.31	6	3	0	3	0	0	18.1	35	25	21	2	1	5	0	11	1
Buces, Union Laguna	0	0	.000	12.38	4	0	0	4	0	0	8.0	14	13	11	2	0	8	0	8	3
Buitimea, MC Tigers	1	1	.500	1.50	4	0	0	4	0	0	12.0	9	2	2	0	0	3	1	6	0
Burke, Veracruz	0	0	.000	21.00	1	0	0	1	0	0	3.0	11	7	7	0	0	0	0	0	0
Calderon, Leon	2	3	.400	5.09	12	3	0	9	0	1	35.1	32	26	20	4	2	23	2	36	2
Camarena, Puebla	8	1	.889	5.90	34	0	0	34	0	1	93.0	130	68	61	9	4	35	4	36	8
Cano, Monclova	1	3	.250	6.68	28	5	2	23	0	1	63.1	71	49	47	11	8	33	2	25	3
Carranza, Nuevo Laredo*	10	4	.714	5.12	37	10	2	27	1	0	96.2	112	65	55	16	4	59	5	62	1
Cartagena, Saltillo	3	5	.375	9.10	31	7	1	24	0	2	60.1	73	66	61	10	2	27	0	36	2
Casas, San Luis	0	2	.000	8.23	15	1	0	14	0	0	42.2	51	40	39	9	2	22	3	21	1
A. Castaneda, 6 Agu-9 Puebla	1	3	.250	4.39	15	6	0	9	0	0	55.1	65	34	27	2	2	32	0	27	3
Mar. Castaneda, Saltillo*	1	0	1.000	5.93	6	1	0	5	0	0	13.2	14	10	9	1	0	11	0	4	1
Max. Castaneda, Union Laguna	0	0	.000	0.90	5	0	0	5	0	0	10.0	13	2	1	0	0	7	0	4	0
Castillejos, Tabasco	5	3	.625	4.97	33	3	0	30	0	4	87.0	121	54	48	12	2	25	1	38	0
H. Castillo, Union Laguna	0	0	.000	13.50	1	0	0	1	0	0	.2	3	1	1	0	0	0	0	2	0
L.T. Castillo, Nuevo Laredo*	6	3	.667	2.93	15	14	5	1	1	1	92.0	89	36	30	10	0	30	0	63	4
R. Castillo, Monterrey	6	2	.750	1.49	33	0	0	33	0	9	66.2	44	13	11	3	2	18	4	70	3
E. Castro, Leon	0	2	.000	5.93	8	0	0	8	0	0	13.2	19	12	9	1	1	11	2	9	2
R. Castro, Monterrey	0	0	.000	13.50	2	0	0	2	0	0	2.2	3	4	4	0	1	2	0	0	1
Chavez, San Luis	11	9	.550	6.49	40	17	5	23	0	3	122.0	162	98	88	16	4	63	9	80	4
Colorado, Cordoba	12	7	.632	3.16	23	23	16	0	3	0	170.2	177	67	60	13	1	26	3	96	0
Contreras, 15 SL-3 MCT-9 Lag	1	10	.091	7.44	27	8	1	19	0	0	75.0	90	72	62	14	3	67	4	51	7
Cordova, 10 Yuc-9 Mon	0	2	.000	7.62	19	3	0	17	0	1	39.0	61	38	33	4	1	18	2	19	0
Cota, San Luis	0	0	.000	6.75	1	0	0	1	0	0	1.1	2	1	1	0	0	1	0	0	0
Ja. Cruz, MC Tigers	0	0	.000	0.00	1	0	0	1	0	0	1.1	0	0	0	0	0	1	0	0	0
Je. Cruz, MC Tigers*	3	0	1.000	5.50	27	0	0	27	0	0	54.0	60	35	33	7	2	24	3	38	5
L.A. Cruz, San Luis	0	0	.000	0.00	2	0	0	2	0	0	1.1	0	0	0	0	0	1	0	2	0
Delgadillo, Aguascalientes	10	6	.625	5.16	31	16	3	15	0	0	129.0	160	84	74	23	6	36	3	40	6
A. Diaz, Leon*	0	0	.000	9.82	5	0	0	5	0	0	7.1	14	9	8	1	1	5	0	3	0
C. Diaz, Yucatan	3	9	.250	6.54	25	17	4	8	0	0	108.2	156	90	79	14	5	48	2	36	1
O. Diaz, 5 Lag-6 SLP-2 Yuc	0	1	.000	6.86	13	2	0	11	0	0	21.0	27	22	16	3	0	35	0	17	6
Dimas, San Luis	8	3	.727	3.97	30	0	0	30	0	0	99.2	106	47	44	8	0	32	3	47	4
Divison, Campeche	4	4	.500	3.10	45	1	1	44	0	16	81.1	79	29	28	4	4	24	7	46	2
Dominguez, Campeche*	15	9	.625	3.39	26	24	10	2	1	0	175.1	167	73	66	11	3	44	1	124	5
Duarte, 14 Le-4 Ve-3 MR-7 Sal	7	8	.429	7.49	28	24	5	4	0	0	139.1	205	119	114	24	9	56	4	49	5
Duran, Campeche	0	0	.000	20.25	2	0	0	2	0	0	2.2	4	7	6	0	0	8	0	1	0
Elvira, Leon*	8	5	.615	4.81	31	19	1	12	0	1	127.1	128	81	68	13	6	84	4	86	8
Enriquez, Leon	3	10	.231	7.49	29	18	2	11	0	0	107.0	149	100	89	13	1	68	11	44	12
Escarrega, Yucatan	1	5	.167	7.52	10	10	1	0	0	0	40.2	67	34	34	7	4	16	0	22	1
Espinosa, San Luis	0	0	.000	10.13	3	0	0	3	0	0	5.1	7	6	6	1	0	3	0	2	2
Esquer, Monterrey*	9	9	.500	4.00	26	26	8	0	4	0	173.1	189	89	77	9	5	49	3	148	14
Evans, Nuevo Laredo	0	0	.000	8.74	9	2	0	7	0	0	22.2	30	23	22	5	2	18	0	17	0
Felix, 11 Agu-6 Cor-17 Leon	0	4	.000	5.65	34	2	0	32	0	5	57.1	62	44	36	5	1	47	2	51	15
Feola, 13 Tab-11 Cordoba	6	11	.353	5.16	24	24	7	0	0	0	129.0	162	90	74	19	5	59	4	50	10
Figueroa, Veracruz	1	9	.100	7.35	26	5	2	21	0	0	78.1	109	72	64	9	4	49	10	28	10
Flores, Campeche	4	7	.364	6.02	25	13	1	12	0	0	89.2	121	64	60	10	1	38	1	37	8
D. Franco, Saltillo	1	10	.091	8.01	24	15	1	9	0	1	96.2	151	94	86	23	3	37	5	39	1
F. Franco, 23 MCR-8 Saltillo	1	9	.100	6.53	31	8	2	23	0	2	82.2	107	67	60	7	6	38	3	30	4
Fuson, Nuevo Laredo	15	4	.789	2.61	22	20	14	2	3	1	162.0	148	56	47	7	1	45	4	114	4
Garces, Saltillo	4	3	.571	6.75	23	2	0	21	0	4	33.1	31	30	25	5	2	39	1	40	3
Jos. L. Garcia, Monclova*	2	1	.667	8.82	27	1	0	26	0	1	16.1	31	18	16	5	0	8	2	13	3
Jor. L. Garcia, Tabasco	7	14	.333	5.58	28	21	4	7	1	0	146.2	172	100	91	16	3	54	1	68	5
Ra. Garcia, Saltillo	11	13	.458	5.59	28	28	12	0	1	0	198.0	210	134	123	30	7	72	2	155	10
Ro. Garcia, Monclova	7	4	.636	5.27	41	0	0	41	0	4	85.1	110	56	50	11	3	40	6	34	7
Garibaldi, Saltillo	0	0	.000	14.25	6	0	0	6	0	0	12.0	21	20	19	3	1	11	0	6	0
Garibay, Nuevo Laredo	0	0	.000	13.50	3	0	0	3	0	0	3.1	7	5	5	2	0	3	0	4	1
Garza, 9 Mon-17 Monclova	0	0	.000	7.92	26	0	0	26	0	1	25.0	38	25	22	1	0	25	3	18	4
Gaxiola, 6 Cor-6 Agu-5 Cam	2	7	.222	5.42	17	16	1	1	0	0	83.0	111	59	50	10	8	32	4	36	6
Gaynor, Union Laguna	4	3	.571	5.21	10	9	3	1	1	0	55.1	73	37	32	6	0	23	1	30	2
Gonzalez, Tabasco	2	2	.500	4.12	9	1	1	8	0	1	19.2	20	9	9	3	0	9	2	9	0
Grajales, Aguascalientes	0	0	.000	2.25	1	0	0	1	0	0	4.0	5	2	1	1	0	1	0	0	0
Granillo, Aguascalientes*	9	6	.600	6.16	38	8	2	30	0	7	87.2	112	72	60	15	3	37	2	63	6
Greer, Mexico City Tigers	0	0	.000	5.40	2	0	0	2	0	0	.2	4	4	4	0	1	2	0	1	0
Guerrero, Aguascalientes	0	0	.000	0.00	1	0	0	1	0	0	.1	0	0	0	0	0	0	0	0	0
Gutierrez, Monterrey	11	6	.647	4.10	25	25	3	0	1	0	136.0	141	70	62	8	4	64	4	85	10
B. Guzman, San Luis	0	0	.000	7.36	3	0	0	3	0	0	3.2	9	3	3	1	0	3	0	1	1
G. Guzman, 1 Mon-20 Cor	3	2	.600	5.89	21	3	1	18	0	0	47.1	47	36	31	5	1	26	0	15	2
J.R. Guzman, Veracruz	0	1	.000	7.50	9	2	0	7	0	0	24.0	42	21	20	5	0	11	0	16	7

Pitcher—Club	W.	L.	Pct.	ERA.	G.	GS.	CG.	GF.	ShO.	Sv.	IP.	H.	R.	ER.	HR.	HB.	BB.	Int. BB.	SO.	WP.
R. Guzman, Monclova	4	2	.667	6.24	44	0	0	44	0	5	70.2	91	54	49	14	0	37	9	35	1
Hann, Nuevo Laredo	0	1	.000	7.30	7	2	0	5	0	0	12.1	11	10	10	0	1	16	1	6	4
Harper, Cordova	2	3	.400	8.14	6	5	1	1	0	0	21.0	32	20	19	2	1	8	0	14	5
Herman, San Luis	10	6	.625	4.25	43	2	1	41	0	4	89.0	112	51	42	6	4	18	1	42	4
Hernandez, Campeche	2	0	1.000	6.14	28	0	0	28	0	1	51.1	70	40	35	14	1	13	1	34	0
Heredia, Monclova	11	9	.550	4.41	24	24	7	0	0	0	157.0	176	93	77	16	1	50	11	98	7
Huerta, Nuevo Laredo	6	6	.500	5.17	21	13	1	8	0	1	95.2	108	60	55	12	2	37	1	41	7
Ibarra, Mexico City Tigers	9	6	.600	5.75	29	20	3	9	1	3	128.1	164	87	82	14	0	41	3	53	8
Inzunza, 17 Cor-4 Saltillo*	2	3	.400	6.82	21	0	0	21	0	1	30.1	37	24	23	10	0	18	2	15	3
Jaime Granillo, 2 MCT-33 Sal	5	4	.556	5.72	35	5	0	30	0	1	74.0	102	59	47	9	2	28	4	30	2
G. Jimenez, Puebla*	17	6	.739	3.37	24	24	14	0	3	0	170.2	183	76	64	9	5	37	2	115	9
I. Jimenez, Puebla*	10	6	.625	5.52	19	19	7	0	0	0	120.2	129	82	74	7	6	96	2	74	13
Keine, Monclova	3	3	.500	7.39	22	0	0	22	0	3	31.2	50	32	26	3	0	6	1	18	1
Kibbe, 7 Lar-14 San Luis	8	11	.421	5.37	21	21	9	0	0	0	122.1	146	84	73	14	1	58	5	74	8
Leal, Cordoba	3	7	.300	4.26	28	12	2	16	1	1	101.1	104	55	48	9	0	53	4	52	4
Ledon, 5 Monclova-8 Monterrey	2	0	1.000	5.87	13	1	0	12	0	0	15.1	25	12	10	1	3	5	0	4	1
Leon, Mexico City Reds	10	6	.625	4.77	21	20	5	1	1	0	122.2	157	75	65	14	3	31	0	43	6
Lizarraga, San Luis	0	1	.000	20.25	3	1	0	2	0	0	2.2	9	8	6	1	0	1	0	0	0
Lomeli, Mexico City Reds	7	3	.700	6.49	42	6	1	36	0	0	97.0	123	77	70	12	2	72	1	49	11
Lopez, Aguascalientes	1	2	.333	5.83	37	1	0	36	0	2	80.1	103	61	52	12	1	41	3	38	2
Low, Union Laguna	3	1	.750	5.18	24	0	0	24	0	2	48.2	51	32	28	8	1	17	1	28	3
Luna, 10 Veracruz-22 Cordoba	4	11	.267	6.11	32	12	3	20	1	0	106.0	134	79	72	9	4	32	4	33	7
Lunar, 13 Agu-18 Leon-8 Lag	10	13	.435	4.35	39	13	2	26	1	6	128.1	131	79	62	4	9	90	8	102	15
MacKenzio, Aguascalientes	6	3	.667	5.31	10	10	1	0	0	0	62.2	76	45	37	9	1	17	2	36	1
Manzanillo, Veracruz	1	3	.250	5.57	5	5	1	0	0	0	21.0	19	16	13	2	0	20	0	16	0
Mariscal, Veracruz	0	0	.000	9.00	2	0	0	2	0	0	2.0	6	2	2	0	0	3	0	2	1
Marquez, San Luis	3	2	.600	5.87	25	15	2	10	1	0	92.0	96	71	60	10	2	69	3	74	5
Martinez, Nuevo Laredo	0	0	.000	4.50	13	1	0	12	0	1	32.0	42	16	16	1	4	13	1	13	2
Mattson, Nuevo Laredo	0	0	.000	7.45	7	0	0	7	0	0	9.2	19	9	8	2	0	8	1	4	0
Matus, 10 Ags-16 Tabasco	6	10	.375	5.90	26	24	4	2	1	0	119.0	162	89	78	16	5	36	2	61	5
Mendez, Mexico City Reds	6	12	.333	5.32	25	23	5	2	2	0	138.2	160	88	82	11	5	50	3	66	2
R. Menendez, 26 Leon-10 Cor	5	6	.455	5.77	36	5	0	31	0	1	101.1	132	74	65	12	4	44	8	30	3
W. Menendez, Tabasco	5	8	.385	5.50	17	16	4	1	0	0	93.1	98	74	57	17	1	59	1	90	13
Meza, Leon	0	1	.000	6.20	8	1	0	7	0	0	24.2	36	22	17	2	0	11	2	9	1
Miranda, Leon	1	1	.500	4.73	18	0	0	18	0	0	32.1	25	21	17	5	3	18	3	20	0
Moncada, Leon	0	0	.000	10.80	2	0	0	2	0	0	5.1	5	7	4	0	0	4	2	0	0
F. Montano, Aguascalientes	12	3	.800	3.57	18	17	3	1	1	0	111.0	134	64	44	9	4	30	2	47	5
N. Montano, Yucatan	1	3	.250	6.29	30	0	0	30	0	0	63.0	88	50	44	4	2	26	2	23	6
Morales, 1 Agu-3 Cor-10 Leon	3	7	.300	6.25	28	6	1	22	0	0	63.1	79	52	44	7	1	36	3	33	3
Ab. Moreno, 5 Leon-14 Agu	0	3	.000	10.55	19	3	0	16	0	0	36.2	56	47	43	2	5	26	1	15	5
An. Moreno, MC Tigers*	14	6	.700	3.94	25	25	12	0	0	0	166.2	169	83	73	10	6	70	4	123	15
J. Moreno, Nuevo Laredo	12	10	.546	5.12	26	26	9	0	2	0	158.1	196	100	90	22	3	49	2	96	1
Moya, Tabasco	10	12	.455	4.76	27	25	11	2	1	1	175.2	174	104	93	19	4	66	2	93	8
Mundo, Monclova	13	9	.591	4.93	27	26	14	1	3	0	177.0	213	112	97	18	9	70	10	53	5
Munoz, Aguascalientes	8	3	.727	6.43	31	13	3	18	0	0	119.0	159	98	85	18	1	38	4	46	3
Murillo, Monterrey	0	0	.000	4.37	12	1	0	11	0	0	22.2	22	13	11	1	1	9	2	14	0
Navarro, Nuevo Laredo	7	10	.412	6.73	30	18	4	12	0	0	116.1	153	101	87	14	0	83	8	89	8
D. Ochoa, 12 Agu-1 Cam	0	2	.000	10.61	13	0	0	13	0	3	9.1	14	12	11	0	0	10	3	5	1
J. Ochoa, Veracruz	0	0	.000	0.00	2	0	0	2	0	0	2.2	3	0	0	0	0	0	0	1	0
P. Ochoa, Nuevo Laredo	4	8	.333	2.39	50	0	0	50	0	8	94.1	80	28	25	10	2	32	8	44	2
Olivares, Campeche*	0	0	.000	9.00	1	0	0	1	0	0	1.0	2	1	1	0	0	2	0	1	0
F. Ontiveros, Veracruz	0	0	.000	6.75	5	0	0	5	0	0	12.0	18	9	9	1	0	8	1	0	0
J. Ontiveros, 2 Pue-23 SLP	1	2	.333	6.78	25	4	0	24	0	1	69.0	98	56	52	10	1	32	8	19	4
J. Orozco, Puebla	12	6	.667	4.10	24	22	15	2	2	1	171.1	193	91	78	23	3	38	4	123	2
O. Orozco, Puebla	13	2	.867	5.80	23	20	5	3	1	0	125.2	172	89	81	13	1	45	5	50	9
Ri. Osuna, Mexico City Reds	0	0	.000	18.00	2	0	0	2	0	0	1.0	1	2	2	0	0	3	0	1	1
Ro. Osuna, Leon	5	6	.455	7.36	39	9	1	30	0	2	96.2	124	85	79	18	1	66	14	63	8
Ortiz, 2 Veracruz-8 Yuc*	1	1	.500	4.62	10	4	1	6	0	1	37.0	40	21	19	7	2	5	1	5	1
Pacheco, Yucatan	0	0	.000	16.20	1	0	0	1	0	0	1.2	5	3	3	2	0	2	0	0	0
Padilla, Saltillo	1	5	.167	8.20	38	1	0	37	0	5	37.1	55	37	34	6	2	33	5	24	4
R. Palacios, Yucatan	1	3	.250	8.51	11	0	0	11	0	0	24.1	42	24	23	5	1	11	1	7	4
V. Palacios, Veracruz	5	14	.263	4.41	23	20	11	3	2	1	138.2	157	75	68	5	4	78	2	121	5
Palafox, Union Laguna	7	8	.467	6.49	23	18	2	5	0	0	105.1	128	81	76	18	7	56	5	39	4
Patterson, Nuevo Laredo	6	3	.667	4.70	16	13	5	3	0	0	76.2	99	49	40	5	1	21	2	36	2
Peralta, Leon*	0	0	.000	6.75	4	0	0	4	0	0	4.0	8	3	3	1	0	3	0	6	1
C. Perez, Puebla*	9	9	.500	6.11	28	25	4	3	0	1	126.2	178	97	86	16	8	56	2	52	8
L. Perez, Leon	3	7	.300	7.05	20	9	2	11	0	0	67.2	90	62	53	4	3	43	6	34	4
Pollorena, Saltillo	5	10	.333	6.98	41	1	0	40	0	1	87.2	124	80	68	8	3	37	4	48	5
Pulido, Mexico City Reds	5	4	.556	5.87	41	0	0	41	0	17	46.0	54	30	30	7	2	13	3	34	5
Purata, San Luis*	6	9	.400	4.89	26	25	4	1	1	1	127.0	145	84	69	14	3	72	3	77	9
Pruneda, Monclova	8	3	.727	4.78	21	16	2	5	1	0	96.0	106	63	51	11	0	52	5	53	9
Quijano, Puebla	4	2	.667	7.06	24	0	0	24	0	2	57.1	88	48	45	11	2	20	4	18	3
A. Ramirez, Leon	1	1	.500	7.71	6	1	0	5	0	0	7.0	8	6	6	1	0	6	1	2	2
R. Ramirez, Veracruz	1	7	.125	7.99	13	8	1	5	0	0	41.2	65	44	37	8	1	30	0	18	5
Raygoza, Campeche	12	11	.522	5.29	30	27	9	3	1	0	161.2	198	110	95	23	8	60	4	79	5
Renteria, Mexico City Tigers	1	2	.333	7.07	4	3	0	1	0	0	14.0	19	11	11	3	1	4	0	5	1
Retes, Mexico City Tigers*	8	1	.889	5.18	35	12	3	23	0	2	92.0	107	62	53	6	3	49	4	50	2
Rice, Monterrey	1	0	1.000	9.26	6	1	0	5	0	0	11.2	18	13	12	1	1	6	0	4	1
Rincon, 8 Veracruz-13 Puebla	6	7	.462	4.73	21	20	6	1	1	0	121.2	136	72	64	12	4	37	3	54	1
H. Rios, 18 Leon-14 MC Reds	9	8	.529	6.71	32	16	0	16	0	1	120.2	183	98	90	8	3	47	7	52	7
J. Rios, Mexico City Tigers	14	9	.609	4.10	28	28	11	0	3	0	180.0	189	89	82	23	4	48	4	145	2
S. Rios, Union Laguna	0	1	.000	5.31	10	0	0	10	0	0	20.1	21	13	12	1	1	10	1	9	3
L. Rivas, Tabasco*	0	0	.000	13.50	1	0	0	1	0	0	1.1	2	2	2	0	0	1	0	0	0
M. Rivas, Mexico City Tigers	2	5	.286	3.32	49	0	0	49	0	23	84.0	84	34	31	6	2	18	2	57	0
Rivera, Union Laguna*	1	3	.250	5.31	10	8	1	2	1	0	39.0	54	28	23	4	2	22	4	21	0
Robles, Saltillo	0	0	.000	5.40	5	0	0	5	0	1	3.1	3	2	2	0	0	2	0	0	1
E. Rodriguez, Saltillo	3	0	1.000	5.98	31	0	0	31	0	2	43.2	57	33	29	16	0	22	2	14	0
M.A. Rodriguez, Aguascalientes	4	10	.286	6.97	28	21	1	7	0	0	121.1	175	112	94	24	6	52	1	78	5
P. Rodriguez, Cordoba	0	0	.000	2.93	11	0	0	11	0	1	15.1	13	5	5	0	0	3	1	5	1
R. Rodriguez, Campeche	2	2	.500	3.97	12	0	0	12	0	0	22.2	25	10	10	2	0	9	0	15	3
Go. Rojo, 20 Tab-32 Ags	5	6	.455	3.67	52	0	0	52	0	10	103.0	110	48	42	11	3	27	3	57	4
Gu. Rojo, Saltillo	0	0	.000	6.75	4	0	0	4	0	0	5.0	4	3	3	1	0	4	1	1	0
Romero, 22 Lag-8 SLP	3	0	1.000	4.66	30	0	0	30	0	1	75.1	101	50	39	9	4	30	3	28	2

Pitcher—Club	W.	L.	Pct.	ERA.	G.	GS.	CG.	GF.	ShO.	Sv.	IP.	H.	R.	ER.	HR.	HB.	BB.	Int. BB.	SO.	WP.
M. Romo, Union Laguna	3	8	.273	8.36	29	9	2	20	0	1	70.0	102	53	65	16	3	40	4	27	4
R. Romo, Campeche	0	0	.000	10.13	5	0	0	5	0	0	5.1	7	6	6	3	0	2	0	3	0
V. Romo, 10 Cor-1 Yuc	4	2	.667	3.59	11	11	1	0	0	0	62.2	61	27	25	3	1	15	0	38	1
Rondon, Veracruz	0	1	.000	4.26	2	2	0	0	0	0	12.2	13	6	6	1	0	2	0	3	0
C. Ruiz, Yucatan*	17	12	.586	4.10	34	25	11	9	2	0	184.1	207	104	84	18	9	91	4	100	9
F. Ruiz, San Luis	0	0	.000	7.36	12	0	0	12	0	0	14.2	24	13	12	4	0	7	1	11	0
P. Ruiz, Monclova*	13	5	.722	4.08	25	25	8	0	0	0	156.2	165	99	71	13	0	77	1	122	4
Salas, 18 Tab-5 Monclova	2	5	.286	7.37	23	9	1	14	0	0	79.1	115	69	65	11	10	37	2	24	5
Saldana, Union Laguna	2	4	.333	6.22	24	9	1	15	0	0	68.0	68	51	47	9	5	63	5	35	2
F. Sanchez, Saltillo	0	0	.000	9.00	7	0	0	7	0	0	8.0	14	8	8	2	0	4	1	5	0
L. Sanchez, Cordoba	0	0	.000	2.25	1	1	0	0	0	0	4.0	3	1	1	0	0	5	0	4	1
Pa. Sanchez, 13 Mo-6 Pu-9 Le*	4	7	.364	8.02	28	9	0	19	0	3	76.1	102	72	68	11	0	40	4	53	6
Pe. Sanchez, Monterrey	0	0	.000	32.40	4	0	0	4	0	0	1.2	2	7	6	0	0	6	1	0	0
Sandate, Campeche*	13	13	.500	3.47	31	26	14	5	4	3	197.0	212	86	76	12	1	48	1	107	5
M. Sarmiento, Cordoba	6	3	.667	4.44	11	11	3	0	2	0	71.0	85	37	35	12	4	22	1	37	5
W. Sarmiento, MC Tigers	3	2	.600	4.65	16	4	0	12	0	2	50.1	70	30	26	4	1	16	3	22	0
Sauceda, Yucatan	0	1	.000	9.00	4	1	0	3	0	0	7.0	18	8	7	4	0	1	0	4	0
Senteney, Tabasco	0	0	.000	3.51	15	0	0	15	0	7	25.2	30	15	10	2	1	10	0	23	1
Serafin, 26 Cor-15 Mon	6	5	.455	5.92	41	5	1	36	0	2	108.0	115	76	71	18	1	52	4	50	7
Serna, Monterrey	12	8	.600	3.88	21	21	8	0	0	0	148.1	161	76	64	8	4	40	2	94	4
Silva, Cordoba	5	9	.357	4.09	42	6	3	36	1	6	105.2	114	52	48	8	3	36	6	60	1
M. Solis, 20 Sal-10 MC Reds	8	10	.444	6.60	30	26	5	4	0	0	178.2	261	143	131	27	12	79	7	53	14
R. Solis, Mexico City Reds*	10	10	.500	4.82	34	29	7	5	2	0	164.1	179	99	88	14	5	53	1	92	3
Sombra, Union Laguna	6	5	.545	5.24	24	20	2	4	0	1	113.1	129	69	66	13	2	60	2	45	7
Sosa, Union Laguna	3	5	.375	7.15	21	9	1	12	0	0	68.0	109	62	54	11	5	19	1	25	4
A. Soto, Puebla	9	4	.692	3.14	44	0	0	44	0	15	77.1	84	29	27	3	1	29	12	29	2
F. Soto, Tabasco	1	1	.500	5.23	11	3	1	8	1	0	32.2	42	21	19	4	1	17	0	15	3
J.L. Soto, Veracruz	1	8	.111	7.76	10	10	1	0	0	0	51.0	73	46	44	12	1	29	2	27	2
Sutton, Leon	0	0	.000	10.80	2	0	0	2	0	0	1.2	3	2	2	1	0	3	0	1	0
Taylor, Leon	0	1	.000	7.54	9	1	0	8	0	0	14.1	23	13	12	2	0	19	2	9	3
Tejeda, Mexico City Reds	6	3	.667	5.57	33	9	4	24	0	0	106.2	133	71	66	12	3	41	2	63	9
Telechea, Monterrey	0	0	.000	18.00	2	0	0	2	0	0	1.0	2	2	2	1	0	2	0	1	2
Tinoco, Nuevo Laredo	0	0	.000	0.00	2	0	0	2	0	0	1.1	0	0	0	0	0	0	0	1	0
Toledo, Veracruz	0	1	.000	9.00	2	1	0	1	0	0	5.0	5	6	5	0	0	5	0	0	0
Torres, Cordoba	7	10	.412	4.59	28	20	8	8	1	2	115.2	123	66	59	10	1	49	1	60	6
Uribe, Yucatan	5	4	.556	5.56	21	14	4	7	0	0	89.0	95	60	55	9	5	62	0	43	7
J. Urrea, Mexico City Tigers	3	1	.750	8.36	6	6	0	0	0	0	28.0	46	27	26	5	0	16	1	15	0
L. Urrea, 11 Mon-24 Yuc	4	4	.500	4.50	35	0	0	35	0	6	50.0	55	26	25	5	5	16	3	27	0
A. Valdez, Mexico City Tigers	2	3	.400	4.92	28	3	0	25	0	2	64.0	77	41	35	8	5	36	4	30	2
E. Valdez, San Luis	11	8	.579	4.60	26	26	5	0	1	0	164.1	176	105	84	17	7	76	4	82	7
H. Valdez, 11 Cam-9 Veracruz	0	2	.000	7.56	20	0	0	20	0	1	33.1	49	30	28	4	2	16	1	11	2
R. Valdez, Campeche	17	7	.708	3.44	29	29	12	0	3	0	204.0	207	90	78	14	1	76	3	131	7
Valencia, Mexico City Tigers	2	3	.400	4.97	7	7	1	0	0	0	29.0	39	25	16	4	1	13	0	12	2
A. Valenzuela, Saltillo*	2	5	.286	4.91	10	9	0	1	0	0	40.1	49	27	22	5	2	28	0	17	0
G. Valenzuela, Leon	8	10	.444	5.27	28	24	9	4	1	1	169.0	231	110	99	22	3	38	5	81	3
H. Valenzuela, MC Tigers	0	0	.000	0.00	1	0	0	1	0	0	1.0	0	0	0	0	0	3	0	1	0
J. Valenzuela, Saltillo	8	7	.533	6.03	25	25	3	0	1	0	152.1	206	112	102	29	6	60	2	53	2
Vaqueiro, Nuevo Laredo	0	1	.000	7.04	12	0	0	12	0	2	7.2	13	6	6	0	0	4	0	5	0
Vargas, Union Laguna	10	6	.625	4.53	51	0	0	51	0	12	113.1	128	65	57	13	5	36	11	68	4
F. Vazquez, Monclova	4	5	.444	7.28	25	10	1	15	0	0	85.1	104	79	69	10	4	61	4	48	9
Vazquez, 6 Cor-5 Agu-2 Lag	1	7	.125	7.88	13	13	1	0	0	0	40.0	48	37	35	5	1	28	0	15	2
I. Velazquez, Yucatan	11	14	.440	5.46	28	23	9	5	1	0	160.0	208	110	97	19	5	50	3	54	4
La. Velazquez, Monclova	10	7	.588	6.58	21	21	5	0	2	0	105.1	121	85	77	17	4	72	2	66	10
Veliz, 2 Cor-24 Mon*	4	6	.400	6.32	26	13	1	13	0	0	78.1	97	65	55	5	4	74	1	47	9
Vidana, Tabasco	4	3	.571	5.14	29	1	0	28	0	2	68.1	86	45	39	9	0	21	3	28	0
Villanueva, Aguascalientes*	8	9	.471	5.52	31	23	5	8	0	0	150.0	200	104	92	19	4	44	3	65	1
Villarreal, 3 Pue-9 MC Reds*	1	2	.333	9.70	12	2	0	10	0	1	21.1	37	24	23	3	1	18	1	11	3
D. Villegas, Yucatan	0	1	.000	12.41	11	0	0	11	0	0	12.1	18	17	17	4	0	14	1	8	6
M. Villegas, Aguascalientes	8	7	.533	5.37	38	11	6	27	0	10	107.1	127	66	64	13	3	33	4	96	1
R. Villegas, Mexico City Tigers	7	4	.636	5.46	24	10	0	14	0	1	84.0	114	55	51	14	0	19	5	42	0
Villela, Mexico City Reds	0	1	.000	10.50	3	0	0	3	0	0	6.0	14	7	7	3	0	2	1	1	1
Vizcarra, Nuevo Laredo	0	1	.000	7.96	22	0	0	22	0	0	26.0	39	30	23	2	1	27	0	14	4
White, Tabasco	1	2	.333	8.24	5	5	0	0	0	0	19.2	24	20	18	4	0	9	0	7	1
Williams, Campeche	0	0	.000	15.75	2	1	0	1	0	0	4.0	9	10	7	0	0	4	0	4	1
Yucupicio, Veracruz	1	1	.500	5.73	38	2	2	36	1	0	75.1	87	57	48	11	2	30	1	37	3
Zamberino, Tabasco	0	0	.000	16.20	3	0	0	3	0	0	1.2	4	3	3	0	0	2	0	2	0
Zamudio, 30 Agu-10 MC Reds	5	9	.357	4.97	40	8	1	32	0	1	108.2	123	74	60	11	5	51	5	63	4

BALKS—Camarena, L.T. Castillo, Delgadillo, Huerta, Ledon, Mundo, Go. Rojo, Salas, 2 each; Duarte, Flores, Fuson, Gaynor, N. Montano, J. Moreno, J. Orozco, O. Orozco, V. Palacios, Palafox, Raygoza, M. Rivas, M. Romo, Sandate, M. Solis, L. Urrea, E. Valdez, F. Vazquez, L.A. Velazquez, M. Villegas, 1 each.

COMBINATION SHUTOUTS—Matus-Granillo, Delgadillo-M. Villegas, Villanueva-M. Villegas, Aguascalientes; Leon-Pulido, Mexico City Reds; Heredia-Jos. L. Garcia, L.A. Velazquez-R. Guzman, Monclova; Escarrega-L. Urrea, Yucatan.

NO-HIT GAMES—K. Angulo, Yucatan, defeated Mexico City Tigers, 8-0 (seven innings), May 4; Dominguez, Compeche, defeated Veracruz, 12-0 (seven innings), May 25.

Pacific Coast League

CLASS AAA

Leading Batter
TY GAINEY
Tucson

League President
BILL CUTLER

Leading Pitcher
DAVE JOHNSON
Hawaii

CHAMPIONSHIP WINNERS IN PREVIOUS YEARS

Year	Club	Pct.
1903	Los Angeles	.630
1904	Tacoma	.589
	Tacoma§	.571
	Los Angeles§	.571
1905	Tacoma	.583
	Los Angeles*	.604
1906	Portland	.657
1907	Los Angeles	.608
1908	Los Angeles	.585
1909	San Francisco	.623
1910	Portland	.567
1911	Portland	.589
1912	Oakland	.591
1913	Portland	.559
1914	Portland	.574
1915	San Francisco	.570
1916	Los Angeles	.601
1917	San Francisco	.561
1918	Vernon	.569
	Los Angeles (2nd) x	.548
1919	Vernon	.613
1920	Vernon	.556
1921	Los Angeles	.574
1922	San Francisco	.638
1923	San Francisco	.617
1924	Seattle	.545
1925	San Francisco	.643
1926	Los Angeles	.599
1927	Oakland	.615
1928	San Francisco*	.630
	Sacramento§§	.626
	San Francisco§§	.626
1929	Mission	.643
	Hollywood*	.592
1930	Los Angeles	.576
	Hollywood*	.650
1931	Hollywood	.626
	San Francisco*	.608
1932	Portland	.587
1933	Los Angeles	.610
1934	Los Angeles z	.786
	Los Angeles z	.689
1935	Los Angeles	.648
	San Francisco*	.608
1936	Portland‡	.549
1937	Sacramento	.573
	San Diego (3rd)†	.545
1938	Los Angeles	.590
	Sacramento (3rd)†	.537
1939	Seattle	.589
	Sacramento (4th)†	.500
1940	Seattle‡	.629
1941	Seattle‡	.598
1942	Sacramento	.590
	Seattle (3rd)†	.539
1943	Los Angeles	.710
	S. Francisco (2nd)†	.574
1944	Los Angeles	.586
	S. Francisco (3rd)†	.509
1945	Portland	.622
	S. Francisco (4th)†	.525
1946	San Francisco‡	.628
1947	Los Angeles††	.567
1948	Oakland‡	.606
1949	Hollywood‡	.583
1950	Oakland	.590
1951	Seattle‡	.593
1952	Hollywood	.606
1953	Hollywood	.589
1954	San Diego y	.604
1955	Seattle	.552
1956	Los Angeles	.637
1957	San Francisco	.601
1958	Phoenix	.578
1959	Salt Lake City	.552
1960	Spokane	.601
1961	Tacoma	.630
1962	San Diego	.604
1963	Spokane	.620
	Oklahoma City a	.632
1964	Arkansas	.609
	San Diego a	.576
1965	Oklahoma City a	.628
	Portland	.547
1966	Seattle a	.561
	Tulsa	.578
1967	San Diego a	.574
	Spokane	.541
1968	Tulsa a	.642
	Spokane	.586
1969	Tacoma a	.589
	Eugene	.603
1970	Spokane a	.644
	Hawaii	.671
1971	Salt Lake City	.534
	Tacoma	.545
1972	Albuquerque	.622
	Eugene	.534
1973	Tucson	.583
	Spokane a	.563
1974	Spokane a	.549
	Albuqerque	.535
1975	Salt Lake City	.556
	Hawaii a	.611
1976	Salt Lake City	.625
	Hawaii a	.531
1977	Phoenix a	.579
	Hawaii	.541
1978	Tacoma b	.584
	Albuquerque b	.557
1979	Albuquerque	.581
	Salt Lake City c	.541
1980	Albuquerque*	.578
	Hawaii	.539
1981	Albuquerque*	.712
	Tacoma	.561
1982	Albuquerque*	.594
	Spokane	.545
1983	Albuquerque	.594
	Portland*	.528
1984	Hawaii	.621
	Edmonton*	.486
1985	Vancouver*	.552
	Phoenix	.563

*Won split-season playoff. †Won four-team playoff. ‡Won pennant and four-team playoff. §Tied for second-half title with Tacoma winning playoff. §§Tied for second-half title, with Sacramento winning playoff. ††Ended regular season in tie with San Francisco and won one-game playoff for pennant, then won four-club playoff. xWon playoff from first-place Vernon and awarded championship. yDefeated Hollywood in one-game playoff for pennant. zWon both halves, no playoff. aLeague was divided into Northern, Southern divisions in 1963, 1969-70-71, and Eastern, Western divisions in 1964 through 1968 and 1972 through 1977, won two-team playoff. bLeague divided into Eastern and Western divisions, Tacoma and Albuquerque declared co-champions following cancellation of four-team playoff due to continuing rain and wet grounds. cWon second-half title and defeated Hawaii in four-team playoff.

STANDING OF CLUBS AT CLOSE OF FIRST HALF, JUNE 21

NORTHERN DIVISION

Club	W.	L.	T.	Pct.	G.B.
Vancouver (Brewers)	42	24	0	.636	....
Calgary (Mariners)	36	35	0	.507	8½
Portland (Phillies)	34	35	0	.493	9½
Tacoma (A's)	32	40	0	.444	13
Edmonton (Angels)	30	39	0	.435	13½

SOUTHERN DIVISION

Club	W.	L.	T.	Pct.	G.B.
Phoenix (Giants)	43	28	0	.606	....
Tucson (Astros)	38	33	0	.535	5
Las Vegas (Padres)	36	34	0	.514	6½
Hawaii (Pirates)	32	40	0	.444	11½
Albuquerque (Dodgers)	28	43	0	.394	15

STANDING OF CLUBS AT CLOSE OF SECOND HALF, SEPTEMBER 1

NORTHERN DIVISION

Club	W.	L.	T.	Pct.	G.B.
Vancouver (Brewers)	43	29	0	.597	....
Tacoma (A's)	40	32	0	.556	3
Edmonton (Angels)	38	34	0	.528	5
Portland (Phillies)	34	38	0	.472	9
Calgary (Mariners)	30	42	0	.417	13

SOUTHERN DIVISION

Club	W.	L.	T.	Pct.	G.B.
Las Vegas (Padres)	44	28	0	.611	....
Phoenix (Giants)	38	33	0	.535	5½
Hawaii (Pirates)	33	39	0	.458	11
Tucson (Astros)	33	39	0	.458	11
Albuquerque (Dodgers)	26	45	0	.366	17½

COMPOSITE STANDING OF CLUBS AT CLOSE OF SEASON, SEPTEMBER 1

NORTHERN DIVISION

Club	Van.	Tac.	Edm.	Port.	Cal.	Phoe.	L.V.	Tuc.	Haw.	Alb.	W.	L.	T.	Pct.	G.B.
Vancouver (Brewers)	....	9	9	10	9	4	12	8	12	12	85	53	0	.616	....
Tacoma (A's)	7	....	8	10	10	9	6	7	7	8	72	72	0	.500	16
Edmonton (Angels)	5	8	....	10	8	8	8	5	8	8	68	73	0	.482	18½
Portland (Phillies)	5	6	6	....	8	7	4	11	11	10	68	73	0	.482	18½
Calgary (Mariners)	7	6	7	8	....	5	6	10	7	10	66	77	0	.462	21½

SOUTHERN DIVISION

Club	Van.	Tac.	Edm.	Port.	Cal.	Phoe.	L.V.	Tuc.	Haw.	Alb.	W.	L.	T.	Pct.	G.B.
Phoenix (Giants)	11	7	8	9	11	....	6	9	9	11	81	61	0	.570	....
Las Vegas (Padres)	4	10	8	10	10	10	....	9	9	10	80	62	0	.563	1
Tucson (Astros)	7	9	11	5	6	7	7	....	7	12	71	72	0	.497	10½
Hawaii (Pirates)	4	9	8	5	9	7	7	9	....	7	65	79	0	.451	17
Albuquerque (Dodgers)	3	8	8	6	6	4	6	4	9	....	54	88	0	.380	27

Hawaii club represented Honolulu, Haw.

Major league affiliations in parentheses.

Playoffs—Las Vegas defeated Phoenix, three games to two; Vancouver defeated Tacoma, three games to none; Las Vegas defeated Vancouver, three games to two, to win league championship.

Regular-Season Attendance—Albuquerque, 235,737; Calgary, 288,197; Edmonton, 229,682; Hawaii, 84,613; Las Vegas, 291,060; Phoenix, 161,583; Portland, 138,677; Tacoma, 247,098; Tucson, 116,117; Vancouver, 231,819. Total, 2,024,583. Playoffs, 39,523.

Managers—Albuquerque, Terry Collins; Calgary, Bill Plummer; Edmonton, Winston Llenas; Hawaii, Tommy Sandt; Las Vegas, Larry Bowa; Phoenix, Jim Lefebvre; Portland, Bill Dancy; Tacoma, Keith Lieppman; Tucson, Carlos Alfonso; Vancouver, Terry Bevington.

All-Star Team—1B—Tim Pyznarski, Las Vegas; 2B—Greg Legg, Portland; 3B—Randy Johnson, Phoenix; SS—Gus Polidor, Edmonton; OF—Glenn Braggs, Vancouver; Mickey Brantley, Calgary; Ty Gainey, Tucson; C—B.J. Surhoff, Vancouver; DH—Mark Ryal, Edmonton; RHP—Mark Grant, Phoenix; LHP—Bob Patterson, Hawaii; Rel P—Chris Bosio, Vancouver; Manager of the Year—Jim Lefebvre, Phoenix; Most Valuable Player—Tim Pyznarski, Las Vegas.

(Compiled by William J. Weiss, League Statistician, San Mateo, Calif.)

CLUB BATTING

Club	Pct.	G.	AB.	R.	OR.	H.	TB.	2B.	3B.	HR.	RBI.	GW.	SH.	SF.	HP.	BB.	Int. BB.	SO.	SB.	CS.	LOB.
Las Vegas	.289	142	4775	720	711	1381	2010	240	67	85	643	71	37	44	19	518	39	789	160	86	1040
Calgary	.288	143	4754	744	804	1367	2115	249	35	143	698	58	60	47	17	471	26	647	116	54	972
Vancouver	.286	138	4543	719	598	1299	1849	211	42	85	653	74	26	55	35	512	32	699	151	74	928
Edmonton	.285	141	4827	757	740	1378	2116	263	50	125	694	67	27	43	17	435	39	707	114	59	960
Phoenix	.284	142	4723	751	684	1342	1991	241	45	106	694	72	42	43	33	483	38	664	91	55	980
Tacoma	.284	144	4834	738	706	1371	1948	255	41	80	675	61	28	69	26	568	27	723	111	55	1071
Tucson	.274	143	4646	666	710	1272	1871	231	58	84	609	62	54	41	22	530	33	817	198	98	959
Albuquerque	.273	142	4810	711	812	1313	1973	253	31	115	651	47	51	55	29	491	43	834	60	52	1001
Portland	.272	141	4713	650	679	1283	1850	238	52	75	603	65	39	47	30	425	30	708	96	77	950
Hawaii	.268	144	4770	606	618	1278	1753	204	56	53	548	59	52	47	23	444	30	687	146	80	1001

INDIVIDUAL BATTING

(Leading Qualifiers for Batting Championship—389 or More Plate Appearances)

*Bats lefthanded. †Switch-hitter.

Player and Club	Pct.	G.	AB.	R.	H.	TB.	2B.	3B.	HR.	RBI.	GW.	SH.	SF.	HP.	BB.	Int. BB.	SO.	SB.	CS.
Gainey, Ty, Tucson*	.351	104	359	72	126	221	22	11	17	63	9	1	0	0	55	5	81	19	8
Ryal, Mark, Edmonton*	.340	127	479	72	163	246	33	4	14	84	9	1	7	1	36	10	50	0	0
Adduci, James, Vancouver*	.339	113	425	71	144	192	26	5	4	53	7	0	3	4	25	6	76	5	5
Johnson, Randall, Phoenix	.332	125	428	62	142	188	23	7	3	68	5	7	4	6	53	3	34	2	4
Pyznarski, Timothy, Las Vegas	.326	135	484	93	158	278	35	8	23	119	14	0	12	1	82	6	127	25	7
Legg, Gregory, Portland	.323	120	461	72	149	204	27	5	6	66	11	1	8	3	41	4	43	8	6
Brantley, Michael, Calgary	.318	106	396	104	126	242	18	4	30	92	12	2	5	1	55	2	51	25	3
Melendez, Francisco, Portland*	.318	96	356	47	113	150	21	2	4	57	7	1	6	1	33	5	33	2	3
Wotus, Ronald, Hawaii	.315	125	419	75	132	174	24	3	4	57	9	6	2	1	58	3	51	7	3
Diaz, Edgar, Vancouver	.315	108	346	44	109	119	2	4	0	43	4	3	5	1	44	0	27	12	7

Departmental Leaders: G—See, 142; AB—Polonia, 549; R—Brantley, 104; H—Polonia, 165; TB—Pyznarski, See, 278; 2B—See, 38; 3B—Gainey, 11; HR—Lancellotti, 31; RBI—Pyznarski, 119; GWRBI—Pyznarski, 14; SH—Dybzinski, 13; SF—Ro. Nelson, 13; HP—Gallego, 8; BB—Watters, 89; IBB—Ryal, 10; SO—Pyznarski, 127; SB—White, 42; CS—Polonia, 21.

(All Players—Listed Alphabetically)

Player and Club	Pct.	G.	AB.	R.	H.	TB.	2B.	3B.	HR.	RBI.	GW.	SH.	SF.	HP.	BB.	Int. BB.	SO.	SB.	CS.
Acker, Larry, Tucson*	.000	46	4	0	0	0	0	0	0	0	0	1	0	0	0	0	4	0	0
Adams, Patrick, Phoenix	.283	96	321	68	91	158	18	2	15	64	6	1	5	5	40	1	87	1	0
Adams, Ricky, Phoenix	.270	18	37	5	10	13	1	1	0	3	0	0	0	1	7	1	8	1	0
Adduci, James, Vancouver*	.339	113	425	71	144	192	26	5	4	53	7	0	3	4	25	6	76	5	5
Aldrete, Michael, Phoenix*	.371	47	159	36	59	91	14	0	6	35	4	1	4	0	36	3	24	0	0

Player and Club	Pct.	G.	AB.	R.	H.	TB.	2B.	3B.	HR.	RBI.	GW.	SH.	SF.	HP.	BB.	Int. BB.	SO.	SB.	CS.
Amelung, Edward, Albuquerque*	.282	82	291	48	82	116	12	2	6	45	4	2	3	0	21	4	30	3	4
Anderson, James, Albuquerque	.247	114	396	53	98	130	20	0	4	38	6	6	4	1	45	1	55	3	3
Asadoor, Randall, Las Vegas	.280	125	396	69	111	186	16	10	13	52	8	2	1	4	66	7	89	6	7
Ashman, Michael, Hawaii*	.159	29	88	6	14	19	5	0	0	6	0	2	0	0	4	0	9	0	0
August, Donald, 24 Tuc-3 Van	.111	27	27	1	3	3	0	0	0	1	0	6	0	0	2	0	13	0	0
Bailey, Mark, Tucson†	.341	35	123	22	42	55	8	1	1	19	2	0	3	0	20	1	22	1	3
Baker, Steven, Albuquerque	.241	27	29	3	7	8	1	0	0	7	2	3	1	0	1	0	9	0	0
Barkley, Jeffrey, 6 LV-4 Port†	.000	10	1	0	0	0	0	0	0	0	0	0	0	0	0	0	1	0	0
Barnes, William, Portland	.369	38	141	21	52	71	8	4	1	29	1	0	6	3	7	0	9	3	4
Bathe, William, Tacoma	.193	40	135	13	26	38	7	1	1	13	1	1	2	0	14	1	27	0	1
Beck, Dion, Portland*	.000	24	2	0	0	0	0	0	0	0	0	1	0	0	1	0	1	0	0
Berra, Dale, Tucson	.244	22	82	8	20	26	3	0	1	9	0	0	0	0	4	0	13	2	3
Bitker, Joseph, Las Vegas	.000	5	8	0	0	0	0	0	0	0	0	0	0	0	0	0	3	0	0
Bittiger, Jeffrey, Portland	.321	27	28	4	9	13	4	0	0	3	0	3	0	0	5	0	7	0	0
Bockus, Randy, Phoenix*	.364	44	22	0	8	10	2	0	0	2	1	2	0	0	1	0	3	0	0
Bonds, Barry, Hawaii*	.311	44	148	30	46	78	7	2	7	37	3	0	3	2	33	0	31	16	5
Booker, Gregory, Las Vegas	.235	36	17	3	4	6	2	0	0	2	0	2	0	0	0	0	2	0	0
Bowden, Mark, Portland*	.000	39	5	0	0	0	0	0	0	0	0	0	0	0	1	0	3	0	0
Braggs, Glenn, Vancouver	.360	90	325	80	117	200	26	6	15	75	9	0	2	5	45	2	32	22	7
Brantley, Michael, Calgary	.318	106	396	104	126	242	18	4	30	92	12	2	5	1	55	2	51	25	3
Braun, Randall, Calgary*	.314	134	507	73	159	260	30	4	21	90	8	2	3	1	39	2	94	6	6
Brown, Darrell, 23 Phx-34 Cal	.261	57	184	33	48	57	4	1	1	21	2	2	2	0	11	1	9	13	7
Brown, Michael, Hawaii	.379	24	87	14	33	44	8	0	1	12	3	0	0	0	9	0	8	0	2
Brummer, Glenn, Hawaii	.235	79	230	18	54	67	9	2	0	28	6	3	1	5	15	0	21	1	0
Bryant, Ralph, Albuquerque*	.237	107	338	56	80	158	17	2	19	55	3	0	5	7	41	9	104	6	5
Bullock, Eric, Tucson*	.384	42	151	28	58	79	8	2	3	21	1	1	2	1	22	5	15	14	8
Bulls, David, Portland	.167	19	6	0	1	1	0	0	0	0	0	1	0	0	0	0	3	0	0
Bundy, Lorenzo, Hawaii*	.306	20	62	7	19	30	1	2	2	9	1	0	1	1	12	2	11	0	0
Calderon, Ivan, Calgary	.333	24	81	17	27	39	3	0	3	18	1	0	3	0	15	1	8	5	1
Calhoun, Jeffrey, Tucson*	.000	22	3	0	0	0	0	0	0	0	0	0	0	0	2	0	2	0	0
Carpenter, Glenn, Tucson	.284	117	401	49	114	154	23	4	3	65	6	2	5	4	23	2	65	1	2
Carrasco, Norman, Edmonton	.301	86	302	38	91	116	14	1	3	34	3	2	0	1	16	0	37	11	8
Cartwright, Alan, Vancouver*	.292	6	24	6	7	12	2	0	1	1	0	0	0	0	2	0	2	0	1
Casey, Patrick, Calgary	.307	116	384	61	118	207	33	4	16	63	5	4	5	2	75	5	71	6	1
Castillo, Juan, Vancouver†	.192	26	73	10	14	17	3	0	0	4	0	2	0	0	8	1	13	3	2
Childress, Rodney, 60 Port-1 Tuc	.000	61	4	0	0	0	0	0	0	0	0	0	0	0	1	0	3	0	0
Cipolloni, Joseph, Portland	.194	10	31	4	6	9	0	0	1	2	1	1	0	0	0	0	4	0	0
Clark, Christopher, Albuquerque†	.292	120	383	50	112	159	22	2	7	55	2	6	8	3	57	5	65	3	2
Clark, Robert, Edmonton	.216	62	213	35	46	84	8	3	8	38	2	1	4	1	35	2	42	0	2
Clark, William, Phoenix*	.250	6	20	3	5	5	0	0	0	1	0	0	0	0	4	0	2	1	1
Cliburn, Stanley, Edmonton	.267	80	258	37	69	125	25	2	9	35	3	0	0	0	23	1	31	0	1
Crone, William, Calgary	.268	102	355	52	95	134	20	5	3	43	3	5	3	1	41	2	48	8	6
Dabney, Ty, Phoenix*	.333	11	36	5	12	20	3	1	1	4	0	0	0	0	3	1	6	0	0
Datz, Jeffrey, Tucson	.200	2	5	0	1	1	0	0	0	0	0	0	0	0	0	0	3	0	0
Davidsmeier, Daniel, Vancouver	.246	91	305	27	75	95	15	1	1	37	4	3	5	3	22	0	36	3	3
Davis, Trench, Hawaii*	.311	104	411	41	128	150	8	7	0	30	3	2	2	0	18	2	25	27	19
Day, Randall, Portland	.230	101	282	41	65	123	24	2	10	41	5	1	2	4	24	2	39	5	2
DeAngelis, Steven, Portland*	.251	101	354	64	89	165	26	4	14	63	7	1	4	5	48	4	75	10	7
Debus, Jon, Albuquerque	.262	93	233	34	61	114	9	1	14	50	5	1	2	0	20	2	49	1	3
deLeon, Jose, Hawaii	.067	15	15	0	1	1	0	0	0	0	0	5	0	0	1	0	5	0	0
Diaz, Carlos, Albuquerque	.000	14	1	0	0	0	0	0	0	0	0	0	0	0	0	0	0	0	0
Diaz, Edgar, Vancouver	.315	108	346	44	109	119	2	4	0	43	4	3	5	1	44	0	27	12	7
Diaz, Mario, Calgary	.282	109	379	40	107	139	17	6	1	41	4	5	4	0	13	2	29	1	3
Dietrick, Patrick, Tacoma	.000	1	4	0	0	0	0	0	0	0	0	0	0	0	0	0	2	0	0
Distefano, Benito, Hawaii*	.259	111	402	58	104	186	25	9	13	57	4	2	4	3	41	6	45	2	4
Dorsett, Brian, Tacoma	.261	117	426	49	111	176	33	1	10	51	4	0	5	3	26	1	82	0	1
Dowell, Kenneth, Portland	.301	141	439	66	132	156	11	5	1	44	6	7	1	1	50	1	64	4	6
Downs, Kelly, Phoenix	.056	18	18	1	1	1	0	0	0	1	0	0	0	0	1	0	7	0	0
Driessen, Daniel, Tucson*	.295	70	237	35	70	106	21	0	5	35	5	0	4	0	41	7	26	3	3
Dybzinski, Jerome, Calgary	.252	115	333	31	84	99	12	0	1	33	2	13	5	1	13	1	30	6	4
Edwards, John, Tucson	.200	2	5	1	1	2	1	0	0	0	0	0	0	0	0	0	2	0	0
Eichhorn, David, Albuquerque†	.000	39	2	0	0	0	0	0	0	0	0	0	0	0	0	0	1	0	0
Engel, Steven, Tucson	.333	7	3	0	1	1	0	0	0	0	0	2	0	0	0	0	1	0	0
Eppard, James, Tacoma*	.274	95	321	39	88	105	15	1	0	34	3	5	4	0	32	0	31	2	3
Espy, Cecil, Hawaii†	.263	106	384	49	101	138	19	3	4	38	5	3	1	0	24	1	83	41	13
Faedo, Leonardo, Albuquerque	.313	15	32	3	10	14	2	1	0	4	0	0	0	0	0	0	3	0	0
Fansler, Stanley, Hawaii	.148	29	27	1	4	4	0	0	0	0	0	3	0	0	2	0	9	0	0
Farmer, Edward, Hawaii	.111	40	9	0	1	1	0	0	0	0	0	0	0	0	0	0	2	0	0
Felder, Michael, Vancouver†	.261	39	153	21	40	54	3	4	1	15	1	0	3	0	17	2	15	4	3
Fermin, Felix, Hawaii	.256	39	125	13	32	37	5	0	0	9	0	1	0	0	7	0	13	1	1
Fimple, John, Albuquerque	.286	92	297	39	85	114	17	3	2	35	2	2	2	1	32	0	50	2	0
Firova, Daniel, Calgary	.249	67	209	19	52	70	9	0	3	22	0	6	3	0	5	1	25	0	1
Ford, Kenneth, Hawaii	.257	49	148	16	38	53	11	2	0	21	1	0	2	0	7	1	28	0	1
Fuentes, Michael, Tucson	.211	9	19	3	4	5	1	0	0	2	0	1	0	0	4	0	4	0	0
Gainey, Ty, Tucson*	.351	104	359	72	126	221	22	11	17	63	9	1	0	0	55	5	81	19	8
Gallego, Michael, Tacoma	.275	132	443	58	122	160	16	5	4	46	5	8	7	8	39	0	58	3	3
Galvez, Balvino, Albuquerque	.400	24	10	1	4	4	0	0	0	0	0	2	0	0	1	0	2	0	0
Garcia, Steven, Las Vegas*	.270	44	115	19	31	37	4	1	0	6	0	3	2	1	12	3	18	12	4
Gerber, Craig, Edmonton*	.239	74	243	32	58	65	5	1	0	15	1	1	2	1	14	2	13	4	3
Gladden, Daniel, Phoenix†	.333	7	27	5	9	13	4	0	0	0	0	0	0	0	2	0	2	0	0
Goldthorn, Burk, Hawaii*	.215	27	65	13	14	22	5	0	1	8	1	0	2	0	19	2	12	0	0
Gomez, Randall, Phoenix	.276	72	243	19	67	87	11	0	3	44	1	0	5	0	13	1	22	1	1
Gonzalez, Arturo, Portland	.158	28	38	4	6	10	1	0	1	6	3	4	0	0	0	0	13	0	0
Gonzalez, Denio, Hawaii	.222	109	379	48	84	128	10	2	10	45	5	0	7	2	44	4	97	10	9
Gonzalez, Jose, Albuquerque	.277	89	303	39	84	128	20	3	6	37	1	3	5	4	16	2	70	11	8
Gorman, Thomas, Portland*	.333	43	3	1	1	2	1	0	0	0	0	0	0	0	0	0	1	0	0
Graham, Everett, Phoenix*	.184	28	76	9	14	21	4	0	1	8	0	1	2	0	8	2	11	4	1
Grant, Mark, Phoenix	.267	29	30	5	8	11	1	1	0	2	0	2	0	0	3	0	7	0	0
Grapenthin, Richard, Las Vegas	.000	39	1	0	0	0	0	0	0	0	0	0	0	0	1	0	0	0	0
Green, Gary, Las Vegas	.250	129	416	42	104	121	11	3	0	41	4	5	3	1	29	1	46	3	0
Gross, Wayne, Tacoma*	.254	62	185	30	47	83	9	0	9	35	3	0	4	0	43	4	24	0	0
Guinn, Brian, Tacoma†	.194	14	36	1	7	8	1	0	0	1	0	0	0	0	3	0	6	0	0
Gulden, Bradley, Phoenix*	.261	20	46	3	12	15	3	0	0	9	1	0	0	0	7	0	4	0	0

Player and Club	Pct.	G.	AB.	R.	H.	TB.	2B.	3B.	HR.	RBI.	GW.	SH.	SF.	HP.	BB.	Int. BB.	SO.	SB.	CS.
Hall, Matthew, Calgary*	.274	58	226	30	62	79	13	2	0	16	1	3	1	1	19	1	30	9	2
Hamilton, Jeffrey, Albuquerque	.313	71	288	40	90	147	21	3	10	42	6	0	1	0	12	2	44	1	1
Haro, Samuel, Hawaii	.253	82	229	33	58	68	4	3	0	9	1	1	1	0	21	3	29	13	5
Hayward, Raymond, Las Vegas*	.367	30	30	5	11	13	2	0	0	4	1	0	0	0	2	0	1	1	1
Heathcock, Jeffrey, Tucson	.171	27	35	2	6	6	0	0	0	0	0	1	0	0	3	0	11	0	1
Hengel, David, Calgary	.285	113	407	73	116	221	22	1	27	94	10	0	9	1	35	1	78	1	0
Hensley, Charles, Phoenix*	.000	44	2	0	0	0	0	0	0	0	0	0	0	0	0	0	1	0	0
Hernandez, Manuel, Tucson	.190	22	21	3	4	7	1	1	0	3	0	3	0	0	2	0	12	0	0
Heuer, Mark, Albuquerque	.130	36	23	2	3	3	0	0	0	0	0	0	0	0	1	0	9	0	0
Hickey, Kevin, Portland*	.182	33	11	2	2	2	0	0	0	1	0	1	0	0	0	0	1	0	0
Hicks, Robert, Portland	.000	29	3	0	0	0	0	0	0	0	0	0	0	0	0	0	3	0	0
Hill, Clay, Calgary	.248	74	226	36	57	84	7	1	6	22	1	9	0	1	25	2	31	2	3
Hillegas, Shawn, Albuquerque	.000	9	6	0	0	0	0	0	0	0	0	0	0	0	0	0	5	0	0
Holton, Brian, Albuquerque	.086	28	35	1	3	3	0	0	0	3	0	2	1	1	0	0	9	0	0
Householder, Paul, Vancouver†	.208	60	212	25	44	63	7	0	4	31	3	0	5	1	23	1	41	9	4
Howell, Jack, Edmonton*	.359	44	156	39	56	88	17	3	3	28	3	0	0	2	38	2	29	1	1
Hummel, Dean, Phoenix*	.500	5	2	1	1	2	1	0	0	0	0	0	0	0	0	0	0	0	0
Huppert, David, Vancouver	.167	12	36	3	6	6	0	0	0	4	1	0	0	0	6	0	10	1	1
Jackson, Charles, Tucson	.306	127	448	83	137	207	27	5	11	62	2	0	3	1	61	1	79	18	14
Jackson, Michael, Portland	.000	17	1	0	0	0	0	0	0	0	0	0	0	0	0	0	0	0	0
James, Christopher, Portland	.241	69	266	30	64	110	6	2	12	41	4	3	2	0	17	1	45	3	6
James, Dion, Vancouver*	.282	130	485	85	157	192	25	6	6	55	6	6	6	3	61	4	66	30	17
Javier, Stanley, Tacoma†	.327	69	248	50	81	113	16	2	4	51	10	0	5	2	47	2	46	18	8
Jeffcoat, Michael, Phoenix*	.400	54	5	0	2	2	0	0	0	0	0	0	0	0	0	0	1	0	0
Jelks, Gregory, Portland	.262	63	206	37	54	92	10	2	8	28	2	0	1	3	16	0	34	3	1
Job, Ryan, Tucson	.263	7	19	1	5	5	0	0	0	0	0	0	0	0	1	0	3	0	1
Johnson, David, Hawaii	.129	22	31	1	4	4	0	0	0	4	0	5	1	0	0	0	14	0	0
Johnson, Randall, Phoenix	.332	125	428	62	142	188	23	7	3	68	5	7	4	6	53	3	34	2	4
Johnson, Roy, Tacoma*	.343	68	248	47	85	140	16	6	9	44	2	0	4	1	32	2	28	4	3
Jones, Barry, Hawaii	.000	35	2	0	0	0	0	0	0	0	0	1	0	0	0	0	2	0	0
Jones, Christopher, Phoenix*	.291	112	364	76	106	168	24	7	8	55	6	2	4	1	44	5	36	5	7
Jones, James C., Las Vegas	.000	28	23	2	0	0	0	0	0	1	1	2	0	0	6	0	9	1	0
Jones, James D., Tacoma	.259	23	58	9	15	19	4	0	0	5	2	1	0	0	10	0	12	0	0
Jones, Ronald, Portland*	.118	11	34	4	4	5	1	0	0	2	0	0	0	1	0	0	1	0	0
Jones, Ross, Calgary	.262	53	187	23	49	75	12	1	4	24	1	1	1	0	21	1	24	3	2
Keedy, Patrick, Edmonton	.203	57	187	27	38	68	7	1	7	22	1	1	1	2	23	0	57	6	3
Kemp, Steven, Las Vegas*	.269	48	160	27	43	72	10	2	5	27	2	0	0	0	26	2	44	2	0
Keough, Matthew, Tucson	.000	8	7	0	0	0	0	0	0	0	0	2	0	0	0	0	1	0	0
Khalifa, Sam, Hawaii	.315	50	200	30	63	73	9	4	1	26	3	4	1	0	18	1	21	4	3
Kiefer, Steven, Vancouver	.268	126	426	67	114	193	22	6	15	69	10	4	8	4	44	3	88	11	5
Klipstein, David, Vancouver	.261	61	134	29	35	47	7	1	1	15	2	2	2	3	21	1	19	10	2
Knight, Timothy, Portland*	.248	131	448	54	111	160	21	8	4	58	6	0	4	1	32	4	80	6	14
Knudson, Mark, 15 Tuc-2 Van	.083	17	12	3	1	1	0	0	0	1	0	4	0	0	1	0	4	0	0
Kramer, Joseph, Tacoma	.000	2	1	1	0	0	0	0	0	0	0	0	0	0	0	0	0	0	0
Krawczyk, Raymond, Hawaii	.000	32	3	0	0	0	0	0	0	1	0	0	0	0	0	0	0	0	0
Kruk, John, Las Vegas*	.464	6	28	6	13	18	3	1	0	9	1	0	0	0	4	2	5	0	1
Kutcher, Randy, Phoenix	.346	55	208	47	72	127	14	4	11	39	4	0	1	0	16	0	28	15	3
Lancellotti, Richard, Phoenix*	.275	122	440	81	121	240	20	3	31	106	11	0	4	6	49	6	79	1	1
Lansford, Joseph, Tacoma	.100	6	20	3	2	3	1	0	0	1	0	0	1	0	3	0	11	1	0
Laskey, William, Phoenix	.063	14	16	1	1	1	0	0	0	0	0	3	0	0	0	0	6	0	0
LeBoeuf, Alan, Portland*	.266	102	252	37	67	101	16	3	4	30	2	0	3	3	27	3	28	1	0
Leeper, David, Hawaii*	.235	57	179	15	42	61	6	2	3	16	3	0	2	0	6	0	21	2	0
Lefebvre, Joseph, Portland*	.200	2	5	1	1	1	0	0	0	1	0	0	0	0	1	0	0	0	0
Legg, Gregory, Portland	.323	120	461	72	149	204	27	5	6	66	11	1	8	3	41	4	43	8	6
Leopold, James, Hawaii	.000	3	1	0	0	0	0	0	0	0	0	0	0	0	0	0	0	0	0
Lerch, Randy, Portland*	.250	15	20	3	5	8	1	1	0	3	0	3	0	0	2	0	3	0	0
Liddle, Steven, Edmonton	.294	63	201	29	59	86	13	1	4	27	3	1	3	0	25	0	34	1	1
Linares, Rufino, Edmonton	.278	85	316	52	88	138	15	7	7	54	6	1	3	0	28	4	32	3	0
Livingston, Dennis, Albuquerque	.333	11	6	1	2	2	0	0	0	0	0	0	0	0	0	0	3	0	0
Loy, Darren, Portland	.269	68	208	22	56	72	8	1	2	22	1	2	0	1	15	0	28	0	3
Mack, Shane, Las Vegas	.362	19	69	13	25	38	1	6	0	6	0	0	0	1	2	0	13	3	4
Maddux, Michael, Portland	.143	14	14	3	2	2	0	0	0	0	0	1	0	0	2	0	4	0	0
Mallicoat, Robin, Tucson*	.500	3	2	0	1	1	0	0	0	0	0	0	0	0	0	0	0	0	0
Mathis, Ronald, Tucson	.154	27	26	1	4	4	0	0	0	0	0	4	0	0	3	0	3	0	0
May, Scott, Albuquerque	.000	32	8	1	0	0	0	0	0	1	0	3	1	0	0	0	2	0	0
McCue, Deron, Phoenix	1.000	1	1	0	1	1	0	0	0	0	0	0	0	0	0	0	0	0	0
McGwire, Mark, Tacoma	.318	78	280	42	89	159	21	5	13	59	5	2	4	2	42	4	67	1	1
McKnight, Jonathan, Phoenix	.120	28	25	3	3	5	0	1	0	2	0	1	0	0	0	0	12	0	0
McLemore, Mark, Edmonton†	.276	73	286	41	79	94	13	1	0	23	3	4	4	0	39	2	30	29	9
Meadows, Michael, Tucson*	.300	82	290	42	87	147	14	8	10	52	11	1	0	1	48	3	53	18	7
Meagher, Adrian, Albuquerque	.000	28	1	0	0	0	0	0	0	0	0	1	0	0	0	0	1	0	0
Meeks, Timothy, Albuquerque	.257	33	35	4	9	9	0	0	0	3	0	2	0	0	1	0	6	0	0
Melendez, Francisco, Portland*	.318	96	356	47	113	150	21	2	4	57	7	1	6	1	33	5	33	2	3
Merrifield, Billie, Edmonton	.282	55	188	32	53	94	12	1	9	38	1	1	3	0	18	0	29	1	0
Meyer, Joe, Vancouver*	.255	126	451	65	115	203	16	0	24	98	9	0	3	6	59	4	116	3	1
Miller, Darrell, Edmonton	.307	63	212	37	65	111	8	7	8	30	4	0	1	0	24	2	46	3	3
Miller, Keith, Portland†	.246	36	130	15	32	42	8	1	0	11	1	0	0	0	21	0	10	6	4
Miller, Stephen, Phoenix*	.217	74	230	16	50	59	5	2	0	23	2	0	1	1	8	1	30	0	0
Miner, James, Tucson	.222	34	9	2	2	2	0	0	0	0	0	2	0	0	1	0	4	0	1
Miscik, Robert, Hawaii	.276	116	399	42	110	146	20	2	4	51	4	5	6	5	51	2	42	5	7
Mizerock, John, Tucson*	.161	20	56	2	9	12	3	0	0	5	0	2	2	1	5	0	8	0	1
Money, Kyle, Portland	.000	7	4	1	0	0	0	0	0	0	0	0	0	0	0	0	1	0	0
Montalvo, Rafael, Tucson	.167	47	6	1	1	1	0	0	0	1	0	1	0	0	0	0	4	0	0
Montgomery, Reginald, Edmonton	.285	127	470	73	134	216	22	3	18	82	11	1	6	4	28	3	75	2	4
Moore, Robert, Phoenix	.286	24	7	0	2	2	0	0	0	0	0	0	0	0	0	0	2	0	0
Moses, John, Calgary†	.324	39	148	31	48	62	3	1	3	18	1	2	1	0	25	0	17	15	2
Moses, Stephen, Portland*	.250	55	108	17	27	34	5	1	0	3	0	2	0	1	9	0	12	4	2
Mulholland, Terence, Phoenix	.115	17	26	2	3	3	0	0	0	1	0	3	0	0	1	0	8	0	0
Nago, Garrett, Vancouver†	.271	28	85	7	23	30	5	1	0	7	1	0	1	0	10	0	20	0	1
Neal, Scott, Hawaii	.000	18	6	0	0	0	0	0	0	0	0	1	0	0	0	0	3	0	0
Nelson, Ricky, Calgary*	.280	81	293	38	82	114	19	2	3	33	1	4	1	1	19	4	49	7	5
Nelson, Robert, Tacoma*	.276	139	508	77	140	234	26	4	20	108	10	0	13	2	62	5	115	3	1
Newell, Thomas, Portland	.333	5	9	0	3	4	1	0	0	1	0	0	0	0	0	0	1	0	0

Player and Club	Pct.	G.	AB.	R.	H.	TB.	2B.	3B.	HR.	RBI.	GW.	SH.	SF.	HP.	BB.	Int. BB.	SO.	SB.	CS.
Newsom, Gary, Albuquerque	.267	12	15	5	4	5	1	0	0	1	0	0	1	0	0	0	2	0	0
Nixon, Donell, Calgary	.343	8	35	3	12	15	1	1	0	1	0	0	0	0	1	0	3	0	0
Noble, Rayner, Tucson†	.200	17	5	0	1	1	0	0	0	0	0	0	0	0	0	0	1	0	0
O'Brien, Charles, Vancouver	.118	6	17	1	2	2	0	0	0	1	0	0	0	0	4	0	4	0	0
Ouellette, Philip, Phoenix†	.313	90	294	48	92	136	21	1	7	41	8	1	0	2	37	5	29	1	0
Paciorek, James, Vancouver	.309	116	408	79	126	180	30	3	6	57	6	1	4	1	62	2	66	8	6
Parent, Mark, Las Vegas	.288	86	267	29	77	110	10	4	5	40	4	1	4	0	23	2	25	0	3
Patterson, Robert, Hawaii	.290	26	31	0	9	9	0	0	0	2	0	1	0	0	0	0	6	0	0
Pederson, Stuart, Albuquerque*	.300	105	357	69	107	166	25	2	10	63	5	0	4	3	52	7	58	5	3
Pena, Adalberto, Tucson	.260	118	457	78	119	181	23	3	11	60	7	2	2	3	37	0	62	18	10
Perlman, Jonathan, Phoenix*	.250	45	12	1	3	3	0	0	0	1	0	0	0	0	0	0	2	0	0
Peters, Richard, Tacoma†	.296	8	27	9	8	13	1	2	0	6	1	0	2	0	6	0	3	2	0
Polidor, Gustavo, Edmonton	.300	119	476	72	143	195	27	5	5	61	4	9	3	1	29	1	41	7	9
Polonia, Luis, Tacoma†	.301	134	549	98	165	202	20	4	3	63	3	2	4	3	52	2	65	36	21
Powell, Dennis, Albuquerque	.200	12	15	1	3	5	0	1	0	1	1	1	0	0	1	0	6	0	0
Pyznarski, Timothy, Las Vegas	.326	135	484	93	158	278	35	8	23	119	14	0	12	1	82	6	127	25	7
Quinones, Luis, Phoenix†	.255	14	55	7	14	20	4	1	0	7	0	0	2	1	4	0	8	0	1
Ramsey, Michael James, Albu†	.385	5	13	3	5	10	2	0	1	2	1	0	0	0	1	0	1	0	1
Ramsey, Michael Jeffrey, Edm†	.364	10	33	4	12	14	2	0	0	5	0	0	0	0	1	0	1	1	2
Ready, Randy, Las Vegas	.368	10	38	5	14	21	4	0	1	8	0	0	0	0	6	0	2	1	1
Reece, Thad, Tacoma*	.282	102	309	47	87	100	9	2	0	27	2	3	2	0	30	0	26	3	5
Reid, Jessie, Phoenix*	.269	120	428	70	115	195	26	6	14	61	7	0	2	3	50	5	86	10	11
Renteria, Richard, Hawaii	.314	112	389	51	122	163	20	9	1	51	5	1	9	2	22	1	29	10	3
Reyes, Gilberto, Albuquerque	.229	104	306	36	70	106	13	1	7	36	2	3	2	2	23	2	54	1	1
Reynolds, Harold, Calgary†	.314	29	118	20	37	47	7	0	1	7	1	1	0	0	20	0	12	10	8
Reynolds, Ronn, Portland	.230	51	165	13	38	61	9	4	2	22	4	1	3	0	11	1	29	1	2
Rodriguez, Edwin, Las Vegas*	.301	105	309	56	93	133	14	7	4	32	4	2	3	1	43	2	44	14	9
Rodriguez, Ruben, Hawaii	.259	30	108	11	28	37	5	2	0	15	1	0	2	2	1	0	18	0	2
Roenicke, Ronald, Tacoma†	.222	20	72	13	16	19	3	0	0	7	0	0	0	0	17	0	13	1	0
Romero, Albert, Edmonton	.220	37	109	17	24	42	3	0	5	14	1	1	1	0	12	0	19	2	1
Rood, Nelson, Tucson	.242	102	310	40	75	90	5	5	0	21	1	6	1	5	41	1	33	15	10
Ross, Mark, Tucson	.000	48	4	0	0	0	0	0	0	0	0	1	0	0	0	0	2	0	0
Rucker, David, Portland*	.375	12	8	0	3	3	0	0	0	1	0	1	0	0	0	0	1	0	0
Ryal, Mark, Edmonton*	.340	127	479	72	163	246	33	4	14	84	9	1	7	1	36	10	50	0	0
Sakata, Lenn, Tacoma	.313	110	399	66	125	164	27	3	2	48	3	1	4	2	52	1	30	11	0
Salava, Randy, Portland*	.273	6	11	1	3	5	2	0	0	1	0	0	0	0	1	0	2	0	0
Santiago, Benito, Las Vegas	.286	117	437	55	125	208	26	3	17	71	6	2	4	1	17	1	81	19	7
Sauveur, Richard, Hawaii*	.071	15	28	2	2	2	0	0	0	0	0	1	0	0	2	0	12	0	0
Schweighoffer, Michael, Albuquerque	.100	49	10	1	1	1	0	0	0	1	0	0	1	0	3	0	4	0	0
See, Laurence, Albuquerque	.289	142	536	83	155	278	38	2	27	106	3	2	8	4	51	4	101	4	0
Seibert, Gibson, Portland	.278	52	158	14	44	54	5	1	1	19	0	0	3	0	15	0	29	5	6
Sherman, James, Tucson	.226	12	31	6	7	14	5	1	0	5	0	0	0	0	4	0	9	1	0
Shipley, Craig, Albuquerque†	.291	61	203	33	59	71	8	2	0	16	0	3	1	2	11	0	23	6	7
Shirley, Steven, Albuquerque*	.200	53	5	0	1	1	0	0	0	0	0	1	0	0	0	0	1	0	0
Simmons, Todd, Las Vegas	.000	20	3	0	0	0	0	0	0	0	0	0	0	0	0	0	3	0	0
Siwy, James, Las Vegas	.042	30	24	2	1	1	0	0	0	0	0	3	0	0	2	0	9	0	0
Smith, Gregory, Las Vegas*	.309	113	320	49	99	150	26	5	5	49	6	1	4	1	29	3	47	4	6
Smith, Keith, Vancouver†	.240	26	75	12	18	22	1	0	1	6	0	2	0	1	17	1	14	7	1
Smith, Raymond, Tacoma	.200	15	40	4	8	8	0	0	0	1	0	0	0	2	4	1	3	1	1
Snyder, Brian, Las Vegas*	.000	45	3	1	0	0	0	0	0	0	0	0	0	0	0	0	1	0	0
Soares, Todd, Portland*	.160	28	75	5	12	18	4	1	0	6	1	0	1	1	6	0	17	0	1
Solano, Julio, Tucson	.000	27	7	0	0	0	0	0	0	0	0	1	0	0	0	0	4	0	0
Sorensen, Lary, Portland	.000	17	5	0	0	0	0	0	0	0	0	0	0	0	1	0	3	0	0
Steels, James, Las Vegas*	.307	126	482	87	148	218	28	9	8	64	7	2	5	2	43	5	48	35	11
Stoddard, Robert, 2 Tac-37 LV	1.000	39	1	0	1	1	0	0	0	0	0	1	0	0	0	0	0	0	0
Stone, Jeffrey, Portland*	.339	31	118	25	40	52	4	1	2	9	0	0	0	1	16	3	20	14	4
Surhoff, William, Vancouver*	.308	116	458	71	141	181	19	3	5	59	6	3	5	2	28	5	31	23	8
Sveum, Dale, Vancouver†	.295	28	105	16	31	41	3	2	1	23	3	0	3	1	13	0	24	0	4
Tatsuno, Derek, Hawaii*	.250	11	4	0	1	1	0	0	0	1	0	1	0	0	0	0	2	0	0
Taylor, Donald, Hawaii	.000	5	2	0	0	0	0	0	0	0	0	0	0	0	0	0	1	0	0
Tellez, Alonso, Albuquerque	.286	2	7	1	2	2	0	0	0	0	0	0	0	0	0	0	0	0	0
Thoma, Raymond, Tacoma	.000	1	1	0	0	0	0	0	0	0	0	0	0	0	0	0	1	0	0
Thomas, James, Tucson	.259	118	378	50	98	116	7	4	1	35	3	4	5	1	30	0	23	23	11
Thompson, Milton, Portland*	.348	41	161	26	56	73	10	2	1	16	2	1	1	1	15	1	20	20	3
Thompson, Scott, Phoenix	.000	1	1	0	0	0	0	0	0	0	0	0	0	0	0	0	1	0	0
Thrower, Keith, Tacoma†	.256	58	203	30	52	67	6	3	1	19	2	4	1	1	23	0	26	17	6
Tillman, Kerry, 2 LV-72 Tac	.314	74	261	42	82	114	19	2	3	42	5	0	6	0	22	3	32	8	1
Toliver, Freddie, Portland	.091	7	11	1	1	1	0	0	0	0	0	1	0	0	0	0	5	0	0
Tunnell, Lee, Hawaii	.107	27	28	3	3	3	0	0	0	0	0	2	0	0	3	0	7	0	0
Tutt, John, Las Vegas	.221	97	231	25	51	58	4	0	1	12	0	2	0	1	19	0	40	8	7
Valle, David, Calgary	.312	105	353	71	110	198	21	2	21	72	7	1	2	7	41	0	43	5	1
Vavra, Joseph, Albuquerque*	.250	38	72	11	18	23	3	1	0	5	1	1	0	0	7	1	8	0	2
Verducci, John, Phoenix	.282	60	174	25	49	63	6	1	2	14	2	2	2	1	12	0	20	2	2
Vila, Jesus, Albuquerque	.000	6	2	0	0	0	0	0	0	0	0	0	0	0	0	0	0	0	0
Vosberg, Edward, Las Vegas*	.235	26	34	3	8	12	4	0	0	6	1	1	0	0	0	0	8	0	0
Walker, Anthony, Tucson	.202	29	84	8	17	22	1	2	0	8	0	0	0	0	11	1	7	7	0
Walker, Duane, Tucson*	.299	81	251	38	75	117	20	5	4	40	3	1	4	0	30	3	48	15	5
Walker, Glen, Edmonton	.280	64	236	36	66	113	14	0	11	43	7	2	4	1	15	2	50	1	0
Waller, Tyrone, Tucson	.246	121	407	45	100	143	14	4	7	56	6	0	4	1	34	3	90	37	7
Ward, Colin, Phoenix*	.080	22	25	0	2	3	1	0	0	2	1	2	0	0	0	0	8	0	0
Washington, U.L., Hawaii	.242	36	120	27	29	42	3	2	2	15	1	0	0	0	24	2	26	7	3
Wasinger, Mark, Las Vegas	.307	103	378	68	116	151	22	5	1	34	2	2	1	4	49	2	36	12	5
Watters, Michael, Albuquerque*	.285	138	508	87	145	177	21	4	1	41	4	7	5	1	89	3	53	12	12
Wellman, Brad, Phoenix	.282	79	262	31	74	99	17	1	2	30	4	2	2	2	24	3	35	3	7
White, Devon, Edmonton†	.291	112	461	84	134	221	25	10	14	60	4	1	1	3	31	8	90	42	12
Willard, Gerald, Tacoma*	.258	22	62	7	16	24	5	0	1	12	0	1	1	0	9	0	11	0	0
Williams, Frank, Phoenix	.250	27	4	0	1	1	0	0	0	2	0	0	0	0	0	0	1	0	0
Williams, Jaime, Tucson	.267	7	15	0	4	4	0	0	0	0	0	0	0	0	1	0	1	0	0
Williams, Reginald, Albuquerque	.295	11	44	6	13	19	1	1	1	4	0	0	0	0	5	1	6	2	0
Williams, Steven, Portland*	.273	41	128	15	35	46	4	2	1	15	1	2	2	0	7	1	26	0	2
Williamson, Mark, Las Vegas	.000	65	5	0	0	0	0	0	0	0	0	2	0	0	0	0	3	0	0
Wilson, Michael, Phoenix	.253	102	360	62	91	111	9	4	1	30	2	5	2	3	38	0	32	28	10
Wine, Robert, Tucson	.228	106	347	42	79	137	24	2	10	44	5	5	6	4	44	0	104	6	2

Player and Club	Pct.	G.	AB.	R.	H.	TB.	2B.	3B.	HR.	RBI.	GW.	SH.	SF.	HP.	BB.	Int. BB.	SO.	SB.	CS.
Wojna, Edward, Las Vegas	.103	25	29	3	3	3	0	0	0	0	0	3	0	0	2	0	14	0	0
Woodard, Michael, Phoenix*	.319	62	248	45	79	90	7	2	0	27	6	6	2	1	19	1	16	10	3
Woods, Gary, Las Vegas	.312	131	462	58	144	174	18	3	2	60	10	1	5	1	52	3	73	13	14
Wotus, Ronald, Hawaii	.315	125	419	75	132	174	24	3	4	57	9	6	2	1	58	3	51	7	3
Zaske, Jeffrey, Hawaii	.182	40	11	2	2	2	0	0	0	0	0	2	0	0	2	0	4	0	0

The following pitchers, listed alphabetically by club, with games in parentheses, had no plate appearances, primarily through use of designated hitters:

ALBUQUERQUE—Silva, Mark (7); Wallace, David (4).

CALGARY—Bartley, Gregory (51); Beattie, James (3); Best, Karl (16); Campbell, Michael (1); Christ, Michael (7); Fireovid, Stephen (14); Forsch, Kenneth (13); Fuson, Robin (6); Grimsley, Ross (3); Guetterman, Lee (4); Martin, Victor (6); Mirabella, Paul (47); Monteleone, Richard (39); Murray, Jed (35); Newman, Randall (34); Nunez, Edwin (6); O'Connor, Jack (23); Reed, Jerry (19); Swift, William (10); Whitmer, Joseph (8); Wilkinson, William (23).

EDMONTON—Bastian, Robert (26); Bryden, Thomas (22); Buice, DeWayne (8); Chadwick, Ray (20); Cliburn, Stewart (20); Cook, Michael (9); Finch, Steven (16); Fischer, Todd (34); Forster, Terry (4); Fossas, Anthony (7); Fowlkes, Alan (21); Fraser, William (6); Gonzalez, Julian (19); Green, Christopher (46); Lugo, Urbano (16); Mack, Tony (27); Romanick, Ronald (8); Ruhle, Vernon (8); Smith, David (36).

HAWAII—Gordon, Kevin (3); Neidlinger, James (4).

PHOENIX—Gott, James (2); Mason, Roger (1); Smith, Stephen (7).

PORTLAND—Shipanoff, David (8).

TACOMA—Akerfelds, Darrel (25); Arroyo, Fernando (15); Bair, Douglas (8); Birtsas, Timothy (19); Broersma, Eric (5); Burns, Todd (11); Citarella, Ralph (11); Dozier, Thomas (19); Kaiser, Jeffrey (34); Kibler, Russell (39); Krueger, William (8); Kyles, Stanley (16); Lambert, Timothy (40); Leiper, David (20); McLaughlin, Joey (44); Mooneyham, William (1); Plunk, Eric (6); Rodriguez, Ricardo (29); Stewart, David (1); Tapani, Kevin (1); Von Ohlen, David (13); Young, Curtis (4).

VANCOUVER—Birkbeck, Michael (23); Bosio, Christopher (44); Ciardi, Mark (26); Clay, David (16); Clutterbuck, Bryan (17); Crews, Timothy (10); Crim, Charles (26); Duquette, Bryan (22); Gibson, Robert (16); Johnson, John Henry (22); Jones, Alfornia (17); Myers, Edward (1); Porter, Charles (19); Searage, Raymond (20); Thompson, Richard (23); Vuckovich, Peter (6); Waits, Richard (28).

GRAND SLAM HOME RUNS—Bryant, Legg, Pena, Ryal, See, 2 each; Aldrete, Bonds, Brantley, Braun, Davidsmeier, DeAngelis, Ro. Johnson, Kiefer, Lancellotti, Melendez, Merrifield, Meyer, Ro. Nelson, Tillman, 1 each.

AWARDED FIRST BASE ON CATCHER'S INTERFERENCE—Amelung 2 (Bailey, Santiago); Ashman 2 (Loy, S. Williams); Hengel 2 (Dorsett, Goldthorn); Wotus 2 (Mizerock, Wine); Bundy (Santiago); Casey (O'Brien); Davidsmeier (Santiago); Firova (Reyes); Gainey (Brummer); Gallego (Rodriguez); Heuer (S. Williams); Householder (Ashman); Patterson (Loy); See (Loy); Steels (Cipolloni); Thrower (Reyes); Wellman (S. Williams).

CLUB FIELDING

Club	Pct.	G.	PO.	A.	E.	DP.	PB.
Calgary	.975	143	3629	1593	133	170	25
Portland	.974	141	3651	1603	139	129	24
Vancouver	.972	138	3568	1425	142	114	23
Edmonton	.972	141	3623	1446	144	143	10
Tacoma	.972	144	3695	1654	156	118	24
Phoenix	.971	142	3628	1547	152	156	8
Hawaii	.971	144	3718	1495	157	131	12
Tucson	.968	143	3664	1556	175	126	19
Las Vegas	.967	142	3650	1627	178	144	20
Albuquerque	.966	142	3690	1708	192	159	27

INDIVIDUAL FIELDING

*Throws lefthanded.

FIRST BASEMEN

Player and Club	Pct.	G.	PO.	A.	E.	DP.
P. Adams, Phoenix	.984	90	714	61	13	90
R. Adams, Phoenix	1.000	2	9	0	0	3
Adduci, Vancouver*	.985	47	311	28	5	17
Aldrete, Phoenix*	.987	10	70	7	1	5
Amelung, Albuquerque*	.818	2	9	0	2	2
Ashman, Hawaii	.913	2	21	0	2	1
Bailey, Tucson	1.000	3	22	1	0	0
Barnes, Portland	1.000	1	9	0	0	0
Braun, Calgary	.984	76	626	53	11	76
Bundy, Hawaii	.977	15	125	5	3	8
Carpenter, Tucson*	.990	87	722	59	8	62
Casey, Calgary	.993	68	632	34	5	72
C. Clark, Albuquerque*	.952	9	57	3	3	4
R. Clark, Edmonton	1.000	2	8	1	0	1
Sta. Cliburn, Edmonton	.957	6	42	2	2	6
Day, Portland	.982	23	193	20	4	16
Debus, Albuquerque	.993	15	125	8	1	13
Distefano, Hawaii*	.986	56	479	31	7	39
Driessen, Tucson	.985	56	495	30	8	37
Eppard, Tacoma*	.989	8	86	7	1	8
Fimple, Albuquerque	1.000	2	8	0	0	0
Gerber, Edmonton	1.000	3	19	2	0	2
Gross, Tacoma	.875	3	6	1	1	1
James, Vancouver*	1.000	4	35	3	0	5
Javier, Tacoma	1.000	2	17	3	0	0
Jelks, Portland	1.000	4	24	2	0	1
Johnson, Phoenix	1.000	8	35	1	0	3
Keedy, Edmonton	.976	29	205	28	1	19
Kruk, Las Vegas*	1.000	1	10	0	0	0
Lancellotti, Phoenix*	.986	49	400	28	6	40
Lansford, Tacoma	1.000	1	8	2	0	1
LeBoeuf, Portland	.983	34	273	9	5	25
Leeper, Hawaii*	1.000	1	5	0	0	0
Liddle, Edmonton	.982	11	101	11	2	10
Meadows, Tucson*	.939	15	81	12	6	10
Melendez, Portland*	.986	91	778	68	12	74
Merrifield, Edmonton	.988	19	146	13	2	21
Meyer, Vancouver*	.982	89	784	41	15	67
Miller, Edmonton	1.000	1	1	0	0	0
Miscik, Hawaii	1.000	8	71	4	0	10
Mizerock, Tucson	1.000	1	6	0	0	0
Nago, Vancouver	1.000	1	11	0	0	0
Nelson, Tacoma*	.9926	134	1228	121	10	100
Paciorek, Vancouver	1.000	10	60	1	0	8
Parent, Las Vegas	.963	11	69	9	3	3
Polidor, Edmonton	1.000	2	11	0	0	0
Pyznarski, Las Vegas	.985	130	1177	77	19	117
Reyes, Albuquerque	.958	14	86	5	4	16
Reynolds, Portland	1.000	3	1	0	0	0
Ryal, Edmonton*	.990	81	632	48	7	73
SEE, Albuquerque	.9931	118	1067	79	8	106
G. Smith, Las Vegas	1.000	10	66	6	0	6
R. Smith, Tacoma	.857	1	10	2	2	0
Wotus, Hawaii	.991	76	583	58	6	63

SECOND BASEMEN

Player and Club	Pct.	G.	PO.	A.	E.	DP.
R. Adams, Phoenix	1.000	1	3	4	0	1
Anderson, Albuquerque	.923	8	11	13	2	5
Berra, Tucson	.977	8	10	32	1	3
Carrasco, Edmonton	.972	47	89	122	6	26
Castillo, Vancouver	.963	26	34	95	5	13
Crone, Calgary	.987	82	183	262	6	76
Davidsmeier, Vancouver	.970	82	150	211	11	47
Diaz, Vancouver	1.000	1	0	1	0	1
Dowell, Portland	1.000	6	13	19	0	6
Dybzinski, Calgary	1.000	12	25	38	0	11
Espy, Hawaii	.833	1	3	2	1	0
Faedo, Albuquerque	1.000	5	5	10	0	2
Fermin, Hawaii	1.000	2	4	4	0	0
Gallego, Tacoma	.952	16	34	45	4	8
Garcia, Las Vegas	.933	22	39	58	7	13
Gerber, Edmonton	.977	23	31	53	2	9
Guinn, Tacoma	1.000	10	17	21	0	5
Job, Tacoma	1.000	3	8	9	0	1
Jones, Calgary	.983	24	42	77	2	18
Khalifa, Hawaii	1.000	5	6	20	0	4
Kiefer, Vancouver	.983	39	71	105	3	15
Kutcher, Phoenix	.956	13	17	26	2	3

SECOND BASEMEN—Continued

Player and Club	Pct.	G.	PO.	A.	E.	DP.
LEGG, Portland	.994	120	265	356	4	76
McLemore, Edmonton	.982	73	173	215	7	55
K. Miller, Portland	.979	19	41	51	2	11
S. Miller, Phoenix	1.000	10	13	31	0	9
Miscik, Hawaii	.977	57	107	149	6	31
Newsom, Albuquerque	.917	4	4	7	1	1
Polidor, Edmonton	1.000	3	5	11	0	2
Reece, Tacoma	.969	25	42	84	4	12
Renteria, Hawaii	.980	42	86	106	4	27
Reynolds, Calgary	.974	29	64	83	4	16
Rodriguez, Las Vegas	.958	70	124	197	14	37

Player and Club	Pct.	G.	PO.	A.	E.	DP.
Rood, Tucson	.968	37	69	113	6	14
Sakata, Tacoma	.978	100	168	286	10	52
Thomas, Tucson	.961	106	207	309	21	66
Vavra, Albuquerque	.923	4	3	9	1	1
Verducci, Phoenix	1.000	9	14	18	0	3
Wasinger, Las Vegas	.976	67	118	202	8	60
Watters, Albuquerque	.947	135	288	442	41	101
Wellman, Phoenix	.970	66	133	195	10	53
Wilson, Phoenix	.846	4	3	8	2	1
Woodard, Phoenix	.974	56	107	151	7	41
Wotus, Hawaii	.986	50	94	116	3	26

THIRD BASEMEN

Player and Club	Pct.	G.	PO.	A.	E.	DP.
R. Adams, Phoenix	1.000	6	5	9	0	0
Anderson, Albuquerque	.933	19	7	35	3	5
Asadoor, Las Vegas	.923	116	75	214	24	22
Barnes, Portland	.908	23	11	48	6	7
Berra, Tucson	.882	9	6	9	2	0
Carrasco, Edmonton	.938	27	24	36	4	2
Casey, Calgary	.500	2	0	1	1	0
Crone, Calgary	.972	18	9	26	1	3
Dabney, Phoenix	.875	7	2	12	2	0
Davidsmeier, Vancouver	.800	8	5	8	0	1
Day, Portland	.983	52	26	87	2	7
Debus, Albuquerque	1.000	2	0	6	0	0
Dybzinski, Portland	.932	80	42	151	14	17
Faedo, Albuquerque	.000	1	0	0	2	0
Fimple, Albuquerque	.939	21	12	34	3	7
Gallego, Tacoma	.962	20	11	40	2	3
Garcia, Las Vegas	1.000	2	2	1	0	0
Gerber, Edmonton	.872	22	14	27	6	5
Gomez, Phoenix	1.000	1	1	4	0	0
Gonzalez, Hawaii	.932	74	49	128	13	8
Gross, Tacoma	.909	8	10	20	3	2
Hamilton, Albuquerque	.909	71	39	151	19	14
Hill, Calgary	.888	58	40	95	17	14
Howell, Edmonton	.933	44	28	84	8	7
Jackson, Tucson	.910	122	91	202	29	22
James, Portland	.927	17	14	37	4	2
Jelks, Portland	.922	16	10	37	4	3
Job, Tucson	1.000	1	1	1	0	0
JOHNSON, Phoenix	.959	121	101	253	15	29
Jones, Calgary	.871	13	3	24	4	2

Player and Club	Pct.	G.	PO.	A.	E.	DP.
Keedy, Edmonton	.979	19	10	36	1	2
Kiefer, Vancouver	.909	79	42	143	19	11
Kutcher, Phoenix	.889	7	7	13	3	4
LeBoeuf, Portland	.919	18	10	24	3	1
McGwire, Tacoma	.877	78	53	126	25	9
Merrifield, Edmonton	.955	35	21	64	4	5
Miller, Portland	.862	13	10	15	4	0
Miscik, Hawaii	.963	27	25	52	3	5
Paciorek, Vancouver	.932	29	21	48	5	5
Polidor, Edmonton	1.000	1	0	2	0	0
Ramsey, Edmonton	.800	4	4	4	2	0
Ready, Las Vegas	1.000	5	2	10	0	1
Reece, Tacoma	.968	40	17	74	3	10
Renteria, Hawaii	.928	46	26	90	9	5
Rodriguez, Las Vegas	1.000	1	3	0	0	0
Rood, Tucson	.882	6	5	10	2	0
Sakata, Tacoma	1.000	3	2	6	0	0
See, Albuquerque	.953	32	22	39	3	7
Seibert, Portland	.903	26	21	63	9	2
G. Smith, Las Vegas	.800	2	0	4	1	1
R. Smith, Tacoma	1.000	2	1	1	0	0
Sveum, Vancouver	.950	28	22	54	4	6
Thomas, Tucson	.750	8	4	2	2	0
Thrower, Tacoma	.889	2	4	4	1	0
Vavra, Albuquerque	.800	14	4	8	3	0
Waller, Tucson	.893	12	8	17	3	1
Wasinger, Las Vegas	.950	25	18	39	3	4
Wellman, Phoenix	.833	6	1	4	1	0
Woodard, Phoenix	.958	9	9	14	1	1

SHORTSTOPS

Player and Club	Pct.	G.	PO.	A.	E.	DP.
R. Adams, Phoenix	.947	5	8	10	1	3
Anderson, Albuquerque	.965	95	181	292	17	85
Barnes, Portland	1.000	5	2	7	0	0
Berra, Tucson	1.000	1	0	4	0	0
Day, Portland	1.000	11	10	24	0	2
E. Diaz, Vancouver	.940	106	173	310	31	54
M. Diaz, Calgary	.969	109	194	302	16	71
Dowell, Portland	.972	136	206	450	19	92
Dybzinski, Calgary	.989	22	30	58	1	9
Faedo, Albuquerque	1.000	1	4	2	0	1
Fermin, Hawaii	.956	37	56	95	7	19
Gallego, Tucson	.966	97	152	332	17	56
Garcia, Las Vegas	.964	11	8	19	1	6
Gerber, Edmonton	.941	26	35	61	6	10
Gonzalez, Hawaii	.898	10	15	29	5	5
Green, Las Vegas	.958	127	158	390	24	81
Guinn, Tacoma	1.000	1	4	2	0	2
Job, Tucson	.917	1	2	9	1	1
Jones, Calgary	.988	17	30	55	1	20
Keedy, Edmonton	.700	3	1	6	3	1
Khalifa, Hawaii	.969	45	76	145	7	24

Player and Club	Pct.	G.	PO.	A.	E.	DP.
Kiefer, Vancouver	.933	10	10	18	2	5
Kutcher, Phoenix	.880	20	32	49	11	13
K. Miller, Portland	1.000	1	3	4	0	0
S. Miller, Phoenix	.954	64	80	167	12	30
Miscik, Hawaii	.962	26	36	64	4	14
Newsom, Albuquerque	.750	3	1	2	1	0
Pena, Tucson	.961	117	206	359	23	65
POLIDOR, Edmonton	.986	111	197	303	7	92
Quinones, Phoenix	.952	14	23	37	3	10
Ramsey, Edmonton	.905	7	10	9	2	2
Reece, Tacoma	.971	14	25	41	2	8
Rodriguez, Las Vegas	.940	17	27	52	5	11
Rood, Tucson	.940	35	44	82	8	12
Siebert, Portland	1.000	1	0	2	0	0
Shipley, Albuquerque	.938	60	99	173	18	30
Smith, Vancouver	.970	25	40	89	4	13
Thrower, Tacoma	.946	36	51	107	9	18
Verducci, Phoenix	.948	48	78	158	13	48
Washington, Hawaii	.906	36	54	90	15	24
Wellman, Phoenix	.943	8	11	22	2	3

OUTFIELDERS

Player and Club	Pct.	G.	PO.	A.	E.	DP.
P. Adams, Phoenix	1.000	1	3	0	0	0
Adduci, Vancouver*	.982	53	107	3	2	1
Aldrete, Phoenix*	1.000	37	61	1	0	0
Amelung, Albuquerque*	.989	80	169	4	2	0
Anderson, Albuquerque	1.000	1	1	0	0	0
Asadoor, Las Vegas	1.000	10	18	0	0	0
Barnes, Portland	1.000	11	22	5	0	1
Berra, Tucson	.900	5	9	0	1	0
Bonds, Hawaii*	.983	44	109	4	2	1
Braggs, Vancouver	.991	90	218	8	2	4
Brantley, Calgary	.981	90	201	9	4	3
Braun, Calgary	.963	14	24	2	1	2
D. Brown, Phoenix-Calgary	.989	43	83	3	1	0
M. Brown, Hawaii	.976	23	38	2	1	1
Bryant, Albuquerque	.928	99	158	10	13	2
Bullock, Tucson*	.987	33	73	2	1	2
Calderon, Calgary	.973	20	34	2	1	1

Player and Club	Pct.	G.	PO.	A.	E.	DP.
Carpenter, Tucson	.988	34	83	1	1	1
Cartwright, Vancouver*	1.000	4	3	1	0	0
Casey, Calgary	1.000	8	11	1	0	0
C. Clark, Albuquerque*	.985	83	124	4	2	1
R. Clark, Edmonton	1.000	41	107	1	0	0
Davis, Hawaii*	.962	102	216	9	9	3
Day, Portland	.800	8	4	0	1	0
DeAngelis, Portland*	.959	96	177	8	8	0
Debus, Albuquerque	1.000	5	2	0	0	0
Distefano, Hawaii*	.978	58	85	6	2	0
Eppard, Tacoma*	.992	77	118	4	1	0
Espy, Hawaii	.978	98	169	6	4	1
Felder, Vancouver	.956	38	83	4	4	1
Fimple, Albuquerque	1.000	1	1	0	0	0
Ford, Hawaii	.935	18	28	1	2	1
Fuentes, Tucson	1.000	7	4	0	0	0
Gainey, Tucson	.949	84	163	4	9	2

OUTFIELDERS—Continued

Player and Club	Pct.	G.	PO.	A.	E.	DP.
Gladden, Phoenix	1.000	7	11	0	0	0
Gonzalez, Albuquerque	.968	84	171	10	6	3
Graham, Phoenix*	.944	27	51	0	3	0
Hall, Calgary*	.951	58	114	2	6	0
Haro, Hawaii	.985	71	134	1	2	1
Hengel, Calgary	.967	105	217	16	8	5
Hill, Calgary	1.000	10	18	0	0	0
Householder, Vancouver	.962	50	96	4	4	0
C. James, Portland	.950	45	69	7	4	2
D. James, Vancouver*	.984	120	313	4	5	1
Javier, Tacoma	.964	66	155	6	6	2
Jelks, Portland	.967	42	59	0	2	0
Johnson, Tacoma*	.950	57	95	1	5	0
C. Jones, Phoenix*	.983	91	177	1	3	0
Ron. Jones, Portland	1.000	9	11	2	0	0
Ros. Jones, Calgary	1.000	3	8	1	0	0
Keedy, Edmonton	.938	6	13	2	1	0
Kemp, Las Vegas*	1.000	24	32	0	0	0
Klipstein, Vancouver	1.000	38	54	4	0	1
Knight, Portland*	.964	118	205	10	8	2
Kramer, Tacoma	1.000	1	1	0	0	0
Kruk, Las Vegas*	1.000	6	12	1	0	0
Kutcher, Phoenix	1.000	20	36	1	0	1
Lancellotti, Phoenix*	.946	56	101	5	6	2
Leeper, Hawaii*	1.000	42	65	0	0	0
Lefebvre, Portland	1.000	2	2	0	0	0
Linares, Edmonton	.833	2	4	1	1	0
Mack, Las Vegas	.956	19	43	0	2	0
Meadows, Tucson*	.977	73	122	3	3	0
Merrifield, Edmonton	1.000	3	4	0	0	0
D. Miller, Edmonton	.950	10	19	0	1	1
K. Miller, Portland	1.000	3	6	0	0	0
Miscik, Hawaii	.923	7	12	0	1	0
Montgomery, Edmonton	.983	125	266	15	5	2
J. Moses, Calgary*	.990	38	93	3	1	1
S. Moses, Portland*	.969	32	61	1	2	0
Nelson, Calgary	1.000	62	120	5	0	0
Newsom, Albuquerque	1.000	1	1	0	0	0
Nixon, Calgary	1.000	7	15	2	0	0
Paciorek, Vancouver	.969	37	61	2	2	0
Pederson, Albuquerque*	.967	95	191	15	7	1
Peters, Tacoma	1.000	7	17	0	0	0
Polonia, Tacoma*	.970	134	318	8	10	4
Pyznarski, Las Vegas	1.000	5	5	0	0	0
Ramsey, Albuquerque*	1.000	5	10	0	0	0
Ready, Las Vegas	1.000	3	10	0	0	0
Reece, Tacoma	1.000	11	13	2	0	0
Reid, Phoenix*	.971	116	227	5	7	2
Roenicke, Tacoma*	.971	20	33	1	1	0
Romero, Edmonton	.962	30	48	3	2	1
Rood, Tucson	.971	25	33	1	1	0
Ryal, Edmonton*	1.000	44	102	2	0	2
Salava, Portland	1.000	3	6	0	0	0
Seibert, Portland	1.000	11	25	3	0	0
Sherman, Tucson	1.000	5	6	0	0	0
G. Smith, Las Vegas	.972	82	134	7	4	1
R. Smith, Tacoma	1.000	2	2	0	0	0
Soares, Portland	1.000	24	50	2	0	0
Steels, Las Vegas*	.953	124	228	16	12	4
Stone, Portland	.984	29	60	0	1	0
Tellez, Albuquerque	1.000	2	3	0	0	0
Thompson, Portland	.990	41	101	1	1	1
Thrower, Tacoma	1.000	14	20	2	0	0
Tillman, Las Vegas-Tacoma	.993	59	128	6	1	0
Tutt, Las Vegas	.991	83	110	6	1	0
Vavra, Albuquerque	1.000	5	1	1	0	0
A. Walker, Tucson	.957	27	62	4	3	1
D. Walker, Tucson*	.984	69	122	5	2	1
G. Walker, Edmonton	.960	62	136	7	6	0
WALLER, Tucson	.985	109	250	16	4	2
White, Edmonton	.982	112	317	16	6	2
Williams, Albuquerque	1.000	11	18	0	0	0
Wilson, Phoenix	.975	88	193	2	5	1
Woods, Las Vegas	.966	125	249	5	9	3

CATCHERS

Player and Club	Pct.	G.	PO.	A.	E.	DP.	PB.
Ashman, Hawaii	.968	24	108	12	4	1	2
Bailey, Tucson	.973	22	98	9	3	0	1
Bathe, Tacoma	.986	26	120	21	2	4	3
Brummer, Hawaii	.986	76	403	33	6	4	6
Carrasco, Edmonton	1.000	1	5	1	0	0	0
Cipolloni, Portland	.977	9	42	1	1	0	2
Sta. Cliburn, Edmonton	.968	61	266	32	10	4	1
Datz, Tucson	1.000	1	5	0	0	0	0
Debus, Albuquerque	.984	27	112	11	2	3	6
Dorsett, Tacoma	.963	91	420	54	18	3	16
Edwards, Tucson	1.000	1	5	1	0	0	0
Fimple, Albuquerque	.994	63	289	44	2	1	4
Firova, Calgary	.978	67	316	46	8	6	14
Goldthorn, Hawaii	.988	27	150	15	2	2	1
Gomez, Phoenix	.992	68	351	42	3	5	4
Gulden, Phoenix	.984	13	56	4	1	0	1
Hill, Calgary	1.000	3	3	0	0	0	0
Huppert, Vancouver	.987	11	72	6	1	0	2
Johnson, Phoenix	1.000	1	8	0	0	0	0
Jones, Tacoma	.989	19	76	13	1	0	3
Kutcher, Phoenix	1.000	1	1	0	0	0	0
Liddle, Edmonton	.967	44	208	30	8	3	2
Loy, Portland	.980	64	309	37	7	3	7
Miller, Edmonton	.950	10	19	0	1	1	0
Mizerock, Tucson	.958	18	81	10	4	0	1
Nago, Vancouver	.982	24	147	14	3	1	6
O'Brien, Vancouver	.926	6	22	3	2	0	0
Ouellette, Phoenix	.981	72	369	50	8	4	3
Parent, Las Vegas	.994	51	275	31	2	2	8
Reyes, Albuquerque	.976	78	337	64	10	7	17
Reynolds, Portland	.992	43	227	23	2	0	1
Rodriguez, Hawaii	.974	30	201	23	6	0	3
Santiago, Las Vegas	.968	99	563	71	21	7	11
Smith, Tacoma	.962	6	22	3	1	0	1
SURHOFF, Vancouver	.989	98	539	70	7	10	15
Valle, Calgary	.987	84	404	61	6	7	11
Willard, Tacoma	.991	17	100	7	1	1	1
J. Williams, Tucson	1.000	6	22	2	0	1	2
S. Williams, Portland	.972	38	191	18	6	2	14
Wine, Tucson	.987	100	459	76	7	10	15

PITCHERS

Player and Club	Pct.	G.	PO.	A.	E.	DP.
Acker, Tucson*	1.000	46	0	5	0	0
Akerfelds, Tacoma	1.000	25	14	17	0	3
Arroyo, Tacoma	.974	15	16	22	1	0
August, Tucson-Vancouver	.952	27	13	27	2	3
Bair, Tacoma	1.000	8	1	2	0	0
Baker, Albuquerque	.958	27	5	18	1	1
Bartley, Calgary	.917	51	2	20	2	1
Bastian, Edmonton	.952	26	9	11	1	1
Beattie, Calgary	.667	3	1	3	2	1
Beck, Portland*	.571	24	1	3	3	0
Best, Calgary	1.000	16	1	1	0	0
Birkbeck, Vancouver	.939	23	11	20	2	0
Birtsas, Tacoma*	1.000	19	2	17	0	0
Bitker, Las Vegas	1.000	5	0	5	0	0
Bittiger, Portland	.862	27	14	11	4	0
Bockus, Phoenix	.970	42	6	26	1	1
Booker, Las Vegas	.895	36	9	25	4	2
Bosio, Vancouver	.900	44	5	4	1	1
Bowden, Portland*	.941	39	3	13	1	0
Broersma, Tacoma	1.000	5	2	1	0	1
Bryden, Edmonton	1.000	22	3	5	0	0
Buice, Edmonton	1.000	8	2	1	0	0
Bulls, Portland	.889	17	9	7	2	1
Burns, Tacoma	1.000	11	1	6	0	1
Calhoun, Tucson*	.909	22	3	7	1	0
Chadwick, Edmonton	.846	20	10	12	4	1
Childress, Portland-Tucson	1.000	61	7	6	0	0
Christ, Calgary	.900	7	6	3	1	1
Ciardi, Vancouver	1.000	26	5	16	0	0
Citarella, Tacoma	1.000	11	5	2	0	0
Clay, Vancouver	1.000	16	2	15	0	1
Ste. Cliburn, Edmonton	.857	20	2	4	1	1
Clutterbuck, Vancouver	1.000	17	3	12	0	0
Cook, Edmonton	1.000	9	2	10	0	1
Crews, Vancouver	1.000	10	2	3	0	0
Crim, Vancouver	1.000	26	4	5	0	0
Day, Portland	1.000	2	0	3	0	0
deLeon, Hawaii	1.000	15	3	7	0	0
Diaz, Albuquerque*	.833	14	2	3	1	0
Downs, Phoenix	.960	18	12	12	1	0
Dozier, Tacoma	.900	19	6	12	2	1
Duquette, Vancouver*	1.000	22	1	3	0	0
Eichhorn, Albuquerque	.967	39	7	22	1	1
Engel, Tucson*	1.000	7	0	5	0	1
Fansler, Hawaii	.885	29	16	30	6	3
Farmer, Hawaii	.833	40	2	13	3	0
Finch, Edmonton	.960	16	5	19	1	1
Fireovid, Calgary	1.000	14	9	15	0	1
Fischer, Edmonton	.778	34	3	4	2	2
Forsch, Calgary	1.000	13	4	5	0	0
Forster, Edmonton*	1.000	4	0	1	0	0
Fossas, Edmonton*	1.000	7	1	5	0	0

PITCHERS—Continued

Player and Club	Pct.	G.	PO.	A.	E.	DP.
Fowlkes, Edmonton	.947	21	8	10	1	1
Fraser, Edmonton	1.000	6	1	6	0	0
Fuson, Calgary	1.000	6	1	6	0	1
Galvez, Albuquerque	.913	18	2	19	2	3
Gibson, Vancouver	1.000	16	15	7	0	1
A. Gonzalez, Portland	.943	28	18	32	3	4
J. Gonzalez, Edmonton	1.000	19	0	7	0	2
Gorman, Portland*	1.000	43	0	16	0	3
Gott, Phoenix	1.000	2	0	1	0	0
Grant, Phoenix	.900	28	17	10	3	2
Grapenthin, Las Vegas	1.000	39	6	12	0	1
Green, Edmonton*	1.000	46	2	8	0	0
Grimsley, Calgary*	1.000	3	0	1	0	1
Guetterman, Calgary*	1.000	4	1	6	0	0
Hayward, Las Vegas*	.915	26	11	32	4	4
Heathcock, Tucson	.967	27	8	21	1	0
Hensley, Phoenix*	1.000	44	1	6	0	3
Hernandez, Tucson	.870	22	9	11	3	0
Heuer, Albuquerque	.913	36	6	15	2	0
Hickey, Portland*	1.000	33	8	9	0	2
Hicks, Portland	.917	29	3	8	1	0
Hillegas, Albuquerque	1.000	9	1	5	0	1
Holton, Albuquerque	.982	27	13	41	1	2
Hummel, Phoenix*	1.000	5	0	1	0	0
Jackson, Portland	1.000	17	2	5	0	0
Jeffcoat, Phoenix*	.941	54	6	10	1	1
D. Johnson, Hawaii	.879	22	7	22	4	2
J.H. Johnson, Vancouver*	1.000	22	1	2	0	0
A. Jones, Vancouver	.800	17	3	1	1	0
B. Jones, Hawaii	.900	35	4	14	2	1
J. Jones, Las Vegas	.973	28	8	28	1	1
Kaiser, Tacoma*	.947	34	10	26	2	1
Keough, Tucson	.900	8	4	5	1	0
Kibler, Tacoma	.938	39	4	11	1	0
Knudson, Tucson-Vancouver	.944	17	4	13	1	0
Krawczyk, Hawaii	1.000	32	4	10	0	1
Krueger, Tacoma*	.909	8	1	9	1	1
Kyles, Tacoma	.833	13	5	5	2	0
Lambert, Tacoma	.931	39	11	16	2	1
Laskey, Phoenix	.867	14	5	8	2	1
Leiper, Tacoma*	1.000	20	1	8	0	0
Leopold, Hawaii	1.000	3	1	3	0	1
Lerch, Portland*	1.000	12	4	10	0	0
Livingston, Albuquerque*	.786	11	2	9	3	0
Lugo, Edmonton	1.000	16	4	19	0	3
Mack, Edmonton	.932	27	18	23	3	2
Maddux, Portland	.875	12	6	8	2	1
Mallicoat, Tucson*	1.000	3	0	4	0	0
Martin, Calgary	1.000	6	2	2	0	0
Mason, Phoenix	1.000	1	1	0	0	0
Mathis, Tucson	.926	26	11	14	2	1
May, Albuquerque	.833	27	6	9	3	0
McKnight, Phoenix	1.000	26	7	9	0	2
McLaughlin, Tacoma	1.000	44	9	12	0	1
Meagher, Albuquerque	1.000	28	1	7	0	0
Meeks, Albuquerque	.952	33	11	29	2	1
Miner, Tucson	.826	34	12	7	4	0
Mirabella, Calgary*	.929	47	5	8	1	0
Money, Portland	1.000	7	1	3	0	1
Montalvo, Tucson	1.000	47	3	17	0	1
Monteleone, Calgary	.917	39	4	18	2	4
Mooneyham, Tacoma	1.000	1	0	1	0	0
Moore, Phoenix	1.000	24	3	9	0	1
Mulholland, Phoenix*	.917	17	9	13	2	0
Murray, Calgary	1.000	35	8	18	0	2
Myers, Vancouver	1.000	1	0	1	0	0
Nago, Vancouver	1.000	1	1	0	0	0
Neal, Hawaii*	1.000	18	2	5	0	0
Neidlinger, Hawaii	1.000	4	0	6	0	0
Newell, Portland	.750	5	3	0	1	0
Newman, Calgary*	.967	34	9	20	1	1
Noble, Tucson*	1.000	17	2	2	0	1
Nunez, Calgary	1.000	6	2	1	0	0
O'Connor, Calgary*	1.000	23	1	5	0	1
Patterson, Hawaii*	1.000	25	13	18	0	1
Perlman, Phoenix	.966	45	8	20	1	3
Plunk, Tacoma	.900	6	3	6	1	0
Porter, Vancouver	.962	19	10	15	1	2
Powell, Albuquerque*	1.000	7	0	13	0	1
Reed, Calgary	.800	19	5	7	3	0
Rodriguez, Tacoma	.953	26	19	22	2	2
Romanick, Edmonton	.900	8	5	4	1	0
Ross, Tucson	1.000	48	5	18	0	2
Rucker, Portland*	.947	12	4	14	1	1
Ruhle, Edmonton	1.000	8	3	1	0	0
Sauveur, Hawaii*	.933	14	8	20	2	1
Schweighoffer, Albuquerque	.972	49	10	25	1	4
Searage, Vancouver*	1.000	20	2	3	0	0
Shipanoff, Portland	.500	8	0	1	1	0
Shirley, Albuquerque*	.917	53	1	10	1	0
Silva, Albuquerque	1.000	7	0	1	0	0
Simmons, Las Vegas	1.000	20	2	7	0	2
Siwy, Las Vegas	.972	30	8	27	1	0
D. Smith, Edmonton	1.000	36	6	15	0	0
S. Smith, Phoenix	1.000	7	1	1	0	0
Snyder, Las Vegas*	.941	45	2	14	1	1
Solano, Tucson	.867	27	1	12	2	0
Sorensen, Portland	.944	17	10	7	1	1
Stewart, Tacoma	1.000	1	2	0	0	0
Stoddard, Tacoma-Las Vegas	.875	39	2	5	1	0
Swift, Calgary	.968	10	9	21	1	4
Tatsuno, Hawaii*	1.000	11	1	6	0	0
Taylor, Hawaii	.833	5	1	4	1	0
Thompson, Vancouver	1.000	23	2	4	0	1
Toliver, Portland	.900	6	1	8	1	1
Tunnell, Hawaii	.946	27	9	26	2	0
Vila, Albuquerque	1.000	6	1	1	0	0
Von Ohlen, Tacoma*	.900	13	3	6	1	0
Vosberg, Las Vegas*	.933	25	10	32	3	2
Vuckovich, Vancouver	1.000	6	1	2	0	0
WAITS, Vancouver*	1.000	28	6	28	0	0
Ward, Phoenix*	.958	22	8	15	1	1
Whitmer, Calgary	1.000	8	1	3	0	0
Wilkinson, Calgary*	.958	23	5	18	1	5
Williams, Phoenix	1.000	27	1	4	0	1
Williamson, Las Vegas	1.000	65	4	8	0	0
Wojna, Las Vegas	.886	25	12	19	4	2
Young, Tacoma*	1.000	4	3	5	0	0
Zaske, Hawaii	.947	40	6	12	1	1

The following players do not have any recorded accepted chances at the positions indicated; therefore, are not listed in the fielding averages for those particular positions: Ashman, ss; Barkley, p; Brummer, of, p; Campbell p; Debus, p; Dietrick, of; Espy, ss; Faedo, of; Garcia, p; Gordon, p; Huppert, of; C. Jackson, of; R. Johnson, p; J. Jones, 3b; Klipstein, p; Leeper, p; Melendez, of; Miscik, c; Pyznarski, 3b; Reece, p; E. Rodriguez, of; Romero, p; Tapani, p; Thoma, 3b; S. Thompson, of; Vavra, 1b; Wallace, p; Watters, of; F. Williams, 3b; S. Williams, 3b; Woods, p.

CLUB PITCHING

Club	ERA.	G.	CG.	ShO.	Sv.	IP.	H.	R.	ER.	HR.	HB.	BB.	Int. BB.	SO.	WP.	Bk.
Hawaii	3.80	144	37	7	22	1239.1	1180	618	523	63	35	540	23	839	68	13
Vancouver	4.00	138	24	10	43	1189.1	1242	598	528	78	20	373	32	741	46	3
Tacoma	4.35	144	17	6	28	1231.2	1271	706	595	92	30	576	43	719	59	17
Portland	4.38	141	19	7	34	1217.0	1232	679	592	92	28	512	38	727	58	11
Las Vegas	4.41	142	16	6	40	1216.2	1309	711	596	92	27	505	38	830	65	18
Phoenix	4.41	142	27	6	42	1209.1	1338	684	593	82	22	501	50	744	51	11
Tucson	4.42	143	14	4	31	1221.1	1427	710	600	72	12	380	26	647	53	9
Edmonton	4.84	141	21	9	30	1207.2	1381	740	649	133	32	462	15	658	37	9
Albuquerque	5.04	142	11	3	22	1230.0	1430	812	689	118	21	529	36	694	51	19
Calgary	5.36	143	21	7	32	1209.2	1474	804	720	129	24	500	36	676	46	22

PITCHERS' RECORDS

(Leading Qualifiers for Earned-Run Average Leadership — 115 or More Innings)

*Throws lefthanded.

Pitcher—Club	W.	L.	Pct.	ERA.	G.	GS.	CG.	GF.	ShO.	Sv.	IP.	H.	R.	ER.	HR.	HB.	BB.	Int. BB.	SO.	WP.
D. Johnson, Hawaii	8	7	.533	3.17	22	22	6	0	1	0	150.1	150	68	53	6	3	35	0	71	0
August, 24 Tuc-3 Van	10	10	.500	3.37	27	27	4	0	0	0	179.0	192	88	67	7	1	51	5	70	7
Patterson, Hawaii*	9	6	.600	3.40	25	21	6	2	1	1	156.0	146	68	59	9	1	44	0	137	3
Siwy, Las Vegas	6	4	.600	3.56	30	19	0	4	0	2	129.0	121	59	51	14	5	47	6	77	2
Wojna, Las Vegas	12	7	.632	3.59	25	25	7	0	1	0	175.1	181	81	70	6	3	50	2	102	7
Fansler, Hawaii	8	9	.471	3.63	29	24	4	0	0	0	156.0	139	83	63	7	7	65	1	77	7

Pitcher—Club	W.	L.	Pct.	ERA.	G.	GS.	CG.	GF.	ShO.	Sv.	IP.	H.	R.	ER.	HR.	HB.	BB.	Int. BB.	SO.	WP.
Holton, Albuquerque	10	10	.500	3.78	27	27	5	0	1	0	182.2	200	90	74	18	0	20	0	105	6
Rodriguez, Tacoma	7	8	.467	3.95	26	19	3	3	1	1	139.0	144	82	61	12	4	59	3	76	3
Ciardi, Vancouver	9	8	.529	4.06	26	25	7	1	2	1	168.1	194	80	76	14	0	35	1	106	7
Bittiger, Portland	13	8	.619	4.15	27	26	6	0	0	0	171.1	181	83	79	15	5	58	3	101	3

Departmental Leaders: G—Williamson, 65; W—Grant, 14; L—Mack, 13; Pct.—Williamson, .769; GS—Six pitchers with 27; CG—Grant, 10; GF—Green, 38; ShO—Chadwick, Grant, 3; Sv.—Bosio, Williamson, 16; IP—Holton, 182.2; H—Heathcock, 211; R—Meeks, 112; ER—Meeks, 98; HR—Meeks, 22; HB—Bastian, 8; BB—Monteleone, 89, IBB—Shirley, 11; SO—Patterson, 137; WP—Zaske, 17.

(All Pitchers—Listed Alphabetically)

Pitcher—Club	W.	L.	Pct.	ERA.	G.	GS.	CG.	GF.	ShO.	Sv.	IP.	H.	R.	ER.	HR.	HB.	BB.	Int. BB.	SO.	WP.
Acker, Tucson*	3	3	.500	4.83	46	0	0	26	0	6	54.0	66	31	29	1	1	21	3	31	3
Akerfelds, Tacoma	8	12	.400	4.74	25	24	2	0	0	0	150.0	158	91	79	12	6	62	3	91	10
Arroyo, Tacoma	7	4	.636	4.34	15	15	2	0	2	0	101.2	112	56	49	7	1	22	1	24	3
August, 24 Tuc-3 Van	10	10	.500	3.37	27	27	4	0	0	0	179.0	192	88	67	7	1	51	5	70	7
Bair, Tacoma	3	1	.750	0.00	8	0	0	8	0	2	12.0	8	3	0	0	1	6	1	13	1
Baker, Albuquerque	6	12	.333	6.21	27	21	2	5	0	1	126.0	174	99	87	9	2	39	2	65	3
Barkley, 6 LV-4 Port	0	0	.000	16.20	10	0	0	1	0	0	10.0	24	19	18	3	0	8	0	9	4
Bartley, Calgary	5	3	.625	5.48	51	0	0	24	0	5	95.1	133	65	58	8	3	47	7	58	3
Bastian, Edmonton	3	12	.200	4.90	26	21	2	1	0	0	125.0	145	74	68	20	8	50	1	58	3
Beattie, Calgary	1	1	.500	5.27	3	3	0	0	0	0	13.2	17	8	8	2	0	6	0	14	0
Beck, Portland*	1	4	.200	3.57	24	0	0	13	0	5	40.1	35	21	16	5	2	18	1	36	1
Best, Calgary	0	1	.000	1.59	16	0	0	12	0	1	17.0	16	6	3	1	0	12	2	20	1
Birkbeck, Vancouver	12	6	.667	4.62	23	23	2	0	0	0	134.1	160	82	69	9	2	39	4	81	6
Birtsas, Tacoma*	3	7	.300	5.07	19	15	2	1	1	0	92.1	94	59	52	6	0	71	1	75	8
Bitker, Las Vegas	2	0	1.000	3.29	5	4	0	0	0	0	27.1	24	10	10	3	2	9	0	19	4
Bittiger, Portland	13	8	.619	4.15	27	26	6	0	0	0	171.1	181	83	79	15	5	58	3	101	3
Bockus, Phoenix	11	6	.647	4.26	42	16	2	21	0	12	122.2	139	69	58	5	2	54	6	55	3
Booker, Las Vegas	8	9	.471	5.25	36	16	2	9	0	4	128.2	148	89	75	4	2	65	1	71	4
Bosio, Vancouver	7	3	.700	2.28	44	0	0	34	0	16	67.0	47	18	17	1	0	13	4	60	0
Bowden, Portland*	4	3	.571	4.48	39	7	0	10	0	2	76.1	73	41	38	7	0	58	5	55	9
Broersma, Tacoma	0	1	.000	6.75	5	0	0	0	0	0	12.0	13	10	9	1	2	3	1	9	0
Brummer, Hawaii	0	0	.000	9.00	1	0	0	1	0	0	1.0	1	1	1	0	0	1	0	0	0
Bryden, Edmonton	1	0	1.000	3.49	22	0	0	10	0	4	38.2	42	16	15	0	2	22	3	34	0
Buice, Edmonton	2	1	.667	0.73	8	0	0	7	0	1	12.1	6	2	1	0	0	3	0	11	0
Bulls, Portland	3	8	.273	5.62	17	12	0	1	0	0	57.2	71	41	36	7	3	24	3	27	4
Burns, Tacoma	0	1	.000	2.16	11	0	0	9	0	2	16.2	11	4	4	1	0	12	1	14	0
Calhoun, Tucson*	1	3	.250	4.38	22	2	0	6	0	2	39.0	29	20	19	2	1	19	1	28	4
Campbell, Calgary	0	1	.000	9.00	1	1	0	0	0	0	3.0	1	3	3	1	0	2	0	3	0
Chadwick, Edmonton	9	9	.500	4.72	20	20	5	0	3	0	124.0	116	66	65	11	3	66	0	89	3
Childress, 60 Port-1 Tuc	5	10	.333	6.80	61	1	0	34	0	13	83.1	99	69	63	7	3	46	8	40	8
Christ, Calgary	1	3	.250	6.49	7	6	1	0	0	0	34.2	47	27	25	5	1	17	0	15	2
Ciardi, Vancouver	9	8	.529	4.06	26	25	7	1	2	1	168.1	194	80	76	14	0	35	1	106	7
Citarella, Tacoma	4	0	1.000	8.21	11	4	0	1	0	0	34.0	42	33	31	5	1	23	1	17	3
Clay, Vancouver	4	3	.571	4.39	16	8	2	3	0	0	69.2	83	38	34	4	3	18	2	28	2
Ste. Cliburn, Edmonton	1	2	.333	6.94	20	0	0	10	0	1	23.1	36	18	18	3	0	7	1	17	1
Clutterbuck, Vancouver	8	5	.615	4.60	17	17	6	0	1	0	115.1	121	60	59	11	2	30	0	63	1
Cook, Edmonton	4	1	.800	5.37	9	9	0	0	0	0	55.1	49	42	33	10	3	24	0	35	3
Crews, Vancouver	2	1	.667	4.05	10	3	0	4	0	1	33.1	39	15	15	1	0	14	3	28	0
Crim, Vancouver	0	3	.000	4.96	26	0	0	8	0	1	45.1	64	32	25	2	1	15	4	26	1
Day, Portland	0	0	.000	0.00	2	0	0	2	0	0	2.0	0	0	0	0	0	0	0	0	0
Debus, Albuquerque	0	0	.000	9.00	2	0	0	2	0	0	3.0	4	3	3	1	0	2	0	0	0
deLeon, Hawaii	5	8	.385	2.46	15	14	7	1	1	0	106.0	87	32	29	5	1	44	3	83	3
Diaz, Albuquerque*	1	4	.200	5.64	14	0	0	7	0	1	22.1	26	17	14	4	0	9	1	10	2
Downs, Phoenix	8	5	.615	3.42	18	18	4	0	0	0	108.0	116	54	41	11	3	28	1	68	6
Dozier, Tacoma	5	3	.625	3.39	19	9	2	5	0	4	74.1	65	31	28	8	1	38	5	49	4
Duquette, Vancouver*	4	0	1.000	7.86	22	0	0	9	0	1	26.1	31	25	23	3	2	17	0	20	2
Eichhorn, Albuquerque	5	6	.455	5.00	39	1	0	24	0	0	63.0	90	46	35	1	1	30	8	30	3
Engel, Tucson*	0	5	.000	8.90	7	6	0	0	0	0	30.1	42	33	30	3	1	16	0	20	2
Fansler, Hawaii	8	9	.471	3.63	29	24	4	0	0	0	156.0	139	83	63	7	7	65	1	77	7
Farmer, Hawaii	4	7	.364	2.57	40	1	0	23	0	8	80.2	63	35	23	3	0	33	4	61	7
Finch, Edmonton	5	3	.625	5.79	16	12	1	1	0	0	74.2	97	58	48	11	3	22	0	29	2
Fireovid, Calgary	6	3	.667	4.70	14	12	1	0	1	0	82.1	93	49	43	5	1	29	3	29	4
Fischer, Edmonton	4	0	1.000	3.83	34	0	0	22	0	7	47.0	36	23	20	2	2	29	1	31	1
Forsch, Calgary	4	3	.571	4.91	13	7	2	2	0	0	55.0	67	31	30	8	1	23	2	23	1
Forster, Edmonton*	0	1	.000	21.00	4	1	0	0	0	0	3.0	9	7	7	1	0	3	0	4	0
Fossas, Edmonton*	3	3	.500	4.57	7	7	2	0	1	0	43.1	53	23	22	4	0	12	0	15	1
Fowlkes, Edmonton	4	5	.444	6.33	21	8	2	6	1	0	69.2	93	54	49	8	3	21	0	36	9
Fraser, Edmonton	4	1	.800	3.15	6	6	2	0	2	0	40.0	25	15	14	5	0	8	0	24	0
Fuson, Calgary	3	2	.600	4.76	6	5	1	1	0	0	28.1	37	18	15	2	0	9	0	20	4
Galvez, Albuquerque	3	6	.333	4.89	18	12	0	2	0	0	81.0	82	50	44	10	1	43	0	32	4
Garcia, Las Vegas	0	0	.000	13.50	1	0	0	1	0	0	2.0	4	3	3	2	0	0	0	0	0
Gibson, Vancouver	10	4	.714	2.78	16	13	0	0	0	0	90.2	81	30	28	3	0	37	1	59	4
A. Gonzalez, Portland	10	11	.476	4.68	28	27	4	1	0	0	179.0	174	102	93	13	4	61	7	90	5
J. Gonzalez, Edmonton	1	0	1.000	6.75	19	0	0	5	0	0	42.2	55	37	32	4	0	31	0	28	0
Gordon, Hawaii	1	2	.333	7.36	3	3	0	0	0	0	14.2	14	12	12	1	2	15	0	8	0
Gorman, Portland*	4	2	.667	2.17	43	0	0	23	0	6	54.0	44	14	13	3	1	27	1	44	3
Gott, Phoenix	0	0	.000	6.75	2	2	0	0	0	0	2.2	2	2	2	0	0	3	0	2	0
Grant, Phoenix	14	7	.667	4.90	28	27	10	0	3	0	181.2	204	105	99	13	3	46	4	93	8
Grapenthin, Las Vegas	3	3	.500	5.01	39	1	0	22	0	2	70.0	92	60	39	4	1	28	7	33	4
Green, Edmonton*	4	5	.444	4.38	46	0	0	38	0	14	63.2	74	37	31	10	0	22	2	44	3
Grimsley, Calgary*	0	0	.000	10.50	3	0	0	2	0	0	6.0	14	8	7	1	0	3	0	0	2
Guetterman, Calgary*	1	0	1.000	5.59	4	4	0	0	0	0	19.1	24	12	12	0	0	7	0	8	0
Hayward, Las Vegas*	9	11	.450	4.63	26	25	1	0	0	0	136.0	156	87	70	10	3	65	1	100	9
Heathcock, Tucson	10	8	.556	5.08	27	27	1	0	0	0	164.2	211	100	93	11	2	42	1	69	3
Hensley, Phoenix*	0	3	.000	2.47	44	0	0	23	0	6	51.0	42	16	14	3	0	27	6	50	2
Hernandez, Tucson	8	7	.533	4.71	22	21	4	1	0	1	128.0	139	79	67	13	2	27	1	84	3
Heuer, Albuquerque	3	5	.375	5.14	36	12	1	5	0	1	119.0	141	78	68	15	4	55	0	50	8
Hickey, Portland*	1	3	.250	6.51	33	5	0	11	0	2	65.0	76	54	47	7	0	29	0	44	2
Hicks, Portland	1	2	.333	4.69	29	0	0	8	0	2	48.0	51	28	25	5	1	20	2	25	2
Hillegas, Albuquerque	1	5	.167	6.17	9	9	1	0	0	0	46.2	48	35	32	1	2	31	2	43	4
Holton, Albuquerque	10	10	.500	3.78	27	27	5	0	1	0	182.2	200	90	74	18	0	20	0	105	6

Pitcher—Club	W.	L.	Pct.	ERA.	G.	GS.	CG.	GF.	ShO.	Sv.	IP.	H.	R.	ER.	HR.	HB.	BB.	Int. BB.	SO.	WP.
Hummel, Phoenix*	2	0	1.000	5.14	5	2	0	2	0	0	14.0	14	8	8	2	0	3	0	8	1
Jackson, Portland	3	1	.750	3.18	17	0	0	10	0	3	22.2	18	8	8	2	1	13	4	23	5
Jeffcoat, Phoenix*	7	2	.778	4.20	54	0	0	18	0	7	75.0	81	40	35	7	2	31	7	57	1
D. Johnson, Hawaii	8	7	.533	3.17	22	22	6	0	1	0	150.1	150	68	53	6	3	35	0	71	0
J.H. Johnson, Vancouver*	2	0	1.000	0.28	22	0	0	13	0	7	32.1	13	1	1	1	0	16	0	35	2
R. Johnson, Phoenix	0	0	.000	0.00	1	0	0	1	0	0	2.0	6	14	0	0	2	8	0	4	0
A. Jones, Vancouver	2	0	1.000	1.50	17	0	0	16	0	7	24.0	20	6	4	1	0	11	4	21	1
B. Jones, Hawaii	3	6	.333	3.56	35	0	0	32	0	7	48.0	41	20	19	3	2	20	4	28	0
J. Jones, Las Vegas	9	10	.474	4.40	28	27	4	0	2	0	157.2	168	84	77	10	1	72	0	114	9
Kaiser, Tacoma*	4	4	.500	4.31	34	18	2	10	1	2	110.2	123	70	53	5	5	52	2	63	6
Keough, Tucson	3	3	.500	3.91	8	8	0	0	0	0	50.2	56	31	22	3	1	21	0	42	5
Kibler, Tacoma	7	6	.538	4.22	39	1	0	26	0	6	64.0	66	37	30	5	1	26	6	28	4
Klipstein, Vancouver	0	0	.000	6.00	2	0	0	2	0	0	3.0	3	2	2	0	1	0	0	1	0
Knudson, 15 Tuc-2 Van	6	6	.500	4.13	17	16	4	0	1	0	106.2	124	54	49	4	0	26	1	63	3
Krawczyk, Hawaii	3	6	.333	4.94	32	0	0	21	0	5	47.1	51	29	26	1	1	21	3	40	4
Krueger, Tacoma*	3	3	.500	4.64	8	8	2	0	1	0	52.1	53	32	27	4	1	27	1	41	2
Kyles, Tacoma	5	2	.714	3.27	13	8	1	4	0	0	52.1	53	22	19	2	0	29	1	30	2
Lambert, Tacoma	1	10	.091	4.96	39	9	0	14	0	2	114.1	119	71	63	13	2	57	7	41	3
Laskey, Phoenix	5	5	.500	3.43	14	13	2	0	0	0	86.2	101	40	33	3	1	22	2	47	1
Leeper, Hawaii*	0	0	.000	0.00	1	0	0	0	0	0	0.2	0	0	0	0	0	1	0	1	0
Leiper, Tacoma*	2	1	.667	4.85	20	0	0	15	0	2	26.0	30	17	14	1	0	9	2	13	3
Leopold, Hawaii	0	1	.000	14.21	3	0	0	1	0	0	6.1	14	11	10	1	0	6	1	2	0
Lerch, Portland*	6	5	.545	3.01	12	12	1	0	1	0	74.2	67	35	25	2	0	27	1	39	5
Livingston, Albuquerque*	3	5	.375	4.93	11	11	0	0	0	0	49.1	39	34	27	5	2	57	0	40	4
Lugo, Edmonton	8	6	.571	4.66	16	16	2	0	0	0	100.1	110	58	52	10	2	41	0	53	7
Mack, Edmonton	7	13	.350	4.77	24	24	5	1	1	0	162.1	206	106	86	18	3	52	5	73	5
Maddux, Portland	5	2	.714	2.36	12	12	3	0	0	0	84.0	70	26	22	5	1	22	0	65	2
Mallicoat, Tucson*	0	2	.000	6.43	3	3	0	0	0	0	14.0	18	14	10	1	0	8	0	9	0
Martin, Calgary	1	4	.200	9.49	6	5	0	1	0	0	24.2	33	32	26	6	0	15	0	21	0
Mason, Phoenix	1	0	1.000	0.00	1	1	0	0	0	0	6.0	2	0	0	0	0	1	0	2	0
Mathis, Tucson	9	8	.529	4.25	26	23	2	1	1	0	144.0	177	83	68	8	1	38	0	64	5
May, Albuquerque	0	7	.000	6.92	27	8	0	12	0	1	65.0	97	59	50	6	2	39	2	57	4
McKnight, Phoenix	6	12	.333	6.61	26	17	1	3	0	0	110.1	147	91	81	16	1	73	6	62	10
McLaughlin, Tacoma	5	2	.714	3.55	44	2	0	23	0	5	83.2	97	38	33	2	4	22	2	49	2
Meagher, Albuquerque	1	3	.250	6.47	28	2	0	16	0	0	48.2	42	40	35	8	0	25	4	39	3
Meeks, Albuquerque	7	11	.389	5.28	33	26	2	4	0	1	167.0	203	112	98	22	4	45	2	80	0
Miner, Tucson	5	4	.556	6.02	34	4	0	5	0	1	80.2	111	66	54	3	0	32	1	43	6
Mirabella, Calgary*	3	4	.429	5.93	47	0	0	22	0	9	68.1	92	48	45	8	2	24	6	42	3
Money, Portland	0	1	.000	4.91	7	1	0	2	0	0	14.2	16	8	8	0	0	11	0	11	1
Montalvo, Tucson	5	3	.625	3.86	47	0	0	29	0	9	77.0	78	39	33	7	0	21	2	31	3
Monteleone, Calgary	8	12	.400	5.28	39	21	0	14	0	5	158.2	177	108	93	16	1	89	5	101	8
Mooneyham, Tacoma	0	1	.000	12.46	1	1	0	0	0	0	4.1	8	6	6	0	0	2	0	4	0
Moore, Phoenix	3	1	.750	4.74	24	1	0	6	0	2	49.1	50	29	26	2	0	26	2	29	3
Mulholland, Phoenix*	8	5	.615	4.46	17	17	3	0	0	0	111.0	112	60	55	6	1	56	4	77	4
Murray, Calgary	8	9	.471	5.14	35	18	2	7	1	1	136.2	183	84	78	18	6	39	2	72	6
Myers, Vancouver	0	1	.000	12.27	1	1	0	0	0	0	3.2	5	5	5	0	1	2	0	3	0
Nago, Vancouver	0	0	.000	16.20	1	0	0	0	0	0	1.2	3	3	3	1	0	1	0	0	0
Neal, Hawaii*	1	1	.500	3.50	18	0	0	8	0	0	36.0	39	15	14	1	2	13	0	16	2
Neidlinger, Hawaii	2	1	.667	3.90	4	4	1	0	0	0	27.2	33	14	12	3	1	9	0	14	0
Newell, Portland	2	2	.500	3.03	5	5	1	0	0	0	32.2	25	14	11	2	1	14	0	25	1
Newman, Calgary*	8	9	.471	5.42	34	22	3	6	1	0	156.0	194	102	94	14	5	56	4	61	5
Noble, Tucson*	3	3	.500	5.40	17	5	0	4	0	0	43.1	56	30	26	3	0	22	5	32	3
Nunez, Calgary	1	2	.333	7.07	6	1	1	4	0	0	14.0	19	13	11	2	0	4	0	17	1
O'Connor, Calgary*	1	6	.143	8.82	23	2	0	15	0	7	32.2	47	33	32	5	0	17	2	30	1
Patterson, Hawaii*	9	6	.600	3.40	25	21	6	2	1	1	156.0	146	68	59	9	1	44	0	137	3
Perlman, Phoenix	7	3	.700	4.31	45	7	1	16	0	2	117.0	149	64	56	3	3	32	7	45	3
Plunk, Tacoma	2	3	.400	4.68	6	6	0	0	0	0	32.2	25	18	17	4	0	33	0	31	3
Porter, Vancouver	6	7	.462	3.59	19	19	2	0	1	0	112.2	118	60	45	5	2	35	2	57	5
Powell, Albuquerque*	3	3	.500	4.10	7	7	0	0	0	0	41.2	45	23	19	3	0	15	0	27	1
Reece, Tacoma	0	0	.000	0.00	3	0	0	2	0	1	3.1	0	0	0	0	0	4	0	1	0
Reed, Calgary	2	1	.667	4.61	19	2	0	10	0	3	41.0	45	24	21	4	0	17	1	20	0
Rodriguez, Tacoma	7	8	.467	3.95	26	19	3	3	1	1	139.0	144	82	61	12	4	59	3	76	3
Romanick, Edmonton	2	3	.400	5.71	8	8	0	0	0	0	52.0	67	39	33	6	1	14	0	17	1
Romero, Edmonton	0	0	.000	9.00	1	0	0	1	0	0	1.0	2	1	1	1	0	0	0	0	0
Ross, Tucson	5	5	.500	4.17	48	0	0	37	0	8	73.1	99	37	34	4	2	20	5	26	1
Rucker, Portland*	3	3	.500	4.26	12	12	1	0	0	0	69.2	71	39	33	1	1	26	0	36	1
Ruhle, Edmonton	0	1	.000	4.15	8	2	0	4	0	0	26.0	30	14	12	2	0	4	0	17	0
Sauveur, Hawaii*	7	6	.538	3.03	14	14	6	0	1	0	92.0	73	40	31	3	6	45	1	68	4
Schweighoffer, Albuquerque	7	3	.700	4.50	49	6	0	12	0	2	112.0	134	68	56	7	1	58	4	26	5
Searage, Vancouver*	2	0	1.000	1.44	20	0	0	12	0	7	25.0	12	5	4	1	0	8	0	20	1
Shipanoff, Portland	1	0	1.000	3.48	8	0	0	6	0	1	10.1	6	7	4	0	1	10	0	10	2
Shirley, Albuquerque*	4	8	.333	3.28	53	0	0	35	0	15	74.0	74	33	27	4	0	40	11	71	1
Silva, Albuquerque	0	0	.000	8.00	7	0	0	2	0	0	9.0	12	9	8	2	0	7	0	3	2
Simmons, Las Vegas	4	2	.667	5.22	20	0	0	8	0	2	29.1	31	21	17	3	1	10	3	29	3
Siwy, Las Vegas	6	4	.600	3.56	30	19	0	4	0	2	129.0	121	59	51	14	5	47	6	77	2
D. Smith, Edmonton	6	7	.462	3.66	36	7	0	15	0	3	103.1	126	50	42	7	2	31	2	39	0
S. Smith, Phoenix	0	0	.000	5.56	7	0	0	2	0	0	11.1	10	9	7	1	0	11	1	11	0
Snyder, Las Vegas*	4	3	.571	5.57	45	1	0	15	0	3	72.2	87	56	45	9	5	35	2	62	5
Solano, Tucson	6	4	.600	1.89	27	6	1	20	0	4	71.1	64	24	15	4	0	27	3	54	4
Sorensen, Portland	5	5	.500	3.77	17	15	3	0	0	0	102.2	112	59	43	8	3	32	3	37	4
Stewart, Tacoma	0	0	.000	0.00	1	0	0	0	0	0	3.0	4	1	0	0	0	1	0	3	0
Stoddard, 2 Tac-37 LV	6	3	.667	4.03	39	0	0	31	0	11	51.1	52	26	23	5	1	19	5	51	4
Swift, Calgary	4	4	.500	3.95	10	8	3	2	1	1	57.0	57	33	25	5	2	22	2	29	2
Tapani, Tacoma	0	1	.000	15.43	1	1	0	0	0	0	2.1	5	6	4	1	0	1	0	1	1
Tatsuno, Hawaii*	2	2	.500	5.52	11	2	1	5	0	0	29.1	23	20	18	3	1	17	2	22	1
Taylor, Hawaii	3	1	.750	2.01	5	5	2	0	1	0	31.1	22	10	7	0	1	12	0	29	6
Thompson, Vancouver	1	1	.500	7.30	23	1	0	6	0	1	40.2	47	35	33	4	4	18	1	24	7
Toliver, Portland	1	3	.250	7.43	6	6	0	0	0	0	26.2	31	23	22	1	1	14	0	15	0
Tunnell, Hawaii	4	11	.267	6.01	27	26	2	0	0	0	142.1	180	106	95	9	5	81	1	95	14
Vila, Albuquerque	0	0	.000	9.22	6	0	0	1	0	0	13.2	11	14	14	2	2	14	0	12	1
Von Ohlen, Tacoma*	2	1	.667	1.77	13	0	0	5	0	1	20.1	15	5	4	0	1	9	4	11	0
Vosberg, Las Vegas*	7	8	.467	4.72	25	24	2	0	1	0	129.2	136	80	68	13	3	64	2	93	9

Pitcher—Club	W.	L.	Pct.	ERA.	G.	GS.	CG.	GF.	ShO.	Sv.	IP.	H.	R.	ER.	HR.	HB.	BB.	Int. BB.	SO.	WP.
Vuckovich, Vancouver	2	1	.667	1.26	6	4	0	2	0	0	28.2	17	6	4	2	1	7	1	19	2
Waits, Vancouver*	11	8	.579	4.42	28	19	3	4	0	1	130.1	145	77	64	13	1	45	3	72	5
Wallace, Albuquerque	0	0	.000	3.00	4	0	0	4	0	0	6.0	8	2	2	0	0	0	0	4	0
Ward, Phoenix*	8	11	.421	5.14	22	21	4	0	0	0	122.2	133	73	70	10	2	63	2	93	7
Whitmer, Calgary	1	1	.500	5.87	8	3	0	1	0	0	23.0	31	16	15	1	1	11	0	7	1
Wilkinson, Calgary*	8	8	.500	4.78	23	23	7	0	0	0	143.0	146	82	76	17	1	51	0	86	2
Williams, Phoenix	1	1	.500	2.13	27	0	0	23	0	13	38.0	28	10	9	0	2	17	2	41	2
Williamson, Las Vegas	10	3	.769	3.36	65	0	0	36	0	16	104.1	103	47	39	10	0	36	10	81	2
Wojna, Las Vegas	12	7	.632	3.59	25	25	7	0	1	0	175.1	181	81	70	6	3	50	2	102	7
Woods, Las Vegas	0	0	.000	36.00	1	0	0	1	0	0	1.0	4	4	4	0	0	0	0	0	1
Young, Tacoma*	4	0	1.000	2.00	4	4	1	0	0	0	27.0	16	7	6	1	0	6	0	28	0
Zaske, Hawaii	5	5	.500	4.12	40	8	2	13	0	1	113.2	104	54	52	8	2	78	3	87	17

BALKS—Newman, 10; Sauveur, Vosberg, 8 each; Holton, J. Jones, Kaiser, 5 each; Meeks, Mulholland, 4 each; Chadwick, Monteleone, Neal, Rodriguez, 3 each; Akerfelds, Baker, Bartley, Bittiger, Bockus, Bowden, Christ, Downs, Fansler, J. Gonzalez, Knudson, Leiper, Lerch, Livingston, Miner, Plunk, 2 each; August, Bastian, Beck, Birtsas, Booker, Clay, Clutterbuck, Cook, deLeon, Eichhorn, Finch, Forsch, Fowlkes, Gibson, Grapenthin, Heathcock, Hernandez, Heuer, Hicks, Jeffcoat, Kibler, Lambert, Maddux, Mallicoat, May, Meagher, Mirabella, Moore, Murray, O'Connor, Ross, Schweighoffer, Siwy, Snyder, Sorensen, Toliver, Vila, Ward, Whitmer, Williamson, 1 each.

COMBINATION SHUTOUTS—Holton-Meagher, Holton-Shirley, Albuquerque; Wilkinson-Murray 2, Monteleone-O'Connor-Bartley, Calgary; Bastian-Green, Edmonton; Tunnell-Farmer, Tunnell-Jones, Hawaii; Bitker-Booker, Siwy-Stoddard, Las Vegas; Laskey-Bockus, Laskey-Hensley, Mason-Hensley-Perlman-Bockus, Phoenix; Bittiger-Childress-Gorman, Bowden-Beck, Lerch-Bowden, Lerch-Childress, Lerch-Childress-Hicks, Sorensen-Hicks-Gorman, Portland; August-Ross, Solano-Acker-Ross, Tucson; Birkbeck-Bosio, Gibson-Searage-Bosio, Gibson-Jones, Porter-Crim-Jones, Vuckovich-Crews, Waits-Bosio, Vancouver.

NO-HIT GAMES—None.

Eastern League

CLASS AA

Leading Batter
JIM OLANDER
Reading

League President
CHARLES ESHBACH

Leading Pitcher
JIM NEIDLINGER
Nashua

CHAMPIONSHIP WINNERS IN PREVIOUS YEARS

Year	Club	Pct.
1923	Williamsport	.661
1924	Williamsport	.654
1925	York§	.583
	Williamsport§	.583
1926	Scranton	.627
1927	Harrisburg	.630
1928	Harrisburg	.603
1929	Binghamton	.597
1930	Wilkes-Barre	.572
1931	Harrisburg	.597
1932	Wilkes-Barre	.561
1933	Binghamton	.690
1934	Binghamton	.694
	Williamsport*	.603
1935	Scranton	.657
	Binghamton*	.580
1936	Scranton*	.609
	Elmira	.629
1937	Elmira†	.622
1938	Binghamton	.622
	Elmira (3rd)‡	.522
1939	Scranton†	.571
1940	Scranton	.568
	Binghamton (2nd)‡	.554
1941	Wilkes-Barre	.630
	Elmira (3rd)‡	.514
1942	Albany	.600
	Scranton (2nd)‡	.593
1943	Scranton	.630
	Elmira (2nd)‡	.568
1944	Hartford	.723
	Binghamton (4th)‡	.474
1945	Utica	.615
	Albany (3rd)‡	.564
1946	Scranton†	.691
1947	Utica†	.652
1948	Scranton†	.636
1949	Albany	.664
	Binghamton (4th)‡	.500
1950	Wilkes-Barre‡	.652
1951	Wilkes-Barre	.612
	Scranton (2nd)†	.562
1952	Albany	.603
	Binghamton (2nd)‡	.562
1953	Reading	.682
	Binghamton (2nd)‡	.636
1954	Wilkes-Barre	.576
	Albany (3rd)‡	.540
1955	Reading	.613
	Allentown (2nd)‡	.565
1956	Schenectady†	.609
1957	Binghamton	.607
	Reading (3rd)‡	.529
1958	Lancaster x	.568
	Binghamton (6th)‡	.493
1959	Springfield†	.607
1960	Williamsport y	.551
	Springfield (3rd)y	.496
1961	Springfield	.612
1962	Williamsport	.593
	Elmira (2nd)‡	.514
1963	Charleston	.593
1964	Elmira	.586
1965	Pittsfield	.607
1966	Elmira	.633
1967	Binghamton z	.586
	Elmira	.532
1968	Pittsfield	.604
	Reading (2nd)‡	.579
1969	York	.640
1970	Waterbury a	.560
	Reading a	.553
1971	Three Rivers	.569
	Elmira b	.561
1972	West Haven b	.600
	Three Rivers	.559
1973	Reading b	.551
	Pittsfield	.551
1974	Thetford Mines (2nd)c	.536
	Pittsfield (2nd)	.496
1975	Reading	.613
	Bristol*	.587
1976	Three Rivers	.601
	West Haven d	.576
1977	West Haven e	.623
	Three Rivers	.551
1978	Reading	.642
	Bristol*	.580
1979	West Haven f	.597
1980	Holyoke*	.561
	Waterbury	.540
1981	Glens Falls	.615
	Bristol*	.577
1982	West Haven*	.614
	Lynn	.590
1983	Lynn	.554
	New Britain‡	.518
1984	Waterbury	.543
	Vermont‡	.536
1985	New Britain	.540
	Vermont‡	.514

*Won split-season playoff. †Won championship and four-team playoff. ‡Won four-team playoff. §Tied for pennant, York winning playoff. xLeague was divided into Northern, Southern divisions and played a split season; Lancaster over-all season leader. yPlayoff finals canceled after one game because of rain with Williamsport and Springfield declared playoff co-champions. zLeague was divided into Eastern, Western divisions; Binghamton won playoff. aTied for pennant, Waterbury winning playoff. bLeague was divided into American, National divisions; won playoff. cLeague was divided into American and National divisions; won four-team playoff. dLeague was divided into Northern, Southern divisions, won playoff. eLeague was divided into New England and Canadian-American divisions; won playoff. fWon both halves of split season (no playoffs). (NOTE—Known as New York-Pennsylvania League prior to 1938.)

STANDING OF CLUBS AT CLOSE OF SEASON, AUGUST 30

Club	Read.	Vrt.	Pitt.	G.F.	Wat.	Alb.	N.B.	Nash.	W.	L.	T.	Pct.	G.B.
Reading (Phillies)	....	12	11	7	15	14	9	9	77	59	0	.566	....
Vermont (Reds)	8	....	10	15	8	10	12	14	77	62	1	.554	1½
Pittsfield (Cubs)	9	10	....	12	10	12	10	13	76	64	0	.543	3
Glens Falls (Tigers)	11	5	8	....	13	10	11	9	67	71	0	.486	11
Waterbury (Indians)	5	11	10	7	....	11	11	11	66	73	1	.475	12½
Albany (Yankees)	6	10	8	10	9	....	9	13	65	74	0	.468	13½
New Britain (Red Sox)	9	8	10	9	9	10	....	9	64	73	0	.467	13½
Nashua (Pirates)	11	6	7	11	9	7	11	....	62	78	0	.443	17

Vermont club represented Burlington, Vt.

Major league affiliations in parentheses.

Playoffs—Vermont defeated Pittsfield, three games to two; Reading defeated Glens Falls, three games to one; Vermont defeated Reading, three games to two, to win league championship.

Regular-Season Attendance—Albany, 316,034; Glens Falls, 70,020; Nashua, 78,103; New Britain, 81,617; Pittsfield, 47,709; Reading, 83,506; Vermont, 77,959; Waterbury, 37,267. Total—792,215. Playoffs, 12,441. All-Star Game, 1,967.

Managers—Albany, Jim Saul; Glens Falls, Bob Schaefer; Nashua, Dennis Rogers; New Britain, Tony Torchia; Pittsfield, Tom Spencer; Reading, George Culver; Vermont, Jay Ward; Waterbury, Orlando Gomez.

All-Star Team—1B-Phil Stephenson, Pittsfield; 2B-Jose Lind, Nashua; 3B-Len Harris, Vermont; SS-Paul Noce, Pittsfield; OF-Dan Boever, Vermont; Jim Olander, Reading; Rafael Palmeiro, Pittsfield; C-Rey Palacios, Glens Falls; DH—Bernardo Brito, Waterbury; RHP-Jim Neidlinger, Nashua; LHP-Steve Searcy, Glens Falls; Reliever-Jeff Gray, Vermont; Most Valuable Player-Rafael Palmeiro, Pittsfield; Pitcher of the Year-Jim Neidlinger, Nashua; Manager of the Year-Bob Schaefer, Glens Falls.

(Compiled by Howe News Bureau, Boston, Mass.)

CLUB BATTING

Club	Pct.	G.	AB.	R.	OR.	H.	TB.	2B.	3B.	HR.	RBI.	GW.	SH.	SF.	HP.	BB.	Int. BB.	SO.	SB.	CS.	LOB.
Waterbury	.266	140	4456	618	617	1185	1608	204	24	57	537	56	50	49	24	458	21	592	89	80	902
Reading	.262	136	4271	648	582	1117	1602	203	42	66	565	70	30	46	39	521	33	674	163	94	881
Pittsfield	.261	140	4488	619	535	1171	1725	227	33	87	560	68	48	63	24	533	38	785	222	79	980
Vermont	.257	140	4396	579	540	1129	1560	178	23	69	526	67	33	44	35	476	29	649	118	62	950
Albany	.251	139	4423	598	629	1111	1625	206	28	84	544	56	37	52	30	516	14	724	97	76	966
New Britain	.248	137	4314	510	526	1070	1523	191	17	76	459	53	38	41	41	498	29	726	112	56	961
Glens Falls	.246	138	4371	573	650	1074	1535	167	27	80	519	62	19	42	30	545	30	805	94	71	941
Nashua	.239	140	4464	471	537	1068	1428	187	25	41	405	53	60	28	37	428	44	720	107	80	945

INDIVIDUAL BATTING

(Leading Qualifiers for Batting Championship—378 or More Plate Appearances)

*Bats lefthanded. †Switch-hitter.

Player and Club	Pct.	G.	AB.	R.	H.	TB.	2B.	3B.	HR.	RBI.	GW.	SH.	SF.	HP.	BB.	Int. BB.	SO.	SB.	CS.
Olander, James, Reading	.325	129	464	77	151	216	33	4	8	68	8	3	5	2	56	3	84	10	15
Noce, Paul, Pittsfield	.307	114	410	87	126	201	26	14	7	56	8	10	7	3	39	1	82	32	5
Palmeiro, Rafael, Pittsfield*	.306	140	509	66	156	225	29	2	12	95	9	1	13	2	54	13	32	15	7
Boever, Daniel, Vermont	.300	124	437	66	131	200	26	2	13	80	10	0	8	3	43	3	46	1	3
Crabbe, Bruce, Pittsfield	.292	121	407	48	119	142	18	1	1	34	3	8	7	1	42	1	64	10	6
Lovell, Donald Waterbury*	.284	135	497	67	141	187	27	2	5	71	8	2	9	0	43	4	27	10	7
Marzano, John, New Britain	.283	118	445	55	126	188	28	2	10	62	11	0	6	12	24	2	66	2	0
Manfre, Michael, Vermont	.282	132	433	69	122	177	18	2	11	63	12	0	5	5	47	2	87	7	7
Lusader, Scott, Glens Falls*	.280	136	479	74	134	196	23	3	11	59	6	1	3	0	69	3	87	13	5
Guzman, Ruben, Glens Falls	.278	108	352	45	98	129	14	4	3	38	2	3	3	2	22	2	84	21	17

Departmental Leaders: G—Palmeiro, Stephenson, 140; AB—D. Jackson, J. Lind, 520; R—Noce, 87; H—Palmeiro, 156; TB—Palmeiro, 225; 2B—Olander, 33; 3B—Noce, 14; HR—Brito, 18; RBI—Palmeiro, 95; GWRBI—Harris, 13; SH—Meleski, 15; SF—Palmeiro, 13; HP—Marzano, 12; BB—Stephenson, 129; IBB—Palmeiro, 13; SO—Brito, 127; SB—Varsho, 45; CS—Barrett, 21.

(All Players—Listed Alphabetically)

Player and Club	Pct.	G.	AB.	R.	H.	TB.	2B.	3B.	HR.	RBI.	GW.	SH.	SF.	HP.	BB.	Int. BB.	SO.	SB.	CS.
Allen, Roderick, Waterbury	.291	31	103	18	30	42	10	1	0	9	1	0	0	1	9	1	10	2	1
Amaral, Richard, Pittsfield	.251	114	355	43	89	101	12	0	0	24	3	5	2	4	39	1	65	25	8
Ashman, Michael, Nashua*	.232	79	267	29	62	86	15	0	3	37	3	2	2	1	31	5	25	1	0
Baker, Kerry, Nashua†	.241	90	241	24	58	85	7	1	6	28	3	2	1	1	29	6	63	1	1
Barrett, Thomas, Albany†	.267	132	498	75	133	166	20	2	3	45	3	11	7	1	48	0	43	34	21
Barton, Shawn, Reading	.071	17	14	3	1	1	0	0	0	1	0	1	0	1	2	0	5	0	0
Beal, Anthony, New Britain	.241	71	170	26	41	70	5	3	6	22	5	2	1	2	17	1	44	8	4
Bean, William, Glens Falls*	.276	80	279	43	77	117	10	3	8	49	6	2	3	4	36	2	27	3	3
Beck, Dion, Reading*	.000	20	1	0	0	0	0	0	0	0	0	0	0	0	0	0	0	0	0
Bell, Jay, Waterbury	.277	138	494	86	137	194	28	4	7	74	9	1	11	0	87	0	65	11	9
Bellaman, Michael, Waterbury	.000	23	1	0	0	0	0	0	0	0	0	0	0	0	0	0	0	0	0
Berge, Jordan, Vermont*	.260	101	292	43	76	107	13	0	6	40	4	1	4	0	44	6	25	1	4
Berger, Michael, Nashua	.265	130	457	58	121	190	26	5	11	60	9	2	3	5	57	8	80	11	11
Bernstine, Nehames, Pittsfield†	.333	21	69	12	23	41	7	1	3	4	1	1	0	1	7	0	11	9	0
Berryhill, Damon, Pittsfield†	.206	112	345	33	71	104	13	1	6	35	3	1	7	1	37	3	54	2	5
Birriel, Jose, New Britain*	.223	114	332	35	74	99	14	1	3	37	7	3	3	2	47	7	43	1	0
Blevins, Bradley, Pittsfield	.333	5	3	0	1	1	0	0	0	1	0	0	0	0	0	0	2	0	0
Boever, Daniel, Vermont	.300	124	437	66	131	200	26	2	13	80	10	0	8	3	43	3	46	1	3
Bombard, Richard, Pittsfield	.000	28	5	0	0	0	0	0	0	0	0	0	0	0	0	0	3	0	0
Boudreaux, Eric, Reading	.100	18	10	1	1	1	0	0	0	0	0	0	0	0	3	0	7	0	0
Bowden, Mark, Reading*	.000	9	2	0	0	0	0	0	0	0	0	0	0	0	0	0	0	0	0
Boyles, John, Vermont	.182	26	22	2	4	5	1	0	0	0	0	3	0	0	1	0	11	0	0
Brake, Gregory, Nashua*	.000	6	1	0	0	0	0	0	0	0	0	0	0	0	0	0	1	0	0
Brink, Bradford, Reading	.000	5	1	0	0	0	0	0	0	0	0	0	0	0	1	0	0	0	0
Brito, Bernardo, Waterbury	.246	129	479	61	118	191	17	1	18	75	8	3	3	3	22	0	127	0	1
Brown, Anthony, Reading*	.289	99	305	49	88	136	19	4	7	58	7	0	3	5	31	3	54	10	6
Brown, Craig, Nashua	.220	99	341	27	75	96	15	0	2	24	6	5	1	1	39	2	65	15	14
Brunenkant, Barry, Waterbury	.278	57	194	24	54	78	9	0	5	26	3	0	1	2	16	0	23	1	0
Burks, Ellis, New Britain	.273	124	462	70	126	194	20	3	14	55	5	3	2	2	44	3	75	31	9
Capel, Michael, Pittsfield	.167	38	6	0	1	1	0	0	0	1	0	0	0	0	0	0	2	0	0
Carpenter, Douglas, Albany	.258	60	178	33	46	61	9	0	2	13	3	0	1	2	34	0	29	5	4
Carrillo, Matias, Nashua*	.154	15	52	3	8	9	1	0	0	0	0	0	0	0	4	1	13	2	4
Carroll, Carson, Albany	.234	99	290	38	68	83	10	1	1	23	4	8	1	2	39	0	53	6	3

Player and Club	Pct.	G.	AB.	R.	H.	TB.	2B.	3B.	HR.	RBI.	GW.	SH.	SF.	HP.	BB.	Int. BB.	SO.	SB.	CS.
Cathcart, Gary, Albany*	.237	42	97	16	23	35	3	0	3	14	1	3	2	2	22	0	18	1	3
Cecena, Jose, Reading	.000	10	2	0	0	0	0	0	0	0	0	0	0	0	0	0	0	0	0
Chambers, Travis, Reading*	.000	5	3	0	0	0	0	0	0	0	0	0	0	0	1	0	1	0	0
Charlton, Norman, Vermont†	.208	22	24	3	5	5	0	0	0	0	0	6	0	0	1	0	8	0	0
Chestnut, Troy, Pittsfield	.077	33	13	0	1	1	0	0	0	0	0	0	0	0	2	0	4	0	0
Ching, Mauricio, Albany*	.227	56	181	27	41	63	10	0	4	30	1	0	1	1	32	1	58	0	1
Corsi, James, New Britain	.333	29	3	0	1	2	1	0	0	0	0	0	0	0	0	0	2	0	0
Crabbe, Bruce, Pittsfield	.292	121	407	48	119	142	18	1	1	34	3	8	7	1	42	1	64	10	6
Crum, George, Waterbury	.254	45	126	16	32	38	6	0	0	10	0	5	0	0	16	0	17	10	5
Cruz, Luis, Pittsfield	.264	43	106	17	28	36	6	1	0	12	2	3	1	0	8	0	18	4	0
Cusack, David, Glens Falls	.213	84	268	36	57	100	13	0	10	41	10	0	1	2	28	1	63	3	1
Daniel, Clay, Vermont†	.043	25	23	0	1	1	0	0	0	0	0	1	0	0	1	0	6	0	0
Darkis, William, Glens Falls	.160	14	50	5	8	16	2	0	2	11	3	0	0	0	9	0	22	0	0
Davidson, Jackie, Pittsfield	.111	13	9	2	1	1	0	0	0	0	0	1	0	0	1	0	2	0	0
Davis, Kevin, Nashua	.248	135	509	57	126	158	22	2	2	46	8	11	3	4	17	2	84	11	10
DeAngelis, Steven, Reading*	.352	30	108	25	38	71	7	1	8	28	3	0	1	0	21	3	9	1	3
DeJesus, Ivan, Vermont	.278	10	36	4	10	14	1	0	1	5	1	0	0	0	3	0	3	1	0
Denbo, Gary, Vermont	.194	35	72	7	14	14	0	0	0	6	0	0	1	0	9	0	12	0	0
Dibble, Robert, Vermont*	.250	31	4	0	1	1	0	0	0	0	0	0	0	0	0	0	2	0	0
Dickerson, James, Pittsfield	.093	17	54	1	5	7	2	0	0	5	0	0	1	0	11	1	15	0	0
Duffy, John, Glens Falls†	.000	42	2	0	0	0	0	0	0	0	0	0	0	0	0	0	1	0	0
Dunlap, Joseph, Vermont	.260	61	208	25	54	69	7	1	2	23	4	2	2	3	13	0	21	4	1
Edge, Gregory, Reading†	.250	1	4	0	1	1	0	0	0	0	0	0	0	0	1	0	1	1	0
Ellsworth, Steven, New Britain	.000	9	2	0	0	0	0	0	0	0	0	1	0	0	0	0	2	0	0
Estrada, Eduardo, New Britain	.193	24	83	7	16	20	4	0	0	4	1	0	0	0	4	0	10	1	0
Ezold, Todd, Albany	.000	3	2	0	0	0	0	0	0	0	0	0	0	0	0	0	1	0	0
Felix, Paul, Glens Falls†	.231	101	295	36	68	116	15	0	11	49	5	0	4	5	34	2	69	1	1
Ficklin, Winston, Waterbury†	.317	92	319	57	101	138	10	6	5	48	5	6	1	2	34	5	39	26	17
Fiepke, Scott, Nashua*	.200	22	15	1	3	3	0	0	0	0	0	0	0	0	3	0	7	0	0
Finley, Brian, Vermont*	.183	43	115	13	21	25	4	0	0	9	1	2	2	7	22	0	15	6	4
Foley, Thomas, Reading*	.182	3	11	2	2	4	2	0	0	0	0	0	0	0	1	0	0	0	0
Ford, Kenneth, Nashua	.256	13	39	0	10	12	2	0	0	9	0	1	0	0	5	3	2	2	1
Fortenberry, Jimmy, Reading*	.333	4	9	2	3	5	2	0	0	2	1	0	1	0	0	0	3	0	0
Freeman, Martin, Glens Falls	.165	30	85	14	14	22	2	0	2	9	1	2	2	1	17	0	18	2	2
Freeman, Marvin, Reading	.226	28	31	0	7	7	0	0	0	3	0	1	0	0	0	0	11	0	0
Frohwirth, Todd, Reading	.000	29	1	0	0	0	0	0	0	0	0	0	0	0	0	0	0	0	0
Gaynor, Richard, Reading	.333	16	3	0	1	1	0	0	0	1	0	0	0	0	2	0	1	0	0
Geren, Robert, Albany	.148	11	27	3	4	5	1	0	0	0	0	0	0	0	6	0	12	0	0
Goff, Michael, New Britain	.222	61	162	17	36	48	9	0	1	13	1	2	3	7	33	0	29	2	0
Gonzalez, Fredi, Albany	.286	18	42	6	12	22	1	0	3	8	0	0	0	1	11	0	10	2	0
Gordon, Kevin, Nashua	.333	19	12	2	4	4	0	0	0	0	0	1	0	0	0	0	2	0	0
Graham, Brian 39 GF-22 Water	.203	61	172	16	35	38	3	0	0	9	1	3	0	1	11	2	32	1	3
Gray, Jeffrey, Vermont	.200	55	5	0	1	1	0	0	0	0	0	1	0	0	0	0	1	0	0
Gregg, Thomas, Nashua*	.268	126	421	55	113	137	13	4	1	29	5	6	1	3	66	3	48	11	8
Gutierrez, Dimas, Nashua	.256	121	394	32	101	135	18	5	2	38	4	2	8	2	21	2	41	9	5
Guzman, Ruben, Glens Falls	.278	108	352	45	98	129	14	4	3	38	2	3	3	2	22	2	84	21	17
Hale, Demarlo, New Britain	.261	110	376	52	98	140	16	1	8	41	4	2	2	4	34	1	47	12	5
Hall, Andrew, Pittsfield*	.125	24	16	2	2	3	1	0	0	1	0	2	1	0	3	0	10	0	0
Hamilton, Carlton, Pittsfield*	.095	28	21	0	2	3	1	0	0	0	0	3	0	0	0	0	9	0	0
Hammonds, Reginald, Nashua	.198	69	167	13	33	45	6	0	2	12	1	3	1	8	15	2	37	5	3
Harper, Milton, Waterbury	.223	50	130	16	29	35	4	1	0	14	1	0	0	0	16	1	23	2	0
Harris, Leonard, Vermont*	.253	119	450	68	114	165	17	2	10	52	13	1	6	6	29	4	38	36	10
Hawley, William, Vermont*	.000	22	8	0	0	0	0	0	0	0	0	1	0	0	0	0	2	0	0
Henderson, Ramon, Reading	.279	85	269	33	75	98	12	1	3	28	4	4	0	1	24	4	37	6	3
Henika, Ronald, Vermont*	.286	61	210	29	60	77	9	1	2	27	2	1	2	1	12	3	19	0	3
Hermann, Jeffrey, Glens Falls*	.235	76	247	28	58	84	12	4	2	31	4	0	3	1	29	1	54	3	3
Hernandez, Martin, Nashua	.000	3	1	0	0	0	0	0	0	0	0	0	0	0	1	0	1	0	0
Hicks, Robert, Reading	.000	10	1	0	0	0	0	0	0	0	0	0	0	0	0	0	0	0	0
Hill, Roger, Waterbury*	.239	81	222	38	53	74	7	4	2	15	4	2	2	0	29	2	33	11	3
Hillman, Thomas, Waterbury	.222	44	108	13	24	27	3	0	0	12	1	4	0	1	21	0	22	0	6
Hoffman, Glenn, New Britain	.250	4	8	1	2	2	0	0	0	1	0	0	0	0	0	0	1	0	0
Hollins, Paul, Glens Falls*	.249	71	221	29	55	92	8	1	9	37	5	0	2	0	32	3	47	0	1
Holman, Shawn, Nashua	.000	25	11	0	0	0	0	0	0	0	0	1	0	0	0	0	7	0	0
Hoppie, Bryan, Reading†	.225	57	151	18	34	42	4	2	0	12	4	3	2	1	12	0	19	0	2
Horn, Samuel, New Britain*	.246	100	345	41	85	122	13	0	8	46	6	0	5	1	49	4	80	1	0
Hughes, Keith, Albany*	.307	94	323	44	99	147	21	3	7	37	5	2	3	1	32	2	53	6	8
Jackson, Darrin, Pittsfield	.267	137	520	82	139	216	28	2	15	64	9	2	8	1	43	1	115	42	10
Jackson, Kenneth, Reading	.229	134	407	76	93	137	16	8	4	33	4	1	5	7	86	3	77	24	15
Jackson, Michael, Reading	.000	30	2	0	0	0	0	0	0	0	0	0	0	0	0	0	2	0	0
Jefferson, James, Vermont	.000	12	2	0	0	0	0	0	0	0	0	0	0	0	0	0	1	0	0
Jelks, Patrick, New Britain	.215	67	181	16	39	58	6	2	3	19	1	0	0	0	17	1	48	2	7
Johnson, Roger, Reading	.222	14	27	4	6	6	0	0	0	3	0	2	1	0	0	0	3	0	0
Jordan, Paul, Reading	.274	133	478	44	131	162	19	3	2	60	8	1	4	3	21	3	44	17	7
Kelly, Roberto, Albany	.291	86	299	42	87	112	11	4	2	43	3	1	5	0	29	0	63	10	5
Kipper, Robert, Nashua	1.000	4	1	1	1	1	0	0	0	0	0	0	0	0	0	0	0	0	0
Knox, Jeffrey, Reading	.250	5	4	0	1	1	0	0	0	0	0	0	0	0	0	0	0	0	0
Kopf, David, Pittsfield	.100	20	10	1	1	1	0	0	0	1	0	1	0	0	1	0	2	0	0
Krawczyk, Raymond, Nashua	.000	5	2	0	0	0	0	0	0	0	0	0	0	0	0	0	2	0	0
Labay, Stephen, Reading	.167	8	6	0	1	2	1	0	0	0	0	0	0	0	2	0	1	0	0
Laird, Anthony, Nashua*	.250	2	4	0	1	1	0	0	0	0	0	0	0	0	0	0	0	0	0
Lancaster, Lester, Pittsfield	.250	14	12	0	3	4	1	0	0	1	0	1	0	0	0	0	5	0	0
Layton, Thomas, Pittsfield*	.250	20	12	1	3	3	0	0	0	1	0	0	0	0	0	0	5	0	0
Leiva, Jose, Reading	.225	53	120	36	27	38	1	2	2	17	1	2	0	1	27	0	24	26	7
Lenderman, David, Pittsfield*	.286	30	7	1	2	3	1	0	0	0	0	1	0	0	0	0	3	0	0
Leopold, James, Nashua	.000	32	4	0	0	0	0	0	0	0	0	0	0	0	1	0	1	0	0
Lind, Jose, Nashua	.263	134	520	58	137	168	18	5	1	33	1	2	2	1	43	5	28	29	12
Lind, Orlando, Nashua	.111	15	9	2	1	1	0	0	0	0	0	1	0	0	1	0	6	0	0
Lindsey, William, Albany	.261	112	376	42	98	157	19	2	12	66	6	0	5	6	52	0	42	1	3
Link, Robert, Waterbury	.000	40	1	0	0	0	0	0	0	0	0	0	0	0	0	0	0	0	0
Long, Bruce, Reading	.000	23	4	0	0	0	0	0	0	0	0	0	0	0	0	0	3	0	0
Loscalzo, Robert, Glens Falls*	.200	10	25	5	5	5	0	0	0	0	0	1	0	0	11	0	8	2	1
Lovell, Donald, Waterbury*	.284	135	497	67	141	187	27	2	5	71	8	2	9	0	43	4	27	10	7

Player and Club	Pct.	G.	AB.	R.	H.	TB.	2B.	3B.	HR.	RBI.	GW.	SH.	SF.	HP.	BB.	Int. BB.	SO.	SB.	CS.
Loy, Darren, Reading	.125	5	16	2	2	2	0	0	0	1	0	0	0	1	0	0	1	0	0
Lundblade, Frederick, Reading	.268	20	56	8	15	26	5	0	2	12	2	1	0	0	8	0	7	0	0
Lusader, Scott, Glens Falls*	.280	136	479	74	134	196	23	3	11	59	6	1	3	0	69	3	87	13	5
Lyden, Mitchell, Albany	.302	46	159	19	48	88	14	1	8	29	5	0	2	2	4	1	39	0	1
Maddux, Gregory, Pittsfield	.200	8	10	1	2	2	0	0	0	0	0	0	0	0	0	0	2	0	0
Manering, Mark, Albany*	.180	19	61	7	11	11	0	0	0	3	0	0	2	0	6	0	9	0	1
Manfre, Michael, Vermont	.282	132	433	69	122	177	18	2	11	63	12	0	5	5	47	2	87	7	7
Martin, Michael, Pittsfield*	.194	56	144	10	28	37	6	0	1	13	5	0	0	3	26	3	26	0	0
Martinez, Carlos, Albany	.277	69	253	34	70	116	18	2	8	39	5	0	2	3	6	0	46	2	3
Marzano, John, New Britain	.283	118	445	55	126	188	28	2	10	62	11	0	6	12	24	2	66	2	0
Masters, Frank, 6 Pitts-10 GF	.246	24	57	7	14	17	1	1	0	6	0	0	1	1	4	1	15	0	1
McAllister, Steven, Nashua	.200	40	90	10	18	20	2	0	0	7	2	3	0	0	12	0	9	1	1
McInnis, William, New Britain*	.254	112	347	38	88	117	17	3	2	22	2	5	1	0	38	4	41	8	10
McKay, Alan, Pittsfield*	.250	49	8	1	2	2	0	0	0	2	0	1	0	0	1	0	2	0	0
McLarnan, John, Reading	.000	7	0	0	0	0	0	0	0	0	0	1	0	0	0	0	0	0	0
Mejia, Oscar, Waterbury	.266	86	252	38	67	83	13	0	1	40	4	6	1	1	32	0	12	0	4
Meleski, Mark, New Britain*	.204	115	294	18	60	63	3	0	0	17	1	15	2	1	38	0	55	0	2
Miller, Keith, Reading†	.263	98	354	57	93	136	14	4	7	57	7	1	6	3	56	5	48	16	7
Mills, Craig, Glens Falls	.204	44	142	18	29	40	5	0	2	9	3	0	1	2	15	1	32	1	2
Monda, Gregory, Vermont*	.263	126	433	39	114	149	18	4	3	43	5	2	2	2	26	2	50	0	1
Money, Kyle, Nashua	.250	27	4	1	1	1	0	0	0	0	0	1	0	0	1	0	0	0	0
Morgan, Christopher, Glens Falls*	.220	27	82	7	18	20	2	0	0	8	0	0	1	2	9	0	14	0	0
Morris, Harold, Albany	.215	25	79	7	17	22	5	0	0	4	0	1	0	1	4	0	10	0	1
Moses, Stephen, Reading*	.282	18	39	3	11	13	2	0	0	2	0	1	0	0	5	1	3	2	1
Moyer, Jamie, Pittsfield*	.143	6	7	0	1	2	1	0	0	0	0	0	0	0	0	0	0	0	0
Nattile, Samuel, New Britain*	.266	92	267	27	71	110	15	0	8	36	3	2	4	2	24	2	34	1	1
Neal, Scott, Nashua	.071	27	14	2	1	1	0	0	0	0	0	1	0	0	0	0	4	0	0
Neidlinger, James, Nashua†	.111	22	18	0	2	2	0	0	0	0	0	3	0	0	0	0	5	0	0
Nichols, Howard, Reading	.266	84	271	39	72	114	15	3	7	51	3	0	3	1	22	1	26	6	4
Noce, Paul, Pittsfield	.307	114	410	87	126	201	26	14	7	56	8	10	7	3	39	1	82	32	5
Olander, James, Reading	.325	129	464	77	151	216	33	4	8	68	8	3	5	2	56	3	84	10	15
Oliver, Joseph, Vermont	.277	84	282	32	78	116	18	1	6	41	4	0	5	0	21	1	47	2	2
Oliverio, Stephen, Vermont	.125	23	16	0	2	2	0	0	0	3	0	2	0	0	6	0	7	0	0
Opie, James, Nashua	.251	133	458	50	115	162	21	1	8	55	6	7	3	1	41	3	112	4	5
Palacios, Rey, Glens Falls	.252	135	461	66	116	192	20	4	16	66	7	0	2	8	81	6	81	6	8
Palmeiro, Rafael, Pittsfield*	.306	140	509	66	156	225	29	2	12	95	9	1	13	2	54	13	32	15	7
Pastornicky, Clifford, Waterbury	.302	73	248	34	75	88	13	0	0	19	2	2	4	1	20	1	18	2	4
Pena, Hipolito, Nashua*	.250	31	12	1	3	4	1	0	0	1	0	1	0	0	0	0	5	0	0
Phillips, James, Pittsfield	.000	15	4	0	0	0	0	0	0	0	0	0	0	0	0	0	2	0	0
Pryor, Buddy, Vermont	.232	76	224	30	52	88	7	1	9	36	3	1	3	0	38	4	70	8	1
Redus, Gary, Reading	.250	6	24	4	6	7	1	0	0	0	0	0	0	0	2	0	6	1	1
Reed, Darren, Albany	.230	51	196	22	45	70	11	1	4	27	2	1	5	1	15	0	24	1	0
Reed, Jody, New Britain	.229	60	218	33	50	64	12	1	0	11	1	3	2	0	52	1	9	10	5
Reynolds, Alfredo, Albany	.000	8	15	1	0	0	0	0	0	0	0	0	0	0	1	0	4	1	0
Rice, Cepedia, Nashua	.400	24	30	7	12	25	4	0	3	7	1	0	0	2	6	0	11	0	0
Riggs, James, Albany*	.207	127	410	57	85	136	14	2	11	75	10	1	9	0	63	4	47	1	0
Ritchie, Wallace, Reading*	.000	28	2	0	0	0	0	0	0	0	0	0	0	0	0	0	0	0	0
Roadcap, Steve, Pittsfield†	.333	2	3	1	1	1	0	0	0	0	0	0	0	0	0	0	1	0	0
Robinson, Brian, Vermont	.204	121	367	43	75	88	8	1	1	24	2	5	2	0	53	2	56	8	7
Rodriguez, Ruben, Nashua	.183	53	169	17	31	45	10	2	0	12	4	3	2	1	9	2	20	0	2
Roman, Miguel, Waterbury	.266	133	477	51	127	172	25	1	6	53	5	10	6	3	25	1	52	3	7
Roman, Ray, Reading	.257	99	300	38	77	102	13	3	2	25	1	3	2	3	26	2	51	3	4
Rooker, David, Nashua	.000	11	3	0	0	0	0	0	0	0	0	0	0	0	0	0	0	0	0
Roomes, Rolando, Pittsfield	.272	79	191	24	52	84	5	3	7	42	6	1	1	1	10	0	54	2	5
Ruffin, Bruce, Reading*	.000	16	6	0	0	0	0	0	0	0	0	1	0	0	2	0	2	0	0
Ruiz, Benny, Glens Falls	.255	110	337	36	86	99	13	0	0	25	4	1	5	0	38	1	65	4	6
Russell, Anthony, Albany†	.263	132	452	75	119	178	18	10	7	44	6	7	4	4	74	3	104	21	19
Rutledge, Jeffrey, Pittsfield	.208	14	48	1	10	12	2	0	0	8	3	0	1	0	8	0	7	1	0
Sambo, Ramon, Vermont†	.294	62	214	39	63	72	1	4	0	23	1	3	0	2	45	0	28	25	10
Sanchez, Juan, Reading	.181	31	72	6	13	19	3	0	1	6	2	0	1	1	6	0	11	0	0
Santiago, Norman, Albany	.273	12	33	2	9	9	0	0	0	3	0	1	0	0	0	0	4	1	0
Sauveur, Richard, Nashua*	.000	5	2	2	0	0	0	0	0	0	0	1	0	1	1	0	0	0	0
Scott, Richard, Albany	.200	10	30	4	6	12	3	0	1	4	0	0	0	1	3	0	6	0	0
Scott, Timothy, Vermont	.500	29	2	0	1	1	0	0	0	0	0	0	0	0	0	0	0	0	0
Shelton, Michael, Reading	.074	38	27	0	2	2	0	0	0	3	0	1	0	0	1	0	15	0	0
Shumake, Brooks, Vermont	.235	103	315	41	74	109	19	2	4	32	3	1	0	5	31	0	63	14	6
Smajstrla, Craig, Waterbury†	.282	42	163	20	46	53	3	2	0	10	1	2	1	3	15	2	14	5	4
Smith, Daniel, Vermont*	.000	41	1	0	0	0	0	0	0	0	0	0	0	0	0	0	0	0	0
Soares, Todd, Reading*	.209	86	254	42	53	79	6	1	6	33	4	0	5	3	36	4	48	12	5
Soper, Michael, Albany	.214	41	131	13	28	37	6	0	1	7	1	1	0	2	7	0	9	1	1
Sosa, Miguel, 50 Alb-32 GF	.231	82	290	29	67	91	9	0	5	28	2	1	6	0	11	0	36	2	3
Soto, Maximilliano, Glens Falls	.250	3	4	0	1	1	0	0	0	0	0	0	0	0	0	0	0	1	0
Spagnola, Glenn, Vermont*	.111	26	27	0	3	5	0	1	0	1	0	0	0	0	3	0	15	0	0
Springer, Gary, Glens Falls*	.253	82	289	41	73	91	13	1	1	25	1	3	4	0	50	2	31	7	4
Stephenson, Phillip, Pittsfield*	.272	140	423	72	115	184	29	2	12	68	6	3	8	2	129	8	67	30	18
Stevens, Michael, Nashua	.116	19	43	3	5	7	2	0	0	0	0	0	0	2	1	0	13	0	0
Syverson, Dain, Waterbury	.254	86	268	36	68	87	12	2	1	29	1	4	6	2	39	2	26	3	5
Taylor, Donald, Nashua	.000	33	3	1	0	0	0	0	0	0	0	1	0	1	0	0	2	0	0
Treadway, Jeffrey, Vermont*	.336	33	122	18	41	54	8	1	1	16	2	0	2	1	23	2	12	3	1
Tremblay, Gary, New Britain	.245	59	188	16	46	63	5	0	4	20	1	0	1	0	22	3	38	2	0
Vargas, Miguel, Reading	.000	11	2	0	0	0	0	0	0	0	0	0	0	0	0	0	1	0	0
Varoz, Eric, Nashua*	.173	44	150	15	26	30	4	0	0	8	0	0	1	3	24	0	26	5	3
Varsho, Gary, Pittsfield*	.266	107	399	75	106	173	18	5	13	44	6	1	3	3	38	4	52	45	11
Wade, Scott, New Britain	.266	123	414	54	110	162	23	1	9	51	4	0	7	8	54	0	102	31	12
Walewander, James, Glens Falls†	.243	124	440	59	107	132	10	6	1	31	3	4	2	2	43	4	54	25	11
Ward, Kevin, Reading	.274	119	398	79	109	169	27	6	7	59	11	1	7	6	66	1	66	28	14
Watts, Leonard, Reading*	.250	22	12	0	3	4	1	0	0	2	0	2	0	0	0	0	3	0	0
Williams, Dana, New Britain	.059	5	17	1	1	1	0	0	0	2	0	0	2	0	1	0	0	0	1
Williams, Edward, Waterbury	.238	62	214	24	51	82	10	0	7	30	3	0	4	4	28	1	41	3	6
Williams, Jeffrey, Glens Falls*	.268	15	41	5	11	11	0	0	0	3	0	0	0	0	7	1	9	1	2
Wilson, Doyle, Waterbury	.231	6	13	0	3	3	0	0	0	0	0	0	0	0	0	0	3	0	0
Winters, Matthew, Albany*	.169	37	118	15	20	37	5	0	4	16	0	0	2	0	22	3	15	2	0

Player and Club	Pct.	G.	AB.	R.	H.	TB.	2B.	3B.	HR.	RBI.	GW.	SH.	SF.	HP.	BB.	Int. BB.	SO.	SB.	CS.
Woods, Tony, Pittsfield	.228	106	356	38	81	134	21	1	10	48	4	1	3	2	33	1	66	5	4
Worden, William, Waterbury	.177	30	79	9	14	20	6	0	0	1	0	1	0	0	2	0	24	0	0
Young, Delwyn, Vermont†	.231	16	52	8	12	15	3	0	0	2	0	0	0	0	5	0	4	2	2

The following pitchers, listed alphabetically by club, with games in parentheses, had no plate appearances, primarily through use of designated hitters:

ALBANY—Blum, Brent (25); Byron, Timothy (17); Christiansen, Clay (11); Christopher, Michael (11); Davidson, Robert (24); Dersin, Eric (22); Easley, Logan (49); Frey, Steven (40); Fulton, William (14); George, Stephen (10); Guercio, Maurice (2); Guidry, Ronald (1); Harrison, Matthew (10); Hellman, Jeffrey (10); Impagliazzo, Joseph (13); Johnson, John (4); Patterson, Scott (15); Pries, Jeffrey (8); Schmidt, Eric (17); Tirado, Aristarco (4); Yaeger, Charles (25).

GLENS FALLS—Barlow, Ricky (28); Cooper, William (14); Fallon, Robert (14); Gibson, Paul (9); Gorman, Michael (31); Heinkel, Donald (10); Hill, Kenneth (1); Jones, Jeffrey (16); Labozzetta, Albert (13); Madden, Morris (38); Minnema, David (17); Pena, Ramon (54); Poissant, Rodney (5); Searcy, Stephen (27); Weissman, Craig (6); Whitehouse, Leonard (15).

NASHUA—Gideon, Brett (4); Marcheskie, Lee (23); Merklen, Edward (10).

NEW BRITAIN—Araujo, Anazario (27); Bast, Steven (9); Cappadona, Anthony (26); Curry, Stephen (24); Davis, Charles (19); Kiecker, Dana (24); Peterson, David (22); Skripko, Scott (15); Slifko, Paul (24); Stewart, Hector (45).

READING—Lachowicz, Allen (9); Sharts, Steve (1).

VERMONT—Brown, Keith (4); Lono, Joel (6); Simpson, Gregory (1).

WATERBURY—Beasley, Christopher (27); Encarnacion, Luis (46); Farrell, John (26); Murphy, Kent (25); Murphy, Michael (25); Sabo, Scott (11); Santarelli, Calvin (44); Smith, Daryl (21); Trudeau, Kevin (4); Whitmyer, Stephen (12).

GRAND SLAM HOME RUNS—Boever, Ching, Cusack, Felix, Harris, Horn, D. Jackson, Nichols, Opie, Palmeiro, Roomes, Winters, 1 each.

AWARDED FIRST BASE ON CATCHER'S INTERFERENCE—Monda 4 (Berryhill, Martin, Palacios, Tremblay); Ashman 3 (Felix 2, Marzano); Stephenson 3 (Marzano, Palacios, Syverson); A. Brown (Tremblay); Carpenter (Oliver); Kelly (Rodriguez); M. Roman (Berryhill).

CLUB FIELDING

Club	Pct.	G.	PO.	A.	E.	DP.	PB.
Pittsfield	.971	140	3586	1601	154	104	16
Nashua	.970	140	3570	1494	157	119	23
Vermont	.969	140	3472	1360	156	92	14
Waterbury	.969	140	3513	1476	161	101	21
Glens Falls	.966	138	3483	1476	172	123	15
Reading	.966	136	3408	1303	167	113	16
New Britain	.963	137	3446	1410	184	94	19
Albany	.963	139	3492	1363	185	119	10

INDIVIDUAL FIELDING

*Throws lefthanded.

FIRST BASEMEN

Player and Club	Pct.	G.	PO.	A.	E.	DP.
Ashman, Nashua	.987	45	361	26	5	39
Baker, Nashua	1.000	5	30	3	0	1
Berge, Vermont	1.000	1	8	1	0	1
Berger, Nashua	.982	81	623	72	13	52
Birriel, New Britain*	.987	89	684	66	10	49
Brown, Reading	1.000	2	12	1	0	0
Brunenkant, Waterbury	1.000	2	11	0	0	0
Carroll, Albany	1.000	5	9	1	0	1
Cathcart, Albany*	.982	14	97	12	2	10
Ching, Albany*	.971	55	402	31	13	47
Cusack, Glens Falls	.985	49	349	33	6	35
Felix, Glens Falls	.983	9	54	4	1	5
Geren, Albany	1.000	3	20	1	0	1
Hale, New Britain	.972	6	31	4	1	4
Harper, Waterbury	.986	8	64	5	1	7
Henika, Vermont	.993	47	360	37	3	23
Hermann, Glens Falls	.987	69	570	54	8	55
Horn, New Britain*	.977	45	356	28	9	26
Hughes, Albany*	1.000	14	99	11	0	7
Jelks, New Britain	.981	11	47	5	1	6
Jordan, Reading	.985	133	1052	87	17	100
Lindsey, Albany	1.000	1	1	0	0	0
Lovell, Waterbury*	.991	133	1110	93	11	82
Lundblade, Reading	1.000	3	21	2	0	1
Manering, Albany*	.994	19	146	14	1	13
McAllister, Nashua	.994	18	141	13	1	17
Monda, Vermont*	.993	94	769	59	6	59
Morgan, Glens Falls	.980	14	97	2	2	7
Morris, Albany	.991	25	203	19	2	19
Nattile, New Britain	1.000	2	8	0	0	0
Opie, Nashua	.929	3	25	1	2	0
Palacios, Glens Falls	.979	12	83	9	2	7
Riggs, Albany	.980	8	45	3	1	0
Santiago, Albany	1.000	7	51	1	0	6
Soares, Reading	.833	2	4	1	1	0
STEPHENSON, Pittsfield*	.996	134	1164	163	5	88
Tremblay, New Britain	1.000	2	15	0	0	0
Varsho, Pittsfield	1.000	4	26	3	0	3
Woods, Pittsfield	.981	9	46	5	1	2

SECOND BASEMEN

Player and Club	Pct.	G.	PO.	A.	E.	DP.
Amaral, Pittsfield	.972	108	228	266	14	57
Barrett, Albany	.954	63	132	156	14	34
Beal, New Britain	1.000	4	1	0	0	0
Carroll, Albany	.987	37	75	76	2	17
Crabbe, Pittsfield	.943	35	54	79	8	15
Crum, Waterbury	1.000	1	1	1	0	0
Cruz, Pittsfield	.962	8	7	18	1	2
Denbo, Vermont	.968	24	48	43	3	7
Dunlap, Vermont	.986	29	61	81	2	16
Estrada, New Britain	.967	23	42	74	4	8
Foley, Reading	1.000	1	0	5	0	1
Goff, New Britain	.968	53	95	145	8	26
Graham, 6 GF-22 Water	.938	28	44	76	8	11
Gutierrez, Nashua	.875	2	4	3	1	0
Hale, New Britain	.946	39	57	83	8	16
Henderson, Reading	.961	30	56	66	5	15
Hillman, Waterbury	.960	28	57	64	5	14
Hoppie, Reading	1.000	7	15	12	0	2
Jackson, Reading	1.000	2	3	4	0	1
LIND, Nashua	.982	130	314	378	13	84
Manfre, Vermont	.500	3	0	1	1	0
McAllister, Nashua	.944	7	9	8	1	1
Mejia, Waterbury	.988	69	142	197	4	34
Meleski, New Britain	.987	41	64	92	2	12
Miller, Reading	.970	97	220	262	15	62
Mills, Glens Falls	1.000	1	1	2	0	0
Reynolds, Albany	1.000	4	9	8	0	5
Ruiz, Glens Falls	1.000	2	5	7	0	3
Sambo, Vermont	.952	59	112	126	12	21
Sanchez, Reading	1.000	5	8	5	0	2
Smajstrla, Waterbury	.984	29	64	60	2	14
Sosa, 45 Alb-22 GF	.968	67	116	184	10	48
Springer, Glens Falls	.991	23	45	65	1	13
Treadway, Vermont	.971	33	68	102	5	21
Varoz, Nashua	1.000	5	9	5	0	0
Walewander, Glens Falls	.972	92	174	241	12	57

THIRD BASEMEN

Player and Club	Pct.	G.	PO.	A.	E.	DP.
Ashman, Nashua	.400	2	0	2	3	0
Barrett, Albany	1.000	2	1	1	0	0
Beal, New Britain	1.000	2	1	0	0	0
Brunenkant, Waterbury	.667	3	2	0	1	0
Carroll, Albany	.983	24	12	45	1	5
Crabbe, Pittsfield	.924	86	63	156	18	8
Cruz, Pittsfield	1.000	5	3	7	0	1
Cusack, Glens Falls	.889	5	4	12	2	1
DeJesus, Vermont	1.000	1	1	1	0	0
Denbo, Vermont	1.000	5	2	4	0	2
Dunlap, Vermont	.902	18	10	27	4	1
Estrada, New Britain	.500	2	1	0	1	0
Felix, Glens Falls	.800	1	1	3	1	0
Graham, Glens Falls	.907	15	14	25	4	1
GUTIERREZ, Nashua	.950	113	76	231	16	23
Hale, New Britain	.882	75	54	111	22	3
Harris, Vermont	.922	116	116	216	28	16
Henderson, Reading	.939	26	18	28	3	1
Hillman, Waterbury	.857	7	4	8	2	0
Hoppie, Reading	.918	35	31	59	8	4
Jackson, Reading	.750	1	0	3	1	0
Leiva, Reading	.810	9	11	6	4	0

THIRD BASEMEN—Continued

Player and Club	Pct.	G.	PO.	A.	E.	DP.
Lindsey, Albany	1.000	1	0	1	0	0
Manfre, Vermont	1.000	5	4	6	0	0
Martin, Pittsfield	1.000	2	0	2	0	0
Martinez, Albany	1.000	5	5	12	0	0
Marzano, New Britain	.800	2	1	3	1	0
Mejia, Waterbury	.842	5	4	12	3	2
Mills, Glens Falls	.935	37	24	63	6	6
Nattile, New Britain	.908	72	50	108	16	15
Nichols, Reading	.862	69	41	90	21	10
Opie, Nashua	.976	35	18	63	2	2
Palacios, Glens Falls	.939	24	17	45	4	4
Pastornicky, Waterbury	.924	72	59	135	16	8
Riggs, Albany	.927	118	90	213	24	22
Robinson, Vermont	1.000	2	1	3	0	0
Sanchez, Reading	.881	21	11	26	5	2
Santiago, Albany	.800	3	4	4	2	1
Sosa, Glens Falls	1.000	3	1	3	0	0
Springer, Glens Falls	.942	44	36	77	7	9
Walewander, Glens Falls	.956	23	27	38	3	6
Williams, Waterbury	.903	56	39	100	15	5
Woods, Pittsfield	.946	64	65	129	11	4

SHORTSTOPS

Player and Club	Pct.	G.	PO.	A.	E.	DP.
Bell, Waterbury	.927	123	197	371	45	57
Carroll, Albany	1.000	35	57	86	0	22
Crabbe, Pittsfield	1.000	2	2	1	0	0
Cruz, Pittsfield	.918	24	32	57	8	10
Davis, Nashua	.934	131	203	318	37	67
DeJesus, Vermont	1.000	9	8	22	0	5
Denbo, Vermont	1.000	1	2	3	0	0
Dunlap, Vermont	.945	16	23	29	3	3
Edge, Reading	1.000	1	3	1	0	0
Foley, Reading	1.000	2	2	6	0	1
Goff, New Britain	.911	14	16	25	4	2
Graham, Glens Falls	1.000	17	21	33	0	9
Hale, New Britain	.667	1	1	1	1	0
Harris, Vermont	1.000	2	3	4	0	1
Henderson, Reading	1.000	1	0	1	0	0
Hillman, Waterbury	.971	7	15	18	1	4
Hoffman, New Britain	1.000	3	0	1	0	0
Hoppie, Reading	1.000	2	1	8	0	1
JACKSON, Reading	.94894	131	186	353	29	68
Leiva, Reading	1.000	1	0	5	0	1
Martinez, Albany	.892	60	115	149	32	35
McAllister, Nashua	.923	10	11	25	3	4
Mejia, Waterbury	.944	7	13	21	2	4
Meleski, New Britain	.951	73	95	175	14	30
Mills, Glens Falls	.938	8	10	20	2	2
Noce, Pittsfield	.94890	108	180	340	28	52
Opie, Nashua	.714	3	6	4	4	0
Reed, New Britain	.956	60	114	190	14	33
Robinson, Vermont	.936	118	186	315	34	47
Ruiz, Glens Falls	.947	107	180	288	26	64
Rutledge, Pittsfield	.978	14	32	55	2	13
Sanchez, Reading	1.000	4	2	7	0	1
Scott, Albany	.885	10	20	26	6	8
Soper, Albany	.941	41	72	102	11	16
Sosa, Glens Falls	.850	8	8	9	3	1
Soto, Glens Falls	.933	2	6	8	1	1
Springer, Glens Falls	.842	6	4	12	3	3
Syverson, Waterbury	.947	4	9	9	1	3
Walewander, Glens Falls	.857	4	6	12	3	2

OUTFIELDERS

Player and Club	Pct.	G.	PO.	A.	E.	DP.
Allen, Waterbury	.980	29	46	3	1	0
Barrett, Albany	.968	12	29	1	1	0
Beal, New Britain	.951	42	93	4	5	0
Bean, Glens Falls*	.985	80	189	4	3	0
Berge, Vermont	1.000	43	64	3	0	1
Berger, Nashua	.981	33	51	1	1	0
Bernstine, Pittsfield	1.000	19	43	0	0	0
Boever, Vermont	.967	122	248	12	9	1
Brito, Waterbury	.986	48	67	1	1	0
A. Brown, Reading	.975	59	113	3	3	1
C. Brown, Nashua	.978	96	213	6	5	1
Burks, New Britain	.985	118	318	5	5	2
Carpenter, Albany	.973	40	70	1	2	0
Carrillo, Nashua*	1.000	11	28	0	0	0
Cathcart, Albany*	.949	27	53	3	3	0
Crum, Waterbury	.979	39	46	0	1	0
Cruz, Pittsfield	1.000	1	2	0	0	0
Cusack, Glens Falls	.950	28	36	2	2	0
Darkis, Glens Falls	1.000	4	8	0	0	0
DeAngelis, Reading*	.955	26	61	3	3	0
Dickerson, Pittsfield	.917	7	11	0	1	0
Duffy, Glens Falls*	1.000	1	1	0	0	0
Felix, Glens Falls	1.000	2	3	0	0	0
Ficklin, Waterbury	.992	91	232	10	2	1
Finley, Vermont*	1.000	40	115	4	0	3
Ford, Nashua	1.000	8	14	0	0	0
Fortenberry, Reading	1.000	1	3	0	0	0
Freeman, Glens Falls	.850	30	47	4	9	0
Graham, Glens Falls	1.000	2	4	0	0	0
Gregg, Nashua*	.982	115	216	7	4	0
Guzman, Glens Falls	.948	98	160	5	9	0
Hammonds, Nashua	.963	38	50	2	2	1
Harper, Waterbury	1.000	19	23	0	0	0
Hill, Waterbury	.986	73	131	8	2	2
Hollins, Glens Falls	.929	6	12	1	1	0
Hoppie, Reading	1.000	1	1	0	0	0
Hughes, Albany*	.957	80	148	6	7	3
Jackson, Pittsfield	.980	137	320	16	7	2
Jelks, New Britain	.957	45	86	3	4	0
Kelly, Albany	.968	86	206	8	7	2
Leiva, Reading	.986	32	71	2	1	0
Loscalzo, Glens Falls*	.889	9	15	1	2	0
Lusader, Glens Falls*	.963	136	275	13	11	1
Manfre, Vermont	.963	127	229	8	9	2
McInnis, New Britain*	.958	99	200	7	9	0
Monda, Vermont*	1.000	13	12	0	0	0
Morgan, Glens Falls	1.000	15	25	4	0	1
Moses, Reading*	1.000	9	14	1	0	1
Nattile, New Britain	1.000	1	1	0	0	0
Nichols, Reading	1.000	10	12	0	0	0
Olander, Reading	.967	125	320	3	11	1
Opie, Nashua	.971	96	158	12	5	3
PALMEIRO, Pittsfield*	.988	130	248	9	3	2
Redus, Reading	.923	6	11	1	1	0
Reed, Albany	.941	36	78	2	5	1
Roman, Waterbury	.977	133	240	11	6	1
Roomes, Pittsfield	.931	55	91	4	7	2
Russell, Albany	.976	117	350	11	9	5
Shumake, Vermont	.971	96	198	6	6	2
Smajstrla, Waterbury	1.000	14	16	0	0	0
Soares, Reading	.975	70	111	5	3	2
Springer, Glens Falls	.952	14	20	0	1	0
Stephenson, Pittsfield*	1.000	2	1	0	0	0
Stevens, Nashua	1.000	10	17	0	0	0
Varoz, Nashua	.976	40	80	2	2	0
Varsho, Pittsfield	.971	95	187	11	6	1
Wade, New Britain	.971	118	255	15	8	1
Ward, Reading	.969	93	155	3	5	0
D. Williams, New Britain	1.000	5	8	0	0	0
J. Williams, Glens Falls*	.880	14	22	0	3	0
Winters, Albany	.984	37	61	1	1	0
Worden, Waterbury	1.000	4	4	0	0	0
Young, Vermont	1.000	15	31	1	0	0

CATCHERS

Player and Club	Pct.	G.	PO.	A.	E.	DP.	PB.
Ashman, Nashua	.986	26	125	12	2	1	3
Baker, Nashua	.982	72	381	66	8	6	13
Berryhill, Pittsfield	.977	102	449	61	12	3	11
Brunenkant, Waterbury	.980	48	267	25	6	2	9
Ezold, Albany	1.000	2	4	0	0	0	0
Felix, Glens Falls	.982	37	153	14	3	0	6
Geren, Albany	1.000	8	31	6	0	2	0
Gonzalez, Albany	.985	15	58	6	1	0	3
Henderson, Reading	.991	22	111	5	1	1	2
Hoppie, Reading	1.000	1	3	0	0	0	0
Johnson, Reading	.964	14	45	9	2	0	1
Lindsey, Albany	.980	92	455	71	11	2	6
Loy, Reading	.955	5	17	4	1	0	0
Lundblade, Reading	.989	15	90	4	1	0	0
Lyden, Albany	.981	31	131	25	3	0	1
Martin, Pittsfield	.984	48	219	30	4	0	5
Marzano, New Britain	.978	100	508	73	13	1	12
Masters, 6 Pitts-11 GF	.971	17	62	2	2	0	3
McAllister, Nashua	1.000	1	3	1	0	0	1
Nattile, New Britain	.917	8	10	1	1	0	0
Nichols, Reading	1.000	1	5	0	0	0	0
Oliver, Vermont	.969	74	383	62	14	4	10
Palacios, Glens Falls	.972	105	603	86	20	8	6
Pryor, Vermont	.978	69	348	53	9	2	4
Roadcap, Pittsfield	1.000	2	11	0	0	0	0
Rodriguez, Nashua	.984	52	318	47	6	4	6
Roman, Reading	.982	99	494	67	10	3	13
SYVERSON, Waterbury	.987	72	383	79	6	5	7
Tremblay, New Britain	.947	36	155	22	10	2	7
Wilson, Waterbury	1.000	6	35	7	0	2	1
Worden, Waterbury	.974	24	98	13	3	1	4

PITCHERS

Player and Club	Pct.	G.	PO.	A.	E.	DP.
Araujo, New Britain	1.000	27	10	20	0	1
Ashman, Nashua	1.000	3	1	0	0	0
Barlow, Glens Falls	1.000	28	11	12	0	1
Barton, Reading*	.958	17	7	16	1	0
Bast, New Britain*	1.000	9	1	6	0	0
Beasley, Waterbury	.964	27	20	34	2	1
Beck, Reading*	1.000	20	0	5	0	0
Bellaman, Waterbury	.824	23	13	15	6	5
Birriel, New Britain*	1.000	2	0	2	0	0
Blevins, Pittsfield	1.000	5	1	1	0	0
Blum, Albany*	.941	25	5	11	1	0
Bombard, Pittsfield	1.000	28	4	13	0	0
Boudreaux, Reading	.950	18	5	14	1	0
Bowden, Reading*	1.000	9	0	5	0	0
Boyles, Vermont	.958	26	7	16	1	2
Brake, Nashua*	1.000	6	1	4	0	2
Brink, Reading	.857	5	2	4	1	1
Brown, Vermont	1.000	4	1	0	0	1
Byron, Albany	.926	17	8	17	2	0
Capel, Pittsfield	.933	38	2	12	1	0
Cappadona, New Britain*	1.000	26	3	10	0	1
Cecena, Reading	1.000	10	1	1	0	0
Chambers, Reading	1.000	5	0	4	0	0
Charlton, Vermont*	.906	22	5	24	3	2
Chestnut, Pittsfield	.897	32	16	19	4	2
Christiansen, Albany	.950	11	10	9	1	1
Christopher, Albany	.909	11	3	7	1	0
Cooper, Glens Falls	1.000	14	11	8	0	0
Corsi, New Britain	1.000	29	2	3	0	0
Curry, New Britain	.891	24	20	29	6	5
Daniel, Vermont*	1.000	25	3	17	0	1
J. Davidson, Pittsfield	.900	12	8	10	2	3
R. Davidson, Albany	.857	24	2	4	1	0
Davis, New Britain	1.000	19	10	13	0	0
Dersin, Albany	.909	22	8	12	2	1
Dibble, Vermont	1.000	31	4	2	0	1
Duffy, Glens Falls*	.950	40	4	15	1	0
Easley, Albany	1.000	49	6	5	0	0
Ellsworth, New Britain	.944	9	2	15	1	1
Encarnacion, Waterbury	1.000	46	4	14	0	1
Fallon, Glens Falls*	.938	14	3	12	1	0
FARRELL, Waterbury	1.000	26	16	25	0	0
Fiepke, Nashua*	1.000	22	5	23	0	1
Freeman, Reading	1.000	27	12	14	0	2
Frey, Albany*	.923	40	4	8	1	0
Frohwirth, Reading	1.000	29	5	8	0	1
Fulton, Albany	.917	14	1	10	1	0
Gaynor, Reading	.800	16	2	2	1	0
George, Albany*	.800	10	4	4	2	1
Gibson, Glens Falls*	1.000	9	1	4	0	0
Gideon, Nashua	.750	4	0	3	1	0
Gordon, Nashua	.800	17	4	16	5	2
Gorman, Glens Falls	1.000	31	10	13	0	0
Graham, Waterbury	.667	1	1	1	1	0
Gray, Vermont	1.000	55	6	14	0	0
Guercio, Albany	.500	2	1	0	1	0
Hall, Pittsfield*	.893	24	4	21	3	0
Hamilton, Pittsfield*	.957	27	10	34	2	0
Harrison, Albany*	1.000	10	7	8	0	0
Hawley, Vermont	1.000	22	7	2	0	1
Heinkel, Glens Falls	1.000	10	4	22	0	1
Hellman, Albany	.000	10	0	0	1	0
Hernandez, Nashua	.500	3	1	0	1	0
Hicks, Reading	.857	9	1	5	1	0
Hill, Glens Falls	1.000	1	1	0	0	0
Holman, Nashua	.917	25	9	13	2	1
Impagliazzo, Albany	1.000	13	1	5	0	1
Jackson, Reading	.909	30	4	6	1	1
Jefferson, Vermont	.800	12	1	3	1	0
Johnson, Albany	1.000	4	0	4	0	0
Jones, Glens Falls	1.000	16	1	3	0	0
Kiecker, New Britain	.946	24	14	21	2	1
Kipper, Nashua*	1.000	4	0	1	0	0
Knox, Reading	1.000	5	1	2	0	0
Kopf, Pittsfield	.893	20	12	13	3	2
Labay, Reading*	1.000	7	4	8	0	0
Labozzetta, Glens Falls*	.882	13	4	11	2	2
Lachowicz, Reading	1.000	9	0	1	0	0
Lancaster, Pittsfield	.944	14	6	11	1	1
Layton, Pittsfield	1.000	20	8	20	0	0
Lenderman, Pittsfield	1.000	30	3	2	0	0
Leopold, Nashua	1.000	32	2	9	0	2
Lind, Nashua	1.000	15	8	8	0	2
Link, Waterbury	.933	40	4	10	1	1
Long, Reading	.714	23	2	3	2	0
Lono, Vermont*	1.000	6	2	3	0	0
Madden, Glens Falls*	.955	35	4	17	1	1
Maddux, Pittsfield	1.000	8	8	13	0	0
Marcheskie, Nashua	.889	23	5	3	1	1
McKay, Pittsfield*	1.000	49	3	7	0	0
McLarnan, Reading	.833	7	1	4	1	0
Meleski, New Britain	1.000	1	1	0	0	0
Merklen, Nashua*	1.000	10	0	3	0	0
Minnema, Glens Falls	1.000	17	4	9	0	0
Money, Nashua	.929	27	4	9	1	0
Moyer, Pittsfield*	1.000	6	3	8	0	1
K. Murphy, Waterbury*	.962	25	5	20	1	1
M. Murphy, Waterbury	.949	25	13	24	2	2
Neal, Nashua*	.941	26	3	13	1	0
Neidlinger, Nashua	.979	22	21	25	1	1
Oliverio, Vermont	.900	23	3	15	2	0
Patterson, Albany	1.000	15	2	5	0	0
H. Pena, Nashua*	.920	31	7	16	2	2
R. Pena, Glens Falls	1.000	54	5	20	0	1
Peterson, New Britain	.900	22	3	6	1	0
Phillips, Pittsfield	.857	15	1	5	1	0
Poissant, Glens Falls	1.000	5	0	2	0	0
Pries, Albany	.778	8	6	1	2	0
Rice, Nashua	.905	12	6	13	2	0
Ritchie, Reading*	1.000	28	4	1	0	0
Rooker, Nashua	1.000	11	3	8	0	1
Ruffin, Reading*	1.000	16	3	18	0	1
Sabo, Waterbury*	.667	11	1	1	1	0
Santarelli, Waterbury	.909	44	4	6	1	0
Sauveur, Nashua*	.941	5	4	12	1	1
Schmidt, Albany	.929	17	6	7	1	1
Scott, Vermont	1.000	29	2	5	0	0
Searcy, Glens Falls*	.978	27	11	33	1	6
Sharts, Reading*	1.000	1	0	3	0	0
Shelton, Reading	.895	37	14	20	4	0
Skripko, New Britain	1.000	10	5	14	0	4
Slifko, New Britain	.889	24	5	19	3	1
Dan. Smith, Vermont*	.929	41	7	6	1	0
Dar. Smith, Waterbury	.960	21	12	12	1	2
Spagnola, Vermont	1.000	25	14	24	0	2
Stewart, New Britain*	1.000	45	3	11	0	1
Taylor, Nashua	.750	33	2	7	3	0
Trudeau, Waterbury	1.000	4	0	1	0	0
Vargas, Reading	1.000	11	2	1	0	0
Watts, Reading*	.824	22	4	10	3	0
Weissman, Glens Falls	1.000	6	2	0	0	0
Whitehouse, Glens Falls*	1.000	15	1	7	0	1
Whitmyer, Waterbury	1.000	12	3	5	0	0
Yeager, Albany*	.955	25	4	17	1	0

The following players do not have any recorded accepted chances at the positions indicated; therefore, are not listed in the fielding averages for those particular positions: Berryhill, of; Birriel, of, c; Brito, ss; Felix, p; Goff, 3b; Graham, 1b; Gregg, 1b; Guidry, p; Gutierrez, ss; Henika, of; Hillman, of; Hollins, c; Jelks, 3b, p; Jordan, of; Krawczyk, p; Lovell, of; Simpson, p; Skripko, 2b; Stephenson, p; Syverson, 3b, of; Tirado, p; Varsho, 2b.

CLUB PITCHING

Club	ERA.	G.	CG.	ShO.	Sv.	IP.	H.	R.	ER.	HR.	HB.	BB.	Int. BB.	SO.	WP.	Bk.
Pittsfield	3.22	140	26	18	35	1195.1	1076	535	427	56	41	501	31	660	48	12
Nashua	3.38	140	22	12	25	1190.0	1053	537	447	55	35	568	26	796	79	11
New Britain	3.42	137	48	11	24	1148.2	1118	526	437	43	23	438	32	636	65	15
Vermont	3.45	140	30	6	32	1157.1	1082	540	444	73	26	506	27	704	63	9
Reading	3.61	136	20	11	43	1136.0	1076	582	456	79	18	521	44	729	48	11
Albany	3.94	139	26	11	27	1164.0	1197	629	509	81	39	469	21	641	73	4
Waterbury	3.95	140	27	13	27	1171.0	1120	617	514	89	43	492	21	742	55	10
Glens Falls	4.16	138	22	10	34	1161.0	1203	650	537	84	35	480	36	767	79	14

PITCHERS' RECORDS

(Leading Qualifiers for Earned-Run Average Leadership — 112 or More Innings)

*Throws lefthanded.

Pitcher—Club	W.	L.	Pct.	ERA.	G.	GS.	CG.	GF.	ShO.	Sv.	IP.	H.	R.	ER.	HR.	HB.	BB.	Int. BB.	SO.	WP.
Neidlinger, Nashua	12	7	.632	2.42	22	22	8	0	2	0	163.2	135	57	44	6	3	44	0	98	5
Curry, New Britain	11	9	.550	2.79	24	24	12	0	2	0	177.1	163	66	55	5	6	76	4	94	7

Pitcher—Club	W.	L.	Pct.	ERA.	G.	GS.	CG.	GF.	ShO.	Sv.	IP.	H.	R.	ER.	HR.	HB.	BB.	Int. BB.	SO.	WP.
Charlton, Vermont*	10	6	.625	2.83	22	22	6	0	1	0	136.2	109	55	43	4	3	74	2	96	8
Spagnola, Vermont	11	10	.524	3.04	25	25	6	0	1	0	169.0	157	67	57	11	1	69	2	76	2
Farrell, Waterbury	9	10	.474	3.06	26	26	9	0	3	0	173.1	158	82	59	15	10	54	2	104	3
C. Davis, New Britain	10	5	.667	3.10	19	19	7	0	2	0	133.2	119	53	46	5	3	48	1	66	4
Chestnut, Pittsfield	9	7	.563	3.15	32	16	3	7	0	2	137.1	137	61	48	7	4	41	1	49	5
Boyles, Vermont	10	9	.526	3.24	26	26	2	0	0	0	161.1	139	71	58	6	3	81	1	115	12
Searcy, Glens Falls*	11	6	.647	3.30	27	27	3	0	0	0	172.0	166	79	63	6	3	74	1	139	12
Shelton, Reading	10	7	.588	3.30	37	18	5	14	0	4	147.1	138	65	54	8	2	44	9	70	3
Hall, Pittsfield*	8	11	.421	3.58	24	24	6	0	3	0	158.1	130	77	63	7	6	84	3	115	10
M. Murphy, Waterbury	8	7	.533	3.58	25	14	5	8	3	1	118.0	107	54	47	3	5	42	2	62	2

Departmental Leaders: G—Gray, 55; W—Gray, 14; L—Fiepke, Holman, Slifko, 13; Pct.—Gray, .875; GS—Freeman, Searcy, 27; CG—Curry, 12; GF—Easley, 45; ShO—Araujo, Farrell, Hall, M. Murphy, 3; Sv.—Easley, Stewart, 18; IP—Curry, 177.1; H—Kiecker, 171; R—Hamilton, 92; ER—K. Murphy, 80; HR—Gorman, 19; HB—Farrell, Hamilton, 10; BB—Freeman, 111; IBB—Long, R. Pena, 10; SO—Searcy, 139; WP—Fiepke, 15.

(All Pitchers—Listed Alphabetically)

Pitcher—Club	W.	L.	Pct.	ERA.	G.	GS.	CG.	GF.	ShO.	Sv.	IP.	H.	R.	ER.	HR.	HB.	BB.	Int. BB.	SO.	WP.
Araujo, New Britain	7	11	.389	3.76	27	18	10	5	3	1	141.1	126	67	59	5	2	53	3	95	9
Ashman, Nashua	0	0	.000	3.00	3	0	0	3	0	0	3.0	5	1	1	0	0	2	0	1	0
Barlow, Glens Falls	5	8	.385	2.63	28	8	2	16	1	4	89.0	82	37	26	2	1	47	2	73	11
Barton, Reading*	8	7	.533	3.79	17	17	3	0	1	0	92.2	92	53	39	10	2	41	2	62	2
Bast, New Britain*	1	3	.250	3.61	9	6	2	2	0	0	42.1	33	21	17	4	2	20	0	27	3
Beasley, Waterbury	8	9	.471	3.82	27	25	5	0	2	0	155.2	152	83	66	10	7	67	2	105	10
Beck, Reading*	1	1	.500	3.67	20	0	0	13	0	7	27.0	23	14	11	3	2	12	1	19	0
Bellaman, Waterbury	6	12	.333	5.34	23	23	0	0	0	0	123.0	146	85	73	6	6	64	2	76	7
Birriel, New Britain*	0	0	.000	4.50	2	0	0	2	0	0	2.0	4	3	1	0	0	1	0	1	0
Blevins, Pittsfield	1	0	1.000	6.55	5	1	0	3	0	0	11.0	9	8	8	3	0	5	0	3	0
Blum, Albany*	9	4	.692	4.36	25	15	0	2	0	0	88.2	102	47	43	9	4	32	1	46	3
Bombard, Pittsfield	3	4	.429	2.94	28	4	0	12	0	1	67.1	83	36	22	2	1	15	7	32	2
Boudreaux, Reading	8	6	.571	4.03	18	17	1	0	0	0	102.2	107	62	46	9	1	42	4	58	4
Bowden, Reading*	0	0	.000	2.45	9	0	0	4	0	2	14.2	16	7	4	0	0	7	0	8	1
Boyles, Vermont	10	9	.526	3.24	26	26	2	0	0	0	161.1	139	71	58	6	3	81	2	115	12
Brake, Nashua*	2	1	.667	7.01	6	4	1	0	0	0	25.2	38	21	20	3	1	10	1	10	0
Brink, Reading	0	4	.000	3.80	5	4	0	0	0	0	23.2	22	12	10	2	1	20	2	8	0
Brown, Vermont	1	1	.500	5.14	4	2	1	0	0	0	14.0	12	10	8	2	0	8	0	11	1
Byron, Albany	1	4	.200	3.48	17	12	0	1	0	0	88.0	99	57	34	7	2	46	3	37	8
Capel, Pittsfield	4	4	.500	1.87	38	0	0	27	0	13	62.2	51	20	13	2	0	22	4	50	1
Cappadona, New Britain*	2	1	.667	2.30	26	1	0	16	0	0	54.2	51	17	14	3	0	16	3	39	1
Cecena, Reading	1	2	.333	7.17	10	2	0	2	0	0	21.1	26	19	17	5	1	16	1	18	2
Chambers, Reading	2	1	.667	1.06	5	2	0	3	0	1	17.0	10	2	2	1	0	5	1	17	1
Charlton, Vermont*	10	6	.625	2.83	22	22	6	0	1	0	136.2	109	55	43	4	3	74	2	96	8
Chestnut, Pittsfield	9	7	.563	3.15	32	16	3	7	0	2	137.1	137	61	48	7	4	41	1	49	5
Christiansen, Albany	4	6	.400	4.52	11	11	5	0	0	0	77.2	88	47	39	3	4	33	0	35	6
Christopher, Albany	3	5	.375	5.04	11	11	2	0	0	0	60.2	75	48	34	6	3	12	1	34	3
Cooper, Glens Falls	5	6	.455	3.50	14	14	2	0	1	0	79.2	73	39	31	10	1	18	1	49	3
Corsi, New Britain	2	3	.400	2.28	29	0	0	19	0	3	51.1	52	13	13	2	1	20	5	38	2
Curry, New Britain	11	9	.550	2.79	24	24	12	0	2	0	177.1	163	66	55	5	6	76	4	94	7
Daniel, Vermont*	7	11	.389	4.04	25	25	5	0	0	0	149.1	149	77	67	16	3	61	3	84	4
J. Davidson, Pittsfield	8	3	.727	3.24	12	12	3	0	2	0	77.2	67	35	28	4	3	27	0	47	2
R. Davidson, Albany	1	1	.500	4.91	24	0	0	12	0	4	36.2	45	23	20	2	1	16	1	25	3
Davis, New Britain	10	5	.667	3.10	19	19	7	0	2	0	133.2	119	53	46	5	3	48	1	66	4
Dersin, Albany	6	10	.375	4.78	22	21	3	1	0	0	124.1	124	70	66	13	3	56	0	55	4
Dibble, Vermont	3	2	.600	3.09	31	1	1	20	0	10	55.1	53	29	19	0	0	28	3	37	5
Duffy, Glens Falls*	3	4	.429	5.99	40	3	1	25	0	6	73.2	98	50	49	9	2	28	4	42	6
Easley, Albany	8	7	.533	1.51	49	0	0	45	0	18	77.2	70	25	13	2	2	20	1	73	4
Ellsworth, New Britain	5	3	.625	1.97	9	9	5	0	1	0	73.0	57	19	16	2	0	18	1	41	5
Encarnacion, Waterbury	8	9	.471	3.99	46	0	0	39	0	10	67.2	58	38	30	6	2	42	5	75	5
Fallon, Glens Falls*	5	2	.714	3.81	14	13	2	0	0	0	82.2	91	43	35	10	0	25	0	40	4
Farrell, Waterbury	9	10	.474	3.06	26	26	9	0	3	0	173.1	158	82	59	15	10	54	2	104	3
Felix, Glens Falls	0	0	.000	15.00	2	0	0	2	0	0	3.0	4	5	5	0	0	3	0	2	0
Fiepke, Nashua*	6	13	.316	4.12	22	20	1	0	0	0	118.0	121	66	54	8	4	69	0	84	15
Freeman, Reading	13	6	.684	4.03	27	27	4	0	2	0	163.0	130	89	73	12	1	111	3	113	11
Frey, Albany*	3	4	.429	2.10	40	0	0	26	0	4	73.0	50	25	17	5	2	18	1	62	2
Frohwirth, Reading	0	4	.000	3.21	29	0	0	23	0	12	42.0	39	20	15	1	2	10	4	23	1
Fulton, Albany	6	6	.500	4.73	14	14	5	0	2	0	80.0	90	46	42	5	1	24	3	46	4
Gaynor, Reading	1	1	.500	3.86	16	1	0	4	0	1	35.0	39	20	15	0	0	9	1	23	1
George, Albany*	1	6	.143	5.68	10	10	1	0	0	0	57.0	62	49	36	5	0	37	1	34	9
Gibson, Glens Falls*	3	1	.750	1.37	9	1	0	3	0	1	19.2	16	3	3	0	0	7	0	21	0
Gideon, Nashua	0	1	.000	3.09	4	2	0	1	0	0	11.2	13	6	4	1	0	5	0	6	1
Gordon, Nashua	4	10	.286	3.47	17	15	1	1	0	0	103.2	96	53	40	7	5	51	3	74	5
Gorman, Glens Falls	8	7	.533	4.39	31	16	2	8	1	2	125.0	142	70	61	19	3	41	3	72	2
Graham, Waterbury	0	0	.000	31.50	1	0	0	1	0	0	2.0	9	9	7	1	0	2	0	0	0
Gray, Vermont	14	2	.875	2.35	55	0	0	42	0	15	84.1	71	24	22	4	6	26	5	65	2
Guercio, Albany	0	0	.000	4.91	2	0	0	1	0	0	7.1	10	5	4	0	1	0	0	2	2
Guidry, Albany*	0	0	.000	3.00	1	1	0	0	0	0	3.0	1	1	1	0	0	2	0	3	0
Hall, Pittsfield*	8	11	.421	3.58	24	24	6	0	3	0	158.1	130	77	63	7	6	84	3	115	10
Hamilton, Pittsfield*	10	10	.500	4.17	27	25	4	2	2	0	155.1	132	92	72	5	10	110	0	92	7
Harrison, Albany*	7	3	.700	2.54	10	10	2	0	1	0	63.2	57	19	18	2	0	15	0	25	2
Hawley, Vermont	4	3	.571	3.36	22	10	1	4	0	2	88.1	96	44	33	7	2	22	3	41	11
Heinkel, Glens Falls	3	5	.375	2.82	10	10	1	0	0	0	67.0	61	30	21	4	0	22	2	49	1
Hellman, Albany	0	0	.000	3.78	10	0	0	4	0	0	16.2	8	9	7	0	0	16	0	18	7
Hernandez, Nashua	1	1	.500	4.91	3	2	0	0	0	0	7.1	7	7	4	0	0	10	0	8	1
Hicks, Reading	2	0	1.000	1.17	9	0	0	3	0	3	15.1	17	8	2	0	1	6	0	5	0
Hill, Glens Falls	0	1	.000	5.14	1	1	0	0	0	0	7.0	4	4	4	1	0	6	0	4	3
Holman, Nashua	4	13	.235	4.77	25	17	1	3	1	0	109.1	108	61	58	9	4	67	3	39	8
Impagliazzo, Albany	1	0	1.000	4.30	13	1	0	4	0	0	23.0	23	12	11	1	1	15	3	15	2
Jackson, Reading	2	3	.400	1.66	30	0	0	23	0	6	43.1	25	9	8	1	1	22	2	42	4
Jefferson, Vermont	1	1	.500	1.93	12	0	0	8	0	2	23.1	16	10	5	2	0	11	1	17	1
Jelks, New Britain	0	0	.000	22.50	1	0	0	0	0	0	2.0	5	6	5	1	0	2	0	1	0
Johnson, Albany	2	2	.500	4.88	4	4	0	0	0	0	24.0	32	14	13	1	3	6	0	10	2
Jones, Glens Falls	2	6	.250	5.28	16	7	3	4	2	1	61.1	57	39	36	4	0	16	3	48	2

Pitcher—Club	W.	L.	Pct.	ERA.	G.	GS.	CG.	GF.	ShO.	Sv.	IP.	H.	R.	ER.	HR.	HB.	BB.	Int. BB.	SO.	WP.
Kiecker, New Britain	7	12	.368	4.14	24	24	7	0	0	0	156.1	171	88	72	8	4	48	3	71	10
Kipper, Nashua*	0	1	.000	3.44	4	4	0	0	0	0	18.1	14	7	7	1	3	3	0	19	1
Knox, Reading	2	1	.667	3.60	5	4	0	0	0	0	25.0	33	13	10	1	0	7	1	15	1
Kopf, Pittsfield	8	2	.800	2.98	20	14	2	2	1	0	99.2	95	44	33	6	3	33	0	34	3
Krawczyk, Nashua	1	0	1.000	0.00	5	2	0	2	0	2	12..2	10	0	0	0	0	1	0	6	0
Labay, Reading*	2	2	.500	3.12	7	6	0	1	0	0	34.2	36	22	12	1	0	17	0	19	5
Labozzetta, Glens Falls*	3	4	.429	6.18	13	9	2	3	1	0	51.0	74	48	35	6	2	23	1	29	3
Lachowicz, Reading	0	2	.000	9.00	9	2	0	3	0	0	10.0	5	15	10	0	2	25	0	4	5
Lancaster, Pittsfield	5	6	.455	4.19	14	14	2	0	0	0	88.0	105	46	41	4	5	34	2	49	2
Layton, Pittsfield	6	4	.600	2.65	20	11	2	3	2	2	91.2	70	31	27	4	4	30	2	38	6
Lenderman, Pittsfield	2	5	.286	5.32	30	0	0	25	0	8	44.0	44	29	26	3	2	24	6	25	4
Leopold, Nashua	4	5	.444	2.76	32	0	0	26	0	7	58.2	49	20	18	3	1	27	5	35	3
Lind, Nashua	4	3	.571	3.59	15	6	0	8	0	4	52.2	56	22	21	1	1	27	0	35	2
Link, Waterbury	6	1	.857	3.68	40	6	1	17	0	3	115.0	103	52	47	11	2	41	1	68	3
Long, Reading	1	3	.250	5.72	23	3	0	0	0	0	45.2	55	32	29	2	1	32	10	36	2
Lono, Vermont*	0	2	.000	9.53	6	3	1	3	0	0	22.2	36	25	24	4	0	7	0	8	2
Madden, Glens Falls*	7	5	.583	4.04	35	8	1	15	0	4	91.1	87	52	41	1	4	55	4	64	14
Maddux, Pittsfield	4	3	.571	2.69	8	8	4	0	2	0	63.2	49	22	19	1	1	15	0	35	1
Marcheskie, Nashua	0	2	.000	3.69	23	0	0	11	0	0	31.2	26	16	13	2	3	12	1	26	4
McKay, Pittsfield*	4	2	.667	2.69	49	5	0	19	0	7	70.1	57	21	21	6	1	39	4	29	2
McLarnan, Reading	0	1	.000	2.87	7	0	0	5	0	3	15.2	11	5	5	3	0	4	1	12	0
Meleski, New Britain	0	0	.000	0.00	1	0	0	0	0	0	1.0	0	0	0	0	0	0	0	0	0
Merklen, Nashua*	1	0	1.000	2.84	10	0	0	6	0	0	12.2	9	4	4	1	0	9	2	16	0
Minnema, Glens Falls	2	9	.182	6.34	17	13	2	0	1	0	76.2	88	63	54	7	8	41	1	30	7
Money, Nashua	3	5	.375	3.74	27	5	3	6	0	0	84.1	76	46	35	2	2	47	5	71	3
Moyer, Pittsfield*	3	1	.750	0.88	6	6	0	0	0	0	41.0	27	10	4	2	0	16	0	42	3
K. Murphy, Waterbury*	13	9	.591	4.43	25	25	3	0	0	0	162.2	168	89	80	13	3	52	1	86	6
M. Murphy, Waterbury	8	7	.533	3.58	25	14	5	8	3	1	118.0	107	54	47	3	5	42	2	62	2
Neal, Nashua*	5	4	.556	3.11	26	8	1	10	1	3	81.0	51	30	28	4	2	38	1	49	4
Neidlinger, Nashua	12	7	.632	2.42	22	22	8	0	2	0	163.2	135	57	44	6	3	44	0	98	5
Oliverio, Vermont	8	9	.471	3.89	23	22	6	1	0	0	132.0	130	63	57	11	3	59	3	81	3
Patterson, Albany	0	0	.000	4.73	15	0	0	6	0	1	26.2	31	15	14	2	2	14	2	22	3
H. Pena, Nashua*	7	4	.636	3.55	31	12	3	10	1	0	99.0	86	47	39	2	3	43	0	76	11
R. Pena, Glens Falls	7	1	.875	2.60	54	1	0	32	0	15	107.1	85	35	31	1	7	39	10	63	8
Peterson, New Britain	4	4	.500	4.90	22	7	0	9	0	1	60.2	69	37	33	3	0	19	2	32	3
Phillips, Pittsfield	1	2	.333	0.77	15	0	0	11	0	2	23.1	19	3	2	0	1	4	2	19	0
Poissant, Glens Falls	0	2	.000	4.15	5	1	1	2	0	0	13.0	9	8	6	2	3	7	0	7	2
Pries, Albany	2	4	.333	4.00	8	6	1	1	1	0	36.0	37	20	16	5	5	27	0	10	7
Rice, Nashua	2	4	.333	3.51	12	12	1	0	0	0	66.2	54	37	26	1	2	49	0	42	10
Ritchie, Reading*	4	1	.800	2.70	28	0	0	15	0	4	30.0	29	13	9	4	1	9	0	13	0
Rooker, Nashua	1	1	.500	4.91	11	3	0	7	0	0	29.1	36	18	16	1	0	17	1	16	0
Ruffin, Reading*	8	4	.667	3.29	16	13	4	0	2	0	90.1	89	41	33	3	0	26	1	68	2
Sabo, Waterbury*	0	1	.000	1.93	11	1	0	4	0	0	23.1	20	7	5	0	0	13	0	17	2
Santarelli, Waterbury	4	10	.286	3.90	44	6	0	32	0	13	92.1	74	52	40	10	5	32	4	70	4
Sauveur, Nashua*	3	1	.750	1.18	5	5	2	0	1	0	38.0	21	5	5	1	1	11	0	28	1
Schmidt, Albany	7	6	.538	3.96	17	17	4	0	2	0	100.0	99	52	44	6	3	33	1	42	1
Scott, Vermont	3	3	.500	4.32	29	3	1	9	0	2	58.1	54	33	28	4	1	21	0	34	4
Searcy, Glens Falls*	11	6	.647	3.30	27	27	3	0	0	0	172.0	166	79	63	6	3	74	1	139	12
Sharts, Reading*	0	0	.000	7.50	1	1	0	0	0	0	6.0	8	5	5	0	0	2	0	1	0
Shelton, Reading	10	7	.588	3.30	37	18	5	14	0	4	147.1	138	65	54	8	2	44	9	70	3
Simpson, Vermont*	0	0	.000	0.00	1	0	0	0	0	0	0.0	3	3	3	0	0	2	0	0	0
Skripko, New Britain	5	3	.625	3.45	10	8	1	1	0	1	57.1	52	25	22	2	1	28	1	34	0
Slifko, New Britain	3	13	.188	4.89	24	21	4	2	1	0	127.0	152	90	69	2	4	57	3	51	13
Dan. Smith, Vermont*	5	3	.625	2.87	41	1	0	23	0	1	62.2	57	29	20	2	4	37	3	39	8
Dar. Smith, Waterbury	4	3	.571	3.54	21	11	4	4	1	0	89.0	71	37	35	8	3	48	0	55	11
Spagnola, Vermont	11	10	.524	3.04	25	25	6	0	1	0	169.0	157	67	57	11	1	69	2	76	2
Stephenson, Pittsfield*	0	0	.000	0.00	3	0	0	3	0	0	4.0	1	0	0	0	0	2	0	1	0
Stewart, New Britain*	7	6	.538	1.97	45	0	0	33	0	18	68.2	64	21	15	1	0	32	6	46	8
Taylor, Nashua	2	2	.500	1.58	33	1	0	24	0	9	62.2	42	13	11	2	0	26	4	57	5
Tirado, Albany	1	0	1.000	1.86	4	0	0	3	0	0	9.2	12	2	2	0	1	3	0	7	0
Trudeau, Waterbury	0	0	.000	6.17	4	1	0	3	0	0	11.2	16	10	8	3	0	7	1	13	0
Vargas, Reading	3	0	1.000	1.89	11	0	0	2	0	0	19.0	20	5	4	3	0	4	1	9	0
Watts, Reading*	9	3	.750	3.61	22	19	3	1	1	0	114.2	106	51	46	10	0	50	0	86	3
Weissman, Glens Falls	0	2	.000	18.26	6	6	0	0	0	0	11.1	31	26	23	2	0	12	0	7	0
Whitehouse, Glens Falls*	2	3	.600	4.45	15	0	0	6	0	1	30.1	35	19	15	0	1	16	4	28	1
Whitmyer, Waterbury	0	2	.000	4.10	12	2	0	5	0	0	37.1	38	19	17	3	0	28	1	11	2
Yaeger, Albany*	3	6	.333	3.69	25	6	3	7	1	0	90.1	82	43	37	7	1	44	3	40	1

BALKS—Curry, Kiecker, 5 each; Gorman, Maddux, 4 each; M. Murphy, 3; Araujo, Beasley, Brake, Gaynor, Hamilton, Kopf, Lono, Minnema, Searcy, Spagnola, Taylor, Watts, 2 each; Barton, Bast, Blevins, Boudreaux, Boyles, Cecena, Chambers, Christiansen, Cooper, Daniel, J. Davidson, Dibble, Duffy, Easley, Ellsworth, Freeman, George, Gideon, Hawley, Hernandez, Jackson, Lancaster, Leopold, Link, Madden, Marcheskie, Money, Moyer, K. Murphy, Neidlinger, Oliverio, R. Pena, Poissant, Sabo, Santarelli, Sauveur, Shelton, Slifko, Weissman, Whitmyer, Yaeger, 1 each.

COMBINATION SHUTOUTS—Byron-Frey, Fulton-Blum-Davidson, Harrison-Easley, Schmidt-Frey, Albany; Heinkel-Duffy-Gorman, Searcy-Barlow, Heinkel-Duffy, Glens Falls; Neidlinger-Leopold, Fiepke-Lind, Neidlinger-Taylor, Holman-Leopold, Money-Neal-Leopold, Fiepke-Leopold, Nashua; Davis-Araujo, Curry-Stewart, New Britain; Moyer-Lenderman, Lancaster-McKay-Capel, Layton-Capel, Kopf-Phillips, Hamilton-McKay, Chestnut-Capel, Pittsfield; Barton-Shelton, Shelton-Beck, Shelton-Frohwirth, Freeman-Ritchie, Long-Chambers, Reading; Daniel-Scott-Gray, Spagnola-Scott-Smith-Gray, Charlton-Hawley, Oliverio-Smith, Vermont; Murphy-Encarnacion, Smith-Link-Encarnacion, Murphy-Santarelli, Link-Santarelli, Waterbury.

NO-HIT GAMES—Neidlinger, Nashua, defeated Glens Falls, 2-0, July 1; Cooper, Glens Falls, defeated Nashua, 4-0 (first game), August 27.

Southern League

CLASS AA

Leading Batter
BRICK SMITH
Chattanooga

League President
JIMMY BRAGAN

Leading Pitcher
ERIC BELL
Charlotte

CHAMPIONSHIP WINNERS IN PREVIOUS YEARS

Year	Club	Pct.
1904	Macon	.598
1905	Macon	.625
1906	Savannah	.637
1907	Charleston	.620
1908	Jacksonville	.694
1909	Chattanooga*	.738
	Augusta	.702
1910	Columbus	.588
1911	Columbus*	.681
	Columbia	.710
1912	Jacksonville*	.679
	Columbus	.632
1913	Savannah	.754
	Savannah	.593
1914	Savannah*	.667
	Albany	.650
1915	Macon	.588
	Columbus*	.686
1916	Augusta*	.617
	Columbia	.631
1917	Charleston	.741
	Columbia*	.667
1918	Did not operate.	
1919	Columbia	.585
1920	Columbia	.633
1921	Columbia	.642
1922	Charleston	.625
1923	Charlotte*	.653
	Macon	.580
1924	Augusta	.612
1925	Spartanburg	.620
1926	Greenville	.662
1927	Greenville	.622
1928	Asheville	.664
1929	Asheville	.605
	Knoxville*	.634
1930	Greenville*	.620
	Macon	.643
1931-35	Did not operate.	
1936	Jacksonville	.652
	Columbus*	.650
1937	Columbus	.572
	Savannah (3rd)†	.565
1938	Savannah	.574
	Macon (2nd)†	.570
1939	Columbus	.601
	Augusta (2nd)†	.597
1940	Savannah	.627
	Columbus (2nd)†	.583
1941	Macon	.643
	Columbia (2nd)†	.636
1942	Charleston	.620
	Macon (2nd)†	.585
1943-45	Did not operate.	
1946	Columbus	.568
	Augusta (4th)†	.547
1947	Columbus	.575
	Savannah (2nd)†	.563
1948	Charleston	.572
	Greenville (3rd)†	.549
1949	Macon‡	.623
1950	Macon‡	.588
1951	Montgomery	.607
1952	Columbia	.649
	Montgomery (3rd)†	.558
1953	Jacksonville	.679
	Savannah (2nd)†	.571
1954	Jacksonville	.593
	Savannah (2nd)†	.571
1955	Columbia	.636
	Augusta (3rd)†	.543
1956	Jacksonville‡	.621
1957	Augusta	.636
	Charlotte (2nd)†	.562
1958	Augusta	.550
	Macon (3rd)†	.500
1959	Knoxville	.557
	Gastonia (4th)†	.504
1960	Columbia	.597
	Savannah (3rd)†	.561
1961	Asheville	.635
1962	Savannah	.662
	Macon (3rd)†	.576
1963	Augusta*	.661
	Lynchburg	.662
1964	Lynchburg	.579
1965	Columbus	.572
1966	Mobile	.629
1967	Birmingham	.604
1968	Asheville	.614
1969	Charlotte	.579
1970	Columbus	.569
1971	Did not operate as league—clubs were members of Dixie Association.	
1972	Asheville	.583
	Montgomery§	.561
1973	Montgomery§	.580
	Jacksonville	.559
1974	Jacksonville	.565
	Knoxville§	.533
1975	Orlando	.587
	Montgomery§	.545
1976	Montgomery x	.591
	Orlando	.540
1977	Montgomery x	.628
	Jacksonville	.522
1978	Knoxville x	.611
	Savannah	.500
1979	Columbus	.587
	Nashville x	.576
1980	Memphis	.576
	Charlotte x	.500
1981	Nashville	.566
	Orlando x	.556
1982	Jacksonville	.576
	Nashville x	.535
1983	Birmingham x	.628
	Jacksonville	.531
1984	Charlotte x	.510
	Knoxville	.483
1985	Charlotte	.545
	Huntsville x	.542

*Won split-season playoff. †Won four-club playoff. ‡Won championship and four-club playoff. §League was divided into Eastern and Western divisions; won playoff. xLeague was divided into Eastern and Western divisions and played split season; won playoff.

STANDING OF CLUBS AT CLOSE OF FIRST HALF, JUNE 19

EASTERN DIVISION

Club	W.	L.	T.	Pct.	G.B.
Jacksonville (Expos)	41	30	1	.577	....
Greenville (Braves)	36	36	0	.500	5½
Charlotte (Orioles)	36	36	0	.500	5½
Orlando (Twins)	31	41	0	.431	10½
Columbus (Astros)	28	41	0	.406	12

WESTERN DIVISION

Club	W.	L.	T.	Pct.	G.B.
Huntsville (A's)	40	29	0	.580	....
Birmingham (White Sox)	38	34	0	.528	3½
Memphis (Royals)	36	36	0	.500	5½
Chattanooga (Mariners)	35	36	1	.493	6
Knoxville (Blue Jays)	35	37	0	.486	6½

STANDING OF CLUBS AT CLOSE OF SECOND HALF, SEPTEMBER 1

EASTERN DIVISION

Club	W.	L.	T.	Pct.	G.B.
Columbus (Astros)	42	29	0	.592	....
Orlando (Twins)	39	32	0	.549	3
Greenville (Braves)	37	35	1	.514	5½
Charlotte (Orioles)	35	37	0	.486	7½
Jacksonville (Expos)	34	38	1	.472	8½

WESTERN DIVISION

Club	W.	L.	T.	Pct.	G.B.
Knoxville (Blue Jays)	39	33	0	.542	....
Huntsville (A's)	38	34	0	.528	1
Memphis (Royals)	33	39	0	.458	6
Birmingham (White Sox)	32	39	0	.451	6½
Chattanooga (Mariners)	29	42	0	.408	9½

COMPOSITE STANDING OF CLUBS AT CLOSE OF SEASON, SEPTEMBER 1

Club	Hunt.	Jax.	Knox.	Grn.	Col.	Char.	Orl.	Birm.	Mem.	Chat.	W.	L.	T.	Pct.	G.B.
Huntsville (A's)	....	10	9	10	6	10	6	10	7	10	78	63	0	.553	....
Jacksonville (Expos)	6	....	10	8	8	8	9	8	8	10	75	68	2	.524	4
Knoxville (Blue Jays)	7	6	....	10	9	3	7	11	10	11	74	70	0	.514	5½
Greenville (Braves)	6	8	6	....	9	12	10	8	11	3	73	71	1	.507	6½
Columbus (Astros)	7	8	7	7	....	6	7	8	9	11	70	70	0	.500	7½
Charlotte (Orioles)	6	8	9	8	10	....	8	7	6	9	71	73	0	.493	8½
Orlando (Twins)	10	7	9	6	9	8	....	7	6	8	70	73	0	.490	9
Birmingham (White Sox)	6	8	5	8	7	9	9	....	7	11	70	73	0	.490	9
Memphis (Royals)	9	8	6	5	7	10	10	9	....	5	69	75	0	.479	10½
Chattanooga (Mariners)	6	5	9	9	5	7	7	5	11	....	64	78	1	.451	14½

Major league affiliations in parentheses.

Playoffs—Columbus defeated Jacksonville, three games to one; Huntsville defeated Knoxville, three games to one; Columbus defeated Huntsville, three games to one, to win league championship.

Regular-Season Attendance—Birmingham, 175,932; Charlotte, 106,426; Chattanooga, 118,684; Columbus, 134,964; Greenville, 203,647; Huntsville, 263,198; Jacksonville, 164,772; Knoxville, 109,731; Memphis, 252,036; Orlando, 75,728. Total—1,604,758. Playoffs—12,323. All-Star Game, 4,181.

Managers—Birmingham, Tom Haller (thru June 9), Bob Bailey (June 10 thru end of season); Charlotte, Greg Biagini; Chattanooga, R.J. Harrison; Columbus, Dave Cripe (thru June 9), Charlie Taylor (June 10), Gary Tuck (June 11 thru end of season); Greenville, Jim Beauchamp; Huntsville, Brad Fischer; Jacksonville, Tommy Thompson; Knoxville, Larry Hardy; Memphis, Tommy Jones; Orlando, George Mitterwald.

All-Star Team—1B-Brick Smith, Chattanooga; 2B-Billy Ripken, Charlotte; 3B-Jeff Reynolds, Jacksonville; SS-Brian Guinn, Huntsville; OF-Glenallen Hill, Knoxville; Alonzo Powell, Jacksonville; Larry Ray, Columbus; Gary Thurman, Memphis; C-Terry Steinbach, Huntsville; DH-Tom Dodd, Charlotte; RHP-Anthony Kelley, Columbus; LHP-Tom Glavine, Greenville; Relief Pitcher-Paul Schneider, Chattanooga; Most Valuable Player-Terry Steinbach, Huntsville; Manager of the Year-Gary Tuck, Columbus.

(Compiled by Howe News Bureau, Boston, Mass.)

CLUB BATTING

Club	Pct.	G.	AB.	R.	OR.	H.	TB.	2B.	3B.	HR.	RBI.	GW.	SH.	SF.	HP.	BB.	Int. BB.	SO.	SB.	CS.	LOB.
Huntsville	.289	141	4764	881	762	1378	1989	231	34	104	789	69	32	57	31	722	24	822	164	74	1113
Orlando	.280	143	4892	726	758	1372	1979	199	39	110	662	59	33	53	44	544	10	674	114	53	1147
Knoxville	.280	144	4929	752	704	1378	2198	236	58	156	676	64	23	60	31	508	17	1017	150	96	1024
Jacksonville	.278	145	4814	722	725	1338	2045	232	35	135	658	69	45	25	46	549	17	703	97	79	1067
Charlotte	.277	144	4953	791	789	1372	2117	246	41	139	729	68	40	49	45	651	32	696	131	61	1135
Columbus	.275	140	4680	725	698	1286	1933	210	40	119	668	66	43	55	31	529	28	795	135	80	994
Chattanooga	.273	143	4691	708	765	1279	1801	224	35	76	650	59	41	57	36	666	20	627	130	61	1117
Birmingham	.272	143	4781	774	780	1301	2006	237	30	136	695	62	39	50	31	644	20	848	127	76	1067
Greenville	.271	145	4778	690	753	1295	1931	239	29	113	615	64	67	39	29	566	24	751	80	52	1077
Memphis	.261	144	4835	717	752	1260	1916	228	40	116	648	61	33	38	46	582	19	992	175	81	1025

INDIVIDUAL BATTING

(Leading Qualifiers for Batting Championship—389 or More Plate Appearances)

*Bats lefthanded. †Switch-hitter.

Player and Club	Pct.	G.	AB.	R.	H.	TB.	2B.	3B.	HR.	RBI.	GW.	SH.	SF.	HP.	BB.	Int. BB.	SO.	SB.	CS.
Smith, Brick, Chattanooga	.344	128	474	80	163	274	38	2	23	101	13	0	7	0	63	5	36	3	1
Steinbach, Terry, Huntsville	.325	138	505	113	164	273	33	2	24	132	13	0	7	5	94	1	74	10	9
Padget, Chris, Charlotte*	.324	127	469	77	152	254	22	7	22	96	9	4	7	3	79	9	66	1	6
Dodd, Thomas, Charlotte	.323	105	399	75	129	238	19	3	28	100	10	0	10	5	54	5	68	3	2
Larkin, Eugene, Orlando†	.321	142	529	85	170	256	29	6	15	104	9	1	13	5	84	2	50	1	0
Trout, Jeffrey, Orlando†	.321	105	390	61	125	176	22	4	7	67	5	0	4	5	54	2	43	1	2
Daugherty, John, Jacksonville†	.317	138	502	87	159	216	37	4	4	63	10	7	3	4	79	1	58	15	6
Palmer, Douglas, Orlando	.317	130	398	51	126	142	9	2	1	41	5	4	3	5	46	0	25	13	5
Tolentino, Jose, Huntsville*	.315	137	540	80	170	246	28	0	16	105	9	2	7	4	53	6	57	7	2
Thurman, Gary, Memphis	.312	131	525	88	164	233	24	12	7	62	9	4	3	0	57	0	81	53	18
Sliwinski, Kevin, Knoxville	.312	142	522	87	163	265	29	5	21	89	6	0	8	7	68	2	97	6	5
Moreno, Armando, Jacksonville	.311	133	456	79	142	223	24	6	15	61	3	2	2	1	90	2	53	3	7
Jones, Gary, Huntsville*	.311	130	450	116	140	177	23	4	2	49	5	8	3	3	128	1	60	34	17
Salinas, Manuel, Birmingham*	.305	119	426	60	130	167	25	0	4	55	2	4	2	0	16	0	24	6	6

Departmental Leaders: G—Tubbs, 144; AB—Hill, 570; R—G. Jones, 116; H—Larkin, Tolentino, 170; TB—Hill, 287; 2B—B. Smith, 38; 3B—Liriano, 15; HR—Hill, 31; RBI—Steinbach, 132; GWRBI—Griffin, 18; SH—Rios, 13; SF—Hill, Larkin, 13; HP—P. Wilson, 9; BB—G. Jones, 128; IBB—Padget, Snider, 9; SO—Hill, 153; SB—Young, 54; CS—Young, 27.

(All Players—Listed Alphabetically)

Player and Club	Pct.	G.	AB.	R.	H.	TB.	2B.	3B.	HR.	RBI.	GW.	SH.	SF.	HP.	BB.	Int. BB.	SO.	SB.	CS.
Afenir, Troy, Columbus	.217	91	313	50	68	131	15	3	14	45	4	4	3	3	22	0	90	0	5
Alcazar, Jorge, Birmingham	.133	5	15	1	2	2	0	0	0	0	0	0	0	0	0	0	9	0	0
Allaire, Karl, Columbus*	.254	119	393	47	100	120	18	1	0	31	4	6	6	0	51	2	52	10	6
Allen, Edward, Memphis	.211	81	251	35	53	66	8	1	1	24	3	1	2	1	45	1	60	18	6

Player and Club	Pct.	G.	AB.	R.	H.	TB.	2B.	3B.	HR.	RBI.	GW.	SH.	SF.	HP.	BB.	Int. BB.	SO.	SB.	CS.
Alvarez, Evelio, Greenville	.125	37	16	1	2	2	0	0	0	0	0	3	0	0	3	0	1	1	0
Amaya, Benjamin, Chattanooga	.194	41	103	13	20	31	2	0	3	14	0	0	2	8	19	1	21	0	0
Aragon, Steven, Orlando	.223	110	310	32	69	101	16	2	4	42	8	4	4	0	32	0	28	3	3
Baker, Mark, Columbus	.000	21	1	0	0	0	0	0	0	0	0	0	0	0	0	0	1	0	0
Balelo, Onesimo, Chattanooga	.204	57	191	24	39	55	8	1	2	16	0	2	5	3	11	0	33	2	1
Barnes, William, Jacksonville	.500	3	8	1	4	4	0	0	0	1	0	0	1	0	1	0	1	0	1
Barrett, Timothy, Jacksonville*	.250	11	4	0	1	1	0	0	0	0	0	0	0	0	0	0	1	0	0
Beamesderfer, Kurt, Charlotte	.290	62	214	35	62	90	13	0	5	36	5	1	2	1	23	1	25	5	1
Beauchamp, Kash, Knoxville	.337	51	193	32	65	101	10	1	8	25	4	0	1	2	17	0	40	5	4
Bell, Terence, 4 Chat-48 Mem	.235	52	136	21	32	41	9	0	0	15	2	2	4	2	29	0	30	1	0
Berroa, Geronimo, Knoxville	.000	1	4	0	0	0	0	0	0	0	0	0	0	0	0	0	1	0	0
Bettendorf, Jeffrey, Columbus	.400	27	5	1	2	2	0	0	0	0	0	1	0	0	0	0	1	0	0
Bierley, Brad, Orlando*	.277	135	501	89	139	234	25	2	22	73	4	3	7	4	58	1	91	8	3
Bishop, James, Knoxville	.211	22	71	7	15	17	0	1	0	5	1	1	1	0	7	0	25	1	1
Blankenship, Kevin, Greenville	.125	38	8	0	1	1	0	0	0	0	0	0	0	0	0	0	4	0	0
Bogener, Terry, Charlotte*	.275	51	153	27	42	46	4	0	0	15	2	1	1	4	22	2	21	5	3
Borders, Patrick, Knoxville	.353	12	34	3	12	19	1	0	2	5	0	2	0	0	1	0	6	0	3
Brilinski, Tyler, Huntsville*	.220	14	50	10	11	22	2	0	3	6	1	0	1	1	5	0	14	0	0
Buss, Scott, Chattanooga	.237	109	321	47	76	102	10	5	2	39	3	6	3	5	44	0	62	11	6
Camelo, Peter, Jacksonville*	.233	129	455	55	106	187	21	3	18	66	9	2	1	3	49	1	88	11	8
Caminiti, Kenneth, Columbus†	.300	137	513	82	154	225	29	3	12	81	5	2	10	1	56	6	78	5	3
Campusano, Silvestre, Knoxville	.256	132	493	89	126	212	32	6	14	59	9	0	4	6	61	2	110	18	10
Capello, Peter, Memphis	.000	3	6	0	0	0	0	0	0	0	0	0	0	0	0	0	3	0	0
Cash, Timothy, Columbus	.000	32	1	0	0	0	0	0	0	0	0	0	0	0	0	0	0	0	0
Cecchini, James, Jacksonville	.247	33	89	10	22	29	4	0	1	7	1	0	0	2	11	0	18	0	1
Childress, Willie, Greenville*	.300	135	486	69	146	217	28	2	13	65	6	8	4	1	54	4	75	5	5
Cimo, Matthew, Charlotte	.242	68	231	39	56	98	7	4	9	29	4	3	1	1	21	0	45	4	4
Cochrane, David, Birmingham†	.272	93	349	66	95	179	23	5	17	74	7	0	6	2	61	4	102	4	4
Coffman, Kevin, Greenville	.000	8	3	0	0	0	0	0	0	0	0	0	0	0	0	0	1	0	0
Colbert, Richard, Orlando	.189	31	90	12	17	24	2	1	1	10	1	0	1	0	20	0	31	0	0
Conklin, Graham, Huntsville	.264	28	91	14	24	38	6	1	2	10	1	0	0	0	8	0	20	0	0
Cook, Kerry, Jacksonville	.000	43	3	0	0	0	0	0	0	0	0	0	0	0	0	0	1	0	0
Cook, Mitchell, Columbus*	.000	21	3	1	0	0	0	0	0	0	0	4	0	0	3	0	1	0	1
Corey, Mark, Jacksonville	.313	90	336	50	105	173	15	1	17	56	4	0	2	4	32	3	64	2	7
Cormack, Terry, Chattanooga*	.400	5	15	3	6	8	2	0	0	2	0	0	0	0	2	0	3	0	0
Coyle, Rock, Huntsville	.291	90	282	53	82	126	15	1	9	51	6	2	5	3	30	3	22	10	3
Criswell, Timothy, Greenville	.500	5	16	3	8	11	1	1	0	1	0	0	0	0	1	0	0	0	0
Cummings, Robert, Chattanooga	.306	41	121	13	37	46	3	0	2	19	1	0	1	0	22	1	14	0	3
Curry, Stephen, Greenville	.230	55	183	18	42	59	6	1	3	16	3	1	0	1	24	2	47	0	1
Cutshall, William, Jacksonville*	.000	18	6	1	0	0	0	0	0	0	0	0	0	0	0	0	1	0	0
D'Alessandro, Salvatore, Greenville	.234	48	154	23	36	47	3	1	2	23	3	2	1	1	29	0	22	0	0
Datz, Jeffrey, Columbus	.325	59	191	26	62	95	13	1	6	25	4	2	1	1	20	2	26	0	1
Daugherty, John, Jacksonville†	.317	138	502	87	159	216	37	4	4	63	10	7	3	4	79	1	58	15	6
David, Amin, Huntsville	.239	42	92	11	22	26	1	0	1	12	2	0	3	1	15	0	19	1	0
David, Brian, Chattanooga	.271	110	399	58	108	129	13	1	2	50	7	7	9	6	65	4	26	22	5
Delgado, Juan, Columbus	.287	58	209	21	60	89	6	4	5	43	5	0	3	1	14	0	27	0	1
DeLosSantos, Luis, Memphis	.303	135	525	72	159	199	21	5	3	84	5	5	7	3	46	1	65	5	1
Denby, Darryl, Greenville	.236	90	280	32	66	113	15	4	8	36	0	2	4	6	9	1	46	5	4
DeWillis, Jeffrey, 49 Mem-26 Knox	.200	75	160	26	32	40	5	0	1	14	1	1	0	5	51	0	39	2	1
Diaz, Jose, Knoxville	.375	11	16	3	6	10	1	0	1	2	0	0	0	0	1	0	4	0	0
Dodd, Thomas, Charlotte	.323	105	399	75	129	238	19	3	28	100	10	0	10	5	54	5	68	3	2
Doerr, Jeffrey, Charlotte	.245	18	53	7	13	15	2	0	0	5	1	1	0	1	7	0	15	0	0
Dowless, Michael, Greenville	.000	8	1	0	0	0	0	0	0	0	0	1	0	0	2	0	1	0	0
Ducey, Robert, Knoxville*	.308	88	344	49	106	167	22	3	11	58	7	0	4	0	29	3	59	7	7
Duncan, John, Chattanooga	.274	92	285	43	78	103	13	3	2	31	4	1	3	2	52	1	42	6	4
Eccleston, Thomas, Chattanooga*	.242	58	182	20	44	57	7	0	2	22	1	2	1	0	29	0	26	4	4
Eichelberger, Juan, Greenville	.000	18	1	0	0	0	0	0	0	0	0	0	0	0	0	0	1	0	0
Engram, Graylyn, Birmingham	.270	49	111	17	30	36	3	0	1	10	1	2	0	0	18	0	11	4	3
Escobar, Jose, Knoxville	.242	19	66	9	16	19	1	1	0	5	0	4	1	1	5	1	6	1	1
Falcone, David, Charlotte*	.292	67	250	39	73	115	15	0	9	37	1	0	1	0	48	4	30	5	3
Falls, Robert, Columbus†	.258	108	368	51	95	142	14	3	9	38	3	5	8	4	23	0	74	17	6
Farmar, Damon, Huntsville†	.275	137	520	94	143	200	18	6	9	88	10	2	5	0	65	3	113	25	8
Fischer, Jeffrey, Jacksonville	.000	11	6	0	0	0	0	0	0	0	0	3	0	0	0	0	1	0	0
Foley, Marvis, Birmingham*	.303	11	33	1	10	13	3	0	0	3	0	0	0	0	8	0	4	0	3
Forrester, Thomas, Birmingham*	.254	137	489	82	124	228	30	1	24	88	5	1	3	0	64	4	97	2	0
Friedrich, Michael, Columbus†	.100	29	10	0	1	1	0	0	0	2	0	1	0	0	0	0	6	0	0
Fuentes, Michael, Columbus	.303	80	241	36	73	134	15	2	14	52	6	0	3	2	33	2	47	1	4
Funderburk, Mark, Orlando	.209	40	148	17	31	56	7	0	6	23	2	0	1	1	15	1	24	1	0
Funk, Thomas, Columbus*	.000	44	1	0	0	0	0	0	0	0	0	0	0	0	0	0	0	0	0
Gardner, Mark, Jacksonville	.182	29	11	0	2	2	0	0	0	0	0	0	0	0	2	0	6	0	1
Garrison, Webster, Knoxville	.000	5	6	0	0	0	0	0	0	0	0	0	0	0	0	0	2	1	0
Gergen, Robert, Charlotte	.347	14	49	7	17	25	5	0	1	7	1	1	1	1	6	0	8	0	0
Gilcrease, Douglas, Memphis	.230	103	318	45	73	108	15	1	6	30	4	2	3	7	28	0	41	8	5
Glavine, Thomas, Greenville*	.286	22	7	2	2	2	0	0	0	0	0	2	0	0	0	0	3	0	0
Gnacinski, Paul, 18 Green-14 Knox	.333	32	3	0	1	1	0	0	0	0	0	0	0	0	0	0	2	0	0
Goff, Timothy, Memphis	.000	4	2	0	0	0	0	0	0	0	0	0	0	0	0	0	2	0	0
Granger, Lee, Charlotte†	.255	76	278	52	71	117	21	5	5	51	2	0	3	1	39	0	63	20	10
Griffin, David, Greenville	.276	137	493	67	136	220	31	1	17	104	18	0	7	6	55	0	85	0	1
Groves, Jeffrey, Greenville	.000	8	6	1	0	0	0	0	0	0	0	0	0	0	1	0	5	0	0
Groves, Larry, Jacksonville	.000	31	2	0	0	0	0	0	0	0	0	0	0	0	0	0	1	0	0
Guerrero, Inocencio, Greenville	.285	98	316	52	90	151	22	3	11	55	4	0	3	0	51	0	57	1	3
Guinn, Brian, Huntsville*	.283	121	463	87	131	176	20	5	5	63	5	9	4	3	52	3	78	19	11
Hall, Matthew, Chattanooga*	.322	74	261	46	84	123	19	4	4	38	3	6	4	5	23	2	23	15	6
Harris, Michael, Birmingham†	.218	42	147	17	32	38	2	2	0	14	1	4	1	0	4	0	27	5	2
Hatcher, Johnny, Greenville	.269	105	383	57	103	132	15	1	4	30	4	9	2	4	18	0	50	10	4
Hill, Glenallen, Knoxville	.279	141	570	87	159	287	23	6	31	96	10	0	13	1	39	3	153	18	18
Hoeksema, David, Memphis	.122	14	41	1	5	6	1	0	0	3	0	0	0	1	5	0	10	0	0
Hollins, Paul, Chattanooga*	.258	46	155	17	40	50	4	3	0	17	1	0	0	0	21	1	26	0	1
Holman, Brian, Jacksonville	.000	27	8	0	0	0	0	0	0	0	0	2	0	0	0	0	4	0	0
Holman, Dale, Greenville*	.273	23	77	10	21	34	6	2	1	8	0	0	1	0	9	0	13	0	0
Holmes, Stanley, Orlando	.246	69	244	34	60	105	8	2	11	46	1	0	4	2	23	2	41	0	0
Holtz, Gerald, Charlotte*	.256	131	485	90	124	170	22	6	4	45	1	4	6	1	111	4	61	30	11
Howard, James, Knoxville	.167	5	6	1	1	3	0	1	0	2	0	0	0	0	0	0	1	0	0

Player and Club	Pct.	G.	AB.	R.	H.	TB.	2B.	3B.	HR.	RBI.	GW.	SH.	SF.	HP.	BB.	Int. BB.	SO.	SB.	CS.
Howe, Gregory, Orlando	.316	37	136	25	43	63	8	3	2	16	0	0	2	2	19	1	19	11	1
Huson, Jeffrey, Jacksonville*	.000	1	4	0	0	0	0	0	0	0	0	0	0	0	0	0	0	0	0
Ingle, Randy, Greenville	.252	65	206	28	52	80	13	0	5	20	2	1	1	0	15	1	33	1	2
Jackson, Vincent, Memphis	.277	53	184	30	51	87	9	3	7	25	4	0	1	5	22	0	81	3	6
Jarrell, Joseph, Memphis	.223	139	534	66	119	224	27	3	24	86	6	0	4	6	22	1	152	4	7
Job, Ryan, Columbus	.244	21	45	7	11	15	1	0	1	5	1	0	0	0	8	0	5	1	0
Johnson, Roy, Huntsville*	.344	52	183	33	63	92	12	1	5	27	1	0	2	0	32	2	20	4	1
Jones, Gary, Huntsville*	.311	130	450	116	140	177	23	4	2	49	5	8	3	3	128	1	60	34	17
Jones, Ross, Chattanooga	.313	70	230	41	72	100	9	2	5	42	8	5	4	1	27	0	34	2	6
Joslyn, John, Memphis*	.500	2	4	0	2	2	0	0	0	0	0	0	0	0	0	0	1	0	0
Karkovice, Ronald, Birmingham	.282	97	319	63	90	165	13	1	20	53	5	2	9	4	61	3	109	2	2
Kelley, Anthony, Columbus	.182	29	11	1	2	4	0	1	0	1	0	1	0	0	1	0	5	0	0
Kinnard, Kenneth, Knoxville	.352	63	230	47	81	125	11	6	7	33	3	1	2	1	16	0	65	16	6
Kramer, Joseph, Huntsville	.329	53	167	29	55	65	8	1	0	16	0	2	3	1	22	1	34	12	4
Larkin, Eugene, Orlando†	.321	142	529	85	170	256	29	6	15	104	9	1	13	5	84	2	50	1	0
Larson, Daniel, Chattanooga	.250	17	56	3	14	14	0	0	0	1	1	1	0	0	3	0	10	3	0
Lawrence, Andy, Jacksonville	.269	41	134	20	36	68	8	0	8	30	2	1	0	2	7	0	17	1	1
Leary, Robert, Jacksonville	.333	1	3	0	1	1	0	0	0	2	0	0	0	0	0	0	1	0	0
Lee, Manuel, Knoxville†	.272	41	158	21	43	48	1	2	0	11	0	0	1	0	20	1	29	8	4
Liriano, Nelson, Knoxville†	.285	135	557	88	159	235	25	15	7	59	5	4	5	3	48	2	63	35	14
Lockwood, Richard, Charlotte†	.167	12	36	4	6	9	1	1	0	0	0	0	0	0	6	1	7	1	1
Longenecker, Jere, Memphis	.260	135	434	74	113	170	28	1	9	65	5	5	5	7	73	0	81	27	7
Loscalzo, Robert, Huntsville*	.065	13	31	4	2	3	1	0	0	5	0	0	0	0	5	0	13	1	1
Mabe, Todd, Memphis†	.228	47	149	29	34	39	5	0	0	12	1	0	0	1	36	1	37	6	4
MacFarlane, Michael, Memphis	.241	40	141	26	34	81	7	2	12	29	2	0	1	2	10	0	26	0	1
Mallicoat, Robbin, Columbus*	.250	10	4	0	1	1	0	0	0	0	0	1	0	0	0	0	3	0	0
Marquardt, John, Orlando	.217	84	258	25	56	71	10	1	1	16	0	4	0	2	18	0	38	2	4
Marte, Alexis, Orlando*	.320	70	284	55	91	105	7	2	1	28	3	4	0	1	30	0	22	42	12
Martinez, Edgar, Chattanooga	.264	132	451	71	119	176	29	5	6	74	6	5	6	2	89	2	35	2	5
Martinez, Reynaldo, Memphis*	.304	93	283	48	86	145	16	5	11	44	3	2	1	2	42	4	58	4	4
Mathews, Charles, Columbus	.200	41	5	0	1	1	0	0	0	0	0	0	0	0	0	0	3	0	0
McDougal, Julius, Orlando†	.377	17	61	9	23	28	2	0	1	7	1	2	0	0	3	0	12	2	0
McGwire, Mark, Huntsville	.303	55	195	40	59	104	15	0	10	53	4	1	6	1	46	0	45	3	0
McKay, Troy, Jacksonville	.250	25	8	2	2	4	2	0	0	0	0	0	0	1	2	0	3	0	0
McMurtry, Craig, Greenville	.500	3	2	0	1	1	0	0	0	0	0	0	0	0	0	0	0	0	0
McNealy, Robert, Chattanooga*	.251	137	537	85	135	160	19	3	0	43	2	4	2	1	74	2	56	47	12
Menendez, Antonio, Birmingham	.000	17	1	0	0	0	0	0	0	0	0	0	0	0	0	0	0	0	0
Mikulik, Joseph, Columbus	.301	130	502	80	151	221	21	11	9	69	4	1	3	7	33	0	92	18	13
Miller, Lemmie, Charlotte	.235	7	17	2	4	4	0	0	0	0	0	0	0	0	3	0	1	0	1
Miller, Michael, Memphis	.249	74	217	41	54	73	13	0	2	23	2	0	1	0	40	1	45	25	9
Moreno, Armando, Jacksonville	.311	133	456	79	142	223	24	6	15	61	3	2	2	1	90	2	53	3	7
Morhardt, Gregory, Orlando*	.279	50	201	35	56	94	9	1	9	43	5	0	2	3	8	0	18	3	3
Moritz, Thomas, Birmingham	.237	57	194	40	46	86	9	2	9	29	3	2	1	6	33	0	37	4	5
Morris, Angel, Memphis	.259	89	247	20	64	89	7	0	6	31	2	3	2	0	26	0	44	0	1
Mueller, Peter, Columbus*	.269	52	167	29	45	64	7	0	4	24	2	1	1	2	18	1	36	1	1
Myers, David, Chattanooga	.289	119	419	60	121	169	24	3	6	66	3	2	3	0	34	0	38	4	6
Nichols, Carl, Charlotte	.269	118	439	63	118	188	26	1	14	72	6	2	2	8	61	1	78	8	2
Nicometi, Anthony, Jacksonville*	.250	41	4	0	1	1	0	0	0	0	0	0	0	0	0	0	0	0	0
Nipper, Michael, Greenville	.268	85	314	35	84	138	19	1	11	36	3	2	1	1	25	4	53	0	2
Nix, David, Huntsville*	.232	61	168	24	39	55	9	2	1	17	2	1	0	0	20	2	22	4	3
Nixon, Donell, Chattanooga	.333	4	18	2	6	7	1	0	0	0	0	0	0	0	2	0	3	2	1
Noble, Rayner, Columbus†	.200	12	5	2	1	1	0	0	0	0	0	0	0	1	2	0	2	0	0
Norman, Daniel, Charlotte	.171	11	41	8	7	14	1	0	2	6	1	0	2	0	1	0	8	2	1
Norman, Nelson, Jacksonville	.289	122	402	53	116	144	19	3	1	45	1	4	4	1	44	4	15	2	3
O'Dell, James, Columbus*	.268	115	392	49	105	160	16	3	11	46	0	2	1	2	45	4	45	3	3
Padget, Chris, Charlotte*	.324	127	469	77	152	254	22	7	22	96	9	4	7	3	79	9	66	1	6
Padia, Steven, Orlando*	.228	49	123	9	28	32	4	0	0	10	2	0	2	0	17	0	27	0	0
Palmer, Douglas, Orlando	.317	130	398	51	126	142	9	2	1	41	5	4	3	5	46	0	25	13	5
Paredes, Johnny, Jacksonville	.286	122	472	86	135	178	15	5	6	34	2	4	1	5	51	0	44	22	10
Parker, Robert, Columbus*	.258	80	236	48	61	67	6	0	0	30	4	7	2	2	53	2	35	24	9
Pino, Rolando, Birmingham	.256	105	308	50	79	114	17	0	6	45	3	4	3	3	65	2	74	16	9
Powell, Alonzo, Jacksonville	.301	105	402	67	121	197	21	5	15	80	12	2	3	4	49	3	78	15	11
Price, Kevin, Jacksonville	.000	60	2	0	0	0	0	0	0	0	0	0	0	0	0	0	1	0	0
Pruitt, Darrell, Birmingham	.273	16	33	3	9	9	0	0	0	3	0	0	0	0	4	0	3	4	2
Ray, Larry, Columbus*	.275	137	494	88	136	233	19	3	24	108	16	1	6	4	75	4	98	1	0
Raymer, Gregory, Jacksonville	.000	32	7	3	0	0	0	0	0	0	0	4	0	0	3	0	3	0	0
Redfield, Joseph, Charlotte	.297	95	344	65	102	168	16	4	14	49	5	1	1	7	38	1	62	8	4
Reynolds, Jeffrey, Jacksonville	.268	143	557	85	149	272	36	0	29	113	17	1	1	6	44	1	106	2	8
Reynolds, Mark, Columbus*	.000	1	1	0	0	0	0	0	0	0	0	0	0	0	0	0	1	0	0
Rincones, Hector, Memphis	.265	67	245	22	65	82	10	2	1	28	1	5	2	2	15	1	13	11	2
Rios, Carlos, Greenville	.302	133	484	78	146	190	25	2	5	60	7	13	5	3	65	2	29	7	3
Ripken, William, Charlotte	.268	141	530	58	142	183	20	3	5	62	4	7	2	1	24	2	47	9	4
Rodriguez, Aristides, Columbus	.333	5	3	0	1	1	0	0	0	0	0	0	0	0	1	0	2	0	0
Rogers, MacArthur, Greenville	.000	16	1	0	0	0	0	0	0	0	0	1	0	0	0	0	0	0	0
Rollin, Rondal, 53-Bir-44 Green	.217	97	345	58	75	142	14	1	17	43	3	0	5	3	27	3	104	5	2
Rossy, Elam, Charlotte	.293	77	232	40	68	97	16	2	3	25	5	8	1	2	26	0	19	13	5
Rypien, Timothy, Knoxville	.400	5	5	1	2	3	1	0	0	1	0	0	0	0	1	0	1	0	0
Salcedo, Ronnie, Charlotte*	.263	123	434	59	114	180	21	3	13	60	5	5	4	8	56	2	26	11	2
Salinas, Manuel, Birmingham*	.305	119	426	60	130	167	25	0	4	55	2	4	2	0	16	0	24	6	6
Samuels, Roger, Columbus*	.000	38	1	0	0	0	0	0	0	0	0	0	0	0	0	0	0	0	0
Santovenia, Nelson, Jacksonville	.306	31	72	15	22	41	7	0	4	11	0	2	0	1	19	0	7	0	1
Scheer, Ronald, Birmingham	.245	20	53	6	13	16	3	0	0	6	2	0	1	1	8	1	8	0	0
Scott, Michael, Greenville	.200	15	5	0	1	1	0	0	0	0	0	1	0	0	0	0	2	0	0
Seilheimer, Ricky, Birmingham*	.256	62	172	21	44	67	6	1	5	23	4	3	2	2	21	0	25	1	0
Seitzer, Kevin, Memphis	.273	4	11	4	3	3	0	0	0	1	0	0	0	0	7	0	1	2	1
Sferrazza, Matthew, Jacksonville	.231	42	156	21	36	40	4	0	0	12	3	4	1	1	16	0	20	12	2
Shaddy, Christopher, Knoxville	.260	123	435	58	113	178	20	6	11	50	5	4	6	2	40	0	98	5	6
Sherlock, Glenn, Columbus*	.308	4	13	4	4	9	0	1	1	5	0	0	0	0	3	0	2	0	0
Sliwinski, Kevin, Knoxville	.312	142	522	87	163	265	29	5	21	89	6	0	8	7	68	2	97	6	5
Smith, Brick, Chattanooga	.344	128	474	80	163	274	38	2	23	101	13	0	7	0	63	5	36	3	1
Smith, David, Charlotte	.241	89	299	14	72	106	15	2	5	34	6	2	5	1	26	0	46	6	1
Smith, Peter, Greenville	.000	24	5	0	0	0	0	0	0	0	0	0	0	0	1	0	1	0	0
Snider, Van, Memphis*	.270	134	492	79	133	248	27	5	26	81	12	4	3	3	48	9	140	7	8

Player and Club	Pct.	G.	AB.	R.	H.	TB.	2B.	3B.	HR.	RBI.	GW.	SH.	SF.	HP.	BB.	Int. BB.	SO.	SB.	CS.
Sorce, Samuel, Orlando	.292	91	336	46	98	152	14	2	12	54	2	2	5	3	21	0	32	1	2
Stark, Matthew, Knoxville	.295	120	424	63	125	197	21	0	17	72	7	2	8	4	47	1	47	1	1
Steinbach, Terry, Huntsville	.325	138	505	113	164	273	33	2	24	132	13	0	7	5	94	1	74	10	9
Strasser, Richard, Columbus	.077	32	13	1	1	1	0	0	0	1	1	2	0	0	1	0	6	0	0
Stringfellow, Thornton, Greenville*	.286	44	7	1	2	2	0	0	0	1	0	2	0	0	0	0	3	0	0
Stromer, Richard, Huntsville	.056	6	18	1	1	1	0	0	0	0	0	0	0	0	3	0	6	0	0
Tatis, Bernardo, Knoxville†	.251	107	355	55	89	145	19	5	9	40	3	2	2	1	43	2	77	25	13
Taylor, Michael, Birmingham	.276	104	333	59	92	146	13	4	11	49	5	0	4	3	47	1	45	20	9
Tejada, Wilfredo, Jacksonville	.270	107	382	49	103	163	11	5	13	46	1	2	2	8	25	1	74	10	8
Thoma, Raymond, Huntsville	.243	112	404	62	98	139	15	4	6	57	4	0	7	0	33	0	82	7	6
Thomas, Troy, Birmingham*	.292	120	391	68	114	155	24	1	5	53	9	4	6	0	96	1	68	16	15
Thurman, Gary, Memphis	.312	131	525	88	164	233	24	12	7	62	9	4	3	0	57	0	81	53	18
Tiburcio, Fredrick, Greenville*	.340	42	162	26	55	66	6	1	1	22	1	1	2	1	19	1	17	9	4
Tolentino, Jose, Huntsville*	.315	137	540	80	170	246	28	0	16	105	9	2	7	4	53	6	57	7	2
Tonucci, Norman, Knoxville	.223	111	382	44	85	153	17	0	17	58	4	2	4	2	47	0	117	2	3
Traen, Thomas, Jacksonville†	.400	14	5	0	2	4	0	1	0	0	0	0	0	0	1	0	1	0	1
Trautwein, John, Jacksonville	.000	12	1	0	0	0	0	0	0	0	0	0	0	0	0	0	1	0	0
Treadway, Andre, Greenville	.000	12	2	0	0	0	0	0	0	0	0	0	0	0	0	0	1	0	0
Trout, Jeffrey, Orlando†	.321	105	390	61	125	176	22	4	7	67	5	0	4	5	54	2	43	1	2
Tubbs, Gregory, Greenville	.269	144	536	95	144	194	21	7	5	56	7	10	3	3	107	2	74	31	22
Tumpane, Robert, Greenville*	.311	55	177	31	55	104	9	2	12	37	3	1	4	1	38	6	23	4	1
Venturini, Peter, Birmingham	.261	70	211	33	55	70	6	3	1	14	0	5	0	0	25	0	28	5	1
Vetsch, David, Orlando*	.250	111	336	50	84	138	15	3	11	40	5	0	2	2	50	0	90	2	3
Wallace, Timothy, Jacksonville	.196	19	56	7	11	15	1	0	1	4	0	2	0	2	7	0	12	0	1
Weinberger, Gary, Jacksonville*	.238	75	261	31	62	82	7	2	3	27	4	3	4	1	17	1	23	2	2
Weiss, Walter, Huntsville†	.250	46	160	19	40	44	2	1	0	13	2	1	1	2	11	0	39	5	1
Wiggins, Kevin, Orlando*	.095	10	21	3	2	2	0	0	0	0	0	0	0	0	3	0	6	0	0
Wilder, David, Huntsville	.301	126	445	91	134	202	23	6	11	85	4	4	3	7	100	2	104	22	8
Williams, Kenneth, Birmingham	.331	68	272	41	90	134	16	5	6	40	7	1	0	5	18	0	48	26	9
Wilson, Phillip, Orlando†	.293	129	526	88	154	200	12	8	6	42	6	9	3	9	43	1	77	24	15
Wilson, Allen, Greenville	.255	22	51	6	13	21	2	0	2	4	0	1	0	0	13	0	16	0	0
Winters, James, Birmingham	.247	66	223	32	55	84	13	2	4	31	2	2	1	1	33	0	27	2	2
Wishnevski, Michael, Chattanooga*	.245	130	461	80	113	191	21	3	17	72	5	0	6	3	84	1	137	7	0
Yastrzemski, Michael, Birmingham†	.285	124	494	76	141	202	21	2	12	73	5	5	7	2	43	1	55	8	2
Yost, Edgar, Greenville	.248	80	254	35	63	97	13	0	7	30	1	6	0	0	19	1	29	3	0
Young, Gerald, Columbus†	.280	136	539	101	151	216	30	4	9	62	7	2	8	1	67	5	57	54	27
Ziem, Stephen, Greenville	.000	31	1	0	0	0	0	0	0	0	0	0	0	0	0	0	0	0	0

The following pitchers, listed alphabetically by club, with games in parentheses, had no plate appearances, primarily through use of designated hitters:

BIRMINGHAM—Burroughs, Darren (24); Cole, Timothy (4); DeVincenzo, Richard (22); Hardy, John (35); Hickey, James (42); Johnson, John (13); Oswald, Steven (16); Pall, Donn (21); Pawlowski, John (23); Peterson, Adam (6); Potestio, Frank (7); Rasmussen, James (11); Reed, Kenneth (10); Thigpen, Robert (25); Walker, Kurt (30); White, David (50); Williams, Mark (13).

CHARLOTTE—Alicea, Miguel (51); Ballard, Jeffrey (10); Bell, Eric (18); Boudreau, James (26); Bowden, Stephen (3); Brown, Mark (27); Fowlkes, Alan (22); Harrington, John (11); Hoover, John (8); Householder, Brian (12); Kucharski, Joseph (26); Lavelle, William (23); Milacki, Robert (1); Oliveras, Francisco (33); Raczka, Michael (32); Rice, Richard (44); Rohan, Edward (1); Steirer, Ricky (5); Stranski, Scott (29); Wilson, Roger (7).

CHATTANOOGA—Baldrick, Robert (27); Bargerhuff, Brian (44); Bryant, James (16); Campbell, Michael (12); Evans, Michael (7); Gunnarsson, Robert (31); Hanson, Erik (3); Luecken, Richard (17); Martin, Victor (19); McDonald, Jeffrey (7); Mendek, William (22); Moore, Richard (27); Schneider, Paul (57); Taylor, Terry (27); Walker, James (13); Whitmer, Joseph (22).

COLUMBUS—Bombard, Richard (15); Cerefin, Michael (1); Dube, Gregory (3); Meads, David (16).

GREENVILLE—Aviles, Brian (1); Benedict, James (7); Cash, Johnny (6); Heise, Larry (31); Jones, Michael (1); Long, Robert (35); Mathews, Edward (2); Morris, David (5).

HUNTSVILLE—Beavers, Mark (7); Belcher, Timothy (9); Brake, Gregory (13); Burns, Todd (20); Cadaret, Gregory (28); Cox, John (18); Criswell, Brian (24); Hilton, Stan (19); Kyles, Stanley (24); Law, Joseph (8); Leonette, Mark (47); McDonald, Kirk (22); Rodriguez, Ricardo (9); Scherer, Douglas (54); Strong, Joseph (6); Tapani, Kevin (1); Whaley, Scott (51); Whitehurst, Walter (19).

JACKSONVILLE—Graves, Joseph (11); Williams, Mark (3).

KNOXVILLE—Alba, Gibson (8); Englund, Timothy (39); Gilliam, Keith (22); Gnacinski, Paul (14); Hogan, Michael (6); Howard, Dennis (25); Hudson, Anthony (23); Klawitter, Thomas (6); McLaughlin, Colin (31); Mesa, Jose (9); Moore, Gregory (28); Mumaw, Stephen (20); Musselman, Jeffrey (7); Peraza, Oswald (26); Segura, Jose (24); Shanks, William (3); Stottlemyre, Todd (18); Walsh, David (11); Wells, David (10); Yearout, Michael (3); Young, Clifford (31).

MEMPHIS—Benedict, James (29); Cato, Keefe (6); Crew, Kenneth (27); Daniel, Jimmy (28); Davis, John (41); George, Phillip (37); Goodin, Richard (22); Martinez, Arthur (2); McKelvey, Mitch (13); Mohr, Thomas (7); Morgan, Eugene (48); Nunez, Jose (13); Rodiles, Jose (33); Sanchez, Israel (28); Sparling, Donald (19).

ORLANDO—Bianchi, Ben (16); Budke, Todd (20); Clemons, Mark (20); Dominguez, Jose (11); Galloway, Troy (5); Gomez, Steven (52); Klink, Joseph (45); Klump, Kenneth (20); Romero, Ramon (30); Shade Michael (17); Smith, Robert (29); Sontag, Alan (26); Taylor, Jeffrey (16); Trudeau, Kevin (15).

GRAND SLAM HOME RUNS—J. Reynolds, Salcedo, 3 each; Cochrane, Dodd, Griffin, Jarrell, Steinbach, 2 each; Allen, Camelo, Coyle, Delgado, DeLosSantos, Denby, Ducey, Engram, Guerrero, Jackson, Lawrence, R. Martinez, Moreno, Myers, Nichols, O'Dell, Padget, Powell, Ray, Redfield, Seilheimer, Shaddy, Sherlock, B. Smith, Stark, Tolentino, Weinberger, Wilder, K. Williams, Wishnevski, 1 each.

AWARDED FIRST BASE ON CATCHER'S INTERFERENCE—Forrester 4 (Cecchini, Cummings, Duncan, Stark); T. Bell 2 (Stark 2); R. Martinez 2 (Sorce, Tejada); Ripken 2 (Colbert, Sorce); Wishnevski 2 (A. Morris, Tejada); Buss (A. Morris); Conklin (Stark); Holtz (Duncan); Karkovice (Cummings); Marquardt (Tejada); McGwire (Sorce); Rollin (D'Alessandro); Sliwinski (Sorce); P. Wilson (Amaya).

CLUB FIELDING

Club	Pct.	G.	PO.	A.	E.	DP.	PB.
Chattanooga	.973	143	3655	1456	141	118	23
Huntsville	.971	141	3636	1580	156	126	28
Greenville	.970	145	3709	1416	157	110	13
Charlotte	.968	144	3799	1457	172	125	22
Jacksonville	.968	145	3697	1349	167	113	20
Orlando	.967	143	3702	1430	175	135	15
Columbus	.966	140	3621	1544	181	134	25
Knoxville	.961	144	3780	1544	215	163	21
Birmingham	.959	143	3709	1382	215	132	15
Memphis	.959	144	3788	1390	224	129	12

INDIVIDUAL FIELDING

*Throws lefthanded.

FIRST BASEMAN

Player and Club	Pct.	G.	PO.	A.	E.	DP.
Afenir, Columbus	.800	2	4	0	1	0
Beamesderfer, Charlotte	.966	7	52	4	2	6
Bell, Memphis	1.000	1	1	2	0	0
Borders, Knoxville	1.000	1	4	0	0	0
Cecchini, Jacksonville	1.000	1	1	0	0	0
Conklin, Huntsville	1.000	6	41	4	0	5
Corey, Jacksonville	.968	4	28	2	1	1
Cummings, Chattanooga	1.000	4	29	0	0	1
Datz, Columbus	1.000	1	11	0	0	1
Daugherty, Jacksonville*	.983	123	1007	64	19	91
DeWillis, 2 Mem-2 Knox	1.000	4	18	2	0	1
Doerr, Charlotte	1.000	5	25	1	0	2
Duncan, Chattanooga	1.000	8	46	2	0	5
Falcone, Charlotte	.988	65	557	34	7	51
Forrester, Birmingham*	.986	133	1077	79	17	110
Fuentes, Columbus	.966	5	28	0	1	3
Funderburk, Orlando	1.000	3	26	2	0	4
Gergen, Charlotte	1.000	1	7	0	0	0
GRIFFIN, Greenville	.995	96	763	58	4	56
Guerrero, Greenville	.975	20	147	6	4	15
Hatcher, Greenville	1.000	1	1	0	0	1
Hoeksema, Memphis	1.000	3	21	0	0	2
Holmes, Orlando	1.000	1	1	0	0	0
Ingle, Greenville	.981	6	47	5	1	5
Joslyn, Memphis*	.800	1	4	0	1	0
Larkin, Orlando	.990	113	922	51	10	87
Lawrence, Jacksonville	.981	19	136	15	3	9
Longenecker, Memphis	.989	131	1039	46	12	101
Miller, Memphis	.857	1	6	0	1	1
Morhardt, Orlando*	.981	27	246	13	5	20
Moritz, Birmingham	.977	11	79	5	2	3
Morris, Memphis	.970	16	58	7	2	7
Mueller, Columbus*	.989	50	442	23	5	40
Myers, Chattanooga	.990	14	96	5	1	13
O'Dell, Columbus*	.988	94	785	58	10	73
Padget, Charlotte	.988	67	540	40	7	49
Paredes, Jacksonville	1.000	1	5	0	0	0
Redfield, Charlotte	.963	3	26	0	1	1
Seitzer, Memphis	.969	4	28	3	1	5
Sliwinski, Knoxville	.987	142	1236	75	17	139
Smith, Chattanooga	.994	127	1023	94	7	88
Steinbach, Huntsville	1.000	6	24	1	0	3
Thomas, Birmingham	1.000	4	6	0	0	1
Tolentino, Huntsville*	.994	134	1253	95	8	112
Tumpane, Greenville*	.987	37	216	20	3	19
Yastrzemski, Birmingham	1.000	1	3	0	0	0

SECOND BASEMEN

Player and Club	Pct.	G.	PO.	A.	E.	DP.
Aragon, Orlando	.981	35	74	85	3	23
Beamesderfer, Charlotte	1.000	1	1	0	0	0
Capello, Memphis	.667	2	0	2	1	1
Childress, Greenville	.972	61	132	148	8	32
Curry, Greenville	.959	54	103	132	10	21
David, Chattanooga	.970	108	225	296	16	71
Engram, Birmingham	.956	15	24	19	2	6
FALLS, Columbus	.973	98	230	276	14	57
Garrison, Knoxville	1.000	5	3	7	0	3
Gilcrease, Memphis	.965	30	64	74	5	18
Guinn, Huntsville	.971	27	55	78	4	23
Harris, Birmingham	.903	7	11	17	3	3
Ingle, Greenville	.961	38	70	79	6	11
Job, Columbus	1.000	10	14	24	0	6
Jones, Huntsville	.981	88	158	245	8	49
Larson, Chattanooga	.911	14	26	25	5	3
Lee, Knoxville	.972	20	45	58	3	20
Liriano, Knoxville	.965	112	231	288	19	75
Mabe, Memphis	.923	38	61	71	11	16
Miller, Memphis	.953	34	67	75	7	18
Moreno, Jacksonville	.970	112	265	279	17	65
Myers, Chattanooga	.975	28	57	62	3	8
Nix, Huntsville	.968	17	25	35	2	5
Norman, Jacksonville	.955	4	10	11	1	2
Palmer, Orlando	.972	119	280	315	17	68
Paredes, Jacksonville	.981	31	76	76	3	17
Parker, Columbus	.966	44	86	111	7	20
Pino, Birmingham	.953	101	233	211	22	62
Redfield, Charlotte	1.000	1	0	1	0	0
Rincones, Memphis	.967	53	98	140	8	32
Ripken, Charlotte	.968	141	305	395	23	79
Rossy, Charlotte	1.000	7	25	10	0	4
Salinas, Birmingham	.987	33	71	81	2	21
Tatis, Knoxville	.963	14	39	38	3	15
Thoma, Huntsville	.957	22	43	46	4	6
Trout, Orlando	1.000	2	0	5	0	0
Yastrzemski, Birmingham	1.000	1	2	0	0	0

THIRD BASEMEN

Player and Club	Pct.	G.	PO.	A.	E.	DP.
Amaya, Chattanooga	.500	3	1	0	1	0
Aragon, Orlando	1.000	20	7	17	0	0
Barnes, Jacksonville	1.000	1	1	0	0	0
Bishop, Knoxville	.958	6	6	17	1	2
Caminiti, Columbus	.924	135	105	299	33	34
Childress, Greenville	.938	41	30	75	7	5
Cochrane, Birmingham	.886	92	82	197	36	20
DeLosSantos, Memphis	.884	131	136	244	50	33
Diaz, Knoxville	1.000	1	0	1	0	0
Dodd, Charlotte	.899	43	26	90	13	8
Doerr, Charlotte	.938	12	13	17	2	3
Engram, Birmingham	.868	17	6	27	5	3
Escobar, Knoxville	.941	14	13	19	2	2
Gergen, Charlotte	.889	3	5	3	1	0
Gilcrease, Memphis	.975	15	6	33	1	4
Griffin, Greenville	.816	20	7	24	7	4
Hoeksema, Memphis	1.000	3	0	12	0	0
Holmes, Orlando	.930	41	38	55	7	8
Howard, Knoxville	1.000	2	0	3	0	0
Huson, Jacksonville	1.000	1	0	1	0	0
Ingle, Greenville	.955	9	5	16	1	2
Job, Columbus	1.000	2	0	1	0	0
Larkin, Orlando	.500	1	1	2	3	0
Liriano, Knoxville	.936	14	8	36	3	10
Lockwood, Charlotte	.870	10	7	13	3	2
Longenecker, Memphis	1.000	1	0	1	0	1
MARTINEZ, Chattanooga	.960	132	94	263	15	26
McGwire, Huntsville	.908	55	34	124	16	6
Miller, Memphis	1.000	1	0	3	0	0
Moritz, Birmingham	1.000	3	2	3	0	0
Myers, Chattanooga	.971	13	6	27	1	1
Nipper, Greenville	.920	82	44	139	16	6
Nix, Huntsville	.913	19	11	31	4	4
Padget, Charlotte	1.000	1	1	4	0	0
Palmer, Orlando	.962	12	6	19	1	0
Paredes, Jacksonville	.875	7	5	2	1	0
Parker, Columbus	.818	5	3	6	2	0
Redfield, Charlotte	.912	74	51	125	17	13
Reynolds, Jacksonville	.926	142	101	263	29	18
Rossy, Charlotte	1.000	11	7	9	0	2
Salinas, Birmingham	.918	42	27	74	9	4
Shaddy, Knoxville	.667	1	2	0	1	0
Tatis, Knoxville	1.000	2	0	1	0	0
Thoma, Huntsville	.945	79	62	180	14	14
Thomas, Birmingham	.667	1	1	1	1	0
Tonucci, Knoxville	.885	106	77	208	37	25
Trout, Orlando	.899	89	55	176	26	23

SHORTSTOPS

Player and Club	Pct.	G.	PO.	A.	E.	DP.
Allaire, Columbus	.933	119	166	349	37	58
Aragon, Orlando	.960	61	84	158	10	30
Balelo, Chattanooga	.971	57	78	186	8	34
Childress, Greenville	.950	12	7	31	2	4
Cochrane, Birmingham	1.000	1	0	4	0	1
Conklin, Huntsville	1.000	2	0	2	0	0
Diaz, Knoxville	1.000	6	7	14	0	3
Escobar, Knoxville	.895	5	4	13	2	7
Falls, Columbus	1.000	6	8	16	0	1
Gilcrease, Memphis	1.000	5	7	16	0	2
Guinn, Huntsville	.937	86	158	256	28	46
Harris, Birmingham	.930	36	53	93	11	25
Ingle, Greenville	.962	6	6	19	1	2
Jarrell, Memphis	.925	131	193	324	42	61
Jones, Chattanooga	.966	67	93	162	9	28
Lee, Knoxville	.944	21	25	59	5	10
Marquardt, Orlando	.950	79	124	221	18	47
McDougal, Orlando	.874	17	31	45	11	10
Myers, Chattanooga	.933	24	29	55	6	9
NORMAN, Jacksonville	.957	112	165	261	19	55
Paredes, Jacksonville	.937	40	46	103	10	17
Parker, Columbus	.926	22	29	58	7	8
Pino, Birmingham	.875	7	6	8	2	0
Redfield, Charlotte	.900	9	9	27	4	5
Rincones, Memphis	.978	14	22	23	1	2
Rios, Greenville	.943	133	190	377	34	67
Rossy, Charlotte	.955	53	84	129	10	26
Salinas, Birmingham	.910	43	78	94	17	19
Shaddy, Knoxville	.939	116	173	383	36	77
Smith, Charlotte	.961	89	129	236	15	44
Thoma, Huntsville	.984	13	27	35	1	7
Venturini, Birmingham	.955	69	100	174	13	29
Weiss, Huntsville	.951	46	72	142	11	36

OUTFIELDERS

Player and Club	Pct.	G.	PO.	A.	E.	DP.
Allen, Memphis	.958	71	181	3	8	1
Barnes, Jacksonville	1.000	1	4	0	0	0
Beamesderfer, Charlotte	1.000	6	6	1	0	0
Beauchamp, Knoxville	.983	47	113	2	2	0
Berroa, Knoxville	1.000	1	2	0	0	0
Bierley, Orlando	.980	129	229	11	5	2
Bogener, Charlotte*	.985	38	62	2	1	0
Buss, Chattanooga	.967	77	144	3	5	1
Camelo, Jacksonville*	.979	125	227	4	5	1
Campusano, Knoxville	.966	131	401	17	15	6
Cecchini, Jacksonville	.875	11	14	0	2	0
Childress, Greenville	1.000	23	38	3	0	0
Cimo, Charlotte	.975	61	112	5	3	0
Conklin, Huntsville	1.000	9	14	1	0	0
Corey, Jacksonville	.963	41	75	3	3	1
Coyle, Huntsville	.983	64	108	6	2	0
Delgado, Columbus	.955	53	103	3	5	0
Denby, Greenville	.981	88	147	9	3	1
Dodd, Charlotte	.958	15	23	0	1	0
Ducey, Knoxville	.970	86	186	10	6	6
Duncan, Chattanooga	1.000	4	6	0	0	0
Eccleston, Chattanooga*	.945	48	98	5	6	0
Engram, Birmingham	1.000	9	13	0	0	0
Farmar, Huntsville	.979	134	316	10	7	0
Fuentes, Columbus	.972	62	98	6	3	1
Funderburk, Orlando	1.000	6	11	0	0	0
Gergen, Charlotte	.958	11	20	3	1	0
Gilcrease, Memphis	.989	45	88	4	1	0
Granger, Charlotte	.962	61	127	1	5	0
Guerrero, Greenville	.333	2	1	0	2	0
Hall, Chattanooga*	.963	72	180	2	7	0
Hatcher, Greenville	.942	98	136	9	9	0
Hill, Knoxville	.919	137	230	9	21	3
Hollins, Chattanooga	.500	1	1	0	1	0
Holman, Greenville	1.000	23	47	1	0	0
Holmes, Orlando	1.000	5	4	0	0	0
Holtz, Charlotte	.975	127	349	5	9	0
Howe, Orlando	.909	9	18	2	2	0
Jackson, Memphis	.947	50	116	8	7	1
Johnson, Huntsville*	.959	48	91	3	4	2
Kinnard, Knoxville	.958	23	44	2	2	0
Kramer, Huntsville	.952	47	76	4	4	0
Lawrence, Jacksonville	1.000	11	10	0	0	0
Longenecker, Memphis	1.000	1	1	0	0	0
Loscalzo, Huntsville*	.933	13	14	0	1	0
Marte, Orlando*	.981	64	142	11	3	3
Martinez, Memphis*	.938	58	115	6	8	1
McNealy, Chattanooga*	.969	135	336	9	11	1
Mikulik, Columbus	.968	127	233	7	8	1
L. Miller, Charlotte	1.000	5	7	0	0	0
M. Miller, Memphis	1.000	5	13	0	0	0
Morhardt, Orlando*	1.000	20	43	1	0	0
Moritz, Birmingham	.930	33	64	2	5	1
Myers, Chattanooga	1.000	4	4	0	0	0
Nichols, Charlotte	.875	4	7	0	1	0
Nixon, Chattanooga	.875	4	7	0	1	0
D. Norman, Charlotte	1.000	11	14	2	0	0
N. Norman, Jacksonville	1.000	4	7	2	0	0
O'Dell, Columbus*	.962	18	21	4	1	1
Padget, Charlotte	1.000	7	12	0	0	0
Paredes, Jacksonville	.955	48	98	8	5	1
Powell, Jacksonville	.989	105	256	4	3	1
Pruitt, Birmingham	1.000	10	22	0	0	0
Ray, Columbus	.904	41	65	1	7	1
Redfield, Charlotte	1.000	2	5	0	0	0
Rollin, 49 Bir-22 Green	.942	71	153	8	10	0
Rossy, Charlotte	1.000	3	5	1	0	0
Salcedo, Charlotte	.957	115	210	12	10	2
Scheer, Birmingham	.957	12	21	1	1	0
Sferrazza, Jacksonville	.971	33	62	4	2	1
Snider, Memphis	.980	129	276	23	6	5
Tatis, Knoxville	.944	11	15	2	1	0
Taylor, Birmingham	.966	46	83	1	3	0
Thoma, Huntsville	1.000	3	2	0	0	0
Thomas, Birmingham	.979	108	220	9	5	0
Thurman, Memphis	.962	99	277	5	11	1
Tiburcio, Greenville*	.943	41	78	5	5	3
TUBBS, Greenville	.990	141	371	7	4	3
Tumpane, Greenville*	.980	28	46	2	1	1
Vetsch, Orlando	.989	92	177	8	2	5
Weinberger, Jacksonville*	.995	71	209	5	1	2
Wiggins, Orlando*	1.000	6	16	0	0	0
Wilder, Huntsville	.977	126	239	13	6	2
Williams, Birmingham	.961	63	192	3	8	1
Wilson, Orlando	.968	114	294	9	10	3
Winters, Birmingham	.965	48	110	1	4	0
Wishnevski, Chattanooga*	.957	101	185	13	9	5
Yastrzemski, Birmingham	.977	79	158	9	4	1
Young, Columbus	.963	136	317	22	13	3

CATCHERS

Player and Club	Pct.	G.	PO.	A.	E.	DP.	PB.
Afenir, Columbus	.976	86	488	38	13	9	18
Alcazar, Birmingham	1.000	2	10	3	0	0	1
Amaya, Chattanooga	.980	37	175	25	4	2	5
Beamesderfer, Charlotte	.988	37	206	33	3	4	8
Bell, 4 Chat-47 Mem	.971	51	276	24	9	3	6
Borders, Knoxville	.939	11	41	5	3	0	5
Cecchini, Jacksonville	.982	10	53	3	1	1	1
Colbert, Orlando	.980	31	166	33	4	4	2
Cormack, Chattanooga	1.000	5	46	3	0	0	1
Criswell, Greenville	1.000	4	28	4	0	1	0
Cummings, Chattanooga	.979	29	132	9	3	1	0
D'Alessandro, Greenville	.989	47	314	39	4	5	5
Datz, Columbus	.994	56	309	39	2	5	7
David, Huntsville	.986	37	132	10	2	0	6
DeWillis, 47 Mem-24 Knox	.982	71	349	41	7	8	4
Duncan, Chattanooga	.988	77	426	56	6	5	12
Foley, Birmingham	1.000	9	41	8	0	0	2
Goff, Memphis	1.000	4	1	1	0	0	0
Hollins, Chattanooga	1.000	2	7	0	0	0	3
Karkovice, Birmingham	.982	92	463	72	10	7	8
Leary, Jacksonville	1.000	1	2	1	0	0	1
Morris, Memphis	.980	79	366	34	8	6	3
Myers, Chattanooga	1.000	6	11	0	0	0	1
Nichols, Charlotte	.982	110	693	110	15	9	14
Padia, Orlando	.973	37	169	14	5	1	4
Rodriguez, Columbus	1.000	5	2	0	0	0	0
Rypien, Knoxville	1.000	5	11	0	0	0	1
Santovenia, Jacksonville	.991	18	97	14	1	0	3
Seilheimer, Birmingham	.993	50	259	16	2	3	4
Sherlock, Columbus	.957	4	19	3	1	2	0
Sorce, Orlando	.978	86	498	35	12	8	9
Stark, Knoxville	.979	118	665	73	16	12	15
Steinbach, Huntsville	.979	122	596	72	14	1	22
Tejada, Jacksonville	.971	106	576	65	19	5	13
Wallace, Jacksonville	.980	18	94	6	2	0	2
Wilson, Greenville	.958	20	108	6	5	0	0
YOST, Greenville	.993	79	502	54	4	3	8

PITCHERS

Player and Club	Pct.	G.	PO.	A.	E.	DP.
Alba, Knoxville*	1.000	8	0	1	0	0
Alicea, Charlotte	1.000	51	5	4	0	1
Alvarez, Greenville	.929	36	14	25	3	2
Baker, Columbus	1.000	21	2	2	0	0
Baldrick, Chattanooga*	.955	27	4	17	1	1
Ballard, Charlotte*	.778	10	0	7	2	0
Bargerhuff, Chattanooga	.909	44	2	8	1	0
Barrett, Jacksonville	.889	11	2	6	1	0
Beavers, Huntsville*	.833	7	0	5	1	0
Belcher, Huntsville	1.000	9	3	7	0	2
Bell, Charlotte*	.960	18	7	17	1	4
Benedict, 29 Mem-7 Green	1.000	36	5	13	0	1
Bettendorf, Columbus	.923	27	4	20	2	1
Bianchi, Orlando	1.000	16	2	16	0	0
Blankenship, Greenville	1.000	38	9	8	0	2
Bombard, Columbus	1.000	15	0	7	0	1
Boudreau, Charlotte*	1.000	26	2	7	0	0
Bowden, Charlotte	1.000	3	0	1	0	0
Brake, Huntsville*	1.000	13	2	7	0	1
Brown, Charlotte	1.000	27	3	3	0	1
Bryant, Chattanooga	1.000	16	6	3	0	0
Budke, Orlando	.957	20	6	16	1	0
Burns, Huntsville	.973	20	10	26	1	2
Burroughs, Birmingham*	1.000	24	2	7	0	0
Cadaret, Huntsville*	.963	28	8	18	1	1
Campbell, Chattanooga	1.000	12	3	6	0	0
T. Cash, Columbus	1.000	32	3	5	0	0
Cerefin, Columbus	.500	1	0	1	1	0
Childress, Greenville	1.000	3	1	1	0	1
Clemons, Orlando	1.000	20	3	15	0	1
Coffman, Greenville	1.000	8	3	6	0	0
Cole, Birmingham*	1.000	4	0	2	0	0
K. Cook, Jacksonville	.857	43	7	11	3	0
M. Cook, Columbus	1.000	21	3	21	0	0
Cox, Huntsville*	1.000	18	2	5	0	0
Crew, Memphis	.969	27	8	23	1	3
B. Criswell, Huntsville*	1.000	24	4	8	0	1
Cutshall, Jacksonville	1.000	18	3	11	0	0
Daniel, Memphis	.920	28	10	13	2	2
Davis, Memphis	1.000	41	6	14	0	0
DeVincenzo, Birmingham*	.933	22	4	10	1	1
Dominguez, Orlando	.750	11	1	2	1	0

PITCHERS—Continued

Player and Club	Pct.	G.	PO.	A.	E.	DP.
Dowless, Greenville	1.000	8	3	3	0	0
Dube, Columbus	1.000	3	2	1	0	0
Eichelberger, Greenville	1.000	18	0	8	0	0
Englund, Knoxville	.931	39	3	24	2	2
Evans, Chattanooga*	1.000	7	0	4	0	0
Fischer, Jacksonville	.818	11	2	7	2	3
Fowlkes, Charlotte	.900	22	3	6	1	2
Friedrich, Columbus	.958	29	8	15	1	0
Funk, Columbus*	1.000	44	0	6	0	0
Galloway, Orlando*	1.000	5	0	3	0	0
Gardner, Jacksonville	.962	29	6	19	1	0
George, Memphis*	.889	37	3	13	2	0
Gilliam, Knoxville*	1.000	22	4	13	0	1
Glavine, Greenville*	1.000	22	6	16	0	1
Gnacinski, 18 Green-14 Knox	.958	32	14	9	1	0
Gomez, Orlando	.900	52	2	7	1	1
Goodin, Memphis*	1.000	22	4	6	0	1
Graves, Jacksonville	1.000	11	0	1	0	0
J. Groves, Greenville	1.000	8	2	4	0	0
L. Groves, Jacksonville	1.000	31	1	6	0	1
Gunnarsson, Chattanooga*	.882	31	4	11	2	0
Hanson, Chattanooga	1.000	3	2	0	0	0
Hardy, Birmingham	1.000	34	2	10	0	2
Harrington, Charlotte	1.000	11	4	6	0	0
Heise, Greenville*	1.000	31	1	1	0	0
Hickey, Birmingham	.920	42	10	13	2	1
Hilton, Huntsville	.846	19	4	7	2	0
Holman, Jacksonville	.893	27	11	14	3	0
Hoover, Charlotte	.889	8	3	5	1	1
Householder, Charlotte*	1.000	12	2	5	0	0
D. Howard, Knoxville	.786	25	6	16	6	3
Hudson, Knoxville	.833	23	0	5	1	1
Ingle, Greenville	1.000	1	1	0	0	0
Johnson, Birmingham	.929	13	3	10	1	1
Jones, Greenville*	1.000	1	1	1	0	0
Kelley, Columbus	.959	29	16	31	2	2
Klawitter, Knoxville*	1.000	6	2	2	0	0
Klink, Orlando*	.909	45	1	9	1	0
Klump, Orlando	1.000	20	2	8	0	0
Kucharski, Charlotte	.875	26	7	14	3	1
Kyles, Huntsville	.938	24	5	10	1	1
Lavelle, Charlotte	1.000	23	6	3	0	2
Law, Huntsville	.900	8	3	6	1	0
Leonette, Huntsville	.833	47	9	11	4	2
Long, Greenville	.875	35	4	3	1	0
Luecken, Chattanooga	.955	17	5	16	1	2
Mallicoat, Columbus*	1.000	10	1	8	0	1
Martin, Chattanooga	.850	19	5	12	3	0
C. Mathews, Columbus	.947	41	3	15	1	3
J. McDonald, Chattanooga	1.000	7	0	1	0	0
K. McDonald, Huntsville	.949	22	13	24	2	3
McKay, Jacksonville	.897	25	12	14	3	1
McKelvey, Memphis	.727	13	1	7	3	0
McLaughlin, Knoxville	.875	31	2	5	1	0
McMurtry, Greenville	1.000	3	1	4	0	0
Meads, Columbus*	1.000	16	0	2	0	0
Mendek, Chattanooga*	1.000	22	1	7	0	0
Menendez, Birmingham	.818	17	6	12	4	0
Mesa, Knoxville	.875	9	4	3	1	0
Milacki, Charlotte	1.000	1	0	3	0	0
Mohr, Memphis*	1.000	7	0	3	0	0
G. Moore, Knoxville	1.000	28	1	9	0	0
R. Moore, Chattanooga	.818	27	3	6	2	1
Morgan, Memphis	.933	48	7	21	2	4
Morris, Greenville	.667	5	0	2	1	0
Mumaw, Knoxville*	.857	20	2	4	1	1
Musselman, Knoxville*	1.000	7	3	10	0	1
NICOMETI, Jacksonville*	1.000	41	7	22	0	2
Noble, Columbus*	1.000	12	3	20	0	1
Nunez, Memphis	.824	13	8	6	3	0
O'Dell, Columbus*	1.000	1	0	1	0	1
Oliveras, Charlotte	.857	33	11	13	4	3
Oswald, Birmingham*	.947	16	7	11	1	0
Pall, Birmingham	.867	21	4	9	2	0
Pawlowski, Birmingham	1.000	23	3	17	0	0
Peraza, Knoxville	.947	26	5	13	1	1
Peterson, Birmingham	.875	6	5	2	1	1
Potestio, Birmingham	1.000	7	1	1	0	0
Price, Jacksonville	.875	60	3	11	2	0
Raczka, Charlotte*	.933	32	6	22	2	1
Rasmussen, Birmingham	.800	11	2	2	1	0
Raymer, Jacksonville	.875	32	11	17	4	0
Reed, Birmingham	.875	10	1	6	1	0
Reynolds, Jacksonville	1.000	4	0	1	0	0
Rice, Charlotte	1.000	44	7	12	0	2
Rodiles, Memphis	1.000	33	6	16	0	1
Rodriguez, Huntsville	1.000	9	1	3	0	0
Rogers, Greenville	1.000	16	2	3	0	1
Romero, Orlando*	.706	30	2	10	5	0
Samuels, Columbus*	.905	38	4	15	2	0
Sanchez, Memphis*	.933	28	5	37	3	1
Scherer, Huntsville	.958	54	7	16	1	0
Schneider, Chattanooga	.950	57	5	14	1	1
Scott, Greenville	.917	15	4	7	1	0
Segura, Knoxville	.864	24	10	9	3	0
Shade, Orlando	.800	17	1	3	1	1
P. Smith, Greenville	1.000	24	7	9	0	0
R. Smith, Orlando	.872	29	10	24	5	1
Sontag, Orlando	.882	26	7	23	4	2
Sparling, Memphis	.923	19	5	7	1	0
Steirer, Charlotte	.800	5	3	5	2	1
Stottlemyre, Knoxville	1.000	18	6	19	0	1
Stranski, Charlotte	.917	29	2	9	1	0
Strasser, Columbus	.947	32	6	30	2	5
Stringfellow, Greenville*	.871	44	4	23	4	1
Strong, Huntsville	1.000	6	1	0	0	1
Tapani, Huntsville	1.000	1	0	1	0	0
J. Taylor, Orlando*	.667	16	0	2	1	1
T. Taylor, Chattanooga	.868	27	9	24	5	4
Thigpen, Birmingham	.875	25	9	19	4	2
Thoma, Huntsville	1.000	5	0	3	0	0
Traen, Jacksonville*	1.000	14	1	5	0	0
Trautwein, Jacksonville	.857	12	1	5	1	0
Treadway, Greenville	.917	12	3	8	1	0
Trudeau, Orlando	.875	15	3	4	1	0
J. Walker, Chattanooga	1.000	13	5	14	0	0
K. Walker, Birmingham	.909	30	3	7	1	0
Walsh, Knoxville*	1.000	11	3	3	0	0
Wells, Knoxville*	1.000	10	0	14	0	0
Whaley, Huntsville	.933	51	5	9	1	0
White, Birmingham	.808	50	6	15	5	0
Whitehurst, Huntsville	.967	19	8	21	1	3
Whitmer, Chattanooga	1.000	22	8	8	0	1
Williams, 13 Bir-3 Jack	.950	16	8	11	1	1
Wilson, Charlotte*	.667	7	0	2	1	0
Yearout, Knoxville*	1.000	3	0	2	0	0
Young, Knoxville*	.930	31	9	31	3	4
Ziem, Greenville	1.000	31	2	10	0	1

The following players do not have any recorded accepted chances at the positions indicated; therefore, are not listed in the fielding averages for those particular positions: Aviles, p; Beamesderfer, p; J. Cash, p; Cato, p; Childress, 1b; Conklin, p; T. Criswell, ss, p; Cummings, of; DeWillis, ss; Dodd, 1b; Falls, of; Gilcrease, p; Hatcher, ss; Hogan, p; Holmes, p; J. Howard, ss, p; Job, ss, p; R. Jones, 2b, of; Liriano, ss; MacFarlane, of; Marquardt, 1b; A. Martinez, p; E. Martinez, 2b; E. Mathews, p; Myers, p; Nix, of; Parker, c; J. Reynolds, of; Rohan, p; Rossy, 1b; Santovenia, of; Scheer, p; Shanks, p; B. Smith, 3b; Sorce, of, p; Steinbach, 3b; Tolentino, p; Venturini, 3b.

CLUB PITCHING

Club	ERA.	G.	CG.	ShO.	Sv.	IP.	H.	R.	ER.	HR.	HB.	BB.	Int. BB.	SO.	WP.	Bk.
Knoxville	3.93	144	10	9	33	1260.0	1273	704	550	99	31	546	18	811	66	14
Columbus	4.38	140	17	6	29	1207.0	1305	698	588	128	40	484	38	768	51	6
Memphis	4.40	144	10	7	30	1262.2	1305	752	618	128	36	608	19	780	50	14
Jacksonville	4.54	145	20	6	34	1232.1	1235	725	621	111	36	672	18	793	77	15
Orlando	4.65	143	27	4	29	1234.0	1314	758	637	130	35	671	12	786	51	15
Greenville	4.73	145	14	3	31	1236.1	1262	753	650	119	45	703	28	908	63	8
Charlotte	4.75	144	17	4	25	1266.1	1349	789	668	156	34	618	9	846	65	8
Birmingham	4.81	143	11	4	36	1236.1	1413	780	661	141	45	578	28	719	67	11
Huntsville	4.89	141	11	10	39	1212.0	1388	762	659	89	34	568	12	709	88	20
Chattanooga	5.07	143	23	9	32	1218.1	1415	765	687	103	34	513	29	805	63	13

PITCHERS' RECORDS

(Leading Qualifiers for Earned-Run Average Leadership—115 or More Innings)

*Throws lefthanded.

Pitcher—Club	W.	L.	Pct.	ERA.	G.	GS.	CG.	GF.	ShO.	Sv.	IP.	H.	R.	ER.	HR.	HB.	BB.	Int. BB.	SO.	WP.
Bell, Charlotte*	9	6	.600	3.05	18	18	6	0	1	0	129.2	109	49	44	7	1	66	0	104	5
White, Birmingham	11	3	.786	3.08	50	3	0	29	0	11	128.2	120	51	44	6	3	62	5	69	5

Pitcher—Club	W.	L.	Pct.	ERA.	G.	GS.	CG.	GF.	ShO.	Sv.	IP.	H.	R.	ER.	HR.	HB.	BB.	Int. BB.	SO.	WP.
Clemons, Orlando	11	5	.688	3.25	20	20	6	0	3	0	135.2	134	58	49	7	1	49	1	91	3
Glavine, Greenville*	11	6	.647	3.41	22	22	2	0	1	0	145.1	129	62	55	14	2	70	3	114	8
Strasser, Columbus	11	5	.688	3.46	32	22	3	2	1	0	164.0	180	75	63	16	10	43	2	87	2
Sanchez, Memphis*	13	7	.650	3.47	28	26	4	0	1	0	184.1	190	97	71	16	7	55	0	141	7
Alvarez, Greenville	11	6	.647	3.55	36	13	6	11	0	1	149.2	123	70	59	11	10	63	4	133	4
Stringfellow, Greenville*	7	8	.467	3.61	44	18	2	10	0	2	147.0	149	81	59	7	4	77	5	96	3
Kelley, Columbus	14	4	.778	3.63	29	29	8	0	3	0	193.1	196	92	78	20	4	35	0	126	3
Burns, Huntsville	7	7	.500	3.75	20	18	5	1	3	0	124.2	122	59	52	16	3	39	1	77	6

Departmental Leaders: G—Price, 60; W—Kelley, 14; L—Young, 14; Pct.—Campbell, .900; GS—Young, 31; CG—Kelley, 8; GF—Schneider, 51; ShO—Burns, Clemons, Kelley, 3; Sv.—Schneider, 24; IP—Young, 203.2; H—Young, 232; R—R. Smith, 123; ER—Raczka, 102; HR—Oliveras, Raczka, 27; HB—Thigpen, 11; BB—Holman, 122; IBB—T. Cash, 8; SO—T. Taylor, 164; WP—T. Taylor, 16.

(All Pitchers—Listed Alphabetically)

Pitcher—Club	W.	L.	Pct.	ERA.	G.	GS.	CG.	GF.	ShO.	Sv.	IP.	H.	R.	ER.	HR.	HB.	BB.	Int. BB.	SO.	WP.
Alba, Knoxville*	0	0	.000	3.72	8	0	0	7	0	1	9.2	6	5	4	0	2	6	0	11	0
Alicea, Charlotte	5	3	.625	3.81	51	1	0	24	0	4	87.1	108	45	37	11	1	20	1	47	3
Alvarez, Greenville	11	6	.647	3.55	36	13	6	11	0	1	149.2	123	70	59	11	10	63	4	133	4
Aviles, Greenville	0	0	.000	9.00	1	1	0	0	0	0	2.0	3	2	2	1	0	0	0	2	0
Baker, Columbus	2	5	.286	5.28	21	0	0	17	0	6	29.0	28	17	17	8	0	16	3	20	2
Baldrick, Chattanooga*	5	9	.357	5.29	27	20	4	2	0	0	129.1	160	85	76	6	1	54	0	65	0
Ballard, Charlotte*	5	2	.714	3.32	10	10	0	0	0	0	59.2	70	29	22	7	1	20	0	35	0
Bargerhuff, Chattanooga	3	6	.333	5.58	44	0	0	19	0	4	92.0	107	62	57	3	6	38	6	36	1
Barrett, Jacksonville	3	4	.429	4.50	11	9	3	0	0	0	60.0	51	30	30	6	1	28	2	31	3
Beamesderfer, Charlotte	0	0	.000	0.00	2	0	0	2	0	0	1.0	1	0	0	0	0	0	0	0	0
Beavers, Huntsville*	1	0	1.000	0.53	7	0	0	3	0	1	17.0	15	2	1	0	0	4	0	10	0
Belcher, Huntsville	2	5	.286	6.57	9	9	0	0	0	0	37.0	50	28	27	3	0	22	1	25	3
Bell, Charlotte*	9	6	.600	3.05	18	18	6	0	1	0	129.2	109	49	44	7	1	66	0	104	5
Benedict, 29 Mem-7 Green	2	3	.400	2.98	36	0	0	25	0	3	54.1	41	24	18	5	0	13	1	47	0
Bettendorf, Columbus	1	5	.167	3.82	27	6	0	6	0	2	73.0	76	42	31	7	2	36	4	47	2
Bianchi, Orlando	5	4	.556	4.88	16	16	2	0	0	0	101.1	97	68	55	11	2	65	1	58	5
Blankenship, Greenville	6	7	.462	4.90	38	13	0	8	0	2	123.0	132	78	67	13	3	84	2	83	5
Bombard, Columbus	2	4	.333	5.46	15	0	0	9	0	1	28.0	37	19	17	1	1	14	5	12	2
Boudreau, Charlotte*	4	2	.667	5.44	26	5	0	7	0	0	48.0	60	38	29	8	3	21	0	28	3
Bowden, Charlotte	0	1	.000	8.22	3	2	0	0	0	0	7.2	11	7	7	0	0	5	0	5	4
Brake, Huntsville*	2	3	.400	5.81	13	3	1	2	1	0	31.0	35	22	20	2	1	17	1	15	2
Brown, Charlotte	2	3	.400	3.97	27	0	0	21	0	2	45.1	45	23	20	6	1	20	1	32	0
Bryant, Chattanooga	2	2	.500	5.92	16	0	0	14	0	2	24.1	24	17	16	1	2	10	1	16	3
Budke, Orlando	7	10	.412	4.87	20	20	5	0	0	0	136.2	146	87	74	19	1	62	1	65	6
Burns, Huntsville	7	7	.500	3.75	20	18	5	1	3	0	124.2	122	59	52	16	3	39	1	77	6
Burroughs, Birmingham*	1	3	.250	7.64	24	3	0	15	0	3	35.1	53	33	30	3	2	21	2	23	2
Cadaret, Huntsville*	12	5	.706	5.41	28	28	1	0	0	0	141.1	166	106	85	6	1	98	0	113	15
Campbell, Chattanooga	9	1	.900	3.48	12	12	1	0	1	0	75.0	69	32	29	5	2	22	0	80	3
J. Cash, Greenville*	1	2	.333	6.33	6	5	0	0	0	0	27.0	38	20	19	3	0	13	1	16	1
T. Cash, Columbus	3	6	.333	3.15	32	0	0	27	0	12	45.2	54	20	16	0	2	17	8	23	1
Cato, Memphis	1	3	.250	6.06	6	6	0	0	0	0	32.2	45	27	22	6	1	7	0	24	2
Cerefin, Columbus	0	0	.000	7.20	1	1	0	0	0	0	5.0	10	8	4	0	0	4	0	3	0
Childress, Greenville	0	0	.000	0.00	3	0	0	2	0	0	2.0	1	0	0	0	0	3	0	0	0
Clemons, Orlando	11	5	.688	3.25	20	20	6	0	3	0	135.2	134	58	49	7	1	49	1	91	3
Coffman, Greenville	3	4	.429	4.44	8	8	0	0	0	0	48.2	43	24	24	4	4	30	0	43	6
Cole, Birmingham*	0	1	.000	12.60	4	1	0	2	0	0	5.0	3	7	7	2	0	10	0	4	0
Conklin, Huntsville	0	0	.000	9.00	1	0	0	1	0	0	1.0	1	1	1	0	0	0	0	1	0
K. Cook, Jacksonville	2	2	.500	4.88	43	0	0	17	0	1	66.1	76	44	36	8	3	43	0	27	8
M. Cook, Columbus	9	9	.500	5.28	21	21	0	0	0	0	105.2	121	70	62	19	1	35	0	71	5
Cox, Huntsville*	1	3	.250	11.49	18	4	0	3	0	1	31.1	49	41	40	6	0	38	0	14	3
Crew, Memphis	8	7	.533	4.77	27	16	1	5	0	2	120.2	124	74	64	15	6	72	2	95	3
B. Criswell, Huntsville*	3	3	.500	4.98	24	2	0	9	0	1	47.0	52	29	26	4	3	26	0	25	3
T. Criswell, Greenville	0	0	.000	40.50	1	0	0	0	0	0	0.2	4	3	3	1	0	1	0	0	1
Cutshall, Jacksonville	8	2	.800	3.20	18	18	0	0	0	0	112.1	93	43	40	3	5	61	1	88	7
Daniel, Memphis	9	13	.409	4.61	28	28	2	0	1	0	166.0	190	106	85	17	5	60	0	94	2
Davis, Memphis	6	6	.500	4.69	41	5	0	24	0	8	111.1	99	63	58	9	4	69	4	70	6
DeVincenzo, Birmingham*	4	2	.667	4.47	22	14	0	3	0	0	86.2	96	51	43	8	0	40	1	46	6
Dominguez, Orlando	0	1	.000	11.72	11	0	0	4	0	0	17.2	34	27	23	4	0	10	0	14	5
Dowless, Greenville	2	3	.400	4.26	8	6	2	0	1	0	44.1	50	21	21	7	0	11	0	28	0
Dube, Columbus	0	1	.000	12.66	3	3	0	0	0	0	10.2	19	16	15	2	1	12	0	5	4
Eichelberger, Greenville	3	3	.500	2.70	18	0	0	13	0	2	23.1	18	8	7	2	0	8	0	25	4
Englund, Knoxville	11	11	.500	4.07	39	20	1	11	0	4	170.1	171	99	77	16	2	41	4	108	7
Evans, Chattanooga*	1	0	1.000	4.26	7	0	0	2	0	0	6.1	11	9	3	0	0	3	1	5	1
Fischer, Jacksonville	5	2	.714	3.69	11	11	3	0	2	0	70.2	70	35	29	9	2	16	1	39	1
Fowlkes, Charlotte	2	2	.500	4.06	22	0	0	12	0	2	31.0	36	23	14	6	0	15	1	25	0
Friedrich, Columbus	8	9	.471	4.35	29	29	5	0	1	0	165.1	161	98	80	17	8	80	2	108	14
Funk, Columbus*	6	2	.750	2.66	44	0	0	19	0	6	64.1	50	23	19	9	2	30	4	58	2
Galloway, Orlando*	0	4	.000	7.17	5	5	0	0	0	0	21.1	27	21	17	3	5	14	0	7	1
Gardner, Jacksonville	10	11	.476	3.84	29	28	3	1	1	0	168.2	144	88	72	8	8	90	1	140	15
George, Memphis*	3	2	.600	4.10	37	2	0	17	0	2	83.1	92	46	38	9	2	34	4	33	5
Gilcrease, Memphis	0	0	.000	15.75	3	0	0	3	0	0	4.0	11	7	7	0	0	2	0	1	0
Gilliam, Knoxville*	4	2	.667	1.43	22	0	0	15	0	5	44.0	31	9	7	0	1	20	4	33	0
Glavine, Greenville*	11	6	.647	3.41	22	22	2	0	1	0	145.1	129	62	55	14	2	70	3	114	8
Gnacinski, 18 Green-14 Knox	4	3	.571	5.01	32	2	0	15	0	0	79.0	84	52	44	9	2	46	1	42	3
Gomez, Orlando	8	8	.500	3.58	52	0	0	40	0	12	75.1	87	38	30	9	3	40	3	50	2
Goodin, Memphis*	1	0	1.000	3.62	22	0	0	12	0	1	54.2	60	24	22	6	2	33	2	24	3
Graves, Jacksonville	0	1	.000	9.22	11	0	0	6	0	2	13.2	18	16	14	2	1	15	1	10	2
J. Groves, Greenville	0	4	.000	7.09	8	7	0	0	0	0	33.0	39	28	26	6	3	23	0	20	4
L. Groves, Jacksonville	5	3	.625	3.88	31	0	0	24	0	7	53.1	53	26	23	7	1	33	2	25	3
Gunnarsson, Chattanooga*	5	11	.313	4.90	31	17	3	6	1	0	136.0	174	83	74	10	1	46	2	78	7
Hanson, Chattanooga	0	0	.000	3.86	3	2	0	1	0	0	9.1	10	4	4	1	2	4	1	11	1
Hardy, Birmingham	6	6	.500	3.63	34	0	0	31	0	10	44.2	47	22	18	6	1	17	6	34	2
Harrington, Charlotte	3	3	.500	6.46	11	11	1	0	1	0	54.1	62	45	39	6	4	32	0	40	5
Heise, Greenville*	2	0	1.000	4.02	31	0	0	17	0	2	31.1	26	17	14	4	1	15	2	27	3
Hickey, Birmingham	6	5	.545	3.17	42	4	0	21	0	7	96.2	94	46	34	6	1	37	2	67	3
Hilton, Huntsville	6	4	.600	6.52	19	19	0	0	0	0	89.2	136	69	65	8	2	22	0	42	11
Hogan, Knoxville	0	1	.000	4.38	6	0	0	4	0	0	12.1	12	7	6	1	0	5	0	5	0

Pitcher—Club	W.	L.	Pct.	ERA.	G.	GS.	CG.	GF.	ShO.	Sv.	IP.	H.	R.	ER.	HR.	HB.	BB.	Int. BB.	SO.	WP.
Holman, Jacksonville	11	9	.550	5.14	27	27	3	0	0	0	157.2	146	111	90	16	0	122	1	118	10
Holmes, Orlando	0	0	.000	0.00	1	0	0	1	0	0	1.0	1	0	0	0	0	0	0	1	0
Hoover, Charlotte	2	4	.333	7.62	8	8	0	0	0	0	39.0	52	35	33	7	2	34	0	9	4
Householder, Charlotte*	1	4	.200	9.20	12	7	0	3	0	0	29.1	35	39	30	3	2	40	0	31	2
D. Howard, Knoxville	5	9	.357	3.85	25	17	2	3	1	0	117.0	136	59	50	7	5	39	1	45	8
J. Howard, Knoxville	0	0	.000	0.00	1	0	0	1	0	0	1.0	1	0	0	0	0	0	0	1	0
Hudson, Knoxville	2	1	.667	2.12	23	0	0	23	0	8	29.2	24	10	7	2	0	7	1	17	0
Ingle, Greenville	0	0	.000	9.00	1	0	0	0	0	0	1.0	2	1	1	0	0	0	0	0	0
Job, Columbus	0	0	.000	45.00	1	0	0	1	0	0	1.0	4	5	5	2	0	2	0	0	0
Johnson, Birmingham	4	5	.444	4.61	13	13	1	0	0	0	80.0	93	49	41	11	2	33	1	37	2
Jones, Greenville*	0	0	.000	0.00	1	0	0	0	0	0	2.0	4	1	0	0	0	0	0	0	0
Kelley, Columbus	14	4	.778	3.63	29	29	8	0	3	0	193.1	196	92	78	20	4	35	0	126	3
Klawitter, Knoxville*	0	1	.000	11.05	6	0	0	1	0	0	7.1	11	9	9	2	2	7	0	2	0
Klink, Orlando*	4	5	.444	2.51	45	0	0	41	0	11	68.0	59	24	19	5	2	37	1	63	1
Klump, Orlando	1	4	.200	6.01	20	9	0	4	0	1	76.1	93	61	51	7	6	58	1	37	1
Kucharski, Charlotte	10	8	.556	4.69	26	23	2	0	0	0	153.2	168	88	80	17	4	43	0	103	7
Kyles, Huntsville	6	1	.857	2.50	24	7	0	13	0	7	72.0	64	28	20	3	5	40	1	44	3
Lavelle, Charlotte	0	2	.000	4.50	23	0	0	10	0	2	38.0	41	21	19	7	1	17	0	26	2
Law, Huntsville	1	4	.200	8.24	8	8	0	0	0	0	39.1	55	37	36	4	0	28	0	12	1
Leonette, Huntsville	6	4	.600	3.78	47	0	0	26	0	11	100.0	108	56	42	7	2	33	2	41	6
Long, Greenville	5	1	.833	2.38	35	0	0	31	0	16	45.1	31	13	12	4	2	28	2	48	1
Luecken, Chattanooga	6	7	.462	5.28	17	14	4	0	2	0	88.2	106	57	52	10	2	42	3	55	2
Mallicoat, Columbus*	0	6	.000	4.81	10	10	1	0	0	0	58.0	61	38	31	2	3	45	1	52	2
Martin, Chattanooga	6	9	.400	6.46	19	19	4	0	0	0	107.1	136	86	77	21	3	46	1	70	9
Martinez, Memphis	0	1	.000	5.40	2	1	0	1	0	0	5.0	5	3	3	2	0	3	0	4	0
C. Mathews, Columbus	5	6	.455	6.01	41	4	0	20	0	0	85.1	121	70	57	6	0	33	5	42	6
E. Mathews, Greenville	0	0	.000	7.71	2	0	0	1	0	0	2.1	2	2	2	0	0	1	0	1	1
J. McDonald, Chattanooga	2	3	.400	7.30	7	6	0	1	0	0	24.2	31	24	20	2	0	22	0	21	1
K. McDonald, Huntsville	12	5	.706	4.68	22	22	2	0	1	0	136.2	165	88	71	5	2	58	0	63	3
McKay, Jacksonville	7	10	.412	4.16	25	25	4	0	1	0	151.1	161	87	70	19	3	59	0	80	7
McKelvey, Memphis	4	5	.444	4.15	13	13	1	0	1	0	84.2	75	49	39	8	2	42	0	57	2
McLaughlin, Knoxville	2	1	.667	3.20	31	0	0	21	0	8	59.0	49	26	21	4	1	21	0	51	6
McMurtry, Greenville	1	1	.500	6.00	3	3	0	0	0	0	15.0	13	10	10	2	0	9	0	12	1
Meads, Columbus*	1	1	.500	4.43	16	0	0	5	0	2	22.1	22	11	11	3	1	13	1	26	0
Mendek, Chattanooga*	0	4	.000	8.23	22	0	0	8	0	1	27.1	36	25	25	4	0	14	2	25	5
Menendez, Birmingham	7	8	.467	5.70	17	17	0	0	0	0	96.1	132	71	61	17	7	50	0	52	14
Mesa, Knoxville	2	2	.500	4.35	9	8	2	1	1	0	41.1	40	32	20	6	2	23	0	30	5
Milacki, Charlotte	0	1	.000	6.75	1	1	0	0	0	0	5.1	7	4	4	0	0	4	0	6	2
Mohr, Memphis*	0	2	.000	9.00	7	1	0	2	0	1	15.0	17	16	15	3	0	17	0	10	0
G. Moore, Knoxville	5	3	.625	3.80	28	0	0	13	0	2	66.1	73	40	28	7	1	19	1	45	6
R. Moore, Chattanooga	3	4	.429	5.45	27	4	0	9	0	1	74.1	101	49	45	7	1	25	4	29	3
Morgan, Memphis	8	5	.615	2.51	48	0	0	39	0	11	82.1	75	29	23	6	2	30	3	52	9
Morris, Greenville	0	1	.000	10.38	5	1	0	0	0	0	13.0	21	16	15	2	1	8	0	3	0
Mumaw, Knoxville*	3	2	.600	4.82	20	0	0	10	0	1	28.0	41	21	15	2	1	16	3	19	1
Musselman, Knoxville*	5	1	.833	2.83	7	7	1	0	1	0	41.1	33	17	13	0	0	25	0	38	3
Myers, Chattanooga	0	0	.000	0.00	1	0	0	1	0	0	2.2	3	0	0	0	0	1	0	0	0
Nicometi, Jacksonville*	2	4	.333	4.33	41	1	0	13	0	2	68.2	80	36	33	6	2	34	2	52	5
Noble, Columbus	6	4	.600	4.52	12	12	0	0	0	0	77.2	86	43	39	7	2	22	0	32	2
Nunez, Memphis	2	6	.250	5.36	13	11	0	2	0	1	48.2	52	43	29	4	1	51	0	36	5
O'Dell, Columbus*	0	0	.000	18.00	1	0	0	1	0	0	1.0	3	2	2	0	0	1	0	0	0
Oliveras, Charlotte	12	9	.571	4.18	33	25	5	3	1	0	194.0	185	112	90	27	5	71	1	127	7
Oswald, Birmingham*	5	4	.556	7.64	16	12	2	1	0	0	68.1	106	64	58	9	5	27	1	36	5
Pall, Birmingham	3	4	.429	4.44	21	9	0	6	0	1	73.0	77	38	36	9	2	27	3	41	5
Pawlowski, Birmingham	6	4	.600	4.91	23	16	0	1	0	0	106.1	111	67	58	15	3	47	2	58	4
Peraza, Knoxville	7	4	.636	4.19	26	16	0	6	0	2	107.1	101	58	50	7	3	54	1	80	2
Peterson, Birmingham	1	3	.250	4.18	6	5	2	0	0	0	32.1	34	16	15	8	0	16	1	21	0
Potestio, Birmingham	0	1	.000	7.71	7	2	0	3	0	0	21.0	27	22	18	3	2	21	0	8	2
Price, Jacksonville	8	6	.571	3.07	60	0	0	47	0	20	93.2	87	36	32	4	2	28	4	63	2
Raczka, Charlotte*	8	7	.533	5.92	32	26	3	3	1	1	155.0	170	114	102	27	3	92	1	107	7
Rasmussen, Birmingham	4	4	.500	3.81	11	9	1	0	0	0	56.2	48	28	24	7	1	32	0	48	3
Raymer, Jacksonville	9	9	.500	6.10	32	21	3	3	0	0	138.2	158	108	94	13	2	86	1	67	10
Reed, Birmingham	1	3	.250	7.47	10	7	0	1	0	0	37.1	55	36	31	6	0	34	1	21	4
Reynolds, Jacksonville	0	0	.000	4.50	4	0	0	4	0	0	4.0	7	2	2	0	1	2	0	2	0
Rice, Charlotte	4	5	.444	4.77	44	1	0	13	0	4	111.1	100	65	59	5	3	65	0	71	7
Rodiles, Memphis	6	12	.333	5.70	33	17	1	7	0	1	132.2	145	96	84	12	1	86	1	68	2
Rodriguez, Huntsville	0	0	.000	5.06	9	0	0	7	0	3	16.0	17	11	9	2	0	7	2	14	2
Rogers, Greenville	3	1	.750	7.52	16	1	0	6	0	0	32.1	48	29	27	4	0	17	0	25	0
Rohan, Charlotte	0	1	.000	9.00	1	1	0	0	0	0	4.0	4	4	4	0	1	2	0	0	0
Romero, Orlando*	8	3	.727	5.50	30	7	0	11	0	1	75.1	78	55	46	11	2	64	2	76	5
Samuels, Columbus*	2	3	.400	5.10	38	3	0	16	0	0	77.2	76	49	44	9	3	46	3	56	4
Sanchez, Memphis*	13	7	.650	3.47	28	26	4	0	1	0	184.1	190	97	71	16	7	55	0	141	7
Scheer, Birmingham	0	0	.000	0.00	1	0	0	0	0	0	0.0	0	4	4	0	0	4	0	0	0
Scherer, Huntsville	2	8	.200	4.59	54	0	0	38	0	11	84.1	101	50	43	5	2	33	1	61	14
Schneider, Chattanooga	3	3	.500	3.42	57	1	0	51	0	24	84.1	79	35	32	4	3	48	4	63	8
Scott, Greenville	2	7	.222	7.87	15	14	2	0	0	0	66.1	69	62	58	6	3	81	0	50	8
Segura, Knoxville	4	7	.364	4.22	24	17	1	3	0	2	106.2	101	72	50	7	6	72	1	55	11
Shade, Orlando	1	1	.500	2.68	17	0	0	6	0	2	43.2	44	17	13	2	1	28	1	36	0
Shanks, Knoxville	1	0	1.000	0.00	3	0	0	0	0	0	6.2	5	0	0	0	0	2	0	1	0
P. Smith, Greenville	1	8	.111	5.85	24	19	0	1	0	0	104.2	117	88	68	11	4	78	0	64	4
R. Smith, Orlando	11	11	.500	4.78	29	29	6	0	0	0	190.0	204	123	101	21	3	84	0	127	8
Sontag, Orlando	9	12	.429	4.84	26	26	7	0	0	0	171.0	188	101	92	17	6	85	1	81	6
Sorce, Orlando	0	0	.000	2.25	2	0	0	2	0	0	4.0	2	1	1	1	0	1	0	4	0
Sparling, Memphis	7	4	.636	4.63	19	18	1	1	0	0	93.1	95	55	48	11	3	39	2	35	4
Steirer, Charlotte	0	3	.000	7.59	5	5	0	0	0	0	21.1	33	26	18	6	1	16	0	11	3
Stottlemyre, Knoxville	8	7	.533	4.18	18	18	1	0	0	0	99.0	93	56	46	5	1	49	1	81	4
Stranski, Charlotte	4	5	.444	2.36	29	0	0	26	0	10	42.0	42	13	11	3	1	28	3	29	3
Strasser, Columbus	11	5	.688	3.46	32	22	3	2	1	0	164.0	180	75	63	16	10	43	2	87	2
Stringfellow, Greenville*	7	8	.467	3.61	44	18	2	10	0	2	147.0	149	81	59	7	4	77	5	96	3
Strong, Huntsville	1	1	.500	5.40	6	0	0	2	0	0	8.1	8	5	5	3	0	7	0	5	0
Tapani, Huntsville	1	0	1.000	6.00	1	1	0	0	0	0	6.0	8	4	4	0	0	1	0	2	0
J. Taylor, Orlando*	0	1	.000	4.50	16	1	0	4	0	0	46.0	44	29	23	5	1	43	0	37	5
T. Taylor, Chattanooga	12	8	.600	4.02	27	27	4	0	1	0	177.0	164	88	79	13	6	90	1	164	16
Thigpen, Birmingham	8	11	.421	4.68	25	25	5	0	0	0	159.2	182	97	83	12	11	54	1	90	4

Pitcher—Club	W.	L.	Pct.	ERA.	G.	GS.	CG.	GF.	ShO.	Sv.	IP.	H.	R.	ER.	HR.	HB.	BB.	Int. BB.	SO.	WP.
Thoma, Huntsville	0	0	.000	3.86	5	0	0	5	0	0	4.2	4	2	2	1	1	0	0	2	1
Tolentino, Huntsville*	0	0	.000	5.40	2	0	0	2	0	0	1.2	4	1	1	0	0	1	0	1	0
Traen, Jacksonville*	3	3	.500	6.85	14	5	1	3	0	1	44.2	56	38	34	7	2	26	0	35	1
Trautwein, Jacksonville	2	1	.667	7.04	12	0	0	6	0	1	23.0	24	19	18	2	3	25	2	14	3
Treadway, Greenville	3	3	.500	6.27	12	9	0	0	0	0	47.1	66	37	33	4	2	16	2	29	2
Trudeau, Orlando	5	4	.556	5.86	15	10	1	3	0	2	70.2	76	48	46	8	2	31	0	39	3
J. Walker, Chattanooga	5	4	.556	3.87	13	13	3	0	0	0	83.2	102	45	36	6	1	19	1	43	1
K. Walker, Birmingham	3	5	.375	5.16	30	3	0	14	0	3	68.0	89	48	39	7	4	29	2	54	4
Walsh, Knoxville*	2	0	1.000	5.65	11	2	0	4	0	0	28.2	30	21	18	3	0	32	0	15	4
Wells, Knoxville*	1	3	.250	4.05	10	7	1	2	0	0	40.0	42	24	18	1	1	18	0	32	4
Whaley, Huntsville	6	5	.545	4.18	51	1	0	18	0	4	118.1	114	57	55	10	5	48	0	88	3
White, Birmingham	11	3	.786	3.08	50	3	0	29	0	11	128.2	120	51	44	6	3	62	5	69	5
Whitehurst, Huntsville	9	5	.643	4.64	19	19	2	0	0	0	104.2	114	66	54	4	7	46	3	54	12
Whitmer, Chattanooga	2	7	.222	7.46	22	8	0	6	0	0	76.0	102	64	63	10	4	29	2	44	2
Williams, 13 Birm-3 Jack	0	2	.000	4.89	16	0	0	6	0	1	46.0	57	36	25	7	1	21	0	12	2
Wilson, Charlotte*	0	2	.000	6.75	7	0	0	3	0	0	9.1	10	9	7	3	0	7	1	10	1
Yearout, Knoxville*	0	1	.000	7.11	3	0	0	2	0	0	6.1	7	5	5	0	0	3	0	3	0
Young, Knoxville*	12	14	.462	3.89	31	31	1	0	0	0	203.2	232	111	88	25	2	71	1	121	3
Ziem, Greenville	7	2	.778	4.70	31	4	0	19	0	6	74.2	73	44	39	7	5	32	6	54	6

BALKS—R. Smith, 7; Young, 5; Martin, K. McDonald, Rodiles, White, 4 each; Bianchi, Burns, Nicometi, Whitehurst, 3 each; M. Cook, Cox, Crew, Cutshall, Gunnarsson, Holman, Householder, Mendek, Pall, Rice, Samuels, Scherer, P. Smith, Sontag, Sparling, Stottlemyre, Stringfellow, T. Taylor, Thigpen, Walsh, Whaley, 2 each; Alicea, Baldrick, Ballard, Barrett, Blankenship, Budke, Cato, Clemons, Daniel, Eichelberger, Fischer, Gardner, Graves, L. Groves, Hanson, Hilton, D. Howard, Kucharski, Kyles, Law, C. Mathews, J. McDonald, Mohr, Morgan, Musselman, Nunez, Oliveras, Oswald, Pawlowski, Peraza, Price, Rasmussen, Rodriguez, Sanchez, Scott, Segura, Strasser, J. Taylor, Traen, Trautwein, Yearout, Ziem, 1 each.

COMBINATION SHUTOUTS—DeVincenzo-Hickey, Johnson-White-Hardy, Thigpen-White, Rasmussen-Hickey, Birmingham; Luecken-Gunnarsson, Campbell-Gunnarsson, Moore-Schneider, Hanson-Bargerhuff, Chattanooga; Strasser-Baker, Columbus; Blankenship-Benedict-Heise, Greenville; Cox-Whaley, Law-Rodriguez, Kyles-Scherer-Tolentino, Hilton-Scherer, Cadaret-Kyles, Huntsville; Gardner-Price, Nicometi-Groves, Jacksonville; Peraza-Walsh, Young-Gilliam, Stottlemyre-McLaughlin, Stottlemyre-Mumaw, Peraza-Segura-Alba, Stottlemyre-Peraza-Shanks-Englund, Knoxville; Crew-Mohr, Sparling-Rodiles-Morgan, George-Nunez, Sanchez-Morgan, Memphis; Sontag-Klink, Orlando.

NO-HIT GAMES—McKay, Jacksonville, tied Chattanooga, 0-0, June 8; McKelvey, Memphis, defeated Columbus, 16-0, July 2.

Texas League

CLASS AA

Leading Batter
STEVE STANICEK
El Paso

League President
CARL SAWATSKI

Leading Pitcher
GEORGE FERRAN
Shreveport

CHAMPIONSHIP WINNERS IN PREVIOUS YEARS

Year	Club	Pct.
1888	Dallas	.671
1889	Houston	.551
1890	Galveston	.705
1892	Houston	.741
	Houston	.613
1895	Dallas	.754
	Fort Worth*	.750
1896	Fort Worth	.757
	Houston*	.679
	Galveston	.548
1897	San Antonio†	.657
	Galveston†	.717
1898	League disbanded.	
1899	Galveston	.632
	Galveston	.762
1900-01	Did not operate.	
1902	Corsicana	.866
	Corsicana	.682
1903	Paris-Waco	.615
	Dallas*	.648
1904	Corsicana*	.615
	Fort Worth	.800
1905	Fort Worth	.545
1906	Fort Worth	.677
	Cleburne x	.609
1907	Austin	.629
1908	San Antonio	.664
1909	Houston	.601
1910	Dallas†	.586
	Houston†	.586
1911	Austin	.575
1912	Houston	.626
1913	Houston	.620
1914	Houston†	.671
	Waco†	.671
1915	Waco	.592
1916	Waco	.587
1917	Dallas	.600
1918	Dallas	.584
1919	Shreveport*	.677
	Fort Worth	.651
1920	Fort Worth	.703
	Fort Worth	.750
1921	Fort Worth	.691
	Fort Worth	.662
1922	Fort Worth	.694
	Fort Worth	.711
1923	Fort Worth	.632
1924	Fort Worth	.689
	Fort Worth	.763
1925	Fort Worth	.711
	Fort Worth y	.653

Year	Club	Pct.
1926	Dallas	.574
1927	Wichita Falls	.654
1928	Houston*	.679
	Wichita Falls	.731
1929	Dallas*	.588
	Wichita Falls	.620
1930	Wichita Falls	.697
	Fort Worth*	.632
1931	Houston a	.625
	Houston	.734
1932	Beaumont*	.640
	Dallas	.727
1933	Houston	.623
	San Antonio (4th)§	.523
1934	Galveston‡	.579
1935	Oklahoma City‡	.590
1936	Dallas	.604
	Tulsa (3rd)§	.519
1937	Oklahoma City	.635
	Fort Worth (3rd)§	.535
1938	Beaumont	.635
1939	Houston	.606
	Fort Worth (4th)§	.540
1940	Houston‡	.652
1941	Houston	.673
	Dallas (4th)§	.519
1942	Beaumont	.605
	Shreveport (2nd)§	.576
1943-44-45	Did not operate.	
1946	Fort Worth	.656
	Dallas (2nd)§	.591
1947	Houston‡	.623
1948	Fort Worth‡	.601
1949	Fort Worth	.649
	Tulsa (2nd)§	.584
1950	Beaumont	.595
	San Antonio (4th)§	.513
1951	Houston‡	.619
1952	Dallas	.571
	Shreveport (3rd)§	.522
1953	Dallas‡	.571
1954	Shreveport	.559
	Houston (2nd)§	.553
1955	Dallas	.581
	Shreveport (3rd)§	.540
1956	Houston‡	.623
1957	Dallas	.662
	Houston (2nd)§	.630
1958	Fort Worth	.582
	Cor. Christi (3rd)§	.507
1959	Victoria	.589
	Austin (2nd)§	.548

Year	Club	Pct.
1960	Rio Grande Valley	.590
	Tulsa (3rd)	.528
1961	Amarillo	.643
	San Antonio (3rd)§	.532
1962	El Paso	.571
	Tulsa (2nd)§	.550
1963	San Antonio	.564
	Tulsa (3rd)§	.529
1964	San Antonio‡	.607
1965	Tulsa	.574
	Albuquerque b	.550
1966	Arkansas	.579
1967	Albuquerque	.557
1968	Arkansas	.586
	El Paso b	.562
1969	Amarillo	.593
	Memphis b	.504
1970	Albuquerque a	.615
	Memphis	.507
1971	Did not operate as league—clubs were members of Dixie Association.	
1972	Alexandria	.600
	El Paso b	.557
1973	San Antonio	.590
	Memphis b	.558
1974	Victoria b	.581
	El Paso	.555
1975	Lafayette c	.558
	Midland c	.604
1976	Amarillo b	.600
	Shreveport	.515
1977	El Paso	.600
	Arkansas d	.485
1978	El Paso d	.593
	Jackson	.567
1979	Arkansas d	.571
	Midland	.563
1980	Arkansas d	.596
	San Antonio	.544
1981	San Antonio	.571
	Jackson d	.507
1982	El Paso	.559
	Tulsa d	.515
1983	Jackson	.507
	Beaumont d	.500
1984	Beaumont	.654
	Jackson d	.610
1985	El Paso	.632
	Jackson d	.537

*Won split-season playoff. †No playoff for title. ‡Finished first and won four-club playoff. §Won four-club playoff. xTitle to Cleburne by default. yTied with Dallas in second half and won playoff for championship. zFort Worth disbanded. aTied with Beaumont at end of first half and won title in best-of-five series played as part of second half schedule. bLeague divided into Eastern, Western divisions; won two-team playoff. cLeague divided into Eastern, Western divisions; declared co-champions when playoffs were not completed. dLeague divided into Eastern and Western divisions and played split-season; won playoffs. NOTE—Championship awarded to winner of four-team playoff, 1933-51; first-place team and playoff winner co-champions, 1952-64.

STANDING OF CLUBS AT CLOSE OF FIRST HALF, JUNE 17

EASTERN DIVISION

Club	W.	L.	T.	Pct.	G.B.
Jackson (Mets)	38	27	1	.585	....
Arkansas (Cardinals)	35	28	1	.556	2
Shreveport (Giants)	33	32	0	.508	5
Tulsa (Rangers)	24	40	0	.375	13½

WESTERN DIVISION

Club	W.	L.	T.	Pct.	G.B.
El Paso (Brewers)	37	29	0	.561	....
Midland (Angels)	35	30	0	.538	1½
Beaumont (Padres)	30	38	0	.441	8
San Antonio (Dodgers)	29	37	0	.439	8

STANDING OF CLUBS AT CLOSE OF SECOND HALF, AUGUST 30

EASTERN DIVISION

Club	W.	L.	T.	Pct.	G.B.
Shreveport (Giants)	47	24	0	.662	....
Jackson (Mets)	34	36	0	.486	12½
Arkansas (Cardinals)	32	39	0	.451	15
Tulsa (Rangers)	25	45	0	.357	21½

WESTERN DIVISION

Club	W.	L.	T.	Pct.	G.B.
El Paso (Brewers)	48	21	0	.696	....
San Antonio (Dodgers)	35	34	0	.507	13
Beaumont (Padres)	30	38	0	.441	17½
Midland (Angels)	27	41	0	.397	20½

COMPOSITE STANDING OF CLUBS AT CLOSE OF SEASON, AUGUST 30

Club	ElP.	Shrv.	Jax.	Ark.	S.A.	Mid.	Beau.	Tul.	W.	L.	T.	Pct.	G.B.
El Paso (Brewers)	....	6	6	6	20	19	22	6	85	50	0	.630	....
Shreveport (Giants)	4	....	20	15	4	7	6	24	80	56	0	.588	5½
Jackson (Mets)	4	12	....	17	8	6	6	19	72	63	1	.533	13
Arkansas (Cardinals)	4	17	15	....	2	4	5	20	67	67	1	.500	17½
San Antonio (Dodgers)	12	6	1	8	....	16	15	6	64	71	0	.474	21
Midland (Angels)	13	3	4	4	16	....	17	5	62	71	0	.466	22
Beaumont (Padres)	10	4	4	5	17	15	....	5	60	76	0	.441	25½
Tulsa (Rangers)	3	8	13	12	4	4	5	....	49	85	0	.366	35½

Arkansas club represented Little Rock, Ark.

Major league affiliations in parentheses.

Playoffs—Jackson defeated Shreveport, two games to one; El Paso defeated Jackson, four games to none, to win league championship.

Regular-Season Attendance—Arkansas, 222,163; Beaumont, 101,060; El Paso, 210,261; Jackson, 118,894; Midland, 129,674; San Antonio, 122,261; Shreveport, 183,560; Tulsa, 162,529. Total—1,250,402. Playoffs, 9,384. All-Star Game, 4,596.

Managers—Arkansas, Jim Riggleman; Beaumont, Steve Smith; El Paso, Duffy Dyer; Jackson, Mike Cubbage; Midland, Joe Maddon; San Antonio, Gary LaRocque; Shreveport, Wendell Kim; Tulsa, Bill Stearns.

All-Star Team—1B—Steve Stanicek, El Paso; 2B—Keith Miller, Jackson; 3B—Tracy Woodson, San Antonio; SS—Kevin Elster, Jackson; OF—Alan Cartwright, El Paso; Mike Devereaux, San Antonio; Shane Mack, Beaumont; C—Charlie O'Brien, El Paso; Mackey Sasser, Shreveport; DH—Kevin King, Midland; P—Charlie Corbell, Shreveport; George Ferran, Shreveport; Shawn Hillegas, San Antonio; Jeff Innis, Jackson; Dan Scarpetta, El Paso; Most Valuable Player—Steve Stanicek, Jackson; Most Valuable Pitcher—George Ferran, Shreveport; Manager of the Year—Wendell Kim, Shreveport.

(Compiled by Howe News Bureau, Boston, Mass.)

CLUB BATTING

Club	Pct.	G.	AB.	R.	OR.	H.	TB.	2B.	3B.	HR.	RBI.	GW.	SH.	SF.	HP.	BB.	Int. BB.	SO.	SB.	CS.	LOB.
El Paso	.302	135	4648	908	716	1405	2162	271	27	144	828	78	19	59	31	688	33	702	87	34	1080
Midland	.294	133	4587	779	766	1349	2059	225	19	149	708	56	19	54	28	479	17	765	106	45	956
Jackson	.262	136	4433	679	628	1163	1687	205	38	81	593	66	53	46	44	569	28	748	100	58	995
Beaumont	.262	136	4639	585	722	1217	1719	222	35	70	514	57	27	38	38	429	24	766	95	73	975
San Antonio	.262	135	4532	577	638	1188	1631	197	27	64	514	60	39	38	27	413	42	624	101	52	922
Arkansas	.260	135	4231	552	573	1101	1554	215	26	62	495	61	54	38	27	421	23	670	148	60	879
Tulsa	.253	134	4326	550	653	1093	1571	191	34	73	499	44	36	26	30	508	15	778	191	89	932
Shreveport	.251	136	4394	589	523	1102	1627	230	41	71	538	72	64	31	34	554	40	822	71	55	1000

INDIVIDUAL BATTING

(Leading Qualifiers for Batting Championship—367 or More Plate Appearances)

*Bats lefthanded. †Switch-hitter.

Player and Club	Pct.	G.	AB.	R.	H.	TB.	2B.	3B.	HR.	RBI.	GW.	SH.	SF.	HP.	BB.	Int. BB.	SO.	SB.	CS.
Stanicek, Stephen, El Paso	.343	127	487	116	167	284	40	1	25	93	15	1	1	5	88	2	70	6	2
Randall, James, Midland†	.331	123	468	90	155	248	23	2	22	93	10	0	9	2	69	6	80	6	6
Miller, Keith, Jackson	.329	94	353	80	116	162	23	4	5	36	0	2	0	7	62	1	55	28	5
O'Brien, Charles, El Paso	.324	92	336	72	109	180	20	3	15	75	6	1	6	6	50	0	30	0	0
Freeman, Lavell, El Paso*	.322	128	515	101	166	249	31	5	14	91	9	2	3	3	59	7	89	15	6
Cartwright, Alan, El Paso*	.321	118	467	90	150	241	27	5	18	84	8	2	5	2	46	2	62	8	3
Tovar, Raul, Midland	.320	90	356	57	114	147	21	3	2	49	5	0	4	2	26	2	40	6	2
Chapman, Christopher, San Antonio*	.305	97	344	50	105	163	19	3	11	55	6	1	5	3	35	4	39	1	2
Cora, Jose, Beaumont†	.305	81	315	54	96	120	5	5	3	41	4	3	3	3	47	3	28	24	11
Browne, Jerome, Tulsa†	.303	128	491	82	149	184	15	7	2	57	8	5	1	0	62	1	61	39	11
Devereaux, Michael, San Antonio	.302	115	431	69	130	186	22	2	10	53	6	1	4	3	58	2	47	31	8
Ortiz, Javier, Tulsa	.302	110	378	52	114	191	29	3	14	65	6	3	1	7	54	2	94	15	10

Departmental Leaders: G—Abner, 134; AB—Freeman, 515; R—Stanicek, 116; H—Stanicek, 167; TB—Stanicek, 284; 2B—Stanicek, 40; 3B—Abner, K. Harvey, 8; HR—King, 30; RBI—Alfaro, Felice, 97; GWRBI—Stanicek, 15; SH—Escobar, 11; SF—Felice, Gibbons, 11; HP—Five players with 7; BB—Stanicek, 88; IBB—Sasser, 13; SO—Cockrell, 126; SB—Johnson, 49; CS—Johnson, 15.

(All Players—Listed Alphabetically)

Player and Club	Pct.	G.	AB.	R.	H.	TB.	2B.	3B.	HR.	RBI.	GW.	SH.	SF.	HP.	BB.	Int. BB.	SO.	SB.	CS.
Abner, Shawn, Jackson	.266	134	511	80	136	223	29	8	14	76	6	2	7	7	23	1	76	8	6
Adamczak, James, Jackson	.500	35	4	1	2	2	0	0	0	1	0	0	0	0	1	0	1	0	0
Adams, Patrick, Shreveport	.340	15	53	12	18	32	6	1	2	8	2	0	0	2	7	1	13	0	3
Agostinelli, Salvatore, Arkansas	.237	58	131	10	31	34	3	0	0	5	1	2	0	2	13	0	10	3	1
Alfaro, Jesus, El Paso	.301	114	448	91	135	206	25	2	14	97	10	1	9	1	53	4	66	1	1
Alicea, Luis, Arkansas†	.235	25	68	8	16	19	3	0	0	3	1	2	2	0	5	0	11	0	3
Allen, Robert, El Paso	.288	68	240	34	69	100	21	2	2	35	2	0	4	1	21	0	35	0	1
Alomar, Santos, Beaumont†	.240	100	346	36	83	112	15	1	4	27	3	2	3	1	15	2	35	2	6
Alvarez, Carmelo, San Antonio†	.125	3	8	0	1	3	0	1	0	2	0	0	0	0	1	0	4	0	0
Amante, Thomas, Arkansas	.242	80	248	33	60	102	10	1	10	45	10	2	3	2	20	2	48	1	1
Arnold, Scott, Arkansas	.000	5	6	0	0	0	0	0	0	0	0	0	0	0	0	0	2	0	0
Bailey, Gregory, Tulsa	.189	83	249	24	47	71	8	2	4	25	2	3	2	1	27	2	78	11	4
Bates, William, El Paso†	.295	122	511	104	151	209	26	4	8	75	2	3	0	2	72	0	64	23	10
Bautista, Jose, Jackson	.000	7	7	0	0	0	0	0	0	0	0	0	0	0	0	0	2	0	0

Player and Club	Pct.	G.	AB.	R.	H.	TB.	2B.	3B.	HR.	RBI.	GW.	SH.	SF.	HP.	BB.	Int. BB.	SO.	SB.	CS.
Bergendahl, Wray, Jackson	.333	22	24	3	8	9	1	0	0	4	0	1	0	0	0	0	8	0	0
Beuerlein, John, El Paso	.242	34	95	13	23	28	5	0	0	13	2	0	3	1	20	0	22	1	0
Bichette, Dante, Midland	.284	62	243	43	69	125	16	2	12	36	1	0	3	2	18	0	50	3	0
Bitker, Joseph, Beaumont	.450	21	20	3	9	10	1	0	0	3	0	0	0	0	3	0	2	1	0
Blair, Paul, Shreveport	.195	21	41	4	8	10	0	1	0	0	0	1	0	1	5	0	9	2	1
Blount, William, Beaumont*	.000	34	2	0	0	0	0	0	0	0	0	0	0	0	0	0	1	0	0
Booker, Roderick, Arkansas*	.318	36	151	20	48	59	7	2	0	20	1	0	1	0	7	1	17	8	5
Bootay, Kevin, Tulsa	.231	97	372	40	86	108	14	1	2	30	1	7	1	2	18	1	35	30	12
Brady, Brian, Midland*	.290	97	355	53	103	157	19	1	11	53	2	0	3	0	27	3	61	3	2
Brantley, Jeffrey, Shreveport	.074	26	27	2	2	2	0	0	0	0	0	4	0	0	1	0	11	0	0
Brassil, Thomas, Beaumont	.239	103	356	30	85	119	18	5	2	38	6	1	7	5	14	3	41	1	2
Brennan, William, San Antonio	.000	26	18	1	0	0	0	0	0	0	0	1	0	0	3	0	10	0	0
Brown, Jeffrey, San Antonio	.232	68	203	25	47	65	9	0	3	17	2	1	2	1	32	3	34	0	1
Brown, Todd, El Paso	.319	43	163	36	52	99	6	1	13	45	4	1	5	0	24	1	29	2	0
Browne, Jerome, Tulsa†	.303	128	491	82	149	184	15	7	2	57	8	5	1	0	62	1	61	39	11
Burkett, John, Shreveport	.053	22	19	4	1	2	1	0	0	0	0	2	0	0	2	0	7	0	0
Burrell, Kevin, Shreveport	.216	63	162	13	35	62	5	2	6	26	4	4	1	2	9	0	31	0	0
Byers, Randall, Beaumont*	.266	121	463	60	123	187	23	4	11	50	8	1	5	1	41	2	71	7	6
Cadahia, Benito, Tulsa	.246	69	199	26	49	78	8	0	7	17	0	1	1	1	31	0	49	2	1
Carmichael, Alan, Jackson	.200	16	40	8	8	10	2	0	0	5	0	1	1	1	8	1	10	0	0
Carrasco, Ernest, Arkansas	.303	28	33	3	10	13	3	0	0	6	0	4	0	0	3	0	14	0	0
Cartwright, Alan, El Paso*	.321	118	467	90	150	241	27	5	18	84	8	2	5	2	46	2	62	8	3
Castro, Frank, Beaumont	.295	102	366	52	108	180	30	3	12	62	4	0	1	1	33	3	50	4	4
Cataline, Daniel, San Antonio	.206	37	107	6	22	30	5	0	1	8	2	0	0	0	12	1	30	1	1
Chapman, Christopher, San Antonio*	.305	97	344	50	105	163	19	3	11	55	6	1	5	3	35	4	39	1	2
Cherry, Paul, Arkansas*	.000	30	5	1	0	0	0	0	0	0	0	0	0	0	2	0	4	0	0
Clark, Jerald, Beaumont	.321	16	56	9	18	24	4	1	0	6	0	1	0	3	5	0	9	1	2
Clements, David, Arkansas	.248	129	440	55	109	154	19	4	6	48	6	3	4	3	30	0	66	10	6
Coachman, Dean, Midland	.349	61	249	53	87	125	17	3	5	35	3	3	1	6	21	0	34	10	6
Cocanower, James, Arkansas	.000	5	4	0	0	0	0	0	0	0	0	0	0	0	0	0	2	0	0
Cockrell, Alan, Shreveport	.258	124	438	66	113	192	31	3	14	78	10	3	3	3	61	3	126	4	2
Contreras, Jouquin, Jackson†	.224	23	76	10	17	24	1	0	2	4	1	1	1	0	8	1	14	3	1
Cora, Jose, Beaumont†	.305	81	315	54	96	120	5	5	3	41	4	3	3	3	47	3	28	24	11
Corbell, Charles, Shreveport	.152	27	33	4	5	5	0	0	0	2	0	4	0	0	5	0	8	0	0
Costello, John, Arkansas	.000	10	1	0	0	0	0	0	0	1	0	0	0	0	0	0	0	0	0
Costello, Michael, Beaumont	.207	27	29	2	6	8	0	1	0	1	0	1	0	0	4	0	13	0	0
Cucjen, Romulo, Shreveport	.167	30	66	4	11	17	2	2	0	8	1	1	2	0	6	2	8	0	0
Davis, Douglas, Midland	.225	48	138	24	31	48	5	0	4	16	2	0	0	0	18	0	32	1	0
DeButch, Michael, Beaumont†	.179	68	212	30	38	51	3	2	2	13	3	0	0	1	31	0	45	17	6
Devereaux, Michael, San Antonio	.302	115	431	69	130	186	22	2	10	53	6	1	4	3	58	2	47	31	8
Devine, Kevin, San Antonio	1.000	38	1	0	1	1	0	0	0	0	0	1	0	0	0	0	0	0	0
Dobie, Reginald, Jackson	.036	29	28	2	1	2	1	0	0	1	0	4	0	0	1	0	15	0	0
Dougherty, Mark, Arkansas	.261	129	426	65	111	166	25	3	8	56	8	6	2	1	50	1	84	31	6
Doughty, Jamie, Tulsa	.244	85	275	42	67	108	7	5	8	33	4	1	0	3	38	1	65	14	8
Doyle, Richard, Beaumont	.000	27	8	0	0	0	0	0	0	0	0	0	0	0	0	0	6	0	0
Edens, Thomas, Jackson	.095	16	21	0	2	2	0	0	0	2	1	8	0	0	2	0	4	0	0
Edwards, Jeffrey, San Antonio*	.000	33	18	1	0	0	0	0	0	0	0	2	0	0	1	0	6	0	0
Eichhorn, David, San Antonio	.000	12	1	0	0	0	0	0	0	0	0	0	0	0	0	0	1	0	0
Elster, Kevin, Jackson	.269	127	435	69	117	148	19	3	2	52	10	4	8	4	61	3	46	7	8
Embser, Richard, Arkansas	.000	14	1	0	0	0	0	0	0	0	0	0	0	0	0	0	0	0	0
Escobar, Angel, Shreveport†	.276	131	439	58	121	149	14	4	2	46	6	11	0	0	60	3	60	15	12
Faedo, Leonardo, San Antonio	.293	65	266	39	78	104	14	0	4	31	2	0	2	1	21	0	10	3	4
Farmer, Albert, Tulsa	.171	10	35	1	6	7	1	0	0	1	0	0	1	0	2	0	3	2	1
Felder, Michael, El Paso†	.452	8	31	10	14	17	3	0	0	2	0	1	1	0	5	1	3	7	0
Felice, Jason, Jackson	.263	125	434	60	114	186	20	2	16	97	12	1	11	2	50	1	62	9	5
Ferran, George, Shreveport	.182	46	22	2	4	4	0	0	0	1	0	1	0	0	1	0	6	0	0
Finley, Brian, El Paso*	.231	53	130	18	30	34	1	0	1	17	1	1	3	3	39	0	18	12	8
Ford, Russell, Beaumont	.000	67	1	0	0	0	0	0	0	0	0	0	0	0	0	0	1	0	0
Francois, Manuel, San Antonio†	.263	9	19	3	5	5	0	0	0	1	0	0	0	0	3	0	5	0	1
Freeland, Dean, Shreveport	.333	7	3	0	1	1	0	0	0	0	0	2	0	0	0	0	2	0	0
Freeman, Lavell, El Paso*	.322	128	515	101	166	249	31	5	14	91	9	2	3	3	59	7	89	15	6
Fultz, William, Jackson	.286	23	14	2	4	5	1	0	0	1	0	1	0	0	0	0	2	0	0
Garcia, Steven, Beaumont*	.340	47	194	26	66	79	9	2	0	11	1	1	0	0	12	4	26	9	3
Gardner, Arthur, Tulsa*	.311	28	90	12	28	49	9	0	4	17	3	0	1	1	8	1	18	1	1
Gergen, Robert, Tulsa	.250	108	368	40	92	144	24	2	8	64	4	0	5	3	43	0	67	5	2
Gibbons, John, El Paso*	.260	109	366	54	95	146	26	2	7	58	6	1	11	2	56	3	54	2	1
Gillaspie, Mark, 68 ElP-35 Bmt†	.294	103	367	81	108	177	26	2	13	60	4	4	3	3	77	6	76	2	1
Gjesdal, Brent, Beaumont	.167	46	132	17	22	39	7	2	2	15	0	0	1	2	15	0	52	1	1
Glynn, Dennis, Jackson	.238	55	84	6	20	21	1	0	0	5	1	3	0	0	9	0	19	0	2
Graham, Brian, El Paso	.000	3	11	1	0	0	0	0	0	0	0	0	0	0	1	0	6	0	0
Graham, Everett, Shreveport*	.292	80	288	54	84	123	20	2	5	42	4	1	2	4	41	1	40	13	9
Grandstaff, Robert, Beaumont	.222	46	144	22	32	54	8	1	4	13	2	2	0	1	15	0	38	0	1
Grimes, John, Shreveport	.199	72	181	24	36	57	12	0	3	19	0	1	3	2	25	2	60	0	0
Gutierrez, Felipe, San Antonio	.228	79	241	28	55	67	7	1	1	25	3	3	4	2	8	0	20	0	0
Gwosdz, Douglas, Jackson	.246	78	232	33	57	99	13	1	9	26	3	1	1	7	40	2	61	0	1
Gwynn, Christopher, San Antonio*	.287	111	401	46	115	157	22	1	6	67	7	1	6	3	16	7	44	2	2
Hamilton, Robert, San Antonio	.130	26	23	2	3	3	0	0	0	0	0	1	0	0	1	0	8	0	0
Hardgrave, Eric, Beaumont	.258	103	364	36	94	122	13	0	5	39	8	0	2	4	29	0	72	1	0
Hartshorn, Kyle, Jackson*	.107	27	28	2	3	3	0	0	0	0	0	3	0	0	3	0	6	0	0
Harvey, Kenneth, San Antonio	.268	113	384	62	103	138	13	8	2	30	4	2	4	3	64	4	59	22	14
Harvey, Randall, Midland*	.833	38	6	3	5	9	2	1	0	2	0	0	0	0	0	0	0	0	0
Hayes, Charles, Shreveport	.247	121	434	52	107	149	23	2	5	45	8	4	4	2	28	3	83	1	4
Heath, David, Midland	.249	91	309	42	77	103	8	0	6	29	2	2	2	4	21	1	65	3	0
Heredia, Hector, San Antonio	.000	39	4	0	0	0	0	0	0	0	0	0	0	0	0	0	2	0	0
Hertzler, Paul, Jackson*	.262	88	294	39	77	112	10	5	5	46	5	2	2	2	31	5	68	6	2
Hill, Bradley, Tulsa*	.177	22	79	5	14	14	0	0	0	6	0	0	1	0	2	1	14	2	1
Hill, Kenneth, Arkansas	.333	3	3	1	1	1	0	0	0	0	0	0	0	0	0	0	2	0	0
Hillegas, Shawn, San Antonio	.158	17	19	1	3	4	1	0	0	1	0	3	0	0	2	0	6	0	0
Hotchkiss, John, Midland	.289	80	218	32	63	81	9	0	3	20	5	5	0	1	27	0	40	1	4
Hummel, Dean, Shreveport*	.350	20	20	3	7	11	1	0	1	1	0	2	0	0	0	0	2	0	0
Huppert, David, El Paso	.200	16	45	9	9	16	1	0	2	9	1	0	1	0	14	0	14	0	0
Innis, Jeffrey, Jackson	.000	56	4	0	0	0	0	0	0	0	0	0	0	0	0	0	4	0	0

Player and Club	Pct.	G.	AB.	R.	H.	TB.	2B.	3B.	HR.	RBI.	GW.	SH.	SF.	HP.	BB.	Int. BB.	SO.	SB.	CS.
Jefferies, Gregg, Jackson†	.421	5	19	1	8	11	1	1	0	7	1	0	0	0	2	1	2	1	0
Johns, Ronald, Arkansas	.277	31	94	8	26	37	8	0	1	17	2	0	1	0	7	0	10	1	1
Johnson, Lance, Arkansas*	.288	127	445	82	128	170	24	6	2	33	4	3	2	1	59	2	57	49	15
Jones, Michael, Shreveport*	.234	108	334	54	78	119	17	6	4	23	1	1	1	6	62	3	56	5	10
Jones, Timothy, Arkansas*	.268	96	284	36	76	99	15	1	2	27	3	3	2	2	42	2	32	7	5
Kable, David, Arkansas*	.246	127	382	47	94	164	23	1	15	67	7	0	2	1	57	6	85	2	2
Keedy, Patrick, Midland	.253	60	233	41	59	100	8	0	11	29	4	0	3	2	37	0	50	12	1
Keener, Jeffrey, Arkansas	.000	62	6	1	0	0	0	0	0	0	0	0	0	0	0	0	1	0	0
Kepshire, Kurt, Arkansas*	.000	9	7	1	0	0	0	0	0	0	0	3	0	0	1	0	2	0	0
Killingsworth, Kirk, Tulsa	.000	36	2	0	0	0	0	0	0	0	0	0	0	0	0	0	1	0	0
King, Kevin, Midland†	.301	112	425	80	128	245	19	4	30	93	8	1	3	3	46	0	123	11	7
Klein, Lawrence, Tulsa	.232	90	298	44	69	84	12	0	1	13	1	5	1	2	32	0	59	10	4
Lachowicz, Allen, Jackson	.000	1	1	0	0	0	0	0	0	0	0	0	0	0	0	0	0	0	0
Lawrence, Andy, Jackson	.292	29	65	9	19	29	1	0	3	15	1	0	0	1	1	0	12	0	2
Ledbetter, Jeffrey, Arkansas*	.180	27	61	9	11	20	1	1	2	8	1	0	1	0	11	0	16	2	0
Lenderman, David, Jackson*	.000	16	5	0	0	0	0	0	0	0	0	3	0	0	0	0	1	0	0
Liddle, Steven, Midland	.300	29	110	10	33	45	7	1	1	19	1	0	1	0	11	0	15	0	1
Little, Scott, Jackson	.208	40	96	15	20	26	6	0	0	8	0	1	0	1	9	0	20	6	3
Litton, Gregory, Shreveport	.246	131	455	46	112	178	30	3	10	55	5	5	2	4	52	4	77	1	2
Livingston, Dennis, San Antonio	.250	29	8	0	2	3	1	0	0	1	0	1	0	0	1	0	1	0	0
Lockwood, Richard, Jackson†	.282	110	372	56	105	164	23	3	10	57	5	1	4	3	52	4	49	2	5
Lubratich, Steven, Beaumont	.265	45	98	8	26	30	4	0	0	9	1	0	2	1	6	0	11	0	3
Lundgren, Kurt, Jackson	.077	18	13	1	1	1	0	0	0	1	0	1	0	0	0	0	9	0	0
Lynch, Joseph, Beaumont	.000	21	1	0	0	0	0	0	0	0	0	1	0	0	0	0	0	0	0
Mace, Jeffrey, Tulsa	.150	25	80	12	12	17	2	0	1	5	0	1	0	1	13	0	12	1	1
Mack, Shane, Beaumont	.281	115	452	61	127	204	26	3	15	68	2	2	3	7	21	2	79	14	9
Madril, Michael, Midland†	.273	47	110	21	30	34	4	0	0	7	1	2	2	2	12	0	13	6	0
Magrane, Joseph, Arkansas	.100	13	10	1	1	1	0	0	0	0	0	1	0	0	0	0	5	0	0
Mancuso, Paul, Beaumont*	.125	43	8	0	1	1	0	0	0	1	0	1	0	0	1	0	4	0	0
Martin, John, Arkansas	.129	22	31	2	4	5	1	0	0	0	0	3	0	0	0	0	13	0	0
May, Scott, San Antonio	.143	4	7	1	1	1	0	0	0	0	0	0	0	0	0	0	0	0	0
Mayberry, Gregory, San Antonio*	.000	3	2	0	0	0	0	0	0	0	0	0	0	0	1	0	2	0	0
McCament, Randall, Shreveport	.000	8	2	0	0	0	0	0	0	0	0	0	0	0	0	0	0	0	0
McClain, Michael, Beaumont	.182	24	11	0	2	2	0	0	0	4	0	1	1	0	3	0	2	0	0
McCue, Deron, Shreveport	.263	111	350	62	92	116	12	6	0	38	3	4	0	2	55	1	68	11	6
McCulla, Henry, Arkansas	.291	66	175	20	51	74	15	1	2	23	1	0	2	4	23	1	35	0	1
McDonald, Thomas, Shreveport	.395	9	38	5	15	19	2	1	0	4	1	0	0	1	1	0	7	5	1
McKnight, Jefferson, Jackson*	.252	132	469	71	118	160	24	3	4	55	6	5	9	3	76	3	58	5	2
McLemore, Mark, Midland†	.316	63	237	54	75	89	9	1	1	29	1	1	4	1	48	1	18	38	8
Medvin, Scott, Shreveport	.000	49	9	0	0	0	0	0	0	0	0	1	0	0	1	0	1	0	0
Melrose, Jeffrey, Tulsa*	.267	80	288	31	77	100	12	4	1	33	4	3	2	1	21	3	42	4	6
Mena, Andres, San Antonio	.000	12	8	0	0	0	0	0	0	0	0	1	0	0	2	0	4	0	0
Merrifield, Billie, Midland	.289	67	253	43	73	116	19	0	8	53	5	0	3	0	32	1	23	2	1
Miller, Keith, Jackson	.329	94	353	80	116	162	23	4	5	36	0	2	0	7	62	1	55	28	5
Miller, Stephen, Shreveport*	.192	12	26	2	5	6	1	0	0	3	0	1	0	0	2	0	3	0	0
Milligan, Randy, Jackson	.316	78	269	53	85	123	11	3	7	53	8	0	1	2	60	3	42	13	6
Mills, Michael, Beaumont	.222	31	18	2	4	5	1	0	0	2	0	3	0	0	3	0	6	0	0
Montanari, David, Midland	.347	28	95	22	33	43	7	0	1	10	1	1	1	0	17	1	9	0	1
Morlock, Allen, Arkansas	.091	15	11	0	1	1	0	0	0	0	0	2	0	0	0	0	1	0	0
Mota, Jose, Tulsa†	.323	41	158	26	51	67	7	3	1	11	1	3	1	0	22	0	13	14	8
Murphy, John, Arkansas	.303	39	132	14	40	44	4	0	0	13	0	0	2	0	8	1	15	10	1
Nago, Garrett, El Paso†	.361	11	36	8	13	17	1	0	1	5	0	0	1	0	10	0	6	1	1
Nandin, Robert, El Paso†	.297	70	236	39	70	77	5	1	0	32	3	2	4	1	36	0	14	7	1
Newsom, Gary, San Antonio	.240	90	287	32	69	80	8	0	1	19	1	4	1	0	20	1	27	11	3
North, Jay, Arkansas	.000	23	4	0	0	0	0	0	0	0	0	1	0	0	0	0	0	0	0
O'Brien, Charles, El Paso	.324	92	336	72	109	180	20	3	15	75	6	1	6	6	50	0	30	0	0
Oakes, Todd, Shreveport	.000	14	1	0	0	0	0	0	0	0	0	0	0	0	0	0	1	0	0
Ohnoutka, Brian, Shreveport	.231	18	13	1	3	4	1	0	0	2	0	2	0	0	1	0	2	0	0
Olson, Gregory, Jackson	.199	64	196	28	39	52	5	1	2	16	1	3	1	1	30	0	16	0	0
Ortiz, Javier, Tulsa	.302	110	378	52	114	191	29	3	14	65	6	3	1	7	54	2	94	15	10
Parsons, Scott, Beaumont	.350	54	206	32	72	102	15	0	5	42	5	0	3	3	16	0	30	0	2
Pequignot, Jonathan, San Antonio*	.241	16	54	7	13	16	3	0	0	6	3	0	0	0	7	1	8	0	0
Peters, Steven, Arkansas*	.316	12	19	3	6	10	1	0	1	3	0	0	0	2	1	0	5	0	0
Pevey, Marty, Arkansas*	.326	55	172	28	56	77	11	2	2	20	6	1	2	1	16	0	18	6	0
Phillips, Stephen, Jackson*	.143	3	7	0	1	1	0	0	0	1	1	0	0	0	1	0	2	0	0
Poole, Mark, Tulsa	.242	58	190	16	46	72	9	1	5	34	4	0	1	2	18	1	26	0	2
Poston, Mark, Beaumont	.222	37	18	2	4	5	1	0	0	0	0	2	0	0	0	0	9	0	0
Pruitt, Edwin, Jackson*	.250	31	4	0	1	1	0	0	0	0	0	0	0	0	0	0	2	0	0
Puikunas, Edmund, Shreveport	.000	48	6	0	0	0	0	0	0	0	0	0	0	0	0	0	5	0	0
Ramsey, Michael, San Antonio	.286	119	427	71	122	156	18	5	2	37	5	9	2	0	40	3	86	21	12
Randall, James, Midland†	.331	123	468	90	155	248	23	2	22	93	10	0	9	2	69	6	80	6	6
Redfield, Joseph, Jackson	.283	15	60	8	17	22	1	2	0	3	0	0	0	0	4	0	10	2	0
Rhodes, Michael, Arkansas*	.000	33	1	0	0	0	0	0	0	0	0	0	0	0	1	0	0	0	0
Robidoux, William, El Paso*	.325	30	114	30	37	76	9	0	10	34	4	0	0	0	25	8	26	0	0
Robinson, Michael, Arkansas	.244	89	176	25	43	64	9	0	4	17	2	3	1	3	11	1	27	4	2
Rodriguez, Jose, Arkansas	.207	71	116	10	24	29	2	0	1	5	1	2	1	2	5	1	18	3	2
Rodriguez, Richard, Jackson*	.200	13	5	1	1	1	0	0	0	0	0	0	0	0	1	0	2	0	0
Romero, Albert, Midland	.222	33	117	19	26	55	5	0	8	20	1	0	3	0	19	0	23	1	1
Rowen, Robert, San Antonio*	.500	3	2	1	1	1	0	0	0	0	0	0	0	0	0	0	1	0	0
Rubel, Michael, 45 Tul.-80 Shreve.	.213	125	413	59	88	176	22	0	22	70	12	1	3	3	86	2	115	3	2
Santiago, Michael, Jackson*	.000	43	4	0	0	0	0	0	0	0	0	1	0	0	0	0	3	0	0
Sasser, Mack, Shreveport*	.293	120	441	52	129	183	29	5	5	72	12	2	9	2	44	13	36	4	0
Schaefer, Jeffrey, Midland	.268	114	406	50	109	146	17	1	6	41	0	4	6	2	14	0	40	1	4
Schroeder, William, El Paso	.231	8	26	5	6	12	3	0	1	2	0	0	0	1	3	1	9	0	0
Schulte, Mark, Arkansas*	.204	21	54	3	11	21	3	2	1	12	1	0	0	0	2	0	5	2	0
Shade, Michael, Arkansas	.000	11	1	0	0	0	0	0	0	0	0	0	0	0	0	0	1	0	0
Sierra, Ulises, Beaumont	.091	16	11	1	1	4	0	0	1	1	0	1	0	0	0	0	9	0	0
Silver, Keith, Shreveport	.250	13	8	1	2	4	0	1	0	1	0	1	0	0	0	0	1	0	0
Simmons, Todd, Beaumont	.000	38	2	0	0	0	0	0	0	0	0	0	0	0	0	0	2	0	0
Smith, Keith, El Paso†	.252	34	123	17	31	45	3	1	3	15	2	0	0	0	11	0	24	2	0
Soff, Raymond, Arkansas	.000	18	1	0	0	0	0	0	0	0	0	0	0	0	0	0	1	0	0
Stanicek, Stephen, El Paso	.343	127	487	116	167	284	40	1	25	93	15	1	1	5	88	2	70	6	2

Player and Club	Pct.	G.	AB.	R.	H.	TB.	2B.	3B.	HR.	RBI.	GW.	SH.	SF.	HP.	BB.	Int. BB.	SO.	SB.	CS.
Stanley, Michael, Tulsa	.294	67	235	41	69	107	16	2	6	35	4	1	4	2	34	1	26	5	3
Stryffeler, Daniel, Arkansas*	.285	40	123	22	35	53	10	1	2	12	1	0	1	0	13	2	16	4	2
Szekely, Joseph, San Antonio*	.244	98	299	28	73	85	7	1	1	23	2	0	2	5	33	7	58	2	0
Tanner, Edwin, Arkansas†	.311	84	270	39	84	105	13	1	2	42	5	3	7	1	23	1	10	5	4
Tate, Stuart, Shreveport	.000	36	3	0	0	0	0	0	0	0	0	0	0	0	0	0	2	0	0
Tejeda, Felix, San Antonio†	.000	34	3	0	0	0	0	0	0	0	0	0	0	0	1	0	2	0	0
Tellez, Alonso, San Antonio	.244	118	434	39	106	143	21	2	4	48	3	3	5	1	17	2	46	3	3
Thomas, Todd, Shreveport*	.256	63	199	24	51	61	6	2	0	17	4	4	1	2	29	2	20	9	3
Thornton, John, El Paso	.143	8	21	1	3	5	2	0	0	1	0	0	0	1	6	0	10	0	0
Torres, Philip, San Antonio	.000	54	4	0	0	0	0	0	0	0	0	0	0	0	0	0	0	0	0
Tovar, Raul, Midland	.320	90	356	57	114	147	21	3	2	49	5	0	4	2	26	2	40	6	2
Triplett, Antonio, Tulsa	.247	91	288	26	71	91	9	4	1	22	1	1	1	1	32	0	45	23	12
Van Cleve, Dandridge, Tulsa*	.183	30	109	9	20	24	4	0	0	7	0	2	2	1	15	1	26	10	2
Varoz, Eric, Beaumont*	.267	83	240	29	64	78	10	2	0	21	2	0	0	1	54	1	49	6	9
Verducci, John, Shreveport	.000	4	5	1	0	0	0	0	0	1	0	0	0	0	5	0	3	0	0
Vila, Jesus, San Antonio	.000	2	2	0	0	0	0	0	0	0	0	1	0	0	0	0	0	0	0
Walker, Glen, Midland	.305	67	259	41	79	143	10	0	18	74	4	0	6	1	16	2	49	2	1
Wallace, Timothy, Arkansas	.212	34	99	5	21	28	4	0	1	10	0	3	2	2	9	2	20	0	3
Ward, Colin, Shreveport*	.000	5	7	1	0	0	0	0	0	0	0	1	0	0	1	0	3	0	0
Weissman, Craig, Arkansas	.000	29	10	0	0	0	0	0	0	0	0	2	0	0	0	0	3	0	0
Weston, Michael, Jackson	.000	34	3	0	0	0	0	0	0	0	0	1	0	0	0	0	1	0	0
Wilson, John, Jackson*	.265	96	238	40	63	84	11	2	2	19	3	1	0	3	32	2	64	10	10
Winters, Daniel, Jackson	.154	6	13	1	2	3	1	0	0	2	1	0	0	0	1	0	1	0	0
Wohler, Barry, San Antonio*	.000	26	12	0	0	0	0	0	0	0	0	2	0	0	1	0	5	0	0
Woodson, Tracy, San Antonio	.269	131	495	65	133	220	27	3	18	90	14	1	1	5	33	7	59	4	1
Wrona, William, Beaumont	.231	124	446	51	103	127	19	1	1	32	7	3	6	3	33	2	50	5	7
Wyatt, David, Jackson	.333	2	3	0	1	1	0	0	0	0	0	2	0	0	0	0	0	0	0
Young, John, Jackson*	.000	3	2	0	0	0	0	0	0	0	0	0	0	0	1	0	1	0	0
Young, Scott, Arkansas	.100	20	30	0	3	4	1	0	0	2	0	5	0	0	2	0	14	0	0

The following pitchers, listed alphabetically by club, with games in parentheses, had no plate appearances, primarily through use of designated hitters:

BEAUMONT—Luebber, Stephen (8).

EL PASO—Aldrich, Jay (40); Clay, David (15); Crews, Timothy (15); Crim, Charles (16); Diaz, Derek (19); Duquette, Bryan (13); Kendrick, Peter (26); Madrid, Alexander (27); Murphy, Daniel (18); Myers, Edward (32); Sadler, Alan (8); Scarpetta, Daniel (27); Stapleton, David (38); Walker, Cameron (13).

JACKSON—Bayer, Christopher (1); Richardson, Jeffrey (1); Wachs, Thomas (1).

MIDLAND—Banning, Douglas (32); Buice, DeWayne (45); Butler, Michael (4); Carter, Richie (4); Cedeno, Vinicio (24); Clark, Terry (57); Cook, Michael (15); Corbett, Sherman (26); Gonzalez, Julian (18); Lovelace, Vance (23); Lugo, Urbano (2); Pimentel, Rafael (29); Price, Bryan (6); Romanovsky, Michael (11); Smith, Lawrence (4); Timberlake, Donald (19); Venturino, Philip (15).

SAN ANTONIO—Legumina, Gary (10).

TULSA—Anderson, Scott (10); Brown, Keith (3); Couchee, Michael (4); Ferlenda, Gregory (21); Harman, David (10); Kilgus, Paul (42); Knapp, Richard (26); Kramer, Randall (26); Loynd, Michael (5); Mielke, Gary (24); Olsson, Daniel (19); Raether, Eric (21); Rodgers, Timothy (36); Rogers, Kenneth (10); Taylor, William (11); Valdez, Efrain (4); Wilson, Stephen (25).

GRAND SLAM HOME RUNS—Walker, 3; Alfaro, E. Graham, Rubel, 2 each; Bates, Bichette, T. Brown, Dougherty, Freeman, Keedy, King, Lawrence, Mack, Merrifield, Ortiz, Stanicek, 1 each.

AWARDED FIRST BASE ON CATCHER'S INTERFERENCE—Amante 3 (Alomar, Cadahia, Davis); Schaefer 2 (Alomar 2); Contreras (Sasser); Gjesdal (J. Brown); Ortiz (Winters); Parsons (Agostinelli); Rubel (Burrell); Stanicek (Alomar).

CLUB FIELDING

Club	Pct.	G.	PO.	A.	E.	DP.	PB.
San Antonio	.975	135	3539	1358	124	122	19
El Paso	.973	135	3516	1485	141	148	13
Jackson	.971	136	3477	1434	146	123	11
Tulsa	.968	134	3398	1340	159	102	11
Shreveport	.967	136	3525	1493	172	127	11
Arkansas	.966	135	3340	1461	167	115	17
Midland	.965	133	3418	1381	173	123	13
Beaumont	.962	136	3591	1564	203	146	10

Triple Play—Midland.

INDIVIDUAL FIELDING

*Throws lefthanded.

FIRST BASEMEN

Player and Club	Pct.	G.	PO.	A.	E.	DP.
Adams, Shreveport	.971	15	127	8	4	13
Alfaro, El Paso	1.000	13	141	10	0	14
Brassil, Beaumont	.985	23	172	20	3	22
Chapman, San Antonio	.994	88	745	34	5	66
Cockrell, Shreveport	.917	1	11	0	1	0
Cucjen, Shreveport	.987	12	71	5	1	10
Gergen, Tulsa	1.000	2	9	1	0	3
Gibbons, El Paso*	.990	14	101	2	1	9
Gillaspie, El Paso	.941	3	29	3	2	1
Glynn, Jackson	1.000	1	1	0	0	0
Grimes, Shreveport	.984	19	170	9	3	12
Gwosdz, Jackson	1.000	4	5	0	0	1
Hardgrave, Beaumont	.989	89	814	46	10	78
Hertzler, Jackson*	.977	21	117	10	3	15
Hill, Tulsa	1.000	1	3	1	0	0
Hotchkiss, Midland	1.000	3	26	2	0	2
Johns, Arkansas	1.000	29	214	14	0	14
Kable, Arkansas*	.988	111	873	51	11	81
Keedy, Midland	1.000	12	90	6	0	10
Lawrence, Jackson	.967	19	108	11	4	8
Ledbetter, Arkansas*	1.000	3	8	1	0	1
Liddle, Midland	.983	7	56	3	1	6
Little, Jackson	1.000	3	18	0	0	1
Lockwood, Jackson	.941	2	12	4	1	2
Lubratich, Beaumont	.992	17	124	3	1	16
McCulla, Arkansas	.976	14	80	1	2	9
McKnight, Jackson	.996	32	213	18	1	14
Melrose, Tulsa*	.992	78	678	32	6	48
Merrifield, Midland	1.000	2	19	1	0	3
Miller, Shreveport	1.000	1	2	0	0	0
Milligan, Jackson	.992	78	684	62	6	66
O'Brien, El Paso	1.000	1	7	0	0	0
Parsons, Beaumont	.984	20	177	7	3	15
Pequignot, San Antonio	.992	14	118	6	1	10
Pevey, Arkansas	1.000	1	1	0	0	0
Poole, Tulsa	1.000	2	20	1	0	2
Randall, Midland*	.988	110	943	72	12	90
Robidoux, El Paso	.996	27	269	11	1	29
RUBEL, 39 Tulsa-80 Shreve	.993	119	1059	79	8	99
Sasser, Shreveport	.983	17	110	6	2	11
Stanicek, El Paso	.993	75	655	30	5	70
Stanley, Tulsa	.992	13	110	9	1	7
Tellez, San Antonio	.987	35	278	19	4	25
Thornton, El Paso	1.000	8	72	4	0	3

Triple Play—Randall.

SECOND BASEMEN

Player and Club	Pct.	G.	PO.	A.	E.	DP.
Alfaro, El Paso	1.000	1	1	0	0	0
Alicea, Arkansas	.971	21	38	61	3	6
Allen, El Paso	.958	7	11	12	1	8
Bates, El Paso	.969	119	286	362	21	96
Blair, Shreveport	.909	3	2	8	1	2
BROWNE, Tulsa	.984	95	234	248	8	56
Clements, Arkansas	1.000	1	2	0	0	0
Coachman, Midland	.964	59	125	171	11	36
Cora, Beaumont	.973	76	206	259	13	66
DeButch, Beaumont	1.000	1	1	1	0	0
Dougherty, Arkansas	.972	121	246	302	16	73
Doughty, Tulsa	1.000	2	5	4	0	2
Escobar, Shreveport	1.000	1	1	1	0	2
Farmer, Tulsa	1.000	2	4	7	0	1
Garcia, Beaumont	.981	40	88	115	4	26
Glynn, Jackson	1.000	14	13	15	0	7
Gutierrez, San Antonio	.957	24	47	42	4	9
Harvey, San Antonio	.979	106	230	282	11	65
Hotchkiss, Midland	.963	13	23	29	2	10
Litton, Shreveport	.963	127	262	369	24	80
McKnight, Jackson	.953	42	89	93	9	18
McLemore, Midland	.964	63	155	194	13	43
K. Miller, Jackson	.961	93	198	272	19	55
S. Miller, Shreveport	1.000	2	4	3	0	1
Montanari, Midland	1.000	1	0	1	0	0
Mota, Tulsa	.949	36	52	98	8	13
Nandin, El Paso	.986	14	31	37	1	7
Newsom, San Antonio	.925	15	38	24	5	7
Phillips, Jackson	.667	1	1	1	1	1
Schaefer, Midland	1.000	1	1	2	0	0
Tanner, Arkansas	.938	7	12	18	2	3
Thomas, Shreveport	.942	13	22	27	3	8
Wrona, Beaumont	.987	24	56	95	2	18

THIRD BASEMEN

Player and Club	Pct.	G.	PO.	A.	E.	DP.
Alfaro, El Paso	.947	83	52	198	14	24
Allen, El Paso	.889	8	3	13	2	1
Beuerlein, El Paso	1.000	1	0	2	0	0
Bichette, Midland	.875	20	15	27	6	2
Blair, Shreveport	1.000	2	1	4	0	1
Brassil, Beaumont	.915	65	49	112	15	9
Brown, San Antonio	1.000	2	1	0	0	0
Clements, Arkansas	.902	128	81	240	35	19
Cucjen, Shreveport	.892	10	10	23	4	3
Davis, Midland	1.000	4	3	6	0	1
DeButch, Beaumont	1.000	1	0	1	0	1
Dougherty, Arkansas	.842	8	5	11	3	0
Doughty, Tulsa	.885	63	41	113	20	12
Faedo, San Antonio	1.000	2	2	4	0	1
Farmer, Tulsa	.846	8	5	6	2	1
Garcia, Beaumont	.813	4	1	12	3	0
Gergen, Tulsa	.943	60	39	93	8	1
Glynn, Jackson	.933	19	5	9	1	2
Grandstaff, Beaumont	.881	39	27	69	13	7
Gutierrez, San Antonio	.875	6	4	10	2	1
Hayes, Shreveport	.933	118	89	259	25	27
Hotchkiss, Midland	.954	27	22	40	3	4
Jefferies, Jackson	.800	3	1	3	1	1
Keedy, Midland	.869	29	16	57	11	7
Lockwood, Jackson	.940	97	71	166	15	8
Lubratich, Beaumont	.909	5	2	8	1	1
Madril, Midland	1.000	1	0	1	0	0
McCulla, Arkansas	1.000	2	0	2	0	0
McKnight, Jackson	.938	21	14	31	3	1
Merrifield, Midland	.936	62	47	114	11	9
Mota, Tulsa	1.000	1	1	4	0	0
Nandin, El Paso	.778	3	1	6	2	0
Pequignot, San Antonio	1.000	1	2	1	0	0
Pevey, Arkansas	.857	4	1	5	1	1
Poole, Tulsa	.778	4	0	7	2	1
Redfield, Jackson	.879	15	10	19	4	3
Stanicek, El Paso	.823	44	25	68	20	8
Tanner, Arkansas	.923	7	5	7	1	0
Thomas, Shreveport	1.000	12	4	21	0	1
Triplett, Tulsa	.960	6	5	19	1	2
Varoz, Beaumont	1.000	1	0	2	0	0
WOODSON, San Antonio	.947	127	135	256	22	25
Wrona, Beaumont	.927	34	19	57	6	7

SHORTSTOPS

Player and Club	Pct.	G.	PO.	A.	E.	DP.
Alicea, Arkansas	.750	3	1	2	1	0
Allen, El Paso	.952	51	81	157	12	33
Alvarez, San Antonio	1.000	3	5	8	0	0
Booker, Arkansas	.949	36	66	121	10	21
Brassil, Beaumont	.957	13	12	32	2	11
Browne, Tulsa	.907	28	48	59	11	12
Cora, Beaumont	.760	6	11	8	6	3
DeButch, Beaumont	.919	62	86	187	24	46
Dougherty, Arkansas	.875	5	8	6	2	1
Doughty, Tulsa	.915	20	24	51	7	8
ELSTER, Jackson	.952	123	196	365	28	83
Escobar, Shreveport	.942	131	184	348	33	76
Faedo, San Antonio	.974	64	96	167	7	31
Francois, San Antonio	.840	7	8	13	4	2
Garcia, Beaumont	1.000	3	2	5	0	0
Gergen, Tulsa	1.000	3	1	0	0	0
Glynn, Jackson	.958	13	14	32	2	7
Graham, El Paso	.923	3	4	8	1	1
Gutierrez, San Antonio	.911	21	25	47	7	11
Hotchkiss, Midland	.964	24	29	52	3	8
Jefferies, Jackson	1.000	3	6	6	0	0
Jones, Arkansas	.946	92	142	277	24	57
Keedy, Midland	1.000	3	3	9	0	2
Klein, Tulsa	.944	90	121	267	23	45
Litton, Shreveport	1.000	1	1	4	0	0
McKnight, Jackson	1.000	5	3	7	0	0
Merrifield, Midland	1.000	1	0	1	0	1
Miller, Shreveport	1.000	1	1	3	0	0
Nandin, El Paso	.933	50	75	177	18	32
Newsom, San Antonio	.933	45	50	132	13	29
Schaefer, Midland	.945	114	191	340	31	68
Smith, El Paso	.982	34	51	111	3	31
Stanicek, El Paso	.833	1	1	4	1	0
Tanner, Arkansas	.931	8	9	18	2	4
Thomas, Shreveport	.900	7	8	10	2	3
Verducci, Shreveport	.833	2	2	3	1	0
Woodson, San Antonio	1.000	1	0	3	0	0
Wrona, Beaumont	.963	70	109	199	12	44

Triple Play—Schaefer.

OUTFIELDERS

Player and Club	Pct.	G.	PO.	A.	E.	DP.
Abner, Jackson	.989	133	338	10	4	3
Amante, Arkansas	.959	44	67	3	3	1
Bailey, Tulsa	.971	75	129	5	4	3
Beuerlein, El Paso	1.000	2	1	0	0	0
Bichette, Midland	.960	46	116	3	5	1
Blair, Shreveport	1.000	7	14	0	0	0
Bootay, Tulsa	.978	96	210	8	5	1
Brady, Midland*	.946	92	169	7	10	2
Brassil, Beaumont	1.000	1	1	0	0	0
J. Brown, San Antonio	1.000	9	15	0	0	0
T. Brown, El Paso	.948	37	72	1	4	1
Burrell, Shreveport	1.000	2	2	0	0	0
Byers, Beaumont	.956	117	204	14	10	3
Cartwright, El Paso*	.965	109	183	9	7	2
Castro, Beaumont	.962	18	25	0	1	0
Cataline, San Antonio	.895	22	33	1	4	0
Clark, Beaumont	.952	15	39	1	2	0
Cockrell, Shreveport	.970	115	192	5	6	1
Contreras, Jackson*	1.000	23	44	1	0	1
Davis, Midland	1.000	2	3	0	0	0
Devereaux, San Antonio	.987	114	292	13	4	0
Doughty, Tulsa	1.000	1	0	1	0	0
Felder, El Paso	1.000	5	14	0	0	0
Felice, Jackson	.975	109	187	8	5	3
Finley, El Paso*	.972	48	104	0	3	0
Freeman, El Paso*	.978	83	165	9	4	3
Gardner, Tulsa*	1.000	1	3	0	0	0
Gergen, Tulsa	.962	24	45	5	2	0
GIBBONS, El Paso*	.996	96	219	8	1	1
Gillaspie, 38 ElP-32-Bmt	.985	70	126	7	2	2
Gjesdal, Beaumont	.904	31	46	1	5	0
Graham, Shreveport*	.989	78	170	5	2	0
Gwosdz, Jackson	1.000	1	1	0	0	0
Gwynn, San Antonio*	.990	107	186	11	2	1
Hardgrave, Beaumont	1.000	1	1	0	0	0
Harvey, Midland*	1.000	2	2	0	0	0
Heath, Midland	1.000	7	6	3	0	0
Hertzler, Jackson*	.969	46	61	1	2	0
Hill, Tulsa	.968	19	30	0	1	0
Hotchkiss, Midland	1.000	3	3	0	0	0
Johnson, Arkansas*	.975	123	262	11	7	1
Jones, Shreveport*	.951	81	129	8	7	1

OUTFIELDERS—Continued

Player and Club	Pct.	G.	PO.	A.	E.	DP.
Kable, Arkansas*	1.000	5	3	0	0	0
Keedy, Midland	1.000	3	5	0	0	0
King, Midland*	.908	36	67	2	7	0
Ledbetter, Arkansas*	1.000	18	16	1	0	0
Liddle, Midland	1.000	2	1	0	0	0
Little, Jackson	.982	28	51	5	1	0
Litton, Shreveport	1.000	1	2	0	0	0
Lockwood, Jackson	1.000	2	2	0	0	0
Lubratich, Beaumont	1.000	2	3	2	0	0
Mace, Tulsa	.909	11	18	2	2	1
Mack, Beaumont	.971	113	255	14	8	4
Madril, Midland	.926	40	70	5	6	0
McCue, Shreveport	.969	102	178	8	6	0
McCulla, Arkansas	1.000	15	17	3	0	1
McDonald, Shreveport	1.000	9	24	0	0	0
McKnight, Jackson	.934	49	81	4	6	1
Montanari, Midland	1.000	19	40	0	0	0
Murphy, Arkansas	1.000	37	60	3	0	0
Newsom, San Antonio	.923	9	11	1	1	1
O'Brien, El Paso	1.000	4	8	0	0	0
Ortiz, Tulsa	.944	96	178	7	11	1
Parsons, Beaumont	.964	29	52	1	2	0
Pevey, Arkansas	1.000	4	3	0	0	0
Ramsey, San Antonio*	.992	109	254	10	2	3
Randall, Midland*	1.000	7	9	1	0	1
Robinson, Arkansas	.955	64	82	2	4	0
Rodriguez, Arkansas	.980	66	90	8	2	3
Romero, Midland	.987	32	76	1	1	0
Sasser, Shreveport	1.000	11	19	1	0	0
Schulte, Arkansas	1.000	16	24	0	0	0
Stanicek, El Paso	1.000	3	2	0	0	0
Stryffeler, Arkansas	.962	34	51	0	2	0
Tanner, Arkansas	.944	70	99	2	6	0
Tellez, San Antonio	.983	58	113	5	2	1
Thomas, Shreveport	1.000	27	62	2	0	1
Tovar, Midland	.978	90	216	7	5	1
Triplett, Tulsa	.960	66	135	8	6	3
Van Cleve, Tulsa	1.000	29	60	3	0	1
Varoz, Beaumont	.967	67	116	2	4	0
Walker, Midland	.978	47	79	12	2	2
Wilson, Jackson	.988	61	74	7	1	0

Triple Play—Madril.

CATCHERS

Player and Club	Pct.	G.	PO.	A.	E.	DP.	PB.
Agostinelli, Arkansas	.980	48	195	45	5	4	7
Alomar, Beaumont	.969	94	505	60	18	5	7
Bailey, Tulsa	1.000	1	11	0	0	0	0
Beuerlein, El Paso	.989	31	156	17	2	1	4
Brown, San Antonio	.984	54	276	34	5	5	5
Burrell, Shreveport	.972	45	225	20	8	1	7
Cadahia, Tulsa	.968	64	347	42	13	4	3
Carmichael, Jackson	.970	14	58	7	2	1	0
Castro, Beaumont	.950	45	265	21	15	1	3
Davis, Midland	.976	43	219	29	6	3	6
Grimes, Shreveport	.972	29	122	16	4	1	0
Gwosdz, Jackson	.990	61	348	29	4	4	4
Heath, Midland	.985	83	406	57	7	3	6
Huppert, El Paso	1.000	16	81	5	0	0	2
Liddle, Midland	.990	19	96	6	1	0	1
McCulla, Arkansas	.958	30	150	10	7	0	6
Nago, El Paso	1.000	7	49	3	0	0	1
O'Brien, El Paso	.991	80	422	43	4	6	6
Olson, Jackson	.990	64	347	49	4	10	7
Pevey, Arkansas	.987	45	206	22	3	1	2
Poole, Tulsa	.990	34	169	23	2	1	4
Rubel, Tulsa	1.000	4	19	2	0	0	0
Sasser, Shreveport	.984	74	448	59	8	4	4
Schroeder, El Paso	1.000	7	26	2	0	0	0
Stanley, Tulsa	.997	44	269	36	1	5	4
SZEKELY, San Antonio	.995	92	508	75	3	9	14
Wallace, Arkansas	.995	30	173	26	1	2	2
Winters, Jackson	.920	5	21	2	2	1	0

PITCHERS

Player and Club	Pct.	G.	PO.	A.	E.	DP.
Adamczak, Jackson	1.000	35	5	8	0	1
Aldrich, El Paso	1.000	40	1	7	0	0
Anderson, Tulsa	1.000	10	2	1	0	0
Arnold, Arkansas	1.000	5	3	4	0	0
Banning, Midland	.917	28	8	14	2	4
Bautista, Jackson	.857	7	0	6	1	0
Bayer, Jackson*	.667	1	1	1	1	0
Bergendahl, Jackson	.870	22	3	17	3	0
Bitker, Beaumont	.885	18	9	14	3	2
Blount, Beaumont*	.900	34	5	4	1	0
Brantley, Shreveport	.900	26	13	23	4	0
Brennan, San Antonio	.946	26	9	26	2	2
Buice, Midland	.870	45	7	13	3	0
Burkett, Shreveport	.964	22	12	15	1	1
Butler, Midland*	1.000	4	0	1	0	0
Carrasco, Arkansas	.887	27	16	31	6	3
Cedeno, Midland	.833	24	2	3	1	0
Cherry, Arkansas*	1.000	30	0	9	0	0
Clark, Midland	.789	57	6	9	4	0
Clay, El Paso	.917	15	4	7	1	0
Cocanower, Arkansas	1.000	5	1	4	0	0
Cook, Midland	.950	15	9	10	1	0
Corbell, Shreveport	.968	26	22	39	2	1
Corbett, Midland*	.947	26	5	13	1	0
J. Costello, Arkansas	.800	10	0	4	1	1
M. Costello, Beaumont	.971	27	5	28	1	2
Couchee, Tulsa	1.000	4	0	1	0	0
Crews, El Paso	1.000	15	2	11	0	3
Crim, El Paso	1.000	16	1	6	0	0
Devine, San Antonio	1.000	38	2	11	0	1
Diaz, El Paso	1.000	19	2	2	0	0
Dobie, Jackson	.871	28	10	17	4	1
Doyle, Beaumont	1.000	27	3	12	0	1
Duquette, El Paso*	1.000	13	0	3	0	0
Edens, Jackson	.964	16	9	18	1	0
Edwards, San Antonio*	1.000	33	5	21	0	1
Eichhorn, San Antonio	1.000	12	1	2	0	1
Embser, Arkansas*	.714	14	0	5	2	1
Ferlenda, Tulsa	1.000	21	8	11	0	0
Ferran, Shreveport	.938	46	13	32	3	3
FORD, Beaumont	1.000	67	4	28	0	2
Freeland, Shreveport	1.000	7	1	6	0	0
Fultz, Jackson	.850	23	5	12	3	2
Gonzalez, Midland	.833	18	1	4	1	0
Hamilton, San Antonio	.972	26	8	27	1	0
Harman, Tulsa	1.000	10	0	6	0	0
Hartshorn, Jackson	.974	27	12	26	1	2
Harvey, Midland*	.923	36	5	7	1	0
Heredia, San Antonio	1.000	39	4	6	0	1
Hill, Arkansas	1.000	3	1	1	0	0
Hillegas, San Antonio	.857	17	15	21	6	0
Hummel, Shreveport*	.864	19	3	16	3	1
Innis, Jackson	1.000	56	7	15	0	1
Keener, Arkansas	.923	62	2	10	1	0
Kendrick, El Paso*	.940	26	10	37	3	3
Kepshire, Arkansas	1.000	9	3	12	0	2
Kilgus, Tulsa*	1.000	41	2	15	0	2
Killingsworth, Tulsa	1.000	36	7	14	0	0
Knapp, Tulsa	.909	26	7	23	3	0
Kramer, Tulsa	1.000	26	1	3	0	0
Legumina, San Antonio*	1.000	10	0	1	0	0
Lenderman, Jackson	1.000	16	3	6	0	0
Livingston, San Antonio*	1.000	29	1	8	0	0
Lovelace, Midland*	.889	23	4	4	1	0
Loynd, Tulsa	1.000	5	4	3	0	0
Luebber, Beaumont	1.000	8	0	2	0	0
Lugo, Midland	1.000	2	3	0	0	0
Lundgren, Jackson	1.000	18	8	9	0	1
Lynch, Beaumont	.900	21	1	8	1	0
Madrid, El Paso	.938	27	6	24	2	4
Magrane, Arkansas*	.964	13	3	24	1	0
Mancuso, Beaumont*	.903	43	10	18	3	1
Martin, Arkansas	.926	22	6	19	2	0
May, San Antonio	.667	4	3	1	2	0
Mayberry, San Antonio	.833	3	2	3	1	0
McCament, Shreveport	1.000	8	1	4	0	0
McClain, Beaumont	.842	23	9	23	6	1
McKnight, Jackson	1.000	5	0	1	0	0
Medvin, Shreveport	1.000	49	4	11	0	1
Mena, San Antonio	.933	12	5	9	1	1
Mielke, Tulsa	.833	24	3	7	2	1
Mills, Beaumont	.969	30	9	22	1	2
Morlock, Arkansas	1.000	15	1	12	0	1
Murphy, El Paso	.850	18	6	11	3	0
Myers, El Paso	1.000	32	2	10	0	1
Newsom, San Antonio	1.000	1	0	1	0	0
North, Arkansas	.875	23	2	5	1	0
Oakes, Shreveport	.857	14	1	5	1	0
Ohnoutka, Shreveport	.913	18	7	14	2	2
Olsson, Tulsa	1.000	19	3	14	0	1
Peters, Arkansas*	1.000	10	0	4	0	1
Pimentel, Midland	1.000	29	4	11	0	1
Poston, Beaumont	.919	37	5	29	3	0
Price, Midland*	1.000	6	2	6	0	1
Pruitt, Jackson*	.882	31	4	11	2	0
Puikunas, Shreveport*	.875	48	5	16	3	0
Raether, Tulsa	1.000	21	1	11	0	3
Rhodes, Arkansas*	1.000	33	0	12	0	1

PITCHERS—Continued

Player and Club	Pct.	G.	PO.	A.	E.	DP.
Richardson, Jackson	1.000	1	0	1	0	0
Rodgers, Tulsa	.947	36	5	13	1	1
J. Rodriguez, Arkansas	1.000	1	0	1	0	0
R. Rodriguez, Jackson*	.900	13	3	6	1	0
Rogers, Tulsa*	1.000	10	1	4	0	0
Romanovsky, Midland*	1.000	11	3	5	0	0
Rowen, San Antonio*	1.000	3	2	1	0	0
Sadler, El Paso	1.000	8	4	7	0	0
Santiago, Jackson*	1.000	43	9	21	0	3
Scarpetta, El Paso*	.963	27	8	18	1	2
Shade, Arkansas	1.000	11	0	1	0	0
Sierra, Beaumont	1.000	16	2	13	0	0
Silver, Shreveport	1.000	13	3	7	0	0
Simmons, Beaumont	1.000	38	3	6	0	1
Soff, Arkansas	1.000	18	1	6	0	0
Stapleton, El Paso*	1.000	38	1	12	0	2
Tate, Shreveport	.846	36	4	7	2	0

Player and Club	Pct.	G.	PO.	A.	E.	DP.
Taylor, Tulsa	.857	11	0	12	2	1
Tejeda, San Antonio*	1.000	34	2	4	0	0
Timberlake, Midland	.840	19	7	14	4	0
Torres, San Antonio	.917	54	3	8	1	2
Valdez, Tulsa*	1.000	4	1	1	0	0
Venturino, Midland	1.000	15	5	6	0	1
Vila, San Antonio	1.000	2	1	0	0	0
Walker, El Paso	1.000	13	3	14	0	0
Ward, Shreveport*	.833	4	0	5	1	1
Weissman, Arkansas	1.000	29	3	6	0	0
Weston, Jackson	1.000	34	6	9	0	1
Wilson, Tulsa*	.867	24	8	18	4	1
Wohler, San Antonio*	.875	26	4	10	2	0
Wyatt, Jackson*	1.000	2	0	1	0	0
J. Young, Jackson*	1.000	3	0	2	0	1
S. Young, Arkansas	1.000	20	8	18	0	1

The following players do not have any recorded accepted chances at the positions indicated; therefore, are not listed in the fielding averages for those particular positions: Bates, of; Bootay, 3b; K. Brown, p; Carter, p; Clements, 1b; Davis, 1b; Gibbons, p; Gutierrez, p; Hotchkiss, p; Kilgus, of; Lachowicz, p; Livingston, of; Peters, of; Ramsey, p; L. Smith, p; Stanley, 3b; Tellez, 3b; Wachs, p; Wallace, of.

CLUB PITCHING

Club	ERA.	G.	CG.	ShO.	Sv.	IP.	H.	R.	ER.	HR.	HB.	BB.	Int. BB.	SO.	WP.	Bk.
Shreveport	3.23	136	25	17	28	1175.0	1022	523	422	60	45	500	11	796	72	17
Arkansas	3.73	135	22	9	36	1113.1	1092	573	461	67	27	468	42	695	58	5
San Antonio	4.21	135	25	7	27	1179.2	1226	638	552	107	15	531	41	758	65	13
Jackson	4.26	136	13	7	39	1159.0	1172	628	549	83	26	501	21	729	82	9
Tulsa	4.50	134	19	6	26	1132.2	1125	653	566	77	44	575	26	787	70	23
Beaumont	4.54	136	9	6	35	1197.0	1323	722	604	80	37	543	39	727	67	14
El Paso	4.80	135	20	7	43	1172.0	1392	716	625	128	22	378	18	698	44	18
Midland	5.19	133	19	9	22	1139.1	1266	766	657	112	43	565	24	685	74	17

PITCHERS' RECORDS

(Leading Qualifiers for Earned-Run Average Leadership — 109 or More Innings)

*Throws lefthanded.

Pitcher—Club	W.	L.	Pct.	ERA.	G.	GS.	CG.	GF.	ShO.	Sv.	IP.	H.	R.	ER.	HR.	HB.	BB.	Int. BB.	SO.	WP.
Ferran, Shreveport	16	1	.941	2.29	46	9	3	17	2	4	153.1	114	45	39	6	8	64	1	147	3
Burkett, Shreveport	10	6	.625	2.66	22	21	4	0	2	0	128.2	99	46	38	7	4	42	0	73	3
Corbell, Shreveport	11	6	.647	2.95	26	26	8	0	4	0	176.2	163	67	58	6	9	36	0	69	5
Hillegas, San Antonio	9	5	.643	3.06	17	17	7	0	1	0	132.1	107	60	45	7	2	58	1	97	7
Carrasco, Arkansas	9	12	.429	3.30	27	26	3	1	0	1	158.1	151	92	58	8	3	61	5	81	6
Martin, Arkansas	7	7	.500	3.38	22	20	3	1	0	1	136.0	140	63	51	14	3	38	4	82	7
Brantley, Shreveport	8	10	.444	3.48	26	26	8	0	3	0	165.2	139	78	64	13	6	68	0	125	11
Bitker, Beaumont	7	7	.500	3.53	18	17	2	1	2	0	114.2	114	55	45	2	6	52	4	91	4
Dobie, Jackson	13	7	.650	3.66	28	27	2	0	1	0	155.0	113	70	63	16	1	94	0	123	15
S. Young, Arkansas	11	3	.786	3.73	20	19	1	1	0	0	125.1	117	56	52	4	3	40	0	48	3

Departmental Leaders: G—Ford, 67; W—Ferran, 16; L—Knapp, 16; Pct.—Ferran, .941; GS—M. Costello, Dobie, Madrid, Scarpetta, 27; CG—Brantley, Corbell, 8; GF—Ford, 54; ShO—Corbell, 4; Sv.—Innis, 25; IP—Corbell, 176.2; H—Madrid, 213; R—Madrid, 119; ER—Madrid, 106; HR—Kendrick, 22; HB—M. Costello, 10; BB—Wilson, 103; IBB—Heredia, 11; SO—Ferran, 147; WP—Dobie, Mills, 15.

(All Pitchers—Listed Alphabetically)

Pitcher—Club	W.	L.	Pct.	ERA.	G.	GS.	CG.	GF.	ShO.	Sv.	IP.	H.	R.	ER.	HR.	HB.	BB.	Int. BB.	SO.	WP.
Adamczak, Jackson	3	6	.333	4.46	35	0	0	16	0	5	68.2	77	39	34	6	2	29	0	31	5
Aldrich, El Paso	3	3	.500	3.48	40	0	0	36	0	20	54.1	60	24	21	4	1	18	3	34	2
Anderson, Tulsa	0	0	.000	1.45	10	0	0	7	0	5	18.2	11	4	3	0	0	8	0	13	0
Arnold, Arkansas	4	1	.800	3.81	5	5	1	0	1	0	28.1	24	15	12	1	1	14	0	23	0
Banning, Midland	4	5	.444	5.38	28	10	1	6	1	0	93.2	107	60	56	10	3	43	2	32	5
Bautista, Jackson	0	1	.000	8.31	7	4	0	0	0	0	21.2	36	22	20	3	1	8	0	13	3
Bayer, Jackson*	0	0	.000	10.38	1	1	0	0	0	0	4.1	9	7	5	1	0	2	0	2	2
Bergendahl, Jackson	6	8	.429	6.28	22	19	0	0	0	0	106.0	121	77	74	10	2	64	0	77	8
Bitker, Beaumont	7	7	.500	3.53	18	17	2	1	2	0	114.2	114	55	45	2	6	52	4	91	4
Blount, Beaumont*	1	2	.333	3.59	34	0	0	13	0	6	47.2	47	24	19	1	3	14	0	25	3
Brantley, Shreveport	8	10	.444	3.48	26	26	8	0	3	0	165.2	139	78	64	13	6	68	0	125	11
Brennan, San Antonio	7	9	.438	3.87	26	21	3	2	0	0	146.2	149	75	63	11	2	61	7	83	7
Brown, Tulsa	0	0	.000	4.50	3	2	0	0	0	0	10.0	9	7	5	0	0	5	0	10	0
Buice, Midland	8	6	.571	3.45	45	0	0	42	0	14	78.1	70	34	30	3	1	22	4	73	6
Burkett, Shreveport	10	6	.625	2.66	22	21	4	0	2	0	128.2	99	46	38	7	4	42	0	73	3
Butler, Midland*	0	0	.000	16.20	4	0	0	0	0	0	5.0	12	9	9	1	0	3	0	2	0
Carrasco, Arkansas	9	12	.429	3.30	27	26	3	1	0	1	158.1	151	92	58	8	3	61	5	81	6
Carter, Midland	0	0	.000	4.82	4	0	0	2	0	1	9.1	10	6	5	1	1	4	1	3	0
Cedeno, Midland	1	4	.200	7.66	24	3	0	7	0	0	47.0	48	43	40	8	2	44	0	27	8
Cherry, Arkansas*	3	4	.429	3.56	30	5	1	7	0	4	55.2	48	26	22	4	2	34	2	53	5
Clark, Midland	9	4	.692	3.29	57	2	0	32	0	4	90.1	98	49	33	6	4	28	3	66	1
Clay, El Paso	5	1	.833	3.42	15	4	0	7	0	1	55.1	53	22	21	7	0	14	2	26	1
Cocanower, Arkansas	1	1	.500	9.35	5	4	0	0	0	0	17.1	23	19	18	0	1	13	2	9	2
Cook, Midland	4	6	.400	3.50	15	15	2	0	0	0	105.1	101	54	41	2	2	52	0	82	10
Corbell, Shreveport	11	6	.647	2.95	26	26	8	0	4	0	176.2	163	67	58	6	9	36	0	69	5
Corbett, Midland*	7	10	.412	4.88	26	24	6	0	0	0	147.2	168	94	80	16	3	56	0	82	6
J. Costello, Arkansas	0	0	.000	5.40	10	0	0	5	0	1	15.0	17	11	9	1	0	6	1	10	1
M. Costello, Beaumont	9	10	.474	5.22	27	27	2	0	0	0	157.0	170	100	91	14	10	88	4	90	10
Couchee, Tulsa	0	1	.000	8.10	4	0	0	3	0	0	3.1	3	3	3	1	1	1	0	2	0
Crews, El Paso	5	5	.500	4.76	15	15	4	0	1	0	90.2	114	53	48	13	0	18	1	50	3
Crim, El Paso	2	4	.333	2.77	16	0	0	13	0	6	39.0	35	16	12	5	2	2	2	32	0
Devine, San Antonio	5	3	.625	4.80	38	3	1	11	0	2	75.0	82	43	40	13	1	30	2	40	2
Diaz, El Paso	1	2	.333	4.59	19	0	0	10	0	3	33.1	33	19	17	1	0	19	5	20	2
Dobie, Jackson	13	7	.650	3.66	28	27	2	0	1	0	155.0	113	70	63	16	1	94	0	123	15
Doyle, Beaumont	3	8	.273	5.68	27	8	0	5	0	0	76.0	89	52	48	5	3	37	2	48	7
Duquette, El Paso*	1	1	.500	6.27	13	1	0	5	0	0	33.0	38	25	23	0	1	19	1	21	2

Pitcher—Club	W.	L.	Pct.	ERA.	G.	GS.	CG.	GF.	ShO.	Sv.	IP.	H.	R.	ER.	HR.	HB.	BB.	Int. BB.	SO.	WP.
Edens, Jackson	9	4	.692	2.55	16	16	4	0	0	0	106.0	76	36	30	4	1	41	1	72	10
Edwards, San Antonio*	9	10	.474	3.77	33	20	4	10	2	4	140.2	128	63	59	14	0	55	1	123	7
Eichhorn, San Antonio	0	1	.000	3.92	12	0	0	5	0	0	20.2	26	13	9	0	0	13	4	6	1
Embser, Arkansas*	3	2	.600	4.91	14	2	0	4	0	1	29.1	30	20	16	1	1	20	2	30	2
Ferlenda, Tulsa	6	13	.316	4.25	21	21	5	0	1	0	125.0	110	70	59	11	0	84	4	91	7
Ferran, Shreveport	16	1	.941	2.29	46	9	3	17	2	4	153.1	114	45	39	6	8	64	1	147	3
Ford, Beaumont	2	9	.182	3.72	67	0	0	54	0	17	82.1	83	45	34	1	2	56	7	64	1
Freeland, Shreveport	1	2	.333	3.78	7	7	0	0	0	0	33.1	31	21	14	1	2	13	0	21	6
Fultz, Jackson	5	4	.556	4.94	23	12	2	3	1	1	89.1	113	59	49	8	2	20	1	34	1
Gibbons, El Paso*	0	0	.000	1.80	2	0	0	2	0	0	5.0	5	1	1	0	0	0	0	2	0
Gonzalez, Midland	1	1	.500	3.42	18	0	0	6	0	0	26.1	31	17	10	5	2	21	1	12	2
Gutierrez, San Antonio	0	0	.000	1.80	2	0	0	2	0	0	5.0	5	1	1	0	0	1	0	2	1
Hamilton, San Antonio	12	5	.706	3.91	26	24	7	0	2	0	147.1	156	76	64	9	2	64	3	67	11
Harman, Tulsa	1	2	.333	3.63	10	1	0	3	0	0	22.1	23	9	9	1	2	9	1	11	3
Hartshorn, Jackson	11	4	.733	3.76	27	26	1	0	0	0	153.1	169	82	64	8	9	58	0	86	5
Harvey, Midland*	2	1	.667	5.61	35	1	1	8	0	2	59.1	61	40	37	9	4	34	3	49	2
Heredia, San Antonio	2	5	.286	3.29	39	0	0	16	0	2	65.2	64	28	24	1	0	37	11	57	4
Hill, Arkansas	1	2	.333	4.50	3	3	1	0	0	0	18.0	18	10	9	0	0	7	0	9	3
Hillegas, San Antonio	9	5	.643	3.06	17	17	7	0	1	0	132.1	107	60	45	7	2	58	1	97	7
Hotchkiss, Midland	0	0	.000	13.06	7	0	0	5	0	0	10.1	20	20	15	1	3	6	0	3	1
Hummel, Shreveport*	5	7	.417	3.28	19	14	1	2	0	0	85.0	66	40	31	7	2	57	1	45	9
Innis, Jackson	4	5	.444	2.45	56	0	0	48	0	25	92.0	69	30	25	2	1	24	3	75	2
Keener, Arkansas	2	6	.250	3.84	62	1	0	40	0	15	82.0	89	37	35	5	1	51	6	64	4
Kendrick, El Paso*	14	6	.700	4.56	26	26	5	0	2	0	169.2	194	98	86	22	1	60	1	98	8
Kepshire, Arkansas	2	4	.333	4.35	9	9	0	0	0	0	51.2	58	34	25	7	1	14	0	28	0
Kilgus, Tulsa*	3	7	.300	3.73	41	7	2	24	0	8	103.2	102	56	43	7	4	36	5	59	4
Killingsworth, Tulsa	10	5	.667	3.77	36	16	3	7	0	1	129.0	122	63	54	7	2	71	3	63	11
Knapp, Tulsa	6	16	.273	5.89	26	26	4	0	1	0	160.1	182	115	105	13	7	67	1	97	5
Kramer, Tulsa	0	3	.000	4.38	26	0	0	17	0	3	39.0	40	22	19	0	2	19	1	32	3
Lachowicz, Jackson	0	1	.000	9.00	1	1	0	0	0	0	3.0	1	4	3	0	0	7	0	1	1
Legumina, San Antonio*	1	1	.500	4.41	10	0	0	4	0	0	16.1	20	9	8	1	0	8	1	12	1
Lenderman, Jackson	3	4	.429	3.68	16	6	1	7	0	1	51.1	50	24	21	0	1	22	1	38	8
Livingston, San Antonio*	1	8	.111	4.48	29	6	1	18	0	9	66.1	59	45	33	7	1	40	1	52	5
Lovelace, Midland*	2	4	.333	8.93	23	6	0	2	0	0	42.1	45	46	42	4	4	58	0	27	13
Loynd, Tulsa	2	1	.667	3.68	5	5	0	0	0	0	29.1	32	12	12	2	0	3	0	31	6
Luebber, Beaumont	0	0	.000	4.29	8	0	0	3	0	0	21.0	20	10	10	4	0	13	0	14	1
Lugo, Midland	1	1	.500	1.64	2	2	0	0	0	0	11.0	9	2	2	0	0	4	0	4	0
Lundgren, Jackson	4	6	.400	4.59	17	9	1	3	0	0	64.2	72	37	33	3	0	25	2	37	2
Lynch, Beaumont	0	2	.000	4.66	21	0	0	6	0	1	38.2	53	26	20	5	0	16	4	29	3
Madrid, El Paso	12	9	.571	6.03	27	27	3	0	1	0	158.1	213	119	106	17	4	51	1	99	3
Magrane, Arkansas*	8	4	.667	2.42	13	13	5	0	2	0	89.1	66	29	24	3	2	31	0	66	8
Mancuso, Beaumont*	4	3	.571	4.78	43	5	0	11	0	2	86.2	112	60	46	6	3	30	2	53	7
Martin, Arkansas	7	7	.500	3.38	22	20	3	1	0	1	136.0	140	63	51	14	3	38	4	82	7
May, San Antonio	2	0	1.000	5.25	4	4	1	0	0	0	24.0	31	15	14	3	1	7	0	12	1
Mayberry, San Antonio	1	2	.333	4.58	3	3	0	0	0	0	17.2	12	9	9	1	0	13	0	10	0
McCament, Shreveport	2	1	.667	2.79	8	0	0	6	0	2	19.1	16	7	6	1	0	4	2	16	1
McClain, Beaumont	6	8	.429	4.73	23	19	1	3	1	1	118.0	115	77	62	4	4	77	5	79	7
McKnight, Jackson	0	0	.000	1.50	5	0	0	5	0	0	6.0	4	1	1	0	0	1	0	1	0
Medvin, Shreveport	8	6	.571	2.40	49	0	0	26	0	6	93.2	71	32	25	1	8	42	2	68	11
Mena, San Antonio	1	8	.111	5.43	12	12	0	0	0	0	69.2	73	48	42	6	2	28	1	34	5
Mielke, Tulsa	2	0	1.000	3.45	24	1	0	12	0	2	47.0	41	22	18	2	2	32	1	48	4
Mills, Beaumont	6	11	.353	5.62	30	26	1	1	0	1	155.1	192	117	97	15	2	64	3	70	15
Morlock, Arkansas	2	5	.286	4.50	15	15	2	0	1	0	78.0	92	46	39	6	3	30	2	48	4
Murphy, El Paso	9	2	.818	4.41	18	18	1	0	0	0	116.1	126	63	57	10	3	40	0	89	4
Myers, El Paso	5	2	.714	7.35	32	0	0	16	0	6	78.1	113	66	64	15	4	21	0	52	3
Newsom, San Antonio	0	0	.000	9.00	1	0	0	1	0	0	2.0	1	2	2	1	0	3	0	0	0
North, Arkansas	2	2	.500	2.89	23	1	0	9	0	0	43.2	36	21	14	0	0	23	2	17	3
Oakes, Shreveport	1	0	1.000	5.64	14	0	0	13	0	1	22.1	32	17	14	0	0	6	0	13	0
Ohnoutka, Shreveport	7	9	.438	4.76	18	18	1	0	1	0	85.0	86	52	45	7	2	52	0	64	4
Olsson, Tulsa	2	8	.200	5.80	19	10	1	4	0	0	76.0	96	57	49	6	6	28	1	52	5
Peters, Arkansas*	3	3	.500	3.81	10	7	2	2	1	1	49.2	50	25	21	6	0	15	2	32	1
Pimentel, Midland	9	8	.529	4.82	29	19	4	3	0	0	130.2	136	81	70	17	0	68	3	94	7
Poston, Beaumont	10	10	.500	4.62	37	19	2	5	1	0	142.1	180	90	73	10	4	28	3	34	6
Price, Midland*	4	1	.800	4.62	6	6	1	0	0	0	37.0	43	19	19	2	2	17	4	21	3
Pruitt, Jackson*	0	1	.000	3.92	31	0	0	11	0	2	41.1	47	19	18	3	0	17	4	36	2
Puikunas, Shreveport*	4	3	.571	3.36	48	1	0	22	0	7	77.2	74	43	29	4	2	31	4	60	8
Raether, Tulsa	3	1	.750	3.21	21	0	0	19	0	4	33.2	24	12	12	1	2	12	2	21	2
Ramsey, San Antonio*	0	0	.000	27.00	1	0	0	1	0	0	1.0	4	3	3	0	0	2	0	0	0
Rhodes, Arkansas*	1	2	.333	3.96	33	1	1	14	0	4	38.2	45	18	17	3	0	13	4	20	2
Richardson, Jackson	0	1	.000	18.00	1	1	0	0	0	0	3.0	6	8	6	0	0	4	0	2	2
Rodgers, Tulsa	4	4	.500	3.44	36	4	0	16	0	3	91.2	97	40	35	5	6	36	3	71	2
J. Rodriguez, Arkansas	0	0	.000	9.00	1	0	0	1	0	0	1.0	0	1	1	0	0	3	0	0	2
R. Rodriguez, Jackson*	3	4	.429	9.00	13	5	1	2	0	0	33.0	51	35	33	5	0	15	2	15	2
Rogers, Tulsa*	0	3	.000	9.91	10	4	0	2	0	0	26.1	39	30	29	4	0	18	1	23	3
Romanovsky, Midland*	3	5	.375	6.12	11	11	2	0	0	0	64.2	85	49	44	8	1	20	0	36	1
Rowen, San Antonio*	1	2	.333	5.40	3	3	0	0	0	0	13.1	17	8	8	0	0	10	0	15	1
Sadler, El Paso	1	3	.250	7.64	8	7	1	0	0	0	35.1	53	34	30	8	0	14	0	14	7
Santiago, Jackson*	6	1	.857	3.71	43	0	0	20	0	3	68.0	63	29	28	4	2	31	4	38	8
Scarpetta, El Paso*	15	6	.714	4.22	27	27	4	0	1	0	158.0	191	91	74	14	1	50	0	83	4
Shade, Arkansas	1	3	.250	7.43	11	1	0	6	0	1	13.1	13	12	11	1	0	15	3	10	3
Sierra, Beaumont	4	5	.444	4.86	16	15	1	0	1	0	90.2	104	53	49	11	0	37	0	60	1
Silver, Shreveport	1	3	.250	5.48	13	8	0	0	0	0	46.0	55	33	28	5	1	28	0	21	6
Simmons, Beaumont	8	1	.889	1.35	38	0	0	25	0	7	66.2	44	13	10	2	0	31	5	70	2
Smith, Midland*	0	2	.000	8.10	4	0	0	1	0	1	3.1	3	3	3	1	0	1	0	2	0
Soff, Arkansas	3	2	.600	1.27	18	0	0	14	0	6	21.1	19	7	3	1	0	7	1	17	0
Stapleton, El Paso*	6	2	.750	3.15	38	0	0	24	0	6	68.2	75	34	24	3	3	22	1	37	4
Tate, Shreveport	5	1	.833	3.39	36	2	0	25	0	8	63.2	56	33	24	2	1	41	1	57	5
Taylor, Tulsa	3	7	.300	3.95	11	11	2	0	1	0	68.1	65	40	30	6	2	37	3	64	3
Tejeda, San Antonio*	2	3	.400	4.96	34	1	0	8	0	2	49.0	61	31	27	5	0	23	3	29	1
Timberlake, Midland	5	7	.417	5.37	19	19	2	0	1	0	104.0	113	76	62	6	7	52	2	37	7
Torres, San Antonio	5	4	.556	3.86	54	0	0	31	0	8	77.0	79	35	33	10	2	27	4	66	7
Valdez, Tulsa*	0	1	.000	5.84	4	2	0	1	0	0	12.1	12	8	8	1	1	6	0	4	0

Pitcher—Club	W.	L.	Pct.	ERA.	G.	GS.	CG.	GF.	ShO.	Sv.	IP.	H.	R.	ER.	HR.	HB.	BB.	Int. BB.	SO.	WP.
Venturino, Midland	2	6	.250	7.21	15	15	0	0	0	0	73.2	106	64	59	12	4	32	1	33	2
Vila, San Antonio	1	0	1.000	6.52	2	2	0	0	0	0	9.2	13	7	7	2	1	7	0	6	0
Wachs, Jackson*	0	0	.000	9.00	1	0	0	1	0	0	1.0	2	1	1	1	0	0	0	0	0
Walker, El Paso	6	4	.600	4.81	13	10	2	2	1	1	76.2	89	51	41	9	2	30	1	41	1
Ward, Shreveport*	1	1	.500	2.55	4	4	0	0	0	0	24.2	20	9	7	0	0	16	0	17	0
Weissman, Arkansas	4	4	.500	3.52	29	3	2	8	1	1	61.1	56	31	24	2	6	33	6	48	2
Weston, Jackson	4	4	.500	4.33	34	4	0	7	0	2	70.2	73	40	34	9	4	27	3	36	3
Wilson, Tulsa*	7	13	.350	4.87	24	24	2	0	0	0	136.2	117	83	74	10	7	103	0	95	12
Wohler, San Antonio*	5	5	.500	5.47	26	19	1	1	1	0	100.1	139	67	61	16	1	44	2	47	4
Wyatt, Jackson*	1	0	1.000	1.50	2	2	1	0	1	0	12.0	8	2	2	0	0	6	0	7	1
J. Young, Jackson*	0	2	.000	6.23	3	3	0	0	0	0	8.2	12	6	6	0	0	6	0	5	2
S. Young, Arkansas	11	3	.786	3.73	20	19	1	1	0	0	125.1	117	56	52	4	3	40	0	48	3

BALKS—Madrid, Wilson, 6 each; Knapp, 5; Killingsworth, Medvin, Scarpetta, 4 each; Bergendàhl, Burkett, Corbett, Edwards, Kendrick, Kilgus, Lynch, 3 each; Banning, Blount, Brantley, Cook, M. Costello, Devine, Ferran, Ford, Hamilton, Hartshorn, Lenderman, Livingston, Lovelace, McClain, Mills, Pimentel, Puikunas, Romanovsky, Sadler, 2 each; Aldrich, Bitker, Brown, Buice, Cedeno, Cherry, Cocanower, Crews, Dobie, Gonzalez, Heredia, Hill, Kramer, Legumina, Loynd, Lundgren, Myers, Oakes, Ohnoutka, Peters, Rhodes, Rogers, Silver, Torres, Valdez, Venturino, Ward, Wohler, 1 each.

COMBINATION SHUTOUTS—Magrane-Soff, Young-Soff, Magrane-Keener-Rhodes-Soff, Arkansas; Costello-Ford, Beaumont; Madrid-Aldrich, El Paso; Edens-Fultz, Dobie-Adamczak, Hartshorn-Innis, Lenderman-Pruitt, Jackson; Banning-Buice, Banning-Clark, Pimentel-Harvey, Cook-Clark, Lovelace-Clark, Lugo-Buice, Pimentel-Buice, Midland; Hamilton-Torres, San Antonio; Burkett-Medvin 2, Hummel-Tate, Ohnoutka-Tate, Ferran-Puikunas, Shreveport; Knapp-Anderson, Killingsworth-Kilgus, Killingsworth-Rodgers, Tulsa.

NO-HIT GAMES—None.

California League

CLASS A

CHAMPIONSHIP WINNERS IN PREVIOUS YEARS

1914—Fresno .571
1915—Modesto .857
1916-40—Did not operate.
1941—Fresno .643
S. Barbara (2nd)* .597
1942—Santa Barbara† .642
1943-44-45—Did not operate.
1946—Stockton‡ .600
1947—Stockton‡ .679
1948—Fresno .607
S. Barbara (3rd)* .529
1949—Bakersfield .612
San Jose (4th)* .543
1950—Ventura .607
Modesto (2nd)* .586
1951—Santa Barbara‡ .599
1952—Fresno‡ .629
1953—San Jose‡ .664
1954—Modesto‡ .623
1955—Stockton .733
Fresno§ .718
1956—Fresno‡ .650
1957—Visalia x .622
Salinas (4th)* .504
1958—Fresno* .639
Bakersfield .672
1959—Bakersfield .592
Modesto§ .643
1960—Reno .614
Reno .657
1961—Reno .743
Reno .643
1962—San Jose§ .686
Reno .587
1963—Modesto .589
Stockton§ .687
1964—Fresno .638
Fresno .600
1965—San Jose .586
Stockton§ .614
1966—Modesto .577
Modesto .671
1967—San Jose§ .676
Modesto .586
1968—San Jose .629
Fresno§ .623
1969—Stockton§ .600
Visalia .614
1970—Bakersfield .667
Bakersfield .671
1971—Visalia§ .583
Fresno .500
1972—Modesto§ .547
Bakersfield .629
1973—Lodi§ .657
Bakersfield .571
1974—Fresno§ .607
San Jose .579
1975—Reno .614
Reno .614
1976—Salinas .650
Reno§ .547
1977—Salinas .564
Lodi§ .579
1978—Visalia§ .698
Lodi .607
1979—San Jose§ .636
Reno .525
1980—Stockton§ .638
Visalia .507
1981—Visalia .621
Lodi§ .521
1982—Modesto§ .671
Visalia .586
1983—Visalia .621
Redwood§ .529
1984—Modesto§ .597
Bakersfield .486
1985—Fresno§ .575
Stockton .566

*Won four-club playoff. †League disbanded June 28. ‡Won championship and four-club playoff. §Won split-season playoff. xWon both halves of split-season.

STANDING OF CLUBS AT CLOSE OF FIRST HALF, JUNE 22

NORTHERN DIVISION

Club	W.	L.	T.	Pct.	G.B.
Salinas (Mariners)	39	32	0	.549	....
Reno (Padres)	38	33	0	.535	1
Stockton (Brewers)	35	36	0	.493	4
Modesto (A's)	33	38	0	.465	6
San Jose (Independent)	28	43	0	.394	11

SOUTHERN DIVISION

Club	W.	L.	T.	Pct.	G.B.
Palm Springs (Angels)	48	23	0	.676	....
Ventura County (Blue Jays)	45	26	0	.634	3
Fresno (Giants)	37	34	0	.521	11
Visalia (Twins)	32	39	0	.451	16
Bakersfield (Dodgers)	20	51	0	.282	28

STANDING OF CLUBS AT CLOSE OF SECOND HALF, AUGUST 31

NORTHERN DIVISION

Club	W.	L.	T.	Pct.	G.B.
Stockton (Brewers)	48	23	0	.676	....
Salinas (Mariners)	38	33	0	.535	10
San Jose (Independent)	37	34	0	.521	11
Modesto (A's)	36	35	0	.507	12
Reno (Padres)	35	36	0	.493	13

SOUTHERN DIVISION

Club	W.	L.	T.	Pct.	G.B.
Visalia (Twins)	43	28	0	.606	....
Palm Springs (Angels)	39	32	0	.549	4
Ventura County (Blue Jays)	30	41	0	.423	13
Fresno (Giants)	29	42	0	.408	14
Bakersfield (Dodgers)	20	51	0	.282	23

COMPOSITE STANDING OF CLUBS AT CLOSE OF SEASON, AUGUST 31

Club	Sto.	Sal.	Reno.	Mod.	SJ.	PS.	VC.	Vis.	Fr.	Bak.	W.	L.	T.	Pct.	G.B.
NORTHERN DIVISION															
Stockton (Brewers)	....	11	15	9	10	6	7	7	7	11	83	59	0	.585	....
Salinas (Mariners)	11	....	8	13	13	6	7	5	5	9	77	65	0	.542	6
Reno (Padres)	7	12	....	10	18	1	3	5	7	10	73	69	0	.514	10
Modesto (A's)	11	7	10	....	9	3	6	8	7	8	69	73	0	.486	14
San Jose (Independent)	6	7	6	11	....	6	10	5	7	7	65	77	0	.458	18
SOUTHERN DIVISION															
Palm Springs (Angels)	6	6	7	9	8	....	13	9	11	18	87	55	0	.613	....
Ventura County (Blue Jays)	7	5	5	8	2	11	....	11	15	11	75	67	0	.528	12
Visalia (Twins)	5	7	7	4	7	11	9	....	11	14	75	67	0	.528	12
Fresno (Giants)	5	7	7	5	5	7	5	11	....	14	66	76	0	.465	21
Bakersfield (Dodgers)	1	3	4	4	5	4	7	6	6	....	40	102	0	.282	47

Major league affiliations in parentheses.

Playoffs—Stockton defeated Salinas, three games to none; Visalia defeated Palm Springs, three games to one; Stockton defeated Visalia, three games to none, to win league championship.

Regular-Season Attendance—Bakersfield, 78,635; Fresno, 100,348; Modesto, 72,757; Palm Springs, 47,547; Reno, 81,397; Salinas, 47,737; San Jose, 87,235; Stockton, 56,129; Ventura County, 38,868; Visalia, 72,962. Total, 683,615. Playoffs, 11,204. All-Star Game, 2,860.

Managers—Bakersfield, Don LeJohn; Fresno, Tim Blackwell; Modesto, Tom Reynolds; Palm Springs, John Kotchman; Reno, Jim Skaalen; Salinas, Greg Mahlberg; San Jose, Harry Steve, Mike Verdi; Stockton, Dave Machemer; Ventura County, Glenn Ezell; Visalia, Dan Schmitz.

All-Star Team—(Northern Division)—1B—Brad Pounders, Reno; 2B—Norio Tanabe, San Jose; 3B—Joe Mitchell, Stockton; SS—Joe Xavier, Modesto; OF—Todd Brown, Stockton; Felix Jose, Modesto; Jerald Clark, Reno; C—Bill McGuire, Salinas; DH—Ty Brilinski, Modesto;

P—Ed Puig, Reno. (Southern Division)—1B—Ty Van Burkleo, Palm Springs; 2B—Ted Holcomb, Bakersfield; 3B—Ty Dabney, Fresno; SS—Tony Perezchica, Fresno; OF—Geronimo Berroa, Ventura County; Tom Thomas, Visalia; T.J. McDonald, Fresno; C—Greg Myers, Ventura County; DH—Mike Burke, Bakersfield; P—Willie Fraser, Palm Springs. Most Valuable Player—Ty Dabney, Fresno; Pitcher of the Year—Jeff Peterek, Stockton; Manager of the Year—Tom Kotchman, Palm Springs.

(Compiled by William J. Weiss, League Statistician, San Mateo, Calif.)

CLUB BATTING

Club	Pct.	G.	AB.	R.	OR.	H.	TB.	2B.	3B.	HR.	RBI.	GW.	SH.	SF.	HP.	BB.	Int. BB.	SO.	SB.	CS.	LOB.
Reno	.290	142	4759	815	789	1378	1996	206	44	108	712	60	43	65	42	527	14	770	124	61	1076
Fresno	.274	142	4667	732	788	1277	1882	267	46	82	643	60	57	49	54	501	29	966	185	104	962
Visalia	.273	142	4636	770	712	1267	1772	213	29	78	682	61	61	64	53	684	38	674	102	72	1097
Ventura County	.272	142	4750	711	676	1291	1969	218	47	122	624	67	22	43	46	476	23	977	204	91	970
Palm Springs	.270	142	4711	813	650	1271	1827	224	46	80	727	79	48	60	37	768	25	1018	133	72	1117
Stockton	.269	142	4553	797	640	1225	1870	234	48	105	719	77	56	51	42	663	23	865	198	83	1018
San Jose	.269	142	4483	547	681	1206	1608	184	34	50	474	58	60	39	21	417	16	728	126	86	969
Salinas	.268	142	4696	681	634	1257	1732	212	49	55	604	65	46	51	34	554	27	736	168	122	1031
Modesto	.265	142	4543	778	759	1205	1756	180	43	95	693	59	46	47	48	743	28	989	139	82	1094
Bakersfield	.247	142	4701	551	866	1159	1593	207	22	61	466	31	56	38	57	524	17	909	77	65	1102

INDIVIDUAL BATTING

(Leading Qualifiers for Batting Championship—383 or More Plate Appearances)

*Bats lefthanded. †Switch-hitter.

Player and Club	Pct.	G.	AB.	R.	H.	TB.	2B.	3B.	HR.	RBI.	GW.	SH.	SF.	HP.	BB.	Int. BB.	SO.	SB.	CS.
Alomar, Roberto, Reno	.346	90	356	53	123	159	16	4	4	49	2	6	7	3	32	2	38	14	8
Dabney, Ty, Fresno*	.343	121	446	75	153	238	36	2	15	107	9	1	6	1	47	8	64	3	8
Jennings, Douglas, Palm Springs*	.317	129	429	95	136	236	31	9	17	89	11	2	8	10	117	7	103	7	11
Wasem, James, Reno	.317	89	344	79	109	132	9	4	2	24	0	4	5	3	45	0	24	18	10
Monico, Mario, Stockton*	.315	104	324	64	102	143	26	3	3	57	3	1	4	1	56	2	40	4	4
Dewolf, Robert, Stockton*	.312	135	500	98	156	225	23	14	6	59	3	10	5	3	77	5	92	51	13
Thomas, Thomas, Visalia*	.310	134	500	96	155	190	18	7	1	44	6	4	8	4	94	3	51	34	19
Krause, Thomas, Salinas*	.309	107	376	43	116	152	15	9	1	48	4	4	5	0	41	2	34	17	11
McDonald, Thomas, Fresno	.308	125	471	95	145	200	30	5	5	54	6	6	7	3	59	3	83	34	15
Tanabe, Norio, San Jose	.306	140	542	76	166	224	23	4	9	64	8	9	8	0	18	1	82	23	12
Garcia, Santiago, Ventura County	.306	105	405	78	124	182	25	3	9	61	8	0	6	2	35	1	54	32	8

Departmental Leaders: G—Tanabe, 140; AB—Yelding, 560; R—Schwarz, 102; H—Tanabe, 166; TB—Pounders, 271; 2B—Dabney, 36; 3B—Dewolf, 14; HR—Pounders, 35; RBI—Van Burkleo, 108; GWRBI—Van Burkleo, 19; SH—Yamano, 15; SF—Van Burkleo, 11; HP—Yanes, 18; BB—Jennings, 117; IBB—Borg, 11; SO—Landrum, 154; SB—Dewolf, 51; CS—Fox, 27.

(All Players—Listed Alphabetically)

Player and Club	Pct.	G.	AB.	R.	H.	TB.	2B.	3B.	HR.	RBI.	GW.	SH.	SF.	HP.	BB.	Int. BB.	SO.	SB.	CS.
Alarid, David, Bakersfield*	.224	71	192	15	43	49	4	1	0	16	1	1	3	1	13	0	30	1	2
Alexander, Tommy, Reno	.000	61	3	0	0	0	0	0	0	0	0	0	0	0	0	0	2	0	0
Alomar, Roberto, Reno	.346	90	356	53	123	159	16	4	4	49	2	6	7	3	32	2	38	14	8
Amaya, Benjamin, Salinas	.333	2	6	1	2	2	0	0	0	2	0	0	0	0	2	0	1	0	0
Anderson, Kent, Palm Springs	.279	69	240	37	67	87	14	0	2	35	3	2	3	3	14	0	28	4	3
Anderson, Michael, Palm Springs	.229	50	157	22	36	49	6	2	1	12	2	4	2	1	13	0	41	9	0
Anderson, Roy, Modesto	.268	71	224	36	60	87	10	1	5	35	2	4	0	2	24	0	70	2	1
Aragon, Joey, Visalia	.253	131	427	54	108	136	9	2	5	50	4	11	9	1	39	1	51	9	5
Baker, Gerald, Palm Springs	.214	5	14	1	3	6	0	0	1	4	0	1	1	0	0	0	7	0	0
Balelo, Onesimo, Salinas	.262	63	229	36	60	84	11	2	3	24	1	1	1	3	22	1	33	11	6
Barton, Shawn, San Jose	.266	101	338	48	90	117	18	3	1	29	3	8	2	0	44	1	18	3	5
Batesole, Michael, Bakersfield	.231	102	350	32	81	125	20	0	8	44	4	4	5	13	30	1	63	9	5
Batiste, Kevin, Ventura County	.180	78	250	29	45	51	6	0	0	9	0	0	0	7	29	1	92	14	4
Bauer, Eric, Reno	.000	22	5	0	0	0	0	0	0	0	0	0	0	0	0	0	2	0	0
Bauer, Mark, San Jose	.000	25	1	0	0	0	0	0	0	0	0	0	0	0	0	0	1	0	0
Bell, Robert, Palm Springs	.153	47	131	15	20	34	6	4	0	12	0	1	3	4	18	1	34	0	0
Benitez, Manuel, Bakersfield	.267	117	420	42	112	170	25	0	11	57	5	2	2	4	26	1	99	2	3
Berroa, Geronimo, Ventura County	.298	128	459	76	137	232	22	5	21	73	11	1	8	5	38	2	92	12	9
Beuerlein, John, Stockton	.233	13	30	4	7	8	1	0	0	3	0	2	1	1	4	1	5	0	0
Bichette, Dante, Palm Springs	.272	68	290	39	79	124	15	0	10	73	13	0	4	3	21	1	53	2	0
Bishop, James, Ventura County	.261	100	326	38	85	119	14	1	6	40	6	1	2	3	60	1	73	6	3
Bispo, Randall, San Jose*	.200	8	15	1	3	3	0	0	0	0	0	0	0	0	1	0	6	0	0
Blair, Paul, Fresno	.308	13	26	2	8	10	0	1	0	3	0	1	1	0	5	1	4	0	5
Blankenship, Lance, Modesto	.292	55	171	47	50	79	5	3	6	25	1	1	0	4	41	0	39	15	5
Bolt, James, San Jose	.125	7	8	1	1	1	0	0	0	0	0	0	0	0	3	0	3	0	0
Borg, Gary, Visalia*	.277	129	444	74	123	201	25	4	15	97	6	3	7	2	73	11	77	4	1
Brake, Gregory, Modesto*	.000	12	1	0	0	0	0	0	0	0	0	0	0	0	0	0	1	0	0
Brilinski, Tyler, Modesto*	.324	89	299	66	97	194	16	0	27	91	8	0	3	3	63	7	83	4	4
Britt, Patrick, Modesto	.327	20	52	5	17	21	1	0	1	6	0	0	0	0	3	0	11	2	0
Brown, Renard, Salinas†	.255	113	385	73	98	125	12	6	1	43	5	5	5	3	79	0	85	34	11
Brown, Todd, Stockton	.290	74	259	52	75	129	17	2	11	44	6	3	6	0	32	2	40	10	4
Bruzik, Robert, Salinas	.287	132	519	86	149	217	28	8	8	82	10	5	9	8	40	2	64	23	15
Burke, Michael, Bakersfield*	.263	131	448	59	118	192	26	6	12	63	4	2	3	2	56	2	105	2	0
Cabrera, Francisco, Ventura County	.167	6	12	2	2	3	1	0	0	3	0	0	0	0	0	0	4	1	0
Calley, Robert, Visalia	.261	43	157	14	41	49	6	1	0	22	0	0	4	0	21	5	11	0	1
Carlucci, David, Bakersfield	.232	78	228	26	53	67	5	0	3	23	1	7	4	2	39	1	45	0	0
Casey, Timothy, Stockton*	.265	99	294	64	78	155	20	3	17	61	7	1	3	3	90	6	74	24	11
Childers, Jeffrey, Reno	.000	6	1	0	0	0	0	0	0	0	0	0	0	0	0	0	0	0	0
Christman, Kevin, San Jose	.119	25	42	4	5	7	2	0	0	1	0	0	1	0	4	0	9	0	0
Cias, Darryl, San Jose	.257	94	269	22	69	96	18	0	3	28	4	2	1	5	19	0	36	1	2
Clark, Daniel, Salinas	.240	116	400	54	96	145	20	7	5	51	11	2	7	4	64	2	87	4	11
Clark, Jerald, Reno	.303	95	389	76	118	179	34	3	7	58	8	0	7	9	29	3	46	5	4
Clark, Robert, San Jose	.286	25	77	7	22	33	2	0	3	10	2	1	0	0	9	0	14	0	3
Clawson, Kenneth, Reno	.385	28	13	3	5	7	2	0	0	1	1	2	0	0	0	0	1	0	0
Coachman, Bobby, Palm Springs	.310	68	274	74	85	114	12	4	3	41	4	2	4	2	51	0	35	29	7
Cook, Dennis, Fresno*	.273	28	11	2	3	3	0	0	0	2	0	0	0	0	0	0	2	0	0
Cormack, Terry, Salinas*	.258	20	66	6	17	22	2	0	1	11	0	0	0	0	5	0	7	1	1
Cortez, David, Reno	.281	94	303	48	85	124	12	3	7	55	6	5	6	5	30	2	70	2	4

Player and Club	Pct.	G.	AB.	R.	H.	TB.	2B.	3B.	HR.	RBI.	GW.	SH.	SF.	HP.	BB.	Int. BB.	SO.	SB.	CS.
Crabtree, Gary, Bakersfield†	.236	69	220	24	52	64	7	1	1	8	0	6	0	1	48	1	35	3	7
Cruz, Todd, San Jose	.208	30	106	5	22	25	0	0	1	10	2	2	0	1	15	0	29	2	3
Cucjen, Romulo, Fresno	.310	81	271	45	84	147	23	5	10	47	8	2	2	2	45	3	58	2	7
Culberson, Charles, Fresno	.275	96	309	54	85	116	19	3	2	32	2	3	2	2	31	0	64	22	7
Dabney, Ty, Fresno*	.343	121	446	75	153	238	36	2	15	107	9	1	6	1	47	8	64	3	8
Davis, Douglas, Palm Springs	.290	31	100	20	29	41	3	0	3	20	0	5	2	0	22	0	26	0	0
Davis, Harry, Fresno	.244	96	275	44	67	98	11	4	4	40	5	5	3	6	30	2	76	18	14
DeButch, Michael, Reno	.165	28	85	9	14	22	2	3	0	6	0	2	1	1	11	0	12	2	1
deMarrais, Scott, Ventura County	.161	21	56	7	9	15	1	1	1	10	0	0	0	1	7	0	24	0	1
Dewolf, Robert, Stockton*	.312	135	500	98	156	225	23	14	6	59	3	10	5	3	77	5	92	51	13
Diaz, Carlos, Ventura County	.400	2	5	1	2	3	1	0	0	0	0	0	0	0	1	0	2	0	0
Dietrick, Patrick, Modesto	.236	59	216	41	51	74	11	3	2	21	2	1	2	2	37	0	52	9	7
DiGioia, John, Palm Springs	.246	74	203	28	50	74	12	0	4	30	3	1	3	1	31	1	64	0	0
Doraf, Mark, Palm Springs	.257	49	171	23	44	61	8	0	3	24	1	0	3	3	19	0	43	1	9
Ducey, Robert, Ventura County*	.337	47	178	36	60	113	11	3	12	38	5	1	2	1	21	2	24	17	5
Duffy, Darrin, Modesto	.150	7	20	1	3	3	0	0	0	1	0	1	0	0	1	0	8	0	0
Duncan, Michael, Modesto*	.248	112	371	67	92	133	15	1	8	54	10	3	4	4	83	3	45	3	8
Duran, Oscar, Stockton*	.238	26	63	9	15	20	3	1	0	3	0	0	0	0	8	0	13	0	0
Eccles, John, Visalia	.263	60	198	32	52	80	6	2	6	36	5	1	3	1	27	2	39	2	3
Edwards, Jovon, Bakersfield*	.249	130	449	54	112	142	15	3	3	44	6	5	3	7	46	3	72	22	6
Erickson, Donald, Fresno†	.286	27	14	2	4	5	1	0	0	4	0	0	0	0	1	0	2	0	0
Escobar, Oscar, Ventura County	.245	17	53	7	13	18	5	0	0	5	0	0	0	0	2	0	9	0	1
Fiala, Michael, Bakersfield*	.000	47	5	0	0	0	0	0	0	0	0	0	0	0	0	0	3	0	0
Filippi, James, Reno†	.500	10	2	1	1	1	0	0	0	0	0	0	0	0	0	0	1	0	0
Flores, Norberto, Bakersfield*	.254	53	189	31	48	68	10	2	2	23	1	1	3	3	31	2	36	6	4
Flowers, Kim, Fresno	.276	26	76	9	21	29	2	0	2	12	2	1	0	0	5	0	18	1	4
Forgione, Christopher, Visalia*	.258	126	426	53	110	143	15	3	4	43	4	6	3	6	29	4	48	7	4
Foster, Kenneth, San Jose	.222	5	18	0	4	6	2	0	0	2	1	0	0	0	3	0	6	0	0
Fox, Eric, Salinas†	.260	133	526	80	137	175	17	3	5	42	3	9	4	1	69	7	78	41	27
Francois, Manuel, Bakersfield†	.253	39	154	18	39	49	7	0	1	5	0	1	0	2	17	0	22	5	3
Fulton, Gregory, Salinas†	.272	127	463	70	126	190	22	6	10	68	4	0	5	1	48	2	51	5	7
Garcaa, Rene, Bakersfield*	.200	21	5	1	1	1	0	0	0	0	0	0	0	0	1	0	1	0	1
Garcia, Santiago, Ventura County	.306	105	405	78	124	182	25	3	9	61	8	0	6	2	35	1	54	32	8
Garner, Michael, Bakersfield†	.163	14	43	8	7	7	0	0	0	2	0	2	0	0	6	0	10	3	4
Gatewood, Henry, Visalia	.290	90	303	35	88	117	17	3	2	39	5	5	4	1	18	1	43	6	3
Gegen, Frederick, Bakersfield*	.266	47	177	26	47	80	10	1	7	26	2	1	2	1	14	0	49	0	3
Geivett, William, Palm Springs	.281	98	320	65	90	122	14	9	0	33	6	5	1	0	67	2	59	20	4
Gilbert, Gregory, Fresno	.222	30	9	2	2	2	0	0	0	0	0	0	0	0	2	0	1	0	0
Gilliam, Darryl, Bakersfield	.221	42	113	11	25	30	2	0	1	8	1	2	2	3	16	0	23	3	1
Ging, Adam, Reno†	.264	132	447	68	118	159	15	4	6	55	7	5	2	0	85	0	64	14	8
Gobbo, Michael, Stockton	.256	96	262	37	67	85	9	0	3	47	3	3	3	3	48	0	29	1	5
Gonzalez, Felipe, Fresno	.269	83	275	28	74	103	15	1	4	43	2	6	3	1	8	0	50	6	3
Grandstaff, Robert, Reno	.262	60	214	34	56	89	10	4	5	37	0	1	7	4	21	0	40	4	1
Grant, Kenneth, Palm Springs	.500	4	10	2	5	7	0	1	0	5	1	0	0	0	6	0	1	1	0
Gray, Jeffrey, Reno	.291	99	347	60	101	125	16	4	0	28	2	3	1	2	23	0	64	22	7
Gray, Lorenzo, San Jose	.274	87	263	38	72	103	17	1	4	28	5	0	3	2	32	4	38	4	1
Greenlee, Robert, Reno*	.000	17	1	0	0	0	0	0	0	0	0	0	0	0	0	0	1	0	0
Guerrero, Epifanio, 39 VC-81 Sto	.293	120	409	61	120	177	28	7	5	61	8	10	8	3	34	1	41	0	8
Hall, Gregory, Reno	.260	88	269	42	70	92	7	0	5	33	2	1	4	3	42	3	58	2	2
Hamm, Timothy, San Jose	.000	10	0	1	0	0	0	0	0	0	0	0	0	0	0	0	0	0	0
Harrison, Ronald, San Jose*	.310	86	300	36	93	130	15	8	2	39	8	5	2	1	13	1	31	9	4
Hartsock, Brian, Palm Springs*	.267	4	15	1	4	4	0	0	0	2	0	0	0	0	1	0	4	0	0
Higgs, Darrell, Salinas	.000	35	1	0	0	0	0	0	0	0	0	0	0	0	0	0	1	0	0
Hinnrichs, David, Fresno	.000	40	8	1	0	0	0	0	0	0	0	0	0	0	0	0	5	0	0
Holcomb, Ted, Bakersfield*	.286	138	514	71	147	172	17	4	0	40	2	9	2	3	74	0	38	15	16
Hornacek, Jay, Bakersfield	.267	48	150	20	40	63	11	0	4	23	1	0	2	2	14	1	39	1	0
Howard, Steven, Modesto	.232	98	302	64	70	116	11	4	9	53	4	0	4	5	100	0	128	13	7
Howard, Thomas, Reno*	.256	61	223	35	57	100	7	3	10	39	7	1	3	0	34	1	49	10	2
Hubbard, Jeffrey, Visalia	.281	58	178	31	50	58	4	2	0	18	2	3	0	2	31	0	28	1	2
Jackson, Ronald, Bakersfield	.231	29	78	10	18	19	1	0	0	6	0	1	1	1	2	0	14	0	1
Jacobo, Edward, Bakersfield	.288	52	184	26	53	79	20	0	2	22	2	1	1	1	18	2	26	0	0
Jennings, Douglas, Palm Springs*	.317	129	429	95	136	236	31	9	17	89	11	2	8	10	117	7	103	7	11
Johnson, Kevin, Modesto†	.000	2	2	1	0	0	0	0	0	0	0	0	0	0	0	0	2	0	0
Jones, Gary, Fresno†	.262	73	195	20	51	75	12	0	4	28	3	2	1	1	26	3	46	1	2
Jones, James, Modesto	.243	72	222	35	54	71	11	0	2	30	2	3	1	5	45	2	46	5	1
Jones, Michael, Ventura County	.271	68	229	28	62	75	6	2	1	21	2	2	1	1	15	0	42	4	5
Jose, Felix, Modesto†	.285	127	516	77	147	227	22	8	14	77	7	3	2	2	36	5	89	14	1
Jurak, Edward, San Jose	.324	28	71	14	23	32	0	0	3	10	2	2	0	0	20	0	13	4	2
Kanter, John, Modesto	.230	77	257	34	59	86	12	0	5	28	2	2	1	7	25	1	55	11	7
Kent, Bernard, Stockton*	.196	120	398	51	78	122	14	3	8	61	6	1	4	1	40	2	83	16	2
Kinnard, Kenneth, Ventura County	.322	34	118	25	38	58	6	4	2	7	1	2	1	1	15	1	27	9	2
Kmak, Joseph, Fresno	.270	60	163	23	44	52	5	0	1	9	1	0	1	3	15	0	38	3	2
Kopetsky, Brian, Bakersfield	.177	76	215	14	38	41	3	0	0	10	1	4	1	2	15	1	45	3	4
Kosco, Andrew, Salinas*	.236	59	199	28	47	57	5	1	1	20	5	0	1	0	12	0	38	2	2
Kramer, Joseph, Modesto	.270	54	189	41	51	83	6	4	6	29	2	3	3	3	32	2	36	13	6
Krause, Thomas, Salinas*	.309	107	376	43	116	152	15	9	1	48	4	4	5	0	41	2	34	17	11
Kroener, Christopher, Visalia	.245	48	159	30	39	57	12	0	2	19	2	1	1	5	13	0	33	2	2
Kubala, Brian, San Jose	.333	31	3	0	1	1	0	0	0	0	0	0	0	0	1	0	1	0	0
Kutsukos, Peter, Reno	1.000	35	1	0	1	1	0	0	0	0	0	0	0	0	1	0	0	0	0
Lambert, Reginald, Palm Springs	.238	98	294	49	70	91	13	1	2	34	1	3	2	3	70	0	75	2	8
Landrum, Darryl, Ventura County	.223	121	421	74	94	177	21	4	18	71	5	0	2	11	69	1	154	20	10
Little, Randy, Salinas	.311	13	45	6	14	16	2	0	0	6	0	1	0	0	6	0	6	1	1
Lynch, Joseph, Reno	.000	33	1	0	0	0	0	0	0	0	0	0	0	0	0	0	0	0	0
Malave, Omar, Ventura County	.234	70	201	29	47	69	8	1	4	30	1	1	3	4	31	1	33	2	3
Marsh, Scott, Reno*	.167	31	6	1	1	1	0	0	0	0	0	1	0	0	1	0	5	0	0
Martig, Richard, Modesto	.271	128	443	63	120	160	15	5	5	76	4	8	5	4	72	2	69	10	5
Martinez, Domingo, Ventura County	.248	129	455	51	113	171	19	6	9	57	5	3	3	4	36	2	127	9	9
Martinez, Ramon, Bakersfield	.100	20	10	1	1	1	0	0	0	0	0	2	0	0	0	0	3	0	0
Martinez, Rey, San Jose*	.265	16	49	8	13	14	1	0	0	1	0	0	0	0	4	0	6	0	0
Mathews, Thomas, Fresno*	.244	115	324	50	79	122	20	1	7	58	6	4	10	4	45	2	57	4	5
Mattox, Frank, Stockton†	.219	55	187	37	41	50	7	1	0	18	3	1	3	0	36	0	27	19	6
McCament, Randall, Fresno	.000	54	1	0	0	0	0	0	0	0	0	0	0	0	0	0	1	0	0
McCatty, Steven, San Jose	.286	17	7	1	2	3	1	0	0	1	0	0	0	0	1	0	2	0	0

Player and Club	Pct.	G.	AB.	R.	H.	TB.	2B.	3B.	HR.	RBI.	GW.	SH.	SF.	HP.	BB.	Int. BB.	SO.	SB.	CS.
McDonald, Thomas, Fresno	.308	125	471	95	145	200	30	5	5	54	6	6	7	3	59	3	83	34	15
McGuire, William, Salinas	.299	116	368	49	110	152	22	1	6	62	5	3	1	4	52	6	60	5	8
Meagher, Thomas, Reno	.250	8	4	1	1	1	0	0	0	2	0	0	0	0	0	0	1	0	0
Mena, Andres, Bakersfield	.000	7	3	1	0	0	0	0	0	0	0	0	0	0	1	0	2	0	0
Mendenhall, Shannon, Modesto	.177	34	79	11	14	17	1	1	0	11	2	1	3	0	16	0	31	2	0
Messier, Thomas, Fresno	.000	29	1	0	0	0	0	0	0	0	0	1	0	0	0	0	0	0	0
Mijares, William, Fresno	.211	10	19	3	4	5	1	0	0	1	0	0	0	0	1	0	8	0	0
Miller, Christopher, Salinas	.101	27	79	8	8	12	2	1	0	3	0	3	0	0	8	0	30	3	1
Milner, Theodore, San Jose*	.214	32	98	12	21	27	2	2	0	11	0	3	2	1	19	1	31	5	5
Mitchell, Joseph, Stockton	.289	106	360	60	104	162	21	5	9	56	8	3	3	7	31	2	64	7	3
Monico, Mario, Stockton*	.315	104	324	64	102	143	26	3	3	57	3	1	4	1	56	2	40	4	4
Montanari, David, Palm Springs*	.277	86	274	23	76	93	10	2	1	33	3	1	2	2	50	4	37	1	2
Moore, Sam, Fresno	.091	38	11	0	1	2	1	0	0	0	0	0	0	0	0	0	8	0	0
Morfan, Arvid, Salinas	.186	15	43	5	8	10	0	1	0	1	0	0	0	0	2	0	12	1	0
Murphy, Dwayne, Modesto*	.200	2	5	1	1	2	1	0	0	0	0	0	0	0	2	0	3	0	0
Murray, Stephen, Salinas†	.257	126	401	48	103	127	20	2	0	48	8	12	4	4	51	2	58	14	15
Myers, Gregory, Ventura County	.295	124	451	65	133	224	23	4	20	79	7	1	5	2	43	5	46	9	4
Nelson, Jeffrey, Bakersfield	.500	24	2	1	1	2	1	0	0	0	0	0	0	0	0	0	0	0	0
Nelson, Kevin, Bakersfield	.000	4	1	1	0	0	0	0	0	1	0	1	0	0	1	0	0	0	0
Nelson, Jerome, Modesto†	.274	97	307	53	84	92	4	2	0	38	3	7	2	2	46	1	53	17	9
Nicolosi, Salvatore, Visalia	.227	48	132	14	30	49	7	0	4	24	1	0	2	0	10	0	26	0	0
Nieporte, James, Reno	.277	102	375	51	104	135	10	3	5	61	8	2	6	2	14	0	53	1	2
Nittoli, Michael, San Jose	.154	52	78	11	12	13	1	0	0	4	1	1	2	0	11	0	23	2	3
Nunez, Dario, Palm Springs	.266	96	334	52	89	101	10	1	0	34	5	9	2	0	23	1	43	1	4
Oakes, Todd, Fresno	.000	12	2	0	0	0	0	0	0	0	0	0	0	0	0	0	0	0	0
O'Connor, William, Visalia	.074	12	27	3	2	2	0	0	0	1	0	0	0	0	6	0	4	0	1
Okubo, Hiromoto, San Jose	.261	127	387	43	101	138	17	1	6	54	4	3	4	2	34	3	52	1	4
Oliva, David, San Jose	.283	93	315	44	89	112	4	2	5	37	3	1	1	1	18	0	53	30	10
Olker, Joseph, Fresno	.200	25	15	2	3	4	1	0	0	0	0	1	0	0	0	0	3	0	0
Pappas, Erik, Palm Springs	.246	74	248	40	61	96	16	2	5	38	3	1	4	1	56	1	58	9	5
Parsons, Scott, Reno	.401	60	217	48	87	144	14	2	13	63	6	0	6	3	21	2	19	7	1
Peguero, Geremia, Modesto	.271	130	442	55	120	137	11	3	0	54	7	3	8	2	21	1	93	10	6
Pena, Daniel, Bakersfield*	.250	14	4	0	1	1	0	0	0	2	0	1	0	0	1	0	1	0	0
Perezchica, Antonio, Fresno	.279	126	452	65	126	199	30	8	9	54	2	10	2	14	35	0	91	18	6
Pettis, Stacey, Palm Springs*	.258	94	299	56	77	114	12	5	5	46	2	2	1	0	53	3	115	28	9
Pohle, Walter, Stockton	.269	109	368	65	99	140	27	1	4	50	4	6	2	12	45	0	62	17	4
Pounders, Bradley, Reno	.288	135	489	101	141	271	21	2	35	104	8	0	6	1	76	1	129	2	2
Puig, Edward, Reno*	.211	25	19	1	4	5	1	0	0	4	0	3	1	0	2	0	2	0	0
Quinones, Hector, Fresno	.197	85	249	35	49	65	5	1	3	26	3	4	2	1	23	1	76	9	4
Rainey, Scott, Reno	.290	80	262	46	76	108	15	1	5	45	3	3	1	5	34	0	45	8	1
Ray, Jay, Bakersfield	.125	43	8	0	1	1	0	0	0	0	0	0	0	0	0	0	2	0	0
Reboulet, Jeffrey, Visalia	.287	72	254	54	73	88	13	1	0	29	3	5	2	1	54	1	33	14	11
Reitz, Kenneth, San Jose	.233	111	356	27	83	109	17	0	3	27	4	4	5	2	24	1	47	2	0
Reyna, Luis, Ventura County*	.291	117	447	66	130	205	28	4	13	66	12	0	4	2	32	3	74	26	8
Reynolds, Mark, Stockton*	.105	7	19	2	2	2	0	0	0	2	0	1	0	1	5	0	7	0	0
Rivera, Pablo, Reno	.288	104	361	56	104	139	15	4	4	47	1	2	2	1	16	0	40	13	8
Rodgers, Darrell, Fresno	.000	3	3	0	0	0	0	0	0	0	0	0	0	0	0	0	1	0	0
Rodriguez, Angel, Stockton	.288	96	337	51	97	155	16	3	12	63	11	5	3	5	19	0	54	4	1
Rowen, Robert, Bakersfield*	.308	19	13	1	4	5	1	0	0	0	0	0	0	0	1	0	4	0	0
Rypien, Timothy, Ventura County	.000	1	3	0	0	0	0	0	0	0	0	0	0	0	0	0	1	0	0
Savage, John, Bakersfield	.333	44	6	1	2	2	0	0	0	0	0	0	0	0	1	0	1	0	0
Savarino, William, Modesto*	.400	3	10	3	4	4	0	0	0	0	0	0	0	0	0	0	2	0	0
Scales, Richard, Reno	.077	7	13	1	1	1	0	0	0	0	0	0	0	0	5	0	2	0	0
Schiffelbein, Gregg, Modesto*	.176	9	17	2	3	3	0	0	0	1	0	2	0	0	3	0	4	1	0
Schwarz, Thomas, Visalia	.298	139	516	102	154	226	34	1	12	101	9	7	8	5	65	3	60	4	3
Sconiers, Daryl, San Jose*	.306	96	317	46	97	140	19	3	6	42	5	1	2	2	45	1	42	12	7
Senne, Timothy, Visalia†	.260	99	258	56	67	100	15	0	6	38	2	9	4	5	76	5	56	3	2
Seoane, Mitchell, Palm Springs	.291	92	361	72	105	122	11	3	0	47	2	8	4	0	34	0	48	8	3
Shanks, William, Ventura County	.000	51	1	0	0	0	0	0	0	0	0	0	0	0	0	0	0	0	0
Sharpnack, Robert, Modesto	.000	25	1	1	0	0	0	0	0	0	0	0	0	0	2	0	1	0	0
Skurla, John, Fresno*	.262	121	420	81	110	178	26	12	6	59	7	2	7	3	45	4	87	21	9
Smith, Bryan, Bakersfield	.167	24	6	1	1	1	0	0	0	0	0	1	0	0	0	0	2	0	0
Smith, Daniel, Bakersfield	.230	83	274	26	63	91	16	0	4	27	0	1	2	2	20	1	73	0	0
Smith, Stephen, Fresno†	.000	23	1	1	0	0	0	0	0	0	0	0	0	0	1	0	1	0	0
Sorrento, Paul, Palm Springs*	.242	16	62	5	15	21	3	0	1	7	0	0	0	0	4	1	15	0	1
Stewart, David, Salinas*	.282	131	479	66	135	197	25	2	11	72	4	0	6	4	40	3	64	5	6
Stewart, Jeffrey, Reno	.200	38	5	1	1	1	0	0	0	0	0	1	0	0	1	0	2	0	0
Stull, Walter, Bakersfield	.250	33	8	2	2	4	0	1	0	0	0	0	0	0	1	0	3	0	0
Tamori, Roymond, San Jose	.000	19	1	0	0	0	0	0	0	0	0	0	0	0	0	0	1	0	0
Tanabe, Norio, San Jose	.306	140	542	76	166	224	23	4	9	64	8	9	8	0	18	1	82	23	12
Tejeda, Gregorio, Bakersfield	.000	5	2	0	0	0	0	0	0	0	0	0	0	0	0	0	2	0	0
Tettleton, Mickey, Modesto†	.238	15	42	14	10	17	1	0	2	8	0	0	0	1	19	1	9	2	0
Thomas, Thomas, Visalia*	.310	134	500	96	155	190	18	7	1	44	6	4	8	4	94	3	51	34	19
Thompson, Scott, Fresno	.271	96	321	52	87	132	17	2	8	31	4	0	0	12	25	0	74	39	5
Thornton, John, Stockton	.288	23	66	16	19	35	5	1	3	11	0	1	1	0	24	1	24	2	4
Thrower, Keith, San Jose†	.286	5	14	2	4	4	0	0	0	0	0	0	0	0	0	0	2	2	0
Van Burkleo, Tyler, Palm Springs*	.268	135	485	94	130	230	28	3	22	108	19	1	11	4	97	3	128	11	6
Van Stone, Paul, Fresno†	.230	60	165	15	38	53	7	1	2	18	0	6	0	1	24	2	26	1	6
Venneri, Anthony, San Jose*	.253	63	158	16	40	54	8	0	2	23	1	1	4	1	23	0	33	2	4
Ventura, Jose, Stockton*	.227	10	22	3	5	5	0	0	0	4	0	1	1	0	1	0	5	3	0
Verducci, John, Fresno	.286	40	133	26	38	43	5	0	0	16	0	2	2	0	25	0	21	3	2
Villa, Michael, Fresno*	1.000	43	1	0	1	1	0	0	0	1	0	0	0	0	1	0	0	0	0
Visor, Michael, Reno	.000	18	4	0	0	0	0	0	0	0	0	1	0	0	1	0	0	0	0
Walters, Darryel, Stockton	.229	123	393	76	90	170	12	1	22	77	6	4	4	1	64	1	139	16	4
Wasem, James, Reno	.317	89	344	79	109	132	9	4	2	24	0	4	5	3	45	0	24	18	10
Wetteland, John, Bakersfield	.000	15	3	0	0	0	0	0	0	0	0	0	0	0	2	0	3	0	0
White, Jerome, San Jose†	.262	40	149	21	39	60	6	6	1	22	2	2	0	0	13	1	15	8	5
White, Michael, Bakersfield	.203	76	236	28	48	66	6	3	2	16	0	1	2	7	28	1	57	2	5
Whitfield, Terry, San Jose*	.391	19	64	18	25	31	3	0	1	6	1	0	0	1	13	2	14	4	4
Wiggins, Kevin, Visalia*	.244	92	262	35	64	80	10	0	2	26	1	2	1	2	33	0	37	5	9
Williams, Fred, Stockton	.208	125	382	62	110	144	12	5	4	55	9	7	4	3	60	0	78	19	15
Wilson, Ricky, Salinas	.284	36	109	22	31	49	9	0	3	22	2	1	3	2	12	0	27	1	0
Xavier, Joseph, Modesto*	.276	104	355	61	98	150	27	8	3	53	3	4	9	2	72	3	60	6	7

Player and Club	Pct.	G.	AB.	R.	H.	TB.	2B.	3B.	HR.	RBI.	GW.	SH.	SF.	HP.	BB.	Int. BB.	SO.	SB.	CS.
Yamano, Kazuaki, San Jose*	.249	135	437	45	109	125	8	4	0	25	2	15	2	2	30	0	120	12	12
Yanes, Edward, Visalia	.281	129	395	87	111	196	22	3	19	95	11	4	8	18	95	2	76	11	6
Yelding, Eric, Ventura County	.280	131	560	83	157	197	14	7	4	40	2	6	2	0	33	3	84	41	18

The following pitchers, listed alphabetically by club, with games in parentheses, had no plate appearances, primarily through use of designated hitters:

BAKERSFIELD—Hardwick, Anthony (9); Naworski, Andrew (20); Young, Raymond (12).

FRESNO—Burkett, John (4); Candelaria, Albert (1); Pilkington, Eric (7).

MODESTO—Applegate, Russell (40); Arroyo, Fernando (1); Balsley, Darren (23); Beavers, Mark (9); Figueroa, Victor (14); Hansen, Darel (30); Harris, Twayne (10); Hogan, Michael (14); Howell, Jay (2); Kent, John (9); Kopyta, Jeffrey (19); Santana, Jose (11); Strichek, James (17); Strong, Joseph (36); Tapani, Kevin (11); Tortorice, Mark (31); Walton, Bruce (28).

PALM SPRINGS—Butler, Michael (33); Candelaria, John (2); Carter, Richard (31); Cook, Larry (34); Dacus, Barry (55); Eggertsen, Todd (22); Fraser, William (19); Garcia, Miguel (43); Harvey, Bryan (43); Lovelace, Vance (6); Lucas, Gary (7); Marrett, Scott (21); Martinez, David (18); McGuire, Stephen (3); Price, Bryan (10); Romanovsky, Michael (14); Shull, Michael (1); Timberlake, Donald (6); Venturino, Philip (8).

RENO—Kristan, Kevin (2).

SALINAS—Barnhouse, Scott (15); Brinkman, Gregory (24); Christ, Michael (19); Givler, Douglas (47); Jones, Calvin (26); Mendek, William (31); Neufelder, Donald (26); Poloni, John (3); Rousey, Stephen (19); Siegel, Robert (1); Snell, David (1); Spratke, Kenneth (26); Swearingen, Douglas (31); White, Logan (40).

SAN JOSE—Arroyo, Fernando (5); Bigusiak, Michael (4); Blobaum, Jeffrey (30); Gallo, Bernard (17); Galloway, Kenneth (2); Garrick, Darren (21); Howe, Steven (14); McCarter, Edward (7); Nakashima, Yoshihiro (33); Norris, Michael (11); Ruhle, Vernon (3); Tinkey, James (41); Yokota, Hisanori (28).

STOCKTON—Ambrose, Mark (10); Brisco, Jamie (8); Diaz, Derek (32); Fleming, Keith (16); Frew, Michael (23); Fulmer, Michael (13); Henderson, Craig (9); Kanwisher, Gary (4); Ludy, John (50); Miglio, John (7); Montano, Martin (42); Norton, Douglas (27); Peterek, Jeffrey (25); Ratliff, Daniel (11); Reece, Jeffrey (24); Sadler, Alan (12); Walker, Cameron (13).

VENTURA COUNTY—Brinson, Hugh (34); Burgos, Enrique (9); Ciprian, Elvis (18); Dickman, Mark (44); Hogan, Michael (10); Mesa, Jose (24); Mumaw, Stephen (6); Musselman, Jeffrey (26); Paris, Zacarias (9); Provence, Todd (27); Reyes, Pablo (32); Stottlemyre, Todd (17); Walsh, David (15); Wasilewski, Thomas (49); Wells, David (5); Wortham, Andrew (2).

VISALIA—Adams, Michael (3); Bianchi, Ben (14); Cardwood, Alfredo (27); Coleman, Dewayne (21); Cramer, Robert (12); Dominguez, Jose (38); Galloway, Troy (18); Hickerson, Bryan (11); Iasparro, Donnie (27); Perry, Jeffrey (14); Pierorazio, Wesley (56); Rohlof, Scott (31); Tabeling, Robert (23); Velasquez, Raymond (44).

GRAND SLAM HOME RUNS—Brilinski, 3; Landrum, Martig, Pounders, Yanes, 2 each; Batesole, Bichette, T. Brown, Cias, Duncan, S. Garcia, Gobbo, Gonzalez, S. Howard, Monico, Okubo, Reyna, J.D. Smith, Van Burkleo, J. White, Yelding, 1 each.

AWARDED FIRST BASE ON CATCHER'S INTERFERENCE—Pohle 5 (Anderson, Davis, Nieporte, Nittoli, Smith); Casey (Diaz); Gegen (Gobbo).

CLUB FIELDING

Club	Pct.	G.	PO.	A.	E.	DP.	PB.
Palm Springs	.970	142	3724	1507	161	132	22
Visalia	.964	142	3630	1480	191	136	18
Stockton	.964	142	3599	1475	192	115	23
Reno	.962	142	3550	1592	201	154	28
Salinas	.961	142	3683	1579	214	141	21
San Jose	.960	142	3483	1448	204	112	21
Fresno	.960	142	3631	1363	201	111	38
Ventura County	.955	142	3651	1329	235	87	13
Modesto	.954	142	3554	1397	238	110	12
Bakersfield	.951	142	3646	1496	266	131	42

Triple Plays—Fresno, Modesto, Salinas.

INDIVIDUAL FIELDING

*Throws lefthanded.

FIRST BASEMEN

Player and Club	Pct.	G.	PO.	A.	E.	DP.
Anderson, Modesto	.986	12	64	4	1	5
Benitez, Bakersfield	1.000	1	6	0	0	0
Bispo, San Jose*	1.000	2	6	0	0	0
Borg, Visalia*	.985	127	964	73	16	101
Brilinski, Modesto*	.981	36	294	24	6	27
Burke, Bakersfield*	.980	121	985	70	22	104
Calley, Visalia	.985	10	62	5	1	6
Christman, San Jose	.875	1	6	1	1	0
Cias, San Jose	.976	6	37	3	1	2
Clark, Salinas	1.000	5	45	4	0	6
Clawson, Reno	1.000	1	1	0	0	0
Cruz, San Jose	1.000	1	4	0	0	0
Cucjen, Fresno	.984	46	335	41	6	30
Dabney, Fresno	.983	8	56	3	1	3
deMarrais, Ventura County	1.000	1	1	0	0	0
DiGioia, Palm Springs	.960	3	23	1	1	4
Ducey, Ventura County	1.000	1	1	0	0	0
Duncan, Modesto*	.984	77	584	50	10	42
Duran, Stockton*	.977	9	40	2	1	5
Fulton, Salinas	.987	26	200	20	3	24
Geivett, Palm Springs	1.000	1	8	0	0	0
Gobbo, Stockton	1.000	1	0	1	0	0
Gray, San Jose	1.000	3	13	0	0	0
Hall, Reno	.975	18	145	8	4	9
Hornacek, Bakersfield	.981	7	49	2	1	2
Hubbard, Visalia	.983	18	107	11	2	7
Jacobo, Bakersfield	.962	23	141	12	6	11
Jones, Fresno	1.000	3	9	1	0	0
Kent, Stockton*	.988	117	963	56	12	77
Kubala, San Jose	1.000	1	10	0	0	1
Malave, Ventura County	1.000	8	31	7	0	6
Martig, Modesto	.966	30	192	8	7	22
D. Martinez, Ventura County	.986	128	1004	79	15	59
Re. Martinez, San Jose*	.923	2	12	0	1	1
Mathews, Fresno	.992	86	612	36	5	48
Mitchell, Stockton	1.000	3	9	0	0	0
Montanari, Palm Springs	.975	15	115	4	3	8
Nicolosi, Visalia	1.000	1	10	1	0	0
Okubo, San Jose	.957	3	22	0	1	1
Pounders, Reno	.988	129	1120	67	15	131
Reitz, San Jose	.984	30	221	23	4	20
Reyna, Ventura County*	.978	11	81	7	2	7
Rodriguez, Stockton	.964	3	27	0	1	2
Sconiers, San Jose*	.988	90	722	37	9	51
Skurla, Fresno*	1.000	5	14	0	0	3
STEWART, Salinas*	.993	117	989	81	8	93
Thornton, Stockton	.981	17	144	10	3	9
Van Burkleo, Palm Springs*	.988	125	1107	73	14	103
Van Stone, Fresno	1.000	10	72	3	0	6
Venneri, San Jose*	.986	19	127	11	2	8
Walters, Stockton	.980	6	49	1	1	5
Wiggins, Visalia*	1.000	1	1	0	0	1
Wilson, Salinas	1.000	1	7	0	0	0
Yanes, Visalia	1.000	1	3	0	0	1

Triple Plays—Mathews, Stewart.

SECOND BASEMEN

Player and Club	Pct.	G.	PO.	A.	E.	DP.
Alomar, Reno	.963	89	198	265	18	75
Aragon, Visalia	.980	59	138	152	6	31
Barton, San Jose	.938	3	9	6	1	1
Blair, Fresno	.900	6	10	8	2	3
Bolt, San Jose	.909	2	3	7	1	1
Bruzik, Salinas	1.000	1	0	1	0	1
Coachman, Palm Springs	.962	65	146	206	14	50
Cortez, Reno	.958	5	11	12	1	2
Crabtree, Bakersfield	.952	4	9	11	1	1
Escobar, Ventura County	.953	13	19	22	2	1
Flowers, Fresno	1.000	5	8	11	0	2
Francois, Bakersfield	.923	3	5	7	1	0
Garcia, Ventura County	.953	103	205	277	24	32
Geivett, Palm Springs	1.000	2	3	8	0	3
Gilliam, Bakersfield	.868	16	27	32	9	4
Ging, Reno	1.000	2	4	7	0	3

SECOND BASEMEN—Continued

Player and Club	Pct.	G.	PO.	A.	E.	DP.
Grant, Palm Springs	1.000	1	3	5	0	1
Gray, San Jose	1.000	1	0	2	0	0
Guerrero, Ven Cnty-Sto	.954	46	67	100	8	24
Holcomb, Bakersfield	.951	128	257	360	32	68
Kanter, Modesto	.981	46	93	116	4	21
Krause, Salinas	.926	25	48	77	10	12
Kroener, Visalia	.951	43	64	110	9	25
Malave, Ventura County	.945	14	17	35	3	5
Martig, Modesto	1.000	1	1	0	0	0
Mattox, Stockton	.949	51	92	132	12	25
Mendenhall, Modesto	.938	7	5	10	1	1
Mijares, Fresno	1.000	7	8	7	0	2
Murray, Salinas	.950	123	304	363	35	86
Nunez, Palm Springs	.970	6	10	22	1	2
Peguero, Modesto	.966	74	180	189	13	33
Pohle, Stockton	.919	8	15	19	3	3
Quinones, Fresno	.942	52	80	82	10	16
Reitz, San Jose	.974	21	24	52	2	8
Scales, Reno	1.000	4	3	7	0	1
Senne, Visalia	.972	49	88	119	6	26
Seoane, Palm Springs	.967	70	146	204	12	34
TANABE, San Jose	.974	120	220	296	14	56
Van Stone, Fresno	.943	49	62	102	10	18
Verducci, Fresno	.958	40	98	106	9	21
Wasem, Reno	.955	46	110	147	12	30
White, San Jose	.833	1	0	5	1	0
Williams, Stockton	.978	67	122	189	7	30
Xavier, Modesto	.969	26	34	61	3	11

Triple Play—Krause.

THIRD BASEMEN

Player and Club	Pct.	G.	PO.	A.	E.	DP.
K. Anderson, Palm Springs	.667	1	2	0	1	0
Batesole, Bakersfield	.927	65	58	108	13	6
Benitez, Bakersfield	.636	3	2	5	4	2
Bichette, Palm Springs	.882	34	14	61	10	5
BISHOP, Ventura County	.935	100	79	165	17	9
Blair, Fresno	.667	4	2	2	2	1
Blankenship, Modesto	.854	15	13	22	6	4
Bolt, San Jose	1.000	4	0	4	0	0
Calley, Visalia	.800	2	1	3	1	0
Carlucci, Bakersfield	.750	5	3	3	2	0
Christman, San Jose	.667	5	2	2	2	0
Cias, San Jose	.600	3	1	2	2	0
Clark, Salinas	.898	90	68	179	28	23
Cortez, Reno	.908	44	35	74	11	8
Crabtree, Bakersfield	1.000	1	0	6	0	0
Cruz, San Jose	.873	26	23	46	10	2
Cucjen, Fresno	.923	24	23	37	5	4
Dabney, Fresno	.890	96	79	107	23	17
Flowers, Fresno	.882	17	9	21	4	2
Fulton, Salinas	.917	49	36	85	11	9
Gegen, Bakersfield	.912	42	30	84	11	10
Geivett, Palm Springs	.945	89	56	150	12	12
Gilliam, Bakersfield	.813	7	4	9	3	1
Ging, Reno	.948	42	29	81	6	8
Grandstaff, Reno	.901	58	43	102	16	13
Grant, Palm Springs	.833	2	0	5	1	0
Gray, San Jose	.908	51	40	79	12	5
Guerrero, Ven Cnty-Sto	.898	57	39	76	13	8
Harrison, San Jose	.500	4	3	2	5	0
Hornacek, Bakersfield	.820	21	12	38	11	0
Hubbard, Visalia	.917	12	4	18	2	1
Jurak, San Jose	1.000	2	7	3	0	0
Kanter, Modesto	.820	28	14	36	11	1
Kopetsky, Bakersfield	.882	10	7	8	2	0
Malave, Ventura County	.865	37	27	63	14	6
Martig, Modesto	.869	97	68	151	33	10
Martinez, Ventura County	.000	1	0	0	1	0
Mendenhall, Modesto	.783	8	6	12	5	2
Mitchell, Stockton	.913	99	74	157	22	20
Morfin, Salinas	1.000	6	2	5	0	0
Murray, Salinas	1.000	1	1	0	0	0
Nunez, Palm Springs	.947	8	6	12	1	1
Okubo, San Jose	.909	15	9	21	3	1
Perezchica, Fresno	.000	1	0	0	1	0
Pohle, Stockton	1.000	1	0	1	0	0
Pounders, Reno	.857	5	4	8	2	0
Quinones, Fresno	.966	12	11	17	1	0
Reitz, San Jose	.948	47	22	88	6	5
Rodriguez, Stockton	.800	2	0	4	1	0
Savarino, Modesto	.778	3	4	3	2	1
Schwarz, Visalia	.921	134	119	243	31	22
Senne, Visalia	1.000	1	0	2	0	0
Seoane, Palm Springs	.915	15	11	32	4	1
Ventura, Stockton	.750	1	0	3	1	1
Wasem, Reno	1.000	1	0	1	0	1
White, San Jose	.500	2	0	1	1	0
Williams, Stockton	.733	4	2	9	4	1
Xavier, Modesto	1.000	7	3	4	0	0

Triple Play—Cucjen.

SHORTSTOPS

Player and Club	Pct.	G.	PO.	A.	E.	DP.
K. Anderson, Palm Springs	.942	60	124	166	18	46
Aragon, Visalia	.936	71	153	186	23	45
Balelo, Salinas	.948	63	87	189	15	37
BARTON, San Jose	.941	98	159	307	29	58
Blair, Fresno	.750	2	1	2	1	0
Bolt, San Jose	.000	1	0	0	2	0
Cortez, Reng	.917	2	5	6	1	2
Crabtree, Bakersfield	.955	62	126	172	14	41
Cruz, San Jose	1.000	1	2	1	0	1
DeButch, Reno	.930	22	33	73	8	13
Duffy, Modesto	.968	7	12	18	1	4
Escobar, Ventura County	1.000	2	0	2	0	0
Francois, Bakersfield	.914	37	67	82	14	19
Fulton$ Salinas	.886	9	11	20	4	4
Gegen, Bakersfield	1.000	1	0	2	0	0
Ging, Reno	.948	81	117	229	19	51
Guerrero, Ven Cnty-Sto	.917	13	15	29	4	3
Holcomb, Bakersfield	.824	4	7	7	3	2
Johnson, Modesto	.750	1	1	2	1	0
Jurak, San Jose	.925	26	48	63	9	13
Kopetscy, Bakersfield	.864	51	67	130	31	20
Krause, Salinas	.938	52	77	134	14	24
Malave, Ventura County	1.000	5	4	8	0	2
Mendenhall, Modesto	.896	18	29	40	8	8
Mijares, Fresno	.889	3	4	4	1	1
Miller, Salinas	.933	27	38	74	8	8
Mitchell, Stockton	.778	2	2	5	2	1
Murray, Salinas	1.000	1	2	2	0	0
Nunez, Palm Springs	.949	82	121	233	19	43
Peguero, Modesto	.934	58	103	150	18	26
Perezchica, Fresno	.928	126	224	303	41	54
Pohle, Stockton	.949	93	139	273	22	45
Quinones, Fresno	.935	22	31	55	6	12
Reboulet, Visalia	.939	71	118	188	20	36
Reitz, San Jose	1.000	2	0	2	0	0
Scales, Reno	.813	3	5	8	3	3
Senne, Visalia	.889	7	6	10	2	1
Seoane, Palm Springs	.895	6	5	12	2	3
Tanabe, San Jose	.918	23	28	39	6	6
Ventura, Stockton	.927	9	14	24	3	2
Wasem, Reno	.938	40	61	120	12	30
Williams, Stockton	.920	42	57	127	16	17
Xavier, Modesto	.922	77	105	180	24	26
Yelding, Ventura County	.899	131	231	284	58	44

Triple Play—Peguero.

OUTFIELDERS

Player and Club	Pct.	G.	PO.	A.	E.	DP.
Alarid, Bakersfield*	.964	58	80	1	3	1
K. Anderson, Palm Springs	1.000	3	5	0	0	0
M. Anderson, Palm Springs	.959	50	90	3	4	1
Batiste, Ventura County	.975	77	189	5	5	0
Benitez, Bakersfield	.925	98	148	12	13	4
Berroa, Ventura County	.935	107	194	9	14	1
Bichette, Palm Springs	.986	35	64	7	1	1
Bispo, San Jose*	1.000	4	2	0	0	0
Blankenship, Modesto	.988	40	75	5	1	0
Borg, Visalia*	1.000	1	1	0	0	0
R. Brown, Salinas	.970	107	154	9	5	1
T. Brown, Stockton	.964	70	133	2	5	0
Bruzik, Salinas	.971	127	215	17	7	6
Casey, Stockton*	.972	78	134	4	4	0
J. Clark, Reno	.966	88	135	6	5	1
R. Clark, San Jose	.963	14	25	1	1	0
Cortez, Reno	.878	23	34	2	5	0
Cruz, San Jose	.833	1	5	0	1	0
Culberson, Fresno	.975	87	150	4	4	1
Davis, Fresno	.956	82	139	12	7	0
DeButch, Reno	.000	1	0	0	1	0
Dewolf, Stockton*	.974	124	249	11	7	4
Dietrick, Modesto	.947	46	121	4	7	1
DiGioia, Palm Springs	1.000	19	21	0	0	0

OUTFIELDERS—Continued

Player and Club	Pct.	G.	PO.	A.	E.	DP.
Doran, Palm Springs	1.000	17	31	1	0	1
Ducey, Ventura County	.980	47	96	3	2	1
Duncan, Modesto*	1.000	17	25	0	0	0
Duran, Stockton*	1.000	7	5	1	0	0
Edwards, Bakersfield*	.973	124	241	12	7	3
Flores, Bakersfield*	.980	49	97	3	2	1
Forgione, Visalia*	.972	124	192	15	6	4
Foster, San Jose	1.000	2	5	0	0	0
Fox, Salinas*	.985	130	314	18	5	7
Fulton, Salinas	.000	3	0	0	1	0
Garner, Bakersfield	1.000	5	8	0	0	0
Gilliam, Bakersfield	1.000	11	7	0	0	0
J. Gray, Reno	.974	93	177	10	5	0
L. Gray, San Jose	.936	26	40	4	3	0
Hall, Reno	.960	22	21	3	1	0
Harrison, San Jose	.959	50	88	5	4	0
Hartsock, Palm Springs	1.000	4	6	0	0	0
S. Howard, Modesto	.929	81	156	2	12	1
T. Howard, Reno	.948	60	104	5	6	0
Jackson, Bakersfield	.909	27	48	2	5	0
Jacobo, Bakersfield	1.000	12	13	1	0	1
Jennings, Palm Springs*	.973	126	205	10	6	1
Jones, Ventura County	.857	14	10	2	2	0
Jose, Modesto	.942	119	215	12	14	1
Kent, Stockton*	1.000	1	2	0	0	0
Kinnard, Ventura County	.986	34	72	1	1	0
Kopetsky, Bakersfield	.958	12	21	2	1	0
Kosco, Salinas	.918	46	51	5	5	1
Kramer, Modesto	.947	51	107	1	6	0
Krause, Salinas	1.000	10	18	0	0	0
Lambert, Palm Springs	.984	96	172	7	3	1
Landrum, Ventura County	.907	89	152	4	16	0
Little, Salinas	1.000	11	13	1	0	0
Malave, Ventura County	1.000	3	4	0	0	0
Martinez, San Jose*	1.000	11	11	0	0	0

Player and Club	Pct.	G.	PO.	A.	E.	DP.
McDonald, Fresno	.960	123	241	26	11	3
Milner, San Jose*	.934	31	66	5	5	2
Monico, Stockton*	.977	72	124	2	3	0
Murphy, Modesto	1.000	2	1	0	0	0
Nelson, Modesto	.975	86	192	7	5	4
Nittoli, San Jose	.667	6	2	0	1	0
O'Connor, Visalia	1.000	12	13	0	0	0
Okubo, San Jose	.714	7	5	0	2	0
Oliva, San Jose	.935	88	165	9	12	3
Parsons, Reno	.976	51	79	3	2	2
Pettis, Palm Springs	.975	94	228	4	6	0
Quinones, Fresno	1.000	1	1	0	0	0
Rainey, Reno	1.000	1	2	0	0	0
Reitz, San Jose	.895	8	15	2	2	0
Reyna, Ventura County*	.930	69	124	8	10	3
Rivera, Reno	.965	100	185	9	7	2
Schiffelbein, Modesto*	1.000	7	11	1	0	0
Sconiers, San Jose*	1.000	2	1	0	0	0
Senne, Visalia	1.000	19	21	2	0	1
SKURLA, Fresno*	.987	114	205	21	3	3
Sorrento, Palm Springs	.944	9	16	1	1	1
Thomas, Visalia	.974	133	290	10	8	1
Thompson, Fresno	.959	54	68	2	3	0
Thornton, Stockton	1.000	1	1	0	0	0
Thrower, San Jose	1.000	5	3	1	0	0
Van Burkleo, Palm Springs*	.944	10	17	0	1	0
Venneri, San Jose*	.921	27	35	0	3	0
Walters, Stockton	.956	78	145	6	7	0
J. White, San Jose	.959	31	45	2	2	0
M. White, Bakersfield	.937	67	97	7	7	0
Whitfield, San Jose	.932	18	38	3	3	1
Wiggins, Visalia*	.937	52	70	4	5	0
Williams, Stockton	1.000	11	15	2	0	0
Yamano, San Jose*	.983	134	289	2	5	1
Yanes, Visalia	.957	122	188	12	9	5

CATCHERS

Player and Club	Pct.	G.	PO.	A.	E.	DP.	PB.
Amaya, Salinas	1.000	2	14	2	0	0	0
Anderson, Modesto	.991	60	293	40	3	6	4
Baker, Palm Springs	1.000	1	2	0	0	0	0
Bell, Palm Springs	.996	42	236	25	1	2	3
Beuerlein, Stockton	.982	12	49	6	1	0	1
Britt, Modesto	.980	19	89	8	2	1	0
Cabrera, Ventura County	.967	5	26	3	1	0	0
Carlucci, Bakersfield	¢982	68	440	53	9	5	16
Christman, San Jose	.977	15	32	10	1	1	2
Cias, San Jose	.988	45	224	32	3	5	7
Cormack, Salinas	.943	14	65	18	5	2	2
Davis, Palm Springs	.990	31	176	20	2	2	6
deMarrais, Ventura County	1.000	20	101	6	0	0	1
Diaz, Ventura County	.952	2	17	3	1	0	0
DiGioia, Palm Springs	1.000	7	32	2	0	0	0
Eccles, Visalia	.974	34	202	25	6	6	7
GATEWOOD, Visalia	.986	88	543	104	9	12	4
Gobbo, Stockton	.982	82	438	74	9	2	14
Gonzalez, Fresno	.973	76	530	76	17	6	18
Hall, Reno	.992	20	120	10	1	5	5

Triple Play—Anderson.

Player and Club	Pct.	G.	PO.	A.	E.	DP.	PB.
Hornacek, Bakersfield	1.000	4	23	5	0	1	1
G. Jones, Fresno	.969	53	281	36	10	4	12
J. Jones, Modesto	.981	68	357	48	8	5	7
Kmak, Fresno	.987	39	203	26	3	3	8
McGuire, Salinas	.975	114	713	83	20	16	14
Mitchell, Stockton	.944	5	27	7	2	0	4
Morfin, Salinas	.939	7	29	2	2	0	2
Myers, Ventura County	.980	124	849	99	19	8	12
Nicolosi, Visalia	.973	33	165	18	5	5	7
Nieporte, Reno	.974	64	323	46	10	3	11
Nittoli, San Jose	.967	26	77	10	3	2	2
Okubo, San Jose	.978	94	472	68	12	8	10
Pappas, Palm Springs	.990	70	445	48	5	3	13
Rainey, Reno	.980	68	401	49	9	8	11
Reynolds, Stockton	.981	7	42	10	1	2	1
Rodriguez, Stockton	.992	52	330	37	3	5	3
Rypien, Ventura County	1.000	1	5	0	0	0	0
J.D. Smith, Bakersfield	.984	80	502	68	9	8	25
Tettleton, Modesto	.956	11	40	3	2	1	1
Wilson, Salinas	.941	17	83	13	6	3	3

PITCHERS

Player and Club	Pct.	G.	PO.	A.	E.	DP.
Adams, Visalia	.750	3	1	2	1	0
Alexander, Reno	.947	61	3	15	1	0
Ambrose, Stockton	1.000	10	9	12	0	2
Applegate, Modesto	.852	39	8	15	4	1
Arroyo, San Jose-Modesto	1.000	6	3	6	0	1
Balsley, Modesto	.760	23	5	14	6	2
Barnhouse, Salinas	.800	15	2	6	2	0
E. Bauer, Reno*	.932	22	8	47	4	1
M. Bauer, San Jose	.964	24	6	21	1	0
Beavers, Modesto*	1.000	9	2	13	0	1
Bianchi, Visalia	1.000	14	2	13	0	0
Bigusiak, San Jose	1.000	4	0	3	0	0
Blobaum, San Jose	.846	30	4	7	2	3
Brake, Modesto*	1.000	12	1	10	0	0
Brinkman, Salinas	.846	24	6	16	4	2
Brinson, Ventura County	.733	34	3	8	4	0
Brisco, Stockton	1.000	8	0	1	0	0
Burgos, Ventura County*	.786	9	4	7	3	2
Burkett, Fresno	.917	4	6	5	1	0
Butler, Palm Springs*	.941	33	5	11	1	1
Candelaria, Palm Springs*	1.000	2	1	0	0	0
Cardwood, Visalia	.880	27	6	16	3	2
Carter, Palm Springs	.933	31	4	10	1	1
Childers, Reno	1.000	6	0	2	0	0
Christ, Salinas	.909	19	15	15	3	1
Christman, San Jose	1.000	5	0	1	0	0
Ciprian, Ventura County	.900	18	2	7	1	0
Clawson, Reno	.918	26	5	40	4	2

Player and Club	Pct.	G.	PO.	A.	E.	DP.
Coleman, Visalia	.923	21	5	7	1	0
D. Cook, Fresno*	.957	27	5	17	1	0
L. Cook, Palm Springs*	.944	34	8	9	1	1
Cortez, Reno	1.000	1	0	1	0	0
Cramer, Visalia*	1.000	12	1	7	0	0
Dacus, Palm Springs	1.000	55	4	9	0	0
Dewolf, Stockton*	1.000	3	1	3	0	0
Diaz, Stockton	1.000	32	1	6	0	0
Dickman, Ventura County	.941	44	4	12	1	0
Dominguer, Visalia	.957	38	6	16	1	2
Eggertsen, Palm Springs	.932	22	13	28	3	0
Erickson, Fresno*	.913	27	5	16	2	2
Fiala, Bakersfield	.947	47	6	12	1	2
Figueroa, Modesto	.933	14	0	14	1	1
Filippi, Reno	1.000	10	0	3	0	0
Fleming, Stockton	1.000	16	1	4	0	0
Fraser, Palm Springs	.950	19	7	12	1	2
Frew, Stockton	.800	23	8	20	7	1
Fulmer, Stockton*	.929	13	4	9	1	0
Gallo, San Jose*	1.000	16	0	3	0	0
Galloway, Visalia*	.917	18	1	10	1	0
M. Garcia, Palm Springs*	.917	43	6	16	2	2
R. Garcia, Bakersfield*	1.000	21	3	14	0	2
Garrick, San Jose	1.000	21	2	5	0	1
Gilbert, Fresno	.949	30	10	27	2	0
Givler, Salinas	1.000	47	3	9	0	1
Greenlee, Reno*	.933	17	5	23	2	3
Hamm, San Jose	.800	8	1	7	2	1

PITCHERS—Continued

Player and Club	Pct.	G.	PO.	A.	E.	DP.
Hansen, Modesto	.914	30	5	27	3	1
Hardwick, Bakersfield*	1.000	9	1	2	0	0
Harris, Modesto	1.000	10	3	10	0	0
Harrison, San Jose	1.000	2	0	1	0	0
Harvey, Palm Springs	1.000	43	2	8	0	0
Henderson, Stockton*	1.000	9	4	11	0	1
Hickerson, Visalia*	.900	11	4	12	2	0
Higgs, Salinas	.917	35	1	10	1	2
Hinnrichs, Fresno	.955	40	8	13	1	0
Hogan, Mod.-Vent. County	1.000	24	4	3	0	0
Howe, San Jose*	.952	14	1	19	1	4
Hubbard, Visalia	1.000	1	1	1	0	0
Iasparro, Visalia	.925	27	8	29	3	1
Jones, Salinas	.944	26	13	21	2	2
Kanwisher, Stockton	1.000	4	4	2	0	0
Kent, Modesto	1.000	9	2	2	0	0
Kopyta, Modesto	.889	19	2	6	1	0
Kubala, San Jose	.929	29	12	14	2	2
Kutsukos, Reno	.952	35	5	15	1	2
Lovelace, Palm Springs*	1.000	6	0	4	0	1
Lucas, Palm Springs*	1.000	7	0	1	0	0
Ludy, Stockton	.931	50	7	20	2	0
Lynch, Reno	.923	33	0	12	1	1
Marrett, Palm Springs	.917	21	10	23	3	0
Marsh, Reno*	1.000	31	2	17	0	2
D. Martinez, Palm Springs	.813	18	1	12	3	2
R. Martinez, Bakersfield	.920	20	4	19	2	0
McCament, Fresno	.913	54	3	18	2	2
McCarter, San Jose	1.000	7	2	10	0	2
McCatty, San Jose	.938	15	3	12	1	1
McGuire, Palm Springs	1.000	3	2	2	0	0
Meagher, Reno	.750	8	3	0	1	0
Mena, Bakersfield	.857	7	2	4	1	0
Mendek, Salinas*	.857	31	0	6	1	0
Mesa, Ventura County	.955	24	8	13	1	0
Messier, Fresno*	.909	29	3	7	1	3
Miglio, Stockton*	1.000	7	0	2	0	0
Montano, Stockton*	.929	42	5	8	1	0
Moore, Fresno	.765	38	7	6	4	0
Mumaw, Ventura County*	.500	6	0	1	1	0
MUSSELMAN, Ventura County*	1.000	26	5	33	0	3
Nakashima, San Jose	.935	32	6	23	2	1
Naworski, Bakersfield	.857	19	2	4	1	0
J. Nelson, Bakersfield	.846	24	4	7	2	1
K. Nelson, Bakersfield	.800	4	1	3	1	0
Neufelder, Salinas*	.980	26	15	35	1	2
Norris, San Jose	.857	11	6	6	2	0
Norton, Stockton	.889	27	6	18	3	1
Oakes, Fresno	.923	12	5	7	1	0
Olker, Fresno*	.947	25	3	15	1	1
Paris, Ventura County	1.000	9	0	1	0	0
Pena, Bakersfield*	.750	14	3	6	3	0
Perry, Visalia	.875	14	6	8	2	0
Peterek, Stockton	.941	25	10	22	2	1
Pierorazio, Visalia*	1.000	56	9	10	0	1
Pilkington, Fresno*	.400	7	1	1	3	0
Poloni, Salinas*	1.000	3	3	2	0	0
Price, Palm Springs*	1.000	10	5	12	0	1
Provence, Ventura County	.947	27	13	23	2	3
Puig, Reno*	.932	25	9	32	3	4
Ratliff, Stockton	1.000	11	2	3	0	0
Ray, Bakersfield	.903	42	7	21	3	0
Reece, Stockton*	.944	24	1	16	1	0
Reyes, Ventura County*	.750	32	3	6	3	2
Rodgers, Fresno	1.000	3	1	6	0	0
Rohlof, Visalia	.900	31	5	13	2	0
Romanovsky, Palm Springs*	.955	14	5	16	1	1
Rousey, Salinas	.952	19	9	11	1	0
Rowen, Bakersfield*	.806	19	6	19	6	3
Ruhle, San Jose	1.000	3	2	3	0	0
Sadler, Stockton	.810	12	6	11	4	0
Santana, Modesto	1.000	11	2	3	0	0
Savage, Bakersfield	.952	44	3	17	1	2
Sconiers, San Jose*	1.000	1	0	1	0	0
Shanks, Ventura County	1.000	51	6	12	0	0
Sharpnack, Modesto	.808	25	8	13	5	1
Shull, Palm Springs	1.000	1	0	1	0	0
B. Smith, Bakersfield*	.923	24	2	10	1	1
S. Smith, Fresno	1.000	23	4	6	0	0
Spratke, Salinas	.938	26	12	18	2	3
Stewart, Reno	.808	38	2	19	5	1
Stottlemyre, Ventura County	.889	17	10	14	3	1
Strichek, Modesto	.917	17	1	10	1	1
Strong, Modesto	1.000	36	0	11	0	0
Stull, Bakersfield	.886	31	10	21	4	0
Swearingen, Salinas*	.931	31	8	19	2	1
Tabeling, Visalia	.781	23	4	21	7	3
Tamori, San Jose	1.000	18	2	7	0	0
Tapani, Modesto	1.000	11	2	10	0	0
Tejeda, Bakersfield	1.000	5	2	3	0	0
Timberlake, Palm Springs	1.000	6	3	3	0	0
Tinkey, San Jose	.957	40	4	18	1	0
Tortorice, Modesto*	1.000	31	4	13	0	2
Velasquez, Visalia	1.000	44	3	3	0	0
Venturino, Palm Springs	1.000	8	1	10	0	1
Verducci, Fresno	1.000	1	0	1	0	0
Villa, Fresno	1.000	43	4	12	0	0
Visor, Reno	1.000	18	0	11	0	3
Walker, Stockton	.813	13	1	12	3	0
Walsh, Ventura County*	1.000	15	2	11	0	1
Walton, Modesto	.932	27	17	24	3	3
Wasilewski, Ventura County	1.000	49	7	9	0	0
Wells, Ventura County*	1.000	5	3	4	0	0
Wetteland, Bakersfield	.778	15	0	7	2	0
White, Salinas	.941	40	4	12	1	1
Wiggins, Visalia*	1.000	1	0	1	0	0
Wortham, Ventura County*	1.000	2	0	1	0	0
Yokota, San Jose	.917	27	3	19	2	2
Young, Bakersfield	.750	12	3	3	2	1

Triple Play—Brake.

The following players do not have any recorded accepted chances at the positions indicated; therefore, are not listed in the fielding averages for those particular positions: R. Anderson, 3b, of; Batesole, ss, of; M. Bauer, 2b; A. Candelaria, p; Cias, of; D. Clark, of; Crabtree, p; Cucjen, ss; DeButch, p; Escobar, of; K. Galloway, p; Geivett, of, p; Gray, p; Howell, p; Kopetsky, p; Krause, 3b; Kristan, p; Kubala, of; D. Martinez, of; Mitchell, p; Quinones, 1b; Reitz, p; Siegel, p; Snell, p; Van Stone, 3b.

CLUB PITCHING

Club	ERA.	G.	CG.	ShO.	Sv.	IP.	H.	R.	ER.	HR.	HB.	BB.	Int. BB.	SO.	WP.	Bk.
Salinas	3.61	142	15	8	40	1227.2	1288	634	492	62	45	475	23	861	71	5
Palm Springs	3.84	142	15	5	35	1241.1	1189	650	532	69	54	596	24	848	83	10
Stockton	3.92	142	23	14	36	1199.2	1215	640	521	53	32	518	29	877	92	14
Ventura County	4.03	142	9	8	30	1217.0	1208	676	545	63	28	565	25	962	80	15
San Jose	4.35	142	45	10	21	1161.0	1268	681	561	81	32	373	9	778	73	14
Visalia	4.44	142	22	10	27	1210.0	1188	712	597	81	49	669	24	888	85	10
Modesto	4.63	142	16	7	26	1184.2	1352	759	610	111	46	498	22	720	56	13
Reno	4.81	142	23	3	26	1183.1	1256	789	632	111	50	656	21	805	79	12
Fresno	4.88	142	12	6	39	1210.1	1238	788	656	115	51	741	11	970	88	11
Bakersfield	5.12	142	15	2	20	1215.1	1334	866	693	89	47	766	52	924	106	18

PITCHERS' RECORDS

(Leading Qualifiers for Earned-Run Average Leadership—114 or More Innings)

*Throws lefthanded.

Pitcher—Club	W.	L.	Pct.	ERA.	G.	GS.	CG.	GF.	ShO.	Sv.	IP.	H.	R.	ER.	HR.	HB.	BB.	Int. BB.	SO.	WP.
Christ, Salinas	7	8	.467	2.69	19	19	5	0	2	0	127.0	132	49	38	3	2	38	3	77	3
Peterek, Stockton	15	6	.714	2.88	25	24	7	0	3	0	168.2	153	63	54	6	1	56	2	113	11
Musselman, Ventura County*	7	7	.500	3.03	26	24	2	0	0	0	154.2	122	67	52	3	1	59	0	165	5
Neufelder, Salinas*	9	9	.500	3.14	26	25	4	0	0	0	163.1	172	80	57	6	12	58	1	110	5
Ludy, Stockton	13	6	.684	3.15	50	8	4	17	1	4	151.1	147	72	53	3	3	46	8	86	6
Provence, Ventura County	6	10	.375	3.39	27	18	2	7	0	3	132.2	141	65	50	7	2	41	3	73	4
Brinson, Ventura County	11	8	.579	3.49	34	18	1	8	0	1	131.2	108	64	51	2	5	83	3	136	12
Ray, Bakersfield	2	13	.133	3.54	42	8	0	26	0	6	139.2	140	65	55	9	2	47	6	125	7
Fraser, Palm Springs	9	2	.818	3.55	19	19	2	0	0	0	124.1	115	60	49	8	7	29	0	99	4
Jones, Salinas	11	8	.579	3.60	26	25	2	0	0	0	157.1	141	76	63	9	4	90	2	137	15
Alexander, Reno	8	5	.615	3.60	61	0	0	46	0	12	132.1	120	69	53	14	3	62	4	131	9

Departmental Leaders: G—Alexander, 61; W—Peterek, 15; L—Sharpnack, 14; Pct.—Peterek, .714; GS—Iasparro, Walton, 27; CG—Yokota, 10; GF—Pierorazio, 49; ShO—Peterek, 3; Sv.—McCament, 19; IP—Puig, 178.2; H—Walton, 204; R—Olker, 116; ER—Olker, 95; HR—Gilbert, 23; HB—Clawson, 13; BB—Erickson, 130; IBB—Savage, 11; SO—D. Cook, 173; WP—Eggertsen, 19.

(All Pitchers—Listed Alphabetically)

Pitcher—Club	W.	L.	Pct.	ERA.	G.	GS.	CG.	GF.	ShO.	Sv.	IP.	H.	R.	ER.	HR.	HB.	BB.	Int. BB.	SO.	WP.
Adams, Visalia	0	2	.000	7.36	3	3	0	0	0	0	11.0	14	10	9	1	0	8	0	1	0
Alexander, Reno	8	5	.615	3.60	61	0	0	46	0	12	132.1	120	69	53	14	3	62	4	131	9
Ambrose, Stockton	7	2	.778	3.39	10	10	1	0	1	0	69.0	57	29	26	2	3	25	2	81	5
Applegate, Modesto	3	8	.273	4.19	39	0	0	20	0	4	92.1	103	58	43	10	7	26	3	55	3
Arroyo, 5 San Jose-1 Mod	2	4	.333	4.01	6	5	2	1	0	0	33.2	33	17	15	2	3	4	0	17	0
Balsley, Modesto	6	5	.545	4.38	23	20	1	1	0	0	115.0	123	76	56	7	3	59	1	71	4
Barnhouse, Salinas	1	1	.500	4.23	15	2	0	3	0	2	38.1	47	27	18	2	3	13	1	15	7
E. Bauer, Reno*	11	5	.688	3.90	22	22	5	0	0	0	147.2	151	76	64	12	5	81	0	100	11
M. Bauer, San Jose	8	7	.533	4.67	24	20	7	3	0	1	135.0	163	72	70	9	4	27	1	111	7
Beavers, Modesto*	6	3	.667	3.23	9	8	1	0	0	0	55.2	57	21	20	2	0	24	0	45	3
Bianchi, Visalia	7	2	.778	2.86	14	5	2	4	0	2	66.0	46	26	21	5	5	38	1	68	9
Bigusiak, San Jose	0	2	.000	18.00	4	0	0	3	0	0	5.0	14	10	10	0	0	3	0	0	0
Blobaum, San Jose	5	5	.500	3.53	30	1	0	20	0	6	51.0	46	25	20	3	3	17	1	30	3
Brake, Modesto*	2	4	.333	5.22	12	5	3	4	1	0	39.2	51	34	23	3	1	20	1	28	0
Brinkman, Salinas	5	8	.385	4.53	24	19	0	3	0	0	119.1	150	82	60	15	7	46	3	71	4
Brinson, Ventura County	11	8	.579	3.49	34	18	1	8	0	1	131.2	108	64	51	2	5	83	3	136	12
Brisco, Stockton	1	1	.500	8.00	8	0	0	3	0	1	9.0	13	11	8	0	0	9	2	8	0
Burgos, Ventura County*	1	3	.250	3.94	9	9	0	0	0	0	45.2	46	27	20	1	0	31	0	37	5
Burkett, Fresno	0	3	.000	5.47	4	4	0	0	0	0	24.2	34	19	15	2	2	8	0	14	3
Butler, Palm Springs*	5	4	.556	3.74	33	9	2	12	0	3	98.2	93	50	41	7	3	41	2	56	2
A. Candelaria, Fresno*	0	0	.000	0.00	1	0	0	1	0	1	1.0	2	1	0	0	0	1	0	2	0
J. Candelaria, P Springs*	0	0	.000	2.57	2	2	0	0	0	0	7.0	4	2	2	0	0	2	0	8	0
Cardwood, Visalia	11	6	.647	3.68	27	26	3	0	1	0	156.1	131	75	64	10	7	96	2	105	3
Carter, Palm Springs	2	4	.333	3.47	31	1	0	14	0	3	57.0	54	27	22	9	1	33	3	45	3
Childers, Reno	1	0	1.000	17.28	6	0	0	1	0	0	8.1	14	16	16	2	1	10	2	5	0
Christ, Salinas	7	8	.467	2.69	19	19	5	0	2	0	127.0	132	49	38	3	2	38	3	77	3
Christman, San Jose	0	0	.000	18.00	1	0	0	0	0	0	2.0	2	4	4	0	0	5	0	0	0
Ciprian, Ventura County	3	7	.300	8.05	18	10	0	6	0	0	53.2	80	56	48	9	2	37	2	33	3
Clawson, Reno	6	9	.400	5.59	26	26	4	0	0	0	148.0	184	109	92	16	13	84	2	61	6
Coleman, Visalia	6	7	.462	6.22	21	21	3	0	1	0	115.2	136	87	80	14	4	69	0	49	6
D. Cook, Fresno*	12	7	.632	3.97	27	25	2	2	1	1	170.0	141	92	75	16	5	100	1	173	7
L. Cook, Palm Springs*	6	3	.667	4.05	34	6	0	9	0	0	102.1	98	56	46	5	3	57	0	73	3
Cortez, Reno	0	0	.000	0.00	1	0	0	1	0	0	1.0	0	0	0	0	0	0	0	0	0
Crabtree, Bakersfield	0	0	.000	9.00	1	0	0	1	0	0	2.0	2	2	2	0	0	1	0	1	0
Cramer, Visalia*	0	1	.000	5.08	12	0	0	5	0	0	33.2	46	31	19	3	1	15	1	16	1
Dacus, Palm Springs	10	10	.500	4.67	55	0	0	28	0	4	79.0	87	57	41	1	5	47	4	54	0
DeButch, Reno	0	0	.000	0.00	1	0	0	1	0	0	0.1	0	0	0	0	0	0	0	0	0
Dewolf, Stockton*	1	0	1.000	2.53	3	1	0	1	0	0	10.2	10	4	3	0	2	5	0	5	3
Diaz, Stockton	1	3	.250	3.38	32	0	0	31	0	9	45.1	42	18	17	1	1	21	3	44	10
Dickman, Ventura County	7	7	.500	6.22	44	9	0	21	0	3	94.0	99	73	65	10	3	67	3	64	16
Dominguez, Visalia	6	6	.500	3.09	38	1	1	16	0	5	105.0	96	47	36	4	3	45	4	92	15
Eggertsen, Palm Springs	5	7	.417	5.74	22	22	0	0	0	0	122.1	120	88	78	11	7	93	1	62	19
Erickson, Fresno*	6	7	.462	5.44	27	21	1	2	0	1	135.2	124	89	82	9	3	130	1	129	10
Fiala, Bakersfield	7	4	.636	5.22	47	0	0	21	0	3	98.1	130	73	57	9	4	42	7	68	7
Figueroa, Modesto	4	5	.444	6.32	14	14	0	0	0	0	72.2	96	57	51	11	2	23	1	41	6
Filippi, Reno	0	1	.000	7.33	10	1	0	4	0	0	27.0	27	28	22	5	0	29	0	21	1
Fleming, Stockton	0	4	.000	4.98	16	0	0	12	0	1	21.2	23	16	12	0	0	10	0	18	2
Fraser, Palm Springs	9	2	.818	3.55	19	19	2	0	0	0	124.1	115	60	49	8	7	29	0	99	4
Frew, Stockton	11	5	.688	3.86	23	22	2	0	1	0	140.0	133	69	60	7	2	61	0	89	13
Fulmer, Stockton*	3	1	.750	5.32	13	6	1	3	0	1	47.1	64	35	28	3	2	12	1	25	3
Gallo, San Jose*	1	3	.250	5.90	16	4	1	7	0	2	39.2	43	29	26	5	1	31	1	31	6
K. Galloway, San Jose*	0	0	.000	33.75	2	0	0	0	0	0	1.1	4	5	5	0	0	4	0	0	0
T. Galloway, Visalia*	6	3	.667	6.97	18	18	1	0	1	0	81.1	101	68	63	4	0	36	0	60	8
M. Garcia, Palm Springs*	8	3	.727	1.61	43	0	0	28	0	9	72.2	59	18	13	2	2	26	6	75	3
R. Garcia, Bakersfield*	3	7	.300	5.12	21	14	3	1	0	0	89.2	101	63	51	10	2	63	0	59	14
Garrick, San Jose	2	2	.500	3.83	21	1	0	12	0	3	42.1	47	30	18	2	2	16	1	25	5
Geivett, Palm Springs	1	0	1.000	5.40	2	0	0	2	0	0	1.2	2	1	1	0	0	2	0	2	0
Gilbert, Fresno	9	13	.409	4.92	30	25	5	0	1	0	162.2	177	109	89	23	8	76	1	93	6
Givler, Salinas	7	3	.700	1.95	47	0	0	40	0	14	74.0	52	18	16	2	0	28	3	66	6
Gray, San Jose	0	0	.000	7.71	5	0	0	3	0	0	7.0	9	6	6	1	0	1	0	3	0
Greenlee, Reno*	6	7	.462	6.08	17	16	0	0	0	0	80.0	94	70	54	5	2	59	0	45	8
Hamm, San Jose	0	3	.000	6.10	8	5	0	1	0	0	20.2	27	23	14	2	0	13	0	9	2
Hansen, Modesto	4	7	.364	4.65	30	9	0	13	0	3	98.2	105	64	51	10	1	48	1	51	4
Hardwick, Bakersfield*	0	3	.000	11.08	9	0	0	5	0	1	13.0	13	22	16	1	2	25	2	14	1
Harris, Modesto	3	5	.375	3.58	10	10	2	0	1	0	55.1	61	25	22	6	0	13	0	38	2
Harrison, San Jose	0	0	.000	20.25	2	0	0	1	0	0	1.1	4	3	3	0	1	0	0	0	1
Harvey, Palm Springs	3	4	.429	2.68	43	0	0	29	0	15	57.0	38	24	17	1	3	38	6	68	2
Henderson, Stockton*	5	2	.714	3.56	9	9	1	0	0	0	60.2	56	24	24	3	1	19	2	61	1
Hickerson, Visalia*	4	3	.571	4.23	11	11	3	0	0	0	72.1	72	37	34	3	1	25	1	69	2
Higgs, Salinas	6	3	.667	2.47	35	0	0	24	0	10	73.0	69	23	20	3	1	18	4	67	8
Hinnrichs, Fresno	5	10	.333	5.22	40	9	0	9	0	2	100.0	127	66	58	10	3	38	0	66	0
Hogan, 14 Mod-10 Ven Cnty	3	2	.600	4.04	24	0	0	12	0	4	42.1	42	21	19	2	3	18	2	26	4
Howe, San Jose*	3	2	.600	1.47	14	8	0	5	0	2	49.0	40	14	8	0	2	5	0	37	1
Howell, Modesto	0	0	.000	13.50	2	2	0	0	0	0	2.0	5	3	3	1	0	1	0	1	0
Hubbard, Visalia	0	0	.000	4.50	1	0	0	1	0	0	4.0	3	2	2	1	0	1	0	2	0
Iasparro, Visalia	11	9	.550	4.45	27	27	4	0	1	0	161.2	136	89	80	12	11	113	2	133	8
Jones, Salinas	11	8	.579	3.60	26	25	2	0	0	0	157.1	141	76	63	9	4	90	2	137	15
Kanwisher, Stockton	0	3	.000	6.23	4	4	0	0	0	0	17.1	21	18	12	4	0	12	1	8	5
Kent, Modesto	0	1	.000	3.75	9	0	0	9	0	3	12.0	15	7	5	0	0	6	0	9	2
Kopetsky, Bakersfield	0	0	.000	2.35	5	0	0	5	0	0	7.2	6	2	2	0	0	5	0	5	0
Kopyta, Modesto	5	2	.714	4.19	19	0	0	10	0	1	43.0	36	28	20	6	0	24	1	31	5
Kristan, Reno	1	0	1.000	4.00	2	2	0	0	0	0	9.0	10	5	4	0	1	2	0	2	0
Kubala, San Jose	9	7	.563	4.30	29	16	5	6	1	0	119.1	119	71	57	9	6	52	0	74	12
Kutsukos, Reno	3	3	.500	5.22	35	5	1	12	1	0	81.0	94	53	47	7	6	34	0	38	3
Lovelace, Palm Springs*	0	1	.000	9.17	6	5	0	1	0	0	17.2	21	23	18	0	1	30	0	16	5
Lucas, Palm Springs*	0	2	.000	5.11	7	0	0	3	0	1	12.1	15	8	7	1	1	1	0	9	2
Ludy, Stockton	13	6	.684	3.15	50	8	4	17	1	4	151.1	147	72	53	3	3	46	8	86	6

Pitcher—Club	W.	L.	Pct.	ERA.	G.	GS.	CG.	GF.	ShO.	Sv.	IP.	H.	R.	ER.	HR.	HB.	BB.	Int. BB.	SO.	WP.
Lynch, Reno	5	3	.625	2.41	33	0	0	33	0	12	56.0	45	18	15	4	1	11	1	43	0
Marrett, Palm Springs	6	6	.500	4.21	21	19	2	1	0	0	119.2	138	69	56	6	9	52	2	56	7
Marsh, Reno*	3	7	.300	5.60	31	13	1	6	0	0	80.1	89	76	50	10	1	64	3	49	14
D. Martinez, Palm Springs	6	4	.600	5.25	18	16	0	0	0	0	94.1	106	63	55	9	3	58	0	41	13
R. Martinez, Bakersfield	4	8	.333	4.75	20	20	2	0	1	0	106.0	119	73	56	3	2	63	2	78	4
McCament, Fresno	4	4	.500	2.49	54	0	0	48	0	19	86.2	87	36	24	4	5	24	1	61	9
McCarter, San Jose	2	3	.400	4.89	7	7	2	0	0	0	46.0	54	31	25	2	2	16	0	21	2
McCatty, San Jose	2	8	.200	4.00	15	11	5	1	1	0	74.1	76	43	33	8	1	18	0	53	4
McGuire, Palm Springs	1	0	1.000	1.86	3	3	0	0	0	0	19.1	15	7	4	1	0	9	0	18	1
Meagher, Reno	3	3	.500	5.57	8	7	3	1	0	0	42.0	42	29	26	5	3	18	0	25	2
Mena, Bakersfield	0	7	.000	7.24	7	7	1	0	0	0	41.0	60	38	33	2	1	16	1	31	1
Mendek, Salinas*	5	4	.556	1.63	31	1	0	23	0	8	49.2	48	14	9	1	0	19	1	55	3
Mesa, Ventura County	10	6	.625	3.86	24	24	2	0	1	0	142.1	141	71	61	6	1	58	0	113	9
Messier, Fresno*	6	5	.545	5.42	29	9	0	8	0	1	76.1	80	55	46	5	2	73	0	59	7
Miglio, Stockton*	1	2	.333	1.26	7	0	0	5	0	2	14.1	12	6	2	0	0	8	1	17	1
Mitchell, Stockton	0	0	.000	0.00	1	0	0	1	0	0	2.1	1	0	0	0	1	2	0	1	0
Montano, Stockton*	3	4	.429	2.95	42	2	0	26	0	9	64.0	61	32	21	2	3	29	1	50	6
Moore, Fresno	7	7	.500	6.15	38	17	0	7	0	1	124.1	125	95	85	13	10	102	1	95	15
Mumaw, Ventura County*	0	0	.000	2.16	6	0	0	2	0	1	8.1	13	2	2	0	0	6	2	6	0
Musselman, Ventura County*	7	7	.500	3.03	26	24	2	0	0	0	154.2	122	67	52	3	1	59	0	165	5
Nakashima, San Jose	3	9	.250	4.79	32	15	6	11	0	1	141.0	175	93	75	11	0	38	1	64	9
Naworski, Bakersfield	0	4	.000	5.54	19	0	0	12	0	1	26.0	36	23	16	3	4	17	3	11	4
J. Nelson, Bakersfield	0	7	.000	6.69	24	11	0	6	0	0	71.1	79	83	53	9	4	84	1	37	10
K. Nelson, Bakersfield	1	2	.333	3.20	4	3	1	1	0	0	25.1	21	10	9	3	0	8	1	14	0
Neufelder, Salinas*	9	9	.500	3.14	26	25	4	0	0	0	163.1	172	80	57	6	12	58	1	110	5
Norris, San Jose	4	3	.571	1.44	11	11	0	0	0	0	56.1	48	18	9	3	0	8	0	62	2
Norton, Stockton	3	3	.500	3.95	27	8	0	14	0	7	84.1	100	44	37	3	3	29	3	52	2
Oakes, Fresno	0	2	.000	3.06	12	0	0	10	0	4	32.1	29	11	11	2	1	7	0	23	0
Olker, Fresno*	7	10	.412	6.58	25	22	2	0	0	0	130.0	152	116	95	18	4	82	0	106	14
Paris, Ventura County	1	1	.500	4.76	9	0	0	5	0	1	11.1	14	8	6	4	0	7	1	10	4
Pena, Bakersfield*	4	4	.500	4.14	14	11	1	2	1	0	58.2	64	36	27	2	3	31	0	53	8
Perry, Visalia	7	2	.778	3.36	14	11	2	2	0	0	80.1	66	38	30	5	3	40	3	63	5
Peterek, Stockton	15	6	.714	2.88	25	24	7	0	3	0	168.2	153	63	54	6	1	56	2	113	11
Pierorazio, Visalia*	8	5	.615	2.18	56	0	0	49	0	13	78.1	72	28	19	4	0	33	5	58	3
Pilkington, Fresno*	1	1	.500	4.66	7	2	1	3	1	0	19.1	15	16	10	1	1	15	0	17	1
Poloni, Salinas*	1	1	.500	1.59	3	1	1	2	0	0	11.1	8	2	2	0	0	3	0	7	0
Price, Palm Springs*	5	2	.714	2.71	10	10	1	0	1	0	63.0	51	23	19	3	6	19	0	55	10
Provence, Ventura County	6	10	.375	3.39	27	18	2	7	0	3	132.2	141	65	50	7	2	41	3	73	4
Puig, Reno*	14	9	.609	4.08	25	25	7	0	2	0	178.2	184	100	81	16	3	58	3	130	8
Ratliff, Stockton	2	2	.500	4.58	11	0	0	6	0	2	19.2	20	10	10	2	1	10	1	13	0
Ray, Bakersfield	2	13	.133	3.54	42	8	0	26	0	6	139.2	140	65	55	9	2	47	6	125	7
Reece, Stockton*	4	8	.333	6.19	24	23	1	0	1	0	109.0	112	93	75	8	3	108	0	104	10
Reitz, San Jose	0	0	.000	0.00	1	0	0	1	0	0	1.0	2	0	0	0	0	0	0	0	0
Reyes, Ventura County*	2	1	.667	6.05	32	0	0	18	0	1	41.2	57	36	28	4	2	23	1	25	4
Rodgers, Fresno	1	1	.500	3.00	3	3	0	0	0	0	18.0	15	13	6	1	1	13	0	17	4
Rohlof, Visalia	3	4	.429	4.57	31	1	0	7	0	1	69.0	74	43	35	6	1	38	1	58	2
Romanovsky, Palm Springs*	9	2	.818	2.86	14	14	4	0	2	0	91.1	85	34	29	3	1	35	0	56	3
Rousey, Salinas	1	2	.333	5.85	19	2	0	3	0	2	47.2	57	33	31	0	3	16	0	25	1
Rowen, Bakersfield*	6	6	.500	3.22	19	14	2	1	0	0	106.1	108	56	38	2	3	52	5	87	9
Ruhle, San Jose	2	1	.667	3.00	3	3	2	0	1	0	21.0	20	10	7	0	1	4	0	16	2
Sadler, Stockton	8	2	.800	3.63	12	12	4	0	1	0	79.1	82	39	32	4	2	26	1	45	9
Santana, Modesto	0	1	.000	6.63	11	0	0	9	0	0	19.0	27	15	14	1	3	14	0	5	2
Savage, Bakersfield	5	8	.385	4.52	44	0	0	32	0	9	77.2	82	45	39	2	7	45	11	77	4
Sconiers, San Jose*	0	0	.000	0.00	1	0	0	1	0	0	1.0	1	0	0	0	0	0	0	0	0
Shanks, Ventura County	2	5	.286	3.18	51	1	0	42	0	18	82.0	88	40	29	3	2	29	3	41	2
Sharpnack, Modesto	5	14	.263	5.58	25	24	4	0	1	0	127.1	151	104	79	19	6	65	2	67	5
Shull, Palm Springs	1	0	1.000	1.29	1	1	1	0	0	0	7.0	6	3	1	0	0	4	0	3	3
Siegel, Salinas	0	0	.000	0.00	1	1	0	0	0	0	4.0	7	0	0	0	0	1	0	4	0
B. Smith, Bakersfield*	3	5	.375	5.40	24	15	0	4	0	0	86.2	91	59	52	3	3	68	5	73	6
S. Smith, Fresno	3	4	.429	3.82	23	5	1	11	1	1	63.2	75	36	27	6	4	23	2	55	2
Snell, Salinas	0	0	.000	0.00	1	0	0	1	0	0	1.0	1	0	0	0	0	0	0	1	0
Spratke, Salinas	13	7	.650	4.23	26	26	2	0	2	0	164.0	182	103	77	8	2	63	3	80	9
Stewart, Reno	8	11	.421	4.39	38	13	1	13	0	2	125.0	125	89	61	7	5	98	5	120	12
Stottlemyre, Ventura County	9	4	.692	2.43	17	17	2	0	0	0	103.2	76	39	28	4	2	36	0	104	7
Strichek, Modesto	3	3	.500	6.25	17	0	0	8	0	1	36.0	46	27	25	5	2	24	4	22	2
Strong, Modesto	2	2	.500	3.42	36	0	0	30	0	11	52.2	43	23	20	5	2	28	4	39	1
Stull, Bakersfield	3	10	.231	5.45	31	15	2	4	0	0	135.1	131	97	82	16	7	96	7	110	12
Swearingen, Salinas*	11	8	.579	4.24	31	20	1	9	0	2	121.0	145	75	57	10	5	43	0	85	5
Tabeling, Visalia	3	11	.214	5.18	23	18	3	2	1	0	120.0	140	86	69	5	7	56	2	54	6
Tamori, San Jose	8	2	.800	3.62	18	8	4	7	2	2	74.2	64	32	30	6	1	18	0	57	1
Tapani, Modesto	6	1	.857	2.48	11	11	1	0	0	0	69.0	74	26	19	2	1	22	1	44	1
Tejeda, Bakersfield	1	2	.333	8.17	5	4	0	0	0	0	25.1	33	26	23	6	0	10	0	16	2
Timberlake, Palm Springs	3	1	.750	3.23	6	6	1	0	0	0	39.0	39	17	14	1	0	9	0	28	2
Tinkey, San Jose	6	6	.500	4.57	40	6	1	11	0	3	102.1	129	59	52	6	3	36	2	85	6
Tortorice, Modesto*	4	4	.500	6.68	31	12	0	11	0	0	94.1	133	86	70	6	6	49	2	49	7
Velasquez, Visalia	3	6	.333	5.50	44	0	0	33	0	6	55.2	55	43	34	4	6	53	2	58	17
Venturino, Palm Springs	7	0	1.000	3.07	8	8	2	0	0	0	55.2	43	20	19	1	2	12	0	24	1
Verducci, Fresno	0	0	.000	0.00	1	0	0	1	0	0	1.0	0	0	0	0	0	1	0	0	0
Villa, Fresno	5	2	.714	4.45	43	0	0	28	0	8	64.2	55	34	32	5	2	48	4	60	10
Visor, Reno	4	6	.400	6.35	18	12	1	1	0	0	66.2	77	51	47	8	6	46	1	35	5
Walker, Stockton	5	5	.500	4.94	13	13	2	0	0	0	85.2	108	57	47	5	4	30	1	57	5
Walsh, Ventura County*	6	3	.667	5.16	15	9	0	4	0	0	59.1	65	41	34	4	3	26	0	43	5
Walton, Modesto	13	7	.650	4.09	27	27	4	0	0	0	176.0	204	96	80	16	9	41	1	107	7
Wasilewski, Ventura County	7	3	.700	4.43	49	1	0	16	0	1	111.2	121	68	55	5	4	52	5	71	3
Wells, Ventura County*	2	1	.667	1.89	5	2	0	1	0	0	19.0	13	5	4	0	0	4	0	26	0
Wetteland, Bakersfield	0	7	.000	5.78	15	12	4	1	0	0	67.0	71	50	43	6	1	46	1	38	10
White, Salinas	0	3	.000	5.14	40	1	0	20	0	2	77.0	77	52	44	3	6	39	2	61	5
Wiggins, Visalia*	0	0	.000	18.00	1	0	0	1	0	0	1.0	2	2	2	0	0	3	0	2	0
Wortham, Ventura County*	0	0	.000	5.40	2	0	0	1	0	0	3.1	2	2	2	0	0	1	0	4	0
Yokota, San Jose	9	10	.474	4.77	27	21	10	4	2	1	139.2	149	86	74	12	3	57	2	85	10
Young, Bakersfield	1	5	.167	9.24	12	8	0	3	0	0	38.0	47	43	39	3	2	47	0	27	7

BALKS—Brinson, Reece, 4 each; E. Bauer, Bianchi, D. Cook, Diaz, Erickson, Olker, Sharpnack, Stull, Tabeling, Tamori, 3 each; Alexander,

Balsley, Blobaum, Cardwood, Clawson, Fiala, Frew, Greenlee, Hamm, Hansen, Jones, R. Martinez, Mendek, Mesa, Norris, Romanovsky, Shanks, B. Smith, Stottlemyre, Visor, Young, 2 each; M. Bauer, Brake, Burgos, Butler, A. Candelaria, Carter, Ciprian, L. Cook, Cramer, Dacus, Dickman, Eggertsen, Figueroa, Gallo, R. Garcia, Hardwick, Henderson, Kubala, Ludy, D. Martinez, Moore, Naworski, Norton, Price, Puig, Ray, Rohlof, Rousey, Rowen, Sadler, Santana, Savage, Strichek, Tinkey, Tortorice, Venturino, Walker, Walsh, Walton, Wasilewski, Wetteland, Yokota, 1 each.

COMBINATION SHUTOUTS—Erickson-Villa, Moore-Oakes, Fresno; Balsley-Hogan, Beavers-Santana, Figueroa-Tortorice-Strong, Walton-Hogan, Modesto; Fraser-Garcia, Price-Dacus-Harvey-Garcia, Palm Springs; Brinkman-Higgs, Jones-Mendek, Siegel-Jones-Snell, Swearingen-Barnhouse, Salinas; Kubala-Garrick-Howe, Norris-Tinkey-Tamori, Yokota-Garrick, San Jose; Ambrose-Diaz, Ambrose-Fleming-Norton, Fulmer-Ludy-Montano, Henderson-Fleming, Peterek-Montano, Reece-Ratliff, Stockton; Musselman-Dickman 2, Brinson-Shanks, Burgos-Shanks, Mesa-Provence, Mesa-Shanks, Wells-Brinson-Shanks, Ventura County; Cardwood-Velasquez-Pierorazio, Cardwood-Bianchi-Velasquez, Cardwood-Dominguez, Hickerson-Pierorazio, Iasparro-Dominguez, Visalia.

NO-HIT GAME—Burgos-Shanks, Ventura County, defeated Visalia, 2-0, August 19.

Carolina League

CLASS A

CHAMPIONSHIP WINNERS IN PREVIOUS YEARS

1945—Danville .681
1946—Greensboro .599
Raleigh (2nd)† .563
1947—Burlington .613
Raleigh (3rd)† .574
1948—Raleigh .592
Martinsville (2nd)† .570
1949—Danville .601
Burlington (4th)† .500
1950—Winston-Salem* .693
1951—Durham .600
Wins-Salem (2nd)† .583
1952—Raleigh .581
Reidsville (4th)† .536
1953—Raleigh .593
Danville (2nd)† .572
1954—Fayetteville* .628
1955—HP-Thomasville .580
Danville (2nd)† .533
1956—HP-Thomasville .591
Fayetteville (4th)† .523
1957—Durham .632
HP-Thomasville .622
1958—Danville .576
Burlington (4th)† .511
1959—Raleigh .600
Wilson (2nd)† .550
1960—Greensboro‡ .636
Burlington .586
1961—Wilson .594
1962—Durham .636
Wilson .600
Kinston (2nd)† .593
1963—Kinston§ .538
Greensboro§ .590
Wilson (2nd)† .535
1964—Kinston§ .572
Winston-Salem§† .590
1965—Peninsula§ .597
Durham§ .580
Tidewater† .528
1966—Kinston§ .547
Winston-Salem§ .586
Rocky Mount† .533
1967—Durham x (West.) .536
Raleigh (East.) .542
1968—Salem (West.) .607
Ral-Dur (East.) .597
HP-Thom. y (W.) .493
1969—Rocky M (East.) .569
Salem (West.) .542
Ral-Dur z (East.) .560
1970—Winston-Salem‡ .586
Burlington .597
1971—Peninsula‡ .647
Kinston .623
1972—Salem‡ .657
Burlington .632
1973—Lynchburg .588
Winston-Salem‡ .557
1974—Salem .671
Salem .582
1975—Rocky Mount .667
Rocky Mount .614
1976—Winston-Salem .618
Winston-Salem .551
1977—Lynchburg .591
Peninsula‡ .556
1978—Peninsula .696
Lynchburg‡ .614
1979—Winston-Salem a .607
1980—Peninsula‡ .714
Durham .600
1981—Peninsula .522
Hagerstown‡ .507
1982—Alexandria‡ .597
Durham .588
1983—Lynchburg‡ .691
Winston-Salem .529
1984—Lynchburg‡ .645
Durham .486
1985—Lynchburg .679
Winston-Salem‡ .417

*Won championship and four-club playoff. †Won four-club playoff. ‡Won split-season playoff. §League was divided into Eastern, Western divisions. xWon eight-club, two-division playoff. yWon eight-club, two-division playoff against Raleigh-Durham. zWon eight-club, two-division playoff against Burlington. aWon both halves of split-season (no playoffs).

STANDING OF CLUBS AT CLOSE OF FIRST HALF, JUNE 19

NORTHERN DIVISION

Club	W.	L.	T.	Pct.	G.B.
Hagerstown (Orioles)	46	24	0	.657	....
Lynchburg (Mets)	38	32	0	.543	8
Prince William (Pirates)	32	38	0	.457	14
Salem (Rangers)	20	49	0	.290	25½

SOUTHERN DIVISION

Club	W.	L.	T.	Pct.	G.B.
Winston-Salem (Cubs)	43	27	0	.614	....
Peninsula (White Sox)	38	32	0	.543	5
Durham (Braves)	32	38	0	.457	11
Kinston (Independent)	30	39	0	.435	12½

STANDING OF CLUBS AT CLOSE OF SECOND HALF, AUGUST 31

NORTHERN DIVISION

Club	W.	L.	T.	Pct.	G.B.
Hagerstown (Orioles)	45	24	0	.652	....
Lynchburg (Mets)	37	33	1	.529	8½
Prince William (Pirates)	35	34	0	.507	10
Salem (Rangers)	25	44	1	.362	20

SOUTHERN DIVISION

Club	W.	L.	T.	Pct.	G.B.
Winston-Salem (Cubs)	39	29	1	.574	....
Durham (Braves)	40	30	1	.571	....
Kinston (Independent)	30	37	0	.448	8½
Peninsula (White Sox)	22	42	0	.344	15

COMPOSITE STANDING OF CLUBS AT CLOSE OF SEASON, AUGUST 31

Club	Hag.	W.S.	Lyn.	Dur.	P.W.	Pen.	Kin.	Sal.	W.	L.	T.	Pct.	G.B.
Hagerstown (Orioles)	....	10	12	13	14	14	14	14	91	48	0	.655	....
Winston-Salem (Cubs)	10	....	13	11	11	10	14	13	82	56	1	.594	8½
Lynchburg (Mets)	8	7	....	11	12	9	14	14	75	65	1	.536	16½
Durham (Braves)	7	9	9	....	11	11	9	16	72	68	1	.514	19½
Prince William (Pirates)	6	9	8	9	....	14	10	11	67	72	0	.482	24
Peninsula (White Sox)	5	9	11	9	5	....	7	14	60	74	0	.448	28½
Kinston (Independent)	6	6	6	11	10	10	....	11	60	76	0	.441	29½
Salem (Rangers)	6	6	6	4	9	6	8	....	45	93	1	.326	45½

Major league affiliations in parentheses.

Playoffs—Winston-Salem defeated Hagerstown, three games to one, to win league championship.

Regular-Season Attendance—Durham, 197,125; Hagerstown, 144,161; Kinston, 48,845; Lynchburg, 87,930; Peninsula, 75,928; Prince William, 117,000; Salem, 87,047; Winston-Salem, 136,841. Total, 894,877. Playoffs, 3,712. All-Star Game, 855.

Managers—Durham, Buddy Bailey; Hagerstown, Bob Molinaro; Kinston, Dave Trembley; Lynchburg, Bobby Floyd; Peninsula, Bob Bailey (thru June 9), Duke Sims (June 10 thru end of season); Prince William, Rocky Bridges; Salem, Mike Bucci; Winston-Salem, Jim Essian.

All-Star Team—1B—Lance Belen, Prince William; 2B—Pete Stanicek, Hagerstown; 3B—Craig Worthington, Hagerstown; SS—Gregg Jefferies, Lynchburg; OF—Doug Dascenzo, Winston-Salem; Sherwin Cijntje, Hagerstown; Ron Scheer, Peninsula; C—Hector Villanueva, Winston-Salem; DH—Gino Gentile, Kinston; LHP—Rob Russell, Prince William; RHP—David Pavlas, Winston-Salem; Most Valuable Player—Gregg Jefferies, Lynchburg; Pitcher of the Year—David Pavlas, Winston-Salem; Manager of the Year—Jim Essian, Winston-Salem.

(Compiled by Howe News Bureau, Boston, Mass.)

CLUB BATTING

Club	Pct.	G.	AB.	R.	OR.	H.	TB.	2B.	3B.	HR.	RBI.	GW.	SH.	SF.	HP.	BB.	Int. BB.	SO.	SB.	CS.	LOB.
Hagerstown	.290	139	4611	842	640	1339	1970	244	45	99	762	76	24	54	45	643	35	676	236	102	980
Lynchburg	.278	141	4752	805	692	1319	1901	222	63	78	712	69	36	44	46	689	32	938	237	77	1137
Winston-Salem	.272	139	4708	748	590	1281	1848	246	30	87	658	71	63	45	33	571	36	778	213	86	1006
Durham	.259	141	4597	771	738	1192	1868	217	30	133	696	64	34	45	61	716	41	859	114	81	1054
Prince William	.255	139	4623	613	626	1177	1693	224	32	76	549	58	32	32	46	457	21	899	187	78	958
Peninsula	.254	134	4508	655	711	1144	1580	208	36	52	574	55	37	45	44	615	27	826	140	77	1032
Salem	.252	139	4512	594	924	1138	1612	199	37	67	523	36	56	35	44	519	25	765	172	95	941
Kinston	.247	136	4455	635	742	1101	1575	187	25	79	548	44	36	32	36	623	29	945	110	71	1009

INDIVIDUAL BATTING

(Leading Qualifiers for Batting Championship—378 or More Plate Appearances)

*Bats lefthanded. †Switch-hitter.

Player and Club	Pct.	G.	AB.	R.	H.	TB.	2B.	3B.	HR.	RBI.	GW.	SH.	SF.	HP.	BB.	Int. BB.	SO.	SB.	CS.
Jefferies, Gregg, Lynchburg†	.354	95	390	66	138	214	25	9	11	80	7	0	5	2	33	3	29	43	8
Dascenzo, Douglas, Winston-Salem†	.327	138	545	107	178	247	29	11	6	83	6	12	5	2	63	5	44	57	13
Villanueva, Hector, Winston-Salem	.318	125	412	58	131	194	20	2	13	100	12	2	12	2	81	3	42	6	4
Stanicek, Peter, Hagerstown†	.317	127	457	115	145	191	24	2	6	67	6	5	3	9	91	1	47	77	17
Farmer, Albert, Salem	.306	111	382	55	117	160	13	6	6	45	2	0	5	4	41	1	34	14	8
Cijntje, Sherwin, Hagerstown*	.303	121	422	79	128	150	10	6	0	43	2	8	2	4	46	2	53	51	18
Cook, Jeffrey, Prince William	.301	128	511	86	154	186	16	5	2	29	1	1	1	3	54	5	77	43	12
Worthington, Craig, Hagerstown	.300	132	480	85	144	226	35	1	15	105	16	0	8	2	82	7	58	7	12
Pruitt, Darrell, Peninsula	.299	105	418	79	125	157	15	4	3	50	2	7	5	3	40	1	64	36	15
Sanchez, Zoilo, Lynchburg	.296	128	459	78	136	215	25	6	14	85	10	0	8	7	53	2	111	13	2
Richardson, Timothy, Hagerstown	.296	124	422	65	125	157	16	8	0	58	3	3	6	3	46	1	27	20	11

Departmental Leaders: G—Lawton, 141; AB—Lawton, 567; R—Lawton, 118; H—Dascenzo, 178; TB—Gant, 271; 2B—Bafia, 36; 3B—Lawton, 16; HR—Gant, 26; RBI—Worthington, 105; GWRBI—Worthington, 16; SH—Dascenzo, 12; SF—H. Villanueva, 12; HP—Stanicek, 9; BB—Lawton, 102; IBB—Gentile, 17; SO—R. Gideon, 133; SB—Stanicek, 77; CS—House, 20.

(All Players—Listed Alphabetically)

Player and Club	Pct.	G.	AB.	R.	H.	TB.	2B.	3B.	HR.	RBI.	GW.	SH.	SF.	HP.	BB.	Int. BB.	SO.	SB.	CS.
Abner, Benjamin, Prince William	.275	57	222	17	61	90	14	0	5	34	2	0	1	1	15	1	26	4	2
Adams, Ralph, Lynchburg	.333	8	3	1	1	1	0	0	0	0	0	0	0	0	3	0	1	0	0
Akers, Howard, Kinston*	.209	110	306	53	64	98	15	2	5	40	5	6	1	6	79	1	94	10	7
Alcazar, Jorge, Peninsula	.260	90	315	45	82	116	16	3	4	52	11	0	4	0	46	2	91	1	3
Allen, James, Salem†	.211	64	152	11	32	43	5	0	2	7	0	1	2	1	21	3	22	0	0
Allen, Larry, Peninsula*	.221	36	113	11	25	30	5	0	0	13	4	0	0	0	8	0	20	0	0
Bafia, Robert, Winston-Salem	.250	132	505	79	126	218	36	4	16	76	7	3	7	1	38	1	115	4	6
Barringer, Reginald, Prince William	.280	38	82	13	23	27	4	0	0	6	1	0	0	3	9	2	8	4	1
Bautista, Jose, Lynchburg	.286	18	21	2	6	9	1	1	0	3	0	2	0	1	0	0	3	0	0
Bayer, Christopher, Lynchburg†	.222	13	9	0	2	2	0	0	0	1	0	3	0	0	0	0	4	0	0
Belen, Lance, Prince William	.293	134	495	76	145	237	32	3	18	88	11	0	4	5	48	4	93	10	3
Bell, Gregory, Winston-Salem*	.286	44	7	0	2	2	0	0	0	0	0	0	0	0	1	0	0	0	0
Bellino, Frank, Hagerstown*	.288	36	118	19	34	58	7	1	5	29	1	0	2	0	11	1	15	2	0
Bernardo, Rick, Salem*	.252	71	234	29	59	85	11	3	3	27	2	2	2	2	22	0	51	4	6
Bertolani, Jerry, Peninsula	.230	68	222	33	51	71	9	1	3	18	1	4	1	2	35	0	50	14	6
Bethel, Donald, Winston-Salem	.000	31	7	0	0	0	0	0	0	0	0	0	0	0	1	0	3	0	0
Billmeyer, Michael, Hagerstown†	.215	68	181	20	39	61	9	2	3	23	4	0	3	2	25	2	42	0	1
Blasucci, Anthony, Prince William*	.000	4	2	0	0	0	0	0	0	0	0	0	0	0	0	0	0	0	0
Blauser, Jeffrey, Durham	.286	123	447	94	128	200	27	3	13	52	3	2	7	7	81	2	92	12	9
Bootay, Kevin, Salem	.304	34	125	25	38	55	7	2	2	20	1	3	2	0	14	0	14	17	7
Borders, Patrick, Kinston	.328	49	174	24	57	85	10	0	6	26	3	0	1	1	10	0	42	0	0
Brooks, Desmond, Lynchburg	.232	36	82	12	19	28	2	2	1	7	2	0	0	3	20	0	24	0	1
Brown, Kevin, Lynchburg*	.231	34	13	0	3	3	0	0	0	1	0	0	0	0	0	0	4	0	0
Caraballo, Wilmer, Lynchburg	.267	94	307	36	82	123	13	2	8	52	5	0	5	0	16	2	50	0	3
Carmichael, Alan, Lynchburg	.294	59	194	28	57	72	12	0	1	31	3	2	2	0	20	0	33	1	0
Cartaya, Joel, Salem†	.287	89	303	35	87	104	12	1	1	37	2	8	4	0	17	0	29	3	2
Cash, Johnny, Durham*	.100	14	10	0	1	1	0	0	0	0	0	1	0	0	0	0	4	0	0
Casteel, Brent, Winston-Salem	.188	10	16	1	3	3	0	0	0	0	0	0	0	0	0	0	3	0	0
Chance, Anthony, Prince William	.233	19	60	5	14	25	1	2	2	11	2	0	0	0	3	0	15	4	2
Cheek, Carey, Prince William	.223	30	103	10	23	31	2	0	2	16	1	0	2	0	18	0	16	0	0
Cijntje, Sherwin, Hagerstown*	.303	121	422	79	128	150	10	6	0	43	2	8	2	4	46	2	53	51	18
Cimo, Matthew, Hagerstown	.237	36	118	15	28	43	3	0	4	18	5	0	2	1	12	1	21	5	3
Ciszkowski, Jeffrey, Lynchburg	.000	11	1	0	0	0	0	0	0	0	0	2	0	0	0	0	1	0	0
Contreras, Jouquin, Lynchburg†	.359	31	117	22	42	62	8	6	0	20	2	0	1	1	10	1	18	19	4
Cook, Jeffrey, Prince William	.301	128	511	86	154	186	16	5	2	29	1	1	1	3	54	5	77	43	12
Criswell, Timothy, Durham	.289	83	263	33	76	91	8	2	1	30	4	4	1	1	27	1	23	11	4
Cron, Christopher, Durham	.208	90	265	26	55	86	10	0	7	34	5	2	2	6	29	0	60	0	2
Cronkright, Daniel, Peninsula*	.211	116	360	46	76	125	16	6	7	45	5	2	3	6	69	6	90	1	4
Dascenzo, Douglas, Winston-Salem†	.327	138	545	107	178	247	29	11	6	83	6	12	5	2	63	5	44	57	13
DelRosario, Maximo, Durham	.333	55	3	0	1	1	0	0	0	0	0	2	0	0	1	0	2	0	0
Delucchi, Ronald, Prince William	.184	30	87	10	16	23	1	0	2	9	0	0	2	0	10	0	20	6	2
Denby, Darryl, Durham	.291	27	103	11	30	43	6	2	1	18	0	0	3	6	3	0	17	4	4
Denson, Andrew, Durham	.234	72	231	31	54	78	6	3	4	23	2	1	0	2	25	0	46	6	1
Dewey, Todd, Durham†	.239	100	306	40	73	107	17	1	5	38	6	2	2	2	35	7	33	1	3
Dial, Bryan, Winston-Salem	.500	11	2	1	1	1	0	0	0	0	0	0	0	0	0	0	1	0	0
DiCeglio, Thomas, Winston-Salem	.333	5	6	1	2	2	0	0	0	0	0	0	0	0	0	0	1	0	0
Dickerson, James, Winston-Salem	.211	72	194	33	41	54	5	1	2	18	2	2	0	2	25	0	41	0	2
Dombek, Damon, Lynchburg†	.000	9	1	0	0	0	0	0	0	0	0	0	0	0	0	0	0	0	0
Drummond, Timothy, Prince William	.000	47	3	0	0	0	0	0	0	0	0	0	0	0	1	0	1	0	0
Duggan, Thomas, Salem	.262	117	336	39	88	138	19	2	9	49	5	1	6	1	37	2	70	0	6
Engram, Graylyn, Peninsula	.203	45	123	21	25	28	3	0	0	10	0	0	2	0	19	0	8	13	4
Epps, Riley, Salem†	.233	33	90	17	21	41	6	1	4	11	1	0	0	5	13	1	30	0	0
Evans, Evan, Kinston	.204	37	98	7	20	26	3	0	1	11	0	0	0	2	15	0	28	4	1
Ewart, Ronald, Winston-Salem*	.241	52	141	24	34	42	5	0	1	15	2	3	3	0	26	0	18	8	3
Falcone, David, Hagerstown*	.359	18	64	22	23	51	4	3	6	27	1	0	0	2	14	3	9	1	0
Farmer, Albert, Salem	.306	111	382	55	117	160	13	6	6	45	2	0	5	4	41	1	34	14	8
Farmer, Bryan, Durham*	.000	8	1	0	0	0	0	0	0	0	0	0	0	0	0	0	0	0	0

Player and Club	Pct.	G.	AB.	R.	H.	TB.	2B.	3B.	HR.	RBI.	GW.	SH.	SF.	HP.	BB.	Int. BB.	SO.	SB.	CS.
Fermin, Felix, Prince William	.280	84	322	58	90	102	10	1	0	26	2	3	1	4	25	0	19	40	12
Ferreiras, Salvador, Prince William	.169	35	83	4	14	20	1	1	1	7	1	1	0	1	6	0	25	0	0
Fredymond, Juan, Durham	.217	94	203	28	44	58	2	3	2	18	1	0	1	2	26	1	47	8	5
Gant, Ronald, Durham	.277	137	512	108	142	271	31	10	26	102	4	2	6	3	78	0	85	35	9
Garcia, Agustin, Lynchburg	.500	16	2	0	1	1	0	0	0	1	0	0	0	0	0	0	1	0	0
Garcia, Cornelio, Peninsula*	.290	33	100	16	29	44	4	4	1	12	0	1	1	2	15	0	19	3	3
Gardner, Jeffrey, Lynchburg*	.272	111	334	59	91	109	11	2	1	39	2	8	3	4	81	3	33	6	4
Gay, Steven, Lynchburg	.400	39	5	0	2	2	0	0	0	0	0	0	0	0	3	0	0	0	0
Gentile, Gene, Kinston*	.267	119	393	74	105	209	25	2	25	85	5	0	3	0	94	17	99	7	5
Giddens, Ronnie, Prince William	.287	36	108	9	31	44	6	2	1	16	0	0	2	1	10	0	17	2	1
Gideon, Brett, Prince William	.286	26	7	2	2	3	1	0	0	1	0	1	0	0	0	0	2	0	0
Gideon, Ronnie, Lynchburg*	.263	118	410	82	108	193	28	3	17	76	9	0	5	5	97	12	133	2	3
Glasker, Stephen, Salem*	.268	109	276	36	74	107	11	8	2	21	0	4	0	1	23	1	81	14	6
Goodwin, Michael, Prince William	.000	4	6	0	0	0	0	0	0	0	0	0	0	0	0	0	1	0	0
Gozzo, Mauro, Lynchburg	.400	61	5	1	2	2	0	0	0	0	0	0	0	0	1	0	2	0	0
Greene, Jeffrey, Durham	.000	25	3	0	0	0	0	0	0	0	0	0	0	0	0	0	3	0	0
Groves, Jeffrey, Durham	.091	25	11	0	1	1	0	0	0	0	0	0	0	0	0	0	5	0	0
Gulliver, Glenn, Hagerstown*	.375	3	8	0	3	3	0	0	0	1	0	0	1	0	1	0	1	0	0
Hardamon, Derrick, Winston-Salem	.327	26	49	11	16	19	3	0	0	8	2	3	0	1	9	0	18	8	2
Harrison, Wayne, Durham	.271	123	388	72	105	189	27	0	19	79	7	0	5	7	72	4	97	4	7
Hatcher, Johnny, Durham	.385	15	52	10	20	26	0	0	2	7	2	0	1	0	1	0	7	5	1
Heise, Larry, Durham*	.500	22	2	0	1	1	0	0	0	1	0	0	0	0	0	0	1	0	0
Hernandez, Martin, Prince William	.000	23	13	0	0	0	0	0	0	0	0	1	0	0	1	0	11	0	0
Hildebrand, Thomas, Peninsula	.227	84	247	24	56	72	8	1	2	24	2	1	6	1	13	1	34	3	1
Hill, Bradley, Salem*	.297	104	340	47	101	152	26	2	7	53	7	2	3	2	27	3	27	7	5
Hopkins, Richard, Winston-Salem*	.268	103	272	43	73	121	16	1	10	37	4	4	4	3	43	4	56	10	5
House, Bryan, Winston-Salem†	.280	130	496	103	139	199	29	2	9	57	4	1	3	8	87	6	88	65	20
Hudson, Lance, Hagerstown†	.261	14	46	6	12	15	3	0	0	4	1	0	0	0	4	0	11	1	3
Ingle, Michael, Kinston†	.247	125	437	58	108	121	10	0	1	45	2	4	3	2	65	4	57	6	8
Jackson, Ronald, Salem	.238	55	126	12	30	40	4	0	2	18	0	2	1	0	12	0	33	6	2
Jefferies, Gregg, Lynchburg†	.354	95	390	66	138	214	25	9	11	80	7	0	5	2	33	3	29	43	8
Jimenez, Cesar, Durham	.083	30	12	1	1	4	0	0	1	3	0	3	0	0	1	0	7	0	0
Johnson, Lindsey, Kinston	.218	79	220	37	48	67	8	1	3	20	4	3	2	6	32	0	61	4	0
Johnson, Roger, Kinston	.231	8	26	3	6	9	3	0	0	2	0	2	0	0	5	1	3	0	0
Jones, Brian, Prince William	.264	127	462	59	122	165	22	6	3	47	6	3	3	2	46	0	83	13	10
Jones, Geary, Lynchburg	.269	26	78	10	21	26	2	0	1	8	0	0	0	3	13	0	31	2	0
Jones, Labarry, Durham*	.148	10	27	2	4	5	1	0	0	3	0	0	0	0	2	0	3	0	2
Justice, David, Durham*	.279	67	229	47	64	111	9	1	12	44	7	1	1	7	46	5	24	2	4
Khoury, Scott, Hagerstown*	.268	109	355	52	95	167	18	3	16	70	8	0	8	4	39	6	51	5	3
Kilner, John, Durham*	.174	23	23	2	4	4	0	0	0	2	0	3	0	0	1	0	7	0	0
King, Jeffrey, Prince William	.235	37	132	18	31	55	4	1	6	20	1	0	0	1	19	2	34	1	1
King, Ronald, Salem*	.233	36	86	17	20	24	4	0	0	9	0	0	0	2	31	1	20	9	3
Koopmann, Robert, Prince William†	.000	7	3	0	0	0	0	0	0	0	0	0	0	0	0	0	2	0	0
Kreuter, Chad, Salem	.220	125	387	55	85	128	21	2	6	49	3	4	4	3	67	2	82	5	5
Lamb, Todd, Durham	.115	36	26	2	3	3	0	0	0	0	0	0	0	0	1	0	9	0	0
Lancaster, Lester, Winston-Salem	.182	14	11	1	2	5	0	0	1	1	0	1	0	0	0	0	4	0	0
Lawton, Marcus, Lynchburg†	.279	141	567	118	158	224	22	16	4	66	3	2	0	2	102	2	111	58	11
Liddell, David, Lynchburg	.103	9	29	5	3	6	0	0	1	3	0	0	0	1	3	0	8	0	0
Little, Scott, Lynchburg	.244	58	172	34	42	67	11	4	2	31	3	1	1	1	29	0	34	5	7
Lynn, Charles, Lynchburg	.222	12	27	6	6	18	3	0	3	4	0	0	0	0	6	0	8	1	0
Magallanes, William, Peninsula	.208	22	77	10	16	28	1	1	3	11	0	0	0	2	4	0	28	2	0
Magrann, Thomas, Hagerstown	.305	74	210	36	64	94	14	2	4	32	1	1	3	2	30	1	34	3	2
Markert, James, Peninsula	.235	44	136	10	32	42	7	0	1	16	3	1	0	1	20	0	25	3	0
Masters, David, Winston-Salem	.179	30	28	5	5	8	1	1	0	2	0	1	0	0	3	0	9	0	0
Maye, Stephen, Winston-Salem	.000	19	4	0	0	0	0	0	0	0	0	0	0	0	0	0	2	0	0
Maynard, Daniel, Salem	.174	35	46	2	8	9	1	0	0	7	0	2	0	1	5	0	14	0	0
McDougal, Julius, Winston-Salem†	.289	103	346	51	100	132	21	4	1	43	7	3	2	3	34	2	61	20	7
McElroy, Glen, Peninsula	.183	42	109	12	20	23	3	0	0	9	1	1	0	1	14	0	20	0	0
McMillan, Timothy, Prince William	.191	67	251	24	48	76	12	2	4	39	5	0	2	2	8	2	97	2	1
McMorris, Mark, Winston-Salem*	.274	72	237	24	65	87	11	1	3	39	5	0	3	2	23	2	24	2	3
McNally, Robert, Durham	.000	2	3	0	0	0	0	0	0	0	0	0	0	0	0	0	1	0	0
Melendez, Jose, Prince William	.040	29	25	1	1	1	0	0	0	0	0	3	0	0	2	0	9	0	0
Melton, Lawrence, Prince William	.050	26	20	2	1	1	0	0	0	0	0	2	0	0	3	0	12	0	0
Melvin, Scott, Kinston	.280	120	425	63	119	168	18	8	5	47	2	2	4	1	64	0	61	3	5
Merullo, Matthew, Peninsula*	.303	64	208	21	63	88	12	2	3	35	3	0	3	1	19	3	16	1	0
Moore, Michael, Peninsula	.241	76	195	23	47	54	5	1	0	17	2	4	0	4	21	0	27	9	6
Moralez, Paul, Kinston	.281	125	462	53	130	168	21	1	5	56	5	2	4	5	20	0	41	5	1
Morelock, Charles, Durham	.143	16	7	0	1	1	0	0	0	0	0	2	0	0	1	0	0	0	0
Morris, David, Durham	.167	37	6	1	1	1	0	0	0	2	0	0	0	0	0	0	1	0	0
Morris, Richard, Durham	.278	72	245	46	68	99	14	1	5	36	2	0	3	2	38	1	41	3	3
Murray, David, Salem	.215	54	158	29	34	42	6	1	0	17	0	5	2	2	40	0	15	13	6
Nichols, Ty, Hagerstown	.271	110	377	63	102	151	15	2	10	58	3	2	4	1	34	1	66	5	8
Nipper, Michael, Durham	.379	52	174	39	66	106	14	1	8	35	4	0	1	3	34	2	31	1	4
Norman, Daniel, Hagerstown	.287	97	341	60	98	164	21	3	13	77	10	0	4	0	54	3	63	5	4
O'Hearn, Robert, Salem	.220	25	50	2	11	14	3	0	0	4	0	1	0	0	8	1	8	0	0
O'Hoppe, Robert, Kinston	.050	7	20	3	1	1	0	0	0	2	0	0	0	0	5	0	9	0	0
Odle, Page, Prince William	.252	128	476	75	120	185	29	6	8	62	8	0	7	4	76	2	100	37	12
Pavlas, David, Winston-Salem	.143	28	21	2	3	3	0	0	0	2	0	0	0	0	0	0	9	0	0
Peluso, Matt, Peninsula	.216	31	97	18	21	30	4	1	1	10	1	0	0	1	14	1	35	3	2
Perez, Hector, Lynchburg*	.273	115	352	61	96	148	21	2	9	66	8	0	4	5	44	2	78	21	10
Phillips, James, Winston-Salem	.333	33	3	0	1	1	0	0	0	0	0	0	0	0	0	0	0	0	0
Phillips, Stephen, Lynchburg*	.289	101	342	62	99	129	13	4	3	49	5	7	3	2	51	2	72	9	8
Pico, Jeffrey, Winston-Salem	.125	27	24	4	3	4	1	0	0	0	0	3	0	0	1	0	5	0	0
Pierce, Chris, Prince William	.183	21	60	3	11	11	0	0	0	3	0	2	1	0	4	0	16	1	0
Posey, Robert, Durham*	.237	58	169	25	40	61	6	0	5	28	2	0	0	2	27	2	37	2	1
Postier, Paul, Salem	.279	13	43	3	12	12	0	0	0	4	1	0	0	0	4	0	10	0	3
Prince, Thomas, Prince William	.253	121	395	59	100	166	34	1	10	47	8	3	2	7	50	1	74	4	5
Pruitt, Darrell, Peninsula	.299	105	418	79	125	157	15	4	3	50	2	7	5	3	40	1	64	36	15
Rauth, Christopher, Lynchburg	.100	12	10	1	1	1	0	0	0	0	0	1	0	0	0	0	3	0	0
Reichel, Thomas, Peninsula	.232	65	237	23	55	68	8	1	1	23	2	2	2	2	25	0	27	4	6
Reimer, Kevin, Salem*	.245	133	453	57	111	184	21	2	16	76	7	2	2	7	61	6	71	4	5
Renfroe, Cohen, Winston-Salem	.200	66	5	1	1	2	1	0	0	0	0	0	0	0	0	0	1	0	0

Player and Club	Pct.	G.	AB.	R.	H.	TB.	2B.	3B.	HR.	RBI.	GW.	SH.	SF.	HP.	BB.	Int. BB.	SO.	SB.	CS.
Reynolds, Michael, Durham*	.248	71	157	33	39	55	5	1	3	17	4	0	0	0	41	5	21	7	7
Rice, Timothy, Winston-Salem	.000	36	6	0	0	0	0	0	0	0	0	0	0	0	0	0	1	0	0
Richardson, Donald, Winston-Salem	.229	16	35	5	8	8	0	0	0	1	0	1	1	0	3	0	3	1	0
Richardson, Jeffrey, Lynchburg	.200	32	25	0	5	5	0	0	0	1	0	1	0	0	2	0	12	0	0
Richardson, Timothy, Hagerstown	.296	124	422	65	125	157	16	8	0	58	3	3	6	3	46	1	27	20	11
Ritter, Christopher, Prince William	.174	27	23	2	4	5	1	0	0	2	0	4	0	0	1	0	7	0	0
Roadcap, Steve, Winston-Salem†	.000	4	3	0	0	0	0	0	0	0	0	0	0	0	2	0	2	0	0
Roberts, Norman, Hagerstown	.305	101	295	56	90	145	19	6	8	67	9	2	2	5	34	2	51	13	4
Robinson, Donald, Prince William	.200	3	5	0	1	2	1	0	0	0	0	0	0	0	0	0	0	0	0
Robinson, Emmett, Kinston	.244	117	373	46	91	119	12	2	4	39	2	7	1	1	50	0	94	25	9
Robles, Gabaliel, Winston-Salem	.222	11	9	1	2	2	0	0	0	0	0	1	0	0	1	0	2	0	0
Rockey, James, Durham	.168	48	125	9	21	24	3	0	0	15	1	2	1	0	22	1	26	1	4
Rodriguez, Richard, Lynchburg*	.000	36	2	0	0	0	0	0	0	0	0	0	0	0	0	0	1	0	0
Rolland, David, Salem	.229	82	175	18	40	65	9	2	4	19	3	4	1	5	18	0	48	6	7
Romagna, Randolph, Kinston	.258	120	422	59	109	152	24	2	5	50	4	0	3	3	45	3	60	7	8
Rooker, David, Prince William	.300	30	10	2	3	4	1	0	0	1	0	0	0	0	0	0	2	1	0
Roomes, Rolando, Winston-Salem	.238	19	63	10	15	36	3	0	6	14	1	0	0	0	5	0	22	1	1
Rosario, Melvin, Kinston	.133	46	120	11	16	24	2	0	2	7	0	3	0	0	11	0	45	2	0
Russell, Robert, Prince William*	.200	30	15	1	3	3	0	0	0	1	0	1	0	0	4	0	7	0	0
Sanchez, Zoilo, Lynchburg	.296	128	459	78	136	215	25	6	14	85	10	0	8	7	53	2	111	13	3
Scheer, Ronald, Peninsula	.292	97	346	69	101	157	28	2	8	54	5	4	3	2	52	7	49	7	4
Schwarz, Jeffrey, Winston-Salem	.000	4	2	0	0	0	0	0	0	0	0	1	0	0	0	0	1	0	0
Scott, Michael, Durham	.091	13	11	0	1	1	0	0	0	1	0	2	0	0	0	0	3	0	0
Sedar, Edward, Peninsula	.287	115	366	83	105	146	24	1	5	54	5	3	7	7	89	2	62	24	8
Shields, Thomas, Prince William	.277	30	112	17	31	43	7	1	1	12	2	1	1	5	9	0	16	4	1
Siebert, Richard, Durham	.200	30	20	4	4	5	1	0	0	3	0	2	0	0	4	0	8	0	0
Smiley, John, Prince William*	.000	48	7	2	0	0	0	0	0	0	0	1	0	0	2	0	3	0	0
Smith, Dana, Hagerstown	.289	89	246	44	71	102	15	2	4	33	2	3	4	5	48	1	48	6	5
Smith, Kenneth, Hagerstown*	.284	30	95	19	27	43	10	0	2	14	1	0	0	0	21	2	23	9	4
Smith, Terrance, Durham	.000	1	1	0	0	0	0	0	0	0	0	0	0	0	0	0	0	0	0
Smith, Todd, Prince William†	.196	19	51	3	10	12	2	0	0	1	0	1	0	1	7	0	20	2	3
Stading, Gregory, Prince William	.000	34	6	0	0	0	0	0	0	0	0	1	0	0	0	0	1	0	0
Stampfl, Eric, Lynchburg	.000	22	7	0	0	0	0	0	0	0	0	2	0	0	0	0	3	0	0
Stanicek, Peter, Hagerstown†	.317	127	457	115	145	191	24	2	6	67	6	5	3	9	91	1	47	77	17
Steen, Scott, Kinston	.221	26	68	11	15	20	2	0	1	7	1	0	0	2	7	0	25	0	1
Stevens, Michael, Prince William	.242	66	186	27	45	83	9	1	9	28	3	0	1	5	14	1	54	2	1
Stiles, William, Lynchburg	.000	26	1	0	0	0	0	0	0	0	0	0	0	0	0	0	1	0	0
Sutryk, Thomas, Peninsula	.329	27	70	9	23	24	1	0	0	6	3	2	0	3	5	0	11	0	1
Tackett, Jeffrey, Hagerstown	.285	83	246	53	70	87	15	1	0	21	2	0	1	5	36	0	36	16	5
Todd, Kyle, Prince William	.261	81	280	28	73	93	14	0	2	43	4	3	2	1	12	1	31	7	9
Toliver, Andre, Peninsula	.136	9	22	1	3	4	1	0	0	3	0	0	1	0	3	1	5	0	1
Trafton, Todd, Peninsula	.290	63	217	37	63	91	12	2	4	37	0	1	4	2	32	3	31	3	0
Tullier, Michael, Winston-Salem*	.230	110	209	37	48	64	9	2	1	22	1	7	2	0	33	2	27	7	6
Valera, Alcadio, 29 Lyn-45 Kin†	.248	74	230	41	57	80	14	3	1	20	2	4	0	1	27	0	72	7	5
Van Cleve, Dandridge, Salem*	.205	92	298	45	61	87	11	3	3	17	0	4	0	0	33	3	71	36	10
Vargas, Jose, Salem†	.243	129	449	58	109	122	9	2	0	33	2	11	1	8	25	1	33	34	14
Venturini, Peter, Peninsula	.220	65	227	18	50	67	9	1	2	26	1	1	2	1	21	0	33	3	4
Villanueva, Hector, Winston-Salem	.318	125	412	58	131	194	20	2	13	100	12	2	12	2	81	3	42	6	4
Villanueva, Juan, Lynchburg	.157	17	51	4	8	8	0	0	0	4	1	0	1	0	9	0	7	1	0
Waggoner, Aubrey, Peninsula*	.194	20	72	7	14	20	0	3	0	9	1	1	0	1	14	0	24	4	3
Wagner, Gerald, Durham	.000	52	0	2	0	0	0	0	0	0	0	1	0	0	2	0	0	0	0
Walker, Darcy, Winston-Salem*	.264	111	356	41	94	147	20	0	11	47	6	0	2	2	36	5	73	4	3
Wellman, Phillip, Durham†	.216	82	236	34	51	89	8	0	10	40	6	0	5	4	54	5	47	5	3
West, David, Lynchburg*	.286	13	14	1	4	5	1	0	0	2	0	1	0	0	0	0	2	0	0
Westbrook, Michael, Lynchburg*	.263	122	419	71	110	133	13	5	0	46	6	1	5	4	55	0	52	54	11
Wetherby, Jeffrey, Durham*	.299	72	261	62	78	124	17	1	9	57	4	0	6	7	48	4	49	6	6
Wheeler, Rodney, Kinston*	.239	92	314	56	75	94	11	1	2	31	2	3	6	6	53	0	58	21	14
Whitaker, Darrell, Salem	.000	52	3	0	0	0	0	0	0	0	0	0	0	0	0	0	2	0	0
Whitfield, Kenneth, Kinston	.223	125	448	53	100	160	13	4	13	68	7	0	4	1	53	3	125	11	10
Wilborn, Thaddeus, Hagerstown†	.315	33	130	33	41	62	6	3	3	15	1	0	1	0	15	1	20	10	2
Williams, Brian, Winston-Salem*	.284	110	401	59	114	143	18	1	3	56	8	5	1	2	31	5	54	15	9
Williams, Roger, Winston-Salem	.231	30	26	3	6	9	3	0	0	5	1	2	0	0	0	0	11	0	0
Wilson, Allen, Durham	.231	27	65	9	15	22	5	1	0	8	0	2	0	0	16	1	22	1	2
Winters, Daniel, Lynchburg	.269	62	193	27	52	65	7	0	2	26	3	1	1	2	25	3	36	0	1
Winters, James, Peninsula	.268	63	231	39	62	95	17	2	4	40	3	2	1	2	37	0	57	6	6
Worthington, Craig, Hagerstown	.300	132	480	85	144	226	35	1	15	105	16	0	8	2	82	7	58	7	12
Wrona, Richard, Winston-Salem	.255	91	267	43	68	95	15	0	4	32	3	8	0	5	25	1	37	5	2
Young, Shane, Lynchburg*	.138	28	29	1	4	4	0	0	0	2	0	2	0	2	1	0	3	0	0

The following pitchers, listed alphabetically by club, with games in parentheses, had no plate appearances, primarily through use of designated hitters:

DURHAM—Clossen, William (3); Coffman, Kevin (3); Rogers, MacArthur (15).

HAGERSTOWN—Alfonzo, Osvaldo (5); Ballard, Jeffrey (17); Boudreau, James (6); Davis, George (1); Dotson, Wayne (6); Dubois, Brian (5); Egelston, Christopher (37); Hoover, John (3); Householder, Brian (16); Lavelle, William (30); Llanes, Pedro (6); Milacki, Robert (13); Palermo, Peter (42); Sanchez, Geraldo (29); Stanhope, Chester (32); Stranski, Scott (24); Talamantez, Gregory (26); Thorpe, Paul (33); Vazquez, Jesse (45); Wilson, Wayne (13).

KINSTON—Ackerman, John (12); Brevell, Ronald (40); Cannon, Scott (30); Cedeno, Vinicio (11); Delzer, Edwin (32); Dowless, Michael (15); Garrick, Darren (21); Heath, Allan (30); Kramer, Randall (17); Larsen, Daniel (11); Lychak, Perry (44); Maye, Stephen (12); McCarter, Edward (14); McLin, Larry (5); Reed, Martin (30); Robles, Gabaliel (11); Schofield, John (26).

LYNCHBURG—Bauer, Peter (4); Marina, Juan (2); Santiago, Michael (10).

PENINSULA—Anderson, Jeffrey (5); Boling, John (2); Conley, Virgil (34); Drees, Thomas (37); Edwards, Wayne (25); Henry, Mark (17); Jefts, Christopher (29); Lahrman, Thomas (34); Little, Douglas (15); Menendez, Antonio (11); Pawlowski, John (8); Peterson, Adam (24); Potestio, Frank (6); Rasmussen, James (10); Reed, Kenneth (18); Renz, Kevin (20); Walker, Kurt (9); Wilson, Eric (45).

SALEM—Barfield, John (13); Dial, Bryan (21); Ferlenda, Gregory (10); Hubbard, Marlon (34); James, Duane (45); Kordish, Steve (7); Kramer, Randall (8); Lankard, Steven (50); Mays, Jeffrey (30); McLoughlin, Timothy (8); Meizoso, Gus (7); Mielke, Gary (37); Mortimer, Robert (7); Olsson, Daniel (9); Rogers, Kenneth (15); Satnat, David (17); Thomas, Mitchell (24); Vlcek, James (18); Williams, Bruce (18); Winbush, Michael (18).

WINSTON-SALEM—Menendez, William (3).

GRAND SLAM HOME RUNS—Roberts, 3; Bellino, Falcone, Lawton, Scheer, 2 each; Bafia, Caraballo, Dewey, Duggan, Gentile, Harrison, House, McMillan, McMorris, Nichols, Perez, Posey, Prince, D. Smith, Wellman, Whitfield, 1 each.

AWARDED FIRST BASE ON CATCHER'S INTERFERENCE—Contreras 6 (Borders 3, Alcazar, Merullo, Prince); Stanicek 3 (Borders, Kreuter, Merullo); Cronkright 2 (L. Johnson, Wrona); Justice 2 (Kreuter, Wrona); Westbrook 2 (Prince, Tackett); Hill (Markert); Norman (Borders); Pruitt (Carmichael); Perez (Kreuter); Todd (Carmichael).

CLUB FIELDING

Club	Pct.	G.	PO.	A.	E.	DP.	PB.
Lynchburg	.970	141	3636	1726	166	138	36
Hagerstown	.966	139	3622	1569	184	136	22
Durham	.963	141	3643	1496	196	116	17
Winston-Salem	.962	139	3699	1585	208	134	9
Prince William	.961	139	3618	1384	202	116	22
Kinston	.961	136	3528	1497	206	157	28
Peninsula	.959	134	3546	1487	215	132	20
Salem	.951	139	3552	1514	259	127	28

Triple Play—Salem.

INDIVIDUAL FIELDING

FIRST BASEMEN

*Throws lefthanded.

Player and Club	Pct.	G.	PO.	A.	E.	DP.
J. Allen, Salem	1.000	10	41	2	0	4
L. Allen, Peninsula*	.971	33	249	21	8	27
Belen, Prince William	.982	119	970	91	19	77
Bernardo, Salem*	.975	71	573	52	16	48
Billmeyer, Hagerstown	.984	24	164	15	3	13
Borders, Kinston	1.000	6	53	2	0	6
Caraballo, Lynchburg	.986	17	119	22	2	14
Casteel, Winston-Salem	.714	1	5	0	2	1
Cheek, Prince William	.990	20	170	19	2	19
Cimo, Hagerstown	.833	1	5	0	1	0
Cron, Durham	.984	69	527	41	9	46
Duggan, Salem	.969	25	119	6	4	15
Falcone, Hagerstown	1.000	8	79	8	0	5
Garcia, Peninsula*	.983	8	57	2	1	5
Gentile, Kinston*	1.000	2	4	0	0	1
Gideon, Lynchburg*	.990	116	1089	75	12	94
Harrison, Durham	.992	89	713	53	6	53
Hill, Salem	.985	23	182	16	3	15
Johnson, Kinston	.966	2	27	1	1	2
Justice, Durham*	1.000	1	1	0	0	0
Khoury, Hagerstown*	1.000	2	17	1	0	3
Lynn, Lynchburg	.974	4	36	1	1	5
McMorris, Winston-Salem*	.987	61	497	32	7	47
Moore, Peninsula	1.000	2	5	0	0	0
Moralez, Kinston	.985	114	983	53	16	105
Norman, Hagerstown	1.000	2	13	3	0	2
Perez, Lynchburg*	.946	9	79	9	5	5
Reimer, Salem	.950	39	318	23	18	26
RICHARDSON, Hagerstown	.992	113	886	85	8	90
Sedar, Peninsula	.992	46	364	28	3	38
D. Smith, Hagerstown	1.000	5	29	0	0	1
K. Smith, Hagerstown	1.000	8	45	3	0	9
Steen, Kinston	.983	22	170	7	3	22
Tackett, Hagerstown	1.000	4	7	0	0	1
Trafton, Peninsula	.980	60	512	27	11	39
Villanueva, Winston-Salem	.995	27	172	18	1	16
Walker, Winston-Salem*	.986	71	573	49	9	51
Wrona, Winston-Salem	1.000	1	3	0	0	0

Triple Play—Reimer.

SECOND BASEMEN

Player and Club	Pct.	G.	PO.	A.	E.	DP.
Allen, Salem	.900	7	5	4	1	2
Bafia, Winston-Salem	1.000	1	2	1	0	0
Barringer, Prince William	1.000	14	15	27	0	6
Bertolani, Peninsula	.969	30	77	81	5	23
Cartaya, Salem	.900	4	5	4	1	0
Engram, Peninsula	.968	13	27	34	2	10
Farmer, Salem	1.000	14	25	22	0	10
Fredymond, Durham	1.000	2	3	3	0	0
Gant, Durham	.960	135	240	384	26	61
GARDNER, Lynchburg	.983	101	212	321	9	65
Giddens, Prince William	.913	6	12	9	2	4
Hildebrand, Peninsula	.970	80	126	161	9	30
Hopkins, Winston-Salem	.975	22	31	46	2	7
House, Winston-Salem	.964	126	243	421	25	64
Ingle, Kinston	.962	21	39	63	4	14
Jackson, Salem	1.000	1	1	2	0	0
Jones, Prince William	.948	126	185	304	27	54
Melvin, Kinston	.964	116	237	330	21	85
Murray, Salem	.962	48	83	121	8	27
Phillips, Lynchburg	.985	49	115	142	4	36
Reichel, Peninsula	.965	16	34	49	3	11
Reynolds, Durham	.932	18	30	39	5	8
Richardson, Hagerstown	.857	2	3	3	1	1
Robinson, Kinston	.875	4	4	3	1	2
Smith, Hagerstown	1.000	21	27	41	0	6
Stanicek, Hagerstown	.969	124	240	357	19	82
Sutryk, Peninsula	.952	22	39	61	5	11
Valera, Kinston	1.000	1	1	7	0	1
Vargas, Salem	.957	81	142	238	17	48
Wilborn, Hagerstown	1.000	1	2	1	0	1

THIRD BASEMEN

Player and Club	Pct.	G.	PO.	A.	E.	DP.
Allen, Salem	.854	27	16	25	7	0
Bafia, Winston-Salem	.904	132	78	204	30	21
Barringer, Prince William	1.000	4	1	1	0	0
Caraballo, Lynchburg	.952	23	18	41	3	2
Criswell, Durham	.889	2	3	5	1	2
Cronkright, Peninsula	.903	107	83	224	33	20
Delucchi, Prince William	.806	13	7	18	6	2
Dewey, Durham	.733	9	5	6	4	1
Duggan, Salem	.940	72	44	129	11	7
Farmer, Salem	.871	60	38	84	18	9
Fredymond, Durham	.857	2	0	6	1	1
Giddens, Prince William	.919	15	12	22	3	4
Hildebrand, Peninsula	.500	1	1	1	2	0
Hopkins, Winston-Salem	.895	9	9	8	2	2
House, Winston-Salem	1.000	2	2	7	0	1
King, Prince William	.904	34	25	50	8	4
Kreuter, Salem	1.000	1	0	1	0	0
Moore, Peninsula	.917	7	7	4	1	0
Morris, Durham	.865	71	60	88	23	6
Murray, Salem	1.000	1	0	3	0	0
Nipper, Durham	.946	52	38	102	8	9
Peluso, Peninsula	.737	18	8	20	10	1
Reichel, Peninsula	.968	11	9	21	1	1
Reynolds, Durham	.914	18	10	22	3	3
Richardson, Hagerstown	.667	1	1	1	1	0
Robinson, Kinston	.893	28	26	41	8	8
Rolland, Salem	.927	17	11	27	3	2
ROMAGNA, Kinston	.954	115	93	262	17	26
Sanchez, Lynchburg	.939	124	88	300	25	24
Smith, Hagerstown	.919	18	10	47	5	4
Todd, Prince William	.912	80	66	141	20	14
Venturini, Peninsula	.714	9	4	6	4	0
Williams, Winston-Salem	1.000	1	0	1	0	0
Worthington, Hagerstown	.914	125	92	249	32	24
Wrona, Winston-Salem	1.000	2	1	3	0	0

Triple Play—Farmer.

SHORTSTOPS

Player and Club	Pct.	G.	PO.	A.	E.	DP.
Barringer, Prince William	.842	11	14	18	6	5
Bertolani, Peninsula	.932	41	83	123	15	20
BLAUSER, Durham	.951	120	167	314	25	59
Cartaya, Salem	.922	82	149	207	30	49
DiCeglio, Winston-Salem	.750	3	1	2	1	0
Fermin, Prince William	.950	84	158	205	19	41
Fredymond, Durham	.896	35	36	84	14	12
Hildebrand, Peninsula	1.000	4	5	7	0	2
Hopkins, Winston-Salem	.939	52	75	141	14	28
Ingle, Kinston	.931	97	136	285	31	77
Jefferies, Lynchburg	.954	89	138	273	20	51
Jones, Prince William	1.000	2	2	4	0	3
McDougal, Winston-Salem	.913	97	171	282	43	74
Murray, Salem	.889	4	5	11	2	4
Nichols, Hagerstown	.932	103	130	297	31	67
O'Hoppe, Kinston	.846	4	4	7	2	0
Phillips, Lynchburg	.890	19	20	45	8	6
Pierce, Prince William	.954	21	35	48	4	9
Postier, Salem	.962	13	19	32	2	6
Reichel, Peninsula	.975	38	49	110	4	15

SHORTSTOPS—Continued

Player and Club	Pct.	G.	PO.	A.	E.	DP.
Reynolds, Durham	.667	5	1	1	1	0
Robinson, Kinston	1.000	1	2	3	0	0
Rolland, Salem	.500	2	2	0	2	0
Shields, Prince William	.967	30	50	67	4	16
Smith, Hagerstown	.944	43	63	123	11	28
Sutryk, Peninsula	.900	3	4	5	1	3
Valera, 26 Lyn-41 Kin	.934	67	86	182	19	36
Vargas, Salem	.907	51	60	126	19	21
Venturini, Peninsula	.958	59	103	171	12	37
Villanueva, Lynchburg	.922	17	26	57	7	17

Triple Play—Vargas.

OUTFIELDERS

Player and Club	Pct.	G.	PO.	A.	E.	DP.
Abner, Prince William	.980	56	143	4	3	1
Akers, Kinston	.969	98	180	9	6	0
Bellino, Hagerstown	.929	33	36	3	3	1
Bootay, Salem	.933	34	54	2	4	1
Borders, Kinston	1.000	1	4	0	0	0
Brooks, Lynchburg	1.000	8	12	1	0	0
Caraballo, Lynchburg	.863	31	43	1	7	0
Chance, Prince William	.875	12	19	2	3	0
Cijntje, Hagerstown*	.946	117	251	10	15	3
Cimo, Hagerstown	1.000	28	55	1	0	0
Contreras, Lynchburg*	.982	31	52	3	1	1
Cook, Prince William	.975	121	259	17	7	5
Criswell, Durham	1.000	9	9	1	0	0
Dascenzo, Winston-Salem*	.975	138	299	15	8	3
Delucchi, Prince William	.846	13	9	2	2	0
Denby, Durham	.974	25	37	1	1	0
Denson, Durham	.890	48	86	3	11	0
Dickerson, Winston-Salem	.941	44	47	1	3	0
Duggan, Salem	.952	24	20	0	1	0
Engram, Peninsula	.923	25	33	3	3	0
Evans, Kinston	.826	17	17	2	4	2
Ewart, Winston-Salem*	.952	49	59	1	3	1
Farmer, Salem	1.000	1	1	0	0	0
Fredymond, Durham	.971	43	66	2	2	0
Garcia, Peninsula*	1.000	6	7	0	0	0
Gentile, Kinston*	.940	41	106	4	7	2
Giddens, Prince William	1.000	2	1	0	0	0
Glasker, Salem*	.937	99	140	8	10	1
Hardamon, Winston-Salem	.935	21	28	1	2	0
Hatcher, Durham	.963	15	26	0	1	0
Hill, Salem	.930	68	87	6	7	1
Hopkins, Winston-Salem	.929	10	12	1	1	0
House, Winston-Salem	1.000	1	1	0	0	0
Hudson, Hagerstown	.963	13	25	1	1	0
Jackson, Salem	1.000	12	6	1	0	0
Jones, Durham	.929	6	11	2	1	0
Justice, Durham*	.994	64	162	5	1	0
Khoury, Hagerstown*	.975	90	149	8	4	2
King, Salem*	.941	36	44	4	3	1
Kreuter, Salem	1.000	1	1	0	0	0
LAWTON, Lynchburg	.983	140	336	17	6	1
Little, Lynchburg	.956	53	76	10	4	2
Lynn, Lynchburg	.500	1	1	0	1	0
Magallanes, Peninsula	.935	21	55	3	4	1
McMillan, Prince William*	.938	66	150	2	10	1
Moore, Peninsula	.940	52	78	1	5	0
Morris, Durham	1.000	2	1	1	0	0
Norman, Hagerstown	.935	48	57	1	4	0
Odle, Prince William	.963	106	177	6	7	1
Perez, Lynchburg*	.938	72	99	6	7	2
Phillips, Lynchburg	.800	4	7	1	2	0
Posey, Durham	.971	43	68	0	2	0
Pruitt, Peninsula	.961	103	203	18	9	3
Reimer, Salem	.875	73	94	4	14	1
Reynolds, Durham	.969	24	29	2	1	1
D. Richardson, Winston-Salem	.929	16	13	0	1	0
T. Richardson, Hagerstown	1.000	12	12	1	0	0
Roberts, Hagerstown	.959	93	161	2	7	0
Robinson, Kinston	.957	71	149	8	7	3
Rockey, Durham	.947	45	86	3	5	0
Rolland, Salem	.973	57	63	10	2	2
Roomes, Winston-Salem	1.000	16	22	0	0	0
Scheer, Peninsula	.930	95	181	18	15	8
Sedar, Peninsula	.976	59	112	8	3	1
K. Smith, Hagerstown	1.000	2	2	0	0	0
T. Smith, Prince William	.947	13	18	0	1	0
Stevens, Prince William	.956	35	62	3	3	1
Sutryk, Peninsula	1.000	2	1	0	0	0
Toliver, Peninsula	.750	2	3	0	1	0
Tullier, Winston-Salem*	.954	96	96	8	5	0
Van Cleve, Salem	.973	91	180	3	5	1
Waggoner, Peninsula	.974	18	37	1	1	0
Walker, Winston-Salem*	.833	5	5	0	1	0
Wellman, Durham	.951	71	130	7	7	4
Westbrook, Lynchburg	.946	112	181	12	11	2
Wetherby, Durham*	.974	72	139	9	4	3
Wheeler, Kinston*	.972	85	199	7	6	3
Whitfield, Kinston	.946	123	211	15	13	5
Wilborn, Hagerstown	.967	32	88	1	3	0
Williams, Winston-Salem	.961	102	189	7	8	2
Winters, Peninsula	1.000	60	130	8	0	1
Wrona, Winston-Salem	1.000	4	4	0	0	0

CATCHERS

Player and Club	Pct.	G.	PO.	A.	E.	DP.	PB.
Alcazar, Peninsula	.980	18	95	5	2	1	2
Billmeyer, Hagerstown	.991	21	95	13	1	0	5
Borders, Kinston	.962	27	154	24	7	0	7
Brooks, Lynchburg	.974	16	70	6	2	1	3
Carmichael, Lynchburg	.987	49	253	43	4	3	12
Casteel, Winston-Salem	1.000	5	15	0	0	0	0
Criswell, Durham	.993	58	356	48	3	9	9
DEWEY, Durham	.9911	72	394	55	4	3	8
Epps, Salem	.974	15	96	16	3	0	6
Ferreiras, Prince William	.970	25	138	24	5	3	7
Goodwin, Prince William	.800	3	3	1	1	0	0
Hopkins, Winston-Salem	1.000	3	1	0	0	0	0
Jackson, Salem	.977	26	120	9	3	1	5
L. Johnson, Kinston	.969	73	363	37	13	7	9
R. Johnson, Kinston	1.000	8	57	6	0	0	2
Jones, Lynchburg	.984	22	108	19	2	1	8
Kreuter, Salem	.972	102	612	113	21	17	11
Liddell, Lynchburg	.972	8	63	7	2	0	0
Magrann, Hagerstown	.975	65	335	56	10	5	11
Markert, Peninsula	.978	43	224	41	6	4	4
Maynard, Salem	.957	23	60	7	3	0	5
McElroy, Peninsula	.991	40	207	21	2	4	3
McNally, Durham	1.000	2	7	1	0	0	0
Merullo, Peninsula	.979	52	225	26	6	3	11
O'Hearn, Salem	.978	10	41	3	1	1	2
Prince, Prince William	.979	120	821	113	20	10	15
Reynolds, Durham	1.000	1	5	0	0	0	0
Roadcap, Winston-Salem	1.000	2	7	0	0	0	0
Rosario, Kinston	.957	44	193	28	10	2	10
Tackett, Hagerstown	.982	72	458	38	9	9	6
Trafton, Peninsula	1.000	1	2	0	0	0	0
Villanueva, Winston-Salem	.9907	78	481	54	5	7	7
Wilson, Durham	.957	25	121	12	6	0	0
Winters, Lynchburg	.988	58	286	46	4	7	13
Wrona, Winston-Salem	.980	79	456	71	11	8	2

PITCHERS

Player and Club	Pct.	G.	PO.	A.	E.	DP.
Ackerman, Kinston	1.000	12	3	4	0	2
Adams, Lynchburg	.875	8	2	5	1	1
Alfonzo, Hagerstown	.714	5	1	4	2	1
Ballard, Hagerstown*	.923	17	5	19	2	2
Barfield, Salem*	1.000	13	4	15	0	0
Bautista, Lynchburg	1.000	18	7	15	0	2
Bayer, Lynchburg	.885	13	12	11	3	0
Bell, Winston-Salem*	.900	44	4	14	2	1
Bethel, Winston-Salem	1.000	31	4	10	0	2
Blasucci, Prince William*	1.000	4	0	1	0	0
Boling, Peninsula*	1.000	2	0	1	0	0
Boudreau, Hagerstown*	1.000	6	0	2	0	0
Brevell, Kinston	.913	40	5	16	2	0
Brown, Lynchburg*	.958	34	3	20	1	0
Cannon, Kinston	1.000	30	0	3	0	0
Cash, Durham*	.500	14	0	3	3	0
Cedeno, Kinston	1.000	11	3	1	0	0
Ciszkowski, Lynchburg	1.000	11	8	14	0	2
Clossen, Durham	1.000	3	1	3	0	0
Coffman, Durham	1.000	3	0	3	0	2
Conley, Peninsula*	1.000	34	0	19	0	3
DEL ROSARIO, Durham	1.000	55	12	32	0	1
Delzer, Kinston*	.944	31	4	13	1	0
Dial, 20 Sal-11 Win-Sal	1.000	31	6	13	0	1
Dombek, Lynchburg*	1.000	9	1	1	0	0
Dotson, Hagerstown	1.000	6	0	1	0	0
Dowless, Kinston	1.000	15	6	5	0	2
Drees, Peninsula*	.870	37	7	13	3	2
Drummond, Prince William	1.000	47	11	14	0	3
Dubois, Hagerstown*	1.000	5	2	7	0	0

PITCHERS—Continued

Player and Club	Pct.	G.	PO.	A.	E.	DP.
Edwards, Peninsula*	.872	24	11	23	5	1
Egelston, Hagerstown	.909	37	6	14	2	1
Farmer, Durham*	1.000	8	2	5	0	0
Ferlenda, Salem	.667	10	2	0	1	0
Garcia, Lynchburg	1.000	16	4	6	0	0
Garrick, Kinston	.889	21	6	10	2	2
Gay, Lynchburg	.955	39	2	19	1	2
Gideon, Prince William	.895	26	7	10	2	0
Gozzo, Lynchburg	.917	60	2	9	1	0
Greene, Durham	.909	25	2	8	1	1
Groves, Durham	.955	25	7	14	1	0
Heath, Kinston*	.919	30	5	29	3	3
Heise, Durham*	1.000	22	2	2	0	1
Henry, Peninsula*	1.000	17	0	9	0	1
Hernandez, Prince William	.941	22	8	8	1	0
Hoover, Hagerstown	.900	3	2	7	1	0
Householder, Hagerstown*	.864	16	5	14	3	1
Hubbard, Salem	.923	34	4	8	1	0
James, Salem	.824	41	8	6	3	1
Jefts, Peninsula	.901	29	21	43	7	1
Jimenez, Durham	.857	30	4	20	4	0
Khoury, Hagerstown*	1.000	3	0	2	0	1
Kilner, Durham*	.905	23	4	15	2	2
Koopmann, Prince William*	1.000	7	3	6	0	0
Kordish, Salem	1.000	7	6	3	0	0
Kramer, 17 Kin-8 Sal	.900	25	2	7	1	1
Lahrman, Peninsula	1.000	34	7	8	0	1
Lamb, Durham	.972	35	11	24	1	1
Lancaster, Winston-Salem	1.000	13	9	12	0	2
Lankard, Salem	.949	50	18	19	2	3
Larsen, Kinston	1.000	11	2	4	0	0
Lavelle, Hagerstown	1.000	30	3	5	0	0
Little, Peninsula	1.000	15	2	4	0	1
Llanes, Hagerstown	1.000	6	1	4	0	0
Lychak, Kinston*	.955	44	4	17	1	2
Marina, Lynchburg	1.000	2	1	0	0	0
Masters, Winston-Salem	.818	30	11	16	6	0
Maye, 12 Kin-19 Win-Sal	.952	31	6	14	1	0
Mays, Salem	.977	30	12	30	1	3
McCarter, Kinston	1.000	14	3	13	0	0
McLin, Kinston*	1.000	5	0	1	0	0
McLoughlin, Salem	1.000	8	1	3	0	0
Meizoso, Salem*	1.000	5	0	3	0	0
Melendez, Prince William	.845	28	13	36	9	3
Melton, Prince William	.933	26	11	17	2	0
Menendez, Peninsula	.800	11	1	7	2	1
Mielke, Salem	.786	37	3	8	3	0
Milacki, Hagerstown	1.000	13	8	8	0	0
Morelock, Durham	1.000	16	6	11	0	1
Morris, Durham	.938	37	2	13	1	1
Mortimer, Salem*	1.000	7	1	4	0	1
Olsson, Salem	1.000	8	1	10	0	0
Palermo, Hagerstown	1.000	42	3	5	0	0
Pavlas, Winston-Salem	.979	28	18	29	1	3
Pawlowski, Peninsula	1.000	8	6	5	0	0
Peterson, Peninsula	.893	24	7	18	3	2
Phillips, Winston-Salem	.889	33	4	12	2	2
Pico, Winston-Salem	.868	27	14	32	7	3
Potestio, Peninsula	1.000	6	2	1	0	0
Rasmussen, Peninsula	1.000	10	3	0	0	0
Rauth, Lynchburg	1.000	12	5	10	0	0
K. Reed, Peninsula	.750	18	1	11	4	1
M. Reed, Kinston*	.935	30	8	35	3	3
Renfroe, Winston-Salem	.926	65	4	21	2	5
Renz, Peninsula	.889	20	5	3	1	0
Rice, Winston-Salem	1.000	36	4	9	0	0
Richardson, Lynchburg	.914	32	12	20	3	0
Ritter, Prince William	.974	27	13	25	1	3
Robinson, Prince William	1.000	3	3	2	0	0
Robles, 11 Kin-10 Win-Sal	.885	21	6	17	3	0
Rodriguez, Lynchburg*	1.000	36	4	7	0	1
K. Rogers, Salem*	.826	12	5	14	4	0
M. Rogers, Durham	1.000	15	2	1	0	0
Rolland, Salem	1.000	2	0	1	0	0
Romagna, Kinston	.917	6	3	8	1	1
Rooker, Prince William	.969	27	10	21	1	1
Russell, Prince William*	.958	29	5	18	1	3
Sanchez, Hagerstown	.968	28	8	22	1	0
Santiago, Lynchburg*	1.000	10	2	3	0	0
Satnat, Salem*	1.000	17	2	4	0	0
Schofield, Kinston	.941	26	6	10	1	1
Schwarz, Winston-Salem	1.000	4	1	1	0	0
Scott, Durham	.846	13	0	11	2	0
Siebert, Durham	.857	30	13	17	5	2
Smiley, Prince William*	1.000	48	6	15	0	1
Stading, Prince William	.864	34	6	13	3	1
Stampfl, Lynchburg	1.000	22	0	9	0	1
Stanhope, Hagerstown	.967	32	12	17	1	0
Stiles, Lynchburg	1.000	26	2	3	0	0
Stranski, Hagerstown	.857	24	3	3	1	0
Talamantez, Hagerstown	.978	26	15	29	1	2
Thomas, Salem	.972	24	12	23	1	2
Thorpe, Hagerstown	1.000	33	6	11	0	1
Vazquez, Hagerstown*	1.000	45	1	6	0	1
Vlcek, Salem	1.000	18	2	3	0	1
Wagner, Durham*	.957	52	8	14	1	2
Walker, Peninsula	.750	9	0	3	1	0
West, Lynchburg*	1.000	13	1	15	0	0
Whitaker, Salem	1.000	52	3	7	0	1
B. Williams, Salem	.667	18	1	1	1	0
R. Williams, Winston-Salem	.965	27	19	36	2	3
E. Wilson, Peninsula	.875	45	4	10	2	0
W. Wilson, Hagerstown	.960	13	4	20	1	4
Winbush, Salem	.885	18	6	17	3	1
Young, Lynchburg*	1.000	27	6	25	0	4

The following players had no recorded accepted chances at the positions indicated; therefore, are not listed in the fielding averages for those particular positions: Anderson, p; Bauer, p; Cartaya, 3b; Davis, p; Epps, 3b; Giddens, p; Glasker, p; James, of; Melvin, 3b; W. Menendez, p; Nichols, of; Peluso, of; S. Phillips, p; Reichel, of; Reynolds, p; T. Richardson, p; D. Smith, of, c; T. Smith, c; Tullier, p.

CLUB PITCHING

Club	ERA.	G.	CG.	ShO.	Sv.	IP.	H.	R.	ER.	HR.	HB.	BB.	Int. BB.	SO.	WP.	Bk.
Winston-Salem	3.56	139	23	8	31	1233.0	1161	590	488	66	46	506	35	913	76	11
Prince William	3.64	139	29	11	34	1206.0	1086	626	488	62	50	573	20	928	67	22
Hagerstown	3.74	139	18	14	50	1207.1	1140	640	502	61	35	605	30	870	70	22
Lynchburg	4.38	141	32	7	23	1212.0	1240	692	590	74	40	612	20	745	94	18
Peninsula	4.41	134	11	3	35	1182.0	1223	711	579	91	43	620	33	744	97	19
Durham	4.78	141	8	6	35	1214.1	1266	738	645	108	44	576	26	853	71	26
Kinston	4.84	136	25	6	22	1176.0	1228	742	632	83	49	627	45	741	96	17
Salem	5.59	139	5	2	24	1184.0	1347	924	735	126	48	714	37	892	123	19

PITCHERS' RECORDS

(Leading Qualifiers for Earned-Run Average Leadership—112 or More Innings)

*Throws lefthanded.

Pitcher—Club	W.	L.	Pct.	ERA.	G.	GS.	CG.	GF.	ShO.	Sv.	IP.	H.	R.	ER.	HR.	HB.	BB.	Int. BB.	SO.	WP.
Ballard, Hagerstown*	9	5	.643	1.85	17	17	5	0	2	0	112.0	106	39	23	3	3	32	1	115	3
Melendez, Prince William	13	10	.565	2.61	28	27	6	0	1	0	186.1	141	75	54	9	2	81	1	146	6
Stanhope, Hagerstown	14	3	.824	2.80	32	18	4	1	1	0	148.0	126	64	46	6	2	52	2	86	3
Russell, Prince William*	13	5	.722	2.90	29	18	5	3	3	0	136.1	110	50	44	7	1	68	3	106	7
Ritter, Prince William	14	9	.609	3.05	27	26	7	1	2	0	177.0	148	88	60	10	10	82	5	149	11
M. Reed, Kinston*	16	6	.727	3.16	30	30	9	0	2	0	196.2	177	89	69	10	7	93	5	98	12
Pico, Winston-Salem	12	8	.600	3.20	27	25	2	1	0	0	166.0	165	75	59	6	5	54	4	116	7
R. Williams, Winston-Salem	12	7	.632	3.28	27	27	8	0	2	0	183.2	168	80	67	11	8	58	6	145	9
Brevell, Kinston	5	2	.714	3.30	40	8	1	12	0	1	120.0	95	52	44	6	1	65	2	58	8
Pavlas, Winston-Salem	14	6	.700	3.84	28	26	5	0	2	0	173.1	172	91	74	8	6	57	2	143	11

Departmental Leaders: G—Renfroe, 65; W—M. Reed, 16; L—Jefts, 13; Pct.—Stanhope, .824; GS—M. Reed, 30; CG—M. Reed, 9; GF—Renfroe, 54; ShO—Russell, 3; Sv.—Renfroe, 21; IP—M. Reed, 196.2; H—Jefts, 207; R—Jefts, 114; ER—Jefts, 101; HR—Jimenez, 18; HB—Masters, 12; BB—Talamantez, 102; IBB—Lankard, 11; SO—Ritter, 149; WP—Masters, 22.

(All Pitchers—Listed Alphabetically)

Pitcher—Club	W.	L.	Pct.	ERA.	G.	GS.	CG.	GF.	ShO.	Sv.	IP.	H.	R.	ER.	HR.	HB.	BB.	Int. BB.	SO.	WP.
Ackerman, Kinston	1	0	1.000	4.19	12	0	0	6	0	0	19.1	20	11	9	2	1	11	3	8	1
Adams, Lynchburg	2	2	.500	7.06	8	4	0	1	0	0	21.2	28	21	17	4	0	15	0	13	1
Alfonzo, Hagerstown	1	0	1.000	5.54	5	2	0	1	0	0	13.0	16	11	8	1	0	8	1	11	4
Anderson, Peninsula	0	1	.000	4.38	5	0	0	2	0	0	12.1	11	6	6	1	1	5	1	8	0
Ballard, Hagerstown*	9	5	.643	1.85	17	17	5	0	2	0	112.0	106	39	23	3	3	32	1	115	3
Barfield, Salem*	2	5	.286	4.98	13	11	0	0	0	0	56.0	71	43	31	7	1	22	0	39	3
Bauer, Lynchburg	1	1	.500	0.00	4	0	0	1	0	0	5.1	3	1	0	0	0	3	0	4	1
Bautista, Lynchburg	8	8	.500	3.94	18	18	5	0	1	0	118.2	120	58	52	12	3	24	1	62	3
Bayer, Lynchburg	7	3	.700	2.78	13	13	6	0	1	0	90.2	91	36	28	5	7	36	1	53	9
Bell, Winston-Salem*	2	0	1.000	2.63	44	0	0	7	0	2	61.2	38	25	18	2	0	39	4	72	4
Bethel, Winston-Salem	2	4	.333	5.98	31	4	0	12	0	0	58.2	83	49	39	4	5	33	3	33	5
Blasucci, Prince William*	1	2	.333	4.26	4	4	0	0	0	0	19.0	19	13	9	0	0	17	1	9	3
Boling, Peninsula*	0	0	.000	0.00	2	0	0	2	0	2	2.2	1	0	0	0	0	1	0	4	0
Boudreau, Hagerstown*	0	0	.000	1.59	6	0	0	4	0	1	5.2	5	1	1	0	0	0	0	7	0
Brevell, Kinston	5	2	.714	3.30	40	8	1	12	0	1	120.0	95	52	44	6	1	65	2	58	8
Brown, Lynchburg*	5	4	.556	4.50	34	13	2	8	0	2	100.0	102	60	50	9	2	50	3	68	9
Cannon, Kinston	2	1	.667	13.50	30	0	0	7	0	0	37.1	63	59	56	2	7	46	2	20	9
Cash, Durham*	7	1	.875	3.84	14	12	0	0	0	0	77.1	79	43	33	5	0	21	0	52	1
Cedeno, Kinston	0	2	.000	9.00	11	0	0	6	0	0	17.0	25	20	17	1	2	12	2	18	5
Ciszkowski, Lynchburg	4	5	.444	5.61	11	11	1	0	0	0	59.1	69	42	37	2	2	45	1	28	9
Clossen, Durham	0	2	.000	6.46	3	3	0	0	0	0	15.1	15	15	11	2	0	14	0	10	1
Coffman, Durham	1	2	.333	7.43	3	3	0	0	0	0	13.1	11	12	11	0	0	17	0	7	4
Conley, Peninsula*	3	4	.429	4.50	34	5	0	11	0	2	84.0	104	51	42	8	3	26	1	55	6
Davis, Hagerstown	0	0	.000	0.00	1	1	0	0	0	0	4.0	3	0	0	0	0	3	0	6	0
DelRosario, Durham	5	8	.385	2.69	55	0	0	38	0	15	93.2	76	30	28	1	3	40	6	65	5
Delzer, Kinston*	5	8	.385	5.51	31	0	0	18	0	2	50.2	56	32	31	5	0	28	3	36	4
Dial, 20 Salem-11 Win-Salem	2	9	.182	6.64	31	17	0	6	0	1	100.1	108	87	74	13	6	71	2	72	7
Dombek, Lynchburg*	0	0	.000	9.31	9	0	0	4	0	0	9.2	16	13	10	0	1	14	0	7	2
Dotson, Hagerstown	0	0	.000	3.38	6	0	0	3	0	2	13.1	14	7	5	3	0	4	0	8	1
Dowless, Kinston	3	5	.375	2.61	15	13	2	0	0	0	89.2	90	36	26	3	3	28	0	67	4
Drees, Peninsula*	5	7	.417	4.75	37	10	1	14	0	2	94.2	108	64	50	5	4	61	1	54	7
Drummond, Prince William	6	4	.600	3.79	47	0	0	35	0	12	73.2	71	39	31	1	4	34	3	55	0
Dubois, Hagerstown*	1	2	.333	7.08	5	5	0	0	0	0	20.1	29	19	16	1	1	11	0	17	2
Edwards, Peninsula*	8	8	.500	4.21	24	21	0	2	0	0	128.1	149	80	60	10	2	68	1	86	8
Egelston, Hagerstown	5	1	.833	4.02	37	4	0	10	0	2	105.1	103	52	47	5	2	43	4	64	6
Farmer, Durham*	2	0	1.000	3.24	8	0	0	2	0	0	16.2	19	7	6	2	0	2	0	13	0
Ferlenda, Salem	2	0	1.000	4.34	10	1	0	5	0	2	18.2	13	9	9	0	0	14	0	31	2
Garcia, Lynchburg	0	0	.000	5.56	16	1	0	7	0	0	22.2	25	20	14	2	0	17	0	7	3
Garrick, Kinston	4	2	.667	5.37	21	7	1	6	0	0	65.1	83	39	39	8	3	22	3	45	3
Gay, Lynchburg	1	5	.167	5.58	39	1	0	4	0	1	71.0	79	50	44	3	0	42	3	41	3
Giddens, Prince William	0	0	.000	0.00	1	0	0	1	0	0	1.0	1	0	0	0	0	0	0	1	0
Gideon, Prince William	1	6	.143	5.50	26	1	0	10	0	3	55.2	60	43	34	3	6	37	1	41	5
Glasker, Salem*	0	0	.000	0.00	1	0	0	1	0	0	1.0	1	0	0	0	0	2	0	1	0
Gozzo, Lynchburg	9	4	.692	3.10	60	0	0	46	0	9	78.1	80	30	27	3	2	35	3	50	4
Greene, Durham	2	2	.500	6.25	25	0	0	9	0	0	44.2	54	38	31	3	0	30	4	35	6
Groves, Durham	5	5	.500	5.97	25	12	0	4	0	0	89.0	98	64	59	10	3	54	3	50	8
Heath, Kinston*	7	7	.500	5.50	30	29	5	0	2	0	149.0	149	103	91	9	2	97	5	113	16
Heise, Durham*	3	3	.500	4.62	22	0	0	15	0	7	25.1	22	14	13	3	0	20	0	30	1
Henry, Peninsula*	1	0	1.000	4.71	17	0	0	5	0	1	28.2	31	18	15	2	2	29	5	24	2
Hernandez, Prince William	6	11	.353	4.51	22	21	3	1	1	0	111.2	118	63	56	10	4	42	2	65	4
Hoover, Hagerstown	2	0	1.000	0.50	3	3	0	0	0	0	18.0	10	2	1	0	0	13	0	13	4
Householder, Hagerstown*	5	4	.556	3.95	16	10	1	3	1	1	68.1	55	39	30	4	5	52	2	58	5
Hubbard, Salem	1	3	.250	3.92	34	0	0	9	0	2	62.0	70	35	27	6	1	32	2	41	9
James, Salem	1	3	.250	6.94	41	4	1	13	0	1	81.2	99	85	63	11	8	86	1	72	18
Jefts, Peninsula	9	13	.409	4.92	29	29	3	0	0	0	184.2	207	114	101	10	5	77	5	85	16
Jimenez, Durham	7	8	.467	5.12	30	22	2	5	2	2	135.1	150	93	77	18	7	49	1	96	5
Khoury, Hagerstown*	0	0	.000	11.57	3	0	0	2	0	0	4.2	8	6	6	1	0	3	0	3	1
Kilner, Durham*	6	8	.429	4.53	23	23	2	0	1	0	141.0	133	79	71	12	7	63	1	89	7
Koopmann, Prince William*	0	6	.000	3.40	7	7	2	0	0	0	39.2	42	21	15	4	0	15	0	19	1
Kordish, Salem	1	3	.250	5.06	7	7	0	0	0	0	32.0	41	29	18	3	1	11	0	25	2
Kramer, 17 Kinston-8 Salem	3	3	.500	4.78	25	1	0	14	0	4	43.1	43	26	23	4	2	28	3	38	4
Lahrman, Peninsula	3	4	.429	3.77	34	3	0	15	0	4	90.2	98	57	38	2	1	48	2	38	7
Lamb, Durham	9	9	.500	5.56	35	20	1	6	0	2	139.1	156	92	86	14	3	60	1	107	7
Lancaster, Winston-Salem	8	3	.727	2.78	13	13	3	0	0	0	97.0	88	37	30	4	2	30	2	52	1
Lankard, Salem	9	9	.500	5.12	50	12	0	29	0	2	114.1	138	86	65	14	3	48	11	72	1
Larsen, Kinston	0	0	.000	11.15	11	0	0	1	0	0	15.1	28	25	19	0	1	19	0	10	6
Lavelle, Hagerstown	2	2	.500	4.21	30	0	0	25	0	16	36.1	30	17	17	3	1	12	3	24	1
Little, Peninsula	0	2	.000	2.32	15	1	0	9	0	3	31.0	28	13	8	0	2	14	2	20	3
Llanes, Hagerstown	2	2	.500	8.10	6	4	0	1	0	0	23.1	29	21	21	4	0	17	2	12	3
Lychak, Kinston*	0	7	.000	2.41	44	0	0	35	0	14	67.1	46	23	18	3	3	36	8	57	7
Marina, Lynchburg	1	1	.500	6.23	2	2	0	0	0	0	8.2	6	7	6	0	0	9	2	7	4
Masters, Winston-Salem	8	9	.471	4.10	30	27	4	2	2	0	158.0	128	86	72	14	12	95	3	125	22
Maye, 12 Kinston-19 Win-Sal	6	7	.462	6.06	31	9	2	4	0	0	87.2	107	75	59	7	5	35	3	43	3
Mays, Salem	9	12	.429	4.91	30	21	1	2	0	0	128.1	136	81	70	15	7	69	3	79	17
McCarter, Kinston	4	7	.364	5.55	14	10	4	3	1	1	71.1	73	51	44	12	6	25	1	42	0
McLin, Kinston*	0	2	.000	19.64	5	1	0	1	0	0	3.2	8	9	8	0	0	7	0	2	1
McLoughlin, Salem	2	1	.667	7.24	8	1	0	2	0	0	13.2	12	12	11	1	3	15	0	8	1
Meizoso, Salem*	0	0	.000	7.63	5	3	0	1	0	0	15.1	23	14	13	1	0	11	0	19	4
Melendez, Prince William	13	10	.565	2.61	28	27	6	0	1	0	186.1	141	75	54	9	2	81	1	146	6
Melton, Prince William	8	9	.471	4.61	26	26	5	0	1	0	158.0	164	102	81	6	7	70	2	134	16
A. Menendez, Peninsula	4	4	.500	4.57	11	10	1	1	1	0	63.0	58	35	32	9	4	29	0	43	6
W. Menendez, Winston-Salem*	0	0	.000	6.00	3	0	0	1	0	0	3.0	2	2	2	0	0	6	0	5	0
Mielke, Salem	4	4	.500	3.93	37	0	0	30	0	11	52.2	48	25	23	4	3	20	2	49	3
Milacki, Hagerstown	4	5	.444	4.75	13	12	1	0	1	0	60.2	69	59	32	4	1	37	2	46	6
Morelock, Durham	2	3	.400	4.50	16	5	0	4	0	0	48.0	44	26	24	3	0	24	0	29	3
Morris, Durham	4	4	.500	5.57	37	3	0	13	0	4	76.0	87	57	47	9	3	40	3	43	5
Mortimer, Salem*	1	2	.333	3.46	7	0	0	3	0	0	13.0	15	10	5	1	0	6	0	12	0
Olsson, Salem	1	3	.250	4.26	8	4	0	0	0	0	31.2	34	22	15	2	0	19	2	30	3
Palermo, Hagerstown	6	3	.667	3.42	42	3	1	17	0	4	79.0	78	40	30	5	3	26	0	61	2
Pavlas, Winston-Salem	14	6	.700	3.84	28	26	5	0	2	0	173.1	172	91	74	8	6	57	2	143	11
Pawlowski, Peninsula	5	2	.714	3.38	8	8	1	0	0	0	48.0	33	21	18	3	4	22	0	30	3

Pitcher—Club	W.	L.	Pct.	ERA.	G.	GS.	CG.	GF.	ShO.	Sv.	IP.	H.	R.	ER.	HR.	HB.	BB.	Int. BB.	SO.	WP.
Peterson, Peninsula	9	8	.529	4.59	24	23	1	1	0	0	147.0	150	92	75	16	3	58	4	84	9
J. Phillips, Winston-Salem	4	3	.571	2.15	33	0	0	15	0	5	62.2	58	16	15	1	2	11	3	54	2
S. Phillips, Lynchburg	0	0	.000	0.00	1	0	0	1	0	0	1.0	1	0	0	0	0	1	0	0	0
Pico, Winston-Salem	12	8	.600	3.20	27	25	2	1	0	0	166.0	165	75	59	6	5	54	4	116	7
Potestio, Peninsula	1	1	.500	11.05	6	5	1	1	0	0	22.0	30	28	27	4	0	27	0	13	4
Rasmussen, Peninsula	1	1	.500	3.27	10	1	0	6	0	2	22.0	27	10	8	3	2	9	2	17	1
Rauth, Lynchburg	4	6	.400	4.92	12	12	3	0	0	0	71.1	75	42	39	3	2	24	0	47	9
K. Reed, Peninsula	4	9	.308	5.79	18	17	3	1	0	0	88.2	89	63	57	11	3	67	2	69	10
M. Reed, Kinston*	16	6	.727	3.16	30	30	9	0	2	0	196.2	177	89	69	10	7	93	5	98	12
Renfroe, Winston-Salem	6	6	.500	2.93	65	0	0	54	0	21	83.0	84	37	27	2	2	27	5	51	6
Renz, Peninsula	2	3	.400	2.86	20	1	0	13	0	3	50.1	41	23	16	2	2	28	2	39	6
Reynolds, Durham	0	0	.000	0.00	3	0	0	3	0	0	2.2	4	0	0	0	0	0	0	0	0
Rice, Winston-Salem	7	1	.875	1.80	36	3	0	16	0	2	55.0	48	13	11	1	1	22	1	34	0
J. Richardson, Lynchburg	13	5	.722	4.21	32	21	6	3	1	1	171.0	183	96	80	9	5	82	2	93	18
T. Richardson, Hagerstown	0	0	.000	9.00	1	0	0	1	0	0	1.0	2	1	1	0	0	2	0	0	0
Ritter, Prince William	14	9	.609	3.05	27	26	7	1	2	0	177.0	148	88	60	10	10	82	5	149	11
Robinson, Prince William	1	1	.500	0.71	3	3	1	0	0	0	12.2	13	7	1	0	0	1	0	13	1
Robles, 11 Kinston-10 Win-Sal.	8	8	.500	4.52	21	21	2	0	0	0	129.1	139	72	65	12	3	52	1	78	4
Rodriguez, Lynchburg*	2	1	.667	3.57	36	0	0	16	0	3	45.1	37	20	18	2	1	19	0	38	4
K. Rogers, Salem*	2	7	.222	6.27	12	12	0	0	0	0	66.0	75	54	46	9	1	26	0	46	2
M. Rogers, Durham	3	0	1.000	2.95	15	0	0	10	0	4	18.1	17	6	6	2	0	4	0	21	1
Rolland, Salem	0	0	.000	6.75	2	0	0	1	0	0	2.2	3	2	2	0	0	3	0	0	1
Romagna, Kinston	1	3	.250	2.37	6	4	0	0	0	0	30.1	24	8	8	0	0	7	2	26	1
Rooker, Prince William	2	2	.500	3.38	27	4	0	8	0	2	74.2	56	34	28	3	4	44	0	45	8
Russell, Prince William*	13	5	.722	2.90	29	18	5	3	3	0	136.1	110	50	44	7	1	68	3	106	7
Sanchez, Hagerstown	13	6	.684	3.97	28	21	2	4	0	1	138.1	140	72	61	9	2	55	2	53	2
Santiago, Lynchburg*	0	1	.000	2.57	10	0	0	4	0	3	14.0	8	7	4	2	0	4	0	10	0
Satnat, Salem*	0	2	.000	4.86	17	1	0	4	0	0	37.0	44	24	20	4	1	17	0	19	1
Schofield, Kinston	2	11	.154	6.23	26	13	0	6	0	0	91.0	113	72	63	7	5	61	3	51	11
Schwarz, Winston-Salem	0	1	.000	7.50	4	2	0	1	0	0	12.0	10	10	10	3	1	12	0	11	3
Scott, Durham	3	1	.750	3.48	13	13	0	0	0	0	62.0	49	24	24	4	7	49	0	56	7
Siebert, Durham	11	9	.550	5.47	30	25	3	3	0	0	151.1	172	103	92	14	11	64	3	104	4
Smiley, Prince William*	2	4	.333	3.10	48	2	0	36	0	14	90.0	64	35	31	2	1	40	1	93	2
Stading, Prince William	0	3	.000	5.76	34	0	0	15	0	3	70.1	79	56	45	7	11	42	1	52	3
Stampfl, Lynchburg	4	3	.571	6.10	22	5	1	7	0	2	48.2	53	34	33	3	6	27	2	27	4
Stanhope, Hagerstown	14	3	.824	2.80	32	18	4	1	1	0	148.0	126	64	46	6	2	52	2	86	3
Stiles, Lynchburg	2	1	.667	4.13	26	0	0	7	0	2	28.1	31	15	13	2	0	16	1	17	2
Stranski, Hagerstown	1	0	1.000	0.31	24	0	0	24	0	19	29.0	9	1	1	0	0	10	0	38	1
Talamantez, Hagerstown	12	6	.667	4.36	26	26	2	0	1	0	148.2	131	93	72	6	5	102	3	124	13
Thomas, Salem	3	12	.200	3.89	24	22	1	0	1	0	136.1	125	75	59	10	4	77	6	109	12
Thorpe, Hagerstown	3	4	.429	5.07	33	0	0	12	0	3	55.0	67	34	31	2	4	30	5	36	6
Tullier, Winston-Salem	0	0	.000	9.00	1	0	0	1	0	0	1.0	1	1	1	0	0	1	0	1	0
Vazquez, Hagerstown	3	3	.500	3.67	45	0	0	13	0	1	49.0	37	22	20	1	5	55	3	55	3
Vlcek, Salem	0	5	.000	11.05	18	8	0	3	0	0	36.2	58	51	45	3	2	45	0	28	5
Wagner, Durham	2	5	.400	3.88	52	0	0	21	0	1	65.0	80	35	28	6	0	25	4	46	6
Walker, Peninsula	2	0	1.000	1.06	9	0	0	7	0	4	17.0	8	2	2	0	0	2	0	21	0
West, Lynchburg	1	6	.143	5.16	13	13	1	0	0	0	75.0	76	50	43	3	3	53	0	70	4
Whitaker, Salem	2	8	.200	5.26	52	3	1	17	0	5	87.1	111	64	51	8	4	22	7	67	6
B. Williams, Salem	0	2	.000	14.23	18	2	0	4	0	0	31.0	50	55	49	10	2	51	0	22	9
R. Williams, Winston-Salem	12	7	.632	3.28	27	27	8	0	2	0	183.2	168	80	67	11	8	58	6	145	9
E. Wilson, Peninsula	3	7	.300	3.22	45	0	0	33	0	12	67.0	50	34	24	5	5	49	5	54	9
W. Wilson, Hagerstown	8	2	.800	4.48	13	13	2	0	1	0	74.1	73	40	37	3	1	38	0	33	4
Winbush, Salem	3	6	.333	6.04	18	12	1	2	0	1	76.0	77	69	51	6	1	63	2	53	20
Young, Lynchburg	11	9	.550	3.94	27	27	7	0	2	0	171.1	157	90	75	10	6	96	1	103	5

BALKS—Hernandez, Siebert, 7 each; Lankard, 6; Jimenez, Lamb, Melendez, Talamantez, 5 each; Mays, Melton, K. Reed, Sanchez, 4 each; Bautista, Greene, Henry, Lahrman, Larsen, Rauth, W. Wilson, 3 each; Ballard, Bell, Cash, Ciszkowski, Delzer, Dowless, Edwards, Egelston, Koopmann, Llanes, Masters, Maye, McCarter, Peterson, M. Reed, J. Richardson, Schwarz, Smiley, Winbush, Young, 2 each; Adams, Barfield, Bauer, DelRosario, Dial, Drees, Dubois, Gideon, Gozzo, Groves, Heath, Heise, Householder, Hubbard, James, Jefts, Kilner, Lancaster, Lychak, Milacki, Mortimer, Palermo, Pavlas, Rasmussen, Renfroe, Ritter, Robles, Rodriguez, K. Rogers, Schofield, Stiles, Thomas, Vlcek, Walker, West, R. Williams, E. Wilson, 1 each.

COMBINATION SHUTOUTS—Morelock-Jimenez, Scott-Morris, Kilner-DelRosario, Durham; Talamantez-Egelston-Vazquez, Ballard-Stranski, Talamantez-Thorpe-Stranski, Davis-Llanes-Vazquez-Lavelle, Stanhope-Lavelle, Householder-Alfonzo-Boudreau, Hoover-Palermo-Vazquez, Hagerstown; Reed-Cedeno, Kinston; West-Gozzo, Rauth-Gozzo, Lynchburg; Pawlowski-Lahrman, Jefts-Wilson, Peninsula; Melendez-Stading, Rooker-Smiley, Russell-Smiley, Prince William; Mays-Ferlenda, Salem; Pico-Renfroe, Pico-Bell, Winston-Salem.

NO-HIT GAMES—None.

Florida State League

CLASS A

CHAMPIONSHIP WINNERS IN PREVIOUS YEARS

Year	Club	Pct.
1919	Sanford*	.605
	Orlando*	.703
1920	Tampa	.654
	Tampa	.722
1921	Orlando	.635
1922	St. Petersburg	.503
	St. Petersburg	.618
1923	Orlando	.667
	Orlando	.678
1924	Lakeland	.695
	Lakeland	.683
1925	St. Petersburg	.667
	Tampa†	.696
1926	Sanford	.647
	Sanford	.623
1927	Orlando†	.600
	Miami	.661
1928-35	Did not operate.	
1936	Gainesville	.542
	St. Augustine (4th)†	.492
1937	Gainesville§	.616
1938	Leesburg	.626
	Gainesville (2nd)‡	.615
1939	Sanford§	.787
1940	Daytona Beach	.619
	Orlando (4th)‡	.507
1941	St. Augustine	.659
	Leesburg (4th)‡	.488
1942-45	Did not operate.	
1946	Orlando§	.681
1947	St. Augustine	.625
	Gainesville (2nd)‡	.584
1948	Orlando	.643
	Daytona Beach (2nd)‡	.616
1949	Gainesville	.635
	St. Augustine (3rd)‡	.556
1950	Orlando	.629
	DeLand (3rd)‡	.590
1951	DeLand§	.643
1952	DeLand x	.704
	Palatka (3rd)‡	.569
1953	Daytona Beach†	.657
	DeLand	.703
1954	Jacksonville Beach	.629
	Lakeland†	.594
1955	Orlando	.671
	Orlando	.643
1956	Cocoa	.614
	Cocoa	.671
1957	Palatka	.629
	Tampa†	.681
1958	St. Petersburg	.732
	St. Petersburg	.681
1959	Tampa	.591
	St. Petersburg†	.612
1960	Lakeland	.731
	Palatka†	.614
1961	Tampa†	.710
	Sarasota	.696
1962	Sarasota	.689
	Fort Lauderdale†	.623
1963	Sarasota	.645
	Sarasota	.667
1964	Fort Lauderdale†	.629
	St. Petersburg	.594
1965	Fort Lauderdale	.627
	Fort Lauderdale	.634
1966	Leesburg†	.781
	St. Petersburg	.700
1967	St. Petersburg y	.691
	Orlando	.638
1968	Miami	.613
	Orlando z	.579
1969	Miami a	.606
	Orlando	.606
1970	Miami b	.662
	St. Petersburg	.600
1971	Miami b	.667
	Daytona Beach	.586
1972	Miami c	.562
	Daytona Beach	.606
1973	St. Petersburg d	.575
	West Palm Beach	.580
1974	West Palm Beach d	.598
	Fort Lauderdale	.626
1975	St. Petersburg d	.652
	Miami	.581
1976	Tampa	.559
	Lakeland d	.536
1977	Lakeland d	.616
	West Palm Beach	.583
1978	Lakeland	.565
	Miami§	.539
1979	Fort Lauderdale	.643
	Winter Haven e	.577
1980	Daytona Beach	.628
	Fort Lauderdale d	.606
1981	Fort Myers	.554
	Daytona Beach f	.504
1982	Fort Lauderdale f	.621
	Tampa	.546
1983	Daytona Beach	.634
	Vero Beach f	.515
1984	Tampa	.532
	Fort Lauderdale f	.521
1985	Fort Myers g	.590
	Fort Lauderdale	.550

*Split-season playoff abandoned after each team won three games. †Won split-season playoff. ‡Won four-club playoff. §Won championship and four-club playoff. xWon both halves of split season. yLeague divided into Eastern and Western divisions with split season. St. Petersburg and Orlando won both halves of split season; St. Petersburg won playoff. zLeague divided into Eastern and Western divisions. Miami won regular-season pennant on basis of highest won-lost percentage. Orlando won four-club playoff involving first two teams in each division. aLeague divided into Southern and Central divisions. Miami won playoff between division leaders. (NOTE—Pennant awarded to playoff winner in 1936.) bLeague divided into Eastern and Western divisions. Miami won regular-season pennant on basis of highest won-loss percentage, and also won four-club playoff involving first two teams in each division. cLeague divided into Eastern and Western divisions. Won four-club playoff involving first two teams in each division. dLeague divided into Northern and Southern divisions. Won four-club playoff involving first two teams in each division. eLeague divided into Northern and Southern divisions. Same two clubs won both halves; won playoffs. fWon split-season playoff. gLeague divided into Western, Central and Southern divisions. Won four-club playoff.

STANDING OF CLUBS AT CLOSE OF SEASON, AUGUST 28

WESTERN DIVISION

Club	W.	L.	T.	Pct.	G.B.
St. Petersburg (Cardinals)	88	48	0	.647	....
Tampa (Reds)	79	57	0	.581	9
Clearwater (Phillies)	63	74	0	.460	25½
Fort Myers (Royals)	50	85	0	.370	37½

SOUTHERN DIVISION

Club	W.	L.	T.	Pct.	G.B.
West Palm Beach (Expos)	80	55	0	.593	....
Fort Lauderdale (Yankees)	80	59	0	.576	2
Miami (Independent)	74	66	0	.529	8½
Vero Beach (Dodgers)	68	70	0	.493	13½

CENTRAL DIVISION

Club	W.	L.	T.	Pct.	G.B.
Winter Haven (Red Sox)	80	47	0	.630	....
Osceola (Astros)	59	78	0	.431	26
Lakeland (Tigers)	54	79	0	.406	29
Daytona Beach (Rangers)	40	97	0	.292	45

COMPOSITE STANDING OF CLUBS AT CLOSE OF SEASON, AUGUST 28

Club	St.P.	WH	WPB	Tam.	Ft.L.	Mia.	VB	Clw.	Osc.	Lak.	Ft.M.	Day.	W.	L.	T.	Pct.	G.B.
St. Petersburg (Cardinals)	....	4	8	11	5	7	7	12	6	6	14	8	88	48	0	.647	....
Winter Haven (Red Sox)	6	....	4	4	6	8	6	6	12	10	5	13	80	47	0	.630	3½
West Palm Beach (Expos)	2	1	....	6	11	11	12	6	8	8	8	7	80	55	0	.593	7½
Tampa (Reds)	9	4	4	....	4	6	6	13	6	6	13	8	79	57	0	.581	9
Fort Lauderdale (Yankees)	5	4	9	6	....	8	13	4	8	8	9	6	80	59	0	.576	9½
Miami (Independent)	3	2	9	4	12	....	7	7	8	7	6	9	74	66	0	.529	16
Vero Beach (Dodgers)	3	4	8	4	7	13	....	5	5	6	6	7	68	70	0	.493	21
Clearwater (Phillies)	7	4	4	7	6	3	5	....	6	6	9	6	63	74	0	.460	25½
Osceola (Astros)	3	8	2	4	2	2	4	4	....	12	6	12	59	78	0	.431	29½
Lakeland (Tigers)	4	6	2	4	1	3	3	4	7	....	4	16	54	79	0	.406	32½
Fort Myers (Royals)	4	4	2	5	1	4	4	11	4	6	....	5	50	85	0	.370	37½
Daytona Beach (Rangers)	2	6	3	2	4	1	3	2	8	4	5	....	40	97	0	.292	48½

Major league affiliations in parentheses.

Playoffs—West Palm Beach defeated Winter Haven, two games to none; St. Petersburg defeated Tampa, two games to one; St. Petersburg defeated West Palm Beach, three games to one, to win league championship.

Regular-Season Attendance—Clearwater, 53,824; Daytona Beach, 42,774; Fort Lauderdale, 43,316; Fort Myers, 42,083; Lakeland, 53,147; Miami, 35,569; Osceola, 36,135; St. Petersburg, 126,242; Tampa, 57,930; Vero Beach, 81,919; West Palm Beach, 97,481; Winter Haven, 21,486. Total—691,906. Playoffs, 5,314. All-Star Game, 2,385.

Managers—Clearwater, Ron Clark; Daytona Beach, Chino Cadahia; Fort Lauderdale, Bucky Dent; Fort Myers, Duane Gustavson; Lakeland, Tom Burgess; Miami, Fred Hatfield, Max Oliveras; Osceola, Tom Wiedenbauer; St. Petersburg, Dave Bialas (thru June 24), Marty Mason (from June 24 to June 29) and Mike Jorgensen (June 30 thru end of season); Tampa, Marc Bombard; Vero Beach, Stan Wasiak; West Palm Beach, Felipe Alou; Winter Haven, Dave Holt.

All-Star Team—1B—Ron Johns, St. Petersburg; 2B—Jim Reboulet, St. Petersburg; 3B—Chris Alvarez, Fort Lauderdale; SS—Esteban Beltre, West Palm Beach; OF—Brady Anderson, Winter Haven; OF—Ron Jones, Clearwater; OF—Jim Fortenberry, Clearwater; OF—Chris Morgan, Lakeland; DH—Tary Scott, Winter Haven; RHP—Rob Lopez, Tampa; RHP—Dody Rather, Fort Lauderdale; LHP—Jeff Fassero, St. Petersburg; LHP—Joel Lono, Tampa; RP—Gary Wayne, West Palm Beach; RP—Ray Perkins, Miami; Most Valuable Player—Ron Jones, Clearwater; Manager of the Year—Dave Holt, Winter Haven.

(Compiled by Howe News Bureau, Boston, Mass.)

CLUB BATTING

Club	Pct.	G.	AB.	R.	OR.	H.	TB.	2B.	3B.	HR.	RBI.	GW.	SH.	SF.	HP.	BB.	Int. BB.	SO.	SB.	CS.	LOB.
Winter Haven	.276	127	4214	646	498	1164	1617	171	54	58	565	67	36	47	42	522	30	623	240	87	958
St. Petersburg	.275	136	4389	681	428	1208	1562	206	29	30	612	78	54	51	27	576	34	558	190	71	1040
Miami	.268	140	4458	586	615	1194	1569	197	29	40	507	60	65	60	35	554	31	605	172	76	1019
Fort Lauderdale	.262	139	4483	683	577	1175	1615	201	43	51	595	71	51	49	27	708	39	762	127	62	1131
Vero Beach	.256	138	4358	627	581	1116	1491	183	57	26	541	54	56	42	36	571	34	686	129	66	994
Daytona Beach	.255	137	4431	526	840	1132	1478	181	33	33	452	35	22	36	36	394	20	623	53	47	921
Osceola	.254	137	4403	567	623	1120	1470	163	47	31	480	48	34	46	31	566	29	734	164	96	1001
Tampa	.254	136	4303	607	548	1092	1400	163	44	19	524	67	50	54	38	587	42	816	245	76	1006
Lakeland	.250	133	4288	532	674	1070	1443	169	42	40	465	50	53	40	37	464	25	627	90	63	926
West Palm Beach	.249	135	4238	533	432	1055	1430	179	29	46	455	69	46	32	32	446	36	663	83	53	938
Fort Myers	.248	135	4218	534	696	1047	1348	150	44	21	453	41	54	46	28	564	24	725	186	72	1011
Clearwater	.246	137	4420	558	568	1088	1494	173	31	57	490	52	61	43	42	425	36	755	137	75	944

INDIVIDUAL BATTING

(Leading Qualifiers for Batting Championship—378 or More Plate Appearances)

*Bats lefthanded. †Switch-hitter.

Player and Club	Pct.	G.	AB.	R.	H.	TB.	2B.	3B.	HR.	RBI.	GW.	SH.	SF.	HP.	BB.	Int. BB.	SO.	SB.	CS.
Jones, Ronald, Clearwater*	.371	108	412	76	153	216	18	12	7	73	11	2	9	4	40	4	30	33	12
Johns, Ronald, St. Petersburg	.333	93	345	47	115	172	27	3	8	81	12	1	5	5	36	3	35	0	1
Reboulet, James, St. Petersburg	.327	127	440	87	144	171	22	1	1	50	3	5	3	0	83	1	40	71	20
Gonzalez, Angel, Winter Haven†	.323	107	387	69	125	169	28	2	4	44	5	2	3	2	46	1	57	31	16
Nunley, Angelo, Tampa	.323	123	446	68	144	169	15	5	0	44	4	3	4	5	54	1	79	28	19
Alvarez, Jesus, Fort Lauderdale*	.322	133	469	79	151	209	30	2	8	90	13	2	5	1	88	5	51	0	6
Anderson, Brady, Winter Haven*	.319	126	417	86	133	210	19	11	12	87	14	7	6	6	107	5	47	44	19
Berry, Mark, Tampa	.315	132	444	76	140	180	20	4	4	73	10	0	10	2	85	10	59	34	11
Morgan, Curt, Miami*	.305	117	328	59	100	137	17	1	6	41	4	2	6	4	97	6	41	3	4
Brock, Norman, Osceola*	.304	115	382	65	116	154	16	8	2	41	4	1	3	3	36	2	48	31	6
Lotzar, Gregory, Winter Haven*	.300	117	446	94	134	179	19	10	2	44	11	6	3	3	58	4	38	42	13
Michel, Domingo, Vero Beach	.300	114	383	64	115	161	25	6	3	58	5	3	9	2	46	2	64	22	5

Departmental Leaders: G—Fishel, 137; AB—St. Laurent, 515; R—Lotzar, 94; H—R. Jones, St. Laurent, 153; TB—R. Jones, 216; 2B—Fishel, 36; 3B—R. Jones, 12; HR—Fortenberry, 18; RBI—Ta. Scott, 93; GWRBI—Ta. Scott, 15; SH—Rowland, 15; SF—Berry, Fishel, Fortenberry, Infante, 10; HP—Tenacen, 13; BB—Br. Anderson, 107; IBB—Fortenberry, 12; SO—Kaye, Randle, 95; SB—Reboulet, 71; CS—Cole, 22.

(All Players—Listed Alphabetically)

Player and Club	Pct.	G.	AB.	R.	H.	TB.	2B.	3B.	HR.	RBI.	GW.	SH.	SF.	HP.	BB.	Int. BB.	SO.	SB.	CS.
Acosta, Carlos, Tampa	.188	13	32	3	6	8	0	1	0	1	0	0	0	0	1	0	6	1	0
Adkins, Todd, Tampa†	.118	25	51	4	6	6	0	0	0	1	0	0	1	0	4	1	7	1	2
Agostinelli, Salvatore, St. Petersburg	.374	27	99	20	37	43	2	2	0	21	4	0	1	0	9	0	6	7	1
Alcala, Julio, Fort Myers	.351	36	148	17	52	64	6	3	0	16	2	0	1	1	5	1	8	11	3
Aleshire, Troy, Osceola	.000	2	5	0	0	0	0	0	0	0	0	0	0	0	0	0	2	0	0
Allen, Edward, Fort Myers	.201	53	169	19	34	44	6	2	0	20	1	1	1	2	35	1	42	15	4
Alvarez, Jesus, Fort Lauderdale*	.322	133	469	79	151	209	30	2	8	90	13	2	5	1	88	5	51	0	6
Amante, Thomas, St. Petersburg	.328	34	122	19	40	64	8	2	4	19	4	0	0	1	7	1	14	1	0
Anderson, Bernard, Lakeland*	.249	125	462	71	115	157	16	10	2	41	5	3	3	2	71	5	55	10	9
Anderson, Brady, Winter Haven*	.319	126	417	86	133	210	19	11	12	87	14	7	6	6	107	5	47	44	19
Anthony, Andrew, Vero Beach*	.226	115	318	63	72	104	10	8	2	38	3	3	2	0	90	6	48	6	7
Arnold, Scott, St. Petersburg	.115	22	26	2	3	3	0	0	0	1	0	3	0	0	1	0	9	0	0
Arnold, Timothy, West Palm Beach	.250	101	308	31	77	91	9	1	1	33	5	8	2	1	26	2	25	1	2
Arnsberg, Timothy, Osceola	.400	27	5	0	2	2	0	0	0	3	0	0	0	0	0	0	1	0	0
Arzola, Ricardo, St. Petersburg*	.245	114	330	58	81	105	20	2	0	43	2	2	2	2	76	4	66	13	1
Ayers, Kevin, Vero Beach	.290	111	321	44	93	106	7	3	0	28	6	9	1	3	23	2	54	9	4
Ayers, Scott, West Palm Beach	.167	4	6	1	1	2	1	0	0	1	0	0	0	0	0	0	1	0	0
Bachman, Kent, West Palm Beach	.262	52	126	21	33	45	5	2	1	17	1	2	0	0	15	0	18	2	1
Barker, Timothy, Tampa	.250	126	460	86	115	150	14	9	1	42	6	3	3	3	94	0	70	64	15
Barrios, Gregg, Winter Haven	.150	7	20	5	3	4	1	0	0	0	0	0	0	0	2	0	6	0	0
Bautista, German, Miami	.133	22	45	3	6	12	1	1	1	7	0	0	1	1	1	0	17	0	1
Bedell, Jeffrey, Fort Myers†	.235	121	426	38	100	118	13	1	1	50	2	7	5	5	25	0	71	5	1
Bellver, Juan, Miami	.250	18	52	7	13	14	1	0	0	3	0	0	1	0	10	0	8	3	1
Beltre, Esteban, West Palm Beach	.242	97	285	24	69	85	11	1	1	20	3	4	1	0	16	2	59	4	2
Bennett, Christopher, Clearwater	.000	4	4	0	0	0	0	0	0	0	0	0	0	0	0	0	2	0	0
Berry, Mark, Tampa	.315	132	444	76	140	180	20	4	4	73	10	0	10	2	85	10	59	34	11
Blaser, Mark, West Palm Beach	.262	92	282	37	74	108	16	0	6	40	6	1	5	3	42	3	43	0	3
Blunt, Bradley, St. Petersburg	.000	3	2	0	0	0	0	0	0	0	0	0	0	0	0	0	2	0	0
Bochesa, Gregory, Winter Haven	.226	81	217	35	49	77	13	0	5	29	1	0	3	6	49	2	37	8	3
Brock, Norman, Osceola*	.304	115	382	65	116	154	16	8	2	41	4	1	3	3	36	2	48	31	6
Brown, Michael, Osceola	.240	77	196	31	47	64	9	1	2	19	1	2	2	2	20	1	29	4	2
Brumfield, Jacob, Fort Myers	.317	12	41	3	13	21	3	1	1	5	0	0	0	0	2	0	11	0	1
Brundage, David, Clearwater*	.211	25	76	9	16	21	1	2	0	6	1	2	1	0	5	3	15	2	1
Buhner, Jay, Fort Lauderdale	.302	36	139	24	42	74	9	1	7	31	7	0	1	0	15	1	30	1	0

Player and Club	Pct.	G.	AB.	R.	H.	TB.	2B.	3B.	HR.	RBI.	GW.	SH.	SF.	HP.	BB.	Int. BB.	SO.	SB.	CS.
Burgos, Francisco, Daytona Beach†	.239	79	268	22	64	78	10	2	0	20	1	3	1	2	8	0	19	1	2
Burke, Donald, West Palm Beach*	.190	19	58	9	11	11	0	0	0	0	0	1	0	0	6	2	11	1	0
Caceres, Edgar, West Palm Beach†	.277	111	382	52	106	125	9	5	0	37	4	4	4	2	24	2	28	25	6
Caffrey, Robert, West Palm Beach	.154	13	26	2	4	7	0	0	1	3	1	0	0	1	5	1	8	0	0
Camp, Scott, Osceola*	.400	16	5	0	2	2	0	0	0	1	0	0	0	0	0	0	0	0	0
Carey, Peter, Fort Myers*	.249	95	301	47	75	95	9	4	1	32	1	3	6	0	52	1	58	20	5
Carpenter, Douglas, Fort Lauderdale	.285	41	130	22	37	50	7	0	2	21	3	1	3	1	31	3	17	4	3
Carrion, Jesus, Osceola	.167	16	36	2	6	7	1	0	0	5	0	0	1	0	9	0	6	0	0
Carson, Henry, St. Petersburg	.091	26	11	2	1	1	0	0	0	0	0	0	0	1	1	0	3	0	0
Carter, Bruce, Clearwater†	.182	6	11	1	2	2	0	0	0	0	0	0	0	0	1	0	2	0	0
Carter, Frederick, Fort Lauderdale	.259	32	116	15	30	48	7	1	3	16	1	2	1	2	10	1	30	0	1
Cash, Timothy, Osceola	1.000	26	1	0	1	1	0	0	0	0	0	0	0	0	0	0	0	0	0
Cathcart, Gary, Fort Lauderdale*	.215	73	256	37	55	80	6	5	3	33	2	3	2	1	38	1	47	18	3
Cecena, Jose, Clearwater	.095	22	21	2	2	2	0	0	0	0	0	1	0	0	0	0	4	0	0
Chambers, Travis, Clearwater*	.071	41	14	0	1	1	0	0	0	0	0	2	0	0	0	0	5	0	0
Cherry, Michael, Vero Beach	.250	8	4	0	1	1	0	0	0	0	0	1	0	0	1	0	1	0	0
Clark, Anthony, Daytona Beach	.267	89	303	38	81	115	15	2	5	39	3	1	3	3	12	0	45	7	6
Cole, Alexander, St. Petersburg*	.343	74	286	76	98	109	9	1	0	26	0	2	1	2	54	1	37	56	22
Collins, Allen, West Palm Beach	.000	26	5	0	0	0	0	0	0	0	0	0	0	0	0	0	1	0	0
Cook, Kerry, West Palm Beach	.000	6	1	0	0	0	0	0	0	0	0	1	0	0	0	0	1	0	0
Costello, John, St. Petersburg	.000	15	8	0	0	0	0	0	0	0	0	0	0	0	0	0	0	0	0
Coveney, Patrick, Clearwater*	.169	87	219	22	37	51	10	2	0	22	0	2	3	3	13	0	36	4	4
Cox, Douglas, Vero Beach*	.071	27	14	1	1	1	0	0	0	0	0	1	0	0	1	0	6	0	0
Crone, Raymond, Miami*	.269	13	26	5	7	7	0	0	0	1	0	2	0	0	3	0	1	2	1
Crosby, Todd, Clearwater†	.243	54	181	18	44	52	3	1	1	11	2	5	0	1	14	1	20	3	3
Cruz, Rafael, Daytona Beach†	.198	42	131	20	26	31	5	0	0	8	0	1	1	0	15	0	36	2	2
Cunningham, William, WPB*	.286	23	14	1	4	4	0	0	0	2	0	1	0	0	2	0	5	0	0
Dale, Philip, Tampa	.308	36	13	1	4	4	0	0	0	0	0	1	0	0	0	0	1	0	0
Dantzler, Shawn, Clearwater	.264	68	227	18	60	76	13	0	1	18	3	1	2	5	10	1	45	3	5
Davis, Robert, Fort Myers	.218	48	147	7	32	35	1	1	0	10	2	2	1	2	11	1	27	0	0
Day, Michael, West Palm Beach*	.314	70	169	21	53	75	6	2	4	28	6	0	2	0	27	2	19	2	0
DeFrancesco, Anthony, Winter Haven	.250	34	88	12	22	26	4	0	0	8	0	1	2	0	13	1	11	1	1
DeLamata, Fred, Miami*	.297	37	111	15	33	48	9	3	0	11	1	1	1	1	7	0	15	1	2
DeLeon, Rafael, Fort Myers	.262	95	324	41	85	101	12	2	0	31	2	6	2	4	14	1	28	7	2
Delgado, Juan, Osceola	.322	48	146	16	47	55	8	0	0	17	0	0	1	1	23	1	34	1	1
Devlin, Robert, West Palm Beach	.286	39	7	0	2	2	0	0	0	0	0	0	0	0	1	0	2	0	0
Dimascio, Daniel, Lakeland	.266	51	143	20	38	57	5	1	4	17	1	2	0	3	11	0	33	2	1
Dixon, Edward, West Palm Beach	.000	43	4	1	0	0	0	0	0	0	0	1	0	0	0	0	3	0	0
Donahue, Charles, Tampa*	.224	25	67	14	15	18	3	0	0	8	0	3	1	0	11	1	18	1	1
Donatelli, Andrew, Clearwater	.228	26	57	5	13	14	1	0	0	3	0	2	1	0	11	0	6	1	1
Dotzler, Michael, Daytona Beach*	.249	103	337	42	84	123	27	6	0	38	1	2	4	3	33	0	68	0	1
Dougherty, Patrick, WPB	.000	7	3	0	0	0	0	0	0	0	0	0	0	0	0	0	1	0	0
Dulin, Timothy, Miami	.257	109	378	51	97	114	15	1	0	29	3	12	7	2	46	1	29	16	9
Dunster, Donald, Osceola	.160	26	25	1	4	6	0	1	0	1	0	0	0	0	1	0	8	0	0
Dunton, Kevin, West Palm Beach	.200	18	60	4	12	16	4	0	0	8	0	0	0	2	1	0	7	0	0
Eagar, Stephen, Lakeland	.183	33	104	16	19	25	3	0	1	8	0	1	0	0	17	0	17	1	0
Edge, Gregory, Clearwater†	.185	60	216	25	40	43	3	0	0	12	2	3	0	1	19	0	10	14	7
Edwards, Todd, Miami	.263	80	217	33	57	68	5	0	2	25	4	6	0	2	23	0	37	12	9
Farwell, Frederick, Vero Beach*	.063	22	16	0	1	1	0	0	0	0	0	3	0	0	0	0	5	0	0
Fassero, Jeffrey, St. Petersburg*	.120	27	25	3	3	3	0	0	0	0	0	10	0	0	0	0	14	0	0
Fischer, Jeffrey, West Palm Beach	.182	14	11	0	2	2	0	0	0	0	0	1	0	0	1	0	2	0	0
Fishel, John, Osceola	.269	137	490	82	132	212	36	4	12	83	6	0	10	5	79	6	69	17	8
Flower, George, West Palm Beach	.248	37	117	16	29	33	4	0	0	5	0	0	0	0	20	0	30	0	1
Foley, Keith, West Palm Beach	.252	90	254	27	64	86	13	0	3	28	7	0	2	3	19	1	28	0	0
Forney, Jeffrey, Tampa	.205	59	151	19	31	36	5	0	0	14	4	1	3	0	21	4	27	4	1
Fortenberry, Jimmy, Clearwater*	.298	122	382	68	114	186	12	3	18	83	11	0	10	2	51	12	51	12	2
Foster, Paul, Lakeland	.121	10	33	1	4	5	1	0	0	3	1	0	0	1	1	0	5	0	0
Freeman, Martin, Lakeland	.136	18	66	7	9	12	1	1	0	4	0	0	0	1	8	0	7	3	0
Fregosi, James, St. Petersburg	.244	121	401	52	98	130	20	3	2	51	9	3	4	2	68	4	67	3	5
Frohwirth, Todd, Clearwater	.000	32	5	0	0	0	0	0	0	0	0	2	0	0	0	0	2	0	0
Fuentes, Roberto, Winter Haven	.220	49	118	15	26	28	0	1	0	9	2	2	0	0	15	0	26	4	0
Garner, Darrin, Daytona Beach	.184	47	147	18	27	31	4	0	0	7	0	3	1	2	29	1	32	0	4
Geist, Peter, Vero Beach	.225	123	383	48	86	113	18	3	1	45	1	9	7	1	42	2	92	4	1
Gonzalez, Angel, Winter Haven†	.323	107	387	69	125	169	28	2	4	44	5	2	3	2	46	1	57	31	16
Gonzalez, Carlos, Fort Myers	.250	2	4	0	1	1	0	0	0	0	0	0	0	0	0	0	3	0	0
Gonzalez, Fredi, Fort Lauderdale	.197	55	157	19	31	47	5	1	3	18	4	4	3	1	29	1	46	4	0
Gonzalez, Otto, Daytona Beach	.260	121	420	54	109	159	22	2	8	63	5	0	4	0	55	2	51	2	3
Gray, Scott, Osceola	.500	2	2	0	1	1	0	0	0	1	0	0	0	0	0	0	0	0	0
Graybill, David, West Palm Beach	.182	18	11	1	2	3	1	0	0	2	1	1	0	0	0	0	5	0	0
Green, Robert, Fort Lauderdale	.214	45	140	18	30	45	10	1	1	16	3	1	5	0	27	3	33	2	0
Green, Terry, Osceola	.274	113	424	41	116	132	10	3	0	47	3	6	3	1	29	0	37	37	16
Guzman, Juan, Vero Beach	.000	26	18	0	0	0	0	0	0	0	0	2	0	0	2	0	7	0	0
Haley, Samuel, West Palm Beach	.235	32	102	17	24	31	4	0	1	6	0	1	0	1	3	0	24	3	1
Hammond, Christopher, Tampa*	.250	5	4	0	1	1	0	0	0	0	0	2	0	0	0	0	1	0	0
Hampton, Anthony, Osceola*	.229	90	218	27	50	65	5	5	0	20	3	2	2	2	21	2	36	12	6
Harris, Tyrone, West Palm Beach	.000	2	2	0	0	0	0	0	0	0	0	0	0	0	0	0	2	0	0
Hartman, Jeffrey, Vero Beach	.215	57	158	16	34	38	4	0	0	18	0	1	1	2	16	1	22	2	1
Hauradou, Yanko, Fort Lauderdale	.348	12	23	5	8	8	0	0	0	2	0	0	0	0	3	1	5	0	1
Hawkins, Johnny, Fort Lauderdale†	.252	59	206	24	52	58	6	0	0	20	1	1	1	1	18	2	15	1	0
Hayward, Jeffrey, Tampa	.000	6	5	0	0	0	0	0	0	0	0	0	0	0	0	0	2	0	0
Hearn, Tommy, Miami	.174	86	161	19	28	31	3	0	0	10	2	4	2	2	19	0	21	1	2
Heist, Charles, Fort Myers*	.223	74	233	34	52	70	6	3	2	21	3	3	0	1	20	2	36	10	4
Henley, Daniel, Vero Beach	.210	43	119	16	25	33	5	0	1	11	2	1	1	2	5	2	17	3	1
Heredia, Geysi, Osceola	.000	9	2	0	0	0	0	0	0	0	0	0	0	0	0	0	1	0	0
Hermann, Jeffrey, Lakeland*	.256	27	78	16	20	39	1	0	6	11	2	0	0	2	17	0	15	0	0
Hernandez, Pedro, Vero Beach	.500	16	2	0	1	1	0	0	0	0	0	0	0	0	1	0	1	0	0
Herzog, Hans, St. Petersburg*	.000	46	2	0	0	0	0	0	0	1	0	1	0	0	1	0	0	0	0
Hibbs, Albert, Clearwater	.192	20	52	3	10	12	2	0	0	3	0	1	0	1	2	0	21	0	0
Higgins, Theodore, Fort Lauderdale*	.265	112	389	66	103	147	17	6	5	52	8	3	5	6	41	5	71	1	7
Hill, Stephen, St. Petersburg*	.200	27	25	3	5	5	0	0	0	4	1	2	0	0	2	0	7	0	0
Hilton, Howard, St. Petersburg	.000	36	5	0	0	0	0	0	0	0	0	1	0	0	1	0	1	0	0
Holmes, Darren, Vero Beach	.250	11	12	1	3	5	0	1	0	1	0	0	0	0	0	0	7	1	0

Player and Club	Pct.	G.	AB.	R.	H.	TB.	2B.	3B.	HR.	RBI.	GW.	SH.	SF.	HP.	BB.	Int. BB.	SO.	SB.	CS.
Hook, Michael, Osceola	.000	1	1	0	0	0	0	0	0	0	0	0	0	0	0	0	1	0	0
Hoskison, Keith, Lakeland	.242	45	128	13	31	42	11	0	0	13	0	3	2	3	7	0	26	0	0
Houston, Melvin, West Palm Beach	.185	108	292	36	54	68	10	2	0	15	3	5	2	2	48	2	51	17	11
Huchingson, Christopher, Osceola	.000	16	3	0	0	0	0	0	0	0	0	1	0	0	1	0	2	0	0
Hudson, Lance, Miami†	.293	108	389	63	114	143	11	3	4	31	2	6	3	4	29	3	53	59	17
Huff, Michael, Vero Beach	.293	113	362	73	106	134	6	8	2	32	5	3	2	5	67	1	67	28	13
Hume, Thomas, Clearwater	.333	9	3	0	1	1	0	0	0	0	0	0	0	0	0	0	0	0	0
Iavarone, Gregory, Fort Lauderdale	.000	2	3	2	0	0	0	0	0	1	0	0	0	1	0	0	1	0	0
Ilsley, Blaise, Osceola*	.000	14	7	0	0	0	0	0	0	0	0	1	0	0	0	0	1	0	0
Infante, Kennedy, St. Petersburg	.295	112	376	57	111	167	30	1	8	78	13	2	10	6	17	3	45	1	1
Jackson, Lavern, Winter Haven	.283	114	353	51	100	133	11	5	4	39	2	2	5	4	53	4	66	20	5
Jacobo, Edward, Vero Beach	.227	52	128	16	29	41	8	2	0	21	2	1	2	1	19	0	22	1	0
Jacobsen, Robert, Vero Beach	.333	44	3	0	1	1	0	0	0	2	0	0	0	0	2	0	0	0	0
James, Calvin, Osceola*	.269	125	424	64	114	136	14	4	0	31	4	4	0	1	81	2	52	25	19
Jefferson, James, Tampa	.000	31	2	0	0	0	0	0	0	0	0	0	0	0	0	0	1	0	0
Jelic, Christopher, Fort Myers	.256	108	348	50	89	125	11	5	5	50	8	4	2	4	83	5	52	13	6
Jester, William, Clearwater*	.077	36	13	0	1	1	0	0	0	1	0	0	0	0	0	0	7	0	0
Job, Ryan, Osceola	.265	63	189	21	50	58	4	2	0	22	3	5	1	2	13	0	25	2	1
Johns, Ronald, St. Petersburg	.333	93	345	47	115	172	27	3	8	81	12	1	5	5	36	3	35	0	1
Johnson, Randall, West Palm Beach	.118	26	17	3	2	2	0	0	0	0	0	2	0	0	0	0	6	0	0
Johnson, Richard, Osceola	.285	69	249	27	71	99	11	1	5	34	3	0	2	1	27	2	54	1	1
Jones, Marshall, Daytona Beach	.000	25	1	0	0	0	0	0	0	0	0	0	0	0	0	0	0	0	0
Jones, Ronald, Clearwater*	.371	108	412	76	153	216	18	12	7	73	11	2	9	4	40	4	30	33	12
Jones, Timothy, St. Petersburg*	.254	39	142	19	36	43	3	2	0	27	3	0	3	1	30	0	8	8	6
Jose, Manuel, Winter Haven†	.279	87	297	46	83	106	10	5	1	34	1	2	4	2	31	1	62	51	13
Juenke, Daniel, Miami*	.286	117	371	46	106	138	17	3	3	37	7	0	5	3	38	4	63	1	2
Kaiser, Bart, Clearwater*	.257	80	253	27	65	90	11	1	4	27	2	5	1	1	24	1	81	6	7
Kaye, Jeffrey, Clearwater	.203	102	316	40	64	112	21	0	9	50	11	2	4	4	51	1	95	1	2
Kearney, William, Clearwater	.212	34	99	10	21	28	4	0	1	12	0	1	0	2	9	1	33	0	2
Kennelley, Steve, Tampa	.053	18	19	5	1	3	0	1	0	1	0	0	0	1	0	0	9	1	0
Kinzer, Matthew, St. Petersburg	.143	22	28	1	4	4	0	0	0	0	0	1	0	0	1	0	13	0	0
Kirby, Wayne, Vero Beach*	.261	114	387	60	101	124	9	4	2	31	5	2	2	1	37	3	30	28	17
Kline, Stewart, Miami†	.344	26	61	8	21	32	6	1	1	8	1	0	1	0	12	0	7	0	0
Knox, Jeffrey, Clearwater	.136	21	22	2	3	3	0	0	0	2	1	5	0	0	1	0	8	0	0
Koslofski, Kevin, Fort Myers*	.254	103	331	44	84	107	13	5	0	29	1	7	4	2	47	2	59	12	6
Kraft, Kenneth, Clearwater	.212	17	52	4	11	14	3	0	0	8	0	0	0	0	7	0	4	2	0
Kramer, Mark, Daytona Beach*	.244	95	312	40	76	101	10	6	1	21	1	3	0	2	33	4	39	4	3
Kwolek, Joseph, Osceola	.218	38	110	10	24	27	1	1	0	10	0	0	1	2	19	0	23	0	1
Ladnier, Deric, Fort Myers†	.197	24	76	4	15	16	1	0	0	8	0	2	1	0	7	0	16	1	1
Lambert, Kenneth, Vero Beach	.177	63	186	20	33	44	5	3	0	20	1	3	0	2	17	1	18	0	0
Lambert, Robert, Fort Lauderdale	.268	23	71	7	19	27	4	2	0	6	0	1	0	1	5	0	16	5	4
Lang, Gary, Daytona Beach	.250	7	12	1	3	4	1	0	0	2	0	1	0	0	0	0	3	0	0
Langdon, Ted, Tampa	.429	48	7	0	3	6	3	0	0	2	0	0	0	0	0	0	1	0	0
Lara, Crucito, St. Petersburg†	.000	1	2	0	0	0	0	0	0	0	0	0	0	0	0	0	0	0	0
Laseke, Eric, Winter Haven	.266	75	214	19	57	62	5	0	0	17	1	6	1	0	16	0	23	7	1
Latmore, Robert, Miami	.242	124	405	32	98	119	12	3	1	43	6	8	3	3	28	0	64	10	8
Lawrence, Andy, West Palm Beach	.226	49	168	19	38	62	9	3	3	20	4	0	1	0	13	2	25	0	0
Leary, Robert, West Palm Beach	.000	2	2	0	0	0	0	0	0	1	0	0	0	1	0	0	0	0	0
Lee, Harvey, Fort Lauderdale	.250	74	208	38	52	68	4	3	2	14	1	0	1	1	33	2	38	18	4
Leiper, Timothy, Lakeland†	.265	107	407	46	108	142	17	4	3	49	9	1	5	1	33	5	21	4	8
Leyritz, James, Fort Lauderdale†	.294	12	34	3	10	13	1	1	0	1	1	0	0	1	4	1	5	0	0
Liebert, Allen, Lakeland*	.225	26	80	8	18	21	3	0	0	4	0	1	0	0	7	0	7	0	1
Livin, Jeffrey, Osceola	.105	26	19	0	2	3	1	0	0	1	0	1	0	0	0	0	5	0	0
Loggins, Michael, Fort Myers†	.289	72	253	51	73	103	11	8	1	18	0	1	2	1	55	0	36	28	11
Lomastro, Gerardo, Miami	.305	40	141	20	43	75	14	0	6	28	1	0	2	2	12	0	17	2	1
Lombardozzi, Christopher, Ft. Laud*	.267	115	326	58	87	117	23	2	1	44	2	5	2	1	88	2	70	6	6
Long, Anthony, Lakeland	.268	33	97	18	26	28	2	0	0	9	2	1	2	1	16	0	10	9	1
Long, Bruce, Clearwater	.000	8	9	0	0	0	0	0	0	0	0	0	0	0	0	0	3	0	0
Lono, Joel, Tampa*	.263	20	19	2	5	5	0	0	0	1	0	3	0	0	0	0	4	0	0
Lopez, Luis, Vero Beach	.286	122	434	52	124	154	21	3	1	60	8	2	4	2	33	3	25	5	7
Lopez, Robert, Tampa*	.130	23	23	0	3	5	0	1	0	3	1	3	0	0	1	0	8	0	0
Lotzar, Gregory, Winter Haven*	.300	117	446	94	134	179	19	10	2	44	11	6	3	3	58	4	38	42	13
Lundblade, Frederick, Clearwater	.259	70	239	32	62	100	17	0	7	31	2	3	2	1	17	2	37	2	2
Maas, Jason, Fort Lauderdale*	.259	110	371	64	96	116	12	4	0	29	2	3	2	0	65	2	50	32	8
Mabe, Todd, Fort Myers†	.251	48	171	25	43	47	4	0	0	16	1	1	3	0	24	1	33	10	7
Madden, Scott, Clearwater	.000	4	1	0	0	0	0	0	0	0	0	0	0	0	0	0	0	0	0
Manering, Mark, Fort Lauderdale*	.241	36	133	17	32	40	4	2	0	23	3	0	0	1	21	1	24	1	1
Mangham, Mark, St. Petersburg	.000	24	4	0	0	0	0	0	0	0	0	2	0	0	0	0	3	0	0
Mangham, Eric, Vero Beach	.238	64	193	27	46	72	8	3	4	19	1	4	1	1	29	1	45	10	5
Mann, Scott, West Palm Beach*	.279	120	390	60	109	162	21	1	10	60	9	2	6	2	55	11	45	3	7
Markert, James, Osceola	.228	48	149	12	34	43	4	1	1	15	5	1	3	2	20	0	32	0	1
Martinez, Carlos, Fort Lauderdale	.063	5	16	1	1	1	0	0	0	0	0	0	0	0	0	0	6	0	0
Martinez, Jose, Miami*	.250	10	32	5	8	8	0	0	0	2	0	0	0	0	3	0	6	1	0
Martinez, Porfirio, Lakeland†	.244	64	213	29	52	68	6	2	2	24	2	2	2	0	13	3	46	4	5
Mason, Martin, St. Petersburg	.000	4	1	0	0	0	0	0	0	0	0	0	0	0	0	0	1	0	0
Masters, Frank, Lakeland	.231	43	130	13	30	36	6	0	0	12	3	1	1	1	19	0	23	1	0
McConnell, Walter, Vero Beach*	.284	126	430	55	122	183	30	5	7	67	8	1	2	7	64	8	70	5	2
McDevitt, Stephen, Clearwater	.000	12	4	0	0	0	0	0	0	1	0	1	0	0	0	0	1	0	0
McGee, Timothy, Winter Haven	.167	48	108	13	18	19	1	0	0	11	3	2	3	0	5	0	9	2	2
McGrath, Charles, St. Petersburg	.000	33	3	0	0	0	0	0	0	0	0	0	0	0	0	0	1	0	0
Meads, David, Osceola*	.000	11	0	0	0	0	0	0	0	0	0	1	0	0	0	0	0	0	0
Melrose, Jeffrey, Daytona Beach*	.320	55	228	33	73	89	9	2	1	19	1	1	0	1	17	5	21	6	2
Mena, Andres, Vero Beach	.000	6	5	0	0	0	0	0	0	0	0	0	0	0	1	0	2	0	0
Menard, Darryl, Osceola	.000	29	1	0	0	0	0	0	0	0	0	0	0	0	0	0	1	0	0
Mendez, Jesus, St. Petersburg	.274	121	445	58	122	155	18	6	1	63	8	3	6	1	30	3	33	8	2
Michel, Domingo, Vero Beach	.300	114	383	64	115	161	25	6	3	58	5	3	9	2	46	2	64	22	5
Miley, David, Tampa*	.000	2	1	0	0	0	0	0	0	0	0	0	0	1	0	0	1	0	0
Millay, Garrick, Daytona Beach	.259	64	212	19	55	71	7	0	3	27	5	0	3	5	15	0	22	0	1
Miller, Michael, Clearwater*	.000	29	22	0	0	0	0	0	0	1	0	2	0	0	0	0	8	0	0
Mills, Craig, Lakeland	.233	53	176	19	41	64	9	1	4	21	3	2	1	4	15	0	32	1	3
Minick, Jeffrey, Lakeland*	.249	104	313	33	78	108	8	5	4	37	4	1	4	2	34	3	63	4	3
Mirabito, Timothy, Tampa	.000	26	22	1	0	0	0	0	0	0	0	2	0	0	2	0	13	0	0

Player and Club	Pct.	G.	AB.	R.	H.	TB.	2B.	3B.	HR.	RBI.	GW.	SH.	SF.	HP.	BB.	Int. BB.	SO.	SB.	CS.
Mitchell, Thomas, Lakeland	.261	82	303	27	79	118	13	7	4	36	3	2	2	2	10	0	48	7	4
Morgan, Curt, Miami*	.305	117	328	59	100	137	17	1	6	41	4	2	6	4	97	6	41	3	4
Morgan, Christopher, Lakeland*	.316	64	228	40	72	99	10	1	5	36	5	1	5	3	38	3	30	0	2
Moritz, Christopher, Winter Haven	.266	112	414	54	110	137	13	4	2	43	1	3	3	7	35	0	68	21	11
Mueller, Peter, Osceola*	.221	65	217	29	48	60	4	1	2	31	3	0	4	1	42	4	42	4	1
Murray, David, Daytona Beach	.289	73	249	34	72	81	4	1	1	17	0	1	2	3	31	1	14	7	10
Murray, Scott, St. Petersburg	.200	24	5	0	1	1	0	0	0	0	0	0	0	0	0	0	3	0	0
Newell, Thomas, Clearwater	.077	22	13	0	1	1	0	0	0	2	0	0	0	0	2	0	2	0	0
Nichols, Scott, St. Petersburg	.217	50	120	14	26	38	2	2	2	18	2	2	2	0	21	0	18	0	0
North, Jay, St. Petersburg	.167	18	6	0	1	1	0	0	0	0	0	1	0	0	0	0	2	0	0
Nunez, Mauricio, St. Petersburg	.240	109	334	42	80	98	10	1	2	35	6	1	9	3	32	6	49	17	7
Nunley, Angelo, Tampa	.323	123	446	68	144	169	15	5	0	44	4	3	4	5	54	1	79	28	19
O'Hoppe, Robert, Fort Myers	.185	78	216	16	40	45	3	1	0	8	1	9	1	0	11	0	43	0	1
Ojeda, Luis, Miami	.295	119	420	56	124	168	20	6	4	57	8	6	3	1	34	2	20	9	3
Owen, Timothy, Daytona Beach	.138	34	80	3	11	12	1	0	0	1	0	0	0	0	7	0	20	0	0
Parker, Richard, Clearwater†	.234	63	218	24	51	65	10	2	0	15	0	3	2	2	21	1	29	8	9
Pena, Alejandro, Vero Beach	.000	4	2	0	0	0	0	0	0	0	0	1	0	0	0	0	0	0	0
Pequignot, Jonathan, Vero Beach*	.304	79	230	44	70	104	18	5	2	50	6	0	5	3	57	2	35	0	3
Perez, Sergio, Clearwater	.250	117	412	68	103	142	19	4	4	39	3	12	1	8	39	1	65	7	4
Perkins, Ray, Miami	.000	59	1	0	0	0	0	0	0	0	0	0	0	0	0	0	0	0	0
Petersen, Geoff, Fort Myers	.238	87	273	33	65	95	19	1	3	36	2	1	2	2	55	2	63	7	2
Petitt, Steven, St. Petersburg	.500	3	2	0	1	2	1	0	0	0	0	0	0	0	0	0	1	0	0
Pliecones, Johnnie, Fort Lauderdale	.233	89	262	27	61	67	2	2	0	22	4	13	2	0	38	0	38	9	3
Postier, Paul, Daytona Beach	.214	39	117	7	25	33	5	0	1	8	1	1	0	0	2	0	18	0	0
Pottinger, Mark, Clearwater†	.252	115	416	49	105	115	6	2	0	26	0	3	0	5	35	4	49	33	7
Powell, Alonzo, West Palm Beach	.329	23	76	20	25	46	7	1	4	18	3	0	1	0	22	0	16	5	1
Prioleau, Thelanious, Lakeland†	.190	47	137	15	26	33	5	1	0	11	1	5	0	1	24	0	36	4	1
Puzey, James, St. Petersburg*	.265	93	260	35	69	88	14	1	1	36	2	2	1	1	42	6	16	0	1
Ramon, Julio, Fort Lauderdale	.400	5	10	3	4	4	0	0	0	4	0	0	0	1	4	0	2	1	0
Ramos, John, Fort Lauderdale	.266	54	184	25	49	67	10	1	2	28	3	4	2	1	26	0	23	8	3
Ramsey, Michael, Tampa*	.220	91	241	35	53	69	9	2	1	21	4	4	2	2	32	5	30	7	2
Randle, Randy, Osceola	.197	128	406	43	80	107	12	6	1	34	3	2	7	4	48	2	95	12	15
Rather, Dody, Osceola	.111	27	9	0	1	1	0	0	0	1	0	3	0	0	2	0	2	0	0
Reboulet, James, St. Petersburg	.327	127	440	87	144	171	22	1	1	50	3	5	3	0	83	1	40	71	20
Rigos, John, St. Petersburg	.154	6	13	2	2	3	1	0	0	2	0	1	0	0	1	0	2	0	0
Riley, Darren, Tampa*	.263	125	438	71	115	160	17	11	2	58	7	2	1	2	70	7	82	50	9
Ritchie, Wallace, Clearwater*	.000	32	6	0	0	0	0	0	0	0	0	0	0	0	0	0	3	0	0
Roberge, Bertrand, West Palm Beach	.000	9	2	0	0	0	0	0	0	0	0	0	0	0	0	0	0	0	0
Roche, Roderick, Vero Beach	.250	33	4	0	1	1	0	0	0	2	0	1	0	0	0	0	2	0	0
Rodriguez, Angel, West Palm Beach	.000	7	2	0	0	0	0	0	0	0	0	0	0	0	0	0	1	0	0
Rodriguez, Ignacio, West Palm Beach	.209	50	153	17	32	38	6	0	0	16	2	0	3	0	11	0	31	1	0
Rogers, Sebastian, Tampa†	.000	24	8	0	0	0	0	0	0	1	0	1	0	0	1	0	2	0	0
Rolland, David, Daytona Beach	.214	30	98	9	21	31	4	0	2	10	1	2	0	1	6	0	22	0	0
Rondon, Isidro, Tampa	.256	34	86	10	22	28	4	1	0	10	1	0	0	2	6	0	17	0	1
Rosario, Victor, 1 Day-19 WH	.218	20	55	6	12	14	2	0	0	5	0	0	0	0	1	0	10	0	0
Rossy, Elam, Miami	.254	38	134	26	34	46	7	1	1	9	1	6	1	1	24	0	8	10	6
Rowland, Donald, Lakeland	.258	123	446	53	115	143	14	4	2	46	4	15	7	7	48	1	40	12	11
Russell, Ronald, Daytona Beach	.241	89	286	23	69	79	10	0	0	26	2	0	3	7	16	0	31	0	0
Samson, Frederick, Daytona Beach	.389	6	18	3	7	10	3	0	0	6	0	1	1	1	0	0	2	0	0
Sanchez, Juan, Clearwater	.242	24	62	8	15	16	1	0	0	2	0	1	1	1	3	1	12	0	1
Santiago, Norman, Fort Lauderdale	.226	56	146	16	33	45	4	1	2	23	5	1	5	0	14	4	13	0	0
Scanlan, Robert, Clearwater	.000	24	16	0	0	0	0	0	0	1	0	0	1	0	2	0	7	0	0
Scanlin, Michael, Daytona Beach*	.242	80	264	33	64	103	9	6	6	42	2	1	4	1	30	1	60	2	2
Schlichting, John, Vero Beach	.229	51	166	21	38	52	7	2	1	27	1	4	2	3	14	0	23	5	0
Schreiber, Martin, Osceola*	.667	54	3	1	2	2	0	0	0	2	0	0	0	0	1	0	0	0	0
Schwartz, Lawrence, Tampa*	.100	19	10	2	1	1	0	0	0	0	0	0	0	0	2	0	4	0	0
Scott, Tary, Winter Haven	.277	114	437	49	121	191	23	1	15	93	15	1	7	3	25	4	81	2	0
Scott, Timothy, Vero Beach	.067	20	15	1	1	1	0	0	0	2	0	0	0	0	0	0	8	0	0
Seay, Mark, Daytona Beach*	.000	3	2	0	0	0	0	0	0	0	0	0	0	0	2	0	1	0	0
Sepanek, Robert, Fort Lauderdale*	.261	116	341	51	89	148	21	4	10	52	4	0	6	1	38	1	72	3	3
Service, Scott, Clearwater	.143	4	7	1	1	1	0	0	0	0	0	0	0	0	0	0	1	0	0
Sferrazza, Matthew, WPB	.162	21	68	9	11	12	1	0	0	5	0	0	0	0	10	0	10	7	4
Shaw, Scott, Fort Lauderdale	.244	47	131	14	32	43	7	2	0	13	1	3	0	2	21	2	24	1	1
Sheffield, Travis, Daytona Beach†	.088	18	34	7	3	3	0	0	0	0	0	0	0	0	3	0	23	1	0
Sherlock, Glenn, Osceola*	.246	59	175	12	43	49	3	0	1	22	2	1	0	0	9	1	18	0	0
Silver, Roy, St. Petersburg†	.294	97	279	49	82	102	13	2	1	43	5	3	2	1	31	1	31	1	0
Silverio, Francisco, Tampa	.194	26	67	13	13	17	4	0	0	6	0	2	1	0	5	0	28	2	0
Singletary, Nathan, St. Petersburg†	.188	27	64	6	12	14	2	0	0	3	0	0	0	0	5	0	15	1	1
Slotnick, Joseph, West Palm Beach	.285	59	186	30	53	74	13	1	2	24	2	1	1	5	7	0	21	3	2
Smith, Jackson, Tampa	.225	123	396	43	89	122	17	2	4	51	9	9	9	0	32	2	93	2	1
Smith, Todd, Miami	.223	93	229	27	51	71	12	4	0	22	2	3	2	1	14	1	68	12	4
Snyder, Doug, Osceola*	.283	115	346	68	98	142	21	7	3	29	7	1	6	2	71	6	82	17	14
Soto, Maximilliano, Lakeland	.256	78	254	26	65	75	8	1	0	16	1	5	0	1	10	0	51	10	8
Soto, Osvaldo, Tampa	.286	4	7	0	2	2	0	0	0	0	0	1	0	0	0	0	1	0	0
Spitale, Benjamin, West Palm Beach*	.357	10	28	3	10	10	0	0	0	5	0	0	0	0	3	1	2	0	0
St. Claire, Steven, West Palm Beach	.235	8	17	1	4	6	0	1	0	1	1	1	0	0	2	0	6	1	0
St. Laurent, James, Daytona Beach*	.297	135	515	62	153	184	21	2	2	58	9	0	6	1	32	5	54	4	5
Steen, Scott, Clearwater	.269	26	67	10	18	20	2	0	0	2	0	0	0	0	12	1	19	0	1
Stevens, Michael, Miami	.231	10	26	1	6	6	0	0	0	6	1	0	2	0	1	0	8	0	1
Stewart, Wayne, Clearwater	.000	2	1	0	0	0	0	0	0	0	0	0	0	0	0	0	0	0	0
Stottlemyre, Melvin, Osceola	.400	9	5	0	2	4	0	1	0	2	0	0	0	0	1	0	1	0	0
Strange, Douglas, Lakeland†	.255	126	466	59	119	162	29	4	2	63	4	7	6	2	65	5	59	18	6
Sudo, Robert, West Palm Beach	.077	9	13	0	1	2	1	0	0	1	1	1	0	0	0	0	4	0	0
Sullivan, Daniel, Winter Haven†	.246	89	284	43	70	115	14	5	7	49	4	0	4	4	40	7	35	2	1
Summers, Thomas, Tampa*	.143	29	14	1	2	2	0	0	0	2	1	0	0	0	1	0	3	0	1
Swob, Timothy, Tampa*	.000	3	5	0	0	0	0	0	0	0	0	3	0	0	0	0	4	0	0
Taveras, Jose, Lakeland†	.500	1	2	0	1	1	0	0	0	0	0	0	0	0	0	0	1	0	0
Taylor, Phil, Miami*	.000	38	1	0	0	0	0	0	0	0	0	0	0	0	0	0	0	0	0
Tejeda, Felix, Vero Beach†	.000	5	3	0	0	0	0	0	0	0	0	0	0	0	1	0	3	0	0
Tenacen, Francisco, Tampa	.266	127	459	61	122	164	22	4	4	67	4	1	7	13	27	2	68	35	8
Thiesen, Michael, St. Petersburg	.208	69	173	29	36	40	4	0	0	10	4	6	2	1	26	1	13	3	3
Thiessen, Timothy, West Palm Beach	.260	122	434	50	113	156	20	4	5	40	6	8	1	7	38	3	72	6	10

Player and Club	Pct.	G.	AB.	R.	H.	TB.	2B.	3B.	HR.	RBI.	GW.	SH.	SF.	HP.	BB.	Int. BB.	SO.	SB.	CS.
Thomas, Christopher, Vero Beach*	.286	32	7	1	2	3	1	0	0	3	0	0	0	0	0	0	2	0	0
Thomson, Robert, Lakeland	.182	8	22	2	4	8	1	0	1	4	0	0	0	0	0	0	2	0	0
Threadgill, George, Daytona Beach	.277	111	394	58	109	140	14	4	3	40	3	1	3	4	48	1	42	17	6
Tomsick, Troy, St. Petersburg	.000	15	5	0	0	0	0	0	0	0	0	0	0	0	1	0	3	0	0
Traen, Thomas, West Palm Beach†	.250	16	8	0	2	3	1	0	0	3	1	0	0	0	2	0	3	0	0
Tucker, Robert, Vero Beach	.148	20	27	2	4	6	0	1	0	4	0	0	1	1	1	0	6	0	0
Turner, Shane, Fort Lauderdale*	.320	66	222	48	71	93	12	2	2	36	3	4	3	3	51	1	35	12	8
Valdez, Sergio, West Palm Beach	.067	24	30	0	2	2	0	0	0	0	0	0	0	0	0	0	14	0	0
Van Blaricom, Mark, Fort Myers	.287	119	411	71	118	158	16	3	6	71	12	4	8	2	77	4	53	40	12
Van Vuren, Robert, Fort Myers*	.000	30	0	0	0	0	0	0	0	0	0	1	0	0	0	0	0	0	0
Vargas, Jose, Osceola	.429	24	14	2	6	8	0	1	0	2	0	1	0	0	2	0	3	0	1
Vargas, Miguel, Clearwater	.000	2	1	0	0	0	0	0	0	0	0	0	0	0	0	0	0	0	0
Vila, Jesus, Vero Beach	.250	21	24	1	6	7	1	0	0	2	0	1	0	0	0	0	3	0	0
Wakamatsu, Donald, Tampa	.277	112	361	41	100	125	18	2	1	66	9	0	8	5	53	2	66	6	1
Walker, Bernard, Tampa*	.159	25	69	9	11	15	1	0	1	3	1	0	0	0	6	0	27	7	1
Walker, Larry, West Palm Beach*	.283	38	113	20	32	61	7	5	4	16	3	0	1	2	26	2	32	2	2
Wallace, Greg, Miami	.249	73	173	14	43	52	9	0	0	18	1	3	2	0	29	1	36	3	1
Watkins, Timothy, Tampa	.000	22	4	0	0	0	0	0	0	0	0	2	0	0	0	0	3	0	0
Watson, De Jon, Fort Myers*	.220	109	346	34	76	103	16	4	1	32	3	2	7	2	41	3	86	7	6
Wayne, Gary, West Palm Beach*	.000	47	3	0	0	0	0	0	0	0	0	0	0	0	1	0	1	0	0
Weatherford, Brant, Tampa	.000	9	2	0	0	0	0	0	0	0	0	0	0	0	0	0	2	0	0
Welter, Andrew, Miami*	.000	2	2	0	0	0	0	0	0	0	0	0	0	0	0	0	1	0	0
Wheeler, Rodney, Clearwater*	.303	22	76	9	23	30	3	2	0	4	0	0	0	1	7	0	9	5	4
Wieligman, Richard, Miami*	.276	103	297	38	82	100	11	2	1	39	3	5	9	4	45	7	31	19	2
Williams, Jaime, Osceola	.151	42	139	13	21	30	3	0	2	6	1	1	0	2	11	0	24	1	3
Williams, Jimmy, Vero Beach*	.000	30	4	1	0	0	0	0	0	0	0	0	0	0	2	0	1	0	0
Williams, Mark, West Palm Beach	.000	10	3	0	0	0	0	0	0	0	0	0	0	0	0	0	0	0	0
Williams, Steven, Clearwater*	.243	66	210	27	51	79	13	0	5	35	3	0	5	0	29	2	30	1	1
Willis, Kenneth, Tampa	.400	6	5	1	2	2	0	0	0	1	0	0	0	0	1	0	3	0	0
Willis, Scott, Tampa	.000	26	3	0	0	0	0	0	0	0	0	0	0	0	2	0	1	0	0
Wilson, Jeff, Tampa	.254	103	283	37	72	81	7	1	0	33	5	2	2	0	73	7	56	2	2
Wilson, Thomas, Tampa	.177	35	79	4	14	21	4	0	1	15	1	2	2	2	3	0	19	0	1
Wisdom, Allen, Clearwater†	.000	7	5	0	0	0	0	0	0	0	0	0	0	0	0	0	3	0	0
Wockenfuss, Johnny, Miami	.269	136	458	58	123	180	27	0	10	80	13	0	9	4	79	6	54	8	2
Zambrano, Roberto, Winter Haven	.279	100	362	49	101	147	8	10	6	53	7	2	3	5	26	1	47	5	2

The following pitchers, listed alphabetically by club, with games in parentheses, had no plate appearances, primarily through use of designated hitters:

CLEARWATER—Befort, Curtis (10); Blackshear, Steven (12); Lachowicz, Allen (1); Tunison, Mark (4).

DAYTONA BEACH—Allison, James (3); Barfield, John (3); Bass, Regan (7); Bryan, Frank (6); Busick, Warren (24); Cerny, Martin (21); Harden, Ty (53); James, Paul (34); Keathley, Robin (6); Larsen, Daniel (29); Linton, David (8); LoSauro, Carmelo (50); Meadows, Jimmy (24); Morse, Scott (10); Mortimer, Robert (34); Odekirk, Richard (20); Pardo, Lawrence (5); Patterson, Glenn (10); Rivera, Lino (1); Shimp, Tommy (5); Soto, Edwardo (2); West, Thomas (26).

FORT LAUDERDALE—Balabon, Richard (15); Blum, Brent (2); Carreno, Amalio (3); Carroll, Christopher (48); Christopher, Michael (15); Clark, David (1); Davidson, Robert (16); Evers, Troy (1); Gay, Scott (8); George, Stephen (15); Giron, Ysidro (7); Guercio, Maurice (37); Harrison, Matthew (15); Hellman, Jeffrey (30); John, Thomas (3); Layana, Timothy (11); Leiter, Alois (22); McClear, Michael (33); Nielsen, Scott (6); Patterson, Kenneth (5); Reker, Timothy (1); Rosenberg, Steven (25); Scurry, Rodney (7); Tirado, Aristarco (21); Torres, Ricardo (11).

FORT MYERS—Alvarez, Evelio (1); Boroski, Stanley (27); DeJesus, Jose (22); Ellis, Rufus (34); Goodenough, Randy (1); Goodin, Richard (2); Hull, Jeffrey (24); Lee, Benjamin (6); McKelvey, Mitch (13); Mulligan, William (42); Nunez, Jose (14); Robinson, Henry (31); Rojas, Ricardo (11); Sanchez, Francisco (1); Schmidt, Gregory (9); Trapp, Michael (4); Watkins, Troy (35); Woyce, Donald (26).

LAKELAND—Agar, Jeffrey (42); Cooper, William (12); Gohmann, Kenneth (32); Labozzetta, Albert (10); Lee, Mark (41); McHugh, Charles (26); Minnema, David (6); Petry, Daniel (3); Poissant, Rodney (22); Raubolt, Arthur (35); Ritz, Kevin (18); Slavik, Joseph (33); Smoltz, John (18); York, Michael (16).

MIAMI—Alfonzo, Osvaldo (4); Boudreau, James (5); Bowden, Stephen (4); Browne, Richard (11); Browning, Michael (51); Concepcion, Carlos (6); Dotson, Wayne (3); Estes, Marcus (5); Gilbert, Jeffrey (19); Harrington, John (15); Hixon, Alan (4); Holm, Michael (14); Hoover, John (2); Leiter, Kurt (7); Llanes, Pedro (21); Mandich, Thomas (3); Milacki, Robert (12); Rasmussen, Eric (5); Rohan, Edward (15); Von Ohlen, David (15); Wilson, Chaunan (11); Wilson, Roger (33).

OSCEOLA—Baker, Mark (1); Durocher, Francois (27); Sheehan, John (7).

VERO BEACH—Devine, Kevin (5); Sepulveda, Jorge (8).

WEST PALM BEACH—Dopson, John (2); Fedor, Francis (1); Kelly, Leonard (8); Robertson, Michael (7); Trautwein, John (10).

WINTER HAVEN—Abril, Ernest (4); Carista, Michael (1); Clarkin, Michael (33); Crouch, Zachary (30); Irvine, Daryl (26); Lockhart, Bruce (34); Magistri, Gregg (29); Manzanillo, Josia (23); Parkins, Robert (25); Sanderski, John (33); Skripko, Scott (8); Snediker, James (28); Vasquez, Luis (31); Williams, Kerman (5).

GRAND SLAM HOME RUNS—Infante, 2; Carey, Clark, Fishel, Foley, O. Gonzalez, Kaye, Kearney, McConnell, Scanlin, Sepanek, Strange, Sullivan, Thiessen, Threadgill, Van Blaricom, T. Wilson, 1 each.

AWARDED FIRST BASE ON CATCHER'S INTERFERENCE—K. Lambert 3 (Dotzler 2, DeFrancesco); P. Martinez 3 (Dotzler, Owen, T. Wilson); Silver 3 (Davis, Leyritz, Wockenfuss); Amante (Davis); Jackson (Berry); Johns (K. Lambert); Lono (Markert); Melrose (Jelic); Strange (Foley); Tenacen (K. Lambert); Thiesen (K. Lambert); T. Wilson (Eager).

CLUB FIELDING

Club	Pct.	G.	PO.	A.	E.	DP.	PB.
St. Petersburg	.971	136	3443	1485	146	127	22
Fort Lauderdale	.969	139	3536	1495	163	119	16
West Palm Beach	.968	135	3376	1450	158	110	19
Miami	.966	140	3572	1647	183	170	18
Vero Beach	.966	138	3449	1412	172	94	25
Winter Haven	.966	127	3303	1370	166	123	14
Clearwater	.962	137	3464	1567	198	139	18
Osceola	.961	137	3494	1503	205	119	29
Lakeland	.960	133	3392	1413	198	125	25
Tampa	.956	136	3447	1389	222	96	22
Fort Myers	.953	135	3306	1280	224	87	19
Daytona Beach	.949	137	3386	1520	262	121	43

Triple Plays—Vero Beach, West Palm Beach.

INDIVIDUAL FIELDING

*Throws lefthanded.

FIRST BASEMEN

Player and Club	Pct.	G.	PO.	A.	E.	DP.
Amante, St. Petersburg	.977	15	108	19	3	13
Anderson, Lakeland*	1.000	1	3	0	0	1
Bautista, Miami	.929	2	12	1	1	5
Bedell, Fort Myers	.991	54	417	40	4	26
Blaser, West Palm Beach	.980	70	581	47	13	44
Brundage, Clearwater*	.857	1	6	0	1	0
Cathcart, Fort Lauderdale*	1.000	1	4	0	0	0
Cerny, Daytona Beach*	1.000	1	1	0	0	0
Clark, Daytona Beach	1.000	1	1	0	0	0
Day, West Palm Beach	.982	24	142	19	3	12

FIRST BASEMEN—Continued

Player and Club	Pct.	G.	PO.	A.	E.	DP.
Dotzler, Daytona Beach	.960	3	21	3	1	3
Dunton, West Palm Beach	.985	16	129	3	2	10
Foley, West Palm Beach	.961	17	91	8	4	5
Fuentes, Winter Haven	1.000	9	26	3	0	5
F. Gonzalez, Fort Lauderdale	1.000	4	32	1	0	3
O. Gonzalez, Daytona Beach	1.000	3	19	1	0	2
Hearn, Miami	1.000	2	3	0	0	1
Hermann, Lakeland	.977	5	38	4	1	8
Hudson, Miami	1.000	1	2	0	0	0
Jacobo, Vero Beach	.989	25	172	11	2	11
Johns, St. Petersburg	.992	89	781	50	7	76
Johnson, Osceola	.984	69	582	43	10	47
Juenke, Miami*	.985	78	642	36	10	74
Kaiser, Clearwater	.969	9	60	3	2	5
Kline, Miami	1.000	1	3	0	0	0
Kwolek, Osceola	.982	5	56	0	1	1
Lawrence, West Palm Beach	.964	26	171	18	7	20
Leiper, Lakeland	.987	104	904	81	13	83
Lopez, Vero Beach	.977	31	236	20	6	15
Lundblade, Clearwater	.983	57	499	28	9	53
Manering, Fort Lauderdale*	.989	21	175	10	2	16
Melrose, Daytona Beach*	.985	54	523	58	9	51
Mendez, St. Petersburg	.988	39	296	22	4	30
Michel, Vero Beach	.981	44	328	27	7	19
Mills, Lakeland	.992	12	107	14	1	11
Morgan, Miami	.987	42	282	29	4	36
Mueller, Osceola*	.988	63	620	48	8	58
Ojeda, Miami	.988	23	152	8	2	24
Owen, Daytona Beach	1.000	2	4	1	0	1
Pequignot, Vero Beach	.993	53	392	36	3	38
Perez, Clearwater	.978	21	162	12	4	14
Randle, Osceola	1.000	1	1	4	0	0
Rodriguez, West Palm Beach	1.000	1	5	0	0	1
Russell, Daytona Beach	.986	29	188	16	3	20
Santiago, Fort Lauderdale	.988	21	153	9	2	21
Scott, Winter Haven	.987	65	519	31	7	61
SEPANEK, Fort Lauderdale*	.989	105	761	54	9	59
Shaw, Fort Lauderdale	1.000	12	103	6	0	6
Silver, St. Petersburg	1.000	2	8	0	0	0
Snyder, Osceola	1.000	3	22	2	0	2
Spitale, West Palm Beach*	1.000	10	73	2	0	10
St. Laurent, Daytona Beach	.981	55	416	42	9	32
Steen, Clearwater	.968	22	177	3	6	16
Strange, Lakeland	.989	12	86	7	1	9
Sullivan, Winter Haven	.992	71	557	45	5	43
Threadgill, Daytona Beach	.750	1	6	0	2	0
Wakamatsu, Tampa	.974	54	394	21	11	30
Wallace, Miami	1.000	4	4	0	0	1
Watson, Fort Myers*	.984	87	656	35	11	47
Wieligman, Miami*	1.000	2	14	0	0	0
Williams, Clearwater	.992	42	351	23	3	33
Wilson, Tampa	.986	99	803	45	12	52
Wockenfuss, Miami	.987	28	226	8	3	22

Triple Plays—Lawrence, Michel.

SECOND BASEMEN

Player and Club	Pct.	G.	PO.	A.	E.	DP.
Adkins, Tampa	1.000	1	2	0	0	0
Alcala, Fort Myers	.961	36	82	90	7	12
Ayers, Vero Beach	.981	73	129	186	6	29
Bachman, West Palm Beach	.900	3	1	8	1	2
Barker, Tampa	.818	10	12	15	6	2
Brown, Osceola	.950	48	80	128	11	17
CACERES, West Palm Beach	.975	100	204	268	12	52
Carter, Clearwater	.733	3	4	7	4	2
Crone, Miami	.969	9	10	21	1	7
Crosby, Clearwater	.975	48	101	132	6	25
Cruz, Daytona Beach	.942	14	19	46	4	13
Donahue, Tampa	.912	12	18	34	5	3
Dulin, Miami	.967	106	253	363	21	95
Edge, Clearwater	.946	35	79	115	11	20
Edwards, Miami	.969	30	51	72	4	16
Fuentes, Winter Haven	.986	13	39	32	1	6
Garner, Daytona Beach	.919	47	82	133	19	17
Gonzalez, Winter Haven	.957	62	133	157	13	34
Green, Osceola	.929	55	99	163	20	28
Hartman, Vero Beach	.923	55	90	139	19	22
Hauradou, Fort Lauderdale	.938	10	14	16	2	4
Hearn, Miami	.882	5	6	9	2	3
Henley, Vero Beach	.946	26	42	46	5	4
Houston, West Palm Beach	.965	48	59	107	6	20
Job, Osceola	.966	48	97	130	8	31
Kennelley, Tampa	.714	7	8	2	4	2
Kirby, Vero Beach	1.000	4	1	3	0	0
Kraft, Clearwater	1.000	2	2	5	0	2
Lambert, Fort Lauderdale	.991	21	47	60	1	17
Lang, Daytona Beach	.808	7	10	11	5	3
Laseke, Winter Haven	.968	72	139	199	11	49
Lombardozzi, Fort Lauderdale	.968	107	204	279	16	53
Long, Lakeland	1.000	6	20	19	0	5
Mabe, Fort Myers	.926	38	68	83	12	19
Martinez, Miami	.833	3	4	6	2	1
Millay, Daytona Beach	1.000	1	0	1	0	0
Mitchell, Lakeland	1.000	5	6	17	0	3
Murray, Daytona Beach	.965	71	165	162	12	38
Nunley, Tampa	.940	116	231	282	33	49
O'Hoppe, Fort Myers	.963	51	83	123	8	19
Perez, Clearwater	.667	1	2	2	2	0
Pliecones, Fort Lauderdale	.963	18	29	49	3	12
Postier, Daytona Beach	1.000	2	4	3	0	2
Pottinger, Clearwater	.973	52	108	178	8	47
Reboulet, St. Petersburg	.972	120	225	371	17	73
Rosario, Daytona Beach	1.000	1	1	4	0	0
Rowland, Lakeland	.972	117	219	336	16	69
Russell, Daytona Beach	1.000	6	19	12	0	1
Sanchez, Clearwater	1.000	4	7	9	0	2
Santiago, Fort Lauderdale	1.000	3	1	0	0	0
Shaw, Fort Lauderdale	.667	2	1	3	2	0
Silver, St. Petersburg	1.000	1	2	3	0	0
Soto, Lakeland	.943	12	19	31	3	11
Thiesen, St. Petersburg	.949	23	31	43	4	8
Thomson, Lakeland	1.000	1	3	4	0	3
Van Blaricom, Fort Myers	.960	20	41	55	4	8

Triple Plays—Ayers, Caceres.

THIRD BASEMEN

Player and Club	Pct.	G.	PO.	A.	E.	DP.
Alvarez, Fort Lauderdale	.913	129	79	225	29	17
Ayers, Vero Beach	1.000	12	3	20	0	1
Barker, Tampa	.916	85	65	164	21	13
Bedell, Fort Myers	.912	50	36	89	12	7
Berry, Tampa	.895	45	47	72	14	7
Blaser, West Palm Beach	.921	18	8	27	3	4
Brown, Osceola	1.000	3	2	3	0	1
Burgos, Daytona Beach	.813	8	3	10	3	1
Caceres, West Palm Beach	.917	8	5	6	1	0
Crosby, Clearwater	1.000	1	3	4	0	1
Donahue, Tampa	.833	10	4	11	3	1
Edge, Clearwater	1.000	1	0	2	0	1
Edwards, Miami	1.000	9	3	7	0	2
Fishel, Osceola	.902	136	99	278	41	20
Fregosi, St. Petersburg	.842	14	8	24	6	2
Fuentes, Winter Haven	.867	10	2	11	2	1
Gonzalez, Winter Haven	.911	36	20	52	7	4
Hearn, Miami	.863	44	26	43	11	6
Infante, St. Petersburg	.943	105	66	165	14	12
Kraft, Clearwater	1.000	2	5	1	0	0
Kwolek, Osceola	1.000	1	0	1	0	0
Ladnier, Fort Myers	.829	15	13	16	6	0
Leiper, Lakeland	.875	3	4	10	2	3
McCONNELL, Vero Beach	.952	122	78	181	13	12
Millay, Daytona Beach	.917	63	59	118	16	15
Mills, Lakeland	.857	5	3	9	2	0
Mitchell, Lakeland	.857	5	7	5	2	0
Moritz, Winter Haven	.955	7	9	12	1	2
Nunley, Tampa	917	6	5	17	2	1
O'Hoppe, Fort Myers	1.000	1	1	1	0	0
Ojeda, Miami	.966	87	60	165	8	15
Pequignot, Vero Beach	957	10	8	14	1	1
Perez, Clearwater	.953	54	57	124	9	10
Pottinger, Clearwater	.933	59	43	123	12	9
Prioleau, Lakeland	1.000	1	0	1	0	0
Rolland, Daytona Beach	.841	22	11	42	10	2
Rossy, Miami	.927	28	14	62	6	4
Russell, Daytona Beach	.904	52	50	128	19	14
Sanchez, Clearwater	1.000	12	7	14	0	3
Santiago, Fort Lauderdale	.950	7	13	6	1	1
Shaw, Fort Lauderdale	.958	10	8	15	1	0
Silver, St. Petersburg	.900	19	13	23	4	1
Soto, Lakeland	1.000	8	5	11	0	2
St. Laurent, Daytona Beach	1.000	2	1	0	0	0
Steen, Clearwater	.750	1	1	2	1	0
Strange, Lakeland	.900	113	116	208	36	20
Sullivan, Winter Haven	1.000	1	0	1	0	0
Thiesen, St. Petersburg	.815	16	3	19	5	4
Thiessen, West Palm Beach	.937	118	73	222	20	18
Thomson, Lakeland	1.000	1	1	1	0	0
Van Blaricom, Fort Myers	.885	74	100	139	31	10
Williams, Clearwater	.821	16	12	20	7	1
Zambrano, Winter Haven	.857	87	67	119	31	9

Triple Play—McConnell.

SHORTSTOPS

Player and Club	Pct.	G.	PO.	A.	E.	DP.
Adkins, Tampa	.849	20	20	42	11	6
Ayers, Vero Beach	.893	23	38	62	12	7
Bachman, West Palm Beach	.922	39	54	99	13	20
Beltre, West Palm Beach	.944	94	116	273	23	38
Berry, Tampa	1.000	1	1	1	0	1
Brown, Osceola	.786	2	4	7	3	3
Brumfield, Fort Myers	.810	8	18	16	8	3
Burgos, Daytona Beach	.882	69	110	182	39	32
Crone, Miami	1.000	1	1	0	0	0
Cruz, Daytona Beach	.892	26	45	87	16	10
DeLeon, Fort Myers	.916	85	121	197	29	27
Edge, Clearwater	.903	23	31	81	12	16
Edwards, Miami	1.000	2	1	5	0	1
Fregosi, St. Petersburg	.947	97	155	311	26	69
Fuentes, Winter Haven	.913	20	32	41	7	12
Geist, Vero Beach	.935	117	169	367	37	54
Gonzalez, Winter Haven	.000	1	0	0	1	0
Green, Osceola	.909	4	4	6	1	1
Hearn, Miami	.939	16	10	21	2	3
Henley, Vero Beach	.909	4	7	3	1	1
Houston, West Palm Beach	.889	17	16	32	6	9
Job, Osceola	.878	11	15	21	5	1
Jones, St. Petersburg	.960	39	67	125	8	19
Kraft, Clearwater	.921	12	20	38	5	4
Kramer, Daytona Beach*	1.000	1	1	1	0	0
Lara, St. Petersburg	1.000	1	0	2	0	0
Latmore, Miami	.942	123	225	424	40	105
Lombardozzi, Fort Lauderdale	.875	5	3	4	1	0
Martinez, Fort Lauderdale	1.000	5	7	18	0	5
McConnell, Vero Beach	1.000	1	0	2	0	0
Mills, Lakeland	.958	28	41	74	5	19
Mitchell, Lakeland	.857	2	4	2	1	1
MORITZ, Winter Haven	.954	101	181	340	25	67
Murray, Daytona Beach	.857	2	2	4	1	2
O'Hoppe, Fort Myers	.872	26	31	51	12	7
Parker, Clearwater	.933	61	94	197	21	35
Perez, Clearwater	.917	39	78	133	19	40
Pliecones, Fort Lauderdale	.964	71	105	213	12	39
Postier, Daytona Beach	.919	35	40	84	11	17
Prioleau, Lakeland	.925	46	86	136	18	31
Randle, Osceola	.917	127	205	324	48	77
Rolland, Daytona Beach	1.000	4	3	6	0	4
Rosario, Winter Haven	.903	18	20	36	6	5
Rossy, Miami	.961	11	16	33	2	11
Rowland, Lakeland	.929	5	7	19	2	4
Russell, Daytona Beach	1.000	6	7	10	0	4
Samson, Daytona Beach	.967	6	11	18	1	0
Sanchez, Clearwater	.857	6	8	16	4	3
Santiago, Fort Lauderdale	.882	4	2	13	2	3
Smith, Tampa	.933	121	184	343	38	49
Soto, Lakeland	.932	62	98	162	19	32
Taveras, Lakeland	1.000	1	1	2	0	0
Thiesen, St. Petersburg	1.000	4	4	4	0	0
Thiessen, West Palm Beach	1.000	2	0	1	0	0
Turner, Fort Lauderdale	.953	64	121	200	16	36
Van Blaricom, Fort Myers	.949	21	34	60	5	9

Triple Play—Bachman.

OUTFIELDERS

Player and Club	Pct.	G.	PO.	A.	E.	DP.
Acosta, Tampa	.850	12	16	1	3	0
Agostinelli, St. Petersburg	1.000	2	2	0	0	0
Allen, Fort Myers	.968	52	147	5	5	1
Amante, St. Petersburg	1.000	15	26	0	0	0
Be. Anderson, Lakeland*	.984	118	298	9	5	2
BR. ANDERSON, Winter Haven*	.997	114	280	5	1	2
Anthony, Vero Beach	1.000	92	164	7	0	1
Arzola, St. Petersburg	.980	91	141	6	3	0
Barker, Tampa	.982	34	51	3	1	0
Barrios, Winter Haven	1.000	5	9	0	0	0
Bellver, Miami	1.000	18	27	1	0	0
Bochesa, Winter Haven	1.000	1	1	0	0	0
Brock, Osceola*	.974	82	147	3	4	1
Brown, Osceola	.967	19	25	4	1	1
Brundage, Clearwater*	.979	21	46	1	1	0
Buhner, Fort Lauderdale	.968	36	84	7	3	0
Burke, West Palm Beach*	.966	19	28	0	1	0
Carey, Fort Myers*	.969	81	148	6	5	1
Carpenter, Fort Lauderdale	.964	36	51	2	2	0
Carter, Fort Lauderdale	.953	29	41	0	2	0
Cathcart, Fort Lauderdale*	.983	73	164	7	3	2
Clark, Daytona Beach	.974	87	143	5	4	0
Cole, St. Petersburg*	.962	74	201	4	8	0
Coveney, Clearwater*	.991	50	112	1	1	0
Dantzler, Clearwater	.979	54	91	2	2	1
DeLamata, Miami*	.942	30	49	0	3	0
Delgado, Osceola	1.000	15	23	1	0	1
Dimascio, Lakeland	.963	20	25	1	1	0
Donatelli, Clearwater	.944	20	33	1	2	0
Edwards, Miami	.964	32	51	2	2	0
Flower, West Palm Beach	.974	27	36	1	1	0
Forney, Tampa	.973	44	70	3	2	2
Fortenberry, Clearwater	.963	101	172	11	7	3
Foster, Lakeland	1.000	10	22	1	0	0
Freeman, Lakeland	.956	18	42	1	2	0
R. Green, Fort Lauderdale	.972	38	68	2	2	0
T. Green, Osceola	.964	48	74	7	3	0
Haley, West Palm Beach	1.000	29	46	0	0	0
Hampton, Osceola*	.973	66	101	7	3	1
Hearn, Miami	1.000	17	16	1	0	0
Heist, Fort Myers	.994	65	175	5	1	1
Hermann, Lakeland	1.000	19	33	1	0	0
Hibbs, Clearwater	1.000	2	3	1	0	0
Higgins, Fort Lauderdale*	.960	104	200	14	9	3
Houston, West Palm Beach	.962	52	72	4	3	1
Hudson, Miami	.975	96	226	10	6	1
Huff, Vero Beach	.996	111	257	10	1	2
Jackson, Winter Haven	.974	104	218	8	6	2
Jacobo, Vero Beach	1.000	13	15	0	0	0
James, Osceola*	.992	121	236	7	2	1
Job, Osceola	1.000	1	1	0	0	0
Jones, Clearwater	.990	97	196	9	2	0
Jose, Winter Haven	.960	68	137	7	6	0
Kaiser, Clearwater	.958	65	131	6	6	1
Kirby, Vero Beach	.986	104	263	15	4	2
Koslofski, Fort Myers	.965	99	178	16	7	4
Kramer, Daytona Beach*	.973	84	165	13	5	2
Kwolek, Osecola	1.000	13	18	0	0	0
Latmore, Miami	1.000	1	1	0	0	0
Lawrence, West Palm Beach	.958	19	23	0	1	0
Lee, Fort Lauderdale	1.000	61	79	4	0	2
Loggins, Fort Myers*	.951	70	149	6	8	1
Lomastro, Miami	1.000	30	55	1	0	0
Long, Lakeland	.935	17	27	2	2	0
Lotzar, Winter Haven*	.973	97	174	4	5	0
Maas, Fort Lauderdale	.960	68	93	4	4	0
Mangham, Vero Beach	.983	52	110	3	2	0
Mann, West Palm Beach	.981	113	149	10	3	3
Martinez, Lakeland	.922	45	80	3	7	0
Mendez, St. Petersburg	.969	82	174	13	6	3
Michel, Vero Beach	.886	28	30	1	4	0
Minick, Lakeland*	.939	39	60	2	4	0
Mitchell, Lakeland	.974	69	141	10	4	2
Ch. Morgan, Lakeland	.970	62	119	9	4	2
Cu. Morgan, Miami	.961	65	94	5	4	0
Moritz, Winter Haven	1.000	7	14	1	0	0
Nunez, St. Petersburg	.992	106	236	13	2	5
Ojeda, Miami	1.000	1	0	1	0	0
Pequignot, Vero Beach	1.000	9	9	0	0	0
Perez, Clearwater	.500	1	1	0	1	0
Petersen, Fort Myers	.983	54	111	4	2	1
Pottinger, Clearwater	1.000	4	9	1	0	1
Powell, West Palm Beach	1.000	22	56	1	0	0
Ramsey, Tampa*	.990	58	102	2	1	0
Rigos, St. Petersburg	.846	4	11	0	2	0
Riley, Tampa	.980	121	290	9	6	5
Rodriguez, West Palm Beach	1.000	45	67	2	0	0
Rolland, Daytona Beach	1.000	1	1	0	0	0
Rondon, Tampa	1.000	2	4	0	0	0
Santiago, Fort Lauderdale	1.000	3	3	0	0	0
Scanlin, Daytona Beach*	.984	80	177	8	3	1
Schlichting, Vero Beach	.955	46	78	6	4	2
Seay, Daytona Beach*	1.000	3	1	0	0	0
Sferrazza, West Palm Beach	1.000	21	34	3	0	0
Sheffield, Daytona Beach	1.000	16	25	2	0	0
Silver, St. Petersburg	1.000	54	81	4	0	0
Silverio, Tampa	.967	23	57	1	2	0
Singletary, St. Petersburg	1.000	21	32	3	0	1
Slotnick, West Palm Beach	.979	58	93	2	2	1
Smith, Miami	.950	88	124	8	7	0
Snyder, Osceola	.989	87	169	10	2	2
St. Claire, West Palm Beach	1.000	8	15	1	0	1
St. Laurent, Daytona Beach	.966	72	136	8	5	4
Stevens, Miami	1.000	10	13	0	0	0
Tenacen, Tampa	.958	124	242	10	11	2
Thiesen, St. Petersburg	1.000	14	20	1	0	1
Threadgill, Daytona Beach	.966	92	165	5	6	3
B. Walker, Tampa	.931	23	26	1	2	1
L. Walker, West Palm Beach	1.000	35	44	5	0	0
Wallace, Miami	.950	14	17	2	1	1
Welter, Miami	1.000	2	1	0	0	0
Wheeler, Clearwater*	1.000	18	40	1	0	0
Wieligman, Miami*	.988	93	154	7	2	2
Zambrano, Winter Haven	1.000	4	1	0	0	0

CATCHERS

Player and Club	Pct.	G.	PO.	A.	E.	DP.	PB.
Agostinelli, St. Petersburg	.975	19	99	16	3	0	1
Aleshire, Osceola	1.000	1	2	0	0	0	0
Arnold, West Palm Beach	.985	97	607	69	10	8	11
Bautista, Miami	1.000	9	20	1	0	0	1
Berry, Tampa	.979	80	428	73	11	5	13
Bochesa, Winter Haven	.983	74	352	47	7	6	5
Brown, Osceola	1.000	4	2	0	0	0	0
Carrion, Osceola	.984	14	54	6	1	1	4
Davis, Fort Myers	.959	35	139	26	7	2	6
Day, West Palm Beach	.961	20	88	10	4	1	3
DeFrancesco, Winter Haven	.954	32	124	21	7	1	3
Dimascio, Lakeland	.941	23	93	19	7	0	7
Dotzler, Daytona Beach	.954	79	366	69	21	9	36
Eagar, Lakeland	.975	32	172	22	5	1	4
Edwards, Miami	1.000	2	1	0	0	0	1
Foley, West Palm Beach	.977	32	197	17	5	2	5
Fregosi, St. Petersburg	1.000	7	34	0	0	0	3
C. Gonzalez, Fort Myers	1.000	1	2	0	0	0	0
F. Gonzalez, Fort Lauderdale	.985	45	231	30	4	2	3
O. Gonzalez, Daytona Beach	.968	42	193	21	7	3	5
Hawkins, Fort Lauderdale	.986	57	327	37	5	5	4
Hearn, Miami	1.000	1	1	0	0	0	0
Hibbs, Clearwater	.963	7	23	3	1	1	2
Hoskison, Lakeland	.988	36	155	14	2	3	2
Iavarone, Fort Lauderdale	1.000	2	7	0	0	0	0
Jelic, Fort Myers	.964	102	482	82	21	3	13
Kaye, Clearwater	.977	93	411	52	11	6	9
Kearney, Clearwater	.975	32	140	16	4	1	4
Kline, Miami	.959	16	55	16	3	0	3
Lambert, Vero Beach	.978	62	269	39	7	2	9
Leary, West Palm Beach	1.000	2	6	0	0	0	0
Leyritz, Fort Lauderdale	.976	7	32	8	1	2	1
Liebert, Lakeland	1.000	15	91	8	0	0	3
Lopez, Vero Beach	.982	81	452	52	9	4	15
Lundblade, Clearwater	1.000	3	20	1	0	0	0
Markert, Osceola	.976	46	244	35	7	1	8
Masters, Lakeland	.967	33	149	26	6	4	7
McGee, Winter Haven	.990	47	181	25	2	2	6
Millay, Daytona Beach	1.000	2	5	0	0	0	1
Nichols, St. Petersburg	.974	43	204	18	6	4	10
Owen, Daytona Beach	.955	26	90	15	5	1	1
PUZEY, St. Petersburg	.993	86	352	45	3	3	8
Ramon, Fort Lauderdale	1.000	5	20	2	0	1	2
Ramos, Fort Lauderdale	.960	30	197	19	9	3	6
Sherlock, Osceola	.983	54	263	33	5	0	7
Thomson, Lakeland	1.000	4	18	2	0	0	2
Tucker, Vero Beach	.952	14	35	5	2	1	1
Wakamatsu, Tampa	.989	48	229	37	3	4	4
Wallace, Miami	.950	51	168	24	10	1	7
J. Williams, Osceola	.978	36	183	39	5	5	10
S. Williams, Clearwater	.984	9	50	10	1	0	3
Wilson, Tampa	.971	21	89	12	3	0	5
Wockenfuss, Miami	.983	96	403	62	8	6	6
Zambrano, Winter Haven	1.000	1	1	0	0	0	0

PITCHERS

Player and Club	Pct.	G.	PO.	A.	E.	DP.
Abril, Winter Haven	1.000	4	2	2	0	1
Agar, Lakeland	1.000	42	5	9	0	0
Alfonzo, Miami	.909	4	5	5	1	0
Alvarez, Fort Myers	1.000	1	1	0	0	0
Arnold, St. Petersburg	.885	22	10	13	3	2
Arnsberg, Osceola	1.000	27	4	7	0	0
Ayers, West Palm Beach	1.000	4	2	4	0	0
Balabon, Fort Lauderdale	.900	15	3	6	1	1
Barfield, Daytona Beach*	1.000	3	2	2	0	0
Bass, Daytona Beach	1.000	7	1	2	0	1
Befort, Clearwater	1.000	10	0	2	0	0
Bennett, Clearwater	.833	4	1	4	1	0
Blackshear, Clearwater*	1.000	12	0	5	0	2
Blunt, St. Petersburg	1.000	3	1	1	0	0
Boroski, Fort Myers	.833	27	5	10	3	1
Boudreau, Miami*	1.000	5	0	1	0	0
Bowden, Miami	1.000	4	0	1	0	0
Brown, Osceola	1.000	3	1	1	0	0
Browne, Miami*	1.000	11	1	4	0	0
Browning, Miami	.952	51	6	14	1	2
Bryan, Daytona Beach	.500	6	0	1	1	0
Busick, Daytona Beach	.667	24	1	7	4	1
Camp, Osceola*	1.000	16	2	9	0	1
Carista, Winter Haven	1.000	1	1	0	0	0
Carreno, Fort Lauderdale	.750	3	1	2	1	0
Carroll, Fort Lauderdale	1.000	48	4	12	0	1
Carson, St. Petersburg	.929	26	10	16	2	3
Cash, Osceola	1.000	26	1	7	0	0
Cecena, Clearwater	1.000	22	6	20	0	3
Cerny, Daytona Beach*	.875	20	1	13	2	0
Chambers, Clearwater	.962	41	6	19	1	0
Cherry, Vero Beach	1.000	8	1	2	0	0
Christopher, Fort Lauderdale	.893	15	13	12	3	0
Clarkin, Winter Haven	1.000	33	7	17	0	0
Collins, West Palm Beach	.923	26	1	11	1	0
Concepcion, Miami	.500	6	0	1	1	0
Cook, West Palm Beach	1.000	6	2	3	0	1
Cooper, Lakeland	1.000	12	5	6	0	0
Costello, St. Petersburg	.938	15	3	12	1	2
Cox, Vero Beach*	1.000	26	9	27	0	1
Crouch, Winter Haven*	.960	30	4	20	1	1
Cunningham, West Palm Beach*	1.000	23	5	28	0	1
Dale, Tampa	.909	36	5	15	2	1
Davidson, Fort Lauderdale	.933	16	5	9	1	0
DeJesus, Fort Myers	.905	22	6	13	2	1
Devine, Vero Beach	.667	5	0	2	1	0
Devlin, West Palm Beach	1.000	39	12	16	0	2
Dixon, West Palm Beach	1.000	43	6	13	0	3
Dopson, West Palm Beach	1.000	2	0	3	0	0
Dotson, Miami	1.000	3	0	1	0	0
Dougherty, West Palm Beach	1.000	7	3	6	0	0
Dunster, Osceola	.905	26	14	24	4	1
Durocher, Osceola	1.000	27	1	5	0	0
Ellis, Fort Myers	.950	34	8	11	1	1
Estes, Miami*	1.000	5	1	2	0	1
Evers, Fort Lauderdale	1.000	1	0	1	0	0
Farwell, Vero Beach	.970	22	7	25	1	4
Fassero, St. Petersburg*	.978	26	13	32	1	1
Fedor, West Palm Beach	1.000	1	0	1	0	0
Fischer, West Palm Beach	1.000	14	5	11	0	1
Frohwirth, Clearwater	1.000	32	3	6	0	0
Gay, Fort Lauderdale	1.000	8	3	13	0	1
George, Fort Lauderdale*	.857	15	2	10	2	0
Gilbert, Miami*	.909	19	12	28	4	2
Giron, Fort Lauderdale	1.000	7	0	4	0	0
Gohmann, Lakeland	.920	32	11	12	2	0
Goodenough, Fort Myers*	1.000	1	0	1	0	0
Goodin, Fort Myers*	1.000	2	0	3	0	0
Graybill, West Palm Beach	1.000	18	10	12	0	0
Guercio, Fort Lauderdale	.867	37	2	11	2	0
Guzman, Vero Beach	.833	26	9	16	5	0
Hammond, Tampa*	1.000	5	1	6	0	0
Harden, Daytona Beach	1.000	53	11	11	0	0
Harrington, Miami	1.000	15	4	4	0	1
Harris, West Palm Beach	.000	2	0	0	1	0
Harrison, Fort Lauderdale*	.824	15	6	8	3	0
Hearn, Miami	1.000	12	0	4	0	0
Hellman, Fort Lauderdale	.833	30	3	7	2	1
Heredia, Osceola	1.000	9	1	2	0	0
Hernandez, Vero Beach	.857	16	2	4	1	0
Herzog, St. Petersburg*	1.000	46	3	23	0	1
Hill, St. Petersburg*	1.000	26	5	17	0	1
Hilton, St. Petersburg	1.000	36	3	5	0	0
Hixon, Miami	.800	4	2	2	1	0
Holm, Miami*	1.000	14	1	4	0	0
Holmes, Vero Beach	.909	11	4	6	1	0
Hook, Osceola*	1.000	1	0	1	0	0
Hoover, Miami	1.000	2	1	1	0	0
Huchingson, Osceola	.900	16	1	8	1	0
Hull, Fort Myers	.947	24	9	9	1	1
Hume, Clearwater	1.000	9	1	1	0	0
Ilsley, Osceola*	.933	14	4	10	1	0
Irvine, Winter Haven	.909	26	8	32	4	1
Jacobsen, Vero Beach	.750	44	5	4	3	0
James, Daytona Beach	.800	34	9	11	5	0
Jefferson, Tampa	.882	31	2	13	2	0
Jester, Clearwater*	1.000	36	6	12	0	0
John, Fort Lauderdale*	1.000	3	2	2	0	0
Johnson, West Palm Beach*	.867	26	5	21	4	0
Jones, Daytona Beach	.958	25	9	14	1	1
Keathley, Daytona Beach	1.000	6	1	5	0	1
Kelly, West Palm Beach	1.000	8	0	1	0	0
Kinzer, St. Petersburg	.933	22	6	22	2	1
Knox, Clearwater	.923	21	4	20	2	1
Labozzetta, Lakeland*	.947	10	5	13	1	0
Langdon, Tampa	.875	48	3	11	2	1
Larsen, Daytona Beach	.857	29	3	9	2	2
Laseke, Winter Haven	1.000	2	0	1	0	1
Layana, Fort Lauderdale	.960	11	7	17	1	0
B. Lee, Fort Myers*	1.000	6	1	2	0	0
M. Lee, Lakeland*	.933	41	6	8	1	0
A. Leiter, Fort Lauderdale*	.974	22	12	26	1	2
K. Leiter, Miami	1.000	7	1	2	0	0
Linton, Daytona Beach*	1.000	8	2	5	0	0
Livin, Osceola	.919	26	15	19	3	2
Llanes, Miami	.813	21	3	10	3	1
Lockhart, Winter Haven*	.842	34	2	14	3	0
Long, Clearwater	.929	8	7	6	1	1
Lono, Tampa*	.939	19	4	27	2	0
Lopez, Tampa	.978	22	8	37	1	1
LoSauro, Daytona Beach	.852	50	12	11	4	1
Magistri, Winter Haven*	.917	29	4	7	1	1

PITCHERS—Continued

Player and Club	Pct.	G.	PO.	A.	E.	DP.
Mandich, Miami	1.000	3	0	1	0	0
Mangham, St. Petersburg	.778	24	1	6	2	0
Manzanillo, Winter Haven	1.000	23	11	27	0	1
Mason, St. Petersburg	1.000	4	1	1	0	0
McClear, Fort Lauderdale	1.000	33	1	8	0	0
McDevitt, Clearwater	1.000	12	1	3	0	1
McGrath, St. Petersburg	.857	33	4	8	2	0
McHugh, Lakeland	.903	26	16	12	3	3
McKelvey, Fort Myers	.857	13	3	3	1	0
Meadows, Daytona Beach	.897	24	10	25	4	1
Meads, Osceola*	.800	11	1	3	1	0
Mena, Vero Beach	.875	6	2	5	1	0
Menard, Osceola	.875	29	1	6	1	0
Milacki, Miami	.857	12	3	9	2	1
Miller, Clearwater*	.970	29	5	27	1	2
Minnema, Lakeland	1.000	6	6	5	0	1
Mirabito, Tampa	.917	26	5	17	2	2
Morse, Daytona Beach	1.000	10	1	6	0	0
Mortimer, Daytona Beach*	1.000	34	3	10	0	3
Mulligan, Fort Myers*	.750	42	3	6	3	0
Murray, St. Petersburg	1.000	24	0	3	0	0
Newell, Clearwater	1.000	22	7	12	0	2
Nielsen, Fort Lauderdale	.889	6	4	4	1	2
North, St. Petersburg	.947	18	1	17	1	1
Nunez, Fort Myers	1.000	14	8	14	0	0
ODEKIRK, Daytona Beach*	1.000	20	10	31	0	2
Pardo, Daytona Beach	1.000	5	1	2	0	0
Parkins, Winter Haven	.909	25	2	8	1	0
G. Patterson, Daytona Beach	1.000	10	0	1	0	0
K. Patterson, Fort Lauderdale*	1.000	5	1	5	0	1
Pena, Vero Beach	.400	4	2	0	3	0
Perkins, Miami	.964	60	6	21	1	2
Petitt, St. Petersburg	1.000	3	1	0	0	0
Petry, Lakeland	1.000	3	1	3	0	0
Poissant, Lakeland	.941	22	7	9	1	0
Rasmussen, Miami	1.000	5	3	6	0	0
Rather, Osceola	.974	27	8	29	1	3
Raubolt, Lakeland	.808	35	9	12	5	1
Ritchie, Clearwater*	1.000	32	6	10	0	0
Ritz, Lakeland	.842	18	3	13	3	0
Roberge, West Palm Beach	.667	9	2	0	1	0
Robertson, West Palm Beach	1.000	7	0	2	0	0
Robinson, Fort Myers	1.000	31	5	10	0	2
Roche, Vero Beach	.800	33	1	11	3	0
Rogers, Tampa*	.962	23	6	19	1	3
Rohan, Miami	.923	15	3	9	1	1
Rojas, Fort Myers	1.000	11	1	5	0	2
Rosenberg, Fort Lauderdale*	1.000	25	0	5	0	0
Sanderski, Winter Haven	1.000	33	5	7	0	0
Scanlan, Clearwater	.853	24	8	21	5	1
Schmidt, Fort Myers	.625	9	3	2	3	0
Schreiber, Osceola*	.971	54	1	32	1	2
Schwartz, Tampa*	.909	19	3	7	1	0
Scott, Vero Beach	.926	20	9	16	2	0
Sepulveda, Vero Beach	1.000	8	1	2	0	0
Service, Clearwater	.875	4	3	4	1	0
Sheehan, Osceola	1.000	7	0	2	0	0
Shimp, Daytona Beach	.750	5	1	2	1	0
Skripko, Winter Haven	1.000	8	5	5	0	1
Slavik, Lakeland*	.815	33	5	17	5	1
Smoltz, Lakeland	.800	18	9	7	4	1
Snediker, Winter Haven	.842	28	5	11	3	1
E. Soto, Daytona Beach	1.000	2	1	0	0	0
O. Soto, Tampa	1.000	4	3	0	0	0
Stewart, Clearwater	.667	2	0	2	1	0
Stottlemyre, Osceola	1.000	9	2	9	0	0
Sudo, West Palm Beach	.947	9	11	7	1	0
Summers, Tampa*	.913	29	3	18	2	0
Swob, Tampa*	1.000	3	3	4	0	0
Taylor, Miami	.973	38	11	25	1	2
Tejeda, Vero Beach*	1.000	5	2	2	0	0
Thomas, Vero Beach	.952	32	8	12	1	2
Tirado, Fort Lauderdale	.900	21	2	7	1	0
Tomsick, St. Petersburg	.857	15	1	5	1	1
Torres, Fort Lauderdale	.938	11	6	9	1	0
Traen, West Palm Beach	1.000	16	4	2	0	0
Trapp, Fort Myers*	1.000	4	2	1	0	0
Trautwein, West Palm Beach	1.000	10	3	4	0	0
Tunison, Clearwater	1.000	4	2	2	0	0
Valdez, West Palm Beach	.871	24	10	17	4	1
Van Vuren, Fort Myers	.889	30	2	6	1	0
J. Vargas, Osceola	.903	24	9	19	3	0
M. Vargas, Clearwater	1.000	2	1	1	0	0
Vasquez, Winter Haven	.938	31	9	21	2	2
Vila, Vero Beach	.833	21	9	11	4	3
Von Ohlen, Miami*	1.000	15	3	14	0	3
Ti. Watkins, Tampa	.800	22	0	4	1	0
Tr. Watkins, Fort Myers	1.000	35	4	11	0	0
Wayne, West Palm Beach*	1.000	47	5	16	0	1
Weatherford, Tampa	1.000	9	1	1	0	0
West, Daytona Beach	.953	26	18	23	2	2
J. Williams, Vero Beach*	.938	30	3	12	1	2
K. Williams, Winter Haven	1.000	5	2	1	0	0
M. Williams, West Palm Beach	.800	10	1	7	2	1
K. Willis, Tampa	1.000	6	1	3	0	0
S. Willis, Tampa	.875	26	1	6	1	0
C. Wilson, Miami	1.000	11	2	7	0	0
R. Wilson, Miami*	.913	32	6	15	2	0
Wisdom, Clearwater*	1.000	7	2	2	0	0
Woyce, Fort Myers	.911	26	13	28	4	3
York, Lakeland	.714	16	1	4	2	2

The following players do not have any recorded accepted chances at the positions indicated: therefore, are not listed in the fielding averages for those particular positions: Allison, p; Arzola, 1b; Baker, p; Bautista, of; Blaser, of; Blum, p; Brown, 1b; Browning, of; D. Clark, p; DeFrancesco, 1b; Donahue, ss; Dulin, of; Edwards, p; Fishel, of; Hauradou, 3b; Hayward, p; Henley, of; Ri. Johnson, of; Juenke, p; Kline, of; Lachowicz, p; Latmore, 2b, 3b; A. Long, 3b; Madden, p, Michel, 3b; Owen, 3b; Petersen, c; Randle, of; Rather, of; Reboulet, 3b; Reker, p; Rivera, p; A. Rodriguez, p; Scurry, p; Silver, c; Thiessen, p; Wakamatsu, 3b; Wallace, 3b; Wieligman, p; Wockenfuss, of, p.

CLUB PITCHING

Club	ERA.	G.	CG.	ShO.	Sv.	IP.	H.	R.	ER.	HR.	HB.	BB.	Int. BB.	SO.	WP.	Bk.
St. Petersburg	2.64	136	22	12	30	1147.2	1066	428	337	26	20	435	38	652	38	6
West Palm Beach	2.77	135	16	21	46	1125.1	934	432	346	43	33	475	15	885	53	16
Winter Haven	3.25	127	14	15	26	1101.0	993	498	397	24	22	538	19	620	46	13
Tampa	3.33	136	34	16	30	1149.0	1074	548	425	34	27	452	37	723	51	14
Clearwater	3.53	137	19	8	35	1154.2	1138	568	453	30	23	494	31	606	46	10
Fort Lauderdale	3.54	139	27	19	27	1178.2	1101	577	464	42	36	603	34	777	60	13
Vero Beach	3.66	138	27	9	28	1149.2	1141	581	467	33	30	575	44	723	80	27
Osceola	3.76	137	20	10	24	1164.2	1217	623	487	36	30	497	26	733	62	12
Miami	3.85	140	15	11	40	1190.2	1197	615	509	35	39	547	67	626	71	13
Fort Myers	4.21	135	27	5	17	1102.0	1130	696	516	43	38	587	19	604	79	13
Lakeland	4.31	133	16	6	26	1130.2	1209	674	541	52	54	530	27	628	72	19
Daytona Beach	5.18	137	12	4	14	1128.2	1261	840	650	54	59	644	23	600	104	18

PITCHERS' RECORDS

(Leading Qualifiers for Earned-Run Average Leadership—112 or More Innings)

*Throws lefthanded.

Pitcher—Club	W.	L.	Pct.	ERA.	G.	GS.	CG.	GF.	ShO.	Sv.	IP.	H.	R.	ER.	HR.	HB.	BB.	Int. BB.	SO.	WP.
Lopez, Tampa	12	5	.706	1.92	22	20	9	1	3	0	150.1	130	51	32	2	3	23	4	97	6
Manzanillo, Winter Haven	13	5	.722	2.27	23	21	3	2	2	0	142.2	110	51	36	3	3	81	0	102	9
Cunningham, W Palm Beach*	10	7	.588	2.37	23	21	3	1	2	1	129.1	94	42	34	8	4	56	1	119	5
Fassero, St. Petersburg*	13	7	.650	2.45	26	26	6	0	1	0	176.0	156	63	48	5	0	56	4	112	5
Valdez, West Palm Beach	16	6	.727	2.47	24	24	6	0	4	0	145.2	119	48	40	9	4	46	0	108	3
Odekirk, Daytona Beach*	5	9	.357	2.62	20	20	7	0	0	0	127.0	125	62	37	9	8	46	0	56	5
Arnold, St. Petersburg	10	5	.667	2.71	22	22	4	0	3	0	136.1	121	57	41	2	4	39	2	85	3
Crouch, Winter Haven*	9	6	.600	2.72	30	19	3	2	1	0	139.0	103	56	42	3	2	64	1	93	4
Hill, St. Petersburg*	10	2	.833	2.76	26	19	2	1	1	0	130.2	123	48	40	6	1	48	1	90	5
Vila, Vero Beach	8	7	.533	2.76	21	12	7	6	2	2	124.0	111	50	38	7	2	36	3	79	5
Kinzer, St. Petersburg	10	7	.588	2.89	22	22	4	0	2	0	134.0	129	49	43	3	4	42	4	80	5

Departmental Leaders: G—Perkins, 59; W—Valdez, 16; L—Meadows, J. Vargas, 13; Pct.—Fischer, Hill, Vasquez, .833; GS—Dunster, Fassero, Johnson, McHugh, 26; CG—Mirabito, 10; GF—Perkins, 44; ShO—Mirabito, Valdez, 4; Sv.—Wayne, 25; IP—Fassero, 176.0; H—Dunster, 185; R—Woyce, 100; ER—Woyce, 79; HR—McHugh, Mirabito, Poissant, 10; HB—Gohmann, 9; BB—Johnson, 94; IBB—Langdon, Taylor, 9; SO—Rather, 151; WP—Guzman, 16.

(All Pitchers—Listed Alphabetically)

Pitcher—Club	W.	L.	Pct.	ERA.	G.	GS.	CG.	GF.	ShO.	Sv.	IP.	H.	R.	ER.	HR.	HB.	BB.	Int. BB.	SO.	WP.
Abril, Winter Haven	2	1	.667	2.45	4	4	0	0	0	0	25.2	21	10	7	0	1	15	0	19	1
Agar, Lakeland	5	4	.556	3.31	42	0	0	37	0	9	73.1	63	34	27	1	4	51	3	57	4
Alfonzo, Miami	1	2	.333	3.16	4	4	1	0	1	0	25.2	19	11	9	1	1	6	0	10	2
Allison, Daytona Beach	0	1	.000	13.50	3	0	0	1	0	0	6.0	8	10	9	0	1	9	0	4	1
Alvarez, Fort Myers	0	0	.000	3.38	1	0	0	0	0	0	2.2	4	1	1	0	0	0	0	1	0
Arnold, St. Petersburg	10	5	.667	2.71	22	22	4	0	3	0	136.1	121	57	41	2	4	39	2	85	3
Arnsberg, Osceola	1	3	.250	4.81	27	1	0	9	0	1	67.1	76	44	36	1	3	39	3	45	9
Ayers, West Palm Beach	2	1	.667	0.92	4	4	0	0	0	0	19.2	14	6	2	0	1	6	0	7	1
Baker, Osceola	0	1	.000	4.50	1	0	0	0	0	0	2.0	1	2	1	0	0	2	0	2	0
Balabon, Fort Lauderdale	4	7	.364	5.64	15	15	1	0	1	0	75.0	81	53	47	6	1	57	1	58	7
Barfield, Daytona Beach*	1	1	.500	4.15	3	3	0	0	0	0	17.1	14	9	8	0	1	1	0	13	0
Bass, Daytona Beach	0	3	.000	6.95	7	4	0	1	0	0	22.0	25	24	17	1	0	20	0	14	2
Befort, Clearwater	0	0	.000	3.00	10	0	0	5	0	2	12.0	8	4	4	1	0	9	2	14	0
Bennett, Clearwater	0	2	.000	3.54	4	3	2	1	0	0	20.1	20	10	8	1	0	8	1	9	0
Blackshear, Clearwater*	1	2	.333	3.00	12	2	1	7	0	4	24.0	30	9	8	0	2	5	1	13	0
Blum, Fort Lauderdale*	0	0	.000	0.00	2	0	0	0	0	0	4.1	7	4	0	0	0	1	0	1	0
Blunt, St. Petersburg	1	2	.333	2.95	3	3	1	0	0	0	21.1	19	8	7	0	0	8	0	12	2
Boroski, Fort Myers	4	7	.364	4.07	27	11	4	5	1	0	95.0	119	72	43	7	3	31	2	38	3
Boudreau, Miami*	2	2	.500	6.35	5	3	0	0	0	0	17.0	24	14	12	0	0	8	2	16	0
Bowden, Miami	1	2	.333	7.27	5	4	1	0	0	0	17.1	18	16	14	1	1	11	2	7	4
Brown, Osceola	0	1	.000	6.75	3	0	0	2	0	0	1.1	2	1	1	0	0	1	0	0	0
Browne, Miami*	2	1	.667	4.13	11	10	0	0	0	0	48.0	52	26	22	2	2	30	6	14	4
Browning, Miami	8	3	.727	2.64	51	2	0	33	0	8	85.1	78	30	25	4	3	35	7	62	5
Bryan, Daytona Beach	0	1	.000	2.57	6	0	0	3	0	0	14.0	17	8	4	0	1	3	0	5	0
Busick, Daytona Beach	2	5	.286	7.04	24	6	0	6	0	0	46.0	51	46	36	1	2	45	3	31	8
Camp, Osceola*	1	1	.500	4.39	16	1	0	5	0	1	41.0	44	23	20	1	3	17	1	20	2
Carista, Winter Haven	0	0	.000	0.00	1	0	0	0	0	0	2.0	3	0	0	0	0	0	0	1	0
Carreno, Fort Lauderdale	1	1	.500	4.02	3	3	1	0	0	0	15.2	16	11	7	0	0	7	1	8	3
Carroll, Fort Lauderdale	5	4	.556	3.52	48	0	0	35	0	10	61.1	61	43	24	0	5	39	4	38	6
Carson, St. Petersburg	10	5	.667	3.35	26	18	2	5	0	0	96.2	95	53	36	1	2	63	2	35	4
Cash, Osceola	3	0	1.000	1.03	26	0	0	24	0	11	26.1	25	7	3	1	1	10	1	17	1
Cecena, Clearwater	8	4	.667	3.34	22	15	2	3	0	0	110.1	97	49	41	6	1	44	2	66	3
Cerny, Daytona Beach*	1	7	.125	4.73	20	8	2	10	1	2	51.1	57	32	27	3	0	26	3	35	5
Chambers, Clearwater	5	7	.417	3.19	41	9	0	22	0	4	101.2	79	41	36	3	3	57	3	78	6
Cherry, Vero Beach	1	3	.250	6.23	8	6	0	1	0	0	26.0	42	23	18	2	2	13	0	9	1
Christopher, Fort Lauderdale	7	3	.700	2.63	15	14	3	0	1	0	102.2	92	37	30	2	1	36	0	56	1
Clark, Fort Lauderdale*	0	0	.000	0.00	1	0	0	1	0	0	1.0	0	0	0	0	0	1	0	0	0
Clarkin, Winter Haven	4	7	.364	3.94	33	6	0	20	0	9	77.2	63	42	34	1	5	33	2	51	4
Collins, West Palm Beach	4	2	.667	3.75	26	4	1	8	0	1	57.2	52	28	24	2	1	31	1	36	5
Concepcion, Miami	0	0	.000	18.36	6	0	0	1	0	0	8.1	10	17	17	0	5	18	0	3	2
Cook, West Palm Beach	0	1	.000	0.87	6	0	0	3	0	1	10.1	5	1	1	0	0	4	1	5	0
Cooper, Lakeland	6	2	.750	3.91	12	12	1	0	0	0	71.1	74	38	31	3	6	26	0	40	4
Costello, St. Petersburg	8	2	.800	2.39	15	12	2	2	1	1	71.2	65	21	19	1	2	24	1	32	0
Cox, Vero Beach*	9	11	.450	4.42	26	25	5	0	0	0	152.2	164	86	75	6	2	79	8	80	8
Crouch, Winter Haven*	9	6	.600	2.72	30	19	3	2	1	0	139.0	103	56	42	3	2	64	1	93	4
Cunningham, W Palm Beach*	10	7	.588	2.37	23	21	3	1	2	1	129.1	94	42	34	8	4	56	1	119	5
Dale, Tampa	5	4	.556	2.80	36	5	1	13	1	3	93.1	87	36	29	2	3	24	4	43	3
Davidson, Fort Lauderdale	4	2	.667	3.99	16	7	1	3	0	0	58.2	65	36	26	2	1	22	4	37	2
DeJesus, Fort Myers	4	9	.308	3.44	22	22	1	0	0	0	110.0	87	64	42	4	4	82	1	97	8
Devine, Vero Beach	2	0	1.000	1.17	5	0	0	1	0	1	15.1	5	3	2	0	0	8	0	14	0
Devlin, West Palm Beach	2	4	.333	3.16	39	2	0	17	0	11	85.1	80	37	30	1	4	30	3	52	2
Dixon, West Palm Beach	5	7	.417	3.36	43	0	0	21	0	4	75.0	66	36	28	1	4	22	0	45	1
Dopson, West Palm Beach	2	0	1.000	0.00	2	2	0	0	0	0	10.2	8	0	0	0	1	4	0	8	0
Dotson, Miami	0	1	.000	7.27	3	3	0	0	0	0	8.2	10	7	7	1	0	8	0	5	1
Dougherty, West Palm Beach	3	1	.750	4.38	7	2	0	3	0	0	24.2	24	14	12	4	0	10	0	22	1
Dunster, Osceola	10	9	.526	4.06	26	26	3	0	2	0	157.1	185	92	71	6	5	41	0	78	6
Durocher, Osceola	0	2	.000	7.03	27	0	0	15	0	1	24.1	35	25	19	0	2	14	2	17	0
Edwards, Miami	0	0	.000	0.00	3	0	0	2	0	0	4.1	4	1	0	0	1	2	0	1	0
Ellis, Fort Myers	6	10	.375	3.92	34	10	3	15	0	2	98.2	86	53	43	5	5	69	4	50	12
Estes, Miami*	0	1	.000	4.73	5	0	0	1	0	0	13.1	11	7	7	0	1	9	1	4	3
Evers, Fort Lauderdale	1	0	1.000	0.00	1	0	0	0	0	0	2.2	2	0	0	0	0	0	0	1	0
Farwell, Vero Beach*	8	5	.615	3.65	22	19	5	3	0	0	123.1	117	58	50	5	3	36	2	62	5
Fassero, St. Petersburg*	13	7	.650	2.45	26	26	6	0	1	0	176.0	156	63	48	5	0	56	4	112	5
Fedor, West Palm Beach	0	0	.000	0.00	1	0	0	0	0	0	1.0	0	0	0	0	0	2	0	0	0
Fischer, West Palm Beach	10	2	.833	1.44	14	14	2	0	2	0	93.2	74	24	15	1	0	20	2	64	2
Frohwirth, Clearwater	3	3	.500	3.98	32	0	0	23	0	10	52.0	54	29	23	1	2	18	2	39	2
Gay, Fort Lauderdale	1	1	.500	3.02	8	8	0	0	0	0	41.2	31	18	14	1	2	30	0	24	3
George, Fort Lauderdale*	6	6	.500	3.22	15	14	6	1	2	0	89.1	83	40	32	4	0	47	1	48	2
Gilbert, Miami*	6	6	.500	3.88	19	17	2	0	0	0	104.1	110	58	45	4	0	44	8	57	3
Giron, Fort Lauderdale	0	1	.000	4.73	7	0	0	4	0	0	13.1	10	8	7	2	0	8	0	6	0
Gohmann, Lakeland	3	4	.429	3.06	32	12	3	13	1	4	123.2	128	58	42	5	9	39	5	59	2
Goodenough, Fort Myers*	0	0	.000	0.00	1	0	0	1	0	0	3.0	1	0	0	0	0	2	0	1	0
Goodin, Fort Myers*	0	2	.000	3.00	2	1	0	1	0	0	9.0	9	5	3	0	0	2	1	8	2
Graybill, West Palm Beach	5	5	.500	3.03	18	17	0	0	0	0	77.1	62	28	26	4	1	32	0	46	4
Guercio, Fort Lauderdale	8	3	.727	2.82	37	6	2	15	0	3	95.2	78	35	30	4	1	40	3	45	6
Guzman, Vero Beach	10	9	.526	3.49	26	24	3	0	0	0	131.1	114	69	51	3	4	90	4	96	16
Hammond, Tampa*	0	2	.000	3.32	5	5	0	0	0	0	21.2	25	8	8	0	1	13	1	5	1
Harden, Daytona Beach	4	9	.308	4.24	53	2	0	41	0	8	80.2	100	57	38	1	2	53	2	49	10
Harrington, Miami	6	2	.750	1.74	15	9	0	3	0	0	67.1	55	17	13	0	1	37	3	44	5
Harris, West Palm Beach	0	0	.000	4.09	2	2	0	0	0	0	11.0	14	7	5	0	0	7	0	5	0
Harrison, Fort Lauderdale*	8	3	.727	3.74	15	15	4	0	3	0	91.1	95	43	38	4	1	32	1	47	3
Hayward, Tampa	0	3	.000	12.12	6	4	0	0	0	0	16.1	29	24	22	0	0	16	0	8	3
Hearn, Miami	1	1	.500	1.35	12	0	0	6	0	0	20.0	22	9	3	0	0	13	1	9	2
Hellman, Fort Lauderdale	4	3	.571	4.42	30	1	0	10	0	3	55.0	53	30	27	3	3	33	5	46	4
Heredia, Osceola	1	4	.200	4.91	9	7	0	0	0	0	33.0	33	20	18	0	0	26	0	16	4
Hernandez, Vero Beach	1	3	.250	3.77	16	4	1	5	0	0	43.0	47	23	18	0	0	19	1	25	2
Herzog, St. Petersburg*	7	5	.583	2.08	46	0	0	30	0	10	56.1	56	19	13	1	0	16	7	31	1
Hill, St. Petersburg*	10	2	.833	2.76	26	19	2	1	1	0	130.2	123	48	40	6	1	48	1	90	5
Hilton, St. Petersburg	4	5	.444	2.44	36	1	0	19	0	3	62.2	53	21	17	1	1	28	5	49	0
Hixon, Miami	0	2	.000	8.27	4	4	0	0	0	0	16.1	25	16	15	0	0	8	0	4	1
Holm, Miami*	1	1	.500	3.97	14	0	0	4	0	1	22.2	30	14	10	2	0	12	4	17	1
Holmes, Vero Beach	3	6	.333	2.92	11	10	0	1	0	0	64.2	55	30	21	0	3	39	2	59	5

Pitcher—Club	W.	L.	Pct.	ERA.	G.	GS.	CG.	GF.	ShO.	Sv.	IP.	H.	R.	ER.	HR.	HB.	BB.	Int. BB.	SO.	WP.
Hook, Osceola*	0	1	.000	3.60	1	1	0	0	0	0	5.0	7	3	2	0	0	2	0	4	0
Hoover, Miami	0	1	.000	22.09	2	2	0	0	0	0	3.2	10	10	9	0	0	8	0	3	0
Huchingson, Osceola	1	2	.333	4.60	16	6	0	7	0	0	47.0	61	33	24	3	0	20	1	20	0
Hull, Fort Myers	2	11	.154	4.73	24	17	2	3	0	0	99.0	115	78	52	3	8	65	1	52	12
Hume, Clearwater	0	1	.000	3.00	9	2	0	4	0	0	24.0	20	13	8	1	0	8	0	15	0
Ilsley, Osceola*	8	4	.667	1.77	14	13	6	1	2	0	86.2	67	24	17	1	0	19	0	74	6
Irvine, Winter Haven	9	8	.529	3.19	26	24	3	0	0	0	161.0	162	73	57	2	7	67	3	73	13
Jacobsen, Vero Beach	5	10	.333	3.12	44	0	0	34	0	14	69.1	59	33	24	3	1	41	8	61	3
James, Daytona Beach	3	2	.600	6.21	34	3	0	12	0	1	66.2	75	52	46	2	4	52	2	32	7
Jefferson, Tampa	4	2	.667	2.37	31	0	0	22	0	12	57.0	48	17	15	0	0	25	7	62	2
Jester, Clearwater*	2	7	.222	3.97	36	2	0	18	0	3	88.1	93	44	39	2	1	25	4	25	2
John, Fort Lauderdale*	2	0	1.000	0.00	3	3	1	0	1	0	13.2	7	2	0	0	1	1	0	7	0
Johnson, West Palm Beach*	8	7	.533	3.16	26	26	2	0	1	0	119.2	89	49	42	3	6	94	0	133	13
Jones, Daytona Beach	2	11	.154	5.08	25	18	1	1	0	0	106.1	117	79	60	7	8	60	3	59	6
Juenke, Miami*	0	0	.000	0.00	6	0	0	4	0	0	8.0	8	5	0	0	0	1	0	3	0
Keathley, Daytona Beach	2	2	.500	3.57	6	5	0	0	0	0	35.1	36	17	14	0	0	14	0	15	1
Kelly, West Palm Beach	1	0	1.000	5.02	8	0	0	4	0	1	14.1	11	8	8	0	0	14	0	14	1
Kinzer, St. Petersburg	10	7	.588	2.89	22	22	4	0	2	0	134.0	129	49	43	3	4	42	4	80	5
Knox, Clearwater	10	11	.476	3.32	21	20	3	0	1	0	138.1	148	68	51	4	4	41	5	64	3
Labozzetta, Lakeland*	5	5	.500	3.23	10	10	1	0	1	0	64.0	61	28	23	1	0	17	0	33	4
Lachowicz, Clearwater	0	0	.000	81.00	1	1	0	0	0	0	0.1	3	3	3	0	0	3	0	0	3
Langdon, Tampa	5	4	.556	2.47	48	0	0	29	0	7	76.2	51	31	21	2	7	60	9	67	7
Larsen, Daytona Beach	1	6	.143	8.69	29	3	0	6	0	0	48.2	68	55	47	2	7	43	0	20	13
Laseke, Winter Haven	1	0	1.000	0.00	2	0	0	2	0	0	2.0	1	0	0	0	0	1	0	0	0
Layana, Fort Lauderdale	5	4	.556	2.24	11	10	3	1	1	1	68.1	59	19	17	1	4	19	1	52	5
B. Lee, Fort Myers*	0	1	.000	1.93	6	2	0	4	0	0	18.2	9	4	4	1	0	13	0	7	0
M. Lee, Lakeland*	2	5	.286	5.17	41	0	0	31	0	10	62.2	73	44	36	4	2	21	8	39	5
A. Leiter, Fort Lauderdale*	4	8	.333	4.05	22	21	1	0	1	0	117.2	96	64	53	2	5	90	1	101	7
K. Leiter, Miami	0	2	.000	6.97	7	0	0	2	0	0	10.1	11	10	8	1	0	8	0	8	1
Linton, Daytona Beach*	0	2	.000	6.87	8	3	0	1	0	0	18.1	19	18	14	1	1	15	0	7	1
Livin, Osceola	8	10	.444	3.97	26	23	4	1	1	0	147.1	156	80	65	7	2	53	0	60	2
Llanes, Miami	7	9	.438	4.87	21	21	2	0	0	0	114.2	126	69	62	3	3	66	5	44	4
Lockhart, Winter Haven*	4	5	.444	3.68	34	1	0	20	0	5	66.0	69	30	27	2	0	31	2	36	1
Long, Clearwater	2	2	.500	4.28	8	6	0	2	0	0	33.2	33	19	16	0	2	20	0	16	2
Lono, Tampa*	12	3	.800	3.14	19	19	6	0	1	0	126.0	141	51	44	8	0	22	1	74	0
Lopez, Tampa	12	5	.706	1.92	22	20	9	1	3	0	150.1	130	51	32	2	3	23	4	97	6
LoSauro, Daytona Beach	3	4	.429	3.28	50	1	0	23	0	2	79.2	82	47	29	2	3	43	5	36	8
Madden, Clearwater*	0	2	.000	5.40	4	3	0	0	0	0	15.0	16	11	9	2	0	9	0	4	2
Magistri, Winter Haven*	2	0	1.000	6.26	29	3	0	12	0	3	50.1	48	40	35	2	1	35	1	32	3
Mandich, Miami	0	1	.000	7.56	3	2	0	1	0	0	8.1	10	7	7	0	0	8	0	8	0
Mangham, St. Petersburg	5	3	.625	1.47	24	2	0	15	0	2	49.0	43	14	8	1	1	11	2	16	1
Manzanillo, Winter Haven	13	5	.722	2.27	23	21	3	2	2	0	142.2	110	51	36	3	3	81	0	102	9
Mason, St. Petersburg	0	1	.000	4.26	4	1	1	0	0	0	12.2	16	7	6	0	0	5	0	6	0
McClear, Fort Lauderdale	4	4	.500	3.36	33	0	0	18	0	3	56.1	52	25	21	2	3	36	6	30	0
McDevitt, Clearwater	3	2	.600	3.89	12	4	1	1	0	0	39.1	30	18	17	3	1	31	0	18	0
McGrath, St. Petersburg	2	2	.500	2.52	33	0	0	12	0	5	53.2	46	17	15	1	3	41	7	36	2
McHugh, Lakeland	8	10	.444	3.54	26	26	6	0	2	0	165.1	174	81	65	10	3	50	3	100	12
McKelvey, Fort Myers	2	6	.250	5.13	13	8	1	0	0	0	54.1	46	37	31	1	4	35	0	49	2
Meadows, Daytona Beach	2	13	.133	5.55	24	23	0	1	0	0	121.2	145	94	75	9	8	51	0	67	9
Meads, Osceola*	2	4	.333	7.63	11	0	0	8	0	1	15.1	24	14	13	0	1	7	2	10	1
Mena, Vero Beach	3	3	.500	3.46	6	6	3	0	1	0	39.0	36	17	15	0	0	22	0	23	4
Menard, Osceola	3	2	.600	2.47	29	1	0	11	0	0	51.0	53	16	14	3	1	19	7	45	3
Milacki, Miami	4	4	.500	3.74	12	11	0	0	0	0	67.1	70	36	28	1	2	27	2	41	6
Miller, Clearwater*	9	10	.474	3.06	29	24	3	1	1	1	156.0	173	82	53	1	0	62	2	51	5
Minnema, Lakeland	2	1	.667	3.14	6	6	2	0	0	0	43.0	40	18	15	2	1	13	1	19	1
Mirabito, Tampa	13	10	.565	3.42	26	25	10	1	4	0	165.2	160	83	63	10	2	39	2	80	3
Morse, Daytona Beach	2	4	.333	5.55	10	10	0	0	0	0	47.0	43	32	29	4	3	25	1	51	3
Mortimer, Daytona Beach*	1	2	.333	6.28	34	3	0	12	0	1	61.2	65	49	43	4	2	42	3	36	1
Mulligan, Fort Myers*	4	5	.444	4.31	42	0	0	32	0	8	56.1	59	35	27	2	1	22	0	41	3
Murray, St. Petersburg	3	1	.750	3.15	24	0	0	19	0	8	34.1	35	14	12	1	0	12	3	15	0
Newell, Clearwater	5	3	.625	2.85	22	12	1	4	0	0	85.1	68	35	27	1	0	46	2	64	4
Nielsen, Fort Lauderdale	4	0	1.000	2.10	6	5	2	0	2	0	34.1	32	12	8	0	1	9	0	10	1
North, St. Petersburg	4	0	1.000	1.95	18	8	0	7	0	0	64.2	57	18	14	2	2	23	0	31	10
Nunez, Fort Myers	8	2	.800	2.47	14	13	5	0	0	0	87.1	73	31	24	1	1	32	0	59	10
Odekirk, Daytona Beach*	5	9	.357	2.62	20	20	7	0	0	0	127.0	125	62	37	9	8	46	0	56	5
Pardo, Daytona Beach	0	1	.000	4.50	5	2	0	2	0	0	14.0	9	10	7	0	2	14	0	10	4
Parkins, Winter Haven	6	3	.667	2.76	25	8	1	11	0	3	75.0	70	33	23	2	0	35	2	39	2
G. Patterson, Daytona Beach	0	1	.000	14.90	10	0	0	0	0	0	9.2	21	29	16	0	2	15	0	7	2
K. Patterson, Fort Lauderdale*	0	2	.000	7.71	5	5	0	0	0	0	18.2	30	20	16	2	3	16	0	13	2
Pena, Vero Beach	0	2	.000	7.47	4	4	0	0	0	0	15.2	22	15	13	1	1	4	0	11	1
Perkins, Miami	9	2	.818	3.23	59	0	0	44	0	24	97.2	92	40	35	3	7	36	4	49	3
Petitt, St. Petersburg	0	0	.000	5.40	3	1	0	0	0	0	11.2	12	7	7	1	0	5	0	6	0
Petry, Lakeland	1	1	.500	6.97	3	3	0	0	0	0	10.1	13	8	8	0	2	1	0	6	0
Poissant, Lakeland	7	11	.389	5.99	22	22	1	0	0	0	112.2	128	93	75	10	8	74	0	67	8
Rasmussen, Miami	1	4	.200	2.92	5	5	3	0	0	0	37.0	23	15	12	1	1	11	0	26	1
Rather, Osceola	12	9	.571	3.21	27	25	4	1	1	0	171.0	154	77	61	2	1	82	1	151	10
Raubolt, Lakeland	1	8	.111	5.82	35	0	0	14	0	1	77.1	95	64	50	2	5	46	5	42	10
Reker, Fort Lauderdale*	0	0	.000	0.00	1	0	0	0	0	0	0.0	0	0	0	0	0	1	0	0	0
Ritchie, Clearwater*	4	1	.800	2.22	32	0	0	22	0	10	52.2	40	15	13	0	0	16	2	39	2
Ritz, Lakeland	3	9	.250	5.57	18	15	0	2	0	1	85.2	114	60	53	3	2	45	1	39	6
Rivera, Daytona Beach	0	0	.000	27.00	1	0	0	0	0	0	2.0	6	6	6	0	0	2	0	0	2
Roberge, West Palm Beach	0	0	.000	3.95	9	0	0	4	0	2	13.2	12	8	6	2	0	2	0	20	1
Robertson, West Palm Beach	0	0	.000	5.19	7	0	0	3	0	0	17.1	22	15	10	3	0	10	0	7	1
Robinson, Fort Myers	3	5	.375	5.11	31	5	1	9	0	0	86.1	110	60	49	3	1	30	0	32	3
Roche, Vero Beach	4	4	.500	4.82	33	4	0	17	0	3	84.0	101	53	45	1	5	33	3	42	8
Rodriguez, West Palm Beach	0	0	.000	3.86	7	0	0	2	0	0	11.2	13	5	5	0	2	6	0	8	1
Rogers, Tampa*	4	6	.400	3.89	23	19	0	3	0	0	90.1	78	53	39	2	5	75	0	88	14
Rohan, Miami	6	3	.667	2.75	15	11	2	1	1	0	75.1	73	31	23	2	3	29	3	37	5
Rojas, Fort Myers	2	5	.286	3.96	11	10	2	0	0	0	52.1	58	34	23	2	0	21	0	33	2
Rosenberg, Fort Lauderdale*	6	1	.857	2.12	25	0	0	15	0	3	29.2	24	7	7	1	0	18	1	26	1
Sanderski, Winter Haven	4	6	.400	2.91	33	7	0	19	0	4	86.2	80	41	28	1	1	49	2	42	4
Scanlan, Clearwater	8	12	.400	4.15	24	22	5	0	0	0	125.2	146	73	58	1	5	45	4	51	4

Pitcher—Club	W.	L.	Pct.	ERA.	G.	GS.	CG.	GF.	ShO.	Sv.	IP.	H.	R.	ER.	HR.	HB.	BB.	Int. BB.	SO.	WP.
Schmidt, Fort Myers	3	1	.750	4.76	9	4	0	0	0	0	28.1	23	18	15	1	1	24	1	9	0
Schreiber, Osceola*	1	5	.167	2.78	54	1	0	31	0	9	87.1	81	30	27	1	2	41	6	45	1
Schwartz, Tampa*	4	7	.364	5.66	19	13	1	2	0	0	76.1	74	53	48	7	0	30	2	50	4
Scott, Vero Beach	5	4	.556	3.40	20	13	3	2	1	0	95.1	113	44	36	2	2	34	2	37	5
Scurry, Fort Lauderdale*	1	0	1.000	3.68	7	0	0	3	0	1	7.1	7	3	3	0	1	7	0	16	1
Sepulveda, Vero Beach	1	0	1.000	9.26	8	0	0	3	0	0	11.2	14	12	12	0	2	16	1	6	1
Service, Clearwater	1	2	.333	3.20	4	4	1	0	1	0	25.1	20	10	9	2	0	15	0	19	1
Sheehan, Osceola	1	0	1.000	2.77	7	0	0	2	0	0	13.0	8	4	4	0	0	5	0	7	1
Shimp, Daytona Beach	2	2	.500	7.88	5	4	1	1	1	0	24.0	33	25	21	2	2	24	0	9	9
Skripko, Winter Haven	6	0	1.000	1.58	8	7	0	1	0	0	40.0	32	7	7	1	0	16	0	15	1
Slavik, Lakeland*	3	8	.273	4.30	33	13	0	7	0	0	104.2	111	62	50	2	4	73	1	51	5
Smoltz, Lakeland	7	8	.467	3.56	17	14	2	0	1	0	96.0	86	44	38	7	5	31	0	47	2
Snediker, Winter Haven	4	3	.571	4.97	28	3	0	17	0	0	58.0	70	40	32	1	1	34	3	17	3
E. Soto, Daytona Beach	0	1	.000	11.81	2	1	0	0	0	0	5.1	7	9	7	0	1	5	0	2	0
O. Soto, Tampa	1	2	.333	3.68	4	3	1	1	0	0	22.0	21	11	9	0	0	9	1	5	1
Stewart, Clearwater	0	0	.000	9.00	2	1	0	1	0	0	5.0	8	5	5	1	0	4	0	2	1
Stottlemyre, Osceola	0	7	.000	7.82	9	8	0	0	0	0	35.2	48	38	31	3	1	26	0	25	5
Sudo, West Palm Beach	5	1	.833	1.15	9	9	1	0	0	0	62.2	38	12	8	0	3	17	2	53	2
Summers, Tampa*	5	4	.556	3.45	29	13	2	2	1	1	99.0	93	53	38	0	2	39	3	42	3
Swob, Tampa*	2	1	.667	1.33	3	3	2	0	2	0	20.1	8	4	3	0	0	6	1	13	0
Taylor, Miami	7	8	.467	3.87	38	14	0	4	0	1	142.0	145	70	61	6	3	36	9	57	6
Tejeda, Vero Beach*	3	1	.750	0.85	5	5	0	0	0	0	31.2	31	7	3	1	0	7	0	28	0
Thiessen, West Palm Beach	0	0	.000	0.00	1	0	0	1	0	0	1.0	0	0	0	0	0	0	0	0	0
Thomas, Vero Beach	4	1	.800	2.44	32	0	0	22	0	8	62.2	63	23	17	1	2	32	8	51	8
Tirado, Fort Lauderdale	3	4	.429	3.88	21	4	0	4	0	2	65.0	68	36	28	4	1	26	2	57	3
Tomsick, St. Petersburg	1	1	.500	2.75	15	1	0	4	0	1	36.0	40	12	11	0	0	14	0	16	0
Torres, Fort Lauderdale	2	2	.500	4.35	11	8	2	2	1	1	60.0	52	31	29	2	2	27	3	50	3
Traen, West Palm Beach*	2	1	.667	2.61	16	3	0	4	0	0	38.0	31	14	11	0	1	21	2	44	3
Trapp, Fort Myers*	2	1	.667	0.00	4	0	0	4	0	0	5.0	6	2	0	0	0	5	2	6	0
Trautwein, West Palm Beach	1	2	.333	5.82	10	0	0	6	0	0	17.0	23	12	11	0	0	6	0	13	4
Tunison, Clearwater	0	0	.000	4.15	4	0	0	3	0	0	4.1	6	4	2	0	0	4	0	3	2
Valdez, West Palm Beach	16	6	.727	2.47	24	24	6	0	4	0	145.2	119	48	40	9	4	46	0	108	3
Van Vuren, Fort Myers	3	4	.429	3.97	30	4	2	15	0	1	79.1	66	44	35	1	4	49	2	47	3
J. Vargas, Osceola	7	13	.350	3.83	24	24	3	0	1	0	152.2	157	90	65	7	8	73	2	97	11
M. Vargas, Clearwater	0	0	.000	0.00	2	0	0	1	0	1	3.2	2	0	0	0	0	0	0	5	0
Vasquez, Winter Haven	15	3	.833	3.39	31	22	4	6	1	2	159.1	145	65	60	6	1	58	3	92	0
Vila, Vero Beach	8	7	.533	2.76	21	12	7	6	2	2	124.0	111	50	38	7	2	36	3	79	5
Von Ohlen, Miami*	6	2	.750	1.62	15	8	2	6	2	1	61.0	54	14	11	3	1	17	2	32	1
Ti. Watkins, Tampa	3	3	.500	4.93	22	3	0	11	0	1	45.2	47	37	25	0	1	31	1	33	3
Tr. Watkins, Fort Myers	1	6	.143	5.42	35	4	2	18	0	5	79.2	87	58	48	3	1	54	5	24	12
Wayne, West Palm Beach*	2	5	.286	1.61	47	0	0	41	0	25	61.1	48	16	11	1	1	25	2	55	3
Weatherford, Tampa	0	0	.000	2.87	9	0	0	2	0	0	15.2	17	7	5	0	0	11	1	14	0
West, Daytona Beach	9	10	.474	4.57	26	18	1	4	0	0	124.0	138	70	63	6	1	36	1	42	7
Wieligman, Miami*	0	0	.000	0.00	1	0	0	0	0	0	0.0	2	3	3	0	0	1	0	0	1
J. Williams, Vero Beach*	1	1	.500	4.35	30	6	0	16	0	0	60.0	47	35	29	1	1	66	2	40	8
K. Williams, Winter Haven	1	0	1.000	5.17	5	2	0	1	0	0	15.2	16	10	9	0	0	19	0	8	1
M. Williams, West Palm Beach	2	3	.400	5.60	10	5	1	1	0	0	27.1	35	22	17	4	0	10	1	21	0
K. Willis, Tampa	4	0	1.000	1.55	6	4	2	1	2	0	29.0	22	6	5	0	2	5	0	12	1
S. Willis, Tampa	5	1	.833	4.12	26	0	0	14	0	6	43.2	43	23	20	1	1	24	0	30	0
C. Wilson, Miami	3	2	.600	5.23	11	7	2	1	1	1	43.0	41	29	25	0	0	24	4	20	2
R. Wilson, Miami*	3	4	.429	3.39	32	3	0	11	0	4	61.0	57	30	23	0	3	34	4	45	7
Wisdom, Clearwater*	2	3	.400	5.54	7	7	0	0	0	0	37.1	44	26	23	0	2	24	1	11	4
Wockenfuss, Miami	0	0	.000	10.13	2	0	0	1	0	0	2.2	7	3	3	0	1	0	0	0	1
Woyce, Fort Myers	6	10	.375	5.19	26	24	4	1	1	1	137.0	172	100	79	9	5	51	0	50	7
York, Lakeland	1	3	.250	6.42	16	0	0	13	0	1	40.2	49	42	29	2	3	43	0	29	9

BALKS—Odekirk, Smoltz, 6 each; Scott, Valdez, Vasquez, 5 each; Johnson, Mirabito, J. Williams, 4 each; Balabon, Cunningham, DeJesus, Fassero, Gohmann, Hernandez, Jacobsen, Lopez, Meadows, Robinson, Sepulveda, Taylor, Thomas, 3 each; Cecena, Cerny, Cox, Crouch, Dunster, Ellis, Gilbert, Guzman, Harrison, Hull, Kinzer, Livin, McHugh, Minnema, Morse, Rather, Raubolt, Rodriguez, Slavik, Snediker, Summers, Wisdom, 2 each; Agar, Alfonzo, Bennett, Blackshear, Browning, Bryan, Busick, Camp, Carson, Cherry, Christopher, Clarkin, Concepcion, Davidson, Graybill, Guercio, Harden, Hearn, Holm, Hume, Ilsley, Irvine, James, Jefferson, Langdon, Layana, B. Lee, A. Leiter, Lono, Magistri, McDevitt, Menard, Mulligan, Parkins, Perkins, Poissant, Rohan, Rosenberg, Scanlan, Schreiber, Scurry, Service, Stottlemyre, Swob, Torres, Van Vuren, J. Vargas, Vila, Wayne, Weatherford, West, R. Wilson, 1 each.

COMBINATION SHUTOUTS—Chambers-Ritchie, Long-Ritchie-Frohwirth, Knox-Ritchie-Frohwirth, Knox-Ritchie, McDevitt-Jester, Clearwater; Meadows-James, West-LoSauro, Daytona Beach; Christopher-Carroll, Balabon-McClear-Carroll, Balabon-Guercio-Carroll, Leiter-Guercio, Gay-Guercio, Gay-Evers-Rosenberg, Fort Lauderdale; DeJesus-Mulligan, Nunez-Watkins, Rojas-Woyce, Fort Myers; McHugh-Gohmann-Slavik, Lakeland; Llanes-Browning, Harrington-Browning, Harrington-Perkins, Harrington-R. Wilson, Rohan-R. Wilson, Gilbert-Perkins, Miami; Rather-Meads, Ilsley-Livin, Ilsley-Menard-Schreiber, Osceola; Carson-Hilton-Herzog-Murray, North-Herzog, Kinzer-Herzog-Murphy-McGrath, Costello-Tomsick, St. Petersburg; Mirabito-Jefferson, Rogers-Langdon, Tampa; Holmes-Roche, Tejada-Farwell, Holmes-Vila, Farwell-Jacobsen, Guzman-Hernandez-Jacobsen, Vero Beach; Valdez-Wayne, Dopson-Cunningham, Johnson-Dixon, Dopson-Devlin, Graybill-Devlin, Johnson-Devlin, Valdez-Cunningham-Dixon-Wayne, Graybill-Traen, Graybill-Wayne, Sudo-Devlin, Sudo-Dixon, Cunningham-Devlin, West Palm Beach; Manzanillo-Lockhart-Clarkin 2, Abril-Sanderski, Crouch-Clarkin, Skripko-Lockhart, Vasquez-Sanderski, Crouch-Sanderski-Magistri-Snediker, Parkins-Sanderski, Crouch-Sanderski, Parkins-Snediker, Vasquez-Clarkin, Winter Haven.

NO-HIT GAME—Crouch, Winter Haven, defeated Miami, 4-0, August 2.

Midwest League

CLASS A

CHAMPIONSHIP WINNERS IN PREVIOUS YEARS

Year	Club	Pct.
1947	Belleville	.667
	Belleville	.672
1948	West Frankfort*	.708
1949	Centralia	.627
	Paducah (4th)†	.454
1950	Centralia‡	.675
1951	Paris§	.700
	Danville (4th)†	.432
1952	Danville x	.685
	Decatur (3rd)†	.584
1953	Decatur*	.576
1954	Decatur	.587
	Danville (2nd)‡	.528
1955	Dubuque*	.587
1956	Paris y	.656
	Dubuque	.603
1957	Decatur y	.683
	Clinton	.623
1958	Michigan City	.623
	Waterloo z	.613
1959	Waterloo	.613
	Waterloo	.613
1960	Waterloo	.629
	Waterloo	.677
1961	Waterloo	.613
	Quincy z	.594
1962	Dubuque z	.667
	Waterloo	.625
1963	Clinton	.710
	Clinton	.629
1964	Clinton	.667
	Fox Cities z	.667
1965	Burlington	.667
	Burlington	.677
1966	Fox Cities z	.689
	Cedar Rapids	.762
1967	Wisconsin Rapids	.685
	Appleton z	.587
1968	Decatur	.656
	Quad Cities z	.648
1969	Appleton	.648
	Appleton	.690
1970	Quincy z	.691
	Quad Cities	.581
1971	Appleton	.642
	Quad Cities a	.548
1972	Appleton	.598
	Danville a	.584
1973	Wisconsin Rapids a	.562
	Danville	.537
1974	Appleton	.593
	Danville a	.517
1975	Waterloo a	.727
	Quad Cities	.624
1976	Waterloo a	.600
	Cedar Rapids	.595
1977	Waterloo	.580
	Burlington a	.511
1978	Appleton a	.708
	Burlington	.500
1979	Waterloo	.600
	Quad Cities a	.579
1980	Waterloo a	.610
	Quad Cities	.532
1981	Wausau a	.636
	Quad Cities	.570
1982	Madison	.626
	Appleton b	.579
1983	Appleton c	.635
	Springfield	.576
1984	Appleton c	.640
	Springfield	.504
1985	Kenosha b	.568
	Peoria	.536

*Won championship and four-club playoff. †Won four-club playoff. ‡Playoff finals canceled because of bad weather. §Won both halves of split-season. xWon first half of split-season and tied Paris for second-half title. yWon first-half title and four-team playoff. zWon split-season playoff. aLeague divided into Northern and Southern divisions and played split-season. Playoff winner. bLeague divided into Northern, Central and Southern. Playoff winner. cLeague divided into Northern, Central and Southern divisions; regular-season and playoff winner. (NOTE—Known as Illinois State League in 1947-48 and Mississippi-Ohio Valley League from 1949 through 1955.)

STANDING OF CLUBS AT CLOSE OF SEASON, SEPTEMBER 1

NORTHERN DIVISION

Club	W.	L.	T.	Pct.	G.B.
Madison (A's)	86	54	0	.614	....
Wausau (Mariners)	73	66	0	.525	12½
Appleton (White Sox)	56	83	0	.403	29½
Kenosha (Twins)	46	92	0	.333	39

CENTRAL DIVISION

Club	W.	L.	T.	Pct.	G.B.
Waterloo (Indians)	78	62	0	.557	....
Beloit (Brewers)	70	69	0	.504	7½
Cedar Rapids (Reds)	70	70	0	.500	8
Clinton (Giants)	63	76	0	.453	14½

SOUTHERN DIVISION

Club	W.	L.	T.	Pct.	G.B.
Springfield (Cardinals)	87	53	0	.621	....
Peoria (Cubs)	77	63	0	.550	10
Burlington (Expos)	69	71	0	.493	18
Quad Cities (Angels)	62	78	0	.443	25

COMPOSITE STANDING OF CLUBS AT CLOSE OF SEASON, SEPTEMBER 1

Club	Spr.	Mad.	Wat.	Peo.	Wau.	Bel.	C.R.	Bur.	Cln.	Q.C.	Apl.	Ken.	W.	L.	T.	Pct.	G.B.
Springfield (Cardinals)	....	7	3	10	8	6	6	12	8	12	9	6	87	53	0	.621	....
Madison (A's)	3	....	6	7	10	4	8	7	7	7	12	15	86	54	0	.614	1
Waterloo (Indians)	7	4	....	6	4	10	13	3	10	7	5	9	78	62	0	.557	9
Peoria (Cubs)	10	3	4	....	9	5	5	12	7	11	7	4	77	63	0	.550	10
Wausau (Mariners)	2	10	6	1	....	4	3	8	6	6	12	15	73	66	0	.525	13½
Beloit (Brewers)	4	6	10	5	6	....	9	4	12	4	4	6	70	69	0	.504	16½
Cedar Rapids (Reds)	4	2	7	5	7	11	....	6	7	7	7	7	70	70	0	.500	17
Burlington (Expos)	8	3	7	8	2	6	4	....	4	12	8	7	69	71	0	.493	18
Clinton (Giants)	2	3	10	3	4	8	13	6	....	4	5	5	63	76	0	.453	23½
Quad Cities (Angels)	8	3	3	9	4	6	3	8	6	....	7	5	62	78	0	.443	25
Appleton (White Sox)	1	8	5	3	8	5	3	2	5	3	....	13	56	83	0	.403	30½
Kenosha (Twins)	4	5	1	6	4	4	3	3	4	5	7	....	46	92	0	.333	40

Quad Cities' home games played in Davenport, Ia.

Major league affiliations in parentheses.

Playoffs—Waterloo defeated Madison, two games to none; Peoria defeated Springfield, two games to none; Waterloo defeated Peoria, three games to none, to win league championship.

Regular-Season Attendance—Appleton, 60,001; Beloit, 101,127; Burlington, 68,457; Cedar Rapids, 131,534; Clinton, 100,326; Kenosha, 57,495; Madison, 118,310; Peoria, 179,183; Quad Cities, 116,062; Springfield, 151,815; Waterloo, 80,124; Wausau, 59,634. Total—1,224,068. Playoffs, 10,149. All-Star Game, 2,276.

Managers—Appleton, Duke Sims (thru June 9), Rico Petrocelli (June 10 thru end of season); Beloit, Gomer Hodge; Burlington, J.R. Miner; Cedar Rapids, Gene Dusan (thru July 27), Paul Kirsch (July 28 thru end of season); Clinton, Jack Mull; Kenosha, Don Leppert; Madison, Jim Nettles; Peoria, Pete MacKanin; Quad Cities, Bill Lachemann; Springfield, Gaylen Pitts; Waterloo, Steve Swisher; Wausau, Bobby Cuellar.

All-Star Team—1B—Mark Grace, Peoria; 2B—Mark Howie, Madison; 3B—Marty Brown, Cedar Rapids; SS—Walt Weiss, Madison; OF—Luis Medina, Waterloo; Dwight Smith, Peoria; Bob Simonson, Beloit; C—Mike Fox, Springfield; DH—Mike Fitzgerald, Springfield; LHP—Dave Otto, Madison; RHP—Jeff Oyster, Springfield; RH Reliever—Paul Wilmet, Springfield; LH Reliever—Tim O'Connor, Kenosha; Most Valuable Player—Luis Medina, Waterloo; Manager of the Year—Gaylen Pitts, Springfield.

(Compiled by Howe News Bureau, Boston, Mass.)

CLUB BATTING

Club	Pct.	G.	AB.	R.	OR.	H.	TB.	2B.	3B.	HR.	RBI.	GW.	SH.	SF.	HP.	BB.	Int. BB.	SO.	SB.	CS.	LOB.
Springfield	.273	140	4629	736	577	1263	1780	213	35	78	657	83	56	61	31	466	15	717	176	50	968
Peoria	.270	140	4598	655	619	1242	1706	222	34	58	575	69	43	42	46	486	24	722	174	84	990
Waterloo	.256	140	4568	701	616	1169	1811	199	22	133	609	69	25	35	31	619	22	899	103	59	1005
Madison	.254	140	4526	716	557	1151	1652	189	30	84	618	71	36	49	46	609	13	991	170	84	1014
Cedar Rapids	.254	140	4535	597	578	1151	1658	161	35	92	510	57	26	36	42	468	18	900	201	115	900
Beloit	.253	139	4591	641	644	1160	1673	182	17	99	557	62	63	44	61	501	18	898	87	45	1032
Quad Cities	.251	140	4349	589	649	1090	1579	200	32	75	528	52	24	35	37	554	16	1030	79	46	978
Burlington	.251	140	4490	658	626	1125	1747	210	29	118	547	55	34	40	47	466	14	989	123	52	906
Wausau	.246	139	4411	653	609	1085	1668	217	18	110	571	68	41	33	61	581	17	1132	129	79	979
Kenosha	.234	138	4535	507	693	1061	1420	179	21	46	440	34	25	29	38	551	23	853	88	49	1075
Appleton	.233	139	4438	525	735	1034	1477	179	24	72	446	49	36	30	49	469	7	1003	116	63	926
Clinton	.232	139	4511	505	580	1046	1429	180	19	55	449	55	35	33	56	404	15	996	164	74	926

INDIVIDUAL BATTING

(Leading Qualifiers for Batting Championship—378 or More Plate Appearances)

*Bats lefthanded. †Switch-hitter.

Player and Club	Pct.	G.	AB.	R.	H.	TB.	2B.	3B.	HR.	RBI.	GW.	SH.	SF.	HP.	BB.	Int. BB.	SO.	SB.	CS.
Grace, Mark, Peoria*	.342	126	465	81	159	242	30	4	15	95	15	2	6	4	60	6	28	6	5
Murphy, John, Springfield	.325	89	348	76	113	176	22	1	13	75	13	1	5	5	32	2	42	37	6
Higgins, Mark, Waterloo	.317	126	448	73	142	247	34	1	23	98	10	0	7	3	64	4	73	0	3
Medina, Luis, Waterloo	.317	136	505	107	160	300	25	5	35	110	14	0	3	4	75	4	109	6	5
Smith, Dwight, Peoria*	.310	124	471	92	146	223	22	11	11	57	9	2	2	3	59	2	92	53	19
Howie, Mark, Madison	.309	130	466	92	144	188	24	4	4	54	4	4	5	5	79	1	52	45	11
Brown, Marty, Cedar Rapids	.299	139	508	85	152	241	19	8	18	83	14	1	6	4	58	4	100	58	20
Fitzgerald, Michael, Springfield	.297	126	498	74	148	243	30	4	19	93	17	0	10	8	19	1	90	1	2
Breedlove, Larry, Springfield	.293	108	362	74	106	126	11	3	1	50	6	11	4	1	65	0	52	3	4
Walker, Larry, Burlington*	.289	95	332	67	96	207	12	6	29	74	6	0	3	9	46	1	112	16	8
Huson, Jeffrey, Burlington*	.289	133	457	85	132	201	19	1	16	72	8	2	3	2	76	4	68	32	6
Hilgenberg, Scott, Cedar Rapids*	.287	115	380	47	109	140	14	1	5	40	2	3	4	5	34	1	56	1	4
Bryant, John, Cedar Rapids	.287	103	363	62	104	144	12	2	8	26	3	1	1	14	48	1	54	31	16

Departmental Leaders: G—Arias, M. Brown, 139; AB—Simonson, 522; R—Medina, 107; H—Medina, 160; TB—Medina, 300; 2B—Higgins, 34; 3B—D. Smith, 11; HR—Medina, 35; RBI—Medina, 110; GWRBI—Fitzgerald, 17; SH—Ventura, 14; SF—Fitzgerald, 10; HP—Nelson, 18; BB—Grant, 95; IBB—Lanoux, 9; SO—Simonson, 145; SB—J. Carter, 60; CS—M. Brown, J. Carter, 20.

(All Players—Listed Alphabetically)

Player and Club	Pct.	G.	AB.	R.	H.	TB.	2B.	3B.	HR.	RBI.	GW.	SH.	SF.	HP.	BB.	Int. BB.	SO.	SB.	CS.
Adkins, Todd, Peoria†	.077	12	26	2	2	2	0	0	0	1	0	0	0	0	1	0	5	2	0
Alfonzo, Edgar, Quad Cities	.215	67	219	21	47	60	8	1	1	12	1	6	0	2	22	0	42	1	1
Alfredson, Thomas, Quad Cities	.228	112	351	48	80	153	14	1	19	52	9	2	2	1	56	4	129	7	3
Allen, Larry, Appleton*	.234	81	299	30	70	89	14	1	1	39	5	1	0	0	29	1	42	5	2
Alvis, David, Waterloo*	.236	93	309	31	73	107	16	0	6	33	3	0	4	0	21	2	42	0	1
Ames, Douglas, Madison	.250	21	4	0	1	2	1	0	0	0	0	1	0	0	0	0	3	0	0
Anders, Scott, Peoria	.211	33	109	9	23	28	2	0	1	11	1	1	2	0	9	0	18	1	0
Arias, Antonio, Madison	.255	139	517	79	132	213	23	2	18	103	10	1	9	9	52	1	116	9	4
Arndt, Larry, Madison	.281	125	445	70	125	195	20	1	16	65	12	0	6	5	52	3	106	12	7
Asbe, Daryl, Burlington	.217	52	152	8	33	47	9	1	1	19	2	1	4	4	10	0	40	1	1
Ashley, Shon, Beloit	.256	95	297	43	76	112	18	0	6	34	3	5	2	2	27	0	69	2	6
Atkinson, Timothy, Springfield	.000	29	2	0	0	0	0	0	0	0	0	0	0	0	0	0	1	0	0
Baker, Gerald, Quad Cities	.238	28	84	17	20	40	3	1	5	11	1	0	1	2	15	0	33	1	0
Ban, Mark, Quad Cities*	.249	64	181	21	45	63	7	1	3	31	1	0	2	3	16	1	27	1	0
Barry, John, Clinton	.243	80	230	21	56	69	13	0	0	20	4	1	1	2	12	1	47	1	2
Bates, Douglas, Springfield*	.000	23	5	0	0	0	0	0	0	0	0	0	0	0	0	0	3	0	0
Bell, Robert, Quad Cities	.234	25	77	12	18	22	4	0	0	3	0	1	2	3	3	0	24	0	0
Bennett, Jose, Wausau	.274	49	168	20	46	77	12	2	5	21	3	2	0	2	10	0	57	1	4
Bennett, Keith, Waterloo	.261	130	471	88	123	147	13	4	1	39	8	8	4	4	83	1	94	46	19
Bernardo, Robert, Wausau	.220	122	423	61	93	167	23	0	17	67	4	0	2	16	57	2	140	9	9
Bernhardt, Cesar, Appleton	.276	19	76	9	21	30	2	2	1	12	1	1	1	1	4	0	11	1	2
Bivens, William, Springfield	.000	16	2	0	0	0	0	0	0	0	0	0	0	0	0	0	2	0	0
Blackwell, Larry, Kenosha	.242	75	265	40	64	89	8	1	5	35	4	0	2	1	48	0	63	15	9
Blair, Paul, Clinton	.214	61	192	20	41	46	5	0	0	15	2	2	2	1	20	0	26	6	4
Blakley, David, Clinton	.000	41	3	0	0	0	0	0	0	0	0	0	0	0	0	0	2	0	0
Blunt, Bradley, Springfield	.000	4	2	0	0	0	0	0	0	0	0	0	0	0	0	0	1	0	0
Bonilla, George, Clinton*	.143	39	7	0	1	1	0	0	0	0	0	0	0	0	0	0	2	0	0
Bosley, Richard, Beloit	1.000	16	1	0	1	1	0	0	0	0	0	0	0	0	0	0	0	0	0
Brandts, Michael, Wausau	.236	52	178	25	42	66	8	2	4	24	1	1	1	4	13	0	53	1	1
Braxton, Glen, Appleton*	.000	4	11	2	0	0	0	0	0	0	0	0	0	1	3	0	5	1	0
Breedlove, Larry, Springfield	.293	108	362	74	106	126	11	3	1	50	6	11	4	1	65	0	52	3	4
Bresnahan, David, Waterloo†	.221	89	281	32	62	92	12	0	6	29	1	0	3	0	56	3	72	2	2
Brown, Kurt, Appleton	.234	65	222	19	52	60	5	0	1	18	4	4	0	4	14	0	41	0	0
Brown, Marty, Cedar Rapids	.299	139	508	85	152	241	19	8	18	83	14	1	6	4	58	4	100	58	20
Brusky, Brad, Cedar Rapids	1.000	45	1	0	1	2	1	0	0	0	0	0	0	0	0	0	0	0	0
Bryant, John, Cedar Rapids	.287	103	363	62	104	144	12	2	8	26	3	1	1	14	48	1	54	31	16
Burcham, Timothy, Quad Cities	.000	27	0	0	0	0	0	0	0	0	0	0	0	0	1	0	0	0	1
Cabrera, Antonio, Madison	.218	65	179	32	39	42	1	1	0	14	1	6	0	3	20	0	23	4	1
Cabrera, Fremio, Wausau	.247	29	89	14	22	25	3	0	0	5	0	1	0	1	15	0	19	2	2
Caci, Robert, Beloit	.150	16	40	3	6	6	0	0	0	0	0	0	0	1	3	0	8	1	0
Cain, Calvin, Cedar Rapids*	.223	85	251	28	56	88	10	5	4	30	3	2	1	1	17	0	55	7	3
Calvert, Christopher, Kenosha	.264	97	333	43	88	124	22	1	4	33	4	0	1	8	46	1	58	2	2
Campbell, Michael, Cedar Rapids	.143	21	7	1	1	1	0	0	0	1	0	2	0	0	3	0	2	0	0
Canan, Richard, Peoria	.251	134	494	53	124	178	31	4	5	68	13	2	6	9	27	0	95	5	6
Canseco, Osvaldo, Madison	.156	42	128	17	20	32	1	1	3	17	1	0	3	0	22	0	47	1	1
Carrasco, Claudio, Waterloo†	.267	121	401	62	107	153	20	4	6	55	3	1	2	2	59	3	77	7	7
Carter, Dennis, Springfield	.270	138	518	82	140	218	27	6	13	82	11	0	6	3	39	2	123	28	8
Carter, Jeffrey, Clinton†	.227	128	472	62	107	135	13	3	3	47	5	3	2	3	58	0	76	60	20
Carter, Ron, Madison	.173	88	255	35	44	70	7	2	5	23	1	3	2	2	45	1	84	10	7
Cash, Todd, Clinton	.238	38	105	11	25	29	4	0	0	8	0	0	1	0	9	0	20	2	1
Casteel, Brent, Peoria	.287	51	150	20	43	51	8	0	0	23	1	1	1	1	7	0	23	2	0
Cento, Anthony, Appleton	.176	7	17	0	3	3	0	0	0	0	0	0	0	1	1	0	3	0	0

Player and Club	Pct.	G.	AB.	R.	H.	TB.	2B.	3B.	HR.	RBI.	GW.	SH.	SF.	HP.	BB.	Int. BB.	SO.	SB.	CS.
Clark, Isaiah, Beloit	.265	32	98	14	26	39	8	1	1	15	0	0	2	1	15	0	15	1	2
Clem, John, Wausau†	.282	112	365	62	103	159	23	0	11	67	13	1	5	1	74	2	87	5	5
Cohoon, Donald, Wausau†	.193	102	342	41	66	87	13	1	2	33	3	3	1	0	34	3	103	7	3
Colbert, Craig, Clinton	.228	72	263	26	60	75	12	0	1	17	2	0	1	3	23	1	53	4	1
Coleman, DeWayne, Peoria	.500	3	4	0	2	2	0	0	0	1	1	0	0	0	1	0	1	0	0
Collins, Anthony, Peoria	.263	17	57	5	15	19	2	1	0	5	1	0	0	2	6	0	10	2	1
Conner, Gregory, Clinton	.275	62	200	27	55	80	10	0	5	29	4	0	0	4	5	0	40	23	5
Converse, Michael, Cedar Rapids	.286	28	14	4	4	8	1	0	1	1	0	0	0	0	1	0	5	0	0
Corcino, Luis, Burlington	.210	55	124	19	26	36	3	2	1	14	1	1	0	1	9	0	34	4	1
Cunningham, Joseph, Springfield	.230	101	291	50	67	100	15	3	4	48	6	7	7	2	47	0	49	8	2
Cupples, Michael, Madison	.224	123	392	41	88	123	11	0	8	53	3	3	4	1	56	0	63	1	3
Damian, Leonard, Peoria	.000	25	13	0	0	0	0	0	0	0	0	1	0	0	1	0	5	0	0
Dandos, Michael, Clinton	.222	18	54	5	12	15	0	0	1	5	1	1	1	1	6	0	11	0	0
Danek, William, Peoria	.143	27	7	1	1	1	0	0	0	0	0	1	0	0	0	0	2	0	0
Dasch, David, Kenosha	.208	57	178	17	37	46	4	1	1	23	5	1	0	0	18	0	36	4	5
Davis, Geffrey, Burlington	.246	111	350	44	86	136	18	1	10	39	3	3	0	2	44	0	78	1	4
Davis, Mark A., Appleton	.228	77	272	37	62	89	10	4	3	22	3	1	0	4	54	0	70	19	8
Davis, Mark J., Springfield*	.333	19	3	0	1	1	0	0	0	0	0	0	0	0	0	0	0	0	0
Deitz, James, Cedar Rapids	.000	45	2	0	0	0	0	0	0	0	0	0	0	0	0	0	1	0	0
Delancer, Julio, Kenosha	.136	9	22	0	3	4	1	0	0	0	0	0	0	0	6	0	5	2	1
DeLima, Rafael, Kenosha*	.029	20	35	2	1	1	0	0	0	0	0	0	0	0	4	0	11	0	0
Diaz, William, Wausau	.273	103	399	55	109	162	26	0	9	60	5	5	5	7	20	1	73	8	9
DiCeglio, Thomas, 51 Ken-10 Peoria	.256	61	203	17	52	65	7	0	2	19	1	4	1	5	8	0	21	3	3
Dietrick, Patrick, Madison	.189	32	90	17	17	24	2	1	1	12	1	2	0	2	13	0	36	5	4
Donahue, Charles, Cedar Rapids*	.191	31	68	1	13	15	2	0	0	5	1	1	0	0	8	0	16	2	1
Duffy, Darrin, Madison	.304	35	112	23	34	51	8	3	1	15	0	1	1	1	27	0	32	8	4
Dull, Michael, Burlington*	.217	83	277	38	60	92	8	3	6	35	4	3	1	1	27	2	54	3	2
Dunlap, Joseph, Cedar Rapids	.232	38	155	25	36	57	9	0	4	19	0	0	3	2	14	1	19	5	4
Ealy, Thomas, Clinton†	.187	31	75	7	14	16	2	0	0	5	0	2	0	2	9	0	21	0	1
Eccleston, Thomas, Wausau*	.306	64	222	49	68	97	16	2	3	24	3	1	1	1	43	1	43	17	6
Escalera, Ruben, Beloit*	.271	119	436	56	118	133	10	1	1	49	6	8	2	6	45	1	54	6	4
Espinoza, Andres, Quad Cities*	.286	124	426	47	122	158	19	1	5	54	2	0	4	2	25	6	70	0	0
Eveline, William, Appleton*	.285	109	411	65	117	164	15	4	8	40	5	3	3	2	40	0	48	12	9
Ewart, Ronald, Peoria*	.276	60	192	28	53	70	10	2	1	23	2	0	6	2	29	0	25	9	4
Fairchild, Glenn, Waterloo†	.191	33	89	7	17	21	4	0	0	7	2	1	0	2	18	0	26	5	2
Fazzini, Frank, Beloit	.157	29	83	8	13	16	1	1	0	11	1	1	1	0	14	0	25	0	1
Fitzgerald, Michael, Springfield	.297	126	498	74	148	243	30	4	19	93	17	0	10	8	19	1	90	1	2
Flowers, Kim, Clinton	.213	37	122	12	26	36	3	2	1	11	0	0	2	0	11	1	22	6	4
Forrest, Christopher, Springfield	1.000	3	1	0	1	1	0	0	0	0	0	0	0	0	0	0	0	0	0
Fox, Michael, Springfield	.278	111	396	47	110	139	21	1	2	51	3	6	6	1	33	1	38	8	3
Freed, Michael, Springfield	.500	29	2	1	1	1	0	0	0	1	0	0	0	0	0	0	0	0	0
Freeland, Dean, Clinton	.167	20	12	1	2	2	0	0	0	2	1	1	0	0	1	0	4	0	0
Frye, Paul, Burlington	.271	17	59	8	16	31	1	1	4	11	2	0	1	4	1	0	14	0	1
Garcia, Cornelio, Appleton*	.261	38	119	24	31	48	9	1	2	17	5	1	2	2	22	1	43	13	2
Gardner, Jimmie, Peoria	.000	9	1	0	0	0	0	0	0	0	0	0	0	0	0	0	1	0	0
Germann, Mark, Cedar Rapids	.267	135	490	62	131	161	16	4	2	43	4	4	2	0	55	1	54	11	9
Gibree, Robert, Wausau	.265	88	279	35	74	105	17	1	4	42	6	4	2	10	47	1	60	3	2
Gilbert, Patrick, Madison	.309	58	217	36	67	85	4	1	4	23	6	1	3	4	22	0	38	2	0
Gill, Turner, Waterloo	.223	70	224	27	50	80	10	1	6	20	1	4	0	1	24	0	55	4	3
Girardi, Joseph, Peoria	.309	68	230	36	71	95	13	1	3	28	4	2	3	3	17	1	36	6	3
Goldstein, Ira, Kenosha*	.239	47	142	14	34	42	5	0	1	17	0	1	3	0	20	0	27	0	0
Gould, Robert, Madison	.262	111	336	69	88	136	23	2	7	54	8	5	7	9	51	0	70	21	16
Grace, Mark, Peoria*	.342	126	465	81	159	242	30	4	15	95	15	2	6	4	60	6	28	6	5
Grant, Kenneth, Quad Cities	.263	107	353	71	93	134	22	2	5	41	5	2	5	1	95	1	88	19	13
Greene, Edward, Beloit	.174	46	121	15	21	23	2	0	0	6	1	0	1	0	12	0	22	2	2
Grimes, Lee, Peoria	.253	79	249	36	63	87	14	2	2	20	0	3	1	2	29	2	33	4	3
Grunhard, Daniel, Quad Cities*	.243	35	111	14	27	37	5	1	1	14	3	1	1	0	25	1	27	6	4
Guillory, Walter, Madison	.194	11	36	3	7	13	3	0	1	8	1	0	0	0	2	0	11	1	0
Haller, Timothy, Appleton	.167	36	84	7	14	18	4	0	0	4	1	0	0	2	12	0	19	1	0
Hamza, Antonio, Peoria	.179	14	28	10	5	12	1	0	2	4	0	0	0	0	11	2	13	1	1
Haney, Joseph, Beloit*	.216	83	264	29	57	62	5	0	0	23	1	7	6	3	19	1	29	5	1
Hanggie, Daniel, Beloit†	.262	128	462	83	121	221	31	0	23	77	8	4	9	7	68	7	88	0	1
Harrison, Brett, Springfield	.280	134	482	70	135	192	17	8	8	65	8	5	8	3	45	2	57	18	5
Hartley, Thomas, Appleton	.174	41	132	15	23	33	2	1	2	8	1	2	0	2	16	0	36	2	2
Heist, Charles, Burlington*	.273	12	44	10	12	18	1	1	1	7	1	2	0	0	6	0	6	3	0
Hemond, Scott, Madison	.306	22	85	9	26	34	2	0	2	13	3	0	1	0	5	0	19	2	1
Henry, Douglas, Beloit	.000	28	1	0	0	0	0	0	0	0	0	0	0	0	0	0	1	0	0
Hernandez, Cesar, Burlington†	.250	38	104	12	26	40	11	0	1	12	0	1	2	4	7	0	24	7	0
Higgins, Mark, Waterloo	.317	126	448	73	142	247	34	1	23	98	10	0	7	3	64	4	73	0	3
Hilgenberg, Scott, Cedar Rapids*	.287	115	380	47	109	140	14	1	5	40	2	3	4	5	34	1	56	1	4
Hillman, Thomas, Waterloo	.107	14	28	3	3	4	1	0	0	0	0	2	0	0	6	0	7	1	0
Hindman, Randall, Cedar Rapids	.227	86	255	25	58	72	10	2	0	20	0	2	1	1	20	0	32	9	5
Hirsch, Jeffrey, Peoria†	.250	47	4	0	1	1	0	0	0	0	0	0	0	0	0	0	1	0	0
Hornsby, David, Clinton	.200	44	105	8	21	31	3	2	1	9	1	3	1	1	7	0	31	0	0
Howie, Mark, Madison	.309	130	466	92	144	188	24	4	4	54	4	4	5	5	79	1	52	45	11
Huff, Marc, Kenosha	.071	9	28	1	2	2	0	0	0	0	0	0	0	0	1	0	3	0	0
Huson, Jeffrey, Burlington*	.289	133	457	85	132	201	19	1	16	72	8	2	3	2	76	4	68	32	6
Isaac, Richard, Appleton	.263	7	19	2	5	8	3	0	0	1	0	0	0	0	2	0	2	2	3
Jacas, Andre, Madison†	.251	53	183	39	46	62	7	3	1	19	2	1	0	4	30	1	32	17	10
Jacas, David, Kenosha	.275	74	298	33	82	96	12	1	0	22	2	2	0	1	19	1	60	10	5
Jackson, Lloyd, Clinton*	.143	36	84	7	12	17	3	1	0	3	0	0	1	0	9	0	28	4	0
Jackson, Mark, Cedar Rapids	.205	106	347	40	71	87	10	0	2	19	2	3	3	3	51	2	92	21	16
Johnigan, Stephen, Waterloo	.091	18	33	1	3	3	0	0	0	3	0	1	1	0	6	0	7	0	0
Johnson, Eric, Kenosha	.134	39	97	3	13	17	2	1	0	4	0	0	1	3	14	0	44	1	2
Johnson, Thomas, Burlington*	.273	129	472	79	129	186	23	2	10	42	5	2	3	4	59	1	98	15	9
Jones, Christopher, Cedar Rapids	.247	128	473	65	117	208	13	9	20	78	9	0	4	3	20	1	126	23	17
Jones, Terence, Burlington*	.244	47	164	25	40	66	11	0	5	17	1	0	3	1	21	0	30	4	1
Jordan, Scott, Waterloo	.249	117	434	88	108	172	17	4	13	55	7	2	3	3	60	0	90	21	8
Kallevig, Gregory, Peoria	.222	25	9	0	2	2	0	0	0	1	0	0	0	0	1	0	0	0	0
Kavanaugh, Timothy, Springfield	.000	33	1	0	0	0	0	0	0	0	0	0	0	0	0	0	0	0	0
Kazmierczak, William, Peoria†	.500	11	2	0	1	1	0	0	0	1	1	1	0	0	0	0	0	0	0
Kindred, Curtis, Cedar Rapids	.000	38	1	0	0	0	0	0	0	0	0	1	0	0	0	0	0	0	0

Player and Club	Pct.	G.	AB.	R.	H.	TB.	2B.	3B.	HR.	RBI.	GW.	SH.	SF.	HP.	BB.	Int. BB.	SO.	SB.	CS.
Kraemer, Joseph, Peoria*	.000	45	1	0	0	0	0	0	0	0	0	0	0	0	0	0	1	0	0
Kroener, Christopher, Kenosha	.194	60	211	13	41	51	4	0	2	17	1	5	0	2	12	0	51	3	0
Laird, Anthony, Quad Cities*	.280	94	314	44	88	135	22	2	7	44	5	0	2	0	34	0	44	0	3
Lambert, Reese, Madison*	.000	25	1	0	0	0	0	0	0	0	0	0	0	0	0	0	1	0	0
Lane, Eric, Waterloo	.252	64	206	36	52	92	7	0	11	32	5	0	0	3	26	1	43	1	0
Lanoux, Marty, Kenosha*	.269	123	442	59	119	189	27	2	13	75	5	0	6	5	55	9	51	0	2
Larson, Daniel, Wausau	.290	76	262	51	76	113	17	1	6	31	5	2	2	1	32	0	52	10	3
Laureano, Francisco, Burlington	.275	130	465	79	128	182	31	1	7	37	5	2	4	3	51	2	64	7	6
Lemons, Timothy, Burlington	.252	121	408	59	103	151	15	3	9	53	6	0	8	1	42	0	79	9	3
Leon, Ronald, Springfield*	.251	82	199	17	50	58	5	0	1	19	0	3	2	0	20	2	28	1	2
Leonard, Andrew, Burlington	.204	98	323	25	66	107	18	1	7	52	5	3	6	1	11	0	114	1	0
Lewis, John, Peoria*	.274	110	358	54	98	117	11	1	2	51	5	3	4	5	54	1	52	28	12
Liddell, David, Peoria	.264	37	125	12	33	48	4	1	3	15	1	1	0	4	15	2	42	0	1
Lincoln, Lance, Beloit	.242	73	240	28	58	64	6	0	0	14	0	6	0	3	30	0	62	4	2
Lockhart, Keith, Cedar Rapids*	.190	13	42	4	8	10	2	0	0	1	0	0	0	1	6	0	6	1	1
Lombarski, Thomas, Peoria*	.231	8	26	7	6	11	2	0	1	3	2	0	0	0	2	0	4	0	0
Mack, Jeremiah, Kenosha	.000	6	17	1	0	0	0	0	0	0	0	0	0	1	3	0	5	0	0
Magallanes, William, Appleton	.252	80	262	37	66	107	15	1	8	27	2	0	2	3	28	0	84	4	2
Maloney, Christopher, Springfield†	.230	68	165	17	38	47	6	0	1	17	1	1	1	1	21	1	31	0	0
Mandeville, Robert, Peoria	.216	31	97	16	21	25	2	1	0	7	1	2	0	0	18	0	13	5	2
Mann, Kelly, Peoria	.462	3	13	4	6	8	2	0	0	4	0	0	0	0	0	0	1	0	0
Manto, Jeffrey, Quad Cities	.247	73	239	31	59	96	13	0	8	49	4	1	2	4	37	0	70	2	1
Manwaring, Kirt, Clinton	.245	49	147	18	36	51	7	1	2	16	2	4	1	1	14	1	26	1	2
Manzon, Howard, Kenosha	.254	101	350	48	89	126	12	8	3	25	2	6	0	3	44	1	60	16	3
Marquez, Edwin, Quad Cities	.280	105	354	58	99	142	18	5	5	43	4	2	2	3	49	0	58	6	1
Martin, Norberto, Appleton†	.303	9	33	4	10	12	2	0	0	2	0	0	0	0	2	0	5	1	0
Martinez, Luis, Madison†	.176	12	34	3	6	10	1	0	1	4	0	0	0	0	10	0	8	0	2
Mattox, Frank, Beloit†	.325	72	295	49	96	118	17	1	1	38	5	5	4	0	24	1	36	19	4
Mauch, Thomas, Springfield*	.200	23	10	3	2	3	1	0	0	0	0	2	0	0	0	0	1	0	0
McCoy, Timothy, Clinton	.000	14	5	1	0	0	0	0	0	0	0	0	0	0	0	0	1	0	0
McCulla, Henry, 5 Spring-22 Bel	.174	27	92	15	16	31	3	0	4	11	0	1	1	3	12	0	22	1	0
McGinnis, Russell, Beloit	.247	124	413	62	102	178	24	2	16	59	6	3	4	12	52	2	79	5	2
McGrew, Charles, Beloit*	.283	118	407	46	115	172	18	0	13	67	9	2	3	3	49	4	93	1	0
McIntosh, Timothy, Beloit	.260	49	173	26	45	64	3	2	4	21	3	0	3	2	18	0	33	0	0
McLaughlin, David, Kenosha*	.271	87	347	41	94	108	9	1	1	17	0	1	1	0	31	5	30	6	3
McMorris, Mark, Peoria*	.268	40	149	18	40	52	9	0	1	15	0	1	0	0	4	0	22	0	0
Mead, Timber, Clinton	.133	27	15	1	2	2	0	0	0	0	0	1	0	0	1	0	6	0	0
Medina, Luis, Waterloo	.317	136	505	107	160	300	25	5	35	110	14	0	3	4	75	4	109	6	5
Meyers, Glenn, Quad Cities	.256	96	348	40	89	120	21	2	2	37	5	0	3	4	16	0	80	5	0
Meyers, Paul, Clinton	.208	73	259	30	54	69	8	2	1	19	3	4	2	1	23	1	41	13	4
Milholland, Eric, Appleton	.250	73	252	28	63	80	6	1	3	31	3	2	0	2	13	0	42	4	3
Miller, Ted, Kenosha	.287	45	122	20	35	41	6	0	0	18	0	1	2	0	21	0	33	3	3
Miller, Todd, Clinton†	.256	113	312	38	80	102	12	2	2	26	7	6	1	8	21	0	73	4	5
Minutelli, Gino, Cedar Rapids*	.308	27	13	1	4	6	2	0	0	0	0	0	0	0	1	0	5	0	0
Moncerratt, Pablo, Wausau*	.266	109	346	51	92	173	14	2	21	64	7	3	1	2	46	2	104	3	5
Morgan, Kenneth, Kenosha*	.214	61	196	23	42	65	12	1	3	22	2	0	1	1	29	3	49	6	0
Moritz, Thomas, Appleton	.320	15	50	11	16	27	2	0	3	13	0	0	0	0	11	2	11	0	1
Murphy, Dwayne, Madison*	.000	1	0	0	0	0	0	0	0	0	0	0	0	0	1	0	0	0	0
Murphy, John, Springfield	.325	89	348	76	113	176	22	1	13	75	13	1	5	5	32	2	42	37	6
Nalls, Gary, Quad Cities	.217	84	254	26	55	66	5	3	0	24	2	1	3	5	23	0	74	5	3
Naveda, Edgar, Kenosha	.233	109	390	40	91	118	21	0	2	31	3	3	3	0	35	0	53	8	5
Nelson, Richard, Clinton	.246	122	406	56	100	162	15	1	15	53	7	0	7	18	48	2	128	15	7
Nettles, James, Madison*	.000	1	1	0	0	0	0	0	0	0	0	0	0	0	0	0	0	0	0
Nix, David, Madison*	.259	26	81	17	21	32	5	0	2	15	0	0	0	0	17	1	15	3	1
Norman, Scott, Springfield	.000	25	2	0	0	0	0	0	0	0	0	0	0	0	0	0	0	0	0
O'Connor, William, Kenosha	.174	13	46	3	8	8	0	0	0	3	0	0	0	0	4	0	6	0	0
Oller, Jeffrey, Burlington*	.125	15	40	3	5	5	0	0	0	0	0	0	0	0	8	1	17	0	1
Olson, Warren, Beloit	.176	29	91	10	16	22	3	0	1	2	1	0	0	7	6	0	26	0	0
Ortman, Douglas, Madison	.333	9	27	5	9	10	1	0	0	0	0	0	0	0	3	0	3	1	0
Oyster, Jeffrey, Springfield	.000	28	29	1	0	0	0	0	0	0	0	0	0	0	1	0	13	0	0
Parker, Stephen, Peoria*	.250	16	4	0	1	1	0	0	0	0	0	0	0	0	0	0	3	0	0
Pawling, Eric, Clinton	.000	2	2	0	0	0	0	0	0	0	0	0	0	0	0	0	1	0	0
Pearson, Darren, Clinton†	.000	30	10	1	0	0	0	0	0	0	0	0	0	0	0	0	3	0	0
Peluso, Matt, Appleton	.053	8	19	1	1	1	0	0	0	2	0	0	0	0	1	0	8	0	0
Pena, Jose, Clinton	.249	102	350	30	87	120	18	0	5	53	7	1	3	2	16	2	61	2	1
Penigar, Charles, Clinton†	.625	21	8	3	5	6	1	0	0	2	1	0	0	0	2	0	0	0	0
Peraza, Luis, Appleton	.115	27	78	1	9	9	0	0	0	4	1	2	0	2	3	0	19	0	2
Perry, Robert, Kenosha	.159	43	132	16	21	37	1	3	3	14	2	0	2	4	26	0	41	2	2
Peters, Steven, Springfield*	.300	16	20	3	6	12	0	0	2	4	1	0	0	0	2	0	5	0	0
Phillips, William, Peoria*	.000	36	2	0	0	0	0	0	0	0	0	0	0	0	0	0	0	0	0
Pilkington, Eric, Clinton*	.125	29	8	0	1	1	0	0	0	0	0	0	0	0	0	0	2	0	0
Pregon, David, Springfield*	.238	70	193	26	46	77	13	0	6	33	2	0	1	2	18	1	48	3	1
Reyes, Giovanny, Quad Cities	.167	12	30	5	5	6	1	0	0	0	0	0	0	0	3	0	4	0	1
Reynolds, David, Appleton	.000	42	1	0	0	0	0	0	0	0	0	0	0	0	0	0	0	0	0
Rivera, Luis, Appleton	.255	30	94	7	24	31	4	0	1	6	2	0	1	0	7	0	17	0	0
Robertson, Douglas, Clinton	.000	27	10	0	0	0	0	0	0	0	0	1	0	0	0	0	6	0	0
Robertson, Michael, Springfield	.000	8	1	0	0	0	0	0	0	0	0	0	0	1	0	0	0	0	0
Robidoux, William, Beloit*	.250	7	16	3	4	6	2	0	0	2	0	0	1	0	9	0	1	0	1
Robles, Gabaliel, Peoria	.000	7	7	0	0	0	0	0	0	0	0	1	0	0	1	0	4	0	0
Rodriguez, Eduardo, Quad Cities	.143	9	21	0	3	3	0	0	0	0	0	2	0	1	3	0	3	0	1
Rodriguez, Ignacio, Burlington	.153	24	59	7	9	16	1	0	2	8	0	3	0	1	5	0	13	2	0
Rodriguez, Jose R., Springfield	.226	43	137	19	31	37	3	0	1	15	2	4	2	0	10	0	13	1	1
Roesler, Michael, Cedar Rapids	.083	32	12	0	1	1	0	0	0	0	0	0	0	0	0	0	7	0	0
Rose, Robert, Quad Cities	.253	129	467	67	118	170	21	5	7	56	7	2	4	0	66	2	116	13	9
Roth, Kris, Peoria	.115	27	26	2	3	4	1	0	0	2	0	2	0	1	2	0	11	0	0
Russ, Kevin, Madison*	.143	4	7	2	1	1	0	0	0	0	0	0	0	0	1	0	4	0	0
Saatzer, Michael, Quad Cities*	1.000	2	1	0	1	2	1	0	0	1	0	0	0	0	0	0	0	0	0
Salazar, Luis, Appleton	.203	21	79	9	16	23	1	0	2	4	0	0	0	1	4	0	18	0	0
Santos, Donaciano, Waterloo	.162	23	68	8	11	23	3	0	3	10	0	0	0	0	5	0	24	0	2
Sassone, Michael, Springfield	.000	14	2	0	0	0	0	0	0	0	0	0	0	0	1	0	0	0	0
Schiffelbein, Greg, Madison*	.194	32	98	11	19	21	2	0	0	5	0	1	1	0	10	0	18	0	0
Schmidt, August, Kenosha	.226	71	243	33	55	75	14	0	2	26	0	0	4	0	54	1	42	4	2

Player and Club	Pct.	G.	AB.	R.	H.	TB.	2B.	3B.	HR.	RBI.	GW.	SH.	SF.	HP.	BB.	Int. BB.	SO.	SB.	CS.
Schulte, Mark, Springfield*	.339	77	271	45	92	129	17	1	6	47	7	3	4	1	22	2	17	2	0
Scruggs, Ronald, Appleton*	.226	110	350	43	79	133	9	0	15	41	6	4	4	1	50	0	128	3	3
Sheldon, David, Appleton	.215	124	396	45	85	124	20	2	5	40	3	5	4	6	41	1	86	1	2
Siegel, Robert, Wausau†	.000	26	1	0	0	0	0	0	0	0	0	0	0	0	0	0	0	0	0
Sigler, Allen, Cedar Rapids*	.274	93	277	42	76	122	8	1	12	41	5	0	2	3	56	3	85	5	7
Silverio, Nelson, Madison	.188	42	112	15	21	25	4	0	0	14	4	5	0	0	27	0	37	0	1
Simonson, Robert, Beloit	.278	133	522	86	145	256	18	6	27	95	12	2	3	7	42	1	145	13	8
Simpson, Gregory, Cedar Rapids*	.111	35	9	0	1	1	0	0	0	1	0	0	1	0	1	0	2	0	0
Slominski, Richard, Wausau	.240	98	321	47	77	149	15	0	19	48	7	4	5	8	35	2	84	3	1
Slotnick, Joseph, Burlington	.256	33	121	23	31	58	8	2	5	18	4	0	2	2	18	0	24	3	3
Slowik, Thaddeus, Peoria	.400	50	5	1	2	2	0	0	0	0	0	1	0	0	0	0	3	0	0
Small, Jeffrey, Peoria	.229	112	397	35	91	128	17	1	6	35	7	6	2	4	21	3	55	8	5
Smith, Dwight, Peoria*	.310	124	471	92	146	223	22	11	11	57	9	2	2	3	59	2	92	53	19
Smith, Gregory, Peoria†	.253	53	170	24	43	61	6	3	2	26	2	2	0	1	19	1	45	9	2
Smith, Michael, Cedar Rapids	.125	30	24	5	3	5	0	1	0	5	0	0	0	1	2	0	11	0	0
Smith, Philander, Beloit	.240	47	179	23	43	58	5	2	2	11	2	2	1	2	25	0	20	18	5
Sorrento, Paul, Quad Cities*	.356	53	177	33	63	96	11	2	6	34	2	0	1	2	24	0	40	0	0
Stolnack, Michael, Kenosha	.216	19	51	0	11	12	1	0	0	4	0	0	0	0	3	0	13	1	1
Sullivan, Carl, Appleton	.209	59	191	12	40	49	6	0	1	20	2	1	5	1	5	0	57	1	2
Swain, Robert, Waterloo	.233	61	150	16	35	43	4	2	0	11	3	2	0	0	13	0	31	0	1
Swan, Russell, Clinton*	.143	7	7	0	1	1	0	0	0	0	0	0	0	0	0	0	5	0	0
Swepson, Lyle, Clinton	.260	104	300	47	78	128	24	1	8	39	4	3	0	3	38	0	91	15	9
Tapias, Luis, Kenosha	.182	17	44	5	8	9	1	0	0	2	0	1	0	0	5	1	15	0	0
Tavarez, Alfonso, Burlington	.209	42	86	9	18	19	1	0	0	6	1	2	0	2	1	0	19	1	1
Thomason, Garrick, Kenosha	.154	45	143	15	22	28	1	1	1	10	0	0	1	4	15	0	36	3	2
Todd, Charles, Waterloo	.231	39	91	10	21	29	2	0	2	13	0	0	0	1	10	1	25	1	0
Toler, Gregory, Cedar Rapids	.242	81	264	29	64	93	10	2	5	28	6	2	3	2	14	1	41	3	1
Toliver, Andre, Appleton	.235	42	136	15	32	43	9	1	0	9	0	2	1	2	7	0	22	0	5
Torres, Eduardo, Quad Cities	.215	26	79	4	17	24	4	0	1	9	1	1	1	3	9	1	22	1	0
Touma, Timothy, Burlington	.229	34	109	12	25	29	4	0	0	8	0	4	0	3	9	1	17	3	2
Townsend, Howard, Clinton†	.000	13	2	0	0	0	0	0	0	0	0	0	0	0	0	0	0	0	0
Traylor, Keith, Springfield	.221	67	163	20	36	48	8	2	0	6	0	3	0	2	21	1	47	19	4
Turner, John, Peoria*	.282	94	294	44	83	103	18	1	0	35	1	2	5	1	46	2	31	13	9
Uribe, Jorge, Wausau	.235	117	371	52	87	113	11	3	3	27	6	5	0	2	61	1	132	28	13
Van Stone, Paul, Clinton†	.240	55	204	18	49	62	5	1	2	18	2	1	1	0	19	3	34	5	2
Velarde, Randy, Appleton	.252	124	417	55	105	177	31	4	11	50	2	1	4	7	58	1	96	13	6
Ventura, Jose, Beloit†	.234	96	304	37	71	76	3	1	0	22	4	14	2	1	32	1	59	10	6
Veras, Camilo, Madison*	.249	111	398	50	99	155	24	4	8	53	4	2	1	0	31	4	107	16	6
Verdugo, Luis, Beloit	.156	20	64	6	10	15	5	0	0	1	0	2	0	1	3	0	14	0	0
Veres, Randolf, Beloit	.000	23	2	0	0	0	0	0	0	0	0	0	0	0	0	0	0	0	0
Vincent, Michael, Cedar Rapids	.260	105	334	46	87	113	11	0	5	40	5	1	3	1	40	3	65	22	8
Vizquel, Omar, Wausau	.213	105	352	60	75	104	13	2	4	28	2	2	5	2	64	1	56	19	6
Waggoner, Aubrey, Appleton*	.181	60	188	25	34	45	2	0	3	7	2	3	0	3	23	1	46	29	4
Wagner, Daniel, Appleton	.243	67	230	22	56	74	8	2	2	29	1	3	3	2	19	0	44	4	5
Walker, Larry, Burlington*	.289	95	332	67	96	207	12	6	29	74	6	0	3	9	46	1	112	16	8
Wallace, Timothy, Peoria	.250	118	392	64	98	126	17	1	3	41	2	5	3	3	46	2	43	19	10
Warmbier, Kenneth, Springfield*	.308	5	13	4	4	4	0	0	0	1	1	0	0	0	1	0	2	2	0
Washington, Glenn, Quad Cities†	.170	51	147	18	25	31	0	3	0	8	0	1	0	0	16	0	47	12	4
Webster, Casey, Waterloo	.259	134	467	65	121	206	23	1	20	69	9	0	5	6	57	2	75	2	2
Webster, Leonard, Kenosha	.154	22	65	2	10	12	2	0	0	8	0	1	0	0	10	0	12	0	0
Weiss, Walter, Madison†	.301	84	322	50	97	128	15	5	2	54	10	0	6	1	33	1	66	12	5
Wellman, Phillip, Kenosha†	.288	45	156	19	45	61	7	0	3	18	3	0	2	1	20	1	32	0	0
Whitt, Micheal, Clinton	.216	95	283	23	61	72	8	0	1	23	1	1	3	3	27	2	80	0	3
Williams, John, Burlington*	.244	104	344	45	84	120	16	4	4	23	1	5	0	2	15	2	84	11	3
Williams, Matthew, Clinton	.240	68	250	32	60	101	14	3	7	29	1	0	3	3	24	1	51	3	3
Wilmet, Paul, Springfield	.000	56	5	0	0	0	0	0	0	0	0	1	0	0	0	0	2	0	0
Wilson, Craig, Springfield	.274	127	496	106	136	168	17	6	1	49	5	9	4	1	65	0	49	44	12
Wilson, Trevor, Clinton*	.000	34	9	0	0	0	0	0	0	0	0	0	0	0	1	0	4	0	0
Woods, Anthony, Wausau†	.188	86	293	30	55	71	6	2	2	30	3	7	3	4	30	1	69	13	10
Workman, Michael, Waterloo	.223	110	363	47	81	92	8	0	1	25	3	4	3	2	36	1	49	7	4
Zeratsky, Rodney, Cedar Rapids	.220	82	245	25	54	83	11	0	6	29	3	3	2	1	19	0	66	2	3
Zottneck, Roger, Quad Cities	.138	48	116	12	16	21	1	2	0	5	0	2	0	1	16	0	32	0	1

The following pitchers, listed alphabetically by club, with games in parentheses, had no plate appearances, primarily through use of designated hitters:

APPLETON—Bartolomucci, Anthony (11); Boling, John (38); Candelaria, Jorge (6); Cortes, Argenis (22); Filippi, James (6); Henry, Mark (6); Hulstrom, Bryce (14); Kershaw, Scott (8); Moran, Steven (29); Ollom, Michael (6); Oswald, Steven (15); Pall, Donn (11); Renz, Kevin (13); Robinson, Randy (8); Sandoval, Jesus (8); Stein, John (30); Stone, George (38); Villanueva, Gilbert (14); Warren, Marty (11).

BELOIT—Brisco, Jamie (42); Cocanower, James (2); Fitzpatrick, Danny (36); Gosling, Mark (2); Henderson, Craig (12); Hunter, James (15); Kleean, Thomas (34); Miglio, John (37); Montano, Martin (4); Moraw, Carl (28); Ojeda, Raymond (6); Reyes, Juan (33); Simmons, Gregory (25); Smith, Jeffery (5); Whitford, Larry (5).

BURLINGTON—Arrington, Thomas (17); Crouch, Matthew (22); Dougherty, Patrick (15); Fedor, Francis (16); Harris, Tyrone (7); Howes, John (15); Hunter, James (9); Kelly, Leonard (12); King, Steven (3); Perez, Melido (28); Robertson, Michael (4); Rodriguez, Jose F. (32); Stauffacher, Stuart (27); Sudo, Robert (16); Sundgren, Scott (18); Trautwein, John (21); Williams, Robert (18).

CEDAR RAPIDS—Belinskas, Dan (38); Bruno, Joseph (9).

CLINTON—Morris, David (41).

KENOSHA—Abbott, Paul (25); Bronkey, Jeffery (14); Bumgarner, Jeffrey (23); Cook, James (19); Craskey, Robert (28); Davis, Mark J. (6); Gasser, Steven (27); Lee, Robert (27); O'Connor, Timothy (38); Perez, Yorkis (31); Redding, Michael (23); Strube, Robert (41).

MADISON—Criswell, Brian (14); Cundari, Philip (15); Deabenderfer, Blaine (18); Hall, Martin (43); Holcomb, Scott (1); Johnson, William (4); Kibler, Russell (9); Krueger, William (1); Law, Joseph (20); McDonald, Kirk (5); Otto, David (26); Sabo, Scott (22); Salcedo, Luis (25); Shaver, Jeffrey (26); Stocker, Robert (11); Walton, Bruce (1); Whitehurst, Walter (8); Williamson, Kevin (22).

PEORIA—Green, John (2); Zarranz, Fernando (15).

QUAD CITIES—Auth, Robert (8); Charland, Colin (10); Collins, Christopher (22); DiMichele, Frank (26); Finley, Charles (10); Franco, Julio (6); Harvey, Randall (5); Johnson, David (26); Kannenberg, Scott (26); Marino, Mark (37); McGuire, Stephen (23); Morehouse, Richard (18); Rivera, Elvin (24); Shull, Michael (35); Smith, Lawrence (24).

SPRINGFIELD—Hartley, Michael (8); Horton, Ricky (1).

WATERLOO—Dube, Gregory (16); Farr, Michael (28); Fedor, Francis (20); Gardner, Myron (6); Ghelfi, Andrew (26); Githens, John (23); Karpuk, Gregory (28); Kuykendall, Kevin (16); LaFever, Gregory (24); Mercado, Manuel (1); Nichols, Rodney (20); Poehl, Michael (18); Scott, Charles (20); Skalski, Joseph (2); Swindell, Gregory (3); Trudeau, Kevin (12); Whitmyer, Stephen (12); Williamson, Greg (16); Winbush, Michael (8).

WAUSAU—Darby, Michael (23); Davis, Bret (24); Fortugno, Timothy (19); Malave, Benito (40); McCorkle, David (23); McLain, Timothy (42); Parker, Clayton (26); Roberts, Jeffrey (21); Schooler, Michael (26); Snell, David (41); Walker, James (15); Zavaras, Clinton (17).

GRAND SLAM HOME RUNS—Medina, 3; Fitzgerald, C. Jones, 2 each; Alvis, Arias, Arndt, Bernardo, Canseco, Conner, Cupples, Dasch, Diaz, Flowers, Gibree, Hemond, Higgins, Huson, Maloney, McGrew, Moncerratt, Morgan, Rose, Santos, Scruggs, D. Smith, Sorrento, Swepson, Woods, 1 each.

AWARDED FIRST BASE ON CATCHER'S INTERFERENCE—Gould 7 (Calvert, G. Davis, Fox, Liddell, McGrew, Slominski, Verdugo); Colbert 2 (Bresnahan, Verdugo); Clem (Goldstein); Dietrick (Fox); Howie (Liddell); J. Murphy (Leonard); Simonson (G. Davis); Slominski (Milholland); D. Smith (Fox).

CLUB FIELDING

Club	Pct.	G.	PO.	A.	E.	DP.	PB.
Madison	.971	140	3595	1477	150	97	9
Cedar Rapids	.967	140	3620	1373	169	110	10
Springfield	.966	140	3590	1458	176	121	23
Beloit	.963	139	3584	1434	195	114	27
Waterloo	.962	140	3598	1473	200	115	19
Clinton	.960	139	3592	1386	206	121	30
Peoria	.958	140	3586	1491	222	140	31
Quad Cities	.958	140	3396	1353	209	99	22
Kenosha	.958	138	3541	1332	215	123	36
Wausau	.956	139	3507	1442	226	113	29
Burlington	.956	140	3512	1385	227	105	18
Appleton	.946	139	3524	1327	278	114	39

Triple Plays—Kenosha, Quad Cities.

INDIVIDUAL FIELDING

*Throws lefthanded.

FIRST BASEMEN

Player and Club	Pct.	G.	PO.	A.	E.	DP.
Alfredson, Quad Cities	1.000	3	36	0	0	2
Allen, Appleton*	.986	79	661	42	10	53
Alvis, Waterloo*	.992	88	725	44	6	63
Arias, Madison	.984	137	1172	79	20	77
Arndt, Madison	1.000	4	19	1	0	1
Asbe, Burlington	.972	27	191	15	6	13
Ban, Quad Cities*	1.000	2	10	2	0	1
Blair, Clinton	1.000	2	11	2	0	0
Brown, Cedar Rapids	1.000	2	2	0	0	0
Canan, Peoria	1.000	2	7	1	0	1
Canseco, Madison	.500	1	1	0	1	2
Casteel, Peoria	1.000	2	14	1	0	1
Clem, Wausau	1.000	12	89	9	0	9
Cohoon, Wausau	.973	12	69	4	2	8
Cunningham, Springfield	.957	4	21	1	1	2
Espinoza, Quad Cities*	.987	84	708	36	10	51
Fitzgerald, Springfield	.979	76	656	39	15	64
Fox, Springfield	.917	1	10	1	1	1
Garcia, Appleton*	.993	37	274	18	2	27
Grace, Peoria*	.988	115	1041	68	13	103
Hamza, Peoria	1.000	1	7	0	0	2
Haney, Beloit	.994	40	311	14	2	25
Hanggie, Beloit	1.000	1	6	0	0	0
Higgins, Waterloo	.991	61	496	29	5	36
HILGENBERG, Cedar Rapids*	.994	104	823	55	5	69
Jones, Burlington*	1.000	6	47	3	0	2
Laird, Quad Cities*	.984	55	417	24	7	39
Lane, Waterloo	1.000	1	1	0	0	0
Lanoux, Kenosha	1.000	2	18	2	0	2
Lemons, Burlington	.990	112	891	63	10	79
Lombarski, Peoria	.950	3	17	2	1	3
Maloney, Springfield	.994	23	151	16	1	16
McCulla, Beloit	.952	4	40	0	2	1
McGinnis, Beloit	.990	101	817	54	9	78
McLaughlin, Kenosha	.981	61	442	25	9	47
McMorris, Peoria*	.988	12	74	5	1	13
Miller, Kenosha	.987	32	205	16	3	29
Moncerratt, Wausau*	.985	90	696	37	11	63
Moritz, Appleton	1.000	3	19	3	0	0
Nelson, Clinton	.988	118	1024	54	13	89
Ortman, Madison	1.000	1	2	0	0	1
Peraza, Appleton	.976	11	81	1	2	3
Perry, Kenosha	.981	39	297	13	6	27
Pregon, Springfield	1.000	49	359	26	0	32
Robidoux, Beloit	1.000	3	12	2	0	1
Schmidt, Kenosha	1.000	1	6	0	0	0
Scruggs, Appleton*	.990	17	94	5	1	9
Silverio, Madison	1.000	3	28	4	0	2
Slominski, Wausau	.979	39	306	13	7	26
Stolnack, Kenosha	.952	13	79	1	4	7
Todd, Waterloo	1.000	3	4	0	0	0
Turner, Peoria*	.984	7	56	5	1	6
Vincent, Cedar Rapids	.987	46	350	21	5	29
Whitt, Clinton	.966	25	191	6	7	15

Triple Plays—Espinoza, Perry.

SECOND BASEMEN

Player and Club	Pct.	G.	PO.	A.	E.	DP.
Adkins, Peoria	1.000	3	5	6	0	2
Alfonzo, Quad Cities	.938	18	32	28	4	9
Alfredson, Quad Cities	1.000	1	4	2	0	0
Barry, Clinton	.667	1	0	2	1	0
Bennett, Waterloo	.965	19	37	46	3	9
Bernhardt, Appleton	.892	14	29	37	8	11
Blair, Clinton	.900	10	21	15	4	4
Breedlove, Springfield	.885	14	26	28	7	6
Bryant, Cedar Rapids	.920	8	13	10	2	4
A. Cabrera, Madison	.989	26	43	50	1	10
F. Cabrera, Wausau	.915	9	25	18	4	2
Caci, Beloit	1.000	1	1	2	0	0
Carrasco, Waterloo	.953	88	158	229	19	43
J. Carter, Clinton	.951	123	221	302	27	67
R. Carter, Madison	1.000	1	2	1	0	0
Cash, Clinton	1.000	9	16	21	0	3
Cunningham, Springfield	1.000	1	5	5	0	3
Delancer, Kenosha	.778	3	5	2	2	0
Diaz, Wausau	.900	3	5	4	1	3
DiCeglio, Kenosha	.909	23	38	42	8	10
Donahue, Cedar Rapids	.914	26	38	47	8	9
Dunlap, Cedar Rapids	.985	31	75	59	2	20
Eveline, Appleton	.933	106	228	231	33	55
Grant, Quad Cities	.963	105	204	270	18	45
Haller, Appleton	.903	22	44	40	9	5
Hillman, Waterloo	1.000	8	7	23	0	4
Hindman, Cedar Rapids	.968	79	125	209	11	43
Howie, Madison	.964	107	221	240	17	48
Huson, Burlington	.750	2	2	1	1	0
Isaac, Appleton	1.000	1	1	0	0	0
Kroener, Kenosha	.973	59	130	155	8	35
Lanoux, Kenosha	1.000	8	14	17	0	4
Larson, Wausau	.927	53	97	131	18	35
Laureano, Burlington	.954	127	226	296	25	70
Lockhart, Cedar Rapids	1.000	9	16	13	0	3
Mack, Kenosha	1.000	1	0	2	0	0
Mandeville, Peoria	.942	22	51	62	7	19
Martinez, Madison	1.000	8	10	24	0	4
Mattox, Beloit	.977	70	146	149	7	51
Miller, Kenosha	.970	7	19	13	1	6
Nalls, Quad Cities	.929	8	11	15	2	4
Naveda, Kenosha	.967	37	86	89	6	19
Nix, Madison	.975	8	17	22	1	5
Reyes, Quad Cities	1.000	3	1	3	0	1
Rodriguez, Quad Cities	1.000	9	13	22	0	1
Rose, Quad Cities	1.000	5	4	4	0	0
Schmidt, Kenosha	1.000	2	1	3	0	2
G. Smith, Peoria	.932	23	33	49	6	6
P. Smith, Beloit	.975	47	78	117	5	18
Swain, Waterloo	.945	51	89	116	12	24
Tapias, Kenosha	.886	9	18	13	4	5
Tavarez, Burlington	.927	24	33	43	6	9
Van Stone, Clinton	1.000	1	2	1	0	1
Ventura, Beloit	.993	25	63	70	1	12
Vizquel, Wausau	.947	3	8	10	1	2
Wallace, Peoria	.954	98	213	286	24	72
WILSON, Springfield	.972	126	292	343	18	86
Woods, Wausau	.960	74	145	191	14	37
Zottneck, Quad Cities	1.000	1	1	0	0	0

Triple Play—Naveda.

THIRD BASEMEN

Player and Club	Pct.	G.	PO.	A.	E.	DP.
Adkins, Peoria	1.000	1	0	1	0	0
Alfonzo, Quad Cities	.972	40	24	80	3	6
Alfredson, Quad Cities	.896	19	8	35	5	2
ARNDT, Madison	.938	113	80	251	22	17
Asbe, Burlington	1.000	1	0	1	0	0
Bell, Quad Cities	.870	20	7	40	7	3

THIRD BASEMEN—Continued

Player and Club	Pct.	G.	PO.	A.	E.	DP.
Bennett, Waterloo	1.000	1	0	1	0	0
Blair, Clinton	.857	6	3	9	2	2
Brandts, Wausau	.855	43	30	94	21	7
Breedlove, Springfield	.907	69	46	160	21	20
Brown, Cedar Rapids	.893	138	84	249	40	20
Cabrera, Wausau	.846	4	5	6	2	0
Caci, Beloit	1.000	1	0	2	0	0
Canan, Peoria	.910	129	88	276	36	29
Carter, Madison	.851	22	9	31	7	1
Cash, Clinton	1.000	2	0	3	0	0
Casteel, Peoria	.625	2	2	3	3	0
Cohoon, Wausau	.872	68	34	116	22	9
Colbert, Clinton	.931	72	49	153	15	17
Cunningham, Springfield	.957	73	39	139	8	15
Dandos, Clinton	.906	10	10	19	3	2
Diaz, Wausau	.868	26	19	47	10	3
Donahue, Cedar Rapids	1.000	3	1	2	0	0
Dull, Burlington	.835	34	39	57	19	3
Fairchild, Waterloo	.667	2	1	1	1	0
Flowers, Clinton	.851	25	12	45	10	4
Frye, Burlington	.936	17	11	33	3	4
Grant, Quad Cities	.667	1	0	2	1	1
Haller, Appleton	.600	4	0	3	2	0
Haney, Beloit	.933	5	3	11	1	0
Hanggie, Beloit	936	123	85	278	25	29
Hindman, Cedar Rapids	1.000	3	1	1	0	0
Huson, Burlington	.868	13	13	20	5	2
Isaac, Appleton	1.000	1	0	1	0	1
Johnson, Kenosha	.867	19	15	24	6	3
Kroener, Kenosha	1.000	1	0	1	0	0
Lanoux, Kenosha	.846	4	3	8	2	2
Larson, Wausau	1.000	4	0	4	0	0
Lockhart, Cedar Rapids	1.000	1	1	2	0	0
Maloney, Springfield	.733	9	2	9	4	1
Mandeville, Peoria	.917	7	6	5	1	1
Manto, Quad Cities	.853	65	48	114	28	5
Marquez, Quad Cities	1.000	1	1	2	0	0
McCulla, Beloit	1.000	2	2	0	0	0
McGinnis, Beloit	.500	4	3	2	5	0
Milholland, Appleton	.739	9	4	13	6	2
Moritz, Appleton	.792	12	2	17	5	0
Naveda, Kenosha	.923	21	14	34	4	1
Nix, Madison	.822	14	9	28	8	0
Oller, Burlington	.730	15	7	20	10	2
Reyes, Quad Cities	.857	2	0	6	1	0
Salazar, Appleton	.906	19	9	39	5	4
Schmidt, Kenosha	.904	68	67	139	22	8
Sheldon, Appleton	.867	95	82	198	43	16
Small, Peoria	.667	1	0	2	1	0
Swain, Waterloo	.900	8	6	12	2	1
Touma, Burlington	.964	34	19	62	3	2
Van Stone, Clinton	.955	31	12	51	3	3
Velarde, Appleton	1.000	8	2	18	0	1
Ventura, Beloit	.800	7	4	8	3	0
Walker, Burlington	.910	36	16	45	6	3
Wallace, Peoria	.900	6	2	7	1	0
Webster, Waterloo	.922	133	98	259	30	30
Wellman, Kenosha	.879	32	30	57	12	4

Triple Plays—Alfonzo, Lanoux.

SHORTSTOPS

Player and Club	Pct.	G.	PO.	A.	E.	DP.
Adkins, Peoria	.882	5	7	8	2	3
Alfonzo, Quad Cities	.886	12	9	30	5	2
Alfredson, Quad Cities	.667	2	1	1	1	0
Barry, Clinton	.915	75	80	188	25	41
Bennett, Waterloo	.920	45	69	115	16	14
Blair, Clinton	1.000	6	3	1	0	1
Breedlove, Springfield	.905	9	9	10	2	3
Cabrera, Madison	.955	26	33	51	4	8
Caci, Beloit	.900	14	11	43	6	2
Canan, Peoria	1.000	2	3	7	0	0
Cash, Clinton	.667	1	2	0	1	0
Corcino, Burlington	.833	32	30	55	17	10
Dandos, Clinton	.947	8	10	26	2	6
Dasch, Kenosha	.926	57	80	144	18	37
Delancer, Kenosha	.944	6	6	11	1	2
Diaz, Wausau	.917	43	81	117	18	21
DiCeglio, 30 Ken-8 Peo	.943	38	50	100	9	22
Duffy, Madison	.959	35	53	110	7	13
Dunlap, Cedar Rapids	.870	7	9	11	3	3
Fairchild, Waterloo	.870	27	46	68	17	20
Germann, Cedar Rapids	.954	134	205	361	27	66
Gill, Waterloo	.899	69	105	196	34	31
Haller, Appleton	.846	7	6	5	2	1
Harrison, Springfield	.930	134	168	379	41	56
Hillman, Waterloo	1.000	5	3	9	0	2
Hindman, Cedar Rapids	.500	1	0	1	1	0
Huson, Burlington	.938	119	168	303	31	52
Johnson, Kenosha	.917	20	16	39	5	7
Larson, Wausau	1.000	1	1	3	0	1
Lincoln, Beloit	.876	70	102	181	40	36
Mandeville, Peoria	.600	1	1	2	2	1
Martin, Appleton	.829	8	13	16	6	2
Naveda, Kenosha	.922	36	55	75	11	14
Peluso, Appleton	.786	5	5	6	3	1
Reyes, Quad Cities	1.000	7	4	20	0	3
Rose, Quad Cities	.921	125	172	293	40	52
Sheldon, Appleton	.894	19	30	54	10	9
Small, Peoria	.915	108	153	330	45	76
Smith, Peoria	.903	23	32	52	9	11
Swain, Waterloo	1.000	3	2	3	0	0
Tapias, Kenosha	.952	4	7	13	1	3
Van Stone, Clinton	.853	8	7	22	5	3
Velarde, Appleton	.901	108	190	282	52	56
Ventura, Beloit	.930	61	97	170	20	23
VIZQUEL, Wausau	.969	101	145	318	15	49
Weiss, Madison	.952	84	143	251	20	37
Williams, Clinton	.960	57	89	150	10	26

OUTFIELDERS

Player and Club	Pct.	G.	PO.	A.	E.	DP.
Alfredson, Quad Cities	.917	72	92	8	9	0
Allen, Appleton*	1.000	1	1	0	0	0
Arias, Madison	1.000	2	1	1	0	1
Asbe, Burlington	1.000	7	11	0	0	0
Ashley, Beloit	.949	63	73	1	4	0
Ban, Quad Cities*	.943	48	62	4	4	1
J. Bennett, Wausau	.917	38	52	3	5	0
K. Bennett, Waterloo	.932	69	102	8	8	1
Bernardo, Wausau	.939	108	152	17	11	2
Blackwell, Kenosha	.948	75	157	8	9	1
Blair, Clinton	.984	40	55	6	1	0
Braxton, Appleton*	1.000	4	6	0	0	0
Breedlove, Springfield	1.000	1	1	0	0	0
Bryant, Cedar Rapids	.978	83	131	3	3	0
Cabrera, Wausau	1.000	2	3	0	0	0
Cain, Cedar Rapids*	.962	68	100	2	4	2
Canseco, Madison	.986	35	71	1	1	0
D. Carter, Springfield	.973	137	237	17	7	0
R. Carter, Madison	.983	46	52	5	1	2
Casteel, Peoria	.958	26	45	1	2	0
Clark, Beloit	.846	11	10	1	2	0
Clem, Wausau	.950	70	102	12	6	1
Collins, Peoria	.938	15	29	1	2	0
Conner, Clinton	.916	55	74	2	7	0
Cupples, Madison	1.000	1	1	0	0	0
Davis, Appleton	.973	75	105	5	3	1
DeLima, Kenosha*	1.000	12	23	0	0	0
Diaz, Wausau	.947	17	17	1	1	0
Dull, Burlington	.941	30	46	2	3	0
Ealy, Clinton	.867	27	23	3	4	0
Eccleston, Wausau*	.971	57	101	1	3	0
Escalera, Beloit*	.967	114	199	6	7	1
Ewart, Peoria*	.957	57	83	6	4	0
Fairchild, Waterloo	1.000	2	1	0	0	0
Fazzini, Beloit	.882	25	29	1	4	0
Flowers, Clinton	.947	10	18	0	1	0
Gilbert, Madison	.955	56	103	3	5	0
Gould, Madison	.984	109	186	3	3	1
Grace, Peoria*	1.000	6	9	1	0	0
Grant, Quad Cities	1.000	1	1	0	0	0
Greene, Beloit	.952	39	59	1	3	0
Grimes, Peoria	.962	71	96	5	4	1
Grunhard, Quad Cities*	.945	35	65	4	4	0
Guillory, Madison	1.000	9	11	0	0	0
Hamza, Peoria	1.000	10	13	0	0	0
Haney, Beloit	.909	33	19	1	2	0
Hartley, Appleton	.988	41	79	0	1	0
Heist, Burlington	.957	11	21	1	1	0
Hernandez, Burlington	.955	38	62	1	3	0
Howie, Madison	.952	12	20	0	1	0
Huff, Kenosha	1.000	8	14	2	0	2
Isaac, Appleton	1.000	4	5	0	0	0
A. Jacas, Madison	1.000	50	104	1	0	0
D. Jacas, Kenosha	.961	74	119	3	5	1
L. Jackson, Clinton*	.902	32	51	4	6	0
M. JACKSON, Cedar Rapids	.985	103	185	7	3	3
Johnson, Burlington*	.927	122	183	7	15	1
C. Jones, Cedar Rapids	.955	118	218	15	11	2
T. Jones, Burlington*	.977	39	84	2	2	0
Jordan, Waterloo	.966	110	212	12	8	1
Laird, Quad Cities*	1.000	2	3	0	0	0
Larson, Wausau	.750	4	3	0	1	0

OUTFIELDERS—Continued

Player and Club	Pct.	G.	PO.	A.	E.	DP.
Leon, Springfield*	.966	41	56	1	2	0
Lewis, Peoria	.969	102	183	3	6	1
Mack, Kenosha	1.000	2	4	0	0	0
Magallanes, Appleton	.907	59	84	4	9	1
Maloney, Springfield	1.000	4	2	0	0	0
Manzon, Kenosha	.978	98	208	10	5	3
McCulla, 1 Spring-8 Bel	.944	9	17	0	1	0
McIntosh, Beloit	.962	39	98	4	4	1
McLaughlin, Kenosha	.975	24	38	1	1	0
Medina, Waterloo*	.977	124	208	8	5	2
G. Meyers, Quad Cities	.935	85	137	7	10	0
P. Meyers, Clinton*	.989	73	169	6	2	0
Miller, Clinton	.964	106	179	9	7	1
Moncerratt, Wausau*	.944	13	17	0	1	0
Morgan, Kenosha*	.894	59	93	0	11	0
Moritz, Appleton	1.000	1	1	0	0	0
D. Murphy, Madison	1.000	1	1	0	0	0
J. Murphy, Springfield	.976	89	201	2	5	0
Nalls, Quad Cities	.936	72	125	6	9	0
Naveda, Kenosha	1.000	22	35	2	0	0
O'Connor, Kenosha	1.000	13	15	0	0	0
Ortman, Madison	1.000	3	5	0	0	0
I. Rodriguez, Burlington	.974	22	36	1	1	0
J. Rodriguez, Springfield	.991	43	106	3	1	1
Russ, Madison*	1.000	4	4	0	0	0
Santos, Waterloo	1.000	21	23	3	0	1
Schiffelbein, Madison*	.950	25	37	1	2	0
Schulte, Springfield	.970	74	156	8	5	1
Scruggs, Appleton*	.917	64	108	3	10	2
Sheldon, Appleton	1.000	7	5	1	0	0
Sigler, Cedar Rapids	.970	67	120	10	4	3
Simonson, Beloit	.964	112	209	7	8	1
Slotnick, Burlington	.982	33	51	4	1	1
Small, Peoria	1.000	1	1	0	0	0
Smith, Peoria	.956	123	272	11	13	2
Sorrento, Quad Cities	.989	47	83	7	1	2
Stolnack, Kenosha	.600	3	2	1	2	0
Sullivan, Appleton	.968	36	58	3	2	2
Swepson, Clinton	.975	96	184	15	5	4
Tavarez, Burlington	.857	11	5	1	1	0
Thomason, Kenosha	.974	42	72	3	2	0
Toliver, Appleton	1.000	27	31	2	0	0
Torres, Quad Cities	.981	26	49	2	1	0
Traylor, Springfield	.969	64	118	5	4	3
Turner, Peoria*	.884	34	37	1	5	0
Uribe, Wausau	.965	117	233	16	9	3
Velarde, Appleton	.867	5	13	0	2	0
Ventura, Beloit	.889	3	8	0	1	0
Veras, Madison*	.971	105	193	9	6	2
Waggoner, Appleton	.930	58	87	6	7	2
Wagner, Appleton	.984	58	121	2	2	1
Walker, Burlington	.960	57	90	6	4	2
Washington, Quad Cities	.955	46	105	1	5	1
Whitt, Clinton	.887	35	46	1	6	0
Williams, Burlington*	.938	85	145	7	10	1
Workman, Waterloo	.984	108	229	13	4	2

CATCHERS

Player and Club	Pct.	G.	PO.	A.	E.	DP.	PB.
Anders, Peoria	.974	32	170	17	5	2	2
Baker, Quad Cities	1.000	4	20	2	0	1	1
Bell, Quad Cities	1.000	6	28	7	0	0	2
Bresnahan, Waterloo	.984	78	503	51	9	8	9
Brown, Appleton	.986	58	382	33	6	5	18
Calvert, Kenosha	.978	89	644	83	16	8	20
Carter, Madison	1.000	3	8	0	0	1	0
Casteel, Peoria	.973	18	105	4	3	1	8
Cento, Appleton	1.000	6	34	3	0	2	2
CUPPLES, Madison	.9910	99	583	78	6	6	4
Davis, Burlington	.986	100	710	78	11	5	10
Fitzgerald, Springfield	.964	35	163	24	7	0	4
Fox, Springfield	.984	105	684	63	12	3	15
Gibree, Wausau	.983	85	587	52	11	4	26
Girardi, Peoria	.989	66	405	34	5	3	13
Goldstein, Kenosha	.981	40	282	29	6	2	15
Hemond, Madison	.985	18	121	11	2	3	1
Hornsby, Clinton	.978	44	250	17	6	0	6
Johnigan, Waterloo	.962	15	66	10	3	1	2
Lane, Waterloo	.989	55	323	23	4	5	8
Leonard, Burlington	.965	49	299	33	12	4	8
Liddell, Peoria	.979	32	206	22	5	3	8
Maloney, Springfield	1.000	3	8	0	0	0	3
Mann, Peoria	.964	3	26	1	1	0	0
Manwaring, Clinton	.982	42	243	31	5	2	9
Marquez, Quad Cities	.984	100	661	83	12	6	15
McCulla, 1 Spring-7 Bel	.978	8	42	3	1	0	0
McGinnis, Beloit	.975	15	109	10	3	1	3
McGrew, Beloit	.988	80	585	60	8	5	16
Milholland, Appleton	.984	55	369	55	7	5	12
Miller, Kenosha	1.000	2	4	0	0	0	0
Olson, Beloit	.986	28	197	12	3	0	6
Pawling, Clinton	1.000	1	1	0	0	0	0
Pena, Clinton	.9908	75	483	57	5	10	14
Rivera, Appleton	.982	29	201	19	4	2	7
Sheldon, Appleton	1.000	1	1	0	0	0	0
Silverio, Madison	.995	32	188	21	1	2	4
Slominski, Wausau	.989	56	421	31	5	4	3
Todd, Waterloo	1.000	4	7	2	0	1	0
Toler, Cedar Rapids	.986	76	511	37	8	1	4
Verdugo, Beloit	.971	14	91	9	3	1	2
Webster, Kenosha	1.000	12	87	9	0	0	1
Zeratsky, Cedar Rapids	.978	75	531	51	13	6	6
Zottneck, Quad Cities	.966	41	183	18	7	3	4

Triple Play—Marquez.

PITCHERS

Player and Club	Pct.	G.	PO.	A.	E.	DP.
Abbott, Kenosha	1.000	25	9	9	0	1
Ames, Madison*	1.000	20	1	14	0	0
Arrington, Burlington	.895	17	3	14	2	1
Atkinson, Springfield	.947	29	7	11	1	0
Auth, Quad Cities	1.000	8	0	1	0	0
Bartolomucci, Appleton*	.750	11	0	3	1	0
Bates, Springfield*	.857	23	0	6	1	0
Belinskas, Cedar Rapids	.917	38	2	9	1	0
Bivens, Springfield	.933	16	5	9	1	1
Blakley, Clinton	.867	41	2	11	2	0
Blunt, Springfield	1.000	4	2	0	0	0
Boling, Appleton*	1.000	38	2	6	0	1
Bonilla, Clinton*	.882	39	3	12	2	1
Bosley, Beloit	1.000	15	4	7	0	0
Brisco, Beloit	1.000	42	3	14	0	0
Bronkey, Kenosha	.917	14	3	8	1	0
Bruno, Cedar Rapids	1.000	9	0	4	0	0
Brusky, Cedar Rapids	1.000	45	7	14	0	1
Bumgarner, Kenosha	.882	23	3	27	4	4
Burcham, Quad Cities	.978	27	12	32	1	4
Campbell, Cedar Rapids	.952	20	9	31	2	2
Candelaria, Appleton	1.000	6	3	4	0	0
Charland, Quad Cities*	.667	10	0	2	1	0
Cocanower, Beloit	1.000	2	1	5	0	1
Coleman, Peoria	1.000	3	0	1	0	0
Collins, Quad Cities	1.000	22	9	14	0	1
Converse, Cedar Rapids	.857	28	10	20	5	3
Cook, Kenosha	1.000	19	0	6	0	0
Cortes, Appleton	.923	22	8	16	2	1
Craskey, Kenosha	.941	28	5	11	1	0
Criswell, Madison*	1.000	14	0	4	0	0
Crouch, Burlington	1.000	20	10	22	0	2
Cundari, Madison	.941	15	6	10	1	0
Damian, Peoria	.933	25	9	19	2	1
Danek, Peoria	.934	27	20	37	4	5
Darby, Wausau	.909	23	3	7	1	0
B. Davis, Wausau*	.833	24	0	5	1	1
M. Davis, 6 Ken-19 Spring*	.727	25	2	6	3	0
Deabenderfer, Madison	.903	18	9	19	3	2
Deitz, Cedar Rapids	.909	45	4	16	2	2
DiMichele, Quad Cities*	.941	26	1	15	1	2
Dougherty, Burlington	1.000	15	3	4	0	0
Dube, Waterloo	1.000	16	6	5	0	0
Farr, Waterloo	1.000	28	1	11	0	0
Fedor, 16 Bur-20 Water	1.000	36	3	14	0	0
Filippi, Appleton	1.000	6	1	2	0	0
Finley, Quad Cities*	.667	10	0	2	1	0
Fitzpatrick, Beloit	1.000	36	3	4	0	0
Forrest, Springfield	1.000	3	0	2	0	0
Fortugno, Wausau*	.750	19	0	3	1	0
Franco, Quad Cities	1.000	6	3	0	0	0
Freed, Springfield	.923	29	5	19	2	1
Freeland, Clinton	1.000	20	5	31	0	1
J. Gardner, Peoria	1.000	9	0	7	0	0
M. Gardner, Waterloo	1.000	6	1	3	0	0
Gasser, Kenosha	.929	27	6	20	2	1
Ghelfi, Waterloo	.957	26	13	31	2	4
Githens, Waterloo	.800	23	4	4	2	0
Gosling, Beloit	1.000	2	0	2	0	0
Hall, Madison	1.000	43	5	8	0	1
Harris, Burlington	.889	7	3	13	2	0
Hartley, Springfield	1.000	8	0	4	0	0
Harvey, Quad Cities*	1.000	5	1	1	0	0
Henderson, Beloit*	.941	12	2	14	1	1
D. Henry, Beloit	.973	27	13	23	1	2
M. Henry, Appleton*	1.000	6	1	6	0	0
Hirsch, Peoria	.941	47	10	6	1	0
Howes, Burlington*	.920	15	2	21	2	1

PITCHERS—Continued

Player and Club	Pct.	G.	PO.	A.	E.	DP.
Hulstrom, Appleton*	1.000	14	1	2	0	0
Hunter, 9 Bur-15 Beloit	.939	24	10	36	3	3
Johnigan, Waterloo	.000	2	0	0	1	0
Johnson, Quad Cities	.833	26	0	5	1	0
Kallevig, Peoria	1.000	25	7	16	0	2
Kannenberg, Quad Cities	.920	26	6	17	2	3
Karpuk, Waterloo	.966	28	13	15	1	0
Kavanaugh, Springfield	.933	33	1	13	1	0
Kazmierczak, Peoria	.909	11	2	8	1	1
Kelly, Burlington	.933	12	5	9	1	0
Kershaw, Appleton	.333	8	1	0	2	0
Kibler, Madison	1.000	9	1	1	0	0
Kindred, Cedar Rapids	1.000	38	5	14	0	0
King, Burlington	1.000	3	3	6	0	1
Kleean, Beloit*	1.000	34	3	8	0	0
Kraemer, Peoria*	1.000	45	4	12	0	2
Kuykendall, Waterloo	.929	16	4	9	1	0
LaFever, Waterloo	.951	24	9	30	2	1
Lambert, Madison*	.947	25	1	17	1	1
Law, Madison	.952	19	6	14	1	1
Lee, Kenosha	.926	27	7	18	2	2
Malave, Wausau	.778	40	5	9	4	1
Marino, Quad Cities	1.000	37	5	14	0	0
Mauch, Springfield	.974	23	7	30	1	0
McCorkle, Wausau	.976	23	11	29	1	1
McCoy, Clinton*	.867	14	2	11	2	0
McDonald, Madison	.923	5	1	11	1	0
McGrew, Beloit	1.000	1	0	1	0	0
McGuire, Quad Cities	.946	23	14	39	3	3
McLain, Wausau	.944	42	4	13	1	1
Mead, Clinton	.828	27	7	17	5	0
Miglio, Beloit*	.882	37	3	12	2	0
Minutelli, Cedar Rapids*	.933	27	11	17	2	1
Montano, Beloit*	1.000	4	0	2	0	0
Moran, Appleton*	.714	29	2	3	2	0
Moraw, Beloit	.949	28	11	45	3	5
Morehouse, Quad Cities	.947	18	8	10	1	2
Morris, Clinton	1.000	41	1	3	0	0
Nichols, Waterloo	.929	20	4	9	1	2
Norman, Springfield	.895	25	4	13	2	0
O'Connor, Kenosha*	1.000	38	1	17	0	3
Ojeda, Beloit*	1.000	6	0	5	0	0
Ollom, Appleton	.500	6	0	1	1	0
Oswald, Appleton*	.700	15	3	11	6	1
Otto, Madison*	.974	26	6	31	1	2
OYSTER, Springfield	1.000	28	22	27	0	1
Pall, Appleton	.967	11	5	24	1	3
C. Parker, Wausau	.966	26	5	23	1	3
S. Parker, Peoria*	1.000	16	10	15	0	1
Pearson, Clinton	.903	30	7	21	3	0
Penigar, Clinton	1.000	21	4	7	0	1
M. Perez, Burlington	.978	28	9	35	1	0
Y. Perez, Kenosha*	.909	31	5	15	2	1
Peters, Springfield*	1.000	15	7	15	0	3
Phillips, Peoria	.917	36	4	7	1	1
Pilkington, Clinton*	.833	29	0	5	1	0
Poehl, Waterloo	.968	18	7	23	1	0
Redding, Kenosha	.909	23	5	15	2	1
Renz, Appleton	1.000	13	5	7	0	2
Reyes, Beloit	.882	33	2	13	2	0
Reynolds, Appleton	.833	41	2	8	2	0
Rivera, Quad Cities	.909	24	1	9	1	0
Roberts, Wausau	.842	21	6	10	3	0
D. Robertson, Clinton	.839	27	9	17	5	0
M. Robertson, 8 Spring-4 Bur	.600	12	1	2	2	0
Robinson, Appleton	1.000	8	0	2	0	0
Robles, Peoria	1.000	7	1	6	0	0
Rodriguez, Burlington	.895	32	8	9	2	1
Roesler, Cedar Rapids	.912	32	7	24	3	1
Roth, Peoria	.975	27	13	26	1	3
Sabo, Madison*	1.000	22	0	3	0	0
Salcedo, Madison	.900	25	3	6	1	2
Sandoval, Appleton	1.000	8	0	2	0	0
Sassone, Springfield	.917	14	4	7	1	1
Schooler, Wausau	.891	26	13	28	5	2
Scott, Waterloo	1.000	20	5	17	0	0
Scruggs, Appleton*	1.000	2	2	0	0	0
Shaver, Madison	.951	26	14	25	2	1
Shull, Quad Cities	.842	35	7	9	3	1
Siegel, Wausau	.848	26	9	30	7	2
Simmons, Beloit	.923	25	3	9	1	0
Simpson, Cedar Rapids*	1.000	35	10	17	0	1
Slowik, Peoria	.882	50	3	12	2	1
J. Smith, Beloit	1.000	5	0	1	0	0
L. Smith, Quad Cities*	1.000	24	0	5	0	0
M. Smith, Cedar Rapids	.934	28	16	41	4	5
Snell, Wausau	1.000	41	6	15	0	1
Stauffacher, Burlington*	.833	23	1	9	2	2
Stein, Appleton	.840	30	5	16	4	1
Stocker, Madison	.929	11	3	10	1	2
Stone, Appleton	.932	38	14	27	3	3
Strube, Kenosha*	.833	41	5	15	4	2
Sudo, Burlington	.941	16	9	39	3	3
Sundgren, Burlington	1.000	17	2	3	0	0
Swan, Clinton*	1.000	7	0	5	0	0
Swindell, Waterloo*	1.000	3	1	2	0	0
Townsend, Clinton*	1.000	13	2	10	0	0
Trautwein, Burlington	.857	21	4	8	2	0
Trudeau, Waterloo	1.000	12	0	5	0	0
Veres, Beloit	.912	23	7	24	3	2
Villanueva, Appleton*	1.000	14	2	9	0	2
Walker, Wausau	1.000	15	0	5	0	1
Walton, Madison	1.000	1	1	0	0	0
Warren, Appleton	.882	11	2	13	2	0
Whitehurst, Madison	.957	8	3	19	1	0
Whitford, Beloit	.800	5	0	4	1	0
Whitmyer, Waterloo	1.000	12	3	4	0	0
Williams, Burlington	.913	18	7	14	2	1
G. Williamson, Waterloo	1.000	16	4	13	0	0
K. Williamson, Madison	.923	22	4	8	1	0
Wilmet, Springfield	1.000	56	6	18	0	2
Wilson, Clinton*	.897	34	11	15	3	2
Winbush, Waterloo	.500	8	1	2	3	0
Zarranz, Peoria	1.000	15	4	13	0	1
Zavaras, Wausau	.857	17	2	10	2	0

Triple Play—Johnson.

The following players do not have any recorded accepted chances at the positions indicated; therefore, are not listed in the fielding averages for those particular positions: Alfredson, c, p; Arias, p; Ban, p; A. Cabrera, of; Canseco, p; Cash, of; Clark, 2b, 3b, ss; Corcino, of; Cunningham, of; DiCeglio, 3b; Green, p; Hemond, of; Holcomb, p; Horton, p; E. Johnson, of; W. Johnson, p; Krueger, p; Lanoux, c; Laureano, 3b; Mercado, p; G. Meyers, p; Te. Miller, 3b, p; Nalls, p; Peluso, of; Pena, of; Peraza, 3b; Reynolds, 3b; Saatzer, p; Skalski, p; Tapias, 3b.

CLUB PITCHING

Club	ERA.	G.	CG.	ShO.	Sv.	IP.	H.	R.	ER.	HR.	HB.	BB.	Int. BB.	SO.	WP.	Bk.
Madison	3.43	140	23	16	34	1198.1	1111	557	457	79	39	508	8	879	64	12
Peoria	3.50	140	19	9	43	1195.1	1147	619	465	62	70	431	16	877	93	14
Clinton	3.55	139	14	12	26	1197.1	1050	580	472	61	45	595	27	950	60	14
Wausau	3.56	139	20	11	35	1169.0	1126	609	462	83	46	496	16	983	105	11
Cedar Rapids	3.63	140	12	12	30	1206.2	1055	578	487	99	34	559	12	1005	91	9
Springfield	3.63	140	32	7	36	1196.2	1151	577	483	99	44	399	13	833	55	13
Waterloo	3.77	140	31	8	28	1199.1	1209	616	502	115	73	347	4	858	76	10
Beloit	3.91	139	18	7	23	1194.2	1169	644	519	81	33	573	45	995	106	20
Burlington	3.96	140	52	13	19	1170.2	1146	626	515	97	30	475	9	971	70	10
Quad Cities	4.12	140	27	11	27	1132.0	1122	649	518	75	45	533	12	861	76	14
Kenosha	4.28	138	24	4	15	1180.1	1137	693	561	104	33	638	21	959	91	8
Appleton	4.35	139	18	8	25	1174.2	1154	735	568	65	53	620	19	959	113	17

PITCHERS' RECORDS

(Leading Qualifiers for Earned-Run Average Leadership—112 or More Innings)

*Throws lefthanded.

Pitcher—Club	W.	L.	Pct.	ERA.	G.	GS.	CG.	GF.	ShO.	Sv.	IP.	H.	R.	ER.	HR.	HB.	BB.	Int. BB.	SO.	WP.
Simpson, Cedar Rapids*	6	4	.600	1.81	35	12	1	10	1	1	119.2	89	32	24	7	1	38	0	78	5
Sudo, Burlington	10	4	.714	1.91	16	16	9	0	1	0	127.0	100	42	27	5	2	38	2	114	6
LaFever, Waterloo	10	5	.667	2.30	24	20	8	4	2	1	152.1	134	49	39	15	5	28	0	108	5
Stone, Appleton	6	7	.462	2.51	38	9	0	20	0	5	125.1	112	62	35	4	6	40	0	84	1

Pitcher—Club	W.	L.	Pct.	ERA.	G.	GS.	CG.	GF.	ShO.	Sv.	IP.	H.	R.	ER.	HR.	HB.	BB.	Int. BB.	SO.	WP.
Otto, Madison*	13	7	.650	2.66	26	26	6	0	1	0	169.0	154	72	50	9	2	71	0	125	6
Freeland, Clinton	7	7	.500	2.85	20	20	6	0	2	0	142.0	101	53	45	6	5	76	3	129	9
Damian, Peoria	12	9	.571	2.85	25	25	7	0	2	0	164.0	140	74	52	8	11	45	1	127	7
C. Parker, Wausau	8	7	.533	2.88	26	26	4	0	0	0	178.0	171	77	57	11	7	39	1	154	13
Oyster, Springfield	17	7	.708	3.03	28	28	10	0	0	0	184.0	170	73	62	14	8	42	2	142	3
Roth, Peoria	11	9	.550	3.22	27	27	2	0	0	0	179.0	164	86	64	7	13	76	0	109	19
M. Smith, Cedar Rapids	10	10	.500	3.35	28	27	4	1	1	0	191.0	155	88	71	12	6	106	1	172	19
Schooler, Wausau	12	10	.545	3.35	26	26	6	0	1	0	166.1	166	83	62	20	4	44	0	171	10

Departmental Leaders: G—Wilmet, 56; W—Oyster, 17; L—Stein, 16; Pct.—Peters, .909; GS—Stein, 30; CG—M. Perez, 13; GF—Wilmet, 46; ShO—DiMichele, Whitehurst, 4; Sv.—Wilmet, 29; IP—M. Smith, 191.0; H—Ghelfi, 198; R—Stein, 118; ER—Lee, Stein, 90; HR—Lee, 21; HB—Ghelfi, 15; BB—Moraw, 108; IBB—Brisco, 13; SO—Gasser, 225; WP—Five pitchers with 19.

(All Pitchers—Listed Alphabetically)

Pitcher—Club	W.	L.	Pct.	ERA.	G.	GS.	CG.	GF.	ShO.	Sv.	IP.	H.	R.	ER.	HR.	HB.	BB.	Int. BB.	SO.	WP.
Abbott, Kenosha	6	10	.375	4.50	25	15	1	7	0	0	98.0	102	62	49	13	2	73	3	73	7
Alfredson, Quad Cities	0	0	.000	0.00	1	0	0	1	0	0	2.0	1	0	0	0	0	0	0	0	0
Ames, Madison*	5	2	.714	4.89	20	4	0	4	0	0	53.1	63	31	29	3	2	15	0	34	4
Arias, Madison	0	0	.000	0.00	1	0	0	1	0	0	2.0	1	0	0	0	0	0	0	1	0
Arrington, Burlington	2	5	.286	5.23	17	11	1	6	0	0	72.1	87	49	42	11	3	23	0	63	4
Atkinson, Springfield	1	4	.200	4.84	29	3	0	14	0	1	57.2	59	38	31	8	1	29	1	44	3
Auth, Quad Cities	0	0	.000	11.17	8	0	0	3	0	0	9.2	13	13	12	1	1	22	0	12	5
Ban, Quad Cities*	0	0	.000	18.00	1	0	0	1	0	0	3.0	5	6	6	2	0	4	0	4	0
Bartolomucci, Appleton*	0	0	.000	6.17	11	0	0	7	0	1	23.1	24	19	16	3	1	25	0	22	8
Bates, Springfield*	3	3	.500	3.61	23	3	0	5	0	0	57.1	70	26	23	3	1	18	2	36	2
Belinskas, Cedar Rapids	4	7	.364	4.82	38	1	0	17	0	2	80.1	77	46	43	9	0	35	2	50	8
Bivens, Springfield	5	7	.417	5.45	16	13	3	0	0	0	77.2	69	53	47	10	3	35	1	49	7
Blakley, Clinton	3	5	.375	2.35	41	0	0	26	0	5	76.2	59	26	20	4	7	44	4	84	1
Blunt, Springfield	0	2	.000	6.48	4	4	0	0	0	0	16.2	16	16	12	2	0	15	0	15	2
Boling, Appleton*	0	2	.000	2.74	38	0	0	30	0	9	49.1	34	18	15	1	1	26	2	57	5
Bonilla, Clinton*	6	5	.545	2.45	39	7	2	21	0	4	92.0	75	32	25	1	0	27	3	73	4
Bosley, Beloit	1	3	.250	6.31	15	0	0	3	0	2	25.2	21	20	18	3	1	23	2	26	5
Brisco, Beloit	13	2	.867	2.43	42	0	0	35	0	10	81.1	72	24	22	5	1	31	13	65	2
Bronkey, Kenosha	4	6	.400	3.83	14	6	1	5	0	0	49.1	41	24	21	5	4	30	3	25	5
Bruno, Cedar Rapids	0	1	.000	5.09	9	0	0	2	0	0	17.2	19	12	10	3	2	6	0	15	1
Brusky, Cedar Rapids	7	4	.636	2.58	45	0	0	38	0	10	73.1	61	29	21	6	2	16	2	63	2
Bumgarner, Kenosha	7	14	.333	3.46	23	23	11	0	1	0	153.1	128	81	59	7	9	80	1	102	19
Burcham, Quad Cities	10	12	.455	4.11	27	27	4	0	1	0	171.0	168	100	78	15	5	86	2	152	7
Campbell, Cedar Rapids	7	5	.583	3.80	20	17	0	1	0	0	104.1	91	50	44	10	6	45	0	82	4
Candelaria, Appleton	4	2	.667	3.96	6	6	0	0	0	0	38.2	35	18	17	1	0	18	0	18	4
Canseco, Madison	1	0	1.000	0.00	2	0	0	1	0	0	4.0	2	0	0	0	0	2	0	3	0
Charland, Quad Cities*	3	4	.429	3.49	10	10	1	0	1	0	59.1	55	29	23	4	1	29	0	61	2
Cocanower, Beloit	2	0	1.000	0.00	2	2	0	0	0	0	15.0	4	1	0	0	1	2	0	12	1
Coleman, Peoria	2	0	1.000	1.20	3	1	0	2	0	0	15.0	8	2	2	0	0	2	0	8	0
Collins, Quad Cities	7	11	.389	5.19	22	20	0	0	0	0	111.0	115	78	64	15	4	36	0	88	11
Converse, Cedar Rapids	7	13	.350	4.28	28	28	3	0	2	0	157.2	134	89	75	11	4	87	1	117	18
Cook, Kenosha	1	3	.250	5.13	19	2	0	11	0	0	47.1	52	32	27	4	2	31	3	26	5
Cortes, Appleton	4	12	.250	5.72	22	21	2	0	1	0	111.2	129	85	71	5	6	78	1	73	16
Craskey, Kenosha	1	1	.500	4.29	28	1	0	15	0	0	56.2	58	37	27	2	1	42	2	52	3
Criswell, Madison*	4	0	1.000	4.31	14	2	0	11	0	4	31.1	27	18	15	1	2	16	0	24	1
Crouch, Burlington	6	6	.500	4.14	20	17	8	1	2	0	117.1	115	62	54	9	4	54	1	81	5
Cundari, Madison	8	2	.800	2.89	15	15	2	0	1	0	93.1	97	41	30	7	0	31	0	51	5
Damian, Peoria	12	9	.571	2.85	25	25	7	0	2	0	164.0	140	74	52	8	11	45	1	127	7
Danek, Peoria	13	8	.619	3.50	27	27	6	0	1	0	174.2	168	89	68	13	7	45	0	117	7
Darby, Wausau	1	1	.500	4.22	23	0	0	13	0	4	32.0	33	19	15	1	2	23	2	28	7
B. Davis, Wausau*	2	1	.667	7.29	24	0	0	12	0	1	33.1	41	30	27	3	1	26	3	29	4
M. Davis, 6 Ken-19 Spring*	5	2	.714	3.36	25	7	1	8	0	0	72.1	74	41	27	6	2	33	1	30	8
Deabenderfer, Madison	3	10	.231	5.66	18	17	2	0	0	0	95.1	88	71	60	6	5	75	0	53	16
Deitz, Cedar Rapids	2	3	.400	3.42	45	0	0	35	0	11	55.1	55	23	21	1	3	26	1	46	1
DiMichele, Quad Cities*	7	10	.412	3.67	26	18	7	5	4	1	122.2	112	72	50	7	3	68	0	64	5
Dougherty, Burlington	4	4	.500	3.29	15	6	2	4	1	1	52.0	52	26	19	5	2	6	0	61	4
Dube, Waterloo	4	4	.500	4.83	16	7	1	6	0	1	69.0	66	41	37	8	6	27	0	44	5
Farr, Waterloo	4	5	.444	2.54	28	0	0	23	0	8	46.0	47	21	13	3	1	14	0	36	6
Fedor, 16 Bur-20 Waterloo	7	4	.636	3.38	36	1	0	29	0	9	64.0	46	26	24	12	3	31	0	72	7
Filippi, Appleton	0	2	.000	10.64	6	2	0	2	0	0	11.0	13	13	13	4	0	13	1	6	1
Finley, Quad Cities*	1	0	1.000	0.00	10	0	0	9	0	6	12.0	4	0	0	0	0	3	0	16	1
Fitzpatrick, Beloit	0	2	.000	3.88	36	1	0	25	0	5	58.0	61	30	25	3	5	42	5	45	2
Forrest, Springfield	2	0	1.000	1.80	3	3	1	0	1	0	20.0	15	4	4	1	1	2	0	7	1
Fortugno, Wausau*	1	1	.500	2.61	19	0	0	13	0	3	31.0	18	17	9	0	0	26	0	38	6
Franco, Quad Cities	1	1	.500	2.77	6	2	0	3	0	0	13.0	14	8	4	0	0	4	0	3	2
Freed, Springfield	10	8	.556	3.42	29	19	4	8	1	3	137.0	144	60	52	11	6	35	2	92	2
Freeland, Clinton	7	7	.500	2.85	20	20	6	0	2	0	142.0	101	53	45	6	5	76	3	129	9
J. Gardner, Peoria	2	2	.500	6.99	9	5	0	0	0	0	28.1	36	24	22	1	3	20	1	21	10
M. Gardner, Waterloo	2	2	.500	8.03	6	0	0	3	0	0	12.1	17	14	11	2	0	6	0	9	3
Gasser, Kenosha	5	10	.333	3.58	27	27	3	0	0	0	188.2	146	88	75	18	2	93	1	225	8
Ghelfi, Waterloo	7	9	.438	4.13	26	26	7	0	0	0	172.0	198	110	79	14	15	42	0	100	8
Githens, Waterloo	4	4	.500	5.36	23	0	0	17	0	2	42.0	42	28	25	7	1	15	0	38	2
Gosling, Beloit	0	1	.000	6.23	2	1	0	1	0	0	4.1	5	4	3	0	0	1	0	1	1
Green, Peoria	0	0	.000	20.25	2	0	0	0	0	0	2.2	5	8	6	0	1	4	0	0	0
Hall, Madison	5	6	.455	4.10	43	0	0	33	0	13	68.0	74	34	31	7	0	36	2	55	4
Harris, Burlington	4	2	.667	1.35	7	6	4	0	3	0	53.1	37	12	8	1	1	15	0	32	2
Hartley, Springfield	0	0	.000	9.60	8	0	0	5	0	1	15.0	22	17	16	4	1	14	1	10	2
Harvey, Quad Cities*	0	0	.000	2.16	5	0	0	3	0	0	8.1	5	2	2	0	0	3	0	8	2
Henderson, Beloit*	6	3	.667	3.08	12	12	2	0	0	0	79.0	66	34	27	7	1	25	0	70	10
D. Henry, Beloit	7	8	.467	4.65	27	24	4	1	1	1	143.1	153	95	74	16	6	56	4	115	9
M. Henry, Appleton*	2	2	.500	5.08	6	6	1	0	0	0	33.2	30	23	19	2	1	16	0	26	3
Hirsch, Peoria	2	4	.333	2.85	47	0	0	34	0	12	66.1	58	24	21	3	7	29	1	59	7
Holcomb, Madison	0	0	.000	9.00	1	0	0	1	0	0	2.0	7	7	2	1	1	0	0	4	0
Horton, Springfield*	0	0	.000	0.00	1	1	0	0	0	0	2.0	2	0	0	0	0	0	0	2	0
Howes, Burlington*	4	5	.444	3.42	15	12	3	3	0	0	84.1	86	36	32	4	0	32	1	62	4
Hulstrom, Appleton*	0	2	.000	4.09	14	3	0	4	0	0	33.0	34	18	15	1	0	24	0	23	1
Hunter, 9 Bur-15 Beloit	6	8	.429	4.02	24	24	3	0	0	0	134.1	143	75	60	5	7	47	3	80	7

Pitcher—Club	W.	L.	Pct.	ERA.	G.	GS.	CG.	GF.	ShO.	Sv.	IP.	H.	R.	ER.	HR.	HB.	BB.	Int. BB.	SO.	WP.
Johnigan, Waterloo	0	0	.000	4.50	2	0	0	2	0	0	2.0	4	2	1	0	0	1	0	0	0
D. Johnson, Quad Cities	3	1	.750	2.29	26	0	0	20	0	4	35.1	42	16	9	2	2	14	1	23	0
W. Johnson, Madison	0	1	.000	3.00	4	0	0	3	0	0	6.0	8	4	2	0	2	6	1	3	1
Kallevig, Peoria	5	9	.357	4.53	25	19	2	3	0	1	119.1	142	83	60	9	7	27	0	66	8
Kannenberg, Quad Cities	4	11	.267	5.39	26	20	4	0	0	0	125.1	156	83	75	12	2	39	0	78	4
Karpuk, Waterloo	7	5	.583	3.41	28	10	3	7	0	1	97.2	100	46	37	3	3	32	1	63	6
Kavanaugh, Springfield	4	2	.667	5.62	33	1	1	17	0	2	49.2	56	36	31	3	2	24	0	29	5
Kazmierczak, Peoria	6	3	.667	4.75	11	10	1	0	0	0	60.2	72	49	32	3	4	36	2	57	6
Kelly, Burlington	4	5	.444	4.07	12	12	2	0	1	0	55.1	46	32	25	5	0	38	0	37	7
Kershaw, Appleton	1	0	1.000	9.00	8	0	0	2	0	0	10.0	10	17	10	1	1	19	0	12	6
Kibler, Madison	2	1	.667	1.65	9	0	0	9	0	4	16.1	13	3	3	0	1	3	0	13	1
Kindred, Cedar Rapids	3	5	.375	3.24	38	4	0	20	0	3	91.2	76	41	33	10	0	44	3	98	4
King, Burlington	1	1	.500	5.29	3	3	1	0	0	0	17.0	22	12	10	2	4	8	0	13	0
Kleean, Beloit*	3	7	.300	5.04	34	8	1	15	0	1	89.1	94	61	50	9	1	39	3	81	12
Kraemer, Peoria*	6	3	.667	1.09	45	0	0	34	0	14	66.1	50	17	8	1	2	19	2	78	6
Krueger, Madison*	0	0	.000	0.00	1	0	0	1	0	0	2.0	1	0	0	0	0	1	0	1	0
Kuykendall, Waterloo	3	2	.600	4.42	16	0	0	12	0	2	38.2	42	24	19	1	3	19	2	27	7
LaFever, Waterloo	10	5	.667	2.30	24	20	8	4	2	1	152.1	134	49	39	15	5	28	0	108	5
Lambert, Madison*	5	3	.625	3.65	25	6	0	10	0	3	69.0	61	31	28	1	4	27	1	53	3
Law, Madison	6	9	.400	3.51	19	18	4	0	1	0	123.0	117	58	48	10	5	61	1	80	5
Lee, Kenosha	5	12	.294	5.70	27	23	2	3	0	1	142.0	166	102	90	21	4	73	0	112	10
Malave, Wausau	5	4	.556	4.23	40	5	1	13	0	3	87.1	76	48	41	4	7	63	3	78	6
Marino, Quad Cities	4	2	.667	4.62	37	1	0	8	0	0	78.0	59	45	40	0	10	63	0	81	9
Mauch, Springfield	9	8	.529	4.46	23	22	4	1	1	0	143.1	151	88	71	16	8	31	1	83	2
McCorkle, Wausau	10	8	.556	3.85	23	23	2	0	2	0	142.2	155	72	61	10	3	35	4	61	12
McCoy, Clinton	5	7	.417	3.46	14	14	1	0	0	0	88.1	68	39	34	5	1	37	1	76	5
McDonald, Madison	2	1	.667	1.15	5	5	1	0	0	0	39.0	23	12	5	0	3	11	0	29	1
McGrew, Beloit	0	0	.000	0.00	1	0	0	1	0	0	1.0	0	0	0	0	0	0	0	1	0
McGuire, Quad Cities	12	10	.545	4.24	23	23	9	0	1	0	155.0	168	86	73	9	6	55	0	115	5
McLain, Wausau	6	2	.750	1.79	42	0	0	37	0	18	55.1	42	16	11	3	0	13	0	43	4
Mead, Clinton	9	6	.600	3.57	27	22	2	4	0	1	141.0	135	70	56	11	7	65	3	125	9
Mercado, Waterloo*	0	0	.000	6.75	1	0	0	1	0	0	1.1	2	1	1	1	0	2	0	1	0
Meyers, Quad Cities	0	0	.000	0.00	1	0	0	0	0	0	0.0	0	4	4	0	0	4	0	0	2
Miglio, Beloit*	6	3	.667	3.38	37	0	0	22	0	1	56.0	49	23	21	1	1	27	7	66	2
Miller, Kenosha	0	0	.000	3.86	3	0	0	3	0	0	7.0	8	4	3	0	0	0	0	4	0
Minutelli, Cedar Rapids*	15	5	.750	3.66	27	27	3	0	2	0	152.2	133	73	62	14	5	76	1	149	16
Montano, Beloit*	2	1	.667	2.41	4	4	0	0	0	0	18.2	17	5	5	1	1	7	0	11	0
Moran, Appleton*	2	3	.400	6.32	29	5	0	10	0	1	72.2	76	61	51	5	5	58	4	74	6
Moraw, Beloit	13	7	.650	3.36	28	28	6	0	1	0	185.0	161	79	69	9	3	108	4	181	19
Morehouse, Quad Cities	6	5	.545	2.76	18	10	1	2	1	2	71.2	60	30	22	1	2	37	0	42	7
Morris, Clinton	7	3	.700	1.75	41	0	0	35	0	10	56.2	28	13	11	2	1	30	5	56	1
Nalls, Quad Cities	0	0	.000	9.00	1	0	0	0	0	0	2.0	2	2	2	0	0	2	0	1	1
Nichols, Waterloo	8	5	.615	4.06	20	20	3	0	1	0	115.1	128	56	52	8	13	21	1	83	3
Norman, Springfield	6	2	.750	3.39	25	8	1	4	0	0	82.1	83	39	31	2	0	33	0	45	2
O'Connor, Kenosha*	5	3	.625	2.28	38	0	0	29	0	12	67.0	51	21	17	4	2	32	4	59	2
Ojeda, Beloit*	0	3	.000	4.63	6	5	0	0	0	0	23.1	22	13	12	0	2	22	0	18	2
Ollom, Appleton	1	4	.200	5.12	6	6	0	0	0	0	31.2	41	23	18	9	4	7	0	17	1
Oswald, Appleton*	5	8	.385	2.35	15	15	3	0	0	0	103.1	92	44	27	4	2	28	0	74	9
Otto, Madison*	13	7	.650	2.66	26	26	6	0	1	0	169.0	154	72	50	9	2	71	0	125	6
Oyster, Springfield	17	7	.708	3.03	28	28	10	0	0	0	184.0	170	73	62	14	8	42	2	142	3
Pall, Appleton	5	5	.500	2.31	11	11	3	0	1	0	78.0	71	29	20	2	4	14	1	51	4
C. Parker, Wausau	8	7	.533	2.88	26	26	4	0	0	0	178.0	171	77	57	11	7	39	1	154	13
S. Parker, Peoria*	6	3	.667	2.84	16	14	0	0	0	0	79.1	82	39	25	6	2	29	0	47	5
Pearson, Clinton	6	4	.600	4.12	30	9	1	6	1	1	98.1	88	55	45	5	9	51	2	48	5
Penigar, Clinton	4	5	.444	4.48	21	10	0	8	0	0	72.1	80	40	36	2	3	47	0	39	4
M. Perez, Burlington	10	12	.455	3.70	28	23	13	5	1	0	170.1	148	83	70	15	3	49	3	153	8
Y. Perez, Kenosha*	4	11	.267	5.15	31	18	3	9	0	0	131.0	120	81	75	9	3	88	1	144	13
Peters, Springfield*	10	1	.909	2.53	15	15	4	0	3	0	103.0	78	32	29	8	5	36	0	99	6
Phillips, Peoria	2	3	.400	4.36	36	0	0	14	0	2	66.0	70	40	32	1	1	25	2	37	7
Pilkington, Clinton*	3	5	.375	3.22	29	8	0	10	0	2	89.1	79	41	32	4	1	53	1	90	4
Poehl, Waterloo	4	6	.400	3.50	18	18	4	0	0	0	105.1	108	55	41	9	5	33	0	64	2
Redding, Kenosha	6	10	.375	4.08	23	20	3	2	0	0	134.2	140	80	61	11	3	44	1	67	11
Renz, Appleton	5	5	.500	4.33	13	10	3	2	0	0	62.1	69	37	30	1	4	15	0	50	2
Reyes, Beloit	4	6	.400	4.02	33	8	0	8	0	3	112.0	107	67	50	8	0	50	1	92	9
Reynolds, Appleton	4	1	.800	5.17	41	0	0	28	0	8	71.1	68	48	41	3	3	48	4	83	8
Rivera, Quad Cities	2	5	.286	5.11	24	8	0	8	0	0	61.2	75	45	35	4	2	22	0	41	5
Roberts, Wausau	6	6	.500	3.13	21	12	3	6	0	1	74.2	73	43	26	4	0	42	0	49	11
D. Robertson, Clinton	3	10	.231	4.56	27	14	0	5	0	1	118.1	117	78	60	7	2	73	3	79	8
M. Robertson, 8 Spr-4 Bur	1	2	.500	4.63	12	1	0	3	0	0	27.2	33	19	14	4	0	13	0	14	2
Robinson, Appleton	1	1	.500	10.07	8	0	0	1	0	0	19.2	31	23	22	2	0	12	0	10	2
Robles, Peoria	4	1	.800	2.25	7	7	1	0	1	0	48.0	37	15	12	4	0	11	1	21	0
Rodriguez, Burlington	4	6	.400	4.14	32	4	1	15	0	2	95.2	103	61	44	13	2	39	0	73	14
Roesler, Cedar Rapids	9	13	.409	4.58	32	24	1	4	0	3	163.0	165	95	83	16	5	80	1	135	13
Roth, Peoria	11	9	.550	3.22	27	27	2	0	0	0	179.0	164	86	64	7	13	76	0	109	19
Saatzer, Quad Cities	0	0	.000	0.00	1	0	0	1	0	0	1.0	2	1	0	0	0	0	0	1	0
Sabo, Madison*	3	4	.429	3.28	22	0	0	17	0	6	35.2	28	14	13	4	0	13	1	44	2
Salcedo, Madison	3	0	1.000	3.00	25	0	0	14	0	3	54.0	55	20	18	5	1	19	1	31	1
Sandoval, Appleton	1	1	.500	7.04	8	0	0	6	0	1	7.2	12	8	6	2	2	6	1	3	1
Sassone, Springfield	7	2	.778	2.69	14	14	3	0	0	0	87.0	85	32	26	6	1	27	0	52	4
Schooler, Wausau	12	10	.545	3.35	26	26	6	0	1	0	166.1	166	83	62	20	4	44	0	171	10
Scott, Waterloo	8	5	.615	4.03	20	19	4	0	2	0	118.1	122	57	53	13	6	21	0	64	4
Scruggs, Appleton*	0	0	.000	9.00	2	0	0	2	0	0	7.0	10	8	7	0	0	5	0	5	1
Shaver, Madison	10	5	.667	3.37	26	26	3	0	1	0	163.0	141	67	61	14	6	61	0	144	5
Shull, Quad Cities	1	5	.167	2.53	35	1	1	27	1	3	57.0	40	25	16	3	3	29	6	41	6
Siegel, Wausau	11	11	.500	3.90	26	26	3	0	0	0	159.1	167	98	69	11	7	74	2	130	11
Simmons, Beloit	3	5	.375	4.62	25	8	0	6	0	0	76.0	85	43	39	7	0	49	2	58	6
Simpson, Cedar Rapids*	6	4	.600	1.81	35	12	1	10	1	1	119.2	89	32	24	7	1	38	0	78	5
Skalski, Waterloo	2	0	1.000	5.68	2	2	0	0	0	0	12.2	15	8	8	2	2	1	0	16	0
Slowik, Peoria	5	5	.500	3.63	50	0	0	30	0	12	72.0	68	36	29	3	8	38	6	78	5
J. Smith, Beloit	0	0	.000	8.31	5	0	0	3	0	0	8.2	12	9	8	0	0	6	0	4	3
L. Smith, Quad Cities*	1	1	.500	0.82	24	0	0	22	0	11	33.0	26	4	3	0	4	13	3	30	2
M. Smith, Cedar Rapids	10	10	.500	3.35	28	27	4	1	1	0	191.0	155	88	71	12	6	106	1	172	19

Pitcher—Club	W.	L.	Pct.	ERA.	G.	GS.	CG.	GF.	ShO.	Sv.	IP.	H.	R.	ER.	HR.	HB.	BB.	Int. BB.	SO.	WP.
Snell, Wausau	5	6	.455	3.32	41	2	1	19	0	2	86.2	76	37	32	8	5	34	1	85	8
Stauffacher, Burlington*	1	3	.250	6.45	23	3	0	10	0	2	51.2	53	46	37	3	2	47	2	43	2
Stein, Appleton	11	16	.407	4.43	30	30	5	0	3	0	183.0	173	118	90	11	7	86	3	170	19
Stocker, Madison	6	2	.750	5.60	11	11	0	0	0	0	53.0	49	39	33	5	4	21	0	33	3
Stone, Appleton	6	7	.462	2.51	38	9	0	20	0	5	125.1	112	62	35	4	6	40	0	84	1
Strube, Kenosha*	1	11	.083	5.23	41	1	0	29	0	2	84.1	101	64	49	7	1	37	1	62	8
Sudo, Burlington	10	4	.714	1.91	16	16	9	0	1	0	127.0	100	42	27	5	2	38	2	114	6
Sundgren, Burlington	2	3	.400	8.74	17	0	0	8	0	2	34.0	51	36	33	2	1	22	0	19	5
Swan, Clinton*	3	3	.500	3.09	7	7	2	0	1	0	43.2	36	18	15	2	1	8	0	37	1
Swindell, Waterloo*	2	1	.667	1.00	3	3	0	0	0	0	18.0	12	2	2	1	0	3	0	25	0
Townsend, Clinton*	1	5	.167	5.81	13	7	0	3	0	0	48.0	58	45	31	6	2	20	1	30	4
Trautwein, Burlington	3	2	.600	1.98	21	0	0	21	0	11	36.1	29	9	8	3	1	10	0	39	0
Trudeau, Waterloo	2	1	.667	1.30	12	0	0	8	0	5	27.2	17	7	4	1	2	10	0	31	2
Veres, Beloit	4	12	.250	3.89	23	22	3	0	1	0	113.1	132	78	49	6	4	52	1	87	13
Villanueva, Appleton*	1	4	.200	6.02	14	6	0	7	0	0	40.1	38	34	27	1	3	44	1	45	11
Walker, Wausau	0	3	.000	5.52	15	2	0	6	0	3	31.0	40	24	19	3	2	10	0	19	2
Walton, Madison	0	0	.000	5.40	1	1	0	0	0	0	5.0	5	3	3	0	0	1	0	1	0
Warren, Appleton	3	6	.333	2.92	11	9	1	0	0	0	61.2	52	29	20	3	3	38	1	56	4
Whitehurst, Madison	6	1	.857	0.59	8	8	5	0	4	0	61.0	42	8	4	1	1	16	0	57	4
Whitford, Beloit	2	1	.667	6.46	5	1	0	1	0	0	15.1	17	11	11	2	1	11	0	10	5
Whitmyer, Waterloo	1	2	.333	4.14	12	5	1	2	0	0	41.1	50	22	19	7	2	9	0	30	7
Williams, Burlington	8	8	.500	4.82	18	17	7	1	1	0	112.0	111	67	60	11	2	44	0	110	4
G. Williamson, Waterloo	4	3	.571	5.43	16	9	0	3	0	0	64.2	66	48	39	10	4	35	0	49	9
K. Williamson, Madison	4	0	1.000	3.74	22	1	0	12	0	1	53.0	55	24	22	5	0	22	1	40	2
Wilmet, Springfield	9	4	.692	2.15	56	0	0	46	0	29	96.1	66	28	23	5	5	33	3	99	4
Wilson, Clinton*	6	11	.353	4.27	34	21	0	7	0	2	130.2	126	70	62	6	6	64	1	84	5
Winbush, Waterloo	2	1	.667	3.67	8	1	0	4	0	0	34.1	29	16	14	4	3	16	0	34	3
Zarranz, Peoria	1	4	.200	5.37	15	5	0	4	0	2	53.2	47	33	32	3	4	25	0	52	6
Zavaras, Wausau	6	6	.500	3.35	17	17	0	0	0	0	91.1	68	45	34	5	8	67	0	98	11

BALKS—Kannenberg, Reyes, 5 each; D. Henry, Stein, Veres, 4 each; Atkinson, Cortes, Danek, Deabenderfer, Freed, Oswald, Pilkington, Sassone, Zarranz, 3 each; Belinskas, Campbell, DiMichele, Ghelfi, Harris, Howes, Hunter, Kallevig, Kavanaugh, Malave, Minutelli, Moraw, Ollom, Roesler, Roth, Salcedo, Schooler, Scott, Shull, Townsend, Wilson, Zavaras, 2 each; Blakley, Bonilla, Bumgarner, Burcham, Coleman, Craskey, Crouch, Damian, M. Davis, Dougherty, Finley, Fitzpatrick, Fortugno, Freeland, Hall, Henderson, M. Henry, Hirsch, Hulstrom, Karpuk, Kindred, Kleean, Kuykendall, Lambert, Law, Lee, Marino, Mauch, McCorkle, McDonald, Morris, Nalls, Nichols, Norman, O'Connor, Ojeda, Otton, C. Parker, Penigar, M. Perez, Y. Perez, Poehl, Redding, Reynolds, Rivera, D. Robertson, Robles, Sabo, Siegel, Snell, Stauffacher, Stocker, Stone, Strube, Sundgren, Swan, Villanueva, G. Williamson, Winbush, 1 each.

COMBINATION SHUTOUTS—Candelaria-Reynolds, Henry-Stone, Renz-Stone, Appleton; Moraw-Brisco-Miglio, Henderson-Reyes, Henry-Brisco, Montano-Brisco, Beloit; Sudo-Perez, Dougherty-Stauffacher, Kelly-Trautwein, Burlington; Minutelli-Brusky 2, Minutelli-Smith, Smith-Deitz-Kindred, Smith-Belinskas-Kindred, Simpson-Brusky, Cedar Rapids; Wilson-Blakley, Pilkington-Bonilla, Mead-Pilkington, Penigar-Blakley, Penigar-Bonilla, Pearson-Robertson, Pearson-Morris, McCoy-Morris, Clinton; Lee-O'Connor, Bumgarner-O'Connor, Redding-O'Connor, Kenosha; Otto-Kibler, Whitehurst-Kibler, Stocker-Criswell, Ames-Hall, Law-Sabo, Shaver-Krueger, Law-Williamson, Williamson-Canseco-Arias, Madison; Damian-Kraemer, Danek-Hirsch, Kazmierczak-Slowik, Damian-Coleman, Parker-Hirsch-Kraemer, Peoria; Morehouse-Marino-Finley, Burcham-Johnson, Quad Cities; Mauch-Hartley, Springfield; Nichols-Farr, Dube-Fedor, Swindell-Kuykendall, Waterloo; Parker-McLain 2, McCorkle-Roberts, Malave-Walker, Schooler-Darby, Schooler-Fortugno, Siegel-McLain, Zavaras-Fortugno, Wausau.

NO-HIT GAMES—Stein, Appleton, defeated Beloit, 5-0, May 26; Converse, Cedar Rapids, defeated Beloit, 2-0, June 6.

NY-Pennsylvania League

CLASS A

CHAMPIONSHIP WINNERS IN PREVIOUS YEARS

Year—Club	Pct.
1939—Olean*	.631
1940—Olean*	.625
1941—Jamestown	.618
Bradford (2nd)†	.549
1942—Jamestown*	.672
1943—Lockport	.591
Wellsville (3rd)†	.532
1944—Lockport	.608
Jamestown (2nd)†	.565
1945—Batavia*	.677
1946—Jamestown‡	.672
Batavia‡	.672
1947—Jamestown*	.690
1948—Lockport*	.603
1949—Bradford*	.635
1950—Hornell	.653
Olean (2nd)†	.568
1951—Olean	.622
Hornell (3rd)†	.568
1952—Hamilton	.659
Jamestown (2nd)†	.643
1953—Jamestown*	.704
1954—Corning*	.621
1955—Hamilton*	.656
1956—Wellsville*	.617
1957—Wellsville	.632
Erie (2nd)†	.598
1958—Wellsville	.556
Geneva (2nd)†	.548
1959—Wellsville†	.635
1960—Erie	.643
Wellsville (2nd)†	.535
1961—Geneva	.616
Olean (4th)†	.512
1962—Jamestown	.580
Auburn (3rd)†	.521
1963—Auburn	.585
Batavia (3rd)†	.485
1964—Auburn§	.622
1965—Binghamton	.677
Binghamton	.607
1966—Auburn x	.620
Binghamton	.646
1967—Auburn	.667
1968—Auburn	.645
Oneonta (2nd)*	.558
1969—Oneonta	.662
1970—Auburn	.623
1971—Oneonta	.662
1972—Niagara Falls	.686
1973—Auburn	.667
1974—Oneonta	.768
1975—Newark	.688
Newark	.714
1976—Elmira	.727
Elmira	.703
1977—Oneonta y	.671
Batavia	.600
1978—Oneonta	.729
Geneva z	.718
1979—Geneva	.725
Oneonta z	.618
1980—Oneonta y	.662
Geneva	.649
1981—Oneonta y	.658
Jamestown	.649
1982—Oneonta	.566
Niagara Falls y	.553
1983—Utica y	.649
Newark	.649
1984—Newark	.622
Little Falls y	.587
1985—Oneonta*	.705
Auburn	.603

*Won championship and four-club playoff. †Won four-club playoff. ‡Jamestown and Batavia declared co-champions; Batavia defeated Jamestown in final of four-club playoff. §Won championship and two-club playoff. xWon split-season playoff. yLeague divided into Eastern and Western Divisions; won playoff. zLeague divided into Wrigley and Yawkey Divisions; won playoff. (NOTE—Known as Pennsylvania-Ontario-New York League from 1939 through 1956.)

STANDING OF CLUBS AT CLOSE OF SEASON, SEPTEMBER 1

YAWKEY DIVISION

Club	W.	L.	T.	Pct.	G.B.
Oneonta (Yankees)	59	18	0	.766	....
Little Falls (Mets)	36	40	0	.474	22½
Watertown (Pirates)	30	48	0	.385	29½
Utica (Phillies)	26	52	0	.333	33½

McNAMARA DIVISION

Club	W.	L.	T.	Pct.	G.B.
Auburn (Astros)	44	32	0	.579	....
Newark (Orioles)	41	37	0	.526	4
Elmira (Red Sox)	39	36	0	.520	4½
Geneva (Cubs)	40	38	0	.513	5

WRIGLEY DIVISION

Club	W.	L.	T.	Pct.	G.B.
St. Catharines (Blue Jays)	48	28	0	.632	....
Erie (Cardinals)	37	40	0	.481	11½
Batavia (Indians)	30	45	0	.400	17½
Jamestown (Expos)	30	46	0	.395	18

COMPOSITE STANDING OF CLUBS AT CLOSE OF SEASON, SEPTEMBER 1

Club	Ont.	St.C.	Aub.	New.	Elm.	Gen.	Eri.	LF.	Bat.	Jam.	Wat.	Uti.	W.	L.	T.	Pct.	G.B.
Oneonta (Yankees)	....	4	5	4	4	4	5	6	5	5	8	9	59	18	0	.766	....
St. Catharines (Blue Jays)	2	....	1	4	4	3	8	5	6	6	4	5	48	28	0	.632	10½
Auburn (Astros)	1	4	....	6	7	6	1	3	3	3	5	5	44	32	0	.579	14½
Newark (Orioles)	2	2	4	....	5	6	2	3	4	3	5	5	41	37	0	.526	18½
Elmira (Red Sox)	2	2	3	5	....	6	3	2	2	4	4	6	39	36	0	.520	19
Geneva (Cubs)	2	3	4	4	4	....	3	4	5	4	1	6	40	38	0	.513	19½
Erie (Cardinals)	1	2	5	4	3	3	....	4	5	5	2	3	37	40	0	.481	22
Little Falls (Mets)	3	1	3	3	3	2	2	....	4	4	7	4	36	40	0	.474	22½
Batavia (Indians)	1	4	3	2	2	1	4	2	....	6	3	2	30	45	0	.400	28
Jamestown (Expos)	1	3	2	3	2	2	5	2	4	....	3	3	30	46	0	.395	28½
Watertown (Pirates)	2	2	1	1	2	5	4	3	3	3	....	4	30	48	0	.385	29½
Utica (Phillies)	1	1	1	1	0	0	3	6	4	3	6	....	26	52	0	.333	33½

Major league affiliations in parentheses.

Playoffs—Newark defeated Oneonta, one game to none; St. Catharines defeated Auburn, one game to none; St. Catharines defeated Newark, two games to one, to win league championship.

Regular-Season Attendance—Auburn, 24,249; Batavia, 34,765; Elmira, 71,463; Erie, 49,411; Geneva, 22,851; Jamestown, 37,009; Little Falls, 40,557; Newark, 17,199; Oneonta, 49,611; St. Catharines, 42,135; Utica, 29,950; Watertown, 35,480. Total—454,680. Playoffs, 3,153.

Managers—Auburn, Keith Bodie; Batavia, Tom Chandler; Elmira, Bill Limoncelli; Erie, Joe Riglio; Geneva, Jay Loviglio; Jamestown, Gene Glynn; Little Falls, Rich Miller; Newark, Art Mazmanian; Oneonta, Buck Showalter; St. Catharines, Cloyd Boyer; Utica, Tony Taylor; Watertown, Ed Ott.

All-Star Team—1B—Hal Morris, Oneonta; 2B—Oscar Escobar, St. Catharines; 3B—Carey Nemeth, Erie; SS—Bien Figueroa, Erie; OF—Barry Shifflett, St. Catharines; Tom Baine, Erie; Ced Landrum, Geneva; C—Todd Zeile, Erie; Fritz Polka, Little Falls; RHP—Alan Koonce, Newark; Dean Wilkins, Oneonta; LHP—Ken Patterson, Oneonta; Joel Estes, Auburn; DH—Frank Bellino, Newark; Rookie of the Year—Hal Morris, Oneonta; Manager of the Year—Cloyd Boyer, St. Catharines.

(Compiled by Howe News Bureau, Boston, Mass.)

CLUB BATTING

Club	Pct.	G.	AB.	R.	OR.	H.	TB.	2B.	3B.	HR.	RBI.	GW.	SH.	SF.	HP.	BB.	Int. BB.	SO.	SB.	CS.	LOB.
Oneonta	.263	77	2539	384	206	667	902	109	27	24	331	53	24	27	34	281	10	433	81	24	590
St. Catharines	.258	76	2586	350	263	668	939	96	17	47	289	41	18	18	22	257	13	581	82	39	545
Elmira	.247	75	2462	298	319	609	797	90	10	26	240	31	33	14	15	261	7	512	59	33	545
Little Falls	.240	76	2499	299	306	600	826	80	19	36	249	32	30	13	18	268	10	522	52	32	526
Auburn	.240	76	2483	356	305	595	859	101	17	43	297	38	12	22	29	299	11	640	172	50	520
Newark	.239	78	2474	321	337	592	807	94	11	33	276	32	17	16	19	360	11	503	120	43	590
Erie	.237	77	2541	360	367	603	854	96	4	49	296	29	18	21	32	330	11	492	116	35	557
Geneva	.235	78	2436	320	303	572	783	107	7	30	267	32	47	22	25	318	17	499	175	52	535
Batavia	.233	75	2454	300	297	572	810	74	7	50	246	21	15	19	35	305	8	593	78	35	570
Jamestown	.228	76	2420	286	342	552	787	98	13	37	227	26	33	11	27	242	14	576	79	39	483
Utica	.219	78	2379	259	410	520	712	76	22	24	215	20	15	15	20	286	7	664	91	71	486
Watertown	.217	78	2549	287	365	552	763	63	20	36	237	27	21	15	44	291	13	633	139	55	537

INDIVIDUAL BATTING

(Leading Qualifiers for Batting Championship—211 or More Plate Appearances)

*Bats lefthanded. †Switch-hitter.

Player and Club	Pct.	G.	AB.	R.	H.	TB.	2B.	3B.	HR.	RBI.	GW.	SH.	SF.	HP.	BB.	Int. BB.	SO.	SB.	CS.
Hinzo, Thomas, Batavia	.333	55	219	35	73	89	7	3	1	15	2	3	0	4	12	1	44	24	8
Landrum, Cedric, Geneva*	.315	64	213	51	67	86	6	2	3	16	0	4	3	3	40	1	33	49	10
Cooper, Gary, Auburn	.313	76	275	52	86	141	16	3	11	54	2	0	2	2	47	0	47	16	4
Escobar, Santiago, St. Catharines	.313	75	320	54	100	140	16	3	6	33	5	0	2	4	22	1	40	13	5
Hubbard, Trent, Auburn†	.310	70	242	42	75	92	12	1	1	32	2	2	2	1	28	0	42	35	5
Twardoski, Michael, Batavia*	.307	63	202	33	62	92	12	0	6	17	3	2	1	0	43	2	25	11	3
Shifflett, Barry, St. Catharines*	.298	65	242	37	72	91	8	1	3	32	6	2	5	0	40	1	36	9	5
Cabrera, Francisco, St. Catharines	.297	68	246	31	73	108	13	2	6	35	10	1	1	4	16	1	48	7	4
Stankiewicz, Andrew, Oneonta	.296	59	216	51	64	78	8	3	0	17	3	4	4	5	38	0	41	14	3
Whited, Edward, Auburn	.292	61	219	34	64	96	15	1	5	36	5	0	3	5	19	0	49	12	4
Weidie, Stuart, Elmira†	.291	62	203	25	59	77	9	3	1	16	2	3	1	3	25	1	59	9	0

Departmental Leaders: G—Bullinger, 78; AB—Escobar, 320; R—Baine, 55; H—Escobar, 100; TB—G. Cooper, 141; 2B—Bullinger, G. Cooper, Escobar, Haggerty, 16; 3B—Alou, 8, HR—Yan, 15; RBI—Zeile, 63; GWRBI—Cabrera, Edwards, 10; SH—Baker, 10; SF—Zeile, 6; HP—Baine, 8; BB—Bullinger, 48; IBB—A. Collins, Edwards, Jeter, 4; SO—Hunter, 87; SB—Landrum, 49; CS—Brumfield, 15.

(All Players—Listed Alphabetically)

Player and Club	Pct.	G.	AB.	R.	H.	TB.	2B.	3B.	HR.	RBI.	GW.	SH.	SF.	HP.	BB.	Int. BB.	SO.	SB.	CS.
Adams, Steven, Watertown	.067	16	15	0	1	1	0	0	0	1	0	0	0	0	1	0	5	0	0
Aleshire, Troy, Auburn	.200	45	130	11	26	37	9	1	0	13	3	0	2	4	13	0	39	3	0
Alicea, Luis, Erie†	.282	47	163	40	46	63	6	1	3	18	2	0	0	1	37	2	20	27	4
Alou, Moises, Watertown	.236	69	254	30	60	103	9	8	6	35	4	0	0	1	22	1	72	14	8
Alvarez, Michael, Erie†	.190	9	21	3	4	5	1	0	0	0	0	0	0	0	1	0	4	0	1
Arendas, Daniel, Oneonta*	.158	9	19	5	3	3	0	0	0	2	0	0	0	0	3	0	2	1	0
Baine, Thomas, Erie	.288	70	250	55	72	97	13	0	4	34	6	1	0	8	37	1	20	5	3
Baker, Michael, Elmira	.284	53	190	27	54	62	8	0	0	8	1	10	0	2	19	1	25	10	3
Balis, Peter, Batavia	.180	28	61	8	11	13	2	0	0	5	0	0	2	3	4	0	19	1	1
Banister, Jeffery, Watertown	.145	41	124	9	18	22	4	0	0	8	0	0	1	1	12	0	27	4	0
Banks, David, 37 Aub-10 One*	.185	47	151	16	28	43	4	1	3	19	6	0	2	2	15	1	41	3	1
Bautista, Bienvenido, Newark†	.255	57	188	20	48	55	2	1	1	12	1	3	1	0	23	1	56	17	4
Becker, Timothy, Oneonta	.226	69	257	34	58	67	5	2	0	29	2	5	1	3	22	0	17	18	6
Befort, Curtis, Utica	1.000	11	1	0	1	1	0	0	0	0	0	0	0	0	0	0	0	0	0
Behnsch, Bobby, Utica*	.276	72	228	30	63	94	9	2	6	33	1	0	2	3	43	2	69	3	7
Behny, Mark, Erie	.000	27	1	0	0	0	0	0	0	0	0	0	0	0	0	0	1	0	0
Bellino, Frank, Newark*	.261	68	234	29	61	112	11	2	12	49	7	0	1	0	25	3	28	3	3
Berge, Louis, Little Falls	.197	27	61	6	12	14	0	1	0	4	1	1	0	0	16	0	20	0	0
Berube, Luc, Oneonta	.242	52	165	19	40	60	8	0	4	25	5	0	2	3	28	3	21	2	1
Blanco, Louis, Oneonta	.161	24	62	8	10	12	2	0	0	6	0	0	1	3	7	0	11	0	0
Blowers, Michael, Jamestown	.253	32	95	13	24	40	9	2	1	6	1	2	0	3	17	2	18	3	2
Bond, Daven, Auburn	.000	14	9	0	0	0	0	0	0	0	0	1	0	0	0	0	7	1	1
Bourne, Kendrick, Elmira	.270	38	122	15	33	48	7	1	2	12	1	0	0	0	13	1	33	1	6
Boyd, Daryl, Watertown	.000	20	6	0	0	0	0	0	0	1	0	0	0	0	0	0	3	0	0
Brady, Lawrence, Watertown	.190	42	84	16	16	20	1	0	1	3	0	2	0	4	28	2	22	4	3
Brantley, Clifford, Utica	.231	11	13	4	3	6	0	0	1	2	1	0	0	0	1	0	2	0	0
Brooks, Damon, Auburn†	.220	44	82	15	18	19	1	0	0	3	0	0	0	0	13	0	31	7	4
Brown, Richard, Little Falls	.100	16	10	1	1	1	0	0	0	1	0	0	0	0	1	0	2	0	0
Brown, Winston, St. Catharines*	.239	43	142	20	34	43	7	1	0	15	4	0	1	0	9	1	33	2	1
Brumfield, Harvey, Utica*	.264	77	288	42	76	111	11	6	4	28	2	0	0	2	40	0	71	32	15
Brunelle, Rodney, Utica	.172	72	244	18	42	57	6	0	3	20	3	0	1	2	29	0	73	11	4
Bruske, James, Batavia	.243	56	181	23	44	59	2	2	3	14	1	0	0	7	21	1	50	7	0
Buheller, Charles, Elmira*	.261	54	184	26	48	51	1	1	0	11	1	4	1	0	29	0	21	16	6
Bullinger, James, Geneva	.246	78	248	35	61	88	16	1	3	33	4	6	2	1	48	3	50	7	5
Burke, Donald, Jamestown*	.266	42	128	23	34	48	14	0	0	13	1	1	0	0	22	0	18	12	3
Burke, Kevin, Newark*	.252	77	246	27	62	86	11	2	3	30	3	1	4	0	40	0	48	6	5
Butts, Randall, Erie*	.200	25	60	8	12	22	1	0	3	12	1	0	1	0	10	1	15	1	1
Cabrera, Francisco, St. Catharines	.297	68	246	31	73	108	13	2	6	35	10	1	1	4	16	1	48	7	4
Calley, Robert, Newark	.273	35	128	13	35	43	8	0	0	11	1	0	1	0	12	0	11	2	0
Calvert, Arthur, Oneonta†	.254	44	142	24	36	60	7	4	3	23	0	1	1	7	14	0	26	8	1
Carganilla, Peter, Batavia	.186	32	102	12	19	23	4	0	0	8	1	1	0	4	20	0	21	2	4
Carter, Frederick, Oneonta	.385	16	65	11	25	35	5	1	1	16	4	0	1	0	2	1	12	1	0
Casteel, Brent, Geneva	.375	3	8	2	3	4	1	0	0	4	0	0	1	0	1	0	0	2	0
Castro, Genaro, 24 LFL-28 Utica	.231	52	143	18	33	49	6	5	0	19	1	1	3	3	28	2	34	2	5
Christian, Ricardo, Erie	.218	53	119	14	26	35	3	0	2	19	2	1	1	0	8	1	32	8	3
Clemo, Scott, Jamestown*	.248	67	238	29	59	83	11	2	3	22	0	2	1	2	36	1	44	4	2
Cloninger, Todd, Geneva*	.154	15	13	2	2	3	1	0	0	1	0	2	0	0	3	0	2	0	0
Close, Casey, Oneonta	.245	67	233	30	57	89	15	4	3	38	8	3	5	5	23	0	40	4	1
Collins, Anthony, Geneva	.256	73	254	30	65	84	13	0	2	42	5	4	4	1	29	4	37	8	5
Collins, Timothy, Utica	.000	24	3	0	0	0	0	0	0	0	0	0	0	0	0	0	2	0	0
Cooper, Gary, Auburn	.313	76	275	52	86	141	16	3	11	54	2	0	2	2	47	0	47	16	4
Cooper, Scott, Elmira*	.288	51	191	23	55	91	9	0	9	43	4	1	4	0	19	2	32	1	4
Copp, William, Watertown	.071	13	14	1	1	1	0	0	0	0	0	3	0	1	3	0	9	0	0

Player and Club	Pct.	G.	AB.	R.	H.	TB.	2B.	3B.	HR.	RBI.	GW.	SH.	SF.	HP.	BB.	Int. BB.	SO.	SB.	CS.
Crofton, Kevin, Oneonta	.124	42	113	12	14	19	5	0	0	5	2	0	0	0	15	0	41	0	0
Crone, Raymond, Newark*	.208	31	72	12	15	16	1	0	0	4	0	1	1	1	13	0	16	7	3
Crosby, Patrick, Little Falls*	.259	62	197	21	51	59	5	0	1	13	3	0	0	0	15	0	26	2	3
Curtis, Michael, Geneva*	.200	14	15	0	3	3	0	0	0	0	0	2	0	0	0	0	2	0	0
DeLaMata, Fred, Newark*	.158	10	19	5	3	6	0	0	1	3	0	0	1	0	7	0	4	0	2
DeLaRosa, Cesar, Utica	.177	64	198	13	35	39	4	0	0	10	1	1	0	0	13	0	60	3	4
DeLaRosa, Juan, St. Catharines	.238	6	21	0	5	5	0	0	0	0	0	0	0	0	0	0	5	0	0
Diaz, Carlos, St. Catharines	.176	24	74	9	13	21	3	1	1	5	1	0	1	2	7	2	18	1	0
DiVincenzo, Mark, Little Falls	.182	53	121	11	22	45	2	0	7	16	2	0	1	1	6	0	29	0	0
Duey, Kody, Jamestown	.133	14	30	2	4	5	1	0	0	0	0	0	0	0	4	0	17	0	0
Duke, Douglas, Jamestown	.233	55	180	17	42	74	8	0	8	26	3	2	1	3	15	1	48	2	0
Dulin, Timothy, Newark	.231	33	121	14	28	36	5	0	1	11	1	1	0	0	23	1	11	6	2
Durant, Richard, Little Falls	.278	14	18	4	5	10	1	2	0	1	0	0	0	0	2	0	6	0	0
Echevarria, Robert, Elmira	.194	15	36	2	7	7	0	0	0	2	1	2	0	0	5	0	11	0	1
Edwards, Jeffrey, Auburn	.241	64	212	25	51	76	7	0	6	33	10	0	2	3	30	4	55	3	3
Elsberry, Russell, Auburn	.000	10	3	0	0	0	0	0	0	0	0	0	0	0	0	0	3	0	0
Escobar, Santiago, St. Catharines	.313	75	320	54	100	140	16	3	6	33	5	0	2	4	22	1	40	13	5
Espinal, Sergio, Geneva	.207	72	208	28	43	60	11	0	2	19	1	3	1	2	31	3	50	15	5
Estes, Joel, Auburn*	.167	23	6	1	1	1	0	0	0	1	0	0	0	0	0	0	3	0	0
Fairchild, Glenn, Batavia†	.192	54	182	32	35	55	2	0	6	17	3	2	2	4	30	1	46	15	5
Farmer, Kennedy, Little Falls	.200	5	15	1	3	3	0	0	0	0	0	1	0	0	0	0	3	1	1
Faryniarz, Tony, Geneva	.000	1	1	0	0	0	0	0	0	0	0	0	0	0	0	0	1	0	0
Faulk, Joel, Utica	.234	54	167	14	39	44	5	0	0	13	0	3	0	3	18	1	45	3	6
Fernandez, Carlos, Batavia	.206	13	34	3	7	8	1	0	0	1	0	0	0	0	2	0	18	0	0
Fiedler, Mark, Little Falls*	.000	6	1	0	0	0	0	0	0	0	0	0	0	0	0	0	1	0	0
Figueroa, Bienvenido, Erie	.237	73	249	31	59	63	4	0	0	30	2	1	3	1	32	1	26	13	4
Forrest, Joel, Watertown*	.125	7	8	0	1	1	0	0	0	0	0	0	0	0	0	0	3	0	0
Fox, Kenneth, Jamestown	.250	6	8	2	2	2	0	0	0	0	0	0	0	0	1	0	2	0	1
Frias-Soto, Adolfo, St. Catharines	.141	36	92	9	13	17	4	0	0	5	0	3	0	1	7	0	37	0	2
Frye, Paul, Jamestown	.329	20	73	13	24	37	1	0	4	16	1	2	0	2	8	1	10	6	2
Galbato, Chan, Jamestown*	.455	11	11	2	5	7	2	0	0	2	0	1	0	0	1	0	2	0	0
Gamba, Thomas, Batavia	.263	55	156	17	41	49	5	0	1	16	1	2	0	0	14	0	22	4	2
Garcia, Victor, Little Falls	.455	10	11	0	5	5	0	0	0	3	0	2	0	0	0	0	2	0	0
Gardner, Jimmie, Geneva	.375	13	8	3	3	3	0	0	0	1	0	0	0	0	1	0	1	0	0
Gaylor, Robert, Jamestown	.264	57	163	19	43	57	8	0	2	11	1	5	0	2	16	2	20	6	5
Glisson, Robert, Erie*	.130	16	23	2	3	3	0	0	0	2	0	0	0	0	1	0	13	0	0
Gonzalez, Clifford, Little Falls*	.222	65	189	24	42	47	5	0	0	14	0	5	3	0	26	2	22	12	7
Graff, Stephen, Erie	.178	25	45	4	8	15	2	1	1	1	0	0	0	2	1	0	15	1	0
Graham, Jeffrey, Erie	.273	3	11	0	3	3	0	0	0	2	0	0	0	0	1	0	3	0	0
Gray, Scott, Auburn	.151	26	53	7	8	12	1	0	1	3	0	1	0	1	9	0	22	1	0
Green, John, Geneva	.125	26	8	1	1	4	0	0	1	2	0	0	0	0	1	0	6	0	0
Griffith, Kerry, Erie	.500	20	4	1	2	2	0	0	0	0	0	1	0	0	0	0	2	0	0
Grimsley, Jason, Utica	.000	14	2	0	0	0	0	0	0	0	0	1	0	1	1	0	0	0	0
Grovom, Carl, Auburn†	.167	17	12	0	2	3	1	0	0	1	0	2	0	1	0	0	5	0	0
Gsellman, Bob, Utica	.185	49	135	14	25	44	7	0	4	15	3	0	1	3	22	1	62	2	2
Gurtcheff, Jefferey, Watertown	.218	53	170	19	37	60	3	1	6	18	3	0	1	2	24	1	45	1	2
Guzman, Hector, Oneonta	.179	23	67	6	12	16	1	0	1	5	1	2	0	0	3	0	21	4	0
Hackett, John, Erie*	.211	15	19	0	4	5	1	0	0	2	1	1	0	0	0	0	7	0	0
Haggerty, Roger, Elmira	.265	70	245	34	65	93	16	0	4	27	6	2	2	1	38	0	41	5	1
Haines, Michael, Jamestown	.286	15	7	0	2	2	0	0	0	0	0	0	0	0	1	0	3	0	0
Hamilton, Scott, Erie	.176	15	17	1	3	3	0	0	0	0	0	0	0	0	0	0	2	1	0
Hamza, Antonio, Geneva	.232	60	181	32	42	62	8	0	4	25	3	7	2	1	38	1	32	33	7
Hansel, Damon, Watertown	.176	16	51	3	9	10	1	0	0	4	0	0	0	1	7	1	22	3	3
Hardamon, Derrick, Geneva	.321	19	28	3	9	13	0	2	0	5	1	2	0	0	2	0	8	5	4
Hardy, Mark, Jamestown	.189	49	143	19	27	37	1	0	3	7	2	0	1	4	7	0	60	12	4
Harris, Robert, Watertown	.172	19	64	6	11	15	0	2	0	1	0	2	0	1	2	0	16	8	2
Harris, Tyrone, Jamestown	.200	4	5	0	1	1	0	0	0	0	0	0	0	0	0	0	2	1	0
Harris, Walter, Newark	.269	55	201	38	54	75	9	3	2	16	3	3	0	3	23	0	45	21	3
Harrison, Keith, Elmira	.178	40	101	12	18	27	3	0	2	10	1	2	0	0	22	1	36	1	0
Harrison, Phillip, Geneva*	.182	16	11	1	2	2	0	0	0	2	1	4	1	0	0	0	3	0	0
Hartman, Edward, Watertown	.163	13	43	5	7	13	0	0	2	5	1	1	0	1	2	0	9	0	0
Harwick, Clinton, Geneva	.181	57	138	9	25	29	4	0	0	9	1	2	3	2	19	1	33	4	0
Hauradou, Yanko, Oneonta	.340	25	94	11	32	44	10	1	0	17	1	1	1	0	6	0	11	0	0
Hawkins, Cedric, Little Falls	.169	41	124	15	21	23	0	1	0	13	2	0	0	2	20	0	28	3	2
Heakins, Craig, Watertown	.208	26	72	6	15	23	5	0	1	9	0	0	0	3	14	0	31	1	0
Hernandez, Robert, Little Falls*	.400	17	20	3	8	11	0	0	1	7	0	1	1	1	0	0	2	0	0
Hershman, William, Erie*	.000	25	3	0	0	0	0	0	0	0	0	1	0	0	0	0	1	1	0
Hill, Anthony, Elmira	.195	49	159	16	31	38	4	0	1	21	1	2	1	1	4	0	48	3	0
Hinzo, Thomas, Batavia	.333	55	219	35	73	89	7	3	1	15	2	3	0	4	12	1	44	24	8
Hithe, Victor, Auburn	.200	5	15	2	3	3	0	0	0	2	0	0	1	1	1	0	4	1	0
Hodo, Edward, Utica*	.292	19	65	10	19	25	1	1	1	9	1	0	2	0	7	1	13	6	2
Hohn, Eric, Erie*	.000	9	3	0	0	0	0	0	0	0	0	0	0	0	0	0	1	0	0
Hollinshed, Joseph, Erie*	.214	20	42	4	9	11	2	0	0	2	0	0	0	0	4	0	13	1	0
Holm, Michael, Newark*	.000	10	1	0	0	0	0	0	0	0	0	0	0	0	0	0	1	0	0
Horton, David, Erie	.272	40	103	6	28	33	5	0	0	7	1	0	2	1	6	0	11	1	2
Howard, Christian, Oneonta	.087	9	23	2	2	2	0	0	0	4	1	0	1	1	5	0	4	1	0
Hubbard, Trent, Auburn†	.310	70	242	42	75	92	12	1	1	32	2	2	2	1	28	0	42	35	5
Hunter, Bertram, Auburn	.236	70	250	39	59	87	11	1	5	27	3	2	1	4	32	2	87	25	8
Ironside, Richard, St. Catharines	.143	16	35	4	5	12	1	0	2	6	0	1	0	0	9	0	13	0	1
Jackson, Gayron, Auburn†	.190	48	121	14	23	33	3	2	1	11	2	1	0	1	16	1	39	15	1
Jacobson, Nels, Jamestown	.333	11	9	2	3	3	0	0	0	3	0	0	0	0	2	0	3	0	0
Jarner, Kenneth, Utica	.264	45	121	16	32	37	1	2	0	13	1	0	2	0	9	0	29	5	4
Jeffers, Steven, Erie†	.226	17	62	6	14	16	2	0	0	3	0	1	0	3	9	1	2	3	1
Jeter, Shawn, St. Catharines*	.237	70	241	29	57	79	5	4	3	19	1	4	0	1	34	4	79	9	6
Jimenez, Alejandro, Little Falls*	.214	11	28	3	6	7	1	0	0	4	1	0	0	0	3	0	8	1	0
Johnson, Christopher, Utica	.000	12	2	0	0	0	0	0	0	0	0	0	0	0	0	0	0	0	0
Jundy, Lorin, Little Falls	.000	15	10	0	0	0	0	0	0	0	0	0	0	0	2	0	6	0	0
Kazmierczak, William, Geneva†	.000	5	6	0	0	0	0	0	0	0	0	0	0	0	2	0	0	0	0
Kelly, Jimy, St. Catharines	.180	60	178	17	32	37	5	0	0	13	0	0	2	2	21	0	57	2	1
Kent, Lewis, Batavia	.199	45	141	13	28	55	3	0	8	21	2	1	0	2	13	0	57	0	0
Khoury, Michael, Watertown*	.191	65	225	19	43	61	8	2	2	14	1	1	2	5	13	1	50	6	4
King, Steven, Jamestown	.111	11	9	2	1	1	0	0	0	1	0	3	0	0	1	0	0	0	0

Player and Club	Pct.	G.	AB.	R.	H.	TB.	2B.	3B.	HR.	RBI.	GW.	SH.	SF.	HP.	BB.	Int. BB.	SO.	SB.	CS.
Kirk, Timothy, Watertown*	.333	22	6	2	2	2	0	0	0	0	0	0	0	1	0	0	1	0	0
Kline, Stewart, Newark†	.170	19	53	8	9	16	1	0	2	8	1	0	0	0	7	0	13	0	1
Kraus, Ralph, Oneonta*	.281	61	224	38	63	81	6	6	0	31	7	1	0	1	27	0	38	9	0
Kryzanowski, Rusty, Auburn	.112	45	116	13	13	30	2	0	5	14	1	0	3	3	15	1	52	0	0
Kuiper, Glen, Erie*	.225	61	129	16	29	30	1	0	0	9	0	5	1	0	18	0	19	3	3
Laboy, Jose, Oneonta	.211	51	166	23	35	50	7	1	2	18	3	0	1	1	11	1	35	0	3
LaMarche, Michel, Utica	.250	25	4	0	1	1	0	0	0	0	0	0	0	0	1	0	1	0	0
Lambert, Robert, Oneonta	.255	31	110	10	28	32	1	0	1	8	2	1	1	1	10	0	28	6	1
Lampkin, Thomas, Batavia*	.258	63	190	24	49	59	5	1	1	20	1	1	1	0	31	3	14	4	3
Landrum, Cedric, Geneva*	.315	64	213	51	67	86	6	2	3	16	0	4	3	3	40	1	33	49	10
Lapenta, Gerald, Geneva*	.259	59	166	20	43	63	8	0	4	21	6	0	0	3	30	3	35	6	1
Lawrence, Scott, Erie	.100	28	10	2	1	1	0	0	0	0	0	0	0	0	3	0	4	1	0
Lemle, Robert, Little Falls	.140	43	107	10	15	22	4	0	1	2	1	4	0	2	9	0	33	2	1
Leyritz, James, Oneonta†	.363	23	91	12	33	50	3	1	4	15	3	2	3	0	5	1	10	1	0
Lockley, Blane, Watertown*	.299	41	117	15	35	55	7	2	3	17	6	1	1	2	17	1	37	1	1
Love, Carl, Utica	.143	3	7	2	1	1	0	0	0	0	0	0	0	0	4	0	2	0	0
Lundahl, Richard, Little Falls	.270	61	230	31	62	105	14	1	9	40	9	0	2	1	17	1	52	0	3
Maas, Kevin, Oneonta*	.356	28	101	14	36	46	10	0	0	18	4	0	1	0	7	1	9	5	1
Machacek, Kenny, Jamestown*	.000	14	4	0	0	0	0	0	0	0	0	0	0	0	0	0	2	0	0
Magee, Warren, Utica†	.333	24	6	2	2	2	0	0	0	0	0	0	0	0	0	0	1	0	0
Mann, Kelly, Geneva	.194	60	191	17	37	44	1	0	2	15	3	0	1	5	18	0	38	3	2
Marchese, Joseph, Elmira	.207	59	213	24	44	63	8	1	3	20	4	2	1	1	12	0	40	3	5
Martineau, Paul, Jamestown*	.191	68	215	22	41	63	9	2	3	19	2	4	3	1	14	1	47	3	0
Matas, James, Geneva	.000	14	4	0	0	0	0	0	0	0	0	1	0	0	1	0	4	0	0
McDevitt, Stephen, Utica	.167	4	6	0	1	1	0	0	0	0	0	0	0	0	0	0	1	0	0
McDonald, James, Jamestown	.000	19	1	0	0	0	0	0	0	0	0	0	0	0	0	0	0	0	0
McElroy, Charles, Utica*	.333	14	18	3	6	6	0	0	0	1	0	0	0	0	1	0	3	0	1
McKinney, John, Utica	.000	14	3	1	0	0	0	0	0	0	0	0	0	0	2	0	1	0	0
McMurtrie, Daniel, Little Falls	.176	15	17	0	3	3	0	0	0	0	0	0	0	0	0	0	3	0	0
Mejias, Simeon, Geneva	.167	3	12	1	2	2	0	0	0	0	0	0	0	0	0	0	2	0	0
Mendez, Eddie, St. Catharines	.176	22	51	6	9	11	2	0	0	1	0	0	0	0	8	0	21	0	0
Mendez, Victor, St. Catharines	.000	8	12	1	0	0	0	0	0	0	0	0	0	0	3	0	6	0	1
Merced, Orlando, Watertown*	.180	27	89	12	16	27	0	1	3	9	0	0	1	2	14	2	21	6	2
Meyer, Brian, Auburn	.143	32	7	1	1	1	0	0	0	0	0	0	0	0	0	0	3	0	0
Meyer, Steven, Erie*	.224	61	205	25	46	78	8	0	8	33	4	2	4	4	15	1	43	1	2
Milstien, David, Elmira*	.271	34	107	15	29	36	4	0	1	6	1	1	0	0	5	0	12	0	2
Mims, Larry, Newark	.222	63	153	29	34	40	4	1	0	15	2	4	0	0	30	0	15	23	8
Moran, Dean, Watertown	.234	55	158	16	37	39	2	0	0	10	0	1	2	0	25	1	37	14	5
Moreno, Douglas, Watertown	.000	6	1	0	0	0	0	0	0	0	0	0	0	0	0	0	0	0	0
Morris, Harold, Oneonta	.378	36	127	26	48	70	9	2	3	30	3	2	1	1	18	2	15	1	1
Morrow, David, Jamestown	.240	47	125	11	30	41	3	1	2	15	2	0	0	1	9	0	21	3	0
Moser, Steven, Watertown	.238	75	282	37	67	78	4	2	1	25	5	5	0	6	32	1	17	12	8
Murphy, Peter, Watertown*	.250	7	8	2	2	2	0	0	0	0	0	0	0	0	0	0	3	0	0
Murrell, Rodney, Little Falls*	.259	71	232	23	60	76	9	2	1	22	2	1	1	0	25	0	32	3	4
Narcisse, Ronald, Little Falls	.240	42	125	15	30	45	7	1	2	11	0	2	0	1	14	1	36	4	3
Natera, Luis, Little Falls	.266	72	248	30	66	81	10	1	1	20	4	4	0	1	31	1	48	7	1
Neel, Troy, Batavia*	.000	4	13	0	0	0	0	0	0	1	1	0	0	0	0	0	8	0	0
Nemeth, Carey, Erie	.264	66	220	29	58	91	12	0	7	29	3	1	1	3	29	0	51	4	2
Nettles, Robert, Erie	.154	16	13	1	2	3	1	0	0	1	0	0	0	1	1	0	1	1	1
Normand, Guy, Auburn	.333	20	6	2	2	5	0	0	1	1	0	1	0	2	1	0	2	0	0
O'Donnell, Glen, Elmira	.290	17	31	4	9	10	1	0	0	1	0	0	0	0	5	0	5	1	0
Ochoa, Steven, Utica	.213	45	136	21	29	45	4	3	2	19	2	1	2	2	30	0	28	10	6
Oertli, Charles, Geneva	.185	42	119	14	22	30	5	0	1	8	0	2	1	2	8	1	21	1	1
Oller, Jeffrey, Jamestown*	.207	66	188	20	39	51	3	0	3	24	2	1	2	2	35	2	52	7	7
Olson, James, Auburn	.077	20	13	1	1	1	0	0	0	0	0	0	0	0	0	0	4	0	0
Otten, Brian, Geneva	.000	29	6	0	0	0	0	0	0	0	0	1	0	0	0	0	3	0	0
Padilla, Livio, Elmira	.241	10	29	7	7	13	3	0	1	3	2	1	1	1	2	0	12	0	0
Pancoski, Tracey, Newark	.146	23	41	4	6	7	1	0	0	1	1	1	0	1	6	0	14	0	0
Parker, Carroll, Erie†	.238	73	239	46	57	78	10	1	3	11	2	2	1	4	39	2	63	33	6
Parker, Olen, Utica†	.250	20	44	6	11	15	2	1	0	2	1	1	0	0	5	0	13	2	4
Perez, Bladimir, Utica	.222	13	9	1	2	2	0	0	0	0	0	0	0	0	0	0	2	0	0
Perez, Francisco, Erie	.189	65	148	13	28	45	5	0	4	14	0	0	0	1	20	0	34	2	1
Perry, Parnell, Geneva	.233	66	223	24	52	66	11	0	1	21	3	2	1	2	7	0	47	19	3
Pilkinton, Lemuel, Elmira	.191	26	68	10	13	19	6	0	0	8	0	0	0	0	21	0	18	3	0
Polka, Fredric, Little Falls*	.284	51	162	28	46	73	7	1	6	28	3	0	1	3	31	2	27	1	1
Posey, John, Newark	.261	75	276	31	72	98	12	1	4	34	4	0	1	3	25	1	42	1	0
Posey, Robert, Newark*	.234	45	141	23	33	59	11	0	5	28	2	0	2	2	28	1	33	0	0
Potts, David, Auburn	.000	16	3	0	0	0	0	0	0	0	0	0	0	0	0	0	1	0	0
Powell, Clyde, Utica	.208	54	149	11	31	41	8	1	0	6	0	0	1	1	13	0	41	8	4
Quintana, Alberto, Watertown	.265	32	117	5	31	39	3	1	1	17	2	0	2	1	4	0	15	3	2
Radzik, Matthew, Newark	.000	9	10	0	0	0	0	0	0	0	0	0	0	0	2	0	4	0	0
Ramos, John, Oneonta	.500	3	8	3	4	8	2	1	0	1	1	0	0	0	2	0	1	0	0
Reese, Kyle, Erie	.174	13	23	2	4	5	1	0	0	0	0	0	0	0	2	0	10	0	0
Richardson, Kerry, Batavia	.246	62	211	25	52	91	9	0	10	40	2	1	3	0	22	0	64	1	0
Rickers, Troy, Jamestown	.193	56	181	18	35	41	2	2	0	7	2	2	0	1	14	1	68	6	4
Robertson, Michael, Jamestown	.000	9	2	1	0	0	0	0	0	0	0	0	0	0	1	0	1	0	0
Robicheaux, Ron, Watertown	.248	29	101	11	25	27	2	0	0	9	0	0	1	1	7	0	19	2	2
Robinson, William, Little Falls	.280	35	82	6	23	29	2	2	0	6	0	1	0	0	8	0	31	0	1
Rockweiler, Dean, Jamestown*	.000	16	1	0	0	0	0	0	0	0	0	0	0	0	1	0	1	0	0
Rodgers, Paul, St. Catharines†	.264	73	269	42	71	95	8	2	4	32	2	1	1	3	26	0	64	19	6
Roebuck, Ron, Auburn†	.143	12	7	0	1	2	1	0	0	1	0	0	0	0	0	0	3	0	0
Rohde, David, Auburn	.261	61	207	41	54	74	6	4	2	22	3	1	2	0	37	1	37	28	9
Rosario, Julio, Elmira†	.241	33	87	9	21	25	2	1	0	13	2	1	1	2	4	0	17	1	1
Rose, Carl, Watertown	.237	43	118	12	28	50	4	0	6	13	3	0	0	0	5	1	56	0	0
Roseboro, Jaime, Little Falls	.269	68	234	26	63	78	5	2	2	17	1	5	2	2	12	3	24	8	2
Runge, Scott, Watertown	.200	10	5	0	1	2	1	0	0	2	0	0	0	0	1	0	2	0	0
Sampen, William, Watertown	.250	9	4	1	1	1	0	0	0	0	0	0	0	0	0	0	0	0	0
Sanchez, Pedro, Auburn†	.241	72	291	32	70	90	10	2	2	21	1	0	1	0	18	1	50	21	10
Sanders, Earl, St. Catharines	.296	39	108	11	32	39	5	1	0	11	0	0	1	1	8	0	27	0	0
Santos, Donaciano, Batavia	.200	47	150	15	30	45	3	0	4	16	2	0	5	3	27	0	43	1	1
Sardinha, Eduardo, Elmira	.286	27	98	15	28	31	1	1	0	9	1	0	0	1	13	0	19	2	2
Schlieper, Joseph, St. Catharines*	.000	7	0	0	0	0	0	0	0	0	0	0	0	0	1	0	0	0	0

Player and Club	Pct.	G.	AB.	R.	H.	TB.	2B.	3B.	HR.	RBI.	GW.	SH.	SF.	HP.	BB.	Int. BB.	SO.	SB.	CS.
Schlopy, Clifford, Watertown*	.000	10	10	1	0	0	0	0	0	0	0	0	0	0	1	0	7	0	0
Schmerer, Dana, Batavia*	.125	14	8	1	1	1	0	0	0	2	0	0	1	0	2	0	1	0	0
Schueler, Russ, Jamestown	.287	23	87	13	25	33	4	2	0	3	1	2	0	1	6	1	17	9	3
Schunk, Jerry, St. Catharines	.276	71	272	39	75	108	12	0	7	33	3	6	3	2	21	2	25	18	6
Seifert, Keith, Batavia	.231	58	195	18	45	60	9	0	2	25	1	1	3	0	18	0	59	2	2
Service, Scott, Utica	.250	10	16	2	4	4	0	0	0	1	0	2	1	0	0	0	2	0	0
Shade, Steven, Erie†	.180	34	61	3	11	12	1	0	0	3	0	0	1	1	5	0	17	3	0
Shannon, Robert, Jamestown	.200	21	45	3	9	15	3	0	1	7	0	1	0	1	0	0	10	0	0
Shea, John, St. Catharines	.000	14	1	0	0	0	0	0	0	0	0	0	0	0	0	0	0	0	0
Shelton, Harry, Geneva*	.252	56	159	23	40	53	8	1	1	14	2	3	1	1	17	0	39	15	5
Shields, Thomas, Watertown	.288	43	153	25	44	64	6	1	4	25	2	1	3	7	17	0	36	15	6
Shifflett, Barry, St. Catharines*	.298	65	242	37	72	91	8	1	3	32	6	2	5	0	40	1	36	9	5
Simon, Richard, Auburn	.000	15	15	1	0	0	0	0	0	0	0	0	0	0	2	0	7	0	0
Sims, Joe, Jamestown	.154	41	104	6	16	23	2	1	1	9	1	1	1	0	8	0	36	0	1
Sims, Mark, Utica*	.077	14	13	2	1	1	0	0	0	0	0	1	0	0	1	0	3	0	0
Skeete, Rafael, Newark*	.244	16	41	6	10	11	1	0	0	2	1	1	0	2	7	0	12	12	1
Slocumb, Heath, Little Falls	.000	25	2	0	0	0	0	0	0	0	0	0	0	0	0	0	2	0	0
Smith, Greg, Erie	.213	36	47	8	10	13	3	0	0	1	0	0	0	0	14	0	10	1	0
Smith, Michael, Utica	.222	40	126	9	28	41	8	1	1	6	1	2	0	1	9	0	35	2	3
Sommers, Scott, Elmira*	.229	64	223	18	51	53	2	0	0	19	3	2	0	3	13	1	25	3	2
St. Claire, Steven, Jamestown	.223	62	229	34	51	78	10	1	5	21	4	0	1	2	12	2	56	5	4
Stankiewicz, Andrew, Oneonta	.296	59	216	51	64	78	8	3	0	17	3	4	4	5	38	0	41	14	3
Stark, Jeffrey, Utica	.209	39	129	9	27	36	4	1	1	13	3	2	2	0	10	0	22	2	3
Stennett, Matthew, Auburn	.163	16	49	6	8	13	0	1	1	4	1	0	1	0	2	0	11	1	0
Strickland, Robert, Geneva*	.244	64	201	23	49	83	14	1	6	28	2	1	1	2	21	0	46	7	4
Strijek, Randy, Newark	.209	72	235	24	49	58	7	1	0	18	1	1	2	3	20	0	70	8	7
Tabaka, Jeffrey, Jamestown	.000	13	7	0	0	0	0	0	0	0	0	1	0	0	0	0	3	0	0
Taylor, Andrew, Little Falls	.000	16	4	1	0	0	0	0	0	1	0	1	0	0	0	0	1	0	0
Taylor, Kenneth, Geneva	.250	1	4	1	1	1	0	0	0	0	0	0	0	0	0	0	1	0	0
Temrowski, Thomas, Auburn*	.250	5	16	3	4	6	2	0	0	3	0	0	0	0	3	0	4	0	0
Thompson, Anthony, Little Falls†	.223	59	184	30	41	67	7	2	5	18	2	1	0	3	16	0	58	7	1
Thornton, Albert, Elmira	.216	20	51	3	11	15	1	0	1	3	0	0	0	0	1	0	22	0	0
Toy, Tracy, Watertown	.000	23	5	0	0	0	0	0	0	0	0	0	0	0	0	0	2	0	0
Travels, Darren, Jamestown	.500	12	4	1	2	2	0	0	0	0	0	1	0	0	0	0	0	0	0
Triplett, Lance, Utica*	.105	30	57	5	6	8	0	1	0	6	0	1	0	0	9	0	23	1	0
Twardoski, Michael, Batavia*	.307	63	202	33	62	92	12	0	6	17	3	2	1	0	43	2	25	11	3
Vaccaro, Salvatore, Jamestown†	.000	11	1	0	0	0	0	0	0	1	0	0	1	0	0	0	0	0	0
Valdez, Mario, Utica	.156	45	109	15	17	23	1	1	1	7	0	0	0	0	4	0	45	0	3
Valverde, Miguel, Watertown†	.178	65	230	33	41	44	3	0	0	11	0	4	1	4	38	1	65	45	7
Vike, James, Auburn	.333	12	6	1	2	3	1	0	0	0	0	1	0	0	2	0	2	0	0
Viltz, Corey, Newark	.212	29	66	12	14	19	2	0	1	9	2	0	0	0	25	1	30	8	1
Walker, Michael, Watertown	.214	16	14	1	3	3	0	0	0	0	0	0	0	0	2	0	1	0	0
Wallen, Walter, Newark	.200	34	110	9	22	29	4	0	1	11	0	1	0	1	9	0	28	2	2
Ward, Turner, Oneonta	.281	63	221	42	62	71	4	1	1	19	2	2	3	2	31	1	39	6	6
Warfel, Brian, Elmira	.178	16	45	3	8	9	1	0	0	3	0	0	1	0	5	0	9	0	0
Wasilewski, Kevin, Auburn	.000	29	2	0	0	0	0	0	0	0	0	0	0	0	0	0	1	0	0
Wedvick, Jeffrey, Jamestown	.274	38	117	14	32	41	6	0	1	13	3	2	0	2	11	0	15	0	1
Weidie, Stuart, Elmira†	.291	62	203	25	59	77	9	3	1	16	2	3	1	3	25	1	59	9	0
Welborn, Anthony, Jamestown	.100	15	10	0	1	2	1	0	0	1	0	0	0	0	0	0	0	0	0
Welborn, Todd, Little Falls	.000	16	4	1	0	0	0	0	0	0	0	0	0	0	0	0	1	0	0
Welter, Andrew, Newark*	.233	23	60	6	14	16	2	0	0	8	1	0	2	1	12	2	12	2	1
Whited, Edward, Auburn	.292	61	219	34	64	96	15	1	5	36	5	0	3	5	19	0	49	12	4
Williams, Michael, Batavia	.118	28	51	3	6	12	0	0	2	3	0	0	0	1	9	0	24	1	1
Williams, Paul, Elmira	.228	28	79	10	18	29	4	2	1	5	0	0	1	0	6	0	27	0	0
Williams, Phillip, Newark	.303	35	76	11	23	25	2	0	0	6	1	0	0	2	22	1	10	2	0
Williams, Rafael, Batavia	.222	32	81	7	18	20	2	0	0	2	0	0	0	1	4	0	6	1	2
Williamson, Raymond, Batavia	.183	58	186	23	34	57	6	1	5	18	1	0	1	6	24	0	58	4	3
Wilson, Randall, Watertown	.000	12	1	0	0	0	0	0	0	0	0	0	0	0	0	0	0	0	0
Wilson, Doyle, Batavia	.187	29	91	8	17	22	2	0	1	5	0	1	0	0	9	0	14	0	0
Winzenread, Richard, Newark	.000	15	2	0	0	0	0	0	0	0	0	0	0	0	1	0	0	0	0
Yan, Julian, St. Catharines	.273	73	282	40	77	133	7	2	15	49	9	0	1	2	25	1	72	2	1
Zaltsman, Stanley, Erie*	.000	29	3	0	0	0	0	0	0	0	0	0	0	0	0	0	0	0	0
Zarranz, Fernando, Geneva	.000	12	11	0	0	0	0	0	0	1	0	1	0	0	1	0	5	1	0
Zeile, Todd, Erie	.258	70	248	40	64	122	14	1	14	63	5	1	6	2	37	1	52	5	1

The following pitchers, listed alphabetically by club, with games in parentheses, had no plate appearances, primarily through use of designated hitters:

AUBURN—Towey, Steve (1).

BATAVIA—Bird, Steven (21); Chambers, Carl (19); Compres, Fidel (18); Egloff, Bruce (12); Gardner, Myron (15); Luckenbill, Kraig (7); Maggard, Kent (24); Shaw, Jeffrey (14); Skalski, Joseph (14); Wickander, Kevin (11).

ELMIRA—Bast, Steven (10); Coffey, Michael (16); Haley, Bart (16); Morrison, James (9); Rawdon, Christopher (10); Ryan, Kenneth (13); Schilling, Curtis (16); Sepela, Thomas (15); Tejada, Joaquin (13); Wacha, Charles (10); Walters, David (15); Warren, Ronald (17); Whiting, Michael (7); Williams, Kerman (14).

ERIE—Becker, Gregory (2); Marte, Roberto (14).

GENEVA—LaPoint, Anthony (21); Soto, Jose (2).

JAMESTOWN—DeBoever, William (11).

LITTLE FALLS—Bauer, Peter (25); Henion, Scott (14).

NEWARK—Beatty, Gordon (15); Borgatti, Michael (16); Bowden, Stephen (13); Carriger, Ricky (3); Cinnella, Douglas (13); Dillard, Gordon (27); Koonce, Alan (13); Mandich, Thomas (6); Peguero, Soto (15); Sonneberger, Steven (20); Williams, Robert (7); Wilson, Chaunan (14).

ONEONTA—Adkins, Steven (14); Azocar, Oscar (10); Balabon, Richard (10); Byrnes, John (17); Layana, Timothy (3); Marris, Mark (7); Patterson, Kenneth (15); Ridenour, Dana (23); Rose, Mark (8); Rosenberg, Steven (4); Rub, Ronald (17); Ryan, Todd (3); Scheid, Richard (15); Voeltz, William (15); Wilkins, Dean (15).

ST. CATHARINES—Blair, William (21); Cavanaugh, Robert (20); Cummings, Steven (18); DeLaCruz, Jose (9); Diaz, Victor (17); Hentgen, Patrick (13); Hernandez, Xavier (14); Jones, Christopher (18); Palma, Ruben (2); Roderick, Morgan (1); Saitta, Patrick (19).

UTICA—Garcia, Rafael (1).

WATERTOWN—Belinda, Stanley (5).

GRAND SLAM HOME RUNS—Zeile, 3; Alou, G. Cooper, Hill, Kent, Nemeth, 1 each.

AWARDED FIRST BASE ON CATCHER'S INTERFERENCE—Banks 2 (J. Posey 2); Lockley 2 (Berge, Polka); Berube (Pa. Williams); Gonzalez (Zeile); Hunter (J. Posey); Thompson (Zeile); Welter (Gurtcheff).

CLUB FIELDING

Club	Pct.	G.	PO.	A.	E.	DP.	PB.
Oneonta	.971	77	1994	853	85	68	20
St. Catharines	.966	76	2042	805	101	57	18
Erie	.963	77	2015	925	113	76	15
Jamestown	.959	76	1938	841	120	74	19
Elmira	.957	75	1947	737	122	53	21
Auburn	.956	76	1986	808	128	62	13
Geneva	.953	78	1994	811	138	63	15
Little Falls	.953	76	1999	815	139	53	18
Batavia	.952	75	1936	766	137	78	20
Utica	.951	78	1934	753	137	57	21
Watertown	.950	78	2073	894	155	77	22
Newark	.949	78	1983	831	151	70	20

Triple Plays—Batavia, Elmira.

INDIVIDUAL FIELDING

*Throws lefthanded.

FIRST BASEMEN

Player and Club	Pct.	G.	PO.	A.	E.	DP.
Banister, Watertown	.973	4	33	3	1	5
Banks, Auburn*	.980	32	226	25	5	19
Behnsch, Utica	.987	31	204	20	3	19
Berge, Little Falls	.944	6	46	5	3	3
Brunelle, Utica	.981	48	398	23	8	25
Burke, Newark*	.987	77	652	38	9	65
Butts, Erie*	.978	15	126	7	3	11
Calley, Newark	1.000	5	14	1	0	1
Carter, Oneonta	1.000	4	30	6	0	5
Casteel, Geneva	1.000	1	9	0	0	0
Cooper, Auburn	.975	5	35	4	1	3
Crosby, Little Falls*	.972	54	421	32	13	30
Diaz, St. Catharines	.952	7	37	3	2	2
Duey, Jamestown	1.000	13	81	6	0	7
Duke, Jamestown	.985	8	63	1	1	8
Edwards, Auburn	.981	11	93	8	2	13
Farmer, Little Falls	1.000	2	16	1	0	1
Garcia, Utica*	1.000	1	2	0	0	1
Graff, Erie	1.000	13	62	5	0	9
Hamza, Geneva	.989	26	166	11	2	18
Hansel, Watertown	.980	15	141	6	3	14
Harwick, Geneva	1.000	5	9	2	0	0
Hawkins, Little Falls	1.000	1	1	0	0	0
Jimenez, Little Falls*	.986	11	63	5	1	7
Kent, Batavia	.952	10	56	4	3	4
Kraus, Oneonta*	.991	14	95	11	1	7
Kuiper, Erie	.984	9	60	3	1	4
Lockley, Watertown	.990	34	282	16	3	23
Lundahl, Little Falls	.985	21	126	9	2	7
Maas, Oneonta*	.996	27	222	19	1	22
Martineau, Jamestown*	.985	65	485	39	8	48
Merced, Watertown	1.000	5	35	1	0	2
Meyer, Erie*	.988	55	544	20	7	40
Moran, Watertown	1.000	2	15	0	0	0
Morris, Oneonta	.991	36	317	26	3	28
Morrow, Jamestown	.938	3	11	4	1	1
Neel, Batavia	1.000	1	2	1	0	0
Oller, Jamestown	1.000	1	2	0	0	0
Pilkinton, Elmira	.988	12	82	3	1	5
Posey, Newark	1.000	1	5	1	0	1
Robicheaux, Watertown	1.000	6	47	1	0	3
Rose, Watertown	.972	20	164	7	5	18
Santos, Batavia	.967	20	140	6	5	8
Seifert, Batavia	.988	52	385	36	5	53
Shannon, Jamestown	1.000	1	6	0	0	0
Shifflett, St. Catharines	1.000	1	7	0	0	0
Sommers, Elmira	.985	61	435	23	7	30
Strickland, Geneva	.987	58	432	30	6	36
Temrowski, Auburn*	.972	4	29	6	1	4
Thornton, Elmira	.968	11	56	4	2	5
Valdez, Utica	1.000	4	14	1	0	2
Ward, Oneonta	1.000	1	1	0	0	0
Whited, Auburn	.986	29	267	20	4	24
Williams, Newark	1.000	2	11	1	0	1
YAN, St. Catharines	.989	70	679	27	8	44

Triple Plays—Seifert, Sommers.

SECOND BASEMEN

Player and Club	Pct.	G.	PO.	A.	E.	DP.
Alicea, Erie	.955	46	94	163	12	38
Baker, Elmira	.950	52	119	126	13	29
Balis, Batavia	.889	3	4	4	1	0
Carganilla, Batavia	.943	7	18	15	2	3
Castro, 23 Little Falls-23 Utica	.911	46	68	95	16	20
Clemo, Jamestown	.974	66	116	178	8	42
Crone, Newark	.965	20	30	53	3	17
Dulin, Newark	.938	33	67	85	10	19
Echevarria, Elmira	.931	9	12	15	2	4
Escobar, St. Catharines	.955	75	117	226	16	31
Espinal, Geneva	.929	68	136	167	23	38
Faulk, Utica	.951	50	68	127	10	16
Frias-Soto, St. Catharines	.909	4	5	5	1	2
Gaylor, Jamestown	.958	14	23	23	2	4
Graff, Erie	1.000	1	1	0	0	0
Gray, Auburn	1.000	2	4	0	0	0
Harwick, Geneva	.900	8	15	12	3	2
Hauradou, Oneonta	1.000	4	9	7	0	1
Hawkins, Little Falls	.960	37	63	81	6	12
Hinzo, Batavia	.954	55	112	135	12	36
Horton, Erie	.857	3	3	9	2	1
Hubbard, Auburn	.930	46	91	107	15	21
Jeffers, Erie	.968	17	32	59	3	5
Kuiper, Erie	.936	20	24	49	5	9
Lambert, Oneonta	.977	20	37	49	2	7
Lundahl, Little Falls	.951	28	44	54	5	11
Marchese, Elmira	.965	19	45	37	3	4
Mejias, Geneva	.900	2	3	6	1	1
Milstien, Elmira	.500	2	0	1	1	0
Mims, Newark	.951	36	68	86	8	16
Moran, Watertown	1.000	7	11	11	0	1
MOSER, Watertown	.982	75	168	221	7	51
Parker, Utica	.951	15	29	29	3	6
Robicheaux, Watertown	.857	1	2	4	1	2
Sanchez, Auburn	.956	40	80	95	8	25
Sardinha, Elmira	1.000	2	0	4	0	1
Shelton, Geneva	.952	7	11	9	1	2
Stankiewicz, Oneonta	.957	54	103	144	11	40
Williams, Batavia	.942	17	26	39	4	11

Triple Plays—Baker, Hinzo.

THIRD BASEMEN

Player and Club	Pct.	G.	PO.	A.	E.	DP.
Balis, Batavia	.860	21	7	36	7	3
Bautista, Newark	.840	18	7	21	5	2
Behnsch, Utica	.849	38	18	44	11	4
Berube, Oneonta	.813	18	10	29	9	1
Blowers, Jamestown	.833	2	2	3	1	0
Calley, Newark	.880	32	23	50	10	5
Carganilla, Batavia	1.000	4	1	10	0	0
Cooper, Elmira	.903	27	22	62	9	2
Crone, Newark	1.000	1	2	0	0	0
DiVincenzo, Little Falls	.900	4	4	5	1	0
Dulin, Newark	1.000	2	0	1	0	0
Frias-Soto, St. Catharines	1.000	6	3	5	0	0
Frye, Jamestown	.789	6	0	15	4	0
Gamba, Batavia	.813	8	4	9	3	0
Gaylor, Jamestown	.909	27	14	46	6	4
Gray, Auburn	.909	4	1	9	1	0
Haggerty, Elmira	.891	43	34	81	14	3
Hartman, Watertown	.500	1	0	1	1	0
Harwick, Geneva	.899	44	40	58	11	7
Hauradou, Oneonta	.814	17	6	29	8	2
Horton, Erie	.956	18	14	29	2	4
Jarner, Utica	.892	17	17	16	4	2
Kryzanowski, Auburn	.932	25	17	51	5	4
Kuiper, Erie	1.000	3	4	4	0	1
Laboy, Oneonta	.958	43	25	88	5	8
Lambert, Oneonta	1.000	3	3	8	0	0
Lapenta, Geneva	.926	47	20	80	8	9
Lundahl, Little Falls	.881	16	5	32	5	1
Mejias, Geneva	1.000	2	2	0	0	0
Merced, Watertown	.796	17	12	27	10	3
Moran, Watertown	.944	32	26	59	5	7
Morrow, Jamestown	1.000	2	2	4	0	1
Murrell, Little Falls	.910	68	53	119	17	5
Nemeth, Erie	.928	60	43	111	12	7
O'Donnell, Elmira	.929	8	1	12	1	2
Oller, Jamestown	.883	45	34	79	15	14
Perry, Geneva	1.000	1	1	0	0	0
Polka, Little Falls	.667	1	0	2	1	0
Posey, Newark	.909	5	3	7	1	0
Powell, Utica	.750	16	10	20	10	2
Quintana, Watertown	.866	29	25	59	13	2
Richardson, Batavia	.906	43	28	59	9	5
Robicheaux, Watertown	.857	6	3	9	2	0
Sanchez, Auburn	.897	23	20	32	6	1

THIRD BASEMEN—Continued

Player and Club	Pct.	G.	PO.	A.	E.	DP.
Sardinha, Elmira	1.000	3	2	6	0	0
SCHUNK, St. Catharines	.955	71	41	127	8	16
Shannon, Jamestown	.923	4	5	7	1	0
Shifflett, St. Catharines	1.000	7	7	12	0	1
Smith, Erie	.500	1	1	0	1	0
Sommers, Elmira	.000	1	0	0	1	0
St. Claire, Jamestown	.000	1	0	0	1	0
Valdez, Utica	.886	15	8	23	4	4
Viltz, Newark	1.000	1	1	0	0	0
Wallen, Newark	.851	33	16	58	13	6
Ward, Oneonta	1.000	1	1	3	0	0
Whited, Auburn	.880	33	19	62	11	5
Williams, Batavia	.800	10	8	8	4	1

Triple Plays—Balis, Cooper.

SHORTSTOPS

Player and Club	Pct.	G.	PO.	A.	E.	DP.
Baker, Elmira	1.000	1	2	0	0	0
BECKER, Oneonta	.958	69	124	196	14	43
Blowers, Jamestown	.885	29	46	70	15	19
Bullinger, Geneva	.923	78	104	207	26	36
Carganilla, Batavia	.912	21	44	59	10	19
Castro, Utica	.750	3	3	6	3	2
Crone, Newark	.881	8	14	23	5	4
DeLaRosa, Utica	.915	64	98	171	25	27
Echevarria, Elmira	.867	6	5	8	2	1
Fairchild, Batavia	.900	52	88	136	25	31
Faulk, Utica	1.000	1	3	1	0	0
Figueroa, Erie	.948	70	123	225	19	41
Frias-Soto, St. Catharines	.890	25	25	64	11	7
Gamba, Batavia	.926	8	9	16	2	4
Gaylor, Jamestown	.965	15	20	35	2	3
Gray, Auburn	.800	8	5	11	4	1
Hartman, Watertown	.882	12	20	40	8	9
Harwick, Geneva	1.000	2	1	3	0	0
Hauradou, Oneonta	1.000	4	4	14	0	4
Horton, Erie	1.000	3	4	8	0	0
Jarner, Utica	.913	17	17	25	4	1
Kelly, St. Catharines	.902	60	86	154	26	22
Kuiper, Erie	1.000	1	0	1	0	0
Laboy, Oneonta	1.000	2	1	2	0	0
Lundahl, Little Falls	.889	8	10	14	3	3
Marchese, Elmira	.861	9	6	25	5	5
Milstien, Elmira	.925	32	28	70	8	8
Mims, Newark	.900	2	2	7	1	1
Moran, Watertown	.862	12	18	32	8	5
Murrell, Little Falls	1.000	3	2	7	0	1
Natera, Little Falls	.917	71	89	211	27	28
Oller, Jamestown	.936	19	33	55	6	9
Parker, Utica	1.000	1	5	2	0	1
Quintana, Watertown	.857	1	4	2	1	2
Robicheaux, Watertown	.871	14	14	40	8	10
Rohde, Auburn	.939	59	90	158	16	33
Rosario, Elmira	.906	23	21	37	6	7
Sanchez, Auburn	.892	15	30	36	8	7
Sardinha, Elmira	.892	21	38	53	11	11
Schueler, Jamestown	.922	23	49	57	9	6
Shields, Watertown	.917	43	74	148	20	26
Smith, Erie	.927	13	12	26	3	9
Stankiewicz, Oneonta	.923	3	4	8	1	1
Strijek, Newark	.905	72	106	198	32	41

OUTFIELDERS

Player and Club	Pct.	G.	PO.	A.	E.	DP.
Alou, Watertown	.952	62	134	6	7	2
Alvarez, Erie*	.500	3	2	0	2	0
Arendas, Oneonta*	1.000	7	14	0	0	0
Baine, Erie	.976	63	76	6	2	1
Banister, Watertown	.750	3	3	0	1	0
Bautista, Newark	.898	41	48	5	6	0
Bellino, Newark	.922	37	46	1	4	1
Bourne, Elmira	.990	38	87	10	1	5
Brady, Watertown	.939	33	45	1	3	0
Brooks, Auburn	.912	24	28	3	3	0
Brown, St. Catharines	.978	33	43	1	1	0
Brumfield, Utica*	.986	77	193	12	3	4
Brunelle, Utica	.917	21	37	7	4	2
Bruske, Batavia	.947	54	85	4	5	2
Buheller, Elmira*	.980	53	145	3	3	0
Burke, Jamestown*	.946	40	66	4	4	0
Calvert, Oneonta	.951	36	36	3	2	1
Carter, Oneonta	1.000	7	6	0	0	0
Casteel, Geneva	1.000	1	1	0	0	0
Christian, Erie	.973	46	69	2	2	1
Close, Oneonta	.989	61	88	0	1	0
Collins, Geneva	.974	70	107	5	3	2
COOPER, Auburn	1.000	67	92	7	0	0
Crosby, Little Falls*	1.000	5	3	0	0	0
DeLaMata, Newark*	.833	7	5	0	1	0
DiVincenzo, Little Falls	1.000	10	9	1	0	0
Edwards, Auburn	.750	5	3	0	1	0
Farmer, Little Falls	1.000	3	7	0	0	0
Fernandez, Batavia	1.000	3	4	0	0	0
Fox, Jamestown	1.000	2	3	1	0	0
Frye, Jamestown	.882	14	13	2	2	0
Gamba, Batavia	.979	35	45	2	1	0
Gonzalez, Little Falls	.947	62	102	6	6	1
Graham, Erie	1.000	3	6	0	0	0
Gray, Auburn	1.000	1	3	0	0	0
Guzman, Oneonta	1.000	23	30	0	0	0
Haggerty, Elmira	1.000	6	14	0	0	0
Hamza, Geneva	.977	29	41	1	1	0
Hardamon, Geneva	1.000	9	11	0	0	0
Hardy, Jamestown	.971	42	62	6	2	2
R. Harris, Watertown	.889	18	23	1	3	0
W. Harris, Newark	.987	55	77	1	1	0
Hill, Elmira	.939	44	75	2	5	0
Hithe, Auburn	1.000	5	12	0	0	0
Hodo, Utica*	.947	19	18	0	1	0
Hollinshed, Erie*	.938	13	13	2	1	1
Horton, Erie	1.000	1	1	0	0	0
Howard, Oneonta*	.833	4	4	1	1	0
Hubbard, Auburn	.935	24	40	3	3	0
Hunter, Auburn	.971	70	129	4	4	0
Jackson, Auburn	.921	40	77	5	7	0
Jarner, Utica	1.000	12	15	1	0	0
Jeter, St. Catharines	.965	69	107	4	4	0
Khoury, Watertown	.949	62	87	6	5	3
Kraus, Oneonta*	.955	49	57	6	3	1
Landrum, Geneva	.927	55	96	5	8	0
Lemle, Little Falls	.955	34	60	3	3	1
Love, Utica	.857	3	5	1	1	0
Marchese, Elmira	.982	27	50	4	1	0
E. Mendez, St. Catharines	.941	11	15	1	1	1
V. Mendez, St. Catharines	1.000	5	2	0	0	0
Merced, Watertown	1.000	3	2	0	0	0
Mims, Newark	1.000	24	41	2	0	0
Narcisse, Little Falls	.889	10	15	1	2	0
Nemeth, Erie	1.000	3	2	0	0	0
Ochoa, Utica	.966	45	81	5	3	2
Pancoski, Newark*	.926	21	24	1	2	0
Parker, Erie	.938	70	85	6	6	0
Perez, Erie	.947	63	105	2	6	1
Perry, Geneva	.961	58	92	6	4	0
Polka, Little Falls	1.000	2	3	1	0	0
Posey, Newark	.972	27	31	4	1	0
Powell, Utica	.889	20	22	2	3	1
Richardson, Batavia	1.000	6	7	0	0	0
Rickers, Jamestown	.966	54	84	2	3	0
Robicheaux, Watertown	1.000	2	4	0	0	0
Robinson, Little Falls	1.000	19	20	1	0	0
Rodgers, St. Catharines	.992	73	122	3	1	1
Rose, Watertown	1.000	1	1	0	0	0
Roseboro, Little Falls	.939	63	90	2	6	0
Santos, Batavia	1.000	20	29	2	0	1
Schueler, Jamestown	1.000	1	1	1	0	0
Shade, Erie	1.000	23	19	2	0	1
Shannon, Jamestown	1.000	1	2	0	0	0
Shelton, Geneva	.906	23	25	4	3	0
Shifflett, St. Catharines	.952	52	76	3	4	0
Sims, Jamestown	1.000	30	42	2	0	0
Skeete, Newark*	.966	14	27	1	1	0
St. Claire, Jamestown	.974	62	106	8	3	2
Stark, Utica	.982	35	53	1	1	0
Stennett, Auburn	1.000	13	21	2	0	0
Thompson, Little Falls	.989	55	85	1	1	0
Triplett, Utica*	.857	13	11	1	2	0
Twardoski, Batavia*	.979	61	89	6	2	2
Valverde, Watertown	.915	64	124	5	12	2
Viltz, Newark*	.886	26	31	0	4	0
Ward, Oneonta	.951	59	95	3	5	1
Warfel, Elmira	1.000	13	26	2	0	1
Wedvick, Jamestown	1.000	1	3	0	0	0
Weidie, Elmira	.951	59	109	8	6	2
Welter, Newark	1.000	18	16	0	0	0
Williams, Batavia	1.000	19	11	0	0	0
Williamson, Batavia	.951	50	55	3	3	2

CATCHERS

Player and Club	Pct.	G.	PO.	A.	E.	DP.	PB.
Aleshire, Auburn	.974	40	245	22	7	0	8
Banister, Watertown	1.000	26	153	18	0	3	5
Behnsch, Utica	1.000	1	2	4	0	1	0
Berge, Little Falls	.979	18	130	9	3	0	5
Blanco, Oneonta	.994	23	156	15	1	1	7
Cabrera, St. Catharines	.988	56	449	50	6	4	15
Casteel, Geneva	.875	2	6	1	1	1	0
Crofton, Oneonta	.985	42	277	42	5	3	7
Diaz, St. Catharines	.992	14	108	11	1	1	1
Duke, Jamestown	.987	35	204	21	3	4	7
EDWARDS, Auburn	.994	45	282	36	2	1	5
Graff, Erie	1.000	9	17	3	0	1	2
Gsellman, Utica	.982	43	302	29	6	7	14
Gurtcheff, Watertown	.961	34	200	20	9	2	7
Harrison, Elmira	.978	38	239	26	6	4	6
Harwick, Geneva	1.000	1	1	1	0	0	0
Heakins, Watertown	.989	22	171	17	2	1	10
Ironside, St. Catharines	1.000	13	86	8	0	1	2
Kent, Batavia	.973	9	63	10	2	1	5
Kline, Newark	1.000	6	39	2	0	0	1
Lampkin, Batavia	.978	41	323	36	8	4	10
Leyritz, Oneonta	.990	20	170	21	2	4	6
Mann, Geneva	.983	54	419	49	8	7	13
Morrow, Jamestown	.973	22	130	15	4	0	7
Narcisse, Little Falls	.974	29	206	17	6	1	6
Nemeth, Erie	1.000	1	4	3	0	0	1
Oertli, Geneva	.978	26	201	18	5	2	2
Padilla, Elmira	1.000	10	49	11	0	0	4
Pilkinton, Elmira	.978	11	83	4	2	0	1
Polka, Little Falls	.972	37	247	28	8	0	7
Posey, Newark	.962	65	453	54	20	1	18
Radzik, Newark	1.000	2	6	0	0	0	0
Ramos, Oneonta	1.000	3	22	0	0	1	0
Reese, Erie	.943	12	30	3	2	0	2
Smith, Utica	.966	38	227	26	9	1	6
Taylor, Geneva	1.000	1	9	0	0	0	0
Valdez, Utica	1.000	1	1	0	0	0	1
Wedvick, Jamestown	.981	29	190	19	4	2	5
Pa. Williams, Elmira	.970	28	144	15	5	4	10
Ph. Williams, Newark	.957	12	77	11	4	1	1
Wilson, Batavia	.989	29	244	33	3	1	5
Zeile, Erie	.983	69	407	66	8	7	10

PITCHERS

Player and Club	Pct.	G.	PO.	A.	E.	DP.
Adams, Watertown	.840	16	3	18	4	1
Adkins, Oneonta*	.923	14	3	9	1	1
Azocar, Oneonta*	1.000	10	2	8	0	0
Balabon, Oneonta	1.000	10	4	9	0	0
Bast, Elmira*	1.000	10	0	7	0	0
Bauer, Little Falls	.833	25	2	3	1	0
Beatty, Newark*	.967	15	2	27	1	2
Becker, Erie*	1.000	2	0	1	0	0
Befort, Utica	.667	11	0	2	1	1
Behny, Erie	.833	27	0	5	1	0
Belinda, Watertown	1.000	5	0	2	0	0
Bird, Batavia	.923	21	4	8	1	2
Blair, St Catharines	1.000	21	2	3	0	0
Bond, Auburn	.938	14	5	10	1	0
Borgatti, Newark	.846	16	5	6	2	0
Bowden, Newark	1.000	13	2	12	0	1
Boyd, Watertown	1.000	20	1	8	0	1
Brantley, Utica	.923	11	5	7	1	1
Brown, Little Falls	1.000	16	6	9	0	1
Byrnes, Oneonta*	1.000	17	2	8	0	0
Carriger, Newark	1.000	3	0	2	0	0
Cavanaugh, St. Catharines	.900	20	1	8	1	0
Chambers, Batavia*	.824	19	4	10	3	4
Cinnella, Newark	.938	12	2	13	1	0
Cloninger, Geneva*	.769	15	5	15	6	2
Coffey, Elmira	.867	16	3	10	2	1
Collins, Utica	.947	24	2	16	1	1
Compres, Batavia	.750	18	4	5	3	1
Copp, Watertown*	.968	13	7	23	1	1
Cummings, St. Catharines	.786	18	4	7	3	0
Curtis, Geneva*	.857	14	1	17	3	1
DeBoever, Jamestown	.875	11	2	5	1	0
DeLaCruz, St. Catharines	1.000	9	1	2	0	1
Diaz, St. Catharines*	.900	17	1	8	1	0
Dillard, Newark*	.923	27	5	7	1	0
Durant, Little Falls	.733	13	5	6	4	0
Egloff, Batavia	.938	12	6	9	1	0
Elsberry, Auburn	.750	10	1	2	1	0
Estes, Auburn*	1.000	23	2	13	0	0
Faryniarz, Geneva	1.000	1	2	4	0	1
Fiedler, Little Falls*	1.000	6	0	6	0	0
Forrest, Watertown*	.833	7	0	10	2	0
Galbato, Jamestown	.833	11	1	4	1	0
Garcia, Little Falls*	1.000	10	5	8	0	0
J. Gardner, Geneva	.875	13	6	15	3	2
M. Gardner, Batavia	.879	15	8	21	4	1
Glisson, Erie*	.844	16	5	22	5	2
Green, Geneva	.810	26	3	14	4	1
Griffith, Erie	1.000	19	0	13	0	0
Grimsley, Utica	.769	14	4	6	3	1
Grovom, Auburn*	.833	17	5	15	4	0
Hackett, Erie*	.882	15	2	13	2	0
Haines, Jamestown	.867	15	3	10	2	2
Haley, Elmira*	.842	16	1	15	3	1
Hamilton, Erie	1.000	15	7	13	0	0
Harris, Jamestown	.900	4	2	7	1	0
Harrison, Geneva*	.897	16	4	22	3	1
Henion, Little Falls	1.000	14	2	4	0	0
Hentgen, St. Catharines	1.000	13	2	5	0	0
R. Hernandez, Little Falls*	.944	16	3	14	1	2
X. Hernandez, St. Catharines	1.000	13	1	16	0	1
Hershman, Erie	1.000	25	1	7	0	0
Hohn, Erie*	1.000	9	3	3	0	0
Holm, Newark*	.750	10	1	2	1	0
Jacobson, Jamestown	.938	10	4	11	1	0
Johnson, Utica*	1.000	12	1	3	0	1
Jones, St. Catharines	.826	18	4	15	4	0
Jundy, Little Falls	.966	15	7	21	1	2
Kazmierczak, Geneva	1.000	5	3	6	0	0
King, Jamestown	.824	11	6	8	3	1
Kirk, Watertown*	.905	22	5	14	2	2
Koonce, Newark	.913	13	9	12	2	2
LaMarche, Utica	1.000	25	4	8	0	2
LaPoint, Geneva	.786	21	2	9	3	0
Lawrence, Erie	.955	27	9	12	1	1
Layana, Oneonta	.875	3	0	7	1	0
Machacek, Jamestown*	1.000	14	0	5	0	1
Magee, Utica	1.000	24	5	5	0	0
Maggard, Batavia	.944	24	7	10	1	2
Mandich, Newark	.500	6	0	1	1	0
Marris, Oneonta	1.000	7	3	3	0	0
Marte, Erie	.500	14	0	2	2	0
Matas, Geneva	.857	14	2	4	1	1
McDevitt, Utica	1.000	4	1	6	0	1
McDonald, Jamestown	1.000	19	1	2	0	0
McELROY, Utica*	1.000	14	3	26	0	1
McKinney, Utica	1.000	14	2	1	0	0
McMurtrie, Little Falls	1.000	15	7	19	0	1
Meyer, Auburn	.692	32	3	6	4	0
Moreno, Watertown	1.000	6	1	3	0	0
Morrison, Elmira	1.000	9	1	3	0	0
Murphy, Watertown	.900	7	2	7	1	0
Nettles, Erie	.867	16	2	11	2	0
Normand, Auburn*	1.000	20	3	6	0	1
Olson, Auburn	1.000	19	2	14	0	0
Otten, Geneva	.947	29	3	15	1	0
Palma, St. Catharines	1.000	2	0	1	0	0
Patterson, Oneonta*	.909	15	8	12	2	2
Peguero, Newark	1.000	15	3	9	0	0
Perez, Utica	.714	13	2	3	2	0
Potts, Auburn	1.000	16	1	8	0	1
Rawdon, Elmira	1.000	10	0	3	0	0
Ridenour, Oneonta	1.000	23	2	5	0	0
Robertson, Jamestown	1.000	9	2	3	0	1
Rockweiler, Jamestown*	1.000	16	1	5	0	0
Roderick, St. Catharines	1.000	1	0	3	0	0
Roebuck, Auburn*	.833	11	1	4	1	0
C. Rose, Watertown	.600	9	2	1	2	1
M. Rose, Oneonta	1.000	8	1	2	0	0
Rosenberg, Oneonta*	1.000	4	1	1	0	0
Rub, Oneonta*	1.000	17	4	10	0	0
Runge, Watertown	.750	10	2	4	2	1
K. Ryan, Elmira	1.000	13	1	4	0	0
T. Ryan, Oneonta	.750	3	2	1	1	0
Saitta, St. Catharines	1.000	19	7	13	0	1
Sampen, Watertown	1.000	9	0	5	0	0
Sanders, St. Catharines	.895	11	2	15	2	2
Scheid, Oneonta*	.971	15	7	26	1	0
Schilling, Elmira	.900	16	5	4	1	1
Schlopy, Watertown*	.929	10	0	13	1	0
Schmerer, Batavia*	1.000	11	1	4	0	0
Sepela, Elmira	1.000	15	2	4	0	0
Service, Utica	1.000	10	4	11	0	1
Shannon, Jamestown	.952	10	6	14	1	1
Shaw, Batavia	.900	14	10	8	2	1
Shea, St. Catharines*	1.000	14	2	5	0	0
Simon, Auburn	1.000	15	7	10	0	0
Sims, Utica*	.897	14	6	20	3	0
Skalski, Batavia	.800	14	3	13	4	0
Slocumb, Little Falls	.818	25	2	7	2	0
Sonneberger, Newark	1.000	20	2	2	0	0
Tabaka, Jamestown*	1.000	13	1	15	0	0
Taylor, Little Falls	1.000	16	2	7	0	0
Tejada, Elmira	1.000	13	0	11	0	0

PITCHERS—Continued

Player and Club	Pct.	G.	PO.	A.	E.	DP.
Toy, Watertown	.833	23	2	3	1	0
Travels, Jamestown	1.000	12	6	12	0	2
Vaccaro, Jamestown*	.909	11	0	20	2	1
Vike, Auburn	.850	12	11	6	3	2
Voeltz, Oneonta*	.889	15	1	7	1	0
Wacha, Elmira	1.000	10	0	3	0	0
Walker, Watertown	.964	16	6	21	1	3
Walters, Elmira	1.000	15	5	9	0	2
Warren, Elmira*	1.000	17	0	6	0	0
Wasilewski, Auburn	1.000	29	6	8	0	3
A. Welborn, Jamestown	.880	15	5	17	3	0
T. Welborn, Little Falls	.833	16	4	11	3	1
Whiting, Elmira	.500	7	0	1	1	0
Wickander, Batavia*	.846	11	2	9	2	0
Wilkins, Oneonta	.880	15	7	15	3	0
K. Williams, Elmira	1.000	14	0	5	0	0
R. Williams, Newark	1.000	7	3	2	0	0
C. Wilson, Newark	.962	14	7	18	1	0
R. Wilson, Watertown	1.000	12	1	1	0	0
Winzenread, Newark	1.000	14	0	6	0	0
Zaltsman, Erie*	.923	29	3	9	1	1
Zarranz, Geneva	1.000	12	5	15	0	0

The following players do not have any recorded accepted chances at the positions indicated; therefore, are not listed in the fielding averages for those particular positions: Brady, p; Bruske, p; Castro, 3b, of; J. DeLaRosa, of; Gaylor, of; Griffith, of; Hardamon, p; K. Harrison, 1b; Jackson, p; Kryzanowski, 2b; Luckenbill, p; O. Parker, 3b; Schlieper, p; Soto, p; Strickland, p; Towey, p; Triplett, p; Vaccaro, of.

CLUB PITCHING

Club	ERA.	G.	CG.	ShO.	Sv.	IP.	H.	R.	ER.	HR.	HB.	BB.	Int. BB.	SO.	WP.	Bk.
Oneonta	2.13	77	12	12	25	664.2	465	206	157	19	27	272	9	634	52	6
St. Catharines	2.74	76	4	8	25	680.2	545	263	207	33	31	275	8	647	38	5
Geneva	2.86	78	15	7	11	664.2	571	303	211	43	24	326	13	635	52	8
Batavia	2.95	75	17	4	10	646.0	542	297	212	45	23	324	8	626	67	3
Little Falls	3.04	76	13	4	14	666.1	573	306	225	50	22	254	12	563	43	4
Newark	3.12	78	21	8	13	661.0	603	337	229	33	24	258	12	572	68	5
Auburn	3.15	76	5	5	22	662.0	567	305	232	40	25	297	13	518	51	2
Elmira	3.33	75	14	10	15	649.0	635	319	240	35	19	262	9	485	42	5
Watertown	3.48	78	12	5	16	691.0	678	365	267	31	33	297	18	514	50	6
Jamestown	3.57	76	14	4	12	646.0	595	342	256	35	22	312	6	502	42	6
Erie	3.97	77	11	8	15	671.0	674	367	296	49	26	258	21	448	38	6
Utica	4.38	78	12	3	9	644.2	654	410	314	22	44	363	3	504	68	8

PITCHERS' RECORDS

(Leading Qualifiers for Earned-Run Average Leadership—62 or More Innings)

*Throws lefthanded.

Pitcher—Club	W.	L.	Pct.	ERA.	G.	GS.	CG.	GF.	ShO.	Sv.	IP.	H.	R.	ER.	HR.	HB.	BB.	Int. BB.	SO.	WP.
Patterson, Oneonta*	9	3	.750	1.35	15	15	5	0	4	0	100.1	67	25	15	2	4	45	0	102	7
Adkins, Oneonta*	8	2	.800	1.68	14	12	2	1	1	1	80.1	59	23	15	1	0	36	2	74	8
Koonce, Newark	7	4	.636	1.75	13	13	7	0	2	0	92.2	84	34	18	4	0	14	1	68	3
Skalski, Batavia	7	6	.538	1.98	14	13	6	0	0	0	104.2	79	34	23	6	1	29	1	130	5
M. Gardner, Batavia	5	8	.385	2.04	15	15	6	0	0	0	110.1	72	35	25	3	2	57	0	87	11
Cummings, St. Catharines	9	5	.643	2.04	18	18	2	0	0	0	110.1	80	36	25	2	6	34	0	86	0
Copp, Watertown*	6	5	.545	2.07	13	13	5	0	3	0	95.2	89	34	22	4	2	21	0	87	4
Beatty, Newark*	11	3	.786	2.11	15	15	8	0	3	0	119.1	98	37	28	6	1	30	3	93	6
Scheid, Oneonta*	9	3	.750	2.23	15	15	3	0	1	0	93.0	62	30	23	2	3	32	1	100	6
Garcia, Little Falls*	3	3	.500	2.23	10	10	1	0	0	0	64.2	61	24	16	1	1	17	0	52	7
Curtis, Geneva*	6	2	.750	2.42	14	14	5	0	2	0	96.2	69	29	26	8	0	43	0	113	6
Shaw, Batavia	8	4	.667	2.44	14	12	3	1	1	0	88.2	79	32	24	5	5	35	0	71	10

Departmental Leaders: G—Meyer, 32; W—Beatty, 11; L—Grimsley, Sims, Walker, 10; Pct.—Wilkins, 1.000; GS—Cummings, Jones, 18; CG—Beatty, 8; GF—Meyer, 28; ShO—Patterson, 4; Sv.—Blair, 12; IP—Beatty, 119.1; H—Walker, 116; R—Walker, 71; ER—Walker, 52; HR—R. Hernandez, McMurtrie, 12; HB—Grimsley, 11; BB—Grimsley, 77; IBB—Green, 6; SO—Skalski, 130; WP—Grimsley, 18.

(All Pitchers—Listed Alphabetically)

Pitcher—Club	W.	L.	Pct.	ERA.	G.	GS.	CG.	GF.	ShO.	Sv.	IP.	H.	R.	ER.	HR.	HB.	BB.	Int. BB.	SO.	WP.
Adams, Watertown	4	3	.571	2.73	16	11	3	3	0	0	82.1	88	35	25	2	4	21	1	36	4
Adkins, Oneonta*	8	2	.800	1.68	14	12	2	1	1	1	80.1	59	23	15	1	0	36	2	74	8
Azocar, Oneonta*	2	0	1.000	2.86	10	1	0	5	0	2	22.0	27	9	7	2	0	9	1	19	1
Balabon, Oneonta	4	3	.571	3.48	10	10	0	0	0	0	51.2	39	26	20	2	3	36	0	43	8
Bast, Elmira*	4	3	.571	1.87	10	3	1	7	0	1	43.1	35	10	9	2	1	12	0	44	1
Bauer, Little Falls	3	3	.500	2.21	25	0	0	18	0	5	40.2	25	14	10	3	4	14	1	58	2
Beatty, Newark*	11	3	.786	2.11	15	15	8	0	3	0	119.1	98	37	28	6	1	30	3	93	6
Becker, Erie*	0	0	.000	10.38	2	0	0	0	0	0	4.1	11	5	5	1	0	4	1	4	0
Befort, Utica	1	2	.333	4.12	11	0	0	7	0	2	19.2	23	11	9	0	1	7	1	14	1
Behny, Erie	3	3	.500	4.74	27	0	0	12	0	4	38.0	43	25	20	4	0	23	4	32	2
Belinda, Watertown	0	0	.000	3.38	5	0	0	5	0	2	8.0	5	3	3	1	0	2	0	5	0
Bird, Batavia	1	4	.200	2.95	21	4	1	15	1	5	58.0	44	24	19	4	0	36	2	53	4
Blair, St. Catharines	5	0	1.000	1.68	21	0	0	18	0	12	53.2	32	10	10	1	0	20	1	55	3
Bond, Auburn	3	3	.500	3.64	14	12	0	1	0	0	59.1	58	33	24	4	1	30	1	34	6
Borgatti, Newark	6	2	.750	2.01	16	5	2	10	1	3	53.2	41	18	12	2	1	16	1	57	3
Bowden, Newark	2	5	.286	3.88	13	6	1	3	0	0	48.2	57	34	21	3	2	22	2	44	9
Boyd, Watertown	1	6	.143	3.66	20	2	0	7	0	0	51.2	51	25	21	3	1	28	2	43	1
Brady, Watertown	0	0	.000	9.00	3	0	0	3	0	0	4.0	6	4	4	0	2	1	0	3	1
Brantley, Utica	3	5	.375	4.30	11	11	0	0	0	0	60.2	68	37	29	5	4	25	1	42	5
Brown, Little Falls	3	4	.429	2.93	16	8	0	2	0	1	61.1	55	30	20	3	2	32	2	54	7
Bruske, Batavia	0	0	.000	18.00	1	0	0	1	0	0	1.0	1	2	2	0	0	3	0	3	2
Byrnes, Oneonta*	4	1	.800	1.80	17	2	0	11	0	3	45.0	39	15	9	2	2	13	0	29	2
Carriger, Newark	1	0	1.000	5.40	3	0	0	0	0	0	3.1	5	2	2	0	1	2	0	5	1
Cavanaugh, St. Catharines	4	4	.500	2.78	20	4	0	12	0	5	64.2	52	21	20	6	4	17	0	56	5
Chambers, Batavia*	1	7	.125	4.67	19	5	0	4	0	0	54.0	41	34	28	5	2	44	1	62	9
Cinnella, Newark	2	6	.250	2.78	12	11	2	0	2	0	68.0	43	36	21	3	8	37	0	57	7
Cloninger, Geneva*	4	5	.444	2.66	15	15	2	0	1	0	98.0	77	43	29	4	4	56	0	96	6
Coffey, Elmira	8	7	.533	2.72	16	16	6	0	2	0	112.1	84	44	34	4	1	34	0	79	8
Collins, Utica	1	6	.143	6.27	24	3	0	12	0	1	47.1	59	50	33	2	4	46	0	38	16
Compres, Batavia	2	5	.286	4.08	18	2	0	7	0	0	39.2	50	29	18	5	4	17	0	34	4
Copp, Watertown*	6	5	.545	2.07	13	13	5	0	3	0	95.2	89	34	22	4	2	21	0	87	4
Cummings, St. Catharines	9	5	.643	2.04	18	18	2	0	0	0	110.1	80	36	25	2	6	34	0	86	0
Curtis, Geneva*	6	2	.750	2.42	14	14	5	0	2	0	96.2	69	29	26	8	0	43	0	113	6
DeBoever, Jamestown	1	2	.333	3.57	11	0	0	6	0	1	22.2	27	12	9	1	3	12	0	21	5
DeLaCruz, St. Catharines	0	0	.000	10.54	9	0	0	8	0	0	13.2	25	17	16	2	3	5	0	9	0

Pitcher—Club	W.	L.	Pct.	ERA.	G.	GS.	CG.	GF.	ShO.	Sv.	IP.	H.	R.	ER.	HR.	HB.	BB.	Int. BB.	SO.	WP.
Diaz, St. Catharines*	2	0	1.000	1.93	17	0	0	10	0	4	37.1	25	11	8	2	1	23	1	41	0
Dillard, Newark*	5	6	.455	4.26	27	7	0	15	0	7	63.1	55	37	30	2	0	34	1	77	11
Durant, Little Falls	5	3	.625	2.68	13	9	3	0	2	0	74.0	61	26	22	6	0	18	2	76	3
Egloff, Batavia	1	2	.333	3.99	12	12	1	0	0	0	70.0	79	42	31	8	3	17	0	62	7
Elsberry, Auburn	1	1	.500	0.41	10	1	1	6	0	2	22.0	10	5	1	0	1	6	2	32	3
Estes, Auburn*	4	3	.571	1.61	23	0	0	11	0	6	44.2	37	11	8	3	1	15	2	30	2
Faryniarz, Geneva	0	1	.000	9.82	1	1	0	0	0	0	3.2	2	4	4	2	0	3	0	2	0
Fiedler, Little Falls*	0	1	.000	3.77	6	2	0	2	0	0	14.1	13	10	6	0	1	8	0	6	1
Forrest, Watertown*	2	3	.400	4.71	7	6	0	0	0	0	36.1	44	25	19	1	1	12	0	23	5
Galbato, Jamestown	1	1	.500	2.39	11	8	0	2	0	0	49.0	35	19	13	2	1	21	0	33	2
Garcia, Little Falls*	3	3	.500	2.23	10	10	1	0	0	0	64.2	61	24	16	1	1	17	0	52	7
J. Gardner, Geneva	2	6	.250	3.15	13	12	1	1	0	0	74.1	66	40	26	4	6	38	2	51	8
M. Gardner, Batavia	5	8	.385	2.04	15	15	6	0	0	0	110.1	72	35	25	3	2	57	0	87	11
Glisson, Erie*	5	2	.714	3.07	16	15	3	0	2	0	91.0	72	41	31	4	6	36	1	64	2
Green, Geneva	4	6	.400	3.00	26	2	0	12	0	0	60.0	60	29	20	5	7	18	6	39	5
Griffith, Erie	3	5	.375	4.26	19	6	2	6	1	0	57.0	74	32	27	5	0	16	2	26	3
Grimsley, Utica	1	10	.091	6.40	14	14	3	0	0	0	64.2	63	61	46	3	11	77	0	46	18
Grovom, Auburn*	4	2	.667	4.16	17	14	0	0	0	0	80.0	70	45	37	5	2	45	1	69	9
Hackett, Erie*	6	5	.545	3.47	15	15	3	0	1	0	93.1	95	41	36	8	1	22	3	48	1
Haines, Jamestown	1	5	.167	4.07	15	8	3	1	0	0	59.2	54	38	27	1	2	30	0	31	4
Haley, Elmira*	5	4	.556	2.76	16	15	3	0	1	0	97.2	97	39	30	5	4	27	0	67	3
Hamilton, Erie	7	6	.538	3.69	15	15	2	0	2	0	100.0	102	49	41	4	1	18	1	67	7
Hardamon, Geneva	0	0	.000	0.00	1	0	0	0	0	0	0.1	0	0	0	0	0	2	0	1	0
Harris, Jamestown	0	2	.000	2.21	4	4	0	0	0	0	20.1	15	8	5	0	0	11	0	16	0
Harrison, Geneva*	10	4	.714	2.57	16	12	4	3	2	0	91.0	80	37	26	3	0	48	1	102	8
Henion, Little Falls	3	2	.600	2.08	14	0	0	13	0	2	17.1	14	5	4	0	0	7	1	15	1
Hentgen, St. Catharines	0	4	.000	4.50	13	11	0	2	0	1	40.0	38	27	20	3	2	30	1	30	3
R. Hernandez, Little Falls	6	6	.500	2.73	16	15	4	1	0	1	99.0	95	44	30	12	4	26	1	81	2
X. Hernandez, St. Catharines	5	5	.500	2.67	13	10	1	3	1	0	70.2	55	27	21	6	6	16	0	69	5
Hershman, Erie	2	2	.500	3.80	25	1	0	8	0	2	47.1	44	24	20	5	3	30	0	44	8
Hohn, Erie*	0	3	.000	6.75	9	3	0	2	0	0	25.1	28	21	19	3	2	11	1	20	1
Holm, Newark*	1	0	1.000	3.60	10	0	0	6	0	1	10.0	13	8	4	1	0	2	0	9	2
Jackson, Auburn	0	0	.000	13.50	1	0	0	0	0	0	2.0	2	3	3	0	0	3	0	3	0
Jacobson, Jamestown	3	4	.429	4.19	10	8	2	1	1	0	53.2	54	31	25	2	1	24	0	58	5
Johnson, Utica*	0	0	.000	5.21	12	0	0	7	0	0	19.0	25	16	11	1	2	12	0	9	3
Jones, St. Catharines	7	4	.636	2.58	18	18	0	0	0	0	101.1	81	36	29	2	1	46	2	103	5
Jundy, Little Falls	4	5	.444	2.86	15	10	0	4	0	0	69.1	71	33	22	4	1	24	1	39	4
Kazmierczak, Geneva	4	0	1.000	2.12	5	5	1	0	0	0	34.0	22	8	8	3	1	19	0	40	3
King, Jamestown	5	6	.455	2.84	11	11	3	0	1	0	66.2	57	34	21	5	3	29	1	54	2
Kirk, Watertown*	4	5	.444	2.98	22	1	0	10	0	3	51.1	43	21	17	0	1	29	5	49	8
Koonce, Newark	7	4	.636	1.75	13	13	7	0	2	0	92.2	84	34	18	4	0	14	1	68	3
LaMarche, Utica	3	1	.750	2.68	25	0	0	18	0	4	43.2	45	21	13	0	7	11	0	45	4
LaPoint, Geneva	1	3	.250	5.54	21	2	0	12	0	0	39.0	50	35	24	3	2	28	1	34	9
Lawrence, Erie	5	6	.455	2.86	27	8	1	16	0	5	85.0	65	39	27	5	9	24	5	48	3
Layana, Oneonta	2	0	1.000	2.37	3	3	0	0	0	0	19.0	10	5	5	1	1	5	0	24	1
Luckenbill, Batavia	0	1	.000	4.82	7	0	0	4	0	0	9.1	13	11	5	3	0	7	0	7	1
Machacek, Jamestown*	3	1	.750	1.19	14	0	0	12	0	6	30.1	16	5	4	2	1	7	0	25	0
Magee, Utica	4	3	.571	4.12	24	0	0	13	0	2	54.2	44	30	25	1	1	29	1	60	2
Maggard, Batavia	2	4	.333	3.15	24	3	0	16	0	4	45.2	35	27	16	0	5	43	4	37	12
Mandich, Newark	0	0	.000	2.35	6	0	0	5	0	1	7.2	7	2	2	0	0	3	0	8	2
Marris, Oneonta	1	1	.500	1.71	7	1	0	2	0	1	21.0	10	5	4	0	0	13	2	14	1
Marte, Erie	0	0	.000	8.24	14	0	0	7	0	0	19.2	28	22	18	2	0	19	0	15	4
Matas, Geneva	2	0	1.000	1.93	14	3	0	6	0	1	37.1	31	16	8	2	0	13	0	42	3
McDevitt, Utica	1	0	1.000	3.20	4	4	0	0	0	0	19.2	10	9	7	0	0	22	0	13	0
McDonald, Jamestown	0	3	.000	4.15	19	0	0	12	0	4	34.2	38	23	16	2	1	8	1	21	1
McElroy, Utica*	4	6	.400	2.95	14	14	5	0	1	0	94.2	85	40	31	4	2	28	0	91	2
McKinney, Utica	0	0	.000	4.56	14	0	0	7	0	0	25.2	30	15	13	2	0	14	0	18	3
McMurtrie, Little Falls	5	7	.417	4.69	15	14	4	0	1	0	86.1	80	48	45	12	7	22	1	50	2
Meyer, Auburn	5	2	.714	1.43	32	0	0	28	0	10	56.2	44	14	9	2	3	10	1	66	0
Moreno, Watertown	0	1	.000	4.30	6	2	0	3	0	0	23.0	13	12	11	0	3	18	2	11	4
Morrison, Elmira	2	2	.500	2.19	9	3	0	2	0	0	24.2	19	13	6	2	1	15	1	15	1
Murphy, Watertown	2	4	.333	4.14	7	7	1	0	0	0	45.2	49	36	21	1	3	14	1	32	3
Nettles, Erie	3	5	.375	4.94	16	14	0	0	0	0	71.0	75	48	39	5	3	41	0	47	4
Normand, Auburn*	4	2	.667	4.28	20	8	2	6	0	1	54.2	53	30	26	2	1	28	0	49	2
Olson, Auburn	4	4	.500	3.45	19	10	0	3	0	0	70.1	62	37	27	2	3	31	2	64	8
Otten, Geneva	1	5	.167	1.71	29	0	0	25	0	10	52.2	45	21	10	3	2	11	3	48	2
Palma, St. Catharines	0	1	.000	2.25	2	0	0	1	0	0	4.0	4	1	1	1	0	3	0	1	0
Patterson, Oneonta*	9	3	.750	1.35	15	15	5	0	4	0	100.1	67	25	15	2	4	45	0	102	7
Peguero, Newark	0	2	.000	7.19	15	6	0	6	0	0	41.1	47	43	33	4	1	35	2	27	9
Perez, Utica	2	5	.286	7.00	13	8	0	1	0	0	45.0	59	39	35	3	2	29	0	25	2
Potts, Auburn	1	0	1.000	2.50	16	0	0	3	0	1	36.0	27	10	10	3	0	9	2	28	5
Rawdon, Elmira	2	1	.667	4.30	10	0	0	6	0	1	14.2	19	11	7	0	0	10	0	12	2
Ridenour, Oneonta	4	2	.667	1.56	23	0	0	20	0	8	34.2	21	6	6	0	1	11	3	47	3
Robertson, Jamestown	5	1	.833	4.08	9	0	0	6	0	0	17.2	15	9	8	3	1	6	0	17	2
Rockweiler, Jamestown*	2	1	.667	4.60	16	1	1	6	1	1	43.0	46	24	22	1	0	25	2	38	4
Roderick, St. Catharines	0	0	.000	0.00	1	0	0	0	0	0	3.0	1	2	0	0	0	1	0	2	0
Roebuck, Auburn*	4	2	.667	1.96	11	8	0	1	0	0	41.1	30	16	9	0	2	26	0	30	4
C. Rose, Watertown	1	0	1.000	3.60	9	0	0	5	0	3	15.0	10	7	6	1	0	4	0	8	2
M. Rose, Oneonta	0	0	.000	0.56	8	0	0	4	0	1	16.0	9	2	1	0	3	7	0	17	0
Rosenberg, Oneonta*	0	0	.000	1.00	4	0	0	4	0	3	9.0	4	1	1	0	0	2	0	10	1
Rub, Oneonta*	3	2	.600	2.12	17	2	0	6	0	3	46.2	25	12	11	2	1	21	0	48	7
Runge, Watertown	1	0	1.000	2.89	10	6	0	2	0	0	37.1	30	13	12	2	3	21	0	23	2
K. Ryan, Elmira	2	2	.500	5.82	13	1	0	10	0	0	21.2	20	14	14	0	1	21	2	22	1
T. Ryan, Oneonta	0	0	.000	5.14	3	1	0	1	0	0	7.0	8	6	4	0	0	11	0	3	1
Saitta, St. Catharines	6	1	.857	2.59	19	2	0	8	0	1	62.2	44	19	18	3	6	14	0	64	8
Sampen, Watertown	0	3	.000	4.25	9	5	0	3	0	2	29.2	27	18	14	0	1	13	0	29	3
Sanders, St. Catharines	6	2	.750	2.08	11	11	1	0	1	0	56.1	53	24	13	1	1	32	2	55	6
Scheid, Oneonta*	9	3	.750	2.23	15	15	3	0	1	0	93.0	62	30	23	2	3	32	1	100	6
Schilling, Elmira	7	3	.700	2.59	16	15	2	1	1	0	93.2	92	34	27	3	2	30	1	75	4
Schlieper, St. Catharines*	1	1	.500	3.86	7	0	0	5	0	2	14.0	11	8	6	2	1	5	1	17	0
Schlopy, Watertown*	5	4	.556	3.81	10	9	1	0	0	0	49.2	55	29	21	4	2	37	1	37	0
Schmerer, Batavia*	0	0	.000	3.93	11	0	0	8	0	1	18.1	19	8	8	2	0	9	0	17	0

Pitcher—Club	W.	L.	Pct.	ERA.	G.	GS.	CG.	GF.	ShO.	Sv.	IP.	H.	R.	ER.	HR.	HB.	BB.	Int. BB.	SO.	WP.
Sepela, Elmira	1	2	.333	6.03	15	1	0	7	0	1	31.1	40	27	21	3	0	12	0	12	4
Service, Utica	5	4	.556	2.67	10	10	2	0	0	0	70.2	65	30	21	1	5	18	0	43	5
Shannon, Jamestown	2	5	.286	3.22	10	7	2	2	0	0	50.1	50	27	18	2	4	12	0	22	1
Shaw, Batavia	8	4	.667	2.44	14	12	3	1	1	0	88.2	79	32	24	5	5	35	0	71	10
Shea, St. Catharines*	3	1	.750	3.67	14	2	0	5	0	0	49.0	44	24	20	2	0	29	0	59	3
Simon, Auburn	4	6	.400	2.92	15	15	1	0	0	0	89.1	76	35	29	9	3	34	0	54	6
Sims, Utica*	1	10	.091	4.25	14	14	2	0	0	0	78.1	78	47	37	0	4	40	0	59	4
Skalski, Batavia	7	6	.538	1.98	14	13	6	0	0	0	104.2	79	34	23	6	1	29	1	130	5
Slocumb, Little Falls	3	1	.750	1.65	25	0	0	13	0	1	43.2	24	17	8	3	0	36	1	41	8
Sonneberger, Newark	0	3	.000	6.59	20	1	0	7	0	0	27.1	36	24	20	4	5	16	1	34	8
Soto, Geneva	0	0	.000	23.14	2	0	0	1	0	0	2.1	3	6	6	0	0	6	0	1	0
Strickland, Geneva	0	0	.000	3.00	3	0	0	3	0	0	3.0	3	1	1	1	0	1	0	4	0
Tabaka, Jamestown*	2	4	.333	4.30	13	9	0	3	0	0	52.1	51	31	25	5	1	34	1	57	5
Taylor, Little Falls	1	1	.500	4.24	16	3	0	5	0	2	46.2	37	26	22	5	0	21	1	44	2
Tejada, Elmira	0	0	.000	3.04	13	1	0	3	0	0	26.2	27	11	9	2	0	19	1	12	3
Towey, Auburn	0	0	.000	27.00	1	0	0	0	0	0	1.0	3	3	3	0	1	4	0	0	0
Toy, Watertown	0	1	.000	4.15	23	0	0	16	0	3	43.1	34	23	20	4	3	19	2	36	4
Travels, Jamestown	2	2	.500	3.77	12	1	0	6	0	0	28.2	32	14	12	3	1	11	1	13	1
Triplett, Utica*	0	0	.000	36.00	2	0	0	1	0	0	1.0	0	4	4	0	1	5	0	1	3
Vaccaro, Jamestown*	0	1	.000	5.12	11	4	0	5	0	0	38.2	46	23	22	4	0	26	0	19	1
Vike, Auburn	3	5	.375	5.29	12	8	1	1	0	0	51.0	58	42	30	7	3	33	1	14	3
Voeltz, Oneonta*	4	1	.800	1.77	15	3	1	8	0	2	35.2	21	9	7	0	1	7	0	24	2
Wacha, Elmira	0	1	.000	4.24	10	1	0	6	0	2	17.0	21	8	8	1	0	3	0	16	2
Walker, Watertown	4	10	.286	4.53	16	16	2	0	0	0	103.1	116	71	52	8	7	46	1	81	8
Walters, Elmira	2	5	.286	4.56	15	14	1	1	0	0	73.0	94	55	37	8	2	34	0	54	10
Warren, Elmira*	5	1	.833	0.99	17	2	1	12	1	6	45.2	39	13	5	1	1	10	1	43	2
Wasilewski, Auburn	7	2	.778	2.85	29	0	0	11	0	2	53.2	37	21	17	3	4	23	1	45	3
A. Welborn, Jamestown	3	8	.273	3.33	15	15	3	0	1	0	78.1	59	44	29	2	3	56	0	77	9
T. Welborn, Little Falls	0	4	.000	3.67	16	5	1	5	0	2	49.0	37	29	20	1	2	29	1	47	4
Whiting, Elmira	0	0	.000	13.50	7	0	0	1	0	0	7.1	14	14	11	0	5	6	0	3	1
Wickander, Batavia*	3	4	.429	2.72	11	9	0	2	0	0	46.1	30	19	14	4	1	27	0	63	2
Wilkins, Oneonta	9	0	1.000	3.13	15	12	1	3	0	1	83.1	64	32	29	5	8	24	0	80	4
K. Williams, Elmira	1	5	.167	4.95	14	3	0	5	0	4	40.0	34	26	22	4	1	29	3	31	0
R. Williams, Newark	0	1	.000	4.66	7	0	0	2	0	1	9.2	11	8	5	1	2	5	0	12	1
C. Wilson, Newark	4	3	.571	2.78	14	14	1	0	0	0	90.2	86	45	28	2	3	30	1	70	2
R. Wilson, Watertown	0	3	.000	3.07	12	0	0	9	0	3	14.2	18	9	5	0	0	11	3	11	1
Winzenread, Newark	2	2	.500	1.78	14	0	0	3	0	0	25.1	20	9	5	1	0	12	0	11	4
Zaltsman, Erie*	3	3	.500	3.00	29	0	0	15	0	4	39.0	37	20	13	3	1	14	3	33	3
Zarranz, Geneva	6	6	.500	2.86	12	12	2	0	0	0	72.1	63	34	23	5	2	40	0	62	2

BALKS—J. Gardner, 4; Behny, 3; Cavanaugh, Cinnella, Durant, Galbato, M. Gardner, X. Hernandez, LaMarche, Scheid, Schilling, Sims, K. Williams, Zarranz, 2 each; Adams, Balabon, Becker, Bond, Brantley, Coffey, Copp, Cummings, Glisson, Harris, Harrison, R. Hernandez, Johnson, King, Kirk, Koonce, Maggard, Marte, McMurtrie, Otten, Patterson, Peguero, Perez, Robertson, Roebuck, Rub, Runge, Service, Shannon, Toy, Walker, Wilkins, C. Wilson, 1 each.

COMBINATION SHUTOUTS—Grovom-Wasilewski, Bond-Estes-Meyer, Bond-Meyer, Roebuck-Wasilewski, Olson-Wasilewski-Elsberry, Auburn; Egloff-Compres, Skalski-Bird, Batavia; Haley-Williams 2, Walters-Bast, Bast-Tejada, Schilling-Warren, Elmira; Glisson-Lawrence, Hamilton-Lawrence, Erie; Kazmierczak-Green-Otten, Matas-Otten, Geneva; Fiedler-Taylor, Little Falls; Patterson-Wilkins, Wilkins-Ridenour, Balabon-Rub-Byrnes, Wilkins-Rub, Adkins-Voeltz-Rub, Scheid-Rose-Byrnes, Oneonta; Jones-Blair 3, Sanders-Cavanaugh, Sanders-Blair, Hernandez-Cavanaugh, St. Catharines; Brantley-Befort, McElroy-Magee, Utica; Copp-Adams, Sampen-Kirk-Boyd-Rose, Watertown.

NO-HIT GAMES—Cinnella, Newark, defeated Oneonta, 1-0, July 23; Cinnella, Newark, defeated Auburn, 3-0, August 3.

Northwest League

CLASS A

CHAMPIONSHIP WINNERS IN PREVIOUS YEARS

1901—Portland .675
1902—Butte .608
1903—Butte .578
1904—Boise .625
1905—Vancouver .586
Everett* .667
1906—Tacoma .600
1907—Aberdeen .625
1908—Vancouver .578
1909—Seattle .653
1910—Spokane .596
1911—Vancouver .628
1912—Seattle .600
1913—Vancouver .600
1914—Vancouver .632
1915—Seattle .564
1916—Spokane .622
1917—Great Falls .592
1918—Seattle .588
1919—Seattle .590
1920—Victoria .600
1921—Yakima .710
Yakima .660
1922—Calgary† .600
1923-36—Did not operate.
1937—Wenatchee .603
Tacoma* .627
1938—Yakima .583
Bellingham (2nd)† .511
1939—Wenatchee .601
Tacoma (2nd)† .533
1940—Spokane .587
Tacoma (4th)† .500
1941—Spokane .669
1942—Vancouver .594
1943-45—Did not operate.
1946—Wenatchee .622
1947—Vancouver .566
1948—Spokane .614
1949—Yakima .660
Vancouver (2nd)† .615
1950—Yakima .613
1951—Spokane .655
1952—Victoria .631
1953—Salem .635
Spokane* .590
1954—Vancouver* .636
Lewiston .629
1955—Salem .646
Eugene* .639
1956—Yakima .691
Yakima .619
1957—Eugene .576
Wenatchee* .647
1958—Lewiston .621
Yakima* .594
1959—Salem .623
Yakima* .563
1960—Yakima .638
Yakima .562
1961—Lewiston* .621
Yakima .600
1962—Wenatchee* .574
Tri-City .580
1963—Lewiston .594
Yakima* .613
1964—Eugene .636
Yakima* .611
1965—Lewiston .667
Tri-City* .681
1966—Tri-City .679
1967—Medford .607
1968—Tri-City .600
1969—Rogue Valley .633
1970—Lewiston a .538
Coos Bay-No. Bend .563
1971—Tri-City a .625
Bend .538
1972—Lewiston a .675
Walla Walla .513
1973—Walla Walla b .638
Portland .563
1974—Bellingham .619
Eugene c .571
1975—Portland .545
Eugene d .684
1976—Portland .556
Walla Walla d .639
1977—Bellingham e .618
Portland .667
1978—Grays Harbor f .671
Eugene .514
1979—Central Oregon d .606
Walla Walla .571
1980—Bellingham g .643
Eugene g .529
1981—Medford d .600
Bellingham .557
1982—Medford .757
Salem d .486
1983—Medford h .735
Bellingham .588
1984—Tri-Cities h .622
Medford .608
1985—Everett h .541
Eugene .541

*Won split-season playoff. †Won four-club playoff. §League disbanded June 18. aLeague divided into Northern and Southern divisions, declared champion under league rules. bLeague divided into Eastern and Western divisions, declared champion under league rules. cLeague divided into Eastern and Western divisions; won two-team playoff. dLeague divided into Northern and Southern divisions; won two-team playoff. eLeague divided into Affiliate and Independent divisions; won two-team playoff. fDeclared league champion after winning one-game playoff. Balance of playoff canceled due to rain and wet grounds. gDeclared co-champion after winning one game. Balance of playoff canceled due to rain and wet grounds. hLeague divided into Washington and Oregon divisions; won two-team playoff. (NOTE—Known as Pacific Northwest League 1901-02, Pacific National League 1903-04, Northwestern League 1905-18, Pacific Coast International League 1919-22 and Western International League 1937-54.)

STANDING OF CLUBS AT CLOSE OF SEASON, AUGUST 31

WASHINGTON DIVISION

Club	Bell	Ev	Spo	TC	Eug	Med	Sal	Bend	W.	L.	T.	Pct.	G.B.
Bellingham (Mariners)	....	14	8	9	3	3	4	4	45	29	0	.608	....
Everett (Giants)	2	....	9	10	4	5	5	5	40	34	0	.541	5
Spokane (Padres)	7	6	....	12	5	3	1	5	39	35	0	.527	6
Tri-Cities (Co-Op)	6	5	4	....	2	2	3	3	25	49	0	.338	20

OREGON DIVISION

Club	Bell	Ev	Spo	TC	Eug	Med	Sal	Bend	W.	L.	T.	Pct.	G.B.
Eugene (Royals)	4	3	2	5	....	7	10	14	45	29	0	.608	....
Medford (A's)	4	2	4	5	8	....	7	13	43	31	0	.581	2
Salem (Angels)	3	2	6	4	6	8	....	9	38	36	0	.514	7
Bend (Phillies)	3	2	2	4	1	3	6	....	21	53	0	.284	24

Tri-Cities represented Richland, Pasco and Kennewick, Wash.

Major league affiliations in parentheses.

Playoff—Bellingham defeated Eugene, one game to none.

Regular-Season Attendance—Bellingham, 14,916; Bend, 29,766; Eugene, 116,286; Everett, 51,131; Medford, 70,590; Salem, 37,279; Spokane, 102,826; Tri-Cities, 30,605. Total, 453,399. Playoff, 1,516.

Managers—Bellingham, Sal Rende; Bend, Ed Pebley; Eugene, Ed Napoleon; Everett, Joe Strain; Medford, Dave Hudgens; Salem, Bruce Hines; Spokane, Rob Picciolo; Tri-Cities, Pat Murphy.

All-Star Team—1B—Nathan Oglesbee, Eugene; 2B—John Toal, Everett; 3B—Anthony Pellegrino, Spokane; SS—Thomas LeVasseur, Spokane; OF—Lee Stevens, Salem; Drew Stratton, Medford; Dave Nash, Everett; C—Mike Knapp, Salem; DH—Carlos Escalera, Eugene; RHP—Gary Blouin, Eugene; LHP—James Pena, Everett; Most Valuable Player—Dave Nash, Everett; Manager of the Year—Sal Rende, Bellingham.

(Compiled by William J. Weiss, League Statistician, San Mateo, Calif.)

CLUB BATTING

Club	Pct.	G.	AB.	R.	OR.	H.	TB.	2B.	3B.	HR.	RBI.	GW.	SH.	SF.	HP.	BB.	Int. BB.	SO.	SB.	CS.	LOB.
Eugene	.275	74	2601	489	400	716	967	129	16	30	416	42	15	30	36	384	12	596	78	29	629
Medford	.269	74	2583	511	433	694	964	146	20	28	404	36	17	35	34	508	13	506	82	29	693
Spokane	.265	74	2575	443	411	683	886	120	16	17	372	31	23	23	24	422	9	449	81	22	658

CLUB BATTING--Continued

Club	Pct.	G.	AB.	R.	OR.	H.	TB.	2B.	3B.	HR.	RBI.	GW.	SH.	SF.	HP.	BB.	Int. BB.	SO.	SB.	CS.	LOB.
Bellingham	.260	74	2421	465	380	630	881	98	27	33	394	37	25	43	34	420	8	536	157	35	592
Everett	.249	74	2519	457	426	627	922	124	15	47	382	35	12	43	29	391	13	531	104	23	595
Salem	.246	74	2517	409	439	618	835	100	9	33	330	31	11	25	32	363	13	532	94	41	586
Bend	.241	74	2509	385	520	605	854	104	14	39	288	17	19	18	27	354	5	623	116	49	569
Tri-Cities	.240	74	2535	390	540	608	834	91	6	41	316	23	32	16	38	408	5	587	78	41	650

INDIVIDUAL BATTING

(Leading Qualifiers for Batting Championship—200 or More Plate Appearances)

*Bats lefthanded. †Switch-hitter.

Player and Club	Pct.	G.	AB.	R.	H.	TB.	2B.	3B.	HR.	RBI.	GW.	SH.	SF.	HP.	BB.	Int. BB.	SO.	SB.	CS.
LeVasseur, Thomas, Spokane	.372	53	191	50	71	79	3	1	1	21	0	2	1	2	47	0	14	28	8
Britt, Patrick, Medford	.352	55	179	46	63	91	14	1	4	34	4	4	5	1	31	1	23	2	3
Toal, John, Everett	.341	59	229	55	78	113	25	2	2	44	4	2	5	7	31	0	36	12	6
Berry, Sean, Eugene	.319	65	238	53	76	115	20	2	5	44	5	1	2	5	44	0	73	10	1
Jaha, John, Tri-Cities†	.318	73	258	65	82	144	13	2	15	67	3	0	2	5	70	4	75	9	4
Howitt, Dann, Medford*	.317	66	208	36	66	97	9	2	6	37	5	1	1	1	49	3	37	5	1
Nash, David, Everett	.313	54	198	42	62	103	14	0	9	37	2	1	1	1	34	1	29	3	0
Escalera, Carlos, Eugene	.312	73	314	62	98	135	15	2	6	69	7	1	4	4	21	4	54	5	2
Bailey, Patrick, Eugene*	.311	64	193	38	60	82	14	1	2	39	1	1	2	6	46	1	48	1	4
Patterson, David, Everett	.305	56	197	34	60	94	16	3	4	42	4	0	7	2	42	3	19	5	2

Departmental Leaders: G—Escalera, Jaha, 73; AB—Escalera, 314; R—McRae, 66; H—Escalera, 98; TB—Jaha, 144; 2B—Toal, 25; 3B—Briley, Disher, Scarsone, Teixeira, 4; HR—Jaha, 15; RBI—Escalera, 69; GWRBI—Cooper, Stevens, 8; SH—Koentopp, 7; SF—Bowie, 11; HP—Toal, 7; BB—Jaha, 70; IBB—Escalera, Jaha, Shultis, 4; SO—Grilione, 76; SB—Te. Williams, 51; CS—K. Greene, 14.

(All Players—Listed Alphabetically)

Player and Club	Pct.	G.	AB.	R.	H.	TB.	2B.	3B.	HR.	RBI.	GW.	SH.	SF.	HP.	BB.	Int. BB.	SO.	SB.	CS.
Allison, Jesse, Bend	.000	16	3	0	0	0	0	0	0	0	0	0	0	0	0	0	3	0	0
Armstrong, Eldridge, Tri-Cities	.000	9	7	0	0	0	0	0	0	0	0	0	0	0	0	0	5	0	0
Asencio, Juan, Bend	.150	38	100	11	15	25	1	0	3	10	1	0	1	0	17	0	37	6	1
Ashby, Andrew, Bend	.250	16	4	0	1	1	0	0	0	0	0	0	0	0	0	0	1	0	0
Austin, James, Spokane	.167	30	6	0	1	1	0	0	0	0	0	1	0	0	1	0	3	0	0
Bailey, Patrick, Eugene*	.311	64	193	38	60	82	14	1	2	39	1	1	2	6	46	1	48	1	4
Bandy, Kenneth, Salem	.207	45	145	20	30	44	6	1	2	9	0	0	0	6	16	1	58	3	2
Barnett, Lance, Bend	.188	13	32	3	6	8	2	0	0	3	0	0	0	1	2	0	11	1	0
Basso, Michael, Spokane	.298	63	225	30	67	90	17	0	2	43	3	0	8	1	32	2	35	1	0
Bell, Robert, Eugene	.219	62	192	42	42	55	4	3	1	28	2	1	4	3	28	0	46	7	2
Bennett, Jose, Bellingham	.357	7	28	4	10	11	1	0	0	2	1	0	0	0	4	0	4	0	0
Berman, Gary, Bend	.295	65	244	36	72	110	17	0	7	45	4	0	3	1	41	1	41	6	1
Berry, Sean, Eugene	.319	65	238	53	76	115	20	2	5	44	5	1	2	5	44	0	73	10	1
Birch, Brock, Everett*	.000	19	4	0	0	0	0	0	0	0	0	0	0	0	0	0	0	0	0
Blankenship, Lance, Medford	.404	14	52	22	21	30	3	0	2	17	2	1	4	0	17	1	9	10	1
Bolar, Wendell, Bellingham	.237	50	152	34	36	59	8	3	3	29	1	5	1	6	28	1	42	18	2
Bones, Ricardo, Spokane	.000	18	3	1	0	0	0	0	0	0	0	0	0	0	1	0	0	0	0
Bonura, Anthony, Salem*	.188	48	144	25	27	30	3	0	0	6	0	1	0	1	23	0	12	4	2
Bordick, Michael, Medford	.257	46	187	30	48	53	3	1	0	19	1	1	1	1	40	0	21	6	0
Bowens, Howard, Tri-Cities	.193	64	197	26	38	51	8	1	1	21	3	4	1	3	30	1	35	12	2
Bowie, James, Bellingham*	.277	72	274	47	76	105	12	1	5	68	7	0	11	2	38	1	53	4	1
Briley, Gregory, Bellingham*	.298	63	218	52	65	106	12	4	7	46	7	0	7	3	50	1	29	26	5
Brito, Jorge, Medford	.153	21	59	4	9	11	2	0	0	5	1	0	1	2	4	0	17	0	2
Britt, Patrick, Medford	.352	55	179	46	63	91	14	1	4	34	4	4	5	1	31	1	23	2	3
Brocail, Douglas, Spokane*	.000	16	11	0	0	0	0	0	0	0	0	1	0	0	2	0	4	0	0
Brooks, Brian, Spokane*	.246	49	134	17	33	39	4	1	0	21	1	0	2	0	14	0	18	3	3
Cabello, Robert, Salem†	.257	40	113	23	29	32	1	1	0	13	1	2	1	0	18	1	21	5	2
Carr, Terence, Salem	.233	48	163	36	38	51	4	0	3	23	2	0	1	6	28	0	41	13	1
Carter, Bruce, Tri-Cities†	.237	51	169	21	40	41	1	0	0	8	1	2	0	4	12	0	38	8	7
Cepeda, Jose, Bend	.176	10	17	0	3	3	0	0	0	2	0	0	0	0	2	0	9	0	0
Cerny, Scott, Salem	.285	70	274	59	78	91	9	2	0	27	1	4	1	2	45	0	28	18	8
Christopher, Frederick, Bend	.000	15	6	0	0	0	0	0	0	0	0	0	0	0	0	0	2	0	0
Church, Scott, Bend	.172	38	99	8	17	20	0	0	1	9	0	1	3	2	9	0	38	1	0
Claudio, Sindulfo, Medford*	.210	46	105	21	22	26	4	0	0	14	1	0	1	0	33	2	32	1	1
Connelly, David, Tri-Cities*	.200	29	50	4	10	14	1	0	1	8	1	0	0	1	3	0	16	0	0
Conner, David, Tri-Cities	.246	31	118	18	29	34	2	0	1	14	2	2	0	0	14	0	18	5	0
Coonan, William, Medford	.100	9	20	1	2	4	0	1	0	1	0	0	1	0	2	1	11	0	0
Cooper, Craig, Spokane	.283	72	286	59	81	114	15	3	4	50	8	0	1	2	45	2	52	4	0
Dean, Jimmie, Spokane†	.000	5	8	0	0	0	0	0	0	0	0	0	0	0	0	0	4	0	0
Disher, Daniel, Bellingham	.231	44	156	19	36	47	3	4	0	22	0	1	1	2	10	0	51	7	2
Dixon, Andrew, Everett*	.220	56	214	48	47	54	4	0	1	15	0	0	0	2	29	0	52	37	5
Duffy, Darrin, Medford	.243	27	103	25	25	33	6	1	0	23	1	0	1	2	19	0	24	12	4
Dyer, Linton, Eugene	.300	6	10	1	3	3	0	0	0	0	0	1	0	0	2	0	5	0	0
Ealy, Thomas, Tri-Cities	.268	41	149	24	40	49	5	2	0	14	1	4	1	5	32	0	28	8	4
Escalera, Carlos, Eugene	.312	73	314	62	98	135	15	2	6	69	7	1	4	4	21	4	54	5	2
Espinosa, Santiago, Salem	.195	52	164	22	32	45	4	0	3	14	2	0	1	2	13	0	38	6	3
Fitzgerald, Kevin, Everett	.225	35	111	13	25	41	5	1	3	15	0	2	1	0	22	0	37	5	0
Fleming, Richard, Everett	.270	23	63	10	17	19	2	0	0	3	1	0	0	0	4	0	16	5	3
Foley, Martin, Bend	.000	2	7	2	0	0	0	0	0	1	0	0	1	1	0	0	4	0	0
Ford, Ondra, Eugene*	.262	50	187	24	49	61	6	0	2	28	3	1	1	1	9	1	68	3	0
Gambee, Bradley, Everett	.143	14	7	1	1	1	0	0	0	0	0	0	0	0	0	0	2	0	0
Gavin, David, Medford	.256	41	117	22	30	37	7	0	0	15	2	0	1	0	15	0	24	3	3
Gay, Jeffrey, Salem*	.278	48	151	22	42	59	8	0	3	22	2	0	3	0	11	0	33	0	0
Gianukakis, John, Bend*	.283	36	92	12	26	34	6	1	0	2	0	0	0	2	19	1	40	4	4
Gilbert, Patrick, Medford	.404	13	52	7	21	33	6	0	2	18	2	0	3	2	8	0	10	2	0
Giles, Troy, Salem	.125	14	24	3	3	7	1	0	1	4	0	0	0	0	2	0	10	0	1
Gilliam, Darryl, Tri-Cities	.272	67	250	45	68	75	7	0	0	20	0	3	0	3	50	0	33	14	8
Gioia, Joseph, Tri-Cities	.212	54	170	27	36	49	5	1	2	16	1	4	1	4	28	0	38	1	4
Glover, Jeffrey, Medford	.000	16	2	0	0	0	0	0	0	0	0	0	0	0	0	0	0	0	0
Goff, Jerry, Bellingham*	.190	54	168	26	32	64	7	2	7	25	1	1	3	4	42	1	55	4	3
Goff, Timothy, Eugene	.312	43	141	27	44	69	8	1	5	29	3	1	2	2	36	1	36	3	2
Gorski, Gary, Salem	.273	49	150	19	41	61	14	0	2	27	2	0	4	2	30	3	41	5	3
Graves, Christopher, Salem	.222	12	36	7	8	10	2	0	0	6	0	0	0	1	6	0	10	3	1
Greene, Keith, Bend†	.249	67	261	40	65	78	8	1	1	14	0	1	1	4	32	0	57	21	14

Player and Club	Pct.	G.	AB.	R.	H.	TB.	2B.	3B.	HR.	RBI.	GW.	SH.	SF.	HP.	BB.	Int. BB.	SO.	SB.	CS.
Greene, Nathaniel, Tri-Cities	.232	56	185	30	43	67	6	0	6	31	3	2	2	3	35	0	46	8	3
Grilione, David, Salem†	.168	51	167	22	28	44	2	1	4	18	3	0	3	1	28	1	76	3	1
Gunn, Clay, Bellingham	.327	33	110	24	36	45	4	1	1	19	0	0	3	2	13	1	16	1	0
Hall, Andrew, Tri-Cities	.217	52	180	21	39	57	9	0	3	24	0	6	4	3	16	0	65	0	1
Hansen, Todd, Tri-Cities*	.500	16	2	0	1	1	0	0	0	1	0	0	0	0	0	0	0	0	0
Harris, Gregory, Spokane	.000	15	8	0	0	0	0	0	0	1	0	1	0	0	0	0	3	0	0
Harrison, Keith, Spokane*	.158	24	38	6	6	6	0	0	0	1	0	0	0	1	11	0	14	1	1
Hibbs, Albert, Bend	.227	44	132	26	30	50	6	1	4	19	1	1	0	3	34	2	43	8	1
Higson, Charles, Everett*	.000	32	4	0	0	0	0	0	0	0	0	0	0	0	0	0	2	0	0
Hodo, Douglas, Bend*	.216	41	148	22	32	40	2	0	2	18	1	1	0	2	14	0	30	12	2
Hoffinger, Glenn, Medford	.206	45	107	21	22	31	9	0	0	13	2	0	2	4	39	1	26	5	2
Holmes, Carl, Spokane	.179	36	106	12	19	30	4	2	1	17	1	1	1	0	11	0	34	1	0
Howard, Thomas, Spokane†	.418	13	55	16	23	38	3	3	2	17	4	0	0	1	3	0	9	2	1
Howitt, Dann, Medford*	.317	66	208	36	66	97	9	2	6	37	5	1	1	1	49	3	37	5	1
Jackson, Gregory, Salem	.246	46	138	25	34	59	7	0	6	34	3	1	3	2	44	0	42	4	3
Jackson, Lloyd, Tri-Cities*	.000	1	4	0	0	0	0	0	0	0	0	0	0	0	0	0	2	0	0
Jackson, Kenneth, Eugene	.223	54	188	29	42	54	8	2	0	24	2	1	2	5	25	1	50	5	2
Jackson, Robert, Tri-Cities	.196	20	46	2	9	10	1	0	0	2	0	0	0	0	12	0	16	0	0
Jaha, John, Tri-Cities†	.318	73	258	65	82	144	13	2	15	67	3	0	2	5	70	4	75	9	4
Johnson, Deron, Bellingham*	.295	57	207	44	61	87	13	2	3	40	5	2	6	1	38	1	43	6	0
Jones, James, Everett†	.209	35	110	21	23	25	2	0	0	8	2	1	1	1	20	0	22	6	1
King, Michael, Spokane*	.224	34	76	10	17	21	4	0	0	5	0	0	1	3	6	0	17	0	0
Kiser, Garland, Bend*	.000	14	5	0	0	0	0	0	0	0	0	2	0	0	0	0	3	0	0
Knapp, Michael, Salem	.295	64	224	31	66	89	12	1	3	39	3	1	3	3	31	1	37	4	4
Koentopp, Kevin, Spokane*	.280	70	264	42	74	84	10	0	0	29	1	7	2	1	44	2	27	6	0
Krafve, Keith, Everett*	.185	34	108	20	20	28	6	1	0	13	2	0	1	0	23	1	31	1	0
Larios, John, Eugene	.267	28	86	16	23	34	6	1	1	15	4	2	2	1	10	0	11	2	1
Larsen, James, Eugene	.152	23	66	8	10	13	3	0	0	5	1	1	0	1	3	0	14	3	1
Lennon, Patrick, Bellingham	.243	51	169	35	41	59	5	2	3	27	3	1	1	0	36	0	50	8	6
Leonard, Mark, Ev. 3-TC 35*	.258	38	128	21	33	51	6	0	4	17	1	0	1	1	27	0	21	4	2
LeVasseur, Thomas, Spokane	.372	53	191	50	71	79	3	1	1	21	0	2	1	2	47	0	14	28	8
Limbach, Chris, Bend*	.000	19	2	0	0	0	0	0	0	0	0	0	0	0	0	0	0	0	0
Little, Randy, Bellingham	.283	47	180	25	51	71	15	1	1	32	6	0	4	0	22	0	15	7	2
Lutticken, Robert, Spokane	.220	39	109	9	24	31	7	0	0	10	0	1	1	4	10	0	27	0	0
MacKenzie, Shaun, Everett	.143	22	7	1	1	1	0	0	0	0	0	0	0	0	2	0	4	0	0
Malone, Charles, Bend	.500	21	2	0	1	1	0	0	0	0	0	1	0	0	0	0	1	0	0
Martinez, Luis, Medford†	.265	33	117	30	31	40	2	2	1	15	0	0	1	3	41	0	25	5	2
Massey, James, Everett	.111	15	9	0	1	1	0	0	0	0	0	1	0	0	0	0	3	0	0
McDevitt, Terrance, Spokane*	.210	54	195	38	41	45	4	0	0	20	2	5	0	3	57	2	35	6	4
McDonald, Michael, Bellingham*	.260	54	169	29	44	56	6	3	0	22	1	0	1	2	30	1	41	4	3
McNamara, James, Everett*	.247	46	158	23	39	68	1	2	8	30	2	0	2	3	18	2	39	0	0
McRae, Brian, Eugene†	.268	72	306	66	82	101	10	3	1	29	3	1	2	5	41	1	49	28	4
Medrano, Felipe, Bend	.000	2	7	0	0	0	0	0	0	0	0	0	0	0	0	0	3	0	0
Mendenhall, Shannon, Medford	.000	1	3	0	0	0	0	0	0	0	0	0	0	0	2	0	3	0	0
Mijares, William, Everett	.202	38	124	16	25	37	10	1	0	10	1	0	1	1	16	1	26	1	0
Miller, Christopher, Bellingham	.556	3	9	5	5	7	0	1	0	1	0	0	0	1	2	0	1	0	0
Miller, Kenneth, Bend	.271	62	214	39	58	79	14	2	1	29	2	2	2	0	43	0	25	8	5
Minch, John, Medford	.200	1	5	1	1	1	0	0	0	1	0	0	0	0	0	0	1	0	0
Minier, Johnny, Medford	.234	33	107	20	25	32	5	1	0	11	0	0	3	6	13	0	16	1	0
Morfin, Arvid, Bellingham	.297	11	37	3	11	16	2	0	1	2	0	0	0	0	3	0	6	0	0
Murphy, Patrick, Tri-Cities	.500	8	2	0	1	1	0	0	0	0	0	0	0	0	0	0	1	0	0
Nash, David, Everett	.313	54	198	42	62	103	14	0	9	37	2	1	1	1	34	1	29	3	0
Navilliat, James, Spokane*	.000	9	4	1	0	0	0	0	0	0	0	0	0	0	1	0	2	0	0
Nelson, Ronald, Bend	.317	17	60	10	19	31	6	0	2	11	0	0	0	0	7	0	13	0	0
Newsome, Warren, Spokane*	.233	54	159	29	37	53	8	1	2	31	3	1	1	0	47	1	37	3	1
Newton, Marvin, Everett	.237	34	118	15	28	38	7	0	1	16	1	0	3	1	16	0	21	0	0
Oglesbee, Nathan, Eugene*	.281	70	256	54	72	102	12	0	6	45	7	0	7	1	55	3	55	1	2
Ortman, Douglas, Medford	.270	40	148	28	40	53	11	1	0	16	0	0	3	1	22	1	34	3	1
Parker, Olen, Bend†	.261	14	46	10	12	13	1	0	0	4	0	0	1	0	5	0	8	8	1
Patterson, David, Everett	.305	56	197	34	60	94	16	3	4	42	4	0	7	2	42	3	19	5	2
Pawling, Eric, Tri-Cities	.188	32	69	8	13	14	1	0	0	5	0	0	0	1	17	0	18	0	0
Pellegrino, Anthony, Spokane	.296	68	267	50	79	116	21	2	4	58	5	0	2	3	45	0	34	6	2
Pena, James, Everett*	.125	14	24	1	3	5	0	1	0	2	0	1	0	0	0	0	5	0	0
Pritikin, James, Bellingham*	.231	60	160	30	37	44	5	1	0	15	1	6	1	4	32	0	40	14	3
Quinzer, Paul, Spokane	.133	16	15	1	2	2	0	0	0	0	0	0	0	0	1	0	6	0	0
Ramirez, Fausto, Bellingham†	.156	20	32	2	5	5	0	0	0	4	0	0	0	0	6	0	15	0	0
Rannow, John, Everett	.259	20	58	7	15	23	5	0	1	15	0	0	2	1	11	0	22	0	0
Rasmus, Anthony, Tri-Cities	.206	52	175	25	36	43	7	0	0	17	2	1	1	3	11	0	38	6	1
Redick, Kevin, Everett	.165	38	121	21	20	27	4	0	1	7	1	1	0	3	13	0	49	5	1
Reiser, James, Medford	.231	40	143	25	33	38	3	1	0	20	0	3	0	1	30	0	25	7	3
Reyes, Giovanny, Salem	.250	67	264	43	66	71	3	1	0	29	3	2	4	3	17	1	12	13	3
Reynolds, William, Medford	.242	30	95	18	23	36	7	0	2	18	3	1	0	1	11	0	31	0	0
Rich, Douglas, Bend*	.000	13	1	0	0	0	0	0	0	0	0	1	0	0	0	0	1	0	0
Riemer, Robin, Everett*	.000	19	2	0	0	0	0	0	0	0	0	0	0	0	1	0	2	0	0
Ritchie, Gregory, Everett*	.250	40	100	36	25	30	3	1	0	11	3	0	3	0	47	0	28	18	2
Roberts, Peter, Spokane*	.000	11	4	0	0	0	0	0	0	1	1	1	0	0	0	0	3	0	0
Robertson, Roderick, Bend	.242	65	248	40	60	72	5	2	1	25	2	5	0	4	28	0	51	18	7
Rodriguez, Edgar, Salem*	.226	37	93	7	21	27	6	0	0	12	1	0	0	1	6	2	24	0	1
Romero, Elvis, Bend	.000	15	5	2	0	0	0	0	0	0	0	1	0	0	2	0	4	0	0
Ronson, Tod, Everett*	.250	57	188	37	47	86	6	0	11	52	5	0	9	4	22	1	40	3	2
Rosso, Pascual, Medford*	.196	19	46	10	9	12	3	0	0	4	0	1	2	1	15	0	20	2	0
Ruckman, Scott, Bend	.252	60	222	29	56	90	14	1	6	26	4	0	1	0	18	1	52	2	4
Sampson, Mark, Spokane	.143	15	7	1	1	1	0	0	0	0	0	0	0	0	1	0	2	0	0
Savarino, William, Medford*	.315	49	168	32	53	83	15	3	3	34	3	1	2	1	21	1	12	3	1
Scarsone, Steven, Bend	.219	65	219	42	48	78	10	4	4	21	2	1	2	4	30	0	51	11	2
Shultis, Christopher, Everett*	.260	59	235	37	61	87	9	1	5	41	4	1	5	3	25	4	20	1	1
Silva, Ryan, Bend	.167	15	30	3	5	14	0	0	3	6	0	0	0	1	2	0	20	0	0
Sossamon, Timothy, Bend	.667	18	3	2	2	3	1	0	0	2	0	0	0	0	1	0	1	0	0
Stark, Jeffrey, Bend	.239	20	67	11	16	25	2	2	1	9	0	0	0	1	11	0	11	0	2
Stevens, Lee, Salem*	.281	72	267	45	75	115	18	2	6	47	8	0	1	2	45	3	49	13	6
Stratton, Drew, Medford	.244	44	176	36	43	69	14	0	4	18	0	0	1	2	27	0	27	4	1
Stubberfield, Kristopher, Everett	.500	18	2	1	1	2	1	0	0	2	0	0	0	0	0	0	0	0	0
Swan, Russell, Everett*	.000	7	8	0	0	0	0	0	0	0	0	1	0	0	1	0	3	0	0

Player and Club	Pct.	G.	AB.	R.	H.	TB.	2B.	3B.	HR.	RBI.	GW.	SH.	SF.	HP.	BB.	Int. BB.	SO.	SB.	CS.
Tartabull, Jose, Bellingham	.186	17	43	10	8	9	1	0	0	6	0	2	0	0	12	0	3	2	1
Tate, Charles, Everett	.000	13	2	0	0	0	0	0	0	0	0	0	0	0	0	0	2	1	0
Taylor, William, Spokane	.282	59	202	38	57	65	6	1	0	20	2	0	1	1	17	0	34	18	2
Teixeira, Vincent, Medford	.274	58	201	50	55	88	13	4	4	40	7	2	2	3	49	2	45	8	2
Tinkle, David, Eugene*	.299	63	251	45	75	94	17	1	0	37	2	1	0	1	29	0	42	5	5
Toal, John, Everett	.341	59	229	55	78	113	25	2	2	44	4	2	5	7	31	0	36	12	6
Ventress, Leroy, Bend	.261	38	115	15	30	35	2	0	1	14	0	2	1	0	13	0	34	6	4
Walker, Matthew, Everett	.247	26	93	15	23	29	4	1	0	7	2	1	0	0	11	0	15	1	0
Walling, Kendall, Tri-Cities	.235	57	221	30	52	76	12	0	4	29	2	1	2	0	20	0	55	3	2
Wentz, Keith, Medford	.284	57	183	26	52	66	10	2	0	31	2	2	0	2	20	0	33	3	2
Williams, Matthew, Everett	.235	4	17	3	4	9	0	1	1	10	0	0	1	0	1	0	4	0	0
Williams, Quinn, Bend	.263	49	118	22	31	44	7	0	2	18	0	1	2	1	24	0	29	4	1
Williams, Ted, Bellingham†	.246	59	224	52	55	57	2	0	0	25	2	5	4	4	38	1	38	51	3
Williams, Troy, Bellingham	.247	30	85	24	21	33	2	2	2	9	2	2	0	3	16	0	34	5	4
Wilson, Todd, Tri-Cities	.239	56	163	23	39	58	7	0	4	24	4	3	2	2	33	0	41	0	3
Wolkoys, Robert, Eugene	.231	50	173	24	40	49	6	0	1	24	2	2	2	1	35	0	45	5	3
Wood, Brian, Spokane*	.200	24	5	1	1	2	1	0	0	0	0	1	0	0	1	0	4	0	0
Young, Michael, Spokane	.000	12	1	0	1	1	0	0	0	0	0	0	0	0	0	0	0	0	0
Yurtin, Jeffrey, Spokane*	.245	50	196	32	48	68	13	2	1	27	0	1	2	2	25	0	31	2	0

The following pitchers, listed alphabetically by club, with games in parentheses, had no plate appearances, primarily through use of designated hitters:

BELLINGHAM—Blueberg, James (14); DeLucia, Richard (13); Fortugno, Timothy (6); Hartnett, David (18); Intorcia, Trent (21); Little, Thomas (31); Mendez, Paul (17); Rohde, Brad (7); Ryan, Jody (7); Simmermacher, Bret (29); Thorpe, Michael (23); Webster, Rudy (10); Wooden, Mark (15).

BEND—Anderson, Glenn (19); Coulter, Darrell (5); Moore, Bradley (16); Myaer, Jeffrey (16).

EUGENE—Adams, Kenneth (15); Blouin, Gary (13); Butcher, Michael (14); Champagne, Brannon (17); Goodenough, Randy (24); Hibbard, James (26); Jones, George (30); Karcher, Kevin (18); McKinzie, Philip (20); Moeller, Dennis (14); Mount, Charles (29); Skodny, Joseph (10); Tresemer, Michael (12).

EVERETT—McClellan, Paul (13); Ricker, Drew (19).

MEDFORD—Beavers, Mark (2); Beck, Rodney (13); Cabrera, Nasual (16); Carroll, James (26); Gilbert, Robbie (11); Hartley, Todd (14); Holcomb, Scott (12); Kent, John (17); Kopyta, Jeffrey (6); Kunkel, Kevin (14); Ritchey, Larry (18); Sanchez, Moises (15); Santana, Jose (3); Stancel, Mark (21); Tapani, Kevin (2); Veres, David (15); Weber, Weston (13).

SALEM—Auth, Robert (9); Bisceglia, James (17); Charland, Colin (5); Fetters, Michael (12); Fix, Gregory (9); Franco, Julio (11); Green, Daryl (14); Hernandez, Roberto (10); Merejo, Luis (20); Mills, Alan (14); Spearnock, Michael (16); Vanderwel, William (13); Vann, Brandy (20); Ward, Colby (27).

SPOKANE—de la Cruz, Francisco (6); Harrison, Brian (8); Vizcaino, Hector (3).

TRI-CITIES—Adriance, Daniel (21); Blasucci, Anthony (3); Brockway, Kevin (19); Collishaw, David (14); Connelly, Daron (20); DeChavez, Oscar (12); Ellis, Douglas (16); Harrison, Brian (14); Naworski, Andrew (17); Smith, Jeffrey (18).

GRAND SLAM HOME RUNS—Jaha 2; Berman, Berry, Blankenship, G. Jackson, McNamara, Ronson, Toal, M. Williams, 1 each.

AWARDED FIRST BASE ON CATCHER'S INTERFERENCE—Ruckman 3 (J. Goff, Hall, Knapp); Q. Williams 3 (Hall 2, Brito); Leonard 2 (J. Goff, Hall); Rannow 2 (Gioia, Hall); Barry (Knapp); Bolar (Gioia).

CLUB FIELDING

Club	Pct.	G.	PO.	A.	E.	DP.	PB.
Everett	.953	74	1957	747	134	57	23
Salem	.951	74	1954	750	138	56	50
Spokane	.949	74	1968	814	150	54	31
Medford	.947	74	1987	810	157	63	29
Eugene	.946	74	1972	781	157	71	43
Bend	.939	74	1935	831	180	71	56
Bellingham	.935	74	1912	763	185	58	27
Tri-Cities	.935	74	1957	874	197	59	30

INDIVIDUAL FIELDING

*Throws lefthanded.

FIRST BASEMEN

Player and Club	Pct.	G.	PO.	A.	E.	DP.
Bailey, Eugene	.978	14	85	6	2	11
Basso, Spokane	.909	2	10	0	1	0
Berman, Bend	.979	64	591	51	14	60
Bowie, Bellingham*	.985	58	496	37	8	40
Brito, Medford	1.000	1	7	0	0	1
Cooper, Spokane	.977	68	622	50	16	49
Escalera, Eugene	.980	23	191	5	4	22
Goff, Eugene	1.000	5	28	0	0	2
Gorski, Salem	.993	16	138	4	1	10
Hoffinger, Medford	.990	14	100	3	1	11
Jackson, Salem	.977	44	319	23	8	27
Jaha, Tri-Cities	.986	38	328	28	5	30
Johnson, Bellingham	.993	18	133	15	1	10
Koentopp, Spokane*	1.000	5	37	3	0	1
Krafve, Everett	.995	36	191	15	1	19
Leonard, Tri-Cities	.909	2	9	1	1	2
Morfin, Bellingham	1.000	1	2	0	0	0
Nelson, Bend	.988	9	79	6	1	9
Newton, Everett	1.000	1	2	0	0	0
Oglesbee, Eugene*	.988	38	307	19	4	30
Ortman, Medford	.992	40	358	10	3	24
PATTERSON, Everett	.996	49	425	37	2	29
Rosso, Medford*	.962	19	124	4	5	14
Silva, Bend	.923	3	11	1	1	0
Stevens, Salem*	.994	22	144	12	1	12
Walling, Tri-Cities	.978	38	322	32	8	24
Wentz, Medford	.989	12	92	2	1	8
Wolkoys, Eugene	1.000	2	3	0	0	0

SECOND BASEMEN

Player and Club	Pct.	G.	PO.	A.	E.	DP.
Bonura, Salem	.960	40	75	91	7	19
Bowens, Tri-Cities	.927	11	20	18	3	3
Briley, Bellingham	.921	60	132	146	24	26
Cerny, Salem	.947	40	83	95	10	19
Conner, Tri-Cities	.895	5	6	11	2	0
Fitzgerald, Everett	.935	19	37	35	5	7
Gilliam, Tri-Cities	.940	65	137	190	21	31
Gioia, Tri-Cities	.667	4	1	1	1	0
Larsen, Eugene	1.000	1	0	1	0	0
Martinez, Medford	.937	33	60	104	11	22
McDevitt, Spokane	.944	52	105	148	15	29
McDonald, Bellingham	.846	3	6	5	2	2
McRAE, Eugene	.965	72	146	214	13	43
Medrano, Bend	1.000	2	3	7	0	0
Minier, Medford	.714	2	2	8	4	0
Parker, Bend	.898	10	16	37	6	5
Pellegrino, Spokane	.936	22	38	64	7	10
Ramirez, Bellingham	.913	10	8	13	2	1
Rasmus, Tri-Cities	.667	3	3	5	4	1
Reiser, Medford	.963	38	61	119	7	18
Robertson, Bend	.875	1	4	3	1	2
Savarino, Medford	.956	7	24	19	2	5
Scarsone, Bend	.919	61	147	182	29	45
Stark, Bend	1.000	1	1	0	0	0
Toal, Everett	.928	56	119	139	20	32
Tr. Williams, Bellingham	.800	12	22	22	11	5
Wolkoys, Eugene	.960	6	9	15	1	1

THIRD BASEMEN

Player and Club	Pct.	G.	PO.	A.	E.	DP.
Basso, Spokane	.933	15	8	20	2	1
Berry, Eugene	.883	64	63	96	21	11
Bolar, Bellingham	.810	47	28	104	31	6
Bowens, Tri-Cities	.000	1	0	0	1	0
Cerny, Salem	.878	33	18	47	9	4
Church, Bend	.865	28	11	34	7	5
Cooper, Spokane	.556	3	0	5	4	0
Dean, Spokane	1.000	2	0	1	0	0
Fitzgerald, Everett	.571	3	0	4	3	0
Fleming, Everett	.889	14	10	22	4	3
Gioia, Tri-Cities	.854	28	21	49	12	2
Gorski, Salem	.919	31	26	42	6	3
Hibbs, Bend	.000	1	0	0	1	0
R. Jackson, Tri-Cities	.500	7	1	3	4	1
Jaha, Tri-Cities	.882	33	24	73	13	4
Johnson, Bellingham	.830	12	10	34	9	2
Knapp, Salem	1.000	1	1	0	0	0
Larios, Eugene	.600	3	1	2	2	0
Lennon, Bellingham	.714	2	3	2	2	0
MacKenzie, Everett	.500	1	1	1	2	0
McDonald, Bellingham	.864	18	17	34	8	3
Minier, Medford	.841	28	8	50	11	2
Pellegrino, Spokane	.875	11	4	24	4	1
Reyes, Salem	.906	21	10	19	3	2
Ruckman, Bend	.853	52	28	88	20	5
Savarino, Medford	1.000	2	1	2	0	0
SHULTIS, Everett	.923	59	41	115	13	9
Teixeira, Medford	.839	17	18	34	10	2
Walling, Tri-Cities	.857	12	7	17	4	0
Wentz, Medford	.853	38	27	60	15	8
Wolkoys, Eugene	.880	9	4	18	3	1
Yurtin, Spokane	.898	48	28	95	14	4

SHORTSTOPS

Player and Club	Pct.	G.	PO.	A.	E.	DP.
Basso, Spokane	.889	4	4	12	2	0
Bordick, Medford	.921	46	68	143	18	25
Bowens, Tri-Cities	.850	5	3	14	3	1
Cabello, Salem	.935	39	52	93	10	19
Carter, Tri-Cities	.869	33	46	73	18	11
Church, Bend	.864	6	5	14	3	3
Conner, Tri-Cities	.921	27	41	87	11	15
Duffy, Medford	.895	27	42	77	14	16
Fleming, Everett	.917	3	7	4	1	1
Foley, Bend	1.000	2	2	9	0	1
Jones, Everett	.874	34	49	103	22	23
Lennon, Bellingham	.850	35	54	88	25	15
LeVasseur, Spokane	.947	47	69	144	12	26
MacKenzie, Everett	.833	1	3	2	1	1
McDonald, Bellingham	.877	33	38	83	17	10
Mendenhall, Medford	1.000	1	3	2	0	0
Mijares, Everett	.934	37	56	100	11	15
Miller, Bellingham	.909	3	5	5	1	2
Pellegrino, Spokane	.908	29	43	75	12	16
Ramirez, Bellingham	.783	9	10	8	5	2
Rasmus, Tri-Cities	.857	17	31	53	14	8
Reiser, Medford	.800	2	1	3	1	0
Reyes, Salem	.935	44	62	124	13	20
ROBERTSON, Bend	.889	63	106	207	39	42
Scarsone, Bend	.889	3	2	6	1	3
Tinkle, Eugene	.880	62	102	176	38	40
Ventress, Bend	1.000	1	0	1	0	0
Williams, Everett	.882	4	5	10	2	2
Wilson, Tri-Cities	1.000	1	0	1	0	0
Wolkoys, Eugene	.867	18	23	29	8	5

OUTFIELDERS

Player and Club	Pct.	G.	PO.	A.	E.	DP.
Armstrong, Tri-Cities	1.000	2	0	0	0	0
Asencio, Bend	.806	22	22	3	6	0
Bailey, Eugene	.921	26	31	4	3	0
Bandy, Salem	.914	41	72	2	7	0
Bell, Eugene	.983	62	108	9	2	0
Bennett, Bellingham	1.000	7	10	0	0	0
Blankenship, Medford	.958	14	22	1	1	1
Bowens, Tri-Cities	.959	42	65	6	3	1
Brooks, Spokane*	.914	37	70	4	7	0
Carr, Salem	.927	35	50	1	4	0
Carter, Tri-Cities	.950	12	18	1	1	0
Cepeda, Bend	.571	2	4	0	3	0
Claudio, Medford*	.900	37	42	3	5	0
Connelly, Tri-Cities*	1.000	9	8	0	0	0
Disher, Bellingham	.961	44	95	4	4	2
Dixon, Everett*	.932	51	80	2	6	0
Ealy, Tri-Cities	.963	41	103	2	4	1
Espinosa, Salem	.896	46	65	4	8	0
Ford, Eugene*	.942	47	44	5	3	0
Gavin, Medford	.958	36	41	5	2	1
Gianukakis, Bend	.967	26	29	0	1	0
P. Gilbert, Medford	1.000	13	18	1	0	0
Giles, Salem	.800	7	6	2	2	0
Gilliam, Tri-Cities	1.000	4	6	3	0	1
Gioia, Tri-Cities	.857	3	5	1	1	0
Goff, Eugene	.923	5	11	1	1	0
Graves, Salem	.963	11	24	2	1	0
Greene, Bend	.939	65	144	9	10	2
Greene, Tri-Cities	.934	38	55	2	4	0
Grilione, Salem	.920	51	76	5	7	1
Harrison, Spokane*	.333	8	1	0	2	0
Hodo, Bend	.971	28	33	0	1	0
Hoffinger, Medford	.964	27	51	2	2	0
Holmes, Spokane	.935	32	54	4	4	0
Howard, Spokane	1.000	13	24	3	0	0
Howitt, Medford	.957	57	83	5	4	2
L. Jackson, Tri-Cities*	1.000	1	2	0	0	0
Jackson, Eugene	.921	53	86	7	8	0
Johnson, Bellingham	1.000	8	7	0	0	0
Koentopp, Spokane*	.977	64	81	5	2	1
Larios, Eugene	.722	20	13	0	5	0
Larsen, Eugene	.944	18	17	0	1	0
Leonard, Everett-Tri-Cities	.947	30	53	1	3	0
R. Little, Bellingham	.983	40	54	4	1	0
Miller, Bend	1.000	27	44	2	0	0
Nash, Everett	.963	43	70	7	3	1
Newson, Spokane*	.950	36	54	3	3	0
Pritikin, Bellingham	.942	57	90	7	6	0
Rasmus, Tri-Cities	.962	24	48	3	2	0
Redick, Everett	.951	35	76	2	4	0
Reyes, Salem	1.000	7	3	0	0	0
Ritchie, Everett*	.961	33	70	3	3	1
Ronson, Everett	.966	46	75	9	3	1
Stark, Bend	1.000	16	22	0	0	0
Stevens, Salem*	.959	47	87	6	4	1
Stratton, Medford	.956	44	100	8	5	0
Tartabull, Bellingham	.920	16	23	0	2	0
Taylor, Spokane	.927	53	113	2	9	0
Teixeira, Medford	.979	31	43	3	1	0
Ventress, Bend	.897	28	33	2	4	0
Walker, Everett	1.000	25	42	1	0	0
Wentz, Medford	1.000	3	1	0	0	0
Williams, Bend	1.000	32	32	2	0	0
TE. WILLIAMS, Bellingham	.992	59	126	0	1	0
Tr. Williams, Bellingham	.889	14	16	0	2	0
Wilson, Tri-Cities	.942	39	63	2	4	0
Wolkoys, Eugene	.893	21	23	2	3	2

CATCHERS

Player and Club	Pct.	G.	PO.	A.	E.	DP.	PB.
Bailey, Eugene	.980	19	128	16	3	2	7
Barnett, Bend	.938	11	56	4	4	0	12
Basso, Spokane	.980	42	318	33	7	0	16
Brito, Medford	.969	20	114	11	4	1	3
Britt, Medford	.985	53	358	37	6	3	11
Coonan, Medford	.894	9	39	3	5	0	4
Dyer, Eugene	.886	6	27	4	4	0	3
Escalera, Eugene	.975	48	380	47	11	4	30
Gay, Salem	.942	21	143	18	10	2	16
Gioia, Tri-Cities	.970	13	56	9	2	1	1
Glover, Medford	1.000	1	1	0	0	0	0
Goff, Bellingham	.964	48	286	35	12	7	23
Goff, Eugene	.992	13	118	9	1	0	3
Gunn, Bellingham	.986	32	186	21	3	2	4
Hall, Tri-Cities	.945	52	296	62	21	4	17
HIBBS, Bend	.990	38	258	38	3	3	27
King, Spokane	.971	12	31	2	1	0	3
Knapp, Salem	.973	54	416	47	13	4	26
Leonard, Tri-Cities	1.000	1	1	0	0	0	0
Lutticken, Spokane	.970	30	208	22	7	0	12
McNamara, Everett	.986	40	266	21	4	1	14
Miller, Bend	.959	23	151	11	7	0	9
Morfin, Bellingham	1.000	2	5	0	0	0	0
Nelson, Bend	1.000	6	57	2	0	0	3
Newton, Everett	.974	29	200	22	6	1	2
Pawling, Tri-Cities	.985	23	122	13	2	1	12
Rannow, Everett	.979	11	90	3	2	2	7
Rodriguez, Salem	1.000	10	44	2	0	1	8
Savarino, Medford	.966	8	46	11	2	0	11
Silva, Bend	1.000	4	22	1	0	0	5

PITCHERS

Player and Club	Pct.	G.	PO.	A.	E.	DP.
Adams, Eugene	.864	15	6	13	3	1
Adriance, Tri-Cities*	1.000	21	5	11	0	0
Allison, Bend	.875	16	4	10	2	0
Anderson, Bend	.778	19	3	4	2	0
Armstrong, Tri-Cities	1.000	6	1	0	0	0
Ashby, Bend	.913	16	7	14	2	1
Austin, Spokane	.800	28	2	6	2	0
Auth, Salem	1.000	9	2	1	0	0
Beavers, Medford*	1.000	2	1	3	0	0
Beck, Medford	.800	13	0	4	1	1
Birch, Everett*	1.000	18	4	6	0	0
Bisceglia, Salem*	1.000	17	1	4	0	0
Blasucci, Tri-Cities*	1.000	3	2	5	0	0
Blouin, Eugene	.909	13	0	10	1	1
Blueberg, Bellingham	.933	14	3	11	1	1
Bones, Spokane	1.000	18	9	11	0	0
Brocail, Spokane	.810	16	6	11	4	0
Brockway, Tri-Cities	.769	19	4	6	3	2
Brooks, Spokane*	1.000	6	1	1	0	0
Butcher, Eugene	.900	14	2	7	1	0
Cabrera, Medford	1.000	16	2	4	0	1
Carroll, Medford	.750	26	3	6	3	0
Champagne, Eugene	.889	17	0	8	1	1
Charland, Salem*	.600	5	1	2	2	0
Christopher, Bend*	.920	15	8	15	2	0
Collishaw, Tri-Cities	.852	14	10	13	4	0
Dar. Connelly, Tri-Cities	.667	20	2	6	4	1
Coulter, Bend	1.000	5	1	0	0	0
DeChavez, Tri-Cities	.900	12	4	14	2	1
de la Cruz, Spokane	1.000	6	0	1	0	0
DeLucia, Bellingham	.905	13	10	9	2	1
Ellis, Tri-Cities	.750	16	2	1	1	0
Fetters, Salem	.762	12	3	13	5	0
Fix, Salem*	1.000	9	0	2	0	0
Fortugno, Bellingham*	1.000	6	0	2	0	0
Franco, Salem	1.000	11	0	1	0	0
Gambee, Everett	.727	14	3	5	3	0
R. Gilbert, Medford	.750	11	2	4	2	0
Glover, Medford	.933	15	6	8	1	0
Goodenough, Eugene*	.750	24	0	6	2	0
Green, Salem	.929	14	4	9	1	1
Hansen, Tri-Cities*	.917	16	9	13	2	2
Harris, Spokane*	.882	15	3	12	2	0
Harrison, Spokane-Tri-Cities*	.737	22	2	12	5	1
Hartley, Medford	.714	14	2	3	2	1
HARTNETT, Bellingham*	1.000	18	11	18	0	0
Hernandez, Salem	1.000	10	5	10	0	0
Hibbard, Eugene*	.778	26	3	4	2	0
Higson, Everett	.917	32	3	8	1	0
Holcomb, Medford*	.000	12	0	0	1	0
Intorcia, Bellingham*	1.000	21	4	10	0	1
Jones, Eugene	1.000	30	3	10	0	1
Karcher, Eugene	.846	18	4	7	2	1
Kent, Medford	1.000	17	0	1	0	0
Kiser, Bend*	.889	14	4	12	2	2
Kopyta, Medford	1.000	6	0	1	0	0
Kunkel, Medford	1.000	14	5	11	0	0
Limbach, Bend*	.778	19	2	5	2	1
T. Little, Bellingham	1.000	31	0	1	0	0
MacKenzie, Everett	.833	20	1	4	1	0
Malone, Bend	.917	21	4	7	1	0
Massey, Everett	.850	15	6	11	3	0
McClellan, Everett	.913	13	8	13	2	0
McKinzie, Eugene*	.929	20	0	13	1	1
Mendez, Bellingham	1.000	17	2	3	0	0
Merejo, Salem	.957	20	4	18	1	1
Mills, Salem	.944	14	6	11	1	2
Moeller, Eugene*	.833	14	4	1	1	1
Moore, Bend	1.000	16	2	7	0	0
Mount, Eugene	.833	29	2	3	1	1
Murphy, Tri-Cities	1.000	7	1	2	0	0
Myaer, Bend	1.000	16	0	8	0	0
Navilliat, Spokane*	1.000	9	3	7	0	0
Naworski, Tri-Cities	.891	15	13	28	5	0
Pena, Everett*	.840	14	3	18	4	0
Quinzer, Spokane	.840	16	5	16	4	2
Rich, Bend*	.667	13	0	2	1	1
Ricker, Everett*	1.000	19	0	5	0	0
Riemer, Everett	.750	19	1	2	1	0
Ritchey, Medford	1.000	18	0	7	0	0
Ritchie, Everett*	1.000	1	0	1	0	0
Roberts, Spokane*	1.000	11	5	10	0	1
Rohde, Bellingham	.750	7	0	3	1	0
Romero, Bend	.889	15	4	20	3	2
Ryan, Bellingham	1.000	7	2	3	0	0
Sampson, Spokane*	.933	15	6	8	1	0
Sanchez, Medford	1.000	15	1	3	0	1
Santana, Medford	.800	3	1	3	1	0
Simmermacher, Bellingham*	.947	29	7	11	1	1
Skodny, Eugene*	1.000	10	0	9	0	0
Smith, Tri-Cities	.889	18	3	5	1	1
Sossamon, Bend	.909	18	3	7	1	0
Spearnock, Salem*	.900	16	3	6	1	0
Stancel, Medford	.778	21	1	6	2	0
Stubberfield, Everett	1.000	18	1	2	0	0
Swan, Everett*	1.000	7	2	6	0	0
Tapani, Medford	1.000	2	0	1	0	0
Tate, Everett	.938	13	6	9	1	0
Thorpe, Bellingham	1.000	23	3	8	0	1
Tresemer, Eugene	.833	12	0	5	1	0
Vanderwel, Salem	.895	13	5	12	2	0
Vann, Salem	.933	20	2	12	1	0
Veres, Medford	.833	15	4	11	3	1
Ward, Salem	1.000	27	4	10	0	0
Weber, Medford	.889	13	4	4	1	0
Webster, Bellingham	.875	10	2	5	1	0
Wood, Spokane	.909	24	3	7	1	0
Wooden, Bellingham	.900	15	6	12	2	1
Young, Spokane*	.625	12	3	2	3	0

The following players do not have any recorded accepted chances at the positions indicated: therefore, are not listed in the fielding averages for those particular positions: Barnett, 1b; Basso, of; Bolar, p; Bowie, of, p; Escalera, of; Gay, 2b; Knapp, 1b; McDevitt, of; Minier, ss; Rodriguez, of; Vizcaino, p; Q. Williams, 3b.

CLUB PITCHING

Club	ERA.	G.	CG.	ShO.	Sv.	IP.	H.	R.	ER.	HR.	HB.	BB.	Int. BB.	SO.	WP.	Bk.
Bellingham	3.70	74	5	4	20	637.1	618	380	262	24	38	302	5	483	46	6
Eugene	3.98	74	2	4	20	657.1	610	400	291	21	27	395	17	649	55	5
Medford	4.33	74	0	3	22	662.1	657	433	319	43	26	369	4	544	50	4
Spokane	4.35	74	6	5	17	656.0	654	411	317	27	33	356	11	566	59	6
Everett	4.48	74	9	4	13	652.1	626	426	325	42	29	451	10	538	56	12
Salem	4.68	74	5	2	15	651.1	624	439	339	31	27	438	3	596	55	7
Bend	5.34	74	0	0	13	645.0	649	520	383	30	37	533	24	511	79	6
Tri-Cities	5.59	74	2	0	9	652.1	743	540	405	50	37	406	4	473	69	12

PITCHERS' RECORDS

(Leading Qualifiers for Earned-Run Average Leadership — 59 or More Innings)

*Throws lefthanded.

Pitcher—Club	W.	L.	Pct.	ERA.	G.	GS.	CG.	GF.	ShO.	Sv.	IP.	H.	R.	ER.	HR.	HB.	BB.	Int. BB.	SO.	WP.
DeLucia, Bellingham	8	2	.800	1.70	13	11	1	1	1	0	74.0	44	20	14	4	1	24	0	69	3
Jones, Eugene	6	1	.857	1.82	30	0	0	16	0	2	59.1	52	22	12	3	4	15	4	45	2
Austin, Spokane	5	4	.556	2.26	28	0	0	19	0	5	59.2	53	24	15	1	1	22	2	74	7
Adams, Eugene	4	2	.667	2.90	15	15	0	0	0	0	80.2	61	42	26	2	1	42	0	71	4
Pena, Everett*	10	2	.833	2.92	14	14	4	0	0	0	101.2	86	40	33	7	0	54	0	92	2
Moeller, Eugene*	4	0	1.000	3.06	14	11	0	0	0	0	61.2	54	22	21	1	2	34	0	65	7
Blouin, Eugene	7	4	.636	3.18	13	12	1	0	0	0	76.1	77	32	27	2	1	25	4	79	4
Veres, Medford	5	2	.714	3.26	15	15	0	0	0	0	77.1	58	38	28	5	3	57	0	60	3
McClellan, Everett	5	4	.556	3.34	13	13	2	0	0	0	86.1	71	39	32	2	0	46	0	74	8
Vanderwel, Salem	8	3	.727	3.38	13	13	0	0	1	0	82.2	73	43	31	4	2	35	0	87	5
Hartnett, Bellingham*	5	4	.556	3.38	18	11	0	4	0	0	77.1	78	43	29	5	5	23	0	64	2
Fetters, Salem	4	2	.667	3.38	12	12	1	0	0	0	72.0	60	39	27	4	3	51	0	72	4

Departmental Leaders: G—Higson, 32; W—Pena, 10; L—Allison, Hansen, 8; Pct.—Pena, .833; GS—Nine pitchers with 15; CG—Pena, 4; GF—Higson, 29; ShO—Six pitchers with 1; Sv.—Little, 13; IP—Pena, 101.2; H—Naworski, 102; R—Gambee, 80; ER—Gambee, 56; HR—Collishaw, 10; HB—Naworski, 12; BB—Gambee, 72; IBB—Sossamon, 7; SO—Pena, 92; WP—Hansen, 15.

(All Pitchers—Listed Alphabetically)

Pitcher—Club	W.	L.	Pct.	ERA.	G.	GS.	CG.	GF.	ShO.	Sv.	IP.	H.	R.	ER.	HR.	HB.	BB.	Int. BB.	SO.	WP.
Adams, Eugene	4	2	.667	2.90	15	15	0	0	0	0	80.2	61	42	26	2	1	42	0	71	4
Adriance, Tri-Cities*	1	5	.167	5.35	21	6	0	12	0	1	74.0	81	53	44	5	0	39	1	47	3
Allison, Bend	0	8	.000	6.39	16	6	0	4	0	1	50.2	62	53	36	3	2	55	0	32	7
Anderson, Bend	0	2	.000	3.86	19	0	0	10	0	0	32.2	35	25	14	3	1	21	1	31	3
Armstrong, Tri-Cities	0	0	.000	3.95	6	0	0	1	0	0	13.2	9	6	6	0	2	15	0	18	4
Ashby, Bend	1	2	.333	4.95	16	6	0	4	0	2	60.0	56	40	33	3	2	34	1	45	3
Austin, Spokane	5	4	.556	2.26	28	0	0	19	0	5	59.2	53	24	15	1	1	22	2	74	7
Auth, Salem	0	2	.000	17.18	9	2	0	2	0	0	11.0	20	25	21	2	3	19	0	7	7
Beavers, Medford*	1	0	1.000	0.00	2	1	0	0	0	0	9.0	1	0	0	0	0	2	0	11	2
Beck, Medford	1	3	.250	5.23	13	6	0	5	0	1	32.2	47	25	19	4	1	11	1	21	4
Birch, Everett*	1	0	1.000	5.75	18	0	0	3	0	1	36.0	35	29	23	2	4	39	1	34	3
Bisceglia, Salem*	2	4	.333	5.54	17	0	0	9	0	0	37.1	33	28	23	4	4	25	0	38	2
Blasucci, Tri-Cities*	0	1	.000	7.20	3	1	0	1	0	0	10.0	12	9	8	0	0	8	0	6	0
Blouin, Eugene	7	4	.636	3.18	13	12	1	0	0	0	76.1	77	32	27	2	1	25	4	79	4
Blueberg, Bellingham	5	6	.455	3.69	14	14	1	0	0	0	70.2	74	46	29	1	8	28	0	48	7
Bolar, Bellingham	0	0	.000	27.00	1	0	0	1	0	0	1.0	3	3	3	1	0	1	0	0	0
Bones, Spokane	1	3	.250	5.59	18	9	0	4	0	0	58.0	63	44	36	3	1	29	1	46	7
Bowie, Bellingham*	0	0	.000	6.00	2	0	0	2	0	0	3.0	5	5	2	0	0	3	0	2	0
Brocail, Spokane	5	4	.556	3.81	16	15	0	1	0	0	85.0	85	52	36	4	6	53	1	77	10
Brockway, Tri-Cities	2	6	.250	6.71	19	5	0	6	0	2	59.0	71	50	44	6	1	34	1	46	5
Brooks, Spokane*	1	0	1.000	4.38	6	0	0	3	0	0	12.1	16	14	6	0	1	11	0	9	2
Butcher, Eugene	5	4	.556	3.86	14	14	1	0	0	0	72.1	51	39	31	2	7	49	0	68	5
Cabrera, Medford	2	3	.400	3.62	16	0	0	5	0	0	27.1	30	14	11	2	1	14	0	14	3
Carroll, Medford	1	2	.333	3.09	26	0	0	11	0	5	55.1	48	33	19	2	1	38	0	54	3
Champagne, Eugene	3	3	.500	8.44	17	6	0	2	0	0	37.1	57	55	35	0	1	34	1	41	5
Charland, Salem*	4	0	1.000	1.45	5	5	0	0	0	0	31.0	16	7	5	0	1	15	0	49	0
Christopher, Bend*	4	6	.400	4.23	15	13	0	0	0	0	78.2	65	55	37	1	6	60	3	54	9
Collishaw, Tri-Cities	3	6	.333	4.46	14	14	0	0	0	0	78.2	83	59	39	10	4	39	0	40	4
Connelly, Dar., Tri-Cities	0	5	.000	8.13	20	4	0	9	0	2	55.1	74	58	50	8	3	37	0	37	1
Coulter, Bend	1	0	1.000	3.00	5	1	0	1	0	0	12.0	12	8	4	1	1	3	0	9	4
DeChavez, Tri-Cities	2	3	.400	5.29	12	10	0	0	0	0	66.1	81	50	39	3	4	38	0	43	7
de la Cruz, Spokane	0	0	.000	5.40	6	0	0	3	0	0	6.2	9	10	4	0	3	7	0	2	0
DeLucia, Bellingham	8	2	.800	1.70	13	11	1	1	1	0	74.0	44	20	14	4	1	24	0	69	3
Ellis, Tri-Cities	3	3	.500	4.38	16	0	0	15	0	0	24.2	24	17	12	0	0	21	0	27	4
Fetters, Salem	4	2	.667	3.38	12	12	1	0	0	0	72.0	60	39	27	4	3	51	0	72	4
Fix, Salem*	1	0	1.000	4.66	9	0	0	5	0	0	9.2	8	8	5	1	0	8	0	13	0
Fortugno, Bellingham*	0	0	.000	1.13	6	0	0	4	0	1	8.0	2	2	1	0	1	12	1	11	1
Franco, Salem	0	0	.000	8.40	11	0	0	6	0	0	15.0	23	15	14	1	0	8	0	7	2
Gambee, Everett	0	6	.000	10.01	14	13	0	0	0	0	50.1	72	80	56	7	4	72	0	51	9
Gilbert, Medford	1	1	.500	7.62	11	5	0	1	0	0	28.1	36	32	24	3	0	26	0	15	2
Glover, Medford	8	2	.800	4.88	15	15	0	0	0	0	83.0	87	56	45	7	2	37	0	63	2
Goodenough, Eugene*	0	3	.000	6.11	24	4	0	5	0	1	45.2	43	35	31	1	0	55	2	51	7
Green, Salem	1	6	.143	5.99	14	14	0	0	0	0	76.2	86	61	51	5	1	54	1	59	5
Hansen, Tri-Cities*	3	8	.273	5.04	16	15	1	0	0	0	89.1	96	76	50	5	6	58	0	51	15
Harris, Spokane*	4	5	.444	6.62	15	10	1	5	0	2	68.0	85	56	50	4	6	30	0	58	5
Harrison, 8 Spokane-14 TC*	3	5	.375	6.20	22	5	0	11	0	2	61.0	66	56	42	5	3	60	1	64	11
Hartley, Medford	2	1	.667	5.82	14	0	0	5	0	1	21.2	26	21	14	0	0	21	1	12	1
Hartnett, Bellingham*	5	4	.556	3.38	18	11	0	4	0	0	77.1	78	43	29	5	5	23	0	64	2
Hernandez, Salem	2	2	.500	4.58	10	10	0	0	0	0	55.0	57	37	28	3	1	42	1	38	6
Hibbard, Eugene*	5	2	.714	3.46	26	1	0	15	0	5	39.0	30	23	15	2	2	19	0	44	0
Higson, Everett	5	4	.556	2.05	32	0	0	29	0	9	44.0	35	12	10	2	0	25	4	44	3
Holcomb, Medford*	1	2	.333	2.94	12	4	0	3	0	0	33.2	30	12	11	2	1	19	1	40	1
Intorcia, Bellingham*	5	2	.714	5.04	21	5	1	8	1	0	55.1	61	46	31	1	1	25	0	29	4
Jones, Eugene	6	1	.857	1.82	30	0	0	16	0	2	59.1	52	22	12	3	4	15	4	45	2
Karcher, Eugene	1	4	.200	4.93	18	1	0	5	0	1	38.1	39	30	21	1	2	30	2	35	7
Kent, Medford	2	0	1.000	2.83	17	0	0	16	0	7	28.2	25	13	9	1	2	15	0	29	1
Kiser, Bend*	4	5	.444	5.48	14	12	0	2	0	0	70.2	79	58	43	4	2	48	2	46	6
Kopyta, Medford	0	0	.000	5.52	6	0	0	3	0	1	14.2	13	12	9	1	0	13	0	12	3
Kunkel, Medford	5	6	.455	6.57	14	13	0	0	0	0	63.0	77	54	46	6	2	19	0	42	8
Limbach, Bend*	0	2	.000	3.89	19	2	0	10	0	2	41.2	38	27	18	2	0	31	2	33	6
Little, Bellingham	4	1	.800	1.10	31	0	0	28	0	13	41.0	29	10	5	0	2	23	2	50	4
MacKenzie, Everett	1	2	.333	3.79	20	1	0	6	0	1	35.2	32	27	15	1	5	27	1	23	1
Malone, Bend	2	6	.250	5.10	21	3	0	11	0	2	54.2	47	38	31	0	2	50	2	60	4
Massey, Everett	2	4	.333	4.76	15	10	0	0	0	0	70.0	81	49	37	5	1	47	2	34	5
McClellan, Everett	5	4	.556	3.34	13	13	2	0	0	0	86.1	71	39	32	2	0	46	0	74	8
McKinzie, Eugene*	2	1	.667	4.44	20	4	0	7	0	1	46.2	53	35	23	4	1	15	1	36	6
Mendez, Bellingham	0	0	.000	5.03	17	0	0	9	0	3	34.0	43	32	19	4	7	17	0	13	1
Merejo, Salem	2	4	.333	2.21	20	0	0	14	0	6	40.2	36	15	10	1	3	22	1	26	2
Mills, Salem	6	6	.500	4.63	14	14	1	0	0	0	83.2	77	58	43	1	5	60	0	50	5
Moeller, Eugene*	4	0	1.000	3.06	14	11	0	0	0	0	61.2	54	22	21	1	2	34	0	65	7
Moore, Bend	2	5	.286	5.88	16	0	0	14	0	4	33.2	32	29	22	4	1	22	5	35	7
Mount, Eugene	3	2	.600	3.35	29	0	0	16	0	8	45.2	31	22	17	1	2	34	0	70	8
Murphy, Tri-Cities	1	0	1.000	2.25	7	0	0	7	0	1	12.0	18	5	3	0	1	3	0	10	2
Myaer, Bend	1	4	.200	6.44	16	8	0	6	0	0	58.2	57	51	42	4	1	58	0	43	4
Navilliat, Spokane*	3	2	.600	5.61	9	5	0	1	0	0	33.2	40	25	21	4	0	22	0	21	1
Naworski, Tri-Cities	6	6	.500	4.99	15	15	1	0	0	0	92.0	102	79	51	8	12	48	1	68	10
Pena, Everett*	10	2	.833	2.92	14	14	4	0	0	0	101.2	86	40	33	7	0	54	0	92	2
Quinzer, Spokane	5	5	.500	3.48	16	15	2	1	1	0	101.0	100	52	39	3	1	29	0	75	4
Rich, Bend*	1	0	1.000	8.15	13	1	0	4	0	0	17.2	20	22	16	0	2	36	0	16	9
Ricker, Everett*	3	1	.750	4.88	19	0	0	10	0	0	31.1	27	23	17	2	5	27	0	28	9
Riemer, Everett	4	4	.500	4.17	19	3	0	5	0	1	49.2	52	30	23	4	1	31	2	38	7
Ritchey, Medford	2	0	1.000	4.78	18	0	0	6	0	1	32.0	29	20	17	1	2	20	0	19	4
Ritchie, Everett*	0	0	.000	0.00	1	0	0	0	0	0	0.1	0	0	0	0	0	2	0	0	0
Roberts, Spokane*	7	2	.778	3.84	11	8	2	3	0	1	68.0	66	29	29	3	2	23	0	61	2
Rohde, Bellingham	0	1	.000	3.75	7	1	0	1	0	0	12.0	11	10	5	0	1	12	0	8	2
Romero, Bend	4	7	.364	4.58	15	15	0	0	0	0	76.2	81	59	39	2	7	64	1	50	9
Ryan, Bellingham	2	2	.500	3.21	7	6	0	0	0	0	28.0	30	12	10	1	0	6	0	16	1
Sampson, Spokane*	3	4	.429	4.15	15	7	1	4	1	3	56.1	47	31	26	3	3	29	1	45	4
Sanchez, Medford	0	1	.000	5.75	15	0	0	6	0	0	20.1	27	23	13	2	1	12	0	12	2
Santana, Medford	1	1	.500	8.71	3	0	0	1	0	1	10.1	15	12	10	1	1	5	0	13	0
Simmermacher, Bellingham*	2	2	.500	3.94	29	0	0	6	0	1	48.0	46	34	21	0	4	32	1	39	8
Skodny, Eugene*	2	1	.667	5.79	10	0	0	4	0	1	18.2	20	13	12	0	1	15	2	16	0

Pitcher—Club	W.	L.	Pct.	ERA.	G.	GS.	CG.	GF.	ShO.	Sv.	IP.	H.	R.	ER.	HR.	HB.	BB.	Int. BB.	SO.	WP.
Smith, Tri-Cities	2	2	.500	7.07	18	2	0	12	0	1	35.2	45	38	28	1	2	29	0	30	8
Sossamon, Bend	1	6	.143	7.53	18	7	0	8	0	2	57.1	65	55	48	3	10	51	7	57	8
Spearnock, Salem*	1	1	.500	6.12	16	0	0	3	0	0	32.1	36	26	22	2	2	26	0	30	2
Stancel, Medford	5	2	.714	3.33	21	0	0	12	0	5	48.2	38	23	18	2	5	29	1	49	6
Stubberfield, Everett	0	1	.000	8.72	18	0	0	13	0	1	21.2	29	23	21	1	2	19	0	14	2
Swan, Everett*	5	0	1.000	2.15	7	7	2	0	0	0	46.0	30	17	11	2	1	22	0	45	1
Tapani, Medford	1	0	1.000	0.00	2	2	0	0	0	0	8.1	6	3	0	0	0	3	0	9	0
Tate, Everett	4	6	.400	5.33	13	13	1	0	0	0	79.1	76	57	47	7	6	40	0	61	6
Thorpe, Bellingham	6	2	.750	4.81	23	2	0	5	0	2	48.2	39	31	26	1	3	48	1	35	7
Tresemer, Eugene	3	2	.600	5.05	12	6	0	2	0	1	35.2	42	30	20	2	3	28	1	28	0
Vanderwel, Salem	8	3	.727	3.38	13	13	3	0	1	0	82.2	73	43	31	4	2	35	0	87	5
Vann, Salem	3	0	1.000	7.06	20	4	0	6	0	0	51.0	56	53	40	0	1	51	0	46	10
Veres, Medford	5	2	.714	3.26	15	15	0	0	0	0	77.1	58	38	28	5	3	57	0	60	3
Vizcaino, Spokane	0	0	.000	5.40	3	0	0	2	0	0	5.0	8	4	3	0	0	6	0	3	0
Ward, Salem	4	6	.400	3.21	27	0	0	24	0	9	53.1	43	24	19	3	1	22	0	74	5
Weber, Medford	5	5	.500	3.44	13	13	0	0	0	0	68.0	64	42	26	4	4	28	0	69	5
Webster, Bellingham	2	3	.400	5.72	10	9	0	0	0	0	45.2	58	39	29	1	3	25	0	35	2
Wood, Spokane	2	2	.500	3.80	24	0	0	15	0	5	64.0	50	37	27	1	6	46	5	72	5
Wooden, Bellingham	6	4	.600	3.77	15	15	2	0	1	0	90.2	95	47	38	5	2	23	0	64	4
Young, Spokane*	2	3	.400	7.58	12	2	0	6	0	1	19.0	13	17	16	0	2	26	1	9	7

BALKS—DeChavez, Harrison, Mendez, Spearnock, 3 each; Birch, Bones, Brockway, Collishaw, Moeller, Naworski, Pena, Stubberfield, Tate, 2 each; Anderson, Ashby, Bisceglia, Blueberg, Brocail, Butcher, Champagne, Christopher, Fetters, Gambee, Glover, Green, Hansen, Hartley, Karcher, Kiser, Malone, Navilliat, Ricker, Riemer, Rohde, Romero, Ryan, Sampson, Swan, Vann, Veres, Weber, 1 each.

COMBINATION SHUTOUTS—Ryan-Hartnett-Little, Bellingham; Butcher-Mount-Skodny, Adams-Karcher, Moeller-Champagne-Jones, Moeller-Jones, Eugene; McClellan-Stubberfield, Pena-Stubberfield-Higson, Riemer-Birch-Ricker, Tate-Ricker, Everett; Veres-Holcomb-Kent, Weber-Carroll, Weber-Sanchez, Medford; Charland-Vann-Ward, Salem; Brocail-Wood, Harrison-Sampson, Quinzer-Wood, Spokane.

NO-HIT GAME—DeLucia, Bellingham, defeated Everett, 1-0 (seven innings, first game), July 17.

South Atlantic League

CLASS A

CHAMPIONSHIP WINNERS IN PREVIOUS YEARS

Year	Club	Pct.
1948	Lincolnton*	.627
1949	Newton-Conover	.667
	Ruth'ford Co. (2nd)†	.627
1950	Newton-Conover	.627
	Lenoir (2nd)†	.626
1951	Morganton	.645
	Shelby (2nd)†	.604
1952	Lincolnton	.649
	Shelby (2nd)†	.645
1953-59	League inactive.	
1960	Lexington	.707
	Salisbury (2nd)†	.650
1961	Salisbury	.627
	Shelby (4th)†	.481
1962	Statesville	.563
	Statesville	.700
1963	Greenville†	.576
	Salisbury	.631
1964	Rock Hill	.672
	Salisbury‡	.631
1965	Salisbury	.641
	Rock Hill‡	.603
1966	Spartanburg	.682
	Spartanburg	.767
1967	Spartanburg	.730
	Spartanburg	.567
1968	Spartanburg	.597
	Greenwood‡	.597
1969	Greenwood‡	.587
	Shelby	.565
1970	Greenville	.576
	Greenville	.619
1971	Greenwood	.631
	Greenwood	.759
1972	Spartanburg‡	.788
	Greenville	.652
1973	Spartanburg‡	.646
	Gastonia	.619
1974	Gastonia	.606
	Gastonia	.672
1975	Spartanburg	.543
	Spartanburg	.614
1976	Asheville	.544
	Greenwood‡	.600
1977	Greenwood	.557
	Gastonia‡	.590
1978	Greenwood	.614
	Greenwood	.565
1979	Greenwood‡	.565
	Spartanburg	.525
1980	Greensboro	.590
	Charleston	.561
1981	Greensboro‡	.695
	Greenwood	.549
1982	Greensboro‡	.681
	Florence	.546
1983	Columbia	.620
	Gastonia‡	.587
1984	Charleston	.549
	Asheville‡	.510
1985	Florence‡	.599
	Greensboro	.540

*Won championship and four-club playoff. †Won four-club playoff. ‡Won split-season playoff. (NOTE—Known as Western Carolina League from 1948 through 1962 and known as Western Carolinas League through 1979.)

STANDING OF CLUBS AT CLOSE OF FIRST HALF, JUNE 19

NORTHERN DIVISION

Club	W.	L.	T.	Pct.	G.B.
Asheville (Astros)	44	26	0	.629	....
Greensboro (Red Sox)	41	29	0	.586	3
Sumter (Braves)	39	30	0	.565	4½
Gastonia (Tigers)	27	43	0	.386	17
Spartanburg (Phillies)	21	47	0	.309	22

SOUTHERN DIVISION

Club	W.	L.	T.	Pct.	G.B.
Columbia (Mets)	48	22	0	.686	....
Savannah (Cardinals)	37	30	0	.552	9½
Charleston (Padres)	36	34	0	.514	12
Macon (Pirates)	27	42	0	.391	20½
Florence (Blue Jays)	25	42	0	.373	21½

STANDING OF CLUBS AT CLOSE OF SECOND HALF, AUGUST 31

NORTHERN DIVISION

Club	W.	L.	T.	Pct.	G.B.
Asheville (Astros)	46	24	0	.657	....
Sumter (Braves)	38	30	0	.559	7
Greensboro (Red Sox)	34	34	0	.500	11
Gastonia (Tigers)	32	37	0	.464	13½
Spartanburg (Phillies)	19	48	0	.284	25½

SOUTHERN DIVISION

Club	W.	L.	T.	Pct.	G.B.
Columbia (Mets)	42	20	0	.677	....
Savannah (Cardinals)	38	30	0	.559	7
Florence (Blue Jays)	31	34	0	.477	12½
Charleston (Padres)	27	35	0	.435	15
Macon (Pirates)	27	42	0	.391	18½

COMPOSITE STANDING OF CLUBS AT CLOSE OF SEASON, AUGUST 31

Club	Col.	Ash.	Sum.	Sav.	Gbr.	Char.	Gas.	Flo.	Mac.	Spar.	W.	L.	T.	Pct.	G.B.
Columbia (Mets)	....	6	8	13	8	10	5	12	16	12	90	42	0	.682	....
Asheville (Astros)	6	....	8	5	13	6	16	8	11	17	90	50	0	.643	4
Sumter (Braves)	4	12	....	8	6	7	12	6	10	12	77	60	0	.562	15½
Savannah (Cardinals)	7	7	3	....	7	11	7	13	15	5	75	60	0	.556	16½
Greensboro (Red Sox)	3	7	14	5	....	8	10	9	6	13	75	63	0	.543	18
Charleston (Padres)	6	6	5	7	4	....	7	11	11	6	63	69	0	.477	27
Gastonia (Tigers)	7	4	8	5	10	5	....	3	4	13	59	80	0	.424	34½
Florence (Blue Jays)	6	4	6	6	3	7	8	....	10	6	56	76	0	.424	34
Macon (Pirates)	3	1	2	5	6	9	8	9	....	11	54	84	0	.391	39
Spartanburg (Phillies)	0	3	6	6	6	6	7	5	1	....	40	95	0	.296	51½

Major league affiliations in parentheses.

Playoffs—Columbia defeated Asheville, three games to one, to win league championship.

Regular-Season Attendance—Asheville, 101,962; Charleston, 131,696; Columbia, 106,403; Florence, 36,010; Gastonia, 79,029; Greensboro, 180,715; Macon, 37,816; Savannah, 44,787; Spartanburg, 16,833; Sumter, 45,290. Total—780,541. Playoffs—3,933. All-Star Game—3,527.

Managers—Asheville, Ken Bolek; Charleston, Pat Kelly; Columbia, Tucker Ashford; Florence, Hector Torres; Gastonia, John Lipon; Greensboro, Doug Camilli; Macon, Mike Quade; Savannah, Mark DeJohn; Spartanburg, Rolando deArmas; Sumter, Brian Snitker.

All-Star Team—1B—Rich Johnson, Asheville; 2B—Dave Gelatt, Columbia; 3B—Carlo Columbino, Asheville; SS—Juan Villanueva, Columbia; OF—Cameron Drew, Asheville; Carlos Quintana, Greensboro; Alan Hayden, Columbia; C—Dan Walters, Asheville; DH—Paul Thoutsis, Greensboro; RHP—Kevin Armstrong, Columbia; LHP—Rob Livchak, Savannah; Most Outstanding Pitcher-Blaise Ilsley, Asheville; Most Valuable Player-Cameron Drew, Asheville; Manager of the Year—Tucker Ashford, Columbia.

(Compiled by Howe News Bureau, Boston, Mass.)

CLUB BATTING

Club	Pct.	G.	AB.	R.	OR.	H.	TB.	2B.	3B.	HR.	RBI.	GW.	SH.	SF.	HP.	BB.	Int. BB.	SO.	SB.	CS.	LOB.
Asheville	.284	140	4764	870	622	1352	2046	253	30	127	735	77	60	33	56	674	16	874	131	52	1133
Columbia	.274	132	4514	836	562	1239	1802	206	39	93	716	70	21	43	55	636	18	819	292	74	1013
Greensboro	.265	138	4650	810	767	1234	1886	210	41	120	713	66	43	61	51	818	13	877	120	49	1225
Sumter	.255	137	4584	731	667	1168	1615	195	21	70	609	62	62	42	46	656	22	891	163	70	1082

Club	Pct.	G.	AB.	R.	OR.	H.	TB.	2B.	3B.	HR.	RBI.	GW.	SH.	SF.	HP.	BB.	Int. BB.	SO.	SB.	CS.	LOB.
Florence	.249	132	4336	641	792	1080	1621	158	34	105	551	49	19	36	36	514	11	1053	167	69	903
Gastonia	.246	139	4452	661	779	1095	1543	175	24	75	547	49	44	32	41	662	16	979	181	63	1031
Macon	.243	138	4468	582	667	1086	1516	187	24	65	516	48	31	44	30	508	14	960	156	52	989
Charleston	.237	132	4223	587	592	1002	1428	165	33	65	498	47	40	37	39	593	14	816	175	80	966
Savannah	.230	135	4272	590	563	982	1361	130	21	69	498	64	51	36	34	708	18	890	168	91	1029
Spartanburg	.224	135	4334	526	823	971	1383	169	21	67	445	38	25	45	46	598	13	988	114	52	1039

INDIVIDUAL BATTING

(Leading Qualifiers for Batting Championship—378 or More Plate Appearances)

*Bats lefthanded. †Switch-hitter.

Player and Club	Pct.	G.	AB.	R.	H.	TB.	2B.	3B.	HR.	RBI.	GW.	SH.	SF.	HP.	BB.	Int. BB.	SO.	SB.	CS.
Colombino, Carlo, Asheville	.339	92	360	77	122	180	35	4	5	58	8	2	2	10	24	4	26	12	7
Drew, Cameron, Asheville*	.326	124	439	77	143	255	26	4	26	117	13	0	5	7	36	3	59	8	3
Quintana, Carlos, Greensboro	.325	126	443	97	144	204	19	4	11	81	10	3	6	4	90	1	54	26	9
Hayden, Alan, Columbia*	.322	109	404	100	130	162	16	5	2	33	0	3	3	5	48	0	36	85	17
Markley, Scott, Asheville*	.315	119	466	113	147	196	23	7	4	47	3	7	2	2	78	0	33	41	4
Johnson, Dodd, Sumter	.302	108	411	69	124	168	20	0	8	66	8	0	5	5	46	3	82	14	9
DeLaCruz, Hector, Florence	.296	94	348	52	103	144	21	1	6	47	4	0	4	1	31	0	82	33	15
Roberts, John, Greensboro	.295	124	478	76	141	204	18	12	7	51	4	5	3	5	68	2	35	32	8
Munoz, Pedro, Florence	.294	122	445	69	131	199	16	5	14	82	7	2	2	5	54	4	100	9	5
Repoz, Craig, Columbia	.292	119	421	80	123	168	22	1	7	78	6	0	7	8	86	3	67	6	5
Perez, Julio, Macon	.292	121	466	67	136	170	18	5	2	45	4	3	2	4	37	0	65	32	7

Departmental Leaders: G—Hood, 135; AB—Hood, 562; R—Markley, 113; H—Markley, 147; TB—Drew, 255; 2B—Colombino, 35; 3B—Roberts, 12; HR—Drew, 26; RBI—Drew, 117; GWRBI—Contreras, Drew, 13; SH—Elliott, 11; SF—Thoutsis, 11; HP—Gelatt, 12; BB—Ashkinazy, 117; IBB—Seven players with 4; SO—Davis, 161; SB—Hayden, 85; CS—McCray, 32.

(All Players—Listed Alphabetically)

Player and Club	Pct.	G.	AB.	R.	H.	TB.	2B.	3B.	HR.	RBI.	GW.	SH.	SF.	HP.	BB.	Int. BB.	SO.	SB.	CS.
Abner, Benjamin, Macon	.333	64	210	35	70	103	17	2	4	31	2	0	4	1	19	0	24	6	1
Abrell, Thomas, Sumter	.000	3	2	0	0	0	0	0	0	1	0	1	0	0	0	0	1	0	0
Akins, Sidney, Sumter	.000	6	6	0	0	0	0	0	0	1	0	2	1	0	0	0	3	0	0
Alva, John, Sumter	.227	129	462	41	105	124	15	2	0	60	3	4	3	3	37	0	71	12	0
Alyea, Brant, Florence	.255	83	322	37	82	125	17	1	8	46	6	3	2	1	23	0	71	3	2
Andersh, Kevin, Macon	.182	27	22	2	4	5	1	0	0	1	0	4	0	0	4	0	11	0	0
Archibald, Jaime, Columbia*	.344	35	125	21	43	59	5	1	3	36	2	0	6	0	21	3	24	2	1
Armstrong, Kevin, Columbia	.185	26	27	3	5	5	0	0	0	0	0	1	0	0	5	0	10	0	0
Arnsberg, Timothy, Asheville	.250	3	4	0	1	1	0	0	0	0	0	0	0	0	0	0	2	0	0
Ashkinazy, Alan, Greensboro	.230	104	387	71	89	98	7	1	0	26	2	7	2	1	117	0	38	31	17
Baerga, Carlos, Charleston†	.270	111	378	57	102	145	14	4	7	41	4	2	5	5	26	1	60	6	1
Bailey, Brandon, Columbia	.234	103	333	57	78	136	16	0	14	48	4	0	4	2	57	1	77	3	3
Baldwin, Jeffrey, Asheville*	.272	118	346	66	94	153	14	3	13	69	7	1	5	5	69	0	64	5	6
Barry, Kirk, Macon	.146	21	41	1	6	6	0	0	0	5	0	0	1	1	3	0	14	1	1
Bastinck, Derek, Gastonia	.238	99	286	39	68	95	11	2	4	39	5	0	3	2	55	0	42	4	1
Batista, Miguel, Charleston	.143	26	63	3	9	9	0	0	0	7	1	0	0	3	5	0	16	1	3
Batiste, Kevin, Florence	.265	49	181	33	48	67	8	1	3	16	1	0	0	2	30	0	56	20	4
Bayer, Christopher, Columbia†	.083	20	12	1	1	1	0	0	0	1	1	2	0	0	2	0	8	0	0
Beck, Dion, Spartanburg*	.500	14	2	1	1	1	0	0	0	1	0	0	1	0	1	0	0	0	0
Bianco, Ronald, Sumter†	.184	56	98	17	18	24	3	0	1	4	2	1	0	0	25	1	34	1	3
Bivens, William, Savannah	.125	5	8	0	1	2	1	0	0	1	0	0	0	0	0	0	4	0	0
Blackmun, Benjamin, Spartanburg	.238	70	256	30	61	80	14	1	1	30	4	0	6	5	26	1	35	15	1
Blount, William, Charleston*	.333	26	3	0	1	2	1	0	0	0	0	0	0	0	0	0	1	0	0
Borders, Patrick, Florence	.375	16	40	8	15	31	7	0	3	9	0	0	0	0	2	0	9	0	0
Bradshaw, Kevin, Gastonia	.269	94	279	50	75	79	4	0	0	22	0	9	2	2	62	0	36	8	7
Brooks, Desmond, Columbia	.356	15	45	8	16	24	1	2	1	8	1	0	0	1	12	0	6	1	0
Brundage, David, Spartanburg*	.239	38	109	12	26	30	4	0	0	11	1	1	2	0	24	0	22	3	2
Brunswick, Mark, Columbia	.272	62	184	20	50	55	5	0	0	25	2	0	0	1	23	2	26	0	1
Cabrera, Victor, Charleston	.183	48	131	6	24	29	3	1	0	6	0	1	1	0	9	1	23	2	1
Callas, Peter, Spartanburg*	.214	119	360	45	77	147	22	0	16	59	4	1	2	1	71	2	104	1	0
Camilli, Kevin, Greensboro*	.200	39	100	12	20	27	7	0	0	7	0	1	1	0	22	0	28	1	0
Camp, Scott, Asheville*	.000	15	10	0	0	0	0	0	0	0	0	2	0	0	1	0	4	0	0
Castro, Genaro, Columbia	.125	2	8	0	1	2	1	0	0	1	0	0	0	0	2	0	1	0	0
Cepeda, Octavio, Macon	.167	29	18	1	3	6	0	0	1	2	0	2	0	0	2	0	8	0	0
Chance, Anthony, Macon	.232	108	366	52	85	154	12	3	17	55	5	5	5	3	38	3	99	18	2
Chapman, Ronald, Gastonia†	.345	10	29	4	10	15	2	0	1	3	0	1	0	0	9	0	2	3	0
Chaves, Rafael, Charleston	.000	39	7	0	0	0	0	0	0	0	0	0	0	0	1	0	2	0	0
Cheek, Carey, Macon	.278	98	356	54	99	132	20	2	3	56	8	0	6	5	45	3	55	5	1
Cisco, Jeffrey, Charleston†	.194	45	124	11	24	28	1	0	1	8	0	1	1	3	15	0	32	3	0
Ciszkowski, Jeffrey, Columbia	.333	9	6	0	2	2	0	0	0	0	0	0	0	0	0	0	2	0	0
Clawson, Christopher, Asheville	.234	64	175	40	41	74	9	0	8	27	2	1	0	3	42	1	48	7	1
Clemente, Roberto, Charleston	.229	31	70	6	16	18	2	0	0	2	2	1	0	0	8	0	20	1	2
Clossen, William, Sumter	.043	23	23	2	1	1	0	0	0	1	0	0	1	0	2	0	14	0	0
Coffman, Kevin, Sumter	.200	19	20	1	4	5	1	0	0	2	0	4	0	1	2	0	8	0	0
Collins, Timothy, Spartanburg	.333	5	3	0	1	2	1	0	0	0	0	0	0	0	0	0	2	0	0
Colombino, Carlo, Asheville	.339	92	360	77	122	180	35	4	5	58	8	2	2	10	24	4	26	12	7
Colpitt, Michael, Spartanburg	.200	37	5	1	1	1	0	0	0	0	0	0	0	0	0	0	1	0	0
Contreras, Joaquin, Columbia†	.321	77	277	67	89	148	15	4	12	66	13	1	2	3	30	2	43	27	2
Credeur, Todd, Asheville*	.125	24	24	3	3	4	1	0	0	0	0	5	0	0	5	0	9	0	0
Crossley, David, Savannah	.000	16	6	0	0	0	0	0	0	0	0	0	0	0	0	0	6	0	0
Cuevas, Angelo, Columbia*	.336	37	128	20	43	55	6	0	2	26	2	0	0	1	23	2	12	0	0
Cuevas, Johnny, Sumter	.257	61	175	18	45	62	5	0	4	22	0	2	1	3	17	1	33	1	2
Daily, Richard, Gastonia†	.230	128	417	60	96	150	17	5	9	68	8	3	3	7	105	4	116	9	3
Dantzler, Shawn, Spartanburg	.333	27	99	13	33	46	6	2	1	17	3	0	3	2	5	1	21	1	1
David, Gregory, Florence*	.241	112	377	61	91	139	13	1	11	47	1	2	7	6	59	3	64	6	4
Davins, James, Macon	.000	44	2	0	0	0	0	0	0	0	0	0	0	0	0	0	0	0	0
Davis, Wayne, Florence	.205	118	439	63	90	151	9	2	16	34	3	1	0	7	28	0	161	18	10
Dean, Roger, Gastonia	.171	10	35	5	6	8	2	0	0	4	0	0	0	0	4	0	11	0	0
DeCordova, David, Savannah*	.111	34	9	0	1	1	0	0	0	0	0	0	0	0	4	0	4	0	0
DeLaCruz, Hector, Florence	.296	94	348	52	103	144	21	1	6	47	4	0	4	1	31	0	82	33	15
DeLeon, Pedro, Asheville	.188	27	32	2	6	8	2	0	0	4	0	4	0	0	0	0	8	0	0

Player and Club	Pct.	G.	AB.	R.	H.	TB.	2B.	3B.	HR.	RBI.	GW.	SH.	SF.	HP.	BB.	Int. BB.	SO.	SB.	CS.
DeLoach, Bobby, Savannah	.194	15	62	7	12	18	2	2	0	4	1	0	0	0	3	0	19	0	0
DeLuca, Kurt, Columbia	.294	86	269	53	79	117	18	4	4	42	10	1	2	1	45	0	38	33	6
Denkenberger, Ralph, Macon*	.203	16	64	3	13	17	4	0	0	4	1	0	0	0	1	0	19	1	1
Diaz, Jose, Florence	.236	61	203	34	48	69	4	1	5	23	3	4	4	2	38	0	39	3	4
Donatelli, Andrew, Spartanburg	.277	95	303	43	84	104	11	3	1	29	4	0	4	1	56	0	28	9	3
Downs, Dorley, Macon	.000	26	4	0	0	0	0	0	0	0	0	1	0	0	0	0	2	0	0
Drew, Cameron, Asheville*	.326	124	439	77	143	255	26	4	26	117	13	0	5	7	36	3	59	8	3
Dumas, Donald, Savannah	.000	14	2	0	0	0	0	0	0	0	0	0	0	0	0	0	2	0	0
Eave, Gary, Sumter	.000	25	4	0	0	0	0	0	0	0	0	0	0	0	0	0	2	0	0
Edge, Gregory, Spartanburg†	.256	53	211	31	54	58	4	0	0	8	0	2	0	0	26	1	11	11	9
Edwards, Jeffrey, Asheville	.278	24	72	15	20	27	1	0	2	6	0	0	0	1	15	0	24	3	0
Elliott, John, Asheville	.288	112	358	98	103	139	21	3	3	31	3	11	2	2	107	0	44	16	7
Fascher, Stanley, Asheville	.143	45	7	0	1	1	0	0	0	1	0	1	0	0	2	0	3	0	1
Ferraro, Carl, Charleston*	.273	27	11	2	3	3	0	0	0	0	0	0	0	0	3	0	3	0	0
Flores, Jose, Greensboro†	.248	80	258	29	64	78	6	4	0	27	1	5	1	4	20	1	56	12	4
Foley, Martin, Spartanburg	.152	50	158	12	24	30	4	1	0	6	0	1	0	4	14	2	51	1	3
Forrest, Christopher, Savannah	.296	24	27	6	8	15	2	1	1	4	0	3	2	0	3	0	7	0	0
Foster, Paul, Gastonia	.219	46	151	22	33	60	3	0	8	25	2	0	1	0	17	2	30	2	1
Fox, Blane, Gastonia*	.280	110	386	71	108	154	25	0	7	49	6	0	4	2	60	1	78	55	3
Franchi, Kevin, Macon*	.300	57	10	1	3	3	0	0	0	0	0	0	0	0	1	0	6	0	0
Frazier, Shawn, Sumter	.214	45	112	13	24	28	2	1	0	8	2	3	0	0	9	0	26	8	3
Gaeckle, Christopher, Greensboro	.238	82	273	33	65	87	8	1	4	41	5	4	3	2	61	0	45	0	0
Gangi, Stephen, Sumter	.203	26	69	10	14	23	3	0	2	13	2	1	0	0	8	0	27	0	0
Garrison, Webster, Florence	.240	105	354	47	85	104	10	0	3	40	4	0	3	2	56	3	53	4	7
Gelatt, David, Columbia	.277	118	415	102	115	155	19	6	3	49	5	1	2	12	89	1	68	56	13
Gellinger, Michael, Gastonia†	.226	35	115	28	26	32	4	1	0	12	1	4	1	0	34	0	20	3	2
Giddens, Ronnie, Macon	.252	69	238	32	60	81	7	4	2	27	6	1	1	1	31	0	38	5	3
Gideon, Brett, Macon	.111	6	9	0	1	1	0	0	0	1	0	0	0	0	2	0	4	0	0
Gilkey, Bernard, Savannah	.235	105	374	64	88	129	15	4	6	36	3	3	3	2	84	1	57	32	15
Givens, Brian, Columbia	.147	27	34	1	5	5	0	0	0	1	0	6	0	1	0	0	13	0	0
Goff, Michael, Greensboro	.292	57	192	48	56	101	18	3	7	35	6	1	3	8	40	0	50	3	0
Gonring, Douglas, Asheville*	.287	60	195	22	56	75	10	0	3	36	4	1	3	1	16	0	22	6	2
Gonzalez, Clifford, Columbia*	.257	25	35	4	9	11	0	1	0	4	0	0	0	0	3	0	7	2	1
Graham, Jeffrey, Savannah	.246	59	183	31	45	62	10	2	1	16	1	3	0	0	24	1	52	8	7
Greene, Nathaniel, Spartanburg	.195	51	113	17	22	32	2	1	2	17	1	0	1	1	24	0	37	1	0
Greene, Jeffrey, Sumter	.000	24	2	0	0	0	0	0	0	0	0	0	0	0	0	0	1	0	0
Greene, Thomas, Sumter	.147	28	34	3	5	7	2	0	0	5	1	4	0	0	4	0	7	0	0
Gsellman, Bob, Spartanburg	.165	36	91	12	15	26	5	0	2	15	0	1	1	1	21	1	39	0	1
Guzman, Rodolfo, Sumter	.000	11	3	0	0	0	0	0	0	0	0	0	0	0	0	0	1	0	0
Hackett, John, Savannah*	.000	6	4	0	0	0	0	0	0	0	0	0	0	0	1	0	2	0	0
Hall, Andrew, Macon	.195	41	128	15	25	42	8	0	3	15	0	0	3	0	10	0	49	1	0
Hansen, Raymond, Greensboro*	.286	91	276	53	79	130	15	0	12	44	5	1	5	1	44	2	53	1	0
Hansen, Todd, Macon*	.083	12	12	0	1	1	0	0	0	0	0	1	0	0	0	0	4	0	0
Harris, Gregory, Charleston	.204	28	49	0	10	13	3	0	0	2	0	2	0	0	3	0	14	0	1
Hartley, Michael, Savannah	.000	39	1	0	0	0	0	0	0	0	0	2	0	0	1	0	1	0	0
Hatfield, Robert, Macon	.050	19	20	0	1	1	0	0	0	0	0	0	0	0	3	0	10	0	0
Hayden, Alan, Columbia*	.322	109	404	100	130	162	16	5	2	33	0	3	3	5	48	0	36	85	17
Hayes, Christopher, Columbia	.111	13	18	3	2	2	0	0	0	0	0	0	0	1	2	0	9	0	0
Hendrix, James, Spartanburg	.286	32	14	1	4	4	0	0	0	0	0	0	0	0	3	0	4	0	0
Henion, Scott, Columbia	.000	5	1	0	0	0	0	0	0	0	0	0	0	0	0	0	0	0	0
Hennessy, Michael, Sumter	.000	34	3	0	0	0	0	0	0	0	0	1	0	0	0	0	2	0	0
Hightower, Barry, Columbia	.125	21	16	2	2	2	0	0	0	1	0	0	0	0	2	0	7	0	0
Hithe, Victor, Asheville	.309	47	149	26	46	63	8	0	3	23	0	0	1	1	10	0	33	4	2
Holyfield, Vince, Spartanburg	.218	118	404	55	88	137	16	3	9	38	4	1	1	6	74	0	103	22	12
Hood, Dennis, Sumter	.253	135	562	104	142	194	25	3	7	42	3	10	4	8	62	1	146	43	17
Horsman, Vincent, Florence	.000	29	1	0	0	0	0	0	0	0	0	0	0	0	0	0	1	0	0
Horta, Neder, Asheville	.223	106	336	46	75	94	9	2	2	30	0	7	0	7	58	2	109	12	4
Housie, Wayne, Gastonia†	.259	90	336	55	87	115	10	6	2	29	2	4	1	4	43	0	85	38	13
Housley, Sterling, Florence	.182	43	121	23	22	32	5	1	1	12	1	1	1	1	17	0	35	6	1
Howey, Todd, Spartanburg*	.214	112	370	41	79	121	17	2	7	47	4	0	10	2	52	3	104	9	4
Hufford, Scott, Spartanburg	.209	101	321	43	67	109	16	1	8	36	2	0	4	5	42	0	95	6	2
Hunter, Bertram, Asheville	.208	54	144	24	30	44	5	3	1	18	4	0	2	1	22	0	50	4	1
Ickes, Michael, Greensboro	.209	64	182	23	38	63	8	1	5	21	1	3	4	1	28	0	50	1	1
Iglesias, Luis, Savannah	.229	102	310	37	71	110	14	2	7	34	5	2	0	8	39	0	72	12	4
Ilsley, Blaise, Asheville*	.407	17	27	5	11	14	3	0	0	6	1	5	0	0	1	0	3	0	0
Jackson, Ruben, Gastonia*	.273	57	176	30	48	58	5	1	1	24	2	0	0	1	22	0	31	0	2
James, Troy, Columbia	.250	47	4	0	1	1	0	0	0	0	0	0	0	0	0	0	2	0	0
Jaster, Scott, Columbia	.252	116	437	71	110	180	20	4	14	87	8	0	4	8	38	0	99	35	6
Jefferies, Gregg, Columbia†	.339	25	112	29	38	61	6	1	5	24	3	0	1	0	9	0	10	13	1
Jimenez, Raul, Savannah	.146	54	137	4	20	23	3	0	0	8	0	0	1	0	17	0	30	1	1
Johnson, Dodd, Sumter	.302	108	411	69	124	168	20	0	8	66	8	0	5	5	46	3	82	14	9
Johnson, Richard, Asheville	.396	68	255	61	101	194	19	1	24	78	9	0	1	2	45	3	51	2	3
Johnson, Roger, Spartanburg	.211	42	128	7	27	32	5	0	0	8	1	2	0	0	14	0	26	0	0
Jones, David, Sumter	.273	42	11	0	3	3	0	0	0	1	0	0	0	0	0	0	2	0	0
Jones, Geary, Columbia	.177	42	130	19	23	36	5	1	2	13	0	0	0	2	22	1	45	1	1
Jones, Labarry, Sumter*	.271	98	288	60	78	107	11	0	6	51	7	2	6	3	56	4	31	17	6
Jones, Michael, Florence	.260	12	50	5	13	19	1	1	1	6	1	0	1	1	3	0	5	6	1
Justice, David, Sumter*	.300	61	220	48	66	112	16	0	10	61	9	0	7	5	48	2	28	10	2
Knabenshue, Christopher, Ch'rlton*	.284	102	335	77	95	153	20	4	10	62	3	2	4	2	82	1	82	36	10
Koopmann, Robert, Macon†	.087	19	23	1	2	2	0	0	0	0	0	2	0	0	3	0	17	0	0
Kwolek, Joseph, Asheville	.319	40	144	27	46	67	6	0	5	28	7	1	1	1	18	0	21	2	1
Lara, Crucito, Savannah†	.231	118	390	47	90	109	11	1	2	40	3	7	3	6	31	0	90	11	5
Lemke, Mark, Sumter†	.272	126	448	99	122	204	24	2	18	66	7	5	4	7	87	3	31	11	7
Lester, James, Charleston	.278	96	299	51	83	109	17	3	1	32	8	4	1	4	75	0	45	6	3
Lewis, James, Charleston	.000	51	9	0	0	0	0	0	0	0	0	0	0	0	0	0	6	0	0
Liddell, David, Columbia	.222	18	54	8	12	20	2	0	2	10	0	0	2	0	12	1	16	0	0
Liebert, Allen, Gastonia*	.327	74	245	28	80	114	10	0	8	44	3	1	2	0	27	4	35	0	1
Livchak, Robert, Savannah*	.206	27	34	6	7	16	0	0	3	7	0	3	1	0	2	0	11	0	0
Love, John, Macon	.291	55	213	26	62	83	11	2	2	26	3	0	1	1	21	0	25	10	6
Luciani, Randall, Gastonia	.224	113	392	59	88	161	18	2	17	54	3	1	1	8	26	1	138	2	4
Lundahl, Richard, Columbia	.000	1	4	0	0	0	0	0	0	0	0	0	0	0	0	0	1	0	0
Machado, Julio, Spartanburg	.000	44	2	1	0	0	0	0	0	0	0	0	0	0	1	0	0	0	0

Player and Club	Pct.	G.	AB.	R.	H.	TB.	2B.	3B.	HR.	RBI.	GW.	SH.	SF.	HP.	BB.	Int. BB.	SO.	SB.	CS.
Madden, Scott, Spartanburg	.000	18	8	0	0	0	0	0	0	0	0	3	0	0	0	0	4	0	0
Maldonado, Peter, Spartanburg	.000	14	1	0	0	0	0	0	0	1	0	0	0	0	0	0	0	0	0
Mantrana, Manuel, Gastonia	.245	64	233	30	57	78	9	3	2	21	3	5	3	2	23	0	45	21	7
Marigny, Ronald, Gastonia	.293	41	133	13	39	46	7	0	0	14	2	1	4	0	21	0	23	7	2
Markley, Scott, Asheville*	.315	119	466	113	147	196	23	7	4	47	3	7	2	2	78	0	33	41	4
Martel, Jay, Savannah	.091	32	11	0	1	1	0	0	0	0	0	2	0	0	0	0	3	0	0
Martin, Albert, Sumter*	.244	44	156	23	38	46	5	0	1	24	0	0	0	0	23	1	36	6	2
Martinez, Julian, Savannah	.258	70	217	31	56	67	5	0	2	25	1	1	0	3	28	2	54	8	4
Martinez, Porfirio, Gastonia†	.140	33	107	7	15	23	2	0	2	6	0	1	0	2	1	0	21	6	2
Marx, William, Charleston	.196	29	46	5	9	11	0	1	0	3	2	1	0	0	1	0	11	0	0
Mathews, Edward, Sumter	.240	30	25	3	6	7	1	0	0	2	0	1	0	0	1	0	6	0	0
Maysey, Matthew, Charleston	.000	18	5	0	0	0	0	0	0	0	0	2	0	0	2	0	2	0	0
McCall, Roy, Spartanburg	.222	58	153	18	34	58	4	1	6	23	2	0	2	2	23	0	40	1	1
McCray, Rodney, Charleston	.257	123	417	88	107	138	13	3	4	33	3	6	2	5	108	2	80	81	32
McMillan, Timothy, Macon	.197	49	173	14	34	52	7	1	3	25	0	0	2	2	8	0	63	0	1
McNally, Robert, Sumter	.233	11	30	4	7	7	0	0	0	5	0	0	0	0	6	0	5	0	0
Meads, David, Asheville*	.400	19	5	1	2	2	0	0	0	1	0	1	0	0	2	0	0	0	0
Meagher, Thomas, Charleston	.077	32	13	0	1	3	0	1	0	2	0	0	0	0	0	0	2	2	0
Merced, Orlando, Macon*	.197	65	173	20	34	46	4	1	2	24	2	0	2	1	12	0	38	5	3
Mercedes, Guillermo, Macon	.000	52	3	0	0	0	0	0	0	0	0	0	0	0	1	0	3	0	0
Merklen, Edward, Macon*	.000	16	2	0	0	0	0	0	0	0	0	0	0	0	0	0	0	0	0
Metoyer, Tony, Asheville	.150	15	20	4	3	9	0	0	2	2	0	1	0	0	0	0	10	0	0
Mitchell, Thomas, Gastonia	.302	24	86	15	26	32	4	1	0	17	2	1	2	0	11	0	20	2	4
Monell, Johnny, Columbia†	.260	86	258	50	67	98	9	2	6	46	7	0	2	0	21	1	38	11	4
Moreno, Douglas, Macon	.200	10	5	1	1	2	1	0	0	0	0	0	0	0	1	0	4	0	0
Moreno, Jaime, Charleston	.174	51	149	14	26	35	3	0	2	19	3	2	1	0	7	0	26	0	1
Morrison, Brian, Florence	.217	119	443	55	96	170	15	4	17	61	3	0	3	2	52	1	156	16	3
Munoz, Pedro, Florence	.294	122	445	69	131	199	16	5	14	82	7	2	2	5	54	4	100	9	5
Muratti, Rafael, Macon	.262	128	405	56	106	160	21	0	11	45	8	0	4	1	68	3	97	6	3
Murphy, Gary, Asheville	.083	18	12	0	1	2	1	0	0	2	1	1	0	0	0	0	6	0	0
Nemeth, Carey, Savannah	.194	11	36	3	7	8	1	0	0	1	0	0	0	0	8	0	13	0	1
Nolte, Eric, Charleston*	.148	26	27	5	4	7	0	0	1	1	0	5	0	1	2	0	5	0	0
Odle, Page, Macon	.333	12	39	11	13	29	4	0	4	16	2	0	0	1	13	0	11	4	0
Ojea, Alexander, Savannah†	.224	125	433	61	97	117	8	0	4	36	7	4	5	4	104	2	75	19	17
Orsag, James, Greensboro*	.271	115	395	82	107	188	20	2	19	79	6	1	3	4	84	3	91	5	3
Paris, Juan, Charleston	.211	82	232	21	49	61	8	2	0	17	2	1	2	0	17	0	41	4	3
Parker, Richard, Spartanburg†	.296	62	233	39	69	97	7	3	5	28	1	2	0	2	36	0	39	14	9
Patton, Claude, Savannah*	.257	97	265	32	68	84	10	0	2	31	4	4	2	1	47	2	38	3	3
Payne, Michael, Sumter	.000	17	8	0	0	0	0	0	0	0	0	3	0	0	0	0	3	0	0
Pena, Feliciano, Gastonia†	.227	96	282	34	64	74	8	1	0	26	2	8	3	0	21	0	59	2	1
Pena, Luis, Macon*	.227	51	66	6	15	22	1	0	2	11	0	0	0	0	3	0	13	1	1
Perdomo, Felix, Columbia	.288	62	208	42	60	105	14	2	9	37	1	0	1	0	23	1	41	4	4
Perez, Francisco, Savannah	.160	10	25	4	4	6	0	1	0	1	0	0	1	1	4	0	14	0	2
Perez, Julio, Macon	.292	121	466	67	136	170	18	5	2	45	4	3	2	4	37	0	65	32	7
Petitt, Steven, Savannah	.100	21	30	2	3	3	0	0	0	3	0	2	0	0	2	0	14	0	0
Pfaff, Robert, Sumter	.257	97	339	43	87	120	12	0	7	48	5	4	1	2	37	2	90	4	6
Picota, Lenin, Savannah	.000	21	10	1	0	0	0	0	0	0	0	1	0	0	4	0	4	0	0
Pimentel, Roberto, Spartanburg†	.198	98	313	29	62	74	6	3	0	20	2	5	3	1	16	0	54	7	1
Pittman, Douglas, Macon	.206	62	194	22	40	59	8	1	3	25	0	0	1	1	21	0	38	6	0
Plante, William, Greensboro	.184	24	49	8	9	14	2	0	1	8	1	0	1	1	13	0	25	0	0
Plesac, Joseph, Charleston	.200	22	20	1	4	5	1	0	0	5	1	1	0	0	0	0	9	0	1
Pratt, Todd, Greensboro	.241	107	348	63	84	136	16	0	12	56	9	4	4	5	74	0	114	0	1
Prioleau, Thelanious, Gastonia†	.205	44	112	15	23	38	7	1	2	13	3	3	0	0	14	0	38	4	1
Pruett, David, Spartanburg	.000	39	10	0	0	0	0	0	0	0	0	0	0	0	0	0	3	0	0
Quintana, Carlos, Greensboro	.325	126	443	97	144	204	19	4	11	81	10	3	6	4	90	1	54	26	9
Rauth, Christopher, Columbia	.095	14	21	1	2	2	0	0	0	0	0	0	0	0	5	0	5	0	0
Raziano, Scott, Savannah	.241	101	328	48	79	110	14	1	5	57	7	5	6	1	68	0	42	4	5
Reese, Kyle, Savannah	.208	14	24	2	5	8	0	0	1	6	0	1	0	0	1	0	8	0	0
Repoz, Craig, Columbia	.292	119	421	80	123	168	22	1	7	78	6	0	7	8	86	3	67	6	5
Reyes, Carlos, Asheville	.234	67	154	23	36	46	7	0	1	20	3	0	2	4	16	1	35	3	2
Reyes, Joselito, Florence	.231	105	342	53	79	124	11	11	4	41	4	1	4	2	36	0	87	29	7
Richardson, Derrick, Spartanburg	.224	70	246	33	55	68	10	0	1	14	1	0	2	5	30	1	48	10	1
Rigos, John, Savannah	.267	113	401	64	107	143	10	4	6	59	9	0	7	2	71	3	59	38	5
Rinehart, Robert, Columbia*	.218	58	147	17	32	40	8	0	0	17	1	1	3	1	18	0	38	3	4
Roberts, John, Greensboro	.295	124	478	76	141	204	18	12	7	51	4	5	3	5	68	2	35	32	8
Robertson, Michael, Savannah	.233	115	387	63	90	137	11	0	12	54	8	1	1	3	70	1	88	21	12
Roby, Ellis, Sumter†	.254	105	358	57	91	114	12	4	1	43	4	5	1	3	45	1	56	13	7
Roca, Gilberto, Macon†	.232	90	285	23	66	86	10	2	2	28	4	1	2	1	15	2	34	1	3
Rockey, James, Sumter	.231	67	225	33	52	66	9	1	1	23	1	2	1	2	38	0	40	8	3
Rodriguez, Aristides, Asheville	.297	32	74	8	22	24	2	0	0	5	0	0	1	3	8	0	10	0	2
Rodriguez, Ramon, Charleston*	.333	25	6	0	2	2	0	0	0	0	0	0	0	0	0	0	2	0	0
Roebuck, Ron, Asheville†	.000	10	1	0	0	0	0	0	0	0	0	0	0	0	0	0	0	0	0
Rogalski, Wayne, Asheville	.239	91	293	44	70	121	14	2	11	53	8	3	4	5	37	0	56	3	3
Romero, Charles, Florence	.242	53	182	19	44	55	4	2	1	13	0	1	2	1	9	0	32	4	3
Rosario, Victor, Greenboro†	.301	26	93	12	28	47	5	1	4	19	1	1	2	1	0	0	14	3	1
Rossum, Floyd, Spartanburg	.000	23	3	0	0	0	0	0	0	1	0	1	1	0	1	0	2	0	0
Rowe, Mathew, Sumter	.000	30	2	0	0	0	0	0	0	0	0	1	0	0	2	0	1	0	0
Russ, Kevin, Charleston*	.230	91	261	29	60	86	6	4	4	32	5	2	0	1	33	2	40	13	4
Rypien, Timothy, Florence	.268	44	127	13	34	44	4	0	2	19	2	1	0	0	14	0	24	2	1
Salisbury, James, Sumter	.188	28	32	4	6	9	3	0	0	0	0	6	0	0	3	0	15	0	0
Sanchez, Juan, Spartanburg	.241	20	87	12	21	31	4	0	2	10	1	0	0	1	4	0	15	2	0
Sardinha, Eduardo, Greensboro	.215	25	79	10	17	19	2	0	0	4	0	2	0	0	4	0	16	0	1
Sarmiento, Ramon, Gastonia	.275	23	80	15	22	36	5	0	3	12	0	0	0	0	9	0	35	6	0
Sassone, Michael, Savannah	.091	14	22	1	2	2	0	0	0	0	0	3	0	0	1	0	8	0	0
Satzinger, Jeffrey, Macon	.167	26	18	4	3	3	0	0	0	0	0	0	0	1	2	0	8	0	0
Schulte, Joseph, Asheville	.333	42	12	4	4	11	1	0	2	3	0	1	0	0	2	0	4	0	0
Seitz, David, Sumter*	.000	23	3	0	0	0	0	0	0	0	0	0	0	0	0	0	0	0	0
Service, Scott, Spartanburg	.000	14	6	0	0	0	0	0	0	0	0	0	0	0	0	0	4	0	0
Sharts, Steve, Spartanburg*	.000	19	11	1	0	0	0	0	0	0	0	1	0	0	1	0	7	1	0
Sheehan, John, Asheville	.250	21	4	1	1	1	0	0	0	0	0	0	0	0	1	0	2	0	0
Siblerud, Daniel, Columbia	.200	22	5	0	1	1	0	0	0	1	0	0	0	0	0	0	2	0	0
Smith, Alexander, Sumter	.284	40	148	20	42	56	8	3	0	17	4	0	4	1	12	0	19	1	1

Player and Club	Pct.	G.	AB.	R.	H.	TB.	2B.	3B.	HR.	RBI.	GW.	SH.	SF.	HP.	BB.	Int. BB.	SO.	SB.	CS.
Smith, Dwayne, Florence*	.239	22	71	10	17	29	1	1	3	13	2	0	0	0	2	0	16	2	1
Smith, Kevin, Asheville	.250	17	8	1	2	2	0	0	0	0	0	0	0	0	0	0	3	0	0
Smith, Terrance, Sumter	.000	3	4	0	0	0	0	0	0	0	0	0	0	0	0	0	4	0	0
Smith, Todd, Macon†	.000	1	1	0	0	0	0	0	0	0	0	0	0	0	0	0	1	0	0
Solano, Ramon, Gastonia	.050	14	20	1	1	1	0	0	0	0	0	0	0	1	2	0	8	1	0
Sparks, Gregory, Charleston*	.235	105	344	40	81	131	18	1	10	59	4	1	2	1	35	1	61	4	3
Steen, Scott, Spartanburg	.070	16	43	1	3	3	0	0	0	0	0	0	0	0	9	0	18	0	0
Stephens, Carl, Savannah	.218	95	325	52	71	120	10	0	13	56	11	1	2	3	57	1	76	2	4
Stevanus, Michael, Macon†	.211	79	237	34	50	58	6	1	0	16	0	5	1	1	33	1	59	10	4
Stevenson, William, Charleston*	.254	102	327	55	83	138	16	3	11	59	5	1	5	6	52	4	76	3	3
Stiles, William, Columbia	.000	27	1	0	0	0	0	0	0	0	0	0	0	0	1	0	0	0	0
Stomp, Mark, Spartanburg*	.500	15	2	1	1	1	0	0	0	0	0	1	0	0	2	0	0	0	0
Stottlemyre, Melvin, Asheville	.000	7	6	0	0	0	0	0	0	0	0	1	0	0	0	0	4	0	0
Swartzlander, Keith, Macon	.188	18	16	0	3	3	0	0	0	0	0	0	0	0	1	0	6	0	1
Takach, David, Savannah*	.125	36	8	0	1	1	0	0	0	0	0	1	0	0	0	0	4	0	0
Talbott, Shawn, Asheville	.000	34	6	0	0	0	0	0	0	0	0	0	0	0	0	0	2	0	0
Tatum, James, Charleston	.260	120	431	55	112	165	19	2	10	62	3	4	5	2	41	2	83	2	4
Temrowski, Thomas, Asheville*	.273	64	231	35	63	90	15	0	4	22	1	0	0	0	42	2	61	2	1
Thomson, Robert, Gastonia	.252	94	298	42	75	100	11	1	4	38	3	1	2	2	48	0	44	1	3
Thoutsis, Paul, Greensboro*	.288	106	364	83	105	172	16	3	15	77	5	1	11	6	77	3	57	0	0
Toale, John, Greensboro*	.278	100	338	42	94	162	27	4	11	72	5	3	6	4	34	1	71	1	1
Tomberlin, Andy, Sumter*	.000	13	1	0	0	0	0	0	0	0	0	0	0	0	1	0	1	0	0
Tonucci, Norman, Florence	.400	3	10	4	4	7	0	0	1	3	1	0	0	0	2	0	3	0	0
Towers, Kevin, Charleston	.250	7	4	1	1	2	1	0	0	0	0	0	0	0	0	0	1	0	0
Traylor, Keith, Savannah	.198	32	86	5	17	23	1	1	1	7	0	1	0	0	13	1	23	2	2
Tunison, Mark, 7 Spart.-20 Macon	.214	27	14	3	3	6	0	0	1	2	0	2	0	0	1	0	4	0	0
Tuozzo, John, Columbia	.231	35	13	2	3	6	0	0	1	1	0	0	0	0	0	0	7	0	0
Valdez, Rafael, Charleston	.212	90	260	25	55	85	15	3	3	27	0	1	5	3	32	0	54	2	5
Van Houten, James, Savannah	.000	47	1	0	0	0	0	0	0	0	0	0	0	0	1	0	1	0	0
Vaughn, Timothy, Macon†	.126	35	103	11	13	14	1	0	0	5	0	0	1	0	19	1	25	2	0
Villanueva, Juan, Columbia	.285	92	333	50	95	140	17	5	6	61	4	1	4	8	31	0	47	10	5
Wachs, Thomas, Columbia*	.000	46	4	0	0	0	0	0	0	0	0	0	0	0	0	0	4	0	0
Walden, Travis, Spartanburg*	.667	29	3	1	2	2	0	0	0	0	0	1	0	0	0	0	0	0	0
Walker, Clifton, Spartanburg	.000	25	9	0	0	0	0	0	0	0	0	2	0	0	1	0	5	0	0
Walters, Daniel, Asheville	.262	101	366	42	96	143	21	1	8	46	3	1	2	1	14	0	59	1	1
Warmbier, Kenneth, Savannah*	.267	34	116	19	31	46	2	2	3	12	4	1	2	0	20	4	9	7	4
Wasem, James, Charleston	.221	27	95	22	21	22	1	0	0	9	0	0	0	2	23	0	7	8	2
Waylock, Edmund, Gastonia	.186	62	204	37	38	63	10	0	5	22	2	0	0	7	41	3	56	6	4
Weiss, Jeffrey, Sumter*	.289	11	38	5	11	17	2	2	0	1	0	0	0	0	3	1	12	2	0
Wells, Terry, Asheville*	.207	31	29	5	6	6	0	0	0	2	0	3	0	0	3	0	9	0	1
West, David, Columbia*	.059	13	17	3	1	1	0	0	0	0	0	2	0	0	5	0	7	0	0
Wetherby, Jeffrey, Sumter*	.297	62	212	46	63	94	13	3	4	34	4	0	3	1	70	1	46	12	1
Whisler, Randy, Florence†	.279	84	280	55	78	112	12	2	6	39	6	3	3	3	58	0	59	6	1
White, Thomas, Gastonia	.200	15	50	1	10	11	1	0	0	5	0	1	0	1	7	1	6	1	2
Wiley, Craig, Charleston†	.187	39	107	13	20	28	3	1	1	10	1	0	3	1	13	0	12	1	1
Willoughby, Mark, Columbia	.125	11	8	2	1	2	1	0	0	0	0	2	0	0	1	0	3	0	0
Wills, Adrian, Sumter*	.280	15	50	8	14	17	3	0	0	8	0	0	0	2	12	1	7	0	1
Wisdom, Allen, Spartanburg†	.091	14	11	0	1	1	0	0	0	0	0	0	0	0	0	0	6	0	0
Wollenburg, Jay, Macon	.269	93	227	31	61	75	11	0	1	28	2	1	7	3	32	1	35	4	2
Zambrano, Eduardo, Greensboro	.238	112	395	68	94	156	16	5	12	65	5	1	6	4	42	0	80	4	3
Zayas, Carlos, Spartanburg	.241	74	245	26	59	88	11	0	6	26	3	0	2	7	21	1	59	0	2
Zellner, Joey, Macon	.239	102	306	56	73	94	15	0	2	23	1	3	1	2	58	0	72	38	12

The following pitchers, listed alphabetically by club, with games in parentheses, had no plate appearances, primarily through use of designated hitters:

ASHEVILLE—Estes, Joel (6).

CHARLESTON—Navilliat, James (10).

FLORENCE—Anderson, Richard (21); Bencomo, Omar (3); Burgos, Enrique (28); Ciprian, Elvis (14); Felden, Keith (28); Guenther, Robert (40); Humphries, Bobbie (20); Johnson, Dane (31); Jones, Christopher (14); Jones, Dennis (17); Kent, Wesley (2); Mejia, Cesar (37); Mumaw, Stephen (15); Saitta, Patrick (8); St. Clair, Kerry (32); Tracy, James (36); Wells, David (4).

GASTONIA—Burduan, Rafael (33); Carter, Richard (15); Cooper, David (40); Friesen, Robert (2); Garces, Robinson (12); Hill, Kenneth (22); Lacko, Richard (11); Nicholson, Keith (30); Nosek, Randall (12); Patenaude, Alain (29); Pifer, Gary (19); Ritz, Kevin (7); Schedeneck, James (5); Schultz, Scott (31); Wetherell, Gerry (22); Williams, Kenneth (28); York, Michael (22).

GREENSBORO—Abbott, John (17); Gabriele, Daniel (27); Gakeler, Daniel (24); Hale, Daniel (48); Kane, Thomas (28); Livernois, Derek (28); McGowan, Donald (38); Peterson, David (5); Revak, Raymond (28); Shikles, Larry (26); Zupka, William (46).

MACON—Reed, Richard (1); Santana, Ernesto (1).

SAVANNAH—Griffith, Kerry (6); Howes, Jeff (5).

SPARTANBURG—Bennett, Christopher (19); Blackshear, Steven (6).

SUMTER—Weems, Danny (8).

GRAND SLAM HOME RUNS—Knabenshue, Rogalski, Sparks, 2 each; Archibald, Bailey, J. Cuevas, Elliott, Gelatt, Gangi, R. Hansen, Hufford, Iglesias, Jaster, Justice, Luciani, Markley, Morrison, Odle, Perdomo, Pratt, Raziano, Reese, J. Reyes, Rigos, Robertson, Stevenson, 1 each.

AWARDED FIRST BASE ON CATCHER'S INTERFERENCE—Repoz 2 (David, Pittman); Bailey (Jimenez); Contreras (J. Cuevas); Ri. Johnson (Hall); Morrison (DeLuca); Traylor (Wiley).

CLUB FIELDING

Club	Pct.	G.	PO.	A.	E.	DP.	PB.
Asheville	.964	140	3643	1491	189	109	22
Sumter	.964	137	3596	1410	187	130	48
Columbia	.961	132	3503	1402	199	100	40
Savannah	.960	135	3507	1499	206	148	27
Gastonia	.958	139	3512	1408	216	136	34
Greensboro	.955	138	3608	1339	235	110	39
Macon	.955	138	3468	1348	229	98	38
Charleston	.954	132	3376	1353	227	107	34
Spartanburg	.953	135	3403	1342	234	115	31
Florence	.943	132	3350	1306	279	108	48

INDIVIDUAL FIELDING

*Throws lefthanded.

FIRST BASEMEN

Player and Club	Pct.	G.	PO.	A.	E.	DP.
Alyea, Florence	.985	83	654	59	11	58
Archibald, Columbia*	.985	31	246	23	4	21
Bailey, Columbia	.984	84	677	52	12	53
Barry, Macon	.958	9	62	6	3	4

FIRST BASEMEN—Continued

Player and Club	Pct.	G.	PO.	A.	E.	DP.
Bastinck, Gastonia	1.000	2	17	3	0	2
Brundage, Spartanburg*	1.000	3	21	1	0	1
Callas, Spartanburg*	.974	103	768	41	22	78
Cheek, Macon	.981	98	721	95	16	52
DAILY, Gastonia	.991	125	1021	57	10	104
DeLaCruz, Florence	.975	50	395	34	11	35
DeLuca, Columbia	.980	22	190	10	4	13
Denkenberger, Macon*	.958	16	104	9	5	11
Foster, Gastonia	1.000	12	78	4	0	7
Gaeckle, Greensboro	1.000	4	27	2	0	4
Gangi, Sumter	.994	17	158	1	1	23
Gonring, Asheville	.991	13	103	12	1	10
Greene, Spartanburg	.963	15	122	7	5	10
Hall, Macon	.889	1	8	0	1	0
Howey, Spartanburg	1.000	1	1	0	0	0
Iglesias, Savannah	.989	70	623	34	7	52
Do. Johnson, Sumter	.990	78	655	52	7	63
Ri. Johnson, Asheville	.992	68	592	37	5	45
Ro. Johnson, Spartanburg	.935	5	27	2	2	0
Kwolek, Asheville	.857	2	6	0	1	3
Lester, Charleston	1.000	2	14	0	0	0
Martin, Sumter*	.975	36	299	12	8	21
McCall, Spartanburg	.986	15	133	5	2	9
Monell, Columbia	.963	3	25	1	1	2
Moreno, Charleston	.889	1	7	1	1	1
Orsag, Greensboro	.986	110	797	54	12	76
Patton, Savannah	1.000	1	1	1	0	0
Perdomo, Columbia	.950	3	16	3	1	1
Pratt, Greensboro	.989	20	166	8	2	9
Quintana, Greensboro	1.000	2	14	0	0	0
Raziano, Savannah	1.000	1	12	0	0	0
Richardson, Spartanburg	1.000	2	9	0	0	0
Robertson, Savannah	.986	73	606	48	9	82
Roca, Macon	1.000	20	154	9	0	12
Rockey, Sumter	1.000	3	12	1	0	0
A. Smith, Sumter	1.000	5	40	2	0	4
D. Smith, Florence*	.909	1	9	1	1	1
Sparks, Charleston*	.982	73	552	34	11	43
Steen, Spartanburg	.900	2	9	0	1	1
Stevenson, Charleston	.981	71	527	34	11	42
Temrowski, Asheville*	.994	61	495	43	3	41
Thomson, Gastonia	1.000	4	28	5	0	5
Toale, Greensboro	.973	7	68	5	2	4
Wetherby, Sumter*	1.000	5	38	1	0	6

SECOND BASEMEN

Player and Club	Pct.	G.	PO.	A.	E.	DP.
Alva, Sumter	.900	4	2	7	1	1
Ashkinazy, Greensboro	.964	103	232	278	19	53
Baerga, Charleston	.955	79	179	205	18	56
Bianco, Sumter	.909	19	32	38	7	10
Castro, Columbia	1.000	2	3	7	0	2
Chapman, Gastonia	.840	5	8	13	4	4
Colombino, Asheville	1.000	5	12	7	0	4
DeLuca, Columbia	1.000	2	6	7	0	0
Edge, Spartanburg	.965	24	67	69	5	16
Elliott, Asheville	.966	67	122	188	11	28
Flores, Greensboro	.932	10	14	27	3	2
Garrison, Florence	.956	97	221	239	21	54
Gelatt, Columbia	.956	111	232	312	25	60
Gellinger, Gastonia	.966	35	87	82	6	26
Giddens, Macon	.951	15	27	31	3	7
Goff, Greensboro	.948	13	26	29	3	10
Housley, Florence	.893	27	39	53	11	13
Lemke, Sumter	.974	50	100	124	6	41
Lester, Charleston	.960	39	68	101	7	20
Lundahl, Columbia	.667	1	0	2	1	0
Mantrana, Gastonia	.946	41	79	114	11	16
Marigny, Charleston	.943	34	76	88	10	25
Martinez, Savannah	.968	13	21	40	2	11
OJEA, Savannah	.974	125	307	355	18	105
Pena, Gastonia	.972	32	76	98	5	23
Perdomo, Columbia	.963	25	48	57	4	16
Perez, Macon	.959	119	237	274	22	56
Pimentel, Spartanburg	.960	49	105	111	9	20
Reyes, Florence	.800	2	3	1	1	0
Richardson, Spartanburg	.923	67	141	170	26	41
Roby, Sumter	.950	78	161	181	18	37
Rogalski, Asheville	.966	74	142	174	11	43
Sardinha, Greensboro	1.000	16	24	43	0	9
Tatum, Charleston	.800	3	2	6	2	0
Valdez, Charleston	.000	1	0	0	1	0
Wasem, Charleston	.978	21	29	62	2	6
Whisler, Florence	.967	16	27	32	2	8
Wollenburg, Macon	.889	16	20	20	5	4

THIRD BASEMEN

Player and Club	Pct.	G.	PO.	A.	E.	DP.
Alva, Sumter	1.000	7	2	11	0	0
Blackmun, Spartanburg	.904	66	65	133	21	10
Colombino, Asheville	.899	77	46	167	24	18
DeLaCruz, Florence	.802	38	32	65	24	10
DeLuca, Columbia	.813	8	3	10	3	1
Flores, Greensboro	1.000	2	1	2	0	0
Foley, Spartanburg	.915	16	11	32	4	1
Gaeckle, Greensboro	.922	20	8	39	4	2
Giddens, Macon	.884	52	33	89	16	12
Goff, Greensboro	.835	42	31	65	19	3
Greene, Spartanburg	.833	3	1	4	1	0
Housley, Florence	.632	5	4	8	7	1
Iglesias, Savannah	.850	20	6	28	6	3
D. Johnson, Sumter	.857	28	18	54	12	5
R. Johnson, Spartanburg	1.000	3	0	1	0	0
Kwolek, Asheville	.906	39	23	73	10	8
Lemke, Sumter	.948	77	34	150	10	12
Lester, Charleston	.912	15	5	26	3	3
Love, Macon	.878	55	38	77	16	6
Mantrana, Gastonia	.782	17	7	36	12	4
Martinez, Savannah	.800	23	16	40	14	5
Merced, Macon	.667	10	5	15	10	0
Mitchell, Gastonia	1.000	2	0	7	0	0
Moreno, Charleston	.950	7	5	14	1	1
Nemeth, Savannah	.844	11	9	18	5	0
Pena, Gastonia	.901	40	28	63	10	5
Perdomo, Columbia	.833	12	3	22	5	3
Pimentel, Spartanburg	.880	21	22	51	10	4
Plante, Greensboro	.545	2	2	4	5	0
Prioleau, Gastonia	.838	13	11	20	6	2
Raziano, Savannah	.916	91	48	214	24	20
REPOZ, Columbia	.914	117	88	229	30	17
C. Reyes, Asheville	.880	41	20	61	11	4
J. Reyes, Florence	.874	40	25	79	15	6
Sanchez, Spartanburg	.909	20	16	34	5	2
Sardinha, Greensboro	1.000	5	1	9	0	1
Smith, Sumter	.914	35	17	68	8	6
Sparks, Charleston*	1.000	1	0	1	0	0
Steen, Spartanburg	.939	10	11	20	2	4
Tatum, Charleston	.892	114	75	214	35	29
Thomson, Gastonia	.902	28	8	38	5	7
Toale, Greensboro	.880	74	44	140	25	14
Tonucci, Florence	1.000	3	0	5	0	0
Wasem, Charleston	1.000	1	1	2	0	0
Waylock, Gastonia	.887	54	32	101	17	7
Whisler, Florence	.905	50	28	105	14	6
Wollenburg, Macon	.877	29	16	41	8	2

SHORTSTOPS

Player and Club	Pct.	G.	PO.	A.	E.	DP.
ALVA, Sumter	.946	122	187	377	32	81
Baerga, Charleston	.875	18	23	40	9	5
bradshaw, Gastonia	.940	94	135	273	26	55
Diaz, Florence	.934	61	80	174	18	29
Edge, Spartanburg	.952	30	49	89	7	20
Elliott, Ashville	.906	44	57	116	18	21
Flores, Greensboro	.893	67	108	159	32	30
Foley, Spartanburg	.828	34	40	80	25	18
Garrison, Florence	.930	12	15	25	3	6
Gelatt, Columbia	.912	9	12	19	3	2
Giddens, Macon	1.000	1	1	1	0	0
Horta, Ashville	.917	106	133	289	38	41
Ickes, Greensboro	.920	62	82	161	21	27
Jefferies, Columbia	.944	25	36	83	7	17
Lara, Savannah	.929	118	164	363	40	82
Lester, Charleston	.892	38	40	101	17	11
Martinez, Savannah	.894	27	26	67	11	13
Parker, Spartanburg	.934	61	87	169	18	30
Pena, Gastonia	.910	21	23	58	8	10
Perdomo, Columbia	.931	15	14	40	4	5
Pimentel, Spartanburg	.873	17	18	30	7	0
Prioleau, Gastonia	.930	31	43	76	9	17
Reyes, Florence	.861	62	88	147	38	26
Roby, Sumter	.919	22	29	50	7	4
Rogalski, Ashville	.750	3	1	2	1	1
Rosario, Greensboro	.919	24	37	65	9	10
Sardinha, Greensboro	.500	1	1	1	2	0
Solano, Gastonia	1.000	5	5	10	0	2
Stevanus, Macon	.921	78	108	197	26	38
Tatum, Charleston	.800	3	4	12	4	2
Valdez, Charleston	.873	78	112	204	46	35
Vaugh, Macon	.934	34	49	79	9	16
Villanueva, Columbia	.903	89	99	246	37	33
Wasem, Charleston	.938	4	3	12	1	2
Waylock, Gastonia	1.000	2	1	2	0	1
Whisler, Florence	.900	6	3	6	1	0
Wollenburg, Macon	.866	33	38	65	16	10

CATCHERS

Player and Club	Pct.	G.	PO.	A.	E.	DP.	PB.
Bastinck, Gastonia	.971	44	258	13	8	3	11
Borders, Florence	1.000	7	21	1	0	0	0
Brooks, Columbia	1.000	3	30	0	0	0	0
Brunswick, Columbia	.985	60	425	33	7	2	10
Cabrera, Charleston	.990	42	282	29	3	3	11
Camilli, Greensboro	.857	1	4	2	1	0	1
Cisco, Charleston	.985	39	237	20	4	1	10
Cuevas, Sumter	.986	53	321	24	5	0	13
David, Florence	.981	100	609	68	13	8	41
DeLuca, Columbia	.984	27	164	21	3	2	9
Edwards, Ashville	.994	24	150	14	1	0	3
Gaeckle, Greensboro	.974	55	401	43	12	6	23
Gonring, Ashville	.978	18	116	16	3	2	6
Gonzalez, Columbia	1.000	1	0	2	0	0	0
Gsellman, Spartanburg	.978	30	164	15	4	0	2
Hall, Macon	.965	37	227	23	9	2	8
Jimenez, Savannah	.966	47	269	17	10	4	10
Johnson, Spartanburg	.976	28	140	16	4	0	4
Jones, Columbia	.997	41	293	30	1	1	14
Liddell, Columbia	.993	18	134	15	1	0	7
Liebert, Gastonia	.994	55	296	33	2	1	9
McCall, Spartanburg	.979	26	130	12	3	0	7
McNally, Sumter	1.000	10	55	2	0	0	4
Moreno, Charleston	.995	33	186	14	1	1	7
Pena, Macon	1.000	4	6	0	0	0	1
Pfaff, Sumter	.978	72	490	51	12	6	22
Pittman, Macon	.994	49	285	34	2	5	17
Pratt, Greensboro	.982	84	660	47	13	9	15
Reese, Savannah	1.000	1	4	1	0	0	0
Robertson, Savannah	.975	9	35	4	1	0	0
Roca, Macon	.990	63	441	51	5	8	12
Rodriguez, Ashville	.971	29	158	11	5	1	1
Rypien, Florence	.980	36	224	20	5	3	7
Smith, Sumter	1.000	1	4	0	0	0	0
Stephens, Savannah	.982	90	570	70	12	6	17
Stevenson, Charleston	1.000	4	17	0	0	0	0
Thomson, Gastonia	.967	57	343	39	13	8	14
WALTERS, Ashville	.992	91	655	62	6	3	12
Wiley, Charleston	.973	31	186	31	6	5	6
Wills, Sumter	.985	15	113	17	2	1	9
Zayas, Spartanburg	.985	59	345	46	6	5	18

OUTFIELDERS

Player and Club	Pct.	G.	PO.	A.	E.	DP.
Abner, Macon	.992	57	121	6	1	2
Archibald, Columbia*	1.000	2	5	1	0	0
Baldwin, Ashville*	.985	108	119	9	2	0
Barry, Macon	1.000	4	4	0	0	0
Batista, Charleston	.917	21	31	2	3	1
Batiste, Florence	.941	49	109	3	7	0
Bianco, Sumter	1.000	3	1	0	0	0
Borders, Florence	1.000	1	1	0	0	0
Brooks, Columbia	1.000	9	12	1	0	0
Brundage, Spartanburg*	1.000	27	70	3	0	0
Chance, Macon	.951	100	181	15	10	0
Clawson, Ashville	.977	47	41	2	1	1
Clemente, Charleston	.963	21	25	1	1	0
Colombino, Ashville	1.000	8	6	0	0	0
Contreras, Columbia*	.971	71	128	8	4	3
Cuevas, Columbia	.971	22	33	1	1	1
Dantzler, Spartanburg	.946	22	34	1	2	0
Davis, Florence	.949	111	213	11	12	2
Dean, Gastonia	.857	9	6	0	1	0
DeLa Cruz, Florence	.500	4	2	0	2	0
DeLoach, Savannah	.964	15	26	1	1	0
DeLuca, Columbia	1.000	26	48	0	0	0
Donatelli, Spartanburg	.965	72	158	6	6	0
Drew, Ashville	.989	96	172	6	2	2
Elliott, Ashville	1.000	2	4	0	0	0
Foster, Gastonia	.96	30	48	2	4	1
Fox, Gastonia*	.961	106	190	9	8	3
Frazier, Sumter	.842	25	32	0	6	0
Gilkey, Savannah	.978	103	220	7	5	1
Gonazlez, Columbia	.895	21	16	1	2	0
Graham, Savannah	.924	49	60	1	5	0
Greene, Spartanburg	1000	9	15	2	0	0
Hansen, Greensboro*	.919	22	34	0	3	0
Harris, Charleston	1.000	1	1	0	0	0
Hayden, Columbia*	.954	91	119	6	6	0
Hithe, Ashville	.877	34	47	3	7	0
Holyfield, Spartanburg	.978	106	258	10	6	3
Hood, Sumter	.963	135	305	11	12	4
Housie, Gastonia	.966	88	214	13	8	3
Housley, Florence	1.000	9	10	2	0	0
Howey, Spartanburg	.974	95	175	13	5	5
Hufford, Spartanburg	.960	85	137	6	6	0
Hunter, Ashville	.988	48	80	4	1	2
Jackson, Gastonia	.943	23	32	1	2	1
Jaster, Columbia	.949	110	215	10	12	1
L. Jones, Sumter	.956	82	127	4	6	0
M. Jones, Florence	1.000	7	18	0	0	0
Justice, Sumter*	.970	59	124	7	4	3
Knabenshue, Charleston	.969	96	205	11	7	1
Luciani, Gastonia	.983	98	165	8	3	0
Mantrana, Gastonia	.917	6	11	0	1	0
MARKLEY, Ashville	1.000	117	281	10	0	3
Martinez, Gastonia	.946	20	33	2	2	0
McCray, Charleston	.980	121	271	17	6	3
McMillan, Macon*	.938	49	102	3	7	0
Merced, Macon	.941	31	48	0	3	0
Mitchell, Gastonia	.963	21	24	2	1	0
Monell, Columbia	.967	53	58	1	2	0
Morrison, Florence	.887	54	97	5	13	1
Munoz, Florence	.959	111	197	14	9	4
Muratti, Macon	.972	122	231	10	7	4
Odle, Macon	.933	12	25	3	2	0
Paris, Charleston	.956	70	104	5	5	2
Patton, Savannah	.928	57	99	4	8	0
Perez, Savannah	.941	9	14	2	1	0
Quintana, Greensboro	.961	124	210	12	9	1
Rigos, Savannah	.981	111	196	8	4	2
Rinehart, Columbia*	.962	36	50	0	2	0
Roberts, Greensboro	.988	120	231	10	3	6
Robertson, Savannah	1.000	28	43	1	0	1
Roca, Macon	1.000	2	1	0	0	0
Rockey, Sumter	.963	63	98	5	4	0
Romero, Florence	.960	52	114	6	5	1
Russ, Charleston*	.959	73	91	3	4	1
Sarmiento, Gastonia	.894	18	41	1	5	0
Smith, Florence*	1.000	14	27	1	0	0
Solano, Gastonia	.667	3	2	0	1	0
Sparks, Charleston*	969	22	31	0	1	0
Thoutsis, Greensboro	.973	74	137	6	4	0
Traylor, Savannah	1.000	27	37	2	0	1
Warmbier, Savannah*	.953	32	40	1	2	0
Waylock, Gastonia	1.000	5	2	1	0	0
Weiss, Sumter*	1.000	11	13	1	0	0
Wetherby, Sumter*	.914	51	61	3	6	0
White, Gastonia	.846	14	22	0	4	0
Zambrano, Greensboro	.965	99	180	11	7	2
Zellner, Macon	.987	55	73	1	1	1

PITCHERS

Player and Club	Pct.	G.	PO.	A.	E.	DP.
Abbott, Greensboro*	1.000	17	0	1	0	0
Abrell, Sumter	1.000	3	0	4	0	0
Akins, Sumter	1.000	6	3	6	0	0
Andersh, Macon*	.967	27	20	39	2	0
Anderson, Florence	.733	21	4	7	4	2
Armstrong, Columbia	.965	26	22	33	2	0
Arnsberg, Asheville	1.000	3	1	3	0	0
Bastinck, Gastonia	1.000	4	1	1	0	0
Bayer, Columbia	.952	20	4	16	1	1
Beck, Spartanburg*	1.000	14	1	8	0	1
Bennett, Spartanburg	1.000	19	1	2	0	0
Bivens, Savannah	1.000	5	0	10	0	0
Blackshear, Spartanburg*	1.000	6	0	2	0	0
Blount, Charleston*	1.000	26	1	5	0	0
Burduan, Gastonia	1.000	33	2	5	0	0
Burgos, Florence*	.929	28	6	20	2	1
Camp, Asheville*	.947	15	4	14	1	3
Carter, Gastonia	1.000	15	5	4	0	0
Cepeda, Macon	.857	29	10	8	3	0
Chaves, Charleston	.813	39	5	8	3	0
Ciprian, Florence	.800	14	2	6	2	0
Ciszkowski, Columbia	.636	9	3	4	4	1
Clossen, Sumter	.867	23	2	11	2	2
Coffman, Sumter	1.000	18	5	10	0	0
Collins, Spartanburg	1.000	5	1	3	0	0
Colpitt, Spartanburg	.714	33	1	4	2	0
Cooper, Gastonia	1.000	40	3	8	0	1
Credeur, Asheville*	.875	24	3	18	3	0
Crossley, Savannah*	.833	16	3	7	2	0
Davins, Macon	1.000	44	5	8	0	0
DeCordova, Savannah*	.905	34	3	16	2	0
DeLeon, Asheville	.853	26	8	21	5	2
Downs, Macon	.900	26	2	7	1	0
Dumas, Savannah	1.000	14	1	6	0	1
Eave, Sumter	.900	25	1	8	1	1
Estes, Asheville*	.833	6	1	4	1	1
Fascher, Asheville	1.000	45	3	7	0	1
Felden, Florence	1.000	28	3	7	0	0
Ferraro, Charleston*	1.000	27	2	7	0	0
Forrest, Savannah	1.000	24	8	25	0	2

PITCHERS—Continued

Player and Club	Pct.	G.	PO.	A.	E.	DP.
Franchi, Macon*	1.000	57	10	10	0	0
Gabriele, Greensboro	1.000	27	15	10	0	0
Gakeler, Greensboro	.939	24	10	21	2	1
Garces, Gastonia*	1.000	12	1	7	0	0
Gideon, Macon	.944	6	8	9	1	0
Givens, Columbia*	.759	27	2	20	7	1
J. Greene, Sumter	1.000	24	4	5	0	0
T. Greene, Sumter	.923	28	6	18	2	0
Griffith, Savannah	1.000	6	0	1	0	0
Guenther, Florence	.933	40	6	8	1	0
Guzman, Sumter	1.000	11	2	6	0	0
Hackett, Savannah*	.750	6	1	2	1	0
Hale, Greensboro	1.000	48	3	15	0	0
Hansen, Macon*	.929	12	0	13	1	0
Harris, Charleston	.968	27	7	23	1	2
Hartley, Savannah	.727	39	2	6	3	0
Hatfield, Macon	.935	19	8	21	2	0
Hayes, Columbia	1.000	12	1	6	0	0
Hendrix, Spartanburg	.955	32	5	16	1	1
Henion, Columbia	1.000	5	0	3	0	0
Hennessy, Sumter	1.000	34	6	4	0	0
Hightower, Columbia*	1.000	21	3	9	0	0
Hill, Gastonia	.958	22	8	15	1	1
Horsman, Florence*	.556	29	0	5	4	1
Howes, Savannah	.750	5	0	3	1	1
Humphries, Florence	.867	20	2	11	2	1
Ilsley, Asheville*	.957	15	5	17	1	1
James, Columbia	1.000	47	3	2	0	0
Johnson, Florence	.840	31	23	19	8	4
C. Jones, Florence	.762	14	5	11	5	0
Da. Jones, Sumter	1.000	42	6	7	0	0
De. Jones, Florence*	1.000	17	1	4	0	0
Kane, Greensboro	.880	28	5	17	3	5
Koopmann, Macon	.909	19	12	28	4	1
Lacko, Gastonia	1.000	11	6	2	0	0
Lewis, Charleston	.900	51	7	11	2	0
Livchak, Savannah*	.906	26	4	25	3	0
Livernois, Greensboro	.708	28	10	7	7	1
Machado, Spartanburg	.889	43	6	10	2	1
Madden, Spartanburg*	.857	18	2	4	1	2
Maldonado, Spartanburg	.750	14	2	1	1	0
Martel, Savannah	1.000	32	7	6	0	0
Marx, Charleston	.927	24	11	27	3	1
Mathews, Sumter	.857	30	14	16	5	1
Maysey, Charleston	1.000	18	4	5	0	1
McGowan, Greensboro	.895	38	4	13	2	1
Meads, Asheville*	1.000	19	1	10	0	1
Meagher, Charleston	1.000	32	6	8	0	0
Mejia, Florence	.905	37	10	9	2	0
Mercedes, Macon	.789	52	3	12	4	1
Merklen, Macon*	1.000	16	1	7	0	0
Metoyer, Asheville	.938	12	5	10	1	0
Moreno, Macon	1.000	10	1	2	0	0
Mumaw, Florence*	1.000	15	2	4	0	0
Murphy, Asheville	.789	18	6	9	4	0
Navilliat, Charleston*	1.000	10	1	3	0	0
Nicholson, Gastonia	.867	30	4	9	2	0
Nolte, Charleston*	.931	26	4	23	2	1
Nosek, Gastonia	.750	12	2	7	3	0
PATENAUDE, Gastonia	1.000	29	14	21	0	0
Patton, Savannah	1.000	1	2	1	0	0
Payne, Sumter	1.000	17	5	11	0	0
Peterson, Greensboro	1.000	5	0	2	0	0
Petitt, Savannah	.893	21	5	20	3	1
Picota, Savannah	.882	21	3	12	2	0
Pifer, Gastonia	.846	19	4	7	2	0
Plesac, Charleston	.892	22	11	22	4	1
Prioleau, Gastonia	1.000	1	0	1	0	0
Pruett, Spartanburg	.920	39	3	20	2	2
Rauth, Columbia	1.000	14	9	8	0	0
Reed, Macon	1.000	1	1	0	0	0
Revak, Greensboro*	1.000	28	2	13	0	0
Ritz, Gastonia	1.000	7	0	2	0	0
Rodriguez, Charleston*	.857	25	1	5	1	0
Roebuck, Asheville*	1.000	10	0	2	0	0
Rossum, Spartanburg	.900	23	5	4	1	0
Rowe, Sumter	.933	30	2	12	1	2
Saitta, Florence	.667	8	0	2	1	0
Salisbury, Sumter	1.000	28	8	24	0	0
Santana, Macon	1.000	1	0	1	0	0
Sassone, Savannah	.923	14	8	16	2	1
Satzinger, Macon	.714	26	7	8	6	0
Schedeneck, Gastonia*	1.000	5	0	1	0	0
Schulte, Asheville	.857	42	7	11	3	0
Schultz, Gastonia	.920	31	3	20	2	2
Seitz, Sumter*	1.000	23	2	10	0	0
Service, Spartanburg	1.000	14	2	5	0	0
Sharts, Spartanburg*	1.000	19	4	23	0	1
Sheehan, Asheville	.875	21	2	12	2	3
Shikles, Greensboro	.871	26	12	15	4	0
Siblerud, Columbia	1.000	22	1	3	0	0
Smith, Asheville	.917	17	3	8	1	0
St. Clair, Florence	.923	32	10	14	2	0
Stiles, Columbia	.857	27	2	4	1	0
Stomp, Spartanburg*	1.000	15	2	5	0	0
Stottlemyre, Asheville	.833	7	1	9	2	0
Swartzlander, Macon	.947	18	6	12	1	2
Takach, Savannah*	.938	36	6	9	1	0
Talbott, Asheville	.882	34	6	9	2	0
Tomberlin, Sumter*	.667	13	2	2	2	0
Towers, Charleston	.875	7	3	4	1	0
Tracy, Florence	.913	36	10	11	2	0
Tunison, 7 Spart-20 Macon	.905	27	9	11	2	0
Tuozzo, Columbia	.960	35	9	15	1	0
Van Houten, Savannah	.900	47	2	7	1	0
Wachs, Columbia*	1.000	46	2	13	0	1
Walden, Spartanburg*	.933	29	3	11	1	2
Walker, Spartanburg	.861	25	12	19	5	3
Weems, Sumter	1.000	8	0	2	0	0
D. Wells, Florence*	1.000	4	1	3	0	0
T. Wells, Asheville*	.964	26	6	21	1	1
West, Columbia*	.960	13	13	11	1	0
Wetherell, Gastonia	.800	22	4	4	2	0
Whisler, Florence	1.000	1	0	1	0	1
Williams, Gastonia	.909	28	5	15	2	3
Willoughby, Columbia*	1.000	11	1	4	0	1
Wisdom, Spartanburg*	.850	14	3	14	3	2
York, Gastonia	1.000	22	0	7	0	1
Zupka, Greensboro	.588	46	7	3	7	0

The following players do not have any recorded accepted chances at the positions indicated; therefore, are not listed in the fielding averages for those particular positions: Bencomo, p; Cabrera, of; Contreras, 1b; Friesen, p; Housey, 3b; Iglesias, p; Jimenez, p; Kent, p; P. Martinez, p; J. Moreno, p; Muratti, 1b; Orsag, ss, of; F. Pena, of; Perdomo, p; Raziano, p; Reese, p; C. Reyes, of; Rogalski, 3b, p; Rosario, 3b; Russ, 1b; Rypien, p; Stevenson, of; Toale, of; Waylock, p.

CLUB PITCHING

Club	ERA.	G.	CG.	ShO.	Sv.	IP.	H.	R.	ER.	HR.	HB.	BB.	Int. BB.	SO.	WP.	Bk.
Savannah	3.33	135	21	12	41	1169.0	1016	563	432	81	42	595	10	842	76	7
Columbia	3.38	132	15	6	31	1167.2	1013	562	439	79	37	546	28	1036	71	10
Asheville	3.65	140	19	12	36	1214.1	1117	622	492	103	44	614	14	1071	96	8
Charleston	3.69	132	19	9	22	1125.1	1055	592	462	75	30	507	27	864	83	17
Sumter	4.15	137	20	8	32	1198.2	1073	667	553	91	44	662	12	965	138	14
Macon	4.22	138	19	7	19	1156.0	1122	667	542	76	38	680	12	934	102	16
Greensboro	4.46	138	23	6	33	1202.2	1324	767	596	87	50	608	18	998	125	11
Gastonia	4.90	139	11	7	26	1170.2	1127	779	637	85	50	782	9	860	109	10
Florence	4.96	132	4	5	22	1116.2	1148	792	616	84	44	708	15	820	105	8
Spartanburg	5.14	135	13	5	19	1134.1	1214	823	648	95	55	665	10	757	87	6

PITCHERS' RECORDS

(Leading Qualifiers for Earned-Run Average Leadership—112 or More Innings)

*Throws lefthanded.

Pitcher—Club	W.	L.	Pct.	ERA.	G.	GS.	CG.	GF.	ShO.	Sv.	IP.	H.	R.	ER.	HR.	HB.	BB.	Int. BB.	SO.	WP.
Ilsley, Asheville*	12	2	.857	1.95	15	15	9	0	3	0	120.0	74	27	26	11	2	23	0	146	2
Harris, Charleston	13	7	.650	2.63	27	27	8	0	2	0	191.1	176	69	56	13	3	54	2	176	6
Livernois, Greensboro	12	7	.632	2.65	28	25	5	0	1	0	159.2	142	72	47	9	4	73	0	164	17
Armstrong, Columbia	17	5	.773	2.72	26	26	6	0	3	0	188.2	161	77	57	12	2	65	2	150	6
Livchak, Savannah*	10	8	.556	2.78	26	25	3	0	0	0	152.1	135	67	47	12	2	77	0	100	11
Hill, Gastonia	9	5	.643	2.79	22	16	1	4	0	0	122.2	95	51	38	4	5	80	0	86	14
Forrest, Savannah	13	6	.684	2.85	24	24	5	0	1	0	157.2	118	58	50	6	5	82	0	102	14
Marx, Charleston	11	9	.550	2.98	24	24	4	0	2	0	166.0	131	76	55	12	2	62	1	133	9

Pitcher—Club	W.	L.	Pct.	ERA.	G.	GS.	CG.	GF.	ShO.	Sv.	IP.	H.	R.	ER.	HR.	HB.	BB.	Int. BB.	SO.	WP.
Koopmann, Macon	5	9	.357	3.07	19	19	6	0	1	0	129.0	131	55	44	11	1	25	2	98	4
Coffman, Sumter	10	3	.769	3.07	18	18	3	0	2	0	114.1	99	56	39	2	7	64	0	120	18
Petitt, Savannah	9	6	.600	3.10	21	21	4	0	1	0	139.1	123	65	48	8	6	76	3	85	9

Departmental Leaders: G—Franchi, 57; W—Armstrong, 17; L—Andersh, 16; Pct.—Bayer, .900; GS—T. Greene, 28; CG—Ilsley, 9; GF—Hale, 46; ShO—Armstrong, T. Greene, Ilsley, Sassone, 3; Sv.—Van Houten, 22; IP—Harris, 191.1; H—Shikles, 182; R—Johnson, 116; ER—Johnson, 96; HR—T. Wells, 20; HB—Plesac, 12; BB—Gabriele, Johnson, 114; IBB—James, 8; SO—Givens, 189; WP—Plesac, 28.

(All Pitchers—Listed Alphabetically)

Pitcher—Club	W.	L.	Pct.	ERA.	G.	GS.	CG.	GF.	ShO.	Sv.	IP.	H.	R.	ER.	HR.	HB.	BB.	Int. BB.	SO.	WP.
Abbott, Greensboro*	0	1	.000	10.04	17	0	0	8	0	0	26.0	43	33	29	2	1	22	1	28	6
Abrell, Sumter	0	1	.000	6.57	3	3	0	0	0	0	12.1	12	9	9	4	4	11	0	7	1
Akins, Sumter	1	3	.250	1.88	6	6	2	0	0	0	38.1	29	8	8	3	1	4	0	41	1
Andersh, Macon*	8	16	.333	4.64	27	27	5	0	2	0	143.2	136	93	74	10	7	87	1	123	16
Anderson, Florence	2	5	.286	5.71	21	7	1	6	0	0	69.1	78	58	44	6	0	35	1	35	6
Armstrong, Columbia	17	5	.773	2.72	26	26	6	0	3	0	188.2	161	77	57	12	2	65	2	150	6
Arnsberg, Asheville	0	0	.000	3.86	3	0	0	1	0	1	11.2	10	5	5	1	1	3	0	14	0
Bastinck, Gastonia	0	0	.000	11.05	4	0	0	4	0	0	7.1	13	11	9	3	0	8	0	3	0
Bayer, Columbia	9	1	.900	2.52	20	9	0	4	0	1	78.2	59	27	22	2	4	32	4	80	10
Beck, Spartanburg*	1	3	.250	1.46	14	0	0	13	0	4	24.2	21	6	4	1	1	8	0	23	0
Bencomo, Florence	0	2	.000	9.00	3	3	0	0	0	0	5.0	9	11	5	1	0	2	0	7	0
Bennett, Spartanburg	1	2	.333	4.40	19	1	1	10	0	0	43.0	58	29	21	5	2	10	0	22	1
Bivens, Savannah	3	1	.750	1.70	5	5	2	0	1	0	37.0	25	7	7	1	0	10	0	19	0
Blackshear, Spartanburg*	0	3	.000	7.43	6	1	0	2	0	0	13.1	22	19	11	1	2	1	0	15	1
Blount, Charleston*	2	3	.400	3.74	26	0	0	23	0	10	33.2	28	14	14	1	1	8	3	36	1
Burduan, Gastonia	2	4	.333	6.24	33	5	0	8	0	1	88.0	82	75	61	7	5	92	0	71	10
Burgos, Florence*	3	8	.273	6.46	28	10	0	6	0	2	85.0	92	76	61	5	2	70	0	71	15
Camp, Asheville*	2	3	.400	3.97	15	8	0	4	0	1	59.0	61	37	26	3	4	22	0	49	3
Carter, Gastonia	2	7	.222	7.42	15	11	0	2	0	0	43.2	55	52	36	7	4	44	0	41	6
Cepeda, Macon	5	3	.625	4.96	29	15	2	3	1	0	103.1	92	64	57	13	0	69	1	97	11
Chaves, Charleston	5	3	.625	3.33	39	2	0	8	0	1	81.0	77	46	30	6	2	37	2	43	1
Ciprian, Florence	4	2	.667	3.66	14	4	0	0	0	0	59.0	54	26	24	4	0	20	0	35	2
Ciszkowski, Columbia	3	3	.500	4.53	9	9	0	0	0	0	53.2	52	35	27	5	5	31	0	43	3
Clossen, Sumter	9	6	.600	4.70	23	23	2	0	2	0	122.2	117	75	64	14	2	75	0	80	18
Coffman, Sumter	10	3	.769	3.07	18	18	3	0	2	0	114.1	99	56	39	2	7	64	0	120	18
Collins, Spartanburg	0	3	.000	11.74	5	5	0	0	0	0	15.1	17	29	20	1	0	28	0	18	2
Colpitt, Spartanburg	0	4	.000	7.88	33	1	0	16	0	0	40.0	43	48	35	6	4	49	3	15	13
Cooper, Gastonia	2	5	.286	3.55	40	0	0	30	0	4	63.1	58	33	25	5	1	31	2	49	0
Credeur, Asheville*	13	2	.867	4.01	24	22	1	0	1	0	130.1	118	69	58	10	0	91	2	147	7
Crossley, Savannah*	3	2	.600	6.28	16	8	0	4	0	0	53.0	60	44	37	8	5	37	1	35	4
Davins, Macon	.3	5	.375	3.81	44	0	0	32	0	5	59.0	49	27	25	2	3	42	0	58	11
DeCordova, Savannah*	2	5	.286	3.38	34	8	0	9	0	2	90.2	96	42	34	8	0	44	0	67	5
DeLeon, Asheville	11	10	.524	4.03	26	25	2	1	0	0	140.2	151	83	63	11	5	67	1	110	22
Downs, Macon	1	4	.200	4.80	26	2	0	9	0	0	45.0	52	30	24	2	3	22	2	24	3
Dumas, Savannah	1	2	.333	6.39	14	0	0	7	0	2	25.1	29	21	18	5	3	13	1	17	0
Eave, Sumter	4	1	.800	2.87	25	0	0	20	0	11	47.0	34	18	15	5	1	21	0	61	6
Estes, Asheville*	0	0	.000	2.79	6	0	0	6	0	1	9.2	10	5	3	0	0	6	0	4	1
Fascher, Asheville	6	6	.500	2.82	45	0	0	35	0	11	79.2	60	33	25	3	5	45	3	90	9
Felden, Florence	7	3	.700	4.86	28	0	0	21	0	4	50.0	53	35	27	0	2	32	2	28	4
Ferraro, Charleston*	5	4	.556	2.57	27	10	0	10	0	0	84.0	78	35	24	7	1	26	5	61	10
Forrest, Savannah	13	6	.684	2.85	24	24	5	0	1	0	157.2	118	58	50	6	5	82	0	102	14
Franchi, Macon*	4	7	.364	3.01	57	0	0	45	0	11	92.2	70	42	31	4	4	62	2	114	4
Friesen, Gastonia	0	0	.000	11.57	2	0	0	0	0	0	2.1	6	6	3	0	1	2	0	0	0
Gabriele, Greensboro	11	6	.647	5.32	27	27	2	0	1	0	159.0	157	113	94	13	5	114	1	149	15
Gakeler, Greensboro	7	6	.538	3.32	24	23	5	1	1	1	154.1	158	73	57	6	4	69	1	154	11
Garces, Gastonia*	2	3	.400	3.22	12	3	1	2	0	1	36.1	26	13	13	2	1	18	0	29	1
Gideon, Macon	5	1	.833	2.63	6	5	3	0	1	0	48.0	33	16	14	0	1	35	0	38	2
Givens, Columbia*	8	7	.533	3.77	27	27	2	0	1	0	172.0	147	89	72	8	4	100	1	189	21
J. Greene, Sumter	2	4	.333	3.05	24	0	0	22	0	8	38.1	34	18	13	6	0	18	3	29	4
T. Greene, Sumter	11	7	.611	4.69	28	28	5	0	3	0	174.2	162	95	91	17	8	82	3	169	15
Griffith, Savannah	1	1	.500	11.37	6	2	0	0	0	0	12.2	15	16	16	3	3	19	0	5	0
Guenther, Florence	3	1	.750	3.16	40	0	0	23	0	3	77.0	67	31	27	4	3	42	2	70	5
Guzman, Sumter	3	0	1.000	4.91	11	1	0	1	0	0	25.2	27	15	14	1	0	16	0	19	5
Hackett, Savannah*	2	2	.500	4.91	6	3	0	0	0	0	18.1	24	19	10	5	0	5	0	22	0
Hale, Greensboro	7	10	.412	3.43	48	0	0	46	0	17	84.0	93	44	32	2	4	38	6	73	13
Hansen, Macon*	1	9	.100	6.02	12	12	0	0	0	0	61.1	70	47	41	4	1	39	0	38	9
Harris, Charleston	13	7	.650	2.63	27	27	8	0	2	0	191.1	176	69	56	13	3	54	2	176	6
Hartley, Savannah	5	7	.417	2.89	39	0	0	25	0	8	56.0	38	31	18	0	7	37	1	55	9
Hatfield, Macon	4	8	.333	3.21	19	19	1	0	0	0	98.0	89	52	35	1	6	66	1	70	10
Hayes, Columbia	5	1	.833	5.59	12	6	0	2	0	1	58.0	66	42	36	6	2	22	1	36	2
Hendrix, Spartanburg	4	7	.364	4.61	32	11	0	8	0	2	105.1	117	68	54	2	8	56	0	58	5
Henion, Columbia	1	0	1.000	0.00	5	0	0	3	0	0	8.2	3	1	0	0	0	3	0	6	0
Hennessy, Sumter	5	0	1.000	3.94	34	0	0	17	0	1	64.0	60	35	28	5	2	24	2	59	4
Hightower, Columbia*	5	4	.556	5.48	20	20	1	0	0	0	87.0	89	62	53	9	6	58	2	94	2
Hill, Gastonia	9	5	.643	2.79	22	16	1	4	0	0	122.2	95	51	38	4	5	80	0	86	14
Horsman, Florence*	4	3	.571	4.07	29	9	1	10	1	1	90.2	93	56	41	8	1	49	0	64	5
Howes, Savannah	0	1	.000	9.82	5	0	0	3	0	0	7.1	15	16	8	1	0	7	1	3	1
Humphries, Florence	3	10	.231	6.24	20	19	0	0	0	0	70.2	93	64	49	7	2	38	0	43	4
Iglesias, Savannah	0	0	.000	18.00	1	0	0	0	0	0	2.0	5	4	4	0	0	1	0	1	0
Ilsley, Asheville*	12	2	.857	1.95	15	15	9	0	3	0	120.0	74	27	26	11	2	23	0	146	2
James, Columbia	13	3	.813	3.25	47	0	0	34	0	9	69.1	61	30	25	5	0	24	8	61	2
Jimenez, Savannah	0	0	.000	10.80	1	0	0	0	0	0	1.2	0	2	2	0	0	5	0	0	1
Johnson, Florence	8	12	.400	6.99	31	24	0	3	0	0	123.2	136	116	96	9	11	114	0	68	18
C. Jones, Florence	1	7	.125	4.28	14	14	0	0	0	0	61.0	54	42	29	5	0	54	1	53	10
Da. Jones, Sumter	10	6	.625	3.84	42	1	0	21	0	7	70.1	64	39	30	6	1	44	1	52	7
De. Jones, Florence*	0	5	.000	5.86	17	14	0	1	0	0	55.1	45	44	36	5	7	49	0	62	8
Kane, Greensboro	3	3	.500	3.87	28	1	0	18	0	2	81.1	95	56	35	6	7	38	1	50	6
Kent, Florence	0	0	.000	4.50	2	0	0	0	0	0	2.0	0	1	1	0	1	1	0	1	3
Koopmann, Macon	5	9	.357	3.07	19	19	6	0	1	0	129.0	131	55	44	11	1	25	2	98	4
Lacko, Gastonia	4	2	.667	3.38	11	11	1	0	1	0	64.0	46	29	24	5	2	30	0	67	3
Lewis, Charleston	4	8	.333	3.43	51	1	1	25	1	4	84.0	87	48	32	4	0	32	4	61	4
Livchak, Savannah*	10	8	.556	2.78	26	25	3	0	0	0	152.1	135	67	47	12	2	77	0	100	11

Pitcher—Club	W.	L.	Pct.	ERA.	G.	GS.	CG.	GF.	ShO.	Sv.	IP.	H.	R.	ER.	HR.	HB.	BB.	Int. BB.	SO.	WP.
Livernois, Greensboro	12	7	.632	2.65	28	25	5	0	1	0	159.2	142	72	47	9	4	73	0	164	17
Machado, Spartanburg	2	5	.286	3.73	43	5	2	28	1	7	79.2	68	39	33	1	8	52	3	81	5
Madden, Spartanburg*	4	9	.308	4.80	18	18	0	0	0	0	95.2	98	70	51	12	0	62	0	44	4
Maldonado, Spartanburg	4	1	.800	0.82	14	0	0	12	0	2	22.0	14	5	2	0	0	10	1	11	0
Martel, Savannah	7	6	.538	4.17	32	11	2	8	1	1	101.1	98	53	47	10	3	41	3	83	4
Martinez, Gastonia	0	0	.000	0.00	4	0	0	3	0	0	6.0	3	1	0	0	2	4	0	2	1
Marx, Charleston	11	9	.550	2.98	24	24	4	0	2	0	166.0	131	76	55	12	2	62	1	133	9
Mathews, Sumter	8	9	.471	4.50	30	19	3	4	0	1	130.0	122	92	65	7	5	73	0	85	10
Maysey, Charleston	3	2	.600	5.02	18	5	0	11	0	1	43.0	43	28	24	5	3	24	2	39	5
McGowan, Greensboro	8	4	.667	5.34	38	14	1	9	1	1	126.1	130	95	75	10	9	88	1	99	16
Meads, Asheville*	4	3	.571	1.99	19	3	0	10	0	3	54.1	51	25	12	4	1	14	1	50	2
Meagher, Charleston	1	7	.125	4.24	32	6	0	22	0	4	70.0	58	41	33	3	2	29	3	61	4
Mejia, Florence	9	7	.563	3.50	37	18	2	9	2	4	131.0	122	61	51	6	6	62	3	122	4
Mercedes, Macon	5	4	.556	4.73	52	1	0	10	0	0	85.2	115	52	45	5	0	32	3	68	5
Merklen, Macon*	0	1	.000	3.03	16	0	0	11	0	2	29.2	25	10	10	3	2	9	0	27	0
Metoyer, Asheville	5	2	.714	3.89	12	12	2	0	0	0	69.1	69	36	30	6	3	38	0	45	10
D. Moreno, Macon	2	1	.667	5.96	10	2	0	1	0	0	22.2	26	19	15	2	3	16	0	17	1
J. Moreno, Charleston	0	0	.000	27.00	1	0	0	1	0	0	1.0	2	3	3	1	0	1	0	1	0
Mumaw, Florence*	1	0	1.000	1.90	15	0	0	10	0	6	23.2	16	5	5	1	0	6	1	20	2
Murphy, Asheville	5	1	.833	4.16	18	12	2	4	0	0	84.1	83	47	39	7	2	52	0	50	4
Navilliat, Charleston*	0	1	.000	0.00	10	0	0	6	0	2	12.1	8	1	0	0	1	10	2	9	0
Nicholson, Gastonia	10	9	.526	4.74	30	19	2	9	0	3	138.2	131	82	73	12	4	71	0	98	8
Nolte, Charleston*	12	9	.571	3.90	26	26	3	0	0	0	164.0	154	80	71	11	1	68	1	121	10
Nosek, Gastonia	4	5	.444	6.02	12	10	0	1	0	0	52.1	56	41	35	4	2	49	0	37	11
Patenaude, Gastonia	6	11	.353	5.44	29	21	3	4	0	0	144.0	150	104	87	7	8	76	1	112	14
Patton, Savannah	0	0	.000	0.00	1	0	0	0	0	0	2.2	1	0	0	0	0	2	0	1	0
Payne, Sumter	5	5	.500	3.32	17	8	1	3	0	2	59.2	45	26	22	5	2	32	1	30	4
Perdomo, Columbia	0	0	.000	18.00	1	0	0	1	0	0	1.0	3	2	2	0	0	1	0	0	0
Peterson, Greensboro	2	0	1.000	3.00	5	0	0	4	0	2	15.0	20	6	5	1	0	2	0	15	1
Petitt, Savannah	9	6	.600	3.10	21	21	4	0	1	0	139.1	123	65	48	8	6	76	3	85	9
Picota, Savannah	6	2	.750	2.00	21	11	0	0	0	0	85.1	55	30	19	4	1	67	0	45	8
Pifer, Gastonia	3	5	.375	5.02	19	7	2	4	0	0	66.1	76	44	37	7	3	30	0	24	8
Plesac, Charleston	5	12	.294	6.00	22	22	2	0	0	0	123.0	131	97	82	9	12	104	1	69	28
Prioleau, Gastonia	0	0	.000	0.00	1	0	0	1	0	0	1.0	0	0	0	0	0	0	0	0	0
Pruett, Spartanburg	6	7	.462	3.94	39	11	3	11	1	2	130.1	128	70	57	11	6	66	2	95	9
Rauth, Columbia	7	4	.636	3.15	14	14	3	0	0	0	94.1	88	48	33	5	3	32	1	68	2
Raziano, Savannah	0	0	.000	0.00	1	0	0	1	0	0	1.0	0	0	0	0	0	0	0	0	0
Reed, Macon	0	0	.000	2.84	1	1	0	0	0	0	6.1	5	3	2	0	0	2	0	1	0
Reese, Savannah	0	0	.000	0.00	1	0	0	0	0	0	0.2	0	0	0	0	0	1	0	1	0
Revak, Greensboro*	9	10	.474	6.61	28	22	2	1	0	1	125.1	173	112	92	16	5	57	2	104	15
Ritz, Gastonia	1	2	.333	4.21	7	7	0	0	0	0	36.1	29	19	17	2	0	21	0	34	6
Rodriguez, Charleston*	1	3	.250	5.13	25	4	0	6	0	0	47.1	59	41	27	1	2	36	1	39	4
Roebuck, Asheville*	0	0	.000	6.28	10	0	0	6	0	2	14.1	12	10	10	0	2	19	0	15	1
Rogalski, Asheville	0	0	.000	0.00	2	0	0	2	0	0	3.0	5	0	0	0	0	1	0	0	0
Rossum, Spartanburg	1	3	.250	8.75	23	5	0	10	0	1	47.1	68	59	46	3	3	35	0	25	3
Rowe, Sumter	3	0	1.000	4.03	30	0	0	9	0	1	58.0	55	34	26	2	5	25	0	47	8
Rypien, Florence	0	0	.000	0.00	1	0	0	1	0	0	2.0	2	3	0	0	0	3	0	0	0
Saitta, Florence	0	1	.000	8.10	8	0	0	4	0	0	20.0	31	21	18	6	0	8	0	11	2
Salisbury, Sumter	5	9	.357	4.22	28	27	4	1	1	0	170.2	142	93	80	12	1	109	1	106	22
Santana, Macon	0	0	.000	0.00	1	0	0	1	0	0	1.0	1	0	0	0	0	0	0	0	0
Sassone, Savannah	7	3	.700	2.29	14	14	5	0	3	0	98.1	68	30	25	4	3	21	0	98	1
Satzinger, Macon	5	8	.385	4.59	26	16	0	1	0	0	100.0	98	59	51	9	1	84	0	83	10
Schedeneck, Gastonia*	0	0	.000	10.80	5	0	0	3	0	1	6.2	6	8	8	1	0	7	0	3	1
Schulte, Asheville	6	4	.600	3.24	42	0	0	23	0	9	100.0	76	44	36	9	6	54	3	102	8
Schultz, Gastonia	6	8	.429	4.28	31	8	1	17	0	4	96.2	109	63	46	4	6	54	3	58	6
Seitz, Sumter*	0	3	.000	6.03	23	3	0	12	0	0	37.1	38	26	25	1	1	27	0	31	7
Service, Spartanburg	1	6	.143	5.83	14	9	1	1	0	0	58.2	68	44	38	3	7	34	0	49	6
Sharts, Spartanburg*	5	8	.385	5.97	19	18	2	0	1	0	110.0	127	76	73	15	4	40	0	75	9
Sheehan, Asheville	4	2	.667	5.19	21	6	0	3	0	1	59.0	60	41	34	9	5	29	0	31	5
Shikles, Greensboro	12	10	.545	4.74	26	26	8	0	2	0	163.1	182	98	86	17	7	68	1	103	12
Siblerud, Columbia	0	1	.000	4.64	22	0	0	11	0	3	33.0	30	24	17	7	2	19	0	29	1
Smith, Asheville	2	4	.333	3.86	17	4	0	2	0	2	51.1	59	27	22	1	0	30	0	25	3
St. Clair, Florence	3	6	.333	4.82	32	9	0	5	0	0	106.1	120	80	57	5	5	68	1	64	10
Stiles, Columbia	4	1	.800	1.45	27	0	0	16	0	2	31.0	19	7	5	1	1	15	2	25	3
Stomp, Spartanburg*	2	3	.400	3.52	15	1	0	4	0	0	30.2	32	17	12	5	0	12	0	31	1
Stottlemyre, Asheville	3	1	.750	2.10	7	7	2	0	1	0	34.1	32	13	8	3	3	12	0	28	2
Swartzlander, Macon	3	6	.333	6.25	18	13	0	2	0	0	67.2	71	59	47	8	2	52	0	38	6
Takach, Savannah*	3	4	.429	4.29	36	3	0	16	0	6	63.0	60	40	30	5	2	27	0	49	5
Talbott, Asheville	5	4	.556	4.13	34	0	0	24	0	5	56.2	61	33	26	5	3	25	4	40	2
Tomberlin, Sumter*	1	0	1.000	4.62	13	0	0	3	0	1	25.1	18	17	13	0	4	27	0	22	6
Towers, Charleston	1	1	.500	4.01	7	5	1	1	1	0	24.2	23	13	11	2	0	16	0	15	1
Tracy, Florence	8	4	.667	5.12	36	0	0	28	0	2	70.1	75	56	40	11	4	43	4	51	7
Tunison, 7 Spart.-20 Macon	4	5	.444	5.40	27	9	2	5	0	2	81.2	82	61	49	4	7	55	1	54	10
Tuozzo, Columbia	3	2	.600	2.32	35	2	0	14	0	6	93.0	74	33	24	4	4	32	1	70	2
Van Houten, Savannah	3	4	.429	1.71	47	0	0	41	0	22	63.1	51	18	12	1	2	23	0	54	4
Wachs, Columbia*	4	4	.500	1.97	46	0	0	30	0	9	73.0	57	22	16	5	0	26	5	61	1
Walden, Spartanburg*	4	5	.444	5.00	29	10	1	6	0	0	93.2	100	66	52	5	1	47	0	71	14
Walker, Spartanburg	2	14	.125	5.94	25	22	1	0	0	0	122.2	127	98	81	14	5	89	0	70	10
Waylock, Gastonia	0	0	.000	18.00	1	0	0	1	0	0	1.0	1	2	2	0	0	2	0	0	0
Weems, Sumter	0	3	.000	9.90	8	0	0	4	0	0	10.0	15	11	11	1	0	10	1	7	2
D. Wells, Florence*	0	0	.000	3.55	4	1	0	0	0	0	12.2	7	6	5	1	0	9	0	14	0
T. Wells, Asheville*	12	6	.667	4.54	26	26	1	0	0	0	136.2	125	87	69	20	2	83	0	125	15
West, Columbia*	10	3	.769	2.91	13	13	3	0	1	0	92.2	74	41	30	4	3	56	1	101	14
Wetherell, Gastonia	2	2	.500	5.91	22	1	0	11	0	3	42.2	36	39	28	3	1	50	2	44	8
Whisler, Florence	0	0	.000	0.00	1	0	0	1	0	0	2.0	1	0	0	0	0	3	0	1	0
Williams, Gastonia	4	10	.286	6.29	28	20	0	4	0	0	117.1	123	91	82	12	3	86	0	75	7
Willoughby, Columbia*	1	3	.250	5.35	11	6	0	2	0	0	33.2	30	22	20	6	1	30	0	23	2
Wisdom, Spartanburg*	2	9	.182	5.18	14	14	2	0	0	0	83.1	83	58	48	8	1	49	0	40	4
York, Gastonia	2	2	.500	3.44	22	0	0	20	0	9	34.0	26	15	13	0	2	27	1	27	5
Zupka, Greensboro	4	6	.400	3.66	46	0	0	28	0	9	108.1	131	65	44	5	4	39	4	59	13

BALKS—T. Greene, 7; Stiles, 6; Horsman, Marx, Petitt, 4 each; Chaves, Downs, Mercedes, Satzinger, 3 each; Andersh, Blount, Credeur, Gakeler, Hennessy, Ilsley, Maysey, Metoyer, Plesac, Revak, Sassone, Shikles, Swartzlander, West, Wetherell, 2 each; Abbott, Bayer, Bencomo, Burduan, Camp, Ciprian, Collins, Cooper, Ferraro, Franchi, Gabriele, Guenther, Hatfield, Hendrix, Hill, Johnson, Da. Jones, Kane, Koopmann, Lewis, Livchak, Livernois, Machado, Martinez, Mathews, McGowan, Nolte, Nosek, Patenaude, Pifer, Pruett, Rodriguez, Salisbury, Seitz, Service, Tomberlin, Wachs, Walden, T. Wells, Williams, 1 each.

COMBINATION SHUTOUTS—DeLeon-Schulte 2, DeLeon-Meads, Murphy-Talbott, Wells-Fascher, Credeur-Schulte, Camp-Fascher, Asheville; Nolte-Blount, Plesac-Meagher, Ferraro-Blount, Charleston; Bayer-Wachs-Stiles-Siblerud, Columbia; Johnson-Tracy, Mejia-Anderson, Florence; Ritz-Hill, Williams-Nicholson, Schultz-Garces, Lacko-Cooper, Pifer-Garces, Schultz-York, Gastonia; Moreno-Davins, Hatfield-Merklen, Macon; Livchak-Van Houten, Forrest-Van Houten-Takach, Picota-Takach-Van Houten, Picota-Hartley, Petitt-Hartley, Savannah; Walden-Maldonado, Madden-Stomp-Maldonado, Spartanburg.

NO-HIT GAMES—Gabriele, Greensboro, defeated Gastonia, 4-0, June 14; Hightower, Columbia, defeated Savannah, 10-2 (first game), August 21; Towers, Charleston, defeated Savannah, 4-0 (first game), August 31.

Appalachian League

SUMMER CLASS A CLASSIFICATION

CHAMPIONSHIP WINNERS IN PREVIOUS YEARS

Year	Club	Pct.
1921	Greenville	.608
	Johnson City*	.627
1922	Bristol	.557
1923	Knoxville	.635
1924	Knoxville*	.642
	Bristol	.607
1925	Greenville	.667
1926-36	Did not operate.	
1937	Elizabethton	.559
	Pennington Gap*	.580
1938	Elizabethton	.664
	Greenville (3rd)†	.571
1939	Elizabethton‡	.597
1940	Johnson City§	.726
	Elizabethton	.750
1941	Johnson City	.614
	Elizabethton*	.661
1942	Bristol	.667
	Bristol x	.660
1943	Bristol	.755
	Bristol y	.617
1944	Kingsport‡	.575
1945	Kingsport‡	.670
1946	New River‡	.675
1947	Pulaski	.648
	New River (3rd)†	.516
1948	Pulaski‡	.680
1949	Bluefield‡	.721
1950	Bluefield	.600
	Bluefield z	.745
1951	Kingsport‡	.659
1952	Johnson City	.595
	Welch (3rd)†	.509
1953	Welch*	.705
	Johnson City	.672
1954	Bluefield‡	.619
1955	Salem**	.689
1956	Did not operate.	
1957	Bluefield	.701
1958	Johnson City	.662
1959	Morristown	.603
1960	Wytheville	.614
1961	Middlesboro	.591
1962	Bluefield	.671
1963	Bluefield	.652
1964	Johnson City	.662
1965	Salem	.614
1966	Marion	.623
1967	Bluefield	.627
1968	Marion	.583
1969	Pulaski a	.576
	Johnson City	.544
1970	Bluefield	.638
1971	Bluefield a	.609
	Kingsport	.559
1972	Bristol a	.588
	Covington	.586
1973	Kingsport	.757
1974	Bristol a	.754
	Bluefield	.536
1975	Marion	.515
	Johnson City a	.603
1976	Johnson City a	.714
	Bluefield	.600
1977	Kingsport	.623
1978	Elizabethton	.594
1979	Paintsville	.800
1980	Paintsville	.657
1981	Paintsville	.657
1982	Bluefield a	.681
	Johnson City	.478
1983	Paintsville	.653
1984	Elizabethton b	.580
	Pulaski	.536
1985	Bristol c	.638

*Won split-season playoff. †Won four-team playoff. ‡Won championship and four-team playoff. §Johnson City, first-half winner, won playoff involving six clubs. xWon both halves and defeated second-place Elizabethton in playoff. yWon both halves, but Erwin won four-team playoff. zWon both halves, but Bristol won two-club playoff. **Salem and Johnson City declared playoff co-champions when weather forced cancellation of final series. aLeague was divided into Northern, Southern divisions; declared league champion, based on highest won-lost percentage. bLeague was divided into Northern, Southern divisions; won one-game playoff for league championship. cBristol declared league champion based on regular-season record.

STANDING OF CLUBS AT CLOSE OF SEASON, AUGUST 29

NORTHERN DIVISION

Club	W.	L.	T.	Pct.	G.B.
Pulaski (Braves)	41	25	0	.621	....
Bluefield (Orioles)	39	29	0	.574	3
Burlington (Indians)	36	31	0	.537	5½
Wytheville (Cubs)	22	46	0	.324	20

SOUTHERN DIVISION

Club	W.	L.	T.	Pct.	G.B.
Johnson City (Cardinals)	44	22	0	.667	....
Elizabethton (Twins)	37	31	0	.544	8
Bristol (Tigers)	35	34	0	.507	10½
Kingsport (Mets)	16	52	0	.235	29

COMPOSITE STANDING OF CLUBS AT CLOSE OF SEASON, AUGUST 29

Club	J.C.	Pul.	Blu.	Eliz.	Bur.	Bri.	Wyt.	Kng.	W.	L.	T.	Pct.	G.B.
Johnson City (Cardinals)	....	6	5	7	5	7	3	11	44	22	0	.667	....
Pulaski (Braves)	2	....	6	3	5	6	11	8	41	25	0	.621	3
Bluefield (Orioles)	2	6	....	5	7	3	11	5	39	29	0	.574	6
Elizabethton (Twins)	5	3	3	....	5	7	6	8	37	31	0	.544	8
Burlington (Indians)	3	7	5	3	....	3	8	7	36	31	0	.537	8½
Bristol (Tigers)	5	2	5	7	4	....	6	6	35	34	0	.507	10½
Wytheville (Cubs)	3	1	3	2	4	2	....	7	22	46	0	.324	23
Kingsport (Mets)	2	0	2	4	1	6	1	....	16	52	0	.235	29

Major league affiliations in parentheses.

Playoffs—Pulaski defeated Johnson City, two games to one, to win league championship.

Regular-Season Attendance—Bluefield, 33,888; Bristol, 15,040; Burlington, 62,701; Elizabethton, 10,338; Johnson City, 23,965; Kingsport, 30,425; Pulaski, 14,040; Wytheville, 18,014. Total, 208,411. Playoffs, 1,975.

Managers—Bluefield, Glenn Gulliver; Bristol, Tom Gamboa; Burlington, Glen Adams; Elizabethton, Fred Waters; Johnson City, Dan Radison; Kingsport, Chuck Hiller; Pulaski, Grady Little; Wytheville, Tony Franklin.

All-Star Team—1B-Chris Hoiles, Bristol; 2B—Geronimo Pena, Johnson City; 3B—Pat Austin, Bristol; SS—Scott Leius, Elizabethton; OF—Jerome Walton, Wytheville; Vince Kindred, Johnson City; Ken Adderly, Bluefield; C—Brian Deak, Pulaski; DH—Scott Johnson, Burlington; RHP—Dave Osteen, Johnson City; LHP—Dave Sala, Johnson City; Player of the Year—Brian Deak, Pulaski; Manager of the Year—Dan Radison, Johnson City.

(Compiled by Howe News Bureau, Boston, Mass.)

CLUB BATTING

Club	Pct.	G.	AB.	R.	OR.	H.	TB.	2B.	3B.	HR.	RBI.	GW.	SH.	SF.	HP.	BB.	Int. BB.	SO.	SB.	CS.	LOB.
Bristol	.273	69	2307	340	354	630	852	77	26	31	289	32	14	20	27	234	11	456	135	37	527
Pulaski	.269	66	2202	413	337	592	892	107	17	53	343	32	14	22	27	318	2	437	99	15	513
Johnson City	.265	66	2252	406	275	597	866	94	14	49	333	31	14	26	35	295	11	392	109	27	531
Bluefield	.257	68	2208	379	344	568	829	95	11	48	325	33	6	23	25	316	7	518	69	40	520
Elizabethton	.242	68	2207	352	362	534	750	82	7	40	280	24	17	21	30	303	4	392	79	24	525
Wytheville	.236	68	2234	312	399	528	697	78	17	19	254	19	27	19	20	257	3	472	89	28	499
Burlington	.231	67	2186	353	320	505	744	90	16	39	276	25	4	25	32	375	9	479	97	30	516
Kingsport	.220	68	2204	294	458	484	698	74	10	40	244	14	10	12	37	269	4	547	97	33	484

INDIVIDUAL BATTING

(Leading Qualifiers for Batting Championship—194 or More Plate Appearances)

*Bats lefthanded. †Switch-hitter.

Player and Club	Pct.	G.	AB.	R.	H.	TB.	2B.	3B.	HR.	RBI.	GW.	SH.	SF.	HP.	BB.	Int. BB.	SO.	SB.	CS.
Clark, Phillip, Bristol	.332	66	247	40	82	102	4	2	4	36	4	1	4	6	19	2	42	12	1
Deak, Brian, Pulaski	.325	62	197	45	64	119	15	2	12	43	3	0	3	3	49	0	57	12	2
May, Derrick, Wytheville*	.320	54	178	25	57	65	6	1	0	23	1	0	1	2	16	1	15	17	4
Hoiles, Chris, Bristol	.320	68	253	42	81	143	19	2	13	57	10	0	2	1	30	3	20	10	1
Austin, Dominic, Bristol	.309	68	256	48	79	104	13	6	0	22	1	1	2	2	31	1	28	48	12
Sims, Kinney, Bluefield*	.308	54	198	38	61	75	5	3	1	21	0	3	2	1	26	0	44	14	4
Randle, Michael, Elizabethton*	.299	58	204	27	61	68	4	0	1	20	2	3	0	4	19	0	15	19	3
Pena, Geronimo, Johnson City	.297	56	202	55	60	84	7	4	3	20	2	1	3	7	46	4	33	27	3
Pennington, Kenneth, Pulaski	.291	58	223	44	65	99	9	2	7	36	3	0	4	5	29	0	25	9	2
Looper, Edward, Johnson City	.290	56	221	38	64	98	9	2	7	41	6	0	2	4	17	1	25	4	1
Hewes, Patrick, Johnson City	.289	60	201	31	58	89	10	0	7	39	2	2	4	2	24	0	35	3	0

Departmental Leaders: G—Austin, Hoiles, 68; AB—Austin, 256; R—Pena, 55; H—Clark, 82; TB—Hoiles, 143; 2B—Hoiles, 19; 3B—Austin, 6; HR—S. Johnson, 14; RBI—Hoiles, 57; GWRBI—Hoiles, 10; SH—Beyeler, 6; SF—DeLima, 6; HP—Pena, 7; BB—Cantrell, 61; IBB—Pena, 4; SO—Reeder, 68; SB—Austin, 48; CS—Austin, 12.

(All Players—Listed Alphabetically)

Player and Club	Pct.	G.	AB.	R.	H.	TB.	2B.	3B.	HR.	RBI.	GW.	SH.	SF.	HP.	BB.	Int. BB.	SO.	SB.	CS.
Abreu, Franklin, Johnson City	.226	48	133	19	30	33	3	0	0	21	0	1	0	1	22	1	22	0	0
Adderly, Kenneth, Bluefield	.282	60	238	42	67	91	7	1	5	32	3	2	3	2	22	0	43	18	7
Akins, Sidney, Pulaski	.000	8	3	0	0	0	0	0	0	0	0	2	0	0	1	0	1	0	0
Alexander, Kent, Wytheville	.000	12	3	0	0	0	0	0	0	0	0	0	0	0	0	0	0	0	0
Almonte, Tobia, Burlington	.138	25	58	4	8	8	0	0	0	4	0	0	1	0	9	0	15	2	0
Alvarez, Michael, Johnson City†	.288	36	111	20	32	49	2	3	3	18	1	1	2	0	10	1	5	5	1
Arias, Pedro, Burlington	.118	37	68	13	8	19	1	2	2	7	1	0	0	4	13	0	30	6	2
Austin, Dominic, Bristol	.309	68	256	48	79	104	13	6	0	22	1	1	2	2	31	1	28	48	12
Baez, Manolo, Johnson City*	.158	13	19	2	3	4	1	0	0	2	0	0	0	0	3	0	13	0	0
Balthazar, Doyle, Bristol	.258	37	120	7	31	39	2	0	2	17	2	0	1	0	14	0	26	2	2
Barr, Jeffrey, Johnson City	.103	18	29	3	3	3	0	0	0	3	0	0	0	0	7	0	9	1	0
Barrs, Stanley, Johnson City	.273	39	110	16	30	42	7	1	1	12	1	1	0	2	12	0	15	7	2
Battaglia, Jeffrey, Burlington	.177	47	124	24	22	47	7	0	6	13	1	0	0	3	21	1	31	6	1
Bautista, Ramon, Burlington	.210	41	105	19	22	25	3	0	0	7	1	0	0	0	35	0	33	8	4
Baxter, James, Burlington	.178	32	90	14	16	19	3	0	0	4	0	0	0	6	17	1	26	2	0
Beasant, Darrel, Kingsport	.228	24	57	9	13	14	1	0	0	5	0	0	0	2	8	1	13	1	0
Berringer, John, Wytheville	.250	26	4	1	1	1	0	0	0	0	0	1	0	0	0	0	0	0	0
Beyeler, Arnold, Bristol	.251	65	223	30	56	64	6	1	0	23	3	6	1	3	30	0	43	20	2
Bohne, Mark, Kingsport	.000	4	2	0	0	0	0	0	0	0	0	0	0	0	0	0	2	0	0
Boskie, Shawn, Wytheville	.250	14	4	1	1	2	1	0	0	0	0	0	0	0	1	0	1	0	0
Boyce, Joseph, Elizabethton*	.197	44	117	31	23	45	7	0	5	22	0	0	5	5	32	1	23	2	3
Browe, Richard, Bristol*	.269	46	130	23	35	64	7	2	6	26	3	1	2	0	20	2	28	2	1
Brown, Jarvis, Elizabethton	.228	49	180	28	41	54	4	0	3	23	2	5	1	4	18	0	41	15	3
Caballero, Eduardo, Wytheville	.000	7	1	0	0	0	0	0	0	0	0	0	0	0	0	0	1	0	0
Cabrera, Basilio, Bristol	.266	47	169	23	45	57	4	4	0	23	1	0	0	1	5	1	32	2	1
Cantrell, Thomas, Pulaski	.276	61	199	45	55	76	11	2	2	25	2	1	2	1	61	1	37	13	2
Carter, Edward, Johnson City*	.275	38	120	22	33	42	4	1	1	12	1	1	1	0	15	0	23	5	2
Carter, Larry, Johnson City	.000	10	7	1	0	0	0	0	0	0	0	0	0	0	2	0	3	0	0
Cartwright, James, Johnson City	.500	4	2	0	1	2	1	0	0	0	0	0	0	0	0	0	1	0	0
Castillo, Axel, Burlington	.208	34	101	16	21	30	3	0	2	16	0	1	2	0	19	0	24	5	0
Castillo, Roberto, Bristol	.286	6	7	1	2	2	0	0	0	0	0	0	0	0	1	0	2	0	0
Clark, Phillip, Bristol	.332	66	247	40	82	102	4	2	4	36	4	1	4	6	19	2	42	12	1
Colavito, Steven, Bluefield†	.228	29	79	9	18	19	1	0	0	8	1	0	0	0	11	0	22	0	1
Corbin, Archie, Kingsport	.000	18	1	0	0	0	0	0	0	0	0	0	0	0	1	0	1	0	0
Courtney, Shawn, Elizabethton	.220	24	82	9	18	19	1	0	0	9	2	0	0	1	12	0	13	0	0
Cramer, Robert, Elizabethton*	.000	2	5	1	0	0	0	0	0	0	0	0	0	0	2	0	2	0	0
Crowley, Terrence, Bluefield	.252	59	214	34	54	65	9	1	0	18	2	0	3	1	19	0	34	10	4
Crowson, David, Kingsport*	.091	13	11	1	1	2	1	0	0	1	0	0	0	0	0	0	1	0	0
Cuyler, Milton, Bristol	.230	45	174	24	40	56	3	5	1	11	1	2	0	5	15	0	35	12	4
Davis, Kenneth, Elizabethton*	.227	58	207	37	47	61	6	1	2	14	3	5	2	0	38	0	25	20	8
Deak, Brian, Pulaski	.325	62	197	45	64	119	15	2	12	43	3	0	3	3	49	0	57	12	2
DeLima, Rafael, Elizabethton*	.228	49	136	20	31	44	7	0	2	21	2	0	6	0	30	2	26	1	4
DeLoach, Bobby, Johnson City	.233	42	133	21	31	49	7	1	3	21	0	0	3	0	9	0	16	5	5
Doster, Zachery, Bristol	.270	65	222	39	60	69	6	0	1	28	1	1	3	3	34	1	60	14	7
Douglas, Arthur, Kingsport	.241	35	112	22	27	38	7	2	0	12	1	1	0	4	13	0	26	6	0
Eggleston, Darren, Wytheville	.188	12	32	4	6	6	0	0	0	2	0	0	0	0	3	0	11	2	0
Elli, Rocky, Kingsport*	.000	16	3	0	0	0	0	0	0	0	0	0	0	0	0	0	1	0	0
Farmer, Joseph, Johnson City	.500	5	2	1	1	1	0	0	0	0	0	0	0	0	0	0	1	0	0
Faron, Robert, Johnson City	.200	14	10	1	2	2	0	0	0	1	0	2	0	0	1	0	2	0	0
Featherstone, Michael, Pulaski	.250	19	4	0	1	1	0	0	0	0	0	0	0	0	0	0	2	0	0
Franco, Alexis, Bluefield†	.259	37	135	23	35	55	9	1	3	22	2	0	0	1	15	1	44	1	3
Garmon, Christopher, Elizabethton*	.266	41	139	15	37	48	5	0	2	21	1	0	0	0	16	1	19	0	0
Geronimo, Angel, Kingsport	.211	43	142	18	30	35	3	1	0	12	0	0	0	0	9	1	25	2	4
Gomez, Henrique, Wytheville	.214	17	14	3	3	4	1	0	0	0	0	1	0	0	0	0	7	0	0
Gomez, Leonardo, Bluefield	.352	27	88	23	31	61	7	1	7	28	1	0	3	1	25	0	27	1	0
Gomez, Patrick, Wytheville*	.250	11	4	0	1	1	0	0	0	0	0	2	0	0	0	0	0	0	0
Gonzalez, Javier, Kingsport	.291	25	55	12	16	35	4	0	5	14	0	0	0	0	14	0	13	0	0
Goodwin, Mark, Bluefield*	.293	50	174	25	51	75	16	1	2	33	3	0	0	1	13	1	11	0	2
Grater, Marc, Johnson City	.500	24	4	1	2	2	0	0	0	0	0	1	0	0	1	0	0	0	0
Hamilton, Michael, Pulaski*	.258	35	93	22	24	40	2	1	4	10	0	0	0	0	18	0	22	0	0
Hannon, Phillip, Wytheville†	.200	43	150	21	30	40	3	2	1	10	1	0	0	2	25	0	31	4	4
Hawkins, Cedric, Kingsport	.284	17	67	9	19	25	4	1	0	7	0	0	0	2	6	0	10	6	1
Height, Ronald, Kingsport	.269	45	119	19	32	40	4	2	0	14	1	0	0	3	20	0	25	7	1
Henry, Michael, Johnson City	.200	9	5	0	1	1	0	0	0	1	0	1	0	0	1	0	3	0	0
Hewes, Patrick, Johnson City	.289	60	201	31	58	89	10	0	7	39	2	2	4	2	24	0	35	3	0
Hildebrandt, Vernon, Elizabethton	.242	14	33	2	8	9	1	0	0	2	0	0	0	1	1	0	10	0	1
Hill, Steven, Wytheville	.286	60	220	37	63	85	10	3	2	25	3	0	1	0	22	1	16	4	1
Hoiles, Chris, Bristol	.320	68	253	42	81	143	19	2	13	57	10	0	2	1	30	3	20	10	1
Jackson, Gregory, Wytheville	.182	41	110	10	20	26	3	0	1	8	1	1	1	0	16	0	39	2	5
Jackson, Ruben, Bristol*	.229	33	96	10	22	33	4	2	1	8	3	0	3	1	11	1	27	4	1

Player and Club	Pct.	G.	AB.	R.	H.	TB.	2B.	3B.	HR.	RBI.	GW.	SH.	SF.	HP.	BB.	Int. BB.	SO.	SB.	CS.
Jeffers, Steven, Johnson City†	.219	29	73	16	16	18	2	0	0	4	0	1	1	0	11	1	4	6	2
Johnson, Jay, Pulaski	.266	58	192	38	51	79	14	1	4	38	4	4	5	2	13	0	26	7	0
Johnson, Lee, Kingsport	.500	19	2	0	1	1	0	0	0	0	0	0	0	1	2	0	0	0	0
Johnson, Scott, Burlington*	.285	66	200	45	57	113	14	0	14	54	4	0	4	2	54	1	49	6	1
Jones-Pointer, Carl, Pulaski	.250	55	196	28	49	71	8	1	4	30	2	1	0	2	15	0	49	10	1
Jose, Elio, Wytheville	.174	41	115	19	20	31	3	1	2	20	1	1	2	3	11	0	33	2	0
Kickbush, Scott, Pulaski	.186	34	86	10	16	19	1	1	0	10	3	0	0	3	15	0	22	3	0
Kindred, Vincent, Johnson City	.329	42	161	37	53	93	8	1	10	41	6	0	3	1	14	1	42	13	1
Kler, William, Bluefield	.124	30	89	9	11	19	2	0	2	14	1	0	1	0	14	0	52	2	0
Klyczek, Christopher, Bluefield†	.286	4	7	2	2	2	0	0	0	1	0	0	0	1	0	0	1	0	0
Lampe, Edward, Johnson City†	.195	29	41	6	8	11	0	0	1	3	0	0	0	4	4	0	14	2	1
Lehman, Michael, Bluefield	.214	28	84	17	18	31	2	1	3	9	0	0	2	2	26	0	30	3	3
Leius, Scott, Elizabethton	.278	61	237	37	66	94	14	1	4	23	1	2	1	3	26	0	45	5	0
LeMasters, James, Pulaski	.000	15	10	0	0	0	0	0	0	0	0	0	0	0	0	0	8	0	0
Lemle, Robert, Kingsport	.340	13	50	8	17	26	2	2	1	12	1	1	0	0	4	0	9	1	1
Lexa, Michael, Elizabethton	.236	31	89	15	21	30	4	1	1	14	0	0	2	3	16	0	12	1	1
Liriano, Julio, Burlington	.287	37	108	13	31	44	3	2	2	11	0	0	1	1	2	0	24	3	2
Looper, Edward, Johnson City	.290	56	221	38	64	98	9	2	7	41	6	0	2	4	17	1	25	4	1
Lora, Julio, Bluefield	.218	34	119	21	26	33	4	0	1	13	2	0	3	3	12	0	27	5	1
Main, Kevin, Wytheville	.000	19	4	0	0	0	0	0	0	0	0	1	0	0	0	0	2	0	0
Mallinak, Michael, Bluefield	.254	43	142	17	36	46	7	0	1	23	4	0	2	0	18	1	39	3	2
Maloney, Richard, Pulaski	.282	59	216	41	61	68	4	0	1	20	1	1	1	0	26	0	20	13	2
Marina, Juan, Kingsport	.167	13	6	1	1	1	0	0	0	0	0	0	0	0	1	0	2	0	0
Martin, Christopher, Elizabethton	.222	31	90	17	20	23	1	1	0	7	0	0	0	0	7	0	28	3	0
Martin, Darryl, Bristol	.256	27	90	11	23	30	4	0	1	12	1	0	0	0	5	0	19	0	4
Martinez, Luis, Burlington	.264	43	140	18	37	55	4	1	4	24	4	0	3	3	6	0	27	5	0
May, Derrick, Wytheville*	.320	54	178	25	57	65	6	1	0	23	1	0	1	2	16	1	15	17	4
May, Lee, Kingsport	.188	52	202	21	38	40	2	0	0	12	1	0	1	4	8	0	59	15	8
McDaniel, Terrence, Kingsport	.246	41	114	24	28	53	5	1	6	21	0	1	3	1	32	0	29	14	3
McGinnis, Shawn, Johnson City*	.245	25	49	5	12	13	1	0	0	6	3	1	2	1	5	0	8	0	1
McNally, Robert, Pulaski	.241	29	58	10	14	20	3	0	1	4	1	0	2	2	18	0	5	2	1
Mejias, Simeon, Wytheville	.305	34	131	23	40	42	2	0	0	9	0	2	0	0	14	0	15	5	2
Melvin, William, Wytheville	.000	14	11	0	0	0	0	0	0	0	0	1	0	0	0	0	7	0	0
Miller, Michael, Wytheville	.236	60	199	26	47	73	12	1	4	31	3	4	4	0	6	0	39	2	2
Minton, Jesse, Pulaski*	.277	63	231	46	64	114	16	5	8	50	6	0	0	3	18	1	49	6	2
Morawski, Mark, Bluefield	.162	11	37	2	6	7	1	0	0	2	1	0	0	0	3	0	11	0	2
Morrisette, James, Kingsport	.217	42	115	14	25	40	3	0	4	9	1	0	0	4	10	0	36	10	3
Mullino, Ray, Wytheville	.000	15	5	0	0	0	0	0	0	0	0	0	0	0	1	0	1	0	0
Murphy, Miguel, Elizabethton	.273	43	132	21	36	55	8	1	3	21	1	1	0	2	10	0	18	8	1
Naughton, Daniel, Kingsport	.250	43	156	22	39	63	9	0	5	19	2	1	2	2	13	0	36	8	2
Nezelek, Andrew, Pulaski*	.000	12	10	1	0	0	0	0	0	0	0	1	0	0	1	0	1	0	0
Nivar, Pedro, Bristol	.246	24	61	14	15	18	0	0	1	4	0	0	0	0	6	0	15	2	0
Nottingham, Daran, Kingsport*	1.000	10	1	0	1	1	0	0	0	0	0	0	0	0	0	0	0	0	0
Nowak, Matthew, Bluefield	.259	50	162	31	42	77	11	0	8	35	2	0	3	5	39	1	32	5	2
O'Keefe, Timothy, Johnson City	.000	16	5	0	0	0	0	0	0	0	0	0	0	0	1	0	4	0	0
O'Quinn, Steven, Pulaski	.333	18	6	0	2	2	0	0	0	1	0	1	0	0	1	0	2	0	0
Oertli, Charles, Wytheville	.158	6	19	2	3	3	0	0	0	4	0	0	1	0	2	0	5	0	0
Olah, Robert, Kingsport	.192	36	120	13	23	26	3	0	0	7	0	0	1	0	6	1	34	1	1
Olmstead, Reed, Johnson City*	.255	58	184	36	47	67	8	0	4	26	4	0	2	6	33	2	42	1	0
Osteen, David, Johnson City	.300	14	10	1	3	4	1	0	0	2	0	0	0	0	1	0	2	0	0
Pancoski, Tracey, Bluefield	.355	15	31	10	11	12	1	0	0	5	0	0	0	1	9	0	5	0	1
Parks, Derek, Elizabethton	.237	62	224	39	53	95	10	1	10	40	5	0	3	5	23	0	58	1	0
Paulino, Ernesto, Bluefield	.265	45	162	29	43	70	6	0	7	28	7	0	0	3	16	0	31	3	1
Pena, Geronimo, Johnson City	.297	56	202	55	60	84	7	4	3	20	2	1	3	7	46	4	33	27	3
Pennington, Kenneth, Pulaski	.291	58	223	44	65	99	9	2	7	36	3	0	4	5	29	0	25	9	2
Perdomo, Soilo, Kingsport	.069	19	29	6	2	2	0	0	0	3	0	0	0	0	5	1	8	0	0
Perez, Michael, Johnson City	.429	18	7	1	3	3	0	0	0	0	0	1	0	0	2	0	2	0	0
Pike, Mark, Burlington	.190	44	121	20	23	33	5	1	1	15	0	0	2	0	20	1	18	10	2
Piskor, Stephen, Kingsport	.197	46	147	20	29	39	4	0	2	19	2	1	2	6	16	0	26	7	2
Polanco, Radhames, Kingsport	.238	62	223	22	53	77	12	0	4	26	2	1	0	3	28	0	56	1	3
Polk, Riley, Burlington	.258	50	159	32	41	58	12	1	1	25	3	1	4	0	33	0	26	10	3
Power, John, Burlington*	.184	46	141	12	26	30	4	0	0	8	1	0	0	1	11	1	27	3	1
Pride, Curtis, Kingsport*	.109	27	46	5	5	8	0	0	1	4	0	0	0	1	6	0	24	5	0
Quiles, Victor, Wytheville	.000	16	1	0	0	0	0	0	0	0	0	1	0	0	0	0	1	0	0
Radcliffe, Ernest, Johnson City	.200	26	70	7	14	21	1	0	2	10	0	0	0	1	4	0	14	0	1
Ragland, William, Pulaski	.300	25	70	7	21	27	3	0	1	12	2	0	1	0	5	0	13	3	0
Randle, Michael, Elizabethton*	.299	58	204	27	61	68	4	0	1	20	2	3	0	4	19	0	15	19	3
Reeder, Michael, Wytheville*	.193	62	197	19	38	48	5	1	1	18	1	1	2	1	38	0	68	4	0
Richardson, James, Burlington	.270	57	189	34	51	70	10	3	1	17	0	0	3	5	36	1	34	5	7
Rincon, Luciano, Johnson City	.000	2	1	0	0	0	0	0	0	0	0	0	0	0	0	0	0	0	0
Rivero, Martin, Wytheville	.148	54	169	16	25	34	4	1	1	20	1	2	2	2	26	1	35	3	0
Rizzo, Paul, Kingsport	.175	54	166	15	29	36	4	0	1	9	0	4	1	0	18	0	25	5	1
Robinson, Lynn, Pulaski	.242	51	132	32	32	59	8	2	5	16	1	0	0	4	23	0	38	15	1
Rocca, Jose, Johnson City	.067	11	15	0	1	1	0	0	0	0	0	0	0	0	1	0	0	0	0
Rosario, David, Wytheville*	.300	17	10	2	3	7	2	1	0	2	0	0	0	0	0	0	0	0	0
Rosario, Francisco, Johnson City	.277	27	65	11	18	24	3	0	1	6	1	0	1	1	5	0	10	3	1
Rountree, Michael, Burlington*	.182	52	132	24	24	37	2	1	3	12	1	1	0	1	35	0	52	11	2
Sala, David, Johnson City*	.250	13	8	2	2	3	1	0	0	0	0	0	0	0	2	0	1	0	0
Sencion, Julio, Wytheville	.221	47	145	16	32	41	7	1	0	13	1	2	1	0	12	0	39	10	5
Senne, Michael, Johnson City	.282	57	206	46	58	93	15	1	6	38	4	0	2	4	35	0	35	21	4
Simmelink, Jeffrey, Burlington*	.194	22	62	8	12	16	4	0	0	8	2	0	0	1	13	0	8	1	1
Sims, Kinney, Bluefield*	.308	54	198	38	61	75	5	3	1	21	0	3	2	1	26	0	44	14	4
Singletary, Nathan, Johnson City†	.250	10	36	6	9	11	2	0	0	4	0	0	0	1	6	0	5	6	2
Sisney, Lorenzo, Kingsport	.241	47	133	19	32	61	6	1	7	26	3	0	1	1	27	0	42	5	3
Smith, Alexander, Pulaski	.357	24	98	20	35	54	7	0	4	34	4	0	3	1	7	0	10	1	0
Smith, Arthur, Pulaski	.211	52	133	19	28	33	5	0	0	10	0	2	1	1	10	0	33	5	2
Snyder, Kendall, Elizabethton	.207	37	111	11	23	39	2	1	4	16	3	1	0	0	16	0	13	2	0
Solano, Ramon, Bristol	.239	62	209	24	50	62	5	2	1	19	2	2	1	4	8	0	62	7	1
Sommer, David, Wytheville	.000	4	1	0	0	0	0	0	0	0	0	0	0	0	0	0	1	0	0
Stewart, John, Pulaski*	.364	16	11	3	4	4	0	0	0	1	0	0	0	0	0	0	3	0	0
Swenson, Lee, Elizabethton	.207	12	29	7	6	8	2	0	0	7	1	0	0	0	11	0	7	0	0
Taveras, Jose, Bristol†	.180	20	50	4	9	9	0	0	0	3	0	0	1	1	5	0	17	0	0
Taylor, Kenneth, Wytheville	.252	37	103	13	26	36	7	0	1	21	1	2	1	3	16	0	28	1	0

Player and Club	Pct.	G.	AB.	R.	H.	TB.	2B.	3B.	HR.	RBI.	GW.	SH.	SF.	HP.	BB.	Int. BB.	SO.	SB.	CS.
Thomas, Orlando, Johnson City	.167	9	12	1	2	3	1	0	0	2	0	0	0	0	1	0	3	0	0
Tomberlin, Andy, Pulaski*	.250	3	4	2	1	1	0	0	0	0	0	0	0	0	2	0	1	0	0
Turner, Matthew, Pulaski	.000	18	5	0	0	0	0	0	0	0	0	0	0	0	3	0	2	0	0
Valera, Julio, Kingsport	.167	13	6	0	1	1	0	0	0	0	0	0	0	0	0	0	1	0	0
Vannucci, Michael, Burlington	.273	24	55	9	15	21	1	1	1	7	0	1	0	1	15	0	13	3	0
Veldez, Frank, Elizabethton	.200	16	40	6	8	10	2	0	0	6	0	0	1	0	4	0	16	1	0
Walker, Abraham, Burlington	.280	47	143	22	40	50	3	2	1	12	2	0	1	3	25	0	12	6	3
Wallen, Walter, Bluefield	.231	20	65	14	15	19	1	0	1	8	1	1	0	2	9	0	8	0	1
Walton, Jerome, Wytheville	.288	62	229	48	66	96	7	4	5	34	1	3	3	6	28	0	40	21	3
Washington, Kirk, Wytheville	.143	17	7	1	1	1	0	0	0	1	0	0	0	0	0	0	3	0	0
Watson, Thomas, Pulaski	.429	20	7	0	3	4	1	0	0	3	0	1	0	0	1	0	2	0	0
Webster, Leonard, Elizabethton	.230	48	152	29	35	48	4	0	3	14	1	0	0	2	22	0	21	1	0
Wenrick, John, Kingsport*	.000	12	3	0	0	0	0	0	0	0	0	0	0	0	5	0	2	0	0
Williams, Edward, Wytheville*	.276	52	156	25	43	53	5	1	1	13	4	2	0	1	19	0	31	12	2
Williams, Walter, Pulaski*	.200	12	10	0	2	2	0	0	0	0	0	0	0	0	1	0	7	0	0
Wills, Adrian, Pulaski*	.000	3	5	0	0	0	0	0	0	0	0	0	0	0	1	0	0	0	0
Wilson, William, Pulaski	.000	12	3	0	0	0	0	0	0	0	0	0	0	0	0	0	2	0	0
Wolton, Brad, Burlington*	.268	61	190	26	51	69	11	2	1	32	5	0	4	1	11	3	30	5	1
Woods, Eric, Wytheville*	.167	13	12	0	2	2	0	0	0	0	0	0	0	0	1	0	3	0	0
Woods, Jason, Kingsport	.190	39	116	14	22	34	0	0	4	12	0	0	1	3	17	0	41	3	0
Young, Ernest, Bluefield†	.223	60	184	33	41	72	6	2	7	24	3	0	1	1	39	3	57	4	6

The following pitchers, listed alphabetically by club, with games in parentheses, had no plate appearances, primarily through use of designated hitters:

BLUEFIELD—Barry, Dale (11); Burdick, Stacey (12); Bushing, Christopher (13); Carriger, Ricky (12); Dubois, Brian (3); Evans, Scott (4); Gast, Joseph (13); Lopez, Craig (9); Ludwig, Frederick (10); Mandich, Thomas (6); McCall, Terrell (1); Michno, Thomas (14); Miller, David R. (13); Severino, Edward (11); Walton, Robert (3); Williams, Steve (23).

BRISTOL—Belcher, Glenn (15); Carter, Richard (11); Falkenhagen, Mickey (11); Foster, Paul (1); Gatchell, Douglas (14); Hursey, Darren (13); Jackson, Paul (4); Lacko, Richard (3); Lott, Henry (1); Nosek, Randall (11); O'Neill, Daniel (19); Parascand, Steven (13); Phillips, Charles (13); Scully, Thomas (1); Strauber, Stephen (5); Wenson, Paul (21); Wetherell, Gerry (15).

BURLINGTON—Baez, Angel (8); Dillmore, Phillip (15); Gilles, Mark (12); Gonzales, Todd (11); Hindulak, James (15); Kuykendall, Kevin (9); Mercado, Manuel (14); Monegro, Juan (2); Ortiz, Angel (11); Scaglione, Anthony (11); Seanez, Rudy (13); Soos, Charles (29); Walker, Michael (14).

ELIZABETHTON—Beattie, Burt (10); Buzzard, Lawrence (13); Cook, James (9); Dyer, Lawrence (14); Heinle, Dana (17); Hernandez, Robert (14); Hoffner, Robert (17); McCall, Terrell (3); Nivens, Toby (13); Pittman, Park (8); Schneider, Steven (7); Stano, Daniel (3); Villanueva, Eric (10); White, Frederick (8).

JOHNSON CITY—Becker, Gregory (22); Diaz, Felix (2).

KINGSPORT—Garcia, Victor (2); Henion, Scott (2); McDonald, Bruce (6); Miller, Larry (18); Newton, Stephen (15); Pena, Jose (14); Stratinsky, Timothy (7).

PULASKI—Miller, David S. (4); Roth, Rex (22); Taylor, Richard (14).

GRAND SLAM HOME RUNS—Deak, L. Gomez, S. Johnson, Jones-Pointer, Jose, Kler, Pennington, E. Williams, 1 each.

AWARDED FIRST BASE ON CATCHER'S INTERFERENCE—Goodwin 2 (Simmelink, Swenson); Barrs (Parks); Douglas (F. Rosario); Hamilton (Simmelink); Height (Parks); Lexa (Paulino); Power (Beasant); Rountree (McNally); E. Williams (Paulino).

CLUB FIELDING

Club	Pct.	G.	PO.	A.	E.	DP.	PB.
Johnson City	.956	66	1712	726	113	52	7
Bluefield	.951	68	1701	666	123	37	14
Bristol	.948	69	1736	719	134	60	17
Elizabethton	.943	68	1711	685	145	57	22
Pulaski	.943	66	1676	637	140	51	9
Wytheville	.943	68	1717	658	144	50	17
Burlington	.941	67	1767	649	152	32	20
Kingsport	.937	68	1700	734	164	46	21

INDIVIDUAL FIELDING

*Throws lefthanded.

FIRST BASEMEN

Player and Club	Pct.	G.	PO.	A.	E.	DP.
Baez, Johnson City*	.958	7	22	1	1	3
Balthazar, Bristol	.967	10	78	11	3	9
Courtney, Elizabethton	1.000	2	10	2	0	1
Cramer, Elizabethton*	1.000	2	21	2	0	1
Garmon, Elizabethton	.977	38	287	12	7	19
Goodwin, Bluefield*	1.000	10	92	5	0	5
HOILES, Bristol	.996	60	515	34	2	45
Jose, Wytheville	.966	16	82	3	3	9
Kickbush, Pulaski	.991	16	98	8	1	8
Martinez, Burlington	.975	28	223	10	6	12
McNally, Pulaski	1.000	2	8	0	0	0
Minton, Pulaski	.976	54	414	33	11	33
Olah, Kingsport	.958	23	195	8	9	16
Olmstead, Johnson City*	.983	58	473	46	9	29
Polk, Burlington	.962	7	48	3	2	2
Power, Burlington*	.979	41	355	21	8	15
Radcliffe, Johnson City	.992	18	121	7	1	12
Reeder, Wytheville*	.980	62	472	21	10	36
Sisney, Kingsport	.959	23	202	9	9	12
Smith, Pulaski	1.000	1	12	0	0	0
Snyder, Elizabethton	.978	35	291	14	7	23
Walker, Burlington	1.000	1	3	0	0	0
Wallen, Bluefield	1.000	4	26	1	0	2
Woods, Kingsport	.970	27	212	13	7	12
Young, Bluefield*	.982	57	448	33	9	27

SECOND BASEMEN

Player and Club	Pct.	G.	PO.	A.	E.	DP.
Abreu, Johnson City	1.000	1	3	3	0	1
Almonte, Burlington	.000	1	0	0	1	0
Arias, Burlington	.898	18	30	23	6	2
Austin, Bristol	1.000	3	4	5	0	0
BEYELER, Bristol	.983	65	119	173	5	36
Brown, Elizabethton	.925	43	83	101	15	16
Cantrell, Pulaski	.935	6	10	19	2	5
Castillo, Bristol	.500	1	1	0	1	0
Courtney, Elizabethton	.914	17	30	44	7	7
Geronimo, Kingsport	.915	38	70	103	16	17
Gomez, Bluefield	.333	2	0	1	2	0
Hawkins, Kingsport	.951	8	12	27	2	2
Height, Kingsport	.877	26	59	55	16	9
Hildebrandt, Elizabethton	.903	10	15	13	3	3
Hill, Wytheville	.940	49	113	122	15	28
Jeffers, Johnson City	.970	14	29	35	2	8
Johnson, Pulaski	.932	52	102	132	17	31
Klyczek, Bluefield	.800	4	2	2	1	0
Lexa, Elizabethton	.850	3	9	8	3	3
Lora, Bluefield	.973	19	31	41	2	4
Mallinak, Bluefield	.956	36	83	90	8	17
Maloney, Pulaski	.964	8	9	18	1	3
Mejias, Wytheville	.909	16	37	33	7	5
Morawski, Bluefield	.943	11	18	32	3	3
Nowak, Bluefield	.800	1	1	3	1	1
Pena, Johnson City	.973	56	108	144	7	27
Perdomo, Kingsport	1.000	3	6	2	0	2
Polk, Burlington	.966	23	56	58	4	5
Ragland, Pulaski	.931	9	12	15	2	1
Sencion, Wytheville	.944	7	13	4	1	0
Taveras, Bristol	.917	4	7	4	1	2
Walker, Burlington	.900	40	94	77	19	16

THIRD BASEMEN

Player and Club	Pct.	G.	PO.	A.	E.	DP.
Abreu, Johnson City	.800	6	1	3	1	0
Austin, Bristol	.867	49	35	95	20	7
Barr, Johnson City	.750	16	6	9	5	0
Barrs, Johnson City	.750	5	0	6	2	0
Boyce, Elizabethton	.860	41	22	76	16	4
Cantrell, Pulaski	.833	2	2	3	1	1
A. Castillo, Burlington	.778	19	7	28	10	3
R. Castillo, Bristol	1.000	3	1	6	0	0
Courtney, Elizabethton	1.000	3	3	12	0	0
Doster, Bristol	.795	16	7	24	8	2
Geronimo, Kingsport	1.000	1	0	2	0	0
Gomez, Bluefield	.911	21	15	36	5	4
Hannon, Wytheville	.769	8	3	7	3	2
Height, Kingsport	.889	12	8	8	2	1
Hildebrandt, Elizabethton	1.000	1	0	1	0	0
Jeffers, Johnson City	1.000	6	2	6	0	0
Jose, Wytheville	.750	1	1	2	1	0
Kickbush, Pulaski	1.000	2	2	3	0	0
Leius, Elizabethton	.750	2	1	2	1	0
Lexa, Elizabethton	.825	27	21	31	11	6
Looper, Johnson City	.873	50	26	98	18	6
Lora, Bluefield	.933	12	11	17	2	0
Mejias, Wytheville	.898	16	17	36	6	2
Miller, Wytheville	.886	17	8	23	4	1
Nowak, Bluefield	.851	25	10	47	10	3
Pennington, Pulaski	.846	53	40	92	24	3
POLANCO, Kingsport	.942	62	44	134	11	4
Ragland, Pulaski	.625	3	1	4	3	0
Richardson, Burlington	.914	53	41	97	13	2
Rivero, Wytheville	.907	30	15	63	8	2
Smith, Pulaski	.789	8	5	10	4	0
Taveras, Bristol	.875	6	1	6	1	1
Wallen, Bluefield	.900	13	9	18	3	2
Walton, Wytheville	.778	1	2	5	2	0

SHORTSTOPS

Player and Club	Pct.	G.	PO.	A.	E.	DP.
Abreu, Johnson City	.911	42	55	129	18	12
Almonte, Burlington	.828	24	11	37	10	5
Austin, Bristol	1.000	1	3	2	0	0
Barrs, Johnson City	.873	33	40	97	20	21
Bautista, Burlington	.893	41	43	115	19	9
Brown, Elizabethton	.800	1	3	5	2	2
Courtney, Elizabethton	.500	1	0	3	3	0
Crowley, Bluefield	.911	59	89	167	25	19
Gomez, Bluefield	1.000	1	0	1	0	0
Hawkins, Kingsport	.895	9	13	21	4	3
Height, Kingsport	.889	2	4	4	1	0
Hill, Wytheville	.818	11	12	24	8	1
Jeffers, Johnson City	1.000	2	4	3	0	4
Johnson, Pulaski	1.000	1	2	1	0	0
Leius, Elizabethton	.931	57	67	174	18	33
Lora, Bluefield	.700	4	0	7	3	0
Mallinak, Bluefield	.917	7	14	30	4	5
Maloney, Pulaski	.917	49	85	125	19	26
Mejias, Wytheville	.625	1	1	4	3	2
Perdomo, Kingsport	.821	13	13	19	7	2
Polk, Burlington	.935	19	25	61	6	4
Ragland, Pulaski	.826	7	7	12	4	4
Rivero, Wytheville	.895	26	39	63	12	12
RIZZO, Kingsport	.933	54	85	164	18	28
Sencion, Wytheville	.871	35	49	99	22	18
Smith, Pulaski	.923	12	20	28	4	10
Solano, Bristol	.894	62	96	166	31	29
Taveras, Bristol	.913	10	13	29	4	7
Veldez, Elizabethton	.822	15	13	24	8	4

OUTFIELDERS

Player and Club	Pct.	G.	PO.	A.	E.	DP.
Adderly, Bluefield	.969	60	122	3	4	0
Alvarez, Johnson City*	.966	28	25	3	1	0
Arias, Burlington	1.000	5	4	0	0	0
Baez, Johnson City*	.000	1	0	0	1	0
Balthazar, Bristol	1.000	2	4	0	0	0
Battaglia, Burlington	.966	42	53	3	2	1
Browe, Bristol	.848	25	28	0	5	0
Brown, Elizabethton	1.000	2	4	1	0	0
Cabrera, Bristol	.933	45	65	5	5	0
Cantrell, Pulaski	.965	51	102	8	4	2
E. Carter, Johnson City*	.960	33	48	0	2	0
L. Carter, Johnson City	1.000	2	2	0	0	0
Castillo, Burlington	.882	11	14	1	2	0
Clark, Bristol	1.000	10	11	0	0	0
Colavito, Bluefield	.977	28	39	3	1	1
Cuyler, Bristol	.960	43	97	0	4	0
Davis, Elizabethton*	.969	56	124	2	4	2
DeLima, Elizabethton*	.978	47	82	5	2	2
DeLoach, Johnson City	.978	38	42	2	1	1
Doster, Bristol	.932	50	75	7	6	1
Douglas, Kingsport	.875	25	34	1	5	0
Franco, Bluefield	.889	18	22	2	3	0
Goodwin, Bluefield*	.920	14	22	1	2	0
Hamilton, Pulaski	.900	20	18	0	2	0
Hannon, Wytheville	.975	36	71	7	2	2
G. Jackson, Wytheville	.889	25	39	1	5	0
R. Jackson, Bristol	.905	30	38	0	4	0
Jeffers, Johnson City	1.000	1	1	0	0	0
J. Johnson, Pulaski	1.000	1	1	0	0	0
S. Johnson, Burlington	.864	16	18	1	3	0
Jones-Pointer, Pulaski	.938	53	81	9	6	1
Jose, Wytheville	.895	12	17	0	2	0
Kickbush, Pulaski	.500	5	2	0	2	0
Kindred, Johnson City	.931	41	81	0	6	0
Kler, Bluefield	.900	27	26	1	3	0
Lampe, Johnson City	.909	13	10	0	1	0
Lemle, Kingsport	.906	11	28	1	3	0
Liriano, Burlington	.929	35	37	2	3	0
Martin, Elizabethton	.903	25	26	2	3	1
D. May, Wytheville	.909	44	47	3	5	0
L. May, Kingsport	.880	49	72	1	10	0
McDaniel, Kingsport	.963	36	68	11	3	1
McGinnis, Johnson City*	1.000	8	5	0	0	0
Miller, Wytheville	1.000	2	1	0	0	0
Morrisette, Kingsport	.917	34	32	1	3	0
Murphy, Elizabethton	.958	34	45	1	2	0
Naughton, Kingsport	.918	40	52	4	5	0
Nivar, Bristol	.826	21	18	1	4	0
Nowak, Bluefield	1.000	5	4	0	0	0
Pancoski, Bluefield*	1.000	14	14	0	0	0
Pike, Burlington	.944	38	67	1	4	0
Pride, Kingsport	1.000	18	17	1	0	0
Ragland, Pulaski	1.000	2	2	0	0	0
Randle, Elizabethton*	.947	56	51	3	3	0
Robinson, Pulaski	.859	45	53	2	9	0
Rountree, Burlington*	.923	50	47	1	4	0
Senne, Johnson City	.976	56	79	4	2	1
Sims, Bluefield*	.948	52	103	6	6	2
Singletary, Johnson City	.833	7	10	0	2	0
Sisney, Kingsport	.923	11	10	2	1	1
Smith, Pulaski	.862	47	46	4	8	0
Walton, Wytheville	.992	61	128	2	1	1
Williams, Wytheville*	.966	44	55	1	2	0
WOLTON, Burlington*	1.000	49	70	2	0	1

CATCHERS

Player and Club	Pct.	G.	PO.	A.	E.	DP.	PB.
Balthazar, Bristol	.971	17	86	13	3	2	2
Baxter, Burlington	.964	32	227	15	9	2	11
Beasant, Kingsport	.961	24	117	7	5	1	3
Clark, Bristol	.971	52	343	25	11	4	14
Deak, Pulaski	.990	50	391	24	4	1	6
Gonzalez, Kingsport	.968	22	124	25	5	3	6
HEWES, Johnson City	.992	50	320	37	3	7	2
Hoiles, Bristol	.963	6	48	4	2	0	1
Kickbush, Pulaski	1.000	4	21	3	0	0	1
Lehman, Bluefield	.976	21	149	14	4	0	6
McNally, Pulaski	.971	18	97	4	3	1	2
Miller, Wytheville	.973	39	207	41	7	3	9
Nowak, Bluefield	.974	13	68	6	2	0	1
Oertli, Wytheville	1.000	6	45	1	0	0	1
Parks, Elizabethton	.979	44	297	36	7	5	17
Paulino, Bluefield	.979	36	259	27	6	1	7
Piskor, Kingsport	.959	35	191	20	9	1	12
Rocca, Johnson City	1.000	6	13	0	0	0	3
Rosario, Johnson City	.979	23	126	13	3	1	1
Simmelink, Burlington	.959	21	134	7	6	0	3
Swenson, Elizabethton	.990	12	86	10	1	0	2
Taylor, Wytheville	.979	32	212	20	5	1	7
Thomas, Johnson City	1.000	7	21	1	0	0	1
Vannucci, Burlington	.978	23	128	6	3	0	6
Webster, Elizabethton	.971	17	88	11	3	1	3
Wills, Pulaski	1.000	1	4	0	0	0	0

PITCHERS

Player and Club	Pct.	G.	PO.	A.	E.	DP.
Akins, Pulaski	1.000	8	2	7	0	0
Alexander, Wytheville	1.000	12	5	4	0	0
Baez, Burlington	1.000	8	1	1	0	0
Barry, Bluefield*	1.000	11	2	7	0	0
Beattie, Elizabethton	.500	10	1	2	3	0
Becker, Johnson City*	1.000	22	0	3	0	1
Belcher, Bristol	1.000	15	2	6	0	2
Berringer, Wytheville	1.000	26	4	12	0	2
Bohne, Kingsport	.500	4	0	2	2	0
Boskie, Wytheville	1.000	14	1	8	0	0
Burdick, Bluefield	.846	12	5	6	2	1
Bushing, Bluefield	1.000	13	0	2	0	0
Buzzard, Elizabethton	.750	13	1	8	3	0
Carriger, Bluefield	1.000	12	4	11	0	0
L. Carter, Johnson City	1.000	8	4	7	0	0
R. Carter, Bristol	.933	11	3	11	1	0
Cartwright, Johnson City	1.000	4	0	3	0	0
Castillo, Bristol	1.000	2	1	2	0	1
Cook, Elizabethton	1.000	9	2	12	0	2
Corbin, Kingsport	1.000	18	1	2	0	1
Crowson, Kingsport	1.000	13	6	12	0	2
Dillmore, Bristol*	1.000	15	2	4	0	0
Dubois, Bluefield*	.750	3	0	3	1	0
Dyer, Elizabethton	1.000	14	3	14	0	0
Elli, Kingsport*	.727	16	2	6	3	0
Evans, Bluefield	1.000	4	0	2	0	0
Falkenhagen, Bristol	1.000	11	3	8	0	0
Farmer, Johnson City	1.000	5	0	2	0	0
FARON, Johnson City	1.000	14	4	15	0	1
Featherstone, Pulaski*	.875	19	1	6	1	2
Garcia, Kingsport*	1.000	2	0	2	0	0
Gast, Bluefield*	.923	13	3	9	1	0
Gatchell, Bristol	1.000	14	3	10	0	0
Gilles, Bristol	1.000	12	8	10	0	0
H. Gomez, Wytheville	.800	16	2	2	1	0
P. Gomez, Wytheville*	.778	11	1	6	2	1
Gonzales, Bristol*	.818	11	1	8	2	0
Grater, Johnson City	1.000	24	5	6	0	0
Heinle, Elizabethton	.778	17	1	6	2	0
Henry, Johnson City	.636	9	0	7	4	1
Hernandez, Elizabethton*	.750	14	2	1	1	0
Hindulak, Bristol*	1.000	15	1	1	0	0
Hoffner, Elizabethton	.846	17	6	5	2	0
Hursey, Bristol*	.941	13	1	15	1	0
Jackson, Bristol	1.000	4	2	3	0	1
Johnson, Kingsport	.933	18	7	7	1	1
Kuykendall, Bristol	.750	9	1	2	1	0
Lacko, Bristol	1.000	3	1	0	0	0
LeMasters, Pulaski	1.000	15	3	6	0	0
Lemle, Kingsport	1.000	1	1	1	0	0
Lopez, Bluefield	1.000	9	1	5	0	0
Ludwig, Bluefield	.429	10	1	2	4	0
Main, Wytheville	.900	19	4	5	1	0
Mandich, Bluefield	1.000	6	1	0	0	0
Marina, Kingsport	.952	13	6	14	1	1
McCall, 1 Blue-3 Eliz*	1.000	4	0	1	0	0
McDonald, Kingsport	.750	6	1	2	1	0
Melvin, Wytheville	.875	13	2	5	1	0
Mercado, Burlington*	.800	14	4	16	5	2
Michno, Bluefield	1.000	14	2	7	0	0
D.R. Miller, Bluefield	.800	13	0	12	3	0
D.S. Miller, Pulaski	1.000	4	0	1	0	0
L. Miller, Kingsport*	1.000	18	0	2	0	0
Mullino, Wytheville	.857	15	3	3	1	1
Newton, Kingsport	.750	15	1	5	2	1
Nezelek, Pulaski	.842	12	3	13	3	0
Nivens, Elizabethton	.868	13	9	24	5	4
Nosek, Bristol	.957	11	8	14	1	0
Nottingham, Kingsport*	1.000	10	0	3	0	0
O'Keefe, Johnson City	1.000	16	3	5	0	0
O'Neill, Bristol*	.600	19	1	2	2	0
O'Quinn, Pulaski	1.000	18	5	6	0	0
Ortiz, Burlington*	.875	11	1	6	1	0
Osteen, Johnson City	.920	14	8	15	2	1
Parascand, Bristol*	.833	13	0	5	1	0
Pena, Kingsport*	1.000	14	0	3	0	0
Perez, Johnson City	1.000	18	8	8	0	0
Phillips, Bristol	.897	13	11	24	4	3
Pittman, Elizabethton	.923	8	3	9	1	1
Quiles, Wytheville	1.000	16	3	4	0	1
Radcliffe, Johnson City	1.000	3	1	0	0	0
Rincon, Johnson City	1.000	1	0	2	0	0
Rosario, Wytheville*	.875	15	3	11	2	0
Roth, Pulaski	.857	22	2	4	1	0
Sala, Johnson City*	.923	13	6	6	1	1
Scaglione, Burlington	.900	11	3	6	1	0
Schneider, Elizabethton	1.000	7	1	1	0	0
Scully, Bristol*	.500	1	1	0	1	0
Seanez, Burlington	.923	13	3	9	1	1
Severino, Bluefield	.500	11	1	0	1	0
Sommer, Wytheville	.909	4	1	9	1	0
Soos, Burlington	1.000	29	1	4	0	0
Stano, Elizabethton*	.000	3	0	0	1	0
Stewart, Pulaski*	.895	16	3	14	2	1
Stratinsky, Kingsport	.750	7	1	2	1	0
Strauber, Bristol*	1.000	5	0	1	0	0
K. Taylor, Wytheville	1.000	1	0	1	0	0
R. Taylor, Pulaski	.667	14	1	1	1	0
Tomberlin, Pulaski*	1.000	3	0	5	0	1
Turner, Pulaski	1.000	18	1	7	0	0
Valera, Kingsport	.960	13	4	20	1	1
Villanueva, Elizabethton*	1.000	10	1	6	0	1
Walker, Burlington	.950	14	6	13	1	0
Walton, Bluefield	1.000	3	0	1	0	0
Washington, Wytheville	.833	17	2	3	1	0
Watson, Pulaski	1.000	20	4	4	0	0
Wenrick, Kingsport	.909	12	2	8	1	0
Wenson, Bristol	.786	21	4	7	3	0
Wetherell, Bristol	1.000	15	2	1	0	0
White, Elizabethton	.750	8	2	1	1	0
S. Williams, Bluefield	.818	23	4	5	2	0
W. Williams, Pulaski*	.750	12	0	3	1	0
Wilson, Pulaski	1.000	12	4	3	0	0

The following players do not have any recorded accepted chances at the positions indicated; therefore, are not listed in the fielding averages for those particular positions: Alexander, of; Arias, ss; Caballero, p; Deak, of; Diaz, p; Henion, p; Hildebrandt, ss; R. Jackson, p; Jeffers, 1b; Lott, p; Martinez, of; McNally, of; Monegro, p; Pennington, of; Radcliffe, of; Richardson, of; Ar. Smith, 2b; Solano, of; Vannucci, 2b; Wallen, of; Wills, of.

CLUB PITCHING

Club	ERA.	G.	CG.	ShO.	Sv.	IP.	H.	R.	ER.	HR.	HB.	BB.	Int. BB.	SO.	WP.	Bk.
Johnson City	3.39	66	14	6	15	570.2	507	275	215	40	31	232	6	460	38	4
Burlington	3.48	67	6	3	13	.589.0	499	320	228	37	25	313	3	474	18	4
Pulaski	4.01	66	7	4	10	558.2	573	337	249	37	31	276	8	486	39	6
Elizabethton	4.31	68	17	5	9	570.1	561	362	273	37	28	304	9	473	52	7
Bluefield	4.30	68	12	5	11	567.0	553	344	271	32	23	258	2	451	52	12
Bristol	4.32	69	8	4	14	578.2	551	354	278	32	34	302	2	467	71	4
Wytheville	4.73	68	5	0	14	572.1	547	399	301	49	39	358	11	460	70	17
Kingsport	5.38	68	7	1	8	566.2	647	458	339	55	22	324	10	422	53	5

PITCHERS' RECORDS

(Leading Qualifiers for Earned-Run Average Leadership—58 or More Innings)

*Throws lefthanded.

Pitcher—Club	W.	L.	Pct.	ERA.	G.	GS.	CG.	GF.	ShO.	Sv.	IP.	H.	R.	ER.	HR.	HB.	BB.	Int. BB.	SO.	WP.
Stewart, Pulaski*	4	2	.667	2.25	16	8	2	1	1	0	64.0	49	21	16	1	2	21	0	75	1
Osteen, Johnson City	9	2	.818	2.26	14	14	8	0	3	0	107.1	81	32	27	9	4	17	1	80	6
Nivens, Elizabethton	9	2	.818	2.62	13	13	7	0	1	0	99.2	76	35	29	3	2	30	0	74	7
Cook, Elizabethton	6	2	.750	2.65	9	8	4	0	0	0	68.0	54	24	20	1	2	22	1	43	4
Hursey, Bristol*	5	3	.625	2.70	13	11	0	0	0	0	66.2	58	29	20	5	0	21	0	44	5
Nezelek, Pulaski	2	4	.333	2.71	12	12	2	0	0	0	66.1	69	36	20	4	9	22	1	55	7
Gilles, Burlington	9	0	1.000	2.76	12	11	1	1	1	0	88.0	72	39	27	5	3	25	0	63	3
Perez, Johnson City	3	5	.375	2.97	18	8	2	6	0	3	72.2	69	35	24	3	5	22	0	72	1
R. Carter, Bristol	5	4	.556	3.05	11	11	3	0	0	0	65.0	48	31	22	0	6	36	0	63	8
Seanez, Burlington	5	2	.714	3.20	13	12	1	1	1	0	76.0	59	37	27	5	3	32	0	56	6

Departmental Leaders: G—Soos, 29; W—Gilles, Nivens, Osteen, Sala, 9; L—Rosario, Valera, 10; Pct.—Gilles, 1.000; GS—Dyer, LeMasters, Mercado, Osteen, 14; CG—Osteen, 8; GF—Soos, 24; ShO—Osteen, 3; Sv.—Berringer, 9; IP—Osteen, 107.1; H—Faron, 93; R—Walker, 65; ER—Melvin, Walker, 46; HR—Marina, Rosario, 11; HB—Henry, 10; BB—Mercado, 74; IBB—Four pitchers with 3; SO—LeMasters, 85; WP—Boskie, 15.

(All Pitchers—Listed Alphabetically)

Pitcher—Club	W.	L.	Pct.	ERA.	G.	GS.	CG.	GF.	ShO.	Sv.	IP.	H.	R.	ER.	HR.	HB.	BB.	Int. BB.	SO.	WP.
Akins, Pulaski	3	2	.600	2.36	8	6	1	1	0	1	42.0	32	14	11	3	1	12	0	39	1
Alexander, Wytheville	3	1	.750	5.46	12	4	1	3	0	0	31.1	33	23	19	3	1	25	3	19	2
Baez, Burlington	0	0	.000	3.68	8	0	0	6	0	0	14.2	12	7	6	1	3	9	0	10	0
Barry, Bluefield*	5	4	.556	3.21	11	11	3	0	0	0	70.0	59	32	25	4	2	27	0	52	3
Beattie, Elizabethton	1	1	.500	9.25	10	0	0	4	0	0	24.1	33	30	25	1	3	23	0	14	3
Becker, Johnson City*	3	0	1.000	2.61	22	0	0	14	0	3	41.1	29	16	12	5	1	8	1	24	1
Belcher, Bristol	0	2	.000	4.93	15	1	0	8	0	3	38.1	45	24	21	2	1	21	0	30	6
Berringer, Wytheville	1	1	.500	3.92	26	0	0	23	0	9	39.0	37	21	17	2	0	23	0	33	4
Bohne, Kingsport	1	2	.333	9.95	4	3	0	0	0	0	12.2	18	17	14	1	4	8	0	6	0
Boskie, Wytheville	4	4	.500	5.33	14	12	1	0	0	0	54.0	42	41	32	4	7	57	1	40	15
Burdick, Bluefield	4	3	.571	6.75	12	12	1	0	0	0	58.2	56	51	44	3	4	51	0	61	5
Bushing, Bluefield	2	0	1.000	1.37	13	1	0	7	0	2	26.1	14	5	4	1	0	12	0	30	4
Buzzard, Elizabethton	2	4	.333	6.55	13	4	1	6	0	2	44.0	52	40	32	2	4	23	1	47	6
Caballero, Wytheville	1	1	.500	0.93	7	1	0	5	0	1	19.1	11	5	2	0	0	6	0	22	1
Carriger, Bluefield	4	0	1.000	2.10	12	5	2	4	2	0	51.1	36	19	12	1	0	23	1	51	4
L. Carter, Johnson City	1	5	.167	3.72	8	8	0	0	0	0	36.1	30	22	15	4	1	18	0	35	1
R. Carter, Bristol	5	4	.556	3.05	11	11	3	0	0	0	65.0	48	31	22	0	6	36	0	63	8
Cartwright, Johnson City	1	0	1.000	4.26	4	3	0	0	0	0	12.2	10	6	6	3	0	15	0	9	1
Castillo, Bristol	0	0	.000	3.38	2	0	0	1	0	0	2.2	2	2	1	0	0	2	0	1	0
Cook, Elizabethton	6	2	.750	2.65	9	8	4	0	0	0	68.0	54	24	20	1	2	22	1	43	4
Corbin, Kingsport	1	1	.500	4.75	18	1	0	9	0	0	30.1	31	23	16	3	0	28	0	30	8
Crowson, Kingsport	2	7	.222	5.23	13	12	2	0	0	0	72.1	83	53	42	10	3	34	0	49	8
Diaz, Johnson City	0	0	.000	11.57	2	0	0	1	0	0	2.1	6	5	3	0	0	1	0	1	1
Dillmore, Burlington*	2	2	.500	5.64	15	2	0	5	0	0	30.1	30	22	19	3	1	21	0	29	3
Dubois, Bluefield*	1	1	.500	0.96	3	1	0	0	0	0	9.1	8	2	1	0	0	2	0	8	1
Dyer, Elizabethton	5	7	.417	3.48	14	14	3	0	1	0	72.1	70	50	28	6	3	42	1	62	5
Elli, Kingsport*	0	2	.000	6.68	16	3	0	3	0	0	33.2	43	34	25	4	1	24	0	28	3
Evans, Bluefield	1	0	1.000	0.00	4	1	1	3	1	1	12.0	8	1	0	0	0	2	0	15	0
Falkenhagen, Bristol	0	1	.000	6.10	11	4	0	1	0	0	31.0	35	28	21	1	1	17	0	16	3
Farmer, Johnson City	1	2	.333	7.50	5	4	0	0	0	0	18.0	18	16	15	1	3	12	0	13	3
Faron, Johnson City	8	1	.889	3.69	14	12	3	0	2	0	83.0	93	39	34	6	1	9	0	46	3
Featherstone, Pulaski*	1	1	.500	7.28	19	1	0	6	0	1	29.2	45	35	24	2	6	13	0	18	1
Garcia, Kingsport*	1	1	.500	2.70	2	2	0	0	0	0	13.1	11	7	4	1	1	2	0	7	2
Gast, Bluefield*	5	3	.625	4.02	13	13	3	0	0	0	80.2	81	49	36	6	3	37	0	44	6
Gatchell, Bristol	4	4	.500	4.43	14	9	0	1	0	0	63.0	63	35	31	6	6	27	0	47	1
Gilles, Burlington	9	0	1.000	2.76	12	11	1	1	1	0	88.0	72	39	27	5	3	25	0	63	3
H. Gomez, Wytheville	2	5	.286	2.81	16	6	1	5	0	2	57.2	55	30	18	3	1	16	0	30	1
P. Gomez, Wytheville*	3	6	.333	5.17	11	11	0	0	0	0	54.0	57	51	31	4	1	46	0	55	13
Gonzales, Burlington*	0	2	.000	2.54	11	3	0	3	0	1	28.1	24	16	8	2	1	16	0	38	0
Grater, Johnson City	5	2	.714	2.40	24	0	0	19	0	8	41.1	25	14	11	2	2	14	3	46	7
Heinle, Elizabethton	2	0	1.000	4.70	17	0	0	13	0	4	30.2	52	22	16	4	0	9	1	18	4
Henion, Kingsport	0	0	.000	2.70	2	0	0	2	0	2	3.1	6	1	1	0	0	1	0	6	0
Henry, Johnson City	3	3	.500	4.28	9	7	0	2	0	0	40.0	37	22	19	3	10	33	1	27	4
Hernandez, Elizabethton*	3	1	.750	3.10	14	0	0	10	0	2	29.0	23	13	10	1	0	15	2	29	5
Hindulak, Burlington*	1	1	.500	2.97	15	0	0	8	0	0	39.1	30	16	13	3	1	12	0	37	0
Hoffner, Elizabethton	4	7	.364	6.05	17	7	1	8	1	1	61.0	67	47	41	8	5	21	3	52	6
Hursey, Bristol*	5	3	.625	2.70	13	11	0	0	0	0	66.2	58	29	20	5	0	21	0	44	5
P. Jackson, Bristol	0	1	.000	8.18	4	2	0	0	0	0	11.0	10	10	10	2	2	9	0	3	3
R. Jackson, Bristol	0	0	.000	0.00	1	0	0	1	0	0	1.0	1	0	0	0	0	0	0	0	0
Johnson, Kingsport	3	5	.375	3.58	18	7	1	6	0	0	65.1	56	38	26	3	1	32	2	43	3
Kuykendall, Burlington	3	0	1.000	1.66	9	0	0	8	0	2	21.2	20	4	4	0	1	9	1	20	0
Lacko, Bristol	1	1	.500	2.84	3	2	0	1	0	0	12.2	5	4	4	1	1	5	0	17	2
LeMasters, Pulaski	7	1	.875	3.38	15	14	0	0	0	0	74.2	68	38	28	8	1	34	0	85	2
Lemle, Kingsport	0	0	.000	0.00	1	0	0	0	0	0	1.0	1	0	0	0	0	3	0	1	0
Lopez, Bluefield	2	5	.286	5.47	9	9	0	0	0	0	51.0	73	41	31	4	2	11	0	31	3
Lott, Bristol*	0	0	.000	0.00	1	1	0	0	0	0	0.1	0	0	0	0	0	0	0	1	0
Ludwig, Bluefield	0	0	.000	9.00	10	0	0	6	0	1	22.0	35	25	22	3	0	5	0	12	3
Main, Wytheville	3	3	.500	4.61	19	2	0	7	0	1	54.2	47	34	28	6	1	37	1	35	2
Mandich, Bluefield	1	1	.500	7.56	6	0	0	4	0	1	8.1	12	7	7	1	0	4	0	8	2
Marina, Kingsport	2	9	.182	4.34	13	13	1	0	0	0	85.0	82	51	41	11	3	37	1	66	5
McCall, 1 Blu-3 Elz	0	1	.000	9.82	4	0	0	2	0	0	3.2	5	8	7	0	1	9	0	3	0
McDonald, Kingsport	0	0	.000	10.50	6	0	0	4	0	1	12.0	22	17	14	1	0	8	1	7	5
Melvin, Wytheville	0	8	.000	7.18	13	12	0	0	0	0	57.2	67	54	46	4	9	42	2	57	10
Mercado, Burlington*	3	6	.333	3.35	14	14	2	0	0	0	78.0	57	46	29	2	2	74	0	62	3
Michno, Bluefield	2	1	.667	2.81	14	1	0	8	0	4	32.0	32	13	10	1	0	15	0	34	7
D.R. Miller, Bluefield	6	4	.600	3.28	13	13	2	0	1	0	82.1	61	37	30	6	5	35	0	63	9
D.S. Miller, Pulaski	2	0	1.000	5.40	4	0	0	4	0	0	5.0	5	3	3	0	0	5	1	4	0
L. Miller, Kingsport*	0	3	.000	6.48	18	0	0	10	0	0	25.0	29	25	18	3	2	25	2	23	2
Monegro, Burlington*	0	0	.000	2.25	2	0	0	0	0	0	4.0	5	3	1	0	0	1	0	2	0
Mullino, Wytheville	0	3	.000	4.46	15	6	1	4	0	0	42.1	41	24	21	4	3	18	0	33	3
Newton, Kingsport	0	2	.000	7.54	15	1	0	8	0	3	22.2	28	27	19	1	2	21	0	19	4
Nezelek, Pulaski	2	4	.333	2.71	12	12	2	0	0	0	66.1	69	36	20	4	9	22	1	55	7
Nivens, Elizabethton	9	2	.818	2.62	13	13	7	0	1	0	99.2	76	35	29	3	2	30	0	74	7
Nosek, Bristol	6	4	.600	4.55	11	11	2	0	0	0	63.1	58	38	32	1	4	45	0	48	12
Nottingham, Kingsport*	0	2	.000	9.00	10	2	0	3	0	1	27.0	39	34	27	6	2	18	0	.18	3
O'Keefe, Johnson City	1	0	1.000	2.36	16	0	0	8	0	1	42.0	44	22	11	2	0	26	0	38	3
O'Neill, Bristol*	0	1	.000	4.45	19	0	0	11	0	3	30.1	31	24	15	0	1	12	1	29	2
O'Quinn, Pulaski	4	4	.500	4.78	18	6	2	6	1	1	49.0	61	29	26	2	2	21	1	22	5
Ortiz, Burlington*	0	2	.000	3.10	11	1	0	5	0	3	29.0	24	13	10	1	0	14	0	26	0
Osteen, Johnson City	9	2	.818	2.26	14	14	8	0	3	0	107.1	81	32	27	9	4	17	1	80	6
Parascand, Bristol*	4	4	.500	3.42	13	7	1	4	1	0	50.0	45	28	19	4	1	23	0	43	2
Pena, Kingsport*	0	1	.000	5.82	14	0	0	9	0	0	17.0	26	19	11	1	0	13	0	11	0
Perez, Johnson City	3	5	.375	2.97	18	8	2	6	0	3	72.2	69	35	24	3	5	22	0	72	1
Phillips, Bristol	6	4	.600	3.97	13	10	2	2	0	1	70.1	83	34	31	5	2	26	0	48	8
Pittman, Elizabethton	3	1	.750	2.45	8	7	1	1	0	0	44.0	31	19	12	2	5	23	0	65	1
Quiles, Wytheville	0	0	.000	7.07	16	0	0	5	0	0	28.0	31	30	22	3	2	20	1	17	5

Pitcher—Club	W.	L.	Pct.	ERA.	G.	GS.	CG.	GF.	ShO.	Sv.	IP.	H.	R.	ER.	HR.	HB.	BB.	Int. BB.	SO.	WP.
Radcliffe, Johnson City	0	1	.000	10.80	3	0	0	1	0	0	5.0	8	7	6	1	0	5	0	3	0
Rincon, Johnson City	0	0	.000	27.00	1	0	0	1	0	0	1.0	4	3	3	0	0	2	0	1	0
Rosario, Wytheville*	3	10	.231	4.29	15	12	1	2	0	0	77.2	71	50	37	11	7	43	1	66	9
Roth, Pulaski	4	3	.571	5.40	22	1	0	13	0	1	36.2	47	32	22	1	1	26	0	29	6
Sala, Johnson City*	9	1	.900	3.86	13	10	1	0	1	0	67.2	53	36	29	1	4	50	0	65	7
Scaglione, Burlington	4	5	.444	3.47	11	11	1	0	0	0	62.1	61	37	24	5	6	31	1	38	1
Schneider, Elizabethton	0	1	.000	4.22	7	2	0	3	0	0	21.1	16	17	10	1	0	26	0	15	4
Scully, Bristol*	0	0	.000	0.00	1	0	0	0	0	0	2.0	2	3	0	0	1	3	0	1	0
Seanez, Burlington	5	2	.714	3.20	13	12	1	1	1	0	76.0	59	37	27	5	3	32	0	56	6
Severino, Bluefield	0	1	.000	12.32	11	1	0	5	0	0	19.0	27	28	26	2	3	12	0	12	3
Sommer, Wytheville	0	2	.000	4.15	4	2	0	1	0	0	13.0	14	7	6	2	1	6	0	5	1
Soos, Burlington	5	5	.500	2.68	29	0	0	24	0	7	47.0	30	15	14	1	0	24	1	51	1
Stano, Elizabethton*	0	0	.000	15.00	3	1	0	1	0	0	3.0	5	7	5	1	1	7	0	2	0
Stewart, Pulaski*	4	2	.667	2.25	16	8	2	1	1	0	64.0	49	21	16	1	2	21	0	75	1
Stratinsky, Kingsport	1	1	.500	1.84	7	0	0	6	0	1	14.2	13	3	3	0	0	10	2	13	2
Strauber, Bristol*	0	1	.000	25.65	5	0	0	2	0	0	6.2	7	19	19	0	7	18	0	6	9
K. Taylor, Wytheville	0	0	.000	11.57	1	0	0	0	0	0	2.1	4	3	3	0	0	1	0	3	1
R. Taylor, Pulaski	6	0	1.000	3.42	14	0	0	9	0	1	23.2	21	12	9	2	1	12	1	18	1
Tomberlin, Pulaski*	2	0	1.000	2.12	3	3	0	0	0	0	17.0	13	4	4	0	0	9	0	15	0
Turner, Pulaski	1	3	.250	4.62	18	5	0	7	0	2	48.2	55	36	25	6	2	28	1	48	2
Valera, Kingsport	3	10	.231	5.19	13	13	2	0	1	0	76.1	91	58	44	5	0	29	2	64	4
Villanueva, Elizabethton*	2	5	.286	5.44	10	6	0	3	0	0	44.2	54	38	27	5	1	34	0	30	5
Walker, Burlington	4	6	.400	5.89	14	13	1	0	0	0	70.1	75	65	46	9	4	45	0	42	1
Walton, Bluefield	1	2	.333	4.15	3	0	0	2	0	0	8.2	9	4	4	0	0	3	0	5	0
Washington, Wytheville	2	2	.500	4.14	17	0	0	8	0	1	41.1	37	26	19	3	6	18	2	45	3
Watson, Pulaski	1	1	.500	2.91	20	1	0	5	0	0	34.0	42	17	11	3	0	15	0	21	2
Wenrick, Kingsport	2	6	.250	5.56	12	11	1	1	0	0	55.0	68	51	34	5	3	31	0	31	4
Wenson, Bristol	3	4	.429	3.82	21	0	0	19	0	7	33.0	28	24	14	2	1	14	0	32	6
Wetherell, Bristol	1	0	1.000	5.17	15	0	0	10	0	0	31.1	30	21	18	3	0	23	1	38	4
White, Elizabethton	0	0	.000	5.11	8	6	0	0	0	0	24.2	24	16	14	2	1	22	0	19	2
S. Williams, Bluefield	5	3	.625	4.08	23	0	0	17	0	2	35.1	41	26	16	0	4	17	1	25	2
W. Williams, Pulaski*	3	2	.600	8.08	12	8	0	0	0	0	45.2	47	46	41	5	4	44	0	35	10
Wilson, Pulaski	1	2	.333	3.63	12	1	0	7	0	3	22.1	19	14	9	0	2	14	3	22	1

BALKS—Severino, 5; Main, Melvin, Nivens, 4 each; Gast, P. Gomez, Washington, 3 each; Burdick, Featherstone, Hursey, Newton, O'Quinn, Osteen, Pittman, 2 each; Baez, Becker, Caballero, Corbin, Dubois, Dyer, Gatchell, H. Gomez, Henry, LeMasters, McDonald, Mercado, D.R. Miller, Monegro, Parascand, Rosario, Roth, Scaglione, Valera, 1 each.

COMBINATION SHUTOUTS—Barry-Williams, Bluefield; Nosek-Belcher-O'Neill, Parascand-Wenson, Carter-Belcher, Bristol; Mercado-Soos, Burlington; Villanueva-Hoffner, White-Heinle, Elizabethton; Stewart-O'Quinn-Turner-Wilson, Stewart-Roth-Miller, Pulaski.

NO-HIT GAME—Seanez, Burlington, defeated Pulaski, 4-0, August 2.

Gulf Coast League

SUMMER CLASS A CLASSIFICATION

CHAMPIONSHIP WINNERS IN PREVIOUS YEARS

Year—Club	Pct.
1964—Sarasota Braves	.610
1965—Bradenton Astros	.632
1966—New York A.L.	.667
1967—Kansas City	.614
1968—Oakland	.650
1969—Montreal	.585
1970—Chicago A.L.	.600
1971—Kansas City	.755
1972—Chicago N.L. a	.651
Kansas City a	.651
1973—Texas	.732
1974—Chicago N.L.	.702
1975—Texas	.774
1976—Texas	.704
1977—Chicago-A.L	.731
1978—Texas	.600
1979—Houston	.635
1980—Kansas City-Blue	.635
1981—Kansas City-Gold	.688
1982—New York-A.L.	.667
1983—Texas	.645
Los Angeles b	.617
1984—White Sox	.651
Rangers b	.571
1985—Yankees c	.705
Rangers	.532

(Note—Known as Sarasota Rookie League in 1964 and Florida Rookie League in 1965.) aDeclared co-champions; no playoff. bLeague divided into Northern and Southern divisions; won one-game playoff for league championship. cYankees declared champion based on winning percentage when one-game playoff against Rangers was rained out.

STANDING OF CLUBS AT CLOSE OF SEASON, AUGUST 31

NORTHERN DIVISION

Club	W.	L.	T.	Pct.	G.B.
Dodgers	33	28	0	.541	....
Expos	33	29	0	.532	½
Rangers	31	31	0	.500	2½
Braves	29	34	0	.460	5
Pirates	24	39	1	.381	10

SOUTHERN DIVISION

Club	W.	L.	T.	Pct.	G.B.
Reds	34	28	0	.548	....
Astros	34	29	0	.540	½
Yankees	33	29	1	.532	1
White Sox	31	32	0	.492	3½
Royals	30	33	0	.476	4½

COMPOSITE STANDING OF CLUBS AT CLOSE OF SEASON, AUGUST 31

Club	Rds.	Dod.	Ast.	Yan.	Exp.	Rng.	W.S.	Roy.	Brv.	Pir.	W.	L.	T.	Pct.	G.B.
Reds	....	4	3	3	4	4	4	3	4	5	34	28	0	.548	....
Dodgers	2	....	1	6	2	3	6	3	5	5	33	28	0	.541	½
Astros	4	6	....	3	6	3	2	3	4	3	34	29	0	.540	½
Yankees	4	1	4	....	2	5	3	6	4	4	33	29	1	.532	1
Expos	3	5	1	4	....	4	5	4	3	4	33	29	0	.532	1
Rangers	3	3	4	2	3	....	5	3	4	4	31	31	0	.500	3
White Sox	3	1	5	4	2	2	....	5	4	5	31	32	0	.492	3½
Royals	4	4	4	1	3	4	2	....	4	4	30	33	0	.476	4½
Braves	3	2	3	3	4	3	3	3	....	5	29	34	0	.460	5½
Pirates	2	2	4	3	3	3	2	3	2	....	24	39	1	.381	10½

Games played at Bradenton and Sarasota, Fla.

Club names are major league affiliations.

Playoffs—Dodgers defeated Reds, one game to none, to win league championship.

Regular-Season Attendance—8,468 total paid for 20 openings (only games for which admission was charged).

Managers—Astros, Julio Linares; Braves, Pedro Gonzalez; Dodgers, Jose Alvarez; Expos, Mike Easom; Pirates, Woody Huyke; Rangers, Rudy Jaramillo; Reds, Sam Mejias; Royals, Luis Silverio; White Sox, Steve Dillard; Yankees, Fred Ferreira.

All-Star Team—1B—John Joslyn, Royals; 2B—Ed Renteria, Astros; 3B—Hensley Muelens, Yankees; SS—Hector Vargas, Yankees; OF—Dan Arendas, Yankees; Sean Ross, Braves; Bernie Williams, Yankees; C—Carlos Gonzalez, Royals; Starting Pitcher—Sam August, Astros; Relief Pitcher—Jose Tapia, Dodgers; Manager—Sam Mejias, Reds.

(Compiled by Howe News Bureau, Boston, Mass.)

CLUB BATTING

Club	Pct.	G.	AB.	R.	OR.	H.	TB.	2B.	3B.	HR.	RBI.	GW.	SH.	SF.	HP.	BB.	Int. BB.	SO.	SB.	CS.	LOB.
Yankees	.260	63	2067	319	275	537	722	74	18	25	284	26	18	24	26	316	7	385	85	48	484
Astros	.247	63	2082	299	273	515	658	76	17	11	244	29	24	20	23	241	13	416	100	33	467
Expos	.246	62	2025	263	272	499	597	61	11	5	219	29	32	18	28	237	6	354	74	27	483
Braves	.242	63	2076	279	263	502	642	66	16	14	239	25	31	28	28	213	13	377	88	41	435
Royals	.240	63	2019	266	297	485	628	66	10	19	211	25	17	14	30	248	6	409	112	54	446
White Sox	.240	63	2121	263	267	509	614	68	11	5	206	24	23	19	24	233	10	343	117	43	469
Dodgers	.236	61	2038	243	231	481	562	65	5	2	194	25	20	15	19	205	12	373	83	29	474
Pirates	.231	64	2015	236	317	465	594	63	18	10	201	20	21	18	27	186	4	437	132	57	397
Reds	.227	62	1986	251	243	451	580	63	15	12	203	30	26	8	11	229	6	440	116	48	394
Rangers	.227	62	1988	244	225	451	543	63	7	5	204	25	23	15	23	291	4	428	132	48	461

INDIVIDUAL BATTING

(Leading Qualifiers for Batting Championship—170 or More Plate Appearances)

*Bats lefthanded. †Switch-hitter.

Player and Club	Pct.	G.	AB.	R.	H.	TB.	2B.	3B.	HR.	RBI.	GW.	SH.	SF.	HP.	BB.	Int. BB.	SO.	SB.	CS.
Joslyn, John, Royals*	.339	55	177	34	60	91	9	2	6	25	1	2	1	0	45	1	28	8	2
Arendas, Daniel, Yankees*	.331	46	157	31	52	62	5	1	1	22	3	1	2	5	22	1	12	9	3
Hernandez, Carlos, Dodgers	.312	57	205	19	64	74	7	0	1	31	6	1	1	2	5	2	18	1	2
Dean, Kevin, Expos	.309	51	181	38	56	69	7	3	0	17	1	1	0	4	30	1	36	16	8
Ross, Sean, Braves*	.305	59	223	43	68	90	9	2	3	35	3	0	10	0	23	1	25	31	7
Valdez, Amilcar, Dodgers	.304	61	227	31	69	83	14	0	0	22	2	3	0	2	30	5	26	2	0
Paredes, Jesus, Expos†	.298	54	171	34	51	53	0	1	0	7	1	4	0	3	27	3	25	19	5
Renteria, Edinson, Astros	.297	52	182	23	54	70	11	1	1	26	5	0	2	1	13	1	9	6	2
Rhodes, Karl, Astros*	.293	62	222	36	65	81	10	3	0	22	3	5	2	0	32	3	33	14	6
Sanchez, Rey, Rangers	.290	52	169	27	49	54	3	1	0	23	4	3	1	3	41	0	18	10	10

Departmental Leaders: G—Rhodes, 62; AB—Ju. Gonzalez, 233; R—Williams, 45; H—A. Valdez, 69; TB—Sosa, 96; 2B—Sosa, 19; 3B—Champion, Jefferson, 5; HR—E. Gonzalez, 9; RBI—E. Gonzalez, 48; GWRBI—E. Gonzalez, Nieto, 8; SH—J. Mota, 6; SF—Ross, 10; HP—Deiley, 9; BB—Joslyn, 45; IBB—A. Valdez, 5; SO—Meulens, 66; SB—Garner, 36; CS—V. Harris, Williams, 12.

(All Players—Listed Alphabetically)

Player and Club	Pct.	G.	AB.	R.	H.	TB.	2B.	3B.	HR.	RBI.	GW.	SH.	SF.	HP.	BB.	Int. BB.	SO.	SB.	CS.
Acosta, Jose, Pirates	.000	21	2	0	0	0	0	0	0	0	0	0	0	0	0	0	1	0	0
Ahearne, Michael, Expos	.000	6	2	0	0	0	0	0	0	0	0	0	0	0	0	0	1	0	0
Alborano, Peter, Royals*	.277	45	137	26	38	48	5	1	1	16	0	0	3	2	24	2	9	10	3
Alcorta, Nicholas, Reds	.000	18	2	2	0	0	0	0	0	0	0	0	0	0	2	0	1	0	0
Almonte, Francisco, Pirates*	.000	4	1	0	0	0	0	0	0	0	0	0	0	0	0	0	0	0	0
Almonte, Heriberto, Astros	.200	14	40	3	8	9	1	0	0	1	0	1	0	0	3	0	13	1	0
Alvarez, Manuel, Expos	.167	34	90	10	15	16	1	0	0	9	1	1	2	1	10	0	17	3	2
Angelero, Jose, Royals	.204	39	93	14	19	20	1	0	0	7	1	1	0	4	10	0	34	1	4
Anthony, Eric, Astros*	.250	13	12	2	3	3	0	0	0	0	0	0	0	1	5	0	5	1	0
Arendas, Daniel, Yankees*	.331	46	157	31	52	62	5	1	1	22	3	1	2	5	22	1	12	9	3
Arteaga, Douglas, Pirates	.000	7	1	0	0	0	0	0	0	0	0	0	0	0	0	0	0	0	0
Audain, Miguel, White Sox	.273	54	150	13	41	48	5	1	0	11	0	6	0	0	7	0	17	4	3
August, Samuei, Astros	.071	13	14	0	1	1	0	0	0	0	0	1	0	0	0	0	4	0	0
Bailey, Jack, White Sox	.250	48	132	14	33	47	6	1	2	17	1	0	1	1	13	1	35	1	0
Barberich, Craig, Dodgers*	.000	17	1	0	0	0	0	0	0	0	0	0	0	0	0	0	0	0	0
Barretto, Saul, Rangers	.202	32	84	10	17	20	3	0	0	8	1	0	2	1	9	0	15	0	3
Bautista, Ruben, Braves†	.264	41	110	7	29	33	1	0	1	11	1	1	1	0	10	0	23	1	3
Bautista, German, Pirates	.286	3	7	1	2	2	0	0	0	1	0	0	0	0	2	0	1	0	0
Beams, Michael, Astros	.209	27	91	10	19	23	4	0	0	10	2	2	2	2	6	1	13	10	1
Beard, Douglas, Reds*	.218	56	188	28	41	68	13	1	4	24	5	0	0	0	29	3	28	5	2
Becker, John, White Sox*	.242	19	33	2	8	9	1	0	0	1	0	0	0	0	2	0	3	0	0
Begeal, John, Yankees	.194	29	67	6	13	13	0	0	0	6	1	3	1	0	15	0	4	1	1
Belinda, Stanley, Pirates	1.000	17	1	1	1	2	1	0	0	0	0	0	0	0	1	0	0	0	0
Bell, Juan, Dodgers	.240	59	217	38	52	62	6	2	0	26	0	0	3	1	29	1	28	12	2
Bell, Rolando, Dodgers	.211	53	147	15	31	33	2	0	0	16	2	1	2	0	8	0	13	4	5
Beltran, Angel, Pirates	.191	23	68	8	13	14	1	0	0	2	1	0	1	0	3	1	9	1	0
Benzo, Luis, Reds†	.267	56	165	20	44	48	4	0	0	8	1	1	0	0	15	1	26	0	4
Bergeron, Gilles, Expos	.000	5	4	0	0	0	0	0	0	0	0	0	0	0	0	0	2	0	0
Bernhardt, Cesar, White Sox†	.184	42	103	6	19	22	3	0	0	10	1	1	2	1	10	3	15	1	1
Bertolani, Jerry, White Sox	.235	7	17	3	4	5	1	0	0	6	1	0	2	0	2	0	1	0	0
Bigden, Maurice, Expos	.185	9	27	4	5	5	0	0	0	1	0	0	0	1	3	0	4	2	0
Bland, Morris, Braves	.196	28	51	8	10	10	0	0	0	1	0	2	0	1	10	0	7	1	1
Bledsoe, James, White Sox	.193	47	109	10	21	26	3	1	0	8	0	1	0	2	18	1	34	6	1
Blowers, Michael, Expos	.217	31	115	14	25	36	3	1	2	17	3	2	0	0	15	0	25	2	0
Bluhm, William, Dodgers	.122	31	41	1	5	6	1	0	0	2	0	0	1	1	0	0	12	0	0
Boagni, Kenneth, Astros*	.111	6	9	0	1	1	0	0	0	0	0	0	0	0	0	0	4	0	0
Bonilla, Carlos, Dodgers	.158	17	19	3	3	3	0	0	0	1	0	0	0	1	4	0	4	0	0
Bottenfield, Kent, Expos	.091	13	22	1	2	2	0	0	0	1	1	0	0	0	2	0	8	0	0
Bottenfield, Keven, Expos	.281	28	64	3	18	22	4	0	0	8	1	1	0	1	4	0	13	0	0
Bouman, Randall, Expos	.333	6	3	0	1	1	0	0	0	0	0	0	0	0	0	0	1	0	0
Bourne, Andrew, Dodgers†	.217	49	157	20	34	37	3	0	0	13	2	1	1	4	14	0	41	13	4
Brian, Braden, Expos*	.197	26	71	8	14	15	1	0	0	5	1	1	2	1	15	0	12	0	0
Brito, Mario, Expos	.143	11	7	0	1	2	1	0	0	1	0	1	0	0	0	0	4	0	0
Brow, Dennis, Yankees	.270	54	159	26	43	64	5	2	4	26	2	0	1	5	29	2	24	6	5
Brown, Keith, Reds	.250	7	8	3	2	2	0	0	0	0	0	0	0	0	1	0	3	0	0
Brown, Kurt, White Sox	.207	26	58	7	12	18	3	0	1	3	0	1	1	0	5	1	5	0	2
Browne, Richard, Braves	.221	28	86	11	19	21	2	0	0	4	1	1	0	1	9	1	17	2	1
Candelino, Anthony, Expos	.218	31	101	8	22	28	6	0	0	9	1	0	1	1	14	0	18	3	1
Canseco, Osvaldo, Yankees	.133	7	15	3	2	6	1	0	1	3	0	0	0	0	5	0	9	0	0
Capello, Peter, Royals	.239	32	92	13	22	27	5	0	0	12	3	2	0	1	16	0	17	4	4
Carr, Charles, Reds	.171	44	123	13	21	26	5	0	0	10	0	5	2	0	10	0	27	9	1
Cento, Anthony, White Sox	.213	28	75	6	16	18	2	0	0	11	1	1	0	0	8	0	15	1	0
Cerefin, Michael, Astros*	.000	3	1	0	0	0	0	0	0	0	0	0	0	0	0	0	0	0	0
Champion, Brian, Braves	.251	56	187	35	47	77	11	5	3	36	5	0	4	5	29	1	37	4	3
Chapin, Darrin, Yankees	.000	13	0	0	0	0	0	0	0	1	1	0	0	0	1	0	0	0	0
Chavez, Samuel, Reds*	.000	9	3	0	0	0	0	0	0	0	0	0	0	0	2	0	2	1	0
Clark, Mark, Braves	.250	12	4	1	1	1	0	0	0	3	0	1	0	0	3	0	2	0	0
Clements, Anthony, Royals	.245	40	143	21	35	41	3	0	1	15	1	0	0	3	19	0	30	8	0
Cole, Lucius, Rangers	.233	29	43	12	10	11	1	0	0	2	0	0	0	0	14	0	14	8	6
Contreras, Carlos, Yankees†	.304	17	46	7	14	15	1	0	0	5	0	0	0	1	3	0	11	0	1
Costello, Fred, Astros	.091	14	11	1	1	1	0	0	0	0	0	2	0	0	0	0	6	0	0
Cota, Christopher, White Sox	.210	48	124	17	26	29	3	0	0	9	2	1	0	2	13	0	19	5	1
Cruz, Rafael, Rangers†	.213	37	89	18	19	26	3	2	0	6	0	2	0	2	24	0	26	14	4
Davis, Michael, Royals	.152	32	99	10	15	22	4	0	1	4	0	1	0	2	4	0	16	2	3
Dean, Kevin, Expos	.309	51	181	38	56	69	7	3	0	17	1	1	0	4	30	1	36	16	8
Deiley, Louis, Astros	.250	42	120	11	30	37	3	2	0	13	1	0	1	9	13	2	22	3	0
DeLaRosa, Carlos, Pirates	.250	6	16	1	4	4	0	0	0	1	0	0	0	0	0	0	4	0	0
Denkenberger, Ralph, Pirates*	.299	50	154	24	46	52	4	1	0	7	0	3	0	1	11	2	20	6	8
Diaz, Rafael, Reds	.111	24	45	4	5	5	0	0	0	2	0	0	0	0	3	0	19	1	0
Doss, Raymond, Pirates	.000	10	3	1	0	0	0	0	0	0	0	2	0	0	1	0	2	0	0
Dotel, Robinson, Expos	.248	39	117	16	29	31	2	0	0	12	2	1	0	2	13	0	29	3	1
Draine, Edward, Pirates*	.275	34	120	11	33	43	6	2	0	10	1	2	0	0	11	0	11	10	3
Duran, Jose, Dodgers	.255	19	47	2	12	16	1	0	1	10	3	1	0	0	7	0	9	0	1
Dyer, Linton, Royals	.143	5	7	2	1	1	0	0	0	0	0	0	0	0	3	0	1	2	0
Eastman, Douglas, Reds	.225	50	151	20	34	45	5	0	2	13	1	2	0	0	11	0	34	17	6
Epps, Ricky, Reds†	.193	42	109	10	21	26	3	1	0	10	0	1	1	2	14	0	27	1	3
Espinal, Arismendy, Reds	.125	14	16	4	2	2	0	0	0	0	0	1	0	0	3	0	5	0	0
Esteban, Philipe, Dodgers	.246	28	69	6	17	20	3	0	0	7	1	3	0	1	5	0	12	1	1
Farmer, Bryan, Braves*	.000	14	2	0	0	0	0	0	0	0	0	0	0	0	0	0	2	0	0
Fernandez, Reynaldo, Yankees*	.178	29	45	7	8	13	0	1	1	5	1	0	0	0	6	0	12	2	0
Fields, Archie, Astros	.000	21	3	0	0	0	0	0	0	0	0	0	0	0	0	0	1	0	0
Finigan, Kevin, Expos	.226	45	106	11	24	30	6	0	0	11	3	3	2	4	7	0	23	9	0
Fontes, Bradley, Rangers	.162	42	117	5	19	19	0	0	0	11	3	2	1	2	7	0	25	1	1
Foster, Albert, Expos	.225	30	89	4	20	23	3	0	0	9	1	2	0	2	2	0	10	0	1
Frazier, Arthur, Astros†	.287	51	178	39	51	65	7	2	1	23	1	3	1	1	32	0	25	17	8
Gangi, Stephen, Braves	.383	18	60	6	23	29	3	0	1	12	2	0	0	4	6	0	12	1	0
Garcia, Victor, Pirates	.208	7	24	2	5	7	0	1	0	3	0	0	1	1	0	0	7	0	1

Player and Club	Pct.	G.	AB.	R.	H.	TB.	2B.	3B.	HR.	RBI.	GW.	SH.	SF.	HP.	BB.	Int. BB.	SO.	SB.	CS.
Garner, Darrin, Rangers	.247	53	174	27	43	49	6	0	0	15	1	1	0	2	41	0	22	36	3
Garrison, James, Dodgers	.226	33	53	9	12	14	2	0	0	5	1	0	1	2	7	0	10	2	1
Gonzalez, Carlos, Royals	.262	54	168	20	44	66	10	0	4	20	1	0	1	3	18	1	43	10	4
Gonzalez, Daniel, Astros	.143	4	7	1	1	1	0	0	0	0	0	0	0	0	1	0	3	0	0
Gonzalez, Eduardo, Yankees	.266	58	203	31	54	93	10	1	9	48	8	0	8	2	33	3	43	2	0
Gonzalez, Jose, Pirates	.147	22	68	5	10	12	2	0	0	3	1	1	0	1	4	0	14	0	1
Gonzalez, Juan, Rangers	.240	60	233	24	56	62	4	1	0	36	5	1	3	1	21	0	57	7	5
Goshay, Henry, Dodgers	.214	58	187	14	40	44	4	0	0	18	2	0	2	1	19	0	36	8	2
Green, Carmelo, Reds	.243	53	181	16	44	54	10	0	0	17	2	0	0	1	9	0	23	9	2
Green, James, Pirates*	.245	48	151	28	37	54	6	4	1	19	3	0	1	1	19	0	43	24	8
Greene, Jeffry, White Sox*	.199	56	161	17	32	44	6	3	0	18	2	1	2	1	12	1	28	0	1
Guerrero, Sixto, Astros	.211	37	109	10	23	33	5	1	1	14	2	1	2	0	10	0	30	6	1
Guzman, Hector, Yankees	.276	11	29	5	8	9	1	0	0	2	0	0	1	1	10	0	6	3	2
Guzman, Jose, Yankees	.167	15	24	4	4	6	0	1	0	1	1	1	0	1	5	0	9	1	0
Haberle, David, Pirates*	.333	7	15	0	5	6	1	0	0	2	0	0	0	0	3	0	5	0	0
Hammond, Christopher, Reds*	.250	7	4	1	1	1	0	0	0	1	0	2	1	0	1	0	2	0	0
Hancock, Kevin, Astros	.087	10	23	0	2	3	1	0	0	2	0	0	0	0	2	0	8	0	0
Hansel, Damon, Pirates	.200	18	65	4	13	16	1	1	0	6	2	0	1	0	6	0	33	7	3
Harris, Robert, Pirates	.255	37	145	23	37	44	2	1	1	11	0	0	2	3	9	0	23	18	5
Harris, Vincent, White Sox†	.221	50	131	28	29	29	0	0	0	7	0	1	1	2	19	0	14	33	12
Hart, Edwin, Dodgers*	.000	15	1	0	0	0	0	0	0	0	0	0	0	0	0	0	0	0	0
Hartman, Edward, Pirates	.242	47	157	17	38	53	9	0	2	22	3	0	3	1	19	1	28	3	6
Henry, Carlos, Astros*	.097	17	31	5	3	3	0	0	0	2	0	0	0	0	8	3	10	4	0
Hernandez, Carlos, Dodgers	.312	57	205	19	64	74	7	0	1	31	6	1	1	2	5	2	18	1	2
Hernandez, Julio, Braves	.115	8	26	3	3	5	0	1	0	2	1	0	0	0	4	1	8	1	2
Herrera, Hector, Astros	.238	13	21	2	5	5	0	0	0	2	0	0	0	0	2	0	11	2	1
Hoffman, Hunter, Royals*	.234	32	77	4	18	26	6	1	0	9	1	0	0	0	15	0	15	0	2
Hook, Michael, Astros	.000	12	6	0	0	0	0	0	0	0	0	0	0	0	0	0	3	0	0
Hornsby, Gregory, Dodgers	.141	34	78	10	11	14	3	0	0	2	0	1	0	0	15	0	28	4	4
Horton, Darryl, White Sox	.146	22	48	6	7	7	0	0	0	2	0	0	0	2	6	0	17	2	0
Howard, Christian, Yankees	.298	43	131	15	39	46	5	1	0	16	0	2	2	2	13	0	25	2	3
Huchingson, Christopher, Astros	.000	8	2	0	0	0	0	0	0	0	0	0	0	0	0	0	2	0	0
Hudson, Scott, Expos*	.000	6	3	0	0	0	0	0	0	0	0	0	0	0	0	0	1	0	0
Hunter, Robert, Yankees	.103	29	29	8	3	5	0	1	0	1	0	0	0	0	4	0	13	4	0
Isaac, Richard, White Sox	.238	53	143	14	34	43	9	0	0	13	1	0	0	1	17	2	22	7	1
Ishmael, Michael, Expos	.290	17	62	4	18	18	0	0	0	11	1	0	2	0	2	0	3	2	1
Jacobson, Nels, Expos	.000	3	2	0	0	0	0	0	0	0	0	1	0	0	1	0	2	0	0
Jefferson, Reginald, Reds*	.260	59	208	28	54	77	4	5	3	33	5	1	2	2	24	1	40	10	9
Jenkins, Mack, Reds	.000	14	8	0	0	0	0	0	0	0	0	0	0	0	0	0	3	0	0
Jerez, Francisco, Royals	.192	30	78	11	15	17	2	0	0	8	3	0	1	0	4	0	12	5	3
Joseph, Miguel, Braves	.000	2	0	0	0	0	0	0	0	0	0	0	0	0	1	0	0	0	0
Joslyn, John, Royals*	.339	55	177	34	60	91	9	2	6	25	1	2	1	0	45	1	28	8	2
Kaiser, Keith, Reds	.000	11	3	0	0	0	0	0	0	0	0	1	0	0	0	0	0	0	0
Kerrigan, Robert, Expos	.143	17	7	0	1	1	0	0	0	1	0	1	0	0	0	0	2	0	0
King, Bryan, Astros†	.296	33	108	24	32	34	2	0	0	8	0	3	0	0	24	0	19	8	3
King, Marc, Expos*	.067	7	15	0	1	1	0	0	0	1	0	0	1	0	2	0	2	0	0
Koller, Mark, Pirates	.000	10	7	0	0	0	0	0	0	0	0	1	0	0	0	0	5	0	0
Kroll, Todd, Dodgers	.000	19	4	0	0	0	0	0	0	0	0	0	0	0	0	0	4	0	0
Kyle, Jeffrey, Braves†	.000	1	0	0	0	0	0	0	0	0	0	0	0	0	1	0	0	0	0
Laboy, Carlos, Astros	.268	44	157	27	42	54	3	3	1	20	3	0	3	2	12	0	41	5	4
Langley, Wesley, Dodgers†	.000	5	1	0	0	0	0	0	0	0	0	1	0	0	0	0	1	0	0
Leary, Robert, Expos	.252	36	115	15	29	33	1	0	1	20	1	0	3	3	12	0	10	1	0
Leon, Danilo, Expos	.000	15	1	0	0	0	0	0	0	0	0	0	0	0	0	0	0	0	0
Lewis, Daniel, Astros*	.293	38	116	22	34	45	4	2	1	18	1	0	2	2	17	1	24	8	3
Lilly, Michael, Dodgers	.455	13	11	4	5	8	1	1	0	2	0	0	0	0	1	0	4	0	0
Lipscomb, Brian, Pirates†	.270	19	37	2	10	10	0	0	0	3	0	0	0	0	5	0	11	3	1
Lockley, Blane, Pirates*	.289	14	38	5	11	19	5	0	1	10	1	0	1	2	9	0	7	1	2
Logan, James, Yankees	.233	13	30	3	7	7	0	0	0	3	0	1	1	0	4	0	3	0	0
Longmire, Anthony, Pirates†	.275	15	40	6	11	15	2	1	0	6	1	0	1	1	2	0	2	1	2
Longuil, Richard, Braves	.154	13	13	1	2	3	1	0	0	0	0	2	0	1	0	0	1	0	0
Lopez, Eduardo, Yankees	.219	13	32	2	7	7	0	0	0	1	0	0	0	0	5	0	9	0	0
Love, John, Pirates	.417	6	12	2	5	5	0	0	0	2	0	0	0	0	3	0	2	0	1
Luckett, Earl, Astros†	.000	11	1	5	0	0	0	0	0	0	0	0	0	0	1	0	0	2	0
Lyden, Mitchell, Yankees	.340	17	50	8	17	33	7	0	3	16	1	0	1	0	7	0	7	0	0
Manering, Mark, Yankees*	.331	32	118	31	39	52	9	2	0	16	1	2	0	0	22	0	13	4	1
Marcano, Antonio, Pirates	.200	6	15	0	3	3	0	0	0	2	0	0	0	2	1	0	5	2	0
Marino, John, Expos*	1.000	21	1	0	1	1	0	0	0	0	0	2	0	0	0	0	0	0	0
Marrero, Miguel, Braves*	.286	18	7	3	2	3	1	0	0	2	0	1	0	0	0	0	1	0	0
Marsh, Quinn, Reds	.000	18	2	1	0	0	0	0	0	0	0	0	0	0	1	0	2	0	0
Martinez, Redy, Royals	.290	47	155	22	45	56	3	4	0	16	1	1	1	0	12	0	36	13	7
Martinez, Ricardo, Yankees	.276	43	145	11	40	46	6	0	0	19	1	1	1	0	11	0	17	3	5
Matos, Ramon, Royals	.176	12	34	3	6	6	0	0	0	0	0	0	0	0	2	0	7	3	1
Maville, Randy, Expos	.040	18	25	1	1	1	0	0	0	2	0	0	0	1	3	0	12	0	0
McClure, Larue, Astros	.000	27	3	0	0	0	0	0	0	0	0	0	0	0	0	0	1	0	0
McCutchon, James, Rangers	.100	12	30	1	3	5	2	0	0	3	1	0	0	0	6	0	12	0	0
McFadden, Charles, Reds	.167	19	30	1	5	5	0	0	0	0	0	0	0	0	1	0	13	0	1
McHugh, Scott, Expos	.214	5	14	2	3	3	0	0	0	1	0	1	0	0	3	0	4	1	0
Mealy, Anthony, Pirates	.210	45	138	20	29	42	2	1	3	12	0	1	1	7	13	0	48	9	1
Mehl, Steven, White Sox	.257	58	152	26	39	43	4	0	0	9	0	2	1	2	18	0	26	29	8
Mendes, Clive, Royals	.263	10	19	3	5	7	2	0	0	0	0	0	0	0	4	0	4	0	0
Mendoza, Jesus, Braves	.213	43	127	14	27	35	2	0	2	12	1	0	0	2	8	0	40	0	2
Mercker, Kent, Braves*	.200	9	5	0	1	1	0	0	0	1	0	2	0	0	0	0	2	0	0
Merejo, Domingo, Pirates*	.190	40	121	13	23	34	2	3	1	11	0	1	1	0	13	0	30	0	6
Meulens, Hensley, Yankees	.233	59	219	36	51	81	10	4	4	31	2	1	1	4	28	0	66	4	2
Miguel, Tamares, Dodgers	.000	13	2	0	0	0	0	0	0	0	0	0	0	0	0	0	2	0	0
Miller, David, Braves	.500	18	4	0	2	3	1	0	0	3	0	0	1	0	1	0	1	0	0
Modica, Joseph, Pirates	.211	5	19	1	4	5	1	0	0	3	0	0	1	0	0	0	2	2	0
Molina, Manual, Pirates	.000	8	4	0	0	0	0	0	0	0	0	0	0	0	0	0	3	0	0
Mora, Juan, Dodgers	.129	18	31	1	4	4	0	0	0	2	0	0	0	0	3	0	8	0	0
Mota, Jose, Braves	.222	59	189	23	42	47	1	2	0	16	0	6	2	0	14	0	28	8	5
Mota, Miguel, Dodgers†	.256	44	176	30	45	48	3	0	0	12	1	0	0	1	11	0	15	30	4
Mullins, Christopher, Braves	.195	36	87	10	17	20	0	0	1	8	1	2	0	3	3	1	14	1	0

Player and Club	Pct.	G.	AB.	R.	H.	TB.	2B.	3B.	HR.	RBI.	GW.	SH.	SF.	HP.	BB.	Int. BB.	SO.	SB.	CS.
Munson, Jay, Expos†	1.000	6	1	1	1	1	0	0	0	0	0	0	0	0	0	0	0	0	0
Murphy, John, Astros	.292	17	24	4	7	8	1	0	0	2	1	0	0	0	6	1	4	0	0
Murphy, Peter, Pirates*	.200	7	10	0	2	2	0	0	0	2	1	1	0	0	0	0	2	0	0
Nelson, Kevin, Dodgers	.000	11	5	1	0	0	0	0	0	1	0	1	0	0	1	0	2	0	0
Nieto, Andres, White Sox	.278	59	180	16	50	59	7	1	0	30	8	3	3	4	11	0	7	4	3
Niewulis, Steven, Yankees*	.136	8	22	2	3	3	0	0	0	2	0	0	0	0	3	0	6	0	0
Nunez, Vinicio, Astros	.000	5	13	1	0	0	0	0	0	0	0	0	0	0	0	0	5	0	0
Ocasio, Javier, White Sox	.225	39	80	14	18	19	1	0	0	2	0	2	0	0	9	0	10	1	2
Oliva, Roberto, Braves	.154	18	26	3	4	4	0	0	0	3	0	1	0	0	3	0	10	0	1
Olivares, Jose, Pirates*	.000	6	1	0	0	0	0	0	0	0	0	1	0	0	0	0	0	0	0
Ortiz, Jacobo, Braves	.000	21	1	0	0	0	0	0	0	0	0	1	0	0	0	0	0	0	0
Palmer, Dean, Rangers	.209	50	163	19	34	43	7	1	0	12	1	0	2	5	22	0	34	6	3
Paredes, Jesus, Expos†	.298	54	171	34	51	53	0	1	0	7	1	4	0	3	27	3	25	19	5
Pearn, Joseph, Rangers	.257	18	35	3	9	10	1	0	0	3	1	2	0	0	14	1	5	1	0
Peel, Jack, White Sox	.195	38	87	8	17	19	0	1	0	5	1	0	1	0	10	0	14	2	4
Peralta, Modesto, Reds	.250	26	4	0	1	1	0	0	0	0	0	1	0	0	0	0	2	0	0
Peraza, Luis, White Sox	.318	7	22	4	7	11	1	0	1	2	0	0	0	0	3	1	8	0	0
Perez, Gorky, Astros*	.202	36	94	8	19	21	2	0	0	11	2	0	1	0	9	0	12	4	2
Pickett, Antoine, Royals†	.246	44	138	15	34	34	0	0	0	16	2	4	2	3	18	0	19	11	5
Pinelli, Willie, Dodgers	.299	38	144	20	43	54	11	0	0	12	2	0	3	1	8	0	27	6	2
Pinol, Juan, Reds	.226	41	124	14	28	36	0	4	0	19	6	4	0	0	17	1	24	8	6
Plumb, David, Braves	.223	41	130	14	29	42	8	1	1	21	3	2	1	0	19	3	21	5	1
Poteet, Donald, Dodgers*	.192	51	156	15	30	38	4	2	0	10	2	0	1	2	32	4	44	0	0
Prescott, Bill, Expos	.455	11	11	0	5	5	0	0	0	0	0	0	0	0	0	0	3	0	0
Pujols, Ruben, Royals	.203	25	64	5	13	18	2	0	1	5	0	2	0	1	10	0	19	1	1
Pulliam, Harvey, Royals	.208	48	168	14	35	50	3	0	4	23	4	2	3	3	8	1	33	3	2
Quintero, Enrique, Pirates	.187	33	91	9	17	22	5	0	0	8	0	4	0	2	12	0	21	3	0
Ramirez, Rodolfo, White Sox	.273	4	11	1	3	3	0	0	0	1	1	0	0	0	0	0	3	0	0
Ramon, Julio, Yankees	.207	34	82	10	17	21	2	1	0	10	0	2	0	1	16	1	21	0	1
Reed, Richard, Pirates	.500	8	2	0	1	1	0	0	0	1	0	0	0	0	0	0	0	0	0
Reeves, Scott, Rangers	.000	17	1	0	0	0	0	0	0	0	0	0	0	0	0	0	1	0	0
Renteria, Edinson, Astros	.297	52	182	23	54	70	11	1	1	26	5	0	2	1	13	1	9	6	2
Rhodes, Karl, Astros*	.293	62	222	36	65	81	10	3	0	22	3	5	2	0	32	3	33	14	6
Richards, Russell, Braves*	.000	14	4	0	0	0	0	0	0	0	0	0	0	0	0	0	1	0	0
Robicheaux, Ron, Pirates	.421	4	19	5	8	9	1	0	0	5	1	0	0	0	0	0	2	2	0
Robinson, Darryl, Royals	.201	47	164	14	33	42	6	0	1	16	1	0	1	3	12	0	34	6	5
Rodriguez, Angel, Expos	.167	11	6	1	1	2	1	0	0	1	0	0	0	0	1	0	1	0	0
Rodriguez, Carlos, Expos*	.000	13	2	0	0	0	0	0	0	0	0	2	0	0	0	0	0	0	0
Rodriguez, Ignacio, Expos	.000	2	1	0	0	0	0	0	0	0	0	0	0	0	0	0	0	0	0
Rogers, Danilo, Braves	.277	54	188	27	52	66	7	2	1	21	2	2	4	2	18	1	23	7	5
Rojas, Melquiades, Expos	.333	13	12	1	4	5	1	0	0	0	0	2	0	0	2	0	4	0	0
Rojas, Ricardo, Dodgers	.059	13	17	1	1	1	0	0	0	0	0	0	0	0	2	0	7	0	1
Romo, Robert, Astros	.294	13	17	2	5	5	0	0	0	2	0	3	0	0	4	0	3	0	0
Rosario, Danilo, Astros	.177	33	96	11	17	21	2	1	0	10	1	0	0	0	10	0	17	3	0
Rosario, Victor, Rangers	.291	45	141	9	41	46	2	0	1	18	2	3	2	0	9	1	9	4	0
Ross, Sean, Braves*	.305	59	223	43	68	90	9	2	3	35	3	0	10	0	23	1	25	31	7
Ruskin, Scott, Pirates†	.355	11	31	3	11	12	1	0	0	4	1	1	1	0	1	0	9	1	0
Sambino, Miguel, Braves*	.288	60	215	38	62	70	6	1	0	9	2	1	1	3	23	3	37	17	7
Samson, Frederick, Rangers	.259	32	85	5	22	25	3	0	0	8	0	1	1	3	9	1	29	2	4
Sanchez, Francisco, Royals†	.208	33	77	20	16	18	2	0	0	4	2	1	0	2	12	0	16	16	3
Sanchez, Rey, Rangers	.290	52	169	27	49	54	3	1	0	23	4	3	1	3	41	0	18	10	10
Santana, Ernesto, Pirates	.000	11	2	0	0	0	0	0	0	0	0	0	0	0	0	0	0	0	0
Sapienza, Richard, Reds	.273	33	110	9	30	34	4	0	0	17	2	1	1	1	6	0	16	3	2
Schlopy, Clifford, Pirates*	.000	1	2	0	0	0	0	0	0	0	0	0	0	0	0	0	2	0	0
Schueler, Russ, Expos	.232	27	99	14	23	29	4	1	0	15	3	1	1	1	4	1	5	5	1
Scieneaux, Desmond, Pirates*	.143	23	70	4	10	13	3	0	0	5	1	1	0	2	3	0	20	0	0
Seay, Mark, Rangers*	.163	52	129	24	21	23	0	1	0	6	2	5	0	1	29	0	55	27	5
Sepulveda, Jorge, Dodgers	.071	16	14	2	1	1	0	0	0	1	0	5	0	0	3	0	9	0	0
Sheffield, Travis, Rangers	.000	10	20	2	0	0	0	0	0	0	0	0	0	0	1	0	12	3	0
Shepherd, Keith, Pirates	.500	9	2	1	1	3	0	1	0	0	0	0	0	1	0	0	0	0	0
Shiverick, William, Reds	.125	14	8	0	1	2	1	0	0	0	0	1	0	0	0	0	2	0	0
Simmons, Robert I., Astros*	.248	32	113	13	28	37	4	1	1	13	3	1	0	0	6	0	24	4	0
Simmons, Robert W., Expos	.211	42	128	19	27	41	6	1	2	21	3	0	1	3	31	1	27	1	0
Simms, Michael, Astros	.260	54	181	33	47	75	14	1	4	37	2	0	4	4	22	1	48	2	1
Sims, Kenneth, Reds*	.240	45	129	14	31	36	5	0	0	18	4	0	0	2	23	0	29	5	2
Slaughter, Garland, Pirates	.500	8	2	1	1	1	0	0	0	0	0	0	0	0	0	0	0	0	0
Smallwood, Douglas, Pirates	.250	9	4	0	1	1	0	0	0	0	0	0	0	0	0	0	0	0	0
Smith, Chad, Braves†	.000	12	9	0	0	0	0	0	0	0	0	1	0	0	0	0	3	0	0
Smith, Willie, Pirates	.250	7	4	1	1	1	0	0	0	1	0	0	0	0	0	0	3	0	0
Snypes, Anthony, Royals*	.246	26	57	7	14	14	0	0	0	8	2	0	1	2	6	1	13	4	0
Sosa, Samuel, Rangers	.275	61	229	38	63	96	19	1	4	28	3	0	2	0	22	0	51	11	3
Spear, Michael, Rangers	.091	25	44	2	4	4	0	0	0	2	0	0	0	1	6	0	5	0	0
Spitale, Benjamin, Expos*	.329	28	82	11	27	34	5	1	0	9	1	0	2	0	8	0	17	1	2
Spurlin, John, Braves	.203	48	128	15	26	36	7	0	1	18	0	0	1	4	10	0	22	5	1
Stoker, Michael, Astros	.222	13	9	1	2	2	0	0	0	0	0	1	0	0	0	0	0	0	1
Stuart, Robert, Braves*	.190	54	184	16	35	45	6	2	0	21	3	5	3	2	17	1	37	4	2
Sullivan, Carl, White Sox	.667	2	6	0	4	4	0	0	0	1	0	0	0	0	0	0	0	1	0
Swob, Timothy, Reds*	.200	11	5	0	1	1	0	0	0	1	1	2	0	0	0	0	0	0	0
Talley, Oscar, Expos*	.294	41	136	24	40	52	6	3	0	18	1	2	1	0	11	0	16	3	4
Tapia, Jose, Dodgers	.000	29	1	0	0	0	0	0	0	0	0	0	0	0	0	0	0	0	0
Taubensee, Edward, Reds*	.196	35	107	8	21	27	3	0	1	11	1	0	0	0	11	0	33	0	1
Thomas, Carl, Dodgers*	.059	15	17	0	1	1	0	0	0	1	1	1	0	0	0	0	7	0	0
Thomas, Keith, Reds†	.214	42	145	24	31	42	1	2	2	13	2	2	1	3	23	0	57	18	6
Thompson, Wayne, Yankees	.231	6	13	1	3	4	1	0	0	0	0	0	0	0	1	0	5	0	0
Torve, Kenton, White Sox*	.000	1	0	0	0	0	0	0	0	0	0	0	0	0	1	0	0	0	0
Touma, Timothy, Expos	.318	27	85	13	27	29	2	0	0	9	2	2	0	0	12	0	2	3	1
Towey, Steve, Astros	.333	13	3	0	1	1	0	0	0	0	0	0	0	0	0	0	2	0	0
Troutman, Keith, Pirates†	.172	32	93	10	16	18	2	0	0	8	0	0	2	1	17	0	16	1	1
Valdez, Amilcar, Dodgers	.304	61	227	31	69	83	14	0	0	22	2	3	0	2	30	5	26	2	0
Valdez, Ramon, Rangers*	.227	38	119	12	27	35	8	0	0	20	1	2	1	0	11	1	25	2	0
Valenzuela, Manuel, Pirates*	.000	3	2	0	0	0	0	0	0	0	0	0	0	0	0	0	1	0	0
Vance, Ricky, Expos	.149	23	47	6	7	8	1	0	0	3	1	1	0	0	3	0	15	0	0

Player and Club	Pct.	G.	AB.	R.	H.	TB.	2B.	3B.	HR.	RBI.	GW.	SH.	SF.	HP.	BB.	Int. BB.	SO.	SB.	CS.
Vargas, Hector, Yankees	.236	61	212	27	50	56	6	0	0	25	3	3	2	3	33	0	28	10	11
Vasquez, Ernesto, Astros	.500	18	2	1	1	1	0	0	0	1	0	0	0	0	1	0	1	0	0
Vaughn, Robin, Pirates	.231	48	182	20	42	48	6	0	0	22	2	1	0	0	12	0	30	24	5
Vaughn, Timothy, Pirates†	.209	20	67	7	14	21	0	2	1	9	1	1	1	1	6	0	13	6	3
Velez, Jose, Rangers	.169	24	83	6	14	15	1	0	0	3	0	1	0	2	5	0	13	0	1
Viltz, Corey, Yankees†	.111	3	9	0	1	1	0	0	0	0	0	0	0	0	1	0	2	1	0
Waggoner, Aubrey, White Sox*	.284	34	81	22	23	35	3	3	1	12	1	0	2	2	27	0	13	18	1
Wagner, Daniel, White Sox	.313	5	16	5	5	8	3	0	0	1	0	0	0	1	1	0	2	0	0
Walker, Bernard, Reds*	.298	30	104	28	31	39	4	2	0	6	0	1	0	0	21	0	21	29	3
Watkins, Darren, Royals	.236	24	72	8	17	24	3	2	0	7	2	1	0	1	6	0	23	5	5
Weems, Danny, Braves	.100	15	10	1	1	1	0	0	0	0	0	0	0	0	1	0	3	0	0
White, James, White Sox	.278	46	108	15	30	32	2	0	0	17	3	2	0	2	11	0	17	2	2
Williams, Bernabe, Yankees	.270	61	230	45	62	79	5	3	2	25	1	1	3	1	39	0	40	33	12
Willis, Kenneth, Reds	.500	7	4	3	2	3	1	0	0	0	0	0	0	0	2	0	1	0	0
Wilson, Randall, Pirates	.000	3	2	0	0	0	0	0	0	0	0	0	0	0	0	0	2	0	0
Wong, Nivaldo, White Sox	.330	40	94	9	31	36	5	0	0	10	1	1	3	1	10	0	18	0	1
Wood, Stephen, Dodgers	.100	10	10	1	1	1	0	0	0	0	0	1	0	0	1	0	6	0	0
Zayas, Pedro, Astros	.206	23	63	4	13	18	2	0	1	7	2	1	0	1	2	0	13	0	0

The following pitchers, listed alphabetically by club, with games in parentheses, had no plate appearances, primarily through use of designated hitters:

ASTROS—Elsberry, Russell (3); Smith, Kevin (1).

BRAVES—Barcelo, Jorge (16); Huff, Roger (2); Mota, Bienvenido (8); Scarborough, Richard (1); Trapasso, Michael (9); West, Matthew (2).

DODGERS—Arzola, Juan (4).

EXPOS—Machacek, Kenny (3).

PIRATES—Balkiewicz, Dennis (1); Forrest, Joel (3); Gobeil, Eric (1); Gonzalez, Pablo (1); Kocis, Timothy (5); Massa, Juan (9); Matos, Jorge (1); Moreno, Douglas (7); Santiago, Delvy (4).

RANGERS—Brown, Kevin (3); Bryan, Frank (14); Burgos, John (12); Busick, Warren (25); Castillo, Felipe (13); Findlay, William (14); Katschke, James (11); Meizoso, Gus (14); Morse, Scott (4); Patterson, Glenn (11); Rivera, Lino (16); Rosenthal, Wayne (23); Shiflett, Christian (1); Soto, Edwardo (9); Vlcek, James (18).

ROYALS—Acevedo, Eugenio (18); Burckhalter, Randall (8); DeLeon, Jesus (12); Gordon, Thomas (9); Lee, Benjamin (10); Maldonado, Carlos (10); Mercado, Daniel (17); Meyers, Brian (12); Nocas, Luke (11); Odom, Timothy (11); Pinto, Francisco (14); Ramirez, Francisco (16); Studeman, Dennis (10); Trapp, Michael (17); Willis, James (7).

WHITE SOX—Babcock, William (4); DeLaCruz, Carlos (14); Hall, Todd (14); Hawkins, Daniel (1); Jensen, Jeffery (15); Kennedy, Benny (10); Kershaw, Scott (16); Kovatch, Edward (12); Maebe, Kelly (14); Martin, Norberto (1); Morgan, Bradford (15); Ollom, Michael (4); Radinski, Scott (7); Robinson, Randy (8); Sandoval, Jesus (15); Tauken, Daniel (17); Villanueva, Gilbert (3).

YANKEES—Azocar, Oscar (6); Brito, Ysaias (6); Carreno, Amalio (7); Clark, David (4); Doyle, Timothy (6); Ezold, Timothy (1); Faccio, Luis (13); Figueroa, Fernando (16); Giron, Ysidro (34); Manon, Ramon (11); Marris, Mark (7); McClear, Michael (6); Morales, Edgar (11); Pardo, Lawrence (3); Rodriguez, Gabriel (19); Ryan, Todd (8); Torres, Ricardo (2).

GRAND SLAM HOME RUNS—Brow, Pulliam, 1 each.

AWARDED FIRST BASE ON CATCHER'S INTERFERENCE—Lackley 4 (Ku. Brown 2, Cento, Zayas); Peel 3 (C. Gonzalez, Leary, Zayas); Becker (Taubensee); Deiley (C. Hernandez); Mehl (C. Gonzalez); Sabino (Zayas); R.W. Simmons (Fontes).

CLUB FIELDING

Club	Pct.	G.	PO.	A.	E.	DP.	PB.
Dodgers	.958	61	1581	740	102	49	8
Royals	.954	63	1612	731	113	51	29
Expos	.953	62	1600	703	113	57	9
Yankees	.952	63	1654	747	120	62	15
White Sox	.952	63	1687	708	122	40	17
Pirates	.951	64	1621	682	119	39	23
Rangers	.950	62	1639	696	124	58	9
Reds	.949	62	1627	775	130	44	18
Astros	.946	63	1630	712	133	52	15
Braves	.937	63	1657	761	162	44	6

Triple Play—Rangers.

INDIVIDUAL FIELDING

*Throws lefthanded.

FIRST BASEMEN

Player and Club	Pct.	G.	PO.	A.	E.	DP.
Bailey, White Sox	.978	34	203	18	5	8
Bautista, Braves	.500	2	1	0	1	0
Beard, Reds	1.000	1	8	1	0	0
Bluhm, Dodgers	.939	8	31	0	2	1
Bottenfield, Expos	.923	4	11	1	1	0
Brow, Yankees	.961	27	204	17	9	17
Davis, Royals	.957	7	66	0	3	4
Denkenberger, Pirates*	.989	33	269	5	3	14
Epps, Reds	.980	7	44	4	1	2
Fernandez, Yankees	.968	5	29	1	1	2
Gangi, Braves	.992	14	111	10	1	9
GREENE, White Sox*	.990	53	360	27	4	27
Hancock, Astros	1.000	1	4	0	0	0
Hansel, Pirates	.969	10	90	5	3	2
Howard, Yankees*	1.000	8	59	2	0	2
Jefferson, Reds*	.989	58	581	36	7	34
Joslyn, Royals*	.987	53	502	25	7	42
King, Expos*	.951	5	38	1	2	1
Leary, Expos	1.000	1	16	1	0	1
Lockley, Pirates	.971	13	100	1	3	7
Manering, Yankees*	.991	32	302	20	3	34
Mendes, Royals	.961	8	48	1	2	3
Mendoza, Braves	.990	41	375	33	4	19
Modica, Pirates*	1.000	3	29	1	0	1
Mullins, Braves	.900	3	18	0	2	2
Pearn, Rangers	1.000	4	25	2	0	3
Peel, White Sox	.800	2	3	1	1	1
Pinelli, Dodgers	1.000	1	1	0	0	0
D. Rosario, Astros	.993	19	132	8	1	14
V. Rosario, Rangers	.994	19	170	5	1	14
Scieneaux, Pirates*	.969	12	92	2	3	8
Simmons, Expos	.994	39	314	24	2	32
Simms, Astros	.985	50	433	28	7	37
Spitale, Expos*	.990	22	189	13	2	14
Spurlin, Braves	.983	16	112	7	2	6
Taubensee, Reds	1.000	3	11	0	0	3
A. Valdez, Dodgers	.987	59	553	34	8	44
R. Valdez, Rangers*	.972	28	199	8	6	14
Velez, Rangers	.980	22	190	11	4	14

Triple Play—R. Valdez.

SECOND BASEMEN

Player and Club	Pct.	G.	PO.	A.	E.	DP.
Audain, White Sox	1.000	1	0	1	0	0
Bautista, Braves	.667	2	1	1	1	0
Beams, Astros	1.000	1	0	1	0	0
Begeal, Yankees	.953	19	30	31	3	6
Bell, Dodgers	1.000	14	29	28	0	5
Benzo, Reds	.899	34	43	64	12	10
Bernhardt, White Sox	.917	30	46	42	8	9
Bertolani, White Sox	958	7	7	16	1	4
Bland, Braves	.903	14	15	13	3	2
Capello, Royals	.971	31	68	98	5	23
Carr, Reds	.941	39	75	100	11	15
Cruz, Rangers	.978	13	21	24	1	6

SECOND BASEMEN—Continued

Player and Club	Pct.	G.	PO.	A.	E.	DP.
Diaz, Reds	.889	3	1	7	1	0
Draine, Pirates	.958	28	60	76	6	14
Eastman, Reds	1.000	1	1	1	0	0
Esteban, Dodgers	.958	26	51	41	4	11
Garner, Rangers	.958	50	111	139	11	27
Garrison, Dodgers	1.000	4	5	8	0	1
Gonzalez, Astros	1.000	4	3	3	0	2
Herrera, Astros	.967	12	15	14	1	4
Ishmael, Expos	.962	10	24	27	2	5
Jerez, Royals	.956	17	37	49	4	16
Joseph, Braves	1.000	2	2	1	0	0
King, Astros	.932	12	28	40	5	6
Logan, Yankees	1.000	11	29	25	0	8
Marcano, Pirates	.852	6	8	15	4	2
Martinez, Yankees	.953	43	99	123	11	28
Mehl, White Sox	.914	13	15	17	3	2
Mota, Braves	.940	55	114	152	17	24
Nieto, White Sox	.963	39	69	86	6	10
Paredes, Expos	.930	52	102	138	18	31
Pinelli, Dodgers	.972	30	64	74	4	15
Quintero, Pirates	1.000	1	3	3	0	1
RENTERIA, Astros	.962	47	99	127	9	28
Robicheaux, Pirates	.900	2	6	3	1	1
Rosario, Rangers	.972	7	20	15	1	4
Samson, Rangers	.500	1	0	1	1	1
F. Sanchez, Royals	.911	21	42	30	7	6
R. Sanchez, Rangers	1.000	4	7	15	0	1
Stuart, Braves	.692	4	3	6	4	0
Touma, Expos	.938	5	6	9	1	1
Vaughn, Pirates	.922	28	47	72	10	12

Triple Play—Garner.

THIRD BASEMEN

Player and Club	Pct.	G.	PO.	A.	E.	DP.
Almonte, Astros	.811	13	14	16	7	2
Angelero, Royals	.933	14	8	20	2	3
Audain, White Sox	.949	13	12	25	2	1
Bautista, Braves	.842	13	4	28	6	3
Beams, Astros	.872	17	15	26	6	2
Beard, Reds	.880	55	34	113	20	4
Becker, White Sox	.913	17	5	16	2	1
Begeal, Yankees	1.000	2	2	0	0	0
Bell, Dodgers	.909	12	14	26	4	0
Bigden, Expos	.773	9	5	12	5	1
Bottenfield, Expos	.889	7	1	15	2	1
Capello, Royals	1.000	2	0	1	0	0
Champion, Braves	.841	41	28	88	22	2
Contreras, Yankees	.692	7	1	8	4	1
Diaz, Reds	.921	19	6	29	3	0
Foster, Expos	.882	21	17	43	8	4
Gangi, Braves	.875	4	2	5	1	0
Garrison, Dodgers	.846	5	0	11	2	0
Hancock, Astros	.882	9	6	9	2	0
Hartman, Pirates	.908	45	38	71	11	3
Hernandez, Dodgers	.667	1	0	2	1	0
Hoffman, Royals	.886	17	10	21	4	0
Isaac, White Sox	.903	37	23	70	10	2
Ishmael, Expos	.967	9	8	21	1	2
Love, Pirates	1.000	3	0	7	0	1
McHugh, Expos	.778	5	5	9	4	0
Meulens, Yankees	.888	58	40	118	20	11
Mullins, Braves	.864	8	8	11	3	0
Nieto, White Sox	.897	16	11	15	3	2
Palmer, Rangers	.885	42	25	75	13	10
Peel, White Sox	.875	3	1	6	1	1
POTEET, Dodgers	.941	48	36	107	9	16
Quintero, Pirates	.941	5	3	13	1	0
Renteria, Astros	.944	5	5	12	1	0
Robinson, Royals	.868	42	21	91	17	5
Rosario, Rangers	.850	9	3	14	3	0
Samson, Rangers	.789	20	7	23	8	2
Schueler, Expos	1.000	1	2	0	0	0
Simmons, Astros	.843	26	15	44	11	3
Spurlin, Braves	.900	10	8	10	2	0
Touma, Expos	.959	18	10	37	2	4
Troutman, Pirates	.952	9	9	11	1	1
R. Vaughn, Pirates	1.000	4	2	8	0	1
T. Vaughn, Pirates	1.000	2	2	5	0	0
Wagner, White Sox	.750	2	1	2	1	1

SHORTSTOPS

Player and Club	Pct.	G.	PO.	A.	E.	DP.
Acosta, Pirates*	1.000	1	2	1	0	0
Angelero, Royals	.944	25	28	74	6	13
Audain, White Sox	.933	41	66	87	11	13
Bautista, Braves	1.000	3	1	0	0	0
Begeal, Yankees	1.000	7	6	13	0	4
Bell, Dodgers	.925	56	78	193	22	27
Benzo, Reds	.850	25	31	65	17	12
Bland, Braves	.886	12	13	26	5	2
Blowers, Expos	.899	31	50	84	15	19
Bonilla, Dodgers	.400	1	0	2	3	0
Champion, Braves	.879	12	15	36	7	5
Clements, Royals	.902	38	53	104	17	17
Cruz, Rangers	.900	19	24	48	8	4
Draine, Pirates	.880	4	11	11	3	0
Fontes, Rangers	1.000	1	1	0	0	0
Foster, Expos	.920	10	8	15	2	4
Frazier, Astros	.872	43	81	131	31	16
Garrison, Dodgers	.815	9	6	16	5	5
Harris, White Sox	.750	1	2	1	1	0
Isaac, White Sox	1.000	1	1	3	0	0
Jerez, Royals	.973	11	10	26	1	5
King, Astros	.914	23	28	68	9	16
Logan, Yankees	1.000	2	1	0	0	0
Luckett, Astros	.000	1	0	0	1	0
Mota, Braves	1.000	2	2	0	0	0
Nieto, White Sox	.889	7	7	9	2	4
Ocasio, White Sox	.917	39	40	59	9	7
Pinol, Reds	.932	41	62	143	15	13
Quintero, Pirates	.945	27	35	68	6	8
Ramirez, White Sox	.800	4	5	7	3	0
Robicheaux, Pirates	.800	2	4	4	2	1
Samson, Rangers	.875	4	4	10	2	2
SANCHEZ, Rangers	.932	46	62	143	15	26
Schueler, Expos	.920	24	32	60	8	11
Stuart, Braves	.833	45	68	116	37	14
Touma, Expos	.947	4	5	13	1	1
Vargas, Yankees	.911	60	90	176	26	36
R. Vaughn, Pirates	.922	15	25	46	6	6
T. Vaughn, Pirates	.961	18	28	70	4	7

OUTFIELDERS

Player and Club	Pct.	G.	PO.	A.	E.	DP.
Alborano, Royals*	.922	42	66	5	6	2
Alvarez, Expos	1.000	29	32	0	0	0
Anthony, Astros*	1.000	3	2	1	0	0
Arendas, Yankees*	.986	44	65	6	1	2
Bautista, Braves	1.000	9	10	1	0	1
Beams, Astros	.889	8	8	0	1	0
Bell, Dodgers	.971	22	33	1	1	1
Bledsoe, White Sox	.943	34	31	2	2	0
Boagni, Astros*	1.000	4	3	0	0	0
Bourne, Dodgers	.961	49	64	10	3	1
Brow, Yankees	.833	12	15	0	3	0
Candelino, Expos	.977	31	40	2	1	0
Canseco, Yankees	.800	7	4	0	1	0
Cole, Rangers	.765	14	12	1	4	0
Cota, White Sox	.986	47	61	7	1	2
Dean, Expos	.970	50	93	5	3	2
DeLaRosa, Pirates	.818	5	8	1	2	1
Denkenberger, Pirates*	.857	9	18	0	3	0
Dotel, Expos	.981	35	50	3	1	2
Eastman, Reds	1.000	47	62	7	0	0
Epps, Reds	.833	10	9	1	2	0
Fernandez, Yankees	1.000	17	19	2	0	1
Finigan, Expos	.978	38	40	5	1	1
Garcia, Pirates	1.000	6	16	1	0	0
E. Gonzalez, Yankees	.931	17	25	2	2	0
J. Gonzalez, Rangers	.941	58	89	6	6	1
Goshay, Dodgers	.957	56	80	9	4	0
C. Green, Reds	.959	49	68	2	3	1
J. Green, Pirates	.930	43	77	3	6	0
Guerrero, Astros	1.000	36	52	3	0	2
H. Guzman, Yankees	.958	10	23	0	1	0
J. Guzman, Yankees	1.000	12	7	3	0	0
R. Harris, Pirates	.973	36	71	2	2	1
V. Harris, White Sox	.963	43	47	5	2	0
Henry, Astros*	1.000	11	12	2	0	0
Hernandez, Braves	1.000	8	13	1	0	0
Hornsby, Dodgers	.962	28	22	3	1	1
Horton, White Sox	.750	4	2	1	1	0
Howard, Yankees*	.936	30	42	2	3	0
Hunter, Yankees	1.000	16	11	0	0	0
Isaac, White Sox	.933	15	14	0	1	0
Laboy, Astros*	.949	37	36	1	2	0
Lewis, Astros*	.929	25	24	2	2	0
Lipscomb, Pirates*	.882	14	12	3	2	0

OUTFIELDERS—Continued

Player and Club	Pct.	G.	PO.	A.	E.	DP.
Longmire, Pirates	.905	9	19	0	2	0
Martinez, Royads	.966	36	56	0	2	0
Matos, Royals	1.000	12	17	0	0	0
McCutchon, Rangers	.929	9	13	0	1	0
Mealy, Pirates	.974	44	108	3	3	0
Mehl, White Sox	.960	42	69	3	3	0
Merejo, Pirates*	.976	36	75	5	2	1
Modica, Pirates*	1.000	1	4	0	0	0
Mota, Dodgers	.967	43	84	5	3	1
Mullins, Braves	1.000	10	12	0	0	0
Nunez, Astros	1.000	4	6	0	0	0
Oliva, Braves	.933	16	14	0	1	0
Peel, White Sox	1.000	29	29	2	0	1
Perez, Astros*	.917	30	42	2	4	1
Pickett, Royals	.960	42	71	1	3	0
Poteet, Dodgers	1.000	1	2	0	0	0
Pulliam, Royals	.944	45	62	5	4	2
RHODES, Astros*	1.000	62	113	6	0	1
Rogers, Braves	.921	53	54	4	5	0
Rojas, Dodgers	1.000	1	1	0	0	0
Ross, Braves*	.956	58	98	11	5	4
Sambino, Braves*	.972	58	100	4	3	1
Seay, Rangers*	.923	50	58	2	5	1
Sheffield, Rangers	.900	7	7	2	1	2
Sims, Reds*	.962	38	42	8	2	2
Snypes, Royals	1.000	14	21	0	0	0
Sosa, Rangers	.944	61	92	9	6	1
Spear, Rangers	1.000	11	6	0	0	0
Sullivan, White Sox	1.000	2	2	0	0	0
Talley, Expos*	.977	30	40	2	1	1
Thomas, Reds	.972	37	65	5	2	0
Vance, Expos	1.000	7	3	1	0	0
Viltz, Yankees*	1.000	1	2	0	0	0
Waggoner, White Sox	.950	33	55	2	3	1
Wagner, White Sox	1.000	3	2	0	0	0
Walker, Reds	.952	30	56	3	3	1
Watkins, Royals	.957	24	41	3	2	1
White, White Sox	.974	32	37	1	1	1
Williams, Yankees	.976	61	117	3	3	0

Triple Play—J. Gonzalez.

CATCHERS

Player and Club	Pct.	G.	PO.	A.	E.	DP.	PB.
Barretto, Rangers	.989	27	167	9	2	0	2
Bautista, Pirates	1.000	2	8	2	0	0	1
Beltran, Pirates	.942	22	78	19	6	1	5
Bottenfield, Expos	.968	12	49	12	2	3	3
Brian, Expos	.960	24	147	20	7	2	3
Brown, White Sox	.962	26	115	13	5	1	0
Browne, Braves	.966	27	176	24	7	3	6
Cento, White Sox	.957	27	130	27	7	1	7
Davis, Royals	.990	18	81	14	1	1	5
Deiley, Astros	.965	41	240	39	10	0	8
Duran, Dodgers	.966	18	96	16	4	1	3
Dyer, Royals	1.000	1	2	0	0	0	0
Fontes, Rangers	.986	41	251	31	4	2	5
C. Gonzalez, Royals	.962	36	192	35	9	1	13
E. Gonzalez, Yankees	.946	11	55	15	4	0	0
J. Gonzalez, Pirates	.963	22	135	19	6	0	11
Haberle, Pirates	.952	6	19	1	1	0	1
Hernandez, Dodgers	.965	39	217	34	9	3	5
LEARY, Expos	.987	34	201	29	3	1	1
Lopez, Yankees	.959	13	59	12	3	1	6
Lyden, Yankees	.972	13	62	8	2	0	1
Maville, Expos	.958	11	21	2	1	0	2
McFadden, Reds	.818	8	25	2	6	0	7
Mora, Dodgers	.961	14	64	10	3	0	0
Murphy, Astros	1.000	17	57	6	0	0	0
Niewulis, Yankees	.962	8	43	8	2	0	1
Pearn, Rangers	1.000	2	7	1	0	0	1
Plumb, Braves	.968	39	234	42	9	3	0
Pujols, Royals	.963	22	89	14	4	0	11
Ramon, Yankees	.985	33	166	37	3	1	7
Rojas, Dodgers	.938	11	29	1	2	0	0
Rosario, Rangers	.980	10	43	5	1	2	1
Sapienza, Reds	.973	31	163	17	5	0	3
Spitale, Expos*	1.000	1	4	1	0	0	0
Taubensee, Reds	.966	32	197	27	8	0	8
Thompson, Yankees	.933	3	13	1	1	0	0
Troutman, Pirates	.983	20	97	16	2	0	5
Wong, White Sox	.982	38	184	30	4	1	10
Zayas, Astros	.953	23	121	21	7	1	7

PITCHERS

Player and Club	Pct.	G.	PO.	A.	E.	DP.
Acevedo, Royals	.800	18	1	3	1	0
Acosta, Pirates*	.900	20	0	9	1	0
Ahearne, Expos	.667	6	1	1	1	1
Alcorta, Reds	1.000	18	5	8	0	1
Almonte, Pirates*	.500	4	0	1	1	0
Arteaga, Pirates	1.000	7	0	3	0	0
Arzola, Dodgers	1.000	4	0	2	0	0
August, Astros	.935	13	11	18	2	1
Azocar, Yankees*	.813	6	2	11	3	2
Babcock, White Sox*	1.000	4	0	1	0	0
Barberich, Dodgers	1.000	16	2	2	0	0
Barcelo, Braves	1.000	16	3	2	0	0
Belinda, Pirates	1.000	17	2	2	0	1
Bergeron, Expos	.727	5	1	7	3	0
Bluhm, Dodgers	1.000	5	0	1	0	1
Ken. Bottenfield, Expos	.893	13	6	19	3	0
Bouman, Expos	.800	6	2	2	1	0
M. Brito, Expos	.917	11	10	12	2	0
Y. Brito, Yankees	1.000	5	2	1	0	0
Kei. Brown, Reds	.789	7	4	11	4	0
Kev. Brown, Rangers	1.000	3	0	1	0	0
Bryan, Rangers	.944	14	2	15	1	1
Burckhalter, Royals	1.000	8	0	1	0	0
Burgos, Rangers*	.941	12	3	13	1	0
Busick, Rangers	.800	25	2	6	2	0
Carreno, Yankees	1.000	7	5	12	0	0
Castillo, Rangers	.500	13	0	2	2	0
Cerefin, Astros	1.000	3	1	0	0	0
Chapin, Yankees	.900	13	7	20	3	1
Chavez, Reds*	1.000	9	2	23	0	2
D. Clark, Yankees*	1.000	4	0	3	0	0
M. Clark, Braves	.800	12	5	7	3	0
Costello, Astros	.810	14	2	15	4	0
DeLaCruz, White Sox	.783	14	2	16	5	0
DeLeon, Royals	1.000	12	3	10	0	0
Denkenberger, Pirates*	1.000	1	1	0	0	0
Doss, Pirates	.882	10	1	14	2	0
Espinal, Reds	.969	14	8	23	1	1
Faccio, Yankees	1.000	13	1	7	0	0
Farmer, Braves*	1.000	14	1	17	0	0
Fields, Astros	1.000	21	5	10	0	0
Figueroa, Yankees*	.938	16	5	10	1	2
Findlay, Rangers*	.571	14	0	4	3	0
Forrest, Pirates*	1.000	3	1	0	0	0
Giron, Yankees	.952	34	4	16	1	2
Gobeil, Pirates	1.000	1	0	1	0	0
Gonzalez, Pirates	1.000	1	0	1	0	0
Gordon, Royals	.900	9	0	9	1	0
Hall, White Sox*	.885	14	2	21	3	0
Hammond, Reds*	.750	7	1	5	2	0
Hart, Dodgers*	.923	15	1	11	1	1
Hook, Astros*	.889	12	3	13	2	1
Huchingson, Astros	1.000	8	2	0	0	0
Hudson, Expos*	.500	6	1	0	1	0
Huff, Braves	1.000	2	2	2	0	0
Jacobson, Expos	1.000	3	2	3	0	0
Jenkins, Reds	1.000	14	3	15	0	3
Jensen, White Sox	.833	15	1	4	1	1
Kaiser, Reds	1.000	11	4	12	0	0
Katschke, Rangers	.923	11	4	8	1	0
Kennedy, White Sox	1.000	10	5	5	0	0
Kerrigan, Expos	.667	17	1	3	2	0
Kershaw, White Sox	.813	16	6	7	3	2
Kocis, Pirates	.600	5	0	3	2	0
Koller, Pirates	1.000	10	1	8	0	0
Kovatch, White Sox	.952	12	7	13	1	0
Kroll, Dodgers	1.000	19	3	12	0	0
Langley, Dodgers*	1.000	5	0	5	0	0
Lee, Royals*	1.000	10	0	7	0	1
Leon, Expos	1.000	15	0	4	0	0
Lilly, Dodgers	1.000	12	1	10	0	0
Longuil, Braves	.879	13	7	22	4	2
Maebe, White Sox*	1.000	14	0	6	0	0
Maldonado, Royals	1.000	10	5	4	0	0
Manon, Yankees	.750	11	2	7	3	0
Marino, Expos*	.875	21	1	6	1	0
MARRERO, Braves*	1.000	18	6	22	0	0
Marris, Yankees	1.000	7	1	2	0	0
Marsh, Reds	1.000	18	1	5	0	0
Massa, Pirates	.889	9	0	8	1	0
Matos, Pirates	.500	1	0	1	1	0
McClear, Yankees	1.000	6	1	6	0	0
McClure, Astros	.857	27	1	5	1	0
Meizoso, Rangers*	.857	14	0	6	1	0
Mercado, Royals	1.000	17	0	5	0	0
Mercker, Braves*	.909	9	1	9	1	0

PITCHERS—Continued

Player and Club	Pct.	G.	PO.	A.	E.	DP.
Meyers, Royals	.947	12	4	14	1	0
Miguel, Dodgers	1.000	13	3	6	0	0
Miller, Braves	1.000	18	3	13	0	0
Molina, Pirates	.923	8	2	10	1	1
Morales, Yankees	1.000	11	1	2	0	0
Moreno, Pirates	1.000	7	0	2	0	0
Morgan, White Sox	.500	15	0	3	3	0
Morse, Rangers	.800	4	1	3	1	0
Mota, Braves	1.000	8	3	5	0	1
Munson, Expos	1.000	6	0	1	0	0
Murphy, Pirates	1.000	7	2	5	0	0
Nelson, Dodgers	.929	11	2	11	1	0
Nocas, Royals	1.000	11	2	8	0	0
Odom, Royals	.941	11	4	12	1	1
Olivares, Pirates*	.750	6	0	3	1	0
Ollom, White Sox	1.000	4	2	4	0	0
Ortiz, Braves	.750	21	1	5	2	0
Patterson, Rangers	.933	11	4	10	1	0
Peralta, Reds	.636	26	2	5	4	0
Pinto, Royals	1.000	14	0	10	0	0
Prescott, Expos	.950	11	3	16	1	0
Radinski, White Sox*	1.000	7	0	3	0	0
Ramirez, Royals	.778	16	1	6	2	0
Reed, Pirates	1.000	8	1	2	0	0
Reeves, Rangers*	.833	17	1	4	1	1
Richards, Braves	1.000	12	2	1	0	0
Rivera, Rangers	.889	16	3	5	1	1
Robinson, White Sox	1.000	8	3	2	0	0
A. Rodriguez, Expos	1.000	11	3	4	0	0
C. Rodriguez, Expos*	1.000	13	0	3	0	0
G. Rodriguez, Yankees	.875	19	0	7	1	2
I. Rodriguez, Expos	1.000	2	0	1	0	0
Rojas, Expos	.917	13	6	16	2	2
Romo, Astros	.864	13	3	16	3	1
Rosenthal, Rangers	.917	23	2	9	1	0
Ryan, Yankees	.818	8	2	7	2	2
Sandoval, White Sox	.875	14	0	7	1	0
Santana, Pirates	.667	11	0	2	1	0
Santiago, Pirates	.667	4	0	2	1	0
Schlopy, Pirates*	1.000	1	0	3	0	0
Sepulveda, Dodgers	.885	14	7	16	3	0
Shepherd, Pirates	.800	8	0	4	1	0
Shiflett, Rangers	1.000	1	1	0	0	0
Shiverick, Reds	1.000	13	6	12	0	0
Simmons, Astros	1.000	2	0	1	0	0
Slaughter, Pirates	1.000	8	0	6	0	0
Smallwood, Pirates	.933	9	2	12	1	2
C. Smith, Braves*	1.000	12	3	12	0	0
W. Smith, Pirates	1.000	7	0	2	0	0
Soto, Rangers	.667	9	0	2	1	0
Stoker, Astros	.818	13	3	15	4	0
Studeman, Royals	1.000	10	1	10	0	1
Swob, Reds*	1.000	11	5	13	0	0
Tapia, Dodgers	1.000	29	0	8	0	0
Tauken, White Sox	.882	18	3	12	2	0
Thomas, Dodgers*	.938	15	1	14	1	0
Torres, Yankees	1.000	2	1	3	0	0
Towey, Astros	1.000	13	1	3	0	0
Trapasso, Braves*	1.000	9	2	2	0	1
Trapp, Royals*	1.000	17	0	9	0	0
Valenzuela, Pirates*	.833	3	0	5	1	0
Vasquez, Astros	1.000	18	4	6	0	1
Villanueva, White Sox*	1.000	3	1	3	0	1
Vlcek, Rangers	.786	18	2	9	3	1
Weems, Braves	.842	15	5	11	3	0
West, Braves	.667	2	1	1	1	0
J. Willis, Royals*	.857	7	0	6	1	0
K. Willis, Reds	.909	7	2	8	1	0
Wood, Dodgers	.857	10	1	11	2	1

The following players do not have any recorded accepted chances at the positions indicated; therefore, are not listed in the fielding averages for those particular positions: H. Almonte, 1b, p; Angelero, 2b; Balkiewicz, p; Beams, p; Bluhm, of; Bonilla, 3b; Carr, ss; Contreras, of; Diaz, of, p; Doyle, p; Elsberry, p; Ezold, p; C. Green, 2b; Hornsby, 3b; Luckett, c; Machacek, p; Mullins, c; Pardo, p; F. Sanchez, 3b; Scarborough, p; Shiverick, of; Sims, p; K. Smith, p; Snypes, 2b; Velez, 2b; Wilson, p.

CLUB PITCHING

Club	ERA.	G.	CG.	ShO.	Sv.	IP.	H.	R.	ER.	HR.	HB.	BB.	Int. BB.	SO.	WP.	Bk.
Rangers	2.62	62	1	7	17	546.1	471	225	159	7	19	221	2	463	41	13
Reds	2.75	62	7	5	16	542.1	450	243	166	6	20	230	24	379	47	7
Dodgers	2.90	61	7	6	18	527.0	427	227	170	12	19	239	16	391	34	14
Braves	2.93	63	3	4	15	552.1	510	267	180	9	16	215	19	397	22	7
White Sox	3.15	63	2	4	13	562.1	484	267	197	13	28	296	0	417	31	12
Astros	3.31	63	7	6	16	543.1	467	273	200	10	40	252	2	418	50	5
Yankees	3.35	63	12	6	8	551.1	526	275	205	11	24	224	5	404	44	11
Royals	3.52	63	3	4	17	537.1	519	297	210	12	19	234	11	363	63	13
Expos	3.54	62	8	6	13	533.1	486	272	210	15	29	264	2	403	28	10
Pirates	3.91	64	5	5	15	540.1	555	317	235	13	25	224	0	327	38	9

PITCHERS' RECORDS

(Leading Qualifiers for Earned-Run Average Leadership — 50 or More Innings)

*Throws lefthanded.

Pitcher — Club	W.	L.	Pct.	ERA.	G.	GS.	CG.	GF.	ShO.	Sv.	IP.	H.	R.	ER.	HR.	HB.	BB.	Int. BB.	SO.	WP.
Rosenthal, Rangers	4	2	.667	0.73	23	3	1	16	1	9	61.2	36	9	5	0	0	11	0	73	4
Espinal, Reds	7	4	.636	1.12	14	14	2	0	1	0	88.1	65	21	11	0	2	28	2	46	3
Giron, Yankees	6	2	.750	1.39	33	0	0	31	0	8	51.2	49	13	8	1	4	17	2	52	2
August, Astros	6	5	.545	1.52	13	13	1	0	0	0	83.0	71	23	14	0	4	20	0	66	6
Burgos, Rangers*	3	3	.500	1.55	12	12	0	0	0	0	63.2	55	18	11	1	0	22	1	53	2
Wood, Dodgers	3	2	.600	1.78	10	9	0	0	0	0	55.2	36	20	11	2	4	18	0	26	3
Stoker, Astros	6	5	.545	1.79	13	11	2	1	1	0	80.1	53	24	16	3	2	39	0	66	5
M. Clark, Braves	6	4	.600	1.86	12	11	0	0	0	0	58.0	44	24	12	0	4	22	0	46	4
Longuil, Braves	4	3	.571	1.91	13	12	1	0	0	0	75.1	65	39	16	1	3	28	1	56	3
Koller, Pirates	4	2	.667	1.94	10	10	1	0	1	0	60.1	62	17	13	0	2	17	0	22	5

Departmental Leaders: G—Giron, 33; W—Thomas, 8; L—DeLeon, C. Smith, 8; Pct.—Thomas, .800; GS—Espinal, Sepulveda, 14; CG—Sepulveda, 5; GF—Giron, 31; ShO—Sepulveda, 3; Sv.—Tapia, 14; IP—Sepulveda, 94.2; H—Figueroa, 77; R—Bottenfield, Chapin, Costello, Marrero, 42; ER—Costello, 35; HR—M. Brito, Marrero, Nocas, 4; HB—Towey, 12; BB—Kershaw, 67; IBB—Tapia, 7; SO—Thomas, 77; WP—Towey, 18.

(All Pitchers—Listed Alphabetically)

Pitcher — Club	W.	L.	Pct.	ERA.	G.	GS.	CG.	GF.	ShO.	Sv.	IP.	H.	R.	ER.	HR.	HB.	BB.	Int. BB.	SO.	WP.
Acevedo, Royals	4	1	.800	2.25	18	0	0	9	0	3	44.0	29	19	11	0	6	25	1	46	5
Acosta, Pirates*	1	2	.333	2.92	20	0	0	16	0	5	24.2	23	13	8	0	0	7	0	18	2
Ahearne, Expos	1	0	1.000	5.28	6	0	0	2	0	1	15.1	8	11	9	0	0	11	0	3	1
Alcorta, Reds	2	1	.667	4.96	18	0	0	10	0	4	32.2	29	21	18	2	2	15	3	19	5
F. Almonte, Pirates*	0	1	.000	7.50	4	0	0	1	0	0	6.0	8	5	5	0	1	2	0	2	0
H. Almonte, Astros	0	0	.000	13.50	1	0	0	0	0	0	0.2	3	7	1	0	0	5	0	0	1
Arteaga, Pirates	1	0	1.000	4.70	7	0	0	1	0	0	15.1	19	9	8	0	0	7	0	11	0
Arzola, Dodgers	0	0	.000	16.62	4	0	0	1	0	0	4.1	14	9	8	2	1	4	0	0	0
August, Astros	6	5	.545	1.52	13	13	1	0	0	0	83.0	71	23	14	0	4	20	0	66	6
Azocar, Yankees*	4	2	.667	3.25	6	5	2	0	1	0	36.0	29	17	13	0	1	12	0	22	3
Babcock, White Sox*	1	0	1.000	1.59	4	0	0	1	0	1	5.2	5	1	1	0	0	0	0	4	0
Balkiewicz, Pirates	0	0	.000	13.50	1	0	0	0	0	0	2.0	2	4	3	1	0	3	0	1	0

Pitcher—Club	W.	L.	Pct.	ERA.	G.	GS.	CG.	GF.	ShO.	Sv.	IP.	H.	R.	ER.	HR.	HB.	BB.	Int. BB.	SO.	WP.
Barberich, Dodgers	0	2	.000	2.19	16	0	0	7	0	0	24.2	25	6	6	0	0	12	2	13	1
Barcelo, Braves	2	3	.400	4.62	16	0	0	6	0	0	25.1	24	13	13	0	0	21	3	30	1
Beams, Astros	0	0	.000	18.00	1	0	0	0	0	0	1.0	3	2	2	0	0	0	0	0	0
Belinda, Pirates	3	2	.600	2.66	17	0	0	15	0	7	20.1	23	12	6	1	1	2	0	17	0
Bergeron, Expos	2	1	.667	1.67	5	4	1	1	1	0	27.0	15	6	5	0	2	15	0	22	1
Bluhm, Dodgers	0	0	.000	4.91	5	0	0	0	0	0	7.1	9	4	4	0	0	3	0	3	0
Ken. Bottenfield, Expos	5	6	.455	3.27	13	13	2	0	0	0	74.1	73	42	27	2	3	30	0	41	0
Bouman, Expos	0	2	.000	3.43	6	6	0	0	0	0	21.0	19	12	8	1	1	18	0	20	1
M. Brito, Expos	5	3	.625	4.10	11	11	1	0	0	0	59.1	58	29	27	4	4	24	0	40	4
Y. Brito, Yankees	0	2	.000	6.75	5	1	0	1	0	0	6.2	11	8	5	0	0	3	0	3	0
Kei. Brown, Reds	4	1	.800	0.95	7	7	1	0	0	0	47.1	29	15	5	0	2	5	1	26	3
Kev. Brown, Rangers	0	0	.000	6.00	3	0	0	0	0	0	6.0	7	4	4	0	0	2	0	1	0
Bryan, Rangers	3	6	.333	2.33	14	13	0	0	0	0	69.2	68	27	18	0	5	18	0	40	5
Burckhalter, Royals	0	1	.000	9.64	8	0	0	3	0	0	14.0	22	18	15	0	0	8	0	4	1
Burgos, Rangers*	3	3	.500	1.55	12	12	0	0	0	0	63.2	55	18	11	1	0	22	1	53	2
Busick, Rangers	1	2	.333	3.38	25	0	0	17	0	2	29.1	28	20	11	0	2	19	0	25	6
Carreno, Yankees	5	0	1.000	1.70	7	7	2	0	1	0	47.2	36	12	9	1	1	12	0	27	1
Castillo, Rangers	0	1	.000	7.98	13	0	0	3	0	0	14.2	22	17	13	0	2	10	0	17	2
Cerefin, Astros	0	0	.000	36.00	3	0	0	0	0	0	3.0	6	12	12	0	6	6	0	0	3
Chapin, Yankees	4	3	.571	3.24	13	13	2	0	2	0	83.1	71	42	30	2	2	27	1	67	10
Chavez, Reds*	3	2	.600	3.18	9	6	1	1	0	0	39.2	45	18	14	2	0	20	3	27	2
D. Clark, Yankees*	0	0	.000	0.00	4	0	0	0	0	0	6.0	6	3	0	0	0	4	0	5	1
M. Clark, Braves	6	4	.600	1.86	12	11	0	0	0	0	58.0	44	24	12	0	4	22	0	46	4
Costello, Astros	4	5	.444	4.75	14	12	1	0	1	0	66.1	74	42	35	1	6	26	0	51	1
DeLaCruz, White Sox	2	4	.333	3.26	14	6	0	5	0	1	47.0	43	25	17	0	1	32	0	46	4
DeLeon, Royals	1	8	.111	3.72	12	10	0	2	0	0	55.2	54	31	23	3	0	22	2	33	3
Denkenberger, Pirates*	0	0	.000	0.00	1	0	0	1	0	0	1.0	0	0	0	0	0	0	0	0	0
Diaz, Reds	0	0	.000	27.00	3	0	0	1	0	0	2.0	4	6	6	0	1	3	0	3	2
Doss, Pirates	2	4	.333	5.50	10	8	0	0	0	0	37.2	34	30	23	0	4	25	0	33	5
Doyle, Yankees*	0	0	.000	7.94	6	0	0	3	0	0	5.2	8	5	5	0	1	2	0	6	0
Elsberry, Astros	0	2	.000	3.00	3	1	0	1	0	1	6.0	6	5	2	0	1	2	0	5	1
Espinal, Reds	7	4	.636	1.12	14	14	2	0	1	0	88.1	65	21	11	0	2	28	2	46	3
Ezold, Yankees	0	0	.000	0.00	1	0	0	1	0	0	1.0	1	0	0	0	0	1	0	1	0
Faccio, Yankees	1	3	.250	5.63	13	2	0	3	0	0	32.0	32	21	20	2	2	21	0	26	6
Farmer, Braves*	1	1	.500	1.93	14	0	0	7	0	2	23.1	29	6	5	0	0	2	0	11	1
Fields, Astros	2	1	.667	2.45	21	0	0	13	0	5	47.2	44	16	13	1	0	17	0	28	1
Figueroa, Yankees*	4	6	.400	2.79	16	11	3	1	0	0	80.2	77	37	25	2	2	29	0	68	7
Findlay, Rangers*	2	0	1.000	1.61	14	0	0	5	0	1	28.0	23	10	5	1	0	15	0	23	2
Forrest, Pirates*	0	2	.000	5.63	3	2	0	0	0	0	8.0	12	8	5	0	0	5	0	5	2
Giron, Yankees	6	2	.750	1.39	33	0	0	31	0	8	51.2	49	13	8	1	4	17	2	52	2
Gobeil, Pirates	0	0	.000	0.00	1	0	0	0	0	0	2.0	1	0	0	0	0	1	0	1	0
Gonzalez, Pirates	0	1	.000	36.00	1	0	0	1	0	0	1.0	5	5	4	0	0	1	0	0	0
Gordon, Royals	3	1	.750	1.02	9	7	2	1	1	1	44.0	31	12	5	0	0	23	1	47	7
Hall, White Sox*	6	2	.750	2.22	14	11	0	2	0	0	73.0	65	32	18	3	2	21	0	58	1
Hammond, Reds*	3	2	.600	2.81	7	7	1	0	0	0	41.2	27	21	13	0	0	17	1	53	5
Hart, Dodgers*	1	1	.500	3.33	15	0	0	2	0	1	24.1	22	12	9	0	0	12	1	26	3
Hook, Astros*	4	2	.667	2.67	12	11	0	0	0	0	64.0	44	23	19	1	0	31	0	50	4
Huchingson, Astros	1	1	.500	5.82	8	1	0	3	0	0	17.0	20	14	11	2	1	2	0	7	0
Hudson, Expos*	0	0	.000	9.58	6	1	0	2	0	0	10.1	12	12	11	1	2	11	0	3	5
Huff, Braves	0	2	.000	4.32	2	2	0	0	0	0	8.1	8	6	4	0	1	7	0	5	0
Jacobson, Expos	1	1	.500	1.06	3	2	1	0	1	0	17.0	7	2	2	0	0	10	0	20	1
Jenkins, Reds	1	6	.143	3.29	14	8	0	3	0	0	52.0	59	24	19	0	3	28	3	38	4
Jensen, White Sox	3	3	.500	3.34	15	1	1	12	0	3	35.0	30	19	13	1	5	13	0	34	0
Kaiser, Reds	0	4	.000	3.18	11	3	0	1	0	0	28.1	28	22	10	0	4	25	1	14	5
Katschke, Rangers	3	3	.500	3.40	11	6	0	3	0	1	45.0	41	22	17	2	1	10	0	35	2
Kennedy, White Sox	0	4	.000	6.38	10	7	0	2	0	1	36.2	47	30	26	1	1	32	0	35	7
Kerrigan, Expos	3	2	.600	4.89	17	1	0	8	0	1	38.2	44	30	21	2	3	18	2	33	5
Kershaw, White Sox	0	6	.000	4.08	16	10	0	3	0	1	57.1	35	35	26	0	11	67	0	29	8
Kocis, Pirates	0	1	.000	2.00	5	1	0	1	0	0	9.0	9	7	2	0	0	10	0	5	1
Koller, Pirates	4	2	.667	1.94	10	10	1	0	1	0	60.1	62	17	13	0	2	17	0	22	5
Kovatch, White Sox	5	2	.714	1.99	12	7	1	3	1	0	54.1	50	15	12	0	0	14	0	42	0
Kroll, Dodgers	3	1	.750	3.40	19	4	0	5	0	2	39.2	38	19	15	1	1	16	2	26	4
Langley, Dodgers*	1	1	.500	1.35	5	5	0	0	0	0	26.2	10	4	4	0	1	20	1	29	2
Lee, Royals*	2	2	.500	5.84	10	0	0	1	0	0	24.2	30	23	16	0	1	13	1	25	1
Leon, Expos	1	2	.333	4.30	15	1	0	8	0	2	29.1	32	18	14	1	3	13	0	21	2
Lilly, Dodgers	2	3	.400	5.58	11	7	0	2	0	0	40.1	44	27	25	1	1	26	1	26	3
Longuil, Braves	4	3	.571	1.91	13	12	1	0	0	0	75.1	65	39	16	1	3	28	1	56	3
Machacek, Expos*	1	0	1.000	3.38	3	0	0	2	0	1	5.1	10	5	2	1	0	1	0	5	0
Maebe, White Sox*	1	0	1.000	3.72	14	0	0	7	0	1	19.1	12	9	8	1	0	19	0	16	4
Maldonado, Royals	0	2	.000	1.83	10	4	0	2	0	1	34.1	29	10	7	1	1	10	1	16	3
Manon, Yankees	0	4	.000	5.14	11	4	0	2	0	0	28.0	31	22	16	0	1	22	1	13	2
Marino, Expos*	0	0	.000	1.99	21	0	0	20	0	7	31.2	24	10	7	0	1	18	0	43	1
Marrero, Braves*	3	3	.500	4.65	18	7	1	7	1	0	62.0	62	42	32	4	2	37	5	39	3
Marris, Yankees	1	1	.500	6.25	7	6	0	0	0	0	31.2	37	24	22	2	3	15	0	14	3
Marsh, Reds	0	2	.000	9.10	18	0	0	9	0	0	28.2	45	31	29	0	1	13	2	19	2
Massa, Pirates	1	3	.250	4.76	9	2	0	2	0	0	34.0	39	19	18	2	3	12	0	28	3
Matos, Pirates	0	0	.000	0.00	1	0	0	1	0	0	1.0	1	1	0	0	1	0	0	0	0
McClear, Yankees	1	2	.333	2.88	6	4	0	1	0	0	25.0	27	11	8	0	0	6	0	15	1
McClure, Astros	4	2	.667	3.12	27	0	0	23	0	7	43.1	36	23	15	1	4	20	1	47	4
Meizoso, Rangers*	1	1	.500	2.53	14	0	0	4	0	1	21.1	21	10	6	0	0	11	0	24	2
Mercado, Royals	2	1	.667	5.46	16	0	0	11	0	2	29.2	38	23	18	0	3	13	0	12	6
Mercker, Braves*	4	3	.571	2.47	9	8	0	1	0	0	47.1	37	21	13	1	0	16	1	42	0
Meyers, Royals	4	5	.444	4.80	12	12	0	0	0	0	50.2	59	37	27	0	0	30	0	24	9
Miguel, Dodgers	0	2	.000	2.08	13	1	0	7	0	0	21.2	12	6	5	0	0	17	0	18	1
Miller, Braves	3	2	.600	1.34	18	0	0	12	0	8	40.1	25	8	6	1	0	7	1	44	2
Molina, Pirates	2	3	.400	1.43	8	8	1	0	0	0	37.2	35	17	6	2	0	10	0	21	1
Morales, Yankees	0	1	.000	5.52	11	0	0	2	0	0	14.2	17	12	9	1	0	12	1	10	1
Moreno, Pirates	1	2	.333	6.04	7	2	0	2	0	1	25.1	27	18	17	2	4	9	0	12	4
Morgan, White Sox	3	2	.600	5.33	15	0	0	10	0	1	27.0	28	20	16	3	1	15	0	17	1
Morse, Rangers	2	1	.667	1.64	4	4	0	0	0	0	22.0	11	4	4	0	0	7	0	20	1
Mota, Braves	0	0	.000	2.76	8	0	0	2	0	0	16.1	15	6	5	0	0	8	0	6	0
Munson, Expos	0	0	.000	3.52	6	0	0	3	0	1	15.1	15	6	6	1	0	8	0	13	1
Murphy, Pirates	2	3	.400	3.54	7	6	0	1	0	0	40.2	48	18	16	2	0	8	0	25	1

Pitcher—Club	W.	L.	Pct.	ERA.	G.	GS.	CG.	GF.	ShO.	Sv.	IP.	H.	R.	ER.	HR.	HB.	BB.	Int. BB.	SO.	WP.
Nelson, Dodgers	2	6	.250	3.72	11	10	1	1	0	1	55.2	59	34	23	2	1	21	0	40	10
Nocas, Royals	5	0	1.000	2.65	11	11	0	0	0	0	51.0	46	19	15	4	2	14	0	39	8
Odom, Royals	2	2	.500	3.72	11	11	1	0	1	0	58.0	60	32	24	1	3	16	0	33	8
Olivares, Pirates*	0	0	.000	2.08	6	0	0	3	0	0	8.2	10	6	2	0	0	3	0	8	0
Ollom, White Sox	0	1	.000	2.74	4	4	0	0	0	0	23.0	21	7	7	0	3	7	0	18	1
Ortiz, Braves	1	0	1.000	3.07	21	1	0	6	0	0	29.1	24	13	10	0	0	17	0	16	1
Pardo, Yankees	0	1	.000	11.25	3	0	0	1	0	0	4.0	6	5	5	0	1	3	0	3	2
Patterson, Rangers	5	3	.625	2.70	11	10	0	1	0	0	53.1	37	18	16	0	3	30	0	65	3
Peralta, Reds	4	2	.667	2.41	26	0	0	23	0	8	41.0	27	16	11	0	2	25	3	20	3
Pinto, Royals	2	1	.667	3.94	14	0	0	3	0	0	32.0	35	22	14	1	0	17	1	17	0
Prescott, Expos	4	5	.444	2.62	11	9	2	0	0	0	65.1	50	22	19	1	3	19	0	52	0
Radinski, White Sox*	1	0	1.000	3.38	7	7	0	0	0	0	26.2	24	20	10	0	0	17	0	18	2
Ramirez, Royals	0	3	.000	5.63	16	1	0	10	0	3	24.0	29	23	15	1	3	11	1	9	3
Reed, Pirates	0	2	.000	3.75	8	3	0	1	0	0	24.0	20	12	10	0	0	6	0	15	0
Reeves, Rangers*	2	1	.667	4.07	17	0	0	3	0	0	24.1	26	12	11	1	0	11	0	19	1
Richards, Braves	0	0	.000	2.33	12	0	0	5	0	1	19.1	17	8	5	0	2	7	2	15	2
Rivera, Rangers	3	2	.600	2.31	16	7	0	0	0	0	50.2	46	19	13	0	2	17	1	29	2
Robinson, White Sox	2	4	.333	2.86	8	5	0	1	0	0	44.0	34	17	14	1	0	13	0	21	0
A. Rodriguez, Expos	3	1	.750	1.46	11	0	0	4	0	0	37.0	30	11	6	0	2	10	0	28	0
C. Rodriguez, Expos*	3	0	1.000	5.57	13	0	0	3	0	0	21.0	15	13	13	1	3	19	0	16	2
G. Rodriguez, Yankees	2	1	.667	2.85	19	0	0	5	0	0	41.0	27	19	13	0	4	24	0	36	3
I. Rodriguez, Expos	0	1	.000	2.70	2	2	0	0	0	0	10.0	11	4	3	0	0	2	0	9	0
Rojas, Expos	4	5	.444	4.88	13	12	1	1	0	0	55.1	63	39	30	0	2	37	0	34	4
Romo, Astros	7	3	.700	2.40	12	12	3	0	0	0	75.0	57	28	20	0	1	38	0	66	5
Rosenthal, Rangers	4	2	.667	0.73	23	3	1	16	1	9	61.2	36	9	5	0	0	11	0	73	4
Ryan, Yankees	3	1	.750	3.43	8	8	2	0	1	0	39.1	54	22	15	0	1	9	0	24	2
Sandoval, White Sox	3	2	.600	2.86	14	0	0	8	0	2	28.1	28	11	9	0	0	8	0	17	0
Santana, Pirates	2	1	.667	6.82	11	6	1	0	0	0	33.0	36	31	25	1	1	34	0	32	5
Santiago, Pirates	0	1	.000	11.25	4	0	0	1	0	0	8.0	17	13	10	0	1	4	0	3	2
Scarborough, Braves	0	0	.000	0.00	1	0	0	1	0	0	1.0	0	0	0	0	0	0	0	0	0
Schlopy, Pirates*	1	0	1.000	3.60	1	1	0	0	0	0	5.0	2	3	2	0	0	3	0	4	0
Sepulveda, Dodgers	7	4	.636	2.57	14	14	5	0	3	0	94.2	65	39	27	2	8	32	1	63	2
Shepherd, Pirates	0	4	.000	6.06	8	2	0	4	0	0	16.1	16	17	11	0	1	15	0	12	3
Shiflett, Rangers	0	0	.000	0.00	1	1	0	0	0	0	3.0	0	0	0	0	0	2	0	6	0
Shiverick, Reds	5	1	.833	2.18	13	7	0	3	0	2	57.2	35	22	14	1	0	27	1	41	7
Simmons, Astros	0	0	.000	5.40	2	0	0	1	0	0	3.1	3	2	2	0	0	0	0	4	0
Sims, Reds*	0	0	.000	3.38	2	0	0	2	0	0	2.2	3	2	1	0	0	2	0	3	0
Slaughter, Pirates	0	1	.000	5.63	8	2	0	1	0	0	24.0	27	16	15	1	2	13	0	12	1
Smallwood, Pirates	3	2	.600	2.50	9	9	2	0	1	0	57.2	47	23	16	1	2	17	0	22	3
C. Smith, Braves*	2	8	.200	3.53	12	12	0	0	0	0	66.1	74	40	26	1	2	25	4	32	1
K. Smith, Astros	0	1	.000	0.00	1	1	0	0	0	0	5.0	2	3	0	0	0	1	0	5	0
W. Smith, Pirates	1	0	1.000	2.49	7	2	0	3	0	1	21.2	16	8	6	0	1	6	0	13	0
Soto, Rangers	1	2	.333	3.00	9	2	0	2	0	1	21.0	17	10	7	1	0	4	0	12	2
Stoker, Astros	6	5	.545	1.79	13	11	2	1	1	0	80.1	53	24	16	3	2	39	0	66	5
Studeman, Royals	1	2	.333	2.59	10	1	0	2	0	0	24.1	23	9	7	0	0	11	1	15	3
Swob, Reds*	2	2	.500	1.03	11	3	2	2	1	2	43.2	22	7	5	0	1	11	3	48	5
Tapia, Dodgers	6	4	.600	2.06	29	0	0	27	0	14	48.0	31	17	11	1	1	16	7	44	3
Tauken, White Sox	4	2	.667	2.48	18	2	0	7	0	2	69.0	52	24	19	3	2	30	0	45	2
Thomas, Dodgers*	8	2	.800	2.36	15	11	1	2	0	0	84.0	62	30	22	1	1	42	1	77	2
Torres, Yankees	2	0	1.000	1.06	2	2	1	0	1	0	17.0	7	2	2	0	1	5	0	12	0
Towey, Astros	0	1	.000	16.80	13	1	0	4	0	1	15.0	18	35	28	0	12	35	0	4	18
Trapasso, Braves*	0	0	.000	4.22	9	0	0	7	0	0	10.2	8	5	5	0	0	6	0	7	1
Trapp, Royals*	4	1	.800	1.82	17	0	0	16	0	7	24.2	19	6	5	0	0	9	2	19	2
Valenzuela, Pirates*	0	1	.000	4.05	3	0	0	2	0	0	6.2	9	4	3	0	0	0	0	1	0
Vasquez, Astros	0	1	.000	2.76	18	0	0	10	0	2	32.2	27	14	10	1	3	10	1	19	1
Villanueva, White Sox*	0	0	.000	0.56	3	3	0	0	0	0	16.0	10	2	1	0	2	8	0	17	1
Vlcek, Rangers	1	4	.200	4.96	18	4	0	7	0	2	32.2	33	25	18	1	4	32	0	21	7
Weems, Braves	3	5	.375	3.78	15	8	1	6	0	4	64.1	73	34	27	1	1	12	2	39	3
West, Braves	0	0	.000	1.80	2	2	0	0	0	0	5.0	5	2	1	0	1	0	0	9	0
J. Willis, Royals*	0	3	.000	3.08	7	6	0	0	0	0	26.1	15	13	9	1	0	12	0	24	4
K. Willis, Reds	3	1	.750	2.45	7	7	0	0	0	0	36.2	32	17	10	1	2	11	1	22	1
Wilson, Pirates	0	1	.000	0.96	3	0	0	2	0	1	9.1	7	1	1	0	1	4	0	4	0
Wood, Dodgers	3	2	.600	1.78	10	9	0	0	0	0	55.2	36	20	11	2	4	18	0	26	3

BALKS—Thomas, 6; Patterson, Stoker, 4 each; DeLaCruz, Marris, Ramirez, Ryan, Tauken, 3 each; Acosta, Arteaga, Burgos, Busick, Findlay, Kaiser, Nocas, Pinto, Prescott, I. Rodriguez, Tapia, Weems, Wood, 2 each; Alcorta, Bergeron, Ken. Bottenfield, M. Brito, Kev. Brown, Bryan, Chapin, Chavez, M. Clark, Doss, Figueroa, Giron, Gordon, Hall, Hart, Kennedy, Kerrigan, Kershaw, Langley, Longuil, Marino, Marsh, McClear, Meizoso, Mercker, Meyers, Miguel, Miller, Morgan, Odom, Olivares, Ollom, Radinski, Reed, A. Rodriguez, G. Rodriguez, Schlopy, Sepulveda, Shepherd, Shiverick, C. Smith, Studeman, Trapp, Vasquez, J. Willis, K. Willis, 1 each.

COMBINATION SHUTOUTS—Hook-Costello-Fields, Hook-McClure, Hook-Elsberry, Romo-McClure, Astros; Clark-Richards-Weems, Clark-Miller, Longuil-Richards-Ortiz, Braves; Kroll-Hart-Tapia, Thomas-Kroll-Tapia, Langley-Nelson, Dodgers; Brito-Ahearn, Prescott-Leon, Brito-Moreno, Rojas-Moreno, Expos; Koller-Slaughter-Acosta, Molina-Acosta, Smallwood-Belinda, Pirates; Morse-Rosenthal-Busick, Burgos-Rivera-Vlcek-Rosenthal-Meizoso-Busick, Rivera-Findlay-Katschke, Patterson-Findlay-Rivera-Busick-Meizoso, Burgos-Soto-Rosenthal, Bryan-Meizoso-Rosenthal, Rangers; Espinal-Peralta, Hammond-Swob-Peralta, Hammond-Swob, Reds; Meyers-Gordon, Nocas-Maldonado, Royals; Kershaw-Babcock-Kovatch, Kovatch-Kennedy, Tauken-DeLaCruz, White Sox.

NO-HIT GAME—Langley-Nelson, Dodgers, defeated Braves, 5-0, August 13.

Pioneer League

SUMMER CLASS A CLASSIFICATION

CHAMPIONSHIP WINNERS IN PREVIOUS YEARS

Year	Club	Pct.
1939	Twin Falls*	.581
1940	Salt Lake City	.608
	Ogden (4th)*	.492
1941	Boise	.623
	Ogden (2nd)*	.598
1942	Pocatello†	.690
	Boise	.683
1943-44-45	Did not operate.	
1946	Twin Falls‡	.585
	Salt Lake City†	.585
1947	Salt Lake City	.618
	Twin Falls†	.600
1948	Pocatello	.611
	Twin Falls (2nd)*	.595
1949	Twin Falls	.624
	Pocatello (3rd)*	.595
1950	Pocatello	.635
	Billings (3rd)*	.571
1951	Salt Lake City	.618
	Great Falls (3rd)*	.559
1952	Pocatello	.595
	Idaho Falls (2nd)*	.573
1953	Ogden	.679
	Salt Lake C. (4th)*	.527
1954	Salt Lake City	.595
	Great Falls (4th)*	.530
1955	Boise	.588
	Magic Valley (4th)*	.489
1956	Boise	.561
1957	Salt Lake City	.650
	Billings†	.582
1958	Great Falls	.582
	Boise†	.615
1959	Boise	.633
	Billings (2nd)*	.523
1960	Boise†	.686
	Idaho Falls	.650
1961	Boise	.638
	Great Falls*	.571
1962	Boise§	.565
	Billings†	.706
1963	Idaho Falls	.702
	Magic Valley†	.643
1964	Treasure Valley	.615
1965	Treasure Valley	.530
1966	Ogden	.591
1967	Ogden	.621
1968	Ogden	.609
1969	Ogden	.620
1970	Idaho Falls	.629
1971	Great Falls	.643
1972	Billings	.694
1973	Billings	.629
1974	Idaho Falls	.569
1975	Great Falls	.577
1976	Great Falls	.577
1977	Lethbridge	.629
1978	Billings x	.735
1979	Helena	.623
	Lethbridge y	.559
1980	Lethbridge y	.743
	Billings	.629
1981	Calgary	.657
	Butte y	.557
1982	Medicine Hat y	.629
	Idaho Falls	.600
1983	Billings y	.614
	Calgary	.600
1984	Billings	.691
	Helena y	.647
1985	Great Falls	.771
	Salt Lake City y	.657

*Won four-club playoff. †Won split-season playoff. ‡Ended first half in tie with Salt Lake City and won one-game playoff. §Ended first half in tie with Billings and Great Falls and won playoff. xBillings (first place) defeated Idaho Falls (second place) in First Place-Second Place playoff. yLeague divided in Northern and Southern divisions; won two-club playoff.

STANDING OF CLUBS AT CLOSE OF SEASON, SEPTEMBER 3

Club	SLC	GF.	Hel.	IF.	Bil.	MH.	W.	L.	T.	Pct.	G.B.
Salt Lake City (Independent)	....	10	8	10	8	9	45	25	0	.643	....
Great Falls (Dodgers)	4	....	7	9	8	12	40	30	0	.571	5
Helena (Brewers)	6	7	....	7	7	11	38	32	0	.543	7
Idaho Falls (Braves)	4	5	7	....	9	7	32	38	0	.457	13
Billings (Reds)	6	6	7	5	....	7	31	39	0	.443	14
Medicine Hat (Blue Jays)	5	2	3	7	7	....	24	46	0	.343	21

Major league affiliations in parentheses.

Playoff—Salt Lake City defeated Great Falls, three games to one, to win league championship.

Regular-Season Attendance—Billings, 95,234; Great Falls, 75,228; Helena, 22,566; Idaho Falls, 43,507; Medicine Hat, 30,671; Salt Lake City, 108,721. Total, 375,927.

Managers—Billings, Jeff Cox; Great Falls, Kevin Kennedy; Helena, Dave Huppert; Idaho Falls, Rod Gilbreath; Medicine Hat, Dennis Holmberg; Salt Lake City, John Freitas and Ruben Rodriguez.

All-Star Team—1B—James Kating, Great Falls; 2B—Keith Lockhart, Billings; 3B—Robert Tinkey, Salt Lake City; SS—Gary Sheffield, Helena; OF—Jeff Weiss, Idaho Falls; Joseph Kesselmark, Great Falls; Darryl Hamilton, Helena; C—Adam Brown, Great Falls; DH—Mathis Huff, Salt Lake City; RHP—Doug Vontz, Salt Lake City; Michael Kolovitz, Salt Lake City; LHP—Joseph Lazor, Billings; Manager of the Year—Rod Gilbreath, Idaho Falls.

(Compiled by William J. Weiss, League Statistician, San Mateo, Calif.)

CLUB BATTING

Club	Pct.	G.	AB.	R.	OR.	H.	TB.	2B.	3B.	HR.	RBI.	GW.	SH.	SF.	HP.	BB.	Int. BB.	SO.	SB.	CS.	LOB.
Helena	.298	70	2459	496	449	733	1099	112	25	68	423	30	21	42	21	306	8	464	132	40	541
Salt Lake City	.273	70	2365	399	358	646	921	108	34	33	330	35	25	26	18	297	8	403	49	31	526
Great Falls	.273	70	2398	432	379	654	927	111	30	34	355	32	47	26	23	324	8	435	107	39	552
Idaho Falls	.272	70	2415	414	468	656	946	94	32	44	358	24	30	19	27	289	10	447	90	27	519
Billings	.269	70	2498	410	423	673	1000	128	35	43	355	24	13	20	13	290	7	529	96	21	538
Medicine Hat	.268	70	2445	366	440	656	904	101	24	33	308	20	14	18	25	236	9	551	105	29	503

INDIVIDUAL BATTING

(Leading Qualifiers for Batting Championship—189 or More Plate Appearances)

*Bats lefthanded. †Switch-hitter.

Player and Club	Pct.	G.	AB.	R.	H.	TB.	2B.	3B.	HR.	RBI.	GW.	SH.	SF.	HP.	BB.	Int. BB.	SO.	SB.	CS.
Hamilton, Darryl, Helena*	.391	65	248	72	97	121	12	6	0	35	1	1	1	1	51	1	18	34	8
Sheffield, Gary, Helena	.365	57	222	53	81	142	12	2	15	71	7	1	7	3	20	2	14	14	4
Weiss, Jeffrey, Idaho Falls*	.362	54	207	56	75	146	11	6	16	56	4	0	4	3	33	3	28	3	4
Kesselmark, Joseph, Great Falls*	.348	70	279	59	97	147	23	6	5	50	5	5	2	5	40	2	34	10	3
Lockhart, Keith, Billings	.347	53	202	51	70	108	11	3	7	31	2	0	3	4	35	0	22	4	2
Martin, Albert, Idaho Falls*	.331	63	242	39	80	121	17	6	4	44	6	0	0	2	20	0	53	11	2
Pearson, Kevin, Billings	.327	59	211	29	69	102	20	2	3	40	6	2	2	2	29	3	29	3	3
Canale, George, Helena*	.326	65	221	48	72	118	19	0	9	49	4	2	5	0	54	0	65	6	4
Tinkey, Robert, Salt Lake City	.315	69	248	50	78	124	19	3	7	43	8	0	8	0	33	1	34	2	1
Brown, Terence, Helena	.314	53	191	44	60	80	9	4	1	24	4	1	2	2	34	1	33	22	3

Departmental Leaders: G—Kesselmark, Van Every, Whiten, 70; AB—Kesselmark, 279; R—Hamilton, 72; H—Hamilton, Kesselmark, 97; TB—Kesselmark, 147; 2B—Kesselmark, 23; 3B—Seven players with 6; HR—Vaughn, Weiss, 16; RBI—Sheffield, 71; GWRBI—Tinkey, 8; SH—T. Anderson, 11; SF—Olson, 9; HP—Butts, Felix, Whiten, 6; BB—Canale, 54; IBB—J. Brown, Pearson, Rodriguez, Weiss, 3; SO—Felix, 84; SB—Felix, 37; CS—Felix, 9.

(All Players—Listed Alphabetically)

Player and Club	Pct.	G.	AB.	R.	H.	TB.	2B.	3B.	HR.	RBI.	GW.	SH.	SF.	HP.	BB.	Int. BB.	SO.	SB.	CS.
Abrell, Thomas, Idaho Falls	.000	10	4	0	0	0	0	0	0	1	0	0	0	0	0	0	2	0	0
Alexander, Eric, Idaho Falls*	.268	52	142	25	38	54	4	3	2	17	0	0	2	1	17	0	38	6	1
Anderson, Daniel, Salt Lake City*	.000	6	1	0	0	0	0	0	0	0	0	0	0	0	0	0	1	0	0
Anderson, Timothy, Great Falls†	.259	67	220	27	57	65	8	0	0	15	0	11	1	1	13	0	29	8	2
Baggott, David, Salt Lake City†	.233	63	240	52	56	86	11	5	3	25	2	5	1	4	45	0	34	9	8
Baldwin, Damon, Salt Lake City*	.200	28	70	7	14	19	3	1	0	5	1	0	1	0	9	0	19	0	1
Bartels, William, Great Falls	.000	19	4	0	0	0	0	0	0	0	0	2	0	0	0	0	2	0	0
Beeler, Robert, Billings	.200	40	130	17	26	40	5	0	3	22	1	0	2	1	9	0	37	2	0
Birchfield, William, Idaho Falls	.000	15	1	0	0	0	0	0	0	0	0	1	0	0	0	0	1	0	0
Bolt, James, Salt Lake City	.207	66	222	30	46	54	6	1	0	20	1	4	2	1	15	0	33	2	1
Boreffi, Francis, Helena*	.319	49	160	30	51	72	6	6	1	18	2	1	1	1	13	0	25	5	1
Brock, Kyle, Great Falls†	.182	12	22	1	4	5	1	0	0	1	0	0	0	0	1	0	6	0	0
Brown, Adam, Great Falls*	.300	64	209	30	63	102	13	1	8	41	0	0	3	4	37	1	62	6	5
Brown, Don, Billings	.268	54	190	43	51	77	7	2	5	25	0	0	2	0	29	0	51	21	4
Brown, Jeffrey, Great Falls*	.282	63	202	46	57	105	16	4	8	57	7	2	4	2	33	3	20	5	2
Brown, Keith, Billings†	.500	4	2	1	1	1	0	0	0	0	0	1	0	0	0	0	0	0	0
Brown, Kevin, Idaho Falls*	.000	12	3	0	0	0	0	0	0	0	0	3	0	0	0	0	1	0	0
Brown, Terence, Helena	.314	53	191	44	60	80	9	4	1	24	4	1	2	2	34	1	33	22	3
Bruno, Joseph, Billings	.000	6	3	0	0	0	0	0	0	1	0	1	0	0	0	0	2	0	0
Bryant, Christopher, Idaho Falls	.219	53	178	20	39	51	4	4	0	17	2	1	3	2	11	0	23	9	2
Butts, David, Idaho Falls*	.285	64	263	50	75	92	9	1	2	32	2	1	1	6	20	1	37	26	3
Calvo, Nelson, Helena	.250	4	4	0	1	1	0	0	0	0	0	0	0	0	1	0	1	0	0
Campbell, Kevin, Great Falls	.000	15	4	0	0	0	0	0	0	0	0	1	0	1	0	0	1	0	0
Campos, Joe, Idaho Falls	.000	4	1	0	0	0	0	0	0	0	0	0	0	0	0	0	1	0	0
Canale, George, Helena*	.326	65	221	48	72	118	19	0	9	49	4	2	5	0	54	0	65	6	4
Casey, Jermaine, Idaho Falls*	.268	49	143	27	39	70	3	2	8	25	1	2	0	0	10	1	31	3	2
Cerny, Christopher, Great Falls*	.000	23	2	0	0	0	0	0	0	0	0	0	0	0	0	0	2	0	0
Chireno, Manuel, Helena	.205	35	112	23	23	35	4	1	2	14	0	2	0	1	9	0	34	7	1
Ciccone, Anthony, Great Falls†	.240	34	75	19	18	19	1	0	0	7	2	3	0	1	10	0	15	5	0
Clark, Isaiah, Helena	.282	68	266	37	75	120	12	0	11	48	2	1	6	4	14	1	27	6	2
Colston, Frank, Salt Lake City*	.311	56	183	25	57	79	11	1	3	22	2	0	1	2	17	1	30	1	0
Cowans, Eddie, Salt Lake City*	.275	48	120	19	33	42	3	3	0	6	0	5	0	0	20	0	16	4	6
Cuevas, Raqueli, Medicine Hat	.200	13	35	5	7	7	0	0	0	8	0	1	2	1	1	0	14	1	2
Czajkowski, James, Idaho Falls	.167	16	12	2	2	2	0	0	0	0	0	1	0	0	2	0	2	0	0
Datin, Joseph, Idaho Falls	.282	53	174	38	49	76	11	2	4	28	3	0	2	4	31	1	39	3	0
Davis, Steven, Billings*	.173	40	110	9	19	33	1	2	3	10	0	0	0	0	12	1	55	4	3
de la Rosa, Juan, Medicine Hat	.225	51	182	19	41	53	8	2	0	15	2	1	0	0	4	0	46	5	3
Del Rosario, Bautista, Medicine Hat	.260	21	77	11	20	32	4	1	2	7	0	0	0	0	6	0	25	1	0
Diaz, Carlos, Medicine Hat	.313	20	83	11	26	35	5	2	0	16	0	0	1	0	6	0	17	1	0
Dodd, William, Billings	.500	22	4	1	2	2	0	0	0	1	0	0	0	0	0	0	1	0	0
Duran, Jose, Great Falls	.000	2	1	0	0	0	0	0	0	0	0	0	0	0	0	0	0	0	0
Dziadkowiec, Andrew, Medicine Hat*	.208	48	168	22	35	46	6	1	1	14	2	1	2	1	20	1	37	0	1
Esteban, Felipe, Great Falls	.250	14	36	3	9	9	0	0	0	7	1	3	1	0	1	0	8	0	2
Falzone, James, Helena	.268	21	56	7	15	17	2	0	0	5	0	0	1	1	1	0	11	0	0
Fazzini, Frank, Salt Lake City	.309	61	220	39	68	117	11	4	10	51	5	0	4	0	33	1	57	2	2
Felix, Junior, Medicine Hat†	.285	67	263	57	75	102	9	3	4	28	3	0	0	6	35	1	84	37	9
Ferradas, Miguel, Great Falls	.200	24	60	4	12	17	3	1	0	6	1	1	0	0	10	0	23	0	0
Foster, Bryan, Helena	.172	24	58	5	10	11	1	0	0	6	0	1	0	0	6	0	16	2	1
Foster, Lindsay, Medicine Hat	.283	40	138	20	39	47	6	1	0	16	0	1	2	1	11	1	23	5	2
Frost, Jerald, Idaho Falls	.263	59	194	25	51	54	3	0	0	13	1	5	2	2	26	0	33	9	8
Gegen, Frederick, Salt Lake City*	.333	24	90	24	30	57	6	3	5	25	2	0	1	0	17	1	18	2	1
Girdner, Troy, Billings	.500	17	8	2	4	4	0	0	0	3	0	0	0	0	0	0	0	0	0
Hackett, Roger, Idaho Falls*	.000	16	5	1	0	0	0	0	0	0	0	0	0	0	0	0	0	0	0
Hamilton, Darryl, Helena*	.391	65	248	72	97	121	12	6	0	35	1	1	1	1	51	1	18	34	8
Hansen, David, Great Falls*	.299	61	204	39	61	77	7	3	1	36	2	1	0	0	27	0	28	9	3
Harris, Rainford, Billings	.307	52	150	26	46	66	5	3	3	32	1	0	1	1	10	0	35	16	1
Hartman, Jeffrey, Great Falls	.200	10	30	4	6	8	2	0	0	2	0	1	0	1	2	0	4	1	0
Hoff, Darren, Salt Lake City	.233	13	30	4	7	7	0	0	0	4	0	0	0	0	4	0	7	0	2
Holland, Troy, Helena*	.156	20	32	5	5	5	0	0	0	5	1	1	0	0	4	0	14	0	0
Huff, Mathis, Salt Lake City	.310	54	197	28	61	88	12	3	3	31	3	1	3	2	16	2	42	5	2
Hughes, Jeffrey, Salt Lake City	.273	69	256	54	70	89	15	2	0	29	4	1	0	5	33	0	23	11	5
Huntington, Ronald, Idaho Falls	.215	46	135	13	29	32	3	0	0	17	1	6	0	0	21	0	29	5	2
Huseby, Kenneth, Billings	.125	14	8	0	1	1	0	0	0	1	0	1	1	0	0	0	3	0	0
Jackson, Ronald, Great Falls	.077	22	39	4	3	3	0	0	0	1	0	1	1	2	2	0	9	2	0
Jones, Robert, Helena	.288	40	132	24	38	56	4	1	4	21	1	1	2	3	16	0	32	4	5
Karasinski, David, Idaho Falls*	.143	12	7	0	1	1	0	0	0	0	0	1	0	0	0	0	1	0	0
Kating, James, Great Falls	.300	69	258	62	77	119	13	4	7	43	5	1	6	4	46	2	27	19	4
Kesselmark, Joseph, Great Falls*	.348	70	279	59	97	147	23	6	5	50	5	5	2	5	40	2	34	10	3
King, Kenneth, Great Falls	.000	23	2	0	0	0	0	0	0	0	0	0	0	0	0	0	1	0	0
Knapp, John, Great Falls	.252	64	234	39	59	90	9	5	4	42	5	1	5	1	29	0	58	10	4
Knorr, Randy, Medicine Hat	.270	55	215	21	58	83	13	0	4	32	1	3	3	0	17	0	53	0	0
Langley, Wesley, Great Falls*	.000	10	2	0	0	0	0	0	0	1	0	0	0	0	1	0	2	0	0
Lazor, Joseph, Billings	.231	12	13	4	3	5	2	0	0	1	0	1	0	0	5	0	5	0	0
Lockhart, Keith, Billings	.347	53	202	51	70	108	11	3	7	31	2	0	3	4	35	0	22	4	2
Lonigro, Gregory, Billings	.274	53	212	36	58	71	9	2	0	17	0	1	0	2	16	0	23	5	0
Lyons, Larry, Idaho Falls	.000	21	2	0	0	0	0	0	0	0	0	0	0	0	1	0	1	0	0
Maldonado, Phillip, Idaho Falls	.250	45	108	20	27	37	7	0	1	18	0	2	1	2	16	1	13	1	0
Marak, Paul, Idaho Falls	.273	12	11	3	3	4	1	0	0	0	0	1	0	0	0	0	4	0	0
Marshall, Gregory, Idaho Falls*	.221	43	104	20	23	33	5	1	1	20	0	0	1	1	28	0	24	4	0
Martin, Albert, Idaho Falls*	.331	63	242	39	80	121	17	6	4	44	6	0	0	2	20	0	53	11	2
Martinez, Luis, Billings†	.205	28	78	11	16	23	2	1	1	11	0	1	2	0	5	0	13	0	1
Maxwell, Scott, Medicine Hat*	.242	36	99	15	24	32	0	1	2	16	2	0	1	1	13	1	23	1	0
McDonald, Raymond, Medicine Hat	.302	68	258	40	78	97	12	2	1	34	4	1	2	3	36	1	40	7	3
Montgomery, Danny, Great Falls†	.215	19	65	8	14	17	1	1	0	6	0	1	0	1	6	0	20	5	3
Moscrey, Michael, Billings	.375	14	8	2	3	3	0	0	0	0	0	0	0	0	0	0	3	0	0
Mullins, Ronald, Billings	.333	26	3	0	1	1	0	0	0	0	0	0	0	0	0	0	0	0	0
Munoz, Michael, Great Falls*	.000	14	10	1	0	0	0	0	0	0	0	1	0	0	1	0	3	0	0
Naumczik, George, Idaho Falls*	.500	17	2	0	1	1	0	0	0	1	0	0	0	0	0	0	0	0	0
Novak, Thomas, Billings	.000	23	3	0	0	0	0	0	0	0	0	0	0	0	0	0	2	0	0
Nowlin, James, Idaho Falls†	1.000	20	1	0	1	1	0	0	0	0	0	0	0	0	0	0	0	0	0
O'Hare, Sean, Billings*	.257	51	144	18	37	50	9	2	0	10	1	0	2	0	35	1	35	4	1

Player and Club	Pct.	G.	AB.	R.	H.	TB.	2B.	3B.	HR.	RBI.	GW.	SH.	SF.	HP.	BB.	Int. BB.	SO.	SB.	CS.
Olson, Warren, Helena	.276	62	217	37	60	99	12	3	7	34	2	2	9	1	13	1	33	1	2
Pearson, Kevin, Billings	.327	59	211	29	69	102	20	2	3	40	6	2	2	2	29	3	29	3	3
Peters, Robert, Salt Lake City†	.246	28	65	8	16	24	2	3	0	7	0	1	1	1	10	1	22	1	1
Pitz, Michael, Great Falls	.143	14	14	0	2	3	1	0	0	0	0	1	0	0	0	0	9	0	0
Poteet, Donald, Great Falls*	.333	2	3	1	1	1	0	0	0	0	0	0	0	0	3	0	2	0	0
Rabb, William, Helena	.000	3	7	1	0	0	0	0	0	1	0	0	1	0	2	0	5	1	0
Ralstin, Randy, Idaho Falls	.143	29	35	5	5	8	0	0	1	8	1	0	2	0	5	0	9	0	0
Richardson, Allen, Helena	.272	58	195	31	53	64	5	0	2	30	1	2	2	0	31	1	45	6	2
Richardson, Jeffrey, Billings	.315	47	162	42	51	73	14	4	0	20	2	0	0	1	17	0	25	12	1
Rivers, Kenneth, Medicine Hat	.290	34	131	14	38	54	6	2	2	21	1	0	0	0	9	0	28	0	0
Rodriguez, Ernie, Idaho Falls*	.289	61	194	38	56	74	7	4	1	23	0	2	0	3	29	3	27	6	3
Rondon, Isidro, Billings	.250	5	20	3	5	6	1	0	0	4	1	0	0	0	4	1	3	0	0
Ryan, Kevin, Great Falls	.000	24	1	0	0	0	0	0	0	0	0	0	0	0	0	0	0	0	0
Samaniego, Jose, Helena	.300	12	20	5	6	6	0	0	0	4	0	0	0	1	1	0	3	0	1
Savage, John, Billings	.250	19	4	0	1	1	0	0	0	0	0	0	0	0	0	0	0	0	0
Scudder, Scott, Billings	.000	12	5	0	0	0	0	0	0	0	0	2	0	0	0	0	4	0	0
Sheffield, Gary, Helena	.365	57	222	53	81	142	12	2	15	71	7	1	7	3	20	2	14	14	4
Shotkoski, David, Idaho Falls	.250	10	4	1	1	1	0	0	0	0	0	1	0	0	0	0	1	0	0
Siler, Michael, Great Falls	.000	21	4	0	0	0	0	0	0	1	0	0	0	0	2	0	1	0	0
Silverio, Francisco, Billings	.281	61	217	30	61	101	10	6	6	28	2	0	1	0	11	0	76	12	4
Sloan, Terry, Idaho Falls*	.276	44	115	19	32	55	5	3	4	24	1	1	0	1	7	0	29	0	1
Smith, Dwayne, Medicine Hat*	.000	1	3	0	0	0	0	0	0	0	0	1	0	0	0	0	0	0	0
Smith, Keith, Idaho Falls	.000	9	9	1	0	0	0	0	0	0	0	1	0	0	2	0	3	0	0
Sobczyk, Robert, Helena	.217	12	23	4	5	5	0	0	0	3	0	0	0	0	3	0	7	1	1
Spagnuolo, Joseph, Great Falls	.266	37	127	32	34	43	5	2	0	18	1	7	0	0	24	0	23	14	5
Stewart, John, Billings	.206	35	107	22	22	38	5	1	3	15	1	0	2	0	25	0	18	4	0
Suero, William, Medicine Hat	.278	64	273	39	76	99	7	5	2	28	0	4	2	3	15	0	36	13	4
Taylor, David, Salt Lake City	.250	49	160	22	40	48	3	1	1	19	1	1	1	0	15	0	22	1	0
Thomas, Kevin, Idaho Falls	.500	11	2	0	1	1	0	0	0	0	0	0	0	0	0	0	0	0	0
Tinkey, Robert, Salt Lake City	.315	69	248	50	78	124	19	3	7	43	8	0	8	0	33	1	34	2	1
Van Every, Lynn, Salt Lake City*	.266	70	263	36	70	87	6	4	1	43	5	7	3	3	30	1	44	10	1
Vaughn, Gregory, Helena	.291	66	258	64	75	140	13	2	16	54	4	5	5	2	30	1	69	23	5
Walker, William, Helena	.158	16	38	6	6	7	1	0	0	2	0	0	0	1	3	0	12	0	0
Ware, Derek, Medicine Hat	.239	46	134	19	32	52	3	1	5	15	0	0	0	2	16	1	52	10	2
Watts, Robert, Medicine Hat	.225	36	111	18	25	31	6	0	0	14	0	0	1	1	17	1	16	2	0
Weiss, Jeffrey, Idaho Falls*	.362	54	207	56	75	146	11	6	16	56	4	0	4	3	33	3	28	3	4
Wenrich, Ronald, Billings*	.252	59	202	30	51	92	11	6	6	48	4	0	0	0	28	2	43	4	1
Wetteland, John, Great Falls	.231	12	13	1	3	5	0	1	0	1	0	2	0	0	0	0	3	0	0
White, Michael A., Great Falls	.000	5	9	1	0	0	0	0	0	0	0	0	0	0	1	0	3	0	0
White, T. Michael, Great Falls*	.287	67	268	51	77	92	8	2	1	26	3	4	3	0	35	0	39	13	6
Whiten, Mark, Medicine Hat†	.300	70	270	53	81	133	16	3	10	44	5	1	2	6	29	2	56	22	3
Williams, Dwayne, Billings	.333	19	3	1	1	1	0	0	0	0	0	0	0	0	0	0	0	0	0
Williamson, Bret, Billings	.274	57	201	24	55	73	10	1	2	24	3	2	1	0	18	0	31	4	0
Wills, Adrian, Idaho Falls*	.241	38	116	11	28	32	4	0	0	14	2	1	1	0	10	0	16	4	0
Wilson, Thomas, Billings	.196	28	97	8	19	28	6	0	1	11	0	0	1	1	2	0	13	1	0
Young-Romero, Charles, Med. Hat†	.000	1	2	0	0	0	0	0	0	0	0	0	0	0	0	0	1	0	0

The following pitchers, listed alphabetically by club, with games in parentheses, had no plate appearances, primarily through use of designated hitters:

GREAT FALLS—Brooks, Billy (26); Nelson, Jeffrey (3); Pena, Daniel (1); Riensche, Kenneth (1); Shea, Kevin (8); Wood, Stephen (4).

HELENA—Ambrose, Mark (3); Anderson, Edwin (18); Bosley, Richard (14); Cangemi, Jamie (28); Carley, David (10); Drahman, Brian (18); Fleming, Keith (11); Gosling, Mark (12); Nelson, Scott (12); Nichols, Oliver (14); Ogawa, Shane (13); Ojeda, Raymond (23); Seaver, George (22); Stone, Brian (14); Wilder, John (5); Woodhouse, David (14).

MEDICINE HAT—Batista, Gabriel (3); Bilawey, John (13); Butler, Alan (20); DePastino, Richard (16); Hall, Darren (17); Kwiatkowski, Glen (2); Maysonet, Geovanny (2); Palma, Ruben (16); Roderick, Morgan (16); Rosenbauer, Patrick (19); Santana, Ramon (25); Ward, Joseph (27); Wortham, Andrew (23).

SALT LAKE CITY—Dunn, Richard (15); Fukuchi, Tsuneto (14); Gold, Mark (18); Humphrey, Michael (16); Kolovitz, Michael (31); Rice, Patrick (18); Shortt, Patrick (2); Sissel, Ronald (2); Smith, Marc (12); Townsend, Howard (15); Vontz, Douglas (12); Yamasaki, Shintaro (14).

GRAND SLAM HOME RUNS—A. Brown, J. Brown, Dziadkowiec, Fazzini, Gegen, Sloan, Vaughn, 1 each.

AWARDED FIRST BASE ON CATCHER'S INTERFERENCE—Casey 3 (Beeler, Diaz, Martinez); Colston 2 (Martinez, Olson); Baldwin (Martinez); Canale (Ferradas); Gegen (Beeler); A. Richardson (Ferradas).

CLUB FIELDING

Club	Pct.	G.	PO.	A.	E.	DP.	PB.
Helena	.953	70	1824	700	125	61	19
Medicine Hat	.950	70	1839	759	138	57	23
Salt Lake City	.948	70	1836	764	143	73	10
Idaho Falls	.947	70	1836	769	146	49	21
Billings	.947	70	1875	747	148	72	14
Great Falls	.946	70	1853	701	147	45	15

INDIVIDUAL FIELDING

*Throws lefthanded.

FIRST BASEMEN

Player and Club	Pct.	G.	PO.	A.	E.	DP.
Baldwin, Salt Lake City	.980	22	191	7	4	14
Brock, Great Falls	1.000	4	26	1	0	1
A. Brown, Great Falls	.939	3	29	2	2	1
CANALE, Helena	.990	65	554	29	6	47
Colston, Salt Lake City	1.000	1	1	0	0	0
Datin, Idaho Falls*	.986	47	395	42	6	27
de la Rosa, Medicine Hat	1.000	1	0	1	0	0
Diaz, Medicine Hat	.947	6	33	3	2	6
Foster, Medicine Hat	1.000	2	3	0	0	0
Gegen, Salt Lake City	1.000	1	10	0	0	0
Harris, Billings	.962	39	274	27	12	30
Huff, Salt Lake City	.980	21	186	12	4	20
Kating, Great Falls	.978	64	538	44	13	39
Knorr, Medicine Hat	.980	55	451	29	10	32
Marshall, Idaho Falls*	1.000	3	3	0	0	0
Martin, Idaho Falls*	.980	31	235	14	5	15
Maxwell, Medicine Hat	1.000	3	21	1	0	1
O'Hare, Billings	.981	48	343	25	7	34
Peters, Salt Lake City	.917	1	8	3	1	0
Tinkey, Salt Lake City	.975	28	247	24	7	32
Walker, Helena	.975	12	68	10	2	6
Watts, Medicine Hat	.987	8	67	11	1	7

SECOND BASEMEN

Player and Club	Pct.	G.	PO.	A.	E.	DP.
Anderson, Great Falls	.948	27	36	73	6	8
Baggott, Salt Lake City	1.000	1	1	0	0	0
Bolt, Salt Lake City	.986	33	48	92	2	20
Butts, Idaho Falls	.947	5	5	13	1	0
Calvo, Helena	1.000	1	2	2	0	0
Chireno, Helena	.894	34	39	79	14	20

SECOND BASEMEN—Continued

Player and Club	Pct.	G.	PO.	A.	E.	DP.
Ciccone, Great Falls	.923	13	18	30	4	4
Clark, Helena	1.000	1	1	2	0	0
Esteban, Great Falls	.962	14	26	25	2	4
Foster, Helena	.800	8	6	6	3	2
Hartman, Great Falls	.936	10	21	23	3	5
Hoff, Salt Lake City	1.000	1	2	7	0	0
Hughes, Salt Lake City	.936	33	64	83	10	19
Huntington, Idaho Falls	.896	27	41	62	12	10
Lockhart, Billings	.931	37	66	110	13	21
Lonigro, Billings	.953	14	27	34	3	7
Montgomery, Great Falls	.920	16	31	50	7	11
Pearson, Billings	1.000	2	1	2	0	0
A. Richardson, Helena	.946	36	77	97	10	22
J. Richardson, Billings	.954	23	45	59	5	14
Rodriguez, Idaho Falls	.946	55	92	134	13	21
Samaniego, Helena	.857	5	3	9	2	0
SUERO, Medicine Hat	.947	63	159	182	19	34
Van Every, Salt Lake City	.894	11	20	22	5	7
Watts, Medicine Hat	.850	7	15	19	6	4

THIRD BASEMEN

Player and Club	Pct.	G.	PO.	A.	E.	DP.
Anderson, Great Falls	.750	1	2	1	1	0
Bolt, Salt Lake City	.929	9	9	17	2	1
BUTTS, Idaho Falls	.937	60	61	131	13	11
Clark, Helena	.879	57	41	83	17	6
Gegen, Salt Lake City	.942	20	16	33	3	6
Hansen, Great Falls	.778	11	6	8	4	0
Harris, Billings	.000	2	0	0	1	0
Hoff, Salt Lake City	.789	10	7	8	4	1
Knapp, Great Falls	.878	61	39	91	18	3
Lockhart, Billings	.932	15	15	40	4	7
Maldonado, Idaho Falls	.760	11	7	12	6	0
Martinez, Billings	.909	5	5	5	1	0
McDonald, Medicine Hat	.911	68	66	129	19	16
Pearson, Billings	.905	24	17	50	7	4
Richardson, Helena	.909	15	10	20	3	2
Rodriguez, Idaho Falls	.857	5	2	10	2	0
Rondon, Billings	.600	1	1	2	2	1
Samaniego, Helena	.250	6	0	1	3	0
Stewart, Billings	.964	28	20	31	8	4
Tinkey, Salt Lake City	.918	27	24	54	7	8
Van Every, Salt Lake City	.944	8	3	14	1	3
Watts, Medicine Hat	1.000	4	3	6	0	0

SHORTSTOPS

Player and Club	Pct.	G.	PO.	A.	E.	DP.
Anderson, Great Falls	.947	41	64	115	10	25
Bolt, Salt Lake City	.929	22	36	68	8	17
Ciccone, Great Falls	.778	2	4	3	2	1
Del Rosario, Medicine Hat	.876	21	46	60	15	10
B. Foster, Helena	.829	16	13	21	7	5
L. Foster, Medicine Hat	.924	36	68	91	13	17
FROST, Idaho Falls	.917	59	99	165	24	24
Huntington, Idaho Falls	.869	18	18	35	8	4
Lonigro, Billings	.939	40	73	96	11	27
Montgomery, Great Falls	1.000	2	2	2	0	1
Pearson, Billings	.911	34	65	79	14	18
A. Richardson, Helena	.938	9	12	18	2	5
J. Richardson, Billings	.889	5	3	5	1	0
Sheffield, Helena	.911	54	97	149	24	34
Spagnuolo, Great Falls	.866	37	53	89	22	8
Van Every, Salt Lake City	.864	49	86	117	32	27
Watts, Medicine Hat	.964	16	19	35	2	4

OUTFIELDERS

Player and Club	Pct.	G.	PO.	A.	E.	DP.
Alexander, Idaho Falls	.923	38	58	2	5	1
BAGGOTT, Salt Lake City	1.000	61	131	2	0	0
D. Brown, Billings	.920	54	79	2	7	1
J. Brown, Great Falls	.926	34	46	4	4	1
T. Brown, Helena	.948	48	85	6	5	1
Bryant, Idaho Falls	.980	51	95	5	2	1
Calvo, Helena	1.000	2	2	0	0	0
Casey, Idaho Falls	.878	25	36	0	5	0
Ciccone, Great Falls	1.000	1	1	0	0	0
Clark, Helena	1.000	6	4	0	0	0
Cowans, Salt Lake City*	.958	45	62	6	3	1
Cuevas, Medicine Hat	.800	10	16	0	4	0
Davis, Billings	.958	39	62	7	3	2
de la Rosa, Medicine Hat	.972	49	90	15	3	1
Fazzini, Salt Lake City	.927	59	95	7	8	1
Felix, Medicine Hat	.970	67	152	8	5	2
HAMILTON, Helena	1.000	63	132	9	0	1
Hansen, Great Falls	.942	36	48	1	3	1
Harris, Billings	1.000	3	3	0	0	0
Holland, Helena*	1.000	16	23	2	0	0
Huff, Salt Lake City	1.000	15	17	2	0	0
Hughes, Salt Lake City	.925	39	57	5	5	2
Jackson, Great Falls	.778	10	7	0	2	0
Jones, Helena	.973	29	34	2	1	1
Kating, Great Falls	1.000	2	2	0	0	0
Kesselmark, Great Falls*	.958	70	131	6	6	4
Marshall, Idaho Falls*	1.000	28	35	1	0	0
Martin, Idaho Falls*	.927	37	37	1	3	1
Maxwell, Medicine Hat	1.000	21	33	3	0	0
Peters, Salt Lake City	.875	15	12	2	2	0
Ralstin, Idaho Falls	1.000	8	5	0	0	0
Silverio, Billings	.977	61	122	6	3	2
Vaughn, Helena	.972	63	99	5	3	1
Ware, Medicine Hat	1.000	8	12	0	0	0
Weiss, Idaho Falls*	.966	53	110	4	4	1
Wenrich, Billings*	.972	46	66	3	2	3
M.A. White, Great Falls	1.000	2	1	1	0	0
T.M. White, Great Falls	.947	67	102	5	6	1
Whiten, Medicine Hat	.923	65	111	9	10	3
Williamson, Billings	.974	50	70	4	2	1
Young-Romero, Medicine Hat	.667	1	2	0	1	0

CATCHERS

Player and Club	Pct.	G.	PO.	A.	E.	DP.	PB.
Anderson, Salt Lake City	1.000	2	3	0	0	0	0
Beeler, Billings	.948	38	258	36	16	3	8
A. BROWN, Great Falls	.989	54	421	31	5	3	11
Colston, Salt Lake City	.935	36	191	24	15	2	4
Diaz, Medicine Hat	.968	9	54	7	2	1	1
Duran, Great Falls	.667	2	2	0	1	0	0
Dziadkowiec, Medicine Hat	.974	37	226	34	7	1	15
Falzone, Helena	1.000	15	75	6	0	0	4
Ferradas, Great Falls	.951	23	140	14	8	1	4
Hansen, Great Falls	1.000	2	0	1	0	0	0
Kating, Great Falls	.939	3	28	3	2	0	0
Maldonado, Idaho Falls	.980	27	137	13	3	0	4
Martinez, Billings	.915	19	69	6	7	1	2
Olson, Helena	.978	59	369	31	9	4	14
Rivers, Medicine Hat	.989	24	147	28	2	2	7
Sloan, Idaho Falls	.950	32	159	13	9	0	12
Sobczyk, Helena	.939	9	29	2	2	0	1
Taylor, Salt Lake City	.988	47	270	49	4	7	6
Wills, Idaho Falls	.966	33	156	15	6	1	5
Wilson, Billings	.981	28	142	16	3	3	4

PITCHERS

Player and Club	Pct.	G.	PO.	A.	E.	DP.
Abrell, Idaho Falls	.818	10	4	5	2	0
Ambrose, Helena	1.000	3	1	5	0	0
D. Anderson, Salt Lake City	.667	4	0	2	1	1
E. Anderson, Helena	.667	18	1	1	1	0
Bartels, Great Falls	.727	19	1	7	3	0
Bilawey, Medicine Hat	.667	13	1	1	1	0
Birchfield, Idaho Falls	1.000	15	4	7	0	2
Bosley, Helena	1.000	14	2	8	0	1
Bolt, Salt Lake City	1.000	1	0	2	0	1
Brooks, Great Falls	1.000	26	1	3	0	0
Kei. Brown, Billings	1.000	4	2	4	0	0
Kev. Brown, Idaho Falls*	.955	12	4	17	1	0
Bruno, Billings	.875	6	2	5	1	0
Butler, Medicine Hat*	.923	20	3	9	1	0
Campbell, Great Falls	.900	15	7	11	2	0
Cangemi, Helena	.923	28	8	16	2	0
Carley, Helena	.857	10	1	5	1	0
Cerny, Great Falls*	.889	23	1	7	1	1
Czajkowski, Idaho Falls	.909	16	10	20	3	1
DePastino, Medicine Hat	.909	16	3	7	1	0
Dodd, Billings	.846	22	7	4	2	0
Drahman, Helena	.963	18	10	16	1	0

PITCHERS—Continued

Player and Club	Pct.	G.	PO.	A.	E.	DP.
DUNN, Salt Lake City	1.000	15	6	11	0	2
Fleming, Helena	1.000	11	2	2	0	0
Fukuchi, Salt Lake City	1.000	14	2	7	0	0
Girdner, Billings	.882	17	4	11	2	1
Gold, Salt Lake City	.846	18	3	8	2	0
Gosling, Helena	1.000	12	5	6	0	0
Hackett, Idaho Falls*	.889	16	5	3	1	0
Hall, Medicine Hat	.818	17	6	12	4	1
Humphrey, Salt Lake City	.826	16	3	16	4	1
Huseby, Billings	.871	14	9	18	4	1
Karasinski, Idaho Falls*	1.000	12	2	6	0	0
King, Great Falls	.875	23	1	6	1	0
Kolovitz, Salt Lake City	.833	31	3	7	2	0
Langley, Great Falls*	1.000	10	3	1	0	1
Lazor, Billings*	.818	12	3	6	2	0
Lyons, Idaho Falls	.833	21	2	3	1	0
Marak, Idaho Falls	.684	12	4	9	6	0
Moscrey, Billings	.909	14	1	19	2	0
Mullins, Billings	1.000	26	3	6	0	0
Munoz, Great Falls*	.867	14	3	10	2	2
Naumczik, Idaho Falls*	1.000	17	2	7	0	1
Nelson, Helena*	.909	12	3	7	1	1
Nichols, Helena	1.000	14	1	2	0	0
Novak, Billings	.933	23	1	13	1	0
Nowlin, Idaho Falls	.500	20	1	1	2	0
Ogawa, Helena	.909	13	5	5	1	1
Ojeda, Helena*	.833	23	1	9	2	0
Palma, Medicine Hat	.900	16	6	3	1	0
Pitz, Great Falls	.917	14	4	18	2	1
Ralstin, Idaho Falls	.667	13	1	1	1	0
Rice, Salt Lake City	.947	18	5	13	1	2
Roderick, Medicine Hat	.778	16	7	7	4	1
Rosenbauer, Medicine Hat	.964	19	8	19	1	2
Ryan, Great Falls	.667	24	1	1	1	0
Santana, Medicine Hat	1.000	25	1	6	0	0
Savage, Billings	1.000	19	8	6	0	0
Scudder, Billings	.857	12	3	3	1	0
Seaver, Helena*	.875	22	4	10	2	1
Shea, Great Falls*	1.000	8	1	0	0	0
Shotkoski, Idaho Falls	.875	10	2	5	1	0
Siler, Great Falls	.867	21	1	12	2	0
Sloan, Idaho Falls	1.000	1	1	1	0	0
K. Smith, Idaho Falls	1.000	9	3	11	0	0
M. Smith, Salt Lake City*	1.000	12	0	4	0	0
Stone, Helena	.955	14	4	17	1	2
Thomas, Idaho Falls	1.000	11	0	1	0	0
Townsend, Salt Lake City*	.667	15	1	3	2	2
Vontz, Salt Lake City	.966	12	9	19	1	4
Ward, Medicine Hat	1.000	27	2	13	0	2
Wetteland, Great Falls	.882	12	5	10	2	0
Wilder, Helena	1.000	5	1	0	0	0
Williams, Billings*	1.000	19	2	6	0	2
Williamson, Billings	1.000	3	0	1	0	1
Wood, Great Falls	1.000	4	0	1	0	0
Woodhouse, Helena	1.000	14	0	2	0	0
Wortham, Medicine Hat*	.905	23	5	14	2	1
Yamasaki, Salt Lake City	.800	14	4	12	4	1

The following players do not have any recorded accepted chances at the positions indicated; therefore, are not listed in the fielding averages for those particular positions: Alexander, ss; Batista, p; Beeler, p; Bolt, of; Boreffi, 2b; Brock, ss; Campos, p; Chireno, of; Datin, p; Hansen, 2b; Jackson, ss; Knapp, ss; Kwiatkowski, p; Maysonet, p; J. Nelson, p; Pena, p; Rabb, of; J. Richardson, 3b; Riensche, p; Shortt, p; Sissel, p; Stewart, 2b.

CLUB PITCHING

Club	ERA.	G.	CG.	ShO.	Sv.	IP.	H.	R.	ER.	HR.	HB.	BB.	Int. BB.	SO.	WP.	Bk.
Salt Lake City	3.91	70	10	7	16	612.0	688	358	266	42	11	201	5	452	35	4
Great Falls	4.12	70	11	5	9	.617.2	638	379	283	38	21	250	11	580	43	4
Billings	4.49	70	1	4	13	625.0	659	423	312	37	25	316	13	468	61	3
Medicine Hat	5.14	70	3	3	7	613.0	646	440	350	50	28	383	4	403	53	8
Idaho Falls	5.31	70	7	1	11	612.0	714	468	361	53	19	270	6	455	56	4
Helena	5.40	70	1	0	20	608.0	673	449	365	35	23	322	11	469	56	6

PITCHERS' RECORDS

(Leading Qualifiers for Earned-Run Average Leadership—56 or More Innings)

*Throws lefthanded.

Pitcher—Club	W.	L.	Pct.	ERA.	G.	GS.	CG.	GF.	ShO.	Sv.	IP.	H.	R.	ER.	HR.	HB.	BB.	Int. BB.	SO.	WP.
Lazor, Billings*	5	1	.833	1.61	12	8	0	2	0	1	61.2	47	21	11	1	0	16	1	75	6
Vontz, Salt Lake City	8	1	.889	2.49	12	12	3	0	2	0	90.1	88	34	25	9	0	30	0	48	4
King, Great Falls	5	1	.833	2.70	23	2	0	5	0	0	56.2	52	27	17	2	1	16	0	59	4
Munoz, Great Falls*	4	4	.500	3.21	14	14	2	0	2	0	81.1	85	44	29	4	1	38	0	49	3
Dunn, Salt Lake City	7	4	.636	3.27	15	13	5	1	3	0	82.2	95	40	30	4	0	9	1	43	1
Siler, Great Falls	3	6	.333	3.32	21	4	2	7	0	2	65.0	79	34	24	5	1	14	1	64	0
Rice, Salt Lake City	1	3	.250	3.34	18	6	0	7	0	0	59.1	67	33	22	1	1	15	0	39	5
Moscrey, Billings	5	6	.455	3.55	14	14	0	0	0	0	88.2	99	52	35	6	4	21	0	62	4
Wortham, Medicine Hat*	3	2	.600	3.60	23	6	0	13	0	3	70.0	64	36	28	4	3	34	0	45	4
Czajkowski, Idaho Falls	7	5	.583	3.65	16	13	3	1	0	0	88.2	90	44	36	5	3	16	0	46	3

Departmental Leaders: G—Kolovitz, 31; W—Kolovitz, Vontz, 8; L—Rosenbauer, 8; Pct.—Vontz, .889; GS—Hall, Rosenbauer, 16; CG—Dunn, 5; GF—Kolovitz, 30; ShO—Dunn, 3; Sv.—Kolovitz, 14; IP—Vontz, 90.1; H—Huseby, 100; R—Huseby, 73; ER—Huseby, 47; HR—Rosenbauer, 10; HB—Ojeda, 9; BB—Butler, 58; IBB—Cangemi, 6; SO—Pitz, 111; WP—Hall, Marak, 12.

(All Pitchers—Listed Alphabetically)

Pitcher—Club	W.	L.	Pct.	ERA.	G.	GS.	CG.	GF.	ShO.	Sv.	IP.	H.	R.	ER.	HR.	HB.	BB.	Int. BB.	SO.	WP.
Abrell, Idaho Falls	1	2	.333	11.16	10	4	0	1	0	0	25.0	43	36	31	6	2	24	1	8	3
Ambrose, Helena	2	0	1.000	0.47	3	3	0	0	0	0	19.0	18	3	1	0	0	1	0	25	1
D. Anderson, Salt Lake City	1	0	1.000	10.61	5	0	0	2	0	0	9.1	18	15	11	1	1	7	0	7	2
E. Anderson, Helena	0	0	.000	9.47	18	1	0	4	0	0	19.0	30	23	20	2	2	21	0	12	2
Bartels, Great Falls	3	1	.750	5.65	19	5	0	3	0	0	43.0	49	34	27	3	2	20	1	39	11
Batista, Medicine Hat	0	0	.000	38.57	3	0	0	1	0	0	2.1	6	10	10	1	0	5	0	1	0
Beeler, Billings	0	0	.000	9.00	2	0	0	2	0	0	3.0	5	3	3	0	0	0	0	1	1
Bilawey, Medicine Hat	0	1	.000	11.51	13	1	0	4	0	0	20.1	34	35	26	3	1	17	0	9	6
Birchfield, Idaho Falls	2	4	.333	3.45	15	0	0	9	0	2	31.1	32	15	12	0	0	9	1	11	0
Bolt, Salt Lake City	0	0	.000	11.25	1	0	0	1	0	0	4.0	10	5	5	0	1	0	0	3	0
Bosley, Helena	0	2	.000	3.45	14	0	0	13	0	5	15.2	13	6	6	1	0	5	0	18	0
Brooks, Great Falls	5	0	1.000	2.27	26	0	0	17	0	6	35.2	20	12	9	0	3	11	1	34	3
Kei. Brown, Billings	2	0	1.000	2.11	4	3	0	1	0	0	21.1	18	6	5	0	1	7	0	14	1
Kev. Brown, Idaho Falls*	3	6	.333	5.03	12	12	1	0	0	0	68.0	65	48	38	5	0	41	0	44	2
Bruno, Billings	0	3	.000	6.25	6	6	0	0	0	0	31.2	41	27	22	2	2	15	1	26	2
Butler, Medicine Hat*	0	4	.000	5.67	20	5	0	8	0	0	46.0	26	34	29	1	3	58	0	49	9
Campbell, Great Falls	5	6	.455	4.66	15	15	3	0	0	0	85.0	99	62	44	5	3	32	0	66	6
Campos, Idaho Falls	0	0	.000	2.00	4	0	0	2	0	1	9.0	2	2	2	0	0	5	0	6	1
Cangemi, Helena	5	5	.500	6.46	28	4	0	13	0	2	54.1	51	42	39	2	1	38	6	46	7
Carley, Helena	3	2	.600	6.31	10	8	0	0	0	0	35.2	41	31	25	3	1	17	0	33	1
Cerny, Great Falls*	1	3	.250	2.79	23	0	0	6	0	0	29.0	25	16	9	1	1	15	1	30	1
Czajkowski, Idaho Falls	7	5	.583	3.65	16	13	3	1	0	0	88.2	90	44	36	5	3	16	0	46	3
Datin, Idaho Falls*	0	0	.000	6.00	1	0	0	1	0	0	3.0	4	3	2	1	0	2	0	0	0
DePastino, Medicine Hat	4	3	.571	5.15	16	10	1	1	1	0	71.2	73	48	41	6	4	44	0	55	8

Pitcher—Club	W.	L.	Pct.	ERA.	G.	GS.	CG.	GF.	ShO.	Sv.	IP.	H.	R.	ER.	HR.	HB.	BB.	Int. BB.	SO.	WP.
Dodd, Billings	5	1	.833	4.05	22	4	0	9	0	0	53.1	57	35	24	3	1	26	1	43	7
Drahman, Helena	4	6	.400	5.92	18	10	0	5	0	2	65.1	79	49	43	4	0	33	1	40	4
Dunn, Salt Lake City	7	4	.636	3.27	15	13	5	1	3	0	82.2	95	40	30	4	0	9	1	43	1
Fleming, Helena	0	0	.000	2.70	11	0	0	11	0	6	16.2	12	7	5	1	0	7	0	23	0
Fukuchi, Salt Lake City	2	4	.333	5.43	14	12	0	0	0	0	66.1	87	54	40	6	2	23	0	40	2
Girdner, Billings	4	3	.571	4.43	17	9	0	5	0	0	61.0	56	39	30	4	5	42	1	38	8
Gold, Salt Lake City	4	0	1.000	3.65	18	1	0	7	0	2	37.0	43	23	15	1	1	18	1	33	1
Gosling, Helena	3	2	.600	4.36	12	7	0	1	0	0	53.2	68	36	26	6	1	11	0	38	8
Hackett, Idaho Falls*	2	1	.667	6.23	16	0	0	5	0	0	30.1	43	29	21	3	2	12	0	21	2
Hall, Medicine Hat	5	7	.417	3.83	17	16	1	0	1	0	89.1	91	64	38	3	3	47	0	60	12
Humphrey, Salt Lake City	5	3	.625	4.17	16	10	0	1	0	0	77.2	87	41	36	4	1	29	1	75	6
Huseby, Billings	3	7	.300	5.47	14	13	1	0	0	0	77.1	100	73	47	6	4	32	1	34	9
Karasinski, Idaho Falls*	4	2	.667	3.72	12	10	1	1	0	1	58.0	53	31	24	6	3	14	0	65	6
King, Great Falls	5	1	.833	2.70	23	2	0	5	0	0	56.2	52	27	17	2	1	16	0	59	4
Kolovitz, Salt Lake City	8	2	.800	2.40	31	0	0	30	0	14	41.1	30	16	11	3	0	17	2	56	2
Kwiatkowski, Medicine Hat	0	2	.000	9.00	2	2	0	0	0	0	4.0	6	8	4	0	2	7	0	2	1
Langley, Great Falls*	0	0	.000	6.87	10	3	0	2	0	0	18.1	18	16	14	1	1	14	1	24	0
Lazor, Billings*	5	1	.833	1.61	12	8	0	2	0	1	61.2	47	21	11	1	0	16	1	75	6
Lyons, Idaho Falls	1	1	.500	6.03	21	0	0	6	0	1	37.1	48	33	25	5	1	16	0	23	6
Marak, Idaho Falls	2	5	.286	5.02	12	12	1	0	0	0	61.0	82	57	34	6	4	25	1	52	12
Maysonet, Medicine Hat	0	0	.000	5.40	1	0	0	1	0	0	1.2	1	1	1	0	0	1	0	0	0
Moscrey, Billings	5	6	.455	3.55	14	14	0	0	0	0	88.2	99	52	35	6	4	21	0	62	4
Mullins, Billings	2	4	.333	4.33	26	0	0	17	0	7	43.2	42	28	21	2	2	38	1	39	5
Munoz, Great Falls*	4	4	.500	3.21	14	14	2	0	2	0	81.1	85	44	29	4	1	38	0	49	3
Naumczik, Idaho Falls*	4	2	.667	4.57	17	3	0	7	0	1	45.1	62	30	23	0	1	16	0	40	1
J. Nelson, Great Falls	0	0	.000	13.50	3	0	0	2	0	0	2.0	5	3	3	0	0	3	2	1	2
S. Nelson, Helena*	3	3	.500	6.35	12	4	0	3	0	0	34.0	41	29	24	3	0	22	0	15	5
Nichols, Helena	1	0	1.000	7.83	14	0	0	5	0	0	23.0	18	22	20	1	3	21	0	13	6
Novak, Billings	2	5	.286	5.33	23	2	0	13	0	2	52.1	69	40	31	3	2	26	5	45	3
Nowlin, Idaho Falls	3	4	.429	4.82	20	0	0	16	0	3	28.0	22	23	15	2	0	21	3	25	4
Ogawa, Helena	5	1	.833	4.52	13	11	1	1	0	0	61.2	58	36	31	3	1	31	1	42	3
Ojeda, Helena*	3	4	.429	5.44	23	3	0	3	0	2	51.1	57	45	31	2	9	33	2	51	8
Palma, Medicine Hat	2	2	.500	6.00	16	0	0	7	0	0	27.0	31	19	18	3	2	21	1	12	2
Pena, Great Falls*	0	0	.000	12.00	1	1	0	0	0	0	3.0	6	4	4	0	0	1	0	5	0
Pitz, Great Falls	4	5	.444	3.67	14	14	3	0	2	0	88.1	81	47	36	7	3	21	1	111	2
Ralstin, Idaho Falls	0	0	.000	11.45	13	0	0	7	0	0	19.2	39	30	25	6	2	15	0	16	3
Rice, Salt Lake City	1	3	.250	3.34	18	6	0	7	0	0	59.1	67	33	22	1	1	15	0	39	5
Riensche, Great Falls	0	0	.000	135.00	1	0	0	0	0	0	0.1	0	5	5	0	0	5	0	1	0
Roderick, Medicine Hat	1	7	.125	4.80	16	14	1	0	0	0	80.2	84	53	43	7	4	50	0	36	3
Rosenbauer, Medicine Hat	2	8	.200	4.26	19	16	0	2	0	0	88.2	92	54	42	10	1	47	0	53	5
Ryan, Great Falls	4	1	.800	2.93	25	0	0	12	0	1	27.2	26	12	9	0	1	16	3	27	3
Santana, Medicine Hat	5	4	.556	6.22	25	0	0	13	0	1	50.2	64	40	35	6	2	28	0	40	2
Savage, Billings	2	3	.400	7.98	19	3	0	7	0	2	44.0	52	43	39	6	1	33	2	24	1
Scudder, Billings	1	3	.250	4.78	12	8	0	1	0	0	52.2	43	34	28	1	3	36	0	38	8
Seaver, Helena*	2	5	.286	6.27	22	5	0	6	0	3	47.1	56	39	33	2	0	27	1	32	3
Shea, Great Falls*	1	0	1.000	6.43	8	0	0	4	0	0	7.0	14	6	5	0	0	2	0	5	0
Shortt, Salt Lake City*	0	0	.000	18.00	2	0	0	1	0	0	1.0	2	2	2	0	0	2	0	1	0
Shotkoski, Idaho Falls	1	3	.250	7.18	10	7	1	2	0	0	36.1	41	32	29	4	1	17	0	29	4
Siler, Great Falls	3	6	.333	3.32	21	4	2	7	0	2	65.0	79	34	24	5	1	14	1	64	0
Sissel, Salt Lake City	0	0	.000	7.71	2	0	0	0	0	0	2.1	2	2	2	0	0	4	0	2	0
Sloan, Idaho Falls	0	0	.000	6.75	1	0	0	0	0	0	4.0	5	3	3	0	0	2	0	3	1
K. Smith, Idaho Falls	2	2	.500	6.35	9	8	0	1	0	0	45.1	59	38	32	3	0	16	0	39	5
M. Smith, Salt Lake City*	1	2	.333	4.76	12	1	0	3	0	0	22.2	23	20	12	0	2	7	0	18	2
Stone, Helena	6	2	.750	4.99	14	14	1	0	0	0	79.1	90	53	44	4	1	32	0	68	6
Thomas, Idaho Falls	0	1	.000	3.74	11	1	0	4	0	2	21.2	24	12	9	0	0	19	0	27	3
Townsend, Salt Lake City*	5	1	.833	2.49	15	1	1	7	0	0	47.0	57	22	13	4	2	9	1	40	4
Vontz, Salt Lake City	8	1	.889	2.49	12	12	3	0	2	0	90.1	88	34	25	9	0	30	0	48	4
Ward, Medicine Hat	2	6	.250	5.19	27	0	0	17	0	3	60.2	73	38	35	6	3	24	3	41	1
Wetteland, Great Falls	4	3	.571	5.45	12	12	1	0	0	0	69.1	70	51	42	8	3	40	0	59	7
Wilder, Helena	0	0	.000	2.84	5	0	0	2	0	0	12.2	14	5	4	0	0	4	0	2	0
Williams, Billings*	0	2	.000	4.35	19	0	0	9	0	1	31.0	27	21	15	2	0	19	0	28	4
Williamson, Billings	0	1	.000	2.70	3	0	0	3	0	0	3.1	3	1	1	0	0	5	0	1	2
Wood, Great Falls	1	0	1.000	9.00	4	0	0	1	0	0	6.0	9	6	6	1	1	2	0	6	1
Woodhouse, Helena	1	0	1.000	6.98	14	0	0	2	0	0	19.1	27	23	15	1	4	19	0	11	2
Wortham, Medicine Hat*	3	2	.600	3.60	23	6	0	13	0	3	70.0	64	36	28	4	3	34	0	45	4
Yamasaki, Salt Lake City	3	5	.375	5.20	14	14	1	0	1	0	71.0	79	51	41	9	0	31	0	47	7

BALKS—Fukuchi, 3; Gosling, Santana, Ward, Wortham, 2 each; Bilawey, Butler, Carley, Dodd, Girdner, Hackett, Huseby, Langley, Marak, Naumczik, Ojeda, Pitz, Siler, Stone, Thomas, Townsend, Wetteland, Woodhouse, 1 each.

COMBINATION SHUTOUTS—Brown-Williams, Girdner-Lazor, Moscrey-Dodd, Moscrey-Girdner, Billings; Pitz-Langley-Bartels-Brooks, Great Falls; Shotkoski-Smith, Idaho Falls; Hall-Wortham, Medicine Hat; Vontz-Kolovitz, Salt Lake City.

NO-HIT GAME—DePastino, Medicine Hat, defeated Salt Lake City, 2-0 (seven innings), August 4.

MIKE SCHMIDT
• PHILLIES •
HOME RUNS (37)
RBIs (119)
SLUGGING PCT. (.547)

TIM RAINES
• EXPOS •
BATTING CHAMPION (.334)
ON-BASE PCT. (.413)

TONY GWYNN
• PADRES •
AT-BATS (642)
HITS (211)
RUNS (107—tie)

1986 N.L. LEADERS

MIKE SCOTT
• ASTROS •
ERA (2.22)
INNINGS (275.1)
STRIKEOUTS (306)
SHUTOUTS (5—tie)

FERNANDO VALENZUELA
• DODGERS •
WINS (21)
COMPLETE GAMES (20)

TODD WORRELL
• CARDINALS •
SAVES (36)

1987 N.L. EAST DIVISION SLATE . . .

1987	EAST					
	AT CHICAGO	AT MONTREAL	AT NEW YORK	AT PHILADELPHIA	AT PITTSBURGH	AT ST. LOUIS
CHICAGO........		April 24, 25, **26** June 29*, 30* July 1* Oct. 2*, 3, **4**	June 23*, 24*, 25 Aug. 6*, 7*, 8*, **9** Sept. 14*, 15*	April 10*, 11*, **12**, 13* Aug. 10*, 11*, 12 Sept. 16*, 17	June 26*, 27*, **28** Aug. 3*, 4*, 5* Sept. 29*, 30* Oct. 1*	April 21*, 22*, 23 June 12*, 13, **14** Sept. 18*, 19*, **20**
MONTREAL	April 17, 18, **19** July 28, 29, 30 Sept. 11, 12, **13**		April 30* May 1*, 2, **3** Aug. 10*, 11*, 12 Sept. 23*, 24*	April 27*, 28*, 29* June 5*, 6*, **7** Sept. 25*, 26*, **27**	June 23*, 24*, 25* Aug. 6*, 7*, 8*, **9** Sept. 14*, 15*	April 14*, 16 June 19*, 20*, **21**, 22* Sept. 29*, 30* Oct. 1*
NEW YORK	June 8, 9, 10 Aug. 13, 14, 15, **16** Sept. 21, 22	June 15*, 16*, 17*, 18* July 31* Aug. 1*, **2** Sept. 16*, 17*		April 14*, 15*, 16* June 26*, 27, **28** Sept. 28*, 29*, 30*	April 20*, 21*, 22* June 12*, 13*, **14** Sept. 18*, 19*, **20**	April 17*, 18*, **19** July 28*, 29*, 30* Oct. 2*, 3, **4**
PHILADELPHIA	June 15, 16, 17, 18 July 31 Aug. 1, **2** Sept. 23, 24	April 20, 22, 23 June 12*, 13*, **14** Sept. 18*, 19*, **20**	June 19*, 20*, **21** Aug. 3*, 4*, 5* Sept. 7*, 8*, 9*		April 17*, 18, **19** July 28*, 29*, 30* Oct. 2*, 3*, **4**	June 23*, 24*, 25* Aug. 13*, 14*, 15*, **16** Sept. 21*, 22*
PITTSBURGH..	April 15, 16 June 19, 20, **21**, 22 Sept. 7, 8, 9	June 8*, 9*, 10* Aug. 13*, 14*, 15*, **16** Sept. 21*, 22*	April 7, 9 June 5*, 6, **7-7** Sept. 25*, 26, **27**	April 24*, 25*, **26** June 29*, 30* July 1* Sept. 11*, 12*, **13**		June 15*, 16*, 17*, 18* July 31* Aug. 1*, **2** Sept. 23*, 24*
ST. LOUIS	April 7, 9 June 4, 5, 6, **7** Sept. 25, 26, **27**	June 26*, 27*, **28** Aug. 3*, 4*, 5* Sept. 7, 8*, 9*	April 24*, 25, **26** June 29*, 30* July 1* Sept. 11*, 12, **13**	June 8*, 9*, 10* Aug. 6*, 7*, 8*, **9** Sept. 14*, 15*	April 10*, 11, **12**, 13 Aug. 10*, 11*, 12* Sept. 16*, 17*	
ATLANTA.......	May 22, 23, **24** Aug. 25, 26, 27	May 11*, 12* July 16*, 17*, 18*, **19**	April 10*, 11, **12** July 20*, 21*, 22	May 13*, 14* July 23*, 24*, 25*, **26**	May 15*, 16*, **17** Aug. 31* Sept. 1*, 2*	May 25*, 26*, 28 Aug. 28*, 29, **30**
CINCINNATI ...	May 19, 20, 21 Sept. 4, 5, **6**	May 13*, 14* July 23*, 24*, 25*, **26**	May 5*, 6* July 16*, 17*, 18*, **19**	May 1*, 2*, **3** July 20*, 21*, 22*	May 29*, 30*, **31** Aug. 24*, 25*, 26*	May 15*, 16*, **17** Aug. 31* Sept. 1*, 2*
HOUSTON.......	June 1, 2, 3 Aug. 21, 22, **23**	May 8*, 9, **10** July 20*, 21*, 22*	April 27*, 28*, 29* July 24*, 25, **26**	May 5*, 6* July 2*, 3*, 4, **5**	May 18*, 19*, 20* Aug. 28*, 29*, **30**	May 29*, 30*, **31** Aug. 24*, 25*, 26
LOS ANGELES	May 4, 5 July 9, 10, 11, **12**	May 15*, 16*, **17** Aug. 18*, 19*, 20*	May 22*, 23, **24** Aug. 24*, 25*, 26*	May 18*, 19*, 20* Aug. 21*, 22, **23**	April 28*, 29*, 30* July 3*, 4, **5**	May 1*, 2*, **3** July 6*, 7*, 8*
SAN DIEGO.....	May 1, 2, **3** July 6, 7, 8	June 2*, 3*, 4* July 3*, 4*, **5**	May 18*, 19*, 20* Aug. 21*, 22*, **23**	May 15*, 16*, **17** Aug. 18*, 19*, 20*	May 12*, 13*, 14* July 10*, 11*, **12**	April 28*, 29*, 30 Sept. 4*, 5*, **6**
SAN FRAN......	April 28, 29, 30 July 3, 4, **5**	May 18*, 19*, 20* Aug. 21*, 22*, **23**	May 15*, 16*, **17** Aug. 18*, 19*, 20	May 22*, 23*, **24** Aug. 24*, 25*, 26*	May 1*, 2*, **3** July 6*, 7*, 8*	May 4*, 5 July 9*, 10*, 11*, **12**
1987	81 HOME DATES 0 NIGHTS	81 HOME DATES 60 NIGHTS	80 HOME DATES 53 NIGHTS	81 HOME DATES 63 NIGHTS	81 HOME DATES 64 NIGHTS	81 HOME DATES 59 NIGHTS

*NIGHT GAME
NIGHT GAME: Any game starting after 5:00 p.m.
HEAVY BLACK FIGURES DENOTE SUNDAY

AND COMPLETE WEST SCHEDULES

1987	WEST AT ATLANTA	AT CINCINNATI	AT HOUSTON	AT LOS ANGELES	AT SAN DIEGO	AT SAN FRANCISCO
CHICAGO........	May 29*, 30*, **31** Aug. 18*, 19*, 20*	May 25, 26*, 27* Aug. 28*, 29*, **30**	May 15*, 16, **17** Aug. 31* Sept. 1*, 2*	May 11*, 12*, 13** July 24*, 25, **26**	May 8*, 9*, **10** July 20*, 21*, 22*	May 6*, 7* July 16*, 17*, 18, **19**
MONTREAL	May 4*, 5*, 6* Sept. 4*, 5*, **6**	April 6, 8 July 9*, 10*, 11*, **12**	April 10*, 11, **12** July 6*, 7*, 8*	May 25*, 26*, 27* Aug. 28*, 29*, **30**	May 22*, 23*, **24** Aug. 25*, 26*, 27*	May 29*, 30, **31** Aug. 31* Sept. 1*, 2
NEW YORK	May 8*, 9, **10** July 6*, 7*, 8*	May 11*, 12* July 2*, 3*, 4*, **5**	May 13*, 14* July 9*, 10*, 11, **12**	June 1*, 2*, 3* Sept. 4*, 5*, **6**	May 29*, 30*, **31** Aug. 31* Sept. 1*, 2*	May 25, 26*, 27 Aug. 28*, 29, **30**
PHILADELPHIA	April 7*, 9* July 9*, 10, 11*, **12**	May 8*, 9, **10** July 6*, 7*, 8*	May 11*, 12* July 16*, 17*, 18*, **19**	May 29*, 30, **31** Aug. 31* Sept. 1*, 2*	May 25*, 26*, 27* Aug. 28*, 29*, **30**	June 1*, 2*, 3 Sept. 4*, 5, **6**
PITTSBURGH..	June 2*, 3*, 4* Aug. 21*, 22*, **23**	May 22*, 23*, **24** Aug. 18*, 19*, 20*	May 25*, 26*, 27* Sept. 4*, 5*, **6**	May 6*, 7* July 16*, 17*, 18*, **19**	May 4*, 5* July 23, 24*, 25*, **26**	May 8*, 9, **10** July 20*, 21*, 22
ST. LOUIS	May 19*, 20*, 21* July 3*, 4, **5**	June 1*, 2*, 3* Aug. 21*, 22*, **23**	May 22*, 23*, **24** Aug. 18*, 19*, 20	May 8*, 9*, **10** July 21*, 22*, 23*	May 6*, 7 July 16*, 17*, 18, **19**	May 12*, 13 July 24*, 25, **26-26**
ATLANTA.......		April 28*, 29*, 30 June 11*, 12*, 13*, **14** Sept. 28*, 29	April 21*, 22*, 23* Aug. 14*, 15*, **16**, 17* Sept. 30* Oct. 1*	June 23*, 24*, 25* Aug. 7*, 8, **9** Sept. 18*, 19*, **20**	June 26*, 27*, **28** Aug. 10*, 11*, 12*, 13 Sept. 16*, 17	April 17*, 18, **19** June 29*, 30* July 1 Oct. 2*, 3, **4**
CINCINNATI ...	April 13*, 14*, 15* June 18*, 19*, 20, **21** Sept. 14*, 15*		April 24*, 25*, **26** June 15*, 16*, 17* Oct. 2*, 3, **4**	June 26*, 27*, **28** Aug. 10*, 11*, 12*, 13 Sept. 17-17	April 20*, 21*, 22*, 23 Aug. 14 (Tn), **16** Sept. 30* Oct. 1	June 23*, 24, 25* Aug. 7*, 8, **9-9** Sept. 19, **20**
HOUSTON.......	May 1*, 2*, **3** July 28*, 29*, 30* Sept. 22*, 23*, 24*	April 17*, 18, **19-19** June 30* July 1* Sept. 25*, 26, **27**		April 13*, 14*, 15* June 11*, 12*, 13*, **14** Sept. 14*, 15*	June 23*, 24*, 25 Aug. 7*, 8*, **9** Sept. 10*, 11*, **13**	June 26*, 27, **28** Aug. 10*, 11*, 12, 13 Sept. 16, 17
LOS ANGELES	June 8*, 9*, 10* July 31* Aug. 1*, **2** Sept. 11*, 12, **13**	June 5*, 6*, **7** Aug. 3*, 4*, 5* Sept. 7, 8*, 9*	April 6*, 7*, 8 June 18*, 19*, 20, **21** Sept. 28*, 29*		April 16, 17*, 18, **19** June 16*, 17 Oct. 2*, 3*, **4**	April 20*, 21*, 22* Aug. 14*, 15, **16** Sept. 21*, 22*, 23*
SAN DIEGO.....	June 5*, 6*, **7** Aug. 4*, 5*, 6* Sept. 7, 8*, 9*	April 10*, 11, **12** July 28*, 29*, 30* Sept. 22*, 23*, 24	June 8*, 9*, 10* July 31* Aug. 1*, **2** Sept. 18*, 19*, **20**	April 24*, 25*, **26** June 29*, 30* July 1* Sept. 25*, 26, **27**		April 6, 7*, 8 June 11*, 12*, 13, **14** Sept. 14*, 15*
SAN FRAN......	April 24*, 25, **26**, 27* June 16*, 17* Sept. 25*, 26*, **27**	June 8*, 9*, 10 July 31* Aug. 1, **2** Sept. 11*, 12*, **13**	June 5*, 6*, **7** Aug. 3*, 4*, 5* Sept. 7*, 8*, 9*	April 9, 10*, 11*, **12** July 27*, 28*, 29* Sept. 30* Oct. 1*	April 13*, 14*, 15* June 18*, 19*, 20*, **21** Sept. 28*, 29*	
1987	81 HOME DATES 61 NIGHTS	80 HOME DATES 54 NIGHTS	81 HOME DATES 61 NIGHTS	80 HOME DATES 60 NIGHTS	80 HOME DATES 57 NIGHTS	79 HOME DATES 39 NIGHTS

JULY 14—ALL-STAR GAME AT OAKLAND

1987 A.L. EAST DIVISION SLATE . . .

1987	EAST						
	AT MILWAUKEE	AT DETROIT	AT CLEVELAND	AT TORONTO	AT BALTIMORE	AT NEW YORK	AT BOSTON
MILWAUKEE...		June 9*, 10*, 11 Sept. 18*, 19, **20**	May 29*, 30, **31** Aug. 17*, 18*, 19*, 20*	June 18*, 19*, 20, **21** Sept. 28*, 29*, 30*	April 13*, 14*, 15* Aug. 13*, 14*, 15*, **16**	June 12*, 13*, **14** Sept. 14*, 15*, 16*	June 22*, 23*, 24* Oct. 2*, 3, **4**
DETROIT.........	June 29*, 30* July 1 Sept. 10*, 11*, 12*, **13**		June 1*, 2*, 3* Aug. 21*, 22, **23**	June 15*, 16*, 17 Sept. 24*, 25*, 26, **27**	June 19*, 20*, **21** Sept. 7*, 8*, 9*	April 20*, 21*, 22* July 31* Aug. 1, **2**	June 4*, 5*, 6, **7** Sept. 21*, 22*, 23*
CLEVELAND ...	May 22*, 23*, **24** Aug. 25*, 26*, 27	May 15*, 16*, **17** Aug. 31* Sept. 1*, 2*, 3*		April 6, 8, 9 July 31* Aug. 1, **2**	April 16*, 17*, 18*, **19** Aug. 10*, 11*, 12*	April 13, 14*, 15* Aug. 14*, 15*, **16**	May 25*, 26*, 27*, 28* Sept. 4*, 5, **6**
TORONTO	June 26*, 27*, **28** Sept. 7, 8*, 9*	June 22*, 23*, 24* Oct. 2*, 3, **4**	April 20*, 21*, 22* Aug. 6*, 7*, 8, **9**		June 11*, 12*, 13*, **14** Sept. 21*, 22*, 23*	June 8*, 9*, 10* Sept. 17*, 18*, 19, **20**	April 10, 11, **12** Aug. 10*, 11*, 12*
BALTIMORE....	April 24*, 25, **26** Aug. 4*, 5*, 6	June 26*, 27*, **28** Sept. 28*, 29*, 30* Oct. 1*	April 10, 11, **12** July 28*, 29*, 30*	June 5*, 6, **7** Sept. 14*, 15*, 16*		June 15*, 16*, 17*, 18* Oct. 2*, 3*, **4**	June 29*, 30* July 1* Sept. 10*, 11*, 12, **13**
NEW YORK	June 4*, 5*, 6*, **7** Sept. 21*, 22*, 23*	April 6, 8, 9 Aug. 6*, 7*, 8, **9**	April 23*, 24*, 25, **26** Aug. 3*, 4*, 5*	June 29*, 30* July 1 Sept. 11*, 12, **13**	June 22*, 23*, 24* Sept. 25*, 26, **27**		June 19*, 20, **21** Sept. 7*, 8*, 9*
BOSTON	April 6, 8*, 9 Sept. 24*, 25*, 26, **27**	June 12*, 13, **14** Sept. 14*, 15*, 16*	June 16*, 17*, 18* Aug. 28*, 29, **30**	April 16*, 17, 18, **19** July 27*, 28*, 29*	June 8*, 9*, 10* Sept. 18*, 19*, **20**	June 26*, 27*, **28** Sept. 28*, 29*, 30* Oct. 1*	
SEATTLE........	May 8*, 9, **10** July 20*, 21*, 22	May 5*, 6 July 16*, 17*, 18*, **19**	June 19*, 20, **21** Sept. 7, 8*, 9*	June 1*, 2*, 3 Sept. 4*, 5, **6**	May 29*, 30*, **31** Aug. 31* Sept. 1*, 2*	May 27*, 28* Aug. 27, 28*, 29*, **30**	May 11*, 12*, 13* July 24*, 25, **26**
OAKLAND	May 12*, 13 July 23*, 24*, 25*, **26**	May 8*, 9*, **10** July 20*, 21*, 22*	June 26*, 27, **28** Sept. 21*, 22*, 23*	May 27*, 28* Aug. 27*, 28*, 29, **30**	June 1*, 2*, 3* Sept. 4*, 5*, **6**	May 29*, 30*, **31** Aug. 31* Sept. 1*, 2*	May 5*, 6* July 16*, 17*, 18, **19**
CALIFORNIA...	May 5*, 6 July 16, 17*, 18*, **19**	May 11*, 12*, 13* July 24*, 25, **26**	June 29*, 30* July 1* Sept. 25*, 26, **27**	May 29*, 30, **31** Aug. 31* Sept. 1*, 2	May 27*, 28* Aug. 27*, 28*, 29*, **30**	June 1*, 2*, 3* Sept. 4*, 5, **6**	May 8*, 9, **10** July 20*, 21*, 22*
TEXAS	April 17*, 18, **19** Aug. 10*, 11*, 12	May 25*, 26*, 27* Aug. 28*, 29*, **30**	May 11*, 12* July 23*, 24*, 25, **26**	May 1*, 2, **3** July 6*, 7*, 8*	April 6, 8, 9* Aug. 7*, 8*, **9**	May 13*, 14 July 2*, 3*, 4, **5**	April 13, 14, 15 Aug. 14*, 15, **16**
KANSAS CITY	June 1*, 2*, 3 Aug. 21*, 22*, **23**	April 24*, 25, **26** Aug. 3*, 4*, 5*	May 8*, 9, **10** July 6*, 7*, 8*	May 11*, 12* July 9*, 10*, 11, **12**	May 13*, 14* July 23*, 24*, 25*, **26**	April 17*, 18, **19** July 28*, 29, 30*	April 20, 21*, 22* Aug. 7*, 8, **9**
MINNESOTA...	June 15*, 16*, 17 Aug. 28*, 29*, **30**	May 29*, 30*, **31** Aug. 18*, 19*, 20	May 19*, 20*, 21* Sept. 11*, 12, **13**	April 28*, 29* July 23*, 24*, 25, **26**	May 11*, 12* July 9*, 10*, 11*, **12**	May 8*, 9*, **10** July 6*, 7*, 8	June 1*, 2*, 3* Aug. 21*, 22, **23**
CHICAGO........	May 19*, 20 July 30*, 31* Aug. 1*, **2**	April 17*, 18, **19** July 27*, 28*, 29*	April 28*, 29* July 2*, 3*, 4, **5**	April 14*, 15* Aug. 13*, 14*, 15, **16**	May 1*, 2*, **3** July 6*, 7*, 8*	May 11*, 12* July 9*, 10*, 11, **12**	May 22*, 23, **24** Aug. 24*, 25*, 26*
1987	81 HOME DATES 50 NIGHTS	81 HOME DATES 55 NIGHTS	81 HOME DATES 53 NIGHTS	81 HOME DATES 47 NIGHTS	81 HOME DATES 65 NIGHTS	81 HOME DATES 57 NIGHTS	81 HOME DATES 50 NIGHTS

*NIGHT GAME
NIGHT GAME: Any game starting after 5:00 p.m.
HEAVY BLACK FIGURES DENOTE SUNDAY

AND COMPLETE WEST SCHEDULES

1987	WEST						
	AT SEATTLE	AT OAKLAND	AT CALIFORNIA	AT TEXAS	AT KANSAS CITY	AT MINNESOTA	AT CHICAGO
MILWAUKEE...	May 1*, 2*, **3** July 6*, 7*, 8*	April 29*, 30 July 9*, 10*, 11, **12**	April 27*, 28* July 2*, 3*, 4*, **5**	April 10*, 11*, **12** July 27*, 28*, 29*	May 15*, 16*, **17** Sept. 1*, 2*, 3*	May 26*, 27*, 28* Sept. 4*, 5*, **6**	April 20*, 21*, 22* Aug. 7*, 8*, **9**
DETROIT.........	April 27*, 28* July 2*, 3*, 4, **5**	May 1*, 2, **3** July 6*, 7*, 8	April 29*, 30* July 9*, 10, 11*, **12**	May 18*, 19*, 20* Sept. 4*, 5*, **6***	April 14*, 15* Aug. 13*, 14*, 15*, **16**	May 22*, 23*, **24** Aug. 24*, 25*, 26*	April 10, 11*, **12** Aug. 10*, 11*, 12
CLEVELAND ...	June 12*, 13*, **14** Sept. 14*, 15*, 16	June 5*, 6, **7** Sept. 29*, 30* Oct. 1	June 8, 9*, 10* Oct. 2*, 3, **4**	May 5*, 6* July 9*, 10*, 11*, **12***	May 1*, 2*, **3** July 20*, 21*, 22*	June 23*, 24*, 25 Sept. 18*, 19, **20**	May 13*, 14* July 16, 17*, 18*, **19**
TORONTO	May 22*, 23*, **24**, 25 Aug. 24*, 25*	May 15*, 16, **17** Aug. 18*, 19, 20	May 18*, 19*, 20* Aug. 21*, 22*, **23**	May 8*, 9*, **10** July 20*, 21*, 22*	May 4*, 5*, 6* July 3*, 4*, **5**	May 13*, 14* July 16, 17*, 18*, **19**	April 24*, 25*, **26** Aug. 3*, 4*, 5*
BALTIMORE....	May 18*, 19*, 20 Aug. 21*, 22*, **23**	May 22*, 23, **24**, 25* Aug. 24*, 25	May 15*, 16, **17** Aug. 18*, 19*, 20*	April 21*, 22*, 23* July 31* Aug. 1*, **2***	April 28*, 29* July 16*, 17*, 18, **19**	May 5*, 6*, 7 July 3*, 4*, **5**	May 8*, 9*, **10** July 20*, 21*, 22*
NEW YORK	May 15*, 16*, **17** Aug. 18*, 19*, 20*	May 18*, 19*, 20* Aug. 21*, 22, **23**	May 22*, 23*, **24**, 25 Aug. 24*, 25*	April 28*, 29* July 16*, 17*, 18*, **19***	April 10*, 11, **12** Aug. 10*, 11*, 12*	May 1*, 2*, **3** July 20*, 21*, 22*	May 4*, 5*, 6* July 24*, 25, **26**
BOSTON.........	April 29*, 30* July 9*, 10*, 11*, **12**	April 27*, 28* July 2*, 3*, 4, **5**	May 1*, 2*, **3** July 6, 7*, 8*	April 24*, 25*, **26** Aug. 3*, 4*, 5*	May 18*, 19*, 20* July 31* Aug. 1*, **2**	May 15*, 16*, **17** Sept. 1*, 2*, 3	May 29*, 30, **31** Aug. 17*, 18*, 19*
SEATTLE........		April 24*, 25, **26** Aug. 3*, 4, 5	April 7, 8*, 9* July 31* Aug. 1*, **2**	June 29*, 30* July 1* Oct. 1*, 2*, 3*, **4**	June 26*, 27*, **28** Sept. 28*, 29*, 30*	April 20*, 21*, 22 Aug. 14*, 15*, **16**, 17*	June 22*, 23*, 24* Sept. 17*, 18*, 19*, **20**
OAKLAND	April 16*, 17*, 18*, **19** Aug. 10*, 11*, 12		April 20*, 21*, 22 Aug. 14*, 15*, **16**, 17*	June 12*, 13*, **14*** Sept. 14*, 15*, 16*	June 15*, 16*, 17* Sept. 18*, 19*, **20**	April 7*, 8*, 9 Aug. 6*, 7*, 8*, **9**	June 29*, 30* July 1* Oct. 2*, 3*, **4**
CALIFORNIA...	April 13*, 14*, 15 Aug. 6*, 7*, 8*, **9**	April 10*, 11, **12** July 27*, 28*, 29		June 22*, 23*, 24* Sept. 18*, 19*, **20**	June 12*, 13*, **14** Sept. 14*, 15*, 16*, 17*	April 23*, 24*, 25*, **26** Aug. 11*, 12*, 13	June 26*, 27, **28** Sept. 29*, 30* Oct. 1*
TEXAS	June 8*, 9*, 10* Sept. 25*, 26*, **27**	June 19*, 20, **21-21** Sept. 7*, 8*, 9	June 15*, 16*, 17* Sept. 10*, 11*, 12*, **13**		May 29*, 30*, **31** Aug. 24*, 25*, 26*, 27*	June 5*, 6*, **7** Sept. 22*, 23*, 24*	May 15*, 16*, **17** Sept. 1*, 2*, 3*
KANSAS CITY	June 4*, 5*, 6*, **7** Sept. 21*, 22*, 23*	June 22*, 23*, 24 Sept. 10, 11*, 12, **13**	June 18*, 19*, 20*, **21** Sept. 7, 8*	May 22*, 23*, **24** Aug. 17*, 18*, 19*		June 8*, 9*, 10* Sept. 25*, 26, **27**	May 25*, 26*, 27* Aug. 28*, 29*, **30**, 31*
MINNESOTA ...	April 10*, 11*, **12** July 27*, 28*, 29	April 13*, 14*, 15 July 31* Aug. 1, **2**	April 17*, 18*, **19** Aug. 3*, 4*, 5	June 26*, 27(Tn), **28*** Sept. 28*, 29*, 30*	June 29*, 30* July 1*, 2* Oct. 2*, 3*, **4**		June 11*, 12*, 13*, **14** Sept. 14*, 15*, 16*
CHICAGO........	June 15*, 16*, 17 Sept. 11*, 12*, **13**	June 8*, 9*, 10 Sept. 24*, 25*, 26, **27**	June 4*, 5*, 6, **7** Sept. 21*, 22*, 23*	June 1*, 2*, 3* Aug. 20*, 21*, 22, **23***	April 6, 8*, 9* Sept. 4*, 5*, **6**	June 19*, 20*, **21** Sept. 7, 8*, 9*	
1987	81 HOME DATES 60 NIGHTS	80 HOME DATES 40 NIGHTS	81 HOME DATES 57 NIGHTS	80 HOME DATES 73 NIGHTS	81 HOME DATES 65 NIGHTS	81 HOME DATES 58 NIGHTS	81 HOME DATES 62 NIGHTS

JULY 14—ALL-STAR GAME AT OAKLAND

DON MATTINGLY
• YANKEES •
HITS (238)
TOTAL BASES (388)
DOUBLES (53)
SLUGGING PCT. (.573)

WADE BOGGS
• RED SOX •
BATTING CHAMPION (.357)
ON-BASE PCT. (.453)
WALKS (105)

JESSE BARFIELD
• BLUE JAYS •
HOME RUNS (40)

1986 A.L. LEADERS

ROGER CLEMENS
• RED SOX •
WINS (24)
ERA (2.48)

JACK MORRIS
• TIGERS •
SHUTOUTS (6)

DAVE RIGHETTI
• YANKEES •
SAVES (46)

Index to Contents

AMERICAN LEAGUE

NATIONAL LEAGUE

1986 Game Scores

1986 Game Scores

NATIONAL ASSOCIATION (MINOR LEAGUE) AVERAGES

Index to Minor League Clubs, Cities

Notes

Notes

NOTES

NOTES